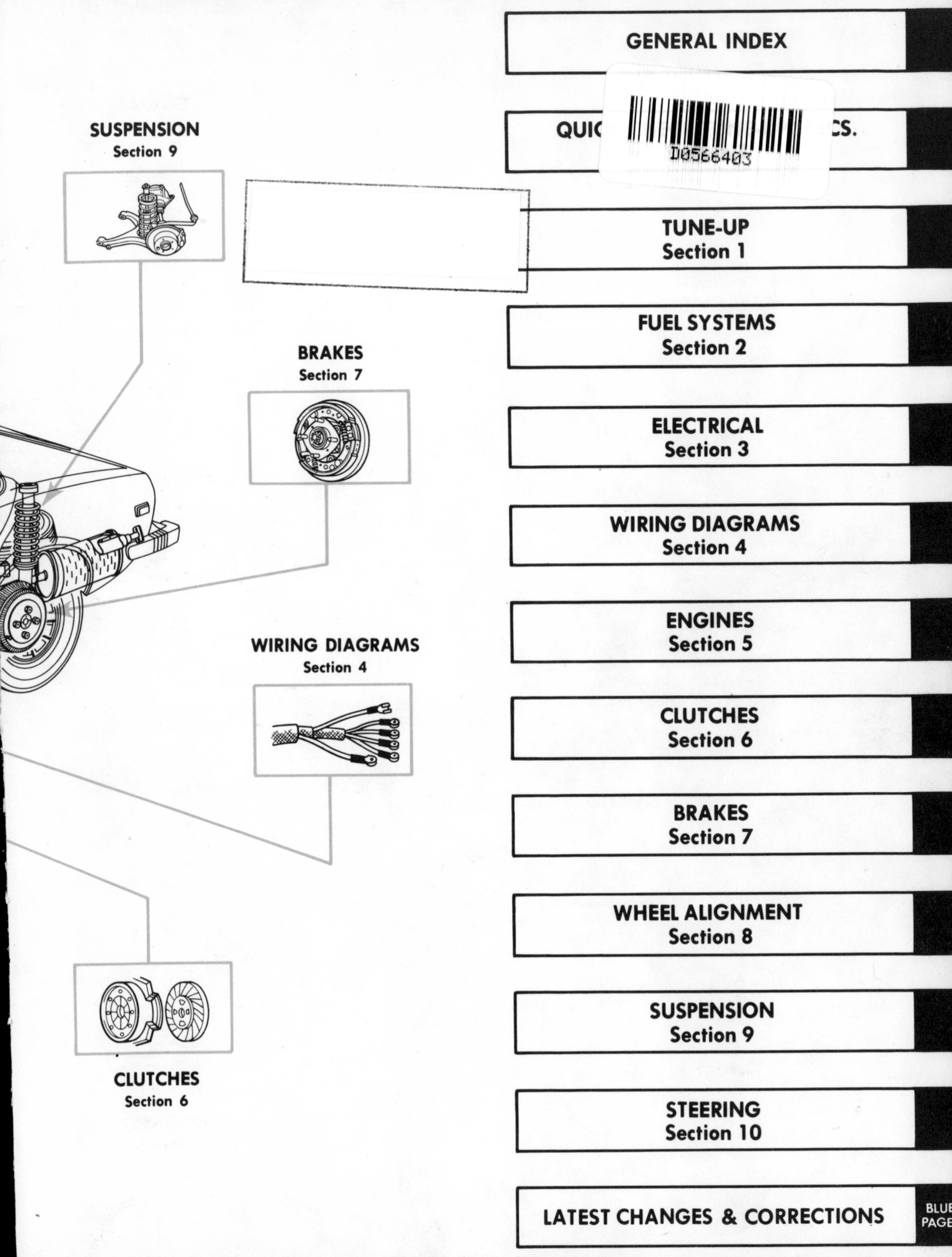

SUSPENSION
Section 9

BRAKES
Section 7

WIRING DIAGRAMS
Section 4

CLUTCHES
Section 6

BLUE
PAGES

D0566403

PREFACE

This is the 1980 edition of Mitchell Manuals'
Imported Car Tune-Up/Mechanical Service and Repair Manual.
This book, like the many Mitchell publications which have preceded it,
represents our commitment to professionalism
in the automotive service market.

The automotive industry advances every year,
and Mitchell Manuals pledges to advance and improve its products
as we maintain the quality and usefulness of all Mitchell Manuals' publications.

We cordially acknowledge the good will
and mutual goals that exist in the automotive business,
and it is in this spirit that we thank the automotive manufacturers,
distributors, dealers and the entire automotive industry
for their fine cooperation and assistance
which have made this publication possible.

1980 IMPORTED CARS & TRUCKS TUNE-UP MECHANICAL SERVICE & REPAIR

National Service Data
Manuals For The Automotive Professional

Published By:
MITCHELL MANUALS, INC.
A Cordura Company
P.O. BOX 26260
SAN DIEGO, CA 9____

ISBN 0-8470-5780-1

©1981 MITCHELL MANUALS, INC. LITHO IN U.S.A.

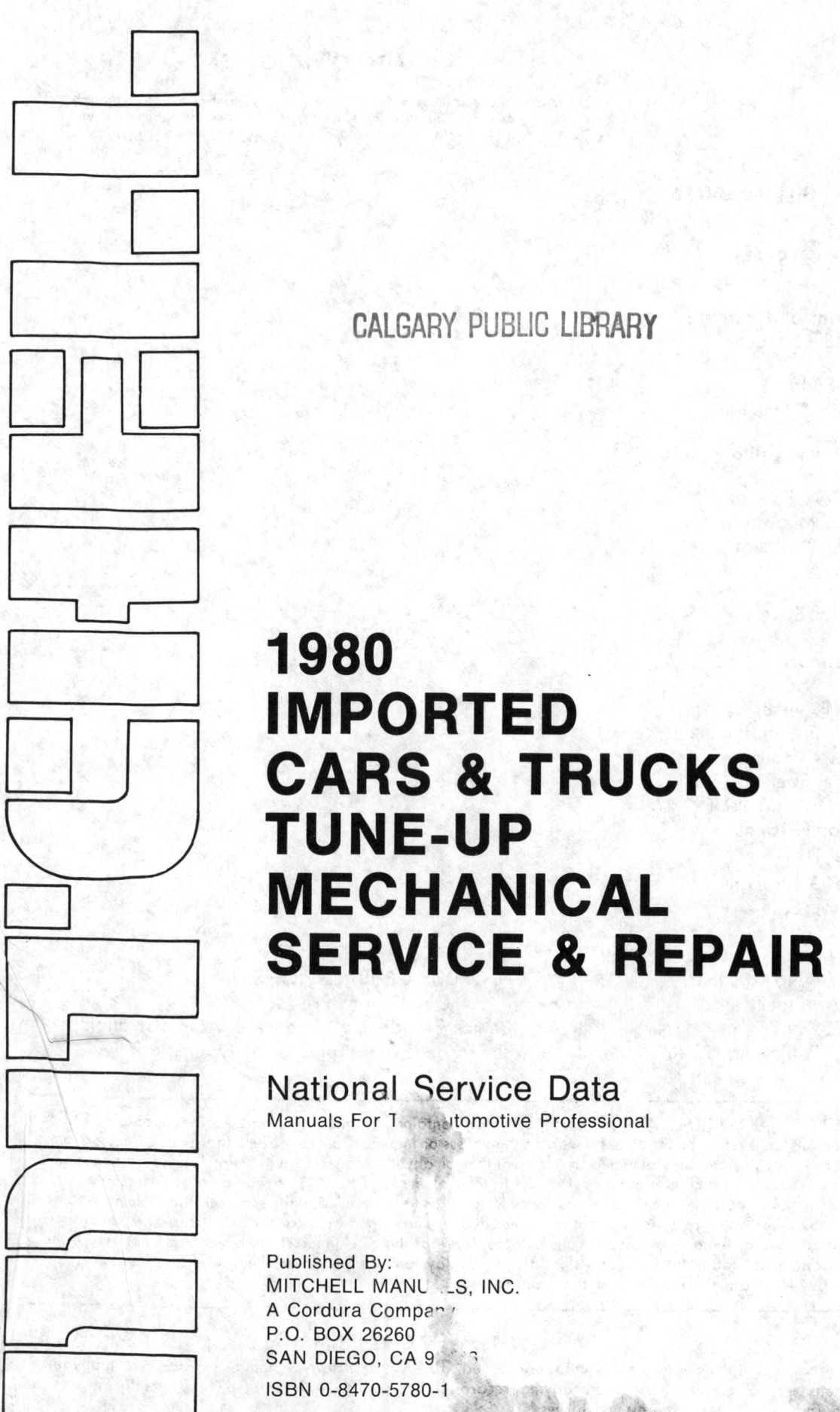

ACKNOWLEDGEMENT

Mitchell Manuals thanks the automotive and equipment manufacturers, distributors, dealers and the entire automotive industry for their fine cooperation and assistance which makes the publication of this manual possible.

MITCHELL MANUALS, INC.

A Cordura Company

Vice President and Publisher
Richard M. Harris

Managing Editor
Kenneth A. Young

Ass't. Managing Editor
Daniel M. Kelley

Composition Manager
Doris J. Williams

Art Director
Eloise S. Stiverson

Technical Editors
Gary L. Haley
Daryl F. Visser
Robert B. Johnson
Steven L. Hansen
Michael Roeder
Terry L. Blomquist
Thomas L. Landis
Daniel D. Fleming
Philip G. Wallan
Alan M. Salo

PUBLISHED BY

MITCHELL MANUALS, INC.
9889 Willow Creek Road
P.O. Box 26260
San Diego, California 92126

a subsidiary of
CORDURA PUBLICATIONS, INC.
C.L. Kobrin, President
John Opelt, Vice President of Finance & Administration
Malcolm Ferrier, Vice President of Operations

Introduction

You now have the most complete and up-to-date Service and Repair Manual currently available to the professional mechanic. Our staff of experts have spent many hundreds of hours gathering and processing service and repair information from sources throughout the automotive world. More than 300 separate articles provide specific, step-by-step testing, adjusting and repair procedures for 1980 Imported Cars and Trucks.

To use this manual in the most efficient and profitable way possible, please take the time to read the following section, "How to Find the Information". This will enable you to quickly locate the model car, and the mechanical procedure you desire, without wasting precious time thumbing through unnecessary pages.

HOW TO FIND THE INFORMATION
3 Quick Steps

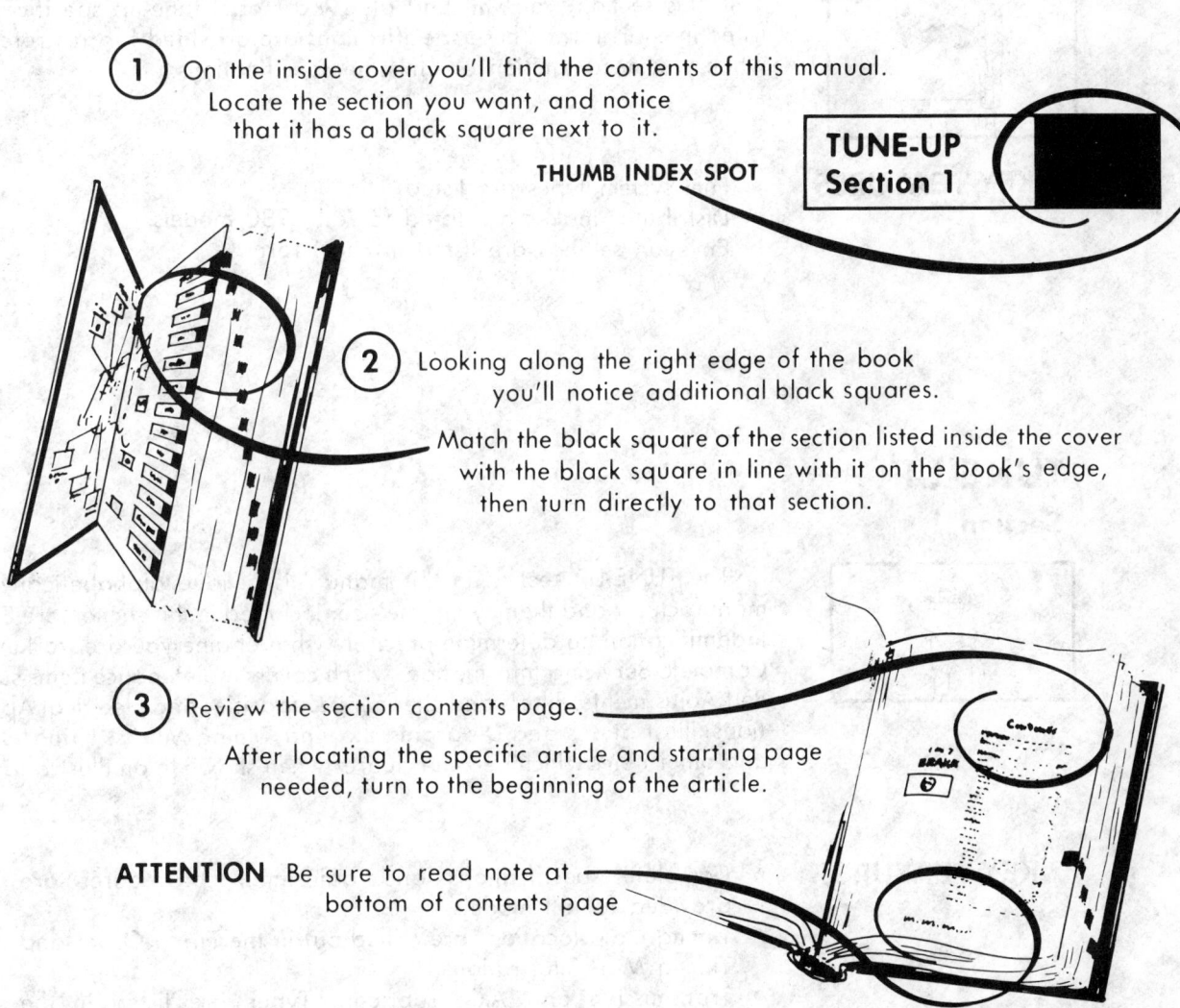

(1) On the inside cover you'll find the contents of this manual. Locate the section you want, and notice that it has a black square next to it.

THUMB INDEX SPOT

TUNE-UP Section 1

(2) Looking along the right edge of the book you'll notice additional black squares.

Match the black square of the section listed inside the cover with the black square in line with it on the book's edge, then turn directly to that section.

(3) Review the section contents page.

After locating the specific article and starting page needed, turn to the beginning of the article.

ATTENTION Be sure to read note at bottom of contents page

OR...

Go directly to the GENERAL INDEX located at the front of the book.
Use this alphabetical index as you would any type of reference index.

Section Highlights

GENERAL INDEX

The first section of the Imported Manual is the GENERAL INDEX. This section is a quick, easy reference to help you locate the information you need. It is arranged alphabetically and is broken down into all of the vehicle's major components and then divided into models under component headings.

TUNE-UP SPECIFICATIONS
Section T

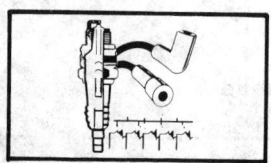

In this section, you will find all 1980 model tune-up specifications listed in chart form. These specifications are provided for fast reference when you need ignition or emission specifications.

KEY FEATURES

- Fuel system types are listed.
- Distributor makes are listed for all 1980 models.
- Emission settings are listed in chart form.

TUNE-UP
Section 1

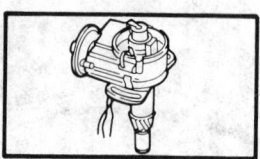

The TUNE-UP section in this manual is divided alphabetically by manufacturer and then by engine size. Included in this section are Engine Indentification, to determine precisely what engine you are working on; Complete Servicing Information, which covers maintenance items such as Belt Adjustments, Filters and Cleaners, Capacities and Electrical Applications; Illustrations and Diagrams showing Timing Marks, Firing Orders and other items which become clearer when shown in an illustration.

KEY FEATURES

- Complete specifications and adjustment procedures are provided for all models.
- Timing mark locations are called out in the Firing Order and Timing Mark illustrations.
- Transmission and Axle Lubricant Types are listed in the Capacities Tables.

FUEL SYSTEMS
Section 2

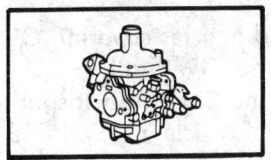

The FUEL SYSTEMS section covers such vital points as, Carburetor and Fuel Injection Trouble Shooting, Carburetor and Fuel Injection (both gasoline and diesel), Adjustment, Inspection and Overhaul procedures. Complete specification tables and exploded views of carburetors are included in this section. The last part of this section is devoted to Electric Fuel Pumps, and includes thorough testing and adjustment procedures.

KEY FEATURES

- Bosch Diesel Injection Systems, including Peugeot 504 and 505.
- Complete coverage of Turbocharging Systems.

ELECTRICAL
Section 3

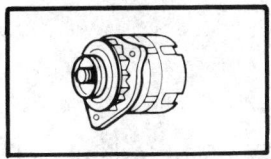

Within the ELECTRICAL section you will find comprehensive Distributor Applications and Specifications. Testing, Adjustment and Overhaul procedures for Ignition Systems, as well as Regulators and Alternators are included here. The last part of the section is comprised of complete data for Switches, Gauges, Speedometers and Instrument Panels.

KEY FEATURES

- Complete Trouble Shooting for Ignition Systems, Alternators and Starters.
- Thorough testing and repair procedures for all Electronic Ignition Systems.
- Starter and Alternator specifications are included.

WIRING DIAGRAMS
Section 4

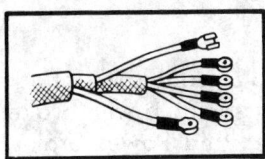

The WIRING DIAGRAM section covers Chassis Wiring for nearly all imported cars, with full schematics spread across several pages for easy reading and comprehension. For your convenience, all Sub-Systems (Fuel Injection, Power Windows, etc.) are now included on the main wiring diagrams. The last part of the section is devoted to Fuses and Circuit Breakers and their applications.

KEY FEATURES

- Many models are covered on detailed 4-page Chassis Wiring Diagrams.
- Diagrams are drawn in a standardized, easy-to-use format.
- A comprehensive Fuse Block, Flasher and Relay location diagram is included.

ENGINES
Section 5

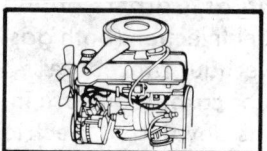

Within the ENGINE section you will find detailed articles covering Oil Pan Removal, Engine Removal, Valve Removal and Overhaul, Crankshaft and Connecting Rod Bearing Fitting and Camshaft Inspection and Replacement. At the end of each individual article you will find tables listing complete Engine Component Specifications as well as Tightening Specifications. This makes it easier to find specifications when procedural information isn't required.

KEY FEATURES

- Complete Gasoline and Diesel Engine Trouble Shooting tables are included.
- Complete specifications and procedures for the Toyota Tercel 4-cylinder engine.
- Coverage of the new Volvo 6-cylinder Diesel engine.

CLUTCHES
Section 6

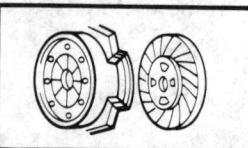

In the CLUTCH section you will find thorough Removal, Adjustment, Overhaul and Installation procedures for all aspects of clutches. This includes Master Cylinders, Release Bearings and Slave Cylinders.

KEY FEATURES

- Descriptions of all clutch systems.
- Complete coverage of the Peugeot 505 clutch system.
- Information and repair procedures for the Volkswagen Jetta clutch system.

BRAKES
Section 7

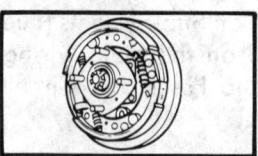

At the beginning of the brake section you will find a Trouble Shooting guide to help you locate and solve most problems associated with brake systems. Individual articles include Master Cylinder and Power Brake Unit coverage, with detailed explanations for Removal, Adjustment, Overhaul and Installation of both drum and disc brake systems. At the end of each article you'll find specifications listed for Disc Brake Rotors and Brake Drums, as well as Tightening Specifications.

KEY FEATURES

- Complete Brake System Bleeding procedures for all models located at the front of this section.
- Coverage of Toyota Tercel brake system.
- Coverage (as available) of proportioning and combination valves.

WHEEL ALIGNMENT
Section 8

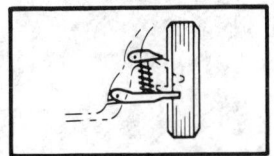

KEY FEATURES

The WHEEL ALIGNMENT section contains a Trouble Shooting Guide and comprehensive Wheel Alignment Specifications at the beginning of the section. Procedures covered include Wheel Alignment, Wheel Bearing Adjustment and Ball Joint Checking. Jacking and Hoisting diagrams are also included.

- Wheel Alignment Specifications are listed in tables.
- Camber and Caster adjustment procedures are provided.
- Riding Height adjustments covered as required for certain models.

SUSPENSION
Section 9

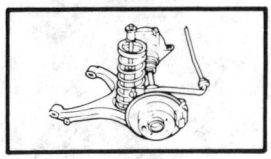

KEY FEATURES

This section covers all front and rear suspension components with complete Removal, Adjustment and Overhaul procedures. Such items as Coil Springs, Strut Assemblies, Stabilizer Bars and Control Arms are given detailed procedural coverage. Large and easy to understand illustrations which show proper positioning of suspension components eliminate guesswork.

- A complete Trouble Shooting Guide at the front of the section saves time.
- Detailed procedures for MacPherson Strut Suspension Overhaul and Adjustment.
- Complete Torque specifications are given.

STEERING
Section 10

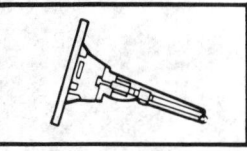

KEY FEATURES

The STEERING section covers all aspects of steering components. Steering Columns and Switches, Steering Gears and Linkage as well as a comprehensive Power Steering section are included. At the start of the section is a Manual and Power Steering Trouble Shooting Guide to help locate problems. Detailed diagrams and illustrations clearly show proper positioning of steering assemblies, and complete Tightening Specifications are given at the end of each article.

- Steering Wheel Removal procedures are provided.
- Complete information on Toyota Tercel Rack and Pinion Steering.
- Coverage of Triumph TR8 Power Rack and Pinion Steering.

LATEST CHANGES and CORRECTIONS

This section is printed on blue paper and contains information on changes and corrections from the car manufacturers which arrived too late to be included among the regular stories. This information also may refer to previous model automobiles which were covered in other editions of Mitchell's Imported Car books.

NOTE — ALSO SEE INDIVIDUAL SECTION CONTENTS PAGE

NOTE – ALSO SEE INDIVIDUAL SECTION CONTENTS PAGE

NOTE – ALSO SEE INDIVIDUAL SECTION CONTENTS PAGE

NOTE — ALSO SEE INDIVIDUAL SECTION CONTENTS PAGE

NOTE — ALSO SEE INDIVIDUAL SECTION CONTENTS PAGE

NOTE — ALSO SEE INDIVIDUAL SECTION CONTENTS PAGE

NOTE — ALSO SEE INDIVIDUAL SECTION CONTENTS PAGE

– F –

FUSES AND CIRCUIT BREAKERS (Cont.)

– G –

GAUGES

–H–

HOISTING

See JACKING.

HORN BUTTON

See SWITCHES

– I –

IGNITION SWITCHES

See SWITCHES

IGNITION SYSTEMS

See Distributors & Ignition Systems.

IGNITION TIMING

INSTRUMENT CLUSTER

See GAUGES.

NOTE — ALSO SEE INDIVIDUAL SECTION CONTENTS PAGE

NOTE – ALSO SEE INDIVIDUAL SECTION CONTENTS PAGE.

NOTE — ALSO SEE INDIVIDUAL SECTION CONTENTS PAGE

— S —   — S —

NOTE — ALSO SEE INDIVIDUAL SECTION CONTENTS PAGE

– S –   **– S –**

NOTE — ALSO SEE INDIVIDUAL SECTION CONTENTS PAGE

NOTE — ALSO SEE INDIVIDUAL SECTION CONTENTS PAGE

– W –

– W –

NOTE — ALSO SEE INDIVIDUAL SECTION CONTENTS PAGE

General Index

Section T

QUICK-CHECK

TUNE-UP SPECS.
1980 Models

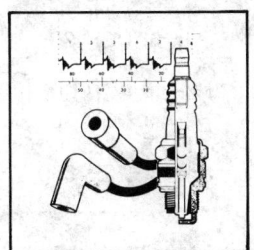

NOTE — ALSO SEE GENERAL INDEX.

1980 Tune-Up Specifications

CAR MODEL	SPARK PLUGS		FUEL SYSTEM	VALVE CLEARANCE		DISTRIBUTOR	No.
	Type	Gap	Make & Model	Int.	Exh.	Make	
AUDI	Bosch						
4000							
4-Cyl.	W7D①	.028"	Bosch CIS Fuel Inj. ④	.010"H	.018"H	Bosch	1
5-Cyl.	W7D①	.028"	Bosch CIS Fuel Inj. ④	.010"H	.018"H	Bosch	2
5000	W7D①	.028"	Bosch CIS Fuel Inj. ④	.010"H	.018"H	Bosch	3
Turbo	WR7DS	.028"	Bosch CIS Fuel Inj. ⑤	.010"H	.018"H	Bosch	4
BMW	Bosch						
320i	WR9DS	.024"	Bosch CIS Fuel Inj.①	.006"C	.006"C	Bosch	5
528i	WR9DS	.024"	Bosch AFC Fuel Inj.①	.010"C	.010"C	Bosch	6
633CSi & 733i	WR9DS	.024"	Bosch AFC Fuel Inj.①	.012"C	.012"C	Bosch	7
CHRYSLER CORP. IMPORTS	NGK						
1400 cc	BPR-6ES-11	.041"	Solex 28-32 DIDTA	.006"H①	.010"H	Mitsubishi	8
1600 cc	BPR-6ES-11	.041"	Solex 28-32 DIDTA	.006"H①	.010"H	Mitsubishi	9
2000 cc	BPR-6ES-11	.041"	Solex 30-32 DIDTA	.006"H①	.010"H	Mitsubishi	10
2600 cc	BPR-5ES-11	.041"	Solex 30-32 DIDTA	.006"H①	.010"H	Mitsubishi	11
COURIER	NGK						
2000 cc	BPR-5ES	.031"	Nikki 2-Bbl.	.012"H	.012"H	Mitsubishi	12
2300 cc	BPR-5EFS	.031"	Hitachi DCS 328 2-Bbl.	.Hyd.	Hyd.	Mitsubishi	13
DATSUN	NGK						
200SX	BP-6ES	.033"	Bosch AFC Fuel Inj.①	.012"H	.012"H	Hitachi	14
210	BP-5ES-11	.041"	Hitachi DCH 306	.014"H	.014"H	Hitachi	15
280ZX	BP-6ES-11	.041"	Bosch AFC Fuel Inj.①	.010"H	.012"H	Hitachi	16
310	BP-5ES-11	.041"	Hitachi DCH 306	.014"H	.014"H	Hitachi	17
510	BP-6ES	.033"	Hitachi DCH 360	.012"H	.012"H	Hitachi	18
810	BP-6ES-11	.041"	Bosch AFC Fuel Inj.①	.010"H	.012"H	Hitachi	19
Pickup	BPS-11	.041"	Hitachi DCH 340	.010"H	.012"H	Hitachi	20
FIAT	Champion						
1500 Carb.	RN9Y	.030"	Weber 28-32 ADHA	.014"H	.018"H	Bosch②	21
1500 F.I.	RN9Y	.030"	Bosch AFC Fuel Inj.①	.014"H	.018"H	Bosch②	22
2000 Carb.	RN9Y	.025"	Weber 28-32 ADHA	.019"H	.021"H	Marelli	23
2000 F.I.	RN9Y	.025"	Bosch AFC Fuel Inj.①	.019"H	.021"H	Marelli	24
FIESTA	Autolite						
1600 cc	AWSF-32	.032"	Weber 740 2-Bbl.	.010"C	.021"C	Motorcraft	25
HONDA	NGK						
Accord & Prelude	B7EB①	.028"③	Keihin 2-Bbl.	.006"C	.011"C	Honda	26
Civic							
1300 cc	②	.039"	Keihin 2-Bbl.	.006"C	.008"C	Honda	27
1500 cc	B7EB-11	.039"	Keihin 2-Bbl.	.006"C	.008"C	Honda	28
JAGUAR	Champion						
XJ6	N12Y	.035"	Bosch AFC Fuel Inj.①	.013"C	.013"C	Lucas	29
LUV	AC						
Pickup	R44XLS	.030"	Hitachi DCH 340	.006"C	.010"C	Nippondenso	30
MAZDA	NGK						
GLC	BP-5ES	.031"	Hitachi 2-Bbl.	.010"H	.012"H	Mitsubishi	31
626	BP-5ES	.031"	Nikki 2-Bbl.	.012"H	.012"H	Mitsubishi	32
RX7	BR-8ET	.039"	Hitachi 4-Bbl.	.....	.....	Mitsubishi	33
B2000 Pickup	BP-5ES	.031"	Nikki 2-Bbl.	.012"H	.012"H	Mitsubishi	34

No.	IGNITION TIMING	HOT IDLE RPM		FAST IDLE RPM	EXHAUST CO READING At Idle Speed	Remarks
		Man. Trans.	Auto. Trans.			
1	3° ATDC	850-1000	850-1000	.....	0.5-0.9%②	① — WR7DS on Calif. models.
2	3° ATDC	.....	800-1000③	.....	0.4-1.2%	② — 0.6-1.0% on Calif. models.
3	3° ATDC	800-1000③	800-1000③	.....	0.4-1.2%	③ — 880-1000 on Calif. models.
4	21° BTDC	.....	880-1000	.....	0.4-1.2%	④ — Calif. models use oxygen sensor.
						⑤ — All models use oxygen sensor.
5	25° BTDC	800-900	900-1000	.....	0.2-1.2%②	① — With oxygen sensor.
6	22° BTDC	850-950	850-950	.....	0.2-0.8%②	② — With oxygen sensor disconnected.
7	22° BTDC	850-950	850-950	.....	0.2-0.8%②	
8	5° BTDC	650-750	.....	.....	0.5-1.5%	① — Set Jet valves to .006"H.
9	5° BTDC	600-700	650-750	.....	0.5-1.5%②	② — Federal Pickup should measure
10	5° BTDC	600-700	650-750	.....	0.5-1.5%②	0.1% after adjustment.
11	7° BTDC	700-800	700-800	.....	0.5-1.5%	
12	8° BTDC	600-700	600-700	.....	2.0-4.0%②	① — With transmission in "D".
13	6° BTDC	750-850	650-750①	.....	3.0-5.0%②	② — With AIR disconnected.
14	8° BTDC②	700	700	.....	0.3-2.3%⑦	① — With oxygen sensor.
15	8° BTDC③	700	650	2300-3200⑤	1.0-3.0%⑧	② — 6° BTDC on Calif. models.
16	10° BTDC	700	700	.....	0.2-1.8%⑨	③ — 10° BTDC on 1200 cc engine.
17	8° BTDC	750	750	2300-3200	1.0-3.0%⑧	④ — 10° BTDC on Calif. Heavy Duty models.
18	8° BTDC②	600	600	.....	0.5-2.5%⑧	⑤ — 2600-3500 RPM on A/T.
19	10° BTDC	700	650	.....	0.2-1.8%⑨	⑥ — 2200-3200 RPM on A/T.
20	12° BTDC④	600	600	1900-2800⑥	0.3-2.7%	⑦ — Less than 4% on Calif. models.
						⑧ — Less than 5% on Calif. models.
						⑨ — Not applicable on Calif. models.
21	5° BTDC	800-900	700-800	.....	1.0-2.0%	① — With oxygen sensor.
22	10° BTDC	800-900	700-800	.....	0.3-0.6%	② — Marelli on some Strada models.
23	10° BTDC	800-900	700-800	.....	1.0-2.5%	
24	10° BTDC	800-900	700-800	.....	0.3-0.6%	
25	12° BTDC	850	.....	2000	.....	
26	TDC④	800	800	2000-3000	.....	① — B7EB-11 on Calif. A/T
						② — Nippondenso W20ES-L11.
27	2° BTDC	750	.....	2500-3500	.....	③ — .039" on Calif. A/T.
28	TDC⑤	750	750	2500-3500	.....	④ — 4° ATDC on Calif. M/T 4-Dr. models.
						⑤ — 15° on Fed. M/T Hatchback, 10° on Wagon.
29	4° BTDC	.....	750-850	.....	0.5-1.5%②	① — With oxygen sensor.
						② — With oxygen sensor disconnected.
30	6° BTDC	850①	950	3400②	.....	① — 900 RPM on Calif. models.
						② — 3200 RPM on A/T models.
31	5° BTDC	650-750	650-750	3000-4000	2.5%②	① — Trailing Timing is 20° ATDC.
32	5° BTDC	600-700	600-700	3000-4000	3.0%②	② — With AIR disconnected.
33	TDC①	725-775	725-775	3200-4000	0.1%	
34	8° BTDC	600-700	.....	3000-4000	3.0%②	

1980 Tune-Up Specifications

CAR MODEL	SPARK PLUGS		FUEL SYSTEM	VALVE CLEARANCE		DISTRIBUTOR	No.
	Type	Gap	Make & Model	Int.	Exh.	Make	
MERCEDES-BENZ	Bosch						
280 Series	W9D	.032″	Bosch CIS Fuel Inj.①	.004″C	.010″C	Bosch	35
450 Series	W9D	.032″	Bosch CIS Fuel Inj.①	Hyd.	Hyd.	Bosch	36
MG	Champion						
MGB	N9Y	.035″	Zen/Strom 175CDST	.013″H	.013″H	Lucas	37
PEUGEOT	Bosch						
505	WR7DS	.024″	Bosch CIS Fuel Inj.①	.004″C	.010″C	Ducellier	38
	Champion						
604	BN9Y	.024″	Solex 34 TBIA②	.004″C	.010″C	Bosch	39
PORSCHE	Bosch						
911SC	W5D	.032″	Bosch CIS Fuel Inj.①	.004″C	.004″C	Bosch	40
924	WR6DS	.028″	Bosch CIS Fuel Inj.①	.008″H	.018″H	Bosch	41
924 Turbo	WR7DS	.024″	Bosch CIS Fuel Inj.①	.008″H	.018″H	Bosch	42
928	WR8DS	.028″	Bosch AFC Fuel Inj.①	Hyd.	Hyd.	Bosch	43
RENAULT	Champion						
Le Car	N12Y①	.024″	Weber 32 DIR	.006″C	.008″C	Ducellier	44
SAAB	NGK						
99	BP-6ES	.026″	Bosch CIS Fuel Inj.①	.009″H	.017″H	Bosch	45
900	BP-6ES	.026″	Bosch CIS Fuel Inj.①	.009″H	.017″H	Bosch	46
900 Turbo	BP-6ES	.026″	Bosch CIS Fuel Inj.①	.009″H	.019″H	Bosch	47
SUBARU	NGK						
W/Cat. Conv.	BP-6ES	.032″	Hitachi DCJ 2-Bbl.	.010″C	.014″C	Nippondenso①	48
W/O Cat. Conv.	BP-6ES	.032″	Hitachi DCP 2-Bbl.	.010″C	.014″C	Nippondenso①	49
TOYOTA	NGK						
Celica	BPR-5EA-L	.031″	Aisan 2-Bbl.	.008″H	.012″H	Nippondenso	50
Corolla	BP-5EA-L11	.043″	Aisan 2-Bbl.	.008″H	.013″H	Nippondenso	51
Corona	BPR-5EA-L	.031″	Aisan 2-Bbl.	.008″H	.012″H	Nippondenso	52
Cressida	BPR-5EA-L	.031″	Bosch AFC Fuel Inj.①	.011″H	.014″H	Nippondenso	53
Land Cruiser	BP-5EA	.031″	Aisan 2-Bbl.	.008″H	.014″H	Nippondenso	54
Pickup	BPR-5EA-L	.031″	Aisan 2-Bbl.	.008″H	.012″H	Nippondenso	55
Supra	BPR-5EA-L	.031″	Bosch AFC Fuel Inj.①	.011″H	.014″H	Nippondenso	56
Tercel	BP-6EKA	.039″	Aisan 2-Bbl.	.008″H	.012″H	Nippondenso	57
TRIUMPH	Champion						
Spitfire	N12Y	.025″	Zen/Strom 150CD4T	.010″C	.010″C	Lucas	58
TR7 Carb.	N12Y	.025″	Zen/Strom 175CDFVX	.008″C	.018″C	Lucas	59
TR7 F.I.	N12Y	.025″	Bosch AFC Fuel Inj.①	.008″C	.018″C	Lucas	60
TR8 Carb.	N12Y	.035″	Zen/Strom 175CDSET	Hyd.	Hyd.	Lucas	61
TR8 F.I.	N12Y	.030″	Bosch AFC Fuel. Inj.①	Hyd.	Hyd.	Lucas	62
VOLKSWAGEN	Bosch						
Dasher	W7D	.028″	Bosch CIS Fuel Inj.①	.010″H	.010″H	Bosch	63
Jetta	W7D	.028″	Bosch CIS Fuel Inj.①	.010″H	.018″H	Bosch	64
Rabbit Carb.	W7D	.028″	Solex 34 PICT-5	.010″H	.018″H	Bosch	65
Rabbit F.I.	W7D	.028″	Bosch CIS Fuel Inj.①	.010″H	.018″H	Bosch	66
Pickup	W7D	.028″	Bosch CIS Fuel Inj.①	.010″H	.018″H	Bosch	67
Scirocco	W7D	.028″	Bosch CIS Fuel Inj.①	.010″H	.018″H	Bosch	68
Vanagon	W8CO	.028″	Bosch AFC Fuel Inj.①	Hyd.	Hyd.	Bosch	69
VOLVO	Bosch						
4-Cyl.	WR7DS	.028″	Bosch CIS Fuel Inj.①	.015″C	.015″C	Bosch	70
6-Cyl.	HR6DS	.028″	Bosch CIS Fuel Inj.①	.005″C	.011″C	Bosch	71

No.	IGNITION TIMING	HOT IDLE RPM		FAST IDLE RPM	EXHAUST CO READING At Idle Speed	Remarks
		Man. Trans.	Auto. Trans.			
35	10° BTDC	.....	700-800	.....	.....	① — With oxygen sensor.
36	5° BTDC	.....	600-700	.....	.....	
37	10° BTDC	750-950	.....	.....	4.5-6.5%①	① — With AIR disconnected.
38	8° BTDC	900-950	900-950	1500-1550	0.5-1.5%	① — With oxygen sensor.
39	10° BTDC	900-950	900-950	1450-1500	3.0-4.0%	② — Primary carb.; Sec. carb. is Solex 35 CEEI.
40	5° BTDC	850-950	.....	.....	0.4-0.8%④	① — With oxygen sensor.
41	TDC	950-1000	950-1000	.....	0.6-1.0%④	② — At 2000 RPM.
42	20° BTDC②	850-950	.....	.....	0.5-1.0%④	③ — At 3000 RPM.
43	23° BTDC③	700-800	700-800	.....	0.4-0.8%④	④ — With oxygen sensor disconnected.
44	3° BTDC	700-800	.....	.....	0.5-2.0%②	① — Bosch WR9DS on Calif.
						② — Not measured for Calif.
45	20° BTDC②	825-925	.....	.....	0.75-1.25%③	① — With oxygen sensor.
46	20° BTDC②	825-925	825-925	.....	0.75-1.25%③	② — At 2000 RPM.
47	20° BTDC②	825-925	825-925	.....	0.75-1.25%③	③ — With oxygen sensor disconnected.
48	8° BTDC	750-850	750-850	.....	1.0-3.0%②	① — Hitachi on 4-WD.
49	8° BTDC	850-950	850-950	.....	3.5-5.5%②	② — With AIR disconnected.
50	8° BTDC	700②	850	2400	.....	① — With oxygen sensor.
51	10° BTDC	700③	750③	2800④	.....	② — 800 RPM on 5-Spd.
52	8° BTDC	700②	850	2400	.....	③ — 850 RPM with power steering.
53	12° BTDC	.....	800	.....	.....	④ — 2600 RPM for Calif. with
54	7° BTDC	850	.....	1800	.....	power steering; 3000 RPM for
55	8° BTDC	800	800	2400	.....	Fed. without power steering.
56	12° BTDC	800	800	.....	.....	
57	5° BTDC	650	800	3600	.....	
58	2° ATDC	800	.....	.....	3.0-7.0%②	① — With oxygen sensor.
59	2° ATDC	800	800	.....	3.0-7.0%②	② — With AIR disconnected.
60	2° ATDC	800	800	.....	0.2%	
61	5° ATDC	800	800	.....	2.5-5.5%②	
62	TDC	800	800	.....	0.2%	
63	3° ATDC	880-1000	880-1000	.....	0.8-1.2%④	① — Calif. models use oxygen sensor.
64	3° ATDC	880-1000	880-1000	.....	0.8-1.2%④	② — 5° ATDC on Calif. models.
65	7.5° BTDC	850-950③	850-950	2350-2450	0.5-1.5%	③ — With idle stabilizer connected.
66	3° ATDC	880-1000	880-1000	.....	0.8-1.2%④	Set to 600-750 with stabilizer
67	3° ATDC	880-1000	880-1000	.....	0.8-1.2%④	disconnected.
68	3° ATDC	880-1000	880-1000	.....	0.8-1.2%④	④ — With oxygen sensor disconnected.
69	7.5° BTDC②	800-950	850-1000	.....	0.5.1.5%⑤	⑤ — Set Calif. models to 0.3-1.1%.
70	8° BTDC	900-1000	900-1000	.....	1.5-3.0%②	① — With oxygen sensor.
71	10° BTDC	900-1000	900-1000	.....	0.7-1.3%②	② — With oxygen sensor disconnected.

Section 1
TUNE-UP

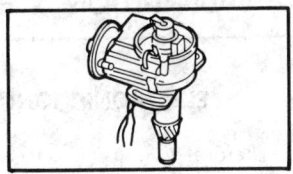

Contents

NOTE – ALSO SEE GENERAL INDEX

Tune-Up

TUNE-UP TROUBLE SHOOTING

CONDITION & POSSIBLE CAUSE	CONDITION & POSSIBLE CAUSE

SPARK PLUG DIAGNOSIS

Normal Spark Plug Condition

- Light tan or gray deposits on insulator.
- Electrode not burned or fouled.
- Gap tolerance not significantly changed.

Cold Fouling or Carbon Deposits

- Over rich air-fuel mixture, possibly from a faulty choke, clogged air cleaner, improper idle adjustment or dirty carburetor.
- Faulty ignition wires.
- Prolonged operation at idle.
- Sticking valves or worn valve guide seals.

Wet Fouling or Oil Deposits

- Worn rings and pistons.
- Excessive cylinder wear.
- Excessive valve guide clearance.
- Worn or loose bearings.

Gap Bridged

- Deposits in combustion chamber becoming fused to electrode under high heat.

Blistered Electrode or Overheating

- Engine overheating.
- Wrong type of fuel.
- Loose spark plugs.
- Over-advanced ignition timing.

Pre-ignition or Melted Electrodes

- Incorrect type of gasoline.
- Incorrect ignition timing.
- Burned valves.
- Engine overheating.
- Wrong type of spark plug, too hot.

Chipped Insulators

- Severe detonation.
- Improper gapping procedure.

Rust Colored Deposits

- Additives in unleaded fuel may create this condition. It may be misdiagnosed as water in the combustion chamber. These deposits do not affect plug performance.

ELECTRONIC IGNITION DIAGNOSIS

Before diagnosing an electronic ignition system, ensure that all wiring is connected properly between distributor, wiring connector and spark plugs. Ignition problems will show up either as: engine will not start or engine runs rough.

Engine Will Not Start

- Open circuit between distributor and bulkhead connector.
- Open circuit between bulkhead connector and ignition switch.
- Open circuit between ignition switch and starter solenoid.

Engine Runs Rough

- Fuel lines leaking or clogged.
- Initial timing incorrect.
- Centrifugal advance malfunction.
- Worn or defective spark plugs.
- Worn or defective secondary wiring.

If the above checks do not locate the problem, check the components listed below.

Component Failure

- Spark arc-over on distributor cap, rotor or coil.
- Defective pick-up coil.
- Defective ignition coil.
- Defective vacuum unit.
- Defective control module.

ELECTRONIC IGNITION DIAGNOSIS BY OSCILLOSCOPE PATTERN

Firing Voltage Lines are the Same, but Abnormally High

- Retarded ignition timing.
- Too lean of a fuel mixture.
- High resistance in coil wire.
- Corrosion in coil tower terminal.
- Corrosion in distributor coil terminal.

Firing Voltage Lines are the Same, but Abnormally Low

- Too rich of a fuel mixture.
- Breaks in coil wire causing arcing.
- Cracked coil tower causing arcing.
- Low coil output.
- Low engine compression.

Tune-Up

TUNE-UP TROUBLE SHOOTING (Cont.)

CONDITION & POSSIBLE CAUSE	CONDITION & POSSIBLE CAUSE

One or More, but Not All Firing Voltage Lines are Higher Than the Others

- Carburetor idle mixture not balanced.
- EGR valve stuck open.
- High resistance in spark plug wire.
- Cracked or broken spark plug insulator.
- Intake vacuum leak.
- Defective spark plugs.
- Corroded spark plug terminals.

One or More, but Not All Firing Voltage Lines are Lower Than the Others

- Curb idle mixture not balanced.
- Breaks in spark plug wires causing arcing.
- Cracked coil tower causing arcing.
- Low compression.
- Defective spark plugs, or spark plugs fouled.

One or More Cylinders Not Firing

- Cracked distributor cap terminals.
- Shorted spark plug wire.
- Mechanical problem in engine.
- Defective spark plugs.
- Spark plugs fouled.

GENERAL DIAGNOSIS

Hard Starting

- Binding carburetor linkage, choke linkage or choke piston.
- Restricted choke vacuum.
- Worn or dirty needle valve and seat.
- Float sticking.
- Incorrect choke adjustment.
- Defective coil.
- Improper spark plug gap.
- Incorrect ignition timing.

Detonation

- Over-advanced ignition timing.
- Defective spark plugs.
- Fuel lines clogged.
- EGR system malfunction.
- PCV system malfunction.
- Vacuum leaks.
- Loose fan belts.
- Restricted air flow.
- Vacuum advance malfunction.

Dieseling

- Binding carburetor linkage, throttle linkage, choke linkage or fast idle cam.
- Defective idle solenoid.
- Improper base idle speed.
- Incorrect ignition timing.
- Incorrect idle mixture setting.

Faulty Acceleration

- Incorrect ignition timing.
- Engine cold and choke too lean.
- Defective spark plugs.
- Defective coil.

Faulty Low Speed Operation

- Clogged idle transfer slots.
- Restricted idle air bleeds and passages.
- Clogged air cleaner.
- Defective spark plugs.
- Defective ignition cables.
- Defective distributor cap.

Faulty High Speed Operation

- Incorrect ignition timing.
- Defective distributor centrifugal advance.
- Defective distributor vacuum advance.
- Incorrect spark plugs or plug gap.
- Faulty choke operation.
- Clogged vacuum passages.
- Improper size or clogged main jet.
- Restricted air cleaner.
- Defective distributor cap, rotor or coil.
- Worn distributor shaft.

Misfire at All Speeds

- Defective spark plugs.
- Defective spark plug wires.
- Defective distributor cap, rotor or coil.
- Cracked or broken vacuum hoses.
- Vacuum leaks.
- Fuel lines clogged.

Hesitation

- Cracked or broken vacuum hoses.
- Vacuum leaks.
- Binding carburetor linkage, throttle linkage, choke linkage or fast idle cam.
- Improper float setting.
- Cracked or broken ignition wires.

TUNE-UP TROUBLE SHOOTING (Cont.)

CONDITION & POSSIBLE CAUSE

Rough Idle, Missing or Stalling

- Incorrect curb idle or fast idle speed.
- Incorrect basic timing.
- Improper idle mixture adjustment.
- Improper feedback system operation.
- Incorrect spark plug gap.
- Moisture in ignition components.
- Loose or broken ignition wires.
- Damaged distributor cap or rotor.
- Faulty ignition coil.
- Fuel filter clogged or worn.
- Damaged idle mixture screw.
- Improper fast idle cam adjustment.
- Improper EGR valve operation.
- Faulty PCV valve air flow.
- Choke binding, or improper choke setting.
- Vacuum leak.
- Improper float bowl fuel level.
- Clogged air bleed or idle passages.
- Clogged or worn air cleaner.
- Faulty choke vacuum diaphragm.
- Exhaust manifold heat valve inoperative.
- Improper distributor spark advance.
- Leaking valves or valve components.
- Improper carburetor mounting.
- Excessive play in distributor shaft.
- Loose or corroded wiring connections.

Engine Surges

- Improper PCV valve air flow.
- Vacuum leaks.
- Clogged main jets.
- Clogged air bleeds.
- EGR valve malfunction.
- Restricted air cleaner.
- Cracked or broken vacuum hoses.
- Cracked or broken ignition wires.
- Vacuum advance malfunction.
- Defective or fouled spark plugs.

CONDITION & POSSIBLE CAUSE

Ping or Spark Knock

- Incorrect ignition timing.
- Distributor centrifugal or vacuum advance malfunction.
- Carburetor setting too lean.
- Vacuum leak.
- EGR valve malfunction.

Poor Gasoline Mileage

- Cracked or broken vacuum hoses.
- Vacuum leaks.
- Defective ignition wires.
- Incorrect choke setting.
- Defective vacuum advance.
- Defective spark plugs.
- Binding carburetor power piston.
- Dirt in carburetor jets.
- Incorrect float adjustment.
- Defective power valves.

Power Not Up to Normal

- Incorrect ignition timing.
- Defective distributor cap, rotor, coil or ignition wires.
- Incorrect spark plug gap.
- Incorrect idle speeds.
- Improper float level.
- Leaking needle valve and seat.
- Choke sticking.

Engine Stalls

- Incorrect idle speed.
- Improper float level.
- Leaking needle valve and seat.
- Sticking choke.
- Carburetor mounting gasket air leaks.
- Vacuum leaks.
- Defective ignition wires, distributor cap or rotor.
- Loose condensor.
- Shorted distributor wires.
- Defective spark plugs.
- Clogged fuel filter.

TUNE-UP

4000

ENGINE IDENTIFICATION

Engine number is stamped on left side of engine block near distributor.

Application	Code
Federal	YG
Calif.	YK

COMPRESSION PRESSURE

Check compression with engine warm, all spark plugs removed, and throttle wide open. Maximum variation permitted between cylinders is 28 psi (2.0 kg/cm²).

NOTE — *On models with electronic ignition, connect coil high tension wire to ground before cranking engine for compression test.*

Application	Standard Pressure psi (kg/cm²)	Minimum Pressure psi (kg/cm²)
All Models	128-185 (9-13)	100 (7)

VALVE CLEARANCE

1) Adjust valves with engine at normal operating temperature. Clearance adjustments are to be checked and made according to firing order sequence (1-3-4-2). Rotate crankshaft until cam lobes for No. 1 cylinder valves point upward, then measure valve clearances of No. 1 cylinder.

NOTE — *When adjusting valves, rotate engine CLOCKWISE only, otherwise timing belt may slip.*

2) If adjustment is necessary, use special tools 10-208 (disc removal tool) and VW546 (tappet depressing tool) to remove and install adjusting discs. Rotate camshaft until cam lobes no longer rest on adjusting discs of cylinder to be adjusted. Turn tappet until notches are at 90° to camshaft. Insert tool VW546 and depress tappet. Using tool 10-208, grasp tappet disc and rotate it out from under camshaft.

3) Thickness is stamped on bottom side of disc. Using clearance measurement, determine thickness of adjusting disc necessary to bring valve clearances within specifications. Discs are available in .0019" (.05 mm) increments from .1181" (3.0 mm) to .1673" (4.25 mm). Reverse removal procedure to install proper disc. Repeat procedure as required for remaining valves.

Valve Clearance

Application	Specification
Intake	①.008-.012" (.2-.3 mm)
Exhaust	①.016-.020" (.4-.5 mm)

① — Adjust with engine warm.

VALVE ARRANGEMENT

E-I-E-I-I-E-I-E (front to rear).

SPARK PLUGS

Application	Gap In. (mm)	Torque Ft. Lbs. (mkg)
All Models	.028 (.7)	22 (3)

Spark Plug Type

Application	Bosch	Champion
Federal	W7D	N8Y
Calif.	WR7DS	N8GY

HIGH TENSION WIRE RESISTANCE

Carefully remove ends of wire from spark plug and distributor. Using an ohmmeter, check resistance of wire while gently twisting wire. If resistance is not to specification, or fluctuates from infinity to any value, replace wire.

Resistance (Ohms) Per Wire

Application	Resistance
Ignition Wire	4800-7400
Coil Wire	1600-2400

DISTRIBUTOR

California models are equipped with electronic ignition systems that use a Hall generator and an idle stabilizer unit. Federal models are equipped with conventional breaker point ignition systems.

Point Gap	.016" (.4 mm)
Cam Angle	44-50°
Condenser Capacity	.22 mfd.

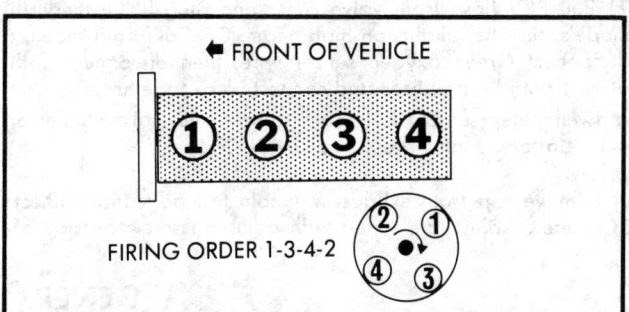

Fig. 1 *Firing Order and Distributor Rotation*

IGNITION TIMING

CAUTION — *Do not connect any test instruments to terminal 15 (+) of ignition coil on vehicles with electronic ignition. Use fuse 10 for connection.*

1) Warm engine to normal operating temperature. On Federal models, turn headlight high beams on. On California models,

1980 Audi 4 Tune-Up

TUNE-UP (Cont.)

stop engine and disconnect oxygen sensor, then disconnect both plugs from idle stabilizer unit and connect them together.

2) On all models, pull PCV hose from valve cover, adjust idle speed, then check ignition timing. Adjust by turning distributor. All vacuum hoses must remain connected.

NOTE — *Electric cooling fan must not run while adjustments are made.*

Ignition Timing Specifications

Application	RPM	Timing
Federal	850-1000	①3° ATDC
Calif.	920-960	①3° ATDC

① — With vacuum hoses connected.

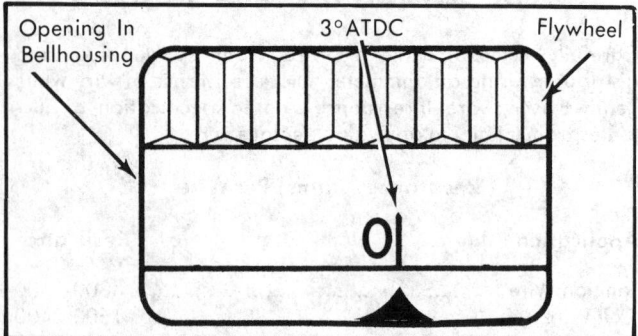

Fig. 2   Ignition Timing Mark Location

IDLE SPEED & MIXTURE

1) With engine at normal operating temperature, check and adjust ignition timing and valve clearances. Engine fan must come on at least once before adjustment, but must not be on during adjustment.

2) Pull PCV hose from valve cover and plug it. On Federal models, turn headlights on high beam. On California models, disconnect Green oxygen sensor wire, then disconnect both plugs from idle stabilizer and connect plugs together. Connect a dwell meter (set to 4-Cyl. scale) to frequency valve connector near battery. Meter should read 40-50°.

3) Remove cap from exhaust manifold test port and connect CO meter. Adjust idle speed with adjusting screw on side of

throttle valve housing. Remove mixture plug from mixture control unit and adjust CO level using Allen wrench tool (P377).

CAUTION — *Do not press down on tool while adjusting CO, and do not accelerate engine with tool in place. Remove tool after each adjustment and accelerate engine briefly before checking CO reading. Always adjust CO level from lean to rich.*

4) On California models, reconnect oxygen sensor wire. Dwell meter reading should begin to vary and CO level should be within 0.4-1.2%. On all models, stop engine and remove test equipment. Reconnect all wiring and hoses.

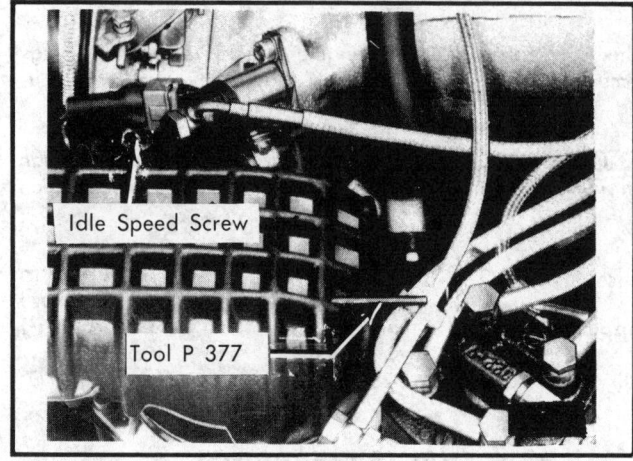

Fig. 3   Adjusting Idle Speed and Mixture

Idle Speed & CO Level

Application	Idle RPM	CO%
Federal	850-1000	0.5-0.9
Calif.	920-960	0.6-1.0

FUEL PUMP PRESSURE & VOLUME

Pressure	64-74 psi (4.5-5.2 kg/cm²)
Volume	1qt. in 40 sec.

EMISSION CONTROL SYSTEMS

See Mitchell Manuals' Emission Control Manual.

GENERAL SERVICING

IGNITION

DISTRIBUTOR

California models are equipped with Bosch breakerless electronic ignition with idle stabilizer unit. Federal models are equipped with Bosch single point distributors.

Other Data & Specifications — *See Tune-Up and Bosch Ignition Systems in ELECTRICAL Section.*

IGNITION COIL

Resistance Specifications

Application	Primary	Secondary
Federal	1.7-2.1	7000-12,000
Calif.	.52-.76	2400-3500

GENERAL SERVICING (Cont.)

FUEL SYSTEMS

FUEL INJECTION

All models are equipped with Bosch Continuous Injection System (CIS). California models use an oxygen sensor system.

Other Data & Specifications — *See Tune-Up and Bosch CIS Fuel Injection in FUEL SYSTEMS Section.*

ELECTRICAL

BATTERY

Application	Amp. Hr. Capacity
Without A/C	45
With A/C	54

Battery Location — Right side of engine compartment.

STARTER

All models are equipped with Bosch Starters.

Other Data & Specifications — *See Bosch Starters in ELECTRICAL Section.*

ALTERNATOR

Application	Rated Amp. Output
Without A/C	55
With A/C	65

Other Data & Specifications — *See Bosch and Motorola Alternators and Regulators in ELECTRICAL Section.*

ALTERNATOR REGULATOR

Motorola and Bosch — Non-adjustable, integral with alternator.

Operating Voltage .... 12.5-14.5 Volts

Other Data & Specifications — *See Bosch and Motorola Alternators and Regulators in ELECTRICAL Section.*

BELT ADJUSTMENT

When depressed with firm thumb pressure, deflection should be 3/8 -9/16" (10-15 mm) for all belts.

FILTERS

Filter	Service Interval (Miles)
Oil Filter	Replace every 15,000
Air Filter	Replace every 30,000
Fuel Filter	Replace every 15,000

CAPACITIES

Application	Quantity
Crankcase (Includes Filter)	3.7 qts.
Cooling System	7.4 qts.
Man. Transaxle (SAE 80W-90)	1.8 qts.
Fuel Tank	15.9 gals.

TUNE-UP

4000 Automatic
5000
5000 Turbo

ENGINE IDENTIFICATION

Engine number is stamped on left side of block near No. 3 cylinder.

Engine Code Numbers

Application	Code
4000 Automatic	WE
5000	
Federal	WD
Calif.	WE
5000 Turbo	WK

COMPRESSION PRESSURE

Check compression pressure with engine at normal operating temperature, all plugs removed, and throttle wide open. Maximum variation permitted between cylinders is 42 psi (3 kg/cm²) on standard engines and 28 psi (2 kg/cm²) on Turbo models.

Application	Standard Pressure psi (kg/cm²)	Minimum Pressure psi (kg/cm²)
All Except Turbo	128-185 (9-13)	100 (7)
Turbo	100-128 (7-9)	

VALVE CLEARANCE

1) Adjust valves with engine at normal operating temperature. Remove accelerator linkage and cylinder head cover. Clearance adjustments are to be checked and made according to firing order sequence (1-2-4-5-3). Rotate crankshaft until cam lobes for No. 1 cylinder valves point upward; then measure valve clearances of No. 1 cylinder.

NOTE — *When adjusting valves, turn engine CLOCKWISE only, or timing belt may slip.*

2) If adjustment is necessary, use special tools US 4476 (disc removal tool) and 2078 (tappet depressing tool) to remove and install adjusting discs. Turn tappet until notches are at 90° to camshaft. Insert tool 2078 and depress tappet. Using tool US 4476, grasp tappet disc and rotate it out from under camshaft.

3) Thickness is stamped on bottom side of disc. Using clearance measurement, determine thickness of adjusting disc necessary to bring valve clearance within specifications. Discs are available in .0019" (.05 mm) increments from .1181-.1673" (3.0-4.25 mm). Repeat procedure as required for remaining valves.

Valve Clearance Specifications①

Application	Clearance
All Models	
Intake	.008-.012" (.2-.3 mm)
Exhaust	.016-.020" (.4-.5 mm)

① — With engine hot.

VALVE ARRANGEMENT

E-I-E-I-I-E-I-E-I-E (front to rear)

SPARK PLUGS

Application	Gap In. (mm)	Torque Ft. Lbs. (mkg)
All Models	.028 (.7)	22 (3)

Spark Plug Type

Application	Bosch	Champion
4000 Automatic & 5000		
Federal	W7D	N8Y
Calif.	WR7DS	N8GY
5000 Turbo	WR7DS	N8GY

HIGH TENSION WIRE RESISTANCE

Carefully remove ends of wire from spark plug and distributor. Using an ohmmeter, check resistance of wire while gently twisting wire. If resistance is not to specification, or fluctuates from infinity to any value, replace wire.

NOTE — *Wire resistance cannot be measured if the wires are marked with this symbol:* —▶◀—

Resistance (Ohms) Per Wire

Application	Resistance
Ignition Wire	4800-7400
Coil Wire	1600-2400

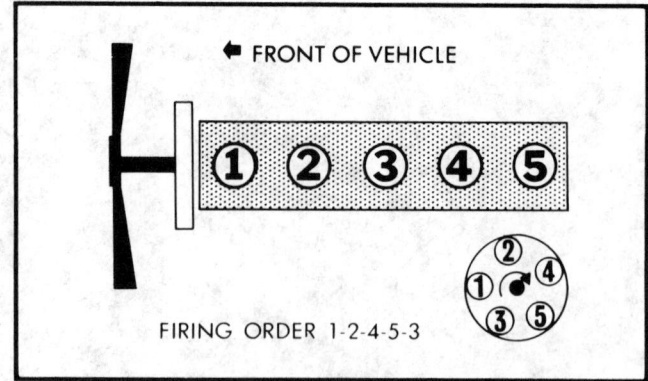

Fig. 1 Firing Order and Distributor Rotation

DISTRIBUTOR

All models are equipped with electronic, breakerless ignition systems. All California models and Federal Turbo models have an idle stabilizer unit which adjusts ignition timing to maintain a constant idle speed.

TUNE-UP (Cont.)

IGNITION TIMING

Turbo — Disconnect and plug both hoses at distributor. With engine at 3000 RPM, adjust timing by turning distributor.

All Except Turbo — Disconnect 2 plugs at idle stabilizer unit (if equipped) and connect them together. Leave vacuum hoses connected at distributor. With engine idling, adjust ignition timing by turning distributor. Reconnect idle stabilizer unit.

Ignition Timing Specifications

Application	RPM	Timing
4000 Automatic & 5000		
Federal	800-1000	3° ATDC
Calif.	880-1000	3° ATDC
5000 Turbo	3000	21° BTDC

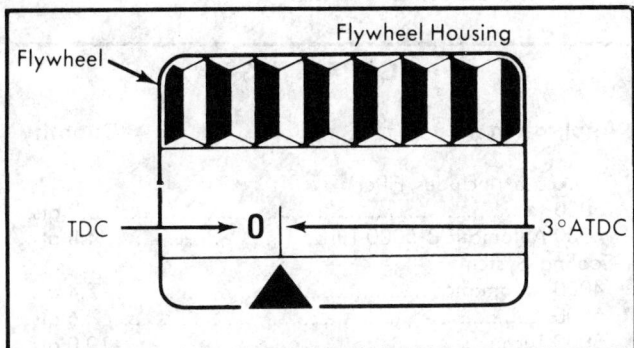

Fig. 2   Ignition Timing Mark Location

IDLE SPEED & MIXTURE

WITHOUT OXYGEN SENSOR

1) With engine at normal operating temperature, check and make sure that ignition timing, valve clearance, spark plug gap and compression pressures are within specifications. Turn headlights on high beam and, if equipped, turn air conditioning off. Disconnect and plug PCV valve hose, then connect CO meter at test port (if equipped) or tailpipe.

NOTE — *Engine cooling fan must not run while adjustments are being made.*

2) Adjust idle speed to specifications by means of the idle control screw at the throttle plate housing.

3) To adjust CO level, remove plug from mixture control unit between fuel distributor and venturi. Insert suitable adjusting tool (P 377) and turn clockwise to raise CO% or counterclockwise to decrease CO% until the specified CO level is obtained.

NOTE — *Engine will stall if pressure is exerted on adjusting tool. Use very small adjustments or CO level will be changed greatly.*

4) Remove adjusting wrench and accelerate engine briefly. Wait until CO meter has stabilized for idle speed reading. Check idle speed and CO level and adjust if necessary.

WITH OXYGEN SENSOR

1) With engine at normal operating temperature, turn all electrical accessories off. With engine stopped, disconnect both plugs from idle stabilizer unit and connect them together. Disconnect and plug PCV valve hose.

2) Check and adjust ignition timing as necessary. Adjust idle speed to specified RPM using adjusting screw on side of throttle valve housing.

NOTE — *Engine cooling fan must not run while adjustments are being made.*

3) Remove cap from CO test receptacle on exhaust manifold and connect CO tester hose directly to test receptacle. Connect a dwell meter to frequency valve electrical connector. Zero dwell meter and set it to the 4-cylinder scale.

4) Disconnect oxygen sensor wire at connector and check dwell meter reading. Meter reading must be constant between 40-50°.

5) Adjust CO level to specifications using adjusting tool (P377). Turn adjusting tool clockwise to increase CO and counterclockwise to decrease CO.

CAUTION — *Do not press down on adjusting tool when adjusting CO level. Also, do not accelerate engine with tool in place. Remove tool after each adjustment and accelerate engine briefly before reading CO level. Always adjust CO level from lean to rich.*

6) Reconnect oxygen sensor wire and check dwell meter reading. Meter reading should now pulsate. Reconnect all hoses and wiring at idle stabilizer, then recheck idle speed.

Idle Speed & CO Level

Application	Idle RPM	CO%
4000 Automatic & 5000		
Federal	800-1000	0.4-1.2
Calif.	880-1000	0.4-1.2
5000 Turbo	880-1000	0.4-1.2

FUEL PUMP PRESSURE & VOLUME

System Pressure
4000 Automatic & 5000 .... 65-75 psi (4.5-5.2 kg/cm)
5000 Turbo .... 72-82 psi (4.9-5.6 kg/cm²)
Volume .... Approx. 1 quart in 40 sec.

EMISSION CONTROL SYSTEMS

See Mitchell Manuals' Emission Control Manual.

1980 Audi 5 Tune-Up

GENERAL SERVICING

IGNITION

DISTRIBUTOR

All models are equipped with electronic ignition. California 4000 and 5000 models, and all Turbo models use an idle stabilizer system in addition to the Hall generator ignition system.

Other Data & Specifications — *See Tune-Up and Bosch Ignition Systems in ELECTRICAL Section.*

IGNITION COIL

Coil Resistance (Ohms@68°F)

Application	Primary (Ohms)	Secondary (Ohms)
4000 Automatic & 5000		
Federal	1.7-2.1	7000-12,000
Calif.	.52-.76	2400-3500
5000 Turbo	.52-.76	2400-3500

FUEL SYSTEMS

FUEL INJECTION

All models are equipped with Bosch CIS Continuous Injection System. All California models and Federal Turbo models are equipped with an oxygen sensor feedback system.

Other Data & Specifications — *See Tune-Up and Bosch CIS or CIS Lambda Fuel Injection in FUEL SYSTEMS Section.*

ELECTRICAL

BATTERY

Application	Amp. Hr. Capacity
All Models	63

Battery Location — On models with factory-installed air conditioning, the battery is located under the left side of the rear seat. On all other models, the battery is located in the engine compartment.

STARTER

All models are equipped with Bosch Starters.

Other Data & Specifications — *See Bosch Starters in ELECTRICAL Section.*

ALTERNATOR

Application	Rated Amp. Output
All Except Turbo	75
Turbo	90

Other Data & Specifications — *See Bosch Alternators & Regulators in ELECTRICAL Section.*

ALTERNATOR REGULATOR

Bosch — Non-adjustable, integral with alternator.

Operating Voltage	12.5-14.5 Volts

Other Data & Specifications — *See Bosch Alternators & Regulators in ELECTRICAL Section*

CAPACITIES

Application	Quantity
Crankcase (Includes Filter)	
5000	5.3 qts.
4000 Automatic & 5000 Turbo	4.8 qts.
Cooling System	
4000 Automatic	7.4 qts.
5000	8.6 qts.
5000 Turbo	10.0 qts.
Man. Transaxle (SAE80W-90)	2.8 qts.
Auto. Trans. (Dexron)	3.2 qts.
Auto. Trans. Final Drive (SAE 90)	1.1 qts.
Fuel Tank	
4000 Automatic	15.9 gals.
5000 & 5000 Turbo	19.8 gals.

BELT ADJUSTMENT

All Models — With a 20 lbs. (9.1 kg) pressure, belt should be able to be depressed 3/8-9/16" (10-15 mm).

FILTERS

Filter	Service Interval (Miles)
Oil Filter①	15,000
Air Filter	30,000
Fuel Filter	15,000

① — Turbo models are equipped with 2 oil filters. Both should be changed at 15,000 mile intervals.

TUNE-UP

5000 Diesel

ENGINE IDENTIFICATION

Engine number is stamped into left side of block near number 3 cylinder.

Engine Code Number

Application	Code
All Models	CN

COMPRESSION PRESSURE

Remove electrical wire from fuel shut-off solenoid on injection pump. Remove injector pipes, injectors and heat shields. Insert old heat shield into head, then adapter (VW 1323/2) and compression tester. Check compression after cranking engine through at least 6 strokes.

Compression Pressure

Application	Pressure psi (kg/cm^2)
Normal (New Engine)	485 (34)
Minimum	400 (28)
Maximum Variation	70 (5)

VALVE CLEARANCE

1) Turn engine clockwise until camshaft lobes for valves to be checked point upwards. Check valve clearance. If not within tolerance, adjusting disc must be changed.

2) Turn crankshaft ¼ turn after TDC (so valves will not hit piston top). Depress cam followers with tool (VW 2078), then remove disc with pliers (VW 4476). Calculate thickness of disc needed, coat with oil and install with marks down.

NOTE — *Discs are available in thicknesses from .120" (3.00 mm) to .167" (4.25 mm) in increments of .002" (0.05 mm).*

3) Check valve clearance on remaining cylinders, proceeding in firing order. Be sure to check valve clearance at TDC, then turn ¼ turn after TDC before depressing valves.

Valve Clearance Specifications

Application	Clearance In. (mm)
Checking	
Cold	
Intake	.006-.010 (.15-.25)
Exhaust	.014-.018 (.35-.45)
Warm	
Intake	.008-.012 (.20-.30)
Exhaust	.016-.020 (.40-.50)
Adjustment	
Cold	
Intake	.008 (.20)
Exhaust	.016 (.40)
Warm	
Intake	.010 (.25)
Exhaust	.018 (.45)

VALVE ARRANGEMENT

E-I-E-I-I-E-I-E-I-E (Front-to-rear)

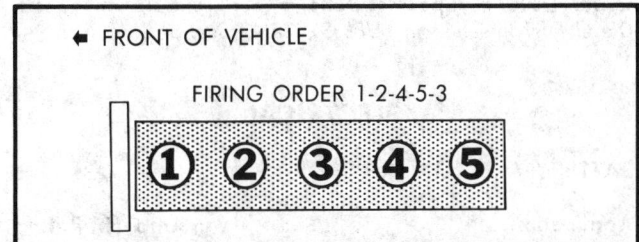

Fig. 1   Firing Order Illustration

GLOW PLUGS

Glow Plug Type

Application	Bosch
All Models	N 019 100 6

IDLE SPEED ADJUSTMENT

1) With engine at normal operating temperature, turn idle speed control knob on dash panel counterclockwise to stop.

2) Connect diesel tachometer (VW 1367) according to instructions from manufacturer. Adjust speed to specifications with idle adjusting screw. Tighten lock nut. *See Fig. 2.*

3) Open throttle fully and quickly adjust maximum speed to specifications using maximum RPM screw. Tighten lock nut.

Fig. 2   Adjusting Idle Speed and Maximum Speed

Idle Speed Specifications

Application	Idle RPM	Maximum RPM
All Models	720-880	5350-5450

GENERAL SERVICING

FUEL INJECTION

All models use Bosch mechanical diesel fuel injection.

Other Data & Specifications — *See Tune-Up and Bosch Diesel Fuel Injection in FUEL SYSTEMS Section.*

ELECTRICAL

BATTERY

Application	Amp. Hr. Rating
All Models	88

STARTER

All models are equipped with Bosch starters.

Other Data & Specifications — *See Bosch Starters in ELECTRICAL Section.*

ALTERNATOR

All models are equipped with Bosch alternators.

Application	Rated Amp. Output
All Models	75

Other Data & Specifications — *See Bosch Alternators & Regulators in ELECTRICAL Section.*

ALTERNATOR REGULATOR

All models are equipped with Bosch non-adjustable voltage regulators with operating voltage of 13.9-14.8 volts.

Other Data & Specifications — *See Bosch Alternators & Regulators in ELECTRICAL Section.*

FILTERS

Filter	Service Interval (Miles)
Oil Filter	Replace every 15,000
Fuel Filter	Drain every 7500
Air Filter	Replace every 30,000

BELT ADJUSTMENT

Adjust belts for deflection of $\frac{3}{16}$-$\frac{3}{8}$" (5-10 mm) when depressed firmly, halfway between pulleys.

CAPACITIES

Application	Quantity
Crankcase (Includes Filter)	5.3 qts.
Cooling System	9.9 qts.
Man. Transaxle (SAE 80)	2.9 qts.
Auto. Trans. (Dexron)	3.2 qts.
Auto. Trans. Final Drive (SAE 90)	1.1 qts.
Fuel Tank	19.8 gals.

TUNE-UP

320i

ENGINE IDENTIFICATION

Engine number is stamped into engine block on left side above starter. Engine can also be identified by first 4 numbers in chassis code, located on sill above right front wheel.

Application	Code
Man. Trans.	1739
Auto. Trans.	1749

COMPRESSION PRESSURE

With battery fully charged, engine at normal operating temperature, throttle fully open and engine at cranking speed, compression pressure should be as follows:

Compression Pressure

Condition	Pressure
Good	Above 149 psi (10.5 kg/cm²)
Normal	135-149 psi (9.5-10.5 kg/cm²)
Poor	Below 128 psi (9.0 kg/cm²)

VALVE CLEARANCE

Adjust valves with engine cold. Remove valve cover, loosen nut on rocker arm, and use a piece of wire to adjust eccentric cam. Adjust valves in firing order sequence at TDC of compression stroke.

Adjust Cylinder at Top Dead Center	When Valves Of Cylinder Overlap
No. 1	No. 4
No. 3	No. 2
No. 4	No. 1
No. 2	No. 3

Valve Clearance Specifications

Application	Clearance In. (mm)
Intake & Exhaust (Cold)	.006-.008 (.15-.20)

VALVE ARRANGEMENT

Left Side — All Intake.
Right Side — All Exhaust.

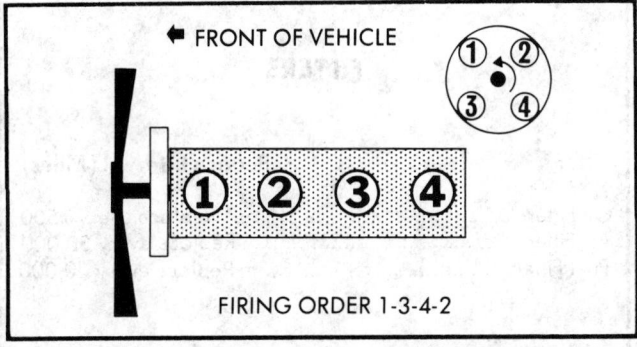

Fig. 1 Firing Order and Distributor Rotation

SPARK PLUGS

Application	Gap In. (mm)	Torque Ft. Lbs. (mkg)
All Models	.024 (.6)	18 (2.5)

Spark Plug Type

Application	Bosch No.
All Models	WR9DS

HIGH TENSION WIRE RESISTANCE

Carefully remove ends of wire from spark plug and distributor. Using an ohmmeter, check resistance of wire while gently twisting wire. If resistance is not to specification, or fluctuates from infinity to any value, replace wire.

Resistance (Ohms) Per Wire

Application	Resistance
All Models	25,000-30,000

DISTRIBUTOR

All models are equipped with Bosch transistorized electronic ignition. No adjustments are necessary.

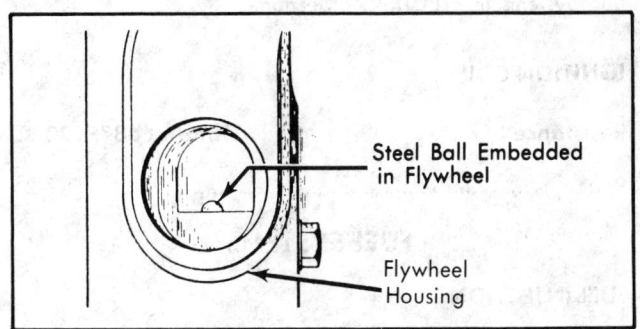

Fig. 2 Ignition Timing Mark Location

IGNITION TIMING

With engine at normal operating temperature, connect a timing light and tachometer to vehicle. Disconnect and plug distributor vacuum line. Start engine and adjust speed to specifications shown in following table. To adjust ignition timing, rotate distributor until center of ball embedded in flywheel is visible at edge of inspection hole.

Ignition Timing Specifications

Application	RPM	Dynamic Timing
All Models	2200	25° BTDC

TUNE-UP (Cont.)

IDLE SPEED & MIXTURE

1) Connect tachometer to engine. Remove caps at exhaust manifold test points and connect CO meter. Warm engine to normal operating temperature and check ignition timing and idle speed. Adjust idle by turning idle air screw on throttle housing.

2) Measure CO level. Disconnect oxygen sensor (plug below distributor on fender panel) and note CO reading. If level changes, adjustment is necessary.

NOTE — *Do not accelerate engine while adjusting CO%.*

3) Adjust mixture with Allen wrench through opening in fuel distributor (remove plug). After adjustment, reconnect oxygen sensor and ensure CO level does not change. Repeat procedure until both mixture and idle speed are correct.

Idle Speed & CO Level

Application	Idle RPM	CO%
Man. Trans.	800-900	①0.2-1.2
Auto. Trans.	900-1000	①0.2-1.2

① — Oxygen sensor disconnected.

FUEL PUMP PRESSURE

Application	psi (kg/cm²)
All Models	64-74 (4.5-5.2)

EMISSION CONTROL SYSTEMS

See Mitchell Manuals' Emission Control Manual.

GENERAL SERVICING

IGNITION

DISTRIBUTOR

All models are equipped with Bosch electronic ignition systems.

Other Data & Specifications — *See Tune-Up and Bosch Ignition Systems in ELECTRICAL Section.*

IGNITION COIL

Resistance	Ohms at 68°F (20°C)
Primary	1.7-2.1

FUEL SYSTEMS

FUEL INJECTION

All models are equipped with Bosch Lambda CIS fuel injection with oxygen sensor.

Other Data & Specifications — *See Tune-Up and Bosch Lambda CIS Fuel Injection in FUEL SYSTEMS Section.*

ELECTRICAL

BATTERY

Application	Amp. Hr. Rating
All Models	55

Battery Location — In engine compartment.

STARTER

All models are equipped with Bosch Starters.

Other Data & Specifications — *See Bosch Starters in ELECTRICAL Section.*

ALTERNATOR

Application	Rated Amp. Output
All Models	55

Other Data & Specifications — *See Bosch Alternators & Regulators in ELECTRICAL Section.*

ALTERNATOR REGULATOR

All models are equipped with Bosch Alternator Regulators with an operating voltage of 13.9-14.2 volts at 68°F (20°C).

Other Data & Specifications — *See Bosch Alternators & Regulators in ELECTRICAL Section.*

FILTERS

Filter	Service Interval (Miles)
Oil Filter	Replace every 7500
Air Filter	Replace every 30,000
Fuel Filter	Replace every 30,000

GENERAL SERVICING (Cont.)

BELT ADJUSTMENT

Application	① Deflection
Alternator Belt	.2-.4" (5-10 mm)
Air Conditioning Belt	.5" (12 mm)

① — Measured with moderate hand pressure applied midway between pulleys on longest belt run.

CAPACITIES

Application	Quantity
Crankcase (Includes Filter)	4.3 qts.
Cooling System (Includes Heater)	7.4 qts.
Man. Trans. (SAE 80)	3.0 pts.
Auto. Trans. (Dexron)	2.1 qts.
Rear Axle (SAE 90)	2.0 pts.
Fuel Tank	15.9 gals.

TUNE-UP

528i
633CSi
733i

ENGINE IDENTIFICATION

All engines have a serial number stamped on block on left side above starter motor. Engines can also be identified by first 4 numbers in chassis code, stamped on sill above right front wheel on 528i, and on firewall on 633CSi and 733i.

Engine Code

Application	Code
528i	
Man. Trans.	3995
Auto. Trans.	3997
633CSi	
Man. Trans.	5235
Auto. Trans.	5245
733i	
Man. Trans.	6633
Auto. Trans.	6643

COMPRESSION PRESSURE

With battery fully charged, engine at normal operating temperature, throttle fully open and engine at cranking speed, compression pressure should be as follows:

NOTE — *Deactivate fuel injection system by pulling off connection "1" at the coil prior to compression test.*

Compression Pressure

Application	Pressure
528i	
Good	Above 156 psi (11 kg/cm²)
Normal	142-156 psi (10-11 kgcm²)
Poor	Below 142 psi (10 kg/cm²)
633CSi & 733i	
Good	Above 142 psi (10 kg/cm²)
Normal	121-142 psi (8.5-10 kg/cm²)
Poor	Below 121 (8 kg/cm²)

VALVE CLEARANCE

With engine cold, loosen nut on rocker arm and adjust position of eccentric cam to obtain proper clearance. Adjust valves in firing order sequence at TDC of compression stroke. Use feeler gauge to measure clearance between rocker arm eccentric and valve stem.

Adjust Cylinder at Top Dead Center	When Valves Of Cylinder Overlap
No. 1	No. 6
No. 5	No. 2
No. 3	No. 4
No. 6	No. 1
No. 2	No. 5
No. 4	No. 3

Valve Clearance Specifications

Application	Clearance In. (mm)
All Models	.010-.012 (.25-.30)

VALVE ARRANGEMENT

Left Side — All Intake.
Right Side — All Exhaust.

SPARK PLUGS

Application	Gap In. (mm)	Torque Ft. Lbs. (mkg)
All Models	.024 (.6)	18 (2.5)

Spark Plug Type

Application	Bosch No.
All Models	WR9DS

HIGH TENSION WIRE RESISTANCE

Carefully remove ends of wire from spark plug and distributor. Using an ohmmeter, check resistance of wire while gently twisting wire. If resistance is not to specification, or fluctuates from infinity to any value, replace wire.

Resistance (Ohms) Per Wire

Application	Resistance
All Models	25,000-30,000

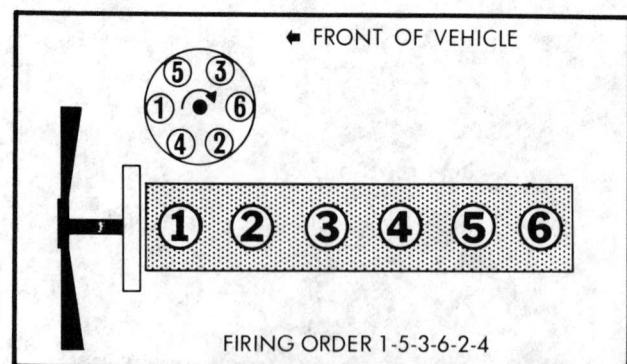

Fig. 1   Firing Order and Distributor Rotation (BMW 528i, 633CSi & 733i)

DISTRIBUTOR

All models use a breakerless, transistorized ignition system.

TUNE-UP (Cont.)

IGNITION TIMING

1) Check and adjust timing with engine at normal operating temperature and distributor vacuum hoses disconnected. Connect timing light, start engine and increase engine speed to specified timing RPM. Steel ball embedded in flywheel (long pin on Auto. Trans. models) should line up with pointer attached to hole in flywheel housing.

2) Loosen distributor clamp, turn distributor until proper timing is achieved and tighten clamp. Connect distributor vacuum hoses and set idle speed to specified RPM.

Ignition Timing Specifications

Application	RPM	Dynamic Timing
528i	2100	22° BTDC
633CSi & 733i	1650	22° BTDC

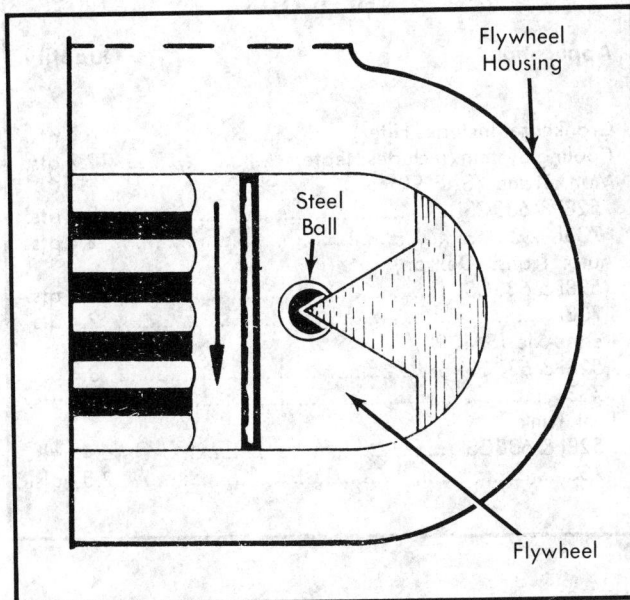

Fig. 2 Ignition Timing Mark In Window of Flywheel Housing

IDLE SPEED & MIXTURE

NOTE — *The following adjustments must be performed with the air filter in good condition, ignition timing and valve clearance adjusted to specifications and engine at normal operating temperature.*

1) Disconnect charcoal canister-to-throttle housing hose at throttle housing, but do not plug port. Connect a tachometer to engine.

2) Connect a CO meter to test points in exhaust manifold. Set idle speed by turning idle adjusting screw (below throttle switch). Read and record CO level. Disconnect oxygen sensor wire in right rear corner of engine compartment. CO reading should not change.

3) If CO reading changes with sensor disconnected, level must be adjusted. Remove plug under left rear corner of air flow meter and adjust with short screwdriver.

4) Check CO readings and adjust until values are within specifications and do not change when sensor is disconnected or connected. Remove test equipment, replace manifold plugs, and connect hose to throttle housing.

Idle Speed & CO Level

Application	Idle RPM	CO%
All Models	850-950	①0.2-0.8

① — With oxygen sensor disconnected.

FUEL PUMP PRESSURE & VOLUME

Pressure	33.4-39.2 psi (2.3-2.7 kg/cm²)
Volume	1.9 pints in 30 seconds

EMISSION CONTROL SYSTEMS

See Mitchell Manuals' Emission Control Manual.

GENERAL SERVICING

IGNITION

DISTRIBUTOR

All models use a Bosch breakerless, transistorized ignition system.

Other Data & Specifications — *See Tune-Up and Bosch Ignition Systems in ELECTRICAL Section.*

IGNITION COIL

Coil Resistance (Ohms@68° F)

Application	Primary	Secondary
All Models	0.4	

FUEL SYSTEMS

FUEL INJECTION

All models are equipped with Bosch AFC electronic fuel injection with oxygen sensor.

Other Data & Specifications — *See Tune-Up & Bosch AFC Fuel Injection in FUEL SYSTEMS Section.*

ELECTRICAL

BATTERY

Application	Amp. Hr. Rating
All Models	66

1980 BMW 6 Tune-Up

GENERAL SERVICING (Cont.)

Battery Location — All models have battery in front left area of engine compartment.

STARTER

All models are equipped with Bosch Starters.

Other Data & Specifications — *See Bosch Starters in ELECTRICAL Section.*

ALTERNATOR

Application	Rated Amp. Output
528i & 733i	65
633CSi	55

Other Data & Specifications — *See Bosch Alternators & Regulators in ELECTRICAL Section.*

ALTERNATOR REGULATOR

All models are equipped with Bosch Alternator Regulators with an operating voltage of 13.5-14.2 volts at 68°F (20°C).

Other Data & Specifications — *See Bosch Alternators & Regulators in ELECTRICAL Section.*

FILTERS

Filter	Service Interval (Miles)
Oil Filter	Replace every 7500
Air Filter	Replace every 30,000
Fuel Filter	Replace every 30,000

BELT ADJUSTMENT

Application	①Deflection
Air Conditioning Belt	.5" (12 mm)
All Others	.2-.4" (5-10 mm)

① — When depressed with firm hand pressure midway between pulleys.

CAPACITIES

Application	Quantity
Crankcase (Includes Filter)	6.1 qts.
Cooling System (Includes Heater)	12.7 qts.
Man. Trans. (SAE 90)	
528i & 633CSi	3.4 pts.
733i	2.4 pts.
Auto. Trans. (Dexron)	
528i & 633CSi	2.1 qts.
733i	2.4 qts.
Rear Axle (SAE 90)	
528i & 633CSi	3.4 pts.
733i	4.0 pts.
Fuel Tank	
528i & 633CSi	16.4 gals.
733i	22.5 gals.

1980 Chrysler Corp. Imports Tune-Up 1-19

T U N E — U P

TUNE-UP

Arrow
Arrow Pickup
Challenger
Champ
Colt
D50 Pickup
Sapporo

ENGINE IDENTIFICATION

Engine model and serial numbers are stamped on top edge of right front side of cylinder block. Engine model and serial numbers are as follows:

Displacement	Engine Model	Serial Number
1400 cc	G12B	12A00101 & Up
1600 cc	G32B	2A00101 & Up
2000 cc	G52B	52A00101 & Up
2600 cc	G54B	54A00101 & Up

COMPRESSION PRESSURE

Check compression pressure with engine at normal operating temperature, choke and throttle valves wide open and engine at cranking speed (250 RPM). Maximum variation between cylinders should not exceed 15 psi (1.1 kg/cm²).

Application	Pressure psi (kg/cm²)
All Models	149 (10.5)

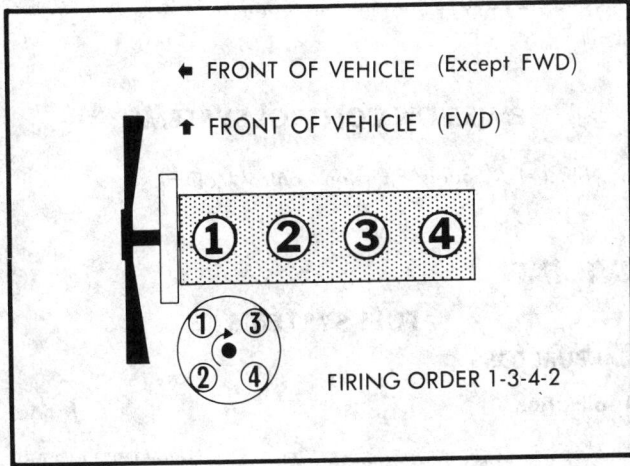

Fig. 1   Firing Order and Distributor Rotation

VALVE CLEARANCE

CAUTION — *Jet valve clearance must be adjusted before adjusting intake valve clearance. Loosen intake valve adjusting screw at least 2 full turns before adjusting jet valve.*

Check or adjust valve clearance with engine off and at normal operating temperature. To adjust valves, loosen lock nut and turn adjusting screw until specified clearance is obtained.

Valve Clearances

Application	Clearance
Jet	.006" (.15 mm)
Intake	.006" (.15 mm)
Exhaust	.010" (.25 mm)

VALVE ARRANGEMENT

Right Side — All Exhaust.
Left Side — All Intake.

SPARK PLUGS

Gap	.039-.043" (1.0-1.1 mm)
Torque	18-21 ft. lbs. (2.5-2.9 mkg)

Spark Plug Type

Application	NGK	Champion
2600 cc	BPR-5ES-11	RN-12Y
All Others	BPR-6ES-11	RN-9Y

HIGH TENSION WIRE RESISTANCE

Carefully remove high tension wires from spark plugs and distributor cap. Using an ohmmeter, check resistance of wire while gently twisting wire. If resistance is not to specification, or fluctuates from infinity to any value, replace wire.

Resistance (Ohms) Per Wire

Application	Resistance
All Models	Less Than 22,000

DISTRIBUTOR

Federal 1400 cc and 1600 cc engines use Mitsubishi single point distributors. California 1400 cc and 1600 cc engines, and all 2000 cc and 2600 cc engines use Mitsubishi Electronic Ignition systems.

Point Gap	.018-.021" (.45-.55 mm)
Cam Angle	49-55°
Breaker Arm Spring Tension	17-21 oz. (482-595 g)
Condenser Capacity	.22 mfd.

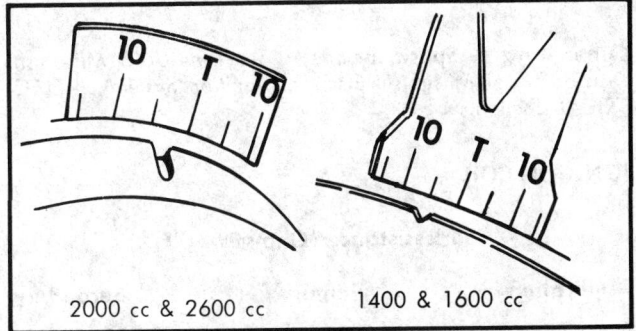

Fig. 2   Ignition Timing Mark Location

TUNE-UP (Cont.)

IGNITION TIMING

1) With engine at normal operating temperature, turn A/C controls and headlights off. Connect tachometer and timing light.

2) Loosen distributor nut and rotate distributor as necessary to adjust timing. Tighten mounting nut when timing is set to basic timing specification.

Ignition Timing Specifications

Application	①Timing
1400 cc	5°BTDC
1600 cc	5°BTDC
2000 cc	5°BTDC
2600 cc	7°BTDC

① — ±1°BTDC.

IDLE SPEED & MIXTURE

All Models (Exc. Federal Pickup with 2000 cc Eng.) — 1) Remove carburetor from engine if equipped with mixture screw caps. Loosen lock screw and remove inner sleeve and snap cap from outer sleeve. Reinstall inner sleeve (without snap cap) to outer sleeve. Tighten lock screw and mount carburetor on intake manifold.

2) Operate engine at idle until coolant temperature reaches 170-190°F. Place transmission in neutral; turn air conditioning and all electrical accessories off. Remove air cleaner-to-reed valve hose and plug air intake of reed valve. Adjust idle speed.

3) Using idle mixture adjusting screw, set mixture to obtain a CO level of .5-1.5%. Unplug reed valve air inlet and reconnect air hose. Reset idle speed with adjusting screw if necessary. Cover mixture screw with snap cap.

Federal Pickup with 2000 cc Eng. — 1) Warm engine to normal operating temperature. Turn air conditioning and all electrical accessories off. Check ignition timing and adjust if necessary.

2) Using idle speed adjusting screw, adjust idle to 80 RPM **above** specified idle speed.

3) Using idle mixture adjusting screw, adjust mixture to obtain a CO level of 1.0%. Use mixture adjusting screw again to lower idle speed to specified RPM.

4) Recheck idle CO%. Reading should now be at specified level. If engine misfires or CO% is incorrect, repeat steps 2) and 3).

Idle Speed (RPM) & CO Level (%)

Application	Idle RPM	①CO%
1400 cc	650-750	.5-1.5
1600 cc & 2000 cc		
Man. Trans.	600-700	②.5-1.5
Auto. Trans.	650-750	②.5-1.5
2600 cc	700-800	.5-1.5

① — Air injection disconnected.
② — Federal Pickup should measure .1% after adjustment.

FUEL PUMP PRESSURE & VOLUME

Pressure (At Idle)
1400 cc & 1600 cc .... 3.7-5.1 psi (.26-.36 kg/cm²)
2000 cc & 2600 cc .... 4.6-6.0 psi (.32-.42 kg/cm²)
Volume (At 5000 RPM)
1400 cc & 1600 cc .... 1.7 pts. in 30 sec.
2000 cc & 2600 cc .... 2.1 pts. in 30 sec.

EMISSION CONTROL SYSTEMS

See Mitchell Manuals' Emission Control Manual.

GENERAL SERVICING

IGNITION

DISTRIBUTOR

Federal 1400 cc and 1600 cc engines use Mitsubishi single point distributors. California 1400 cc and 1600 cc engines, and all 2000 cc and 2600 cc engines use Mitsubishi Electronic Ignition systems.

Other Data & Specifications — See Tune-Up & Mitsubishi Distributors or Mitsubishi Electronic Ignition Systems in ELECTRICAL Section.

IGNITION COIL

Coil Resistance (Ohms@68° F)

Application	Primary	Secondary
Conventional	0.95-1.15	15,000-20,000
Electronic	0.70-0.85	9000-11,000

FUEL SYSTEMS

CARBURETORS

Application	Model
All Models	Solex DIDTA 2-Bbl.

Other Data & Specifications — See Tune-Up and Solex Carburetors in FUEL SYSTEMS Section.

ELECTRICAL

BATTERY

Application	Amp. Hr. Rating
Challenger, Colt Wagon, Sapporo	65
All Other Models	45

Battery Location — Front left side of engine compartment.

GENERAL SERVICING (Cont.)

STARTER

All models use Mitsubishi overrunning clutch type starters.

Starter Testing Specifications

Application	Volts	Amps	Test RPM
1400 cc & 1600 cc			
Man. Trans.	11.5	53	6800
Auto. Trans.	11.5	60	6600
2000 cc & 2600 cc			
Man. Trans.	11.5	60	6600
Auto. Trans.	11.5	90	3300

Other Data & Specifications — *See Mitsubishi Starters in ELECTRICAL Section.*

ALTERNATOR

All 1600 cc engines (except Challenger and Sapporo) use Nippondenso alternators. All other models (including Challenger and Sapporo) use Mitsubishi Alternators.

Application	Rated Amp. Output
1400 cc & 1600 cc	45
2000 cc & 2600 cc	
Arrow, Challenger & Sapporo	50
All Others	45

Other Data & Specifications — *See Mitsubishi and Nippondenso Alternators and Regulators in ELECTRICAL Section.*

ALTERNATOR REGULATOR

All 1600 cc engines (except Challenger and Sapporo) use Nippondenso alternator regulators. Regulators are mounted externally to the top rear half of Nippondenso alternators. All other models (including Challenger and Sapporo) use Mitsubishi alternator regulators with the regulator mounted internally to the brush holder.

Operating Voltage .... 14.1-14.7@68°F (20°C)

Other Data & Specifications — *See Mitsubishi and Nippondenso Alternators and Regulators in ELECTRICAL Section.*

BELT ADJUSTMENT

Pull belt between alternator and water pump pulley, using 22 lbs. force. Belt should deflect ¼ -⅜" (7-10 mm).

FILTERS

Filter	Service Interval (Miles)
Oil Filter	①Replace every 15,000
Air Filter	Replace every 30,000
Fuel Filter	Replace every 15,000
Canister Filter	Replace every 30,000

① — At first 7,500 miles, then every other oil change.

CAPACITIES

Application	Quantity
Crankcase (Includes Filter)	
1400 cc	3.7 qts.
1600 cc	4.2 qts.
2000 cc	4.5 qts.
2600 cc	4.5 qts.
Cooling System (Includes Heater)	
1400 cc	4.7 qts.
1600 cc	
Arrow	8.1 qts.
All Others	4.7 qts.
2000 cc & 2600 cc	9.7 qts.
Manual Transmission (SAE 90)	
4-Speed	2.2 qts.
5-Speed	
1600 cc	2.1 qts.
2000 cc & 2600 cc	2.4 qts.
Manual Transaxle (SAE 80)	2.4 qts.
Automatic Transaxle (Dexron)	6.0 qts.
Automatic Transmission (Dexron)	7.2 qts.
Rear Axle (SAE 80W-90)	
Pickup	2.8 pts.
All Others	2.4 pts.
Fuel Tank	
Arrow & Colt Wagon	13.2 gals.
Challenger & Sapporo	15.8 gals.
Champ & Colt Hatchback	10.6 gals.
Pickup (Arrow & D50)	15.1 gals.

TUNE-UP

Courier

ENGINE IDENTIFICATION

The engine identification number is stamped on right side of engine block below distributor and on model identification plate attached to body at right rear corner of engine compartment. Engine model code is the fourth character of identification number.

Application	Code
2000 cc	C
2300 cc	B

MODEL IDENTIFICATION

VEHICLE IDENTIFICATION NUMBER

Vehicle identification number is stamped on model identification plate which is attached to body at right rear corner of engine compartment.

COMPRESSION PRESSURE

Check compression pressure with engine at normal operating temperature, all spark plugs removed, throttle valve wide open and engine at cranking speed. Compression pressure is within specifications if lowest reading cylinder is more than 75% of highest.

VALVE TAPPET CLEARANCE

NOTE — *2300 cc engines are equipped with hydraulic valve lifters which require no adjustment during engine tune-up.*

Application	Clearance
2000 cc	
Intake & Exhaust .... ①.012" (.3 mm)	

① — Adjust with engine off and at normal operating temperature.

VALVE ARRANGEMENT

2000 cc
 Right Side — All Exhaust
 Left Side — All Intake
2300 cc — E-I-E-I-E-I-E-I

SPARK PLUGS

Application	Gap In. (mm)	Torque Ft. Lbs. (mkg)
All Models	.029-.033 (.7-.8)	10-16 (1.4-2.2)

Spark Plug Type

Application	NGK No.
2000 cc	BPR5ES
2300 cc	BPR5EFS

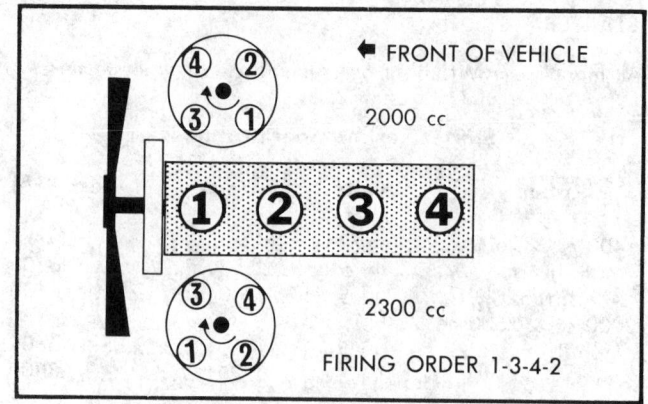

Fig. 1   Distributor Rotation and Firing Order

DISTRIBUTOR

All models are equipped with breakerless, electronic ignition systems.

Armature Tooth-to-Magnetic
 Pickup Gap .... .008-.024" (.2-.6 mm)

HIGH TENSION WIRE RESISTANCE

Carefully remove ends of wire from spark plug and distributor. Using an ohmmeter, check resistance of wire while gently twisting wire. If resistance exceeds 570 ohms per inch of wire or fluctuates from infinity to any value, replace wire.

IGNITION TIMING

Check or adjust ignition timing with engine at normal operating temperature, at correct idle speed, and with distributor vacuum advance line disconnected and plugged.

Ignition Timing Specifications

Application	Timing
2000 cc	8°BTDC
2300 cc	6°BTDC

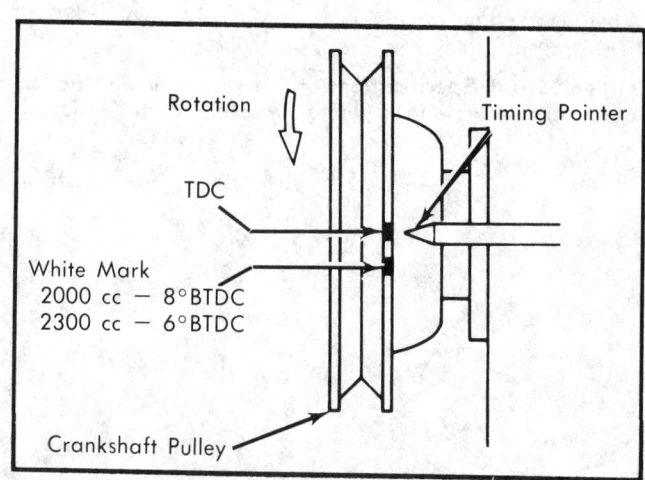

Fig. 2   Ignition Timing Mark Locations

TUNE-UP (Cont.)

IDLE SPEED & MIXTURE

1) With engine at normal operating temperature and automatic transmission in "D", connect a tachometer and detach purge hose between canister and air cleaner. Adjust curb idle RPM to specifications using curb idle adjusting screw.

2) Stop engine. Disconnect hose between air pump and check valve at check valve, and plug check valve port. Start engine and turn idle mixture adjusting screw in or out to obtain specified CO level.

3) Reconnect hoses. Recheck idle speed and readjust if necessary.

Idle Speed & CO Level

Application	RPM	①CO%
2000 cc	600-700	2.0-4.0
2300 cc		
Man. Trans.	750-850	3.0-5.0
Auto. Trans.	②650-750	3.0-5.0

① — With air injection disconnected.
② — Transmission in "D".

COLD (FAST) IDLE RPM

With choke valve fully closed, position fast idle screw on highest step of fast idle cam. Measure clearance between lower edge of throttle valve and wall of throttle bore. If clearance is not within specifications, adjust by turning screw clockwise to increase clearance, counterclockwise to decrease clearance.

Fast Idle Specifications

Application	Clearance
2000 cc	.055" (1.4 mm)
2300 cc	.062" (1.6 mm)

DASHPOT ADJUSTMENT

NOTE — Engine idle speed and carburetor mixture must be properly set before dashpot is adjusted.

1) With engine at normal operating temperature, remove air cleaner and attach a tachometer to engine. With engine running, move throttle lever until it contacts dashpot rod. Engine speed should be within specifications.

2) If engine speed is not within specifications, loosen dashpot lock nut. Hold throttle lever to maintain correct engine speed, then turn dashpot until dashpot rod contacts throttle lever. Tighten lock nut and recheck dashpot adjustment.

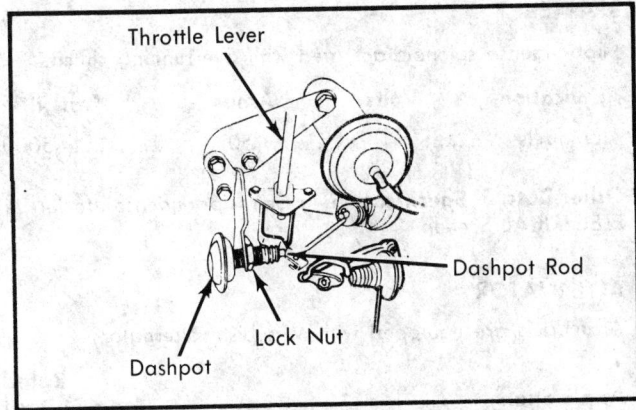

Fig. 3 Adjusting Dashpot

Dashpot Adjustment Specifications

Application	RPM
Federal	2400-2600
Calif.	2100-2300

FUEL PUMP PRESSURE & VOLUME

Pressure	2.8-3.6 psi (.20-.25 kg/cm²)
Volume	1 pt. in 30 sec.

EMISSION CONTROL SYSTEMS

See Mitchell Manuals' Emission Control Manual.

GENERAL SERVICING

IGNITION

DISTRIBUTOR

All models are equipped with Mitsubishi breakerless, electronic ignition system.

Other Data & Specifications — See Mitsubishi Distributors in ELECTRICAL Section.

IGNITION COIL

Coil Resistance (Ohms)

Application	Primary	Secondary
All Models	0.9	7,000

FUEL SYSTEMS

CARBURETORS

Application	Model
2000 cc	Nikki 2-Bbl.
2300 cc	Hitachi DCS 328 2-Bbl.

Other Data & Specifications — See Tune-Up and Hitachi or Nikki Carburetors in FUEL SYSTEMS Section.

GENERAL SERVICING (Cont.)

ELECTRICAL

BATTERY

Application	Amp. Hr. Rating
All Models	
Standard	45
Optional	70

STARTER

Nippondenso solenoid-actuated with overrunning clutch.

Application	Volts	Amps.	Test RPM
All Models	11	50	5000

Other Data & Specifications — *See Nippondenso Starters in ELECTRICAL Section.*

ALTERNATOR

All models are equipped with Mitsubishi alternators.

Application	Rated Amp. Output
All Models	35

Other Data & Specifications — *See Mitsubishi Alternators and Regulators in ELECTRICAL Section.*

ALTERNATOR REGULATOR

All models are equipped with externally mounted Mitsubishi regulators having an operating voltage of 14.5-15.8 volts.

Other Data & Specifications — *See Mitsubishi Alternators and Regulators in ELECTRICAL Section.*

FILTERS

Filter	Service Interval (Miles)
Oil Filter	Replace every 7500
Air Filter	①Replace every 30,000
Fuel Filter	Replace every 15,000
PCV Valve	②Replace every 30,000

① — Inspect and clean every 15,000 miles.
② — 2300 cc engine models only.

BELT ADJUSTMENT

Application	①Deflection New Belt	①Deflection Used Belt
2000 cc		
Alternator	0.3-0.4" (8-10 mm)	0.5-0.6" (13-15 mm)
Air Pump	0.4-0.6" (10-15 mm)	0.6-0.7" (15-18 mm)
2300 cc		
Alternator	0.4-0.45" (10-11 mm)	0.45-0.5" (11-13 mm)
Air Pump	0.6-0.7" (15-18 mm)	0.8-0.9" (20-23 mm)

① — Deflection is with 22 lbs. (10 kg) pressure applied midway on longest belt run.

CAPACITIES

Application	Quantity
Crankcase (Includes Filter)	
2000 cc	4.7 qts.
2300 cc	5.0 qts.
Cooling System	
2000 cc	7.6 qts.
2300 cc	8.8 qts.
Man. Trans.(SAE 90 with EP)	
4-Speed	1.5 qts.
5-Speed	1.8 qts.
Auto. Trans. (Type F Trans. Fluid)	6.6 qts.
Rear Axle (Hypoid Gear Lubricant)	2.8 pts.
Fuel Tank	
Standard	15.0 gals.
Optional	17.5 gals.

TUNE-UP

200SX
210
310
510
Pickup

ENGINE IDENTIFICATION

Engine model number followed by engine serial number is stamped on left side of cylinder block for 200SX and 510 models and on right side of cylinder block for all other models, just below cylinder head mating surface. Model numbers are as follows:

Application	Model No.
200SX	Z20E
210	
Man. Trans.	A12A, A14
Auto. Trans.	A15
310	A14
510	Z20S
Pickup	L20B

MODEL IDENTIFICATION

VEHICLE IDENTIFICATION NUMBER

Vehicle identification number is stamped on a plate attached to instrument panel and is visible through windshield from outside of vehicle. Number on Pickup is on upper face of right side member. An identification plate also is found inside the engine compartment.

COMPRESSION PRESSURE

Check compression pressure with engine at normal operating temperature, all spark plugs disconnected, electrical lead to anti-dieseling solenoid disconnected, choke and throttle valves wide open and engine at cranking speed.

Lowest cylinder pressure should be at least 80% that of the highest cylinder pressure. Compression pressure should be as follows:

**Compression Pressure
@350 RPM**

Application	Psi (kg/cm²)
A12A, A14 & A15	178-192 (12.5-13.5)
L20B, Z20E & Z20S	128-171 (9-12)

VALVE CLEARANCE

On all engines, start and run engine to normal operating temperature. Turn engine off, remove valve cover and adjust clearances immediately. Do not allow engine to cool before or during adjustment, or incorrect valve clearances may be obtained.

A12A, A14 & A15 ENGINES

1) Rotate crankshaft to bring No. 1 piston to TDC on compression stroke. Adjust intake valves on cylinders No. 1 and No. 2, and adjust exhaust valves on cylinders No. 1 and No. 3.

2) Rotate crankshaft 360° to bring No. 4 piston to TDC on compression stroke. Adjust intake valves on cylinders No. 3 and No. 4, and adjust exhaust valves on cylinders No. 2 and No. 4.

L20B ENGINES

1) Rotate crankshaft to bring the first cam lobe to a straight up position. Adjust intake valves on cylinders No. 2 and No. 4, and exhaust valves on cylinders No. 1 and No. 3.

2) Rotate crankshaft 360° to bring the first cam lobe to a straight down position. Adjust intake valves on cylinders No. 1 and No. 3, and exhaust valves on cylinders No. 2 and No. 4.

Z20E & Z20S ENGINES

1) Rotate crankshaft to bring the first cam lobe to a straight up position. Adjust intake valves on cylinders No. 3 and No. 4, and exhaust valves on cylinders No. 1 and No. 2.

2) Rotate crankshaft 360° to bring the first cam lobe to a straight down position. Adjust intake valves on cylinders No. 1 and No. 2, and exhaust valves on cylinders No. 3 and No. 4.

Valve Clearance Specifications

Application	Intake In. (mm)	Exhaust In. (mm)
A12A, A14 & A15	.014 (.35)	.014 (.35)
L20B	.010 (.25)	.012 (.30)
Z20E & Z20S	.012 (.30)	.012 (.30)

VALVE ARRANGEMENT

Z20E & Z20S
  Right Side — All Intake.
  Left Side — All Exhaust.
All Other Engines — E-I-I-E-E-I-I-E (front to rear).

SPARK PLUGS

Application	Gap In. (mm)	Torque Ft. Lbs. (mkg)
200SX & 510	.031-.035 (0.8-0.9)	11-14 (1.5-2.0)
210, 310 & Pickup	.039-.043 (1.0-1.1)	11-14 (1.5-2.0)

Spark Plug Type

Application	NGK No.
200SX & 510	BP6ES
210 & 310	BP5ES-11
Pickup	BPS-11

TUNE-UP (Cont.)

HIGH TENSION WIRE RESISTANCE

Remove distributor cap from distributor but do not disconnect high tension wires from cap. Disconnect high tension wires from spark plugs. Using an ohmmeter, check resistance from contact at spark plug end of wires to contact inside of distributor cap. Resistance should be less than 30,000 ohms. If resistance is more, disconnect wire from cap and recheck resistance. Replace wire if resistance still exceeds specification.

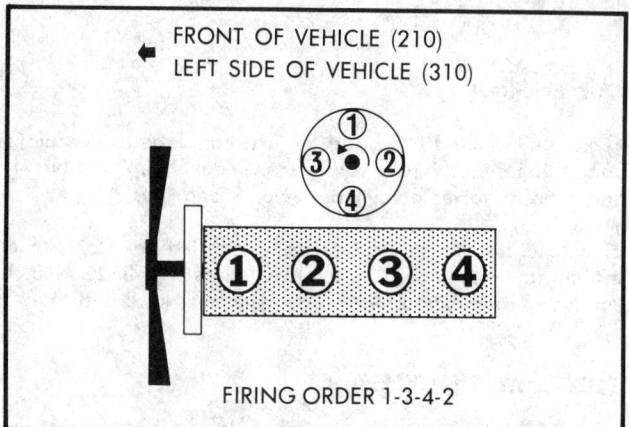

Fig. 1   Firing Order and Distributor Rotation (210 and 310 Models)

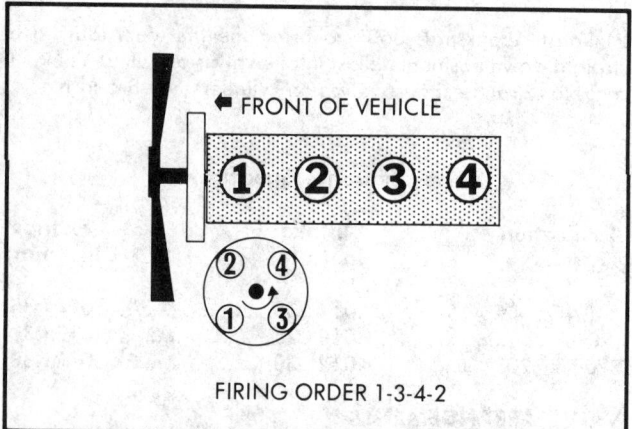

Fig. 2   Firing Order and Distributor Rotation (Federal 200SX and 510 Models and All Pickup Models)

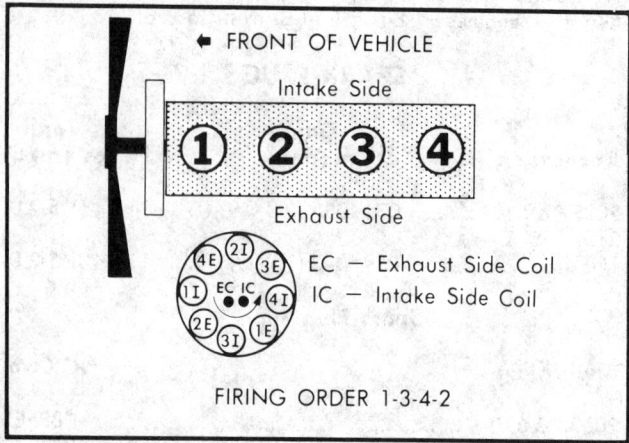

Fig. 3   Firing Order and Distributor Rotation (California 200SX and 510 Models)

DISTRIBUTOR

All models are equipped with breakerless, transistorized ignition systems. California 200SX and 510 models have 2 spark plugs per cylinder and the distributor is equipped with 8 secondary wires and a dual level rotor which fires both spark plugs at the same time.

Air Gap .... .012-.020" (.3-.5 mm)

IGNITION TIMING

Check and adjust ignition timing with engine at normal operating temperature, air gap set within specifications and engine idle speed correct. On all models except 200SX and California Pickup, disconnect and plug distributor vacuum hose. To adjust, loosen distributor set screw and rotate distributor until correct timing is achieved. Tighten set screw, recheck timing and reconnect distributor vacuum hose (if removed).

Ignition Timing Specifications

Application	Man. Trans.	Auto. Trans.
200SX & 510		
Federal	8° BTDC	8° BTDC
California	6° BTDC	6° BTDC
210		
1200 cc Eng.	10° BTDC	
1400 cc Eng.	8° BTDC	
1500 cc Eng.		8° BTDC
310	8° BTDC	
Pickup	①12° BTDC	12° BTDC

① — California Heavy Duty — 10° BTDC.

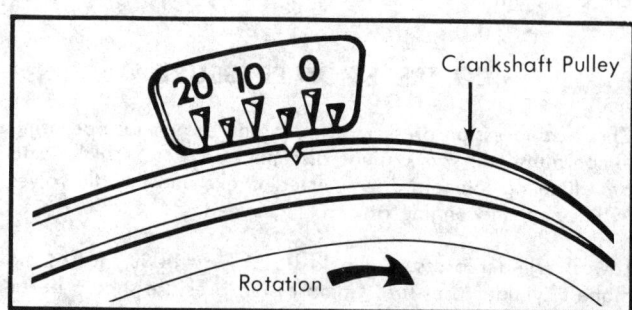

Fig. 4   Ignition Timing Mark Location (210 and 310 Models)

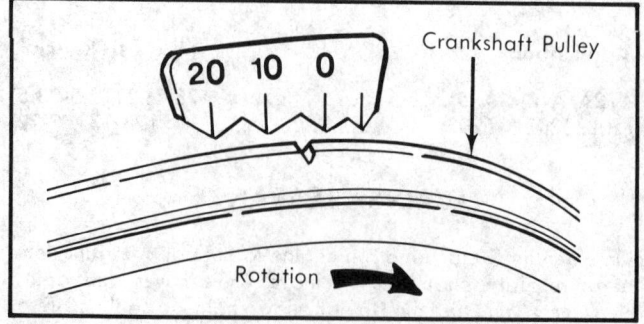

Fig. 5   Ignition Timing Mark Location (200SX, 510 and Pickup Models)

TUNE-UP (Cont.)

IDLE SPEED & MIXTURE

EXHAUST GAS ANALYZER METHOD

NOTE — *The following adjustment procedures should be performed with engine at normal operating temperature, air conditioning "OFF" (if equipped), ignition timing set to specifications and air cleaner installed. Set parking brake, block drive wheels and on models with automatic transmission, place gear selector in "D" position.*

All Models Except 200SX

NOTE — *CO meter probe must be inserted into tail pipe more than 8" on Pickups and 16" on all other models.*

1) Run engine at 2000 RPM for 2 minutes (5 minutes on Pickups) to stabilize engine condition, connect CO meter and tachometer and return engine to idle. On 510 models, disconnect and plug air induction and distributor hoses. On all other models, disconnect air injection hose (Calif.) or air induction and distributor hoses (Federal).

NOTE — *If air induction hose is removed, cap air induction pipe. If air injection hose is removed, cap check valve on air injector gallery.*

2) Accelerate engine to 2000-3000 RPM several times under no load, then run engine at idle for one minute and check ignition timing. Adjust to specifications if necessary.

3) On 210 and 310 models, reconnect distributor vacuum hose. Accelerate engine to 2000-3000 RPM several times and return to idle. On all models, check idle speed and adjust to specifications if necessary.

4) With idle speed correct, check CO level. Adjust idle mixture adjusting screw to obtain specified CO valve (if necessary).

5) After setting CO level, install new seal cap (California models). If limiter cap was removed (Federal and all Pickup models), reposition on adjusting screw to ensure screw can be rotated 1/8 turn counterclockwise and press cap onto screw.

NOTE — *California models (except Pickups) are equipped with a steel cup plug covering mixture screw. To remove, remove carburetor and drill a small hole in plug near side. DO NOT allow drill to contact mixture adjusting screw below plug. Install self-tapping screw into hole and pull plug from bore.*

Idle Speed & CO Level
(All Models Except 200SX)

Application	Idle RPM	CO%
210		
Federal	①700	2.0
California	①700	Less than 5.0
310		
Federal	750	2.0
California	750	Less than 5.0
510		
Federal	600	0.5-2.5
California	600	Less than 5.0
Pickup	600	0.3-2.7

① — Set Auto. Trans. models to 650 RPM.

6) Accelerate engine several times and recheck CO level. Reconnect all hoses and reset idle speed (if necessary).

200SX Models

NOTE — *CO meter probe must be installed into tail pipe more than 16".*

1) Run engine at 2000 RPM for 2 minutes to stabilize engine condition, then connect CO meter and tachometer.

2) Disconnect air induction hose and plug induction pipe. Accelerate engine 2-3 times under no-load and return engine to idle for 1 minute. Adjust idle speed and ignition timing (if necessary).

NOTE — *On California models, air by-pass screw in air flow meter is covered by a steel plug. To remove plug, remove air flow meter and drill a small hole in plug. DO NOT allow drill to contact by-pass screw. Install self-tapping screw into hole and pull plug from bore.*

3) With engine idling, check CO level. Adjust air by-pass screw in air flow meter to obtain specified CO level (if necessary). Turn by-pass screw clockwise to richen mixture and counterclockwise to lean mixture. On Federal models, adjust CO level according to altitude at which vehicle is to be operated.

Idle Speed & CO Level
(200SX Models)

Application	Idle RPM	CO%
200SX		
Federal		
To 2000 feet	700	0.3-2.3
2000-4000 feet	700	2.7
4000-6000 feet	700	3.8
Above 6000 feet	700	5.0
California	700	Less than 4

COLD (FAST) IDLE RPM

210, 310 & Pickup Models — Adjust fast idle speed with engine at normal operating temperature, transmission in neutral and fast idle speed screw on 2nd highest step of fast idle cam.

510 Models — Carburetor must be removed from vehicle to set fast idle. Place upper side of fast idle screw on 1st step of fast idle cam. Measure throttle valve clearance. Clearance should be .030-.035" (.76-.90 mm) on manual transmission models and .038-.043" (.96-1.1 mm) on automatic transmission models. If not, adjust clearance by turning fast idle screw.

Fast Idle RPM

Application	Man. Trans.	Auto. Trans.
210		
Federal	2400-3200	2700-3500
California	2300-3100	2600-3400
310		
Federal	2400-3200	....
California	2300-3100	....
Pickup	1900-2800	2200-3200

TUNE-UP (Cont.)

DASHPOT ADJUSTMENT

With engine at normal operating temperature and idle speed and mixture correctly set, turn throttle valve by hand and read engine speed when dashpot just contacts adjusting screw on stop lever. Turn adjusting screw on stop lever to obtain specified engine speed. Accelerate engine and release. When dashpot plunger contacts stop lever, engine should decelerate smoothly from 2000 RPM to 1000 RPM in about 3 seconds.

Dashpot Adusting Specifications

Application	Man. Trans. (RPM)	Auto. Trans. (RPM)
210 & 310	1900-2100	1900-2100
510		1400-1600
Pickup		1650-1850

FUEL PUMP PRESSURE & VOLUME

Pressure	
200SX	①30 psi (2.1 kg/cm²)
All Other Models	3.0-3.8 psi (.21-.27 kg/cm²)
Volume (at 1000 RPM)	
210 & 310	1 pt. per minute
510	3.7 pts. per minute
Pickup	2.2 pts. per minute

① — Measured between fuel filter and fuel delivery line at idle. Pressure should increase to 37 psi (2.2 kg/cm²) when accelerator pedal is fully depressed.

NOTE — *When performing tests on fuel pump output volume and output pressure, use a fuel line with an inside diameter of ¼" (6 mm). Improper size of test hose could cause incorrect delivery pressure and volume.*

EMISSION CONTROL SYSTEMS

See Mitchell Manuals' Emission Control Manual.

GENERAL SERVICING

IGNITION

DISTRIBUTOR

All models are equipped with Hitachi breakerless, transistorized ignition systems.

Other Data & Specifications — *See Tune-Up & Hitachi Ignition Systems in ELECTRICAL Section.*

IGNITION COIL

Coil Resistance (Ohm@68° F)

Application	Primary	Secondary
200SX & 510		
Federal	.84-1.02	8,200-12,400
California	1.04-1.27	7,400-11,000
All Other Models	.84-1.02	8,200-12,400

FUEL SYSTEMS

CARBURETORS

Application	Model
210 & 310	Hitachi DCH 306
510	Hitachi DCR 360
Pickup	Hitachi DCH 340

Other Data & Specifications — *See Tune-Up & Hitachi Carburetors in FUEL SYSTEMS Section.*

FUEL INJECTION

200SX models are equipped with Bosch AFC electronic fuel injection.

Other Data & Specifications — *See Tune-Up & Bosch Fuel Injection in FUEL SYSTEMS Section.*

ELECTRICAL

BATTERY

Application	Amp. Hr. Rating
All Models	60

Battery Location — Engine Compartment.

STARTER

Hitachi solenoid actuated with overrunning clutch.

Application	Volts	Amps	Test RPM
All Models	11.5	60	7000

Other Data & Specifications — *See Hitachi Starters in ELECTRICAL Section.*

ALTERNATOR

Application	Rated Amp. Output
200SX & 310	60
210 & 510	50
Pickup	
Standard	35
Heavy Duty	38

Other Data & Specifications — *See Hitachi Alternators & Regulators in ELECTRICAL Section.*

ALTERNATOR REGULATOR

All Models use a Hitachi alternator regulator with an operating voltage of 14.4-15.0 volts at 68°F (20°C).

Other Data & Specifications — *See Hitachi Alternators & Regulators in ELECTRICAL Section.*

GENERAL SERVICING (Cont.)

FILTERS

Filter	Service Interval (Miles)
Oil Filter	Replace every 7500
Air Filter	Replace every 30,000
Fuel Filter	Replace every 30,000
PCV Filter	Replace every 30,000
Canister Filter	Replace every 30,000

BELT ADJUSTMENT

Application	①Deflection
All Models	
All Belts	⁵⁄₁₆-¼" (8-12 mm)

① — Deflection is with 22 lbs. (10 kg) pressure applied midway on longest belt run.

CAPACITIES

Application	Quantity
Crankcase (Includes Filter)	
200SX & 510	4.4 qts.
210 & 310	3.4 qts.
Pickup	4.5 qts.
Cooling System (Includes Heater)	
210 & 310	6.3 qts.
All Others	9.5 qts.
Man. Trans (SAE 80W-90/API GL-4)	
200X	4.3 pts.
210	
4-Speed	
1200 cc	2.5 pts.
1400 cc	2.8 pts.
5-Speed	2.5 pts.
310	4.9 pts.
510	
4-Speed	3.1 pts.
5-Speed	3.7 pts.
Pickup	
4-Speed	3.7 pts.
5-Speed	4.3 pts.
Auto. Trans. (Dexron)	
All Models	5.9 qts.
Rear Axle (SAE 80W-90/API GL-5)	
200SX & 510	2.4 pts.
210 & 310	1.9 pts.
Pickup	2.6 pts.
Fuel Tank	
200SX	
Hardtop	14.0 gals.
Hatchback	15.9 gals.
210, 310 & 510	13.3 gals.
Pickup	
Shortbed①	13.3 gals.
Longbed②	16.9 gals.

① — Includes King Cab model.
② — Includes Cab & Chassis model.

1980 Datsun 6 Tune-Up

TUNE-UP

280ZX
810

ENGINE IDENTIFICATION

Engine serial number is stamped on right rear side of cylinder block at cylinder head contact surface. Serial number is preceded by engine model number.

Engine Model Number

Application	Model No.
280ZX	L28E
810	L24

COMPRESSION PRESSURE

Test compression with engine at normal operating temperature, spark plugs removed, throttle and choke open, and engine at cranking speed. Lowest reading cylinder must be at least 80% of highest reading cylinder. Compression pressure should be as follows at 300-400 RPM:

Application	Min. Pressure psi (kg/cm²)	Max. Pressure psi (kg/cm²)
280ZX	128 (9)	171 (12)
810	128 (9)	171 (12)

VALVE TAPPET CLEARANCE

Adjust valves with engine off and at normal operating temperature. Insert feeler gauge between heel of cam and pivot arm from valve side of head. Use suitable wrench (ST1064001) to loosen pivot locking nut and a second wrench to turn pivot adjuster until specified clearance is obtained. Tighten locking nut and recheck clearance.

Valve Clearance Specifications

Application	Intake	Exhaust
All Models	.010" (.25 mm)	.012" (.30 mm)

VALVE ARRANGEMENT

E-I-I-E-I-E-E-I-E-I-I-E (front to rear).

SPARK PLUGS

Application	Gap In. (mm)	Torque Ft. Lbs. (mkg)
All Models	.039-.043 (1.0-1.1)	11-14 (1.5-2.0)

Spark Plug Type

Application	NGK No.
280ZX & 810	BP6ES-11

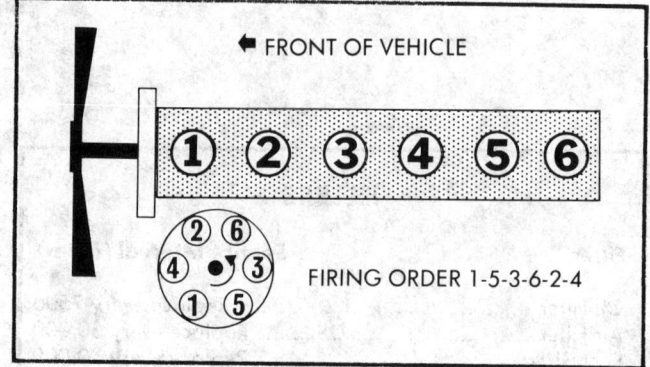

Fig. 1   Firing Order and Distributor Rotation

HIGH TENSION WIRE RESISTANCE

Remove distributor cap from distributor but do not disconnect high tension wires from cap. Disconnect high tension wires from spark plugs. Using an ohmmeter, check resistance from contact at spark plug end of wires to contact inside of distributor cap. Resistance should be less than 30,000 ohms. If resistance is more, disconnect wire from cap and recheck resistance. Replace wire if resistance still exceeds specifications.

DISTRIBUTOR

All models use a single pick-up transistor ignition system with no point set. The only adjustment needed is for air gap between the reluctor and pick-up coil.

Measure air gap using a non-magnetic feeler gauge. If gap is not to specifications, loosen pickup coil screws and adjust gap.

Air Gap .... .012-.020" (.3-.5 mm)

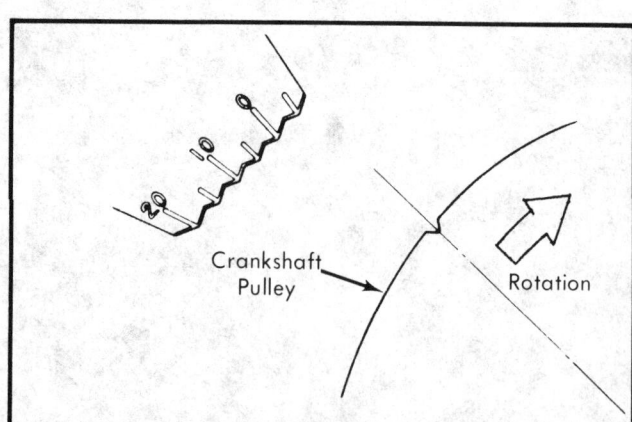

Fig. 2   Ignition Timing Mark Location

IGNITION TIMING

With engine at normal operating temperature, connect a timing light and tachometer to engine. Check air gap and idle speed and adjust to specifications if necessary. With Man. Trans. in neutral or Auto. Trans. in "D", adjust timing by loosening set screw and rotating distributor until timing is set to specifications. Tighten set screw and recheck timing.

TUNE-UP (Cont.)

Ignition Timing Specifications

Application	①Timing
All Models	10°BTDC

① — Auto. Trans. in "D".

IDLE SPEED & MIXTURE

NOTE — *Ignition switch must be "OFF" before disconnecting fuel injection system component harness connectors. Engine should be at operating temperature. Be sure CO meter is fully warmed up before check.*

FEDERAL MODELS

1) Connect a tachometer to engine and run at 2000 RPM for 5 minutes to stabilize operating condition. Accelerate engine 2-3 times and return to idle. Turn idle speed adjusting screw to obtain specified idle RPM.

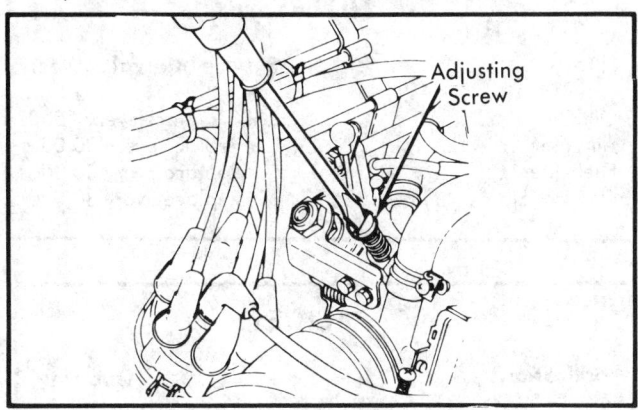

Fig. 3   Adjusting Idle Speed

2) Turn ignition switch off and disconnect throttle valve switch harness connector. Position harness connector at least 4" away from any secondary ignition wires.

3) Disconnect and plug distributor vacuum hose. Disconnect air induction hose and canister purge hose at intake manifold. Plug air induction pipe and purge hose fitting on intake manifold. Start engine, accelerate 2-3 times and allow to idle for 1 minute.

4) Check ignition timing and reset idle speed screw to obtain 700 RPM. Connect a jumper wire between throttle valve switch harness connector terminals No. 24 and No. 30. *See Fig. 4.*

NOTE — *Connecting jumper wire between connector terminals signals the control unit of a full throttle condition which allows the idle mixture to run at full load enrichment. This step is necessary to enrichen the CO% level at idle enough to be read by the CO meter.*

5) Insert CO meter probe into tail pipe (at least 16"), and measure CO level. If necessary, remove air by-pass screw plug from air flow meter and adjust by-pass screw to obtain specified CO level (according to altitude in which vehicle is operated). Turn air by-pass screw clockwise to richen mixture or counterclockwise to lean mixture.

6) Stop engine and remove jumper wire from throttle valve switch harness connector. Reconnect harness and all hoses. Reset idle speed to specified RPM.

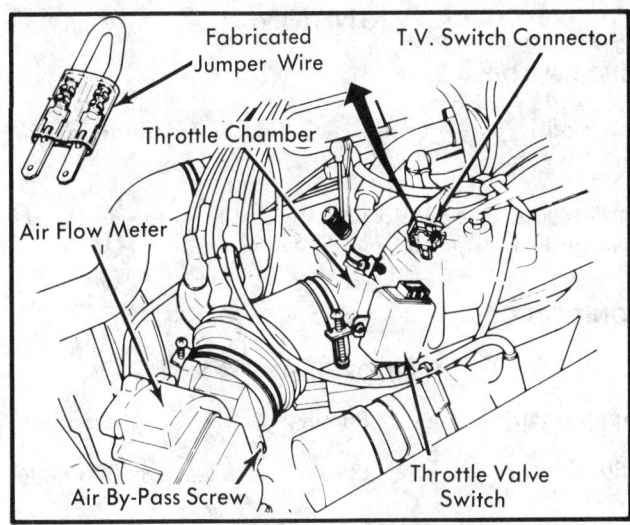

Fig. 4   Idle Mixture Adjustment (CO%)
(280ZX Shown — 810 Similar)

CALIFORNIA MODELS

1) Start engine and run to normal operating temperature. Accelerate and run engine at 2000 RPM for 5 minutes to stabilize operating condition.

Idle Speed & CO Level

Application	Idle RPM①	CO%
280ZX & 810		
Federal		
0-2000 feet	②700	0.2-1.8
2000-4000 feet	②700	2.4
4000-6000 feet	②700	3.5
Above 6000 feet	②700	4.7
California	②700	③

① — Auto. Trans. in "D".
② — Set 810 model with Auto. Trans. at 650 RPM.
③ — See adjustment procedure.

2) Accelerate engine 2-3 times and allow to idle. Turn idle speed adjusting screw to obtain specified idle RPM. Check ignition timing and reset if necessary. Raise engine speed to 2000 RPM and observe inspection light on bottom of EFI computer.

3) Light should blink more than 5 times in 10 seconds, indicating mixture is correct and is being controlled by the computer. If not, refer to *Mixture Control Components Test* in *Bosch AFC Fuel Injection* article in *FUEL SYSTEMS* Section for repair and testing of system.

FUEL PUMP PRESSURE

Pressure .... 36.3 psi (2.6 kg/cm²)

EMISSION CONTROL SYSTEMS

See Mitchell Manuals' Emission Control Manual.

1980 Datsun 6 Tune-Up

GENERAL SERVICING

IGNITION

DISTRIBUTOR

All models are equipped with Hitachi Transistor Ignition System.

Other Data & Specifications — *See Tune-Up and Hitachi Ignition Systems in* ELECTRICAL *Section.*

IGNITION COIL

Coil Resistance (Ohms@68° F)

Application	Primary	Secondary
280ZX & 810	.84-1.02	8,200-12,400

FUEL SYSTEMS

FUEL INJECTION

All models are equipped with Bosch AFC Fuel Injection System.

Other Data & Specifications — *See Tune-Up and Bosch AFC Fuel Injection in* FUEL SYSTEMS *Section.*

ELECTRICAL

BATTERY

Application	Amp. Hr. Rating
All Models	
Battery Type	
N50Z	60
N70Z	70

Battery Location — Right side of engine compartment.

STARTER

Hitachi	Overrunning Clutch
Free Speed Voltage	12 at 4300 RPM
Free Speed Amperage	100 (Max.) at 4300 RPM

Other Data & Specifications — *See Hitachi Starters in* ELECTRICAL *Section.*

ALTERNATOR

Application	Rated Amp. Output
All Models	60

Other Data & Specifications — *See Hitachi Alternators & Regulators in* ELECTRICAL *Section.*

ALTERNATOR REGULATOR

All models use a Hitachi alternator regulator with an operating voltage of 14.3-15.3 volts at 68°F (20°C).

Other Data & Specifications — *See Hitachi Alternators & Regulators in* ELECTRICAL *Section.*

BELT ADJUSTMENT

Application	①Deflection
All Belts	$5/16$-$1/2$" (8-12 mm)

① — Deflection is with 22 lbs. (10 kg) pressure applied midway on belt run.

FILTERS

Filter	Service Interval (Miles)
Oil Filter	Replace every 7500
Air Filter	Replace every 30,000
Fuel Filter	Replace every 30,000
Canister Filter	Replace every 30,000

CAPACITIES

Application	Quantity
Crankcase (Includes Filter)	
280ZX	4.8 qts.
810	5.9 qts.
Cooling System (Includes Heater)	
280ZX	
With Reservoir	11.1 qts.
Without Reservoir	10.3 qts.
810	11.0 qts.
Man. Trans. (API GL-4/SAE 80)	
280ZX & 810	
4-Speed	3.6 pts.
5-Speed	4.3 pts.
Auto. Trans. (Dexron)	5.9 qts.
Rear Axle (API GL-5/SAE 80-90)	
280ZX	
Model R-180	2.1 pts.
Model R-200	2.8 pts.
810	2.1 pts.
Fuel Tank	
280ZX	21.1 gals.
810 Sedan	15.9 gals.
810 Station Wagon	14.5 gals.

TUNE-UP

Brava
Spider 2000
Strada
X1/9

ENGINE IDENTIFICATION

Brava & Spider Models — Engine code and identification numbers are stamped on crankcase near oil filter mount.

Strada & X1/9 Models — Engine code and identification numbers are stamped on crankcase (flywheel end).

Application	Code
Brava & Spider	
With Fuel Injection	132C3.031
With Carburetor	132C3.040
Strada X1/9	
With Fuel Injection	138B2.031
With Carburetor	138B2.040

VALVE CLEARANCE

Application	①Intake In. (mm)	①Exhaust In. (mm)
Brava & Spider	.019 (.48)	.021 (.53)
Strada & X1/9	.014 (.35)	.018 (.45)

① — Set valves with engine hot.

VALVE ARRANGEMENT

Brava & Spider Models
  Right Side - All Exhaust
  Left Side - All Intake
Strada & X1/9 — E-I-I-E-E-I-I-E

SPARK PLUGS

Application	Gap In. (mm)	Torque Ft. Lbs. (mkg)
Brava & Spider	.025 (.64)	25 (3.5)
Strada & X1/9	.030 (.76)	25 (3.5)

Spark Plug Type

Application	Champion No.	Bosch No.
All Models	RN9Y	WR7D

HIGH TENSION WIRE RESISTANCE
Resistance (Ohms) Per Wire

Application	Resistance
All Models	25,000-30,000

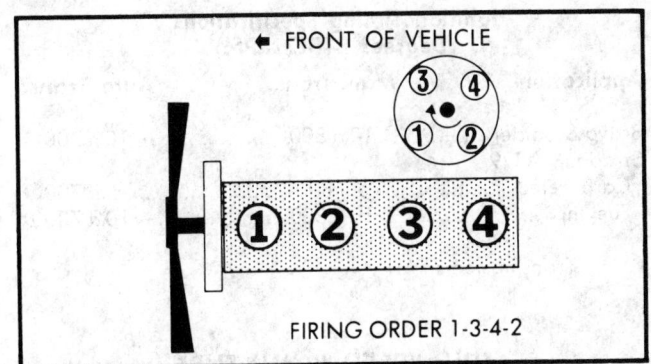

Fig. 1 Firing Order and Distributor Rotation (Brava & Spider — 2000 cc)

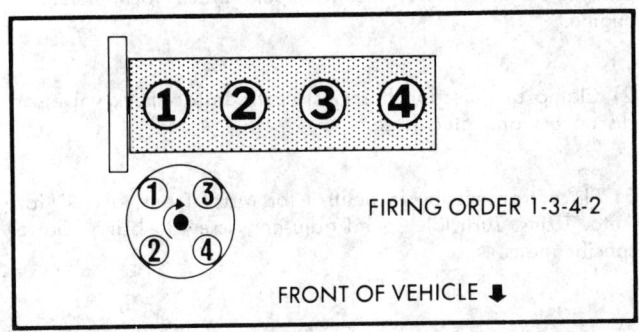

Fig. 2 Firing Order and Distributor Rotation (Strada & X1/9 — 1500 cc)

DISTRIBUTOR

All models are equipped with breakerless, electronic ignition systems. Brava and Spider use a Marelli system, and Strada and X1/9 use a Bosch unit. Some Strada models may be equipped with the Marelli system.

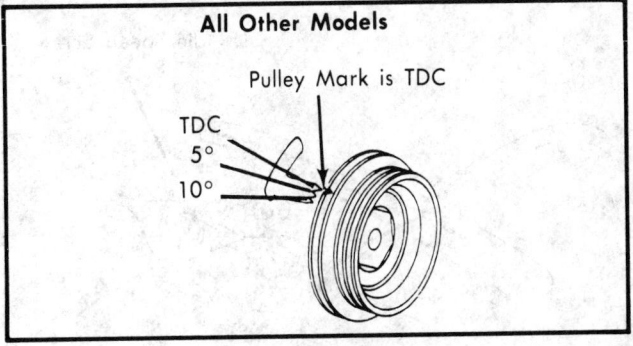

Fig. 3 Ignition Timing Mark Location

IGNITION TIMING

Check or adjust ignition timing with engine at normal operating temperature, Man. Trans. in neutral or Auto. Trans. in "D" and idle speed set to specifications. To adjust timing, align mark on drive pulley or flywheel with specified pointer by turning distributor.

TUNE-UP (Cont.)

Ignition Timing Specifications
(Degrees BTDC@RPM)

Application	Man. Trans.	Auto. Trans.
Brava & Spider	10@800	10@700①
Strada & X1/9		
Carbureted	5@800	5@700①
Fuel Inj.	10@800	10@700①

① — Transmission in "D".

IDLE SPEED & MIXTURE

CARBURETED MODELS

1) With engine at normal operating temperature, insert CO analyzer pickup tube into tailpipe. Attach tachometer to engine.

2) Clamp air injection hose just upstream of check valve, or disconnect and plug hose.

3) Place transmission in neutral for Man. Trans. or "D" for Auto. Trans. Turn idle speed adjusting screw to bring idle to specifications.

4) Using mixture screw, set CO level to specification. Recheck idle speed. If it has changed, repeat entire adjustment until both are as specified.

FUEL INJECTION MODELS

1) Warm engine to operating temperature (electric fan has cycled twice). Place manual transmission in neutral or automatic in "D". Wait until electric fan is off to adjust idle.

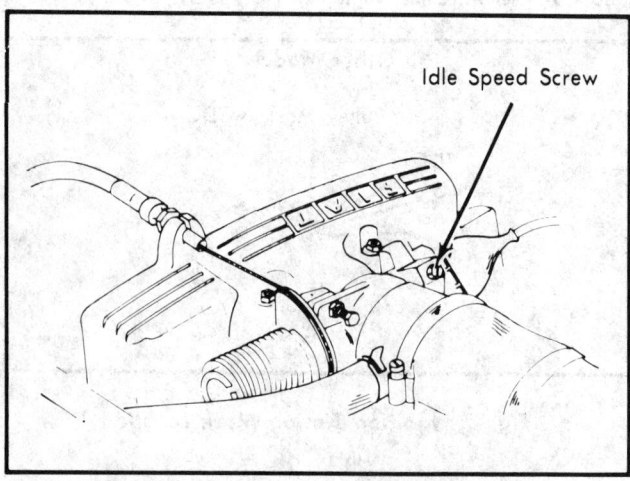

Fig. 4   Fuel Injection Idle Speed Adjustment

2) Turn air bypass screw on top of intake manifold to adjust idle speed to specifications. See Fig. 4.

3) Connect CO meter to pipe tap in front of catalytic converter. Disconnect plug from oxygen sensor and ensure that neither side is grounded. Remove plug from airflow meter and adjust CO to 0.5-0.9%. See Fig. 5.

4) Ground control unit side of oxygen sensor connector. CO level should rise to at least 1.5%. Reconnect oxygen snesor and check for CO level of 0.3-0.6%. Remove test equipment and plug air flow meter screw. See Fig. 5.

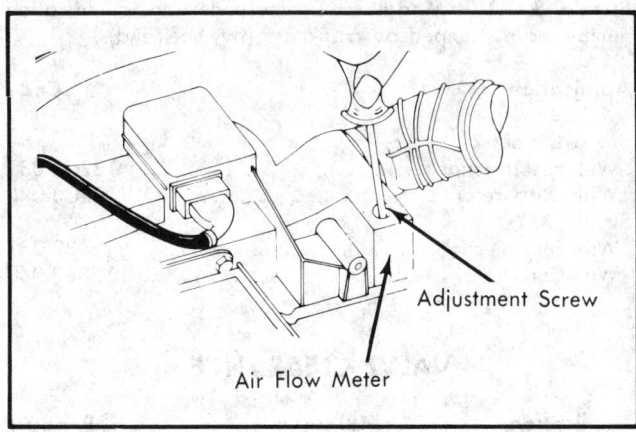

Fig. 5   Fuel Injection Mixture Adjustment

Idle Speed & CO Level

Application	Idle RPM	CO%
Carbureted Models		
Brava & Spider		
Man. Trans.	800-900	1.0-2.5
Auto. Trans.①	700-800	1.0-2.5
Strada & X1/9		
Man. Trans.	800-900	1.0-2.0
Auto. Trans.①	700-800	1.0-2.0
Fuel Injected Models		
All Man. Trans.	800-900	0.3-0.6
All Auto. Trans.①	700-800	0.3-0.6

① — With transmission in "D".

FUEL PUMP PRESSURE

Carbureted Models
  Pressure .... 3.5-4.3 psi (.25-.30 kg/cm²)
Fuel Injection Models
  Pressure① .... 39-45 psi (2.74-3.16 kg/cm²)

① — Disconnect hose to pressure regulator.

EMISSION CONTROL SYSTEMS

See Mitchell Manuals' Emission Control Manual.

GENERAL SERVICING

IGNITION

DISTRIBUTOR

All models are equipped with breakerless, electronic ignition systems. Brava and Spider use a Marelli system, and Strada and X1/9 use a Bosch unit. Some Strada models may be equipped with the Marelli system.

IGNITION COIL

Coil Resistance (Ohms@68°F)

Application	Primary	Secondary
Bosch Coil	1.1-1.7	6,000-10,000
Marelli Coil	.75-.81	10,000-11,000

Other Data & Specifications — *See Tune-Up and Bosch or Marelli Ignition Systems in ELECTRICAL Section.*

FUEL SYSTEMS

CARBURETORS

Application	Model
All Models	Weber 28/32 ADHA

Other Data & Specifications — *See Tune-Up and Weber Carburetors in FUEL SYSTEMS Section.*

FUEL INJECTION

Application	Model
All Models	Bosch AFC

Other Data & Specifications — *See Tune-Up and Bosch AFC Fuel Injection in FUEL SYSTEMS Section.*

ELECTRICAL

BATTERY

Application	Amp Hr. Rating
All Models	60

Battery Location — Battery is located in engine compartment on all except Spider 2000 models. On these models, battery is located in trunk.

STARTER

Brava and Spider 2000 models are equipped with Fiat starters. Strada and X1/9 models use Bosch starters on Man. Trans. models and Marelli starters on Auto. Trans. models.

Starter Specifications

Application	Volts	Amps	Test RPM
Brava & Spider	12	12	4700-5700
Strada & X1/9			
Man. Trans.	11.5	35-55	6000-8000
Auto. Trans.	11.5	30-40	5500-6500

Other Data & Specifications — *See Bosch or Fiat Starters in ELECTRICAL Section.*

ALTERNATOR

All models are equipped with Bosch alternators.

Application	Rated Amp. Output
Brava, Spider & Strada①	55
X1/9	65

① — Strada with air conditioning rated 65 amperes.

Other Data & Specifications — *See Bosch Alternators and Regulators in ELECTRICAL Section.*

ALTERNATOR REGULATOR

All models have alternators with internal regulators. With headlights on and heater fan on high speed, operating voltage should be 12.5-14.5 volts at 2500 RPM.

Other Data & Specifications — *See Bosch Alternators and Regulators in ELECTRICAL Section.*

CAPACITIES	
Application	Quantity
Crankcase (Includes Filter)	
Brava, Spider & X1/9	4.3 qts.
Strada	4.6 qts.
Cooling System	
Brava	8.5 qts.
Spider	8.0 qts.
Strada	7.5 qts.
X1/9	12.2 qts.
Man. Trans. (SAE 90)	
All Models	3.5 pts.
Auto. Trans. (Dexron)	
Brava, Spider & Strada	6.0 pts.
Rear Axle (SAE 90)	
Brava & Spider	1.4 qts.
Transaxle (SAE 90)	
X1/9	3.2 qts.
Strada	3.5 qts.
Fuel Tank	
Brava & Strada	12.1 gals.
Spider	11.4 gals.
X1/9	12.2 gals.

1980 Fiat 4 Tune-Up

GENERAL SERVICING (Cont.)

BELT ADJUSTMENT

Application	①Deflection
All Drive Belts	.4-.6″ (10-15 mm)

① — Deflection is with 22 lbs. (10 kg) pressure applied midway on longest belt run.

FILTERS

Filter	Service Interval (Miles)
Oil Filter	Replace every 7,500
Air Cleaner	Replace every 15,000
Fuel Filter	Replace every 15,000

TUNE-UP

Hatchback

ENGINE IDENTIFICATION

Engine identification code is located on bottom line of vehicle identification plate, which is riveted on the panel above right front headlight just under hood.

Application	Code
1600 cc	L4

COMPRESSION PRESSURE

Check compression pressure with engine at normal operating temperature, all spark plugs removed, throttle valve wide open and engine at cranking speed. Compression pressure is within specifications if lowest reading cylinder is at least 75% of highest reading cylinder.

VALVE CLEARANCE

Adjust valves with engine cold. To adjust, turn adjusting screw until correct clearance is obtained.

NOTE — *Do not use go/no-go type feeler gauge. Check clearance fore and aft parallel to crankshaft centerline. Any other method will result in an incorrect reading.*

Adjust valves in the following sequence.

Valves Open	Adjust Valves
No. 1 & 6	No. 3 & 8
No. 2 & 4	No. 5 & 7
No. 3 & 8	No. 1 & 6
No. 5 & 7	No. 2 & 4

Valve Clearance

Application	Clearance
Intake	①.010″ (.25 mm)
Exhaust	①.021″ (.53 mm)

① — Adjust with engine cold.

VALVE ARRANGEMENT

E-I-I-E-E-I-I-E

SPARK PLUGS

Application	Gap In. (mm)	Torque Ft. Lbs. (mkg)
All Models	.032 (.8)	15 (2.1)

Spark Plug Type

Application	Autolite No.
All Models	AWSF-32

HIGH TENSION WIRE RESISTANCE

Remove distributor cap from distributor, but do not disconnect high tension wires from cap. Disconnect high tension wires from spark plugs. Using an ohmmeter, check resistance from contact at spark plug end of wires to contact inside of distributor cap. Resistance should be less than 4100 ohms per inch. If not, disconnect wire from cap and recheck. Replace wire if not within specifications.

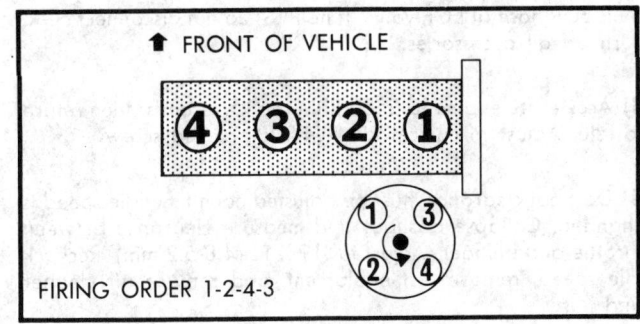

Fig. 1   Firing Order and Distributor Rotation

DISTRIBUTOR

All models are equipped with Dura Spark II ignition system. No adjustments are required.

IGNITION TIMING

Check and adjust ignition timing with engine at normal operating temperature, idle speed set to specification and distributor vacuum hose disconnected and plugged.

Ignition Timing Specifications

Application	Timing
All Models	12° BTDC

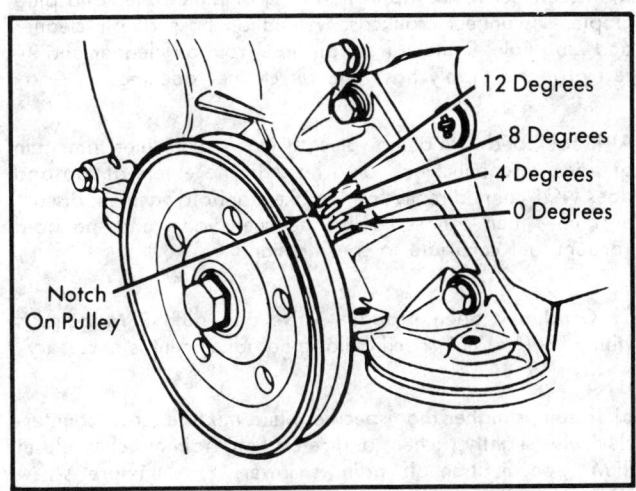

Fig. 2   Ignition Timing Mark Location

1980 Fiesta 4 Tune-Up

TUNE-UP (Cont.)

HOT (SLOW) IDLE RPM

1) With engine at normal operating temperature, connect tachometer and install jumper wire across fan switch so fan runs constantly. Remove air cleaner. If equipped with a spark delay valve in distributor vacuum line, remove valve and connect hoses together.

2) If equipped with EGR ported vacuum switch, disconnect and plug EGR hose at EGR valve. If no PVS, do not disconnect EGR. Turn off all accessories.

3) Accelerate engine to 2500 RPM for 15 seconds, then return to idle. Adjust to correct RPM with idle speed screw.

4) Dashpot clearance must be adjusted each time idle speed is changed. Collapse dashpot and measure clearance between throttle and plunger. Adjust to .19-.21" (4.8-5.2 mm). Recheck idle speed, remove test equipment, and replace air cleaner and hoses.

Idle Speed

Application	Curb Idle RPM
All Models	850

IDLE MIXTURE

PROPANE ENRICHMENT PROCEDURE

1) Apply parking brake and block drive wheels. Air cleaner may be removed as necessary to make adjustments; however, be sure to remove No. 3 and 4 spark plug wires from snorkel first.

2) Connect suitable tachometer and bring engine to normal operating temperature. Disconnect radiator fan switch and attach a jumper wire so fan operates continuously.

3) Disconnect fuel evaporation hose at air cleaner and plug nipple. Disconnect crankcase ventilation hose at air cleaner and plug hole. Remove fresh air hose from air cleaner and insert propane supply hose into air cleaner opening.

4) If equipped with dump valve having vacuum lines coming in at sides, disconnect and plug lines. If line enters at top and does NOT come directly from intake manifold vacuum, disconnect line, then connect a line between valve and manifold vacuum. Set curb idle to specification.

5) Gradually open propane valve and note RPM gain. If within "RPM Gain" specifications, no adjustment is necessary.

6) If gain is higher than specified, turn mixture screw counterclockwise slightly (richen) and retest until gain matches "Reset RPM" specification. If gain is lower, turn mixture screw clockwise (lean) and retest until gain matches "Reset RPM" speed.

7) When RPM gain is set correctly, install cap on mixture screw. Reconnect vacuum hoses, check idle speed, and remove test equipment.

Propane Enriched Mixture Specifications

Application	RPM Gain	Reset RPM
All Models	100-130	115

COLD (FAST) IDLE RPM

1) With engine at normal operating temperature, disconnect and plug all hoses at air cleaner and remove air cleaner. Connect tachometer and install a jumper wire across fan switch so fan runs constantly.

2) If equipped with spark delay valve in distributor vacuum line, remove valve and connect hoses together. If equipped with EGR ported vacuum switch, disconnect and plug vacuum hose at EGR valve. If no EGR PVS, DO NOT disconnect EGR valve.

3) With engine running at normal operating temperature, ensure that choke plates are fully opened. Place fast idle screw on kickdown step (against shoulder of highest step) of fast idle cam.

NOTE — *Cam steps are visible through hole in choke housing.*

4) Check fast idle RPM. If not within 100 RPM of specification, loosen fast idle screw lock nut and turn screw as necessary to obtain specified RPM. Tighten lock nut.

5) Run engine at 2500 RPM for several seconds. Recheck RPM and readjust if necessary. Restore all hoses and components to original positions.

Fast Idle RPM

Application	RPM
All Models	2000

AUTOMATIC CHOKE SETTING

Application	Setting
All Models	INDEX

FUEL PUMP PRESSURE & VOLUME

Pressure (At Idle) .... 3.5-6.0 psi (.25-.42 kg/cm²)
Volume (At Idle) .... 1 pt./min.

EMISSION CONTROL SYSTEMS

See Mitchell Manuals' Emission Control Manual.

GENERAL SERVICING

IGNITION

DISTRIBUTOR

All models are equipped with Motorcraft Dura-Spark II breakerless, electronic ignition system.

Other Data & Specifications — *See Motorcraft Ignition Systems in ELECTRICAL Section.*

IGNITION COIL

Coil Resistance (Ohms@68° F)

Application	Primary	Secondary
All Models	1.13-1.23	7700-9300

FUEL SYSTEMS

CARBURETORS

Application	Model
All Models	Weber Model 740 2-Bbl.

Other Data & Specifications — *See Tune-Up and Weber Carburetors in FUEL SYSTEMS Section.*

ELECTRICAL

BATTERY

Battery Location — Battery is located at right front corner of engine compartment.

Application	Amp. Hr. Rating
All Models	43

STARTER

Bosch Pre-Engaged Type.

Maximum Current Draw .... 350 Amps.

Other Data & Specifications — *See Bosch Starters in ELECTRICAL Section.*

ALTERNATOR

Air conditioned models are equipped with Bosch alternators. All other models are equipped with Motorcraft alternators.

Application	Rated Amp. Output
Bosch	55
Motorcraft	
Color Code Orange	40
Color Code Green	60

Other Data & Specifications — *See Bosch or Motorcraft Alternators & Regulators in ELECTRICAL Section.*

ALTERNATOR REGULATOR

Air conditioned models are equipped with Bosch alternator regulators. All other models are equipped with Motorcraft alternator regulators.

Operating Voltage 13.6-14.5

Other Data & Specifications — *See Bosch or Motorcraft Alternators and Regulators in ELECTRICAL Section.*

ENGINE

BELT ADJUSTMENT

Belts with a span of more than 12 inches should deflect ⅛-½" (3-12 mm) when depressed firmly with thumb. Belts with shorter span should deflect ⅛-¼" (3-6 mm).

FILTERS

Filter	Service Interval (Miles)
Oil Filter	Replace every 7500
Air Filter	Replace every 30,000

CAPACITIES

Application	Quantity
Crankcase (Includes filter)	3.3 qts.
Cooling System (Includes heater)	7.6 qts.
Transaxle (ATF)	5.0 pts.
Fuel Tank	10.0 gals.

1980 Honda 4 Tune-Up

TUNE-UP

Accord
Civic
Prelude

ENGINE IDENTIFICATION

Engine serial number is stamped on a machined surface at rear of engine, near starter. Engine serial number is preceded by engine model number. Model numbers are as follows:

Application	Model Code
Accord & Prelude	EK1
Civic	
1300	EJ1
1500	EM1

COMPRESSION PRESSURE

Check compression with engine at normal operating temperature, air cleaner and spark plugs removed, throttle and choke valve wide open.

Compression Pressure @ 400 RPM

Application	Pressure
Accord & Prelude	128-156 psi (9-11 kg/cm²)
Civic	
1300	128-156 psi (9-11 kg/cm²)
1500	156-185 psi (11-13 kg/cm²)

VALVE CLEARANCE

1) Adjust valves with engine cold. Remove valve cover and set No. 1 piston at TDC. Cutaway notch in camshaft belt pulley should be at top (Civic) or word "UP" should be at top (Accord and Prelude). Adjust valves for No. 1 cylinder.

2) Repeat procedure for remaining valves in firing order sequence, rotating crankshaft 180° counterclockwise after each adjustment to position piston of next cylinder in sequence at TDC of compression stroke.

Valve Clearance Specifications

Application	Clearance
Accord & Prelude	
Intake & Auxiliary	.005-.007" (.12-.17 mm)
Exhaust	.010-.012" (.25-.30 mm)
Civic	
Intake & Auxiliary	.005-.007" (.12-.17 mm)
Exhaust	.007-.009" (.17-.22 mm)

VALVE ARRANGEMENT

All Models
Left Side — I-E-E-I-I-E-E-I
Right Side — All Auxiliary.

SPARK PLUGS

Application	Gap In. (mm)	Torque Ft. Lbs. (mkg)
Accord & Prelude		
Calif. Auto.	.039 (1.0)	17 (2.3)
All Others	.028 (.7)	17 (2.3)
Civic	.039 (1.0)	13 (1.8)

Spark Plug Type

Application	Nippondenso	NGK
Accord & Prelude		
Calif. Auto.		B7EB-11
All Others		B7EB
Civic		
1300	W20ES-L11	
1500		B7EB-11

HIGH TENSION WIRE RESISTANCE

Carefully remove ends of wire from spark plug and distributor. Using an ohmmeter, check resistance of wire while gently twisting wire. If resistance is not to specification, or fluctuates from infinity to any value, replace wire.

Resistance (Ohms) Per Wire

Application	Resistance
All Models (2 ft. length)	25,000 Max.

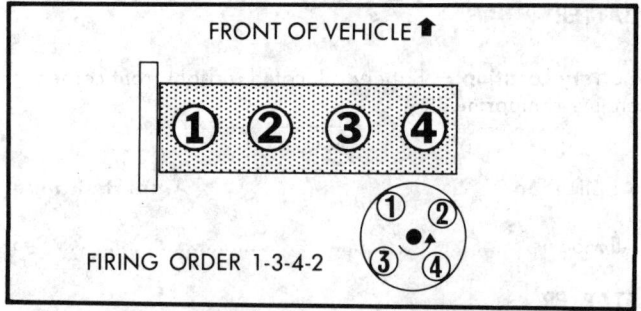

Fig. 1 Firing Order and Distributor Rotation (Accord, Civic and Prelude)

DISTRIBUTOR

All models are equipped with electronic breakerless ignition systems. California Accord and Prelude with automatic transmission use the same system as all Civic models. All other Accord and Prelude models use a different system, with igniter module mounted on firewall.

IGNITION TIMING

1) Remove rubber inspection cap from window on cylinder block. Attach timing light. Engine should be idling at normal operating temperature.

2) Timing is correct if specified mark on flywheel is aligned with index pointer on crankcase.

TUNE-UP (Cont.)

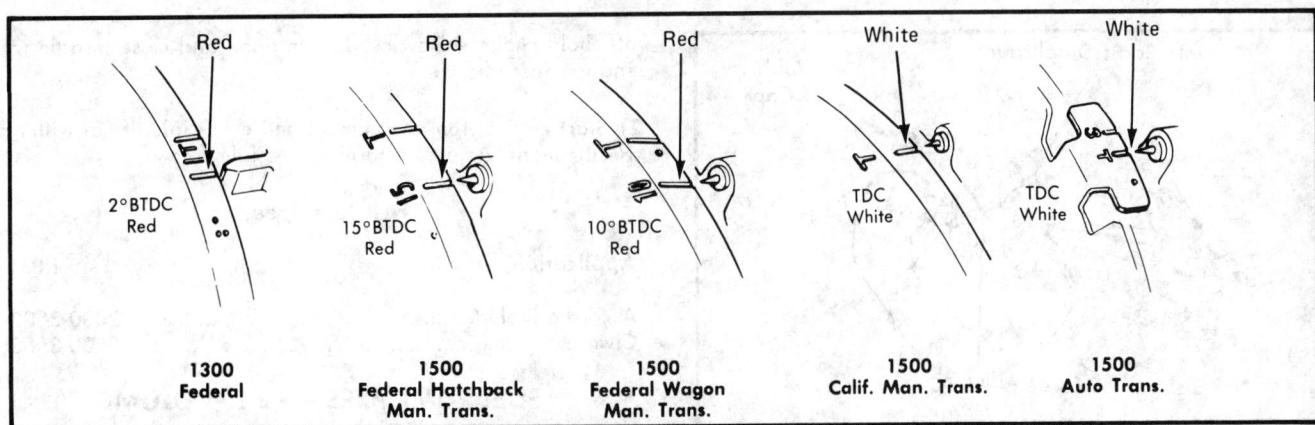

Fig. 3 Ignition Timing Mark Location
(Civic 1300 & 1500)

3) To adjust, loosen distributor bolt and turn body counterclockwise to retard timing and clockwise to advance timing.

Ignition Timing Specifications

Application	Man. Trans.	Auto. Trans.
Accord & Prelude .... ①TDC .... TDC		
Civic		
1300 .... 2°BTDC		
1500		
Federal .... ②15°BTDC .... TDC		
Calif. .... TDC .... TDC		

① — Set Calif. 4-Dr. to 4°ATDC.
② — Set wagon to 10°BTDC.

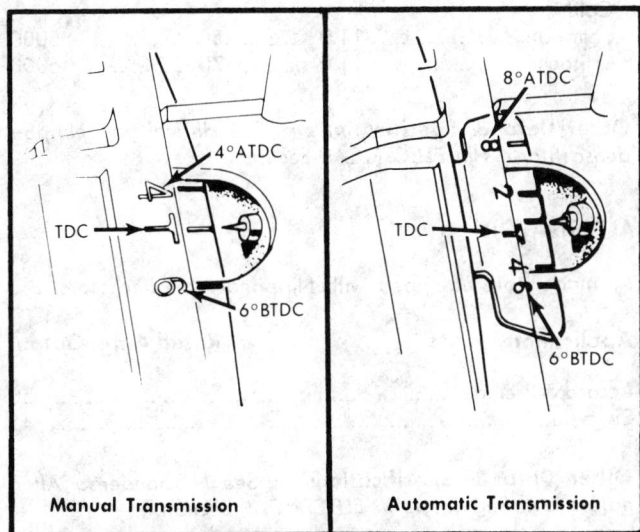

Fig. 2 Ignition Timing Mark Location
(Accord & Prelude)

IDLE SPEED & MIXTURE

PROPANE ENRICHMENT PROCEDURE

1) Start engine and warm up to normal operating temperature. Remove vacuum tube from hot air door on air cleaner and plug tube. Connect tachometer and check idle speed with all electrical accessories off.

2) If necessary, adjust idle speed with throttle screw. If equipped with air conditioning, turn system on. Idle speed should not change. If necessary, turn adjusting screw on idle boost diaphragm to return idle to specification.

3) Pull air cleaner intake tube from air duct near radiator. Insert propane hose 4" into air intake tube and slowly open valve. Engine should be idling (in Drive on automatics).

4) Engine speed should increase by amount listed in table. If increase is not as specified, idle mixture must be adjusted. If peak RPM is below specification, lean out mixture. If above specification, enrich mixture.

NOTE — *California and High Altitude vehicles have a shield over the mixture screw. Remove screw, swing tab out of the way, and use special tool 07974-6890200 to adjust mixture.*

5) Turn mixture screw clockwise to increase RPM; counterclockwise to lower RPM. Run engine at 2500 RPM for 10 seconds to stabilize mixture, then test again. Repeat procedure until idle speed and increase are correct.

6) Remove propane equipment and reconnect vacuum hose to air cleaner hot air door. Recheck idle speed with air conditioning on, and adjust with idle boost diaphragm screw.

Idle Speed & Enriched Speed

Application	Idle RPM	Enriched RPM
Accord & Prelude		
Man. Trans. 800 870		
Auto. Trans.① 800 850		
Civic		
1300 .... 750 870		
1500		
Man. Trans. 750 850		
Auto. Trans.① 750 800		

① — With Auto. Trans. in Drive.

1980 Honda 4 Tune-Up

TUNE-UP (Cont.)

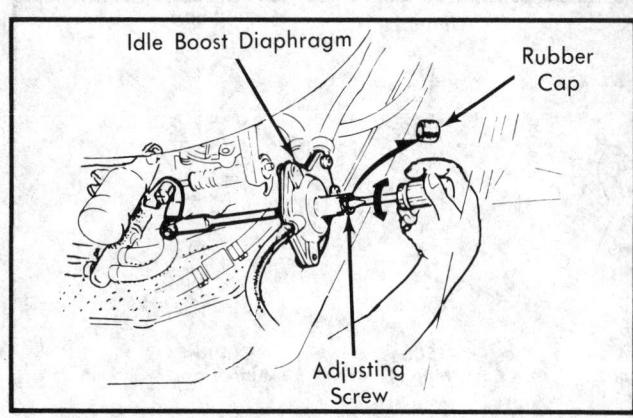

Fig. 4   Adjusting Idle Boost Diaphragm

COLD (FAST) IDLE RPM

All Models — 1) Connect tachometer to engine. Disconnect and plug vacuum hose to fast idle unloader. With the engine off, hold choke valve closed, then open and close throttle to engage fast idle cam.

2) Start engine, run one minute, and check idle. If not within specifications, adjust by turning fast idle screw.

Fast Idle Speed

Application	RPM
Accord & Prelude	2000-3000
Civic	2500-3500

FUEL PUMP PRESSURE & VOLUME

Pressure	2-3 psi (.13-.18 kg/cm²)
Volume	1.4 pts. in 30 sec.

EMISSION CONTROL SYSTEMS

See Mitchell Manuals' Emission Control Manual.

GENERAL SERVICING

IGNITION

DISTRIBUTOR

All models are equipped with Honda electronic ignition.

Other Data & Specifications — *See Honda Distributors and Ignition Systems in ELECTRICAL Section.*

IGNITION COIL

Coil Resistance (Ohms@68° F)

Application	Primary	Secondary
Accord & Prelude		
Calif. Auto.	1.06-1.24	7400-11,000
All Others	1.78-2.08	8800-13,200
Civic	1.00-1.30	7400-11,000

FUEL SYSTEMS

CARBURETORS

Application	Model
All Models	Keihin 2-Bbl.

Other Data & Specifications — *See Tune-Up and Keihin Carburetors in FUEL SYSTEMS Section.*

ELECTRICAL

BATTERY

Application	Amp. Hr. Rating
All	47

Battery Location — In engine compartment.

STARTER

Testing Specifications

Application	Volts	Amps	Test RPM
Accord & Prelude	11.5	90	3500
Civic			
Fed.	11.5	90	3000
Calif.			
Nippon.	11.0	50	5000
Hitachi	11.0	70	6000

Other Data & Specifications — *See Hitachi and Nippondenso Starters in ELECTRICAL Section.*

ALTERNATOR

All models are equipped with Nippondenso alternators.

Application	Rated Amp. Output
Accord & Prelude	50
Civic	45

Other Data & Specifications — *See Nippondenso Alternators and Regulators in ELECTRICAL Section.*

ALTERNATOR REGULATOR

All models are equipped with Nippondenso alternator regulators with an operating voltage of 13.5-14.5 volts.

Other Data & Specifications — *See Nippondenso Alternators and Regulators in ELECTRICAL Section.*

GENERAL SERVICING (Cont.)

FILTERS

Filter	Service Interval (Miles)
Oil Filter	Replace every 7500
Air Filter	Replace every 30,000

BELT ADJUSTMENT

All Models — Deflection of belt should be .5-.7" (12-17 mm) when 22 lbs. (10 kg) pressure is applied to belt midway between alternator and fan pulleys.

CAPACITIES

Application	Quantity
Crankcase (Including Filter)	
Accord & Prelude	3.8 qts.
Civic	3.2 qts.
Cooling	
Civic 1300	5.2 qts.
All Others	6.4 qts.
Man. Transaxle (SAE 10W-40)	2.5 qts.
Auto. Transaxle (Dexron II)	
Drain & Refill	2.6 qts.
Overhaul	① 5.2 qts.
Fuel Tank	
Accord & Prelude	13.2 gals.
Civic	10.8 gals.

① — Hondamatic 2-Spd., 4.4 qts.

1980 Jaguar 6 Tune-Up

TUNE-UP

XJ6L

ENGINE IDENTIFICATION

Engine number is stamped on top of cylinder block at rear of engine. Number is also stamped on Commission Plate, which is located in the engine compartment. Suffix following engine number indicates compression ratio, "L" — Low.

COMPRESSION PRESSURE

Check compression pressure with engine at normal operating temperature, throttle valve wide open, all spark plugs removed and coil wire disconnected. Compression pressure is normal if all cylinders are within 5 psi (.35 kg/cm²) of each other.

VALVE CLEARANCE

Valve Clearance Specifications

Application	Clearance (Cold)
Intake	.012-.014" (.30-.35 mm)
Exhaust	.012-.014" (.30-.35 mm)

VALVE ADJUSTMENT

1) With camshaft covers removed, rotate camshafts and record clearance between heel of each cam lobe and its respective tappet. If adjustment is necessary, rotate camshaft and install valve timing gauge (C.3993) before removing final camshaft retaining nut. If required, disconnect sprockets from camshafts.

NOTE — *DO NOT rotate engine while camshaft sprockets are disconnected.*

2) Remove camshaft bearing caps and lift off camshaft. Remove each tappet that requires adjustment and note its location for reassembly in its original position. Remove adjusting pad and measure thickness.

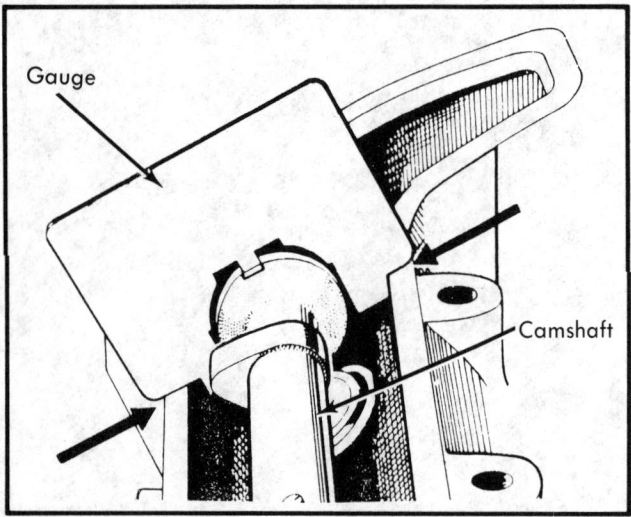

Fig. 1   Position of Valve Timing Gauge

3) Use measured pad thickness and difference between measured valve clearance and specified clearance to calculate required thickness of new adjusting pad. Adjusting pads are available in increments of .001" (.03 mm) from .085" (2.16 mm) to .110" (2.79 mm) and are marked with letters from "A" to "Z" respectively.

4) Insert correct adjusting pads and install tappets. Attach camshafts (using timing gauge). Torque camshaft bearing cap nuts to 9 ft. lbs. (1.2 mkg), connect camshaft sprockets, and install camshaft covers.

VALVE ARRANGEMENT

Left Side — All Exhaust
Right Side — All Intake

SPARK PLUGS

Application	Gap In. (mm)	Torque Ft. Lbs. (mkg)
All Models	.035 (.9)	27 (3.7)

Spark Plug Type

Application	Champion No.
All Models	N12Y

HIGH TENSION WIRE RESISTANCE

Carefully remove high tension wires from spark plugs and distributor cap. Using an ohmmeter, check resistance of each wire while gently twisting wire. If resistance is not to specifications, or fluctuates from infinity to any value, replace wire.

Resistance (Ohms) Per Wire

Application	Resistance
All Models	25,000-30,000

DISTRIBUTOR

All models are equipped with a breakerless, electronic ignition system.

Air Gap .... ①.014-.016" (.36-.41 mm)

① — Measured between timing rotor and pick-up module.

IGNITION TIMING

Check or adjust ignition timing with engine at normal operating temperature, idle speed set to specification and distributor vacuum line connected. If timing is not correct, loosen distributor clamp bolt and rotate distributor to achieve specified timing. Then tighten clamp bolt.

Ignition Timing Specifications

Application	Timing
All Models	4°BTDC

TUNE-UP (Cont.)

Fig. 2   Ignition Timing Mark Location

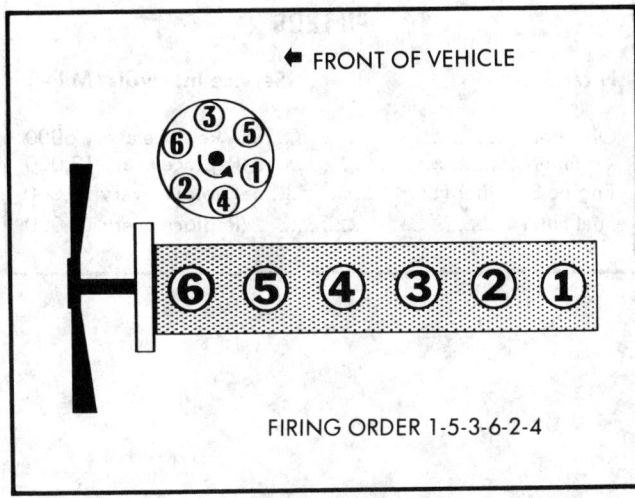

FIRING ORDER 1-5-3-6-2-4

Fig. 3   Firing Order and Distributor Rotation

IDLE SPEED & MIXTURE

1) Connect a tachometer and CO% meter to engine (at exhaust manifold test points). Run engine until normal operating temperature is reached.

2) Adjust idle with air volume screw at overrun valve housing. Use $7/32$" Allen wrench and turn clockwise to lower idle; counterclockwise to raise engine idle.

3) Remove plastic plug on airflow meter to locate mixture adjustment screw. Disconnect oxygen sensor and allow engine to idle for 1 minute to stabilize mixture.

4) Turn mixture screw clockwise to richen mixture and counterclockwise to lean mixture. If correct setting cannot be attained, check all electrical connections and all hoses for proper location.

5) Replace oxygen sensor lead and disconnect test instruments.

Idle Speed & CO Level

Application	Idle RPM	CO %
All Models	750-850	.5-1.5

FUEL PUMP PRESSURE

Pressure .... 36 psi (2.5 kg/cm²)

EMISSION CONTROL SYSTEMS

See Mitchell Manuals' Emission Control Manual.

GENERAL SERVICING

IGNITION

DISTRIBUTOR

All models are equipped with Lucas Opus Electronic Ignition System.

Other Data & Specifications — *See Tune-Up and Lucas Ignition Systems in ELECTRICAL Section.*

FUEL SYSTEMS

FUEL INJECTION

All models are equipped with Lucas-Bosch fuel injection.

Other Data & Specifications — *See Tune-Up and Bosch Fuel Injection in FUEL SYSTEMS Section.*

ELECTRICAL

BATTERY

Battery Location — Battery is located in right rear corner of engine compartment.

Application	Amp. Hr. Capacity
All Models	66

STARTER

All models are equipped with Lucas pre-engaged Starters.

Free Speed Amperage
All Models .... 100 at 5000-6000 RPM

Other Data & Specifications — *See Lucas Starters in ELECTRICAL Section.*

GENERAL SERVICING (Cont.)

ALTERNATOR

Application	Rated Amp. Output
All Models	65

Other Data & Specifications — *See Lucas Alternators and Regulators in* ELECTRICAL *Section.*

ALTERNATOR REGULATOR

Lucas — Non-Adjustable; Integral with Alternator.

Other Data & Specifications — *See Lucas Alternators and Regulators in* ELECTRICAL *Section.*

CAPACITIES

Application	Quantity
Crankcase (Includes Filter)	8.7 qts.
Cooling System	19.5 qts.
Auto. Trans. (ATF Type F)	7.5 qts.
Rear Axle (SAE 90 EP)	3.3 pts.
Fuel Tank	
Right Side	12.6 gals.
Left Side	12.6 gals.

BELT ADJUSTMENT

Belt	① Deflection
Fan/Steering Pump	Self-Adjusting
Alternator	.15" (3.8 mm)
A/C Compressor	.17" (4.3 mm)

① — Deflection is with pressure applied midway on longest belt run.

FILTERS

Filter	Service Intervals (Miles)
Oil Filter	Replace every 6000
Air Filter	Replace every 12,000
Engine Breather Filter	Replace every 12,000
Fuel Filter	Replace every 12,000

TUNE-UP

Pickup

ENGINE IDENTIFICATION

Engine serial number is stamped on pad between distributor and cylinder head.

MODEL IDENTIFICATION

VEHICLE IDENTIFICATION NUMBER

Vehicle Identification Number is stamped on a plate attached to driver's door lock pillar.

COMPRESSION PRESSURE

Test compression with engine at normal operating temperature, spark plugs removed, throttle valve wide open and engine at cranking speed. Maximum variation between cylinders should not exceed 8.5 psi (.6 kg/cm²).

Compression Pressure @ 300 RPM

Application	Min. Pressure psi (kg/cm²)	Std. Pressure psi (kg/cm²)
All Models	120 (8.4)	170 (12)

VALVE CLEARANCE

NOTE — *Before adjusting valve tappet clearance, check torque of cylinder head and camshaft bolts. Valves should be adjusted every 15,000 miles.*

1) Measure valve clearance between rocker arm and valve stem. Position piston number one on compression stroke at TDC. Adjust intake valves 1 and 2 and exhaust valves 1 and 3.

2) Turn crankshaft one full turn until number four cylinder is at TDC. Adjust intake valves 3 and 4 and exhaust valves 2 and 4.

Valve Tappet Clearance

Application	Clearance (Cold)
Intake	.006" (.015 mm)
Exhaust	.010" (.025 mm)

VALVE ARRANGEMENT

All Models
  Right Side — All Intake
  Left Side — All Exhaust

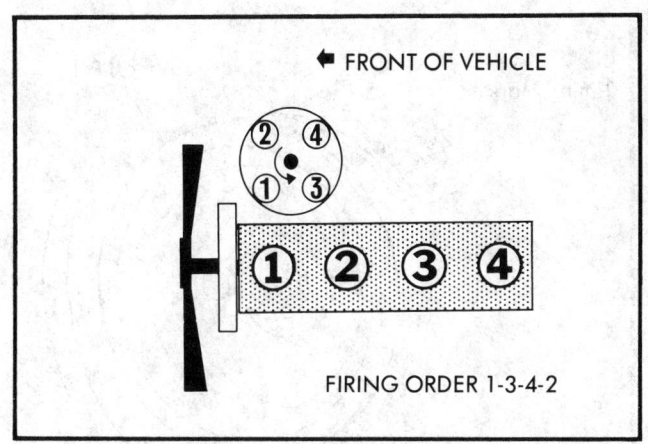

Fig. 1   Firing Order and Distributor Rotation

FRONT OF VEHICLE

FIRING ORDER 1-3-4-2

SPARK PLUGS

Gap	.030" (.8 mm)
Torque	18-25 ft. lbs. (2.5-3.5 mkg)

Spark Plug Type

Application	AC	NGK
All Models	R44XLS	BPR6ES

HIGH TENSION WIRE RESISTANCE

Carefully remove high tension wires from spark plugs and from distributor cap. Using an ohmmeter, check resistance of wire while gently twisting wire. If resistance is not to specification, or fluctuates from infinity to any value, replace wire.

Resistance (Ohms)

Application	Resistance
All Models	25,000-30,000

DISTRIBUTOR

Point Gap	.016-.020" (.41-.51 mm)
Cam Angle	47-57°
Breaker Arm Spring Tension	14-19 ozs. (400-540 g)
Condenser Capacity	.20-.24 mfd.

IGNITION TIMING

With engine at normal operating temperature and idle speed set to specification, connect a timing light to No. 1 or No. 4 cylinder. Disconnect distributor vacuum line and plug end. Check timing with marks on crankshaft pulley and rotate distributor to adjust timing.

TUNE-UP (Cont.)

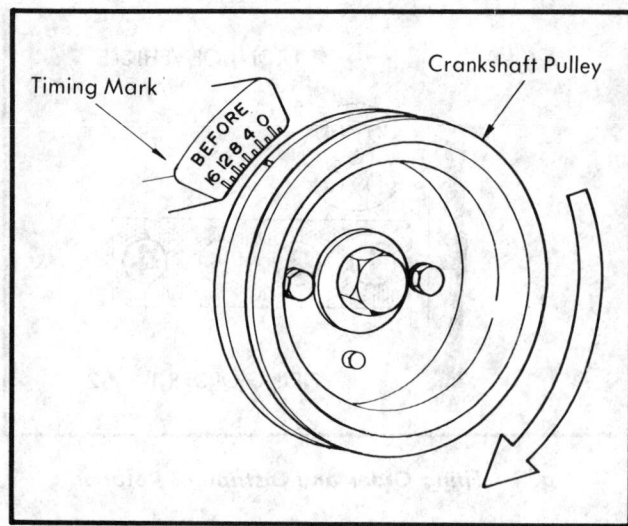

Fig. 2   Ignition Timing Mark Location

Ignition Timing Specifications

Application	Timing
All Models	①6° BTDC

① — With distributor vacuum hose disconnected and plugged.

IDLE SPEED & MIXTURE

Set idle with engine at normal operating temperature, valve clearance correctly set and ignition timing to specifications. Choke should be open, air conditioning off and air cleaner installed. Disconnect and plug vacuum lines for distributor, hot idle compensator, and EGR valve. Then proceed as follows:

1) Turn idle mixture adjusting screw fully in, then back out 3 turns (Federal) or 1½ turns (Calif.). Set throttle adjusting screw to obtain specified curb idle.

2) Reset idle mixture screw to obtain maximum RPM, then reset throttle adjusting screw to achieve specified curb idle. Turn idle mixture screw clockwise (lean) until speed drops to specified lean drop RPM.

4) On California models only, turn mixture screw out ¼ turn, then reset throttle adjusting screw to obtain curb idle.

5) If equipped with air conditioner, turn on to maximum cooling and high blower. Open throttle slightly to allow solenoid to extend, then close throttle. Adjust solenoid screw to give 900 RPM idle.

Idle Speed & Mixture Adjustment

Application	Idle RPM	Lean Drop RPM
Federal		
Man. Trans.	850	800
Auto. Trans.	950	900
Calif.	900	850

COLD (FAST) IDLE RPM

Automatic choke fast idle is adjusted by opening angle of throttle valve on carburetor, rather than by engine speed. Adjust valve opening at 1st step of fast idle cam to 16-18°.

Disconnect and plug distributor, hot idle compensator and EGR valve vacuum hoses after engine warm-up. Fast idle speed should be as follows:

Fast Idle Specifications

Application	Engine Speed
Man. Trans.	3400 RPM
Auto. Trans.	3200 RPM

AUTOMATIC CHOKE

Automatic choke is correctly set when thickest line on the thermostat housing is aligned with index mark on thermostat cover.

FUEL PUMP PRESSURE

Pressure .... 2.4-3.3 psi (.17-.23 kg/cm²)

EMISSION CONTROL SYSTEMS

See *Mitchell Manuals' Emission Control Manual.*

GENERAL SERVICING

IGNITION

DISTRIBUTOR

All Models are equipped with a Nippondenso single point distributor.

Other Data & Specifications — *See Tune-Up and Nippondenso Distributors in ELECTRICAL Section.*

IGNITION COIL

Coil Resistance (Ohms@68° F)

Application	Primary	Secondary
All Models	1.13-1.53	10,200-13,800

GENERAL SERVICING (Cont.)

FUEL SYSTEMS

CARBURETORS

Application	Model
All Models	Hitachi 2-Bbl.

Other Data & Specifications — *See Tune-Up and Hitachi Carburetors in FUEL SYSTEMS Section.*

ELECTRICAL

BATTERY

Application	Amp. Hr. Rating
All Models	50

Battery Location — Engine compartment, left side of engine.

STARTER

Hitachi	Overrunning Clutch

Starter Specifications

Application	Volts	Amps	Test RPM
All Models	12	60	6000

Other Data & Specifications — *See Hitachi Starters in ELECTRICAL Section.*

ALTERNATOR

Application	Rated Amp. Output
All Models	35

Other Data & Specifications — *See Hitachi Alternators and Regulators in ELECTRICAL Section.*

ALTERNATOR REGULATOR

All models utilize a Hitachi adjustable alternator regulator with an operating voltage of 13.8-14.8 volts.

Other Data & Specifications — *See Hitachi Alternators and Regulators in ELECTRICAL Section.*

BELT ADJUSTMENT

Belt deflection for all drive belts should be .4" (10 mm) with pressure applied midway on belt run.

FILTERS

Filter	Service Interval (Miles)
Oil Filter	①Replace every 15,000
Air Filter	Replace every 30,000
Fuel Filter	Replace every 15,000
PCV Valve	Replace every 15,000

① — Replace at 7500 miles and then every 15,000 miles.

CAPACITIES

Application	Quantity
Crankcase (Includes Filter)	4.2 qts.
Cooling System	6.4 qts.
Auto. Trans. (Dexron II)	
Refill	3.5 qts.
Overhaul	5.0 qts.
Man. Trans. (SAE 30)	
Except 4x4	2.7 pts.
4x4	5.3 pts.
Front Axle (SAE 90)	1.7 pts.
Rear Axle (SAE 90)	2.7 pts.
Fuel Tank	13.2 gals.

TUNE-UP

GLC
626
B2000 Pickup

ENGINE IDENTIFICATION

Engine serial number and model code are stamped on right front upper wall of cylinder block.

Application	Code
GLC	UC
626	MA
B2000	MA

COMPRESSION PRESSURE

Check compression pressure with engine at normal operating temperature, spark plugs removed, throttle valve wide open and engine at cranking speed. Crank engine until maximum pressure is reached at each cylinder. Compression is normal if lowest cylinder reading is at least 75% of highest reading.

Compression Pressure @300 RPM

Application	Min. Pressure psi (kg/cm^2)	Max. Pressure psi (kg/cm^2)
GLC	112 (7.9)	149 (10.5)
626 & B2000	128 (9.0)	171 (12.0)

VALVE CLEARANCE

Application	Intake In. (mm)	Exhaust In. (mm)
GLC	.010 (.25)	.012 (.30)
626 & B2000	.012 (.30)	.012 (.30)

Adjust valves with engine at normal operating temperature.

VALVE ARRANGEMENT

All Models
    Right Side — All Exhaust.
    Left Side — All Intake.

SPARK PLUGS

Application	Gap In. (mm)	Torque Ft. Lbs. (mkg)
All Models	.031 (.8)	13 (1.8)

Spark Plug Type

Application	Nippondenso	NGK
All Models	W16EXR-U	①BP-5ES

① — Use BPR-5ES where required for suppression of radio interference.

HIGH TENSION WIRE RESISTANCE

Carefully remove high tension wires from spark plugs and distributor cap. Using an ohmeter, check resistance of wires while gently twisting wire. If resistance is not to specification, or fluctuates from infinity to any value, replace wire.

Resistance (Ohms) of Wire

Application	Resistance
All Models	3300-7000 Ohms per Foot

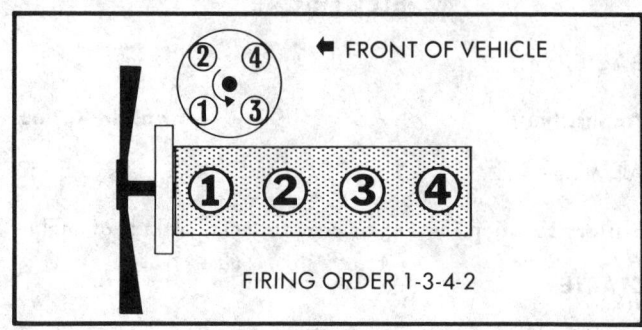

Fig. 1   Firing Order and Distributor Rotation (GLC)

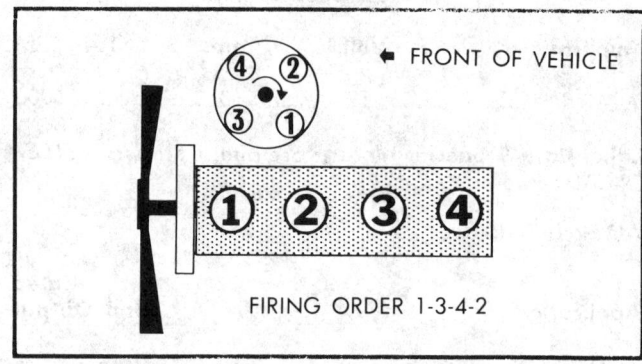

Fig. 2   Firing Order and Distributor Rotation (626 & B2000)

DISTRIBUTOR

All models are equipped with a Mitsubishi breakerless electronic ignition system.

Air Gap
GLC .... .012" (0.30 mm)
626 & B2000 .... Nonadjustable

IGNITION TIMING

With engine at normal operating temperature, idle speed set to specification and Man. Trans. in neutral or Auto. Trans. in "D", connect timing light, start engine and rotate distributor until specified mark on crankshaft pulley aligns with indicator pin.

Ignition Timing Specifications

Application	Timing
GLC & 626	5°BTDC
B2000	8°BTDC

TUNE-UP (Cont.)

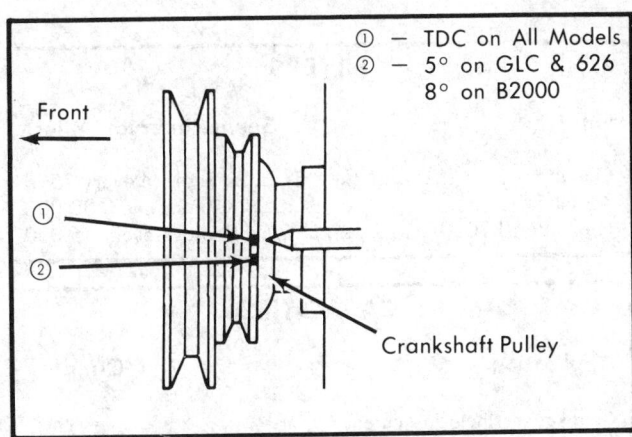

① — TDC on All Models
② — 5° on GLC & 626
    8° on B2000

Front

① ②

Crankshaft Pulley

Fig. 3   Mazda Ignition Timing Marks

IDLE SPEED AND MIXTURE

1) Connect tachometer. Start engine, warm to operating temperature, and run at 2000 RPM for 3 minutes. On B2000, disconnect canister purge hose at air cleaner. On all models, adjust idle speed with throttle adjust screw.

2) Connect CO meter at tailpipe. Disconnect air hose between air pump and air cleaner, or reed valve and air cleaner. Plug check valve or reed valve port.

3) Check CO level. If necessary, adjust by turning mixture adjust screw with screwdriver or special tool (498343869). Reconnect hoses and check idle speed. Repeat procedure if idle speed changed during adjustment. Remove test equipment.

Idle Speed & CO Level

Application	Idle RPM	CO%
GLC	650-750	1.0-4.0
626 & B2000	600-700	2.0-4.0

COLD (FAST) IDLE RPM

1) After adjusting curb idle and mixture, remove air cleaner. Hold throttle valve slightly open and push choke closed. Release throttle valve, then choke valve.

2) Start engine without touching accelerator. Check to see that engine speed increases to 3000-4000 RPM. If not, adjust using fast idle adjusting screw located on linkage below choke housing.

FUEL PUMP PRESSURE & VOLUME

Pressure (At Idle)
  GLC .... 2.8-3.8 psi (.20-.27 kg/cm²)
  626 & B2000 .... 2.8-3.6 psi (.20-.25 kg/cm²)

Volume (At Idle)
  GLC .... .7 pts. in 30 seconds
  626 & B2000 .... .8 pts. in 30 seconds

EMISSION CONTROL SYSTEMS

See Mitchell Manuals' Emission Control Manual.

GENERAL SERVICING

IGNITION

DISTRIBUTOR

All models are equipped with a Mitsubishi breakerless electronic ignition system.

Other Data & Specifications — *See Tune-Up and Mitsubishi Ignition Systems in ELECTRICAL Section.*

IGNITION COIL

Coil Resistance (Ohms@68°F)

Application	Primary	Secondary
GLC	1.28	13,500
626 & B2000	.81-.99	7000

FUEL SYSTEMS

CARBURETORS

Application	Model
GLC	Hitachi 2-Bbl.
626	Nikki 2-Bbl.
B2000	Nikki 2-Bbl.

Other Data & Specifications — *See Tune-Up and Hitachi or Nikki Carburetors in FUEL SYSTEMS Section.*

ELECTRICAL

BATTERY

Application	Amp. Hr. Rating
GLC	
Federal	45
California	33
626	45
B2000	45

STARTER

Mitsubishi .... Overrunning Clutch

Starter Specifications

Application	Volts	Amps	Test RPM
626 Auto Trans.	11.5	60	6600
All Other Models	11.5	53	6800

Other Data & Specifications — *See Mitsubishi Starters in ELECTRICAL Section.*

1980 Mazda 4 Tune-Up

GENERAL SERVICING (Cont.)

ALTERNATOR

All models are equipped with Mitsubishi alternators.

Application	Rated Amp. Output
GLC	30
626	45
B2000	30

Other Data & Specifications — *See Mitsubishi Alternators & Regulators in ELECTRICAL Section.*

ALTERNATOR REGULATOR

All models are equipped with a Mitsubishi adjustable alternator regulator with an operating voltage of 14-15 volts.

Other Data & Specifications — *See Mitsubishi Alternators & Regulators in ELECTRICAL Section.*

BELT ADJUSTMENT

Application	① Deflection
Alternator Belt	.3-.4" (8-10 mm)
Air Conditioner Belt	.6-.7" (15-18 mm)
Air Pump Belt	
GLC	.3-.4" (8-10 mm)
626 & B2000	.4-.6" (10-15 mm)

① — Deflection is with 22 lbs. (10 kg) pressure applied midway on longest belt run.

FILTERS

Filter	Service Interval (Miles)
Oil Filter	Replace every 7500
Air Filter	Replace every 30,000
Fuel Filter (B2000)	Replace every 15,000

CAPACITIES

Application	Quantity
Crankcase (Includes Filter)	
GLC	3.2 qts.
626 & B2000	4.1 qts.
Cooling System (Includes Heater)	
GLC	5.8 qts.
626	7.9 qts.
B2000	7.6 qts.
Man. Trans. (SAE 80W-90)	
4-Speed	1.5 qts.
5-Speed	1.8 qts.
Auto. Trans. (Type "F")	
All Except 626	6.0 qts.
626	6.6 qts.
Rear Axle (SAE 80W-90)	
GLC (Exc. Sta. Wagon)	2.2 pts.
GLC (Sta. Wagon)	1.6 pts.
626	2.6 pts.
B2000	2.8 pts.
Fuel Tank	
GLC (Exc. Sta. Wagon)	10.6 gals.
GLC (Sta. Wagon)	11.9 gals.
626	14.5 gals.
B2000	
Standard Bed	14.8 gals.
Long Bed	17.4 gals.

TUNE-UP

RX-7

ENGINE IDENTIFICATION

Engine type code is stamped on rear rotor housing, to the rear of oil filter. Engine serial number is stamped on front rotor housing behind distributor. Engine type codes are as follows:

Engine Type Codes

Application	Code
All Models	12A

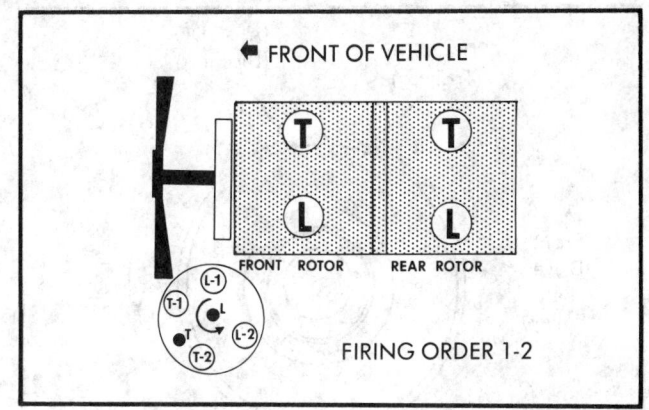

Fig. 1 Firing Order and Distributor Rotation

COMPRESSION PRESSURE

Application	Pressure
All Models	①85 psi (6 kg/cm²)

① — At 250 RPM. Maximum variation allowable between chambers is 21 psi (1.5 kg/cm²).

SPARK PLUGS

Application	Gap In. (mm)	Torque Ft. Lbs. (mkg)
All Models	.039 (1.0)	11 (1.5)

Spark Plug Type

Application	Nippondenso	NGK
All Models	W25EBR	BR8ET

HIGH TENSION WIRE RESISTANCE

Carefully remove high tension wires from spark plugs and distributor cap. Using an ohmmeter, measure resistance of wires while gently twisting wires. If resistance is not to specifications, or fluctuates from infinity to any value, replace high tension wire(s).

Resistance (Ohms) Per Wire

Application	Resistance
All Models	3300-7000 Ohms per foot

DISTRIBUTOR

All models are equipped with electronic ignition with 2 pick-up coils. Air gap is non-adjustable but should measure .008-.024" (0.2-0.6 mm).

IGNITION TIMING

NOTE — *On vehicles equipped with automatic transmission, place selector lever in "D" position and block the wheels.*

1) Warm engine to normal operating temperature. Connect a tachometer, then connect timing light to leading (lower) spark plug of front rotor. Start engine and run at idle speed.

2) Check ignition timing and rotate distributor to correct if necessary. Tighten distributor lock nut and recheck timing.

3) Connect timing light to trailing (upper) plug of front rotor. Start engine and check timing. If not correct, loosen vacuum unit attaching screws and move vacuum unit in or out to adjust trailing timing. Remove test equipment.

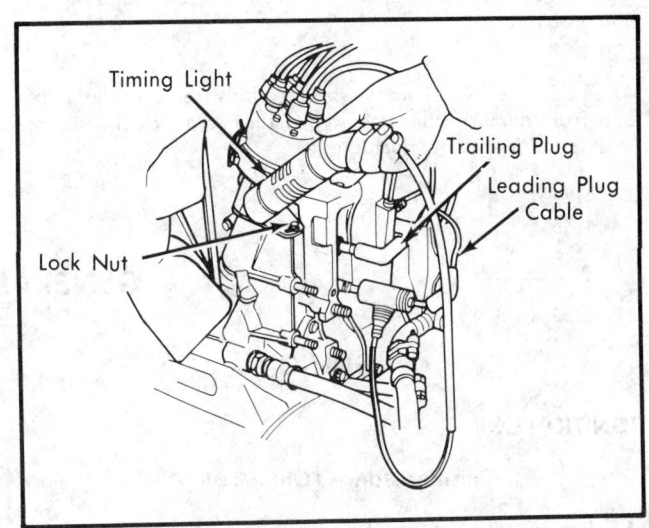

**Fig. 2 Connecting Timing Light
(Shown Connected to Leading Plug Wire)**

TUNE-UP (Cont.)

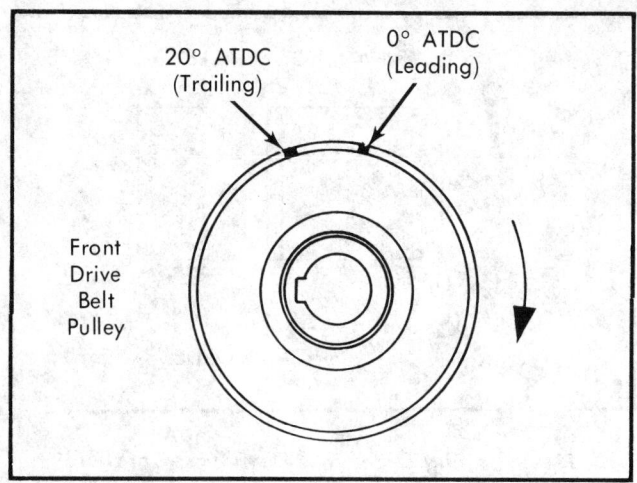

Fig. 3 Ignition Timing Mark Location

Ignition Timing Specifications

Application	Timing
Leading	TDC
Trailing	20°ATDC

IDLE SPEED & MIXTURE

1) Ensure engine is warmed up to normal operating temperature. Run engine at 2000 RPM for about 3 minutes.

2) Turn OFF all accessories. Unhook and plug idle compensator hose. Remove fuel filler cap. Connect exhaust gas analyzer to exhaust pipe and tachometer to engine.

3) With Man. Trans. in neutral or Auto. Trans. in "D", turn air adjustment screw (located on carburetor body above mixture screw) to obtain specified idle speed. Check CO level. If within specifications and idle speed is stable, mixture adjustment is not required.

4) If CO level is not within specifications, remove idle limiter cap from mixture adjusting screw. Turn screw clockwise until idle speed begins to fluctuate.

5) Slowly turn mixture adjusting screw counterclockwise until maximum specified CO level is obtained. Then, turn mixture screw an additional ½ turn counterclockwise. Recheck idle speed and readjust if necessary. Replace idle mixture limiter cap and restore all components to original positions.

Idle Speed (RPM) & CO (%)

Application	RPM	CO%
All Models	725-775	0.1

COLD (FAST) IDLE RPM

1) Connect a tachometer to engine and run engine until normal operating temperature is reached. Stop engine.

2) Pull choke knob out fully. Restart engine. Engine speed should reach RPM shown in chart within 10 seconds of starting.

3) If fast idle speed is not within specifications, remove carburetor from engine. With carburetor removed, be sure choke valve is held fully closed.

4) Measure clearance between PRIMARY throttle valve and wall of throttle bore. Clearance should be as shown in chart. If not, bend fast idle rod until correct clearance is reached.

Fast Idle Specifications

Application	RPM	Bore Clearance
All Models	3200-4000	.051-.059" (1.3-1.5 mm)

FUEL PUMP PRESSURE & VOLUME

Pressure	3.7-4.7 psi (.26-.33 kg/cm²)
Volume	1.16 qts. per min.

EMISSION CONTROL SYSTEMS

See Mitchell Manuals' Emission Control Manual.

GENERAL SERVICING

IGNITION

IGNITION COIL

Coil Resistance (Ohms@68°F)

Application	Primary	Secondary
All Models	0.81-0.99	.....

DISTRIBUTOR

All models are equipped with Mitsubishi electronic ignition systems.

Other Data & Specifications — *See Tune-Up and Mitsubishi Ignition Systems in ELECTRICAL Section.*

GENERAL SERVICING (Cont.)

FUEL SYSTEMS

CARBURETOR

Application	Model
All Models	Hitachi 4-Bbl.

Other Data & Specifications − *See Tune-Up & Hitachi Carburetors in FUEL SYSTEMS Section.*

ELECTRICAL

BATTERY

Application	Amp. Hr. Capacity
All Models	45

Battery Location − In engine compartment.

STARTER

Mitsubishi	Overrunning Clutch

Test Specifications

Application	Volts	Amps	Test RPM
Man. Trans.	11.5	50	5600
Auto. Trans.	11.5	100	6600

Other Data & Specifications − *See Mitsubishi Starters in ELECTRICAL Section.*

ALTERNATOR

Application	Rated Amp. Output
All Models	55

Other Data & Specifications − *See Mitsubishi Alternators in ELECTRICAL Section.*

ALTERNATOR REGULATOR

All models are equipped with Mitsubishi adjustable alternator regulators with an operating voltage of 14-15 volts.

Other Data & Specifications − *See Mitsubishi Alternator Regulators in ELECTRICAL Section.*

FILTERS

Filter	Service Interval (Miles)
Oil Filter	Replace every 15,000
Air Filter	Replace every 30,000

BELT ADJUSTMENT

Application	①Deflection
Alternator Belt	.5-.7″ (13-17 mm)
Air Pump Belt	.4-.5″ (11-13 mm)
A/C Belt	.3-.4″ (8-10 mm)

① − Deflection is with 22 lbs. (10 kg) pressure applied midway on longest belt run.

CAPACITIES

Crankcase (Includes Filter)	5.5 qts.
Cooling System (Includes Heater)	10.0 qts.
Man. Trans. (SAE 90)	3.6 pts.
Auto. Trans. (ATF Type F)	6.6 qts.
Rear Axle (SAE 90)	2.6 pts.
Fuel Tank	14.5 gals.

TUNE-UP

240D
300 Series

ENGINE IDENTIFICATION

First six digits of engine identification number, located on a tag at the rear, left side of engine crankcase, identify engines as follows:

Model	Code
240D	616.912
300D, CD & TD	617.912
300SD (Turbocharged)	617.950

COMPRESSION PRESSURE

Check compression pressure with engine at normal operating temperature and throttle valve fully open. Crank engine through at least 8 revolutions.

Application	Pressure psi (kg/cm²)
Normal	319-348 (22.5-24.5)
Minimum	218 (15.0)
Maximum Variation Between Cylinders	44 (3.0)

VALVE CLEARANCE

Valves must be adjusted at ignition TDC and in firing order of individual cylinders. With engine cold, measure clearance between rocker arm and base circle of cam. Adjust valves to following specifications:

Valve Clearance Specifications

Application	Intake	Exhaust
Cold	.004″ (.10 mm)	①.012″ (.30 mm)
Warm	.006″ (.15 mm)	②.014″ (.35 mm)

① — 300 SD models: .014″ (.35 mm).
② — 300 SD models: .016″ (.40 mm)

VALVE ARRANGEMENT

4-Cylinder
E-I-I-E-E-I-I-E (front-to-rear)
5-Cylinder
E-I-I-E-E-I-I-E-E-I (front-to-rear)

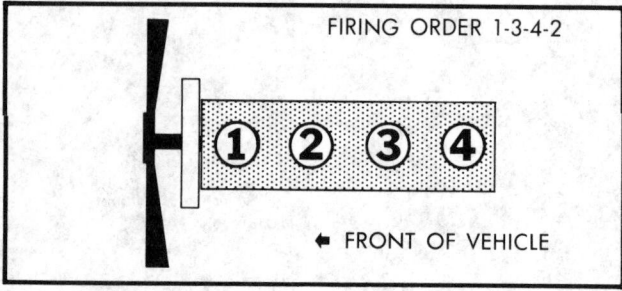

Fig. 1   240D Firing Order Illustration

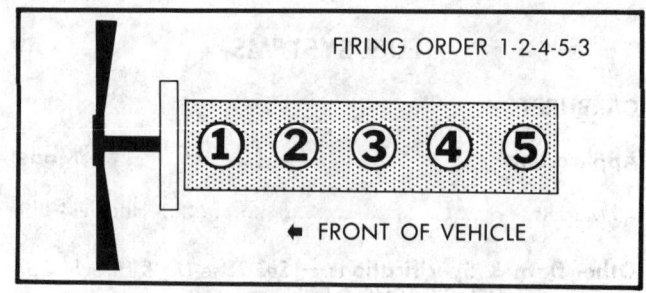

Fig. 2   300 Series Firing Order Illustration

GLOW PLUGS

Type	Bosch 0 100 221 107
Torque	15-22 ft. lbs. (2-3 mkg)

IDLE SPEED ADJUSTMENT

1) Start engine and run until normal operating temperature is reached, at least 176° F (80° C) oil temperature. If equipped, turn idle adjusting knob on dashboard clockwise to stop.

2) Disconnect throttle linkage push rod at angle lever. Check idle speed. If necessary, loosen lock nut and adjust with idle adjusting screw.

3) Reconnect push rod and adjust so clearance between lever cam and switch-over valve actuator(s) is 0.20″ (0.5 mm). Be sure speed control cable has a small amount of slack. Place transmission selector in "D", turn on air conditioning, and turn wheels to full lock. Engine must run smoothly. If not, raise idle slightly.

CAUTION — *If engine speed is adjusted too high, it will be above governor control range and could increase to maximum RPM when engine is not loaded.*

Idle Speed Specifications

Application	Idle RPM
300SD	650-850
All Others	700-800

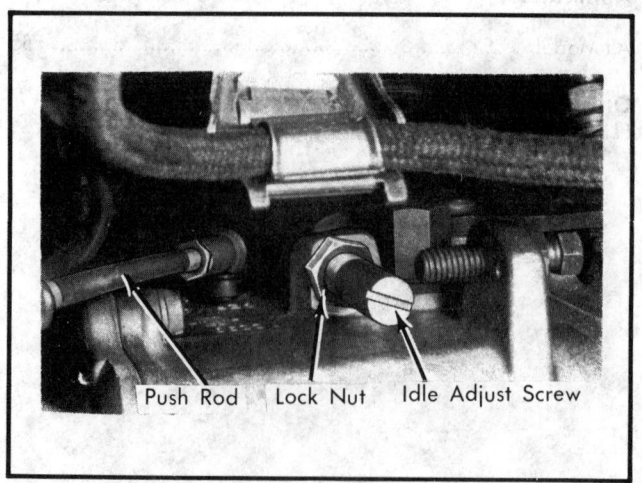

Fig. 3   Diesel Idle Adjustment Locations

GENERAL SERVICING

FUEL SYSTEMS

FUEL INJECTION

All Models use Bosch Diesel Fuel Injection.

Other Data & Specifications — *See Tune-Up and Bosch Diesel Fuel Injection in FUEL SYSTEMS Section.*

ELECTRICAL

BATTERY

Application	Amp. Hr. Rating
All Models	88

STARTER

All models are equipped with Bosch Starters.

Starter Specifications

Application	Volts	Amps	Test RPM
All Models	11.5	65-95	6500

Other Data & Specifications — *See Bosch Starters in ELECTRICAL Section.*

ALTERNATOR

Application	Rated Amp. Output
All Models	55

Other Data & Specifications — *See Bosch Alternators & Regulators in ELECTRICAL Section.*

ALTERNATOR REGULATOR

Bosch — Non-Adjustable; integral with alternator.

Other Data & Specifications — *See Bosch Alternators & Regulators in ELECTRICAL Section.*

CAPACITIES

Application	Quantity
Crankcase (Includes Filter)	
300SD	7.9 qts.
All Others	7.0 qts.
Cooling System (Includes Heater)	
240D	10.6 qts.
300SD	12.7 qts.
All Others	11.6 qts.
Man. Trans. (SAE 10W-20)	3.4 pts.
Auto. Trans. (Dexron)	
300SD	5.6 qts.
All Others	5.0 qts.
Rear Axle (SAE 90)	2.1 pts.
Fuel Tank	
240D	17.2 gals.
300TD	18.5 gals.
300D, 300CD	21.1 gals.
300SD	21.6 gals.

FILTERS

Filter	Service Interval (Miles)
Oil Filter	Replace every 5000
Air Filter	Replace every 30,000
Fuel Filter	Replace every 30,000

BELT ADJUSTMENT

Application	①Deflection
Power Steering Belt	.40" (10 mm)
All Other Belts	.20" (5 mm)

① — Deflection is with a pressure of 13 lbs. (6 kg) applied midway on longest belt run.

TUNE-UP

280 Series

ENGINE IDENTIFICATION

First six digits of engine identification number, located on tag on front left side of engine crankcase, identify engine as follows:

Engine Identification

Application	Code
280 E, CE	110.984
280 SE	110.985

COMPRESSION PRESSURE

Check compression pressure with engine at normal operating temperature and throttle valve fully open. Crank engine a minimum of eight revolutions to obtain following specifications:

Compression Pressure

Application	Pressure
Normal Pressure	130-144 psi (9-10 kg/cm²)
Minimum Pressure	108 psi (7.5 kg/cm²)
Maximum Variation	21 psi (1.5 kg/cm²)

VALVE CLEARANCE

Engine Temp.	Intake	Exhaust
Cold	.004″ (.10 mm)	.010″ (.25 mm)
Warm	.006″ (.15 mm)	.012″ (.30 mm)

VALVE ARRANGEMENT

All Models
 Right Side — All Exhaust.
 Left Side — All Intake.

SPARK PLUGS

Application	Gap In. (mm)	Torque Ft. Lbs. (mkg)
All Models	.032 (.8)	22 (3.0)

Spark Plug Type

Application	Bosch No.	Champion No.
All Models	W9D	N12Y

HIGH TENSION WIRE RESISTANCE

Carefully remove high tension wires from spark plugs and distributor cap. Using an ohmmeter, measure resistance while gently twisting wire. If resistance is not to specifications or fluctuates from infinity to any value, replace wire(s).

Resistance (Ohms) Per Wire

Application	Ohms
All Models	25,000-30,000

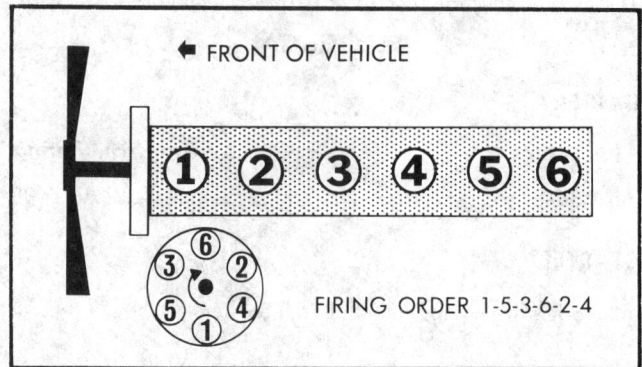

Fig. 1   Firing Order and Distributor Rotation

DISTRIBUTOR

All models are equipped with Bosch breakerless electronic ignition systems.

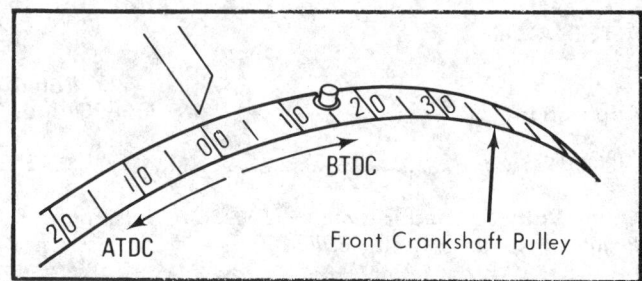

Fig. 2   280 Series Ignition Timing Marks

IGNITION TIMING

Check or adjust ignition timing with engine at normal operating temperature, idle speed set to specifications and distributor vacuum lines connected.

Ignition Timing Specifications

Application	RPM	Timing
All Models	750	10° BTDC

IDLE SPEED & MIXTURE

NOTE — *Be sure spark plug gap and ignition timing are to specifications, and check air intake system for leaks. Turn off air conditioning system when making adjustment.*

1) Connect tachometer and run engine until normal operating temperature is reached. Turn all accessories off.

TUNE-UP (Cont.)

2) Remove cover from diagnostic plug and connect negative lead of needle-type voltmeter to pin "3". Connect positive lead to battery voltage. Be sure throttle lever is against stop and cruise control cable is tension free. If not, adjust as necessary.

3) Check and adjust idle speed using idle air adjustment screw (on air housing near ignition distributor).

4) Disconnect plug from oxygen sensor in exhaust manifold. Note indicated value on voltmeter and mark dial with tape or ink. Reconnect oxygen sensor plug and check voltmeter reading.

5) Remove rubber plug in air cleaner top and insert Allen wrench. Press down on wrench until screw is engaged, then adjust until voltmeter needle fluctuates evenly around the mark

on voltmeter dial. Remove wrench, accelerate engine, and recheck. Adjust speed and mixture again if necessary.

Idle Speed

Application	RPM
All Models	700-800

FUEL PUMP PRESSURE & VOLUME

Pressure .... 72-81 psi (5.0-5.6 kg/cm²)
Volume .... 1 qt. in 30 sec.

EMISSION CONTROL SYSTEMS

See *Mitchell Manuals' Emission Control Manual.*

GENERAL SERVICING

IGNITION

DISTRIBUTOR

All models are equipped with Bosch breakerless, transistorized distributors.

Other Data & Specifications — *See Tune-Up and Bosch Ignition Systems in ELECTRICAL Section.*

IGNITION COIL

Coil Resistance (Ohms@68° F)

Application	Primary	Secondary
All Models	.38-.42	8000-11,000

FUEL SYSTEMS

FUEL INJECTION

All models are equipped with Bosch Lambda CIS fuel injection systems with oxygen sensor.

Other Data & Specifications — *See Tune-Up and Bosch Lambda CIS Fuel Injection in FUEL SYSTEMS Section.*

ELECTRICAL

BATTERY

Application	Amp. Hour Rating
All Models	55

Battery Location — In engine compartment.

STARTER

All models are equipped with Bosch starters.

Starter Specifications

Application	Volts	Amps	Test RPM
All Models	11.5	50-80	8300

Other Data & Specifications — *See Bosch Starters in ELECTRICAL Section.*

ALTERNATOR

Application	Rated Amp. Output
All Models	55

Other Data & Specifications — *See Bosch Alternators & Regulators in ELECTRICAL Section.*

ALTERNATOR REGULATOR

All models are equipped with Bosch electronic voltage regulators with an operating voltage of 13.0-14.5 volts.

Other Data & Specifications — *See Bosch Alternators & Regulators in ELECTRICAL Section.*

FILTERS

Filter	Service Interval (Miles)
Oil Filter	Replace every 7500
Air Filter	Replace every 30,000
Fuel Filter	Replace every 30,000
Auto. Trans. Filter	Replace every 30,000

GENERAL SERVICING (Cont.)

BELT ADJUSTMENT

Application	①Deflection
Power Steering Belt	.40″ (10 mm)
All Other Belts	.20″ (5 mm)

① — Deflection with 12 lbs. pressure applied midway on belt run.

CAPACITIES

Application	Quantity
Crankcase (Includes Filter)	6.3 qts.
Cooling System (Includes Heater)	
280E, 280CE	10.6 qts.
280SE	11.6 qts.
Auto. Trans (Dexron)	5.6 qts.
Rear Axle (SAE 90)	2.1 pts.
Fuel Tank	
280E, 280CE	21.1 gals.
280SE	25.4 gals.

TUNE-UP

450 Series

ENGINE IDENTIFICATION

First 6 digits of engine identification number (located on left rear side of block) are used to identify engine as follows:

Application	Code
450 SEL	117.986
450 SL	117.985
450 SLC	117.985

COMPRESSION PRESSURE

Check compression pressure with engine at normal operating temperature and throttle valve fully open. Crank engine a minimum of eight revolutions to obtain following specifications:

Application	Pressure
Normal Pressure	130-144 psi (9-10 kg/cm²)
Minimum Pressure	108 psi (7.5 kg/cm²)
Maximum Variation	21 psi (1.5 kg/cm²)

VALVE CLEARANCE

Mercedes-Benz V8 engines use hydraulic valve lifters and no adjustment is necessary.

VALVE ARRANGEMENT

450 Series
  Right Bank — E-I-E-I-E-I-I-E (front to rear).
  Left Bank — E-I-I-E-I-E-I-E (front to rear).

SPARK PLUGS

Application	Gap In. (mm)	Torque Ft. Lbs. (mkg)
All Models	.032 (.8)	22 (3.0)

Spark Plug Type

Application	Bosch No.	Champion No.
All Models	W9D	N12Y

HIGH TENSION WIRE RESISTANCE

Carefully remove high tension wires from spark plugs and distributor cap. Using an Ohmmeter, check resistance of wires while gently twisting wire. If resistance is not to specifications, or fluctuates from infinity to any value, replace wire(s).

Resistance (Ohms) Per Wire

Application	Ohms
All Models	25,000-30,000

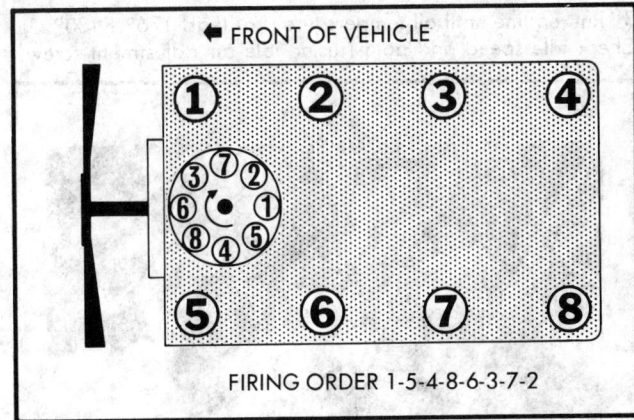

Fig. 1   Firing Order and Distributor Rotation

DISTRIBUTOR

All models feature a breakerless, transistorized ignition system.

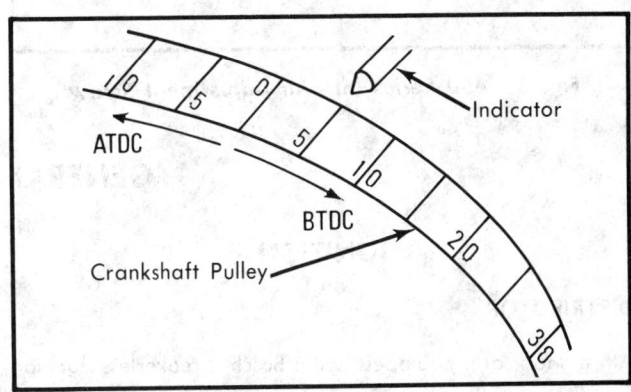

Fig. 2   450 Series Ignition Timing Marks

IGNITION TIMING

Check or adjust ignition timing with engine at normal operating temperature, idle speed set to specifications and distributor vacuum lines connected.

Ignition Timing Specifications

Application	RPM	Timing
All Models	600-700	5° BTDC

IDLE SPEED & MIXTURE

NOTE — *Be sure spark plug gap and ignition timing are to specifications, and check air intake system for leaks. Turn off air conditioning system when making adjustments.*

1) Connect tachometer and oil temperature gauge. Start engine and run in neutral with all accessories off.

2) Remove cover from diagnostic plug and connect negative lead of needle-type voltmeter to pin "3". Connect positive lead to battery voltage. Check to ensure that throttle valve lever is against stop, and cruise control cable is tension free. If not, adjust as necessary.

TUNE-UP (Cont.)

3) Run engine until oil temperature is at least 176° F (80° C). Check idle speed and adjust using idle air adjustment screw.

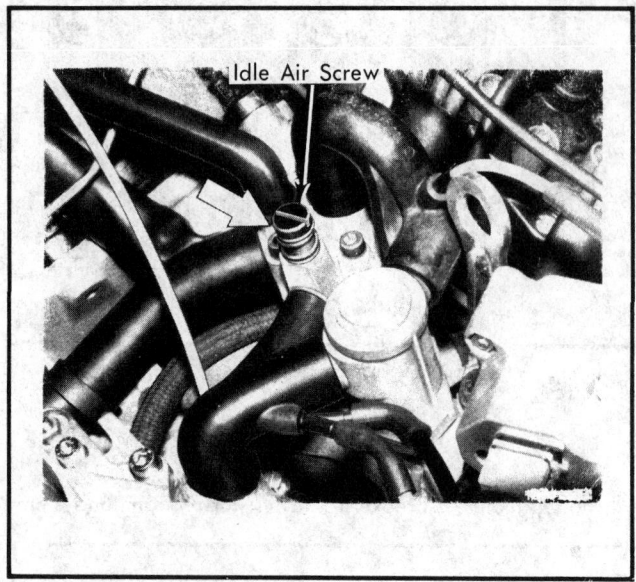
Idle Air Screw

Fig. 3   450 Series Idle Air Adjustment Screw

4) Disconnect plug from oxygen sensor. Note indicated value on voltmeter and mark dial with tape or ink. Reconnect oxygen sensor and check voltmeter reading.

5) Remove rubber plug in air cleaner top and insert Allen wrench. Press down on wrench until screw is engaged, then adjust until voltmeter needle fluctuates evenly around the mark on voltmeter dial. Remove wrench, accelerate engine, and recheck. Adjust speed and mixture again if both are not correct.

Idle Speed

Application	RPM
All Models	600-700

FUEL PUMP PRESSURE & VOLUME

Pressure .... 72-81 psi (5.0-5.6 kg/cm²)
Volume .... 1 qt. in 30 sec.

EMISSION CONTROL SYSTEMS

See *Mitchell Manuals' Emission Control Manual.*

GENERAL SERVICING

IGNITION

DISTRIBUTOR

All models are equipped with Bosch breakerless ignition system.

Other Data & Specifications — *See Tune-Up & Bosch Ignition Systems in ELECTRICAL Section.*

IGNITION COIL

Coil Resistance (Ohms@68° F)

Application	Primary	Secondary
All Models .... .38-.42 8000-11,000		

FUEL SYSTEMS

FUEL INJECTION

All models use Bosch Lambda Continuous Injection System fuel injection.

Other Data & Specifications — *See Tune-Up and Bosch Lambda CIS Fuel Injection in FUEL SYSTEMS Section.*

ELECTRICAL

BATTERY

Application	Amp. Hr. Rating
450SL, 450SLC	88
450SEL	88

Battery Location — Battery is located in engine compartment on 450SEL models, and in right side of trunk on 450SL and 450SLC models.

STARTER

All models are equipped with Bosch starters.

Starter Specifications

Application	Volts	Amps	Test RPM
All Models .... 11.5 .... 50-80 8300			

Other Data & Specifications — *See Bosch Starters in ELECTRICAL Section.*

ALTERNATOR

Application	Rated Amp. Output
All Models	70

Other Data & Specifications — *See Bosch Alternators & Regulators in ELECTRICAL Section.*

ALTERNATOR REGULATOR

All models use Bosch integral alternator regulators with an operating voltage of 13.0-14.5 volts.

Other Data & Specifications — *See Bosch Alternators & Regulators in ELECTRICAL Section.*

GENERAL SERVICING (Cont.)

BELT ADJUSTMENT

Application	① Deflection
Power Steering Belt	.40" (10 mm)
All Other Belts	.20" (5 mm)

① — Deflection with 12 lbs. pressure applied midway on belt run.

FILTERS

Filter	Service Interval (Miles)
Oil Filter	Replace every 7500
Air Filter	Replace every 30,000
Fuel Filter	Replace every 30,000
Auto. Trans. Filter	Replace every 30,000

CAPACITIES

Application	Quantity
Crankcase (Includes Filter)	8.4 qts.
Cooling System (Includes Heater)	15.8 qts.
Auto. Trans. (Dexron)	8.3 qts.
Rear Axle (SAE 90)	2.7 pts.
Fuel Tank	
450SL, 450SLC	23.8 gals.
450SEL	25.4 gals.

TUNE-UP

MGB

ENGINE IDENTIFICATION

MGB number is stamped on a plate attached to right side of cylinder block. Engine may be identified by prefix of engine number as follows:

Application	Engine Code
MGB	18V

COMPRESSION PRESSURE

Application	Pressure
MGB	①130 psi (9.1 kg/cm²)

① — Minimum.

VALVE CLEARANCE

Remove valve cover and observe opening and closing of valves. Measure clearance between rocker arms and valve stems for a "sliding" fit. To check clearance, turn crankshaft until first valve listed is open, then check or adjust second valve listed. Adjust in following order: 8 (open) - 1 (adjust), 6-3, 4-5, 7-2, 1-8, 3-6, 5-4, 2-7.

NOTE — *Count valves from front to rear.*

Valve Clearance

Application	①Clearance
MGB (Hot)	.013″ (.33 mm)

① — Intake and exhaust valves set to same clearance.

VALVE ARRANGEMENT

E-I-I-E-E-I-I-E (front to rear).

SPARK PLUGS

Application	Gap In. (mm)	Torque Ft. Lbs. (mkg)
All Models	.035 (.9)	.... 18 (2.5)

Spark Plug Type

Application	Champion No.
MGB...	N-9Y

HIGH TENSION WIRE RESISTANCE

Remove high tension wires from spark plugs and distributor cap. Using an ohmmeter, check high tension wire resistance while gently twisting wire. If resistance is not to specifications, or fluctuates from infinity to any value, replace wire(s).

Resistance (Ohms) Per Wire

Application	Ohms
All Models	25,000-30,000

DISTRIBUTOR

All models are equipped with breakerless, electronic ignition systems.

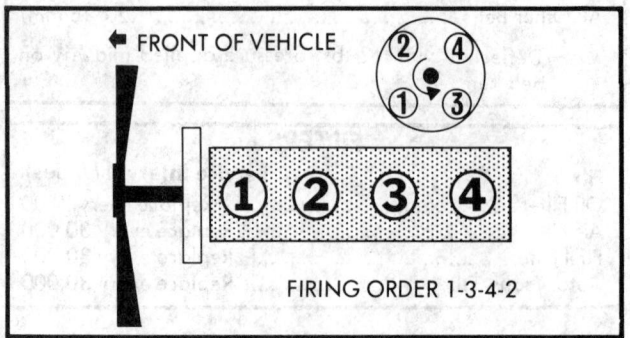

Fig. 1   MGB Firing Order and Distributor Rotation

IGNITION TIMING

Check or adjust engine timing with engine speed as specified. Rotate distributor to obtain correct timing.

Ignition Timing Specifications

Application	RPM	Timing
MGB	1500	.... 10°BTDC

Fig. 2   MGB Ignition Timing Mark Location

IDLE SPEED & MIXTURE

NOTE — *Before checking idle speed and CO% level, be sure valve clearance, spark plug gap and ignition timing are to specifications. Install tachometer on engine.*

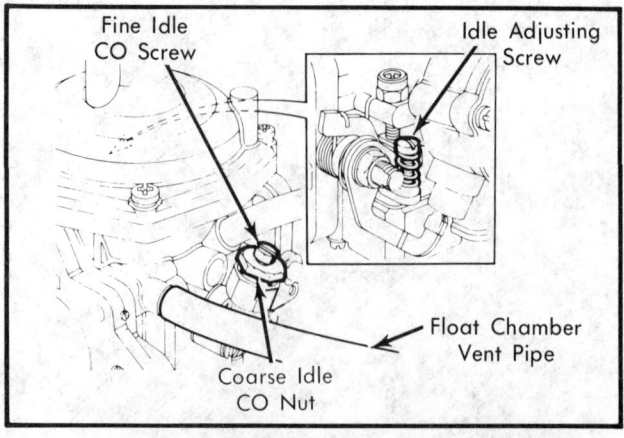

Fig. 3   Adjusting Idle Speed & CO%

TUNE-UP (Cont.)

1) Top up carburetor damper piston with engine oil and run engine until it reaches operating temperature.

2) Disconnect air manifold hose from check valve and plug hose. Disconnect float chamber vent pipe from carburetor. See Fig. 3.

3) Run engine at 2500 RPM for 30 seconds and check idle speed. Adjust idle speed to specifications, using idle adjusting screw.

4) Connect an exhaust gas analyzer to vehicle. If CO% level is not within specifications, turn FINE idle CO screw clockwise to enrich and counterclockwise to weaken mixture.

5) If correct CO level cannot be obtained by means of the fine idle CO screw, remove piston damper and insert adjusting tool (BLT 2010) into dashpot. Ensure that outer tool is engaged in piston and inner tool engages hexagon hole in needle adjuster plug.

6) Hold outer tool firmly and turn inner tool clockwise to enrich or counterclockwise to weaken mixture. After each adjustment, top up piston with engine oil, reinstall damper and recheck CO level. When proper CO level is obtained, recheck idle speed. Restore all components to original positions.

Idle Speed & CO Level

Application	Idle RPM	①CO%
MGB	750-950	4.5-6.5

① — With air injection disconnected.

COLD (FAST) IDLE RPM

1) All models are equipped with automatic chokes for fuel enrichment. To check and adjust, remove carburetor. Open throttle butterfly and wedge open. Remove bolt and washer holding water jacket and three screws retaining heat mass.

2) Rotate the operating arm and check vacuum kick piston and rod for full, free movement; fast idle cam and thermostat lever freeness to pivot; and spring operation on cam and lever.

3) Remove wedge from throttle opening.

4) Set gap between choke and throttle levers to proper clearance. Adjust by turning idle speed screw.

5) Adjust throttle stop screw to obtain proper clearance between end of fast idle pin and cam. Lock adjusting screw with lock nut.

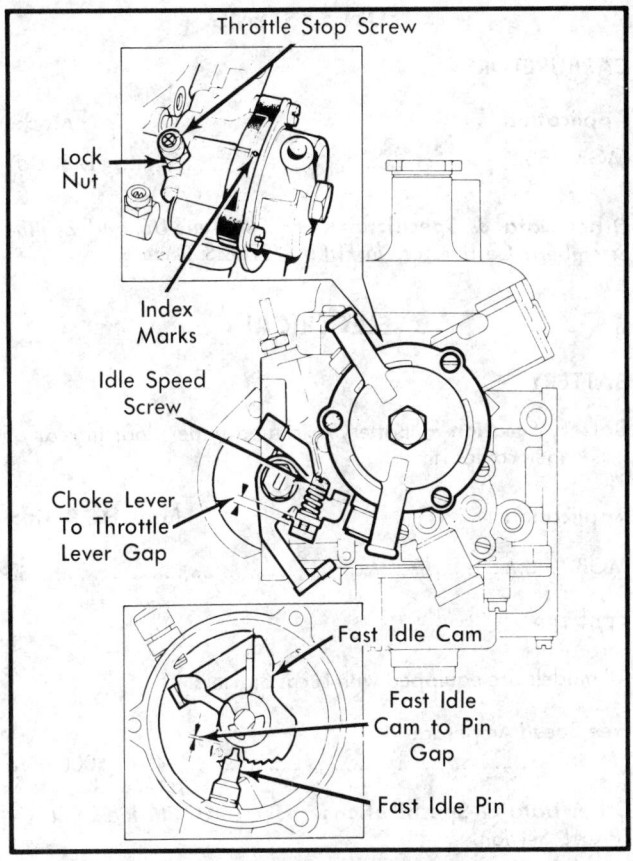

Fig. 4 Setting Fast Idle Clearances

6) Install parts previously removed, being sure to align index marks on heat mass and automatic choke body. Reinstall carburetor and check or adjust idle speed and CO% level.

Fast Idle Gap Settings

Application	Clearance
Choke Lever-to-Throttle Lever	.094" (2.4 mm)
Fast Idle Pin-to-Cam	.025" (.6 mm)

FUEL PUMP PRESSURE & VOLUME

Pressure (At Idle)	2.8-3.8 psi (.20-.27 kg/cm²)
Volume	1 pint in 30 sec.

EMISSION CONTROL SYSTEMS

See Mitchell Manuals' Emission Control Manual.

GENERAL SERVICING

IGNITION

DISTRIBUTOR

All models are equipped with Lucas Opus breakerless, electronic ignition systems.

Other Data & Specifications — See Tune-Up and Lucas Ignition Systems in ELECTRICAL Section.

IGNITION COIL

Coil Resistance (Ohms@68° F)

Application	Primary	Secondary
All Models	1.43-1.58	

1980 MG 4 Tune-Up

TUNE-UP (Cont.)

FUEL SYSTEMS

CARBURETORS

Application	Model
MGB 1-Bbl.	175CD5T

Other Data & Specifications — *See Tune-Up and Zenith-Stromberg Carburetors in FUEL SYSTEMS Section.*

ELECTRICAL

BATTERY

Battery Location — Battery is located under floor in rear of passenger compartment.

Application	Amp. Hr. Rating
MGB	66

STARTER

All models are equipped with Lucas Starters.

Free Speed Amperage
MGB...	40 at 6000 RPM

Other Data & Specifications — *See Lucas Starters in ELECTRICAL Section.*

ALTERNATOR

Application	Rated Amp. Output
MGB	45

Other Data & Specifications — *See Lucas Alternators and Regulators in ELECTRICAL Section.*

ALTERNATOR REGULATOR

Lucas — Non-Adjustable; Integral with Alternator.

Other Data & Specifications — *See Lucas Alternators and Regulators in ELECTRICAL Section.*

BELT ADJUSTMENT

Adjust belts to give ½″ deflection when depressed with moderate hand pressure on longest belt span.

FILTERS

Filter	Service Interval (Miles)
Oil Filter	Replace every 6,500
Air Filter	Replace every 12,500
Fuel Filter	Replace every 12,500

CAPACITIES

Application	Quantity
Crankcase (Includes Filter)	3.6 qts.
Cooling System (Includes Heater)	7.2 qts.
Man. Trans. (SAE 20W-50)	3.6 pts.
Rear Axle (SAE 90)	2.0 pts.
Fuel Tank	13.0 gals.

TUNE-UP

505

ENGINE IDENTIFICATION

Engine in all 505 models is referred to as XN6 version. Engine codes are stamped on camshaft tunnel on left side of block.

505
  Man. Trans. .... M5 BVM
  Auto. Trans. .... M3 BVA

VALVE CLEARANCE

Valves must be set with engine cold. To adjust valves, rotate crankshaft until valve listed in first column of table is fully open, then adjust valves listed in second column of table. Note that valves (and cylinders) are numbered from REAR to FRONT.

Valve Open	Valves to Adjust
No. 1 Exh.	No. 3 Int. & No. 4 Exh.
No. 3 Exh.	No. 4 Int. & No. 2 Exh.
No. 4 Exh.	No. 2 Int. & No. 1 Exh.
No. 2 Exh.	No. 1 Int. & No. 3 Exh.

Valve Clearance

Valve	①Clearance
Intake	.004″ (.1 mm)
Exhaust	.010″ (.25 mm)

① — +.002″ (.05 mm)

VALVE ARRANGEMENT

All Models
  Right Side — All Exhaust.
  Left Side — All Intake.

SPARK PLUGS

Gap .... .024″ (.6 mm)

Spark Plug Type

Application	Bosch No.
All Models	WR7DS

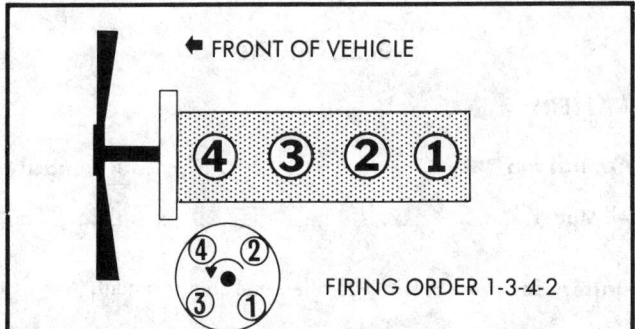

Fig. 1   Firing Order and Distributor Rotation

HIGH TENSION WIRE RESISTANCE

Carefully remove high tension wires from spark plugs and distributor cap. Using an ohmmeter, check high tension wire resistance while gently twisting wire. If resistance is not to specification, or fluctuates from infinity to any value, replace wire(s).

Resistance (Ohms) Per Wire

Application	Ohms
All Models	6000

DISTRIBUTOR

All models use a Ducellier single pickup breakerless distributor in conjunction with an AC Delco coil and transistorized amplifier module. The only adjustment provided is for air gap between the reluctor and pickup coil in the distributor. Measure gap using a non-magnetic feeler gauge. If gap is not to specifications, loosen pickup coil screws and adjust gap.

Air Gap .... .012-.020″ (.30-.50 mm)

IGNITION TIMING

1) Disconnect vacuum advance hose and plug it. Connect timing light, dwell meter and tachometer. Start engine and check dwell angle.

2) With engine idling at 900 RPM, check ignition timing. The 8° reference mark should align with notch on pulley. To adjust timing, loosen distributor flange and turn distributor until timing is to specifications. Tighten flange. Reconnect vacuum hose to distributor.

Ignition Timing Specifications

Application	RPM	Timing
All Models	900	8°BTDC

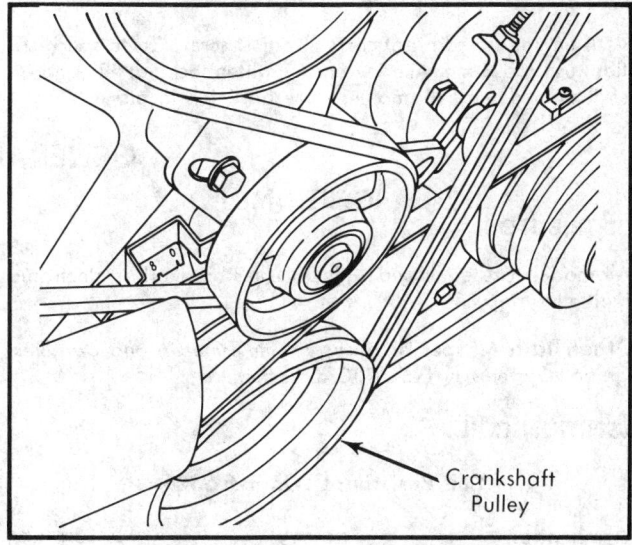

Fig. 2   Timing Marks Illustrated

IDLE SPEED & MIXTURE

1) With engine at normal operating temperature, turn off all electrical accessories and air conditioning. Connect tachometer, and connect CO meter to front tap in catalytic converter.

TUNE-UP (Cont.)

2) With transmission in neutral and air cleaner in place, adjust idle speed at air bleed screw on throttle housing using special tool 8.0141 BA. Accelerate engine and return to idle, then check CO level.

3) If CO is incorrect, disconnect wire from air slide valve thermal switch (top rear of engine). Disconnect and plug vacuum supply hose to canister purge valve and air injection hose at diverter valve. Use Allen wrench to adjust mixture after removing plug from fuel distributor (below brake master cylinder).

NOTE — *Do not push down on wrench while adjusting or readings will be incorrect. Remove wrench and plug access hole before accelerating engine or checking CO level.*

4) Accelerate engine and recheck CO%. If not correct, repeat adjustment. Remove equipment and reconnect thermal switch wire, canister purge hose and air injection hose.

Idle Speed & CO Level

Application	RPM	CO%
All Models	900-950	0.5-1.5

COLD (FAST) IDLE RPM

1) With engine at operating temperature and idle correctly adjusted, place transmission in neutral and turn off all accessories. Stop engine.

2) Disconnect hose with green ring from vacuum "T" near Solex valve (right fender panel). Disconnect hose with red ring from Solex valve and connect it to "T". This applies vacuum to idle speed diaphragm.

3) Remove domed nut "1" in *Fig. 3*. Loosen lock nut "2" and start engine. Engine speed should be 1500-1550 RPM.

4) If engine speed is not correct, adjust screw "3" to specification, using a 3 mm Allen wrench. Tighten lock nut "2" and install domed nut "1", making sure gasket is in place.

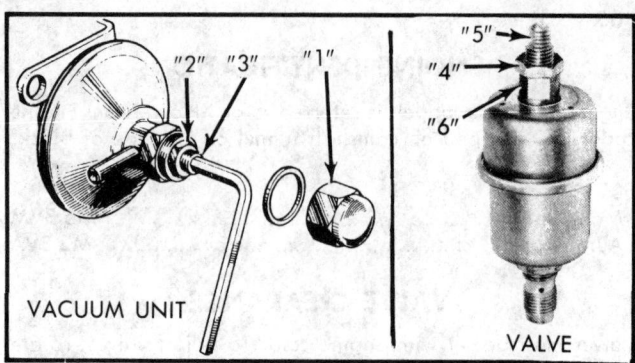

Fig. 3   Adjusting Fast Idle at Deceleration Vacuum Unit

5) Return vacuum hoses to original locations. Loosen lock nut "4" on Solex valve (not vacuum unit). Screw in threaded rod "5" to obtain 1500 RPM idle.

NOTE — *Always hold part "6" with wrench when loosening or tightening lock nut on deceleration valve, so as not to exert force on diaphragm.*

6) Increase engine speed to 3000 RPM without load, and allow engine speed to decrease. Unscrew threaded rod "5" one-half a turn at a time until normal idle (900 RPM) is obtained.

7) Then unscrew threaded rod one additional half turn and tighten lock nut.

Fast Idle RPM

Application	RPM
All Models	1500-1550

EMISSION CONTROL SYSTEMS

See Mitchell Manuals' Emission Control Manual.

GENERAL SERVICING

IGNITION

DISTRIBUTOR

All models are equipped with Ducellier breakerless electronic ignition systems.

Other Data & Specifications — *See Tune-Up and Ducellier Ignition Systems in ELECTRICAL Section.*

IGNITION COIL

Coil Resistance (Ohms@68°F)

Application	Primary	Secondary
All Models	.48-.61	9000-11,000

FUEL SYSTEMS

FUEL INJECTION

All models are equipped with Bosch Lambda Continuous Injection System (CIS) fuel injection with oxygen sensor.

Other Data & Specifications — *See Tune-Up and Bosch Lambda CIS Injection Systems in FUEL SYSTEMS Section.*

ELECTRICAL

BATTERY

Application	Amp. Hour Capacity
All Models	60

Battery Location — Left side of engine compartment.

STARTER

All models use Paris Rhone starters.

Other Data & Specifications — *See Paris Rhone Starters in ELECTRICAL Section.*

GENERAL SERVICING (Cont.)

ALTERNATOR

All models are equipped with Paris Rhone Alternators.

Application	Rated Amp. Output
All Models	75

ALTERNATOR REGULATOR

A solid state, integral alternator regulator is used on all models.

FILTERS

Filter	Service Interval (Miles)
Oil Filter	Replace every 10,000
Fuel Filter	Replace every 30,000
Air Filter	Replae every 30,000

BELT ADJUSTMENT

Loosen idler pulley mounting bolts and apply 36 ft. lbs. (5 mkg) to pivot nut above idler pulley. Tighten bolts, then turn engine one revolution. Loosen bolts and apply 58 ft. lbs. (8 mkg) to pivot nut. Tighten idler pulley mounting bolts.

Air conditioning belt is tightened by pivoting compressor. The belt from crankshaft pulley to water pump is a force-fit and no adjustment is possible.

CAPACITIES

Application	Quantity
Crankcase (Includes Filter)	4.2 qts.
Cooling System	7.6 qts.
Man. Trans. (SAE 10W-40)	3.4 pts.
Auto. Trans. (Dexron)	5.4 qts.
Rear Axle (SAE 80)	3.2 pts.
Fuel Tank	18.0 gals.

TUNE-UP

504 Diesel
505 Diesel

ENGINE IDENTIFICATION

Engine number is stamped on left side of block just below cylinder head. The engine number is followed by the VIN number. Numbers for the 1980 XD2 engines begin at 1080373 for 505 models, and 3375001 for 504 models.

COMPRESSION PRESSURE

With engine at normal operating temperature, disconnect injection lines, then remove return lines and nozzle holders. Lock pump stop control in off position. Connect pressure gauge and crank for 4 seconds at 300 RPM. Compression pressure should be as follows:

**Compression Pressure
@300 RPM**

Application	Pressure
All Models	435-580 psi (30.6-40.7 kg/cm²)

VALVE CLEARANCE

Valves must be set with engine cold. To adjust valves, rotate crankshaft until valve listed in first column of table is fully open, then adjust valves listed in second column of table. Note that valves (and cylinders) are numbered from REAR to FRONT.

Valve Adjustment Sequence

Valve Open	Valves to Adjust
No. 1 Exh.	No. 3 Int. & No. 4 Exh.
No. 3 Exh	No. 4 Int. & No. 2 Exh.
No. 4 Exh.	No. 2 Int. & No. 1 Exh.
No. 2 Exh.	No. 1 Int. & No. 3 Exh.

Valve Clearance

Application	Clearance
Intake	.006-.008″ (.15-.20 mm)
Exhaust	.010-.012″ (.25-.30 mm)

VALVE ARRANGEMENT

All Models — I-E-E-I-I-E-E-I (rear to front)

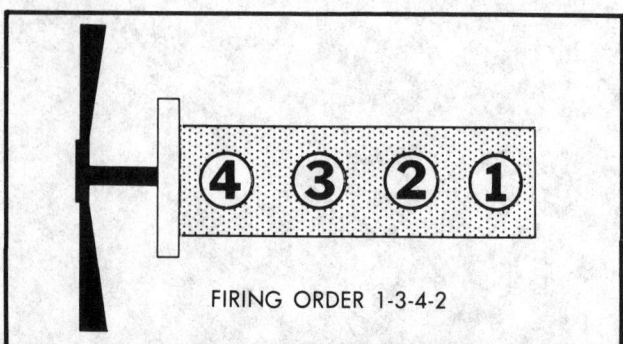

FIRING ORDER 1-3-4-2

Fig. 1   504 & 505 Diesel Firing Order

GLOW PLUGS

Torque .... 33 ft. lbs. (4.5 mkg)

SLOW IDLE RPM

With engine at normal operating temperature, adjust idle speed using idle speed screw.

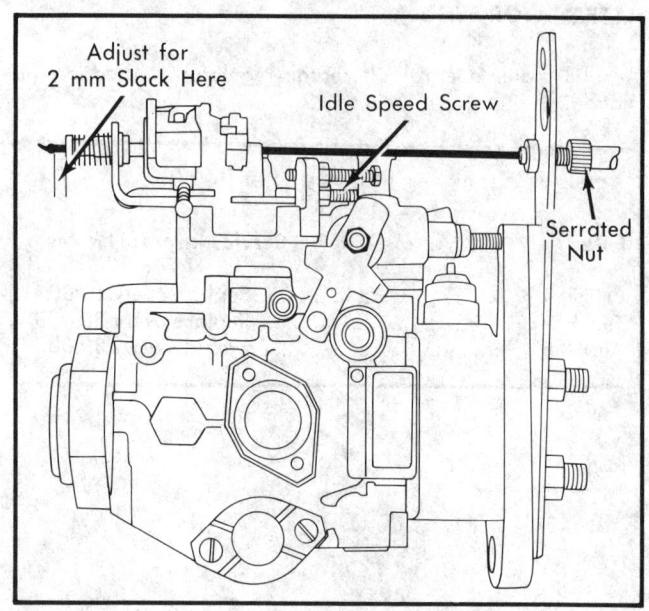

Fig. 2   Diesel Idle Adjustment Locations

FAST IDLE RPM

Adjust cable tension so cable end has .08″ (2 mm) free play. Start engine and pull spool to maximum travel. Adjust engine RPM by rotating serrated nut where cable passes through mounting bracket. Recheck free play in cable.

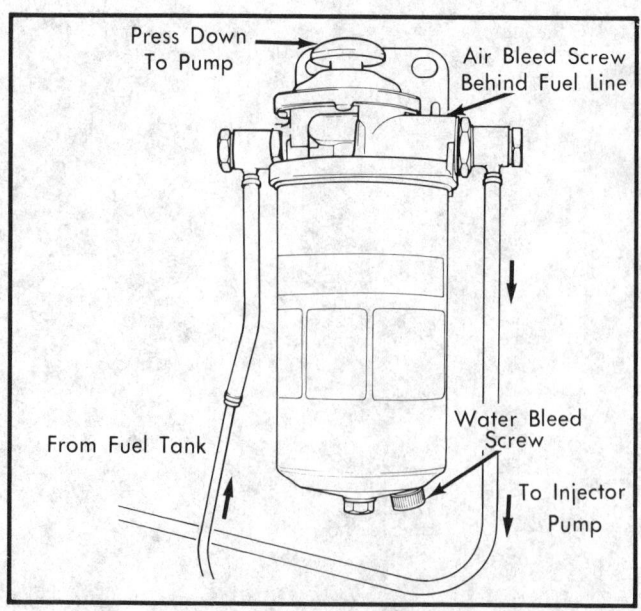

Fig. 3   Fuel System Bleeding Locations

TUNE-UP (Cont.)

Slow & Fast Idle RPM

Application	Slow RPM	Fast RPM
All Models		
Without A/C	780-830	1200-1300
With A/C	830-860	1200-1300

BLEEDING & PRIMING FUEL SYSTEM

1) Loosen bleed screw at bottom of filter bowl. Pump lever or button on top of filter to force out water. Retighten bleed screw and loosen air bleed screw. Pump button until resistance is felt, then tighten air bleed screw.

2) If vehicle ran out of fuel and injector pump is dry, continue to pump fuel filter button approximately 40 times. Turn key on and activate starter for 15 seconds, then press accelerator until engine starts.

GENERAL SERVICING

FUEL SYSTEMS

FUEL INJECTION

All models use Bosch Diesel Injection Systems with the VE4/9 F2250 R50 pump.

Other Data & Specifications — *See Tune-Up and Bosch Diesel Fuel Injection in FUEL SYSTEMS Section.*

ELECTRICAL

BATTERY

Application	Amp. Hour Capacity
All Models	90

Battery Location — In engine compartment.

STARTER

All Models	Bosch, Ducellier or Paris-Rhone

Other Data & Specifications — *See Bosch, Ducellier or Paris-Rhone Starters in ELECTRICAL Section.*

ALTERNATOR

All models are equipped with a Paris Rhone alternator rated at 75 amperes.

ALTERNATOR REGULATOR

All models are equipped with a Paris Rhone integral alternator regulator.

FILTERS

Filter	Service Interval (Miles)
Air Filter	Replace every 12,500
Oil Filter	Replace every 3000
Fuel Filter	Replace every 12,500

BELT ADJUSTMENT

Tighten belts until deflection on longest span is approximately $\frac{1}{4}$-$\frac{3}{8}$" when depressed with thumb pressure.

CAPACITIES

Application	Quantity
Crankcase (Includes Filter)	5.3 qts.
Cooling System	10.5 qts.
Man. Trans. (SAE 10W-40)	2.4 pts.
Auto. Trans. (Dexron)	5.4 qts.
Rear Axle (SAE 80)	3.3 pts.
Fuel Tank	18.0 gals.

1980 Peugeot V6 Tune-Up

TUNE-UP

604

ENGINE IDENTIFICATION

Engine number is stamped on left side of engine block, directly in front of oil filter. Engine codes are as follows:

Engine Code Numbers

Application	Code Number
All Models	
174" (2849 cc) V6	
Manual Transmission	151.9 ZM
Automatic Transmission	151.9 ZA

COMPRESSION PRESSURE

With engine at normal operating temperature, disconnect and plug fuel line to carburetor. Lock throttle plate fully open and remove all spark plugs. Crank engine for four seconds on each cylinder to obtain an accurate compression reading. Compression pressure should check approximately as shown in table, with a maximum variation between cylinders of 14.5 psi (1.0 kg/cm^2).

Compression Pressure

Application	Pressure psi (kg/cm^2)
All Models	160 (11.2)

VALVE CLEARANCE

1) Valves must be set with engine cold. Bring piston of No. 1 cylinder to TDC on ignition stroke. Align distributor rotor with timing mark on distributor housing. Check that slot in crankshaft pulley aligns with "0" mark on timing plate. Adjust the following valves:

Adjustment Sequence

Exhaust Valves	Intake Valves
No. 1, No. 3, & No. 6	No. 1, No. 2, & No. 4

2) Bring piston of No. 1 cylinder to TDC at end of exhaust stroke. Rotate crankshaft one full turn. Distributor rotor should now point 180° away from housing timing mark. Slot of crankshaft pulley should again align with "O" mark on timing plate. Adjust valves:

Adjustment Sequence

Exhaust Valves	Intake Valves
No. 2, No. 4, & No. 5	No. 3, No. 5 & No. 6

Valve Clearance Specifications

Valves	Clearance
Intake	.004" (.10 mm)
Exhaust	.010" (.25 mm)

VALVE ARRANGEMENT

Intake Valves — Center of "V" (Inner Row of Valves in Each Head)

Exhaust Valves — Outer Row of Valves in Each Head

SPARK PLUGS

Application	Gap In. (mm)	Torque Ft. Lbs. (mkg)
All Models	.024 (.6)	13 (1.8)

Spark Plug Type

Application	Champion No.
All Models	BN9Y

HIGH TENSION WIRE RESISTANCE

Carefully remove high tension wires from spark plugs and distributor cap. Using an ohmmeter, check high tension wire resistance while gently twisting wire. If resistance is not to specification, or fluctuates from infinity to any value, replace wire(s).

Resistance (Ohms) Per Wire

Application	Ohms
All Models	7000-12,000

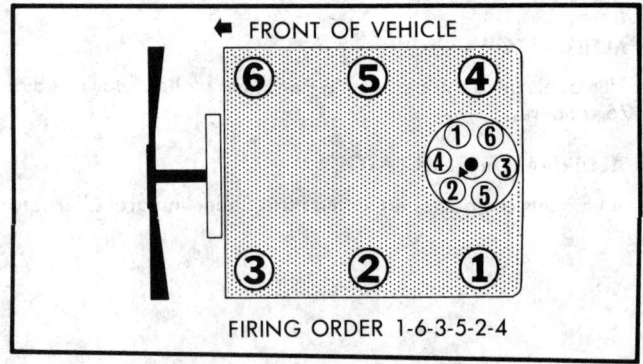

← FRONT OF VEHICLE

FIRING ORDER 1-6-3-5-2-4

Fig. 1   Firing Order and Distributor Rotation

DISTRIBUTOR

All models are equipped with breakerless ignition system.

IGNITION TIMING

1) With engine at normal operating temperature, but not running, connect wires 152 and 152A from air injection electrovalves to ground with jumper wires.

TUNE-UP (Cont.)

NOTE — *These electrovalve terminals are connected to the thermoswitch, not to the in-line fuse.*

2) Be sure idle at this time is within 800-850 RPM. Disconnect and plug advance unit vacuum line. Connect high-voltage sensor of timing light to No. 1 cylinder or No. 6 cylinder.

3) Start engine and adjust timing mark (if necessary) on crankshaft pulley with 10° BTDC mark on timing plate. To adjust, move distributor until marks align. Tighten distributor flange after adjustment.

4) Reconnect line for vacuum advance and remove jumper wire from electro valve leads. Idle speed should now be 900-950 RPM.

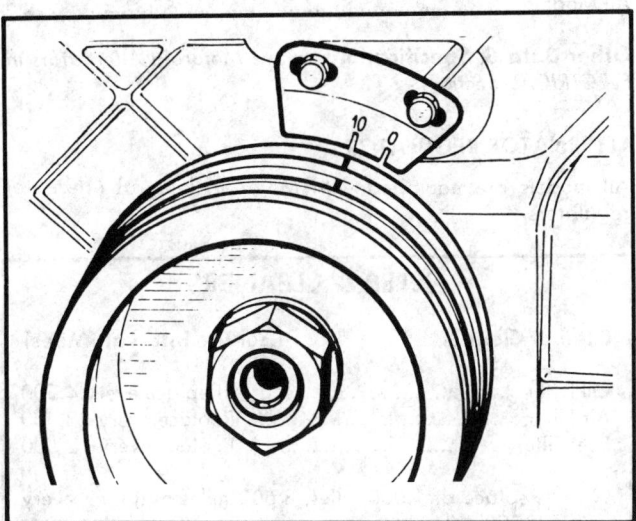

Fig. 2   Timing Mark Location for 604

Ignition Timing Specifications

Application	Timing
All Models	10° BTDC

IDLE SPEED & MIXTURE

1) Warm engine to normal operating temperature. Connect wires 152 and 152A at air injection system electrovalves to ground with jumper wire. Connect tachometer and insert CO meter probe in tailpipe. Remove air filter and disconnect canister purge hose at valve. Turn air conditioning off.

2) Adjust idle speed to 800-850 RPM with idle speed screw. Adjust idle mixture screw to obtain proper CO%. Repeat procedure as necessary to have both speed and mixture correct.

NOTE — *Idle adjustments are made using screws on primary carburetor ONLY. DO NOT touch screws on secondary carburetor.*

3) Remove ground wire from electrovalves and adjust idle speed if necessary to 900-950 RPM. Reconnect canister purge hose and install air cleaner.

Idle Speed & CO Level

Application	RPM	CO%
All Models	900-950	3.0-4.0

DECELERATION VALVE

1) Check engine for idle speed of 900-950 RPM with engine at normal operating temperature. Disconnect the vacuum line (with red ring) from the deceleration vacuum unit. Check for 1 mm play between throttle lever and screw.

2) If there is no play present, loosen locknut adjust screw. Then loosen domed nut "1" (See Fig. 3), saving gasket.

3) Disconnect vacuum line (with green ring) from "T" connector leading to deceleration valve. Connect this line to the deceleration vacuum unit where line with red ring was previously removed.

4) Start the engine. Fast idle speed should be within a range of 1450-1500 RPM (1450 RPM preferred). If not within this range, loosen lock nut "2", and adjust screw "3" using a 3 mm Allen wrench.

5) When to specification, tighten locknut "2". Install gasket and domed nut "1". Then remove and reinstall vacuum lines to previous locations (green line to "T" connector of deceleration valve and red line to deceleration vacuum unit).

NOTE — *Always hold part "6" on deceleration valve whenever tightening or loosening lock nut "4" to prevent damage to valve diaphragm.*

6) Loosen lock nut "4" on deceleration valve. Turn threaded rod clockwise until engine speed reaches 1500 RPM. Accelerate engine several times to ensure 1500 RPM speed.

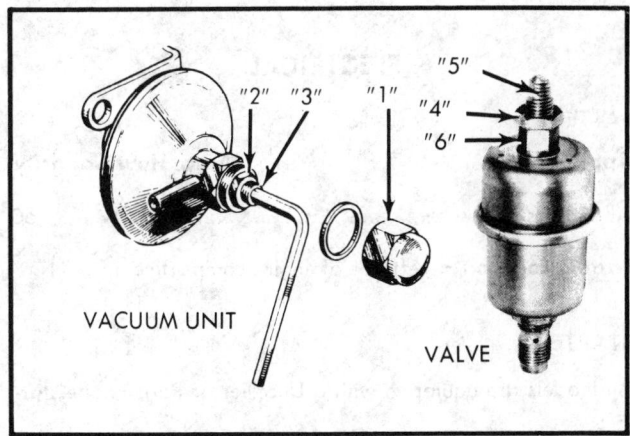

Fig. 3   Adjusting Fast Idle at Deceleration Vacuum Unit and Valve

7) Increase engine speed to 3000 RPM and allow it to decrease. Unscrew threaded rod "5" one-half turn at a time until idle speed returns to 900-950 RPM (900 preferred). Then, turn threaded rod one additional half turn. Tighten lock nut "4".

TUNE-UP (Cont.)

FUEL PUMP PRESSURE

Pressure .... 3.6 psi (.25 kg/cm²)

EMISSION CONTROL SYSTEMS

See *Mitchell Manuals' Emission Control Manual.*

GENERAL SERVICING

IGNITION

DISTRIBUTOR

The 604 SL is equipped with a Bosch breakerless distributor, electronic module and coil.

Other Data & Specifications — See *Tune-Up & Bosch Breakerless Distributors in ELECTRICAL Section.*

IGNITION COIL

Coil Resistance (Ohms@68° F)

Application	Primary	Secondary
All Models	.33-.46	7000-12,000

FUEL SYSTEMS

CARBURETORS

Application	Model
All Models	
Manual Transmission	
Primary Carburetor	Solex 34 TBIA PEU 262
Secondary Carburetor	Solex 35 CEEI PEU 264
Automatic Transmission	
Primary Carburetor	Solex 34 TBIA PEU 263
Secondary Carburetor	Solex 35 CEEI PEU 264

Other Data & Specifications — See *Tune-Up & Solex Carburetors in FUEL SYSTEMS Section.*

ELECTRICAL

BATTERY

Application	Amp. Hour Capacity
All Models	60

Battery Location — Left side of engine compartment.

STARTER

All models are equipped with a Ducellier or Paris Rhone starter.

Other Data & Specifications — See *Ducellier or Paris Rhone Starters in ELECTRICAL Section.*

ALTERNATOR

All models are equipped with Motorola alternators.

Application	Rated Amp. Output
All Models	55

Other Data & Specifications — See *Motorola Alternators in ELECTRICAL Section.*

ALTERNATOR REGULATOR

All models are equipped with Motorola integral alternator regulators.

FILTER & CLEANERS

Filter or Cleaner	Service Interval (Miles)
Oil Filter	①Replace every 4,500
Air Filter	Replace every 12,500
Fuel Filter	Replace every 12,500

① — Replace at 1,000 miles, 3,500 miles and then every 4,500 miles.

BELT ADJUSTMENT

When installing or replacing belt, make two marks on belt 3.93" (100 mm) apart. Then tighten belt until marks are 3.99" (101.5 mm) apart for a used belt or 4.01-4.04" (102-102.5 mm) apart for new belts.

CAPACITIES

Application	Quantity
Crankcase (Includes Filter)	6.3 qts.
Cooling System	11.0 qts.
Man. Trans. (SAE 10W-40)	3.9 pts.
Auto. Trans. (Dexron)	6.1 qts.
Rear Axle (SAE 80)	3.2 pts.
Fuel Tank	18.5 gals.

TUNE-UP

924

ENGINE IDENTIFICATION

Engine identification number is located on the left side of the engine crankcase next to the clutch housing.

Application	Displacement	Code
924	1984 cc	VC
Turbo	1984 cc	3102

COMPRESSION PRESSURE

Test compression pressure with fully open throttle, oil temperature above 140° F (60° C), all spark plugs removed and engine at cranking speed. Each cylinder should be allowed about 12 compression strokes. Differences between cylinders should not exceed 43 psi (3 kg/cm²).

Application	Stand. Pressure psi (kg/cm²)	Min. Pressure psi (kg/cm²)
All Models	142-184 (10-13)	107 (7.5)

VALVE CLEARANCE

It is recommended that valve clearances be checked and adjusted with engine oil temperature at 176° F (80° C). To adjust, remove cylinder head cover and turn crankshaft until cam lobes of cylinder to be adjusted point upward.

NOTE — *On Turbo, remove pressure duct and top cover of air cleaner to remove cylinder head cover.*

Check valve clearance. Correct by making complete turns of adjusting screw, using US 8005 adjusting tool. *See Fig. 1.* One turn changes clearance by .002" (.05 mm). Various adjusting screws are available. Camshaft must be removed to replace screws.

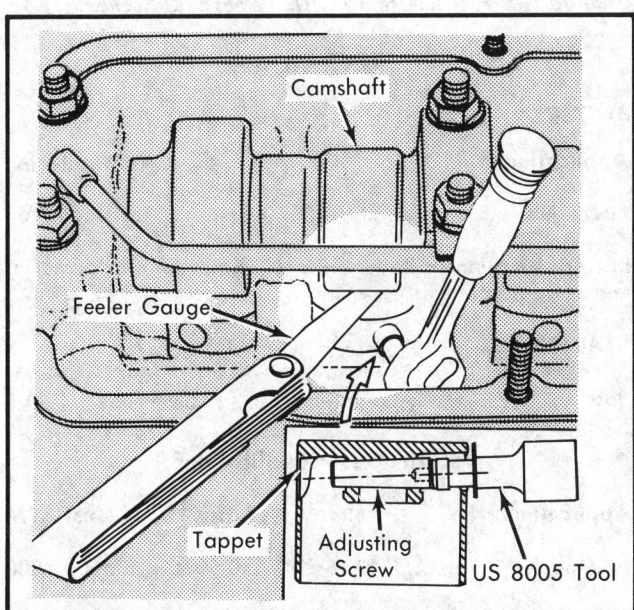

Fig. 1   Adjusting Valve Clearance

Valve Clearance Specifications

Application	Clearance
Intake	①.008" (.20 mm)
Exhaust	①.018" (.45 mm)

① — Adjust with engine at normal operating temperature.

VALVE ARRANGEMENT

I-E-I-E-I-E-I-E (front to rear).

SPARK PLUGS

Application	Gap In. (mm)	Torque Ft. Lbs. (mkg)
924	.028 (.7)	22 (3)
Turbo	.024 (.6)	22 (3)

Spark Plug Type

Application	Bosch	Champion
924	WR6DS	.....
Turbo	WR7DS	N8GY

HIGH TENSION WIRE RESISTANCE

Carefully remove high tension wires from spark plugs and distributor cap. Using an ohmmeter, check resistance of high tension wires while gently twisting wire. If resistance is not to specification, or fluctuates from infinity to any value, replace high tension wire(s).

Resistance (Ohms) Per Wire

Application	Ohms
All Models	6,000

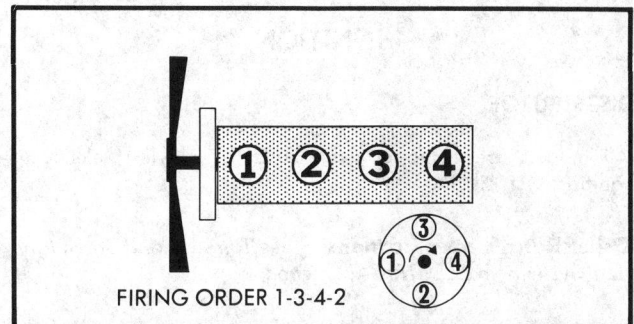

Fig. 2   Firing Order and Distributor Rotation

DISTRIBUTOR

All models are equipped with a breakerless, electronic ignition system.

Air Gap (Rotor-to-Stator) .... .010" (.25 mm)

IGNITION TIMING

924 — Adjust timing with engine idling at specified RPM and both distributor vacuum hoses connected. Turn distributor until mark on flywheel aligns with reference edge on clutch housing.

TUNE-UP (Cont.)

Turbo — Adjust ignition timing with engine at normal operating temperature. Disconnect and plug both hoses at distributor and raise engine speed to 2000 RPM. Adjust timing by turning distributor until mark on flywheel aligns with reference edge on clutch housing.

Ignition Timing Specifications

Application	RPM	Timing
924	900-1000	TDC
Turbo	2000	20°BTDC

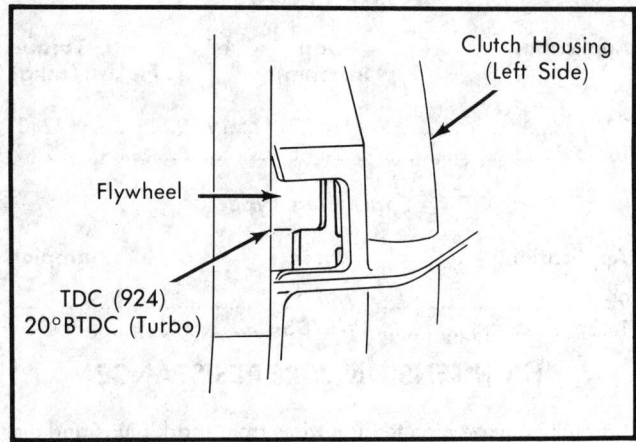

Fig. 3 Flywheel Ignition Timing Marks

IDLE SPEED & MIXTURE

1) Remove rubber cap from oxygen sensor plug (on frame rail) and disconnect plug. Connect exhaust probe to connection point on catalytic converter and calibrate CO tester. Connect a tachometer to engine.

2) With engine idling at normal operating temperature and engine fan off, turn control screw or bypass screw on throttle housing until correct idle speed is obtained.

3) If mixture must be adjusted, remove cap from top of mixture control unit and insert adjusting tool. Turning tool clockwise richens mixture; turning tool counterclockwise leans mixture. Always adjust from lean to rich.

NOTE — *Do not press down on tool while adjusting mixture. Be sure to remove tool and replace cap before accelerating engine or taking a CO reading.*

4) Accelerate engine briefly and allow to return to idle. Check CO level and adjust until correct. Recheck idle speed. Reconnect oxygen sensor plug and cap test port on catalytic converter.

Idle Speed & CO Level

Application	Idle RPM	CO%
924	950-1000	0.6-1.0
Turbo	850-950	0.5-1.0

FUEL PUMP PRESSURE & VOLUME

Two electric fuel pumps are used, one in fuel tank and one in right rear fender.

Pressure	65-75 psi (4.6-5.3 kg/cm²)
Volume	1 qt. in 40 sec.

EMISSION CONTROL SYSTEMS

See Mitchell Manuals' Emission Control Manual.

GENERAL SERVICING

IGNITION

DISTRIBUTOR

All models are equipped with Bosch breakerless, electronic ignition systems.

Other Data & Specifications — *See Tune-Up and Bosch Ignition Systems in ELECTRICAL Section.*

IGNITION COIL

Coil Resistance (Ohms@68° F)

Application	Primary	Secondary
All Models	1.0-1.35	5500-8000

FUEL SYSTEMS

FUEL INJECTION

All models are equipped with Bosch Lambda CIS fuel injection with oxygen sensor.

Other Data & Specifications — *See Tune-Up and Bosch Lambda CIS Fuel Injection in FUEL SYSTEMS Section.*

ELECTRICAL

BATTERY

Application	Amp. Hr. Rating
All Models	63

Battery Location — Battery is located at right rear corner of engine compartment.

STARTER

Bosch	Overrunning Clutch

Starter Test Specifications

Application	Volts	Amps	Test RPM
All Models	11.5	30-50	5500-7500

Other Data & Specifications — *See Bosch Starters in ELECTRICAL Section.*

GENERAL SERVICING (Cont.)

ALTERNATOR

Application	Rated Amp. Output
All Models	75

Other Data & Specifications — *See Bosch Alternators in ELECTRICAL Section.*

ALTERNATOR REGULATOR

All models are equipped with Bosch alternator regulators. With rear window defogger and headlights turned on, operating voltage should be 13.5-14.5 volts at 2000 RPM.

Other Data & Specifications — *See Bosch Alternator Regulators in ELECTRICAL Section.*

BELT ADJUSTMENT

Tension is correct when center portion of belt can be depressed approximately $3/16$ to $3/8$" (5-10 mm) by firm thumb pressure. Adjustment is made by shifting position of alternator. Remove small plate from alternator cover for access to adjustment lock screw.

FILTERS

Filter	Service Interval (Miles)
Oil Filter	
924	Replace every 15,000
Turbo	Replace every 7500
Air Filter	Replace every 30,000
Fuel Filter	Replace every 30,000

CAPACITIES

Application	Quantity
Crankcase (Includes Filter)	
924	5.3 qts.
Turbo	5.8 qts.
Cooling System (Includes Heater)	8.4 qts.
Manual Transaxle (SAE 90)	2.6 qts.
Auto. Transaxle (Dexron)	
Drain & Refill	3.0 qts.
Overhaul	6.4 qts.
Differential (SAE 90)	1.1 qts.
Fuel Tank	①16.4 gals.

① — Includes approximately 1.3 gals. reserve.

1980 Porsche 6 Tune-Up

TUNE-UP

911SC

ENGINE IDENTIFICATION

Engine identification number is stamped on engine crankcase near oil temperature sensor. The first three digits in engine number identify engine type and year.

Application	Engine Type	Code
911SC	930/07	640

COMPRESSION PRESSURE

Perform compression test with wide open throttle and oil temperature not less than 140°F (60°C). Remove all spark plugs and allow about 12 piston strokes per cylinder test. Pressure difference between cylinders should not exceed 22 psi (1.5 kg/cm²).

VALVE CLEARANCE

Adjust valve clearance to specifications with engine cold.

Valve Clearance Specifications

Application	Clearance
All Models (Intake & Exhaust)	.004" (.1 mm)

VALVE ARRANGEMENT

Engine cylinders have individual heads and contain one intake and one exhaust valve per head. Upper valves are intake and lower valves are exhaust.

SPARK PLUGS

Application	Gap In. (mm)	Torque Ft. Lbs. (mkg)
911SC	.032 (.8)	22 (3)

Spark Plug Type

Application	Bosch No.
911SC	W5D

HIGH TENSION WIRE RESISTANCE

Carefully remove high tension wires from spark plugs and distributor cap. Using an ohmmeter, check high tension wire resistance while gently twisting wires. If resistance is not to specifications, or fluctuates from infinity to any value, replace high tension wire(s).

Resistance (Ohms) Per Wire

Application	Ohms
All Models	25,000-30,000

DISTRIBUTOR

All models use Bosch breakerless electronic distributors. No adjustments are necessary.

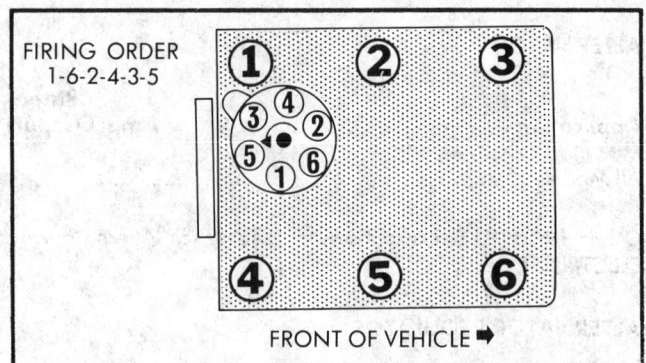

Fig. 1 Firing Order and Distributor Rotation

IGNITION TIMING

Warm engine to normal operating temperature and disconnect both distributor vacuum lines. Connect tachometer and timing light. With engine idling, rotate distributor until mark on pulley is lined up with reference mark on blower housing.

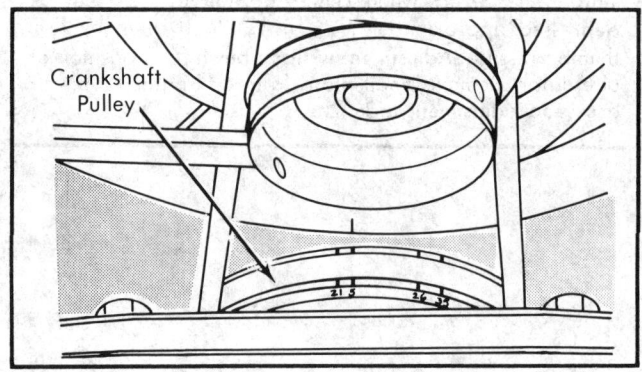

Fig. 2 911 Ignition Timing Marks

Ignition Timing Specifications

Application	RPM	Timing
911SC	850-950	5° BTDC

IDLE SPEED & MIXTURE

1) Engine should be at normal operating temperature and oil filler cap must be tightly sealed. Connect CO level meter to pickup point on catalytic converter and connect tachometer to ignition control box black/purple wire.

2) Disconnect plug from oxygen sensor (left side of engine compartment). Turn idle by-pass screw on throttle housing to obtain correct idle RPM. If mixture must be adjusted, remove plug from mixture control unit.

3) Insert adjusting tool and rotate clockwise to richen mixture; counterclockwise to lean mixture. Turn tool in small amounts without pressing down. Be sure to remove tool and plug opening before accelerating engine or testing mixture.

TUNE-UP (Cont.)

4) Accelerate engine briefly, then allow idle to stabilize before taking readings. When CO level is correct, check idle speed and readjust if necessary. Remove test equipment, coat threads of test point cap (on converter) with anti-seize compound, and reconnect oxygen sensor.

Idle Speed & CO Level

Application	Idle RPM	CO%
All Models	850-950	0.4-0.8

FUEL PUMP PRESSURE & VOLUME

Pressure .... 64-74 psi (4.5-5.2 kg/cm²)
Volume .... 1.5 pts. in 30 sec.

EMISSION CONTROL SYSTEMS

See Mitchell Manuals' Emission Control Manual.

GENERAL SERVICING

IGNITION

DISTRIBUTOR

All models are equipped with Capacitive Discharge Ignition systems with Bosch breakerless distributors.

Other Data & Specifications — See Tune-Up and Bosch Ignition Systems in ELECTRICAL Section.

IGNITION COIL

Coil Resistance (Ohms@68°F)

Application	Primary	Secondary
All Models	0.4-0.6	600-790

FUEL SYSTEMS

FUEL INJECTION

All models are equipped with Bosch Lambda Continuous Injection System (CIS) with oxygen sensor.

Other Data & Specifications — See Tune-Up and Bosch Lambda CIS Injection System in FUEL SYSTEMS Section.

ELECTRICAL

BATTERY

Application	Amp. Hr. Rating
All Models..................	66

Battery Location — Battery is located on left in front luggage compartment, under the floor mat.

STARTER

Bosch...................................... Overrunning Clutch

Starter Specifications

Application	Volts	Amps	Test RPM
911SC	11.5	50-80	7300-9300

Other Data & Specifications — See Bosch Starters in ELECTRICAL Section.

ALTERNATOR

Application	Rated Amp. Output
All Models	70

Other Data & Specifications — See Bosch or Motorola Alternatorw and Regulators in ELECTRICAL Section.

ALTERNATOR REGULATOR

All models are equipped with Bosch or Motorola alternator regulators with an operating voltage of 14.2 volts at 2500 RPM.

Other Data & Specifications — See Bosch or Motorola Alternators and Regulators in ELECTRICAL Section.

BELT ADJUSTMENT

Belt should deflect from ¼-½" (5-10 mm) when light thumb pressure is applied halfway between pulleys. Adjustment is made by removing or adding spacers between pulley halves. Rotate belt several times and recheck adjustment after changing spacers.

FILTERS

Filter	Service Interval (Miles)
Oil Filter	Replace every 15,000
Air Cleaner	Replace every 30,000
Fuel Filter	Replace every 30,000

CAPACITIES

Application	Quantity
Crankcase	
Total Capacity	13.7 qts.
Oil Change	10.6 qts.
Transaxle (SAE 90)	
911SC	3.2 qts.
Fuel Tank	①21 gals.

① — Includes 2.1 gals. in reserve.

1980 Porsche V8 Tune-Up

TUNE-UP

928

ENGINE IDENTIFICATION

The engine identification number is stamped on the front reinforcing rib in the top half of the crankcase, directly behind the fan. The first 3 digits in engine number identify type and model year.

Application	Engine Type	Code
928		
Man. Trans.	M28/13	810
Auto. Trans.	M28/14	810

COMPRESSION PRESSURE

With engine at normal operating temperature, remove all plugs and allow 12 compression strokes per cylinder. Pressure should not vary more than 21 psi (1.5 kg/cm²) between cylinders.

VALVE TAPPET CLEARANCE

Porsche 928 models are equipped with hydraulic valve lifters and no adjustments are necessary.

VALVE ARRANGEMENT

Both Banks — I-E-I-E-I-E-I-E (front to rear)

SPARK PLUGS

Application	Gap In. (mm)	Torque Ft. Lbs. (mkg)
All Models	.028 (.7)	18 (2.5)

Spark Plug Type

Application	Bosch
All Models	WR8DS

HIGH TENSION WIRE RESISTANCE

Carefully remove high tension wires from spark plugs and distributor cap. Using an ohmmeter, check resistance of high tension wires while gently twisting wires. If resistance is not to specification, or fluctuates from infinity to any value, replace wires.

Resistance (Ohms) Per Wire

Application	Ohms
All Wires	2,500

DISTRIBUTOR

All models use Bosch breakerless electronic ignition and no adjustment in distributor is necessary.

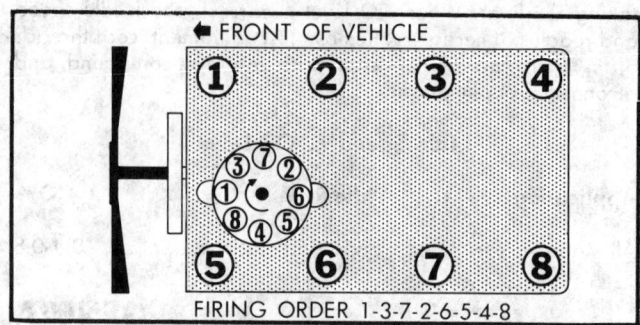

Fig. 1   Firing Order and Distributor Rotation

IGNITION TIMING

1) With engine at normal operating temperature, disconnect hoses at distributor advance unit. Stop engine and connect timing light to No. 1 cylinder and tachometer to connection stud near ignition control unit in engine compartment.

CAUTION — *Ignition must be off when attaching test equipment, as extremely high voltage can cause severe shock when ignition is on.*

2) Start engine and increase speed to 3000 RPM. Timing should be as specified. Adjust if necessary by turning distributor. Return engine to idle and connect vacuum hoses. Timing should now read TDC to 7° BTDC. If not, distributor should be removed and tested.

Ignition Timing Specifications

Application	RPM	Timing
All Models	3000	①23° BTDC

① — With distributor vacuum hoses disconnected.

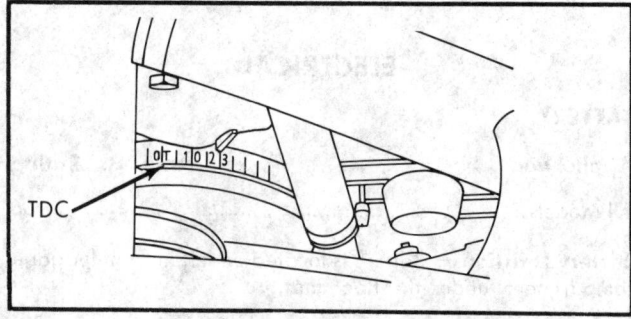

Fig. 2   Timing Marks on Crankshaft Pulley

IDLE SPEED & MIXTURE

1) Fold up foot support on passenger side under dashboard. Disconnect plug for oxygen sensor (left side of footwell). Connect CO meter to test point on catalytic converter and connect tachometer.

2) Adjust idle speed using screw in front of throttle housing. If mixture must be adjusted, insert tool through opening in air flow sensor. Turn clockwise to richen mixture and counterclockwise to lean mixture.

TUNE-UP (Cont.)

3) When idle mixture and speed are correct, remove test equipment. Connect oxygen sensor plug and coat threads of catalytic converter test cap with anti-seize compound.

Idle Speed & CO Level

Application	Idle RPM	CO%
All Models	700-800	①0.4-0.8

① — With oxgen sensor disconnected.

FUEL PUMP PRESSURE & VOLUME

Pressure (At Idle) .... 26-32 psi (1.8-2.2 kg/cm²)
Volume .... 1.2 qts. in 30 sec.

EMISSION CONTROL SYSTEMS

See Mitchell Manuals' Emission Control Manual.

GENERAL SERVICING

IGNITION

DISTRIBUTOR

All models are equipped with Bosch transistorized ignition systems.

Other Data & Specifications — See Tune-Up and Bosch Ignition Systems in ELECTRICAL Section.

IGNITION COIL

Coil Resistance (Ohms@68°F)

Application	Primary	Secondary
All Models	0.4-0.6	650-790

FUEL SYSTEMS

FUEL INJECTION

All models are equipped with Bosch AFC Lambda fuel injection system with oxygen sensor.

Other Data & Spefications — See Tune-Up and Bosch AFC Fuel Injection in FUEL SYSTEMS Section.

ELECTRICAL

BATTERY

Application	Amp. Hr. Rating
All Models	88

Battery Location — Battery is located under spare tire in rear of passenger compartment.

STARTER

Bosch .... Overrunning Clutch

Starter Test Specifications

Application	Volts	Amps	Test RPM
All Models	11.5	55-85	8500-10,500

Other Data & Specifications — See Bosch Starters in ELECTRICAL Section.

ALTERNATOR

Application	Rated Amp. Output
All Models	90

Other Data & Specifications — See Bosch or Motorola Alternators in ELECTRICAL Section.

ALTERNATOR REGULATOR

All Models use Bosch or Motorola solid state alternator regulators.

Other Data & Specifications — See Bosch or Motorola Regulators in ELECTRICAL Section.

BELT ADJUSTMENT

Tension is correct when belts can be depressed .4" (10 mm) by thumb pressure on center portion of belt.

FILTERS

Filter	Service Interval (Miles)
Oil Filter	Replace every 15,000
Air Filter	Replace every 30,000
Fuel Filter...........................	Replace every 30,000

CAPACITIES

Application	Quantity
Crankcase (Includes Filter)	8.5 qts.
Cooling System	17.0 qts.
Man. Transaxle (SAE 75W-90)	4.0 pts.
Auto. Trans. (Dexron)	6.4 qts.
Differential (SAE 90)	2.1 qts.
Fuel Tank	23.0 gals.

TUNE-UP

Le Car

ENGINE IDENTIFICATION

Type of vehicle and engine number is marked on a number plate riveted to the left rear side of the engine block. Plate is located just below cylinder head mating surface. First five digits indicate engine type.

Engine Codes

Application	Code
Le Car	847-25

VALVE CLEARANCE

Application	Intake	Exhaust
Le Car	①.006" (.15 mm)	①.008" (.20 mm)

① — Set valves with engine cold.

VALVE ARRANGEMENT

E-I-I-E-E-I-I-E (Front to Rear)

SPARK PLUGS

Application	Gap In. (mm)	Torque Ft. Lbs. (mkg)
All Models	.024 (.6)	20 (2.8)

Spark Plug Type

Application	Bosch	Champion
Federal		N12Y
Calif. .... WR9DS ....

HIGH TENSION WIRE RESISTANCE

Carefully remove high tension wires from spark plugs and distributor cap. Using an ohmmeter, check resistance of high tension wires while gently twisting wires. If resistance is not to specification, or fluctuates from infinity to any value, replace high tension wire(s).

Resistance (Ohms) Per Wire

Application	Ohms
All Models	25,000-30,000

DISTRIBUTOR

All models are equipped with dual pick-up electronic ignition distributors. Trigger plate gap is adjustable and should be set to .012-.024" (.3-.6 mm).

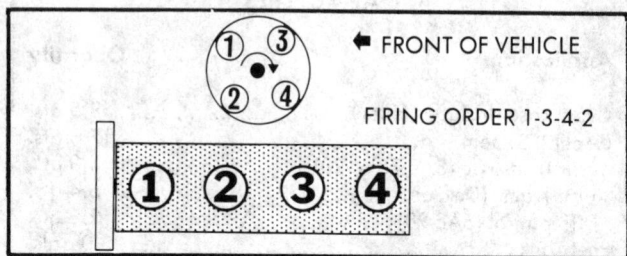

Fig. 1   Le Car Firing Order and Distributor Rotation

IGNITION TIMING

Check or adjust ignition timing with vacuum line disconnected and plugged and engine running at idle speed. To adjust, turn distributor until specified mark on flywheel is aligned with specified graduation mark on clutch housing. Reconnect distributor vacuum hose.

Ignition Timing Specifications

Application	Timing
All Models	3° BTDC

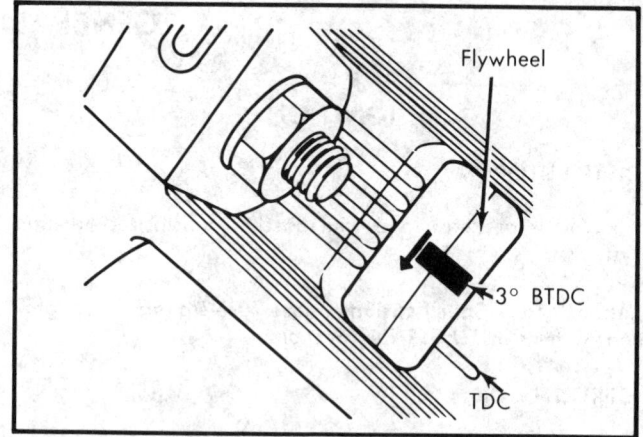

Fig. 2   Le Car Timing Mark Location

IDLE SPEED & MIXTURE

Federal — 1) Clamp, or disconnect and plug air pump hose to injection manifold. Connect tachometer.

2) Adjust idle speed screw to obtain 675-725 RPM idle. Remove cap and adjust fuel metering screw to obtain 0.5-2.0% CO level. Repeat procedure if necessary to have both speed and mixture correct.

3) Reconnect air injection. Idle speed must be 700-800 RPM. If not, adjust with idle speed screw. Remove test equipment.

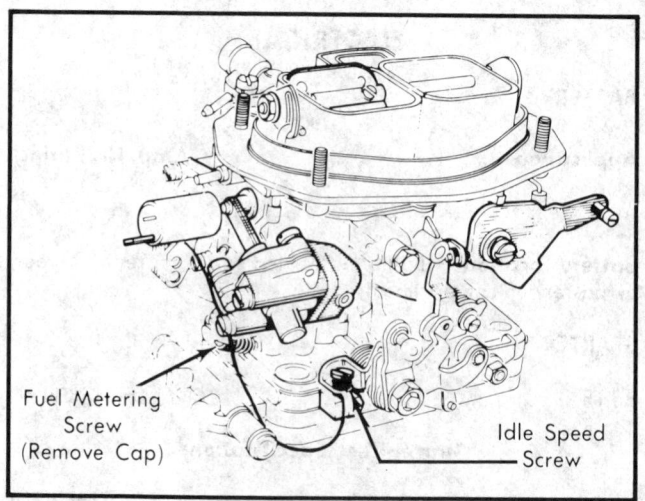

Fig. 3   Carburetor Adjustment Locations (Federal Models)

TUNE-UP (Cont.)

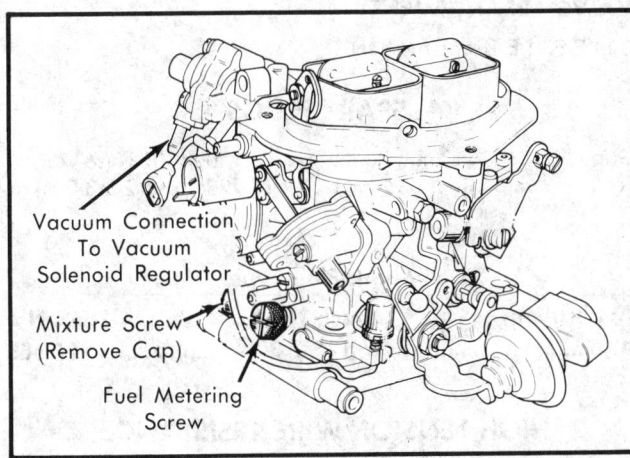

Fig. 4   Carburetor Adjustment Locations (Calif. Models)

Vacuum Connection
To Vacuum
Solenoid Regulator

Mixture Screw
(Remove Cap)

Fuel Metering
Screw

California — 1) Start engine and bring to normal operating temperature. Stop engine and connect timing light. Using a "T" connector, connect accurate vacuum gauge to line between carburetor and vacuum solenoid regulator.

2) Start engine and adjust idle speed with fuel metering screw to 700-800 RPM. Vacuum gauge should indicate 1.5±1.2 in. Hg.

3) If vacuum reading is not correct, remove brass cap from mixture screw. Adjust carefully until vacuum reading is within specifications. Remove test equipment.

Idle Speed & CO Level

Application	Idle RPM	CO%
Federal	700-800	①0.5-2.0
Calif.	700-800	②

① — Air injection disconnected.
② — CO% not measured.

FUEL PUMP PRESSURE

Pressure .... 2.5-4.0 (.18-.28 kg/cm²)

EMISSION CONTROL SYSTEMS

See *Mitchell Manuals' Emission Control Manual.*

GENERAL SERVICING

IGNITION

DISTRIBUTOR

All models are equipped with Ducellier electronic distributors.

Other Data & Specifications — *See Tune-Up and Ducellier Ignition Systems in ELECTRICAL Section.*

IGNITION COIL

All models use an ignition coil which is mounted in an aluminum housing together with the electronic control module.

FUEL SYSTEMS

CARBURETORS

Application	Model
Federal	Weber 32 DIR 82
Calif.	Weber 32 DIR 80

Other Data & Specifications — *See Tune-Up and Weber Carburetors in FUEL SYSTEMS Section.*

ELECTRICAL

BATTERY

Battery Location — Battery is located in right front corner of engine compartment.

Application	Amp. Hr. Rating
Le Car	50

STARTER

All models are equipped with a Paris Rhone starter.

Other Data & Specifications — *See Paris Rhone Starters in ELECTRICAL Section.*

ALTERNATOR

All models are equipped with Paris Rhone alternators.

ALTERNATOR REGULATOR

All models are equipped with Paris Rhone alternator regulators.

BELT ADJUSTMENT
Tension With Strand Tension Gauge

Application	Lbs. (kg)
Alternator Belt	80-90 (36-41)
Air Pump Belt	75-80 (34-36)
A/C Compressor Belt	80 (36)

FILTERS

Filter	Service Interval (Miles)
Oil Filter	Replace every 6,250
Air Filter	Replace every 12,500
Air Pump Filter	Replace every 12,500

CAPACITIES

Application	Quantity
Crankcase (Includes Filter)	3.4 qts.
Cooling System (Includes Heater)	6.3 qts.
Manual Transaxle (SAE 80)	3.8 pts.
Fuel Tank	10.0 gals.

1980 Saab 4 Tune-Up

TUNE-UP

99
900

ENGINE IDENTIFICATION

Engine number is stamped on a machined pad on engine block below CIS throttle housing.

Application	Code
99	BI 20 P04
900	
Man. Trans.	BI 20 P11
Auto. Trans.	BI 20 P12
Turbo	BSI 20 P02

VALVE CLEARANCE

Bring camshaft into correct position for checking valves. Using a suitable go and no-go feeler gauge, check that clearance between valve tappet and heel of cam is to specifications given under "Preliminary Check." If within specifications, no further adjustment is necessary. If not, proceed as follows:

NOTE — *Turbo valve clearances are critical. Use only specifications listed for Turbo.*

1) Using special tool (8391450) and a dial indicator, measure clearance of each valve. With measuring point of dial indicator resting on tip of cam, zero dial indicator.

2) Lift valve depressor with special tool and note movement of dial indicator, indicating present valve clearance. Any valve not within "Adjustment Limit" specifications should be adjusted as follows:

3) Remove camshaft, valve depressors and adjusting pads of valves needing adjustment. Measure thickness of adjusting pad with special tool (8391633) and calculate thickness of new pad required to bring valve clearance within "Adjustment Limit" specifications.

4) Measured valve clearance plus adjusting pad thickness equals total distance between valve and cam. This total distance less the specified valve clearance, determines thickness of new adjusting pad to be installed.

5) Install new adjusting pad, valve depressors, and camshaft and recheck that clearances are correct.

Valve Clearances①

Application	Clearance
Preliminary Check	
Intake	.006-.012" (.15-.30 mm)
Exhaust	
All Exc. Turbo	.014-.020" (.35-.50 mm)
Turbo	.016-.020" (.40-.50 mm)
Adjustment Limit	
Intake	.008-.010" (.20-.25 mm)
Exhaust	
All Exc. Turbo	.016-.018" (.40-.45 mm)
Turbo	.018-.020" (.45-.50 mm)

① — When checked 30 minutes after driving vehicle at normal operating temperature.

VALVE ARRANGEMENT

E-I-I-E-E-I-I-E (front to rear).

SPARK PLUGS

Gap	.024-.028" (.6-.7 mm)
Torque	18-22 ft. lbs. (2.5-3.0 mkg)

Spark Plug Type

Application	Bosch No.	NGK No.
All	W 175 T 30	BP-6ES

HIGH TENSION WIRE RESISTANCE

Carefully remove high tension wires from spark plugs and distributor cap. Using an ohmmeter, check high tension wire resistance while gently twisting wires. If resistance is not to specifications, or fluctuates from infinity to any value, replace high tension wire(s).

Resistance (Ohms) Per Wire

Application	Ohms
All Models	
Wires to Cylinder 1 & 2	2600-3900
Wires to Cylinder 3 & 4	2400-3600
Wire from Coil to Distributor	800-1200

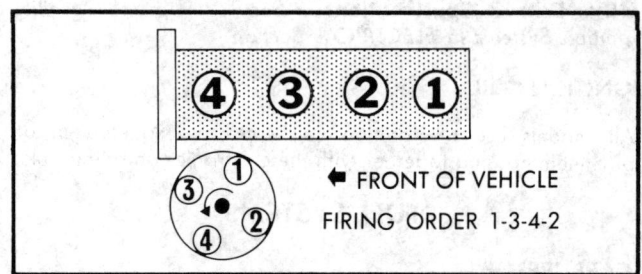

Fig. 1   Firing Order and Distributor Rotation

DISTRIBUTOR

All models are equipped with Bosch breakerless electronic ignition systems. No adjustments are required for distributor.

IGNITION TIMING

1) Connect tachometer and timing light. Disconnect vacuum hose and place transmission in neutral position. Check timing at 2000 RPM.

2) If not within specifications, loosen distributor retaining screw and rotate distributor housing. Turn clockwise for earlier ignition; counterclockwise for later.

3) Reconnect vacuum hose and adjust engine idle speed.

TUNE-UP (Cont.)

Ignition Timing Specifications

Application	RPM	Timing
All Models	2000	20° BTDC

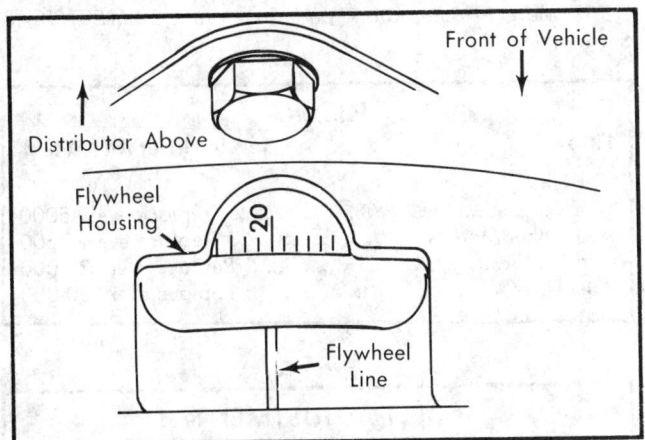

Fig. 2   Saab Timing Mark Location

IDLE SPEED & MIXTURE

1) Warm engine to normal operating temperature. Connect a CO meter to the plug in exhaust manifold pipe. Disconnect wire to oxygen sensor.

CAUTION — *Do not allow disconnected wire from Lambda oxygen sensor to touch an engine or chassis ground.*

2) Check and adjust engine idling speed by turning idle adjusting screw on throttle valve housing. Accelerate engine, then return to idle. Recheck idle speed.

3) Check CO level. Accelerate engine, then allow to run at stable idle for 30 seconds before reading CO level. Adjust with Allen wrench, using screw underneath plug in fuel distributor. Turn clockwise to richen mixture, counter clockwise to lean mixture.

CAUTION — *Remove Allen "T" wrench from adjustment screw after each adjustment. If key is left in screw and engine is accelerated, lever could be damaged.*

4) When mixture and idle adjustments are correct, remove CO probe, replace plug in manifold, and connect oxygen sensor wire. Insert CO meter probe into tailpipe and check CO with oxygen sensor connected. CO level should be less than 0.4%.

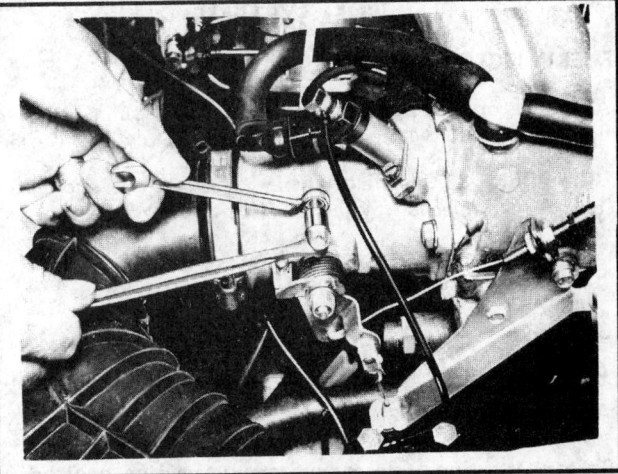

Fig. 3   Adjusting Idle Speed

Idle Speed & CO Level

Application	RPM	CO%
All Models	825-925	①.75-1.25

① — With oxygen sensor disconnected. With sensor connected, maximum level is 0.4%.

DASHPOT

1) With engine at normal operating temperature, connect tachometer and check idle speed. Adjust if necessary. Rotate throttle lever and check that dashpot rod strikes the stop at 2400-2600 RPM. If not, adjust by turning dashpot.

2) Accelerate engine to 3000 RPM and measure time from release of throttle until engine reaches idle speed. Deceleration time should be 3-6 seconds. If not, turn dashpot in towards stop to lengthen delay, or away from stop to shorten delay time.

FUEL PUMP PRESSURE & VOLUME

Pressure .... 64-72 psi (4.5-5.1 kg/cm²)
Volume .... ①1.9 pts. in 30 sec.

① — Measured in return fuel line

EMISSION CONTROL SYSTEMS

See Mitchell Manuals' Emission Control Manual.

GENERAL SERVICING

IGNITION

DISTRIBUTOR

All models are equipped with Bosch electronic breakerless distributors.

Other Data & Specifications — *See Tune-Up and Bosch Ignition Systems in ELECTRICAL Section.*

IGNITION COIL

Coil Resistance (Ohms@75°F)

Application	Primary	Secondary
All Models	1.05-1.35	5500-8500

1980 Saab 4 Tune-Up

TUNE-UP (Cont.)

FUEL SYSTEMS

FUEL INJECTION

All models are equipped with Bosch Lambda Continuous Injection System (CIS) with oxygen sensor and catalytic converter.

Other Data & Specifications — *See Tune-Up and Bosch Lambda CIS Injection System in FUEL SYSTEMS Section.*

ELECTRICAL

BATTERY

Application	Amp. Hr. Rating
All Models	60

Battery Location — In engine compartment on right side.

STARTER

Bosch	Overrunning Clutch

Starter Specifications

Application	Volts	Amps	Test RPM
All Models	11.5	35-55	6500-8500

Other Data & Specifications — *See Bosch Starters in ELECTRICAL Section.*

ALTERNATOR

99 models are equipped with Marchal or Bosch alternators. 900 models are equipped with Motorola or Bosch alternators.

Application	Rated Amp. Output
99	55
900	70

Other Data & Specifications — *See Bosch, Motorola, or S.E.V. Marchal Alternators and Regulators in ELECTRICAL Section.*

ALTERNATOR REGULATOR

All models are equipped with Bosch, Motorola, or S.E.V. Marchal alternator regulators.

Other Data & Specifications — *See Bosch, Motorola, or S.E.V. Marchal Alternators and Regulators in ELECTRICAL Section.*

FILTERS

Filter	Service Interval (Miles)
Oil Filter	
Turbo	Replace every 5000
All Other Models	Replace every 7500
Air Filter	Replace every 30,000
Fuel Filter	Replace every 30,000

BELT ADJUSTMENT

Application	①Deflection
Alternator Belt	.4" (10 mm)

① — Deflection is with 3.3 lbs. (1.5 kg) pressure applied midway on longest belt run.

CAPACITIES

Application	Quantity
Crankcase (Includes Filter)	
Turbo	4.5 qts.
All Other Models	4.0 qts.
Cooling System	
99	8.5 qts.
900 & Turbo	10.5 qts.
Man. Trans. (SAE 10W-30)①	3.0 qts.
Auto. Trans. (ATF Type F)	8.5 qts.
Auto. Trans. Final Drive (SAE 80)	1.3 qts.
Fuel Tank	14.5 gals.

① — Including Final Drive.

TUNE-UP

1600
1800

ENGINE IDENTIFICATION

Engine can be identified by a letter-number combination stamped on machined pad on side of engine, near distributor (below carburetor). Engine codes are as follows:

Application	Code
2-WD	
Federal	
Man. Trans.	E71AA3, E71GA3A
Auto. Trans.	E81TA
Calif.	
Man. Trans.	E71AC3
Auto. Trans.	E81TC
4-WD	
Federal	E71WA3, E71WA4
Calif.	E71WC3, E71WC4

COMPRESSION PRESSURE

Check pressure with engine warm, plugs removed, throttle valve wide open and engine at cranking speed. Pressure should be as specified with a variation of 7 psi (.5 kg/cm²) maximum between cylinders.

Compression Pressure
@350 RPM

Application	Pressure psi (kg/cm²)
All Models	156 (11)

VALVE CLEARANCE

With engine cold, bring piston to be checked to top dead center of compression stroke. Loosen lock nuts and turn adjusting screws to proper clearance. Adjust valves in firing order sequence (1-3-2-4) using valve clearance adjusting tool 398760100 (or equivalent).

Valve Clearance Specifications

Application	Clearance
Intake	.010″ (.25 mm)
Exhaust	.014″ (.35 mm)

VALVE ARRANGEMENT

I-E-E-I (both banks, front to rear).

Application	Gap In. (mm)	Torque Ft. Lbs. (mkg)
All Models	.032 (.8)	18 (2.1)

Spark Plug Type

Application	NKG	Nippondenso
All Models	BP6ES	W20EP

HIGH TENSION WIRE RESISTANCE

Carefully remove high tension wires from spark plugs and ignition coil. Remove distributor cap with wires still in place. Using an ohmmeter, check high tension wire resistance between free end of wire and distributor cap electrode. If resistance is not to specifications, or fluctuates from infinity to any value, replace high tension wire(s).

Resistance (Ohms) Per Wire

Application	Ohms
All Models	25,000

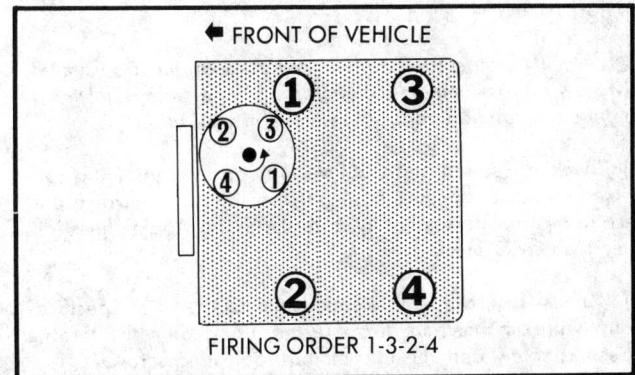

Fig. 1 Firing Order and Distributor Rotation

DISTRIBUTOR

All models are equipped with breakerless, electronic ignition systems.

Air Gap	
Nippondenso	.008-.016″ (.2-.4 mm)
Hitachi	.012-.016″ (.3-.4 mm)

IGNITION TIMING

Adjust timing with engine at normal operating temperature and transmission in neutral. Disconnect and plug vacuum hoses at distributor. With engine at idle, check timing and turn distributor to adjust.

Ignition Timing Specifications

Application	Timing
All Models	8° BTDC

1980 Subaru 4 Tune-Up

TUNE-UP (Cont.)

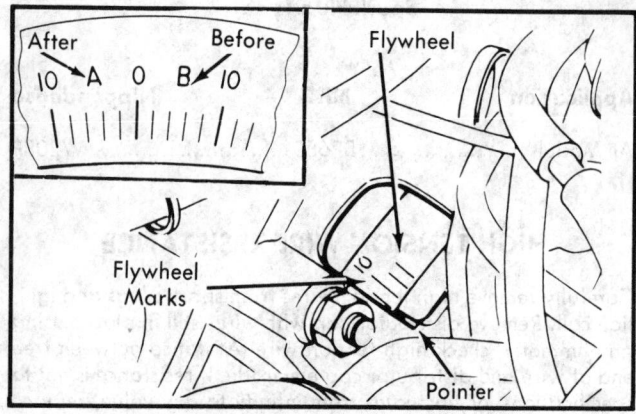

Fig. 2   Subaru Timing Mark Location

IDLE SPEED & MIXTURE

NOTE — *Ignition timing and valve clearances must be correct and engine must be at normal operating temperature prior to adjusting idle speed and mixture.*

1) Disconnect fuel evaporation purge hose at purge check valve and plug manifold hose. Start engine and allow to warm up for 5 minutes.

NOTE — *If engine stalls and is restarted during adjustment, always wait for 5 minutes after starting to perform adjustment, as timer of ignition control system is in operation.*

2) Check idle speed and CO level with air injection (AIR) connected. Next, disconnect hose between air suction valve and secondary air filter assembly and plug hose. Again check idle speed and CO level.

3) If necessary, adjust idle speed and CO level to specifications, with air injection disconnected, using both the throttle adusting screw and the idle mixture adjusting screw.

NOTE — *On California models only, spring pin in throttle body must be removed to gain access to idle mixture adjusting screw. After adjustment is completed, spring pin must be reinstalled.*

4) Reconnect air suction valve-to-secondary air filter hose. Recheck idle speed and CO level with air injection connected and adjust as necessary to obtain specified settings with air injection connected.

Idle Speed & CO Level

Application	RPM	CO%
W/Cat. Converter		
AIR Connected	750-850	0-1.0
AIR Disconnected	750-850	1.0-3.0
W/O Cat. Converter		
AIR Connected	850-950	0-2.0
AIR Disconnected	850-950	3.5-5.5

COLD (FAST) IDLE RPM

With cam adjusting lever on first step of fast idle cam, primary throttle valve opening angle and clearance should be as follows. If not, adjust fast idle screw.

Fast Idle Specifications

Application	Throttle Valve Opening Angle	Clearance Valve-to-Body
Man. Trans.		
Fed. W/Converter	14°	.041" (1.05 mm)
Fed. W/O Converter	16°	.050" (1.27 mm)
Calif.	17°	.051" (1.31 mm)
Auto. Trans.	19°	.060" (1.53 mm)

FUEL PUMP PRESSURE & VOLUME

Pressure	1.9-2.6 psi (.13-.18 kg/cm²)
Volume	0.9 pts./min.

EMISSION CONTROL SYSTEMS

See Mitchell Manuals' Emission Control Manual.

GENERAL SERVICING

IGNITION

DISTRIBUTORS

Breakerless, electronic ignition systems are used on all models. Hitachi systems are used on four-wheel-drive models, and Nippondenso systems are used on all other models.

Other Data & Specifications — *See Tune-Up and Hitachi and Nippondenso Ignition Systems in ELECTRICAL Section.*

IGNITION COIL

Coil Resistance (Ohms@68°F)

Application	Primary	Secondary
Hitachi	1.17-1.43	7800-11,600
Nippondenso	1.33-1.63	12,600-15,400

FUEL SYSTEMS

CARBURETORS

Application	Model
W/Cat. Converter	Hitachi DCJ 2-Bbl.
W/O Cat. Converter	Hitachi DCP 2-Bbl.

Other Data & Specifications — *See Tune-Up and Hitachi Carburetors in FUEL SYSTEMS Section.*

ELECTRICAL

BATTERY

Application	Amp. Hr. Capacity
Federal 1800	65
All Other Models	60

GENERAL SERVICING (Cont.)

Battery Location — Engine compartment; front.

STARTER

Nippondenso.. Magnetic Switch Type

Starter Test Specifications

Application	Volts	Amps	Test RPM
Federal 1800	11.5	90	4100
All Others	11.0	50	5000

Other Data & Specifications — *See Nippondenso Starters in ELECTRICAL Section.*

ALTERNATOR

Application	Rated Amp. Output
4-WD Station Wagon	55
All Other Models	50

Other Data & Specifications — *See Hitachi Alternators and Regulators in ELECTRICAL Section.*

ALTERNATOR REGULATOR

All models are equipped with Hitachi alternator regulators with an operating voltage of 14.0-14.5 volts.

Other Data & Specifications — *See Hitachi Alternators and Regulators in ELECTRICAL Section.*

ENGINE

BELT ADJUSTMENT

Application	①Deflection
All Belts	.51-.55" (13-14 mm)

① — Deflection is with 22 lbs. (10 kg) pressure applied midway on longest belt run.

FILTERS

Filter	Service Interval (Miles)
Oil Filter	Replace every 7500
Air Filter	Replace every 30,000
Fuel Filter	Replace every 15,000

CAPACITIES

Application	Quantity
Crankcase (Includes Filter)	
1600	3.7 qts.
1800	4.2 qts.
Man. Transaxle (SAE 85W-90)	
2-WD	2.9 pts.
4-WD	3.2 pts.
Rear Differential (4-WD)	1.6 pts.
Auto. Trans. (Dexron)	5.9-6.3 qts.
Front Differential (SAE 85W-90)	2.6 pts.
Fuel Tank	
2-WD	13.2 gals.
4-WD	11.9 gals.

1980 Toyota 4 Tune-Up

TUNE-UP

Celica
Corolla
Corona
Pickup
Tercel

ENGINE IDENTIFICATION

Each engine serial number contains an identifying code for engine identification. All numbers are stamped on the left side of engine block. Engine codes are also provided on decal at front edge of valve cover.

Engine Identification Codes

Application	Code
Celica, Corona, Pickup	20R
Corolla	3T-C
Tercel	1A-C

COMPRESSION PRESSURE

With engine at normal operating temperature, spark plugs removed, throttle valve wide open and engine at cranking speed, compression pressures should be as follows with a maximum variation between cylinders of 14 psi (1 kg/cm²):

Compression Pressure

Application	Standard psi (kg/cm²)	Minimum psi (kg/cm²)
Celica, Corona, Pickup	156 (11.0)	128 (9.0)
Corolla	163 (11.5)	128 (9.0)
Tercel	177 (12.5)	128 (9.0)

VALVE CLEARANCE

Check or adjust valve clearance with engine warm. Remove valve cover and set number 1 cylinder at TDC. On Corolla models, adjust valves 1,2,4 & 5 (counting from front to back), turn crankshaft 360°, and adjust valves 3,6,7 & 8. On all other models, adjust 1,2,4 & 6, turn crankshaft 360°, then adjust valves 3,5,7 & 8.

Valve Clearance Specifications

Application	Intake	Exhaust
Corolla	.008″ (.20 mm)	.013″ (.33 mm)
All Other Models	.008″ (.20 mm)	.012″ (.30 mm)

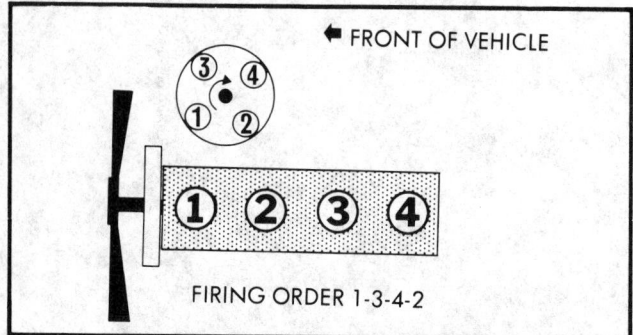

Fig. 1 Firing Order and Distributor Rotation (Corolla)

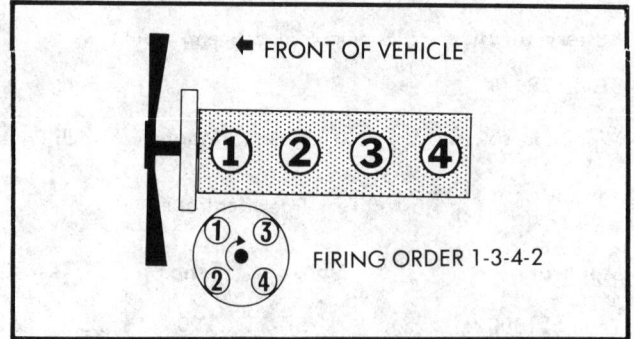

Fig. 2 Firing Order and Distributor Rotation (Celica, Corona and Pickup)

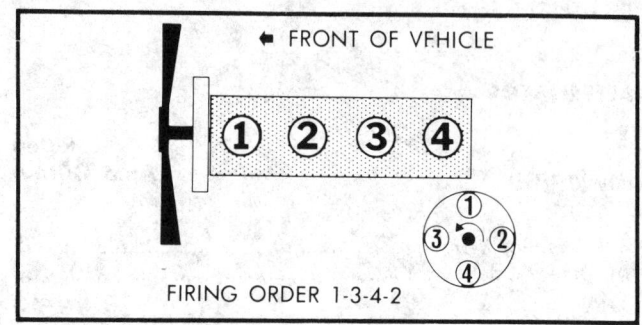

Fig. 3 Firing Order and Distributor Rotation (Tercel)

VALVE ARRANGEMENTS

Tercel — I-E-E-I-I-E-E-I

All Other Models
Right Side — All Intake
Left Side — All Exhaust

SPARK PLUGS

Application	Gap In. (mm)	Torque Ft. Lbs. (mkg)
Celica, Corona, Pickup	.031 (.8)	11-15 (1.5-2.1)
Corolla	.043 (1.1)	11-15 (1.5-2.1)
Tercel	.039 (1.0)	11-15 (1.5-2.1)

Spark Plug Type

Application	NGK No.	Nippondenso No.
Celica, Corona, Pickup	BPR5EA-L	W16EXR-U
Corolla	BP5EA-L11	W16EX-U11
Tercel	BP6EKA	W20ETS

HIGH TENSION WIRE RESISTANCE

Carefully remove high tension wires from spark plugs and distributor cap. Using an ohmmeter, check high tension wire resistance while gently twisting wires. If resistance is not to specifications, or fluctuates from infinity to any value, replace high tension wire(s).

TUNE-UP (Cont.)

Resistance (Ohms) Per Wire

Application	Ohms
All Models	25,000 Maximum

DISTRIBUTOR

All models use transistorized ignition which eliminates breaker points. Reluctor-to-pickup air gap is the only adjustment. Measure air gap with a non-magnetic feeler gauge and move pickup if necessary to correct air gap.

Air Gap .... .008-.016" (.2-.4 mm)

IGNITION TIMING

1) Connect tachometer and timing light to engine. The positive lead of tachometer is connected to the (−) terminal of coil on all models except Tercel and Federal Corolla. On these models, connect tachometer positive lead to service connector located at coil (covered with rubber cap).

2) With engine at normal operating temperature, be sure all hoses are connected and all accessories are turned off. Adjust idle speed to specifications.

3) On models with dual diaphragm distributors, disconnect and plug hose at sub-diaphragm (closest to distributor body). On all models, check timing and adjust by turning distributor. When sub-diaphragm hose is connected, timing should advance 8-10°.

Ignition Timing Specifications

Application	Timing
Celica, Corona, Pickup	①8°BTDC
Corolla	①10°BTDC
Tercel	①5°BTDC

① — With distributor sub-diaphragm hose disconnected.

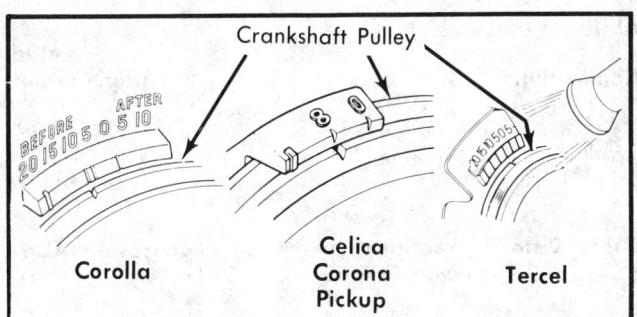

Fig. 4   Ignition Timing Marks

IDLE SPEED & MIXTURE

1) With air cleaner installed, engine at normal operating temperature, all accessories off and vacuum lines connected, be sure timing is set.

2) Set transmission in "N" and check that fuel level in carburetor sight glass is about mid-way.

3) On California vehicles, use special tool (09243-00020) to remove idle mixture screw protective cover and to adjust mixture screw.

4) Remove idle limiter caps, if installed, and adjust idle speed to specifications.

5) Turn idle mixture adjusting screw to obtain maximum RPM. Now, turn idle speed screw until IDLE MIXTURE SPEED is obtained. Repeat adjustments again, turning idle mixture screw to maximum RPM, then idle speed screw to idle mixture speed. Repeat until highest RPM is obtained before setting final idle mixture speed.

6) Once idle mixture speed is set after the highest possible RPM is obtained using the above procedure, turn in idle mixture adjusting screw until normal IDLE SPEED is obtained.

7) Install replacement mixture screw caps. On California models, install protective cover.

Idle Speed and Mixture Specifications

Application	Idle Mixture RPM	Idle Speed RPM
Celica, Corona		
4 Spd.	750	700
5 Spd.	870	800
Auto. Trans.	920	850
Corolla		
Man. Trans.①	760	700
Auto Trans.①	810	750
Pickup	870	800
Tercel		
Man. Trans.	750	650
Auto Trans.	900	800

① — With power steering, set to 920/850 RPM.

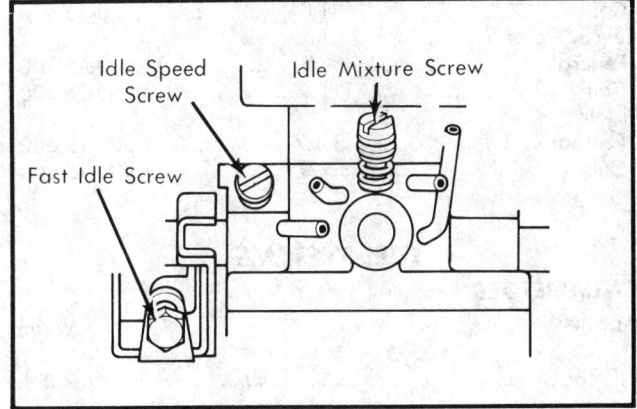

Fig. 5   Carburetor Adjusting Screws (All Models)

COLD (FAST) IDLE RPM

1) After setting idle mixture and speed, stop engine. Remove air cleaner. On Corolla, plug HIC hose after removing air cleaner, and disconnect and plug hose from choke opener.

1980 Toyota 4 Tune Up

TUNE-UP (Cont.)

2) On Tercel, disconnect hose from port "M" of TVSV and plug port, then disconnect and plug hose from EGR valve. On Celica, Corona, and Pickup, disconnect and plug hoses at distributor advance, and EGR valve.

Fast Idle Speed

Application	RPM
Celica, Corona, Pickup	2400
Corolla	
Federal①	3000
Calif.①	2800
Tercel	3600

① — If equipped with power steering, set fast idle speed 200 RPM lower.

3) With engine stopped, open throttle, pull open choke linkage, and set screw on high step of fast idle cam. Without touching accelerator, start engine.

4) Set fast idle speed to specifications. On Corolla, reconnect hose to choke opener diaphragm and check for idle speed to drop to 1800 RPM or less. Reconnect hoses on all models.

FUEL PUMP PRESSURE & VOLUME

Pressure	2.1-4.3 psi (.15-.3 kg/cm²)
Volume	1 pint in 30 seconds

EMISSION CONTROL SYSTEM

See Mitchell Manuals' Emission Control Manual.

GENERAL SERVICING

IGNITION

DISTRIBUTOR

All models are equipped with transistorized ignition systems.

Other Data & Specifications — See Tune-Up & Nippondenso Electronic Ignition Systems in ELECTRICAL Section.

IGNITION COIL

Coil Resistance (Ohms@68°F)

Application	Primary	Secondary
Tercel	.4-.5	8500-11,500
Corolla		
Federal	.4-.5	8500-11,500
Calif.	.8-1.0	11,500-15,500
Celica, Corona		
Federal	.5-.6	11,500-15,500
Calif.	.8-1.0	11,500-15,500
Pickup		
Federal	1.3-1.7	12,000-16,000
Calif.	.8-1.0	11,500-15,500

FUEL SYSTEMS

CARBURETORS

Application	Make
All Models	Aisan 2-Bbl.

Other Data & Specifications — See Tune-Up and Aisan Carburetors in FUEL SYSTEMS Section.

ELECTRICAL

BATTERY

Application	Amp. Hr. Rating
Standard	50
Optional	60

Battery Location — In engine compartment.

STARTER

All models are equipped with Nippondenso starters.

Starter Specifications

Application	Volts	Amps	Test RPM
Tercel			
Conventional	11.0	50	5000
Reduction	11.5	90	3000
Corolla	11.5	90	3000-3500
All Others			
Conventional	11.0	50	5000
Reduction	11.5	90	3500

Other Data & Specifications — See Nippondenso Starters in ELECTRICAL Section.

ALTERNATOR

Application	Rated Amp. Output
Tercel	50
Corolla	50, 55
Celica, Corona, Pickup	40, 50

Other Data & Specifications — See Nippondenso Alternators and Regulators in ELECTRICAL Section.

ALTERNATOR REGULATOR

All models are equipped with Nippondenso alternator regulators. Separate alternator regulators have an operating voltage of 14.0-14.7 volts. Integral regulators have an operating voltage of 13.8-14.8 volts.

Other Data & Specifications — See Nippondenso Alternators and Regulators in ELECTRICAL Section.

GENERAL SERVICING (Cont.)

BELT ADJUSTMENT

Tension Using Tension Gauge

Application	New Belt Lbs. (kg)	Used Belt Lbs. (kg)
All Models	100-150 (45-68)	60-100 (27-45)

FILTERS

Filter	Service Interval (Miles)
Oil Filter	Replace every 10,000
Air Filter	Replace every 30,000
Fuel Filter	Replace every 30,000

CAPACITIES

Application	Quantity	Application	Quantity
Crankcase (Includes Filter)		Differential (SAE 90)	
Celica, Corona, Pickup	4.9 qts.	Celica, Corona	2.6 pts.
Corolla	4.0 qts.	Corolla	2.2 pts.
Tercel	3.7 qts.	Tercel (with Auto. Trans.)	2.0 pts.
Cooling System (Includes Heater)		Pickup	
Celica, Corona, Pickup	8.9 qts.	2-WD	3.6 pts.
Corolla	8.4 qts.	4-WD Front	4.8 pts.
Tercel	5.4 qts.	4-WD Rear	4.6 pts.
Man. Trans. (SAE 90)		Fuel Tank	
Celica, Corona	2.8 qts.	Celica	16.1 gals.
Corolla	1.8 qts.	Corolla	
Pickup		Station Wagon	12.4 gals.
4 Spd.	2.0 qts.	Except Station Wagon	13.2 gals.
5 Spd.	2.8 qts.	Corona	
Man. Transaxle (SAE 90)		Station Wagon	15.6 gals.
Tercel	3.5 qts.	Except Station Wagon	16.1 gals.
Auto. Trans. (ATF Type F)		Tercel	11.9 gals.
Tercel	2.3 qts.	Pickup	
All Other Models	2.5 qts.	Short Bed	13.5 gals.
Transfer Case (SAE 90)	3.4 pts.	Long Bed	16.0 gals.

TUNE-UP

Cressida
Land Cruiser
Supra

ENGINE IDENTIFICATION

Engines can be identified by prefix of engine serial number, stamped on right side of engine block. Engine code can also be found on front of valve cover.

Engine Model Number

Application	Engine Number
Cressida & Supra	4M-E
Land Cruiser	2F

COMPRESSION PRESSURE

Check compression pressure with engine at normal operating temperature, all spark plugs removed, throttle valve wide open and engine at cranking speed. Maximum variation between cylinders should not exceed 14 psi (1.0 kg/cm^2). Standard and minimum pressures are as follows:

Compression Pressure

Application	Standard psi (kg/cm^2)	Minimum psi (kg/cm^2)
Cressida & Supra	156 (11.0)	128 (9.0)
Land Cruiser	149 (10.5)	114 (8.0)

VALVE CLEARANCE

NOTE – Check or adjust valve clearance with engine at normal operating temperature.

Valve Clearance Specifications

Application	Intake	Exhaust
Cressida & Supra	.011" (.28 mm)	.014" (.36 mm)
Land Cruiser	.008" (.21 mm)	.014" (.36 mm)

VALVE ARRANGEMENT

Cressida & Supra
Left Side – All Intake
Right Side – All Exhaust

Land Cruiser – E-I-I-E-E-I-I-E-E-I-I-E

SPARK PLUGS

Application	Gap In. (mm)	Torque Ft. Lbs. (mkg)
All Models	.031 (.8)	10-15 (1.4-2.1)

Spark Plug Type

Application	NGK	Nippondenso
Cressida & Supra	BPR5EA-L	W16EXR-U
Land Cruiser	BP5EA	W14EX-U

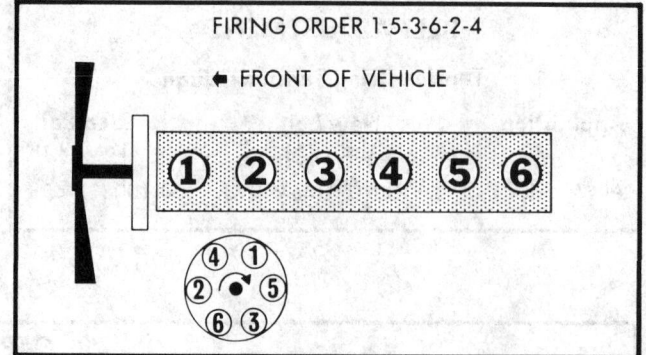

Fig. 1   Firing Order and Distributor Rotation (Cressida & Supra)

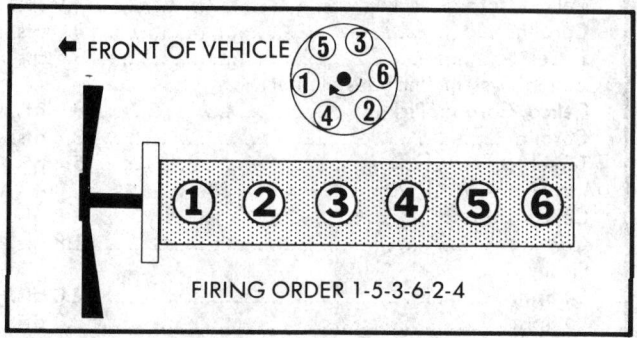

Fig. 2   Firing Order and Distributor Rotation (Land Cruiser)

HIGH TENSION WIRE RESISTANCE

Carefully remove high tension wires from spark plugs and distributor cap. Using an ohmmeter, check high tension wire resistance while gently twisting wires. If resistance is not to specifications, or fluctuates from infinity to any value, replace high tension wire(s).

Resistance (Ohms) Per Wire

Application	Ohms
All Models	16,000-25,000

DISTRIBUTOR

All models with 6-cylinder engines are fitted with Nippondenso Transistorized Electronic Ignition Systems. The only in-service adjustment possible is to set the air gap.

Air Gap .... .008-.016" (.2-.4 mm)

IGNITION TIMING

Check or adjust ignition timing with engine at normal operating temperature and choke fully open. Adjust idle speed. On Land Cruiser, disconnect distributor sub-diaphragm hose (farthest from distributor body). Turn distributor to adjust timing.

TUNE-UP (Cont.)

CAUTION — *Do not allow tachometer connector at distributor (−) terminal to touch ground or damage may occur to system.*

Ignition Timing Specifications

Application	RPM	Timing
Cressida & Supra	800	12° BTDC
Land Cruiser	800	7° BTDC

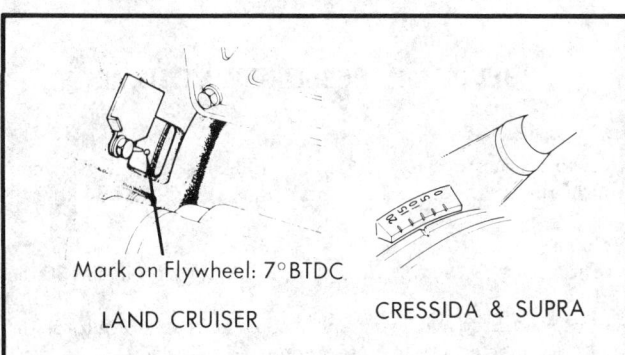

Fig. 3   Ignition Timing Marks

IDLE SPEED & MIXTURE

CARBURETED MODELS

1) With engine at normal operating temperature, choke valve fully open, all accessories off, all vacuum lines connected, ignition timing set to specifications and transmission in neutral, check that fuel level is aligned with dot on sight glass of carburetor float bowl. Adjust float level if necessary.

2) With air cleaner installed, adjust idle mixture screw until fastest idle RPM is obtained. Then, adjust idle speed screw until specified mixture adjustment RPM is achieved.

3) Repeat procedure until RPM cannot be increased by adjusting mixture screw. Set idle to specified initial idle RPM by adjusting idle speed screw in a clockwise direction.

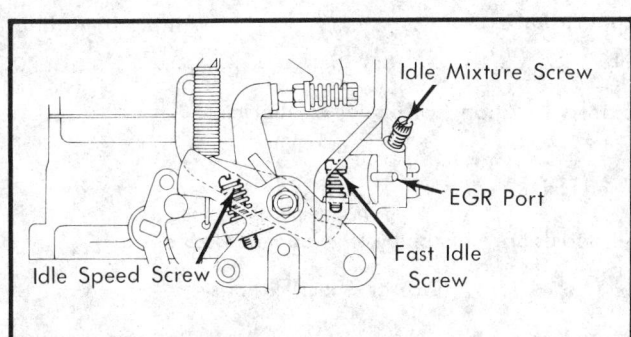

Fig. 4   Carburetor Adjustment Screw Locations

FUEL INJECTED MODELS

1) Remove rubber cap from the service connector at left front fender and connect an EFI Idle Adjusting Wiring Harness to it (Toyota 09842-14010).

2) Connect a voltmeter to the special wiring harness. Positive probe should go to the red lead; negative probe to black lead.

CAUTION — *Do not connect the voltmeter probes directly to the service connector.*

3) Warm up engine at 2500 RPM for 2 minutes. Voltmeter needle should fluctuate. If not, adjust idle mixture needle until it does. See *Fig. 5*.

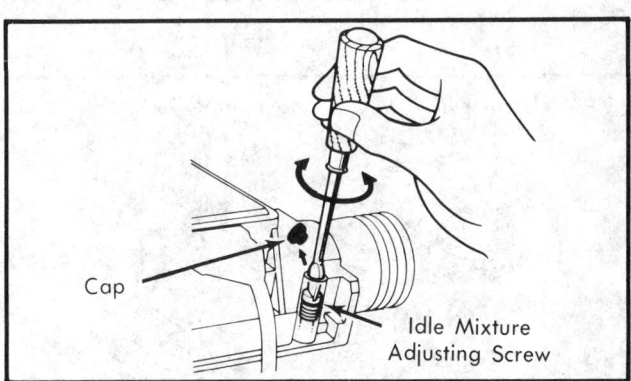

Fig. 5   Idle Mixture Adjusting Screw (Fuel Injected Models)

4) Set the idle speed to 800 RPM with idle speed adjusting screw. See *Fig. 6*.

5) Remove rubber cap from idle adjusting connector and short both terminals with a jumper wire. Warm engine at 2500 RPM for 2 minutes. Note voltage reading with engine at idle.

6) Remove the short-circuit wire and race engine to 2500 RPM once. Adjust idle mixture screw until the voltmeter needle fluctuation is centered on the voltage reading noted in step **5)**.

7) Remove voltmeter and wiring harness and replace rubber caps on connectors.

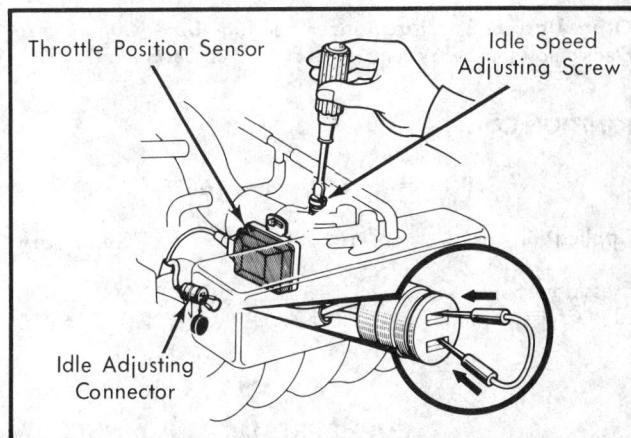

Fig. 6   Idle Speed Adjusting Screw and Connector (Fuel Injected Models)

Idle Speed Specifications

Application	Man. Trans.	Auto. Trans.
Cressida		800
Supra	800	800
Land Cruiser	850	

TUNE-UP (Cont.)

COLD (FAST) IDLE RPM

NOTE — *There is no fast idle speed adjustment for Electronic Fuel Injection equipped vehicles.*

Land Cruiser — 1) Pull choke knob out fully. Disconnect and plug hose to distributor main diaphragm (hose closest to distributor cap). Disconnect hoses to VCV post "S" and EGR valve port "P". Use one hose to connect VCV pipe to EGR pipe. See Fig. 8.

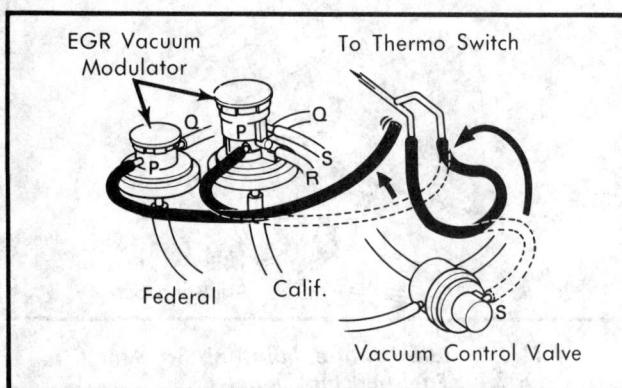

Fig. 7   Land Cruiser Vacuum Hose Routing for Fast Idle Adjustment

2) Start engine and adjust engine speed with fast idle screw. Engine should return to normal idle when choke knob is pushed in all the way. Reconnect hoses.

Fast Idle Specifications

Application	RPM
Land Cruiser	①1800

① — EGR, EVAP, and distributor diaphragm disconnected.

FUEL PUMP PRESSURE & VOLUME

Pressure
Cressida & Supra	①33-38 psi (2.3-2.7 kg/cm²)
Land Cruiser	3.4-4.8 psi (.24-.34 kg/cm²)

Volume
Land Cruiser	2.5 pints in 30 sec.

① — Measured with vacuum hose at pressure regulator disconnected. With hose connected, 28 psi (2.0 kg/cm²)

EMISSION CONTROL SYSTEMS

See Mitchell Manuals' Emission Control Manual.

GENERAL SERVICING

IGNITION

DISTRIBUTOR

All models are equipped with Nippondenso Transistorized Electronic Ignition Systems.

Other Data & Specifications — *See Tune-Up & Nippondenso Electronic Ignition Systems in ELECTRICAL Section.*

IGNITION COIL

Coil Resistance (Ohms @ 68°F)

Application	Primary	Secondary
Cressida & Supra	.5-.6	11,500-15,500
Land Cruiser	1.3-1.7	12,000-16,000

FUEL SYSTEMS

CARBURETORS

Application	Model
Land Cruiser	Aisan 2-Bbl.

Other Data & Specifications — *See Tune-Up and Asian Carburetors in FUEL SYSTEMS Section.*

FUEL INJECTION

Cressida and Supra Models are equipped with Bosch AFC fuel injection with oxygen sensor.

Other Data & Specifications — *See Tune-Up and Bosch AFC Fuel Injection in FUEL SYSTEMS Section.*

ELECTRICAL

BATTERY

Application	Amp. Hr. Rating
All	70

Battery Location — In engine compartment.

STARTER

All models are equipped with Nippondenso Starters.

Starter Specifications

Application	Volts	Amps	Test RPM
Cressida & Supra			
Conventional	11.0	50	5000
Reduction	11.5	90	3500
Land Cruiser	11.0	50	5000

Other Data & Specifications — *See Nippondenso Starters in ELECTRICAL Section*

GENERAL SERVICING (Cont.)

ALTERNATOR

Application	Rated Amp. Output
Cressida	55
Land Cruiser	
With Integral Regulator	55
With External Regulator	40
Supra	60

Other Data & Specifications — *See Nippondenso Alternators and Regulators in ELECTRICAL Section.*

ALTERNATOR REGULATOR

All models are equipped with Nippondenso alternators and regulators. Some alternators are equipped with integrated circuit regulators (mounted integrally with alternator). Operating voltage for these regulators is 14.0-14.7 volts. Operating voltage for externally mounted regulators is 13.8-14.8 volts.

Other Data & Specification — *See Nippondenso Alternators and Regulators in ELECTRICAL Section.*

BELT ADJUSTMENT

Application	①Deflection
Alternator Belt	
Cressida & Supra	.4-.55" (10-14 mm)
Land Cruiser	.5-.6" (13-15 mm)
Air Pump Belt	
Land Cruiser	.3-.4" (8-10 mm)
Air Conditioning Belt	
Cressida & Supra	.4-.5" (10-13 mm)
Land Cruiser	.6-.7" (15-18 mm)
Power Steering Belt	
Cressida & Supra	.4-.5" (10-13 mm)
Land Cruiser	.43-.55" (11-14 mm)

① — Deflection is with 22 lbs. (10 kg) pressure applied midway on longest belt run.

FILTERS

Filter	Service Interval (Miles)
Oil Filter	
Cressida & Supra	Replace every 10,000
Land Cruiser	Replace every 7500
Air Filter	Replace every 30,000
Fuel Filter	Replace every 60,000

CAPACITIES

Application	Quantity
Crankcase (Includes Filter)	
Cressida & Supra	4.9 qts.
Land Cruiser	8.2 qts.
Cooling System	
Cressida & Supra	11.6 qts.
Land Cruiser (Includes Heater)	
Station Wagon	17.4 qts.
All Others	16.9 qts.
Man. Trans. (SAE 80W-90)	
Land Cruiser	6.6 pts.
Supra	5.6 pts.
Auto. Trans. (ATF Type F)	2.5 qts.
Differential (SAE 90)	
Cressida & Supra	3.0 pts.
Land Cruiser	5.2 pts.
Transfer Case (SAE 90)	3.6 pts.
Fuel Tank	
Cressida	
Sedan	17.2 gals.
Station Wagon	16.2 gals.
Land Cruiser	
Station Wagon	21.7 gals.
All Others	22.4 gals.
Supra	16.1 gals.

1980 Triumph 4 Tune-Up

TUNE-UP

Spitfire
TR7

ENGINE IDENTIFICATION

Engine number is stamped on engine boss on left side of block below number four spark plug on Spitfire models and is stamped on the cylinder head between carburetors on TR7 models. The following engine codes (prefix letters) denote engines designed specifically for the USA market.

Engine Identification

Application	Code
Spitfire	FM XXXXXX UE
TR7	
Carb. Models	CV XXXXXX U
Fuel Inj. Models	CK XXXXXX UC

COMPRESSION PRESSURE

Check compression with engine at normal operating temperature, spark plugs removed and throttle wide open. Crank engine through four compression strokes before taking reading. On Spitfire models, minimum pressure is 145 psi (10.2 kg/cm^2). On both Spitfire and TR7 models, lowest pressure should be at least 85% that of highest cylinder.

VALVE CLEARANCE

Spitfire — 1) Disconnect battery, then remove valve cover and spark plugs. Check valve clearance with engine cold. Adjust valves in outlined sequence (numbered front to rear):

Valves Open	Adjust Valves
No. 8 & No. 6	No. 1 & No. 3
No. 4 & No. 7	No. 5 & No. 2
No. 1 & No. 3	No. 8 & No. 6
No. 5 & No. 2	No. 4 & No. 7

2) Turn crankshaft until appropriate valves in first column open. Then check and adjust valves listed in second column.

3) To adjust, loosen lock nut and turn slotted adjusting pin clockwise to decrease clearance and counterclockwise to increase clearance. Tighten lock nut when correct.

TR7 — 1) Disconnect battery and remove camshaft cover. Loosen camshaft bearing cap nuts and retighten to 10-14 ft. lbs. (1.4-1.9 mkg). Rotate engine. Check and record clearance between cam heel and tappet. Maximum clearance is present when cam is in vertical position.

2) If clearance is not within specifications, remove camshaft and individually lift out each tappet and adjusting shim.

3) Using a micrometer, measure thickness of adjusting shim removed. Add to this the measured valve clearance and subtract the specified clearance from the total. This will offer you the thickness of adjusting shim necessary to bring the clearance within specifications.

4) Install tappets and add shims as needed. Install camshaft and tighten bearing caps. Recheck valve clearance, and, when correct, replace camshaft cover.

Valve Clearance Specifications

Application	Clearance (Cold)
Spitfire	
Intake & Exhaust	.010" (.25 mm)
TR7	
Intake	.008" (.20 mm)
Exhaust	.018" (.50 mm)

VALVE ARRANGEMENT

E-I-I-E-E-I-I-E (front to rear).

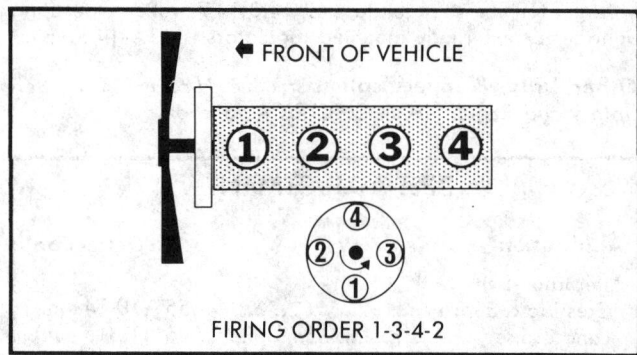

Fig. 1 *Firing Order and Distributor Rotation (Spitfire)*

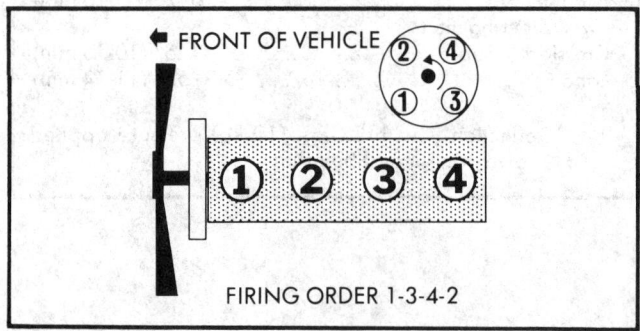

Fig. 2 *Firing Order and Distributor Rotation (TR7)*

SPARK PLUGS

Application	Gap In. (mm)	Torque Ft. Lbs. (mkg)
All Models	.025 (.64)	20 (2.8)

Spark Plug Type

Application	Champion No.
All Models	N12Y

TUNE-UP (Cont.)

HIGH TENSION WIRE RESISTANCE

Carefully remove high tension wires from spark plugs and distributor cap. Using an ohmmeter, check high tension wire resistance while gently twisting wires. If resistance is not to specifications, or fluctuates from infinity to any value, replace high tension wire(s).

Resistance (Ohms) Per Wire

Application	Ohms
All Models	25,000-30,000

DISTRIBUTOR

All models are equipped with Opus Electronic Ignition System and the only adjustment required is adjusting the Pick-Up Module air gap.

CAUTION — *DO NOT insert feeler gauge into pick-up air gap when the ignition circuit is energized.*

Air Gap .... ①.010-.017" (.25-.43 mm)

① — Measured between timing rotor and pick-up module.

IGNITION TIMING

Check or adjust engine timing with engine idling at normal operating temperature. If correction is needed, rotate distributor.

Ignition Timing Specifications

Application	RPM	Timing
All Models	800	2° ATDC

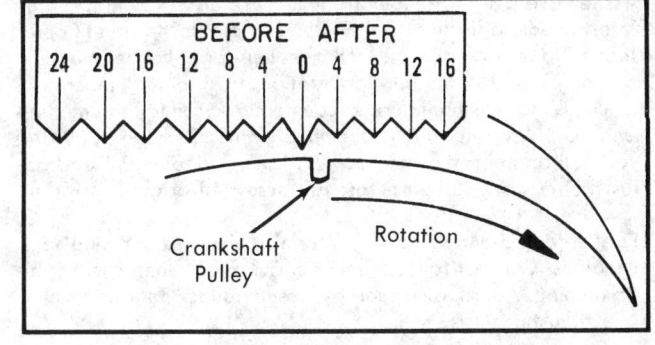

Fig. 3 Ignition Timing Mark Location

IDLE SPEED & MIXTURE

Carbureted Models — **1)** Remove air cleaner and fresh air duct, then ensure oil in carburetor damper is ¼" below top of damper tube. Connect tachometer and CO meter to vehicle, then warm to operating temperature. Unscrew fast idle screw until it does not contact fast idle cam (note amount required).

2) On models with a single carburetor, adjust idle speed to specifications by adjusting throttle adjusting screw. On models with dual carburetors, use an air flow balance meter and synchronize carburetors, then adjust idle speed to specifications by adjusting throttle adjusting screw on each carburetor an equal amount.

3) On all models, stop engine and disconnect and plug air pump outlet hose. Start engine and check CO level. If CO level is not within specifications, adjust idle trim screw(s) clockwise to richen mixture or counterclockwise to lean mixture until CO level is within specified limit. If CO level cannot be adjusted within correct limits by adjusting the idle trim screw(s), proceed to step **4)**.

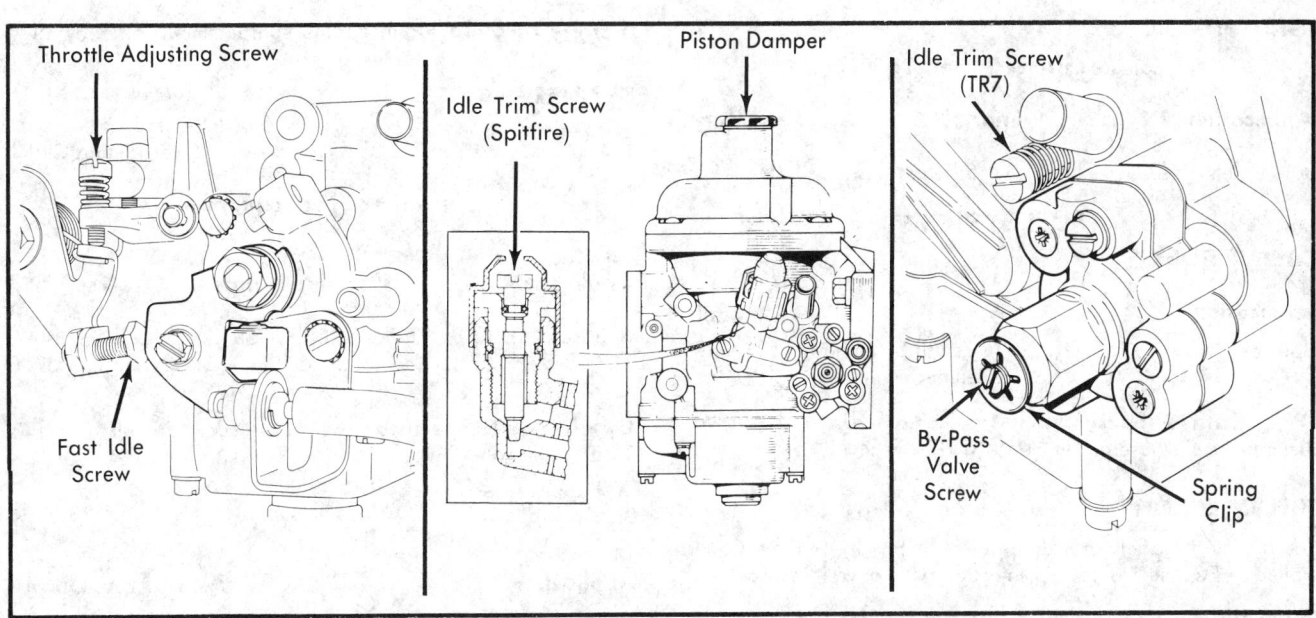

Fig. 4 Screws for Adjusting Idle Speed, Mixture, & Decel Valve (Carbureted Models Only)

TUNE-UP (Cont.)

4) Remove piston damper from carburetor(s). Then, carefully insert needle adjusting tool (BLT 2010) into dashpot until outer tool engages air valve and inner tool engages hexagon in needle adjuster. Hold outer tool stationary and turn inner tool clockwise to richen mixture or counterclockwise to lean mixture until CO level is within specified limits. Remove tool and reinstall damper, then recheck CO level and idle RPM and adjust as necessary. Return fast idle screw to original position.

Fuel Injected Models — 1) Warm engine to operating temperature. Connect tachometer and CO meter, then check ignition timing. Adjust idle speed by loosening lock nut and turning idle adjustment screw.

2) Check CO level. If not correct, remove plug from air flow meter. Turn adjustment screw until specified reading is obtained. Replace plug, recheck idle speed, and remove test equipment.

Idle Speed & CO Level

Application	Idle RPM	CO%
Spitfire	700-900	① 3.0-7.0
TR7		
Carb. Models	700-900	① 3.0-7.0
Fuel Inj. Models	700-900	0.2

① — Air pump disconnected.

DECEL VALVE ADJUSTMENT

CARBURETED MODELS ONLY

Spitfire — With engine warm, disconnect and plug distributor retard line. Engine speed should increase to 1300 RPM. If speed increases to 2000-2500 RPM, decel valve needs to be adjusted. Turn by-pass screw until speed drops to 1300 RPM, then turn screw an additional ½ turn to fully seat valve. Reconnect vacuum retard line at distributor.

TR7 — Turn decel valve screw on rear carburetor clockwise until engine speed increases, then turn counterclockwise 3 turns. Repeat procedure on front carburetor, but turn screw counterclockwise 2 turns. Turn screw on rear carburetor counterclockwise 1 additional turn.

FUEL PUMP PRESSURE

Pressure	
Spitfire	2.5-3.8 psi (.17-.26 kg/cm²)
TR7 Carb. Models	2.5-3.5 psi (.17-.24 kg/cm²)
TR7 Fuel Inj. Models	36 psi (2.5 kg/cm²)

EMISSION CONTROL SYSTEMS

See *Mitchell Manuals' Emission Control Manual.*

GENERAL SERVICING

IGNITION

DISTRIBUTOR

All models are equipped with Lucas Opus Electronic Ignition System.

Other Data & Specifications — *See Tune-Up and Lucas Ignition Systems in ELECTRICAL Section.*

IGNITION COIL

Coil Resistance (Ohms@68°F)

Application	Primary	Secondary
All Models	1.3-1.5	

FUEL SYSTEMS

CARBURETORS

Application	Model
Spitfire	1 Zenith-Stromberg 150 CD4T
TR7	2 Zenith-Stromberg 175 CDFVX

Other Data & Specifications — *See Tune-Up and Zenith-Stromberg Carburetors in FUEL SYSTEMS Section.*

FUEL INJECTION

Fuel injected models are equipped with Bosch Air Flow Controlled (AFC) electronic fuel injection with oxygen sensor.

Other Data & Specifications — *See Bosch AFC Fuel Injecton Systems in FUEL SYSTEMS Section.*

ELECTRICAL

BATTERY

Application	Amp. Hr. Capacity
Spitfire	40
TR7	50

Battery Location — In engine compartment, on firewall.

STARTER

Lucas .... Overrunning Clutch

Starter Specifications

Application	Volts	Amps	Test RPM
Spitfire	12	65	8000
TR7	12	40	6000

Other Data & Specifications — *See Lucas Starters in ELECTRICAL Section.*

ALTERNATOR

Application	Rated Amp. Output
Spitfire	36
TR7	65

GENERAL SERVICING (Cont.)

Other Data & Specifications — *See Lucas Alternators and Regulators in ELECTRICAL Section.*

ALTERNATOR REGULATOR

Lucas — Non-Adjustable, integral with alternator, with an operating voltage of 13.6-14.4 volts.

Other Data & Specifications — *See Lucas Alternators and Regulators in ELECTRICAL Section.*

BELT ADJUSTMENT

Application	① Deflection
Fan Belt	.75-1.0" (19-25 mm)
Air Pump Belt	.25-.50" (6-13 mm)

① — Deflection is with pressure applied midway on longest belt run.

FILTERS

Filter	Service Interval (Miles)
Oil Filter	Replace every 7500
Air Filter	Replace every 36,000
Fuel Filter	Replace ever 36,000

CAPACITIES

Application	Quantity
Crankcase (Includes Filter)	4.8 qts.
Cooling System (Includes Heater)	
Spitfire	5.6 qts.
TR7	7.8 qts.
Man. Trans. (SAE 75)	
Spitfire	
Without Overdrive	1.8 pts.
With Overdrive	3.3 pts.
TR7	3.3 pts.
Rear Axle (SAE 75)	
Spitfire	1.2 pts.
TR7	2.4 pts.
Fuel Tank	
Spitfire	8.7 gals.
TR7	14.4 gals.

TUNE-UP

TR8

ENGINE IDENTIFICATION

Engine number is stamped on left side of block near No. 3 spark plug. The following code prefixes designate US models:

Application	Code
TR8 Carb.	10E, 12E
TR8 Fuel Inj.	14E

COMPRESSION PRESSURE

Check compression with engine warm, spark plugs removed, and throttle wide open. Crank engine through at least 4 compression strokes before taking reading. Minimum pressure should not be less than 135 psi (9.5 kg/cm²).

VALVE CLEARANCE

TR8 engines are equipped with hydraulic valve lifters and no adjustment is necessary.

VALVE ARRANGEMENT

E-I-E-I-I-E-I-E

SPARK PLUGS

Application	Gap In. (mm)	Torque Ft. Lbs. (mkg)
Carb. Models	.035 (.9)	12 (1.7)
Fuel Inj. Models	.030 (.8)	12 (1.7)

Spark Plug Type

Application	Champion No.
All Models	N12Y

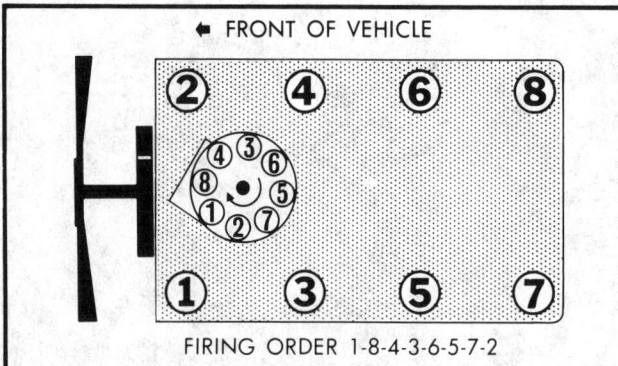

Fig. 1   TR8 Firing Order and Distributor Rotation

(image text: ← FRONT OF VEHICLE; 2 4 6 8; 1 3 5 7; FIRING ORDER 1-8-4-3-6-5-7-2)

HIGH TENSION WIRE RESISTANCE

Carefully remove high tension wires from spark plugs and distributor cap. Using an ohmmeter, check high tension wire resistance while gently twisting wires. If resistance is not to specifications, or fluctuates from infinity to any value, replace high tension wire(s).

Resistance (Ohms) Per Wire

Application	Ohms
All Models	25,000-30,000

DISTRIBUTOR

All models are equipped with Lucas electronic breakerless ignition systems. The only maintenance is adjusting air gap between timing rotor and pick-up module.

CAUTION — *DO NOT insert feeler gauge into pick-up air gap when the ignition circuit is energized.*

Air Gap .... .012-.017" (.3-.4 mm)

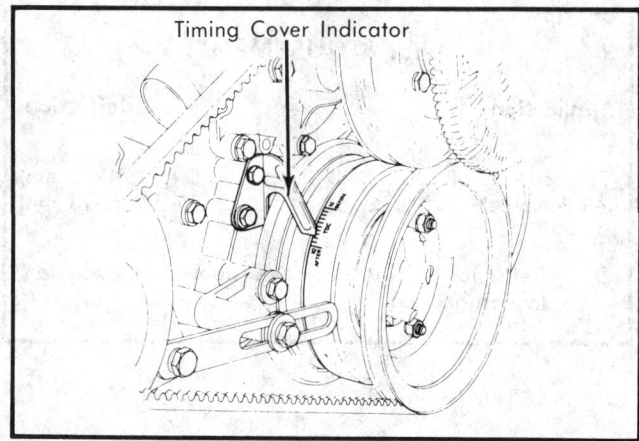

Timing Cover Indicator

Fig. 2   TR8 Ignition Timing Mark Location

IGNITION TIMING

Check or adjust ignition timing with engine at normal operating temperature, idle speed set to specification, and distributor hoses disconnected. If adjustment is necessary, rotate distributor.

Ignition Timing Specifications

Application	RPM	Timing
Carb. Models	750-900	5° ATDC
Fuel Inj. Models	750-900	TDC

IDLE SPEED & MIXTURE

Carbureted Models — 1) Connect tachometer to engine, then check ignition timing. Warm engine to normal operating temperature and remove air cleaners. Disconnect throttle rod and connecting rod between carburetors.

2) Turn linkage adjusting screw until it is clear of spring-loaded pad. Check to ensure automatic choke is off, then adjust idle speed and balance using air flow meter and idle adjusting screws. Reconnect carburetor connecting rod, then hold left carburetor throttle lever against stop. Turn linkage adjusting screw until it hits spring-loaded pad.

3) Connect throttle rod and install air cleaners. Run engine at 2000 RPM for 30 seconds, then disconnect hoses from air pump and clamp ends of hoses. DO NOT plug air pump outlets. Insert CO meter probe into either tailpipe at least 18 inches.

TUNE-UP (Cont.)

4) Check CO level. If adjustment is necessary, remove piston damper caps. Insert special tool BLT 2010 into damper and hold outer part engaged. Turn inner part of tool clockwise to richen and counterclockwise to lean mixture. Adjust both carburetors evenly until mixture is within specifications.

5) Remove tool, fill pistons with oil, and replace caps. Run engine at 2000 RPM for 30 seconds, then recheck mixture and idle speed. Remove test equipment and reconnect air pump hoses.

Fuel Injected Models — 1) Adjust timing and run engine until normal operating temperature is reached. Connect tachometer and connect CO meter to manifold test points. Loosen lock nut and turn idle adjustment screw (on air flow meter) to adjust idle speed.

2) To adjust mixture, remove plug from air flow meter. Turn adjustment screw until mixture is correct, then replace plug. Recheck idle speed and remove test equipment.

Idle Speed & CO Level

Application	RPM	CO%
Carb. Models	800	2.5-5.5
Fuel Inj. Models	800	0.2

COLD (FAST) IDLE RPM

Fast idle cam gap adjustment is factory set and should not be changed.

FUEL PUMP PRESSURE

Pressure (At Idle)
Carb. Models .... 2.5-3.5 psi (.18-.24 kg/cm²)
Fuel Inj. Models .... 36 psi (2.5 kg/cm²)

EMISSION CONTROL SYSTEMS

See *Mitchell Manuals' Emission Control Manual.*

GENERAL SERVICING

IGNITION

DISTRIBUTOR

All models are equipped with Lucas Opus Electronic Ignition System.

Other Data & Specifications — *See Tune-Up and Lucas Ignition Systems in* ELECTRICAL *Section.*

IGNITION COIL

Coil Resistance (Ohms @ 68°F)

Application	Primary	Secondary
All Models	.9-1.1	....

FUEL SYSTEMS

CARBURETORS

Application	Model
TR8	2 Zenith-Stromberg CDSET

Other Data & Specifications — *See Tune-Up and Zenith-Stromberg Carburetors in* FUEL SYSTEMS *Section.*

FUEL INJECTION

All models are equipped with Bosch Air Flow Controlled fuel injection systems with oxygen sensor.

Other Data & Specifications — *See Bosch AFC Fuel Injection in* FUEL SYSTEMS *Section.*

ELECTRICAL

Battery Location — Battery is located in trunk.

Application	Amp. Hr. Capacity
All Models	68

STARTER

Lucas .... Overrunning clutch

Starter Specifications

Application	Volts	Amps	Test RPM
All Models	12	65	6000

Other Data & Specifications — *See Lucas Starters in* ELECTRICAL *Section.*

ALTERNATOR

Application	Rated Amp. Output
All Models	65

Other Data & Specifications — *See Lucas Alternators and Regulators in* ELECTRICAL *Section.*

ALTERNATOR REGULATOR

All models are equipped with Lucas integral alternator regulators.

Other Data & Specifications — *See Lucas Alternators and Regulators in* ELECTRICAL *Section.*

BELT ADJUSTMENT

Application	①Deflection
Alternator	.5-.75″ (13-19 mm)
A/C & Power Steering	.75-1.0″ (19-25 mm)

① — Deflection is with moderate pressure applied midway on longest belt run.

1980 Triumph V8 Tune-Up

GENERAL SERVICING (Cont.)

FILTERS

Application	Service Interval (Miles)
Oil Filter	Replace every 7500
Air Filter	Replace every 36,000
Crankcase Breather Filter	Replace every 36,000
Fuel Filter	Replace every 36,000

CAPACITIES

Application	Quantity
Crankcase (Includes Filter)	5.4 qts.
Cooling System (Includes Heater)	11.5 qts.
Man. Trans. (SAE 75)	3.3 pts.
Rear Axle (SAE 75)	3.3 pts.
Fuel Tank	14.4 gals.

TUNE-UP

Dasher   Rabbit Pickup
Jetta   Scirocco
Rabbit   Vanagon

ENGINE IDENTIFICATION

Engine code prefixes are placed in the following locations:

Vanagon — Engine serial number is stamped on right side of crankcase joint behind fan housing.

All Other Models — Engine serial number is stamped on left side of engine near ignition distributor.

Engine Codes

Application	Code
Dasher	
Man. Trans.	YG
Auto. Trans.	YH, YK
Jetta, Rabbit, Scirocco (F.I.)	EJ
Rabbit (Carb.)	FX
Rabbit Pickup	EH
Vanagon	CV

COMPRESSION PRESSURE

Check compression with engine warm, all spark plugs removed, and throttle wide open. Maximum variation permitted between cylinders is 42 psi (3.0 kg/cm²).

CAUTION — *On models with electronic ignition, connect coil high tension wire to ground before cranking engine.*

Application	Standard Pressure psi (kg/cm²)	Minimum Pressure psi (kg/cm²)
Vanagon	85-135 (6.0-9.5)	71 (5.0)
All Others	142-184 (10.0-13.0)	107 (7.5)

VALVE CLEARANCE

Vanagon — No adjustment is needed as engine is equipped with hydraulic valve lifters.

All Other Models — Remove distributor cap and set engine at TDC. Align distributor rotor with No. 1 cylinder mark on distributor body. Adjust by replacing tappet discs. Discs are available in 26 thicknesses from .119-.166" (3.0-4.25 mm). Adjust valves in firing order, 1-3-4-2, with engine at normal operating temperature.

NOTE — *Use special tool VW546 to press down cam follower, so that adjusting disc can be readily removed with tool US 4476. When depressing cam followers, turn so that openings are at 90° angle to cam.*

Valve Clearance Specifications

Application	Intake	Exhaust
All Except Vanagon	.008-.012" (.2-.3 mm)	.016-.020" (.4-.5 mm)

VALVE ARRANGEMENT

Vanagon — E-I-I-E (Both banks)
All Others — E-I-E-I-I-E-I-E (front-to-rear).

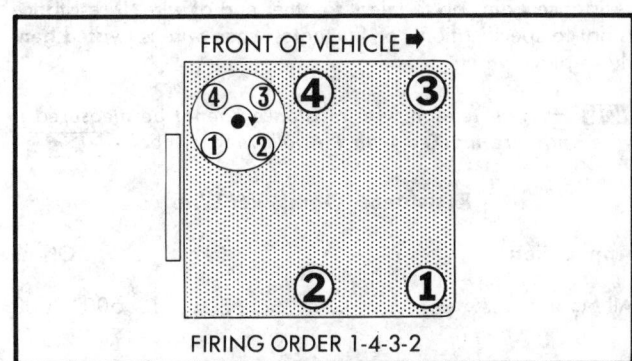

Fig. 1   *Firing Order & Distributor Rotation (Vanagon)*

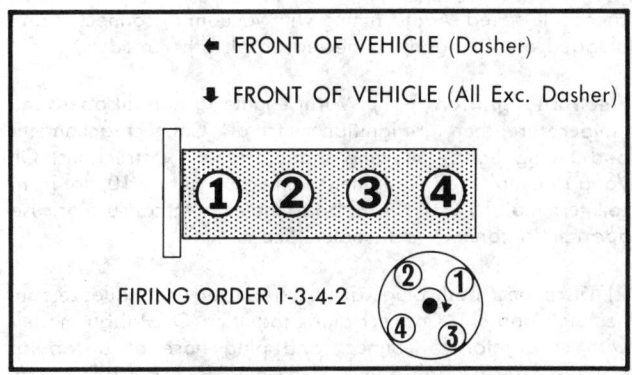

Fig. 2   *Firing Order & Distributor Rotation (All Except Vanagon)*

DISTRIBUTOR

All carbureted Rabbit models and all California vehicles have electronic, breakerless ignition systems. Federal fuel injected models use conventional Bosch single point distributors.

Point Gap	.016" (.4 mm)
Dwell Angle	44-50°
Breaker Arm Tension	14-21 ozs. (450-600 g)
Condenser Capacity	.20 mfd.

SPARK PLUGS

Application	Gap In. (mm)	Torque Ft. Lbs. (mkg)
All Models	.028 (.7 mm)	22 (3.0)

Spark Plug Type

Application	Bosch	Champion
Vanagon	W8CO	N288
All Others	W7D	N8Y

TUNE-UP (Cont.)

HIGH TENSION WIRE RESISTANCE

Remove distributor cap and disconnect high tension wires from spark plugs (not distributor cap). Using an ohmmeter, measure resistance from cap terminal to other end of wire. If resistance is not to specifications, or fluctuates when wire is twisted gently, replace wire(s).

NOTE — *High tension wire resistance cannot be measured if wire ends are marked with the following symbol:* —▭▸◂▭

Resistance (Ohms) Per Wire

Application	Ohms
All Models	5000-7000

IGNITION TIMING

Breaker Point Ignition — Connect tachometer and timing light. Warm engine to normal operating temperature and check idle speed. Adjust timing with vacuum disconnected and plugged on Vanagon; connected on all other models.

Electronic Ignition — 1) Warm engine to normal operating temperature, then turn ignition switch off. Connect tachometer and timing light, following manufacturer's instructions. On Vanagon, make test equipment connection at fuse 10, not from coil terminal 15 (+). On Rabbit models with carburetor, use adapter to connect tachometer. *See Fig. 4.*

2) Disconnect both plugs at idle stabilizer unit (squeeze connector to loosen). Connect plugs together. On Rabbit models with carburetor, disconnect and plug hose at distributor vacuum retard diaphragm. On all models, check idle speed, then adjust timing by turning distributor.

Ignition Timing Specifications

Application	RPM	Timing
Vanagon		
Fed.	850-950	7.5°BTDC
Calif.	850-950	5°ATDC
Rabbit (Carburetor)	800-1000	7.5°BTDC
All Other Models	850-1000	3° ATDC

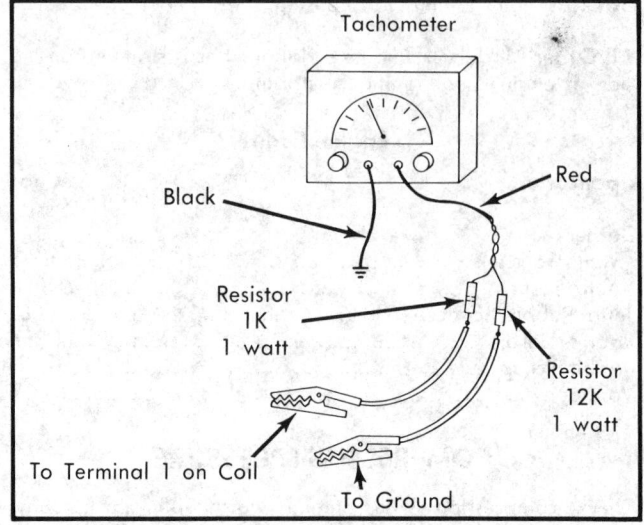

Fig. 4 Tachometer Adapter for Rabbit Carbureted Models

IDLE SPEED & MIXTURE

Vanagon — 1) With engine at normal operating temperature, connect CO tester at probe receptacle on exhaust

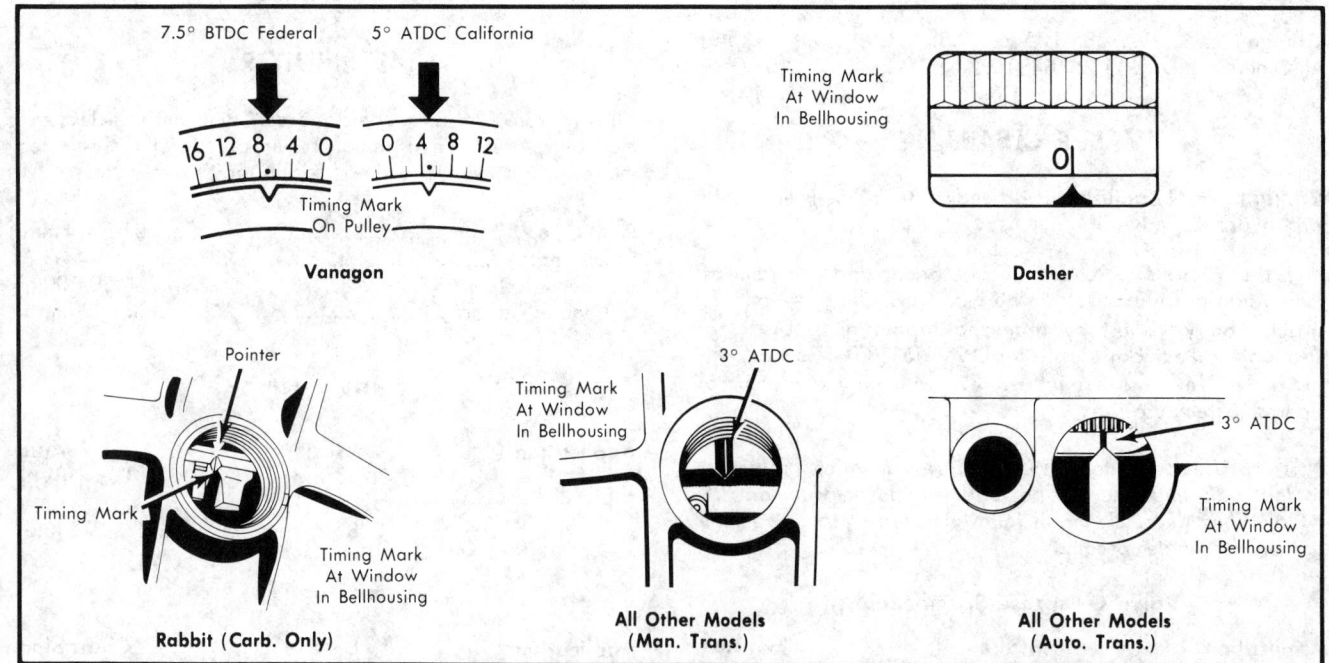

Fig. 3   Ignition Timing Mark Locations (All Models)

TUNE-UP (Cont.)

pipe in front of catalytic converter. Connect tachometer. Disconnect and plug charcoal canister hose at air cleaner.

2) Adjust idle speed with idle screw. Check CO reading, and if incorrect, turn engine off and disconnect oxygen sensor (Calif. models). Disconnect idle stabilizer plugs (Calif. models) and connect together.

3) Start engine and adjust CO at screw on throttle housing. Allow engine to stabilize between readings. When CO is correct, stop engine, reconnect plugs, and remove test equipment.

Rabbit Carbureted Models — 1) With engine at normal operating temperature, disconnect crankcase ventilation hose, fuel evaporation hose, and air injection hoses. Plug openings on air intake (where hoses were removed) and plug both air injection check valves.

2) Turn off all electrical accessories. Connect CO meter to receptacle in manifold, and connect tachometer using adapter. See *Fig. 4.*

3) Start engine and check idle and CO reading. If not to specifications, stop engine. Disconnect plugs at idle stabilizer and connect together. Disconnect and plug vacuum advance and retard hoses at distributor. Start engine and adjust idle speed with idle speed screw.

NOTE — *Engine cooling fan must not run while CO adjustment is being made.*

4) If mixture must be adjusted, reconnect vacuum advance and retard, then adjust CO with CO adjusting screw (below idle speed screw). Stop engine, disconnect test equipment, and reconnect all hoses.

All Other Models — 1) Warm engine to normal operating temperature, then stop engine. Turn off all accessories and connect dwell meter to Blue/Brown wire near right shock tower. Set meter at 4-cylinder scale. Connect tachometer to terminal 1 at ignition coil, then disconnect both plugs from idle stabilizer unit and connect them together (Calif. models only).

2) Start engine and raise RPM until alternator light on dash goes out, then return to idle. Frequency valve must make buzzing sound and dwell meter needle must fluctuate. Adjust idle speed.

NOTE — *Engine fan must not be running when adjusting idle speed and mixture.*

3) Disconnect PCV valve hose from valve cover and plug hose. Locate hose at bottom of charcoal canister (under front body panel) and pull loose end of hose from hole in body panel. Do not plug hose.

4) Disconnect oxygen sensor and position wires so neither end can touch ground. Remove cap from test port on exhaust manifold and connect CO meter to it. Start engine and check idle speed. Adjust if necessary.

5) Dwell meter reading should be 43-47°. Check CO level and adjust by using screw under rubber cap on mixture control unit. Reconnect oxygen sensor and recheck readings. Dwell meter must fluctuate and CO level should be between 0.3-1.2%.

6) Remove test equipment. Reconnect PCV hose, canister hose, and idle stabilizer (if equipped).

Idle Speed & CO Level

Application	Idle RPM	CO%
Vanagon		
Federal		
Man. Trans.	800-950	0.5-1.5
Auto. Trans.	850-1000	0.5-1.5
Calif.	850-950	0.3-1.1
Rabbit (Carburetor)	①850-950	0.5-1.5
All Other Models		
Federal	850-1000	0.8-1.2
Calif.	880-1000	0.8-1.2

① — Idle speed when checking. Adjust to 600-750 when idle stabilizer is disconnected.

COLD (FAST) IDLE RPM

Rabbit (Carburetor) — With engine at normal operating temperature, timing set and idle speed set, place fast idle adjusting screw on 3rd step of choke lever. Open choke valve fully by hand and check idle speed. Adjust if necessary.

Fast Idle RPM

Application	RPM
Rabbit (Carburetor)	2350-2450

EMISSION CONTROL SYSTEMS

See *Mitchell Manuals'* Emission Control Manual.

GENERAL SERVICING

IGNITION

DISTRIBUTOR

All carbureted Rabbit models and all California vehicles have electronic ignition. Federal fuel injected models use a conventional breaker point ignition system.

Other Data & Specifications — *See Tune-Up and Bosch Ignition Systems or Distributors in ELECTRICAL Section.*

FUEL SYSTEMS

CARBURETOR

Rabbit — Carbureted models use a Solex 34 PICT-5 carburetor.

Other Data & Specifications — *See Tune-Up and Solex Carburetors in FUEL SYSTEMS Section.*

GENERAL SERVICING (Cont.)

FUEL INJECTION

Vanagon — All models use Bosch AFC Electronic Fuel Injection.

Dasher, Jetta, Rabbit, Rabbit Pickup & Scirocco — All models use Bosch Continuous Injection System (CIS).

Other Data & Specifications — *See Tune-Up and Bosch AFC or CIS Fuel Injection Article in FUEL SYSTEMS Section.*

ELECTRICAL

BATTERY

Application	Standard Amp. Hr.	Optional Amp. Hr.
Vanagon	54	
Rabbit (Carb.)	45	
Scirocco	65	
All Other Models	45	54

Battery Location — Battery is located under right front seat on Vanagon models, and in engine compartment on all other models.

BELT ADJUSTMENT

Application	① Deflections
All Models	.4-.6" (10-15 mm)

① — Deflection is with thumb pressure, about 16.5 lbs. (7.5 kg), applied midway on longest belt run.

FILTERS

Filter	Service Interval (Miles)
Oil Filter	Replace every 15,000
Air Filter	Replace every 30,000
Fuel Filter	Replace every 15,000

STARTER

All models are equipped with Bosch starters.

Other Data & Specifications — *See Bosch Starters in ELECTRICAL Section.*

ALTERNATOR

Application	Rated Amp. Output
Convertible, Scirocco, Vanagon	65
Dasher, Pickup, Rabbit (F.I.)	55, 65
Jetta	45, 65
Rabbit (Carburetor)	35

Other Data & Specifications — *See Bosch & Motorola Alternators & Regulators in ELECTRICAL Section.*

ALTERNATOR REGULATOR

Bosch & Motorola — Non-Adjustable; integral with alternator.

Other Data & Specifications — *See Bosch & Motorola Alternators & Regulators in ELECTRICAL Section.*

CAPACITIES

Application	Quantity
Crankcase (Including Filter)	
Dasher	3.2 qts.
All Other Models	3.7 qts.
Cooling System	
Dasher	6.3 qts.
All Other Models	4.9 qts.
Man. Transaxle (SAE 80W-90)	
Vanagon	3.7 qts.
All Other Models	
4 Speed	1.6 qts.
5 Speed	2.1 qts.
Auto. Transmission (Dexron)	
All Models	3.2 qts.
Auto. Trans. Differential (SAE 90)	
Vanagon	3.0 pts.
All Other Models	1.6 pts.
Fuel Tank	
Dasher	11.9 gals.
Rabbit Pickup	15.0 gals.
Vanagon	16.0 gals.
All Others Models	10.5 gals.

TUNE-UP

Dasher
Rabbit
Rabbit Pickup

ENGINE IDENTIFICATION

First 2 letters of engine identification code are used to identify engine models. Code is stamped on cylinder block below No. 3 glow plug and is as follows:

Application	Code
All Models	CK

COMPRESSION PRESSURE

Remove electrical wire from fuel shut-off solenoid on injection pump. Insulate wire end and remove injection pipes. Disconnect fuel return hoses. Remove injectors with tool US 2775 (or equivalent). Remove heat shields from injectors and place in cylinder as it is being tested. Install test gauge adapter (VW 1323/2) and test gauge (VW 1323) to glow plug hole, operate starter and read compression. Install new injector heat shields when reinstalling injectors.

Application	Pressure
New	483 psi (34 kg/cm²)
Wear Limit	398 psi (28 kg/cm²)
Maximum Variation	71 psi (5 kg/cm²)

VALVE CLEARANCE

CAUTION — *When adjusting valves, pistons MUST NOT be at TDC. Turn crankshaft ¼ turn past TDC so valves do not hit pistons when tappets are depressed.*

CAUTION — *When adjusting valves, do not rotate crankshaft by turning camshaft pulley. This will stretch the drive belt. Place vehicle in 4th gear and push to turn crankshaft.*

1) Valves must be checked with engine warm, coolant above 95° F (35° C). Check valve clearance in firing order, 1-3-4-2.

2) Measure between cam lobes and adjusting disc, when both lobes to be checked point upward. Adjust clearance to specifications by changing disc thickness. Twenty six discs are available in thicknesses from .118-.167" (3.00-4.25 mm).

3) To remove adjusting discs, use a 10-208 removal tool, while holding cam follower down with special tool VW 546 (10-209).

Valve Clearance Specifications

Application	Clearance
Engine Warm	
Intake	.008-.012" (.20-.30)
Exhaust	.016-.020" (.40-.50)

VALVE ARRANGEMENT

All Models — E-I-E-I-I-E-I-E

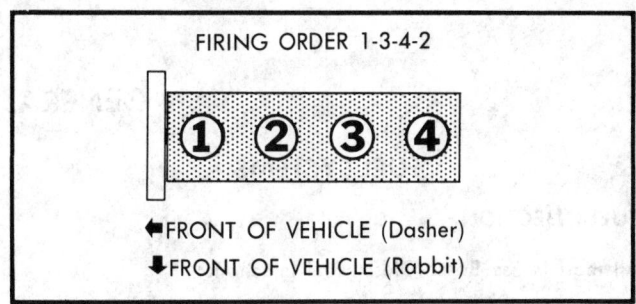

FIRING ORDER 1-3-4-2

① ② ③ ④

← FRONT OF VEHICLE (Dasher)
↓ FRONT OF VEHICLE (Rabbit)

Fig. 1   Diesel Firing Order Illustration

IDLE SPEED ADJUSTMENT

Run engine until warm. Mount tachometer sensor (US 1324) on valve cover and connect to battery. Attach tachometer to sensor and check idle speed. If adjustment is needed, loosen locknut on idle screw. Turn in to increase idle, out to decrease. Apply thread sealer and tighten locknut.

Idle Speed Specifications

Application	Idle RPM
All Models	800-850

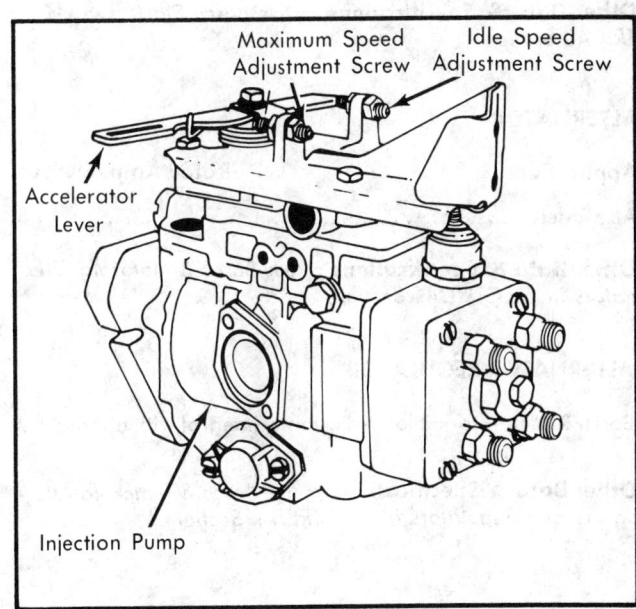

Maximum Speed Adjustment Screw

Idle Speed Adjustment Screw

Accelerator Lever

Injection Pump

Fig. 2   Idle and Maximum Speed Adjustment

MAXIMUM SPEED ADJUSTMENT

Run engine until warm and install tachometer sensor (US 1324). Connect tachometer and set idle speed. Accelerate

TUNE-UP (Cont.)

engine briefly to full throttle. If maximum speed does not match specifications, loosen speed locknut and adjust. Turning screw out raises speed, turning screw in lowers speed. Apply thread sealer and tighten locknut.

Maximum Speed Specifications

Application	Maximum RPM
All Models	5500-5600

GENERAL SERVICING

FUEL SYSTEMS

FUEL INJECTION

All models use Bosch Diesel Fuel Injection.

Other Data & Specifications — *See Tune-Up and Bosch Diesel Fuel Injection in FUEL SYSTEMS Section.*

ELECTRICAL

BATTERY

Battery Location — Battery is located in engine compartment.

Application	Amp. Hr. Rating
All Models	63

STARTER

All models are equipped with Bosch Starters.

Other Data & Specifications — *See Bosch Starters in ELECTRICAL Section.*

ALTERNATOR

Application	Rated Amp. Output
All Models	55

Other Data & Specifications — *See Bosch & Motorola Alternators in ELECTRICAL Section.*

ALTERNATOR REGULATOR

Bosch & Motorola — Non-Adjustable; integral with alternator.

Other Data & Specifications — *See Bosch & Motorola Alternators and Regulators in ELECTRICAL Section.*

FILTERS

Filter	Service Interval (Miles)
Oil Filter	Replace every 7500
Air Filter	Replace every 15,000
Fuel Filter	Replace every 15,000

CAPACITIES

Application	Quantity
Crankcase (Includes Filter)	①3.7 qts.
Cooling System	
Dasher	6.3 qts.
Rabbit	7.3 qts.
Manual Transaxle (SAE 80W-90)	
4-Speed	1.6 qts.
5-Speed	2.1 qts.
Fuel Tank	
Dasher	11.9 gals.
Rabbit	10.5 gals.

① — 3.2 quarts without filter.

BELT ADJUSTMENT

Application	①Deflection
All Belts	3/8 - 5/8" (10-15 mm)

① — Measured between longest span and depressed with firm thumb pressure.

1980 Volvo 4 Tune-Up

TUNE-UP

DL
GL
GT

ENGINE IDENTIFICATION

B21F engine identification number is stamped on left side of engine block.

Application	Code
Man. Trans.	498-848
Auto. Trans.	498-849

COMPRESSION PRESSURE

With engine at normal operating temperature, spark plugs removed, throttle valve wide open and cranking speed at 250-300 RPM, compression should be as follows:

Application	Pressure psi (kg/cm²)
All Models	128-156 (9-11)

VALVE CLEARANCE

1) Valve clearance is adjusted with engine shut off and either warm or cold. Remove valve cover. Turn crankshaft center bolt until camshaft is in position for firing No. 1 cylinder. Both cam lobes should point up at equally large angles. Pulley timing mark should be at 0°.

2) Check valve clearance of No. 1 cylinder, using a feeler gauge between camshaft lobe and adjusting discs. Intake and exhaust valves have same clearances.

3) If clearances are incorrect adjust by changing thickness of discs, which are available in .05 mm increments from 3.30 to 4.50 mm. Use tools 5022 and 5026 to depress and remove discs.

4) After valves for No. 1 cylinder are properly adjusted, rotate crankshaft to firing position for No. 3, No. 4, and No. 2 cylinders in sequence and complete adjustment.

Valve Clearance Specifications

Application	Cold In. (mm)	Hot In. (mm)
Intake and Exhaust		
Checking	.010-.018 (.25-.45)	.012-.020 (.30-.50)
Setting	.014-.016 (.35-.40)	.016-.018 (.40-.45)

VALVE ARRANGEMENT

E-I-E-I-E-I-E-I (front to rear).

SPARK PLUGS

Application	Gap In. (mm)	Torque Ft. Lbs. (mkg)
All Models	.028 (.7)	15 (2.0)

Spark Plug Type

Application	Bosch No.
All Models	WR7DS

DISTRIBUTOR

All models are equipped with Breakerless Electronic Ignition System and no adjustments are required.

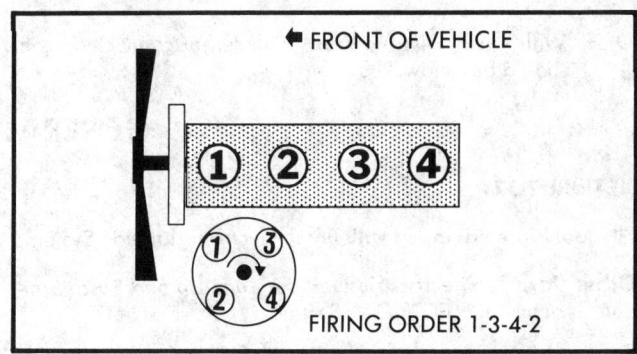

Fig. 1   Firing Order and Distributor Rotation

IGNITION TIMING

Connect timing light and tachometer. Disconnect and plug vacuum hose at distributor. Use idle air adjusting screw to set idle speed to specified timing RPM. Rotate distributor to set timing, then reconnect vacuum hose and reset idle.

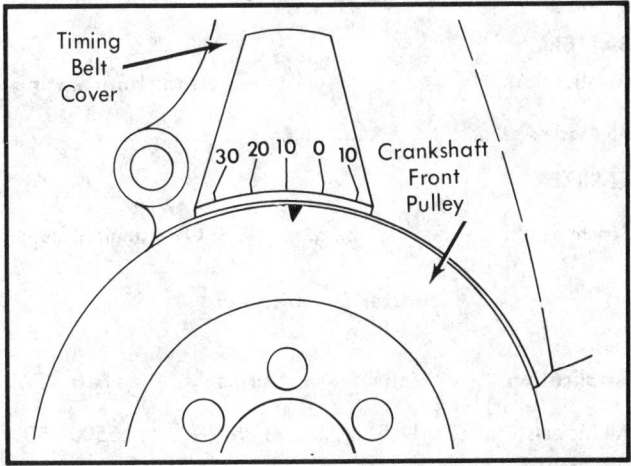

Fig. 2   Timing Mark Location

Ignition Timing Specifications

Application	RPM	Timing
All	700-800	①8°BTDC

① — With distributor vacuum hose disconnected and plugged.

IDLE SPEED & MIXTURE

1) Disconnect oxygen sensor wire at connector. Attach CO meter at fitting on exhaust pipe before catalytic converter. Adjust idle with knob on throttle body.

1980 Volvo 4 Tune-Up

TUNE-UP (Cont.)

2) Check CO level. If necessary, adjust with Allen wrench through hole in fuel distributor. Reconnect oxygen sensor wire and check that CO level drops below 1%. Readjust idle speed if necessary, then remove test equipment.

Idle Speed & CO Level

Application	RPM	CO%
All Models	900-1000	①1.5-3.0

① — With sensor disconnected. With sensor connected, level should be below 1%.

GENERAL SERVICING

DISTRIBUTOR

All models are equipped with Bosch Electronic Ignition System.

Other Data & Specifications — See *Tune-Up and Bosch Ignition Systems in ELECTRICAL Section.*

FUEL SYSTEM

FUEL INJECTION

All models are equipped with Bosch Lambda CIS fuel injection with oxygen sensor.

Other Data & Specifications — See *Tune-Up and Bosch Lambda CIS Fuel Injection in FUEL SYSTEMS Section.*

ELECTRICAL

BATTERY

Application	Amp. Hour Rating
All Models	70

STARTER

Bosch	Overrunning Clutch

Starter Specifications

Application	Volts	Amps	Test RPM
All Models	11.5	30-50	5500-7500

Other Data & Specifications — See *Bosch Starters in ELECTRICAL Section.*

ALTERNATOR

All models are equipped with Bosch alternators.

Application	Rated Amp. Output
All Models	55

Other Data & Specifications — See *Bosch Alternators and Regulators in ELECTRICAL Section.*

ALTERNATOR REGULATOR

All models are equipped with Bosch alternator regulators with an operating voltage of 13.0-15.0 volts.

FUEL PUMP PRESSURE

Pressure .... 64-74 psi (4.5-5.2 kg/cm²)

EMISSION CONTROL SYSTEMS

See *Mitchell Manuals' Emission Control Manual.*

Other Data & Specifications — See *Bosch Alternators and Regulators in ELECTRICAL Section.*

BELT ADJUSTMENT

Application	①Deflection
All Belts	.2-.4" (5-10 mm)

① — Deflection is with thumb pressure applied midway on longest belt run.

FILTERS

Filter	Service Interval (Miles)
Oil Filter	Replace every 7500
Air Filter	Replace every 30,000
Fuel Filter	Replace every 15,000
Fuel Tank Filter	Replace every 30,000

CAPACITIES

Application	Quantity
Crankcase	4.0 qts.
Cooling System (Includes Heater)	10.0 qts.
Man. Trans. (ATF Type F)	
With Overdrive	2.4 qts.
Without Overdrive	1.6 pts.
Auto. Trans. (ATF Type F)	7.3 qts.
Rear Axle (SAE 90)	3.4 pts.
Fuel Tank	15.8 gals.

TUNE-UP

GLE
Coupe

ENGINE IDENTIFICATION

B28F engine identification number is stamped in lower left front corner of block above oil pan.

Engine Identification

Application	Code
Federal	
Man. Trans.	498-628
Auto. Trans.	498-629
Calif.	
Man. Trans.	498-630
Auto Trans	498-631

COMPRESSION PRESSURE

With engine at normal operating temperature, spark plugs removed, throttle valve wide open and cranking speed at 250-300 RPM, compression should be as follows:

Compression Pressure

Application	Pressure psi (kg/cm²)
All Models	114-156 (8-11)

VALVE CLEARANCE

1) Adjust valves with engine cold. Rotate crankshaft so No. 1 cylinder is at TDC of ignition stroke (both rocker arms for No. 1 cylinder have clearance).

NOTE — *Crank pulley has 2 notches. When No. 1 cylinder is at TDC, upper notch will align with "0" notch on timing marker and lower crank pulley notch will be 150° counterclockwise from upper notch. (Second notch is TDC for No. 6 cylinder when aligned with "0" on timing marker).*

2) Adjust valves in sequence as follows:

Intake	Exhaust
Cyl. 1	Cyl. 1
Cyl. 2	Cyl. 3
Cyl. 4	Cyl. 6

3) Rotate crankshaft 360°. This will set No. 1 cylinder at TDC of exhaust stroke (rocker arms for No. 1 cylinder indicating no clearance). Adjust valves in following sequence:

Intake	Exhaust
Cyl. 3	Cyl. 2
Cyl. 5	Cyl. 4
Cyl. 6	Cyl. 5

Valve Clearance Specifications

Application	Clearance
Intake	.004-.006" (.10-.15 mm)
Exhaust	.010-.012" (.25-.30 mm)

VALVE ARRANGEMENT①

Right Bank: E-I-E-I-E-I (front to rear).
Left Bank: I-E-I-E-I-E (front to rear).

① — Intake valves are inside the engine's "V"; exhaust valves are on outer sides of heads.

SPARK PLUGS

Application	Gap In. (mm)	Torque Ft. Lbs. (mkg)
All Models	.028 (.7)	7 (1.0)

Spark Plug Type

Application	Bosch No.
All Models	HR6DS

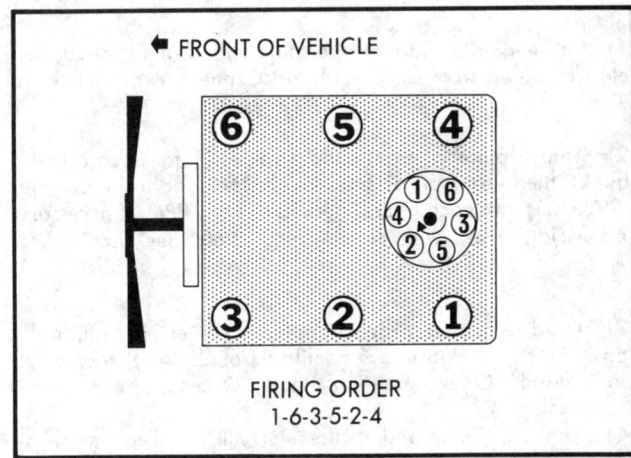

Fig. 1 Firing Order and Distributor Rotation

DISTRIBUTOR

All models are equipped with Breakerless Solid State Ignition System and no adjustments are required.

IGNITION TIMING

Connect a timing light and tachometer. Disconnect and plug distributor vacuum hose. Use idle air adjusting screw to set idle speed to specified timing RPM. Rotate distributor to set timing to specifications. Reconnect distributor vacuum hose.

1980 Volvo V6 Tune-Up

TUNE-UP (Cont.)

Ignition Timing Specifications

Application	RPM	Timing
All Models	700-800	①10°BTDC

① — With distributor vacuum hose disconnected and plugged.

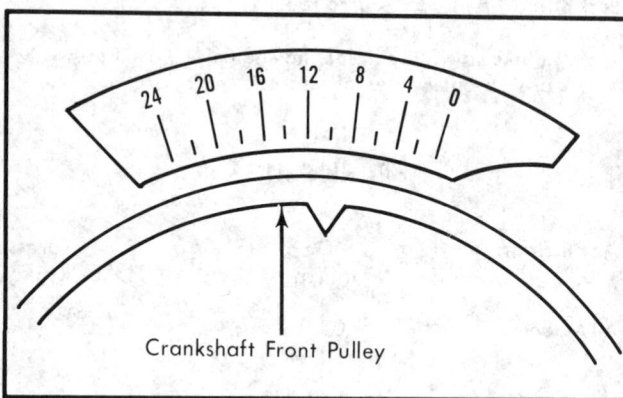

Fig. 2   Ignition Timing Mark Location

IDLE SPEED & MIXTURE

1) With engine at normal operating temperature, disconnect electrical lead from oxygen sensor. Connect a tachometer to engine.

2) Remove plugs at front exhaust pipes (1 for each cylinder bank), then insert probe from CO meter dual probe adapter (9995151) into each pipe. Check idle speed RPM. If necessary, adjust idle speed with air adjusting screw. See *Fig. 3.*

3) Set valve of dual probe adapter to center position. In this position, exhaust gases are admitted from both cylinder banks for a total CO level reading. Read CO level.

4) With CO meter and tachometer still installed, install air cleaner and connect all hoses. To adjust CO level, remove plug and copper washer from CO adjustment hole on top of mixture control unit.

5) Insert special adjusting wrench (5102) and adjust CO level to specifications. Turn tool counterclockwise to decrease CO level or clockwise to increase CO level.

NOTE — *After each adjustment, the adjusting wrench must be removed and the hole covered to prevent a lean mixture while taking CO reading.*

6) Mixture must be adjusted for strength and balance between both banks. After adjusting mixture strength, check balance.

7) Turn dual probe adapter valve toward left cylinder bank and check CO level. If left bank CO level is not within specifications, correct by adjusting balance screw "2". See *Fig. 3.*

8) Next, turn valve towards right bank and check CO level. If right bank CO level is not within specifications, correct by adjusting balance screw "1". See *Fig. 3.*

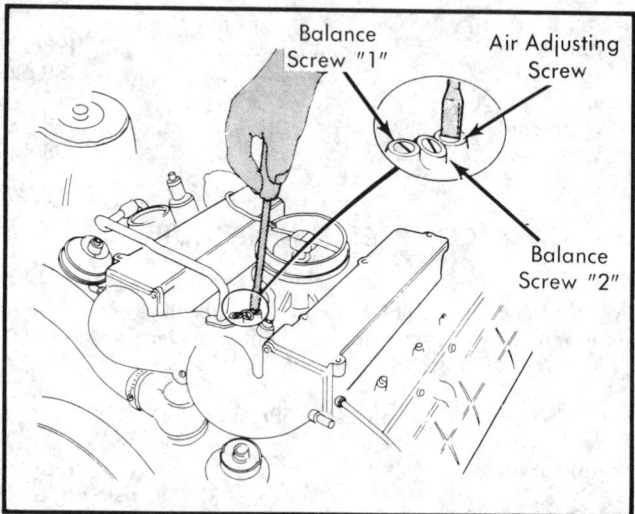

Fig. 3   Idle and Mixture Adjusting Screws

NOTE — *CO reading should be equal for both banks and correct for the total system. Also, left side intake manifold goes to right bank and right side manifold to left bank.*

9) Recheck CO level with dual probe adapter valve in center position. If necessary, repeat adjustment procedure. Reconnect electrical lead to oxygen sensor.

10) Finally, recheck idle speed RPM and correct as necessary. Remove tachometer and CO meter. Reinstall exhaust pipe plugs.

Idle Speed & CO Level

Application	RPM	CO%
All Models	900-1000	①0.7-1.3

① — With oxygen sensor connected, CO level should drop below 1.0%.

FUEL PUMP PRESSURE

Pressure .... 64-74 psi (4.5-5.2 kg/cm²)

EMISSION CONTROL SYSTEMS

See Mitchell Manuals' Emission Control Manual.

GENERAL SERVICING

IGNITION

DISTRIBUTOR

All models are equipped with Bosch Breakerless Solid State Ignition System.

Other Data & Specifications — *See Tune-Up and Bosch Ignition Systems in ELECTRICAL Section.*

FUEL SYSTEM

FUEL INJECTION

All models are equipped with Bosch Lambda/CIS fuel injection systems.

Other Data & Specifications — *See Tune-Up and Bosch Lambda/CIS Fuel Injection System in FUEL SYSTEMS Section.*

ELECTRICAL

BATTERY

12 Volt — Negative Ground.

Application	Amp. Hr. Rating
All Models	70

Battery Location — In engine compartment on right side.

STARTER

Bosch .... Overrunning Clutch

Starter Specifications

Application	Volts	Amps	Test RPM
All Models	11.5	30-50	5500-7500

Other Data & Specifications — *See Bosch Starters in ELECTRICAL Section.*

ALTERNATOR

All models are equipped with SEV Marchal alternators.

Application	Rated Amp. Output
All Models	70

Other Data & Specifications — *See SEV Marchal Alternators in ELECTRICAL Section.*

ALTERNATOR REGULATOR

All models are equipped with Bosch regulators with an operating voltage of 13.0-15.0 volts at 4000 RPM.

Other Data & Specifications — *See Bosch Regulators in ELECTRICAL Section.*

FILTERS

Filter	Service Interval (Miles)
Oil Filter	Replace every 7500
Air Filter	Replace every 30,000
Fuel Filter	Replace ever 15,000
Fuel Tank Filter	Replace every 60,000

BELT ADJUSTMENT

Application	①Deflection
All Belts	.2-.4" (5-10 mm)

① — Deflection is measured with thumb pressure applied at midpoint of longest belt run.

CAPACITIES

Application	Quantity
Crankcase (Includes Filter)	6.9 qts.
Cooling System (Includes Heater)	11.5 qts.
Man. Trans. with Overdrive (ATF Type F)	2.4 qts.
Auto. Trans. (ATF Type F)	7.3 qts.
Rear Axle (SAE 90)	1.7 qts.
Fuel Tank	15.8 gals.

TUNE-UP

Diesel

ENGINE IDENTIFICATION

D24 diesel engine identification numbers are stamped on left side of block under vacuum pump. Engines are identified by the following codes:

Model	Code
Man. Trans.	498704
Auto. Trans.	498705

COMPRESSION PRESSURE

Disconnect wire at stop valve on injection pump. Remove vacuum pump and pump plunger. Clean fuel delivery pipes, remove pipes, and plug all openings. Remove injectors and heat shields. Place heat shield back in injector opening, followed by adapter 5191. Connect compression gauge and test compression.

Compression Pressure

Application	Pressure psi (kg/cm^2)
Normal (New Engine)	485 (34.0)
Minimum	400 (28.0)
Maximum Variation	70 (5.0)

VALVE CLEARANCE

1) Turn engine using wrench on crankshaft pulley until No. 1 cylinder is at TDC on compression stroke. Remove valve cover. Both cam lobes should point upwards at equal angles.

2) Check valve clearance for No. 1 cylinder. If not correct, turn crankshaft ¼ turn ATDC (so valves will not hit piston top). Depress cam followers with tool 5196. Using pliers (tool 5195), remove disc. Calculate thickness of disc needed, coat with oil, and install.

NOTE — *New discs are available in thicknesses from .130" (3.30 mm) to .167" (4.25 mm) in increments of .002" (.05 mm). New discs should be positioned with marks down.*

3) Check valve clearance on remaining cylinders, proceeding in firing order. Be sure to check valve clearance at TDC and turn ¼ turn after TDC before depressing valves.

Valve Clearance Specifications

Application	Clearance In. (mm)
Checking	
Cold	
Intake	.006-.010 (.15-.25)
Exhaust	.014-.018 (.35-.45)
Warm	
Intake	.008-.012 (.20-.30)
Exhaust	.016-.020 (.40-.50)
Adjustment	
Cold	
Intake	.008 (.20)
Exhaust	.016 (.40)
Warm	
Intake	.010 (.25)
Exhaust	.018 (.45)

VALVE ARRANGEMENT

E-I-E-I-E-I-I-E-I-E-I-E

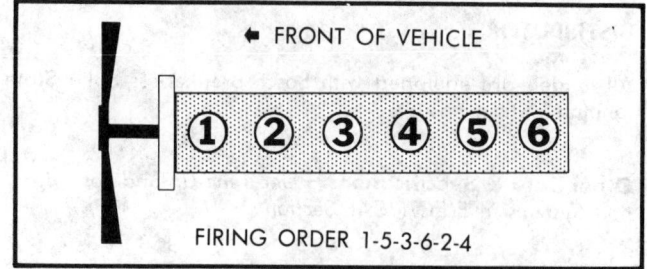

Fig. 1 Firing Order Illustration

GLOW PLUGS

Glow Plug Type

Application	Volvo Part No.
All Models	1257141-0

IDLE SPEED ADJUSTMENT

1) Connect photo-electric tachometer. Warm engine to normal operating temperature. Adjust low idle speed to 750-850 RPM. Check maximum engine speed and adjust if necessary to 5100-5300 RPM. *See Fig. 2.*

2) Stop engine and disconnect link rod at lever on injection pump. Adjust throttle cable by turning cable sheath nut. Cable should be tight but not move pulley. Depress accelerator pedal and ensure that pulley touches full speed stop.

3) On automatic transmission models, depress accelerator to floor. Kickdown cable should move 2.05" (52 mm) between end positions. In idle position, cable should be stretched and clearance between clip and cable sheath should be .01-.04" (.25-1.0 mm)

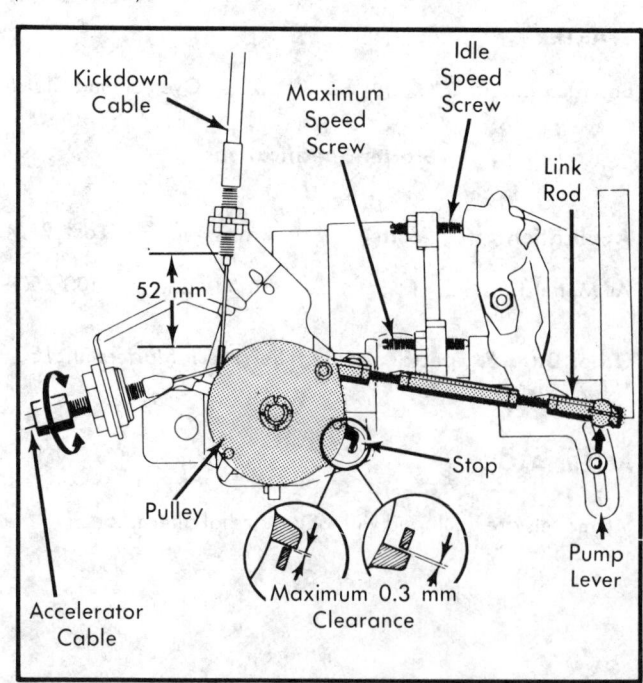

Fig. 2 Adjusting Idle Speed and Throttle Linkage

TUNE-UP (Cont.)

4) Connect link rod to injection pump lever. Turn pulley to maximum throttle position and adjust length of link (by rotating) until lever touches maximum speed screw.

5) Return pulley to idle position and move link rod ball joint in lever slot until lever touches idle adjusting screw. Recheck adjustments and repeat if necessary until idle speed and throttle positions are correct.

NOTE — *A clearance of .012" (.3 mm) is permissible between pulley and stop.*

Idle Speed Specification

Application	Idle RPM	Maximum RPM
All Models	750-850	5100-5300

GENERAL SERVICING

FUEL INJECTION

All models use Bosch diesel fuel injection.

Other Data & Specifications — *See Tune-Up and Bosch Diesel Fuel Injection in FUEL SYSTEMS Section.*

ELECTRICAL

BATTERY

Application	Amp. Hr. Rating
All Models	88

STARTER

All models are equipped with Bosch starters.

Other Data & Specifications — *See Bosch Starters in ELECTRICAL Section.*

ALTERNATOR

All models are equipped with Bosch alternators.

Application	Rated Amp. Output
All Models	55

Other Data & Specifications — *See Bosch Alternators & Regulators in ELECTRICAL Section.*

ALTERNATOR REGULATOR

All models are equipped with Bosch non-adjustable voltage regulators with operating voltage of 13.9-14.8 volts.

Other Data & Specifications — *See Bosch Alternators & Regulators in ELECTRICAL Section.*

FILTERS

Filter	Service Interval (Miles)
Oil Filter	①Replace every 15,000
Fuel Filter	Drain every 7500
	Replace every 15,000
Air Filter	Replace every 30,000

① — First change at 7500 miles.

BELT ADJUSTMENT

Adjust belts for deflection of $\frac{3}{16}$-$\frac{3}{8}$" (5-10 mm) when depressed firmly halfway between pulleys.

CAPACITIES

Application	Quantity
Crankcase (Includes Filter)	7.4 qts.
Cooling System (Includes Heater)	10.0 qts.
Man. Trans. (ATF Type F)	2.4 qts.
Auto. Trans. (ATF Type F)	7.3 qts.
Rear Axle (SAE 90)	1.7 qts.
Fuel Tank	15.8 gals.

Section 2
FUEL

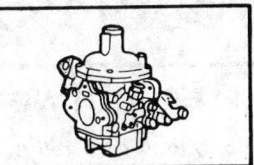

Contents

NOTE — ALSO SEE GENERAL INDEX.

CARBURETION TROUBLE SHOOTING

NOTE — *This is a general troubleshooting guide. Not all steps will apply to all carburetors. When using this guide, locate the symptom in column one that corresponds to your problem and determine the possible causes in column two. Match the number of the possible cause with the same number in column three, and you will have the correction required.*

CONDITION	POSSIBLE CAUSE	CORRECTION
COLD STARTING SYMPTOM		
▶ Engine cranks but will not start	1) Choke not closing (frozen)	1) Inspect choke plate and coil; free up and adjust
	2) Choke cable or linkage binding or out of adjustment	2) Free up and adjust
	3) Faulty cold start or thermo-start valve	3) Test, replace if needed
	4) No fuel to carburetor	4) Add fuel if needed, check for pinched or blocked fuel line or filter
	5) Faulty fuel pump	5) Test and/or replace
▶ Flooding	1) Faulty fuel inlet needle and/or seat	1) Replace
	2) Dirt holding needle off seat	2) Clean and reinstall
	3) Excessive fuel pump pressure	3) Test, replace if needed
	4) Improper fuel/float level (too high)	4) Adjust float level and drop
	5) Restricted (dirty) air cleaner	5) Clean and/or replace
	6) Ruptured, split internal carburetor seals or gaskets	6) Replace as needed
	7) Choke plate setting (vacuum kick) too narrow	7) Adjust, check linkage
	8) Wrong fast idle cam index	8) Check linkage, adjust fast idle cam setting
	9) Fast idle RPM too low	9) Adjust RPM
▶ Engine stalls after starting	1) Choke plate setting (vacuum kick) too wide	1) Adjust, check linkage
	2) Fast idle RPM too low	2) Adjust RPM
	3) Wrong fast idle cam index	3) Check choke control lever; set cam index correctly
	4) Vacuum leak	4) Locate and repair
	5) Low fuel pump output	5) Test and/or replace
	6) Fuel/float level too low	6) Adjust float level and float drop
	7) Faulty intake manifold gasket	7) Replace gasket
	8) Incorrect fuel/air mixture setting	8) Adjust fuel/air mixture
	9) Faulty idle fuel shut off valve	9) Replace shut off valve
	10) Idler jet blocked	10) Clean
	11) Damaged idle adjust screw	11) Replace screw
▶ Engine starts; idles rough and erratic	1) Flooding in carburetor	1) *See Flooding in this table*
	2) Vacuum leak	2) Locate and correct
	3) Incorrect idle RPM	3) Adjust fast idle RPM
	4) Damaged idle adjust screw	4) Replace screw
	5) Clogged slow jet	5) Clean
	6) Incorrect fast idle cam index setting	6) Adjust fast idle cam setting
	7) Carburetor seals leaking	7) Locate and replace
	8) Carburetors not synchronized; dual carburetor models only	8) Synchronize carburetors
	9) Incorrect fuel/float level	9) Adjust float drop and float setting
	10) Idling air and/or bypass holes blocked	10) Clean
	11) Faulty anti-dieseling solenoid valve	11) Replace solenoid
	12) Worn throttle shafts	12) Replace
	13) Stuck anti-stall dashpot	13) Replace dashpot

CARBURETION TROUBLE SHOOTING (Cont.)

CONDITION	POSSIBLE CAUSE	CORRECTION
HOT STARTING SYMPTOM		
▶ Engine cranks but will not start	1) Engine flooded, fuel level too high	1) Adjust float drop and setting; inspect needle and seat for proper seating; check for dirt
	2) Fuel vapors in carburetor bowl	2) Inspect bowl vent operation and correct
	3) Fuel line hot, touching engine block or exhaust	3) Inspect and reroute fuel line
COLD ENGINE DRIVEABILITY SYMPTOM		
▶ Engine stalls when put in gear	1) Incorrect choke vacuum kick setting	1) Inspect and correct
	2) Fast idle RPM too low	2) Adjust fast idle RPM
	3) Incorrect fast idle cam setting	3) Correct cam positioning
	4) Improper choke adjustment	4) Adjust choke
▶ Hesitation, stalling during acceleration

Backfire

Stumble | 1) Defective choke control switch | 1) Test, replace if needed |
	2) Incorrect choke vacuum kick setting	2) Adjust vacuum kick
	3) Low fuel/float level	3) Adjust float drop and setting; check fuel level
	4) Faulty accelerator pump or blocked pump discharge	4) Inspect, adjust pump stroke, plunger; test fuel discharge quantity; check pump spray direction
	5) Secondary throttle not closed, wrong lockout adjustment	5) Adjust secondary throttles
	6) Bypass holes and ducts blocked	6) Clean preheater assembly
	7) Incorrect intake air preheater setting	7) Set to proper season
	8) Incorrect carburetor synchronization; on dual carburetor models	8) Synchronize carburetors
	9) Main and/or air corrector jets blocked	9) Inspect and clean
	10) Faulty power valve	10) Replace
	11) Plugged heat crossover system	11) Clean and test heat crossover valve; clean passages
WARM ENGINE DRIVEABILITY SYMPTOM		
▶ Low power, Surging high speed operation	1) Main jets clogged	1) Clean
	2) Fuel filter dirty (restricted)	2) Replace filter
	3) Pinched, blocked fuel line	3) Inspect and repair
	4) Air cleaner dirty (restricted)	4) Replace air cleaner
	5) Faulty power valve	5) Adjust or replace
	6) Throttle linkage out of adjustment; not opening fully	6) Inspect and adjust linkage
	7) Low fuel pump output	7) Replace after testing
	8) Improper fuel level	8) Adjust float/fuel level
	9) Carburetor seals leaking	9) Replace seals, gaskets
▶ Carburetors cannot be synchronized

(Dual Carburetor models) | 1) Weak return springs | 1) Replace springs |
	2) Linkage binding, needs adjusting	2) Inspect, clean and adjust
	3) Blocked idler jets	3) Clean jets
	4) Faulty mixture control screw(s)	4) Replace screw(s)
	5) Faulty carburetor seals	5) Replace seals as needed
	6) Vacuum leak(s); Check for leak at brake unit	6) Locate and correct leak
	7) Carburetors not tightened to intake manifold properly	7) Evenly tighten carburetor screws; check torque

CARBURETION TROUBLE SHOOTING (Cont.)

CONDITION	POSSIBLE CAUSE	CORRECTION
► High fuel consumption	1) Fuel system leak 2) Wrong size jets 3) Faulty fuel inlet needle and/or seat 4) Fuel mixture setting incorrect 5) Dirty air cleaner 6) Excessive accelerator pump discharge 7) Intake air preheater not ON or OFF according to season 8) Enrichment system does not switch off 9) Choke valve not opening all the way 10) Secondary throttle opens too early	1) Locate and repair leak 2) Install correct jets 3) Replace needle and seat 4) Adjust idle RPM and mixture 5) Clean or replace 6) Test and adjust fuel discharge quantity 7) Temperature above 50°F (10°C), preheater should be OFF 8) Free up vacuum plunger 9) Adjust choke valve 10) Inspect secondary throttle linkage, adjust or repair as needed

GASOLINE FUEL INJECTION TROUBLE SHOOTING

CONDITION	POSSIBLE CAUSE	CORRECTION
COLD START SYMPTOM ► Engine cranks, will not start	1) Fuel pump not working 2) "Cold" control pressure incorrect (CIS) 3) Auxiliary air valve does not open 4) Cold start valve does not operate 5) Cold start valve leaking 6) Sensor plate stop set incorrectly (CIS) 7) Sensor plate and/or plunger sticking 8) Vacuum leak 9) Fuel system leak 10) Faulty Thermo Time switch 11) Distributor triggering contacts (AFC 12) Temperature sensors 1 & 2 (AFC	1) Check fuel pump and double fuse relay, replace as necessary 2) Replace warm-up regulator if pressure not to specification 3) Replace valve 4) Check electrical power to valve, replace valve if necessary 5) Replace valve 6) Adjust to specifications 7) Free up or replace as needed 8) Repair vacuum leaks 9) Repair fuel leaks 10) Replace switch 11) Repair or replace as needed 12) Replace as necessary
► Engine hard starting	1) "Cold" control pressure incorrect (CIS) 2) Auxiliary air valve does not open 3) Cold start valve does not open 4) Cold start valve leaking 5) Sensor plate stop set incorrectly (CIS) 6) Sensor plate and/or plunger stuck (CIS) 7) Vacuum leak(s) 8) Fuel leak(s) 9) Thermo Time switch does not close	1) Replace warm-up regulator 2) Replace valve 3) Check for electrical power to valve, replace valve if necessary 4) Replace cold start valve 5) Adjust sensor plate stop to specifications 6) Free up or replace as necessary 7) Repair vacuum leak(s) 8) Repair fuel leak(s) 9) Replace Thermo Time switch

GASOLINE FUEL INJECTION TROUBLE SHOOTING (Cont.)

CONDITION	POSSIBLE CAUSE	CORRECTION
HOT STARTING SYMPTOM ▶ Engine cranks, will not start	1) Electric fuel pump not operating 2) "Warm" control pressure incorrect (CIS) 3) Sensor plate stop adjustment incorrect (CIS) 4) Sensor plate and/or plunger stuck (CIS) 5) Vacuum leak(s) 6) Fuel system leak(s) 7) Injectors leaking 8) Idle mixture out of adjustment	1) Check fuel pump and relay fuse, replace as needed 2) Replace warm-up regulator 3) Adjust sensor plate stop 4) Free up or replace 5) Repair vacuum leak(s) 6) Repair fuel leak(s) 7) Clean or replace as necessary 8) Adjust mixture to specifications
▶ Engine Hard Starting (Long Cranking Time)	1) "Warm" control pressure incorrect (CIS) 2) Auxiliary air valve does not close 3) Sensor plate stop adjustment incorrect (CIS) 4) Sensor plate and/or plunger stuck (CIS) 5) Vacuum leak(s) 6) Fuel system leaks 7) Injectors leaking 8) Idle mixture out of adjustment	1) Replace warm-up regulator 2) Replace valve 3) Adjust to specification 4) Free up or replace as necessary 5) Repair vacuum leak(s) 6) Repair fuel leak(s) 7) Clean or replace as necessary 8) Adjust mixture to specifications
SYMPTOM ▶ Rough Idle During Warm-Up	1) "Cold" control pressure incorrect (CIS) 2) Auxiliary air valve does not close 3) Auxiliary air valve does not open 4) Cold start valve leaking 5) Vacuum leak 6) Fuel system leak(s) 7) Injectors leaking	1) Replace warm-up regulator 2) Replace valve 3) Replace valve 4) Clean or replace valve 5) Repair vacuum leaks 6) Repair fuel leaks 7) Clean or replace as necessary

GASOLINE FUEL INJECTION TROUBLE SHOOTING (Cont.)

CONDITION	POSSIBLE CAUSE	CORRECTION
HOT ENGINE DRIVEABILITY SYMPTOM		
▶ Rough idle with warm engine	1) "Warm" control pressure incorrect (CIS) 2) Auxiliary air valve does not close 3) Faulty cold start valve 4) Sensor plate and/or plunger stuck (CIS) 5) Vacuum leak(s) 6) Fuel system leak(s) 7) Injectors leaking 8) Idle mixture out of adjustment	1) Replace warm-up regulator 2) Replace air valve 3) Clean or replace as necessary 4) Free up or replace as necessary 5) Repair vacuum leak(s) 6) Repair fuel leak(s) 7) Clean or replace injectors 8) Adjust mixture to specifications
▶ CO level too high at idle	1) "Warm" control pressure incorrect (CIS) 2) Cold start valve leaking 3) Sensor plate and/or plunger stuck (CIS) 4) Fuel system leaking 5) Idle mixture out of adjustment	1) Replace warm-up regulator 2) Replace valve 3) Free up or replace as necessary 4) Repair fuel leak(s) 5) Adjust mixture to specifications
▶ CO level too low at idle	1) "Warm" control pressure incorrect (CIS) 2) Vacuum leak 3) Idle mixture out of adjustment	1) Replace warm-up regulator 2) Repair vacuum leak(s) 3) Adjust mixture to specifications
▶ Poor engine performance	1) "Warm" control pressure incorrect (CIS) 2) Cold start valve leaking 3) Sensor plate and/or plunger stuck (CIS) 4) Idle mixture out of adjustment 5) Throttle valve does not open completely	1) Replace warm-up regulator 2) Clean or replace valve 3) Free up or replace as necessary 4) Adjust mixture to specifications 5) Check and adjust as necessary
▶ Excessive fuel consumption	1) "Warm" control pressure incorrect (CIS) 2) Cold start valve leaks 3) Fuel system leaking 4) Idle mixture out of adjustment	1) Replace warm-up regulator 2) Clean or replace as necessary 3) Repair fuel leak(s) 4) Adjust mixture to specifications
▶ Engine misfire at high speed	1) Loose electrical contact at fuel pump 2) Primary pressure too low or too high 3) Fuel system leaking	1) Check and repair as necessary 2) Check pressure and adjust if not within specifications 3) Repair fuel leak(s)
▶ Engine "Diesels"	1) Sensor plate and/or plunger stuck (CIS) 2) Injectors leaking 3) Faulty cold start valve	1) Free up or replace as necessary 2) Clean or replace as necessary 3) Clean or replace as necessary

GASOLINE FUEL INJECTION TROUBLE SHOOTING (Cont.)

CONDITION	POSSIBLE CAUSE	CORRECTION
► Idle Speed Too High and Cannot Be Adjusted Lower	1) Auxiliary air valve does not close	1) Replace valve
► Engine Backfires into Intake Manifold	1) "Warm" control pressure incorrect (CIS) 2) Vacuum leak(s) 3) Idle mixture out of adjustment	1) Replace warm-up regulator 2) Repair vacuum leaks 3) Adjust mixture to specifications
► Engine Backfires into Exhaust Manifold	1) "Warm" control pressure incorrect (CIS) 2) Cold start valve leaks 3) Fuel system leaking 4) Idle mixture out of adjustment	1) Replace warm-up regulator 2) Clean or replace as necessary 3) Repair fuel leaks 4) Adjust mixture to specifications

DIESEL FUEL INJECTION TROUBLE SHOOTING

CONDITION	POSSIBLE CAUSE	CORRECTION
HARD STARTING SYMPTOMS ► Engine cranks but will not start:	1) Incorrect fuel or no fuel 2) Glow plug not working properly 3) Air in fuel system 4) Faulty injector(s) 5) Injection pump faulty	1) Fill or replace fuel as necessary 2) Repair or replace as necessary 3) Bleed fuel system 4) Repair or replace 5) Repair as necessary
► Engine starts but will not run:	1) Air in fuel system 2) Modulator valve out of adjustment 3) Fuel lines, filter or tank plugged 4) Idle speed adjustment incorrect	1) Bleed fuel system 2) Adjust modulator valve 3) Clear fuel system 4) Adjust as necessary
LOW SPEED DRIVEABILITY SYMPTOM ► Engine runs rough:	1) Air or dirt in fuel system 2) Fuel system leak 3) Fuel flow uneven 4) Incorrect fuel 5) Governor or timing incorrect	1) Clean or Bleed fuel system 2) Repair fuel leaks 3) Repair as necessary 4) Change to correct fuel 5) Adjust to specifications
► Engine idle speed too high:	1) Idle speed set incorrectly 2) Modulator valve jammed 3) Governor improperly adjusted 4) Vacuum leaks in manifold	1) Adjust to specifications 2) Repair as necessary 3) Adjust to specifications 4) Repair vacuum leaks
► Poor acceleration:	1) Incorrect fuel 2) Timing device stuck in idle position 3) Fuel pump not operating correctly	1) Change to correct fuel 2) Repair as necessary 3) Repair or replace
► Engine knocks:	1) Incorrect fuel 2) Air in fuel system 3) Incorrect injection timing 4) Dirt in pump or injectors	1) Change to correct fuel 2) Bleed fuel system 3) Adjust timing 4) Clean and replace filter

DIESEL FUEL INJECTION TROUBLE SHOOTING (Cont.)

CONDITION	POSSIBLE CAUSE	CORRECTION
HIGH SPEED DRIVEABILITY SYMPTOM ▶ Engine smokes:	1) Incorrect fuel 2) Air leak in fuel system 3) Injection pump misadjusted	1) Change to correct fuel 2) Repair air leak 3) Adjust to specifications
▶ Engine has power loss:	1) Throttle valve not fully open 2) Clogged air filter 3) Badly worn pump plungers 4) Low fuel pressure 5) Timing device stuck in idling position 6) Control rod stuck 7) Incorrect fuel	1) Adjust as necessary 2) Replace filter 3) Replace injection pump 4) Repair or replace fuel pump or injector pump 5) Repair 6) Repair 7) Change to correct fuel
▶ Engine exceeds maximum permissible speed:	1) Maximum speed stop misadjusted 2) Faulty governor 3) Control rod sticks open 4) Vacuum leaks	1) Adjust to specifications 2) Repair or replace 3) Repair or replace 4) Repair vacuum leaks
▶ Engine will not stop:	1) Stop cable broken or misadjusted 2) Idle speed misadjusted 3) Governor malfunction	1) Replace or Repair 2) Adjust to specifications 3) Repair or replace

ELECTRIC FUEL PUMP TROUBLE SHOOTING

NOTE — *This is a general trouble shooting guide. Not all steps will apply to all fuel pumps. Most electrical fuel pumps are sealed units and must be replaced if found defective.*

CAUTION — *Be sure to relieve fuel pressure on systems which maintain fuel pressure at all times. Do not allow smoking, open flames or sparks in area while performing work on any fuel system components. Fuel vapors may be present and danger of fire or explosion exists. Disconnect battery while working on fuel system.*

CONDITION	POSSIBLE CAUSE	CORRECTION
▶ Pump motor not operating; no fuel output:	1) Check wiring to pump, check for blown pump fuse 2) Check for damaged pump body	1) Repair wiring, ensure proper electrical current to pump 2) Replace if damaged
▶ Pump operating; low fuel output:	1) Check for restricted fuel line, filter or accumulator 2) Check fuel tank venting (may cause vacuum in tank if blocked) 3) Check for air leak on inlet side of pump	1) Repair or replace 2) Repair tank venting system. Test pump output with gas cap removed to check venting. 3) Repair air leak

ELECTRIC FUEL PUMP TROUBLE SHOOTING (Cont.)

CONDITION	POSSIBLE CAUSE	CORRECTION
► Pump operating; no fuel output	1) Check fuel supply 2) Check for pinched or blocked fuel line from pump to carburetor 3) Check for blocked fuel filter 4) Check fuel cut-off valve 5) Check contact points in pump	1) Add fuel 2) Locate and repair 3) Replace 4) If blocked, disconnect outlet hose at valve and apply low air pressure to valve to reseat check ball. Recheck pump output. 5) Clean or replace points
► Pump noisy	1) Check for air leak on inlet (suction) side of pump 2) Pump loose, vibrating against other parts 3) Pump lines (metal) touching body parts 4) Check foam rubber insulation at pump mounting	1) Locate and repair leak 2) Tighten pump evenly 3) Reroute lines for clearance 4) Position insulation correctly or replace
► Excessive pump pressure	1) Defective pressure relief valve	1) Replace pump assembly

TURBOCHARGER TROUBLE SHOOTING

CONDITION	POSSIBLE CAUSE	CORRECTION
► Compressor noise or vibration	1) Poor lubrication of turbocharger shaft bearing 2) Leakage in induction or exhaust system 3) Unbalanced turbocharger shaft due to damage	1) Check oil pressure to turbocharger 2) Tighten connections and replace gaskets or seals 3) Replace turbocharger
► Insufficient charge pressure	1) Leakage between compressor or turbine and cylinder head 2) Incorrect setting of charge pressure 3) Charge pressure regulator stuck in open position 4) Partially clogged exhaust system 5) Clogged air cleaner 6) Binding turbocharger shaft	1) Tighten leaking connections. Replace seals and gaskets 2) Adjust charge pressure regulator spring tension 3) Overhaul regulator 4) Clean or replace exhaust system 5) Change air filter 6) Replace turbocharger
► Metallic noise from regulator	1) Play in regulator valve 2) Spring insufficiently offset in regulator	1) Overhaul regulator 2) Adjust postion of spring

TURBOCHARGER TROUBLE SHOOTING (Cont.)

CONDITION	POSSIBLE CAUSE	CORRECTION
▶ Excessive charge pressure	1) Leakage at exhaust pressure line connection	1) Tighten connections
	2) Clogged exhaust pressure line	2) Remove and clean
	3) Damaged diaphragm in charge pressure regulator	3) Replace diaphragm or regulator
	4) Valve in charge pressure regulator stuck in closed position	4) Overhaul regulator
	5) Ice formation in exhaust pressure line	5) Avoid heavy loading of engine after cold start
	6) Incorrect setting of charge pressure regulator	6) Adjust regulator
▶ Engine knocking	1) Excessive charge pressure	1) Adjust charge pressure
	2) Fuel octane too low	2) Change fuel
	3) Ignition setting too far advanced	3) Adjust timing
▶ Oil leakage at turbo shaft (oil fumes in exhaust)	1) Poor return oil flow from turbocharger	1) Check oil return line, crankcase ventilation, and air filter
	2) Turbocharger seals damaged	2) Replace turbocharger

AISAN 2-BARREL – TOYOTA 1A-C ENGINE

Tercel

DESCRIPTION

Carburetor is of 2-barrel, downdraft design and is equipped with automatic choke which is heated by an electrically operated bimetal heating coil. A piston type accelerator pump is incorporated into the primary barrel and an auxiliary accelerator pump system aids in cold engine acceleration. Other equipment includes diaphragms which open secondaries at high speed and full throttle operation. Other features include dash pot, mixture control, choke breaker, choke opener, deceleration fuel cut, hot idle compensation and high altitude compensation (Federal) devices.

CARBURETOR IDENTIFICATION

Application	Part No.
Federal	
Man. Trans. (4-speed)	21100-15080
With High Altitude Comp.	21100-15130
Man. Trans. (5-speed)	21100-15090
With High Altitude Comp.	21100-15140
Auto. Trans.	21100-15100
With High Altitude Comp.	21100-15150
California (All Models)	21100-15120

ADJUSTMENTS

NOTE – *It is recommended that Toyota carburetor adjusting kits 09240-00014 and 09240-00020 be used to make the following adjustments.*

HOT (SLOW) IDLE RPM

See appropriate TUNE-UP SERVICE PROCEDURES article.

IDLE MIXTURE

See appropriate TUNE-UP SERVICE PROCEDURES article.

COLD (FAST) IDLE RPM

See appropriate TUNE-UP SERVICE PROCEDURES article.

FLOAT LEVEL ADJUSTMENT

NOTE – *When top and bottom lever positions are properly adjusted, float will maintain specified fuel level (glass level mark) when engine is running.*

Hold air horn upside-down. Allow float to hang by its own weight. Measure gap between float lip and air horn gasket surface (gasket removed). Bend float by inserting suitable tool in hole until gap is correct. See *Fig. 1 and 2.*

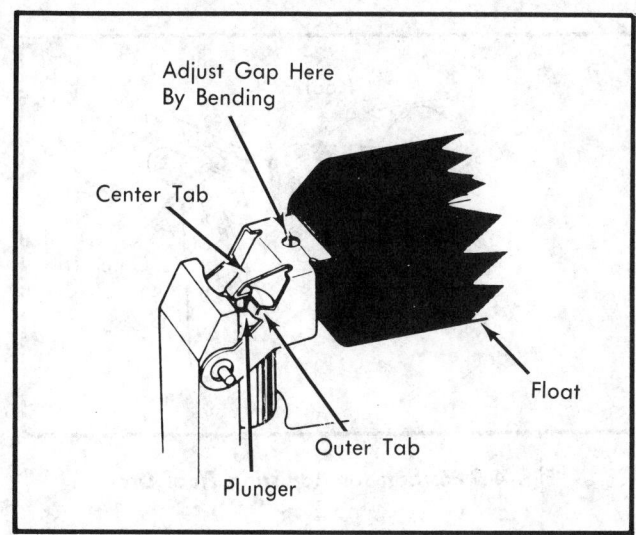

Fig. 1 *Adjusting Carburetor Float Level*

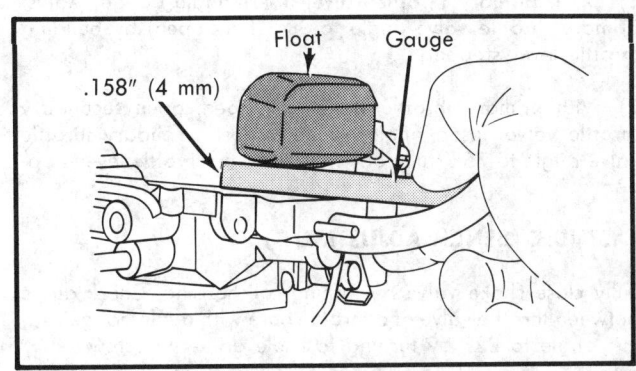

Fig. 2 *Float Level Measurement Points and Gauge*

FLOAT DROP ADJUSTMENT

Lift up float. Measure gap between needle valve and float lip. Bend float outer tab until gap is correct. See *Fig. 3 and 4.* After adjustment ensure plunger moves smoothly.

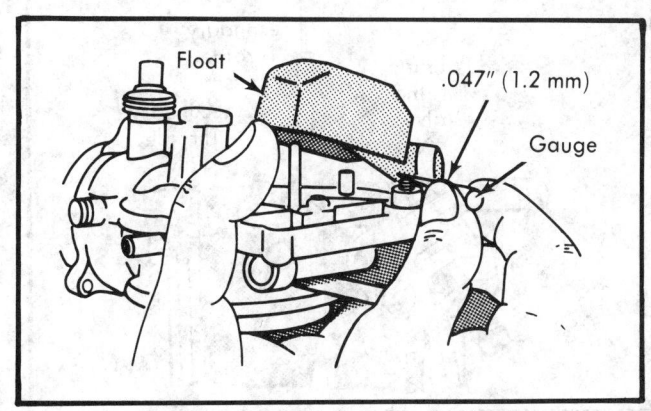

Fig. 3 *Float Drop Measurement Points and Gauge*

1980 Aisan Carburetors

AISAN 2-BARREL — TOYOTA 1A-C ENGINE (Cont.)

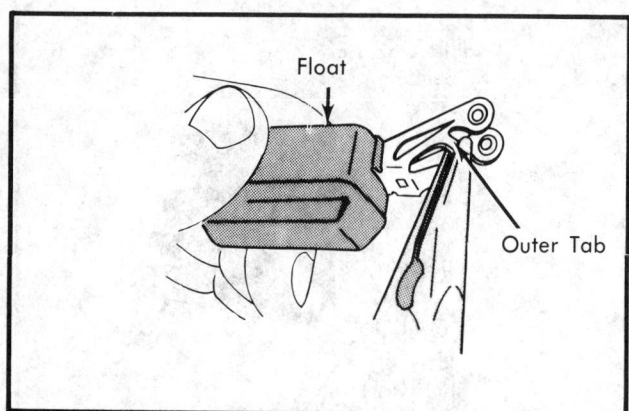

Fig. 4   Position for Adjusting Float Drop

PRIMARY & SECONDARY THROTTLE VALVES

1) Open primary throttle valve. Insert angle gauge. Adjust primary throttle valve angle to 90° (fully open) by bending throttle lever stopper.

2) With primary throttle valve fully open, open secondary throttle valve. Insert angle gauge. Adjust secondary throttle valve angle to 75° (fully open) by bending throttle lever stopper.

FAST IDLE (BENCH ADJUSTMENT)

Fully close choke valve by turning coil housing. Check angle between throttle valve and throttle bore with angle gauge. Adjust angle to 22° by turning fast idle adjusting screw.

SECONDARY THROTTLE OPENING ANGLE (KICK-UP)

Bend secondary throttle lever to obtain .013-.0177" (.33-.45 mm) clearance between secondary throttle valve and bore when primary valve is fully open. See Fig. 5.

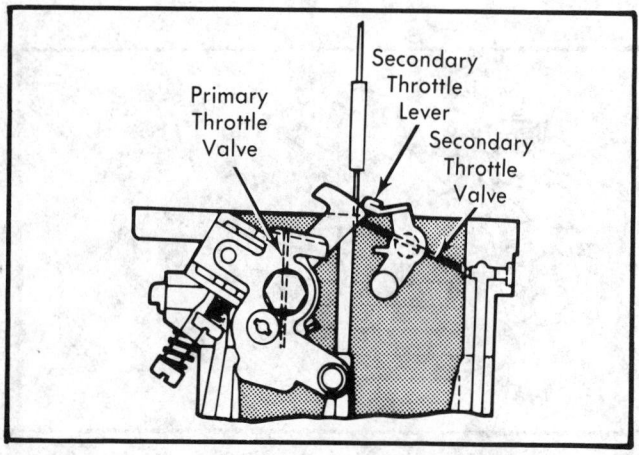

Fig. 5   Carburetor Kick-Up Adjustment

CHOKE UNLOADER ADJUSTMENT

Insert angle gauge. Adjust angle of choke valve so it will be 47° from fully closed position when primary throttle valve is fully open. Bend fast idle cam follower to obtain correct angle. See Fig. 6.

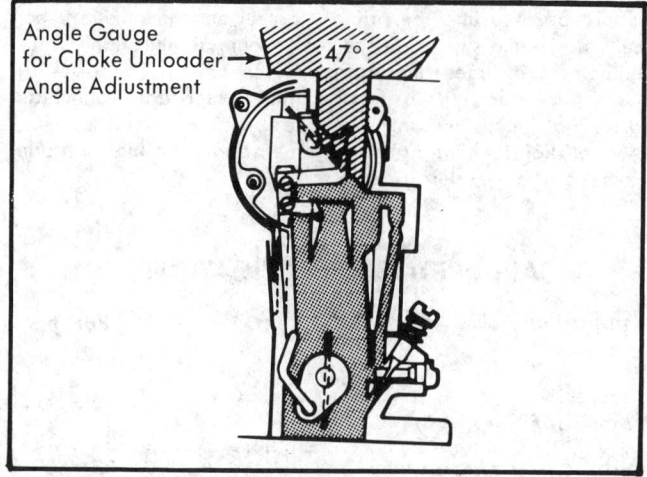

Fig. 6   Adjusting Choke Unloader Angle with Gauge

CHOKE BREAKER ADJUSTMENT

Fully close choke valve by turning coil housing. Connect hoses to breaker vacuum diaphragm and apply vacuum. With vacuum applied, adjust choke angle to 39° by bending release tang.

CHOKE OPENER ADJUSTMENT

Fully close choke valve by turning coil housing. Connect hose to opener diaphragm and apply vacuum. With vacuum applied, adjust choke angle to 72° (between choke valve and bore) by bending relief lever tang.

DASH POT ADJUSTMENT

1) Connect tachometer. With engine at normal operating temperature, disconnect and plug vacuum hose at EGR valve. Disconnect dash pot vacuum hose.

NOTE — *Dash pot setting speed must be done with engine cooling fan "OFF".*

2) Open throttle valve until dash pot adjusting screw does not rest on stopper. See Fig. 7. Plug dash pot diaphragm port.

3) Release throttle valve and check dash pot setting speed. Set engine speed to 3000 RPM when adjusting screw rests on stopper by turning adjusting screw. Reconnect dash pot diaphragm vacuum hose. Open throttle valve and check smooth operation of dash pot linkage.

4) Open throttle valve until dash pot adjusting screw does not rest on stopper. Release throttle valve. After adjusting screw touches stopper, stopper should return to idle position within 1-4 seconds. If not, check and/or replace diaphragm.

AISAN 2-BARREL — TOYOTA 1A-C ENGINE (Cont.)

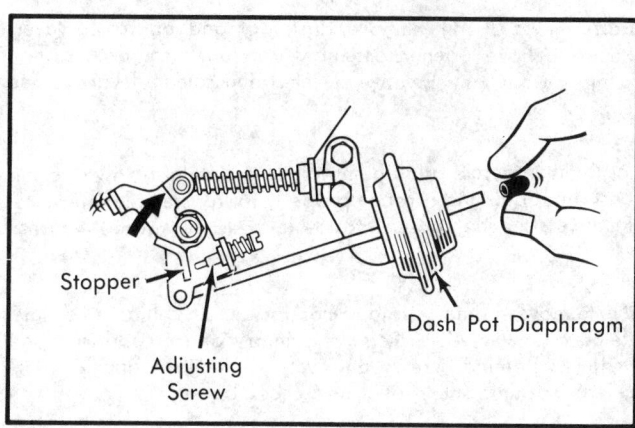

Fig. 7 Adjusting Dash Pot Setting Speed

AUTOMATIC CHOKE ADJUSTMENT

Set coil housing scale to center line of thermostat case. Turn coil housing and adjust engine starting mixture to conform with vehicle operating conditions. When mixture for starting is too rich, turn clockwise; when too lean, turn counterclockwise.

NOTE — *Choke valve fully closes at atmospheric temperature of 86°F (30°C).*

ACCELERATOR PUMP STROKE ADJUSTMENT

Place a straightedge on top of air horn and measure full travel of pump plunger. Make measurement at boot end. Adjust travel distance to .118″ (3.0 mm) by bending accelerator pump actuating rod at existing bend. See Fig. 8.

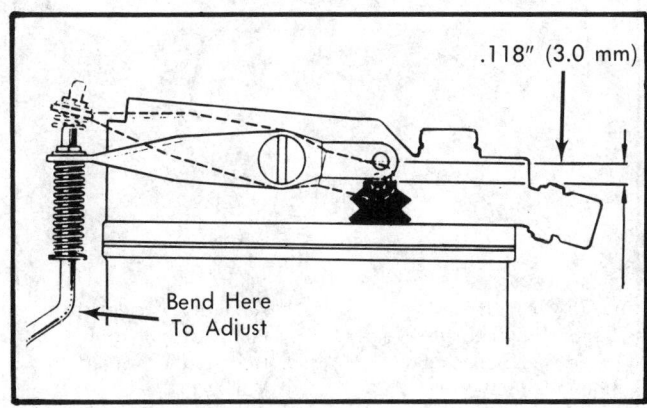

Fig. 8 Carburetor Accelerator Pump Stroke Adjustment

OVERHAUL

NOTE — *It is recommended that Toyota carburetor driver kit 09860-11011 be used during carburetor overhaul.*

DISASSEMBLY

Air Horn — 1) Remove accelerator pump retaining screw and connecting link. Remove pump lever and connecting rod. Remove circlip from fast idle lever and disconnect lever. Remove choke opener lever circlips and lever. See Fig. 9.

2) Remove fuel inlet fitting and line. Remove 8 air horn retaining screws and auxiliary mounting clips. Remove air horn from carburetor body.

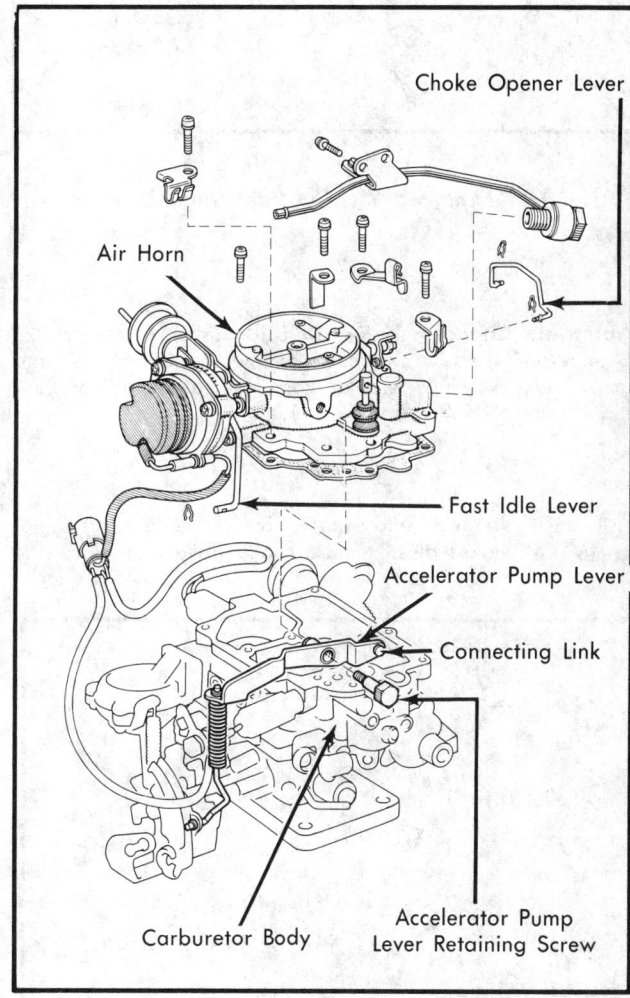

Fig. 9 Exploded View of Carburetor Air Horn

Float Parts — 1) Remove pump plunger and float retaining pin and float. Remove needle valve pin, spring and valve. Remove power piston retaining screw and clip. Remove power piston and spring assembly. See Fig. 10.

2) Using appropriate driver from carburetor kit, remove needle valve seat and filter. Remove and discard gasket. Clean gasket mounting surface.

AISAN 2-BARREL — TOYOTA 1A-C ENGINE (Cont.)

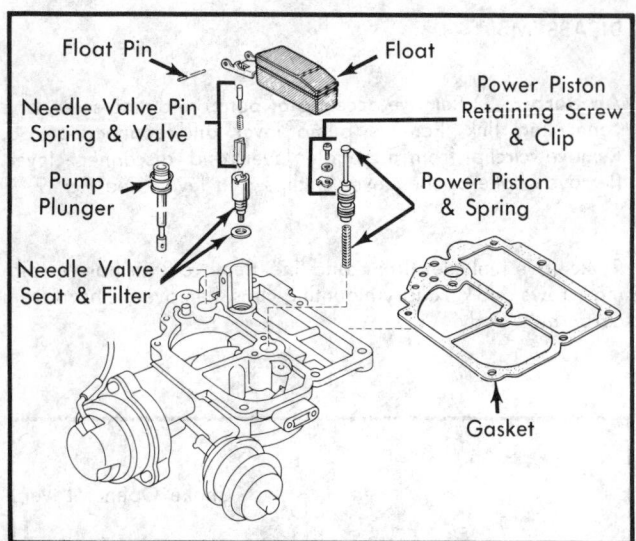

Fig. 10 **Exploded View of Carburetor Float Parts**

Automatic Choke — 1) Remove coil housing. Remove choke lever retaining screw and lever. Remove thermostat case and gasket. Remove choke breaker cam, lever and choke breaker diaphragm assembly. See *Fig. 11*.

2) Remove relief lever and cam. Remove choke valve retaining screws and choke valve. Remove choke valve shaft.

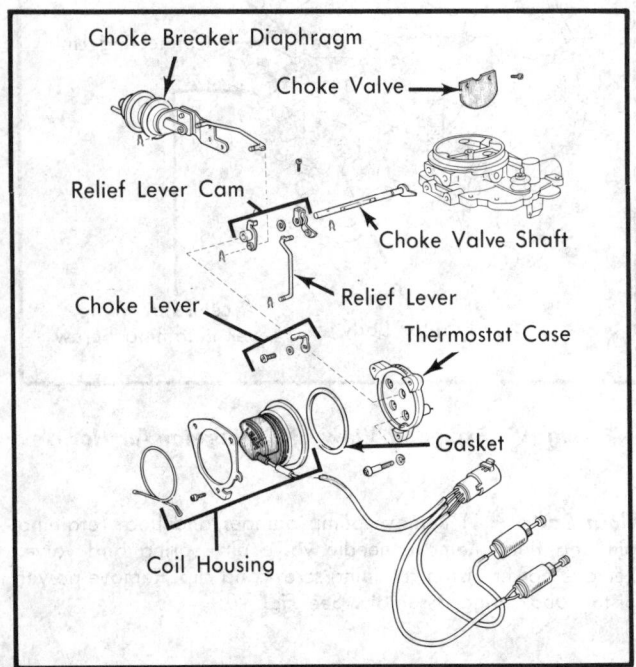

Fig. 11 **Exploded View of Automatic Choke Assembly**

Body Parts — 1) Remove dash pot and operating lever. Remove choke opener assembly and auxiliary acceleration pump diaphragm. Remove deceleration solenoid valves. See *Fig. 12*.

2) Remove acceleration pump discharge weight, valve, spring and check ball and arrange properly for reassembly reference. Remove slow jet. Loosen throttle lever set nut about 4 turns.

3) Remove primary and secondary main plugs and jets. Remove power valve. Remove primary and secondary small venturi retaining screws and venturi. Remove auxiliary accelerator pump inlet valve and check ball.

4) Remove auxiliary accelerator pump outlet plug, then remove spring and checkball. Remove inlet pump retainer with tweezers, then remove inlet valve, spring and check ball. Remove secondary throttle valve diaphragm assembly.

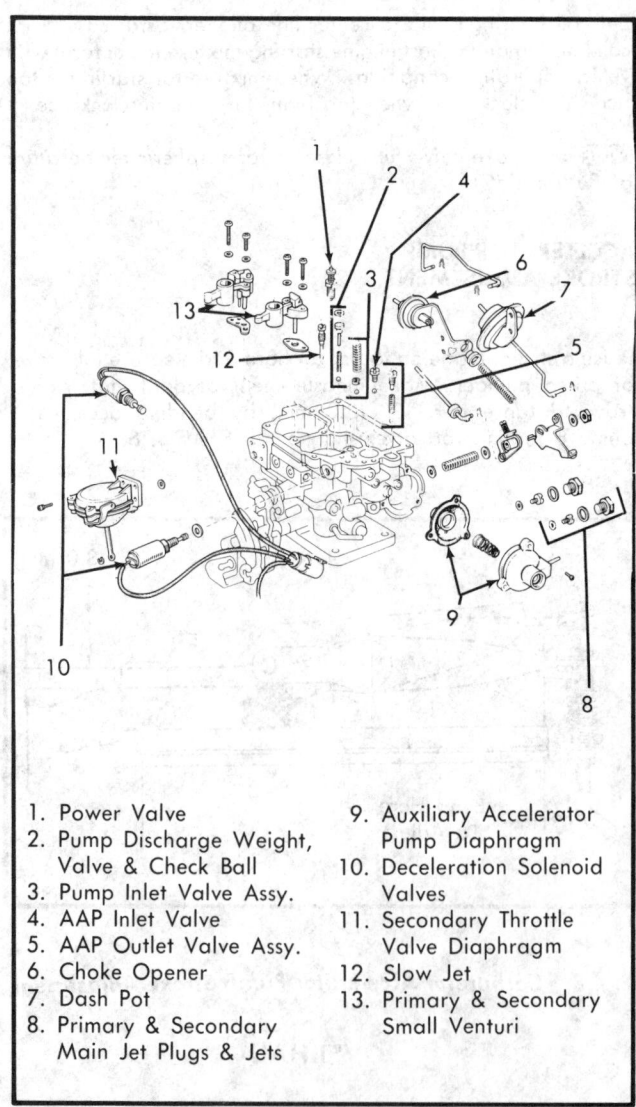

1. Power Valve
2. Pump Discharge Weight, Valve & Check Ball
3. Pump Inlet Valve Assy.
4. AAP Inlet Valve
5. AAP Outlet Valve Assy.
6. Choke Opener
7. Dash Pot
8. Primary & Secondary Main Jet Plugs & Jets
9. Auxiliary Accelerator Pump Diaphragm
10. Deceleration Solenoid Valves
11. Secondary Throttle Valve Diaphragm
12. Slow Jet
13. Primary & Secondary Small Venturi

Fig. 12 **Exploded View of Carburetor Body Parts**

AISAN 2-BARREL — TOYOTA 1A-C ENGINE (Cont.)

Flange Parts — 1) Remove vacuum passage bolts and flange retaining bolts. Note position of vacuum passage bolt with hole. Using appropriate idle screw wrench, remove idle adjusting screw. *See Fig. 13.*

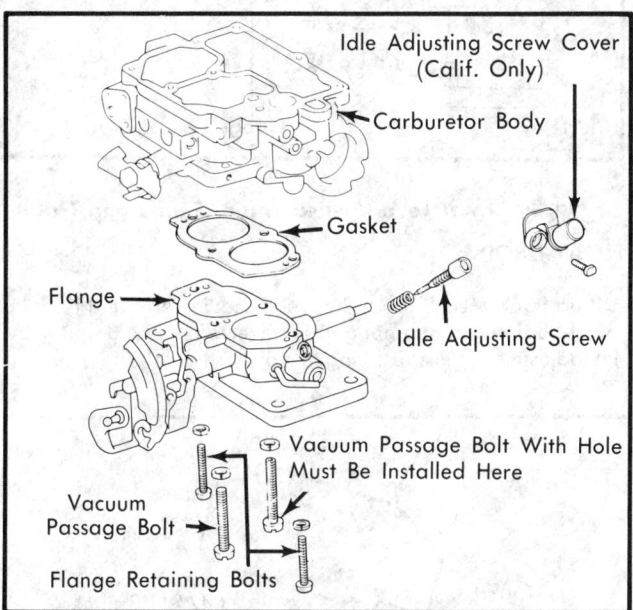

Fig. 13 Exploded View of Carburetor Flange Parts

NOTE — *Idle adjusting screw cover must be removed on California models to gain access to idle adjusting screw.*

2) Separate flange from carburetor body and discard gasket. Clean all gasket surfaces.

CLEANING & INSPECTION

Clean all parts in suitable solvent (carburetor cleaner) and blow dry. Do not attempt to clean jets or other passages with wire or other metal objects. Inspect all parts for wear or damage and replace necessary parts.

REASSEMBLY

Use all new gaskets, reverse disassembly procedure and note the following:

1) When assembling flange assembly, install vacuum passage bolt with hole in correct position. *See Fig. 13.* California models must have idle adjusting screw cover installed.

2) When installing main jets, primary jet is "brass" colored and secondary jet is "chrome" colored. When assembling accelerator pump components, ensure check balls are positioned correctly.

3) When assembling air horn, tighten 8 retaining screws in criss-cross pattern. Tighten each screw a little at a time to prevent damage.

	CARBURETOR ADJUSTMENT SPECIFICATIONS							
Application	Idle Speed (Engine RPM)		Float Level Setting In. (mm)	Float Drop In. (mm)	Fast Idle Opening Angle	Choke Unloader Angle	Accel. Pump Stroke In. (mm)	Dash Pot Setting Speed (Eng. RPM)
	Hot	Fast						
Tercel	650①②	3600①③	.158 (4)	.047 (1.2)	22°	47°	.118 (3)	3000①③

① — Cooling fan "OFF".
② — Auto. Trans. (Neutral) 800 RPM.
③ — EGR Off.

1980 Aisan Carburetors

AISAN 2-BARREL — TOYOTA 3T-C ENGINES

DESCRIPTION

Carburetor is of 2-barrel, downdraft design and is equipped with automatic choke which is heated by an electrically operated bimetal heating coil. A piston type accelerator pump is incorporated into the primary barrel and an auxiliary accelerator pump system aids in cold engine acceleration. Other equipment includes diaphragms which open secondaries at high speed and full throttle operation. Other features include mixture control (except Federal Auto. Trans.), throttle positioner, choke breaker, choke opener, deceleration fuel cut, hot idle compensation and high altitude compensation (Federal option) devices.

CARBURETOR IDENTIFICATION

Application	Part No.
Federal	21100-28080
With High Altitude Comp.	21100-28110
California	21100-28090

ADJUSTMENTS

NOTE — *It is recommended that Toyota carburetor adjusting kits 09240-00014 and 09240-00020 be used to make the following adjustments.*

HOT (SLOW) IDLE RPM

See appropriate *TUNE-UP SERVICE PROCEDURES* article.

IDLE MIXTURE

See appropriate *TUNE-UP SERVICE PROCEDURES* article.

COLD (FAST) IDLE RPM

See appropriate *TUNE-UP SERVICE PROCEDURES* article.

FLOAT LEVEL

Hold air horn upside-down. Allow float to hang by its own weight. Measure gap between float tip and air horn gasket surface (gasket removed). Bend float by inserting suitable tool in hole until gap is correct. See *Fig. 1 and 2.*

NOTE — *After April 1980 (Engine number 3T-4749400), float level specification changed to .362" (9.2 mm).*

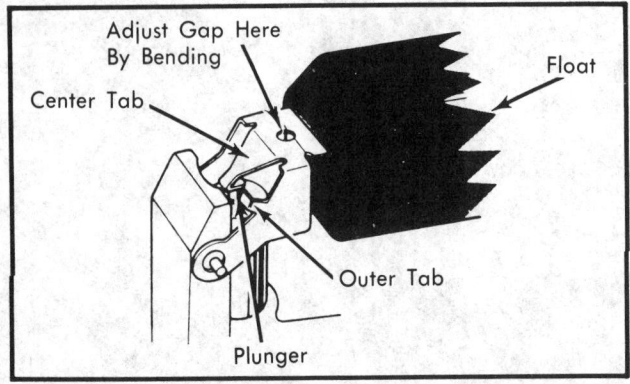

Fig. 1   Point for Adjusting Carburetor Float Level

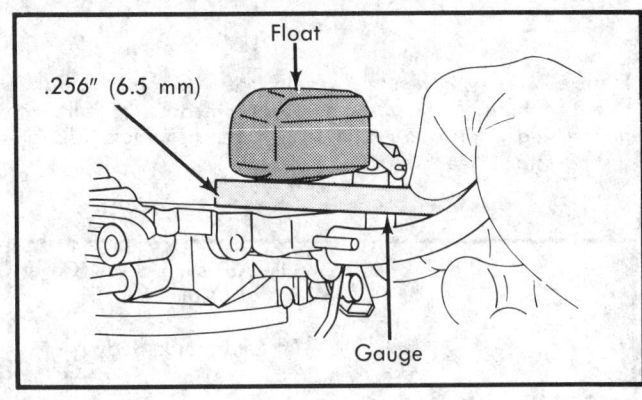

Fig. 2   Float Level Measurement Points and Gauge

FLOAT DROP

Lift up float. Measure gap between needle valve and float lip. Bend float outer tab until gap is correct. See *Fig. 3 and 4.* After adjustment, ensure plunger moves smoothly.

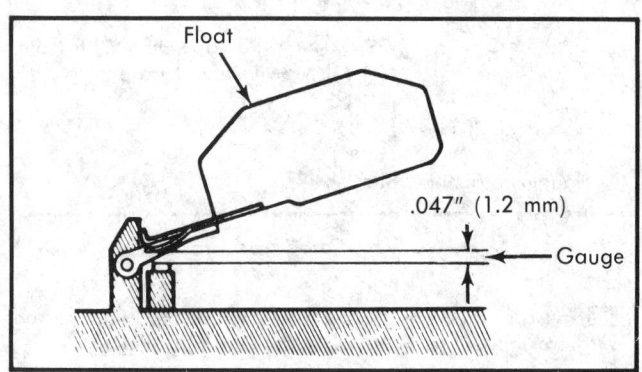

Fig. 3   Float Drop Measurement Points and Gauge

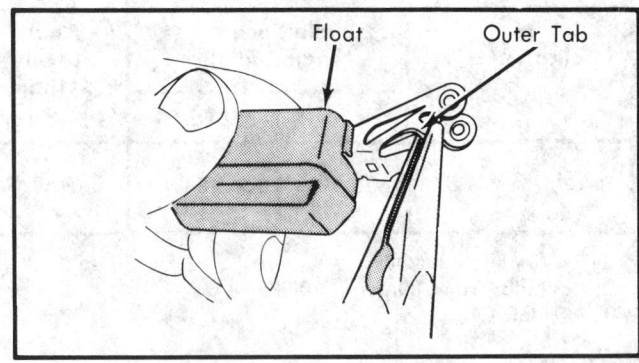

Fig. 4   Position for Adjusting Float Drop

PRIMARY & SECONDARY THROTTLE VALVES

When primary throttle valve is fully opened (90°), secondary throttle valve should also be completely open (80°). If adjustment is necessary, bend throttle shaft link.

NOTE — *The secondary throttle valve should begin to open when primary throttle valve is open 57° from bore surface.*

AISAN 2-BARREL – TOYOTA 3T-C ENGINES (Cont.)

FAST IDLE (BENCH ADJUSTMENT)

Fully close choke valve by turning coil housing. Check angle between thottle valve and throttle bore with angle gauge. Adjust angle to 24° by turning fast idle adjusting screw.

SECONDARY THROTTLE OPENING ANGLE (KICK-UP)

Bend secondary throttle lever to obtain .0059" (.15 mm) clearance between secondary throttle valve and bore when primary throttle valve is open between 64° and 90° (fully open). See Fig. 5.

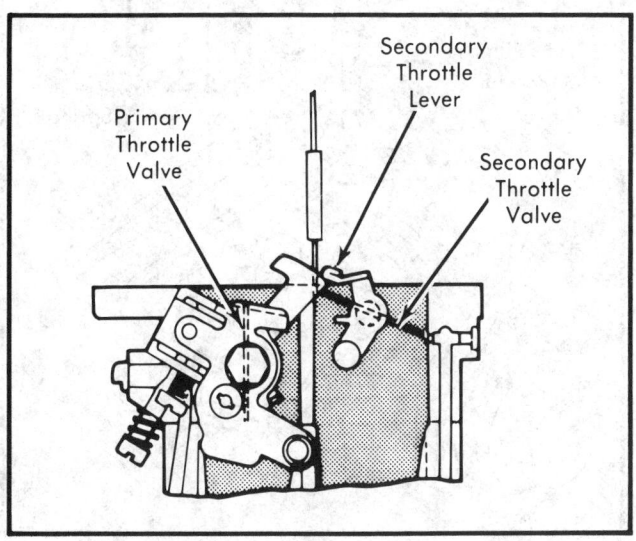

Fig. 5 Carburetor Kick-Up Adjustment

CHOKE UNLOADER

Insert angle gauge. Adjust angle of choke valve so it will be 47° from fully closed position when primary throttle valve is fully open. Bend fast idle cam follower to obtain correct angle. See Fig. 6.

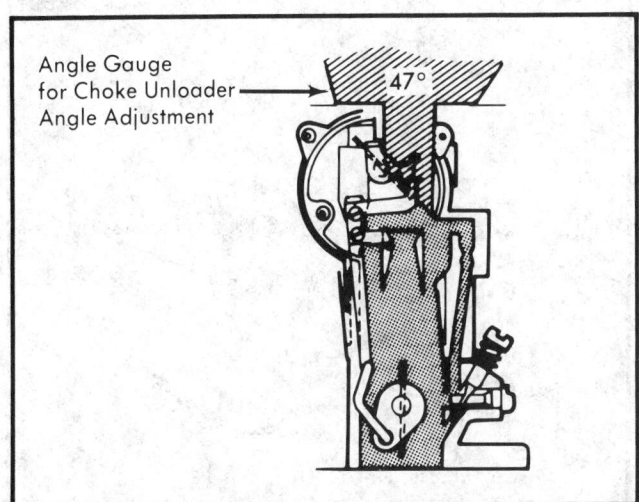

Fig. 6 Adjusting Choke Unloader Angle with Gauge

CHOKE BREAKER

Fully close choke valve by turning coil housing. Connect hoses to breaker vacuum diaphragm and apply vacuum. With vacuum applied, adjust choke angle to 40° (42° Calif.) by bending release tang.

CHOKE OPENER

Fully close choke valve by turning coil housing. Connect hose to opener diaphragm and apply vacuum. With vacuum applied, adjust choke angle to 85° (between choke valve and bore) by bending relief tang.

AUTOMATIC CHOKE

Set coil housing scale to center line of thermostat case. Turn coil housing and adjust engine starting mixture to conform with vehicle operating conditions. When mixture for starting is too rich, turn clockwise; when too lean, turn counterclockwise.

NOTE – *Choke valve fully closes at atmospheric temperature of 77°F (25°C).*

THROTTLE POSITIONER

Turn carburetor upside-down and place throttle positioner adjusting screw against tab on throttle lever. Check angle between throttle valve and bore. Adjust angle to 17° (16.5° Calif.) by turning throttle positioner adjusting screw. See Fig. 7.

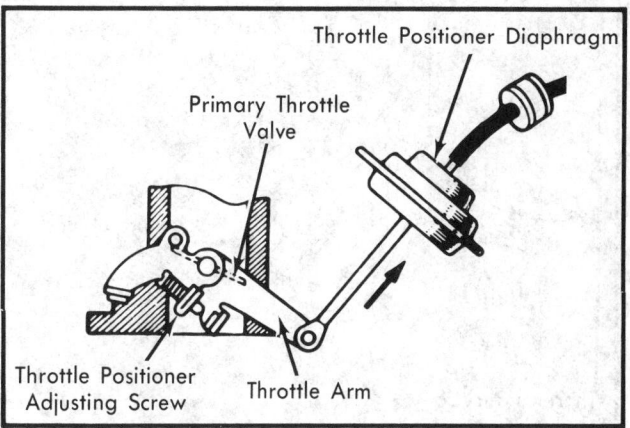

Fig. 7 Making Throttle Positioner Adjustment

ACCELERATOR PUMP

Place a straight edge on top of air horn and measure full travel of pump plunger. Make measurement at boot end. Adjust travel distance to .197" (5.0 mm) by bending accelerator pump actuating rod at existing bend.

OVERHAUL

NOTE – *It is recommended that Toyota carburetor driver kit 09860-11011 be used during carburetor overhaul.*

AISAN 2-BARREL – TOYOTA 3T-C ENGINES (Cont.)

DISASSEMBLY

Air Horn – 1) Disconnect choke breaker vacuum hose. Remove pump lever connecting link and pump lever. Remove fast idle cam link circlip and throttle valve return spring.

2) Remove terminal from thermostatic coil connector. Remove all fittings from air horn. Remove 8 air horn retaining screws and carefully lift off air horn.

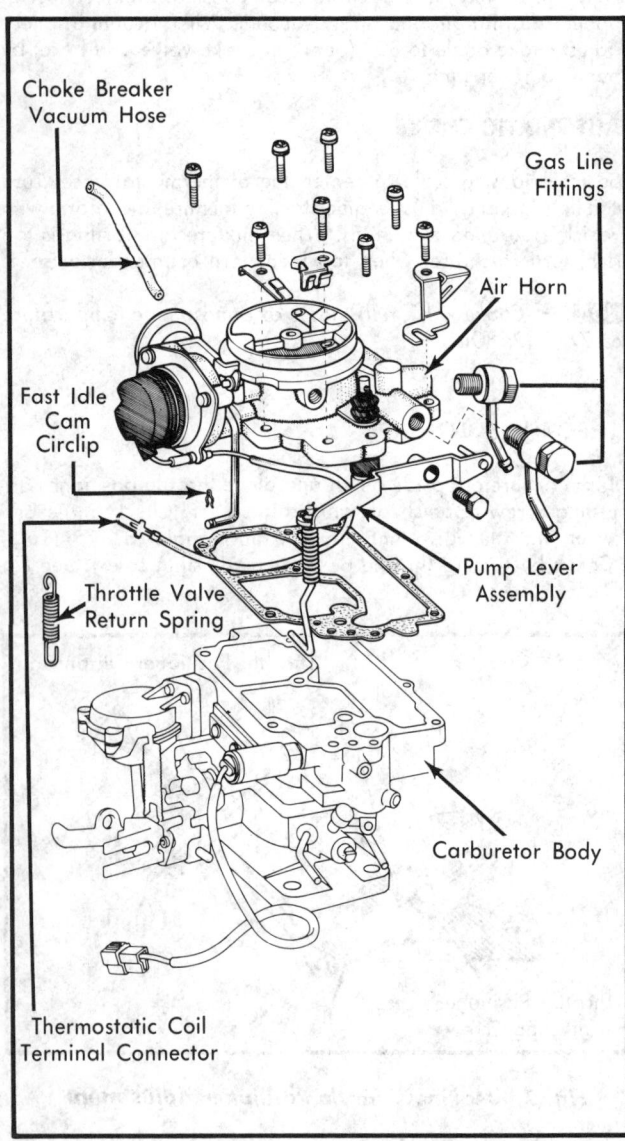

Fig. 8   Exploded View of Air Horn Assembly

Float Parts – Remove pump plunger, float assembly and needle valve pin, spring and valve assembly. Using appropriate driver, remove needle valve seat. Remove power piston retaining clip and screw. Remove power piston and spring assembly.

Automatic Choke Parts – Remove coil housing, then remove choke lever retaining screw and lever. Remove thermostat case and gasket, choke breaker diaphragm, relief lever, choke valve retaining screws and choke valve and choke shaft.

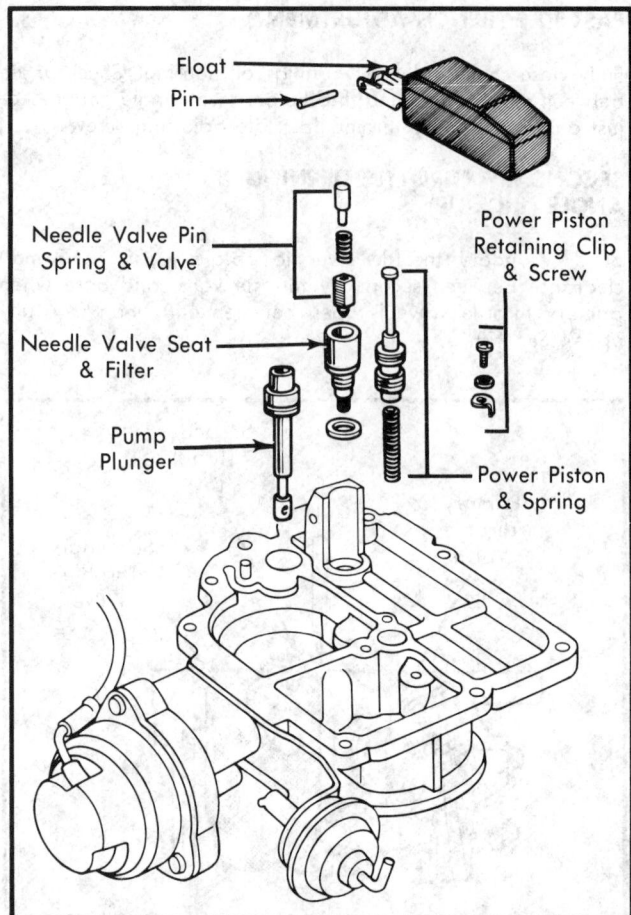

Fig. 9   Exploded View of Float Parts

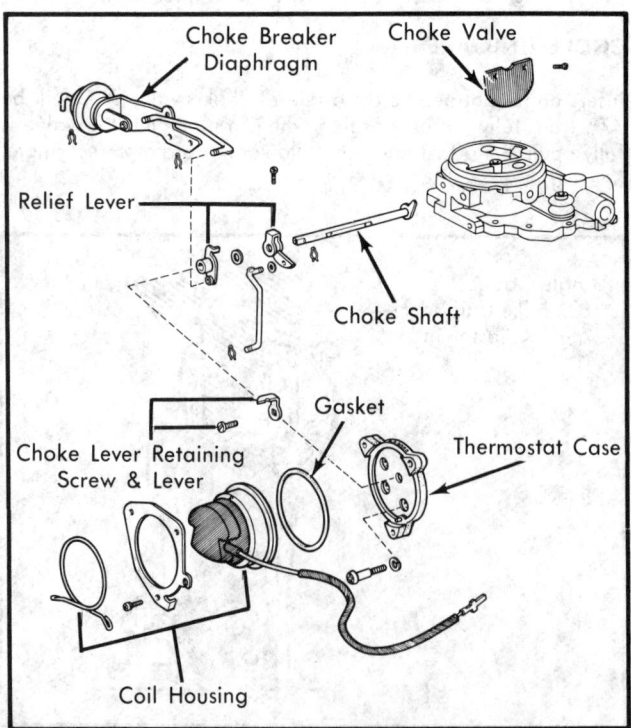

Fig. 10   Exploded View of Automatic Choke Parts

AISAN 2-BARREL — TOYOTA 3T-C ENGINES (Cont.)

Body Parts — 1) Remove throttle positioner assembly, auxiliary accelerator pump (AAP) diaphragm, and fuel cut solenoid.

2) Remove acceleration pump nozzle, discharge weight, valve, spring and check ball. Arrange in order of removal for reassembly reference. *See Fig. 11.*

3) Remove slow jet, primary and secondary main jet plugs and jets, power valve and primary and secondary venturi. Remove AAP inlet valve plug and check ball, then remove AAP outlet valve plug, spring and check ball.

4) Remove pump inlet valve retainer with tweezers, then remove check ball. Remove secondary throttle valve diaphragm and carefully remove gasket. Remove hot idle compensator assembly (Federal models).

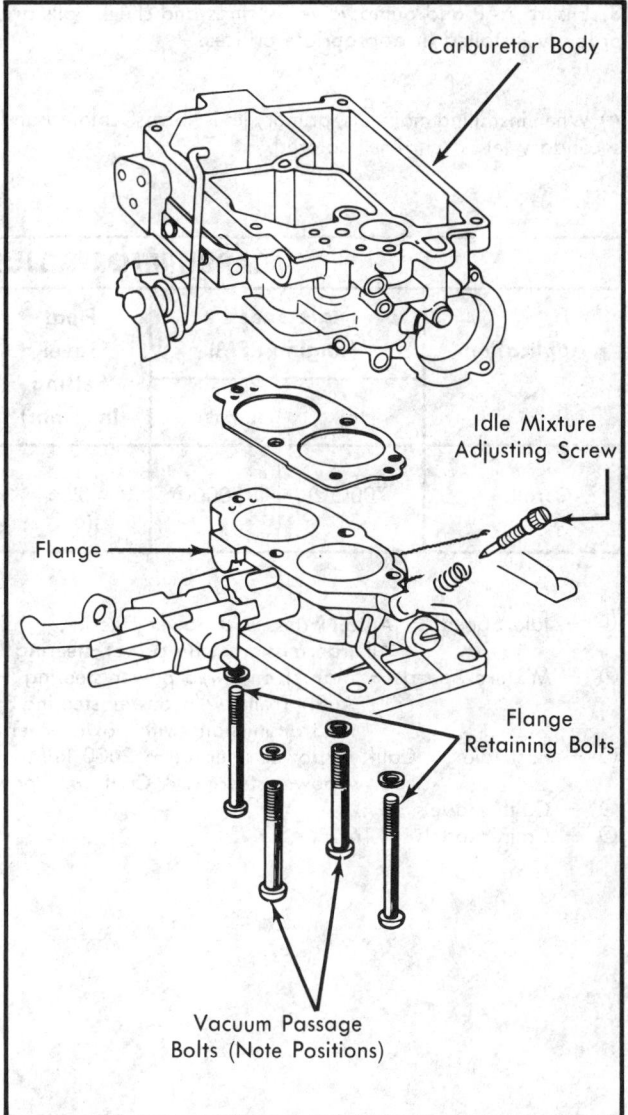

Fig. 12 *Exploded View of Carburetor Flange Parts*

CLEANING & INSPECTION

Clean all parts in suitable solvent (carburetor cleaner) and blow dry. Do not attempt to clean jets or other passages with wire or other metal objects. Inspect all parts for wear or damage and replace necessary parts.

REASSEMBLY

Use all new gaskets, reverse disassembly procedure and note the following:

1) When assembling flange parts, ensure vacuum passage bolts are installed in correct position.

2) When assembling secondary throttle valve diaphragm, ensure gasket is properly installed and seated.

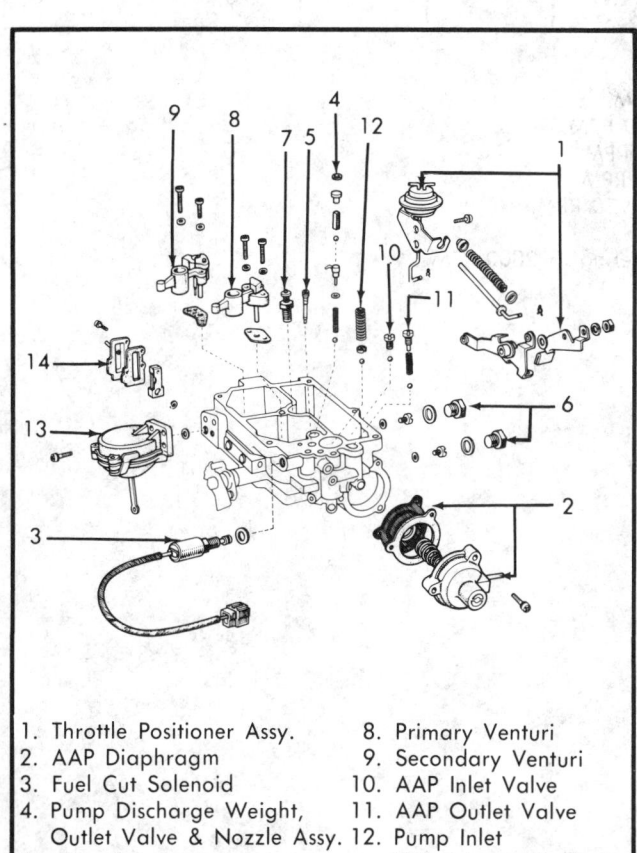

1. Throttle Positioner Assy.
2. AAP Diaphragm
3. Fuel Cut Solenoid
4. Pump Discharge Weight, Outlet Valve & Nozzle Assy.
5. Slow Jet
6. Primary & Secondary Main Jet Plugs & Jets
7. Power Valve
8. Primary Venturi
9. Secondary Venturi
10. AAP Inlet Valve
11. AAP Outlet Valve
12. Pump Inlet Valve Assembly
13. Secondary Throttle Valve Diaphragm
14. Hot Idle Compensator

Fig. 11 *Exploded View of Carburetor Body Parts*

Flange Parts — Remove vacuum passage bolts and arrange in proper order for reassembly reference. Remove flange retaining bolts and separate flange and carburetor body. Discard gasket. Remove idle mixture adjusting screw with appropriate tool (09243-00010).

1980 Aisan Carburetors

AISAN 2-BARREL — TOYOTA 3T-C ENGINES (Cont.)

3) Ensure AAP and pump valves, springs and check balls are properly installed in appropriate orifices.

4) When installing main jets, primary jet is "brass" colored and secondary jet is "chrome" colored.

5) When installing pump discharge weight and outlet valve assembly, ensure all components are installed in correct order. See *Fig. 11*.

6) After installing power piston retaining clip and screw, check power piston for smooth operation.

	CARBURETOR ADJUSTMENT SPECIFICATIONS							
Application	Idle Speed (Engine RPM)		Float Level Setting In. (mm)	Float Drop In. (mm)	Fast Idle Angle	Choke Breaker Opening Angle	Accel. Pump Stroke In. (mm)	Throttle Positioner Angle
	Hot	Fast						
Corolla	700①②	3000③	.256 (6.5)	.047 (1.2)	24°	40°④	.197 (5.0)	17°⑤

① — Idle Speed — Auto. Trans. w/o power steering — 750 RPM.
            All transmissions with power steering — 850 RPM.
② — Mixture Speed — Man. Trans. w/o power steering — 760 RPM.
            Auto. Trans. w/o power steering — 810 RPM.
            All transmissions with power steering — 920 RPM.
③ — Fast Idle — Calif. w/power steering — 2600 RPM.
            Fed. w/power steering & Calif. w/o power steering — 2800 RPM.
④ — Calif. models — 42°.
⑤ — Calif. models — 16.5°.

AISAN 2-BARREL — TOYOTA 20R ENGINE

Celica
Corona
Pickup

DESCRIPTION

Carburetor is a two barrel downdraft design with primary and secondary venturi. An automatic choke containing a bi-metal spring heated by coolant provides proper air/fuel mixture control during engine warm-up. Secondary throttle valve is actuated by a vacuum diaphragm unit with a kick-up (open) lever. Secondary valve begins to open when primary throttle valve opening exceeds 59°. During deceleration, a throttle positioner opens primary throttle valve slightly to maintain proper combustion of air/fuel mixture (except Federal Auto. Trans. pickup). A thermostatic valve provides air flow under secondary throttle valve when ambient air temperature is high to maintain proper combustion. Other features include choke breaker, auxiliary accelerator pump, secondary slow circuit fuel cut system (except Federal pickup), fast idle cam breaker (except Federal pickup) and deceleration fuel cut (except Federal pickup).

CARBURETOR IDENTIFICATION

Application	Part No.
Celica & Corona	
Federal①	21100-38311
Calif.	21100-38331
Pickup	
Federal②	21100-38351
Calif.	21100-38371

① — 4-speed Man. Trans. — 21100-38440.
② — Auto. Trans. pickup — 21100-38361.

ADJUSTMENTS

HOT (SLOW) IDLE RPM

See appropriate TUNE-UP SERVICE PROCEDURES article.

IDLE MIXTURE

See appropriate TUNE-UP SERVICE PROCEDURES article.

COLD (FAST) IDLE RPM

See appropriate TUNE-UP SERVICE PROCEDURES article.

NOTE — It is recommended that Toyota carburetor adjustment kit 09240-00011 be used to make the following adjustments.

ACCELERATOR PUMP STROKE ADJUSTMENT

Place a straightedge on top of air horn and measure full travel of pump plunger. Make measurement at boot end. Adjust travel distance to .154″ (3.9 mm) by bending accelerator pump actuating rod at existing bend. See Fig. 1.

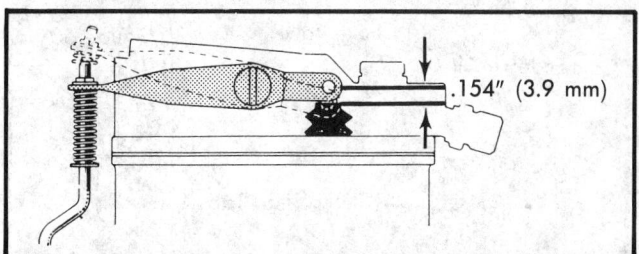

Fig. 1   Accelerator Pump Adjustment and Measurement

FLOAT LEVEL ADJUSTMENT

Allow float to hang down by its own weight. Adjust clearance between float tip and air horn to .276″ (7 mm) by bending float lip (A). See Fig. 2.

NOTE — Measurement must be made without gasket on air horn.

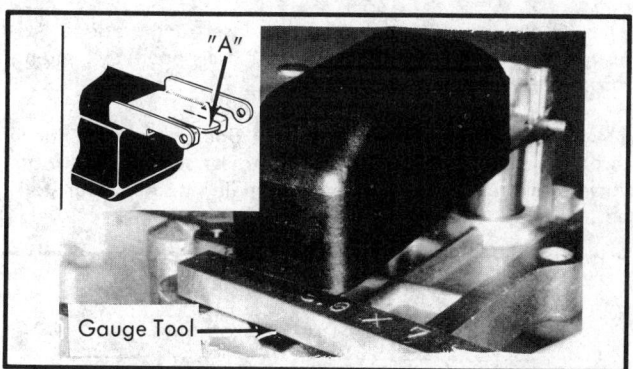

Fig. 2   Adjustment Points for Float Level

FLOAT DROP ADJUSTMENT

Lift up float. Adjust clearance between needle valve plunger and float lip to .04″ (1 mm) by bending float tab (B). See Fig. 3.

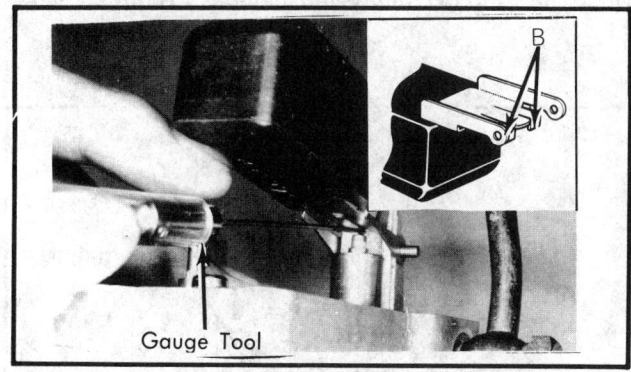

Fig. 3   Float Drop Adjustment Using Angle Gauge

UNLOADER ADJUSTMENT

Fully open primary throttle valve. Insert angle gauge. Adjust choke valve angle to 50° by bending fast idle cam follower lip. See Fig. 4.

1980 Aisan Carburetors

AISAN 2-BARREL — TOYOTA 20R ENGINE (Cont.)

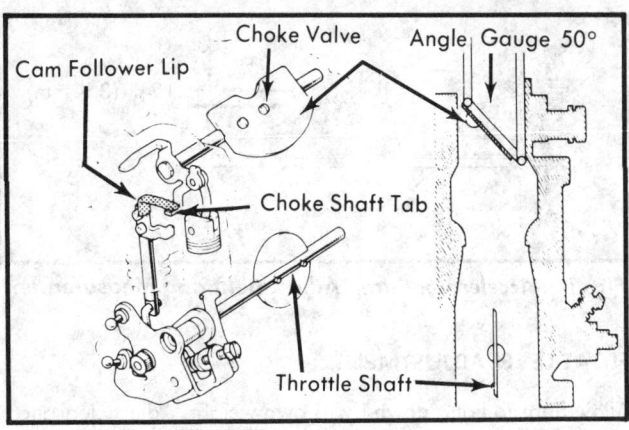

Fig. 4   Choke Unloader Adjustment Points and Measurements

PRIMARY & SECONDARY THROTTLE VALVE ADJUSTMENT

1) Fully open primary throttle valve. Insert angle gauge. Adjust primary throttle valve angle to 90° (fully open) by bending throttle lever stopper.

2) With primary throttle valve fully open, open secondary throttle valve. Insert angle gauge. Adjust secondary throttle valve angle to 75° (fully open) by bending throttle lever stopper. See Fig. 5.

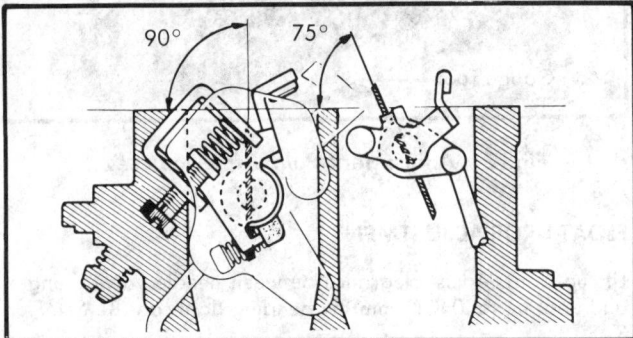

Fig. 5   Adjusting Primary and Secondary Throttle Valves

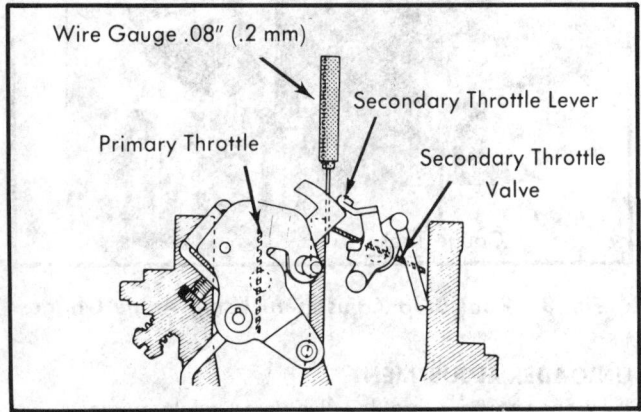

Fig. 6   Secondary Kick-Up Measurement and Adjustment

SECONDARY THROTTLE KICK-UP

Fully open primary throttle valve. Check secondary throttle valve opening. Clearance between secondary throttle valve and bore should be .008" (.2 mm). See Fig. 6. Bend secondary throttle lever.

AUTOMATIC CHOKE (ON VEHICLE)

With engine cold and stopped, remove air cleaner. Depress and release accelerator. Choke valve should be almost closed. Start engine and after warm-up, choke valve should be open.

FAST IDLE (BENCH ADJUSTMENT)

With choke valve fully closed, check clearance between primary throttle valve and throttle bore. If clearance is not to specifications found in Fig. 7, adjust by turning fast idle screw.

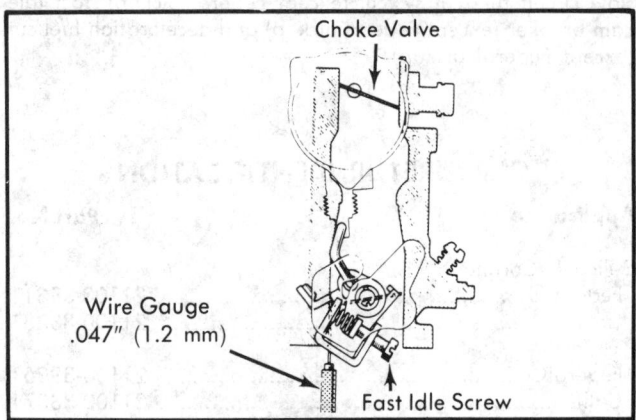

Fig. 7   Bench Adjustment of Carburetor Fast Idle

CHOKE BREAKER ADJUSTMENT

Push (depress) choke breaker rod to open choke valve. Check choke valve angle (38° from bore). Bend relief lever until correct measurement is obtained.

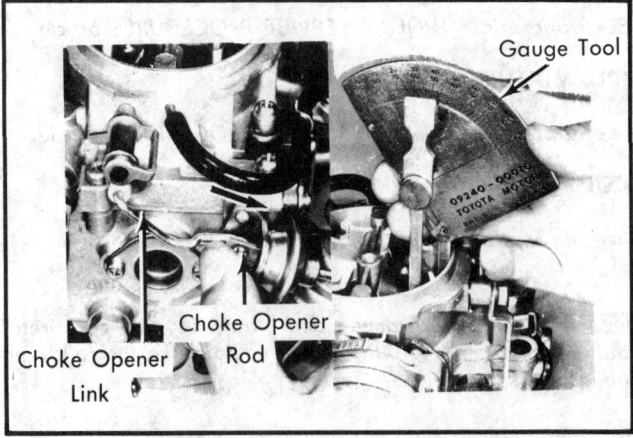

Fig. 8   Choke Opener Adjustment

CHOKE OPENER ADJUSTMENT

Push in choke opener rod. Bend choke opener link until choke valve angle is 55° (measured from bore). See Fig. 8.

AISAN 2-BARREL — TOYOTA 20R ENGINE (Cont.)

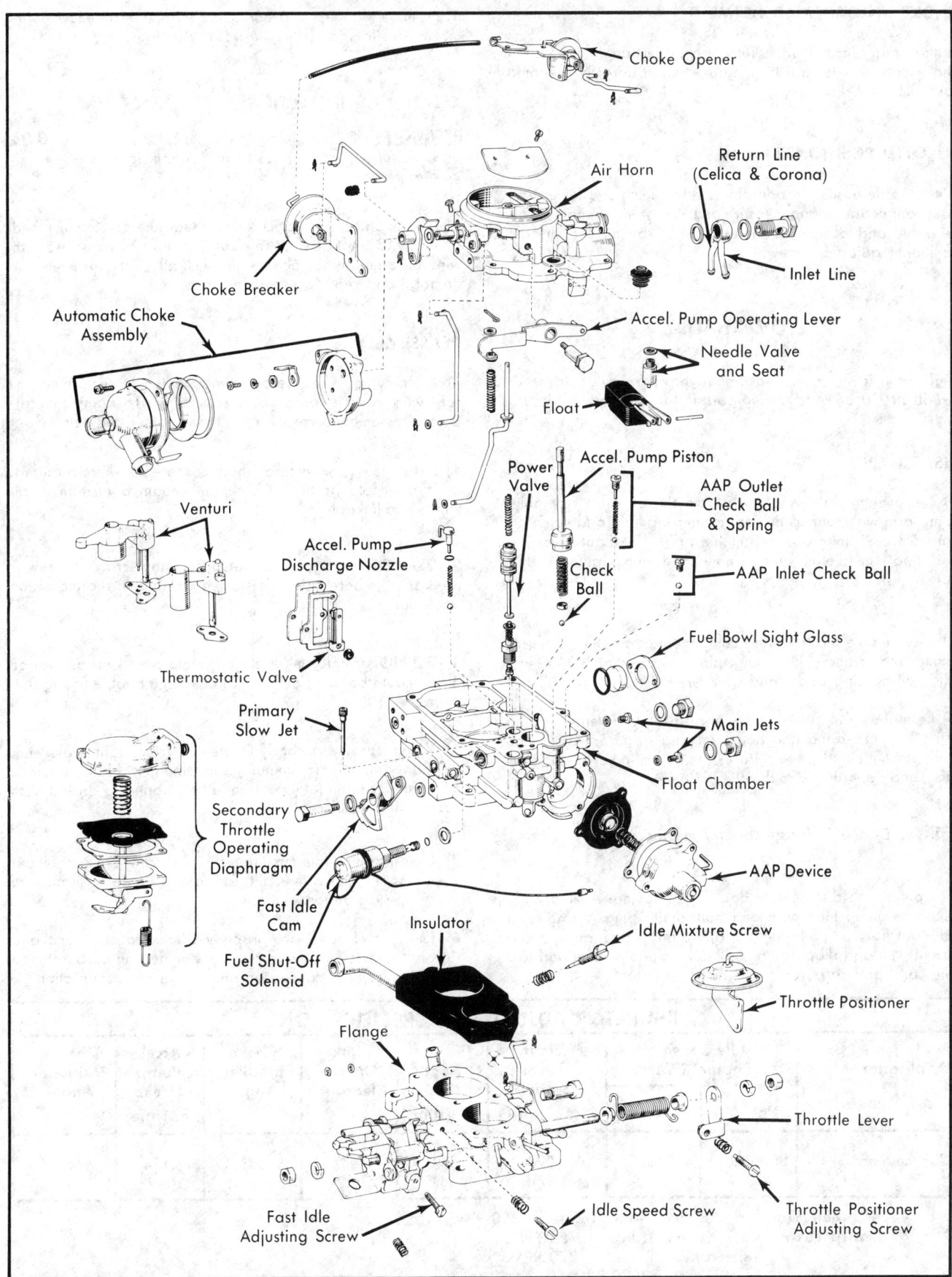

Choke Opener

Air Horn

Return Line (Celica & Corona)

Inlet Line

Choke Breaker

Automatic Choke Assembly

Accel. Pump Operating Lever

Needle Valve and Seat

Float

Venturi

Power Valve

Accel. Pump Piston

AAP Outlet Check Ball & Spring

Accel. Pump Discharge Nozzle

Check Ball

AAP Inlet Check Ball

Thermostatic Valve

Fuel Bowl Sight Glass

Primary Slow Jet

Main Jets

Float Chamber

Secondary Throttle Operating Diaphragm

AAP Device

Fast Idle Cam

Insulator

Idle Mixture Screw

Fuel Shut-Off Solenoid

Throttle Positioner

Flange

Throttle Lever

Fast Idle Adjusting Screw

Idle Speed Screw

Throttle Positioner Adjusting Screw

Fig. 9   Exploded View of Toyota 20R Engine Carburetor

AISAN 2-BARREL — TOYOTA 20R ENGINE (Cont.)

CHOKE UNLOADER ADJUSTMENT

With primary throttle valve fully open, insert angle gauge. Set choke valve angle to 50° (measured from bore) by bending fast idle lever.

THROTTLE POSITIONER

With throttle positioner adjusting screw on center of lever tab, insert angle gauge and measure angle between primary throttle valve and bore. Set angle to 16.5° by turning throttle positioner adjusting screw.

OVERHAUL

NOTE — *It is recommended that Toyota carburetor driver kit 09860-11010 be used during carburetor overhaul.*

DISASSEMBLY

1) Remove the following parts from the air horn assembly: Pump arm with connecting rod; connecting links and seven air horn screws; choke opener; air horn (lift off); float pivot pin and float; needle valve assembly; and pump plunger and power piston.

2) Disassemble the following components from the automatic choke: Water and coil housing, plate and gasket; choke lever and coil housing body; and breaker, relief lever and link.

3) From the main body remove or disassemble: Venturi; pump jet, "O" ring, spring and ball; damping spring, retainer and ball; slow jet and power valve; thermostatic valve and "O" ring; and sight glass and throttle positioner.

NOTE — *DO NOT disassemble thermostatic valve.*

4) Continue to disassemble body by removing: Auxiliary accelerator pump inlet plug and ball; outlet plug, spring, and ball; auxiliary pump housing; diaphragm, spring, and gasket; spring, link and diaphragm assembly; solenoid valve and fast idle cam; and carburetor body and insulator.

5) From the flange, remove: Mixture screws; throttle lever, spring and collars; and throttle positioner lever.

CLEANING & INSPECTION

CAUTION — *Do not immerse synthetic components (gaskets, plastics, rubber) or thermostat and diaphragm valves in carburetor cleaner.*

Clean all parts in suitable solvent (carburetor cleaner) and blow dry. Do not attempt to clean jets or other passages with wire or other metal objects. Inspect all parts for wear or damage and replace necessary parts.

REASSEMBLY

Reassembly of carburetor components is performed by following reverse order of disassembly. To complete carburetor assembly correctly, refer to the notes listed below:

1) Install new gaskets throughout carburetor where required. Discard all old gaskets. Check for smooth operation of all valves and linkage.

2) DO NOT overtighten power piston stop screw. If screw is too tight, the bore may be distorted resulting in sticking piston operation.

3) DO NOT install fuel level gauge glass backwards. Dot on glass should be to inside of float bowl and bubble facing outward.

4) When carburetor body is viewed from sight glass end, secondary main jet (aluminum) is located in right side opening and primary main jet (brass) in left side opening. Install both jets with flat washers.

5) After installing idle mixture adjusting screw, back screw out 1½ turns (1⅓ turns on Calif. Celica and Corona) for mixture screw preset position.

6) Ensure fuel hoses are properly connected on Celica and Corona models. Arrow marks are stamped on carburetor to identify inlet hose connection and return hose connection.

CARBURETOR ADJUSTMENT SPECIFICATIONS

Application	Idle Speed (Engine RPM)		Float Level Setting In. (mm)	Float Drop In. (mm)	Choke Opener Clearance	Choke Breaker Angle	Accel. Pump Stroke In. (mm)	Throttle Positioner Angle
	Hot	Fast						
20R Engine	800①②	2400③	.276 (7)	.040 (1)	.047 (1.2)	38°	.154 (3.9)	16.5°

① — 4-speed Man. Trans. — 700 RPM; Auto. Trans. — 850 RPM.
② — Mixture speeds — 4-speed Man. Trans. — 750 RPM.
                  5-speed Man. Trans. — 870 RPM.
                  Auto. Trans. — 920 RPM.
③ — With EGR disconnected, vacuum advance cut and fast idle cam breaker disconnected.

AISAN 2-BARREL — TOYOTA 2F ENGINE

Land Cruiser

DESCRIPTION

Carburetor is a 2-barrel, downdraft type with vacuum operated choke breaker to improve cold engine operation. A secondary slow port helps fuel mixing at start of secondary valve opening. Improvement of operation is noticed during low speed load. A piston type accelerator pump is incorporated into the primary barrel and an auxiliary accelerator pump system aids in cold engine operation. Other equipment includes a diaphragm to open secondary valve at high speed and full throttle operation and a throttle positioner to prevent complete closing of throttle during deceleration. A throttle stop solenoid is also used to prevent dieseling during engine shut down.

CARBURETOR IDENTIFICATION

Application	Part No.
Federal	21100-61025
California	21100-61065

ADJUSTMENTS

NOTE — *It is recommended that Toyota carburetor adjusting kits 09240-00014 and 9240-00020 be used to make the following adjustments.*

HOT (SLOW) IDLE RPM

See appropriate TUNE-UP SERVICE PROCEDURES article.

IDLE MIXTURE

See appropriate TUNE-UP SERVICE PROCEDURES article.

COLD (FAST) IDLE RPM

See appropriate TUNE-UP SERVICE PROCEDURES article.

FLOAT LEVEL ADJUSTMENT

Turn air horn assembly upside-down. Measure clearance between upper surface of float and gasket surface of air horn. Bend center float tab until float level is correct. *See Fig. 1*

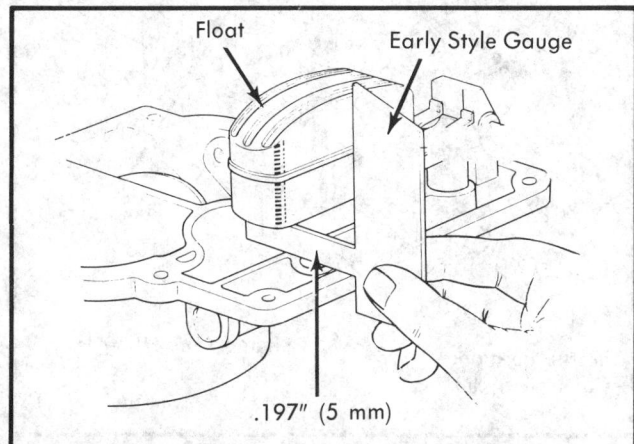

.197" (5 mm)

Fig. 1 Float Level Measurement Points

FLOAT DROP ADJUSTMENT

Lift up float assembly and measure clearance between needle valve plunger and float lip. Adjust clearance to specification by bending both outside float tabs. *See Fig. 2.*

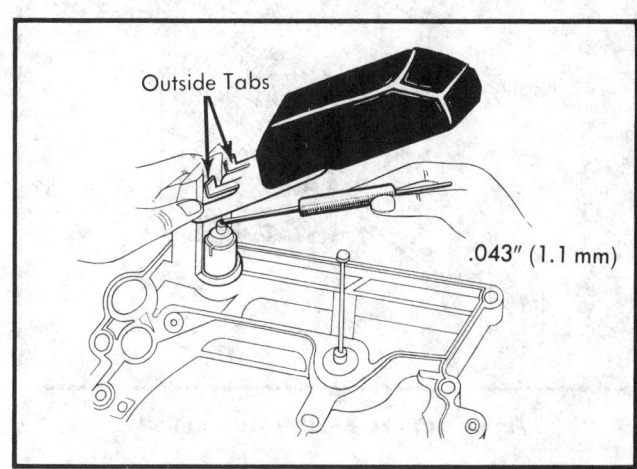

Outside Tabs

.043" (1.1 mm)

Fig. 2 Measuring Carburetor Float Drop with Gauge

PRIMARY & SECONDARY THROTTLE VALVE ADJUSTMENT

1) Open primary throttle valve. Then, open secondary throttle valve. Make sure valves are perpendicular to flange surface when fully opened.

2) Bend throttle lever stopper(s) until proper opening is obtained.

FAST IDLE (BENCH ADJUSTMENT)

Fully close choke valve. Check clearance between throttle bore and primary throttle valve. Adjust clearance to .051" (1.3 mm) by turning fast idle adjusting screw. *See Fig. 3.*

Gauge

Adjustment Screw

Fig. 3 Making Fast Idle Measurement and Adjustment

CHOKE BREAKER ADJUSTMENT

Push choke vacuum breaker diaphragm rod to open choke valve. Insert angle gauge. Set choke valve angle to 45° by bending choke-to-vacuum breaker diaphragm rod at existing bend. After adjustment, ensure smooth operation of choke valve. *See Fig. 4.*

AISAN 2-BARREL — TOYOTA 2F ENGINE (Cont.)

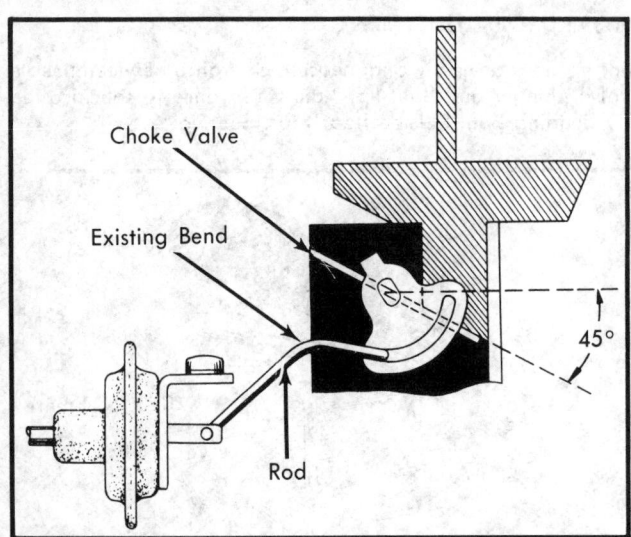

Fig. 4 Choke Breaker Adjustment

THROTTLE POSITIONER ADJUSTMENT

Turn carburetor upside-down and place throttle positioner adjusting screw against tab on throttle lever. Check clearance between throttle bore and primary valve. Adjust clearance to .031″ (.8 mm) by turning throttle positioner adjusting screw. See Fig. 5.

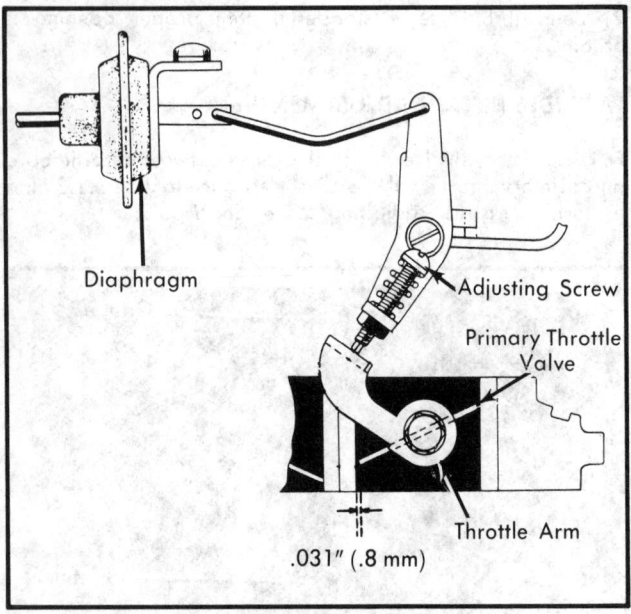

Fig. 5 Making Throttle Positioner Adjustment

SECONDARY THROTTLE OPENING ANGLE (KICK-UP)

Bend secondary throttle lever to obtain 25° angle between secondary throttle valve and bore when primary valve is fully open. See Fig. 6.

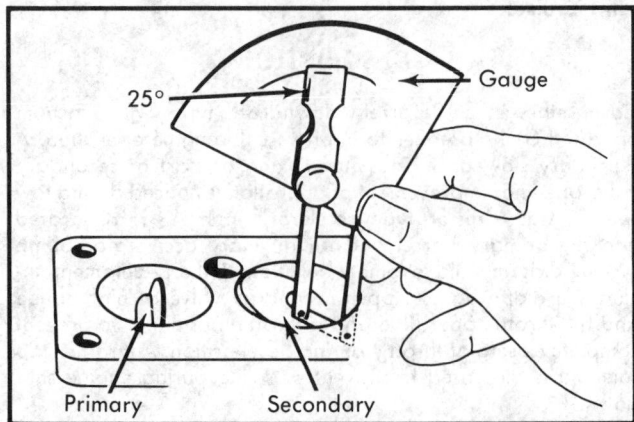

Fig. 6 Adjusting Secondary Throttle Opening Angle (Kick-Up)

OVERHAUL

NOTE — It is recommended that Toyota carburetor driver kit 09860-11011 be used during carburetor overhaul.

DISASSEMBLY

Body and Air Horn — Remove pump arm, pump connecting link, choke breaker connecting link, fast idle connecting link and throttle positioner assembly. See Fig. 7. Remove screws securing air horn to carburetor body and carefully lift off air horn assembly.

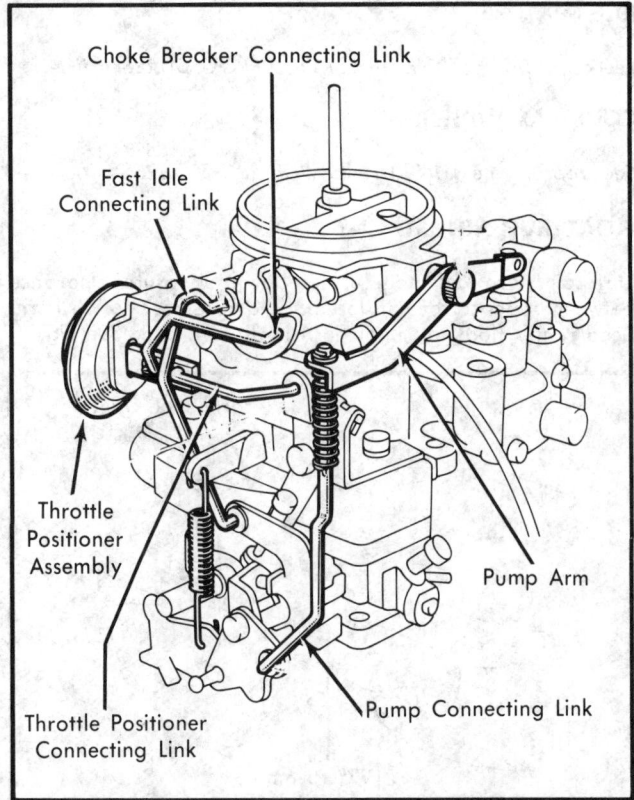

Fig. 7 Air Horn and Carburetor Body

AISAN 2-BARREL — TOYOTA 2F ENGINE (Cont.)

Air Horn — 1) Remove float assembly, needle valve and seat and pump plunger. Remove power piston retaining screw and retaining clip, then remove power piston and spring. Remove fuel shut-off solenoid. *See Fig. 8.*

NOTE — *Perform step 2 only if required.*

2) File off peened part of valve set screw and remove choke valve. Disconnect choke shaft return spring and pull out choke shaft.

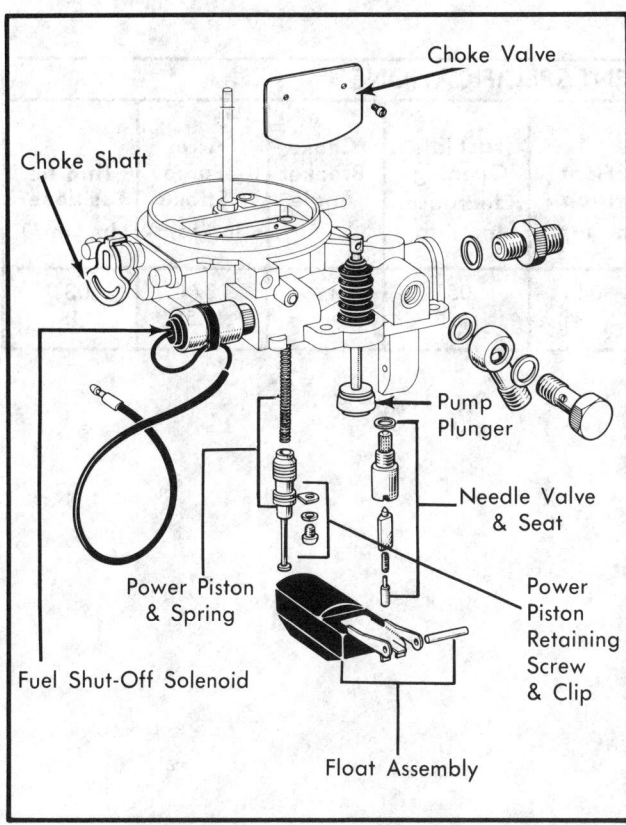

Fig. 8 *Exploded View of Air Horn Assembly*

Body Parts — 1) Remove pump outlet check ball and spring, pump dampening spring and inlet check ball and slow metering jets. *See Fig. 9.*

2) Loosen auxiliary accelerator pump (AAP) outlet screw plug, then remove outlet spring and check ball. Loosen AAP inlet screw plug, then remove check ball. Note size of check balls for reassembly reference.

3) Remove power valve. Remove primary and secondary main jet plugs and jets. Remove primary (triple venturi) and secondary (double venturi) venturi. Remove AAP diaphragm without turning adjusting screw. Remove secondary throttle valve diaphragm. Remove flange from carburetor body.

Flange Parts — Remove only those parts which are necessary for proper cleaning and inspection.

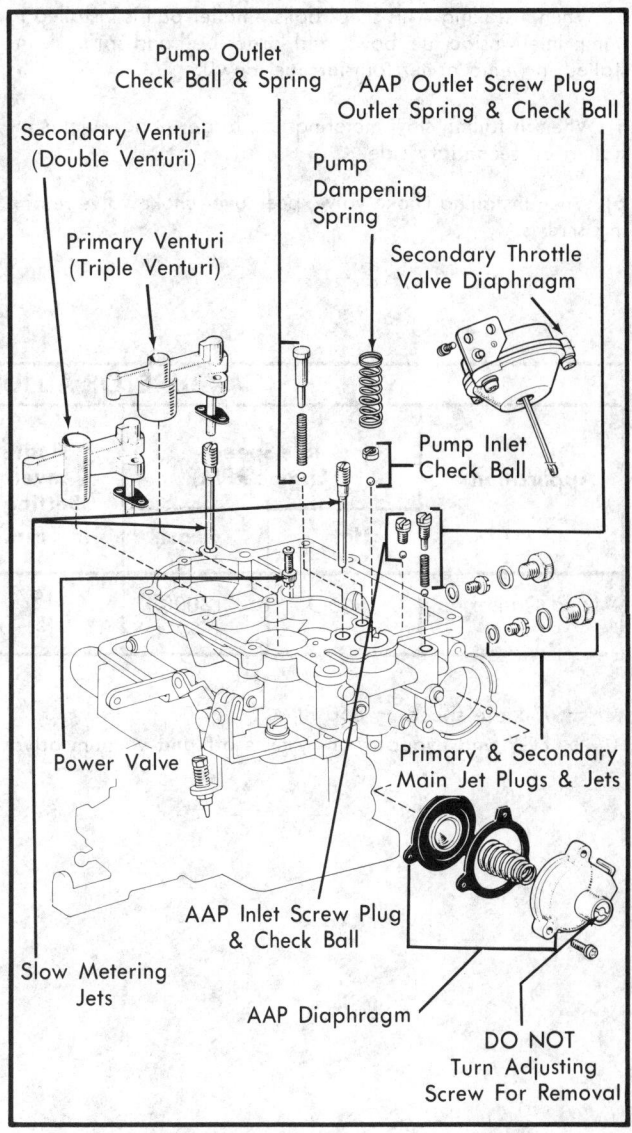

Fig. 9 *Exploded View of Carburetor Body Parts*

CLEANING & INSPECTION

Clean all parts in suitable solvent (carburetor cleaner) and blow dry. Do not attempt to clean jets or other passages with wire or other metal objects. Inspect all parts for wear or damage and replace necessary parts.

REASSEMBLY

1) When assembling AAP diaphragm, spring should be installed with small end away from diaphragm or toward cover.

2) When installing venturi, primary venturi is triple venturi and secondary is double venturi.

3) When installing primary and secondary main jets, primary jet is "brass" colored and secondary jet is "chrome" colored.

1980 Aisan Carburetors

AISAN 2-BARREL — TOYOTA 2F ENGINE (Cont.)

4) When installing AAP check balls, smaller ball is installed in pump inlet (inside fuel bowl) and larger ball and spring is installed in pump outlet (outside fuel bowl).

5) When installing slow metering jets, larger (longer) jet is installed on secondary side.

6) When installing choke valve, peen over choke valve retaining screws.

7) Make sure power piston operates smoothly after installing retaining clip and screw.

8) Make sure that needle valve, spring and plunger are properly installed in correct order. Float must be correctly adjusted.

9) When installing air horn to main body, take care not to damage pump plunger leather.

	CARBURETOR ADJUSTMENT SPECIFICATIONS							
Application	Idle Speed (Engine RPM)		Float Level Setting In. (mm)	Float Drop In. (mm)	Fast Idle Opening Clearance In. (mm)	Choke Breaker Angle	Accel. Pump Stroke In. (mm)	Throttle Positioner In. (mm)
	Hot	Fast						
Land Cruiser	800①	1800②	.197 (5)	.043 (1.1)	.051 (1.3)	45°	.374 (9.5)	.031 (.8)

① — Mixture speed — 850 RPM.
② — EGR and evaporation systems off and vacuum advance cut.

HITACHI DCG 306, DCH 306, DCJ 306 & DCP 306 2 BARREL

Datsun 210 & 310
Mazda GLC
Subaru

DESCRIPTION

Carburetor is a two barrel downdraft design with primary and secondary throttle systems. A choke valve and idle circuit are used in primary system only. Both primary and secondary venturis have main fuel nozzles. When the primary throttle valve is nearly wide open, secondary throttle valve begins to open. An auxiliary throttle valve, located above secondary throttle valve, provides smooth operation as secondary begins to open. A mechanical accelerator pump and vacuum operated power valve are used for increased fuel requirements. An anti-dieseling solenoid valve is used to stop fuel flow in idle circuit (on some models) when the ignition switch is turned off. To control exhaust emissions, Subaru uses a coasting by-pass system, Mazda an anti-afterburn valve and throttle opener system, and Datsun uses a throttle opener control system (except on California models). All models use an electric choke system. Some models use an altitude compensation device to maintain optimum air/fuel ratio at higher altitudes as the air becomes less dense.

CARBURETOR IDENTIFICATION

Hitachi Carb. No.

Application	Man. Trans.	Auto. Trans.
Datsun		
210 Models		
1237 cc		
Federal	DCH306-105	
Calif.	DCH306-115	
1397 cc		
Federal	DCH306-100	
Calif.	DCH306-110	
1488 cc		
Federal		DCH306-101
Calif.		DCH306-111
310 Models		
1397 cc		
Federal	DCH306-102	
Calif.	DCH306-112	
Mazda GLC	DCG306	DCG306
Subaru		
Federal	①DCP306-4	②DCP306-3
	③DCJ306-15	④DCP306-5
Calif.	DCP306-1	DCP306-2

① — Hatchback, Sedan and Hardtop.
② — Except Station Wagon.
③ — Except Hatchback, Sedan and Hardtop.
④ — Station Wagon only.

ADJUSTMENTS

HOT (SLOW) IDLE RPM

See appropriate TUNE-UP SERVICE PROCEDURES article.

IDLE MIXTURE

See appropriate TUNE-UP SERVICE PROCEDURES article.

COLD (FAST) IDLE RPM

See appropriate TUNE-UP SERVICE PROCEDURES article.

FLOAT LEVEL

NOTE — *Float level may be checked through the sight glass of the float chamber. If fuel is not within .06" (1.5 mm) of the mark with engine idling, remove air horn and proceed according to the following steps.*

1) With air horn removed and inverted, raise float and lower it slowly until it just touches needle valve. Measure distance between float and air horn gasket surface (gasket removed).

2) Bend tang to adjust to specifications. *See Carburetor Adjustment Specifications table for correct specifications.*

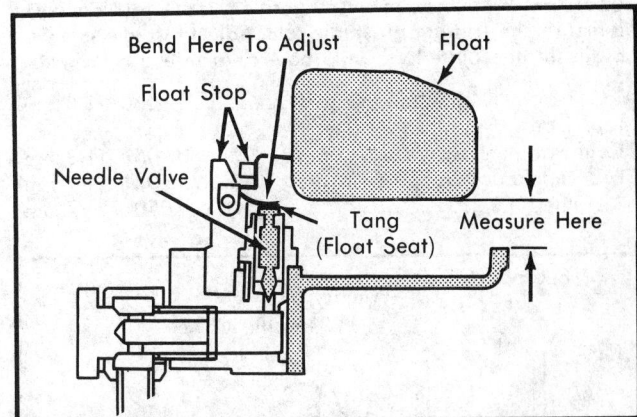

Fig. 1 *Float Level Measurement and Adjustment Points*

FLOAT DROP

After checking float level, raise float until float stop contacts air horn projection. With float held up in this position, measure clearance between float tang and needle valve seat. If clearance is not to specifications, adjust by bending float stop. *See Carburetor Adjustment Specifications table for correct specifications.*

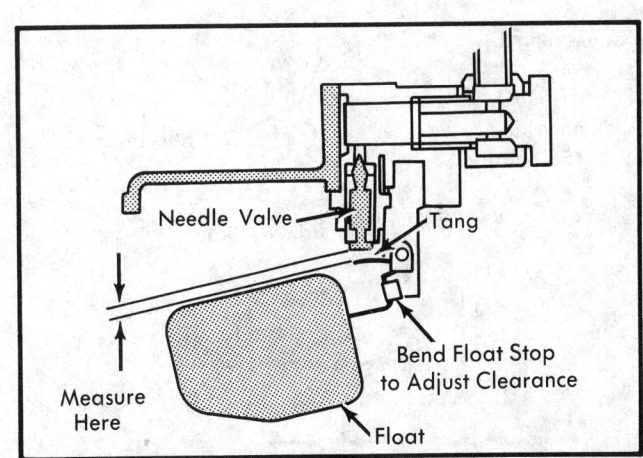

Fig. 2 *Float Drop Measurement and Adjustment Points*

HITACHI DCG 306, DCH 306, DCJ 306 & DCP 306 2-BARREL (Cont.)

FAST IDLE (OFF CAR)

Datsun — With choke cover removed, place fast idle adjusting screw on second step of fast idle cam and measure clearance between primary throttle plate and throttle bore. See *Fig. 3*. To adjust, turn fast idle screw to the following specifications:

DCH306-105 .... .025-.032" (.63-.80 mm)
DCH306-101 and DCH306-111 .... .039-.046" (.98-1.17 mm)
DCH306-100, DCH306-102,
  and DCH306-112 .... .028-.035" (.72-.89 mm)

Mazda — Ensure that long arm of cam lever is on high (first) step of fast idle cam and hold choke fully in closed position. Measure clearance of .054" (1.37 mm) between throttle plate and bore wall. If necessary to adjust, turn screw clockwise to increase or counterclockwise to decrease clearance.

Subaru — With choke in closed position, place fast idle lever on first (highest) step of fast idle cam. Adjust fast idle screw to obtain throttle plate-to-throttle bore clearance as follows:

Auto. Trans. .... .060" (1.5 mm)
Man. Trans.
  Calif. .... .052" (1.3 mm)
  Fed. Hatchback, Sedan & Hardtop .... .041" (1.1 mm)
  All Others .... .050" (1.27 mm)

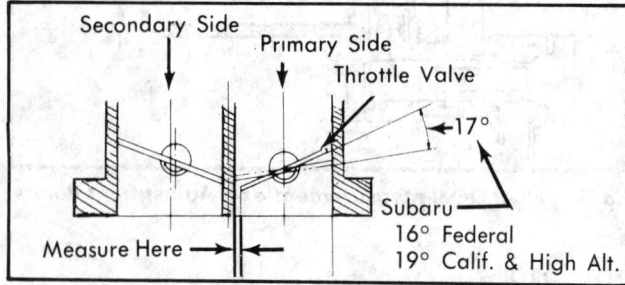

Fig. 3   Fast Idle Bench Adjustment

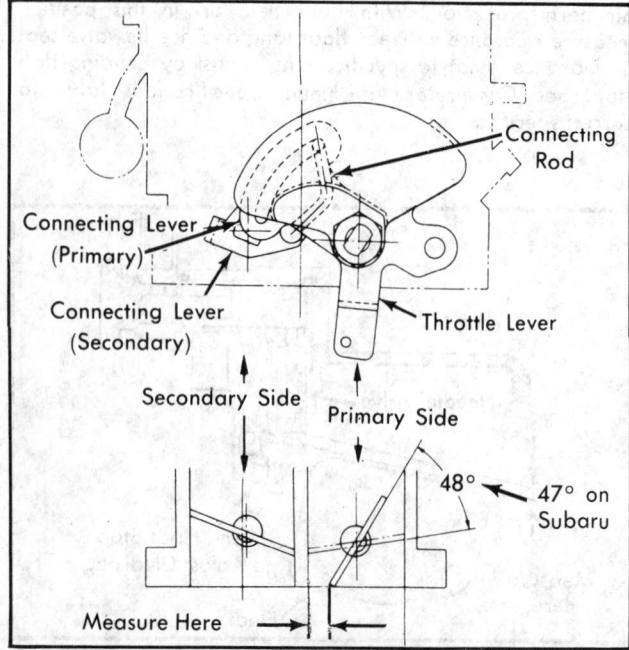

Fig. 4 Secondary Throttle Initial Opening Adjustment

SECONDARY THROTTLE INITIAL OPENING

All Models — With primary-to-secondary throttle connecting rod contacting end of slot in primary throttle lever, measure clearance between primary throttle plate and bore. If adjustment is necessary, bend connecting rod to obtain specified clearance. See *Carburetor Adjustment Specifications* table for correct specifications. See *Fig. 4*.

VACUUM BREAK

All Models — Open throttle and close choke. Release throttle lever first, to trap choke closed. Remove choke cover, and using rubber band, hold choke valve closed. Manually pull vacuum break diaphragm stem out fully (keep straight) in order to compress diaphragm. Measure clearance between choke valve and air horn wall. If adjustment is necessary, bend vacuum break connecting rod. See *Fig. 5*.

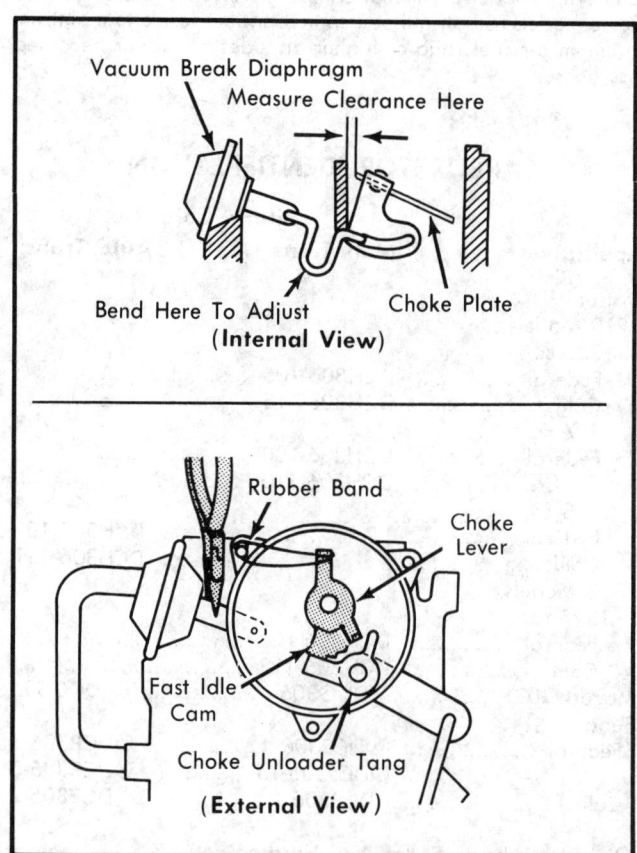

Fig. 5   Vacuum Break Adjustment

CHOKE UNLOADER

All Models — Open throttle valve to wide open position. Hold choke valve closed with rubber band (see *Fig. 9*). With throttle wide open and choke closed with rubber band, measure clearance between choke valve and air horn wall. If adjustment is necessary, bend choke unloader tang. See *Carburetor Adjustment Specifications Table* for correct specifications. See *Fig. 9*.

HITACHI DCG 306, DCH 306, DCJ 306 & DCP 306 2-BARREL (Cont.)

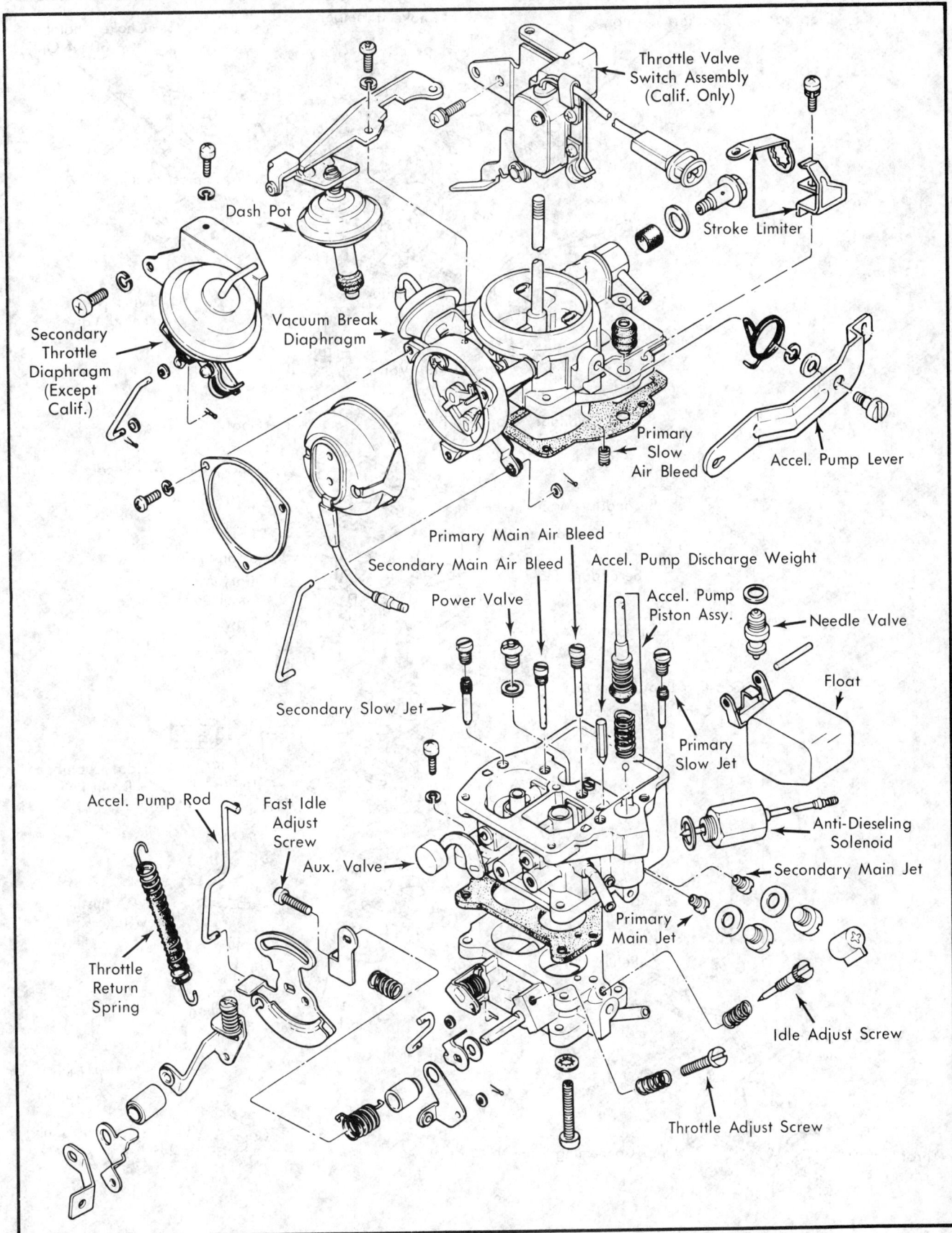

Throttle Valve Switch Assembly (Calif. Only)

Stroke Limiter

Dash Pot

Secondary Throttle Diaphragm (Except Calif.)

Vacuum Break Diaphragm

Primary Slow Air Bleed

Accel. Pump Lever

Primary Main Air Bleed

Secondary Main Air Bleed

Accel. Pump Discharge Weight

Power Valve

Accel. Pump Piston Assy.

Needle Valve

Float

Secondary Slow Jet

Primary Slow Jet

Anti-Dieseling Solenoid

Accel. Pump Rod

Fast Idle Adjust Screw

Aux. Valve

Secondary Main Jet

Primary Main Jet

Throttle Return Spring

Idle Adjust Screw

Throttle Adjust Screw

Fig. 6 *Exploded View of Datsun 210 and 310 Hitachi DCH 306 Carburetor*

1980 Hitachi Carburetors

HITACHI DCG 306, DCH 306, DCJ 306 & DCP 306 2-BARREL (Cont.)

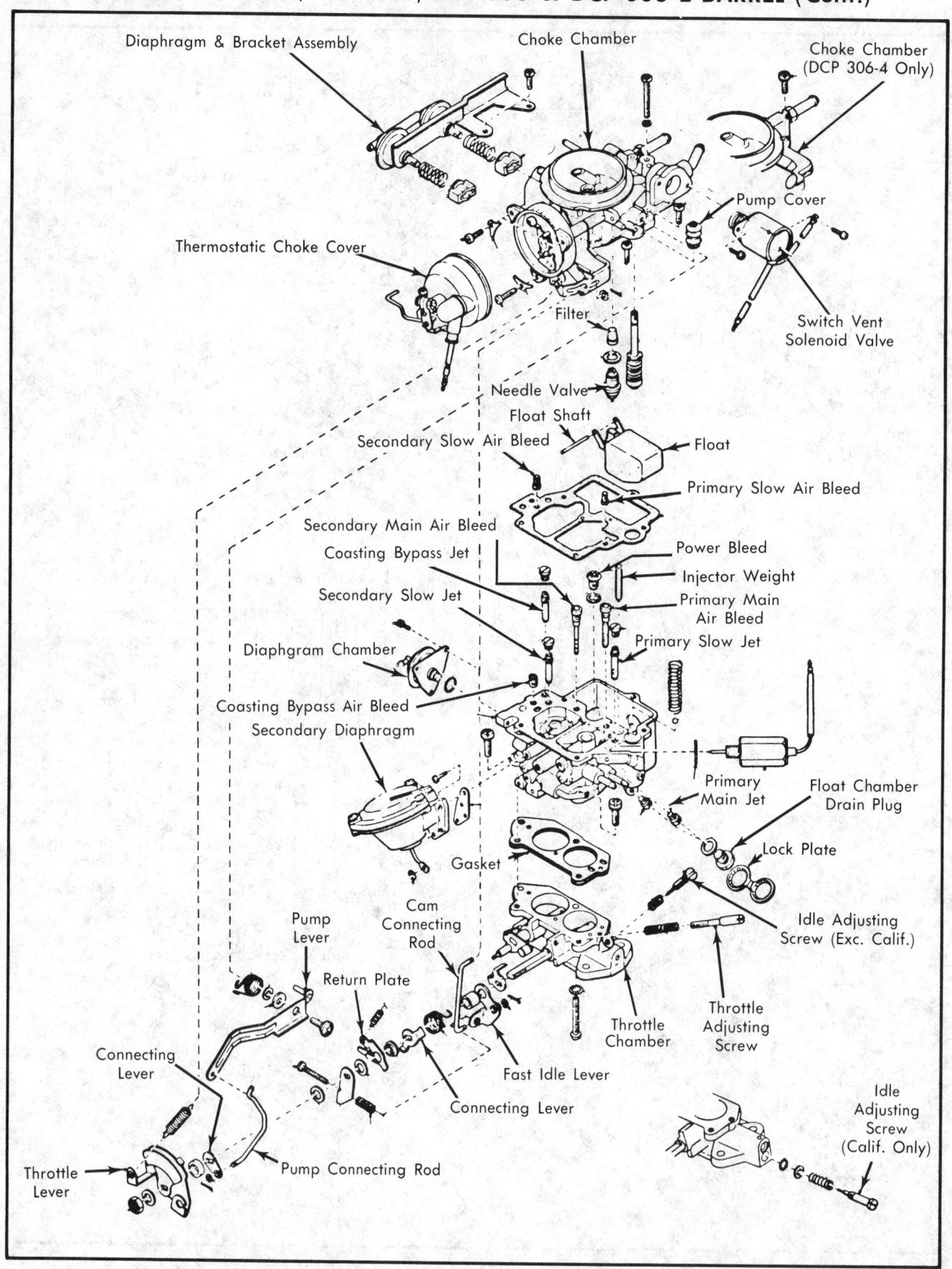

Fig. 7 Exploded View of Subaru Hitachi DCP 306 Carburetor (DCJ 306 Similar)

HITACHI DCG 306, DCH 306, DCJ 306 & DCP 306 2-BARREL (Cont.)

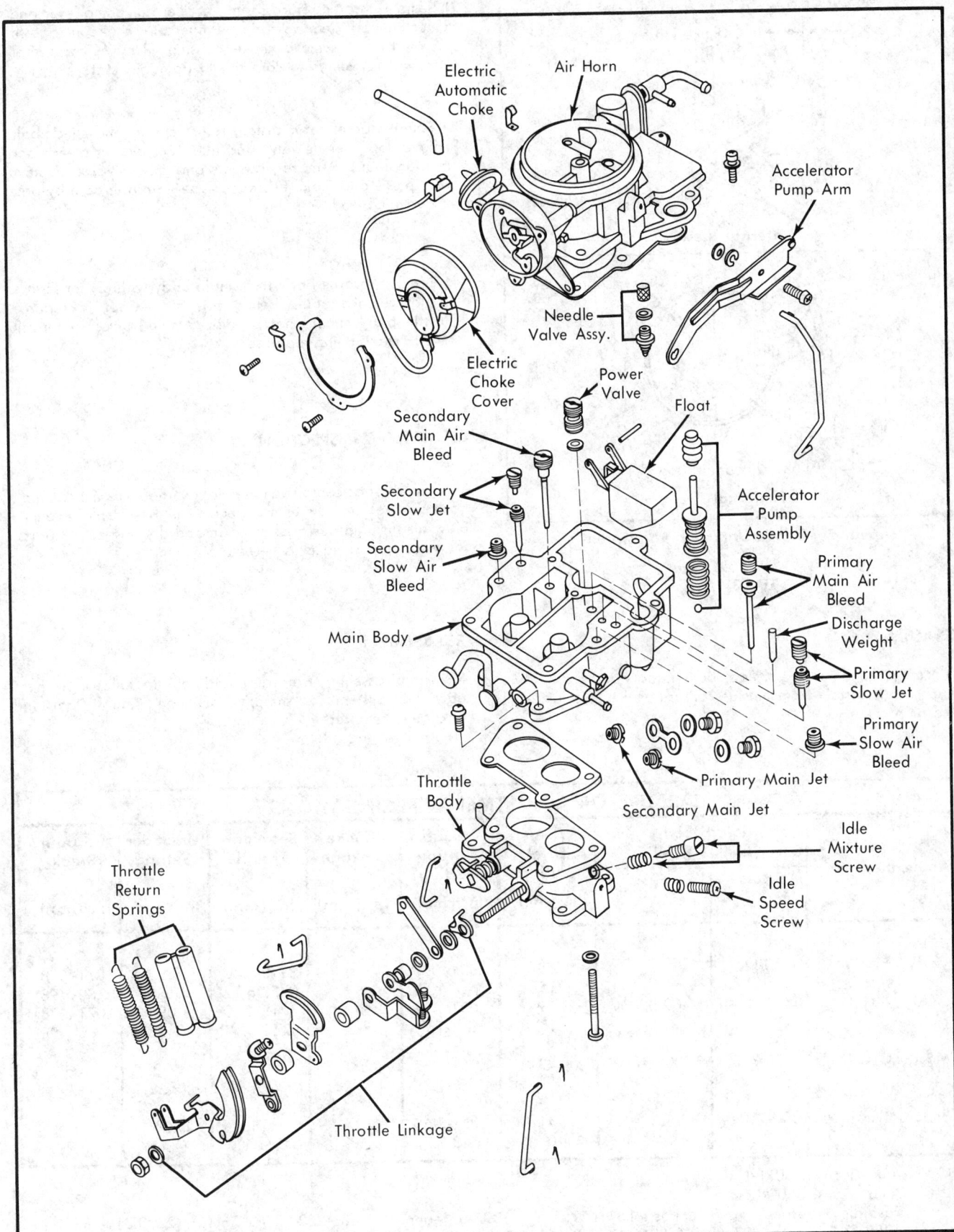

Electric Automatic Choke

Air Horn

Accelerator Pump Arm

Needle Valve Assy.

Electric Choke Cover

Power Valve

Float

Accelerator Pump Assembly

Secondary Main Air Bleed

Secondary Slow Jet

Secondary Slow Air Bleed

Main Body

Primary Main Air Bleed

Discharge Weight

Primary Slow Jet

Primary Slow Air Bleed

Primary Main Jet

Secondary Main Jet

Throttle Body

Idle Mixture Screw

Idle Speed Screw

Throttle Return Springs

Throttle Linkage

Fig. 8   Exploded View of Mazda GLC Hitachi DCG 306 Carburetor

1980 Hitachi Carburetors

HITACHI DCG 306, DCH 306, DCJ 306 & DCP 306 2-BARREL (Cont.)

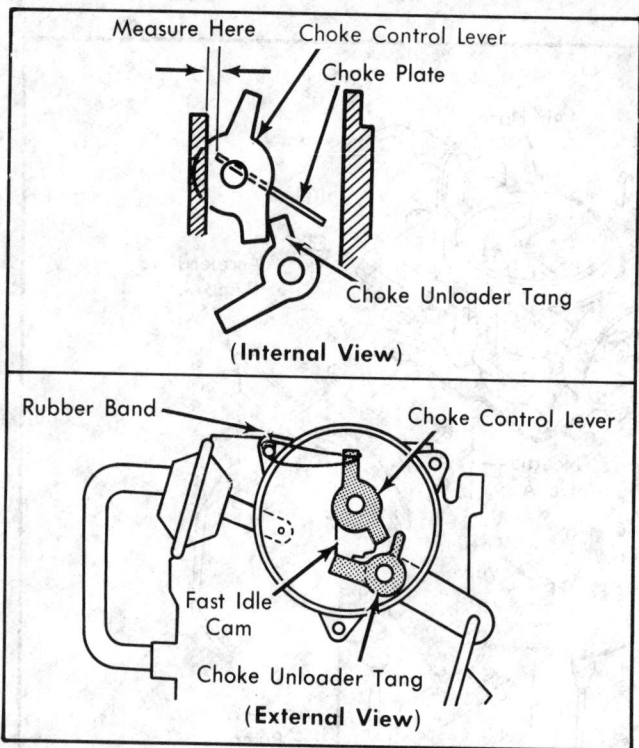

(Internal View)

(External View)

Fig. 9 Choke Unloader Adjustment

OVERHAUL

DISASSEMBLY

1) Main jets and needle valves on both primary and secondary sides are accessible from outside carburetor. Remove for service as necessary.

2) Remove throttle return spring, accelerator pump lever and connecting rod. Remove spring hanger and choke linkage (if equipped) and remove choke housing. Remove carburetor main body cover using care not to damage float.

3) Remove accelerator piston, return spring and check ball. Remove float, needle valve and filter. Remove air bleeds and emulsion tubes. Remove slow jets and power valve. Remove drain plugs and main jets. Remove servo diaphragm by-pass jet and air bleed.

4) Remove throttle body from main body with (3) set screws. Do not remove anti-dieseling solenoid except to replace. Throttle body should not be disassembled unless a throttle valve or rod is being replaced.

CLEANING & INSPECTION

Replace all parts contained in service overhaul kits. Soak metal parts (except anti-dieseling solenoid) in a suitable cleaner. Blow air through passages to clean and dry. Inspect all parts for wear and replace as necessary.

REASSEMBLY

Reverse disassembly procedure and note the following: Check each link system for smooth operation. Adjust float and linkage as required.

Application	Idle Speed (Engine RPM)		Float Level Setting	Float Drop Setting	Choke Linkage	Secondary Throttle	Unloader Setting	Vacuum Break
	Hot	Fast	In. (mm)	In. (mm)	In. (mm)	In. (mm)	In. (mm)	In. (mm)
Datsun 210	700②	③	.59 (15)	.051-.067 (1.3-1.7)	.....	.218-.240 (5.53-6.12)	.093 (2.36)	.071-.078 (1.80-1.98)
310	750	2400-3200④	.59 (15)	.051-.067 (1.3-1.7)	.....	.218-.240 (5.53-6.12)	.093 (2.36)	.071-.078 (1.80-1.98)
Mazda GLC	650-750	3000-4000	.43 (11)	.051-.067 (1.3-1.7)	.....	.240 (6.12)	.09 (2.28)	.05 (1.3)
Subaru	850-950⑤	.....	.41 (10.5)	.051-.067 (1.3-1.7)	.....	.240 (6.12)	.04 (1.11)	.067 (1.7)

CARBURETOR ADJUSTMENT SPECIFICATIONS

① — Auto. Trans. in DRIVE.
② — Auto. Trans. 650 RPM.
③ — Fast idle on second step of cam as follows: 1237 cc & 1397 cc Federal — 2400-3200 RPM, Calif. — 2300-3100 RPM; 1488 cc Federal — 2700-3500 RPM, Calif. — 2600-3400 RPM.
④ — Calif. Models — 2300-3100 RPM.
⑤ — Hatchback, Sedan and Hardtop — 750-850 RPM.

HITACHI DCH 340 2-BARREL

Datsun Pickup
LUV Pickup

DESCRIPTION

Carburetor is a 2-barrel downdraft type equipped with piston type accelerator pump. Carburetor consists of low speed (primary) barrel and high speed (secondary) barrel integrated into a single unit with common fuel bowl. Secondary throttle is actuated by vacuum diaphragm when primary throttle is opened a predetermined amount. Additional equipment includes an anti-dieseling solenoid, electric choke, by-pass air control valve (Datsun), coasting richer solenoid (LUV), idle compensator (Datsun), dashpot (Calif. Auto. Trans. Datsun), and an altitude compensator (Calif. Datsun).

CARBURETOR IDENTIFICATION

	Carburetor No.	
Application	Man. Trans.	Auto. Trans.
Datsun Pickup		
Federal	DCH340-113	DCH340-114
Calif.	DCH340-111	DCH340-112
LUV Pickup		
Federal	DCH340-207	DCH340-208
Calif.	DCH340-209	DCH340-210

ADJUSTMENTS

HOT (SLOW) IDLE RPM

See appropriate TUNE-UP SERVICE PROCEDURES article.

IDLE MIXTURE

See appropriate TUNE-UP SERVICE PROCEDURES article.

COLD (FAST) IDLE RPM

See appropriate TUNE-UP SERVICE PROCEDURES article.

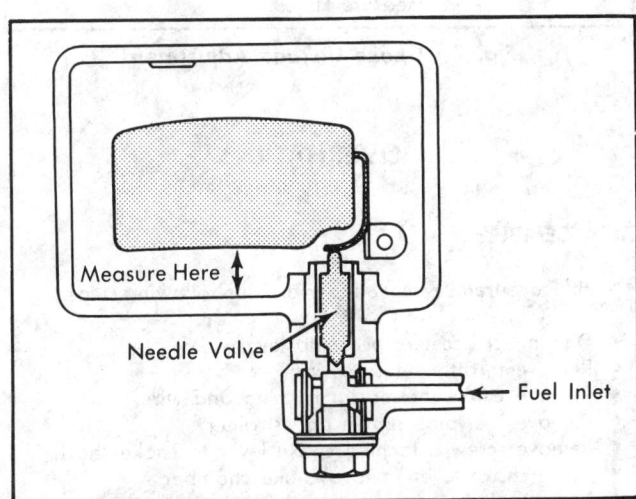

Fig. 1   Float Level Measurement Point

FLOAT LEVEL

NOTE – Fuel bowl is equipped with a sight glass. Line on sight glass indicates proper fuel level. If adjustment must be made to correct improper level, use following procedure.

Datsun – With sight glass removed and carburetor main body inverted, measure distance from top of float to top of float bowl. Set clearance to .283" (7.2 mm) by bending float tang. See Fig. 1.

LUV – With sight glass removed and carburetor main body inverted, bend float tang until float is parallel with top of float bowl.

FLOAT DROP

With float bowl removed and held upright, measure clearance between needle valve and float tang. If clearance is not .059" (1.5 mm), adjustment will be necessary. Adjust by bending float tang which contacts needle valve. See Fig. 2.

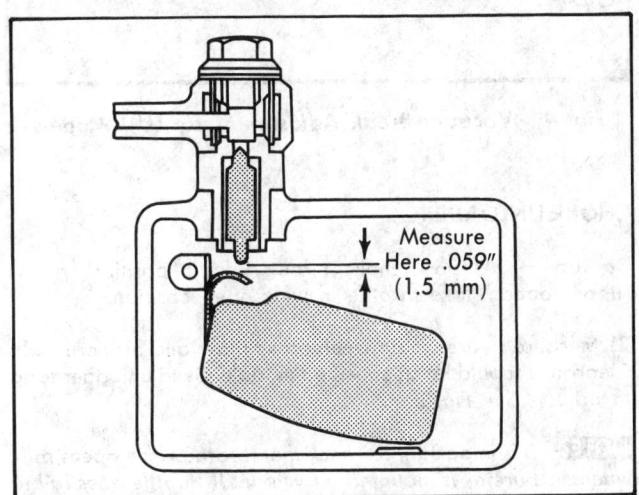

Fig. 2   Float Drop Measurement Point

VACUUM BREAK

Datsun – Close choke and hold closed with rubber band stretched between choke piston and stationary part of car-

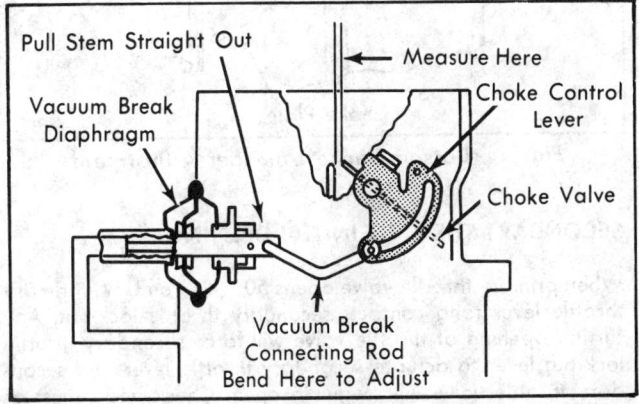

Fig. 3   Vacuum Break Adjustment for Datsun Models

1980 Hitachi Carburetors

HITACHI DCH 340 2-BARREL (Cont.)

buretor. Grip stem of vacuum break diaphragm and pull straight outward (stem extended). Adjust gap between choke plate and air horn wall to .109" (2.76 mm) by bending vacuum break rod. See Fig. 3.

LUV — Fully depress vacuum break diaphragm stem and measure distance between choke plate and air horn wall. Adjust gap to .11-.29" (2.7-3.5 mm) by bending vacuum break rod. See Fig. 4.

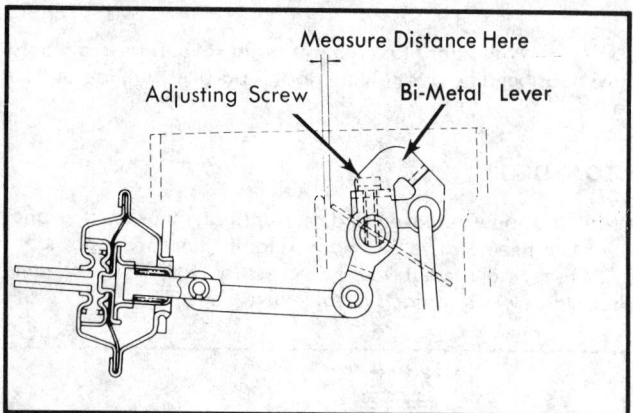

Fig. 4   Vacuum Break Adjustment for LUV Models

CHOKE UNLOADER

Datsun — **1)** Close choke plate. Hold in position with a rubber band. Place throttle in wide open position.

2) Measure clearance between choke plate and air horn wall. Clearance should be as specified in table. Bend unloader tang to adjust. See Fig. 5.

NOTE — It is important to check that throttle valve opens fully when carburetor is mounted on vehicle. If throttle does fail to open, unloader becomes inoperative.

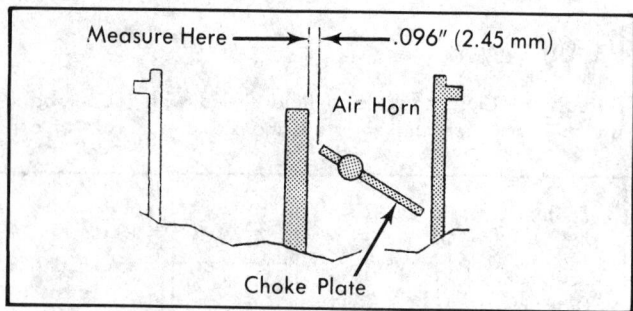

Fig. 5   Datsun Choke Unloader Adjustment

SECONDARY THROTTLE INITIAL OPENING

When primary throttle valve opens 50° (47° on LUV), primary throttle lever tang contacts secondary throttle lock-out. Any further opening of throttle valve will force secondary throttle lock-out lever to actuate secondary throttle lever and secondary throttle valve will begin to open. Check and adjust as follows:

Open primary throttle valve until it is observed that secondary is just begining to open. Hold throttle in this position and measure clearance between primary throttle valve and throttle bore. If clearance is not to specifications, adjust by bending primary throttle tang. See Fig. 6.

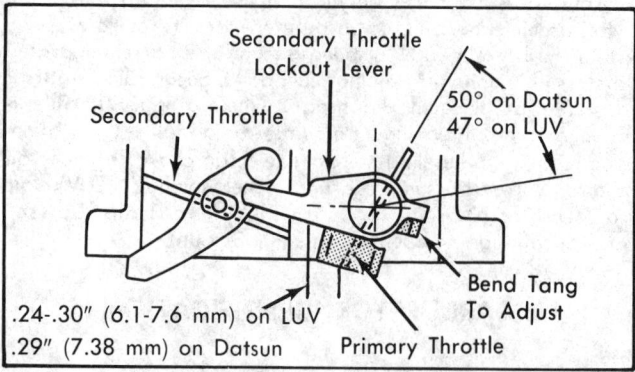

Fig. 6   Secondary Throttle Initial Opening Adjustment

CHOKE LINKAGE (FAST IDLE BENCH)

With fast idle speed screw on 1st step of fast idle cam (2nd on Datsun), invert carburetor and close choke valve. Measure clearance (angle) between throttle plate and throttle bore. If adjustment is necessary, turn fast idle speed screw. Set clearance to .032-.037" (.81-.95 mm) on Datsun Man. Trans. or .040-.046" (1.02-1.17 mm) on Datsun Auto. Trans. Set angle to 16-18° on LUV. See Fig. 7.

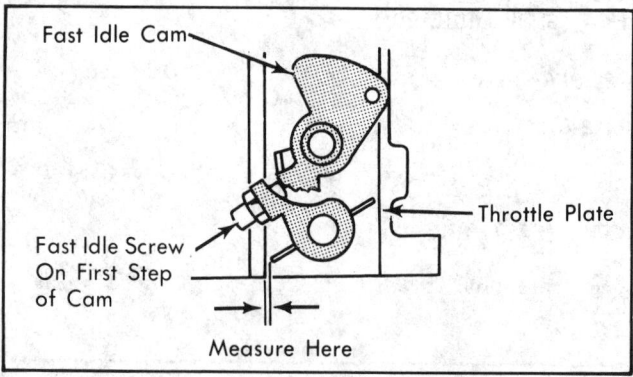

Fig. 7   Choke Linkage Adjustment

OVERHAUL

DISASSEMBLY

1) With carburetor removed, perform the following steps:

- Disconnect accelerator pump lever.
- Remove throttle return spring.
- Remove choke thermostat housing and wire.
- Remove fuel pipe nipple and strainer.
- Remove screw attaching choke lever to choke shaft.
- Move choke lever toward choke chamber.
- Remove choke connecting rod from counter lever.
- Disconnect vacuum hose from float chamber.

HITACHI DCH 340 2-BARREL (Cont.)

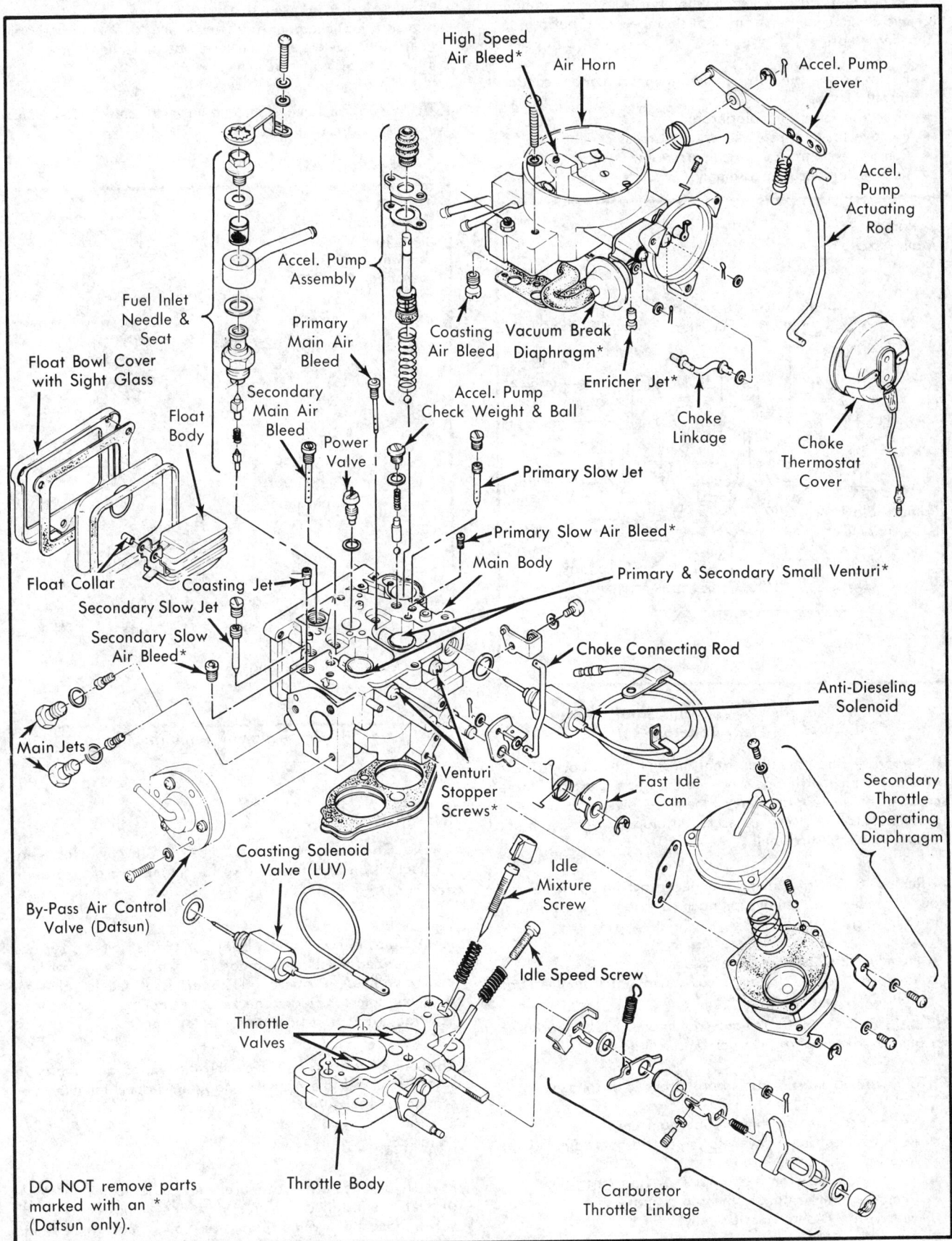

High Speed Air Bleed*

Air Horn

Accel. Pump Lever

Accel. Pump Actuating Rod

Accel. Pump Assembly

Primary Main Air Bleed

Fuel Inlet Needle & Seat

Coasting Air Bleed

Vacuum Break Diaphragm*

Float Bowl Cover with Sight Glass

Secondary Main Air Bleed

Accel. Pump Check Weight & Ball

Enricher Jet*

Choke Linkage

Choke Thermostat Cover

Float Body

Power Valve

Primary Slow Jet

Float Collar

Coasting Jet

Primary Slow Air Bleed*

Main Body

Primary & Secondary Small Venturi*

Secondary Slow Jet

Secondary Slow Air Bleed*

Choke Connecting Rod

Anti-Dieseling Solenoid

Main Jets

Venturi Stopper Screws*

Fast Idle Cam

Secondary Throttle Operating Diaphragm

By-Pass Air Control Valve (Datsun)

Coasting Solenoid Valve (LUV)

Idle Mixture Screw

Idle Speed Screw

Throttle Valves

Throttle Body

Carburetor Throttle Linkage

DO NOT remove parts marked with an * (Datsun only).

Fig. 8   Exploded View of Hitachi DCH Carburetor Assembly

1980 Hitachi Carburetors

HITACHI DCH 340 2-BARREL (Cont.)

2) Remove bolts attaching choke chamber from float chamber. Remove choke chamber from float chamber, then perform the following steps:

- Remove cotter pin between diaphragm rod and secondary throttle lever.
- Separate lever and diaphragm.
- Remove the two solenoid valve harness clips.
- Remove diaphragm attaching screws.
- Remove diaphragm assembly.

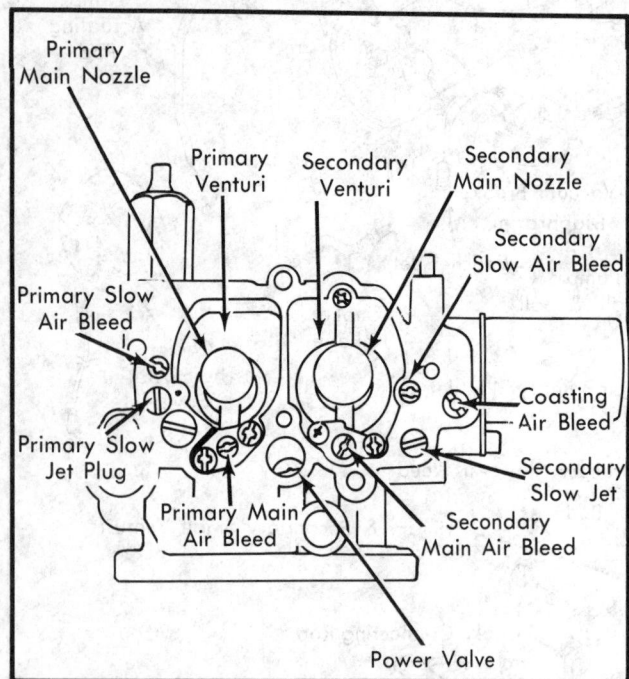

Fig. 9   Location of Jets and Small Venturi in Float Chamber

3) Separate float chamber from throttle valve body. These parts are attached by one screw on the upper part and three screws on the lower part. One of the three lower screws is used to remove the negative pressure developed in the venturi. Remove this screw carefully.

4) Remove accelerator pump plunger attaching screws. Invert float chamber and remove plunger assembly. Then perform the following:

- Remove float needle valve assembly.
- Remove float level gauge cover. Do not lose the float collar.

CAUTION — DO NOT remove automatic choke body or vacuum break diaphragm from Datsun models.

5) To disassemble rest of carburetor, proceed as follows:

- Remove screws attaching diaphragm cover.
- Remove diaphragm cover, spring and diaphragm. Do not lose ball and small spring.
- Remove all jets from upper part of float chamber.
- Remove small venturi from both primary and secondary venturi (on Federal models only).
- Invert float chamber.
- Remove small venturi from both primary and secondary venturi (LUV only).

- Remove injector weight plug.
- Invert float chamber and remove injector weight and ball.
- Remove power jet, main jet plugs and main jets.
- Remove primary vacuum jet.

NOTE — Do not remove throttle valves or choke valve unless components are damaged.

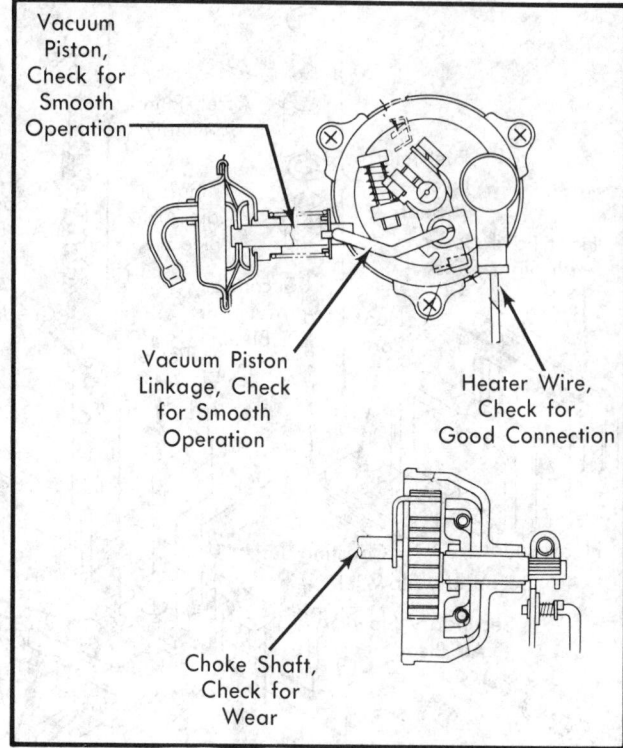

Fig. 10   Inspection of Automatic Choke

INSPECTION

Choke Chamber — Inspect choke shaft holes for wear, vacuum piston and choke valve for smoothness of operation. See Fig. 10.

Float Chamber — Inspect body for cracks, jointing surfaces and threaded holes for damage. Check power valve for leaks and smoothness of operation. Inspect float needle valve and float pin hole for wear. Check accelerator pump plunger for damage, wear and smoothness of operation.

Throttle Chamber — Check throttle valves and shafts for wear, slow and idle ports for clogging. Inspect mixture screw seating and mixture screw for step wear.

REASSEMBLY

Reverse disassembly procedures and note following: Make sure jets are installed in correct positions. If choke and throttle valves have been removed, install valves making necessary adjustments and seal screws with a suitable sealer. Check accelerator pump operation by filling cylinder with gasoline and operating plunger by hand.

HITACHI DCH 340 2-BARREL (Cont.)

Application	Idle Speed (Engine RPM)		Float Level Setting In. (mm)	Float Drop Setting In. (mm)	Choke Linkage Setting In. (mm)	Secondary Throttle In. (mm)	Unloader Setting In. (mm)	Vacuum Break In (mm)
	Hot	**Fast**						
Datsun	600①	1900-2800②	.283 (7.2)	.059 (1.5)	.032-.037③ (.81-.95)	.291 (7.4)	.096 (2.5)	.109 (2.8)
LUV	850④	3400⑤	⑥	.059 (1.5)	16-18°	.24-.30 (6.1-7.6)	.....	.11-.29 (2.7-3.5)

CARBURETOR ADJUSTMENT SPECIFICATIONS

① — Auto. Trans. in "D" range.
② — Auto. Trans. in neutral — 2200-3200 RPM.
③ — Auto. Trans. — .040-.046" (1.02-1.17 mm).
④ — Federal Auto. Trans. — 950 RPM; All Calif. models — 900 RPM.
⑤ — Auto. Trans. — 3200 RPM.
⑥ — Float parallel with top of float bowl. See adjustment procedure.

HITACHI DCR 360 2-BARREL

Datsun 510

DESCRIPTION

Carburetor is a 2-barrel, downdraft type equipped with automatic choke which is heated by an electrically operated bimetal heating coil. A piston type accelerator pump is incorporated into the primary barrel and a high speed enricher system in secondary barrel to improve engine performance during high speed driving. The primary barrel also includes a power valve to supply additional fuel under heavy load driving conditions. Other equipment includes a diaphragm which opens secondary at high speed and full throttle operation; slow economizer for stable low speed performance; anti-dieseling solenoid; dash pot (Auto. Trans.) or fast idle breaker (Man. Trans.) and altitude compensator (Calif.).

CARBURETOR IDENTIFICATION

Application	Carburetor No. Man. Trans.	Auto. Trans.
Datsun 510		
Federal	DCR360-54	DCR360-56
With A/C	DCR360-55	.....
Calif.	DCR360-51	DCR360-53
With A/C	DCR360-52	.....

ADJUSTMENTS

HOT (SLOW) IDLE RPM

See appropriate TUNE-UP SERVICE PROCEDURES article.

IDLE MIXTURE

See appropriate TUNE-UP SERVICE PROCEDURES article.

COLD (FAST) IDLE RPM

See appropriate TUNE-UP SERVICE PROCEDURES article.

FLOAT LEVEL

NOTE — Fuel bowl is equipped with a sight glass. Line on sight glass indicates proper fuel level. If adjustment must be made to correct improper level, use following procedure.

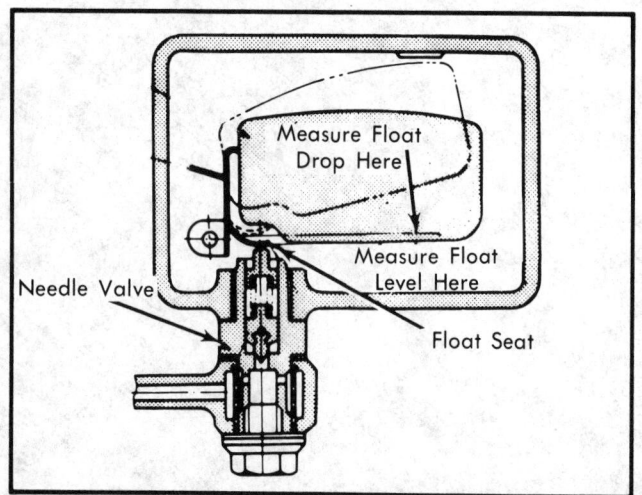

Fig. 1   Float Level and Float Drop Measurement Points

With sight glass removed and carburetor body inverted measure distance from top of float to top of float bowl. Adjust clearance to .283" (7.2 mm) by bending float seat. See Fig. 1.

FLOAT DROP

With float bowl removed, hold float upright and measure clearance between needle valve and float seat. Adjust clearance to .051-.067" (1.3-1.7 mm) by bending float stopper. See Fig. 1.

VACUUM BREAK

NOTE — Vacuum break adjustment must be done when ambient temperature is 77°F (25°C).

Close choke and hold closed with rubber band stretched between choke control lever and stationary part of carburetor. Grip stem of vacuum break diaphragm and pull straight out (stem extended). Adjust gap between choke valve and air horn wall to .103-.127" (2.62-3.22 mm) on Federal or .123-.147" (3.12-3.72 mm) on California, by bending vacuum break rod at existing bend. See Fig. 2.

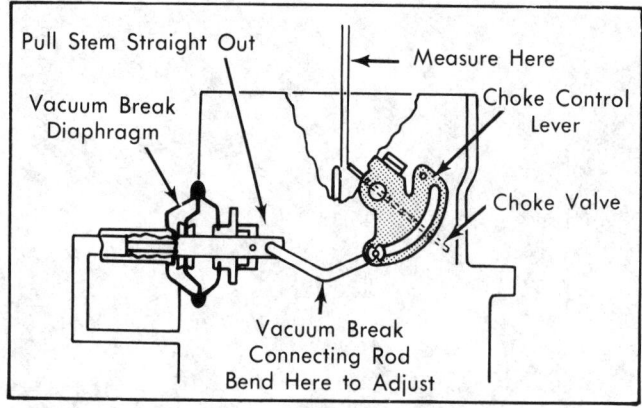

Fig. 2   Vacuum Break Adjustment for Datsun 510

CHOKE UNLOADER

Fully close choke and hold in position with a rubber band. Fully open throttle valve. Adjust clearance between choke valve and air horn wall to .081-.112" (2.05-2.85 mm) by bending unloader tang. See Fig. 3.

NOTE — It is important to check that throttle valve opens fully when carburetor is mounted on vehicle. If throttle fails to open, unloader becomes inoperative.

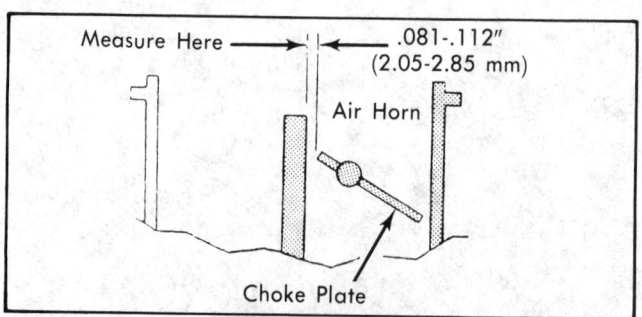

Fig. 3   Adjusting Choke Unloader

HITACHI DCR 360 2-BARREL (Cont.)

SECONDARY THROTTLE INITIAL OPENING

1) When primary throttle valve opens 50°, primary throttle lever tang contacts secondary throttle lock-out. Any further opening of throttle valve will force secondary throttle lock-out lever to actuate secondary throttle lever and secondary throttle valve will begin to open. Check and adjust as follows:

2) Open primary throttle valve until it is observed that secondary is just beginning to open. Hold throttle in this position and measure clearance between primary throttle valve and throttle bore. Adjust clearance to .271-.310" (6.88-7.88 mm) by bending connecting link. See Fig. 4.

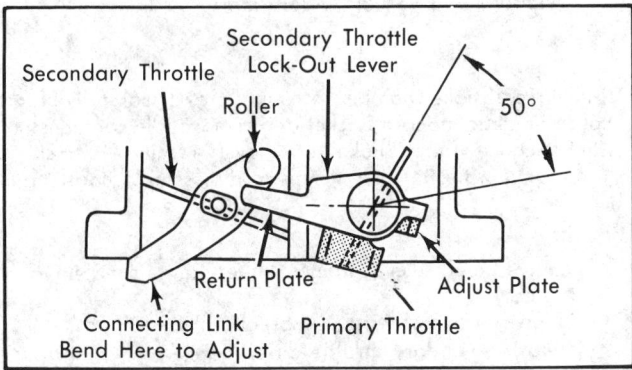

Fig. 4 Secondary Throttle Initial Opening Adjustment

FAST IDLE (BENCH ADJUSTMENT)

With fast idle speed screw on 2nd step of fast idle cam, invert carburetor and close choke valve. Set clearance between throttle valve and throttle bore to .030-.035" (.76-.90 mm) on Man. Trans. or .038-.043" (.96-1.10 mm) on Auto. Trans. by turning fast idle speed screw. See Fig. 5.

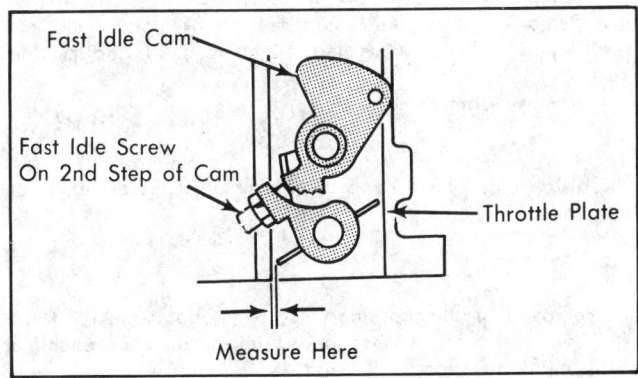

Fig. 5 Fast Idle Adjustment and Measurement Points

AUTOMATIC CHOKE

Choke Mechanism — 1) Before starting cold engine, fully depress and release accelerator. Ensure choke valve is closed and center index mark on bi-metal cover is aligned with center mark on thermostat housing. Check proper electrical connections. Start engine.

2) After warming up engine, ensure choke valve is fully open. If choke heater wiring is normal and choke valve does not fully open, replace bi-metal cover.

Choke Heater Circuit — 1) With engine off, connect ohmmeter to electrical connector under instrument panel. Continuity should exist between terminals "A" and "B". See Fig. 6.

2) Start engine and run at idle speed. Voltmeter should read 12 volts across terminals "A" and "B". If voltage readings are not as described, check for open circuit, faulty connector or faulty choke relay. Replace defective parts.

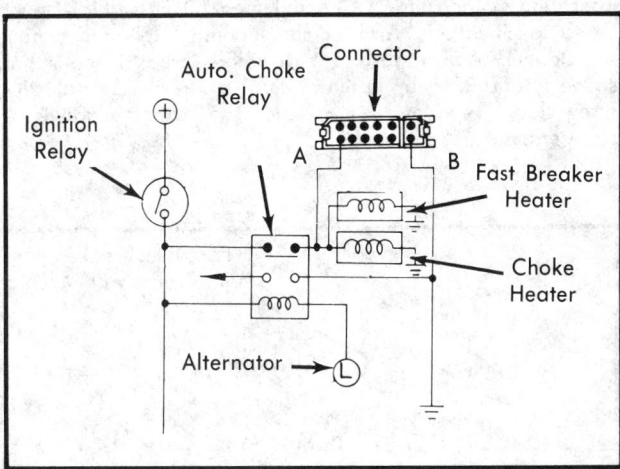

Fig. 6 Checking Choke Heater Circuit

Choke Relay — Remove choke relay from relay bracket near battery. Connect ohmmeter and check continuity between terminals. See Fig. 7. With no battery power applied, continuity should exist between terminals No. 2 and No. 4. Apply battery power to terminals No. 5 and No. 6. Continuity should not exist between terminals No. 2 and No. 4. If relay does not perform as described, replace choke relay.

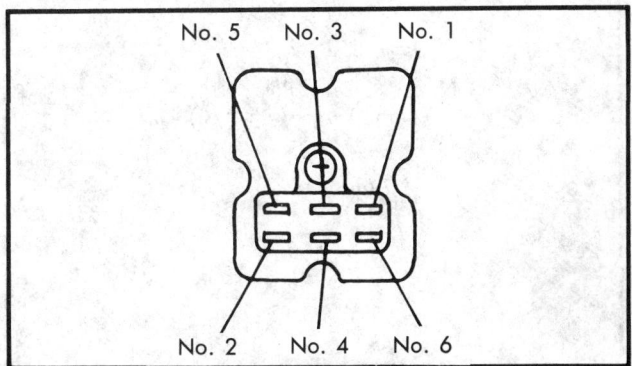

Fig. 7 Checking Automatic Choke Relay

FAST IDLE BREAKER (MAN. TRANS. WITH A/C)

Fast idle breaker is used in conjunction with the automatic choke to gradually decrease engine speed during warm-up mode without touching accelerator. *Test fast idle breaker in same manner as "Dash Pot" in this article. Replace unit as an assembly if defective.*

HITACHI DCR 360 2-BARREL (Cont.)

DASH POT
(AUTO. TRANS. WITH A/C)

Dash Pot Position — With engine at normal operating temperature and idle speed set to specifications, turn air conditioning "OFF". Turn throttle valve by hand and read engine speed when dash pot just touches stopper lever. Adjust position of dash pot until engine speed is 1400-1600 RPM, by turn adjusting screw. When properly adjusted, engine speed should drop from 2000 RPM to 1000 RPM within 3 seconds.

Dash Pot Operating Speed — With engine at normal operating temperature, air conditioning "OFF" and idle speed set to specifications. Turn air conditioning "ON" and remove air cleaner. Adjust dash pot (fast idle breaker) operating speed to 800 RPM, by turning adjusting screw. Turn adjusting screw clockwise to lower engine speed and counterclockwise to raise engine speed. *See Fig. 8.*

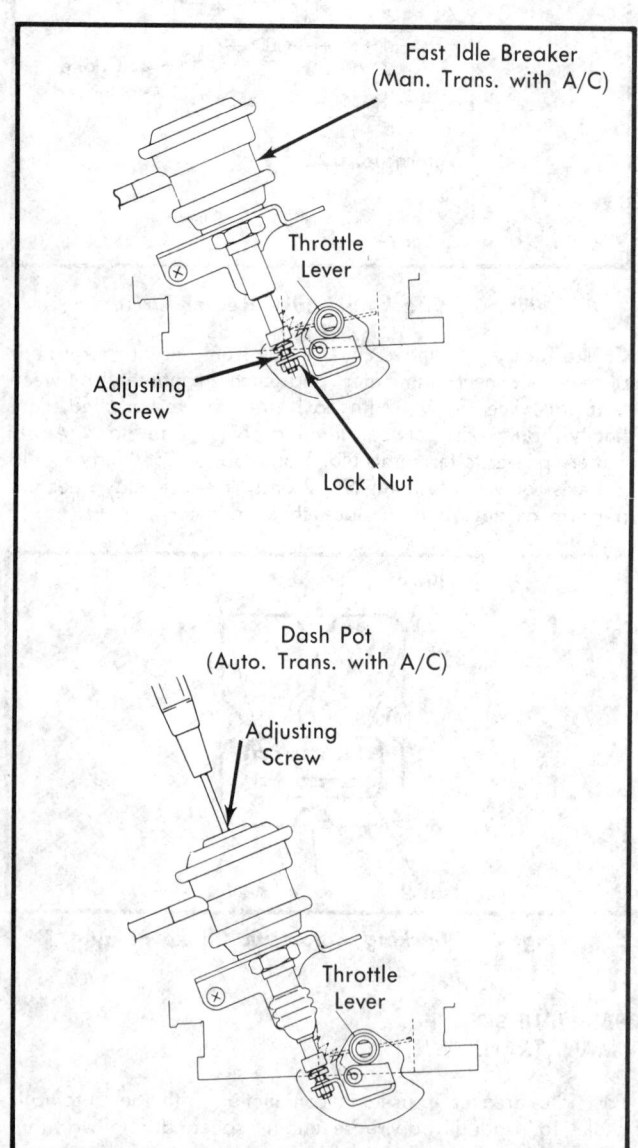

Fig. 8   Adjusting Dashpot (Fast Idle Breaker)

OVERHAUL

DISASSEMBLY

1) With carburetor removed, perform the following steps:

- Disconnect accelerator pump lever and choke connector rod.
- Remove throttle return spring.
- Remove vacuum breaker diaphragm hose.
- Remove choke bi-metal housing, wire, choke lever and cam, thermostat housing, fast idle breaker heater (if equipped) and vacuum diaphragm.

2) Remove 4 choke chamber retaining screws. Carefully lift off choke chamber, discard gasket and remove idle compensator (Calif.), choke plate, choke shaft lever, retainer and choke shaft. Perform the following steps to disassemble float chamber:

- Remove fuel inlet retainer, filter and needle valve assembly.
- Remove dash pot (fast idle breaker), if equipped.
- Remove secondary throttle diaphragm.
- Remove anti-dieseling solenoid.
- Remove by-pass air control valve.
- Remove float level gauge cover. Do not lose float collar.
- Remove float assembly.

3) Remove accelerator pump plunger retaining screws. Invert float chamber and remove plunger assembly. Then perform the following:

- Remove power valve, primary and secondary main air bleeds.
- Remove secondary slow jet plug and jet.
- Remove secondary slow air bleed.
- Remove primary and secondary main jet plugs and jets.
- Remove auxiliary accelerator pump plug and plunger assembly.
- Remove primary slow jet.

CAUTION — *DO NOT remove venturi stopper screws or small venturi.*

4) Remove fast idle cam and throttle linkage. Remove 3 throttle body retaining screws and note position of each for reassembly reference.

NOTE — *One throttle body retaining screw has a hole for fit of power valve mechanism. Note position of this screw for reassembly reference.*

5) Remove throttle adjusting screw and spring. Remove idle limiter cap (blind plug on Calif. models) and remove idle adjusting screw and spring. Remove throttle valves and shaft assemblies.

HITACHI DCR 360 2-BARREL (Cont.)

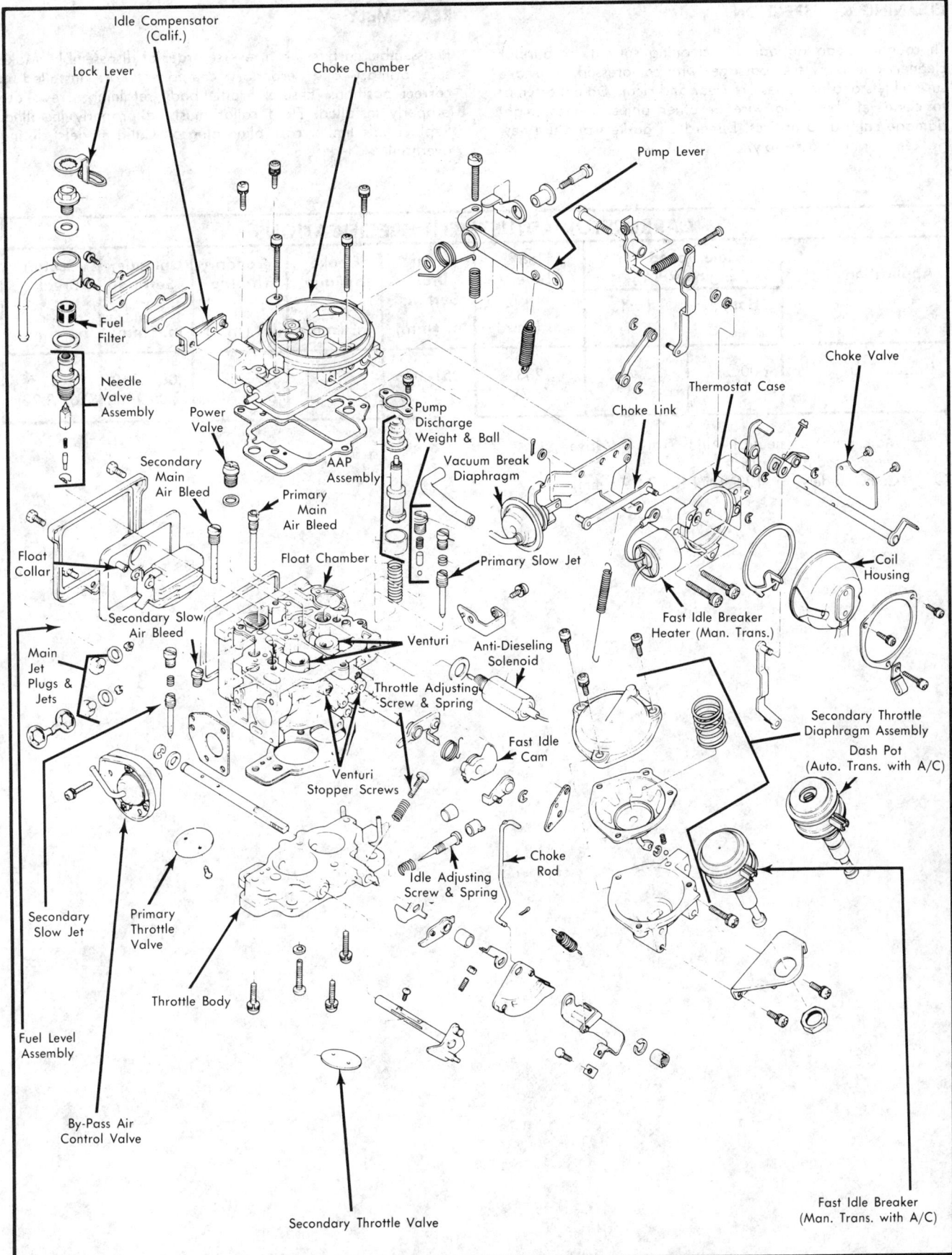

Fig. 9   Exploded View of Hitachi DCR360 2-Barrel Carburetor

1980 Hitachi Carburetors

HITACHI DCR 360 2-BARREL (Cont.)

CLEANING & INSPECTION

Thoroughly clean all parts in cleaning solvent (carburetor cleaner) and blow fuel passages with compressed air. Make sure all jets and passages are clear and clean. Do not attempt to clean jets by using wire or other objects which might damage calibrated orifices. Discard all gaskets and use new gaskets during reassembly.

REASSEMBLY

Reassemble carburetor in reverse order of disassembly. Make sure primary and secondary components are installed in correct positions. Ensure throttle body retaining screws are properly installed. Float collar must be properly installed. Replace idle limiter cap (blind plug on Calif. models) during overhaul.

Application	Idle Speed (Engine RPM)		Float Level Setting	Float Drop Setting	Choke Linkage	Secondary Throttle	Unloader Setting	Vacuum Break
	Hot	Fast	In. (mm)	In. (mm)	In. (mm)	In. (mm)	In. (mm)	In. (mm)
Datsun 510	600①	②	.283 (7.2)	.051-.076 (1.3-1.7)	.....	.271-.310 (6.88-7.88)	.081-.112 (2.05-2.85)	.103-.127③ (2.62-3.22)

CARBURETOR ADJUSTMENT SPECIFICATIONS

① — Man. Trans. in neutral. Auto. Trans. in drive.
② — See procedure in article.
③ — Calif. models — .123-.147" (3.12-3.72 mm)

HITACHI DCS 328 2-BARREL

Ford Courier (2300 cc)

DESCRIPTION

Carburetor is a 2-stage, 2-barrel downdraft type. The primary stage includes a curb idle system, a piston-type accelerator pump system, idle transfer system, main metering system and power enrichment system. The secondary stage includes an idle transfer system and main metering system. An electric heater warms a bi-metal connected to the choke valve, controlling choke valve and throttle valve position automatically. Carburetor also features a coasting richer (deceleration) valve, slow fuel cut valve, secondary throttle diaphragm and dash pot (Calif. Man. Trans.).

CARBURETOR IDENTIFICATION

Application	Carburetor No.
2300 cc	
Federal	DCS328-1
Calif.	
Man. Trans.	DCS328-5
Auto. Trans.	DCS328-6

ADJUSTMENTS

HOT (SLOW) IDLE RPM

See appropriate *TUNE-UP SERVICE PROCEDURES* article.

IDLE MIXTURE

See appropriate *TUNE-UP SERVICE PROCEDURES* article.

COLD (FAST) IDLE RPM

See appropriate *TUNE-UP SERVICE PROCEDURES* article.

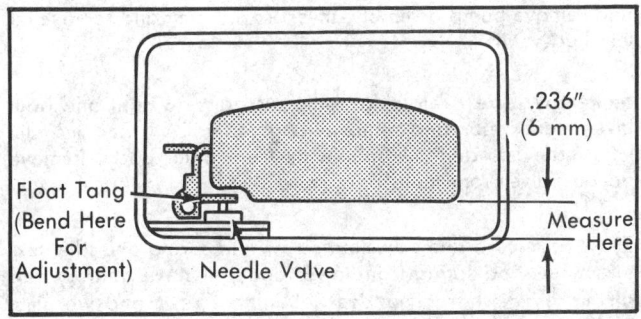

Fig. 1 *Measurement for Float Level Adjustment (Carburetor Upside-Down)*

FLOAT LEVEL

With engine running, check fuel level in bowl sight glass. If fuel level is not within specified range, remove carburetor from engine. Remove fuel bowl cover and invert carburetor. Allow float to lower by its own weight. Measure clearance between float and edge of bowl. If clearance is not to specifications, bend float tang to achieve proper clearance. *See Fig. 1.*

FAST IDLE CAM ADJUSTMENT

Close choke valve fully. Place fast idle screw on the high (1st) step of fast idle cam. Adjust throttle valve opening clearance by turning fast idle adjusting screw clockwise to increase or counterclockwise to decrease the opening clearance. *See Fig. 2.* Clearance should be .058-.066" (1.47-1.67 mm).

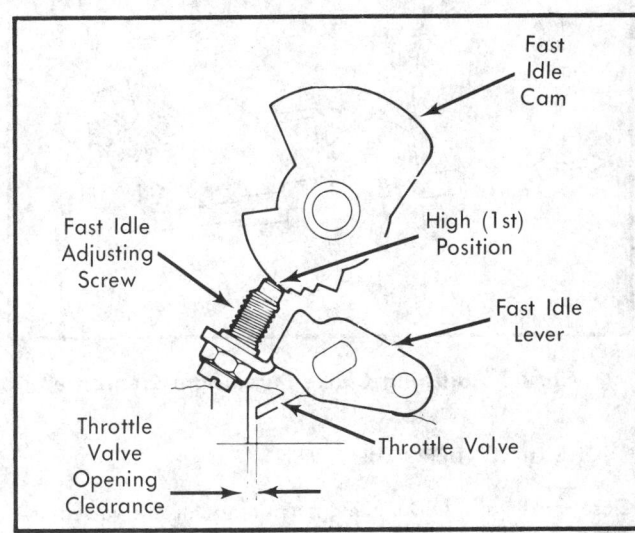

Fig. 2 *Adjusting Fast Idle Cam*

CHOKE VALVE OPENING ANGLE ADJUSTMENT

Adjust fast idle cam. Position fast idle adjusting screw on 2nd step of fast idle cam. *See Fig. 3.* Adjust choke valve opening clearance by bending starting arm. Clearance should be .039-.051" (.99-1.29 mm). If a large adjustment is required, bend choke rod.

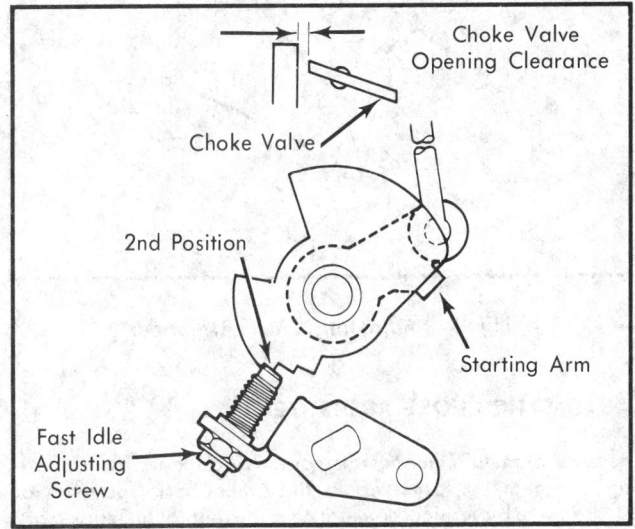

Fig. 3 *Adjusting Choke Valve Opening Clearance*

HITACHI DCS 328 2-BARREL (Cont.)

CHOKE DIAPHRAGM ADJUSTMENT

Apply approximately 15.6" (400 mm) Hg vacuum to choke diaphragm vacuum tube. See *Fig. 4*. Check that fast idle cam is on high (1st) position. Press choke valve slightly, then adjust choke valve opening by bending choke lever. Clearance should be .051-.071" (1.31-1.81 mm).

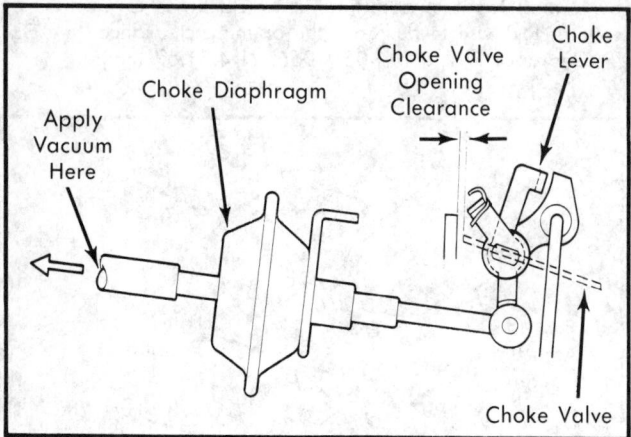

Fig. 4 Adjusting Choke Diaphragm Clearance

CHOKE UNLOADER ADJUSTMENT

Close choke valve fully. Then open primary throttle valve fully. Measure choke valve opening clearance. See *Fig. 5*. Bend unloader adjusting nail to obtain .090-.110" (2.29-2.79 mm) clearance.

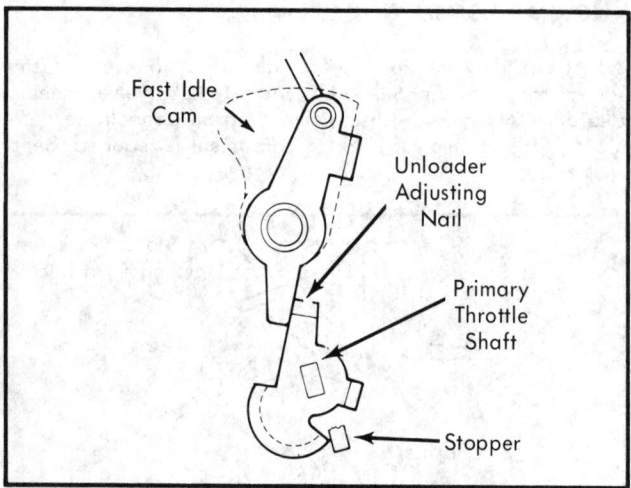

Fig. 5 Adjusting Choke Unloader

AUTOMATIC CHOKE ADJUSTMENT

Be sure bi-metal (thermostat) cover is positioned over choke arm so bi-metal spring hooks the arm. Check operation of choke valve by turning bi-metal cover. To set, align index mark on bi-metal cover with center mark on choke housing. Tighten attaching screws. See *Fig. 6*.

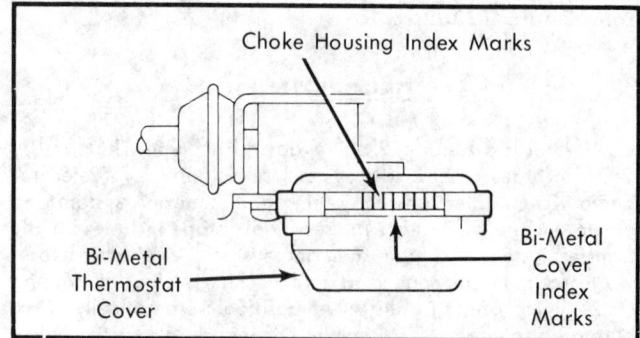

Fig. 6 Adjusting Automatic Choke

OVERHAUL

DISASSEMBLY

1) Disconnect accelerating pump connecting rod from pump lever. Remove pump lever from main body. Disconnect throttle return spring. Disconnect fast idle rod from lever. Do not lose spring and washer. Remove automatic choke thermostat cover, choke housing and cotter pin and washer from rod selector.

2) Unhook unloader return spring from unloader lever and choke diaphragm bracket. Remove coasting richer (deceleration) valve assembly. Disconnect lead at quick disconnect. Disconnect secondary throttle rod from secondary throttle shaft. Remove secondary throttle actuator from main body.

3) Unscrew slow fuel cut valve (solenoid) from main body. Remove left rear screw attaching air horn to body. Remove bolt lock from fuel inlet assembly. Remove two remaining air horn attaching screws and remove air horn.

4) Remove bolt, fuel strainer, fuel inlet fitting, fuel inlet bolt and needle valve assembly. Remove fuel bowl sight glass cover, gasket and glass assembly.

5) Remove float lever pin collar, then remove float. Do not lose float collar. Remove accelerating pump cover from main body and remove pump assembly. Invert carburetor and remove inlet check ball.

6) Remove screw retaining pump discharge weight and ball. Invert carburetor and remove weight and ball. Remove idle jets, main jets and all air bleeds from main body. Remove power valve from main body.

7) Remove curb idle adjusting screw and spring and idle mixture screw and spring from lower body. Remove primary and secondary discharge nozzles, retaining screws and washers. Remove air bleed screws from discharge nozzles and remove air emulsion tubes.

8) Remove lower body from main body. Remove retaining nut and washer from end of primary throttle shaft, and remove throttle operating lever washer and servo diaphragm operating lever, if so equipped.

9) Remove accelerating pump actuating lever, choke actuating lever, throttle return lever and idle adjusting lever.

HITACHI DCS 328 2-BARREL (Cont.)

10) Mark the primary throttle plate location in reference to its bore and to its relative position on throttle shaft. Remove throttle plate and shaft from lower body.

INSPECTION & CLEANING

Clean all parts thoroughly in solvent and check all passages and parts for wear or damage. Make sure that all jets are clear and clean. Do not attempt to clean jets by using wire or other objects which might damage calibrated orifices. Discard old gaskets and use new gaskets for assembly.

REASSEMBLY

Reassemble carburetor in reverse order of disassembly. Make sure that primary and secondary components are installed in their correct locations. When installing throttle valve or choke valve, make sure to eliminate gap between valve and wall of carburetor. When assembling float, ensure float collar is installed.

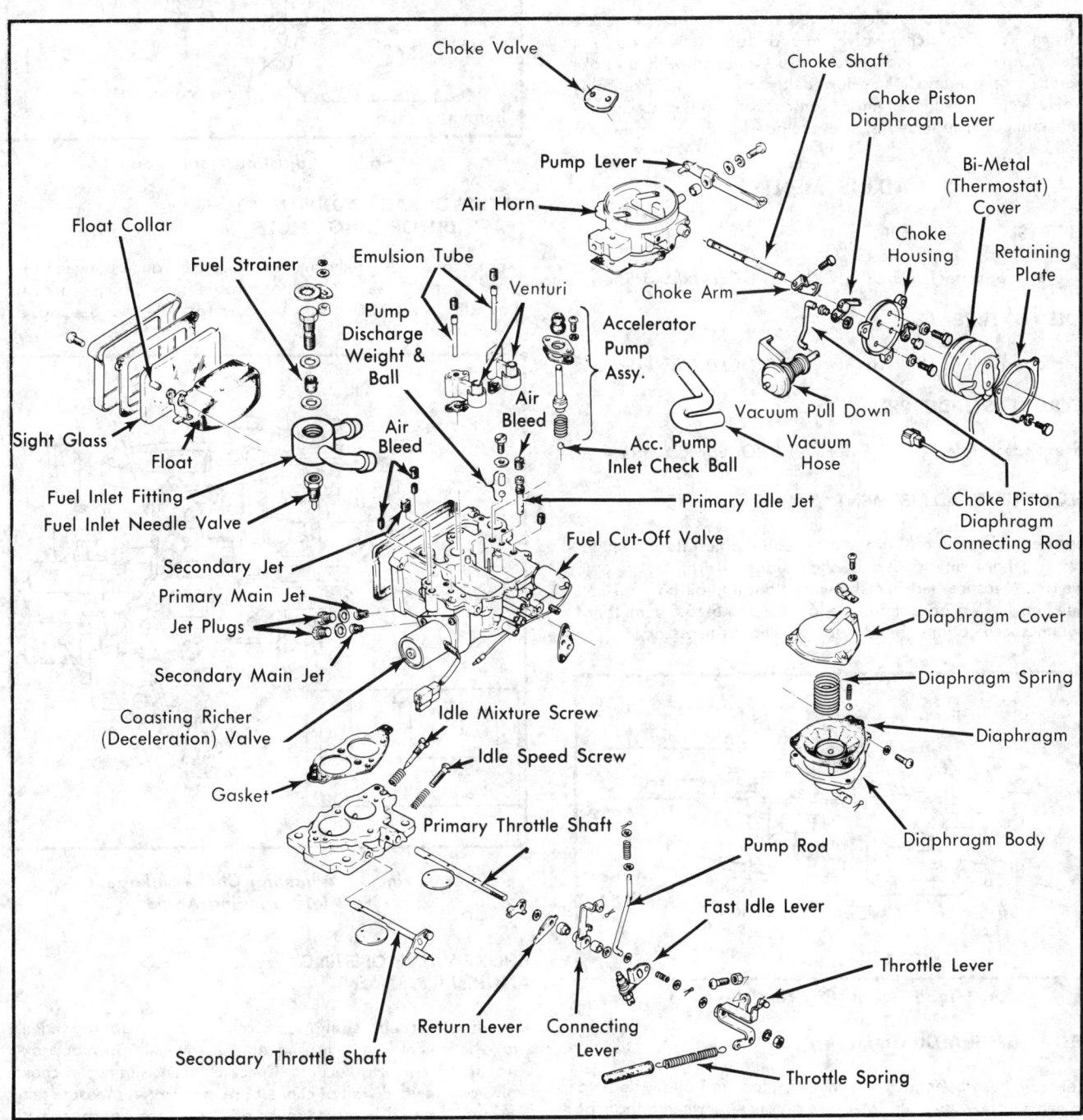

Fig. 7 Exploded View of Hitachi DCS 328 2-Barrel Carburetor (Ford Courier 2300)

1980 Hitachi Carburetors

HITACHI 4-BARREL

Mazda RX7

DESCRIPTION

Carburetor is of 4-barrel, 2-stage design. Primary stage includes idle system, slow speed circuit, accelerator pump system and main metering system. In addition, on vehicles so equipped (Federal), fluid from sub-zero starting device and oil from metering oil pump is admitted into primary stage. Secondary stage contains secondary vacuum diaphragm operating system, stepping circuit, and main metering system. Choking is accomplished through a semi-automatic choke.

Manual transmission vehicles are equipped with an electric idle switch, coasting richer valve, and a dashpot with dashpot delay valve. California vehicles are equipped with a choke return diaphragm, choke return delay valve, and choke delay valve. Vehicles with automatic transmissions, as well as California manual transmissions, are equipped with an accelerator sensor.

ADJUSTMENTS

HOT (SLOW) IDLE RPM

See *appropriate TUNE-UP SERVICE PROCEDURES* article.

IDLE MIXTURE

See *appropriate TUNE-UP SERVICE PROCEDURES* article.

COLD (FAST) IDLE RPM

See *appropriate TUNE-UP SERVICE PROCEDURES* article.

FLOAT LEVEL ADJUSTMENT

Before assembling air horn to main body, adjust float level. Invert air horn on stand and allow float to drop by its own weight. Measure clearance between float and air horn gasket. See *Fig. 1.* Clearance should be .61-.65" (15.5-16.5 mm). If not within specifications, bend float seat lip as necessary.

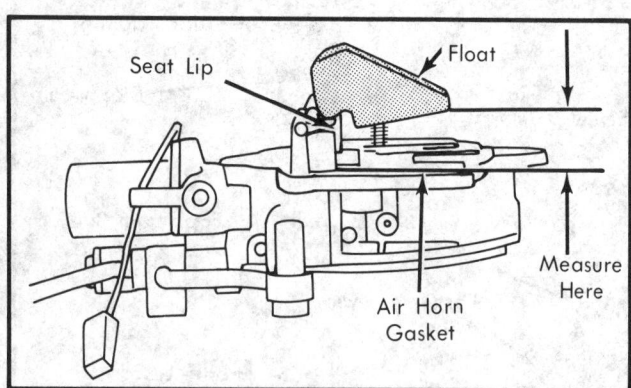

Fig. 1   Adjusting Float Level

FLOAT DROP ADJUSTMENT

Turn air horn over to its normal position and allow float to lower by its own weight. Measure distance between bottom of float and air horn gasket. See *Fig. 2.* Distance should be 1.98-2.03" (50.5-51.5 mm). If not, bend float stopper to obtain proper distance.

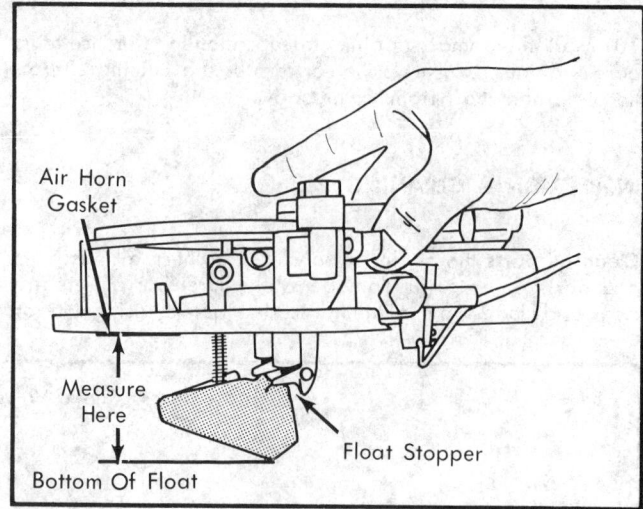

Fig. 2   Adjusting Float Drop

CHOKE LINKAGE ADJUSTMENT (FAST IDLE OPENING ANGLE)

Close choke valve fully and measure clearance between primary throttle valve and wall of throttle bore. Set clearance to .051-.059" (1.3-1.5 mm) by bending fast idle rod. See *Fig. 3.*

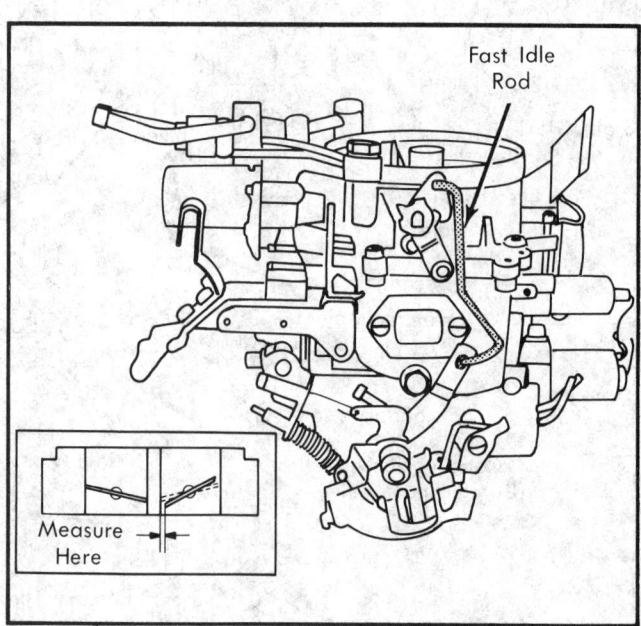

Fig. 3   Adjusting Choke Linkage Fast Idle Opening Angle

CHOKE VALVE OPENING ANGLE ADJUSTMENT

Disconnect vacuum sensing tube from vacuum diaphragm. Pull choke lever link out fully and hold in place. Apply approximately 19.7 in. Hg vacuum. Check clearance between choke valve and inward wall of choke bore. See *Fig. 4.* Measure temperature around bi-metal cover and compare clearance with chart in *Fig. 5.* If not to specifications, adjust by turning adjusting nut on end of vacuum diaphragm shaft at bi-metal housing.

HITACHI 4-BARREL (Cont.)

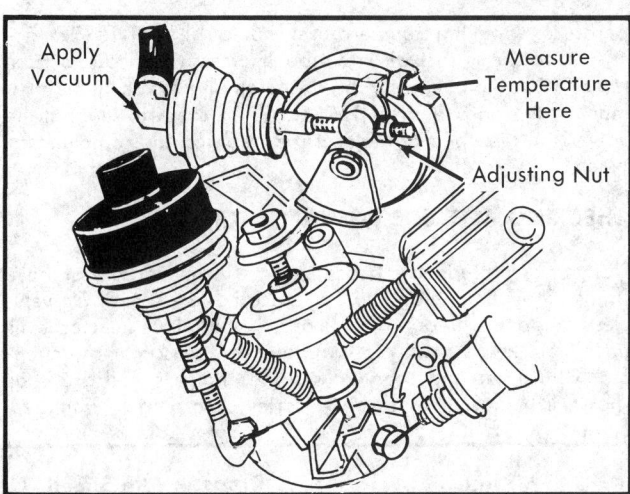

Fig. 4 Adjusting Choke Valve Opening Angle

Labels in figure: Apply Vacuum; Measure Temperature Here; Adjusting Nut

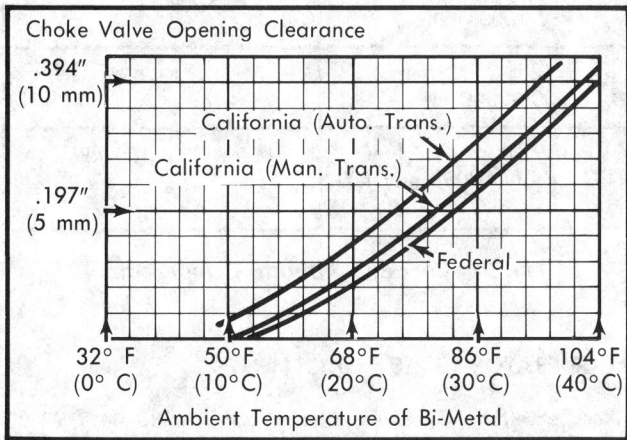

Fig. 5 Determining Choke Valve Opening Clearance Based on Bi-Metal Ambient Temperature

CHECKING NO. 2 CHOKE DIAPHRAGM OPERATION (FEDERAL ONLY)

1) Disconnect No. 2 choke diaphragm connecting link and install small spring scale. Slowly pull spring scale. Diaphragm shaft should begin to move with a pulling force of 1.2-1.8 oz.

2) Continue pulling spring scale. When the diaphragm shaft is pulled out .12-.14" (3-3.6 mm), reading should be 1.9-2.9 oz.

3) Remove spring scale and reconnect diaphragm connecting link. Fully pull out and hold choke lever link. Apply more than 17.7 in. Hg vacuum to No. 2 choke diaphragm and push diaphragm shaft (plastic shaft) in with finger.

4) Measure clearance between upper end of choke plate and inward wall of choke bore. Clearance should be .07-.116" (1.78-2.94 mm). With vacuum still applied, pull out diaphragm and again measure clearance at choke plate. Clearance should be .04-.054" (1.02-1.8 mm).

CHECKING NO. 1 CHOKE DIAPHRAGM OPERATION

Remove air cleaner assembly. Start engine and run at idle speed. Disconnect vacuum sensing tube from choke diaphragm. Diaphragm shaft should move outward from diaphragm.

CHECKING CHOKE DELAY VALVE OPERATION

Warm engine to normal operating temperature. Stop engine and remove air cleaner assembly. Disconnect vacuum sensing tube from No. 1 choke diaphragm. Start engine and run at idle speed. Diaphragm shaft should move fully inward within 10-20 seconds after reconnecting vacuum sensing tube to choke diaphragm.

NOTE — *Automatic transmission must be in Neutral.*

CHECKING CHOKE RETURN DELAY VALVE OPERATION (CALIF. ONLY)

Warm up engine to normal operating temperature. Stop engine and remove air cleaner assembly. Disconnect vacuum sensing tube from choke return diaphragm. With automatic transmission in Neutral, start engine and run at idle speed. Reconnect vacuum sensing tube to choke return diaphragm. Diaphragm shaft should be fully pulled into diaphragm within 20-70 seconds.

CHECKING CHOKE RETURN SOLENOID VALVE (FEDERAL ONLY)

1) Disconnect vacuum sensing tubes from choke return diaphragm and solenoid valve. Blow through diaphragm hose. Air should pass through valve and escape at solenoid filter.

2) Disconnect coupler from solenoid valve and apply battery voltage to solenoid valve terminal. Blow through hose again. Air should escape at solenoid vacuum port.

CHECKING AUTOMATIC CHOKE RELEASE

1) With engine cold and ignition off, pull out fully on choke knob and release. Knob should return automatically and freely. Connect a tachometer to engine.

2) Start engine with choke knob pulled fully out. Knob should return halfway automatically within 48-72 seconds (20-70 seconds on Calif.) after starting. Set engine speed at 2000 RPM with choke knob. Let engine run and when temperature reaches range indicated in Fig. 6, choke knob should automatically return completely inward.

3) Stop engine and pull choke knob fully out with ignition switch on. Choke knob should be held in this position (should not return).

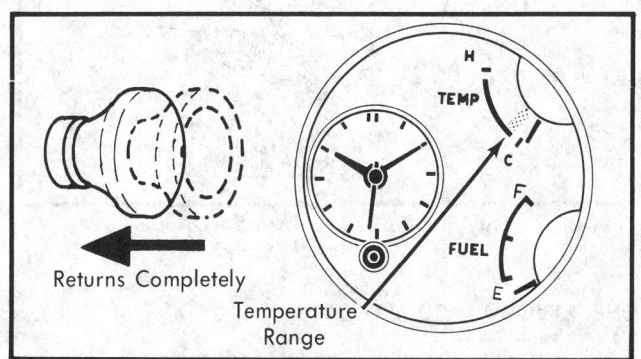

Fig. 6 Checking Automatic Choke Release

HITACHI 4-BARREL (Cont.)

HOT START ASSIST CABLE ADJUSTMENT

Remove lock spring of hot start assist cable from cable bracket. Slowly pull outer cable until hot start lever just touches stopper lever. Check clearance between cable bracket and lock nut on cable. *See Fig. 7.* Clearance should be .02-.08" (0.5-2.0 mm). If not within specifications, adjust by turning lock nut. Then install lock spring securely on cable.

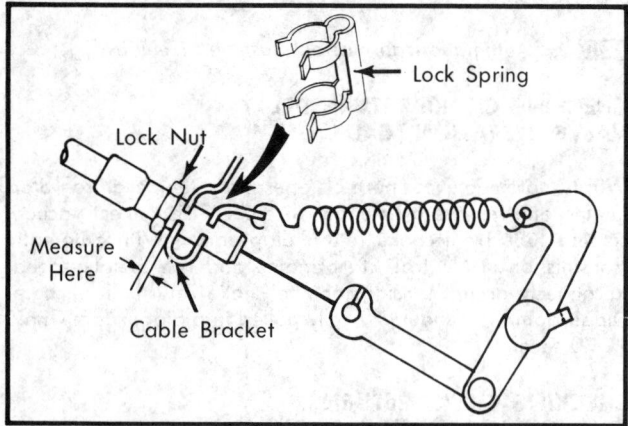

Fig. 7   Adjusting Hot Start Assist Cable

THROTTLE OPENER ADJUSTMENT (A/C MODELS ONLY)

Turn off all accessories. Disconnect vacuum tube at idle compensator (in air cleaner). Plug end of tube. Connect tachometer to engine and warm engine to normal operating temperature. Turn off air conditioner switch. Disconnect coupler from air conditioning solenoid valve. Connect battery power to one terminal and ground to second terminal. Check to see that throttle opener operates and engine speed increases to 1150-1250 RPM in Neutral. If engine speed is not within specification, turn adjusting nut. *See Fig. 8.*

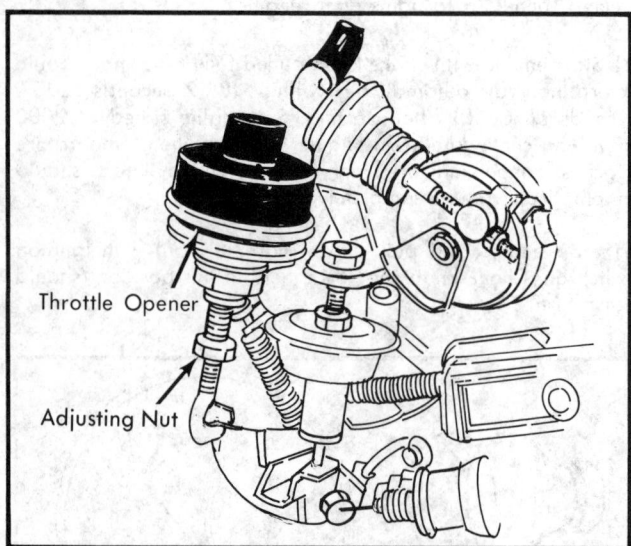

Fig. 8   Adjusting Throttle Opener (A/C Models Only)

CHECKING IDLE COMPENSATOR

Check that valve (located in air cleaner) is in closed position when bi-metal temperature is lower than operating tem-

perature. Opening temperature should be 141-157°F (61-69°C). To check, suck air into tube. If excessive leakage occurs, replace idle compensator as an assembly. When bi-metal is more than approximately 159°F (69°C), check to see that the valve is in the open position. If not, replace idle compensator assembly.

CHECKING ALTITUDE COMPENSATOR

Disconnect altitude compensator hose from carburetor hose fitting. Start engine and run at specified idle speed. On vehicles equipped with automatic transmission, place selector lever in "N" or "P" position. Close altitude compensator hose opening with finger and check to see the engine speed drops as shown in *Fig. 9.* Engine speed varies according to altitude.

Altitude	Drops in Idle Speed
0-3280 feet (0-1000 meters)	10-100 RPM
3280-6560 feet (1000-2000 meters)	50-200 RPM
More Than 6560 feet (More than 2000 meters)	More Than 100 RPM

Fig. 9   Checking Altitude Compensator

ACCELERATOR CABLE ADJUSTMENT

Check accelerator pedal position. Pedal should be 1.5-1.9" (37-47 mm) lower than brake pedal. *See Fig. 10.* If necessary, adjust nut "A" to obtain correct position. Check cable free play

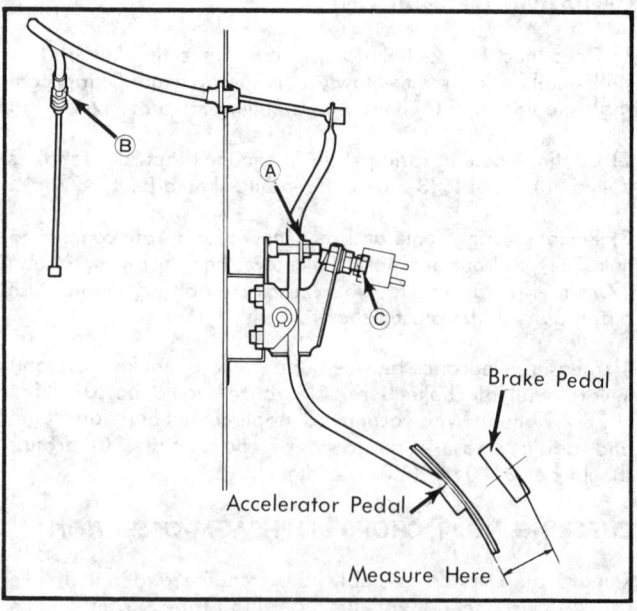

Fig. 10   Adjusting Accelerator Cable And Pedal Height

HITACHI 4-BARREL (Cont.)

at carburetor for .04-.12" (1-3 mm). To adjust cable free play, adjust nut "B". Depress accelerator all the way to the floor and check that throttle valves are wide open. If necessary, adjust stopper bolt "C".

DASHPOT ADJUSTMENT (MAN. TRANS. ONLY)

1) Remove air cleaner and check all sensing tubes for damage or mislocation. Be sure dashpot does not keep throttle lever from returning to idle stop. Quickly operate throttle lever fully and make sure dashpot extends quickly.

2) Release throttle lever and make sure lever returns slowly to idle position after it has touched dashpot rod. Connect a tachometer to engine and warm to normal operating temperature. Be sure engine operates at specified idle speed.

3) Operate throttle lever until it is away from dashpot rod. Slowly decrease engine speed. The throttle lever should contact the dashpot rod when engine speed is 3500-3900 RPM. If not, loosen lock nut and rotate dashpot diaphragm to obtain specified engine speed. Tighten lock nut.

OVERHAUL

NOTE – *Disassembly and assembly procedures will vary somewhat from vehicle to vehicle, depending upon sales area (Federal or California) and type of transmission. Therefore, some carburetors may not have all parts referred to in the following procedures.*

1) Remove carburetor from vehicle and begin disassembly with semi-automatic choke housing and air horn. Remove choke return delay valve (Calif. only) and choke delay valve. Remove heater lead and choke return solenoid (Federal only).

2) Remove throttle opener and bracket assembly. Remove dashpot diaphragm (Man. Trans. only). Remove throttle return spring, sub-return spring and semi-automatic choke housing. From air horn, remove "E" clip, choke lever, choke return diaphragm and bracket, hot start assist lever spring, fast idle rod and bracket. Remove No. 2 choke diaphragm (Federal only).

3) Remove air horn assembly from main body. Disconnect float pin, and remove float, needle valve, spring and retainer. From main body, remove accelerator pump rod, secondary throttle valve rod, idle switch return spring and idle switch (Man. Trans. only), and main body attaching screws.

4) Remove secondary throttle attaching screws, cover, return spring, pin and clip, diaphragm, housing and gasket. Remove "E" clip, washer and shaft, accelerator pump lever, attaching screws, cover, diaphragm and return spring.

5) From main body, remove accelerator pump injection screw, nozzle, gasket, weight, outlet check valve, check valve seat, weight and inlet check valve. Remove retainer, blind plug and washer, primary main jet and secondary main jet.

6) Remove the following jets or air bleeds (*Fig. 11*):

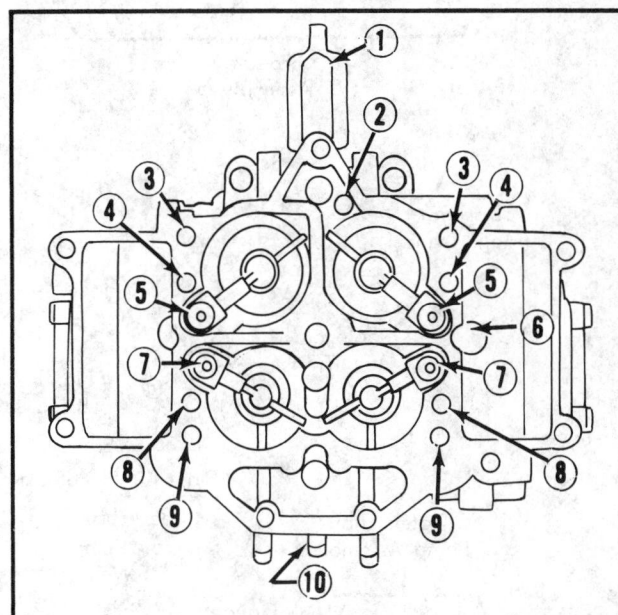

1. Coasting richer (Man. Trans. only)
2. Richer jet (Man. Trans. only)
3. Secondary No. 2 step air bleed
4. Secondary step jet
5. Secondary main air bleed
6. Power jet (Auto. Trans. & Calif. Man. Trans.)
7. Primary main air bleed
8. Primary slow jet
9. Primary No. 2 slow air bleed
10. Sub-zero starting assist fluid inlet (Federal only)

Fig. 11 Removing Jets and Air Bleeds Hitachi 4-Bbl. Carburetor

PRIMARY THROTTLE VALVE INITIAL OPENING ANGLE ADJUSTMENT

NOTE – *The following adjustment should be made when throttle body, throttle lock lever or lock lever adjusting screw have been replaced.*

Loosen lock nut and back off adjusting screw from lock lever. Close throttle valve completely and turn screw in gradually until it just touches throttle lock lever. Then turn adjusting screw "A" an additional 1/8 - 3/8 turn. Tighten lock nut. Throttle valve clearance should be .002" (.05 mm) and initial throttle opening angle should be 1°. See *Fig. 13*.

1980 Hitachi Carburetors

HITACHI 4-BARREL (Cont.)

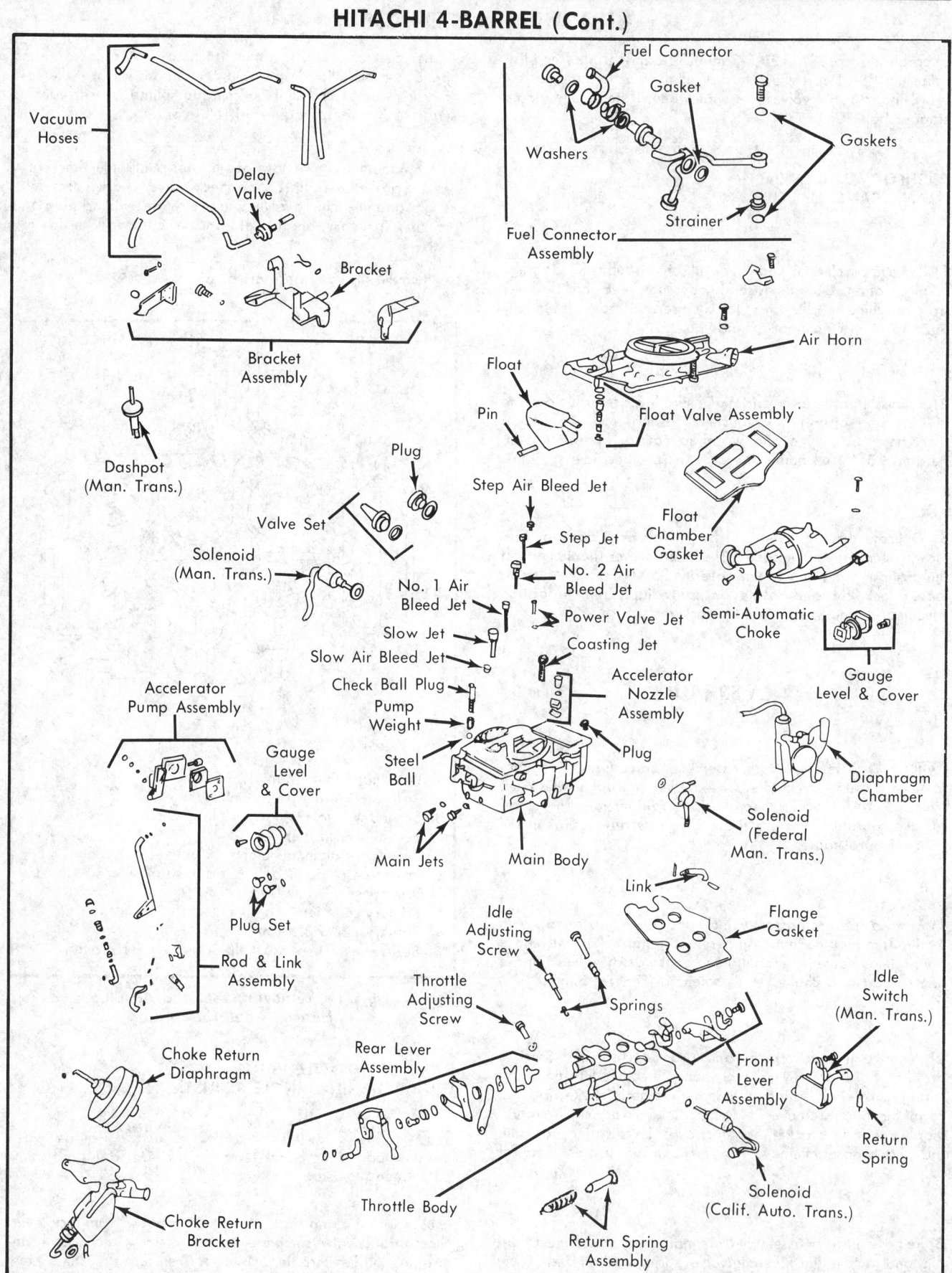

Fig. 12 *Exploded View of Hitachi 4-Bbl. Carburetor (Mazda RX7)*

HITACHI 4-BARREL (Cont.)

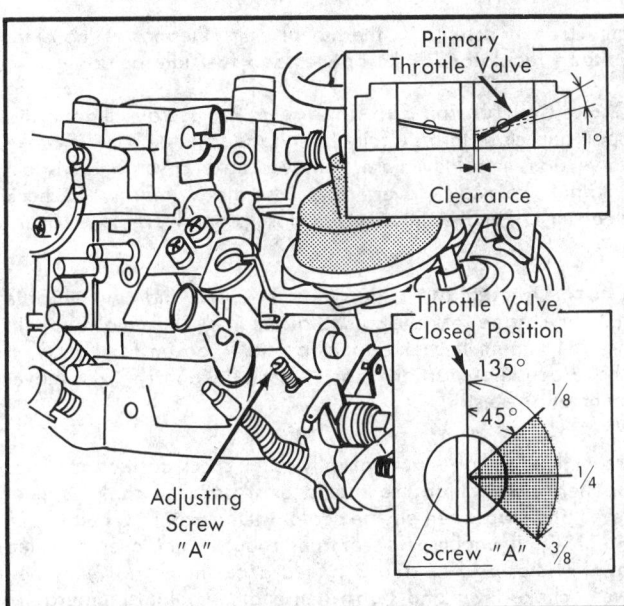

Fig. 13 Adjusting Primary Throttle Valve Initial Opening Angle

INSPECTION

Wash all parts in clean solvent, blow fuel passages with compressed air and remove dirt. Never use wire for cleaning jets. Inspect air horn, main body and throttle body for cracks or breakage. Inspect choke shaft and throttle shaft for wear, linkage and connecting rods for bends, and return springs for damage. Inspect for damage. Inspect float, needle valve and seat and strainer. Check air vent solenoid valve, richer solenoid valve (Man. Trans.), power valve solenoid (Auto. Trans. & Calif. Man. Trans.) for proper operation.

REASSEMBLY

To assemble, reverse disassembly procedure. Discard all old gaskets, using new ones. Clean and inspect all parts. Prevent primary and secondary system parts from becoming mixed. When installing bi-metal spring housing, fit choke shaft lever to bi-metal spring by closing choke valve and pulling vacuum diaphragm shaft.

	CARBURETOR ADJUSTMENT SPECIFICATIONS						
Application	Idle Speed (Engine RPM)		Float Level Setting In. (mm)	Float Drop Setting In. (mm)	Choke Linkage (Off Car) In. (mm)	Accelerator Cable Free Play	Choke Valve Opening In. (mm)
	Hot	Fast					
RX-7	750±25	①	.61-.65 (15.5-16.5)	1.8-2.2 (46-56)	.051-.059 (1.3-1.5)	.04-.12 (1-3)	②

① — Manufacturer does not supply fast idle speed. See Choke Linkage (Fast Idle Opening Angle).

② — Varies with ambient temperature. See Fig. 5.

1980 Keihin Carburetors

KEIHIN 2-BARREL – HONDA CVCC ENGINE

Accord
Civic
Prelude

DESCRIPTION

Carburetor is a two barrel, three venturi downdraft design. Carburetor contains two systems, primary and auxiliary. Primary system utilizes primary and secondary venturi, float system, accelerator pump system, and an idle system. Auxiliary system utilizes an auxiliary venturi with a float and idle system. Auxiliary system provides fuel to the pre-combustion chamber.

Carburetor components include electrically heated, automatic choke, choke opener diaphragm, secondary throttle opener diaphragm, fuel shut-off solenoid, primary/secondary main fuel cut-off solenoid, primary slow mixture cut-off solenoid, fast idle unloader and air jet controller (Calif. and high altitude models).

CARBURETOR IDENTIFICATION

Application	Carburetor No.	
	Man. Trans.	Auto. Trans.
Civic 1300	CB11A	
Civic 1500		
Sedan		
Federal	CB13A	CB13B
All Others①	CB14A	CB14B
Station Wagon		
Federal	CB13C	CB13D
All Others	CB14A	CB14B
Accord LX		
Federal	CB23A	CB23B
Calif	CB21A	CB27A
High Altitude	CB25A	CB25B
Accord (Sedan) & Prelude		
Federal	CB22A	CB22B
Calif.	CB20A	CB26A
High Altitude	CB24A	CB24B

① – High altitude GL sedan (5-speed) – CB14B

ADJUSTMENTS

HOT (SLOW) IDLE RPM

See appropriate TUNE-UP SERVICE PROCEDURES article.

IDLE MIXTURE

See appropriate TUNE-UP SERVICE PROCEDURES article.

COLD (FAST) IDLE RPM

See appropriate TUNE-UP SERVICE PROCEDURES article.

AUTOMATIC CHOKE

Both the choke valve setting and fast idle position are controlled during engine warmup by the automatic choke. It consists of a 5 ohm resistor on the firewall, an air intake sensor in air cleaner assembly, thermovalve in thermostat housing, voltage regulator, choke opener and fast idle unloader.

Choke Coil Tension and Linkage — Remove air cleaner and open and close throttle fully to engage fast idle cam. If choke valve does not fully close, remove choke cover and inspect linkage. Reinstall cover, aligning index marks. Recheck clearance. If choke still does not close properly, replace cover.

Choke Opener and Linkage — 1) Open and close throttle fully to engage fast idle cam. Start engine. Choke valve should partially open. If choke opens partially, go on to step 3). If choke does not partially open, check linkage for free movement and retest.

2) If choke still does not partially open, check position of choke opener lever. Clearance should exist between choke opener lever and stop when engine coolant temperature is below 52° F (11°C). If engine stalls or runs rough when lever is pulled against stop, go to step 3). Clearance should not exist between choke lever and stop when engine coolant temperature exceeds 66°F (19°C). If clearance exists, go on to step 4).

3) With coolant temperature below 52°F (11°C), disconnect choke opener-to-thermostatic valve tube at choke opener. If choke opener lever moves away from stop, replace thermostatic valve and repeat test. If lever touches stop, clean choke opener joint orifice with .02" (.5 mm) drill bit (or equivalent) and repeat test. If lever is still against stop, check for broken diaphragm, misaligned choke cover or defective bimetal choke spring.

4) With coolant temperature above 66°F (19°C), disconnect and plug choke opener-to-thermostatic valve tube at choke opener. Lever should touch stop. If lever does not touch stop, choke opener has air leak. If lever touches stop, the tube is leaking or thermostatic valve is defective.

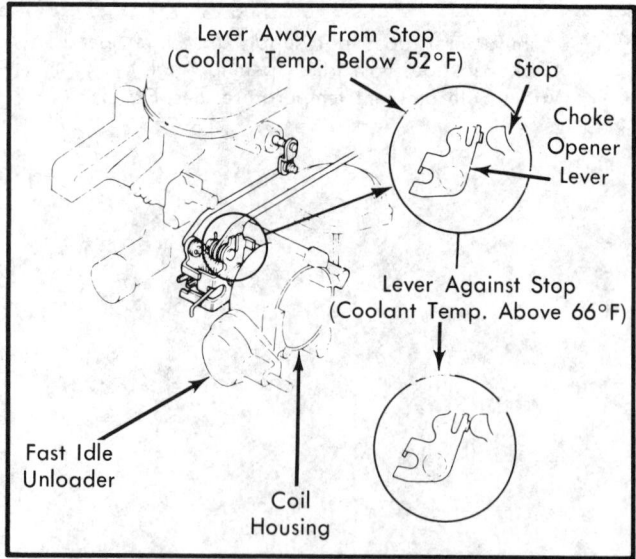

Fig. 1 Checking Choke Opener Lever Position

Choke Valve Opening Adjustment — 1) Remove choke cover. Fully close choke valve. Fully open, then close throttle valve. Disconnect choke opener tube and apply 85 psi (6 kg/cm²) air to choke opener.

KEIHIN 2-BARREL — HONDA CVCC ENGINE (Cont.)

2) Push choke opener rod in towards diaphragm until it stops. Measure choke valve clearance. Adjust clearance to .030-.036" (.76-.90 mm) on Civic or .265-.271" (.61-.75 mm) on all other models. See *Fig. 2.*

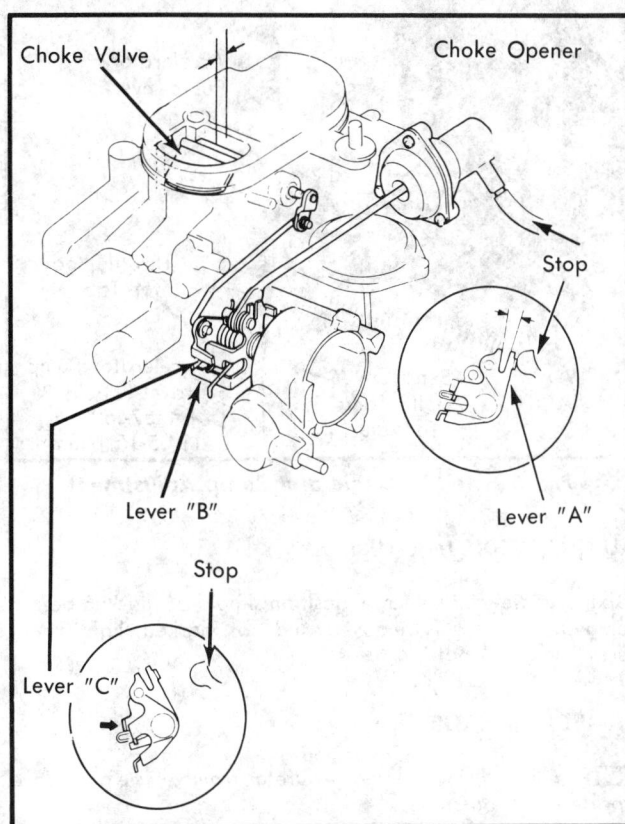

Fig. 2   Measuring Choke Valve Opening

3) Reconnect choke opener tube. With lever "B" held against stop, push choke opener rod in until it stops. Adjust clearance to .054-.062" (1.39-1.57 mm) on Federal Civic 1500, Accord and Prelude or .062-.070" (1.58-1.76 mm) on all other Civic models by bending opener lever "A".

4) Following step **3)**, immediately release lever "B" and adjust choke clearance to .13-.15" (3.4-3.8 mm) on Federal Civic 1500; .15-.17" (3.9-4.3 mm) on all other Civic models or .073-.089" (1.85-2.25 mm) on Accord and Prelude, by bending lever "C".

Choke Coil Tension and Heater — 1) As engine warms up, choke valve should fully open. If choke does not open at all, check voltage across connectors of choke cover. If no voltage, check external resistor for 4.5-5.5 ohms resistance, fuses, voltage regulator and wiring. If voltage, check for 18-26 ohms resistance across choke cover leads. If resistance exceeds specifications, replace choke cover assembly and recheck.

2) If choke does not open fully, inspect linkage. Disconnect air sensor wires, start engine and measure for 9.5-12 volts across choke cover leads. If more than 12 volts, replace external resistor. If still ineffective, replace choke cover assembly.

Fast Idle Unloader — 1) Connect tachometer to cold engine. Start engine and allow to reach operating temperature. Do not manually open throttle. As engine warms up, speed should drop below 1400 RPM.

2) If engine speed does not drop below 1400 RPM, disconnect fast idle unloader hose and check for vacuum. If vacuum is present, check diaphragm for leaks and free movement of unloader rod and retest.

3) If no vacuum is present, test voltage at unloader solenoid valve-to-emission control box connector. If no voltage is present, replace unloader solenoid and retest.

4) On all models except Calif. Civic 1500, if voltage is present, replace thermosensor and retest. On Calif. Civic 1500, disconnect thermosensor connector. If voltage at connector disappears, replace thermosensor. If voltage remains, replace diode in emission control box and retest.

NOTE — *Diode should have continuity in one direction only; from yellow wire to yellow/red wire on Calif. Civic 1500.*

Air Temperature Sensor — Disconnect and remove sensor from air cleaner. Check continuity across sensor lead wires. Continuity should be present at 57-73° F (14-23° C), but absent below this temperature range. Replace sensor if not to specifications.

Thermovalve — Drain engine coolant until level is below distributor holder. Remove distributor holder and thermovalve. Suspend thermovalve in cold water with vacuum pump attached to thermovalve. Slowly heat water and note temperature and vacuum readings. Valve should open below 60°F (15°C) and not hold vacuum. Valve should close above 77°F (25°C) and hold vacuum. See *Fig. 3.*

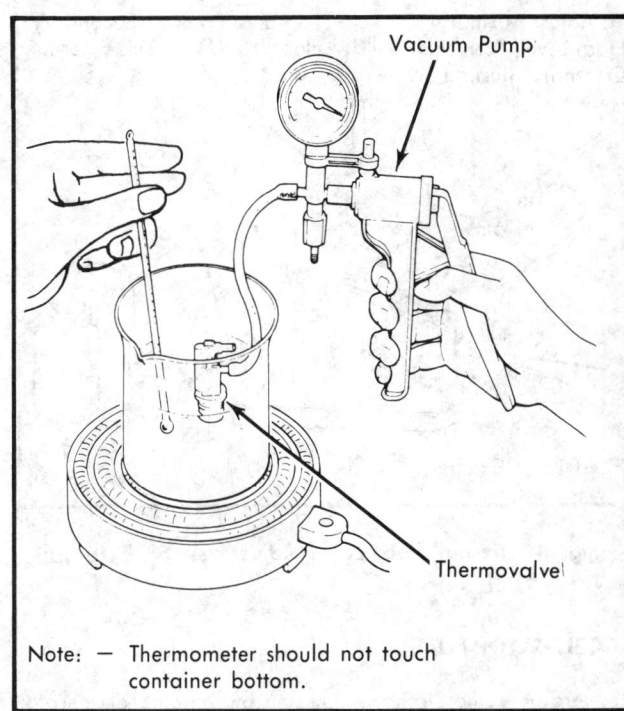

Note: — Thermometer should not touch container bottom.

Fig. 3   Testing Automatic Choke Thermovalve

KEIHIN 2-BARREL – HONDA CVCC ENGINE (Cont.)

THROTTLE CABLE

1) Check that throttle cable operates smoothly with no binding or sticking. Check cable free play at linkage. Adjust cable deflection to .16-.40" (4-10 mm) by turning adjusting nut. Tighten lock nut.

2) Throttle valve should open fully when accelerator pedal is depressed and return to idle position when pedal is released.

FLOAT LEVEL

NOTE – Be sure to use correct float gauge and catch tray when checking float level. Use Float Level Gauge 07501-6950100 for all models. Use Catch Tray 07501-6950202 for Civic and 07501-6950201 for Accord and Prelude models. Gauge includes a see through adapter, with a red line as a fuel level indicator. Gauge is installed where primary main cut-off solenoid, auxiliary main jet plug and air vent cut-off diaphragm mount to carburetor body.

1) With air cleaner removed and carburetor installed on vehicle, remove primary main cut-off solenoid, auxiliary main jet plug and air vent cut-off diaphragm. Attach special float level gauge, catch tray and drain bottle to carburetor.

2) Start engine and allow it to stabilize. Float level should remain at red line on gauge. If not, adjustment is made by turning external float level adjusting screws. See Fig. 4.

3) Allow time for fuel level to stabilize and check again. When correct float level is achieved, paint adjusting screws to keep adjustment from changing.

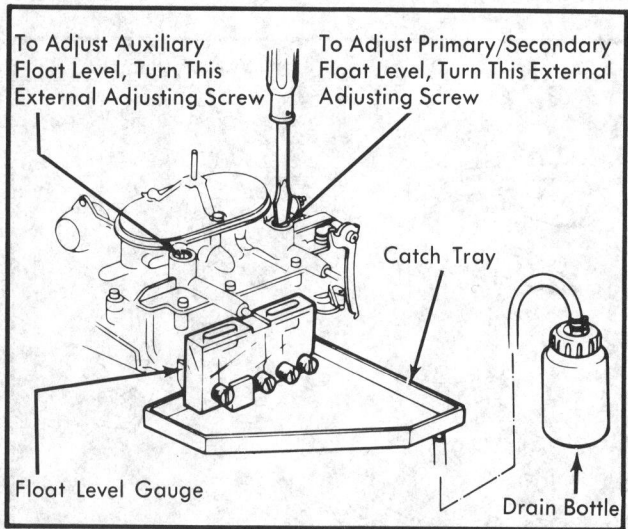

Fig. 4   Keihin Float Level Adjustment – External

ACCELERATOR PUMP

Accelerator pump stroke is adjusted by bending accelerator pump lever tang to get a clearance of .57-.60" (14.5-15.1 mm) between tang and throttle body stop tab. See Fig. 5.

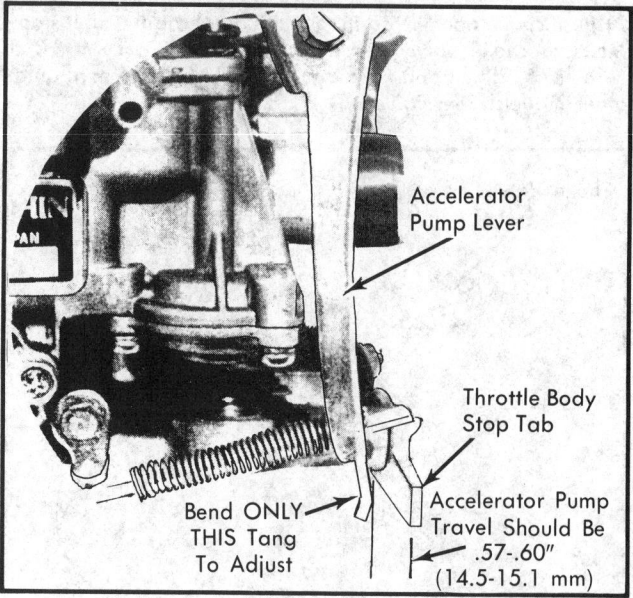

Fig. 5   Keihin Accelerator Pump Adjustment

AUXILIARY IDLE MIXTURE

Auxiliary idle mixture screw position should be marked before removal. If screw is removed and not marked, lightly seat screw then back out 1¾ turns.

LAMBDA LINKAGE

NOTE – To adjust, remove carburetor from vehicle and place upside down on stand.

1) Back out throttle stop screw. Install dial indicator holder (07974-6570501) then mount dial indicator. See Fig. 6. Loosen linkage adjustment screw lock nut. See Fig. 8.

2) Tighten adjustment screw until primary throttle plate just opens. At this point, set dial indicator to zero. Loosen adjustment screw until dial indicator has a reading of .004±.0004" .10±.01 mm). See Fig. 8.

3) Tighten lock nut without changing position of adjustment screw. Readjust throttle stop screw when carburetor is installed on vehicle.

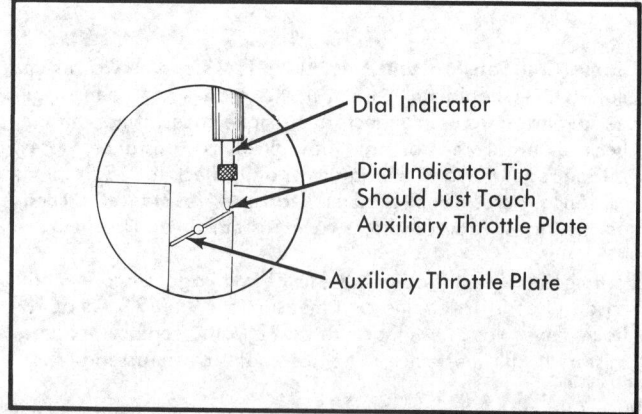

Fig. 6   Positioning Dial Indicator on Throttle Plate

KEIHIN 2-BARREL – HONDA CVCC ENGINE (Cont.)

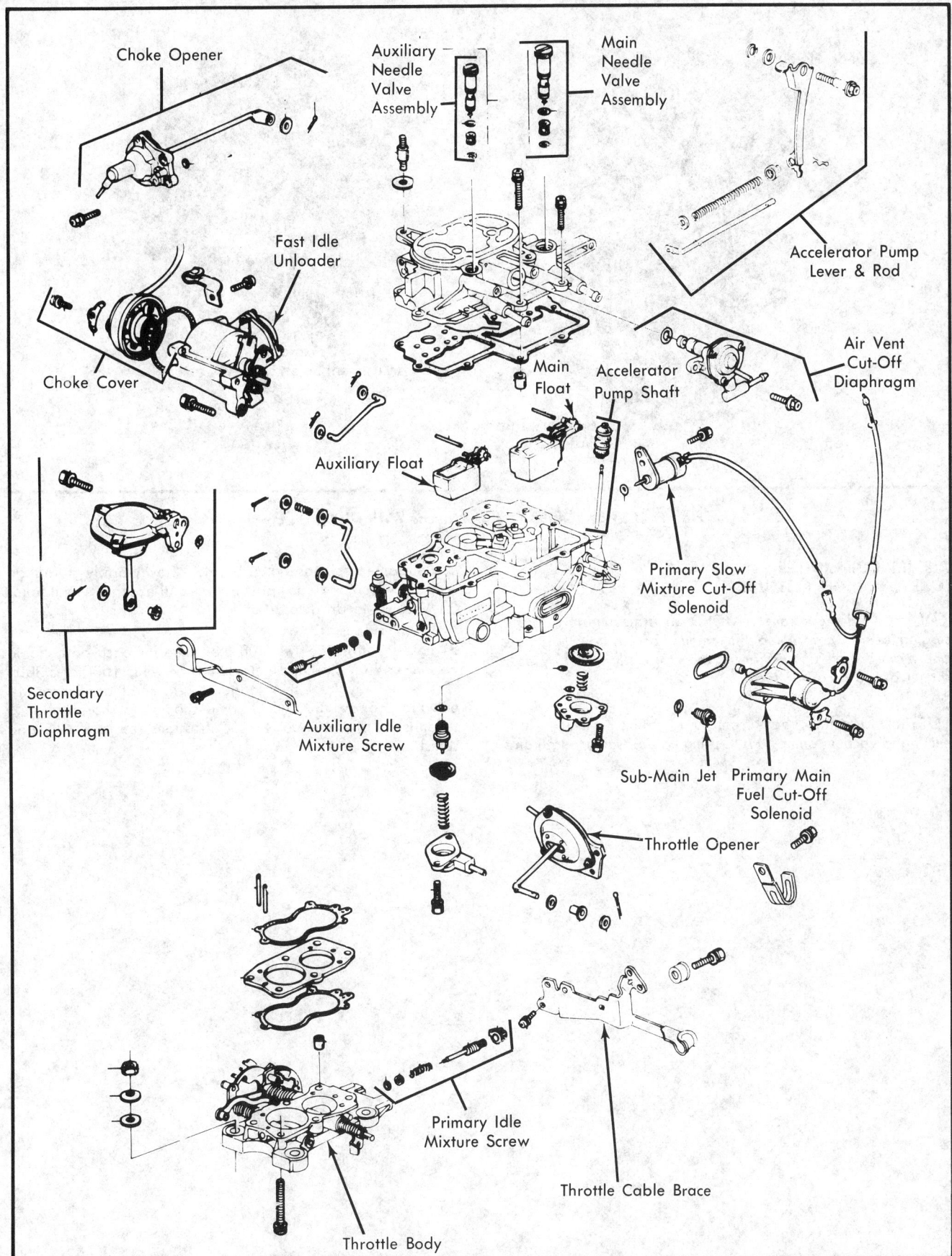

Fig. 7 Exploded View of Keihin Carburetor

1980 Keihin Carburetors

KEIHIN 2-BARREL — HONDA CVCC ENGINE (Cont.)

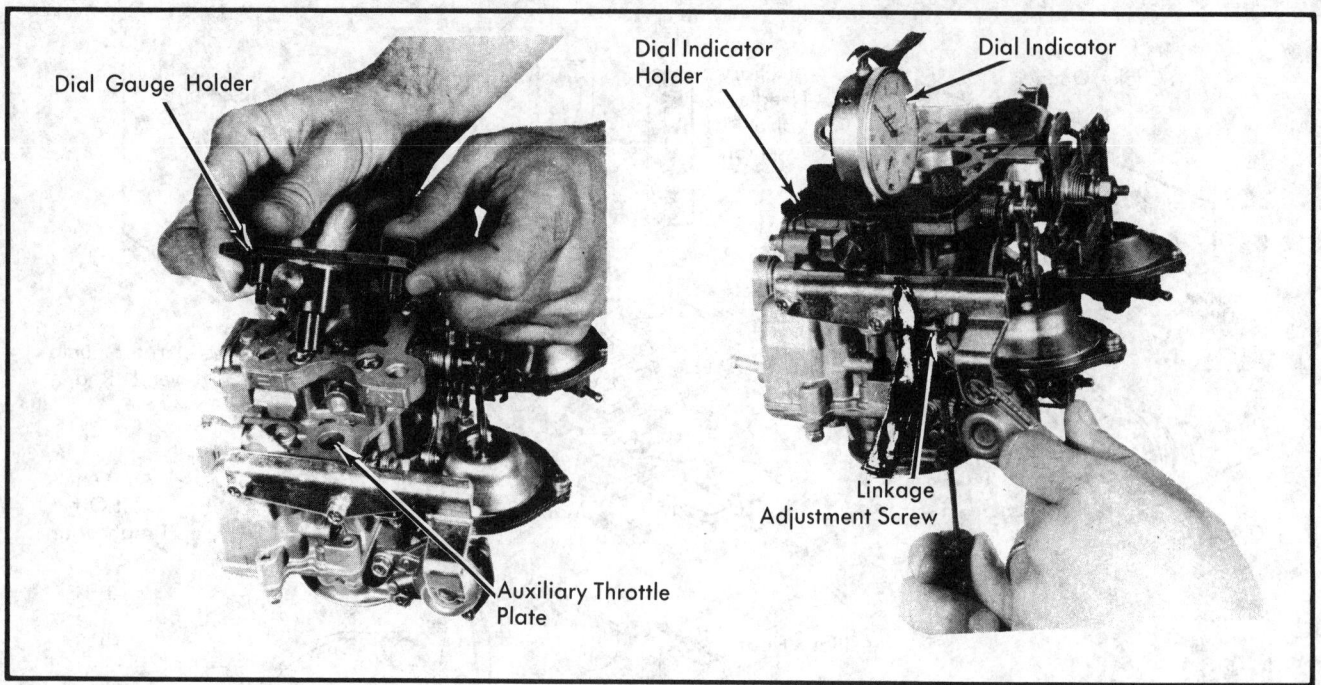

Fig. 8   Lambda Linkage Adjustment With Dial Indiactor

AIR JET CONTROLLER (CALIF. & HIGH ALTITUDE)

NOTE — *Air jet controller (AJC) is an atmospheric pressure sensing device, controlling the amount of air flow into slow and main air jets of auxiliary carburetor and secondary slow air jet of main carburetor.*

1) To test, disconnect hose from air jet controller (AJC). Connect hand vacuum pump to AJC using hose of same length and inside diameter as hose to carburetor. Slowly apply more than 8 in. Hg vacuum to each port in turn and observe time it takes for vacuum to drop to zero.

2) For elevations below 1500 feet, time for each port should be longer than 5 seconds; elevations between 1500 and 3000 feet, time may be either longer or shorter than 5 seconds; elevations above 3000 feet, time should be shorter than 5 seconds. If any are not to specifications, replace AJC and retest.

NIKKI 2-BARREL

Ford Courier (2000 cc)
Mazda B2000

DESCRIPTION

Carburetor is a Nikki 2-barrel, downdraft type, 2-stage design. It is equipped with an electric automatic choke and a slow fuel cut valve (throttle solenoid). The primary stage includes a curb idle system, accelerator pump system, idle transfer system, main metering system and power enrichment system. The secondary stage includes an idle transfer system and main metering system.

For deceleration control, Federal vehicles make use of an anti-afterburn valve and throttle positioner system; California vehicles, an air bypass valve and throttle positioner system.

ADJUSTMENTS

HOT (SLOW) IDLE RPM

See appropriate TUNE-UP SERVICE PROCEDURES article.

IDLE MIXTURE

See appropriate TUNE-UP SERVICE PROCEDURES article.

COLD (FAST) IDLE RPM

See appropriate TUNE-UP SERVICE PROCEDURES article.

AUTOMATIC CHOKE SETTING

Align index mark on thermostat cover with center of choke housing index mark. See Fig. 1. Tighten attaching screws.

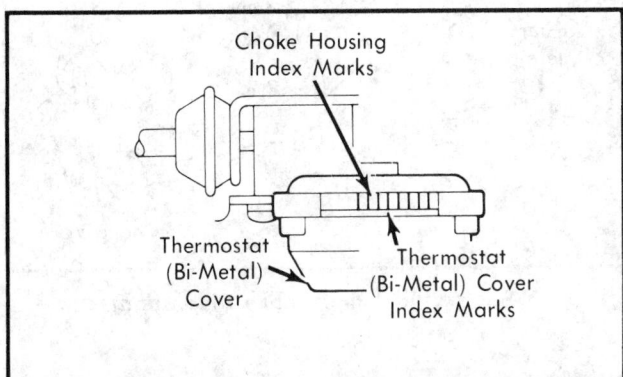

Fig. 1   Choke Thermostat Cover Index Marks

THROTTLE VALVE OPENING ANGLE

1) Close choke valve fully. Place fast idle screw on high (1st) step of fast idle cam. See Fig. 2. Adjust throttle valve opening clearance by turning the adjusting screw clockwise to increase or counterclockwise to decrease the opening clearance.

2) Measure throttle valve opening clearance between throttle bore wall and lower edge of throttle plate. Clearance should be .051-.059" (1.3-1.5 mm).

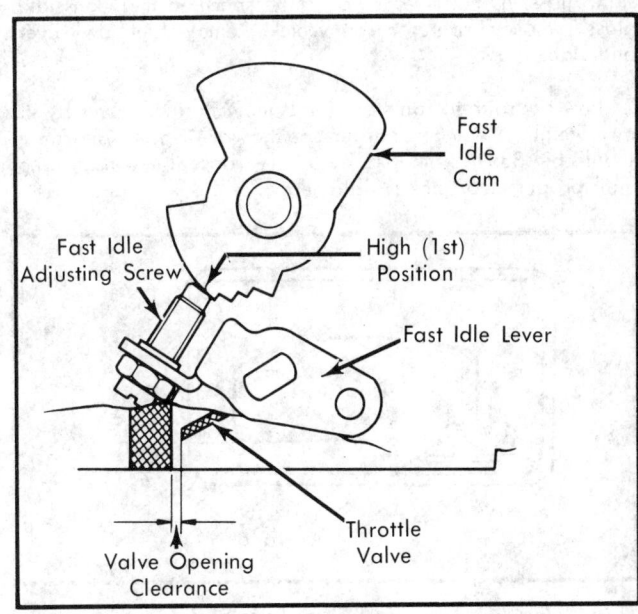

Fig. 2   Measuring Throttle Valve Opening Angle

CHOKE VALVE OPENING ANGLE

1) Place fast idle screw on 2nd step of fast idle cam. See Fig. 3. Adjust choke valve opening clearance by bending starting arm. If a large adjustment is necessary, bend choke rod.

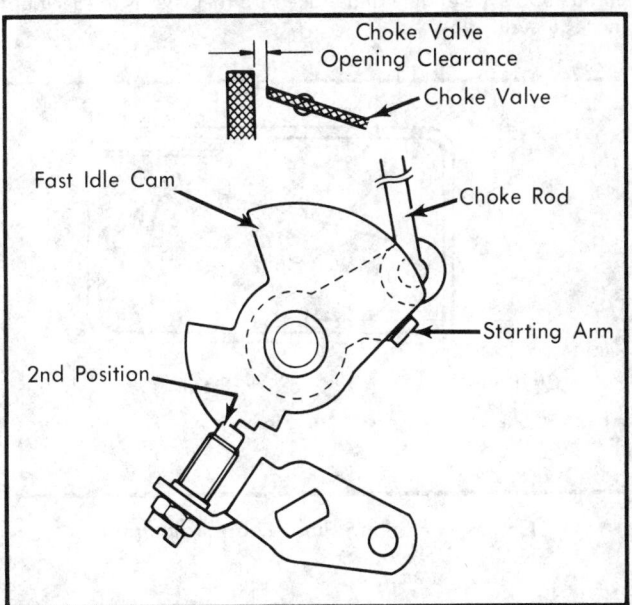

Fig. 3   Adjusting Choke Valve Opening Angle

2) Choke valve opening clearance, measured between choke valve bore and upper edge of valve, should be .016-.028" (.40-.70 mm).

NIKKI 2-BARREL (Cont.)

FLOAT LEVEL ADJUSTMENT

1) With the engine running, check the fuel level in the fuel bowl sight glass. If fuel level is not to the specified mark on sight glass, remove carburetor from vehicle. Remove fuel bowl cover and sight glass.

2) Invert carburetor on stand and allow float to lower by its own weight. Measure clearance as shown in *Fig. 4*. Clearance should be .335″ (8 mm). To adjust clearance, bend float tang until proper clearance is obtained.

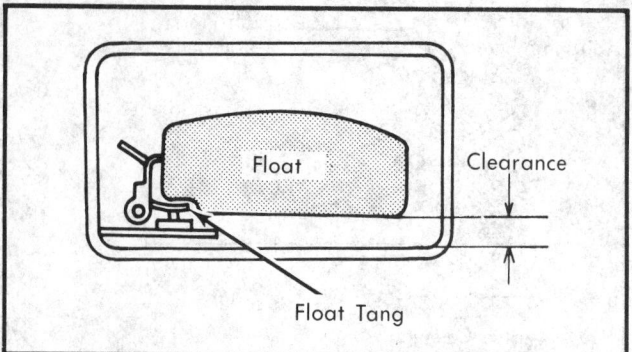

Fig. 4 Checking Float Level Adjustment

3) Turn carburetor to its normal position (not inverted). Allow float to lower by its own weight. Measure clearance between bottom of bowl and float. *See Fig. 5*. Clearance should be .039″ (1 mm). If not, bend float stopper until proper clearance is obtained.

4) Install fuel bowl sight glass and install carburetor on engine. Operate engine and make sure fuel level is to specified mark in sight glass.

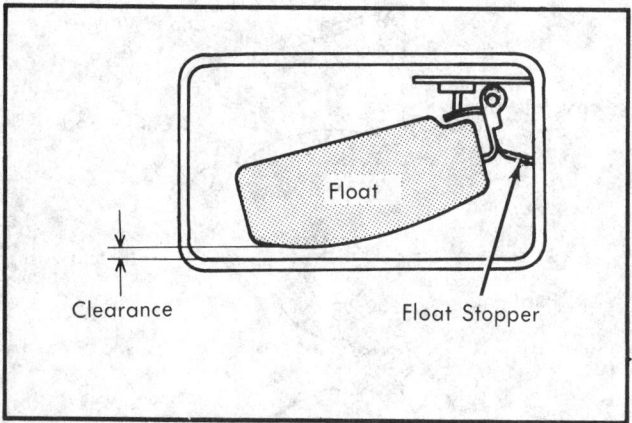

Fig. 5 Checking Float Drop Adjustment

CHOKE UNLOADER ADJUSTMENT

Close choke valve fully and then open primary valve fully. Measure choke valve clearance between air horn and choke valve. *See Fig. 6*. Clearance should be .079-.099″ (2.0-2.5 mm). To adjust clearance, bend throttle adjusting arm.

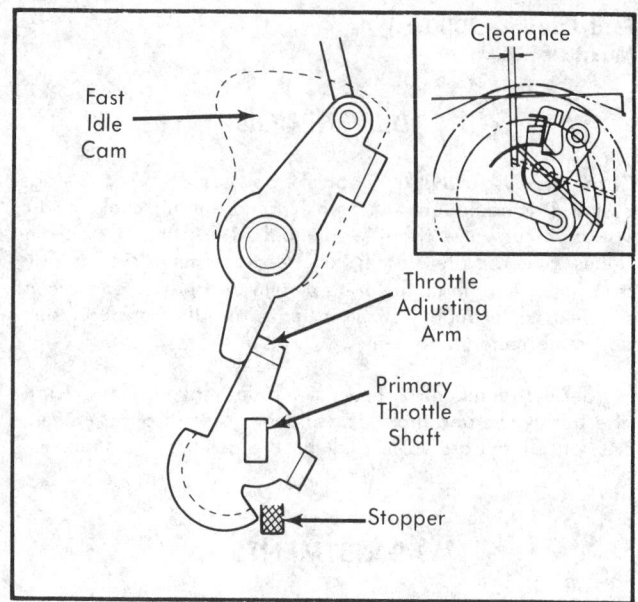

Fig. 6 Adjusting Choke Unloader

CHOKE DIAPHRAGM ADJUSTMENT

Place fast idle screw on high (1st) step of fast idle cam. Apply approximately 15.7 in. Hg vacuum to choke diaphragm. Press choke valve slightly to closed position and measure clearance between choke valve and air horn. Adjust clearance to .047-.067″ (1.2-1.7 mm) by bending choke lever. *See Fig. 7*.

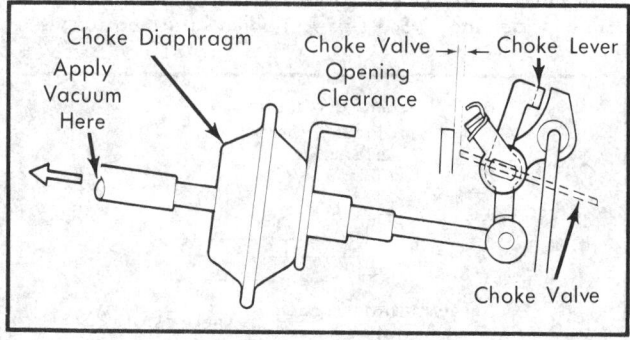

Fig. 7 Adjusting Choke Diaphragm

ACCELERATOR PEDAL HEIGHT ADJUSTMENT

1) To adjust accelerator pedal height, loosen lock nuts on longer linkage rod ("A" in *Fig. 9*). Rotate rods in sockets until proper accelerator travel from idle to wide-open-throttle is obtained. Tighten lock nuts.

2) On Mazda B2000 vehicles, accelerator pedal should be 1.57-1.97″ (40-50 mm) lower than brake pedal height. Throttle valves should be wide open when accelerator pedal is against the floor. No specification was available for the Courier.

NIKKI 2-BARREL (Cont.)

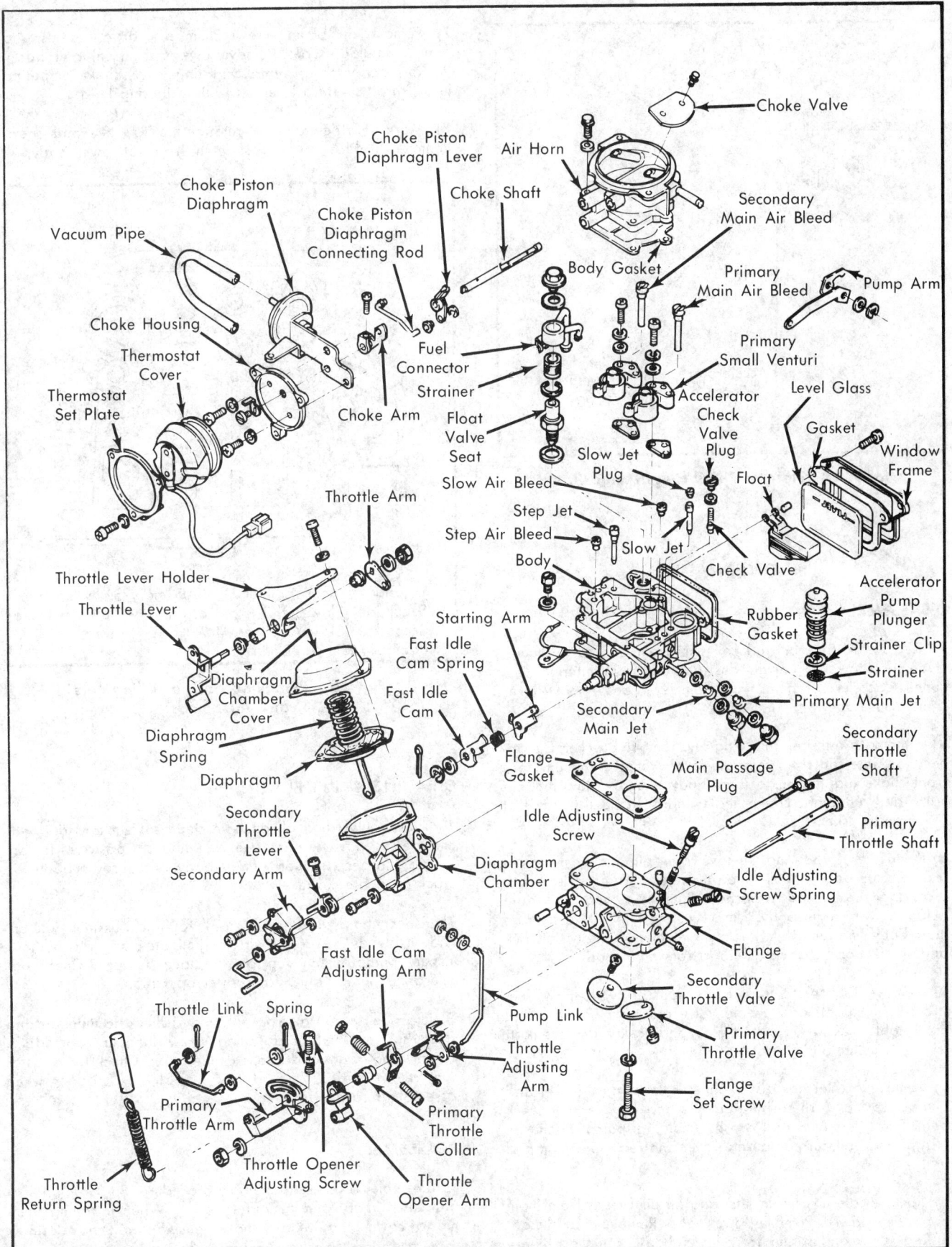

Fig. 8   Exploded View of Nikki 2-Bbl. Carburetor (Ford Courier 2000 cc and Mazda B2000)

NIKKI 2-BARREL (Cont.)

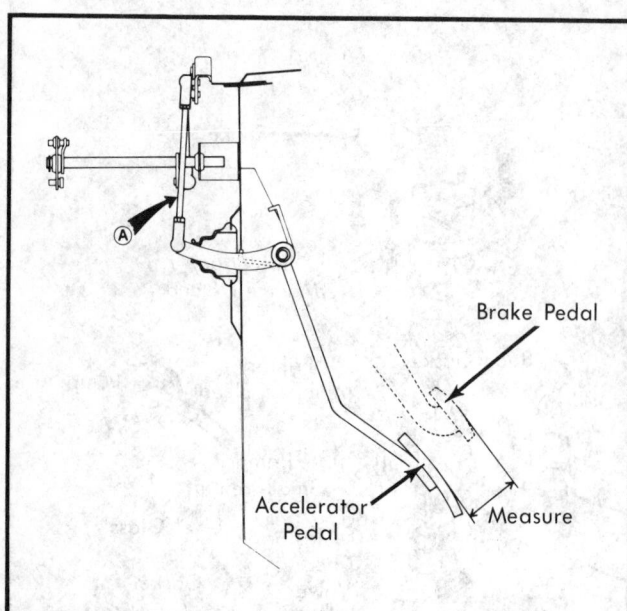

Fig. 9   Accelerator Pedal Height Adjustment

OVERHAUL

DISASSEMBLY

1) Remove carburetor and cover intake manifold port with clean shop towel to prevent dust and dirt from entering. Disconnect accelerator pump rod from lever and remove lever from main body. See *Fig. 10.*

2) Unhook throttle return spring and remove bracket. Disconnect fast idle rod from fast idle lever. Remove vacuum hose from choke diaphragm to main body. Remove slow fuel cut valve and automatic choke heater leads. Remove thermostat cover and gasket.

3) Remove choke housing. Remove cotter pin and washer from rod selector and unhook unloader return spring. Disconnect secondary throttle rod from shaft. Remove secondary throttle actuator from main body. Unscrew slow fuel cut valve from main body and remove it. Remove fuel inlet assembly bolt lock and spacer, and detach air horn from main body.

4) Remove fuel inlet fitting from main body. Remove fuel strainer, inlet bolt and needle valve assembly. Remove fuel bowl sight glass cover, gasket, glass and gasket. Remove float lever pin collar and float.

5) Remove accelerator pump plunger cover and gasket and plunger spring. Turn carburetor over and remove inlet check ball. Remove screw and washer holding pump discharge weight and ball, turn carburetor over and remove weight and ball.

6) Remove idle jets, main jets, and all air bleeds from main body. See *Fig. 10.* Remove power valve. Remove curb idle adjusting screw and spring from lower body. Remove primary and secondary discharge nozzles, retaining screws and washers. Remove nozzles and gaskets.

7) Remove air bleed screws from discharge nozzles and remove emulsion tubes. Remove lower body from main body. Remove accelerating pump actuating lever, choke actuating lever, throttle return lever and idle adjusting lever.

8) Mark throttle valve in relationship to bore and shaft. Remove throttle valve and slide shaft out of lower body.

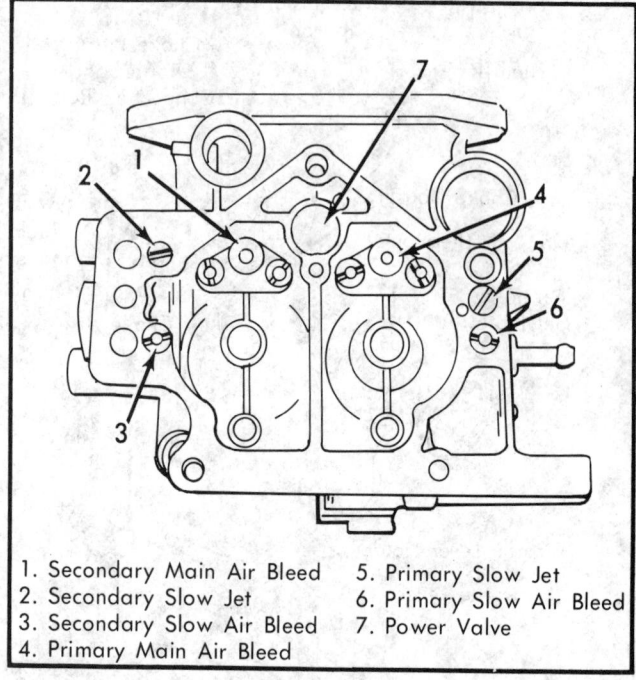

1. Secondary Main Air Bleed
2. Secondary Slow Jet
3. Secondary Slow Air Bleed
4. Primary Main Air Bleed
5. Primary Slow Jet
6. Primary Slow Air Bleed
7. Power Valve

Fig. 10   Removing and Installing Jets and Air Bleeds

CLEANING & INSPECTION

1) Thoroughly clean all parts in clean solvent and dry with compressed air. Use care when blowing out passages in carburetor. Inspect air horn, main body and throttle body for cracks and breakage.

2) Inspect choke and throttle shafts for wear. Examine all jets and air bleeds. Never use wire to eliminate clogged condition. Inspect pump piston cup and replace if worn. Check accelerating pump valves for proper operation.

3) Examine power valve operation and check float needle and float. Inspect mixture adjusting screw for burrs or ridges. Check diaphragm and solenoid operation. Check for clogs at fuel return orifice. Discard and use all new gaskets when assembling carburetor.

REASSEMBLY

To assemble, reverse disassembly procedure. Be careful not to mistake primary and secondary parts. When installing thermostat cover on automatic choke housing, hook choke arm to bimetal spring. Check correct operation of the choke valve by turning thermostat cover. Then align index mark on cover with center mark on choke housing. Tighten screws.

NIKKI 2-BARREL

Mazda 626

DESCRIPTION

Carburetor is a Nikki 2-barrel downdraft type. It is equipped with an electric automatic choke, fuel cut solenoid valve, an air by-pass valve for deceleration control, an idle compensator, high altitude compensator and throttle positioner system for air conditioned models. A double venturi provides for high air flow velocity at the venturi under all operating conditions, resulting in more efficient atomization of fuel for smooth combustion.

ADJUSTMENTS

HOT (SLOW) IDLE RPM

See appropriate *TUNE-UP SERVICE PROCEDURES* article.

IDLE MIXTURE

See appropriate *TUNE-UP SERVICE PROCEDURES* article.

COLD (FAST) IDLE RPM

See appropriate *TUNE-UP SERVICE PROCEDURES* article.

AUTOMATIC CHOKE SETTING

Before starting engine, fully depress accelerator pedal to ensure choke valve closes properly. Push choke valve with finger to check for binding. Be sure thermostat cover index mark is set at center of choke housing index mark. See *Fig. 1*. Warm engine and check that choke valve is fully open. Tighten all attaching screws after aligning index marks.

NOTE – *Do not set thermostat cover index mark at any position except center of choke housing index mark.*

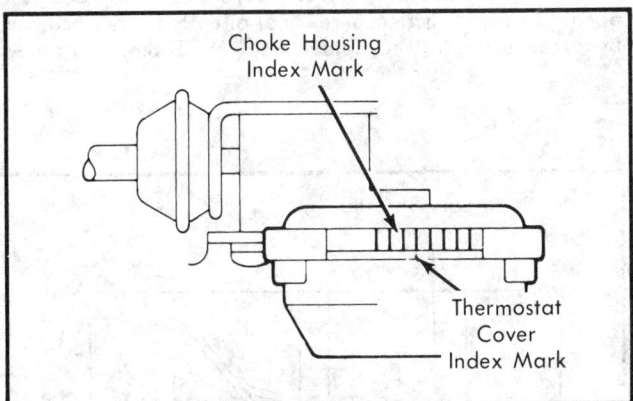

Fig. 1   Adjusting Automatic Choke

FLOAT LEVEL ADJUSTMENT

Remove air horn from carburetor. Invert air horn on stand and allow float to lower by its own weight. Measure clearance between float and air horn bowl. If clearance is not .433" (11 mm), bend float seat lip to obtain proper clearance. See *Fig. 2*.

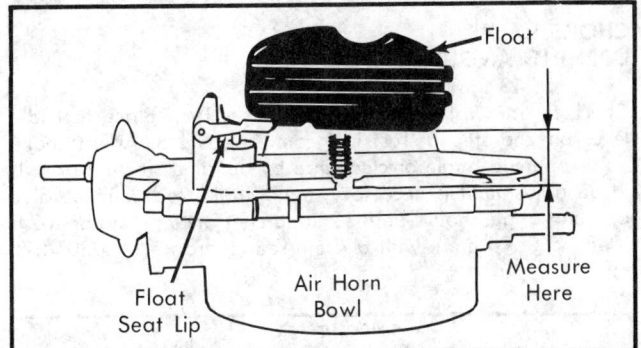

Fig. 2   Adjusting Float Level

FLOAT DROP ADJUSTMENT

Adjust float level and turn air horn over to its normal position. Make adjustment without gasket on air horn. Allow float to lower by its own weight. See *Fig. 3*. Measure distance between bottom of float and air horn bowl. If clearance is not 1.811" (46 mm), bend float stopper to obtain proper clearance.

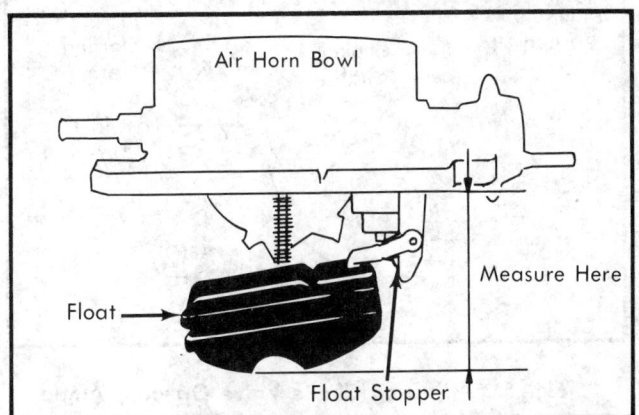

Fig. 3   Adjusting Float Drop

THROTTLE VALVE OPENING ANGLE

Close choke valve fully. Check that fast idle lever is on second position of fast idle cam. See *Fig. 4*. Adjust throttle valve opening angle or clearance by turning fast idle adjusting screw. Turn screw clockwise to make angle larger, counterclockwise to make angle smaller. Clearance should be .020-.026" (.50-.66 mm).

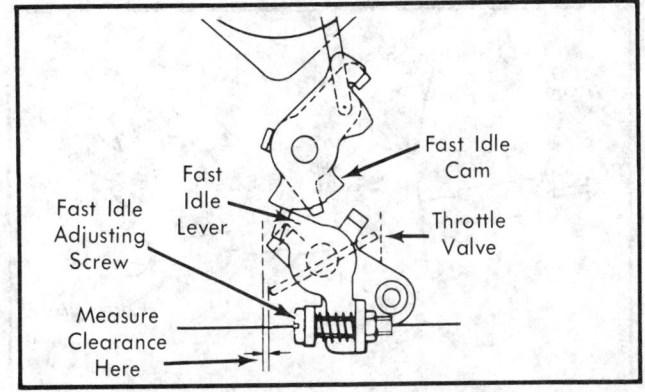

Fig. 4   Adjusting Throttle Valve Opening Angle

1980 Nikki Carburetors

NIKKI 2-BARREL (Cont.)

CHOKE VALVE OPENING ANGLE

Check throttle valve opening clearance. Then place fast idle lever on 2nd step of fast idle cam. See *Fig. 5*. Adjust choke valve opening angle or clearance by bending starting arm. If large adjustment is necessary, bend choke rod. Choke valve opening angle should be 8-12° and clearance should be .024-.038″ (.60-.95 mm), with a preferred clearance of .030″ (.75 mm).

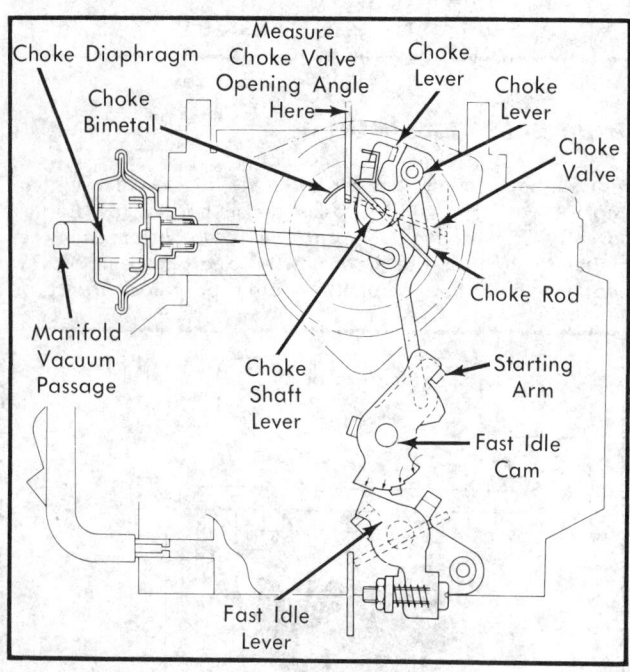

Fig. 5 Adjusting Choke Valve Opening Angle

CHOKE DIAPHRAGM ADJUSTMENT

Apply approximately 15.7 in. Hg vacuum from the choke diaphragm vacuum tube. Fast idle lever should be on high step of cam. Press choke valve slightly and check choke valve opening angle or clearance. Opening angle should be 17-21° and clearance should be .063-.079″ (1.6-2.0 mm) with a preferred clearance of .071″ (1.8 mm). If not within specifications, bend choke lever. See *Fig. 6*.

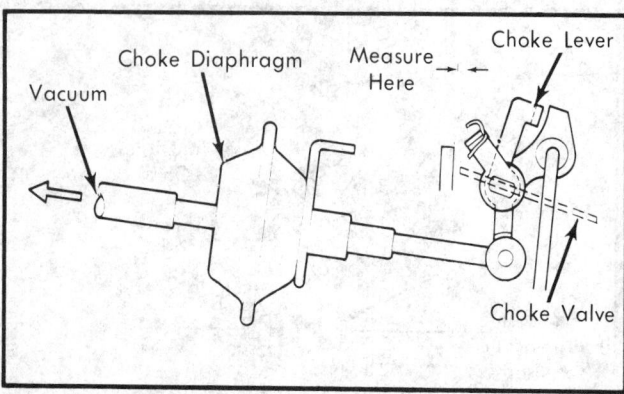

Fig. 6 Adjusting Choke Diaphragm

CHOKE UNLOADER ADJUSTMENT

Close choke valve fully and then open primary throttle valve fully. Measure choke valve opening angle or clearance. Opening angle should be 27-33° with a clearance of .102-.134″ (2.6-3.4 mm). If not within specifications, adjust by bending tab. See *Fig. 7*.

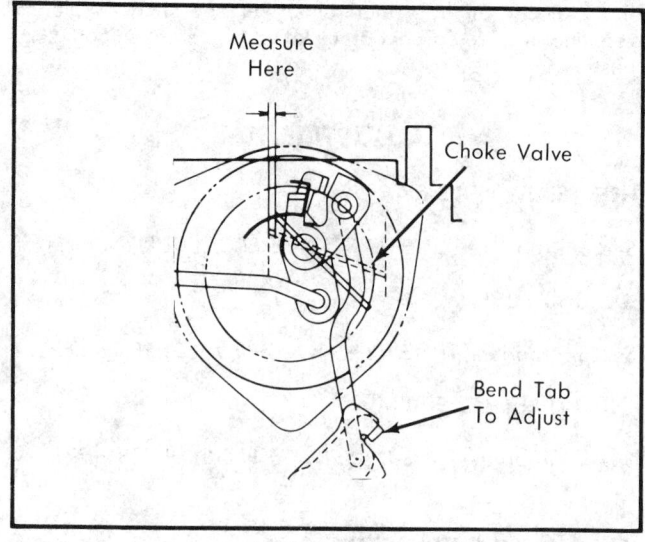

Fig. 7 Adjusting Choke Unloader

SECONDARY THROTTLE VALVE OPENING ANGLE

The secondary valve should begin to open when primary throttle valve opens 45° and should be fully open when primary valve fully opens. Check clearance of primary throttle valve and wall of throttle bore as secondary throttle valve begins to open. See *Fig. 8*. If clearance is not already to specifications, bend connecting rod to obtain .266″ (6.75 mm) clearance.

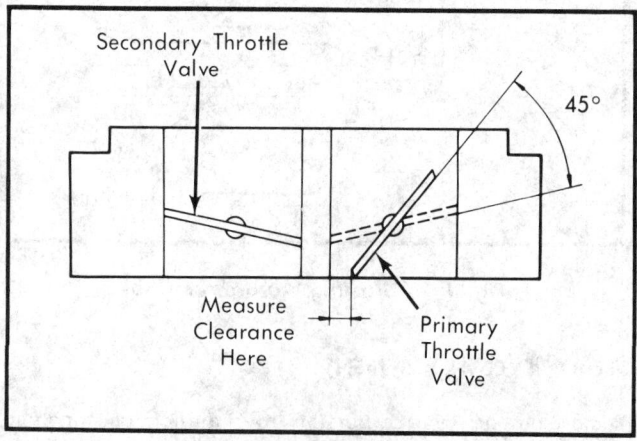

Fig. 8 Adjusting Secondary Throttle Valve Opening Clearance

NIKKI 2-BARREL (Cont.)

ACCELERATOR PEDAL HEIGHT ADJUSTMENT

Accelerator pedal should be 1.5-1.9" (40-50 mm) lower than brake pedal. Adjust rod "A" in *Fig. 9* to obtain correct adjustment. Cable free play at carburetor should be .04-.12" (1-3 mm). If free play is not to specifications, adjust nut "B" on cylinder head cover. As final check, press accelerator pedal all the way to floor and check that throttle valves are wide open. If necessary, adjust stopper bolt "C".

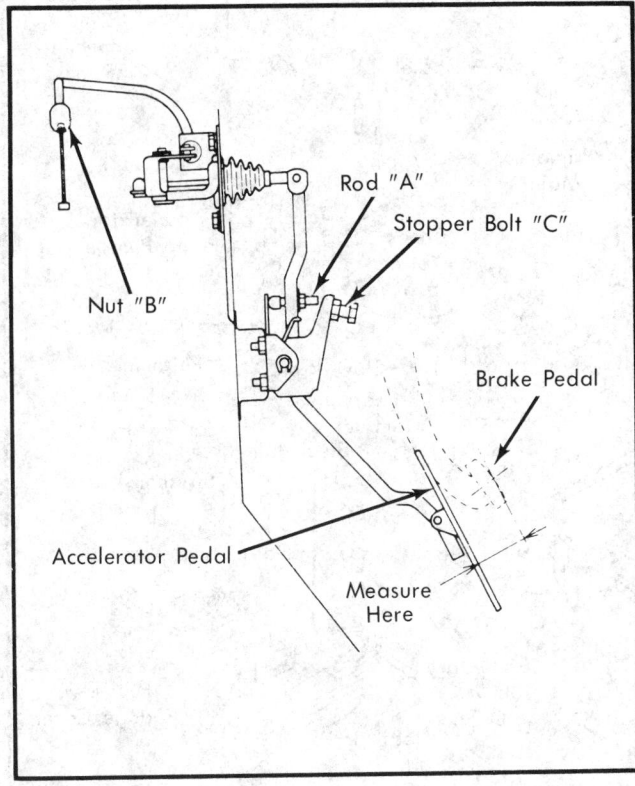

Fig. 9   Adjusting Accelerator Pedal Height

THROTTLE OPENER ADJUSTMENT (A/C MODELS ONLY)

1) Connect tachometer to engine, warm up engine and run at idle speed. *See Fig. 10*. Stop engine and remove air cleaner. Disconnect vacuum sensing tube (servo diaphragm to 3-way solenoid valve) at servo diaphragm.

2) Disconnect evaporative shutter valve vacuum hose from intake manifold. Connect servo diaphragm directly to intake manifold vacuum supply.

3) Start engine and increase speed to 2000 RPM. Turn A/C "ON". Decrease engine speed and check for 1150-1200 RPM, preferably 1200 RPM. If speed is not within specifications, turn throttle opener adjusting screw in or out to achieve 1200 RPM setting.

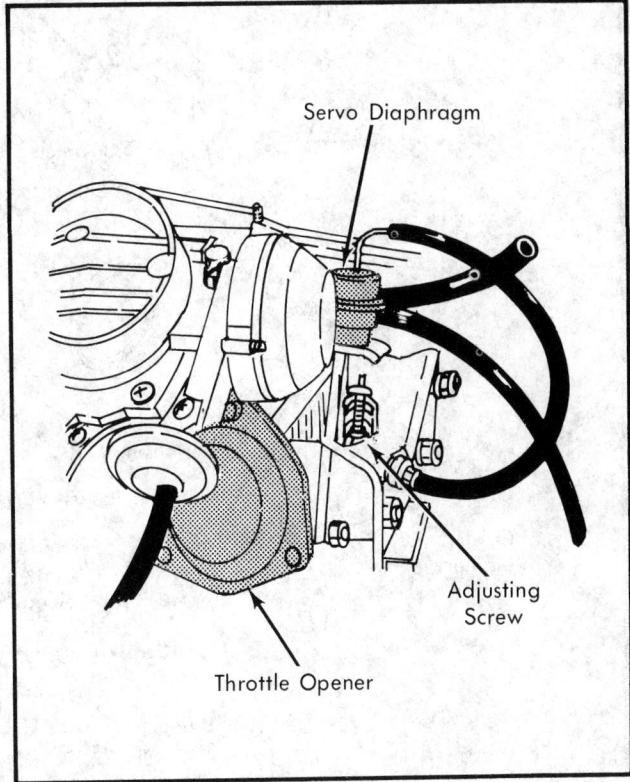

Fig. 10   Adjusting Throttle Opener (A/C Models Only)

OVERHAUL

DISASSEMBLY

1) Remove carburetor and cover intake manifold port with clean shop towel. When disassembling automatic choke and air horn, remove vacuum tube, throttle return spring, accelerator pump connecting rod and arm. Remove choke rod, air horn, automatic choke and gasket. Remove fuel inlet fitting.

2) Remove accelerator pump plunger assembly from main body. Remove retaining clip and turn main body over. Remove strainer and accelerator pump inlet check ball. Remove check valve plug and washer. Remove accelerator pump outlet check ball and spring. Remove slow fuel cut solenoid valve and gasket.

3) Disconnect throttle link and vacuum diaphragm connecting rod. Remove vacuum diaphragm and main body from throttle body.

NOTE – *One bolt attaching main body is inside the throttle body.*

4) Remove air bleeds and jets as shown in *Fig. 12*. Note the size of all jets and air bleeds so they may be reinstalled in correct position.

5) Remove throttle hanger, but do not remove throttle valve and shaft, venturi, and choke valve and shaft. Remove float and collar and needle valve assembly.

1980 Nikki Carburetors

NIKKI 2-BARREL (Cont.)

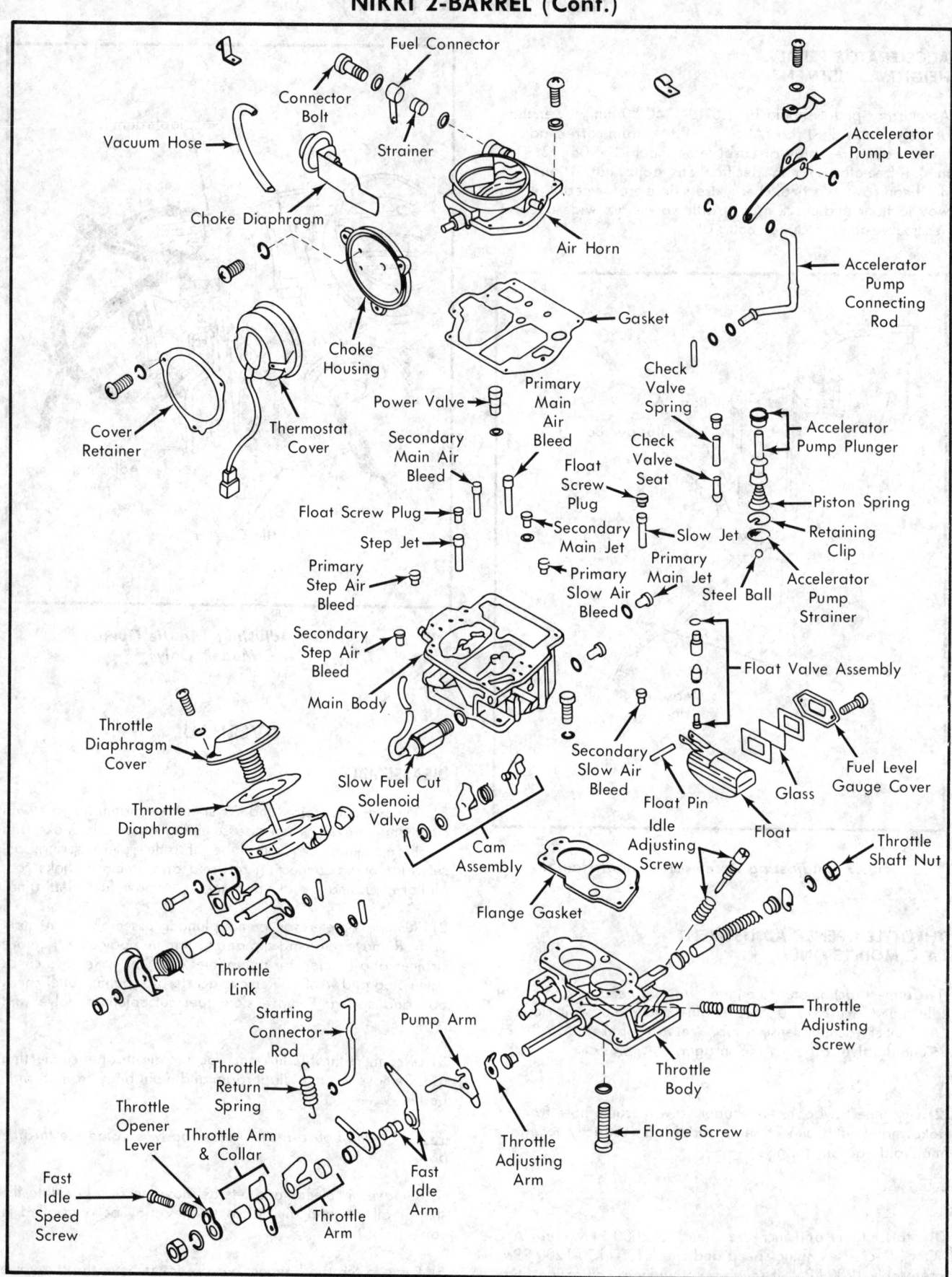

Fig. 11 *Exploded View of Nikki 2-Bbl. Carburetor (Mazda 626)*

NIKKI 2-BARREL (Cont.)

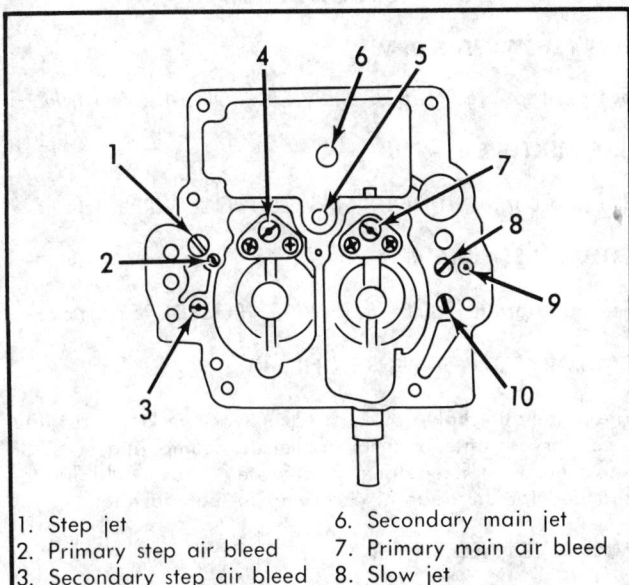

1. Step jet
2. Primary step air bleed
3. Secondary step air bleed
4. Secondary main air bleed
5. Power valve
6. Secondary main jet
7. Primary main air bleed
8. Slow jet
9. Primary slow air bleed
10. Secondary slow air bleed

***Fig. 12   Removing Air Bleeds and Jets
(Nikki 2-Bbl. Carburetor, Mazda 626)***

INSPECTION

1) Wash all parts in clean gasoline and blow out fuel passages with compressed air. Never use wire for cleaning jets. Inspect air horn, main body and throttle body for cracks and breakage.

2) Check float needle and seat for wear and float for damage. Inspect choke shaft and throttle shaft for wear. Examine all jets and air bleeds for clogs. Inspect accelerator pump plunger for wear or damage. Check diaphragms and inspect mixture adjusting screws.

3) Test solenoid valve operation by grounding body while terminal is touched to battery positive post. Valve stem should pull into solenoid body.

REASSEMBLY

Use all new gaskets and use care not to mix primary and secondary barrel parts. Before attaching air horn, check float level and float drop and adjust as necessary. After carburetor is assembled, make other adjustments as necessary.

1980 Solex Carburetors

SOLEX (MIKUNI) DIDTA 2-BARREL

Arrow
Arrow Pickup
Challenger
Champ

Colt
D50 Pickup
Sapporo

DESCRIPTION

The Solex (Mikuni) 28-32 DIDTA Carburetor is used on all 1400 cc and 1600 cc models and the 30-32 DIDTA on all 2000 cc and 2600 cc models. These 2-barrel, 2-stage carburetors utilize primary and secondary circuits. Components include a conventional accelerator pump, a vacuum-actuated secondary throttle diaphragm, a sub-EGR valve system, fully automatic choke, vacuum kick (choke breaker), and an air switching valve and coasting air valve. The 2600 cc models (also the 1600 cc engine used in Champ and Colt front wheel drive vehicles with automatic transmissions) feature a fuel cut-off solenoid. The 1400 cc and 1600 cc engines used in the front wheel drive models have a throttle opener. Other models with air conditioning may also have a throttle opener as part of an add-on kit.

CARBURETOR IDENTIFICATION

Champ and Colt Carburetor No.
(Front Wheel Drive)

Application	Man. Trans.	Auto. Trans.
1400 cc		
Federal	28-32 DIDTA-191	
Calif.	28-32 DIDTA-190	
1600 cc		
Federal	28-32 DIDTA-195	28-32 DIDTA-196
Calif.	28-32 DIDTA-193	28-32 DIDTA-294

Arrow, Challenger
Colt & Sapporo Carburetor No.

Application	Man. Trans.	Auto. Trans.
1600 cc		
Federal	28-32 DIDTA-92	28-32 DIDTA-93
Calif.	28-32 DIDTA-90	28-32 DIDTA-91
2600 cc		
Federal	30-32 DIDTA-192	30-32 DIDTA-197
Calif.	30-32 DIDTA-190	30-32 DIDTA-191

D50 & Arrow Pickup Carburetor No.

Application	Man. Trans.	Auto. Trans.
2000 cc		
Federal	30-32 DIDTA-85	30-32 DIDTA-86
Calif.	30-32 DIDTA-83	30-32 DIDTA-84
2600 cc		
Federal	30-32 DIDTA-185	30-32 DIDTA-186
Calif.	30-32 DIDTA-183	30-32 DIDTA-184

ADJUSTMENTS

HOT (SLOW) IDLE RPM

See appropriate TUNE-UP SERVICE PROCEDURES article.

IDLE MIXTURE

See appropriate TUNE-UP SERVICE PROCEDURES article.

COLD (FAST) IDLE RPM

See appropriate TUNE-UP SERVICE PROCEDURES article.

FACTORY ADJUSTMENTS ONLY

The automatic choke, choke breaker (vacuum kick), fast idle, secondary throttle opener, accelerator pump and sub-EGR valve have all been factory-calibrated and should not be changed for any reason, according to manufacturer.

FUEL LEVEL ADJUSTMENT

Bring engine to normal operating temperature while operating at idle speed, in "Neutral", and with all accessories off. Fuel level should be .15" (4 mm) above or below dot on sight glass. See Fig. 1. If not within this range, adjust by adding or subtracting packing shims at the needle valve assembly. Adding shims lowers fuel level, removing shim raises level. Each shim changes float height by .09" (2.5 mm). Always make sure there is at least one shim present to serve as a gasket in preventing leaks.

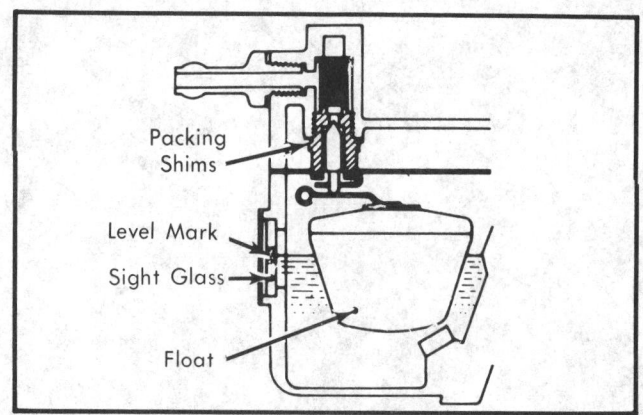

Fig. 1 Adjusting Fuel Level

THROTTLE VALVE INITIAL OPENING ANGLE ADJUSTMENT

Check initial opening angle or clearance between throttle bore and valve with fast idle screw on high (1st) step of fast idle cam. If not to specifications, turn fast idle adjusting screw in clockwise direction to increase opening, counterclockwise to decrease opening. See Fig. 2.

Throttle Valve Initial Opening Angle (Degrees)

Application	Man. Trans.	Auto. Trans.
1600 cc	12°	13°
2000 cc	12°	13°
2600 cc	13°	14°

SOLEX (MIKUNI) DIDTA 2-BARREL (Cont.)

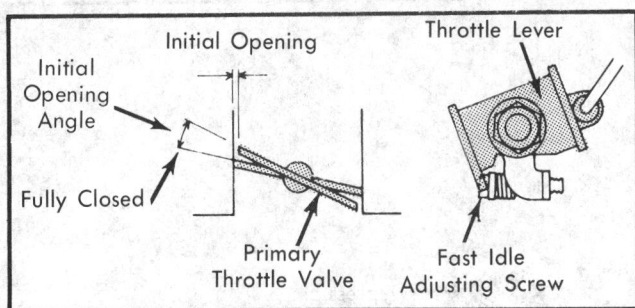

Fig. 2 Adjusting Throttle Valve Initial Opening Angle

ACCELERATOR PEDAL & CABLE ADJUSTMENT

Colt, Arrow, Challenger and Sapporo — To provide proper pedal-to-floor clearance, adjust stopper bolt so .75" (19 mm) extends through support arm and rests against stopper. See Fig. 3.

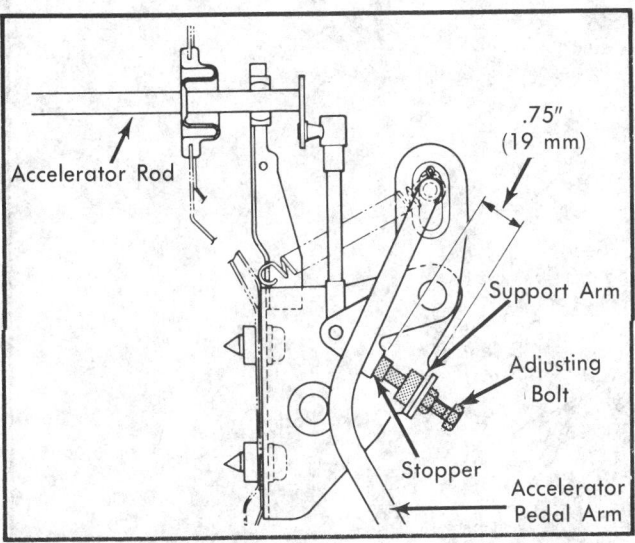

Fig. 3 Adjusting Accelerator Pedal Clearance (Arrow, Challenger, Colt & Sapporo)

Champ and Colt Front Wheel Drive — With engine at normal operating temperature, turn adjusting screw to adjust accelerator cable free play to .04" (1 mm). Tighten lock nut. Operate accelerator pedal to be sure throttle valves open and close smoothly and fully. See Fig. 4

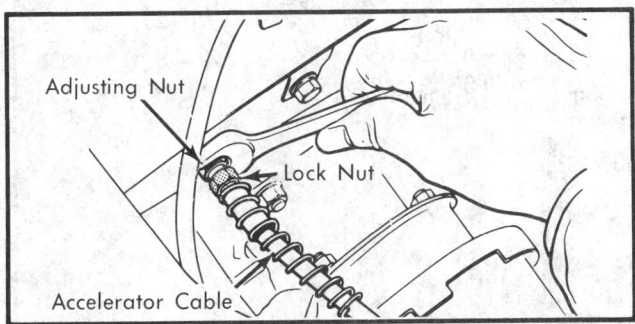

Fig. 4 Adjusting Accelerator Cable Free Play (Champ & Colt)

D50 and Arrow Pickups — Adjust cable holder to limit free play of accelerator pedal to .04" (1 mm). Operate pedal to be sure throttle valves open and close smoothly and fully. See Fig. 5.

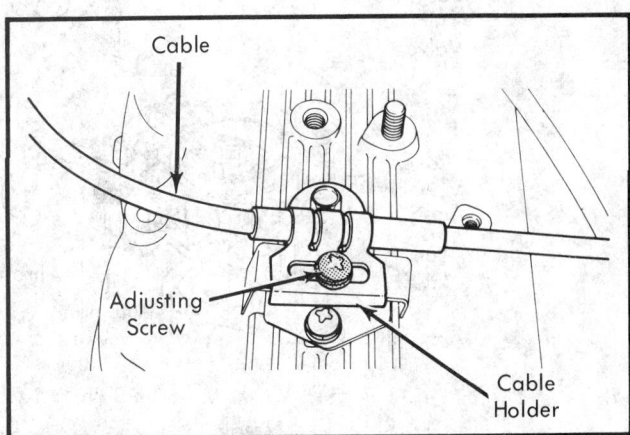

Fig. 5 Adjusting Accelerator Cable Free Play (D50 & Arrow Pickup)

OVERHAUL

DISASSEMBLY

1) Remove carburetor and disconnect water hose from choke body. Remove throttle return spring and damper srping. Remove throttle adjusting lever spring and secondary return spring. Remove choke unloader link, vacuum hose, diaphragm chamber link and chamber. On Champ and Colt front wheel drive models, remove throttle opener. Remove air switching valve. See Fig. 6.

2) Remove float chamber cover from main body, using a plastic hammer or handle of screwdriver to tap it free. Do not pry on cover when removing. Remove gasket.

NOTE — *Do not turn carburetor over with cover removed, as discharge check ball and weight may be lost from accelerator pump.*

3) Remove float lever pin, float and related parts. Remove needle valve assembly, gasket and filter. Remove coasting air valve, leaving orifice in place. Do not remove automatic choke system. Turn main body upside down and remove pump discharge check ball and weight.

4) Remove fuel cut-off solenoid, main jets and pilot jets, using a screwdriver blade that matches the groove of jets. See Fig. 7. Do not tamper with factory pre-set bypass screw or adjusting screw, both of which have white paint on their heads.

5) Remove enrichment assembly, disconnect pump rod from throttle shaft lever, and remove accelerator pump assembly. Remove sub-EGR valve link clip and the washer and spring. Disconnect link. Do not touch EGR adjusting screw (factory preset). Do not distort sub-EGR valve link when removing it.

6) Remove main body from throttle body. Remove gasket and idle speed adjusting screw, spring and washer.

1980 Solex Carburetors

SOLEX (MIKUNI) DIDTA 2-BARREL (Cont.)

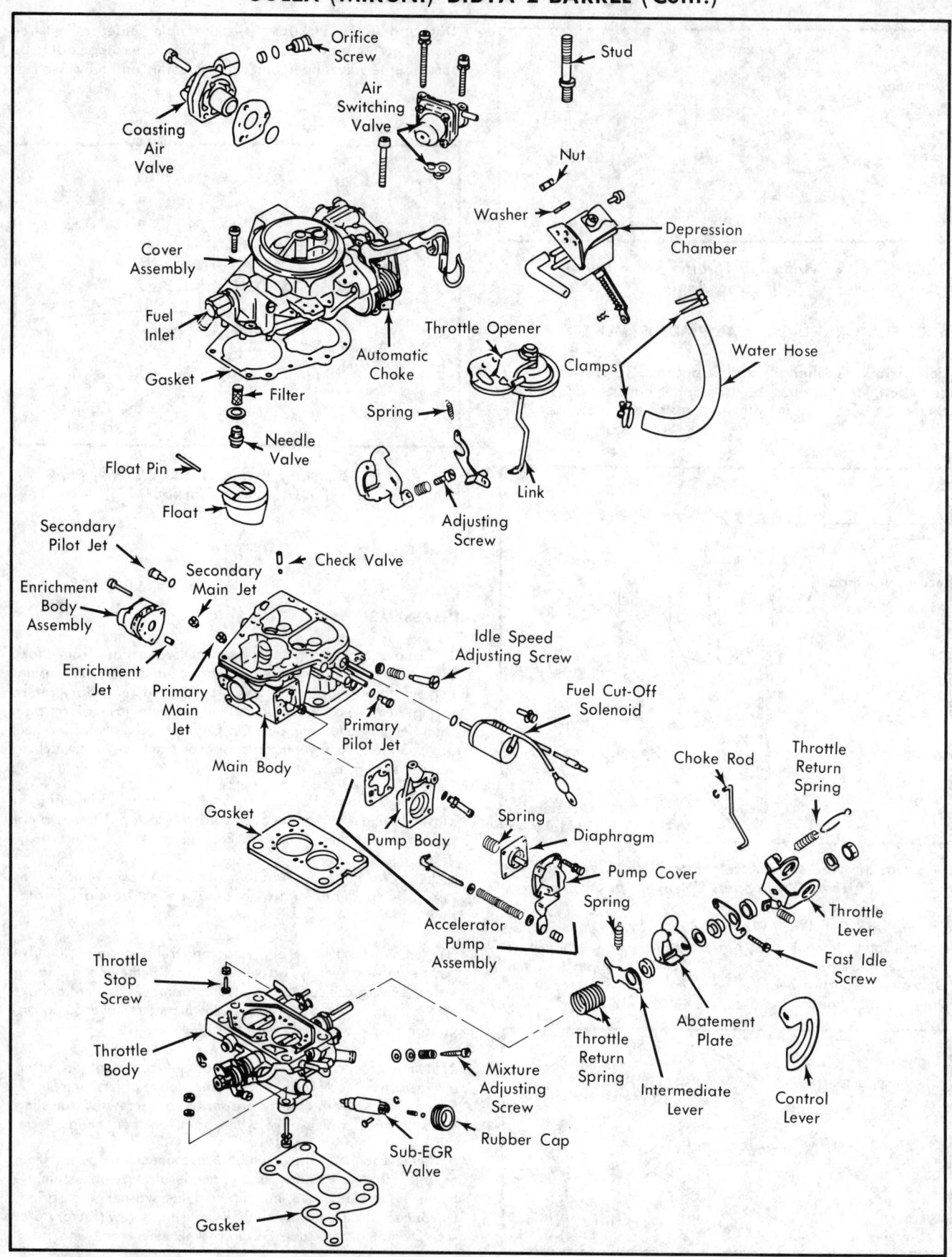

**Fig. 6 Exploded View of Solex (Mikuni) DIDTA
2-Barrel Carburetor**

SOLEX (MIKUNI) DIDTA 2-BARREL (Cont.)

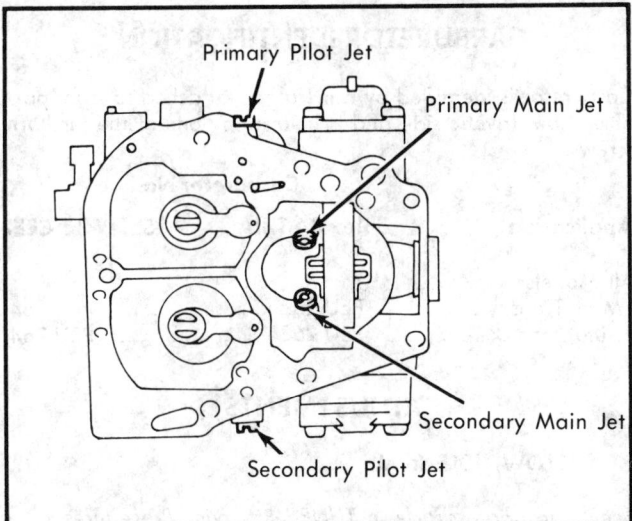

Fig. 7 *Location of Primary and Secondary Jets*

Primary Pilot Jet
Primary Main Jet
Secondary Main Jet
Secondary Pilot Jet

INSPECTION

Clean all parts removed, using care not to damage diaphragms with solvent. Check throttle valve and choke valve shafts for operation. Check jets for damage or clogging using compressed air, never use wire. Check idle mixture adjusting screw for grooves, ridges or other damage. Check needle valve assembly, strainer screen and vacuum chamber. Check fuel cut-off solenoid operation, using battery. Solenoid needle should move in when attached to battery, out when disconnected. Thoroughly inspect carburetor main body, throttle body and float chamber cover for cracks or other damage.

REASSEMBLY

1) Install the idle mixture adjusting screw, spring, washer and packing in throttle body. Turn screw lightly against its seat with fingers (do not use screwdriver). Turn idle mixture screw 1½ turns counterclockwise on 1400 cc and 1600 cc engines as a starting point; ¾ turn counterclockwise on 2000 cc and 2600 cc engines.

2) Using a new gasket, install throttle body to main body and tighten screws. Connect sub-EGR valve link to lever and install spring, washer and retaining clip. Connect accelerator pump rod to throttle shaft lever.

3) Install main jets and pilot jets. Install fuel cut-off solenoid. Using a new gasket, install enrichment valve assembly to main body. Install accelerator pump assembly, pump discharge check ball and weight.

4) Install steel ball to bottom of float chamber. Be sure brass blade is facing downward. Install filter and gasket and then needle valve assembly. Install float assembly to float chamber cover.

5) Place a new gasket on main body, install float chamber cover assembly and tighten screws. Install new gasket on float chamber cover and install coasting air valve. Using new gasket, install air switching valve on float chamber cover.

6) Install return springs and connect water hose.

SOLEX 34 TBIA 1-BARREL & SOLEX 35 CEEI 2-BARREL

Peugeot 604

DESCRIPTION

The carburetion for the 1980 Peugeot 604 is composed of a 1-barrel primary carburetor (34 TBIA) and a 2-barrel secondary unit (35 CEEI). These carburetors are mounted inline and are both of downdraft design.

The secondary 2-barrel unit is vacuum-controlled, while the primary carburetor operates directly from the throttle linkage. Opening of the secondary carburetor is progressive. With only slight depression of the accelerator pedal, only the 1-barrel carburetor functions, a mechanical stop preventing the secondary carburetor from opening.

As pedal depression increases, stop moves and allows the 2-barrel carburetor to begin operation. Vacuum pick-up for secondary carburetor operation is located at the main venturi of both the carburetors.

The idle system on both carburetors operates continually to ensure smooth transfer of operation when secondary carburetor begins to open. The 34 TBIA unit has an anti-dieseling solenoid cut-off valve. The 35 CEEI has an idle compensating solenoid for vehicles with air conditioning. High altitude models have different internal jets to compensate for differences in air density.

The 34 TBIA features a choke pull-off system, consisting of a cam-lever-link mechanism that is operated by the throttle linkage, intake manifold coolant temperature, engine vacuum, and an expanding type wax element in the choke housing. The choke pull-off offers 2 choke positions during cold engine operation. At idle, choke opening is maintained at a smaller controlled opening; at cold engine acceleration and cruise conditions, a second choke opening provides smooth throttle response and improves fuel economy and emission levels.

The 35 CEEI features a delayed throttle opening to improve cold starting and driveaway performance. It improves fuel economy by avoiding overrich mixtures at idle speed. The system is controlled and actuated by an electro-valve installed in the vacuum feed line to the carburetor's vacuum motor and by a coolant temperature switch, located in the intake manifold passage. The temperature switch is connected to the electro-valve.

When engine temperature is below 104°F (40°C), the vacuum control electro-valve is energized and valve plunger partially closes the vacuum feed line. The vacuum restriction to the vacuum motor produces a delay in throttle plate opening. When temperatures are above 104°F (40°C), the coolant temperature switch cuts off electrical flow to the electro-valve and the plunger returns to the seated position. With full vacuum to the vacuum motor, carburetor throttle plates now open normally in response to both vacuum and mechanical linkage.

Both the 34 TBIA and 35 CEEI carburetors require idle position throttle plate angle adjustment. If the adjustment of the 35 CEEI is incorrect, throttle plate operation and position can be hindered or adversely affected.

CARBURETOR IDENTIFICATION

Carburetor is identified by a metal tag attached to front part of unit on driver's side and is held on by one of the air horn screws.

Carburetor No.

Application	Solex 34 TBIA	Solex 35 CEEI
All Models		
Man. Trans.	PEU 262	PEU 264
Auto. Trans.	PEU 263	PEU 264

ADJUSTMENTS

HOT (SLOW) IDLE RPM

See appropriate article in TUNE-UP Service Procedures.

IDLE MIXTURE

See appropriate TUNE-UP SERVICE PROCEDURES article.

THROTTLE CONTROL

1) Rotate throttle drum to full open position. Stop should be against washer to opposite side of flat area.

2) Loosen lock nuts and turn throttle link to adjust. Clearance of .067" (1.7 mm) should exist between fixed stop and movable stop.

3) With engine warmed up, bring release lever against its stop in clockwise direction. Do not allow 1-barrel carburetor throttle plate to open.

4) Clearance of .157" (4 mm) should exist between control quadrant stop and return link.

THROTTLE CABLE

1) Operate engine until it reaches normal operating temperature. Shut off engine. Press accelerator pedal down completely (wide open throttle).

2) Check throttle plate of primary carburetor. Plate should be in wide open throttle position. Adjust throttle cable so cable stop has a .08" (2 mm) clearance when primary carburetor throttle plate is in wide open position.

FLOAT LEVEL

1) Fabricate a float position measurement gauge to dimensions shown in *Fig. 1*. Position gauge over float, allowing float weight to gently compress needle valve ball. Note position of float gauge and float.

2) Float should just contact gauge with gauge feet resting upon fuel bowl cover sealing surface. There should be no gap between float and gauge or between gauge feet and fuel bowl cover. DO NOT apply excessive pressure on float gauge to force gauge feet to contact fuel bowl cover.

SOLEX 34 TBIA 1-BARREL & SOLEX 35 CEEI 2-BARREL (Cont.)

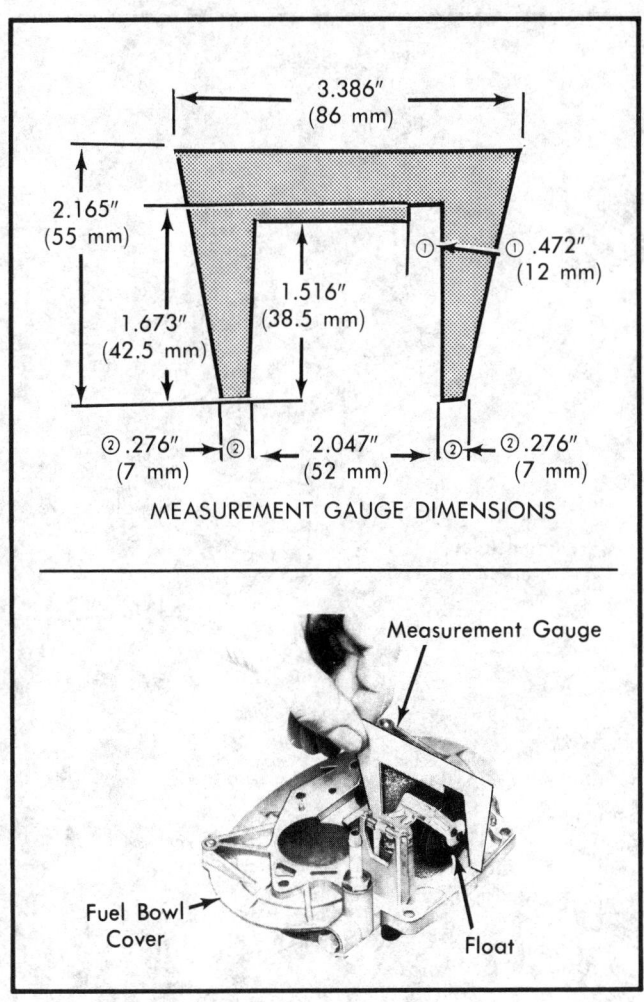

MEASUREMENT GAUGE DIMENSIONS

Fig. 1   Float Level Adjustment Showing Fabricated Measurement Gauge

NOTE – *Illustration for checking float level shows 35 CEEI carburetor fuel bowl cover as example. Appearance of 34 TBIA is different, but manner in which float level is checked is identical.*

3) Adjust float to desired position by bending hinge, using 2 pairs of long-nosed pliers. DO NOT bend at or near float, as this can cause incorrect float alignment in fuel bowl or crack float causing it to leak.

CHOKE PULL-DOWN
(34 TBIA ONLY)

1) Remove air cleaner and choke linkage cover plate. Place special tool (Part No. 9763.43) on linkage roller (roller in notch in tool). See *Fig. 2*. Tool should be against upper housing.

2) With tool in place, insert drill (.295″ or 7.5 mm) between choke flap and (flat against) air horn wall. To adjust, loosen lock nut and turn screw. Tighten lock nut when specified clearance is obtained.

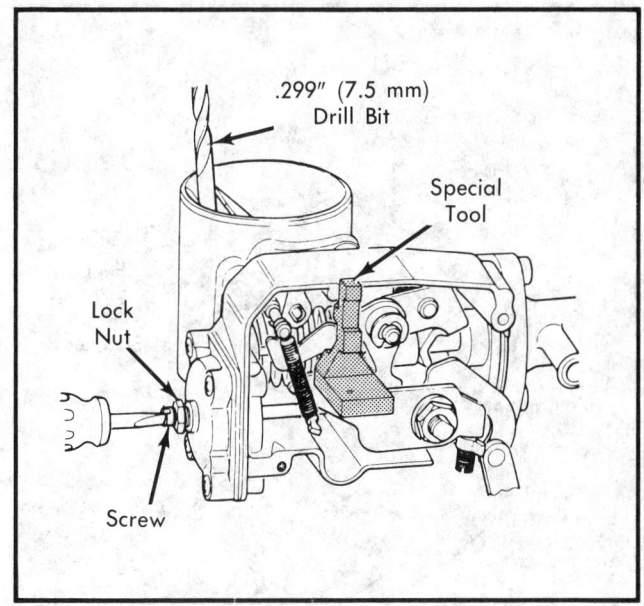

Fig. 2   Installing Special Tool for Choke Pull-Down Adjustment

CHOKE PLATE OPENING POSITION
(34 TBIA ONLY)

1) Adjust pivoting roller position by turning adjusting screw to obtain a clearance of .08″ (2 mm) between intermediate lever and choke housing. See *Fig. 3*. Install special tool in reverse position. See *Fig. 5*. Turn cam adjusting screw until the roller engages in notch of special tool.

2) Remove special tool and turn cam adjusting screw in one complete additional turn.

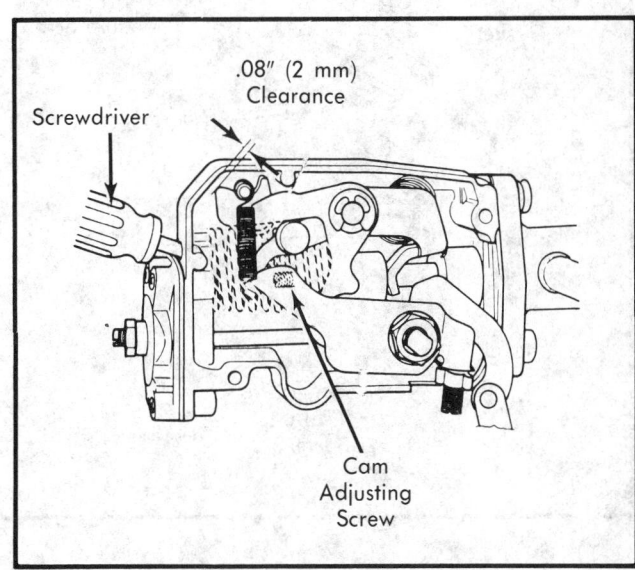

Fig. 3   Adjusting Choke Pivoting Roller Position

1980 Solex Carburetors

SOLEX 34 TBIA 1-BARREL & SOLEX 35 CEEI 2-BARREL (Cont.)

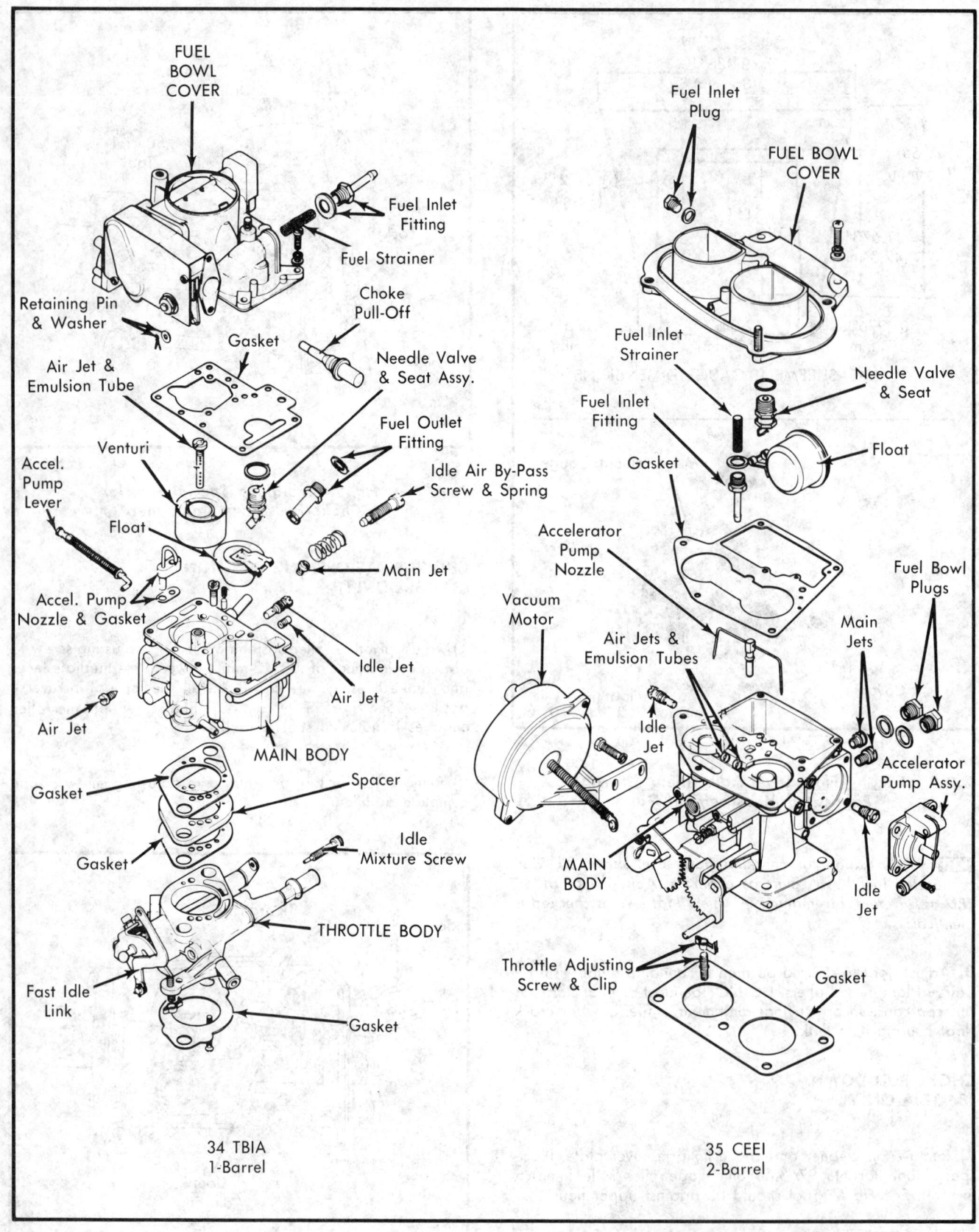

Fig. 4 *Exploded View of Solex Models 34 TBIA and 35 CEEI Carburetors*

SOLEX 34 TBIA 1-BARREL & SOLEX 35 CEEI 2-BARREL (Cont.)

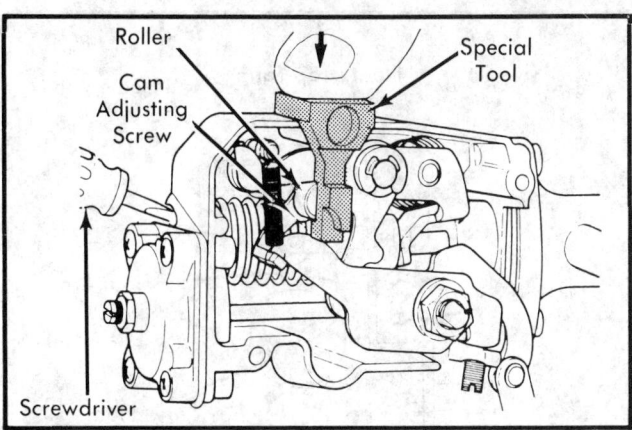

Fig. 5   Adjusting Choke Plate Opening Position

COLD (FAST) IDLE

1) Disconnect spring and push lever downward, but do not force. See *Fig. 6.*

2) Start engine and check speed (at normal operating temperature). Adjust to 3100-3200 RPM by turning screw on linkage at bottom of carburetor. Replace choke linkage cover.

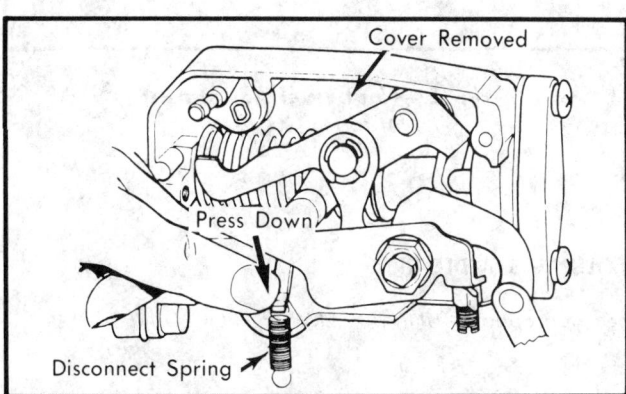

Fig. 6   Fast Idle Adjustment

ACCELERATOR PUMP STROKE

1) Back off accelerator pump adjusting rod nut. Turn carburetor upside down and insert a .197" (5 mm) diameter drill bit or gauge between throttle plate and throttle bore wall.

2) Adjust accelerator pump adjusting rod nut until nut just contacts accelerator pump arm.

ACCELERATOR PUMP NOZZLE (34 TBIA ONLY)

1) Fill carburetor fuel bowl ½ full of gasoline. Operate throttle and note direction of fuel spray from pump nozzle.

2) If spray direction was toward base of main well housing, nozzle position is correct. If not, bend nozzle to obtain desired spray direction.

THROTTLE PLATE ANGLE

Adjustment of throttle plate angle, as given by manufacturer, requires purchase of special tools, including a special dial in-dicator and accessories. Angle should be 3° 20' for the 34 TBIA or 45° for the 35 CEEI carburetor.

OVERHAUL

DISASSEMBLY

34 TBIA — 1) Remove fuel bowl cover attaching screws. Remove cotter pin attaching fast idle link to throttle and remove fuel bowl cover. Remove screws attaching throttle body to main body and separate assemblies.

2) Remove choke pull-down diaphragm cover, spring and diaphragm. Remove fuel float and fuel inlet valve, seat and gasket. Remove main body gasket, fuel inlet fitting, fuel strainer and inlet fitting gasket.

3) Remove emulsion tube and air jet assembly, and remove main jet from fuel bowl. Remove acclerator pump nozzle, carrier, and gasket. Remove idle shut-off solenoid, idle jet, idle mixture and idle speed control screws, and constant CO idle circuit jet.

4) Disconnect accelerator pump arm at throttle lever rod. Remove pump, spring and diaphragm as an assembly. Remove pump valve and valve holder as an assembly.

5) Remove throttle body from main body. Remove spacer plate, gaskets and idle adjusting screw.

35 CEEI — 1) Remove fuel bowl cover from main body. Remove fuel inlet fitting, gasket and strainer. Remove fuel inlet plug and gasket. Remove hinge pin and float. Remove needle valve, seat assembly and gasket. Set main body gasket.

NOTE — *Do not attempt to remove air correction jets or emulsion tube assemblies, as these parts are pressed into the main body to a precise depth.*

2) Remove the following parts in order: fuel bowl plugs and gaskets, main jets, idle jets, accelerator pump valve, nozzle carrier, pump housing and diaphragm, throttle motor cover, vacuum diaphragm spring and motor diaphragm, and air conditioning compensating solenoid.

CLEANING & INSPECTION

- Use regular carburetor cleaning solution. Soak components long enough to thoroughly clean all surfaces and passages of foreign matter.

- Do not soak any components containing rubber, leather or plastic materials.

- Remove any residue after cleaning by rinsing components and passages in a suitable solvent.

- Blow out all passages with dry compressed air.

REASSEMBLY

To assemble carburetor, reverse disassembly procedure, using new gaskets and seals. Make sure that all linkage operates smoothly and is not binding or sticking (pay extra attention to full throttle position for sticking or binding). Do not over tighten fuel bowl cover attaching screws.

1980 Weber Carburetors

WEBER 28/30 DHTA 2-BARREL

Fiat
Strada
X1/9

DESCRIPTION

Carburetor is two barrel downdraft design. This unit uses a diaphragm type accelerator pump, a crankcase ventilation device, carbon monoxide idling control device, excess fuel recycling device (from carburetor to fuel tank), anti-dieseling solenoid and a dashpot. A choke unloader is used to prevent excessively rich mixtures when cold starting. This system operates both by vacuum and mechanical lever and spring action. Also featured is a coolant-heated automatic choke system.

CARBURETOR IDENTIFICATION

Carburetor numbers are located on the lower edge of main body. Refer to chart in right hand column for carburetor numbers and application.

Carburetor Identification Numbers

Application	Carburetor No.
Strada	
Federal Only	
Man. Trans.	28/30 DHTA 5/180
	28/30 DHTA 5/280
Auto. Trans.	28/30 DHTA 6/180
	28/30 DHTA 6/280
X1/9	
Federal Only	
With Air Conditioning	28/30 DHTA 7/180
Without Air Conditioning	28/30 DHTA 7/280

ADJUSTMENTS

HOT (SLOW) IDLE RPM

See appropriate *TUNE-UP SERVICE PROCEDURES* article.

IDLE MIXTURE

See appropriate *TUNE-UP SERVICE PROCEDURES* article.

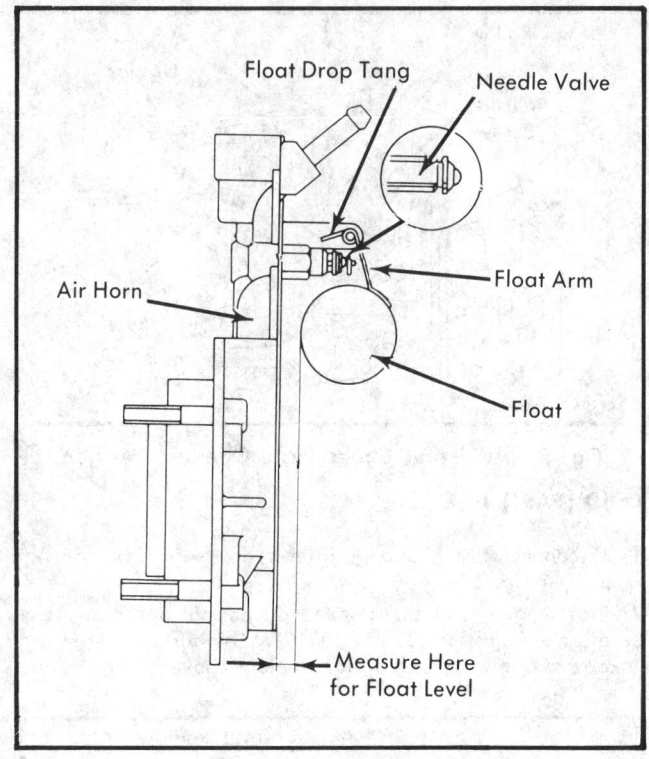

*Fig. 1   Float Level Adjustment
(Strada & X1/9)*

COLD (FAST) IDLE RPM

See appropriate *TUNE-UP SERVICE PROCEDURES* article.

FLOAT LEVEL

Remove air horn. With gasket in place on underside of air horn, hold vertically so weight of float closes needle valve gently. Measure distance from surface of gasket to float. This measurement should be .265-.285 (6.75-7.25 mm). If adjustment is needed, bend tang beneath float arm and recheck measurement.

WEBER 28/32 ADHA 2-BARREL

Fiat
Brava
Spider 2000

DESCRIPTION

Carburetor is a two stage, two barrel downdraft type unit. Primary stage is mechanically operated by accelerator linkage. Secondary stage is operated by mechanical linkage and a vacuum diaphragm. Primary stage includes idle and transition, main metering system and acceleration system. Secondary stage includes power enrichment, secondary main metering and transfer circuits. A single fuel bowl supplies fuel for both stages. A coolant heated choke bi-metal spring operates the choke plate through linkage and is completely automatic. An idle stop solenoid shuts off fuel supply when ignition switch is in "OFF" position.

CARBURETOR IDENTIFICATION

Carburetor number is located on lower edge of main body base on the side facing the engine. It can be quickly found by looking just above the gasket between main body and throttle plate housing.

Application	Carburetor
Brava	
Federal Only	
Man. Trans	28/32 ADHA 5/180
	28/32 ADHA 5/280
Auto. Trans	28/32 ADHA 6/180
	28/32 ADHA 6/280
Spider 2000	
Federal Only	
Man. Trans.	28/32 ADHA 7/180
	28/32 ADHA 8/180

ADJUSTMENTS

HOT (SLOW) IDLE RPM

See appropriate *TUNE-UP SERVICE PROCEDURES* article.

IDLE MIXTURE

See appropriate *TUNE-UP SERVICE PROCEDURES* article.

COLD (FAST) IDLE RPM

See appropriate *TUNE-UP SERVICE PROCEDURES* article.

FLOAT LEVEL

Remove air horn from carburetor. Hold vertical and ensure gasket is in place. Weight of float should gently depress needle valve. Measure distance between top of float and gasket surface. Distance should be .236-.275" (6-7 mm). If adjustment is needed, bend float arm where it joins float.

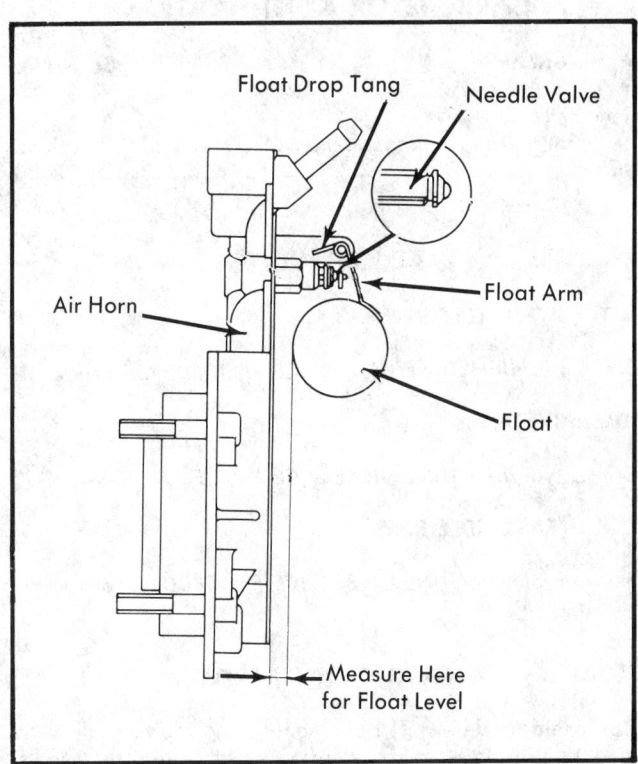

Fig. 1   Float Level Adjustment
(Fiat Brava & Spider 2000)

1980 Weber Carburetors

WEBER 32 DIR 2-BARREL

Renault
Le Car

DESCRIPTION

The Weber 32 DIR carburetor is a 2-barrel downdraft type. The carburetor base is heated by engine coolant flowing through it.

The California model has a fuel feedback system, a fast idle (throttle opener) system, a dashpot, idle cut-off, an electromagnetic vent cut-off valve and a cold start system (manual choke).

The Federal model has a throttle plate opener, an electromagnetic vent valve, idle cut-off and manual choke, but has no dashpot or fuel feedback system.

CARBURETOR IDENTIFICATION

Application	Carb. No.
Renault Le Car	
Federal	32 DIR 82
Calif.	32 DIR 80

ADJUSTMENTS

HOT (SLOW) IDLE RPM

See appropriate *TUNE-UP SERVICE PROCEDURES* article.

IDLE MIXTURE

See appropriate *TUNE-UP SERVICE PROCEDURES* article.

COLD (FAST) IDLE RPM

See appropriate *TUNE-UP SERVICE PROCEDURES* article.

FLOAT LEVEL & FLOAT DROP (TRAVEL)

California Models — 1) Hold the fuel bowl top vertically with its gasket in place, so that the float weight closes the needle without pushing the ball inward.

2) Check dimension between bowl gasket and float, float level dimension "A" in *Fig. 1*, against specifications. To adjust bend float arm "1" until inner tab "2" resting against needle, is perpendicular to needle. Tab "3" should permit float travel, dimension "B", as noted in specifications.

Federal Models — 1) Remove float bowl and hold top in vertical position. *See Fig. 2.* Allow weight of float to close needle without allowing ball to enter valve.

2) Measure dimension "A" in *Fig. 2* to check float level. If necessary, adjust by bending float arm. Measure dimension "B" for float drop or travel. If necessary, adjust by bending float tab.

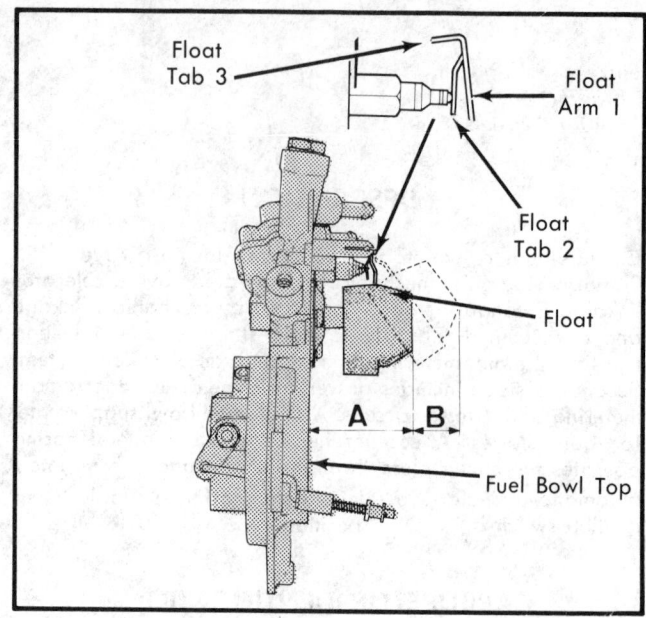

Fig. 1 *Float Level and Drop (Travel) Adjustment (California Models)*

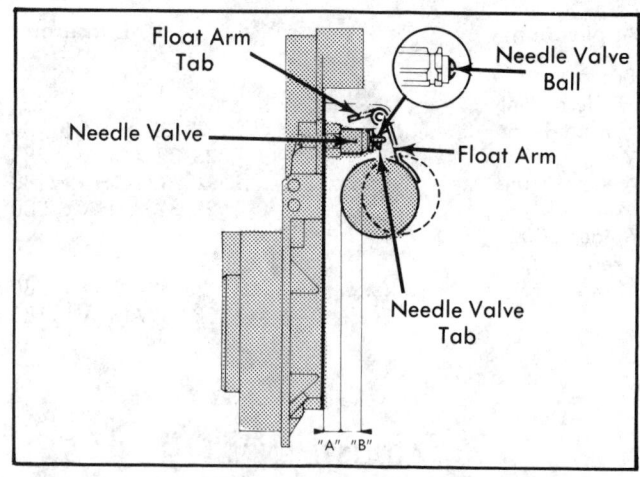

Fig. 2 *Float Level and Drop (Travel) Adjustment (Federal Models)*

INITIAL THROTTLE VALVE OPENING ADJUSTMENT

1) Put choke lever in cold start position. Measure initial opening of first barrel throttle, using feeler gauges (MS 787).

2) To adjust, remove plastic cap and turn adjusting screw until specification is reached. *See Fig. 3.* After adjustment, tighten lock nut (if equipped) and install new plastic cap over adjusting screw.

NOTE — *To remove brass cap, drill a .118" (3 mm) hole and insert screw in hole and lift off.*

WEBER 32 DIR 2-BARREL (Cont.)

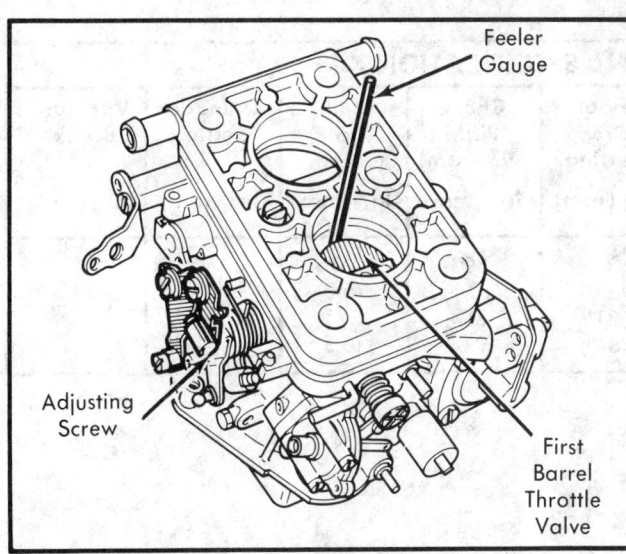

Fig. 3   Initial Throttle Valve Opening Adjustment (California Model Shown)

INITIAL CHOKE VALVE MECHANICAL OPENING ADJUSTMENT

With choke valve fully closed, push on sleeve until it contacts cam lever. Measure opening at bottom of choke valve. Measurement should be as noted in specifications. If adjustment is needed, bend link as shown in *Fig. 4.*

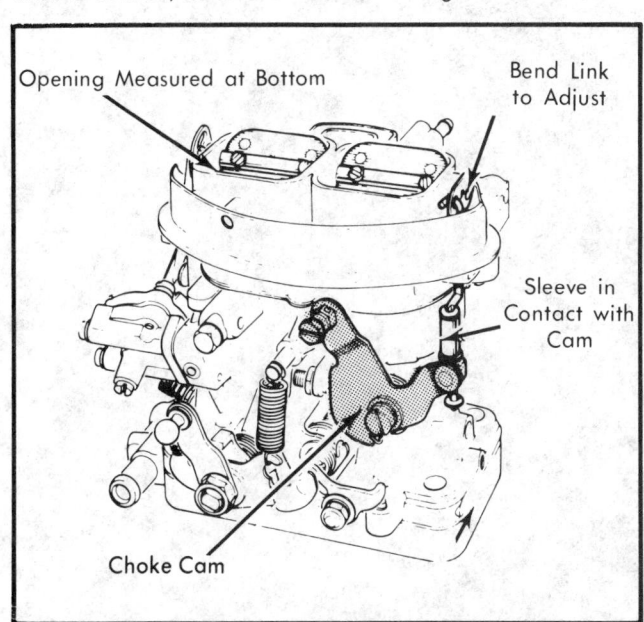

Fig. 4   Initial Choke Valve Mechanical Adjustment (Federal Model Shown)

INITIAL CHOKE VALVE VACUUM OPENING ADJUSTMENT

California Models — 1) Place choke lever in cold start position. Push in diaphragm link until it is against stop. Measure initial opening of choke valve on the large section side. *See Fig. 5.* Measure at bottom of valve.

2) Remove brass cap from adjusting screw. Turn screw, as necessary, to obtain specified valve vacuum opening.

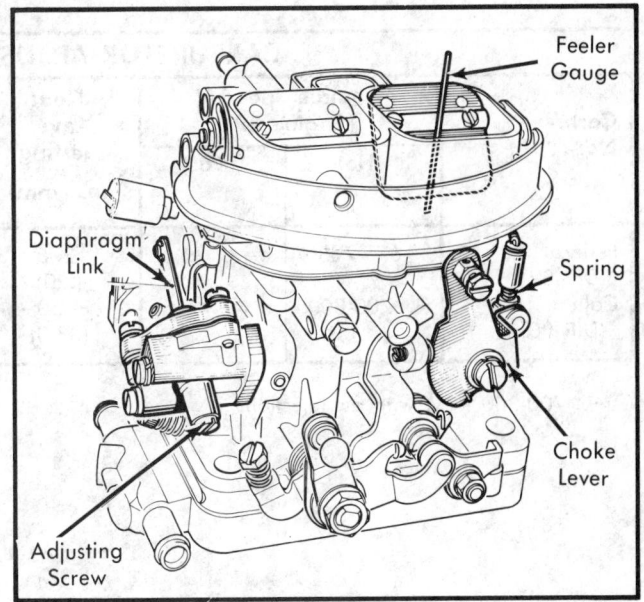

Fig. 5   Initial Choke Valve Vacuum Adjustment (California Model Shown)

NOTE — *To remove brass cap, drill a .118" (3 mm) hole and then insert a screw in cap hole and lift off.*

Federal Models — 1) Push diaphragm link in as far as possible. Now close choke valves with choke lever until spring on link is slightly compressed. Measure opening at bottom of choke valve.

2) Measurement should be as specified. If adjustment is needed, remove screw from end of diaphragm and turn set rew until choke valve vacuum opening is correct.

DASHPOT ADJUSTMENT (CALIFORNIA MODELS ONLY)

1) Install .059" (1.5 mm) feeler gauge as shown in *Fig. 3* to maintain the initial opening of the first barrel throttle plate.

2) Cut plastic cover off dashpot assembly to gain access to adjustment screw. *See Fig. 6.* Position dashpot so that it just contacts the throttle lever. Install new cover, and lock it in place by driving pin in dashpot bracket hole provided for locking purposes.

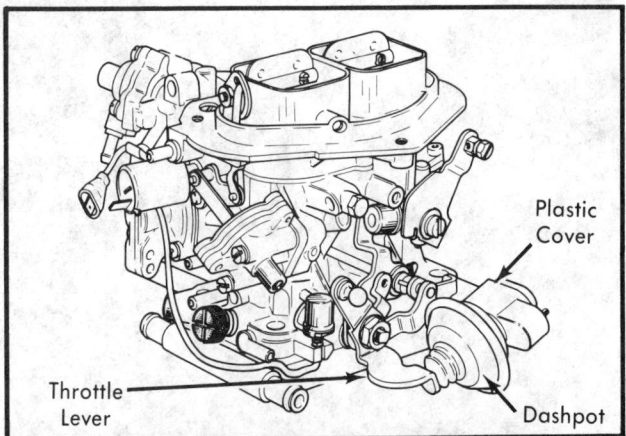

Fig. 6   Dashpot Adjustment (California Only)

1980 Weber Carburetors

WEBER 32 DIR 2-BARREL (Cont.)

CARBURETOR ADJUSTMENT SPECIFICATIONS								
Carb. No.	Idle Speed (Engine RPM)		Float Level Setting	Float Drop Setting	Choke Plate (Vacuum)	Choke Plate (Mech.)	Unloader Setting	Vacuum Break
	Hot	Fast	In. (mm)	In. (mm)	In. (mm)	In. (mm)	In. (mm)	In. (mm)
Federal (DIR 82)	675-725①	.....	.276 (7.0)	.315 (8.0)	.393 (10.0)	.236 (6.0)	.....	.....
Calif. (DIR 80)	700-800	.....	1.50 (38.0)	.315 (8.0)	.354 (9.0)	.25 (6.5)	.....	.....

① — 700-800 RPM with air injection

WEBER 740 2-BARREL

Fiesta

DESCRIPTION

The Weber Model 740 2-bbl. carburetor is a 2-stage, 2-venturi downdraft unit. Primary and secondary bores are the same size, 1.260" (32 mm). The primary throttle plate is operated directly by the throttle linkage. Secondary throttle plate is connected by linkage to primary plate.

The Model 740 has 4 basic metering systems, including idle and main metering systems, acceleration and power enrichment. Vacuum ports for distributor vacuum advance and EGR system are located in the primary bore area of the carburetor. The Model 740 is equipped with an automatic electric choke.

CARBURETOR IDENTIFICATION

Application	Carburetor No.
Federal	801F9510GA
Calif.	801F9510HB

TESTING

AUTOMATIC ELECTRIC CHOKE

1) Bring engine to normal operating temperature and turn off engine. Remove air cleaner and plug vacuum hoses to air cleaner. Check all vacuum hoses, solenoids and choke wires for proper connections. Be sure all linkage operates freely.

2) Be sure choke cap is properly aligned with index mark. Choke plates should be fully open. If not, disconnect electric choke lead from cap terminal and connect to test light. Ground second test light lead. With engine running, if light does not light, suspect faulty alternator or open circuit in choke lead. If light glows, replace choke cap.

3) Hold throttle ¼ open and move choke plates to closed position. Release plates. They should return to fully open position. If not, clean or repair choke system.

4) Using an LRE-34618 Rotunda Choke Tester or its equivalent, cool choke bi-metal. Hold throttle open and insert tester into choke housing's fast idle speed screw opening. Apply cool air for 8 minutes or until choke plates seat themselves lightly in air horn. If seating does not occur in this time, clean and repair choke system.

5) Hold choke plates ¼ open and remove tester. Allow throttle to close. Choke plates should remain partially open and throttle will be in kickdown position. Without touching throttle, start and run engine. Open throttle momentarily and then release it. Choke plates should be vertical and engine speed should drop to normal idle. If not, replace electric choke cap unit.

6) Turn off engine, remove test equipment and reinstall all components.

FUEL BOWL VENT

NOTE — *Before removing air cleaner, be sure to remove No. 3 and 4 spark plug wires from clip attached to air cleaner. Disconnect vacuum, evaporative and air pump hoses and electrical connections.*

1) Apply parking brakes and block wheels. Remove air cleaner. Remove bowl vent hose from canister. Check fuel bowl vent solenoid for external damage and electrical connections. Attach a Rotunda T75L-9487-A tool or equivalent to end of canister hose.

2) Turn ignition switch off and hold choke plates open. Force air into fuel bowl vent system by squeezing tool's rubber bulb. If no fuel is displaced through metering system, start engine and run for 2 minutes. Turn off engine, and repeat test.

3) If fuel is still not displaced, remove carburetor air horn. Switch ignition on and off. Solenoid plunger should retract when switch is on and extend when off. If so, replace bowl vent plunger seal. If not, replace solenoid, plunger, seal and plunger spring. Reassemble carburetor.

4) With ignition switch on and tool still connected, again force air into fuel bowl vent system. If rubber bulb resists rapid squeezing (pressure build up), bowl vent is working properly. If not, disconnect electrical lead to bowl vent solenoid and connect it to test light. Ground second test light lead.

5) Turn ignition switch on. If test light does not glow and battery is okay, solenoid lead has an open circuit. Repair or replace. If light glows, remove test light and reconnect lead to solenoid. Remove all test equipment and reassemble all components. Install air cleaner and check all hose connections. Start and run engine at 2500 RPM for 15 seconds and turn off engine.

ADJUSTMENTS

HOT (SLOW) IDLE RPM

See appropriate *TUNE-UP SERVICE PROCEDURES* article.

IDLE MIXTURE

See appropriate *TUNE-UP SERVICE PROCEDURES* article.

COLD (FAST) IDLE RPM

See appropriate *TUNE-UP SERVICE PROCEDURES* article.

CHOKE PLATE VACUUM PULL-DOWN

NOTE — *DO NOT perform this adjustment unless replacement choke pull-down adjusting screw SEAL is available.*

1) Remove carburetor from vehicle.

2) Remove (3) choke retaining screws, ring, housing and heat shield.

3) Open throttle to wide open position.

4) Close choke valve.

5) Place fast idle adjusting screw on FIRST step of fast idle cam and close throttle.

6) Using an outside vacuum source of 17 in. Hg, hook vacuum pump into vacuum channel on pump bore under base of carburetor.

7) Measure clearance between LOWER edge of choke plate and bore wall.

NOTE — *Make measurement using applied vacuum of 17 in. Hg and light thumb pressure closing choke plates.*

NOTE — *Modulator spring should NOT be compressed.*

1980 Weber Carburetors

WEBER 740 2-BARREL (Cont.)

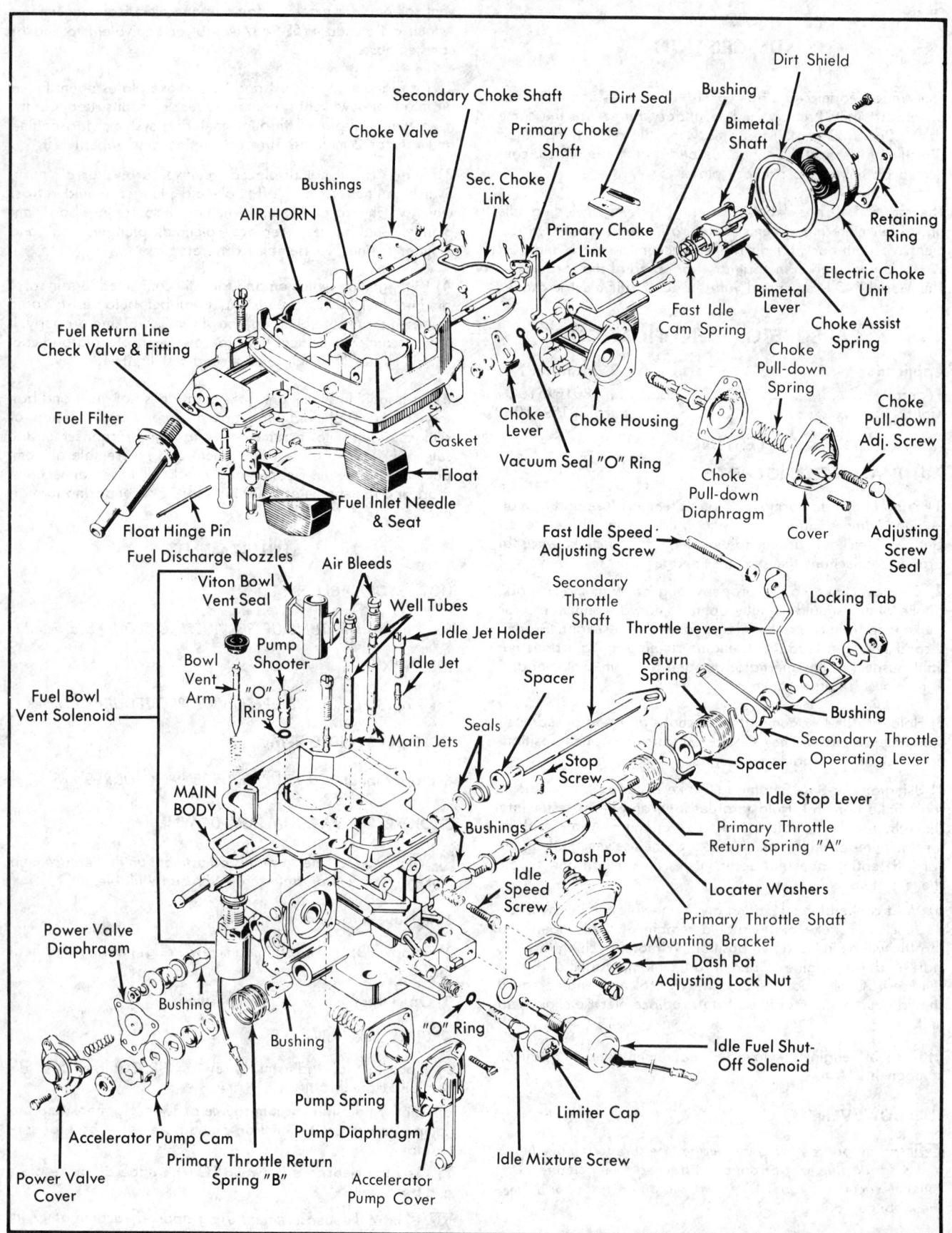

Fig. 1 Exploded View of Weber Model 740 2-Bbl. Carburetor

WEBER 740 2-BARREL (Cont.)

8) If adjustment is needed, turn vacuum diaphragm adjusting screw in or out as required.

9) When correct clearance has been obtained, install carburetor on engine.

10) Reinstall dirt shield, choke cap, ring and (3) screws.

FLOAT LEVEL

1) Remove air cleaner.

2) Remove carburetor air horn from carburetor main body.

3) Remove gasket from air horn.

4) Hold carburetor in vertical position. *See Fig. 2.*

NOTE — *Needle and seat assembly are spring loaded. Air horn must be held vertically to obtain accurate float setting.*

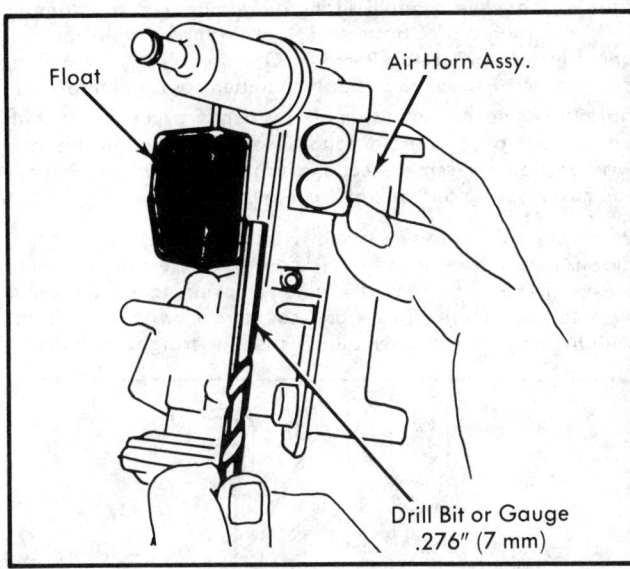

**Fig. 2 Float Level Adjustment
(Hold Air Horn As Shown)**

5) Insert drill bit or pin gauge of correct size (.276" or 7 mm) between float and air horn casting gasket surface. To adjust, bend float arm as necessary, at float.

OVERHAUL

DISASSEMBLY

NOTE — *To prevent damage to throttle plates, install carburetor legs or four 2¼" bolts into base, using eight nuts. Use separate containers for parts removed from various assemblies.*

Bowl Cover — 1) Remove fuel filter. Remove bowl cover screws and washers. Remove cover.

2) Remove float hinge pin, float and inlet needle. Remove inlet needle seat and gasket, bowl cover gasket and fuel return line check valve and fitting.

Automatic Electric Choke — 1) Remove bowl cover. Open throttle plate to clear fast idle screw. Remove 3 choke cap retaining screws, retaining ring, cap unit and dirt shield.

2) Remove three screws securing choke housing to bowl cover and disengage choke link. Remove "O" ring from vacuum passage.

3) Remove three choke pull down cover screws. Remove cover, spring and diaphragm assembly.

Accelerator Pump — 1) Remove four pump cover screws and cover, pump diaphragm and pump return spring.

2) To remove internal pump shooter, the bowl cover must be removed. Remove "O" ring with shooter.

Main Body — 1) Remove idle fuel shut-off solenoid and washer. Remove fuel bowl vent solenoid and washer. Remove three power valve cover screws, power valve cover, spring, and diaphragm.

2) Remove dash pot (if so equipped). Remove throttle kicker (air conditioned cars only). Remove idle limiter cap, mixture screw and spring.

3) Remove fuel discharge nozzles, primary idle jet holder, secondary idle jet holder and high speed air bleeds.

NOTE — *Idle jets are located in bottom of holders. The air bleeds, main well tubes and main jets are a press fit assembly, but may be removed and assembled by hand.*

Idle Fuel Shut-Off Solenoid — Remove solenoid, using a spanner wrench (Rotunda No. TBE). When installing, torque to 38-42 INCH lbs. (43.8-48.4 cmkg).

INSPECTION

Thoroughly clean all parts and use compressed air to clean jets and fuel ports. Do not use wire brush. Check parts for wear or damage and replace plastic or rubber parts if questionable. Check all diaphragms for cracks or other defects.

REASSEMBLY

To assemble carburetor, reverse disassembly procedure, noting the following. Do not intermix parts. Replace gaskets, seals and "O" rings with new ones, and check that all linkage moves freely without binding or sticking. Do not overtighten attaching screws.

CARBURETOR ADJUSTMENT SPECIFICATIONS

Ford Carb. Number	Idle Speed (Engine RPM)		Fast Idle Cam Setting	Accel. Pump Setting	Float Level Setting	Choke Pull-Down Setting	Unloader Setting	Auto. Choke Setting
	Hot	Fast						
801F9510GA 801F9510HB	①	2000 RPM②	.....	.....	.276"③ (7 mm)	.236"④ (6 mm)	.276"⑤ (7 mm)	INDEX

① — See Emission Control Tune-Up Decal.
② — ±100 RPM.
③ — ±.031" (.8 mm).
④ — ±.020" (.5 mm).
⑤ — Minimum.

1980 Zenith-Stromberg Carburetors

ZENITH-STROMBERG CD TYPE 1-BARREL

MGB (Federal)
Triumph (Federal)

DESCRIPTION

Stromberg CD type carburetor is a constant depression carburetor, which operates on the principle of varying effective areas of choke and jet openings. This variation depends upon the degree of throttle opening, engine speed and engine load requirements. The MG and Spitfire models have single carburetors, and the TR-7 and TR-8 have twin carburetors. All carburetors feature automatic chokes. MGB and Spitfire models are not available in California in 1980, and all California TR-7 and TR-8 models are equipped with fuel injection.

CARBURETOR IDENTIFICATION

Application	Type No.
MGB	175 CD5T
Triumph	
Spitfire	150 CD4T
TR-7	Two 175 CDFVX
TR-8	Two 175 CDSET

ADJUSTMENTS

HOT (SLOW) IDLE RPM

See appropriate *TUNE-UP SERVICE PROCEDURES* article.

IDLE MIXTURE

See appropriate *TUNE-UP SERVICE PROCEDURES* article.

COLD (FAST) IDLE RPM

See appropriate *TUNE-UP SERVICE PROCEDURES* article.

FLOAT

With float cover removed and carburetor body inverted, measure distance from gasket surface of body to highest point of float. This distance should be .624-.672" (16-17 mm).

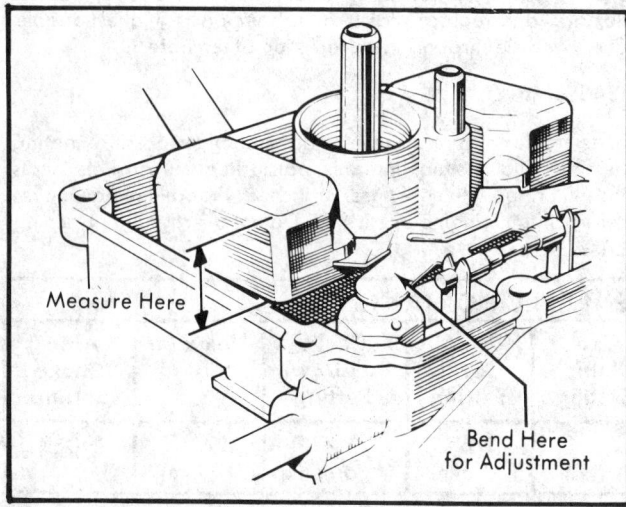

Measure Here

Bend Here for Adjustment

Fig. 1   Float Level Adjustment Points

NOTE — *Use care to prevent misaligning floats when making adjustment. If necessary to adjust, bend float tab that contacts fuel inlet needle. Be sure tab rests on needle valve at a 90° (right) angle. See Fig. 1.*

OVERHAUL

NOTE — *The following overhaul procedure is generally applicable to all Stromberg CD type carburetors, although minor variations may exist from carburetor to carburetor. Internal and external components of some models may vary slightly.*

1) With carburetor removed, unscrew the damper cap. Reach in through air filter side of carburetor bore and with finger, raise piston while carefully lifting oil retainer cap (on damper rod). Pull plug out of bottom of float chamber and drain fuel and oil from carburetor. Remove "O" ring on float bowl plug. Remove screws securing float chamber to bottom of carburetor. Remove float assembly by gently prying float shaft out of clip on carburetor body. Remove needle valve and washer. Remove screws securing top cover to body. Remove top cover, spring and air valve assembly.

2) From air valve assembly, remove screws securing diaphragm and retaining ring. Loosen set screw holding needle in air valve and insert needle removing tool (S353) into stem of air valve. Turn tool counterclockwise two turns, withdrawing needle assembly by pulling straight upward.

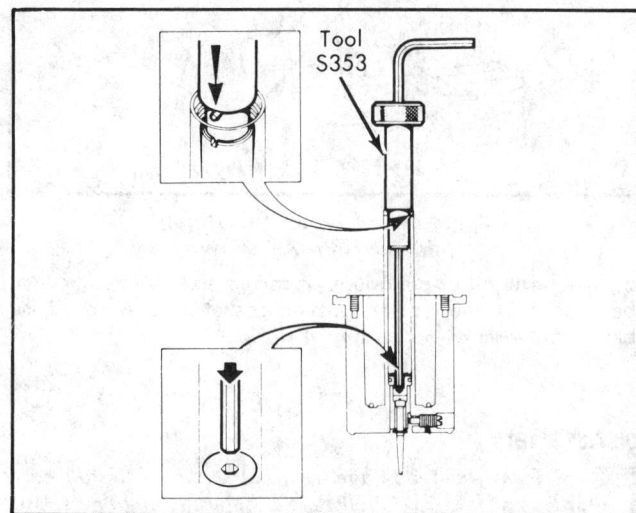

Tool S353

Fig. 2   Removing Needle Valve with Special Tool

3) Remove choke retaining screws and remove choke assembly from side carburetor body. From removed choke assembly, remove EGR air bleed valve, nut and lock washer from choke spindle, choke cable lever, fast idle cam, and choke (starter) disc.

4) Remove screws securing idle air regulator. Remove screws securing deceleration by-pass valve. From deceleration by-pass valve body, remove screws in base plate, spring, valve and gaskets. Remove star washer to release adjustment screw from valve housing. Remove "O" ring seal from adjustment screw and unscrew lock nut. Remove split pin and withdraw clevis pin and washers to disconnect throttle linkage from throttle spindle lever. Remove throttle lever.

ZENITH-STROMBERG CD TYPE 1-BARREL (Cont.)

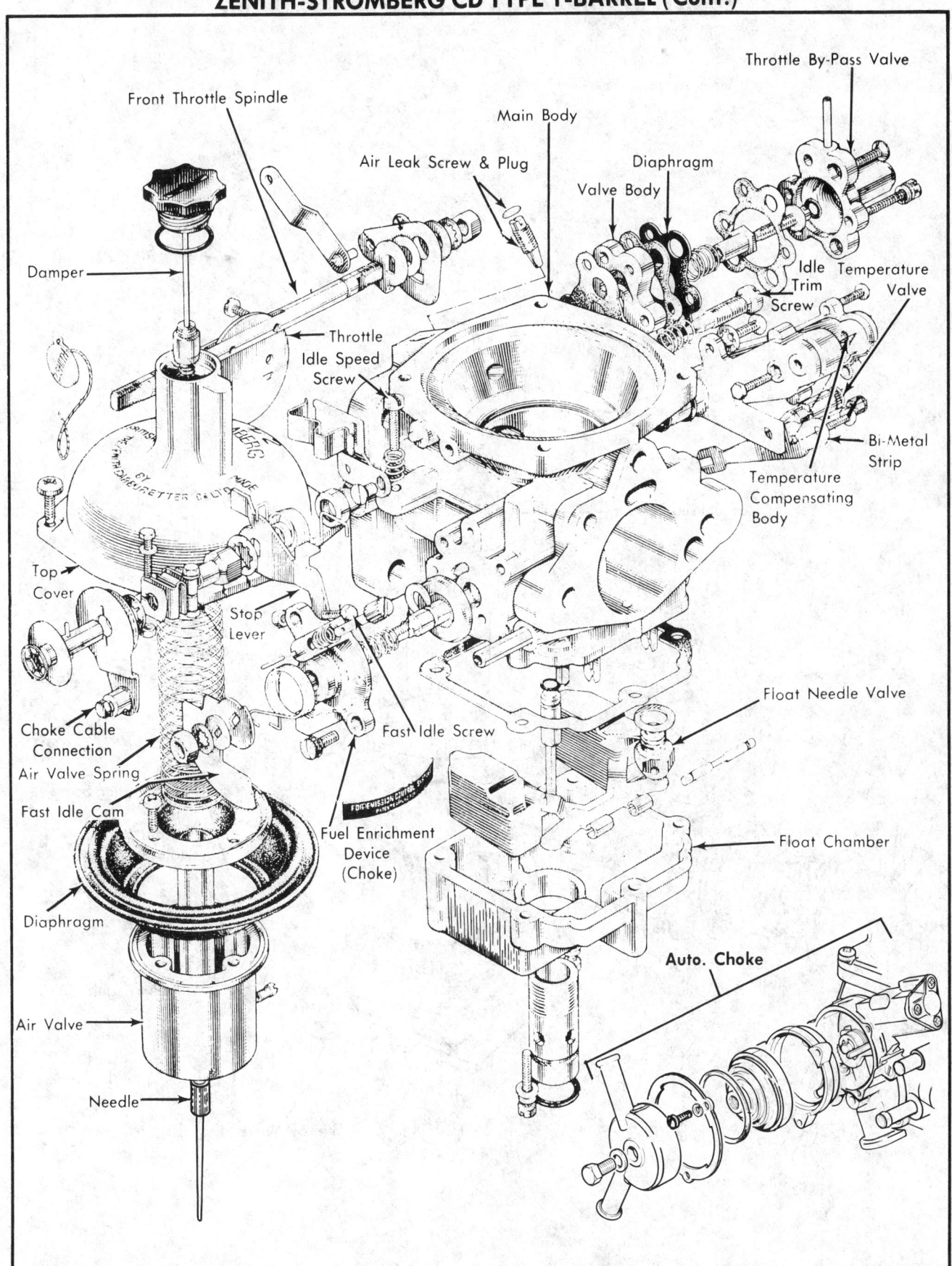

Fig. 3 Exploded View of Stromberg 175 CDFVX Carburetor

ZENITH-STROMBERG CD TYPE 1-BARREL (Cont.)

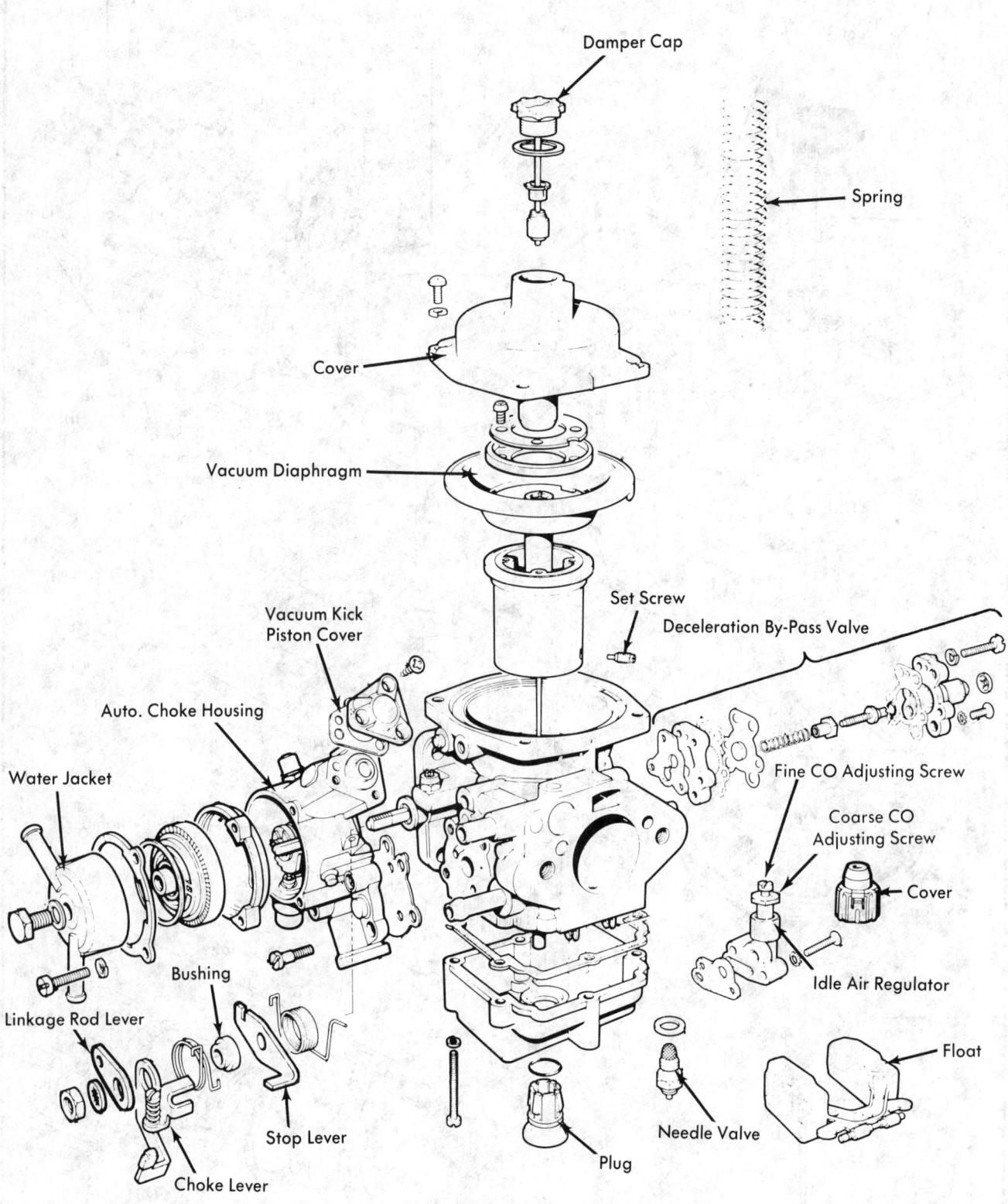

Fig. 4 Exploded View of CD4T Carburetor Assembly

ZENITH-STROMBERG CD TYPE 1-BARREL (Cont.)

CLEANING & INSPECTION

Wash all components in clean fuel or suitable carburetor solvent and blow dry with compressed air. Examine all parts for wear, paying particular attention to needle and seat, air valve and diaphragm.

NOTE — *The parts previously mentioned should be replaced, unless all are in excellent condition.*

REASSEMBLY

Reverse disassembly procedures and note the following:

1) When fitting deceleration valve, ensure that register for the spring is toward the valve body.

2) Refit disc assembly to choke body, ensuring that lug with detent ball is between slot of disc and largest series of holes. Refit cam lever and choke cable lever (to choke body) ensuring that cam lever is located on detent ball.

3) When installing air valve needle assembly with tool S353, make sure tool is turned clockwise to engage threads of needle valve assembly with adjusting screw. Continue to turn until slot in needle housing is aligned with set screw. Tighten set screw carefully.

4) When fitting diaphragm to air valve, locate inner tag of diaphragm into recess of air valve. Now fit diaphragm retaining ring and secure with screws. Fit air valve assembly to carburetor body, by locating outer tag and rim of diaphragm with complimentary recesses of body. Fit carburetor top cover with bulge on housing neck toward air intake.

5) Fill carburetor damper dashpot with lightweight engine oil or Dexron automatic transmission fluid. Fill until resistance is felt to insertion of damper piston when screw cap of damper piston is about .25" (6 mm) above top cover.

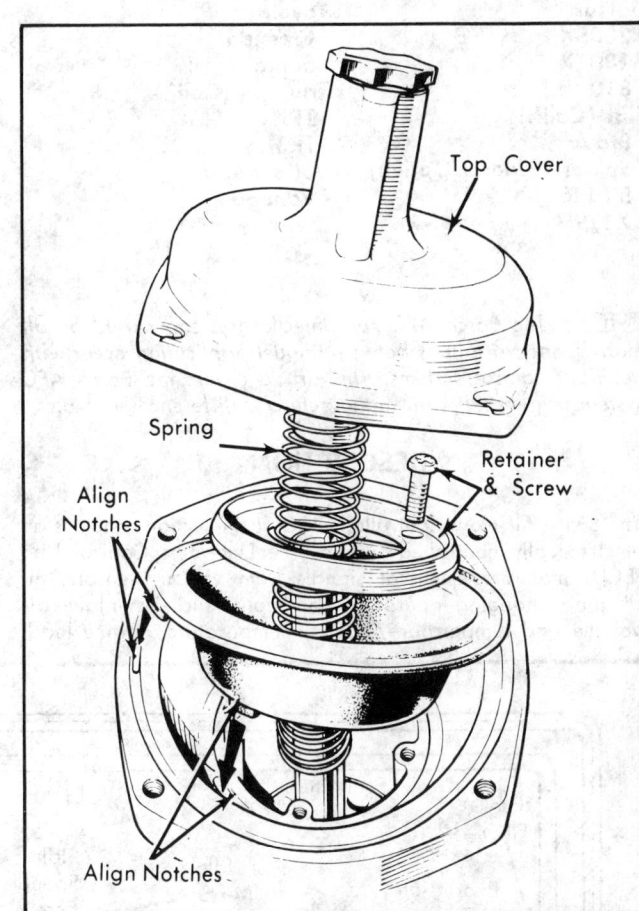

Fig. 5 Expanded View of Vacuum Piston and Diaphragm

1980 Bosch Fuel Injection

BOSCH AFC FUEL INJECTION SYSTEM

BMW
528i
633CSi
733i
Datsun
200SX
280ZX
810
Fiat (Calif.)
Brava
Spider (Federal Option)
Strada
X1/9

Jaguar
XJ6
Porsche
928
Toyota
Cressida
Supra
Triumph (Calif.)
TR7
TR8
Volkswagen
Vanagon

NOTE — *The Bosch AFC Fuel Injection system is used on all models and variations between model application occur with auxiliary control systems. This article covers the Bosch AFC system in general, with manufacturer's differences noted.*

DESCRIPTION

The Bosch Air Flow Controlled (AFC) fuel injection system is an electronically controlled system. The Electronic Control Unit (ECU) monitors electrical signals from various sensors, indicating changing operating conditions; such as intake air volume and temperature, coolant temperature, engine load, acceleration/deceleration and exhaust gas oxygen content (some models). The ECU analyzes these signals and determines the fuel injection duration necessary for optimum air/fuel ratio. *See Fig. 1.*

An air flow meter, mounted between the throttle chamber and air cleaner, is the major control unit in addition to the ECU. The air flow to the engine is monitored by the ECU and fuel is adjusted accordingly by timing injector delivery. Injector delivery is based upon amount of intake air required for one engine rotation. The AFC system maintains constant fuel pressure and maintains proper air/fuel mixture by adjusting quantity of fuel to amount of intake air.

A "Closed Loop" feedback system is incorporated into the Bosch AFC fuel injection system by various manufacturers. The system consists of an oxygen sensor (2 on TR8) mounted in the exhaust manifold, special 3-way catalytic converter and special electronic control unit with feedback monitor system. Some systems also employ a modulating valve or frequency valve. Oxygen sensor feedback systems are used on the following models:

- All BMW Models
- Calif. Datsun 280ZX & 810
- Calif. Fiat Brava, Strada & X1/9
- All Fiat Spider 2000

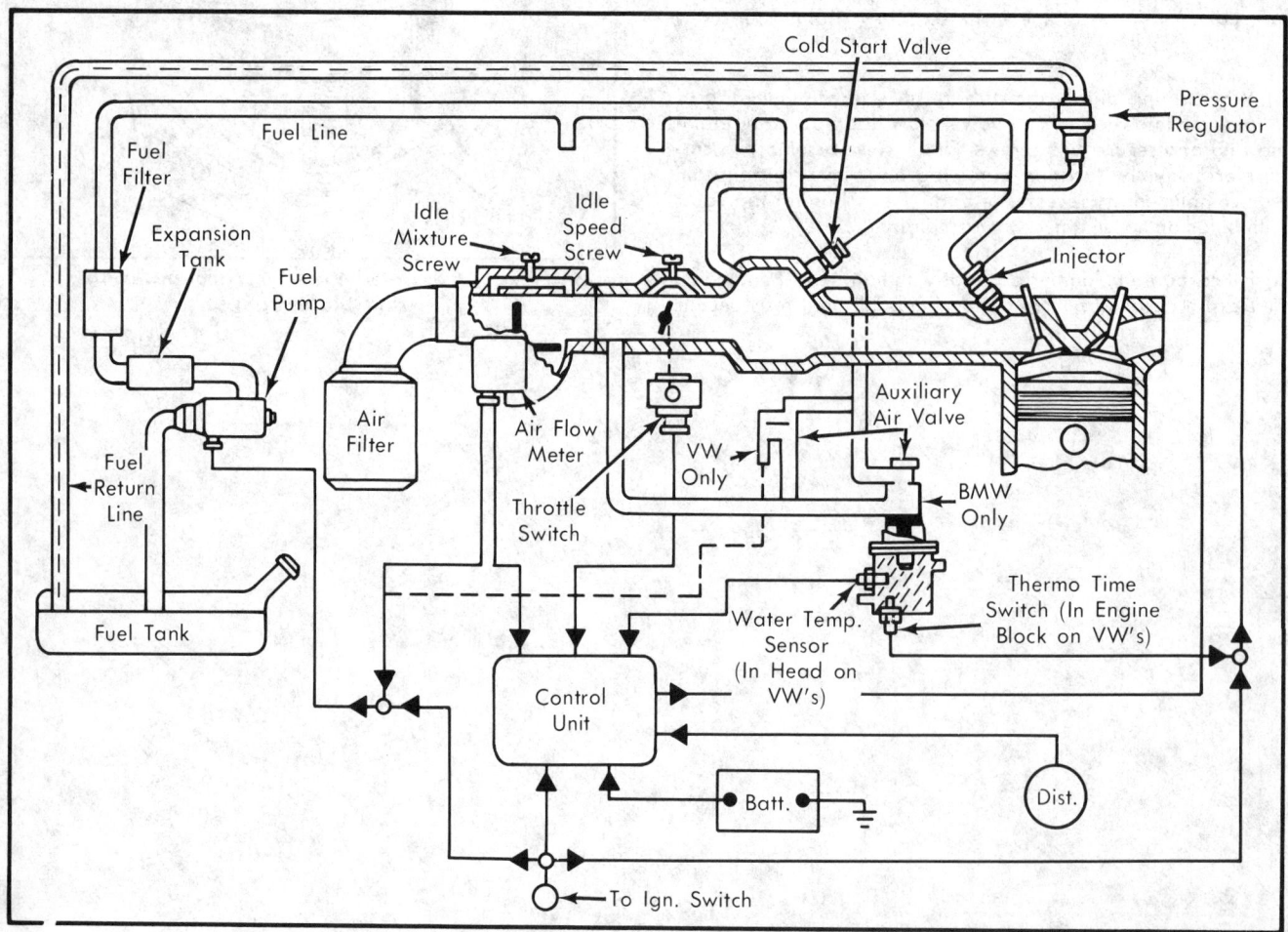

Fig. 1 Diagram of Bosch AFC Fuel Injection System (Exc. Datsun 280ZX & 810)

BOSCH AFC FUEL INJECTION SYSTEM (Cont.)

- All Jaguar Models
- All Porsche 928
- Calif. Toyota Cressida & Supra
- All Triumph Models
- Calif. Volkswagen Vanagon

OPERATION

FUEL SYSTEM

Fuel under pressure from electric fuel pump, flows through a pulsation damper (some models) to a pressure regulator. The pressure regulator consists of a sealed, spring loaded diaphragm with a connection for intake manifold vacuum. Fuel pressure differential is maintained at approximately 36 psi (2.5 kg/cm²) between fuel pressure and intake manifold vacuum to ensure amount of fuel injected is solely dependent upon injector "open" time. Fuel in excess of fuel differential is returned to the fuel tank. To aid in cold engine starting, a cold start valve (injector) is activated by a thermo-time switch (except Datsun 200SX) to increase quantity of fuel to combustion chambers.

FUEL INJECTORS

A fuel rail links the fuel pressure regulator with fuel injectors. Each cylinder is provided with a solenoid operated injector, mounted to directly spray fuel towards back of each inlet valve. Each injector is energized through the distributor (coil) and grounded through the ECU to complete the electrical cir-

cuit. Each injector is linked in series to a resistor (except TR7 and all Fiat models) which reduces operating voltage of the injector and also protects injector from power surges. The ECU controls the electrical pulsations required to open each injector and the length of time each injector is open. Therefore, no fixed relationship exists between injector timing and ignition timing or valve timing. The time that the injectors are open governs the amount of fuel delivered and the time is controlled by interpretation of sensor impulses received by the ECU. Each injector opens at the same time to deliver ½ the fuel required for ideal combustion with each engine revolution.

AIR FLOW SYSTEM

Air is drawn in through air cleaner and is measured by the air flow meter. Air then travels through throttle chamber and into intake manifold. A throttle valve in the chamber controls air flow while driving. At idle, throttle valve is almost closed and air is drawn through a by-pass port in throttle chamber. Idle speed adjusting screw controls quantity of air intake at idle. During warm-up operation, extra air is by-passed through air regulator to increase engine RPM.

The oxygen sensor detects the amount of oxygen in the exhaust gases. If the sensor senses too much or too little oxygen in the exhaust gases, a change in voltage is produced in the sensor and is transmitted to the ECU. The ECU then changes the amount of fuel injected by using the modulating valve to vary

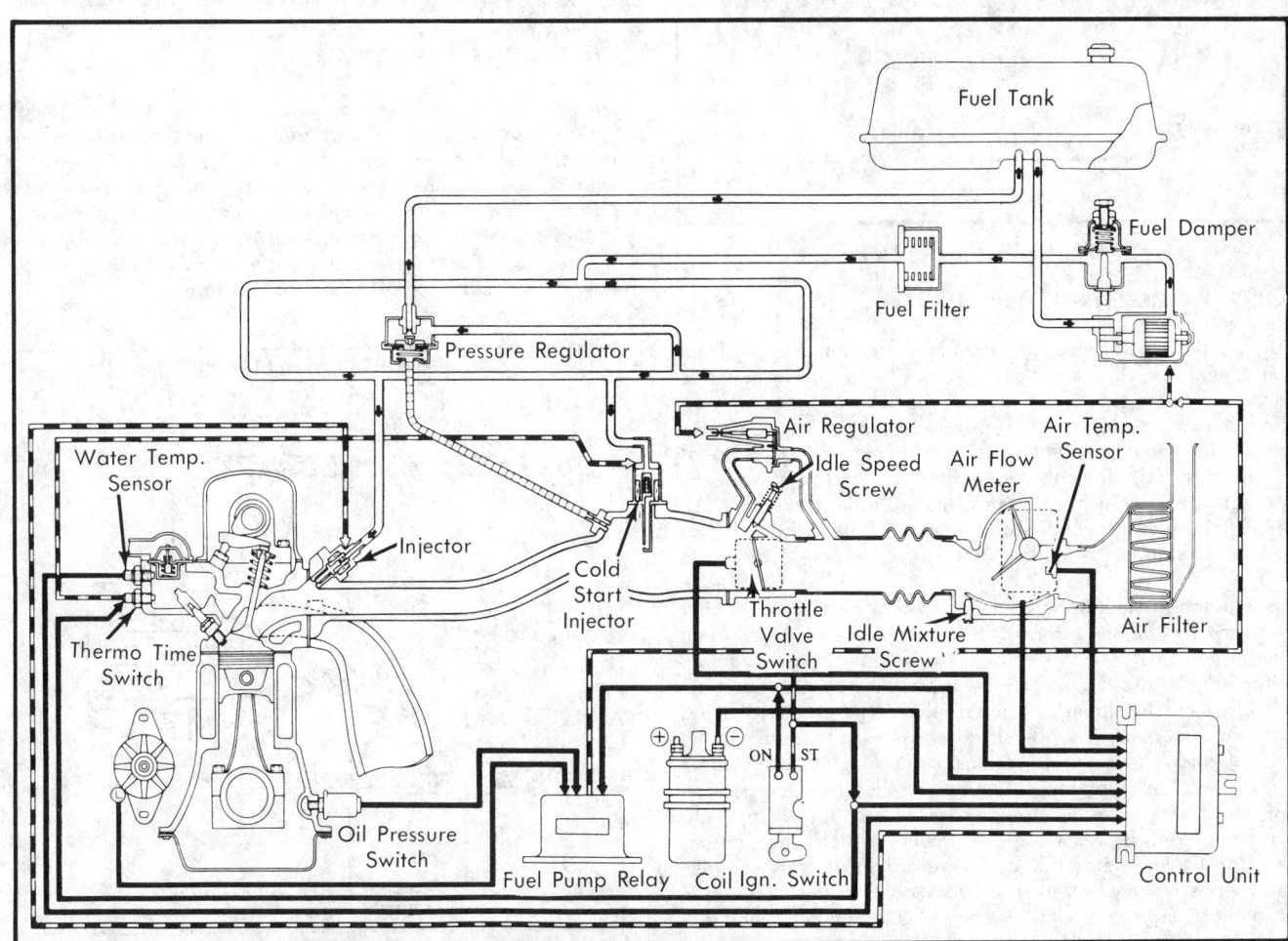

Fig. 2   Diagram of Bosch AFC Fuel Injection System (Datsun 280ZX & 810)

BOSCH AFC FUEL INJECTION SYSTEM (Cont.)

the length of time injectors are on. This varying injection time leans or richens the air/fuel ratio, keeping the air/fuel ratio very close to the stoichiometric value of 14.5 to 1.

ELECTRONIC CONTROL UNIT (ECU)

All components of the control system are electrically connected to the electronic control unit. See *Fig. 3.* The ECU is a pre-programmed computer which receives and interprets data from various sensors to calculate the amount of fuel required by the engine to maintain maximum efficiency with minimum exhaust contamination. The ECU controls the injection pulses and injects the correct amount of fuel by controlling length of time injectors are held open. An automatic function of the ECU is to provide fuel enrichment whenever engine is cranked, regardless of engine temperature. This is activated by a direct electrical connection from the starter circuit to the ECU.

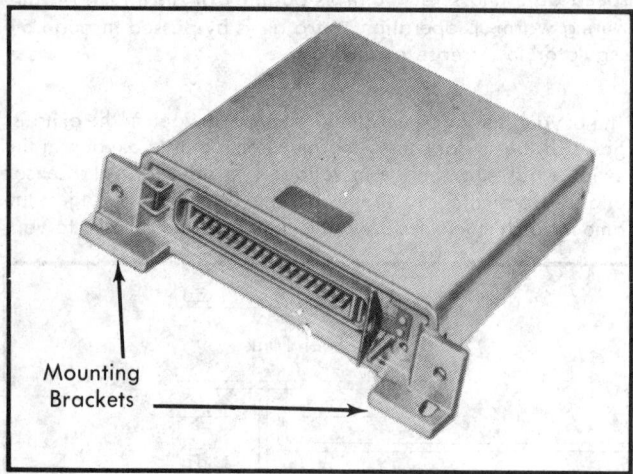

Fig. 3   Electronic Control Unit (ECU)

AIR FLOW METER & POTENTIOMETER

The air flow meter measures the amount of air entering from air cleaner to the throttle housing. The air flow meter is basically a tunnel with a similarly shaped measuring flap and dampening flap (offset 90° on same casting). The measuring flap swings on an axis in air stream against reverse pressure of a spiral spring. The measuring flap is linked to a variable potentiometer which regulates the voltage sent to ECU, depending upon angular displacement of flap as it opens and closes in relation to air flow. See *Fig. 4.*

In addition to monitoring air flow, the air flow meter also controls the fuel pump (except Datsun models) and idling. Within the potentiometer is an electrical contact for fuel pump relay. With engine stopped, no air flow is present, fuel pump contact is open and fuel pump is inoperable. While engine is being started, fuel pump is supplied power from starter relay via the combination relay. Once engine starts, fuel pump contact closes and fuel pump operation is controlled by open position of air flow measuring flap. If flap closes, fuel pump contacts open and power is cut to fuel pump. At idle, the measuring flap is almost closed due to spiral spring pressure. An idle air by-pass channel receives air from main air flow through a small hole, the size of which is controlled by the idle speed adjusting screw. The idle speed adjusting screw also controls quantity of air and exhaust emissions during idle speeds.

NOTE — *Datsun fuel pumps operate on same basic principle, except engine operating mode is sensed by engine oil pressure and alternator output. BOTH oil pressure and alternator output must be lost to break fuel pump relay. Manufacturer recommends thorough test of system to preclude faulty diagnosis of related fuel system components.*

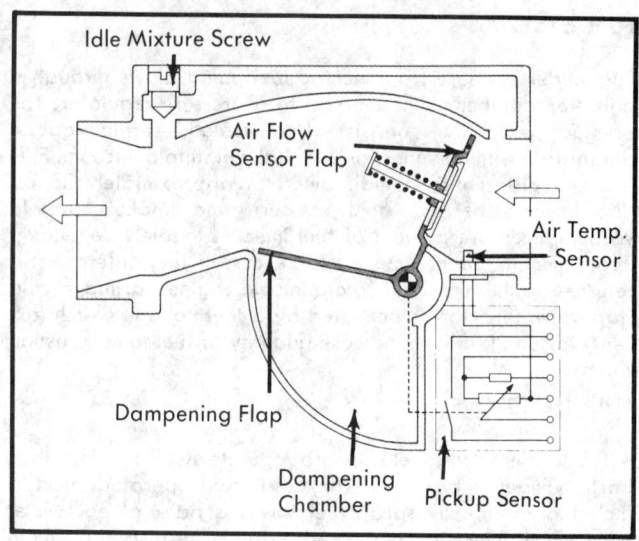

Fig. 4   Air Flow Meter Schematic

AIR TEMPERATURE SENSOR

The air temperature sensor provides the control unit with voltage signals. The temperature of incoming air is converted to electrical impulses which are used by the ECU to adjust engine fuel requirements. The higher the intake air temperature, the lower the electrical impulse; less fuel is required at higher temperatures because of the vaporization ability of warm air. The air temperature sensor is integral with the air flow meter and cannot be serviced or repaired.

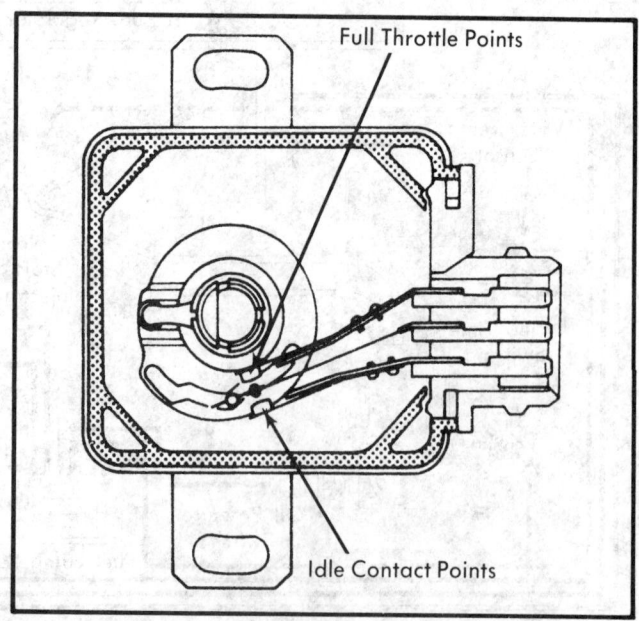

Fig. 5   Typical Contact Type Throttle Switch

BOSCH AFC FUEL INJECTION SYSTEM (Cont.)

THROTTLE VALVE SWITCH

A potentiometer type throttle switch is installed on throttle chamber of TR8 models and a contact type is used on all other models. Both throttle switches send electrical impulses to ECU with information on throttle position. On contact type switch, signals are sent to ECU when throttle is fully open or fully closed. See Fig. 5. The potentiometer type monitors the throttle plate angle at all times and through variable resistance, electrical impulses are sent to ECU. The throttle switch on Porsche models deactivates the oxygen sensor during vehicle coasting and when throttle valve is opened more than 30°. This lowers exhaust gas temperatures.

ENGINE COOLANT SENSOR

This sensor provides ECU with engine temperature information relating to cold starting and warm-up enrichment operation. The coolant sensor operates in conjunction with cold start system and auxiliary air valve to provide same function as an automatic choke on carbureted engines. As coolant temperature increases, enrichment decreases until engine reaches normal operating temperature.

NOTE — *Any reference made to coolant temperature implies cylinder head temperature for Volkswagen.*

AUXILIARY AIR REGULATOR

The auxiliary air regulator provides additional air required to aid in cold engine starting and initial warm-up. The valve consists of an electrically heated bi-metal strip, movable disc and air by-pass channel. The bi-metal strip is wrapped with a heater coil which is energized by the fuel pump relay. Control of the bi-metal plate is done by engine coolant temperature (except Datsun models). The air by-pass channel is open when engine is cold and closes gradually as temperature rises. At predetermined temperatures, air by-pass channel is blocked and additional air flow stops. See Fig. 6.

NOTE — *Control of Datsun auxiliary air regulator is by monitoring engine oil pressure and alternator output. For more information see "Air Flow Meter" in this article.*

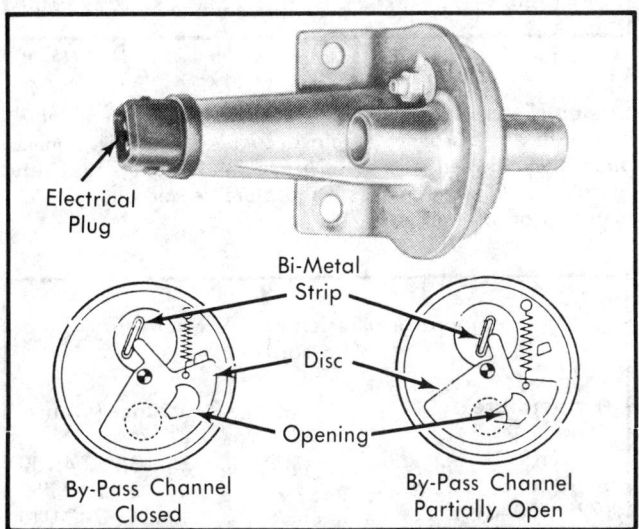

Fig. 6 Typical Auxiliary Air Regulator

THERMO-TIME SWITCH

For cold starting, additional fuel is injected into intake manifold by the cold start injector (valve). This cold start aid is controlled by the thermo-time switch. The switch has a bi-metal contact, surrounded by a heating coil which is energized during cranking. Thermo-time switch limits cold start relay to 5-20 seconds under extreme cold engine starts. When engine coolant temperature is above 95°F (35°C), bi-metal contact breaks ground circuit of cold start injector (valve) and cold start enrichment is by-passed.

NOTE — *Datsun 200SX is not equipped with cold start aid.*

VACUUM SWITCH

All Datsun, Jaguar, Toyota and Triumph models are equipped with a switch to compensate for high load/low manifold vacuum conditions when full throttle contacts have not been activated. Upon acceleration, additional fuel is required and is provided by this switch.

ELECTRICAL RELAYS

Various relay combinations are used by model application. However, most common relays are main relay which activates the ECU, injector circuit and starting circuit when ignition is switched to start mode and fuel pump relay which activates fuel pump during engine start mode and is then controlled by air flow during operating mode (except Datsun models). Datsun models are equipped with a fuel pump control relay which monitors engine oil pressure and alternator output for deactivating fuel pump upon engine failure when ignition switch is left "ON".

TESTING

NOTE — *This fuel injection system maintains constant fuel pressure in fuel lines and component parts at all times. Be sure to relieve pressure before attempting to open system at any point for testing. Do not allow fuel to flow onto engine or electrical parts. Do not allow open flame in area while testing fuel system components.*

ELECTRONIC CONTROL UNIT (ECU)

Do not attempt to test electronic control unit, as permanent damage could result. It is possible to check plug wires for continuity. The electronic control unit should only be judged faulty after compression is checked, the ignition system (particularly breaker points) has been tested and found problem-free, and all other fuel injection components have been thoroughly tested (including wiring).

FUEL PRESSURE

BMW, Fiat, Porsche & VW — 1) Disconnect negative battery cable and release fuel system pressure. Connect fuel pressure gauge between fuel rail and fuel pressure regulator.

2) Disconnect vacuum line at pressure regulator. Reconnect battery and start engine (operate starter on Fiat). Read pressure. On all models except Fiat, reconnect vacuum hose.

BOSCH AFC FUEL INJECTION SYSTEM (Cont.)

With vacuum hose connected, pressure should read approximately 28 psi (2.0 kg/cm²). If pressure is not as specified, ensure proper operation of fuel pump and replace pressure regulator and repeat test.

3) On Fiat models, if pressure reading is lower or higher than specified, pinch return fuel line. If pressure increases, replace regulator. If pressure remains constant, check fuel pump operation and fuel line. If no reading is measured, replace fuel pump and repeat test.

NOTE — On BMW 733i, detach plugs at air sensor. Connect terminals 36 and 39 with jumper wire. Turn ignition ON. A click indicates pump relay is good; a humming sound means fuel pump is running. If no fuel is delivered, the pressure relief valve or check valve in fuel pump is defective. Fuel pump pressure should be 34-38 psi (2.4-2.7 kg/cm²).

Jaguar & Triumph — 1) Release pressure from main fuel line at cold start injector and connect fuel pressure gauge. Disconnect negative lead from ignition coil and turn ignition switch "ON".

2) Note pressure reading. Slow pressure drop is permissible; sudden pressure drop requires check of entire fuel system.

3) On Jaguar only, operate fuel change-over switch on dash and recheck reading. Reading from both fuel tanks should agree. On all models, if pressure reading is not to specifications, replace fuel pressure regulator.

NOTE — Datsun recommends using Kent-Moore Electronic Fuel Injection Analyzer (J-25400) to perform tests on any component of fuel injection system. Follow manufacturers' instructions.

Datsun & Toyota — 1) Disconnect negative battery cable. On Toyota, disconnect electrical connector at cold start injector. On all models, release fuel line pressure. Install fuel pressure gauge to cold start injector (Toyota) and between fuel rail and fuel filter hose (Datsun).

2) Start engine. On Toyota, disconnect and plug vacuum hose at pressure regulator. On all models, note pressure reading. If pressure reading is higher than specified, replace regulator and repeat test. If pressure is lower, check fuel line, fuel filter and fuel pump.

3) On Toyota, reconnect vacuum hose at pressure regulator. Fuel pressure reading should stabilize at 28 psi (2.0 kg/cm²). If above specification, replace pressure regulator. Stop engine. If fuel pressure drops quickly, check fuel pump, pressure regulator and/or injectors.

Fuel Pressure Specifications

Application	Pressure
BMW①	34-38 psi (2.4-2.7 kg/cm²)
Datsun	30 psi (2.1 kg/cm²)
Fiat①	35 psi (2.5 kg/cm²)
Jaguar & Triumph	35.5-37 psi (2.5-2.6 kg/cm²)
Porsche & VW	35 psi (2.5 kg/cm²)
Toyota②	33-38 psi (2.3-2.7 kg/cm²)

① — Vacuum line disconnected at regulator.
② — Regulator vacuum line disconnected and plugged.

4) On Datsun, quickly depress accelerator pedal fully. Fuel pressure reading should immediately read approximately 37 psi (2.6 kg/cm²). If not, replace regulator and repeat test.

NOTE — Record outside temperature before testing air temperature sensor.

AIR TEMPERATURE SENSOR

NOTE — Testing procedures not available for Porsche.

BMW & Fiat — Turn ignition switch off and disconnect electrical connector at ECU and connect ohmmeter between terminals 6 and 27. Readings should be as follows. If not, replace temperature sensor and air flow meter as an assembly.

Temperature/Resistance Relationship (BMW & Fiat)

Temperature	Resistance (Ohms)
14°F (-10°C)	8,260-10,560
68°F (20°C)	2,280-2,720
122°F (50°C)	760-970

Jaguar & Triumph — Disconnect negative battery cable and air flow meter connector. Connect ohmmeter leads to terminals 6 and 27 on potentiometer connector. Readings should be as follows. If not, replace temperature sensor and air flow meter as an assembly.

Temperature/Resistance Relationship Jaguar & Triumph

Temperature	Resistance (Ohms)
14°F (-10°C)	9,200
32°F (0°C)	5,900
68°F (20°C)	2,500
104°F (40°C)	1,180
140°F (60°C)	600

Datsun (Federal 280ZX & 810, all 200SX) — Turn ignition switch off and disconnect electrical connector at ECU. Connect ohmmeter between terminals 25 and 34. Readings should be as follows. If not, replace temperature sensor and air flow meter as an assembly.

Temperature/Resistance Relationship (Datsun)

Temperature	Resistance (Ohms)
50°F (10°C)	3,250-4,150
68°F (20°C)	2,250-2,750
122°F (50°C)	740-940

BOSCH AFC FUEL INJECTION SYSTEM (Cont.)

Toyota — Disconnect air flow meter multi-pin connector and record ambient air temperature. Connect ohmmeter leads to terminals E_2 and THA on potentiometer connector. Ohmmeter readings should be as follows, if not, replace temperature sensor and air flow meter as an assembly.

Temperature/Resistance Relationship	
Temperature	**Resistance (Ohms)**
−4°F (−20°C)	10,000-20,000
32°F (0°C)	4,000-7,000
68°F (20°C)	2,000-3,000
104°F (40°C)	900-1,300

Volkswagen — Turn ignition switch off and disconnect electrical connector at ECU. Connect ohmmeter between terminals 6 and 27. Readings should be 2,500 ohms maximum at 68°F (20°C). If not, replace temperature sensor and air flow meter as an assembly.

AIR FLOW METER & POTENTIOMETER

NOTE — *Testing procedures not available for BMW, Jaguar, Porsche or Triumph models.*

Fiat — Turn ignition switch off and disconnect electrical connector at ECU. Connect ohmmeter between terminals as shown in table and note readings. If readings are not to specifications, replace air flow meter. If readings are correct, check fuel injection system.

Air Flow Meter Resistance (Fiat)	
Terminal No.	**Resistance (Ohms)**
6 & 8	180
7 & 8	150
8 & 9	100

Datsun (Federal 280ZX & 810; All 200SX) — Turn ignition switch off and disconnect electrical connector at ECU. Connect ohmmeter between terminals shown in table and note readings. If readings are not to specifications, replace air flow meter. If readings are correct, check fuel injection relays.

Air Flow Meter Resistance (Federal 280ZX & 810, All 200SX)	
Terminal No.	**Resistance (Ohms)**
33 & 34	100-400
34 & 35	200-500
32 & 33①	Except 0 & Infinity

① — 200SX terminals 32 & 34 with same results.

Toyota — Turn ignition switch off and disconnect air flow meter connector at ECU. Connect ohmmeter between terminals shown in table and note readings. If readings are not to specifications, replace air flow meter.

Air Flow Meter Resistance (Toyota)	
Terminal No.	**Resistance (Ohms)**
E_2 & Vs	20-100
E_2 & Vc	100-300
E_2 & Vb	200-400
E_1 & Fc	Infinity

Volkswagen — Disconnect electrical connector at air flow meter and connect ohmmeter between terminals shown in table. Note readings. If readings are not to specifications, replace air flow meter.

Air Flow Meter Resistance (Volkswagen)	
Terminal No.	**Resistance (Ohms)**
6 & 9	200-400
6 & 8	130-260
8 & 9	70-140
6 & 7	40-300
7 & 8	100-500

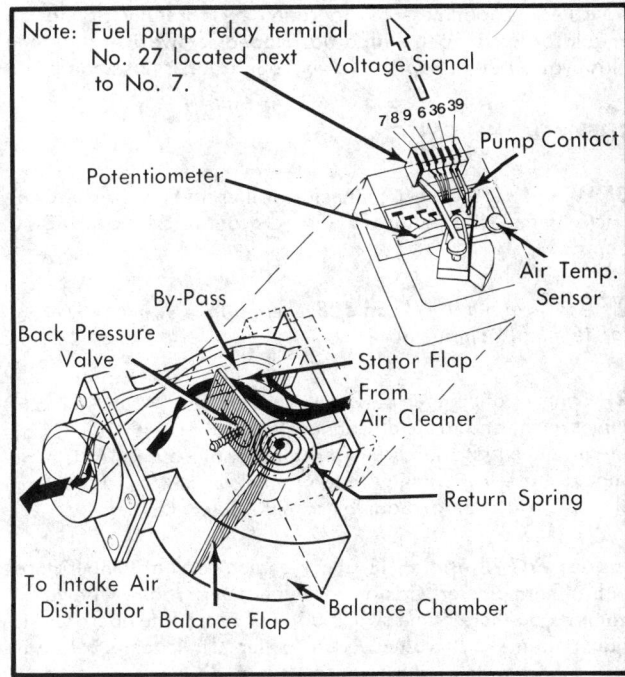

Note: Fuel pump relay terminal No. 27 located next to No. 7.

Fig. 7 Air Flow Meter & Potentiometer (Volkswagen Shown — Others Similar)

BOSCH AFC FUEL INJECTION SYSTEM (Cont.)

AUXILIARY AIR REGULATOR

NOTE — *Testing procedures not available for Porsche.*

BMW — With engine at normal operating temperature and idle speed set to specifications, turn air conditioner "ON". Connect ohmmeter to black wire of valve connector. Voltage should be registered and air should flow through valve. Turn air conditioner "OFF". No voltage or air should flow through valve. If valve does not function as described, replace air regulator.

Jaguar & Triumph — 1) Remove auxiliary air regulator connector and connect an ohmmeter to both terminals. Resistance should read approximately 33 ohms. If not, replace auxiliary air regulator.

2) Remove valve from inlet manifold and immerse mounting plate in cold water, avoiding contact of terminals and by-pass channel with water. The movable plate should fully expose air by-pass channel. Gradually heat water and as water temperature increases, channel should be blocked. If not, replace valve.

Datsun, Fiat, Toyota & VW — 1) With engine warm and at idle speed, pinch-off hose between throttle chamber and air regulator. Engine speed should drop. If not, proceed to next step.

2) Unhook hoses at each end of regulator. Visually check opening in valve. Valve should be open when cold, and close as temperature increases.

3) Check continuity of air regulator at electrical connector. If continuity does not exist, air regulator is defective and should be replaced.

4) Check smoothness of operation by carefully prying air regulator valve open with a flat bladed screwdriver and then close valve again. Replace valve if operation is not smooth.

THERMO-TIME SWITCH

BMW — 1) Disconnect connector at thermo-time switch. Connect ohmmeter to terminal "G" and ground. Check for 40-70 ohms.

NOTE — *Terminal "W" on 528i thermo-time switch is connector terminal number 86c.*

2) Connect ohmmeter between terminal 85 ("W" on thermo-time switch) and ground. Connect terminal 86 with 30 ("G" on thermo-time switch). For temperatures above 59°F (15°C), you should have an infinity reading. Below 59°F (15°C), you should have a zero reading for 0 to 8 seconds.

Jaguar & Triumph — 1) Check engine coolant temperature with a thermometer. Compare coolant temperature with value stamped on thermotime switch body. If coolant temperature is higher than switch value go on to step **2)**. If temperature is lower than switch value, go on to step **3)**.

2) If coolant temperature is higher than switch value, connect an ohmmeter between terminal "W" and ground. A very high

resistance (open circuit) should be obtained. If not, replace switch.

3) If coolant temperature is lower than switch value, connect an ohmmeter between terminal "W" and ground. A very low resistance (closed circuit) should be obtained. Connect battery voltage via an isolating switch to terminal "G" of thermo-time switch. Using a stop watch, check delay time as ohmmeter changes between high and low resistance. Delay period should be as specified in table. If not, replace switch.

Coolant/Delay Time Relationship (Jaguar & Triumph)	
Temperature (Coolant)	**Delay (Seconds)**
-4°F (-20°C)	8
32°F (0°C)	4.5
50°F (10°C)	3.5
95°F (35°C)	0

Datsun (Except 200SX) — 1) Disconnect negative battery cable and switch connector. Connect ohmmeter between terminal 45 and ground. Check for 40-70 ohms. Connect ohmmeter between terminal 46 and switch body.

2) Ohmmeter reading should show full continuity (0 ohms) at 57°F (14°C) and infinity reading at 77°F (25°C). If readings are not as specified, replace thermo-time switch.

Fiat — 1) Disconnect connector from cold start injector. Connect test light between terminals, operate starter and note time test light stays lit. No light should be present if coolant temperature is above 95°F (35°C) and should glow for 1-8 seconds at temperatures below 95°F (35°C).

2) If light does not perform as described, check relay and wiring. If good, replace thermo-time switch.

Toyota — 1) Disconnect thermo-time switch connector. Connect ohmmeter between terminal STA and STJ on thermo-time switch and measure resistance. Then, measure resistance between terminal STA and ground.

2) Resistance between terminal STA and ground should be 20-80 ohms. Resistance between terminal STA and STJ should be 20-40 ohms with coolant temperature below 95°F (35°C) and 40-60 ohms with coolant temperature above 95°F (35°C).

Volkswagen — 1) Ensure engine coolant temperature is below 95°F (35°C). Disconnect electrical connector at cold start valve. Disconnect and tape ignition primary wire from terminal 1 of ignition coil to prevent engine starting.

2) Attach test light to switch terminals and operate starter. Light should glow from 2-11 seconds at temperatures ranging from -4°-104°F (-20°C-40°C). If light does not glow or perform as described, check wiring harness and replace switch. Test lamp should not glow at temperatures above 104°F (40°C).

BOSCH AFC FUEL INJECTION SYSTEM (Cont.)

COLD START VALVE

NOTE — *Testing procedures not available for Porsche or VW.*

BMW — 1) With ignition switch "OFF", disconnect electrical connector from cold start valve. Release pressure from fuel system and remove cold start valve with fuel lines connected.

2) Place container under cold start valve. Disconnect air flow meter connector and connect jumper wire between terminals 36 and 39. Connect another jumper wire between cold start relay terminals 87 and 30. Turn ignition switch "ON". Cold start valve should spray fuel. If not, replace cold start valve.

NOTE — *On 528i, connect lead 61 1 440 to cold start valve, then connect terminal "B+" to ground after jumping air flow connector.*

Jaguar & Triumph — 1) Remove electrical connector from cold start valve and connect voltmeter across connector terminals. Crank engine with ignition switch. Battery voltage should be read.

2) Release fuel system pressure and remove cold start valve with fuel lines connected. Reconnect coupler and place cold start valve in container. As cold engine is cranked with ignition switch, fuel spray should be observed until thermo-time switch cuts off relay. When the engine is warm, no fuel spray should occur during cranking. If valve does not perform as described, replace cold start valve.

Datsun (Except 200SX) — 1) Disconnect battery ground cable. Remove cold start valve with fuel lines connected and place tip in glass container.

2) Disconnect oil pressure switch connector or alternator "L" terminal. Connect battery ground cable. Turn ignition switch "ON". Cold start valve should NOT inject fuel.

3) Turn ignition switch off. Using 2 jumper wires, connect cold start valve to battery. Fuel should be injected. If not, replace cold start valve.

Fiat — 1) Release fuel system pressure and remove cold start valve from intake manifold without removing fuel lines or connector. Place cold start valve in glass container.

2) Turn ignition switch to "START" and crank engine. With engine coolant temperature below 95°F (35°C), fuel should be sprayed for 1-8 seconds; above 95°F (35°C), no fuel should be sprayed.

3) If valve sprays continuously, drips or does not spray fuel at temperature below 95°F (35°C), replace cold start valve.

Toyota — 1) Remove cold start injector from inlet chamber with fuel lines and coupler connected. Remove coupler and install test coupler to valve. Position cold start valve in glass container and keep valve away from electrical connectors.

2) Turn ignition switch "ON" but do NOT start engine. Connect jumper wire to fuel pump check connector terminals (located in wiring harness near air flow meter). Connect test coupler to battery voltage. Fuel should be injected.

3) Disconnect test coupler from battery and check that valve does not leak fuel. Remove jumper wire at fuel pump check connector and test coupler from valve. Connect ohmmeter to cold start valve terminals and check for 3-5 ohms. If cold start valve does not perform as described, replace cold start valve.

WATER TEMPERATURE SENSOR

All Models — Disconnect plug and connect an ohmmeter between temperature sensor II (engine coolant sensor) and ground. Sensor is temperature sensitive; as temperature increases, resistance will decrease. Readings should be as specified in following tables:

Temperature/Resistance Relationship (Jaguar, Toyota, Triumph & VW)	
Temperature (Coolant)	**Resistance (Ohms)**
-22° F (-30° C)	20,300-33,000
14° F (-10° C)	7,600-10,800
50° F (10° C)	3,250-4,150
68° F (20° C)	2,250-2,750
122° F (50° C)	740-940
176° F (80° C)	290-360

Temperature/Resistance Relationship (BMW, Fiat & Datsun)	
Temperature (Coolant)	**Resistance (Ohms)**
14°F (-10°C)	7,000-11,600
68°F (20°C)	2,100-2,900
176°F (80°C)	270-390

MIXTURE CONTROL COMPONENTS

Datsun 280ZX & 810 Models (Calif. Only) — 1) Start engine and warm to normal operating temperature. Accelerate and run engine at 2000 RPM for 5 minutes to stabilize operating condition.

2) Accelerate engine 2-3 times and allow to idle. Turn idle speed adjusting screw to obtain 700 RPM. Check ignition timing and adjust if necessary. Raise engine speed to 2000 RPM and observe inspection light on bottom of EFI control unit.

3) Light should blink more than 5 times in 10 seconds, indicating mixture is correct and is being controlled by the computer. If light is blinking properly, system is functioning and no adjustment is required.

4) If not, turn ignition switch off, disconnect negative battery cable and 35 pin connector from control unit. Disconnect exhaust gas sensor harness connector. Ground sensor terminal of connector.

5) Check for continuity between terminal No. 31 of control unit connector and chassis ground. If circuit is open, repair or

BOSCH AFC FUEL INJECTION SYSTEM (Cont.)

replace EFI harness and repeat test procedure. If continuity exists, reconnect control unit harness and battery negative cable.

6) Start engine, run at 2000 RPM and observe inspection light on control unit. With exhaust sensor terminal grounded, light should glow. Remove ground wire from sensor terminal and light should go out. If not okay, replace control unit and repeat all test procedures. If okay, proceed to next step.

7) Turn ignition switch off, disconnect throttle valve switch harness connector and connect a jumper wire between harness connector terminals No. 24 and No. 30. Position harness connector at least 4" away from any secondary ignition wires.

8) Disconnect and plug distributor vacuum hose. Disconnect air induction hose and canister purge hose at intake manifold. Plug air induction pipe and purge hose fitting on intake manifold. Start engine, accelerate 2-3 times and allow to idle.

9) Insert CO meter probe into tail pipe (a minimum of 16") and measure CO level. Idle CO level should be less than 5%. If CO level is okay and engine runs smoothly, replace exhaust gas sensor and repeat all test procedures. If CO level is incorrect or if CO level is correct, but engine does not run smoothly, proceed to next step.

10) Turn ignition switch off and remove air flow meter. Drill a small hole in steel plug covering air by-pass screw. Install a self-tapping screw into hole and remove plug. Reinstall air flow meter, start engine and run to normal operating temperature.

11) With engine idling, adjust air by-pass screw to obtain a 0.2-1.8% reading on CO meter. If mixture will not adjust, repair or replace air flow meter or other defective EFI components and repeat all test procedures.

12) If mixture adjusts correctly, replace steel plug in air flow meter and reconnect all hoses and harness connectors. Repeat all test procedures.

REMOVAL & INSTALLATION

NOTE — *This fuel injection system maintains constant fuel pressure in fuel lines and component parts at all times. Be sure to relieve pressure before attempting to open system at any point for testing. Do not allow fuel to flow onto engine or electrical parts. Do not allow open flame or sparks in area while servicing or testing fuel system components.*

AIR FLOW METER & AIR CLEANER

Removal (BMW & Fiat) — Disconnect electrical plug and loosen clamps on both sides of air flow meter. Remove air cleaner and lift air flow meter out of its holder.

Installation (BMW & Fiat) — To install, reverse removal procedure.

Removal (Datsun, Jaguar & Triumph) — Disconnect battery ground cable. Disconnect rubber hose from both sides of air flow meter. Disconnect air flow meter ground cable and remove bolts securing air flow meter to bracket. Move air flow meter upward, disconnect electrical connector and remove air flow meter.

Installation (Datsun, Jaguar & Triumph) — To install, reverse removal procedure.

NOTE — *Removal procedures not available for Porsche.*

Removal (Toyota) — Remove air cleaner inlet pipe, cover and filter element. Remove 4 nuts attaching air cleaner to air flow meter. Remove bracket bolt, hose clamp and hose from end of meter. Disconnect electrical connector and remove air flow meter.

Installation (Toyota) — To install, reverse removal procedures, making sure gasket between air flow meter and air cleaner assembly is properly positioned.

Removal (Volkswagen) — 1) Remove air cleaner top and filter, then carefully remove electrical connector from sensor. Loosen hose clamp then disconnect elbow duct from sensor.

2) Remove nuts securing air cleaner body to vehicle chassis. Remove sensor and air cleaner body as a unit. Now remove sensor from air cleaner body.

Installation (Volkswagen) — To install sensor, reverse removal procedure. Make sure sensor is properly adjusted after installation.

THROTTLE VALVE HOUSING

Removal (BMW & Fiat) — 1) Disconnect and remove air cleaner assembly. Remove engine valve cover. Remove throttle linkage and throttle cable (automatic transmission).

2) Disconnect all vacuum hoses. Always mark or note where vacuum hose was removed from for correct replacement. Disconnect throttle valve switch connector.

3) Drain vehicle coolant below auxiliary air valve or pinch water hoses going to air valve with clamps. Remove hoses from auxiliary air valve. Remove throttle valve mounting bolts and throttle valve.

Installation (BMW & Fiat) — Use new gasket for throttle body, then reverse removal procedure for installation.

Removal (Datsun) — Disconnect battery ground cable. Remove rubber hoses from throttle chamber. Remove throttle valve switch and disconnect BCDD device (if equipped). Disconnect rod from auxiliary throttle shaft. Remove four screws securing throttle chamber to intake manifold. Throttle chamber can now be removed together with dashpot and BCDD device (if equipped).

Installation (Datsun) — To install, reverse removal procedure.

Removal (Toyota) — Drain coolant from radiator. Remove air intake connector, throttle link, water and vacuum hoses. Remove electrical connectors from throttle body. Remove 4 throttle body attaching bolts and throttle body from air intake chamber.

Installation (Toyota) — Reverse removal procedure, using a new throttle body gasket.

Removal (Volkswagen) — 1) Remove intake air sensor and air cleaner as a unit. Loosen clamp and remove elbow ducting from top of throttle valve housing.

2) Disconnect throttle return spring from bracket on EGR valve body. Detach operating rod from EGR valve. Disconnect throttle linkage from arm on throttle valve shaft. Detach upper end of ball link from arm.

BOSCH AFC FUEL INJECTION SYSTEM (Cont.)

3) Disconnect vacuum hoses from throttle valve housing, mark hoses for correct position when installing. Remove screws securing throttle valve housing to manifold and remove throttle valve housing.

Installation (Volkswagen) — To install throttle valve housing, reverse removal procedure. Always use a new gasket when installing housing.

CONTROL UNIT (ECU)

Removal (BMW) — Disconnect negative battery cable. ECU is located behind cover at right kick panel on 733i and in glove compartment on all other models. Press back on clip located on wire end of electrical connector and swing cable assembly to right while removing. Remove ECU retaining screws and remove control unit.

Installation (BMW) — To install, reverse removal procedure.

NOTE — *Plug connector on left rear side of harness MUST be connected for BMW vehicles registered in Colorado.*

Removal (Jaguar & Triumph) — Disconnect negative battery cable. ECU is located in glove compartment on TR7; below glove compartment on TR8; and at forward end of luggage compartment on Jaguar. Remove ECU cover, retainer band and cable clamp clip. Unclip end cover and lift out ECU. Disconnect pin connector and remove ECU.

Installation (Jaguar & Triumph) — To install, reverse removal procedure, making sure pin connector is installed squarely and securely.

Removal (Datsun & Toyota) — Turn ignition switch "OFF", then disconnect battery negative cable. Remove left kick panel. Remove cover and 3 bolts securing control unit to side panel bracket. Carefully disconnect pin connector(s) and remove control unit.

Installation (Datsun & Toyota) — To install, reverse removal procedure.

Removal (Fiat) — Disconnect negative battery cable. Under dash panel, press back on clip located on wire end of electrical connector and swing cable to right while removing. Remove ECU retaining screws and remove control unit.

Installation (Fiat) — To install, reverse removal procedure.

Removal (Porsche) — Disconnect negative battery cable. At right kick panel, disconnect connector retainer clamps and remove connector. Remove ECU retaining bolts and remove contol unit.

Installation (Porsche) — To install, reverse removal procedure.

Removal (Volkswagen) — Disconnect negative battery cable. In luggage compartment, near distributor, remove ECU connector by carefully using screwdriver. Position connector where it cannot be damaged physically or electrically. Remove control unit.

Installation (Volkswagen) — To install ECU, reverse removal procedure. Make sure cable plug is carefully and completely engaged in ECU. Be sure new ECU has same part number as one removed. Reattach battery ground cable.

COLD START VALVE

Removal (All Models, Except 200SX) — Disconnect battery ground cable and remove connector at cold start valve. Release fuel line pressure and remove cold start valve retaining screws. Remove cold start valve.

Installation — To install, reverse removal procedure.

AUXILIARY AIR REGULATOR

Removal (Jaguar, Toyota & Triumph) — 1) Disconnect negative battery cable. Disconnect air hoses from auxiliary air valve.

NOTE — *Auxiliary air valve is installed in engine cooling system.*

2) When removing auxiliary air valve from cooling system, either have another valve ready for immediate installation or drain cooling system below level of valve. Remove valve retaining screws and remove auxiliary air valve.

Installation (Jaguar, Toyota & Triumph) — To install, reverse removal procedure.

Removal (All Others) — Disconnect battery ground cable. Remove electrical connector and air hoses at air regulator. Remove retaining screws and remove auxiliary air regulator.

Installation (All Others) — To install, reverse removal procedure.

WATER TEMPERATURE SENSOR

NOTE — *Removal of water temperature sensor should be done only when engine is cold. Removal of sensor requires having replacement sensor ready for immediate installation or draining cooling system below level of sensor.*

Removal (All Models) — Disconnect negative battery cable. Drain coolant and disconnect sensor electrical connector. Loosen and remove engine coolant temperature sensor.

Installation — To install, reverse removal procedure using suitable liquid sealer on sensor threads. Replace sealing washers, if equipped.

THERMO-TIME SWITCH

NOTE — *Thermo-time switch removal should be done only when engine is cold. Removal of switch requires having replacement switch ready for immediate installation or draining cooling system below level of switch.*

Removal (All Models, Except 200SX) — Disconnect negative battery cable and drain radiator coolant (except VW). Disconnect electrical connector from switch and remove switch.

Installation (All Models, Except 200SX) — To install, reverse removal procedure, using suitable liquid sealer on switch threads.

PRESSURE REGULATOR

NOTE — *Throttle body must be removed on Toyota models before removing pressure regulator.*

BOSCH AFC FUEL INJECTION SYSTEM (Cont.)

Removal (All Models) — Disconnect negative battery cable and relieve fuel system pressure. Disconnect fuel lines and vacuum line at regulator. Remove pressure regulator (separating from bracket, if installed).

Installation — To install, reverse removal procedure.

INJECTORS

NOTE — *Removal procedures not available for Porsche models.*

Removal (BMW) — 1) Disconnect negative battery cable and relieve pressure in fuel system. Remove electrical connectors from injectors, fuel line at pressure regulator and fuel return line. Remove injector mounting bolts. Remove fuel rail and injectors as an assembly.

2) Remove injector-to-fuel rail sleeve by cutting sleeve. Remove injector from fuel rail by burning hose with a soldering gun, until assembly can be removed from fuel rail.

Installation (BMW) — To install, reverse removal procedure and ensure new hose is sealed at fuel rail with new sleeve.

Removal (Jaguar & Triumph) — 1) Disconnect negative battery cable and depressurize fuel system. Disconnect electrical connectors at injectors. Remove 2 screws attaching fuel rail to intake manifold.

2) Release clips holding fuel supply and return rails. Remove manifold pressure pipe. Remove 6 nuts and washers from injector clamps and lift off fuel rail with injectors. Loosen injector clamps and remove injectors from fuel rail.

Installation (Jaguar & Triumph) — To install, reverse removal procedure, making sure electrical connectors are properly installed on injectors before installing fuel rail assembly to manifold.

Removal (Datsun) — 1) Disconnect negative battery cable and depressurize fuel system. On 200SX, remove accelerator cable and vacuum control valve hose. On all models, disconnect electrical connectors from injectors and cold start valve (except 200SX). Disconnect harness from fuel rail wire clamp. Remove blow-by hose at rocker cover side (except 200SX). Remove air regulator pipe. Disconnect pressure regulator vacuum hose.

2) Disconnect fuel feed and return lines from fuel rail. Remove fuel rail and pressure regulator mounting bolts and all injector retaining screws. Remove fuel rail, pressure regulator and injectors as an assembly. Remove fuel injectors by removing hose clamp on injector and pulling injector from hose.

Installation (Datsun) — To install, reverse removal procedure.

Removal (Fiat) — Disconnect negative battery cable and depressurize fuel system. Disconnect electrical connectors at all injectors. Remove fuel supply hose from fuel rail, fuel return line from pressure regulator, fuel line from cold start valve and vacuum line from pressure regulator. Remove fuel rail mounting bolt and 4 injector retaining nuts. Remove fuel rail, injectors and pressure regulator as an assembly. Remove injectors from fuel rail by pulling off fuel hoses.

Installation (Fiat) — To install, reverse removal procedure.

Removal (Toyota) — 1) Disconnect battery ground cable and drain coolant. Disconnect (after marking for installation) all vacuum, fuel and water hoses connected to intake air chamber. Remove cold start injector, EGR pipe and throttle link from air chamber. Remove air intake chamber.

2) Unplug electrical connectors from injectors and remove 2 injector harness clamps from fuel delivery pipe. Remove 4 fuel delivery pipe bolts and remove fuel delivery pipe with injectors attached.

Installation (Toyota) — To install, reverse removal procedure, using new "O" rings and seals.

Removal (Volkswagen) — 1) Remove the large air duct between fan housing and heat exchangers on exhaust system. Disconnect battery and relieve pressure in fuel system.

2) Disconnect electrical connector and fuel lines from injectors to be removed. Remove screw securing injector to intake manifold. Remove injector with seals and retainer plate.

Installation (Volkswagen) — To install injectors, reverse removal procedure.

ADJUSTMENTS

HOT (SLOW) IDLE RPM

See appropriate *TUNE-UP SERVICE PROCEDURES* article.

IDLE MIXTURE

See appropriate *TUNE-UP SERVICE PROCEDURES* article.

OXYGEN SENSOR WARNING LIGHT

1) All vehicles equipped with oxygen sensors are also equipped with an oxygen sensor maintenance interval light. This light is located on the dash panel of all models. Light will come on after a predetermined number of miles, indicating need for oxygen sensor replacement.

2) Service interval is 12,500 for Jaguar and 30,000 miles for all other models. After oxygen sensor replacement, reset the oxygen sensor warning light switch, except Datsun models. On BMW, switch is located on left side of engine near transmission (in line with speedometer cable). On British Leyland, Fiat and VW, switch is on control box located on speedometer cable. On Porsche, switch is located to right of passenger seat. On Toyota, switch is located beneath switch cover on pedal assembly, below instrument panel.

THROTTLE VALVE SWITCH

BMW — 1) Connect Bosch tester (0684 100 202) to ECU. Set cylinder selector switch to "6" and program selector switch to "5". Turn ignition on. Tester gauge should read 0 ohms with throttle valve at idle position; infinite for partial throttle valve position and 0 ohms for full throttle valve position.

2) If throttle valve switch does not perform as described, loosen throttle switch screws and place throttle valve in idle position. At idle, tester reading should be 0 ohms. When throttle valve is moved .118-.157" (3-4 mm), tester reading should read infinity. If relocating throttle switch does not produce above results, replace throttle switch.

BOSCH AFC FUEL INJECTION SYSTEM (Cont.)

NOTE — *Throttle switch contacts can be tested for continuity on 633CSi and 733i models with an ohmmeter. With ohmmeter connected between terminal 18 (center) and 2 (top), 0 ohms should be measured with throttle at idle. With ohmmeter connected between terminal 18 and 3 (bottom), 0 ohms should be measured with throttle at full throttle position.*

Triumph (TR8) — Disconnect electrical connector at throttle switch and connect throttle gauge connector (60973067). With engine at normal operating temperature and idle speed set, adjust until green light glows on throttle gauge. Remove gauge and reconnect harness.

Datsun — 1) With engine running at idle, disconnect throttle valve switch connector. Connect ohmmeter leads to terminals 29 and 30 of throttle valve switch.

NOTE — *Do not connect ohmmeter to throttle valve switch wire connector or damage to ohmmeter may result.*

2) With engine operating at idle, 0 ohms should register on ohmmeter. Loosen throttle switch retaining screw and increase engine idle speed to 900 RPM (770 RPM on 200SX). Adjust location of switch so that ohmmeter reading goes from 0 ohms to infinity. If ohmmeter registers correctly, proceed to step **4)**. If ohmmeter readings are not correct, proceed with next step.

3) Turn engine OFF and set clearance between throttle valve shaft lever and stopper screw to .020" (.5 mm) on 280ZX and 810 or .012" (.3 mm) on 200SX. Adjust throttle switch position until ohmmeter reading goes from 0 ohms to infinity. If switch does not perform as described, replace throttle switch.

4) To check full throttle contact, disconnect negative battery cable and throttle valve switch connector. Connect ohmmeter between terminals 24 and 30. Continuity should not exist when throttle valve is in idle position. Depress accelerator to full throttle position. Continuity should exist between terminals. If not, replace throttle switch.

Fiat — 1) Before adjusting throttle valve switch, ensure engine idle speed is set to specifications. With engine OFF, remove connector from throttle switch, loosen 2 screws and connect an ohmmeter between terminals 18 (center) and 2 (right of center).

2) Rotate switch clockwise until ohmmeter reading is 0 ohms. Tighten mounting screws at point ohmmeter reading registers 0 ohms. If throttle valve switch cannot be adjusted as described, replace switch.

NOTE — *Adjustment procedures not available for Porsche or VW.*

Toyota — 1) Construct an angle gauge as shown in *Fig. 8*. Insert in throttle valve to obtain either a 55° or a 65° throttle angle. Check continuity between each terminal of switch (IDL-TL, IDL-PSW and PSW-TL).

2) At 55° throttle opening, there should be no continuity between any terminals. And at 65° throttle opening, there should be continuity between PSW and TL terminals only. If incorrect, proceed to step **3)**.

3) To adjust switch, loosen adjustment screws and insert a .020" (.52 mm) feeler gauge between throttle stop screw and lever. Connect ohmmeter to terminals IDL and TL (ohmmeter should show continuity). Gradually turn switch assembly

counterclockwise until ohmmeter deflects and tighten screws. Remove feeler gauge.

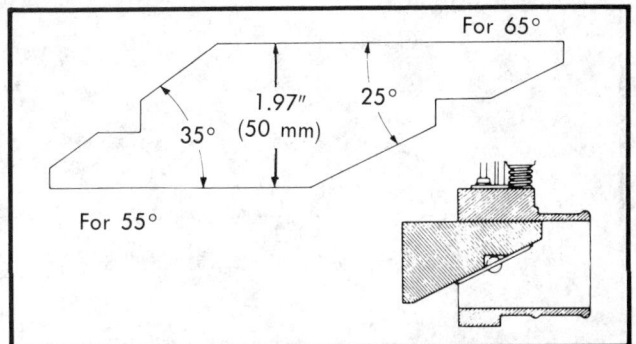

Fig. 8 Angle Gauge Dimensions for Adjusting Toyota Throttle Valve Switch

4) To recheck, insert a .017" (.44 mm) feeler gauge between throttle stop and lever. Ohmmeter should show continuity. Now, replace this feeler gauge with one that is .026" (.66 mm) and check continuity. There should be no continuity.

THROTTLE VALVE (JAGUAR ONLY)

1) Remove air intake hose and elbow to expose throttle valve. Loosen throttle valve lock nut on stop screw and loosen stop screw. Ensure throttle valve fully closes.

2) Insert .002" (.05 mm) feeler gauge between throttle valve and throttle housing bore. *See Fig. 9*. With feeler gauge in position, adjust stop screw so it just touches stop arm. Tighten locknut. Press stop arm against stop screw and remove feeler gauge.

3) Seal threads of adjusting screws and lock nuts with paint spots. Install hose and elbow. Check operation of throttle linkage and adjust if required.

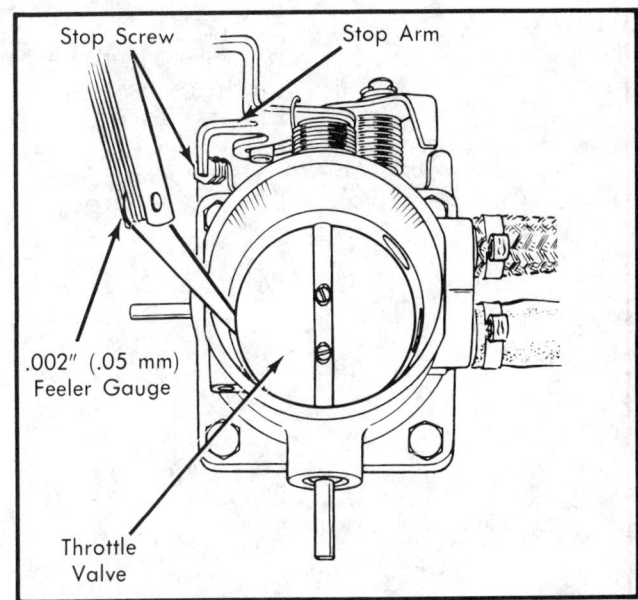

Fig. 9 Adjusting Throttle Valve Clearance (Jaguar Models Only)

BOSCH AFC FUEL INJECTION SYSTEM (Cont.)

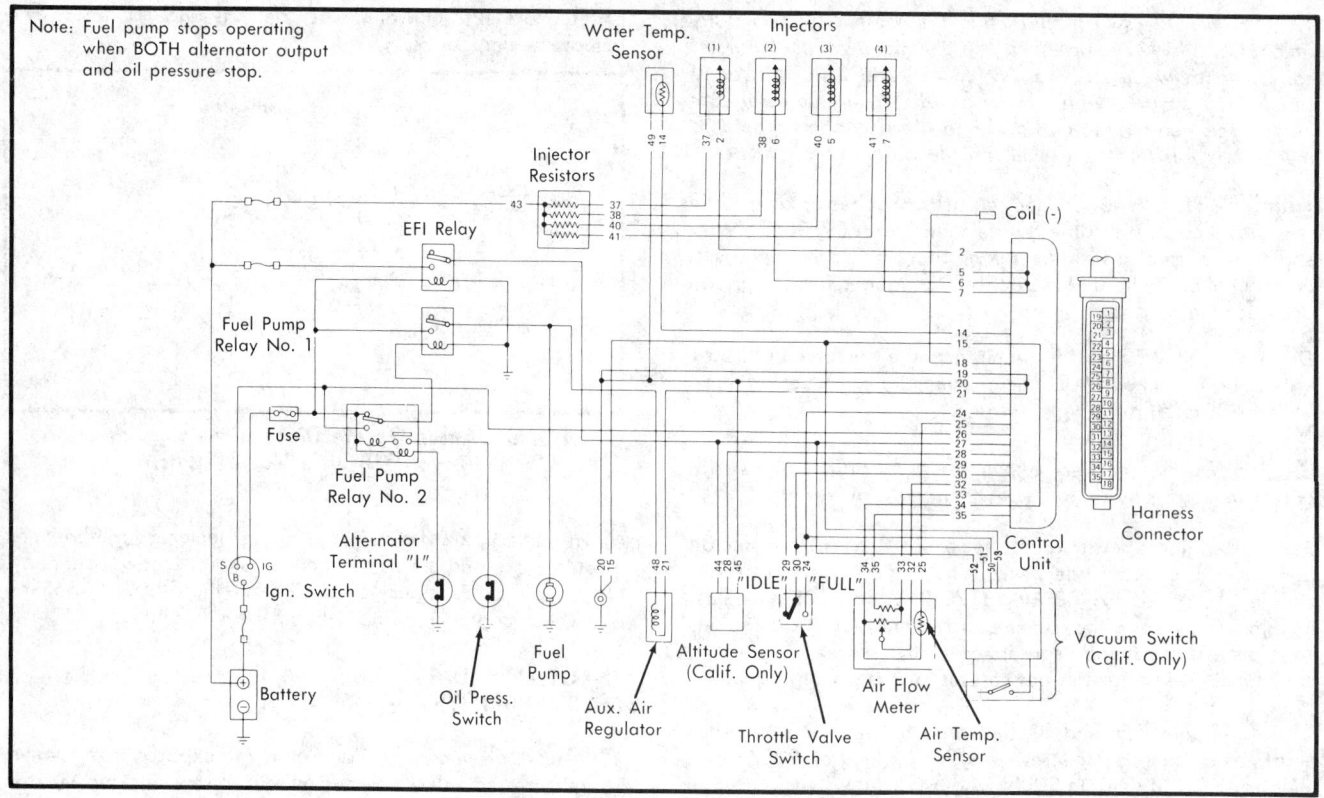

Fig. 10   Electronic Fuel Injection Wiring Diagram (Datsun 200SX)

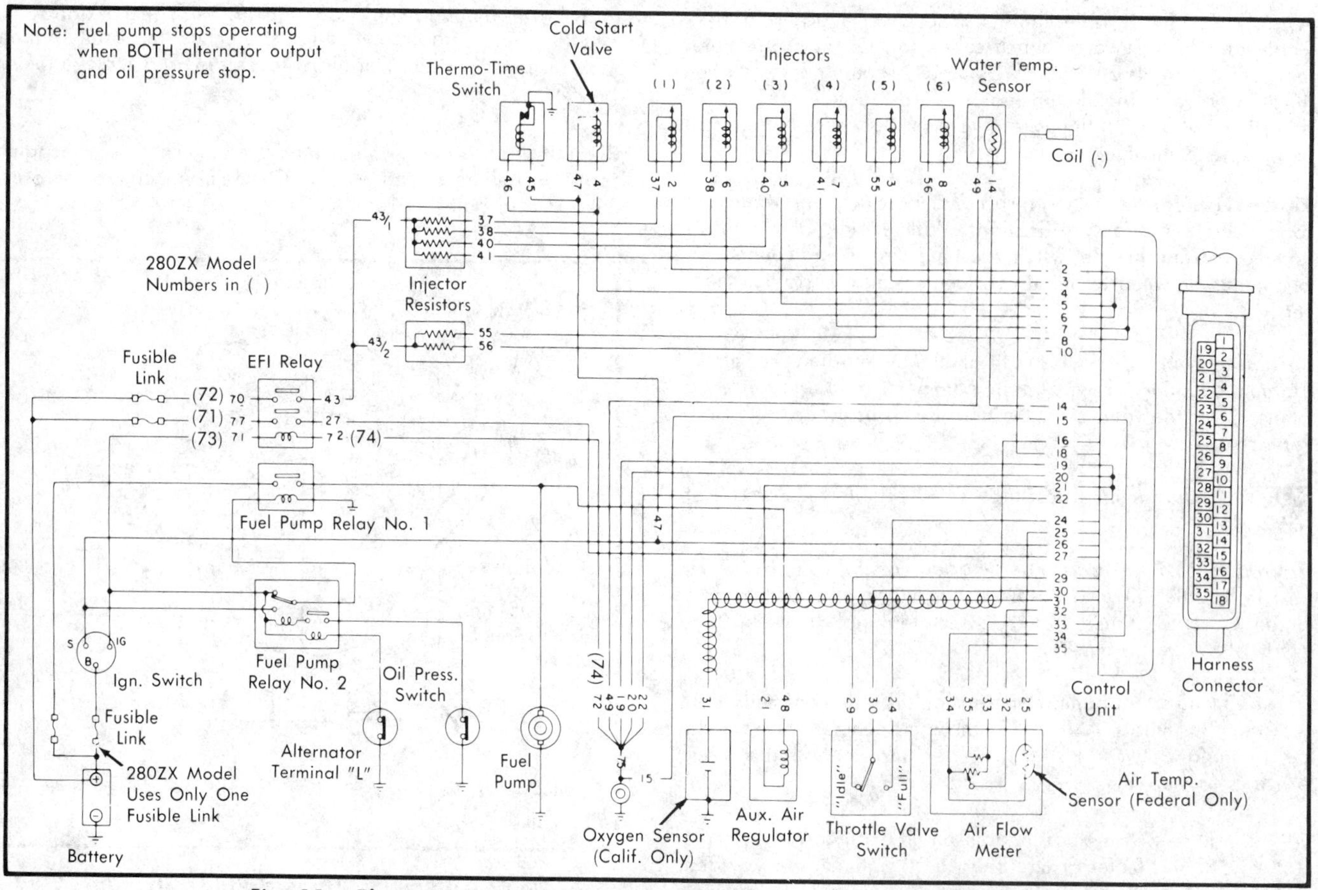

Fig. 11   Electronic Fuel Injection Wiring Diagram (Datsun 280ZX & 810)

BOSCH AFC FUEL INJECTION SYSTEM (Cont.)

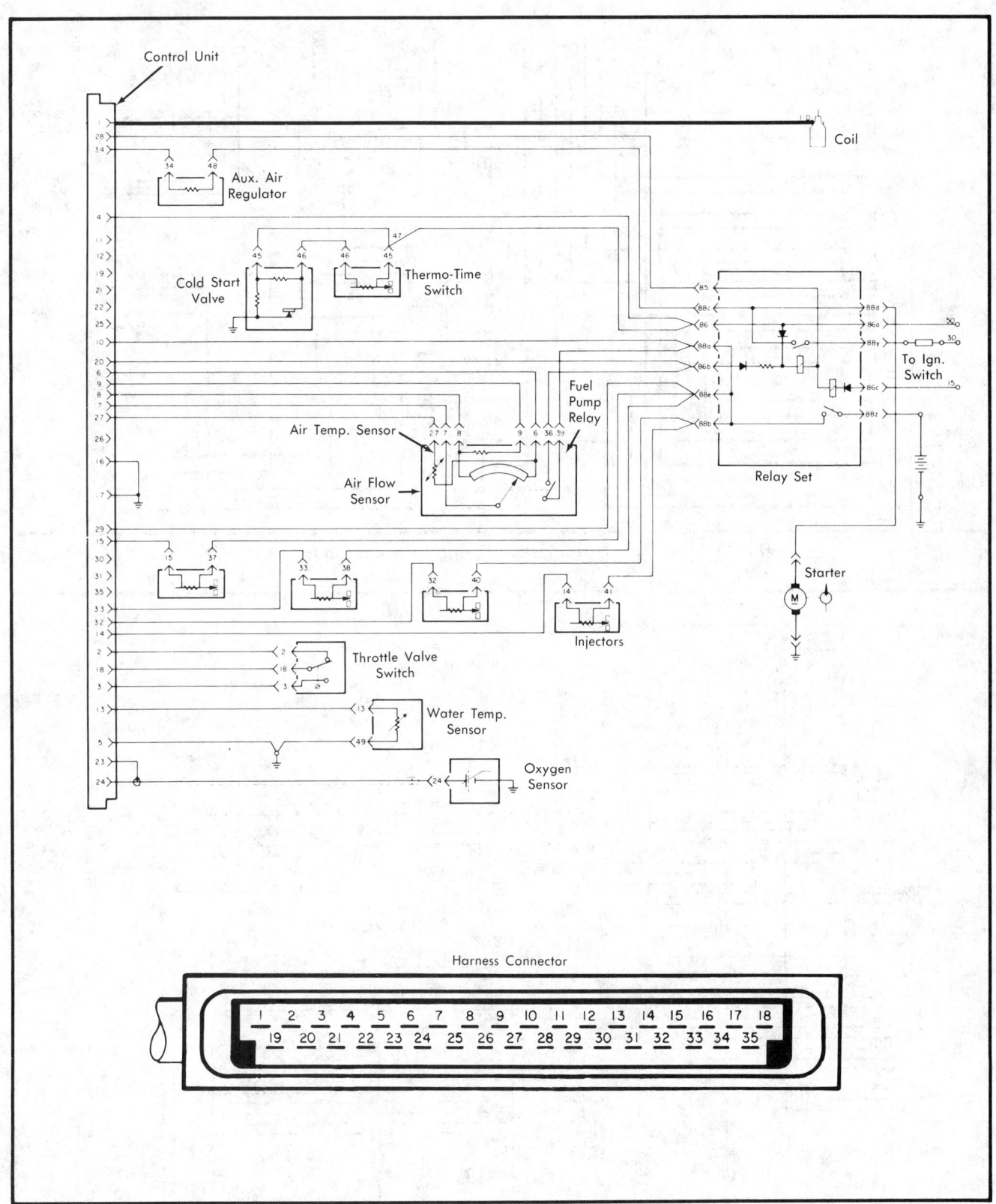

Fig. 12 *Electronic Fuel Injection Wiring Diagram (Fiat Models)*

1980 Bosch Fuel Injection

BOSCH AFC FUEL INJECTION SYSTEM (Cont.)

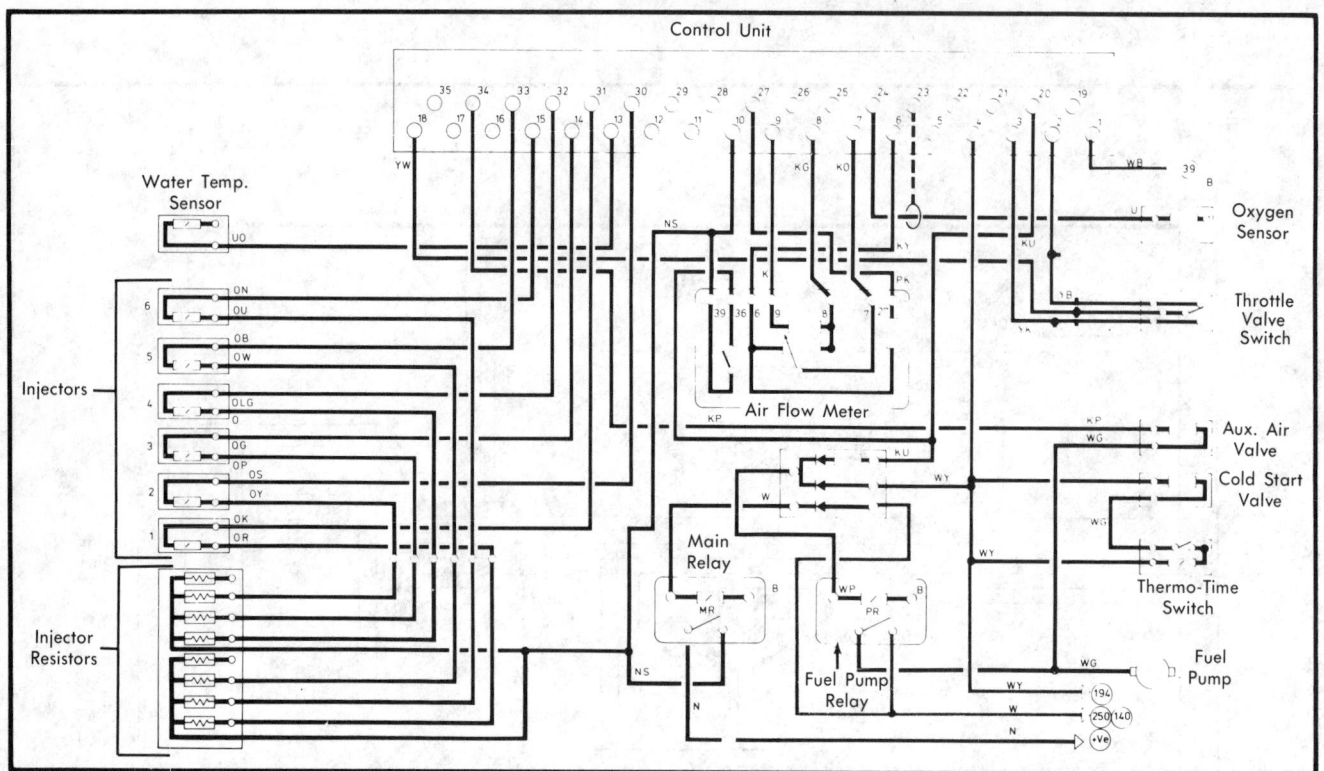

Fig. 13 *Electronic Fuel Injection Wiring Diagram (Jaguar XJ6L)*

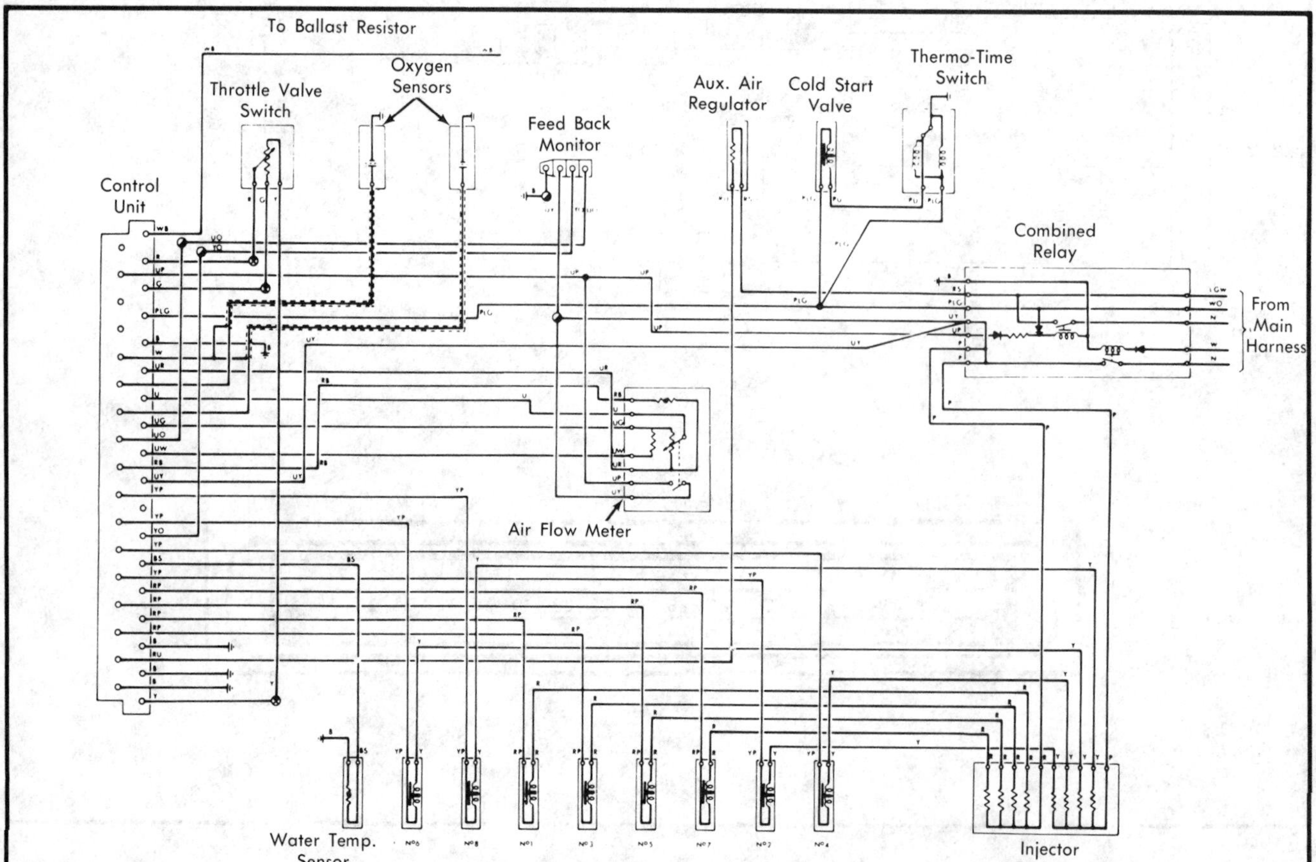

Fig. 14 *Electronic Fuel Injection Wiring Diagram (TR8)*

BOSCH AFC FUEL INJECTION SYSTEM (Cont.)

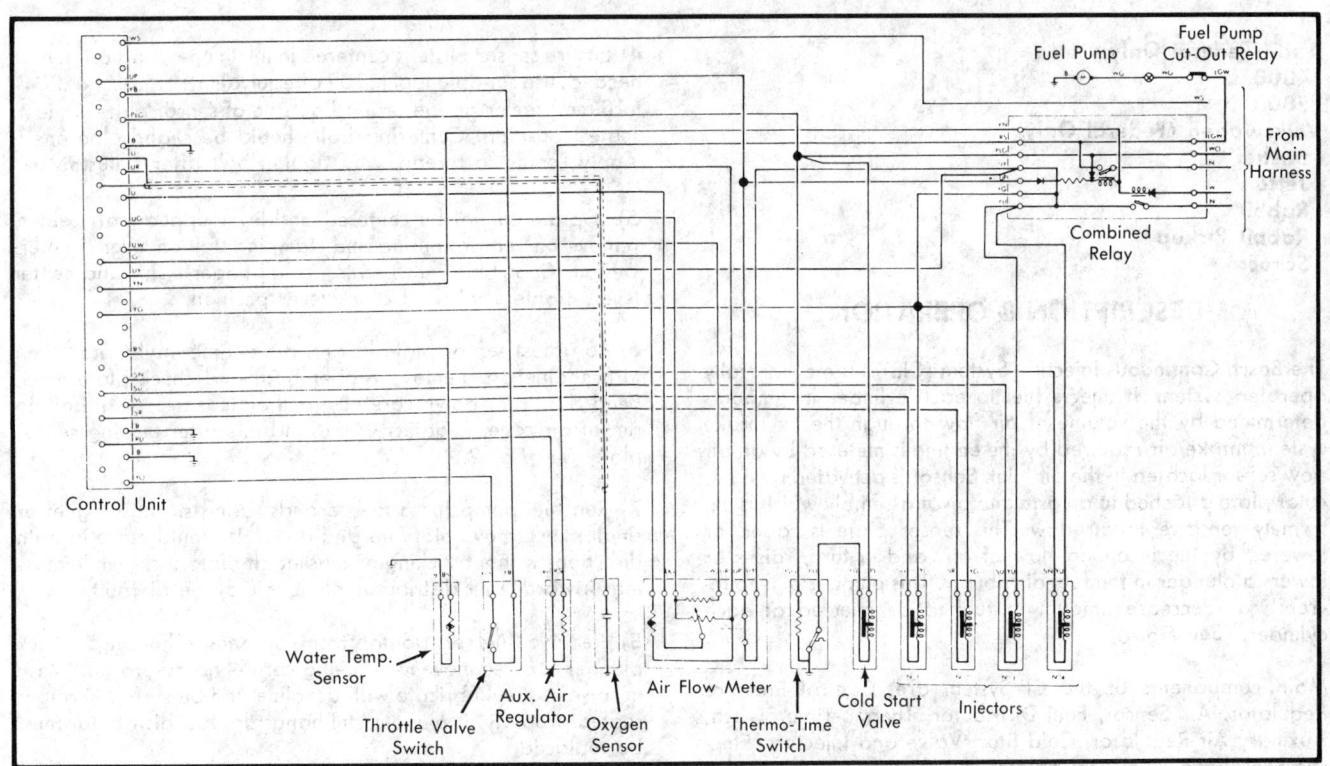

Fig. 15 Electronic Fuel Injection Wiring Diagram (TR7)

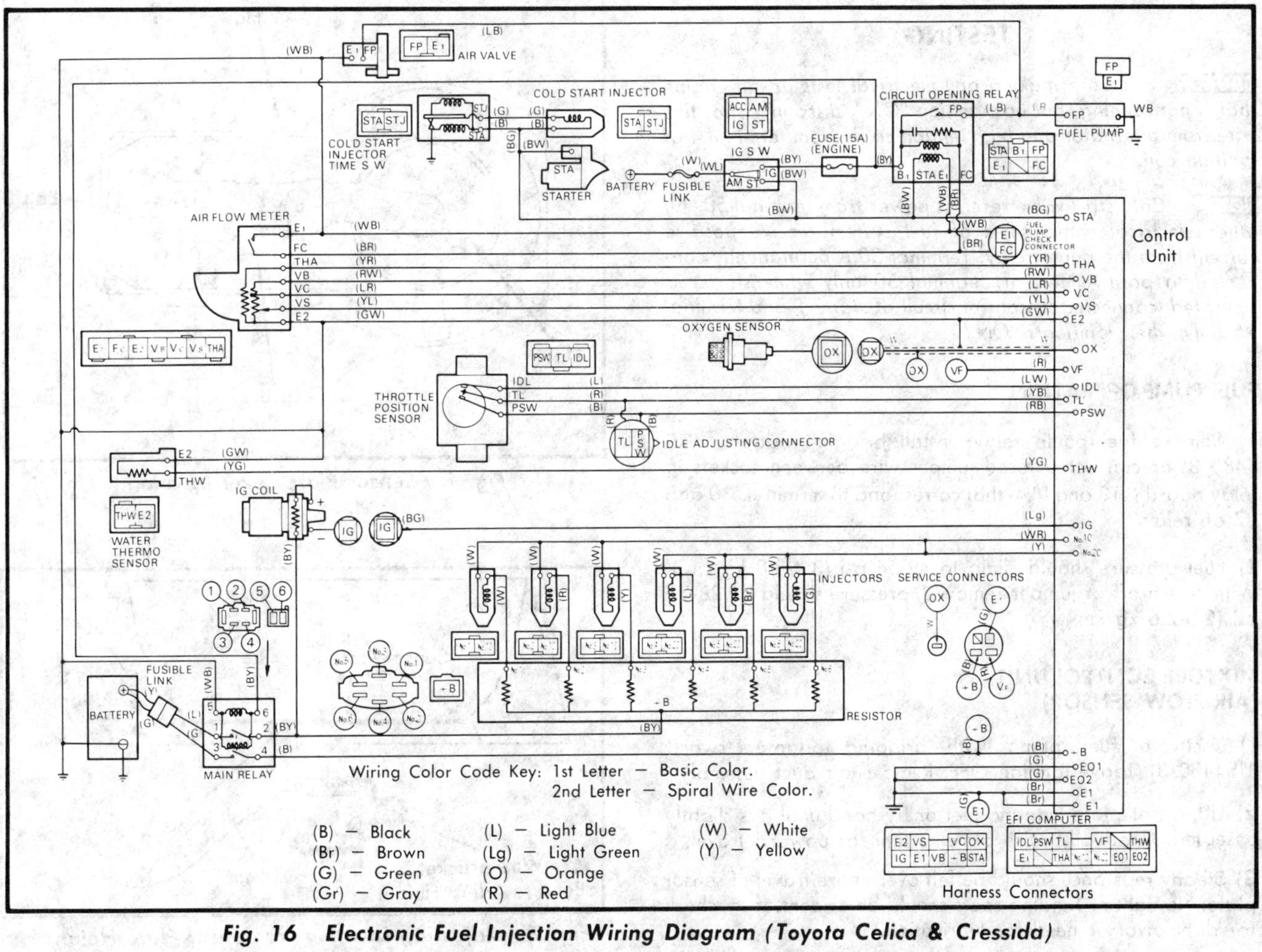

Fig. 16 Electronic Fuel Injection Wiring Diagram (Toyota Celica & Cressida)

BOSCH CIS INJECTION SYSTEM — AUDI & VOLKSWAGEN

Audi (Federal Only)
  4000
  5000
Volkswagen (Federal Only)
  Dasher
  Jetta
  Rabbit
  Rabbit Pickup
  Scirocco

DESCRIPTION & OPERATION

The Bosch Continuous Injection System (CIS) is a mechanically operated system. It injects fuel to each cylinder in amounts determined by the volume of air flow through the air intake system. Intake air required by the engine is metered by an air flow sensor located in the air inlet. Sensor is activated by a circular plate attached to an arm and pivot assembly which is extremely sensitive to air flow. This sensor plate is raised or lowered by the incoming flow of air, and in turn, raises or lowers a plunger in the fuel distributor. This plunger acts to increase or decrease amount of fuel to be injected at each cylinder. *See Fig. 6.*

Main components of the CI System are: Control Pressure Regulator, Air Sensor, Fuel Distributor, Thermo-Time Switch, Auxiliary Air Regulator, Cold Start Valve and Injectors, Electric Fuel Pump, Fuel Accumulator, Auxiliary Air Valve and a hot start pulse relay.

TESTING

CAUTION — *Before making any electrical tests on an engine that is not running, but has ignition "ON", disconnect positive wire from alternator and high tension cable from terminal 4 of ignition coil.*

NOTE — *Cold start valve receives power from terminal 50. All other electrical components of fuel system receive positive current from the pump relay. Terminal 30 is permanently connected to positive current, terminal 50 only while starter is operated (connected to control circuit of starter); and terminal 15 only when ignition is ON.*

FUEL PUMP OPERATION

1) Remove fuel pump relay. Install bridging adaptor (US 4480/3) or connect a fused jumper wire between sockets in relay board (L13 and L14) that correspond to terminals 30 and 87 on relay.

2) Fuel pressure should climb to 49-54 psi (3.4-3.8 kg/cm²). With switch off or jumper removed, pressure should be 28-37 psi (2.0-2.6 kg/cm²).

MIXTURE CONTROL UNIT (AIR FLOW SENSOR)

1) Activate fuel pump with bridging adaptor switch (US4480/3). Leave ignition OFF. Remove air duct assembly.

2) Lift sensor plate with magnet or by hand until it is slightly unseated. Gradually raise plate to limit of upward travel.

3) Steady resistance should be felt over entire travel of sensor plate. No tight or binding spots should be evident. If so, check for dirty pivot or need for lubrication.

4) Ensure sensor plate is centered in inlet cone. If adjustment is needed, use suitable tool (1109 or equivalent) or insert a .004" (.10 mm) feeler gauge around outside of sensor plate while in seated position. Centering bolt should be slightly loosened. Apply Loctite to threads and tighten bolt after adjustment.

5) If plate cannot be centered and lever appears off center, remove air sensor housing and clamping bolt on lever counterweight. Coat bolt with Loctite, install finger tight, and center lever. Tighten bolt and check lever position.

6) To adjust sensor plate height, run engine until warm, then turn engine off. Remove rubber boot and check plate level. Bend clip up or down carefully until plate is even with bottom rim of air cone. Readjust CO% and idle after moving sensor plate. *See Fig. 2.*

7) Run fuel pump for a few seconds. Using strong magnet or small pliers, move plate up and down. It should move in both directions without sticking or binding. If plate sticks while moving upward, fuel distributor plunger may be at fault.

8) Remove fuel distributor from air sensor housing. Check plunger for free movement, being careful not to drop it. Wash in solvent, then lubricate with gasoline and be sure "O" ring is seated properly. If plunger still hangs up, fuel distributor must be replaced.

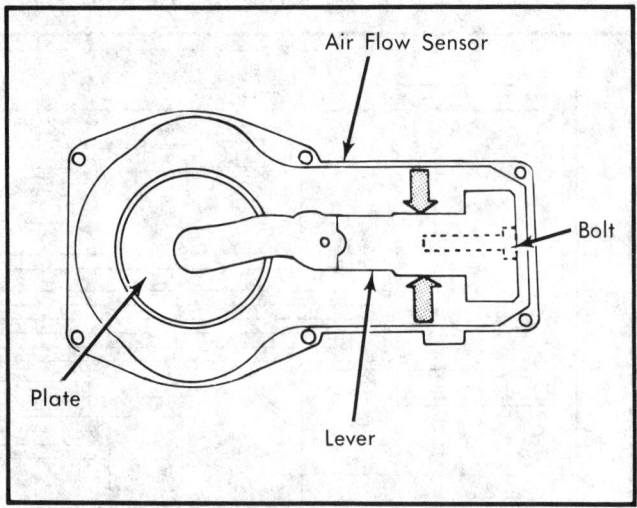

Fig. 1   Sensor Plate Lever Location

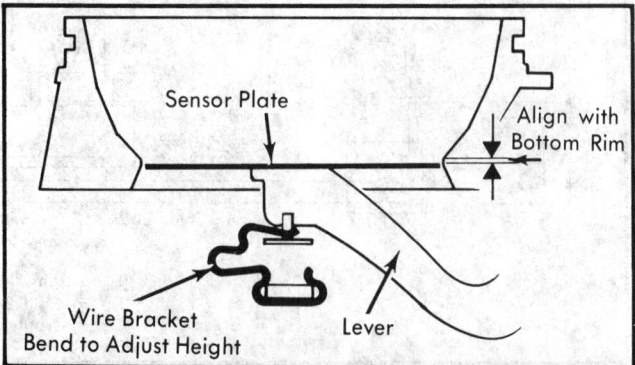

Fig. 2   Adjusting Location for Sensor Plate Height

BOSCH CIS INJECTION SYSTEM — AUDI & VOLKSWAGEN (Cont.)

INSTALLING AND BLEEDING PRESSURE GAUGE AND VALVE

NOTE — *Before any pressure tests can be completed, it is necessary to install and bleed air from a gauge and valve, such as VW1318 or P378.*

1) Although pressure testing valves and gauges may appear identical to those pictured in this article, DISREGARD handle position shown when making pressure tests on fuel system.

NOTE — *Valves from the same manufacturer may appear the same, but may vary in interior design. When checking rest pressure or control pressure (either cold or warm), be sure valve on tester is OPEN. When checking system (line) pressure, be sure valve is CLOSED.*

2) Install gauge and valve between control pressure regulator and fuel distributor, with valve toward control pressure regulator.

3) To bleed air from valve, hang gauge downward below valve and connecting lines. Open and close valve 4 or 5 times at 10 second intervals. Raise gauge so that it is now above valve and lines and proceed with testing.

COLD ENGINE CONTROL PRESSURE TEST

NOTE — *Engine must be cold for this test, preferably having set overnight at test site without operation.*

1) Install pressure gauge and valve in fuel line between fuel distributor and control pressure regulator.

2) Valve assembly should be on control pressure regulator side of gauge. See *Fig. 3* .

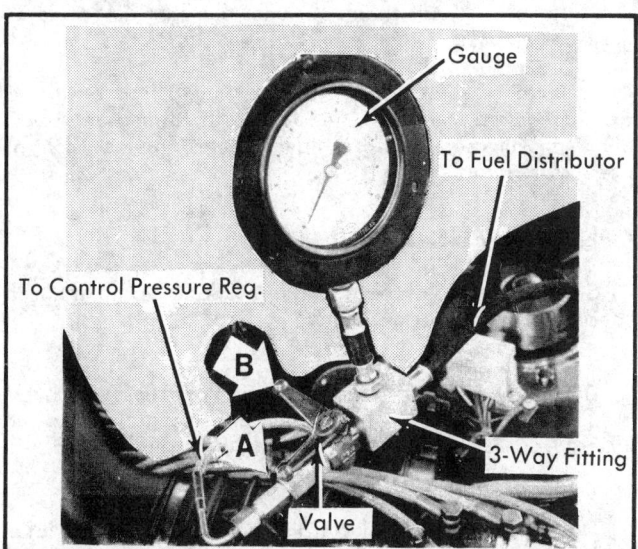

Fig. 3   Connecting Fuel Pressure Gauge and Valve To Test Control Pressure

3) Turn ignition ON. With fuel pump running, bleed and then OPEN valve.

4) Unplug electrical connectors from control pressure regulator and auxiliary air regulator. Start engine and idle for maximum of one minute.

5) Note control pressure and refer to graph in *Fig. 4*. At normal room temperature, about 68° F (20° C), pressure should read between 18-24 psi (1.3-1.7 kg/cm²).

6) If pressure does not read within specifications, replace control pressure regulator.

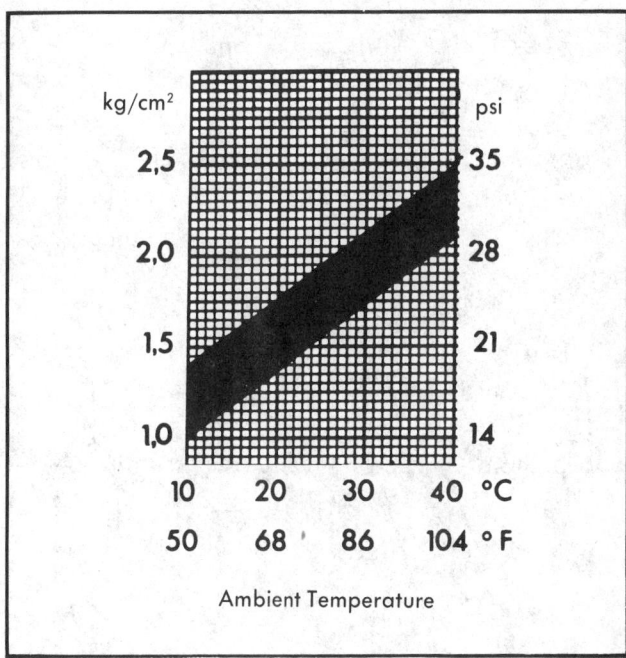

Fig. 4   Graph Showing Cold Control Pressure at Various Temperatures

WARM ENGINE CONTROL PRESSURE TEST

NOTE — *Connect pressure testing gauge and valve in same manner as for Cold Engine Control Pressure Test. Keep pump relay bridged.*

1) Be sure to connect control pressure regulator electrical plug, previously removed. OPEN valve. See *Fig. 3*.

2) Start engine and idle until fuel pressure stabilizes. Reading should be 48-54 psi (3.4-3.8 kg/cm²).

NOTE — *On Audi 5000, pressure should be 49-53 psi (3.5-3.8 kg/cm²) with control pressure regulator vacuum hose connected; 39-43 psi (2.8-3.1 kg/cm²) with hose disconnected.*

3) If control pressure does not increase enough, remove plug from control pressure regulator and connect a test lamp across terminals. If lamp does not light, either power or ground connection is bad. If lamp lights with engine idling and pressure is too low, replace regulator.

SYSTEM (LINE) PRESSURE TEST

NOTE — *Connect and bleed pressure gauge and valve in same manner as for Control Pressure Test. Keep fuel pump relay bridged. Be sure electrical plugs are connected to control pressure regulator and auxiliary air regulator.*

1) Ensure electric fuel pump activates when ignition switch is turned ON and that fuel filter is clean.

BOSCH CIS INJECTION SYSTEM — AUDI & VOLKSWAGEN (Cont.)

2) CLOSE valve *(Fig. 3)*. Start engine and run at idle.

3) System (line) pressure should be 64-74 psi (4.5-5.2 kg/cm²). If not within specifications, clean, check and adjust fuel distributor pressure regulator (relief) valve.

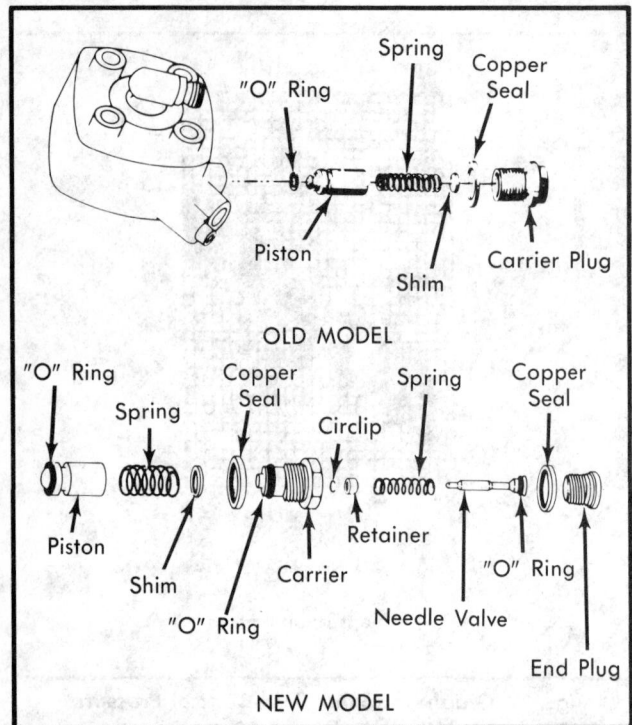

OLD MODEL

NEW MODEL

Fig. 5   Components of Pressure Regulator Valve

4) System pressure may be adjusted by adding to or removing shims from valve. *See Fig. 5.* Pressure will be changed 1 psi (.06 kg/cm²) by a .004" (.1 mm) shim or 4 psi (.3 kg/cm²) by a .020" (.5 mm) shim.

5) If system pressure is low, check for leaks between fuel pump and control pressure regulator. Also check for defective fuel pump.

LEAK AND FLOW RATE TEST

1) Check for correct system (line) pressure, bleed pressure gauge, then move lever to OPEN position. Gauge should read 49-54 psi (3.4-3.8 kg/cm²). Turn engine "OFF"; pressure should drop to a maximum of 37 psi (2.6 kg/cm²).

2) If pressure is too high, readjust system pressure and retest. Pressure should hold at a minimum of 26 psi (1.8 kg/cm²) after 10 minutes, and 23 psi (1.6 kg/cm²) after 20 minutes.

3) If pressure drops too much, restart and warm-up engine. Turn engine off, pinch off hose between fuel tank and pump, and recheck pressure drop. If pressure is now okay, pump check valve is leaking. If not, check relief valve in mixture control unit, or leaking injectors or cold start valve.

4) Test fuel pump flow rate by removing return line at fuel distributor and placing open end in container. With pump running for exactly 30 seconds, flow should measure 24 oz. (750 cc)

on pump with push-on terminals, or 30 oz. (900 cc) on pump with bolt-on terminals.

PULSE RELAY & COLD START VALVE

1) Disconnect high tension wire 4 from distributor and connect to ground. Remove cold start valve, but leave fuel line and wiring connected. Point valve into container.

2) With engine coolant below 90°F (35°C), crank engine with starter. Valve should spray for 1-8 seconds in cone-shaped pattern, then stop spraying momentarily. Valve should continue to spray periodically in pulses as starter is operated.

3) With engine warmed up, valve should spray fuel after 2 seconds, then stop. It will begin to spray periodically in pulses if the engine is still cranked.

4) If spray does not pulse, check for open or shorted wires. If wiring is good, replace pulse relay.

AUXILIARY AIR REGULATOR

NOTE — *Test must be performed on cold engine only.*

1) Remove electrical connector from auxiliary air regulator. Start engine and run at idle. Pinch either hose at auxiliary air regulator. Idle speed should drop slightly.

2) Reconnect plug at auxiliary air regulator and warm up engine. Pinch either hose at regulator; idle speed should not change.

3) If idle speed decreases when hose is pinched, disconnect electrical connector and connect a test lamp across terminals. If test lamp is lit with engine running, auxiliary air regulator must be replaced.

4) If voltage is reaching regulator plug, check resistance across regulator terminals. Resistance should measure 16-22 ohms on all models. If resistance varies, replace control pressure regulator.

CONTROL PRESSURE REGULATOR

1) Check control pressure regulator (cold and warm). If not to specifications, replace regulator.

2) Disconnect electrical plug from air flow sensor and the positive wire from alternator. Install pressure gauge and set valve to open. Turn ignition ON without starting engine.

3) Disconnect electrical plug from control pressure regulator and measure voltage at plug. If none, check power relay and pump relay. If voltage is available at pump relay, problem lies with wire connecting control pressure regulator and pump relay.

4) If voltage is reaching regulator plug, check resistance across regulator terminals for 20 ohms. If resistance varies greatly, replace control pressure regulator.

BOSCH CIS INJECTION SYSTEM – AUDI & VOLKSWAGEN (Cont.)

INJECTOR NOZZLES

NOTE – *Do not allow open flame or sparks in area while testing and servicing fuel system components, to avoid possibility of fire or explosion.*

1) Remove one injector from manifold tube, leaving fuel hose attached to injector. Pull injector straight out. Disconnect high tension cable from terminal 4 of ignition coil to prevent engine from starting.

2) Point injector into a glass jar. Have someone operate starter for 15 seconds while you observe spray pattern, which should be steady and cone-shaped.

3) Turn ignition switch OFF. Hold injector horizontally. No fuel should drip from injector nozzle. If injector does not perform to specifications, replace it. Repeat test for each injector.

NOTE – *When installing injectors, soak rubber seals in gasoline briefly. Be sure injectors are fully pressed into seat.*

REMOVAL & INSTALLATION

MIXTURE CONTROL UNIT

CAUTION – *On all models, disconnect battery ground cable and relieve fuel pressure before removing mixture control unit.*

1) Clean all fuel connections completely and disconnect them, tagging each one to insure correct installation later.

2) Disconnect air duct from air sensor and throttle valve housing.

3) Use tip of screwdriver to snap loose the retainers holding bottom part of air cleaner. Prevent unit from falling. Carefully remove mixture control unit, taking care that fuel does not spill on engine or electrical connections.

4) To install, reverse removal procedure. Use new gasket beneath upper section of mixture control unit.

FUEL DISTRIBUTOR

CAUTION – *On all models, disconnect battery ground cable and relieve fuel pressure before removing fuel distributor.*

1) Clean and remove fuel lines at fuel distributor. Remove fuel distributor retaining bolts.

2) Carefully lift fuel distributor up and away. Use care to avoid control plunger falling out from underside of fuel distributor.

3) If control plunger has been removed, dampen with fuel before installing.

NOTE – *Small shoulder of plunger must be inserted first.*

4) Install fuel distributor using new O-rings.

CONTROL PRESSURE REGULATOR FOR WARM RUNNING COMPENSATION

CAUTION – *On all models, disconnect battery ground cable and relieve fuel pressure before removing control pressure regulator.*

1) Clean fuel lines and disconnect. Remove electrical connections to regulator.

2) Remove two screws holding regulator to engine block. Remove regulator and gasket.

3) To install, reverse removal procedure, using new gasket.

AUXILIARY AIR REGULATOR

1) Remove vacuum hose connections to valve. Remove electrical connection(s).

2) Remove two screws holding regulator to No. 4 cylinder manifold tube of the intake air distributor.

3) To install, reverse removal procedure.

THERMO-TIME SWITCH

1) Relieve any cooling system pressure and drain enough coolant from system to bring level below that of time switch.

2) Switch is located on coolant adaptor on engine block. Unplug electrical harness plug from thermo-time switch.

3) Using a deep socket (to avoid damaging electrical terminals on top of switch), remove thermo-time switch.

4) To install switch, reverse removal procedure. Suitable sealing compound may be needed to ensure proper seal of new switch.

COLD START VALVE

CAUTION – *On all models, disconnect battery ground cable and relieve fuel pressure before removing cold start valve.*

1) Cold start valve is bolted to intake manifold behind throttle valve housing. Clean around fuel line and remove line from valve.

2) Remove electrical connector from cold start valve.

3) Remove bolt(s) holding cold start valve and lift out valve.

4) To install, reverse removal procedure.

INJECTORS

CAUTION – *On all models, disconnect battery ground cable and relieve fuel pressure before removing injectors.*

1) Clean fuel line connection at injector thoroughly. Remove fuel line from injector with special tool (P384) or equivalent.

2) Pull steadily upward on injector to remove.

3) To install, reverse removal procedure. Be sure "O" rings are soaked in gasoline for a few minutes prior to installation.

BOSCH CIS INJECTION SYSTEM — AUDI & VOLKSWAGEN (Cont.)

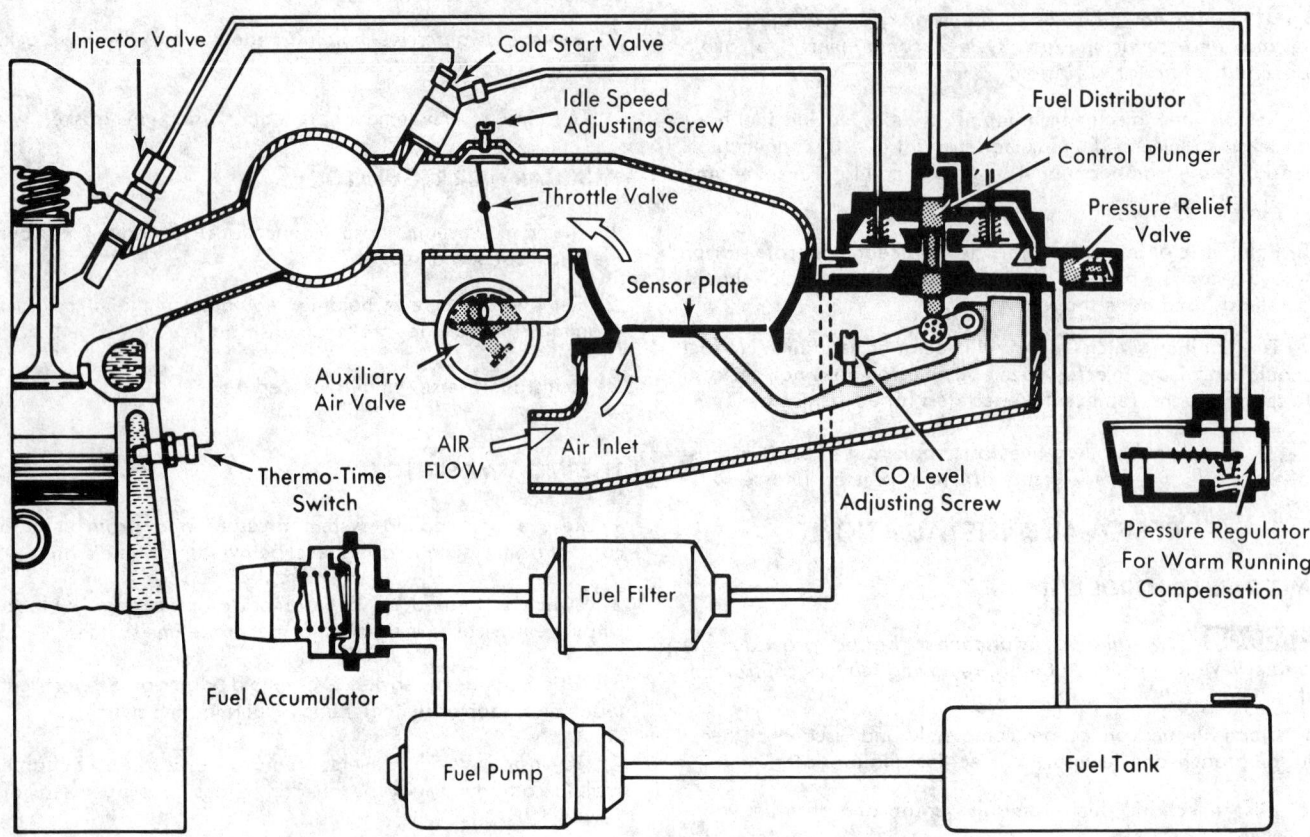

Fig. 6 Functional Diagram of Volkswagen & Audi Bosch CIS Fuel Injection System

BOSCH LAMBDA CIS INJECTION SYSTEM – ALL MODELS

Audi
  4000 (Calif. Only)
  5000 (Calif. Only)
  5000 Turbo
BMW 320i
Mercedes-Benz
  280 Series
  450 Series
Peugeot 505
Porsche
  911SC
  924
  924 Turbo

Saab
  99
  900
  900 Turbo
Volkswagen (Calif. Only)
  Dasher
  Jetta
  Rabbit
  Scirocco
  Rabbit Pickup
Volvo
  All Models

The system consists of the mixture control unit (air flow sensor and fuel distributor), control pressure regulator, auxiliary air valve, cold start valve, thermo-time switch, injector nozzles, fuel pump, filter, oxygen sensor, electronic control unit, frequency valve, and catalytic converter. Some models use additional components, such as a thermo-vacuum valve or hot start pulse relay.

DESCRIPTION

The Bosch Continuous Injection System is a mechanical fuel injection system operated by incoming air flow. The Lambda system is a feedback control capable of measuring air/fuel ratios and correcting them constantly. The combination of the 2 systems makes it possible to obtain good economy and performance while minimizing exhaust emissions.

OPERATION

MIXTURE CONTROL UNIT

The air flow sensor contains a plate mounted on a hinged lever which moves in a cone shaped venturi. All engine air is drawn through this sensor. The plate moves as air passes through, pulling the hinged lever up or down. This raises or lowers a fuel control plunger in the fuel distributor, determining the amount of fuel to be injected into each cylinder. The movement of the plate is controlled by air flow, cone shape of venturi, a balance weight, and fuel pressure.

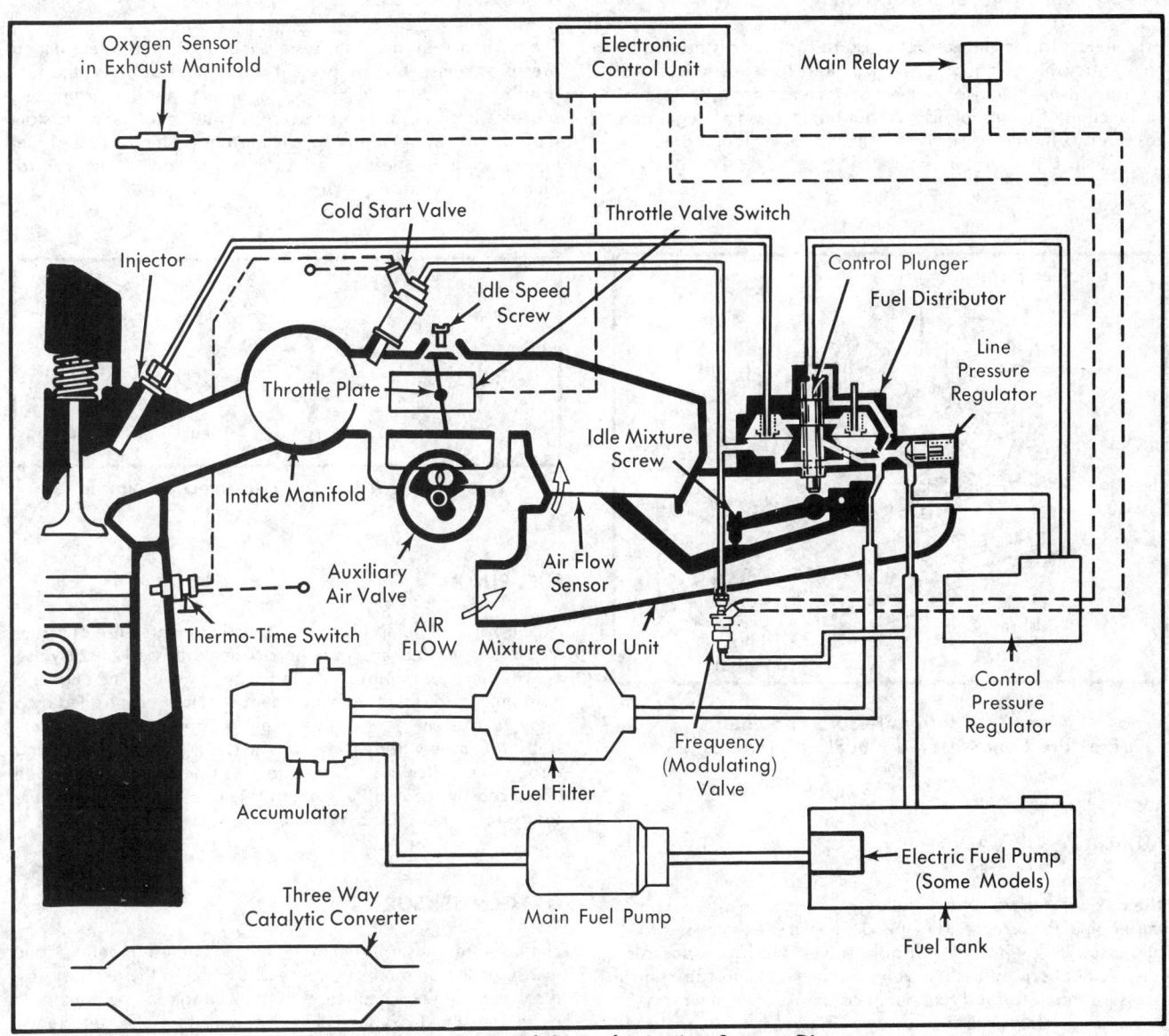

Fig. 1 Bosch CIS Lambda Fuel Injection System Diagram
(Typical of All Models – Details May Vary)

BOSCH LAMBDA CIS INJECTION SYSTEM — ALL MODELS (Cont.)

NOTE — *Air flows UP through the sensor on most inline engines, and DOWN through the sensor on V6, V8, and turbocharged engines. The direction of air flow does not affect system operation, it is changed for convenience of routing air flow.*

Fuel distribution can be equal only if the pressure to each injector is equal. Pressure regulating valves in the fuel distributor equalize system pressure. These valves are adjusted during assembly of distributor and cannot be adjusted in service.

CONTROL PRESSURE REGULATOR

The control pressure regulator provides fuel pressure to the top of the plunger in the fuel distributor. Reduced pressure allows the plate to move farther with the same air flow. This supplies more fuel to the cylinders to improve warming up. As the engine reaches operating temperature (or a pre-determined time elapses) the control pressure regulator increases control pressure, leaning the air/fuel mixture.

A bi-metal strip in the control pressure regulator is heated by an electric coil. As it heats up, it gradually increases the control pressure. If the electrical connections are not good, the warm-up function of the regulator will not operate. Some regulators have an altitude-sensitive function that compensates for changes in barometric pressure.

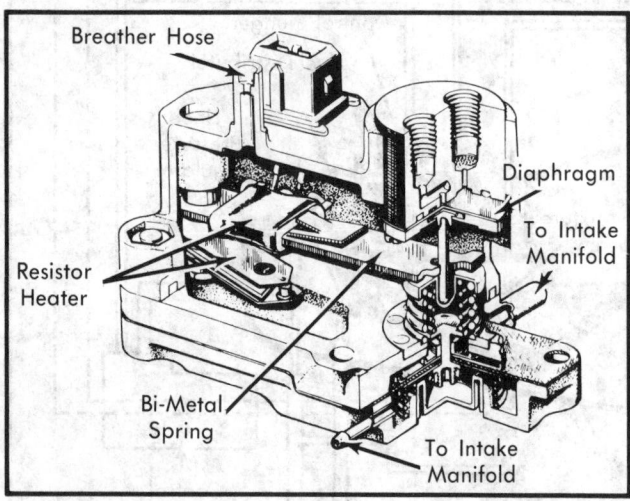

Fig. 2   Control Pressure Regulator
(Pressure Compensated Model — Others Similar)

AUXILIARY AIR VALVE

The auxiliary air valve, or regulator, provides additional air to the engine to increase idle speed when the engine is cold. It allows air to by-pass the throttle valves which are closed at idle. A heating coil in the valve is connected to the control pressure regulator and fuel pump circuit. As the coil warms up, it gradually closes the air passage. The valve is calibrated to keep idle smooth without a large speed change as the engine is warming up.

COLD START VALVE

The cold start valve is located in the intake manifold and sprays fuel during starting. It enrichens the mixture so the engine will start easily. The valve is powered through the starter circuit and grounded through the thermo-time switch so it operates for only a short time while the engine is being cranked.

THERMO-TIME SWITCH & HOT START RELAY

The thermo-time switch is affected by coolant or block temperature and starter current. Depending on engine temperature, the switch will take from 3-10 seconds to open. Injection through the cold start valve will then stop. Some models use a hot start pulse relay to improve hot starting. The relay will operate the cold start valve in short pulses after it would normally have been turned off by the thermo-time switch.

INJECTOR NOZZLES

The injectors in the CIS system open at a predetermined pressure. Fuel is always present in the lines between the fuel distributor and the injectors, to ensure good starting. As pressure in the distributor increases (when the engine is started), the valves open and spray constantly. The amount of fuel injected will be determined by the position of the control plunger and control pressure.

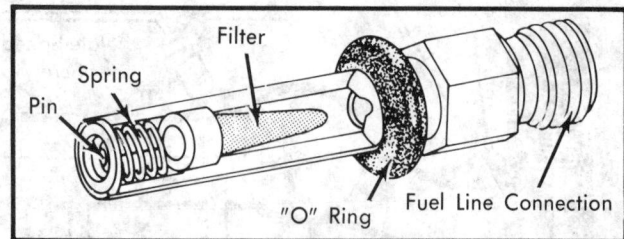

Fig. 3   Bosch CIS Lambda Injection Nozzle

FUEL PUMP

An electric fuel pump is used to provide fuel pressure of about 60-80 psi (4.1-5.5 kg/cm²). An accumulator and check valve operate to maintain pressure in the system when the engine is not running, to aid in starting. The fuel pump is controlled by a relay to prevent it from continuing to operate if the engine stalls. It can be wired in several ways, the most common being through a switch on the air flow sensor or through a coil energized by the ignition system. When testing the system, the safety relay must be bypassed.

OXYGEN SENSOR

The oxygen sensor is located in the exhaust manifold and measures the amount of unburned oxygen in the exhaust gas. If oxygen is low (rich mixture) a high voltage will be generated by the sensor. If oxygen is high (lean mixture) the voltage will be low. The signal from the oxygen sensor goes to an electronic control unit which determines engine mixture.

BOSCH LAMBDA CIS INJECTION SYSTEM — ALL MODELS (Cont.)

ELECTRONIC CONTROL UNIT & FREQUENCY VALVE

The electronic control unit is designed to continually correct the air/fuel mixture, based on signals from the oxygen sensor. It sends a series of pulses to a frequency valve. The frequency valve is located in a fuel line that connects the upper and lower halves of the fuel distributor.

When the frequency valve is closed, fuel pressure to the injectors is determined by a spring in each pressure regulating valve. When the frequency valve is open, fuel pressure decreases in the lower half of the fuel distributor, the tension on the spring is relieved, and more fuel goes to the cylinders.

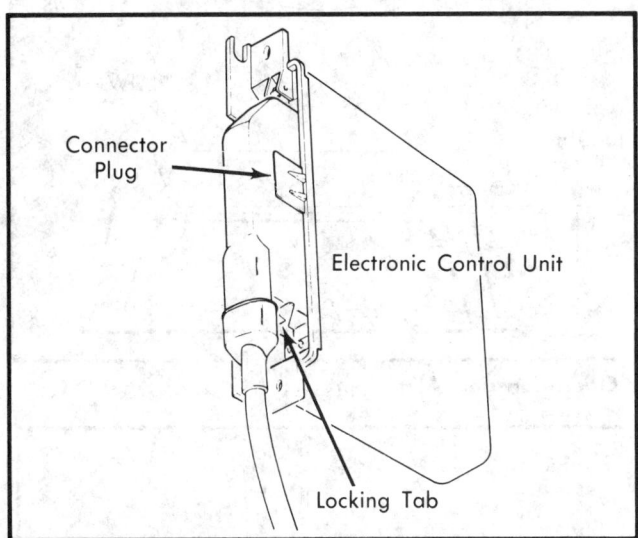

Fig. 4 Bosch CIS Lambda Electronic Control Unit

The electronic control unit opens and closes the frequency valve many times a second to ensure a smooth regulation of fuel pressure and mixture. When the engine is cold, the ratio of valve open to valve closed is about 50%. After the engine warms up, the voltage produced by the oxygen sensor determines the amount of time the frequency valve must be open or closed. This ratio can be read with a special tester or with a dwell meter (on most models). A dwell reading of 45° indicates a ratio of 50% open, 50% closed.

CATALYTIC CONVERTER

CIS Lambda systems can control air/fuel ratios within .02%. This close regulation allows the use of a 3-way catalyst that can decrease NOx, HC, and CO emissions. The converter can be damaged by improper adjustment of the system or by the use of leaded fuels.

TESTING

NOTE — *Testing procedures described below will apply to all models using the CIS Lambda system unless otherwise noted. Not all models will use all components.*

PREPARATION FOR TESTING

1) All CIS systems are very sensitive to air leaks. Check condition of rubber boots, hoses, and gaskets. Other areas of leakage are injectors, cold start valve, and PCV system (filler cap and dipstick).

2) A pressure gauge must be installed to perform fuel pressure tests. On all models, pressure gauge is installed between the control pressure regulator and the center fitting on fuel distributor.

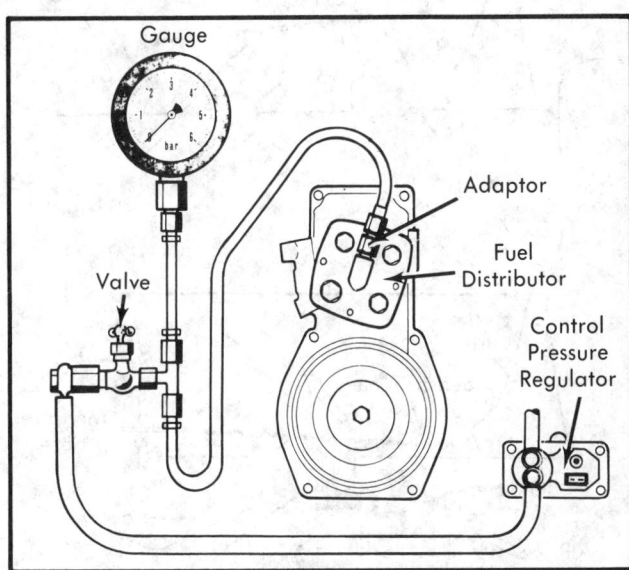

Fig. 5 Pressure Gauge Installation

3) To operate fuel pump with engine off, disconnect fuel pump relay from relay panel (VW, Porsche, Audi, Saab, Mercedes Benz). Insert a jumper wire into sockets that correspond to terminals 30 and 87 on relay. On Peugeot, remove steering wheel and lower left dash panel. Install switch and harness (8.0141 P) to tachymetric relay connector, or jumper across 30 and 87B. On Volvo, Mercedes-Benz, and other models so equipped, disconnect safety switch connector on air flow sensor.

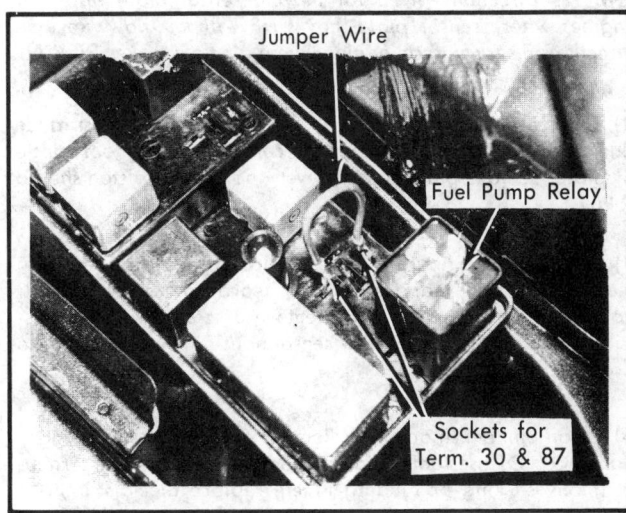

Fig. 6 Fuel Pump Jumper Wire For Testing (Saab Shown, Others Similar)

4) Operate fuel pump on Peugeot by depressing switch on harness. On all other models, turn ignition on. Place pressure gauge as low as possible in engine compartment, then open and close valve 5 times to bleed gauge. Place valve in open position and hang in convenient location. Turn pump off.

BOSCH LAMBDA CIS INJECTION SYSTEM — ALL MODELS (Cont.)

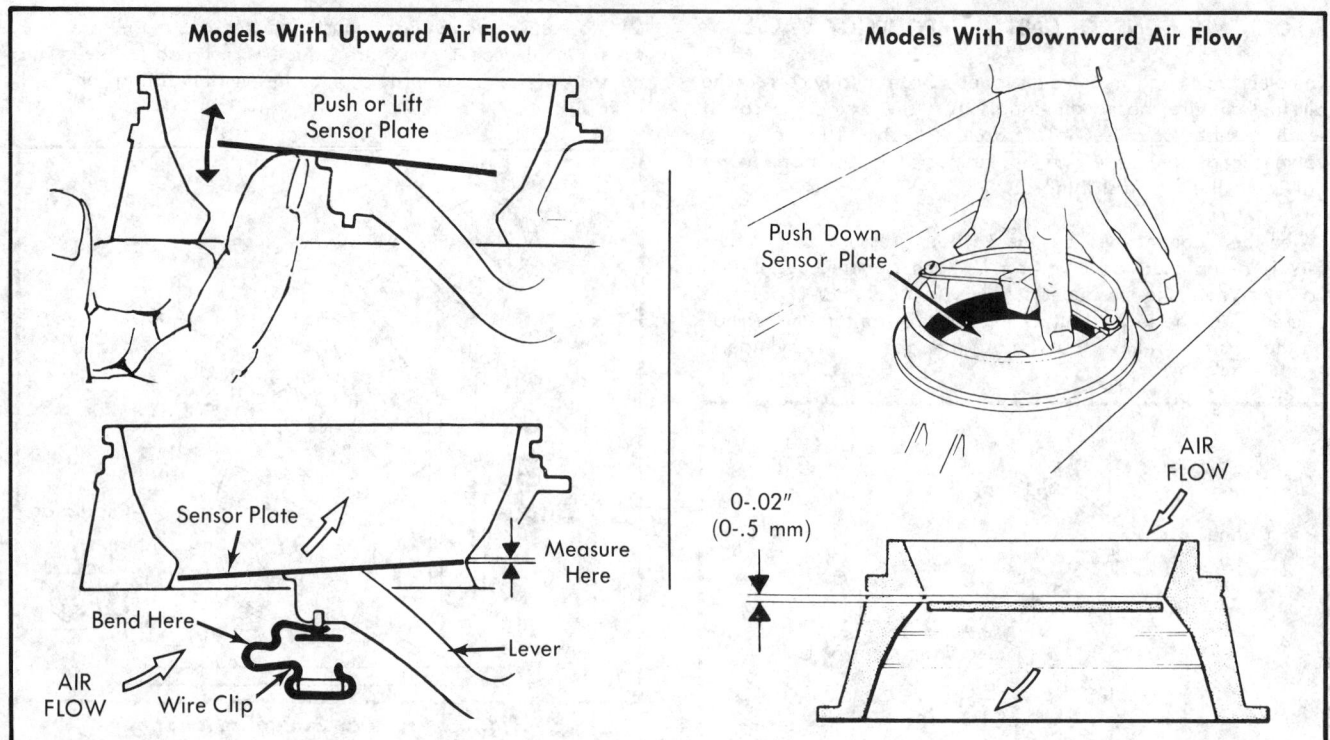

Models With Upward Air Flow

Push or Lift Sensor Plate

Sensor Plate

Measure Here

Bend Here

Lever

AIR FLOW

Wire Clip

Models With Downward Air Flow

Push Down Sensor Plate

AIR FLOW

0-.02"
(0-.5 mm)

Fig. 7   Checking Air Flow Sensor Operation and Alignment

AIR/FUEL MIXTURE CONTROL (AIR FLOW SENSOR)

1) Remove rubber bellows to expose plate in sensor. Disconnect electrical connectors on auxiliary air valve and control pressure regulator, then operate fuel pump for ten seconds to build up control pressure.

NOTE — *Directions given for moving sensor plate apply to engines where sensor plate moves UP with air flow. Reverse directions if servicing an engine where air flow moves DOWN.*

2) Lift sensor plate slowly with magnet or pliers. Resistance due to control pressure should be constant throughout range of plate. Release plate slowly, lever and control piston should follow.

3) Lift plate, then return it rapidly to lower position. The piston moves more slowly and should be heard hitting the lever. If not, control piston is sticking. Remove 3 screws from fuel distributor and lift off of air flow sensor housing. Be careful not to drop control piston.

4) Clean plunger in gasoline. Remove any deposits with finger nail; DO NOT use tools. Slide plunger in and out while turning it. If any sticking or binding is felt, replace fuel distributor.

5) Reinstall fuel distributor. Check air flow sensor plate alignment. Plate should be even with bottom rim or 0.02" (0.5 mm) lower. If not, bend spring to correct, or reposition stop pin (tap lightly with punch).

6) Plate should be centered in housing. If not, loosen center screw and align plate with 0.004" (0.1 mm) feeler gauge at four points around rim. Apply Loctite and tighten screw.

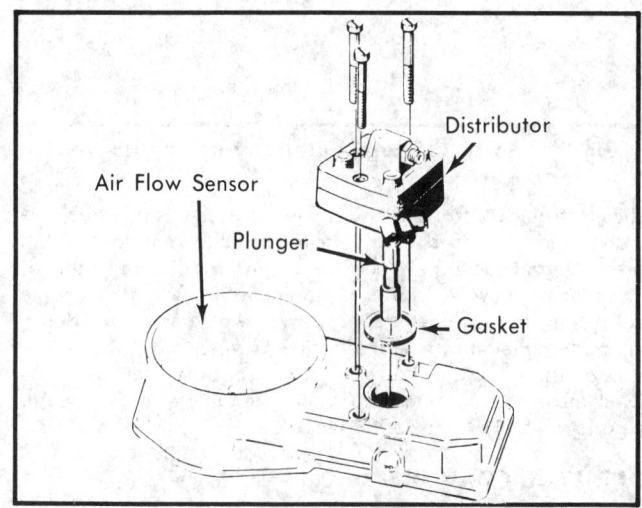

Distributor

Air Flow Sensor

Plunger

Gasket

Fig. 8   Checking Fuel Distributor Plunger

COLD ENGINE CONTROL PRESSURE TEST

1) Testing must be done on cold engine. Unplug connectors at auxiliary air valve and control pressure regulator. Place valve on pressure gauge in open position and operate fuel pump.

2) Check pressure quickly. Reading should fall in shaded area of graph. Be sure to check air temperature and read correct area of graph.

3) If control pressure is not correct, retest with new control pressure regulator. No servicing is possible.

NOTE — *Some models have a control pressure regulator with atmospheric pressure compensation. Pressures may vary slightly on these models.*

BOSCH LAMBDA CIS INJECTION SYSTEM – ALL MODELS (Cont.)

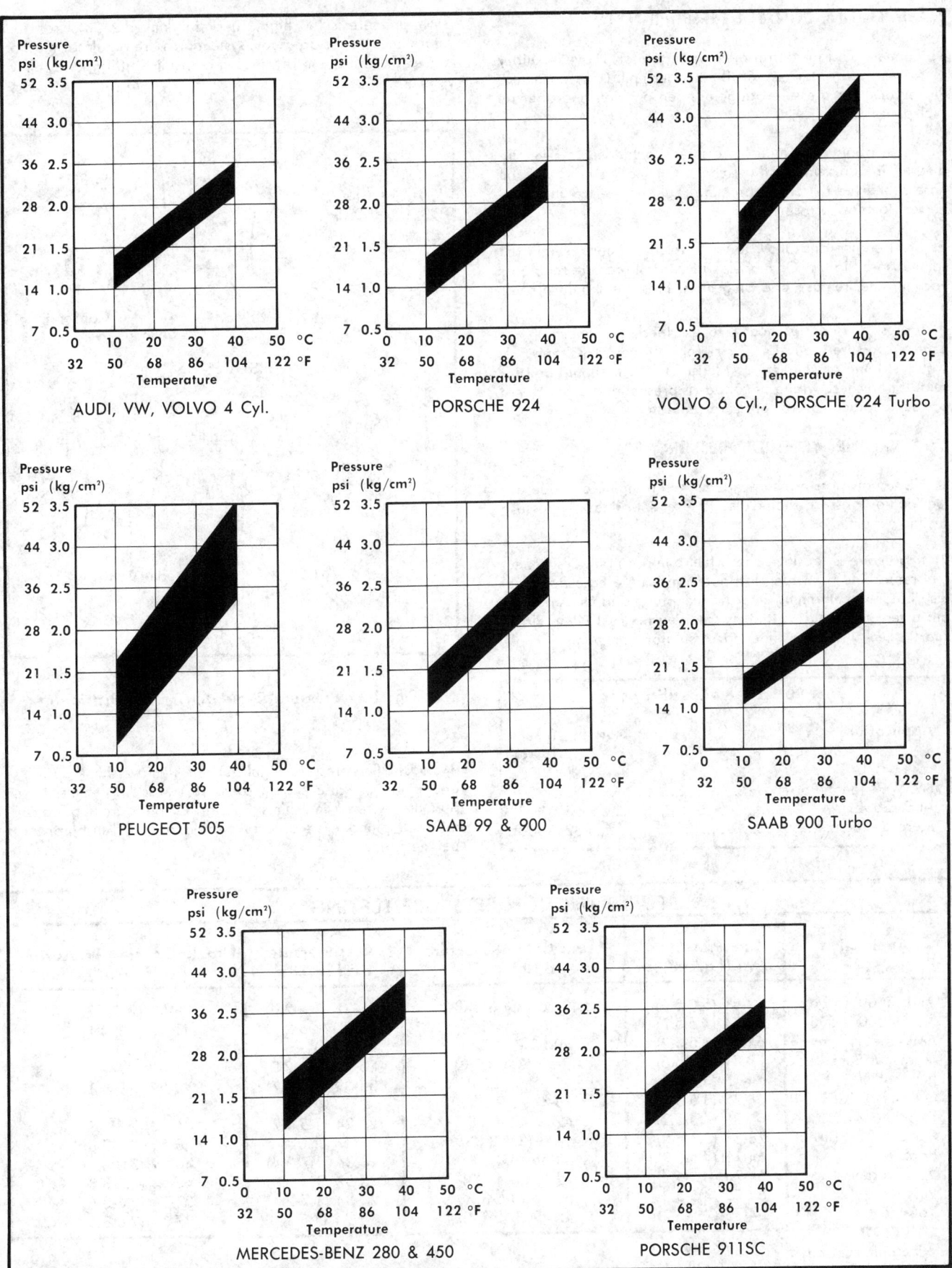

Fig. 9 Cold Engine Control Pressure Test Graphs

BOSCH LAMBDA CIS INJECTION SYSTEM — ALL MODELS (Cont.)

WARM ENGINE CONTROL PRESSURE TEST

1) Connect plug to control pressure regulator. Leave auxiliary air valve and air flow sensor (if equipped) plugs disconnected. Place valve for pressure gauge in open position and operate fuel pump.

2) After about 5 minutes, pressure should rise to level indicated in "Pressure Testing" chart. On models with vacuum hose connected to control pressure regulator, leave hose connected to read pressure.

3) Start engine and allow to idle. Pressure should remain the same or rise slightly. On models with control pressure regulator vacuum line, remove and plug hose. Pressure should drop.

4) If pressure does not reach level specified, disconnect plug at control pressure regulator. Check for voltage across terminals with test lamp or voltmeter. At least 11.5 volts should be present. If not, check wiring. If voltage is present and pressure not correct, replace control pressure regulator.

SYSTEM (LINE) CONTROL PRESSURE TEST

1) Close valve on pressure gauge. With engine off, operate fuel pump. Pressure should rise to level specified in "Pressure Testing" chart.

2) If pressure is too low, check fuel pump output. Disconnect fuel return line from fuel distributor and run a hose from fuel distributor to container. Operate fuel pump and measure output after 30 seconds. If not as specified in "Fuel Pump Flow" chart, check fuel lines, filter, accumulator and pump.

3) If pressure is too high, check for kinked or blocked fuel return line. If lines are clear, system pressure regulator must be adjusted. Turn pump off, loosen return line fitting, and relieve pressure.

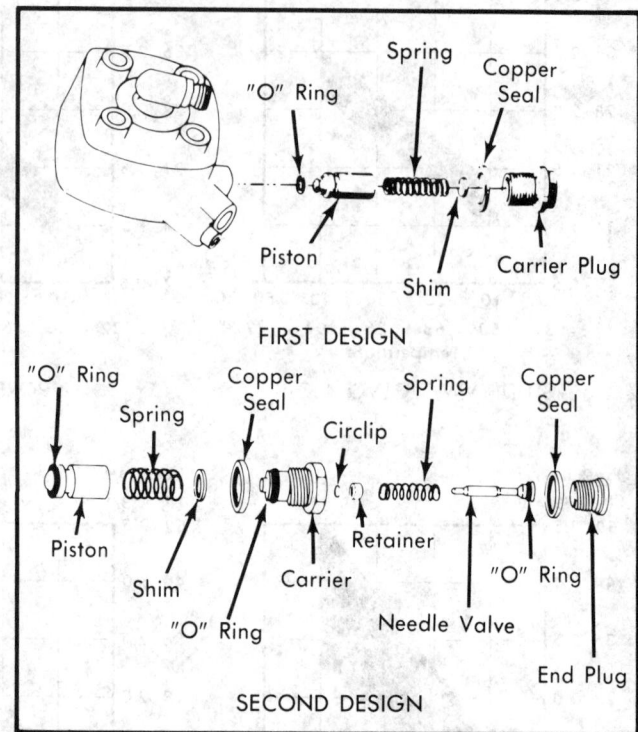

Fig. 10   Pressure Regulator in Fuel Distributor

4) Loosen line pressure regulator nut. Remove shims, spring(s) and plunger. Raise system pressure by adding shims; lower pressure by removing shims. Be sure "O" rings are in good condition. If plunger is scored or damaged, fuel distributor must be replaced.

Fuel Pump Flow Specifications

Application	Flow in 30 Sec. oz. (cc)
BMW, Peugeot, Porsche	24 (750)
Audi, Saab, VW	30 (900)
Mercedes-Benz	32 (1000)

FUEL INJECTION PRESSURE TESTING

Application	Line Pressure psi (kg/cm²)	Warm Control Pressure psi (kg/cm²)	Rest Pressure psi (kg/cm²)	Nozzle Opening Pressure psi (kg/cm²)
Audi 5000 Turbo	72-81 (5.0-5.6)	49-55 (3.4-3.8)①	23-37 (1.6-2.6)	38-53 (2.7-3.7)
Audi 4000, 5000	64-74 (4.5-5.2)	49-55 (3.4-3.8)	23-37 (1.6-2.6)	41-59 (2.9-4.1)
BMW 320i	64-75 (4.5-5.2)	49-55 (3.4-3.8)	24 (1.7)	44 (3.1)
Mercedes-Benz	72-81 (5.0-5.6)	49-55 (3.4-3.8)①	36-41 (2.5-2.8)	43 (3.0)
Peugeot 505	64-75 (4.5-5.2)	49-55 (3.4-3.8)	38-39 (2.6-2.7)	43-59 (3.0-4.1)
Porsche 911SC	64-75 (4.5-5.2)	38-44 (2.7-3.1)	②	②
Porsche 924	64-75 (4.5-5.2)	49-55 (3.4-3.8)	21-24 (1.5-1.7)	36-52 (2.5-3.6)
Porsche 924 Turbo	78-87 (5.4-6.0)	49-55 (3.4-3.8)③	14 (1.0)	38-55 (2.7-3.8)
Saab	64-75 (4.5-5.2)	49-55 (3.4-3.8)	24-34 (1.7-2.4)	43-59 (3.0-4.1)
Volkswagen	64-75 (4.5-5.2)	49-55 (3.4-3.8)	23-37 (1.6-2.6)	46-54 (3.2-3.8)
Volvo 4 Cyl.	64-75 (4.5-5.2)	50-56 (3.5-3.9)	24-34 (1.7-2.4)	37-51 (2.6-3.6)
Volvo 6 Cyl.	64-75 (4.5-5.2)	45-49 (3.1-3.4)	24 (1.7)	37-51 (2.6-3.6)

① Vacuum connected.
② Not available.
③ No vacuum applied.

BOSCH LAMBDA CIS INJECTION SYSTEM — ALL MODELS (Cont.)

REST PRESSURE & LEAK TEST

1) After correct warm engine control pressure has been obtained, stop fuel pump and note pressure drop. Valve should be in open position. Minimum pressure after 20 minutes must be as specified in "Pressure Testing" chart.

2) If pressure drops too rapidly, run pump again and close valve. Stop pump and observe pressure. If values are now correct, control pressure regulator is faulty and must be replaced.

3) If pressure still drops, check all connections, fuel pump check valve, cold start valve, and fuel injectors.

COLD START VALVE, THERMO-TIME SWITCH & HOT START PULSE RELAY

1) If engine coolant is below 85°F (30°C), disconnect plug on cold start valve and connect test lamp across terminals. Remove coil high tension wire to prevent starting. Operate starter.

2) On models without hot start pulse relay, test lamp will light for several seconds, then go out. On models with relay, lamp will continue to flash off and on.

3) If lamp does not light, test thermo-time switch for continuity below opening temperature. If good, check wiring to starter terminal.

4) Remove cold start valve from manifold but leave fuel line connected. Place valve in a container. Connect a jumper wire from one terminal to ground, and from other terminal of cold start valve to a switch. The other side of switch should be connected to battery voltage.

CAUTION — *Do not connect wire directly to battery. Extreme fire danger is present due to atomized fuel. Sparks may result if wire is touched to battery.*

5) Operate fuel pump. Turn switch to "ON" position. Cold start injector should spray. Turn switch "OFF", but leave fuel

pump running. Injector should not spray. Wipe off nozzle and check for leakage. With pump running, no drops should form within one minute.

6) Replace cold start valve if faulty. Reinstall original valve if good, making sure that "O" ring is properly positioned.

FUEL INJECTORS

1) Remove injectors but leave hoses connected. Place injectors in individual measuring containers. Operate fuel pump to build up pressure, then turn pump off.

2) Lift air flow sensor plate half-way to operate injectors until one container has filled to 3.4 oz. (100 cc). Other container volume should not vary more than 10-20°.

3) If one injector is outside specifications, swap hoses from it and one good injector at fuel distributor and retest. If same container is low, injector is faulty. If other container is low, fuel distributor must be replaced.

4) Relieve system pressure and remove pressure testing gauge. Turn on pump to build up pressure. Injectors may leak slightly, but no drops should form in less than 15 seconds. If drops form, check air flow sensor plate height, sticking fuel distributor plunger, or injector opening pressure.

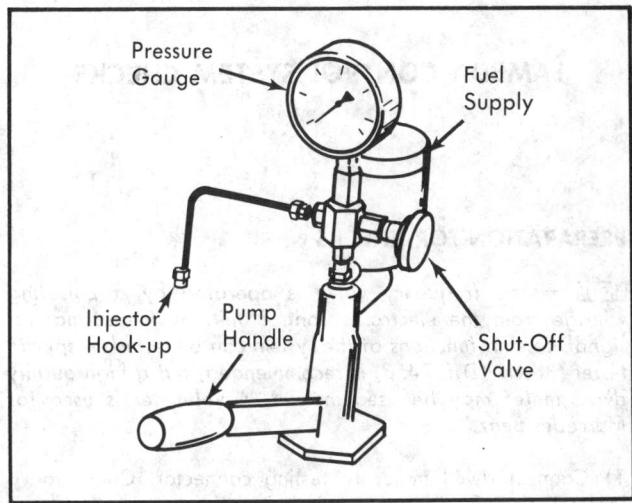

Fig. 12   Fuel Injector Tester

5) Remove injectors from vehicle and use injector tester to determine opening pressure. Check specifications in "Pressure Testing" chart and replace injectors if faulty.

AUXILIARY AIR VALVE

1) Disconnect hoses from auxiliary air valve. Shine a light through valve. At room temperature, valve should be slightly open. Turn ignition "ON" (disconnect wires from air flow sensor, if equipped) and see that opening is closed in less than 5 minutes. Tap valve slightly to assist in closing.

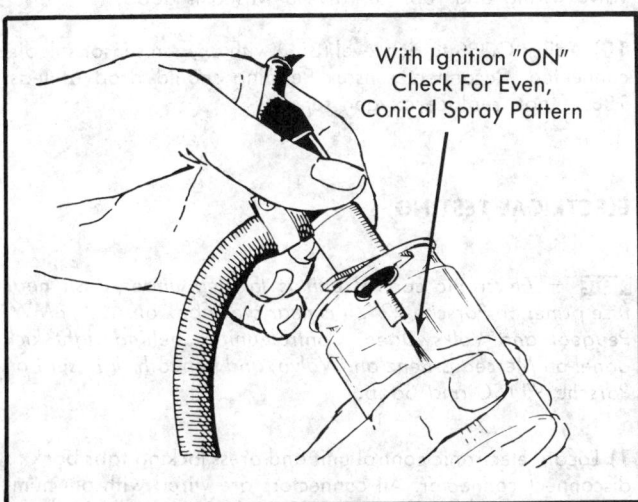

Fig. 11   Testing Cold Start Injector Valve

BOSCH LAMBDA CIS INJECTION SYSTEM — ALL MODELS (Cont.)

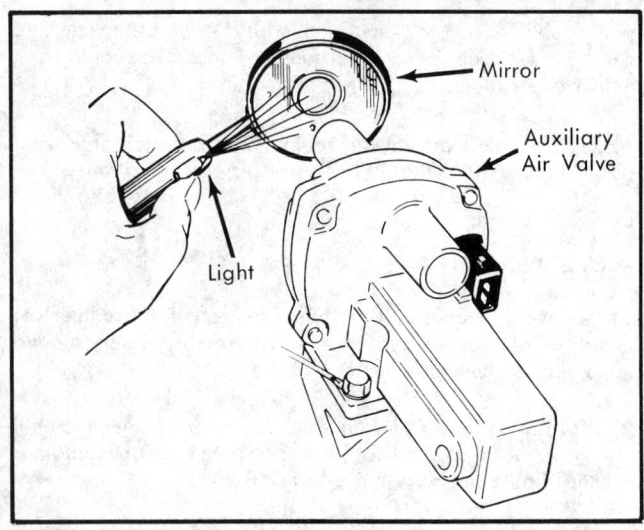

Fig. 13 Checking Auxiliary Air Valve Operation

2) If valve does not operate properly, check for power at connector with engine running. Connect a test lamp across connector terminals. If lamp does not light, check fuse and wiring. If lamp lights, check resistance of auxiliary air valve. If no resistance is measured, valve is bad. If resistance is measured, clean terminals and make sure connection is good.

LAMBDA CONTROL SYSTEM CHECKS

PREPARATION FOR CHECKS

NOTE — *The frequency valve is operated by a pulsating voltage from the electronic control unit. By measuring this signal, certain functions of the system can be tested. A special tester (Bosch KDJE 7453) is recommended, but a high quality dwell meter may be used instead. A voltmeter is used for Mercedes-Benz.*

1) Connect dwell meter to testing connector. Connector is located on left side near windshield washer container on Peugeot, beside brake booster on Volvo, and to left of fuse and relay panel on Saab. Connector is behind throttle valve housing on Volkswagen and Audi. Set meter on 4-cyl. scale.

2) On Mercedes-Benz, remove cap from diagnostic plug connector (rear of left fender panel). Connect positive lead of voltmeter to battery and negative lead to pin 3 of diagnostic plug. Start engine and run until warm. Disconnect oxygen sensor and observe needle (should not fluctuate). Place a piece of tape on meter face to indicate 50% position.

OPERATION CHECK

1) Remove fuel pump relay and connect jumper wire across sockets corresponding to terminals 30 and 87. If equipped, remove plug at air flow sensor. Turn ignition "ON".

2) Frequency valve should operate, making a buzzing noise. Dwell meter should indicate 45-65°. Disconnect wire from oxygen sensor and touch wire end to ground. Readings on dwell meter should rise. Ground one end of a 1.5 volt flashlight battery, and touch positive end to sensor wire. Readings should drop to less than 15°.

3) On models with throttle enrichment switch, operate throttle. Readings should be higher at idle or wide open throttle. See *wiring diagram for enrichment switches used.*

4) If engine is cold, enrichment switches will be closed. Disconnect lead at temperature sender. Readings should drop slightly. If engine is hot, connect temperature sender lead to ground. Reading should rise. See *wiring diagram for enrichment switches used.*

5) If starter enrichment relay is used, disconnect high tension lead at coil and crank engine. Readings should rise above normal level. If vacuum switches are used, apply vacuum to switch and note readings. Level should be higher with switch closed, and lower with switch open.

6) Connect oxygen sensor and start engine. With cold engine, dwell reading should be stable. When engine warms up, meter needle should fluctuate 10-20°. It may be necessary to run engine faster than idle to heat oxygen sensor and cause needle fluctuation.

7) Connect a CO meter to exhaust test point. With oxygen sensor disconnected, reading should be stable on dwell meter. Note CO%. With sensor lead grounded, reading should rise and CO% increase. With lead connected to flashlight battery, reading and CO% should decrease.

8) If dwell reading does not rise with sensor grounded, check sensor wiring (see "Electrical Testing"). If wiring is good, replace control unit. If dwell rises, but CO% does not, check frequency valve and wiring (see "Electrical Testing"). Replace if necessary.

9) If dwell does not decrease with battery connected to sensor lead, check sensor wiring and replace control unit if wires are good. If dwell decreases but CO% does not, check frequency valve wiring and replace valve if wiring is good.

10) Adjust CO% to rich level (3%) with oxygen sensor still disconnected. Reconnect sensor. Reading should drop at least 1%. If not, replace oxygen sensor.

ELECTRICAL TESTING

NOTE — *Electronic control unit is located under dash near fuse panel on Porsche 924. It is near glove box on Audi, BMW, Peugeot and Volkswagen. Control unit is behind right kick panel on Mercedes-Benz and Volvo, and beneath right seat on Porsche 911SC and Saab.*

1) Locate electronic control unit and press locking tabs back to disconnect connector. All connectors are wired with pin numbers in the same location. Obtain a high-quality volt-ohmmeter for testing.

BOSCH LAMBDA CIS INJECTION SYSTEM — ALL MODELS (Cont.)

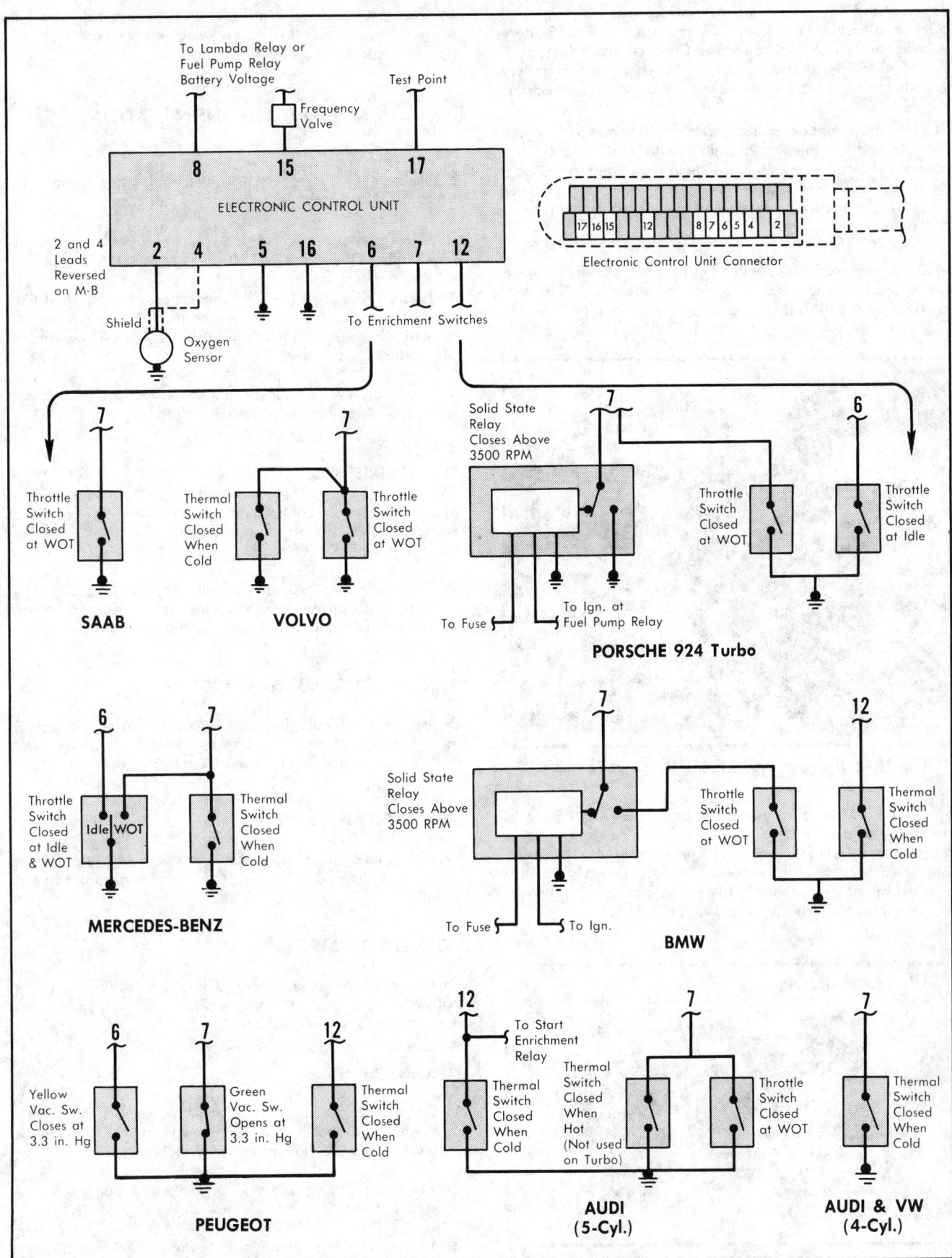

Fig. 14 Bosch CIS Lambda Electronic Control Unit Wiring Diagram

BOSCH LAMBDA CIS INJECTION SYSTEM — ALL MODELS (Cont.)

2) Refer to wiring diagram for pin locations. With ignition "ON" and fuel pump jumper wire in place, check for battery voltage at terminals 8 and 15. Connect ground lead of voltmeter to terminals 5 and 16 while checking for battery voltage to ensure these wires make a good ground connection.

3) If battery voltage is not available at terminal 8, check Lambda and fuel pump relays. If no voltage at 15, check frequency valve connector. One wire should have battery voltage; the other wire should have continuity to terminal 15. Frequency valve should have 2-3 ohms resistance. Repair or replace as necessary.

4) Disconnect oxygen sensor and check for continuity between sensor lead and terminal 2 (4 on Mercedes-Benz). No continuity should exist between ground and lead wire.

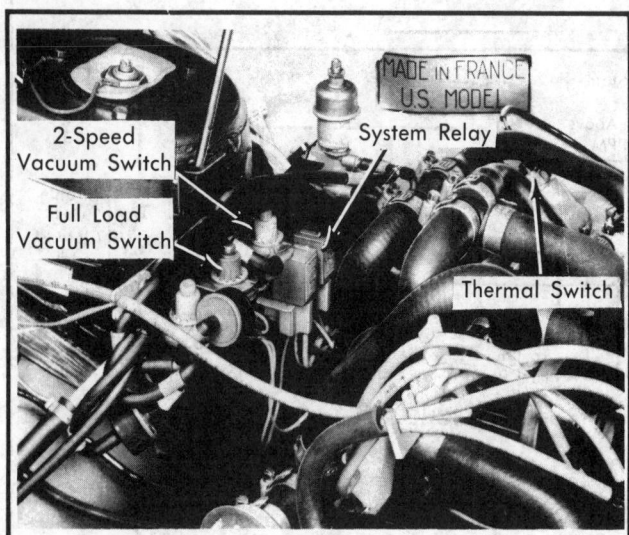

Fig. 15 Peugeot Enrichment Vacuum Switches

5) All models use enrichment switches. All switches provide continuity to ground when switch is closed. Actuate throttle to test throttle switches. Apply vacuum to switches to test vacuum enrichment switches on Peugeot. Thermal switches can be checked by removing switch and heating in water. Repair wiring or replace switches as necessary.

Fig. 16 Throttle Enrichment Switches (Porsche 924 Turbo Shown)

6) After testing is completed, reconnect electronic control unit, oxygen sensor, and all switches. Remove fuel pump relay jumper wire and testing equipment.

REMOVAL & INSTALLATION

CAUTION — *On all models, disconnect battery and relieve fuel pressure before removing component parts.*

MIXTURE CONTROL UNIT

1) Clean around all fuel line connections. Remove fuel lines and wipe up any spilled fuel. Disconnect electrical wiring and remove rubber boot to manifold. Remove Allen screws and lift off mixture control unit.

2) To install, reverse removal procedure. Replace gaskets and seals and check for leaks after installation.

FUEL DISTRIBUTOR

1) Remove mixture control unit. Remove 3 screws from top of fuel distributor. Lift off carefully, ensuring that plunger does not fall out of distributor.

2) Only pressure regulator shims may be exchanged. If plunger or piston is scored, replace fuel distributor. Be sure "O" ring is in place and in good condition when replacing unit.

CONTROL PRESSURE REGULATOR

Disconnect electrical plug and vacuum lines (if equipped). Remove fuel lines and wipe up any spilled fuel. Remove bolts and regulator. To install, reverse removal procedure.

AUXILIARY AIR VALVE

Remove and plug hoses. Disconnect electrical plug. Remove mounting bolts and air valve. Reverse removal procedure to install.

COLD START VALVE

Remove electrical connector and fuel line. Loosen mounting bolts and remove cold start valve. Check "O" ring and replace if necessary when reinstalling valve.

FUEL INJECTORS

1) Clean area around valves. On BMW, remove intake cowl and pipes at number 2 and 3 cylinders. Hold valve and remove fuel line fitting. Do not allow valve to turn.

2) Remove retaining plate if present, and pull valves out carefully. Do not remove insulator sleeve if possible.

3) To install, reverse removal procedure. Replace "O" rings and lubricate with a drop of oil. Place injectors in sleeve and press until seated. Tighten fuel lines and check for leaks.

BOSCH LAMBDA CIS INJECTION SYSTEM — ALL MODELS (Cont.)

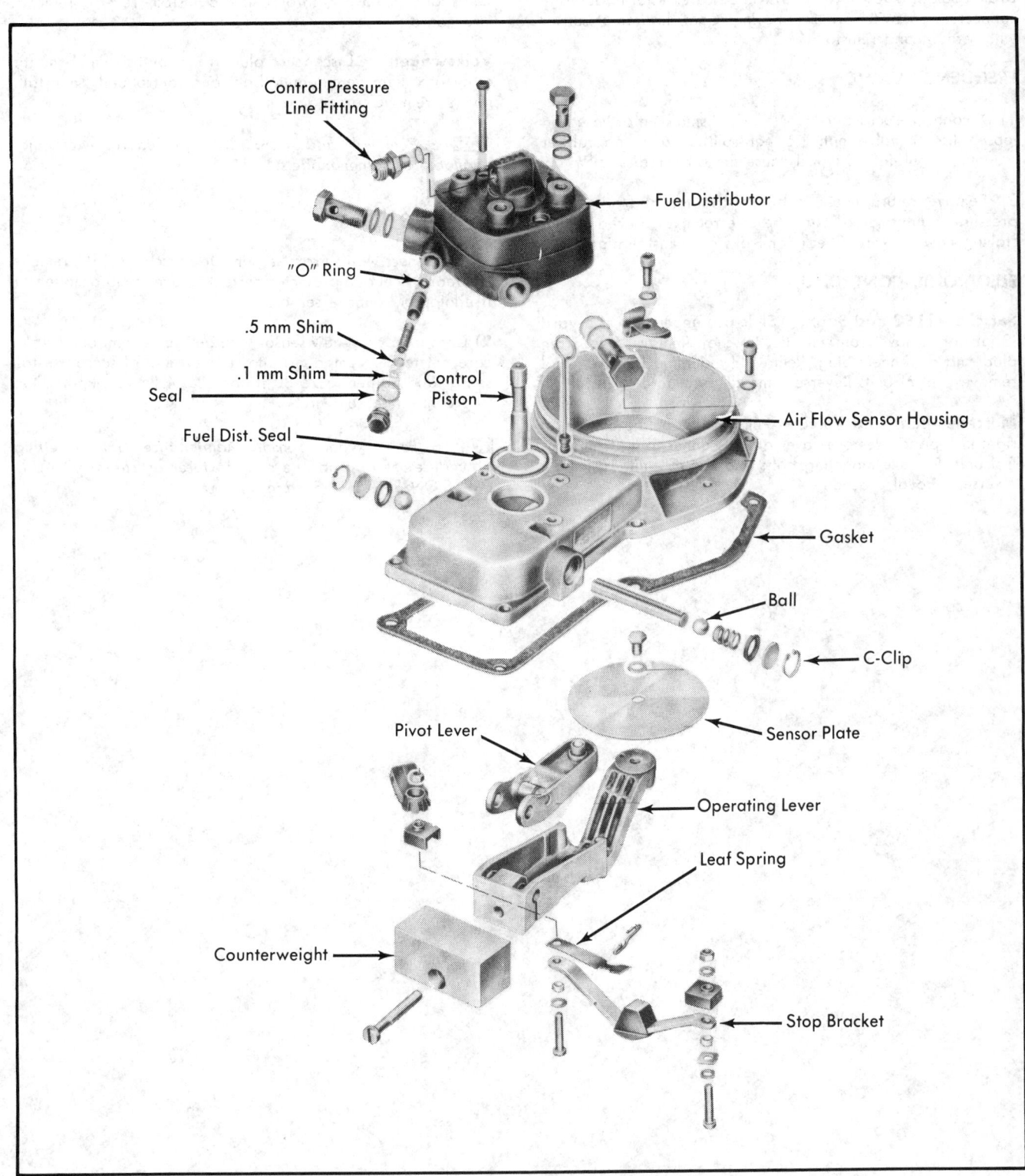

Fig. 17 *Exploded View of Mixture Control Unit for Porsche 924 Model*

BOSCH LAMBDA CIS INJECTION SYSTEM — ALL MODELS (Cont.)

THERMAL SWITCH

Drain coolant below level of switch. Be careful not to damage connectors on switch while removing. Coat threads of sensor with sealant and reinstall.

FREQUENCY VALVE

1) Disconnect electrical connector. Hold small nut at hose and loosen larger valve nut. Do not spill gasoline on rubber mounting insulator as it will cause the rubber to swell.

2) Remove return lines at fuel distributor and/or control pressure regulator. To install, reverse removal procedure, installing new gaskets. Check for leaks after installation.

ELECTRONIC CONTROL UNIT

Porsche 911SC and Saab — Slide passenger seat rearward (Saab) or remove from vehicle (Porsche). Remove cover from plug and disconnect plug. Remove 3 mounting fasteners and remove control unit. Reverse removal procedure to install.

Mercedes-Benz and Volvo — Pull back carpeting or trim on right kick panel. Remove cover and disconnect plug from control unit. Remove mounting bolts and control unit. To install, reverse removal procedure.

Peugeot — Remove glove box, support, and heater hose. Disconnect plug from control unit. Remove 2 nuts from mounting studs and remove control unit. To install, reverse removal procedure.

Volkswagen — Disconnect plug from control unit beneath glove box. Remove mounting bolts and control unit. To install, reverse removal procedure.

NOTE — *Removal and installation procedures were not available for other models.*

OXYGEN SENSOR

1) Disconnect wiring from sensor. On Porsche 911SC, remove left rear wheel and protector plate. Remove shield from sensor if equipped. Remove sensor.

2) Coat threads of new sensor with anti-seize compound. Take care not to get compound into slots on end of sensor. Install sensor and tighten to 25-30 ft. lbs. (3.5-4.1 mkg). Refit shield and connect sensor wire.

NOTE — *For Oxygen Sensor Maintenance Light resetting procedure see appropriate manufacturer article in EXHAUST EMISSION SYSTEMS Section.*

BOSCH DIESEL FUEL INJECTION – AUDI & VOLKSWAGEN

Audi
5000
Volkswagen
Dasher
Rabbit
Pickup

DESCRIPTION

Diesel fuel injection systems consist of the fuel tank, fuel filter, distributor-type injection pump, glow plugs, throttle pintle injection nozzles and a centrifugal governor. See *Fig. 1.*

A vane-type fuel pump, built into the injection pump, supplies fuel from tank to fuel filter to injection pump. See *Fig. 2.* Injection pump supplies fuel to nozzles under high pressure, according to the firing sequence (1-3-4-2 on Volkswagen and 1-2-4-5-3 on Audi). Excess fuel is returned to fuel tank by return lines.

SYSTEM COMPONENTS

FUEL INJECTION PUMP

The Bosch single plunger mechanical pump consists of a low-pressure, vane-type fuel pump, a high-pressure distributor plunger injection pump, a centrifugal governor, an injection timing mechanism, and an electrical fuel shut-off solenoid. See *Fig. 1.*

As the vane pump rotor turns, centrifugal force holds the vanes against the walls of the pump's pressure chamber. The off-center design of the rotor and pressure chamber squeezes trapped fuel between vanes and forces it out the delivery port. Vane pressure is 42.7-99.6 psi (3-7 kg/cm^2).

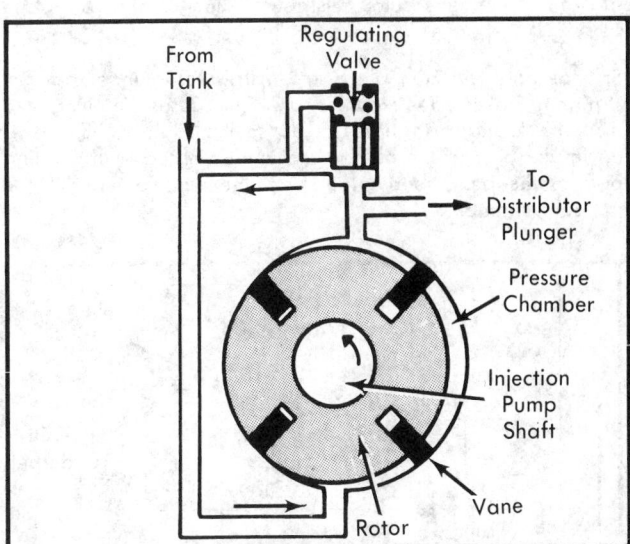

Fig. 2   Vane-Type Fuel Pump Components

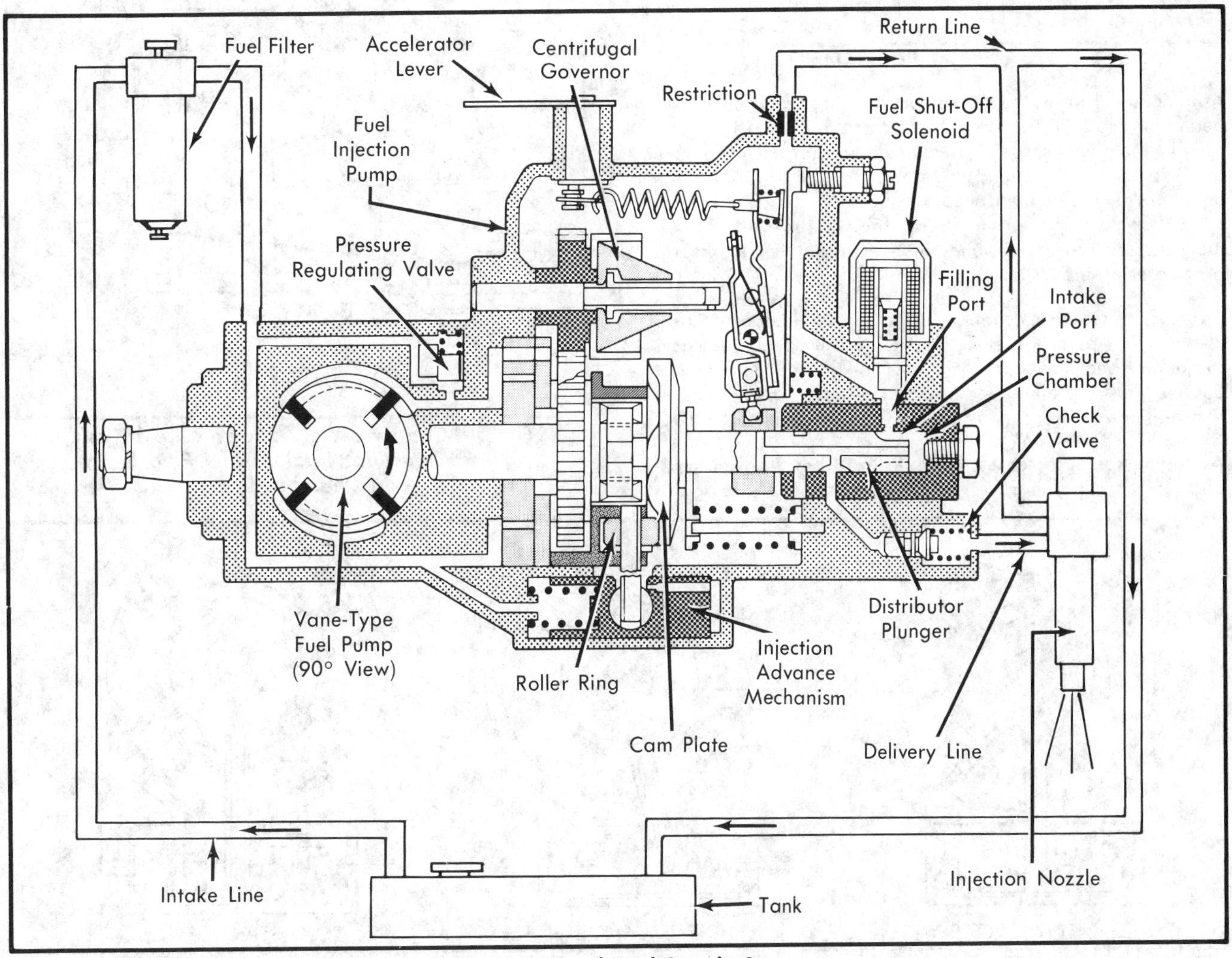

Fig. 1   Diesel Fuel Supply System

BOSCH DIESEL FUEL INJECTION – AUDI & VOLKSWAGEN (Cont.)

The vane pump is driven by the camshaft at one-half engine speed. See Fig. 2. It lubricates all moving parts of the injection pump with diesel fuel, supplies fuel to the distributor plunger for pressurization and use by injection nozzles, and controls injection timing advance mechanism. The injection pump drive shaft turns the vane pump, distributor plunger and cam plate as a unit.

Springs hold the cam plate and distributor plunger against stationary rollers. See Figs. 1 and 3. This causes the plunger to move back and forth in its cylinder as it also turns. Whenever an intake port in the plunger becomes aligned with a filling port in the pump body, fuel from the vane pump fills the pressure chamber.

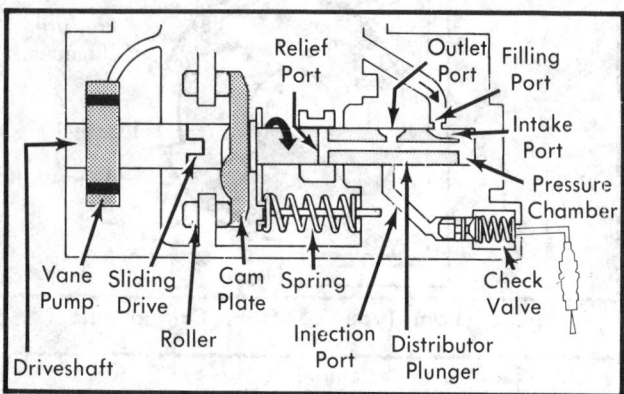

Fig. 3   Operation of Distributor Plunger

As the plunger turns, the intake port is covered and fuel is trapped in the pressure chamber. As the cam plate and rollers push against the plunger, fuel is pressurized to approximately 1800 psi (126 kg/cm²). As the plunger continues to turn, the single outlet port in the plunger becomes aligned with one of the 4 or 5 injection ports in the pump body. This pressurized fuel opens the check valve and supplies high pressure fuel to the appropriate injection nozzle.

An injection timing mechanism is located on the lower side of the injection pump. See Fig. 4. As engine speed increases, stroke time becomes shorter and injection time becomes longer. Burning must therefore begin sooner to ensure peak combustion pressures still occur at the most efficient point after TDC.

As engine speed increases, fuel pressure from the vane pump also increases, pushing the hydraulic piston to the side against

its spring. This causes the roller housing to turn slightly as the peg is moved. Since the cam plate is turning in the opposite direction, the ramps on the cam plate engage the roller sooner.

For cold start and warm-up periods, a lever and cam act against the hydraulic piston, advancing injection timing approximately 5°. See Fig. 4. This provides more time for fuel to burn, improving performance and preventing black exhaust smoke during cold start and warm-up periods.

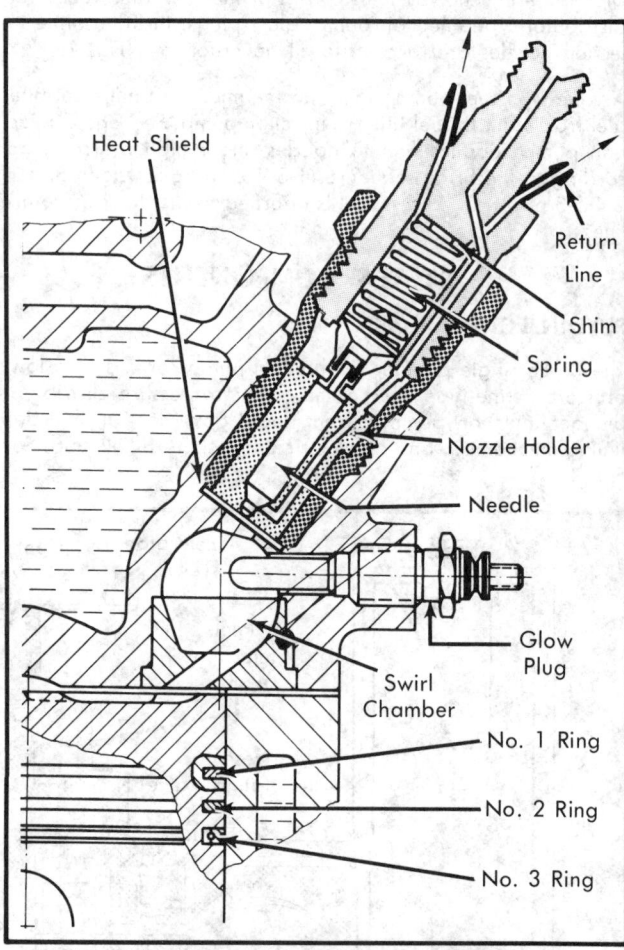

Fig. 5   Cutaway View Showing Relationship of Injection Nozzle, Glow Plug & Swirl Chamber to Piston

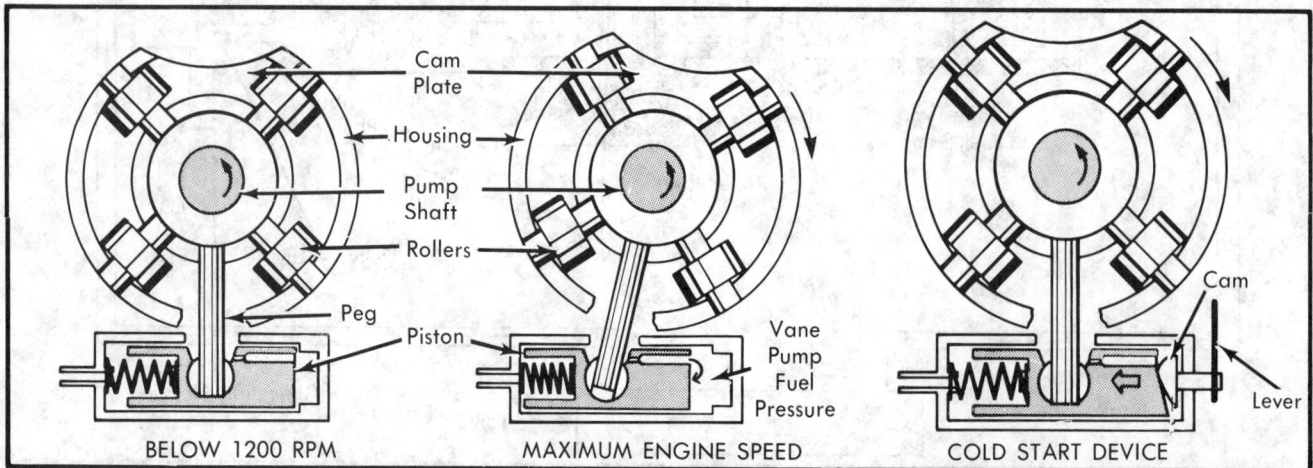

Fig. 4   Injection Timing Mechanism & Cold Start Device

BOSCH DIESEL FUEL INJECTION – AUDI & VOLKSWAGEN (Cont.)

INJECTION NOZZLES

Bosch DNOSD 193 injection nozzles, mounted in KDA SD 27/4 sockets, inject fuel at 1706-1850 psi (120-130 kg/cm²). *See Fig. 5.*

A pressurized mist of fuel is injected into a round swirl chamber. Fuel swirls around the chamber, mixing with hot air, compressed at a 23:1 ratio. Heat shields protect each injector.

Combustion begins in rich swirl chamber, continues on through a small passageway and into a leaner main chamber. As peak cylinder pressures build in swirl chamber, rather than main chamber, loads on connecting rods and crankshaft are reduced.

GLOW PLUGS

During cold starts, glow plugs are used to preheat swirl chambers. *See Fig. 5.* When current is applied, glow plugs become red hot. A temperature sensor connected to a time circuit in a relay controls pre-heating time.

To start a cold engine, pull out cold start knob to left of steering column (Volkswagen only). Turn ignition switch to glow plug position (No. 2). When light goes out, crank the engine. At below freezing temperatures, depress accelerator pedal while cranking. About 2 minutes after engine starts, push cold start knob in fully. When starting a warm engine, do not use glow plugs.

NOTE — *Cold starting device of Audi 5000 is automatically controlled by engine coolant passing over a thermostat. When engine is cold, thermostat pulls on advance lever advancing injection timing.*

FUEL FILTER

The fuel filter allows unrestricted flow of fuel from the tank to the injection pump, but stops any dirt or water. A replaceable element, similar to an oil filter cartridge, threads onto a removable flange. *See Fig. 6.*

To drain water from filter, open vent screw on top of filter flange. If there is no vent screw, remove fuel return line at injection pump. Remove flange mounting nuts and lift filter. Open water drain on bottom of filter. Drain until clean fuel runs out. Close water drain and vent screw (or reattach return line).

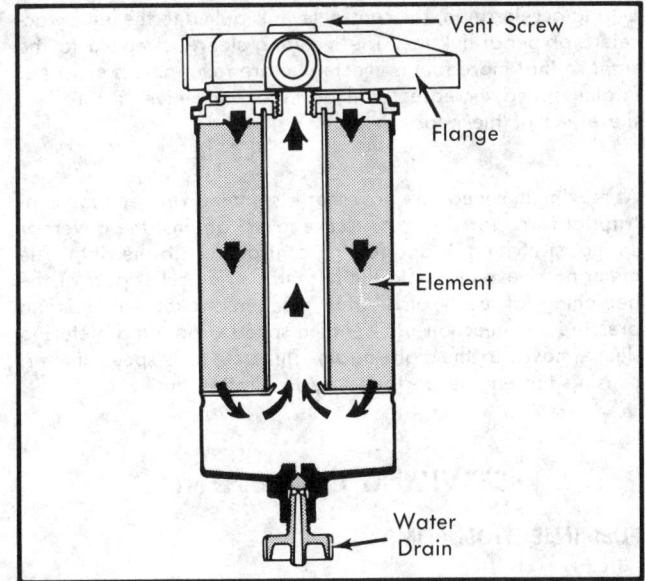

Fig. 6 Components of Fuel Filter

CENTRIFUGAL GOVERNOR

The amount of fuel injected is controlled by changing the injection cut-off point according to engine speed and load conditions. The cut-off point is controlled by the position of the metering sleeve around the distributor plunger. The sleeve normally covers a relief port in the plunger. Uncovering the port, stops injection.

The position of the metering sleeve is controlled by linkage connected to the centrifugal governor and accelerator pedal. *See Fig. 7.* When engine is starting, leaf spring presses starting lever to left, so metering sleeve moves right. Injection lasts longer, as the plunger must move further before uncovering the relief port. More fuel is supplied during starting.

At idle speed, governor weights are partly expanded. The governor sleeve moves to the right, starting lever is pushed against control lever, and metering sleeve moves to the left. The distributor plunger moves only a short distance before relief port is uncovered, stopping injection. A small amount of fuel is supplied at idle.

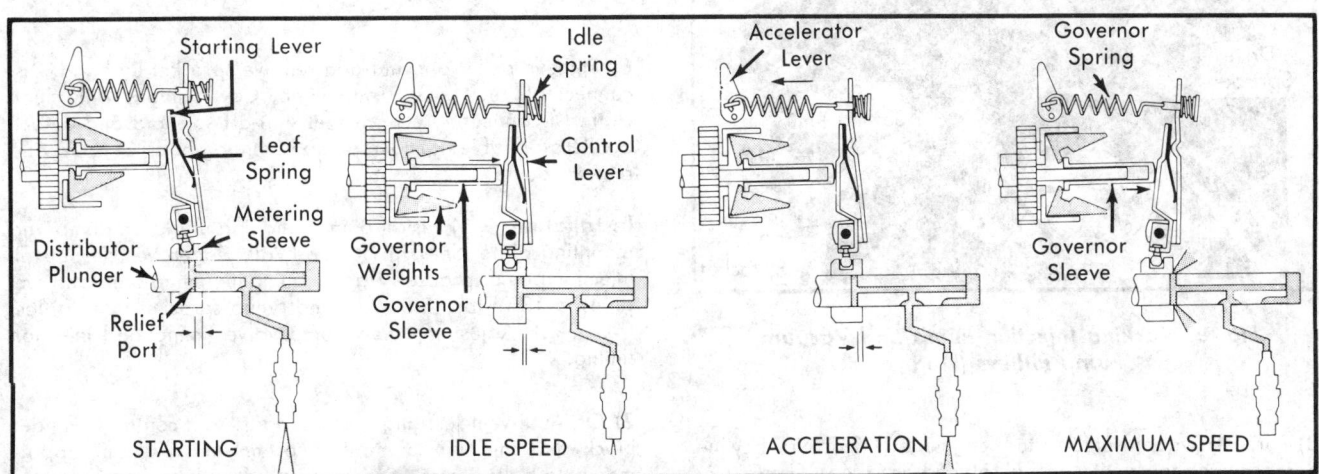

Fig. 7 Operation of Injection Pump Centrifugal Governor

BOSCH DIESEL FUEL INJECTION – AUDI & VOLKSWAGEN (Cont.)

During acceleration, the control lever is pulled to the left by accelerator pedal linkage. The metering sleeve is moved to the right so that more fuel is injected before relief port is exposed. Engine speed increases until governor movement neutralizes the effect of the pedal linkage.

At maximum speed, the governor is spinning with enough centrifugal force for governor sleeve to act against the governor spring, stretching it, and forcing control lever to the right. The metering sleeve moves to the left uncovering relief port at the beginning of each distributor plunger stroke. There is no pressure for injection until engine speed drops and metering sleeve moves to the right again. This acts as a speed limiter, causing the engine performance to "flatten out".

SERVICING COMPONENTS

FUEL INJECTION PUMP

NOTE – *When working on an injection system, keep all components clean. Clean injection line unions before loosening.*

Removal – 1) If injection pump is faulty, it must be replaced. Special test equipment and service tools are necessary for making repairs. For Audi vehicles, continue to step **2).** For Volkswagen vehicles, proceed to step **3).**

2) For Audi vehicles, remove vacuum pump pulley and drive belt and injection pump drive belt cover. Set crankshaft at TDC for No. 1 cylinder and align marks on flywheel and clutch housing and injection pump sprocket and mounting plate. Install special tool (2064) to lock injection pump sprocket securely. Lock vacuum pump belt pulley and injection pump drive sprocket with special tool (3036). *See Fig. 8.* Loosen and remove retaining bolt and remove drive sprocket and drive belt. Proceed to step **4).**

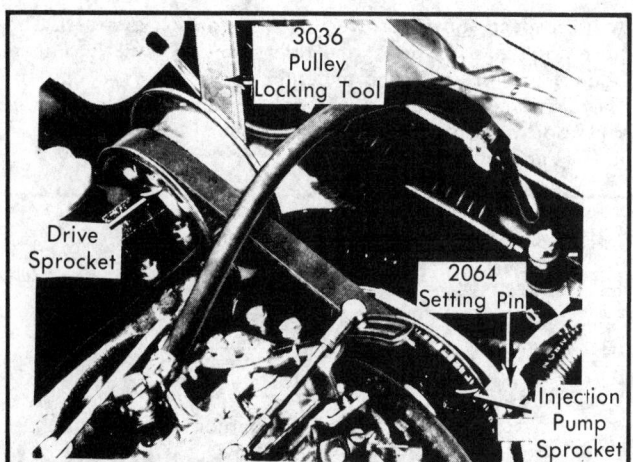

Fig. 8   Locking Injection Pump and Vacuum Pump Pulleys (Audi)

3) For Volkswagen vehicles, turn engine to TDC on No. 1 cylinder. Lock camshaft with special setting bar (2065). *See Fig. 9.* Remove drive belt. Proceed to step **4).**

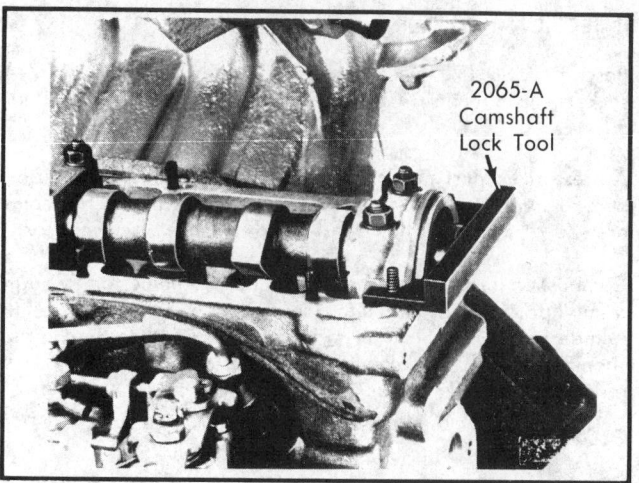

Fig. 9   Camshaft Locking Tool Installation (Volkswagen Shown)

4) Loosen injection pump sprocket retaining nut approximately one turn. On Audi vehicles, remove special tool (2064) from sprocket.

5) Attach puller (VW203b for Volkswagen; 3032 for Audi) to injection pump sprocket and apply light tension to puller. *See Fig. 10.* Tap lightly on puller spindle head until sprocket loosens from pump shaft.

Fig. 10   Fuel Injection Pump Gear Removal (Audi Shown)

6) Remove puller and nut and remove sprocket by hand. Disconnect all fuel pipes from pump. Cover unions with clean cloth. Disconnect wire from fuel shut-off solenoid and detach accelerator cable. Remove pump mounting bolts. Support and remove pump.

Installation – 1) Install pump, aligning marks on pump and mounting plate. *See Fig. 11.* For Volkswagen vehicles, install injection pump sprocket. Tighten pump mounting bolts and fuel pipes to 18 ft. lbs. (2.5 mkg) and pump sprocket to 33 ft. lbs. (4.5 mkg). Adjust injection pump/valve timing and injection timing.

2) On Audi vehicles, align rear support so it contacts cylinder block and injection pump free of tension. Tighten support mounting bolts. Install injection pump sprocket and turn it until marks on sprocket and mounting plate are in line.

BOSCH DIESEL FUEL INJECTION – AUDI & VOLKSWAGEN (Cont.)

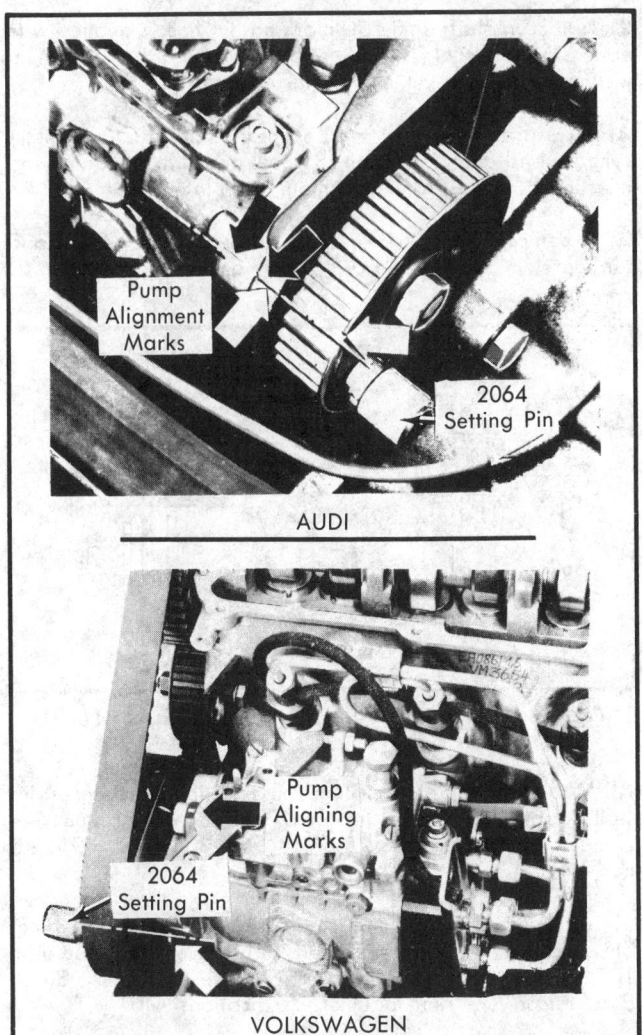

Fig. 11 *Aligning Reference Marks on Injection Pump*

3) Lock pump with special tool (2064) and tighten retaining nut to 33 ft. lbs. (4.5 mkg). Install drive belt and injection pump drive sprocket. Tighten drive sprocket retaining bolt so that sprocket can still be turned by hand. Check drive belt tension with VW 210 scale. Value should register 12-13 on scale.

4) If not, adjust drive belt tension by loosening bolts and moving mounting plate with pump. Check if TDC mark on flywheel is still aligned with reference mark. Tighten injection pump drive sprocket using special tool (3036), tightening bolt to 72 ft. lbs. (9.95 mkg). Remove special tool (2064). Check injection pump/valve timing and injection timing.

5) Reinstall fuel pipes, drive belt cover, and vacuum pump pulley and drive belt. Reattach accelerator cable and wire to fuel shut-off solenoid.

INJECTION NOZZLES

Injection nozzle problems usually are accompanied by knocking in one or more cylinders, engine overheating, loss of power or performance, black exhaust smoke and increased fuel consumption. To locate and correct faulty injectors, proceed as follows:

1) Loosen line unions on each injection nozzle, one at a time with engine running at fast idle. If engine speed remains constant with line removed, that nozzle is defective.

2) To remove nozzle, detach injector line. Use special tool (US 2775) to remove injection nozzles. To install, insert new heat shield with recess pointing upward. Tighten nozzles to 51 ft. lbs. (7.0 mkg) and lines to 18 ft. lbs. (2.5 mkg). Bleeding is not necessary.

FUEL FILTER

Service is limited to replacing filter at proper interval and draining water, when present. Bleeding is not required.

ADJUSTMENTS

ACCELERATOR CABLE

Place accelerator pedal in full throttle position. Adjust cable with nuts until pump lever contacts stop free of strain. *See Fig. 12.* Be sure ball pin on pump lever is pointing upward and touching end of elongated hole. Accelerator cable should be attached at upper hole in bracket. *See Fig. 13.*

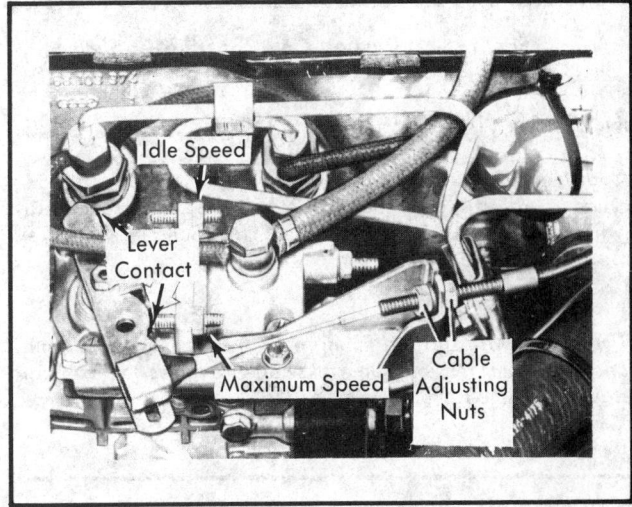

Fig. 12 *Adjusting Points for Accelerator Cable*

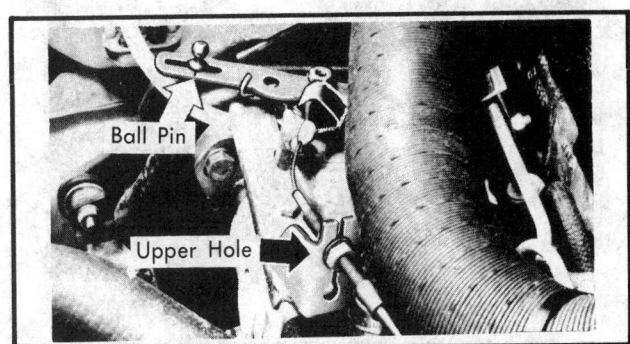

Fig. 13 *Accelerator Cable Attaching Points*

BOSCH DIESEL FUEL INJECTION — AUDI & VOLKSWAGEN (Cont.)

COLD STARTING CABLE

On Volkswagen vehicles, insert washer onto cable and install cable into bracket with rubber bushing. See *Fig. 14.* Insert cable into pin. Install lock washer and move lever as far as possible in direction of arrow. Pull cable tight and secure pin with clamping screw.

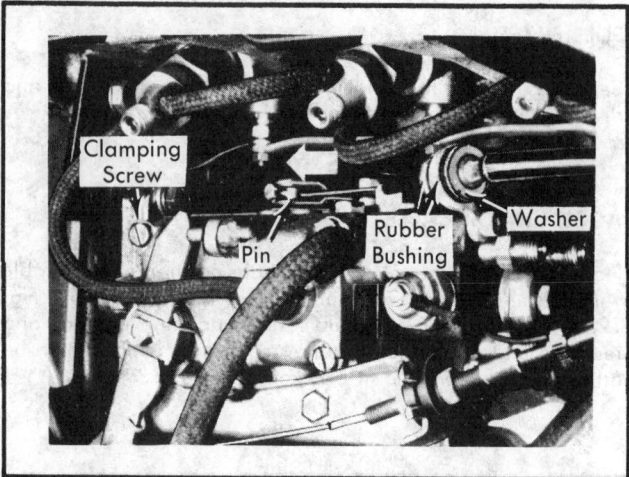

Fig. 14   Adjusting Cold Starting Cable

INJECTION PUMP TIMING

Audi (Engine Removed) — 1) Set engine to TDC on No. 1 cylinder. Adjust special tool (2068/A) to 125.5 reference mark (white arrow), left notch of vernier scale. See *Fig. 15.* Screw tool in as shown.

NOTE — *Before starting timing procedure, check valve timing and drive belt tension. On Volkswagen engines, be sure cold start knob is pushed fully inward.*

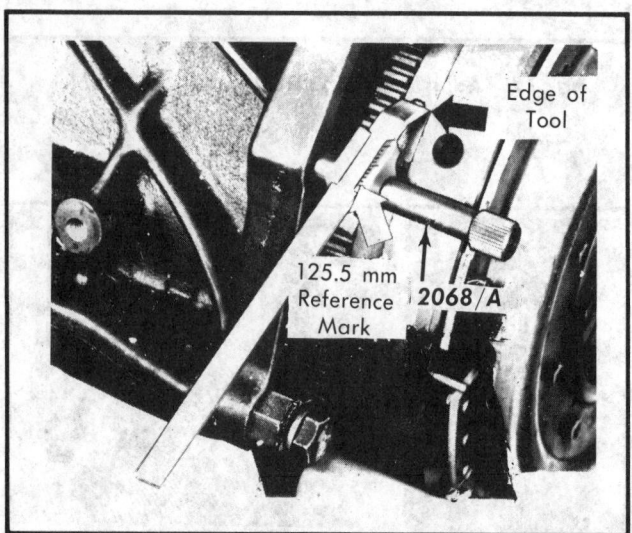

Fig. 15   Adjusting No. 1 Cylinder to TDC With Engine Removed (Audi Shown)

2) Turn crankshaft until TDC mark on flywheel is aligned with edge of special tool (2068/A) at black arrow and marks on injection pump sprocket align with mounting plate.

Audi (Engine Installed) — 1) Set crankshaft to TDC on No. 1 cylinder and align marks on flywheel and clutch housing and injection pump sprocket and mounting plate.

2) Loosen cold start device cable by loosening screw No. 1 and turning clamp 90°. See *Fig. 16.* Do not loosen screw No. 2.

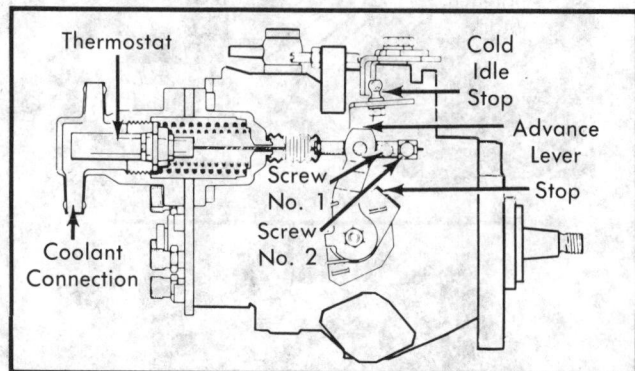

Fig. 16   Loosening Cold Start Device Screw No. 1

All Models — 1) Remove plug from injection pump cover. Install adaptor and dial indicator (2066) in place of plug. See *Fig. 17.* Preload indicator (0-0.118" or 0-3 mm) to .097" (2.5 mm).

2) Turn engine slowly counterclockwise until dial indicator needle stops moving. Zero indicator. Turn engine clockwise until TDC mark on flywheel is aligned with reference mark. Check dial indicator reading against specifications.

Fig. 17   Preloading Injection Pump With Dial Indicator (2066)

3) If necessary, loosen bolts on mounting plate and support. Set lift to specifications by turning pump and retightening bolts. Recheck dial indicator reading against specifications.

4) On Audi vehicles, turn clamp on cold start device back 90° to original setting and tighten screw No. 1.

BOSCH DIESEL FUEL INJECTION – AUDI & VOLKSWAGEN (Cont.)

Injection Pump Timing Specifications

Application	Dial Indicator Reading
Audi	.033" (.85 mm)
Volkswagen	
Rabbit①	.045" (1.15 mm)
All Others	.035" (.88 mm)

① — Only those models with yellow paint mark on pump advance cover.

MEASURING ENGINE SPEED

When measuring engine speed use the VW 1324 senser with Volkswagen vehicles or VW 1367 tester or Siemans 451 with Audi. Use Bosch Dwell-Tach (EFAW 166C) or the Sun Dwell-Tach (TDT-12) as an alternate.

IDLE SPEED

Audi – 1) Warm engine to normal operating temperature (oil temperature of 122-158°F or 50-70°C). Turn idle speed control knob on instrument panel counterclockwise to stop.

2) Connect VW 1367 tester or use Siemans 451 according to instructions. Adjust speed to 720-880 RPM by loosening lock nut, and turning adjusting screw in to raise idle speed and out to lower idle speed. Retighten lock nut. See Fig. 18.

Fig. 18 Adjusting Idle and Maximum Speeds (Audi Vehicles)

Volkswagen – 1) Warm engine to normal operating temperature (oil temperature of 122-158°F or 50-70°C). Adjust idle speed to 770-870 RPM.

2) To adjust, loosen lock nut and turn screw in to raise idle speed and out to lower it. See Fig. 19. Retighten lock nut with paint.

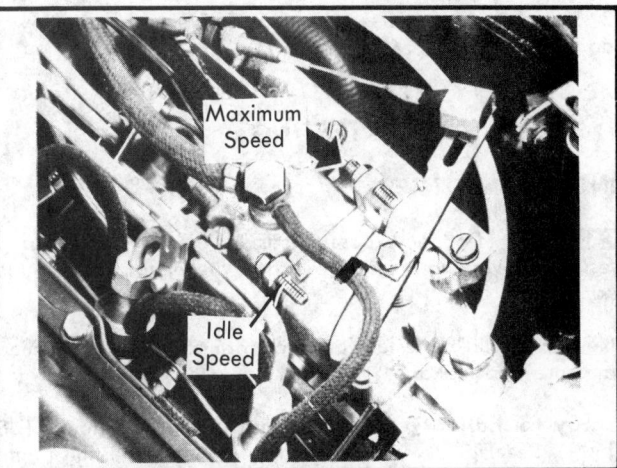

Fig. 19 Adjusting Idle and Maximum Speeds (Volkswagen Vehicles)

MAXIMUM SPEED

Adjust idle speed to proper setting and then open throttle fully. Maximum speed for Audi should be 5330-5450 RPM; for Volkswagen, 5500-5600 RPM. To adjust, loosen lock nut and turn screw out to raise maximum speed and in to lower it. See Figs 18 and 19. Tighten lock nut when adjustment is completed. Seal lock nut and screw with paint.

INJECTION NOZZLES

1) To disassemble nozzles, place upper part in vise and loosen lower part. To prevent parts from falling out, then reverse position with lower part in vise. Carefully disassemble, keeping all individual parts together. See Fig. 20. Do not interchange parts from one nozzle to another.

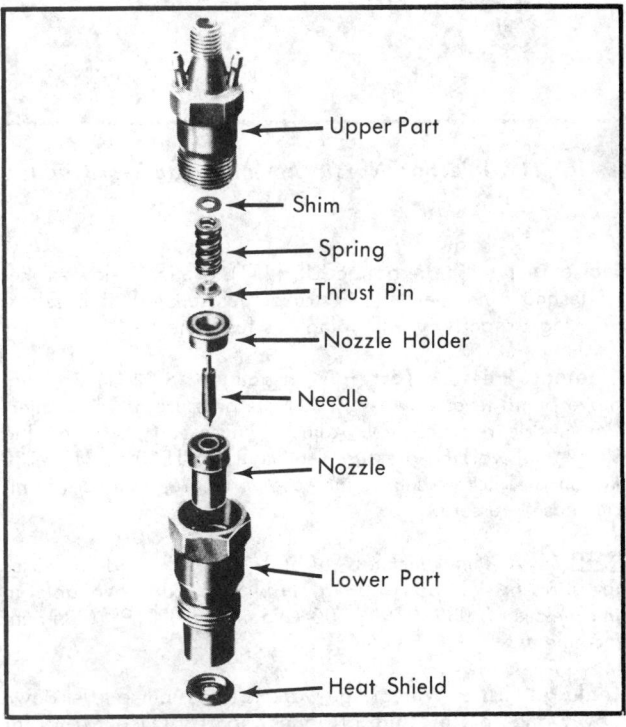

Fig. 20 Exploded View of Injection Nozzle

BOSCH DIESEL FUEL INJECTION — AUDI & VOLKSWAGEN (Cont.)

2) To reassemble, reverse procedure. Tighten upper and lower parts to 51 ft. lbs. (7.0 mkg).

TESTING

INJECTION NOZZLES

CAUTION — *Do not expose hands to injector spray during testing, as working pressure will cause fuel oil to penetrate the skin.*

Nozzles should be tested for spray formation, noise, opening pressure and leakage.

Spray Formation Test — Isolate special testing gauge (US 1111). See *Fig. 21*. Use short rapid strokes of testing pump lever (4-6 strokes per second). Spray should be even and stop cleanly. Nozzles should not drip.

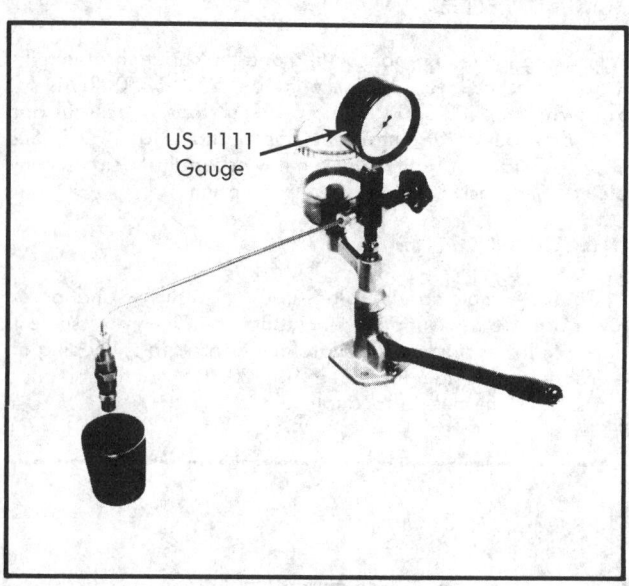

Fig. 21 Injection Nozzle Assembled to Test Gauge

Noise Test — Isolate gauge (US 1111). Use long, slow strokes of testing pump lever (1-2 strokes per second). If nozzle is working properly, it will "ping" as fuel emerges.

Opening Pressure Test — With gauge (US 1111) working, move pump lever down slowly. Note pressure at which injection nozzle releases fuel. Adjust, if necessary, by changing shims until working pressure reaches 1706-1850 psi (120-130 kg/cm²). Thicker shims increase pressure, thinner shims decrease pressure.

NOTE — *A shim thickness of .0019" (0.05 mm) increases pressure by 71 psi (5.0 kg/cm²). Shims are available in thicknesses of .039-.070" (1.00-1.95 mm) in .0019" (0.05 mm) increments.*

Leakage Test — With gauge working, press pump lever down slowly and hold pressure at about 1564 psi (110 kg/cm²) for 15 seconds. No fuel should leak from nozzle tip.

GLOW PLUGS

1) To check glow plug condition, remove glow plug wire and bus bar connector. Connect test lamp between glow plugs (one at a time) and battery positive terminal. See *Fig. 22*. Test lamp will light if plugs are good. If not, replace glow plugs.

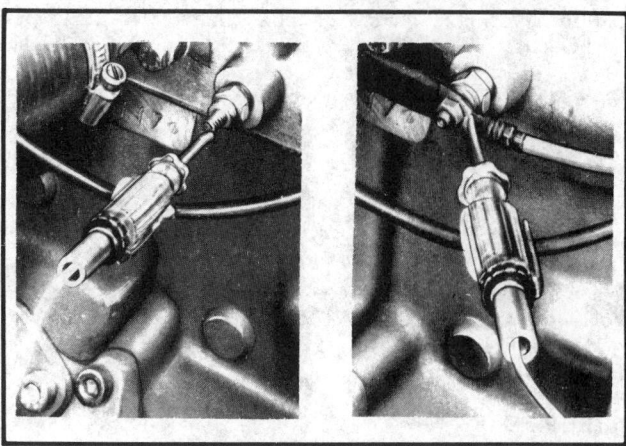

Fig. 22 Checking Glow Plug Condition (Left) and Current Supply to Glow Plugs (Right)

2) To check current supply to glow plug, reinstall wires and bus bar connector. Connect test lamp between glow plug to No. 4 cylinder and ground. See *Fig. 22*. Turn ignition switch to glow plug position and lamp should light. If not, check wiring or check for a defective glow plug fuse (80 amp.) located to the left of steering column behind instrument panel.

3) If fuse is OK, check terminal 30 of glow plug relay for voltage. If voltage is not present, check terminal connections or defective relay. If voltage is present at terminal 30, relay is not working.

4) Connect test lamp to terminal 86 and turn ignition key to glow plug position. If test lamp lights, repair connection from relay terminal 86 to ground or replace relay. If test lamp does not light, check connection between relay terminal 86 and board terminal 86 or replace board.

TIGHTENING SPECIFICATIONS

Application	Ft. Lbs. (mkg)
Injection Pump Mounting Bolts	18 (2.5)
Fuel Injection Line Unions	18 (2.5)
Fuel Injection Pump Gear Nut	33 (4.5)
Camshaft Gear Bolt	33 (4.5)
Injection Nozzle-to-Socket	51 (7.0)
Nozzle (Upper-to-Lower Part)	51 (7.0)
Injection Pump Drive Gear	72 (100)

BOSCH DIESEL INJECTION – MERCEDES-BENZ

**Mercedes-Benz
240 Series
300 Series**

DESCRIPTION

Fuel injection system consists of the following components. See *Fig. 1*:

- Pre-filter
- Main Fuel Filter
- Fuel Injection Pump with Fuel Pump
- Mechanical Centrifugal Governor
- Automatic Altitude Compensating Device
- Vacuum Control Unit
- Injection Nozzles
- Glow Plugs
- Key-starting System

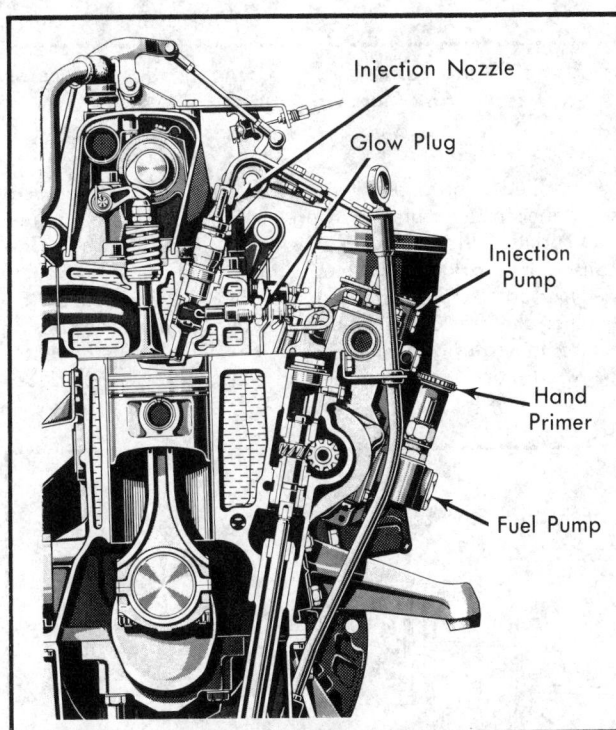

Fig. 1 Components of Typical Bosch Diesel Fuel Injection System for Mercedes-Benz

OPERATION

Fuel is pumped from fuel tank, through a pre-filter and main fuel filter into suction chamber of injection pump. Pump's camshaft operates injection pump plungers, which force fuel through delivery valves, reverse-flow dampening valves, and pressure lines to fuel injection nozzles.

When pressure stroke is completed, spring-loaded valves close pressure lines. Plungers return to original position.

TESTING

Manufacturer recommends that ALL tests be conducted on an injection pump test stand, using tests sheets furnished by manufacturer.

SYSTEM COMPONENTS

FUEL INJECTION PUMP

Injection pumps used on 240 and 300 series diesel engines are similar. *See Fig. 2*. The major difference is the number of pumping elements, five on the 300 series and four on the 240D — one for each cylinder.

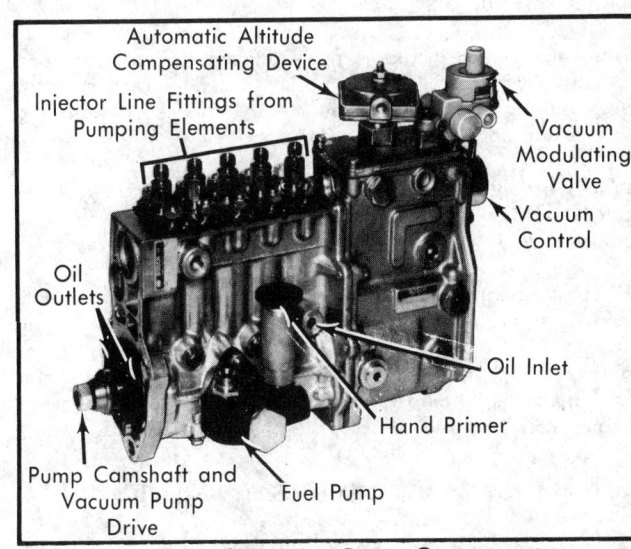

Fig. 2 Fuel Injection Pump Components

Built-in mechanical centrifugal governor has eliminated need for previously-used throttle valve in intake manifold. Engine shut-off is achieved by vacuum control unit. Pumps are lubricated by engine lubrication system. Note oil inlet and outlets. *See Fig. 2*.

An automatic altitude compensating device has been added to governor housing to meet exhaust emission standards at varying altitudes.

Fuel pump, attached to fuel injection pump, is driven by injection pump camshaft and features a hand primer pump.

Injection pumps feature new control levers, full load stop screws and idle adjusting screws. *See Fig. 3*. On the 240D engine, control pressure rod for automatic transmission is connected to end of control lever. *See arrow in Fig. 3*.

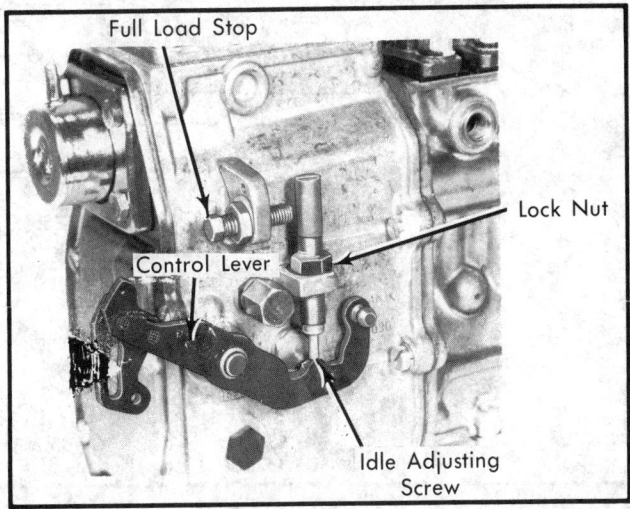

Fig. 3 Control Lever and Adjusting Screws

BOSCH DIESEL INJECTION – MERCEDES-BENZ (Cont.)

GOVERNOR

Governor is an idle-maximum RPM control. *See Fig. 4*. Springs are designed and adjusted so no regulating takes place in intermediate range except for compensation. Between idle and maximum RPM cutout, main rack is operated only by accelerator pedal. Pedal is connected, through linkage, with fulcrum lever of governor.

When engine RPM increases, flyweights move outward as soon as centrifugal force exceeds spring pressure. Movement of flyweights is transmitted through the angle lever, adjusting screws and control lever to main rack.

When reaching maximum RPM, main rack is moved toward the cutout position, reducing the amount of fuel and limiting engine RPM. As engine RPM decreases, the function is reversed.

Through governor action, engine RPM is held constant at idle speed, regardless of engine operating conditions — cold engine, air conditioner operation, power steering, or automatic transmission. At 5000-5100 RPM, governor limits RPM by pulling main rack back, until balance exists between engine RPM and fuel delivery.

AUTOMATIC ALTITUDE COMPENSATING DEVICE

Governor is equipped with an automatic altitude compensating device to control exhaust emissions at varying altitudes. On the 300SD (turbocharged engine) models, this aneroid is equipped with an inlet from the intake manifold to sense increased (boosted) manifold pressure. *See Figs. 5 and 6.*

With increasing altitude, atmospheric pressure is decreased. This causes two aneroid (non-fluid) compensators to expand.

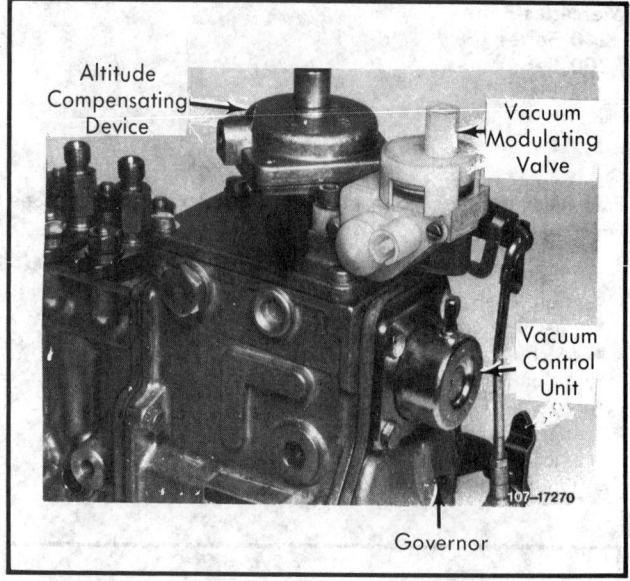

Fig. 5 Automatic Altitude Compensating Device and Vacuum Control Unit

At specified atmospheric pressure, internal force of compensators becomes greater than pretension of aneroid compression spring. Push rod moves downward, moving linkage. This causes main rack to move in direction "d", allowing less fuel to be injected. During increased manifold pressures on 300SD engines, the pressure in the aneroid cavity is increased causing the compensator and main rack to move in opposite direction, allowing more fuel to be injected while turbocharger boosts engine compression. *See Fig. 6.*

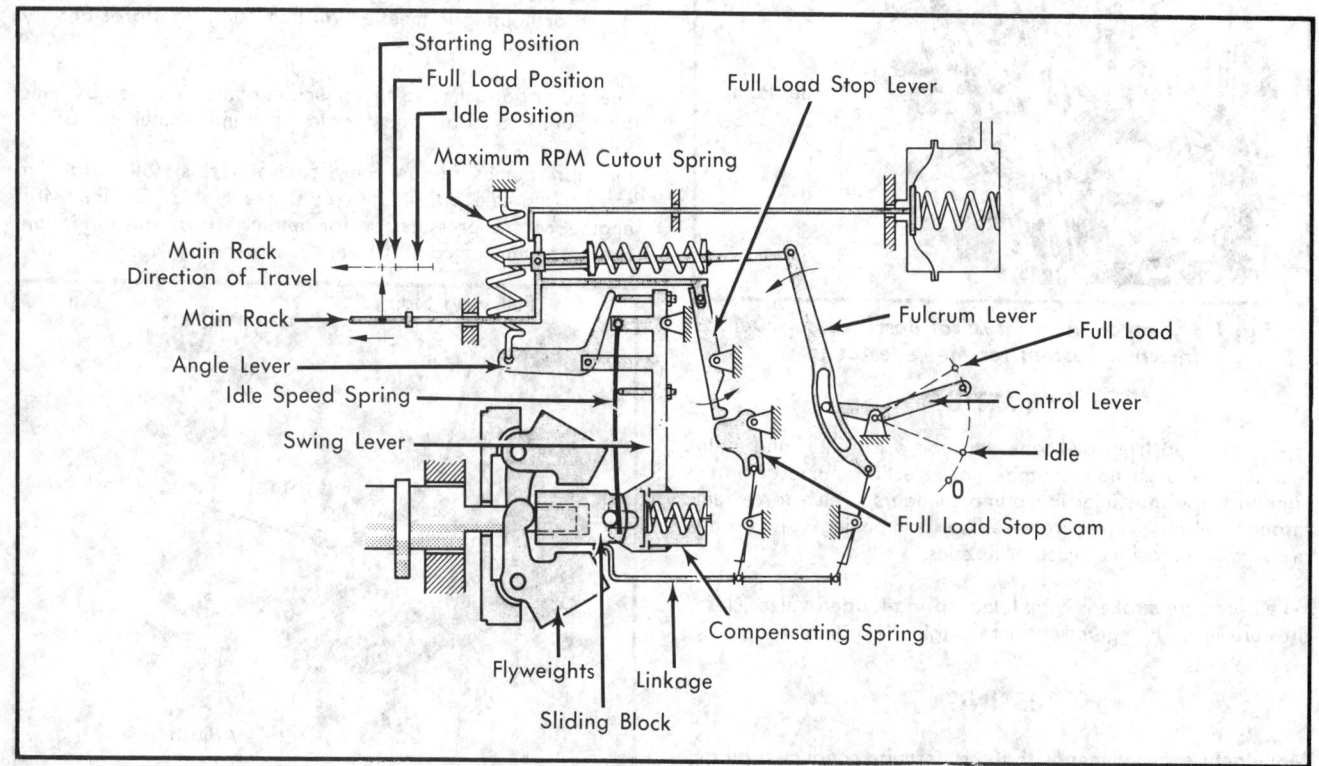

Fig. 4 Typical Governor Linkage for Mercedes-Benz (Start Position Illustrated)

BOSCH DIESEL INJECTION – MERCEDES-BENZ (Cont.)

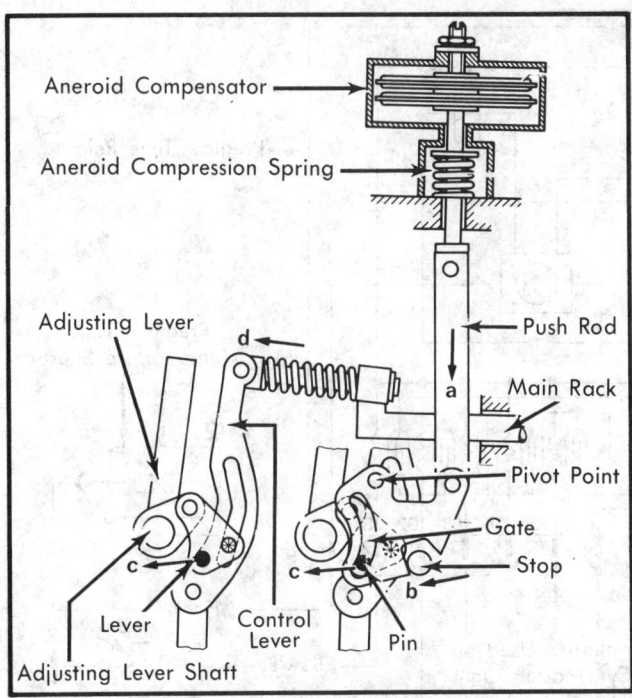

Fig. 6   Diagram of Automatic Compensating Device and Linkage

As adjusting lever moves closer to idle stop, compensating adjustment in partial load range is gradually reduced. At idle it is almost completely eliminated. At low altitudes, governor settings are not affected by compensators.

MAIN FUEL FILTER

Main fuel filter is composed of a throwaway-type filter element, which is part of lower filter housing. See *REMOVAL AND INSTALLATION*.

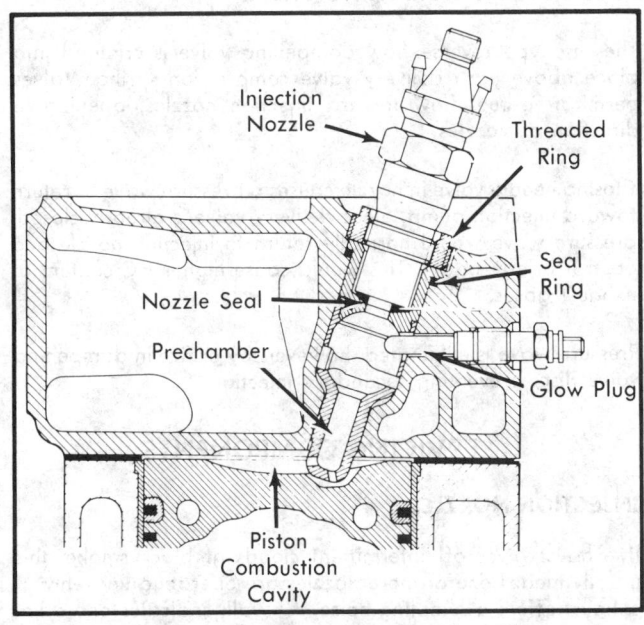

Fig. 7   View Showing Injector, Glow Plug and Prechamber

INJECTION NOZZLES

Injection nozzles are used to spray fuel into the cylinder under the proper pressure and spray pattern for optimum combustion. See *Fig. 7.*

PRE GLOW SYSTEM

All engines are equipped with pin-type glow plugs which are connected in parallel. The parallel connection allows glow plugs to operate independently of each other and provides 11 volts to each plug during the preglow process. A dual material heating element which consists of a heating coil and a control coil has allowed the heating process to be shortened to 5-7 seconds at 32°F (0°C). See *Fig. 8.*

NOTE – *This type plug is called the "Quick-Preglow" plug and is identified by a brass hexagon. It must not be interchanged with glow plugs used in previous models.*

These glow plugs are grounded directly to the cylinder head through plug body. Each receives separate power directly from preglow time relay (total initial current draw is approximately 200 amperes).

The preglow time relay is located on the left inner fender of engine compartment. This relay is protected by an 80 ampere fusible link mounted on its cover. It is equipped with a safety cutout circuit to turn off preglow current if no attempt to start vehicle is made within 40-60 seconds after turning ignition to position "2, Preglowing".

Certain malfunctions of preglow system are indicated through preglow indicator light on instrument panel as follows:

1) Preglow light blinks for approximately 30 seconds with ignition switch in position "2" — Main power circuit is interrupted. Blown 80 ampere fusible link or defective power relay in preglow time relay.

2) Preglow light fails to light but engine can be started — Inspect preglow indicator light circuit and check for open in circuit between temperature sensor and preglow time relay.

3) Preglow light blinks for approximately 30 seconds after engine is started — Disconnect 8-pin plug from preglow time relay and measure ohms between engine ground and harness terminals leading to glow plugs. High or infinite ohm reading indicates open in glow plug, cable to glow plug or terminal connections.

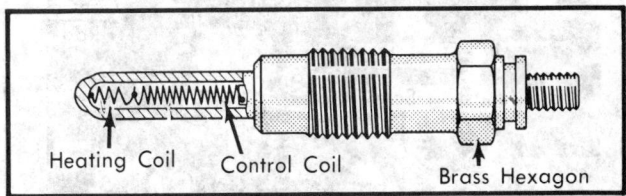

Fig. 8   Quick Preglow Pin-Type Glow Plug

ENGINE SHUT-DOWN
(All Models)

To shut off engine, turn key to position "1" or "0". A cam-operated valve, attached to starter switch opens, connecting the vacuum line from the vacuum pump to the injection pump. See *Fig. 11.*

1980 Bosch Diesel Fuel Injection

BOSCH DIESEL INJECTION – MERCEDES-BENZ (Cont.)

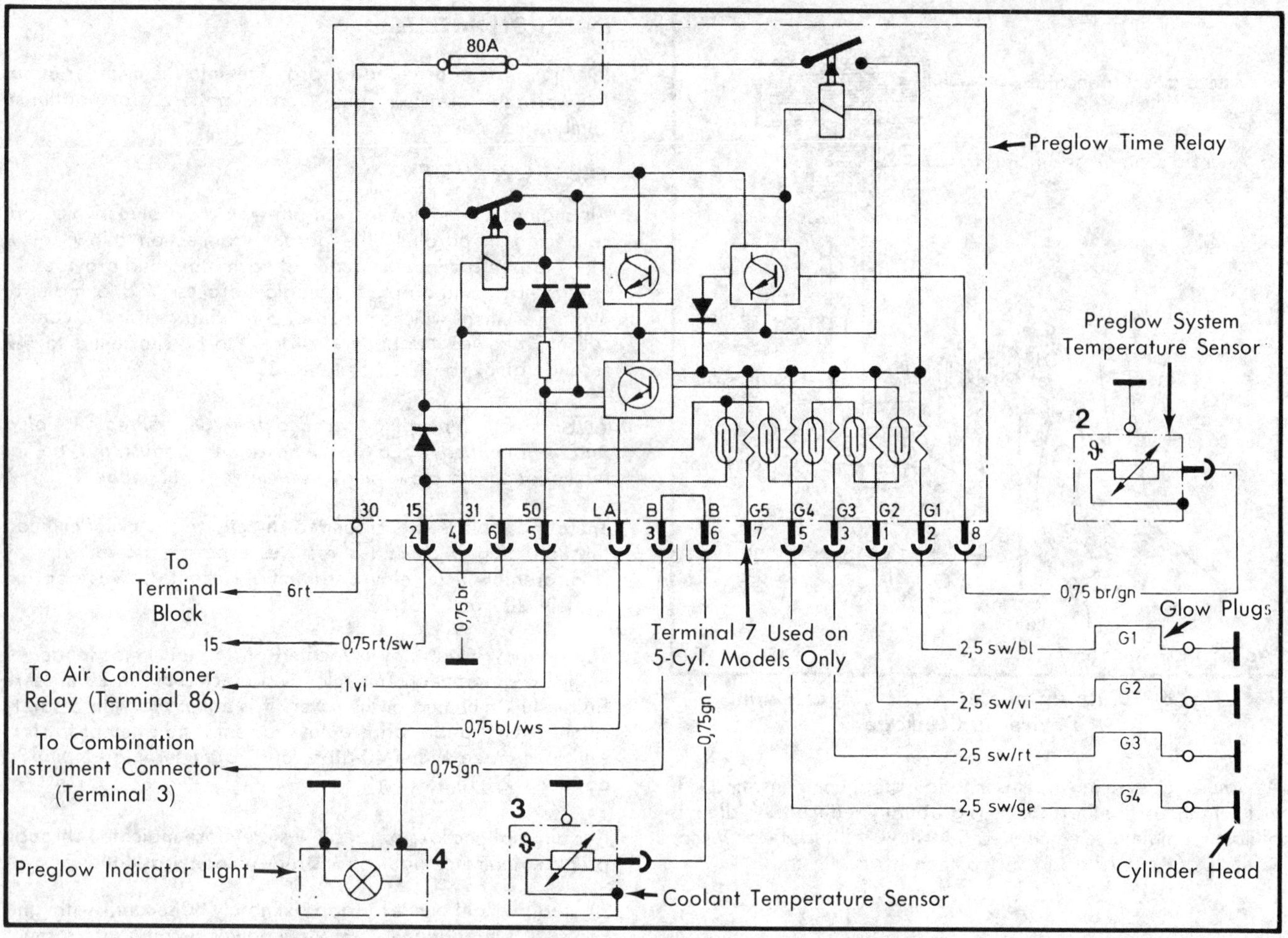

80A

Preglow Time Relay

Preglow System Temperature Sensor

2

30 15 31 50 LA B B G5 G4 G3 G2 G1

2 4 6 5 1 3 6 7 5 3 1 2 8

0,75 br

To Terminal Block ← 6rt

15 ← 0,75 rt/sw

To Air Conditioner Relay (Terminal 86) ← 1 vi

To Combination Instrument Connector (Terminal 3) ← 0,75 gn

0,75 bl/ws

0,75 gn

Terminal 7 Used on 5-Cyl. Models Only

0,75 br/gn

Glow Plugs

2,5 sw/bl — G1

2,5 sw/vi — G2

2,5 sw/rt — G3

2,5 sw/ge — G4

Cylinder Head

Preglow Indicator Light → 4

3

Coolant Temperature Sensor

Fig. 9   Wiring Diagram of "Quick-Preglow" System

Diaphragm of pump-mounted vacuum control unit reacts, pulling main rack to "stop" position.. If engine fails to stop, push "stop" lever on cylinder head. This manually moves main rack to "stop" position. See *REMOVAL AND INSTALLATION, VACUUM CONTROL UNIT and Fig. 10.*

Fig. 10   Manual "Stop" Lever Controlling Injection Pump Main Rack

Bell Crank Lever

Control Rod

Lock Nut

Idle Adjusting Screw

Starting Lock Position

To lock engine, so vehicle cannot be started by towing or coasting downhill, remove key or turn key to position "1" or

"0". Vacuum control unit will then pull main rack to "stop" position.

REVERSE FLOW DAMPENING VALVE

The disc-type reverse flow dampening valve is crimped into place above each delivery valve compression spring. Valves permit free fuel flow toward injection nozzles, opening in direction of nozzles.

Closing needle valve in nozzle causes a pressure wave to return toward injection pump. Since delivery valve is already closed, pressure wave would normally return to injection nozzle and open it briefly again. This would cause higher HC content of exhaust gases.

Pressure wave is eliminated, however, by orifice in dampening valve disc, preventing secondary injection.

SERVICING COMPONENTS

INJECTION NOZZLES

If exhaust gives off intermittent clouds of black smoke, this usually means one or more nozzles are operating unevenly. If exhaust offers a rumbling noise, it usually indicates one cylinder is partly or completely out of action. To determine problem, check injection nozzles as follows:

BOSCH DIESEL INJECTION — MERCEDES-BENZ (Cont.)

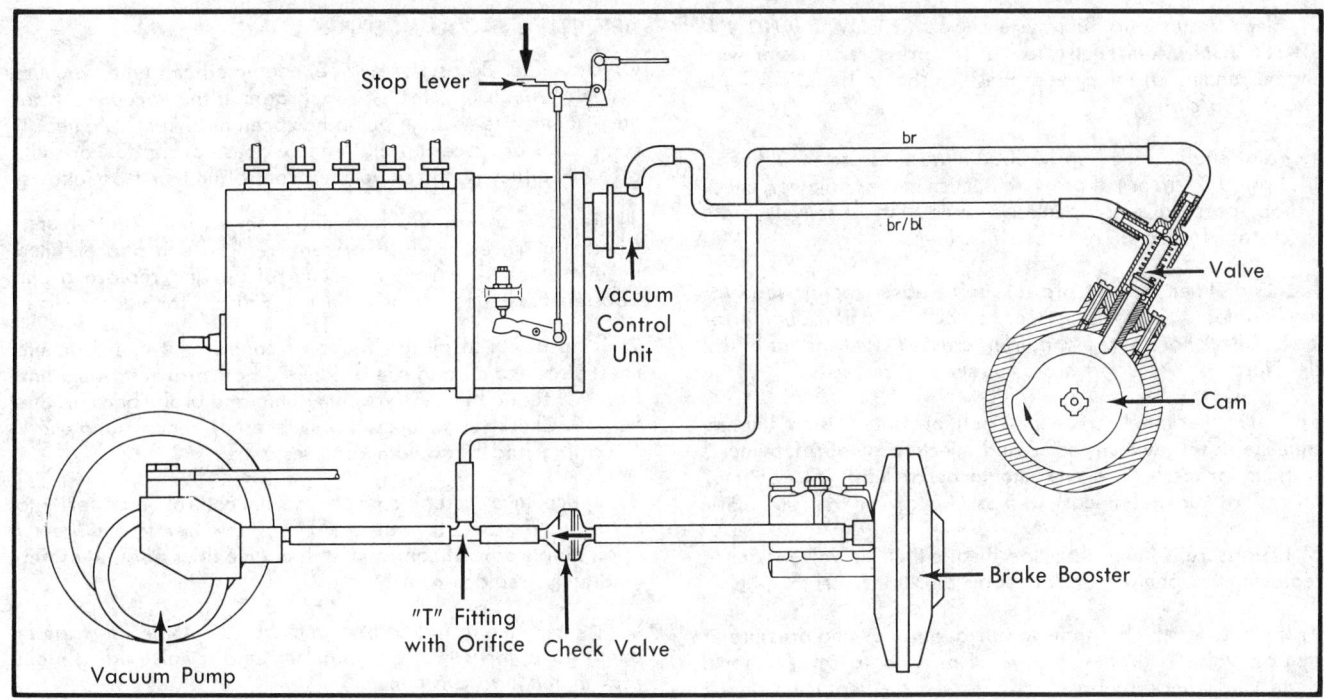

Fig. 11   Vacuum Diagram Showing Vacuum Pump, Valve, and Vacuum Control Unit on Injection Pump

1) At idle, loosen each injection pipe cap nut (in turn) one-half turn. If sound of engine does not change, part of problem is a defective nozzle or inadequate sealing between pipe union and nozzle holder.

2) Raise engine RPM above idle speed and repeat test procedure. If engine still does not run erratically with nut loosened, repair or replace that particular nozzle. If engine runs erratically when nut is loosened, nozzle is operating properly. Tighten one-half turn and check next nozzle.

Nozzle Opening Pressures

The DNOSD 240 nozzles used on unsupercharged engines should have an opening pressure of 1668-1784 psi (115-123 kg/cm^2) for new nozzles and at least 1450 psi (100 kg/cm^2) for used nozzles. Turbocharged models use DNOSD 2400 nozzles with opening pressure of 1958-2074 psi (135-143 kg/cm^2) for new nozzles and at least 1740 psi (120 kg/cm^2) for used nozzles. Difference in opening pressures in one engine should not exceed 71 psi (5 kg/cm^2).

When testing injection nozzles, the most important factors in order of importance are:

- Correct nozzle opening pressure setting.
- Tightness of valve seat to minimum 280 psi (19.7 kg/cm^2) below opening pressure of nozzle.
- Correct spray pattern.

Always install new seal between nozzle and prechamber. Tighten nozzles to specified torque. Use accurate torque wrench so seals and nozzles are not damaged. Coked-up seals speed clogging of nozzle throttling gaps, causing distorted spray pattern and diesel knock.

FUEL PUMP

Fuel pump must deliver fuel under constant pressure and without bubbles. Insufficient pressure could cause engine problems. Pressure is kept constant by a by-pass valve which does not open until specified pressure is reached.

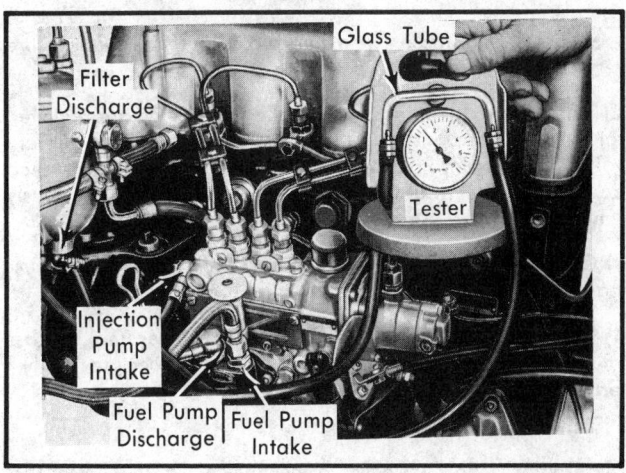

Fig. 12   Pressure Tester (000 589 49 21 00) Hook-Up (Earlier Model Injection Pump Shown)

Checking Delivery Pressures

1) Install a suitable tester (000 589 49 21 00) between main fuel filter and fuel injection pump. See *Fig. 12*. Check for proper delivery pressure, delivery end (final) pressure, and opening pressure of by-pass valve.

2) Using tester's glass tube, check for air bubbles in fuel at same time pressure is read.

BOSCH DIESEL INJECTION — MERCEDES-BENZ (Cont.)

3) Bleed tester and fuel system. *See REMOVAL AND IN-STALLATION, Main Fuel Filter.* Check pressure at tester with engine running at idle speed. Pressure should be 8.5-11.4 psi (0.6-0.8 kg/cm²).

4) Raise engine speed up to 3000 RPM. Pressure should read 11.4 psi (0.8 kg/cm²). If pressure is much higher or lower, check that by-pass valve is opening properly. If excessively high, check for crushed or restricted fuel lines.

NOTE — *When making pressure tests, observe glass tube for air bubbles. If bubbles appear, check system thoroughly for leaks. Check hose porosity, hairline cracks in fuel lines or hoses, deteriorated or scuffed hoses, or slack hose clips.*

5) Next, check delivery end (final) pressure. Using fingers, squeeze hose between tester and injection pump. If pump is working properly, pressure should be at least 15.6 psi (1.1 kg/cm²) at idle and at least 18.5 psi (1.3 kg/cm²) at 3000 RPM.

6) If pressure is lower than specified, either the valve requires replacing, or pump requires repair or replacement.

7) If pressure is higher than specified, and opening pressure of by-pass valve is greater than 11.4 psi (0.8 kg/cm²), remove, clean and check by-pass valve for leaks. Replace valve if necessary.

LEAKING FUEL LINE FITTINGS

If external fuel leakage occurs between pipe connection fitting (union) and adjusting plate of injection pump, install new "grooved" fittings.

1) If pump is equipped with non-grooved fittings, replace ALL fittings with new "grooved" fittings. If equipped with "grooved" fittings, replace only leaking fittings.

NOTE — *Do not loosen adjusting plate, as this would require recalibration of injection pump on a test stand.*

2) Whenever new fittings are installed or fittings are removed for any purpose, install new copper gaskets under delivery valve carriers. Grooved end of valve carrier should be installed downward. Reinstall other valve components previously removed.

3) Oil fitting threads and tighten to 29-36 ft. lbs. (4-5 mkg), using one continuous motion.

4) Install injection lines and operate hand primer until by-pass valve opens (audible sound). Run engine and check for further leaks.

DIESEL KNOCK

Diesel knock can be traced to mechanical causes, diesel fuel properties, or a combination of both. Knock is a pinging noise caused by excessive combustion pressure.

To eliminate or reduce knock, use fuel best suited for your area and check and correct the following:

- Beginning of fuel delivery to assure optimum compression temperature and air charge.
- Valve lash.
- Correct nozzle spray pattern and opening pressure.
- Reverse flow dampening valve for proper operation.
- Insufficient compression pressure (compression check and cylinder leak test).

DEFECTIVE VACUUM CONTROL UNIT

On 5-cylinder 300 series engine, engine oil can enter vacuum system through a defective diaphragm in the vacuum control unit. Sometimes vacuum pump has been mistakenly blamed. If complaints are received that engine does not shut off or shuts off with difficulty, check vacuum control unit first as follows:

1) Remove brown and blue line from vacuum control unit. Check for traces of oil. If present, replace unit and oil-filled vacuum lines. Also repair vacuum pump and replace brake booster if oil is found at connecting fitting for vacuum line.

2) If no traces of oil are found at control unit or in vacuum lines, start engine and run at idle. Pull off brown vacuum line from "T" fitting between vacuum pump and brake booster. *See Fig. 10.* Check for vacuum. If none present, remove and check "T" fitting and clean with compressed air.

3) If vacuum is present, connect vacuum control unit directly to "T" fitting (by-pass the valve). Pump is now free to act directly upon diaphragm of control unit. If engine does not shut off immediately, replace control unit.

NOTE — *When installing new unit, be sure control linkage in pump governor is properly engaged and is not holding main rack in full-load position.*

4) If engine shuts off immediately, vacuum control unit is not to blame. Problem could then be jammed vacuum valve in steering lock.

5) Be sure all vacuum lines are connected as shown in *Fig. 10.* Start engine, check vacuum control unit, valve in steering lock and injection pump for leaks.

INJECTION TIMING ADVANCE MECHANISM

In order to comply with stricter emission standards, the advancement range for injection timing has been changed to 7.5° for all models. In addition, the front plate for the vacuum pump drive has been changed from internal drive teeth to a plate with an axial lift cam. This is due to a change from a twin-diaphragm to a piston type pump.

CAUTION — *This injection timing advance mechanism can NOT be installed on previous model engines.*

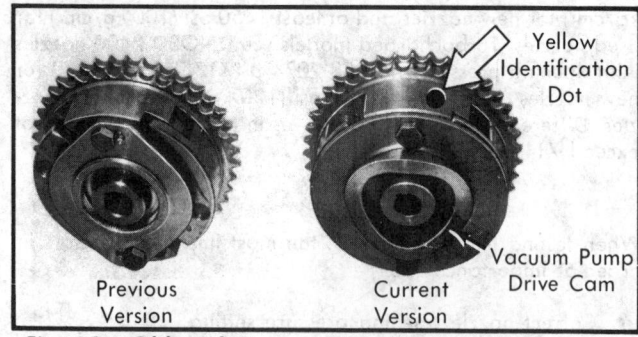

Fig. 13   Old and New Timing Advance Mechanisms

REMOVAL AND INSTALLATION

FUEL INJECTION PUMP

Removal — 1) Remove battery and battery frame. Clean pump and fuel lines to prevent entrance of dirt into system. Disconnect all injection, vacuum, fuel and oil lines at injection pump. Plug injection lines and fuel hose unions at pump.

BOSCH DIESEL INJECTION — MERCEDES-BENZ (Cont.)

2) Detach connecting rods and all cables from pump.

3) Remove mounting nuts at rear support and front flange, using a 13 mm (45° rebent) box wrench. Lift injection pump rearward from crankcase.

NOTE — *If drive collar is to be replaced, observe markings on flange, collar, and pump shaft for reassembly reference.*

Installation — 1) Remove plug and fill injection pump with ½ pint of engine oil. Turn crankshaft in direction of rotation until 45° BTDC mark aligns with pointer. Piston of No. 1 cylinder must be in compression stroke.

2) Slide coupling sleeve onto drive collar of injection pump. Now, slide coupling forward onto drive shaft in crankcase.

3) Set injection pump to "start delivery" position by turning pump shaft until drive collar tooth gap aligns with pump shaft and pump flange marks. See *Fig. 14.*

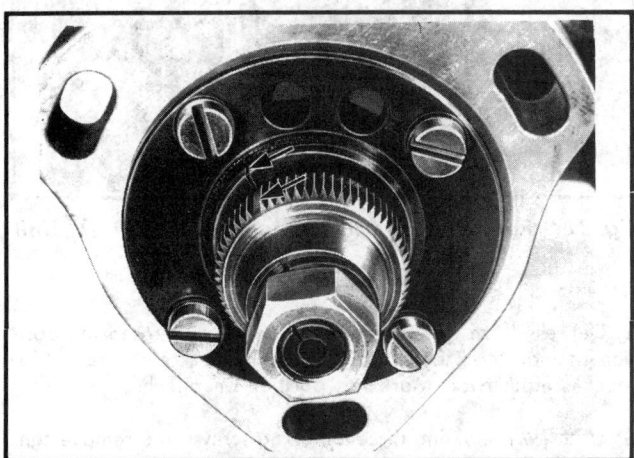

Fig. 14   Aligning Marks on Injection Pump Shaft Drive Collar and Flange

4) When applying light counterclockwise pressure (opposite direction of rotation) to drive collar, cam pressure action causes drive collar to jump back two teeth to cam base circle. Second tooth must then coincide with marking on injection pump housing.

NOTE — *Before installing pump, be sure piston of No. 1 cylinder is in compression stroke and crankshaft is 45° BTDC.*

5) Apply grease to either side of new paper gaskets and place gaskets on crankcase. Install injection pump in coupling sleeve. Be sure stud bolts are centrally positioned within slotted holes. This permits later alignment in either direction.

NOTE — *After aligning injection pump, there must be a clearance of 3.15" (80 mm) between crankcase and center of injection line fitting. This is to permit glow plug removal.*

6) Place washers in position and slightly tighten injection pump nuts.

NOTE — *Use special spacer washer (116 990 14 40) and M8 x 16 hex head screw to fasten rear support bracket.*

Checking for Start of Delivery

1) Turn crankshaft further in direction of rotation, until 24° BTDC mark aligns with pointer. Piston of No. 1 cylinder must again be in compression stroke position.

2) Screw out pipe connection fitting (union) of first pumping element and remove valve parts. Reinstall fitting and attach overflow pipe.

NOTE — *During test adjust control lever on injection pump to full throttle (full-load) position.*

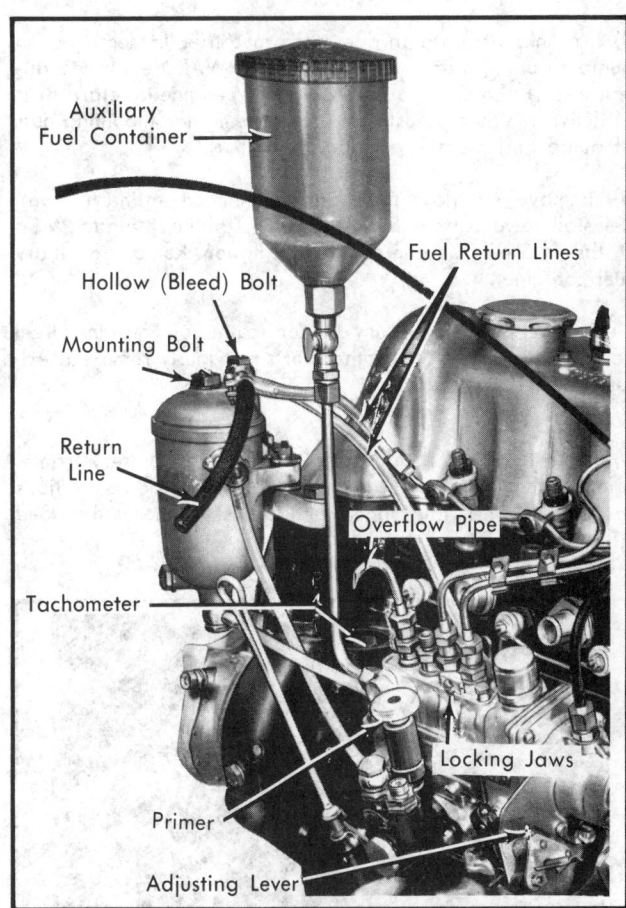

Fig. 15   Installing Auxiliary Fuel Container on Injection Pump (Typical)

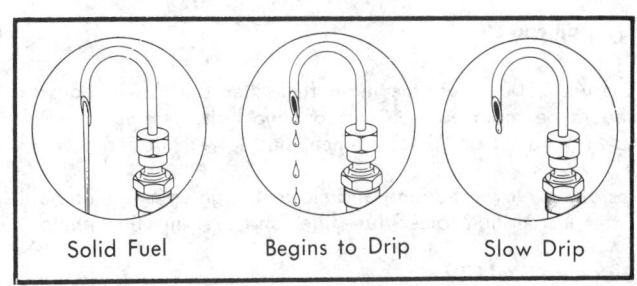

Fig. 16   Checking Fuel Dripping From Overflow Pipe

BOSCH DIESEL INJECTION — MERCEDES-BENZ (Cont.)

3) Connect auxiliary fuel container (000 589 05 23 00) to injection pump. *See Fig. 15.* Turn engine over slowly in normal direction of rotation until fuel stream from overflow pipe stops dripping. *See Fig. 16.*

NOTE — *Another drop may follow 10-15 seconds later, but this is normal.*

4) Start of delivery should occur when pipe stops dripping Crankshaft pointer should then be on 24° BTDC mark. Turn crankshaft two more full turns. Fuel should stop dripping again at end of second full turn. If so, tighten injection pump in this position.

5) If crankshaft position does not prove true, loosen injection pump mounting nuts and turn pump TOWARD engine to advance start of delivery and AWAY FROM engine to retard start of delivery. When adjustment is correct, tighten mounting nuts of pump and recheck position.

6) Remove overflow pipe and connection fitting (union). Reinstall valve parts using new gasket. Tighten fitting to 29-36 ft. lbs. (4-5 mkg) in one continuous motion. Remove auxiliary fuel container.

7) Connect all fuel, vacuum and lubricating oil lines. Install all control rods, cables, and other parts previously removed. Adjust as necessary.

8) Bleed fuel system and install battery and battery frame. Bring engine to operating temperature. Check all connections for leaks. Check idle speed and adjust as necessary. See *ADJUSTMENTS.*

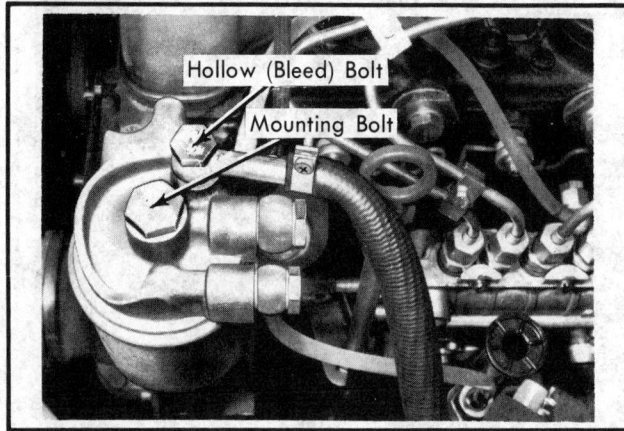

Fig. 17   Removing, Installing and Bleeding Fuel Filter

FUEL FILTER

Every 37,500 miles, the main fuel filter and lower housing should be replaced. Loosen mounting bolt. *See Fig. 17.* Pull downward on one-piece element and lower housing.

Install new lower housing and element. Tighten mounting bolt. After installation, bleed fuel filter and fuel injection pump.

Bleeding Fuel Filter

Loosen hollow bolt. *See Fig. 17.* Pump hand primer pump until fuel emerges free of bubbles. Retighten hollow bolt.

Bleeding Injection Pump

Pump hand primer until by-pass valve on injection pump opens. You will hear a buzzing sound when this occurs. Run engine and check for leaks.

VACUUM CONTROL UNIT

Removal — 1) Unscrew lower right-hand mounting screw from vacuum control unit. *See Fig. 18.*

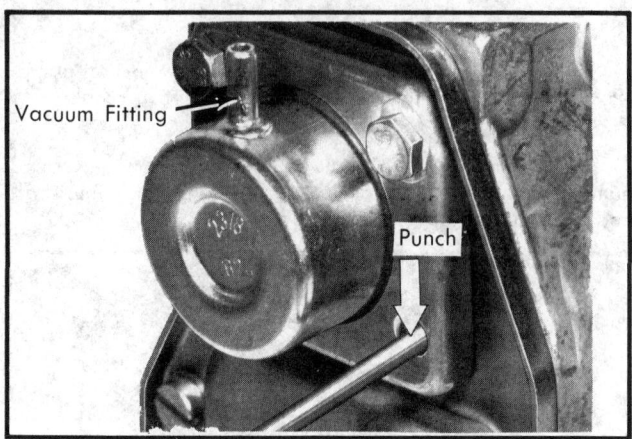

Fig. 18   Removing and Installing Vacuum Control Unit

2) Depress "stop" lever on cylinder head cover. Measure position of main rack by inserting punch into screw bore until it touches main rack. Mark this position on punch.

3) Unscrew remaining three mounting screws and remove control unit.

Installation — 1) Install new gasket and steel ring. Make sure tang on vacuum control unit engages in main rack. Install last three mounting screws removed.

2) Insert punch in lower right-hand screw bore. Check main rack position with mark on punch. When punch touches main rack, press lightly on punch and move control lever on injection pump from "stop" position to "full load" stop. Punch must follow the main rack smoothly. If correct, install remaining screw.

AUTOMATIC ALTITUDE COMPENSATING DEVICE

NOTE — *Do not attempt to remove upper cover of governor housing. Governor linkage is assembled to altitude compensating device.*

Removal — Hold altitude compensating device by small nut, while loosening larger nut. *See Fig. 19.* Unscrew altitude compensating device and remove shims.

Installation — Using previously removed shims, screw compensating device into place. Be sure vent tube is positioned at lowest point to drain off any possible condensation. Hold small nut and tighten large nut.

BOSCH DIESEL INJECTION — MERCEDES-BENZ (Cont.)

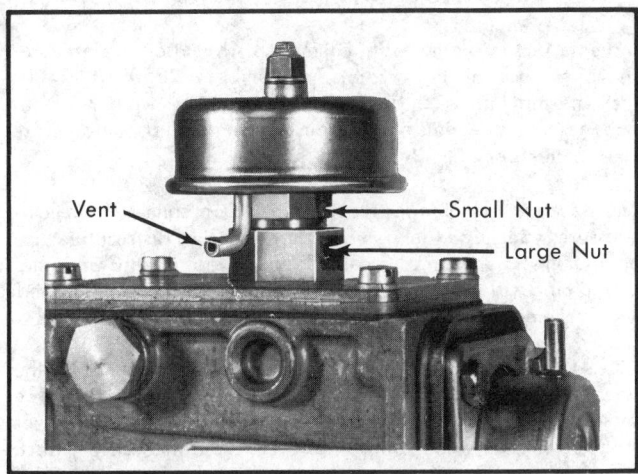

Fig. 19 *Removing and Installing Automatic Altitude Compensating Device*

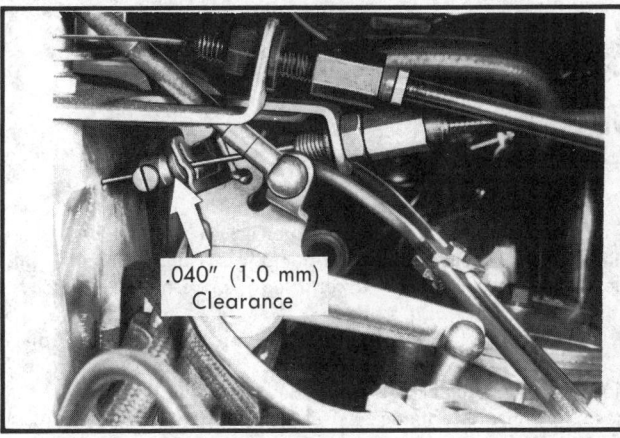

Fig. 20 *Measuring Distance Between Collar and Spring*

ADJUSTMENTS

IDLE SPEED AND IDLE SPEED REGULATOR

1) Check throttle linkage for free movement and wear. Run engine until oil temperature reaches 140-176°F (60-80°C). Turn idle speed regulator knob on dashboard clockwise to stop (Non-turbocharged models) and measure distance between collar and spring. Adjust collar as necessary to obtain .040" (1.0 mm). *See Fig. 20.*

NOTE — *Due to further technological development, the idle speed adjustment knob on Turbo-Diesels has been eliminated.*

2) Depress "stop" lever. *See Fig. 10.* Bowden cable of cruise control should rest tension-free against bell crank. If necessary, adjust cable with adjusting nut. Release "stop" lever. Cable should have play.

3) Disconnect control rod at bellcrank lever and check idle speed with tachometer. Loosen lock nut and adjust idle speed to 700-800 RPM with adjusting screw. *See Fig. 3.* Reconnect control rod so that it is free of tension and adjust throttle linkage if necessary.

CAUTION — *If engine speed is adjusted higher, it will be above controlled idle speed range of governor. Engine speed could automatically increase up to maximum RPM (without load).*

TIGHTENING SPECIFICATION

Application	Ft. Lbs. (mkg)
Rocker Arm Cover	3.6 (0.5)
Glow Plugs	36.0 (5.0)
Precombustion Chamber	118.5 (16.5)
Nozzle-to-Holder	54.0 (7.5)
Nozzle Holder-to-Head	54.0 (7.5)
Nozzle Holder Connector	54.0 (7.5)
Injection Pump Shaft Nut	50.6 (7.0)
Connecting Fitting (Union)	29.0-36.0 (4.0-5.0)
Injection Pipe Cap Nuts	18.0 (2.5)

SYSTEM SPECIFICATIONS

Application	Specifications
Idle Speed	700-800 RPM
Fuel Pump	
Delivery Pressure	
Idle Speed	8.5-11.4 psi (0.6-0.8 kg/cm²)
3000 RPM	11.4 psi (0.8 kg/cm²)
Fuel Pump	
Final Delivery Pressure	
Idle Speed	15.6 psi (1.1 kg/cm²)
3000 RPM	18.5 psi (1.3 kg/cm²)
Start of Delivery	24° BTDC (In Compression Stroke)
Nozzle Opening Pressure	
240D & 300D	1668-1784 psi (115-123 kg/cm²)
300SD Turbo	1958-2074 psi (135-143 kg/cm²)

1980 Bosch Diesel Fuel Injection

BOSCH DIESEL FUEL INJECTION — PEUGEOT & VOLVO

Peugeot
504
505
Volvo

DESCRIPTION

The diesel fuel injection systems consist of the fuel tank, fuel filter, distributor-type injection pump, glow plugs, throttle pintle injection nozzles and a centrifugal governor. See *Fig. 1*.

A vane-type fuel pump, built into the injection pump, supplies fuel from tank to fuel filter to injection pump. See *Fig. 2*. Injection pump supplies fuel to nozzles under high pressure, according to firing sequence (1-3-4-2 on Peugeot and 1-5-3-6-2-4 on Volvo). Excess fuel is returned to fuel tank by return lines.

SYSTEM COMPONENTS

FUEL INJECTION PUMP

Peugeot vehicles use a Bosch VE 4/9 F2250 R50 pump; Volvo, a Bosch VE 6/10 F2400 L32 (manual transmission) or L32-1 (automatic transmission). Pumps are distributor-type pumps, signified by the "V" designation. The letter "E" is the power rating of the pump. The numbers "4" and "6" denote the number of outlets or engine cylinders. The numbers "9" and "10"

indicate piston diameter in millimeters. The letter "F" indicates use of a mechanical governor. The numbers "2250" or "2400" indicate maximum adjusted load speed and the letters "L" or "R" indicate direction of rotation. The remaining numbers are design numbers.

The Bosch single plunger mechanical pump consists of a low-pressure, vane-type fuel pump, a high-pressure distributor-type plunger injection pump, a centrifugal governor, and an injection timing advance mechanism. Both pumps are equipped with an electrical fuel shut-off solenoid. See *Fig. 1*.

As the vane type pump rotor turns, centrifugal force holds the vanes against the walls of the pump's pressure chamber. The offset design of the rotor and pressure chamber, squeezes trapped fuel between vanes and forces it out the delivery port. Vane pressure of the Peugeot pump is 65-73 psi (4.6-5.1 kg/cm²) at 1600 RPM or 87-94 psi (6.1-6.6 kg/cm²) at 2200 RPM.

NOTE — *Vane pressures are given at pump speed, not engine speed and were not available for Volvo models.*

The injection pump drive shaft turns the vane-type fuel pump, distributor plunger and cam plate as a unit. The injection pump is driven by the camshaft at one-half engine speed. The fuel pump lubricates all moving parts of the injection pump with diesel fuel and supplies fuel to the distributor plunger for pressurization and metering to injection nozzles.

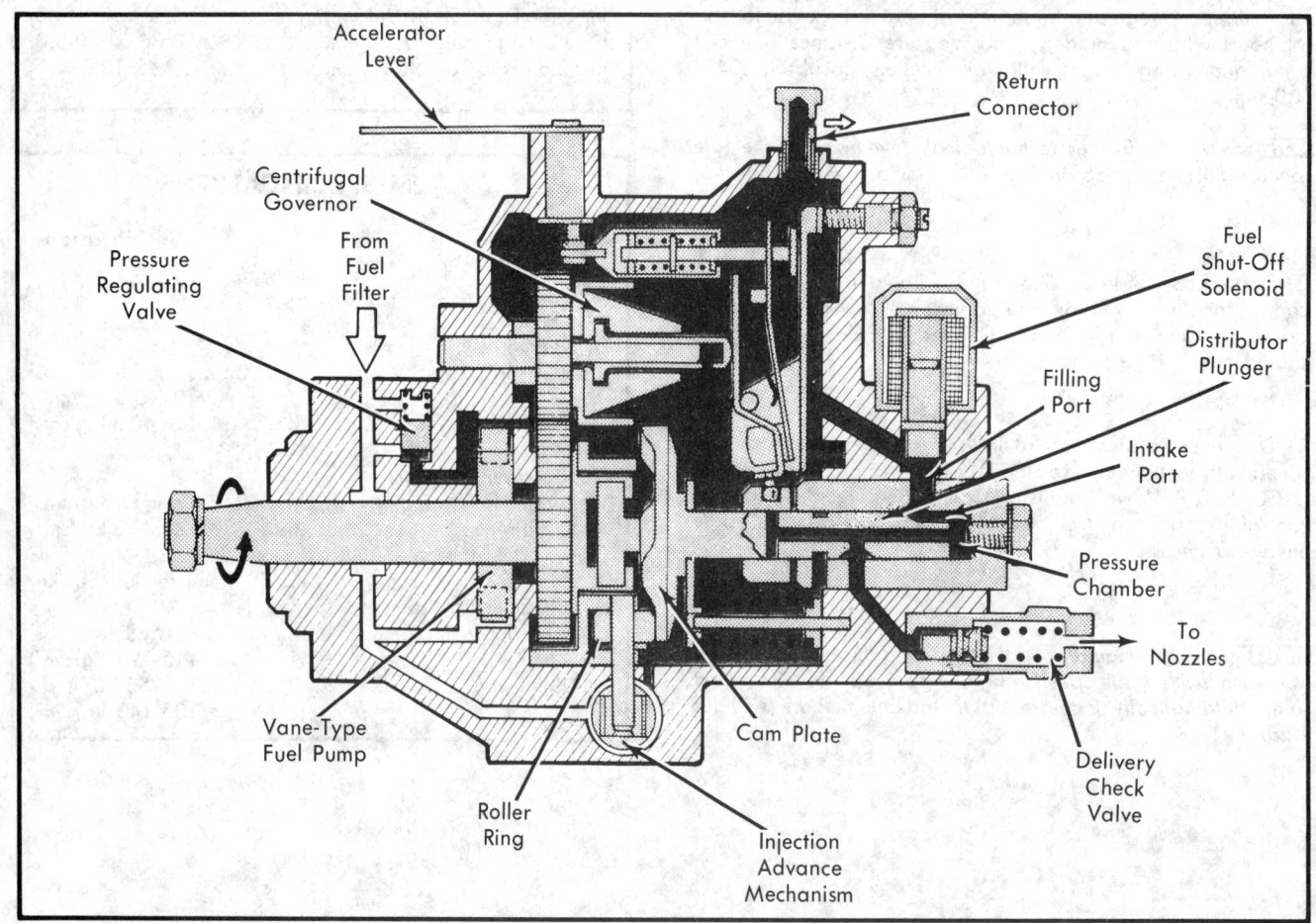

Fig. 1 Cutaway View of Volvo Fuel Injection Pump

BOSCH DIESEL FUEL INJECTION — PEUGEOT & VOLVO (Cont.)

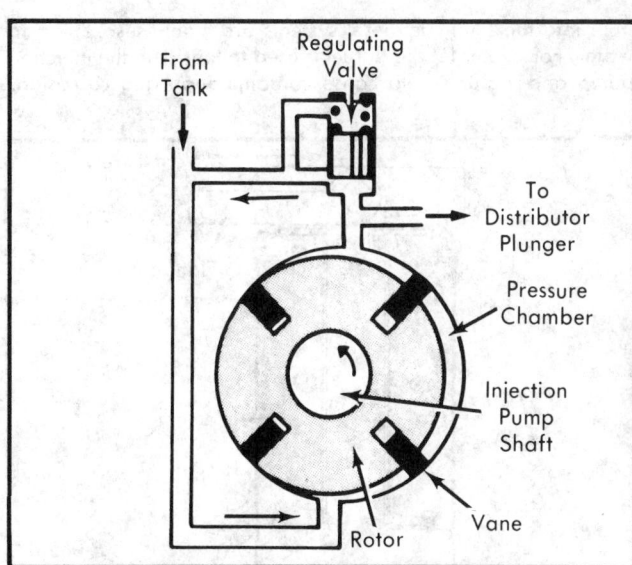

Fig. 2   Vane-Type Fuel Pump

Springs hold the cam plate and distributor plunger against stationary rollers. See *Figs. 1 and 3*. This causes the plunger, not only to rotate, but also move back and forth in its cylinder. Whenever an intake port in the plunger becomes aligned with a filling port in the pump body, fuel from the vane-type fuel pump fills the pressure chamber.

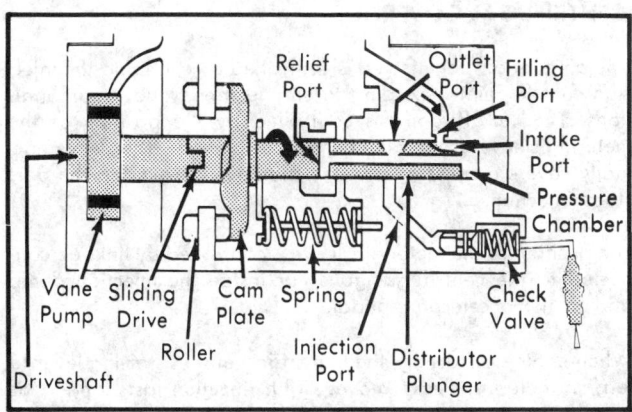

Fig. 3   Operation of Distributor Plunger

As the plunger rotates, the intake port is covered and fuel is trapped in the pressure chamber. As the cam plate and rollers push against the distributor plunger, the fuel is pressurized to approximately 1800 psi (126.6 kg/cm²). As the plunger continues to turn, the single outlet port in the plunger becomes aligned with one of the 4 or 6 injection ports in the pump body (one per cylinder). This pressurized fuel opens the delivery check valve and supplies high pressure fuel to the appropriate injection nozzle.

An injection timing mechanism is located on the lower side of the injection pump. See *Fig. 4*. As engine speed increases, stroke time becomes shorter and injection time becomes longer. Burning must therefore begin sooner and ensure peak combustion pressures still occur at the most efficient point after TDC.

As engine speed increases, fuel pressure from the vane pump also increases, pushing the hydraulic piston to the side against its spring. This causes the roller housing to turn slightly as the peg is moved. Since the cam plate is turning in the opposite direction, the ramps on the cam plate engage with the rollers sooner.

For cold start and warm-up periods, a lever and cam act against a hydraulic piston, advancing injection timing. See *Fig. 4*. This provides more time for fuel to burn, improving performance and preventing black exhaust smoke during cold start and warm-up periods.

INJECTION NOZZLES

The Peugeot engines use DNO SD 1510 nozzles with KCA 17S38/4 holders. Opening pressure is 1668-1813 psi (117.3-127.5 kg/cm²). Volvo uses DNO SD 193 nozzles with KCA 30 SD 27/4 holders. Opening pressure is 1706-1849 psi (120-130 kg/cm²).

A pressurized mist of fuel is injected into a round swirl chamber. See *Fig. 5*. Fuel swirls around the chamber, mixing with hot air, compressed at a 23:1 ratio for Peugeot or 23.5:1 for Volvo.

Combustion actually begins in the rich swirl chamber and continues on through a small passageway and into the leaner main chamber. As peak cylinder pressures build in swirl chamber, rather than main chamber, loads on connecting rods and crankshaft are reduced.

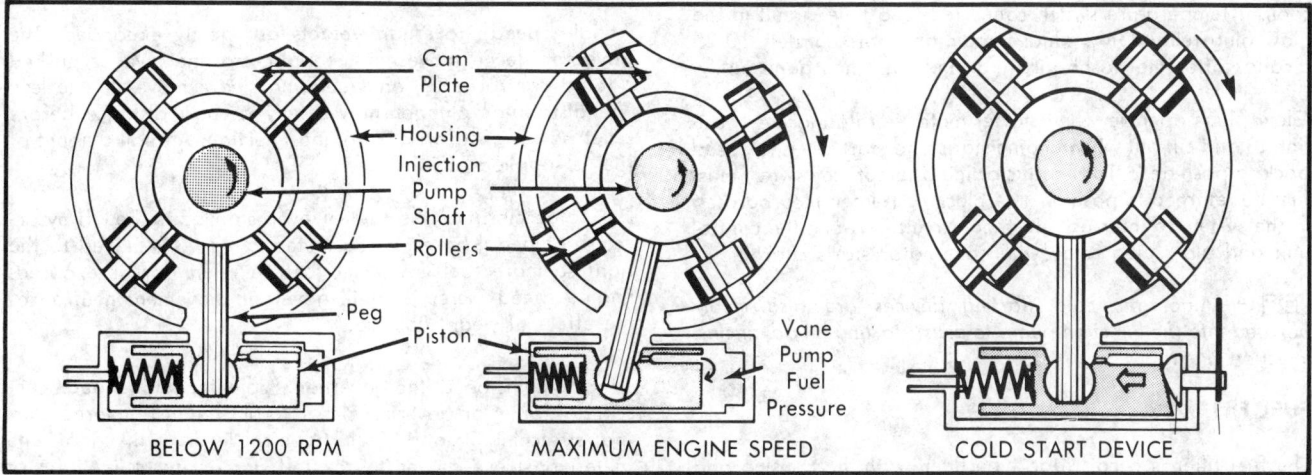

Fig. 4   Injection Advance Mechanism and Cold Start Device

BOSCH DIESEL FUEL INJECTION — PEUGEOT & VOLVO (Cont.)

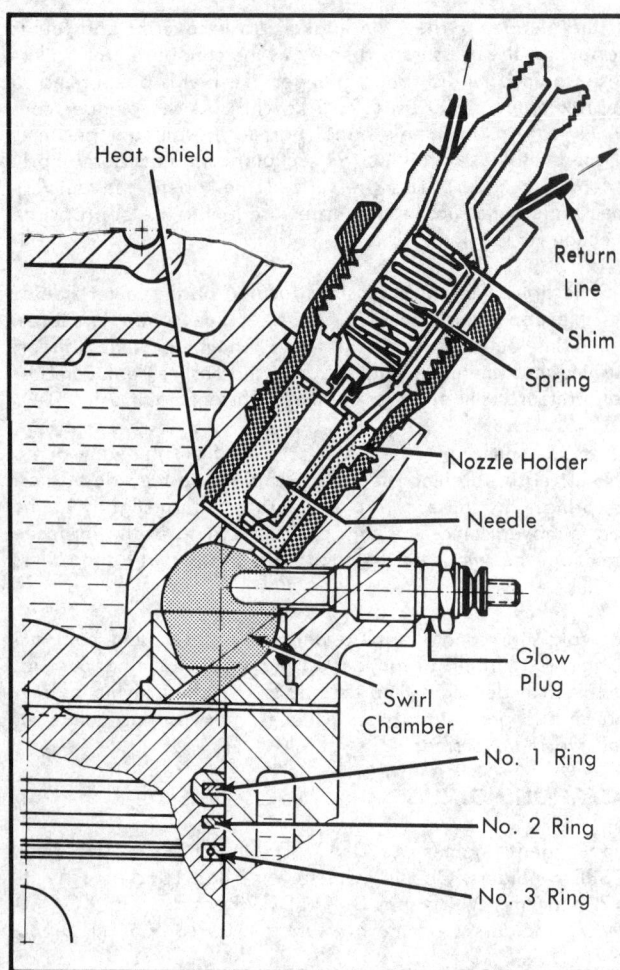

Fig. 5   Cutaway View Showing Relationship of Injection Nozzle, Glow Plug and Swirl Chamber to Piston

GLOW PLUGS

Glow plugs are used during cold starts to preheat swirl chambers. See *Fig. 5*. The system is switched "ON" when the key switch is turned to position 2. Preheating time depends on a coolant temperature switch connected to a time circuit in the glow plug relay. Glow plugs remain on approximately 10-25 seconds after the dashboard indicator light has gone out.

Glow plugs operate when starter motor is rotating (key position 3) and cut out when engine starts and start key is released back to position 2. To repeat starting attempt, key switch must first be returned to position 1. A blocking relay is incorporated in the system to interrupt electrical circuit between the control unit and glow plug relay when alternator starts charging.

NOTE — *Automatic cold starting devices are also incorporated into the injection pump to assist starting by advancing injection timing.*

FUEL FILTER

The fuel filter is a cartridge type filter, with the housing and filter being replaced as a unit. See *Fig. 6*. A water separator is

built into the filter, as diesel systems are highly susceptible to water. For example, diesel fuel is used to lubricate the injection pump and water would cause contamination and corrosion.

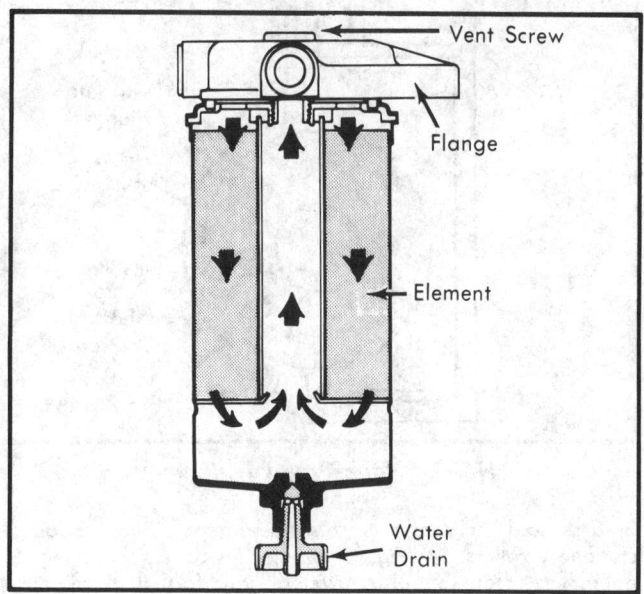

Fig. 6   Components of Fuel Filter

CENTRIFUGAL GOVERNOR

The amount of fuel injected is controlled by changing the injection cut-off point according to engine speed and load conditions. The cut-off point is controlled by the position of the metering sleeve around the distributor plunger. The sleeve normally covers a relief port in the plunger. Uncovering the port stops injection.

The position of the metering sleeve is controlled by linkage connected to the centrifugal governor inside the injection pump and to the accelerator pedal. See *Fig. 7*.

When engine is starting, the leaf spring pushes starting lever to left, so metering sleeve moves right. Injection lasts longer, as the plunger must move further before uncovering relief port in plunger. More fuel is supplied during starting.

At idle speed, governor weights are partly expanded. The governor sleeve moves to the right, starting lever is pushed against control lever, and metering sleeve moves to the left. The distributor plunger moves only a short distance before relief port is uncovered, stopping injection. A small amount of fuel is supplied at idle speed.

During acceleration the control lever is pulled to the left by accelerator pedal linkage. The metering sleeve is moved to the right so more fuel is injected before relief port is exposed. Engine speed increases until governor movement neutralizes the effect of pedal linkage.

At maximum speed, the governor is spinning with enough centrifugal force for governor sleeve to act against governor spring, stretching it, and forcing control lever to the right. The metering sleeve moves to the left uncovering relief port at beginning of each distributor plunger stroke. There is no

BOSCH DIESEL FUEL INJECTION – PEUGEOT & VOLVO (Cont.)

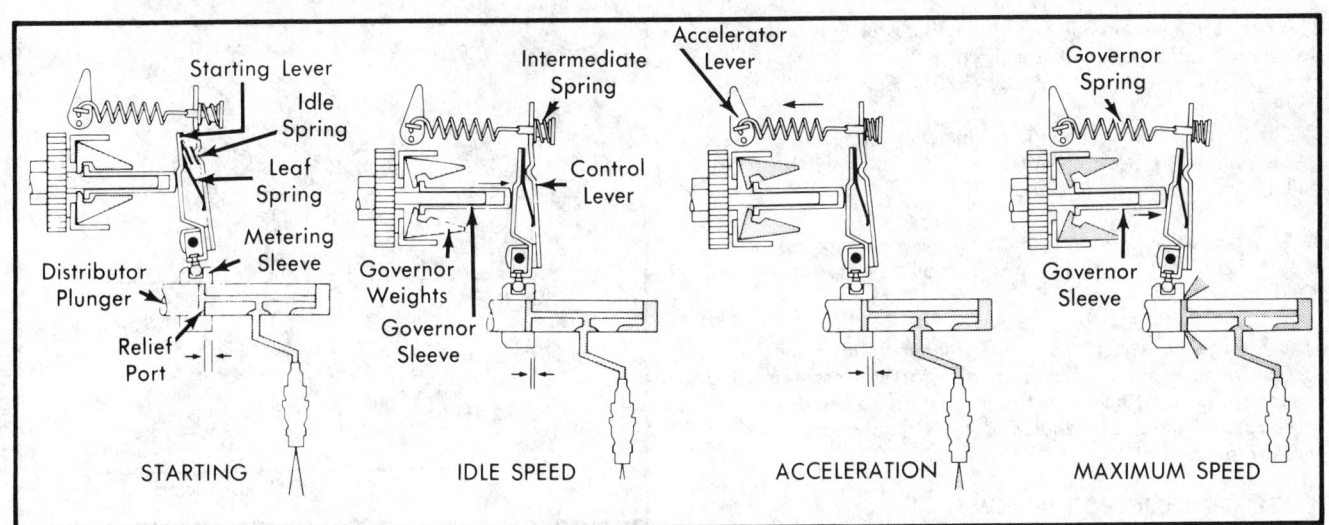

Fig. 7 *Operation of Injection Pump Centrifugal Governor*

pressure for injection until engine speed drops and metering sleeve moves to the right again. This acts as a speed limiter, causing the engine performance to "flatten out."

SERVICING COMPONENTS

VOLVO FUEL INJECTION PUMP

NOTE — *As injectors are manufactured to extremely small tolerances (pump cylinder and bore clearance is .00004-.00008" or .001-.002 mm), extreme cleanliness is a necessity. Clean all injection pump and nozzle unions before removal.*

Removal — **1)** Use clamping pliers to pinch off coolant hoses for cold start device. Disconnect hoses at cold start device. Disconnect accelerator cable and kickdown cable (automatic transmission) from cable pulley. Disconnect wire at fuel shut-off solenoid.

2) Remove rear timing gear cover. Clean fuel line connections at injection pump. Disconnect fuel supply and return lines at pump. Plug open connections to prevent dirt from entering fuel system.

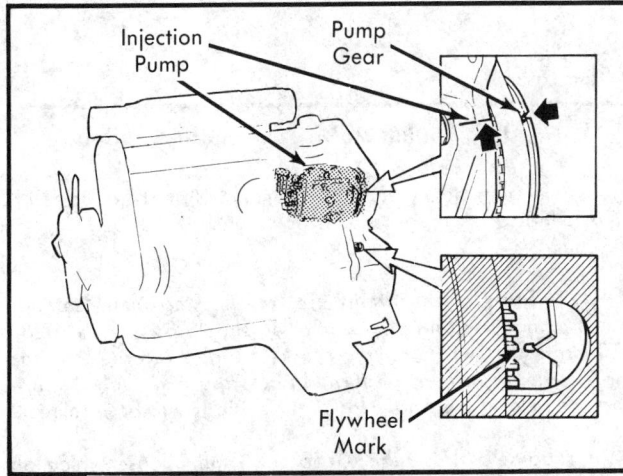

Fig. 8 *Aligning Timing Marks Prior to Fuel Injection Pump Removal*

3) Remove vacuum pump and pump plunger. Remove injection pump delivery pipes. Plug all openings. Set cylinder No. 1 at TDC and injection. See *Fig. 8*. Timing marks should align.

4) Remove injection pump drive belt, after relieving tension by loosening injection pump bracket bolts. Tighten one bolt to retain injection pump in upper position.

5) Loosen camshaft rear gear, using special tool (5199) to hold gear while loosening with special tool (5201). Camshaft must not rotate. Loosen bolts only enough to let gear rotate on camshaft.

6) Lock injection pump gear with stop (5193) See *Fig. 9*. Remove gear nut with special tool (5201). Remove pump gear with puller (5204). Remove injection pump front bracket bolts and rear pump retaining bolts. Lift off pump and front bracket.

Fig. 9 *Removing Injection Pump Gear*

Installation — **1)** Position injection pump. Install retaining bolts finger tight, so pump position can still be adjusted. Set pump so mark on injection pump and pump bracket align. Tighten retaining bolts.

BOSCH DIESEL FUEL INJECTION — PEUGEOT & VOLVO (Cont.)

2) Make sure injection pump shaft key is correctly installed. Install gear, washer and nut. Lock gear with special tool (5193) and tighten nut with special tool (5201). *See Fig. 9.*

3) Set injection pump timing. Fill injection pump with diesel fuel if pump has been emptied or a new pump is being installed. Install rear timing gear cover.

4) Connect fuel supply and return lines. Do not mix connection screws. Screw for return line has a small hole and is marked "OUT".

5) Install fuel delivery pipes. Install vacuum pump plunger and vacuum pump. Connect hoses to cold start devices, removing clamping pliers. Attach wire to fuel shut-off solenoid, connect accelerator cable and, if equipped, the kickdown cable. Adjust accelerator control.

PEUGEOT FUEL INJECTION PUMP

NOTE — *No information was available at time of publication on correct removal and installation of the Peugeot fuel injection pump.*

INJECTION NOZZLES

Problems with injection nozzles usually are accompanied by knocking in one or more cylinders, engine overheating, loss of power or performance, black exhaust smoke and increased fuel consumption. To locate and correct faulty injectors, proceed as follows:

1) Remove vacuum pump and vacuum pump plunger. Loosen line unions on each injection nozzle, one at a time with engine running at fast idle. If engine speed remains constant with line removed, that nozzle is defective.

2) To remove nozzle, detach injector line after cleaning connection. Plug all openings to keep dirt out of fuel system. Remove injectors and heat shields. When installing injection nozzles, use new heat shields with recess pointing upward. Install delivery pipes. Install vacuum pump plunger and vacuum pump.

FUEL FILTER

Service is limited to draining water periodically and normal filter replacement. *See Fig. 6.*

To drain water from filter, place a tray under filter drain screw in bottom of filter. Loosen bleed screw on top several turns with a screwdriver. Loosen drain screw by hand. Drain until only clean fuel runs out. Tighten drain screw and bleed screw and remove tray.

ADJUSTMENTS

FUEL INJECTION PUMP TIMING

Volvo — 1) Remove rear timing gear cover. Disconnect cold start device by loosening screw "1", pushing lever forward and rotating it 90°. *See Fig. 10.* Do NOT touch screw "2". If it is loosened, cold start device must be reset on a test bench.

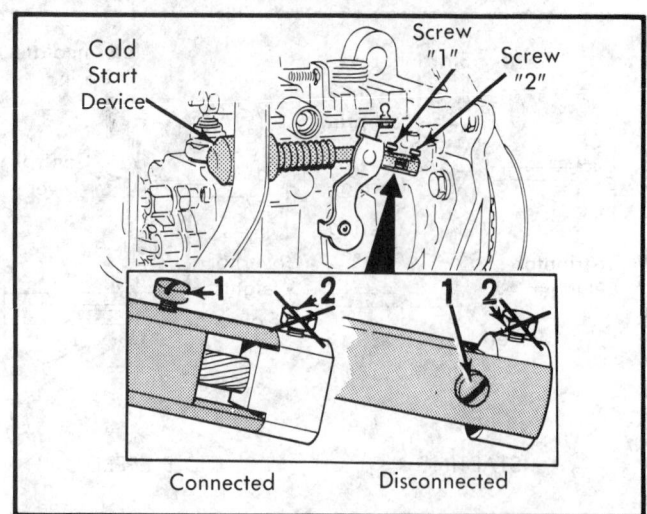

Fig. 10   Disconnecting and Connecting Cold Start Device

2) Set cylinder No. 1 at top dead center and injection. *See Fig. 8.* Both cam lobes should point up at equally large angles. Flywheel timing mark should be at "0".

3) Remove the plug from injection pump cover. Install dial indicator holder (5194) and a 0-.12" (0-3 mm) dial indicator gauge. *See Fig. 11.* Preset indicator to approximately .08" (2 mm). Turn engine counterclockwise until indicator gauge is at minimum. Set gauge to zero.

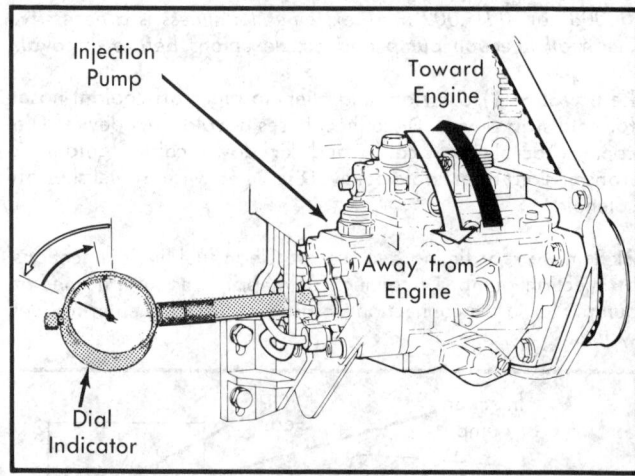

Fig. 11   Timing Volvo Fuel Injection Pump

4) Turn engine clockwise until flywheel "0" mark aligns with arrow. Indicator gauge should now read .0256-.0287" (.65-.73 mm).

NOTE — *These specifications are for checking pump setting. When actually setting pump, reading should be exactly .028" (.70 mm). Also, when making check, if engine is turned too far past "0" mark, it must be turned back approximately ¼ turn and then clockwise again to "0" or settings will be incorrect.*

5) If reading is less than .0256" (.65 mm), loosen injection pump retaining bolts. Turn injection pump inward until .028" (.70 mm) is indicated on gauge. Tighten retaining bolts.

BOSCH DIESEL FUEL INJECTION — PEUGEOT & VOLVO (Cont.)

6) If reading is more than .0287" (.73 mm), loosen injection pump retaining bolts. Turn injection pump outward until reading is approximately .0236" (.60 mm) and then turn pump inward until it is at .028" (.70 mm). Tighten injection pump retaining bolts.

CAUTION — *If adjusting allowances in steps* **5)** *and* **6)** *are insufficient, do not tap or knock injection pump to change setting. It may be camshaft is not in proper relationship to crankshaft and/or front or rear drive belts may be improperly tensioned. Correct this and then set injection timing.*

7) After adjusting injection pump setting, turn engine twice and recheck setting. See *Fig. 11.* Readjust as necessary. Remove dial indicator and holder. Install rear timing gear cover.

8) Reconnect cold start device, remembering not to touch screw "2". Push lever forward and turn sleeve 90° and tighten screw "1". See *Fig. 10.*

Peugeot — 1) Remove valve cover and glow plugs. Rotate engine until cylinder No. 1 exhaust valve just begins to open (flywheel end). Using valve spring compressor, remove No. 4 exhaust valve rocker arm without altering its adjustment.

2) Slide rocker arm rearward and direct its nose upward. Disconnect and remove valve spring. Rotate engine clockwise until No. 1 exhaust valve closes and No. 1 intake valve opens (overlap).

3) Attach dial indicator support to front valve cover stud. Attach dial indicator with feeler squarely on top of exhaust valve stem. Add approximately .39" (10 mm) preload. Rotate engine counterclockwise, lowering the piston .28" (7 mm) from TDC. The gauge will read .12" (3 mm).

4) Using a second dial indicator with adapters, install dial indicator in timing plug opening in hydraulic head of injection pump. Loosen pump mounting bolts, move pump fully away from the engine. Lightly tighten mounting bolts. This is BDC at the pump. Adjust a .039" (1 mm) preload on pump dial indicator.

5) Rotate engine clockwise until exhaust valve dial indicator matches specifications in table.

Exhaust Valve Dial Indicator Specifications①

Peugeot Engine	Inches (mm)
Federal	.34 (8.65)②
Calif.	.36" (9.03)③

① — ±.0008" (.02 mm).
② — .053" (1.35 mm) BTDC.
③ — .038" (.97 mm) BTDC.

6) Rotate pump toward the engine until pump dial indicator reads .059" (1.50 mm), an actual lift of .020" (.50 mm). Tighten pump mounting bolts.

7) Rotate engine counterclockwise .275" (7 mm) from TDC (.12" or 3 mm indicated). Rotate engine clockwise while observing pump dial indicator until exactly .059" (1.50 mm) is shown. This again is .020" (.50 mm) lift.

8) Check exhaust valve dial indicator again according to table. A tolerance of .0008" (.02 mm) is permitted. Remove dial indicators, reinstall valve components and pump cover plug.

VOLVO ENGINE CONTROLS

1) Disconnect cold start device. See *Fig. 10.* Disconnect link rod at lever on injection pump. Adjust accelerator cable by turning sheath until cable is stretched, but does not influence pulley position. Pulley should touch idle stop. See *Fig. 12.*

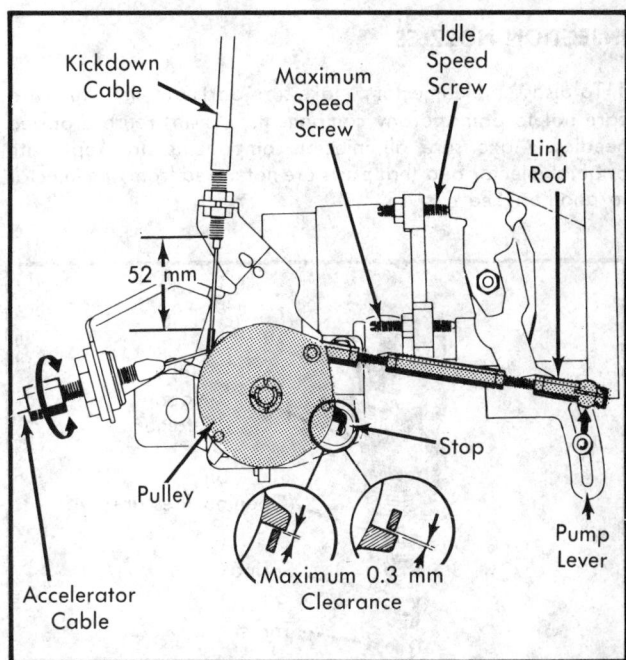

Fig. 12 Adjusting Engine Controls (Volvo Shown)

2) Depress accelerator pedal fully. Pulley should touch full speed stop. Adjust kickdown cable on automatic transmission models. Depress accelerator pedal to floor. Kickdown cable should move approximately 2.05" (52 mm) between end positions. In idle position, kickdown cable should be stretched and distance between kickdown cable clip and cable sheath should be .01-.04" (.25-1.0 mm).

3) Connect link rod to injection pump lever. Adjust link rod in maximum position by turning pulley to maximum position. Adjust link rod length so injection pump lever touches the maximum speed adjusting screw.

4) Adjust link rod in idle position by returning pulley to idle stop. Move link rod ball joint in oblong hole in injection pump lever until lever touches idle adjusting screw.

5) Readjust link rod by repeating steps **3)** and **4)**. A clearance of .012" (.3 mm) is permitted between pulley and maximum speed stop. Reconnect cold start device.

MEASURING VOLVO ENGINE SPEED

Use a Volvo Monotester and adapter (9950) or a photoelectric tachometer. Always check and adjust engine controls after adjustment.

BOSCH DIESEL FUEL INJECTION — PEUGEOT & VOLVO (Cont.)

VOLVO IDLE SPEED

Run engine to normal operating temperature. Check low idle speed for 750-850 RPM. Adjust outer screw to obtain correct speed. Apply tamperproof seal on screw and lock nut after adjustment.

VOLVO MAXIMUM SPEED

Maximum speed setting should be 5100-5300 RPM. Adjust inner screw to obtain high idle speed. Apply tamperproof seal on screw and lock nut after adjustment.

INJECTION NOZZLES

1) To disassemble injectors, make sure parts are clean and use care not to damage any components. Do not reuse dropped needles. Make sure all injector components are kept with original injector and that parts are not mixed from one injector to another. See *Fig. 13.*

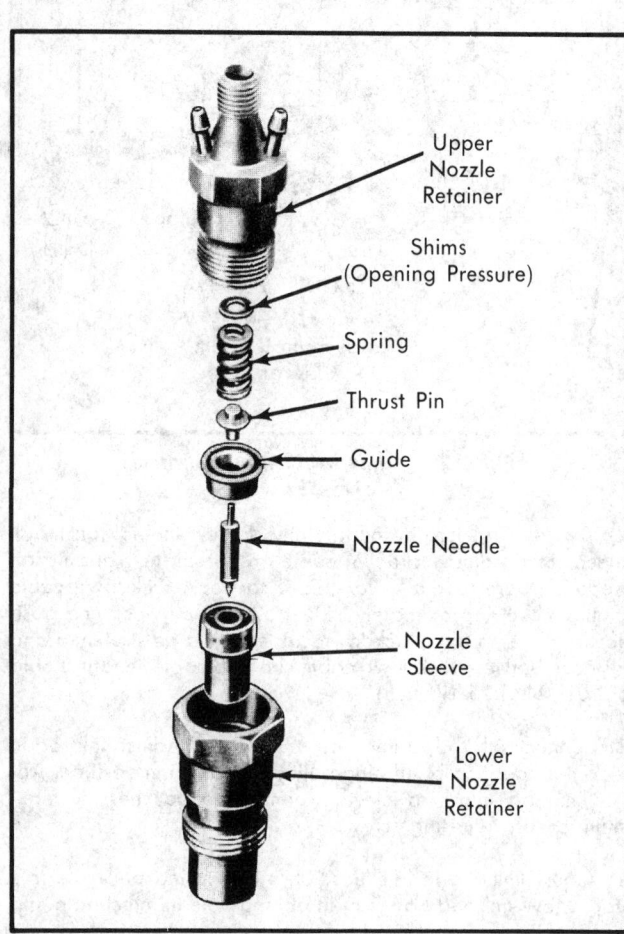

Fig. 13   Disassembling Injection Nozzles

Upper Nozzle Retainer
Shims (Opening Pressure)
Spring
Thrust Pin
Guide
Nozzle Needle
Nozzle Sleeve
Lower Nozzle Retainer

2) Clean all parts in diesel oil. Use nozzle cleaner tool to clean nozzle needle and nozzle sleeve. Replace damaged parts. Nozzle needle and sleeve are matched assemblies and must both be replaced, if one requires replacement.

3) To assemble injectors, clean new parts with gasoline to remove storage grease. Immerse new parts in diesel oil prior to

assembly. Assemble injectors in correct order. Test injectors after reassembly.

TESTING

INJECTION NOZZLES

CAUTION — *Do not expose hands to injector spray during testing, as working pressure will cause fuel oil to penetrate the skin.*

Injection nozzles should be tested for spray pattern, injection sound, opening pressure, and leakage.

Spray Pattern — Install injector in tester. See *Fig. 14.* Seal fuel return lines with rubber plugs and hose clamps. Disengage pressure gauge. Pump lever with short, quick strokes (4-6 per second). Spray jet should be compact and stop abruptly. Injector must not drip.

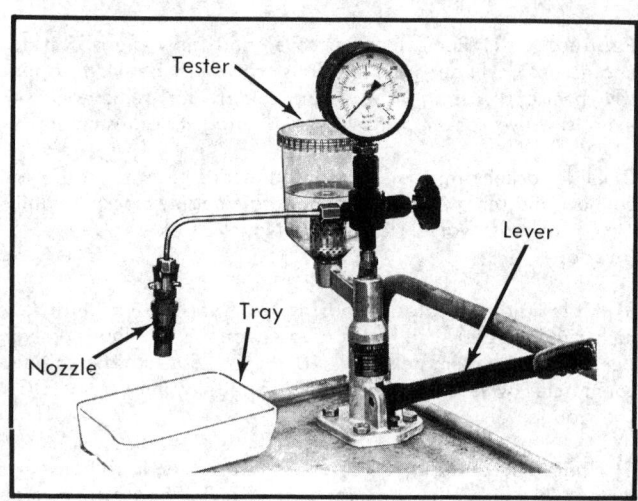

Tester
Lever
Nozzle
Tray

Fig. 14   Testing Injection Nozzles

Injection Sound — With gauge still disengaged, slowly depress tester lever fully (1-2 strokes per second). A good injector will whir during spray (buzzing sound).

Opening Pressure — Engage pressure gauge. Slowly depress lever and read injector opening pressure. Nozzle should open at 1668-1813 psi (117.3-127.5 kg/cm²) for Peugeot and 1706-1849 psi (120-130 kg/cm²) for Volvo. If opening pressure is incorrect perform leak test before adjusting.

Leak Test — With pressure gauge still engaged, wipe injector nozzle. Pump pressure up to 1560 psi (109.7 kg/cm²) and hold for 10 seconds. There must be no fuel drip from nozzle, although a moist nozzle is acceptable.

Adjusting Opening Pressure — To adjust opening pressure change shim thickness. Thicker shims will increase opening pressure; thinner shims will decrease it. Shims are available in thicknesses from .040-.077" (1.00-1.95 mm) in increments of .002" (.05 mm).

NOTE — *A .002" (.05 mm) shim will increase opening pressure by approximately 71 psi (4.992 kg/cm²).*

BOSCH DIESEL FUEL INJECTION — PEUGEOT & VOLVO (Cont.)

VOLVO COLD START DEVICE

NOTE — *The cold start device can only be tested on a test bench together with the injection pump, but a simple check can be made of its operation.*

1) Cold start malfunction usually is indicated by hard starting of a cold engine, failure of engine to start below 14°F (−10°C), or blue-white exhaust smoke. *See Fig. 15.* Check idle speed with engine cold and at normal operating temperature.

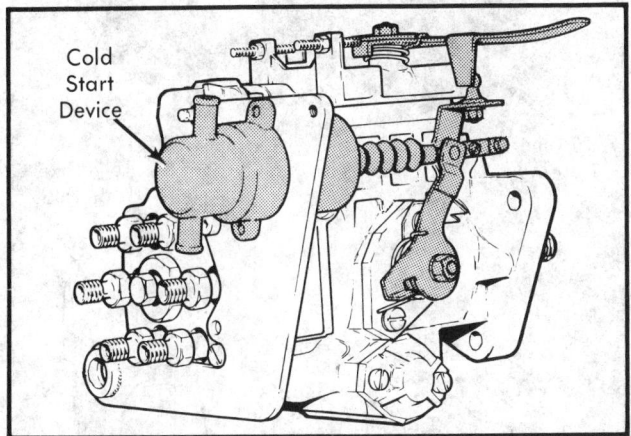

Cold Start Device

Fig. 15 Testing Cold Start Device (Volvo Shown)

2) With cold engine, below 70°F (20°C), engine should idle at approximately 950 RPM. With engine at normal operating temperature, idle speed should be lower, approximately 750-800 RPM. The cold start lever should clear lever on injection pump. If idle speeds do not vary as specified, cold start device is defective.

VOLVO GLOW PLUG SYSTEM

1) Connect 12-volt test lamp across glow plug terminal and ground. *See Fig. 16.* Check test lamp and indicator light on instrument panel. If indicator light and test lamp are both out, control unit is defective. If indicator light is on, but test light is not, glow plug relay is defective. If indicator light is out, but test light is on, check coolant temperature sender or control unit.

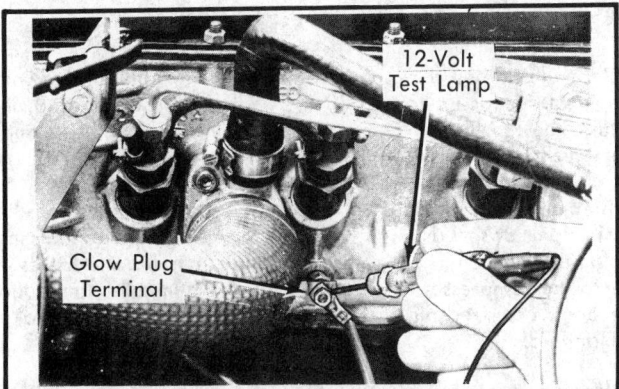

12-Volt Test Lamp

Glow Plug Terminal

Fig. 16 Testing Glow Plugs with Test Lamp

2) If both indicator light and test lamp are on, check length of time light and lamp are on. Indicator light should vary with coolant temperature. Test lamp should stay on 10-25 seconds after indicator light goes out. If too short a time is observed, try a new control unit or temperature sender.

3) Check operation with starter motor operating. Test lamp should light, indicating voltage at glow plugs. If not, check voltage with test lamp at terminal 50 (blue-yellow wire) of control unit. If there is voltage, control unit is defective. If no voltage, check for open circuit between connector and control unit.

4) If test light was on during starter operation, check glow plugs one at a time. Place key switch in position "0". Remove bar between glow plug terminals. Connect test lamp across battery positive terminal and one glow plug. If light is out at one or more glow plugs, glow plugs are faulty. If test lamp and indicator fail to light, replace control unit.

5) If indicator light and test lamp are both out, make progressive voltage checks as indicated:

- Terminal 15 (blue-red wire) of control unit. If no voltage, check for open circuit between fuse box and control unit.
- Terminal 31 (black wire) of control unit (test lamp connected to battery positive terminal and terminal 31). If no voltage, check for faulty ground. If voltage, check for defective control unit.

6) If indicator light is on, but test lamp is out, make the following progressive voltage checks:

- Terminal 86 (red wire) of glow plug relay (test lamp connected to battery positive terminal and terminal 86). Voltage indicates faulty glow plug relay. No voltage indicates incorrect ground connection.
- Terminal G (blue wire) of control unit. No voltage indicates faulty control unit.
- Terminal 30 (blue wire) of blocking relay. No voltage indicates open circuit in wire between control unit and blocking relay.
- Terminal 87 (red wire) of blocking relay. Voltage indicates open circuit in wire between blocking relay and glow plug relay.
- Terminal 86 (blue-red wire) of blocking relay. No voltage indicates open circuit in wire between fuse box and blocking relay.
- Terminal 85 (red wire) of blocking relay (connect test lamp between fuse box positive and terminal 85). No voltage indicates faulty blocking relay. Voltage indicates open circuit in wire between blocking relay and instrument panel or defect in instrument panel printed circuit.

7) If indicator light is out, but test lamp is on, this usually indicates a failure of either the temperature sender or control unit. Disconnect wire at temperature sender. Indicator light should now be on. If so, this indicates circuit from sender to indicator light is OK, but sender is defective.

8) Check ground connection at terminal K (yellow wire) of control unit. Connect test lamp from battery positive terminal to terminal K. If voltage is indicated, indicator light on instrument panel is defective, there is a defective wire between control unit and indicator light or printed circuit is faulty. If no voltage exists, either the control unit is defective or wire between temperature sender and control unit is grounded.

9) If indicator light comes on when engine is warm, disconnect wire at temperature sender and ground it. Turn key switch to driving position "2" and check indicator light. If light is on, there is an open circuit in wire between temperature sender and control unit or control unit is defective. If indicator light is out, temperature sender is faulty.

AUDI TURBOCHARGING SYSTEM

**Audi
5000 Turbo**

DESCRIPTION

The Audi 5000 Turbo uses a Kuhnle, Kopp, Kausch turbocharger with a small diameter turbine and impeller. It is bolted directly to the front of the exhaust manifold to make best use of exhaust energy. A wastegate, a valve preventing excessive boost pressure, is attached to the back of the manifold. *See Fig. 1.*

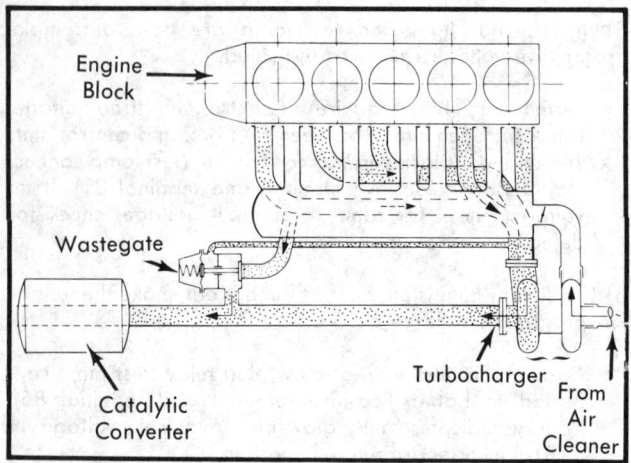

Fig. 1   Components of Audi Turbocharger System

Other components of the turbocharging system include an additional safety switch that prevents excessive boost pressure in the event of wastegate failure; an oil cooler mounted behind the right side of the front spoiler that stabilizes oil temperatures during hard driving an an injector cooling fan.

The Audi 5000 engine has been modified to match the additional power output, as have other vehicle components including the automatic transmission, chassis, tires, front and rear suspension and brakes.

Among the engine changes are the following: The cylinder block has a fitting for the turbo oil return line, a modified oil filter flange to accommodate the oil cooler thermostat, and a piston cooling system. Pistons are cooled by jets which spray engine oil on the inside of the piston anytime oil pressure reaches 36 psi (2.53 kg/cm²). Pistons have a deep-dished recess in their tops to reduce compression ratio to 7.0:1. The piston skirt is notched on one side to clear the piston cooler spray jets, and larger piston pins are used. Exhaust valves are sodium filled to withstand higher exhaust temperatures.

OPERATION

At idle and light throttle, the Turbo engine operates like any other engine. When more power is required, the usually wasted exhaust gases from the exhaust manifold enter the turbocharger's turbine housing and flow through the turbine blades. *See Fig. 2.*

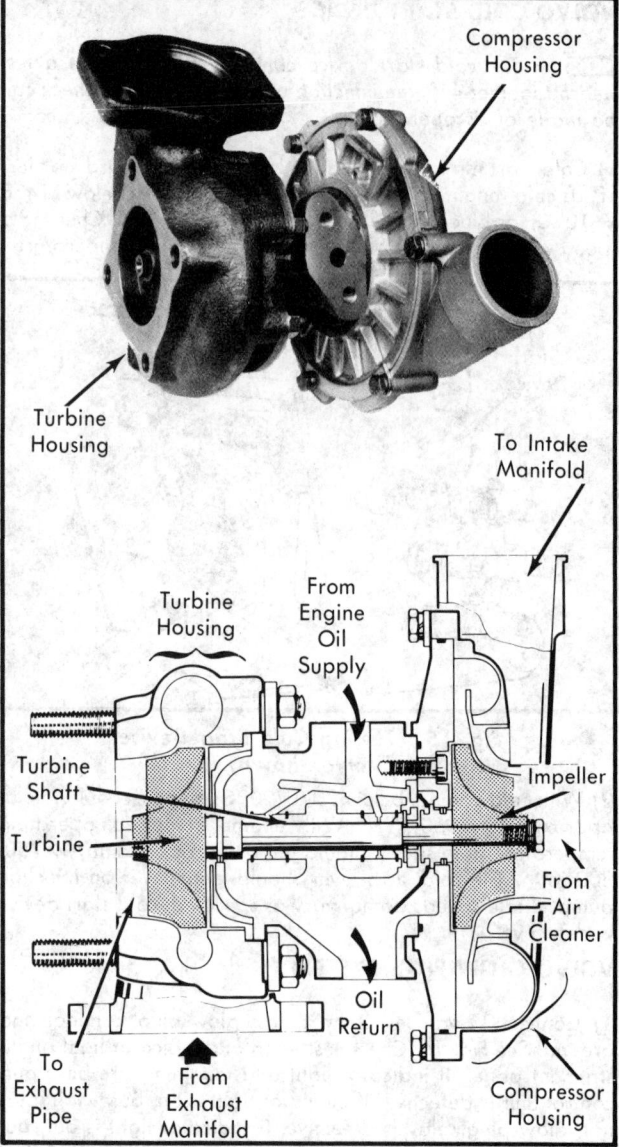

Fig. 2   Cutaway View of Turbocharger

Depending upon the amount of exhaust flow, the turbine will spin at speeds up to 90,000 RPM. The exhaust flow and, in turn, the turbine RPM increases as the throttle is opened and engine speed increases.

The impeller is mounted on the turbine shaft and therefore, it also spins at speeds up to 90,000 RPM. As the impeller turns inside the turbocharger compressor, it draws in air and forces it into the compressor housing. The faster the impeller turns, the more pressurized air (boost pressure) is forced into the intake manifold.

If boost pressures produced in the turbocharger were allowed to go too high, serious engine damage could result. The wastegate, mounted at the rear of the exhaust manifold prevents this from occurring.

When boost pressure created by the turbocharger exceeds a predetermined limit, a valve inside the wastegate begins to

AUDI TURBOCHARGING SYSTEM (Cont.)

open. *See Fig.* 3. This permits some of the exhaust gases to bypass the turbocharger and flow directly from the exhaust manifold to the exhaust system through the wastegate.

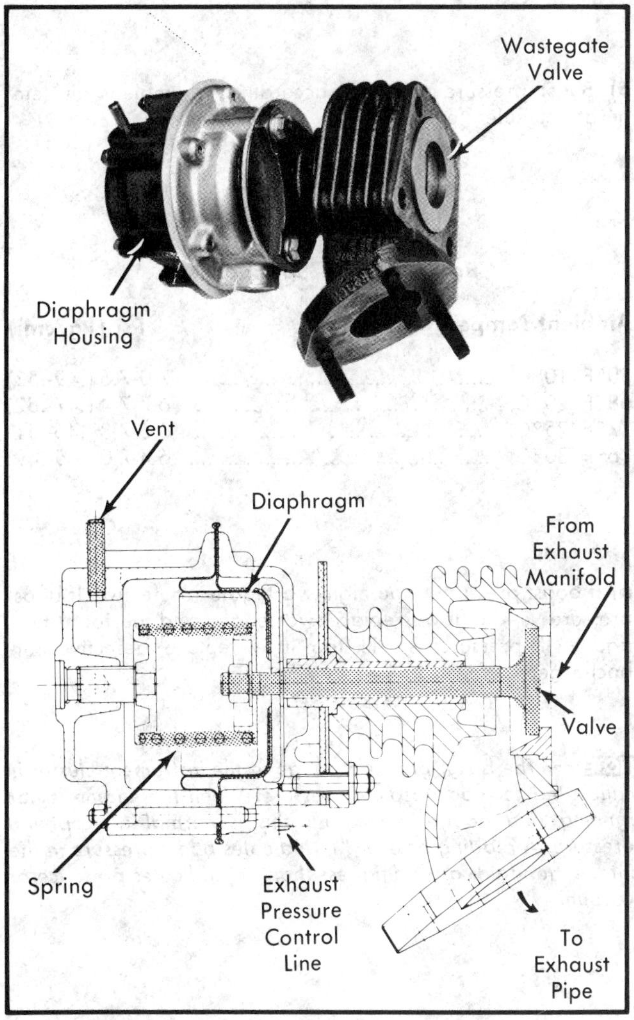

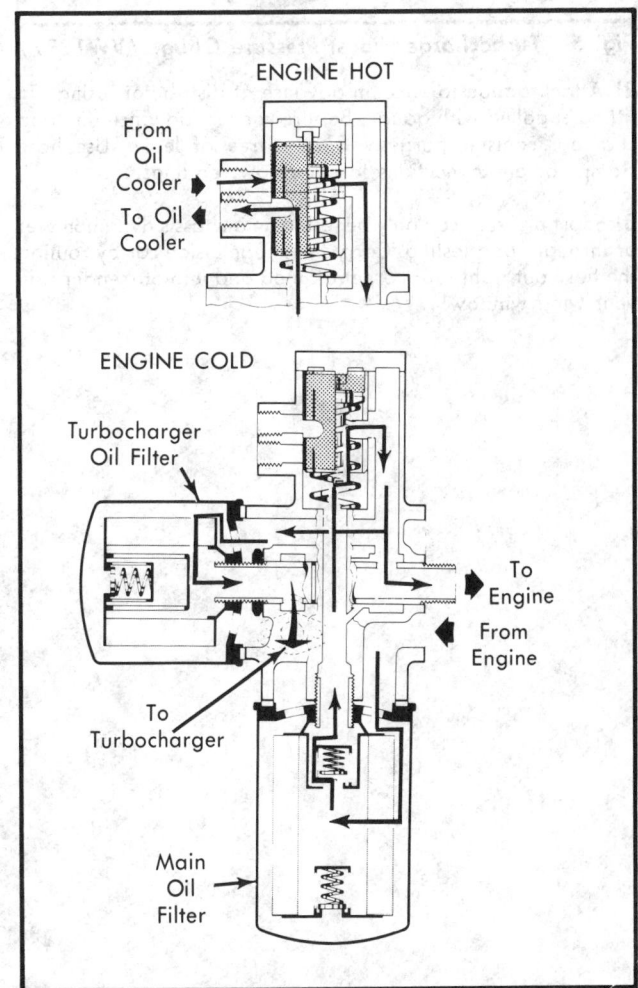

Fig. 3   Cutaway View of Wastegate

The wastegate consists of a valve, attached to a diaphragm. The valve is normally held closed by a spring. A small diameter control line connects the chamber below the diaphragm with the exhaust manifold. When exhaust pressure in this chamber exceeds the tension of the spring, the valve opens.

When the valve in the wastegate is closed, all of the exhaust gases power the turbocharger; when it is open, bypassing the gases limits boost pressure produced in the turbocharger.

Should the wastegate fail, a boost pressure safety switch mounted on a hose leading to the intake manifold, opens and shuts off the fuel pump. The switch is energized whenever boost pressure exceeds 11.6 psi (.82 kg/cm²).

The fuel pump relay is grounded through the safety switch. When boost pressure exceeds the specified limit, the switch opens removing the ground and opening the pump relay.

To prevent vapor lock, a thermo-switch controls an electric blower fan which cools injectors at the cylinder head. The fan

comes on (with or without ignition being on) whenever manifold temperatures reach 212°F (100°C).

LUBRICATION

The turbine shaft runs in plain bearings, which must be pressure lubricated. Finely filtered oil from the engine lubrication system enters the top of the turbocharger and is distributed to the bearings. The oil returns to the engine oil pan through a large line attached to the bottom of the turbocharger.

An oil filter and thermostat assembly is attached to the engine block. *See Fig.* 4. Oil from the oil pump flows through the main oil filter and to the thermostat housing. When the engine is cold, the oil bypasses the oil cooler and flows directly to the engine and the turbocharger oil filter. When the engine is hot, a thermostat opens the control piston. Oil from the main filter then flows through the oil cooler before going to the engine and turbocharger oil filter. The oil cooler is located behind the right side of the front spoiler.

Fig. 4   Cutaway View of Oil Filter Assemblies

AUDI TURBOCHARGING SYSTEM (Cont.)

TESTING

1) To test the turbocharging system, use a pressure gauge (VW1397) calibrated in both psi and bar. The gauge is equipped with a valve which locks pressure measurement when closed. See *Fig. 5.*

Fig. 5   Turbocharger Boost Pressure Gauge (VW1397)

2) Attach gauge to vacuum advance at distributor, using "T" fitting supplied with gauge. Be sure vacuum advance unit and charcoal canister purge valve are free of leaks. Use hose clamps at all connections to avoid low readings.

3) Boost pressure can only be tested on a chassis dynamometer or through road testing. Carry the gauge inside car by routing the hose out right rear corner of hood and into passenger side vent wing window.

4) Accelerate engine to full throttle in drive position "2". Hold vehicle speed constant with foot brake, when engine speed reaches 4000 RPM. Wait 2 seconds and close gauge valve by pulling sleeve away from dial.

5) Boost pressure will vary according to ambient air temperature. Refer to table.

Boost Pressure Specifications

Ambient Temperature	Psi (kg/cm²)
50°F (10°C)	7.0-7.6 (.49-.53)
68°F (20°C)	6.7-7.4 (.47-.52)
77°F (25°C)	6.6-7.3 (.46-.51)
86°F (30°C)	6.4-7.0 (.45-.49)

6) If boost pressure is too high, wastegate is defective. If boost pressure is too low, replace wastegate and perform tests again. If pressure is still too low, replace defective turbocharger.

NOTE — *The boost pressure gauge in the instrument cluster is calibrated to read absolute pressure. When the engine is not running and gauge reads "1", this is normal atmospheric pressure. A reading of over "1" indicates boost pressure in the intake manifold; a reading less than "1" indicates presence of vacuum.*

MERCEDES-BENZ DIESEL TURBOCHARGING SYSTEM

**Mercedes-Benz
300 SD**

DESCRIPTION

The Diesel turbocharged engine (617.950) is basically the same design as the naturally aspirated engine (617.912). See *Fig. 1*. Installation of the Garret turbocharger produced an increase to 110 SAE net brake horsepower at 4200 RPM.

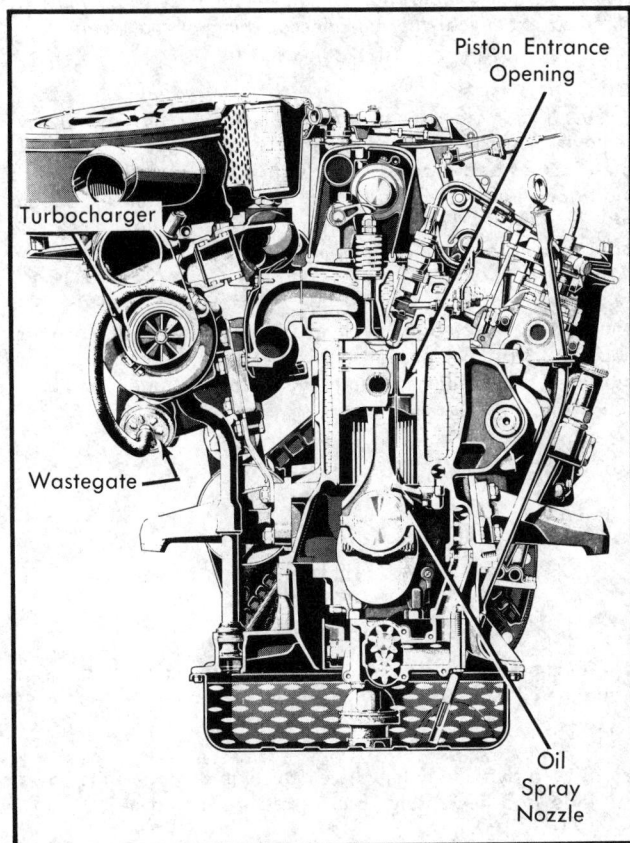

Fig. 1   Cutaway View of Mercedes 300 SD
Turbocharged Engine

This increased power output required modifications of engine and vehicle components, including redesign of the crankcase, pistons, valve train, lubrication system, cooling system and fuel injection system.

The turbocharger delivers pre-compressed air to the engine, providing a higher air charge in the cylinders and creating higher pressures and temperatures in the combustion chambers.

The system includes a turbocharger which consists of a turbine, compressor and a wastegate that prevents excessive boost pressures from damaging the engine. See *Fig. 2*.

The turbocharger's turbine wheel and compressor wheel are mounted on a common shaft and turn at the same speed. The turbocharger is mounted between the exhaust manifold and the exhaust pipe and is connected directly to the engine for lubrication and cooling. The wastegate is attached to the turbine housing. Should its boost pressure control valve malfunction, an engine overload protection system will prevent engine damage.

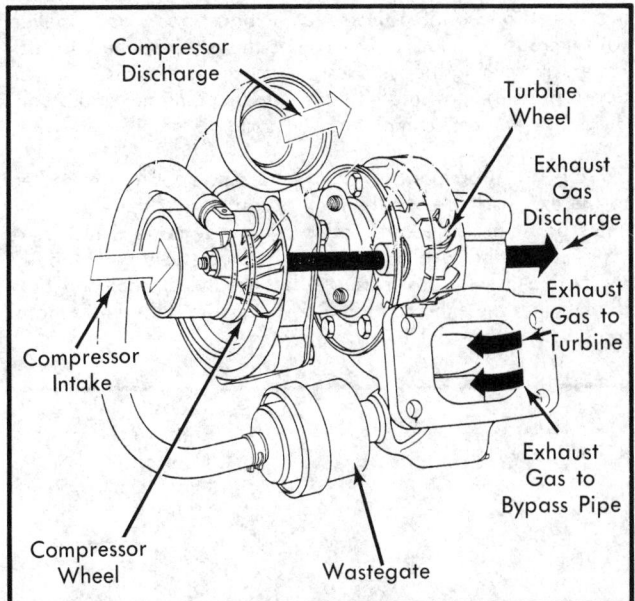

*Fig. 2   Cutaway View of Garret Turbocharger
Used in Mercedes 300 SD*

OPERATION

Exhaust gases leaving the cylinders flow through the exhaust manifold directly into the turbocharger's turbine housing. The force of the gases turns the turbine wheel, which in turn spins the compressor wheel at the same speed. Turbine and compressor wheel speeds can reach up to 100,000 RPM. *See Figs. 2 and 3.*

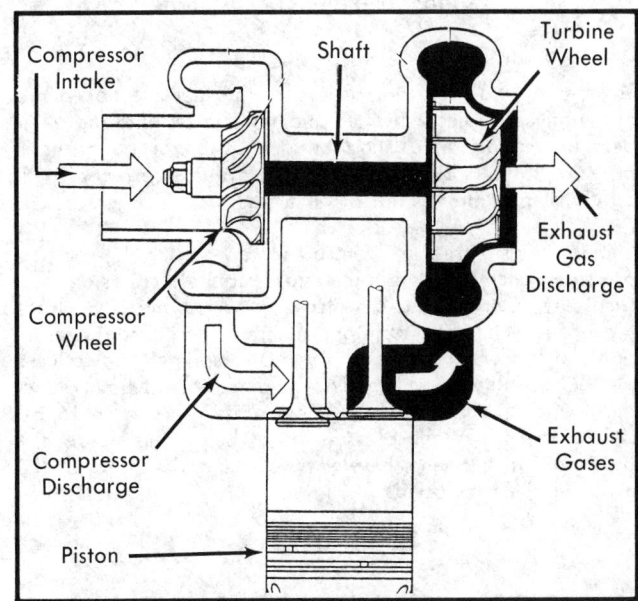

Fig. 3   Airflow Pattern with Garret Turbocharger

The fresh air drawn in by the compressor wheel is compressed and delivered to the combustion chamber above the pistons. At idle speed, the engine operates like any other. However, with

MERCEDES-BENZ DIESEL TURBOCHARGING SYSTEM (Cont.)

increasing load and engine speed, exhaust gases are expelled with increasing velocity. This causes the turbine wheel to turn faster, increasing boost pressure at the compressor wheel. Boost pressure is routed to the intake manifold and to individual cylinders, completing the cycle.

Exhaust gases passing through the turbine housing are routed to the exhaust pipe. As the cycle is continuous, the wastegate limits boost pressure, preventing engine damage. See Fig. 4. Installed on the turbine housing, the wastegate valve opens, permitting the exhaust gases to bypass the turbine and flow directly into the exhaust pipe. Boost pressure is therefore maintained at a constant level.

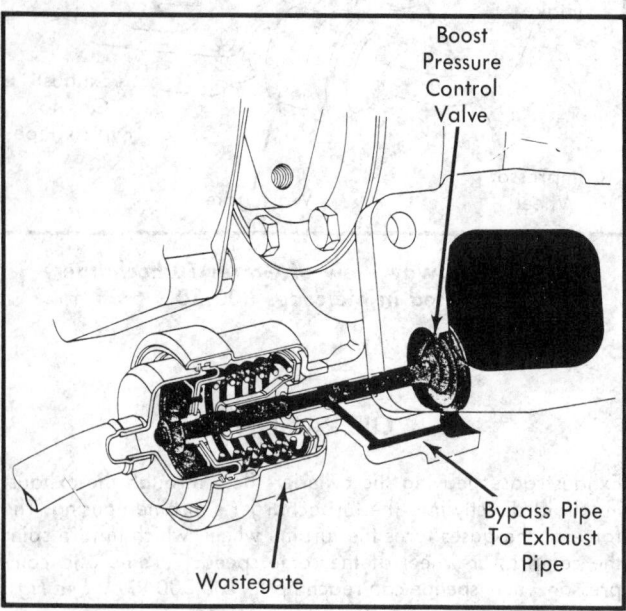

Boost Pressure Control Valve

Bypass Pipe To Exhaust Pipe

Wastegate

Fig. 4   Cutaway View of Wastegate Valve

The aneroid compensator on top of the fuel injection pump automatically adjusts the fuel quantity injected into the cylinders depending on existing boost pressure or atmospheric pressure in the intake manifold. Therefore, the correct air-fuel relationship is maintained at all times.

Should boost pressure control valve (wastegate) fail, a pressure switch installed in the intake manifold closes an electrical circuit, energizing a switch-over valve. This valve closes the pressure line to the intake manifold and simultaneously opens the aneroid compensator to atmosphere. This reduces the fuel quantity being injected. The pressure switch only functions when intake manifold boost pressure reaches 16 psi (1.125 kg/cm²). When pressure drops below this figure, the pressure switch opens the electric circuit and venting of the pressure line is stopped.

LUBRICATION

The exhaust gas turbocharger and piston cooling systems increased the total capacity of the lubrication system to 9.0 quarts (7.9 quarts for an oil and filter change).

Oil is supplied to the turbocharger for lubrication and cooling from the rear cover of the oil filter. The oil return line runs from the turbocharger back to the upper oil pan housing. Oil spray

nozzles for cooling the pistons are connected internally to the engine lubrication system's main oil gallery. See Fig. 1. Check valves in the oil spray nozzles open at engine oil pressure of 21.8 psi (1.53 kg/cm²). An oil stream is sprayed directly into the piston entrance openings for the ring passages and travels around the piston crown and returns to the oil pan. The spray nozzles close at 14.5 psi (1 kg/cm²) oil pressure.

NOTE — *The direction of oil nozzle spray should be checked during assembly operations on the engine, as spray must be directed exactly at the entrance opening of the piston.*

CAUTION — *When removing and installing pistons, always remove oil spray nozzles first. They should be reinstalled only after pistons and connecting rods have been installed. Nozzles must not be interchanged from cylinder to cylinder and should be carefully checked for damage before installation. Nozzle bores should only be cleaned with air pressure applied in the direction of oil travel.*

The engine is equipped with an oil cooler with a .75 quart capacity. Oil flow through the cooler is controlled by a thermostat in the oil filter housing. The thermostat opens at 203°F (95°C).

TESTING

1) To check turbocharger boost pressure, connect pressure gauge (617 589 02 21 00) to intake manifold after removing plug.

2) Using a dynamometer, drive vehicle in driving range "S" at full load and 4000 RPM. Boost pressure should be 10.1-11.6 psi (.71-.82 kg/cm²).

3) If boost pressure is too low, check air filter and air intake shroud duct for obstructions. Check turbocharger for leaks between manifold and turbine housing, compressor housing discharge and intake manifold, and between intake or exhaust manifold and cylinder head.

4) Check pressure line between intake manifold and aneroid compensator and overload switch-over valve. To check valve, turn ignition switch to position "2". Disconnect plug on valve and check for battery voltage at black/red wire. If not present, check fuse number 4 or wiring. Check for ground condition of brown/black wire. There should be no ground connection below boost pressure of 16 psi (1.13 kg/cm²). If ground exists, check pressure switch in intake manifold or its wiring.

5) Other possible causes of low boost pressure would be a defective wastegate, requiring turbocharger replacement, or problems with the fuel injection pump, requiring removal, testing, and repair.

6) If boost pressure control valve (wastegate) does not open, causing boost pressure at full load operation to exceed 16 psi (1.13 kg/cm²), check hose between compressor housing and wastegate. If hose is leaking or is kinked, replace the hose. If not, replace turbocharger.

MERCEDES-BENZ DIESEL TURBOCHARGING SYSTEM (Cont.)

NOTE — *When dynamometer test is complete, road test vehicle with tester inside the vehicle. Drive vehicle in driving range "L" or "S" at 4000 RPM. Fully depress accelerator pedal and hold engine speed at 4000 RPM with brakes (short test duration only). Boost pressure should be 10.1-11.6 psi (.71-.82 kg/cm²). If not, repeat steps* **3)** *through* **6)**.

REMOVAL & INSTALLATION

Removal — **1)** Remove air filter and disconnect electrical cable from coolant temperature switch.

2) Loosen hose clamp at air intake duct. Remove vacuum line, crankcase breather pipe, air filter housing and air intake duct. Disconnect engine oil supply line to turbocharger. Remove air filter mounting bracket and disconnect exhaust flange.

3) Disconnect and remove exhaust bracket on automatic transmission. Press exhaust pipe to the rear. Remove mounting bracket for intermediate flange and four mounting nuts on the turbocharger.

4) Lift off turbocharger and remove intermediate flange and disconnect oil return pipe at turbocharger.

Installation — **1)** Install all parts in reverse order of removal. Before mounting the turbocharger, install intermediate flange and oil return pipe. Install flange gasket between turbocharger and exhaust manifold with reinforcing bead towards the exhaust manifold.

2) Use only heatproof nuts and bolts when installing turbocharger. Fill center turbocharger housing with approximately ¼ pint of engine oil through the engine oil supply bore, before operating turbocharger. Be sure "O" rings are mounted correctly when installing air intake duct.

PORSCHE TURBOCHARGING SYSTEM

**Porsche
924 Turbo**

DESCRIPTION

The turbocharger used on the 924 Turbo is mounted on the right side of the engine under the exhaust manifold. Components include the turbine, compressor wheel, rotor shaft, bearings and housings. *See Fig. 1.* A wastegate, located near the right side of the bell housing prevents excessive boost pressure. Should it fail, a boost pressure safety switch turns off the fuel pumps.

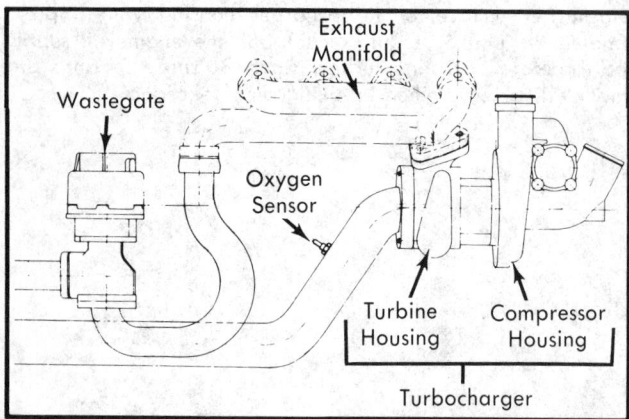

Fig. 1   Porsche Turbocharging System

OPERATION

The turbocharger is driven by exhaust gases being expelled from the cylinder combustion chambers. At idle speeds there is no pressurization of incoming air, and the engine operates like a normally aspirated engine.

At partial load, the throttle valve is open and more fuel-air mixture is drawn into the combustion chamber. Speed and volume of exhaust gases increase, in turn. The increasing volume of exhaust gases causes the turbocharger turbine to turn with greater speed. *See Fig. 2.* The compressor, mounted on the same shaft turns at the same speed as the turbine, producing boost pressure for incoming air. Opening the throttle valve reduces manifold vacuum, closing the pop-off valve located in the compressor housing between the inlet and outlet.

At full load, a large volume of exhaust gases are fed to the turbine, increasing speed of both the turbine and compressor wheels. Boost pressure will then reach the maximum. When it increases to 7.5 psi (.52 kg/cm²), the wastegate (boost pressure control valve) opens. Part of the exhaust gases are now routed directly into the main exhaust pipe, bypassing the turbine wheel. The turbocharger speed and boost pressure remain almost constant at 7.5 psi (.52 kg/cm²).

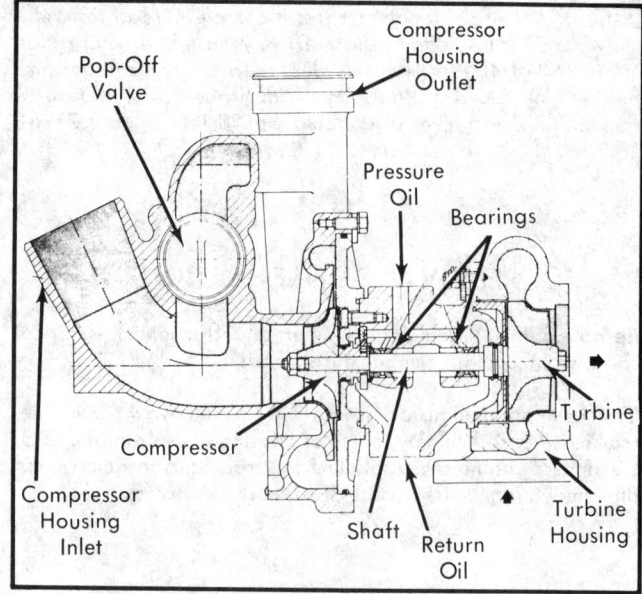

Fig. 2   Cutaway of Porsche Turbocharger

Should the wastegate fail to function properly, an electric boost pressure safety switch located in the compressor discharge pressure duct turns off the electric fuel pumps. Fuel shut-off occurs as boost pressure reaches 16-20 psi (1.1-1.4 kg/cm²). This prevents engine damage from excessive pressures.

During deceleration, the throttle valve is closed. The turbocharger now operates against a closed throttle valve, which could damage the turbocharger. To prevent this from occurring, the pop-off valve located between the pressure and intake duct opens due to intake manifold vacuum. This sets up a bypass circuit between pressure and intake ducts. Since the wastegate valve is shut, all exhaust gases are routed to the turbocharger turbine upon acceleration.

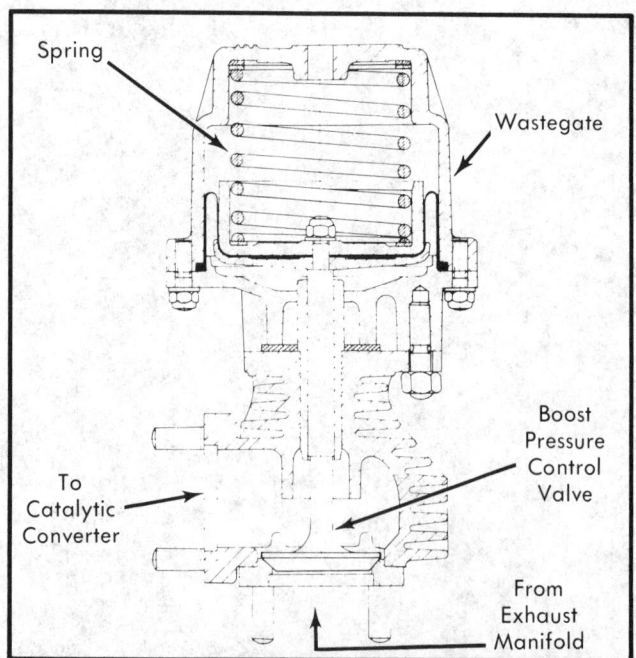

Fig. 3   Cutaway View of Porsche Wastegate

PORSCHE TURBOCHARGING SYSTEM (Cont.)

LUBRICATION

The oil filter houses a thermostat which opens at 189°F (87°C). This channels the oil either to the oil cooler or directly to the turbocharger, depending upon oil temperature. Return oil from the turbocharger flows back to the oil pan by gravity.

The oil cooler is located directly behind the air ducts in the front spoiler.

REMOVAL & INSTALLATION

TURBOCHARGER ASSEMBLY

Removal — 1) Remove engine guard and rubber cap from oxygen sensor and plug. Remove starter and disconnect and remove bypass line between exhaust manifold and wastegate.

2) Remove nuts between turbine housing and exhaust pipe. Remove bolts from flange between front and rear mufflers. Loosen muffler suspension bracket and remove rear muffler. Loosen heat shields over bypass line and loosen pipe clamp.

3) Disconnect control line at wastegate and remove entire exhaust line with wastegate. Be careful not to damage oxygen sensor.

NOTE — *Some vehicles will have a vent line for the wastegate. This can only be removed after lowering exhaust line.*

4) Disconnect oil lines leading to engine oil cooler and oil feed line for turbocharger. Plug oil lines at oil filter flange. Disconnect and remove oil filter flange, catching the escaping oil. Loosen oil clamps and pull out oil lines from the front.

5) Remove pressure duct and take off air cleaner upper and lower sections. Remove mounting nuts from bottom of fuel distributor. Loosen hose clamps on dust cover and move fuel distributor to one side.

6) Unscrew mounting bolt on pressure duct and take off pressure duct. Remove nuts holding exhaust manifold and turbocharger. Unscrew Allen head nuts. Loosen hose clamp. Disconnect both sides of stabilizer. Disconnect steering gear from control arm.

7) Disconnect turbocharger base and remove turbocharger with console toward front. Pull off hose from wastegate connection.

Installation — 1) Install components in reverse order of removal. Loosen Allen head bolts of the base before attempting to install turbocharger on engine. While positioning turbocharger against engine, push hose on turbocharger. Tighten mounting nuts of exhaust manifold and turbocharger and then the base.

2) Always use new seals on oil lines. Make sure that round seal fits properly on pressure duct. Install both pressure ducts before tightening bolt. Tighten steering gear bolts to 14-17 ft. lbs. (1.94-2.35 mkg).

3) Before starting engine for first time, prime turbocharger with lubricating oil for 15 seconds by pulling plugs off manifold pressure limiting switch and operating starter.

SAAB TURBOCHARGING SYSTEM

**Saab
900 Turbo**

DESCRIPTION

Saab uses the Garret turbocharger, with turbine and compressor impellers (wheels). *See Fig. 1.* Exhaust gases drive the turbine, which turns the compressor forwarding air under pressure to the throttle valve.

Excessive pressures are prevented by a charge pressure regulator (boost pressure control valve or wastegate). A back-up safety device, a pressure switch, prevents engine damage in case there is failure of the charge pressure regulator.

The Saab Turbo is designed to operate at low engine speeds to provide increased torque at typical vehicle driving speeds. The turbine shaft, which is delicately balanced, is mounted in a floating, sliding-contact bearing having a high oil flow. The shaft actually floats on oil during operation.

Lubrication is supplied by the engine lubrication system. The shaft is sealed against bearing housings with sealing rings installed in shaft grooves.

OPERATION

As engine operation begins, exhaust gases flow through the turbocharger's turbine impeller, causing it to rotate. Gases are expelled through the turbine to the exhaust pipe. As the turbine spins, its shaft turns the compressor impeller, compressing the intake air.

At idle speeds, the air compression has little effect upon its operation. However, as engine speed is increased (partial load), the pressurized air enters the system faster, and exhaust gases are expelled faster. The more exhaust gases passing over the turbine impeller, the faster it turns, and the more pressurized air is delivered to the engine.

At full load, the throttle valve is fully open and charge pressure increases. At 6.4-7.8 psi (.45-.55 kg/cm^2), the valve in the charge pressure regulator opens permitting exhaust gases to flow directly to the exhaust pipe, bypassing the turbine impeller.

In the event the valve sticks and does not open, charge pressure increases to 8.6-11.4 psi (.6-.8 kg/cm^2). This causes a pressure switch to break current flow to the fuel pump, thereby preventing engine damage.

The charge pressure regulator is located on the exhaust side of the engine and its valve is held closed by a spring-loaded diaphragm.

CAUTION — *Never increase the preset charge pressure regulator limit.*

TESTING

CHARGE PRESSURE REGULATOR

1) Connect a pressure gauge (83 92 813) between nipple on inlet manifold and line to pressure switch. Run hose into passenger compartment and place gauge on left hand corner of instrument panel.

2) Warm up engine, and drive vehicle in 3rd gear at an engine speed lower than 1500 RPM. Then accelerate at full throttle by pressing pedal to the floor. As engine speed approaches 3000 RPM, apply brakes while still keeping accelerator pedal pressed down.

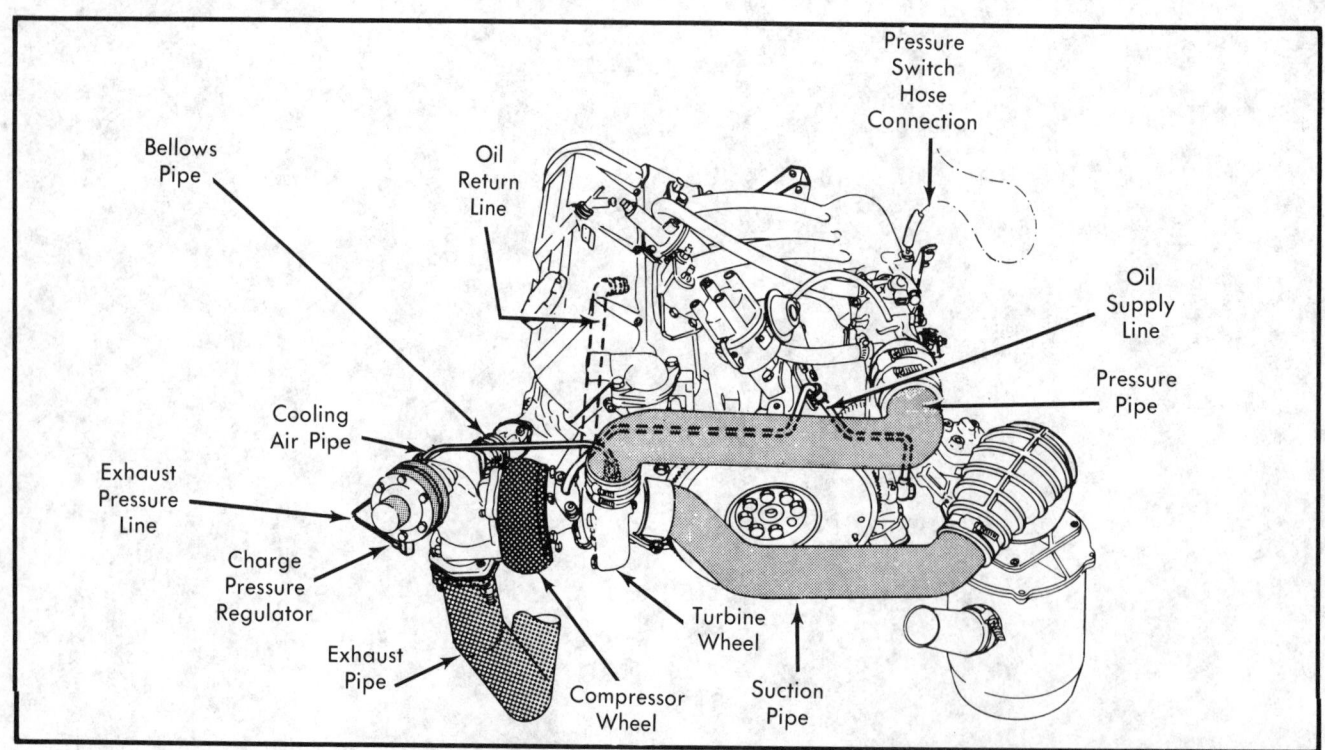

Fig. 1   Components of Saab Turbocharging System

SAAB TURBOCHARGING SYSTEM (Cont.)

3) Note maximum pressure indicated with vehicle under full load at 3000 RPM. Charge pressure should be 6.4-7.8 psi (.45-.55 kg/cm²).

4) To adjust charge pressure, disconnect exhaust line from the charge pressure regulator and remove its diaphragm housing cover. See Fig. 2. Loosen the lock nut, using a 10 mm spanner wrench. Grip the spring seat with adjustable pliers.

Fig. 2   Adjusting Charge Pressure Regulator

5) Adjust spring tension by rotating spring seat clockwise or counterclockwise according to table. Be sure valve does not turn. Tighten lock nut after adjustment. Replace diaphragm cover and gasket and install exhaust line. Seal the charge pressure regulator.

Charge Pressure Adjustment

Gauge Reading While Driving — Psi (kg/cm²)	Spring Seat Turns
9.57 (.67)	1 out
8.99 (.63)	¾ out
8.41 (.59)	½ out
7.83 (.55)	¼ out
7.25 (.51)	Correct setting ①
6.67 (.47)	¼ in
6.09 (.43)	½ in
5.51 (.39)	¾ in
4.93 (.35)	1 in

① — If reading is 6.4-7.8 psi (.45-.55 kg/cm²), no adjustment is necessary.

PRESSURE SWITCH

1) Start the engine and run it at idle. Disconnect hose from pressure switch at inlet manifold. Connect pressure gauge and suitable pump (cooling system tester) to pressure switch hose.

2) Increase pressure with pump and check pressure at which engine cuts out. Reading should be 8.6-11.4 psi (.6-.8 kg/cm²). If not, replace pressure switch.

TURBO PRESSURE GAUGE

To check the pressure gauge on the instrument panel, use the same procedure as for the pressure switch. At maximum charge pressure, the needle should be within the wide orange range. At pressure switch actuating pressure, the needle should be in front of the limit between the orange and red zones. If not, replace gauge.

NOTE — Late model 1980 Saabs have the pressure switch located inside the vehicle, under the instrument panel.

REMOVAL & INSTALLATION

TURBOCHARGER

Removal — 1) Remove charge pressure regulator and blank off exhaust pipe. Disconnect hose between compressor and throttle housing.

2) Disconnect oil supply and return lines at turbocharger. Remove bolts securing turbocharger to exhaust manifold and remove turbocharger. Plug all holes in turbocharger.

Installation — 1) Attach turbocharger unit to exhaust manifold, using a new gasket between mating flanges. Fill lubricating inlet of turbocharger with engine oil and connect oil return line at turbocharger, using new gasket.

2) Connect the oil supply line, using new gasket and new seals. Attach the hose between the compressor and throttle housing and the hose between the air flow meter and compressor.

3) Attach the charge pressure regulator, using new gaskets and locking plates. Turn engine on starter for about 30 seconds with terminal 15 on ignition coil disconnected. This fills the turbocharger's lubrication system before engine runs.

CHARGE PRESSURE REGULATOR

Removal — 1) Disconnect exhaust and cooling air lines from charge pressure regulator. Remove bolts from exhaust manifold flange. Save the taper seal ring and plug the exhaust pipe.

2) Remove bolts from bellows pipe and from the turbocharger. Lift off charge pressure regulator.

Installation — 1) Attach charge pressure regulator to turbocharger, using a new gasket. Attach bellows pipe, locking bolts in place with locking plate. Remove plug from exhaust pipe and connect the pipe with taper seal ring to the charge pressure regulator housing.

2) Connect exhaust and cooling air lines. Use "Never Seize" or Molycote 1000 or equivalent on exhaust pressure line. Test drive vehicle and check charge pressure. Adjust as necessary. Seal charge pressure regulator and attach heat shield.

BOSCH ELECTRIC FUEL PUMPS

Audi
BMW
Fiat
  Gasoline Injected Models
Jaguar
  XJ6
Mercedes Benz
  Gasoline Injected Models

Peugeot
Porsche
Saab
Triumph
  TR7 & TR8
Volkswagen
  Gasoline Injected Models
Volvo

DESCRIPTION

Bosch electric fuel pumps are positive displacement roller cell type, operated on 12 volts. Operating pressure is determined by one or more external fuel regulators in engine compartment. Pumps include an internal fuel pressure relief valve and an external, replaceable discharge check valve to prevent fuel from returning to tank when pump is off. Some pumps may also incorporate a damper chamber on discharge outlet to prevent pulsations in fuel lines.

OPERATION

Pumps are activated by relays when ignition switch is in "START" or "RUN" position, and are protected from circuit overload by fuses and/or fuseable links. Fuel is circulated through pump rotor and brushes to discharge outlet. Pumps are a non-servicable component and should be replaced if not operating properly. *Refer to appropriate Fuel Injection article in FUEL SYSTEMS Section for testing and diagnostic procedures.*

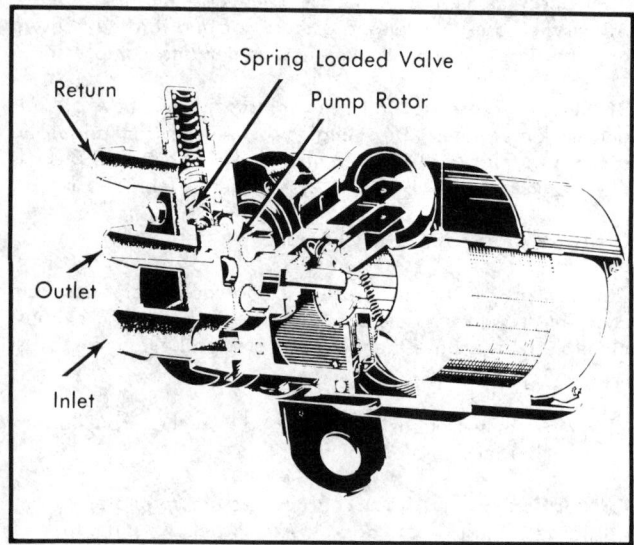

Fig. 1   Return Line Type Fuel Pump

TESTING

NOTE — *Refer to appropriate Fuel Injection article in FUEL SYSTEMS Section for Testing and Diagnostic procedures.*

REMOVAL & INSTALLATION

FUEL PUMP

CAUTION — *Do not allow smoking, open flame or sparks in area while servicing fuel system components. Disconnect bat-*

tery ground terminal prior to removing pump. Danger of fire or explosion exists.

Removal — 1) Fuel pressure must be relieved prior to any component removal. Carefully remove and plug fuel lines to prevent spillage. Disconnect electrical connections.

NOTE — *Depending on make and model, it may be necessary to jack car up or remove carpeting and panels in order to gain access to fuel pump.*

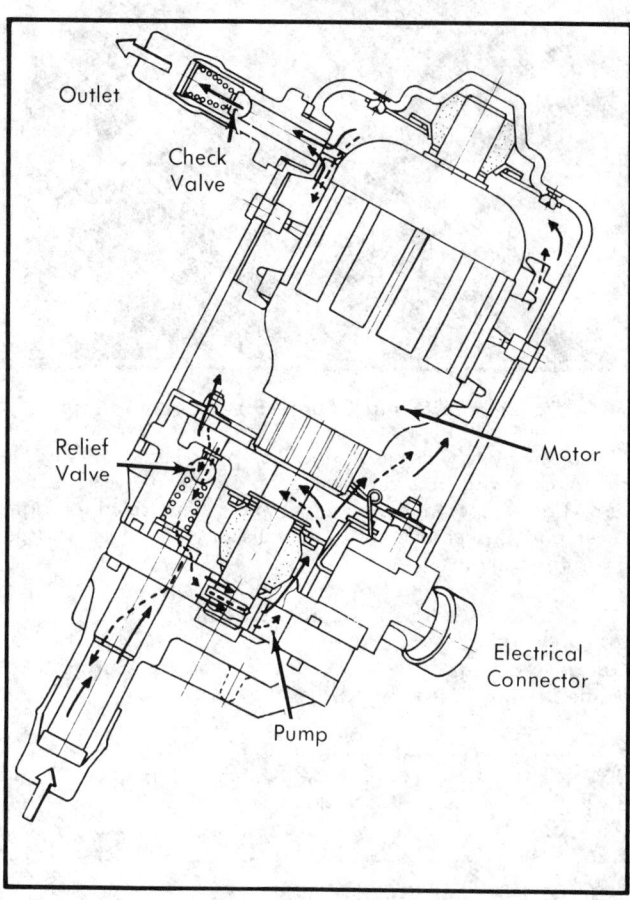

**Fig. 2   Non-Return Type Fuel Pump
(Datsun Shown)**

2) Remove mounting bolts and retain rubber insulating grommets for reinstallation. Tip pump as required to clear chassis and remove from car.

Installation — Reverse removal procedure while noting the following:

1) Be sure rubber grommets and insulation are installed correctly or noise and vibration will result.

2) Hook all fuel lines and return lines to proper fittings and be sure they are tight to avoid air and/or fuel leaks.

3) Route fuel lines so they will not vibrate or rub against other body parts.

4) Test system for leaks with engine running.

COURIER & MAZDA ELECTRIC FUEL PUMPS

Courier
  Pickup
Mazda
  626
  RX7
  B2000 Pickup

DESCRIPTION

Pulsating electric powered fuel pump is mounted near fuel tank on frame member.

OPERATION & TESTING

NOTE — *In line fuel filter must be changed within recommended mileage interval before performing tests. If in doubt, install new filter.*

Electrical power is supplied when ignition switch is in "RUN" position. This circuit is protected by a 15 amp fuse (20 amp on RX7) at fuse panel.

Pressure Test — **1)** Remove air cleaner assembly and disconnect fuel line at carburetor. Connect suitable pressure gauge with restrictor and a flexible hose as illustrated in *Fig. 2.*

2) Turn ignition on and briefly vent the system into container by opening hose restrictor. Pressure should stabilize within specifications. If not within specifications and lines and filter are in satisfactory condition, pump must be replaced.

Volume Test — With fuel pressure within limits, open restrictor for one minute and measure fuel expelled. If not within specifications, check for restrictions in tank, line or filter. Replace pump if required.

REMOVAL & INSTALLATION

NOTE — *Negative cable should be disconnected at battery when working on fuel pump.*

1) On 626 and RX7 models, open trunk lid, lift mat and disconnect fuel pump electrical lead. Raise rear of vehicle and support on stands. Remove fuel pump cover attaching bolts and cover.

2) On all models, disconnect inlet and outlet hoses and wiring connector. Remove attaching bolts and nuts and take pump off vehicle. To install, reverse removal procedure.

SPECIFICATIONS

Application	Pressure (psi)	Volume
Courier	2.8-3.6	2 pints/minute
626	2.8-3.6	1.6 pints/minute
RX7	3.7-4.7	2.4 pints/minute
B2000	2.8-3.6	1.6 pints/minute

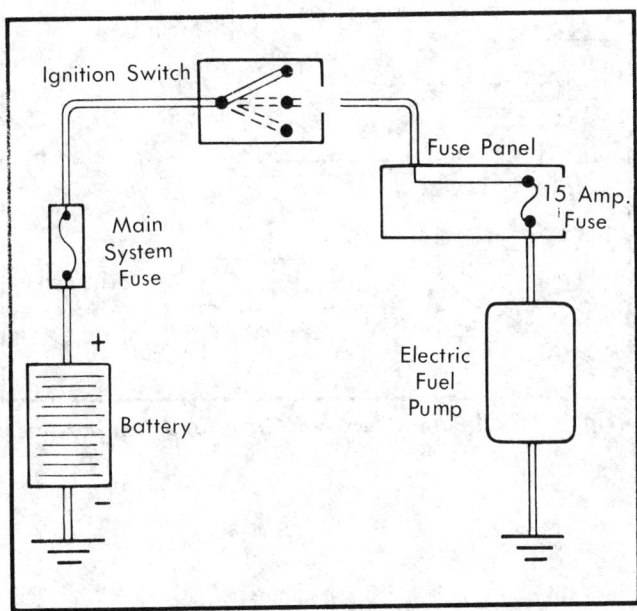

Fig. 1 Fuel Pump Circuit Schematic

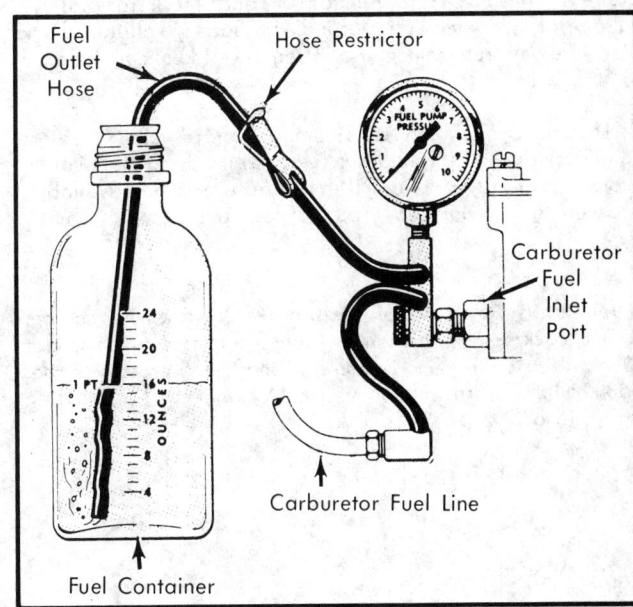

Fig. 2 Fuel Pump Pressure and Volume Test

1980 Electric Fuel Pumps

HONDA ELECTRIC FUEL PUMPS

Accord
Civic
Prelude

DESCRIPTION

Electric fuel pump is located near gas tank at left side of vehicle. On all models, fuel pump is mounted to fuel pump cover and cover is bolted directly to fuel tank bracket and frame. Fuel pump is a sealed unit and is serviceable as an assembly only.

OPERATION & TESTING

A solid-state relay senses negative pulsations at the ignition coil and switches the pump on when the engne is running or the starter is engaged. Relay is located under dash panel at left side of driver's cmpartment. Circuit is protected by fuse in fuse box as well as main in-line fuse.

Electrical Testing — 1) With ignition switch OFF, connect positive probe of voltmeter to black/yellow wire terminal of fuel pump relay connector, and negative probe to ground (black) terminal. Turn ignition switch on and check for voltage. If no voltage, check fuse and continuity of black/yellow wire.

2) If voltage is available, connect the positive probe of voltmeter to blue wire at pump cut-off relay and negative probe to ground. Turn ignition on and check for battery voltage. If voltmeter does not indicate battery voltage, check blue wire between connector and negative side of coil. Proceed to step **3)**.

3) Disconnect relay connector, jumper 2 black/yellow wires of connector and turn ignition. If fuel pressure is now available, replace fuel cut-off relay. If fuel pressure is not available, proceed to fuel pump operational testing.

Fuel Pump Operational Testing — 1) Attach jumper between black/yellow wires in fuel pump cut-off relay connector. Disconnect fuel hose to carburetor and install pressure gauge to fuel hose. Turn ignition switch ON and check for normal pressure of 2-3 psi (.13-.18 kg/cm²)

2) Remove pressure gauge and hold measuring beaker under fuel hose. Turn ignition on and measure amount of fuel flow in 60 seconds. With 10 volts minimum battery voltage, flow should be as indicated in chart.

SPECIFICATIONS

Application	Pressure psi (kg/cm²)	Volume oz./minute
Accord	2-3 (.14-.21)	21
Civic	2-3 (.14-.21)	17
Prelude	2-3 (.14-.21)	23

REMOVAL & INSTALLATION

FUEL PUMP

Raise vehicle and support on jack stands. Disconnect electrical leads at pump and clamp fuel lines between pump and tank. Remove fuel pump cover bolts and lift off cover and pump as an assembly. Disassemble pump from cover. To install, reverse removal procedure.

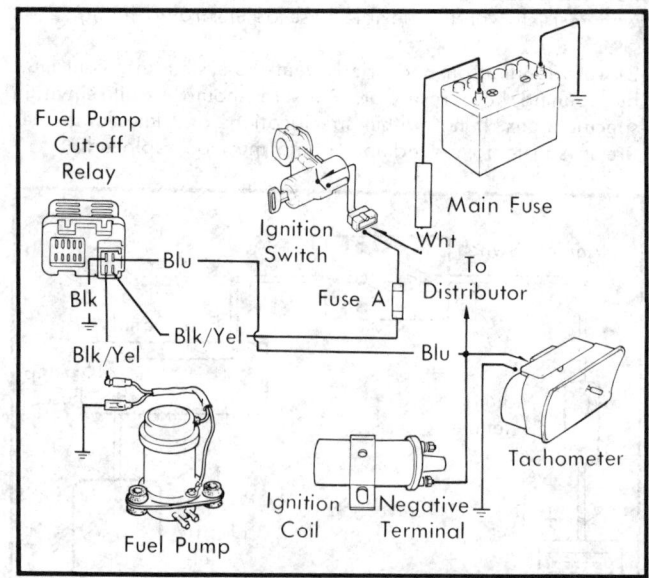

Fig. 1 Fuel Pump Electrical Circuit and Components

LUV ELECTRIC FUEL PUMPS

Pickup

DESCRIPTION

Electric fuel pump is mounted to left side frame rail adjacent to fuel tank. Pump is cylindrical in shape, with electrical lead, fuel inlet fitting and fuel outlet fitting located on same side. No internal pump components are serviceable, and entire pump should be replaced if found defective.

OPERATION

The 12-volt electrical circuit is protected by fuses No. 4 and No. 5 and is controlled by fuel pump relay mounted on inner right front fender. *See Fig. 1.* This relay is controlled by alternator output when engine is running. When engine is off, power is fed through transmission switch (when closed for starting) directly to fuel pump circuit of relay.

NOTE — *Entire pump should be replaced in event of faulty operation. Pump is totally enclosed and should not be disassembled.*

REMOVAL & INSTALLATION

FUEL PUMP

Remove electrical lead and fuel lines from tank and carburetor. Remove mounting bolts and nuts and take pump off frame. To install, reverse removal procedure.

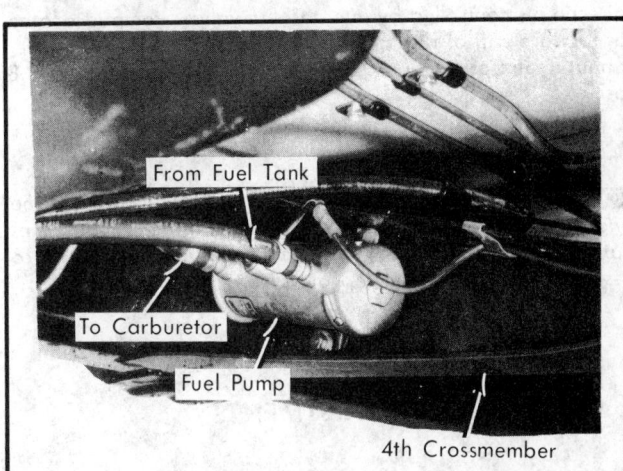

Fig. 2   Fuel Pump Installed Position

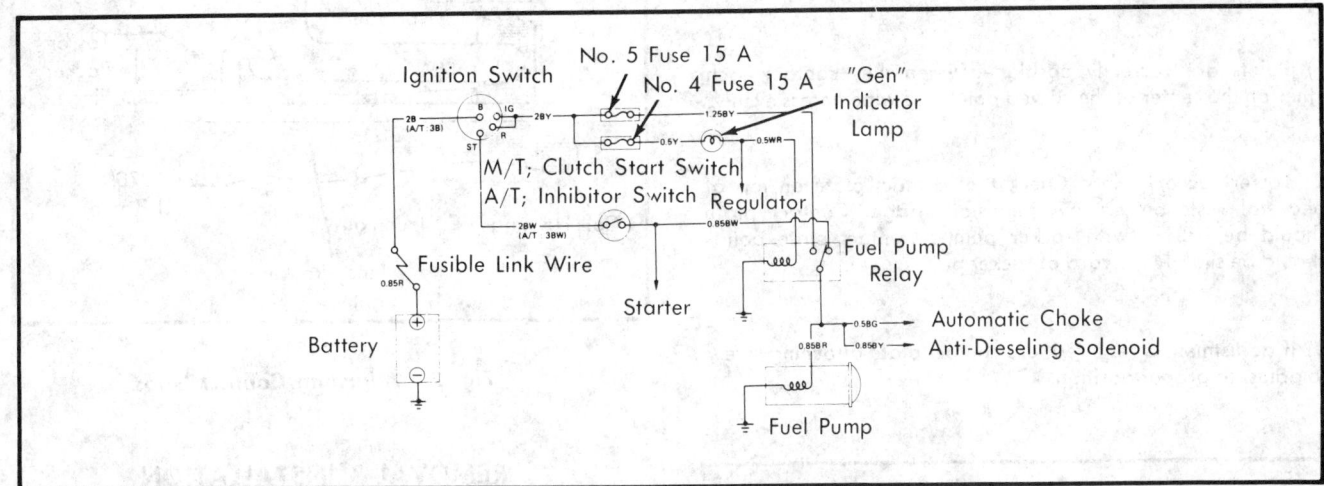

Fig. 1   Fuel Pump Electrical Circuit

S.U. AUF TYPE ELECTRIC FUEL PUMPS

MGB

DESCRIPTION

Diaphragm type pump is operated by electro-magnetic plunger controlled by adjustable contact points. Fuel flow direction is controlled by internal disc valves. Pump is located at forward end of fuel tank on right side. Pump should deliver about 1 pint of fuel in 30 seconds with a pressure of 2.3-3.8 psi.

NOTE — *A fuel pump inertia (safety) valve is located in the engine compartment next to the brake master cylinder. This cut-off valve is activated in the event of collision or roll-over. To reset, depress button on top of valve.*

ADJUSTMENTS

CONTACT PLATE POSITIONING

1) Points are correctly positioned when they contact each other on the center of the curved point and wipe across evenly.

2) Lower rocker points. Check that contact plate on top of pedestal rests on narrow pedestal bridge. Contact plate should be square with rocker points. Contact plate points should be slightly forward of rocker points.

3) If adjustment is required, use contact plate attaching screw to adjust to proper position.

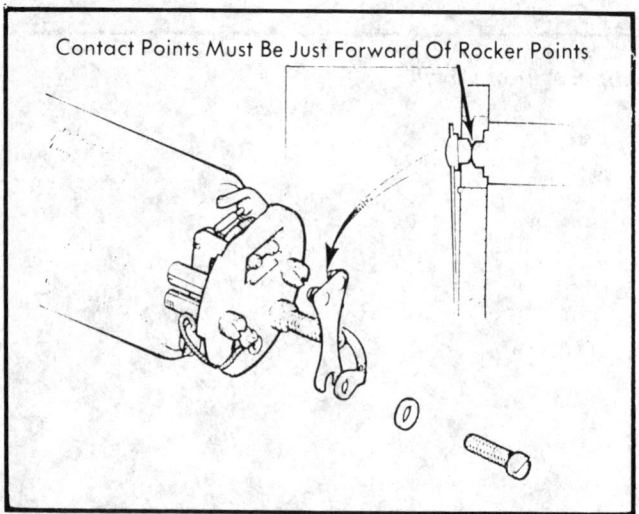

Fig. 1   Correct Contact Point Alignment

SETTING CONTACT GAPS

1) Ensure rocker points are touching contact plate points. Measure distance contact points are pushed (lifted) above pedestal when cycled. Lift should be .035" (.9 mm).

2) Adjust by bending upper rocker finger beneath pedestal.

3) Now check gap between lower rocker finger and housing. Gap should be .070" (1.8 mm). To adjust, upper rocker finger may again need to be bent. **NOTE** — *Both adjustments require bending same upper rocker finger. Be careful because this finger is used to set both adjustments and they must be proportioned correctly.*

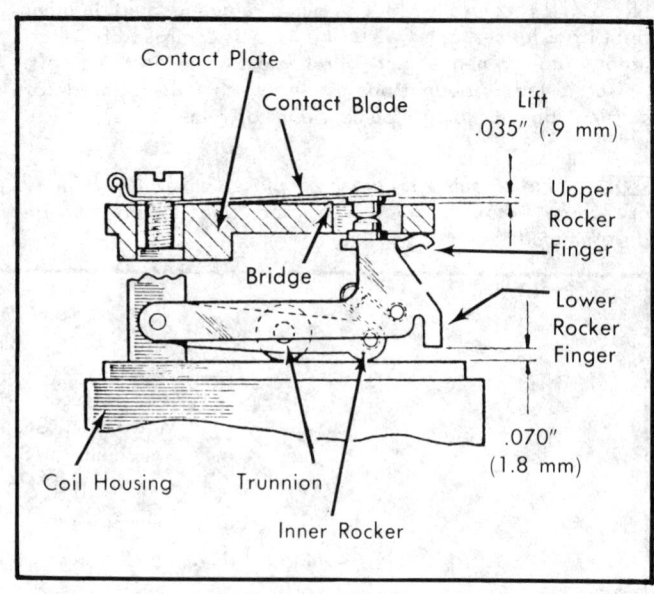

Fig. 2   Adjusting Contact Gaps

REMOVAL & INSTALLATION

FUEL PUMP

Removal —1) Disconnect battery. From inside trunk, remove retaining screws and take off fuel pump guard.

2) Loosen clamp retaining pump in supporting rubber insulator. Disconnect electrical terminal from pump.

3) Working under car, disconnect inlet and outlet lines, breather pipe and electrical connection. Remove pump from support.

Installation — Reverse removal procedure, ensuring that pump tubing connections are fitted at the proper angle.

TOYOTA ELECTRIC FUEL PUMPS

**Corona
Celica
Pickup**

DESCRIPTION

Fuel pump is located inside gas tank and is serviced only as a unit. *See Fig. 1.* If electric pump becomes defective, it must be replaced.

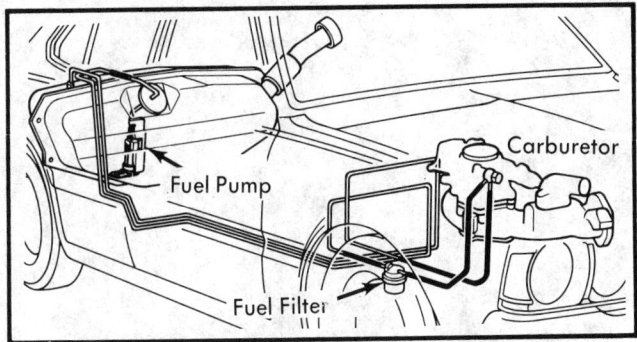

Fig. 1   Toyota Electric Fuel Pump System

Fuel pump assembly is composed of pump, filter, cover, cushion, and relief valve. *See Fig. 2.* Fuel pump operates when starter is turning and when oil pressure is present.

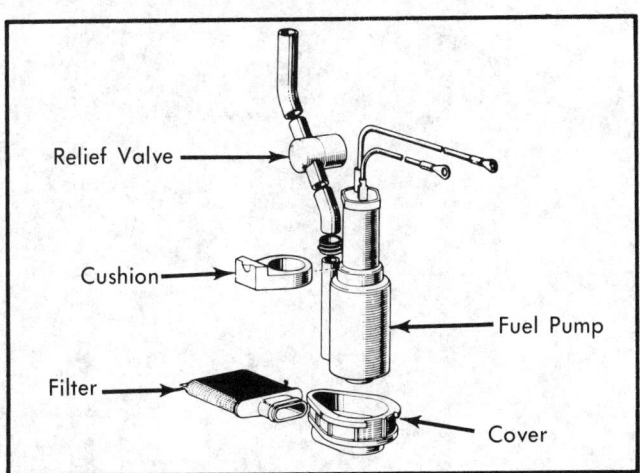

Fig. 2   Exploded View of Electric Fuel Pump

TESTING

CAUTION — *Do not operate electric fuel pump unless it is immersed in gasoline. Do not attempt to test pump without resistor.*

PUMP OPERATION CHECK

1) Check oil pressure switch operation.

2) Disconnect connector from oil pressure switch, to operate fuel pump relay. *See Fig. 3.*

3) Turn ignition key to ON position.

4) Check pump for steady, smooth operation. Replace pump if abnormal noise is present. If pump does not run, check pump resistor, relay and pump.

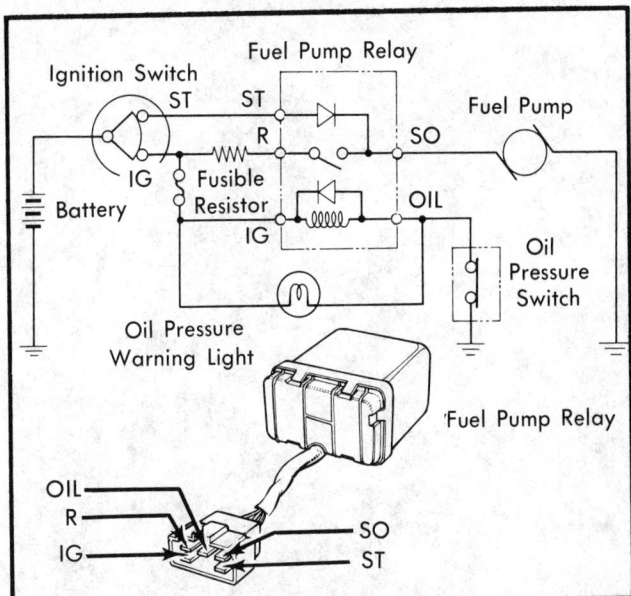

Fig. 3   Fuel Pump Control System Circuit

DISCHARGE CAPACITY TEST

1) Connect a short test hose to fuel filter outlet.

2) Turn ignition key to ON position. Measure discharge capacity. Pump should discharge 1.3 quarts per minute.

3) If below specification, check fuel lines, hoses, and filter for restrictions. Replace fuel pump, if necessary.

DISCHARGE PRESSURE TEST

1) Connect pressure gauge to fuel filter outlet.

2) Turn ignition key to ON position. Measure discharge pressure at gauge. Reading should be 2.1-4.3 psi (0.15-0.30 kg/cm²). If not within specified limits, check fuel level. Replace pump if necessary.

COMPLETING TESTS

After tests, necessary repairs or replacement of parts, turn off ignition. Reconnect fuel hoses and lead to oil pressure switch.

REMOVAL & INSTALLATION

Removal — Remove fuel pump from tank. On pickup, remove fuel tank. Remove negative battery cable.

Installation — Install fuel pump into tank, using a new gasket. Reconnect electrical leads and fuel lines. Connect negative battery cable and check fuel system for leaks.

FUEL PUMP RESISTOR TEST

Check for continuity between two terminals of resistor connector. If no continuity, replace resistor and check fuel pump. Resistance of 1.4 ohms required.

Section 3
ELECTRICAL

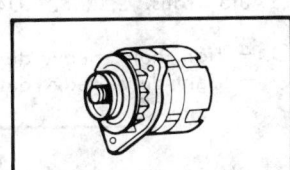

Contents

NOTE — ALSO SEE GENERAL INDEX.

1980 Distributor Specifications

DISTRIBUTOR APPLICATION TABLES

AUDI

Application	Fed.	Calif.
Bosch		
4000		
4 Cyl.	049 505 205A	049 905 205Q
5 Cyl.	035 905 205J	035 905 205J
5000		
Turbo	035 905 205H	035 905 205H
All Others	035 905 205B	035 905 205B

BMW

Application	Fed.	Calif.
Bosch		
320i	0237 002 049	0237 002 049
528i	0237 304 006	0237 304 006
633CSi	0237 304 002	0237 304 002
733i	0237 304 002	0237 304 002

CHRYSLER CORP. IMPORTS

Application	Fed.	Calif.
Mitsubishi		
Colt, Champ (FWD)		
Man. Trans.	T3T05776	T4T60272
Auto. Trans.	T3T05771	T4T60272
D50 & Arrow Pickup		
2.0 Liter		
Man. Trans.	T4T60174	T4T60175
Auto. Trans.	T4T60175	T4T60175
2.6 Liter	T4T60171	T4T60171
All Others		
1.6 Liter	T3T05771	T4T60272
2.6 Liter	T4T60171	T4T60171

COURIER

Application	Fed.	Calif.
Mitsubishi①		
2000 cc	D97Z-E	D97Z-E
2300 cc	D97Z-C	D97Z-A

① — Ford basic part number is 12127. Distributor advance specifications are not available for Courier.

DATSUN

Application	Fed.	Calif.
Hitachi		
200SX		
Man. Trans.	D4K9-09	D4N9-05
Auto. Trans.	D4K9-09	D4N9-04
210		
Man. Trans.	D4K9-05	D4K9-12
Auto. Trans.	D4K9-04	D4K9-06

DATSUN (Cont.)

Application	Fed.	Calif.
510		
Man. Trans.	D4K9-08	D4N9-01
Auto. Trans.	D4K9-08	D4N9-02
810		
Man. Trans.	D6K9-10	D6K8-01
Auto. Trans.	D6K9-07	D6K8-01
280ZX		
Man. Trans.	D6K9-10	D6K8-22
Auto. Trans.	D6K9-09	D6K8-22
Pickup		
Man. Trans.	D4K9-01①	D4K8-08②
Auto. Trans.	D4K9-02	D4K9-02

① — Light duty. Heavy duty is D4K9-03.
② — Light duty. Heavy duty is D4K8-10.

FIAT

Application	Fed.	Calif.
Bosch		
X1/9	4452749	4430227
Strada		
With A/C	4443054	4430226
Without A/C	4452750	4430226
Marelli		
Brava	4387796	4430224
Spider 2000	4387796	4430224

FIESTA

Application	Fed.	Calif.
Ford Distributors①		
All Models	D8RZ-A	D8RZ-A

① — Ford basic part number is 12127. Distributor advance specifications are not available for Fiesta.

HONDA

Application	Fed.	Calif.
Hitachi①		
1300 Hatchback	PA6-662	PA6-662
1500 Hatchback		
Man. Trans.	PA6-662	②PA6-015
Auto. Trans.	PA6-912	②PA6-912
1500 Wagon		
Man. Trans.	PA6-015	②PA6-912
Auto. Trans.	PA6-912	②PA6-692
Accord & Prelude		
Man. Trans.	②689-662	689-782
Auto. Trans.	②689-662	689-791

① — Honda part number prefix is 30100.
② — High Altitude also.

DISTRIBUTOR APPLICATION TABLES (Cont.)

JAGUAR

Application	Fed.	Calif.
Lucas		
XJ6L	45DM6	45DM6

LUV

Application	Fed.	Calif.
Nippondenso		
Man. Trans.	029100 5970	029100 6000
Auto. Trans.	029100 5990	029100 5980

MAZDA

Application	Fed.	Calif.
Mitsubishi		
GLC	891418200	891418200
626	823918200	823918200
B2000	868218200A	868218200A
RX-7		
Man. Trans.	834118200	834118200
Auto. Trans.	834218200	834218200

MERCEDES-BENZ

Application	Fed.	Calif.
Bosch		
280 Series	0237 304 003	0237 304 003
450 Series	0237 405 012	0237 405 012

MG

Application	Fed.	Calif.
Lucas		
MGB	45DE4	

PEUGEOT

Application	Fed.	Calif.
Bosch		
604	0237 402 015	0237 402 015
Ducellier		
505	525213A	590241

PORSCHE

Application	Fed.	Calif.
Bosch		
911SC	0237 304 016	0237 304 016
924 & Turbo	477 905 205A	477 905 205A
928	0237 405 010	0237 405 010

RENAULT

Application	Fed.	Calif.
Ducellier		
LeCar	7700668704	7700668704

SAAB

Application	Fed.	Calif.
Bosch		
99	0237 002 023	0237 002 023
900	0237 002 023	0237 002 023
900 Turbo	0237 003 014	0237 003 014

SUBARU

Application	Fed.	Calif.
Hitachi		
4WD Models	D4H9-02	D4H9-02
Nippondenso		
2WD Models	029100-6060	029100-6060

TOYOTA

Application	Fed.	Calif.
Nippondenso①		
Tercel	15030	15030
Corolla	28030	28040
Celica	38210	38220
Corona	38240	38250
Pickup	②38260	38250
Cressida & Supra	45190	45190
Land Cruiser	61101	61101

① — Nippondenso basic part number is 19100.
② — 19100-38250 for cab and chassis models.

1980 Distributor Specifications

DISTRIBUTOR APPLICATION TABLES (Cont.)

TRIUMPH

Application	Fed.	Calif.
Lucas		
Spitfire	45DE4	
TR7	47DE4	47DE4
TR8	35DE8	35DE8

VOLKSWAGEN

Application	Fed.	Calif.
Bosch		
Dasher	049 905 205Q	049 905 205Q
Rabbit & Pickup		
Carburetor	055 905 205AA	055 905 205AA
Fuel Injection	049 905 205Q	049 905 205Q

VOLKSWAGEN (Cont.)

Application	Fed.	Calif.
Scirocco	049 905 205Q	049 905 205Q
Vanagon	022 905 205S	071 905 205

VOLVO

Application	Fed.	Calif.
Bosch		
4 Cyl.	0237 002 038	0237 002 039
6 Cyl.	0237 406 004	0237 402 013

BOSCH DISTRIBUTOR ADVANCE & RETARD SPECIFICATIONS

NOTE – FOR DISTRIBUTOR RPM & DEGREES, DIVIDE SPECIFICATIONS BELOW BY 2

Distributor Part No.	Rot. ①	Centrifugal Advance (Engine Degrees @ RPM)			Vacuum Advance (Engine Degrees @ In. of Hg)			Vacuum Retard (Engine Degrees @ In. of Hg)		
022 905 205S	C	0 / 1000	9-14 / 1600	21-25 / 3400	0 / 3.15	....	8-12 / 7.87	....	....	....
035 905 205B	C	0 / 1000	17-23 / 2500	21-25 / 4500	3.15 / 6.5	....	4.8 / 8.66	8-10 / 5.5	....	....
035 905 205H	C	0 / 1050	2-14 / 1400	10-18 / 2000	0 / 2.36	....	11-15 / 5.3	16-18 / 7.4	....	1.5
035 905 205J	C	0 / 1050	17-22 / 2500	26-30 / 7000	4.13 / 0	....	10-14 / 7.1	8.10 / 5.3	....	1.18
049 505 205A	C	....	15-20 / 2200	26-30 / 5000	7.87 / 0	....	4.8 / 11	8-10 / 8.3	....	3.94
049 905 205Q	C	0 / 1050	15-20 / 2200	26-30 / 5000	0 / 3	....	10-12 / 7②	8-10 / 5.3	....	1.8
055 905 205AA	C	1400	15-19 / 2100	26-30 / 5000	0 / 7.28	3	11-15 / 13	9-11.5 / 9.1	....	0 / 3
071 905 205	C	0 / 1050	9-13 / 1600	21-25 / 3400	0 / 3	....	9-12 / 7.1	11-13 / 5.9	....	2.75
0231 176 084	C	14-20 / 2000	24-30 / 3000	....	0 / 7.1	....	4-6 / 10.4	7-9 / 6.7	....	1.8
0231 305 059	C	14-17 / 1000	23-27 / 2000	26-30 / 2300	0 / 3.15	....	17 / 8.7	13-17 / 9.84	....	0 / 3.15
0231 305 070	C	11-14 / 1000	15-21 / 2000	26-32 / 3600	0 / 2.75	....	17 / 8.8	10-14 / 8.27	....	0 / 2.75
0237 002 023	CC	0 / 680	2 / 1500	9.4 / 2500	0 / 4.9	13.6 / 7.4	17 / 11.4	....	....	....
0237 002 038	C	5 / 1800	10 / 2800	30 / 3900	3.1 / 5	6.7 / 5.3	17 / 8.7	....	....	....
0237 002 039	C	4 / 1200	10 / 1800	16 / 2350	0 / 4.1	12 / 5.3	17 / 8.8	....	....	....
0237 002 049	CC	10-14 / 2000	16-20 / 2500	20-24 / 2600	2.69 / 5.38	7 / 3	10.74 / 20	....	....	....
0237 003 014	CC	0-4 / 2000	4-8 / 3000	12-17 / 5000	0 / 1.8	16 / 1-3	20	3-7 / 5.8②	0-3 / 4.1②	3.48②
0237 011 002	CC	7 / 2000	15.4 / 3000	34 / 5000	0 / 1.8	32 / 16	40 / 9.1	14 / 5.8②	11 / 4.1②	6.2 / 3.77②
0237 304 002	C	9-12 / 1000	17-23 / 2000	26-32 / 3500	0 / 5.12	7.87 / 2.76	8-12 / 8.58	13-17 / 9.84	....	0 / 2.75
0237 304 002③	C	6-9 / 1000	14-20 / 2000	26-32 / 3500	0 / 5.12	7.87 / 2.76	8-12 / 8.58	13-17 / 9.84	....	0 / 2.75

① – C (Clockwise), CC (Counterclockwise), viewed from rotor end.
② – These figures represent psi because of the turbo boost pressure.
③ – Calif. models only.
④ – Fiat part numbers.

BOSCH DISTRIBUTOR ADVANCE & RETARD SPECIFICATIONS (Cont.)

NOTE – FOR DISTRIBUTOR RPM & DEGREES, DIVIDE SPECIFICATIONS BELOW BY 2

Distributor Part No.	Rot. ①	Centrifugal Advance (Engine Degrees @ RPM)				Vacuum Advance (Engine Degrees @ In. of Hg)			Vacuum Retard (Engine Degrees @ In. of Hg)		
0237 304 003	C	15-25 / 1500	..... /	..... /	22-28 / 5500	.....	.....	.....	.....	.....	.....
0237 304 006	C	13-19 / 1500	..... /	..... /	26-32 / 3000	0 / 2.68	.....	13-17 / 7.68	0 / 4.13	.....	6-10 / 9.17
0237 304 016	C	9 / 1800	15 / 2400	13.6 / 4800	20 / 6400	3.3 / 3.2	5.2 / 4.1	7 / 4.35②	3.42② / 3.9②	.....	8 / 4.93②
0237 402 013	C	9 / 1400	20 / 2600	28 / 4700	26 / 6000	0 / 3.77	2 / 8	17 / 11.8	.....	.....	.....
0237 402 015	C	12 / 2000	20 / 3000	28.8 / 4000	32 / 4400	5.9 / 2	7.7 / 9.0	17 / 15.7	.....	.....	.....
0237 405 010	C	17 / 2400	15.6 / 4000	20 / 5000	26 / 6200	9 / 5	12 / 9	15.7 / —	2.47② / 2.76②	2 / 3.0②	4 / 3.48②
0237 405 012	C	7-13 / 1500	..... /	..... /	22-28 / 3500	1.7 / 2.3	5 / 2.8	9 / 3.3	.....	.....	.....
0237 406 004	C	10 / 1500	13 / 3100	24 / 4000	22 / 6000	0 / 4.7	4 / 6.3	10 / 16.5	0 / .8	4 / 2.4	12 / 5.9
477 905 205A	C	..... /	19-25 / 2500	..... /	29-35 / 4500	.....	.....	.....	.....	.....	.....
4430226④	C	..... /	..... /	..... /	..... /	.....	.....	.....	.....	.....	.....
4430227④	C	7 / 1500	12.5 / 3000	18 / 4000	25 / 5500	0 / 8	.....	8 / 16	.....	.....	.....
4443054④	C	4 / 1500	8.5 / 2000	16 / 3000	18 / 3500	3 / 3.9	.....	5 / 5.5	.....	.....	.....
4452749④	C	4 / 1500	8.5 / 2000	16 / 3000	18 / 3500	3.2 / 5	.....	8 / 8	.....	.....	.....
4452750④	C	4 / 1500	8.5 / 2000	16 / 3000	18 / 3500	3.2 / 6	.....	8 / 8	.....	.....	.....

① – C (Clockwise), CC (Counterclockwise), viewed from rotor end.
② – These figures represent psi because of the turbo boost pressure.
③ – Calif. models only.
④ – Fiat part numbers.

DUCELLIER DISTRIBUTOR ADVANCE & RETARD SPECIFICATIONS

NOTE — FOR DISTRIBUTOR RPM & DEGREES, DIVIDE SPECIFICATIONS BELOW BY 2

Distributor Part No.	Rot.①	Centrifugal Advance (Engine Degrees @ RPM)	Vacuum Advance (Engine Degrees @ In. of Hg)	Vacuum Retard (Engine Degrees @ In. of Hg)
525213A	C	0@1300, 8@1800, 14@3000, 28@4000, 32@5000	0@3.5, 4@5.9, 9@7.9, 14@9.8	……
590241	C	0@1300, 8@1800, 14@3000, 28@4000, 32@5000	0@3.5, 4@5.9, 9@7.9, 14@9.8	……
7700668704②	C	0@1000, 14@2200, 20@3200, 25@4200, 31@5000	0@3.2, 6.1@5.9, 15@9.8, 20@12.8	……

① — C (Clockwise), CC (Counterclockwise), viewed from rotor end.
② — Renault part number.

FORD DISTRIBUTOR ADVANCE & RETARD SPECIFICATIONS

NOTE — DISTRIBUTOR ADVANCE SPECIFICATIONS FOR FORD ARE NOT AVAILABLE FROM MANUFACTURER

HITACHI DISTRIBUTOR ADVANCE & RETARD SPECIFICATIONS

NOTE — FOR DISTRIBUTOR RPM & DEGREES, DIVIDE SPECIFICATIONS BELOW BY 2

Distributor Part No.①	Rot.②	Centrifugal Advance (Engine Degrees @ RPM)	Vacuum Advance (Engine Degrees @ In. of Hg)	Vacuum Retard (Engine Degrees @ In. of Hg)
30100 PA6 015	CC	0@800, 16.4@2900, 21@4500	0@2.1, 11@4.2	……
30100 PA6 662③	CC	0@950, 13@1750, 28@4300	0@2.2, 11@4.2	……
30100 PA6 662④	CC	0@800, 16.4@2900, 21@4500	0@2.2, 8@5.9	……
30100 PA6 692	CC	0@1300, 14.4@2900, 21@4500	0@2.2, 7@4.1	……
30100 PA6 912	CC	0@800, 16.4@2900, 21@4500	0@2.2, 7@4.1	……
30100 689 662	CC	0@1100, 20@2600, 30@3600	0@7, 16@10.8	……
30100 689 782	CC	0@1400, 13@3400, 24@5000	5.5, 14@12.8	0@2.36, 8@4.3
30100 689 791	CC	0@900, 14@3400, 30@3600	……	……

① — Honda part numbers.
② — C (Clockwise), CC (Counterclockwise), viewed from rotor end.
③ — 1300 Hatchback.
④ — Federal 1500 Hatchback with manual transmission.

HITACHI DISTRIBUTOR ADVANCE & RETARD SPECIFICATIONS (Cont.)

NOTE – FOR DISTRIBUTOR RPM & DEGREES, DIVIDE SPECIFICATIONS BELOW BY 2

Distributor Part No.	Rot. ①	Centrifugal Advance (Engine Degrees @ RPM)			Vacuum Advance (Engine Degrees @ In. of Hg)		Vacuum Retard (Engine Degrees @ In. of Hg)	
D4H9-02	CC	0 / 1000	17 / 2900	28 / 4800	0 / 1.97	20 / 11.8	0 / 3.2	14 / 10.6
D4K8-08	CC	0 / 1200		22 / 3900	0 / 2.76	25 / 9.8		
D4K8-10	CC	0 / 1200		22 / 3900	0 / 3.9	13 / 9.8		
D4K9-01	CC	0 / 1200		22 / 3900	0 / 4.3	30 / 10.6		
D4K9-02	CC	0 / 1200		22 / 3900	0 / 4.3	15 / 9.8		
D4K9-03	CC	0 / 1200		22 / 3900	0 / 3.9	5 / 7.87		
D4K9-04	CC	0 / 1120	6.4 / 2000	24 / 5600	0 / 3.2	24 / 10.4		
D4K9-05	CC	0 / 1120	6.4 / 2000	24 / 5600	0 / 3.2	29 / 13		
D4K9-06	CC	0 / 1120	6.4 / 2000	24 / 5600	0 / 3.2	30 / 10.4		
D4K9-08	CC	0 / 1500	7 / 2300	12 / 4000	0 / 2.76	25 / 7.87		
D4K9-09	CC	0 / 1400	6 / 2000	12 / 3200	0 / 2.76	20 / 9.8		
D4K9-12	CC	0 / 1120	6.4 / 2000	24 / 5600	0 / 4.1	24 / 11.8		
D4N9-01	CC	0 / 1400		10 / 5400	0 / 2.76	25 / 7.87		
D4N9-02	CC	0 / 1400		10 / 5400	0 / 2.76	25 / 11.8		
D4N9-04	CC	0 / 1400	7 / 2200	10 / 3000	0 / 2.76	20 / 9.8		
D4N9-05	CC	0 / 1800		10 / 3000	0 / 2.76	20 / 9.8		
D6K8-01	CC	0 / 1220		17 / 2500	0 / 2.76	30 / 11		
D6K8-22	CC	0 / 1200		17 / 2500	0 / 5.9	30 / 11.8		
D6K9-07	CC	0 / 1180		17 / 2500	0 / 3.94	20 / 11.8		
D6K9-09	CC	0 / 1200		17 / 2500	0 / 5.9	15 / 11		
D6K9-10	CC	0 / 1180		17 / 2500	0 / 3.94	20 / 11.8		
D6K9-10②	CC	0 / 1200		17 / 2500	0 / 5.9	18 / 12.2		

① – C (Clockwise), CC (Counterclockwise), viewed from rotor end.
② – 280 ZX models only.

LUCAS DISTRIBUTOR ADVANCE & RETARD SPECIFICATIONS

NOTE — FOR DISTRIBUTOR RPM & DEGREES, DIVIDE SPECIFICATIONS BELOW BY 2

Distributor Part No.	Rot. ①	Centrifugal Advance (Engine Degrees @ RPM)				Vacuum Advance (Engine Degrees @ In. of Hg)				Vacuum Retard (Engine Degrees @ In. of Hg)			
35DE8	C	.....	.....	.....	.....	.....	.....	.....	.....	.....	.....	.....	.....
45DE4 MGB	CC	0 / 850	15 / 2000	30 / 3500	35 / 4500	0	.....	24 / 11.0	.....	.....	.....	.....	.....
Spitfire	CC	10 / 1600	13 / 2600	14 / 3200	14 / 5000	3.0	15.0	20.0	.....	12	12	.....	0
45DM6	CC	0 / 880	.....	.....	.....	1.0	.....	.....	.....	.....	.....	.....	.....
47DE4	CC	8 / 1500	11 / 2100	19 / 3800	22 / 4500	.....	.....	.....	.....	0 / 3.0	12 / 11.0	12 / 15.0	15.0

① — C (Clockwise), CC (Counterclockwise), viewed from rotor end.

MARELLI DISTRIBUTOR ADVANCE & RETARD SPECIFICATIONS

NOTE — FOR DISTRIBUTOR RPM & DEGREES, DIVIDE SPECIFICATIONS BELOW BY 2

Distributor Part No.	Rot. ①	Centrifugal Advance (Engine Degrees @ RPM)					Vacuum Advance (Engine Degrees @ In. of Hg)				Vacuum Retard (Engine Degrees @ In. of Hg)			
4387796②	C	0 / 1000	8 / 1800	12.4 / 2500	15.8 / 3000	18 / 3500	0	6	12	15	.....	.....	.....	.....
4430224②	C	0 / 1000	10 / 2000	15.8 / 3000	20.5 / 4000	28 / 5200	4	7 / 8	10	12 / 14	.....	.....	.....	.....

① — C (Clockwise), CC (Counterclockwise), viewed from rotor end.
② — Fiat part numbers.

MITSUBISHI DISTRIBUTOR ADVANCE & RETARD SPECIFICATIONS

NOTE — FOR DISTRIBUTOR RPM & DEGREES, DIVIDE SPECIFICATIONS BELOW BY 2

Distributor Part No. [1]	Rot. [2]	Centrifugal Advance (Engine Degrees @ RPM)				Vacuum Advance (Engine Degrees @ In. of Hg)				Vacuum Retard (Engine Degrees @ In. of Hg)
T3T05771 [3]	C	0 / 1000			20 / 4400	0			23 / 11.0	
T3T05776 [3]	C	0 / 1000			20 / 4400	3.2			28 / 9.5	
T4T60171 [3]	C	0 / 1200	12 / 2800		20 / 6000	0			15 / 11.8	
T4T60174 [3]	C	0 / 1200	12 / 2800		20 / 6000	5.1			23 / 11.0	
T4T60175 [3]	C	0 / 1200	12 / 2800		20 / 6000	0			20 / 14.2	
T4T60272 [3]	C	0 / 1000			20 / 4400	3.2			20 / 14.2	
891418200 [4]	C	0 / 1400	5 / 2000	10 / 3000	16 / 4000	0 / 2.9	6 / 7.87	11 / 11.8	14 / 13.8	
823918200 [4]	C	0 / 1100		10 / 2400	14 / 4000	0 / 2.95	4 / 6.3	11.4 / 8.66	14 / 13.8	
868218200A [4]	C	0 / 1500	5 / 2000	10 / 2500	14 / 3400	0 / 2.4	3.6 / 3.9	/ 7.87	18 / 11.8	
834118200 [4] Leading	C	0 / 1000	5 / 1500	10 / 2000	15 / 2500	0 / 3.9	5 / 7.9	10 / 11.8	15 / 15.7	
834118200 [4] Trailing	C	0 / 1000	5 / 1500	10 / 2000	15 / 2500	0 / 7.9	10 / 9.8	25.4 / 13.8	30 / 15.7	
834218200 [4] Leading	C	0 / 1000	5 / 1500	10 / 2000	15 / 2500	0 / 3.9	5 / 7.9	10 / 11.8	15 / 15.7	
834218200 [4] Trailing	C	0 / 1000	5 / 1500	10 / 2000	15 / 2500	0 / 7.9	10 / 9.8	25.4 / 13.8	30 / 15.7	

[1] — No distributor advance specifications are available for Ford Courier from manufacturer.
[2] — C (Clockwise), CC (Counterclockwise), viewed from rotor end.
[3] — Chrysler Corp. Imports.
[4] — Mazda part numbers.

NIPPONDENSO DISTRIBUTOR ADVANCE & RETARD SPECIFICATIONS

NOTE – FOR DISTRIBUTOR RPM & DEGREES, DIVIDE SPECIFICATIONS BELOW BY 2

Centrifugal Advance cells are given as **degrees @ RPM**; Vacuum Advance and Vacuum Retard cells are given as **degrees @ In. of Hg**.

Distributor Part No.	Rot. ⊖	Centrifugal Advance (Engine Degrees @ RPM)					Vacuum Advance (Engine Degrees @ In. of Hg)				Vacuum Retard (Engine Degrees @ In. of Hg)			
		1	2	3	4	5	1	2	3	4	1	2	3	4
19100 15030	CC	0 @ 1200	3.8 @ 1928	10 @ 2800	15 @ 4500	13.6 @ 6000	0 @ 2.4	9.4 @ 4.1	20 @ 6.7	26 @ 12.2	…	…	…	…
19100 28030	C	0 @ 1400	3.8 @ 1910	10 @ 2600	…	18 @ 6000	0 @ 2.8	18.4 @ 6.5	…	30 @ 9.5	…	…	…	…
19100 28040	C	0 @ 1400	3.8 @ 1910	10 @ 2600	16 @ 5600	15.6 @ 6000	0 @ 3.9	15.2 @ 5.4	…	24 @ 7.1	…	…	…	…
19100 38210	C	0 @ 1100	4.6 @ 1576	12.8 @ 2300	21 @ 5000	20 @ 6000	0 @ 3.9	16.2 @ 8.4	…	28 @ 12.6	…	…	…	…
19100 38220	C	0 @ 1100	4.6 @ 1576	12.8 @ 2300	21 @ 5000	20 @ 6000	0 @ 3.9	10.6 @ 7.4	…	20 @ 11.8	…	…	…	…
19100 38240	C	0 @ 1100	4.6 @ 1576	12.8 @ 2300	21 @ 5000	20 @ 6000	0 @ 3.9	16.2 @ 8.4	…	28 @ 12.6	…	…	…	…
19100 38250	C	0 @ 1100	4.6 @ 1576	12.8 @ 2300	21 @ 5000	20 @ 6000	0 @ 3.9	10.6 @ 7.4	…	20 @ 11.8	…	…	…	…
19100 38260	C	0 @ 1100	4.6 @ 1576	12.8 @ 2300	21 @ 5000	20.2 @ 6000	0 @ 3.9	10.8 @ 7.2	…	20 @ 11.8	…	…	…	…
19100 45190	C	0 @ 1100	2.4 @ 1512	6 @ 2000	12 @ 4000	10 @ 6000	0 @ 3.9	7 @ 5.9	18 @ 9.8	22 @ 11.8	…	…	…	…
19100 61101	C	0 @ 1200	10 @ 1800	12.4 @ 2736	17 @ 3800	15 @ 6000	0 @ 3.9	8.6 @ 5.9	…	32 @ 8.3	…	…	…	…
029100 5970	CC	0 @ 1250	7 @ 2000	13 @ 2800	16 @ 3500	19.8 @ 4400	0 @ 2	9 @ 4.7	13.6 @ 8.3	17.6 @ 10.6	…	…	…	…
029100 5980	CC	0 @ 1250	7 @ 2000	13 @ 2800	16 @ 3500	19.8 @ 4400	0 @ 2	8 @ 5.1	11.2 @ 7.1	13.6 @ 8.3	…	…	…	…
029100 5990	CC	0 @ 1250	7 @ 2000	13 @ 2800	16 @ 3500	19.8 @ 4400	0 @ 3.1	3 @ 4.3	8 @ 7.1	10.8 @ 8.3	…	…	…	…
029100 6000	CC	0 @ 1250	7 @ 2000	13 @ 2800	16 @ 3500	19.8 @ 4400	0 @ 2	10 @ 4.7	17 @ 7.9	23 @ 10.2	…	…	…	…
029100 6060	CC	0 @ 1000	10 @ 2000	16 @ 3000	24 @ 4000	28 @ 4800	0 @ 2	9 @ 5.5	16 @ 8.8	20 @ 11.8	0 @ 3.1	5.6 @ 5.5	10 @ 7.9	15 @ 11

⊖ – C (Clockwise), CC (Counterclockwise), viewed from rotor end.

Distributors & Ignition Systems

IGNITION SECONDARY QUICK CHECK CHART

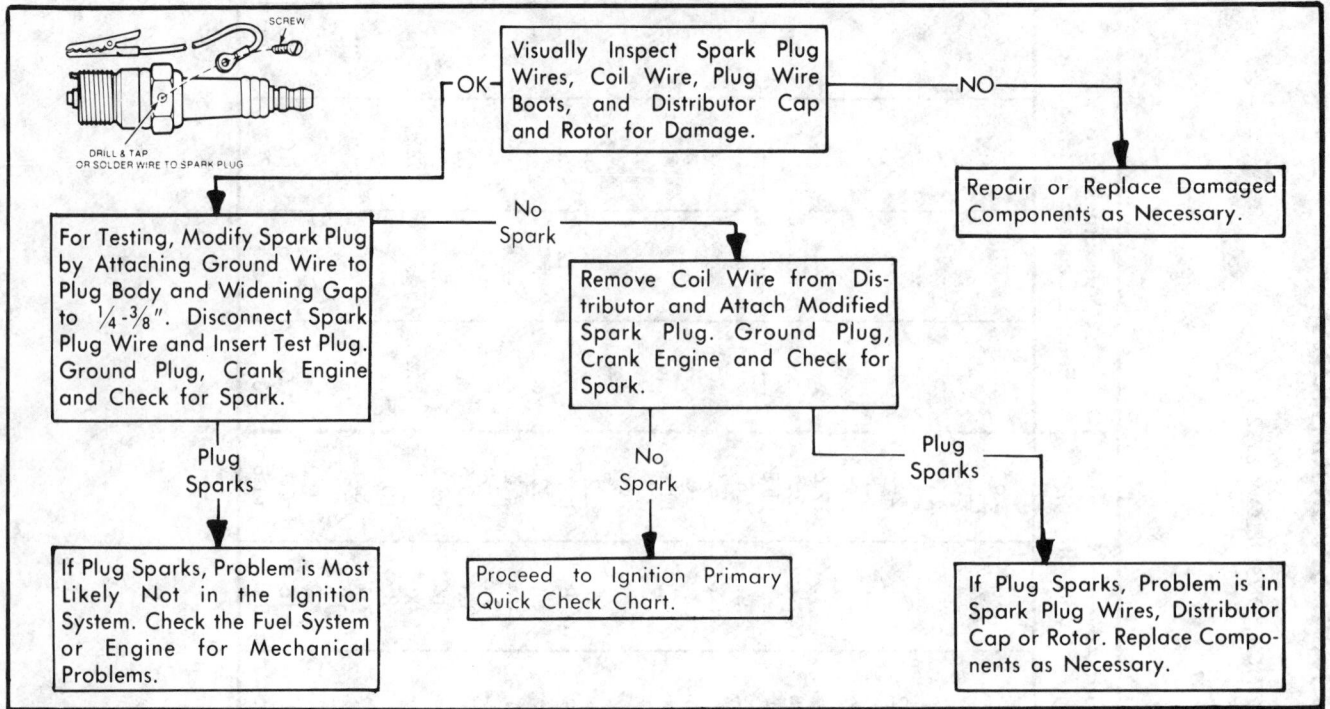

Visually Inspect Spark Plug Wires, Coil Wire, Plug Wire Boots, and Distributor Cap and Rotor for Damage.

—OK→ / —NO→

Repair or Replace Damaged Components as Necessary.

For Testing, Modify Spark Plug by Attaching Ground Wire to Plug Body and Widening Gap to ¼-⅜". Disconnect Spark Plug Wire and Insert Test Plug. Ground Plug, Crank Engine and Check for Spark.

No Spark →

Remove Coil Wire from Distributor and Attach Modified Spark Plug. Ground Plug, Crank Engine and Check for Spark.

Plug Sparks ↓

No Spark ↓ / Plug Sparks ↓

If Plug Sparks, Problem is Most Likely Not in the Ignition System. Check the Fuel System or Engine for Mechanical Problems.

Proceed to Ignition Primary Quick Check Chart.

If Plug Sparks, Problem is in Spark Plug Wires, Distributor Cap or Rotor. Replace Components as Necessary.

DRILL & TAP OR SOLDER WIRE TO SPARK PLUG

SCREW

IGNITION PRIMARY QUICK CHECK CHART

Inspect All Ignition Secondary Wiring for Broken, Frayed, Split or Cut Wires. Also Check for Loose, Corroded or Disconnected Connectors.

—OK→ / —NO→

Repair or Replace Components as Necessary.

Check Battery Voltage. Should Be 11.5 Volts or Above.

NO ↓ / —OK→

Check for Battery Voltage at Positive Terminal of Coil.

Replace or Recharge Battery.

—OK→ / —NO→

Check Air Gap of Pick-Up Coil in Distributor.

OK ↓ / —NO→

Check Wires from Battery/Ignition Switch to Coil. Also Check Coil Primary and Secondary Resistance.

←OK—

Check Resistance of Ballast Resistor (If Used) for Correct Value.

NO ↓

Check Pick-Up Coil Resistance for Correct Value.

Adjust or Repair as Necessary.

Replace Ballast Resistor if Value is Not to Specification.

NO ↓ / —OK→

Check Control Module for Good Ground Connections.

Replace Pick-Up Coil if Not to Specifications.

OK ↓

If Vehicle Still Fails to Run, Turn to Appropriate Article in this Manual for Complete Primary Ignition Checks with Specifications.

BOSCH ELECTRONIC IGNITION SYSTEM

BMW	**Porsche**
320i	911SC
528i	924
633CSi	928
733i	**Saab**
Fiat	99
Strada	900
X1/9	**Volvo**
Mercedes-Benz	DL
280 Series	GL
450 Series	GT
Peugeot	GLE
604	Coupe

DESCRIPTION

The Bosch electronic ignition system consists of a control module, a breakerless distributor, a single or dual resistor (some models may have a resistor wire), a high output ignition coil, an ignition switch and battery. Standard centrifugal and vacuum advance mechanisms are used. See *Fig. 1*.

NOTE — *Some Strada models are equipped with the Marelli Electronic Ignition system.*

OPERATION

Inside the distributor, a trigger wheel turns with the distributor shaft. The trigger wheel has one tooth or lug for each engine cylinder. As the trigger wheel rotates past the lugs of the magnetic pick-up coil, a magnetic field is built up that continually builds and collapses. This produces a low voltage electrical signal.

This signal passes to the control module, which controls the dwell angle and at the same time interrupts the ignition coil's primary current. This induces the high secondary coil output voltage that fires the spark plugs.

SPECIFICATIONS

Dwell Angle — *Controlled by Electronic Control Module. Not adjustable. See table later in this article.*

Centrifugal & Vacuum Advance (and/or Retard) — *See Specifications Tables in this section.*

ADJUSTMENT

NOTE — *No adjustment should be attempted on ignition system except spark plug gap and ignition initial timing. Air gap should be visually checked when testing, but if specified clearance does not exist, replace components. Air gap is non-adjustable.*

TESTING

NOTE — *Before testing ignition system, be sure battery is fully charged and in good condition, that all wires are sound and connections are good. Due to high voltage, use care when working on electronic ignition system.*

SYSTEM SPARK TEST

1) If starter turns, but engine will not start or it fails to develop sufficient power, hold distributor end of coil wire about $\frac{3}{8}$" (10 mm) from engine block and crank engine. See *Fig. 2*.

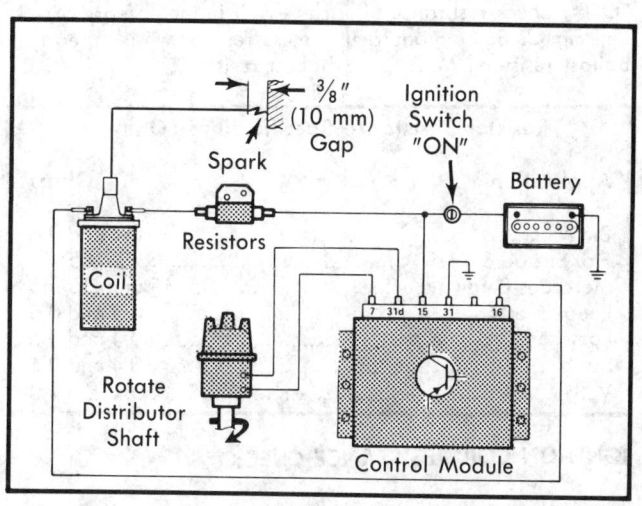

Fig. 2 Coil Wire Hookup for Making System Spark Test

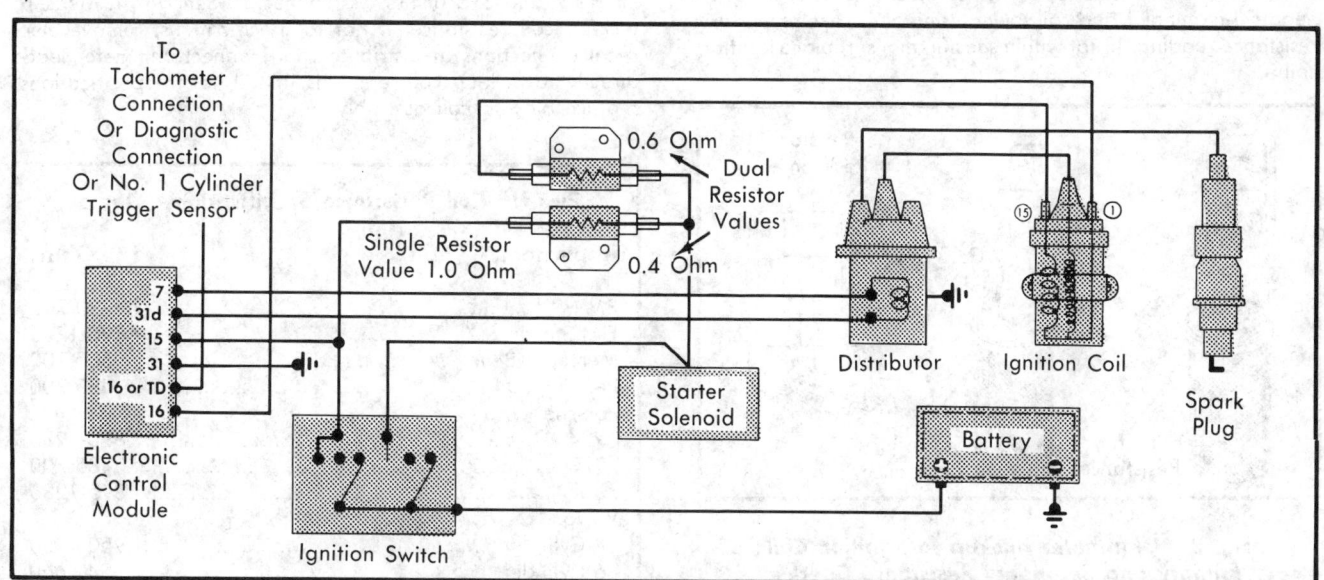

Fig. 1 Wiring Diagram of Typical Bosch Electronic Ignition System

BOSCH ELECTRONIC IGNITION SYSTEM (Cont.)

2) If spark jumps gap, check distributor cap, rotor, cables and spark plugs. Be sure ignition timing and fuel system are OK. If no sparks occur, perform the following tests

ROTOR RESISTANCE CHECK

Set an ohmmeter to the x1000 scale. With ignition switch "OFF", attach ohmmeter leads to rotor. Resistance should be approximately 5,000 ohms.

SPARK PLUG WIRE RESISTANCE

If spark plug connectors have sheet metal jackets carrying the following symbol (—▆◀—), they contain "air gap" resistors. Wires cannot then be checked for resistance using an ohmmeter. An oscilloscope must be used.

RESISTOR RESISTANCE CHECK

Set an ohmmeter in the low scale. Be sure ignition switch is "OFF". Check resistance of each resistor in the primary circuit. See Fig. 3. Some manufacturers use resistor wires instead of ballast resistors. Most use 2 ballast resistors.

Resistor Resistance Specifications (Ohms)	
Application	**Ohms**
BMW	0.4 and 0.6
Fiat Strada & X1/9	.85-.95
Mercedes-Benz	.35-.45 and .55-.65
Peugeot 604	0.5 and 0.5
Porsche	0.4 and 0.6
Saab	0.4 and 0.6
Volvo	1.0

IGNITION COIL RESISTANCE CHECK

Turn ignition switch "OFF". Using an ohmmeter set at the low scale, attach leads to ignition coil primary terminals 1 and 15 (wires removed). See Fig. 3. Take primary resistance reading. Set ohmmeter to x1000 scale, then connect ohmmeter leads to negative terminal 1 and coil tower terminal 4. Take secondary resistance reading. If not within specifications, replace ignition coil.

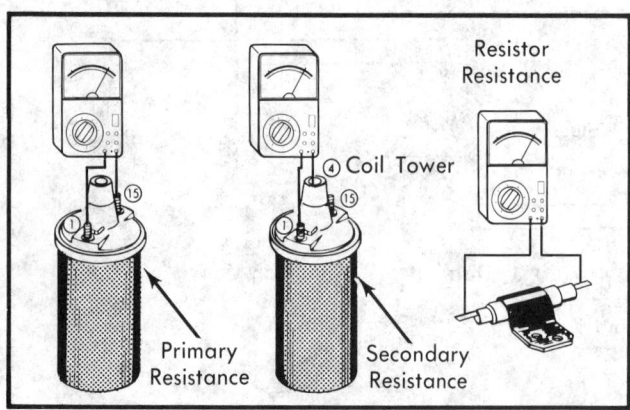

Fig. 3 Ohmmeter Hookup for Ignition Coil Primary and Secondary Resistance Checks and for Resistor Resistance Check

Ignition Coil Resistance Specifications (Ohms)		
Application	**Primary**	**Secondary**
BMW	.4	.....
Fiat Strada & X1/9	1.1-1.7	6,000-10,000
Mercedes-Benz	.38-.42	8,000-11,000
Peugeot 604	.33-.46	7,000-12,000
Porsche		
924	1.0-1.35	5,500-8,000
928	.33-.46	7,000-12,000
Saab	1.05-1.35	5,500-8,500
Volvo	1.0-2.0	

IGNITION COIL VOLTAGE CHECK

1) Connect voltmeter positive lead to positive coil terminal 15. Connect negative lead to terminal 1. Turn ignition switch "ON". A reading of 4-7 volts should be indicated. If less, check wires, connections at ignition switch, resistors, coil and control unit to eliminate voltage drop.

2) Connect voltmeter positive lead to negative coil terminal 1, and negative lead to a good ground. Reading should be 0.5-2.0 volts (maximum 2.0 volts). If previous tests and pick-up coil resistance, starting voltage and control module voltage checks prove OK, substitute a known good control module. If system is now operative, install new module.

STARTING VOLTAGE CHECK

Disconnect line leading to starter terminal 15a at the .4 ohm resistor (most models). Attach voltmeter and crank engine. Voltage should be the same as battery voltage. If not, check for break in electrical supply line or contact 15a in starter relay.

PICK-UP COIL RESISTANCE CHECK

Turn ignition switch "OFF". Disconnect connector from control module and attach ohmmeter leads (set in x100 scale) to terminals 7 and 31d of harness connector. See Fig. 4. Measure pick-up coil resistance. If not to specifications, remove electrical connections at distributor and connect ohmmeter leads directly to pick-up coil terminals. If still not to specifications, replace pick-up coil assembly.

Pick-Up Coil Resistance Specifications (Ohms)	
Application	**Ohms**
BMW	520-700
Fiat Strada & X1/9	890-1285
Mercedes-Benz	500-700
Peugeot 604	485-700
Porsche	
924	890-1285
928	485-700
Saab	895-1285
Volvo	
4-Cylinder	950-1250
6-Cylinder	540-660

BOSCH ELECTRONIC IGNITION SYSTEM (Cont.)

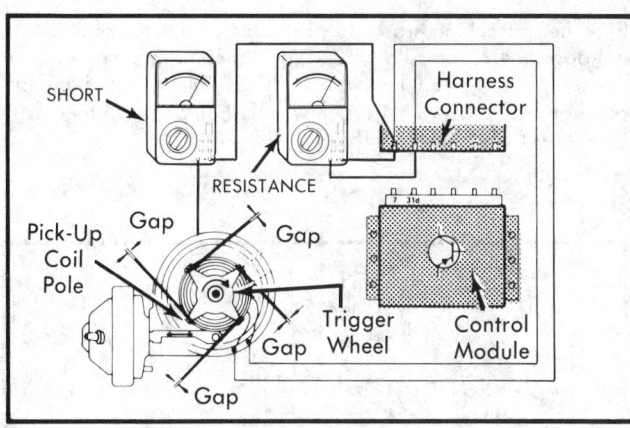

Fig. 4 Ohmmeter Hookups for Pick-Up Coil Resistance and Short Checks

PICK-UP COIL SHORT CHECK

Turn ignition switch "OFF". Connect an ohmmeter to control module harness terminal 7 and ground and then to terminal 31d and ground. Resistance reading should be infinity. If not, make same check at distributor connector. If infinity reading is not obtained, replace pick-up coil assembly. If infinity is shown, replace harness.

DWELL ANGLE CHECK AND VISUAL CHECK OF PICK-UP COIL ASSEMBLY

Check trigger wheel and pick-up coil assembly for damage. Also check visually for air gap between trigger wheel and pick-up coil. See Fig. 4. If damaged or if air gap is not to specifications, replace distributor (if components cannot be replaced individually). Check dwell angle and compare with specifications. If not within specifications, repeat Pick-Up Coil

Dwell Angle & Air Gap Specifications

Application	Dwell Angle	Air Gap
BMW	32-53°@1500 RPM	.014-.028" (.36-.72 mm)
Fiat Strada & X1/9	②	.011-.019" (.3-.5 mm)
Mercedes-Benz		
280 Series	33-51°@1500 RPM	②
450 Series	25-39°@1500 RPM	②
Peugeot 604		
Cyls. 1, 2 and 3	41-64°@1500 RPM	②
Cyls. 4, 5 and 6	25-34°@1500 RPM	②
Porsche		
911SC	②	②
924	52-70°@1500 RPM	.010" (.25 mm)
928	25-39°@1500 RPM	.010" (.25 mm)
Saab	60-80°①	②
Volvo		
4-Cylinder	45-63°@1500 RPM	②
6-Cylinder	45-63°@1500 RPM	②

① — No speed specified by manufacturer.
② — Specification not available from manufacturer. Be sure there is clearance and that no parts are damaged.

Resistance, Short and Visual Checks. If OK, then replace control module.

CONTROL MODULE VOLTAGE

Disconnect connector from control module and turn ignition switch "ON". Attach voltmeter positive lead to terminal 15 of control module harness connector. Connect negative lead to ground. Battery voltage should be shown. If not, check for voltage drop in harness between ignition switch and control module.

CONTROL MODULE GROUND CHECK

Disconnect connector at control module. Turn ignition switch "ON". Connect voltmeter positive lead to terminal 31 of control module (not harness). Connect negative lead to ground. Reading should be zero (0) volts. Check module ground wire and repair as necessary if reading is not zero (0).

FINAL CONTROL MODULE OR IGNITION COIL CHECK

If ignition coil is suspected of being defective, substitute a known good coil and attempt to start vehicle. If it starts, reinstall old coil and start vehicle. If it then fails to start, replace with new coil. If control module is suspected, substitute a known good module and start vehicle. If it starts, reinstall original module. If vehicle fails to start now, install new control module. If system still fails to operate, disconnect tachometer connector at instrument cluster. Attempt to start engine. If engine now starts, replace tachometer.

OVERHAUL

Disassembly — 1) Remove distributor cap, rotor and dust cover. Remove vacuum unit screws and lock clasp screws. Remove screws securing electrical leads and remove leads by carefully pulling straight out.

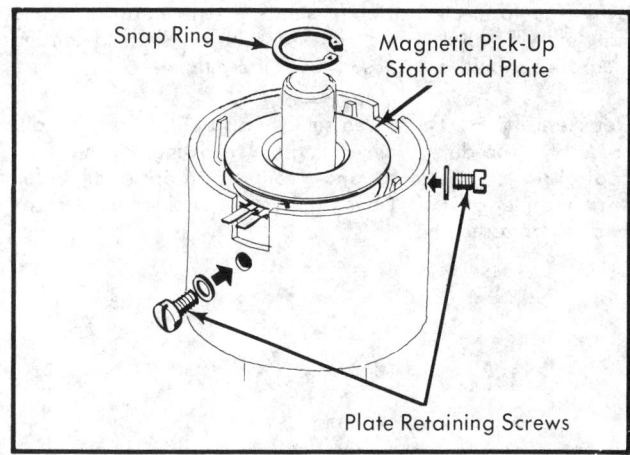

Fig. 5 Removing or Installing Pick-Up, Stator and Carrier Plate

NOTE — *Keep screws with component they attach, as screws are different lengths and damage could result if installed in wrong location.*

BOSCH ELECTRONIC IGNITION SYSTEM (Cont.)

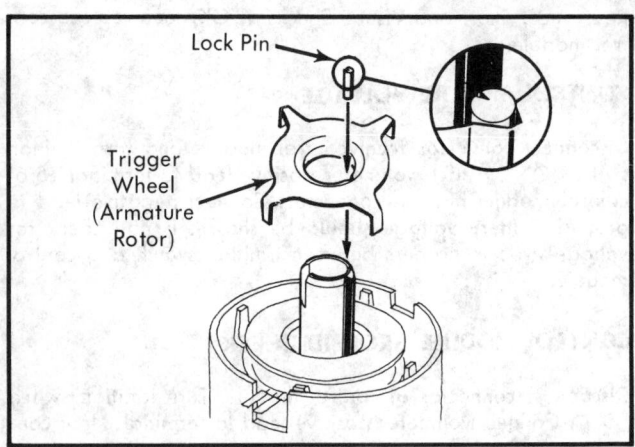

**Fig. 6   Installing Trigger Wheel (Armature)
and Lock Pin**

2) Remove trigger wheel snap ring and then shims. Using 2 screwdrivers, carefully pry upward on trigger wheel. Remove trigger wheel and lock pin. Remove screws securing pick-up coil and stator assembly carrier plate. Remove snap ring and retaining clips. Lift carrier plate and stator straight up off shaft. Remove 3 screws to separate stator winding from carrier plate.

3) Disconnect springs to centrifugal governor. Mark drive shaft relationship to distributor shaft and then secure drive shaft in a soft-jawed vise. Carefully tap on distributor housing with a plastic mallet until circlip releases. If equipped, remove triggering contacts and attaching screws.

4) Remove resilient ring. Mark location of flange to distributor shaft. Support distributor shaft and using a pin punch, remove pin. Remove flange and distributor shaft. Remove lock springs for centrifugal weights and then weights.

Inspection — Springs for weights must not be deformed or damaged. Holes in centrifugal governor weights must not be oval or deformed. Distributor shaft-to-cam clearance should not exceed .004" (.1 mm). Distributor shaft-to-housing clearance should not exceed .008" (.2 mm).

Reassembly — 1) To reassemble distributor, reverse disassembly procedure, while noting the following: Place a light coat of grease on weights and a couple of drops of oil on felt wick in center of shaft. Do not get grease or oil on pick-up coil and stator assembly.

2) When attaching stator to plate, the connector pins should be positioned opposite and above the attachment ear for carrier plate. Install lock pin with lift facing ridge on distributor shaft. Slot on trigger wheel should be aligned with groove on distributor shaft.

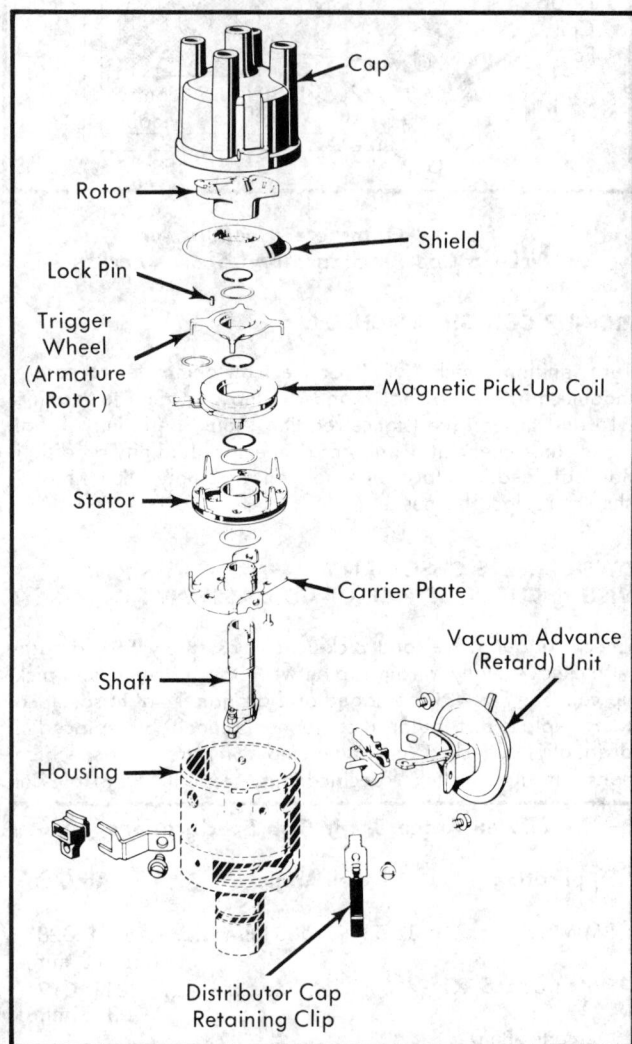

**Fig. 7   Exploded View of Bosch
Breakerless Distributor**

BOSCH HALL EFFECT ELECTRONIC IGNITION SYSTEM

Audi
Volkswagen
  All Calif. Models
  Federal Models
    Rabbit with Carburetor

DESCRIPTION

The Bosch Hall Effect electronic ignition system consists of a breakerless Hall Effect distributor, an ignition control unit, ignition coil, ignition switch, and battery.

Closely allied with the ignition system is an idle stabilizer, a solid state control unit located between the ignition control unit and the distributor. It replaces the distributor in sending signals to the ignition control unit when engine speeds fall below 940 RPM.

The Hall Effect distributor has normal centrifugal and vacuum advance mechanisms. *See Figs. 1 and 10.*

OPERATION

The Hall sending unit (pick-up coil) is mounted inside the distributor on a switch plate. A trigger wheel (segmented shutter) attached to the distributor shaft under the rotor, passes in and out of the air gap of the Hall sending unit.

At speeds greater than 940 RPM, the Hall sending unit signals the ignition control unit to make and break the primary circuit current flow in the ignition coil. There is one trigger wheel shutter or tooth for each cylinder of the engine. Shutter width determines dwell, which is not adjustable.

As the ignition control unit breaks the primary circuit through the coil, secondary voltage is released through high tension wiring, distributor cap and rotor to spark plugs. *See Fig. 1.*

If engine speed drops below 940 RPM, the idle stabilizer takes over the duty of producing the signal to the ignition control unit, instead of the Hall sending unit. Mounted between the

distributor and the ignition control unit, the idle stabilizer senses engine speed earlier, causing ignition timing to advance. Advancing ignition timing causes idle speed to increase, and the Hall sending unit to resume its normal operation.

SPECIFICATIONS

Centrifugal & Vacuum Advance − *See Specifications Pages in this section.*

ADJUSTMENTS

Hall Effect Air Gap − Air gap is pre-set and cannot be adjusted.

TESTING

NOTE − *Be sure battery is at full charge and in good condition before making tests. Check all wiring harnesses, ignition switch, ignition coil, spark plug cables and connectors.*

TESTING PRECAUTIONS

CAUTION − *Do not connect any 12 volt test instruments on terminal 15 of ignition coil, as this could damage electronic components. Do not connect any condenser/suppressor or powered test light to terminal 1 of ignition coil. Only connect and disconnect test instruments when ignition is turned "OFF".*

TACHOMETER ADAPTER

1) An adapter is necessary when attaching a conventional tachometer into the Hall Effect electronic ignition system. *See Fig. 2.* Tachometer black lead is attached to engine ground. Attach adapter to tachometer red lead.

2) Adapter is formed from 2 wires soldered together at one end. One wire (leading to coil terminal 1) must be equipped with a 1000 ohm, 1 watt resistor. The second wire (also leading to engine ground) must be equipped with a 12,000 ohm, 1 watt resistor. Both resistors should be soldered to attaching wires.

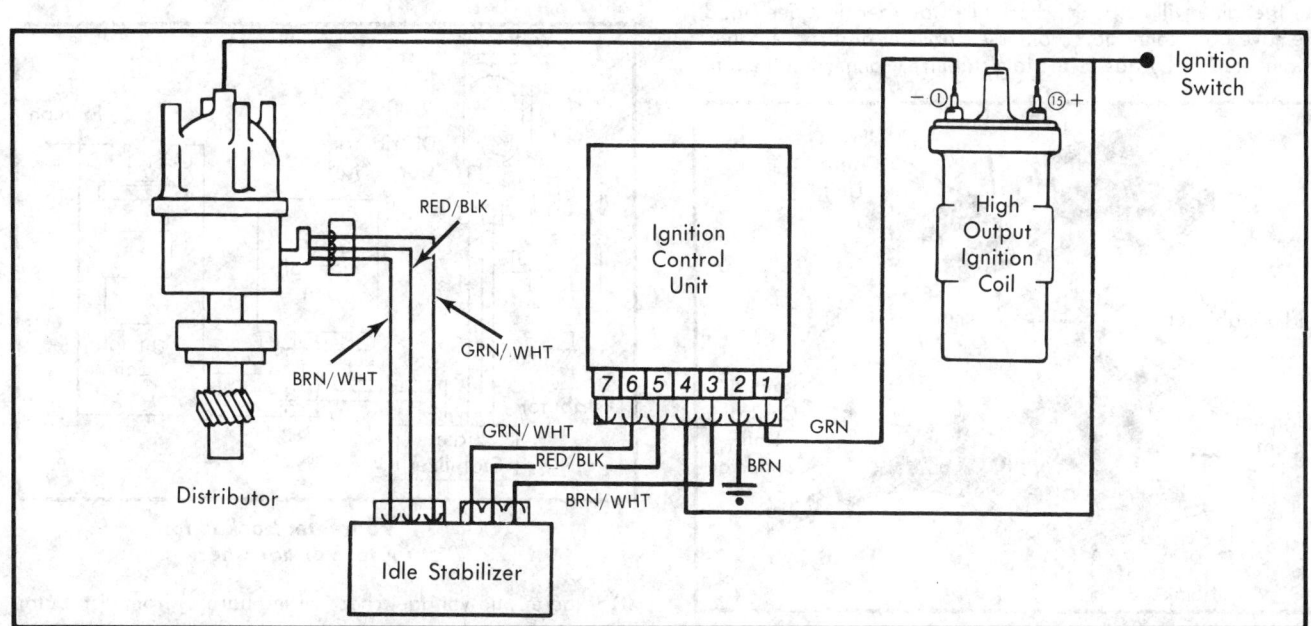

Fig. 1 *Schematic Diagram of Bosch Hall Effect Electronic Ignition System*

BOSCH HALL EFFECT ELECTRONIC IGNITION SYSTEM (Cont.)

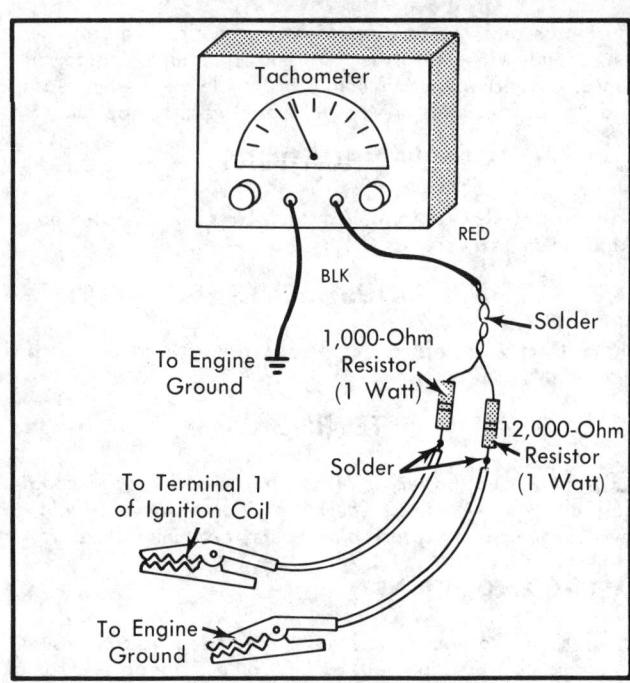

Fig. 2   Assembling Tachometer Adapter

SYSTEM SPARK CHECK

1) If vehicle will not start, check for secondary voltage. Remove coil high tension wire from distributor cap. Hold wire approximately ¼" (6 mm) from engine ground, using insulated pliers.

2) Crank engine and check for a constant blue spark at gap to ground. If there is a good spark, check distributor cap, rotor, spark plug wires, spark plugs, fuel system and engine mechanical components. If there is no spark or only a very weak spark, perform the following checks.

IDLE STABILIZER CHECK

1) If engine will not start, check idle stabilizer first. *See Fig. 3.* Remove both connectors from idle stabilizer and connect them together. This by-passes the idle stabilizer connecting the igni-

tion control unit directly to the distributor. If engine now starts, idle stabilizer is defective.

2) In other cases where engine starts but idle stabilizer is suspected, by-pass the stabilizer by removing the 2 connectors and connecting them together. Turn off all electrical accessories and set idle speed and timing.

3) Then, reconnect the idle stabilizer. Ignition timing at idle may fluctuate, but should be between 3° ATDC (±3°). Turn all power accessories in step **2)** back on. Ignition timing should be advanced to keep engine speed to specifications. If not, replace idle stabilizer.

NOTE — *An alternative manner of checking idle stabilizer can be used. With engine oil temperature above 140° F (60° C), connect test equipment according to manufacturer's instructions. Start engine and slowly increase engine speed while applying foot brake. Let engine idle. On vehicles with manual transmission, engage 4th gear and release clutch slowly. On vehicles with automatic transmission, move selector into "DRIVE" position. As engine load increases, ignition timing must advance. If not, idle stabilizer control unit is defective and must be replaced.*

SPARK PLUG WIRE RESISTANCE

If spark plug connectors have sheet metal jackets carrying the following symbol (▬►◄▬), they contain "air gap" resistors. Wires cannot then be checked for resistance using an ohmmeter. An oscilloscope must be used.

ROTOR RESISTANCE CHECK

Connect leads of an ohmmeter set in x1000 scale to distributor rotor. Resistance should be approximately 1000 ohms. If not to specification, replace rotor.

DISTRIBUTOR VOLTAGE CHECK

1) Remove connector from distributor and connect voltmeter leads to each of the two outer terminals. See *Fig. 4.* Turn ignition switch "ON". Battery voltage should be read on voltmeter.

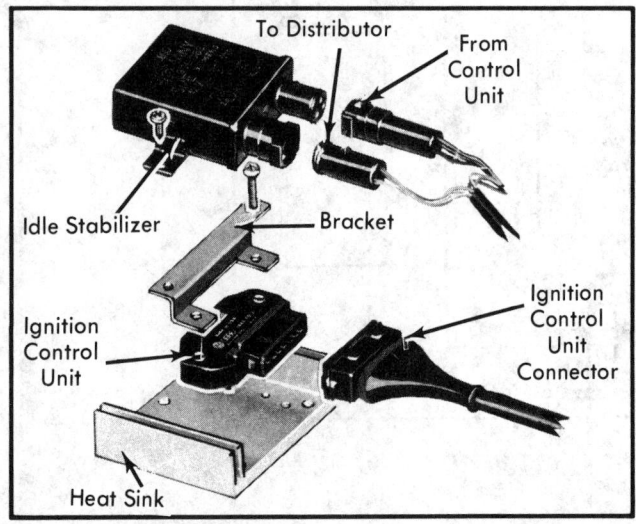

Fig. 3   Idle Stabilizer and Ignition Control Unit

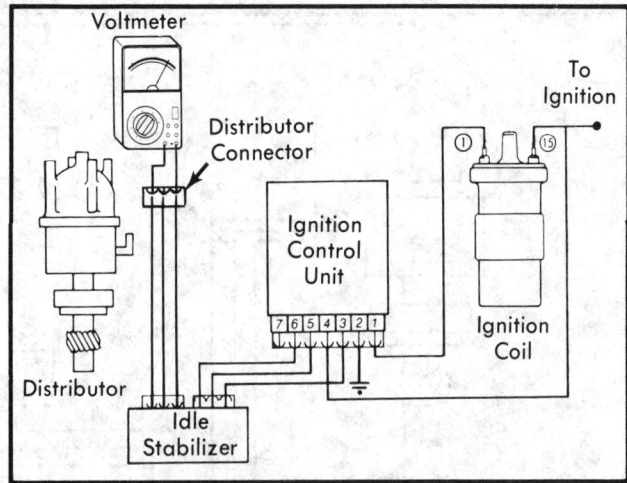

Fig. 4   Voltmeter Hookup for Distributor Voltage Check

2) If there is no voltage, check wiring harness from distributor to control unit before proceeding to Control Unit Voltage Check.

BOSCH HALL EFFECT ELECTRONIC IGNITION SYSTEM (Cont.)

CONTROL UNIT VOLTAGE CHECK

1) Disconnect connectors from idle stabilizer and connect them to each other. Reconnect connector to distributor. Remove connector from electronic ignition control unit. See *Fig. 5*. Connect positive voltmeter lead to terminal 4 of control unit harness connector. Attach negative lead to terminal 2 (ground).

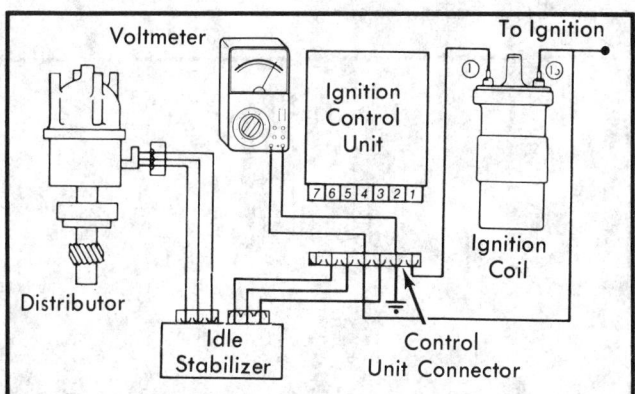

Fig. 5   Voltmeter Hookup for Control Unit Voltage Check

2) Turn ignition switch "ON". Voltmeter should register approximately 12 volts. If voltage at connector is within specification, replace defective control unit. If not within specification, check wiring circuit.

IGNITION COIL RESISTANCE CHECK

1) Remove all wires from ignition coil. Set an ohmmeter in the low scale and attach its leads to ignition coil primary terminals 1 and 15. See *Fig. 6*. Coil primary resistance should be .52-.76 ohm.

NOTE — *It may be impossible to check primary resistance with ordinary shop equipment. If electronic ignition checks OK, but there is no spark available at high tension wire, replace ignition coil and retest.*

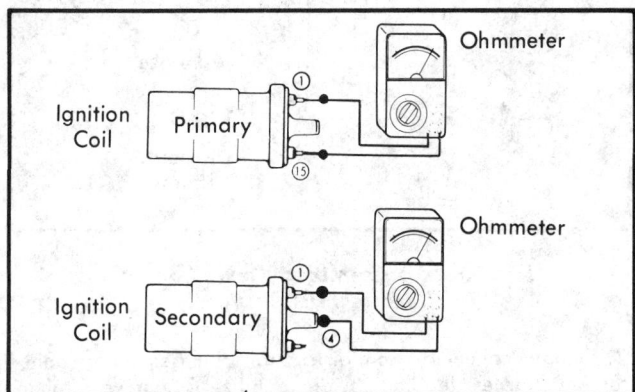

Fig. 6   Ohmmeter Hookups for Coil Resistance Checks

2) Reset ohmmeter to x1000 scale and connect leads to primary terminal 1 and to coil tower, terminal 4. See *Fig. 6*. Resistance should read 2400-3500 ohms.

3) If either reading is not to specification, replace ignition coil.

IGNITION CONTROL UNIT CHECK

Vanagon Only — 1) Remove connector from distributor. Connect positive lead of voltmeter to terminal 15 of ignition coil. Connect negative lead to terminal 1 of coil. See *Fig. 7*. Turn ignition switch "ON".

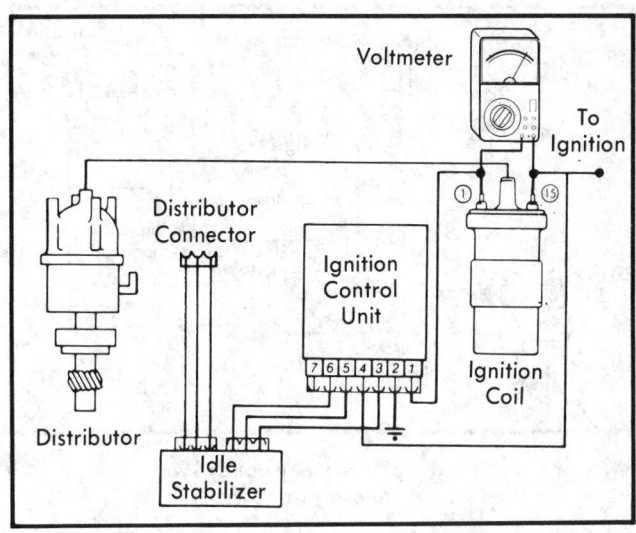

Fig. 7   Voltmeter Hookup for Ignition Control Unit Operation Check (Vanagon)

2) Voltage should be approximately 6 volts and then drop to zero (0) volts within 1 or 2 seconds. If not, replace ignition control unit. Also check ignition coil.

All Except Vanagon — 1) Disconnect both plugs at idle stabilizer control unit and connect them together. Attach positive lead of voltmeter to terminal 15 and negative lead to ground. Turn ignition switch "ON". Voltage must be present.

2) Disconnect coil high tension wire from distributor cap. Disconnect connector at distributor. Connect positive terminal of voltmeter to terminal 1 of ignition coil and negative lead to ground. Turn ignition switch "ON". A voltage reading of at least 12 volts should be read. If voltage drops below 12 volts within 1 second, turn ignition switch "OFF" and replace defective ignition control unit.

3) Disconnect green/white wire at connector on distributor and ground the wire. Voltage reading must be approximately 12 volts. Disconnect green/white wire from ground and voltage must drop shortly to 6 volts.

4) If voltage does not drop, replace defective ignition control unit. Connect voltmeter positive lead to red wire (connected to terminal 5) at distributor connector. Attach negative lead to brown wire (connected to terminal 3). Turn ignition switch "ON". Voltmeter must read about 10 volts. If not, replace ignition control unit.

5) If other tests fail to locate defective components, substitute a known good ignition control unit and retest for secondary voltage spark.

BOSCH HALL EFFECT ELECTRONIC IGNITION SYSTEM (Cont.)

HALL SENDING UNIT (GENERATOR) CHECK

1) Reconnect the control unit harness connector to control unit. See Fig. 8. Pull back rubber boot on connector. Attach voltmeter positive lead to connector terminal 6 and negative lead to terminal 3. Make sure connector is attached securely to control unit.

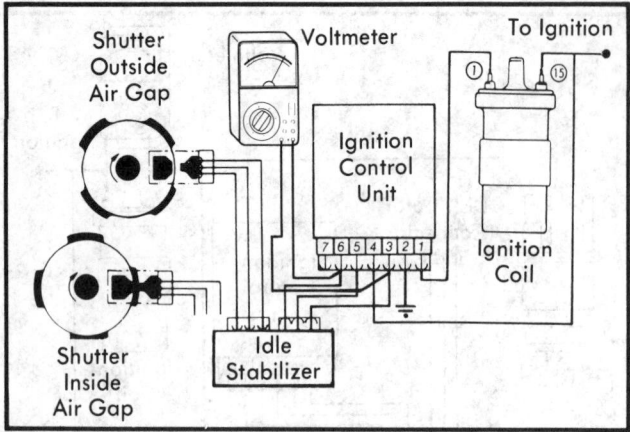

**Fig. 8   Voltmeter Hookups for
Hall Sending Unit Check**

2) Turn ignition switch "ON". With trigger wheel shutter outside Hall sending unit air gap, check voltage reading. It should be 0.4 volts or less.

3) Now turn distributor until trigger wheel shutter is inside Hall sending unit air gap. See inset in Fig. 8. Voltmeter reading should increase to 9 volts.

4) Connect voltmeter leads in same manner to terminals 3 and 5 of control unit. See Fig. 9. Turn ignition switch "ON". Voltage should be a minimum of 7.5 volts.

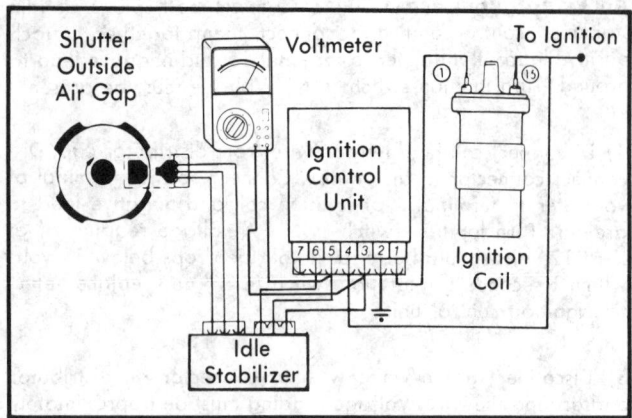

**Fig. 9   Voltmeter Hookup for Final
Hall Sending Unit Check**

5) If any of the above voltage readings are incorrect, replace the Hall sending unit.

ALTERNATIVE HALL SENDING UNIT OPERATION CHECK

1) Disconnect high tension wire at distributor and connect it to ground. Connect a test light (4-24V) between terminal 1 and 15 of ignition coil. Crank engine with starter for approximately 5 seconds.

2) Test light must flicker. If not, replace Hall sending unit in distributor.

OVERHAUL

Disassembly — 1) Loosen ground strap and remove static shield from distributor cap. See Fig. 10. Remove cap, rotor, carbon brush and spring. Remove dust cover.

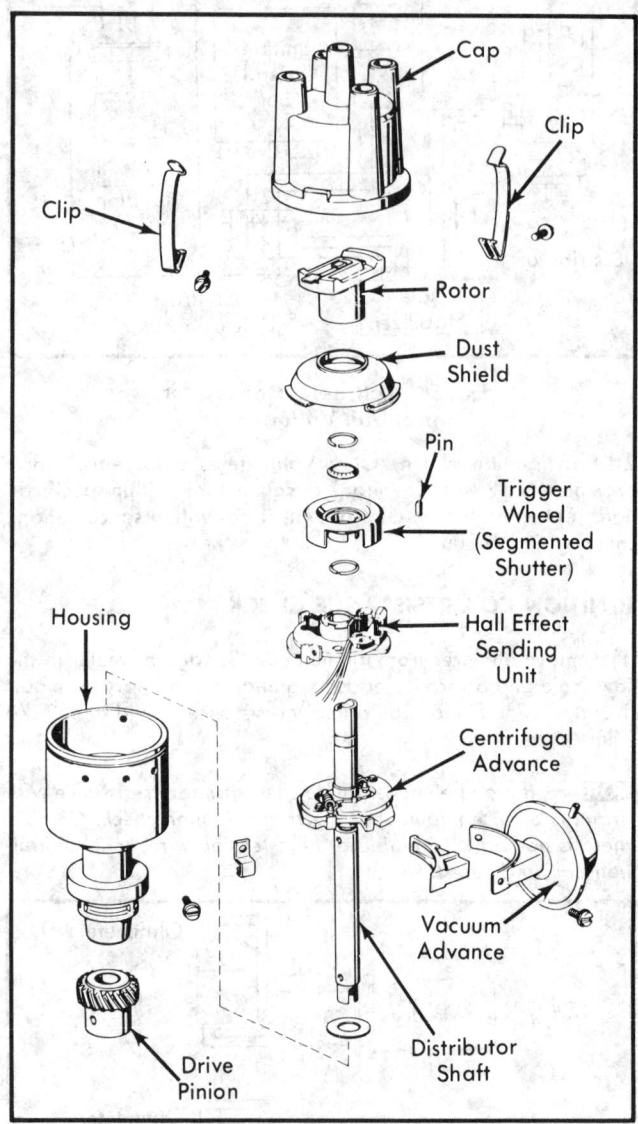

**Fig. 10   Disassembled View of Bosch
Hall Effect Distributor**

2) Remove connector from distributor (Hall generator connector and harness leading to idle stabilizer). Remove retaining snap ring and trigger wheel (segmented shutter). Remove washers. Remove screws and lift out Hall sending unit and connecting socket.

3) Remove base plate and vacuum unit. Remove pin and distributor drive pinion and shims.

Reassembly — To reassemble, reverse disassembly procedure. Replace seals and check components for cracks, corrosion and wear. Clean cap before installing.

ELECTRICAL

BOSCH SINGLE BREAKER DISTRIBUTOR

Volkswagen (Federal)
Except Rabbit (Carburetor Model)

DESCRIPTION

Conventional single breaker distributor with centrifugal advance and vacuum advance and/or retard unit. Vacuum units may be single or dual diaphragm and are linked to the moveable portion of the breaker plate assembly to advance or retard spark.

NOTE — *Some distributors may use a dual diaphragm unit to provide retard only (vacuum advance side not used.)*

SPECIFICATIONS

Point Gap & Cam Angle — *See Tune-Up Data on Car Model Tune-Up Pages.*

Centrifugal & Vacuum Advance (Or Retard) — *See Specification Tables in this section.*

ADJUSTMENT

Point Gap, Alignment, & Cam Angle — With rubbing block on high point of cam lobe, insert a feeler gauge blade between contacts and check reading against specification. To correct, loosen retaining screw and move stationary contact point until correct gap is obtained, then tighten screw. Align points if necessary by bending stationary contact support only. Check cam angle with a dwell meter; compare indicated reading with specification and correct if necessary.

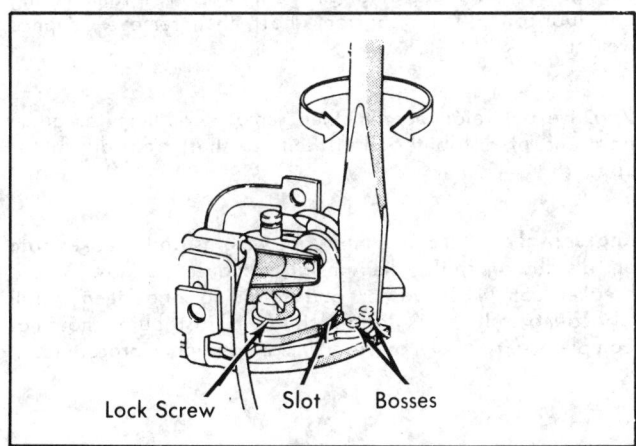

Fig. 1   Adjusting Contact Points

Lock Screw   Slot   Bosses

Breaker Arm Spring Tension — To check spring tension, place hook end of spring scale as close as possible to the movable breaker point. Pull scale at a right angle (90 degrees) to the movable arm and note reading just as points begin to open.

Centrifugal Advance — 1) Check distributor in test stand according to test equipment manufacturer's instructions. Operate distributor both up and down the RPM range and check advance at all RPM settings specified. Adjust or replace springs, weights or cam as necessary.

2) If distributor has adjustable driving collar for centrifugal advance, disassemble and lift shaft out. *See Fig. 2.* It is not necessary to remove breaker cam assembly from shaft. To adjust, loosen screws retaining driving collar. If collar is turned in direction of rotation, the advance curve rises. Turning collar in opposite direction of rotation will lower the curve.

CAUTION — *Centrifugal advance curve must not be adjusted by bending spring clamps of driving collar.*

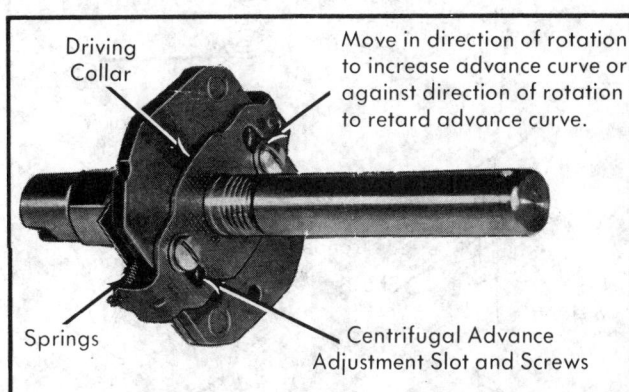

Driving Collar

Move in direction of rotation to increase advance curve or against direction of rotation to retard advance curve.

Springs

Centrifugal Advance Adjustment Slot and Screws

Fig. 2   Centrifugal Advance Adjustment (Driving Collar)

3) If distributor does not have adjustable driving collar, adjustment may be made by bending spring anchor tabs to modify spring tension (see illustration). To adjust for low speed operation, bend primary spring anchor tab outward to decrease advance, and inward to increase advance. For high speed operation, bend secondary spring anchor tab in or out to obtain specified settings.

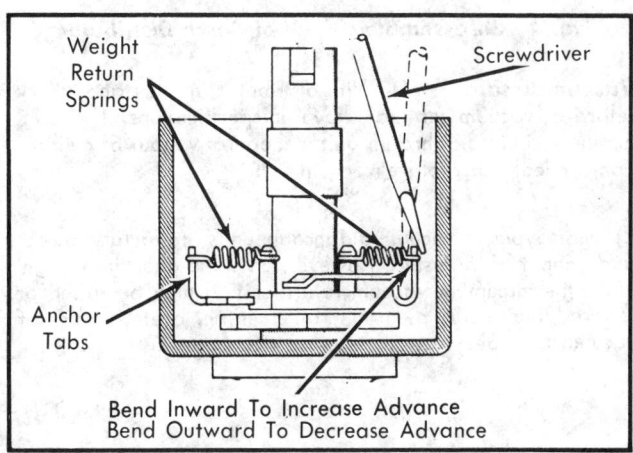

Weight Return Springs

Screwdriver

Anchor Tabs

Bend Inward To Increase Advance
Bend Outward To Decrease Advance

Fig. 3   Centrifugal Advance Adjustment (Spring Anchor Tabs)

Vacuum Advance — 1) With distributor in test stand, check advance at vacuum settings shown in specifications. If tests indicate vacuum diaphragm unit is inoperative, out of calibration, or leaking, replace vacuum unit.

2) Most types of vacuum diaphragm units are factory pre-set and cannot be adjusted. However, on some dual diaphragm vacuum units, the vacuum advance may be increased or decreased by turning an Allen screw located in end of diaphragm unit.

BOSCH SINGLE BREAKER DISTRIBUTOR (Cont.)

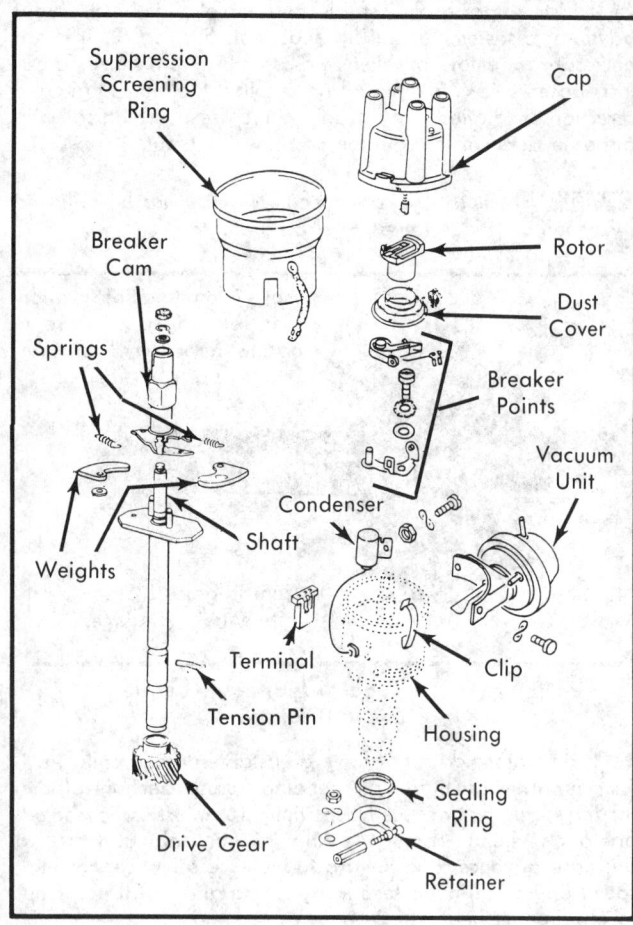

Fig. 4   Disassembled View of Bosch Distributor

Fig. 5   Adjusting Maximum Vacuum Retard (Eccentric Location)

OVERHAUL

Vacuum Retard — 1) With distributor in test stand, check retard at vacuum setttings shown in specifications. If tests indicate vacuum diaphragm unit is inoperative, out of calibration, or leaking, replace vacuum unit.

2) Most types of vacuum diaphragm units are factory pre-set and cannot be adjusted. However, on some dual diaphragm units, the maximum vacuum retard setting may be raised or lowered if necessary by turning an eccentric, located at side of vacuum unit. See *Fig. 5*.

NOTE — *All parts should be marked or set aside separately or in groups so that same combination can be reinstalled. Keep screws with the component they attach, as screws are different lengths and damage could occur if installed in wrong position.*

Disassembly — 1) Disconnect and remove vacuum unit. Remove breaker points and condenser, then remove breaker assembly. Note positioning of centrifugal advance parts and mark for assembly reference. Disconnect and remove centrifugal advance springs (do not distort). Using 2 screwdrivers, carefully pry upward on the lower edge of breaker cam to disengage cam retaining ring. Lift cam, washer, retaining ring and lubricating felt pad from shaft, then remove advance weights.

2) Drive out retaining pin, then remove coupling (or gear) from end of distributor shaft. Remove shaft from distributor housing.

Reassembly — Install centrifugal weights and breaker cam on distributor shaft, then install advance springs. Secure breaker cam with washer and retaining ring, then install lubricating felt pad. Install shaft in distributor housing. Complete reassembly by reversing disassembly procedure.

DUCELLIER ELECTRONIC IGNITION SYSTEM – PEUGEOT

505

DESCRIPTION

The Ducellier electronic ignition system consists of a Ducellier breakerless distributor, a Delco-Remy ignition coil and amplifier module, an ignition switch and necessary wiring.

The distributor contains both centrifugal and vacuum advance mechanisms, a pick-up coil and a reluctor (polarity wheel). See Fig. 1. The ignition coil and amplifier are both mounted to a common light alloy base that provides both good grounding and cooling of the amplifier module. Silicone grease, which comes with the module and is applied between the module and base, gives improved heat transfer. Since both units are grounded through the common base, all mounting bolts should be snug.

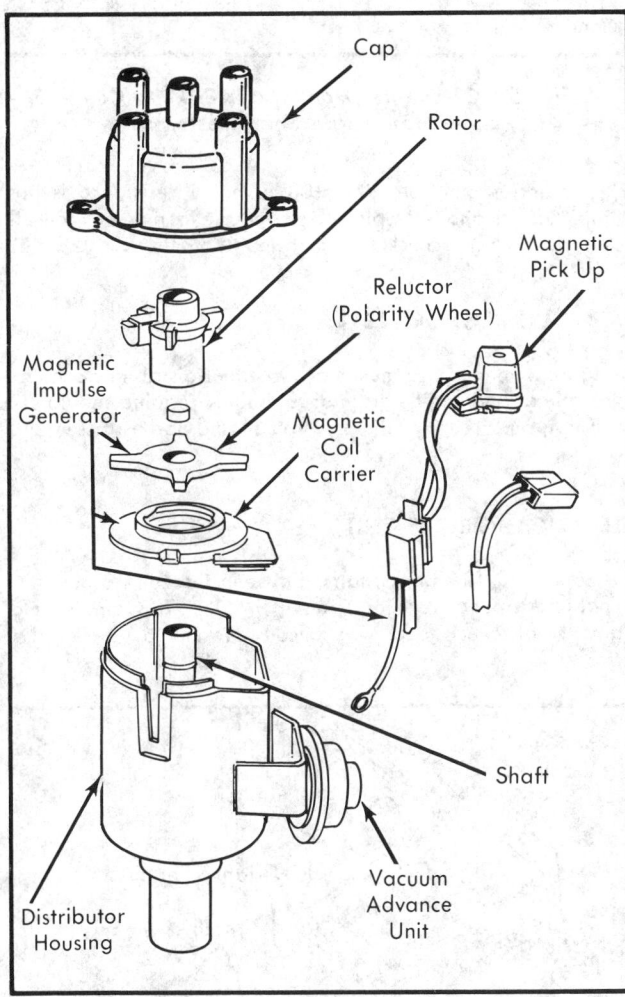

Fig. 1 Exploded View of Ducellier Breakerless Distributor

The ignition coil is encased in epoxy resin instead of oil. The amplifier module receives, amplifies and sends electronic signals to provide proper spark timing.

OPERATION

The distributor contains an electronic pulse generator, consisting of a pick-up coil and a reluctor (polarity wheel). As the

distributor shaft turns, the reluctor teeth approach and pass the magnetic pick-up coil. This causes signals to be transmitted to the amplifier module, which in turn opens and closes a transistorized switch in the module. This turns the primary circuit of the ignition coil on and off. When the primary circuit is switched off, a high voltage surge occurs in the secondary circuit, firing the spark plugs.

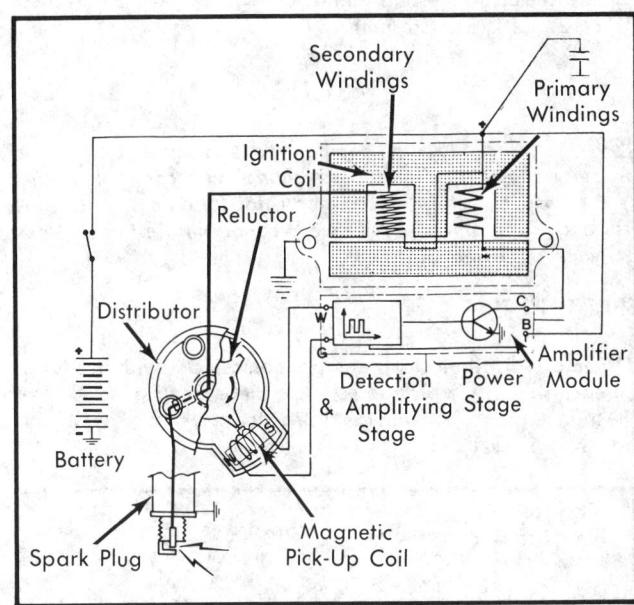

Fig. 2 Schematic of Ducellier Electronic Ignition System

The amplifier module has 4 terminals. Terminals "W" and "G" are connected to the distributor magnetic pulse generator (pick-up coil). Terminal "B" is connected to the coil positive terminal, and terminal "C" to the coil negative terminal. See Fig. 3. The unit is grounded through one of its mounting bolts through the alloy base.

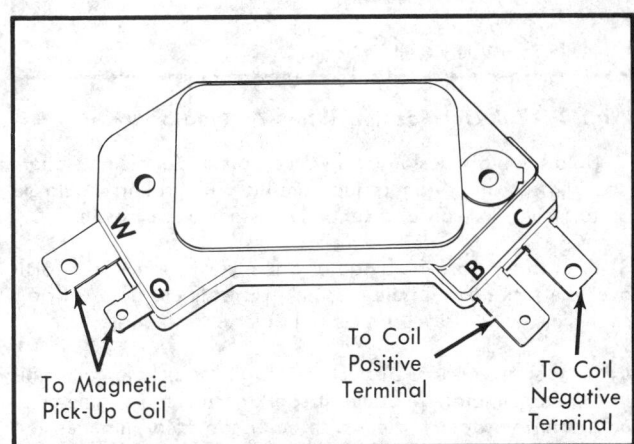

Fig. 3 Amplifier Module Connector Terminals

SPECIFICATIONS

Centrifugal & Vacuum Advance – See Specifications Tables in this section.

DUCELLIER ELECTRONIC IGNITION SYSTEM — PEUGEOT (Cont.)

ADJUSTMENTS

Reluctor-to-Pick-Up Coil Air Gap — Loosen both magnetic pick-up coil mounting screws. See Fig. 4. Position reluctor tooth in line with pick-up coil pole piece. Insert a non-magnetic feeler gauge of the proper thickness (.016" or .40 mm) between one reluctor tooth and pole piece. Pivot pick-up coil against feeler gauge and tighten both screws. Air gap should be .012-.020" (.30-.50 mm).

TESTING

NOTE — Before testing components, be sure battery is properly charged, all wires are sound, and connections are secure. Inspect distributor cap and rotor for cracks or carbon-tracking. Turn ignition "OFF" when connecting test equipment or when replacing parts.

SPARKING TEST

1) Remove distributor cap and position reluctor with one tooth on each side of the pick-up coil pole piece. See Fig. 4. Remove the high tension lead from the distributor cap and turn the ignition switch "ON".

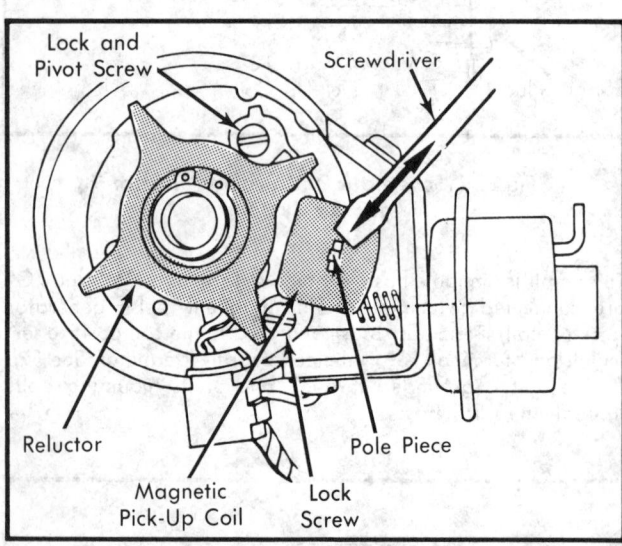

Fig. 4   Reluctor Position When Making Sparking Test

2) Hold the high tension lead with a pair of electrician's pliers about .4" (10 mm) from a good ground. The ground should be as far from the coil and amplifier assembly as possible.

3) Alternately pass the blade of a screwdriver back and forth over the pick-up coil pole piece. A spark should occur at gap each time screwdriver passes pole piece.

4) If no spark occurs, suspect the magnetic pick-up coil, ignition coil or amplifier module. If spark occurs, but engine does not perform properly, check distributor cap, rotor, high tension cables and battery condition.

PICK-UP COIL RESISTANCE TEST

1) Turn ignition switch "OFF". Disconnect connector for terminals "W" and "G" at amplifier module. Using an ohmmeter set in the x100 scale, check the resistance between distributor connector terminals. See Fig. 5.

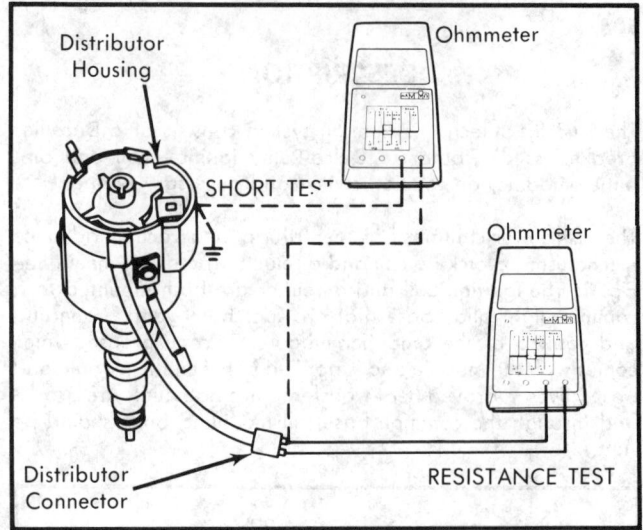

Fig. 5   Ohmmeter Hookup for Pick-Up Coil Resistance and Short Tests

2) Reading should be 900-1100 ohms. If resistance is not within specifications, replace the magnetic pick-up coil. If resistance is high, check for corroded contacts.

PICK-UP COIL SHORT TEST

Using an ohmmeter, connect leads to either distributor connector terminal and engine ground. An infinity reading should exist. If not, replace magnetic pick-up coil and harness assembly. See Fig. 5.

ELECTRICAL CIRCUIT TEST

1) Connect a 12-volt test lamp between the coil positive terminal and ground. Turn ignition switch "ON". Test lamp should light. If not, check feed wire to coil. See Fig. 6.

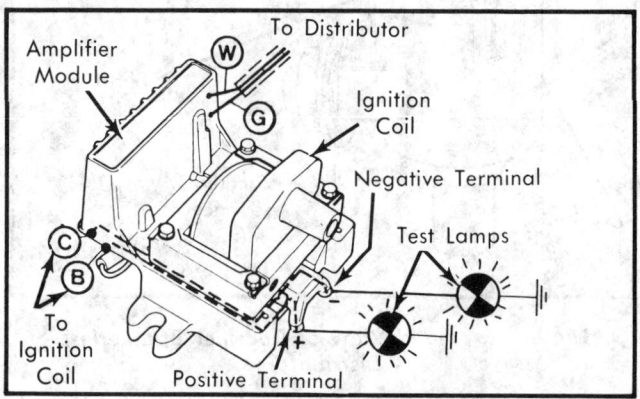

Fig. 6   Test Lamp Hookup for Electrical Circuit Test

2) Connect test lamp between the coil negative terminal and ground. Turn ignition switch "ON". Test lamp should again light. If not, check if coil primary circuit is broken or if amplifier module's power transistor is shorted.

DUCELLIER ELECTRONIC IGNITION SYSTEM – PEUGEOT (Cont.)

IGNITION COIL RESISTANCE TEST

1) Using an ohmmeter set in the low scale, connect leads to coil primary (positive and negative) terminals. Resistance should be .48-.61 ohms. *See Fig. 7.*

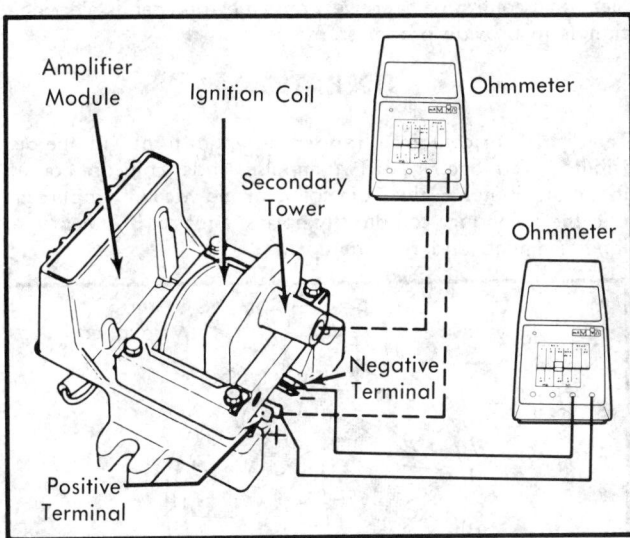

Fig. 7   Ohmmeter Hookup for Making Ignition Coil Resistance Tests

2) Connect ohmmeter set in the x1000 scale to the coil positive terminal and its secondary tower. Reading should be 9,000-

11,000 ohms. If either reading is not to specifications, replace ignition coil.

AMPLIFIER MODULE TEST

1) Disconnect distributor harness connector from amplifier module "W" and "G" terminals. Disconnect the high tension lead from distributor cap. Turn ignition switch "ON". Hold high tension lead with a pair of electrician's pliers and position it .4" (10 mm) from good engine ground away from amplifier. The ground should be as far from the coil and amplifier module assembly as possible.

2) Use a jumper wire to feed terminal "G" of amplifier module with successive impulses from battery positive terminal. At each impulse, a spark should jump the gap to ground. If not, repeat same test with a new amplifier module. If spark jumps gap, replace with new module.

OVERHAUL

Disassembly – 1) Remove distributor cap, rotor, and plastic protector. Remove screw in the side of distributor. Pull upward on electrical connector to remove it from distributor housing. Remove 2 screws securing magnetic pick-up coil. *See Fig. 1.*

2) Lift out pick-up coil assembly. Remove reluctor, vacuum advance unit, electromagnetic coil carrier. Remove drive pinion from distributor shaft and pull shaft and centrifugal advance mechanism from housing.

Reassembly – To install, reverse removal procedure.

DUCELLIER ELECTRONIC IGNITION SYSTEM — RENAULT

Le Car

DESCRIPTION

The Ducellier electronic ignition system consists of a Ducellier breakerless distributor, a Delco-Remy ignition coil, an electronic control unit, ignition switch and necessary wiring.

The distributor contains both centrifugal and vacuum advance mechanisms, main and secondary impulse sender coils (pick-up coils), a trigger (reluctor), seal, rotor and cap. *See Fig. 1.*

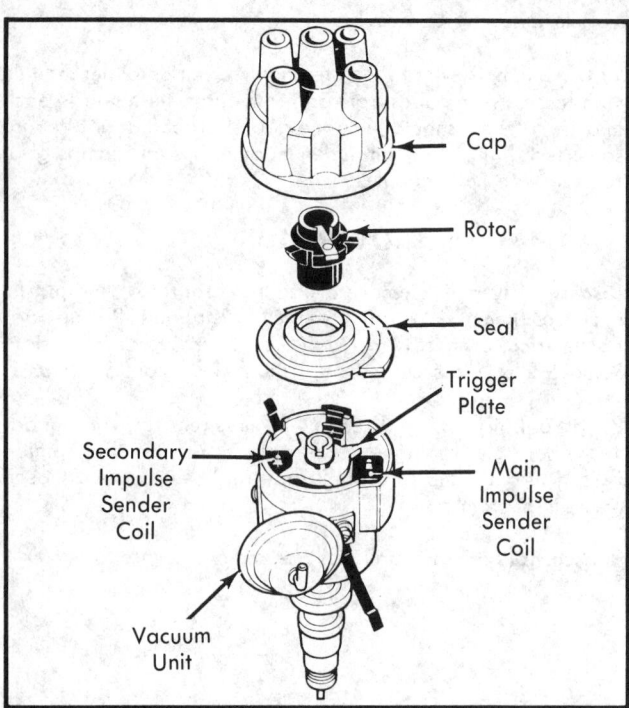

Fig. 1   Exploded View of Ducellier Electronic Distributor

The ignition coil and electronic control unit are mounted to a common support that provides both good grounding and cooling of the electronic control unit. *See Fig. 2.* Silicone grease,

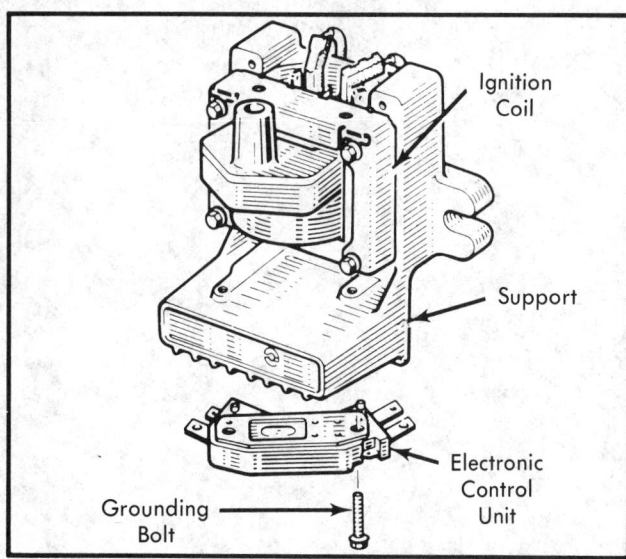

Fig. 2   Ignition Coil and Electronic Control Unit Assembly

which comes with each electronic control unit, is applied between the unit and support to provide improved heat transfer. Since both units are grounded through the common support base, all mounting bolts should be snug.

The ignition coil is encased in epoxy resin instead of oil. The electronic control unit receives, amplifies and sends electronic signals to provide proper spark timing.

OPERATION

The distributor contains a trigger plate that turns with the distributor shaft. *See Fig. 3.* Two impulse sender coils are housed in the distributor — the main coil near the vacuum diaphragm and the secondary coil directly opposite (offset 3° for proper ignition timing during warm-up).

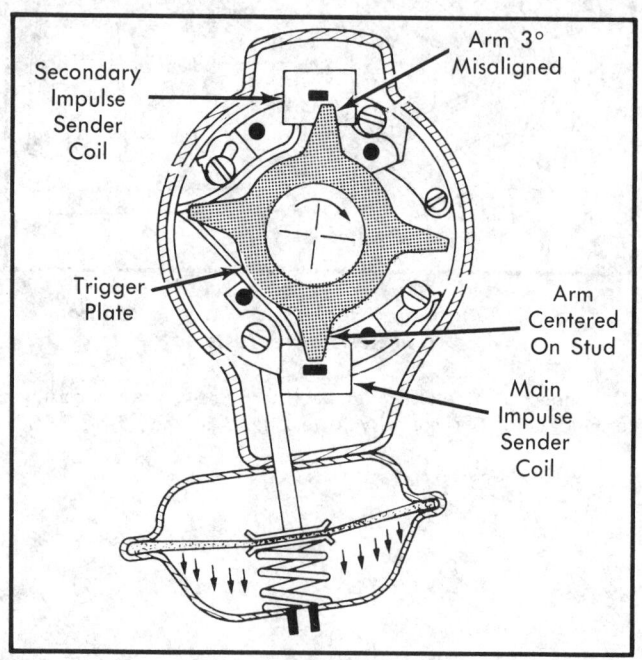

Fig. 3   Ducellier Internal Distributor Components

When oil temperature is below 59° F (15° C), the secondary impulse sender operates to provide 3° additional advance (6° total). When oil temperature reaches 59° F (15° C) or higher, a relay switches operation to the main impulse sender which takes over the function from the secondary. Ignition timing returns from 6° to 3° BTDC. The two impulse senders never operate simultaneously.

As the rotating trigger plate approaches and passes the proper impulse sender coil, a magnetic field builds and collapses, sending a signal to the electronic control unit. This signal opens and closes a transistor in the electronic control unit, turning the primary circuit in the ignition coil on and off.

When the primary coil circuit is turned off, a high voltage surge occurs in the coil secondary circuit, providing spark to the spark plugs through the distributor rotor, cap and secondary wires.

The electronic control unit has 4 terminals. *See Fig. 4.* Terminals "W" and "G" are connected to the distributor impulse sender coils, terminal "G" through a relay switch that activates either the main or secondary impulse sender coil. Terminal "B" is connected to the coil positive terminal and terminal

DUCELLIER ELECTRONIC IGNITION SYSTEM – RENAULT (Cont.)

"C" to the coil negative terminal. The unit is grounded through one of its mounting bolts to the support shared with the ignition coil.

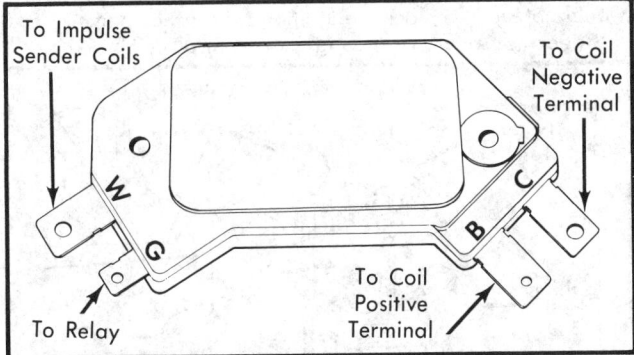

Fig. 4   Electronic Control Unit Terminals

SPECIFICATIONS

Centrifugal & Vacuum Advance – See *Specifications Tables* in this section.

ADJUSTMENTS

Trigger Plate-to-Impulse Sender Coil Air Gap – Loosen screws "A" and "B". See *Fig. 5*. Place an .018" (.45 mm) feeler gauge between either pick-up coil stud and one arm of the trigger plate. See *Fig. 6*. Move slotted coil base on screw "B" until stud on top of coil touches feeler gauge. Tighten screws "A" and "B". Check air gap at all 4 arms of trigger plate. If

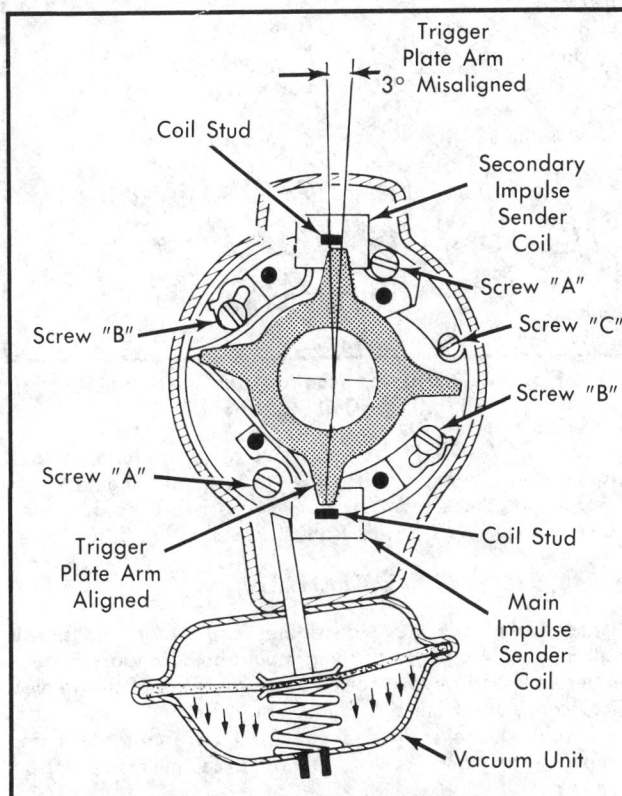

Fig. 5   Adjusting Ignition Timing by Misaligning Trigger Plate Arm 3°

gap is not within .012-.024" (.3-.6 mm) range for any arms of trigger plate and cannot be adjusted correctly, replace distributor.

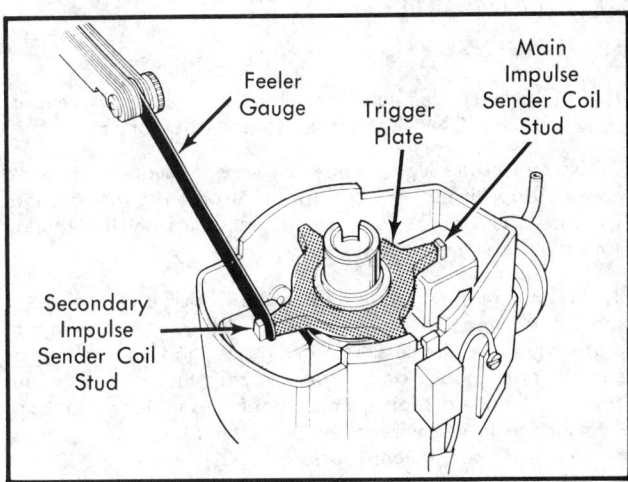

Fig. 6   Adjusting Distributor Air Gap

Ignition Timing of Secondary Impulse Sender – Set trigger plate-to-impulse sender coil air gap. Loosen screw "B" (for secondary sender) and screw "C". See *Fig. 5*. Align one trigger plate arm with main impulse sender coil stud. Then, move secondary impulse sender coil so that the center of its stud aligns with edge (not center) of trigger plate arm. Tighten screws "B" and "C". This provides 3° additional advance when engine oil temperature is below 59° F (15° C).

TESTING

NOTE – *Before testing components, be sure battery is properly charged, all wires are sound and connections are secure. Inspect distributor cap and rotor for cracks or carbontracking. Turn ignition "OFF" when connecting test equipment or when replacing parts.*

CAUTION – *Before replacing "defective" parts such as the ignition coil, distributor or electronic control unit, check that the electrical system is operative. Particularly check the oil thermoswitch on the right-hand side of the oil pan and the relay which it controls. Also check all wiring and connectors.*

ENGINE STARTS WHEN COLD BUT STALLS WHEN IT WARMS UP

If engine starts normally and runs well, but stalls when oil temperature reaches 59° F (15° C), the main impulse sender coil is defective. Both impulse coils must be replaced.

IGNITION DEFECT OCCURS DURING ENGINE OPERATION

If ignition defect occurs during normal engine operation, check condition of spark plug wires, coil high tension wire and spark plugs. If engine surges or misfires due to ignition malfunction, and wires and spark plugs are not defective, replace electronic control unit.

NOTE – *Never disconnect spark plug wires when engine is running. This may cause high voltage to seek ground through distributor body, causing trigger plate deterioration.*

DUCELLIER ELECTRONIC IGNITION SYSTEM — RENAULT (Cont.)

TESTING SYSTEM WHEN ENGINE WILL NOT START

In cold start situations where the engine will not start, perform the following tests.

SPARKING TEST

1) With engine oil temperature below 59° F (15° C), turn ignition switch to "ON" position. Remove distributor cap.

2) Disconnect the high tension coil wire from distributor and hold it approximately ¼" (6 mm) from a good ground. Ground should be as far away as possible from the ignition coil and electronic control unit.

3) Move a magnet in a spiral motion back and forth over secondary impulse sender stud (furthest from vacuum diaphragm). A spark should jump the gap to ground as magnet passes back and forth over coil stud. If it does, but engine will not start, problem probably lies in distributor cap, rotor or spark plug wires or in fuel system. If no spark occurs, proceed with component checks.

IMPULSE SENDER COIL CHECK

NOTE — *Do not use a test light to check distributor impulse sender coil. High voltage may damage the coil.*

1) Be sure impulse sender coil feed wires have not been cut. Disconnect the 5-wire relay connector and the 3-wire distributor connector (2 black wires, 1 gray). See *Fig. 7.*

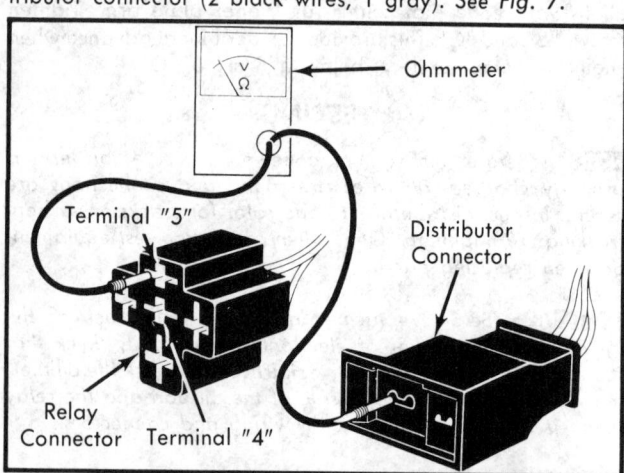

Fig. 7 Ohmmeter Hookup for Checking Impulse Sender Coils

2) Connect one lead of an ohmmeter to terminal 5 of the 5-wire relay harness connector. Connect other ohmmeter lead to double black wire terminal of distributor connector. Then move ohmmeter lead from terminal 5 to terminal 4.

3) The needle should move in each instance. If not, replace both impulse sender coils as an assembly.

4) To check impulse sender coils for shorts, connect one ohmmeter lead to terminal 5 (and then terminal 4) with second ohmmeter lead connected to distributor body. The needle should not move in either instance. If it does, replace both impulse sender coils as an assembly.

IGNITION COIL AND ELECTRONIC CONTROL UNIT CHECK

1) Turn the ignition switch to the "ON" position. Connect positive voltmeter lead to ignition coil positive terminal. Con-

nect remaining lead to ignition coil negative terminal. See *Fig. 8.*

2) Quickly move a magnet back and forth over the secondary impulse sender coil. If the voltmeter needle moves, but engine would not start, replace the ignition coil. If the voltmeter needle does not move, replace ignition control unit.

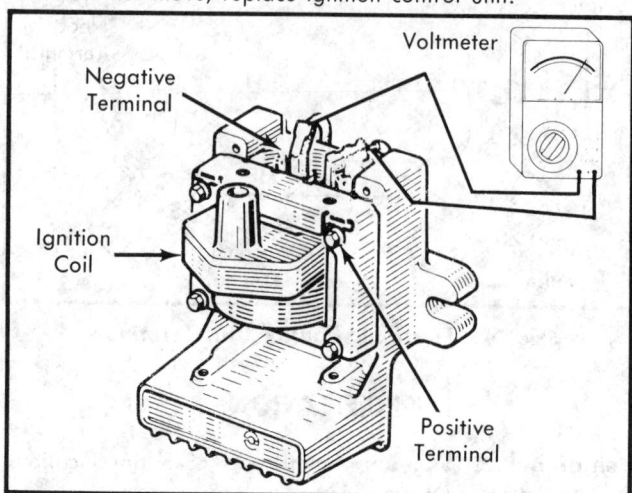

Fig. 8 Voltmeter Hookup for Checking Ignition Coil & Electronic Control Unit

ELECTRICAL CIRCUIT TEST

1) Connect a 12-volt test light between the coil positive terminal and ground. Turn ignition switch "ON". Test light should light. If not, check feed wire to coil. See *Fig. 9.*

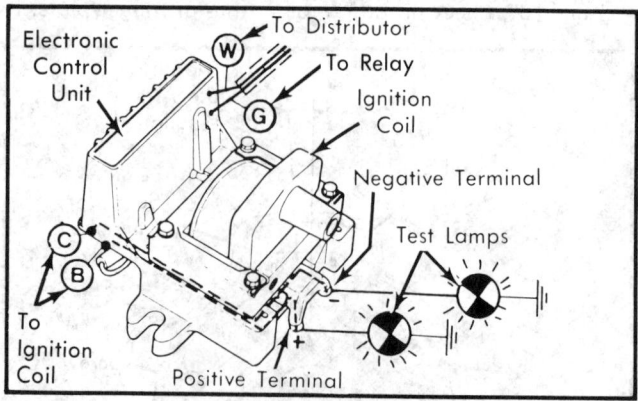

Fig. 9 Test Lamp Hookup for Checking Ignition Coil Voltage

2) Connect test light between coil negative terminal and ground. Turn ignition switch "ON". Test light should again light. If not, check if coil primary circuit is broken or if electronic control unit's power transistor is shorted.

OVERHAUL

Disassembly — Remove distributor cap, rotor and plastic seal. Remove 4 screws attaching main and secondary impulse sender coils and remove coils and trigger plate. Remove electrical connector from distributor body. Remove vacuum advance unit. Remove drive pinion from distributor shaft and remove shaft and centrifugal advance mechanism from housing.

Reassembly — Reverse disassembly procedure, adjusting air gap and ignition timing at secondary impulse sender coil.

HITACHI ELECTRONIC IGNITION SYSTEMS – DATSUN

200SX	510
210	810
280ZX	Pickup
310	

DESCRIPTION

Two different systems are used on Datsun models in 1980, however the principle of operation is the same. Both systems use an electronic distributor, an IC ignition unit, ignition coil(s), battery and wiring harnesses. *See Figs. 1 through 4.*

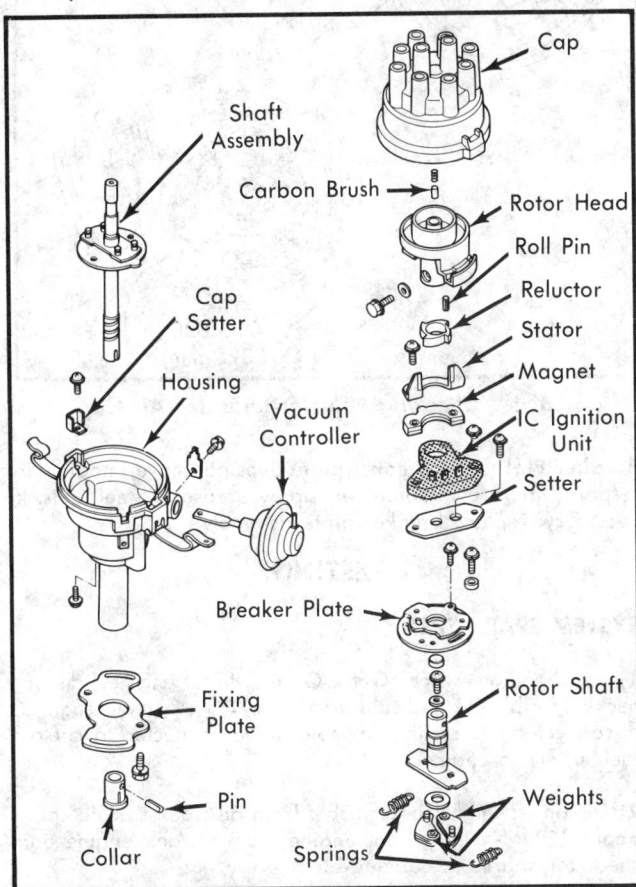

**Fig. 1 Disassembled View of Hitachi Distributor
(Calif. 510 and 200SX Models)**

The system for all models except California 510 and 200SX is similar to the 1979 system. California 510 and 200SX have 4-cylinder engines with 8 spark plugs. Therefore they have a special distributor cap (8 spark plug wire outlet terminals and 2 coil wire inlet terminals). These models also use 2 ignition coils, one for the spark plugs on the exhaust side of the engine and one for the spark plugs on the intake side.

California 510 and 200SX models also differ in that the IC ignition unit is located inside the distributor, stator and magnet assembly has a different shape, IC ignition unit has a 3-pin connector rather than a 2-pin connector, and IC ignition unit contains only 4 internal circuits and 2 transistors, instead of 5 circuits found on other models.

All models except California 510 and 200SX have IC ignition unit mounted externally on distributor housing. Unit is connected with 2 wires to pick-up coil located inside distributor. These models also have a fusible link between battery and ignition

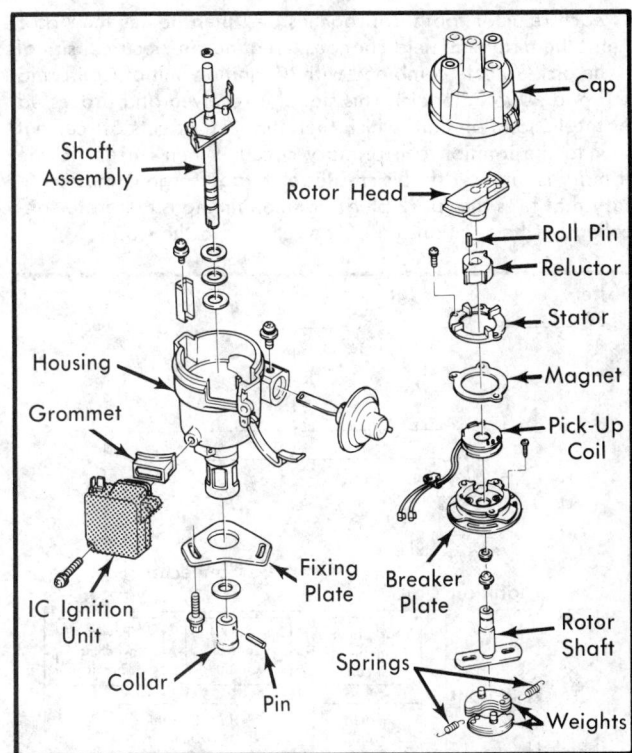

**Fig. 2 Disassembled View of Hitachi Distributor
(All Models Except Calif. 510 and 200SX)
(280ZX and 810 – 6-Tooth Reluctors and Stators)**

switch. The 280ZX and 810 models, which have 6-cylinder engines, feature reluctors and stators with 6 teeth, while other models have 4-cylinder engines with 4-tooth reluctors and stators.

OPERATION

Regardless of model, all distributors are equipped with a reluctor and stator, although the shapes may differ. The reluctor, which is mounted on the rotor shaft assembly, turns with the distributor shaft inside the stator.

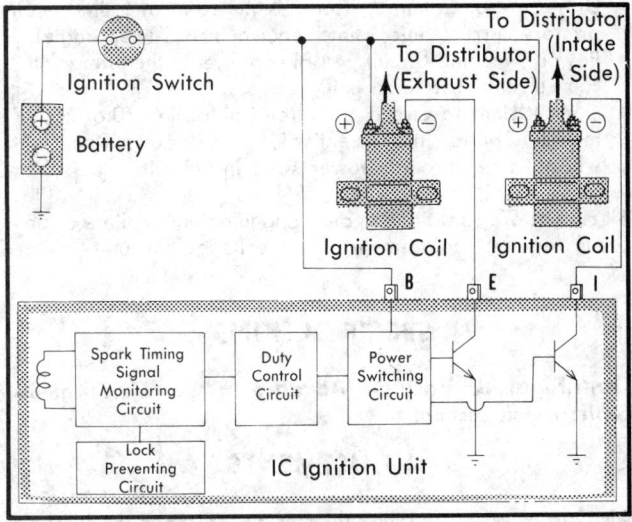

**Fig. 3 IC Ignition Unit Circuit Diagram
(Calif. 510 and 200SX Models)**

HITACHI ELECTRONIC IGNITION SYSTEMS — DATSUN (Cont.)

As each reluctor tooth approaches and then passes the stator teeth, the magnetic field changes, creating an electrical signal in the pick-up coil (combined with IC ignition unit of California 510 and 200SX models). This signal is received and processed by the IC ignition unit, which then turns on or cuts off current flow to the ignition coil primary circuit. When current to the primary is turned off, this creates a voltage surge in the secondary that fires the spark plugs. Ignition timing is therefore controlled by the relationship of the reluctor to the stator.

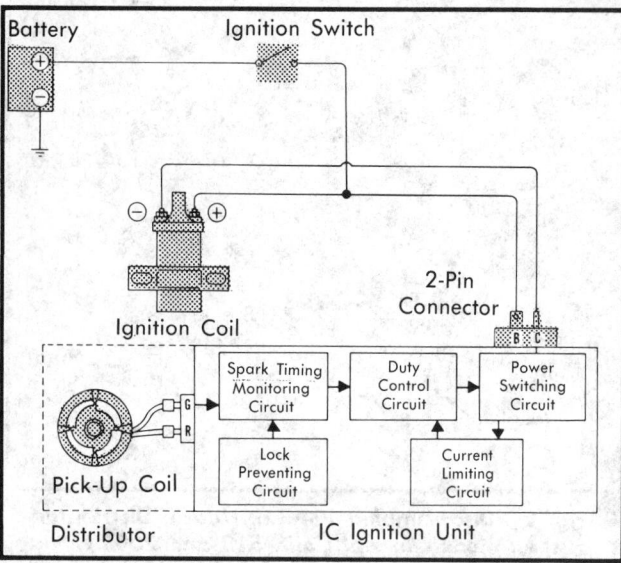

Fig. 4   IC Ignition Unit Circuit Diagram (All Models Except Calif. 510 and 200SX)

The IC ignition unit contains 5 circuits on most models (4 circuits and 2 transistors on California 510 and 200SX models). These circuits perform the following functions. See *Figs. 3 and 4.*

- Spark Timing Signal Monitoring Circuit — Monitors and amplifies signal from distributor pick-up coil.
- Lock-Preventing Circuit — Cuts off ignition coil primary current when ignition switch is "ON" and engine is not running.
- Duty Control Circuit — Controls the ratio of ignition coil primary current on-off time (equivalent to dwell angle).
- Power Switching Circuit — Makes or breaks the primary circuit current of ignition coil.
- Current Limiting Circuit — Not on California 510 or 200SX models. Controls the current value so that excessive current will not flow through power switching circuit.

All circuits are contained in one IC ignition unit. Failure of any circuit requires replacement of entire IC ignition unit.

SPECIFICATIONS

Centrifugal & Vacuum Advance — See *Specifications Tables* in this section.

ADJUSTMENTS

Air Gap — When installing reluctor and stator or checking air gap, loosen screws and center stator around reluctor so that there is equal air gap between each set of reluctor teeth and matching stator teeth. See *Fig. 5.* Then tighten screws securing stator. Standard air gap is .012-.020" (.3-.5 mm).

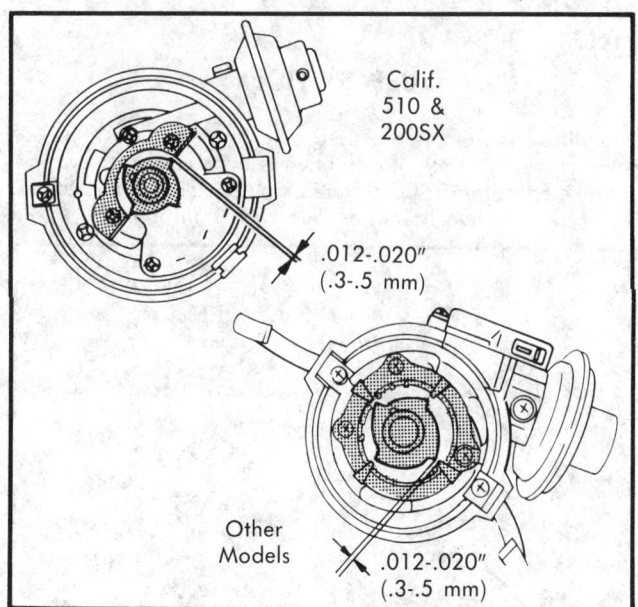

Fig. 5   Checking Reluctor-to-Stator Air Gap

Breaker Plate — If breaker plate does not move smoothly in response to vacuum controller, apply grease to steel balls. If necessary, replace breaker plate assembly.

TESTING

SYSTEM SPARK TEST

1) Turn ignition switch "OFF". On 6-cylinder engines, disconnect EFI fusible link and cold start valve. On 4-cylinder engines, disconnect anti-dieseling solenoid valve connector to cut off fuel supply to engine.

2) Disconnect high tension cable from distributor. Hold cable about ¼" (4-5 mm) from engine block. Crank engine and check for sparks at cable-to-block gap.

3) If sparks occur, the IC ignition system is OK and no further ignition checks are required. If no sparks occur, proceed with tests that follow.

BATTERY VOLTAGE CHECK

1) Turn ignition switch to "OFF" position. Connect positive lead of voltmeter to battery positive terminal. Connect negative lead to battery negative terminal. Read and record battery voltage. If below 11.5 volts, battery charging or starting system is faulty.

2) With ignition switch still "OFF" and voltmeter still hooked to battery, remove coil wire from distributor and connect it to a good ground. Crank engine and record cranking voltage registered on voltmeter. If voltage reading is less than 9.6 volts, battery charging or starting system is faulty.

SECONDARY WIRING CHECK

Connect an ohmmeter, in turn, to each spark plug wire. Attach one lead to terminal inside distributor cap and other lead to

HITACHI ELECTRONIC IGNITION SYSTEMS — DATSUN (Cont.)

other end of wire. Resistance reading should be less than 30,-000 ohms. If resistance is higher, replace high tension cables and/or distributor cap.

IGNITION COIL RESISTANCE CHECK

Primary Resistance — 1) Turn ignition switch "OFF". Remove coil wires to isolate coil from system. See *Fig. 6*. Set ohmmeter to x1 range. Connect ohmmeter leads to two primary terminals of coil. California 510 and 200SX models should show a resistance reading of 1.04-1.27 ohms. All other models should read 0.84-1.02 ohms.

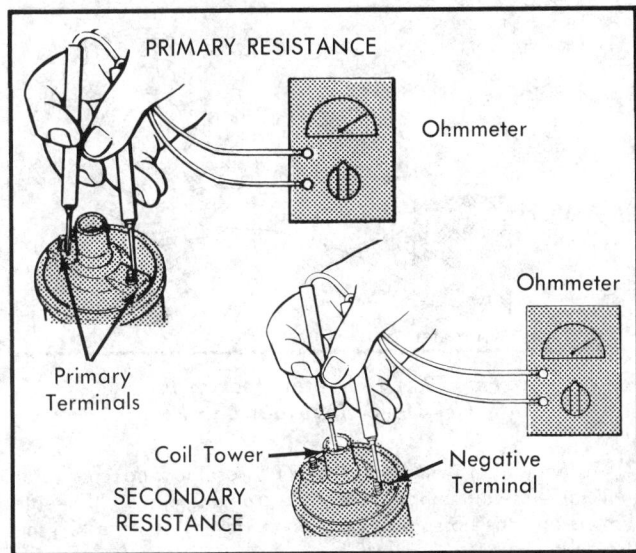

Fig. 6   Ohmmeter Hookup for Coil Resistance Checks

2) If resistance reading is OK, but engine will not start, check ignition switch and wiring from switch to coil and IC ignition unit. If reading is not within specifications, replace ignition coil.

Secondary Resistance — With ignition switch "OFF", set an ohmmeter to the x1000 range. Connect one lead to coil negative terminal and other lead to coil tower. See *Fig. 6*. Resistance for California 510 and 200SX models should be 7,400-11,000 ohms. All other models should be 8,200-12,400 ohms. If not, replace ignition coil.

POWER SUPPLY CIRCUIT CHECK

California 510 and 200SX — Connect a voltmeter positive lead to connector removed from "B" terminal of IC ignition unit inside distributor. See *Fig. 7*. Connect voltmeter negative lead to side of distributor. Turn ignition switch "ON". If reading is less than 11.5 volts, check wiring from ignition switch to IC ignition unit.

All Other Models — 1) Connect voltmeter positive lead to "B" terminal (black and white wire) of IC ignition unit connector. See *Fig. 8*. Connect negative lead to side of distributor. Turn ignition switch "ON". If below 11.5 volts, check wiring from ignition switch to IC ignition unit.

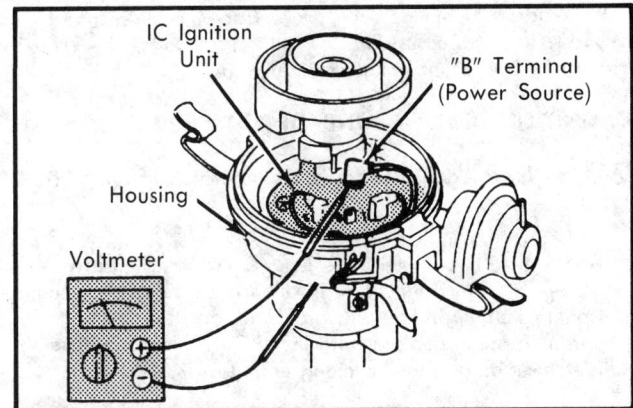

Fig. 7   Voltmeter Hookup for Power Supply Check (Calif. 510 & 200SX Models)

2) To check power supply while cranking engine, remove high tension wire from distributor and ground it. Connect voltmeter positive lead to "B" terminal (black and white wire) of IC ignition unit connector. Connect negative lead to side of distributor. Turn ignition switch to "START" position. Note voltmeter reading.

3) If voltage reading is more than 1 volt below battery CRANKING voltage and/or is below 8.6 volts, check ignition switch and wiring from switch to IC ignition unit.

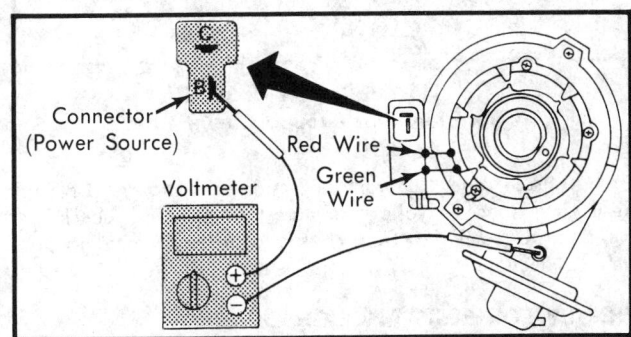

Fig. 8   Voltmeter Hookup for Power Supply Check (All Models Except Calif. 510 & 200SX)

IGNITION PRIMARY CIRCUIT CHECK

NOTE — *This test does not apply to California 510 and 200SX models.*

1) Connect voltmeter positive lead to "C" terminal (blue wire) of IC ignition unit connector. See *Fig. 9*. Attach negative lead to side of distributor. Turn ignition switch "ON".

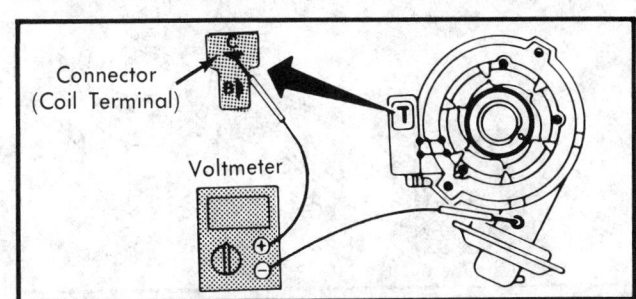

Fig. 9   Voltmeter Hookup for Ignition Primary Circuit Check

HITACHI ELECTRONIC IGNITION SYSTEMS — DATSUN (Cont.)

2) If voltage is 11.5-12.5 volts, proceed to IC Unit Ground Circuit Test. If voltage reading is below 11.5 volts, check Coil Primary Resistance, if not previously done.

IC IGNITION UNIT GROUND CIRCUIT CHECK

NOTE — *This test does not apply to California 510 and 200SX models.*

1) Connect voltmeter negative lead to battery negative terminal. *See Fig. 10.* Connect positive lead to exterior of vacuum controller. Pull high tension wire from distributor cap and ground it. Turn ignition switch to "START" position and observe voltmeter reading while cranking engine.

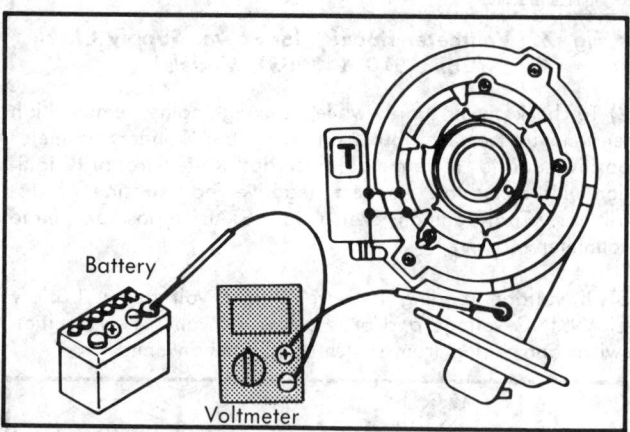

**Fig. 10   Voltmeter Hookup for
IC Ignition Unit Ground Circuit Check**

2) If voltage reads 0.5 volts or less, proceed to Pick-Up Coil Resistance Check. If voltage is more than 0.5 volts, check distributor ground wiring from chassis to battery, including battery connections.

PICK-UP COIL RESISTANCE CHECK

NOTE — *This test does not apply to California 510 and 200SX models.*

1) For this test, engine should be at operating temperature. Turn ignition switch "OFF". Connect an ohmmeter set to x100 scale to pick-up coil terminals (red and green wires). *See Fig. 11.*

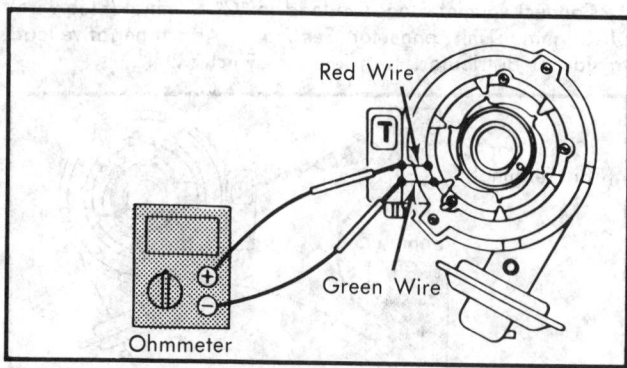

**Fig. 11   Ohmmeter Hookup for
Pick-Up Coil Resistance Check**

2) If ohmmeter reading is approximately 400 ohms, proceed to Pick-Up Coil Output Check. If ohmmeter reading varies widely from 400 ohms, check pick-up coil and wires leading to it.

PICK-UP COIL OUTPUT CHECK

NOTE — *This test does not apply to California 510 and 200SX models.*

1) Engine should be at operating temperature. Connect a voltmeter, set at the low scale (0-5 volt), with positive lead connected to pick-up coil terminal with red wire. *See Fig. 12.* Attach negative lead to side of distributor.

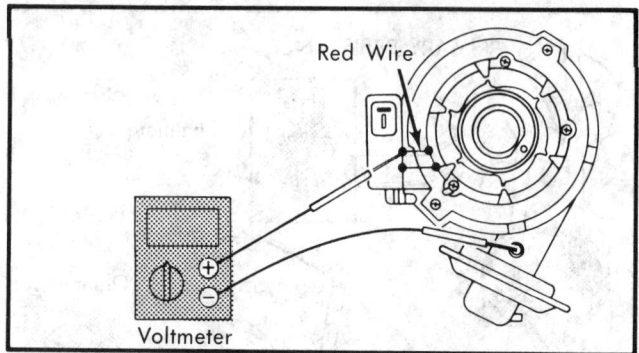

**Fig. 12   Voltmeter Hookup for
Pick-Up Coil Output Check**

2) Turn ignition switch to "START" position and check for movement of voltmeter needle while cranking engine. If needle wavers and the no spark condition still exists, replace IC ignition unit.

3) If needle is steady, check physical condition of pick-up coil and reluctor. Check wiring and connector between pick-up coil and IC ignition unit.

OVERHAUL

Disassembly (Calif. 510 and 200SX) — **1)** Remove distributor cap and rotor head. Pry reluctor from rotor shaft assembly. Use care not to damage teeth.

2) Remove IC ignition unit and unit setter. Remove stator and magnet. Remove vacuum controller and breaker plate. Mark housing and fixing plate. Remove fixing plate and collar. Remove rotor shaft and drive shaft. Mark rotor shaft and drive shaft. Remove packing from top of rotor shaft and remove rotor shaft from drive shaft.

3) Mark one governor spring and its bracket and one weight and its pivot pin. Remove springs and weights and apply grease to weights.

Disassembly (All Other Models) — **1)** Remove distributor cap and rotor head. Remove IC ignition unit by disconnecting harness connector, removing screws and disconnecting pick-up coil wires.

2) Remove stator and magnet. Remove vacuum controller and carefully pry reluctor from shaft. Remove roll pin, pick-up coil assembly and breaker plate assembly. Remove pin and pinion gear. Remove rotor shaft and drive shaft assembly.

HITACHI ELECTRONIC IGNITION SYSTEMS — DATSUN (Cont.)

3) Mark rotor and drive shafts for later assembly. Remove packing and rotor shaft set screw. Mark one of governor springs and its bracket; also one weight and its pivot pin. Remove weights and springs.

Reassembly (All Models) — 1) To assemble, reverse disassembly procedure, noting the following if it applies. Clean surfaces of IC ignition unit and distributor before assembling. Be sure pick-up coil leads (if equipped) are securely attached to IC ignition unit terminals. *See Fig. 13.*

2) Align match marks so parts are assembled in original positions. Be sure reluctor is centered in stator, before tightening stator screws. Drive in roll pin with its slit toward outer end of shaft. Grease top of rotor shaft. Check governor operation before installing distributor.

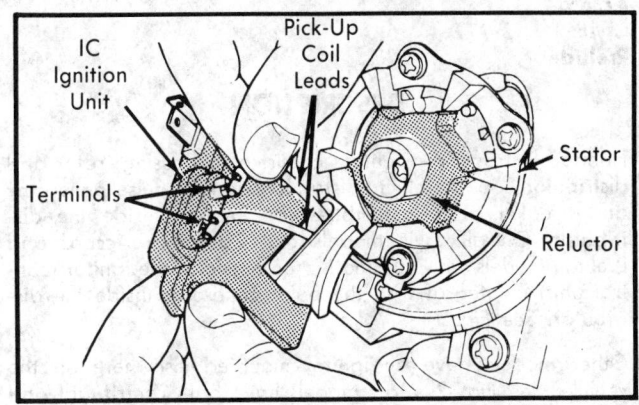

**Fig. 13 Connecting Pick-Up Coil Terminals
(All Models Except Calif. 510 & 200SX)**

HITACHI ELECTRONIC IGNITION SYSTEMS – HONDA

Accord
Civic
Prelude

DESCRIPTION

Honda electronic distributors consist of a housing, rotor and distributor cap. A reluctor, stator, magnets, pulse generator and breaker plate assemblies are located inside the distributor. On all Civic models and California Accord and Prelude models with automatic transmissions, the ignitor (control unit) is integral with the pulse generator inside the distributor. See *Fig. 1*

Other models have an ignitor mounted elsewhere on the vehicle. See *Fig. 2*. Most models have both centrifugal and vacuum advance/retard mechanisms. California Accord and Prelude models with automatic transmissions have no vacuum advance/retard mechanism.

OPERATION

The reluctor is mounted on the distributor rotor shaft and turns with the distributor shaft. See *Figs. 1 and 2*. It is secured to the shaft with a roll pin. As the reluctor turns, its 4 external teeth come in line with the 2 stator upright teeth. As the reluctor approaches and passes the stator teeth, variations occur in the magnetic field around them.

This causes the pulse generator, located inside the distributor housing, to signal the ignitor (mounted inside the distributor and integral with pulse generator on Civic models and California Accord and Prelude models with automatic transmission; mounted remote from distributor on other models). See *Figs. 3 and 4*.

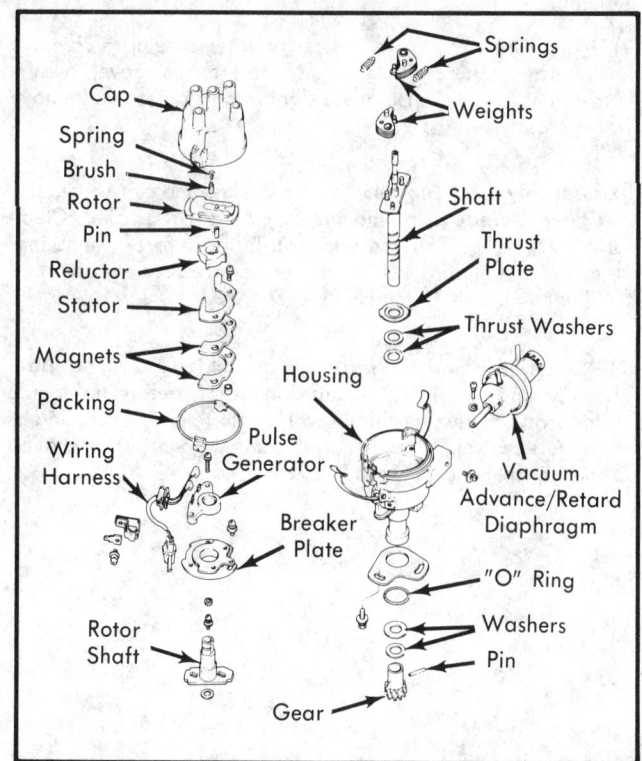

**Fig. 2   Disassembled View of Hitachi Distributor
(Accord & Prelude — Calif. Man. Trans.
& All Federal)**

Each time the reluctor teeth come in line and then pass the stator teeth, transistors inside the ignitor are turned off and on. This results in a magnetic field building and collapsing in the

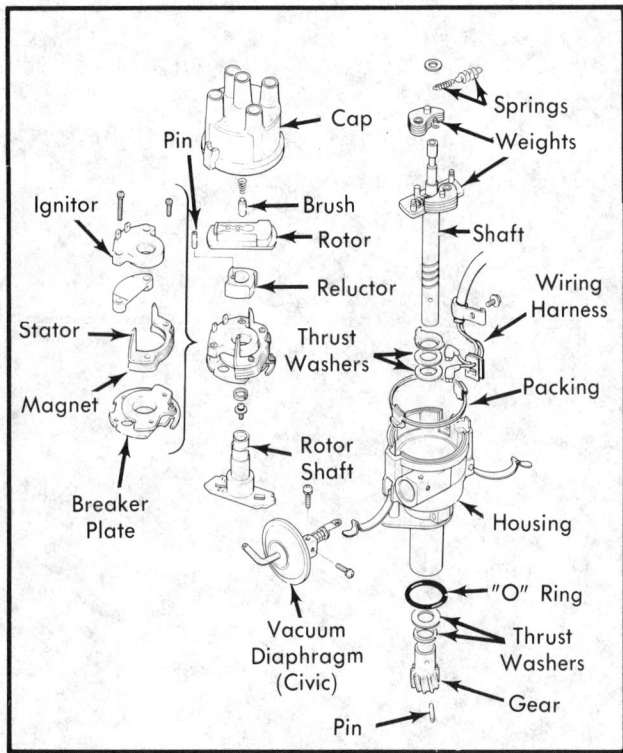

**Fig. 1   Disassembled View of Hitachi Distributor
(All Honda Civics — Other Calif. Auto. Trans. Similar)**

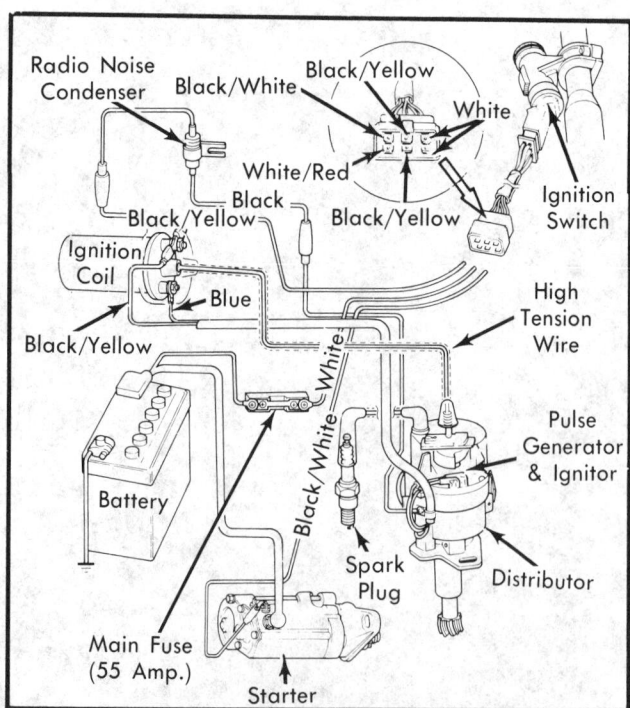

**Fig. 3   Schematic of Ignition System
(Civic & Calif. Accord & Prelude Auto. Trans.)**

HITACHI ELECTRONIC IGNITION SYSTEMS – HONDA (Cont.)

primary circuit of the ignition coil. When this field collapses, a voltage surge occurs in the secondary circuit of the ignition coil.

When this occurs, a high voltage spark is fed from the coil, through the distributor's rotor and cap to the secondary wiring and spark plugs.

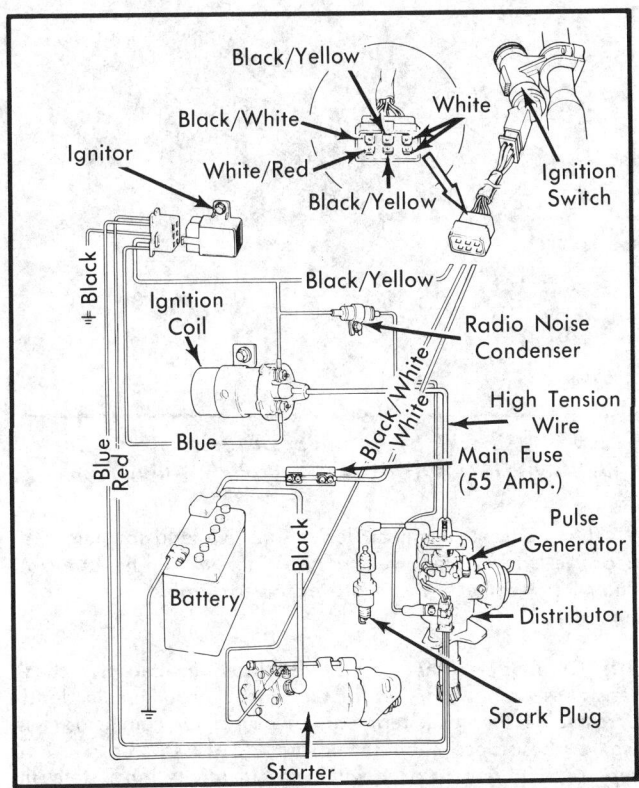

Fig. 4 Schematic of Ignition System (Accord & Prelude – Calif. Man. Trans. & All Federal)

On models with pulse generator/ignitor assemblies, two wires lead from the ignitor to the ignition coil. On models with only an internal pulse generator (an external ignitor), two wires lead from the pulse generator to the ignitor. The ignitor then is connected with 2 additional wires to the ignition coil. A fifth wire from the ignitor leads to ground.

SPECIFICATIONS

Centrifugal & Vacuum Advance/Retard — See Specifications Pages in this section.

ADJUSTMENT

CAUTION — To avoid damaging the ignition system, never reverse battery polarity. Do not let pulse generator wires touch ignition wires. Do not do anything that would produce abnormal pulses. Always connect pulse type tachometers to negative terminal of ignition coil. Make sure all wires and cables are connected properly.

Cam Angle — Cam angle (dwell) is automatically set and manual adjustment is not required.

Reluctor-To-Stator Air Gap — Align 2 teeth of reluctor with 2 teeth of stator and check air gap. Check air gap at all teeth as

reluctor is rotated. See Fig. 5. There should be equal air gap at all 4 teeth. If necessary to adjust, loosen 2 screws securing stator and reposition stator to provide equal air gaps. Tighten 2 screws.

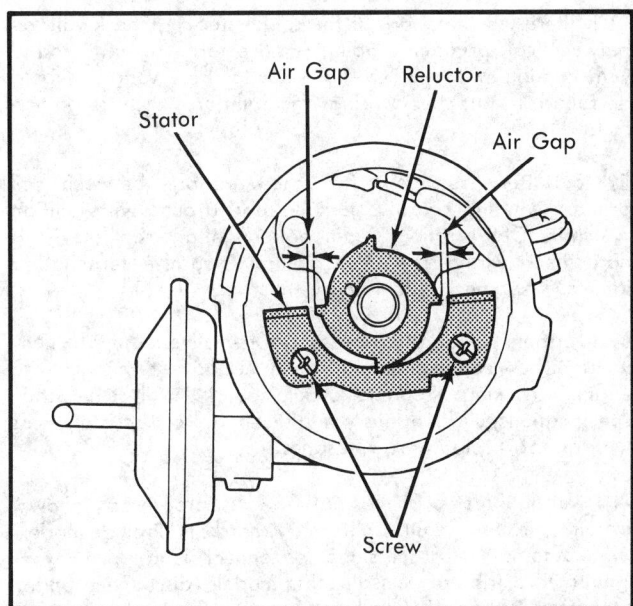

Fig. 5 Adjusting Reluctor-To-Stator Air Gap

Rotor-to-Distributor Cap Terminal — Check occasionally for rough or pitted rotor or cap terminals. Scrape or file off carbon deposits. Smooth rotor terminal with an oil stone or No. 600 sandpaper if roughness exists.

Centrifugal Advance — Disconnect vacuum advance hoses from distributor. Connect timing light and start engine. Increase engine speed. Timing mark (T) should appear to move past pointer toward firewall, indicating an increase in ignition advance. If not, check centrifugal advance mechanism for sticking or binding.

Vacuum Advance — Remove distributor cap. Disconnect vacuum hoses from distributor vacuum advance or advance/retard diaphragm. Connect vacuum pump to diaphragm. Gradually draw a vacuum while watching breaker plate movement. Check for smooth operation without binding. If pump indicates a loss of vacuum, replace diaphragm unit. Turn breaker plate right and left to check for free movement.

TESTING

BASIC SYSTEM TEST

1) If engine will not start and starter will not crank engine, check battery, main fuse and electrical wiring. Check starter circuit wiring and ignition switch. If engine will not start, but starter cranks engine, hold coil wire ¼" from coil tower while cranking engine.

2) If there is spark from coil, then hold spark plug wire terminal ¼" from spark plug while cranking engine.

3) If there is no spark at the plug, check spark plug wire condition, inspect distributor cap and rotor, and as a last resort on

HITACHI ELECTRONIC IGNITION SYSTEMS – HONDA (Cont.)

Civic models and California Accord and Prelude models with automatic transmission, replace ignitor in distributor. On all models, if spark exists at the plug, check fuel system, spark plugs, ignition timing or valve timing.

4) If there was no spark at the coil in step **1)**, check voltage between coil primary winding positive terminal and ground with ignition switch in "ON" position. Battery voltage should be found. If not, check wiring from ignition switch to ignition coil.

5) If battery voltage exists, check voltage between coil primary winding negative terminal and ground with ignition switch in "ON" position. Again, battery voltage should exist. If not, check wiring from coil primary negative terminal to igniter. Also check coil primary resistance.

6) If battery voltage was present at negative terminal, check voltage between coil positive and negative terminals with engine cranking. Reading should be 1-3 volts. If within specifications, check primary and secondary coil resistance, as well as spark plug wire resistance.

7) If voltage in step **6)** was not 1-3 volts, proceed as follows. On all Civic models and California Accord and Prelude models with automatic transmissions, disconnect lead wires from ignitor in distributor. On all other models, disconnect ignitor connector. See Fig. 6. Check voltage on coil side of connector, first between blue wire and black (ground) wire and then between black/yellow wire and black (ground) wire. Battery voltage should exist with ignition switch "ON".

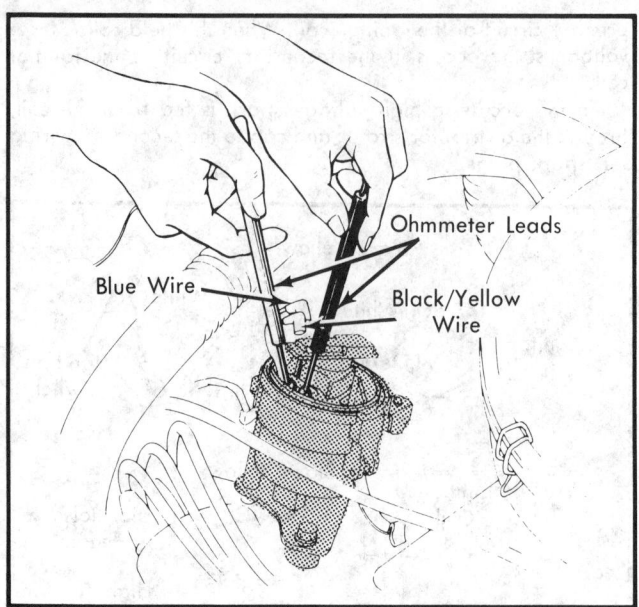

Fig. 7 Checking Continuity at Ignitor Terminals (All Civics & Calif. Accord & Prelude Auto. Trans.)

9) Then, reverse ohmmeter leads (positive lead to blue wire, negative lead to black/yellow wire). There should now be continuity. If incorrect results are obtained, replace ignitor and repeat test.

10) On models other than those listed in step **8)**, check resistance of pulse generator by connecting ohmmeter leads across blue and pink terminals at distributor connector. See Fig. 8. Resistance should measure 800-1200 ohms. If not, replace pulse generator. If within specifications, but system still does not operate, replace ignitor and repeat test.

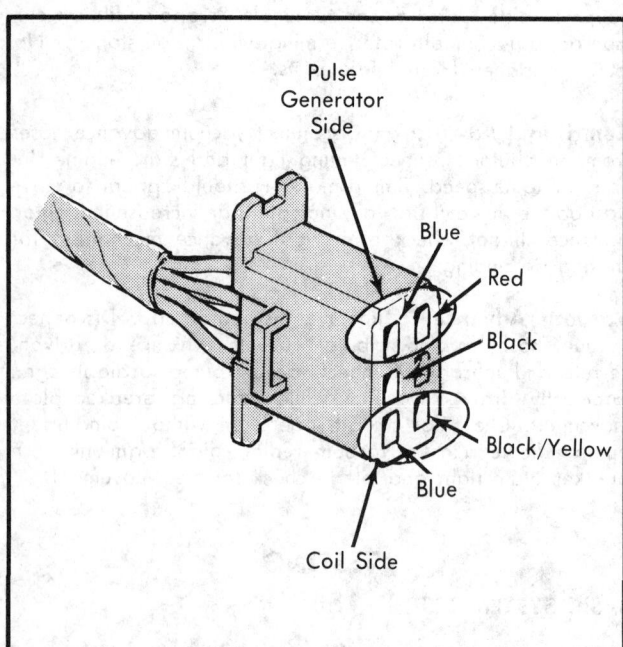

Fig. 6 Checking Voltage at Ignitor Connector

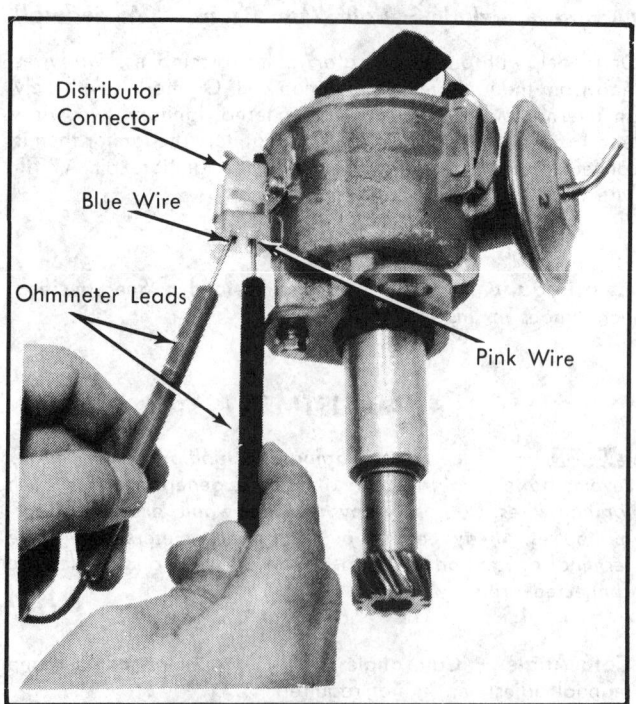

Fig. 8 Checking Pulse Generator Resistance (Models with Externally Mounted Ignitors)

8) If not, check wiring from ignition coil to ignitor. On Civic models and California Accord and Prelude models with automatic transmissions, check continuity between ignitor terminals. See Fig. 7. Set ohmmeter to x100 range. Attach positive lead to black/yellow wire and negative lead to blue wire. There should be no continuity.

HITACHI ELECTRONIC IGNITION SYSTEMS – HONDA (Cont.)

COMPONENT TESTS

Ignition Coil Primary Resistance – Turn ignition switch "OFF" and remove positive and negative wires from ignition coil terminals. Connect an ohmmeter set in the x1 range with one probe touching each primary terminal. See *Fig. 9*. On California Accord and Prelude models with automatic transmission, the reading should be 1.06-1.24 ohms. On other Accord and Prelude models, the reading should be 1.78-2.08 ohms, and on Civic models, 1.0-1.3 ohms. If not, replace ignition coil.

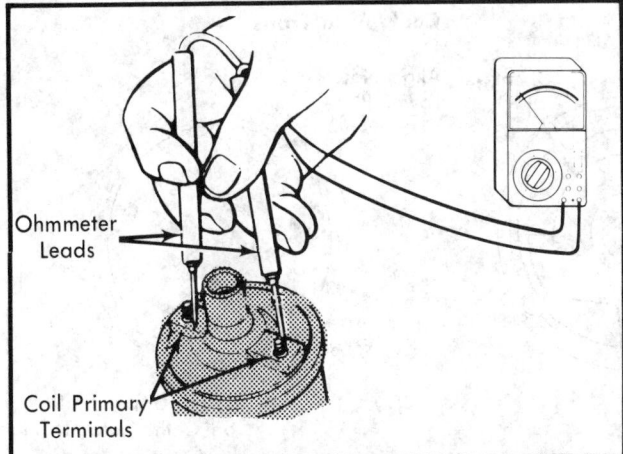

Fig. 9   Checking Ignition Coil Primary Resistance

Ignition Coil Secondary Resistance – Turn ignition switch "OFF". Set ohmmeter in x1000 range. Connect ohmmeter probes to ignition coil negative terminal (wire removed) and coil tower terminal. See *Fig. 10*. On Civic models and California Accord and Prelude models with automatic transmission, the reading should be 7,400-11,000 ohms. On all other models, resistance should read 8,800-13,200 ohms. If not, replace ignition coil.

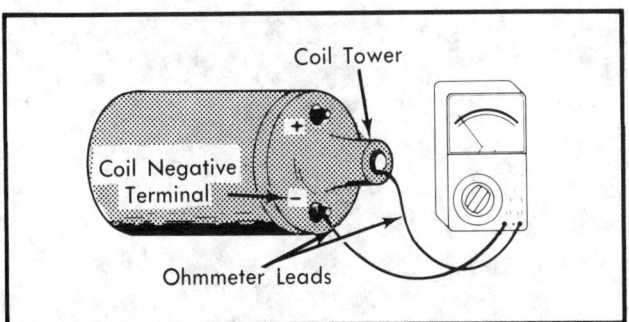

Fig. 10   Checking Ignition Coil Secondary Resistance

Condenser Capacity – Using a condenser tester, check for 0.38-0.56 microfarads.

Pulse Generator Resistance – Disconnect connector from distributor. Connect ohmmeter probes (set to x100 range) across blue and pink wire terminals on distributor side of connector. Resistance should be 800-1200 ohms. If not, replace pulse generator. If resistance is correct, but system still will not operate, replace ignitor and recheck system operation.

Ignition Wire Resistance – Carefully remove wires by pulling on their rubber boots. Do not bend wire or conductor may be broken. Check for corroded condition, cleaning if necessary. Connect ohmmeter probes (set in x1000 scale) to each end of ignition wires. Resistance reading should be less than 25,000 ohms. If not, replace wires.

OVERHAUL

Disassembly – 1) Remove spark plug wires and vacuum hoses from distributor. Remove distributor cap. Remove condenser ground wire and disconnect pulse generator connector or lead wires from ignitor in distributor. Remove hold-down bolt, lifting distributor from cylinder head.

2) Carefully pry upward on reluctor with 2 screwdrivers, cushioned with rags to prevent damage to distributor housing. See *Fig. 11*. Use care not to damage reluctor or stator. When installing reluctor, drive roll pin in place with its gap away from distributor shaft.

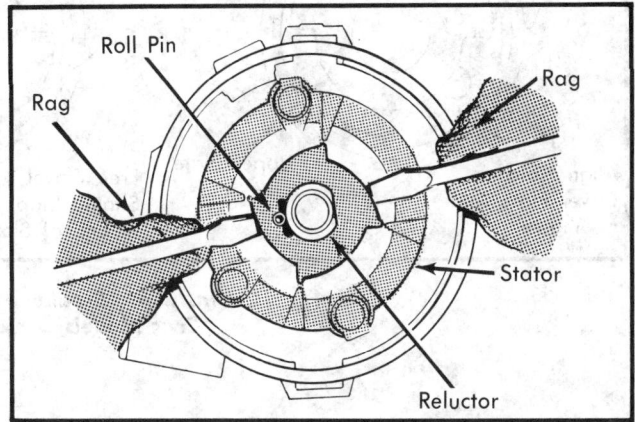

Fig. 11   Removing Reluctor From Shaft

3) On California Accord and Prelude models with manual transmission, remove advance/retard diaphragm mount screw. Pull out on diaphragm unit, while pushing down on arm. California models with automatic transmission have no vacuum advance mechanism.

4) On other models, including the Civic, remove advance diaphragm mount screws. Pull diaphragm arm out of housing, while lifting up on end of arm.

5) On all models, drive roll pin from distributor shaft. Remove shaft and gear from housing. Inspect and replace parts as necessary.

Installation – 1) Install centrifugal advance weights and springs. Install thrust plate and 2 washers on shaft. Grease shaft and install in housing. Put 2 washers and gear on lower end of shaft. Line up holes in gear shoulder with hole in shaft. Drive in new roll pin.

2) Rotate gear until mark on gear shoulder lines up with mark on housing. Hold gear in line with mark and install rotor shaft on top of main shaft. Flat surface should face vacuum advance side of housing.

3) Be sure holes in rotor shaft arms fit over pins in centrifugal advance weights. Install screw with lock washer in top of shaft.

4) Align breaker plate in distributor housing. See *Fig. 12*. Check that upper plate moves freely (California Accord and

HITACHI ELECTRONIC IGNITION SYSTEMS — HONDA (Cont.)

Prelude models with automatic transmission have no upper plate). Be sure diaphragm arm attachment hole (California Accord & Prelude models with manual transmissions) or pin (other models) does not rotate past end of slot in lower plate.

5) If such condition exists, adjust range of free travel by forcibly rotating plate past its limit in opposite direction. Recheck hole and pin positions.

6) Check reluctor-to-stator air gap and rotor-to-terminal surfaces. Install diaphragm assembly. Crank engine until No. 1 piston is at TDC. Install new "O" ring on distributor housing. Line up mark on distributor gear shoulder with mark on housing. Insert distributor straight into final position. Rotor will turn itself to No. 1 firing position.

7) Install hold-down bolt and tighten temporarily. Set ignition timing and tighten hold-down bolt securely. Install distributor cap, aligning mark on cap (near clamp lug) with rotor.

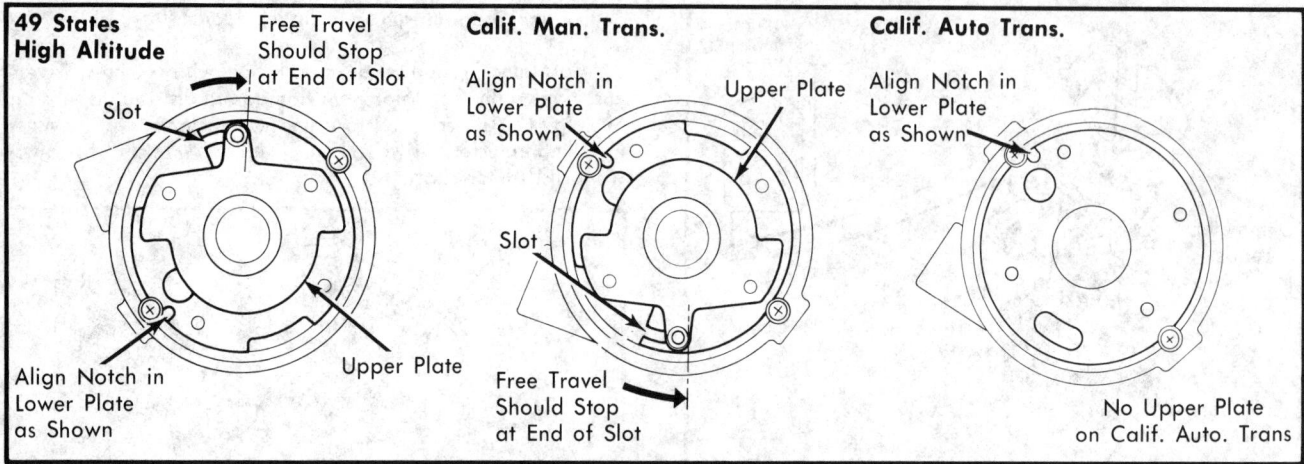

**Fig. 12   Installing Breaker Plate on Accord & Prelude Models
(Civic Models Same as Center Illustration)**

HITACHI ELECTRONIC IGNITION SYSTEM — SUBARU

1600 (4-WD Models)

DESCRIPTION

The Hitachi electronic distributor consists of a housing, rotor and distributor cap. See *Fig. 1*. A reluctor, mounted on the shaft and governor assembly, combines with the pick-up coil to replace the conventional cam and breaker points. With the ignition switch "ON", the distributor reluctor rotates past the pick-up coil. As each tooth of the reluctor approaches and passes the pick-up coil, a signal is sent to the ignition control unit. The control unit then turns the primary circuit in the ignition coil on and off as each tooth passes the pick-up coil. This causes a build-up and collapse of a magnetic field in the coil, resulting in a high voltage surge in the coil's secondary circuit. This fires the spark plugs. See *Fig. 2*.

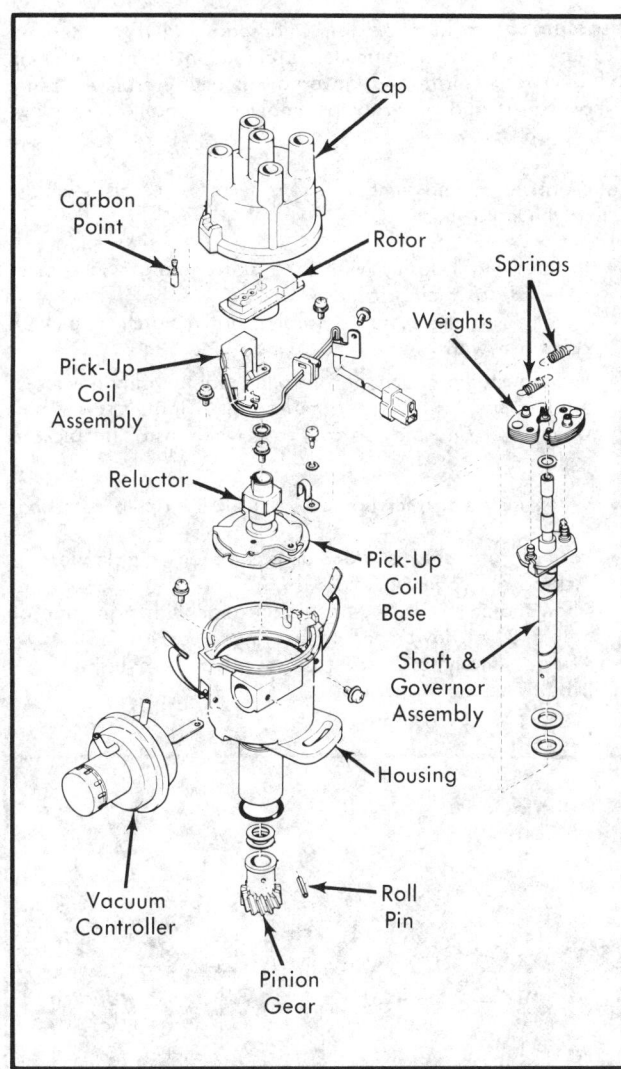

Fig. 1   Disassembled View of Hitachi Distributor for Subaru 4-Wheel Drive Vehicles

SPECIFICATIONS

Centrifugal & Vacuum Advance — See *Specification Tables in this section.*

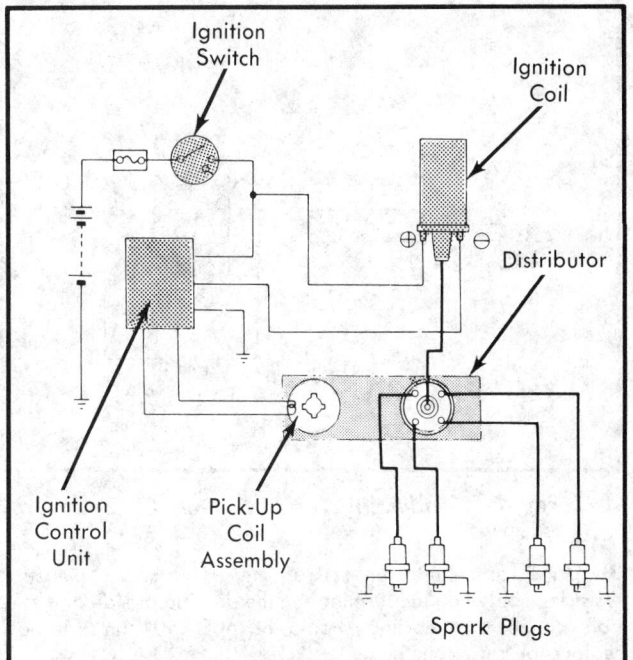

Fig. 2   Schematic of Ignition Circuit for Subaru 4-Wheel Drive Vehicles

ADJUSTMENTS

Air Gap — Align tooth of reluctor with pole piece of pick-up coil. Loosen pick-up coil hold-down screw. Insert a .014" (.35 mm) feeler gauge between tooth and pole piece. Move pick-up coil against gauge and tighten hold-down screw. Air gap should be .012-.016" (.3-.4 mm). See *Fig. 3*.

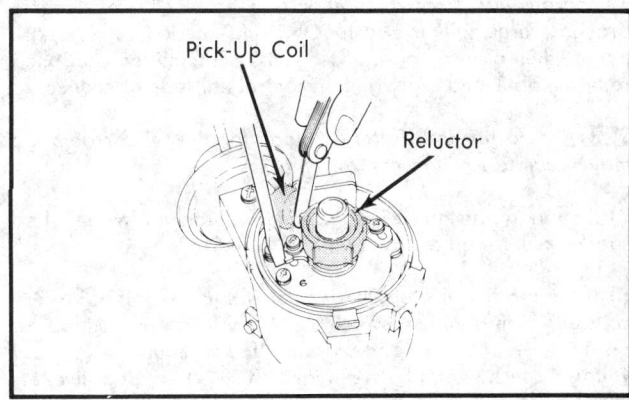

Fig. 3   Adjusting the Air Gap

TESTING

1) Turn ignition switch "ON". Connect negative lead of voltmeter to ground and positive lead to negative terminal of ignition coil. Voltage should be within 1 volt of battery voltage. If not, proceed to step **8)**.

2) If reading was within 1 volt of battery voltage, turn ignition switch "OFF" and disconnect 2-pole connector. See *Fig. 4*.

HITACHI ELECTRONIC IGNITION SYSTEM — SUBARU (Cont.)

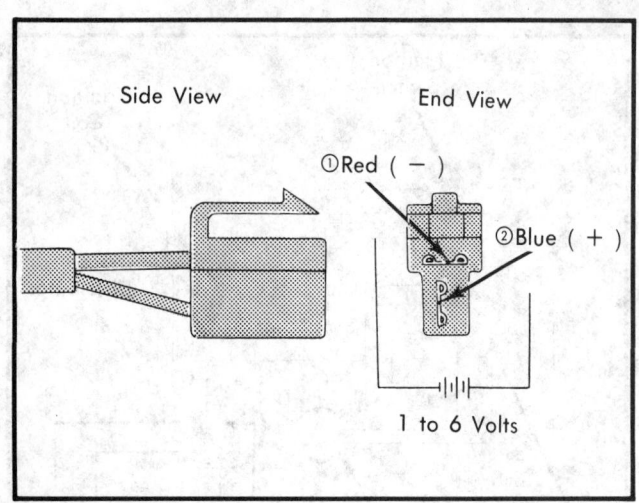

Fig. 4   Conducting Tests at 2-Pole Connector

3) Using an ohmmeter set at the x100 scale, measure resistance between the terminals in the distributor side of the 2-pole connector. Reading should be 600-850 ohms. If not, replace pick-up coil.

4) If reading was within specifications, turn ignition switch "OFF". Using an ohmmeter set to the x1 scale, measure resistance between ground and ignition control unit side. Resistance should be less than .5 ohm. If not, check ground wire at regulator mounting screw.

5) If less than .5 ohm, turn ignition switch "OFF" and check air gap between reluctor and pick-up coil. Adjust as necessary.

6) If air gap was originally within specifications, turn ignition switch "OFF" and disconnect 2-pole connector. Disconnect secondary wire from distributor and hold ¼" from engine ground. Turn ignition switch "ON" and check whether spark jumps when a small voltage (1-6 volts) is intermittently applied to terminals 1 and 2 on ignition control unit side of connector.

NOTE — *Do not use battery voltage for this test or damage may occur to ignition control unit.*

7) If spark occurs, there is no trouble with ignition system. If no spark occurs, replace ignition control unit.

8) If the reading in step **1)** was not within 1.0 volt of battery voltage, turn ignition switch "ON" and check voltage at positive terminal of ignition coil. If not equal to battery voltage, check wiring between ignition switch and positive terminal of ignition coil. Repair or replace as necessary. If OK, check connector, switch, fuse and wiring back to the battery.

9) If reading at coil positive terminal was within 1.0 volt of battery voltage, disconnect the lead at negative terminal (coming from ignition control unit). Turn ignition switch "ON". Voltage at negative terminal should be within 1.0 volt of battery voltage.

10) If voltage is within 1.0 volt of battery voltage, but engine will not start, replace ignition control unit. If not within 1.0 volt, remove lead from tachometer (if equipped) at ignition coil. Turn ignition switch "ON" and again check voltage at negative terminal of coil.

11) If reading is now correct, but engine will not start, check wiring harness from negative terminal of coil to tachometer for short circuit. If in step **10)**, reading was still not within 1.0 volt of battery voltage, replace ignition control unit.

12) If ignition coil is suspected of being defective, check primary and secondary coil resistance. To check primary coil resistance, attach leads of an ohmmeter set in x1 range to coil primary terminals. Reading should be 1.17-1.43 ohms.

13) To check secondary resistance, set ohmmeter in x1000 range and attach leads to coil negative terminal and coil tower. Reading should be 7,800-11,600 ohms. If either reading is not to specifications, replace ignition coil.

OVERHAUL

Disassembly — Remove distributor cap and rotor. Remove pick-up coil, vacuum controller, and pinion. Remove pick-up coil base and shaft and governor assembly from housing. Remove shaft and governor assembly and finally the springs and weights.

Reassembly — Reassemble in reverse order of disassembly, noting the following:

- Install weight spring with longest free length to shorter hole side of timing lever.
- When installing rotor assembly, match notch in pick-up coil base with groove end of housing.
- When installing vacuum controller, tighten only the screw holding the controller to the housing. Tighten screw between lever and pick-up coil base when installing pick-up coil.
- When installing pick-up coil, adjust air gap to specifications.
- Position rotor shaft so flat side is centered on pole piece of pick-up coil. See *Fig. 5.*
- Align match mark "A" on pinion gear with right side of notch "B" on lower end of housing. See *Fig. 5.*
- After assembly, check centrifugal advance by using a distributor tester.

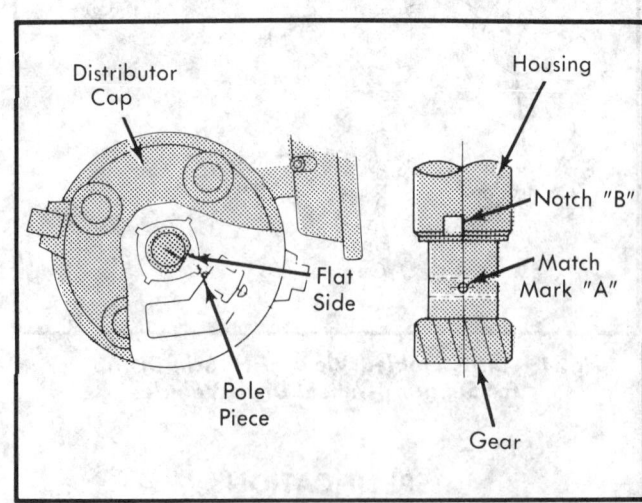

Fig. 5   Aligning Rotor Shaft With Pole Piece and Pinion Gear With Housing

LUCAS "OPUS" ELECTRONIC IGNITION SYSTEM

Jaguar
  XJ6
MG
  MGB
Triumph
  Spitfire
  TR7
  TR8

DESCRIPTION

Although the principle of operation of all Lucas "OPUS" electronic ignition systems is similar, variations do occur between models. *See Fig. 1.*

For example, the XJ6 features a remote electronic control module (amplifier), while the TR8 has the control module mounted inside its distributor. Other models have the module mounted externally on the distributor housing. *See Figs. 4, 5 and 6.*

The XJ6 distributor is equipped with a gear-type reluctor (timing rotor) with one tooth for each cylinder. Other models use a timing rotor with ferrite iron rods (one for each cylinder) imbedded in its outside circumference. In all cases, the reluctor or timing rotor, mounted on the distributor shaft, rotates adjacent to a magnetic pick-up coil (module). The reluctor or timing rotor combines with the pick-up coil to generate signals to the electronic control module (amplifier).

All distributors feature centrifugal advance mechanisms and either vacuum advance or retard units. Some models, such as the TR8, feature ballast-drive resistor assemblies, while others such as the TR7, Spitfire and MGB use ballast wires during normal engine operation.

Other system components include the battery, ignition switch, and ignition coil.

OPERATION

With the ignition switch turned "OFF" and the engine stopped, the distributor reluctor or timing rotor is normally positioned so the teeth or iron rods do not align with the iron core of the pick-up coil. When the ignition switch is turned "ON", a power transistor in the electronic control module (amplifier) completes the ignition coil primary winding circuit.

At the same time a pulsating alternating current voltage is applied by the module to the distributor pick-up coil windings. A small alternating current voltage is produced, and pick-up coil windings are magnetically balanced.

NOTE — *The pick-up coil is magnetically balanced at the factory and the setting must not be changed. The sealed adjusting screw must not be disturbed.*

The voltage at the pick-up coil is applied to the amplifier unit, but is insufficient to affect the transistor controlling the ignition coil primary circuit.

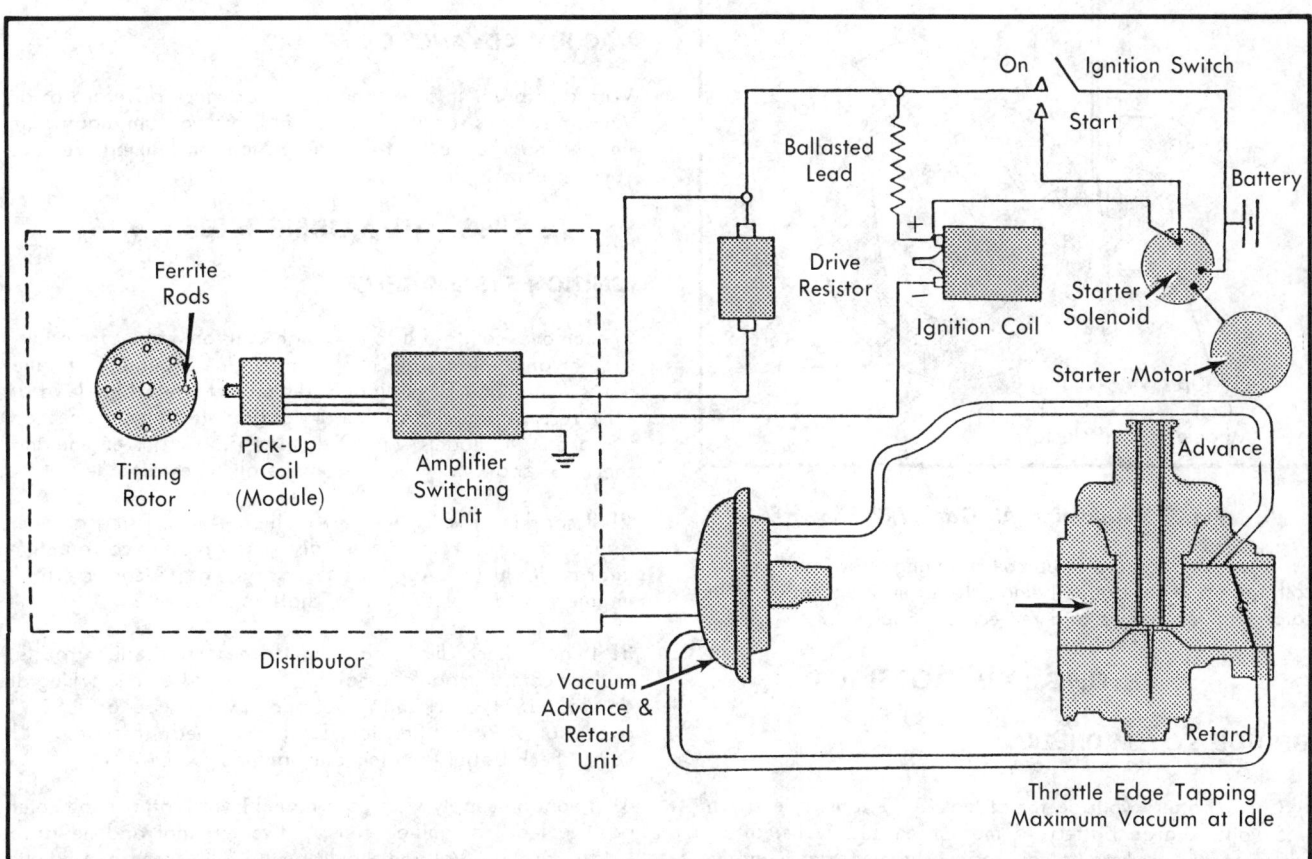

Fig. 1 Typical Lucas "OPUS" Electronic Ignition System (TR8 Shown)

LUCAS "OPUS" ELECTRONIC IGNITION SYSTEM (Cont.)

As the engine is cranked, the teeth or the iron rods come in alignment with the iron core of the pick-up coil. This causes a magnetic unbalancing and voltage increases to maximum as each tooth or rod passes the pick-up coil. The higher voltage signal is then transmitted to the control module. The transistor is switched off and the coil primary windings' magnetic field collapses.

This results in a high voltage surge in the secondary, which is transmitted to each spark plug by the distributor rotor.

SPECIFICATIONS

Centrifugal and Vacuum Advance (or Retard) — See *Specifications Tables in this section.*

ADJUSTMENT

Reluctor (Timing Rotor)-to-Pick-Up Coil Air Gap — 1) Disconnect battery ground cable. Remove distributor cap and rotor and anti-flash cover, if equipped. Using a non-magnetic feeler gauge, check for .014-.016" (.35-.40 mm) air gap (.006-.008" or .15-.20 mm air gap for XJ6 models). *See Fig. 2.* Measurement should be made between timing rotor at iron rod (or reluctor teeth) and center core of pick-up coil.

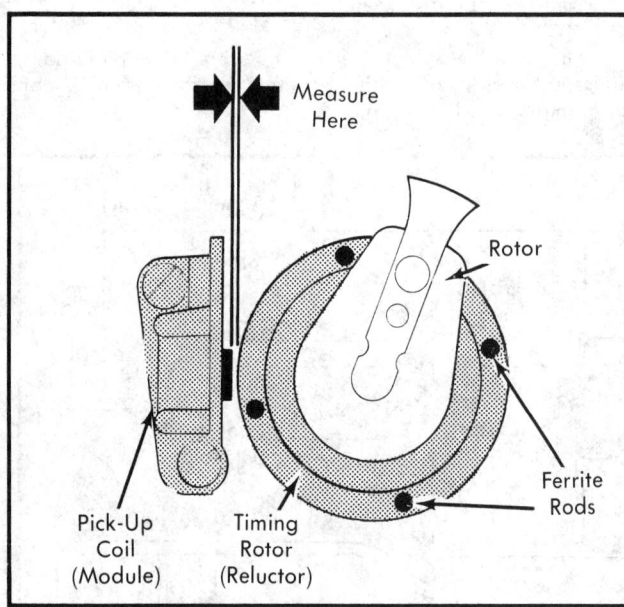

Fig. 2   Adjusting Air Gap (TR7 Shown)

2) To adjust, loosen pick-up coil mounting screws and position coil against feeler gauge being held against reluctor or timing rotor. Tighten screws and recheck air gap.

TESTING (XJ6 MODELS)

IGNITION SYSTEM CHECK

1) Check battery voltage for at least 11.5 volts. If less than 11.5 volts, charge battery. If more than 11.5 volts, attach voltmeter positive lead to coil positive terminal and negative lead to ground. Voltage should be within 1 volt of battery voltage.

2) If incorrect reading is obtained, check wiring between coil positive terminal and ignition switch. If voltage was within 1 volt of battery voltage, attach positive voltmeter lead to coil negative terminal and negative lead to ground. Voltage reading should be more than 2 volts.

3) If voltage is incorrect, disconnect wire leading to control module (amplifier) at coil negative terminal. Again check voltage at coil negative terminal. If less that 2 volts, replace ignition coil. If more than 2 volts, replace control module.

4) If voltage in step **2)** was correct (more than 2 volts), disconnect control module from distributor. Turn ignition switch "OFF" and attach leads of an ohmmeter (set to high scale) to distributor pick-up coil leads. Resistance reading should be 2200-4800 ohms. If not, replace pick-up coil.

5) If pick-up coil resistance is correct, connect control module to distributor. Attach voltmeter positive lead to coil negative terminal and negative lead to ground. Measure voltage. Then crank engine and voltage should fall. If not, replace control module.

6) If voltage fell in step **5)**, but system still is not operating properly, check high tension wires, ignition coil secondary, rotor arms, distributor cap and spark plugs.

CENTRIFUGAL ADVANCE

Check distributor in test stand according to test equipment manufacturer's instructions. Operate distributor up and down the RPM range and check advance at all RPM settings specified.

VACUUM ADVANCE OR RETARD

With distributor in test stand, check advance or retard at all vacuum settings specified. If tests indicate vacuum diaphragm unit is inoperative, out of calibration or leaking, replace vacuum unit.

TESTING (ALL MODELS EXCEPT XJ6)

IGNITION SYSTEM CHECK

1) Remove coil-to-distributor high tension cable from distributor and hold ¼" (6 mm) from engine ground. Turn ignition switch "ON". If equipped, disconnect white/blue lead at drive resistor and check for spark at gap each time connection is broken. On models without drive resistor, crank engine and check for sparks at gap. Reconnect all wires after test.

2) If sparking results, turn off ignition switch. Using a feeler gauge, check air gap between distributor pick-up coil and timing rotor (reluctor). Adjust as necessary. If gap is correct, crank engine to see that distributor shaft rotates.

3) If not, check distributor and drive. If shaft does rotate, replace control module (amplifier). If there was no sparking at gap in step **1)**, check supply voltage at white wire (or at "SW" connector of Ballast Resistor 9BR, if equipped). If less than 11 volts, check battery, wiring and ignition switch.

4) If voltage supply was more than 11 volts, attach voltmeter positive lead to ignition coil positive terminal and negative lead to ground. Voltage should be 11 volts or more (4-8 volts on ballasted models). If voltage is zero (0) or extremely low, check ballast resistor, coil and wires.

LUCAS "OPUS" ELECTRONIC IGNITION SYSTEM (Cont.)

5) If voltage is normal or high, attach voltmeter positive lead to coil negative terminal and negative lead to ground. If voltage reads more than 2 volts, check drive resistor. Turn ignition switch "OFF" and attach ohmmeter leads to drive resistor and check for 9-11 ohms resistance. If not to specifications, replace drive resistor. If OK, check control module and distributor grounds. If OK, but engine does not perform properly, replace control module.

6) If voltage at coil negative terminal was less than 2 volts, disconnect white/blue wire at drive resistor (if equipped). Check voltage again at coil negative terminal. If voltage is now more than 9 volts, check high tension leads, substitute a new ignition coil and replace amplifier, in turn, until problem is corrected.

7) If voltage in step **6)**, was less than 9 volts, disconnect coil negative lead and recheck voltage at coil negative terminal. If now less than 9 volts, replace coil. If more than 9 volts, replace control module (amplifier).

BALLAST RESISTOR CHECK (MODEL 9BR)

1) Some models such as the TR8 may be equipped with the Model 9BR Ballast Resistor, a unit consisting of 4 resistors and a printed wiring board mounted in an aluminum heat sink. One side of resistor is connected to (1) starter solenoid ignition terminal, (2) ignition switch and (3) to tachometer. The other side has 2 connections to distributor pick-up coil and 2 connections to primary terminals of ignition coil.

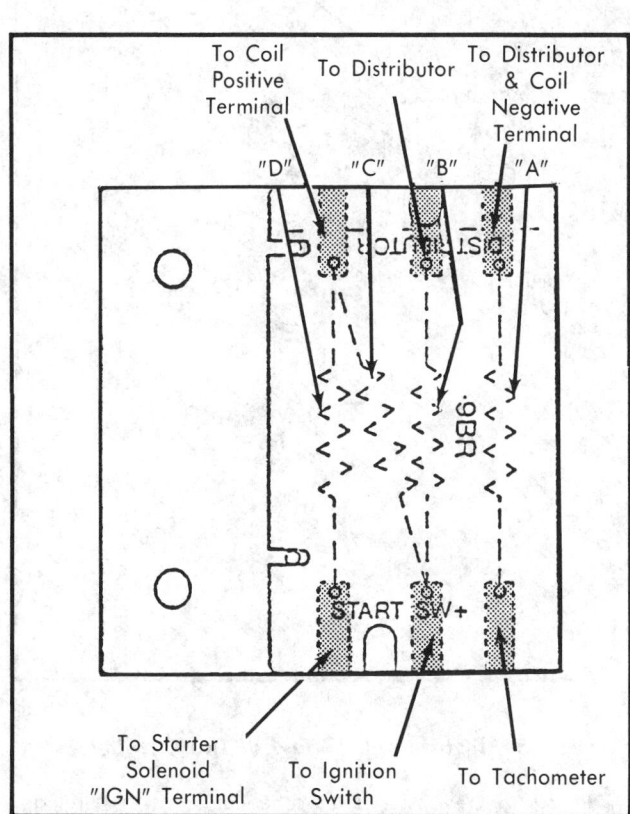

Fig. 3   Model 9BR Ballast Resistor Connections

2) Turn ignition switch "OFF". Connect ohmmeter leads to each set of terminals shown in *Fig. 3*. Resistor reading "A" (tachometer connection) should be 9,000-11,000 ohms. Reading "B" (drive resistor) should be 0.5 ohm; reading "C" (ballast ignition resistor) should be 1.62-1.80 ohms, and reading "D" (ballast resistor) should read 0.25-0.28 ohm. If not, replace ballast resistor assembly.

BALLAST WIRE CHECK

1) On most models, such as the TR7, a pink/white ballast resistance wire is built into the wiring harness leading to the ignition coil. The wire causes a voltage drop so the 12-volt supply may be used to power the 6-volt ignition coil. During engine start, the resistor is bypassed to apply 12 volts reduced by starter load directly to the coil.

2) To check resistor wire, turn ignition switch "OFF" and attach ohmmeter leads to each end of pink/white wire. Resistance should be 1.3-1.5 ohms. If not, replace ballast resistor wire.

DRIVE RESISTOR CHECK

1) A drive resistor is used on some models, such as the TR7, and is mounted externally near the distributor control module (amplifier). This is due to its size and heat dissipating requirements.

2) To check, disconnect connectors from resistor. With ignition switch "OFF", attach ohmmeter leads to each resistor terminal. Resistance should be 9.5-11.5 ohms. If not, replace drive resistor.

IGNITION COIL RESISTANCE

1) Connect ohmmeter leads to positive and negative primary terminals of ignition coil. Be sure ignition is "OFF" and coil wires are removed.

2) Primary resistance should read 1.30-1.45 ohms. If not, replace ignition coil.

OVERHAUL

MGB, SPITFIRE AND TR7 MODELS

Disassembly — 1) Disconnect battery and remove distributor from vehicle. Remove cap, rotor, anti-flash cover and felt pad. Remove screws and washers from magnetic pick-up coil (pick-up module). Do not remove pick-up coil at this time.

2) Remove screws securing amplifier to distributor. Hold amplifier while removing screw from bottom of housing. Carefully disengage vacuum unit from movable plate.

3) Remove wire grommet, amplifier housing, and pick-up coil with lead. Remove spring clips. Tap out roll pin securing vacuum unit and remove unit. Remove external snap ring from distributor shaft and carefully remove timing rotor, washer and "O" ring.

4) Remove 2 Phillips head screws and lift out base plate with movable plate attached. Remove springs carefully, noting positions of 2 different springs.

LUCAS "OPUS" ELECTRONIC IGNITION SYSTEM (Cont.)

TR8 MODELS

Disassembly – 1) Remove negative battery cable and then remove distributor from vehicle. Remove cap, rotor, anti-flash cover and felt pad.

2) Remove snap ring, plain washer and rubber "O" ring. Remove timing rotor carefully. Remove 3 screws, spring washers and washer. Remove wire grommet and electronic control module assembly as a unit.

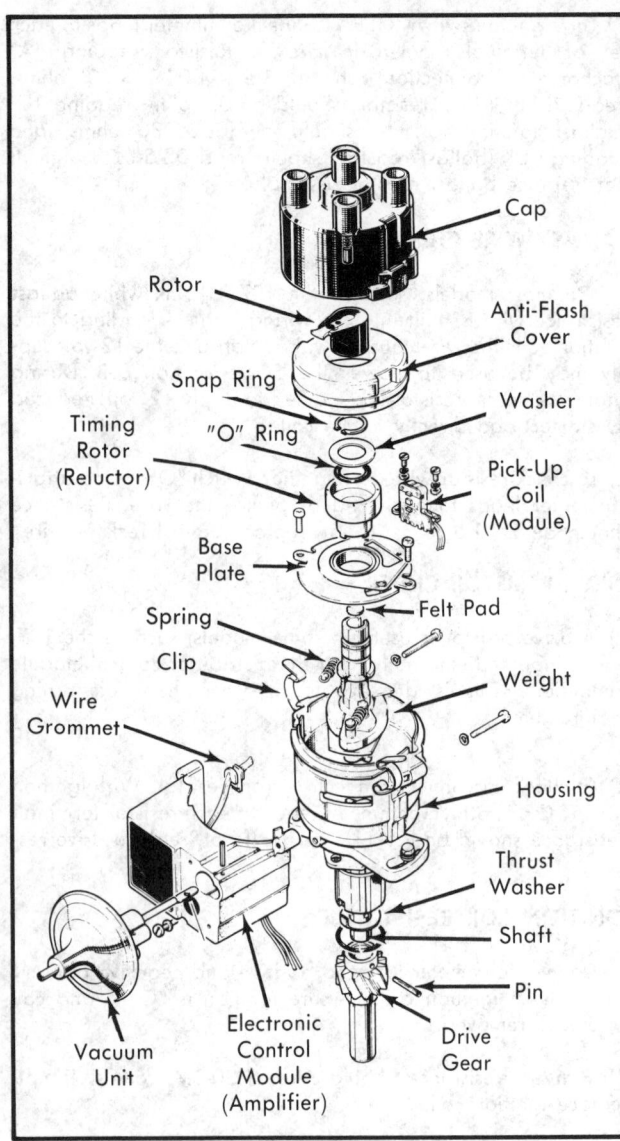

Fig. 4   Disassembled View of TR7 Distributor (MGB and Spitfire Similar)

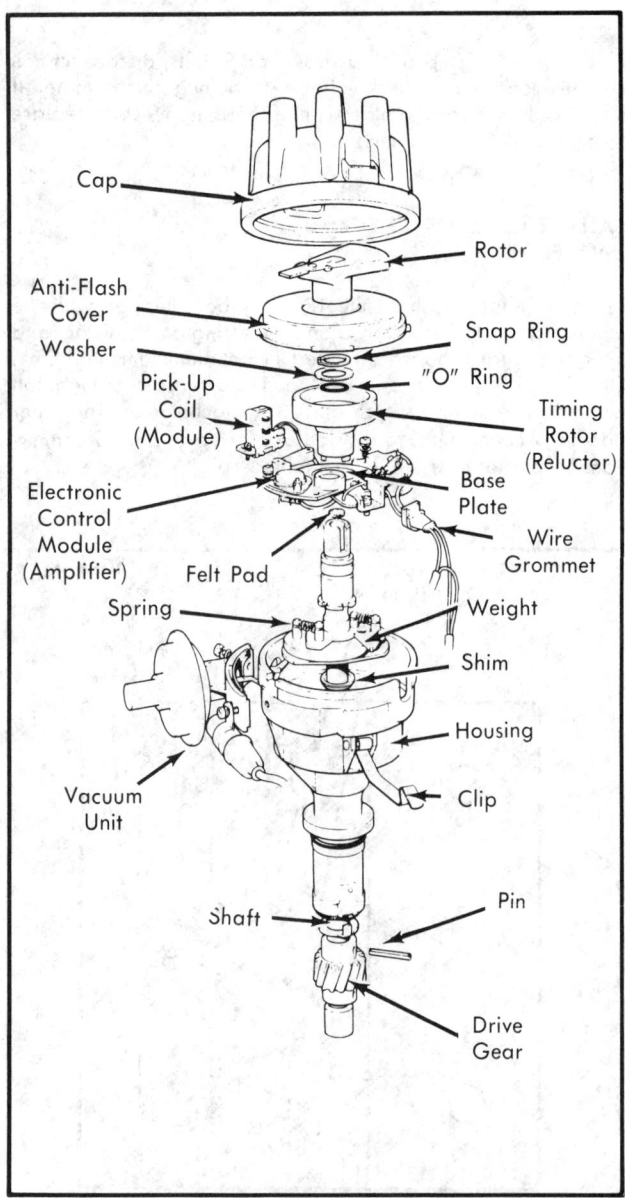

Fig. 5   Disassembled View of TR8 Distributor

5) Drive out pin securing drive collar to distributor shaft. Remove drive collar and thrust washer. Remove shaft from housing, along with shim. Detach return springs.

Inspection – Check control springs for proper length. Check pivot holes in weights for wear or deformation. Check distributor shaft for excessive play.

NOTE – *If any part of the distributor body assembly is found to be defective, the complete assembly must be replaced.*

Reassembly – To reassemble distributor, reverse disassembly procedure noting the following. Lubricate weight assembly, shaft and moving plate with Rocol "Moly Pad" or equivalent. Make sure vacuum link is properly attached to moving plate pin. Timing rotor tang must fit into slot on shaft. With distributor assembled and replaced in vehicle, set air gap and ignition timing to specifications.

3) Remove 2 screws, 2 spring washers and washer to release vacuum unit, rubber gasket and capacitor. Tap out drive gear pin. Remove drive gear and thrust washer. Be sure shaft is free of burrs, and remove shaft from housing.

LUCAS "OPUS" ELECTRONIC IGNITION SYSTEM (Cont.)

4) Remove plastic collar and control springs, but do not attempt to disassemble further.

Reassembly — To reassemble distributor, reverse disassembly procedure, noting the following. Lubricate weight assembly, shaft and moving plate with Rocol "Moly Pad" or equivalent. Make sure vacuum link is properly attached to moving plate pin. Timing rotor tang must fit into slot on shaft. With distributor assembled and installed in vehicle, set air gap and ignition timing to specification.

JAGUAR XJ6 MODELS

Disassembly — **1)** Disconnect negative battery cable and remove distributor from vehicle. Remove distributor cap, anti-flash cover and rotor. Remove snap ring, plain washer and "O" ring. Remove felt pad from end of shaft.

2) Remove reluctor gear from distributor shaft. Remove pick-up coil assembly, and base plate assembly. Remove vacuum unit from housing. Drive pin from drive collar and after checking shaft for burrs, remove distributor shaft from housing. Disassemble auto-advance mechanism as necessary.

Reassembly — **1)** To reassemble distributor, reverse disassembly procedure. Check parts for wear and lubricate weight assembly, shaft and moving plate with Rocol "Moly Pad" or equivalent. Be sure all parts are properly assembled and move freely.

2) Install distributor in vehicle and adjust air gap and ignition timing to specifications.

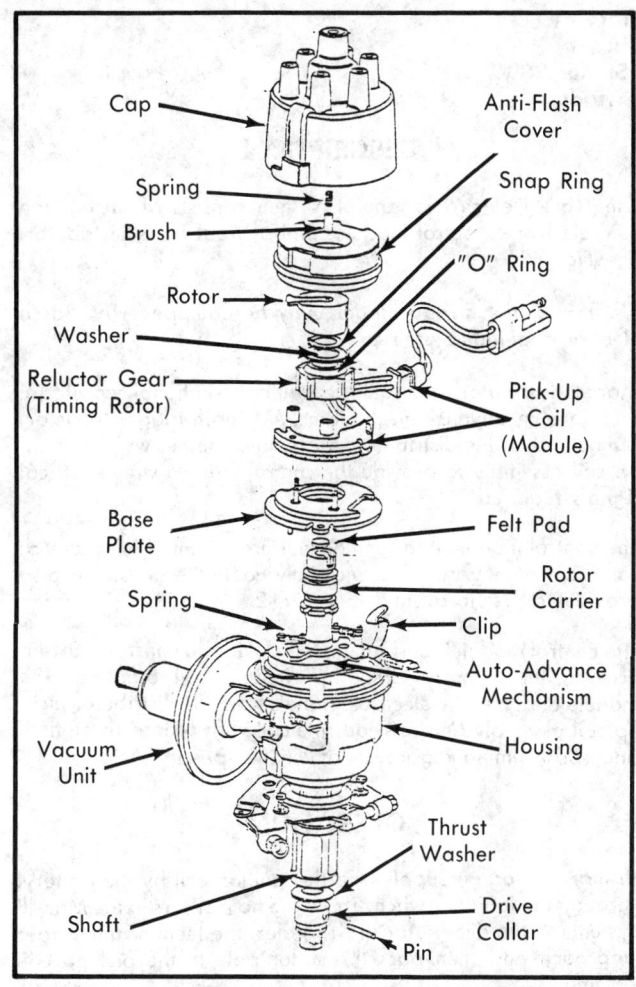

Fig. 6 Disassembled View of XJ6 Distributor

MARELLI ELECTRONIC IGNITION SYSTEM

Fiat
Brava
Spider 2000
Strada

DESCRIPTION

The Marelli electronic ignition system consists of an ignition coil, electronic control module, and a breakerless distributor. See Fig. 1.

NOTE — Some Strada models may be equipped with Bosch electronic ignition systems.

Marelli distributors are equipped with conventional centrifugal and vacuum advance mechanisms. A 4-tooth trigger (reluctor) is mounted on the distributor shaft and combines with the pick-up coil assembly to provide the control module with electrical signals required.

The control module and ignition coil are mounted on a finned, cast aluminum base which not only cools the units, but also provides a system ground. See Fig. 2.

The control module's current limiter provides a constant current flow to the primary circuit, preventing coil damage. The module analyzes the electrical signals from the distributor pick-up coil assembly and provides the coil with proper dwell time and spark timing regardless of engine speed.

OPERATION

Primary voltage is supplied to the ignition coil by the battery, through the ignition switch. There are no resistors in the Marelli system. As the distributor shaft rotates, the teeth of the trigger approach and then pass the stator pole in the pick-up coil assembly.

This creates and collapses a magnetic field, causing an electrical signal or impulse, which is fed to the control module. As this signal is received, the control module opens and closes the ignition coil primary circuit. This causes a high voltage surge in the coil secondary windings, firing the spark plugs.

SPECIFICATIONS

Centrifugal & Vacuum Advance — See Specifications Pages in this section.

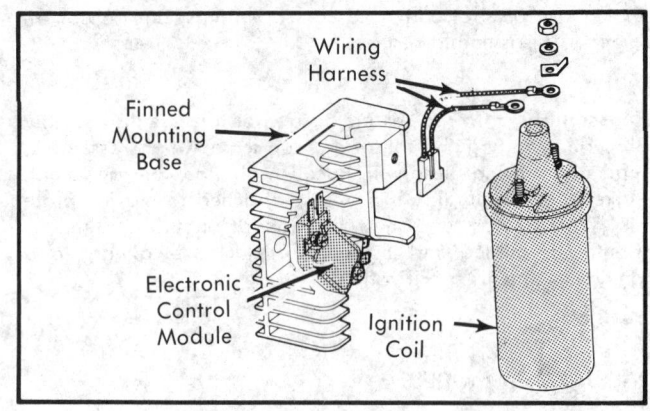

Fig. 2   Ignition Coil, Control Module and Base Assembly

ADJUSTMENT

Trigger-to-Pick-Up Coil Air Gap — Check air gap between trigger and stator pole piece of pick-up coil assembly, using a non-magnetic feeler gauge. Air gap should be .020-.024" (.5-.6 mm). If not to specification, loosen retaining screws and move advance plate to adjust gap. Tighten retaining screws and recheck air gap.

TESTING

CAUTION — When working around coil, do not ground wire lead to tachometer. Be careful not to disconnect high tension terminal of coil with engine running. Make all resistance checks with the ignition switch "OFF".

ROTOR RESISTANCE CHECK

Using an ohmmeter set at the x1000 scale, check the rotor resistance for 4,000-6,000 ohms. Replace if resistance varies considerably.

IGNITION SYSTEM CHECK

With ignition system in the "MAR" (Run) position, inspect wiring and connectors. Be sure heat dissipater (module and coil base), power unit, and battery are properly grounded. Be sure coil and distributor connectors are firmly attached to control module terminals.

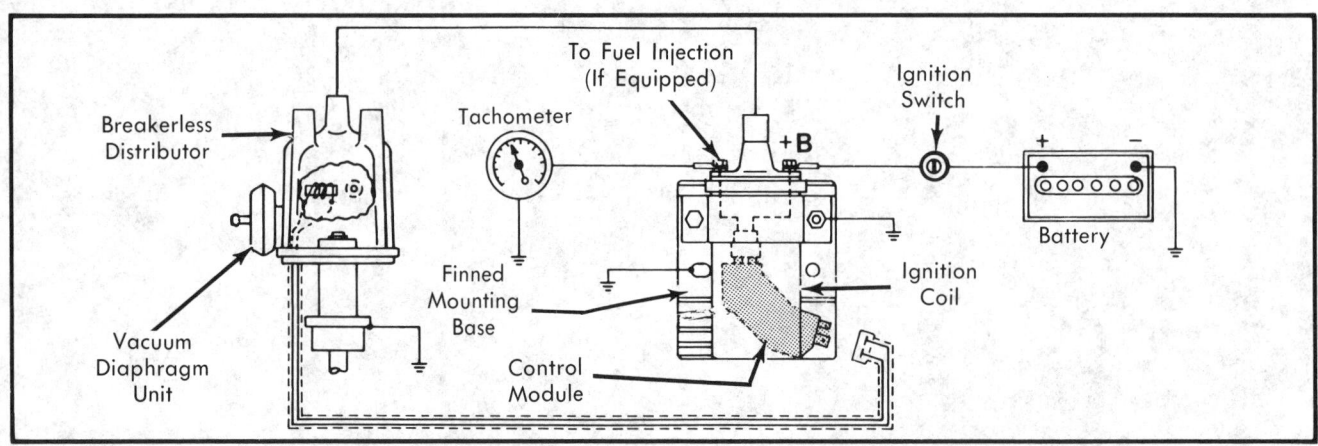

Fig. 1   Schematic of Marelli Electronic Ignition System

MARELLI ELECTRONIC IGNITION SYSTEM (Cont.)

SYSTEM INPUT VOLTAGE CHECK

1) With the ignition key in the "MAR" (Run) position and engine shut off, attach positive voltmeter lead to ignition coil positive (+B) terminal. Attach negative lead to ground. Voltage should be 12 volts. See Fig. 3. If not, check battery, ignition switch, wires and connectors.

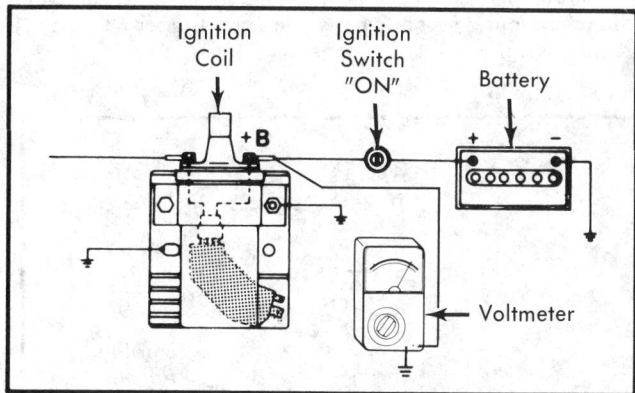

**Fig. 3   Voltmeter Hookup for
System Input Voltage Check**

2) Move positive voltmeter lead to ignition coil negative terminal. Voltage should be within 0.3 volts of voltage recorded at coil positive terminal. If not as specified, make Ignition Coil Resistance Check.

GROUND CIRCUIT CHECK

1) Turn ignition switch "OFF". Connect ohmmeter leads to battery ground terminal and ignition coil ground stud. See Fig. 4.

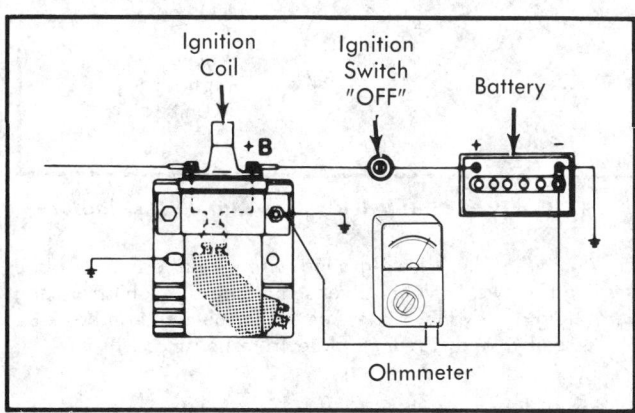

**Fig. 4   Ohmmeter Hookup for
Ground Circuit Check**

2) Resistance reading should be less than 0.2 ohms. If resistance is higher, check support, mounting and battery ground connections. Also check that control module casing is clean and that all mounting bolts are clean and tight.

IGNITION COIL RESISTANCE CHECK

1) Using an ohmmeter set in the low scale, connect the leads to the positive and negative primary terminals of the ignition coil. See Fig. 5. Resistance reading should be .75-.81 ohm.

2) Change ohmmeter to the x1000 scale and connect leads to coil negative terminal and coil center tower. See Fig. 5. Resistance should be 10,000-11,000 ohms.

3) If either reading is not to specifications, replace ignition coil.

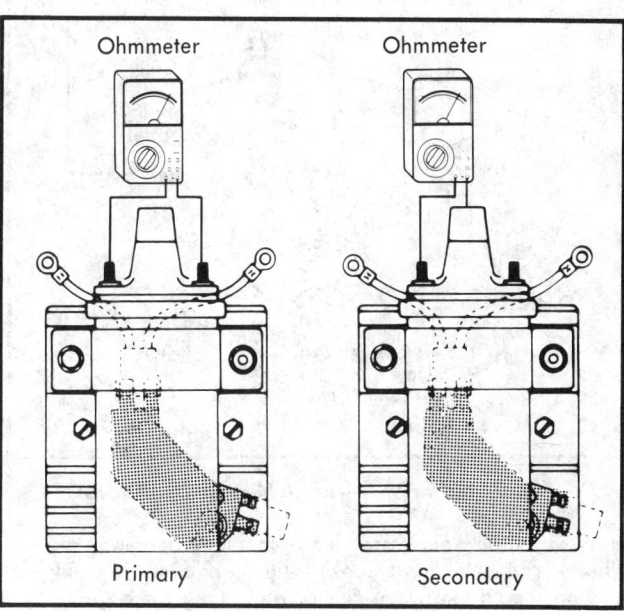

**Fig. 5   Ohmmeter Hookup for Ignition Coil
Primary and Secondary Resistance Check**

PICK-UP COIL RESISTANCE AND SHORT CHECK

1) Turn the ignition switch "OFF". Disconnect 2-wire distributor connector. Connect an ohmmeter set in the x100 scale with one lead touching each terminal of distributor harness connector. See Fig. 6.

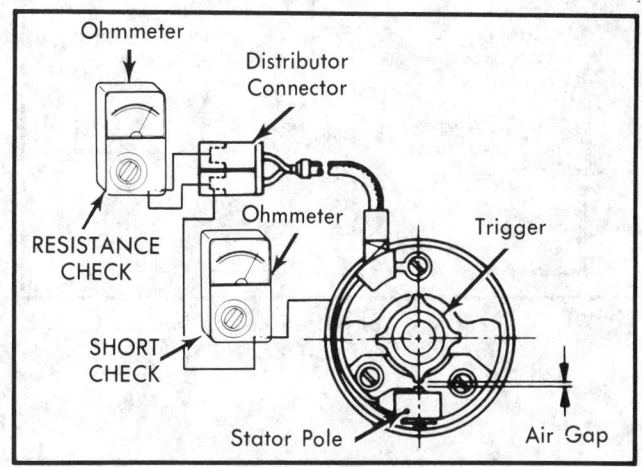

**Fig. 6   Ohmmeter Hookups for Pick-Up Coil
Resistance and Short Check**

2) Pick-up coil resistance should be 700-800 ohms. If not, replace pick-up coil assembly. If system works intermittently, be sure pick-up coil wire in distributor is properly grounded. See Fig. 7.

MARELLI ELECTRONIC IGNITION SYSTEM (Cont.)

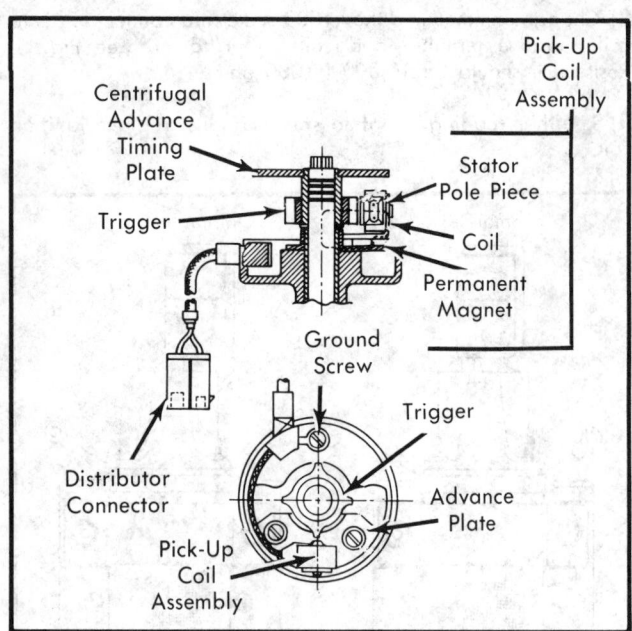

Fig. 7   Interior View of Marelli Distributor

3) Next, attach ohmmeter leads to either terminal of distributor connector and to distributor housing. An infinity reading should exist. See *Fig. 6*. Also check air gap.

CONTROL MODULE CHECK

1) Be sure all ignition system wires and connectors are properly connected. Disconnect coil-to-distributor high voltage wire at the distributor. Hold wire about ¼" (5-6 mm) from a good engine ground, using insulated pliers. See *Fig. 8*.

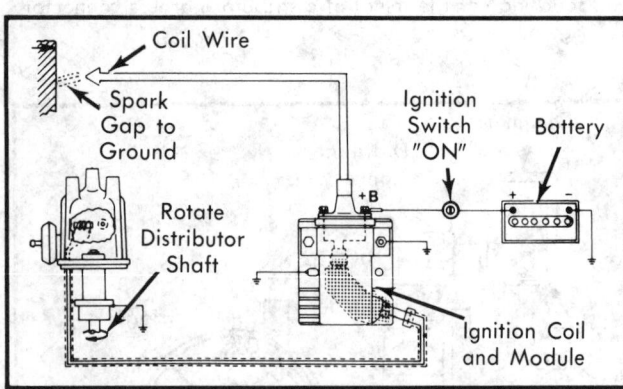

Fig. 8   Coil Wire Hookup for Making Control Module Check

2) Crank engine and check for sparks at gap to ground. If previous tests have disclosed no problem and no spark exists at gap, replace control module.

OVERHAUL

Disassembly – 1) Remove distributor cap and rotor. *See Fig. 9*. Remove pin securing pinion gear and lift shaft and centrifugal advance mechanism (with integral trigger or reluctor) from housing.

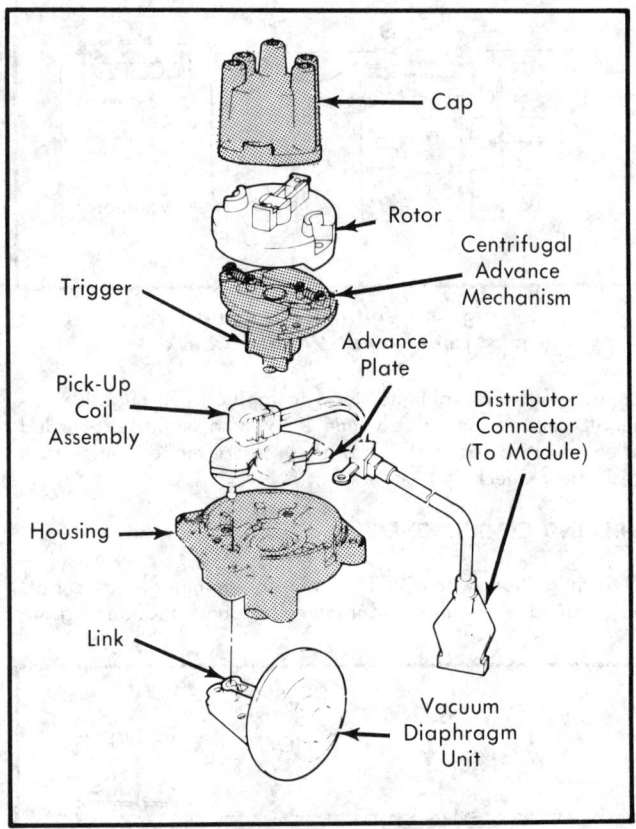

Fig. 9   Disassembled View of Marelli Distributor

2) Remove pick-up coil ground screw and advance plate retaining screws. Disconnect vacuum diaphragm unit from peg on bottom of advance plate. Remove vacuum unit and pick-up coil assembly and advance plate from housing.

Reassembly – Install parts in reverse order of disassembly. Be sure pick-up coil ground screw is tight and that vacuum unit is secured to peg on bottom of advance plate.

MITSUBISHI ELECTRONIC IGNITION SYSTEM

Arrow
  All 2600 cc
  Calif. 1600 cc
Arrow Pickup
Champ & Colt Hatchback
  Calif. Only
Challenger

Colt Wagon
Courier
Mazda
  GLC
  626
  B2000 Pickup
Sapporo

DESCRIPTION

Mitsubishi transistorized breakerless ignition consists of an electronic control module (ignitor), ignition coil and distributor. On some models, the control module was mounted with the ignition coil on the left fender apron. See *Fig. 1*. On others, such as Chrysler Corp., Courier 2000 cc, and Mazda 626 and B2000 Pickup, the control module was mounted on the outside of the distributor housing. See *Fig. 2*.

The GLC utilizes a dual timing ignition system to control spark timing. The system consists of two water thermo switches and a timer unit. See *Fig. 8*. Within a 2 minute period after starting the engine, timing is retarded when the coolant temperature range is 50-122° F (10-50° C). Advance timing is 5° BTDC; retard timing is 1° BTDC. As the engine warms to normal operating temperature, timing will advance to 5° BTDC.

The Mazda 626 utilizes a water thermo valve to cut advance when the engine is cold. Federal B2000 Pickups use a vacuum delay valve during acceleration, and Calif. B2000 Pickups use both a water thermo valve and vacuum delay valve. On Calif.

models, vacuum advance is cut when engine is cold and delayed during acceleration.

OPERATION

Whenever the ignition switch is "ON", the primary circuit of the ignition coil is energized. As the distributor shaft rotates, the armature (reluctor) rotates inside the magnetic pick-up coil (stator) assembly. See *Fig. 2*. As the teeth of the armature pass the pegs of the pick-up coil and breaker plate assembly, a signal is sent to the control module (ignitor). The module then breaks the primary circuit in the coil, inducing high voltage in the secondary circuit firing the spark plugs.

SPECIFICATIONS

Centrifugal & Vacuum Advance — See *Specifications Pages* in this section.

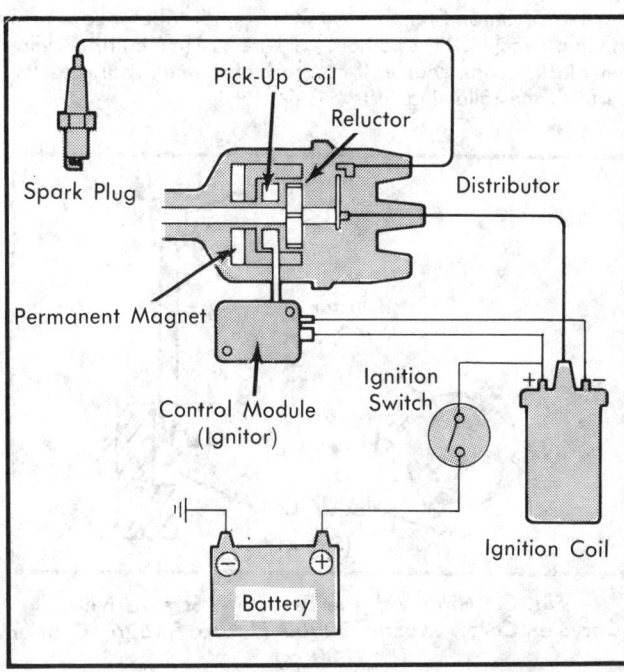

Fig. 2   Wiring Schematic of Mitsubishi Transistorized Breakerless Ignition System (Chrysler Corp., Courier 2000 cc, Mazda 626 & B2000 Pickup)

ADJUSTMENTS

NOTE — *There is no air gap adjustment possible on Chrysler Corp. Imports, Mazda B2000 Pickup & 626, or Courier 2000 cc engines.*

Armature-to-Pick-Up Coil Air Gap — Align teeth of armature (reluctor) with pegs of pick-up coil and breaker plate assembly. Using a feeler gauge, check for air gap of .008-.024" (.2-.6 mm) on Courier 2300 cc engine or .010-.014" (.25-.35 mm) on GLC. To adjust gap, loosen set screws and move pick-up coil.

NOTE — *No other adjustments should be attempted on the ignition system except armature-to-pick-up coil air gap, spark plug gap and initial ignition timing.*

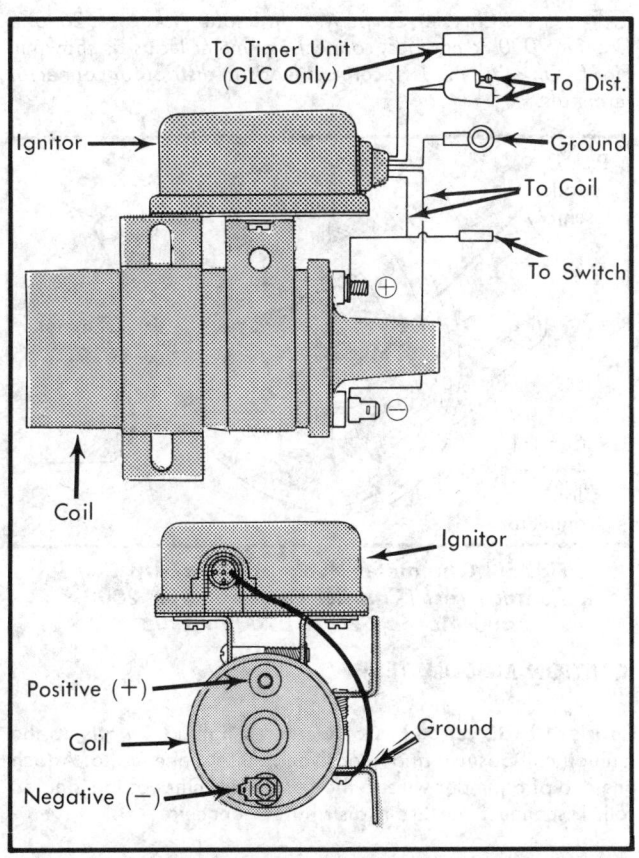

Fig. 1   Control Module & Coil Wiring Connections (GLC & Courier 2300 cc)

Distributors & Ignition Systems

MITSUBISHI ELECTRONIC IGNITION SYSTEM (Cont.)

TESTING

NOTE — *Be sure battery is at full charge and in good condition before making any tests. Check all wiring harnesses, ignition switch, coil and spark plug cables and connectors.*

HIGH VOLTAGE TEST

Chrysler Corp., Courier 2000 cc, & Mazda B2000 Pickup & 626 — Remove distributor cap and remove rotor assembly. Turn ignition switch "ON". Disconnect coil wire from distributor cap and hold its end ¼" (6 mm) from cylinder block. Insert a conventional screwdriver blade between the armature (reluctor) and magnetic pick-up coil. See *Fig. 3*. If no spark is produced at gap, suspect a defective control unit, pick-up coil assembly, ignition coil or secondary cables.

Other Models — Connect a remote starter switch in the starting circuit and remove coil wire from distributor cap. Turn ignition switch "ON" and hold coil wire ¼" (6 mm) from cylinder block. Crank engine. If no spark or a weak spark results, perform the following tests.

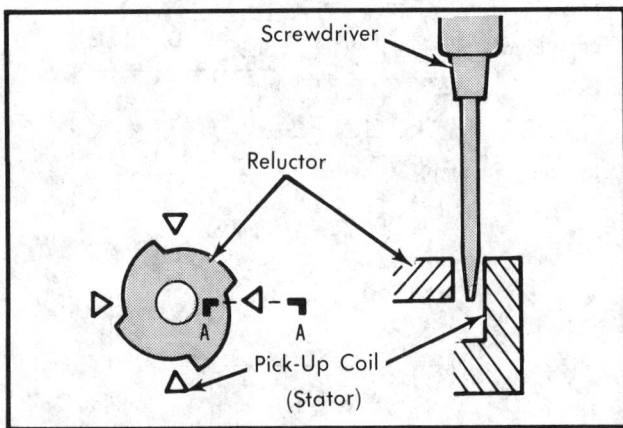

Fig. 3 High Voltage Test with Screwdriver (Chrysler Corp., Mazda B2000 Pickup & 626, Courier 2000 cc)

IGNITION COIL RESISTANCE TEST

1) Turn ignition switch "OFF". Set an ohmmeter in the low scale and attach its leads to the coil positive and negative terminals. Coil should be isolated from rest of system. Check primary resistance reading. Replace coil if not to specifications. See *Fig. 4*.

2) Set ohmmeter in x1000 scale and attach leads to positive primary terminal and secondary tower. Check secondary resistance reading. Replace coil if not to specifications.

Ignition Coil Resistance Specifications (Ohms)

Application	Primary	Secondary
Chrysler Corp.	.70-.85	9,000-11,000
Courier	.81-.99	6,800-9,200
Mazda GLC	1.28	13,500
Mazda 626 & B2000	.81-.99	7,000

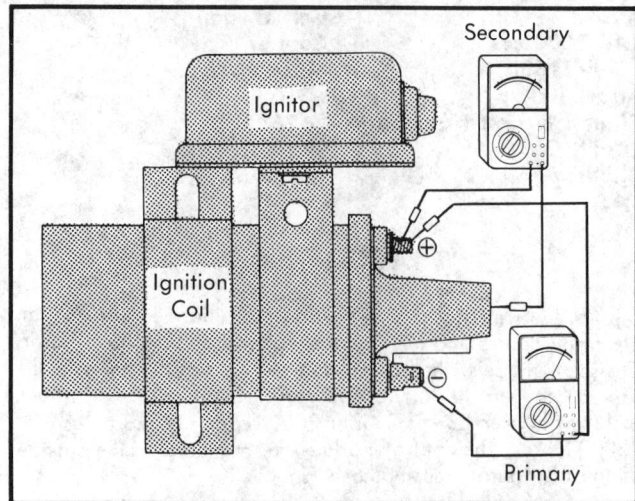

Fig. 4 Ohmmeter Hookup for Ignition Coil Primary & Secondary Resistance Test

MAGNETIC PICK-UP COIL RESISTANCE TEST

Turn ignition switch "OFF". Set an ohmmeter in the x100 scale. Attach its leads to pick-up coil's distributor connector terminals. Resistance reading for Chrysler Corp., Courier 2000 cc, and Mazda B2000 Pickup & 626 should be 1,000-1,100 ohms. Courier 2300 cc resistance should read 760-840 ohms; Mazda GLC, 670-790 ohms. If not to specifications, replace pick-up coil assembly.

NOTE — *On Chrysler Corp., Mazda B2000 Pickup & 626, and Courier 2000 cc engines, connect ohmmeter leads as shown in Fig. 5. On other models, connect leads to distributor connector terminals.*

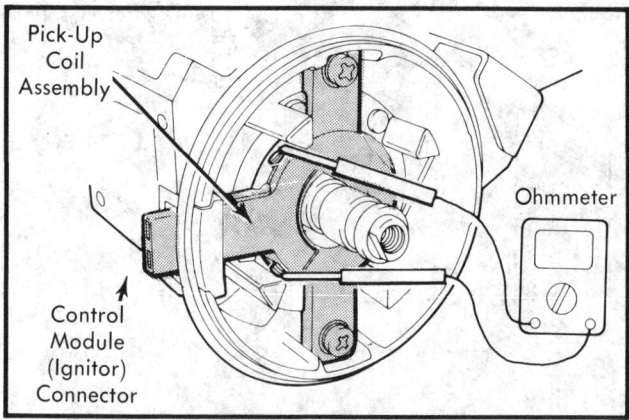

Fig. 5 Ohmmeter Hookup for Pick-Up Coil Resistance Test (Chrysler Corp., Courier 2000 cc and Mazda 626 & B2000 Pickup)

IGNITION MODULE TEST

Courier (2300 cc) — 1) Connect a test light (3.4 watts) to the ignition coil positive and negative terminals. See *Fig. 6*. Attach one end of a jumper wire to the positive terminal of the ignition coil. Disconnect the 2-pin distributor connector.

2) Attach other end of jumper wire to the red wire terminal on the module side of the connector. Turn the ignition switch

MITSUBISHI ELECTRONIC IGNITION SYSTEM (Cont.)

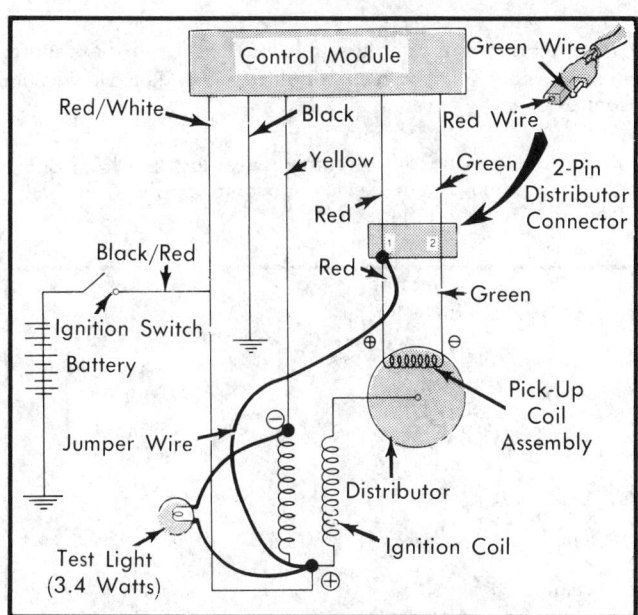

Fig. 6   Courier Ignition Control Module Test (2300 cc engine)

"ON". The test light should come on. The light should go out when the jumper wire is disconnected.

3) If test light does not function as stated, retest to make sure bulb is OK and that all connections are tight. If results are still improper, replace control module and retest.

Chrysler Corp., Courier 2000 cc, and Mazda B2000 Pickup and 626 – 1) Turn ignition switch "OFF". Using an ohmmeter, check for continuity between terminal "C" of the control module (ignitor) and its metallic reverse surface. See Fig. 7. If the module is installed on the distributor, make check between terminal "C" and distributor housing (ground).

2) Perform test in same manner as a diode test, alternately switching the leads of the ohmmeter. If there is continuity or if there is an open circuit in both directions, the control module is defective and must be replaced.

NOTE – Only the transistors in the switching section of control module are evaluated by this test. The module may still

be defective, even if the test shows good. If control module checks OK, but system does not operate properly, substitute a known good module and attempt to start vehicle.

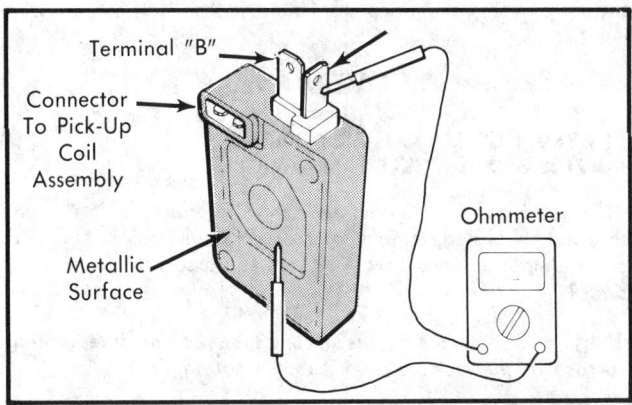

Fig. 7   Checking Transistors in Switching Section of Control Module/Ignitor (Chrysler Corp., Courier 2000 cc, Mazda B2000 Pickup and 626)

SECONDARY WIRE RESISTANCE TEST

Test coil and spark plug cables with an ohmmeter. Do not puncture secondary wires when making the resistance check. Connect leads to each end of the cable. Resistance for Courier should not exceed 570 ohms per inch; for Mazda vehicles, resistance should not exceed 16,000 ohms for each 39" (1 m); and Chrysler Corp. vehicles should not exceed 22,000 ohms per cable.

TIMER TEST (GLC ONLY)

1) To check timer (located under instrument panel on left side panel), connect wires to terminals "A", "B", and "C" of timer. See Fig. 8. Connect a wire with a 30,000 ohm resistor to terminal "D". Connect a wire with a 3.4 watt test lamp to terminal "E". Connect a voltmeter to terminal "D" and to negative battery terminal.

2) Connect wires from terminals "A", "D", and "E" to battery positive terminal. Connect wire from terminal "C" to battery negative terminal. Voltmeter should show more than 6 volts.

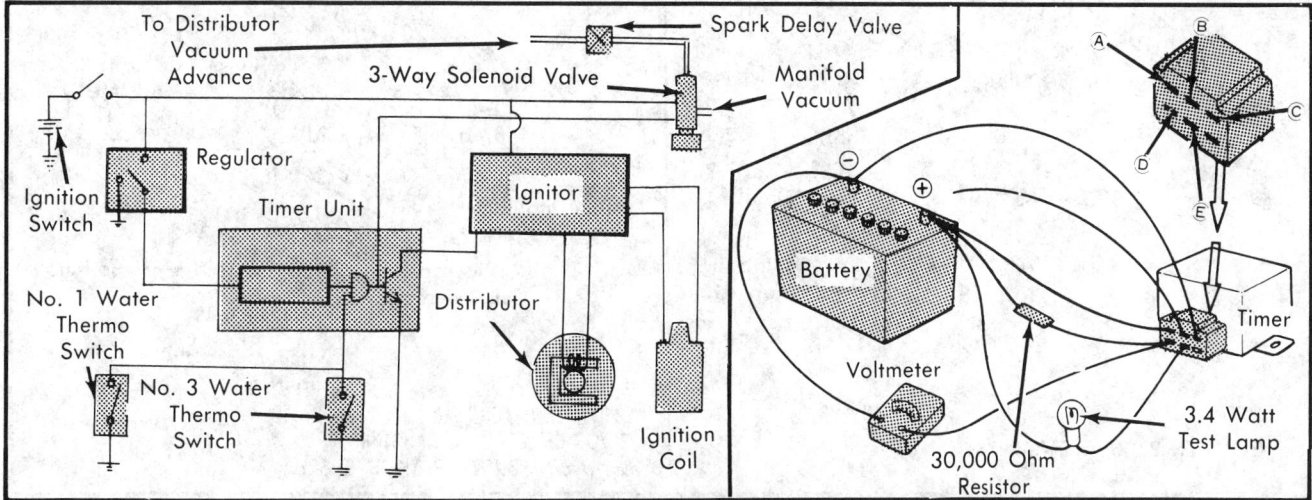

Fig. 8   Schematic of GLC Dual Timing System and Voltmeter Hookup for Timer Test

MITSUBISHI ELECTRONIC IGNITION SYSTEM (Cont.)

3) Then, connect wire from terminal "B" to battery positive terminal. Instantly, voltmeter should show less than 1 volt and test lamp should light. After approximately 105-135 seconds from showing 1 volt, voltmeter should indicate 8 volts. If not, replace timer.

OVERHAUL

**CHRYSLER CORP., COURIER 2000 cc
MAZDA B2000 PICKUP AND 626**

Disassembly — 1) To remove control module (ignitor) from distributor housing, remove 2 screws and pull straight outward on module to unplug it from pick-up coil assembly. *See Figs. 9 and 10.*

NOTE — *Do not remove the silicone grease from either mating surface of the module or distributor housing.*

2) Remove distributor cap by inserting screwdriver in screw heads, depressing and turning retaining lugs. Remove rotor assembly, governor assembly with reluctor and then remove pick-up coil assembly.

3) Remove vacuum control unit screws and "E" ring from vacuum link. Lift out vacuum control unit. Remove breaker plate assembly, spring pin securing driven gear and remove plate and shaft from housing.

Reassembly — Reverse removal procedure. Inspect cap and rotor for cracks and deposits on inside surfaces. Check driven gear for wear and shaft for play in thrust direction.

**COURIER 2300 cc
AND MAZDA GLC**

Disassembly — 1) Remove distributor cap and rotor. *See Fig. 7 and 8.* Remove cover, gasket and grommet. Remove clips.

Drive roll pin from armature (reluctor) and remove armature. Remove clip holding vacuum diaphragm link. Remove vacuum control unit.

2) Remove pick-up coil assembly. Drive lock pin from driven gear and remove gear. Remove governor and shaft assembly from distributor housing.

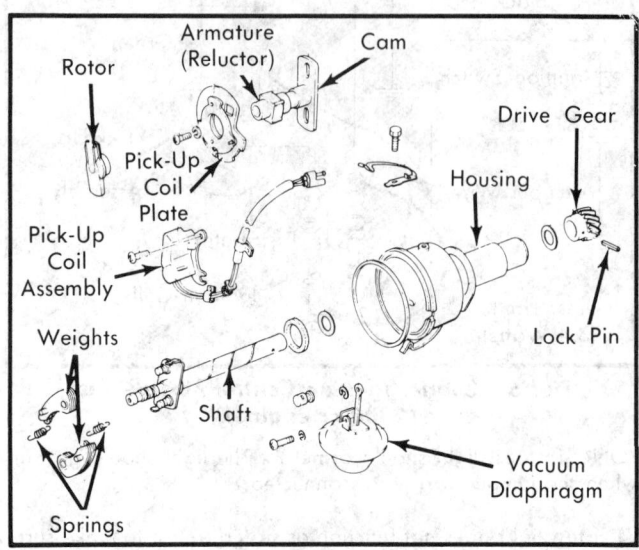

**Fig. 10   Disassembled View of Distributor
(Mazda GLC)**

Reassembly — Reverse disassembly procedure. When installing cam, align marks on distributor housing and gear. Align rotor metal end with clip mounting lug on side of distributor with mounting slot.

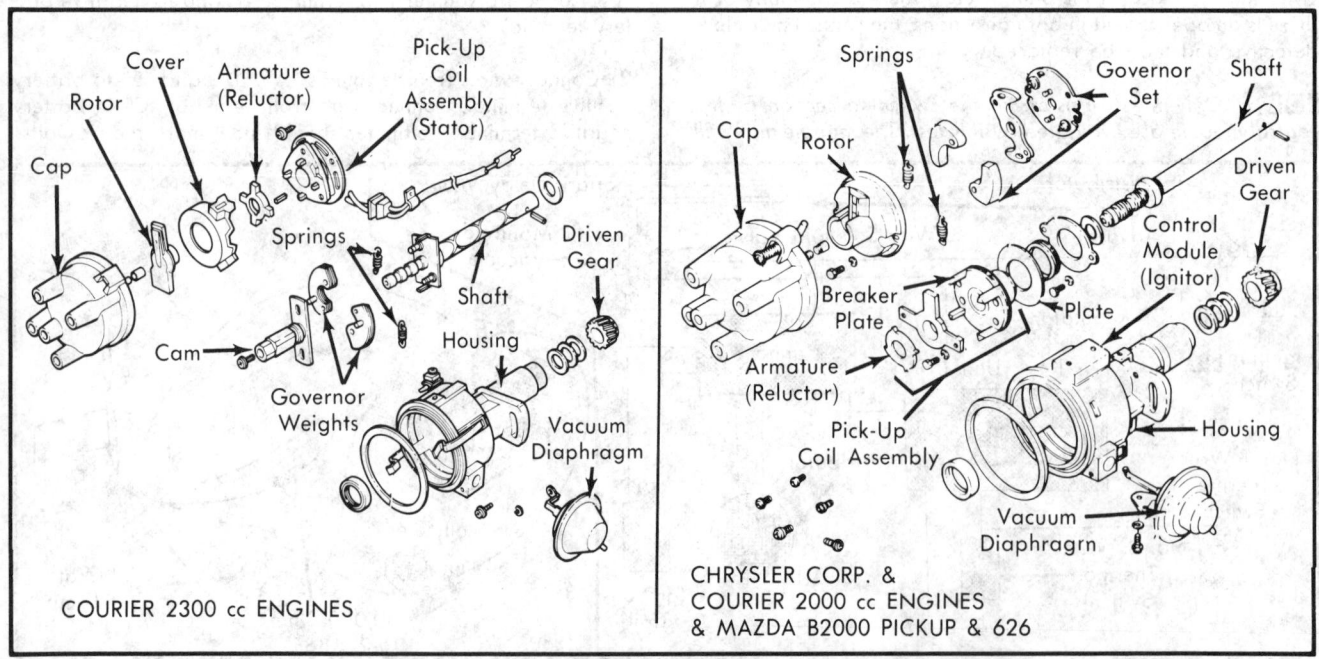

COURIER 2300 cc ENGINES

CHRYSLER CORP. &
COURIER 2000 cc ENGINES
& MAZDA B2000 PICKUP & 626

Fig. 9   Disassembled View of Courier, Mazda (Except GLC) & Chrysler Corp. Distributors

MITSUBISHI ELECTRONIC IGNITION SYSTEMS – ROTARY ENGINE

Mazda RX7

DESCRIPTION

The Mitsubishi electronic ignition system used on the Mazda RX7 rotary engine is unique in that it has 2 sets of spark plugs (leading and trailing) with one set in the front rotor housing and one in the rear rotor housing. See Fig. 1. There are also 2 ignition coils, 2 pick-up coils in the distributor, and 2 coil-to-distributor high tension wires.

There are 2 separate ignitors, mounted on a common base, one for leading side and one for the trailing side. Other system components include a battery, ignition switch, ignition control switches (water temperature, altitude, etc.), and various relays.

All models are equipped with an ignition control system and centrifugal advance mechanisms. All models have vacuum control units on both trailing and leading sides, except automatic transmission models which have no trailing vacuum control unit.

OPERATION

A reluctor (signal rotor) is mounted on the rotor shaft and turns inside 2 magnetic pick-up coils, one for the leading side and one for the trailing side. See Fig. 2. As each tooth of the reluctor approaches and then passes the leading pick-up coil, a signal is generated that is sent to the leading ignitor, which breaks the primary circuit in the leading ignition coil. As each tooth passes the leading pick-up coil, the previous passing tooth approaches and becomes aligned with the trailing pick-up coil. This triggers a signal to the trailing ignitor, which breaks the primary circuit in the trailing ignition coil.

Therefore, immediately after the leading spark plug fires, the trailing spark plug also fires, providing more complete and efficient combustion and reducing HC and CO emissions.

As the primary circuit is broken in the leading and trailing ignition coils, a voltage surge occurs in the secondary circuit of the ignition coils. This high voltage is transmitted through the leading and trailing high tension wires to the distributor, rotor and spark plugs.

An emission control unit is also included in the ignition control system along with different sensing switches to provide proper timing under varying engine operating conditions.

SPECIFICATIONS

Centrifugal & Vacuum Advance (or Retard) – See Specifications Tables in this section.

ADJUSTMENTS

Reluctor-to-Pick-Up Coil Air Gap – 1) Remove distributor cap and rotor. Turn distributor shaft until the extended tooth of the reluctor (signal rotor) aligns with core of pick-up coil. See Fig. 2.

2) Using a feeler gauge, check for .008-.024" (.2-.6 mm) air gap. If gap is incorrect, replace pick-up coil and bearing assembly or distributor drive shaft, if necessary.

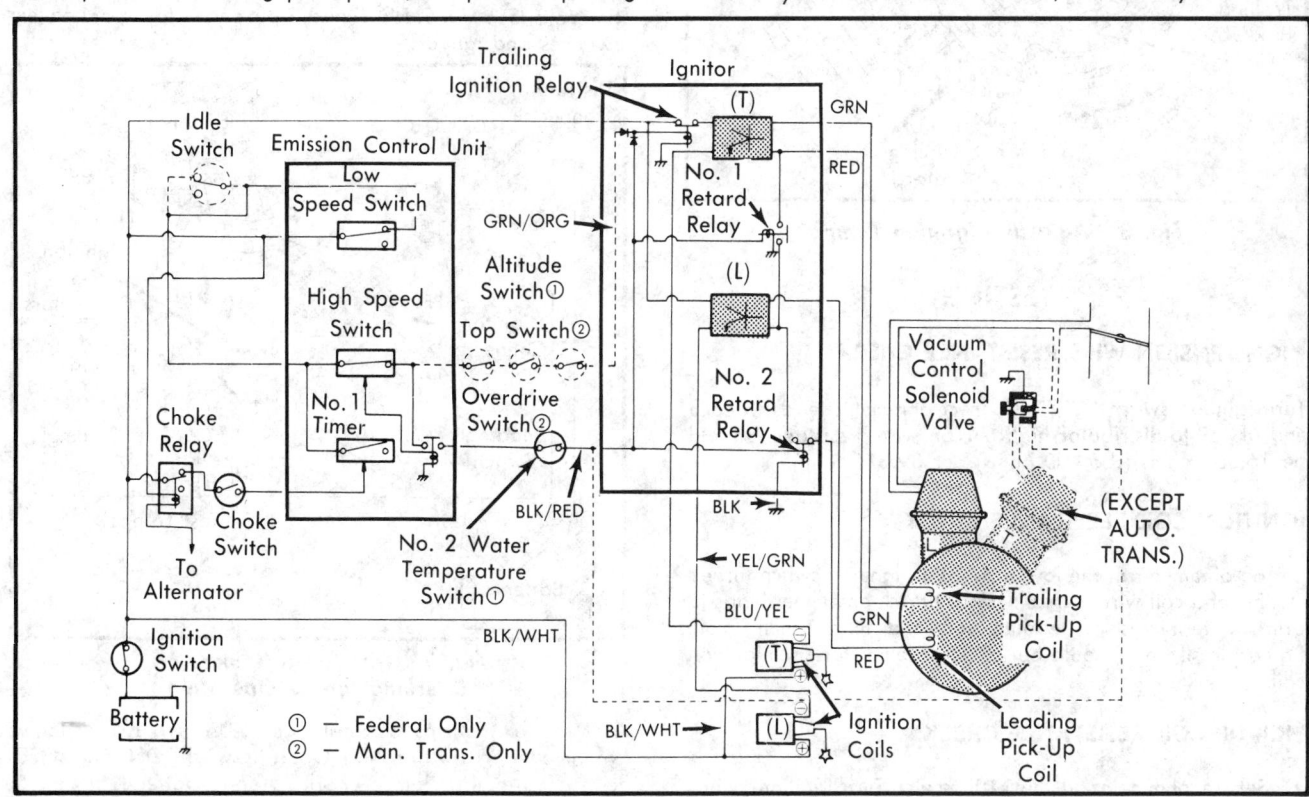

Fig. 1 Schematic of RX7 Ignition System

Distributors & Ignition Systems

MITSUBISHI ELECTRONIC IGNITION SYSTEMS – ROTARY ENGINE (Cont.)

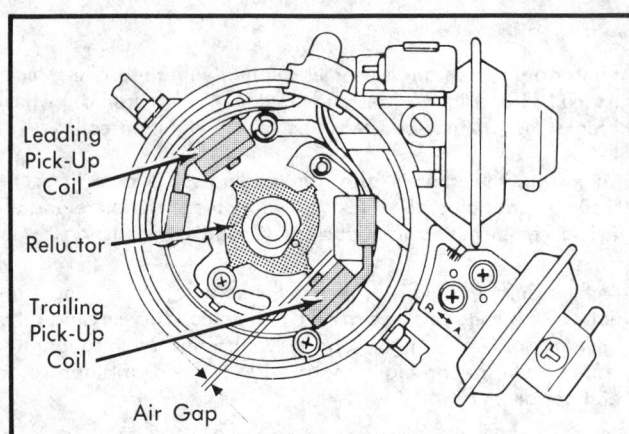

Fig. 2   Adjusting Distributor Air Gap

Ignition Timing – **1)** Leading timing is adjusted by loosening distributor lock nut and rotating distributor housing until correct timing is obtained. *See Fig. 3.*

2) Trailing timing is changed by loosening the screws securing the vacuum unit and moving the vacuum unit outward (to advance) or inward (to retard). Retighten screws when correct timing is obtained.

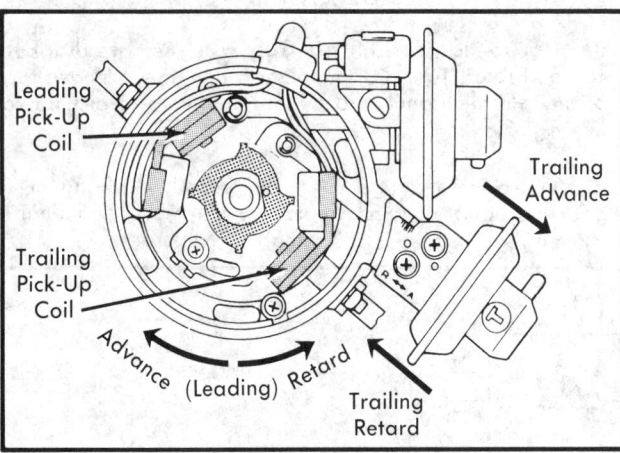

Fig. 3   Adjusting Ignition Timing

TESTING

HIGH TENSION WIRE RESISTANCE CHECK

Turn ignition switch "OFF". Connect ohmmeter leads to each end of coil-to-distributor high tension wire. Resistance should be 16,000 ohms (±6,400 ohms) per 39.37" (1 m).

IGNITION COIL RESISTANCE CHECK

Set an ohmmeter in the low scale. With ignition switch turned "OFF", and coil wires disconnected, attach ohmmeter leads to primary terminals of leading coil and then trailing coil. Primary resistance should be 1.22-1.48 ohms for each ignition coil.

PICK-UP COIL RESISTANCE CHECK

1) Set an ohmmeter in the x100 scale. Turn ignition switch "OFF". Disconnect connector between ignitor and distributor. *See Fig. 4.*

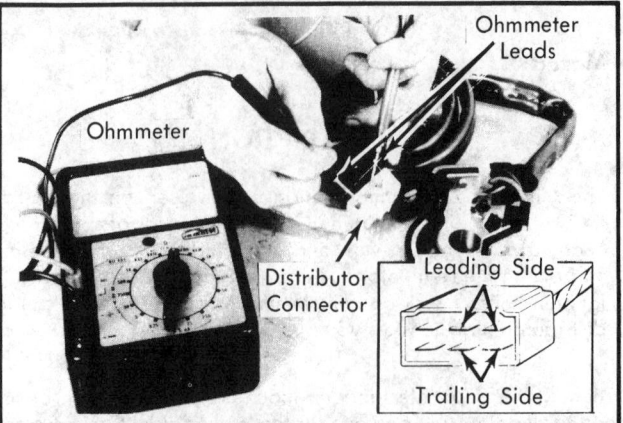

Fig. 4   Ohmmeter Hookup for Pick-Up Coil Resistance Check

2) Connect ohmmeter leads to leading terminals and then to trailing terminals. Resistance should be 600-700 ohms at 68° F (20° C) for each set of pick-up coils. If not, replace pick-up coil and bearing assembly.

PICK-UP COIL OPERATION CHECK

1) With distributor connector still disconnected, touch ammeter leads to leading terminals and then to trailing terminals.

2) Place a screwdriver against core of pick-up coil being tested. Indicator of meter should move each time screwdriver is taken quickly away from core. If not, replace pick-up coil and bearing assembly.

IGNITOR CHECK

1) Disconnect connectors from pick-up coil lead and from ignition coils. *See Fig. 5.* Disconnect 2-pin connector from between switches and ignitor.

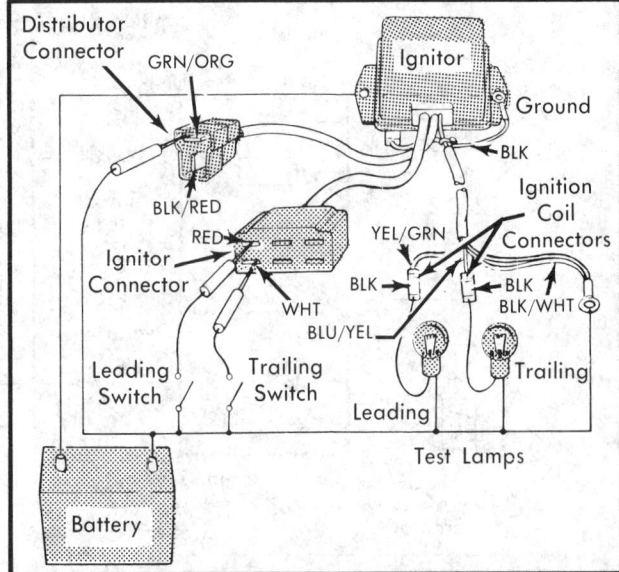

Fig. 5   Test Lamp Hookup for Checking Ignitor Operation

2) Make a circuit as shown in *Fig. 5*. Use two 12 volt lamps with less than 10 watt rating. Operate switch "ON" and "OFF" to be sure test lamps work. Apply battery power to green/orange wire in 2-pin connector. Operate trailing side switch "ON" and "OFF". Trailing side lamp should not flash.

MITSUBISHI ELECTRONIC IGNITION SYSTEMS — ROTARY ENGINE (Cont.)

3) Now apply battery power to black/red wire in same connector. Operate trailing side switch "ON" and "OFF". Test lamp of leading lamp should flash. If test results differ, replace ignitors.

4) To replace ignitors, disconnect couplers from ignitor leads and remove ignitor assembly. See *Fig. 6*. Grip coupler (not wires) and remove from each ignitor. Loosen ignitor attaching screws. Insert thin screwdriver between ignitor and aluminum base plate (on end of ignitor opposite coupler connections), and pry upward on ignitor a little at a time. Remove from plate. Clean ignitor and plate mounting surfaces and install

new ignitor. Tighten attaching screws to 10-17 INCH lbs. (12-20 cmkg). Reinstall ignitor assembly on front of shock absorber housing and connect couplers to ignitor leads.

OVERHAUL

Disassembly — 1) Remove distributor cap, rotor and seal cover. See *Fig. 7*. Remove clips holding vacuum diaphragm links. Remove screws attaching vacuum control units to distributor housing. Remove vacuum control units and condenser.

2) Remove reluctor (signal rotor) shaft attaching screw from end of shaft. Remove pick-up coil base bearing attaching screws. Remove reluctor, reluctor shaft, pick-up coils and coil base bearing assembly from top of distributor drive shaft.

3) Remove reluctor from reluctor shaft, using suitable puller. Remove spring pin. Remove governors by removing springs. Drive lock pin out of driven gear, using a small drift. Remove gear and washers. Remove drive shaft through top of distributor housing.

Reassembly — Inspect distributor cap and rotor for cracks, carbon tracks, and burned or corroded terminals. Assemble distributor in reverse order of disassembly, noting the following: Install reluctor shaft onto distributor drive shaft, engaging slots of reluctor shaft and governor pins. Install pick-up coil and coil base bearing assembly and tighten attaching screws. Install reluctor on shaft, driving spring pin in with a suitable punch.

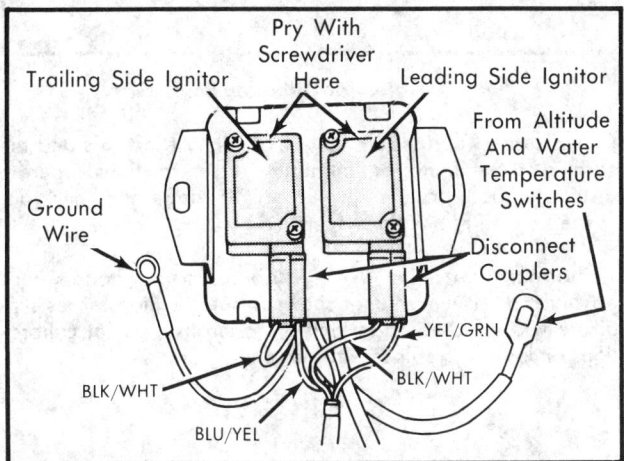

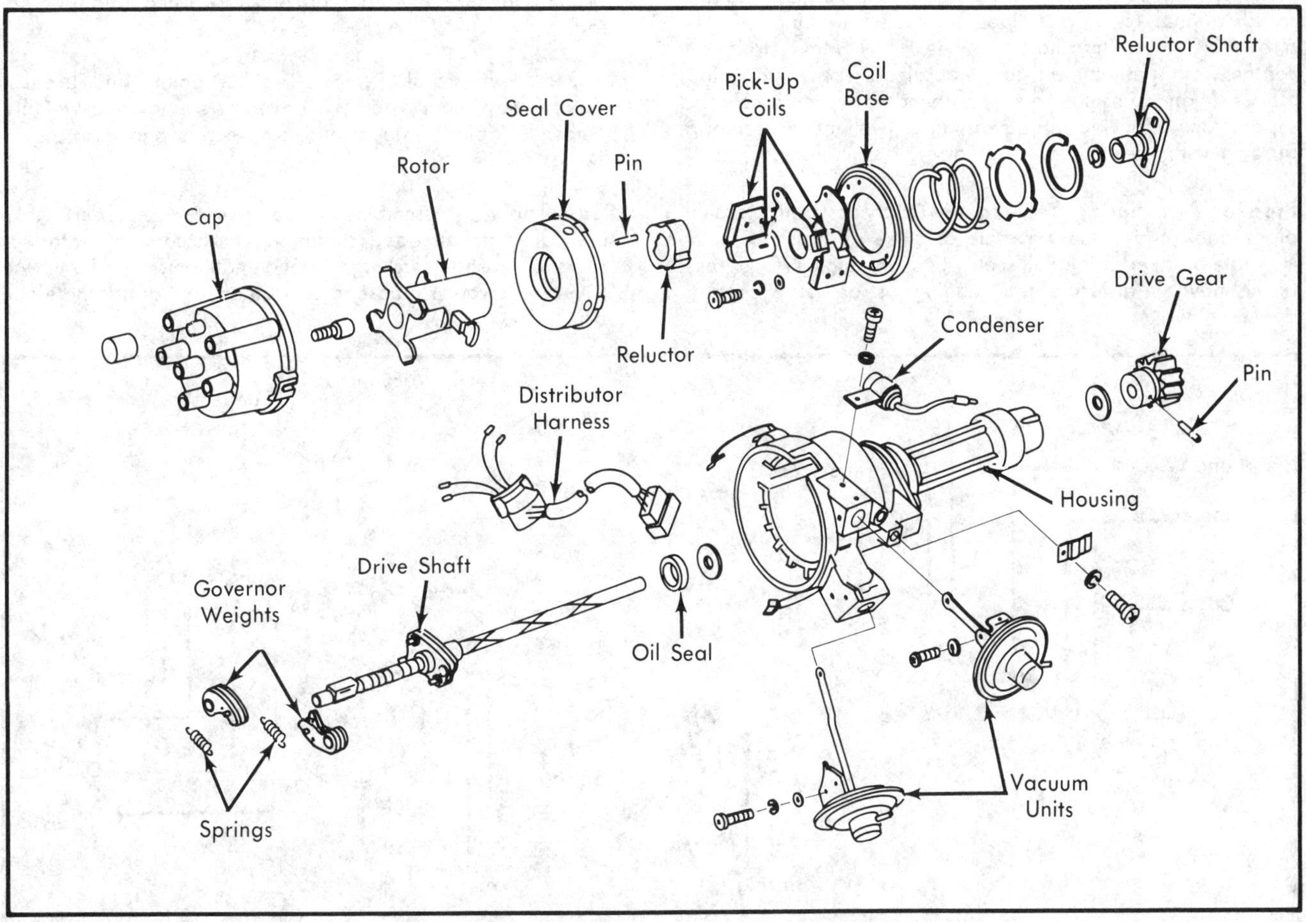

Fig. 6 Removing Ignitors from Base

Fig. 7 Disassembled View of RX7 Distributor

Distributors & Ignition Systems

MITSUBISHI BREAKER TYPE DISTRIBUTOR

Chrysler Corp. Imports
 Arrow
  1600 cc (Federal)
 Champ & Colt Hatchback
  1400 cc (Federal)
  1600 cc

DESCRIPTION

Mitsubishi distributors are fully automatic and of conventional design. Breaker plate assembly consists of a fixed lower plate, with breaker points mounted on movable upper plate. Centrifugal advance is conventional type with weights and springs. Vacuum advance/retard is controlled by a vacuum diaphragm unit mounted on distributor housing and linked to movable portion of breaker plate assembly.

SPECIFICATIONS

Point Gap, Cam Angle & Breaker Arm Spring Tension — *See Tune-Up Data on Car Model Tune-Up Pages.*

Centrifugal & Vacuum Advance — *See Specification Tables in this section.*

ADJUSTMENT

Point Gap, Alignment & Cam Angle — Turn engine over until points are as wide open as possible. Insert a suitable feeler gauge between contacts and check reading against specifications. To correct, loosen lock screws and insert a screwdriver blade into hole "A". See *Fig. 1.* Move stationary contact point until correct gap is obtained. Then, tighten lock screws. Align points if necessary by bending stationary contact support only. Check cam angle using a dwell meter. Compare reading with specification and correct if necessary.

Breaker Arm Spring Tension — To check spring tension, place hook end of spring scale as close as possible to the movable breaker point. Pull scale at a right angle (90 degrees) to the movable arm and note reading just as points begin to open.

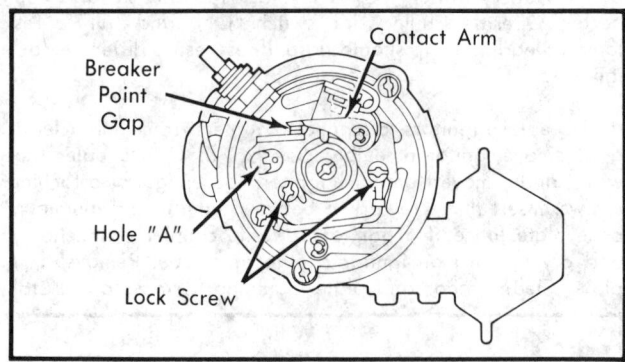

Fig. 1 Adjusting Breaker Point Gap

Centrifugal Advance — Check distributor in test stand according to test equipment manufacturers instructions. Operate distributor both up and down the RPM range and check advance at all RPM settings specified.

Vacuum Advance — With distributor in test stand, check advance at vacuum settings shown in specifications. If tests indicate vacuum diaphragm unit is inoperative, out of calibration, or leaking, replace vacuum unit.

OVERHAUL

Disassembly — 1) Remove cap, rotor and condenser. Remove snap ring from breaker plate spindle. Remove screws securing vacuum advance unit and disconnect ground and primary leads.

2) Remove terminal. Remove breaker points and breaker plate. Remove cam assembly, governor springs and weights. Remove lock pin from gear and remove gear and shaft assembly.

Reassembly — Assemble distributor in reverse order. Make sure points are in good condition, check cap and rotor for cracks or carbon-tracking. Apply small amount of MOPAR DCG or equivalent grease to distributor cam, arm spindle and vacuum link.

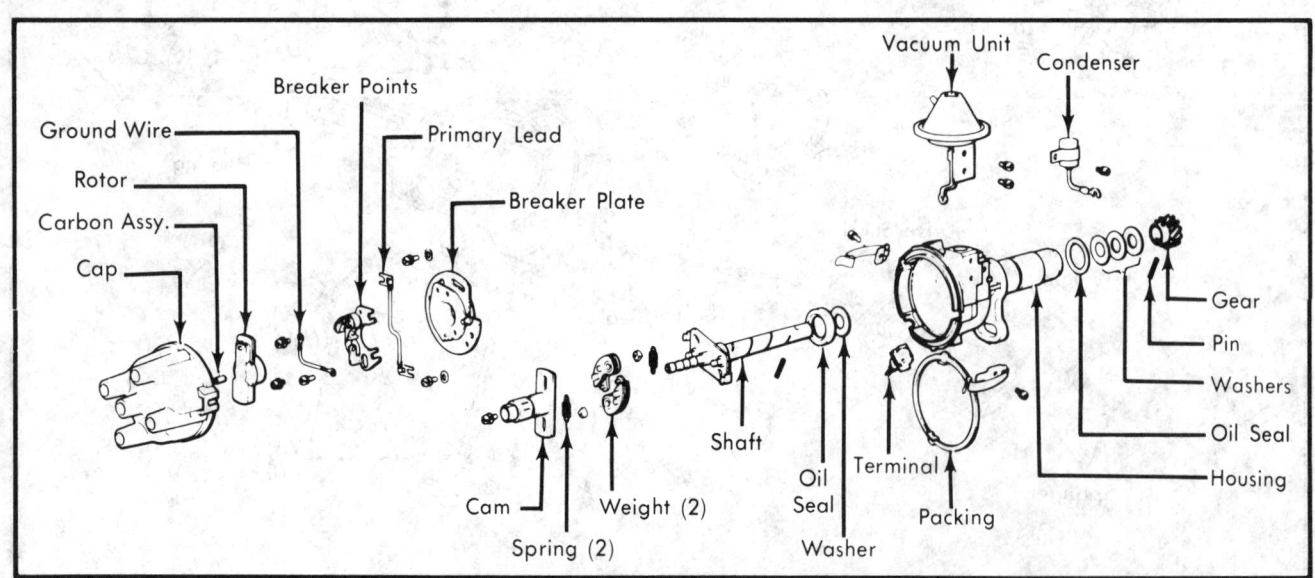

Fig. 2 Exploded View of Typical Mitsubishi Distributor

MOTORCRAFT DURA-SPARK II ELECTRONIC IGNITION SYSTEM

Fiesta

DESCRIPTION

The Dura-Spark II ignition system is basically a solid state system, using a larger rotor, distributor cap and adapter, secondary wires and wide gap spark plugs to take advantage of the higher energy produced.

OPERATION

The Dura-Spark II system contains a distributor, electronic control module and ignition coil. *See Fig. 1.* An armature (reluctor) with 4 teeth (one for each cylinder) rotates with the distributor shaft past a stator (pick-up coil). As the teeth pass the pick-up coil, a signal is sent to the electronic control module.

The module then determines when to turn current off and on in the primary windings of the ignition coil. This current collapse in the primary causes a high voltage surge in the secondary, firing the spark plugs. System components include the following:

Electronic Control Module — Each Dura-Spark II module has 6 wires (a 2-wire connector and a 4-wire connector). *See Fig. 2.* The red and white wires are the ignition feed wires — the white for cranking, the red after the engine begins to run. The red wire circuit contains a 1.1 ohm wire resistor. The current in the primary circuit of the ignition coil is turned off and on by the green wire. The orange and purple wires transmit signals to the module from the armature and pick-up coil in the distributor. The black wire is used to ground the distributor. The module is "ON" whenever the ignition switch is in the "RUN" or "START" position.

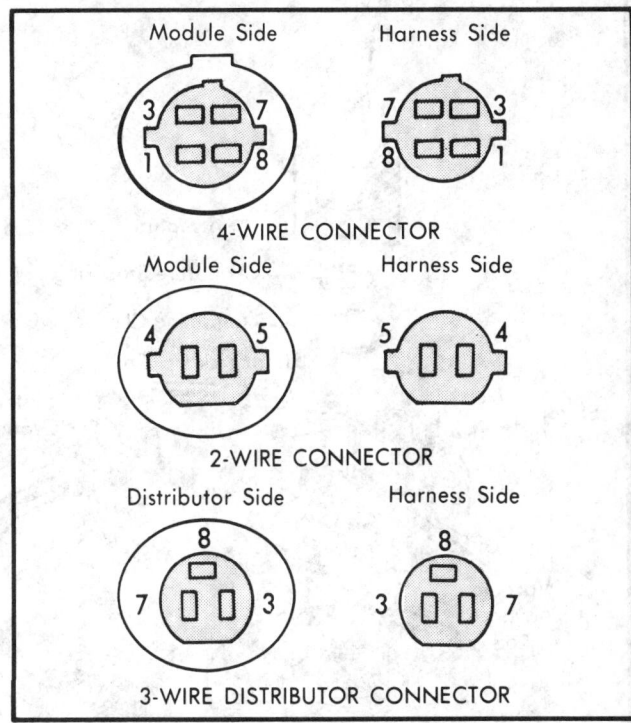

Fig. 2 Control Module and Distributor Connectors for Dura-Spark II

Distributor — A 4-tooth armature (reluctor) and a stator (pick-up coil) combine to signal the control module when to turn the ignition coil off and on. *See Fig. 3.* The distributor has both centrifugal and vacuum advance mechanisms for altering spark timing.

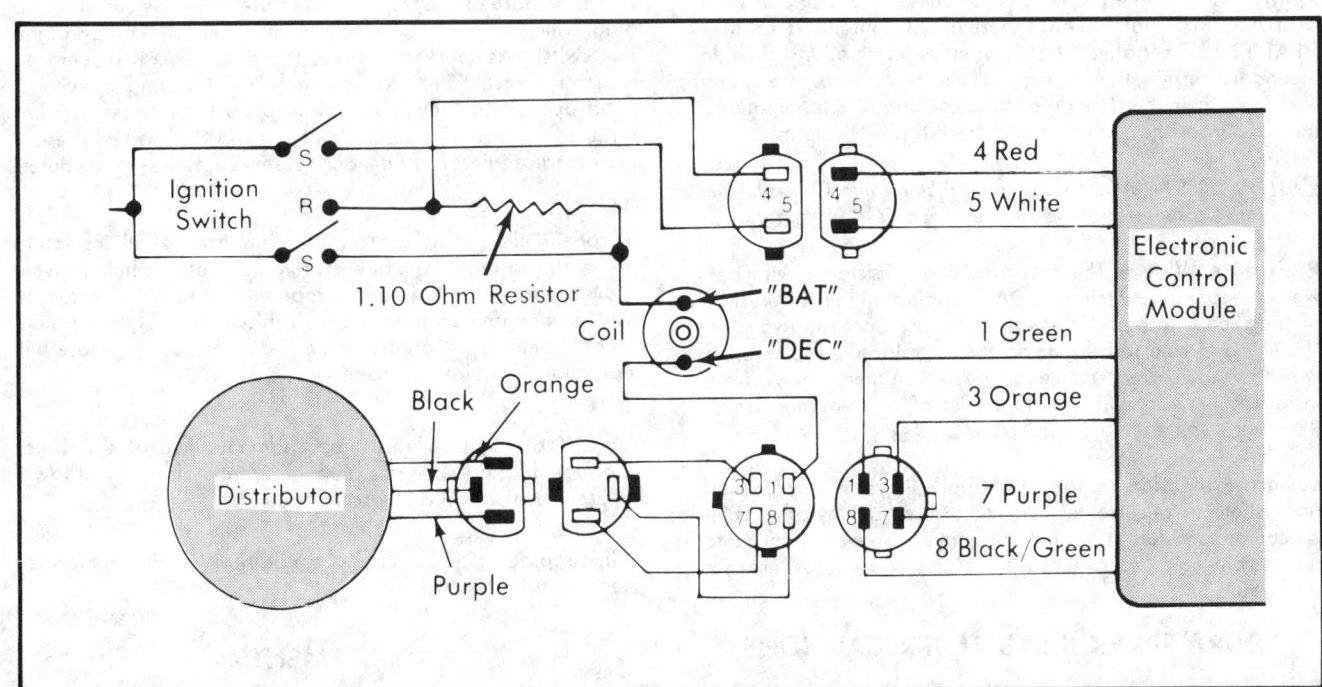

**Fig. 1   Dura-Spark II Ignition System
Wiring Diagram**

MOTORCRAFT DURA-SPARK II ELECTRONIC IGNITION SYSTEM (Cont.)

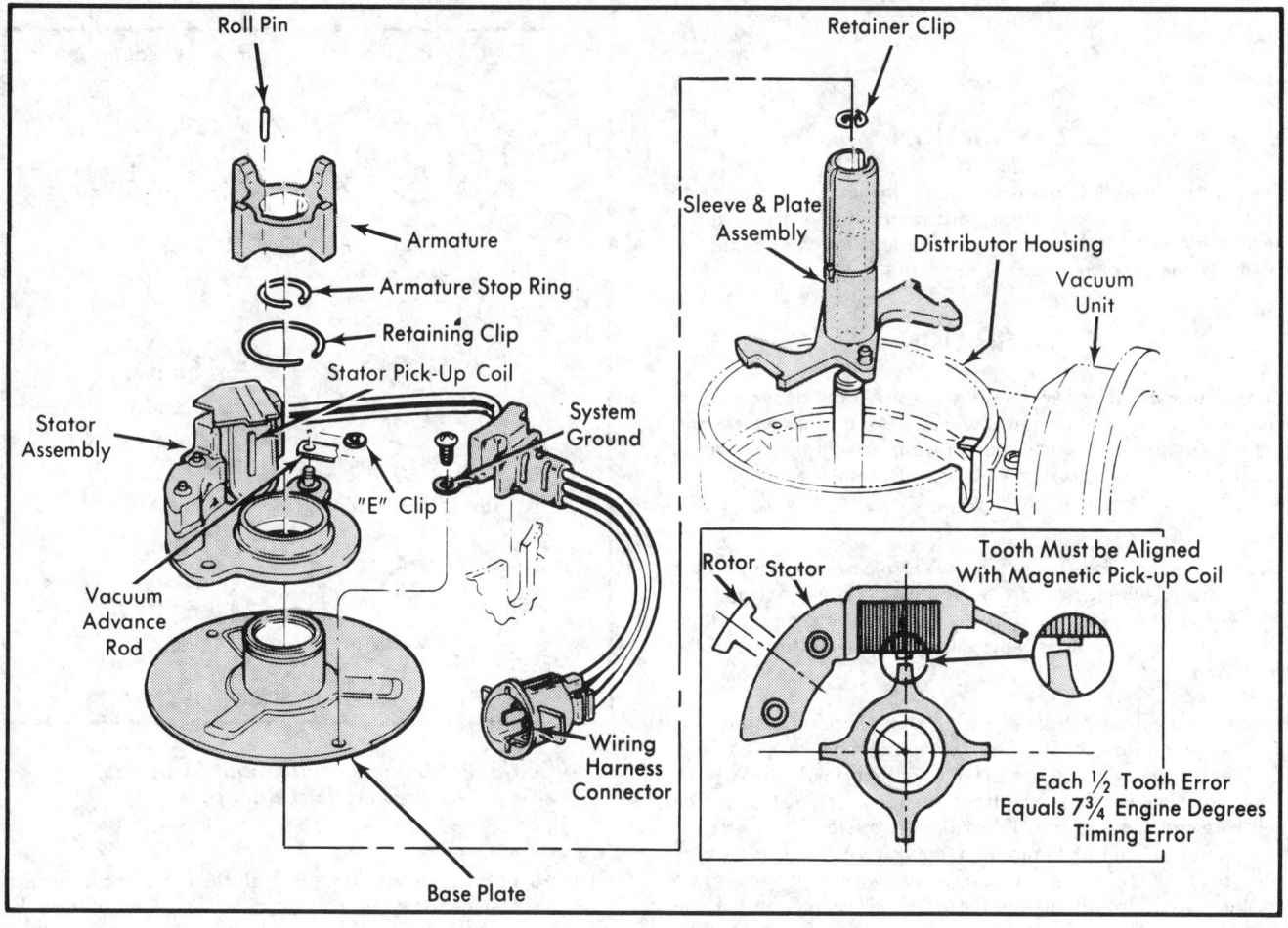

Fig. 3   Components of Dura-Spark II Distributor

Ignition Coil — The coil is "ON" whenever the ignition switch is in the "RUN" or "START" position. It contains a positive ("BAT") and a negative ("DEC") primary terminal and a single secondary terminal. A special connector attaches the green wire from the control module to the coil negative terminal and the wire from the ignition switch to the positive terminal.

NOTE — "DEC" refers to Distributor Electronic Control. This terminal is also referred to as the "Tach Test" terminal.

Resistance Wire — The special ignition resistance wire between the ignition switch and "BAT" terminal of the coil must be of specified length and diameter to reduce operating voltage. Under no circumstances should it be replaced by any other wire than the correct service resistor wire. When a new wire is installed, the old wire should be isolated from the system. Resistance value is 1.05-1.15 ohms.

System Protection — The Dura-Spark II system is protected against electrical currents produced or used by any other vehicle component during normal operation. However, damage to the system can occur if proper testing procedures are not followed.

DURA-SPARK II SYSTEM PRECAUTIONS

Since the electronic control module and ignition coil are "ON" whenever the ignition switch is in the "RUN" or "START" position, the system will generate a spark whenever the ignition

switch is turned "OFF." This feature may be used as a diagnostic tool to check for continuity of circuit, coil and ignition switch. As spark may occur if distributor cap is removed with the switch "ON", keep switch "OFF" during under-the-hood operations, unless you plan to start the engine or perform a test requiring the switch to be "ON". This will prevent accidental engine rotation during service or test procedures.

Silicone dielectric grease must be applied to all insulating areas at distributor, coil and spark plug boots. To help prevent radio frequency interference, coat the entire brass rotor tip with silicone dielectric grease to a thickness of $\frac{1}{32}$" (.75 mm). Do not remove this grease, even if discolored, as grease will maintain its insulating properties.

A $\frac{3}{4}$" (18 mm) clearance must be maintained at distributor cap mounting edge, spark plug wire terminals and coil tower to prevent high voltage arc to ground.

When replacing spark plug wires, be sure to use the specified Fiesta spark plug wires.

ADJUSTMENTS

No adjustments are to be made to the ignition system, except initial engine timing and spark plug gap.

MOTORCRAFT DURA-SPARK II ELECTRONIC IGNITION SYSTEM (Cont.)

TESTING

CAUTION — *When checking the secondary voltage, do not remove the No. 1 or 3 spark plug wires while the engine is running.*

Perform the following tests using an oscilloscope which has inductive type clamps. Always follow the scope manufacturer's instructions. Also use suitable grounding probes and insulated pliers where necessary.

NOTE — *On vehicles with catalytic converters, do not run the engine for more than 30 seconds with a spark plug wire removed.*

Coil Reserve Voltage — **1)** Clamp secondary voltage pick-up over coil-to-distributor high voltage wire. Run engine at 1000 RPM and check engine operation and read scope pattern. With engine running at 1000 PRM, remove one spark plug wire without letting it arc to ground.

2) Read the highest open circuit voltage indicated on scope. Reserve voltage should be 28,000 volts minimum. Regardless of reading, continue with other tests. Using an ohmmeter, check resistance of coil-to-distributor high voltage wire. Resistance should be 3,500 ohms per foot. Replace if required.

Rotor-to-Cap Voltage Drop — Connect high voltage pick-up to coil-to-distributor secondary wire. Remove one spark plug wire momentarily and ground the wire to the engine. Run engine at idle speed, without letting a spark gap appear between engine and spark plug wire. High voltage reading should be 8,000 volts maximum. If voltage fails to meet specifications, check rotor, adapter and distributor cap.

Spark Plug Required Voltage — **1)** Make this test with engine running at 2000 RPM and with secondary voltage probe connected over coil-to-distributor high voltage wire. Read the highest spark plug high voltage requirement for each cylinder. Readings should be 6,000-20,000 volts. If measured voltage is too low, remove probe from coil wire and connect it in turn to each spark plug wire to determine which spark plug is low.

2) When measuring required voltage on individual plug wires, the minimum voltage is reduced to 6,000 volts. If less than 6,000 volts for any cylinder, remove spark plug and check for closed or bridged gap, fouled insulator nose or cracked ceramic.

3) If measured voltage is higher than 20,000 volts (or 50% or more higher than other cylinders), check individual spark plug wires with probe. When problem cylinder is located, check spark plug and its wire. Inspect especially for burned or excessively worn electrodes and high resistance between terminal and center electrode.

Spark Plug Wire Resistance — Check spark plug wire resistance using an ohmmeter. Remove spark plug wire and boot from spark plug, but leave wire attached to distributor cap. Resistance should not exceed 4,100 ohms from boot terminal to internal distributor cap terminal.

IGNITION COIL RESISTANCE CHECK

Primary Resistance — Remove connector from coil's positive and negative primary terminals. Be sure ignition switch is "OFF". Set an ohmmeter on the low scale and connect ohmmeter leads to primary terminals of ignition coil. Ohmmeter reading should be 1.13-1.23 ohms at 75° F (24° C). With temperature of coil at 200° F (93° C), a 1.5 ohm reading is acceptable.

Secondary Resistance — Be sure ignition switch is still "OFF". Set ohmmeter to high scale (x1000) and connect one lead to coil negative terminal and other lead to coil tower (remove coil secondary wire first). Ohmmeter reading should be 7,700-9,300 ohms with coil temperature at 75° F (24° C). With coil temperature at 200° F (93° C), a maximum reading of 12,000 ohms is acceptable.

BASIC SYSTEM CHECK

1) Connect a scope with clamp-on pick-ups to coil high voltage wire, according to manufacturer's specifications. If a scope is not available, remove coil wire from distributor and insert a modified spark plug into coil wire. See *Fig. 4*.

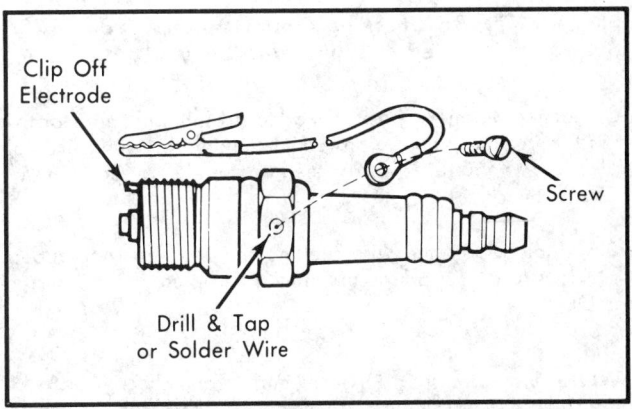

Fig. 4   Modified Spark Plug Tester

NOTE — *To modify spark plug, cut off side electrode and solder or tap and screw a ground lead to spark plug case. Ground wire and insert plug terminal into coil wire.*

2) Turn ignition switch to "RUN" position and tap distributor base with a screwdriver handle. Check for sparks while tapping (visible by checking scope trace or at modified spark plug gap). If spark occurs, see Control Module Feed Check, White Wire Circuit.

3) If no spark, turn ignition switch "OFF". Crank engine to approximately align engine timing pointer with initial timing degree line on damper. Turn key to "RUN" position and repeat tapping of distributor, checking again for sparks. Then proceed to next check.

CONTROL MODULE FEED CHECK

Red Wire Circuit — **1)** If no spark occurred in step **3)** of Basic System Check, measure battery voltage. Then using a straight pin, puncture red wire of control module's 2-wire harness (between module and connector). See *Fig. 5*.

MOTORCRAFT DURA-SPARK II ELECTRONIC IGNITION SYSTEM (Cont.)

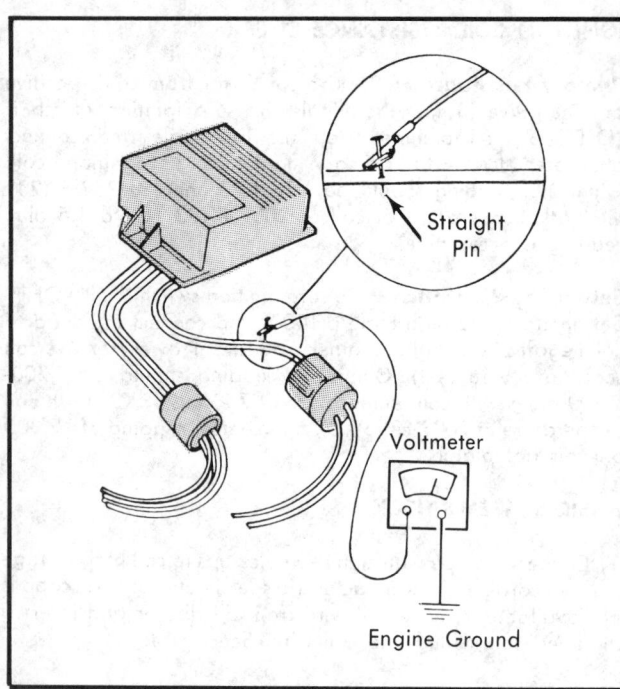

**Fig. 5   Checking Control Module Feed
(Red or White Wire Circuits)**

2) Connect voltmeter positive lead to straight pin and negative lead to ground. Voltage on red wire should be within 1.0 volt of battery voltage. If so, proceed to step **1)** of Coil Primary Circuit Check.

3) If not, repair the wire feeding the red wire and repeat previous tests. If spark occurs at modified plug, ignition system is OK.

White Wire Circuit — 1) Crank engine and check for sparks. If sparks occur, ignition system is OK. Check fuel system instead. If no sparks occur, measure battery voltage while cranking engine. Then, without disconnecting the control module's 2-wire connector, measure voltage on white wire while cranking engine.

2) Using a straight pin, puncture white wire between control module and connector. See Fig. 5. Voltage should equal battery cranking voltage. If so, proceed to step **3)**. If not equal, repair wire feeding the control module white wire, and repeat test.

3) If voltage in step **2)** was equal to battery cranking voltage, or if no spark occurred after repairing wire feeding white wire, connect positive lead of voltmeter to ignition coil positive ("BAT") terminal and negative lead to ground. Measure voltage while cranking engine. Battery voltage should exist. If so, proceed to step **4)**. If not, repair wire feeding coil positive ("BAT") terminal and repeat test. If still no sparks occur, see Intermittent Operation Check.

4) If voltage at coil positive ("BAT") terminal was equal to battery voltage, but problems still exist, substitute but do not install a known good control module and repeat the test. If sparks occur, reconnect original module to check if it is faulty. Repeat test. If no sparks, replace module.

COIL PRIMARY CIRCUIT CHECK

1) Refer to step **1)** of Control Module Feed Check for red wire circuit. If voltage was within 1.0 volt of battery voltage, turn ignition switch from "RUN" to "OFF". A spark should be seen each time ignition switch is turned "OFF". Then return ignition switch to "RUN" position. If modified plug sparks, proceed to Control Module & Stator Check. If no spark occurs, proceed to next step.

2) Connect positive lead of voltmeter to ignition coil positive ("BAT") terminal and negative lead to ground. Reading should be 6-8 volts. If so, proceed to step **11)**. If less than 6 volts, proceed to step **10)**.

3) If voltage in step **2)** is battery voltage, disconnect 4-wire connector at control module. Insert a jumper wire (paper clip) into the 4-wire harness connector's terminals that mate with the control module's green and black wires (terminals 1 and 8).

4) Connect voltmeter positive lead to ignition coil positive ("BAT") terminal and negative lead to ground. Measure voltage. If battery voltage, proceed to step **6)**.

5) If voltage now reads 6-8 volts, substitute (but do not install) a known good control module. Repeat previous tests. If no spark, see Intermittent Operation Check. If sparks occur, reconnect original module and retest. If no spark now occurs, replace control module.

6) If voltage in step **4)** was battery voltage, make sure coil connector is fully engaged on primary terminals of ignition coil. Ground the "Tach Test" terminal of coil. See Fig. 6. Connect voltmeter positive lead to coil's positive ("BAT") terminal and negative lead to ground.

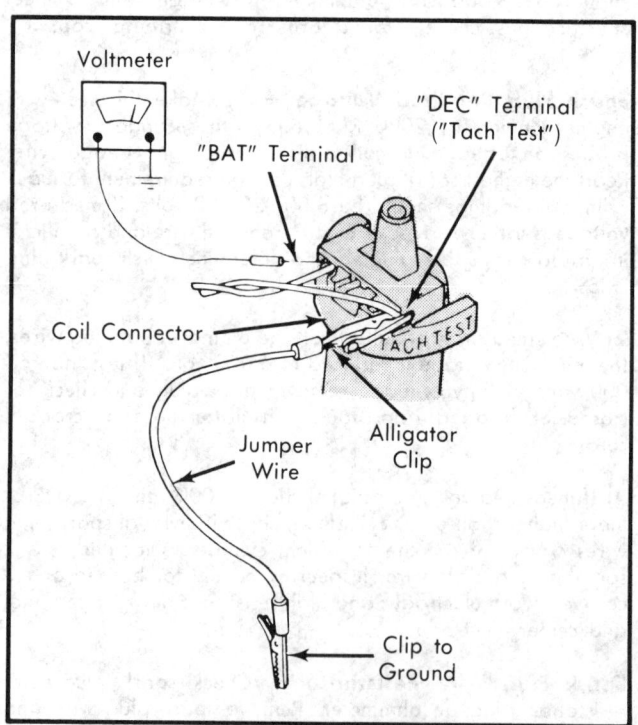

**Fig. 6   Grounding "Tach Test" Terminal
In Coil Primary Circuit Check**

MOTORCRAFT DURA-SPARK II ELECTRONIC IGNITION SYSTEM (Cont.)

7) If reading is now 6-8 volts, remove ground wire from "Tach Test" terminal of coil connector. Ground jumper wire (paper clip) in 4-wire connector. Again measure voltage at coil positive ("BAT") terminal. Reading should be approximately 6-8 volts. If so, proceed to step **9)**.

8) If not, repair wire from control module to coil (mates with green wire, terminal 1). Remove jumper wire (paper clip) from 4-wire connector. Reconnect control module and retest system. If sparks occur at modified plug, system is OK. If not, see Intermittent Operation Check.

9) If voltage in step **7)** was 6-8 volts, repair the ground circuit (black wire, terminal 8) from control module to distributor. Remove jumper wire (paper clip) from 4-wire connector and retest system. If sparks occur at modified plug, system is OK. If not, see Intermittent Operation Check.

10) If voltage in step **2)** was less than 6 volts, repair wire feeding the ignition coil positive ("BAT") terminal. Retest system and if spark occurs at modified plug, system is OK. If not, see Intermittent Operation Check.

11) If voltage in step **2)** was 6-8 volts but engine would not run, or if voltage in step **6)** was battery voltage, remove paper clip and reconnect control module. Substitute (but do not install) a known good ignition coil and repeat system test. If spark occurs, reconnect original coil and retest. If sparks now occur, see Intermittent Operation Check. If no spark results, replace ignition coil.

12) If no sparks occurred with substitute coil, connect original ignition coil and be sure connector is fully engaged over terminals. Substitute (but do not install) a known good control module and repeat tests. If sparks occur, reconnect original module and retest. If no spark now occurs, replace control module.

CONTROL MODULE & STATOR CHECK

1) Refer to step **1)** of Coil Primary Circuit Check. If modified plug sparked, but engine would not run, substitute any known good distributor (not limited to 4-cylinder). Attach distributor connector to control module harness connector. Run 15" ground wire from vacuum unit screw to engine ground. Spin drive gear and check for sparks.

2) If sparks occur, reconnect original distributor to check if it is damaged. Repeat tests to check for sparks. If sparks now occur, see Intermittent Operation Check. If no sparks occur, replace distributor stator assembly.

3) If no sparks occurred when gear of good distributor was spun, disconnect 3-wire distributor connector and 4-wire control module connector. Check harness wires as shown in steps **4)** through **8)**.

4) Turn ignition switch "OFF". Connect ohmmeter leads to ends of each wire, one at a time. Wire mating with control module black wire (terminal 8) grounds the distributor. Wires mating with control module orange wire (terminal 3) and purple wire (terminal 7) signal control module as to when coil primary circuit should be shut off and on. Continuity should exist at each wire.

5) Then connect ohmmeter leads to harness wires mating with orange and purple wires of control module. There should be no continuity between these 2 wires.

6) Then connect one ohmmeter lead to ground and touch other lead in turn to wires mating orange and purple control module wires. An open condition should exist.

7) If harness checks OK, reconnect distributor connector and substitute a known good control module and repeat system tests. If no spark occurs, see Intermittent Operation Check. If sparks occur, reconnect original control module and retest. If no sparks occur now, replace control module.

8) If harness proved defective in step **4)** through step **6)**, repair wires or connectors as necessary and retest for spark at modified plug.

INTERMITTENT OPERATION CHECK

1) If the ignition system becomes operative during testing without a repair having been made, attempt to recreate the original problem. With the engine running, wiggle the wires at the coil, module, distributor and other harness connectors. Check connections first that you have previously disconnected.

2) Check the ground connection in the distributor. Then turn engine off, heat the stator pick-up coil by placing a 250 watt heat lamp approximately 1-2 inches (25-50 mm) from its top surface. Apply heat for 5-10 minutes, while checking pick-up coil resistance at the distributor connector terminals 3 and 7 (orange and purple wires). Resistance should be 400-1000 ohms. Tapping with screwdriver may also be helpful.

3) With the engine running, heat control module in the same manner. Do not let module temperature exceed 212°F (100°C). If ignition system malfunctions, substitute (but do not install) a new control module. If malfunction is corrected, recheck old control module before replacing it.

OVERHAUL

Disassembly — 1) Remove distributor cap and rotor. Disconnect distributor wiring harness connector. Using a small gear puller or 2 screwdrivers, carefully pry armature (reluctor) from sleeve and plate assembly. Remove spring pin.

NOTE — *When removing armature with screwdrivers, lever against lower plate only (not upper plate). Lower plate is supported by base casting.*

2) Remove snap ring, washer and wave washer. Remove ground screw and stator (pick-up coil) assembly. Remove vacuum diaphragm attaching screws and remove unit by tilting downward to disengage link from the advance plate.

Reassembly — Reverse disassembly procedure, but use new spring pin and install pin in groove 180° from original location.

CAUTION — *Do not pinch stator (pick-up coil) wires when removing armature.*

NIPPONDENSO ELECTRONIC IGNITION SYSTEM

Subaru
  1600 (Except 4-WD)
  1800
Toyota
  Celica
  Corolla

Corona
Cressida
Land Cruiser
Pickup
Supra
Tercel

DESCRIPTION

Nippondenso electronic ignition system includes a breakerless distributor, an ignitor (ignition control unit), a special ignition coil, an ignition signal generating mechanism (pick-up coil assembly) and ignition switch.

The distributor consists of a housing, rotor and cap. It contains a timing rotor (reluctor), magnet, and pick-up coil assembly. A transistorized ignitor is separate from the distributor. See Fig. 1. Distributors contain conventional centrifugal and vacuum advance mechanisms.

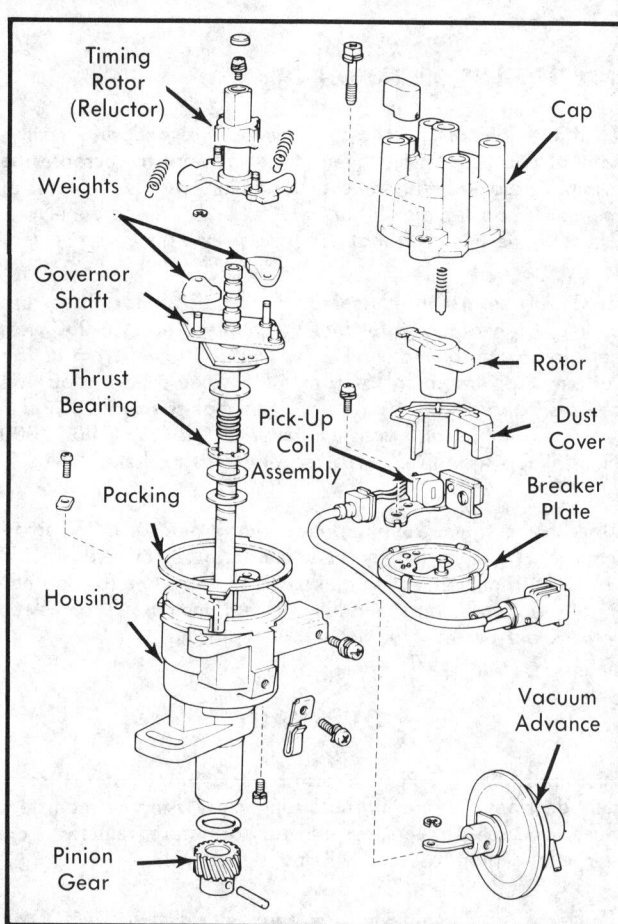

Fig. 1 Disassembled View of Nippondenso Distributor (Toyota Model Shown)

OPERATION

As the timing rotor turns with the distributor shaft, its teeth (one for each engine cylinder) pass the pick-up coil assembly. See Fig. 2. As the air gap changes with the approach and passing of each tooth, the magnetic field varies. This creates a signal in the pick-up coil assembly.

The ignitor senses this signal and turns the ignition coil primary circuit on and off. This causes voltage to build and collapse, resulting in a voltage surge in the secondary that fires the spark plugs.

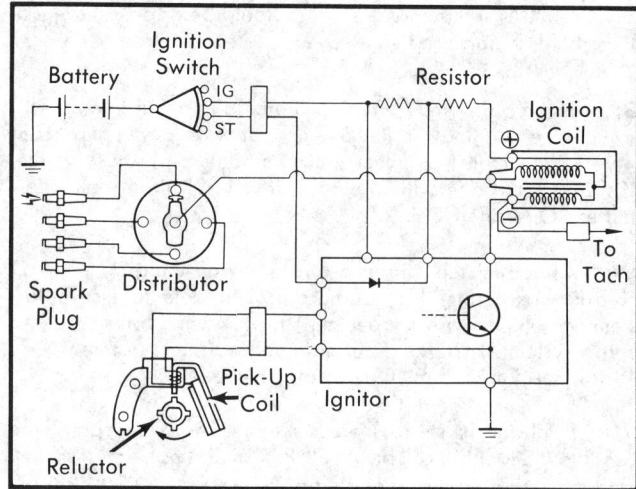

Fig. 2 Schematic of Typical Toyota Electronic Ignition Circuit (Federal Celica and Corona)

SPECIFICATIONS

Centrifugal & Vacuum Advance — See Specifications Tables in this section.

ADJUSTMENT

Timing Rotor (Reluctor)-to-Pick-Up Coil Air Gap — Using a flat feeler gauge, check air gap. Gap should be .008-.016" (0.2-0.4 mm). If not, loosen screws and move pick-up coil against feeler gauge of proper thickness. Tighten screws and recheck air gap.

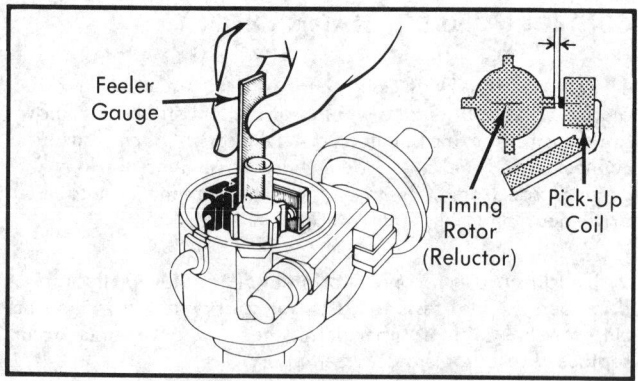

Fig. 3 Checking Timing Rotor-to-Pick-Up Coil Air Gap (Toyota Shown)

TESTING

CAUTION — Be sure all connections are correct, as reverse battery polarity within the system will damage the ignitor (ignition control unit). Do not disconnect battery while engine is running or transistors may be damaged. Do not allow water to enter ignitor. If a tachometer is connected to system, connect tachometer positive lead to coil negative terminal.

NIPPONDENSO ELECTRONIC IGNITION SYSTEM (Cont.)

CAUTION — *Be especially careful when checking Toyota systems, as a variety of ignition coil, ignitor, and resistor combinations are used. Connectors and wire colors also vary from model to model. Illustrations are for typical systems only.*

IGNITION COIL TEST

NOTE — *All tests on the ignition coil are made with an ohmmeter with the ignition switch in the "OFF" position. If the resistance for any test is not within specifications, replace ignition coil.*

Primary Coil Resistance — Connect an ohmmeter set in x1 range so leads touch coil positive and negative primary terminals (or connector terminals leading to them). See *Ignition Coil Resistance chart.*

Secondary Coil Resistance — Set an ohmmeter in the x100 range. Connect leads to coil primary terminal and to coil tower (high tension terminal). See *Ignition Coil Resistance chart.*

Resistor Resistance — Connect an ohmmeter, set in the x1 range, so that leads are connected to each side of resistor (or resistance wire), if equipped. See *Ignition Coil Resistance chart.*

Ignition Coil Resistance (Ohms)		
Application	Primary Resistance	Secondary Resistance
Toyota		
Tercel①	0.4-0.5	8,500-11,500
Corolla		
Federal①	0.4-0.5	8,500-11,500
Calif.①	0.8-1.0	11,500-15,500
Celica & Corona		
Federal②	0.5-0.6	11,500-15,500
Calif.②	0.8-1.0	11,500-15,500
Pickup		
Federal③	1.3-1.7	12,000-16,000
Calif.①	0.8-1.0	11,500-15,500
Supra & Cressida①	0.5-0.6	11,500-15,500
Land Cruiser③	1.3-1.7	12,000-16,000
Subaru③	1.33-1.63	12,600-15,400

① — No external resistor or resistance wire.
② — Resistor resistance is 1.2-1.4 ohms.
③ — Resistor resistance is 1.1-1.3 ohms.

Insulation Resistance — Connect ohmmeter leads between coil positive terminal and mounting bracket of coil. Reading on all models should exceed 10,000 ohms (infinity).

High Tension Wire Resistance — Connect an ohmmeter, set in x1000 range, so that leads touch each end of high tension wires. Readings should not exceed 25,000 ohms. If so, replace wires.

IGNITOR TESTS

CAUTION — *Be especially careful when checking Toyota systems, as 2 different procedures are used, depending upon vehicle model.*

Federal Celica, Corona and Pickup Models — 1) Turn ignition switch on. Connect voltmeter negative lead to a good ground. On Celica and Corona models connect the positive voltmeter lead to the resistor positive terminal. On Pickup models, unplug harness connector at the ignitor and touch positive voltmeter lead, in turn, to each terminal (A and B). All readings should be 12 volts.

2) Unplug the wiring connector from the distributor. Using a 1.5 volt dry cell battery, connect the positive battery pole to the White wire terminal and the negative battery terminal to the Pink wire terminal. Connect negative voltmeter lead to ground and positive lead to ignition coil negative terminal.

3) Voltmeter reading should be 12 volts. Reverse battery connections and recheck voltage at coil negative terminal. It should be 1-2 volts. If not, replace ignitor.

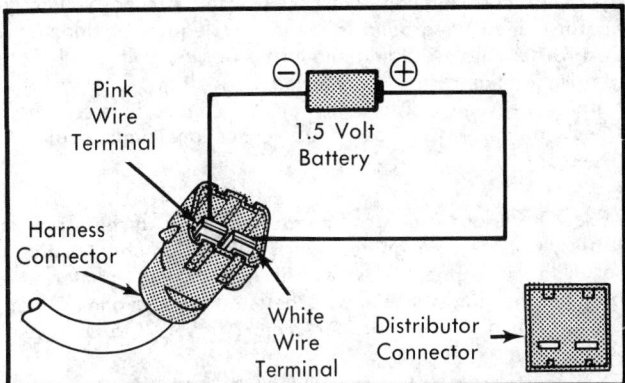

Fig. 4 Checking Ignitor Operation with 1.5 Volt Battery (Toyota Celica, Corona & Pickup Models Shown — Others Have Connections Reversed)

Other Toyota Models — 1) Turn ignition switch on. Connect negative voltmeter lead to a good ground and positive lead to ignition coil positive terminal. Voltage reading should be 12 volts.

2) Next, connect voltmeter positive lead to ignition coil negative terminal, with negative lead still connected to ground. Voltage should still be 12 volts.

3) Unplug wiring connector from distributor. Using a 1.5 volt dry cell battery, connect battery positive pole to Pink wire terminal and negative pole to White wire terminal. Do NOT apply voltage for more than 5 seconds. Voltage at negative terminal of ignition coil should now read 5 volts less than battery voltage. If not, replace ignitor.

IGNITION SYSTEM TEST

NOTE — *Although this information applies basically to Subaru models, the same principle applies to Toyota models with resistors or resistance wires.*

1) Turn ignition switch "ON". Connect negative lead of a voltmeter to ground and positive lead (in turn) to each of the resistor terminals "a" and "b". One reading should be battery voltage, the other reading should be one half that voltage. If so, proceed to step **10**).

2) If there was no voltage at either terminal in step **1**), check wiring harness, connector, ignition switch and fuse between

NIPPONDENSO ELECTRONIC IGNITION SYSTEM (Cont.)

battery and resistor. Check for broken wires, poor connections, and battery condition.

3) If there was voltage at only one of the resistor terminals in step **1)**, turn ignition switch "ON" and disconnect lead wire from terminal having no voltage. Check resistor terminal for voltage. If none, replace resistor. If voltage now exists, check wiring harness between resistor and positive terminal of ignition coil for short circuit. Repair or replace as necessary.

4) If there was voltage at both terminals, but one was not about one-half battery voltage, turn ignition switch "ON". Connect voltmeter negative lead to ground and positive lead to ignition coil negative terminal. Reading should be battery voltage.

5) If not, turn ignition switch "ON" and connect voltmeter negative lead to ground and positive lead to ignition coil positive terminal. Reading should be battery voltage. If not, replace ignition coil. If battery voltage is shown, check wiring harness between resistor and ignition coil positive terminal. Check for broken wires, poor connections and repair as necessary.

6) If voltage at ignition coil negative terminal in step **4)**, was battery voltage, turn ignition switch "OFF". Using an ohmmeter set in the x1 range, measure resistance between ignitor side and ground. Resistance should be less than 0.5 ohm. If not, check ground wire for proper contact at regulator bracket

7) If resistance was less than 0.5 ohm in step **6)**, proceed to the next step, step **8)**.

8) Turn ignition switch "OFF". Disconnect 2-pin (Toyota) or 3-pin (Subaru) distributor connector. Disconnect high tension wire at distributor and hold it about ¼" (6 mm) from engine block. Turn ignition switch "ON". Check if spark jumps when a small voltage (1-6 volts) is applied intermittently on terminals "1" (pink wire) and "2" (white wire) on ignitor side of connector. See *Fig. 6*.

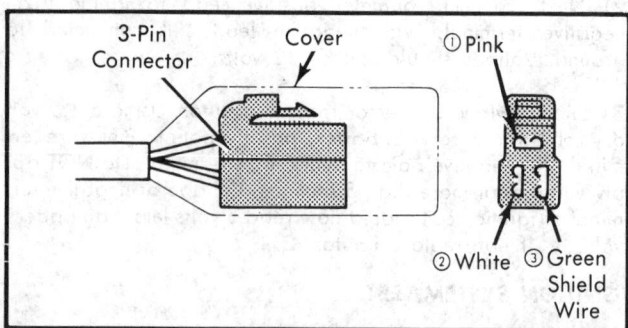

**Fig. 5   Conducting Tests at Distributor Connector
(Subaru Shown)**

CAUTION — *Do not use battery voltage (12 volts) for this test or ignitor may be damaged.*

9) If spark jumps gap, there is no problem with the ignition system. If no spark occurs, replace ignitor.

10) If in step **1)**, the voltage at one resistor terminal was one-half that of the other, turn ignition switch "ON". See *Fig. 3*. Connect negative lead of voltmeter to a good ground and

positive lead to ignition coil negative terminal. If reading is not below 0.5 volt, check wiring harness for shorts, check loose connections at coil negative terminal and repair as necessary. If no problem is found, perform steps **8)** and **9)** again.

11) If in step **10)** reading was below 0.5 volts, turn ignition switch "OFF" and disconnect 2-pin connector. Using an ohmmeter set to the x100 range, connect leads to terminals "1" (pink wire) and "2" (white wire) on distributor side of 2-pin (Toyota) or 3-pin (Subaru) connector. Reading should be 130-190 ohms for all models.

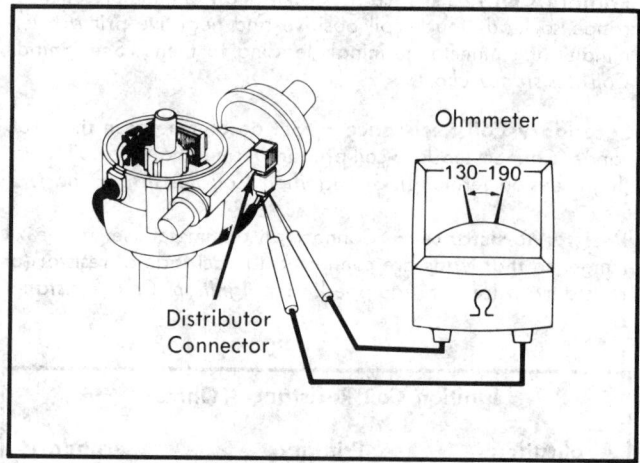

**Fig. 6   Checking Pick-Up Coil Resistance
(Toyota Shown)**

12) If resistance reading is incorrect, replace pick-up coil assembly. If correct, turn ignition switch "OFF" and check timing rotor (reluctor)-to-pick-up coil air gap. If not .008-.016" (0.2-0.4 mm), adjust as necessary. If air gap is correct, perform steps **8)** and **9)** again.

OVERHAUL

Disassembly — 1) Remove distributor cap rotor, dust cover, and packing. Remove pick-up coil assembly, vacuum advance mechanism, breaker plate and drive pinion.

2) Remove 2 screws from bottom of distributor housing and using a plastic hammer, carefully drive out shaft. Remove thick washer, bearing, thin washer, spring, and blue washer from shaft.

3) Remove governor springs, cam cap, timing rotor (reluctor), weight snap ring and weights.

Reassembly — Assemble in reverse order, noting the following:

- Lightly grease timing rotor (reluctor) inner surface. Install on shaft aligning mark on stopper plate ("15.5" mark on Subaru; "10" mark on Celica, Corona, and Pickups; and "13.5" on Corolla) with stopper.
- When installing breaker plate, align 4 clips of plate with 4 grooves in housing.
- When replacing pinion, replace pin and pinion as a set.
- Adjust air gap between timing rotor and pick-up coil.

NIPPONDENSO BREAKER TYPE DISTRIBUTOR

LUV

DESCRIPTION

Single breaker, fully automatic type of conventional design. Breaker points are mounted on movable portion of breaker plate assembly. Centrifugal advance is conventional type with weights and springs. Vacuum advance is controlled by a vacuum diaphragm unit mounted on distributor housing and linked to movable portion of breaker plate assembly.

SPECIFICATIONS

Point Gap, Cam Angle & Breaker Arm Spring Tension — *See Tune-Up Data on Car Model Tune-Up Pages.*

Centrifugal & Vacuum Advance — *See Specifications Tables in this section.*

ADJUSTMENT

Point Gap, Alignment, & Cam Angle — With rubbing block on high point of cam lobe, insert a feeler gauge blade between contacts and check reading against specification. To correct, loosen retaining screws and move stationary contact point until correct gap is obtained, then tighten screws. Align points if necessary by bending stationary contact support only. Check cam angle using a dwell meter; compare indicated reading with specification and correct if necessary.

Breaker Arm Spring Tension — To check spring tension, place hook end of spring scale as close as possible to the movable breaker point. Pull scale at a right angle (90 degrees) to the movable arm and note reading just as points begin to open.

Centrifugal Advance — Check distributor in test stand according to test equipment manufacturers instructions. Operate distributor both up and down the RPM range and check advance at all RPM settings specified.

Vacuum Advance — With distributor in test stand, check advance at vacuum settings shown in specifications. If tests indicate vacuum diaphragm unit is inoperative, out of calibration, or leaking, replace vacuum unit.

OVERHAUL

Disassembly — 1) Remove cap, rotor, dust cover and terminal with insulation. Remove condenser, snap ring retaining vacuum advance rod. Remove vacuum advance. Remove dust gaskets. Remove breaker points and damper spring. Remove cap clamps and lead wire.

NOTE — *Record the quantity, type, sequence, and thickness of washers in use at each location during disassembly.*

2) Remove breaker plate assembly. Note positioning of cam, springs and weights on distributor shaft, then remove attaching screw, cam, governor springs and weights. Mark position of driven gear on shaft for reassembly reference. Remove retaining pin, then remove collar from end of shaft. Remove shaft from distributor housing.

Reassembly — Reassemble distributor in reverse order of disassembly, lubricating shaft, cam, damper spring and breaker arm slightly.

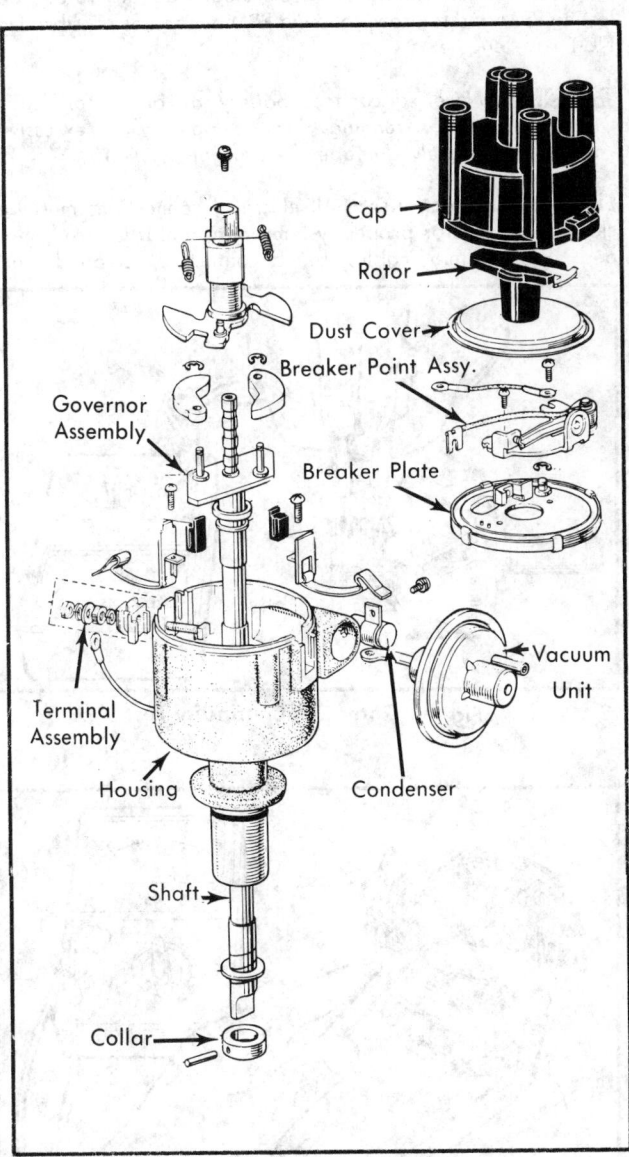

Fig. 1 Disassembled View of Nippondenso Breaker Type Distributor

Alternators & Regulators

GENERAL SERVICING

TESTING

In order to properly diagnose charging system performance, the following conditions and precautions should be observed:

Battery Voltage — Battery must be fully charged before conducting alternator test. Charge or replace battery as necessary.

Battery Charging — Both battery cables should be disconnected if using a Quick Charger in order to prevent damage to alternator and regulator components.

Battery Boost (For Engine Start) — Do NOT use a Quick Charger to provide starting voltage. Booster battery must be connected with negative lead to negative terminal of vehicle battery and positive lead to positive terminal of battery.

On Car Testing — Perform tests at normal operating temperatures. Engine should be accelerated gradually to desired testing RPM and returned to lower RPM as soon as possible. Do NOT race engine.

CAUTION — *Never disconnect battery or alternator leads while alternator is running. Reverse polarity or excessive voltage will severely damage the charging system.*

Electrical Connections — All electrical connections must be clean and snug for proper system operation. It is recommended that battery cables be disconnected, cleaned and tightened whenever performing charging system maintenance. Regulator must be properly grounded also.

Component Replacement — In order to prevent stray voltage or shorts, always disconnect battery prior to alternator or regulator removal.

Drive Belt — Drive belts must not be cracked, glazed or oily, and must be set at proper tension. A glazed belt may slip even though belt is not loose.

NOTE — *Excessive drive belt tension can cause bearing or case failure. Do NOT overtighten to correct for slippage.*

Disassembly — Case halves and stator should be scribed prior to separation for proper orientation when reassembling.

Diode Test and Replacement — Never use a high voltage source to test diodes. Use a low voltage source to check for one-way current flow. If replacement is required, soldering operations must be performed quickly to prevent diode damage. Diode lead should be pinched with pliers to prevent heat transfer to diode.

Rotor and Stator Testing — Continuity with minimum resistance should be noted between slip rings. No continuity should exist between either slip ring and rotor core or shaft. Stator conduction is normal when there is continuity between leads of stator coil but NOT between stator coil leads and stator core.

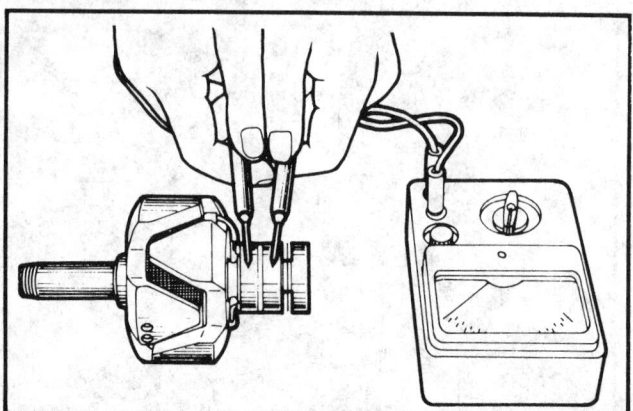

Fig. 1   *Rotor Coil Continuity Test*

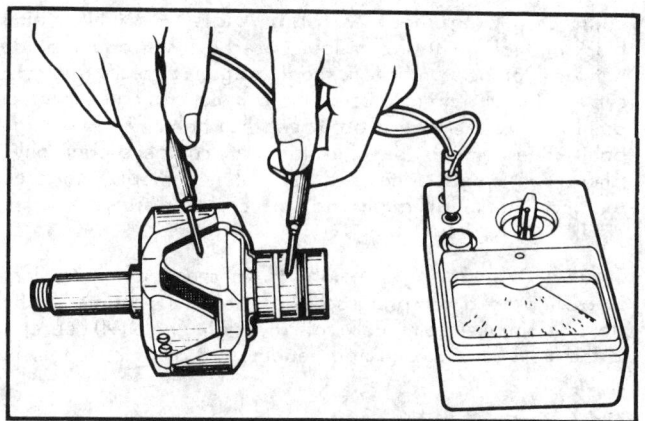

Fig. 3   *Rotor Coil Ground Test*

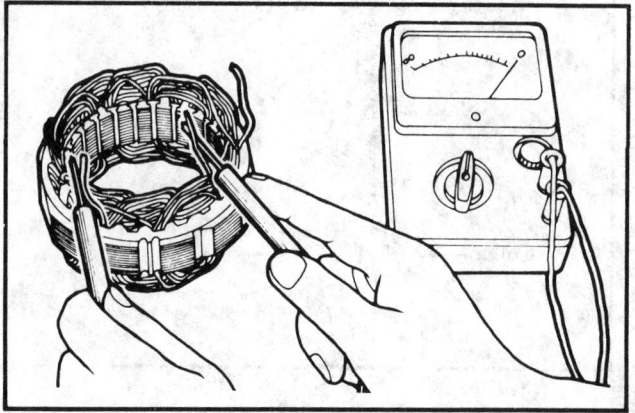

Fig. 2   *Stator Coil Continuity Test*

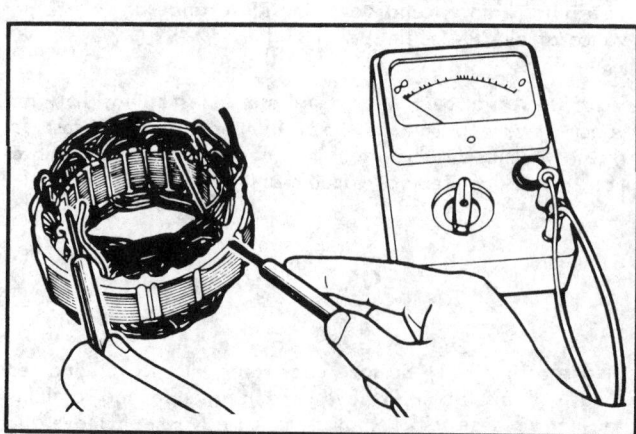

Fig. 4   *Stator Coil Ground Test*

GENERAL SERVICING (Cont.)

CHARGING SYSTEM TROUBLE SHOOTING

CONDITION	POSSIBLE CAUSE	CORRECTION
▶ No output	1) Sticking brushes. 2) Dirty brushes and slip rings. 3) Loose or dirty connections. 4) Broken leads. 5) Open stator winding. 6) Open rotor winding. 7) Open diodes. 8) Shorted rotor. 9) Shorted stator. 10) Grounded terminal. 11) Broken fan belt. 12) Blown fuse or defective contact.	1) Replace brushes and springs. 2) Clean. 3) Clean and tighten. 4) Replace. 5) Repair or replace stator. 6) Replace rotor. 7) Replace diodes. 8) Replace rotor. 9) Replace or repair stator. 10) Replace insulator. 11) Replace belt. 12) Replace or repair.
▶ Excessive output	1) Broken neutral wire. 2) Defective voltage regulator. 3) Poor ground of alternator and regulator terminals. 4) Broken ground wire.	1) Replace wire. 2) Check and repair or replace. 3) Clean and tighten mountings and terminals. 4) Replace wire.
▶ Low output	1) Loose or worn fan belt. 2) Sticking brushes. 3) Low brush spring tension. 4) Defctive regulator. 5) Dirty slip rings. 6) Partial short, ground, or open in stator winding. 7) Partial short, ground or open in rotor winding. 8) Open diode.	1) Adjust or replace belt. 2) Correct or replace brushes and/or springs. 3) Replace springs. 4) Adjust or replace. 5) Clean. 6) Replace stator. 7) Replace rotor. 8) Replace diode.
▶ Noisy alternator	1) Loose mounting. 2) Loose drive pulley. 3) Defective alternator bearing. 4) Brushes improperly seated.	1) Tighten mounting bolts. 3) Tighten pulley. 3) Replace bearing. 4) Seat brushes correctly.

Alternators & Regulators

BOSCH ALTERNATORS

Audi   Porsche
BMW   Saab
Fiat   Volkswagen
Fiesta   Volvo
Mercedes-Benz

DESCRIPTION

Bosch alternators are conventional 3 phase, self rectifying type alternators. Nine rectifier diodes are connected to stator windings (3 to each phase lead). Diodes change alternator A.C. voltages to D.C. voltages coming out of the "B+" and the "D+" terminals of the alternator.

APPLICATION

Model	Volts/Amps	① Bosch Part No.
Audi		
4000		
Standard	14/55	469 520
Heavy Duty	14/65	489 713
California	14/35	469 502
5000		
Gasoline & Diesel	14/35	469 502
Gasoline Only	14/55	489 653
Gasoline & Diesel	14/65	489 613
All With A/C	14/90	489 514
BMW		
320i	14/65	489 718
528i, 633CSi, 733i	14/65	489 619
Fiat		
Brava & Spider		
Standard	14/55	489 743
With A/C	14/65	489 824
Fiesta	14/55	489 667
Mercedes-Benz		
240D	14/55	489 556
280 Series	14/35	489 751
300 Series	14/55	489 527
300 Turbo	14/55	489 683
450 Series	14/70	489 898
Porsche 924	14/75	469 502
Saab		
99	14/55	489 783
900	14/55	489 735
Volkswagen		
Dasher		
Gasoline	14/55	489 622
Diesel	14/55	489 520
Calif. & All With A/C	14/65	489 713
Jetta, Rabbit & Scirocco		
Standard	14/45	489 858
With A/C	14/65	489 713
Rabbit Diesel		
Standard	14/35	489 799
With A/C	14/65	489 712
Vanagon	14/65	489 913
Volvo		
DL & GT		
Standard	14/55	400 933
Heavy Duty	14/70	450 009
Diesel	14/55	② 1257294

① — Bosch part numbers are preceded by 0 120 for alternators. Integral regulator models are numbered 469 and 489, while separate regulator models are numbered 400 and 450.

② — Volvo part number.

ON VEHICLE TESTING

NOTE — *Off vehicle testing is included in Overhaul procedures in this article.*

WIRING CONTINUITY TEST

Disconnect terminal plug from rear of alternator and connect a voltmeter negative terminal to ground. With ignition "ON", connect positive lead to each of the connector wires in turn. Voltmeter should read battery voltage as each positive connection is made. If proper voltage is not read, trace each wire to find fault.

VOLTAGE DROP TEST — GROUND SIDE

Connect voltmeter between negative terminal of battery and alternator housing. Start engine and run at approximately 3000 RPM. If voltmeter reading exceeds .25 volt, a high resistance in negative side of charging circuit is indicated. If so, check for loose, dirty or corroded connections.

OUTPUT TEST

Disconnect terminal plug from rear of alternator and connect ammeter in series between alternator center terminal and corresponding socket in terminal plug. Connect a jumper lead between the "D+" terminal and its corresponding socket in terminal plug. Start engine and run at approximately 3000 RPM. Turn on headlights and leave on for 5 minutes. Ammeter should read maximum alternator amperage at normal operating temperature.

REGULATOR CONTROL VOLTAGE TEST

Connect voltmeter between battery terminals. Connect ammeter in series between "B+" terminal of alternator and corresponding terminal of connector plug. Connect a jumper lead between alternator "D+" terminal and corresponding terminal of connector plug. Start engine and increase speed to approximately 3000 RPM. Run engine until charging rate falls below 3-5 amps. Voltmeter should then read 13.7-14.4 volts. If these readings are not obtained, replace regulator.

NOTE — *Test cables should not be removed or load excessively reduced during testing procedure. Considerable load variations may damage the diodes. Control lamp should not go on at any time during the test.*

OVERHAUL

DISASSEMBLY

1) Scribe mark for alignment on front and rear alternator housing. Remove nut, pulley, fan and key. Unscrew brush plate assembly and remove from alternator. Remove frame bolts and separate rear frame from front frame with rotor. Press rotor from frame and bearing from rotor. Remove insulation from wires and cut wires as close to soldered joints as possible.

NOTE — *On 4XX 6XX series alternators, lift and secure brushes prior to disassembly.*

BOSCH ALTERNATORS (Cont.)

2) Diodes may be tested at this point without further disassembly. Use care with insulating bushings under positive diode carrier. To remove negative carrier, extract threaded studs. When one diode has been damaged due to short circuiting, the 3 complementing diodes must also be replaced. Unscrew nuts on both "B+" terminal bolts and lift positive carrier (heat sink) up and back.

TESTING AND REPAIRING

Diode Assemblies — Test diodes with suitable tester before dismantling slip ring end frame. DO NOT lay positive diode carrier on housing or a false reading will obtained. Disconnect conductor from "D+" to exciter diodes at heat sink. Unscrew spring and brush holder and remove from alternator. Unsolder stator lead and negative diode connections. Unscrew exciter diodes heat sink and remove together with positive diodes heat sink. Clean all components with gasoline or trichlorethylene prior to further testing.

Stator — Test stator for short circuits to ground. Tester voltage should be 40V AC. Measure resistance of stator windings between phase connections. Fiesta should indicate .14-.16 ohms, with all remaining models showing .20 to .22 ohms.

Rotor — Test claw pole rotor for short circuits to ground using 40V AC tester. Measure resistance of exciter (field coil) in rotor with ohmmeter across slip rings. Resistance should be 4.0-4.4 ohms. If necessary, turn slip rings in a lathe, noting maximum runout of .001" (.03 mm) and minimum diameter of 1.25" (31.5 mm). Maximum pole wheel runout should not exceed .002" (.05 mm).

Diode Replacement — In case diodes are found to be defective, entire diode plate assembly should be replaced. Care must be exercised in soldering near diodes due to possible damage from excess heat. Use flat jawed pliers as heat sink applied to leads when soldering diode connections.

Drive End Frame — Check ball bearings for wear and replace as necessary. Lubricate ball bearings on one side. Press ball bearing into drive end frame with shielded side downward. Screw on retainer plate. Press ball bearing on slip ring end of rotor and press drive end frame onto drive end of rotor.

Carbon Brushes — Minimum brush length is .2" (5 mm). If replacement is required, grip brush with flat-jawed pliers and unsolder brushes. Do not allow solder to run into strands of brush leads. Brush must be free to slide in holder with normal spring tension of 10-14 ozs. (283-397 g).

REASSEMBLY

1) Solder stator and diode connections using caution not to overheat diodes. Place stator and diode assembly in rear housing and secure with screws.

2) Lubricate new rear bearing and press onto rotor shaft, assuring that shielded side of bearing faces slip rings. Place front bearing in housing with shielded side rearward. Install retainer plate.

3) Place spacer ring on rotor shaft and install rotor assembly into front housing. Press front bearing retaining ring over shaft and into front housing with a socket.

4) Coat bearing bore of rear housing with grease and install spring washer. Assemble front housing with rotor to rear housing, using a turning or twisting motion to seat rear bearing. Line up scribed alignment marks and install screws through housing.

5) Install shaft key, washer, fan, spacer, pulley, lock washer and nut. Install brush and connector plug assembly and retain with screws.

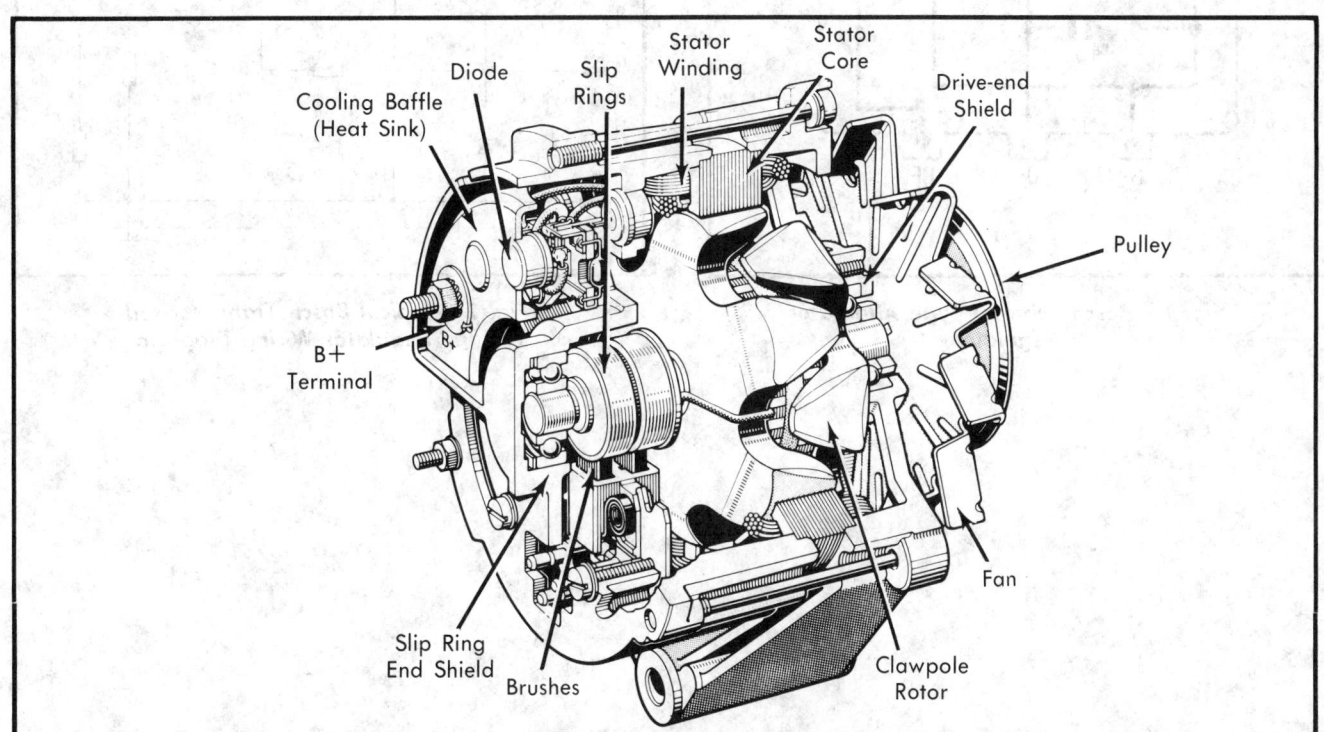

Fig. 1   Cutaway View of Bosch Alternator

BOSCH REGULATORS

Audi
BMW
Fiat
Fiesta
Mercedes-Benz

Porsche
Saab
Volkswagen
Volvo

DESCRIPTION

Bosch regulators are provided in either transistorized solid state or the vibrating contact type. Vibrating type is mounted separate from alternator. Solid state type may be integral with alternator or separately mounted. Vibrator model is designated "ADN" and externally mounted solid state type is designated "ED". Integral mounted solid state regulator is designated "EE".

NOTE — For Regulator Applications and additional Testing procedures, see Bosch Alternators in this Section.

TESTING

ON CAR TEST

Vibrator Type — Install a battery post adapter at the positive post of the battery. Connect voltmeter across battery. Connect a tachometer to ignition system. Make sure all electrical acessories are turned off. Start engine with battery post adapter switch closed; open switch as soon as engine is started. With engine speed at 4000 RPM, after voltage reading stabilizes, any reading between 13.7 and 14.8 volts is satisfactory.

Transistorized (Solid State) Regulators — All applicable regulators are designed to maintain from 13.7 to 14.5 volts at a load current of 5 to 7 amps. Alternator should be driven at 4000 RPM and load current set at load current rating. Resistance and speed of alternator may be readjusted if necessary. Read voltage within 1 minute. If not within specifications, regulator requires replacement.

ADJUSTMENT

NOTE — If regulator fails to keep voltage within specified limits, it must be replaced. No adjusting procedures are recommended.

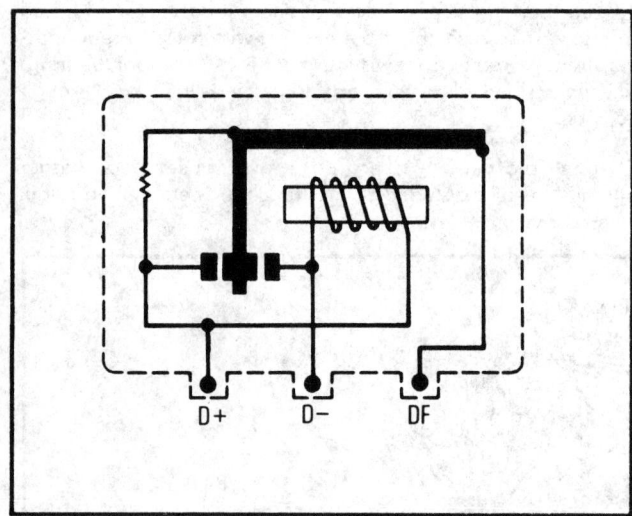

Fig. 1   Bosch Vibrator Type Alternator
Regulator

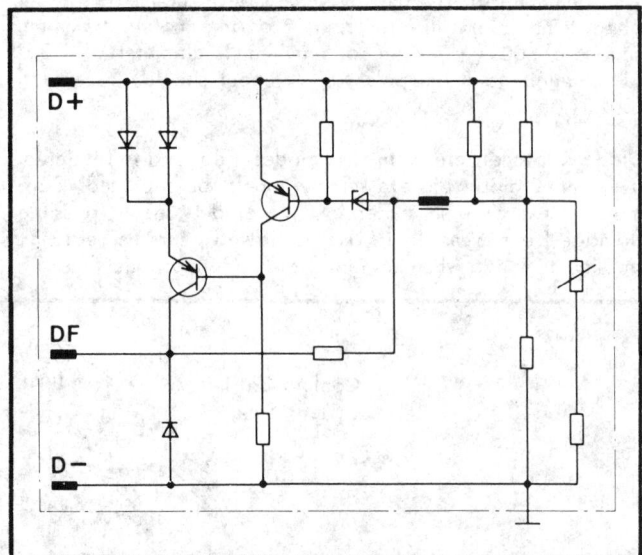

Fig. 2   Typical Bosch Transistorized
Voltage Regulator Wiring Diagram

HITACHI ALTERNATORS

Datsun (With IC Regulator)
LUV
Subaru

DESCRIPTION

Hitachi alternators are conventional 3 phase, self rectifying type alternators. Six diodes (3 positive and 3 negative) are used to rectify current.

APPLICATION

Model	Hitachi Type No.
Datsun	
200SX	LR160-47
210	LR150-36
310	LR160-46
510	LR150-52
280ZX & 810	LR160-42B
Pickup	
Standard	LR135-44
Heavy Duty	LR138-01
LUV	LT135-30
Subaru	
Exc. Sta. Wagon	LT150-113
Station Wagon	LT150-114B

SPECIFICATIONS

Output@2500 Alternator RPM

Alternator	Amps	Volts
LT135-30	28	14
LT135-44	27.5	14
LR138-01	30	14
LR150-36	40	14
LR150-52	40	14
LT150-113	42	14
LT150-114B	50	14
LR160-42B	50	14
LR160-46	45	14
LR160-47	45	14

Nominal Output@5000 Alternator RPM

Alternator	Amps	Volts
LT135-30	35	12
LT135-44	35	12
LR138-01	38	12
LR150-36	50	12
LR150-52	50	12
LT150-113	50	12
LT150-114B	55	12
LT160-42B	60	12
LR160-46	60	12
LR160-47	60	12

TESTING

NOTE — *Some testing is described as part of Overhaul procedure in this article. The following testing is performed with alternator on the vehicle.*

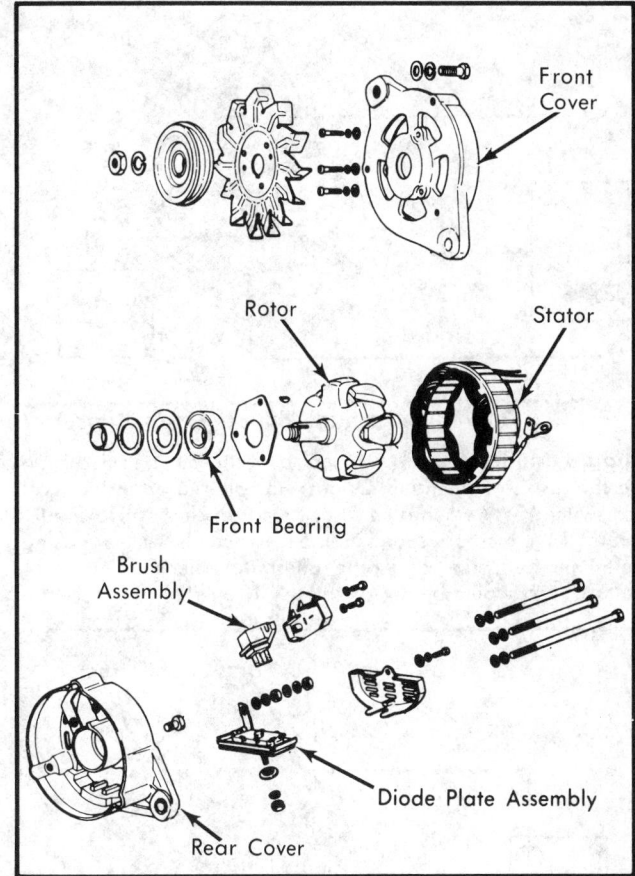

Fig. 1 Disassembled View of Typical Hitachi Alternator

ALTERNATOR TEST ON VEHICLE

Datsun Models — Ensure that battery has a full charge, then connect 30-volt voltmeter as illustrated in *Fig. 2*. Turn ignition switch "ON" and test as follows:

1) If charge light remains OFF, disconnect connector from rear of alternator and ground "L" lead wire. If light remains OFF, replace indicator bulb. If light is ON, reconnect connector and ground "F" terminal by touching brush with grounded wire. If light stays on, replace IC regulator. If light goes out, remove and repair alternator.

2) If light came ON when ignition was turned "ON", start and idle engine. If light is dim, flickers or remains bright, remove and repair alternator. If light went off at idle, run engine at 1500 RPM and turn headlights on high beam. If charge light is on dim, idle engine and measure voltage between terminals "B" and "L". If less than .5 volt, alternator is OK. If more than .5 volt, remove and repair alternator.

NOTE — *Terminals "S", "L", "BAT" and "E" are marked on rear cover of alternator.*

3) If charge light went OFF at 1500 RPM with lights on high beam, measure "B" voltage. If more than 15.5 volts, replace IC regulator. If 13 to 15 volts, idle engine and check indicator light. If OFF, system is OK. If ON, repair faulty alternator.

Alternators & Regulators

HITACHI ALTERNATORS (Cont.)

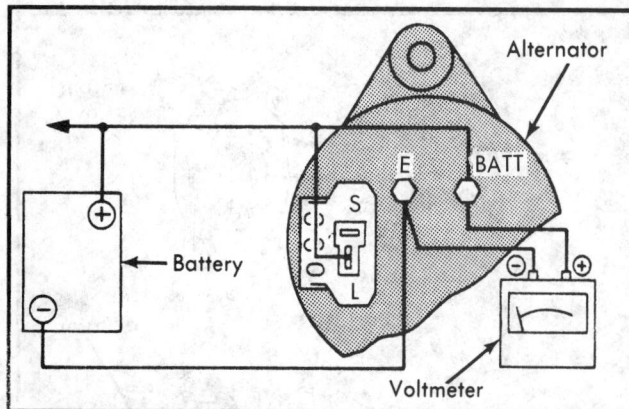

Fig. 2   Alternator Testing Connections for Datsun

Subaru Models — 1) Connect a voltmeter and leads to battery as shown in *Fig. 3*. Operate the alternator and turn off the switch "SW" when alternator speed reaches approximately 800 RPM. Increase speed in small increments while watching voltmeter deflection and read alternator speed when at 14 volts. Speed should be approximately 1000 RPM.

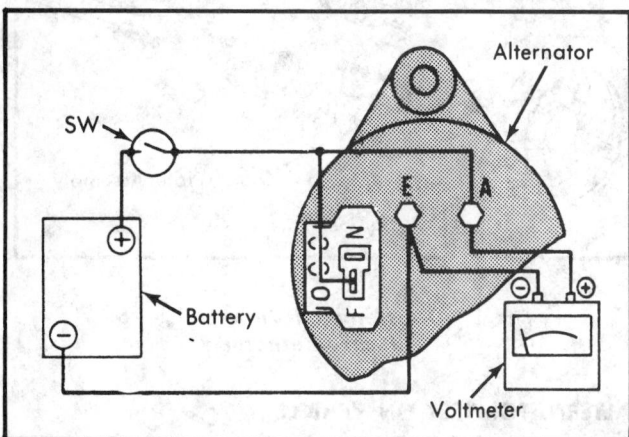

Fig. 3   Alternator Cut-In Speed Test Connections (Subaru)

2) Make test connections using a 30-50 ampere variable resistor, battery, ammeter, and voltmeter as shown in *Fig. 4*. Operate alternator with switch "SW-1" closed. When alternator speed reaches approximately 800 RPM, set the variable resistor to maximum and turn on switch "SW-2". Increase alternator speed while maintaining a constant 14 volts by adjusting resistance. Read current at 2500 RPM and 5000 RPM. Readings should be 37-43 amperes at 2500 RPM and 48-54 at 5000 RPM.

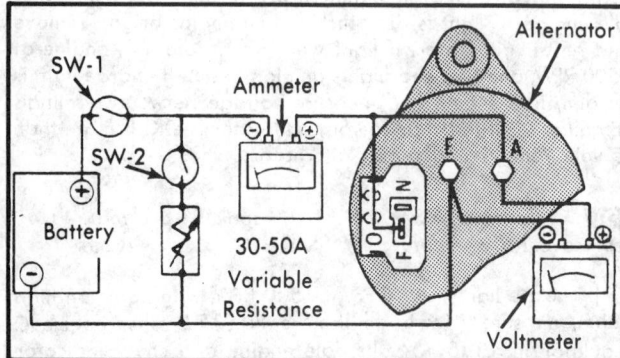

Fig. 4   Alternator Output Test Connections for Subaru

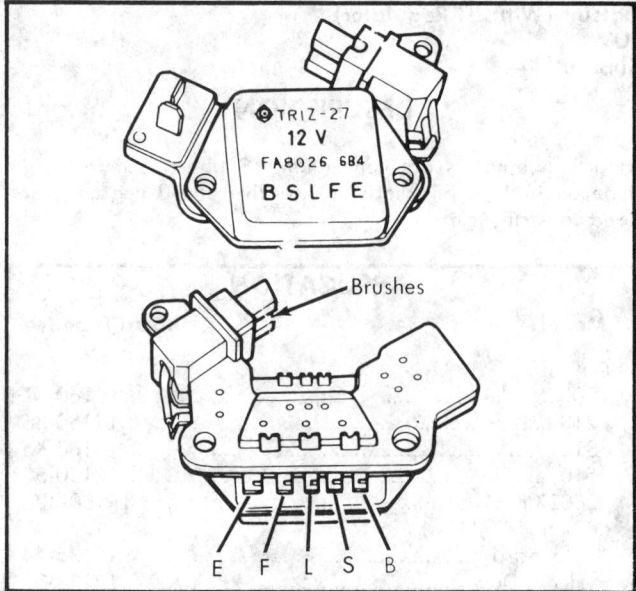

Fig. 5   Front and Rear Views of IC Regulator (Datsun)

RESISTANCE & CONTINUITY TESTING

All Models — 1) Measure resistance, using an ohmmeter, across "F" and "E" terminals for rotor coil resistance. Rotor coil circuit is normal if resistance is 4-5 ohms. If resistance is high, there is poor contact between brushes and commutator. If no continuity exists between "F" and "E" terminals, there is either an open rotor coil circuit, brush sticking or a broken lead wire. If resistance is low, it indicates a rotor coil layer short or grounded circuit.

NOTE — *The following test will not indicate an open state of the diodes. Tester will indicate continuity regardless of diode conditions if tester leads are connected to the terminals with polarity reversed.*

2) Connect positive lead of tester to alternator "N" terminal, and tester negative lead to alternator "A" terminal. If tester shows continuity, one or more positive diodes are shorted.

3) Next, connect positive lead of tester to alternator "E" terminal, and tester negative lead to alternator "N" terminal. If continuity is indicated, one or more of the negative diodes are shorted.

INTEGRATED CIRCUIT (IC) REGULATOR

An integrated circuit regulator is used on all Datsun models. The voltage regulator is soldered to the brush assembly and mounted inside the alternator.

Testing — 1) Remove brush assembly and with suitable tester, connect wiring as shown in *Fig. 6*. If V-1 voltage is not within 10-13 volts, charge or replace battery as necessary. Disconnect lead at terminal "S" and check voltage between terminals "F" and "E". If less than 2.0 volts, regulator is functioning properly.

2) Measure total voltage (V-3) of batteries 1 and 2. If not within 20-26 volts, recharge or replace. Gradually decrease variable resistance (Rv) from 300 ohms and check voltage (V-2) between terminals "E" and "F". At some point, V-2 should increase to equal V-1 measured in step 1). If no V-2 variation occurs as described, regulator is defective.

HITACHI ALTERNATORS (Cont.)

3) Measure voltage (V-4) between center tap of variable resistor (Rv) and terminal "E". With resistance set as in previous step, voltage should be $14.7\pm.5$ volts at 68°F (20°C). At extremely high case temperatures, voltage may be 1 volt lower, while at extremely cold temperatures, voltage may be 1 volt higher.

4) Remove test lead from terminal "S" and connect to terminal "B". Repeat steps 2) and 3) and check for voltage (V-4) .5-2.0 volts higher than in step 3). If testing specifications are not met, it will be necessary to replace the IC regulator/brush assembly.

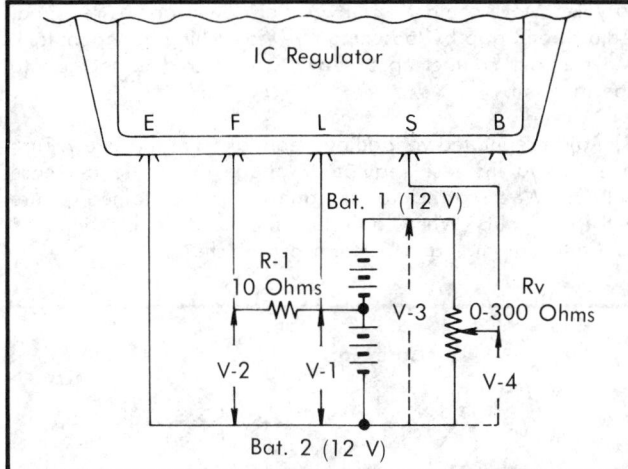

Fig. 6   Regulator Test Arrangement

OVERHAUL

DISASSEMBLY

1) Remove nut and take off pulley, fan, and washers. Pull out spacer. Remove screws securing brush holder and brush holder cover, leaving "N" lead wire connected to stator coil lead.

2) Unscrew through bolts and separate front and rear housings. Remove 3 set screws from bearing retainer and separate rotor from front cover. Pull rear bearing from rotor assembly if replacement is required.

3) Remove diode cover and disconnect stator coil lead wire from diode terminal using a soldering iron. Remove the diode assembly by unscrewing the terminal nut and diode setting nuts. Remove stator from rear cover.

INSPECTION & REPAIR

Rotor — Apply tester to slip rings of rotor. If ohm reading is within specifications, rotor conduction is satisfactory. If not, an open connection to the field coil may exist. Next, apply probes to slip ring and rotor core to check for ground. If conduction exists, replace rotor assembly.

Stator — The stator is normal when there is conduction between individual stator core terminals. When there is no conduction between terminals, cable is broken and stator must be replaced. If each lead wire of stator coil (including neutral wire) is not conductive with stator core, condition is satisfactory. If conduction exists, stator is grounded and must be replaced.

Diodes — 1) Perform a conduction test on all diodes in both directions using an ohmmeter. Test the conduction between

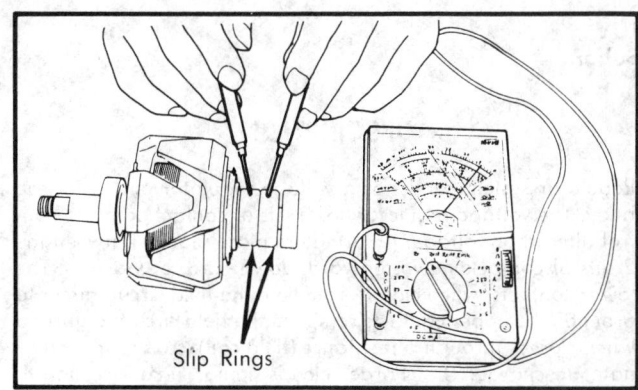

Fig. 7   Rotor Field Coil Conduction Test

each terminal and plate. Diode installed on a "+" plate is a positive diode which allows current to flow from terminal to "+" plate only. Current does NOT flow from "+" plate to the terminal. A diode installed on the "−" plate is a negative diode and allows current to flow from the "−" plate to the terminal only. Current does NOT flow from the terminal to the "−" plate.

2) If current flows in both directions, the diode is shorted. If current does not flow in either direction, the diode is open. If any diode is defective, replace the entire diode assembly (individual diodes are not serviceable).

Brushes & Brush Springs — Inspect brushes for freedom of movement in holder. Clean brush holder if necessary. Check brushes for cracks and wear; replace if beyond limits (.28" or 7.0 mm for LT135-30, LT150-21 and LR160-42; .30" or 7.5 mm for all others). Check brush springs for corrosion, damage and proper tension (9-12.2 oz. with .08" or 2 mm protrusion from holder). Test brush holder to assure that no continuity exists between holders; replace if required.

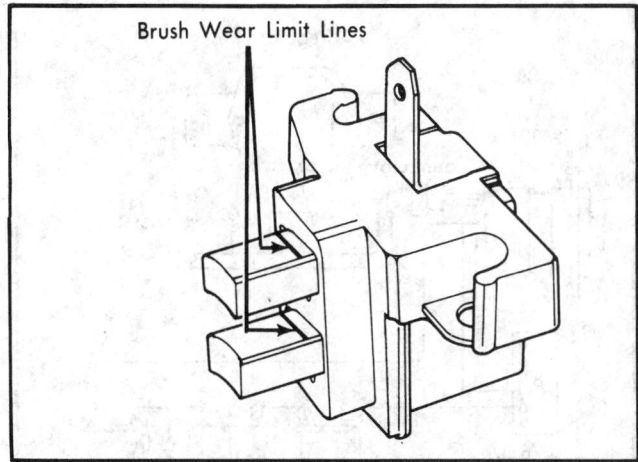

Fig. 8   Brush Assembly with Wear Indicators

REASSEMBLY

Reinstall diode assembly and stator to rear cover. Connect lead wires of stator coil to terminals of diode assembly. Reinstall diode cover. Reinstall rotor to front cover. Place assembly in vise and replace pulley and components. Insert and tighten housing through bolts. Assemble brushes to brush holder and insert holder into alternator.

NOTE — *Soldering must be done quickly to avoid damage to diodes.*

HITACHI REGULATORS

LUV
Subaru

DESCRIPTION

Regulator system consist of a voltage regulator and a charge relay. The voltage regulator has 2 sets of contact points to control alternator voltage. An armature plate placed between the 2 sets of contacts moves upward, downward, or vibrates. The lower contacts, when closed, complete the field circuit direct to ground. The upper contacts complete the field circuit to ground when closed, through a resistance (field coil), causing the alternator to charge. The charge relay is similar in construction to the voltage regulator. When upper contacts are closed, the ignition warning light goes on.

APPLICATION

Model	Hitachi No.
LUV	TLIZ-87
Subaru	TLIZ-94E

TESTING

VOLTAGE REGULATOR

1) Connect voltmeter and ammeter as illustrated. Start and maintain engine speed at 2500 RPM for a few minutes, then check that ammeter reading is 5 amps or less. If ammeter remains higher than 5 amps, disconnect battery in use and connect a battery known to be fully charged. Recheck to ensure that ammeter reading is less than 5 amps.

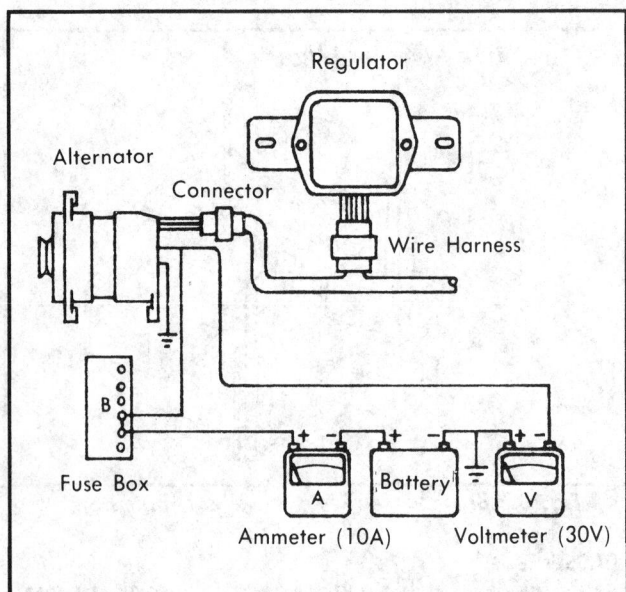

Fig. 1   Test Connections for Voltage Regulator

2) Lower engine speed to idle and again increase it gradually to 2500 RPM, then note voltmeter reading. Function of regulator is normal if measured value is within specified regulating voltage. If voltmeter reading deviates from specified range, regulator is in need of adjustment.

ADJUSTMENT

NOTE – Charge relay is adjusted in same manner as voltage regulator.

1) Disconnect and remove voltage regulator from vehicle. If contact points are roughened, smooth with fine sandpaper. Check and adjust core gap first, then point gap. Yoke gap adjustment may be unnecessary on some models.

2) Adjust core gap by loosening screws attaching contact set to yoke. Move contact set upward or downward as required. Adjust point gap by loosening screw attaching upper contact. Move upper contact up or down as required to set gap to specification.

3) Adjust regulated voltage by means of adjusting screw. Turn screw in to increase regulated voltage or out to decrease voltage. When correct voltage adjustment is obtained, secure with lock nut. When adjustment procedure is complete, reinstall regulator and perform on car check.

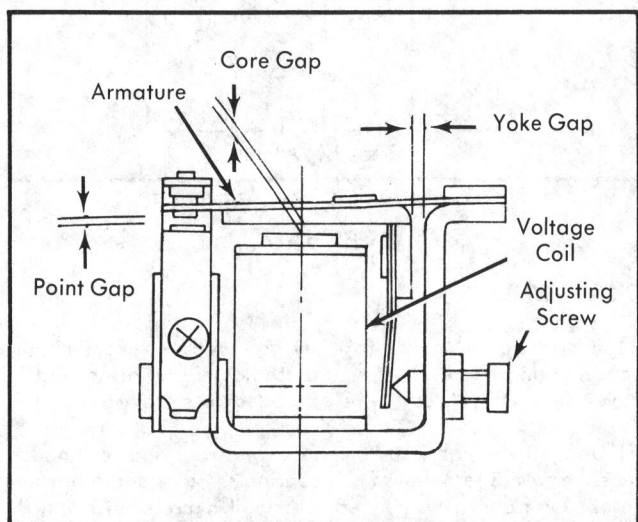

Fig. 2   Adjustment Points for Charge Relay

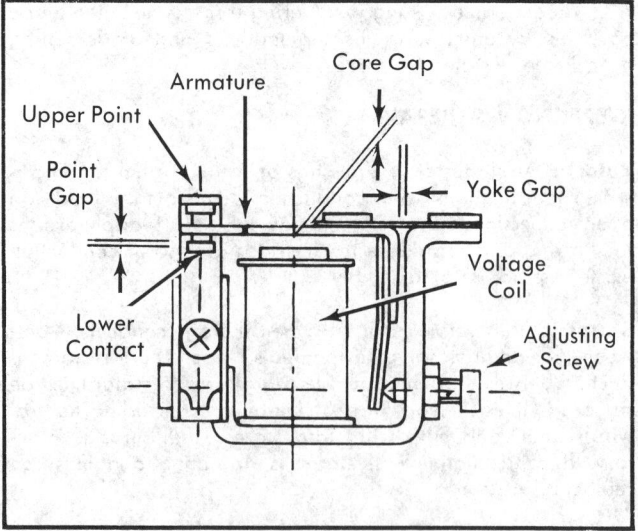

Fig. 3   Adjustment Points for Voltage Regulator

ELECTRICAL

HITACHI REGULATORS (Cont.)

VOLTAGE REGULATOR SPECIFICATIONS

Regulator	Battery Voltage	Regulated Voltage	Voltage Coil Resistance (Ohms)	Yoke Gap In. (mm)	Core Gap In. (mm)	Point Gap In. (mm)
TLIZ-87	12	13.8-14.8	10.3	①	.024-.039(.6-1.0)	.012-.016 (.30-.40)
TLIZ-94E	12	14.0-15.0	10.3	.035(.9)	.024-.039(.6-1.0)	.014-.018 (.35-.45)

① — No yoke gap adjustment required.

VOLTAGE RELAY SPECIFICATIONS

Regulator	Released Voltage	Voltage Coil Resistance (Ohms)	Yoke Gap In. (mm)	Core Gap In. (mm)	Point Gap In. (mm)
TLIZ-87	5②	31.9	①	.032-.039(.8-1.0)	.016-.024(.41-.61)
TLIZ-94E	8-10	32.1	.035(.9)	.032-.039(.8-1.0)	.016-.024(.41-.61)

① — No yoke gap adjustment required.

② — Measured at "A" terminal.

LUCAS ALTERNATORS

Jaguar
XJ6
MGB
Triumph
TR7
TR8

DESCRIPTION

Lucas ACR model alternators have an integral voltage regulator mounted in the slip ring end bracket. The stator consists of star-connected, 3 phase windings on a ring end cover and drive end bracket. The rotor is either an 8 or 12 pole type with the field windings connected to 2 face-type slip rings. It is supported in the drive-end bracket by ball bearings and in the end cover by needle roller bearings. One positive and one negative carbon brush ride against concentric brass slip rings. The heatsink-rectifier, terminal block assembly incorporates 6 silicon diodes, forming a full wave rectifier bridge circuit, and 3 diodes which supply current to the rotor windings.

APPLICATION

Model	Type No.
Jaguar XJ6	25 ACR
MGB	18 ACR
Triumph	
Spitfire	16 ACR
TR7	25 ACR
TR8	
Without Air Cond.	17 ACR
With Air Cond.	25 ACR

SPECIFICATIONS

Nominal Output

Alternator	Amps@6000 RPM	Voltage
16 ACR	24	 14
17 ACR	36	 14
18 ACR	45	 14
25 ACR	66	 14

TESTING

ON CAR TESTING

NOTE — *Alternator drive belt must be properly adjusted, battery and connections in good condition and charge warning bulb and circuit continuous in order to test charging system. Polarity of alternator and battery terminals MUST be observed to prevent system damage. Warm engine 3-4 minutes before testing. (Output may be slightly higher when alternator is cold.) Battery ground cable should be disconnected when attaching jumper wires to alternator and regulator.*

Alternator Output Test — 1) Disconnect multi-socket connector and remove molded cover from rear of alternator. (Cover may be pierced with a probe on some models in order to ground the field winding brush and by-pass the regulator.) Provide a test circuit as illustrated.

2) Start engine and run to give 1,500 alternator RPM (approximately 650-800 engine RPM). Test circuit bulb should be out.

3) Increase engine speed to 2500-3,000 RPM to give 6,000 alternator RPM. Adjust variable resistor so voltmeter reads 14 volts and note ammeter reading equal to the nominal output rating for the appropriate alternator. If readings are not correct, alternator requires overhaul or replacement.

NOTE — *Do not connect variable resistor across battery for longer than is necessary to complete the test.*

Regulator Test — 1) Provide Regulator Test Circuit as shown and gradually increase engine speed to approximately 640 RPM (1,550 alternator RPM). Test lamp should go out.

2) Increase engine speed to approximately 2,500 RPM (6,000 alternator RPM). Voltmeter should be steady at 13.6-14.4 volts. If reading is not steady and satisfactory Output Test has been performed, regulator should be replaced.

NOTE — *Up to 10 milliamp battery drain is normal, even with the ignition in the "OFF" position.*

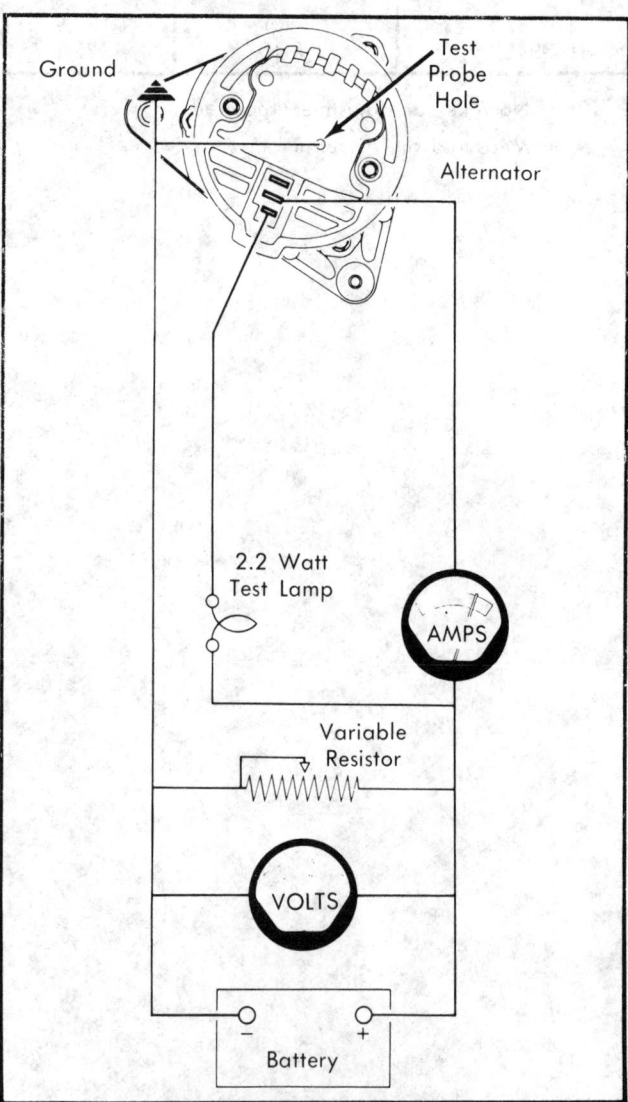

Fig. 1 Alternator Output Test Circuit
(Spitfire Shown)

LUCAS ALTERNATORS (Cont.)

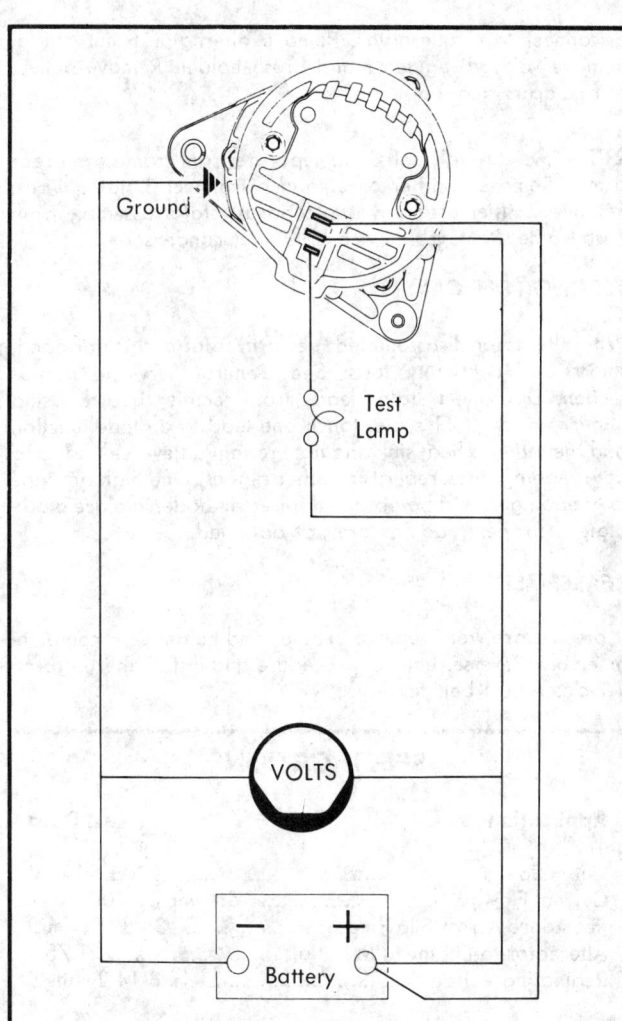

**Fig. 2   Regulator Test Circuit
(Spitfire 1500 Shown)**

OVERHAUL

DISASSEMBLY

1) Remove end cover and note wire positions and color. Remove screws attaching surge protection diode and brush assembly. Lift out brush assembly and surge protection diode. Regulator may be removed if desired.

2) Unsolder stator wire connections and remove rectifier pack grounding strip. Withdraw rectifier pack. Remove through bolts.

CAUTION — *When necessary to solder or unsolder leads from diodes, use pliers as a heat sink by pinching diode pin with jaws of pliers. Solder connections quickly to prevent heat damage to diodes.*

3) Remove through bolts from alternator frame and carefully slip end bracket and stator off of rotor. (It may be necessary to tap lightly on an extractor or tube placed against outer bearing journal to separate rotor from end bracket.)

4) Complete disassembly, if required, by removing pulley and drive key. Press rotor from drive end bracket and remove screws retaining end bearing in position. Replace as necessary.

NOTE — *Position of all washers, spacers and insulators must be noted for proper assembly.*

TESTING

Rotor — Connect an ohmmeter and read resistance of field coil (across slip rings). Using a 110-volt A.C. supply and a 15-watt test lamp, check for insulation between one of the slip rings and any rotor pole. If lamp lights, rotor is shorted.

Stator — Connect 12-volt battery and 36-watt test lamp to 2 of the stator connections. Repeat test using any other combination of 2 of the 3 connections. If lamp fails to light in either test, stator has an open coil. Using 110-volt/15-watt test lamp, check for insulation between any one of the 3 stator connections and stator laminations. If lamp lights, stator should be relaced.

Diodes — Connect a 12-volt battery and a 1.5-watt test lamp in turn to each of the 9 diode pins and its corresponding heat sink on the rectifier pack, then reverse the connections. Lamp should light (with current flow) in one direction only. If lamp lights in both directions or fails in either, rectifier pack must be renewed.

PARTS REPLACEMENT

Regulator — Aluminum casing of control unit must not make contact with alternator body when installed. (Shorted field circuit could result in maximum alternator output at all times regardless of battery condition.)

Diodes — In event of defective diodes, heatsink and rectifier assembly should be replaced. Protect diodes from excess heat when soldering by using pliers on diode pin as a thermal shunt.

Brushes — Installed brushes must extend at least .2" (5 mm) from housing and springs should indicate 9-13 oz. tension when brush is pushed back flush with housing. If beyond limits, replace brush assembly.

REASSEMBLY

Reverse disassembly procedure and note the following: When intalling slip ring end bearing, ensure that it is fitted with open side facing rotor and that it is seated fully. When replacing rotor to drive end bracket, support inner track of bearing with suitable piece of tubing. DO NOT use drive end bracket as the only support for the bearing when fitting rotor.

MARELLI ALTERNATORS

Fiat
Strada

DESCRIPTION

Marelli alternators are conventional 3-phase, self-rectifying type alternators. The externally mounted rectifier contains a silicon diode pack connected to form a full-wave, 3-phase rectifying bridge. An integral voltage regulator, also mounted on the rear of the alternator, controls charging rate.

APPLICATION

Model	Type
Strada (W/O Air Cond.)	A125/14V/55A

TESTING

NOTE – *Prior to performing any testing, ensure that alternator drive belt tension is properly adjusted and that battery condition, water level and connections are good. Some testing is done as part of Overhaul procedure.*

ENGINE CRANK TEST

Disconnect distributor connector and connect voltmeter to battery. Crank engine 3 to 4 seconds and note voltmeter reading. A reading of less than 9 volts indicates possible faulty battery.

VOLTAGE TEST

Set engine speed at 2500 RPM with headlights on and heater fan on high speed. Voltmeter should read at least 12.5 but no more than 15.0 volts.

REGULATOR/ALTERNATOR CHECK

If voltage is not as specified, disconnect battery ground cable and remove regulator from alternator. Install known good voltage regulator, connect battery and repeat voltage test. If voltage is now within specifications, original regulator is defective. If voltage still is below specifications, repair or replace alternator.

MOUNTING CHECK

Remove rear shield and check that mounting screws for voltage regulator and brush holder are tight and free of corrosion.

EXCITOR SYSTEM CHECK

Turn ignition switch "ON" and check for charge indicator light. If no light, check bulb, wiring or alternator brushes. If indicator lights, start engine and check that light goes out. If light remains ON, check for short in excitor system wiring.

OVERHAUL

DISASSEMBLY

1) Disconnect battery ground cable and remove rear shield from alternator. Mark electrical leads for identification and disconnect from alternator. Remove alternator from vehicle. Remove voltage regulator and brush holder. Remove pulley, fan, spacers and key.

2) Remove through bolts and separate front frame from rear frame. Remove rectifier cover and disconnect 3 stator wires. Remove rectifier assembly and separate stator assembly from rear frame. Remove screw and lift out condenser.

TESTING (OFF CAR)

With alternator disassembled, perform rotor and stator open, shorts and continuity tests. *See General Servicing in this section.* Disconnect stator leads from rectifier board. Using ohmmeter set to X1 scale, touch one lead to a diode junction and the other to heat sink and note reading. Reverse leads and note reading, then repeat for other diodes. One high and one low reading should be obtained for each diode. Replace diode plate if proper readings are not obtained.

REASSEMBLY

If brushes are worn replace brushes and holder as a complete assembly. Reverse removal procedure and install alternator on vehicle. Adjust belt tension.

SPECIFICATIONS

Application	Test Data
Cut-in Speed	900±50 RPM
Current Flow	55 amps.@7000 RPM
Resistance Across Slip Rings	3.1±.1 ohm①
Alternator-to-Engine RPM Ratio	1.75:1
Regulating Voltage	13.8-14.2 volts①

① – At 77° F.

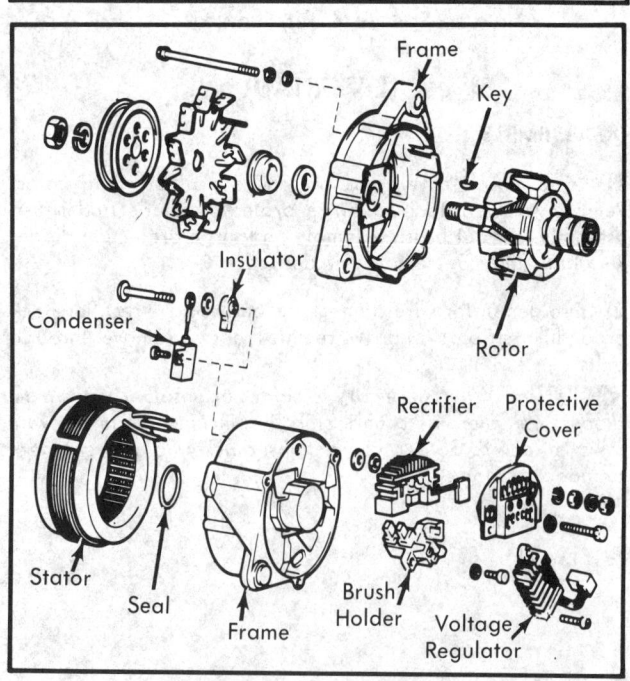

Fig. 1   Disassembled View of Marelli Alternator

MITSUBISHI ALTERNATORS

Chrysler Corp. Imports
 Arrow & Colt (2600 cc)
 Arrow & D50 Pickups
 Champ, Challenger, Colt Hatchback & Sapporo
Courier
Mazda
 GLC
 RX7
 626
 B2000 Pickup

DESCRIPTION

Mitsubishi alternators are conventional 3-phase, self-rectifying type units containing 6 diodes (3 positive and 3 negative) which are used to rectify current. A case mounted Integrated Circuit (IC) regulator is used on all except Courier, Mazda GLC and B2000 models.

APPLICATION

Model	Type or Part No.
Arrow, Challenger, Sapporo	
2600 cc	AQ2250G1
Champ and Colt	
Hatchback	A2T16371
Colt Wagon, D-50 and Arrow Pickup	
2000 and 2600 cc	A2T16471
Courier	①D47Z-10346-A
Mazda	
GLC	8317-18-300
626	8356-18-300
RX7	8871-18-300
B2000 Pickup	0571-18-300A

① — Ford part number. Check number stamped on housing for individual application.

SPECIFICATIONS

Nominal Output@2500 RPM

Application	Amps.	Voltage
AQ2250G1	41-50	.... 13.5
A2T16371	37-42	.... 13.5
A2T16471	37-42	.... 13.5
D47Z-19346-A	35	 14
8317-18-300	30	 14
8356-18-300	42	.... 13.5
8871-18-300	39	.... 13.5
0571-18-300A	30	 14

Brush Wear Limit — To limit line, .22" (5.5 mm), or when one third of original length has worn away, whichever is greater.

Brush Spring Pressure — Standard tension should be 12-16 oz. Replace if less than 8 oz. or if springs are corroded.

TESTING

NOTE — *Some testing is done as part of Overhaul procedure.*

ON CAR TEST

CAUTION — *DO NOT short across any alternator terminals nor run vehicle with any wires disconnected.*

Output Test — With ignition switch off and battery ground cable disconnected, connect ammeter between alternator terminal "B" and cable. Connect voltmeter between "B" (+) terminal and ground. Connect ground cable and observe battery voltage. Start engine and turn all lights on. Run engine to produce alternator RPM specified and check ammeter for specified output.

NOTE — *Alternator RPM is approximately twice engine RPM.*

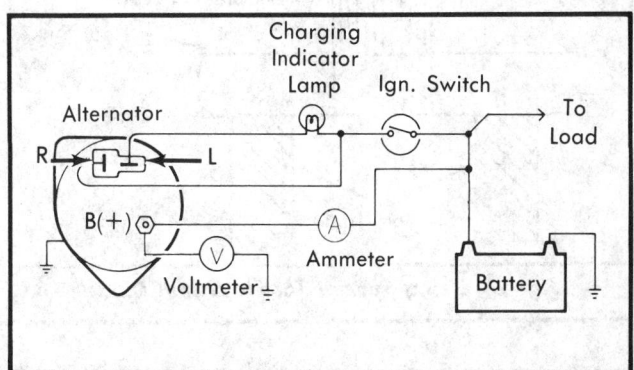

Fig. 1 Alternator Output Test Arrangement

OVERHAUL

DISASSEMBLY

1) Remove brush cover and through bolts. Separate diode end housing from drive housing by tapping front bracket lightly with a soft mallet.

2) Place rotor shaft in padded vise, using caution. Remove pulley nut, pulley, fan, and spacer. Remove rotor drive end housing by lightly tapping end housing with a soft mallet.

3) To separate stator from diode end housing, unsolder three negative diode leads and connections between diodes.

TESTING

Diode Assemblies — Disconnect heat sink and check each diode with tester on continuity in forward or reverse direction. If the diode shows large resistance in one direction and small resistance in other direction, diode is normal. If it shows small resistance in both directions it is shorted. If large resistance is shown in both directions, diode is open.

MITSUBISHI ALTERNATORS (Cont.)

CAUTION — *If excessive temperature is allowed, diode will become inoperative.*

Rotor Field Continuity — Check continuity across field coil slip rings. No continuity indicates broken wire. Rotor must be replaced.

Rotor Field Coil Ground — Check continuity between individual slip rings and rotor core/shaft. If there is continuity, coil or slip ring is grounded. Rotor must be replaced.

Stator Coil Ground — Check to ensure no continuity between stator coil leads and stator core.

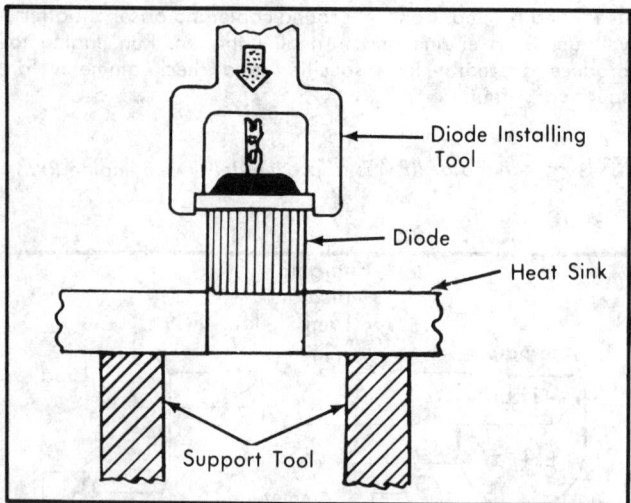

Fig. 2   Using Special Tool to Install Diode

Stator Coil Continuity — Check continuity between leads of stator coil. If there is no continuity, coil has broken wire and must be replaced.

NOTE — *See General Servicing in this section.*

PARTS REPLACEMENT

Diodes — To remove diode, use a suitable tool to support heat sink and remove diode by use of a suitable press. Press out carefully to avoid damaging mounting bore of heat sink. To install diode, support heat sink as in removal. Select correct type diode (positive diodes have red markings; negative diodes have black markings), and press diode into heat sink.

CAUTION — *Do not strike diodes to remove them since shock may damage other diodes.*

Drive End Bearing — Remove bearing retainer by unscrewing set screws and press out bearing, using a suitable press.

Rear Bearing — Remove rear bearing from housing assembly, using a suitable press or bearing puller.

REASSEMBLY

Reassemble by reversing disassembly procedures, making sure polarity of diodes is correct.

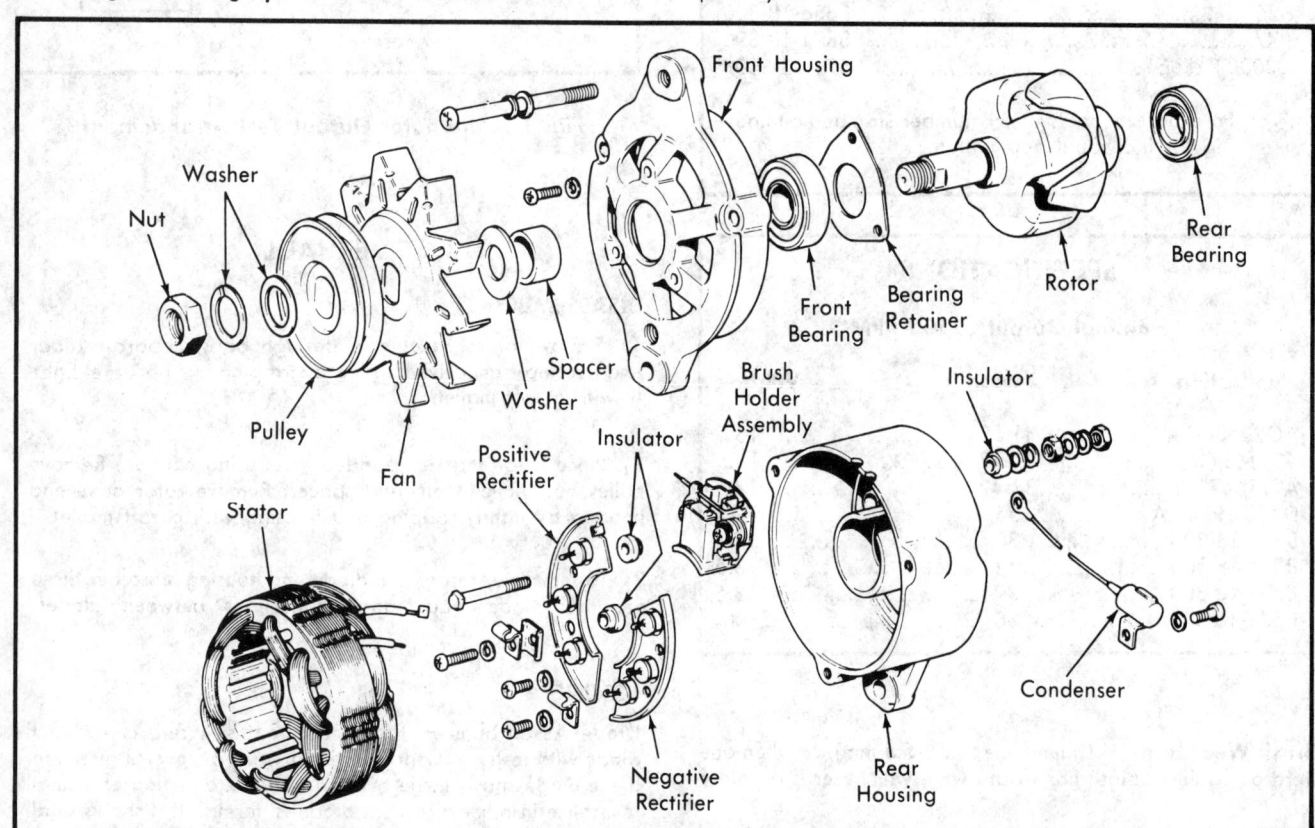

Fig. 3   Exploded View of Mitsubishi Alternator (Courier Application Shown)

MITSUBISHI REGULATORS

Courier
Mazda

DESCRIPTION

Regulator consists of a constant voltage relay and a pilot lamp relay. Both relays consist of an electromagnet, contacts, frame, moving element and coil side plate. This regulator has a temperature compensation gradient incorporated to automatically lower the adjusted value of the constant voltage relay in warm weather and to increase it in cold temperatures.

APPLICATION

Model	Part. No.
Courier	D97Z-10316-A
Mazda	8914 18 391

TESTING

CAUTION — Ensure that voltage regulator protecting fuse is functional before conducting any charging system diagnosis. Verify condition by substituting known good fuse.

To check adjusted value of constant voltage relay, connect a voltmeter between terminal "A" and E" of the regulator. Place generator at no load by disconnecting one of the battery terminals during operation at idling speed, then increase alternator speed to approximately 4000 RPM (Approximately 2000 engine RPM). In this condition, satisfactory voltage is 14.5-15.8 volts.

ADJUSTMENT

NOTE — Adjustment procedures furnished for Mazda only. Manufacturers recommend installation of new regulator when tolerance not within limits for other models.

Adjust voltage of the constant voltage relay by bending end of coil side plate up or down as shown in illustration. If plate is bent up, the adjusted value becomes higher. If it is bent down, value becomes lower. Adjust pilot lamp relay by same method.

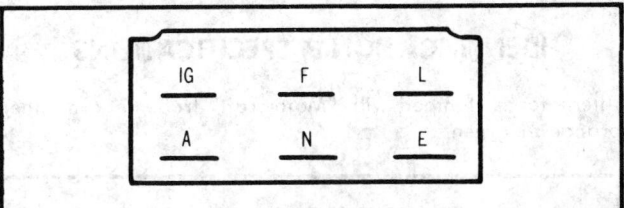

Fig. 1   Regulator Harness Connector

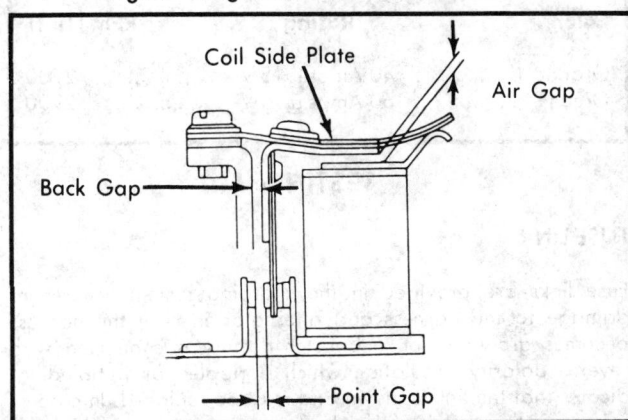

Fig. 2   Voltage Adjustment Point

	MITSUBISHI ALTERNATOR REGULATOR SPECIFICATIONS						
Reg. No.	VOLTAGE REGULATOR				PILOT LAMP RELAY		
	Output Volts	Air Gap in. (mm)	Back Gap in. (mm)	Point Gap in. (mm)	Air Gap in. (mm)	Back Gap in. (mm)	Point Gap in. (mm)
891418391	14-15	.028-.051 (.71-1.3)	.028-.059 (.71-1.5)	.012-.018 (.31-.45)	.039-.059 (1.0-1.5)	.028-.059 (.71-1.5)	.020-.035 (.71-1.1)

MOTORCRAFT ALTERNATORS

Fiesta

DESCRIPTION

Alternator is belt driven from engine. An external regulator controls charging rate by switching rotor field current in and out as required through brushes contacting slip rings. Alternating current is produced and converted to direct current by the diode rectifier assembly.

IDENTIFICATION & SPECIFICATIONS

Alternator is stamped with "Motorcraft" trademark in either orange or green.

APPLICATION		
Color	Rating	RPM (Hot)
Orange	40 Amps@15 V	2900
Green	60 Amps@15 V	2900

TESTING

FUSE LINK

Fuse links are provided in the charging system to prevent damage to the harness and alternator in case the harness becomes grounded or a booster battery is connected with reverse polarity. Insulation which is rippled or bubbled indicates that the link is blown and must be replaced. In case of vehicles with two fuse links, check the accessories link by turning headlamps or an accessory on. If fuses are not blown and they still fail to function, the link is probably blown and must be replaced.

INDICATOR LIGHT

Warning light should come on when starting engine and go off after engine is idling. If no light, check bulb and replace if burned out. If bulb is not burned out check for open circuit between switch and regulator. If light does not go out until engine reaches high RPM, check 15 ohm resistor connected in parallel with light.

VOLTAGE OUTPUT TEST

1) Attach voltmeter to battery and record voltage. Start engine and increase engine speed to 1500 RPM when normal operating temperature is reached. With NO electrical load on system, voltage should increase to at least 1 volt but not more than 2 volts above original reading.

2) Turn on heater blower motor to high speed and headlights to high beam. Increase engine speed to 2000 RPM and note battery voltage at least 0.5 volt above original reading with engine off.

3) If no-load voltage in step 1) exceeds 2 volts, assure that ground connections between regulator, alternator and engine are tight. Disconnect wiring plug Afrom regulator and recheck no-load voltage. If voltmeter now indicates battery voltage throughout the test, replace voltage regulator and recheck.

4) If voltage increase is excessive with regulator disconnected, repair shorted wiring harness between alternator and regulator.
NOTE — *If harness is shorted, regulator will have been damaged and must be replaced.*

5) If load voltage in step 2) did not increase or increase was less than 0.5 volt, check battery voltage at alternator "BAT" terminal. Disconnect regulator plug and check battery voltage at "A" terminal. If no voltage present at these terminals, repair wiring and repeat output test.

6) If battery voltage is present at both "BAT" and "A" terminals, connect jumper across "A" and "F" terminals of regulator plug. If field circuit is grounded, jumper will spark and heat. Check field circuit for ground and regulator for open before continuing.

7) To check field circuit, measure resistance between "F" terminal on regulator plug and negative battery cable clamp. Ohmmeter should read between 4 ohms and 250 ohms. No resistance indicates that the field circuit is grounded and requires alternator removal and repair.

8) Check resistance between "I" and "F" terminals with plug removed. Ohmmeter should indicate zero resistance. A reading of 10 or more ohms indicates an open connection in the regulator. Replace regulator and repair alternator field circuit.

9) If load voltage is still less than specified, remove jumper from regulator wiring plug and install a jumper between alternator "BAT" and "FLD" terminals. Repeat output test. If results are satisfactory, wiring harness is at fault and must be repaired or replaced. If load voltage increase is still less than 0.5 volt, alternator must be removed from vehicle for bench testing.

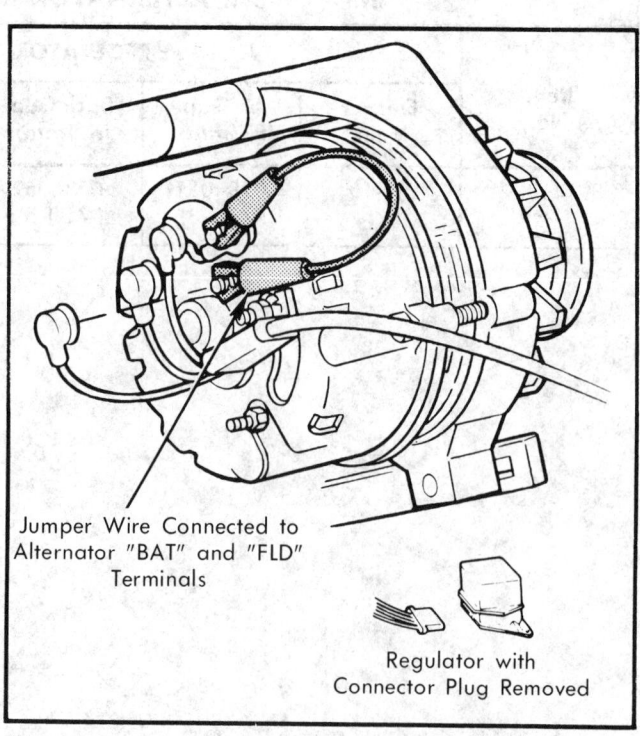

Jumper Wire Connected to Alternator "BAT" and "FLD" Terminals

Regulator with Connector Plug Removed

Fig. 1 Alternator with Jumper for Testing

MOTORCRAFT ALTERNATORS (Cont.)

OVERHAUL

DISASSEMBLY

1) Scribe mark across front and rear housings and stator for alignment during reassembly. Remove through bolts and separate front housing and rotor from rear housing and stator.

2) Remove terminal nuts and insulators from rear housing and separate stator/rectifier assembly from housing. Remove brushes and brush holder.

3) To remove stacked type rectifier, remove stator terminal screw and grounded screw by turning them ¼ turn to unlock from rectifier. Unsolder leads from rectifier using caution not to overheat rectifier assembly. To remove flat type rectifier, remove stator terminal screw by pressing straight out of rectifier. Do NOT turn screw or remove grounded screws. Unsolder leads from rectifier.

4) Remove front pulley and fan, then separate rotor from housing and bearing. Bearing may be replaced by removing retainer screws and retainer.

TESTING

1) Using 12 volt test lamp, check rotor continuity at slip rings and absence of ground between slip ring and rotor shaft. With ohmmeter, check for resistance of 4.0 to 4.4 ohms between slip rings.

2) Check resistance of .14 to .16 ohms between stator wires with ohmmeter. Check that windings are not grounded and have winding continuity with 12 volt test lamp.

3) Check diodes for continuity (approximately 60 ohms) in one direction only. If no continuity is observed in either direction, diode is open. If continuity is observed in both directions, diode is shorted. Rectifier assembly must be replaced if open or shorted diodes are found.

REASSEMBLY

1) Install bearing and retainer in front housing. Install rotor in housing to stop-ring, then install spacer, fan, pulley and nut with lock washer.

2) Assemble brush holder with brushes and springs, holding brushes in retracted position by inserting length of wire (paper clip) in holder. Solder leads from stator to rectifier pack and reverse disassembly procedure noting that scribe marks are aligned.

3) Remove brush retracting wire (paper clip) and seal hole with waterproof cement. Install and test alternator.

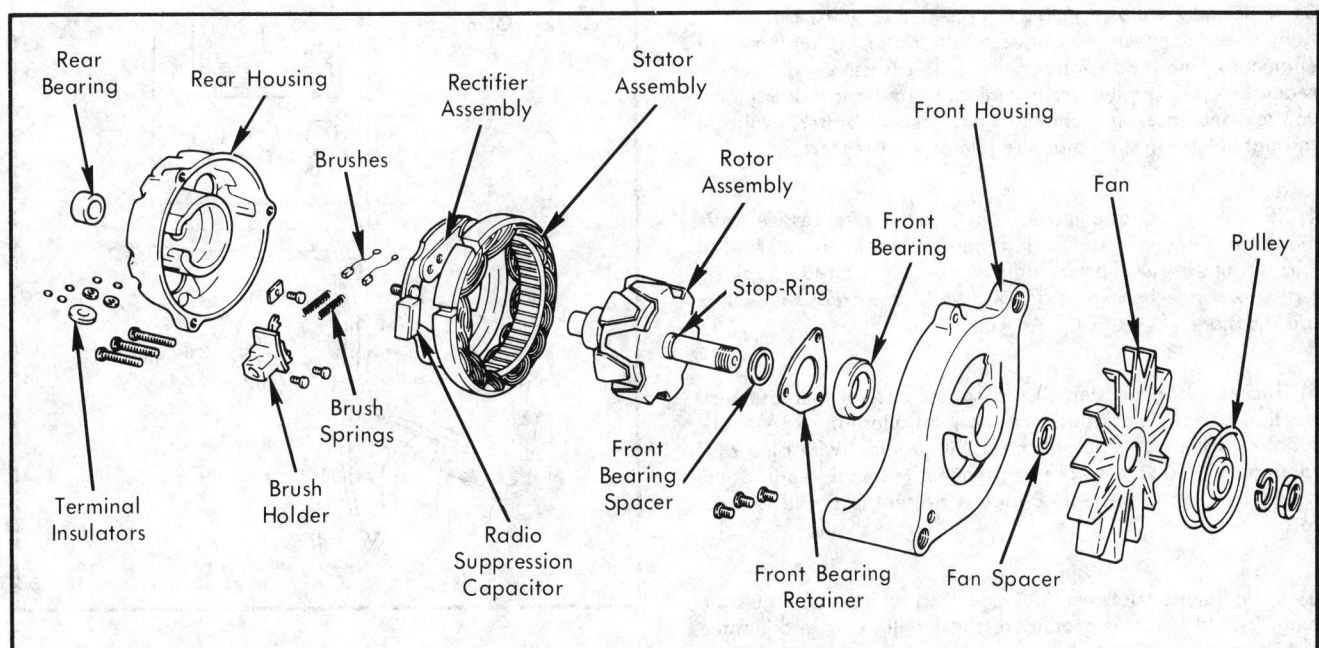

Fig. 2 Exploded View of Motorcraft Alternator

Alternators & Regulators

MOTORCRAFT REGULATORS

Fiesta

DESCRIPTION

Fiesta models equipped with Motorcraft 40 or 60 amp alternators have an externally mounted regulator. The regulator controls charging rate by switching rotor field current in and out as required.

TESTING

ON CAR TEST

NOTE — *Battery must be charged to at least 1.200 specific gravity before beginning test. All lights and electrical components must be OFF.*

1) Connect voltmeter to battery and note voltage for reference. Connect tachometer to engine and slowly increase engine RPM to about 1500 RPM as engine reaches normal operating temperature. With no electrical load, voltage should increase to at least one but not more than 2 volts higher than reference voltage. This is no-load voltage.

2) If voltage increase is within 1-2 volts, turn heater blower on high and headlights on high beam. Increase engine speed to about 2000 RPM and look for a voltage increase of at least .5 volt. This is load voltage. If both no-load and load voltage increases are within specifications, charging system is operating properly.

3) If no-load voltage increase exceeded 2 volts, clean and tighten all connections between alternator, regulator and engine. If no-load voltage is still excessive, disconnect regulator wiring plug from regulator and recheck no-load voltage increase. If voltmeter now reads battery voltage throughout the test, replace regulator and recheck.

4) If no-load voltage increase in step **3)** is excessive with regulator disconnected, wiring harness between alternator and regulator is shorted and must be repaired. Replace regulator and check that no-load voltage increase is within specifications.

5) If load voltage in step **2)** did not increase or increase was less than .5 volt, check battery voltage at alternator "BAT" terminal and then at regulator plug "A" terminal with plug disconnected. If no voltage present at either terminal, repair open wiring and repeat test. If voltage is present, proceed to step **6)**.

6) Install jumper between "A" and "F" terminals of regulator plug. If field circuit is grounded, spark will occur and jumper will heat when connected. If this happens, check field circuit for

ground and regulator for open before continuing. Leave jumper out of plug and check field circuit as follows: Set ohmmeter on low range and check for 4 to 250 ohms between "F" terminal on regulator plug and negative battery cable clamp. If no resistance, field circuit is grounded and alternator must be repaired or replaced.

7) Connect an ohmmeter between "I" and "F" terminal of regulator with plug removed. Ohmmeter should read zero resistance. If ohmmeter reads approximately 10 ohms, regulator has an open curcuit and must be replaced.

8) If field circuit test is satisfactory (step **6)**, leave jumper in place and perform voltage output test. If test results are now satisfactory, replace regulator and retest. If load voltage increase is still less than specified, remove jumper from plug and install between alternator "BAT" and "FLD" terminals. Repeat voltage output test. If test results are now satisfactory, wiring harness is at fault and must be repaired or replaced. If load voltage increase is still less than .5 volt, fault is in alternator.

NOTE — *There are no recommended adjustment procedures for this regulator. If not within specifications, regulator must be replaced.*

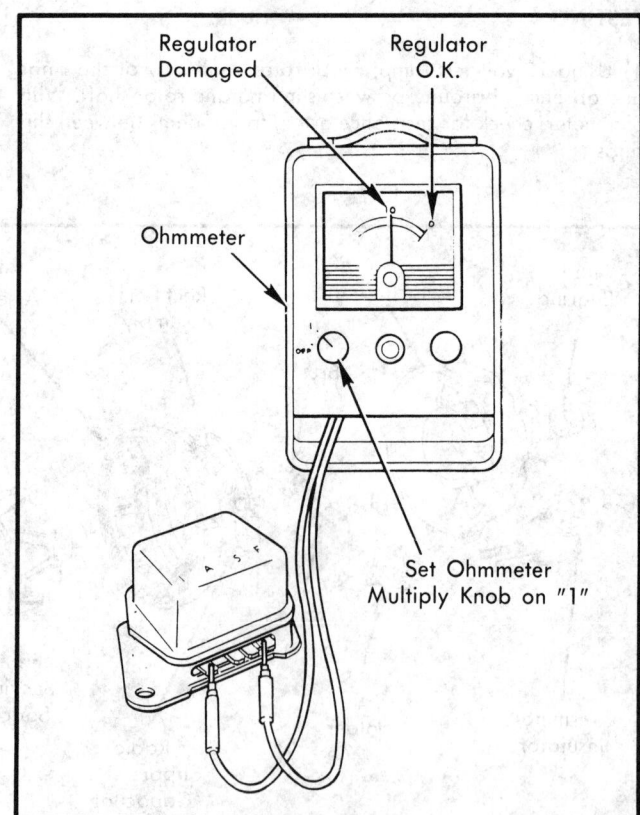

Fig. 1   Regulator Open Wire Test

NIPPONDENSO ALTERNATORS

Chrysler Corp. Imports
  Arrow (1600 cc)
Honda
  Accord
  Civic
  Prelude
Toyota
  Celica

Corolla
Corona
Land Cruiser
Pickup
Supra
Tercel

DESCRIPTION

Nippondenso alternators are conventional 3-phase alternators utilizing 6 diodes (3 positive and 3 negative) to rectify current. Charge control may be either integrated circuit (IC) or externally mounted contact point type.

APPLICATION

Model	Amps	①Part No.
Arrow	45	100211 0140
Honda		
Accord	50	31100-689-014
Civic	45	31100-PA0-662
Prelude	50	31100-689-014
Toyota		
Celica	55	27020 28012
Corolla	50	27020 26101
Corona	55	27020 28012
Land Cruiser		
Standard	40	27020 61013
Optional	55	27020 61071
Pickup		
Standard	40	27020 38104
Optional	55	27020 38111
Supra	60	27020 45140
Tercel		
Standard	50	27020 15040
Optional	55	27020 15050

① — Vehicle manufacturer part number.

TESTING

ON CAR TEST

Preliminary Inspection — Check alternator mounting and drive belt tension. Inspect turn signal and gauge fuses. Check alternator and regulator wire connections for tightness. Battery must be fully charged prior to beginning test.

No Load Test — 1) Connect a suitable test meter (09081-00010 alternator tester for models with special connector from regulator, or a common regulator tester) as shown in illustrations. Start engine and increase speed gradually to 2000-2300 RPM. Read "B" terminal voltage. Voltage should be 13.5-14.8 with a current draw of not more than 10 amps. If current is over specifications, battery is discharged or internally shorted.

2) If voltage is not steady, dirty regulator points or defective connection at "F" terminal may be the cause.

3) If voltage reading is too high, one of the following problems may be indicated: Regulator low speed gap too wide. High speed point gap too wide. High speed point gap resistance too high. Open circuit regulator coil or voltage relay coil. Open circuit regulator "N" terminal or "B" terminal. Low speed point contact tension too heavy. Loose regulator ground connection.

"F" Terminal Voltage Test — 1) With regulator tester, stop engine, disconnect alternator wiring connector, turn ignition switch to "ON" and measure voltage between "F" and "E" terminals of connector. Voltage should be 12 volts. If voltage is zero or very low, note the following possible causes; blown fuse, regulator "IG" terminal open, or regulator high speed points are burned.

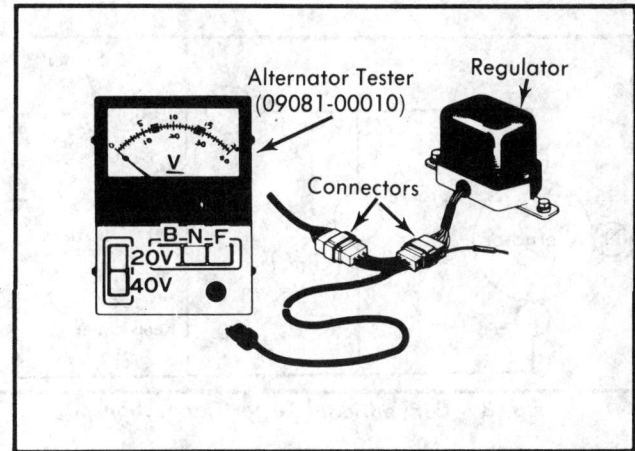

Fig. 1   Connections for Tester 0981-00010

2) With alternator tester (09081-00010) connected and engine idling, press switch "F" on tester. Gradually increase engine speed to 2300 RPM. Needle on tester should deflect in small steps from 12-7 volts, 6-4 volts and 3-1 volts. If voltage does not drop as specified, regulator is defective or out of adjustment.

Regulator Circuit Resistance — Disconnect regulator connector plug and check resistance between regulator "IG" and "F" terminals with an ohmmeter. If any resistance is shown, the low speed contact in the regulator is defective.

Load Test — With regulator tester connected as illustrated, start engine and turn on all lights and accessories. Run engine at 1100 RPM and check amperage and voltage. If reading is low due to fully charged battery, it may be necessary to crank engine (with coil disconnected) for about 15 seconds to discharge battery. If amperage is low when rechecking, rectifiers are open or shorted, or stator coil is open or shorted.

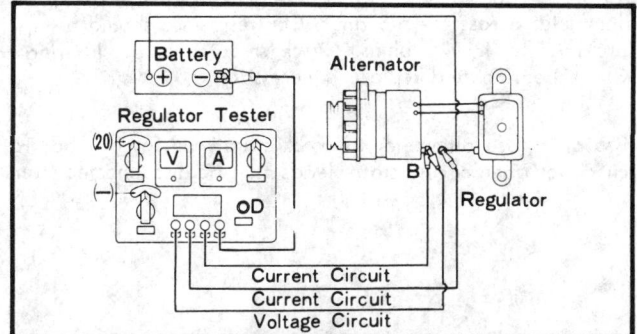

Fig. 2   Connections for Regulator Tester

NIPPONDENSO ALTERNATORS (Cont.)

Performance Test Using Conventional Tester — 1) Attach tester as illustrated and increase engine speed until reverse current (approximately 2.5 amp.) ceases to flow to rotor field coil.

2) Turn off No. 1 switch and increase speed until voltmeter indicates 14V. If speed is under 1000 RPM, alternator performance is satisfactory.

3) Increase load resistance to near maximum so that nearly no current will flow. Close switches 1 and 2 while gradually increasing speed. Rated output should be reached by approximately 5000 RPM with satisfactory alternator.

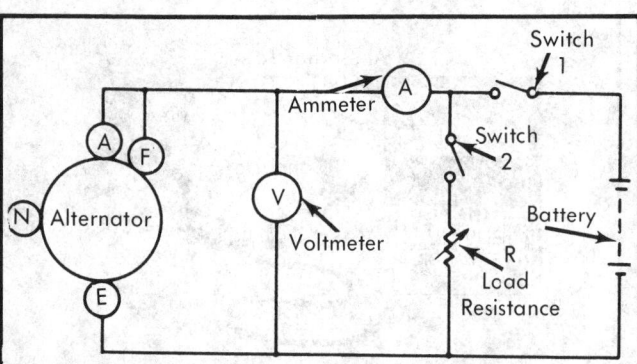

Fig. 3 Conventional Tester Connections

OVERHAUL

DISASSEMBLY

1) Remove retaining screws and pry drive end frame from stator with screwdriver. If necessary, tap lightly on drive end frame with mallet. Secure rotor core in padded vise and remove pulley attaching nut. Withdraw pulley, fan and spacer. Press rotor from drive end frame. Remove bearing retainer from end frame, then remove bearing, felt cover and felt ring.

2) Remove rectifier holder securing nuts and brush holder attaching screws. Separate stator with rectifier holders and brush holders from rectifier end frame. Remove brush lead terminal and stator coil "N" terminal from brush holder using a small screwdriver. When removing brush holder assembly, DO NOT cut "N" terminal lead or melt the solder.

TESTING

Rotor — Check rotor for open field windings using an ohmmeter across the slip rings. Coil resistance should be approximately 4.1-4.3 ohms. Check smoothness of slip rings. Check bearing and replace if necessary.

Stator — Use ohmmeter to check stator coil for ground. To check for open circuit, stator leads must be disconnected from diode leads. To disconnect leads from diodes, unsolder as quickly as possible with a low watt iron. Check 4 leads of stator coil for continuity between each lead. If no continuity or if resistance is noted, stator coil must be replaced.

Diode Test — With diode assembly on bench, contact diode plate with one probe and each of 3 diode leads with other probe. Note ohmmeter reading, then reverse probes and repeat test. Check both positive and negative diodes in this manner. All diodes should show a low reading in one direction and NO reading in the opposite direction. If any rectifier (diode) is defective, replace holder assembly.

NOTE — *Also see General Servicing in this section.*

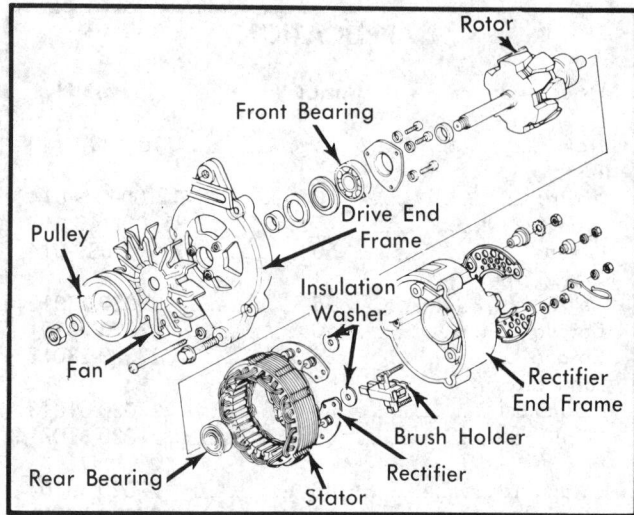

Fig. 4 Disassembled View of Nippondenso Alternator

PARTS REPLACEMENT

Brushes — Check for cracks and minimum length of .22" (5.5 mm). If damaged or worn beyond limit, replace brushes. Brushes should slide smoothly in holders. Install new spring when replacing brush. Solder brush wire keeping brush protruded length to .51" (13 mm). For heavy duty alternators, brush should protrude .73" (18.5 mm) from holder.

REASSEMBLY

1) Press brushes into holder against spring tension. Insert a retaining wire through access hole in rectifier end frame and into brush holder to prevent brushes from falling. Remove wire after assembly to end frame is completed.

2) Pack multipurpose grease into rear bearing and press bearing onto rotor shaft. Pack drive end bearing with grease and install in drive end frame. Install felt ring, cover and bearing retainer.

3) Ensure that drive end frame with rotor and rectifier end frame with stator are assembled in original alignment. Tighten body screws and remove brush retaining wire.

Alternators & Regulators

NIPPONDENSO REGULATORS

Honda   Corolla
  Accord   Corona
  Civic   Cressida
  Prelude   Land Cruiser
Toyota   Pickup
  Celica

DESCRIPTION

Nippondenso regulators may be either single or double element type. Single element type has a voltage regulator element only while 2 element type has both voltage regulator and a voltage warning relay. Single element type is normally fitted to units with an ammeter, while double element type normally has a charge warning light.

APPLICATION

Model	Part No.①
Honda (All Models)	SAO 672
Toyota	
Celica	27700 38100
Corolla	27700 26030
Corona	27700 38100
Cressida	27700 41050
Land Cruiser	27700 24020
Pickup	27700 38120

① — Vehicle manufacturer part number. Some regulators are integrated circuit (IC) type. Part number furnished for information only.

TESTING

VOLTAGE REGULATOR

NOTE — Substitution of a known good regulator for one suspected of malfunctioning will frequently save time during testing.

Toyota — Disconnect wire from "B" terminal of alternator and connect to negative of ammeter. Connect test lead from ammeter positive terminal to "B" terminal of alternator. With engine running at varying speeds from idle to 2000 RPM, voltage should be 13.8-14.8 volts and amperage should be less than 10 amps. If not within specifications, adjust or replace regulator as required. See ADJUSTMENT.

NOTE — If a battery/alternator tester is available, connect and test according to tester manufacturer's instructions.

Honda — Connect voltmeter across battery terminals and ammeter between positive terminal and main fuse. (Main fuse wire from battery disconnected.) Ensure that all lights and accessories are OFF and disconnect negative cable from battery with engine idling. Vary engine speed from 2000 to 4000 RPM and note voltage reading between 13.5 and 14.5 volts. If not within specifications, adjust or replace regulator as required. See ADJUSTMENT.

CAUTION — If engine stops when battery negative cable is removed, DO NOT attempt to restart engine until cable is connected.

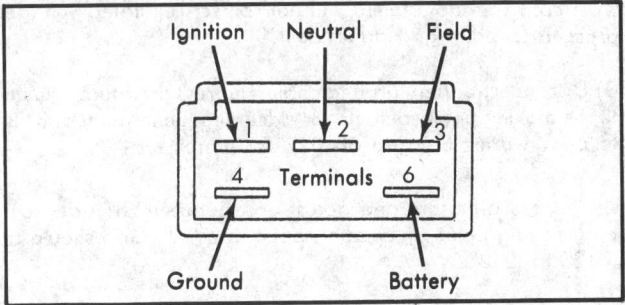

Fig. 1   Terminal Positions for Honda Connector

ADJUSTMENT

NOTE — Adjustments are not applicable to sealed units. If points are slightly oxidized or pitted, dress contacts with sandpaper (400 grit or finer). If points are oxidized or pitted excessively, replace regulator assembly.

Voltage Relay — Connect voltmeter between "N" terminal (white wire) and ground then increase engine speed gradually. Voltmeter reading should be 4.0-5.8 volts when indicator light goes out. Adjust cut-in voltage by adjusting armature core gap and point gap using following procedures.

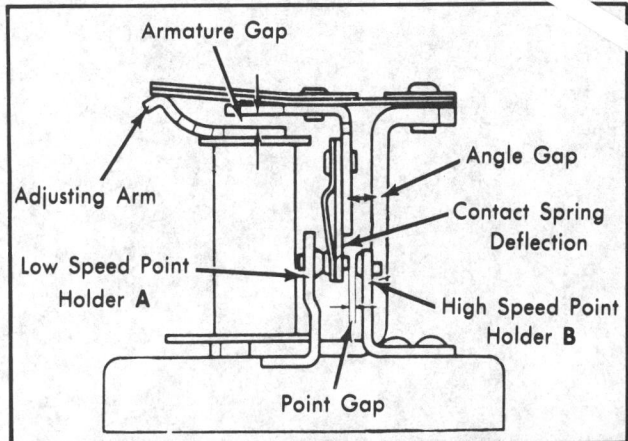

Fig. 2   Adjustments for Voltage Relay

1) If cut-in voltage is too high, adjust by bending core adjusting arm down. Bend arm up if cut-in voltage is too low.

2) If adjustment of core arm does not correct cut-in voltage, proceed with point gap adjustment. Disconnect negative cable from battery. Check armature core gap with armature depressed until moving point is in contact with "B" side point. Armature core gap should be .012" or more. Adjust by bending point arm "B".

3) Release the armature and adjust the gap between the "B" side point and the moving point by bending point arm "A". Point gap should be .016" to .047".

4) After point gap adjustment, recheck cut-in voltage. If not within 4.0-5.8 volts, repeat cut-in voltage adjustment.

Voltage Regulator — If the no load regulated voltage is not within the 13.8-14.8 volt range, adjust regulator as follows:

1) If regulated voltage is too high, adjust by bending armature adjusting arm down. If voltage is too low, bend arm up.

NIPPONDENSO REGULATORS (Cont.)

2) If core arm adjustment will not correct regulated voltage, proceed to point gap adjustment.

3) Disconnect battery ground cable. Depress armature arm until the moving point contacts "B" side point. Bend point arm "B" to obtain armature gap of .012" or more.

4) Release armature and adjust gap between "B" side point and moving point by bending point arm "A". Gap should be .012" to .018".

5) After gap adjustment is made, recheck no load regulated voltage under operating test. Repeat core arm adjustment if necessary.

NOTE — *Regulator cover must be installed after adjustments prior to further testing.*

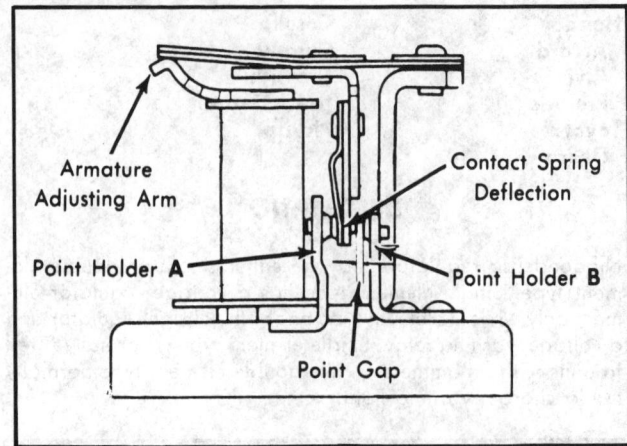

Fig. 3   Adjustments for Voltage Regulator

SEV MARCHAL ALTERNATORS

Renault
 Le Car
Volvo
 DL
 GL
 GT

DESCRIPTION

Alternator is a conventional three-phase, self-rectifying type. Six silicon rectifier diodes are connected to form a full-wave, three-phase rectifying bridge. Three exciter diodes are connected to stator windings and have a common junction point.

APPLICATION

Model	Rating	Part No.
Renault	50	7701 389 063
Volvo	70	1258 995

OVERHAUL

DISASSEMBLY

1) Remove brush holder attaching screws and carefully remove brush holder. Scribe a mark on end frames for reassembly reference, then remove four through bolts. Separate end frames by inserting two screwdrivers into notches on sides of alternator.

CAUTION — *Do not insert screwdrivers deeper than .08" (2 mm) or damage may occur to stator windings.*

2) Remove nuts and washers for positive and negative diode holders from end frame. Carefully remove stator from end frame. Hold rotor in a vise using special wood blocks so no damage will occur to rotor. Remove nut, washer, pulley, fan, key and spacer.

NOTE — *Check direction spacer under pulley fan faces for assembly reference.*

3) Remove three attaching screws for bearing cap, then push rotor shaft from end frame. Press bearing from end frame. Use a puller to remove bearing from slip ring end of rotor.

BENCH TESTING

NOTE — *Use 40V AC for testing rotor and stator only.*

Rotor — Check rotor winding resistance across slip rings with ohmmeter and insulation between slip rings and rotor with test lamp. Replace rotor if grounded or if resistance is greater than 4.4 ohms.

Stator — Check stator coils for resistance with leads disconnected using an ohmmeter. Check for shorts between core and leads with test lamp. Replace stator if grounded or if resistance is greater than .15 ohm.

Diodes — Use ohmmeter to perform conduction test on diodes. Observe current flow in one direction only from terminal to plate for positive diodes and from plate to terminal for negative diodes. If open or shorted, replace entire diode assembly.

NOTE — *Diodes may be either cylindrical or spherical in construction. Terminals must be disconnected during testing.*

REASSEMBLY

1) Press on inner race of bearing to position bearing on slip ring end of rotor shaft. Press on outer race to press bearing into end frame. Install bearing cap and three attaching screws. Press end frame with bearing assembly firmly onto rotor shaft. Install spacer, key, fan, pulley, washer and nut onto rotor shaft. Tighten nut to 29 ft.lbs. (4 mkg).

2) Install insulating washers and sleeves onto positive diode holder, then install stator to end frame while inserting brush holder through opening in end frame. Install nuts and washers to secure diode holders. Check that "O" ring in end frame bearing seat does not block vent hole.

3) Assemble two end frames along with stator and rotor assemblies together, then secure with four through bolts. Install brush holder attaching screws and tighten.

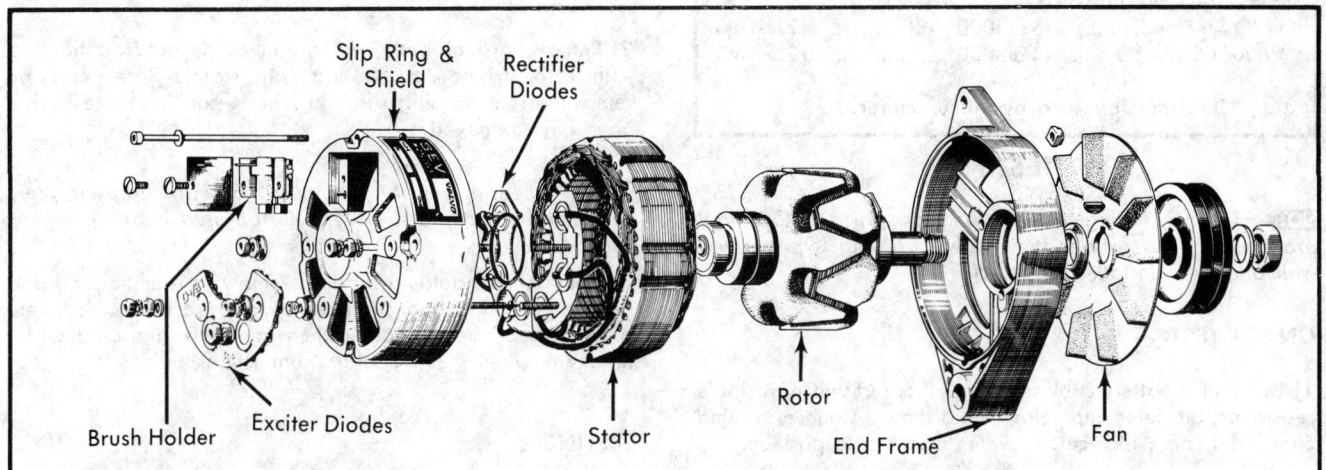

Fig. 1   *Exploded View of Alternator*

SEV MOTOROLA ALTERNATORS

Peugeot	Volkswagen
604	Dasher
Porsche	Jetta
911SC	Rabbit
924	Rabbit Pickup
928	Scirocco

DESCRIPTION

SEV Motorola alternators are conventional three-phase, self-rectifying type alternators. Six silicon diodes (three positive and three negative) are used to rectify AC current.

NOTE — *Either SEV Motorola or Bosch alternators may be used. Due to the wide variance in application and output for the various models, not all individual part numbers and ratings may be shown. Always check identification plate attached to housing.*

APPLICATION

Model	Amp Rating	①Part No.
Peugeot 604	55	5702.52
Porsche		
911SC	70	911 603 120 02
924	75	063 903 017
928	90	928 603 113 03
Volkswagen (All Models)		
W/O Air Cond	55	049 903 015X
	65	055 903 017X
W/Air Cond	65	055 903 017AX

① — Vehicle manufacturer part number.

SPECIFICATIONS

Application	Amps/RPM	Voltage
Peugeot 604	55@4000	14
Porsche (All Models)	①	14
Volkswagen (All Models)		
W/O Air Cond	25@3000	12.5-14.5
W/Air Cond	44@3000	12.5-14.5

① — Data not furnished by manufacturer.

TESTING

NOTE — *Some testing is described as part of Overhaul procedure in this article. The following testing is performed with alternator installed on vehicle.*

ON CAR TEST

1) Disconnect battery cables and install cutout switch, variable resistance, ammeter and voltmeter as shown. Connect ground cable and check that cutout switch is in closed position.

2) Start engine and run at test RPM. Adjust variable resistance to give amperage readings as follows: Type 1 and models with air conditioning — 45 Amps, Type 2 — 30 Amps, other VW's without air conditioning and Audi Fox — 25 Amps. Open battery cutout switch, separating battery from test circuit. Load current is now determined by variable resistance.

3) Readjust variable resistance to provide Test Output Amperage. Voltage should be as specified.

CAUTION — *Never run alternator without battery connected unless variable resistor is installed to provide load. Alternator or regulator or both could be severely damaged without providing current load.*

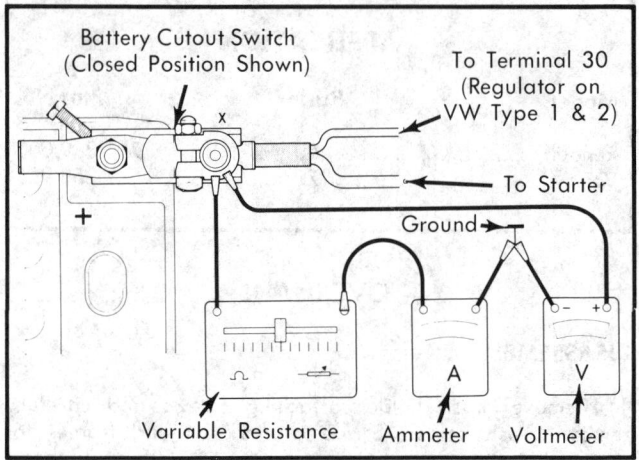

Fig. 1   Alternator Testing Set-Up

OVERHAUL

NOTE — *Since battery current reaches the alternator when the ignition is not on, battery ground strap should be disconnected when removing or installing alternator.*

DISASSEMBLY

1) Remove drive pulley and cooling fan. Remove regulator and brush assembly. Mark front and rear housing along with stator for proper orientation during reassembly.

2) Remove through bolts and carefully separate front housing with rotor from rear housing with stator. Rotor may be removed from housing after bearing retaining plate screws have been removed.

NOTE — *Bearings must be removed and installed using press with suitable adaptors. Never reinstall used bearings.*

3) Remove nuts holding diode assembly to rear housing and separate housing and stator. If diodes are faulty, complete assembly must be replaced rather than individual diodes. Use heat sink when making solder connections.

TESTING

Stator — Check stator for short circuits. If one or more coils are burned, stator shows evidence of shorts. Connect 12 volt,

SEV MOTOROLA ALTERNATORS (Cont.)

brush holder frame and "−" brush. Lamp should give steady light. If test results are not satisfactory or brush length is less than ³⁄₁₆" (5 mm), replace brush holder.

CAUTION − *Use only specified test lamp. DO NOT use 110 or 220 volt test lamp on this or any other alternator test procedure.*

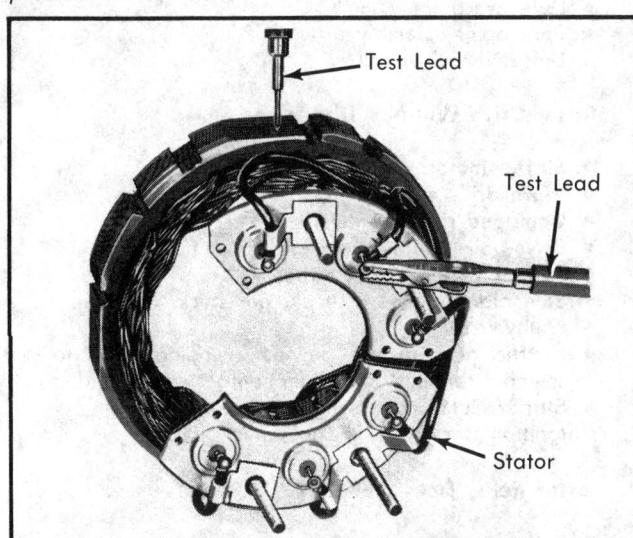

Fig. 2   Checking Stator for Shorts

Diodes − Check diodes with a diode tester for shorts or open circuits. If any diode is defective, entire diode holder with diodes installed must be replaced. If diode tester is not available, diode leads should be quickly and carefully unsoldered and tested with an ohmmeter. Diodes should show low resistance in flow direction and high resistance in reverse direction.

Rotor − Check that slip rings are not dirty or burned. Check winding for breakage or damaged isolation. Measure resistance between slip rings. Normal resistance should be approximately 4.5 ohms. If winding is faulty, rotor must be replaced.

NOTE − *It is recommended that bearings be replaced whenever alternator is disassembled.*

Brush Holder − Connect a test lamp between brushes. Lamp should NOT light. Connect test lamp between "DF" terminal and "+" brush. Lamp should give steady light even if brush and/or terminal cable is moved. Connect test lamp between

2-5 watt test lamp between stator plates and a terminal on stator. If lamp lights, isolation between stator winding and stator plates is defective and stator should be replaced.

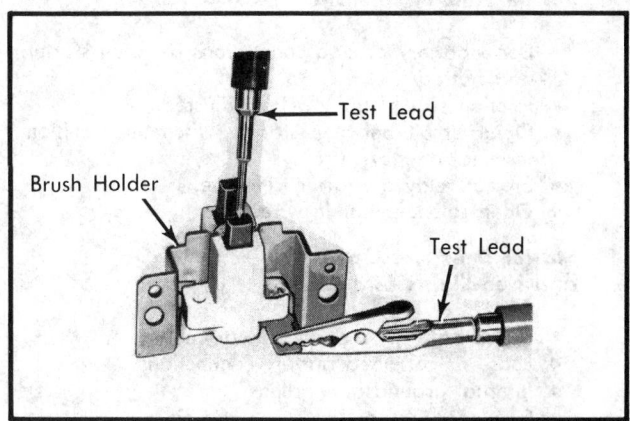

Fig. 3   Checking Brush Holder

NOTE − *Brush length is measured between brush contact surface and holder, with brush resting against spring.*

PARTS REPLACEMENT

Diodes − Mark leads connecting stator to diodes, then quickly and carefully unsolder leads. Place new diode holder in exact position of holder being replaced. Solder new leads while holding with pliers acting as a heat sink. Use minimum 100-watt, well heated soldering iron. Never change places of diode holders. Positive holder is isolated from frame by means of isolation washers and sleeves, and its diodes are marked in red. Negative holder is not isolated and its diodes are marked in black.

CAUTION − *Heat sink must be used during soldering to avoid damage to diodes from overheating.*

REASSEMBLY

Alternator is assembled by reversing disassembly procedures while noting the following: Rotor must be pressed into drive end shield. Connect test lamp between "B+" terminal and alternator frame, then reverse connections. Lamp should light only in one direction. After completion of assembly, test run alternator on bench using same procedure as described for On Car Testing.

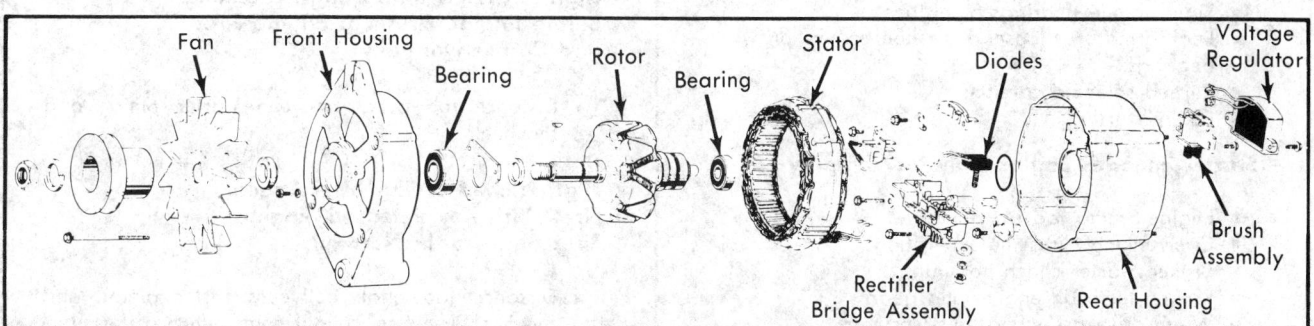

Fig. 4   Disassembled View of SEV Motorola Alternator
(Volkswagen Shown)

Starters

STARTING SYSTEMS TROUBLE SHOOTING

CONDITION & POSSIBLE CAUSE	CONDITION & POSSIBLE CAUSE

Starter Fails to Operate

- Dead battery or bad connections between starter and battery.
- Ignition switch faulty or misadjusted.
- Open circuit between starter switch and ignition terminal on starter relay.
- Starter relay or starter defective.
- Open solenoid pull-in wire.

Starter Does Not Operate and Headlights Dim

- Weak battery or dead battery cell.
- Loose or corroded battery connections.
- Internal ground in windings.
- Grounded starter fields.
- Armature rubbing on pole shoes.

Starter Turns but Engine Does Not Rotate

- Starter clutch slipping.
- Broken clutch housing.
- Pinion shaft rusted or dry.
- Engine basic timing incorrect.
- Broken teeth on engine ring gear.

Starter Will Not Crank Engine

- Faulty overrunning clutch.
- Broken clutch housing.
- Broken ring gear teeth.
- Armature shaft sheared or reduction gear teeth stripped.
- Weak battery.
- Faulty solenoid.
- Starter spins slowly and draws high current.
- Poor grounds.
- Engine siezed.
- Ignition switch faulty or misadjusted.

Starter Cranks Engine Slowly

- Battery weak or defective.
- Engine overheated.
- Engine oil too heavy.
- Poor battery-to-starter connections.
- Current draw too low or too high.
- Tight engine bearings or pistons.
- Bent armature, loose pole shoe screws or worn bearings.
- Burned solenoid contacts.
- Faulty starter.

Starter Engages Engine Only Momentarily

- Engine timing too far advanced.
- Overrunning clutch not operating.
- Broken starter clutch housing.
- Broken teeth on engine ring gear.
- Weak drive assembly thrust spring.
- Weak hold-in coil.

Starter Drive Will Not Engage

- Defective point assembly.
- Poor point assembly ground.
- Defective pull-in coil.

Starter Drive Will Not Disengage

- Starter motor loose on mountings.
- Worn drive end bushing.
- Damaged ring gear teeth.
- Drive yolk return spring broken or missing.
- Faulty ignition starter switch.
- Solenoid contact switch plunger stuck.
- Faulty relay.
- Insufficient clearance between winding leads to solenoid terminal and main contact in solenoid.
- Starter clutch not disengaging.
- Ignition starter switch contacts sticking.

Starter Relay Does Not Close

- Dead battery.
- Faulty wiring.
- Neutral safety switch faulty.
- Starter relay faulty.

Starter Relay Operates but Solenoid Does Not

- Faulty solenoid switch, switch connections or switch wiring.
- Broken lead or loose soldered connections.

Solenoid Plunger Vibrates When Switch is Engaged

- Weak battery.
- Solenoid contacts corroded.
- Faulty wiring.
- Broken connections inside switch cover.
- Open hold-in wire.

Low Current Draw

- Worn brushes or weak brush springs.

High Pitched Whine During Cranking Before Engine Fires but Engine Fires and Cranks Normally

- Distance too great between starter pinion and flywheel.

High Pitched Whine After Engine Fires With Key Released. Engine Fires and Cranks Normally

- Distance too small between starter pinion and flywheel. Flywheel runout contributes to the intermittent nature.

BOSCH

Audi   **Peugeot**
BMW   **Porsche**
Fiat   **Saab**
Fiesta   **Volkswagen**
Mercedes-Benz   **Volvo**

DESCRIPTION

Starter is a brush type, series wound electric motor equipped with an overrunning clutch. Integral solenoid mounted on the starter engages starter pinion gear with flywheel ring gear when starter is engaged. Field frame is enclosed by commutator end frame and drive bushing and carries pole shoes and field coils. A spline on the drive end of the armature shaft carries the overrunning clutch and pinion assembly. Armature shaft is supported in sintered bronze bushings in the commutator end frame and drive end housings.

APPLICATION

Model	①Bosch Part No.
Audi	
4000	211 218
5000	311 122
5000 Diesel	362 069
BMW	
320i	311 100
528i, 633CSi & 733i	314 025
Fiat Strada & X1/9	212 210
Fiesta	211 227
Mercedes-Benz	
240 & 300 Series	362 047
280 & 450 Series	314 018
Peugeot	
504	362 044
505 Diesel	362 045
505 Gasoline	208 211
604	311 124
Porsche	
911SC	312 100
924	311 122
924 Turbo (Standard)	208 221
924 Turbo (Heavy Duty)	311 134
928	312 102
Saab 99, 900 & 900 Turbo	311 108
Volkswagen	
Dasher	
Gasoline	211 218
Diesel	314 014
Jetta, Rabbit & Scirocco (Gasoline)	
Man. Trans.	211 223
Auto. Trans.	212 206
Rabbit (Diesel)	
Man. Trans.	314 012
Auto. Trans.	312 105
Vanagon	
Man. Trans.	211 221
Auto. Trans.	212 208
Volvo	
DL, GL & GT	311 103
GLE & Coupe	311 105
Diesel	②1257325

① — Bosch starter basic part number is 0 001.
② — Volvo part number.

TESTING

Lock Test— Mount starter in a test stand to allow starter torque measurement (follow manufacturers instructions). With voltage adjusted to specifications, ammeter reading and starter torque should be within specifications.

Free Running Test— With starter in test bench, take readings of starter current, voltage and RPM. Readings should be within specifications.

NOTE — Starter must be mounted to prevent meshing of pinion and ring gear even in engaged position. If starter has warmed up during previous tests, RPM will be higher.

SPECIFICATIONS

Brush Length & Spring Tension

Application	In.(mm)	Lbs. (g)
208 xxx	.52 (13)	2.5-3.1(1150-1350)
211 xxx	.52 (13)	2.5-2.9(1150-1300)
212 xxx	.52 (13)	2.4-2.7(1080-1220)
311 xxx	.39 (10)	2.5-2.9(1150-1300)
312 xxx	.39 (10)	1.8-2.0(800-900)
314 xxx	.52 (13)	2.5-2.9(1150-1300)
362 xxx	.61 (15.5)	2.5-2.9(1150-1300)

OVERHAUL

DISASSEMBLY

1) Clamp starter in vise and remove nut and washer from solenoid main terminal connection. Remove solenoid mounting screws and guide solenoid body away from drive end housing and plunger. Disconnect plunger from actuating lever.

2) Remove screws and cap with rubber seal from commutator end housing. Wipe grease from armature shaft and remove "C" clip with shims. Remove through bolts or nuts from studs and lift off commutator end housing.

3) Lift springs clear of brushes and slide brushes from holders. Remove brush plate from housing. Separate drive end housing and armature assembly from yoke by tapping apart.

4) Remove armature assembly from drive end housing while at the same time uncoupling actuating arm. If necessary to remove actuating arm, first remove rubber insert from drive end housing. Remove pivot arm screw and nut and extract actuating arm.

5) To remove drive pinion assembly from armature shaft, separate thrust collar from over "C" clip. Remove "C" clip from its groove and drive pinion assembly off armature shaft.

BOSCH (Cont.)

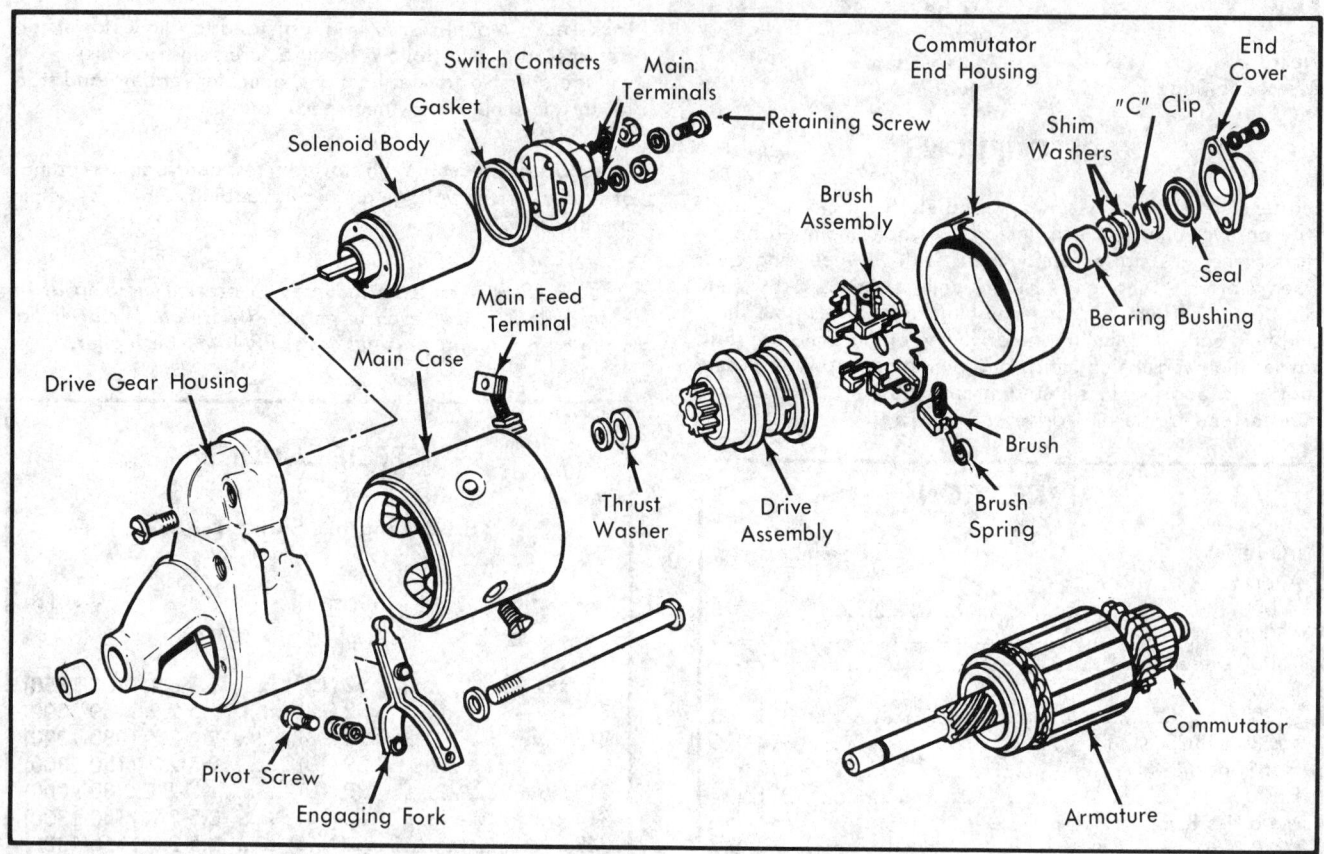

Fig. 1 Disassembled View of Typical Bosch Starter

CLEANING & INSPECTING

Clean all parts with suitable cleaning agent. Inspect for wear or damage, then apply thin coat of oil to running surfaces.

PARTS REPLACEMENT & TESTING

Brushes & Springs —Check brush spring pressure with suitable spring scale. Check brushes for minimum length and freedom of movement in holders. If replacement is necessary, replace all brushes by cutting old brush leads midway between connection and old brush. Solder new brushes to original leads.

Armature — **1)** Check commutator to shaft (or core) for short circuit with 110 volt AC test lamp. Test lamp should not light, however slight glow may occur due to dampness. Check armature coils for short circuit between windings using an armature growler.

2) Check commutator for pits, burns or rough surface. If out of round exceeds .002" (.05 mm), or grooves or burned spots cannot be removed with fine crocus cloth, commutator must be tur-

ned. Undercut insulation between commutator bars to a maximum depth of .024" (.6 mm).

NOTE — *Never use emery cloth or a file on commutator; turn on a lathe only.*

Bushings — Self-lubricating bushings should be replaced only when worn or damaged. Force out bushings with suitable mandrel. Clean hole and remove burrs. Before pressing new bushing in place, soak bushing in suitable lubricant for at least 30 minutes.

Drive Assembly — Replace drive when damaged or teeth are worn. *See Disassembly.*

Solenoid Plunger (Armature) — Plunger must move in and out of solenoid body when disconnected from pinion drive lever. If corroded, clean thoroughly before proceeding with tests.

Solenoid Pull-In Coil — Connect jumper wires between a 12 volt battery and the solenoid as shown in *Fig. 2.* Armature should pull in suddenly and return when electrical connection is broken.

BOSCH (Cont.)

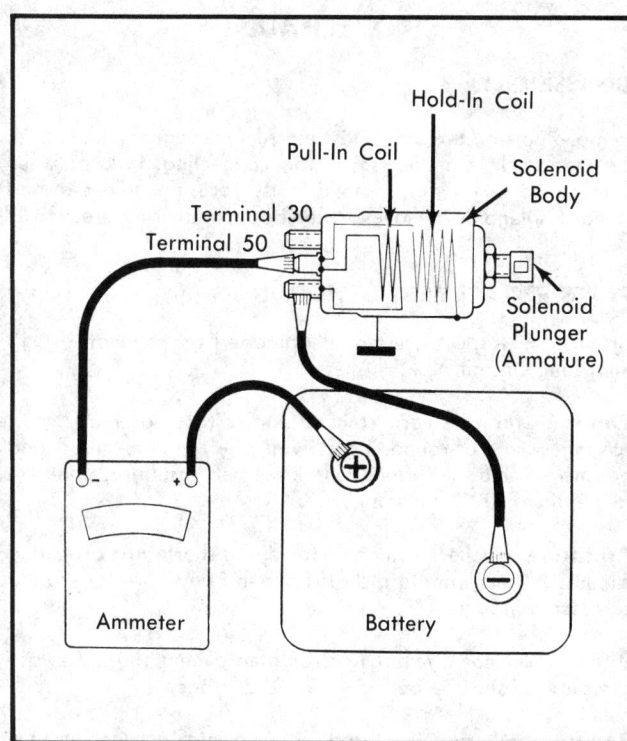

Fig. 2 Typical Connections for Pull-In Test

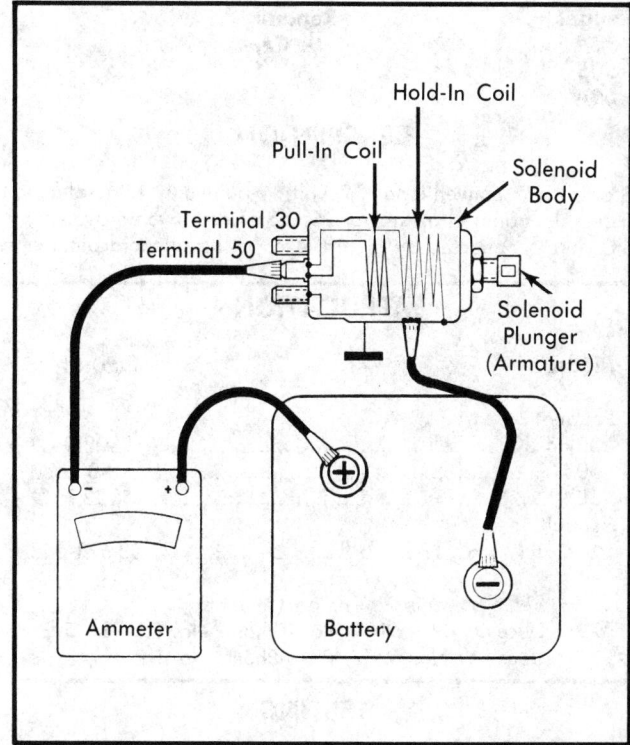

Fig. 3 Typical Connections for Hold-In Test

Hold-In Coil — Connect jumper wires as shown in *Fig. 3* while pressing armature into solenoid by hand. Armature should remain held in. Disconnect jumper terminal 50 and armature should immediately return to its outer position.

NOTE — *Do not attempt to repair solenoid. If either test is unsatisfactory, install new solenoid.*

REASSEMBLY

1) Slide drive pinion assembly and thrust washer onto armature shaft. Install "C" clip into groove in armature shaft and pull thrust washer up over clip. Align fork in drive end housing and insert pivot pin. Slide armature assembly into drive end housing, coupling the shift fork onto the drive pinion flange.

2) Install rubber insert in drive end housing. Guide yoke assembly over armature while aligning notch with rubber insert. Tap yoke into full contact with drive end housing.

3) Install brush assembly noting that cutouts in brush plate slide over through bolts on models so equipped. On models with screws, brush plate cutouts align with loops in field windings. Plates are properly positioned when screws are installed in commutator end housing. Install brushes and springs assuring that field winding brush leads do not contact yoke.

4) Slide commutator end housing into position and secure with nuts and washers or screws, as appropriate. Install drive end housing. Install shims onto armature shaft at commutator end to eliminate end play and install "C" clip in groove.

5) Install bearing cap seal on commutator end housing. Lubricate end of armature shaft with lithium based grease and install bearing cap. Lubricate plunger hook and place in position over shift fork in drive end housing. Install solenoid body with return spring properly positioned, then tighten mounting screws and field connections.

STARTER PERFORMANCE SPECIFICATIONS

Model	No Load Test		Amps.	Lock Test Volts	Torque	Solenoid Pull-In Volts
	Amps.	RPM				
208 xxx	35-55	6000-8000	320-410	8.5	9.4 ft.lbs.	7.5
211 xxx	35-55	6000-9000	340-430	8.5	8.7 ft.lbs.	8.0
212 xxx	35-55	6000-8000	320-410	8.5	9.4 ft.lbs.	7.5
311 xxx	30-50	5500-7500	350-450	8.5	13.0 ft.lbs.	7.5
312 xxx	55-85	8500-10,500	650-730	6.0	13.7 ft.lbs.	8.0
314 xxx	50-80	7300-9300	690-780	6.0	16.6 ft.lbs.	7.5
362 xxx	65-95	6500-8500	1100-1300	7.0	32.5 ft.lbs.	7.5

Starters

DUCELLIER & PARIS-RHONE

Peugeot	Renault
504	Le Car
505	
604	

DESCRIPTION

Starter is a conventional 12 volt, 4 pole unit with solenoid assembly mounted on starter case. Starters have an overrunning clutch connected by a shift lever to the solenoid plunger.

APPLICATION	
Model	①**Part No.**
Peugeot	
504 & 505 Diesel	5802.04②
505	5802.20
604	5802.17③
Renault	
Le Car	77 00 671 608

① — Vehicle manufacturer part number.
② — Ducellier No. 6109, Paris-Rhone No. D11 E 159.
③ — Ducellier No. 6237, Paris-Rhone No. D9 E 14.

TESTING

Lock Test (Le Car) — Follow instructions and procedures outlined in manual furnished with tester. Use a fully charged battery and carry out the test at a temperature of 77°F. Starter torque should be 9 ft. lbs. at 400 amps.

Operational Test (Peugeot) — Disconnect coil high tension wire (except diesel) and connect tachometer to engine. Connect ammeter between battery and starter and energize starter for maximum of 15 seconds. Gasoline engine should turn at 120 RPM with a maximum draw of 250 amperes. Diesel engine should turn at 120 RPM with a maximum draw of 350 amperes.

NOTE — *Further test procedures not furnished by manufacturer.*

OVERHAUL

DISASSEMBLY

Remove nuts on through bolts and remove rear shield. Lift out brushes and retaining shaft for connecting fork between solenoid and pinion. Remove bolts securing solenoid and remove solenoid. Remove starter body and armature.

PARTS REPLACEMENT & TESTING

Brushes — Inspect brushes. If damaged or less than $\frac{5}{16}$" (8 mm) long, install new brushes.

Commutator — Check commutator surface for burns, pits, scoring or out-of-round. Dress with a lathe if required and polish with fine sandpaper. Check segment insulators undercut to depth of .020" (.5 mm).

Armature — Check armature for open, shorted or grounded circuits. Inspect armature shaft for bend and core for scoring or loose windings.

NOTE — *Do not attempt to straighten a bent shaft. Replace armature if shaft is bent or core is damaged.*

Bearings — Inspect front and rear bearings for wear and excessive clearance with armature shaft. Replace if damaged or in case of excess clearance.

REASSEMBLY

1) Clean all parts and coat sliding surfaces with multi-purpose grease. Assemble in reverse order of disassembly and check pinion clearance.

2) Disconnect starter field terminal from solenoid and energize solenoid with 12 volt battery. Measure clearance of pinion gear to stop collar. Clearance should be .02-.10" (.5-2.5 mm). Adjust to proper clearance by screwing plunger fork or adjusting screw in or out.

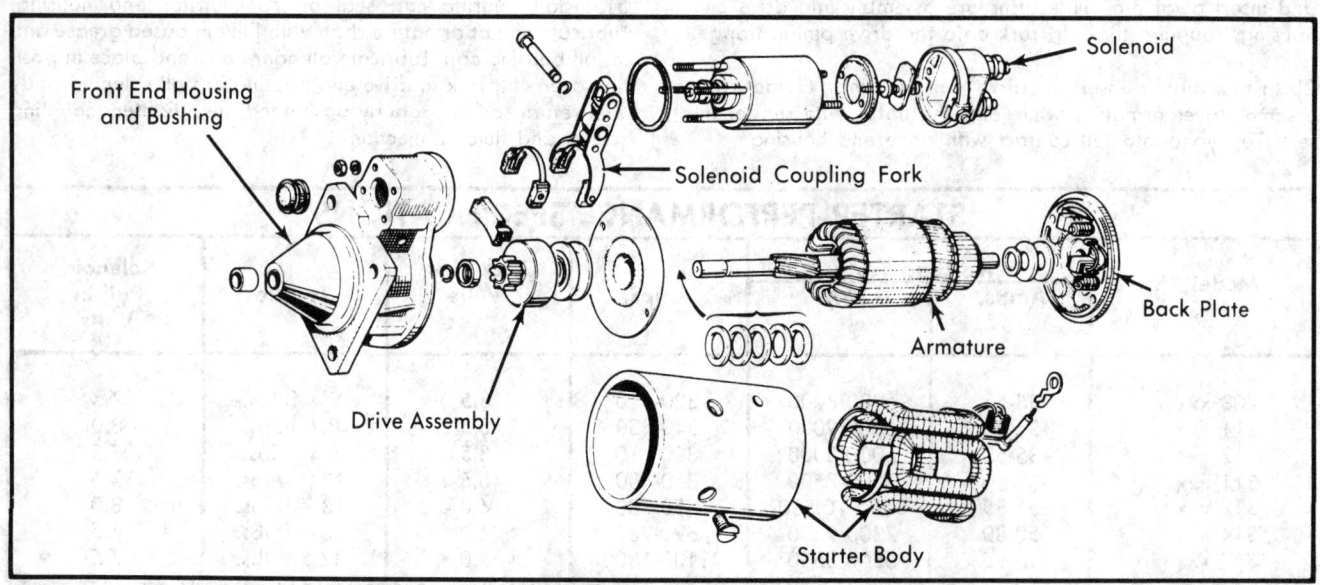

Fig. 1   Disassembled View of Paris Rhone Starter

FIAT

Brava
Spider 2000

DESCRIPTION

Fiat starter is a 12 volt, brush type, 4-pole system with field windings in series. Integral solenoid is mounted on starter housing and causes starter pinion to engage flywheel ring gear when starter is energized. Overrunning clutch pinion drive is mounted directly on drive end of armature shaft.

APPLICATION

Model	Fiat No.
Brava & Spider 2000	E 100-1.3/12

TESTING

PERFORMANCE TESTS

Mount starter in suitable test stand and perform running test, no load test and stall (lock) test. Starter should develop 2.78± .14 ft. lbs. torque while drawing 280 amps at 1500-1700 RPM, 9.5 volts. At 12 volts, 28 amps under no load conditions, armature speed should be 5200±500 RPM. Stall torque test should produce 12.58±.7 ft. lbs. torque at 12 volts, 28 or less amps.

OVERHAUL

DISASSEMBLY

1) With metal band (dust cover) removed from commutator end frame, disconnect solenoid terminal lead and remove nuts from solenoid mounting bolts. Remove solenoid. Remove nuts from through bolts and slide off end frame while holding brushes off of commutator.

2) Remove pinion end frame while disengaging shifter fork from overrunning clutch. If pinion drive assembly is to be removed, slide back stop ring and remove lock ring from armature shaft. Remove overrunning cluch/pinion drive assembly.

CLEANING

Use dry compressed air to blow dirt and worn brush dust from starter. Do not immerse starter components in solvent. Use brush dipped in cleaning solvent to clean drive unit, then blow dry with air.

PARTS REPLACEMENT

To replace field coils, mount starter frame in press-type screwdriver stand and remove pole piece attaching screws. Remove pole pieces and field coils. Heat replacement field coils to about 128°F in order to obtain added flexibility and ease in installation. Install pole shoes and tighten screws. Inner diameter of pole shoes should be 2.675-2.677" (67.95-68.00 mm) to assure proper air gap between armature and shoes.

REASSEMBLY

Lubricate inner splined face of drive assembly with SAE 10 motor oil before installing drive on armature shaft. Reverse disassembly procedure to complete overhaul.

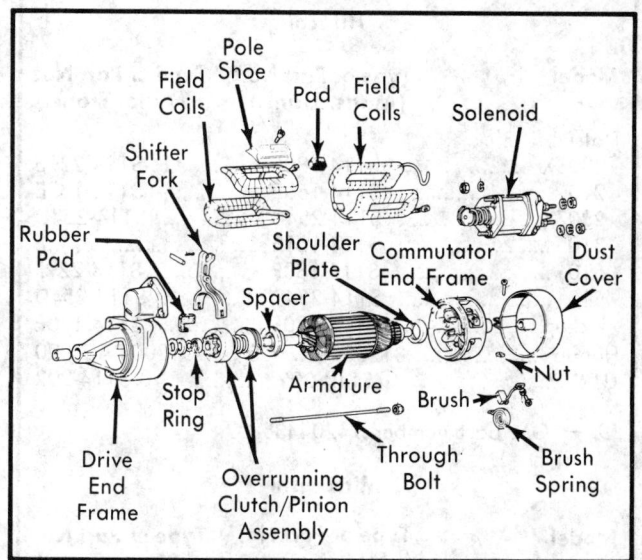

Fig. 1 Disassembled View of Fiat Starter Motor

HITACHI & MITSUBISHI

Chrysler Corp. Imports	310
Arrow	510
Arrow Pickup	810
Champ	Pickup
Challenger	Honda
Colt	Civic (Calif.)
D50 Pickup	LUV
Sapporo	Mazda
Datsun	626
200SX	GLC
210	RX7
280ZX	B2000 Pickup

DESCRIPTION

Starter is a conventional 12-volt, 4-pole brush type motor. May be either direct or reduction gear drive. Solenoid mounted on starter shifts overrunning clutch and pinion to flywheel when starter is energized.

APPLICATION

Hitachi

Model	Type or Part No. (Mans. Trans.)	Type or Part No. (Auto. Trans.)
Datsun		
200SX	S114-180F	S114-229E
210	S114-160E	S114-163E
280ZX	S114-254D	S114-254D
310	S114-161E	
510	S114-180F	S114-229F
810	S114-254D	S114-254D
Pickup	S114-180F	S114-170E
Honda	31200 PAO 000	31200 PAO 000
LUV	① S114-202	① S114-202

① — GM part number 94204438.

Mitsubishi

Model	Type or Part No. (Man. Trans.)	Type or Part No. (Auto Trans.)
Chrysler Corp. Imports		
1400 cc	M3T22581	
1600 cc	M3T22581	M3T25781
2000 cc	M3T25781	M2T53081
2600 cc	M3T25781	M2T53081
Mazda		
626	8088 18 400A	8964 18 400
RX7	1757 18 400D	8872 18 500A
GLC	8131 18 400	0324 18 400B
B2000 Pickup	8088 18 400A	

TESTING

STARTER PERFOMANCE TESTS

No Load Tests — Connect starter in series with a 12 volt battery and an ammeter capable of at least a 1000 ampere reading. Connect voltmeter as shown in *Fig. 1* and compare readings with *Starter Performance Specifications* as shown.

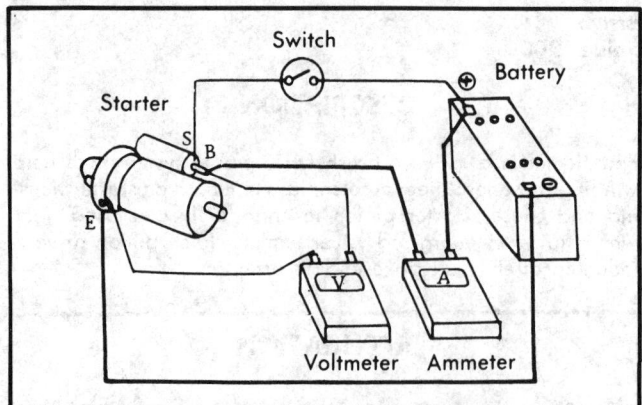

Fig. 1   Connections for No Load Test

Lock (Torque) Test — Mount starter in a test stand to perform torque measurement test. Follow manufacturer's instructions for test stand operation. With voltage adjusted, ammeter reading and torque should be within specifications.

SOLENOID TESTS

NOTE — *Make tests with solenoid removed from starter or remove solenoid lead to starter before testing. Ensure that solenoid plunger and sleeve are clean and dry before performing tests.*

Pull-In Coil Test — Connect jumper between negative post of 12 volt battery and "S" terminal. Connect a second jumper to positive battery terminal and touch "M" (MT) terminal. Plunger should pull in immediately.

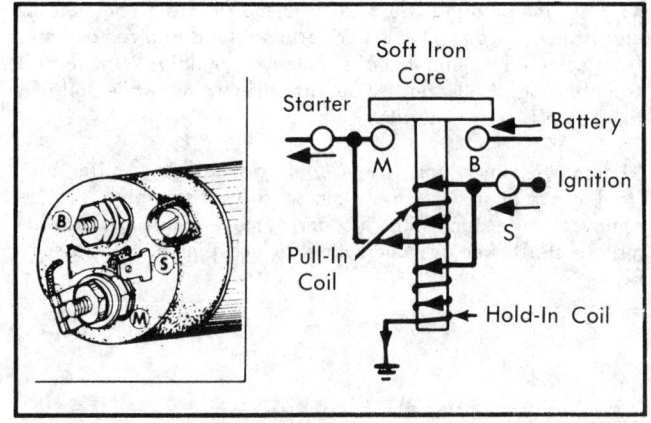

Fig. 2   Starting Circuit Diagram and Solenoid Terminals

Hold-In Coil Test — Connect a ground lead between the "M" (MT) terminal and the solenoid case. Apply 8 volts to the "S" terminal to pull in the plunger. Disconnect lead to "M" (MT) terminal and plunger should remain in.

Return Test — Push plunger into solenoid body by hand. Apply 12 volts between "M" (MT) terminal and the solenoid case. If the case is short circuited, the plunger will be attracted. If nothing happens, the solenoid is satisfactory.

HITACHI & MITSUBISHI (Cont.)

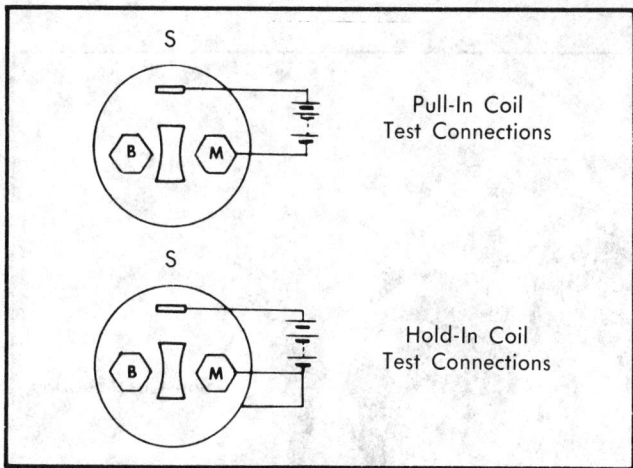

Fig. 3   Test Connections for Pull-In Coil and Hold-In Coil

OVERHAUL

DISASSEMBLY

1) Loosen nut securing connecting plate to magnetic switch "M" terminal. Remove screws securing magnetic switch and remove switch (solenoid) assembly. Remove through bolts and brush cover assembly, then tap yoke assembly loose with wooden mallet. Remove yoke, armature assembly and pinion shift lever.

2) Remove pinion stop ring from end of armature shaft by pushing stop ring to clutch side. Remove snap ring and overrunning clutch assembly from armature shaft.

PARTS REPLACEMENT & TESTING

Brushes & Springs — Check brush spring tension using a suitable spring scale. Check brush contact surface condition and brush length. Check lead clip and wire conections and condition of brush holders. Replace as required. *See Brush Spring Tension and Brush Length (Minimum).*

Brush Spring Tension	
Application	**Lbs. (kg)**
Chrysler Corp. Imports	3.3 (1.5)
Datsun	①3.1-4.0 (1.4-1.8)
Honda, LUV, Mazda	3.5 (1.6)

① — Reduction gear starter brush spring tension should be 3.5-4.4 lbs. (1.6-2.0 kg).

Brush Length (Minimum)	
Application	**In. (mm)**
Chrysler Corp. Imports & Mazda	.45 (11.5)
Datsun	①.47 (12.0)
Honda	.16 (4.0)
LUV	.47 (12.0)

① — Reduction gear starter minimum length should be .043" (11.0 mm).

Armature — Check external condition of armature for scoring or other damage. Measure shaft distortion with dial indicator. Replace armature if shaft bend exceeds .003" (.08 mm) on Datsun, .006" (.15 mm) on LUV, and .004" (.10 mm) on all other models.

Commutator — Inspect commutator for roughness, grooves, burns or pitting. Sand lightly with 500 grit sandpaper if necessary. Check commutator for out-of-round and mica insulators undercut to a depth of .020-.031" (.5-.8 mm). If necessary, commutator may be turned less than .04" (1 mm) from original size and mica undercut. Replace if excessively worn.

Field Coil — Check field coil continuity by connecting test probe of circuit tester or an ohmmeter to the field coil positive terminal and brush holder. If circuit is open, replace field coil. Check for grounding of field coils by placing one probe of circuit tester on starter housing and other probe to field coil positive terminal. If little or no resistance, field coil is grounded and must be replaced.

Overrunning Clutch Assembly — Inspect pinion assembly and sleeve. Sleeve should slide freely on armature shaft and spline. If damage or resistance is noted, replace assembly. Check pinion and flywheel teeth for excessive rubbing or damaged teeth. Replace as required.

Pinion Gear Clearance — The clearance between the pinion gear and stop collar should be .012-.059" (.30-1.52 mm) on Hitachi and .02-.08" (.51-2.03 mm) on Mitsubishi when solenoid is engaged. Adjust as necessary by changing shims between solenoid and starter yoke. See Fig. 4.

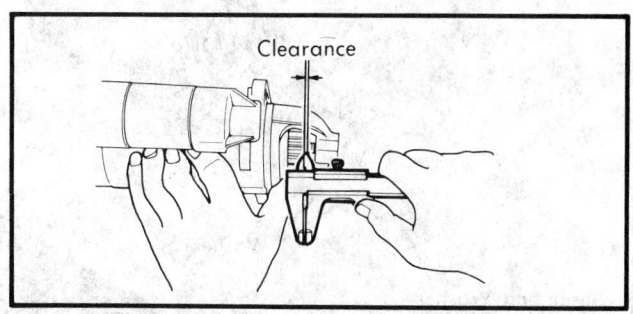

Fig. 4   Measuring Pinion Edge-to-Pinion Stopper Clearance

Pinion Case Bearing — Inspect bearing for wear and check side play. If clearance exceeds .008" (.2 mm), replace bearing. New bearing clearance should be .001-.004" (.025-.10 mm) for Hitachi or .002-.004" (.05-.10 mm) for Mitsubishi starters.

NOTE — *Ensure that bearing is installed so that end of bearing is flush with gear case end.*

CLEANING & INSPECTION

Clean all disassembled parts. Do not use grease dissolving solvent on overrunning clutch, armature assembly, solenoid assembly or field coils due to possible damage. Inspect all parts for damage or wear and replace as required.

REASSEMBLY

To reassemble, reverse disassembly procedure. Fill rear case on reduction gear models with grease. Lightly oil pinion and all bearing surfaces.

Starters

HITACHI & MITSUBISHI (Cont.)

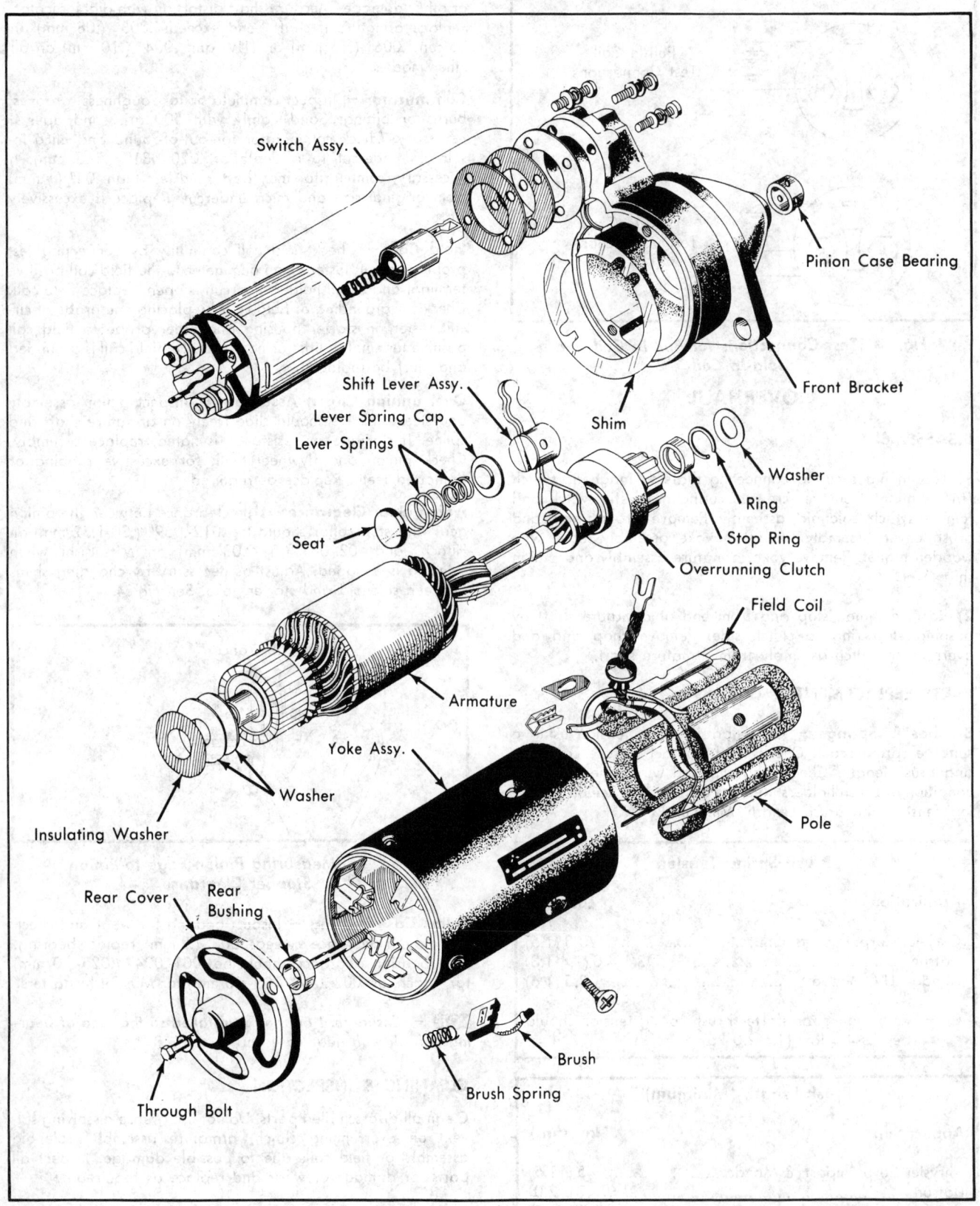

Fig. 5 *Disassembled View of Typical Mitsubishi Starter*

HITACHI & MITSUBISHI (Cont.)

Type or Part No.	No Load Test		Load Test		
	Amps. (Maximum)	RPM	Amps. (Maximum)	Volts	Torque (Ft. Lbs.) (Minimum)
STARTER PERFORMANCE SPECIFICATIONS					
HITACHI					
S114-160B	60	7000	.....	.....	.....
S114-161E	60	7000	.....	.....	.....
S114-163E	60	7000	.....	.....	.....
S114-170E	60	7000	.....	.....	.....
S114-180F	60	6000	.....	.....	.....
S114-202	60	6000	330	5.0	5.8
S114-229E & F	60	7000	.....	.....	.....
S114-254B	100	3900	.....	.....	.....
31200-PAO-000	70	6000	200	8.0	3.3
MITSUBISHI					
M2T 53081	90	3300	.....	.....	.....
M3T 22581	53	6800	.....	.....	.....
M3T 25781	60	6600	.....	.....	.....
0324 18 400B	53	6800	310	5.0	5.4
1757 18 400D	50	5600	600	5.0	6.9
8088 14 400A	53	6800	310	5.0	5.4
8131 18 400	53	6800	310	5.0	5.4
8872 18 400A	100	6600	1050	5.0	15.9
8964 18 400	60	6600	500	5.0	8.3

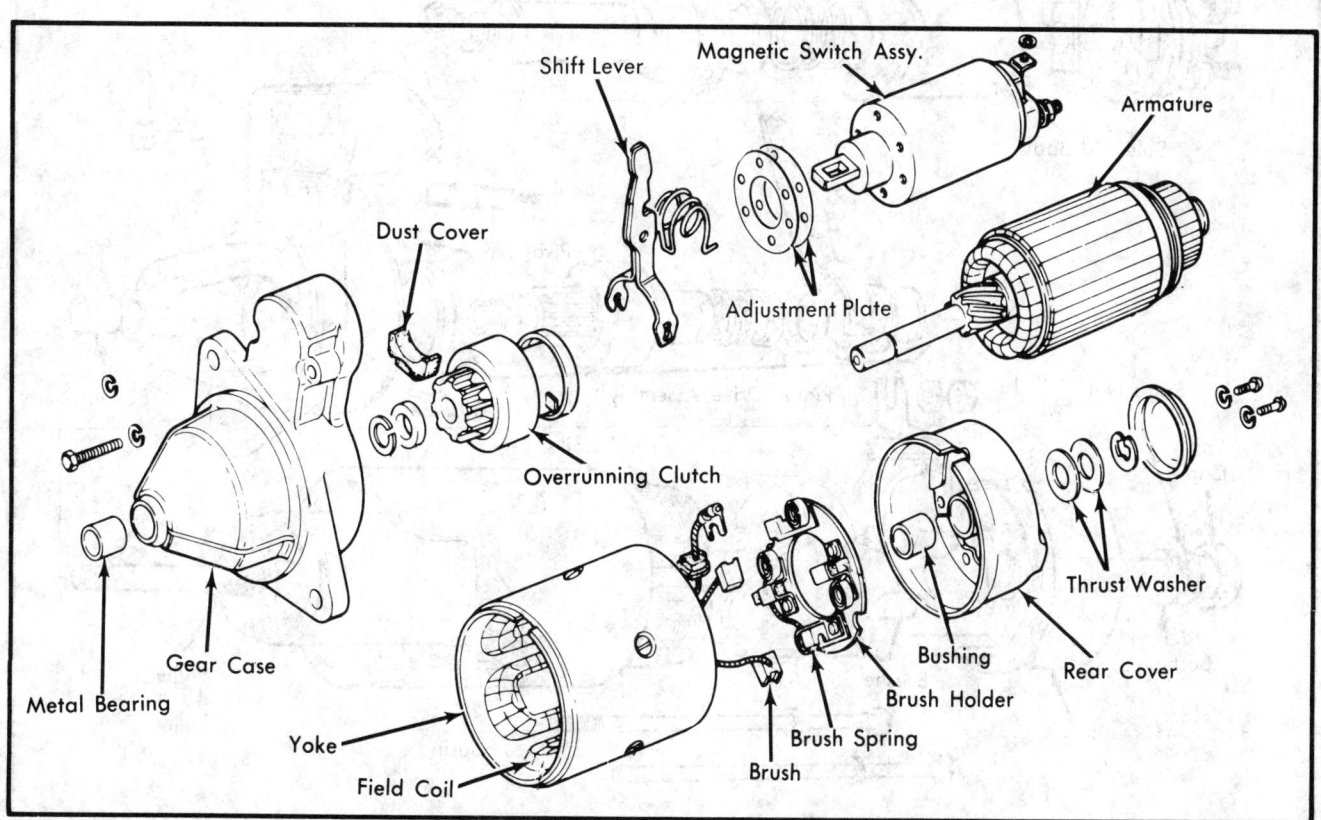

Fig. 6 Disassembled View of a Typical Hitachi Starter

LUCAS

Jaguar
XJ6
MGB
Triumph
Spitfire
TR7
TR8

DESCRIPTION

Starter is a series wound 4-pole, 4-brush motor, using either wedge shaped or conventional brushes. A housing mounted solenoid shifts the roller type starter clutch and pinion to engage the ring gear when starter is energized.

APPLICATION		
Car Model	**Lucas No.**	**Type**
Jaguar XJ6		3M100
MGB		2M100
Triumph		
Spitfire	25149	.... M35J
TR7	25703	.... 3M100
TR8	25724	.... 3M100

TESTING

PERFORMANCE TESTS

No Load Test — With starter on bench and using a good 12-volt battery, connect an ammeter in series to starter. Starter should rotate smoothly at specified RPM and current draw.

Lock Test — Use suitable tester and set up according to instructions. With starter locked in test stand and voltage adjusted, ammeter and starter torque readings should be as specified. *See Starter Performance Specifications.*

OVERHAUL

DISASSEMBLY

1) Disconnect electrical link between solenoid and starting motor. Remove nuts securing solenoid to end bracket and lift off solenoid, leaving plunger attached to engagement lever. Pry off end cap and spire nut (locking washer). Remove through bolts and end cover with brush holder.

2) Carefully remove brushes from holder. Remove seal between drive end bracket and starter housing. Remove engagement lever pivot pin and separate armature with drive assembly from drive end bracket. If removing drive assembly, remove thrust collar and lock ring from armature shaft and take drive assembly off of armature.

PARTS RELACEMENT AND TESTING

Armature — Check armature for open, shorted or grounded circuits. Check for lifted commutator segments and loose turns in armature winding. Check armature for scoring. A scored armature could indicate a loose pole shoe or a bent armature shaft. Do not attempt to true a distorted shaft or machine armature core; replace if damaged.

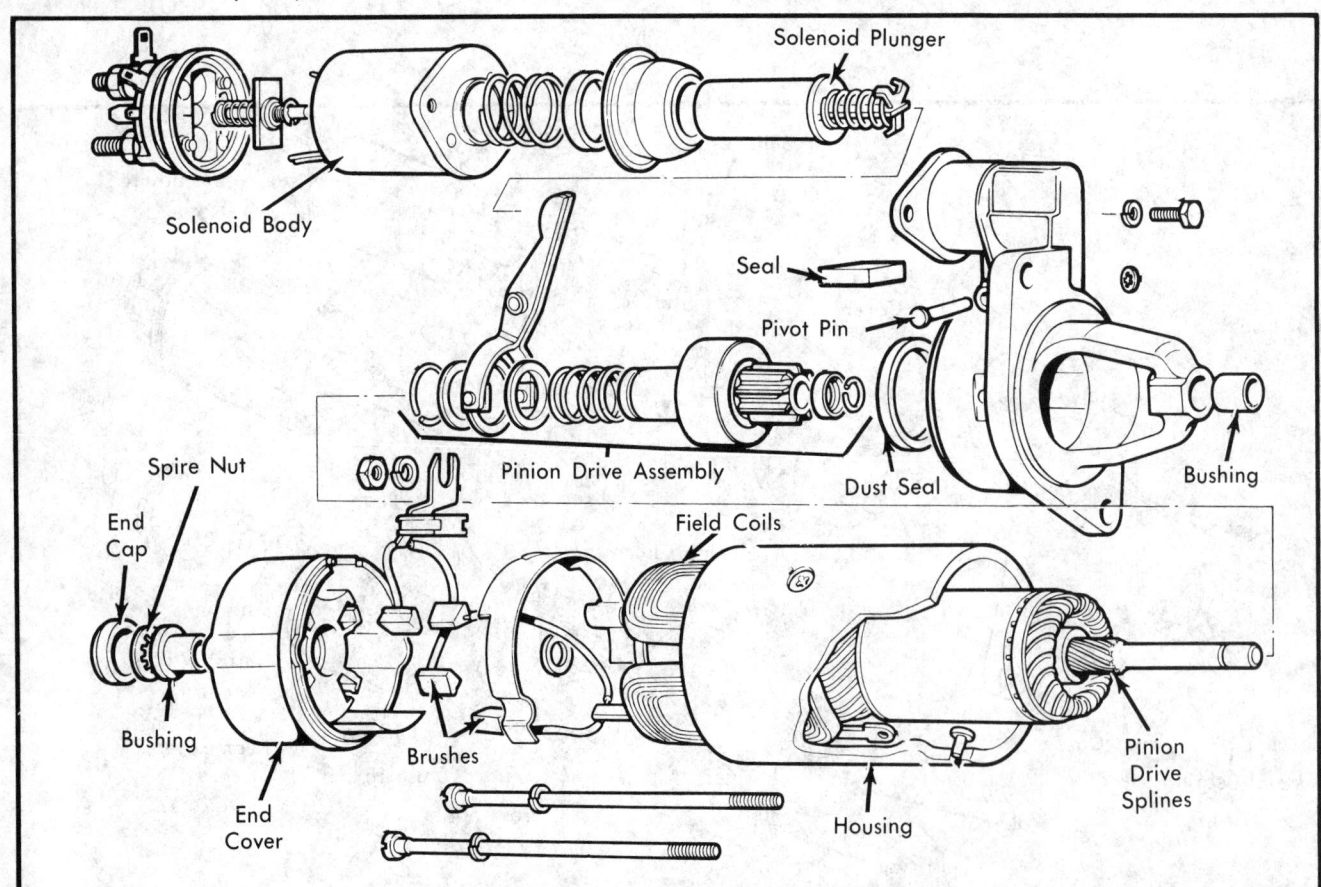

Fig. 1 Exploded View of Lucas 2M100 Starter

LUCAS (Cont.)

Commutator — Clean commutator with cloth moistened in suitable solvent and, if necessary, with fine sandpaper. If further clean up is necessary, turn down in a lathe, removing only as much metal as is absolutely necessary. Do NOT undercut insulators between commutator segments.

Brushes & Springs — Check that brushes move freely in holders by holding back brush springs and pulling gently on connecting wires. If movement is sluggish, remove brush from holder and clean with solvent moistened cloth. Replace brushes if less than 3/8" (9.5 mm) long and springs if tension is less than 36 ozs. (800 g).

Field Coils — Check for open or grounded coils using test lamp or voltmeter and battery connected in series. If any coil is defective, replace all coils. Mark housing and pole shoes for installation in original position. Remove pole piece screws and pry pole shoes, coils and insulation pieces from housing. To install, reverse removal procedure.

Bushings — In event of excessive wear or damage, remove old bushings with suitable mandrel or extractor. Ensure that new porous bronze bushings have been soaked in light engine oil for at least 24 hours and press into position. Fit new bushing using highly polished mandrel .0005" (.013 mm) larger than diameter of shaft.

NOTE — *Do NOT ream bushing after fitting due to possible damage to porosity of new bearing.*

Starter Solenoid — 1) With all cables and connectors disconnected from solenoid, connect a 12 volt power supply between starter terminal and small unmarked solenoid terminal. Connect a test lamp across main terminals and note test lamp lighted, indicating contacts are closed. Disconnect power from small solenoid terminal and lamp should go out, indicating contacts have been opened.

2) To check winding continuity, connect ohmmeter between starter terminal and ground on solenoid body. Resistance should be 1.01-1.07 ohms. To check pull-in winding, check across small unmarked terminal and starter terminal. Resistance should be .36-.42 ohms for Jaguar and .25-.27 ohms for other models.

3) To check hold in winding, connect ohmmeter between ground on solenoid body and unmarked terminal. Resistance for Jaguar should be 1.49-1.71 ohms and .76-.80 ohms for remaining models.

REASSEMBLY

Ensure that all parts are clean and reverse disassembly procedure, using new lock ring and spire nut. Lightly lubricate bearing surfaces and pivot pin. Armature end play should be adjusted to maximum end play of .010" (.25 mm) by driving retaining ring (spire nut) to proper position.

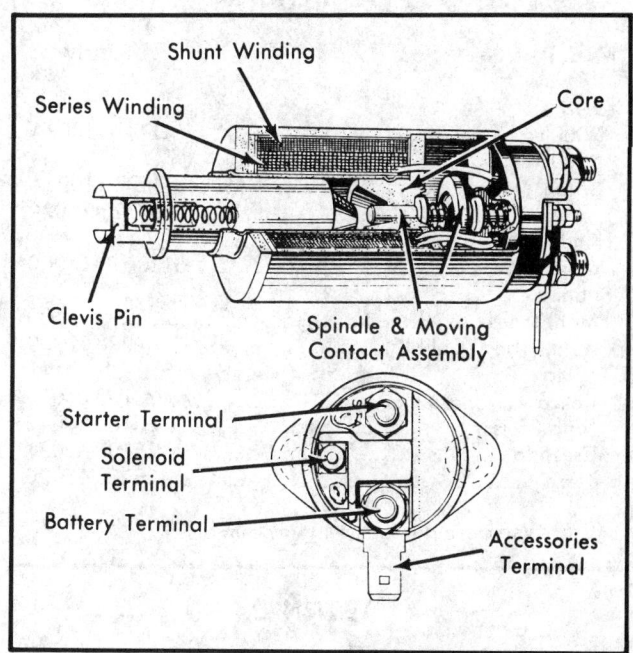

Fig. 2 Lucas Starter Solenoid

STARTER PERFORMANCE SPECIFICATIONS					
	No Load Test ①		Lock Test		
Model	Amps.	RPM	Amps.	Volts	Torque
2M100 3M100	100	6,000	463	①	14.4 ft. lbs.
XJ6	100	5,000-6,000	940	①	29.0 ft. lbs.
TR8	65	6,000	545	①	16.5 ft. lbs.
M35J	65	8,000-10,000	350-375	①	7 ft. lbs.

① — Use 12 volt fully charged battery.

Starters

NIPPONDENSO DIRECT DRIVE

Courier
  Pickup
Honda
  Civic (Calif.)
Subaru
  1600
  1800

Toyota
  Celica
  Corona
  Land Cruiser
  Pickup
  Tercel

DESCRIPTION

Nippondenso direct drive starter is conventional 12 volt, 4-pole, brush type starter. Integral solenoid is attached to drive housing and causes starter pinion to engage flywheel ring gear when starter is energized. Overrunning clutch pinion drive is mounted directly on drive end of armature shaft.

APPLICATION

Model	①Part No.
Courier	
2000 cc	D97Z 11002A
2300 cc	
Man. Trans.	D77Z 11002A
Auto. Trans.	D77Z 11002B
Honda	
Civic (Calif.)	31200 PAO 000
Subaru	
Man. Trans.	8299 18600
Auto. Trans. (Calif.)	4299 17200
Toyota	
Celica, Corona & Pickup	28100 34070
Land Cruiser	28100 60042
Cressida	28100 42021
Tercel	28100 15020

① — Vehicle manufacturer part number.

TESTING

PERFORMANCE TESTS

No Load Test —With starter on bench and using a fully charged 12 volt battery, make connections as shown in *Fig. 1.* Starter should rotate smoothly at specified RPM and current draw indicated in *Starter Performance Specifications.*

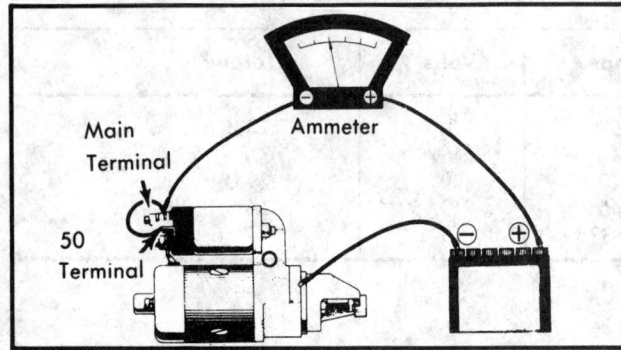

Fig. 1   Circuit for No Load Test

Lock Test — To perform lock test, follow procedures outlined in tester instruction manual. With starter locked in test stand and voltage adjusted as specified, ammeter and torque should be within limits.

SOLENOID TESTS

NOTE — *Tests must be performed with starter assembled and "M" (field) lead from starter disconnected at the solenoid. Plunger and sleeve must be clean and dry.*

Pull-In Test — Apply 8 volts momentarily between the "S" terminal and "M" terminal of solenoid. If plunger is pulled in strongly, pull-in coil is satisfactory.

Hold-In Test — Connect leads from an 8 volt source to solenoid case and "M" terminal. Connect a jumper wire between "M" terminal and "S" terminal to pull in plunger. Disconnect jumper wire from "M" terminal and plunger should remain held in. If plunger does NOT stay in, hold-in coil is defective and solenoid must be replaced.

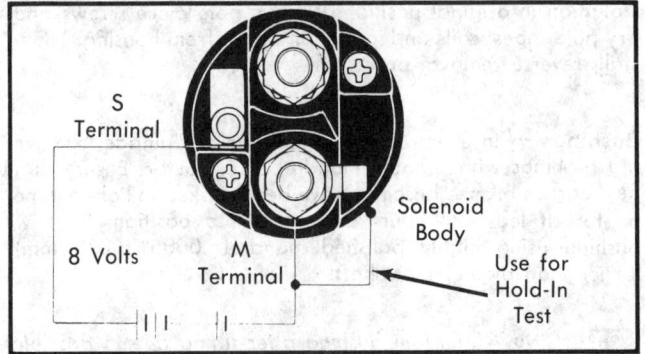

Fig. 2   Test Connections for Pull-In and Hold-In Coils

Plunger Return Test — Apply 12 volts between "M" terminal and solenoid case. Pull out starter pinion gear with fingers until it stops. If plunger returns to original position when pinion is released, solenoid is satisfactory.

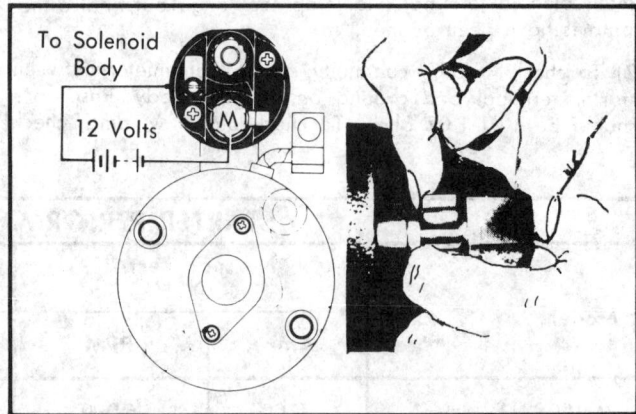

Fig. 3   Test Connections for Plunger Return

OVERHAUL

DISASSEMBLY

1) Disconnect field coil wire from starter solenoid main terminal and remove solenoid attaching bolts. Remove solenoid by moving it up and down to unhook unit from drive lever.

2) Remove bearing cover and pull out armature shaft lock plate, washer, seal and spring. Remove through bolts, commutator end frame, brush holder and yoke.

NIPPONDENSO DIRECT DRIVE (Cont.)

3) Remove drive lever set bolt, rubber piece, plate, armature and drive lever from housing. Remove pinion stop collar from armature shaft end and remove starter clutch.

PARTS REPLACEMENT & TESTING

Armature — Check armature for open, shorted or grounded circuits. Check armature shaft for bend. Inspect bushings for condition and maximum clearance of .008"(.20 mm). Replace if required.

NOTE — *Do NOT attempt to straighten a bent armature shaft. Replace if bent.*

Commutator — Clean contact surface and polish with fine sandpaper if required. If surface is scored, burned, out-of-round or pitted, dress in a lathe only enough to restore smooth concentric surface. Out-of-round should not exceed .004" (.10 mm) and mica depth should be .008-.032" (.20-.80 mm). Undercut to give correct depth of .020-.032" (.50-.80 mm).

Brushes & Springs — 1) Check brush holder insulation. Connect one lead of ammeter to brush holder positive side and other lead to negative side. If test needle moves, brush holder is shorted and must be replaced.

2) Check brush length and if less than .51" (13 mm) for Land Cruiser, .47" (12 mm) for Cressida, or .39" (10 mm) for all others, replace brushes. Check minimum spring tension of 21 ozs. (595 g) with brush installed. New brush springs should have 37-48 ozs. (1050-1360 g) tension. Brushes must move freely in holders.

Starter Solenoid — Test pull-in motion of solenoid by connecting test leads to the "50" terminal and the main "F" terminal. Plunger should be pulled in. If plunger does not pull in, switch is defective. Disconnect "F" terminal lead and plunger should remain pulled in if switch is satisfactory. Test plunger return movement by connecting battery positive lead to "F" terminal and negative lead to switch body. Depress plunger by hand, then release it. Switch is satisfactory if plunger returns to original position.

Field Coils — Connect one prod of circuit tester lead to field coil and other to soldered portion of brush lead. If meter does not register, field coil is open and must be repaired or replaced. Check field coil for ground by connecting one test prod to field coil lead and other to starter housing. If meter registers, coil is grounded and must be repaired or replaced.

REASSEMBLY

Clean all parts and coat sliding surface of armature shaft splines, starter clutch bushing, drive lever and moving stud with multipurpose grease. Reassemble in reverse order of disassembly and note the following: After completing reassembly, between pinion gear and stop collar. If clearance is not .080-.160" (.20-.40 mm) for Courier or .004-.160" (.10-4.0 mm) for all other models, adjust by lengthening or shortening plunger shaft.

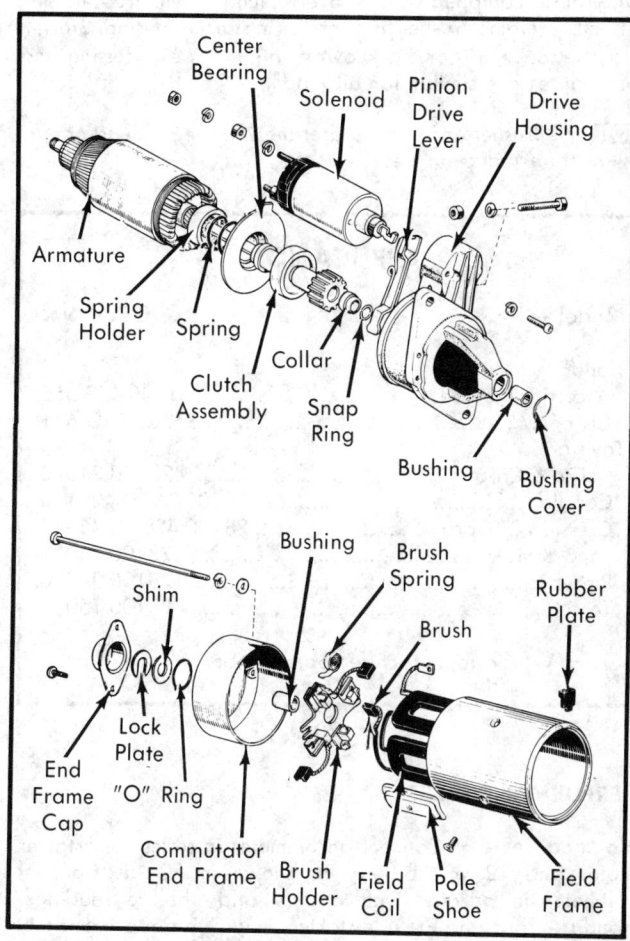

Fig. 4   Disassembled View of Typical Nippondenso Direct Drive Starter Motor

	STARTER PERFORMANCE SPECIFICATIONS				
	No Load Test		Lock Test		
Part No.	Amps.	RPM	Amps.	Volts	Torque (Ft. Lbs.)
D77Z, D97Z (All)	50	5000	.....	.....	.....
31200 PAO 000	50	5000	200	11	3.3
8299 18600	50	5000	600	7.7	9.0
4299 17200	50	5000	600	7.0	13.0
28100 (All)	50	5000	.....	.....	.....

Starters

NIPPONDENSO REDUCTION GEAR

Honda
  Accord
  Civic (Exc. Calif.)
  Prelude
Toyota
  Celica

Corolla
Cressida
Land Cruiser
Pickup
Supra
Tercel

DESCRIPTION

Starter is a 12 volt, 4 brush, solenoid actuated, gear reduction type and is equipped with an overrunning clutch. Brush holder assembly retains brushes and springs in starter housing. Starter may be .8, .9, 1.0 or 1.4 kilowatt rated, however testing and procedures are similar for all models.

NOTE — *Brushes and commutator may be on gear end or end away from reduction gear.*

APPLICATION

Model	①Part No.
Honda	
Accord & Prelude	31200 689 662
Civic	31200 PAO 671
Toyota	
Celica & Corona	28100 34070
Corolla	28100 26070, 26110
Cressida & Supra	28100 42021, 45033
Land Cruiser	28100 34070
Pickup	28100 34070
Tercel	28100 15011

① — Vehicle manufacturer part number.

TESTING

PERFORMANCE TESTS

No Load Tests — Connect an ammeter in series with starter motor and 12 volt battery as shown in *Fig. 1*. Connect voltmeter in parallel with battery and observe readings. Honda Accord and Prelude starter should give approximately 3500 RPM at 90 amps, 11.5 volts. Civic starter should give approximately 3000 RPM. Toyota starter RPM is not specified, however starter should spin smoothly with no more than 90 amps.

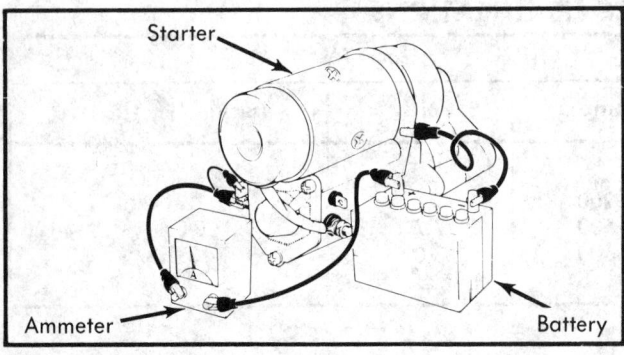

Fig. 1   Ammeter Hook-Up for No Load Test (Toyota Shown)

OVERHAUL

DISASSEMBLY

1) With starter removed from vehicle, disconnect wire(s) to magnetic switch. Remove bolts and remove field frame with armature from magnetic switch. Remove "O" ring and felt seal.

2) Remove screws and then remove starter gear housing from magnetic switch. Pull out clutch assembly and gears. Remove ball from clutch shaft hole or from magnetic switch. Remove brushes from brush holder then pull armature out of field frame.

3) Use low pressure air and soft bristle brush to clean brush dust from field frame assembly and armature. Use care to prevent dust from contaminating front and rear bearings or it may be necessary to replace them.

NOTE — *Complete immersion of starter and/or components in solvent is not recommended.*

PARTS REPLACEMENT & TESTING

Brushes & Springs — If brush spring length is less than .33" (8.5 mm) on Honda or .39" (10 mm) on Toyota, replace brushes. Replace brush springs if tension is not between 2.6 lbs. (1.2 kg) and 4.3 lbs. (1.96 kg). Check condition of brush holders, spring clip and insulation between positive and negative brush holders and repair or replace as needed.

Commutator — Inspect commutator for roughness, if surface is pitted or grooved, it should be sanded lightly with a no. 500 emery paper. Also check commutator for being out-of-round. If out-of-round is more than .002" (.05 mm), turn commutator in a lathe until out-of-round is less than .002" (.05 mm). Insulating mica should be undercut to a depth of .024-.035" (.6-.9 mm) if it is less than .008" (.2 mm). Wear or cutting limit of commutator is 1.14" (29 mm).

Armature Coil — Check commutator and armature coil core for continuity, if continuity exists, replace armature. Check armature with an armature tester (growler) for shorts, if shorts exist, replace armature. Check for continuity between segments on commutator, if no continuity exists replace armature.

Field Coil — Check field coil for open circuits. There should be continuity between lead wire and field coil brush lead, if not, replace field coil. Check for no continuity between field coil end and end frame, if continuity exists, replace field coil.

Overrunning Clutch Assembly — Inspect gear teeth for wear and damage. Replace gears if damaged. Also, if gears are damaged, check flywheel ring gear. Rotate pinion. Pinion should rotate freely in a clockwise direction and lock up in a counterclockwise direction.

Bearings — Turn each bearing by hand, replace bearings if they stick or have a high resistance to turning.

NIPPONDENSO REDUCTION GEAR (Cont.)

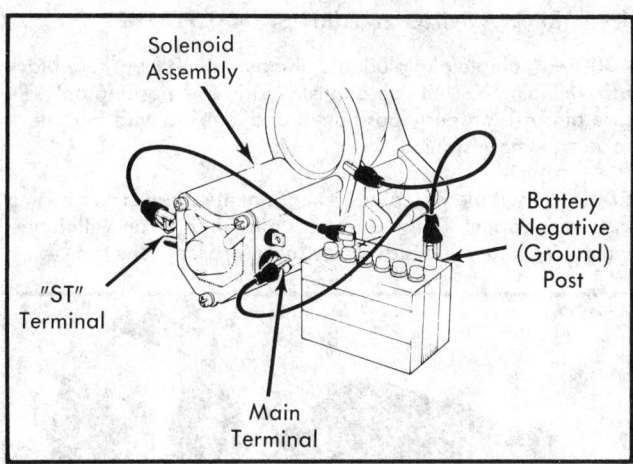

Fig. 2   Solenoid Pull-In Coil Test

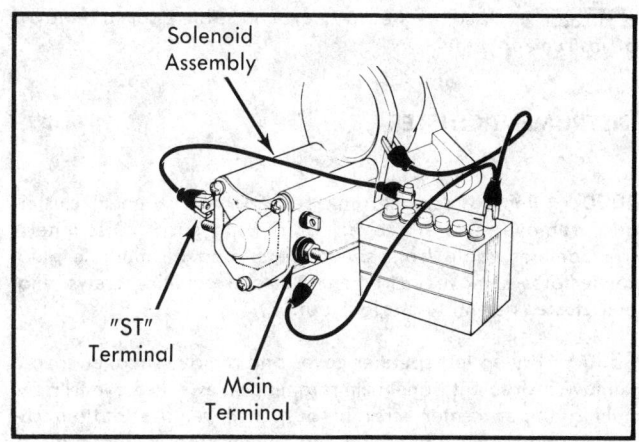

Fig. 3   Solenoid Hold-In Coil Test

Solenoid Assembly — Connect a 12 volt battery to solenoid "ST" terminal, main terminal and ground (Fig. 2). Plunger should extend firmly. If not, replace solenoid. Next, disconnect battery from main terminal (Fig. 3). Plunger should remain extended. If not, replace solenoid.

REASSEMBLY

To reassemble, reverse disassembly procedures and note the following: Coat all sliding or moving surfaces of shaft splines, bushings and solenoid with multi-purpose grease. Apply grease to clutch assembly cavity to retain steel ball when assembling.

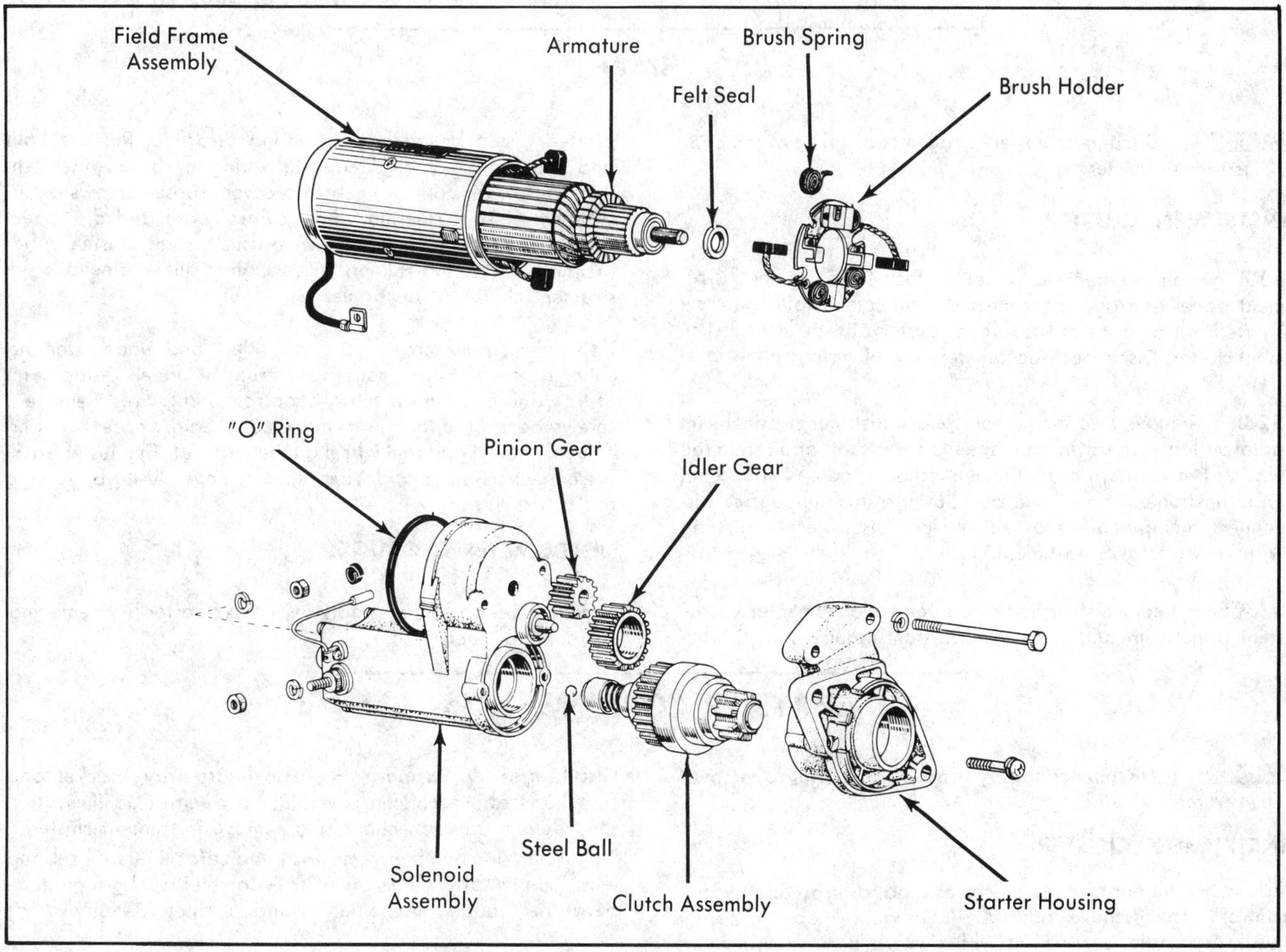

Fig. 4   Exploded View of Nippondenso Reduction Gear Starter

AUDI

CAUTION — *Disconnect battery ground cable prior to removal of instrument panel.*

INSTRUMENT CLUSTER

4000 — Remove screw from each side of instrument cluster and remove cluster cover and trim strip. Disconnect speedometer cable from speedometer and all multiple plug connectors. Remove instrument cluster retaining screws and pull cluster assembly straight out.

5000 — Pry up left speaker cover and remove speaker cover. Remove instrument panel trim retaining screws. Remove trim by pulling upper center straight out, then remove bottom by grasping on each side of steering column and pulling straight out. Loosen cluster mounting screws, detach speedometer cable from speedometer and all multiple plug connectors. Carefully pull cluster assembly straight out.

SPEEDOMETER, CLOCK & GAUGES

Speedometer, clock and all gauges may be removed after first removing instrument cluster from panel.

HAZARD WARNING & TURN SIGNAL FLASHER

4000 — Multiple pin, plug-in unit mounted on front fuse block at terminal "N". Unit can be installed in one position only. Be sure pins are properly positioned and indexed with fuse block sockets when installing.

5000 — Multiple pin, plug-in unit mounted in bracket behind instrument panel. Unit must be installed in bracket with lettering facing mounting side of retainer bracket. See *Fig. 1*.

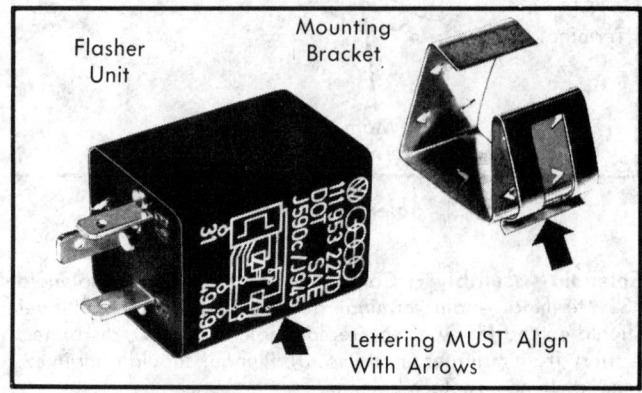

Fig. 1   Mounting Position of 5000 Flasher Unit

BMW

CAUTION — *Disconnect battery ground cable prior to removal of instrument cluster.*

INSTRUMENT CLUSTER

320i — Remove steering wheel. Detach lower center instrument panel trim and disconnect speedometer cable. Unscrew knurled nut at base of instrument cluster and pull out instrument cluster. Disconnect tachometer and all wiring connectors.

528i — Remove steering wheel. Detach instrument panel trim at lower left corner. Unscrew speedometer shaft and retain felt washer between upper and lower sections. Loosen knurled nut under instrument panel and pull cluster out far enough to disconnect multiple plugs at either side. Disconnect remaining wires and remove instrument cluster.

633CSi — Remove steering wheel. Detach lower center instrument panel trim and remove mask from inquiry unit. Detach printed circuit board leaving wiring attached. Remove light and fog light switch; disconnect wiring at back of switch. Remove left air control knob and cover. Loosen screws on instrument cluster, steering wheel control base and disconnect speedometer cable. Press down on instrument cluster upper section and steering column far enough to allow removal of instrument cluster at an angle.

733i — Loosen screws at bottom left and under steering column attaching trim panel to instrument panel. Detach trim at tray and disconnect window control cutout wires. Remove 3 screws beneath upper instrument panel trim. Loosen steering column control and pull wheel all the way out. Tip cluster back, disconnect all plugs and wires, then remove cluster by turning out to right rear.

SPEEDOMETER & GAUGES

Speedometer and gauges may be removed after first removing instrument cluster.

CHRYSLER CORP. IMPORTS

CAUTION — *Disconnect battery ground cable prior to removal of instrument cluster.*

INSTRUMENT CLUSTER

Arrow — Pull out air intake control knob, ashtray and heater control knobs. Remove radio (AM/FM) tuning knob and 2 ring nuts. (AM radio is removed with cluster). Remove attaching screws from around panel and pull panel out far enough to disconnect speedometer, radio and electrical connections. Remove instrument cluster.

Challenger & Sapporo — Remove ash tray bracket and panel just above column cover. Remove lenses as illustrated, then detach all connections and remove instrument cluster.

To further disassemble, remove all indicator lights, bezel and lens. Remove attaching nuts of speedometer, fuel gauge, temperature gauge, tachometer and ammeter. Remove as required.

CAUTION — *Handle cluster with care to avoid damaging printed circuit board. Do not overtighten nuts when reassembling.*

CHRYSLER CORP. IMPORTS (Cont.)

Champ & Colt Hatchbacks — Remove instrument panel hood attaching screws. Remove corner panels. Pull out hood connector and push claw to release connector. Remove hood and instrument panel. Disconnect speedometer and electrical connections.

Colt Station Wagon — Remove instrument panel hood by lifting at an angle, using caution to prevent catching and bending clock and odometer knobs. Disconnect speedometer cable and all gauge connections. Remove peripheral mounting screws and lift cluster away from instrument panel. Further disassembly requires removal of clock knob and instrument cluster glass.

Pickups — Remove heater fan switch knob, heater control knobs, ashtray and radio knobs. Remove 4 attaching screws and pull out instrument cluster bezel. Disconnect speedometer cable from speedometer and all electrical connections. Remove instrument cluster. To further disassemble cluster, remove 6 lens retaining screws and remove lens and bezel. Remove fasteners from printed circuit board and remove speedometer, tachometer and gauges.

HAZARD WARNING & TURN SIGNAL FLASHERS

Separate hazard warning and turn signal flasher units are mounted below instrument panel on driver's side with a single screw. Champ and Colt Hatchbacks have individual flashers which are held in position by plastic claws. Clamp claws together to remove or install either flasher.

COMBINATION GAUGE (CONSOLE MOUNTED)

Arrow — Remove 2 combination gauge panel mounting screws. From rear of gauge, disconnect electrical connections and remove gauge by pulling straight out.

Pickups — Remove screws securing console and pull console rearward. Working behind the console, remove 3 mounting screws and remove combination gauge from console. Disconnect electrical plug from combination gauge.

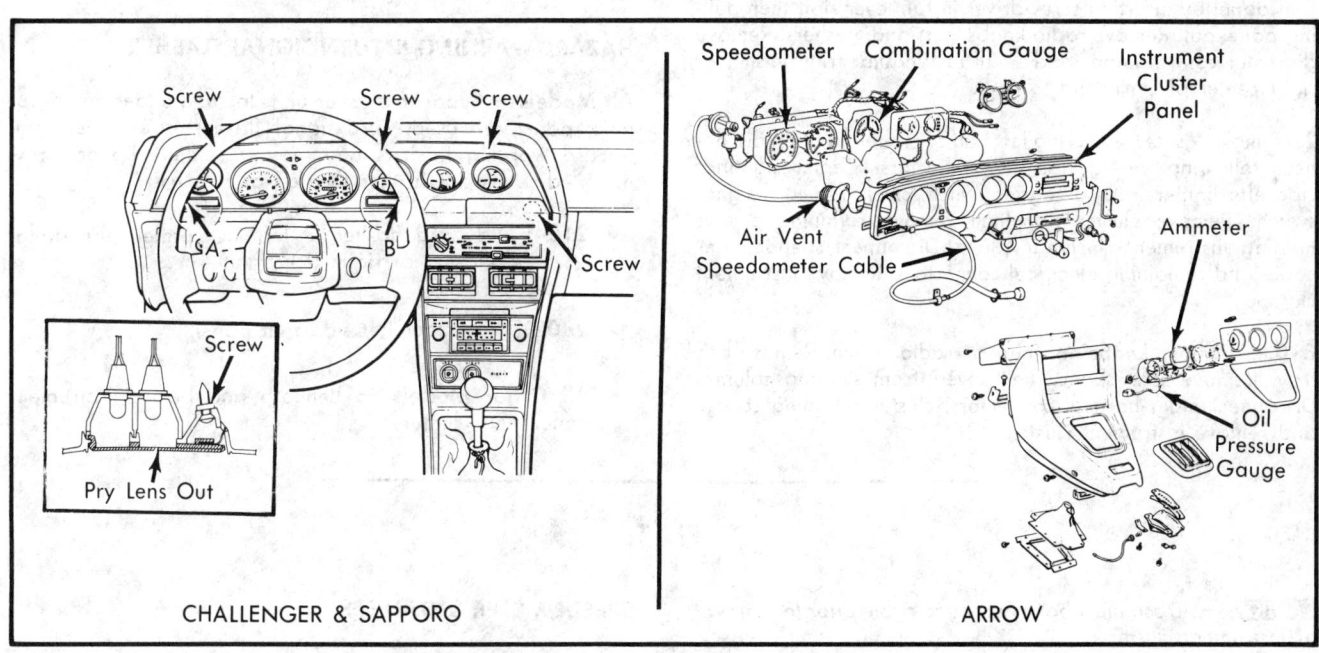

Fig. 2   Chrysler Corp. Import Instrument Cluster Arrangements

COURIER

CAUTION — *Disconnect battery ground cable prior to removal of instrument cluster.*

INSTRUMENT CLUSTER

Remove meter hood. Remove screws securing cluster to instrument panel. Pull cluster out sufficiently to gain access and disconnect speedometer cable and wiring. Remove cluster from vehicle.

SPEEDOMETER & GAUGES

Speedometer and all gauges may be removed after first removing instrument cluster.

HAZARD WARNING & TURN SIGNAL FLASHER

Combination flasher is located to the left of the steering column beneath instrument panel. Unit is secured by clamp with a single screw and connected by a multiple connector type plug.

DATSUN

CAUTION — *Disconnect battery ground cable prior to removal of instrument cluster.*

INSTRUMENT CLUSTER

200SX — Remove steering wheel and column covers. Remove all knobs and nuts. Remove upper and lower screws from instrument cluster. Pull cluster forward and disconnect wiring connectors, speedometer cable and remove rear window defogger switch. Remove instrument cluster.

210 & 310 — Remove steering wheel and column covers. On 310, remove instrument lower cover on left side. On all models, remove knobs and nuts from switches and radio controls. Remove ashtray, cover and meter retaining screws. Remove cluster cover retaining screws; pull cover out slightly and disconnect electrical connections. Remove cluster cover. Remove instrument cluster retaining screws. Pull cluster out slightly and remove speedometer cable and electrical connections. Remove instrument cluster assembly.

510 — 1) Remove steering column covers and disconnect hazard warning switch connector. Pull out ash tray and heater control knobs. Remove wiper control switch. Remove heater trim panel by inserting screwdriver in fan lever slot, then pulling panel out. Remove radio knobs, nuts and washers. Remove defroster control knobs and small rectangular trim finisher at right center of cluster lid.

2) Remove 9 screws securing left half of cluster lid, then disconnect following wiring harness connectors: Center lighting, cigarette lighter, rear defogger switch, clock and turn signal switch. Remove cluster lid, then remove retaining screws holding instrument cluster in place. Disconnect speedometer cable and remaining electrical connectors. Remove instrument cluster.

810 — Remove knobs and nuts on radio switch. Remove ash tray. Remove screws and shell covers from steering column. Disconnect main harness connectors, cluster retaining screws and remove instrument cluster.

280ZX — Remove steering wheel, column covers and dimmer/wiper combination switch. Remove instrument lower cover on left side. Disconnect speedometer cable at intermediate connection. Remove cluster retaining screws and pull cluster out sufficiently to disconnect all electrical connections. Remove instrument cluster.

Pickups — Remove screws securing cluster to instrument panel and from under panel remove screw securing cluster to dash. Withdraw cluster slightly, then from behind cluster disconnect speedometer cable and wiring. Remove screws securing cluster cover to cluster and remove cluster assembly.

SPEEDOMETER & GAUGES

280ZX — Speedometer and tachometer may be removed after removing instrument cluster. To remove gauges, remove glove box door, disconnect electrical connections and remove retaining screws. Carefully pull gauge assembly toward glove box while pushing out toward front of car. Do not damage printed circuit board or clock knob.

All Others — Speedometer and all gauges may be removed after removing instrument cluster.

HAZARD WARNING & TURN SIGNAL FLASHER

All Models — Separate flasher units located under the instrument panel are used. Turn signal flashers are larger than hazard warning flashers and may be either clip or screw mounted. Units are further located as follows:

- **210** — Hazard flasher at left kick panel, turn signal flasher at right kick panel.

- **280ZX** — Under left side trim panel.

- **All Other Models** — Beneath and behind instrument panel, near center.

FIAT

CAUTION — *Disconnect battery ground cable prior to removal of instrument cluster.*

INSTRUMENT CLUSTER

Disconnect battery. Remove 5 screws holding cluster to panel. Slide cluster forward and disconnect electrical connections and speedometer cable. Remove instrument cluster.

SPEEDOMETER & GAUGES

Speedometer and all gauges may be removed after removing instrument cluster.

FIESTA

CAUTION — *Disconnect battery ground cable prior to removal of instrument cluster.*

INSTRUMENT CLUSTER

1) Disconnect battery. Snap off upper steering column shroud, then remove screws below dashboard storage space and drop lower panel (where applicable). Reach behind cluster and snap off speedometer cable locking catch with thumb, then pull cable off speedometer.

2) Pull instrument bezel off with fingers. Remove 4 screws from front of cluster and pull assembly out. Disconnect multiplug connectors and remove cluster.

FIESTA (Cont.)

SPEEDOMETER & GAUGES

Speedometer, tachometer (if equipped), and gauges may be removed after first removing instrument cluster.

HAZARD WARNING & TURN SIGNAL FLASHER

Single flasher unit is mounted on relay bracket under dash panel to left of steering column.

HONDA

CAUTION — *Disconnect battery ground cable prior to removal of instrument cluster.*

INSTRUMENT CLUSTER

Accord — Remove steering column lower cover and steering column. Detach speedometer cable from speedometer by reaching under panel. Remove 2 screws from under cluster. Disconnect wiring harness connections from rear of cluster and remove cluster assembly.

Civic — Remove steering column covers and steering column. Remove bulb access panel and 2 upper cluster mounting screws after removing access panel. Remove lower cluster mounting bolt and screw. Disconnect speedometer cable, tachometer (if equipped) and all electrical connections from back of cluster. Remove instrument cluster.

Prelude — Remove steering wheel and coin box. Remove 3 screws from panel cover. Disconnect warning light connector. Remove panel cover, steering column covers and headlight dimmer/washer combination switch. Remove mounting bolts and disconnect speedometer cable and electrical connections. Remove instrument cluster.

SPEEDOMETER, TACHOMETER & GAUGES

Speedometer, tachometer (if equipped) and all other gauges may be removed after first removing instrument cluster.

HAZARD WARNING & TURN SIGNAL FLASHER

Individual flasher units are mounted on relay bracket under dash panel to left of steering column.

JAGUAR

CAUTION — *Disconnect battery ground cable prior to removal of instrument cluster.*

INSTRUMENT CLUSTER

NOTE — *Instruments are removed individually from instrument cluster.*

SPEEDOMETER & TACHOMETER

Speedometer and tachometer may be removed by pressing on rim and turning counterclockwise until free of locking tabs in panel. Disconnect speedometer cable and electrical connections, then remove from panel.

HAZARD WARNING & TURN SIGNAL FLASHERS

Individual flasher units are mounted on relay bracket under center of dash panel.

LUV

CAUTION — *Disconnect battery ground cable prior to removal of instrument cluster.*

INSTRUMENT CLUSTER

Disconnect speedometer cable from speedometer. Remove wing nuts on rear side of instrument cluster, pull cluster out to gain access to electrical harnesses. Disconnect electrical harnesses and remove instrument cluster.

SPEEDOMETER & GAUGES

Speedometer and all gauges may be removed after first removing instrument cluster.

HAZARD WARNING & TURN SIGNAL FLASHER

Individual flasher units are mounted on relay bracket under center of dash panel.

MAZDA

CAUTION — *Disconnect battery ground cable prior to removal of instrument cluster.*

INSTRUMENT CLUSTER

RX-7 & 626 — Remove steering wheel, column cover and instrument cluster cover. Remove light control switches (if necessary). Remove cluster attaching screws, then tip cluster to disconnect speedometer cable and multiple connectors. Remove instrument cluster.

GLC & Pickup — Remove screws holding meter hood to panel and remove hood. Remove center panel and crash pad. Disconnect speedometer cable, remove mounting screws and tip out instrument cluster. Remove multiple connector plugs from rear of unit and remove cluster.

SPEEDOMETER & GAUGES

Speedometer and all gauges can be removed when cluster is removed.

MERCEDES-BENZ

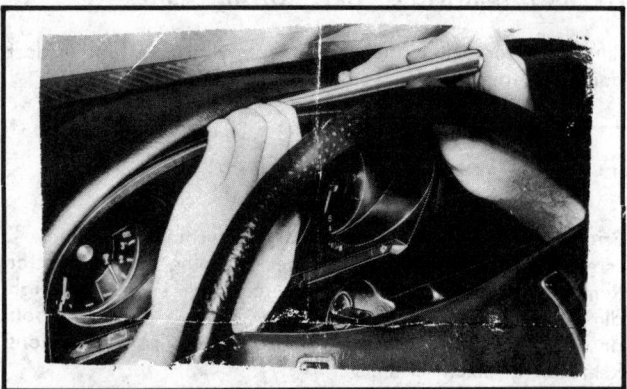

Fig. 3   Instrument Cluster Removal

INSTRUMENT CLUSTER

Instrument cluster is held in a recess by a rubber section. Remove instrument plate glass, prying out and lifting up, using a non-metallic device to prevent damage to the glass.

Remove the speedometer shaft from the cable strap under the left floormat. Pull instrument cluster out, loosen speedometer shaft, electrical connections and oil pressure line. Remove the instrument cluster sideways and to the right.

SPEEDOMETER & GAUGES

Speedometer and all gauges may be removed after removing instrument cluster.

MG

CAUTION — *Disconnect battery ground cable prior to removal of any gauges.*

SPEEDOMETER & TACHOMETER

Remove lower left instrument panel cover. Unscrew knurled nut and disconnect speedometer cable. Push in and turn speedometer clockwise about 30° until 3 body studs on speedometer clear locking tabs on dash. Pull from dash and disconnect speedometer cable and tachometer electrical harness.

GAUGES

Temperature gauge removal requires removal of speedometer first. Then remove knurled nuts, pull gauge from dash and disconnect wiring. All other gauges may be removed by removing knurled nuts, pulling gauge from dash and disconnecting wiring.

PORSCHE

CAUTION — *Disconnect battery ground cable prior to removal of instrument cluster.*

INSTRUMENT CLUSTER

928 Models — Disconnect battery ground lead. Remove steering wheel, steering column switch and instrument cover mounting screws. Disconnect both 12 pin connector plugs at instrument cluster. Lift instrument cover carefully and tilt to rear. Unscrew mounting bolt and remove instrument cluster.

SPEEDOMETER, TACHOMETER & GAUGES

928 Models — Instruments may be removed from assembly individually with cluster out of car. Use caution so that printed circuit board is not damaged when disassembling cluster.

924 Models — Disconnect battery. Put hand underneath instrument panel to back of instrument to be removed. Press in-strument forward out of instrument panel. Disconnect wiring or speedometer cable.

NOTE — *Remove tachometer and combination gauge before removing speedometer.*

911 Models — 1) Connecting terminals and wires of all instruments are accessible from luggage compartment side of instrument panel after luggage compartment carpet is removed.

2) Disconnect and detach all connections from instrument to be removed. To remove speedometer, remove knurled nut and withdraw speedometer shaft. Remove knurled nuts from instrument, remove retaining clamp and take instrument out from passenger side of instrument panel.

TURN SIGNAL FLASHER (911 MODELS)

Plug-in type flasher is located next to fuse block in luggage compartment.

RENAULT

CAUTION — *Disconnect battery ground cable prior to removal of instrument cluster.*

INSTRUMENT CLUSTER

Le Car — Disconnect speedometer cable in engine compartment. Unclip instrument panel cowl and remove. Press left and right side clips until support plate is cleared and remove instrument panel. Disconnect 2 electrical junction blocks and speedometer cable.

SPEEDOMETER & GAUGES

Speedometer and all gauges may be removed after instrument cluster is removed.

SAAB

CAUTION — *Disconnect battery positive cable prior to removal of instrument cluster.*

INSTRUMENT CLUSTER

99 Models — Remove safety padding. Remove 4 self-tapping screws. Disconnect speedometer cable and wiring. Remove bulb holders. Lift out instrument cluster.

900 Models — Remove steering wheel. Remove 4 switch panel screws and properly mark location for reinstallation. Tilt switch panel back out of way. Remove left speaker and defroster grill. Reach behind instrument cluster and disconnect electrical connections and speedometer cable. Remove cluster retaining screws and remove cluster assembly.

SPEEDOMETER & GAUGES

Speedometer and all gauges may be removed after first removing instrument cluster.

TURN SIGNAL FLASHER

Located under instrument panel on left hand side of steering column.

SUBARU

CAUTION — *Disconnect battery ground cable prior to removal of instrument cluster.*

INSTRUMENT CLUSTER

Dual Meter — Remove trim panel, then remove 5 cluster retaining screws. Partially pull out cluster, disconnect speedometer cable and all electrical connections. Remove instrument cluster.

Triple Meter — Remove 7 cluster retaining screws. Remove plug and attaching screw from under lighting switch. Remove passing light switch (if equipped). Remove ventilation knob. Remove center vent cover and left vent cover. Remove screws and disconnect electrical wiring from all switches. Disconnect speedometer cable and pull out instrument cluster.

SPEEDOMETER & GAUGES

Speedometer and all gauges may be removed after first removing instrument cluster.

HAZARD WARNING & TURN SIGNAL FLASHER

Located under instrument panel.

TOYOTA

CAUTION — *Disconnect battery ground cable prior to removal of instrument cluster.*

INSTRUMENT CLUSTER

NOTE — *Removal procedures are similar for all models, however all steps may not apply to each model.*

Loosen instrument cluster trim panel screws. Remove radio and heater control knobs (if required) and remove trim panel. Loosen steering column clamp bolts (if required). Remove screws, bolts or nuts mounting cluster to instrument panel. Disconnect speedometer cable and all wiring connectors. Remove instrument cluster.

SPEEDOMETER & GAUGES

Speedometer and all gauges may be removed after removal of cluster.

HAZARD WARNING & TURN SIGNAL FLASHER

Mounted near steering column, behind instrument panel center.

TRIUMPH

CAUTION — *Disconnect battery ground cable prior to removal of instrument cluster.*

INSTRUMENT CLUSTER

Spitfire — Disconnect battery and remove heater control knobs. Remove four screws and cup washers and lower cluster. Remove bulb holders, disconnect wiring and remove cluster.

TR7 & TR8 — Remove radio speaker grille and top instrument panel trim pad. Remove steering column shrouds, loosen odometer reset knob and remove knob with cable. Loosen clock reset knob and remove with cable. Disconnect speedometer cable, remove retaining screws and pull out instrument cluster slightly. Disconnect all wiring connectors and remove cluster.

TACHOMETER

Tachometer may be removed after removing instrument cluster.

SPEEDOMETER

Spitfire — Disconnect battery. Lower center dash, remove tachometer and depress lever releasing catch from annular

TRIUMPH (Cont.)

groove in the boss. Detach speedometer cable, unscrew trip reset and remove two knurled nuts. Disconnect two connectors, bulb holders and remove speedometer.

TR7 & TR8 — Speedometer may be removed after removing instrument cluster.

GAUGES

All gauges may be removed after removing instrument cluster.

HAZARD WARNING & TURN SIGNAL FLASHER

Spitfire — Separate units are mounted under dash and held in position by spring clips.

TR7 & TR8 — Separate turn signal and hazard units are mounted behind lower panel at rear of glove box. To gain access, open glove box and remove cover panel.

VOLKSWAGEN

CAUTION — *Disconnect battery ground cable prior to removal of instrument cluster.*

INSTRUMENT CLUSTER

All Others — Remove trim plate for fresh air control and remove radio or dash plate. Disconnect speedometer cable and wiring. Remove retaining screw on right side of cluster, swtiches and bulb holders. Remove cluster.

Dasher — Remove radio (if equipped) or shelf. Remove fresh air control and fan knobs. Remove fresh air control trim panel. Remove 6 retaining screws. Disconnect and remove light switch, hazard switch and rear window defogger switch. Disconnect fresh air fan electrical connection. Remove cluster

cover. Remove cluster screws, detach speedometer cable and electrical connections. Remove cluster.

Vanagon — Grasp rear of cluster cover with fingers, pull up on cover and remove. Push hazard warning switch and brake warning light housing forward. Remove 4 cluster retaining screws. Disconnect speedometer cable and wiring connectors. Remove cluster.

SPEEDOMETER

All Models — Speedometer can be removed after removing instrument cluster and speedometer retaining screws.

HAZARD WARNING & TURN SIGNAL FLASHER

All Models — Flasher is a plug-in unit on fuse block.

VOLVO

CAUTION — *Disconnect battery ground cable prior to removal of instrument cluster.*

INSTRUMENT CLUSTER

All Models — Remove steering column shrouds. Loosen bracket screw and allow bracket to drop down steering column. Remove instrument cluster mounting screws. Disconnect speedometer cable. Press upward on back of speedometer until snap lock on upper edge releases. Lift cluster forward and disconnect wiring. Disconnect tachometer and remove cluster.

SPEEDOMETER & GAUGES

All Models — Speedometer and all gauges can be removed after removing instrument cluster.

HAZARD WARNING & TURN SIGNAL FLASHER

DL, GL, GT — Flasher is mounted behind left kick panel.

Coupe, GLE, Diesel — Flasher is mounted behind instrument cluster.

Section 4
WIRING DIAGRAMS

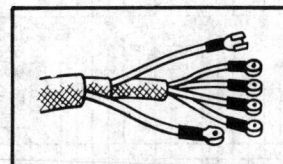

Contents

FUSES & CIRCUIT BREAKERS

FUSE, FLASHER AND RELAY LOCATIONS

FUSES AND CIRCUIT BREAKERS

NOTE – ALSO SEE GENERAL INDEX

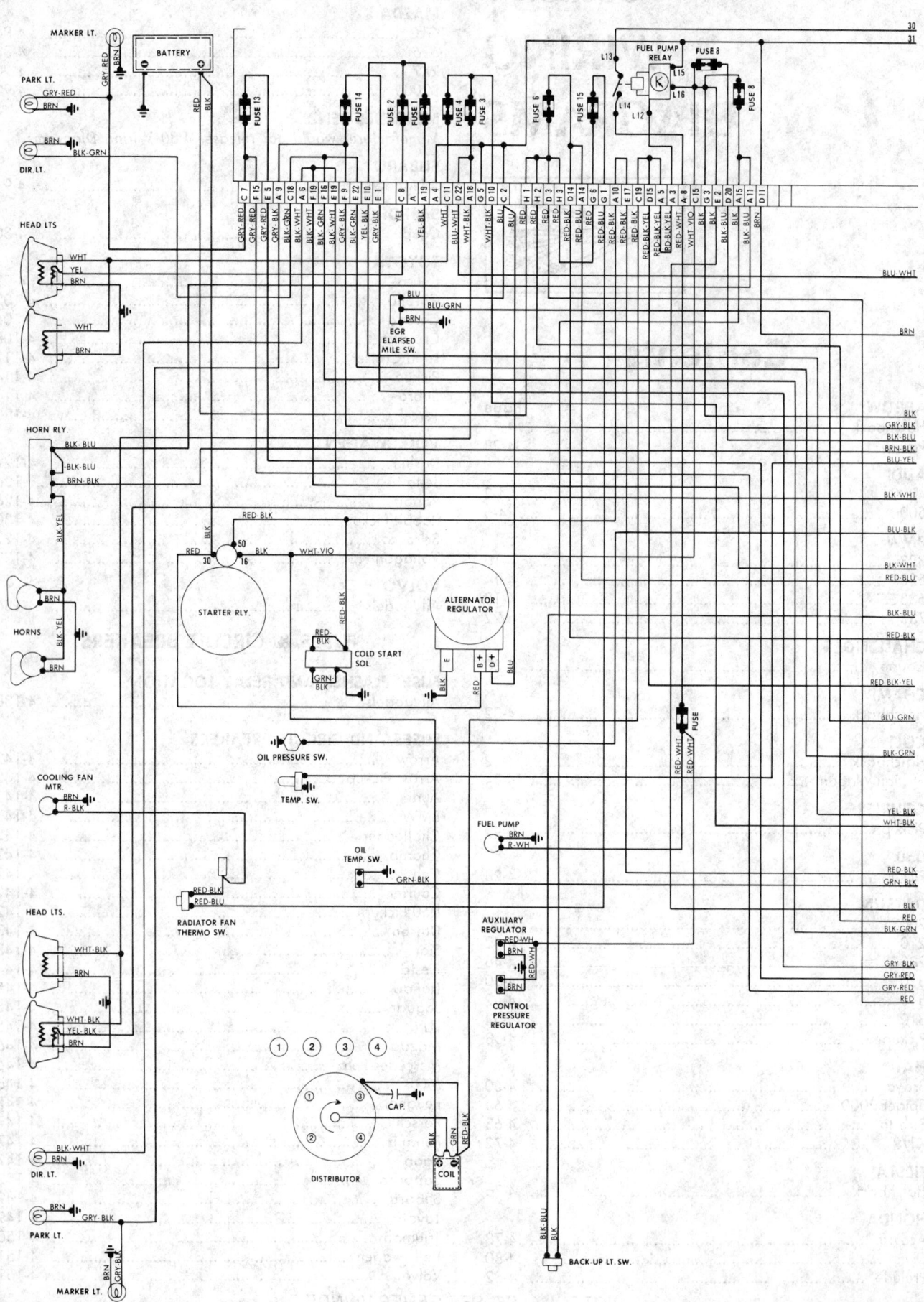

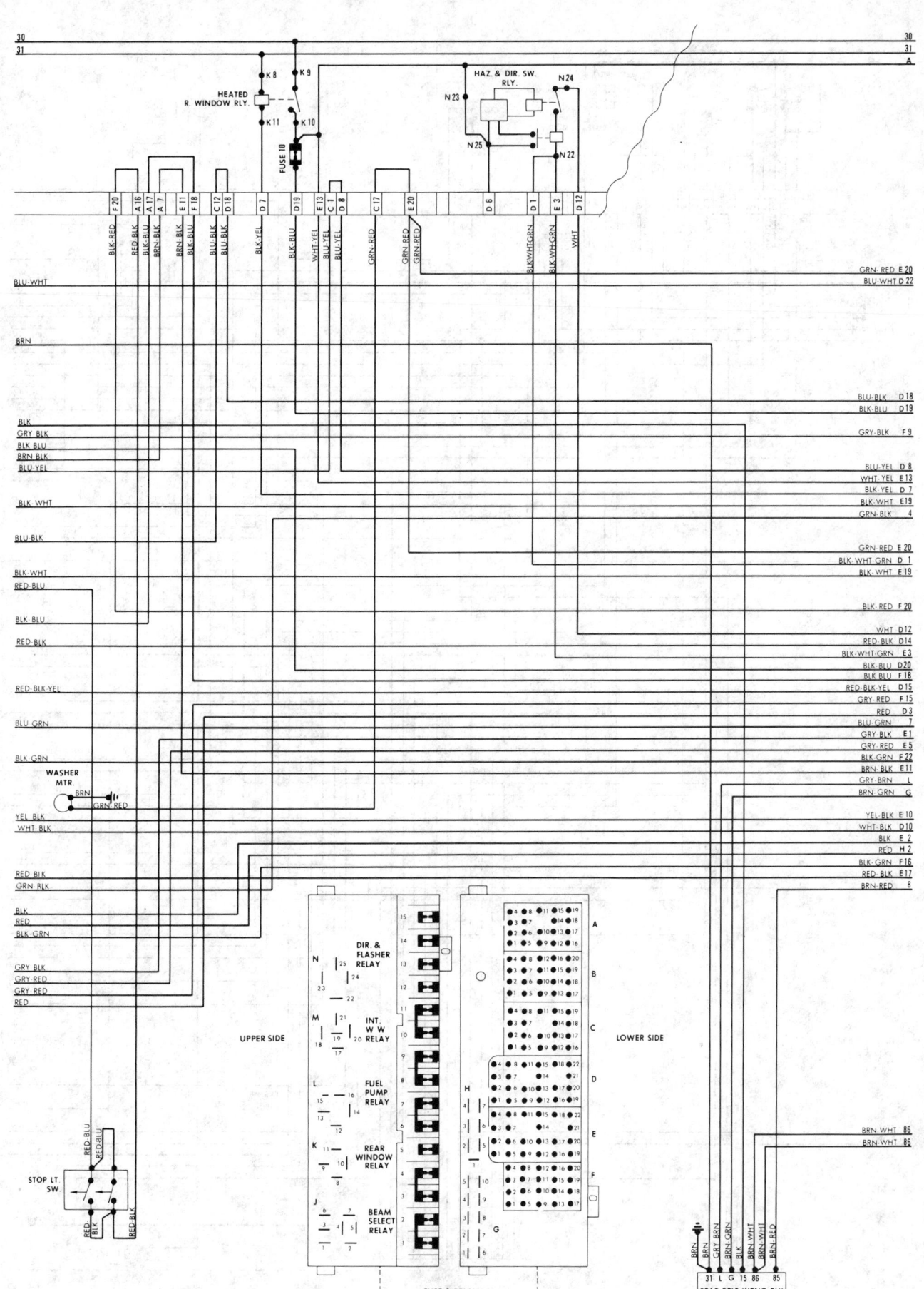

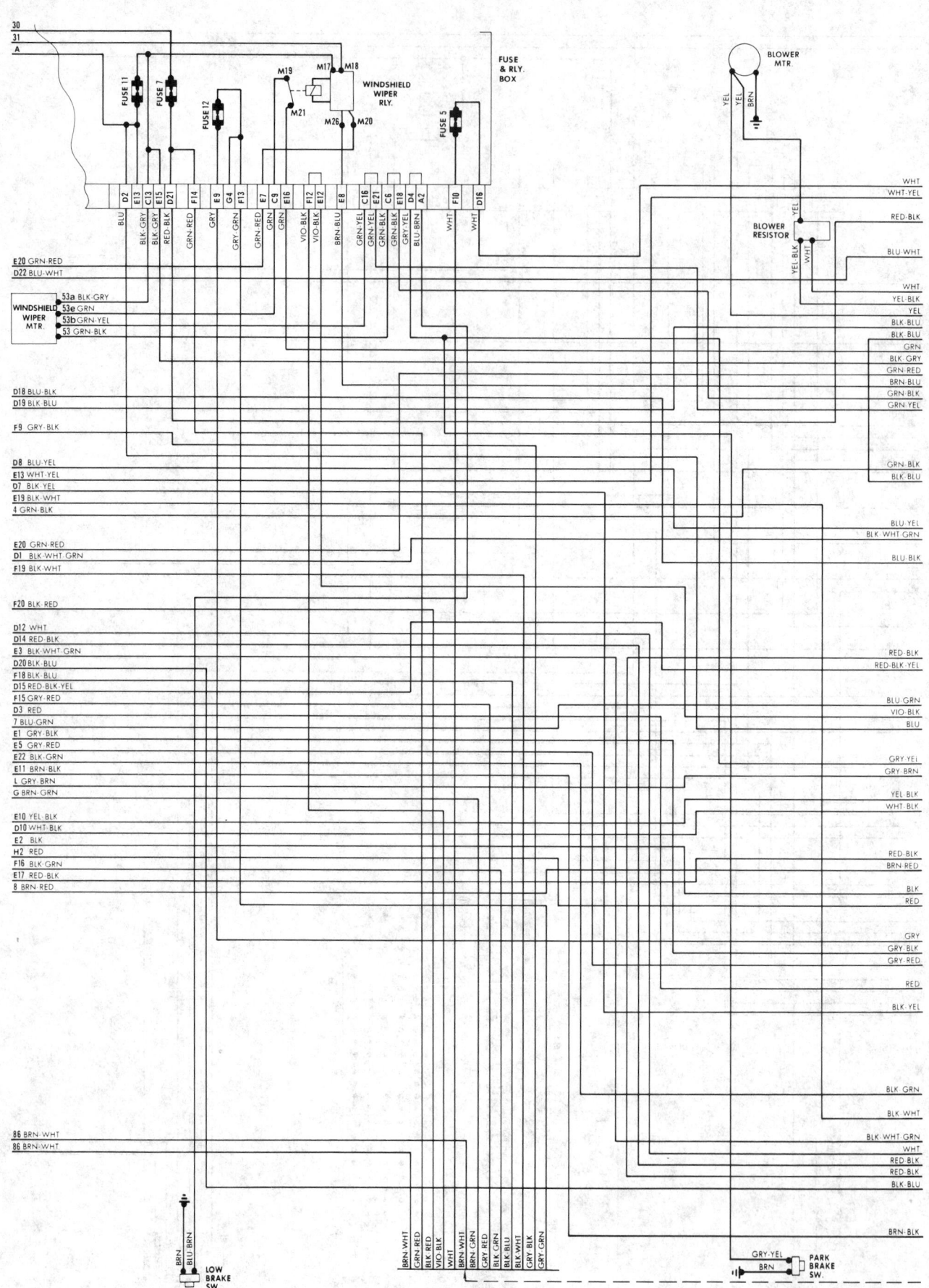

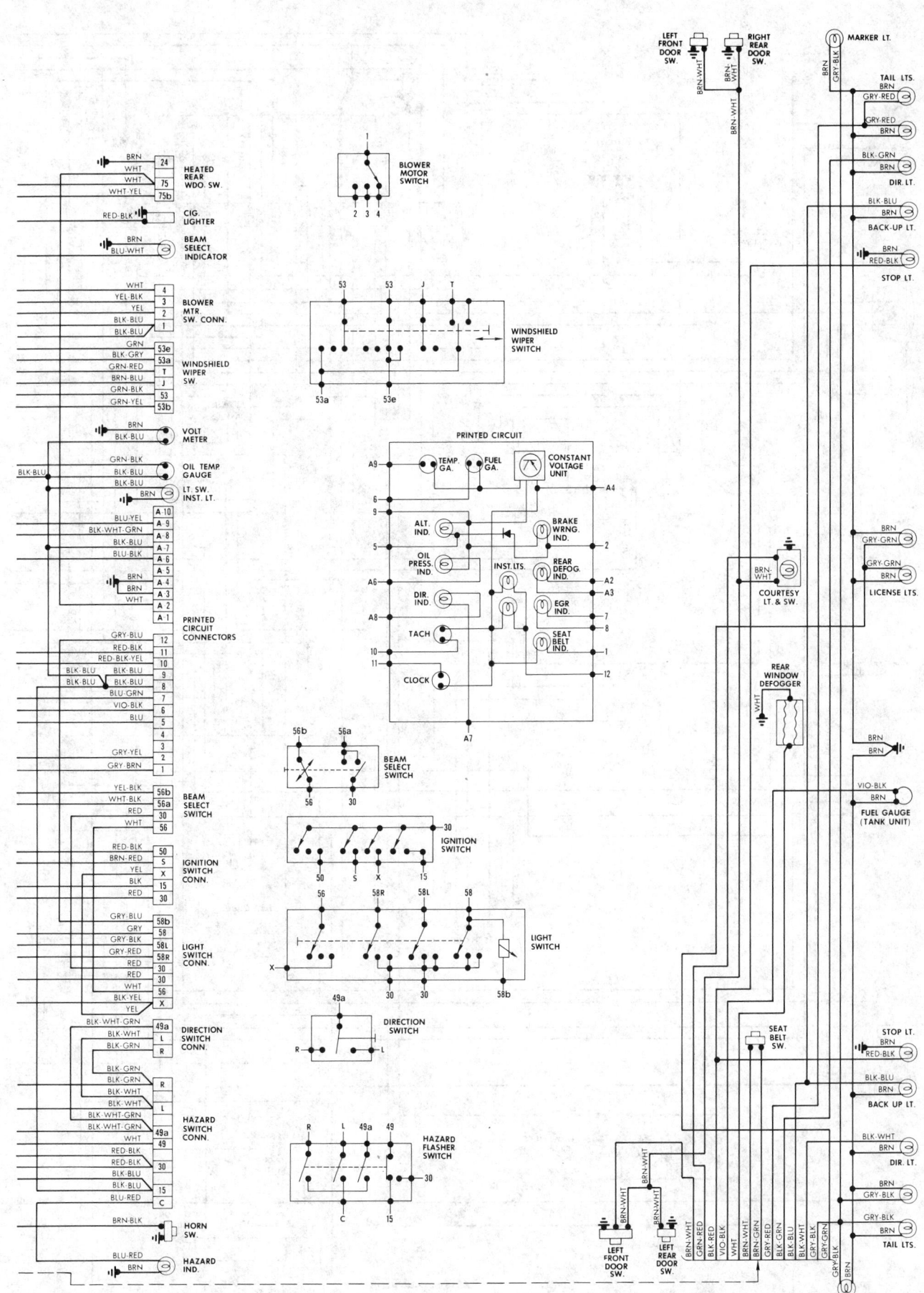

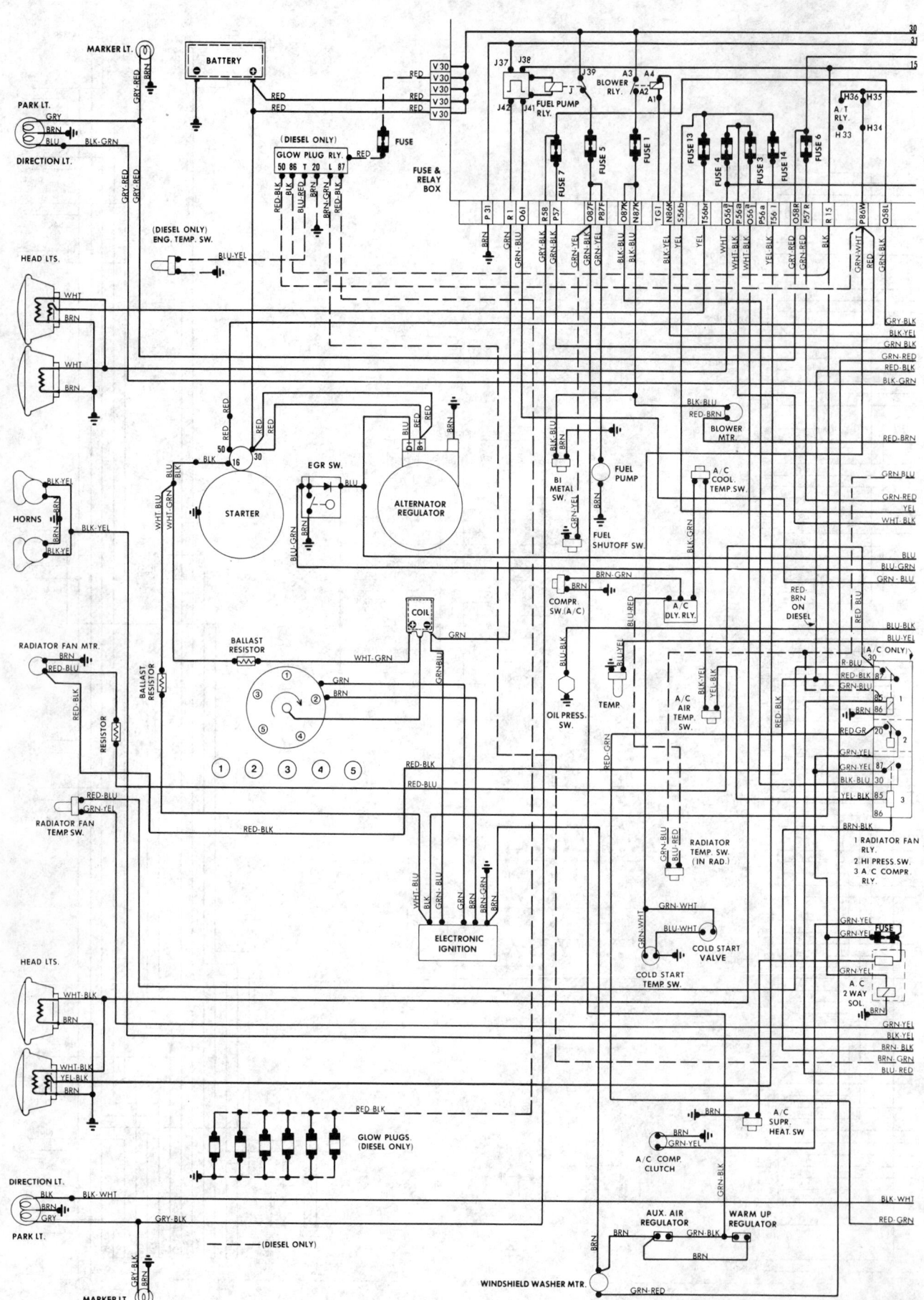

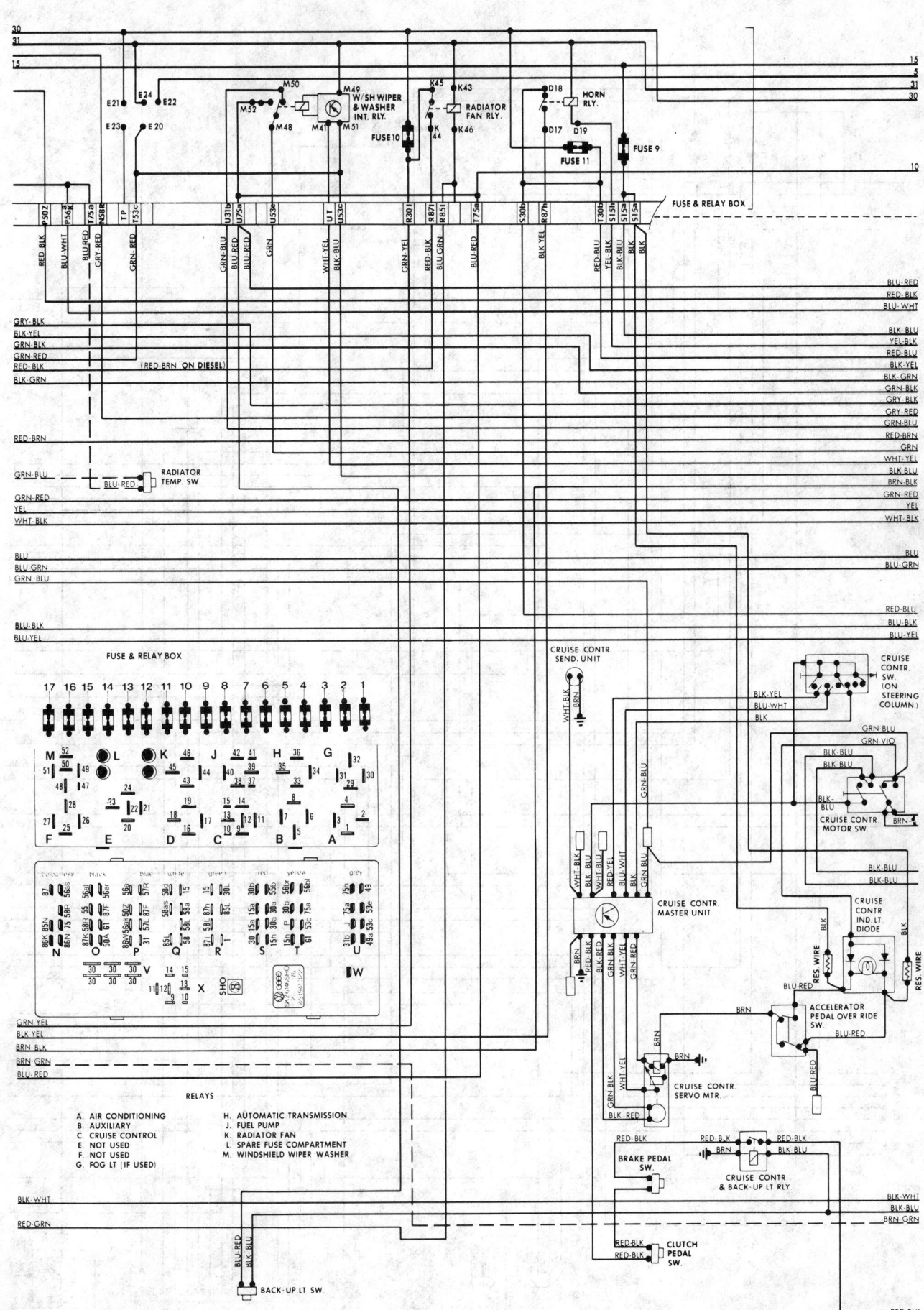

1980 Audi

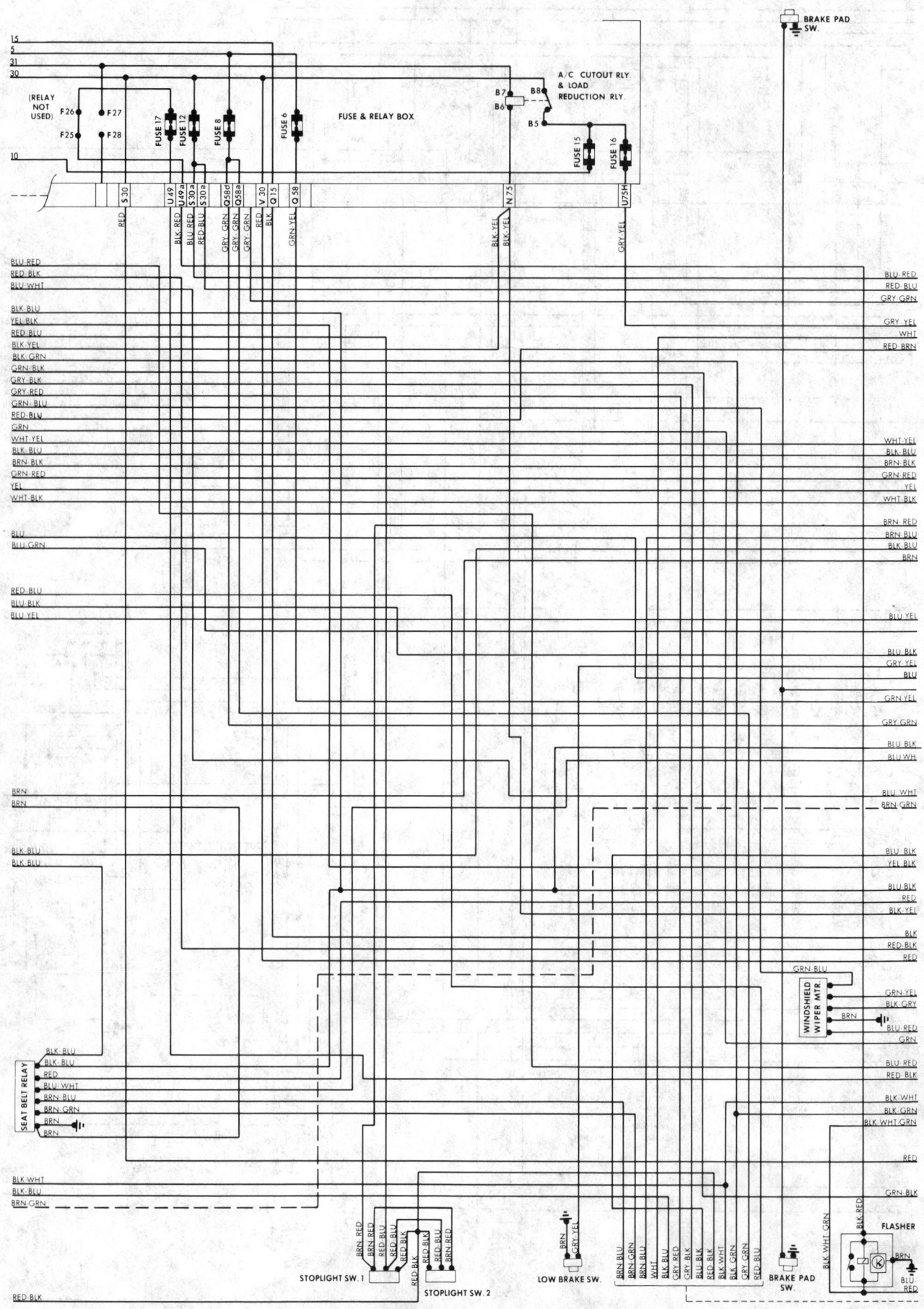

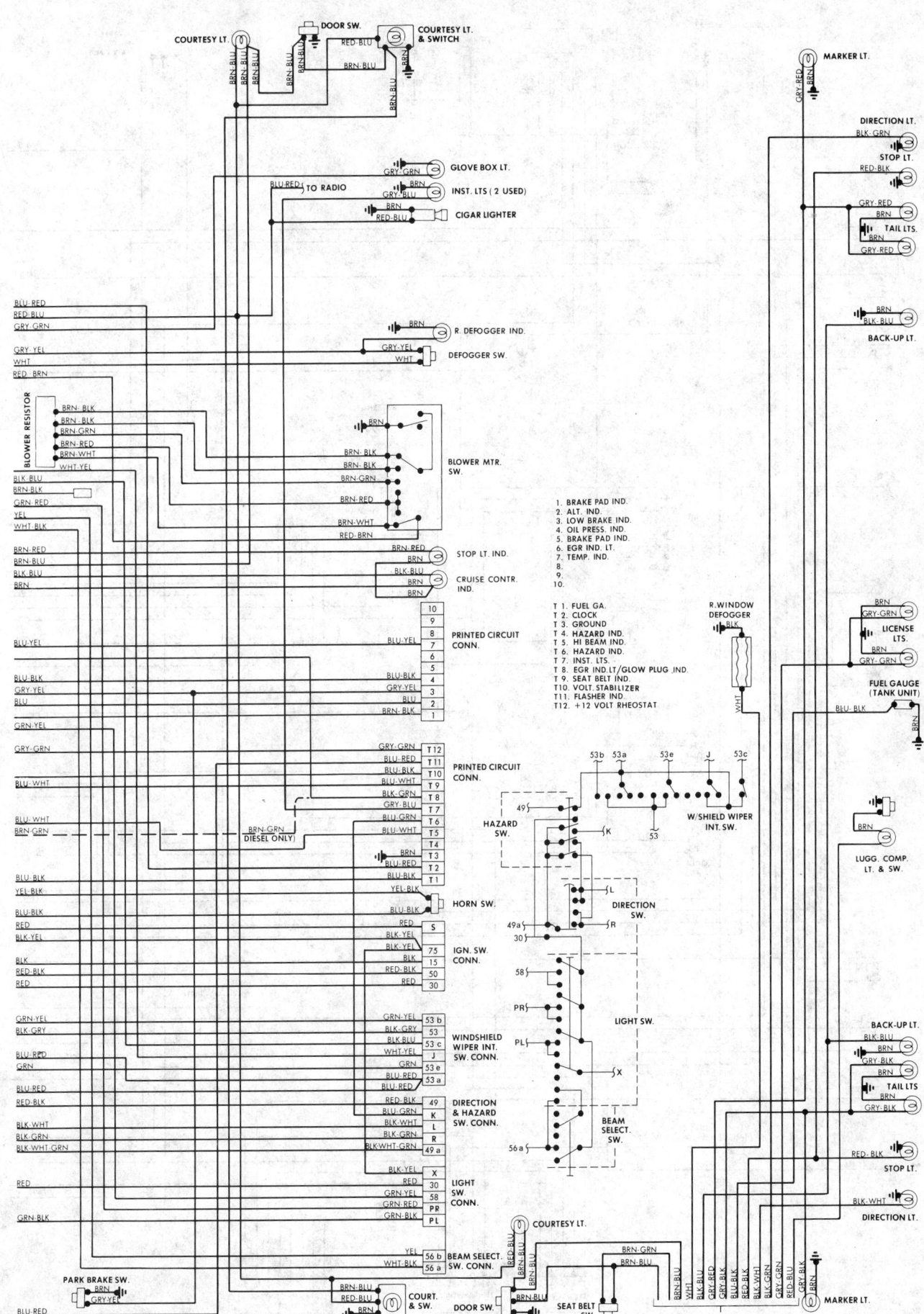

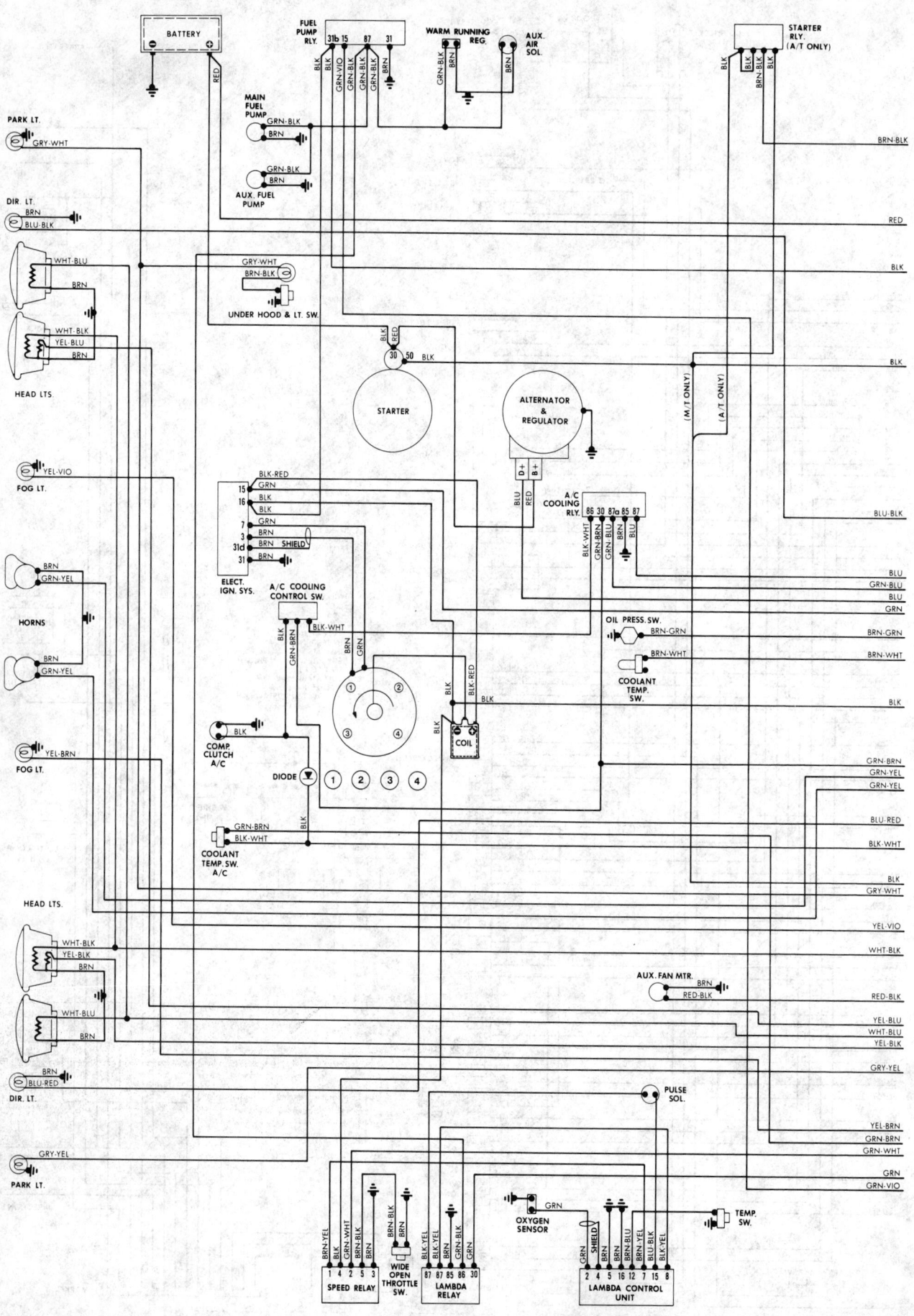

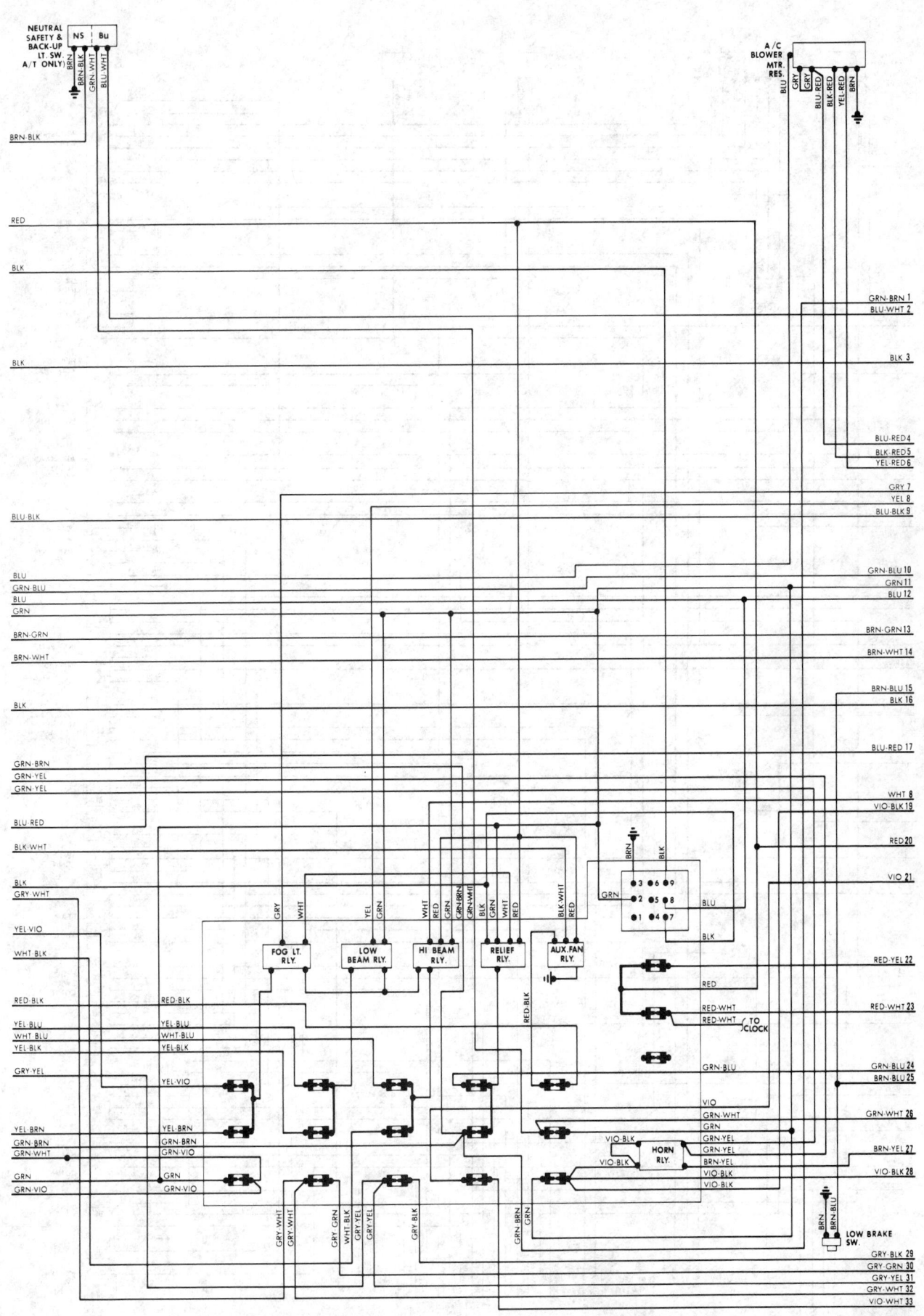

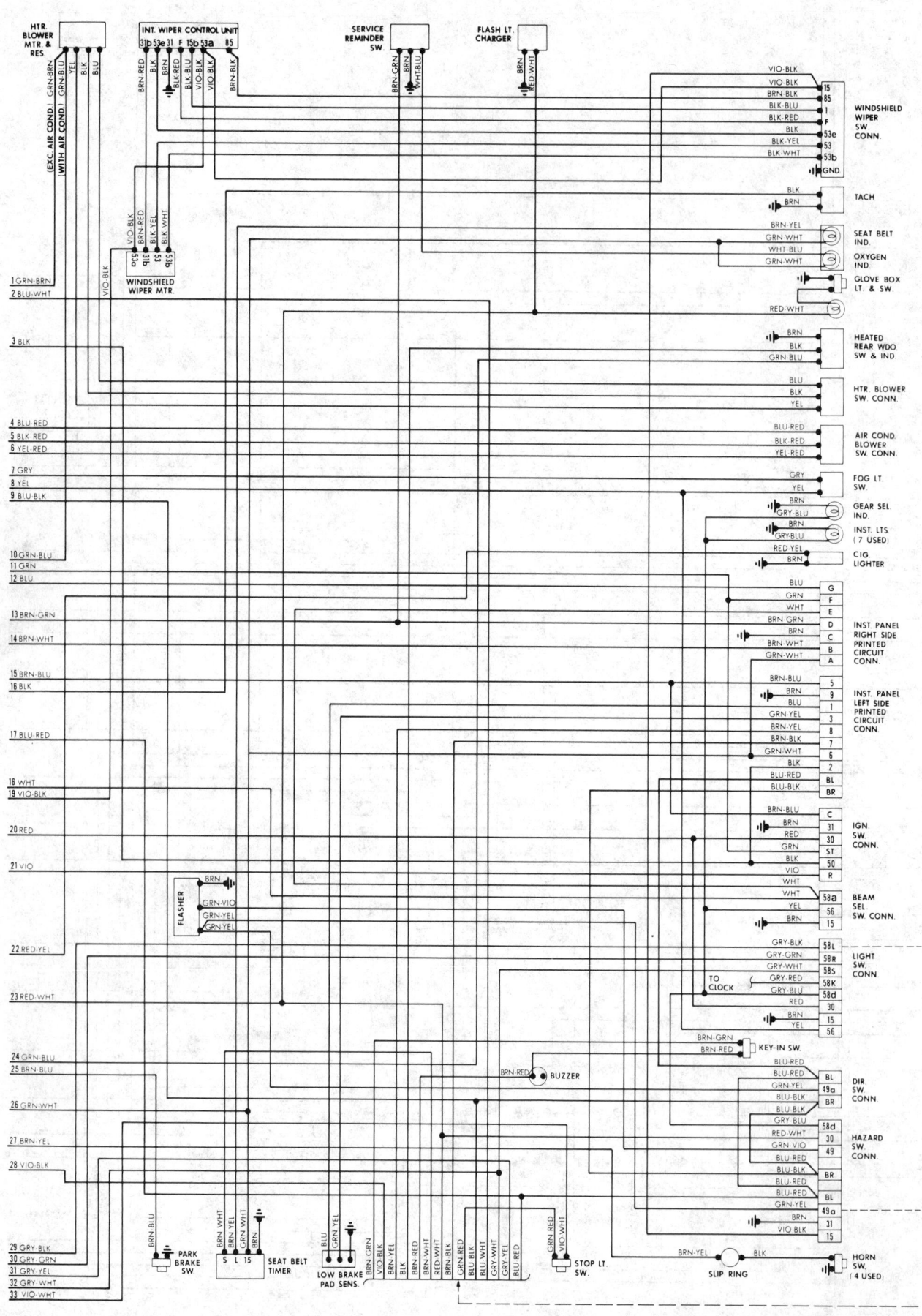

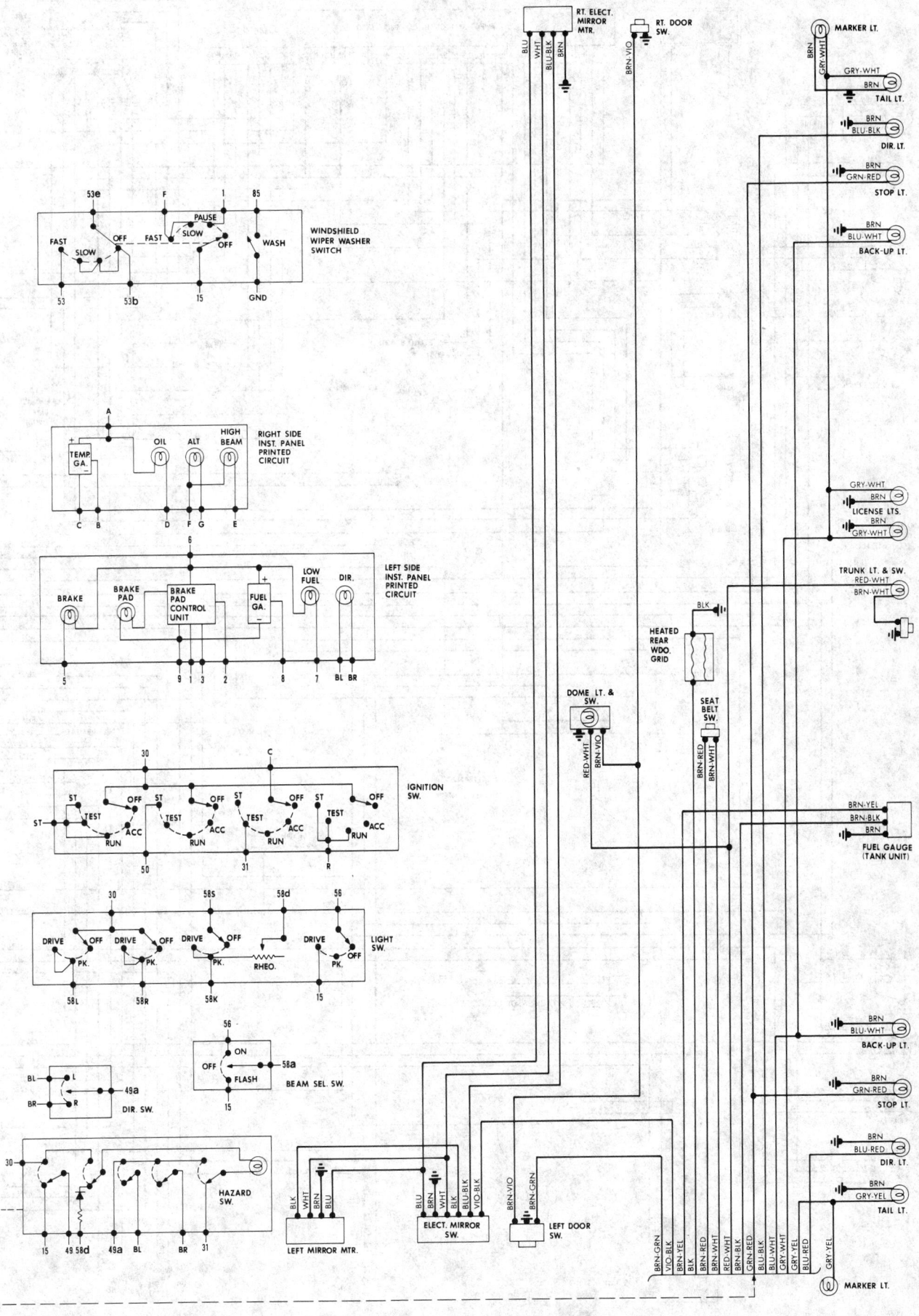

1980 BMW

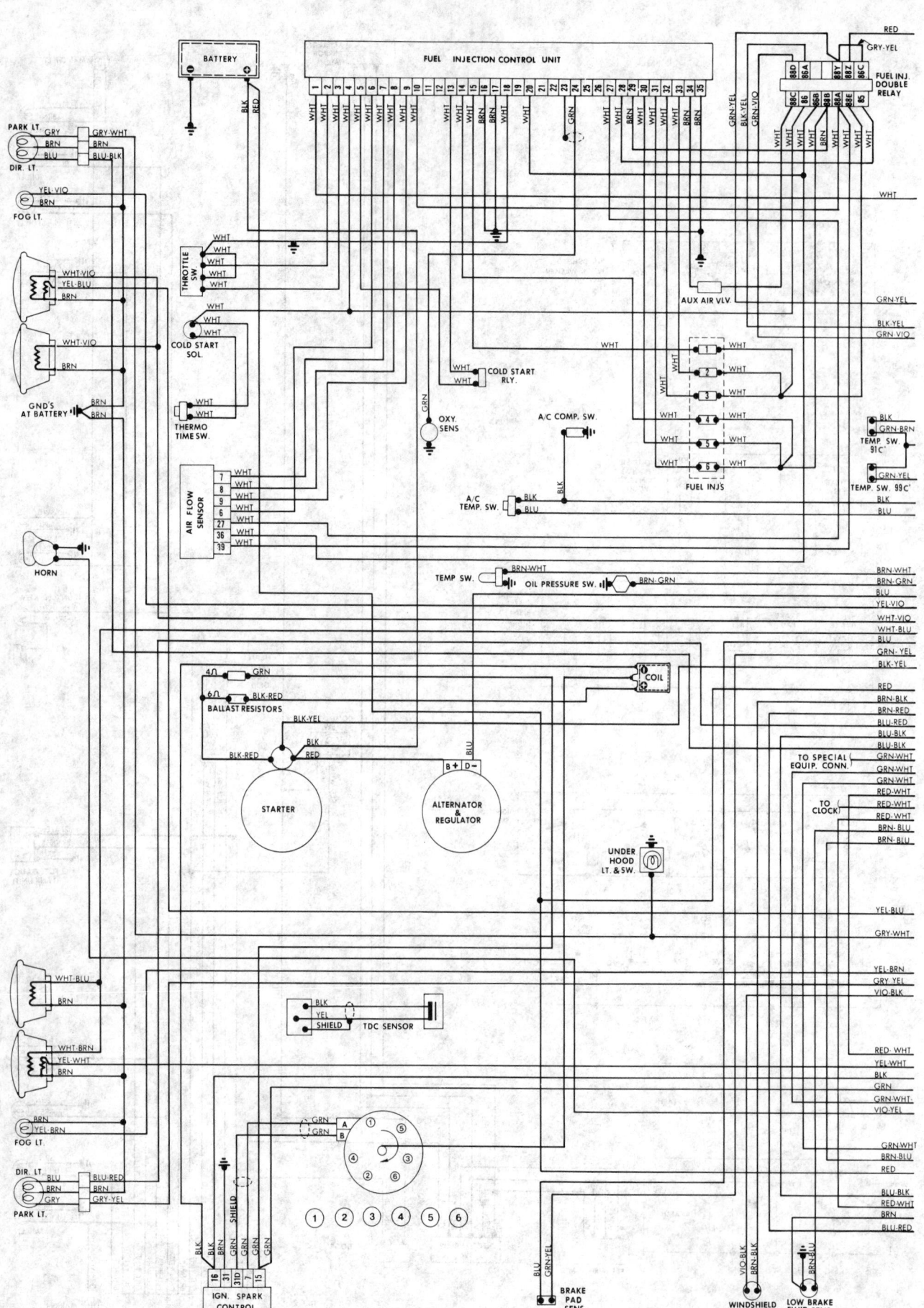

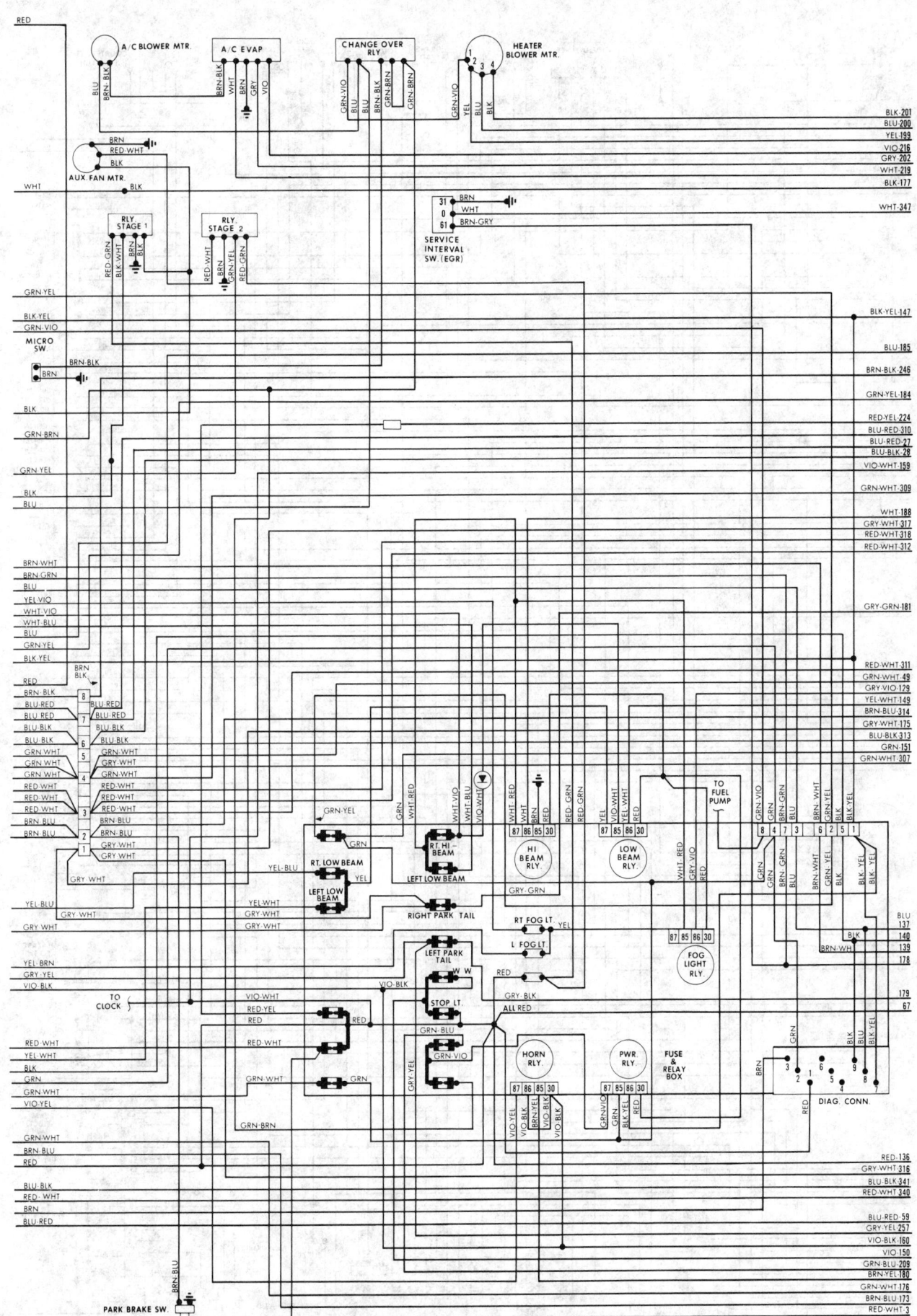

1980 BMW

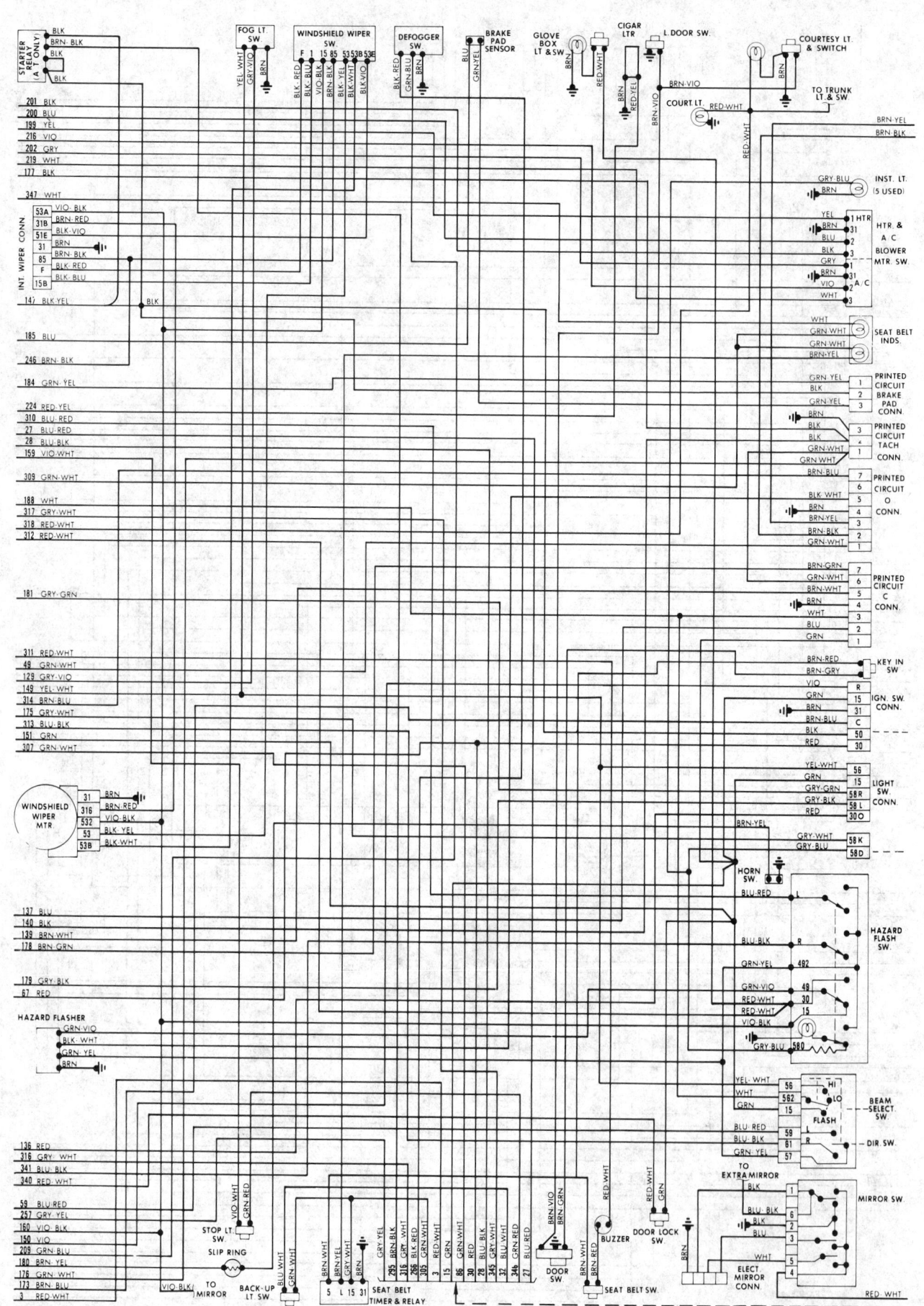

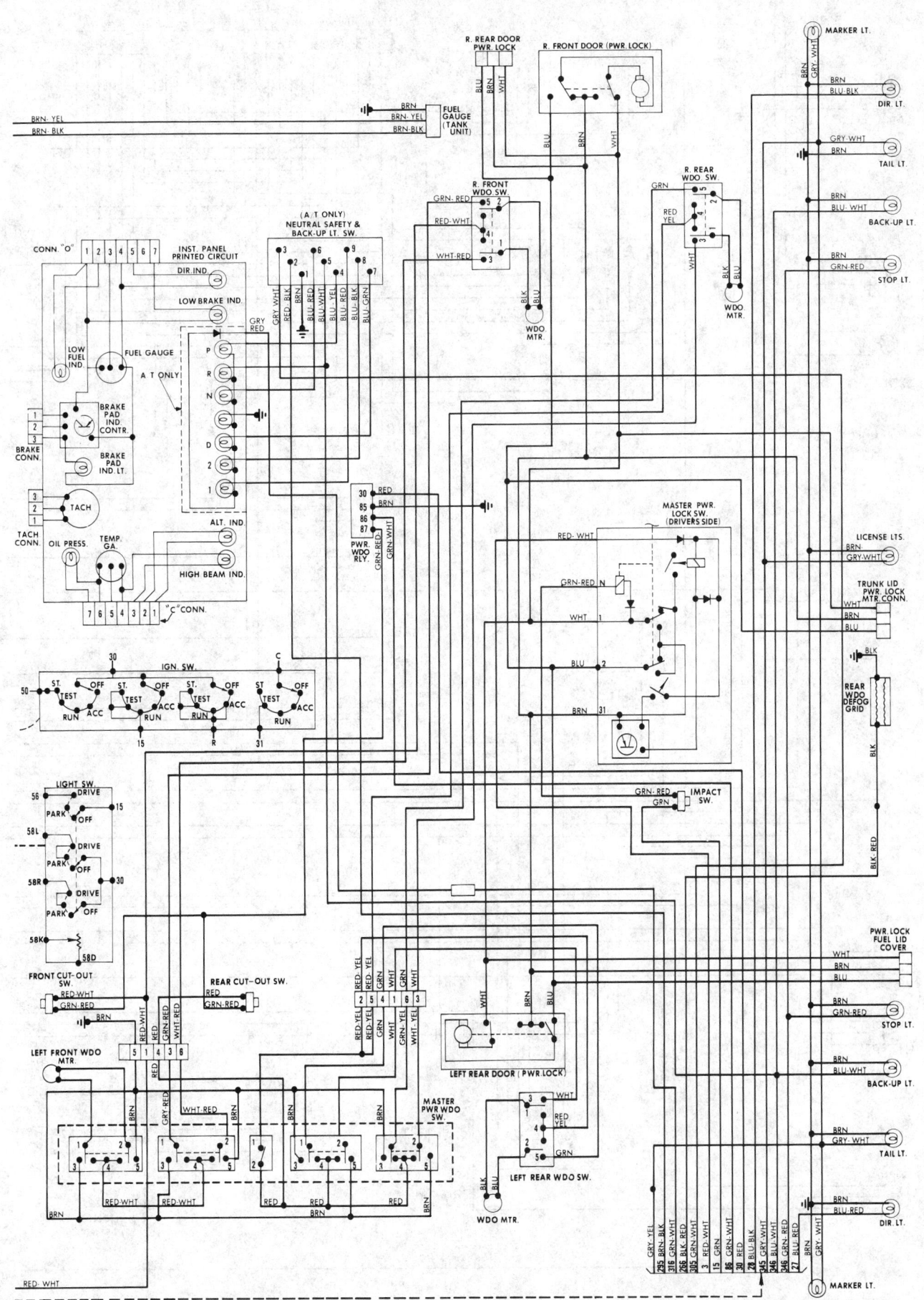

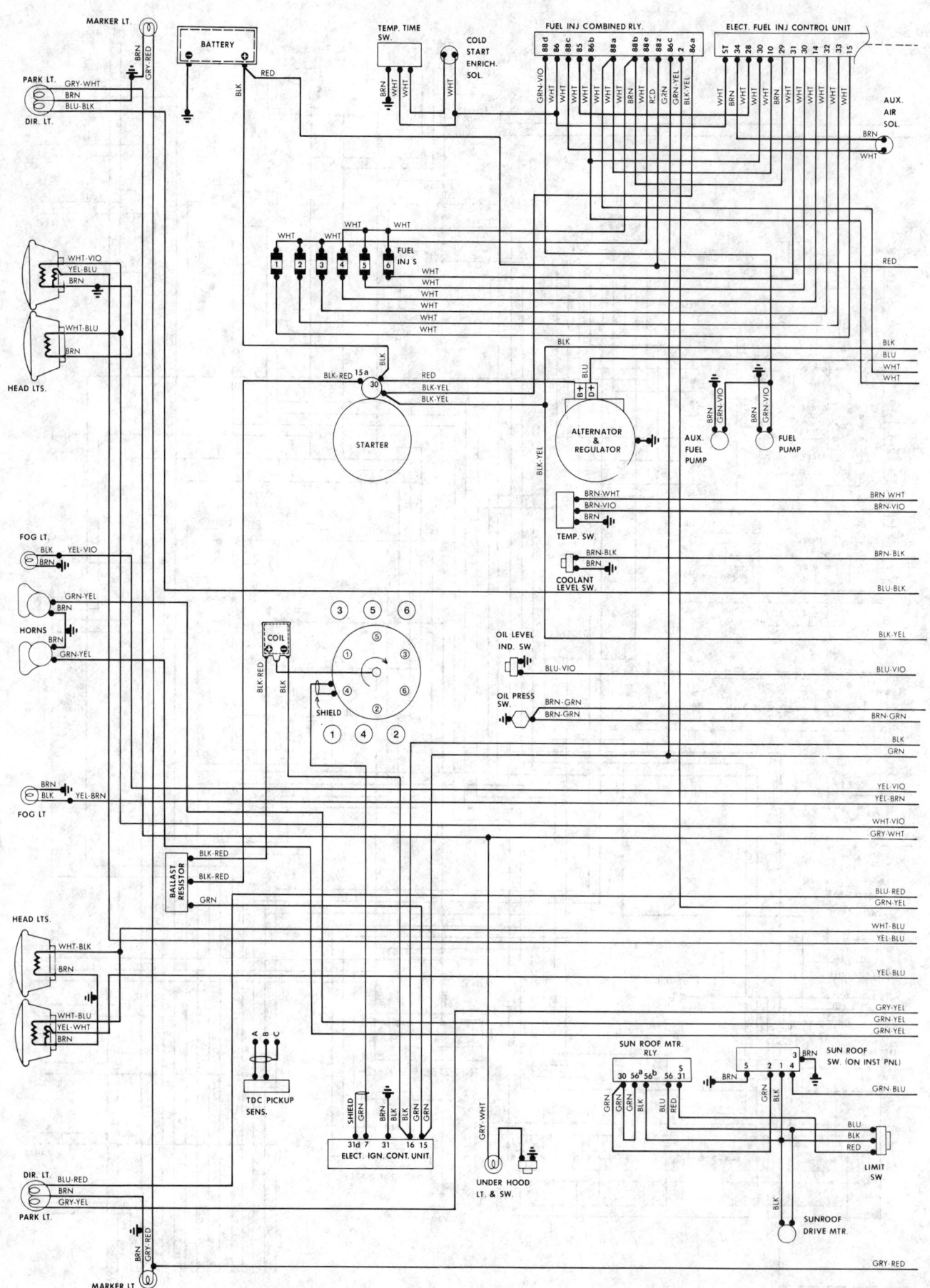

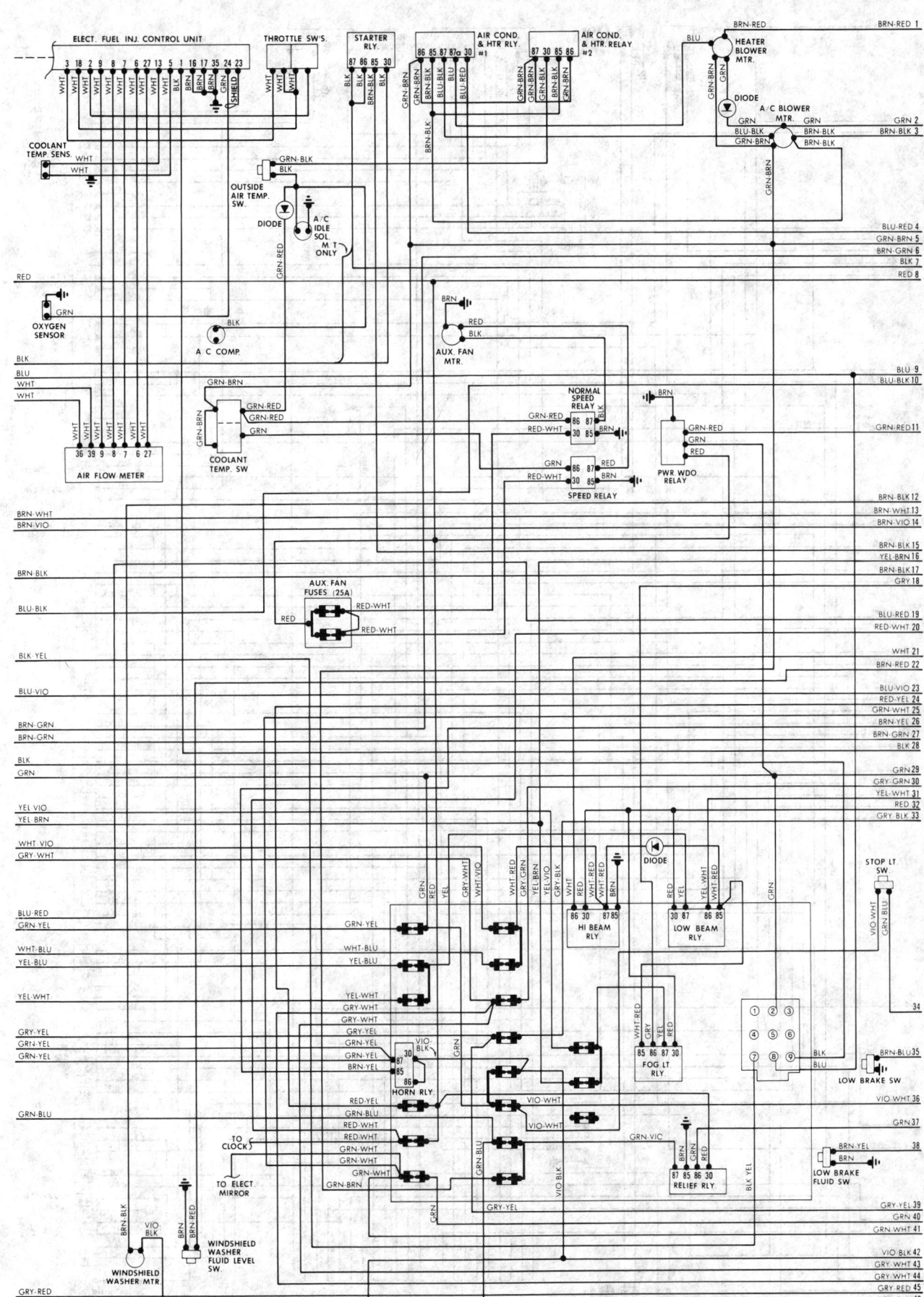

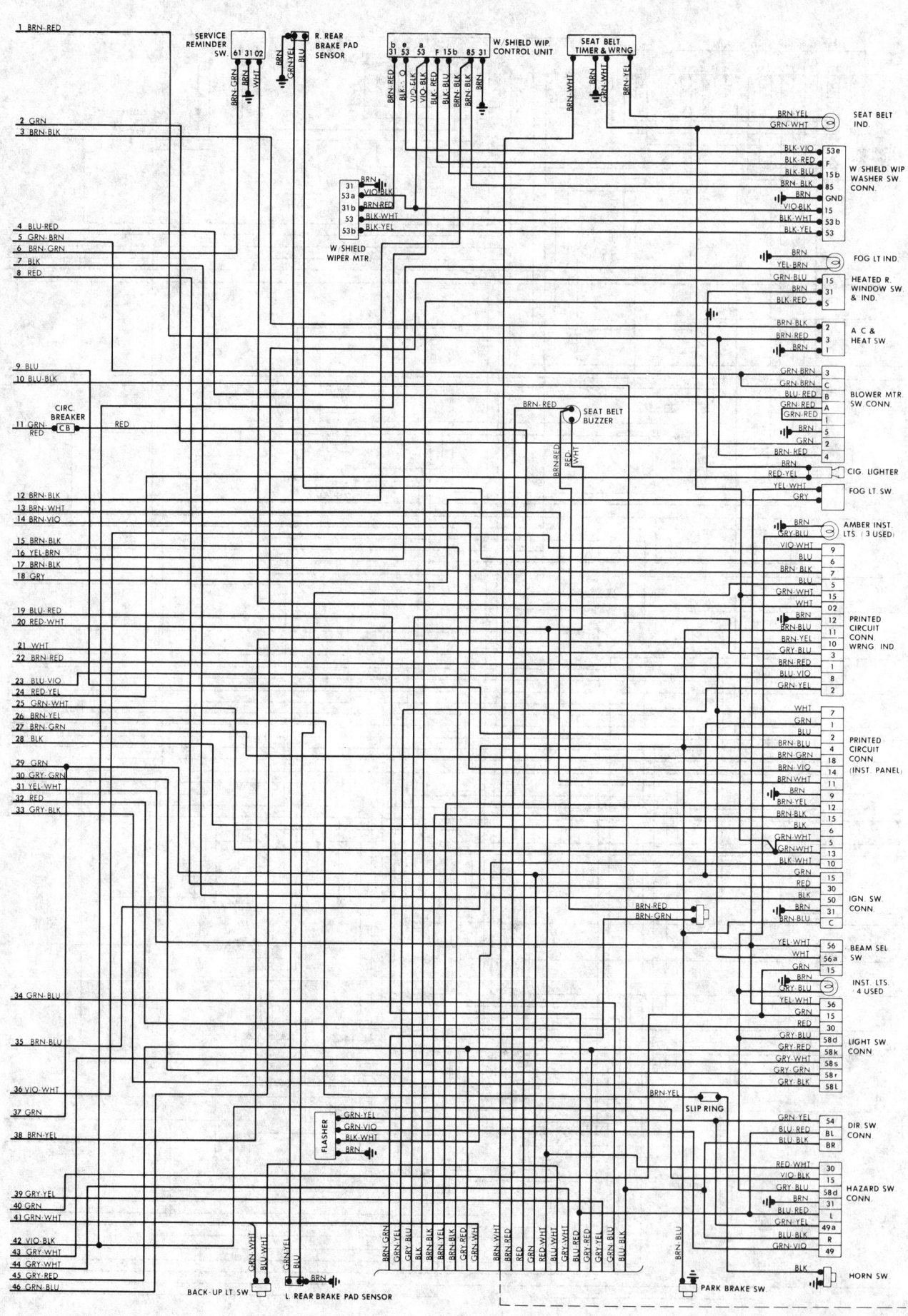

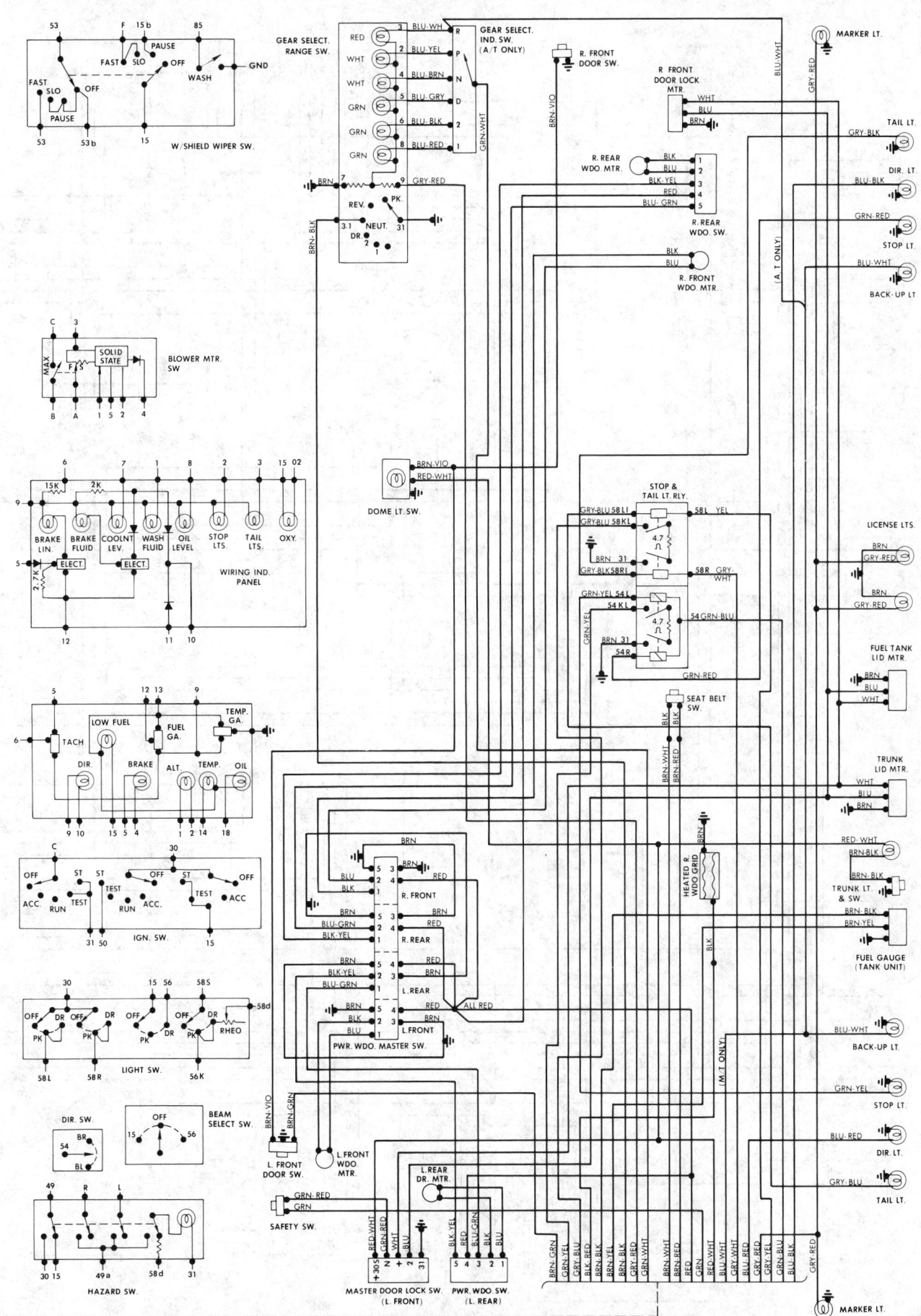

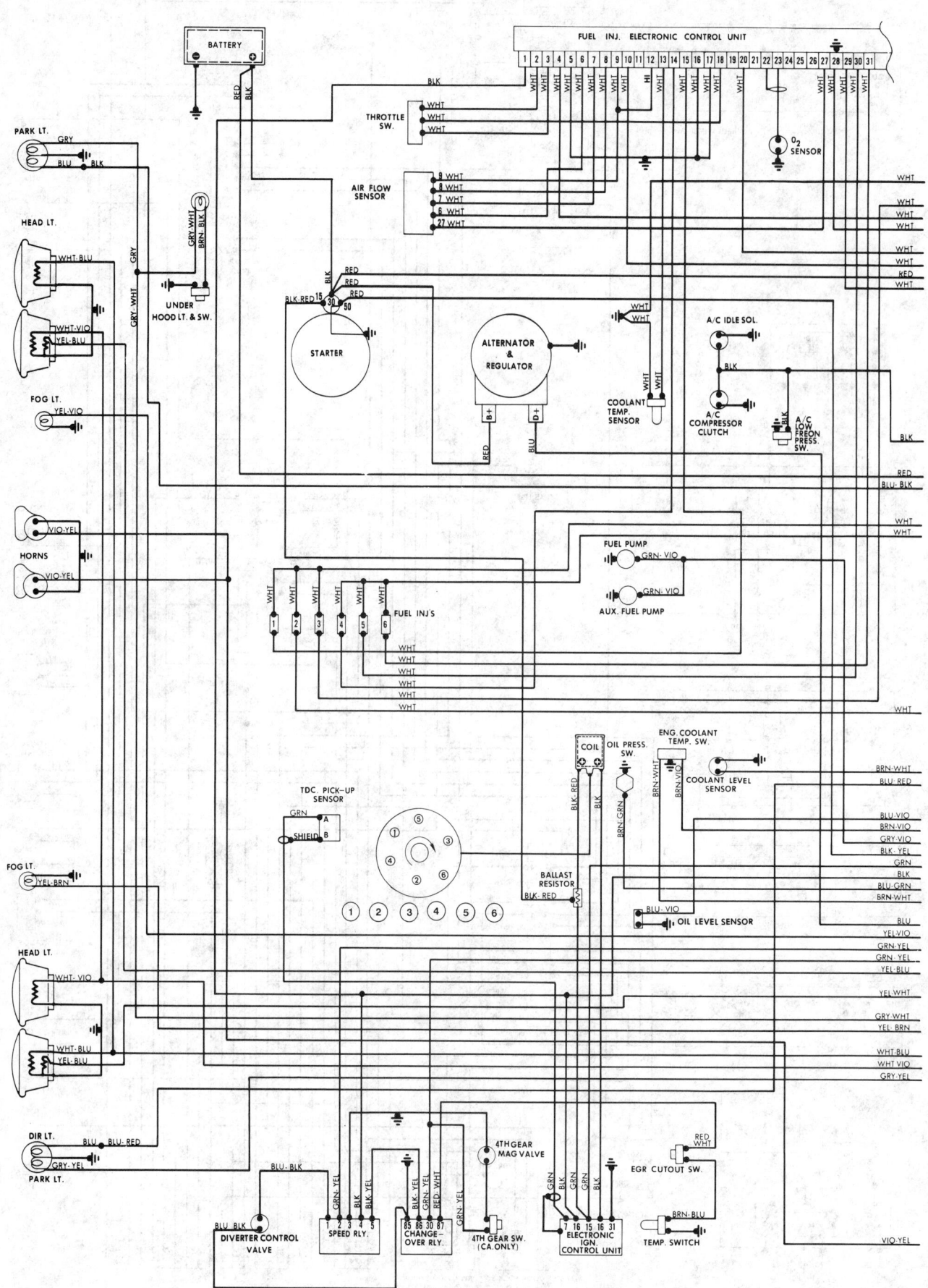

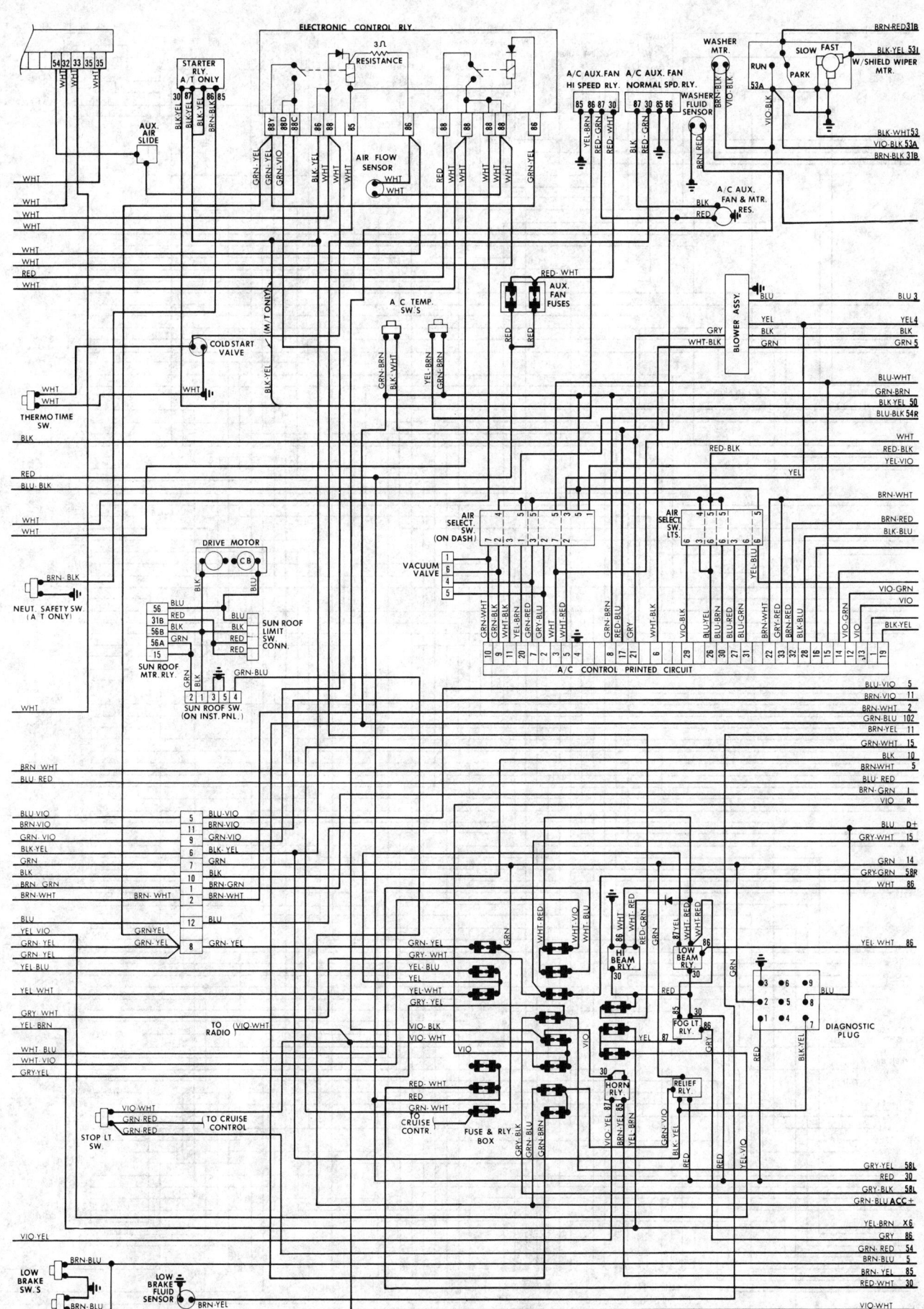

1980 BMW

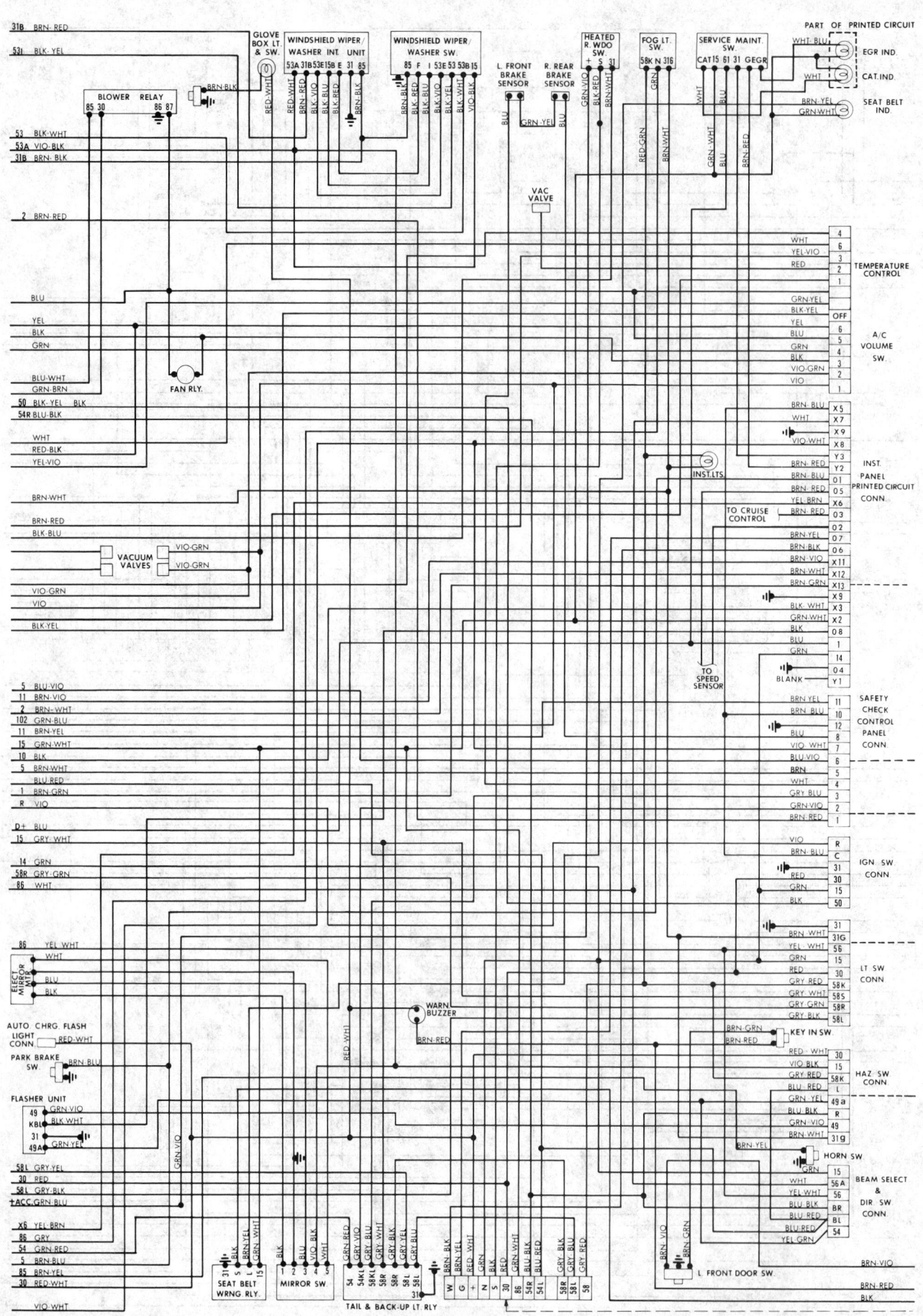

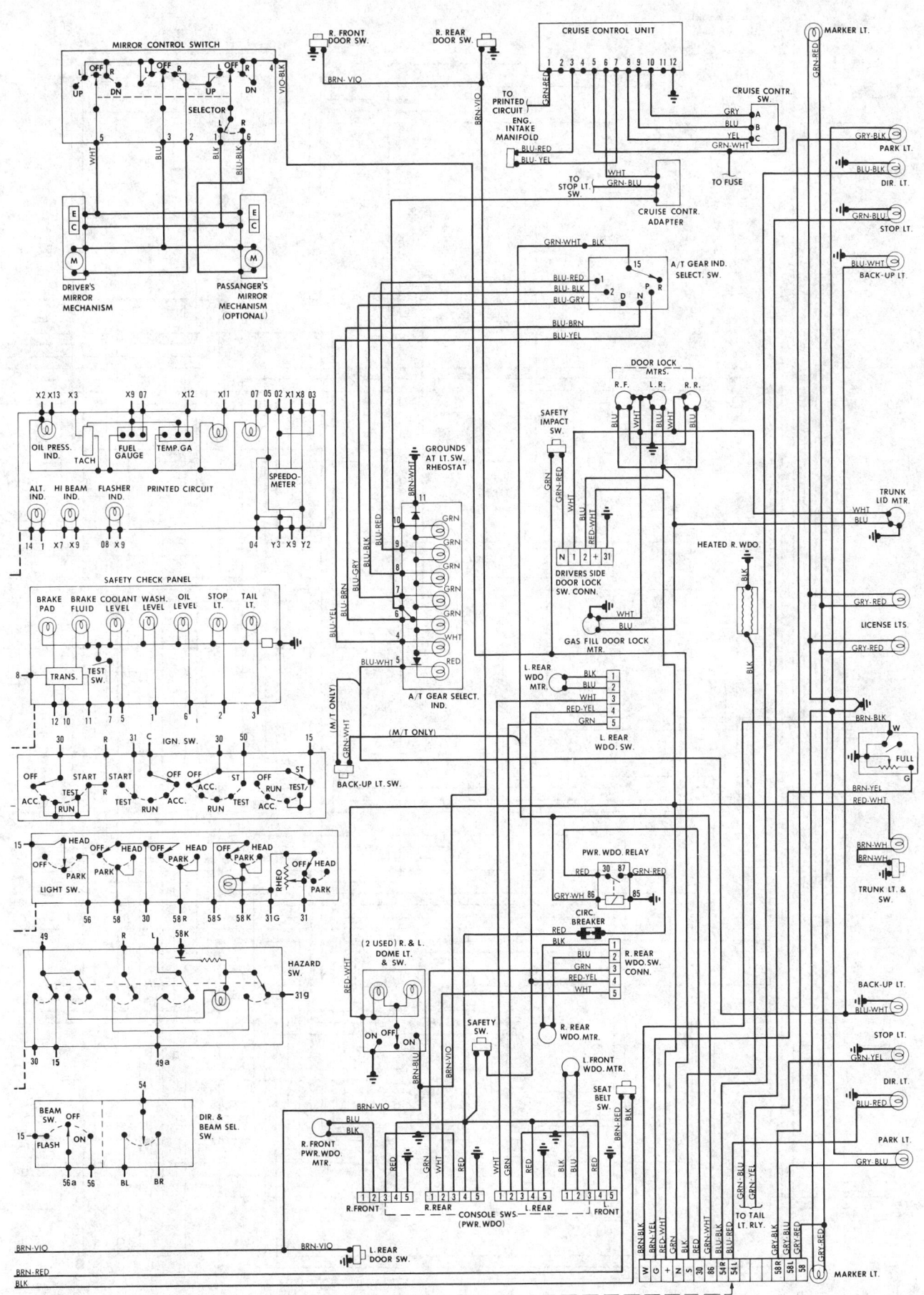

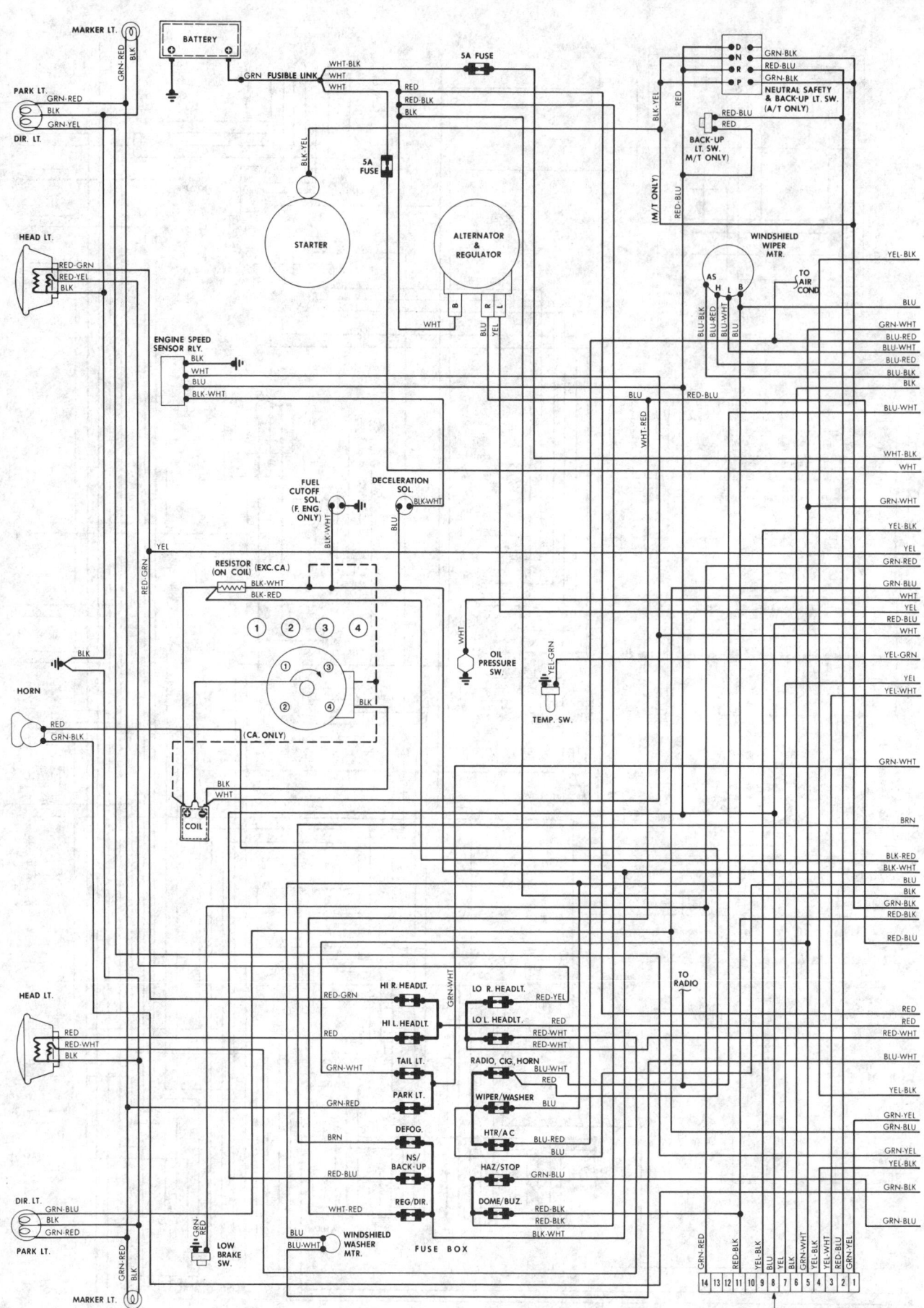

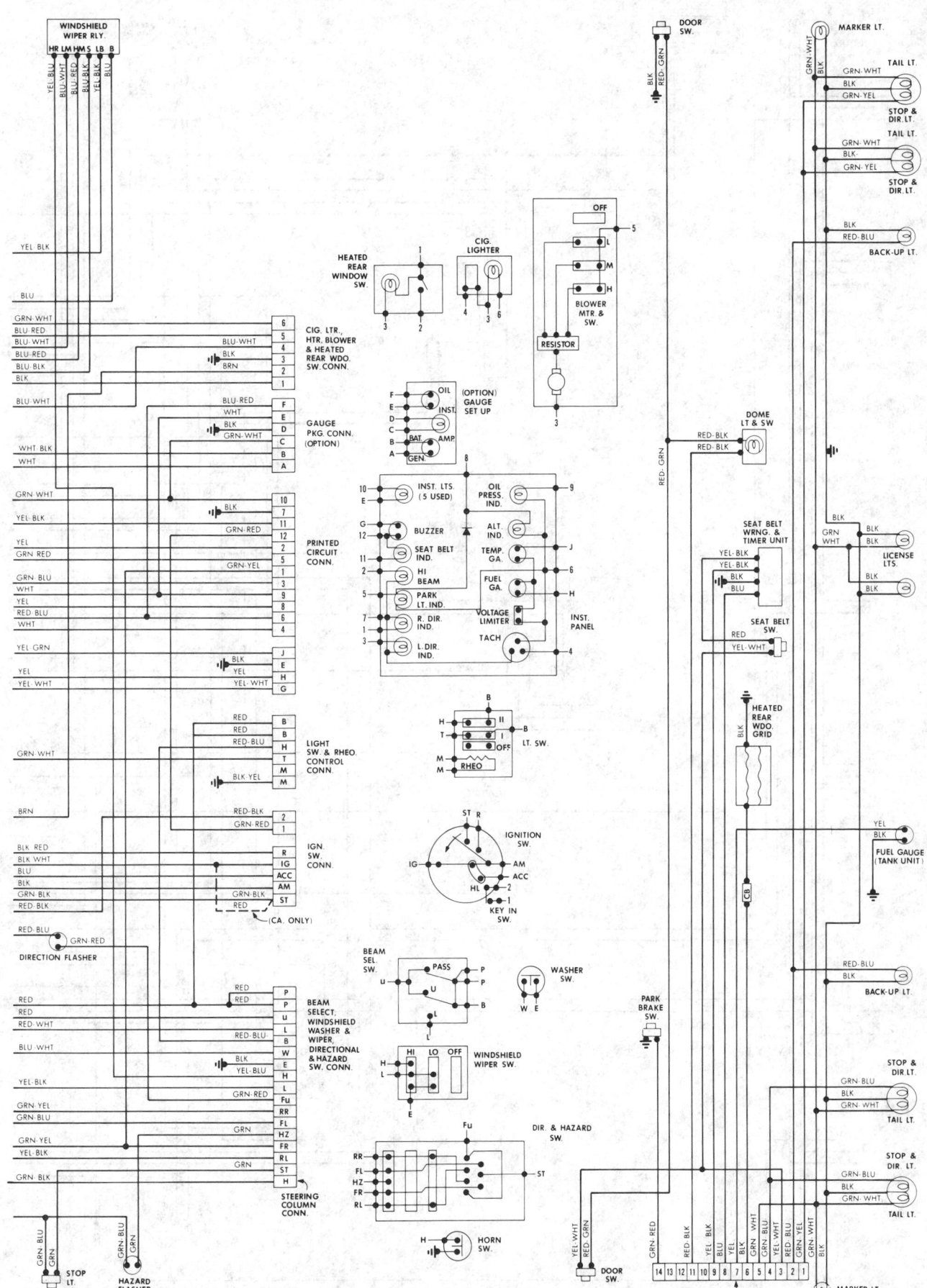

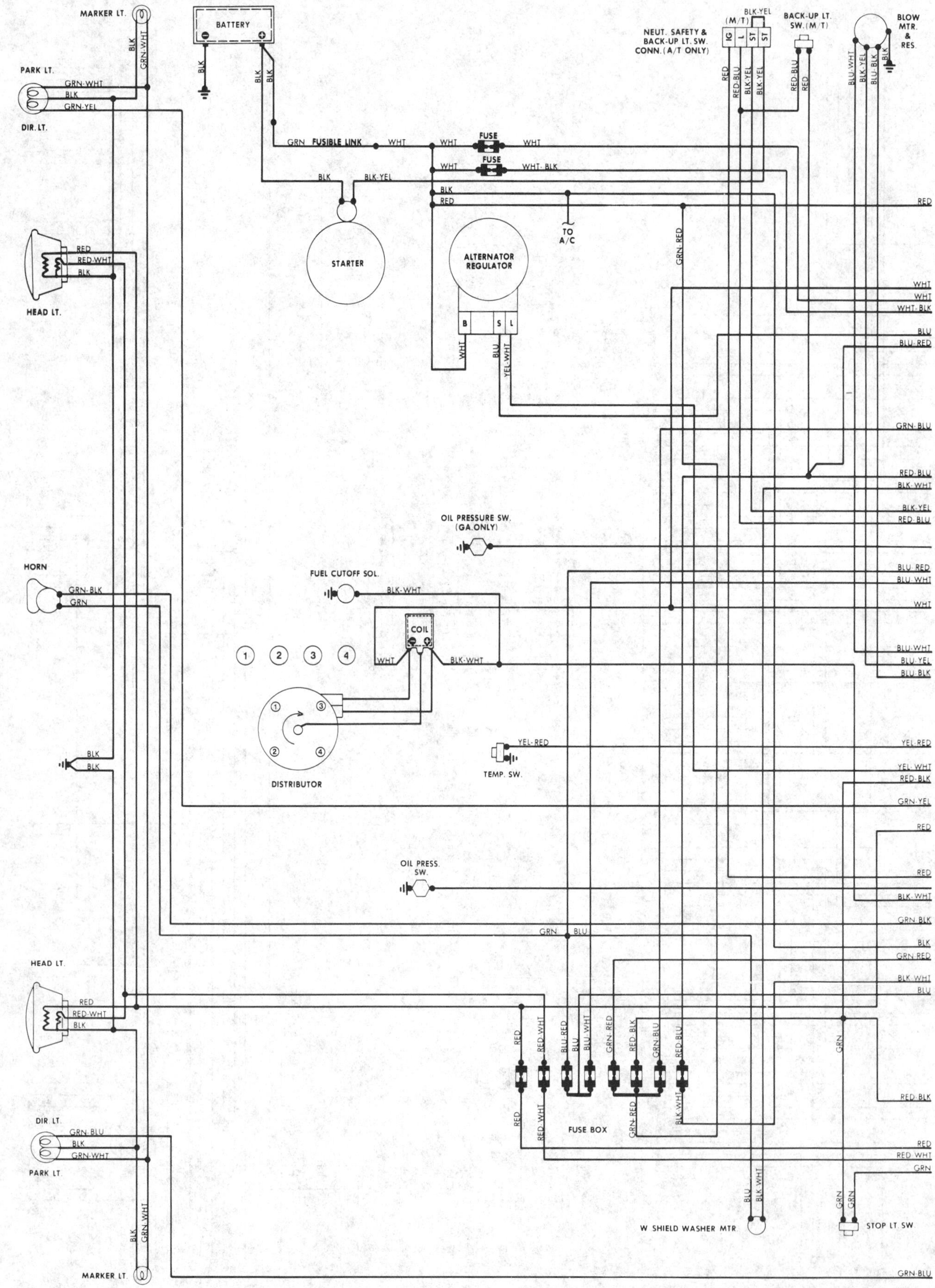
MARKER LT.
BATTERY
NEUT. SAFETY & BACK-UP LT. SW. CONN. (A/T ONLY)
(M/T)
BLK-YEL
IG
L
ST
ST
BACK-UP LT. SW. (M/T)
BLOW MTR. & RES.
PARK LT.
DIR. LT.
GRN-WHT
BLK
GRN-YEL
GRN
FUSIBLE LINK
WHT
FUSE
WHT-BLK
BLK-YEL
RED
TO A/C
STARTER
ALTERNATOR REGULATOR
B
S
L
HEAD LT.
RED-WHT
GRN-RED
WHT
BLU
BLU-RED
GRN-BLU
RED-BLU
BLK-WHT
OIL PRESSURE SW. (GA. ONLY)
HORN
GRN-BLK
FUEL CUTOFF SOL.
COIL
1
2
3
4
DISTRIBUTOR
BLU-WHT
BLU-YEL
BLU-BLK
YEL-RED
TEMP. SW.
YEL-WHT
RED-BLK
OIL PRESS. SW.
FUSE BOX
W SHIELD WASHER MTR
STOP LT SW

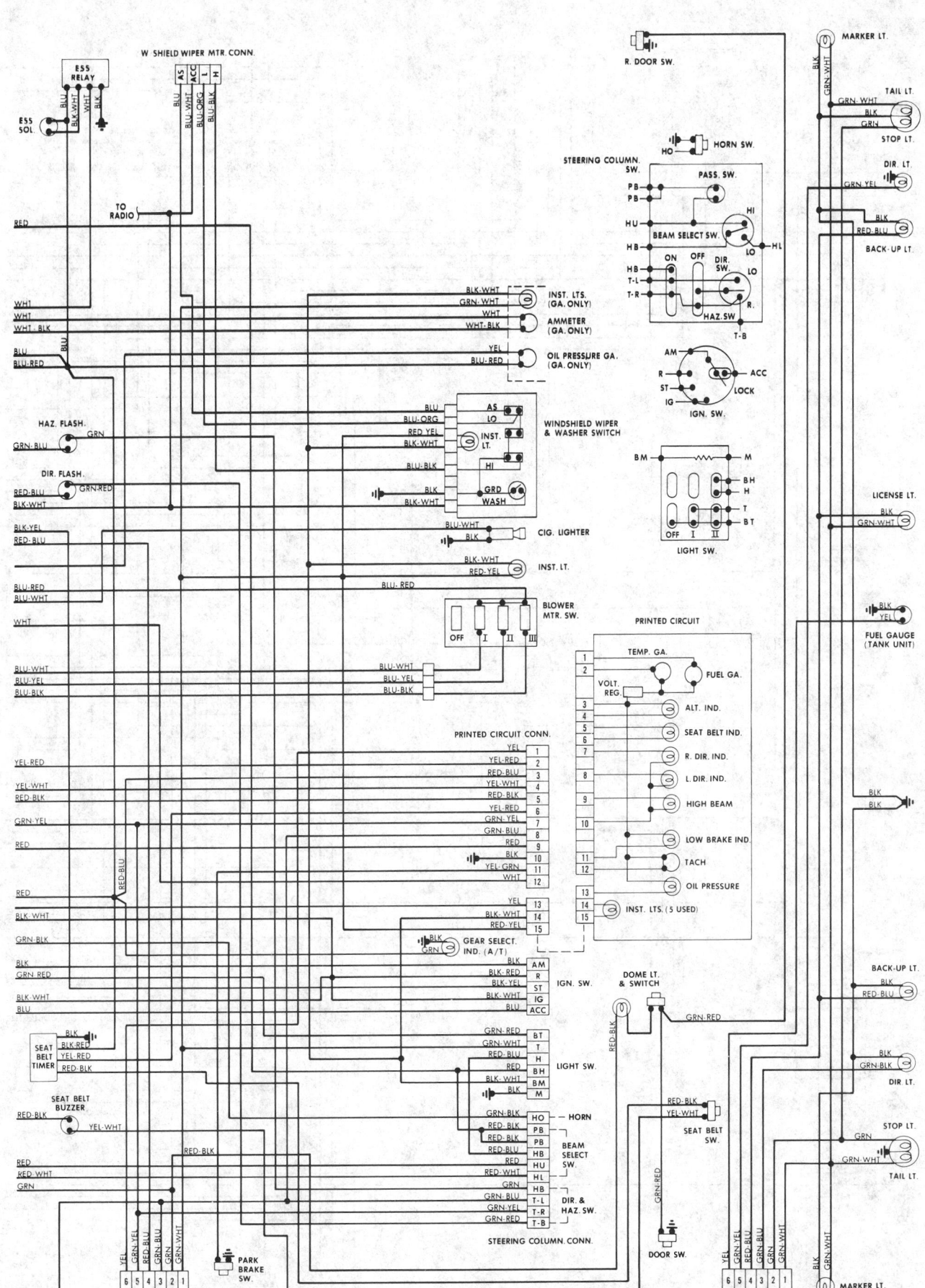

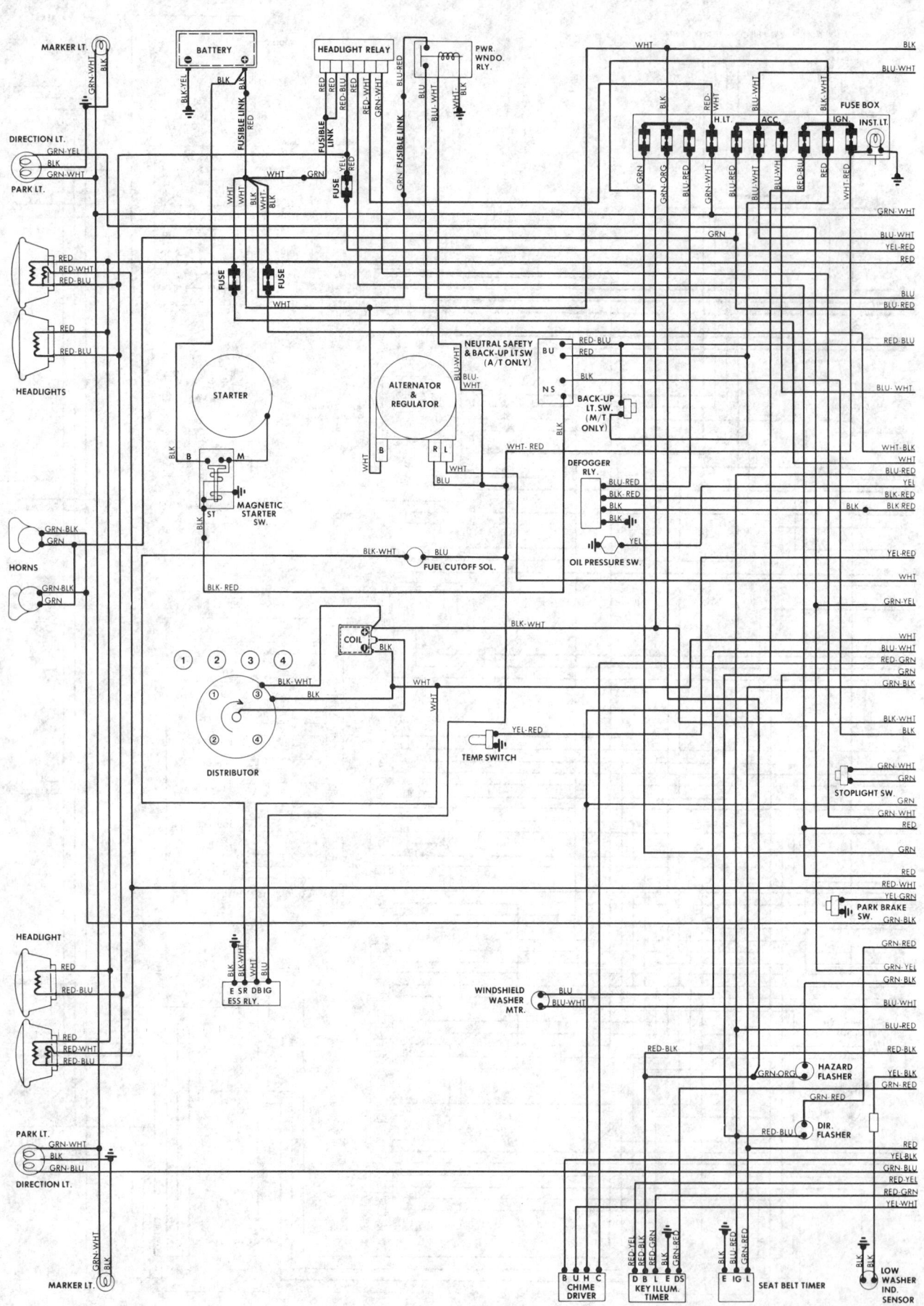

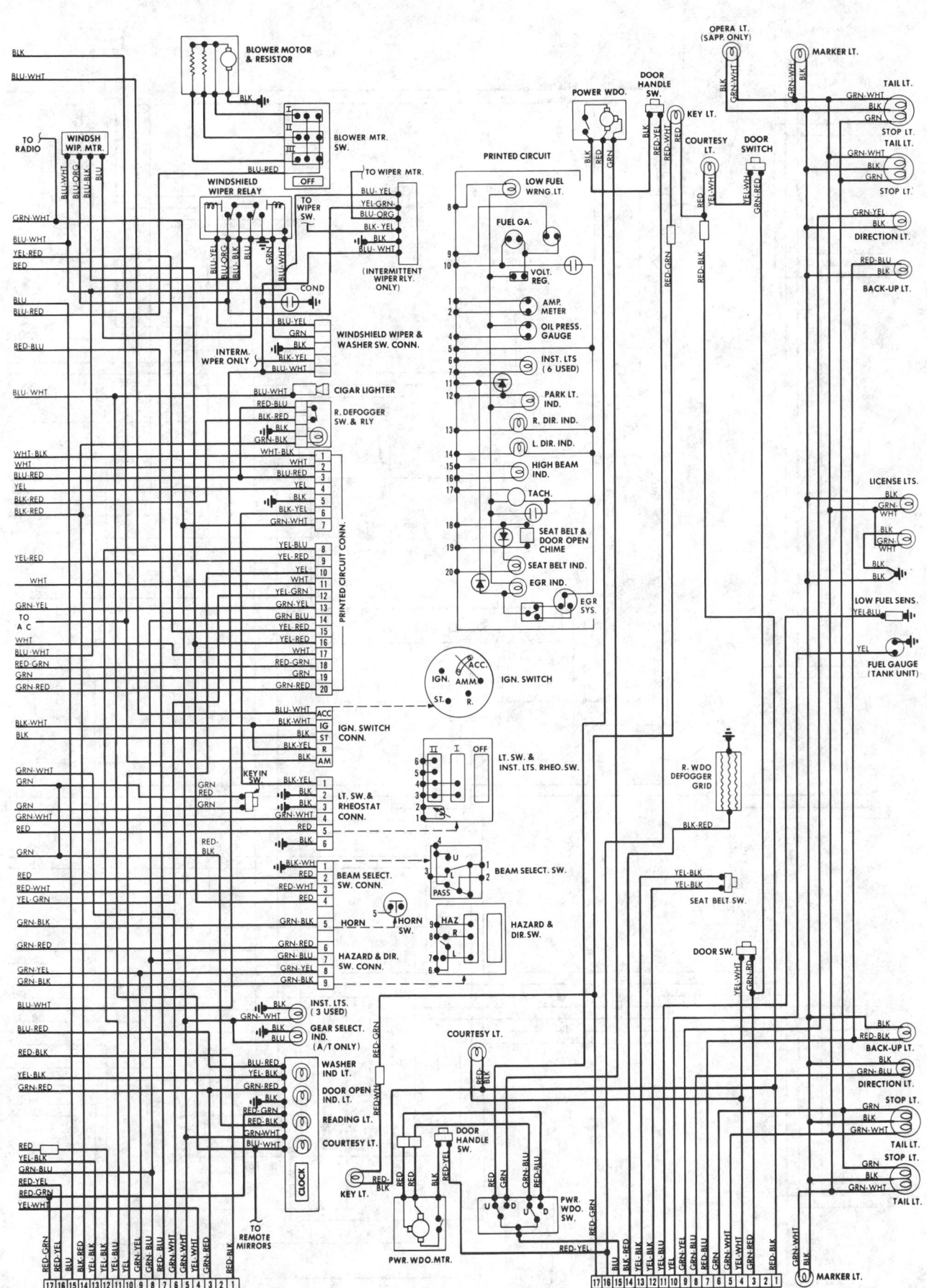

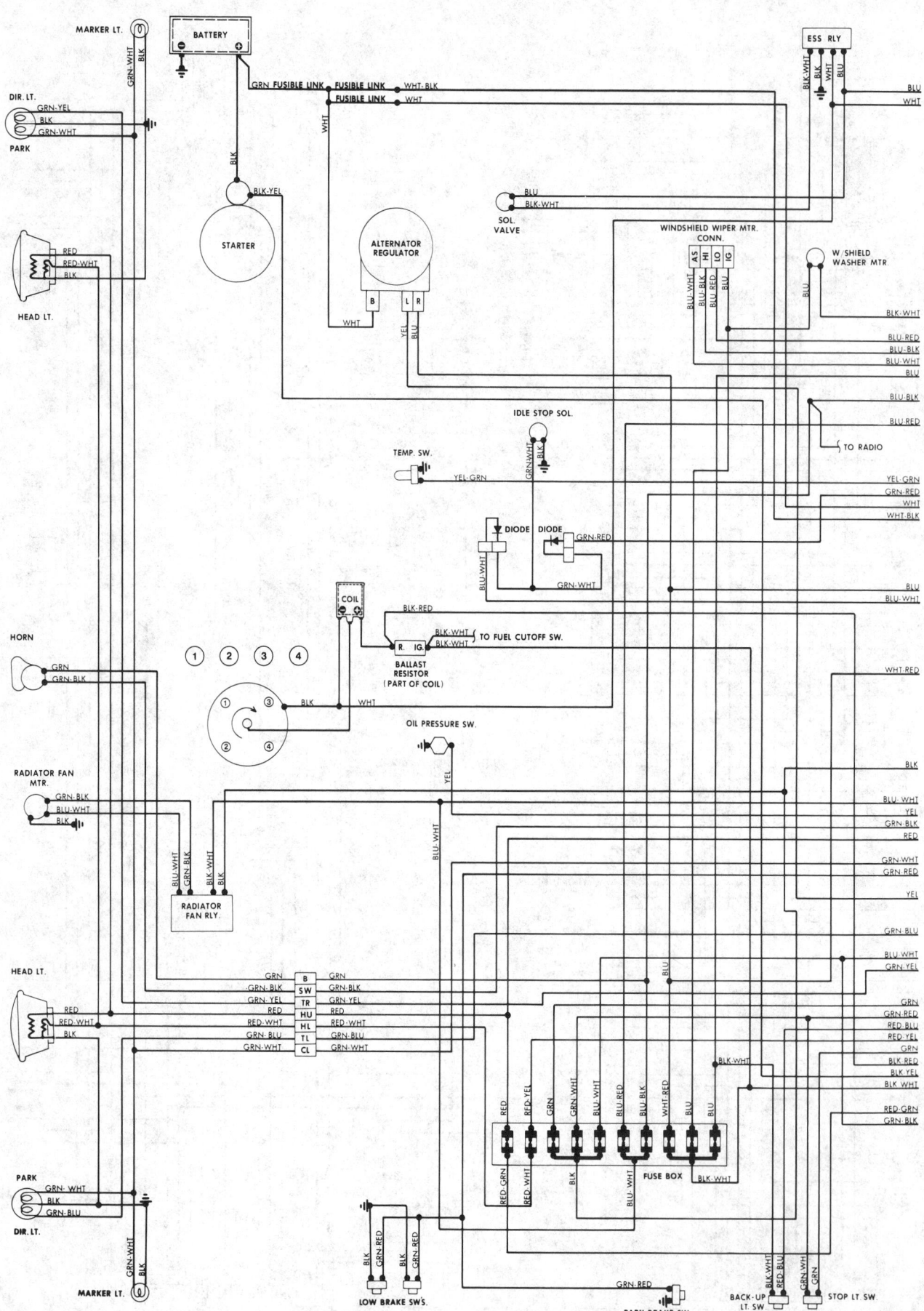

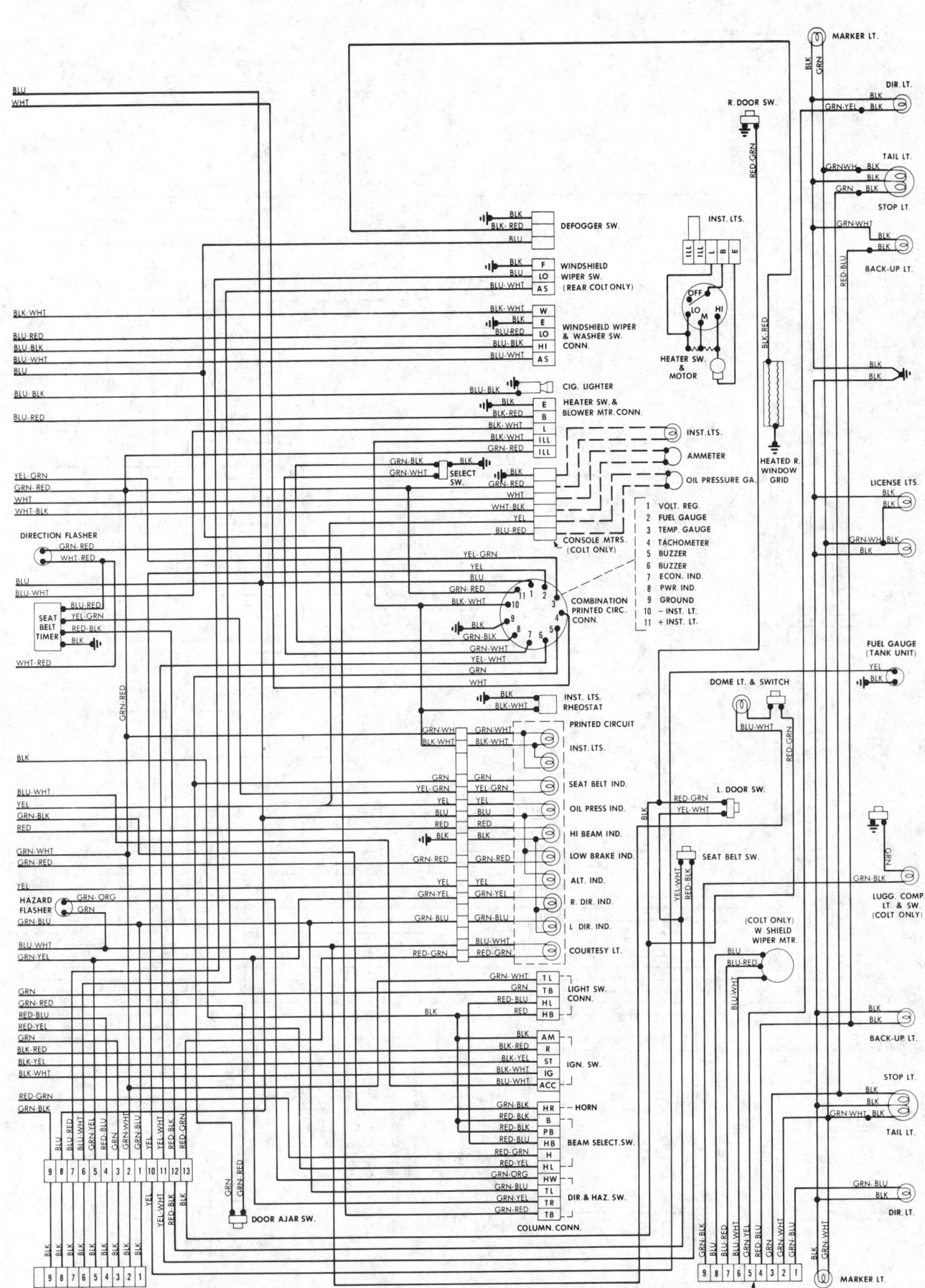

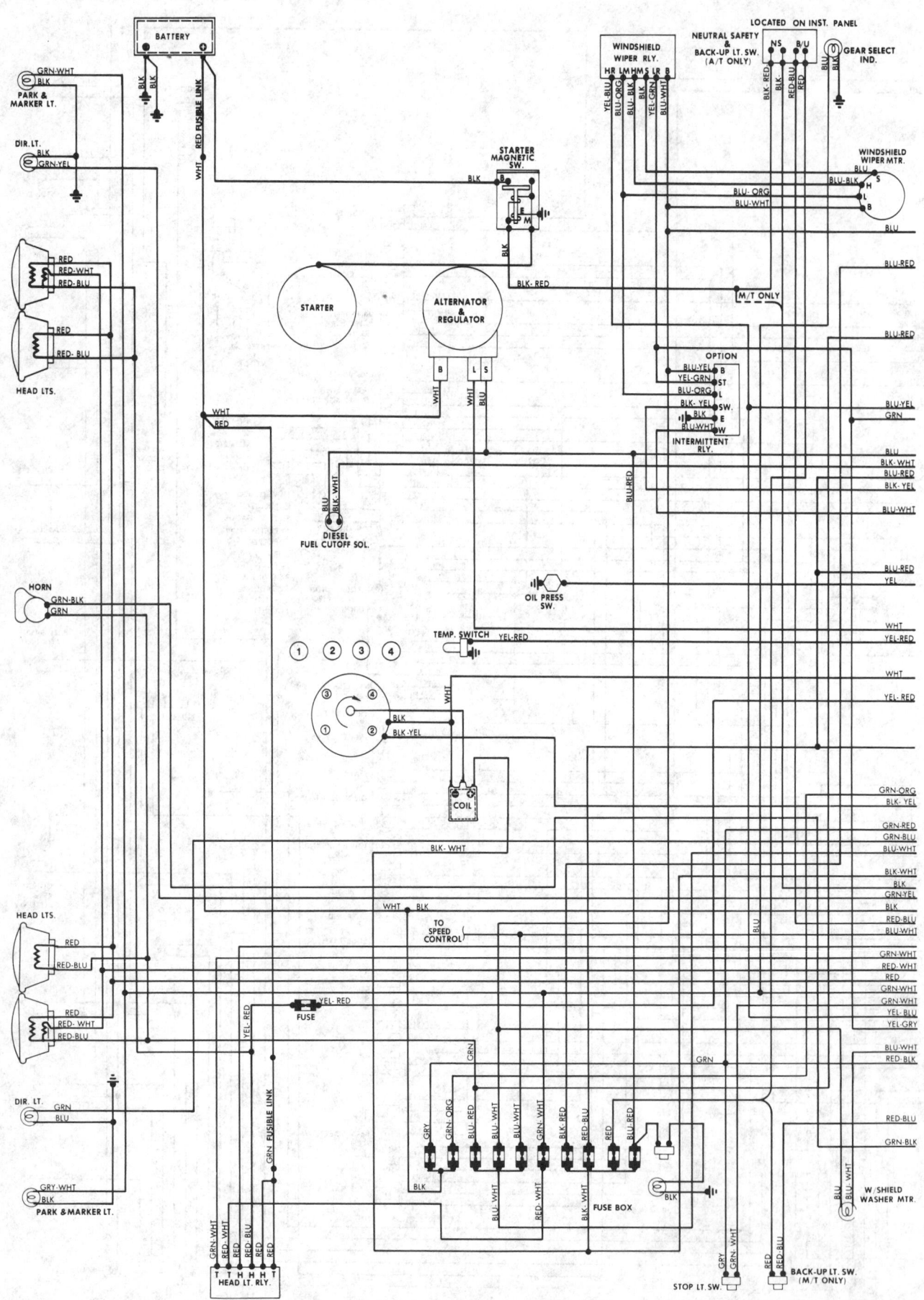

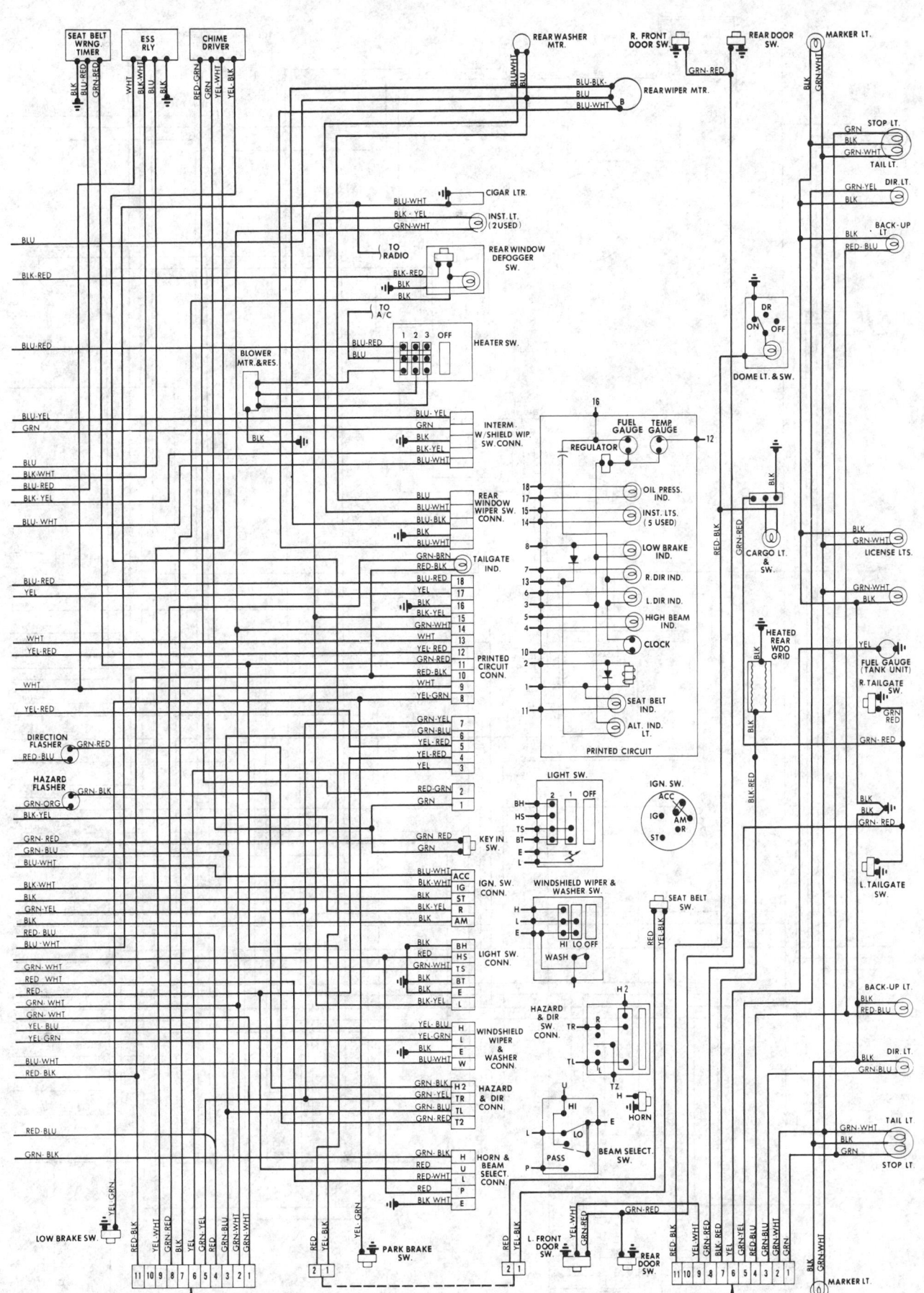

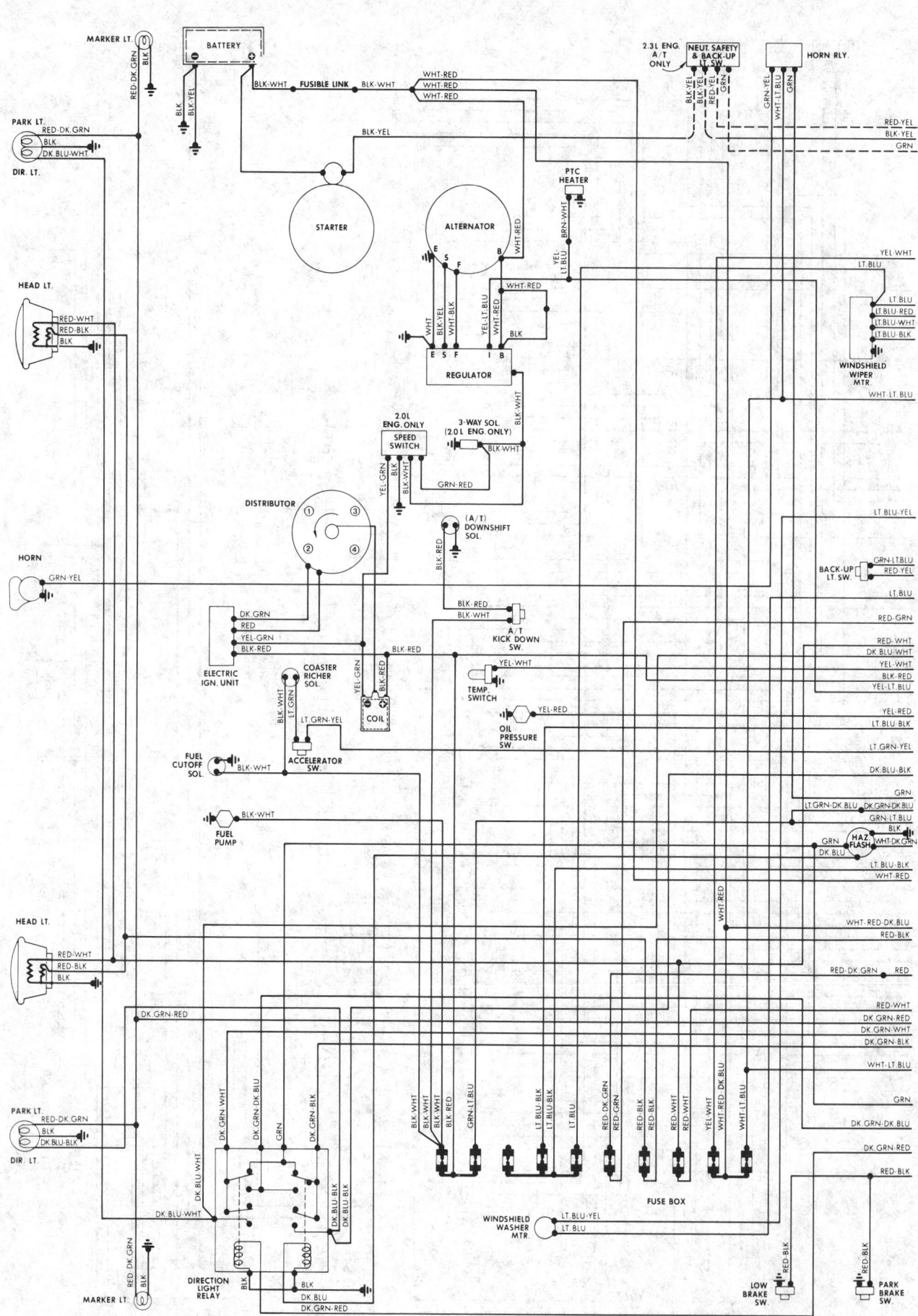

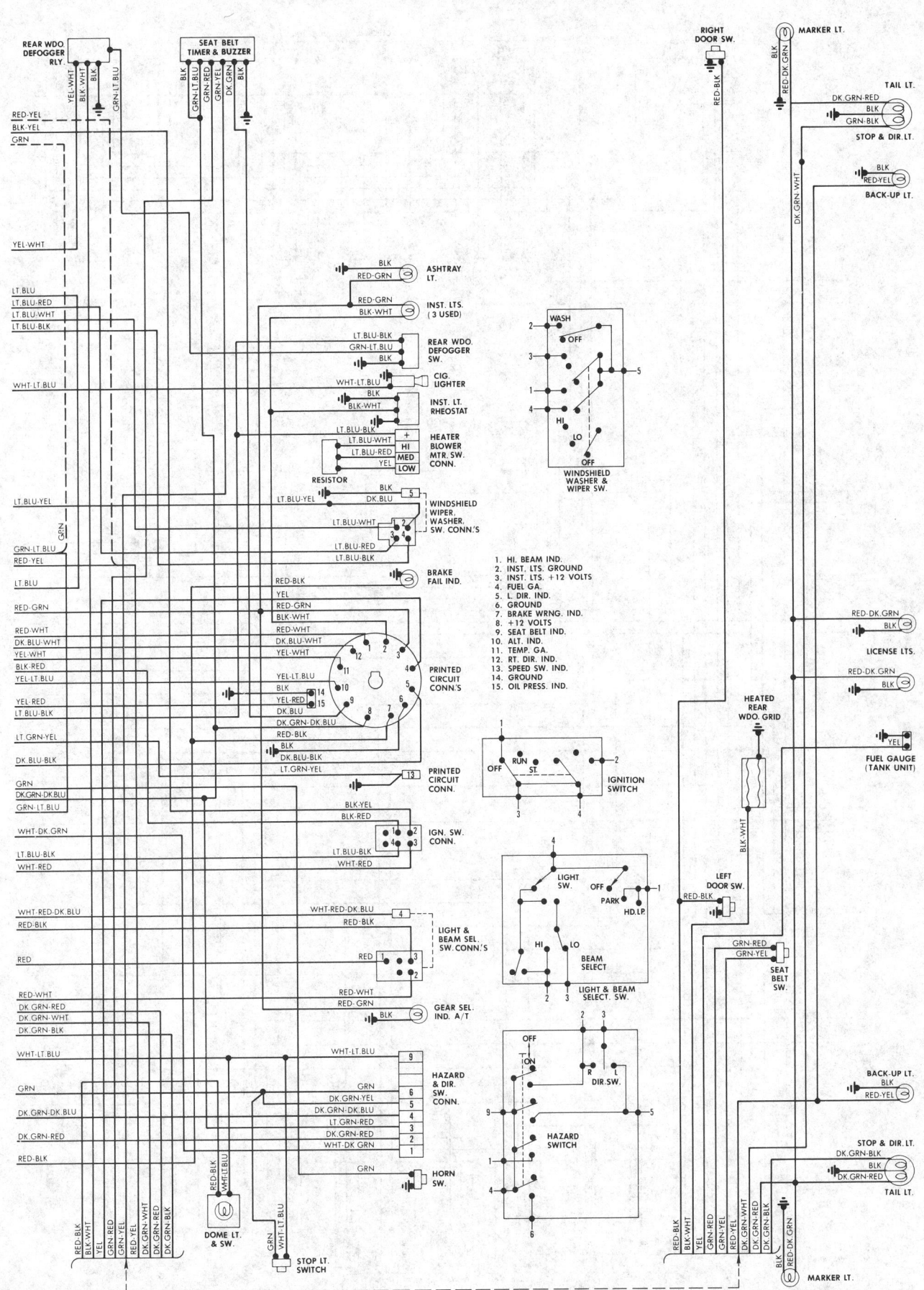

1980 Datsun

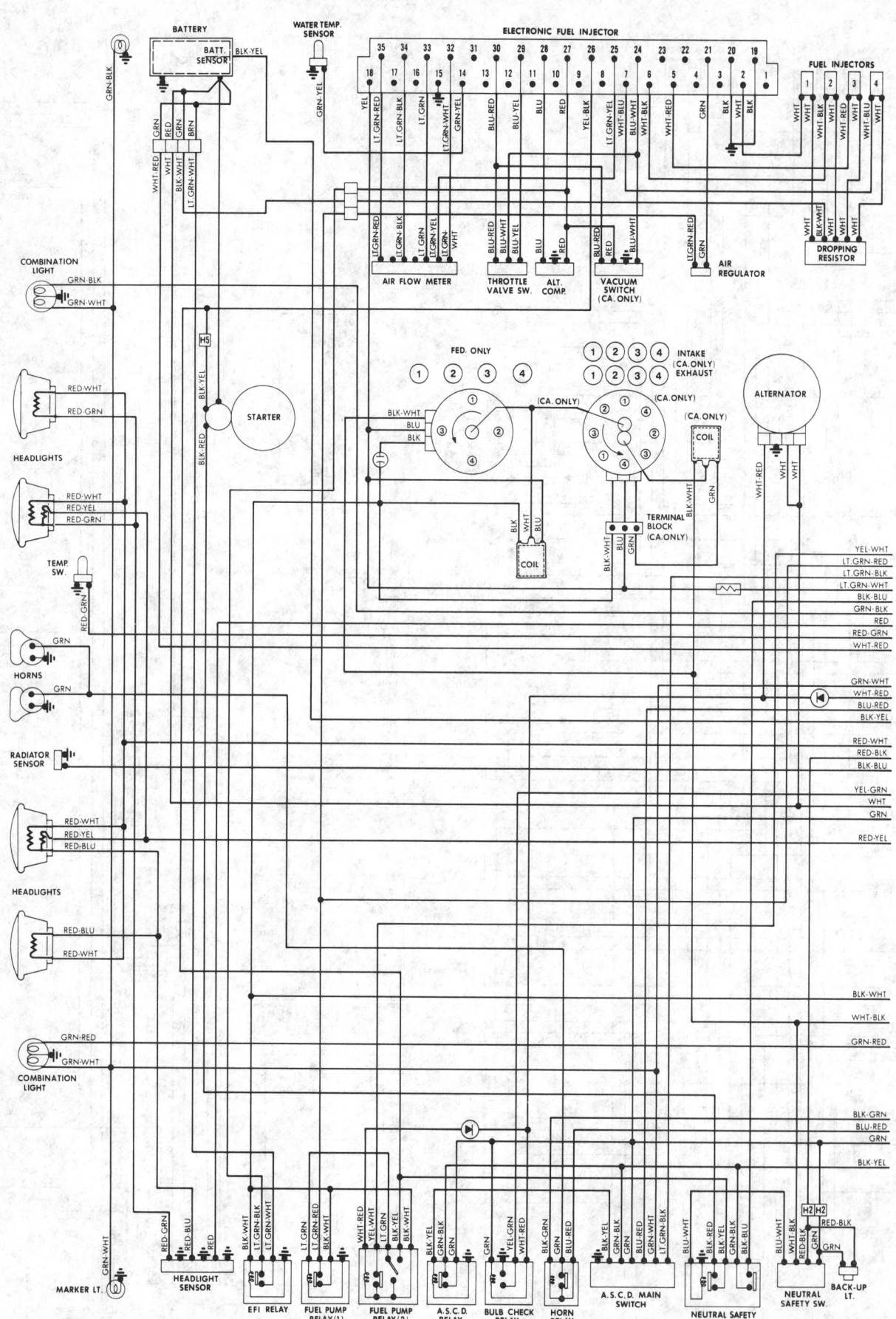

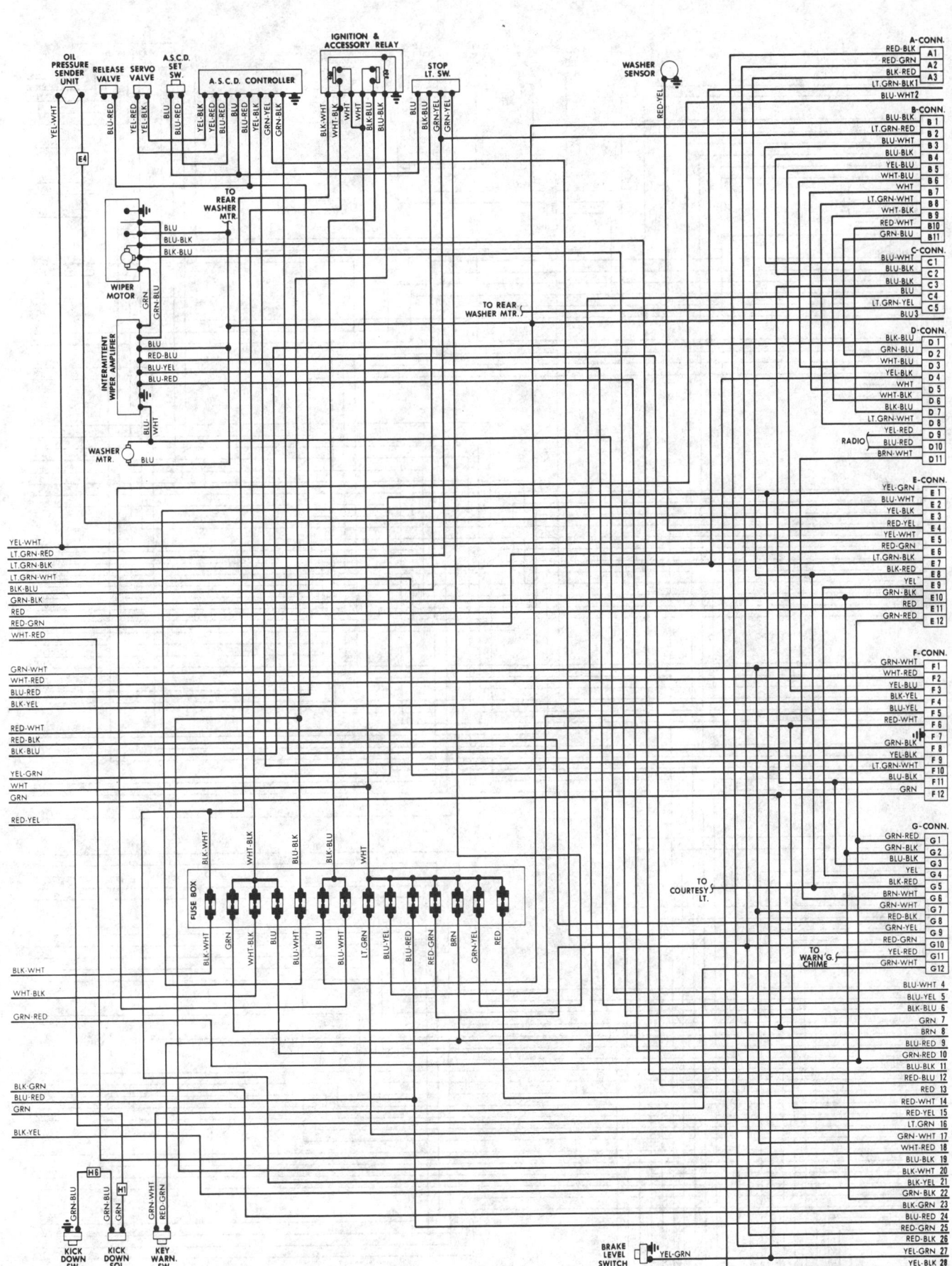

1980 Datsun

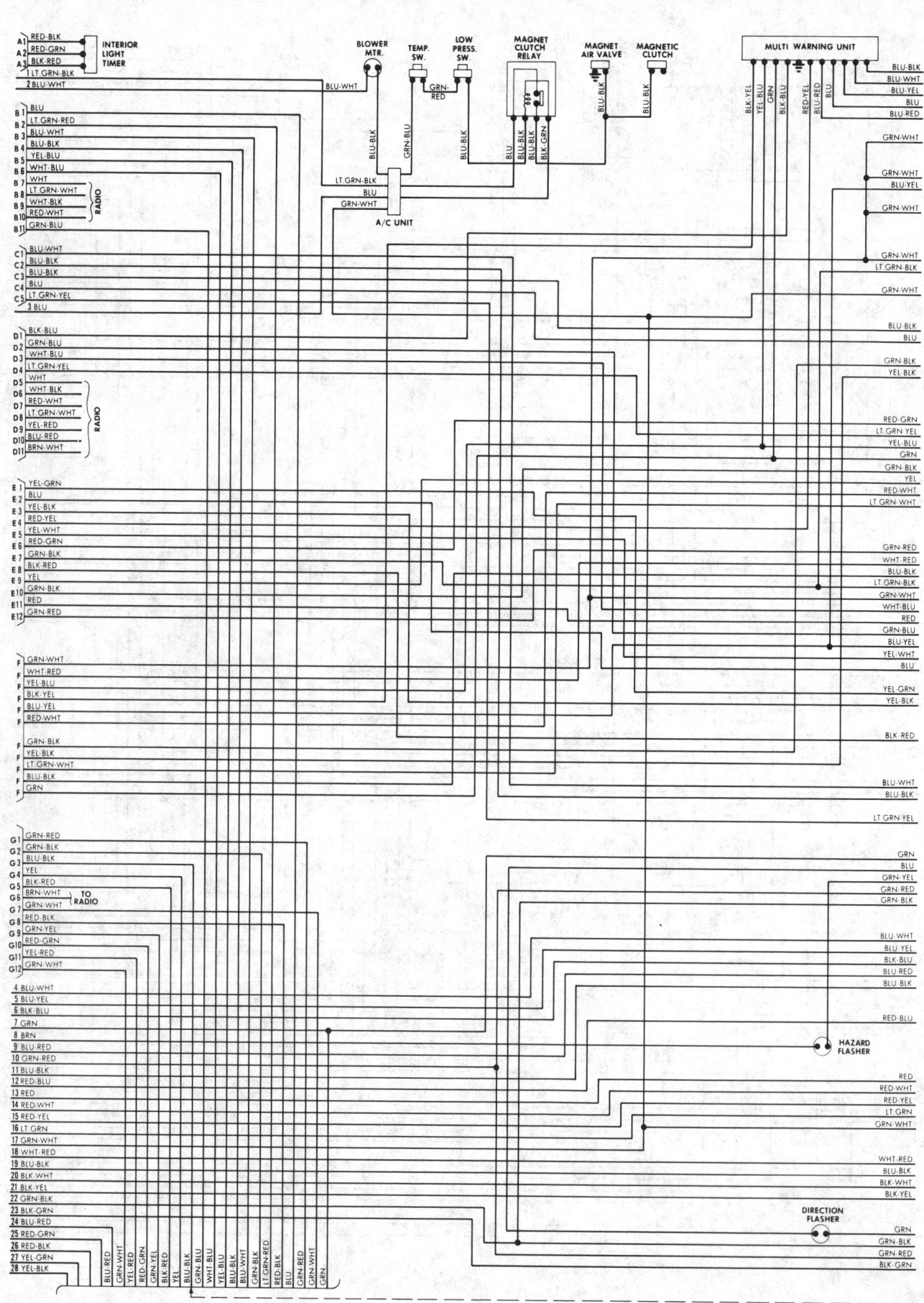

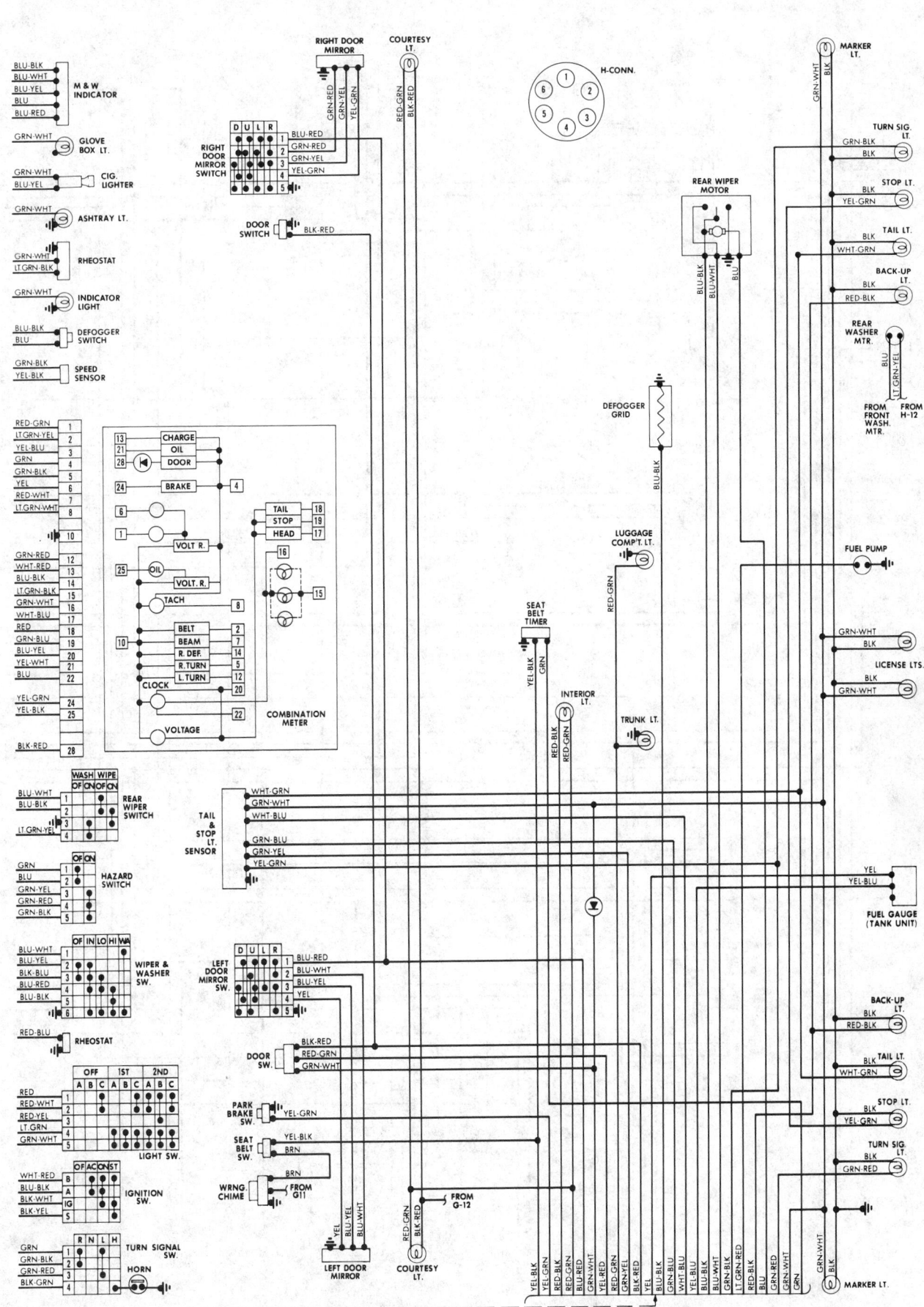

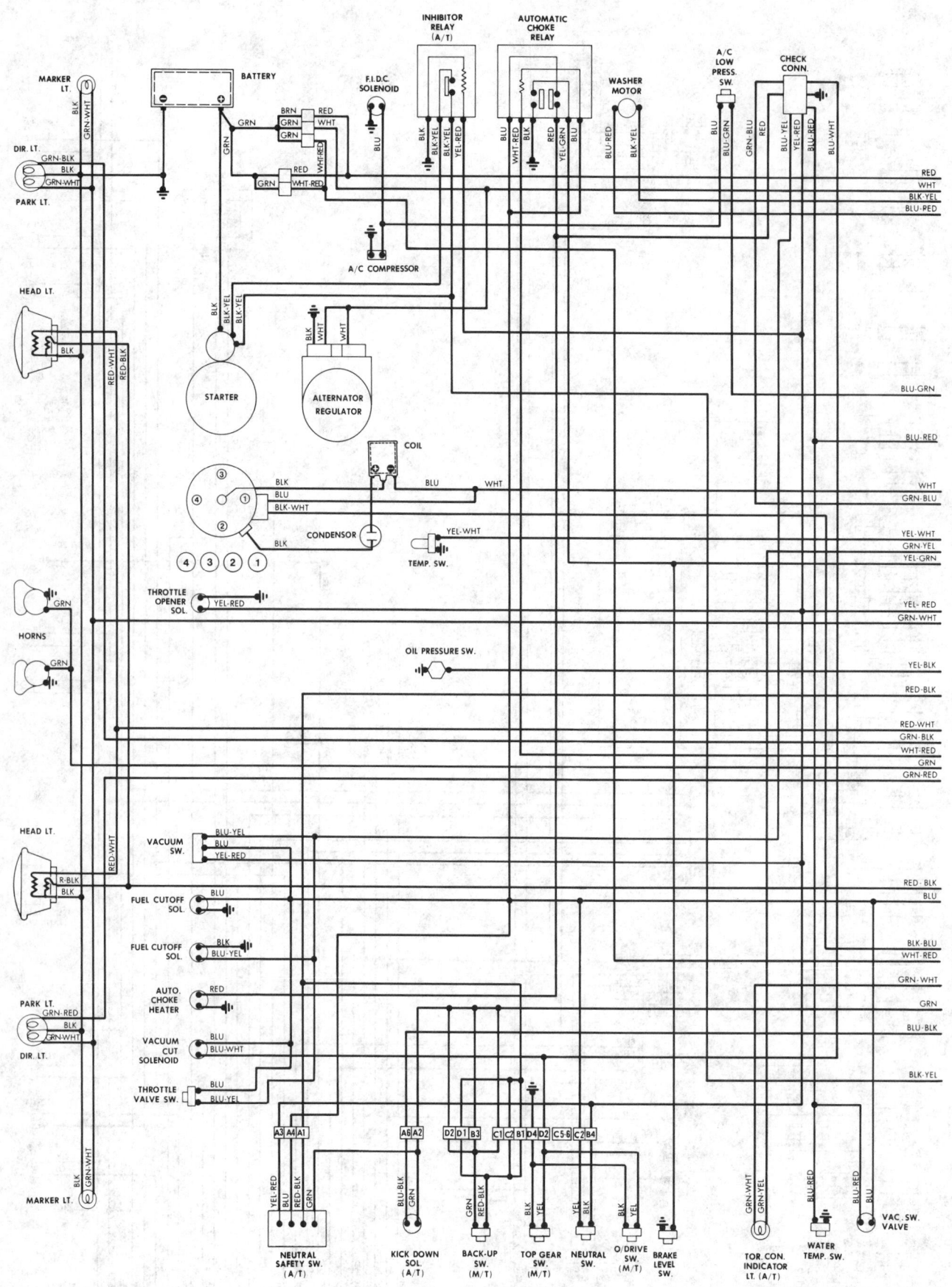

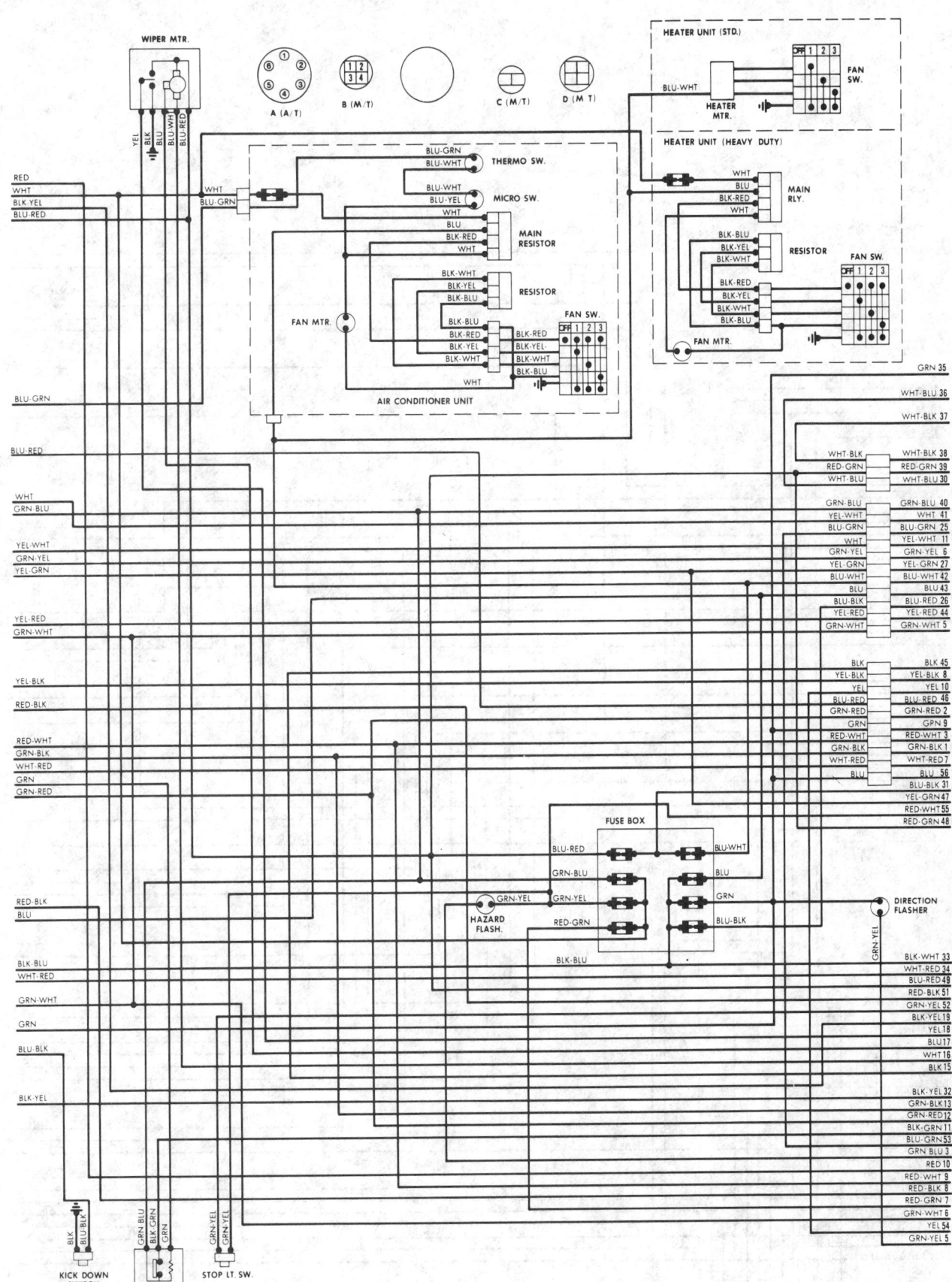

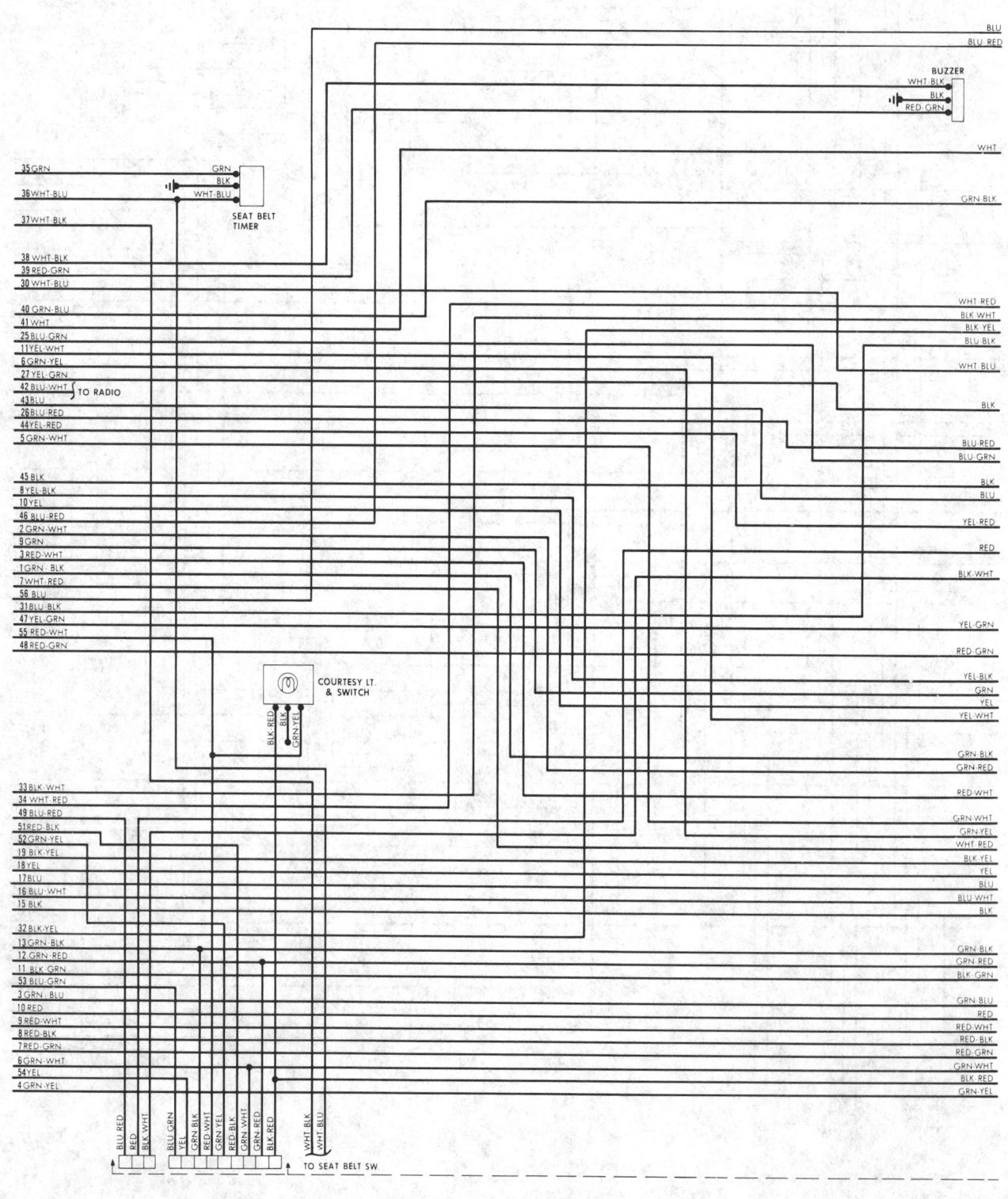

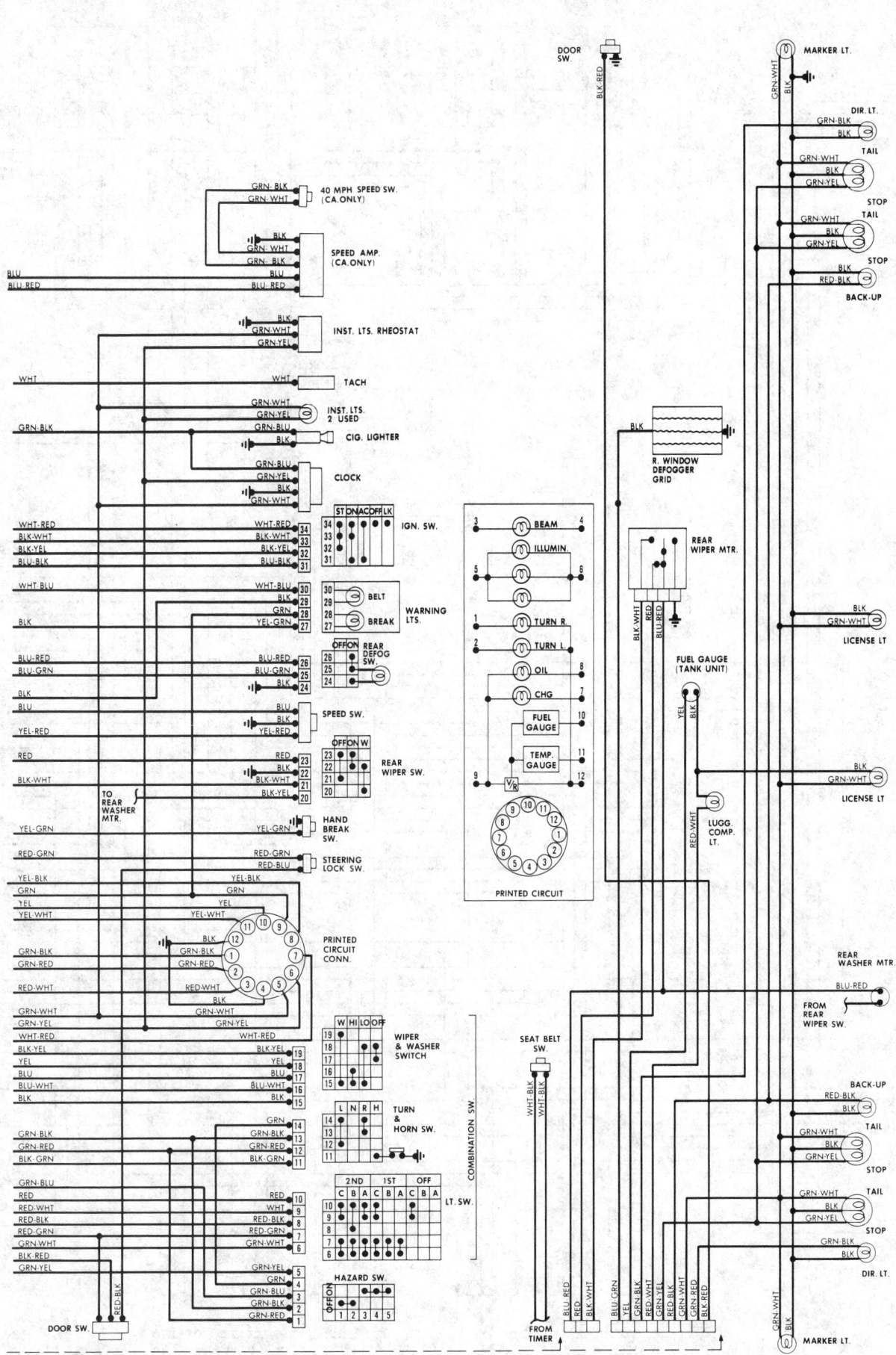

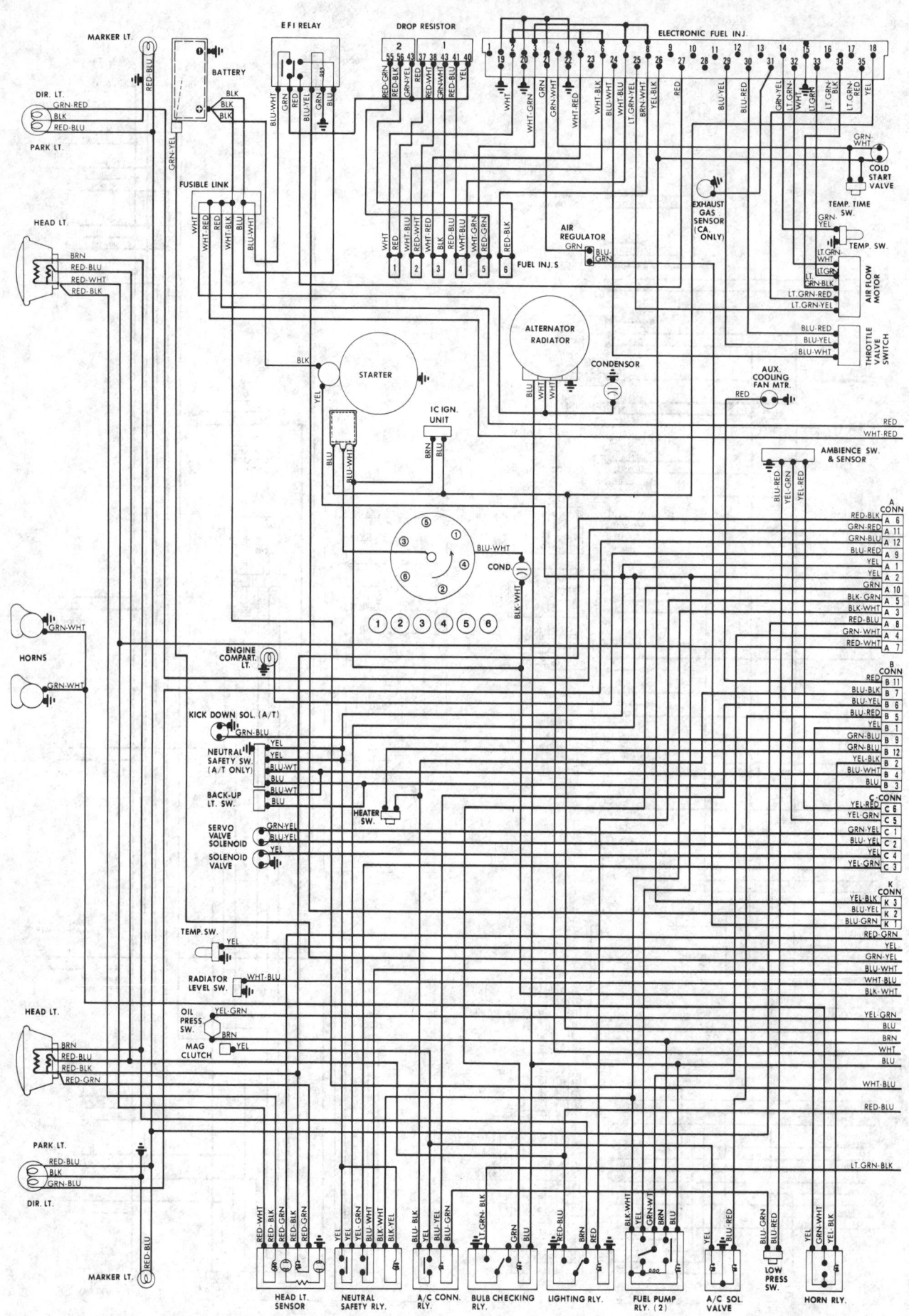

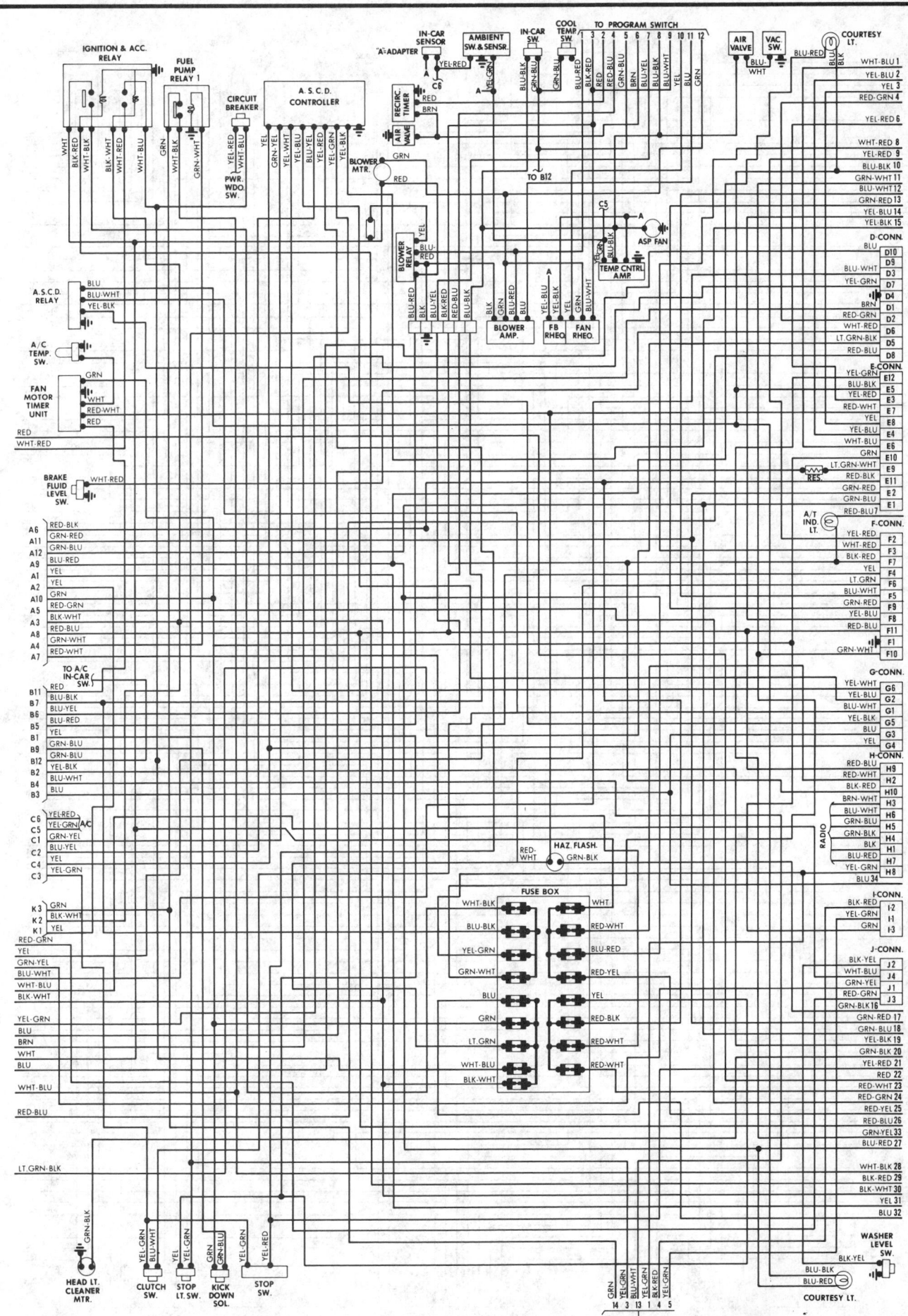

1980 Datsun

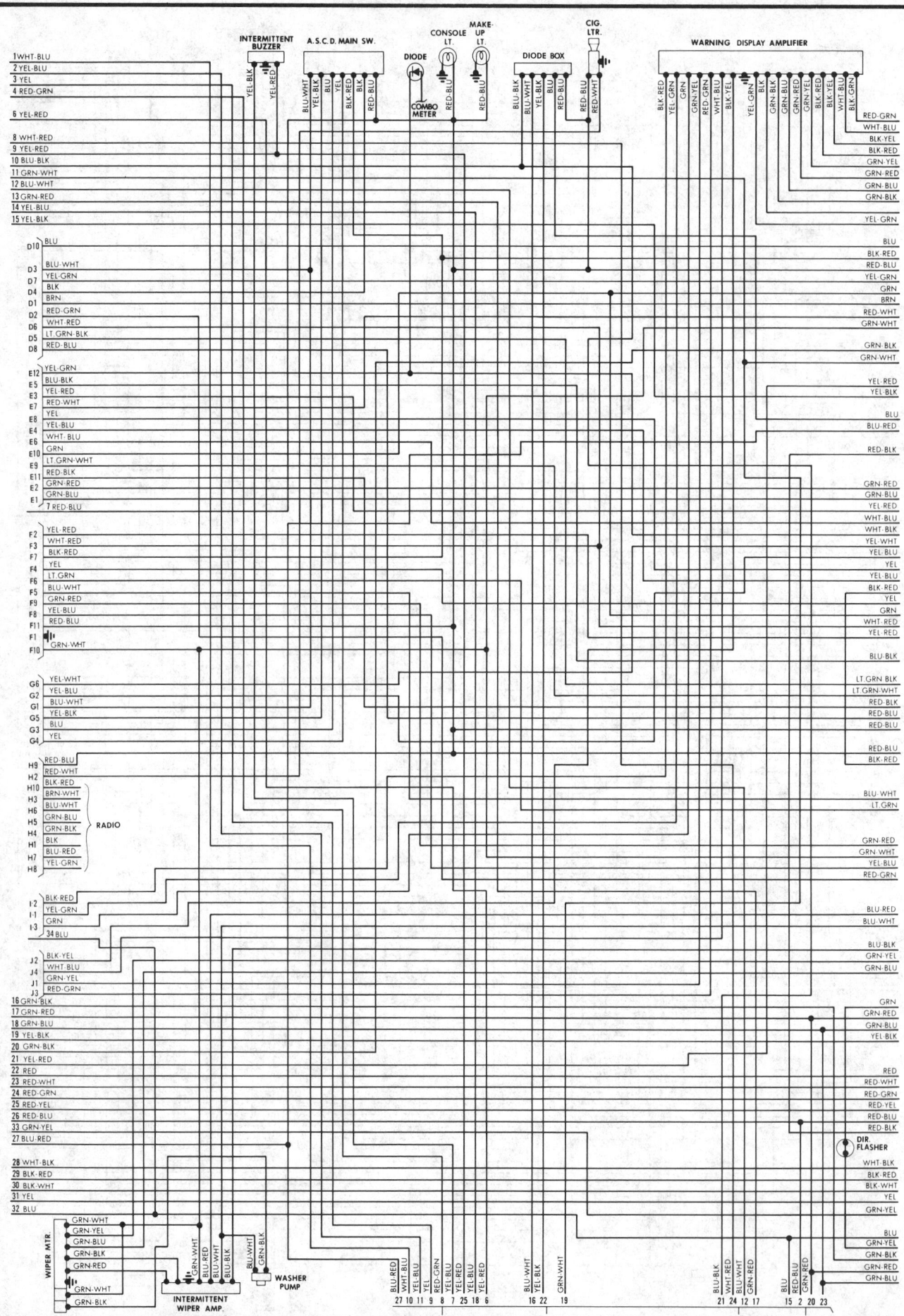

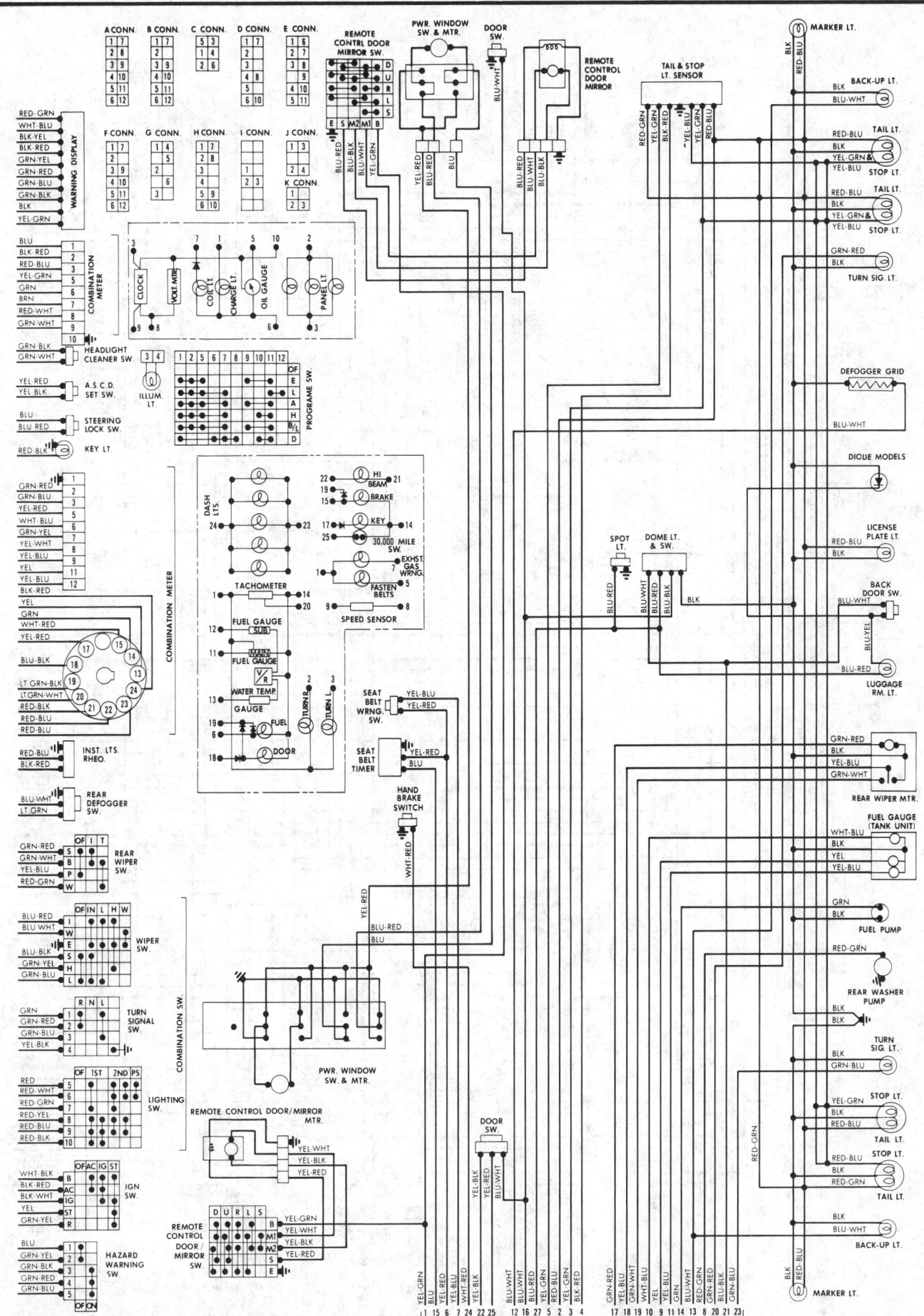

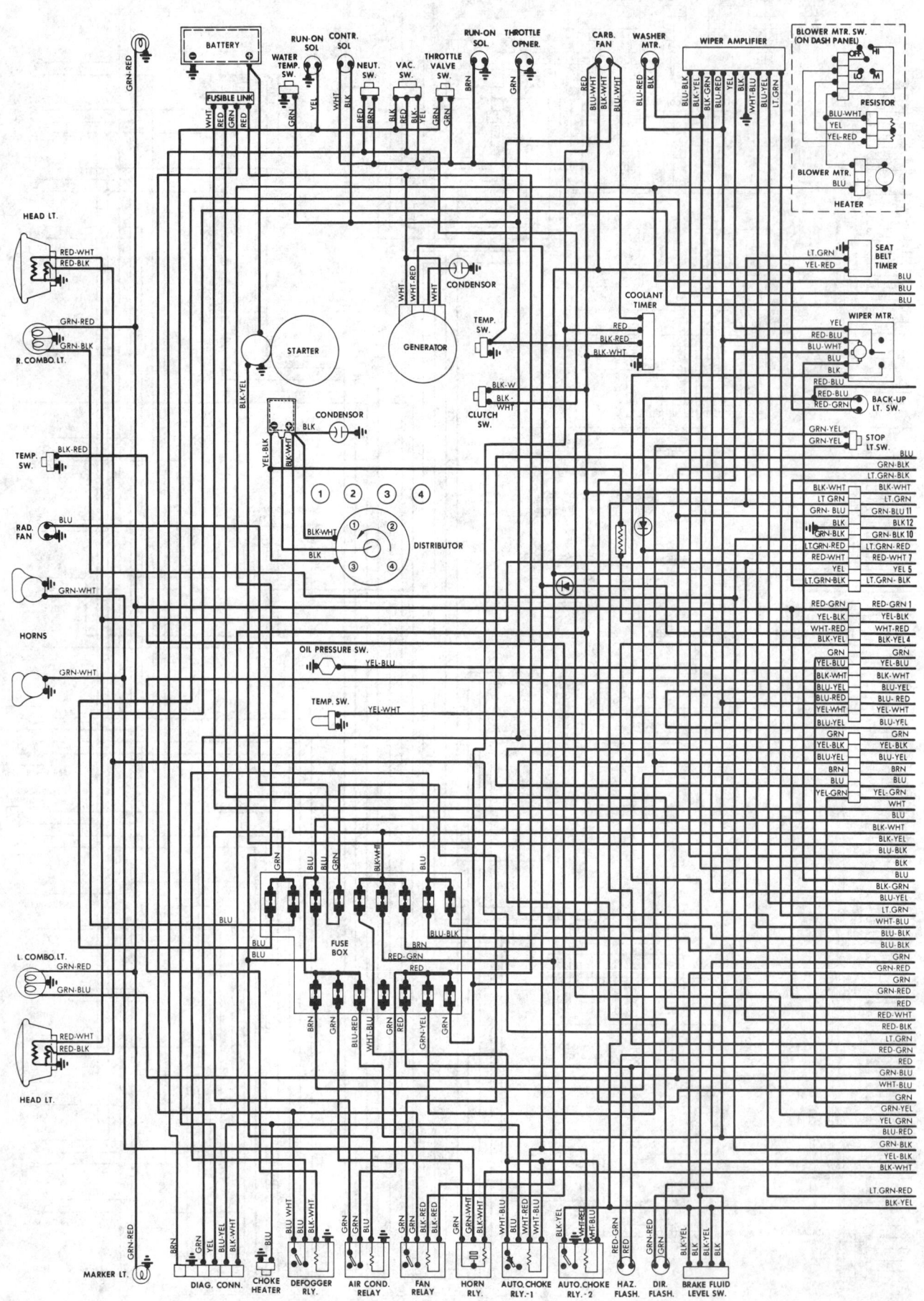

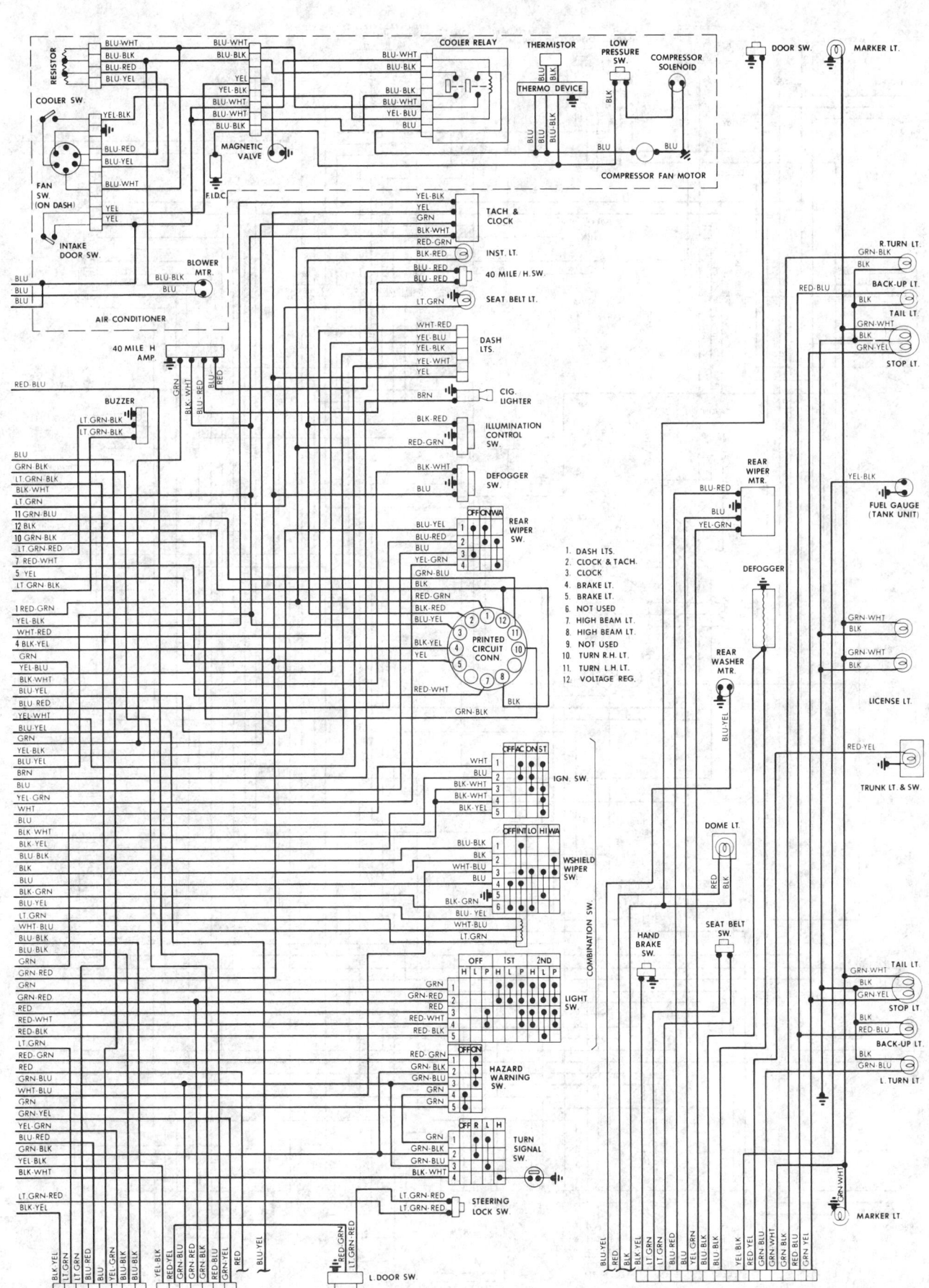

1980 Datsun

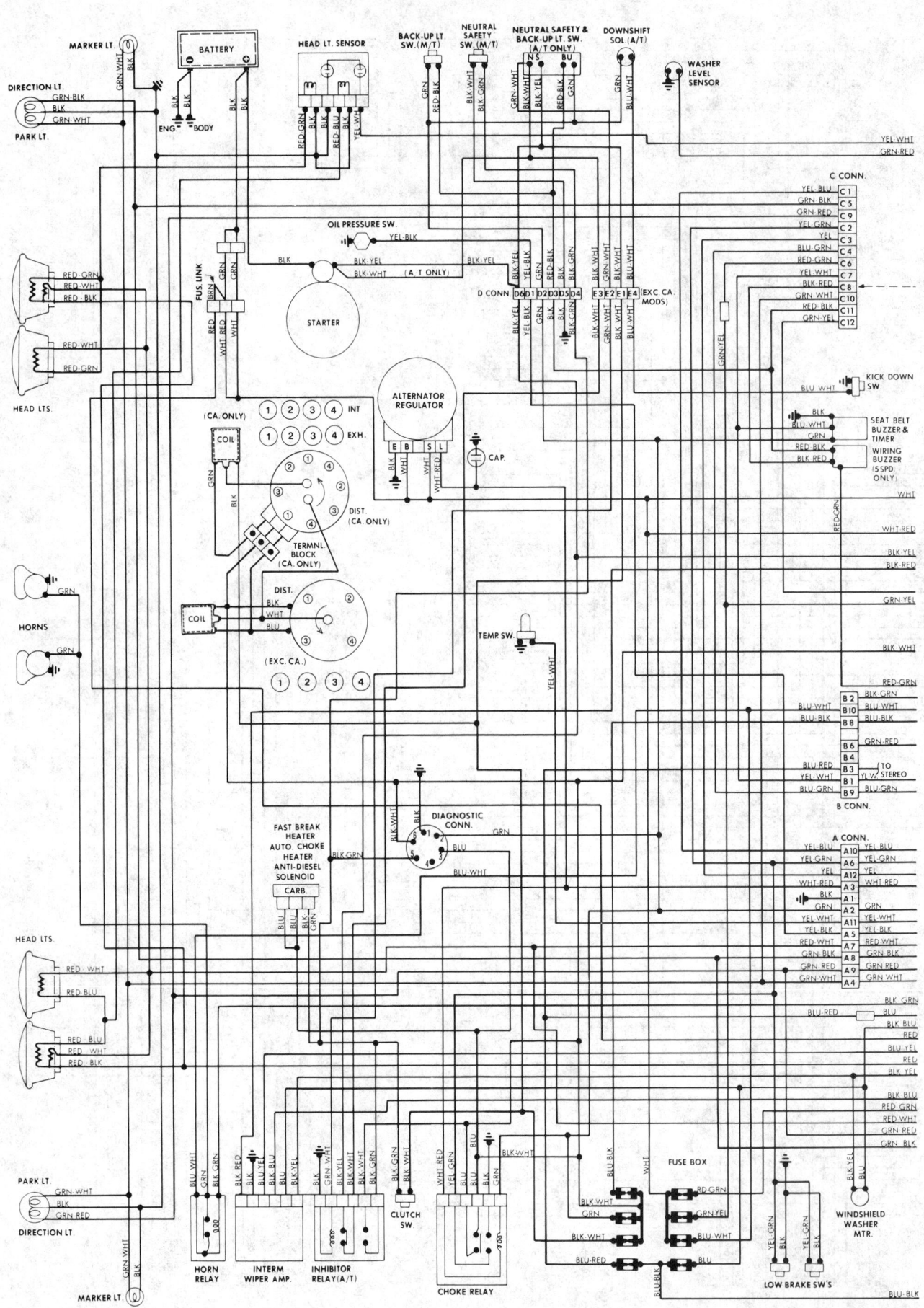

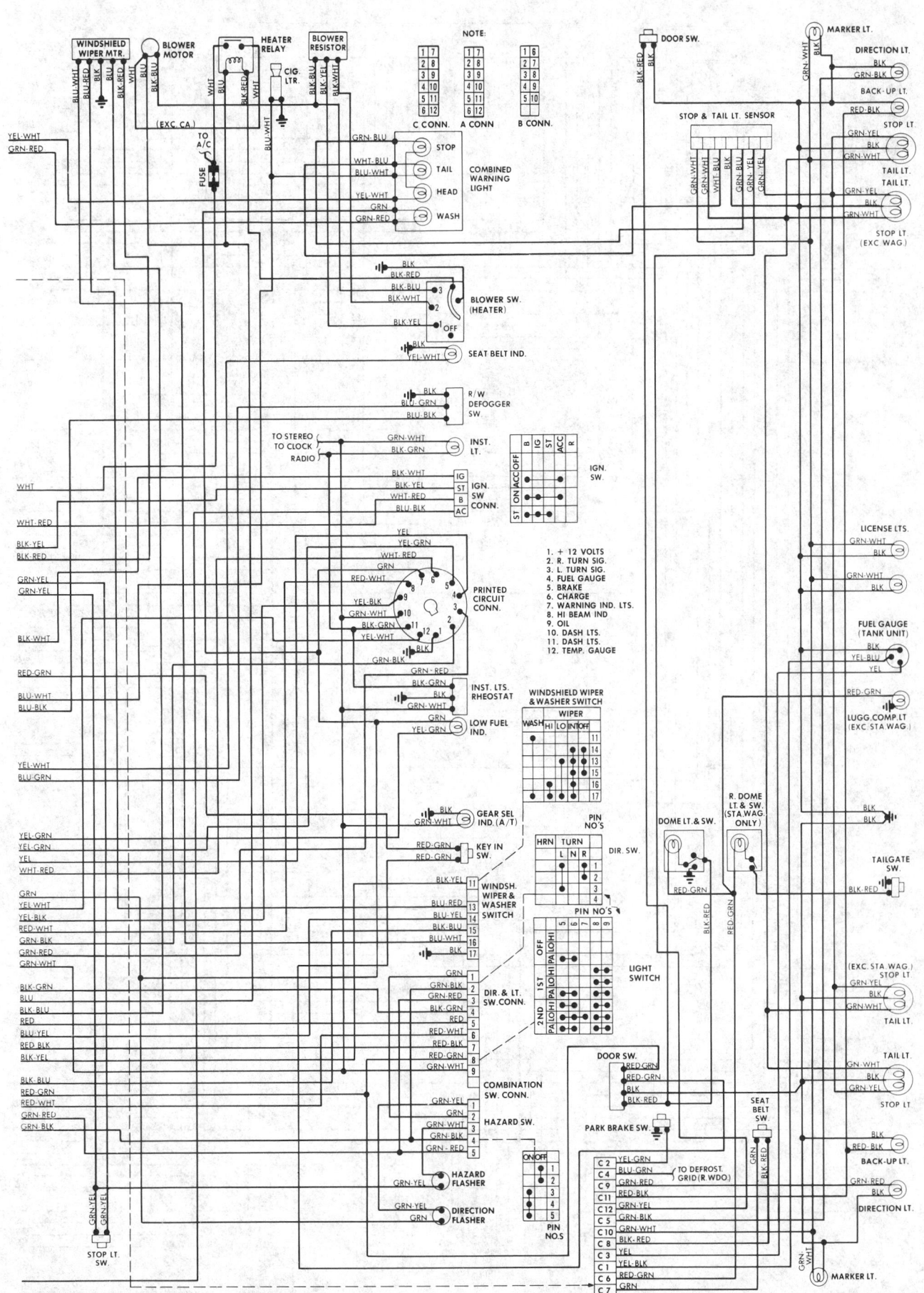

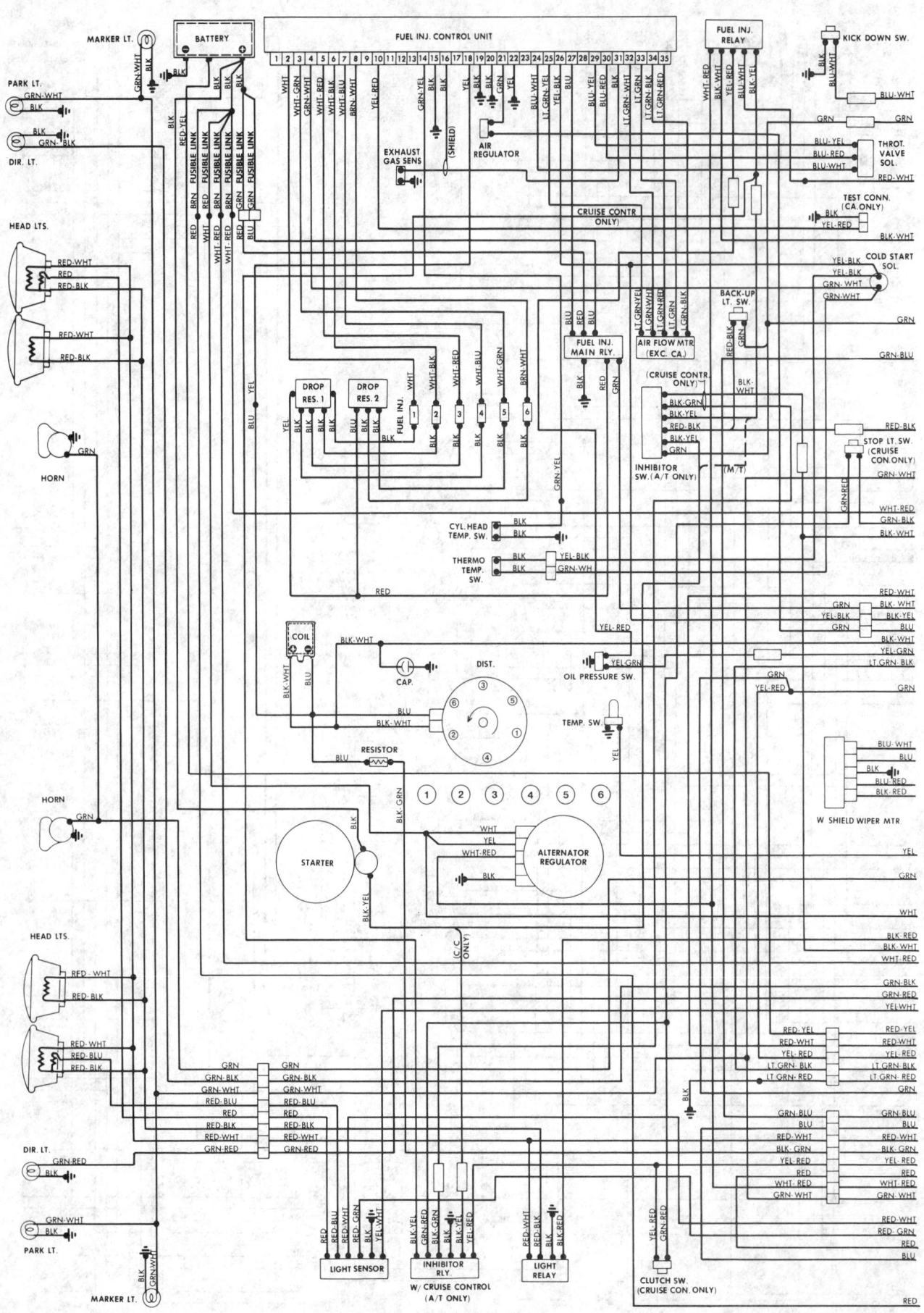

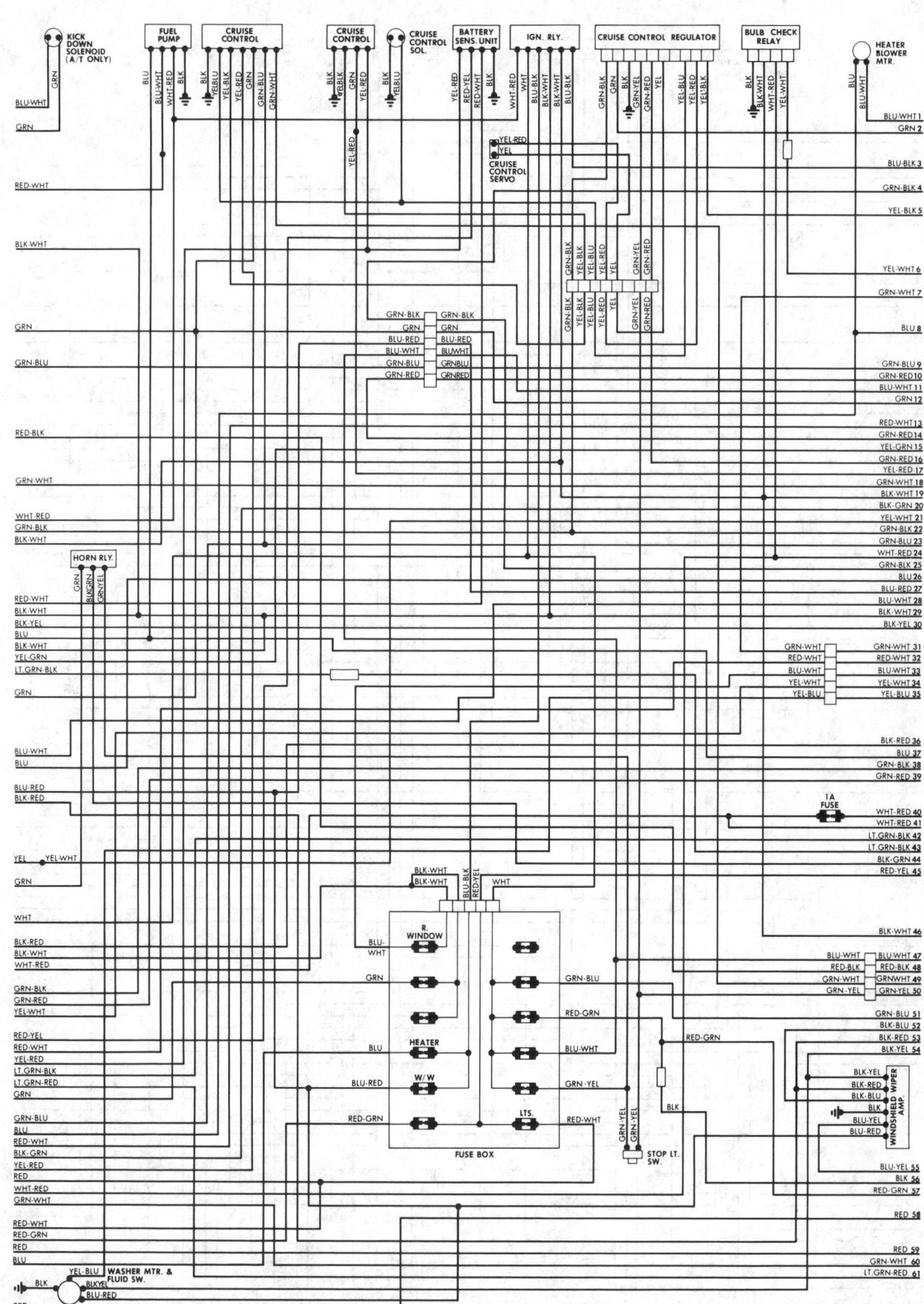

1980 Datsun

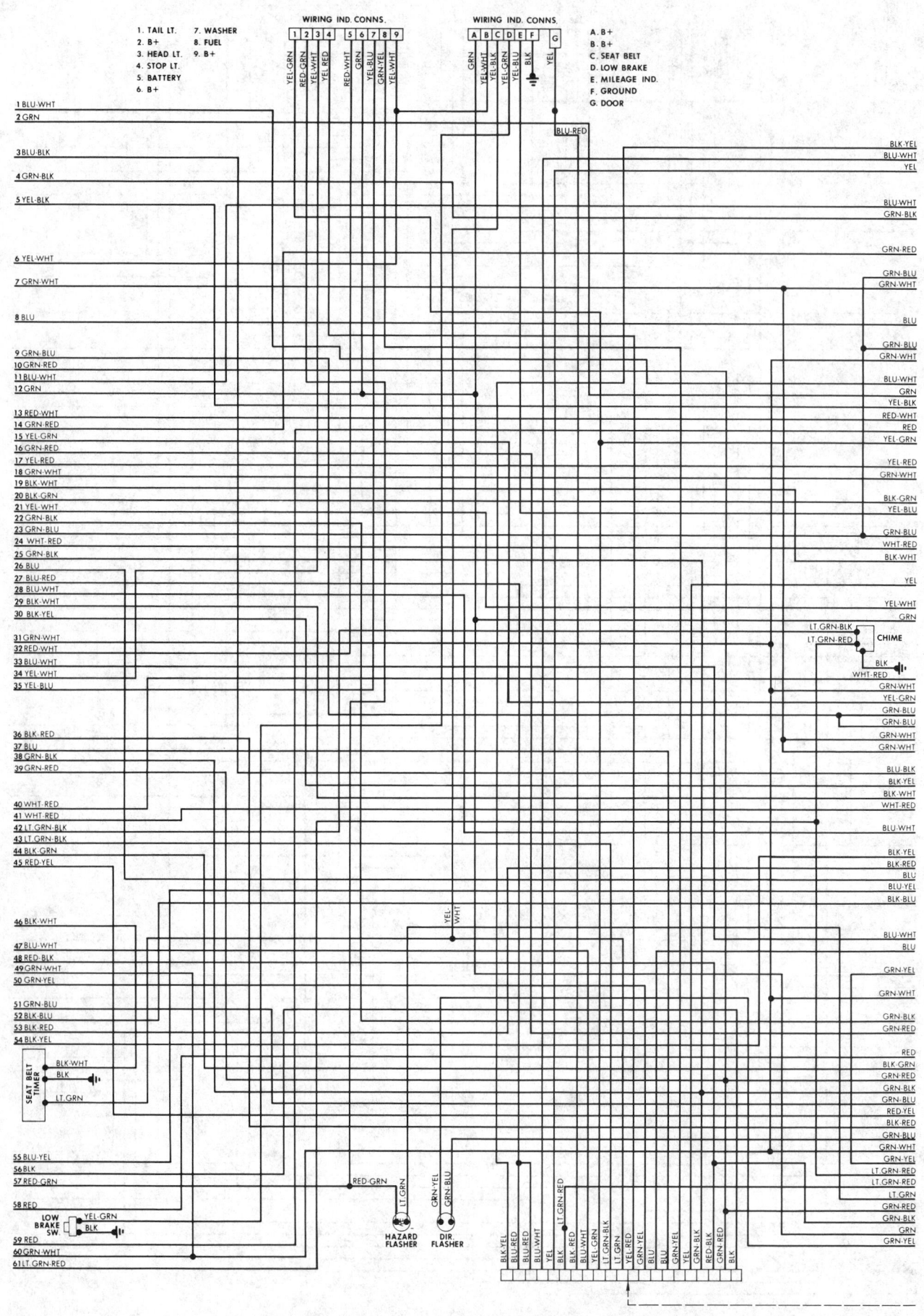

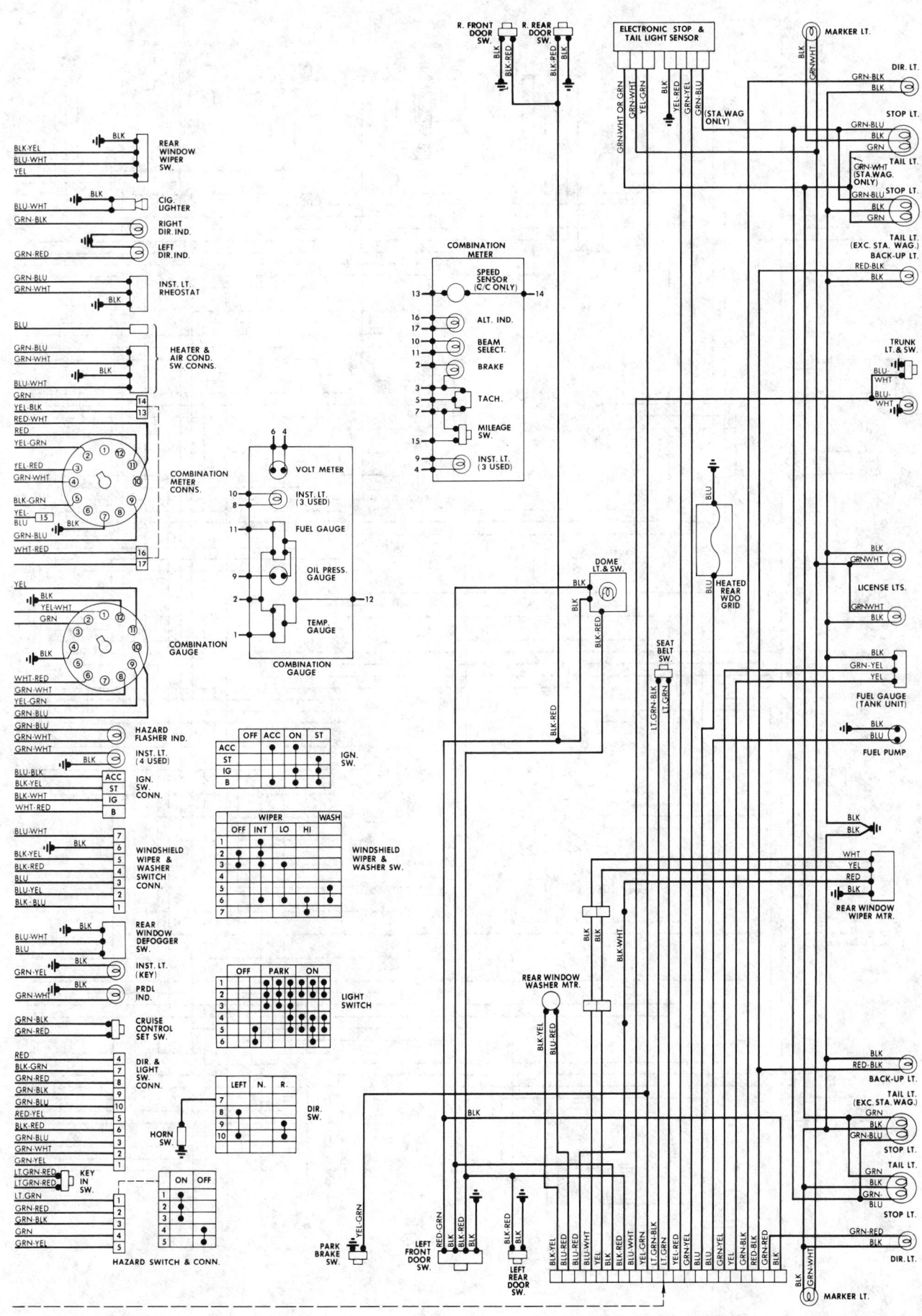

1980 Datsun

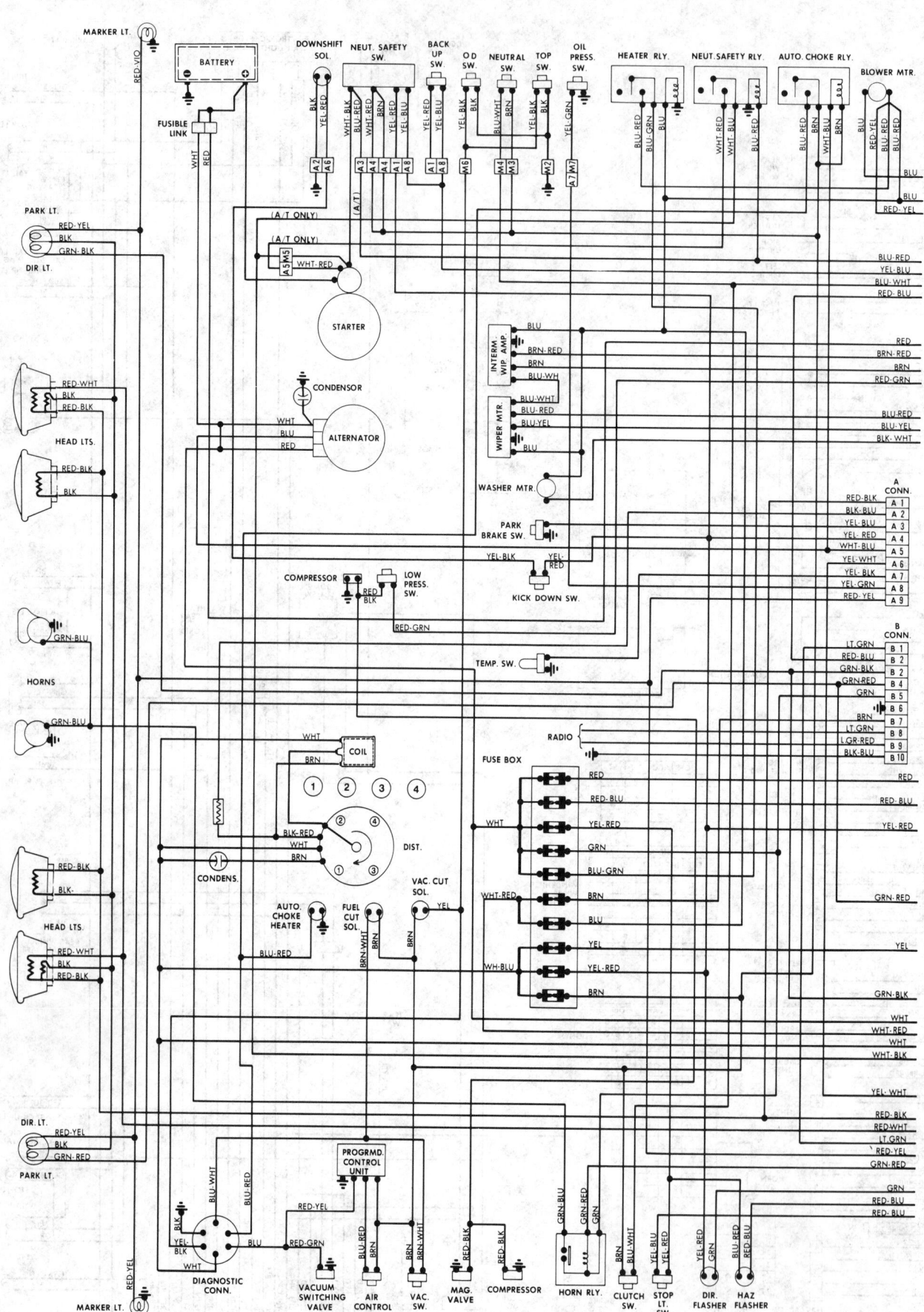

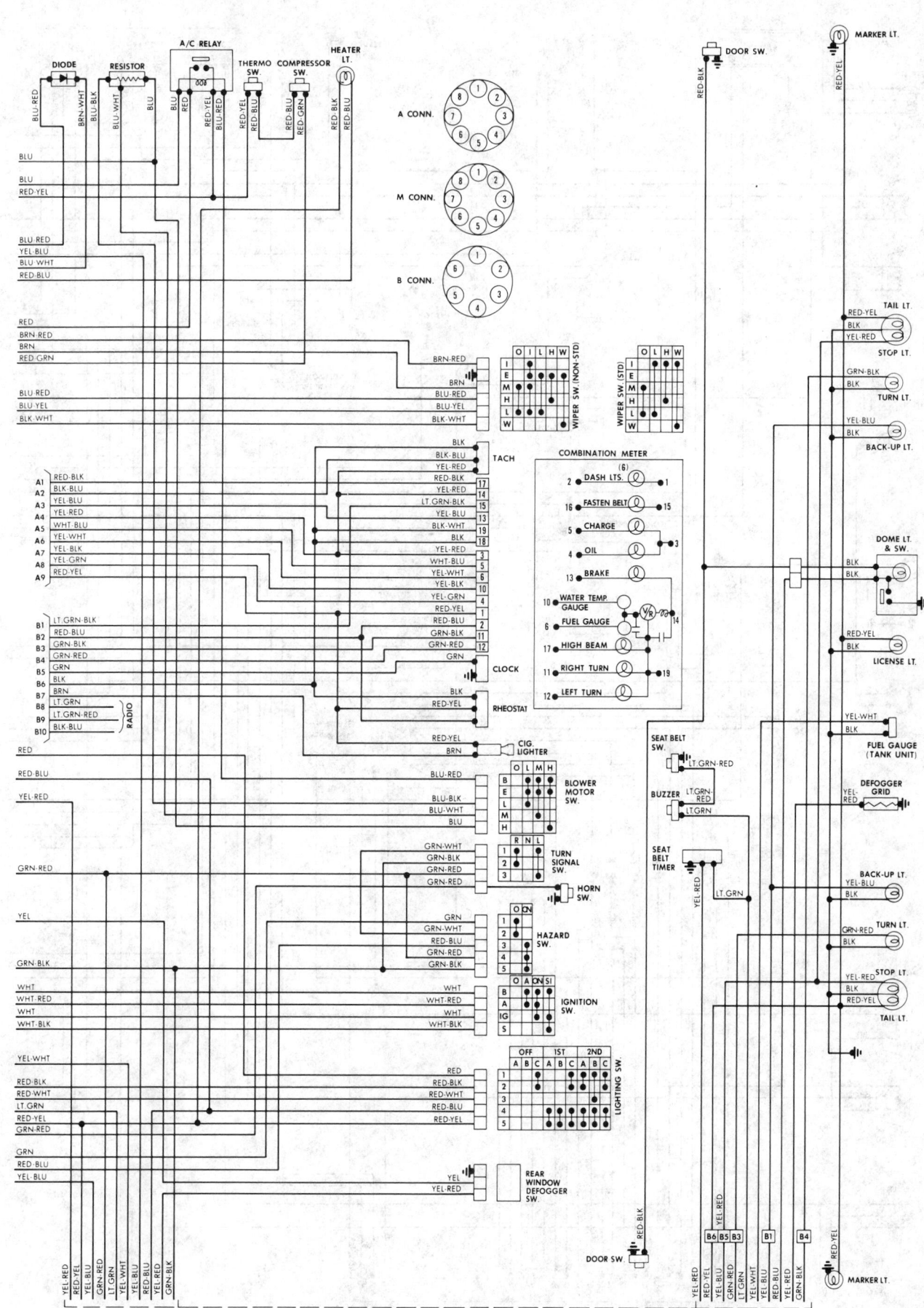

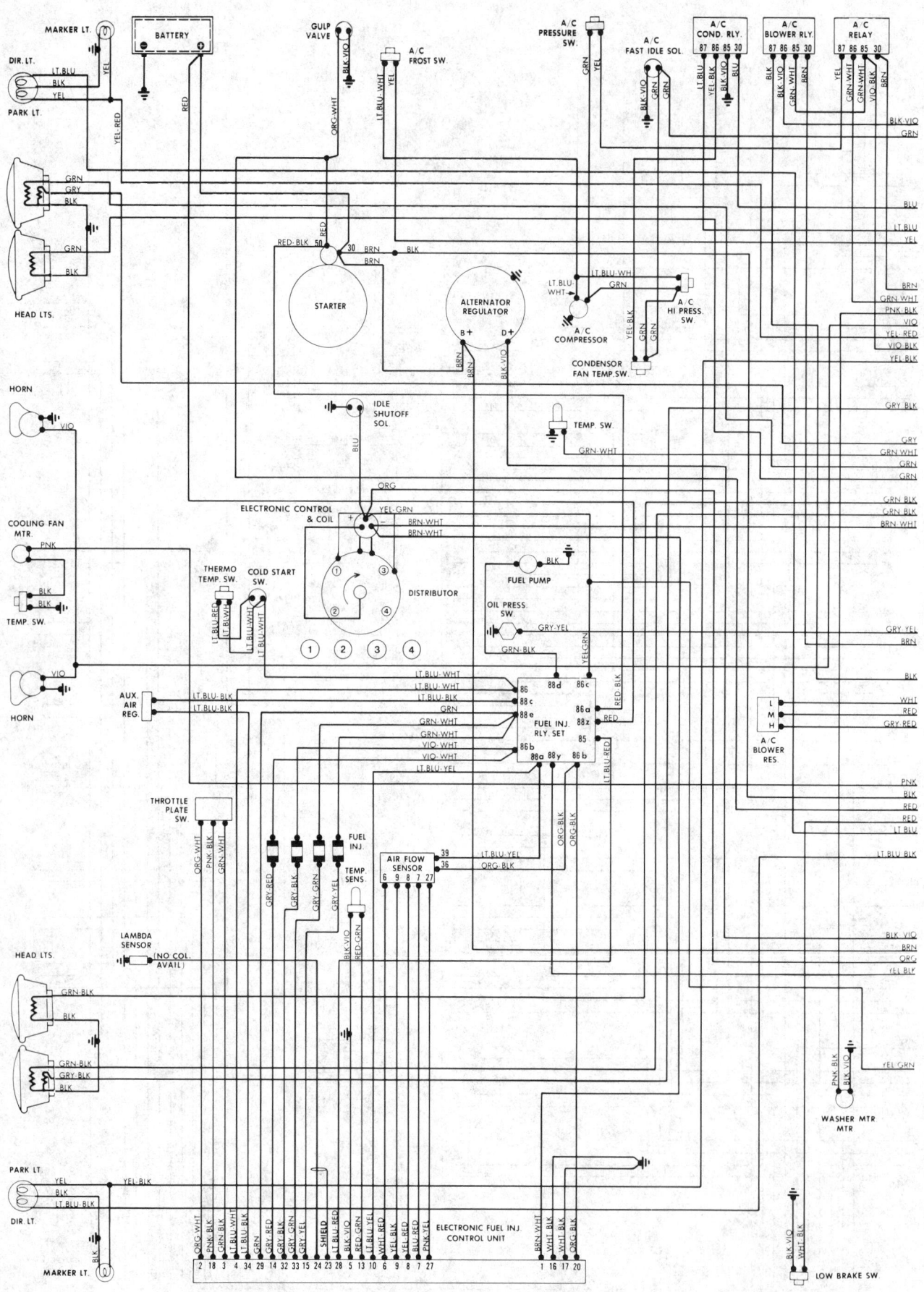

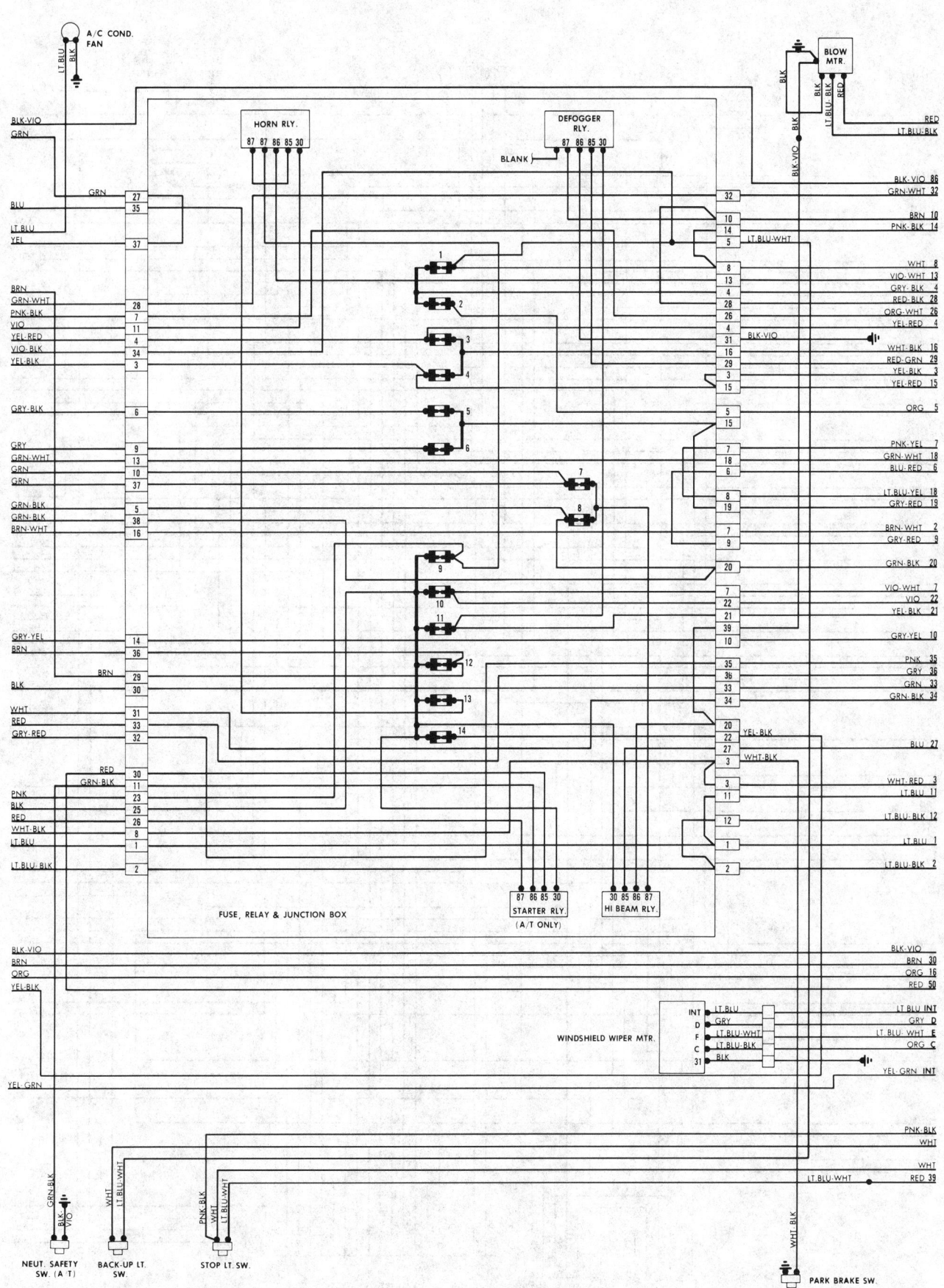

1980 Fiat

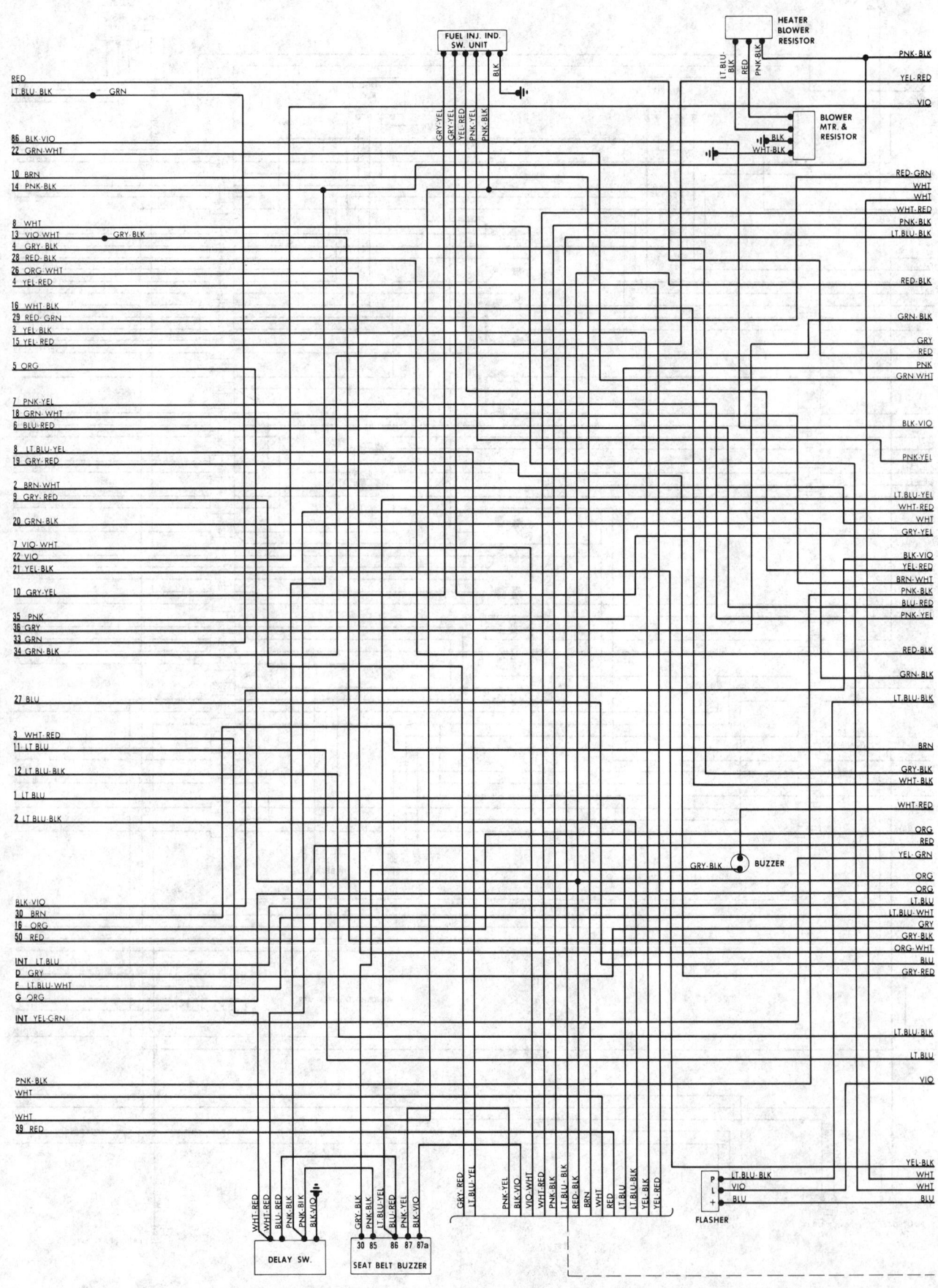

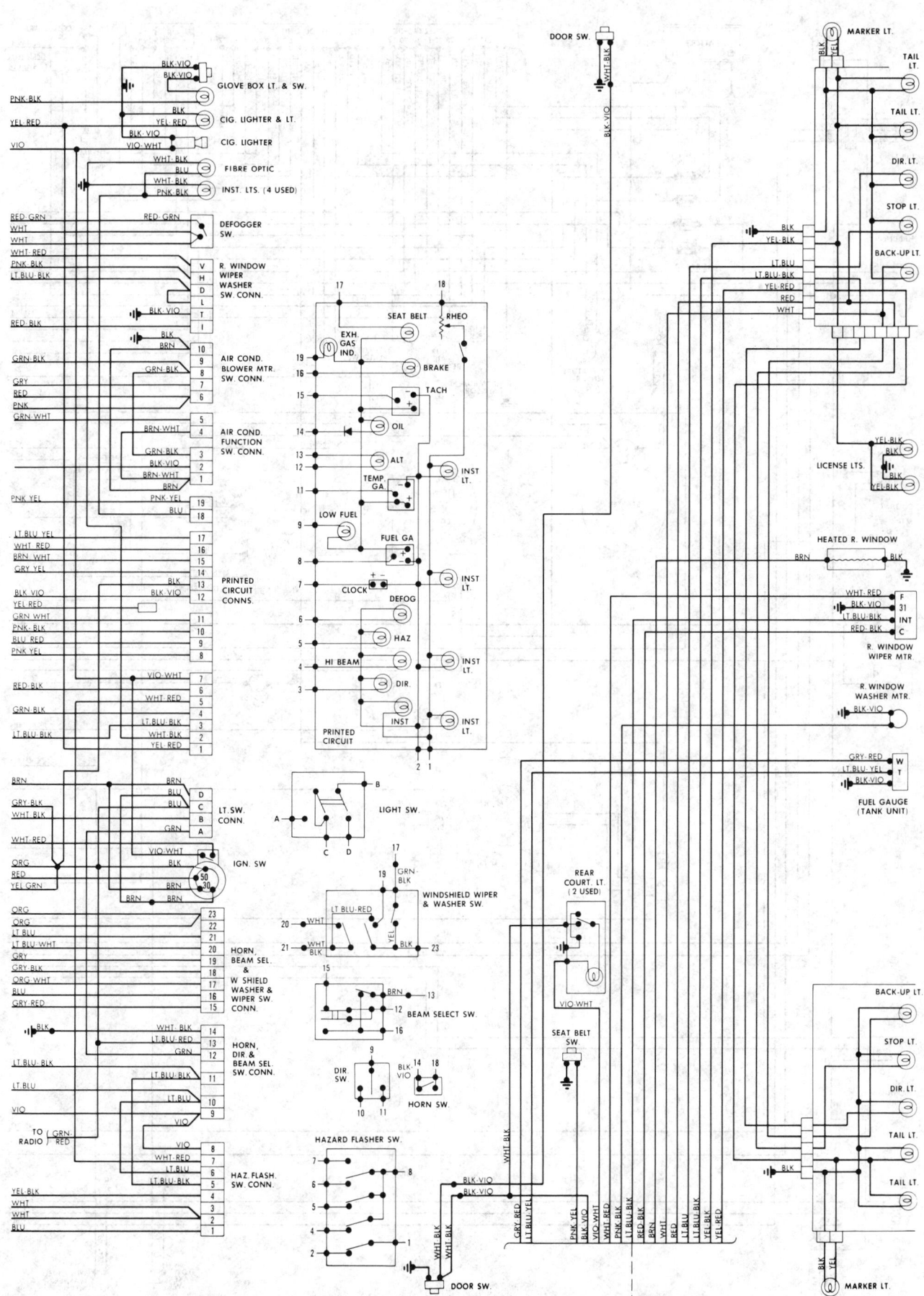

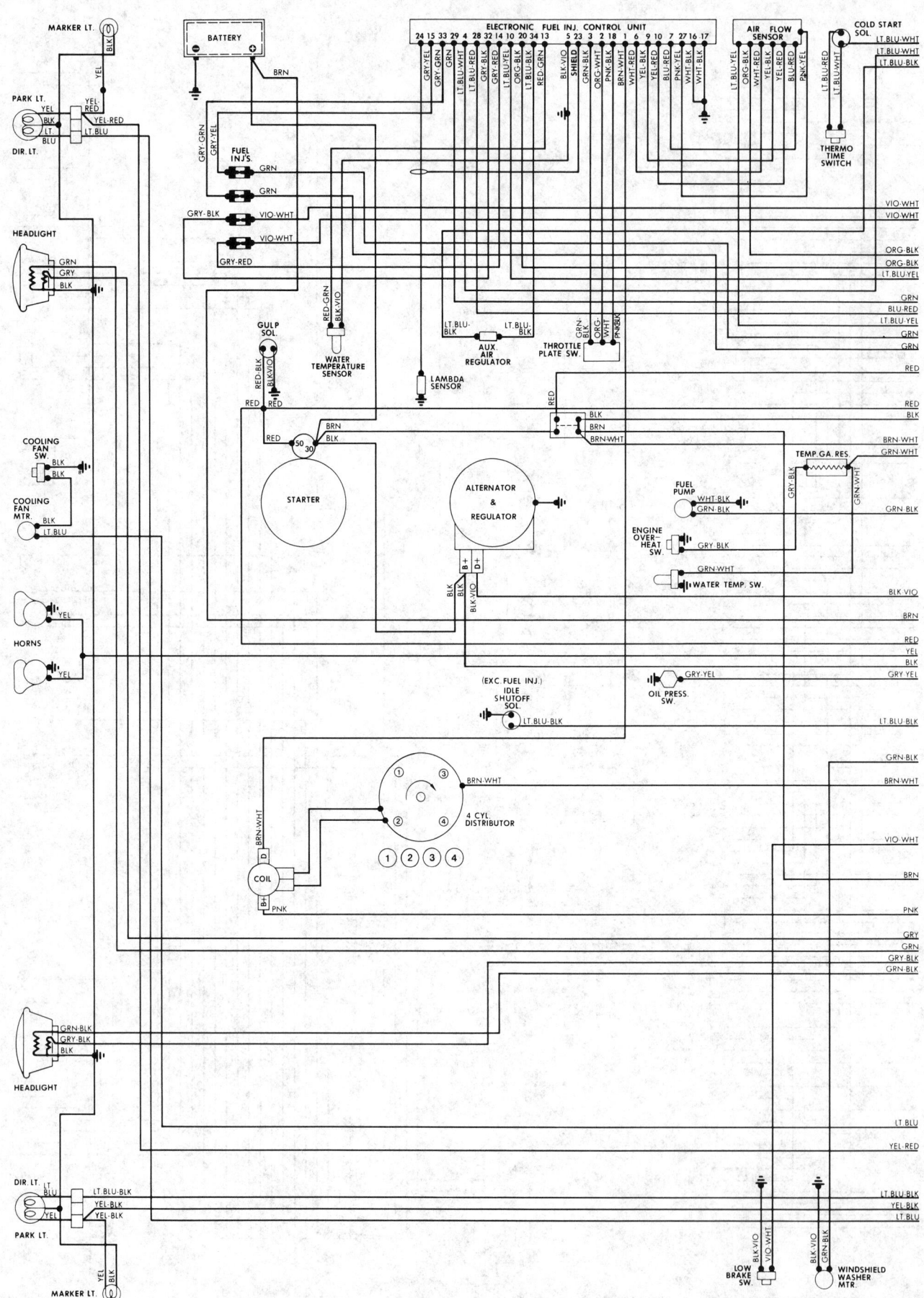

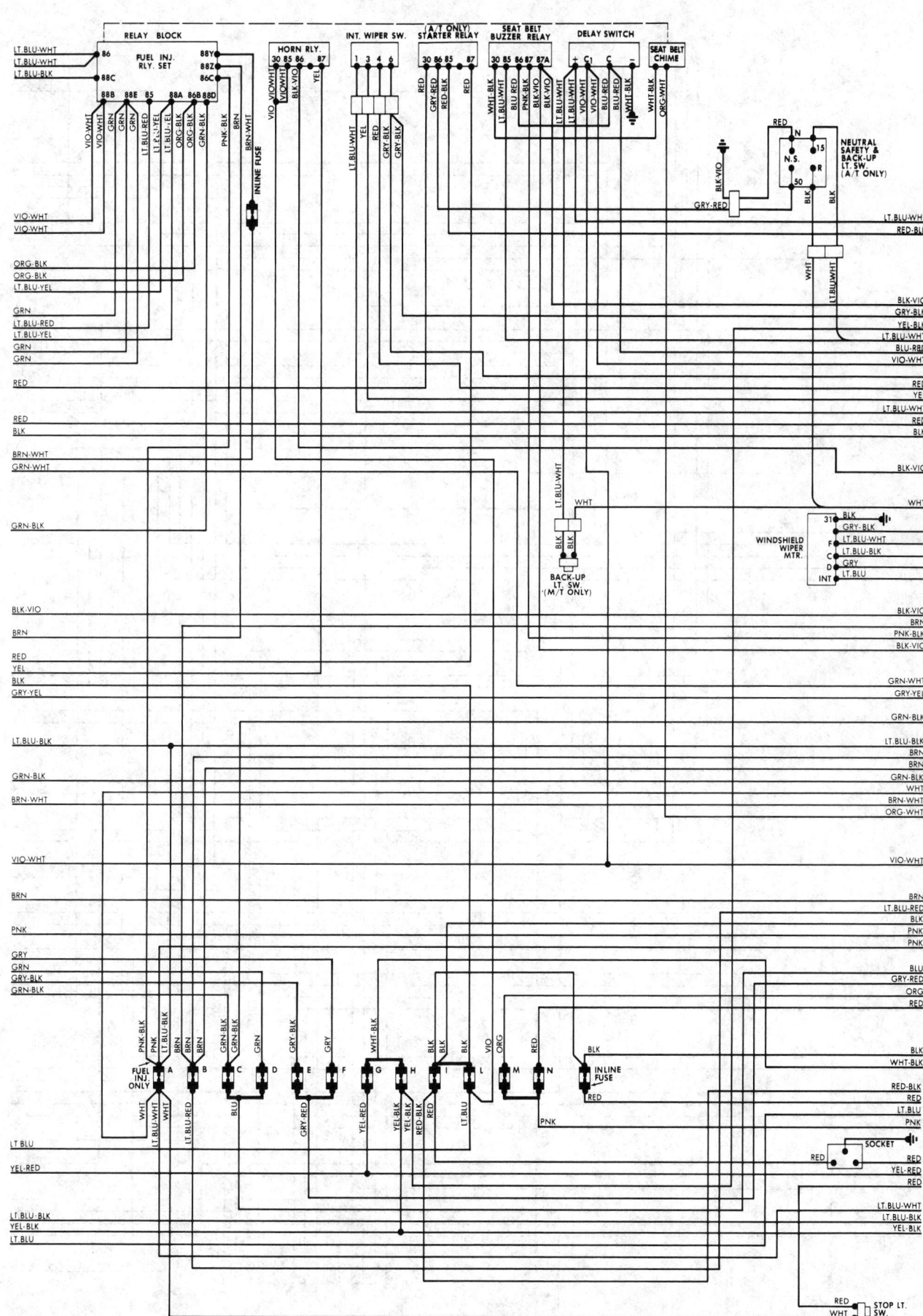

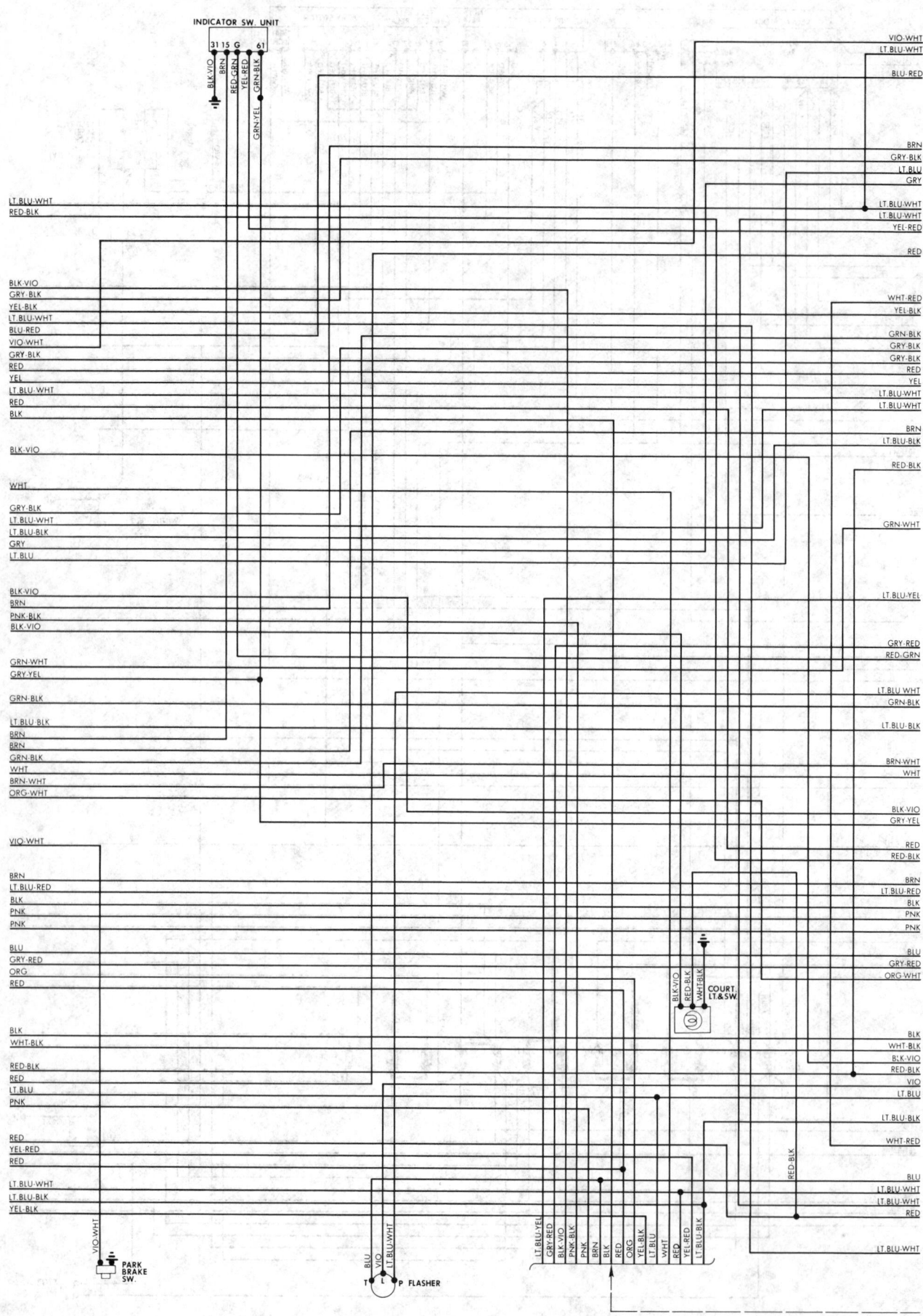

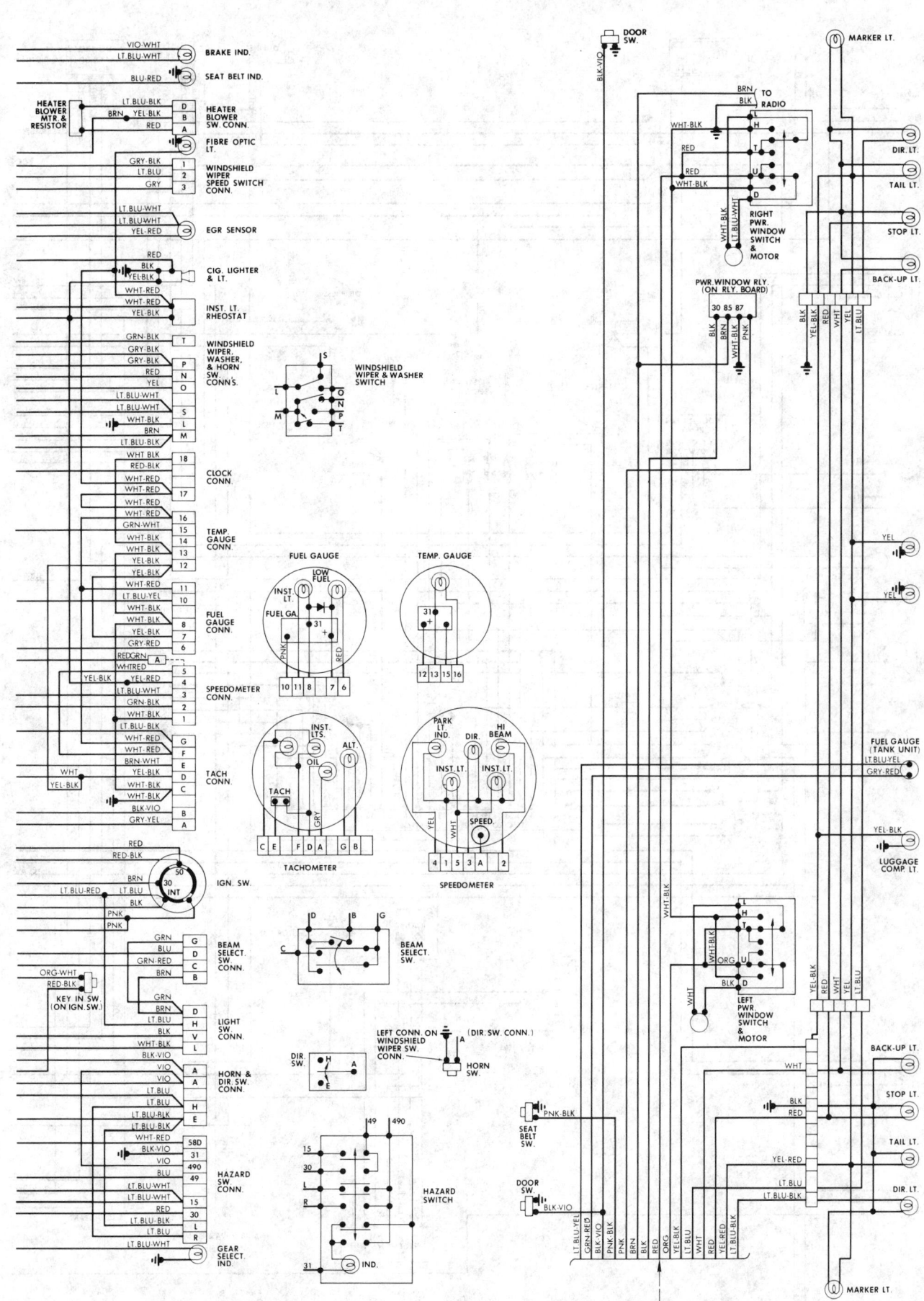

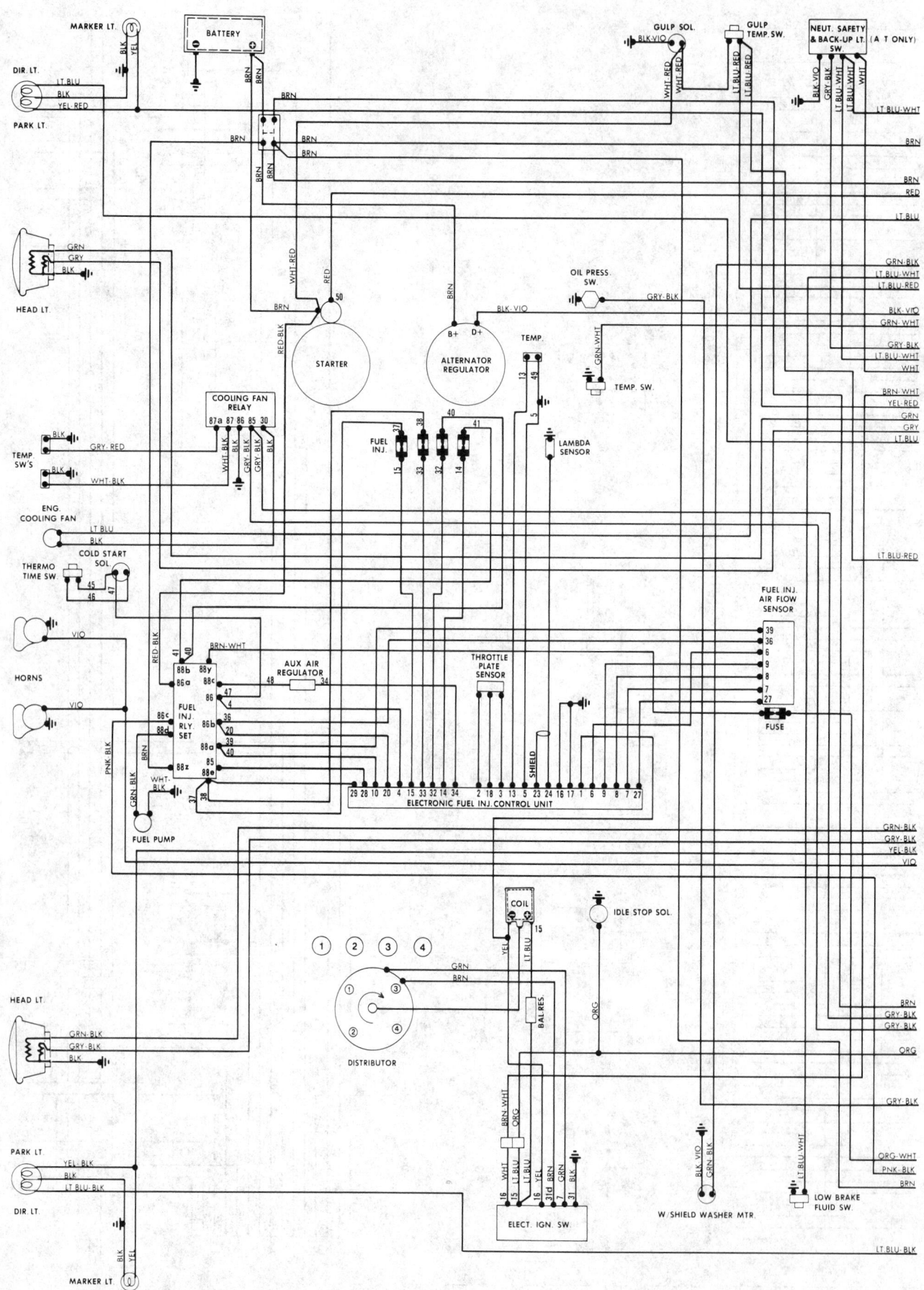

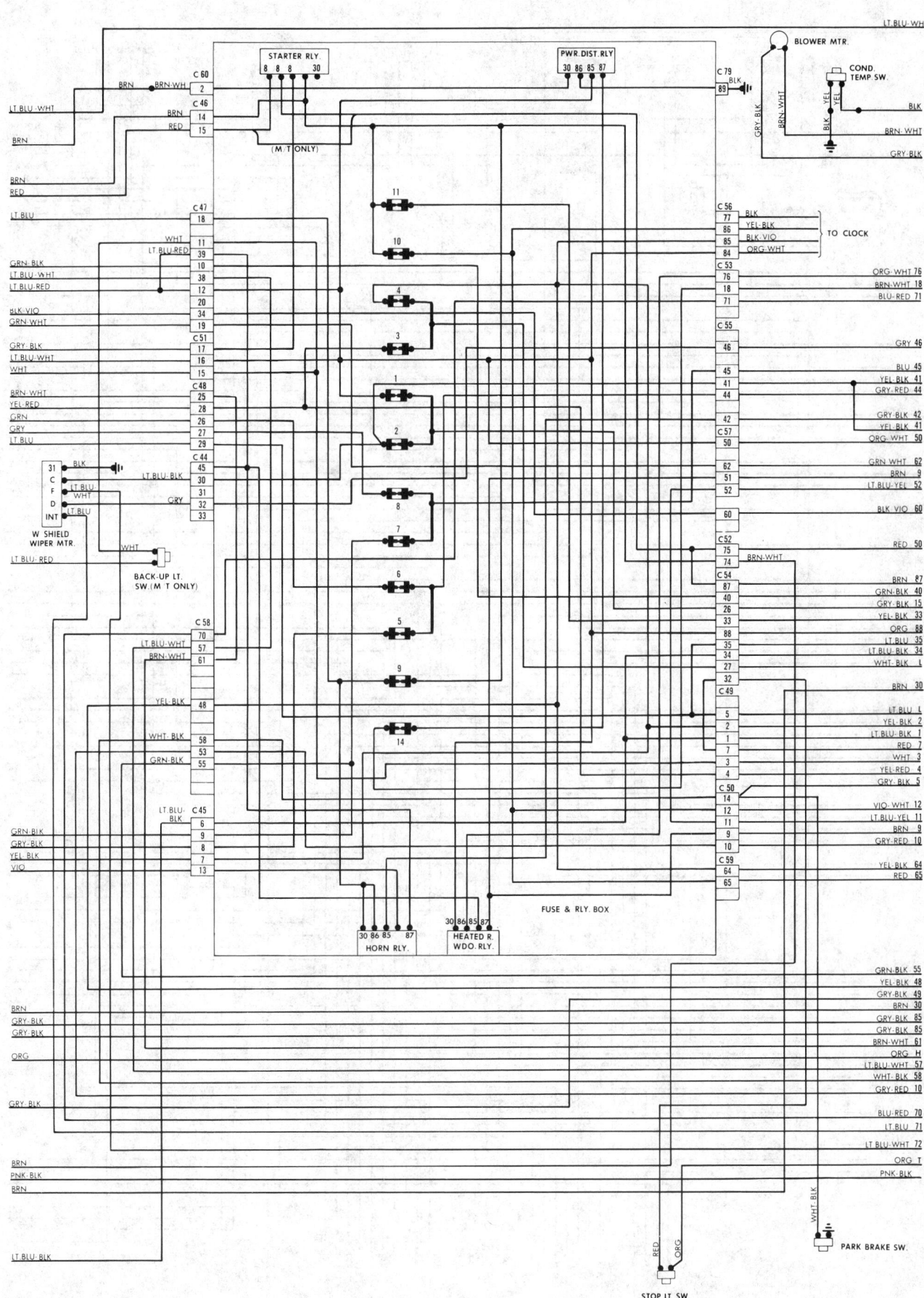

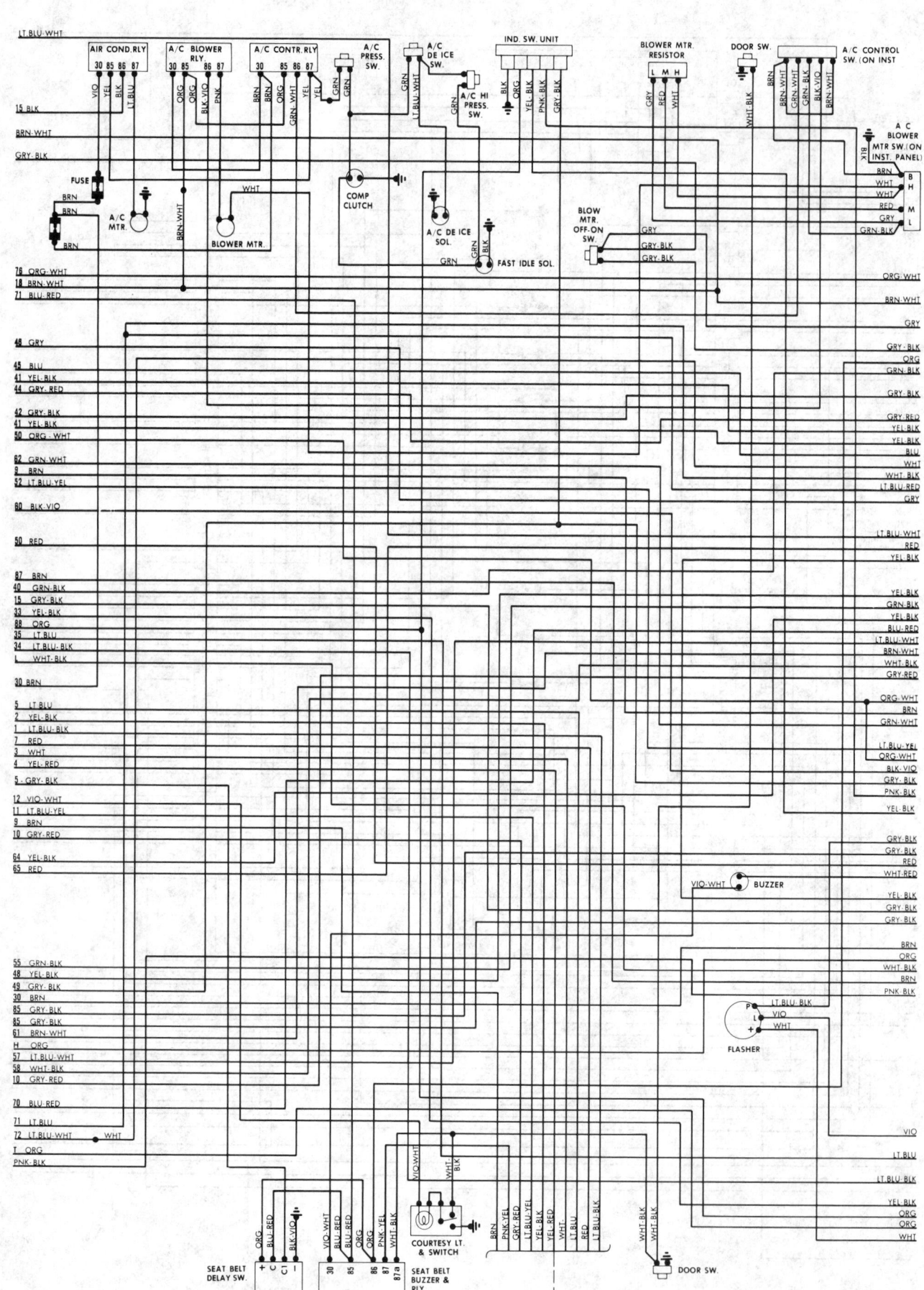

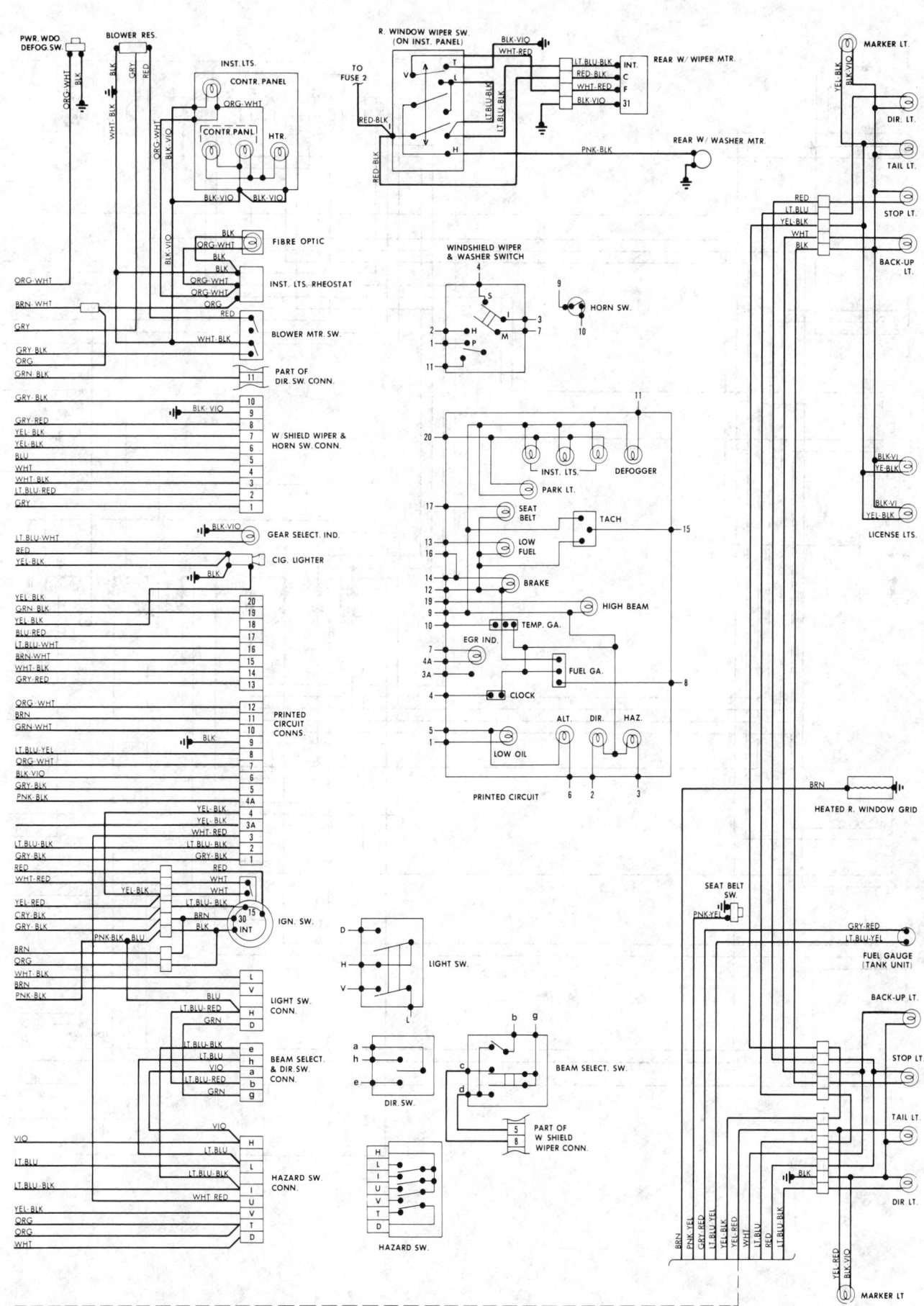

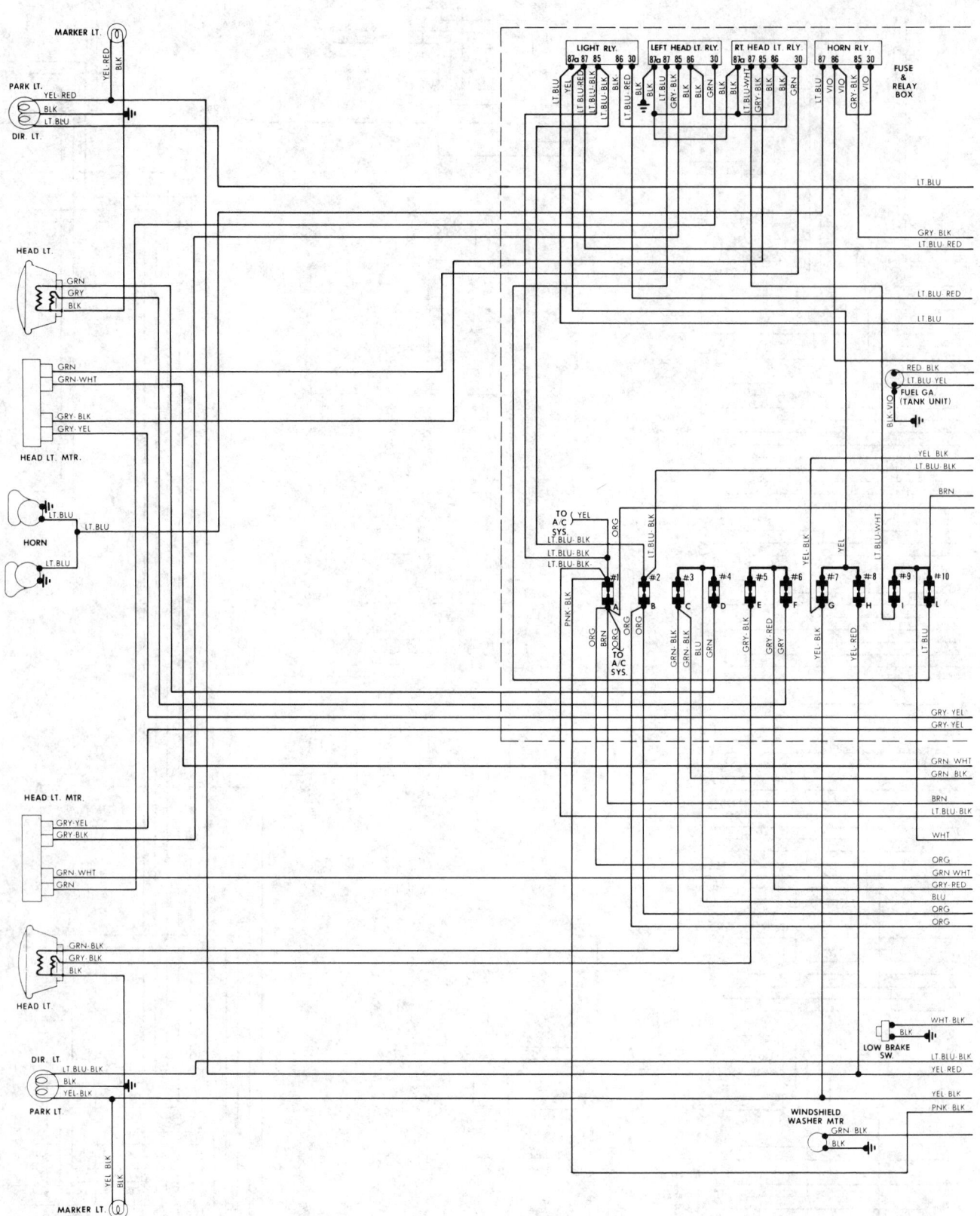

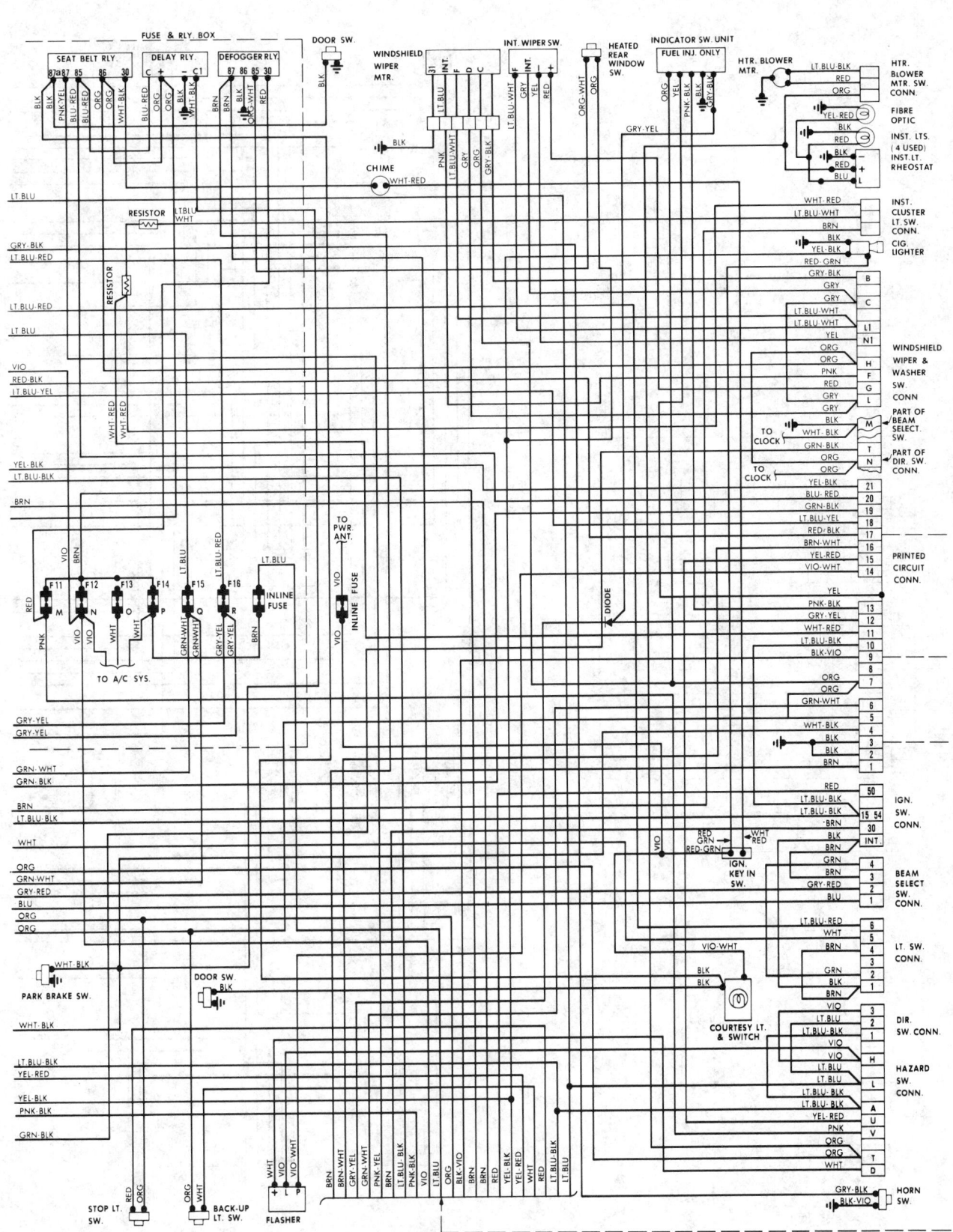

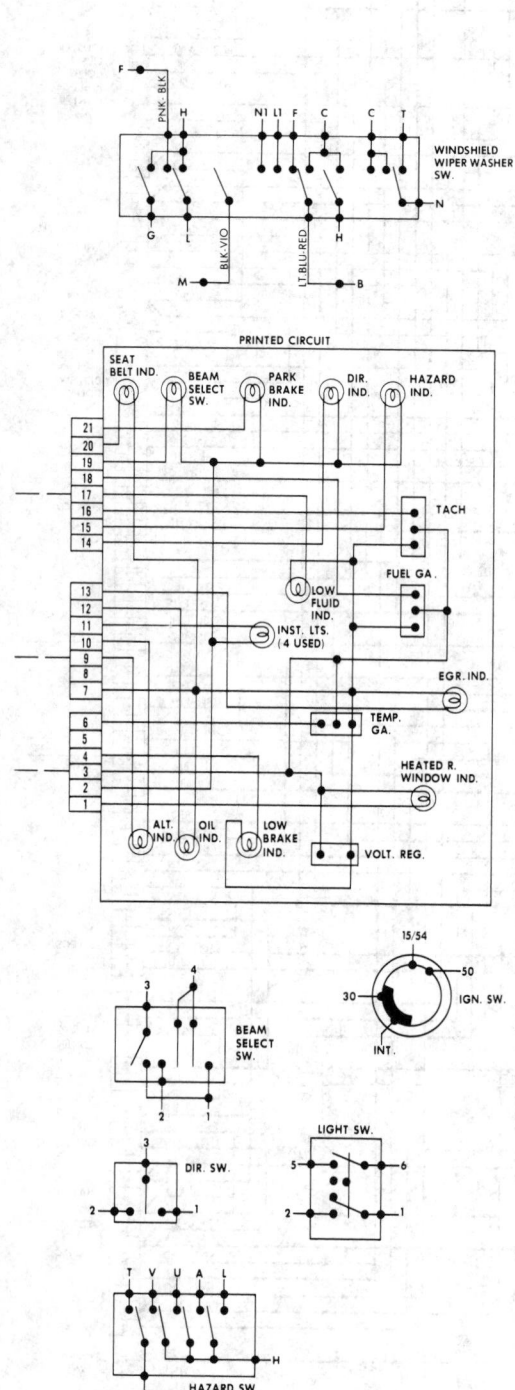

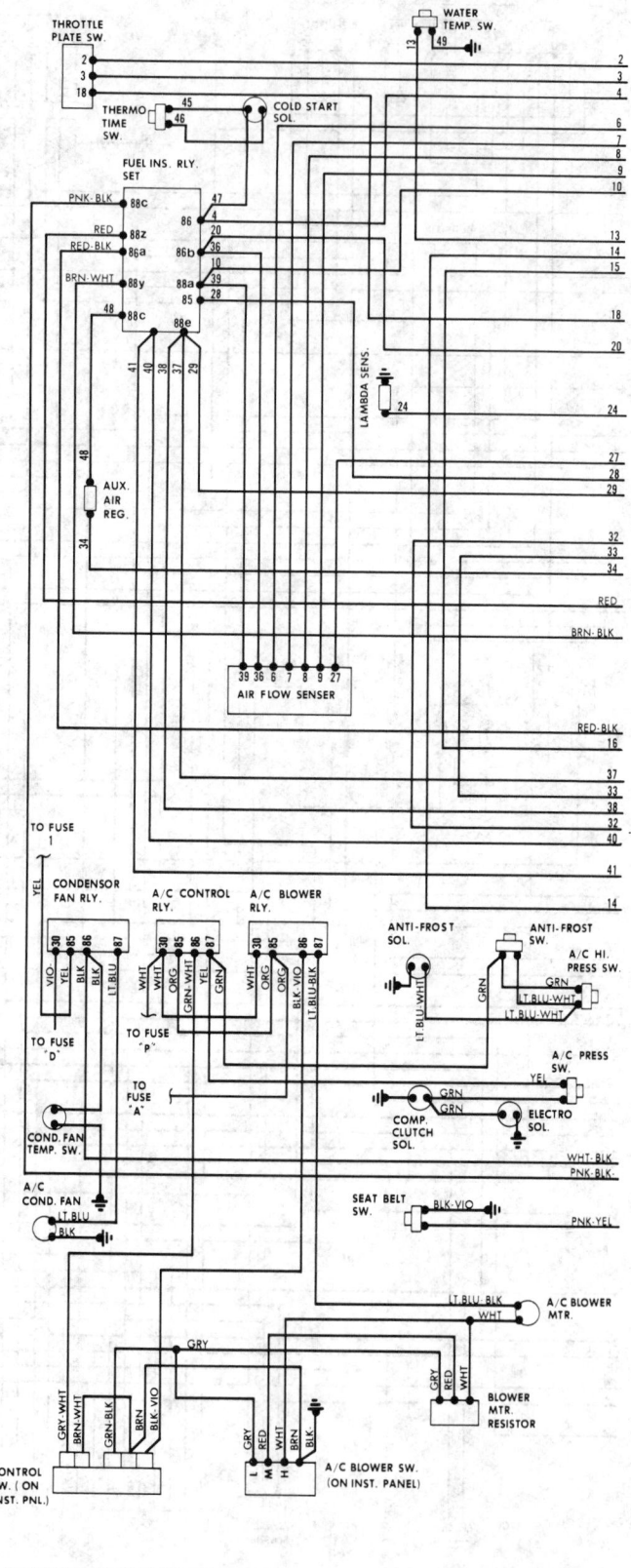

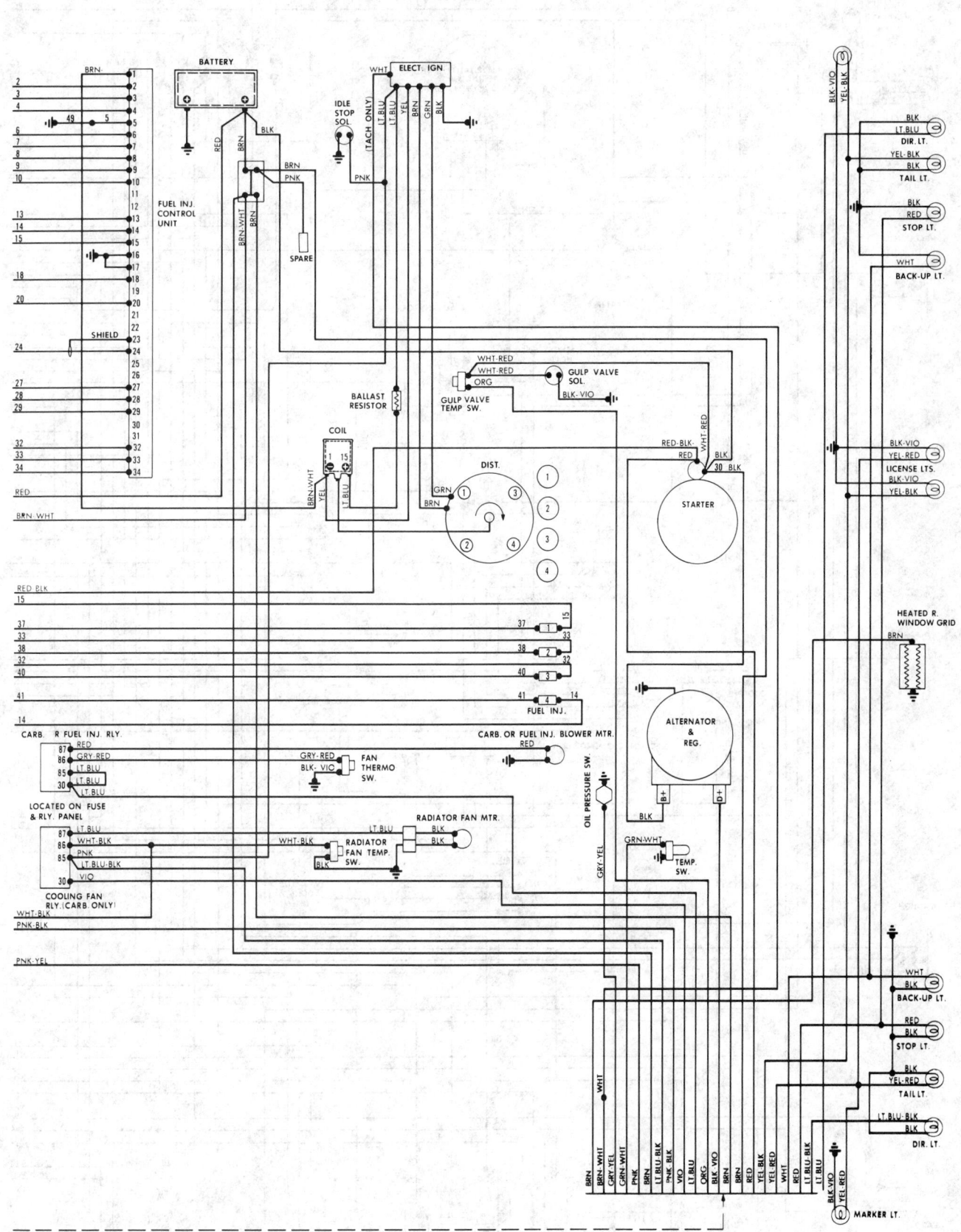

1980 Fiesta

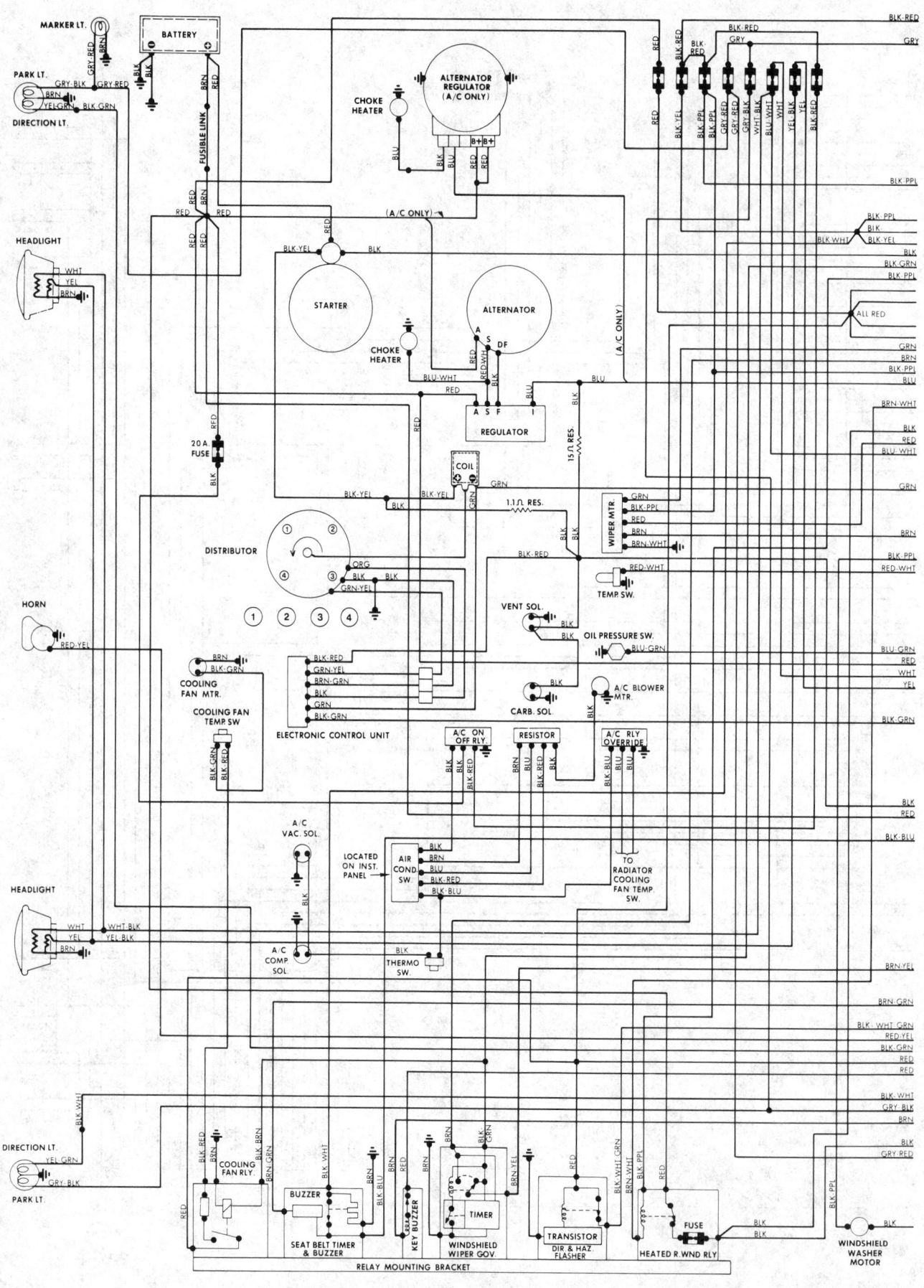

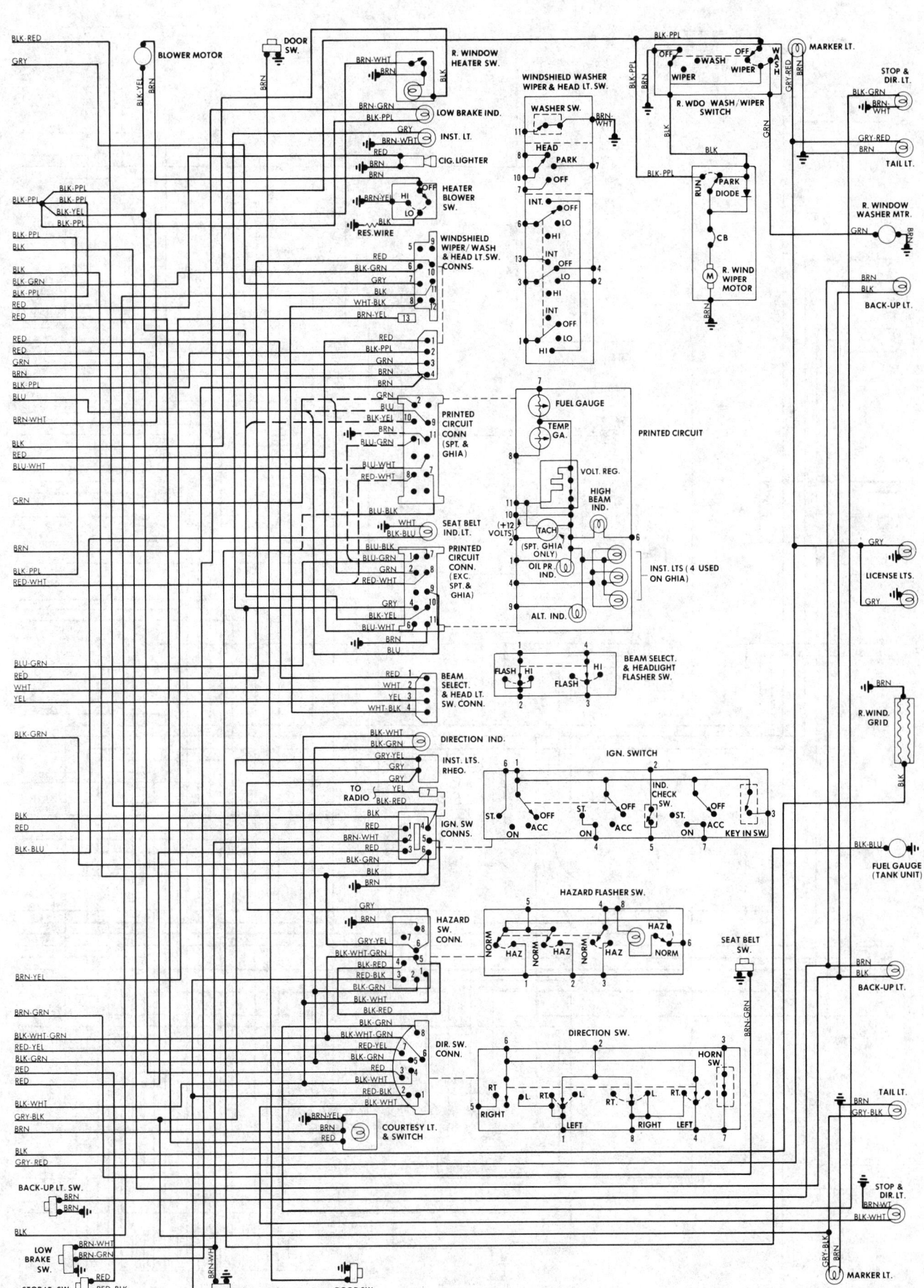

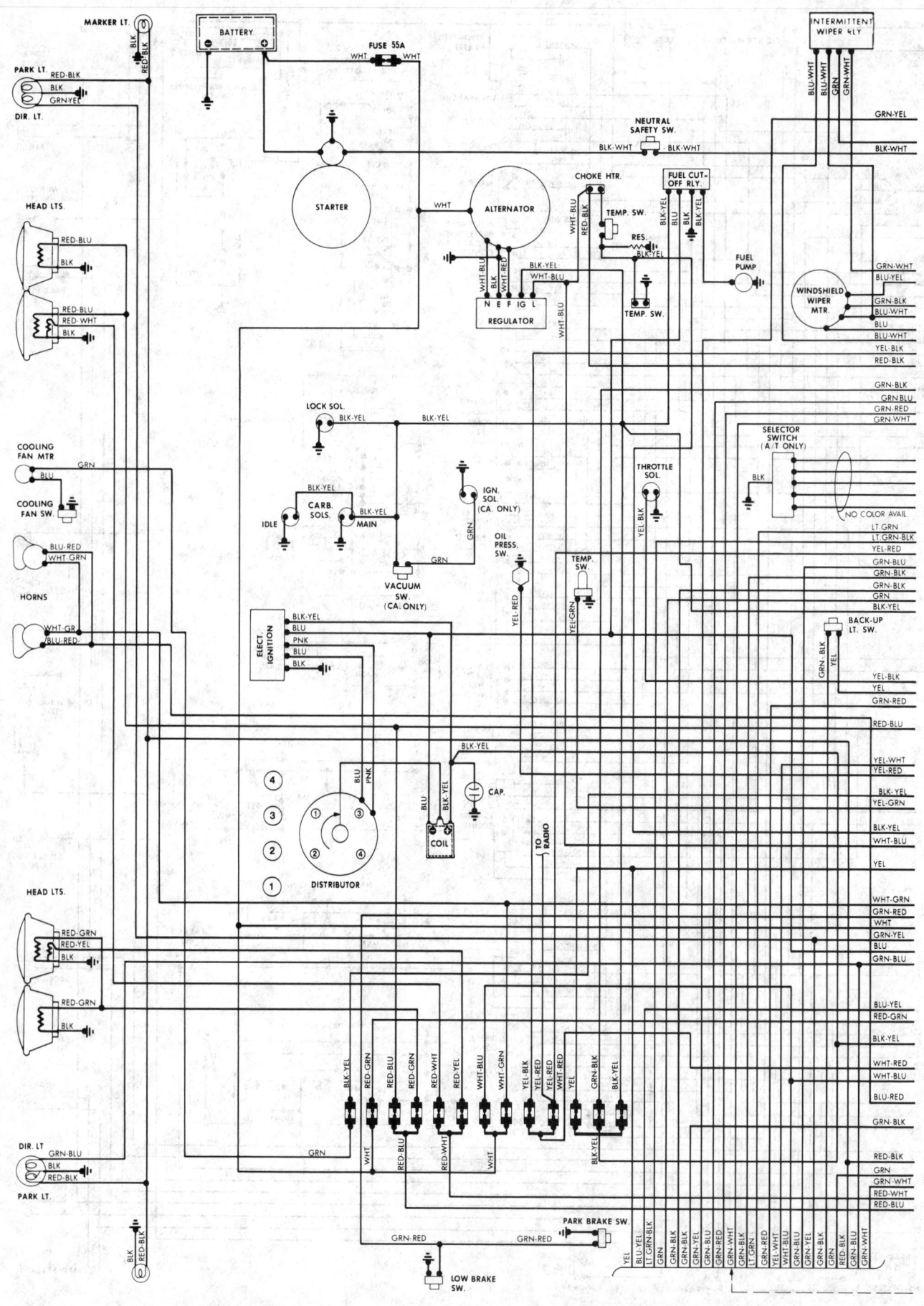

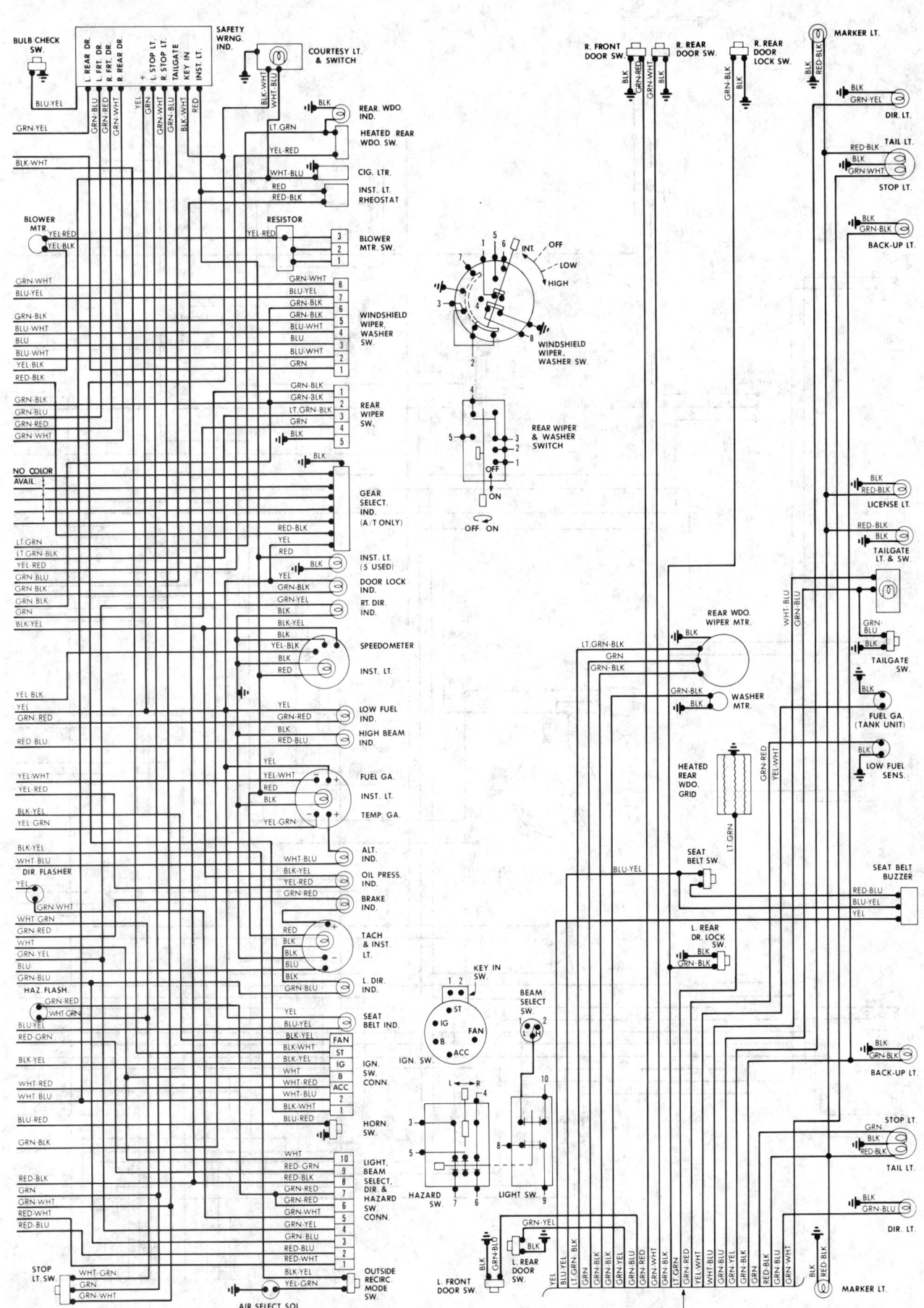

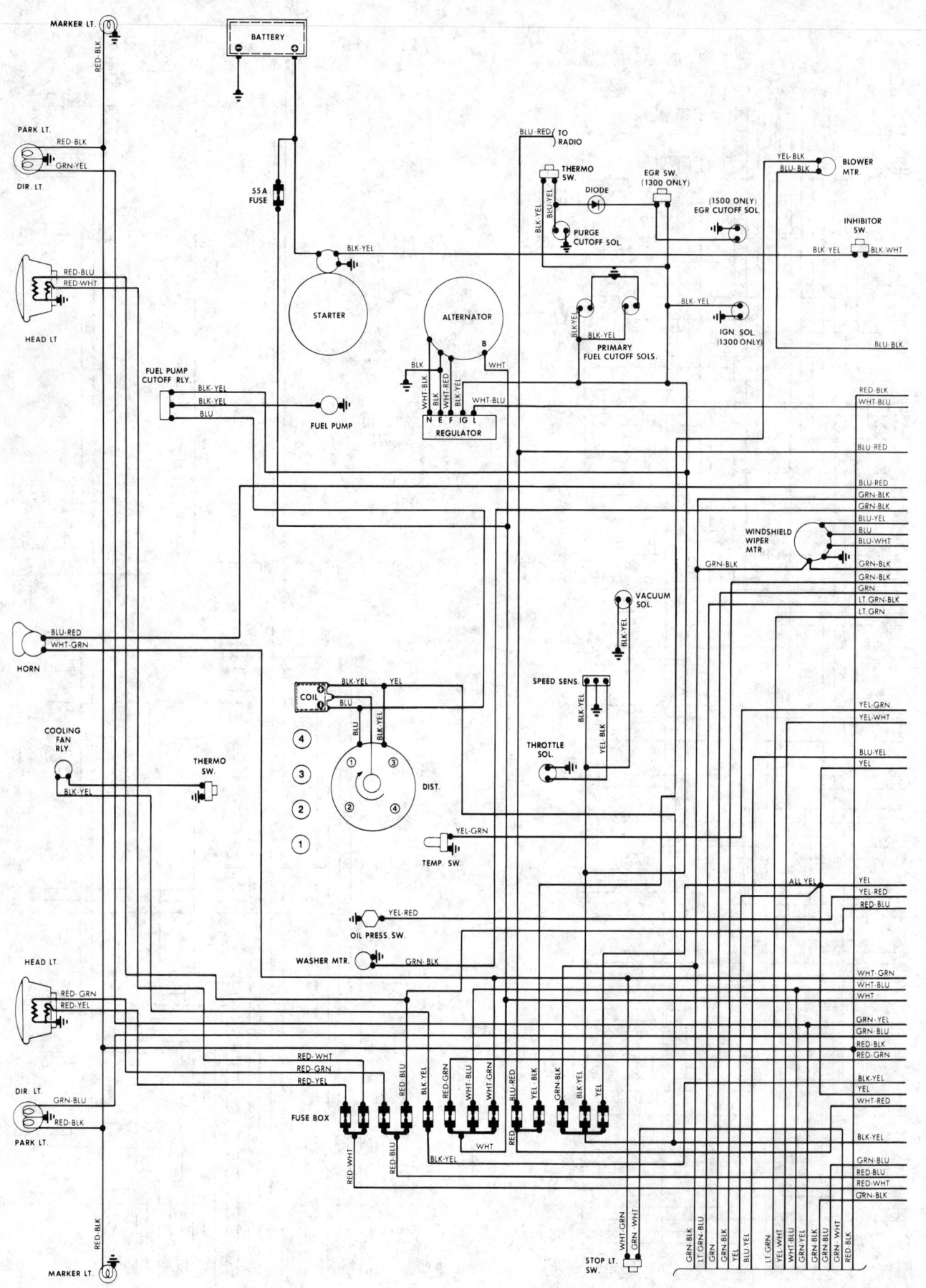

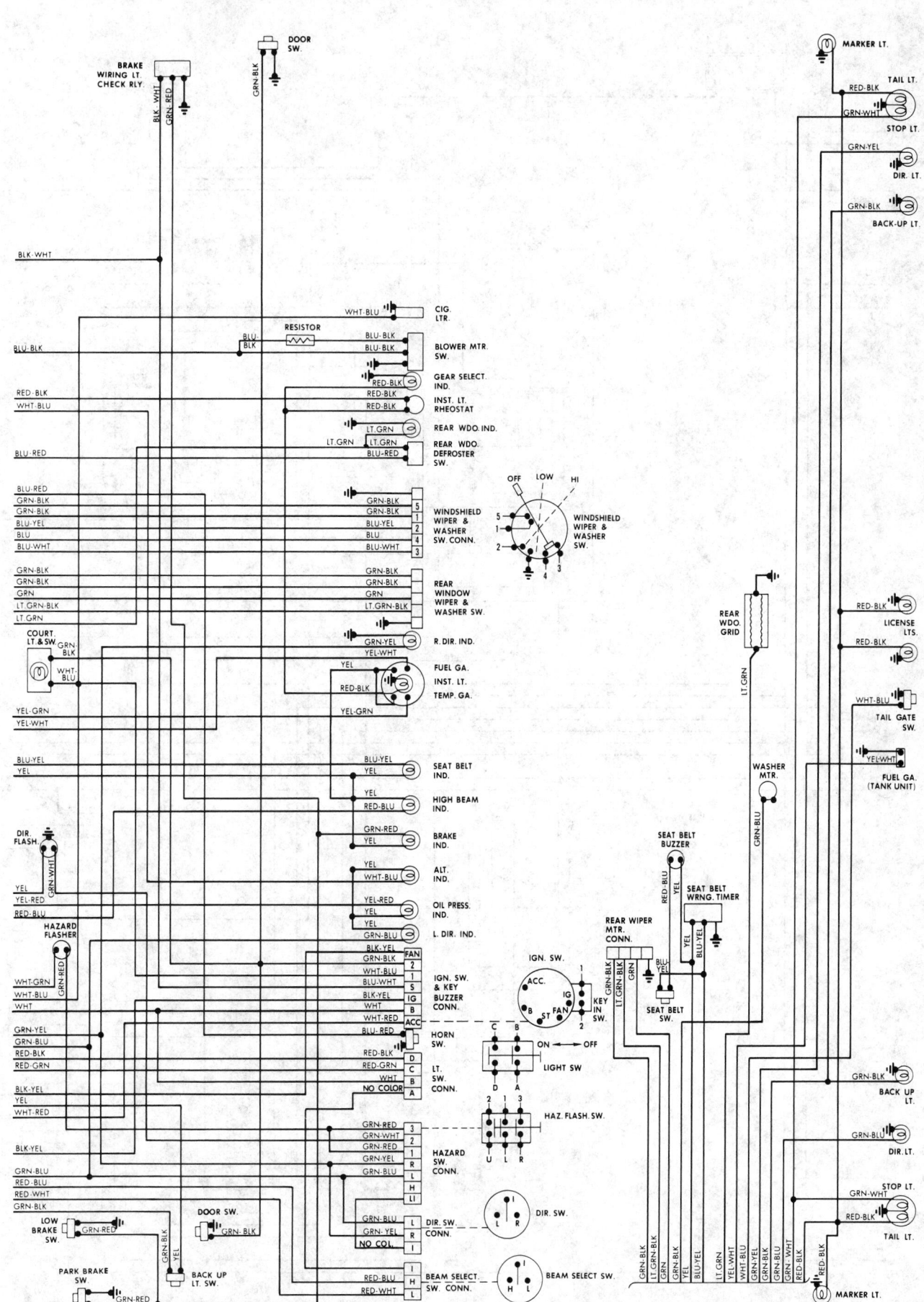

1980 Honda

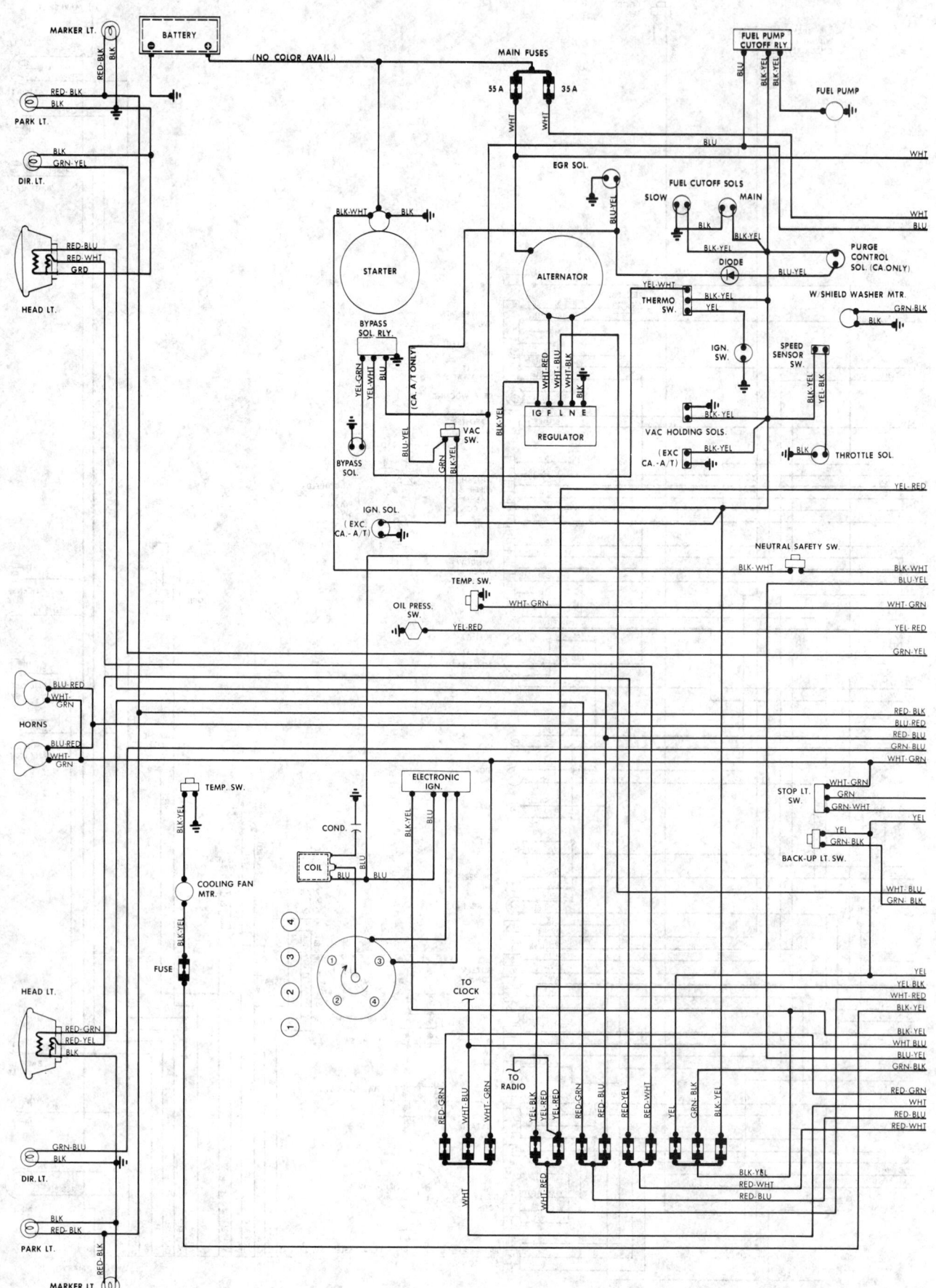

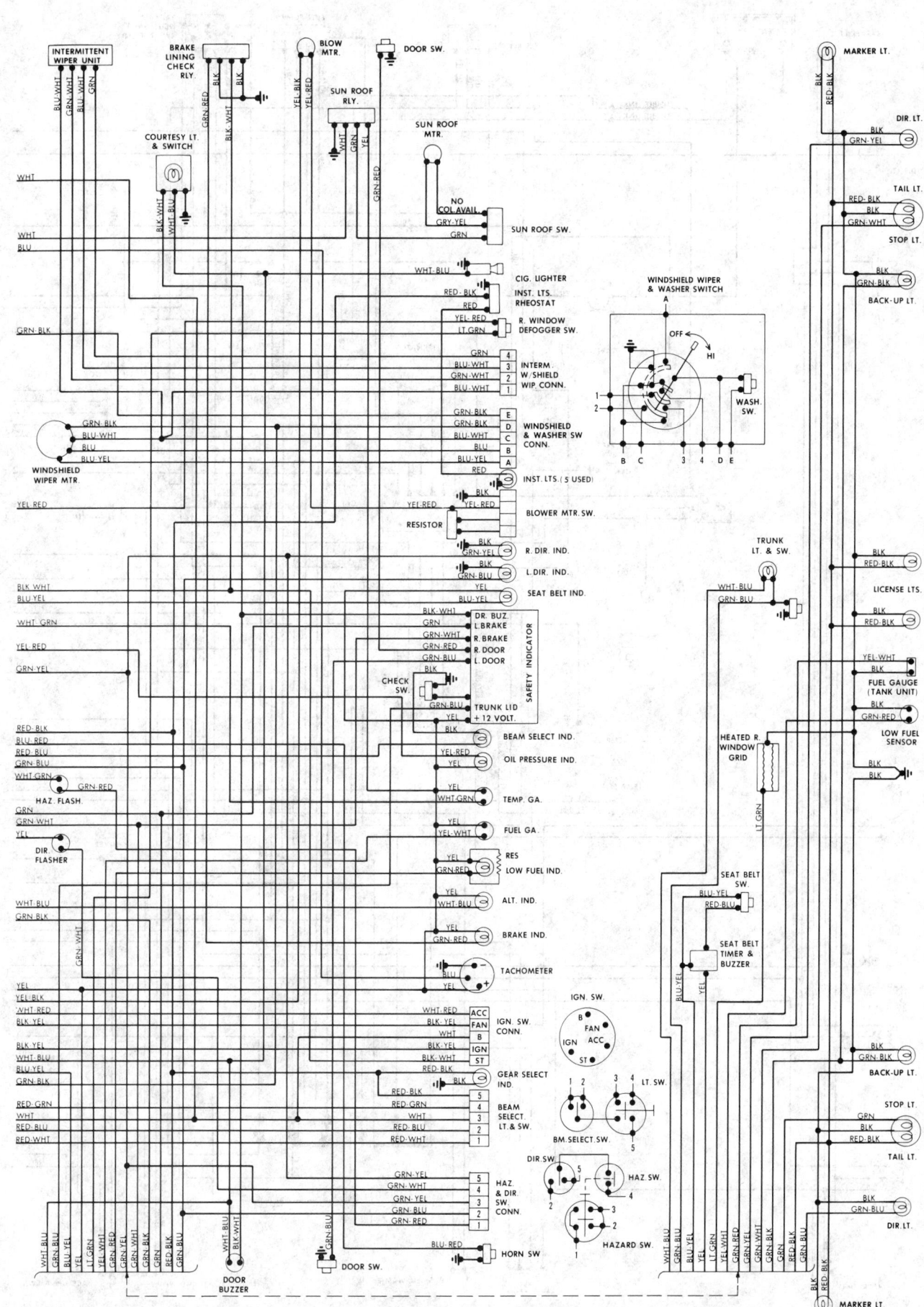

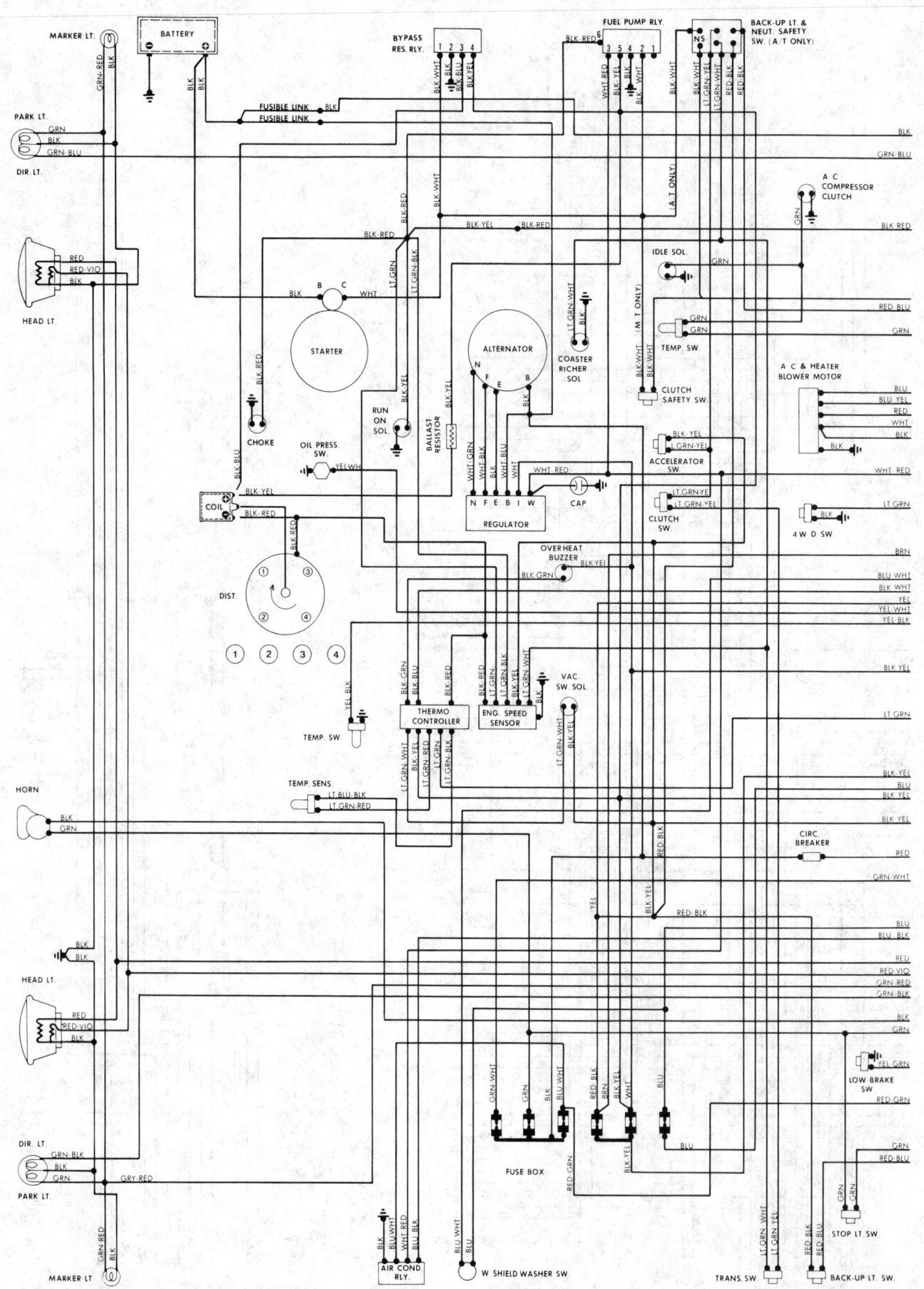

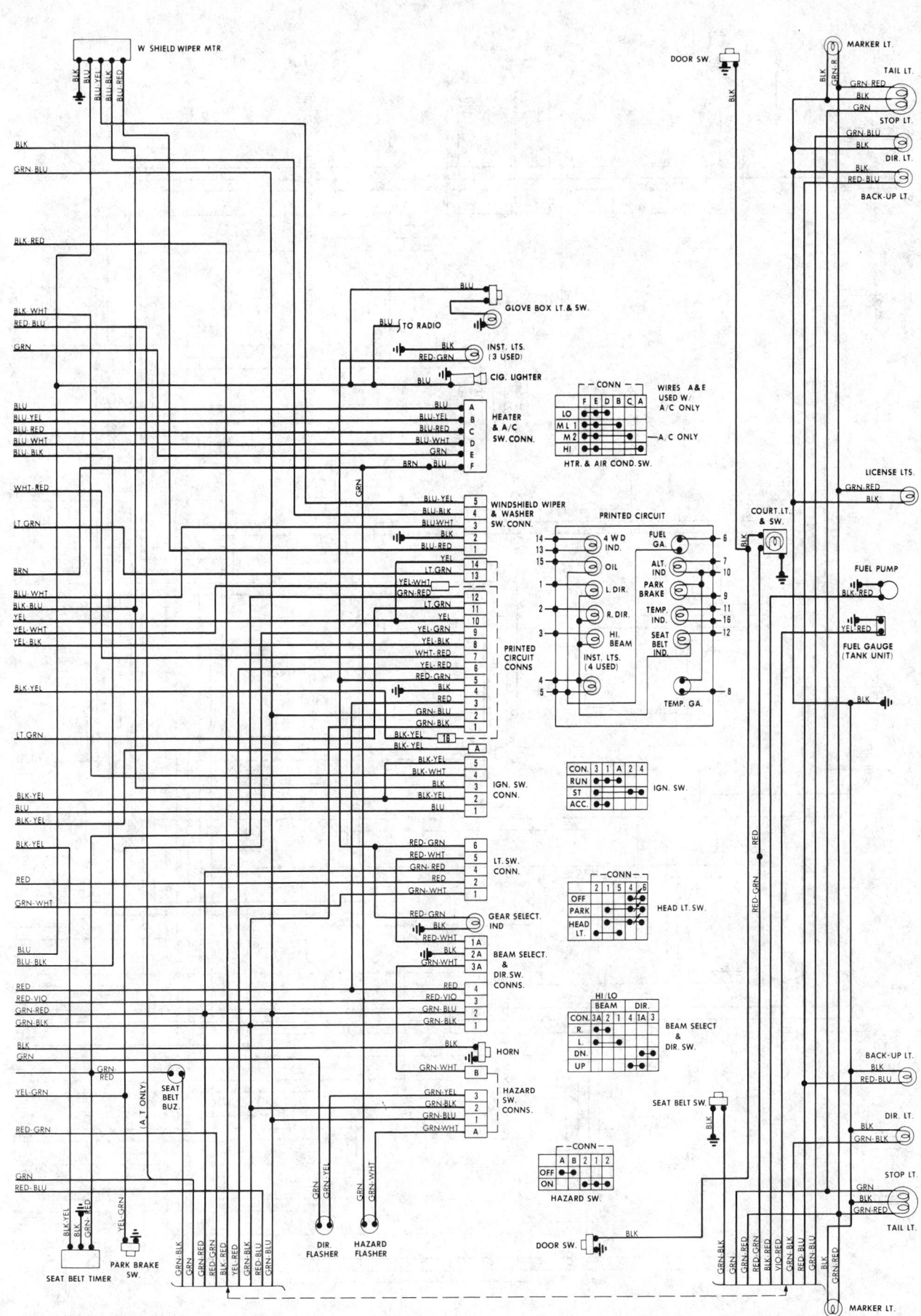

1980 Mazda

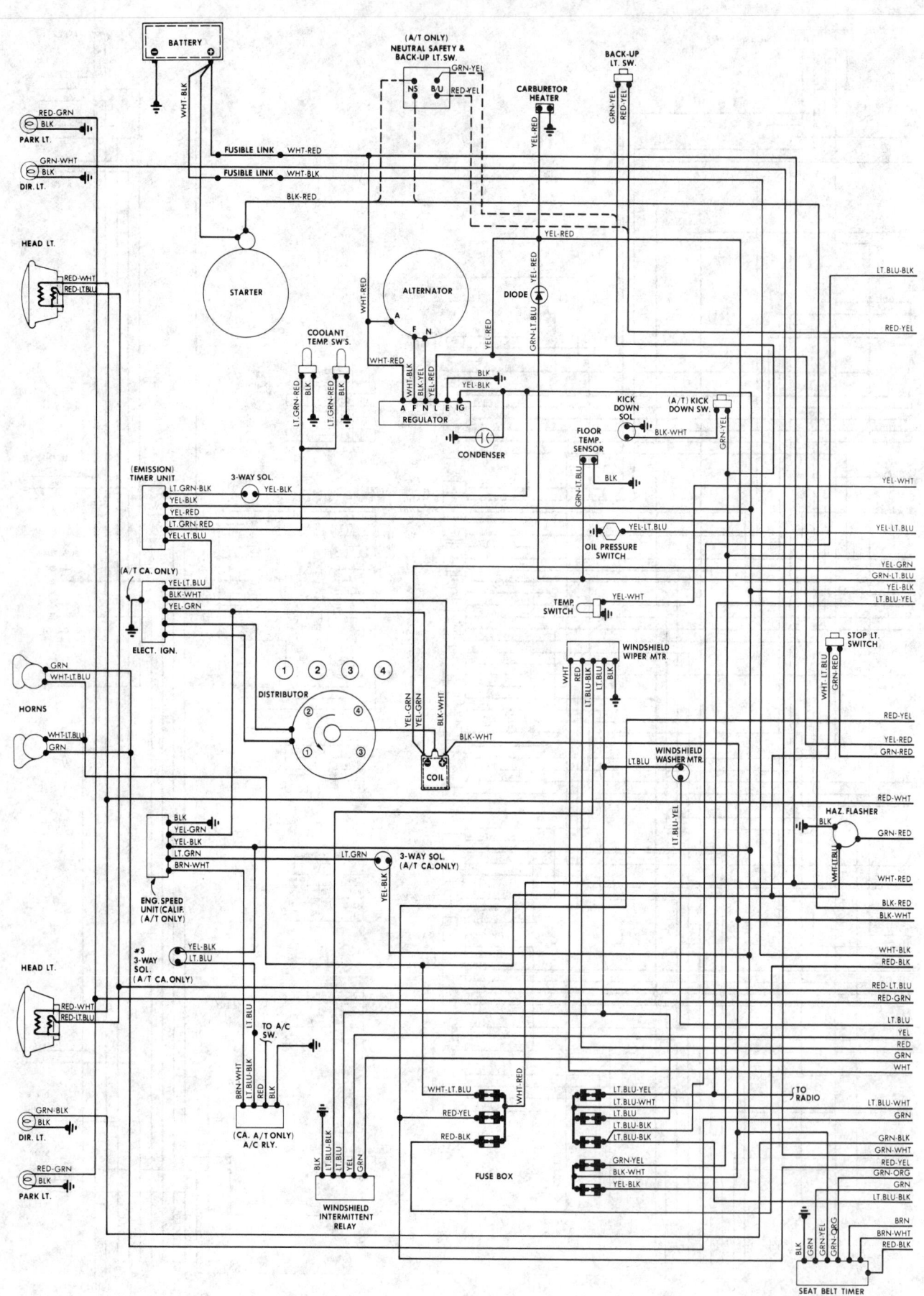

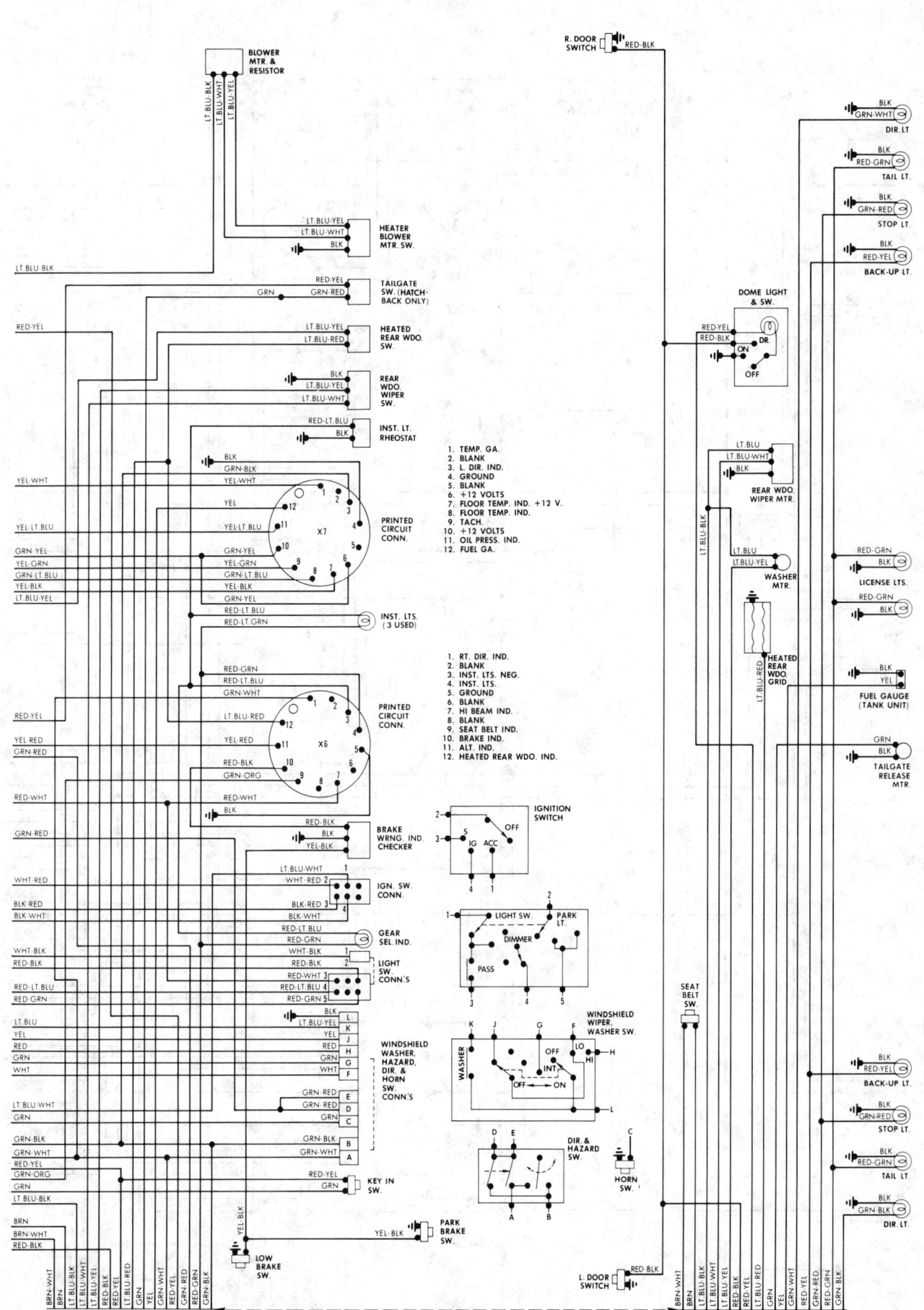

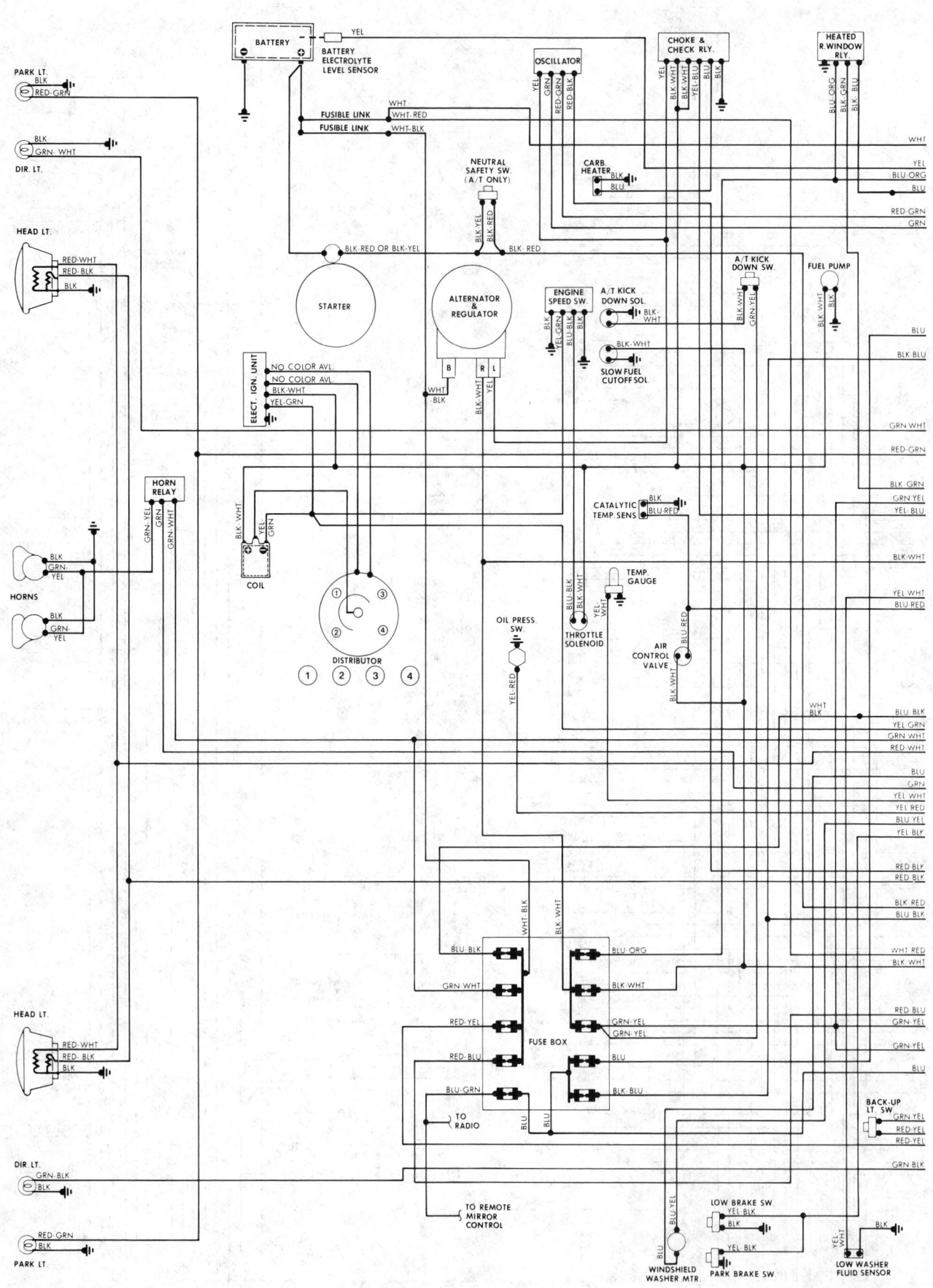

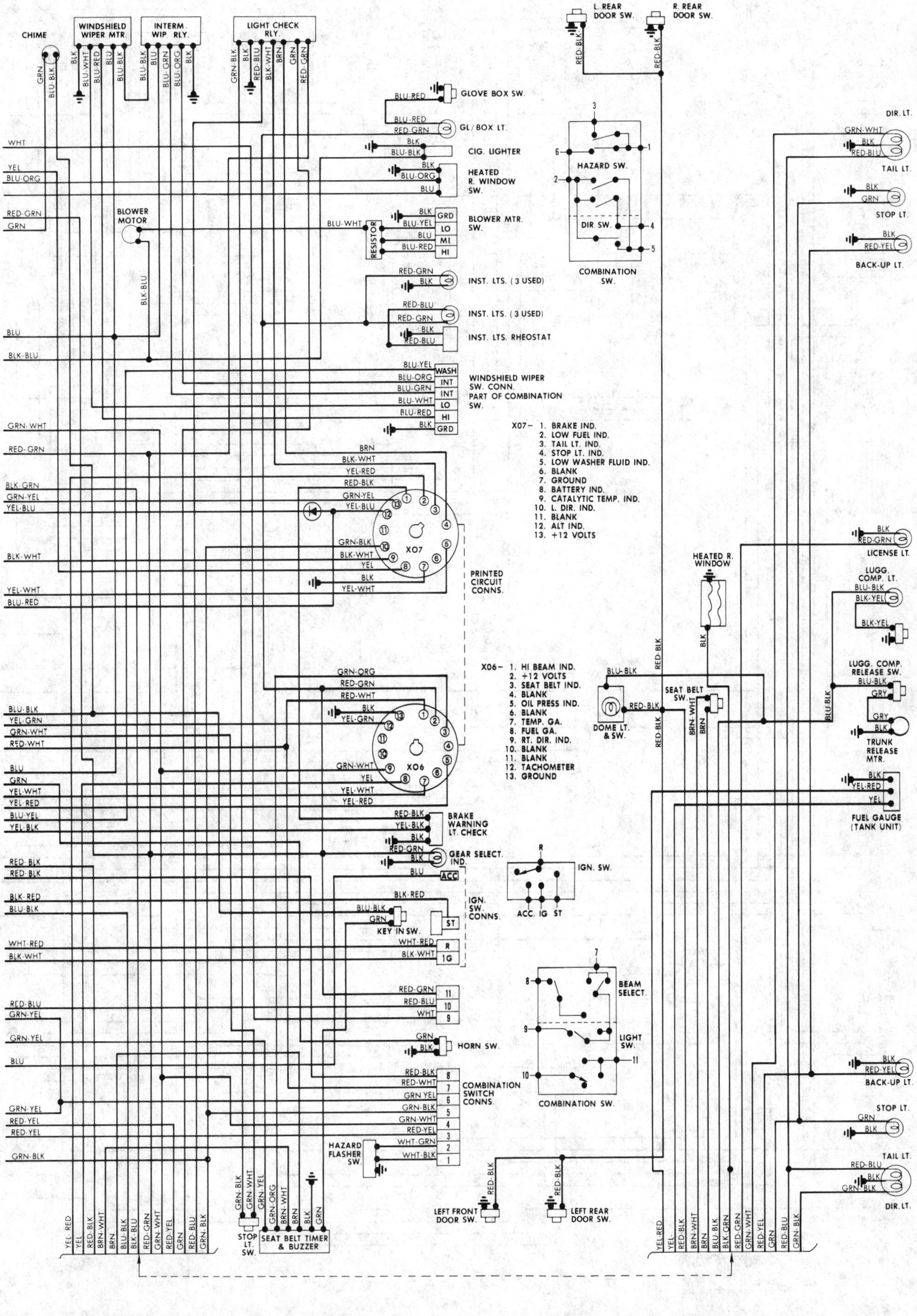

CHIME

WINDSHIELD WIPER MTR.

INTERM. WIP. RLY.

LIGHT CHECK RLY.

L. REAR DOOR SW.

R. REAR DOOR SW.

GLOVE BOX SW.

GL./BOX LT.

CIG. LIGHTER

HEATED R. WINDOW SW.

BLOWER MTR. SW.

RESISTOR

GRD / LO / MI / HI

HAZARD SW.

DIR. SW.

COMBINATION SW.

INST. LTS. (3 USED)

INST. LTS. (3 USED)

INST. LTS. RHEOSTAT

DIR. LT.

TAIL LT.

STOP LT.

BACK-UP LT.

WINDSHIELD WIPER SW. CONN. PART OF COMBINATION SW.

WASH / INT / INT / LO / HI / GRD

X07 — 1. BRAKE IND.
2. LOW FUEL IND.
3. TAIL LT. IND.
4. STOP LT. IND.
5. LOW WASHER FLUID IND.
6. BLANK
7. GROUND
8. BATTERY IND.
9. CATALYTIC TEMP. IND.
10. L. DIR. IND.
11. BLANK
12. ALT IND.
13. +12 VOLTS

PRINTED CIRCUIT CONNS.

X07

BLOWER MOTOR

HEATED R. WINDOW

LICENSE LT.

LUGG. COMP. LT.

X06 — 1. HI BEAM IND.
2. +12 VOLTS
3. SEAT BELT IND.
4. BLANK
5. OIL PRESS IND.
6. BLANK
7. TEMP. GA.
8. FUEL GA.
9. RT. DIR. IND.
10. BLANK
11. BLANK
12. TACHOMETER
13. GROUND

X06

DOME LT. & SW.

SEAT BELT SW.

LUGG. COMP. RELEASE SW.

TRUNK RELEASE MTR.

FUEL GAUGE (TANK UNIT)

BRAKE WARNING LT. CHECK

GEAR SELECT. IND.

IGN. SW.

ACC. IG. ST

IGN. SW. CONNS.

ACC / ST / R / 1G

KEY IN SW.

BEAM SELECT.

LIGHT SW.

COMBINATION SW.

HORN SW.

COMBINATION SWITCH CONNS.

HAZARD FLASHER SW.

STOP LT. SW.

SEAT BELT TIMER & BUZZER

LEFT FRONT DOOR SW.

LEFT REAR DOOR SW.

BACK-UP LT.

STOP LT.

TAIL LT.

DIR. LT.

1980 Mazda

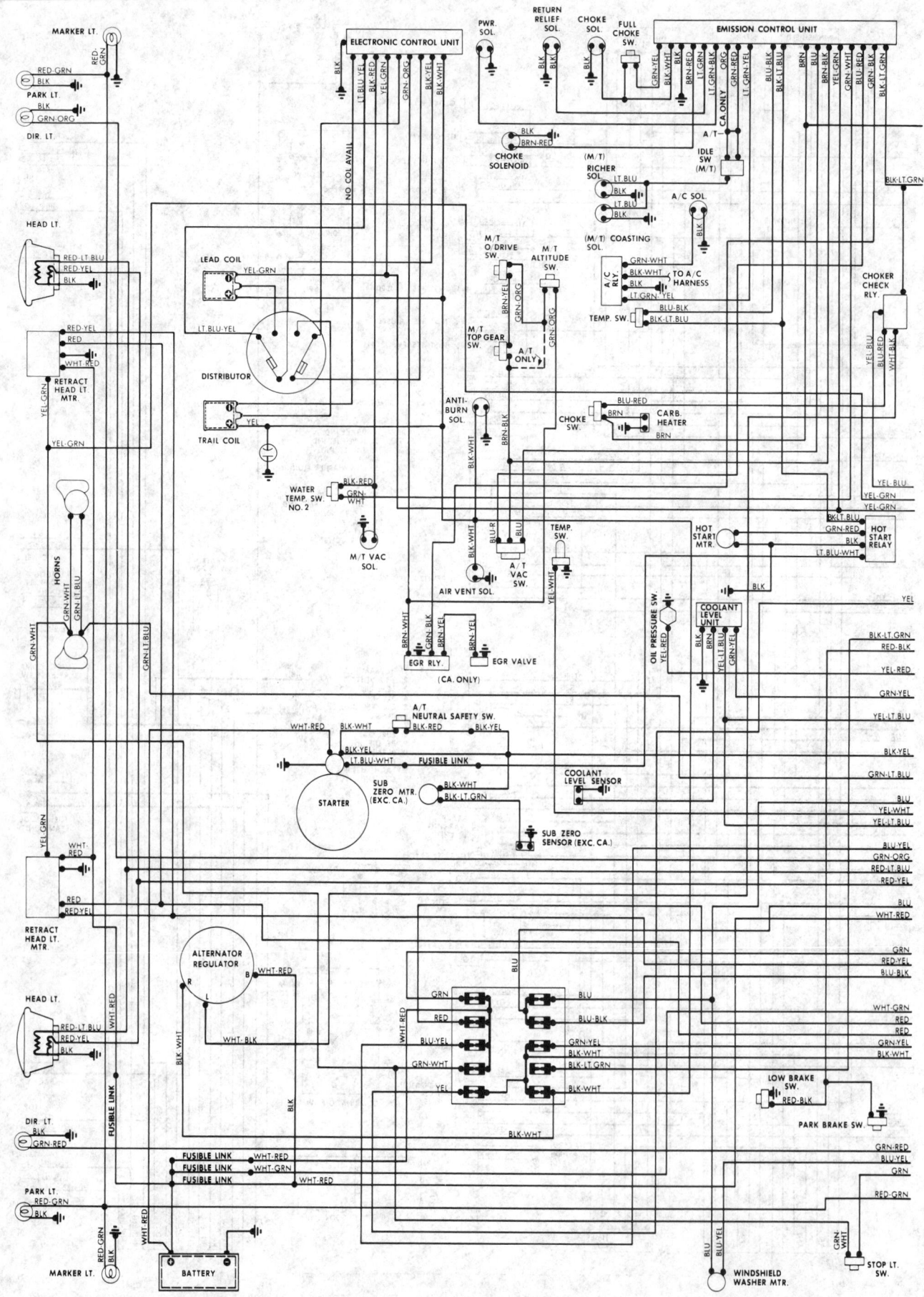

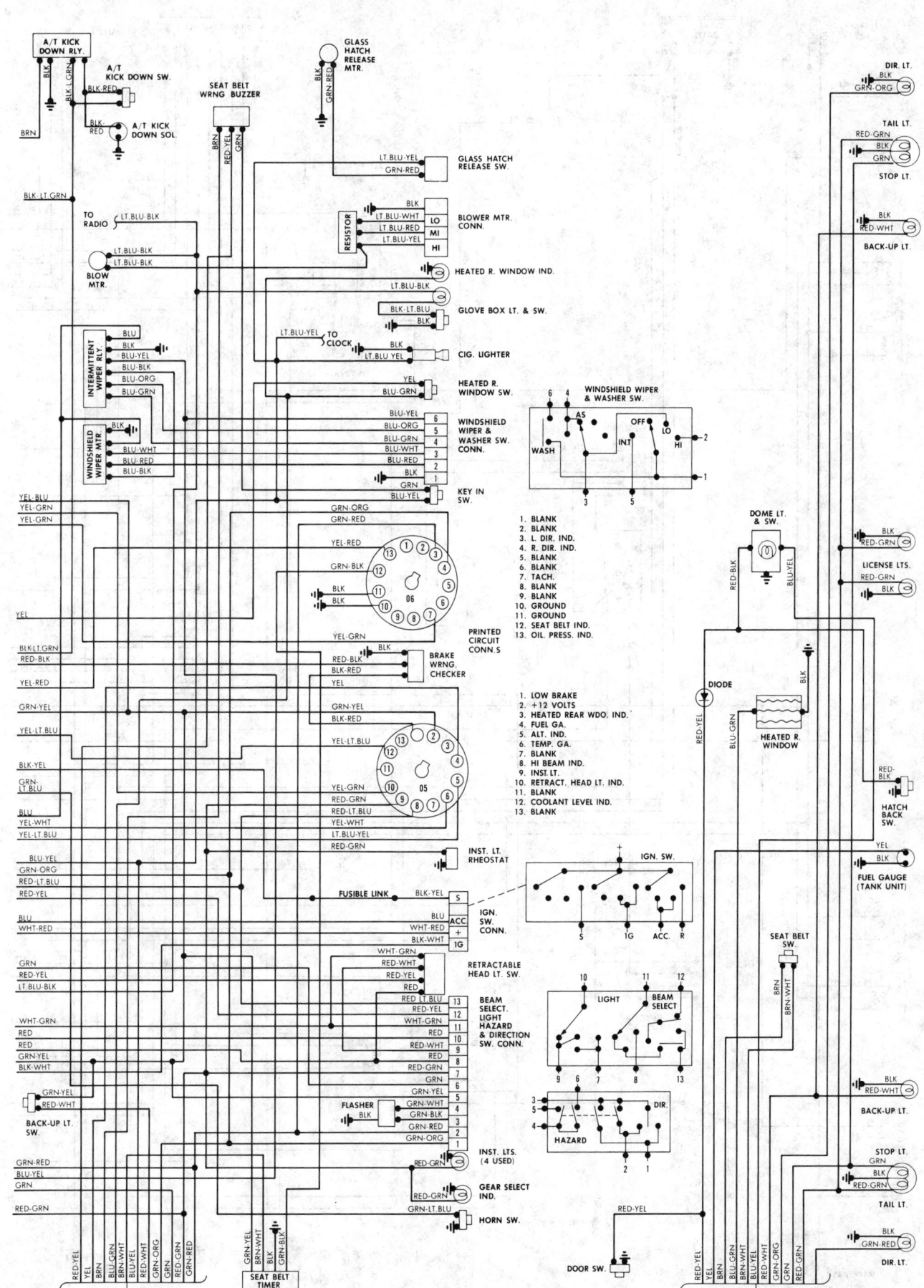

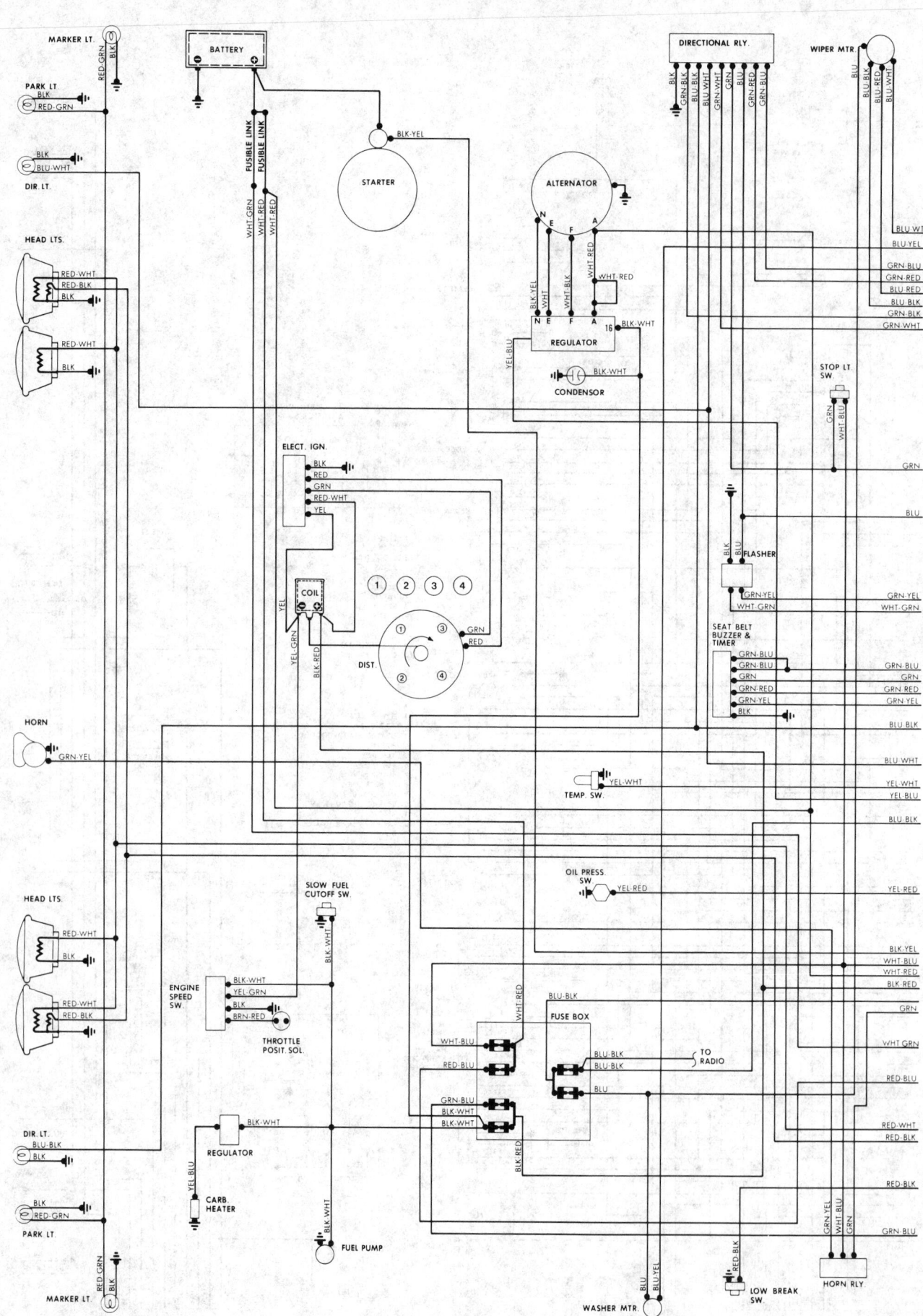

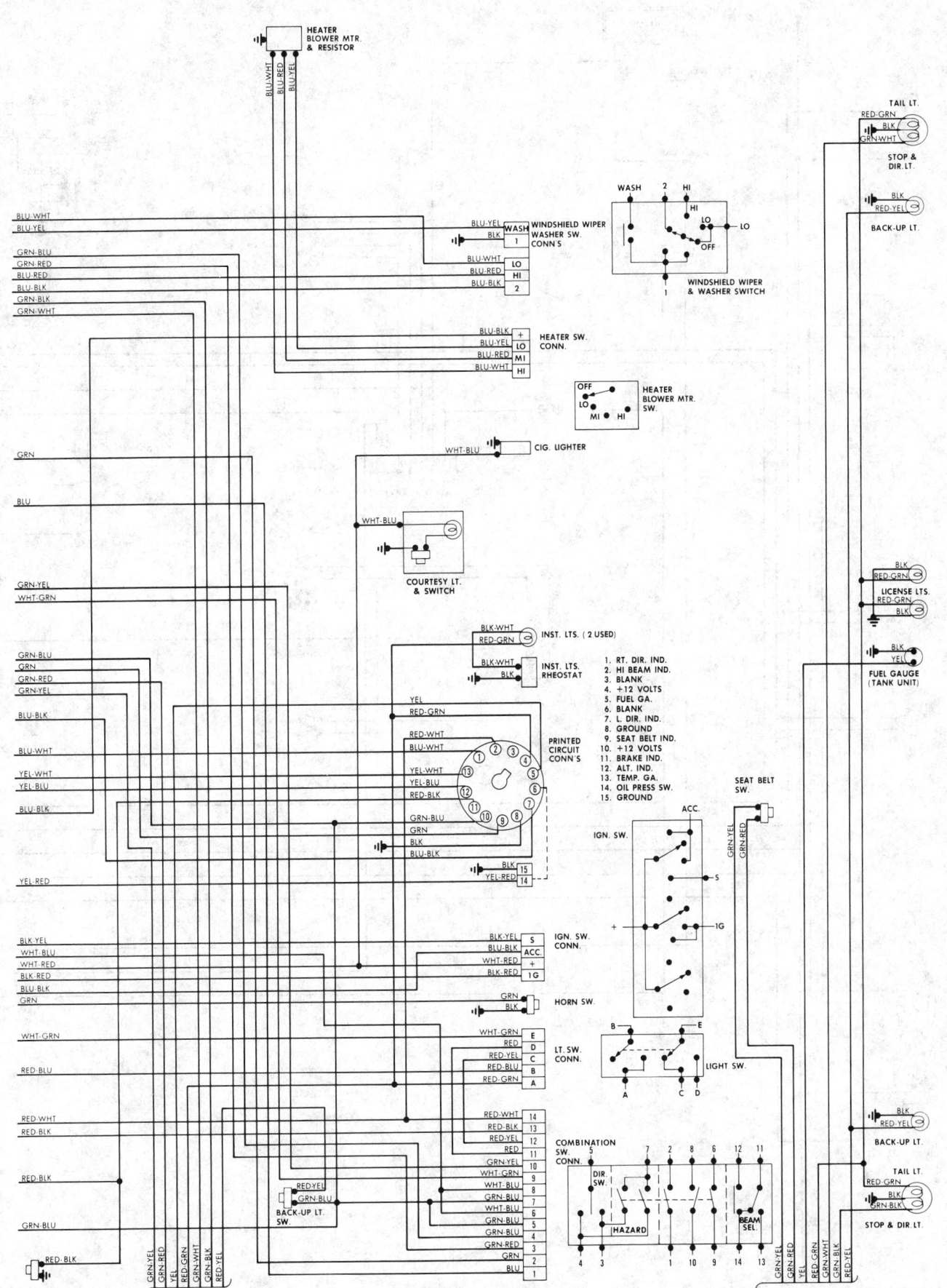

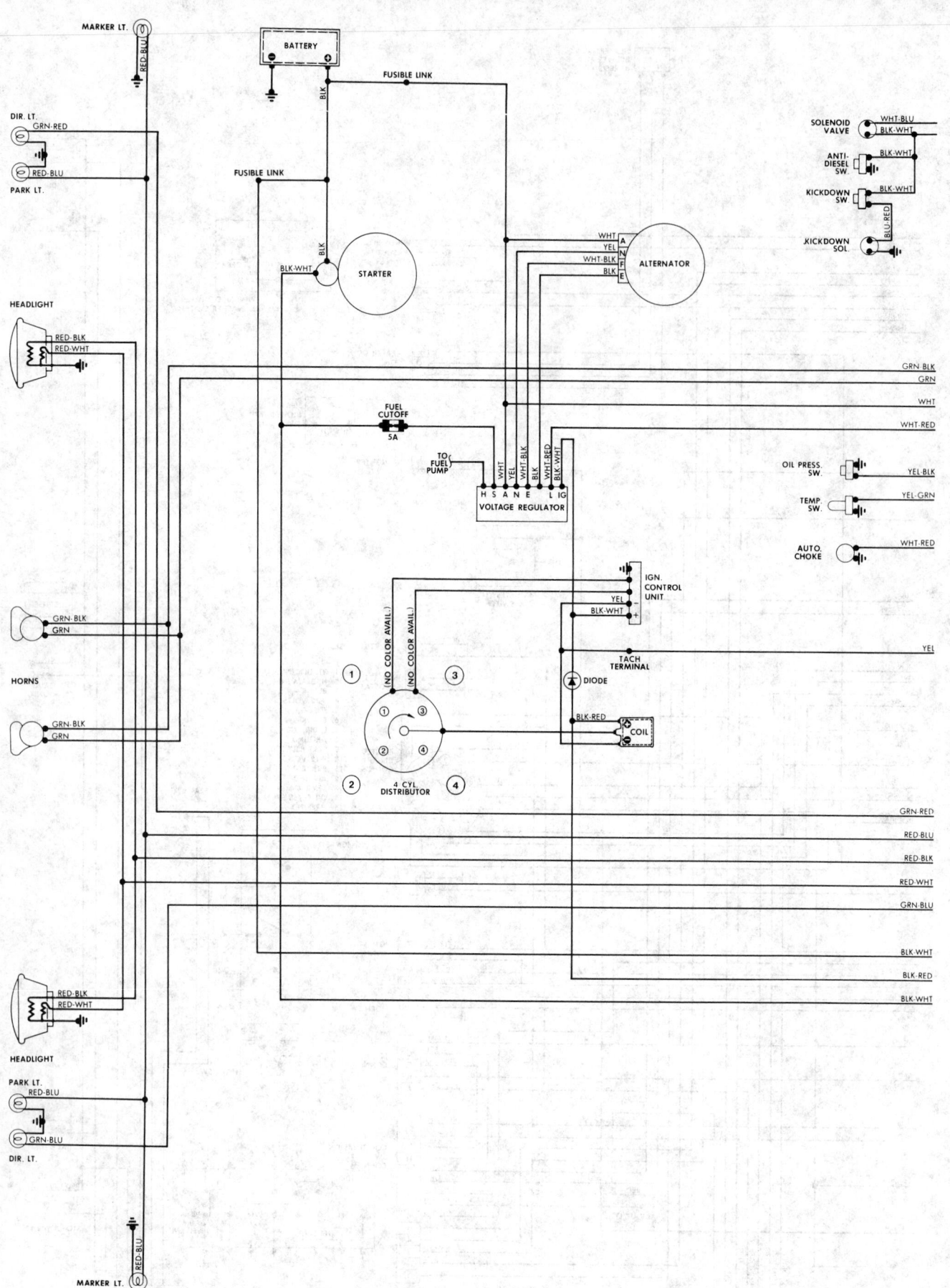

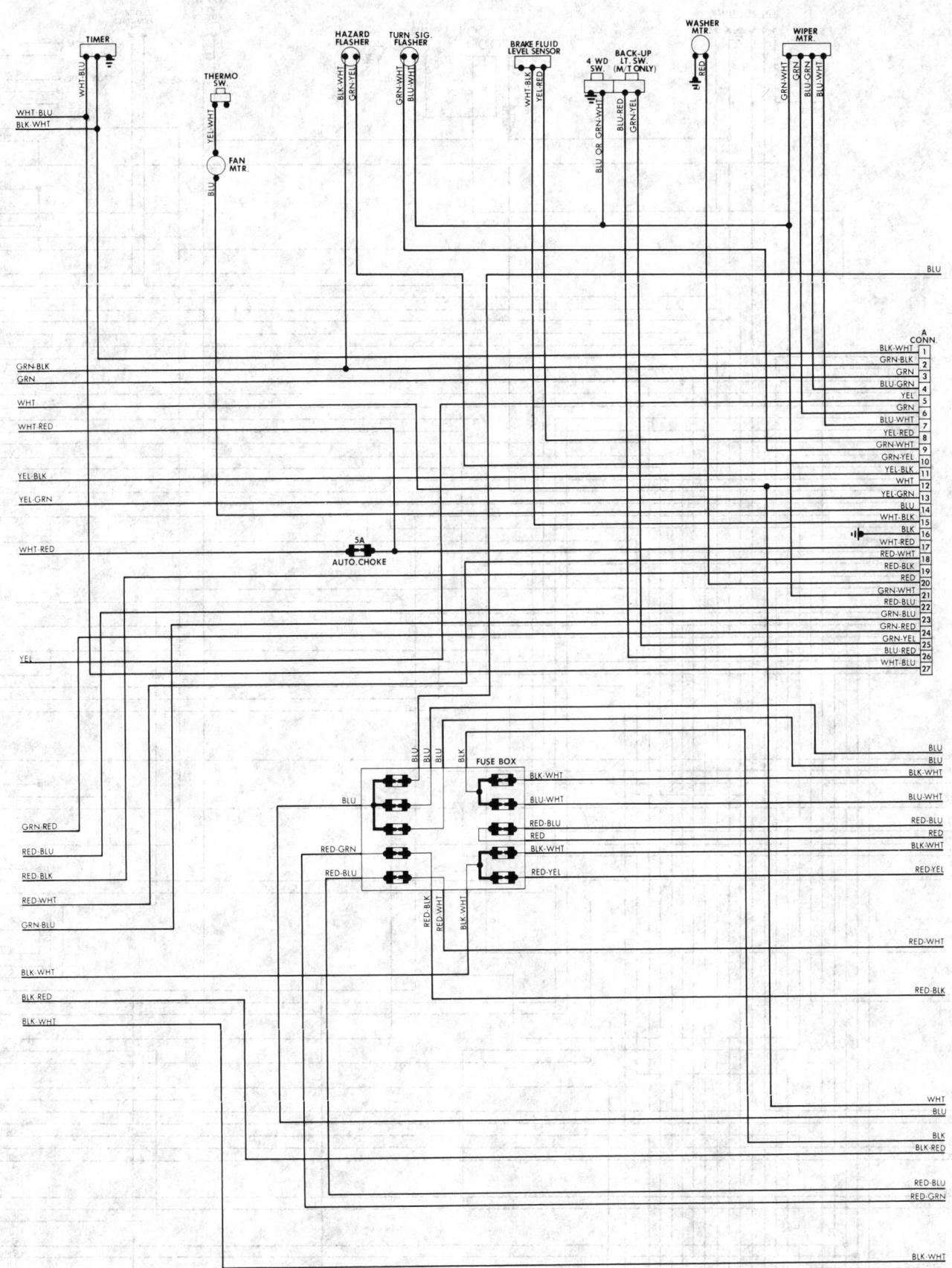

1980 Subaru

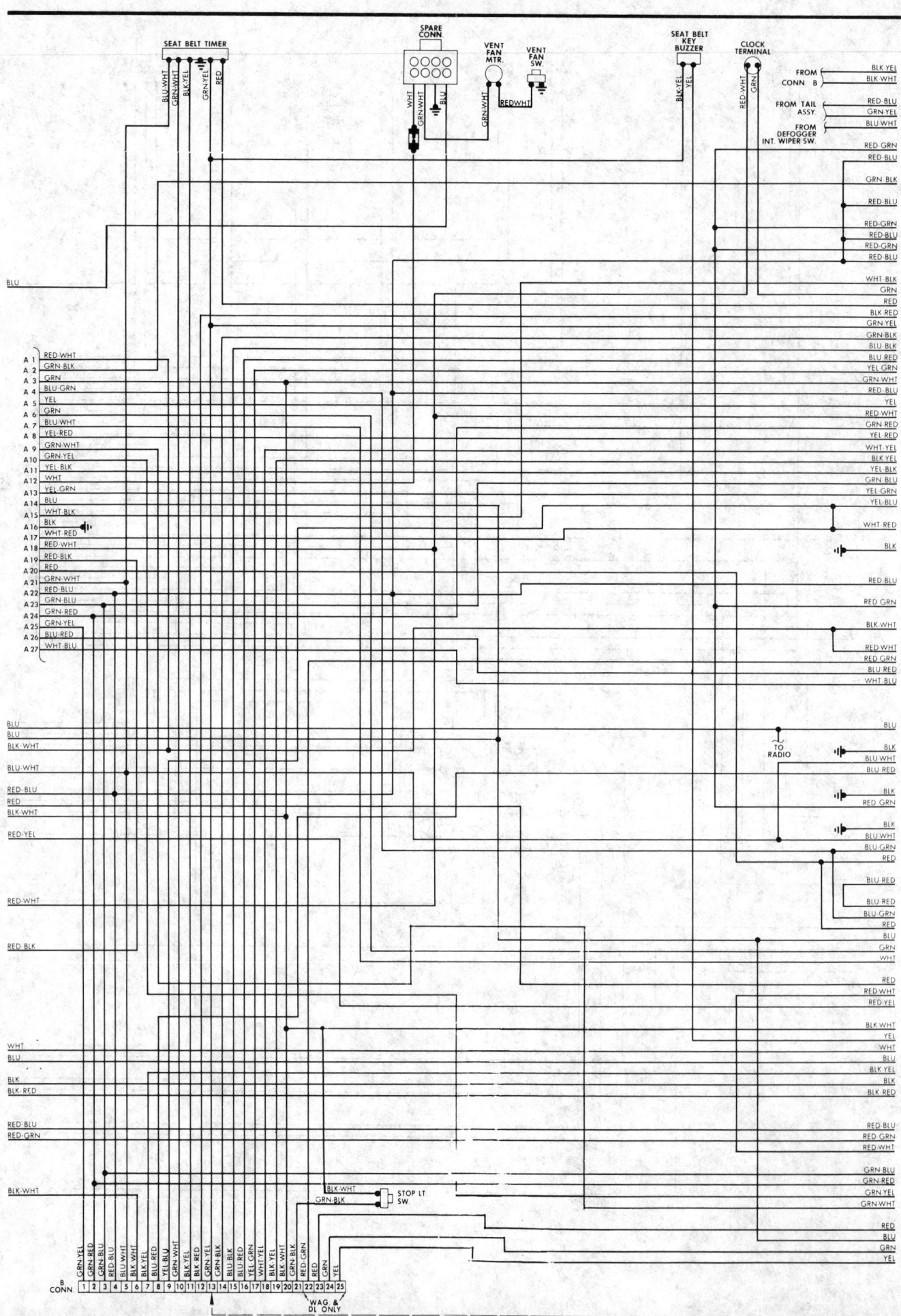

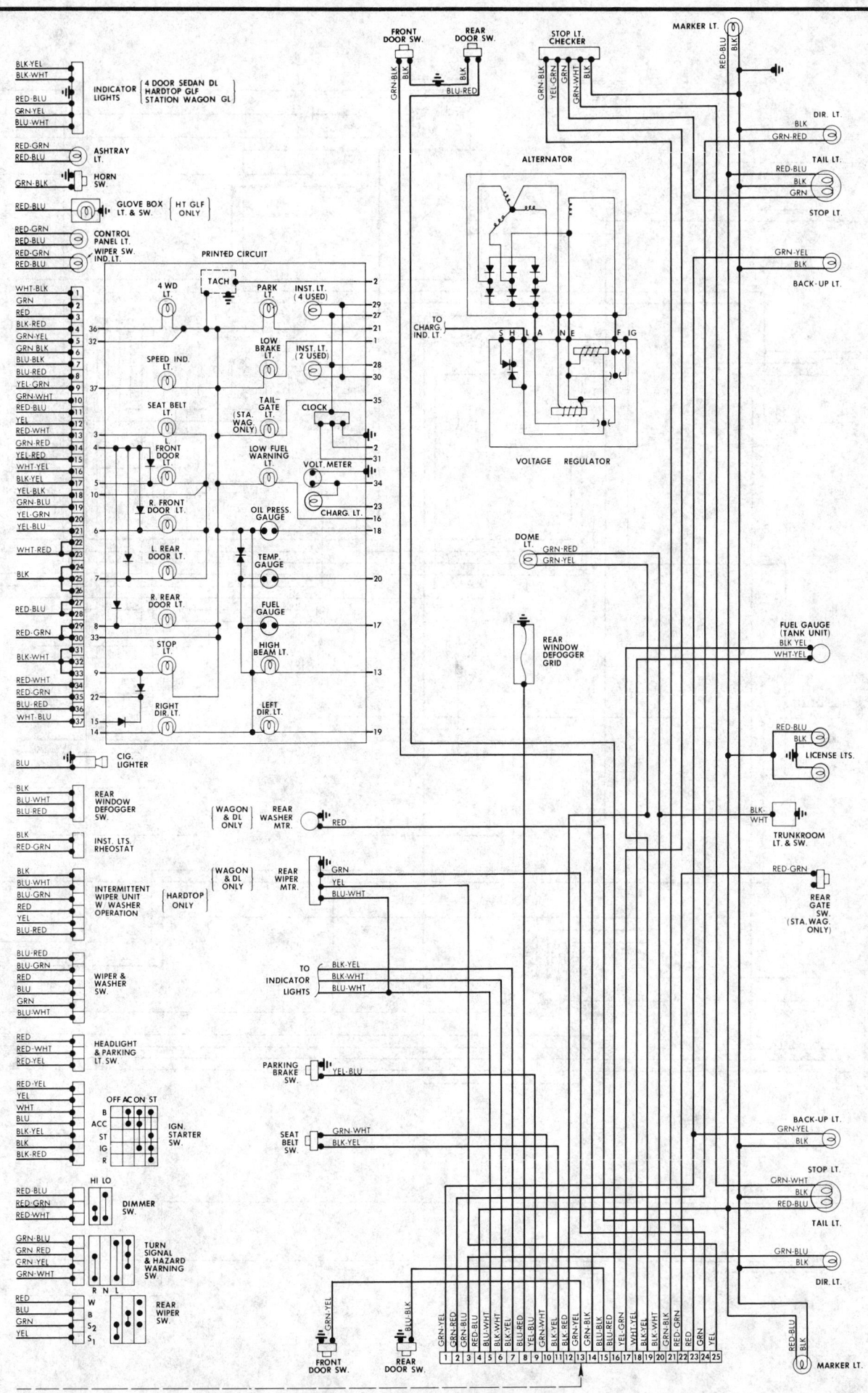

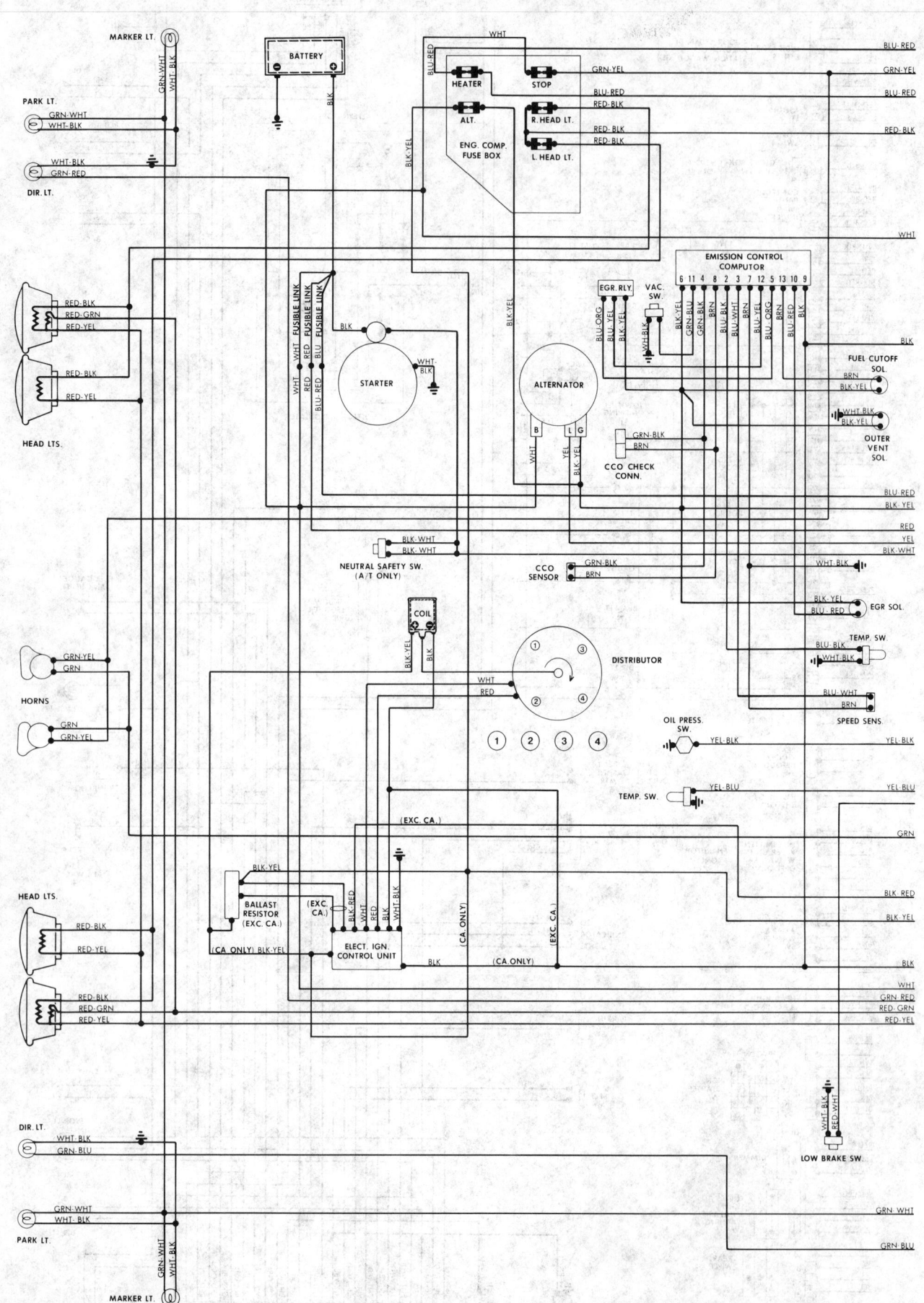

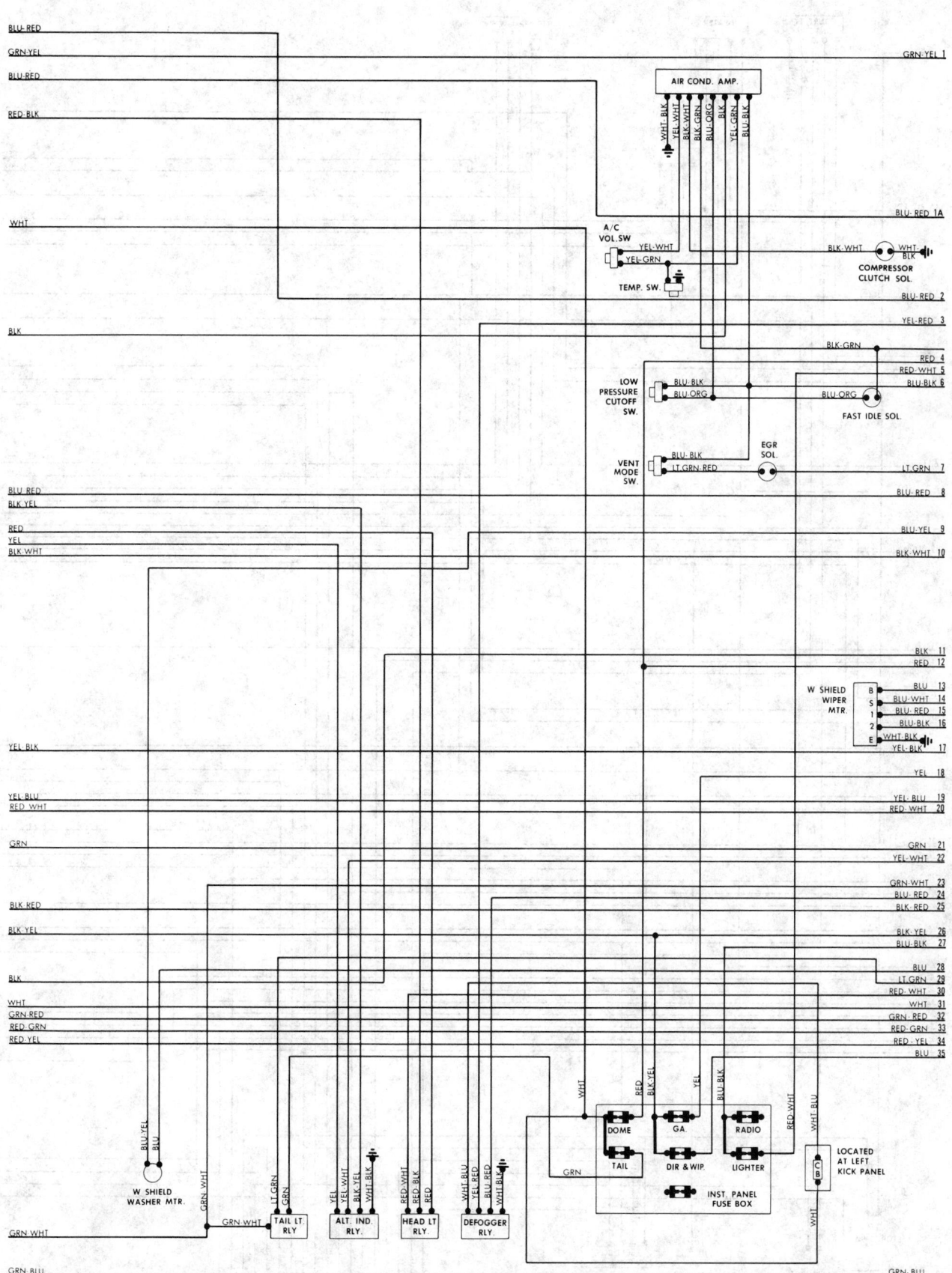

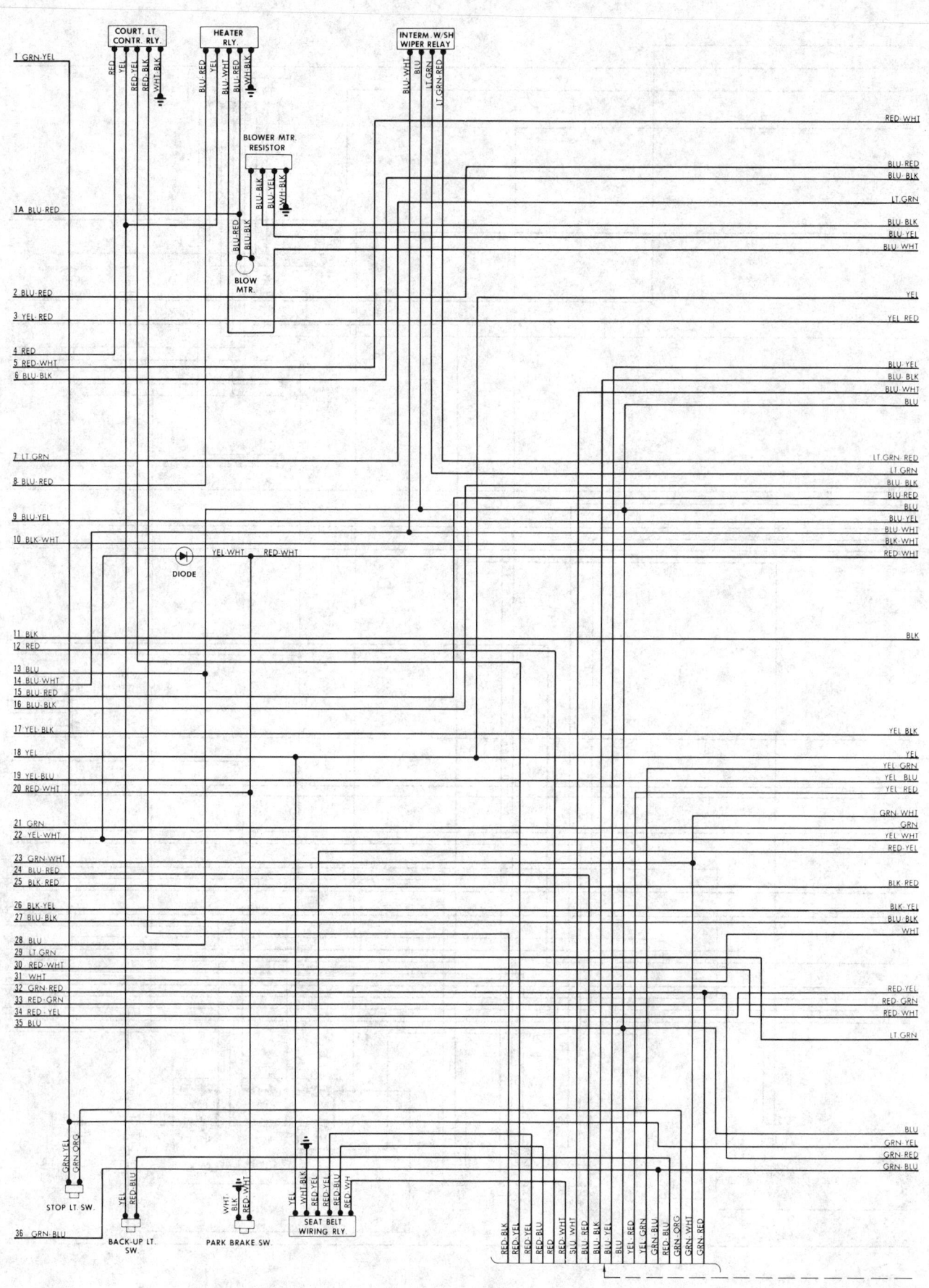

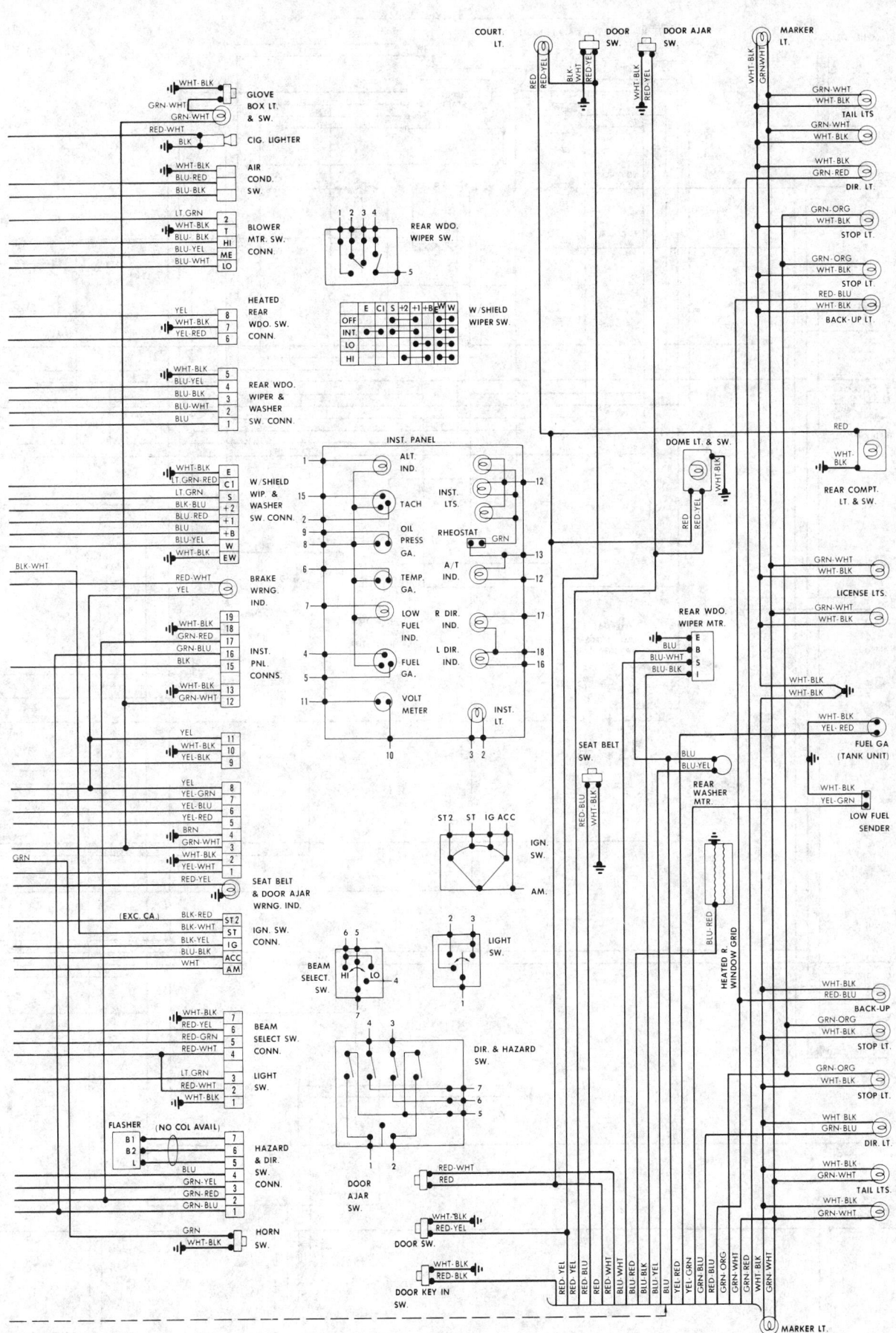

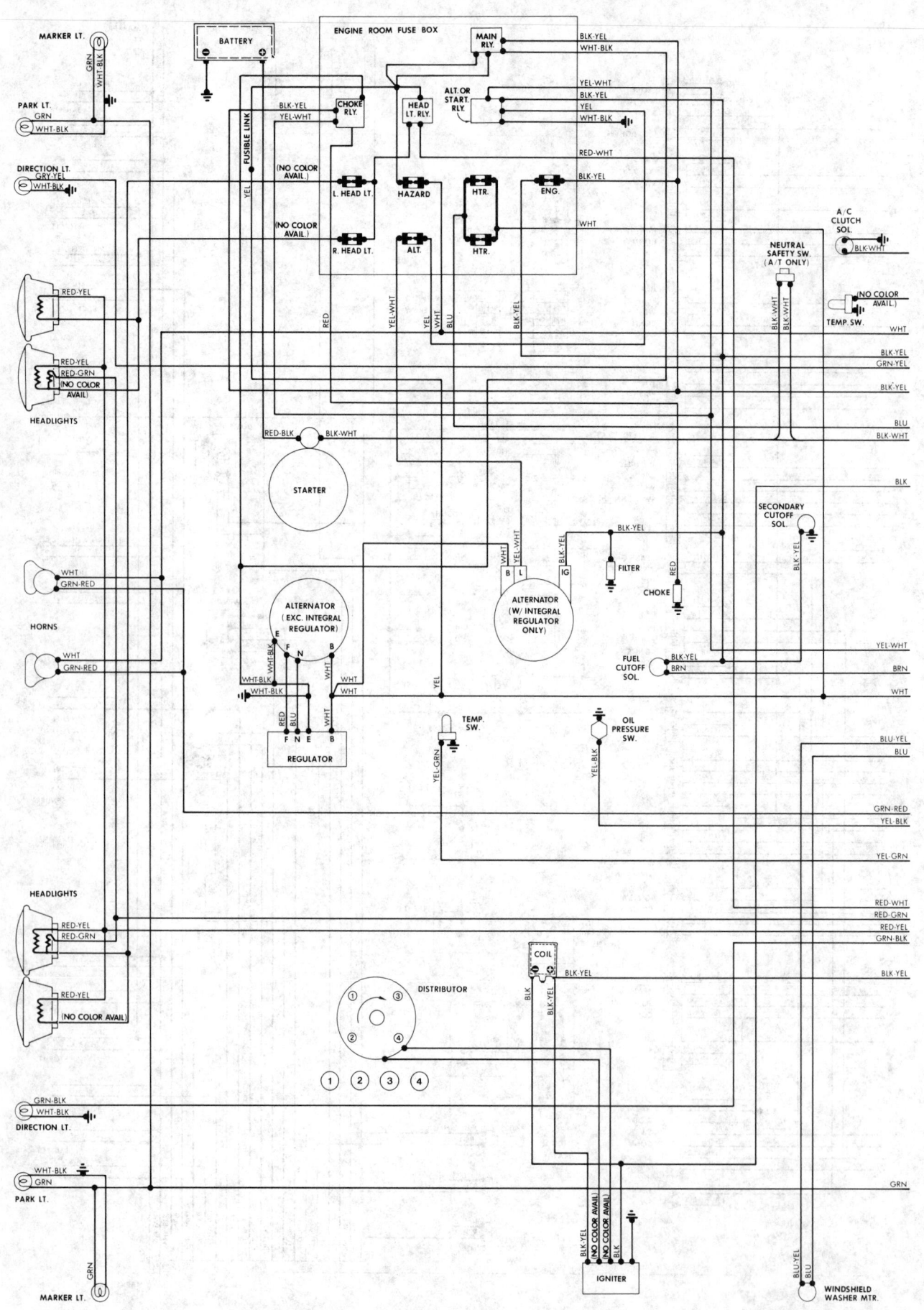

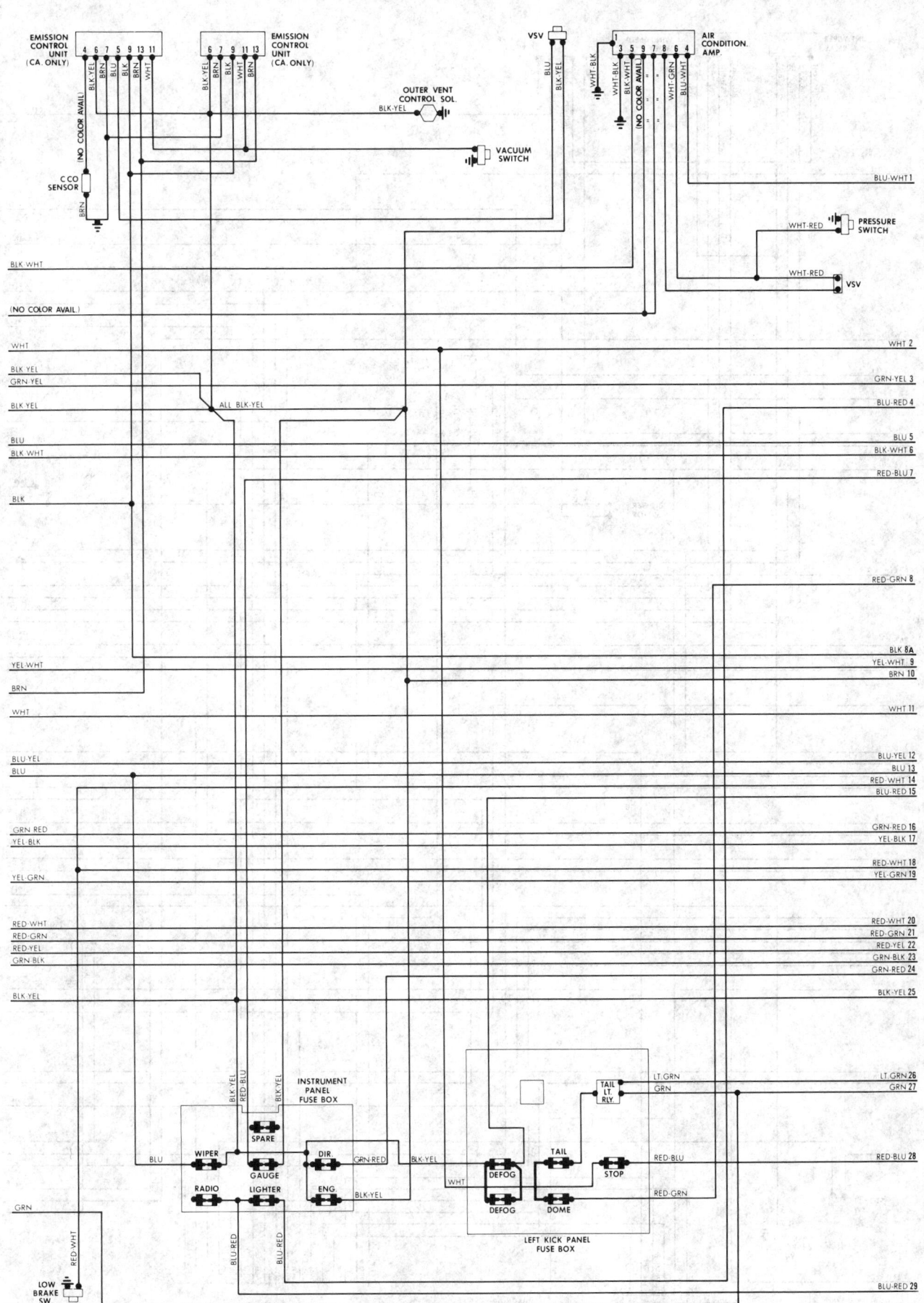

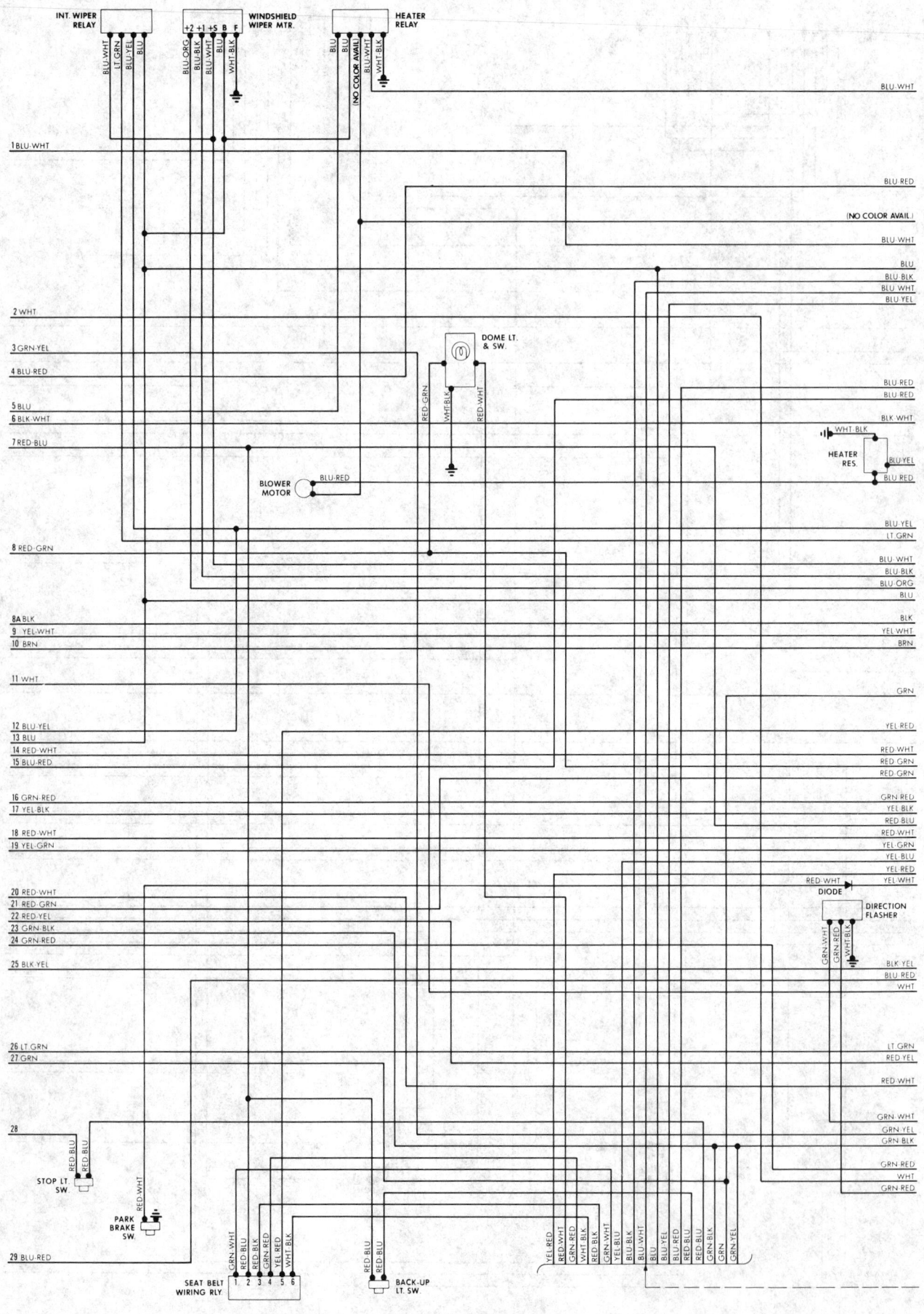

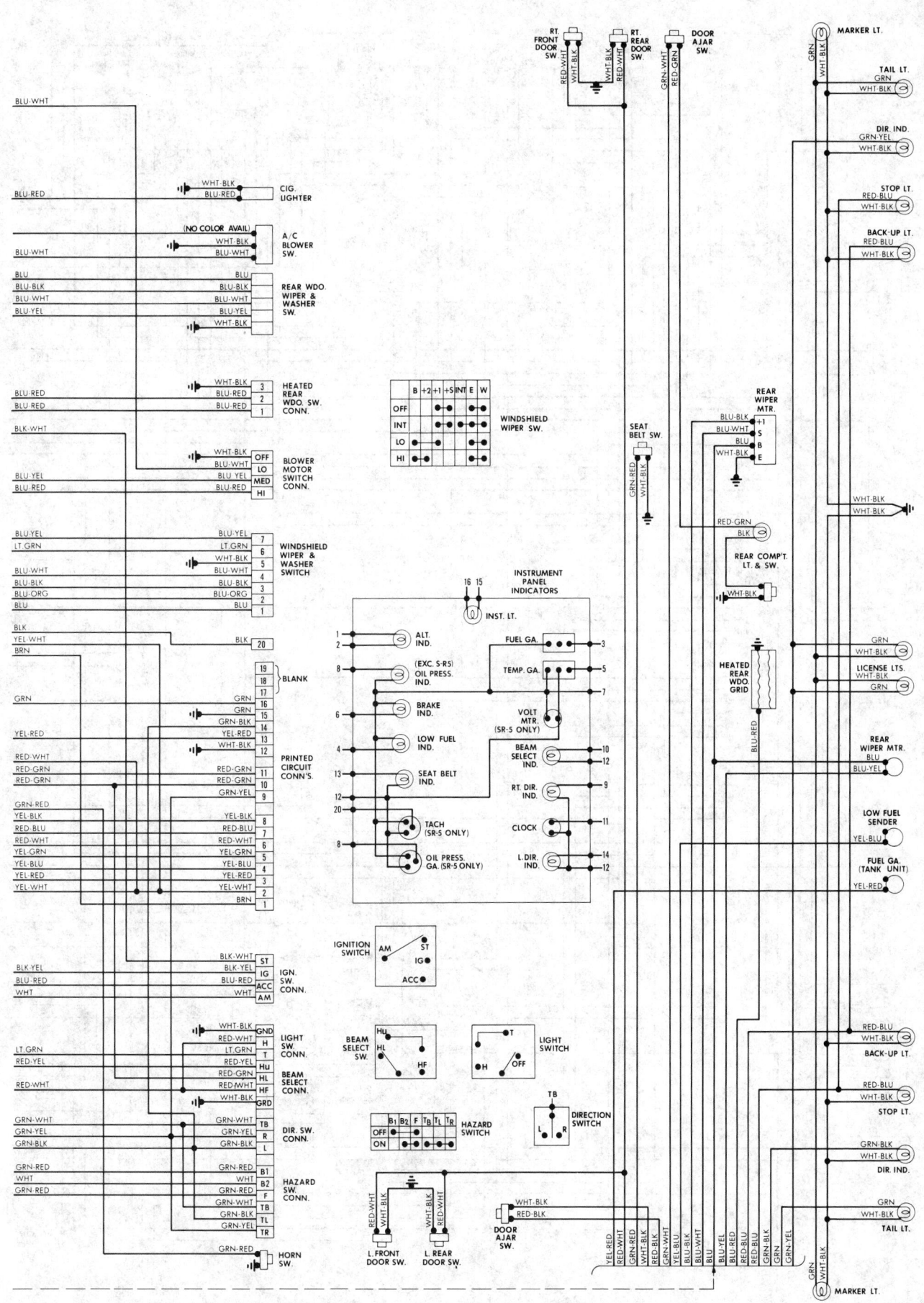

1980 Toyota

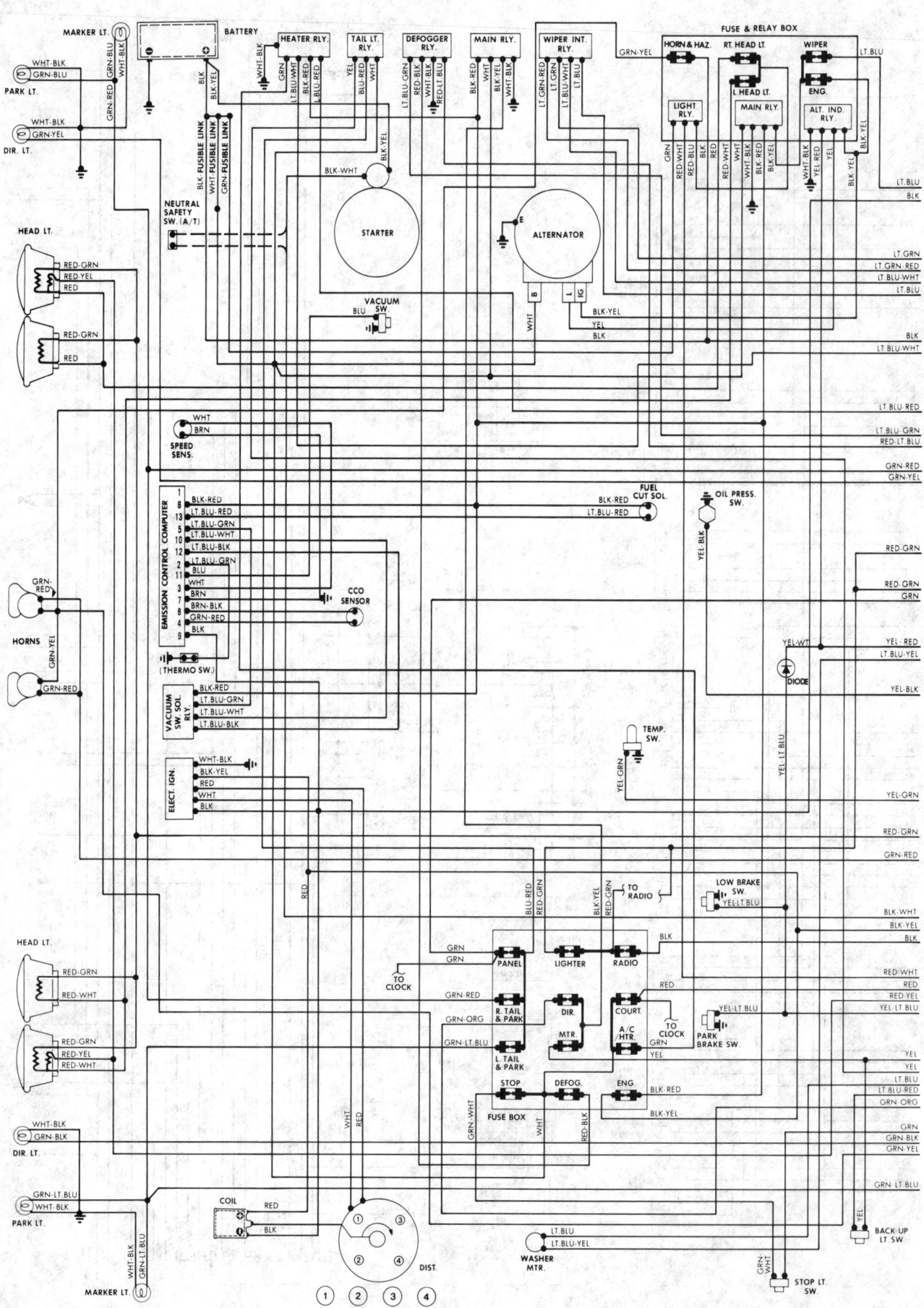

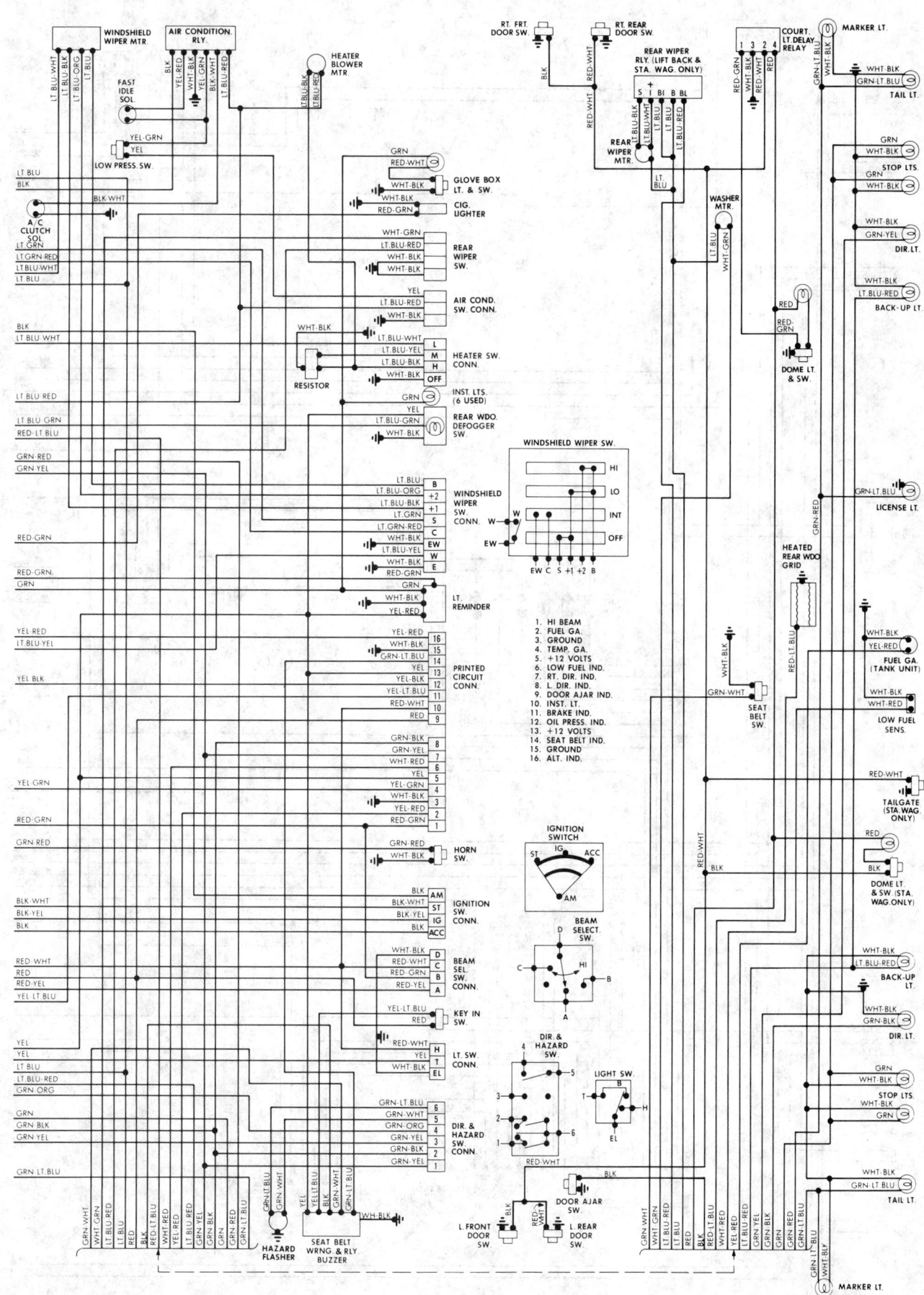

1980 Toyota

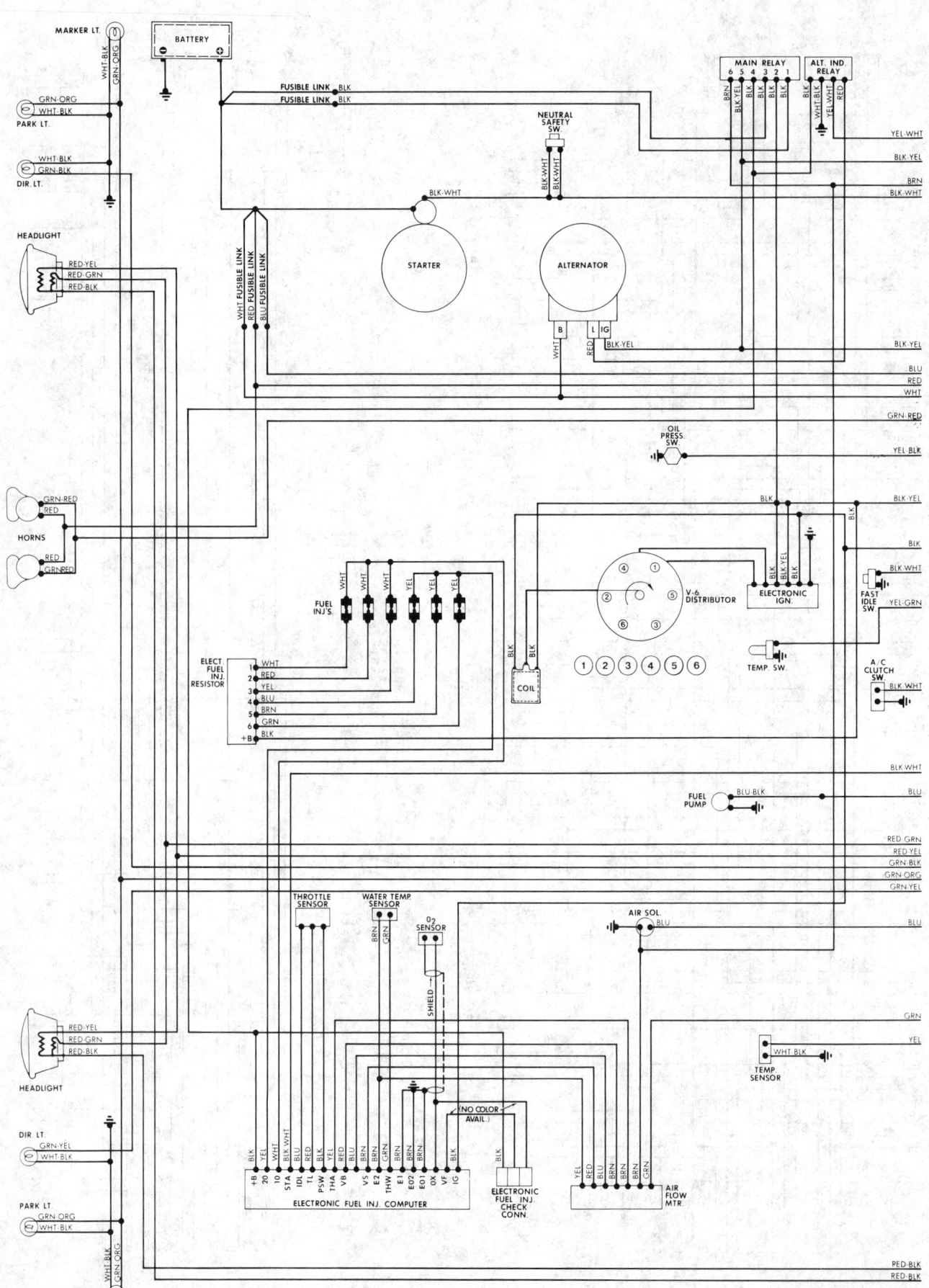

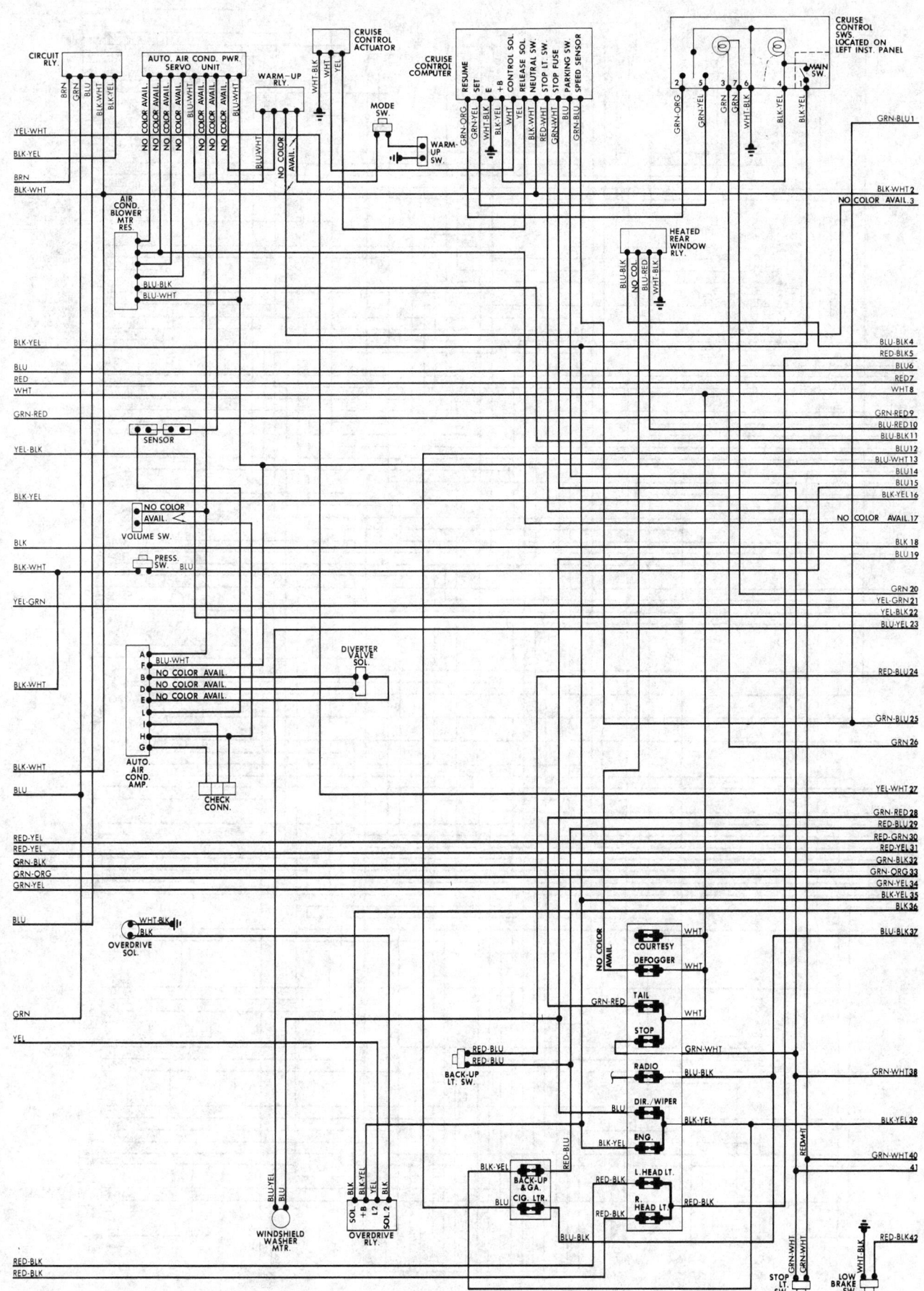

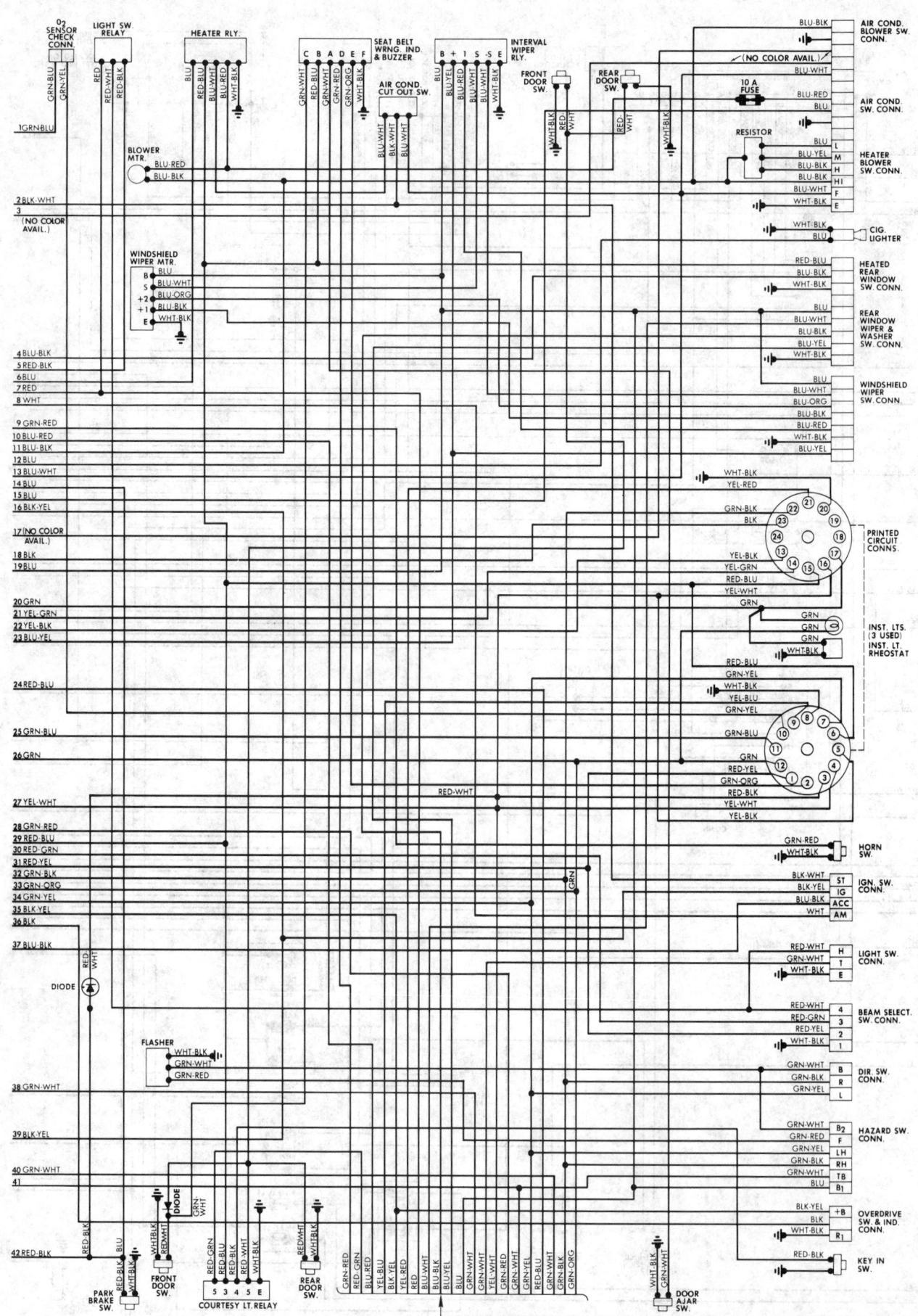

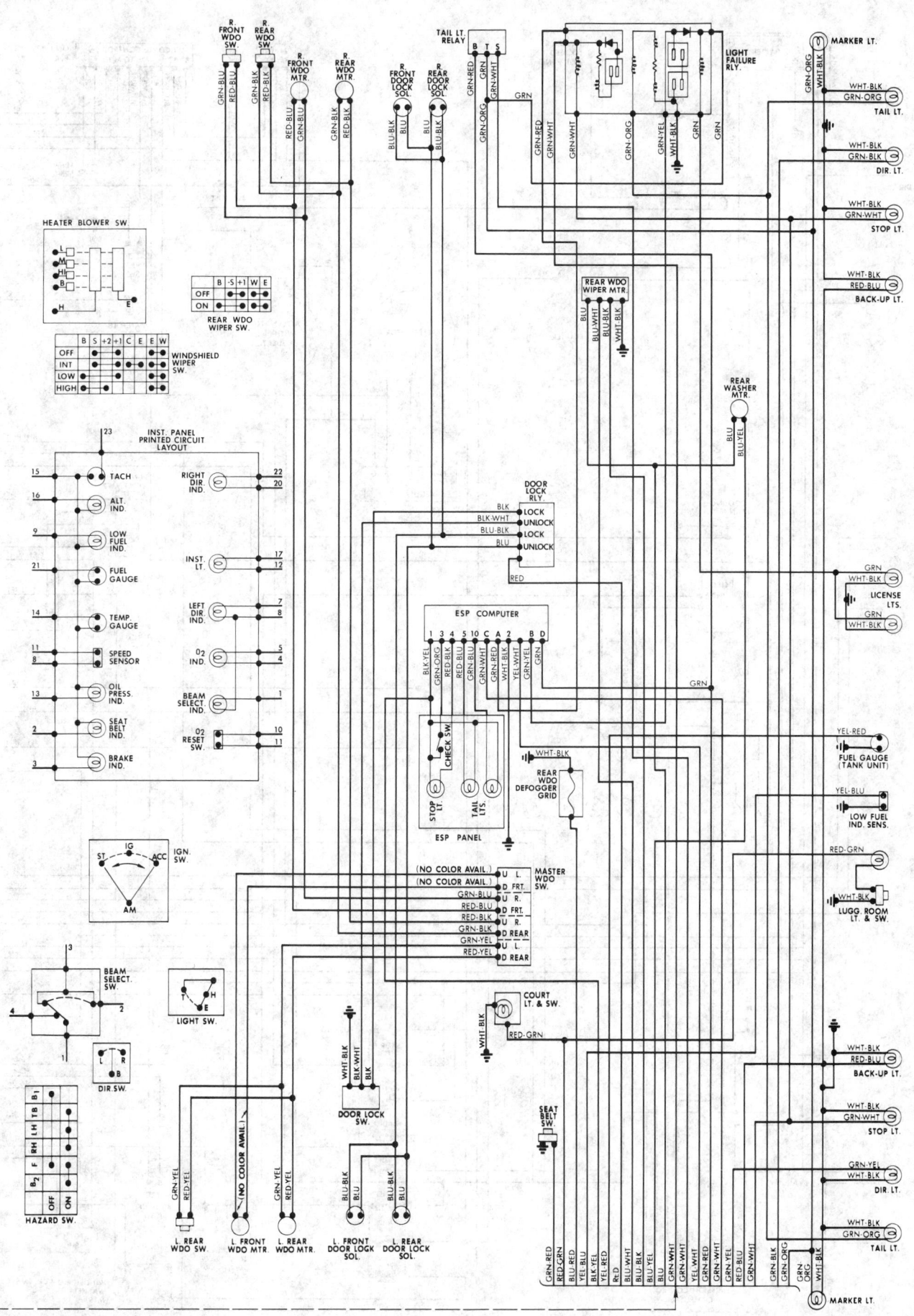

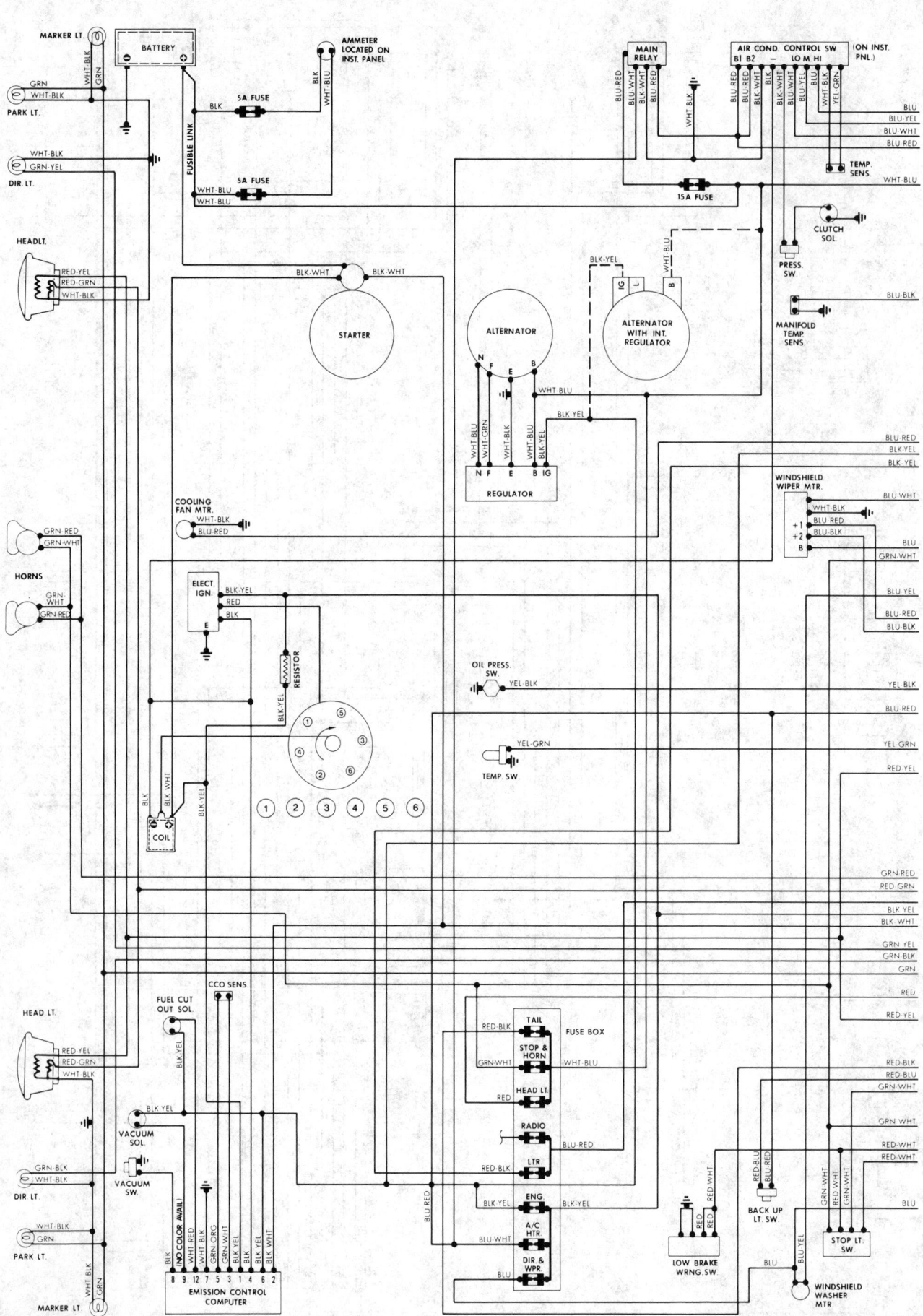

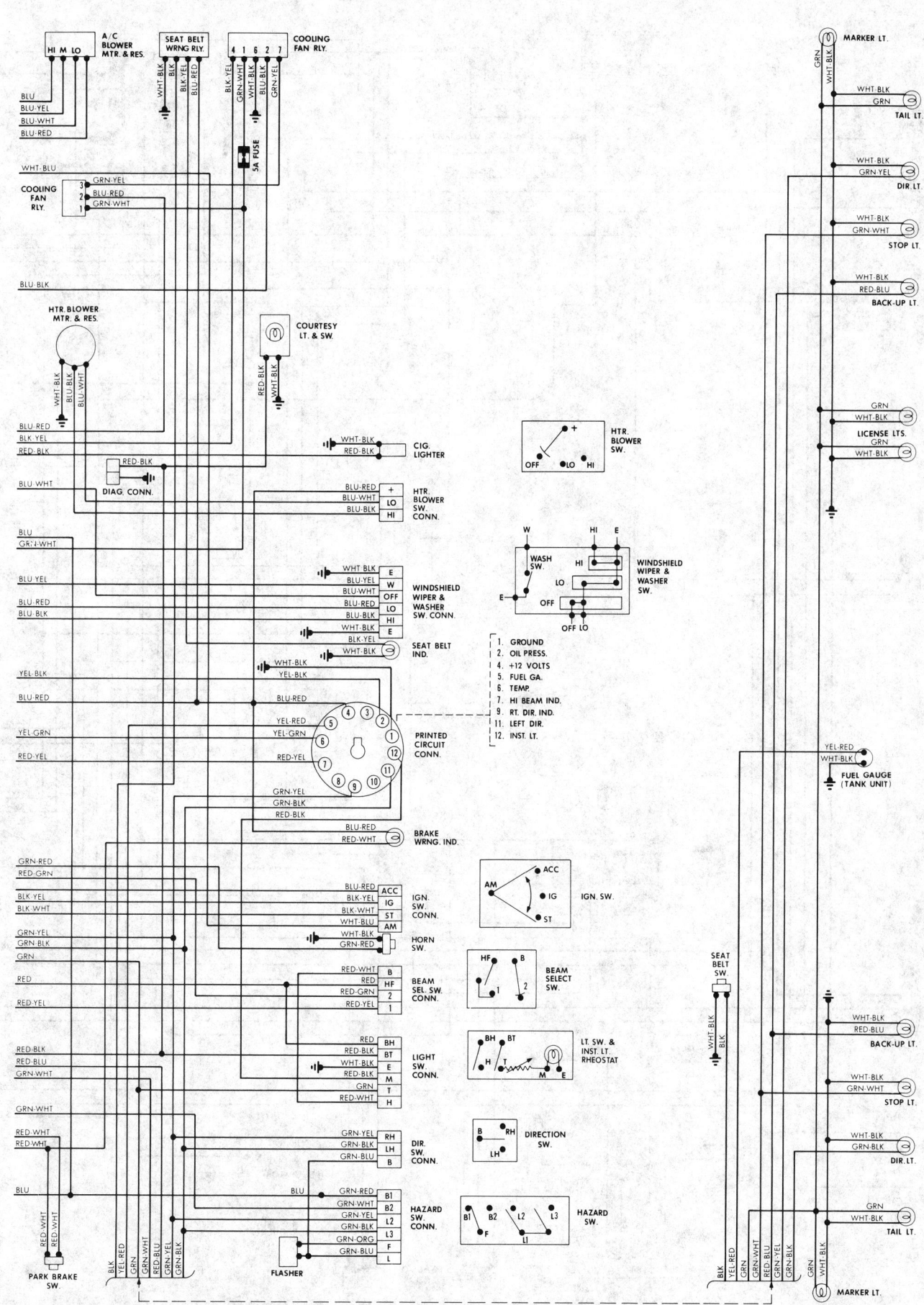

1980 Toyota

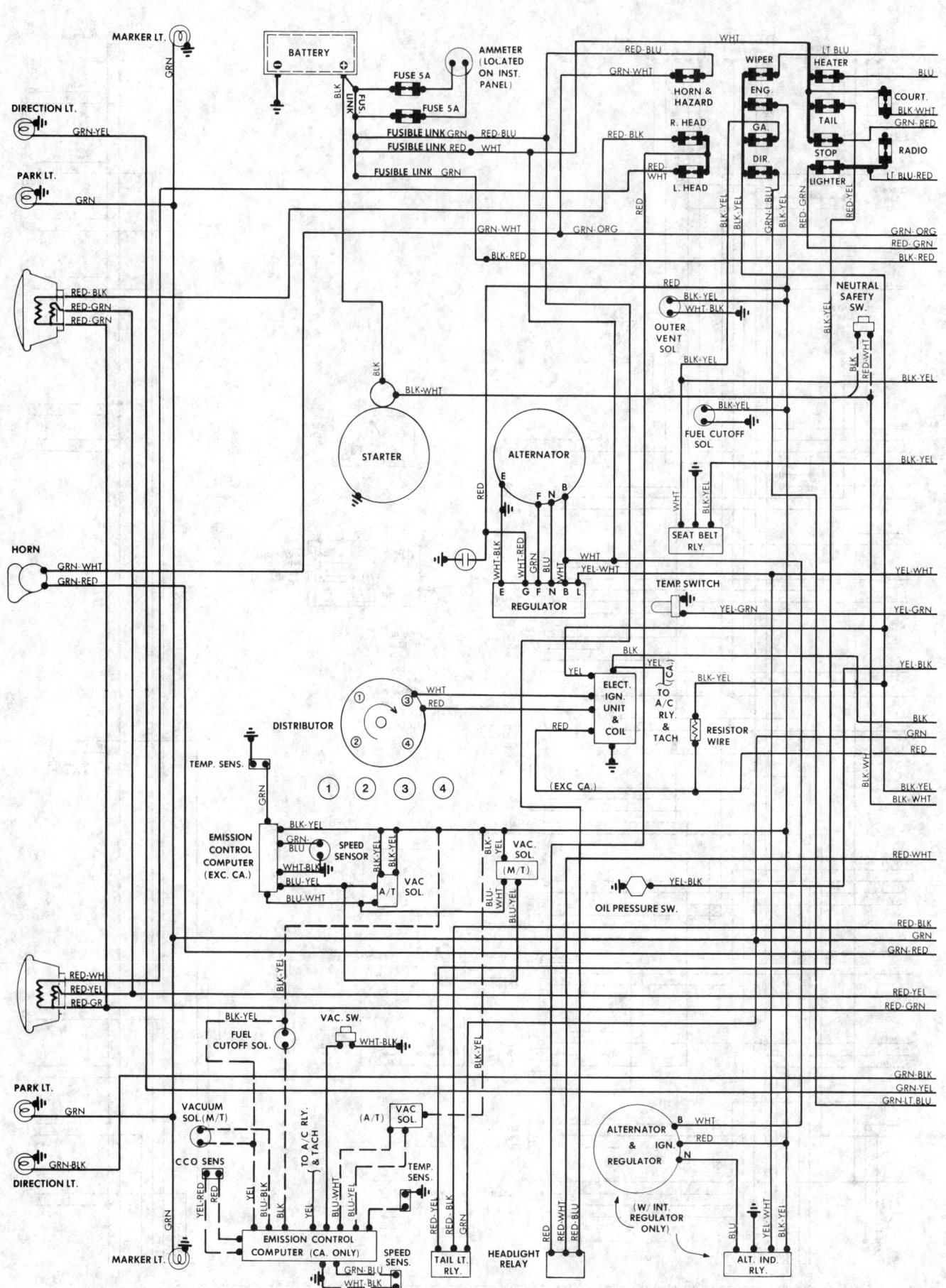

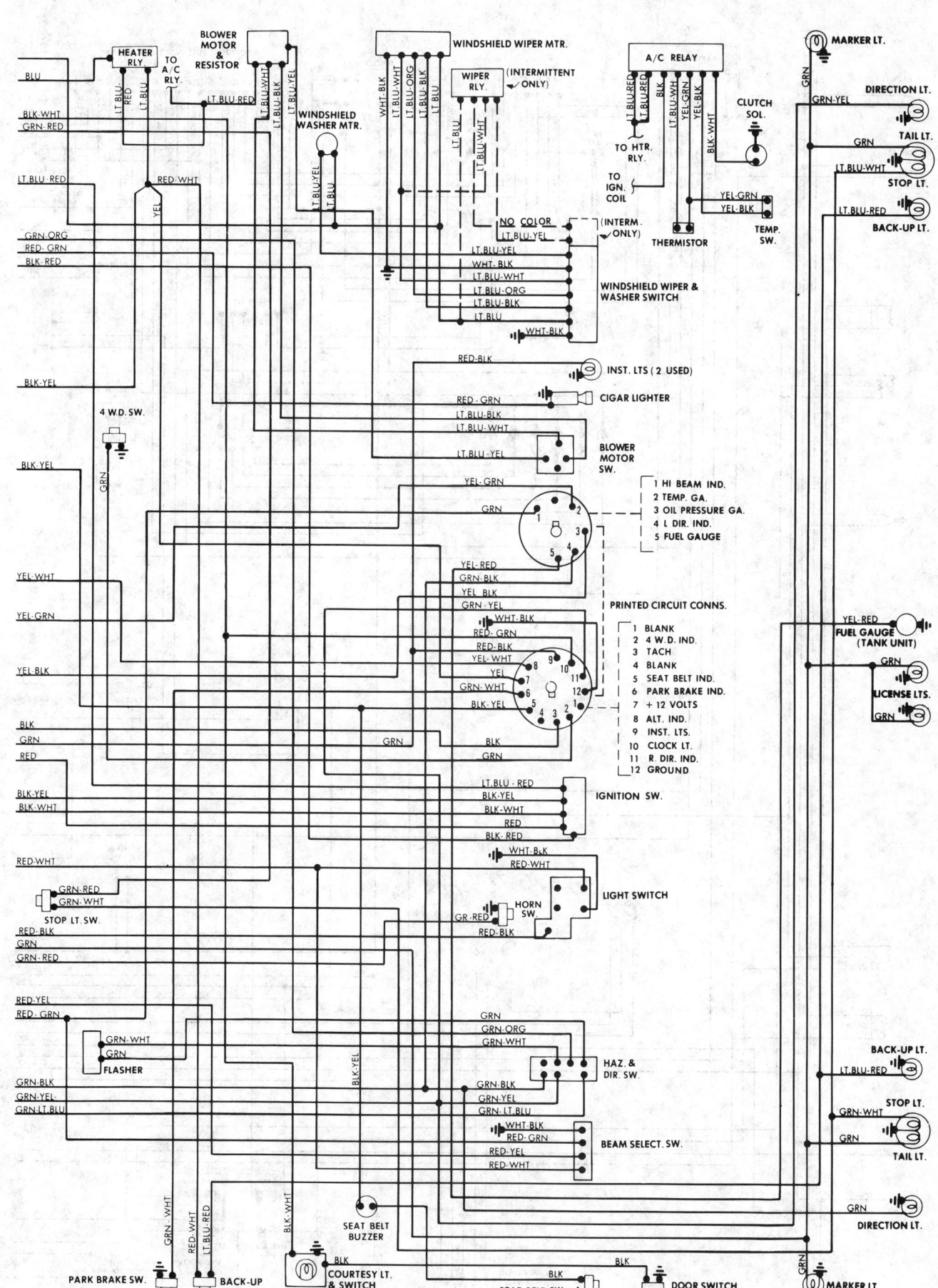

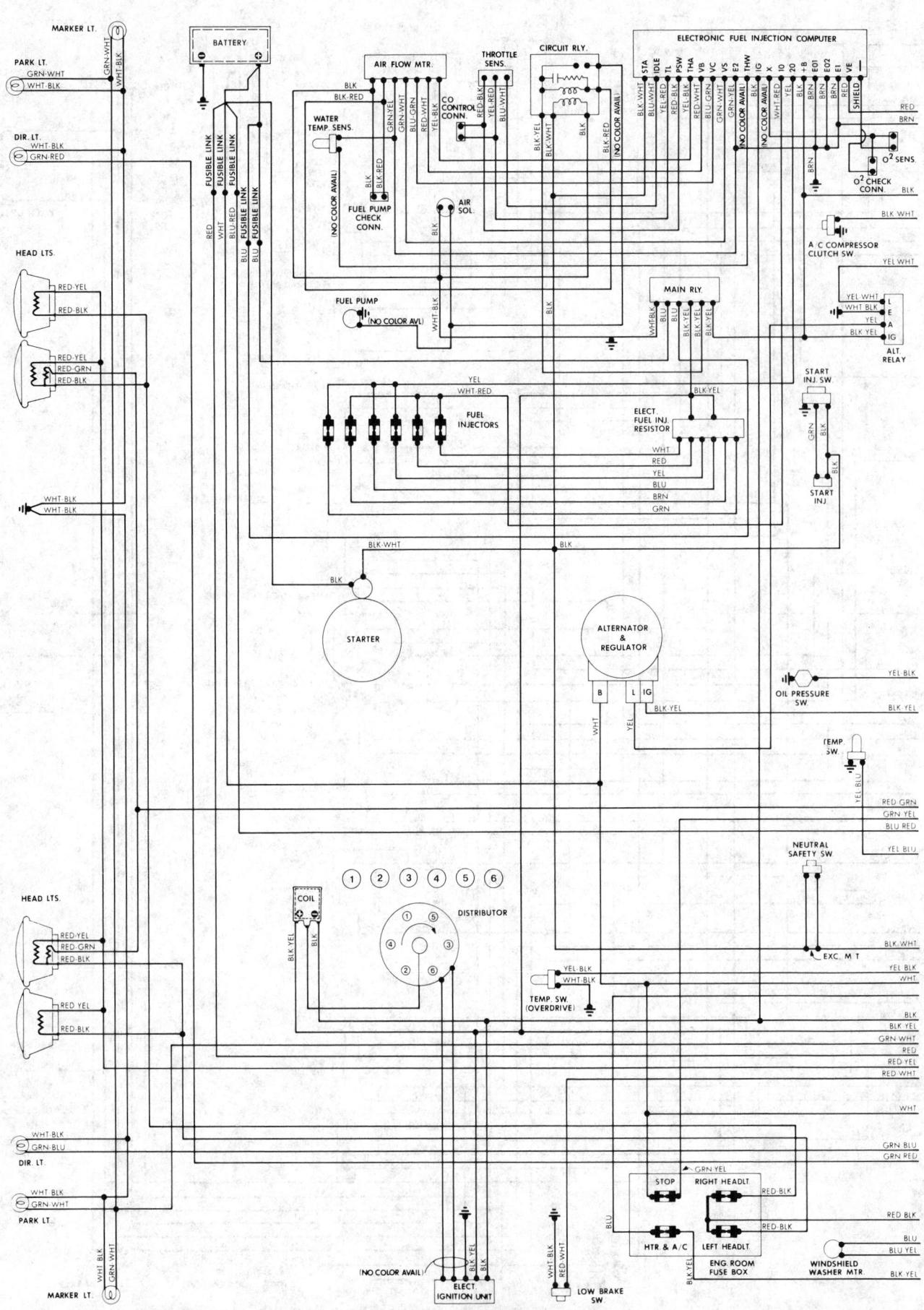

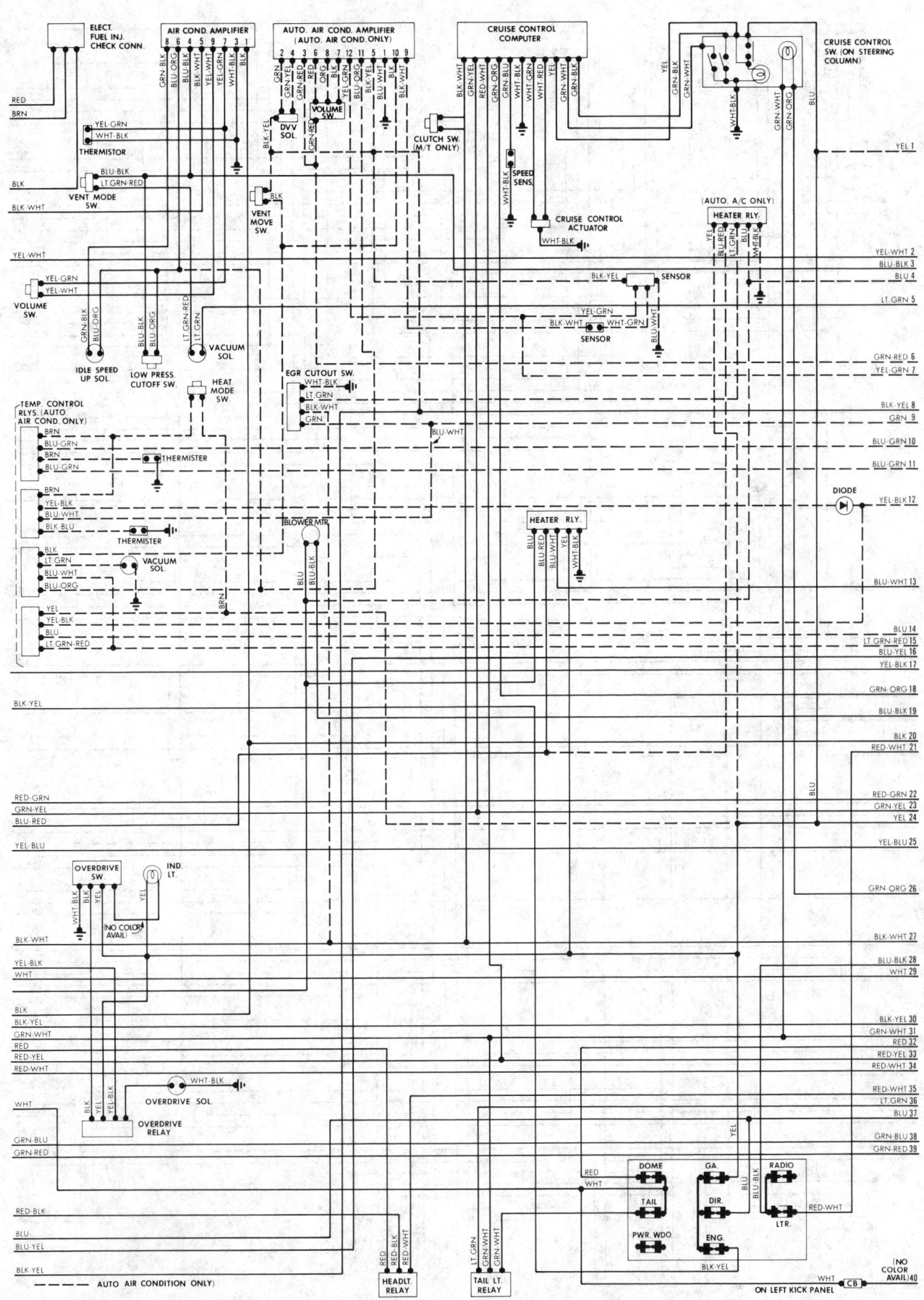

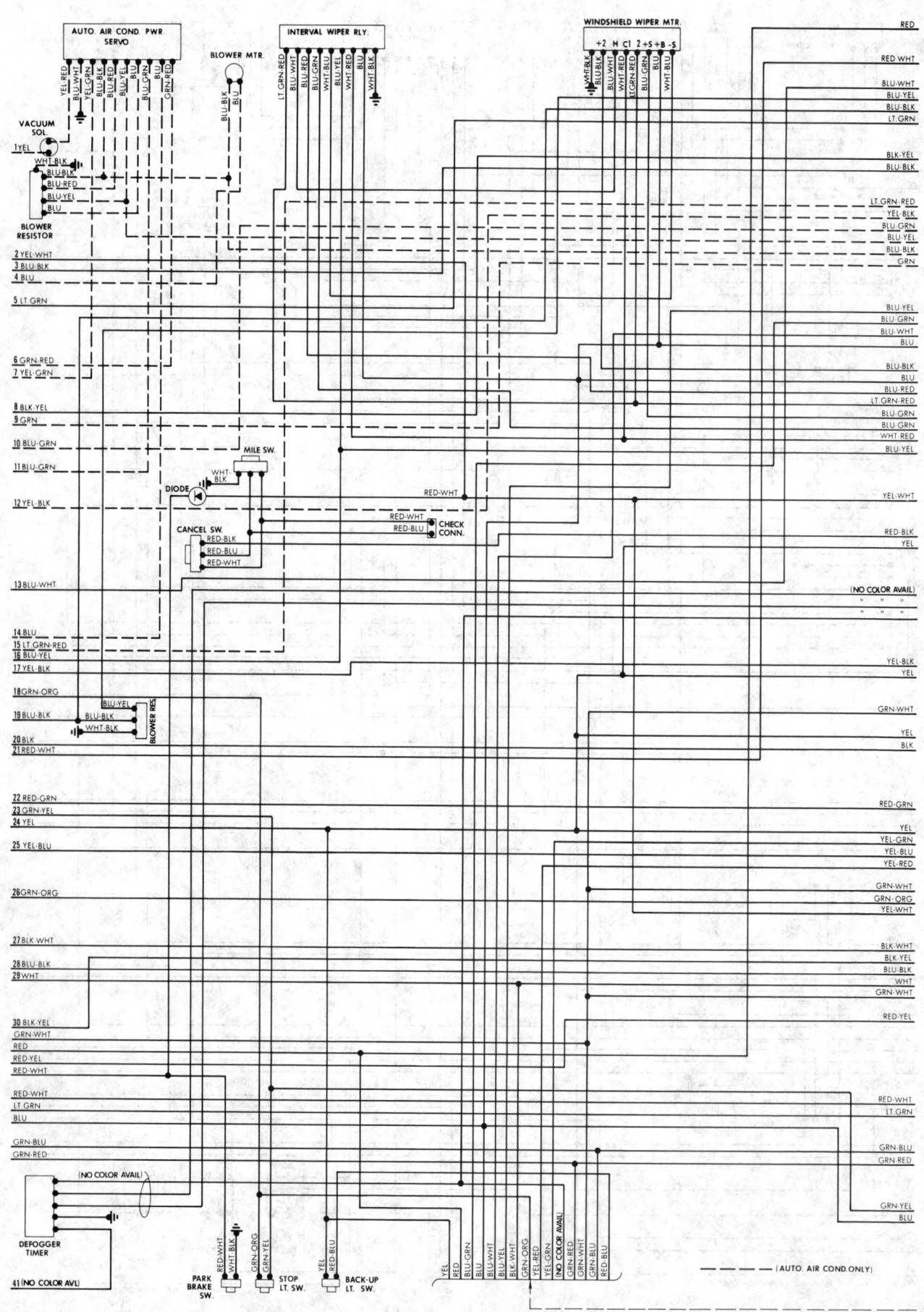

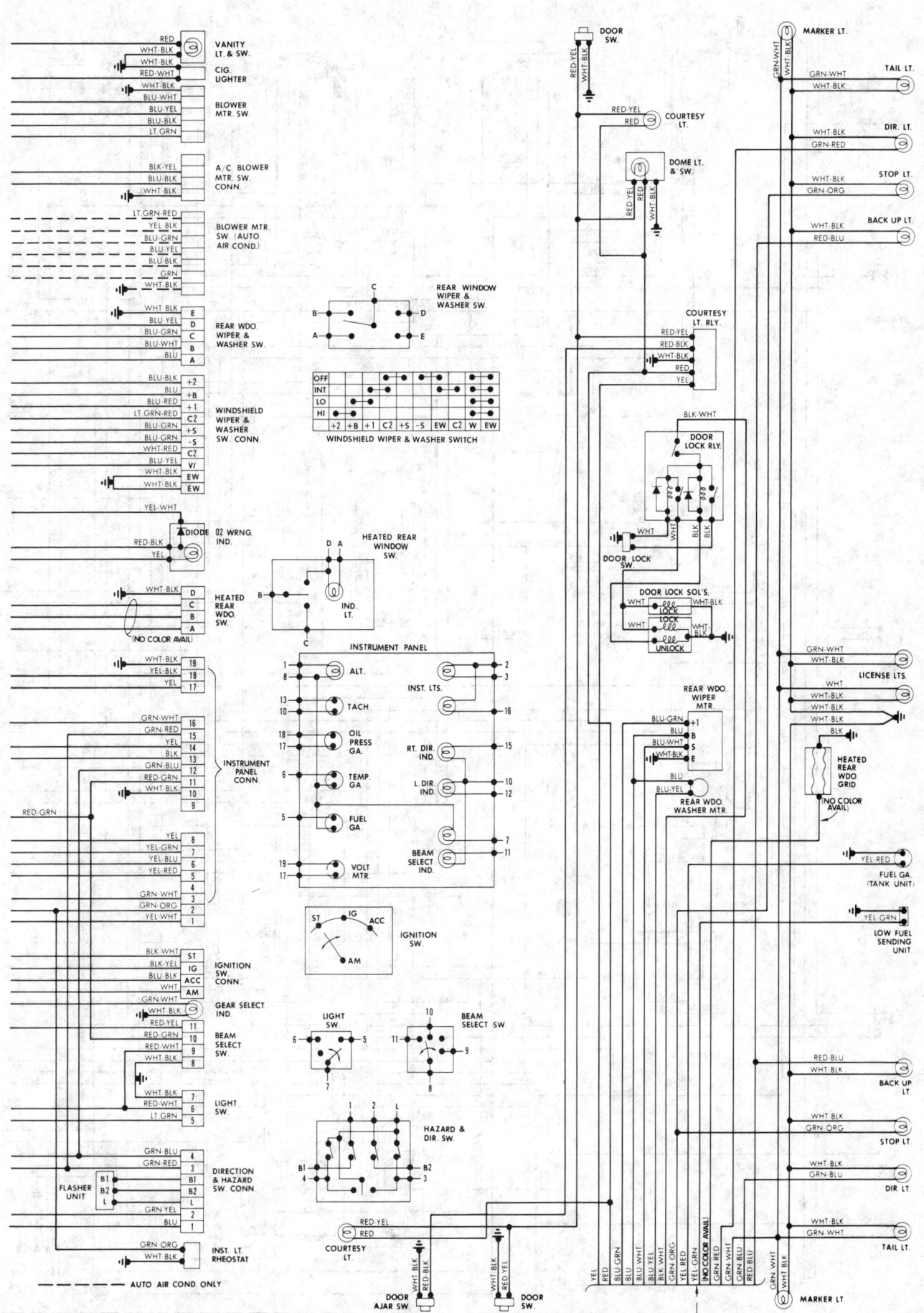

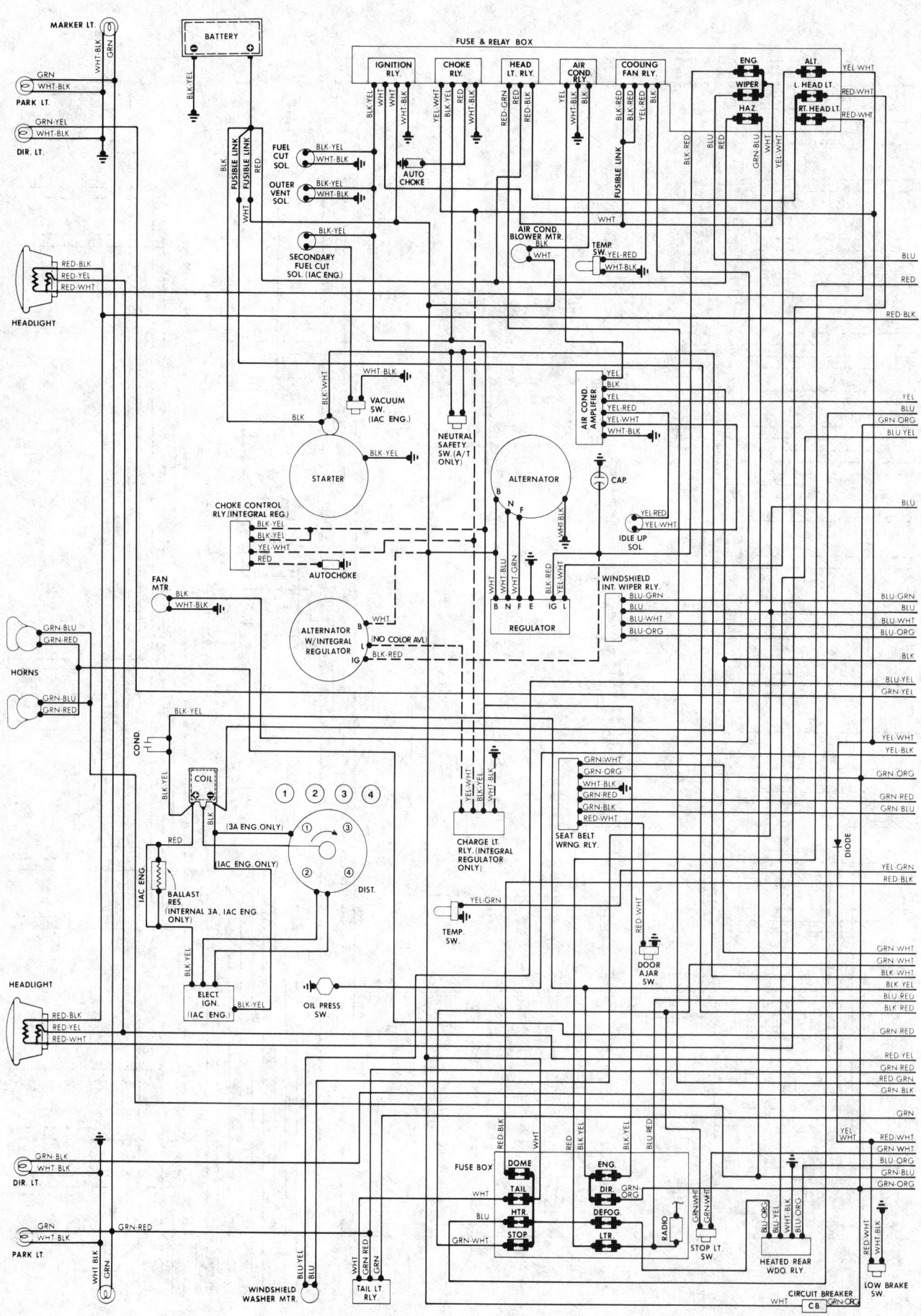

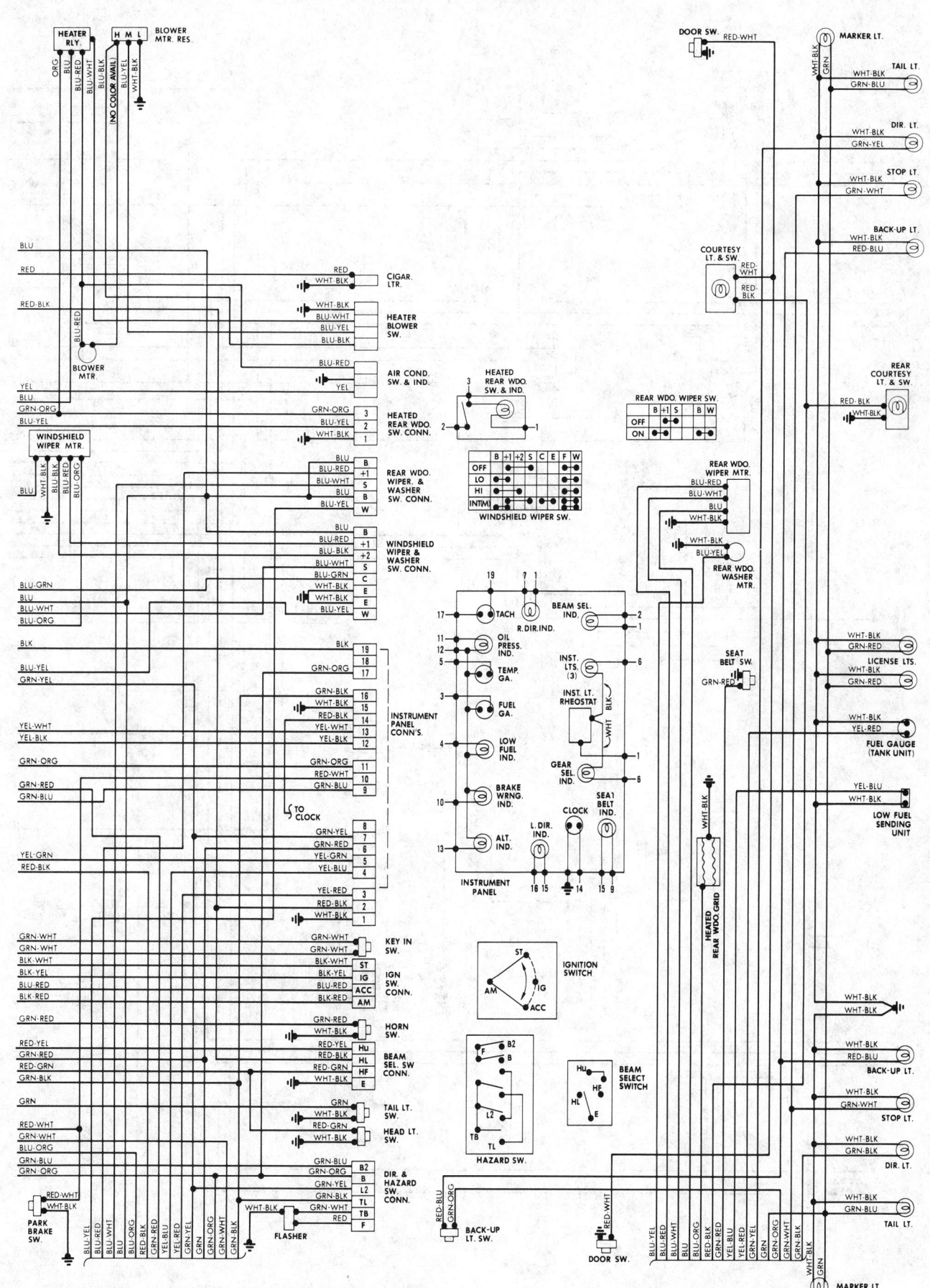

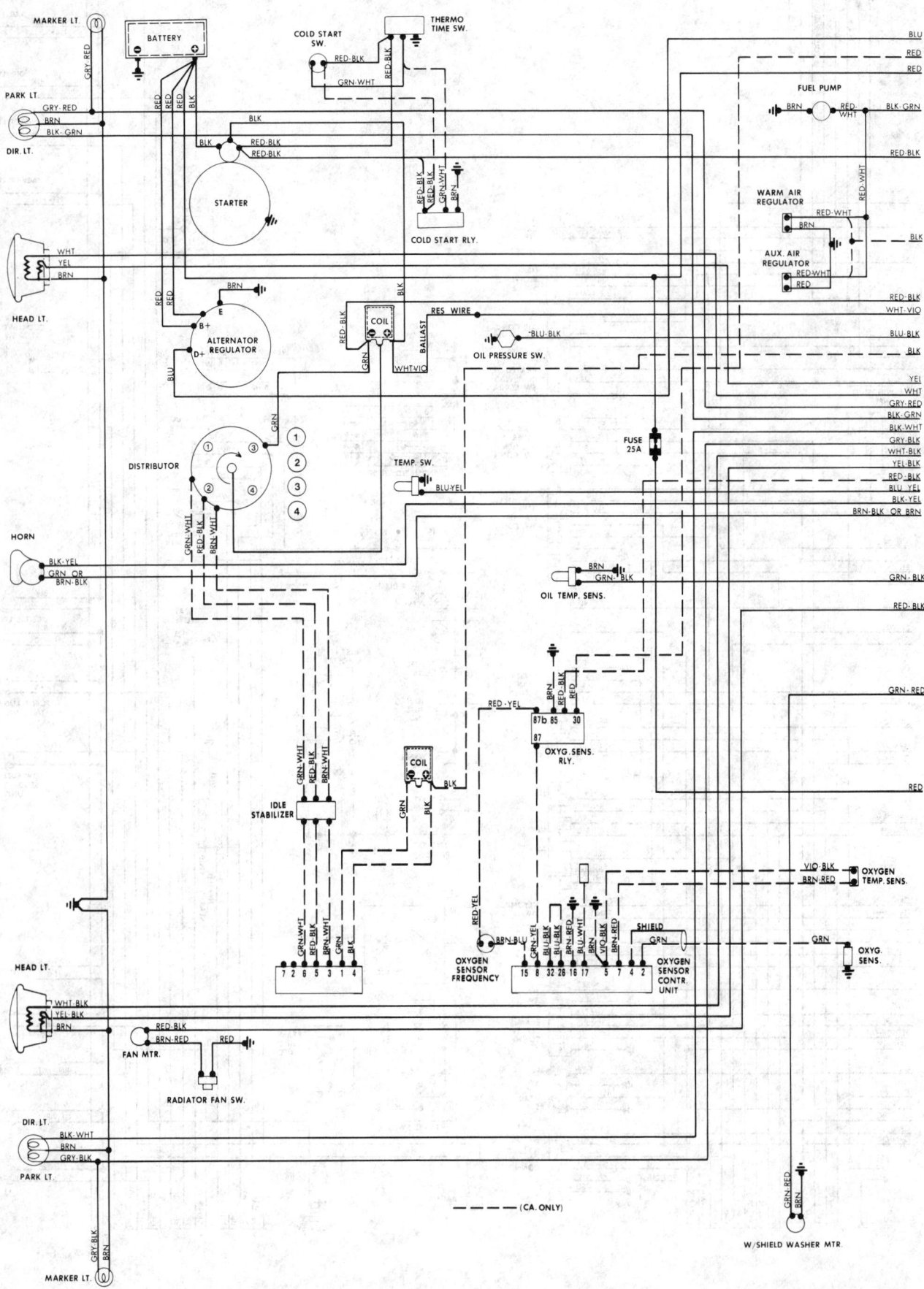

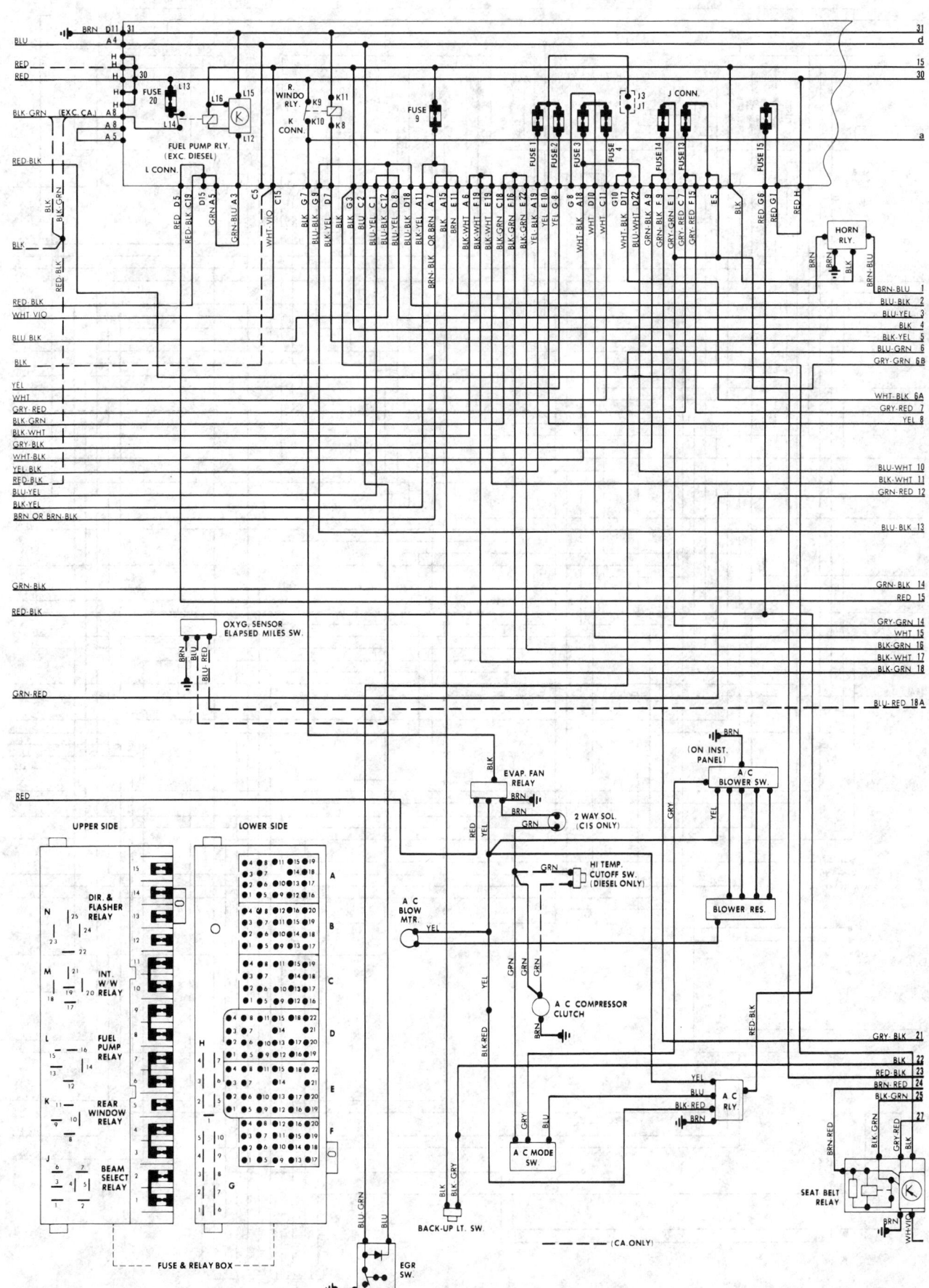

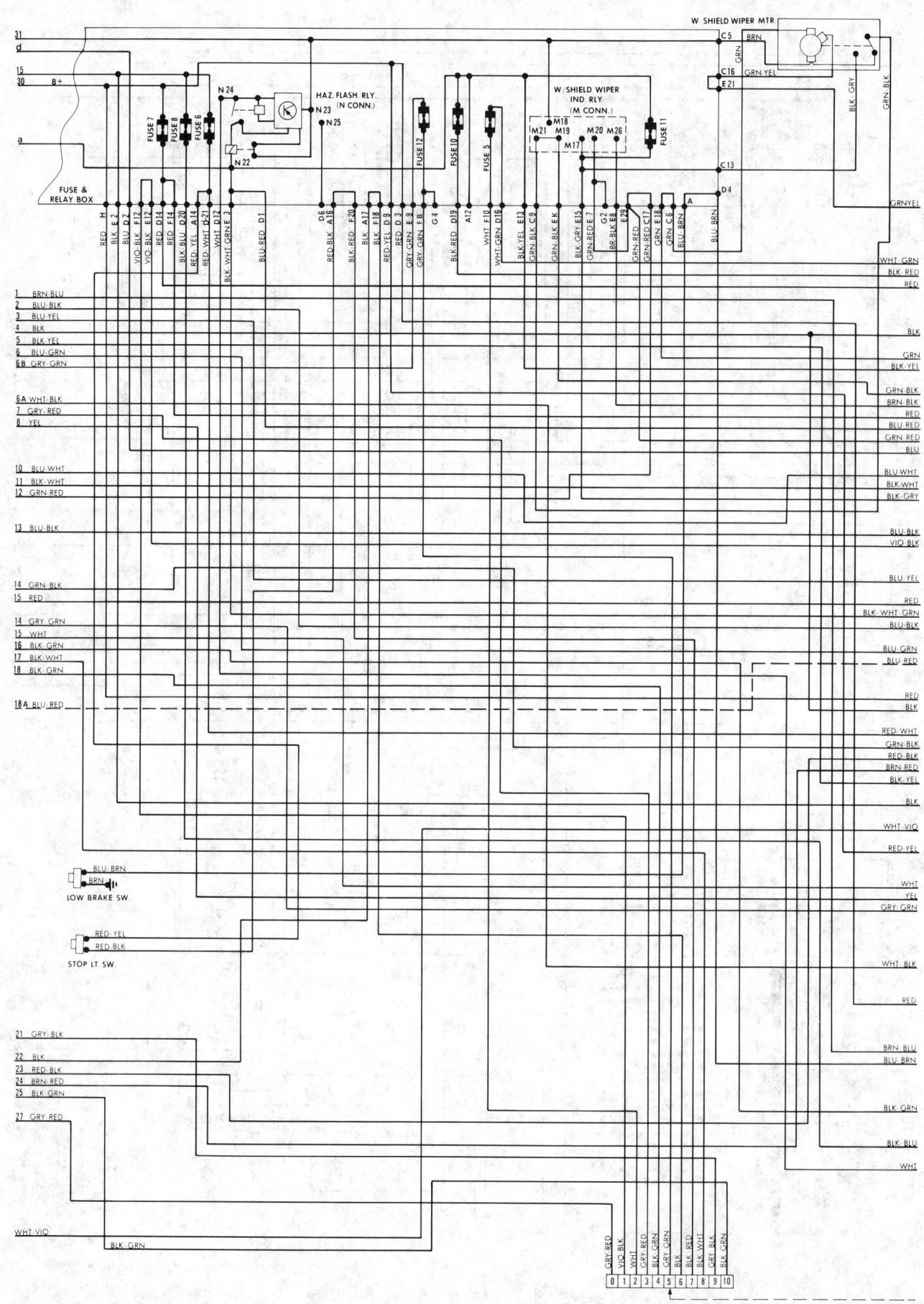

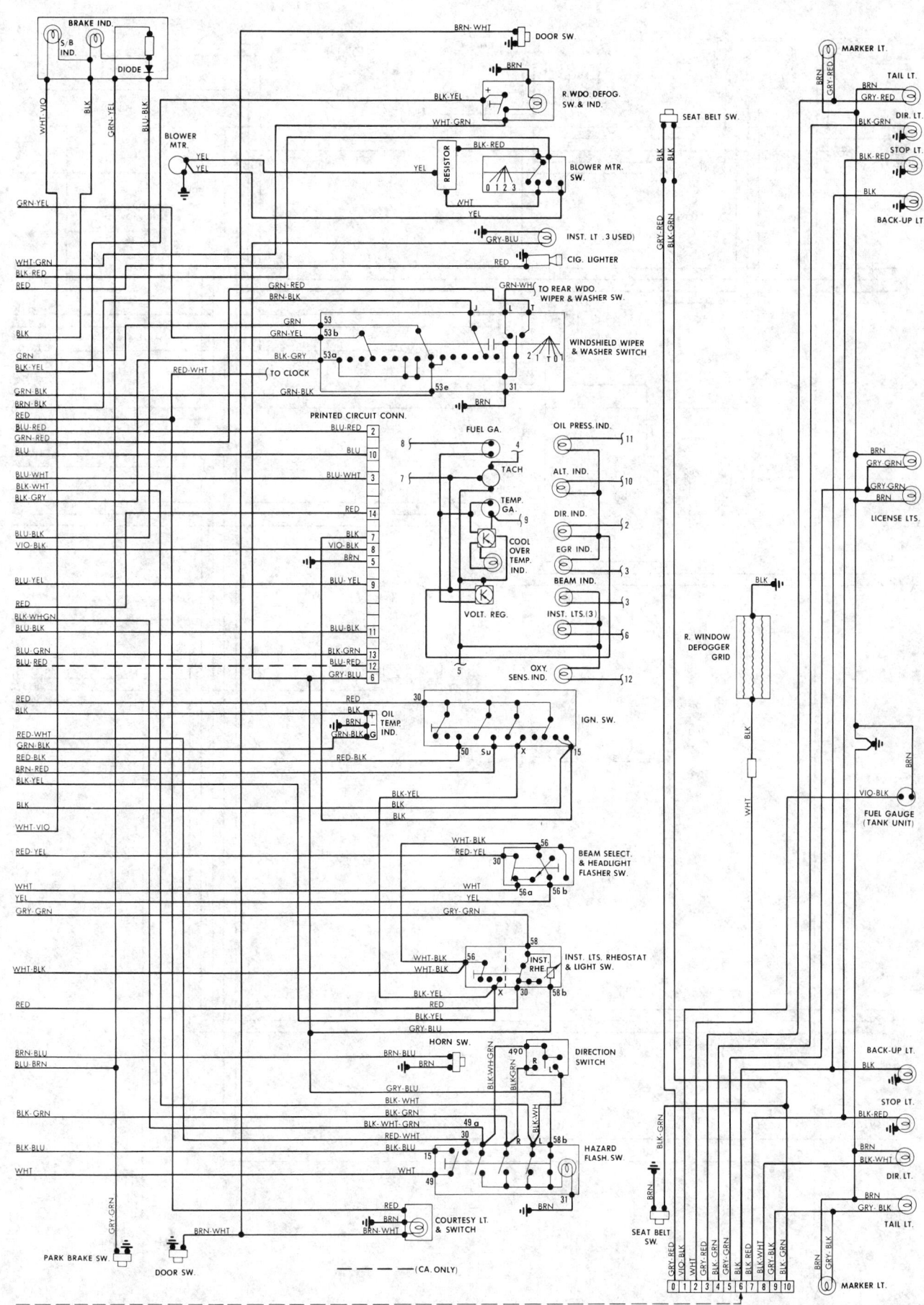

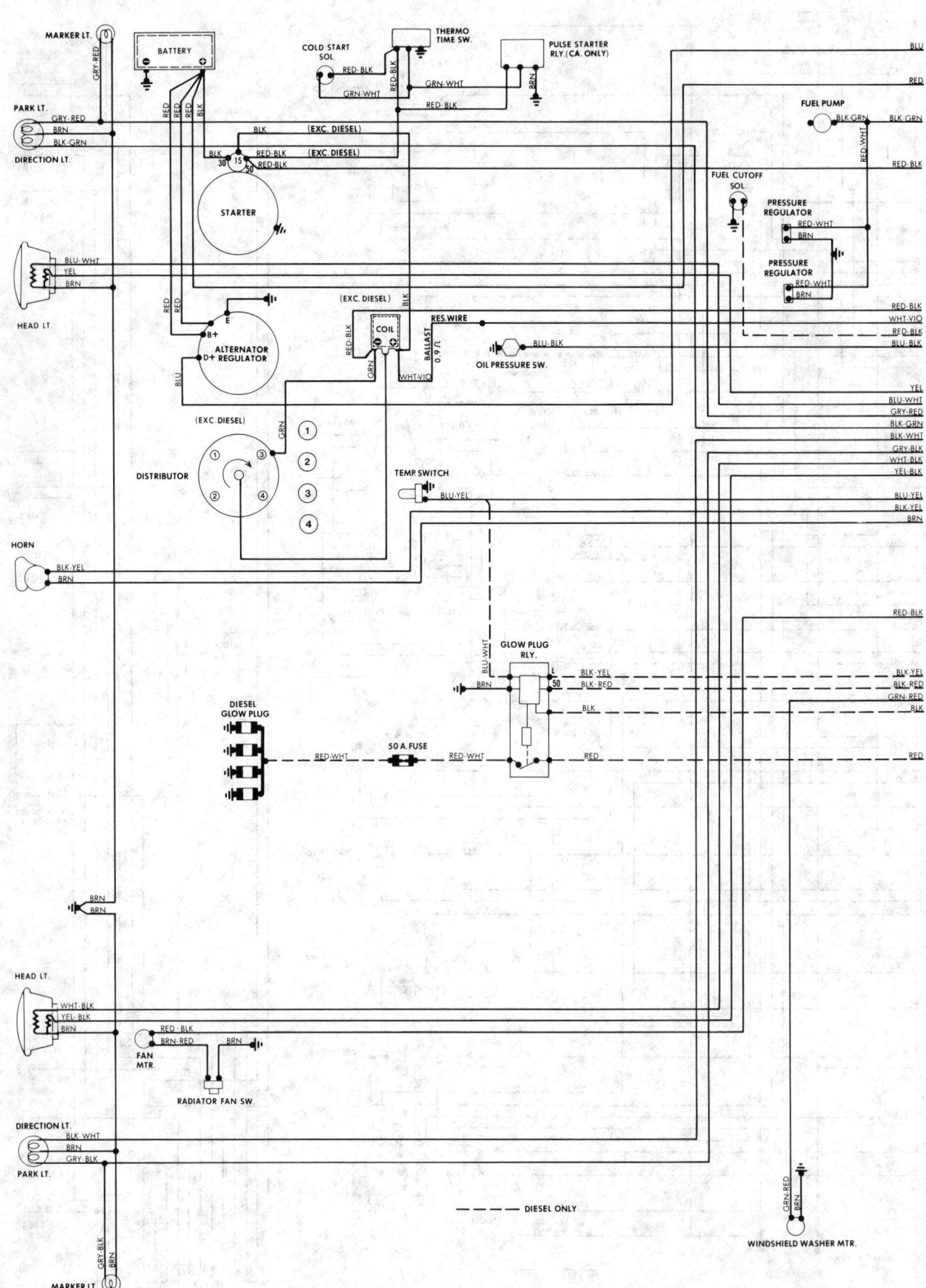

MARKER LT.

BATTERY

COLD START SOL.

THERMO TIME SW.

PULSE STARTER RLY.(CA. ONLY)

PARK LT.

DIRECTION LT.

STARTER

FUEL PUMP

FUEL CUTOFF SOL.

PRESSURE REGULATOR

PRESSURE REGULATOR

HEAD LT.

ALTERNATOR REGULATOR

COIL

BALLAST 0.9 Ω

RES.WIRE

OIL PRESSURE SW.

DISTRIBUTOR

TEMP SWITCH

HORN

DIESEL GLOW PLUG

GLOW PLUG RLY.

50 A. FUSE

HEAD LT.

FAN MTR.

RADIATOR FAN SW.

DIRECTION LT.

PARK LT.

MARKER LT.

------ = DIESEL ONLY

WINDSHIELD WASHER MTR.

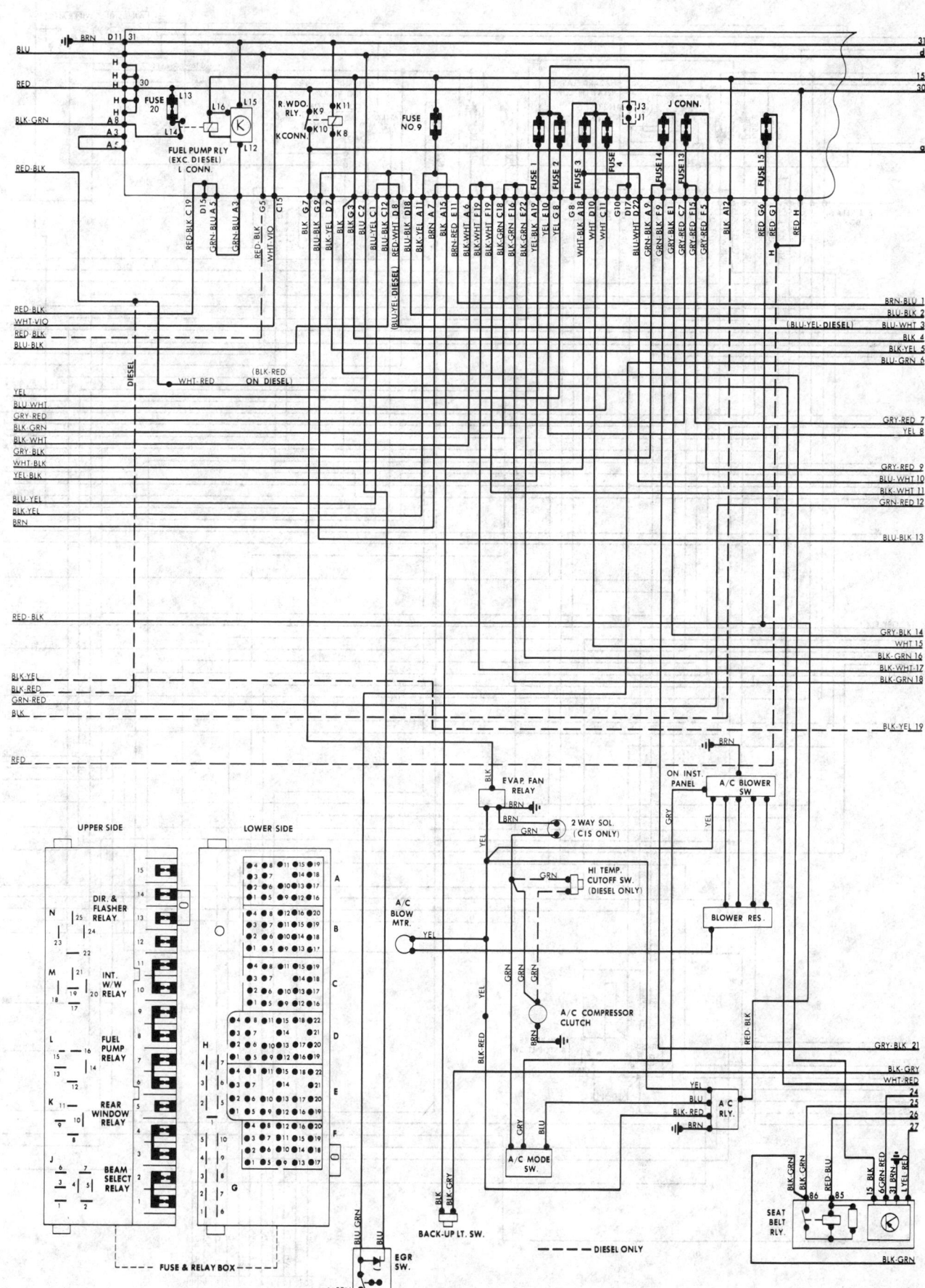

1980 Volkswagen

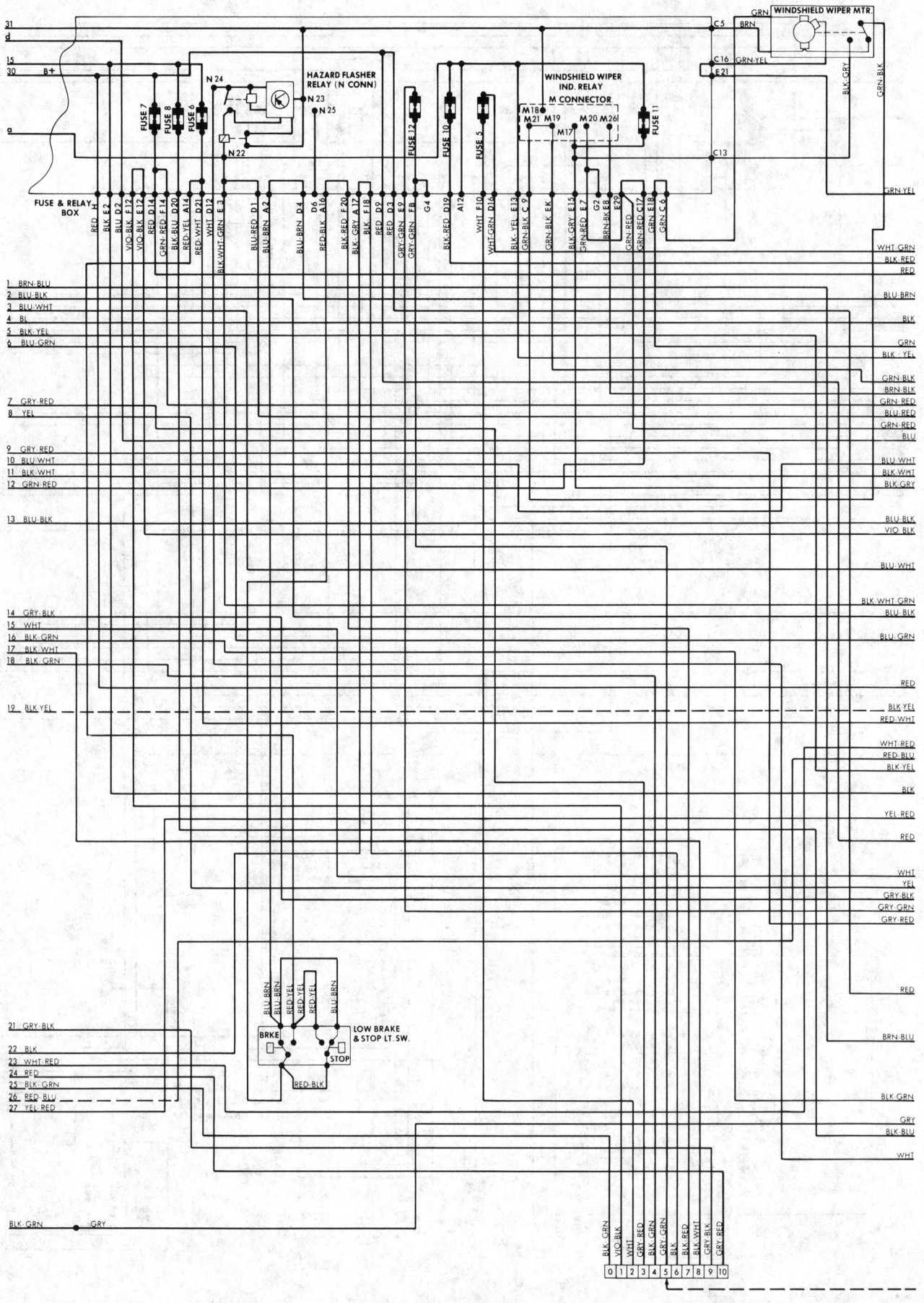

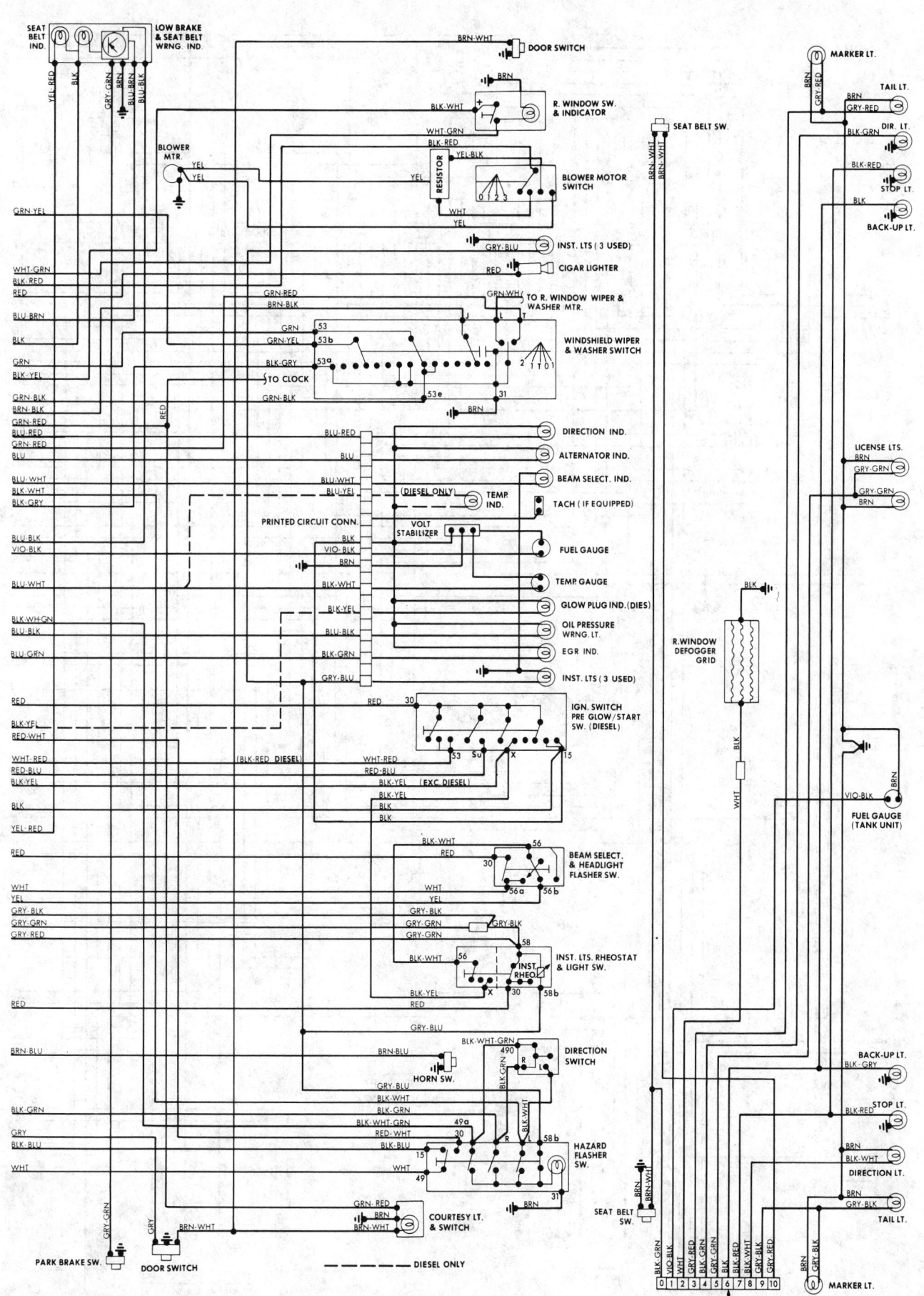

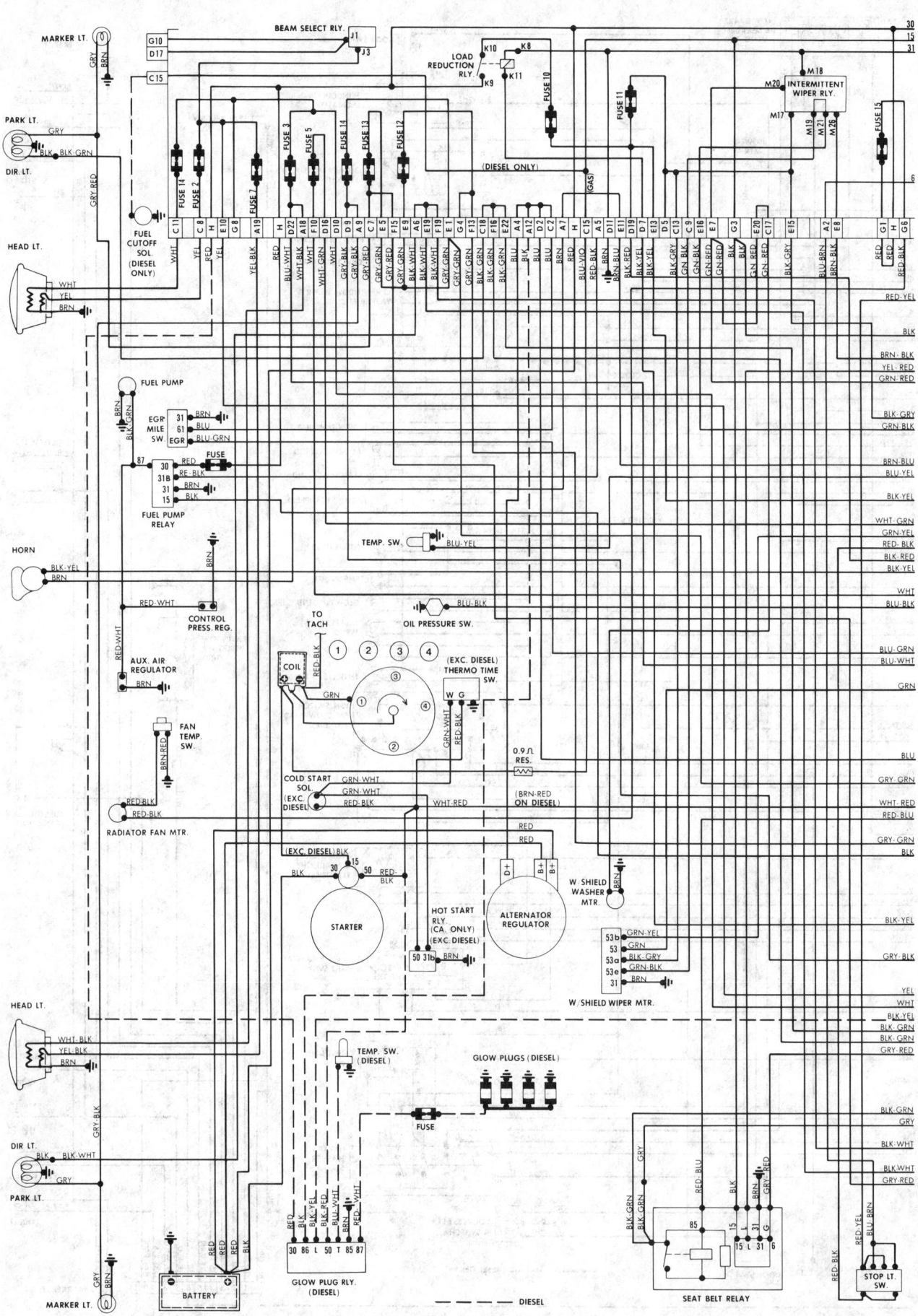

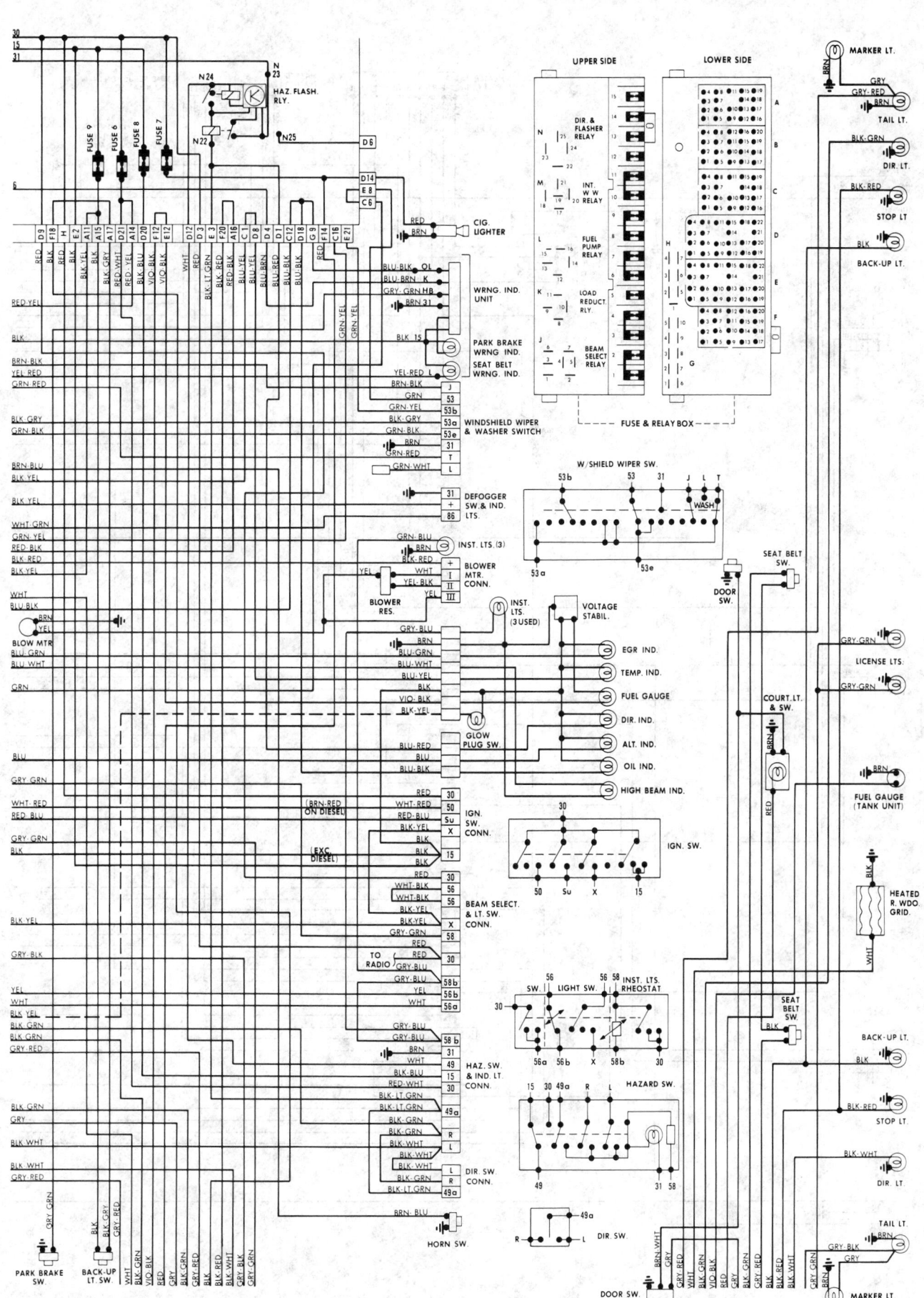

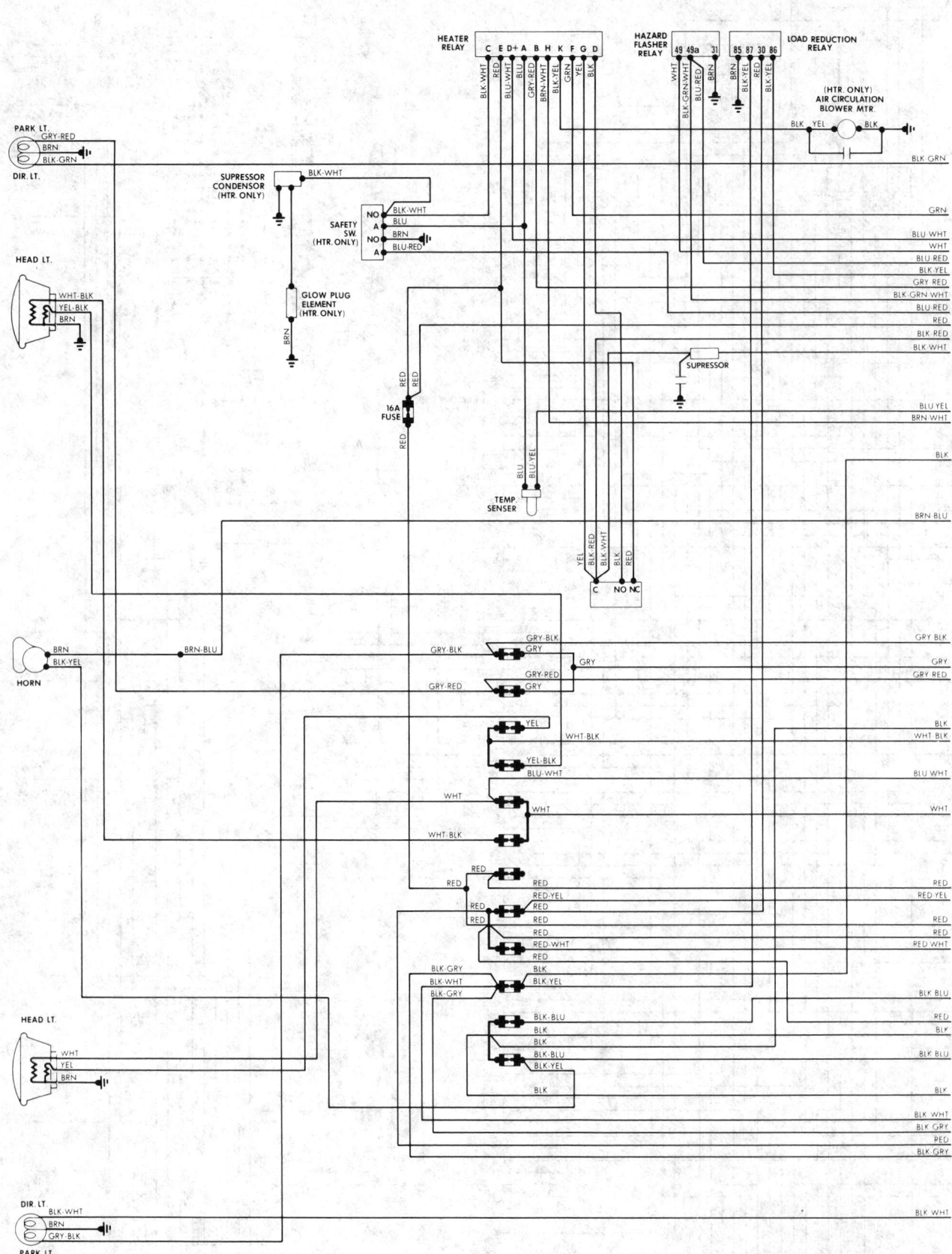

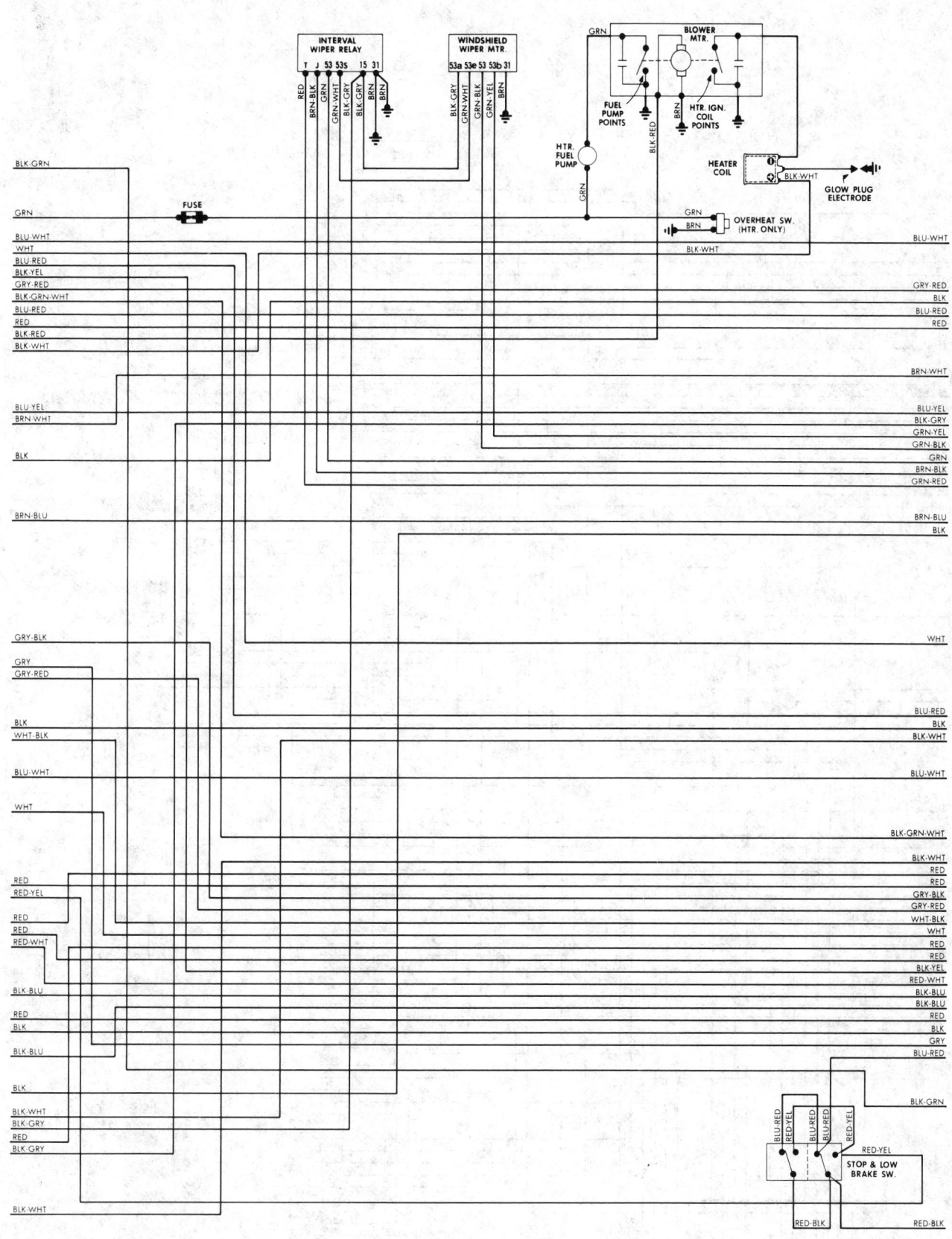

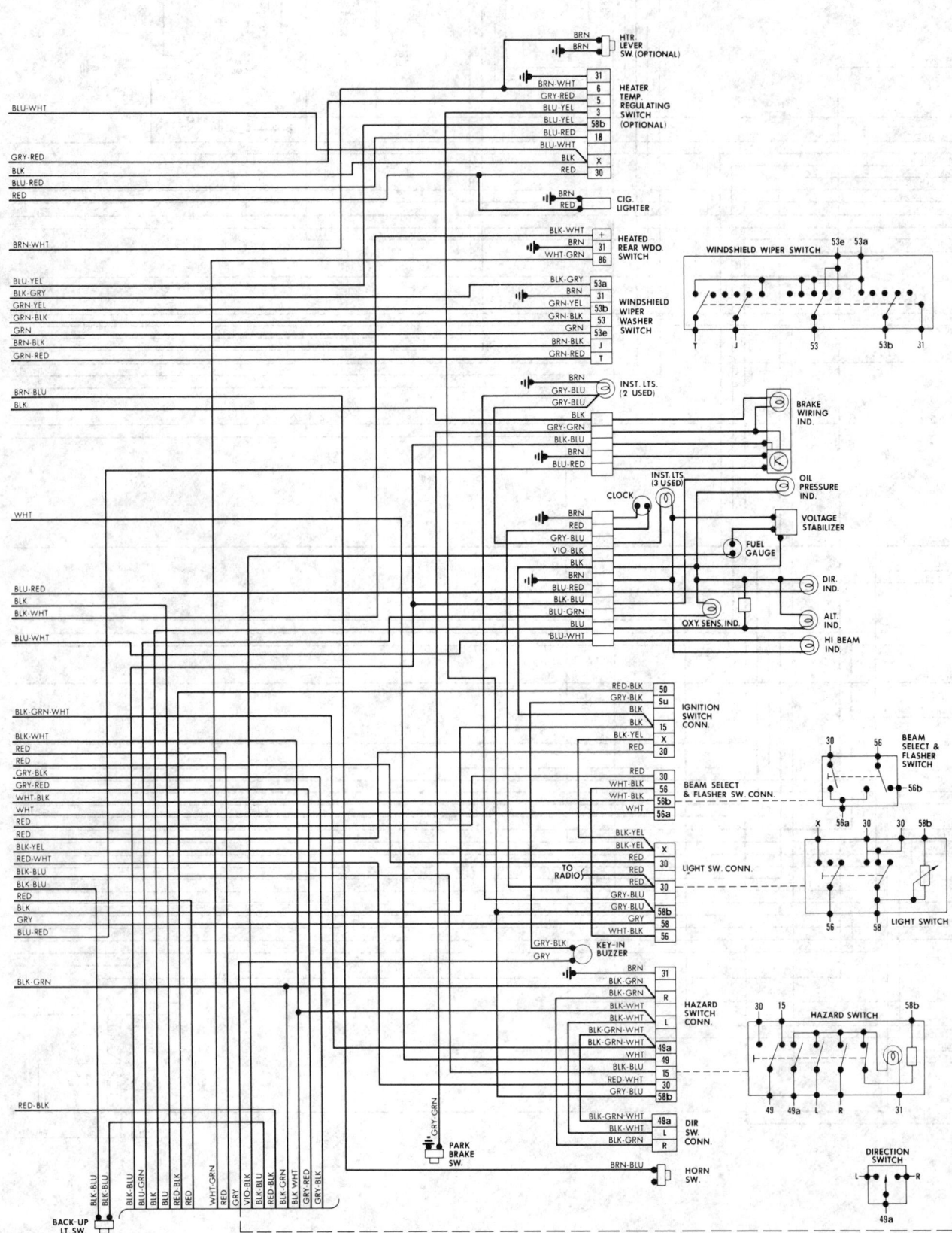

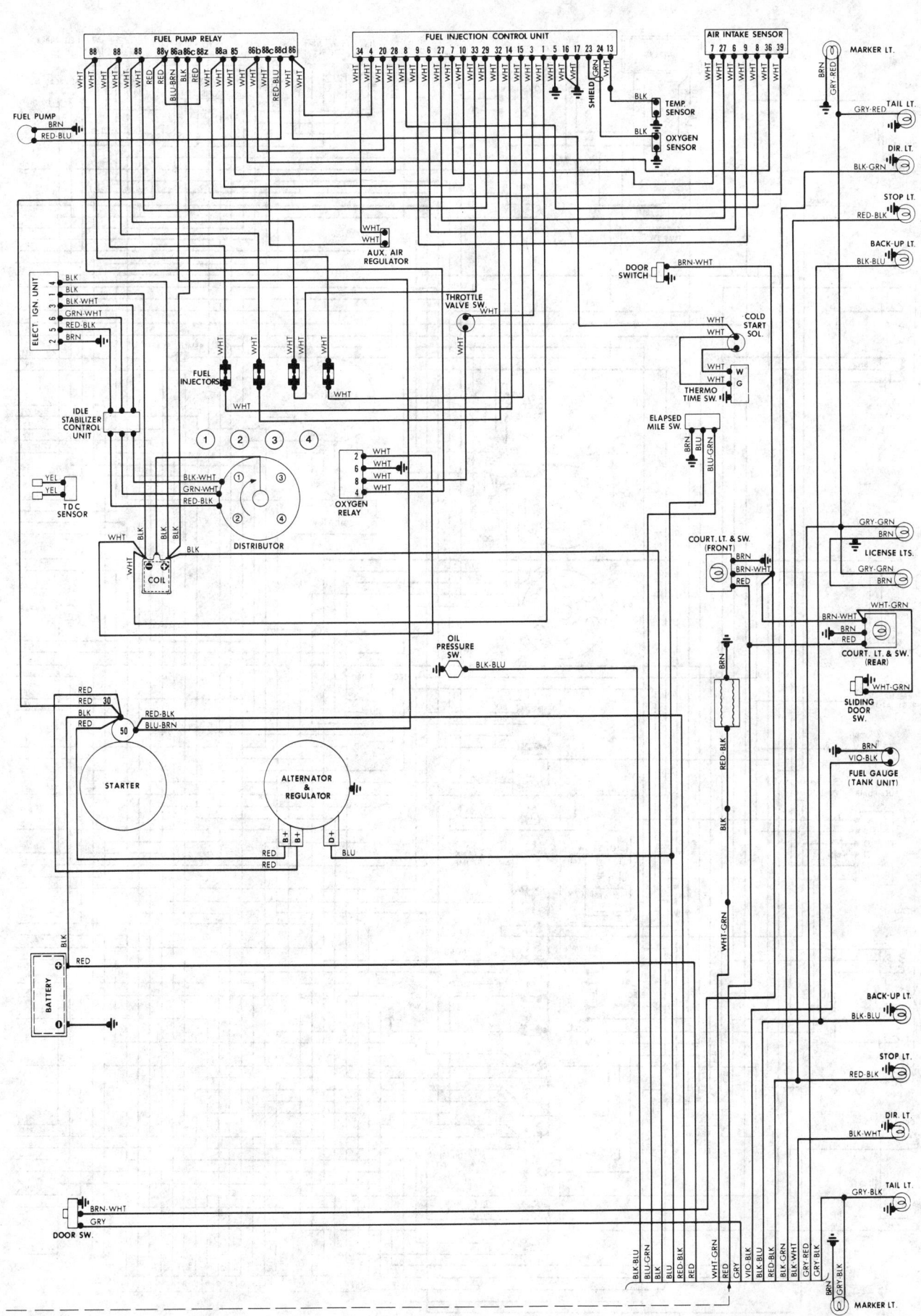

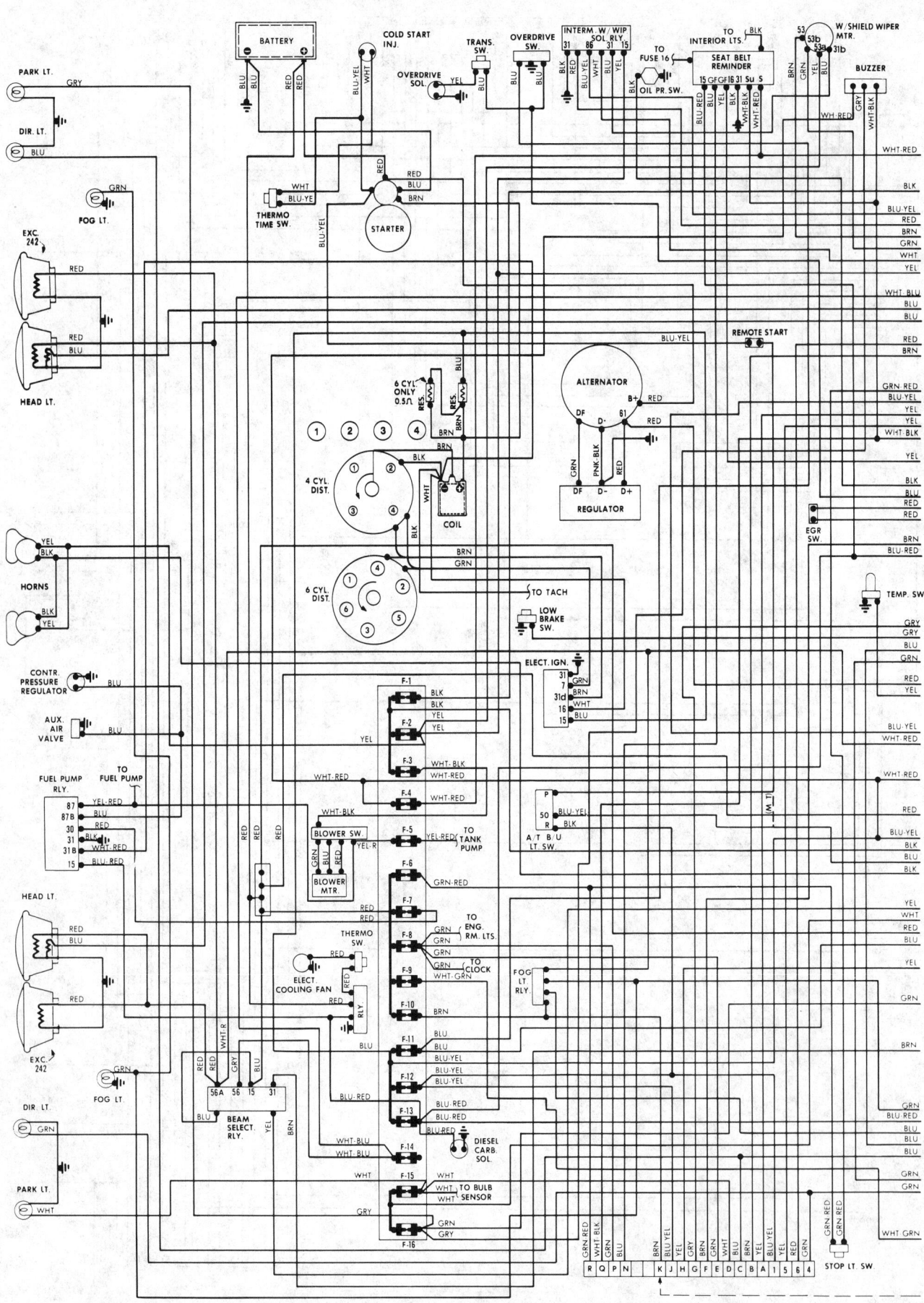

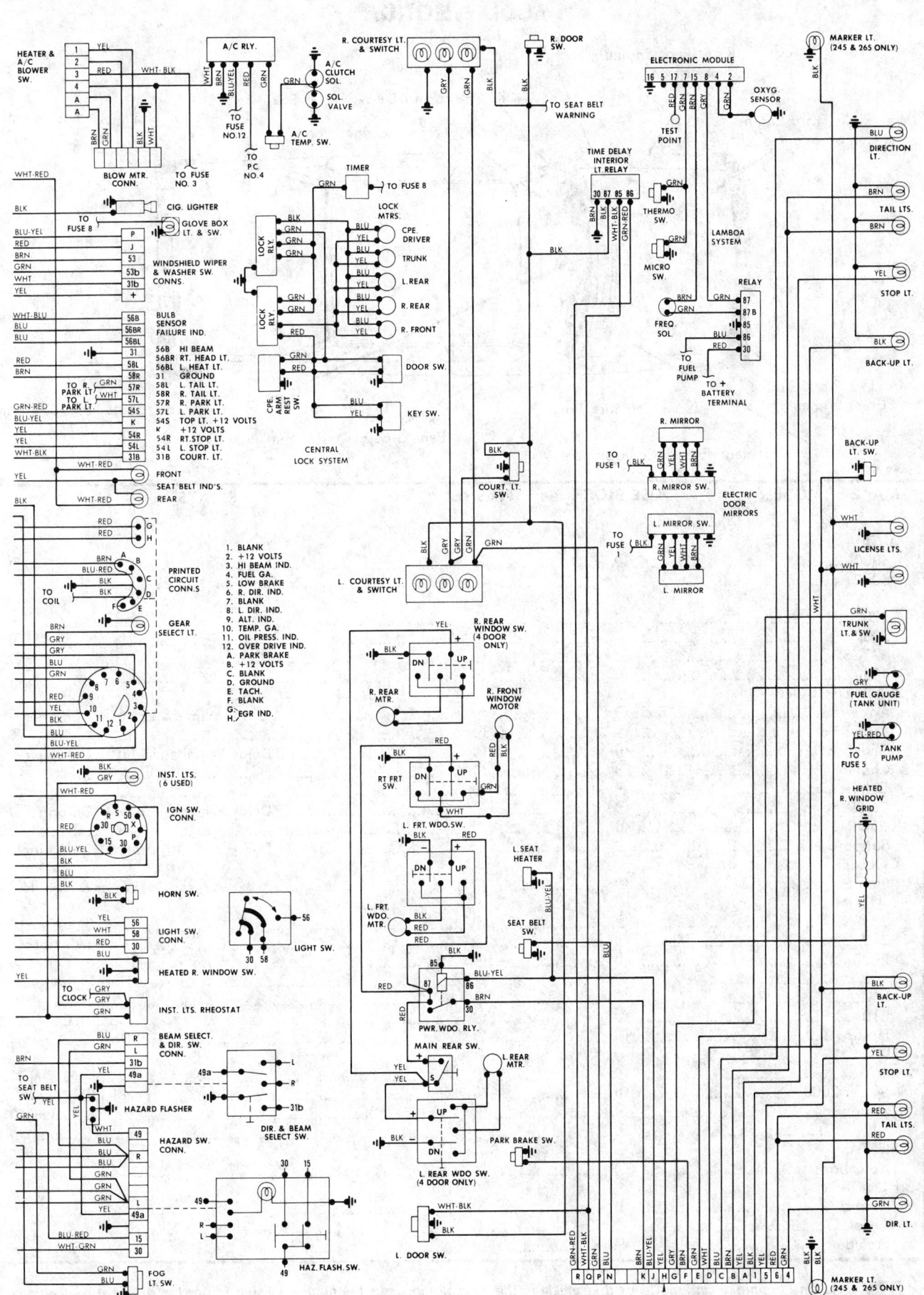

AUDI – HONDA

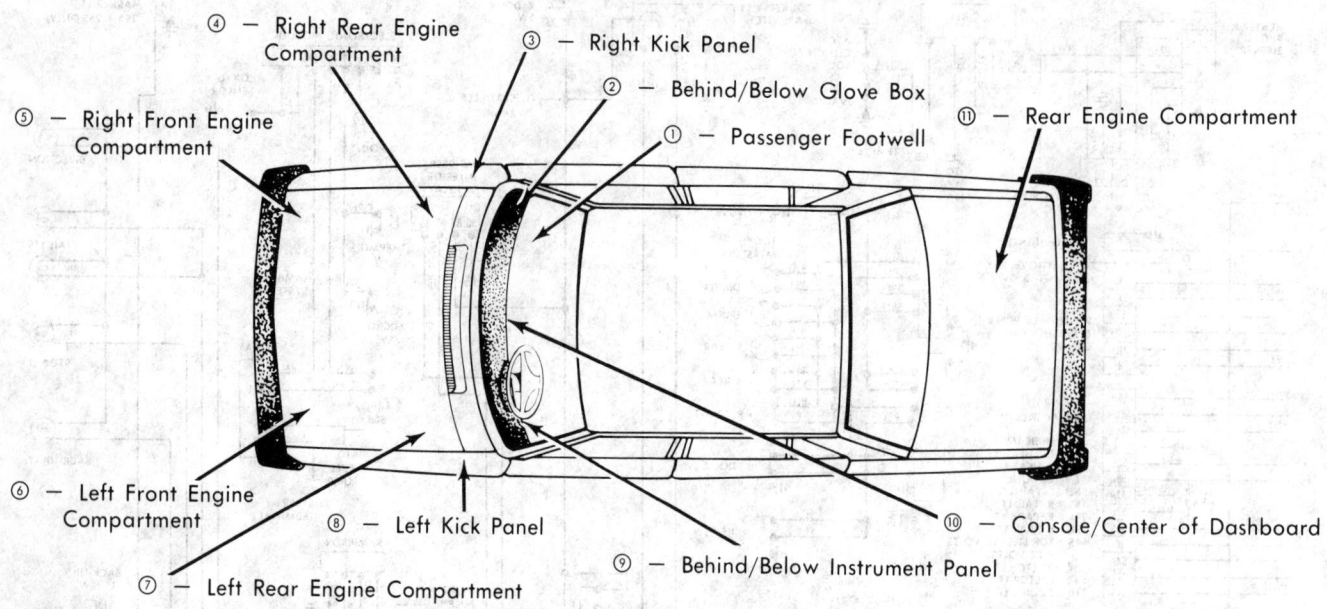

④ — Right Rear Engine Compartment
③ — Right Kick Panel
② — Behind/Below Glove Box
⑤ — Right Front Engine Compartment
① — Passenger Footwell
⑪ — Rear Engine Compartment
⑥ — Left Front Engine Compartment
⑧ — Left Kick Panel
⑩ — Console/Center of Dashboard
⑦ — Left Rear Engine Compartment
⑨ — Behind/Below Instrument Panel

MAKE – MODEL	FUSE BLOCK	FLASHER	RELAYS	
AUDI				
4000	⑨	⑨		⑨
5000	⑦	⑦		⑦
BMW				
320i	⑥	⑥		⑥
528i	⑥	⑥		⑥
633CSi	⑦	⑦		⑦
733i	⑥	⑥		⑥
CHRYSLER CORP.				
Arrow	⑨	⑨	Wiper & Lights⑥, Defogger⑩	
Arrow Pickup	⑧	⑨		⑨
Challenger	⑨	⑨	Delay Wiper⑤, Lights⑥, Defogger⑩	
Champ	⑨	⑨		⑨
Colt Hatchback	⑨	⑨		⑨
Colt Wagon	⑨	⑨	Delay Wiper⑤, Lights⑥, Defogger⑩	
D50 Pickup	⑧	⑨		⑨
Sapporo	⑨	⑨	Delay Wiper⑤, Lights⑥, Defogger⑩	
COURIER				
Pickup	⑦	⑨	Horn⑥, Wiper & Signals⑨	
DATSUN				
200SX	⑨	⑨	Ign. ③, Others⑤	
210	⑧	⑨	Choke⑤, Horn⑨	
280ZX	③	⑨	Ign. & Fuel Pump③, Others⑤	
310	⑧	③⑧	Choke & Horn⑤, Others⑧	
510	⑧	⑨		⑤
810	⑨	⑨	Ign.③, Others⑤	
Pickup	⑧	⑨	Horn⑨, Others⑧	
FIAT				
Brava	②	⑨	Fuel Inj.⑦	
Spider 2000	⑨	⑨	Fuel Inj.⑨, Others②	
Strada	⑨	⑨	Fuel Inj.⑦	
X1/9	②	②		②
FIESTA				
Hatchback	⑨	⑨		⑨
HONDA				
Accord	⑨	⑨		⑨
Civic	⑨	⑨		⑨
Prelude	⑨	⑨		⑨

NOTE — *Locate the make and model of the vehicle in the left column. Take the numbers listed under the appropriate column (Fuse Blocks, Flashers or Relays) and refer to the illustration above to find component.*

JAGUAR — TOYOTA

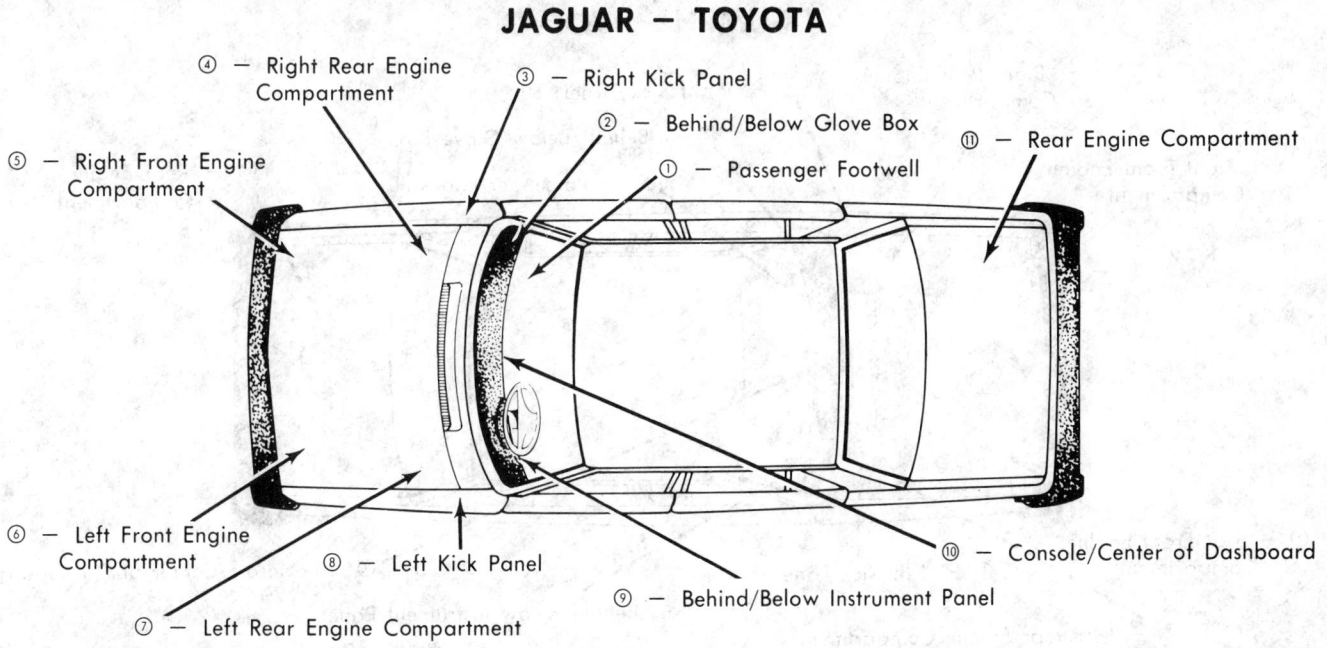

④ — Right Rear Engine Compartment
③ — Right Kick Panel
② — Behind/Below Glove Box
① — Passenger Footwell
⑪ — Rear Engine Compartment
⑤ — Right Front Engine Compartment
⑥ — Left Front Engine Compartment
⑧ — Left Kick Panel
⑩ — Console/Center of Dashboard
⑨ — Behind/Below Instrument Panel
⑦ — Left Rear Engine Compartment

MAKE — MODEL	FUSE BLOCK	FLASHER	RELAYS
JAGUAR			
XJ6	②⑨⑤⑥	⑨	Cold Start & Fuel Pump④
LUV			
Pickup	⑦	⑨	Horn⑥, Others④
MAZDA			
GLC	⑨	⑨	⑦
626	⑨	⑧	Choke⑥, Others⑧
RX7	⑨	⑨	⑦⑨
B2000	⑦	⑨	Horn⑥, Others⑨
MERCEDES-BENZ			
450SL & 450SLC	①	⑨	.....
All Others	⑦	⑨	
MG			
MGB	⑤	②	⑤
PEUGEOT			
504	⑨	⑩	⑨
505	⑦	⑩	⑦
604	⑨	⑩	Fan⑤, Bal. Resistor⑤, Others⑨
PORSCHE			
911SC	⑥⑪	.....	⑥⑪
924	⑨	⑨	⑨
928	①	①	①
RENAULT			
LeCar	⑩	⑨	.....
SAAB			
99	④	④	④
900	⑦	⑦	⑦
SUBARU			
All Models	⑨	⑨	.....
TOYOTA			
Celica	⑨⑥	⑨	⑨
Corolla	⑨⑧⑥	⑨	Heater & Wiper②, Others⑥
Corona	⑨⑤	⑨	Lights & Charging⑤, Others⑨
Cressida	⑨⑧③	⑨	⑧③
Land Cruiser	⑨④	⑨	⑨
Pickup	⑨	⑨	⑦
Supra	⑨⑤	⑨	Lights & Wiper②, Others⑨
Tercel	⑨⑥	⑨	Choke④, Fan⑦, Others⑨

NOTE — *Locate the make and model of the vehicle in the left column. Take the numbers listed under the appropriate column (Fuse Blocks, Flashers or Relays) and refer to the illustration above to find component.*

Fuse Blocks, Flashers & Relays

TRIUMPH — VOLVO

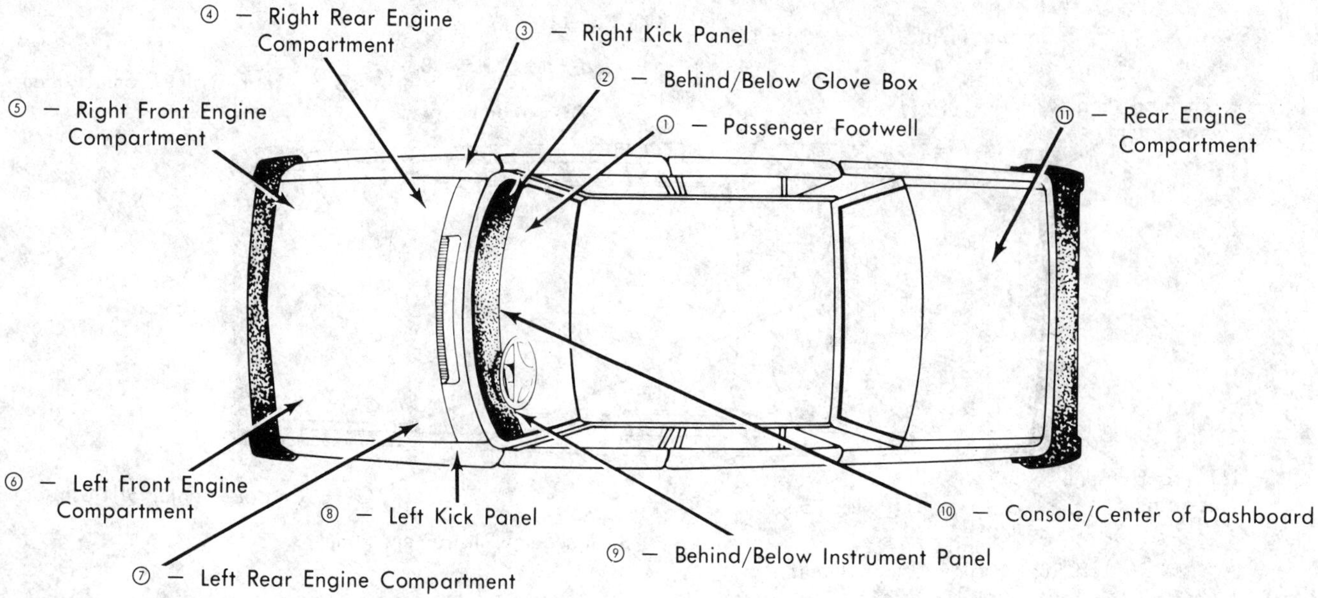

④ — Right Rear Engine Compartment
③ — Right Kick Panel
② — Behind/Below Glove Box
① — Passenger Footwell
⑪ — Rear Engine Compartment
⑤ — Right Front Engine Compartment
⑥ — Left Front Engine Compartment
⑧ — Left Kick Panel
⑩ — Console/Center of Dashboard
⑨ — Behind/Below Instrument Panel
⑦ — Left Rear Engine Compartment

MAKE — MODEL	FUSE BLOCK	FLASHER	RELAYS
TRIUMPH			
Spitfire	⑦	⑨	
TR7	②	⑨②	
TR8	②	②	②
VOLKSWAGEN			
Dasher	⑨	⑨	⑨
Jetta	⑨	⑨	⑨
Rabbit	⑨	⑨	⑨
Rabbit Pickup	⑨	⑨	⑨
Scirocco	⑨	⑨	⑨
Vanagon	⑨②	⑨	⑨
VOLVO			
DL, GL, GT	⑧	⑩	⑨⑩
GLE, Coupe	⑧	⑩	⑨⑩
Diesel	⑧	⑩	⑨⑩

NOTE — *Locate the make and model of the vehicle in the left column. Take the numbers listed under the appropriate column (Fuse Blocks, Flashers or Relays) and refer to the illustration above to find component.*

AUDI

FUSE BLOCK

4000 — Fuse block is located at left side of dashboard behind storage bin. It contains 15 fuses arranged horizontally. Circuits protected are as follows:

① — 8 Amp. Low Beam Left
② — 8 Amp. Low Beam Right
③ — 8 Amp. High Beam Left
④ — 8 Amp. High Beam Right
⑤ — 16 Amp. Rear Window Defogger
⑥ — 8 Amp. Stop lights, Turn Signals
⑦ — 8 Amp. Cigar Lighter, Radio, Glove Box Light
⑧ — 8 Amp. Instrument Panel Lights
⑨ — 8 Amp. Back-Up Lights, Horn
⑩ — 25 Amp. Fresh Air Fan
⑪ — 8 Amp. Windshield Wiper Washer
⑫ — 8 Amp. License Plate Light
⑬ — 8 Amp. Tail, Parking & Side Marker Lights (Right)
⑭ — 8 Amp. Tail, Parking & Side Marker Lights (Left)
⑮ — 25 Amp. Radiator Fan

5000 Models — Fuse block is located in engine compartment left rear corner. Fuses are numbered from 1 to 17, with 17 closest to the front of the car and 1 nearest the rear. Circuits protected are:

① — 25 Amp. A/C, Heater Fan, Tachometer
② — Not Used
③ — 8 Amp. High Beam Headlight, Left
④ — 8 Amp. High Beam Headlight, Right
⑤ — 16 Amp. Fuel Pump
⑥ — 8 Amp. Right Marker, Tail Lights
⑦ — 8 Amp. Left Marker Lights, Engine Comp. Light
⑧ — 8 Amp. Instrument Panel, Glove Compartment, License Plate Lights
⑨ — 16 Amp. Horn, Instruments, Power Windows, Sunroof
⑩ — 25 Amp. Radiator Fan
⑪ — 16 Amp. Brake Lights
⑫ — 16 Amp. Lighter, Radio, Antenna, Clock, Dome Light
⑬ — 8 Amp. Low Beam Headlight, Right
⑭ — 8 Amp. Low Beam Headlight, Left
⑮ — 16 Amp. Back-up Lights, Wipers
⑯ — 25 Amp. Rear Window Defogger
⑰ — Flashers

BMW

FUSE BLOCK

320i — Fuse block is located at left front corner of engine compartment. Fuses are arranged in 6 rows of 3, with first row toward battery. Number 1 fuse is next to front relay. Protected circuits are:

① — 8 Amp. Right Fog Light
② — 8 Amp. Left Fog Light
③ — 16 Amp. Fuel Pump
④ — 8 Amp. Right Low Beam
⑤ — 8 Amp. Left Low Beam
⑥ — 8 Amp. Dash Lights, Right Park and Taillights, Hood Light
⑦ — 16 Amp. High Beam
⑧ — 16 Amp. High Beam
⑨ — 8 Amp. Left Park and Taillights
⑩ — 16 Amp. Defogger
⑪ — 25 Amp. Heater Fan, A/C Fan
⑫ — 8 Amp. Brake Lights, Radio, Tachometer
⑬ — 25 Amp. Auxiliary Fan
⑭ — 16 Amp. Back-up Lights, Gauges, Warning Lights
⑮ — 16 Amp. Horn, Wipers, Washer, Power Mirror
⑯ — 16 Amp. Lighter
⑰ — 8 Amp. Turn Signals, Hazard Flashers, Clock, Buzzers
⑱ — Spare

528i, 633CSi and 733i — All models have fuse block at left front corner of engine compartment. Fuses are located in 3 rows with 6 in first row, 8 in second row, and 2 or 3 in third row. Fuses are numbered from center of car toward left side, and protect the following circuits:

① — 8 Amp. (528i), 16 Amp. (633CSi and 733i) Fuel Pump, Emission Controls
② — 8 Amp. Right Low Beam
③ — 8 Amp. Left Low Beam
④ — 16 Amp. Lighter
⑤ — 8 Amp. Clock, Interior Lights, Trunk Light, Warning Buzzer, Locking System, Hazard Lights, Glove Box Light (528i Only), Turn Signals (733i Only)
⑥ — 8 Amp. Warning Lights, Instruments, Back-Up Lights, Transmission Indicator Light, Power Windows, Cruise Control (733i Only)
⑦ — 8 Amp. Right High Beam
⑧ — 8 Amp. Left High Beam
⑨ — 8 Amp. Right Parking and Marker Lights, Instrument Panel and Console Lights
⑩ — 8 Amp. Left Parking and Marker Lights
⑪ — 16 Amp. Wipers, Washers, Power Mirrors, Turn Signals (528i)
⑫ — 8 Amp. Radio, Brake Lights, Clock (Exc. 528i). (733i Only) Safety Check Panel, Speedometer and Cruise Control
⑬ — 16 Amp. Defogger, Sun Roof
⑭ — 25 Amp. A/C, Heater Fan, Auxiliary Fan Relay
⑮ — 8 Amp. Right Fog Light
⑯ — 8 Amp. Left Fog Light
⑰ — 25 Amp. (2 on 633CSi and 733i) Auxiliary Fan

Fuses & Circuit Breakers

CHRYSLER CORP. IMPORTS

FUSE BLOCK

Arrow — Fuse block is located on left kick panel. Fuse circuits and ratings are listed on cover. Fuses are numbered from front to rear, top row first, then bottom. Circuits protected are as follows:

① — 10 Amp. Right High Beam
② — 10 Amp. Left High Beam
③ — 10 Amp. Taillights, Marker Lights, License
④ — 5 Amp. Parking Lights
⑤ — 15 Amp. Defogger
⑥ — 10 Amp. Back-up Lights
⑦ — 10 Amp. Voltage Regulator, Turn Signals
⑧ — 10 Amp. Right Low Beam
⑨ — 10 Amp. Left Low Beam
⑩ — 15 Amp. Radio, Horn, Lighter
⑪ — 15 Amp. Wiper, Washer
⑫ — 15 Amp. Heater, Air Conditioner
⑬ — 15 Amp. Hazard Flashers, Stop Lights
⑭ — 5 Amp. Dome, Buzzer, Indicators

Arrow Pickup, Dodge D50 Pickup — Fuse block is located beneath instrument panel on left side. Fuses are numbered with first fuse at bottom right side of block and last fuse on top left. Circuits protected are:

① — 15 Amp. High Beams
② — 15 Amp. Low Beams
③ — 15 Amp. Heater, Windshield Washer
④ — 15 Amp. Wipers, Radio, Lighter
⑤ — 15 Amp. Taillights, Parking Lights
⑥ — 15 Amp. Stop Lights, Dome
⑦ — 15 Amp. Hazard Flashers
⑧ — 15 Amp. Turn Signal, Backup Lights

Challenger, Sapporo — Fuse block is underneath dash on driver's side. Fuses are arranged in one row with first fuse to right side. A check lamp system is provided. With ignition "ON" headlight switch at first position, check light should come on for each circuit as knob is moved along top of fuse panel. If light is not lit, fuse is blown. Be sure to return knob to rest position to avoid draining battery. Circuits protected are:

① — 15 Amp. Stop Lights, Dome
② — 15 Amp. Hazard Flashers, Courtesy Lights
③ — 20 Amp. Defogger
④ — 15 Amp. Taillights, Instrument Lights
⑤ — 15 Amp. Heater, A/C, Horn
⑥ — 15 Amp. Wiper, Washers
⑦ — 15 Amp. Lighter, Radio
⑧ — 10 Amp. Turn Signals, Dash Warning Lights
⑨ — 10 Amp. Backup Lights
⑩ — 10 Amp. Voltage Regulator

Champ, Colt Hatchback — Fuse block is located beneath instrument panel on left side. Fuses are numbered from right to left, and protect the following circuits:

① — 15 Amp. Backup Lights, Gauges, Defogger
② — 15 Amp. Wipers, Washers
③ — 15 Amp. Turn Signals, Indicators
④ — 15 Amp. Lighter, Radio
⑤ — 15 Amp. Heater
⑥ — 15 Amp. Hazard Flashers, Dome Light
⑦ — 15 Amp. Stop Lights
⑧ — 15 Amp. Taillights, Parking Lights
⑨ — 15 Amp. Low Beams
⑩ — 15 Amp. High Beams

Colt Station Wagon — Fuse block is underneath dash on driver's side. Fuses are arranged in order with first fuse to right side. A check lamp system is provided. With headlights and ignition "ON", check light should come on for each circuit as knob is moved across top of panel. If light is not lit, fuse is blown. Be sure to return check knob to rest position to avoid draining battery. Fuses protect circuits as listed:

① — 15 Amp. Stop, Dome, Seat Belt Warning
② — 15 Amp. Hazard Flashers
③ — 15 Amp. Heater, A/C, Horn
④ — 15 A. Wipers, Washers
⑤ — 15 Amp. Radio, Lighter
⑥ — 15 Amp. Taillights, Meter
⑦ — 15 Amp. Defogger
⑧ — 15 Amp. Turn Signals, Gauges
⑨ — 10 Amp. Backup Lights
⑩ — 10 Amp. Voltage Regulator

COURIER

FUSE BLOCK

Fuse block is located in engine compartment on left side near windshield. Fuses are numbered with first fuse in back row toward outside, and last fuse in front row toward engine. Fuses and circuits protected are:

① — 15 Amp. Horn, Stop Lights, Hazard Warning Flasher, Interior Light, Cigar Lighter
② — 15 Amp. Hood & Glove Box Light, Electric Rear Window Defroster
③ — Blank
④ — 15 Amp. Headlights (High Beam)
⑤ — 15 Amp. Headlights (Low Beam)
⑥ — 10 Amp. Tail, License, Front Parking, Front Side Marker, Instrument Lights
⑦ — 10 Amp. Windshield Wipers/Washers
⑧ — 15 Amp. Heater/Defroster Blower Motor, Radio
⑨ — 10 Amp. Front & Rear Turn Signal Lights, Fasten Seat Belt, Oil Pressure & Brake Warning Lights, Fuel Gauge, Temperature Gauge, Back-Up Lights
⑩ — 15 Amp. Engine

DATSUN

FUSE BLOCK

200SX — Fuse block is located under dash at left side. It contains 13 fuses which protect the following circuits:

① — 20 Amp. Headlights
② — 20 Amp. Heater, Air Conditioning
③ — 20 Amp. Rear Window Defogger
④ — 15 Amp. Stop Lights
⑤ — 15 Amp. Clearance, Tail Lights
⑥ — 15 Amp. Wiper/Washer
⑦ — 15 Amp. Coil Injector
⑧ — 10 Amp. Hazard Lights
⑨ — 10 Amp. Horn
⑩ — 10 Amp. Cigar Lighter, Clock
⑪ — 10 Amp. Dome, Step Light
⑫ — 10 Amp. Engine Control
⑬ — 10 Amp. Turn Signal, Meter

210 — Fuse block is located on left kick panel under hood release handle. A single inline fuse of 20 Amp. capacity protects the air conditioner circuit, while 8 fuses in the block protect the following circuits:

① — 10 Amp. Wipers, Washers
② — 15 Amp. Horn, Lighter
③ — 15 Amp. Stop Lights, Courtesy Lights
④ — 15 Amp. Taillights
⑤ — 15 Amp. Heater, Radio
⑥ — 10 Amp. Engine
⑦ — 10 Amp. Flashers, Meter
⑧ — 20 Amp. Defogger

280ZX — Fuse block is located in right kick panel and contains 12 fuses, which protect the following circuits:

① — 10 Amp. Right Headlight
② — 10 Amp. Left Headlight
③ — 20 Amp. Stop Lights, Horn
④ — 15 Amp. Marker Lights, Taillights
⑤ — 10 Amp. Courtesy Lights
⑥ — 20 Amp. Hazard Flashers
⑦ — 20 Amp. Air Conditioner
⑧ — 10 Amp. Radio
⑨ — 15 Amp. Wipers, Washers
⑩ — 10 Amp. Turn Signals
⑪ — 10 Amp. Gauges
⑫ — 20 Amp. Defogger

310 — Fuse block is mounted on left kick panel below hood release handle. Circuits protected are:

① — 10 Amp. Defogger
② — 10 Amp. Voltage Regulator, Fuel Cut-Off
③ — 10 Amp. Turn Signals, Backup Light, Gauge Lights
④ — 10 Amp. Radiator Fan Motor
⑤ — 10 Amp. Heater, A/C, Radio

⑥ — 10 Amp. A/C Fan Motor
⑦ — 10 Amp. Right Taillight, Dash Light
⑧ — 10 Amp. Left Taillight, License Plate Light
⑨ — 10 Amp. Stop Lights, Clock
⑩ — 10 Amp. Hazard Flashers, Courtesy Lights
⑪ — 10 Amp. Wipers, Washers
⑫ — 10 Amp. Horn
⑬ — 10 Amp. Lighter

510 — Fuse block is located under instrument panel near hood release handle. A separate 20 Amp. inline fuse protects the air conditioner circuit. Circuits protected through the fuse block include:

① — 15 Amp. Horn, Lighter
② — 15 Amp. Stop Lights, Courtesy Lights
③ — 15 Amp. Taillights
④ — 15 Amp. Heater, Radio
⑤ — 10 Amp. Wipers, Washers
⑥ — 10 Amp. Engine Controls
⑦ — 10 Amp. Flashers, Meter
⑧ — 20 Amp. Defogger

810 — Fuse block is located behind cover in right kick panel. A single 20 Amp. inline fuse protects air conditioner, while the following circuits are protected through fuse block:

① — 20 Amp. Stop Lights, Horn
② — 10 Amp. Courtesy Lights
③ — 10 Amp. Taillights, Side Marker Lights
④ — 15 Amp. Heater, Radio
⑤ — 10 Amp. Wipers, Washers
⑥ — 10 Amp. Right Headlight
⑦ — 10 Amp. Left Headlight
⑧ — 10 Amp. Flashers, Meter
⑨ — 20 Amp. Defogger

Pickup — Fuse block is beneath headlight switch, under left side of dash. Two inline fuses (each 15 Amp.) protect the air conditioner, lighter and clock. Fuses in the fuse block protect the following circuits:

① — 20 Amp. Headlights
② — 10 Amp. Tail, License, Marker, Gauges & Interior Lights
③ — 15 Amp. Hazard & Stop Lights
④ — 10 Amp. Horn, Clock
⑤ — 15 Amp. Radio, Cigar Lighter
⑥ — 15 Amp. Wipers, Washer, Heater, Air Conditioning
⑦ — 20 Amp. High Powered Heater
⑧ — 15 Amp. Gauges, Hazard, Turn Signals
⑨ — 10 Amp. Engine Control

FUSIBLE LINK

All Models — Fusible link is located in wire between battery and alternator near the battery. Its purpose is to protect the alternator and related circuits.

FIAT

FUSE BLOCK

Brava — Fuse block is positioned in box underneath glove compartment. Fuses are numbered from right to left (1-12 in bottom row, 13 and 14 in top row) and protect the following circuits:

① — 8 Amp. Left Front and Right Rear Tail and Marker Lights, Instrument Panel Illumination
② — 8 Amp. Left Rear and Right Front Tail and Marker Lights, License Plate Lights
③ — 16 Amp. Optional Accessory Circuit
④ — 8 Amp. Wipers, Washers

FIAT (Cont.)

⑤ — 8 Amp. Stop and Backup Lights, Gauges, Heater Fan, A/C Relay, Defogger Relay, Warning Buzzers

⑥ — 16 Amp. A/C Condenser Motor

⑦ — 16 Amp. A/C Compressor, Fast Idle Electrovalve

⑧ — 16 Amp. Defogger, Hazard Flashers

⑨ — 8 Amp. Clock, Courtesy Lights, Lighter, Antenna

⑩ — 16 Amp. Horns, Engine Fan Motor

⑪ — 8 Amp. Left Low Beam

⑫ — 8 Amp. Right Low Beam

⑬ — 8 Amp. Left High Beam, High Beam Indicator

⑭ — 8 Amp. Right High Beam

Spider 2000 — Fuse block is placed under dash on left side of steering column. One fuse (8 Amp.) is located in separate inline holder and powers Lighter. Other fuses in block are numbered from right to left and protect the following circuits:

① — 8 Amp. Dashboard Indicators, Seat Belt Timer & Relay, Stop & Back-up Lights, Gauges, Tachometer, Turn Signals

② — 8 Amp. Wiper/Washer, Heater Fan Switch, Lambda Sensor

③ — 8 Amp. Left High Beam

④ — 8 Amp. Right High Beam

⑤ — 8 Amp. Left Low Beam

⑥ — 8 Amp. Right Low Beam

⑦ — 8 Amp. Left Side Marker, Tail & License Lights

⑧ — 8 Amp. Right Side Marker, Tail & License Lights, Dashboard Lights, Lights On Indicator

⑨ — 8 Amp. Courtesy & Hazard Lights, Clock, Seat Belt Chimes, Power Antenna, High-Low Headlight Switch

⑩ — 16 Amp. Horns, Engine Fan

⑪ — 16 Amp. Optional Left Power Window

⑫ — 16 Amp. Optional Right Power Window

Strada — Fuse block is under dashboard on left side. All fuses are in the fuse block and are numbered right to left, protecting these circuits:

① — 8 Amp. Heater Fan, Warning Buzzers, Switch Illumination

② — 16 Amp. Engine Fan, Horn & Relay Winding

③ — 8 Amp. Left Headlight Low Beam

④ — 8 Amp. Right Headlight Low Beam

⑤ — 8 Amp. Left Headlight High Beam & High Beam Indicator

⑥ — 8 Amp. Right Headlight High Beam

⑦ — 8 Amp. Windshield Wiper/Washer, Rear Window Wiper

⑧ — 8 Amp. Stop Light, Back-Up Lights, GULP Valve, Heater Fan, Defogger Relay, Turn Signals, Gauges, Tachometer, Dashboard Indicators

⑨ — 8 Amp. Front Right & Left Rear Parking, Tail & Marker Lights

⑩ — 8 Amp. Instrument Lights, License Light, Cigar Lighter & Clock Lights, Front Left & Right Rear Parking, Tail & Marker Lights

⑪ — 8 Amp. Clock, Front & Rear Courtesy Lights, Cigar Lighter & Warning Buzzers

⑫ — 16 Amp. Hazard Lights, Rear Window Defogger

X1/9 — Fuse block is located in swing-down panel below glove compartment. One inline (8 Amp.) fuse protects Lighter, Clock, Courtesy Lights, and Buzzers. All other fuses are in block, numbered from left to right:

① — 8 Amp. Turn Signals, Stop Lights, Heater Fan, Defogger Relay, Switch Indicator Lights

② — 8 Amp. Gauges, Dashboard Indicators, Clock Light, Wiper/Washer, Delay Circuit, Back-Up Lights

③ — 8 Amp. Left High Beam, High Beam Indicator

④ — 8 Amp. Right High Beam

⑤ — 8 Amp. Left Low Beam

⑥ — 8 Amp. Right Low Beam

⑦ — 8 Amp. Front Left & Right Rear Marker Lights, Front Left Parking Light, Right Rear Tail Light, License Light, Cigar Lighter, Spot Light

⑧ — 8 Amp. Right Front Parking Light, Left Rear Tail Light, Clock Dimming, Right Front & Left Rear Marker Lights

⑨ — 16 Amp. Right Headlight Motor

⑩ — 16 Amp. Left Headlight Motor

⑪ — 16 Amp. Rear Defogger, Hazard Lights

⑫ — 16 Amp. Horn & Relay, Engine Fan

⑬ — 16 Amp. Spare Fuse

⑭ — 3 Amp. Spare Fuse

⑮ — 3 Amp. Headlight Closing Control Switch

⑯ — 3 Amp. Headlight Raising Control Switch

FIESTA

FUSE BLOCK

Fuse block is located under left side of instrument panel. Additional fuses are located inline to radio (2 Amp.), under cover of Defogger Relay (16 Amp.) and Cooling Fan Relay (16 Amp.). Fuses are numbered from left to right and protect the following circuits:

① — 16 Amp. Courtesy Lights, Horn, Flashers, Lighter, Stop & Turn Signal Lights

② — 8 Amp. Back-Up Lights, Heater Motor, Windshield Washer, Gauges, Warning Lights & Buzzer

③ — 16 Amp. Wipers, Rear Wiper Washer

④ — 16 Amp. Rear Window Defogger

⑤ — 8 Amp. Engine Fan, Air Conditioning

⑥ — 8 Amp. Right Side Parking, Marker & Tail Lights, License Lights

⑦ — 8 Amp. Left Side Parking, Marker & Tail Lights, Instrument Cluster Lights

⑧ — 8 Amp. High Beam Indicator Light

⑨ — 8 Amp. Low Beam Headlights

HONDA

FUSE BLOCK

Accord — Fuse block is located in a swing-down panel to left of steering column. Fuses are arranged in 2 rows. Moving from right to left, short row first, protected circuits are:

① — 10 Amp. Right High Beam
② — 10 Amp. Left High Beam
③ — 10 Amp. Right Low Beam
④ — 10 Amp. Left Low Beam
⑤ — 10 Amp. Optional A/C
⑥ — 15 Amp. Cooling Fan
⑦ — 15 Amp. Wipers, Washer
⑧ — 10 Amp. Regulator, Fuel Pump
⑨ — 10 Amp. Turn Signals, Back-Up Lights, Fuel Gauge
⑩ — 20 Amp. Heater
⑪ — 15 Amp. Radio, Defogger
⑫ — 15 Amp. Tail Lights, Gauge Light, License Light
⑬ — 10 Amp. Courtesy Light, Clock, Lighter, Horn
⑭ — 15 Amp. Hazard Flashers, Stop Lights

Civic — Fuse block is located in front of the right door hinge pillar. Block contains 13 fuses. Circuits protected are, from right to left:

① — 10 Amp. Right Low Beam Headlight
② — 10 Amp. Left Low Beam Headlight
③ — 10 Amp. Right Headlight High Beam, High Beam Indicator
④ — 10 Amp. Left Headlight High Beam
⑤ — 15 Amp. Tail, Side Marker, License, Gauge, Heater Control, Ignition Switch & Dashboard Control Lights
⑥ — 10 Amp. Courtesy Light, Trunk Light, Cigar Lighter, Clock, Warning Buzzers
⑦ — 15 Amp. Stop Lights, Horn, Hazard Flashers

⑧ — 15 Amp. Rear Defogger, Radio
⑨ — 15 Amp. Blower Motor & Resistor
⑩ — 15 Amp. Cooling Fan & Thermoswitch
⑪ — 10 Amp. Turn Signal Relay, Switch & Lights, Hazard Switch, Back-Up Lights, Gauges, Warning Indicators, Clock
⑫ — 10 Amp. Voltage Regulator, Carburetor Solenoids, Fuel Pump Cut-Off Relay & Pump
⑬ — 15 Amp. Wiper/Washer Switch, Wiper/Washer Motors

Prelude — Fuse block is located in swing-down panel to left of steering column. Fuses are arranged in 2 rows. Moving from right to left, short row first, protected circuits are:

① — 10 Amp. Right High Beam, High Beam Indicator
② — 10 Amp. Left High Beam
③ — 10 Amp. Right Low Beam
④ — 10 Amp. Left Low Beam
⑤ — 15 Amp. Heater Fan
⑥ — 15 Amp. Defogger, Radio
⑦ — Blank for Accessories
⑧ — 15 Amp. Wipers, Washers
⑨ — 10 Amp. Fuel Pump, Engine Controls
⑩ — 10 Amp. Backup Lights, Gauges, Warning Lights, Turn Signals, Buzzers, Sunroof Relay
⑪ — 15 Amp. Engine Fan
⑫ — 15 Amp. Tail, License, Side Marker, Gauge, Glove Box & Switch Lights
⑬ — 10 Amp. Courtesy Lights, Cigar Lighter, Clock, Trunk Light, Door Buzzer
⑭ — 15 Amp. Horn, Stop Lights, Hazard Lights

IN-LINE FUSES

One or two main fuses are installed near the battery to protect entire electrical system. A spare fuse is provided inside fuse block cover.

JAGUAR

FUSE BLOCK

XJ6 Models — Fuse block is located behind instrument panel. Access to fuses is obtained by turning access panel retaining pin counterclockwise until it unlocks. Panel will then drop slightly and bottom edge may be lifted clear of opening. Circuits protected are as follows:

① — 20 Amp. Fog Lights
② — 15 Amp. Hazard Warning System, Electronic Control Unit

③ — 35 Amp. Courtesy Lights, Cigar Lighter, Clock, Trunk Light, Power Antenna
④ — 15 Amp. Back-Up Lights, Gauges, Warning Indicators
⑤ — 35 Amp. Rear Window Defogger
⑥ — 20 Amp. Windshield Wipers
⑦ — Not Used
⑧ — 15 Amp. Instrument Panel Lights
⑨ — 10 Amp. Rear Fog Lights
⑩ — 15 Amp. Turn Signals
⑪ — 35 Amp. Engine Fan, Horn Relay, Windshield Wipers, Stop Lights, Mileage Counter
⑫ — 2 Amp. Cruise Control

LUV

FUSE BLOCK

Fuse block is located in engine compartment on left inner valance panel. Fuse block contains 6 fuses and 4 spares. Circuits protected by fuses are as follows:

① — 15 Amp. Tail Lights, Instrument Lights

② — 15 Amp. Horn, Stop Lights
③ — 15 Amp. Dome Light, Air Conditioning
④ — 15 Amp. Heater, Back-Up Lights, Turn Signals
⑤ — 15 Amp. Fuel Pump, Ignition Coil, Voltage Regulator
⑥ — 15 Amp. Radio, Windshield Wiper/Washer, Cigar Lighter

Fuses & Circuit Breakers

MAZDA

FUSE BLOCK

626 — Fuse block is located beneath dashboard on left side of steering column. Fuse capacities and circuits protected are marked on fuse block cover.

GLC — The fuse block is located under the instrument panel and contains 10 fuses. Circuits protected are as follows:

① — 15 Amp. Horn, Stop & Hazard Lights
② — 15 Amp. Interior Light, Cigar Lighter, Clock, Reminder Buzzer, Liftgate Release
③ — 15 Amp. Tail & License Lights, Parking & Side Marker Lights, Instrument Lights
④ — Not Used
⑤ — Not Used
⑥ — 10 Amp. Rear Window Defogger, Radio
⑦ — 10 Amp. Wipers, Washers
⑧ — 15 Amp. Rear Wiper, Washer
⑨ — 10 Amp. Back-Up Lights, Kickdown Switch, Warning Lights, Gauges, Seat Belt Warning Light, Turn Signal Lights, Tachometer
⑩ — 10 Amp. Heat Hazard Warning Light, Emission Devices, Regulator

Pickup — Fuse block is located in left rear corner of engine compartment and contains six fuses. Circuits protected by fuses in block are as follows:

① — 15 Amp. Horn, Stop Lights, Interior Light, Cigar Lighter, Hazard Flashers
② — 10 Amp. Front Parking Lights, Side Lights, License Light, Tail Lights, Instrument Panel Lights
③ — 10 Amp. Back Up Lights, Warning Lights, Fuel Gauge, Water Temperature Gauge, Turn Signals
④ — 15 Amp. Choke Switch, Voltage Regulator, Fuel Pump, Fuel Cut
⑤ — 15 Amp. Heater, Radio
⑥ — 10 Amp. Windshield Wipers & Washer

RX-7 — Fuse Panel is located beneath instrument panel on left side near kick panel. Starting from top row, right side and moving to left, circuits protected are:

① — 15 Amp. Hazard Flashers
② — 15 Amp. Dash Lights, Tail Lights, Marker Lights, License Light
③ — 20 Amp. Courtesy Light, Cigar Lighter, Liftgate Release, Buzzer
④ — 15 Amp. Horn, Stop Lights
⑤ — 15 Amp. Rear Window Defogger
⑥ — 15 Amp. Wiper/Washer
⑦ — 20 Amp. Heater, Radio
⑧ — 15 Amp. Gauges, Indicator Lights, Back-Up Lights,
⑨ — 15 Amp. Kickdown, Choke Relay
⑩ — 15 Amp. Ignition, Emission Controls, Fuel Pump

IN-LINE FUSES

A fuse block containing large in-line fuses is installed in engine compartment near battery. Fuse amperage and circuits protected is printed on fuse block cover.

MERCEDES-BENZ

FUSE BLOCK

All (Exc. 450 SL & SLC) — Main fuse block is located under hood on left inner fender panel. Fuse capacities and circuits protected are marked on fuse block cover.
450 SL & SLC — Main fuse block is located on right side kick panel. Fuse capacities and circuits protected are marked on fuse block cover.

IN-LINE FUSES

Additional fuses for optional equipment and/or standard extras such as sliding sun roof, heated rear window, radio, automatic antenna, electric windows and air conditioning are located in engine compartment.

MGB

FUSE BLOCK

Fuse block is located on right hand side of engine compartment. Fuse block contains four 35 Amp. fuses and two spares. Circuits protected are, from top to bottom:

① — 35 Amp. One Parking Light, One Tail Light, One License Plate Light, One Front & Rear Side Marker Light
② — 35 Amp. One Parking Light, One Tail Light, One Licence Plate Light, One Front & Rear Side Marker Light
③ — 35 Amp. Turn Signal Indicator, Stop Lights, Back-Up Lights, Seat Belt & Brake Warning Lights
④ — 35 Amp. Horn, Interior & Luggage Compartment Lights, Headlight Flasher, Cigar Lighter

IN-LINE FUSES

Auxiliary Equipment — A 35 Amp. in-line fuse located below fuse block protects Windshield Wiper/Washer, Heater Blower Motor and Radio.

Fan Thermostat — A 35 Amp. in-line fuse protects the fan thermostat circuit.

Hazard Warning — A 35 Amp. in-line fuse located behind Hazard Warning Switch protects Warning Lights.

Radio — A separate additional in-line fuse protects Radio.

PEUGEOT

FUSE BLOCK

504 — Fuse block is located behind lower left corner of instrument panel. Fuses are arranged in a single row and numbered from left to right. Circuits protected are:

① — 15 Amp. Parking, Marker, License & Dashboard Lights
② — 10 Amp. Clock, Courtesy Lights, Trunk Light, Horn, Cigar Lighter, Hazard Flashers, Ignition Buzzer
③ — 10 Amp. Back-Up, Stop & Low Fuel Lights, Preheat Relay, Pre-Heat Indicator Light, Temperature Indicator, Engine Fan, Tailgate Wipers, Seat Belt Buzzer & Light, Fuel Cut-Off
④ — 15 Amp. Rear Window Defogger, Windshield Wiper Motor & Relay, Washer Pump
⑤ — 10 Amp. Warning Indicators, Turn Signals, Gauges, Heater Blower Motor, Radio

505 — Fuse block is located on top of left front inner fender. Fuses are arranged in two rows with seven fuses in each row. Circuits protected are, from left to right, top row first:

① — 16 Amp. Fuel Pumps, Auxiliary Air Device, Control Pressure Regulator, Electronic Box Relay, Exhaust Overheat Warning
② — 16 Amp. Accessories, Air Conditioning, Temperature Gauge, Warning Indicators, Windshield/Washer, Turn Signals
③ — 10 Amp. Left High Beam Headlight & High Beam Indicator

④ — 5 Amp. Spare Fuse
⑤ — 10 Amp. Right Low Beam Headlight
⑥ — 16 Amp. Power Windows & Sunroof
⑦ — 16 Amp. Rear Window Defogger
⑧ — 16 Amp. Heater Blower
⑨ — 10 Amp. Stop Lights, Back-Up Lights, Engine Fan, Idle Vacuum Switch, Tachometer & Relay, Seat Belt Warning Buzzer
⑩ — 10 Amp. Parking Lights & Indicator, Instrument Panel Lights, License Lights
⑪ — 10 Amp. Right High Beam Headlight
⑫ — 10 Amp. Left Low Beam Headlight
⑬ — 15 Amp. Not Used
⑭ — 10 Amp. Clock, Cigar Lighter, Courtesy Lights, Trunk Light, Glove Box Light, Key Chime
⑮ — 16 Amp. Horns, Hazard Warning Lights

604 — Fuse block is located behind cover on left end of instrument panel. Fuses are arranged in 2 rows and numbered from left to right, top row first. Protected circuits are:

① — 10 Amp. Lighter, Horns, Flashers, Courtesy Light
② — 10 Amp. Stop and Backup Lights, Gauges, Indicator Lights, Starter Switch
③ — 16 Amp. Defogger, Indicator Lights, Accessories
④ — 16 Amp. A/C Fan, Wipers, Washers, Sunroof
⑤ — 10 Amp. Parking and Marker Lights, Dash Lights
⑥ — 16 Amp. Heater Fan and A/C Compressor Relays
⑦ — 16 Amp. Power Windows
⑧ — 16 Amp. Rear Window Lockout

PORSCHE

FUSE BLOCK

924 — Fuse block is located under instrument panel on left of steering column. First row is below relays, second row is above relays. Fuses are numbered from left to right, lower row first.

① — 8 Amp. Left Headlight (Low Beam)
② — 8 Amp. Right Headlight (Low Beam)
③ — 8 Amp. Left Headlight (High Beam)
④ — 8 Amp. Right Headlight (High Beam)
⑤ — Not Used
⑥ — 8 Amp. Interior Lights, Retractable Headlights, Brake Warning
⑦ — 8 Amp. Emergency Flashers, Clock
⑧ — 8 Amp. Turn Signal Indicators
⑨ — 8 Amp. Backup Lights, Rear Wiper, Mirrors
⑩ — 16 Amp. Fresh Air Blower
⑪ — 8 Amp. Windshield Wipers
⑫ — 8 Amp. License Plate & Luggage Compartment Lights
⑬ — 8 Amp. Side Marker Light (Right)
⑭ — 8 Amp. Side Marker Light (Left)
⑮ — 16 Amp. Fog Lights
⑯ — 8 Amp. Horn
⑰ — 16 Amp. Fuel Pump
⑱ — 16 Amp. Engine Fan, Antenna
⑲ — 25 Amp. Defogger
⑳ — 16 Amp. A/C Condenser Fan
㉑ — 25 Amp. A/C Compressor, Fresh Air Fan
㉒ — Blank
㉓ — 25 Amp. Power Windows
㉔ — Blank

911SC — Main fuse block is located inside luggage compartment on left side and contains 21 fuses. An additional fuse block is located in engine compartment on left side under regulator cover. Secondary fuse block protects Heater Fan Relay (5 Amp.), Heater Fan (25 Amp.) and Rear Window Defogger and Wiper Return (25 Amp.). Main Fuses, numbered from front of car to rear, protect the following circuits:

① — 16 Amp. Fog Lamps
② — 5 Amp. License Plate Light
③ — 5 Amp. Right Front and Rear Parking Lights
④ — 5 Amp. Left Front & Rear Parking Lights
⑤ — 8 Amp. Right Headlight Low Beam
⑥ — 8 Amp. Left Headlight Low Beam
⑦ — 8 Amp. Right Headlight High Beam
⑧ — 8 Amp. Left Headlight High Beam, High Beam Indicator
⑨ — 5 Amp. Right Front Flasher Light
⑩ — 5 Amp. Left Front Flasher Light
⑪ — 16 Amp. Flasher Relay, Stop and Backup Lights, Speed Control
⑫ — 25 Amp. Defogger Indicator and Relay, Fresh Air Blower
⑬ — 25 Amp. Windsield Wiper, Washer
⑭ — 25 Amp. Sunroof, Mirrors, Rear Wiper
⑮ — 16 Amp. Cigar Lighter, Blower Switch Control Light
⑯ — 25 Amp. Fuel Pump
⑰ — 16 Amp. Emergency Flasher
⑱ — 5 Amp. Interior, Glove Compartment, and Luggage Compartment Lighting, Clock
⑲ — 16 Amp. Headlight Washer
⑳ — 25 Amp. Blower for Air Conditioner
㉑ — 25 Amp. Power Windows

PORSCHE (Cont.)

928 — Fuse block is located in the passenger foot well and contains 34 fuses and 22 relays. Circuits protected by fuses are as follows, from left to right:

1 — 16 Amp. Fog Lights
2 — Not Connected
3 — 8 Amp. License Light, Engine Compartment Light
4 — 8 Amp. Switch Illumination Light
5 — 16 Amp. Cigar Lighter
6 — 16 Amp. Windshield Wipers
7 — Not Used
8 — 16 Amp. Sliding Roof
9 — 8 Amp. Back Up Lights, Outside Mirror
10 — 8 Amp. Brake Lights, Automatic Speed Control
11 — 8 Amp. Instrument Panel Lights
12 — 8 Amp. Instrument Warning Lights
13 — Not Connected
14 — 25 Amp. Power Seats
15 — 16 Amp. Power Antenna, Horn, Rear Wiper
16 — 25 Amp. Electric Radiator Fan
17 — 25 Amp. Heater, Air Conditioning Blower
18 — 25 Amp. Rear Window Defogger
19 — 16 Amp. Headlight Motor
20 — 16 Amp. Headlight Washer
21 — 25 Amp. Power Windows
22 — 16 Amp. Fuel Pump
23 — 8 Amp. Interior Lights, Clock
24 — 8 Amp. High Beam Headlights Left
25 — 8 Amp. High Beam Headlights Right
26 — 8 Amp. Low Beam Headlights Left
27 — 8 Amp. Low Beam Headlights Right
28 — 8 Amp. Left Side Markers
29 — 8 Amp. Right Side Markers
30 — 8 Amp. Front Left Turn Signal
31 — 8 Amp. Rear Left Turn Signal
32 — 8 Amp. Front Right Turn Signal
33 — 8 Amp. Rear Right Turn Signal
34 — Not Connected

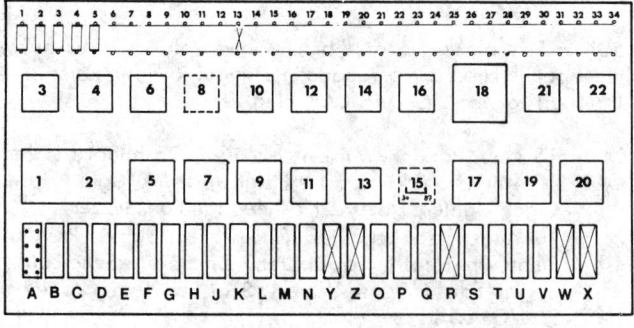

Fig. 1   Porsche 928 Fuse and Relay Block

Relay circuits are located below the fuses on the block.

① - ② — Rear Defogger
③ — Not Used
④ — Not Used
⑤ — Hazard Flasher Unit
⑥ — Window Controls
⑦ — Headlight Washer Pump
⑧ — Not Used
⑨ — Not Used
⑩ — Horns
⑪ — Not Used
⑫ — Fog Lights
⑬ — Intermittent Wiper Speed Control
⑭ — Starter Relay Bridge
⑮ — Washer Pump
⑯ — Not Used
⑰ — Fuel Pump
⑱ — Extra Cooling Fan for Air Conditioning
⑲ - ⑳ — Retractable Headlight Relay
㉑ — Fresh Air Fan
㉒ — Defroster

RENAULT

FUSE BLOCK

LeCar — Fuse block is located underneath dashboard on right side of steering column. Fuses are numbered from left to right and protect these circuits:

① — 5 Amp. Left Side Parking Lights, Dash Lights

② — 5 Amp. Lighter, Right Parking Lights
③ — 8 Amp. Wipers, Washers
④ — 5 Amp. Courtesy Light
⑤ — 8 Amp. Heater Fan, Radio
⑥ — 5 Amp. Turn Signals
⑦ — Blank
⑧ — 16 Amp. Backup Lights, Defogger, Brake Lights, Rear Wiper, A/C Relay, Speed Sensor

SAAB

FUSE BLOCK

99 Models — Electrical system is protected by 12 fuses. Fuse block is mounted on the right wheel housing in the engine compartment. All parts of the system are fused except the headlights and the ignition system. A label by the fuse box shows which fuses protect which circuits.

900 Models — Fuse block is located in engine compartment near left rear corner. Fuse capacities and circuits protected are as follows:

① — 8 Amp. Right High Beam
② — 8 Amp. Left High Beam
③ — 8 Amp. Right Low Beam
④ — 8 Amp. Left Low Beam
⑤ — 16 Amp. Engine Fan
⑥ — 16 Amp. Defogger
⑦ — 5 Amp. Interior Lights
⑧ — 16 Amp. Fuel Pump, Injection Engines
⑨ — 8 Amp. Hazard Flashers
⑩ — 5 Amp. Stop Lights
⑪ — 16 Amp. A/C Fan
⑫ — 5 Amp. Right Parking and Taillights

SAAB (Cont.)

⑬ — 5 Amp. Left Parking and Taillights
⑭ — 8 Amp. Horn
⑮ — Blank
⑯ — 16 Amp. Heated Driver's Seat
⑰ — 25 Amp. Heater Fan

⑱ — 8 Amp. Spare
⑲ — 8 Amp. Warning Lights
⑳ — 8 Amp. Turn Signals
㉑ — 8 Amp. Wipers
㉒ — 8 Amp. Cornering Lights

SUBARU

FUSE BLOCK

The fuse block is located underneath dashboard on left side. The heater is protected by a 15 Amp. inline fuse. All other circuits are fuses through the block. Protected circuits are:

① — 25 Amp. Fan Motor
② — 15 Amp. Radio, Cigar Lighter
③ — 15 Amp. Wipers, Cooling Fan

④ — 15 Amp. Low Beam Headlights
⑤ — 15 Amp. High Beam Headlights
⑥ — 15 Amp. Ignition Coil, Fuel Pump, Warning & Indicator Lights, Gauges
⑦ — 15 Amp. Turn Signals, Back-Up Lights, Defogger
⑧ — 15 Amp. License, Tail & Illumination Lights
⑨ — 15 Amp. Horn, Stop Lights, Hazard Lights, Dome & Trunk Light, Door Ajar Warning
⑩ — 25 Amp. Tail & Parking Lights

TOYOTA

FUSE BLOCK

Celica — Main fuse block is located on left side of instrument panel behind conver. In addition, a smaller fuse block is located in engine compartment on left side. Fuses in main block are arranged in three rows. Fuses in engine fuse block are arranged in two rows. Moving from top-to-bottom, and left-to-right, fuses are as follows:

Main Block

① — 5 Amp. Courtesy Lights, Trunk Light, Clock
② — 15 Amp. Tail, Parking, License, Glove Box, Transmission Selector, Instrument Panel, Heater Panel & Marker Lights. Cigar Lighter
③ — 15 Amp. Gauges, Warning Indicators, Back-Up Lights
④ — 15 Amp. Turn Signals, Wiper/Washer
⑤ — 15 Amp. Alternator, Emission Controls
⑥ — 7.5 Amp. Radio & Tape Player
⑦ — 15 Amp. Cigar Lighter

Engine Fuse Block

① — 15 Amp. Heater, Air Conditioning
② — 5 Amp. Discharge Warning Light, Charge Relay, Electric Choke Relay
③ — 15 Amp. Horn, Stop Lights, Hazard Flashers
④ — 15 Amp. Right Side Headlights
⑤ — 15 Amp. Left Side Headlights

Corolla — Main fuse block is located on left side of instrument panel. In addition, two other fuse blocks are used. One is located on left side kick panel and contains five fuses. The other is located in the engine compartment on left side, and contains seven fuses. Left side kick panel fuse block has circuits protected listed on block cover. Other fuse blocks protect the following circuits, starting from top-to-bottom, left-to-right.

Main Fuse Block

① — 20 Amp. Wiper/Washer, Rear Wiper/Washer, Wiper Indicator Light
② — 5 Amp. Radio & Tape Player

③ — Not Used
④ — 10 Amp. Gauges, Warning Indicator, Back-Up Lights
⑤ — 10 Amp. Cigar Lighter, Clock
⑥ — 5 Amp. Turn Signals, Turn Signal Indicators
⑦ — 10 Amp. Discharge Warning Light, Main Relay, Choke Relay, Canister Control Valve, Emission Control Computer, Cooling Fan Relay

Engine Fuse Block

① — 15 Amp. Left Side Head Lights
② — 15 Amp. Right Side Head Lights
③ — 10 Amp. Hazard Warning Flashers, Horn
④ — 10 Amp. Discharge Warning Light, Charge Light Relay, Choke Relay
⑤ — 15 Amp. (2) Heater Relay, Heater Motor, Air Conditioning
⑥ — 10 Amp. Voltage Regulator, Charge Relay, Fuel Cut Solenoid, Vacuum Switching Valve

Corona — Fuses are located in 2 separate fuse blocks, one near battery in engine compartment, and one on left side of dashboard. Circuits protected are:

Engine Compartment

① — 15 Amp. Right Headlights
② — 15 Amp. Left Headlights
③ — 20 Amp. Wipers, Washers (Front and Rear)
④ — 10 Amp. Engine Voltage Regulator
⑤ — 10 Amp. Horns, Hazard Flashers

Dashboard

① — 10 Amp. Stop Lights
② — 5 Amp. Panel Lights
③ — 5 Amp. Right Marker and Taillights
④ — 5 Amp. Left Marker and Taillights
⑤ — 15 Amp. Lighter, Clock, Antenna, Light Reminder
⑥ — 10 Amp. Turn Signals
⑦ — 10 Amp. Gauges, Warning Lights, Backup Lights
⑧ — 20 Amp. Defogger
⑨ — 5 Amp. Radio
⑩ — 5 Amp. Clock, Courtesy Lights
⑪ — 20 Amp. Heater Fan, A/C Compressor Clutch
⑫ — 10 Amp. Engine and Main Relays

TOYOTA (Cont.)

Cressida — Fuse panel is behind cover on left side of instrument panel. Circuits protected by inline fuses are Lighter and Antenna (15 Amp.), Backup Lights, Gauges, Overdrive, Warning Lights (15 Amp.), Clock, Courtesy Lights (5 Amp.) and Air Conditioner (10 Amp.). Fuses in block are numbered from left to right and protect the following circuits:

① — 30 Amp. Rear Window Defogger
② — 15 Amp. Tail, Marker, Parking, Glove Box & Instrument Panel Lights. Gauges
③ — 15 Amp. Stop Lights, Hazard Flashers, Key Buzzer
④ — 5 Amp. Radio, Tape Player, Clock
⑤ — 15 Amp. Turn Signals, Wipers, Washers
⑥ — 15 Amp. Engine Controls
⑦ — 15 Amp. Left Headlight
⑧ — 15 Amp. Right Headlight

Pickup — Fuse block is located on left side of drivers compartment under instrument panel. Circuits protected are:

① — 10 Amp. Right Headlight
② — 10 Amp. Left Headlight
③ — 15 Amp. Horn, Hazard Flashers
④ — 10 Amp. Turn Signals
⑤ — 10 Amp. Gauges, Heater Relay, Backup Lights
⑥ — 15 Amp. Engine Controls, Fuel Pump
⑦ — 15 Amp. Wipers, Washers
⑧ — 10 Amp. Lighter
⑨ — 10 Amp. Stop Lights
⑩ — 15 Amp. Taillights, Dashboard Lights, Marker Lights
⑪ — 15 Amp. Heater, A/C
⑫ — 5 Amp. Radio, Tape Player
⑬ — 5 Amp. Courtesy Light, Clock

Land Cruiser — Main fuse block is located under left side of instrument panel. Two 5 Amp. Ammeter fuses are located near battery, the 15 Amp. A/C fuse is near heater fan motor, and the 5 Amp. Engine Fan fuse is behind instrument panel. Fuses and circuits in the main block are:

① — 15 Amp. Tail, Parking, Marker, License, Dome & Instrument Panel Lights.
② — 15 Amp. Horn, Stop Lights, Hazard Flashers, Engine Fan
③ — 15 Amp. Headlights
④ — 5 Amp. Radio
⑤ — 15 Amp. Lighter
⑥ — 20 Amp. Heater Fan, Gauges, Backup Lights, Buzzers
⑦ — 20 Amp. Turn Signals, Wipers, Washers, Tailgate Relay
⑧ — 15 Amp. Engine Controls

Supra — Main fuse block is located on left side of instrument panel. An additional fuse block is located on right side of engine compartment. The rear window defogger is protected by a circuit breaker located in right side kick panel. Fuses in block are arranged in three rows. Starting from left-to-right, top-to-bottom, circuits protected are as follows:

Main Fuse Block

① — 5 Amp. Interior Lights, Luggage Compartment Light & Clock
② — 15 Amp. Tail Lights Relay, Tail Lights, Parking Lights, License Lights, Glove Box Light, Lighter, Heater Control Light, Transmission Indicator Light, Map Light, Instrument Panel Lights, Marker Lights
③ — 30 Amp. Power Windows
④ — 15 Amp. Gauges, Warning Indicators, Cruise Control, Defogger Switch, Illuminated Entry Relay, Overdrive Solenoid, Heater Relay, Back-Up Lights
⑤ — 15 Amp. Turn Signals, Wipers, Washer
⑥ — 15 Amp. Alternator, Discharge Warning Light Relay, Electronic Fuel Injection Relay, Emission Control System
⑦ — 7.5 Amp. Radio & Tape Player
⑧ — 15 Amp. Cigar Lighter

Engine Fuse Block

① — 15 Amp. Stop Lights, Horn, Flashers
② — 15 Amp. Heater, Air Conditioning
③ — 15 Amp. Right Side High & Low Headlights
④ — 15 Amp. Left Side High & Low Headlights

Tercel — Main fuse block is located at left side of instrument panel. In addition, a fuse block is located on left side of engine compartment, and circuits protected and fuse amperage are shown on fuse block cover. Circuits protected in main fuse block are as follows, from left-to-right, top-to-bottom.

① — 5 Amp. Radio
② — 10 Amp. Cigar Lighter
③ — 30 Amp. Rear Window Defogger
④ — 10 Amp. Turn Signals, Back-Up Lights, Gauges, Warning Indicators, Heater & Defogger Relays
⑤ — 5 Amp. Ignition Relay, Fuel Cut Solenoid
⑥ — 10 Amp. Stop Lights
⑦ — 20 Amp. Heater, Air Conditioning
⑧ — 15 Amp. Tail, License & Instrument Panel Lights
⑨ — 5 Amp. Dome Light, Trunk Light, Clock
⑩ — 10 Amp. Right Side Headlight
⑪ — 10 Amp. Left Side Headlight
⑫ — 5 Amp. Discharge Warning Light
⑬ — 15 Amp. Hazard Flasher, Horn
⑭ — 20 Amp. Wiper/Washer, Rear Wiper/Washer
⑮ — 20 Amp. Alternator Regulator, Engine Cooling Fan

FUSIBLE LINKS

All Models — A fusible link is located in main battery feed wire near the battery. Protects all circuits except for starter motor.

TRIUMPH

FUSE BLOCK

Spitfire — Fuse block is mounted on left hand side of firewall in engine compartment, adjacent to clutch master cylinder. Block contains 3 fuses and 2 spares. Circuits protected are as follows:

① — 35 Amp. Windshield Wipers, Gauges, Stop & Reverse Lights, Turn Signals, Seat Belt Warning Light
② — 10 Amp. Side Marker Lights, Front Parking Lights, Tail Lights, License Light, Instrument Panel Lights
③ — 35 Amp. Headlight Flasher, Courtesy Light, Horn, Key & Hazard Warning Lights

TRIUMPH (Cont.)

TR7 & TR8 — Fuse block is located on a relay plate and is accessible after removal of cover panel at front of glove box. Fuses are arranged in two rows of six. Circuits protected, from top left to right are as follows:

① — 25 Amp. Left Headlight Low Beam
② — 25 Amp. Back-Up Lights, Wiper Motor
③ — 25 Amp. Left Headlight High Beam
④ — 35 Amp. Air Conditioning Clutch Relay, Blower Fan
⑤ — 25 Amp. Right Headlight High Beam

⑥ — 25 Amp. Right Headlight Low Beam
⑦ — 35 Amp. Air Conditioning Fan Relay
⑧ — 15 Amp. Rear Window Defogger
⑨ — 50 Amp. Horn, Cigar Lighter, Hazard Warning, Courtesy Lights, Fog Lights, Power Antenna
⑩ — 15 Amp. Front Right Parking & Marker Lights, Instrument Panel Dimmer
⑪ — 15 Amp. Front Left Parking & Marker Lights
⑫ — 35 Amp. Air Conditioning Fan Relay

VOLKSWAGEN

FUSE BLOCK

All Models Except Vanagon — Fuse block is located under dashboard on left side and contains 15 fuses in one centralized unit. In addition, fuses are located above the fuse block to protect the following circuits: Rear Window Wipers (8 Amp. Rabbit & Scirocco), Electric Fuel Pump (16 Amp. All Models), Air Conditioning (25 Amp. All Models), Radio (5 Amp. Rabbit & Pickup). Circuits protected by fuses in block are as follows:

① — 8 Amp. Left Headlight Low Beam
② — 8 Amp. Right Headlight Low Beam
③ — 8 Amp. Left Headlight High Beam and Indicator
④ — 8 Amp. Right Headlight High Beam
⑤ — 16 Amp. Rear Window Defogger (Not Used on Pickup)
⑥ — 8 Amp. Stop Lights, Hazard Warning Flasher
⑦ — 8 Amp. Interior Lights, Clock, Cigar Lighter
⑧ — 8 Amp. Turn Signal System
⑨ — 8 Amp. Back-Up Lights, Horn, Transmission Shift Indicator (Dasher), Choke (Rabbit)
⑩ — 16 Amp. Fresh Air Fan
⑪ — 8 Amp. Windshield Wiper & Washer
⑫ — 8 Amp. Luggage Compartment & License Plate Lights

⑬ — 8 Amp. Right Parking, Tail & Side Marker Lights
⑭ — 8 Amp. Left Parking, Tail & Side Marker Lights
⑮ — 25 Amp. Radiator Fan

Vanagon — Fuse block is located under dashboard on left side of steering column. Fuse block contains 12 circuits. In addition, a 16. Amp fuse is located at right side of fuse panel to protect blower fan. Circuits protected in main fuse block are as follows:

① — 8 Amp. Left Tail, Parking & Marker Lights
② — 8 Amp. Right Tail, Parking, Marker & License Lights
③ — 8 Amp. Low Beam Headlight Left
④ — 8 Amp. Low Beam Headlight Right
⑤ — 8 Amp. Left High Beam Headlight & Indicator
⑥ — 8 Amp. Right High Beam Headlight
⑦ — 8 Amp. Accessories
⑧ — 8 Amp. Cigar Lighter, Stop Lights, Interior Lights
⑨ — 16 Amp. Hazard Warning Lights
⑩ — 16 Amp. Windshield Wiper/Washer, Rear Window Defogger
⑪ — 8 Amp. Turn Signals
⑫ — 8 Amp. Horn, Back-Up Lights

VOLVO

FUSE BLOCK

All Models — Fuse block is located in left kick panel behind cover. Fuses are numbered from top to bottom and space is provided for spare fuses at bottom of block. Circuits protected are as follows:

① — 8 Amp. Lighter, Rear Wipers, Mirrors, Radio, Cruise Control
② — 16 Amp. Horn, Wipers, Washers
③ — 16 Amp. Heater Fan
④ — 8 Amp. Warning Buzzers
⑤ — 8 Amp. Fuel Pump (Feed Pump)
⑥ — 8 Amp. Brake Lights, Courtesy Light Relay

⑦ — 16 Amp. Main Fuel Pump
⑧ — 8 Amp. Courtesy Lights, Power Antenna, Locking System
⑨ — 8 Amp. Hazard Flashers
⑩ — 16 Amp. Power Windows, Heated Driver Seat
⑪ — 16 Amp. Overdrive, Defogger
⑫ — 8 Amp. Backup Lights, Power Window Relay, Heated Driver's Seat, A/C
⑬ — 8 Amp. Gauges, Turn Signals, Belt Warning, Fuel Injection Relay
⑭ — Spare
⑮ — 8 Amp. Left Parking and Marker Lights, License Light
⑯ — 8 Amp. Right Parking and Marker Lights, Headlight Buzzer, Instrument Panel Lights

Section 5
ENGINES

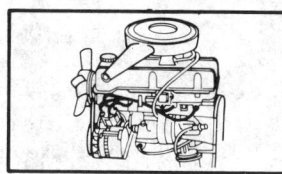

Contents

NOTE — ALSO SEE GENERAL INDEX.

Engine Trouble Shooting

GASOLINE ENGINE TROUBLE SHOOTING

The following Trouble Shooting guide covers all mechanical problems which relate to all engines in general. For specific Trouble Shooting problems relating to Diesel engines, see Diesel Engine Trouble Shooting in this section. For Carburetor or Ignition problems in all engines, see Tune-Up Trouble Shooting in Section 1.

CONDITION & POSSIBLE CAUSE	CONDITION & POSSIBLE CAUSE

Engine Lopes While Idling

- Intake manifold-to-head leaks.
- Blown head gasket.
- Worn timing gears, chain or sprocket.
- Worn camshaft lobes.
- Overheated engine.
- Blocked crankcase vent valve.
- Leaking EGR valve.
- Faulty fuel pump.

Engine Has Low Power

- Leaking fuel pump.
- Sticking valves, weak valve springs, incorrect valve timing or worn camshaft lobes.
- Excessive piston-to-bore clearance.
- Blown head gasket.
- Improper power steering glow control valve operation.
- Clutch slipping on manual transmission.
- Engine overheating.
- Improper pressure regulator valve operation on automatic transmission.
- Improper automatic transmission fluid level.
- Improper operation of diverter valve.
- Vacuum leaks.
- Leaking piston rings.

Faulty High Speed Operation

- Low fuel pump volume.
- Leaking engine valves, or faulty valve springs.
- Incorrect valve timing.
- Intake manifold restricted.
- Worn distributor shaft.

Faulty Acceleration

- Improper fuel pump stroke.
- Incorrect basic ignition timing.
- Inoperative pump discharge check ball or needle.
- Faulty elastomer valve.
- Worn or damaged pump diaphragm or piston.
- Leaking engine valves.

Intake Backfire

- Improper ignition timing.
- Faulty accelerator pump discharge.
- Improper choke operation.
- Defective EGR valve.
- Too lean fuel mixture.
- Initial choke valve clearance too large.

Exhaust Backfire

- Vacuum leak.
- Faulty diverter valve.
- Faulty choke operation.
- Exhaust system leak.

Engine Detonation

- Overadvanced timing or faulty ignition system.
- Spark plugs loose or cracked.
- Fuel lines, fuel filter or fuel pump clogged or faulty.
- EGR valve inoperative.
- PCV system inoperative.
- Vacuum leaks.
- Excessive combustion chamber deposits.
- Leaking, sticking or broken valves.

External Oil Leakage

- Improperly seated fuel pump, or worn gasket.
- Improperly seated or broken push rod cover gasket.
- Improperly seated or broken oil filter gasket.
- Improperly seated or broken oil pan gasket, or bent oil pan gasket surface.
- Improperly seated or broken timing chain cover gasket.
- Improperly seated or worn rear main bearing oil seal.
- Loose oil line plugs.
- Improperly seated oil pan drain plug.
- Obstructed camshaft rear bearing drain hole.
- Loose rocker arm cover, or broken cover gasket.
- Oil pressure sending switch leaking.

GASOLINE ENGINE TROUBLE SHOOTING (Cont.)

CONDITION & POSSIBLE CAUSE	CONDITION & POSSIBLE CAUSE

Excessive Oil Consumption

- Intake or exhaust valve "O" ring seal damaged or has excessive looseness.
- Worn valve stems or guides.
- Plugged oil drain back holes.
- Improper PCV valve operation.
- Engine oil level too high.
- Engine oil too thin.
- Valve stem oil deflectors missing or damaged.
- Piston rings improperly installed or incorrect size.
- Piston rings out-of-round, broken or scored.
- Piston ring gaps not staggered.
- Piston ring tension insufficient due to engine overheating.
- Piston ring grooves or oil return slots clogged.
- Piston rings sticking in ring grooves.
- Ring grooves worn excessively.
- Compression rings installed upside down.
- Excessively worn or scored cylinder walls.
- Mismatch of oil ring expander and rail.
- Intake gasket dowels too long.
- Excessive main or connecting rod bearing clearance.

No Oil Pressure

- Low oil level.
- Oil pressure gauge or sending unit broken.
- Oil pump malfunction.
- Oil pressure relief valve sticking.
- Oil passages on pressure side of pump blocked.
- Oil pickup screen or tube blocked.
- Loose oil inlet tube.
- Excessive clearance at main or connecting rod bearing.
- Loose camshaft bearings.
- Internal leakage at oil passages.

Low Oil Pressure

- Low engine oil level, or engine oil too thin.
- Oil pressure relief spring weak or stuck.
- Oil pickup tube and screen blocked, or has air leak.
- Excessive oil pump clearance.
- Excessive main, rod or camshaft bearing clearance.

High Oil Pressure

- Improper grade of oil.
- Oil pressure gauge or sending unit inaccurate.
- Oil pressure relief valve sticking closed.

Noisy Main Bearings

- Inadequate oil supply.
- Excessive main bearing clearance.
- Excessive crankshaft end play.
- Loose flywheel or torque converter.
- Loose or damaged vibration damper.
- Eccentric or out-of-round crankshaft journals.
- Excessive belt tension.

Noisy Connecting Rods

- Inadequate oil supply.
- Excessive bearing clearance or missing bearing.
- Crankshaft connecting rod journal out-of-round.
- Misaligned connecting rod or cap.
- Improperly tightened connecting rod bolts.

Noisy Pistons and Rings

- Excessive piston-to-cylinder wall clearance.
- Cylinder walls excessively tapered or out-of-round.
- Piston ring broken.
- Piston pin loose or seized.
- Connecting rods misaligned.
- Piston ring side clearance excessively loose or tight.
- Excessive carbon build-up on piston.

Noisy Valve Train Components

- Insufficient oil supply.
- Worn or bent push rods.
- Worn rocker arms, or bridged pivots.
- Dirt or chips in hydraulic valve lifters.
- Excessive valve lifter leak down.
- Valve lifter face worn.
- Broken or cocked valve springs.
- Excessive valve stem-to-guide clearance.
- Valve bent.
- Loose rocker arms.
- Excessive valve seat runout.
- Missing valve lock.
- Push rod rubbing or contacting cylinder head.

Engine Trouble Shooting

GASOLINE ENGINE TROUBLE SHOOTING (Cont.)

CONDITION & POSSIBLE CAUSE	CONDITION & POSSIBLE CAUSE

Noisy Valve Train Components (Cont.)

- Excessively worn camshaft lobes.
- Plugged valve lifter oil feed holes.
- Faulty valve lifter check ball.
- Rocker arm retaining nut installed upside down.
- Valve lifters incorrectly fitted to bore size.
- Faulty valve lifter plunger, or push rod seat.

Noisy Valves

- Improper valve lash.
- Excessively worn, dirty or faulty valve lifters.
- Worn valve guides.
- Excessive runout of valve seat or valve face.
- Worn camshaft lobes.
- Loose rocker arm studs.
- Bent push rods.
- Broken valve springs.

Burned, Sticking or Broken Valves

- Weak valve springs.
- Improper valve lifter clearance.
- Improper valve guide clearance, or worn guides.

- Out-of-round valve seats, or improper valve seat width.
- Deposits or gum formation on valve stems, seats or guides.
- Warped valves or faulty valve forgings.
- Exhaust back pressure.
- Improper spark timing.

Broken Pistons and/or Rings

- Undersize pistons.
- Wrong type or size of rings.
- Tapered or eccentric cylinder bore.
- Improper connecting rod alignment.
- Excessively worn ring grooves.
- Improperly assembled piston pins.
- Insufficient ring gap clearance.
- Engine overheating.
- Incorrect ignition timing.

Excessive Exhaust Noise

- Leaks at exhaust pipe joints.
- Burned or blown out muffler or exhaust pipe.
- Exhaust pipe leaking at manifold flange.
- Exhaust manifold cracked or broken.
- Leak between manifold and cylinder head.
- Obstruction in muffler or tail pipe.

DIESEL ENGINE TROUBLE SHOOTING

Diesel engine mechanical diagnosis is the same as that for gasoline engines for such items as noisy lifters, rod bearings, main bearings, valves, rings and pistons. The following trouble shooting guide cover those items which apply only to diesel engines.

Engine Does Not Crank

- Loose or corroded battery cables, or dead batteries.
- Loose starter connections or faulty starter.

Engine Cranks Slowly but Does Not Start

- Loose or corroded battery cables, or batteries do not have a sufficient charge.
- Wrong weight engine oil in engine.

Engine Cranks Normally but Does Not Start

- Glow plugs not functioning.
- Glow plug control system not functioning.
- Fuel not being injected into cylinders.
- No fuel going to injection pump.
- Fuel filter blocked.
- Fuel tank filter blocked.
- Fuel pump not operating.
- Fuel return system blocked.
- No voltage to fuel solenoid.
- Incorrect or contaminated fuel.

DIESEL ENGINE TROUBLE SHOOTING (Cont.)

CONDITION & POSSIBLE CAUSE	CONDITION & POSSIBLE CAUSE

Engine Cranks Normally but Does Not Start (Cont.)

- Incorrect injection pump timing.
- Low compression.
- Injection pump malfunction.

Engine Starts but Will Not Run at Idle

- Incorrect slow idle adjustment.
- Fast idle solenoid not functioning.
- Fuel return system blocked.
- Glow plugs turning off too soon.
- Injection pump timing incorrect.
- Insufficient fuel going to injection pump.
- Incorrect or contaminated fuel.
- Low compression.
- Injection pump malfunction.
- Fuel solenoid closes in "RUN" position.

Engine Starts and Idles Rough Without Abnormal Smoke or Noise

- Incorrect slow idle adjustment.
- Injection line fuel leaks.
- Fuel return system blocked.
- Air in fuel system.
- Incorrect or contaminated fuel.
- Injector nozzle malfunction.

Engine Starts and Idles Rough Without Abnormal Smoke or Noise, but Clears After Warm-Up

- Injection pump timing incorrect.
- Engine has not fully broken in.
- Air in fuel system.
- Injector nozzle malfunction.

Engine Misfires Above Idle but Idles Correctly

- Blocked fuel filter.
- Injection pump timing incorrect.
- Incorrect or contaminated fuel.

Engine Will Not Return to Idle

- External linkage binding or adjusted wrong.
- Fast idle adjustment incorrect.
- Internal injection pump malfunction.

Fuel Leaking on Ground

- Loose or broken fuel line or connection.
- Internal injection pump seal leak.

Knocking Noise from Cylinders

- Injector nozzles sticking open.
- Very low nozzle opening pressure.

Noticeable Loss of Engine Power

- Restricted air intake.
- EGR valve malfunction.
- Restricted or damaged exhaust system.
- Blocked fuel tank filter
- Blocked fuel filter, or fuel tank vacuum vent in gas cap.
- Restricted fuel supply from tank to injection pump.
- Restricted fuel return system.
- Incorrect or contaminated fuel.
- External compression leaks.
- Blocked injector nozzles.
- Low compression.

Excessive Black Smoke and Loud Engine Noise

- Basic timing incorrect.
- EGR valve malfunction.
- Injector pump housing pressure not to specifications.
- Internal injection pump malfunction.

Engine Overheating

- Cooling system leaks.
- Belt slipping or damaged.
- Thermostat stuck closed.
- Head gasket leaking

Oil Light On at Idle

- Oil cooler, or oil cooler line restricted.
- Low oil pump pressure.

Engine Will Not Shut Off

- Injector pump fuel solenoid doesn't return fuel valve to "OFF" position.

VACUUM PUMP DIAGNOSIS

Excessive Noise

- Loose screws between pump and drive assembly.
- Loose tube on pump assembly.
- Valves not functioning properly.

Oil Leakage

- Loose end plug.
- Bad crimp.

4000 4 CYLINDER

ENGINE CODING

ENGINE IDENTIFICATION

Engine number is stamped on side of engine block near distributor. Number prefix indicates the following application:

Engine Identification Codes	
Application	**Engine Code**
Federal .... YG	
Calif. .... YK	

ENGINE & CYLINDER HEAD

ENGINE

NOTE — *Unless otherwise specified, leave all fuel injection lines connected to components.*

Removal — 1) Disconnect battery ground strap. Remove grille, condenser from radiator, and air duct from throttle valve housing. Remove hose from air duct to auxiliary air regulator. Remove fuel distributor, air flow sensor, fuel injectors, and air cleaner as one unit. Remove cold start valve.

NOTE — *Cap or plug fuel injectors and cold start valve.*

2) Remove front engine mount. Loosen nuts on outer half of crankshaft pulley and remove "V" belt. Discharge refrigerant from air conditioning system and remove air conditioning lines from compressor. Support bracket and plug all open connections.

3) Disconnect wire to compressor clutch. Remove crankcase vent hose connection from valve cover and move air conditioning hoses to one side, away from engine. Remove upper compressor mounting bolts and 3 lower compressor mounting bolts. Remove compressor from vehicle.

4) Open heater control valve fully. Remove cap from coolant expansion tank. Drain coolant from engine by removing hoses, saving coolant for later installation. Remove upper radiator hose from engine, lower radiator hose from radiator, and plug from radiator fan.

5) Disconnect plug from radiator thermo switch. Remove both rubber mounts and lift radiator, fan and fan shroud out of vehicle as an assembly.

6) Disconnect clutch cable. Disconnect wiring. Remove control pressure regulator, leaving fuel lines connected. Remove air hose, if equipped. Unplug blue wire from alternator at plug between battery and rear of engine. Remove charcoal filter hose at intake air duct.

7) Disconnect wiring on oil pressure switch and coolant temperature gauge sender. Remove wires from ignition coil. Remove heater hoses.

8) Remove throttle cable. Remove vacuum hoses from the following:

- Ignition distributor retard unit (clear hose).
- Ignition distributor advance unit (violet hose), leading to charcoal filter.

- Throttle valve housing (gray hose) leading to vacuum amplifier.
- EGR temperature control valve (blue angled connection) to vacuum amplifier.
- Throttle valve housing stage 1 (red hose) to vacuum amplifier.
- Intake manifold (hose leading to brake booster).

9) Pull out fuel injectors and remove cold start valve. Disconnect hose from auxiliary air duct. Remove 3 upper engine-to-transmission bolts. Remove right and left engine mount nuts. Remove exhaust pipe attaching nuts from manifold and remove pipe. Remove cover plate.

10) Remove front engine mount. Disconnect starter cables and label for later installation. Remove starter. Remove 2 lower engine-to-transmission bolts. Loosen right and left engine mount nuts on subframe.

11) Remove bolt for front exhaust pipe support. Install transmission support tool. Install engine lift chain (US 1105). Lift engine until weight is taken off engine mounts. Adjust support bar to contact transmission.

12) Pry engine apart from transmission. Carefully lift engine out of engine compartment, using caution not to damage transmission mainshaft, clutch and body. Mount engine on stand.

Installation — To install engine, reverse removal procedure. When tightening engine mount and subframe bolts, run engine at idle speed. Tighten front mount bolts to 18 ft. lbs. (2.5 mkg) and right and left mount nuts to 25 ft. lbs. (3.5 mkg). Adjust throttle and clutch cables, align exhaust system components and refill coolant expansion tank.

CYLINDER HEAD

Removal & Installation — 1) Disconnect battery ground cable. Drain coolant system and disconnect hoses which are connected to cylinder head. Disconnect exhaust pipe and electrical wires. Disengage accelerator linkage and disconnect at holder. Loosen alternator tensioner and remove "V" belt and camshaft drive belt.

2) Loosen head bolts in reverse of tightening sequence shown in *Fig. 1.* To install, ensure that cylinder head and block mating surfaces are clean. Install cylinder head gasket DRY, using no sealant. Use only polygon cylinder head bolts. Install bolts 8 and 10 first to center cylinder head. Tighten head bolts in sequence illustrated as follows: Step 1 — 29 ft. lbs. (4.0 mkg); Step 2 — 43 ft. lbs. (6.0 mkg); Step 3 — 54 ft. lbs. (7.5 mkg) plus ¼ turn (90°) more.

NOTE — *DO NOT torque polygon cylinder head bolts after first 1000 miles, nor after 1000 miles following repair.*

3) When installing "V" belt, adjust tension so that thumb pressure permits ⅜-⁹⁄₁₆" (10-15 mm) deflection of belt inward, midway between alternator and crankshaft belt pulley. When installing camshaft timing belt, adjust tensioning arm until belt can be turned 90° with thumb and index finger at a point midway between camshaft sprocket and intermediate sprocket.

4000 4 CYLINDER (Cont.)

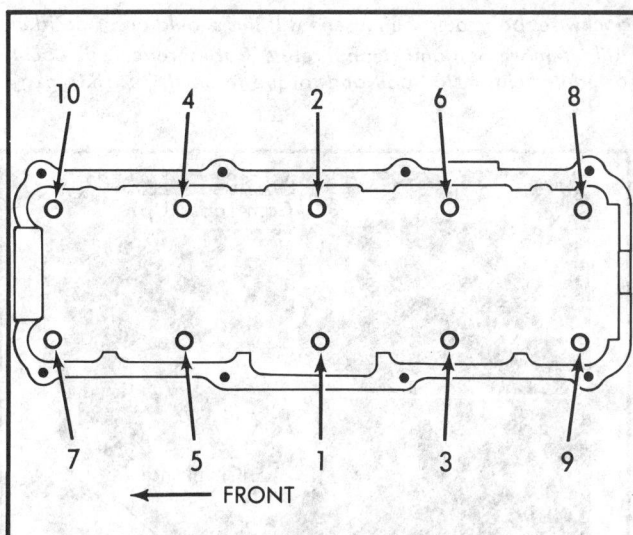

**Fig. 1   Cylinder Head Tightening Sequence
(Reverse Sequence When Removing)**

CAMSHAFT

TIMING BELT

1) Remove radiator grille. Loosen alternator mounting bolts and remove "V" belt. Remove camshaft belt guard. Loosen mounting nut of camshaft belt tensioner arm and remove tension from belt. Slide belt forward off camshaft sprocket.

2) Install new belt and adjust tensioner arm until belt can be turned 90° with thumb and index finger at a point midway between camshaft sprocket and intermediate sprocket. Check valve timing.

CAMSHAFT

Removal — Remove bearing caps 1, 3, and 5. Diagonally loosen bearing caps 2 and 4 in steps. Remove caps and lift out camshaft.

Installation — To install, lubricate bearing shells, journals and contact faces of caps. Install caps 1, 3, and 5, observing off-center bearing position. See *Fig*. 2. Numbers on bearing caps are not always on same side. Tighten bearing caps diagonally. Install caps 2 and 4 and tighten diagonally.

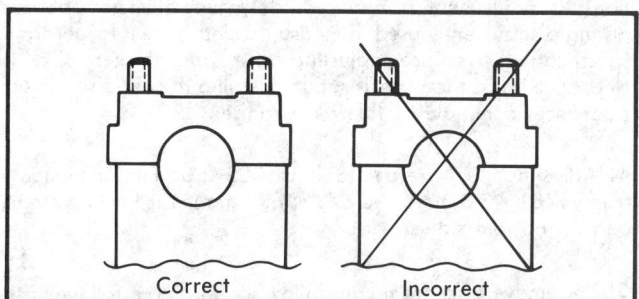

Fig. 2   Checking Bearing Cap Alignment

CAMSHAFT OIL SEAL

Removal — Remove upper drive belt cover. Set crankshaft to TDC on cylinder 1. Loosen drive belt and remove camshaft

sprocket. Remove Woodruff key. Using special tool (10-219), remove oil seal.

Installation — Install protective sleeve (10-203) over camshaft. Push seal over sleeve, and using remainder of special tool (10-203), press seal in until flush. Check camshaft end play with cam followers removed. Maximum end play is .006" (.15 mm). Reinstall cam followers.

VALVE TIMING

1) Turn camshaft sprocket until punch mark on rear of camshaft sprocket is aligned with upper edge of lower drive belt cover (arrow) or valve cover gasket on left side of engine. See *Fig*. 3.

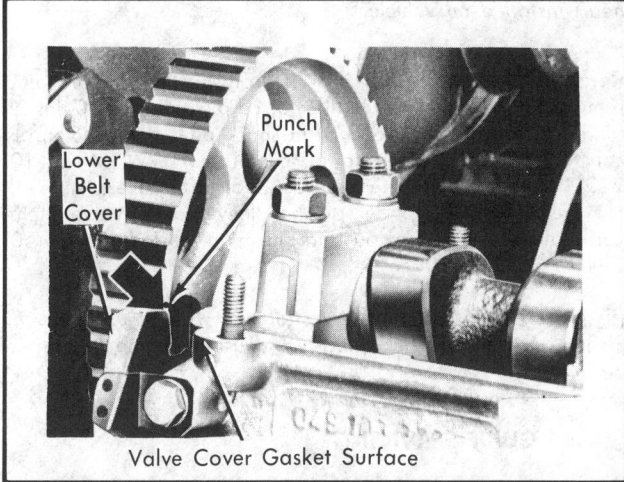

Fig. 3   Camshaft Drive Sprocket Timing Mark Alignment

2) Turn crankshaft pulley and intermediate shaft sprocket until notch in crankshaft pulley is aligned with punch mark on intermediate shaft sprocket. See *Fig*. 4. Slide camshaft drive belt in place and adjust tension, as previously described.

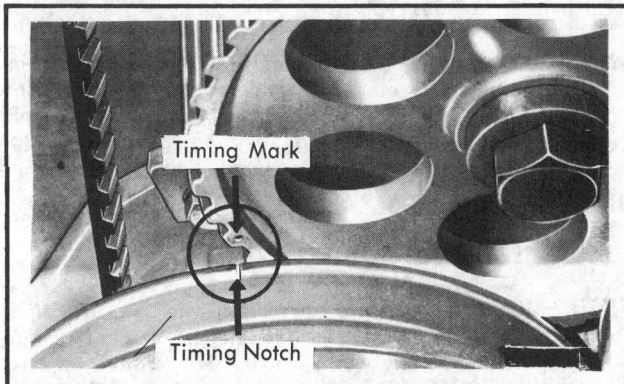

**Fig. 4   Intermediate Shaft Sprocket Aligned with
TDC Notch in Crankshaft Pulley**

VALVES

VALVE ARRANGEMENT

E-I-E-I-I-E-I-E (front to rear).

Audi Engines

4000 4 CYLINDER (Cont.)

VALVE SPRINGS

With cam followers removed, install valve spring compressor tool (10-210). Compress springs and remove valve keepers and collar. Lift out valve springs. To install, reverse removal procedure.

MECHANICAL VALVE LIFTER ASSEMBLY

With camshaft and adjusting discs removed, lift out cam followers. Inspect for wear or damage. Replace as necessary. Lightly oil cam followers and replace in original location.

VALVE STEM OIL SEALS

NOTE — Valve stem oil seals may be replaced with cylinder head installed on vehicle.

Removal & Installation — With camshaft and spark plug removed, turn crankshaft until affected piston is at BDC. Install air hose adapter (VW 653/3) in spark plug hole and apply constant pressure. Using spring compressor (VW 541 or 10-210), remove valve keepers. Lift seal off valve stem with remover (10-218). Slide plastic sleeve onto valve stem. Lubricate new seal and push in place with installing tool (10-204).

NOTE — Do not attempt to install seal without using plastic sleeve, or seal will be damaged, causing engine to use excessive oil.

VALVE GUIDE SERVICING

1) Before taking measurements, clean valve guides with a cleaning broach. To measure, attach a suitable device with a dial indicator (VW 387 or US 4420A) to mounting surface of cylinder head. Insert a new valve into valve guide until stem is flush with end of guide. Rock valve against dial indicator and check amount of guide-to-stem clearance. Maximum valve rock should not exceed .039" (1.0 mm) for intake valves or .051" (1.3 mm) for exhaust valves.

2) Use suitable press and adaptor (10-206) to remove and install valve guides. Press worn guides out from combustion chamber side. Coat new guide with oil and press into cold cylinder head from camshaft side. Do not use more than 1 ton of pressure or guide shoulder may break. Ream guide by hand to proper size.

VALVE CLEARANCE ADJUSTMENT

NOTE — Cold settings are given for reference as initial settings after engine work. Final adjustments are to be made with engine moderately warm (coolant temperature approximately 95° F (35° C).

1) Remove accelerator linkage, upper drive belt cover and cylinder head cover. Turn crankshaft pulley bolt in a clockwise direction until cam lobes of cylinder to be adjusted point upward. See Fig. 5.

NOTE — Do not turn camshaft by mounting bolt as this will stretch drive belt. If crankshaft sprocket bolt is turned counter-

clockwise, bolt could be loosened. If this should occur accidentally, remove bolt and clean threads. Coat threads with Loctite or equivalent, install bolt and torque to 58 ft. lbs. (8.0 mkg).

Fig. 5   Adjusting Valve Clearance

2) Adjust valve clearances in firing order (1-3-4-2). Using a feeler gauge, measure valve clearance of each cylinder in turn. If clearance is within .002" (.05 mm) of specification, no adjustment is necessary.

Valve Clearance Specifications	
Application	**In. (mm)**
Intake	
Hot	.008-.012 (.20-.30)
Cold	.006-.010 (.15-.25)
Exhaust	
Hot	.016-.020 (.40-.51)
Cold	.014-.018 (.36-.46)

3) Compare measured clearance for each valve to specifications. If adjustment is required, determine thickness of adjusting disc currently used. If measured clearance is larger than specifications, replace adjusting disc with thicker disc. If clearance is less than specification, install a thinner disc. Adjust clearance to middle of tolerance range.

4) Adjusting discs are available in .002" (.05 mm) increments from .1181" (3.0 mm) to .1673" (4.25 mm). Thickness is stamped on bottom side of disc.

5) To remove discs from cam followers, turn cam followers so that they are adjacent to each other between cam lobes. Insert cam follower tool (VW 546) and depress cam followers. Remove adjusting discs with special tool (US 4476 or 10-208). To install discs, depress cam followers and slip discs into place with side indicating thickness downward. Remove tool. Repeat procedure until all valves are properly adjusted.

4000 4 CYLINDER (Cont.)

PISTONS, PINS & RINGS

OIL PAN

Drain engine oil. Attach a suitable lifting device to engine and apply supporting tension to engine. Remove front sub frame attaching bolts at left and right. Remove cover plate. Unscrew oil pan bolts and remove pan. When installing, use a new gasket, installing it dry without adhesive. Install oil pan bolts and tighten in a crisscross pattern.

PISTON & ROD ASSEMBLY

1) Before removing connecting rods, mark rod, cap and piston for proper installation. Remove nuts from connecting rod bolts, remove caps, and carefully push piston and rod assemblies out top of cylinders.

2) On reassembly of piston and rod assemblies, forged marks on rod and cap, as well as locating projections on bearing inserts, should face toward timing gear at front of engine. See Fig. 6. All connecting rods must be of same weight class. Weight class numbers are stamped on bottom of connecting rod caps. Using a ring compressor tool (US 1008A), install piston and rod assemblies with arrow on top of piston facing timing gear (front of engine).

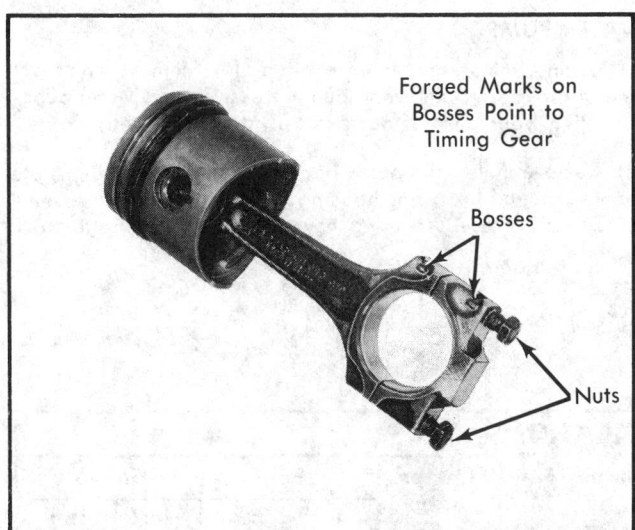

Forged Marks on Bosses Point to Timing Gear

Bosses

Nuts

Fig. 6   Identification Marks on Connecting Rod Bosses

FITTING PISTONS

1) Measure cylinder at three points: .39" (10 mm) from top and bottom, and at center of cylinder bore. Take measurements in line with thrust face and at 90° to thrust face.

2) Measure piston diameter at .39" (10 mm) from bottom of piston skirt (measuring at 90° to pin bore). Combining this measurement with measurement of corresponding cylinder bore, if piston-to-cylinder clearance exceeds .003" (.07 mm), oversize pistons must be installed.

NOTE — Top of piston is marked with an arrow, denoting direction piston is to be installed in cylinder, and with a 4-digit number indicating piston diameter in millimeters (for example, 79.48).

3) Place piston rings squarely in top of cylinder bore (above ring ridge) and measure end gap; replace as necessary. Measure ring side clearance; replace rings and/or pistons if clearance exceeds .006" (.15 mm). Install rings on piston with end gaps 120° offset to each other and stamped word "TOP" on rings facing upward.

PISTON PINS

Use pin-drift to lift circlip from piston groove. Use tool (VW 207c) to remove and install piston pins. If pins are too tight it may be necessary to warm pistons to about 140°F (60°C) for removal and replacement.

CRANKSHAFT MAIN & CONNECTING ROD BEARINGS

MAIN & CONNECTING ROD BEARINGS

1) Push crankshaft toward one end and measure crankshaft end play at No. 3 (thrust) bearing. Main bearing caps are stamp-numbered "1" to "5" from timing gear end to flywheel end. They must be installed in original positions upon reassembly. Measure connecting rod side play. Remove rod and main bearing caps and check bearing clearance, using Plastigage method.

2) Measure crankshaft journals with a micrometer to determine if crankshaft is out-of-round. Maximum ovality permissible is .0012" (.03 mm). Install main inserts with bearing half having oil groove into block. Lubricate bearings and install caps.

Crankshaft Journal Diameters		
Size	Main Bearing Inches (mm)	Connecting Rod Inches (mm)
Stud	2.124 (53.97)	1.809 (45.97)
1st US	2.114 (53.72)	1.799 (45.72)
2nd US	2.104 (53.47)	1.789 (45.47)
3rd US	2.094 (53.22)	1.779 (45.22)

REAR MAIN BEARING OIL SEAL

Rear main bearing oil seal may be replaced with engine in vehicle, if transmission and flywheel are removed. Carefully pry oil seal from crankcase. Install guide tool (2003/2A) on crankshaft and press seal into position as far as possible by hand. Press seal in until properly seated with installing tool (2003/1).

INTERMEDIATE SHAFT OIL SEAL

Press seal out of flange. Coat new seal lips with oil and press new seal into flange, using suitable tool (10-203). Press until flush.

FRONT MAIN BEARING OIL SEAL

1) Remove "V" belt and upper drive belt cover. Set crankshaft to TDC. Remove "V" belt pulley from crankshaft and loosen

Audi Engines

4000 4 CYLINDER (Cont.)

drive belt sprocket. To remove drive belt sprocket bolt, engage 4th gear and apply foot brake. Have assistant remove water pump pulley and lower drive belt cover. Then loosen drive belt and remove drive belt sprocket.

2) Pry old seal out of front cover with extractor tool (10-219). Using installation tool (10-203), press new seal into place after coating seal lips with oil. Press in until flush and then to a depth of .080" (2 mm) below outer edge of cover.

NOTE — *When pressing seal into place, install washer from socket bolt between tool (10-203) and bolt head.*

3) To install remaining components, reverse removal procedure and check valve timing.

ENGINE OILING

Crankcase Capacity — 3.2 qts. (3.7 qts. with filter).

Oil Filter — Replaceable, spin-on type. Hand-tighten.

Normal Oil Pressure — 28 psi (1.97 kg/cm²) at 2000 RPM with oil temperature at 176° F (80° C).

ENGINE OILING SYSTEM

Oiling system is a pressure feed system. A gear type oil pump lifts oil from oil pan and pressure feeds it to crankshaft journals, camshaft bearings and intermediate shaft. Other parts of system receive oil mist or splash for lubrication.

OIL PUMP

Remove oil pan and two oil pump mounting bolts. Pull pump straight down and out of engine. Remove two pump cover bolts and separate cover from pump body. Ensure that oil pump gear backlash is .002-.008" (.05-.20 mm). Check that gear end clearance is not more than .006" (.15 mm). Remove pump drive shaft and gears. Bend up metal edges and remove filter screen. To assemble, reverse disassembly procedure.

ENGINE COOLING

Cooling System Capacity — With air conditioning — 7.4 qts.; without air conditioning — 6.5 qts.

Thermostat — Arrow should point toward fender when installed. Begins to open at 194°F (90°C); opening ends at 216°F (102°C).

Expansion Tank Cap — Pressure relief valve opens at 17-19 psi (1.20-1.33 kg/cm²)

Cooling Fan — Begins to operate at 199-208° F (93-98° C); shuts down at 190-199° F (88-93° C). Switch located in radiator.

WATER PUMP

1) Drain coolant and remove alternator. Remove camshaft belt guard, hose clamps and pump hoses. Remove water pump mounting bolts and lift out pump by turning slightly.

2) Remove pulley and pump body mounting screws. Separate pump assembly from housing. To reassemble, reverse diassembly procedure using new gasket and pump-to-block seal.

ENGINE SPECIFICATIONS

GENERAL SPECIFICATIONS										
Year	Displ.		Carburetor	HP at RPM	Torque (Ft. Lbs. at RPM)	Compr. Ratio	Bore		Stroke	
	cu. ins.	cc					in.	mm	in.	mm
1980	97	1588	Fuel Inj.	76@5500	82.7@3200①	8.2:1-	3.13	79.5	3.15	80.0

① — Calif. models — 84.1@3200.

VALVES							
Engine & Valve	Head Diam. In. (mm)	Face Angle	Seat Angle	Seat Width In. (mm)	Stem Diameter In. (mm)	Stem Clearance In. (mm)	Valve Lift In. (mm)
1588 cc Intake	1.338 (34)	45°	45°	.079 (2.0)	.314 (7.98)	.008-.012 (.20-.30)	.....
Exhaust	1.220 (31)	45°	45°	.094 (2.4)	.313 (7.95)	.016-.020 (.40-.51)	.....

4000 4 CYLINDER (Cont.)
ENGINE SPECIFICATIONS (Cont.)

PISTONS, PINS, RINGS

| Engine | PISTONS | PINS | | RINGS | | |
	Clearance In. (mm)①	Piston Fit In. (mm)	Rod Fit In. (mm)③	Rings	End Gap In. (mm)④	Side Clearance In. (mm)⑤
1588 cc	.0011 (.028)	②	.0011-.0034 (.028-.086)	Comp.	.012-.018 (.30-.46)	.0008-.002 (.02-.05)
				Oil	.010-.016 (.25-.40)	.0008-.002 (.02-.05)

① — Wear limit .003" (.07 mm). ② — Push fit at 140°F (60°C). ③ — Wear limit .004" (.12 mm).
④ — Wear limit .040" (1.0 mm). ⑤ — Wear limit .006" (.15 mm).

CRANKSHAFT MAIN & CONNECTING ROD BEARINGS

| Engine | MAIN BEARINGS | | | | CONNECTING ROD BEARINGS | | |
	Journal Diam. In. (mm)	Clearance In. (mm)①	Thrust Bearing	Crankshaft End Play In. (mm)②	Journal Diam. In. (mm)	Clearance In. (mm)③	Side Play In. (mm)
1588 cc	2.125 (53.97)	.001-.003 (.025-.076)	No. 3	.003-.007 (.077-.178)	1.810 (45.97)	.0011-.0034 (.028-.086)	.015 (.38)

① — Wear limit .007" (1.7 mm). ② — Wear limit .015" (.37 mm). ③ — Wear limit .004" (.12 mm).

TIGHTENING SPECIFICATIONS

Application	Ft. Lbs. (mkg)
Head Bolts (Cold Only)	
Step 1	29 (4.0)
Step 2	43 (6.0)
Step 3	54 (7.5) Plus 90°
Main Bearing Caps	47 (6.5)
Connecting Rod Caps	33 (4.5)
Flywheel (Use Loctite)	54 (7.5)
Intermediate Shaft Sprocket	58 (8.0)
Crankshaft Drive Belt Sprocket	58 (8.0)
Oil Pan Bolts	7 (1.0)
Exhaust Manifold	18 (2.5)
Intake Manifold	18 (2.5)
Camshaft Bearing Caps	14 (2.0)
Camshaft Sprocket	58 (8.0)
Front Engine Mount Bolts	18 (2.5)
Right & Left Engine Mount Nuts	25 (3.5)
Cover Plate Bolts	7 (1.0)
Engine-to-Transmission Bolts	40 (5.5)
Drive Belt Tensioner Nut	33 (4.5)
Crankshaft "V" Belt Pulley	14 (2.0)
Exhaust Pipe-to-Manifold	22 (3.0)

VALVE SPRINGS

| Engine | Free Length In. (mm) | PRESSURE Lbs. @ In. (kg @ mm) | |
		Valve Closed	Valve Open
1588 cc Inner	.....	.....	46-51 @ .72 (21-23 @ 18.3)
Outer	.....	.....	96-106 @ .92 (44-48 @ 22.3)

4000 & 5000 5 CYLINDER

ENGINE CODING

ENGINE IDENTIFICATION

Engine number is stamped on left side of block near control pressure regulator.

Engine Identification Codes	
Application	**Code**
2144 cc	
Federal CIS	WD
Calif. CIS	WE
Turbo	WK

ENGINE & CYLINDER HEAD

ENGINE

Removal (5000) — 1) Disconnect battery ground cable. Remove coolant expansion tank cap. Disconnect hose from bottom of expansion tank and drain. Place temperature lever in "COLD" position if vehicle is equipped with air conditioning.

2) Disconnect coolant hoses and drain coolant. DO NOT disconnect any fuel lines. Remove control pressure regulator, cold start valve, and fuel injectors. Loosen air duct and vacuum hoses from throttle valve assembly. Remove air cleaner cover with filter.

3) Pull hood latch cable guide from bracket. Remove radiator cowl, shroud, electric fan and radiator, if necessary for clearance. On air conditioned vehicles, remove grille and tilt condenser outward.

4) Remove power steering pump, leaving hoses connected. Remove vacuum amplifier, ignition coil and EGR control valve. Remove windshield washer and power steering reservoirs from holders. Remove distributor cap, rotor and ignition wires.

5) Remove circlip to remove throttle cable (manual transmission). Remove throttle push rod (automatic transmission). Disconnect electrical connections on distributor. Disconnect wiring to oil pressure and water temperature senders.

6) Remove air conditioning compressor, leaving hoses connected. Tie back compressor with wire. Remove exhaust pipe from manifold and from transmission bracket. Remove front engine mount, starter and alternator.

7) Remove torque converter mounting bolts (automatic transmission) from drive plate, doing so through starter mounting hole. Remove lower engine-to-transmission bolts. Install transmission support tool (VW 785/1). Remove upper engine-to-transmission bolts.

8) Remove left engine bracket and loosen right engine bracket from engine mount. With engine lifting device securely attached, lift engine until "V" belt pulley is behind grille opening. Lift transmission with support tool. Detach engine from transmission.

9) Lift engine upward, turning front of engine toward right as engine is lifted. Remove engine, using care that all wires, hoses and vacuum lines are free. Mount engine on stand (VW 540).

Installation — 1) To install engine, reverse removal procedure, noting the following: Tighten starter cable, so cable cannot touch engine. Metal lip of gasket between exhaust manifold and exhaust pipe faces exhaust pipe. Adjust power steering pump, alternator, and air conditioning compressor belt tension.

2) Attach vacuum hoses to EGR control valve with straight adapter installed to EGR valve and angled adapter to vacuum amplifier. Refill coolant expansion tank. Adjust accelerator cable.

3) Tighten engine mounting bolts with engine running at idle speed.

Removal (4000) — 1) Disconnect battery ground cable. Open heater control valve fully. Open cap on coolant expansion tank and drain coolant. Remove engine-to-transmission bolt holding coolant pipe. Remove upper coolant hose from pipe on left side of engine.

2) Remove upper radiator cover and upper radiator hose from engine. Remove vacuum hose at brake booster and at cruise control unit. Remove power steering pump and place in cowl.

3) Detach coolant hose at thermostat housing. Disconnect wires from oil pressure switch and control pressure regulator. Remove throttle push rod and control pressure regulator, leaving fuel lines connected.

4) Remove remaining coolant hose. Remove alternator adjusting bolt and mounting bolt and place alternator into lower radiator cover. Remove alternator bracket from engine block and remove front stop.

5) Loosen clamps and remove air duct. Disconnect plugs from frequency valve and ground point. Remove distributor vacuum unit hoses. Disconnect plugs at cold start valve, auxiliary air regulator and throttle switch. Remove coil high tension wire at ignition coil.

6) Pull out fuel injectors and remove cold start valve. Leave all fuel lines connected, protecting injectors and valve with caps. Remove fuel distributor with air flow sensor plate. Disconnect fuel feed and return lines. Pull PCV valve hose from valve cover.

7) Loosen upper air filter housing clips and housing bolt. Disconnect oxygen sensor, thermo switch, thermo-time switch, temperature sending unit, and ignition distributor connectors.

8) On air conditioned vehicles, remove coolant hoses at oil cooler. Remove heater hoses. Remove hose flange from engine block and remove cover for right engine mount. Loosen left and right engine mounts. Detach ground strap from mounting bracket. Remove upper engine-to-transmission bolts, leaving one easy-to-reach bolt installed.

9) Loosen "V" belt adjusting bolts for air conditioner compressor. Disconnect wire from oil temperature switch. Remove compressor clamping bolt, bracket from engine block, and wire from compressor clutch. Remove upper compressor mounting bolt and wire compressor out of way, leaving hoses connected.

10) Disconnect starter cables. Remove both front subframe bolts. Remove exhaust pipe attaching nuts from manifold. Remove bolt from exhaust pipe support. Remove starter.

4000 & 5000 5 CYLINDER (Cont.)

11) Working through starter mounting hole, remove 3 torque converter mounting bolts from drive plate. Remove lower engine-to-transmission bolts. Unhook shift rod clip. Install transmission support tool (VW 785/1).

12) Attach engine sling (US 9010 and US 1105) to engine. Adjust support bar to contact transmission. Remove upper engine-to-transmission bolt, left in earlier. Lift engine slightly and pry engine away from transmission. Continue to lift engine, while turning it toward the left.

13) Use care when guiding engine out of engine compartment. Be sure all wires, hoses, and vacuum lines have been removed. Secure torque converter so it does not fall out. Mount engine on stand (VW 540).

Installation — To install engine, reverse removal procedure, noting the following: Attach starter cable so that it does not touch engine, causing a short circuit. Align exhaust system and refill coolant tank. Tighten engine mounting bolts while engine is running at idle speed.

CYLINDER HEAD

Removal — 1) Disconnect battery ground strap and drain cooling system. Disconnect coolant hoses from head and exhaust pipe from manifold. Remove electrical and vacuum leads from distributor. Disconnect accelerator linkage, fuel and vacuum lines and air filter from manifold.

2) Remove valve cover and timing belt cover. Rotate crankshaft so that number 1 cylinder is at TDC on firing stroke. Remove drive belt sprocket from camshaft, but do NOT separate from timing belt. Loosen head bolts in reverse order of tightening sequence and lift off head.

Installation — 1) Install head gasket DRY (no adhesive) with part number facing upward. Guide pins may be used at opposite corners of head to ease alignment. Be sure cylinder head and block mating surfaces are clean.

2) Install head using only polygon cylinder head bolts. Install bolts 9 and 11 to center head, then tighten bolts in sequence shown in *Fig. 1.*

3) Tighten bolts in three steps with engine cold first to 29 ft. lbs. (4.0 mkg), then 43 ft. lbs. (6.0 mkg) and finally to 54 ft. lbs. (7.5 mkg) plus an additional ¼ (90°) turn. DO NOT retorque bolts after first 1,000 miles nor after first 1,000 miles following repair.

4) Complete assembly in reverse order of removal and ensure that all timing marks are properly positioned.

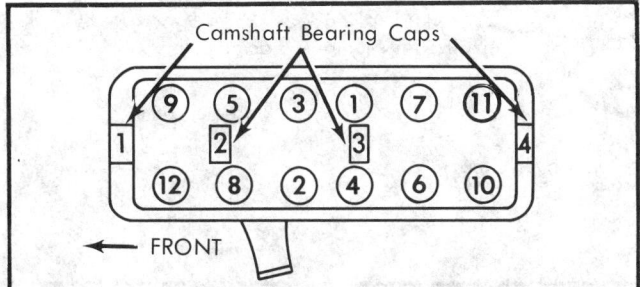

Fig. 1   Tighten Cylinder Head in Sequence Shown (Loosen in Reverse Order)

CAMSHAFT

DRIVE (TIMING) BELT

Remove "V" belts and take off drive belt cover. Engine should be in number 1 cylinder firing position (TDC). Loosen water pump bolts and turn pump counterclockwise to loosen belt. Install new belt and adjust by turning water pump clockwise to tighten. Ensure that valve timing is correct. Belt is properly adjusted when it can just be twisted 90° with thumb and index finger between camshaft and water pump sprockets.

CAMSHAFT

Diagonally loosen bearing caps 2 and 4 and remove caps. Diagonally loosen bearing caps 1 and 3 and remove caps. Remove camshaft from head. When installing, caps must be installed in original position. Lubricate bearings and journals and install caps with off-center position properly aligned. See *Fig. 2.* Tighten caps 2 and 4 diagonally and then caps 1 and 3.

CAUTION — *Front oil seal must not be installed beyond flush position or oil return will be blocked.*

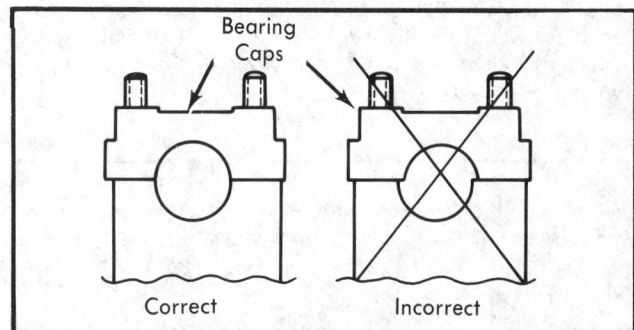

Fig. 2   Camshaft Bearing Caps with Proper Off-Center Position

VALVE TIMING

Rotate crankshaft until notch on "V" belt pulley aligns with mark on oil pump housing (engine out of vehicle) or TDC "0" mark on flywheel aligns with lug cast on clutch housing (engine installed). Fully loosen drive belt tension by loosening and turning water pump counterclockwise. Turn camshaft sprocket so that punch mark on rear aligns with valve cover gasket (upper edge of belt cover) on left side of engine. Install and adjust belt by turning water pump clockwise to tighten.

VALVES

VALVE ARRANGEMENT

E-I-E-I-I-E-I-E-I-E (front to rear).

VALVE GUIDE SERVICING

1) With head disassembled, insert new valve and check for wear with dial indicator. See *Fig. 3.* If wear exceeds .039" (1.0 mm) for intake, or .051" (1.3 mm) for exhaust valve, guides should be replaced.

4000 & 5000 5 CYLINDER (Cont.)

2) Press worn guides out of head from combustion chamber side with suitable tool (10-206). Coat new guides with oil and press into cold head from camshaft side. Press guides in as far as they will go, but DO NOT use more than 1 ton pressure once shoulder is seated. Ream guide by hand to proper size.

VALVE STEM OIL SEALS

NOTE — *Valve stem seals may be replaced with cylinder head installed on vehicle.*

With camshaft and followers removed, remove spark plug and turn crankshaft until piston of cylinder concerned is at BDC position. Install pressure hose (VW 653/3) in spark plug hole and apply low pressure air to keep valve seated. Remove valve springs with compressor (VW 451/1 or 2036) and lift off seal with pliers (10-218). Place seal protector over valve stem, lubricate seal and push seal in place with installing tool (10-204).

VALVE SPRINGS

With camshaft and followers removed, compress spring with suitable tool (US 1020 and 1020/1 or 2037) and remove valve locks (keepers). Lift off valve springs. If required, valve spring seats may be removed using pliers (10-218). To install, reverse removal procedure.

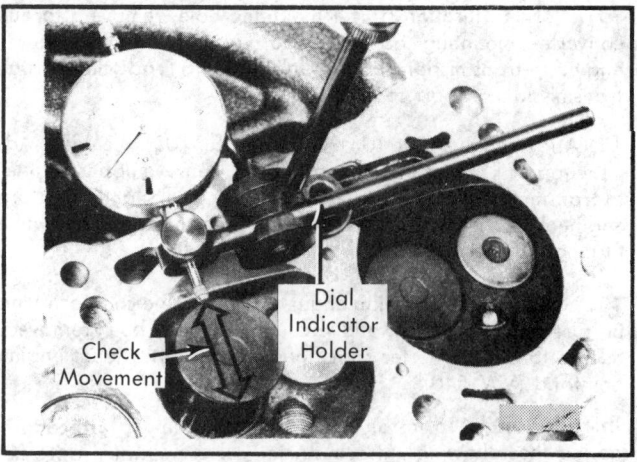

Fig. 3   Checking Valve Guide for Wear

CAM FOLLOWERS (TAPPETS)

With camshaft removed, lift off followers and adjusting discs. Inspect for wear or damage and replace as necessary.

NOTE — *Cam followers and valve system components must be kept in order and installed in original positions. Coat with oil when installing.*

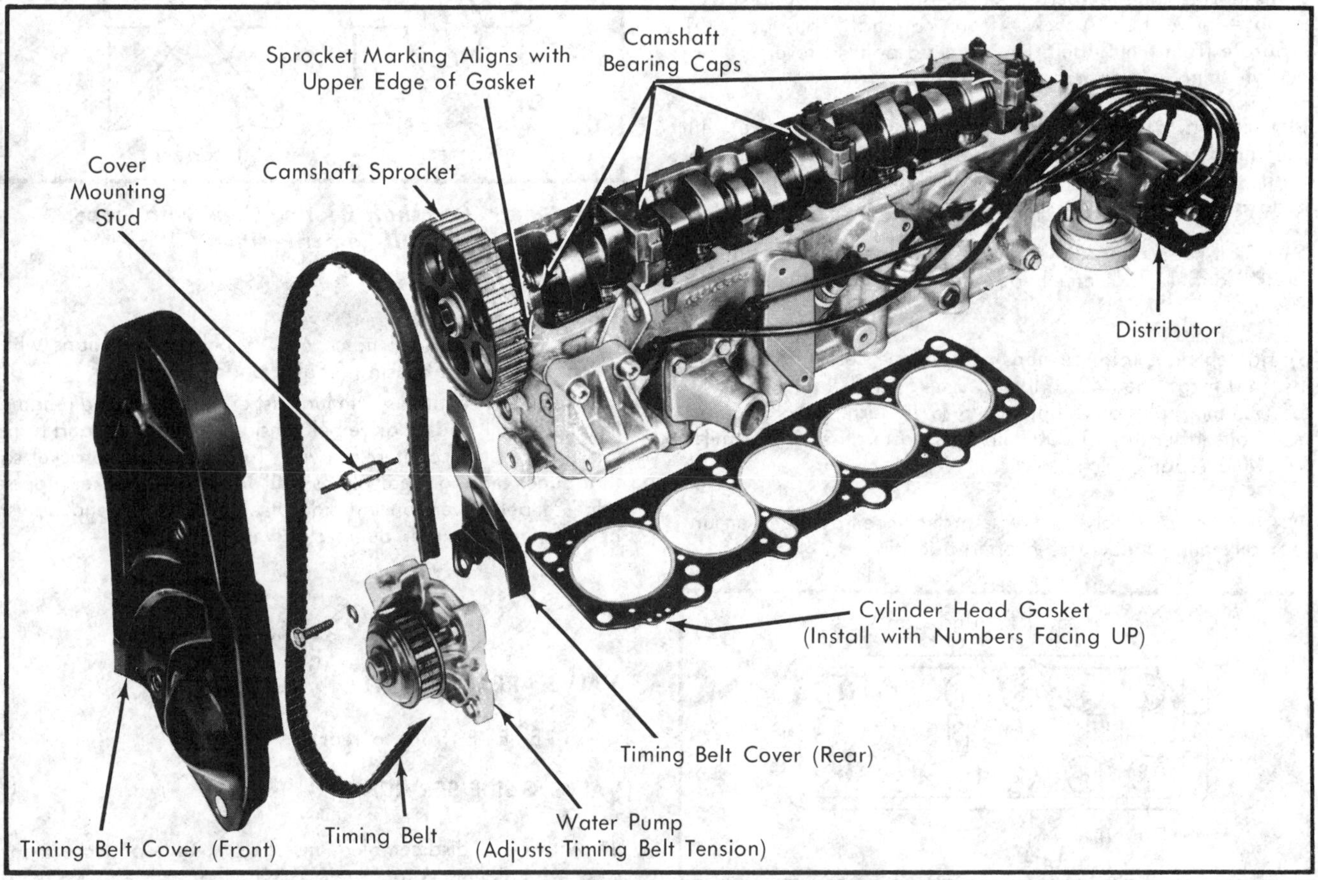

Fig. 4   Cylinder Head and Camshaft Assembly with Drive (Timing) Belt and Cover

4000 & 5000 5 CYLINDER (Cont.)

VALVE CLEARANCE ADJUSTMENT

1) Disconnect accelerator linkage and remove valve cover. Turn crankshaft so that both cam lobes of cylinder to be adjusted point upward. Check valve clearances between cam and follower in firing order (1-2-4-5-3). If clearance is greater than .002" (.05 mm) from specifications, select thicker or thinner disc.

2) To replace valve adjusting discs, use follower depressor tool (2078) to press follower down, then remove adjusting disc with tool (10-208 or US4476). Insert appropriate disc and recheck clearance. Discs are available in .0019" (.05 mm) increments from .1181" (3.0 mm) to .1673" (4.25 mm). Thickness is etched on bottom of disc; discs should be assembled with etched mark toward follower.

Valve Clearances

Application	Hot In. (mm)	Cold In. (mm)
Intake	.008-.012 (.20-.30)	.006-.010 (.15-.25)
Exhaust	.016-.020 (.40-.50)	.014-.018 (.35-.45)

NOTE — *Cold settings are given for reference as initial setting after engine rework. Final adjustments are to be made after engine is warm (at least 95 °F or 35 °C), and checked again after 1000 miles.*

PISTONS, PINS & RINGS

OIL PAN

Removal & Installation — Oil pan may be removed while engine is installed. Remove 2 front bolts in subframe and drain engine oil. Turn flywheel so that recesses point down and remove both rear pan bolts. Remove remaining pan bolts and lower pan from engine. To install, use new pan gasket and tighten pan bolts in a criss-cross pattern.

PISTON & ROD ASSEMBLY

Removal & Installation — Note that rod cap and rod are marked for proper installation. Remove cap nuts and push piston/rod assembly out of cylinder from bottom. When assembling, note that arrow on piston top points to crankshaft pulley (front of engine). Valve detents will be at left side of block. Raised casting marks on connecting rod and cap must face oil filter side of engine and point toward timing gear (front of engine).

FITTING PISTONS

1) Measure cylinder at 3 points: 3/8" (10 mm) from top and bottom, and at center of bore. Measure in line with and at 90° to thrust face. Wear limit is .003" (.08 mm).

NOTE — *Do not measure when block is mounted in repair stand with adapter VW 540 due to possible distortion.*

2) Measure pistons 5/8" (16 mm) from bottom of piston skirt, 90° to pin bore. Subtract this measurement from that of corresponding cylinder bore and note piston-to-cylinder clearance. If clearance exceeds .0028" (.07 mm), oversize pistons must be installed.

3) Place each piston ring squarely into bottom of cylinder about 5/8" (16 mm) and measure end gap. Reading should be .010-.020" (.25-.50 mm). Measure ring side clearance in pistons using a feeler gauge. Ring clearance should be .0008-.0030" (.02-.08 mm) with a wear limit of .004" (.1 mm)

4) Install rings on pistons with "TOP" mark facing piston crown. Recessed edge on outside of center ring must face toward piston pin. Oil scraper ring with spring can be placed in either way. Ring gaps should be spaced 120° apart. Use suitable compressor (US 1008 A) and install piston and rod assemblies.

PISTON PINS

Removal & Installation — Use pin type drift to pry circlip from pin boss. Press out pin with suitable driver (VW 207 C). If pin is too tight, heat piston to approximately 140° F (60° C) prior to removal. Assemble piston and connecting rod assembly so that arrow on piston top faces forward when installed. Use new circlips to retain pins.

CRANKSHAFT MAIN & CONNECTING ROD BEARINGS

MAIN & CONNECTING ROD BEARINGS

Check crankshaft end play at number 4 main bearing with feeler gauge. Check main and connecting rod bearing clearance using Plastigage method. Main bearings are numbered 1 through 6 with 1 at drive belt end and 6 at flywheel end. Install bearing shells with lubrication grooves in block and shells without grooves in bearing caps. All bearing shells must be installed in original position if they are not being replaced. Use new connecting rod cap nuts.

Crankshaft Journal Diameters

Size	Main Bearing In. (mm)	Connecting Rod In. (mm)
Std.	2.282 (57.97)	1.810 (45.97)
1st US	2.272 (57.72)	1.800 (45.72)
2nd US	2.263 (57.47)	1.790 (45.47)
3rd US	2.253 (57.22)	1.780 (45.22)

NOTE — *Bearing clearance may be checked with engine installed in vehicle. DO NOT turn crankshaft when checking with Plastigage.*

CRANKSHAFT REAR OIL SEAL

Removal & Installation — With flywheel removed, use tool (2086) to pry old seal from sealing flange. Coat lips and outer edge of new seal with oil push seal into position by hand, then use installing tool (2003/1) to press in until properly seated.

CRANKSHAFT FRONT OIL SEAL

Removal & Installation — With front crankshaft pulley removed, pry old seal from housing using puller (2086). Coat seal lip and outer edge lightly with oil and start into position. Use pulley bolt and tool (2080) to press seal in until seated.

Audi Engines

4000 & 5000 5 CYLINDER (Cont.)

ENGINE OILING

Crankcase Capacity — 4.8 quarts (5.3 quarts with filter change); Turbo models, 4.3 quarts (4.8 quarts with filter change).

Oil Filter — Replaceable, spin-on type.

Normal Oil Pressure — 14 psi (.98 kg/cm²) at idle speed or 85 psi (5.98 kg/cm²) at 5500 RPM measured with oil temperature at 176°F (80°C).

OIL PUMP

1) Gear type pump is mounted at front of engine, driven by crankshaft with oil suction pipe extending into oil pan. To remove, loosen pulley bolt, take off timing belt cover, loosen

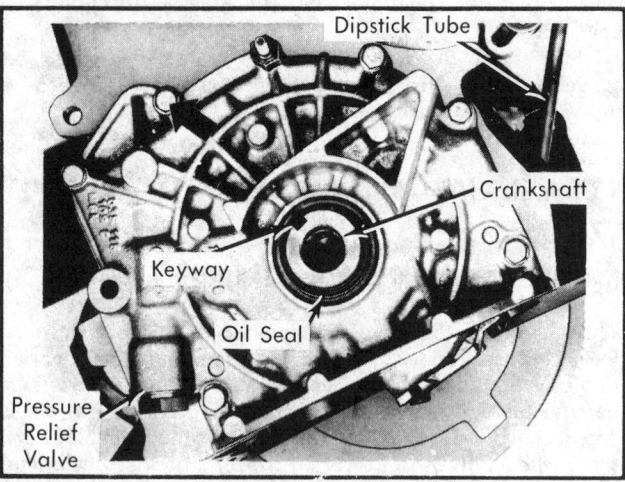

Fig. 5 Engine Oil Pump with Crankshaft Oil Seal

water pump bolts and turn pump counterclockwise, and remove front "V" belt pulley and drive belt sprocket. Drain engine oil and remove oil pan and oil suction pipe.

2) Unbolt pump and remove from front of engine. Inspect end cover, housing and gears for wear or scoring. Replace pump gears in pairs only, with triangle marking toward end cover (rear). To install, reverse removal procedure.

ENGINE COOLING

Cooling System Capacity — 8.6 quarts.

Thermostat — Begins to open at 194° F (90° C). Opening ends at 216° F (102° C).

Expansion Tank Cap — Relief valve opens at 17-19 psi (1.20-1.33 kg/cm²).

Radiator — Cross flow type with electric cooling fan and coolant expansion tank. Fan cuts in at 194-203° F (90-95° C) and cuts off at 185-194° F (85-90° C). Switch controlling fan is located in radiator. On air conditioned vehicles, temperature switch in supply hose controls compressor. It cuts in at 223-232° F (106-111° C) and cuts off at 244-253° F (118-123° C).

WATER PUMP

Water pump is driven by timing belt and is mounted at lower left front of engine block. To remove, drain cooling system and remove timing belt cover. Loosen and remove water pump mounting bolts. Remove pump and check for wear. To install, use new "O" ring and reverse removal procedure. Add coolant mixture until tank is full and replace cap. Run engine until cooling fan turns on. Check coolant level and top off if necessary.

ENGINE SPECIFICATIONS

GENERAL SPECIFICATIONS											
Year	Displ.		Carburetor	HP at RPM	Torque (Ft. Lbs. at RPM)	Compr. Ratio	Bore		Stroke	
	cu. ins.	cc					in.	mm	in.	mm
1980 Turbo	130.8	2144	Fuel Inj.	130@5400	142.0@3000	7.0:1	3.13	79.5	3.40	86.4
Others	130.8	2144	Fuel Inj.	103@5300	112.4@4000	8.0:1	3.13	79.5	3.40	86.4

① — Push fit at 140° F (60° C).

VALVES							
Engine & Valve	Head Diam. In. (mm)	Face Angle	Seat Angle	Seat Width In. (mm)	Stem Diameter In. (mm)	Stem Clearance In. (mm)①	Valve Lift In. (mm)
2144 cc Intake	1.496 (38.0)	45°	45°	.079 (2.0)	.314 (7.97)	.039 (1.0)	.....
Exhaust	1.220 (31.0)	45°	45°	.094 (2.4)	.313 (7.95)	.051 (1.3)	.....

① — Maximum allowable clearance.

Audi Engines

4000 & 5000 5 CYLINDER (Cont.)

ENGINE SPECIFICATIONS (Cont.)

	PISTONS	PINS		RINGS		
		PISTONS, PINS, RINGS				
Engine	Clearance In. (mm)	Piston Fit In. (mm)	Rod Fit In. (mm)	Rings	End Gap In. (mm)②	Side Clearance In. (mm)③
2144 cc	.001-.003 (.025-.080)	①	.....	All	.010-.020 (.25-.50)	.0008-.003 (.02-.08)

① — Push fit at 140°F (60°C).   ② — Wear limit .040" (1.0 mm).   ③ — Wear limit .004" (.1 mm).

CRANKSHAFT MAIN & CONNECTING ROD BEARINGS

	MAIN BEARINGS				CONNECTING ROD BEARINGS		
Engine	Journal Diam. In. (mm)	Clearance In. (mm)	Thrust Bearing	Crankshaft End Play In. (mm)	Journal Diam. In. (mm)	Clearance In. (mm)	Side Play In. (mm)
2144 cc	2.282 (57.97)	.0006-.003① (.016-.075)	No. 4	.003-.010 (.08-.25)	1.810 (45.97)	.0006-.002② (.015-.62)	.016 (.40)

① — Wear limit .005" (.12 mm).
② — Wear limit .006" (.16 mm).

TIGHTENING SPECIFICATIONS

Application	Ft. Lbs. (mkg)
Head Bolts	
Cold (In 3 Steps)①	55 (7.5)
Warm (Hex Socket Head Only)	61 (8.5)
Main Bearing Caps	47 (6.5)
Connecting Rod Caps	36 (5.0)
Flywheel/Drive Plate (Use Loctite)	54 (7.5)
Crankshaft Pulley/Sprocket	235 (35)
Oil Pan Bolts	7 (1.0)
Exhaust Manifold	18 (2.5)
Intake Manifold	18 (2.5)
Camshaft Bearing Caps	14 (2.0)
Camshaft Sprocket	58 (8.0)
Oil Pump Mounting Bolts	
Short	7 (1.0)
Long	14 (2.0)
Timing Belt Cover	7 (1.0)
Cylinder Head Cover	7 (1.0)
Water Pump Mounting Bolts	14 (2.0)
Engine Mount Bolts	33 (4.5)
Starter Mounting Bolt	40 (5.5)
Alternator Mounting Bolt	33 (4.5)
Oil Drain Bolt	29 (4.0)

① — After 3rd step, tighten polygon socket head bolts ¼ turn (90°) past specified torque. DO NOT retighten after 1,000 miles.

Audi Engines

5000 5 CYLINDER DIESEL

ENGINE CODING

ENGINE IDENTIFICATION

Engine number is stamped on a raised pad at the top of the block on the left side between number 2 and 3 cylinder.

Engine Identification	
Application	Code
1986 cc	CN

ENGINE & CYLINDER HEAD

ENGINE

NOTE — *Engine is removed from car with hood and transmission remaining installed.*

Removal — 1) Disconnect battery ground strap and remove air cleaner. Remove front grille and cover plates under engine/transmission. Detach and lay aside windshield washer reservoir and hydraulic fluid reservoir. Drain cooling system and disconnect water hoses attached to engine.

2) Remove power steering pump with hoses connected and lay aside. If equipped with A/C, loosen condenser and tilt outward. Remove auxiliary radiator. Disconnect wiring harness, overheating fuse connector, temperature sender wire, and wires connected to starter.

3) Remove upper part of fuel filter and loosen fuel return pipe on injection pump. Detach accelerator cable and disconnect idle speed control cable from injection pump lever. Remove right engine mount cover plate and remove front engine mount from crossmember. If equipped with A/C, remove compressor from engine leaving hoses attached.

4) Remove alternator mounting bracket and remove exhaust pipes from manifold and transmission bracket. Remove body ground strap and lower engine/transmission bolts. Remove flywheel cover plate from transmission and install supporting tool (VW785/1) with slight preload. Install engine lifting tool (US 1105 or equivalent).

5) Loosen right engine bracket from engine mount and remove left engine bracket. Lift engine/transmission up until transmission housing touches steering housing. Turn disc of supporting tool until it touches transmission housing and remove upper engine/transmission bolts.

6) Pry engine/transmission apart and turn engine to right while lifting. Turn engine 90° so that left side of engine is toward front of car and lift out. Use caution not to damage transmission main shaft, clutch and body.

Installation — To install engine, reverse removal procedures and note that metal lip on exhaust manifold flange gasket must face exhaust pipe. After installing upper transmission/engine bolts, remove supporting tool (VW785/1). It is recommended that engine mountings be tightened while engine is running at idle speed.

CYLINDER HEAD

Removal — 1) Disconnect battery ground strap and drain cooling system. Disconnect coolant hoses from head and exhaust pipe from manifold. Remove feed pipes from injectors and disconnect wire to glow plug feed. Disconnect temperature sender wire and any other wires which could interfere with removal of cylinder head.

2) Remove valve cover and front timing belt cover. Remove vacuum pump "V" belt at rear of engine. Remove injection pump belt cover and set crankshaft to TDC on number 1 cylinder. Align marks on flywheel/clutch housing and injection pump sprocket mounting plate.

3) Lock injection pump sprocket in position with tool (2064). Hold vacuum pump pulley and injection pump drive sprocket with tool (3036) and remove retaining bolt. Remove "V" belt pulley and injection pump sprocket along with drive belt. Note number and position of spacer washers on "V" belt pulley.

4) Remove front camshaft sprocket and timing belt but DO NOT separate sprocket from belt. Loosen and remove head bolts in reverse order of tightening sequence. Lift off cylinder head with camshaft installed.

Installation — 1) Ensure that mating surfaces of engine block and cylinder head are clean. Use gasket with same identification notches as original if installing on original piston and block assembly. To determine proper gasket for new assemblies, measure piston height above top surface of engine block and select gasket from following table:

Available Cylinder Head Gaskets

Piston Projection in Inches (mm)	Gasket Number	Identification Notches
.026-.031 (.67-.80)	069 103 383	1
.032-.035 (.81-.90)	069 103 383A	2
.036-.040 (.91-1.02)	069 103 383B	3

2) Install guide pins in right front and left rear cylinder head bolt holes and place DRY gasket in position with numbers facing UP. Do NOT use sealer. Install head bolts and tighten in three steps following the sequence illustrated in Fig. 1: Step 1 — 35 ft. lbs. (4.8 mkg); Step 2 — 50 ft. lbs. (6.9 mkg); Step 3 — 65 ft. lbs. (9.0 mkg). Run engine to operating temperature of 122°F (50°C). Stop engine and repeat tightening sequence, again torquing bolts to 65 ft. lbs. (9.0 mkg).

NOTE — *After approximately 1000 miles, retorque cylinder head bolts in sequence, loosening them one at a time 30°, and then retightening to 65 ft. lbs. (9.0 mkg).*

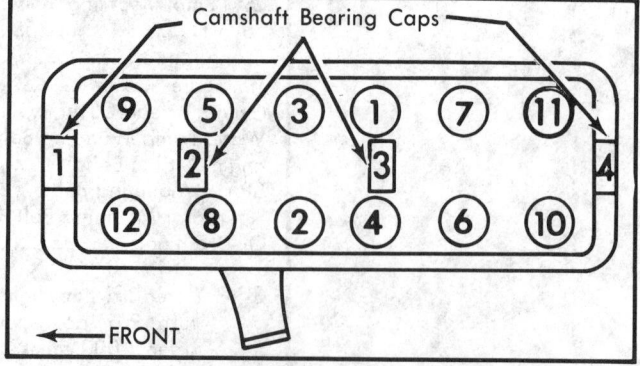

Fig. 1   Cylinder Head Tightening Sequence (Loosen in Reverse Order)

5000 5 CYLINDER DIESEL (Cont.)

CAMSHAFT

TIMING BELTS

Removal — 1) Remove alternator "V" belt and outer half of vacuum pump pulley and "V" belt. Remove drive belt covers and cylinder head cover. Set crankshaft at TDC on No. 1 cylinder and align marks on flywheel/clutch housing and injection pump sprocket mounting plate.

2) Lock injection pump sprocket with pin (2064) and hold inboard half of vacuum pump pulley and injection pump drive sprocket with tool (3036). Remove center retaining bolt and pulley half along with pump sprocket and injection pump drive belt.

3) Lock camshaft with tool (2065 A) and loosen drive belt by loosening water pump. Remove crankshaft pulley, camshaft drive belt and drive belt sprocket.

Installation — 1) Ensure that crankshaft is still at TDC on No. 1 cylinder and install injection pump drive sprocket with drive belt. Tighten injection pump drive retaining bolt until it is just possible to turn sprocket on camshaft by hand. Check belt tension and adjust by moving mounting plate and injection pump.

2) Tighten drive sprocket bolt and remove setting pin from injection pump. Attach crankshaft pulley, camshaft drive belt and camshaft sprocket. Tension belt by moving water pump. To complete installation, reverse removal procedure.

NOTE — *Belt should be tensioned so that scale on tool (VW 210) reads 12 to 13. Tension may also be checked by twisting belt 90° between pulleys using thumb and index finger. If belt twists more than 90°, tension is too loose. If belt will not twist 90°, tension is too tight.*

CAMSHAFT

To check camshaft end play, camshaft followers must be removed and camshaft free of tension. Check for maximum end play of .006" (.15 mm) with dial indicator. To remove camshaft, first remove camshaft drive belt and injecton pump drive belt. Remove outer bearing caps (1 and 4) first, loosen nuts of caps 2 and 3 alternately and diagonally, and lift off cam shaft. To install, reverse removal procedures, installing bearing caps 2 and 3 first, then caps 1 and 4.

VALVE TIMING

See *TIMING BELT* procedures in this article.

INJECTION PUMP TIMING

1) To check injection pump timing, set crankshaft to TDC on No. 1 cylinder. Align marks on flywheel/clutch housing and injection pump sprocket/mounting plate. Loosen cold start cable clamp screw nearest to lever and turn clamp 90°. *Do NOT loosen clamp screw at end of cable.*

2) Install dial indicator with adaptor on injection pump cover with .10" (2.5 mm) preload between plunger and pump shaft. Slowly turn crankshaft counterclockwise until indicator stops moving, then zero the dial indicator with about .04" (1 mm) preload.

3) Turn crankshaft clockwise so TDC mark is aligned with reference mark. Dial indicator should show lift of .033" (.85 mm). If necessary, loosen injection pump bolts and turn pump to set .033" (.85 mm) lift. Tighten mounting bolts and turn clamp on cold start device cable back 90° to tension cable. Tighten screw. Remove dial indicator and replace plug on injection pump.

VALVES

VALVE ARRANGEMENT

E-I-E-I-I-E-I-E-I-E (front to rear).

VALVE GUIDE SERVICING

1) With head disassembled, insert new valve in guide which has been cleaned of carbon deposits. With end of stem flush with end of guide, check back and forth travel of head with dial indicator. Maximum reading for intake and exhaust valve is .051" (1.3 mm).

2) Before replacing worn guides, ensure that valve seats can be refaced and that head is not cracked. Use tool (10-206) and press worn guides out from combustion chamber side. Oil new guides and press in up to shoulder from camshaft side. DO NOT use more than 1 ton pressure or guide shoulder may break. Ream guides by hand and reface valve seats.

VALVE STEM OIL SEALS

Removal & Installation — 1) Seals may be replaced with cylinder head installed or removed from engine. Remove camshaft drive belt and injection pump drive belt. Remove camshaft and cam follower. Turn crankshaft until piston of cylinder concerned is at TDC. Remove valve springs, allowing valve to rest on piston crown.

2) Using special pliers (10-218), pull valve stem seals off. To install new seal, slide plastic sleeve from gasket set onto valve stem. Lubricate new seal and place in installer tool (10-204). Push seal carefully onto valve guide and reverse removal procedure.

VALVE SPRINGS

Removal & Installation — With camshaft and followers removed, compress spring with suitable tool (US 1020 and 1020/1 or 2037) and remove valve locks (keepers). Lift off valve springs. Valve spring seats may be removed with pliers (10-218) if required. To install, reverse removal procedure.

CAM FOLLOWERS (TAPPETS)

Removal & Installation — With camshaft removed, lift off followers and adjusting discs. Mark all components for installation in original position and inspect for wear or damage. To install, coat with oil and replace in original position.

VALVE CLEARANCE ADJUSTMENT

1) With cylinder head cover removed, turn crankshaft so that cam lobes of cylinder to be checked point upward. Check for specified clearance. If not within tolerances given, replace adjusting disc to mid-point of clearance range. Adjusting discs are available in .0019" (.05 mm) increments from .1181" (3.0 mm) to .1673" (4.25 mm).

5000 5 CYLINDER DIESEL (Cont.)

2) To replace disc, turn crankshaft so piston is NOT at TDC so that valves do not contact pistons when cam followers are pressed down. Use follower depressor tool (2078) to press follower down, then remove adjusting disc with tool (10-208 or US 4476). Insert required disc with etched marking downward (toward cam follower).

3) Rotate crankshaft so that lobes point upward and recheck clearance. Start and run engine until coolant temperature is warmed to approximately 95°F (35°C) and recheck clearance.

NOTE — *Valve clearances must be checked and adjusted after 1000 miles following cylinder head, camshaft or valve replacement or grinding.*

Valve Clearances

Application	Hot In. (mm)	Cold In. (mm)
Intake	.008-.012 (.20-.30)	.006-.010 (.15-.25)
Exhaust	.016-.020 (.40-.50)	.014-.018 (.35-.45)

NOTE — *Cold settings are given for reference as initial setting after engine rework.*

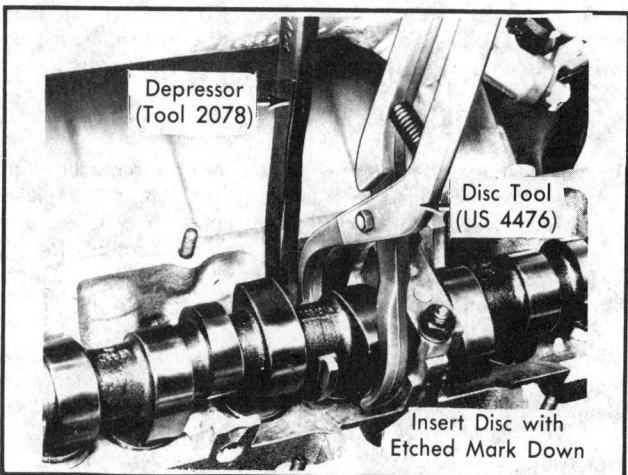

Depressor (Tool 2078)

Disc Tool (US 4476)

Insert Disc with Etched Mark Down

Fig. 2   Adjusting Valve Clearance

PISTONS, PINS & RINGS

OIL PAN

Removal & Installation — Oil pan may be removed while engine is installed. Remove 2 front bolts in subframe and drain engine oil. Turn flywheel so that recesses point down and remove both rear pan bolts. Remove remaining pan bolts and lower pan from engine. To install, use new pan gasket and tighten pan bolts in a criss-cross pattern.

PISTON & ROD ASSEMBLY

Removal & Installation — Note that rod cap and rod are marked for proper installation. Remove cap nuts and push piston/rod assembly out of cylinder from bottom. When assembling, note that arrow on piston top points to crankshaft pulley (front of engine). Valve detents will be at left side of block. Raised casting marks on connecting rod and cap must face oil filter side of engine.

FITTING PISTONS

1) Measure cylinder at 3 points: ⅜" (10 mm) from top and bottom, and at center of bore. Measure in line with and at 90° to thrust face.

NOTE — *Do not measure when block is mounted in repair stand with adapter VW 540 due to possible distortion.*

2) Measure pistons at 9/16" (15 mm) from bottom of piston skirt, 90° to pin bore. Subtract this measurement from that of corresponding cylinder bore and note piston-to-cylinder clearance. If clearance exceeds .027" (.07 mm), oversize pistons must be installed.

3) Place each piston ring squarely into bottom of cylinder about 9/16" (15 mm) and measure end gap. Measure ring side clearance in pistons with feeler gauge.

4) Install rings on pistons with "TOP" mark facing piston crown. Ring gaps should be spaced 120° apart. Use suitable compressor (US 1008 A or equivalent) and install piston/rod assemblies.

PISTON PINS

Removal & Installation — Use pin type drift to pry circlip from pin boss. Press out pin with suitable driver (10-508). If pin is too tight, heat piston to approximately 140°F (60°C) prior to removal. Assemble piston/connecting rod assembly so that arrow on piston top faces forward when assembly is correctly installed. Use new circlips to retain pins.

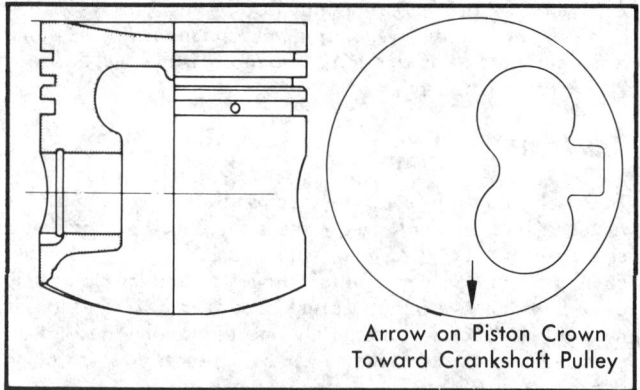

Arrow on Piston Crown Toward Crankshaft Pulley

Fig. 3   Side and Top View of Diesel Piston

CRANKSHAFT MAIN & CONNECTING ROD BEARINGS

MAIN & CONNECTING ROD BEARINGS

Check crankshaft end play at number 4 main bearing with feeler gauge. Check main and connecting rod bearing clearance using Plastigage method. Main bearings are numbered 1 through 6 with 1 at drive belt end and 6 at flywheel end. Install bearing shells with lubrication grooves in block and shells without grooves in bearing caps. All bearing shells must be installed in original position if they are not being replaced. Use new connecting rod cap nuts.

NOTE — *Bearing clearance may be checked with engine installed in vehicle. DO NOT turn crankshaft when checking with Plastigage.*

5000 5 CYLINDER DIESEL (Cont.)

CRANKSHAFT REAR OIL SEAL

Removal & Installation — With flywheel removed, use tool (2086) to pry old seal from sealing flange. Coat lips and outer edge of new seal with oil. Push seal into position by hand, then use installing tool (2003/1) to press in until properly seated.

CRANKSHAFT FRONT OIL SEAL

Removal & Installation — With front crankshaft pulley removed, pry old seal from housing using puller (2086). Coat seal lip and outer edge lightly with oil and start into position. Use pulley bolt and tool (2080) to press seal in until seated.

NOTE — *When installing crankshaft pulley bolt, coat threads and contact surface of bolt head with Loctite 573 or equivalent.*

ENGINE OILING

Crankcase Capacity — 5.3 quarts with filter; 4.8 quarts without filter change.

Oil Filter — Replaceable spin-on type filter is mounted on right side of engine block.

Normal Oil Pressure — Minimum of 28 psi (1.97 kg/cm^2) at 2000 RPM with engine at normal operating temperature.

OIL PUMP

Gear-type pump is mounted at front of engine and is driven by the crankshaft. The oil suction tube extends from the oil pump base to the oil pan. The pump is non-serviceable, and must be replaced as an assembly if defective.

Removal — Remove front crankshaft pulley and "V" belts. Remove camshaft drive belt and cover. Drain engine oil and remove oil pan and oil suction pipe. Unbolt pump and remove from engine.

Installation — Ensure that driving dog on crankshaft engages pump gear properly and reverse removal procedure. Align drive belt sprocket with Woodruff key and apply Loctite 573 (or equivalent) to threads and contact surface of pulley bolt before installing.

ENGINE COOLING

Cooling System Capacity — 9.9 quarts.

Thermostat — Opens at 188°F (87°C).

Expansion Tank Cap — Relieves pressure at 18 psi (1.27 kg/cm^2).

Radiator — Diesel models use a main and an auxiliary radiator, both cross flow type, and a coolant expansion tank. An electric cooling fan is actuated by a thermoswitch at temperatures above 200°F (93°C) and turned off at lower temperatures.

WATER PUMP

Removal & Installation — Allow engine to cool, then drain cooling system. Remove "V" belts, timing belt and drive belt covers. See *TIMING BELT* procedures in this article. Remove retaining bolts and water pump. To install, use new "O" ring on pump and reverse removal procedure.

ENGINE SPECIFICATIONS

		GENERAL SPECIFICATIONS								
Year	Displ.		Carburetor	HP at RPM	Torque (Ft. Lbs. at RPM)	Compr. Ratio	Bore		Stroke	
	cu. ins.	cc					in.	mm	in.	mm
1980	121	1986	Fuel Inj.	67@4800	90@3000	23.0:1	3.01	76.5	3.40	86.4

VALVES In. (mm)							
Engine & Valve	Head Diam.	Face Angle	Seat Angle	Seat Width	Stem Diameter	Stem Clearance	Valve Lift
1986 cc Diesel Intake	1.417 (36.0)	45°	45°	.078 (2.0)	.314 (7.97)	.051 (1.3)	.....
Exhaust	1.220 (31.0)	45°	45°	.096 (2.4)	.313 (7.95)	.051 (1.3)	.....

Audi Engines

5000 5 CYLINDER DIESEL (Cont.)
ENGINE SPECIFICATIONS (Cont.)

PISTONS, PINS, RINGS						
	PISTONS	PINS		RINGS		
Engine	Clearance In. (mm)①	Piston Fit In. (mm)	Rod Fit In. (mm)	Rings	End Gap In. (mm)②	Side Clearance In. (mm)
1986 cc Diesel	.011 (.03)	Push Fit	.....	Upper	.012-.020 (.30-.50)	.002-.004③ (.06-.09)
				Center	.012-.020 (.30-.50)	.002-.003③ (.05-.08)
				Oil	.010-.016 (.25-.40)	.001-.002④ (.03-.06)

① — Wear Limit — .027″ (.07 mm). ③ — Wear Limit — .008″ (.2 mm).
② — Wear Limit — .040″ (1.0 mm). ④ — Wear Limit — .006″ (.15 mm).

CRANKSHAFT MAIN & CONNECTING ROD BEARINGS						
	MAIN BEARINGS				CONNECTING ROD BEARINGS	
Engine	Journal Diam. In. (mm)	Clearance In. (mm)①	Thrust Bearing	Crankshaft End Play In. (mm)②	Journal Diam. In. (mm)	Clearance In. (mm)	Side Play In. (mm)③
1986 cc Diesel	2.28 (57.96)	.0006-.003 (.016-.075)	No. 4	.003-.007 (.07-.18)	1.88 (47.77)	.0005-.0024 (.015-.06)	.016 (.40)

① — Wear Limit .006″ (.16 mm). ② — Wear Limit .01″ (.25 mm). ③ — Wear Limit .015″ (0.4 mm).

TIGHTENING SPECIFICATIONS

Application	Ft. Lbs. (mkg)
Head Bolts	
Step 1	35 (4.8)
Step 2	50 (6.9)
Step 3	65 (9.0)
Camshaft Bearing Caps	14 (2.0)
Main Bearing Caps	47 (6.5)
Connecting Rod Caps	33 (4.5)
Flywheel (Use Loctite)	54 (7.5)
Crankshaft Pulley (Use Loctite)	250 (35.0)
Oil Pan Bolts	14 (2.0)
Oil Pump Mounting Bolts	7 (1.0)
Oil Pump Pickup Tube	7 (1.0)
Timing Belt Cover	7 (1.0)
Cylinder Head Cover	7 (1.0)
Water Pump Mounting Bolts	14 (2.0)
Camshaft Sprocket Bolt	
Front	33 (4.5)
Rear	72 (10.0)
Exhaust Manifold	18 (2.5)
Exhaust Manifold Flange	22 (3.0)
Intake Manifold	22 (3.0)
Injectors	51 (7.0)
Injector Pipes	18 (2.5)
Engine Mounting Bolts	33 (4.5)
Engine to Transmission	43 (6.0)

320i 4 CYLINDER

ENGINE CODING

ENGINE IDENTIFICATION

Engine identification number is on engine block at left hand side above starter motor.

ENGINE & CYLINDER HEAD

NOTE — *Transmission must be removed prior to removing engine.*

MANUAL TRANSMISSION

Removal — **1)** Remove all mounting bolts accessible from above. Remove exhaust support and exhaust pipe at manifold. Tighten compressing strap (261012) around front rubber coupling until bolts attaching rubber coupling to transmission output flange can be removed.

2) Detach center bearing bracket from body after removing heat shield to gain access. Pull down on propeller shaft at center bearing to disengage shaft from transmission flange. Remove speedometer cable and disconnect back-up light switch.

3) Remove center console from transmission, remove circlip and washer, pull out selector rod. Remove clutch slave cylinder, support transmission with jack or stand. Remove crossmember and remaining transmission mounting bolts. Remove transmission towards rear of vehicle.

Installation — To install, reverse removal procedure and note the following: When installing propeller shaft, push center bearing bracket forward .08" (2 mm) to preload center bearing and tighten nuts.

AUTOMATIC TRANSMISSION

Removal — **1)** Remove accelerator cable. Remove all mounting bolts accessible from above. Remove oil filler neck and drain oil. Remove exhaust support and exhaust pipe at manifold. Remove speedometer drive cable. Tighten compressing strap (261012) around front rubber coupling until bolts attaching rubber coupling to transmission output flange can be removed.

2) Detach center bearing bracket from body after removing heat shield to gain access. Pull down on propeller shaft at center bearing to disengage shaft from transmission flange.

3) Remove drive plate bolts from torque converter. Remove transmission oil cooler lines. Support transmission with jack or stand, then remove crossmember at body. Remove remaining transmission mounting bolts. Remove transmission and torque converter from vehicle.

Installation — To install, reverse removal procedure, ensuring that torque converter is properly positioned on drive plate. When installing propeller shaft, push center bearing bracket forward .08" (2 mm) to preload center bearing and tighten nuts.

ENGINE

Removal — **1)** Remove transmission. Drain cooling system and disconnect hoses. Remove fan shroud and radiator. Disconnect and remove battery. Remove intake cowl and disconnect wires and fuel lines to injection system. Detach and suspend A/C compressor (if equipped). DO NOT disconnect hoses.

2) Disconnect wires, fuel and coolant lines and control cables between engine and chassis. Install engine sling (110000) to eyes at front and rear of engine. Detach left engine mount and upper engine damper. Detach right engine mount and lift engine from vehicle.

Installation — To install, reverse removal procedure and note the following: When filling with coolant, set heater control to "warm" and fill radiator slowly. Bleed system after engine is warm by turning cap to catch 1, then remove cap and fill radiator.

CYLINDER HEAD

Removal — **1)** Pull off breather tube, then pull hose with connector out of tube. Dismantle air cleaner assembly. Disconnect ground lead from battery. Drain cooling system. Disconnect accelerator cable. Remove cylinder head cover (rocker arm cover).

2) Remove lines to injection valves (mark for reassembly). Remove pressure converter hoses, water hoses at cylinder head and crankcase hoses at throttle housing and thermo valve (marking for reassembly). Remove upper timing case cover, disconnect plug connectors and ignition coil wires. Remove distributor cap and pull plugs off cold start valve, auxiliary air valve and timing valve. Disconnect oil pressure switch wire.

3) Set piston of No. 1 cylinder at TDC, (rotor points to notch in distributor housing, indicator points to notch in pulley). Remove timing chain tensioner and timing chain sprocket. Remove exhaust pipe at manifold and holder to transmission. Remove cylinder head bolts in reverse sequence of tightening, remove cylinder head.

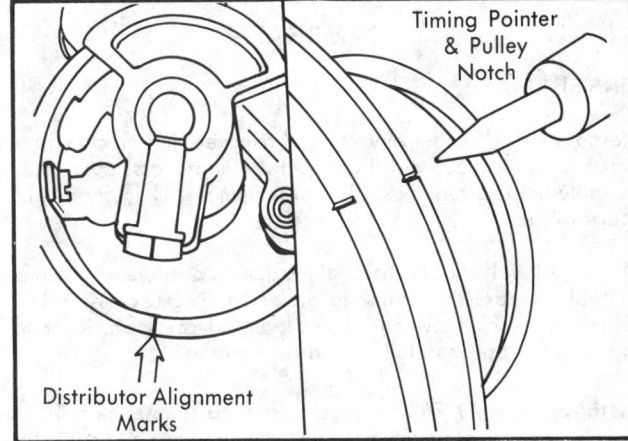

Timing Pointer & Pulley Notch

Distributor Alignment Marks

Fig. 1   Correct Procedure to Set No. 1 Piston at TDC

Installation — **1)** Measure dowel (installation guide) projection above cylinder head mounting surface. See *Fig. 3*. Maximum projection should not exceed .197" (5 mm). Ensure that there is no oil in cylinder head bolt blind holes or head bolts will not be able to exert required holding force on head.

2) Replace cylinder head and components in reverse of removal procedure. Tighten head bolts in 3 steps according to sequence illustrated in *Fig. 2*. See *TIGHTENING SPECIFICATIONS*. Start and run engine until normal operating temperatures are reached, then allow to cool to about 95°F (35°C) and tighten to final torque.

320i 4 CYLINDER (Cont.)

NOTE — *Head bolts should be re-checked for final torque after 600 miles. Always check torque with engine cool.*

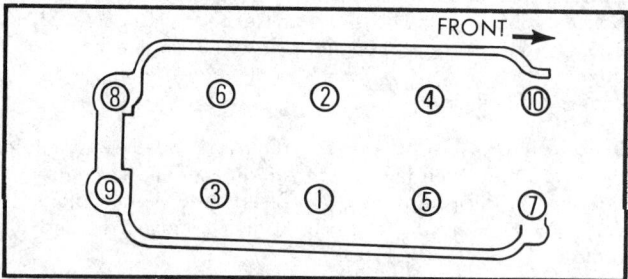

Fig. 2   Tighten Cylinder Head in Sequence Shown (Remove in Reverse Sequence)

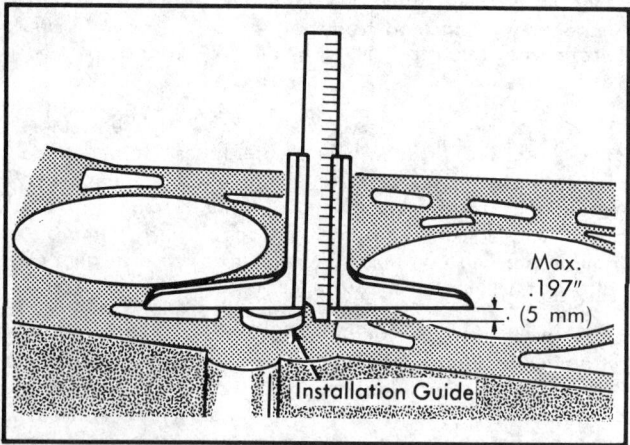

Fig. 3   Measure Dowel Projection as Shown

CAMSHAFT

CAMSHAFT

Removal — 1) With cylinder head removed, loosen clamping screw and pull out distributor. Attach head assembly to a suitable holding tool (No. 11 1 040). Remove oil line and cold start valve.

2) Adjust valve clearance to maximum possible. Attach a suitable compression frame to preload the rocker assembly. Check end play between guide plate and camshaft. Remove guide plate and carefully withdraw camshaft.

Installation — 1) When replacing camshaft, note the following: After guide plate has been installed, it must be possible to easily rotate the camshaft. Make sure that notch in flange aligns with cast tab on cylinder head. Adjust valve clearances, note position of oil pipe sealing rings.

2) When replacing distributor, turn rotor counterclockwise by about 1.4" (35 mm) from notch in distributor housing, bring distributor drive into mesh with camshaft drive. Ensure vacuum advance has been located in original position. Adjust ignition timing.

ENGINE FRONT COVER

Upper Cover — Remove cylinder head cover and detach EGR check valve pipe from exhaust manifold. Take out bolts (8) at-

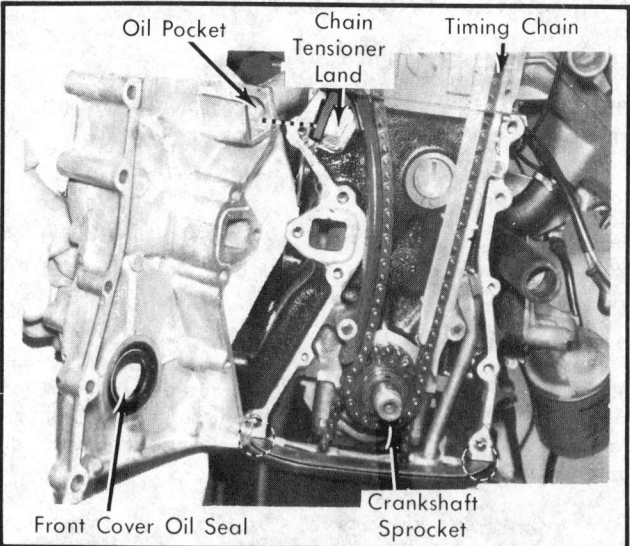

Fig. 4   Timing Chain with Lower Case and Cover

taching cover to head and block. Remove, clean and inspect cover. To install, use new gasket and apply suitable sealant to mating surfaces. Place cover in position and insert all bolts, tightening lower bolts at block slightly. Tighten bolts evenly to specifications starting at lower head and finishing with bolts fastening cover to block.

Lower Timing Case Cover — 1) Disconnect battery ground cable and remove water pump. Remove upper timing case cover and chain tensioner piston. Remove alternator with bracket and tensioning bar. Remove air pump and bracket with tensioning bar.

2) Take off front pulley and remove bolts on timing case cover and front of oil pan. Carefully separate oil pan gasket from timing case cover with knife blade and remove lower cover.

3) To install, apply sealant and new gaskets. Ensure that chain tensioner take-up land is in oil pocket and reverse removal procedures.

TIMING CHAIN REPLACEMENT

Removal & Installation — 1) Remove distributor cap, set piston of No. 1 cylinder at TDC. Remove upper and lower timing case covers. Remove sprocket. Remove circlip and unscrew pivot pin until guide rail rests on cylinder head gasket. Remove timing chain from sprocket and crankshaft. Remove guide rail by pulling down and swinging to the right.

2) If timing chain sprockets need replacing. Remove oil pan, remove sprocket from oil pump. Remove timing chain. Remove sprocket with suitable puller (No. 11 2 000). To install: Heat sprocket, reverse removal procedure.

VALVE TIMING

Rotate engine to TDC of No. 1 piston. Position camshaft so that timing mark on camshaft flange is straight up and locating pin hole is straight down. Without moving crankshaft or camshaft, install camshaft sprocket so that it engages locating pin hole in camshaft flange.

320i 4 CYLINDER (Cont.)

TIMING CHAIN TENSIONER SERVICE

1) Use caution due to high spring pressure and unscrew tensioner plug. Remove piston and spring. Press piston out of sleeve, remove ball bearing and perforated disc, and clean all parts thoroughly. Reassemble parts in order, ensuring that perforated disc does not block bleed slots.

2) Install piston in tensioner body. Place spring with tapered end facing tensioner plug. Screw plug slightly into tensioner body. Fill oil pocket with engine oil and move tensioner rail back and forth until oil comes out around plug threads. Tighten tensioner plug.

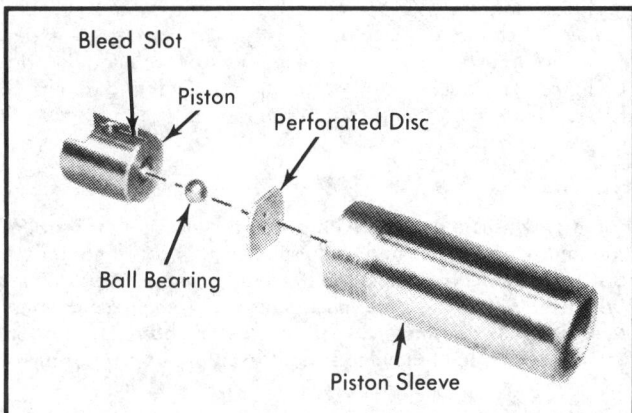

Fig. 5 Exploded View of Chain Tensioner Piston Assembly

VALVES

VALVE ARRANGEMENT

Right Side — All exhaust.

Left Side — All intake.

ROCKER ARM ASSEMBLY

Removal — With camshaft removed, push back thrust ring and rocker arm so rocker shaft circlip may be removed . Remove distributor mounting flange. Drive out rocker arms from rear using drift (11 3 040). Retain all springs, washers, rocker arms and thrust rings in proper order for assembly.

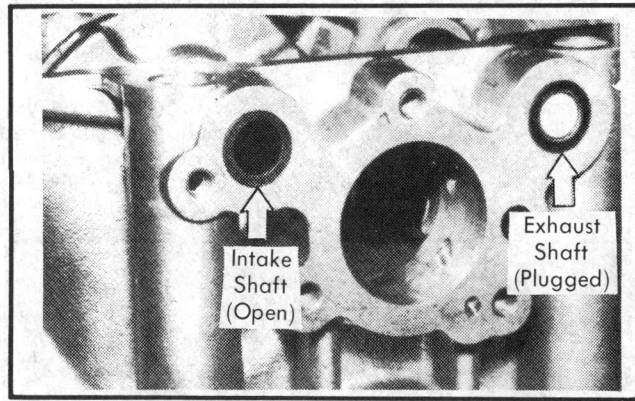

Fig. 6 Rear View of Head Showing Plug in Exhaust Rocker Shaft

Installation — Install all parts in original location. Replace worn rocker arms and shafts, and any rocker arms with loose

contact pads. When installing rocker arm shafts, notches must be aligned to allow cylinder head bolts to fit in openings. Install circlip and ensure that plug in exhaust side rocker shaft is tight.

NOTE — *Rocker arm shaft on intake side is open. Exhaust rocker shaft is plugged.*

VALVE SPRING SERVICE

Compress spring and remove keepers. Remove spring and retainer. Check spring free length and pressure and replace as required. Install springs with tight winding (painted mark) facing cylinder head. Install retainers and keepers.

VALVE GUIDE SERVICE

1) Check valve guide for wear. If replacement is necessary, press out guide toward combustion chamber. Measure guide bore in cylinder head. If bore exceeds .5512" (14 mm), ream head and install oversize guide.

2) Heat cylinder head to 428-482°F (220-250°C) and press in new guide from top side until tapered groove end protrudes .591" (15 mm) for standard guide, or .531" (13.5 mm) for modified guide. Ream guide to obtain specified clearance. Valve guides are available in the following sizes:

Valve Guide Sizes

Application	Guide O.D. In. (mm)
Standard	.5532 (14.05)
1st Oversize	.5551 (14.10)
2nd Oversize	.5590 (14.20)
3rd Oversize	.5630 (14.30)
Standard Length	2.047 (52.0)
Modified Length	1.988 (50.5)

VALVE SEAT SERVICE

Refer to illustration and note minimum valve seat and valve head thicknesses. If either specification is not met, replace necessary component. When replacing valve seat, remove old seat by turning out with suitable cutting tool. Drill out bore to appropriate oversize: note valve seat oversize to be used and rebore head allowing for shrink-fit of replacement seat. When installing new seat, heat head to approximately 392°F (200°C) and chill valve seat to approximately −94°F (−70°C). Replacement seats are available in the following oversizes:

Replacement Valve Seat Rings

Application	Measurement In. (mm)
Intake	
1st Oversize	1.864 (47.35)
2nd Oversize	1.872 (47.55)
Exhaust	
1st Oversize	1.589 (40.35)
2nd Oversize	1.596 (40.55)

320i 4 CYLINDER (Cont.)

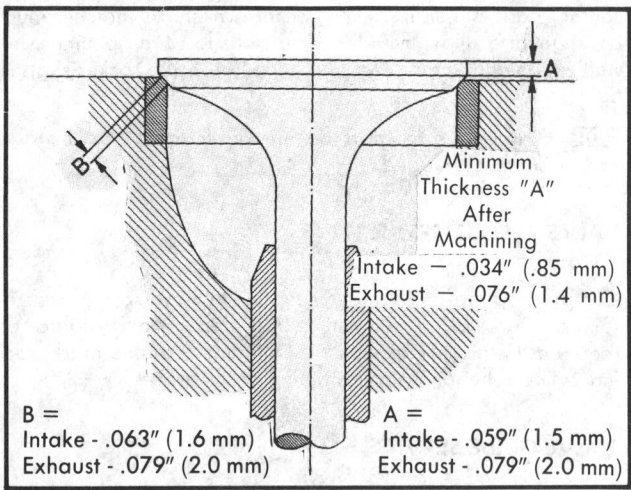

B =
Intake - .063" (1.6 mm)
Exhaust - .079" (2.0 mm)

A =
Intake - .059" (1.5 mm)
Exhaust - .079" (2.0 mm)

Minimum Thickness "A" After Machining
Intake — .034" (.85 mm)
Exhaust — .076" (1.4 mm)

Fig. 7   Checking Valve Head and Seat Thickness

VALVE CLEARANCE ADJUSTMENT

Adjust valves in firing order sequence (1-3-4-2) with No. 1 cylinder at TDC of compression stroke. Using a feeler gauge between rocker eccentric and valve stem, set clearance to .008-.010" (.20-.25 mm) with engine hot or to .006-.008" (.15-.20 mm) with engine cold. Loosen nut of rocker eccentric, insert a rod in eccentric hole and rotate until proper clearance is obtained. *See Fig. 8.*

NOTE — *Never measure or adjust valve clearance between camshaft and rocker arm pad.*

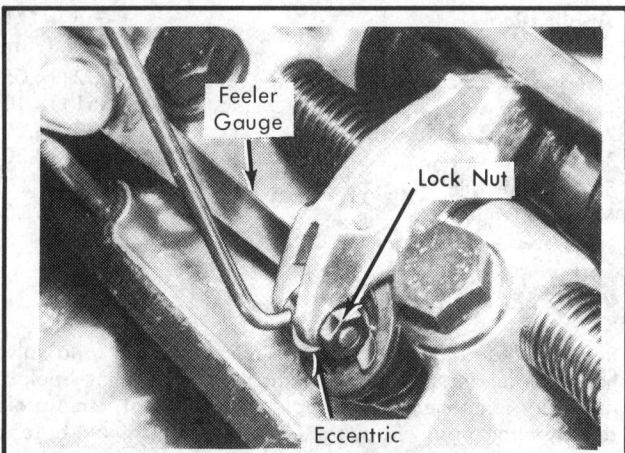

Feeler Gauge

Lock Nut

Eccentric

Fig. 8   Correct Procedure to Perform Tappet Adjustment

PISTONS, PINS & RINGS

OIL PAN

With engine installed, remove bolts securing steering to front axle carrier, move steering out of way. Drain oil, remove bolts securing oil pan, swing pan down. Turn crankshaft and remove oil pan. Coat crankcase ends where timing cover and rear main bearing cover join crankcase with sealing compound before reassembly.

PISTON & ROD ASSEMBLY

Removal — After removing oil pan and cylinder head, rotate crankshaft to BDC of piston and rod assembly to be removed. Unscrew connecting rod cap nuts and push assembly out top

---

of engine. Replace worn or damaged parts as necessary, according to appropriate service procedure indicated in this article.

Installation — Place rings on piston with marking "TOP" facing upward and ring end gaps 120° apart. Install piston with arrow facing forward and oil hole in wrist pin end of connecting rod facing timing chain. Ensure connecting rod and bearing cap numbers match, with No. 1 rod nearest the timing chain.

CONNECTING ROD BUSHING

Wrist pins and pistons are matched to each other and must be replaced together. To remove piston pin from assembly, remove circlip and push out wrist pin. In event of excess clearance, new wrist pin bushing may be pressed in rod. Bushing seam should be at 90° to oil bore. Drill and deburr oil holes, then ream bushing so that pin is a light push fit through connecting rod.

FITTING PISTONS

Piston crowns are marked with arrow for direction of installation and a "+", "-" or no sign to show weight classification. All pistons should have same weight mark. Measure piston and cylinder diameter to determine clearance (see specifications). Measure piston diameter at 90° to wrist pin bore near bottom of piston skirt, see following table for distance from bottom of piston.

Piston Measuring Location

Piston	①In. (mm)
Mahle	.630 (16.0)
KS	.959 (24.35)

① — Distance from bottom of piston.

Piston Sizes

Application (Grade)	Diameter In. (mm)
Standard	3.5027 (88.97)
Intermediate	3.5059 (89.05)
No. 1 Oversize	3.5126 (89.22)
No. 2 Oversize	3.5224 (89.47)

CRANKSHAFT MAIN & CONNECTING ROD BEARINGS

MAIN BEARING SERVICE

Plastigage method is used to determine connecting rod and main bearing journal clearances. Standard or undersize crankshafts are marked red or blue. Color coded inserts must agree with crankshaft color code as illustrated. The following tables show color code and undersizes available:

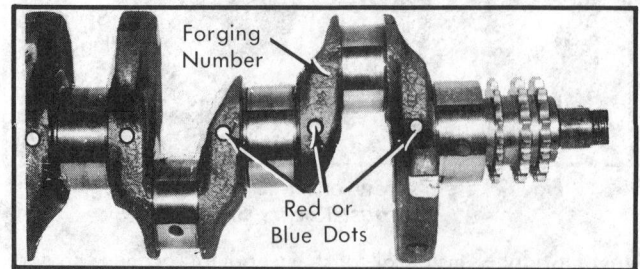

Forging Number

Red or Blue Dots

Fig. 9   View Showing Original Crankshaft Marks

320i 4 CYLINDER (Cont.)

Main Bearing Journal

Application	In. (mm)
Original	2.165 (55.0)
1st Stage	2.156 (54.75)
2nd Stage	2.146 (54.50)
3rd Stage	2.136 (54.25)

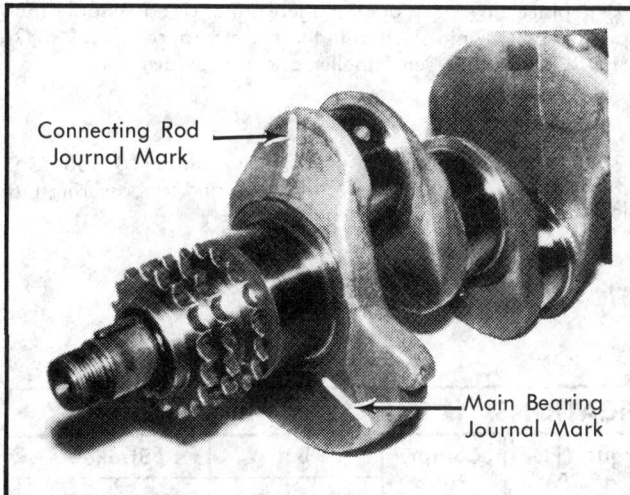

Fig. 10   View Showing Undersize Crankshaft Marking

Connecting Rod Journal

Application	In. (mm)
Original	1.889 (48.0)
1st Stage	1.879 (47.75)
2nd Stage	1.870 (47.50)
3rd Stage	1.860 (47.25)

CAUTION — *Crankshaft should only be factory ground.*

THRUST BEARING ALIGNMENT

Attach a dial indicator to crankcase with shaft touching flywheel. Move flywheel in and out to determine endplay of crankshaft. If endplay is excessive, replace center main bearing inserts.

REAR MAIN BEARING OIL SEAL SERVICE

With flywheel removed, unscrew six attaching bolts from rear crankshaft seal holder. Carefully run a knife blade between seal holder and oil pan gasket to break seal. Remove seal holder and press out old seal, press in new seal. Coat oil pan gasket at either side with sealing compound and replace seal holder.

FRONT COVER OIL SEAL

Seal may be replaced with engine in car. Remove radiator and fan belt. Lock flywheel with suitable tool (11 2 100), remove front pulley nut and take off pulley. Remove seal and inspect pulley for wear. Pack lips of new radial seal with grease and install with suitable tool (11 1 270). Position Woodruff key correctly and install pulley.

ENGINE OILING

ENGINE OILING SYSTEM

A chain driven rotor type oil pump pressure feeds oil to a full-flow oil filter. From oil filter, oil is circulated through passages to all moving parts of the engine.

Crankcase Capacity — 4.25 qts. (4.0 liters) with filter.

Oil Filter — Full-Flow

Oil Pressure — 57psi@4000 RPM

Pressure Regulator Valve — Non-adjustable

OIL PUMP

1) Remove oil pan and oil pump sprocket. Remove bolts attaching pump pick-up. Remove two bolts mounting pump to crankcase and lift out pump.

2) Unscrew union and remove spring and plunger from pump body. Remove pick-up tube and cover from pump body.

3) Measure clearance between outer rotor-to-pump body, rotor-to-rotor and rotor face-to-pump body flange (see specifications).

4) Using suitable puller, remove drive flange from rotor shaft. Press drive flange on new rotor shaft to a distance of 1.68" (42.7 mm) between flange and rotor face (See Fig. 11).

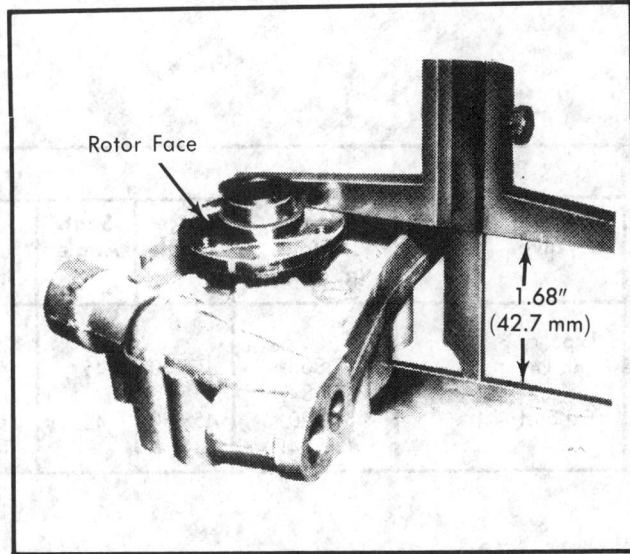

Fig. 11   Measuring Distance Between Flange and Rotor Face

Oil Pump Specifications

Application	Measurement In. (mm)
Rotor-to-Pump Body	.006-.011 (.150-.275)
Inner-to-Outer Rotor	.0047-.0079 (.12-.20)
Cover-to-Rotor	.0014-.0037 (.035-.095)
Pressure Relief Spring	
Free Length	2.677 (68.0)
Installed Length	2.618 (66.5)

BMW Engines

320i 4 CYLINDER (Cont.)

5) To install, reverse removal procedure noting that normal length (colored red) and extra long (colored green) chains are available. Further adjustment is possible by using shims between pump body and block. Oil hole in shims must line up with oil hole in pump. Chain tension is correct if chain gives under slight thumb pressure.

ENGINE COOLING

Thermostat — Opens at 176°F (80°C).
Cooling System Capacity — 7.4 qts. (7 liters)

WATER PUMP

1) Loosen alternator bracket. Remove fan and drive belt. Loosen hose clamps and remove water pump.

2) Using a suitable puller, remove fan hub from impeller shaft. Extract circlip and spacer ring from front of pump.

3) Press impeller off shaft and pump bearing out of housing. Drive friction seal out of housing and lift out cover ring.

4) Replace any worn or damaged parts. Using suitable tool, press impeller onto shaft until there is clearance of .039-.047" (1.0-1.2 mm) between impeller and pump face.

5) Press fan hub onto shaft until shaft extends .118-.138" (3.0-3.5 mm) beyond hub face. Install pump and fan, assuring that lockplates are crimped fan bolts.

ENGINE SPECIFICATIONS

GENERAL SPECIFICATIONS

| Year | Displ. | | Carburetor | HP at RPM | Torque (Ft. Lbs. at RPM) | Compr. Ratio | Bore | | Stroke | |
	cu. ins.	cc					in.	mm	in.	mm
1980	107.7	1766	Fuel Inj.	102 @ 5800	100 @ 4500	8.8:1	3.504	89	2.795	71

VALVES

Engine & Valve	Head Diam. In. (mm)	Face Angle	Seat Angle	Seat Width In. (mm)	Stem Diameter In. (mm)	Stem Clearance In. (mm)	Valve Lift In. (mm)
1766 cc							
Intake	1.805 (45.84)	45° 30'	45°	.059-.083 (1.50-2.10)	.3134-.3139 (7.960-7.975)	.0010-.0020 (.025-.055)	.....
Exhaust	1.490 (37.84)	45° 30'	45°	.061-.081 (1.55-2.05)	.3129-.3134 (7.945-7.960)	.0015-.0030 (.040-.070)	.....

VALVE SPRINGS

| Engine | Free Length In. (mm) ① | PRESSURE Lbs. @ In. (kg @ mm) | |
		Valve Closed	Valve Open
1766 cc	1.712 (43.5)	64 @ 1.48 (29 @ 37.6)	154 @ 1.12 (70 @ 28.5)

VALVE TIMING

| Engine | INTAKE | | EXHAUST | |
	Open (BTDC)	Close (ABDC)	Open (BBDC)	Close (ATDC)
1766 cc	4°	52°	52°	4°

① — May be 1.811" (46.0 mm) for some springs.

320i 4 CYLINDER (Cont.)
ENGINE SPECIFICATIONS (Cont.)

PISTONS, PINS, RINGS

Engine	PISTONS	PINS		RINGS		
	Clearance In. (mm)	Piston Fit In. (mm)	Rod Fit In. (mm)	Rings	End Gap In. (mm)	Side Clearance In. (mm)
1766 cc	.0018 (.045)	①.0008-.0024 (.002-.006)	.0001-.0004 (.003-.010)	No.1 No.2 No.3	①.012-.020 (.30-.50) .008-.016 (.20-.40) .010-.016 (.25-.40)	.0024-.0036 (.06-.092) ②.0016-.0028 (.040-.072) ②.0012-.0024 (.030-.062)

① — Mahle Pistons — .0004-.0020" (.001-.005 mm)
② — Mahle Pistons No. 2 — .0012-.0024" (.030-.062 mm)
　　 No. 3 .0008-.0020" (.020-.052 mm)

CRANKSHAFT MAIN & CONNECTING ROD BEARINGS

Engine	MAIN BEARINGS				CONNECTING ROD BEARINGS		
	Journal Diam. In. (mm)	Clearance In. (mm)	Thrust Bearing	Crankshaft End Play In. (mm)	Journal Diam. In. (mm)	Clearance In. (mm)	Side Play In. (mm)
1766 cc Red	2.165 (55.0)	.0012-.0027 (.030-.070)	Center	.0033-.0068 (.085-.174)	1.8898 (48.0)	.0012-.0027 (.030-.070)	.....
Blue	2.165 (55.0)	.0012-.0026 (.030-.068)	Center		1.8898 (48.0)	.0012-.0026 (.030-.068)	.....

CAMSHAFT

Engine	Journal Diam. In. (mm)	Clearance ①In. (mm)	Lobe Lift In. (mm)
1766 cc No. 1	1.3769-1.3795 (34.975-35.041)	.0013-.0029 (.033-.074)	6.95-7.11 (.273-.278)
No. 2	1.6525-1.6551 (41.975-42.041)	.0013-.0029 (.033-.074)	6.95-7.11 (.273-.278)
No. 3	1.6919-1.6945 (42.975-43.041)	.0013-.0029 (.033-.074)	6.95-7.11 (.273-.278)

① — End play is .0008-.005" (.020-.127 mm).

TIGHTENING SPECIFICATIONS

Application	Ft. Lbs. (mkg)
Cylinder Head Studs ①	
Step 1	25-32 (3.5-4.5)
Step 2	49-52 (6.8-7.2)
Step 3	56-59 (7.8-8.2)
Main Bearing Caps	42-46 (5.8-6.3)
Connecting Rod Bolts	38-41 (5.2-5.7)
Flywheel-to-Crankshaft ②	76-83 (10.5-11.5)
Rocker Arm Lock Bolts	7-8 (0.9-1.1)
Oil Pan Bolts	7-8 (0.9-1.1)
Camshaft Oiler (Hollow Bolt)	8-9 (1.1-1.3)
Crankshaft Pulley	101-108 (14-15)
Fuel Pump	7-10 (1.0-1.4)
Timing Cover	7-8 (0.9-1.1)

① — With engine cool, 95°F (35°C).
② — Coat bolts with Loctite.

BMW Engines

528i, 633CSi, & 733i 6 CYLINDER

ENGINE CODING

ENGINE IDENTIFICATION

Engine serial number is same as chassis serial number. Engine serial number is stamped in crankcase above starter.

ENGINE, CYLINDER HEAD & MANIFOLDS

NOTE — *Transmission (manual or automatic) must be removed prior to removing engine.*

MANUAL TRANSMISSION

Removal — **1)** Remove exhaust system and support brackets from vehicle. Pull up boot from shift lever, remove circlip and pull shift lever up and out. Disconnect drive shaft at transmission and loosen threaded coupling off drive shaft at rear of center bearing.

2) Remove center support bearing and pull drive shaft from transmission. Remove speedometer cable and disconnect backup light switch connection. Disconnect transmission from clutch housing. Support engine at front, remove transmission crossmember and transmission.

Installation — To install, reverse removal procedure. When installing drive shaft, push center support bearing forward .08" (2 mm) to preload bracket and tighten nuts.

AUTOMATIC TRANSMISSION

Removal — **1)** Disconnect exhaust system and remove support brackets. Disconnect accelerator cable at transmission and take off of counterholder. Drain transmission and remove filler tube. Plug filler tube opening and disconnect oil cooler lines at transmission. Remove web from bottom of drive shaft tunnel and disconnect wire harness to transmission.

2) Rotate torque converter and remove 4 bolts securing converter to drive plate. Disconnect shift rod from lever. Disconnect drive shaft coupling at rear of transmission and loosen threaded coupling at rear of center support bearing.

3) Remove center support bearing and pull drive shaft down and out to remove. Disconnect speedometer cable and backup light connection. Remove transmission crossmember, allowing engine oil pan to rest on front axle crossmember.

4) Place a jack under transmission and remove ground strap. Separate transmission from engine, making sure torque converter stays in housing in transmission. Remove transmission.

Installation — Reverse removal procedures and note that center support of torque converter is below edge of transmission. Push center support forward .08" (2 mm) to preload center bearing and tighten nuts. Adjust accelerator cable lever.

ENGINE

Removal — **1)** Drain cooling system and disconnect battery ground cable. Remove hood and radiator. Remove air cleaner with fuel injection air volume control unit. Remove distributor cap and secondary wiring. Disconnect vacuum line from distributor and primary wires from ignition coil.

2) Disconnect fuel feed hose at fuel filter, vapor hose at charcoal filter, and vacuum hoses from brake booster. Disconnect all remaining coolant and fuel hoses from engine. Remove engine ground cable and disconnect plug from fuel injection control unit. Pull control harness into engine compartment from glove box.

3) Mark for identification and disconnect all remaining electrical connections to engine. Detach air conditioner compressor (if equipped) and suspend from wire. Do NOT disconnect hoses. Disconnect wires from starter and alternator. Detach power steering pump from engine, leaving hoses connected.

4) Disconnect accelerator linkage from engine and remove nuts from engine mounts. Remove protective cover from under engine. Attach a hoist to lifting holes at front and rear of engine. On manual transmission models, push back rubber boot on slave cylinder, remove circlip and pull slave cylinder out toward front. Remove throw-out-bearing lever and bearing from clutch housing.

5) On all models, gradually lift engine and turn as necessary to clear vehicle. If disassembling engine, mount on engine support tool and adapter (00 1 500 and 11 0 130).

Installation — On manual transmission models, lubricate contact surfaces of throw-out-bearing lever with suitable lubricant. To install engine on all models, reverse removal procedures. Ensure that all hoses, lines and electrical connections are restored to original position.

INTAKE MANIFOLD

NOTE — *Throttle housing, air collector and intake pipes may be separated individually.*

Removal — **1)** Disconnect battery ground cable and remove cylinder head cover. Disconnect throttle linkage and detach throttle housing from collector, leaving water hose connected.

2) Mark for identification and remove hoses, lines and wires from intake system. Detach support bracket and press away from collector. Detach collector from intake pipes and remove collector.

Installation — Use all new gaskets and reverse removal procedure. Ensure that all hoses, lines and electrical connections are installed in correct locations.

CYLINDER HEAD

Removal — **1)** Disconnect battery ground cable and drain cooling system. Remove air cleaner, spark plug wire tube and valve cover. Disconnect fuel line at fuel pump.

2) Disconnect all fuel and vacuum lines, along with all wiring from injection system and cylinder head. Disconnect accelerator linkage.

3) Remove upper front cover. See *Engine Front Cover & Oil Seal.* Bend back lock tabs and remove camshaft sprocket bolts and sprocket. Remove timing chain tensioner plug, spring and piston. Disconnect water hoses at base of intake manifolds.

528i, 633CSi, & 733i 6 CYLINDER (Cont.)

4) Disconnect exhaust pipes. Remove cylinder head bolts and install aligning pins to keep rocker arm shafts from moving. Remove cylinder head.

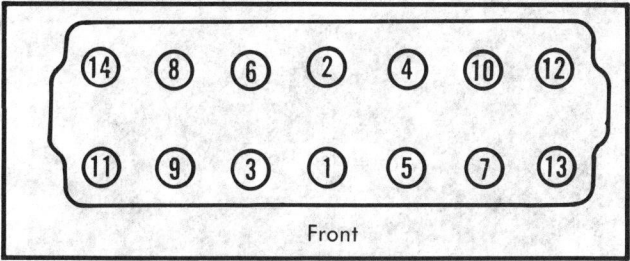

Fig. 1   Cylinder Head Tightening Sequence

Installation − 1) Ensure that there is no oil or fluid in recesses of block and insure that all mating surfaces are clean. Install new head gasket ensuring that openings for coolant flow are aligned. Install head and tighten head bolts in 3 steps in sequence illustrated. *See Tightening Specifications.*

NOTE − *Never loosen bolts during tightening sequence; turn only in tightening direction.*

2) Install camshaft sprocket and timing chain. *See Timing Chain Replacement.* Install valve cover and complete installation in reverse order of removal. Retighten cylinder head bolts after engine has been run and allowed to cool to approximately 100°F (38°C).

CAMSHAFT

ENGINE FRONT COVER AND OIL SEAL

Upper Front Engine Cover − 1) Remove distributor cap and valve cover. Remove thermostat housing and thermostat. Rotate crankshaft untill number one cylinder is at TDC of compression stroke. Distributor rotor should point at notch in distributor.

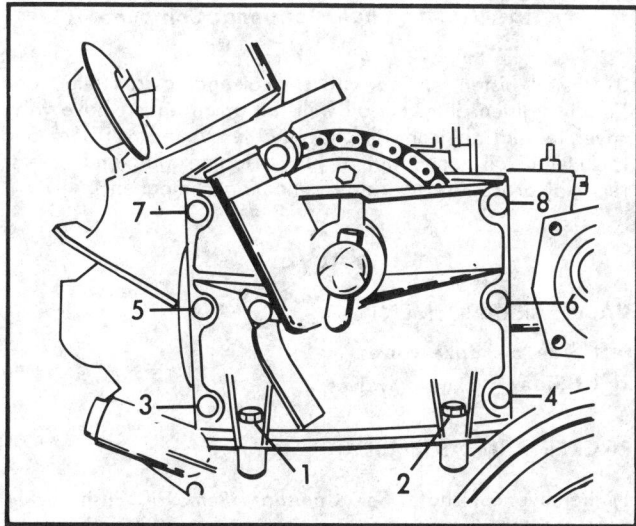

Fig. 2   Upper Front Cover Tightening Sequence

2) Disconnect vacuum lines to distributor. Loosen pinch bolt on distributor mounting and pull out distributor. Remove guard

and upper timing cover bolts. Take off cover with distributor drive gear.

3) To install, thoroughly clean all mating surfaces, fill bores of timing cover with Dirco (or equivalent) sealer, replace cord seal around distributor drive gear, and replace cover with new gasket and sealer. Turn distributor rotor counterclockwise so that rotor tip is about 1½" (38 mm) from notch in distributor housing and guide distributor into position. Note that vacuum advance unit is aligned approximately 90° to valve cover when installed properly.

4) Lightly tighten bolts one and two (see illustration), then tighten remaining bolts to specification in sequence shown in illustration. Tighten bolts one and two to specification. To install remaining components, reverse removal procedure.

Lower Front Engine Cover − 1) Remove upper front engine cover as previously outlined. Remove timing chain tensioner piston, fan clutch and crankshaft pulley. Remove lower front engine cover.

2) Replace oil seal. To install cover, reverse removal procedure. Thoroughly clean mating surfaces and use new gasket with sealer. Tighten bolts to specification.

NOTE − *Oil seal can be replaced without removing lower front engine cover.*

Timing Case Cover Oil Seal − 1) Remove lower flywheel cover and install suitable ring gear lock. Remove fan housing and all drive belts. Unscrew crankshaft nut and remove vibration damper with hub. Pry out radial seal.

2) Pack lips of new radial seal with grease. Press seal in with installing tool (11 1 280). Install components in reverse order of removal and remove lock on flywheel.

CAMSHAFT

Removal − 1) Cylinder head must be removed from engine. Remove coolant hose. Loosen bolts holding oil distribution line to rocker arm supports and remove line. Loosen all valve adjustments to maximum clearance position.

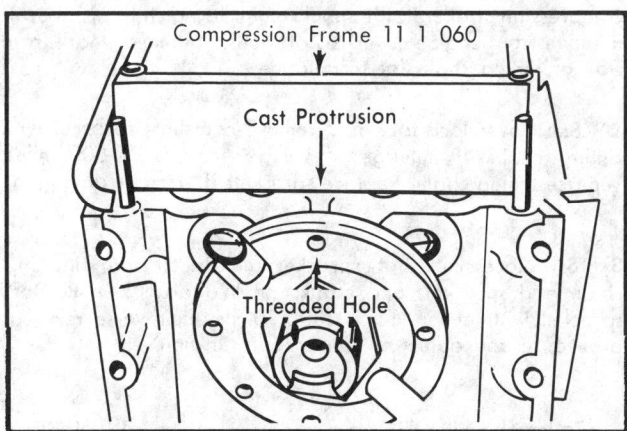

Fig. 3   Position of Camshaft with No. 6 Valves in Overlap Position

528i, 633CSi, & 733i 6 CYLINDER (Cont.)

2) Rotate camshaft from TDC position of No. 1 cylinder toward intake approximately .59" (15 mm) and install compression tool (11 1 060). Tighten exhaust side nuts on tool to stop, then intake side nuts. Remove camshaft retaining bolts and pull out camshaft.

Installation — 1) Install camshaft in head and tighten thrust plate bolts. Cam must turn easily without excess end play. Turn camshaft to No. 6 overlap position as illustrated and remove compression tool.

2) Install oil line so that oil bores will give off spray between rocker arms and cams of intake and exhaust valves. Ensure that seals are used between line and rocker supports as well as under head of attaching bolts. Continue assembly in reverse order of removal.

CAMSHAFT END PLAY

Check camshaft end play with a feeler gauge. If end play exceeds .001-.007" (.03-.18 mm), replace camshaft thrust plate.

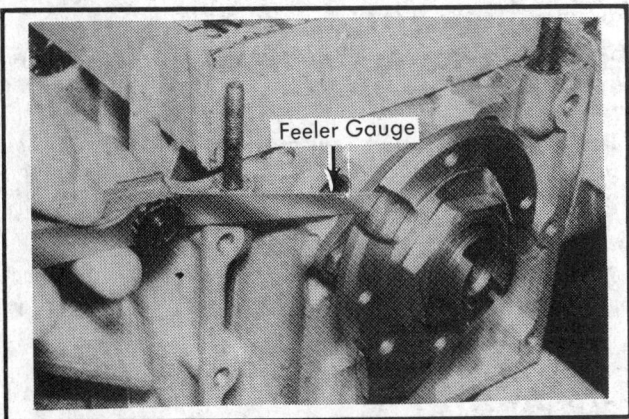

Fig. 4   Checking Camshaft End Play with Feeler Gauge

TIMING CHAIN REPLACEMENT

1) Rotate crankshaft until number one cylinder is at TDC of compression stroke. Rotor should point to notch in distributor. Remove front engine covers as previously outlined. Mark front side of timing chain for installation.

2) Bend over lock tabs and remove camshaft sprocket with timing chain. If mileage of vehicle exceeds 30,000 miles, replace timing chain. Replace sprockets if worn or damaged.

3) To replace crankshaft sprocket, remove oil pan, oil pump chain and sprocket, and crankshaft Woodruff key. Pull off sprocket with puller (11 2 000). To install, reverse removal procedure and adjust oil pump chain tension.

4) To install timing chain, reverse removal procedure, making sure number one cylinder is at TDC of compression stroke. Line up tapped hole in sprocket hub with cast protrusion in cylinder head and install timing chain and sprocket.

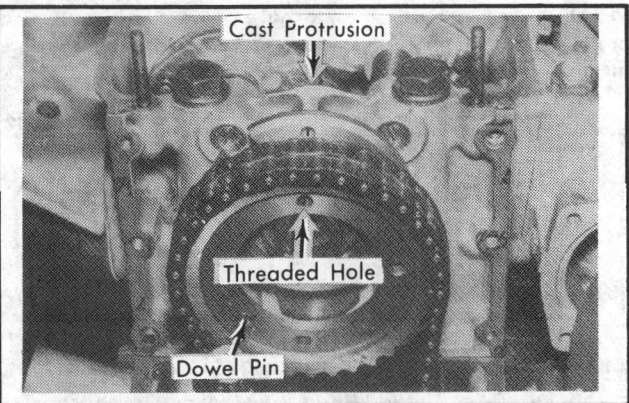

Fig. 5   Camshaft, Sprocket and Timing Chain Alignment for Installation

TIMING CHAIN TENSIONER

1) Remove tensioner plug, spring and piston. Check length of spring and piston assembly. Length of spring should be 6.122" (155.5 mm). Piston assembly length should be 2.441" (62.0 mm)

2) Check piston with compressed air to see if air vent slots (see illustration) are plugged. Clean slots if air does not pass through. When assembling piston, do not block air vents with disc.

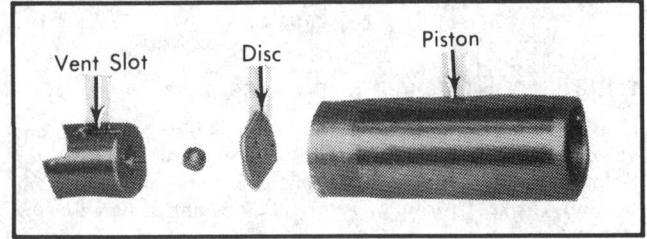

Fig. 6   Timing Chain Tensioner Components

3) Install piston, spring with conical end toward plug and slightly tighten plug. Fill oil well full of oil and remove valve cover to vent air from piston. Move tensioning rail back and forth until oil comes out at plug. Tighten plug and reverse removal procedure to install remaining components.

VALVES

VALVE ARRANGEMENT

Left Side — Intake valves.
Right Side — Exhaust valves.

ROCKER ARM ASSEMBLY

1) Remove camshaft. *See Camshaft Removal.* Push rocker arms and thrust rings against springs and remove circlips from front rocker arm shafts.

2) Remove two countersunk rocker arm shaft locking bolts next to number one bearing bore of camshaft. Install a suitable

528i, 633CSi, & 733i 6 CYLINDER (Cont.)

removing tool (No. 11 3 060) in shaft and pull out of cylinder head. Remove rocker arms, thrust rings, springs and disc.

3) Check rocker arms and shaft for excessive play. Normal shaft diameter should be at least .609" (15.466 mm) and maximum bushing bore in rocker arms should not exceed .611" (15.518 mm). Check cam follower pads on rocker arms for wear and security. If loose, replace rocker arms.

4) Install spring, disc, rocker arm and thrust ring. Install rocker arm shafts and adjust so that recesses in shafts are aligned with cylinder head bolt holes in cylinder head.

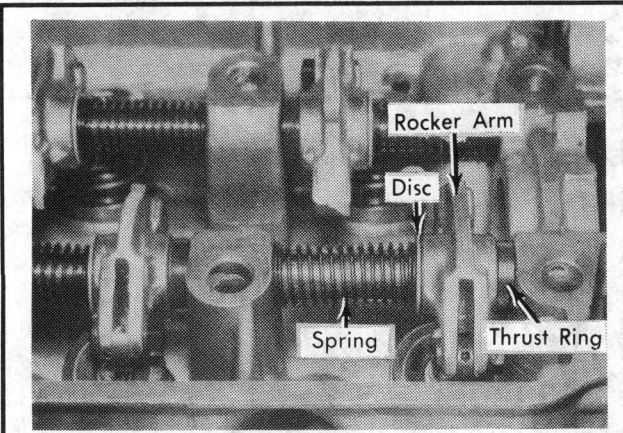

Fig. 7   Installed View of Rocker Arm Assembly

5) To disassemble rear rocker arm assemblies, remove rear cover on cylinder head. Use same procedure for rear shafts as used for front. Install self sealing discs on bolts for rear cover plate and use Cabritol sealer on plate gasket.

VALVE GUIDE SERVICING

1) With valve removed, check inside diameter of valve guide. If size exceeds specifications, drive guide out through combustion chamber with a suitable driver (No. 11 1 100).

2) Check size of valve guide bore in cylinder head. If size exceeds .5519" (14.018 mm), an oversize guide must be installed. If guide or bore condition warrant, the following sizes of guides are available for service replacement: .5551" (14.10 mm), .5591" (14.20 mm), and .5630" (14.30 mm).

3) Guides require a .0006-.0019" (.015-.044 mm) press fit in cylinder head with head heated to 430-480°F (220-250°C). Ream head bores according to guide size being installed.

4) Using suitable driver (No. 11 1 120), drive guide into cylinder head from top until top of guide protrudes .591" (15.0 mm) for standard guide, or .531" (13.5 mm) for modified guide. Ream valve guide until correct clearance with valve is obtained.

VALVE SPRING

With rocker arms and shafts removed, compress valve spring with suitable tool (11 1 060) and remove keepers. Remove valve spring and retainer and check spring free length. Check

compressed length and pressure in a suitable tester. Replace defective springs and assemble with paint stripe (tight coil end) against head. Install retainer and keepers.

VALVE STEM OIL SEALS

To replace valve stem oil seals, use guide or tape over stem grooves to prevent damage to new seals. Lubricate seal and press into position with suitable tool (11 1 130).

VALVE CLEARANCE ADJUSTMENT

Remove valve cover and turn crankshaft so that No. 1 cylinder is at TDC on firing stroke. Assure that engine temperature is cool (max. 95°F, 35°C) and use feeler gauge to check clearance between valve and adjusting eccentric. Clearance for both intake and exhaust valves should be .010-.012" (.25-.30 mm). To adjust clearance, loosen nut on rocker arm and rotate eccentric.

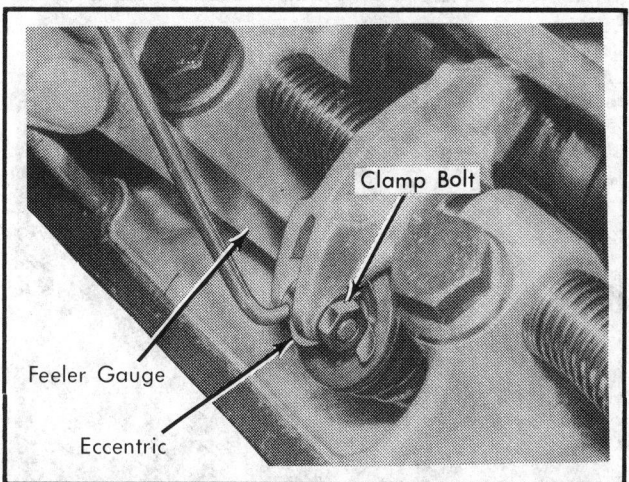

Fig. 8   Valve Clearance Adjustment Procedure

PISTONS, PINS & RINGS

OIL PAN

Drain engine oil and remove wires from oil level switch (if equipped). Remove power steering pump but do NOT disconnect hoses. Remove alternator and loosen mounting pad bolts enough to allow access to pan bolts. Remove bottom rear bolt of mounting pad and unscrew pan bolts. Turn crankshaft so that No. 6 connecting rod is above crankcase sealing surface and remove pan. On 733i, it may be necessary to detach engine mounts and lift engine slightly to completely remove pan. To install, use new gaskets and apply Atmosit sealer (or equivalent) to all junctions of block, pan and end covers. Continue in reverse order of removal.

PISTON & ROD ASSEMBLY

With cylinder head, oil pan and oil pump removed, remove connecting rod cap. Push piston and rod assembly up and out through top of block. To install, ensure that ring gaps are offset 120° to each other. Apply ring compressor and insert bearing halves in rod and cap. Install with arrow on piston top facing timing chain. Assemble cap to rod with numbers matching and tighten cap.

528i, 633CSi, & 733i 6 CYLINDER (Cont.)

PISTON PIN REPLACEMENT

1) With piston and rod assembly removed, remove circlips from piston pin hole in piston. Drive out piston pin and separate piston from connecting rod. Thoroughly clean and inspect rod and piston.

Piston Pin Class Designation

Application	Pin Diameter In. (mm)
White	.8660-.8661 (21.997-22.000)
Black	.8659-.8660 (21.994-21.997)
Blue	.8661-.8663 (22.000-22.005)

2) Pistons and pins are installed as a matched set only. Pin class may be coded by white or black marking for standard or blue for oversize pins.

Fig. 9   View Showing Connecting Rod Cap Installation

3) Classes of pins and pistons must not be interchanged. If piston or pin is replaced, it must be replaced with one of a corresponding class and weight. Weight classification is designated by a "+" or "−" stamped in top of piston.

4) Check pin-to-piston clearance, if clearance exceeds that specified and pin is not worn, replace piston. Check pin-to-rod clearance, if clearance exceeds that specified, depending on pin class, new bushing must be installed.

5) Press out old bushing and install new one with split in bushing rotated 90° from oil hole in connecting rod. Drill through oil hole in connecting rod. Ream bushing to specified clearance with piston pin.

6) If connecting rod is replaced, replace with rod which is within 4 grams of rod being replaced. Position piston on connecting rod with arrow on piston facing in same direction as oil hole in connecting rod. Lubricate and install piston pin and circlips.

FITTING PISTONS

1) With piston removed and disassembled from connecting rod, measure diameter of piston. Measure with micrometer positioned 90° from pin hole and at a point measured from bottom of piston skirt. (Distance "A" in *Fig. 10.*)

NOTE — *Distance depends on engine and manufacturer of pistons.*

Application	Manufacturer	Distance "A"
528i, 633CSi	Mahle	.630" (16.0 mm)
528i, 633CSi	KS	.947" (24.05 mm)
733i	Mahle	1.024" (26.0 mm)
733i	KS	1.340" (34.05 mm)

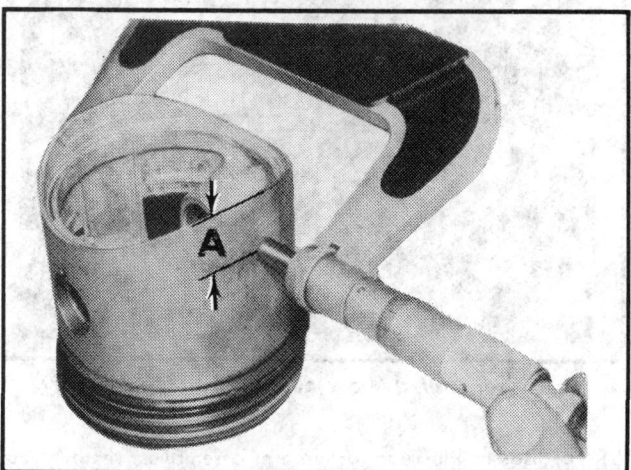

Fig. 10   Measuring Piston Diameter

2) Measure inside diameter of bore in crankcase. If clearance exceeds specification, crankcase must be bored for next oversize piston. Pistons are available in .010" (.25 mm) and .020" (.50 mm) oversize.

3) Check piston ring side clearance and end gap. If new rings are installed, install with word "TOP" stamped in ring toward top of piston.

CRANKSHAFT MAIN & CONNECTING ROD BEARINGS

MAIN & CONNECTING ROD BEARING SERVICE

1) With engine removed, remove clutch, flywheel, cylinder head, oil pan and timing chain. See *Timing Chain Replacement.* Remove rear main bearing oil seal mount.

2) Remove pistons and connecting rods. Remove main bearing caps and lift out crankshaft. Thoroughly clean and inspect crankshaft. Blow out oil passages with compressed air.

3) Main bearing journals are manufactured in 2 standard sizes. Sizes are designated by a colored dot on crankshaft balance weight next to individual journal. See *Fig. 11.*

528i, 633CSi, & 733i 6 CYLINDER (Cont.)

4) Check main and connecting rod bearing clearance using Plastigage method. If clearance will not meet specifications when installing new bearings, it will be necessary to exchange crankshaft. Crankshaft is tenifer treated and may only be reground at the factory.

5) Install bearing halves in crankcase and bearing caps. Lubricate crankshaft bearing journals and install crankshaft in crankcase.

NOTE — *In the event of a crankshaft of a different colorcode than the crankcase, use one blue and one red bearing shell for each journal. Make sure that all red or all blue shells are installed facing up and the remaining color facing down.*

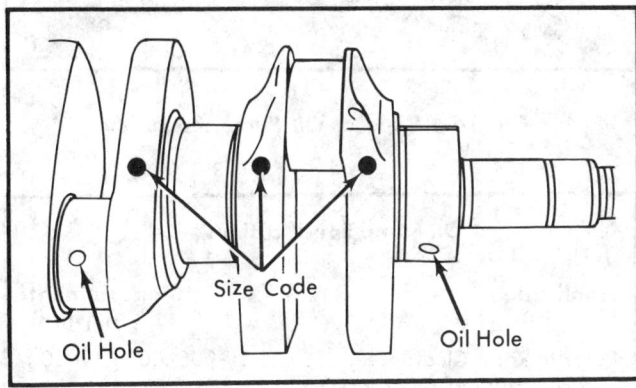

Fig. 11 Crankshaft Color Code Markings

6) Install bearing caps with numbers on caps running from one through six in order from front to rear. Install caps with bearing locks on same side as bearing locks in crankcase.

7) Tighten caps to specifications. Check crankshaft endplay. *See Thrust Bearing Alignment.* To install remaining components, reverse removal procedure.

NOTE — *Crankshafts which have been ground undersize are marked with painted stripes. See Illustration.*

Fig. 12 View Showing Crankshaft Undersize Markings

Crankshaft Journal Sizes

Connecting Rod	In. (mm)
Standard	1.888-1.889 (47.97-47.99)
1 paint stripe	1.852-1.853 (47.72-47.74)
2 paint stripes	1.851-1.852 (47.48-47.49)
3 paint stripes	1.850-1.851 (47.22-47.24)
Main Bearings Red Code	**In. (mm)**
Standard	2.361-2.362 (59.98-59.99)
1 paint stripe	2.324-2.325 (59.73-59.74)
2 paint stripes	2.323-2.324 (59.48-59.49)
3 paint stripes	2.322-2.323 (59.23-59.24)
Main Bearings Blue Code	**In. (mm)**
Standard	2.361-2.362 (59.98-59.99)
1 paint stripe	2.324-2.325 (59.72-59.73)
2 paint stripes	2.323-2.324 (59.47-59.48)
3 paint stripes	2.322-2.323 (59.22-59.23)

THRUST BEARING ALIGNMENT

Check axial play prior to disassembly by attaching dial indicator to block and moving flywheel to front and rear. If play exceeds .007" (.174 mm), check and replace main bearings as required.

REAR MAIN BEARING OIL SEAL REPLACEMENT

NOTE — *To replace rear main bearing oil seal in vehicle, transmission must be removed.*

1) Remove clutch and flywheel and drain engine oil. Remove bolts securing oil pan to rear main bearing oil seal mount.

2) Pry oil pan down at area around seal mount, taking care not to damage gasket. Remove bolts securing seal mount to crankcase and remove mount.

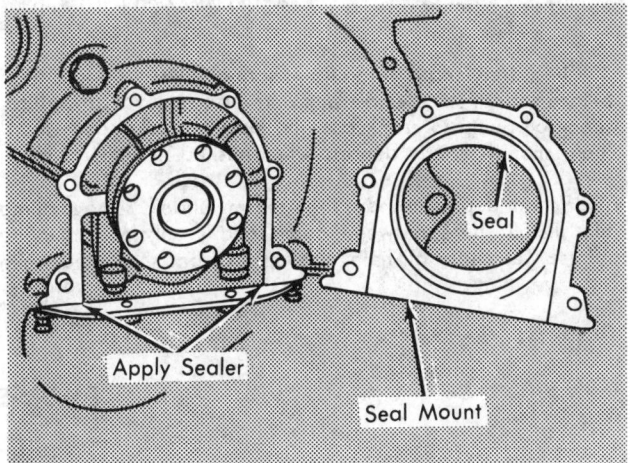

Fig. 13 Installing Crankshaft Rear Oil Seal

3) Pry old seal from mount and install new one using driver and adapter (00 5 500 and 11 1 260). Use guide (11 2 213) when replacing mount to prevent damage to seal. Pack seal lips with grease and apply Atmosit (or equivalent) sealer to junction of oil pan and seal mount. Reverse removal procedure to complete installation.

528i, 633CSi, & 733i 6 CYLINDER (Cont.)

ENGINE OILING

ENGINE OILING SYSTEM

Full pressure oil system, utilizing a chain driven Eaton type oil pump, a full flow filter and a pressure regulator valve.

Crankcase Capacity — 6 quarts including filter.

Oil Filter — Full-flow, paper element type.

Normal Oil Pressure — 7-28 psi (.5-2.0 kg/cm²) at idle and 71 psi (5.0 kg/cm²) at max. RPM.

Pressure Regulator Valve — Mounted in oil pump. *See Oil Pump Removal.*

OIL PUMP

1) Remove oil pan, front engine covers and timing chain as previously outlined. Remove oil pump drive sprocket and chain. Remove oil pump.

2) Remove pressure regulator plug, spring and piston. Remove pump cover and thoroughly clean and inspect all components. Check clearance between inner and outer rotors. If clearance exceeds maximum specified, replace rotors.

3) Check clearance between outer rotor and pump body and clearance between rotor sealing face and mating surface of pump body and pump cover. If either clearance exceeds maximum specified, replace pump body.

4) To remove sprocket flange, pull with suitable tool. Install flange so that distance between sprocket side of flange and sealing side of inner rotor is 1.744±.004″ (44.30±.10 mm).

5) Check free length of regulator spring, if less than specified, replace spring. To assemble pump, reverse removal procedure. Attach oil pump to crankcase and install sprocket and chain. Chain should slightly depress when pushed in with thumb.

6) If chain depresses more than recommended, remove pump and install shims between pump and crankcase mounting points. Make sure oil holes line up on front shim. Rear shim must be same thickness as front. To install remaining components, reverse removal procedure.

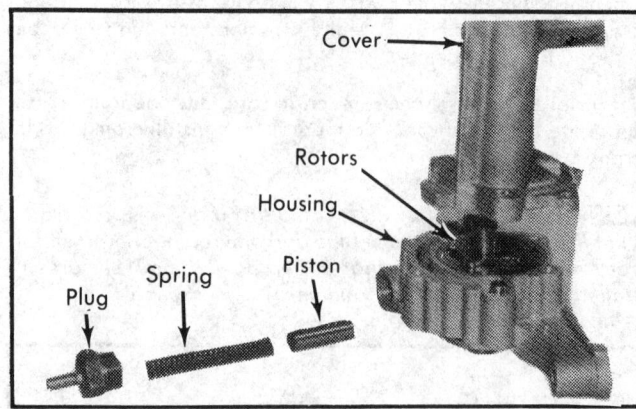

Fig. 14   View of Oil Pump Assembly

Oil Pump Specifications	
Application	**Measurement In. (mm)**
Rotor-to-Rotor Clearance	.005-.008 (.12-.20)
Rotor-to-Housing Clearance	
Radial	.006-.011 (.150-.275)
Axial	.0014-.0037 (.035-.095)
Regulator Spring Free Length	2.677 (67.99)

ENGINE COOLING

WATER PUMP

Remove clutch fan, pulley, side bar and connecting hose. Remove water pump. To install, reverse removal procedure. Use new gaskets and sealer.

Thermostat — Opens at 176°F (80°C).

Cooling System Capacity — 12.7 qts.

ENGINE SPECIFICATIONS

GENERAL SPECIFICATIONS										
Year	**Displ.**		**Carburetor**	**HP at RPM**	**Torque (Ft. Lbs. at RPM)**	**Compr. Ratio**	**Bore**		**Stroke**	
	cu. ins.	cc					in.	mm	in.	mm
1980										
528i	170	2788	Fuel Inj.	169@5500	170@4500	8.2:1	3.386	86	3.150	80
633CSi	196	3210	Fuel Inj.	177@5500	195@4000	8.4:1	3.504	89	3.386	86
733i	196	3210	Fuel Inj.	174@5200	188@4200	8.0:1	3.504	89	3.386	86

528i, 633CSi, & 733i 6 CYLINDER (Cont.)
ENGINE SPECIFICATIONS (Cont.)

VALVES							
Engine & Valve	Head Diam. In. (mm)	Face Angle	Seat Angle	Seat Width In. (mm)	Stem Diameter In. (mm)	Stem Clearance In. (mm)	Valve Lift In. (mm)
2788 cc & 3210cc Intake	1.811 (46.0)	45°30'	45°	.063-.079 (1.6-2.0)	.3134-.3140 (7.960-7.975)	.0010-.0022 (.025-.055)	.....
Exhaust	1.496 (38.0)	45°30'	45°	.079-.095 (2.0-2.4)	.3128-.3134 (7.945-7.960)	.0016-.0027 (.040-.070)	.....

VALVE SPRINGS			
Engine	Free Length In. (mm)	PRESSURE Lbs. @ In. (kg @ mm)	
		Valve Closed	Valve Open
2788 cc & 3210 cc	①1.712 (43.5)	64±2.5@1.480 (29.0±1.2@37.6)	154±6@1.122 (70.0±2.8@28.5)

① — Some springs are 1.811" (46.0 mm), depending on manufacturer.

PISTONS, PINS, RINGS						
	PISTONS	PINS		RINGS		
Engine	Clearance In. (mm)	Piston Fit In. (mm)	Rod Fit In. (mm)	Rings	End Gap In. (mm)	Side Clearance In. (mm)
2788 cc & 3210 cc	.0016-.0018 (.040-.045)	0-0002 (0-.005)	①.0002-.0005 (.005-.013) ②.0003-.0006 (.008-.016)	No. 1 No. 2 Oil	.012-.020 (.30-.50) .008-.016 (.20-.40) .010-.016 (.25-.40)	③.002-.004 (.06-.09) ③.001-.002 (.03-.06) ③.0008-.002 (.02-.06)

① — White color code.   ② — Black color code.   ③ — Mahle specifications shown; For KS, No. 1 .002-.004" (.06-.09 mm), No. 2 .002-.003" (.04-.07 mm), Oil .001-.002 (.03-.06 mm).

CRANKSHAFT MAIN & CONNECTING ROD BEARINGS						
	MAIN BEARINGS				CONNECTING ROD BEARINGS	
Engine	Journal Diam. In. (mm)	Clearance In. (mm)	Thrust Bearing	Crankshaft End Play In. (mm)	Journal Diam. In. (mm)	Clearance In. (mm)	Side Play In. (mm)
2788 cc & 3210 cc Red Code	2.3614-2.3618 (59.98-59.99)	.0012-.0028 (.030-.070)	No. 4	.0033-.0069 (.085-.174)	1.8888-1.8894 (47.975-47.991)	.0009-.0027 (.023-.069)	.....
Blue Code	2.3610-2.3614 (59.97-59.98)	.0012-.0027 (.030-.068)					

BMW Engines

528i, 633CSi, & 733i 6 CYLINDER (Cont.)

ENGINE SPECIFICATIONS (Cont.)

CAMSHAFT			
Engine	Journal Diam. In. (mm)	Clearance In. (mm)	Lobe Lift In. (mm)
2788 cc & 3210 cc		.0013-.003 (.03-.075)	.2802 (7.12)
No. 1	1.3764-1.3770 (34.96-34.98)		
No. 2	1.7304-1.7310 (43.95-43.97)		
No. 3	1.7704-1.7710 (44.97-44.98)		
No. 4	1.8094-1.8100 (45.96-45.97)		

VALVE TIMING				
	INTAKE		EXHAUST	
Engine	Open (BTDC)	Close (ABDC)	Open (BBDC)	Close (ATDC)
2788 cc ①	47°	51°	51°	47°
②	18°	62°	62°	18°
3210 cc ①	14°	54°	54°	14°
②	26°	66°	66°	26°

① — With .020" (.51 mm) clearance between heel of camshaft and rocker pad.
② — With .014" (.37 mm) clearance between heel of camshaft and rocker pad.

TIGHTENING SPECIFICATIONS

Application	Ft. Lbs. (mkg)
Cylinder Head Bolts①	
1st Stage	26-32 (3.5-4.5)
2nd Stage	49-52 (6.8-7.2)
3rd Stage	56-59 (7.8-8.2)
Main Bearing Bolts	42-45 (5.8-6.3)
Rod Cap Nuts	38-41 (5.3-5.7)
Camshaft Thrust Plate	101-108 (14.0-15.0)
Upper Front Engine Cover	7-8 (0.9-1.1)
Lower Front Engine Cover	7-8 (0.9-1.1)
Oil Pan Bolts	7-8 (0.9-1.1)
Timing Chain Tensioner Plug	22-29 (3.0-4.0)
Rocker Arm Clamp Bolt	6.5-8.0 (0.8-1.1)
Flywheel Bolts ②	72-84 (10.0-11.6)
Crankshaft Pulley Nut	318-333 (44.0-46.0)
Oil Pump Regulator Plug	26-30 (3.6-4.1)
Camshaft Oil Line Hollow Bolt	8-9 (1.1-1.3)

① — With engine cool — Max. 95°F (33°C).
② — Coat threads with Loctite.

1400, 1600, 2000 & 2600 cc 4 CYLINDER

ENGINE CODING

ENGINE IDENTIFICATION

Engine model code and serial number is stamped on engine block just below number 1 spark plug on right side of block. Model codes are as follows:

Engine Identification		
Application In. (cc)	Engine Model	Model Code
86.0 (1400) .... J G12B
97.5 (1600) .... K G32B
121.7 (2000) .... U G52B
155.9 (2600) .... ①F G54B

① — Code "W" for Pickup models.

ENGINE & CYLINDER HEAD

ENGINE

Removal (Rear Wheel Drive Models) — **1)** Drain cooling system, remove battery and remove engine hood. Disconnect ground strap, wiring from ignition coil, vacuum control solenoid valve, fuel cut-off solenoid valve, generator, starter, transmission switch, back-up light switch, water temperature gauge and oil pressure switch.

2) Remove air cleaner and disconnect attaching hoses. Disconnect accelerator linkage and heater hoses. Unbolt and separate exhaust pipe from manifold. Disconnect pipe mounting bracket at transmission.

3) Disconnect hose between fuel filter and fuel pump return pipe. Remove radiator and radiator shroud. If equipped with automatic transmission, remove oil cooler pipe and tie rod when removing radiator.

4) Remove console box, then detach control lever assembly from transmission. Remove hood. Disconnect speedometer cable and back-up light switch wiring from transmission. Disconnect clutch cable from shift lever and then disconnect cable from its bracket (if equipped with manual transmission). Drain transmission. If equipped with transmission dynamic vibration damper, remove damper, remove locking bolts for attaching flange yoke at rear of propeller shaft, then draw shaft out of transmission.

5) Support transmission on a suitable jack and remove front and rear mount bolts. Remove rear engine support bracket. Attach suitable lifting device to front and rear engine hangers. Lift engine-transmission assembly at an angle, upward and out of engine compartment.

NOTE — *Keep transmission lower than engine when removing. If lower part of bell housing interferes with relay rod, raise rear of transmission to clear rod, then remove engine-transmission assembly.*

Removal (Front Wheel Drive Models) — **1)** Drain cooling system and remove battery and tray. Remove air cleaner assembly. Remove purge control valve bracket from battery support and disconnect vacuum hose from valve. Remove windshield washer tank and coolant reservoir.

2) Remove radiator assembly and cooling fan. Disconnect the following from engine-transaxle: clutch, accelerator and speedometer cables; heater hose, fuel hoses, VCU vacuum hose, idle up switch vacuum hose; wires from starter, engine ground, alternator, coolant temperature, ignition coil, high-temp sensor, back-up light and oil pressure switch.

3) Remove ignition coil. From under vehicle, remove under-cover and drain transaxle. Remove right and left drive shafts from transaxle case and suspend with wire to prevent damaging joints. Cover holes in transaxle case to prevent entry of foreign matter.

NOTE — *Drive shaft retainer rings should be replaced whenever drive shafts are removed from transaxle.*

4) Remove assist rod, control rod and range selector cable from transaxle. Disconnect and suspend exhaust pipe. Remove front roll rod bolts and loosen transaxle mounting bracket attaching nuts. Remove bolts and nuts from front and rear engine insulators and disconnect rear roll rod.

5) Suspend engine from chains attached to hoisting brackets and remove mounting bracket nuts loosened previously. Lift engine-transaxle assembly from vehicle using care that assembly does not hit battery bracket during removal.

Installation (All Models) — Reverse removal procedures and tighten mounting bolts and nuts to specifications with weight of engine on insulators. Replace all fluids and adjust all cables and linkages.

CYLINDER HEAD & INTAKE MANIFOLD

Removal — **1)** Drain cooling system. Disconnect water hoses at cylinder head, manifold and carburetor. Remove breather and purge hose, vacuum hose at distributor and purge control valve.

2) Disconnect accelerator linkage, spark plug wires, water temperature gauge unit and exhaust manifold flange. Remove air cleaner, fuel line, distributor and fuel pump. Remove exhaust manifold, then intake manifold and carburetor assembly.

3) Remove rocker cover and breather. On 1400 and 1600 cc engine, remove timing belt upper front cover. Turn crankshaft so number 1 piston is at TDC on compression stroke. Mark belt (1400 or 1600 cc) or chain (2000 and 2600 cc) with suitable marker in line with sprocket mark. On 1400 cc engine, move timing belt tensioner fully toward water pump and slide belt off camshaft sprocket.

4) Except on 1400 cc engine, remove camshaft sprocket from camshaft. On 1600 cc engine, remove timing belt upper inner cover. Remove cylinder head bolts in 2 or 3 stages according to sequence shown in *Fig. 2*, loosening high numbers first. Lift off head using caution to avoid twisting sprocket and chain (or belt).

1400, 1600, 2000 & 2600 cc 4 CYLINDER (Cont.)

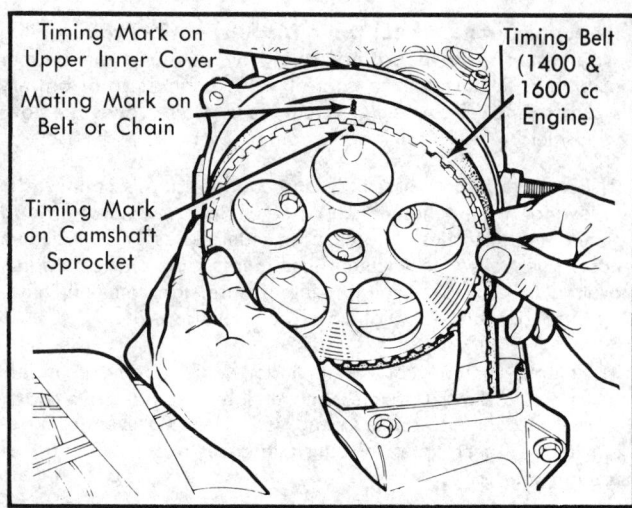

Fig. 1   Aligning Timing Marks at TDC (1400 & 1600 cc Engine Shown)

Installation — 1) To install, reverse removal procedure. Gasket surfaces must be clean and NEW gaskets must be used. Use sealer ONLY at points where cylinder head joins front cover case (2000 and 2600 cc engines) and to intake manifold gasket around water passages (all models). On 1400 cc engine, ensure that timing belt tensioner is properly adjusted.

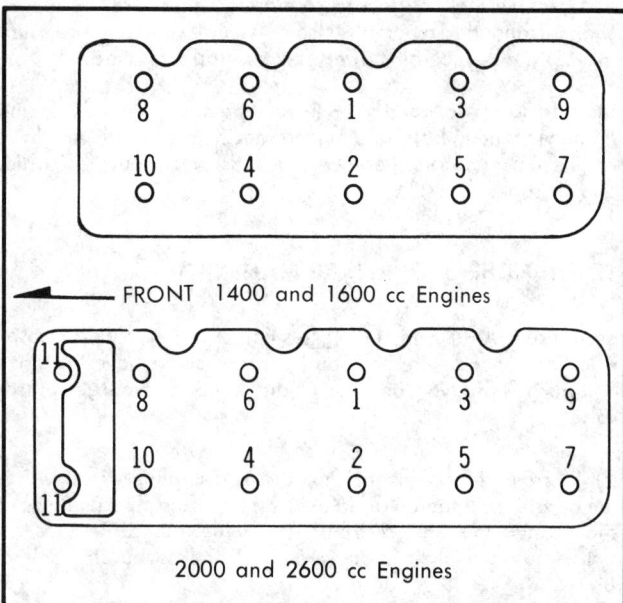

Fig. 2   Cylinder Head Bolt Tightening Sequence (Remove in Reverse Order)

NOTE — *Avoid sliding cylinder head when installing in order to prevent damage to gasket and aligning dowels (when installed). Engine should not be run with rocker cover off due to oil spray from rocker arms.*

2) Tighten cylinder head bolts to initial torque (25 ft. lbs. for 1600 cc, 35 ft. lbs. for others) according to sequence shown in *Fig. 2*. Repeat the procedure, retightening all cylinder head bolts to specified torque.

3) Temporarily set valve clearance to cold engine settings, then readjust to hot engine settings after engine is at normal operating temperature. Install rocker cover, air cleaner and breather hoses.

CAMSHAFT

ROCKER ARMS & SHAFTS (1400 cc)

Removal & Installation — Remove air cleaner, breather hose to rocker cover and rocker cover. Remove rocker shaft mounting bolts and lift off rocker shaft, rocker arms and rocker arm springs as an assembly. Remove bolts from shafts and slide off springs and rocker arms. To install, ensure that short springs are used on right hand rocker arm and reverse removal procedure.

CAMSHAFT (1400 cc)

Removal — 1) Remove rocker arms and shafts as previously described. Remove timing belt cover and move belt tensioner fully toward water pump, ensuring that camshaft sprocket mark is aligned with head timing mark. Remove timing belt and camshaft sprocket from camshaft.

2) Remove distributor and fuel pump. Remove camshaft rear cover from rear of head and thrust case tightening bolt from top of head. Tap sprocket end of shaft with brass drift and remove camshaft from rear of head.

3) Check thrust case for camshaft end play. If excessive, replace thrust case and recheck. If rear of camshaft journal is badly worn, replace camshaft.

Installation — To install, thoroughly lubricate camshaft and seal lips and reverse removal procedure.

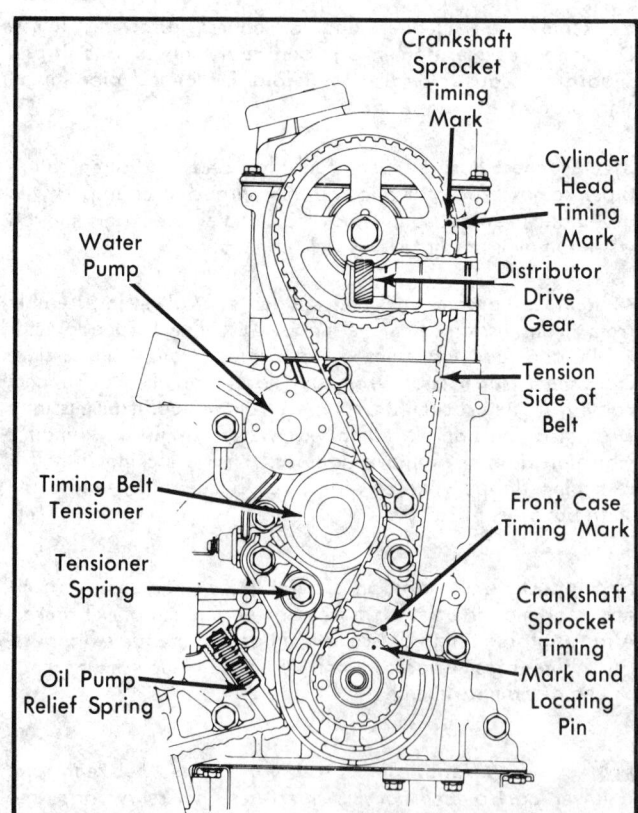

Fig. 3   View of 1400 cc Timing Belt Installation

1400, 1600, 2000 & 2600 cc 4 CYLINDER (Cont.)

ROCKER ASSEMBLY & CAMSHAFT (1600, 2000 & 2600 cc)

Removal — 1) Remove air cleaner, breather hoses and purge line. Remove fuel pump and line (2000 and 2600 cc engines). Disconnect spark plug wires and remove rocker cover. Remove breather and semicircular seal (2000 and 2600 cc engines). Slightly loosen camshaft sprocket bolt and turn engine to TDC of compression stroke on number 1 cylinder.

2) Make mating mark on timing belt or chain and camshaft sprocket. Remove camshaft sprocket and hang sprocket on sprocket holder provided on timing belt or chain lower front cover. Remove distributor drive gear (2000 and 2600 cc engines). Remove camshaft spacer and upper under cover (1600 cc engines).

NOTE — If there is a large gap between camshaft sprocket and sprocket holder, insert a 2" (50 mm) piece of timing belt or similar material into the gap to prevent belt from disengaging from crankshaft sprocket or oil pump sprocket.

3) Remove camshaft bearing caps, rocker arms and rocker shafts as an assembly. Remove oil seal and distributor drive gear from camshaft (1600 cc engine). Remove camshaft.

NOTE — If front and rear bearing caps are left inserted, rocker shaft assembly can be removed without separation of pieces.

Installation — 1) Lubricate camshaft lobes and camshaft bearing journals and install camshaft to cylinder head. Install distributor drive gear (1600 cc engine). Install rocker arm assembly to cylinder head. Camshaft should be positioned with keyway at 41° position (1600 cc engine), or dowel in the 12 o'clock position (2000 & 2600 cc engines). See Figs. 4 and 5.

2) Insert camshaft bearing cap bolts and tighten to 7 ft. lbs. (1 mkg) in sequence of center, 2, 4, front and rear. Repeat sequence, tightening to specified torque. Install camshaft sprocket and distributor drive gear to camshaft (2000 & 2600 cc engines). Using seal installer (MD998284) drive camshaft oil seal in until installer touches distributor drive gear (1600 cc engine). To complete installation, reverse removal procedure.

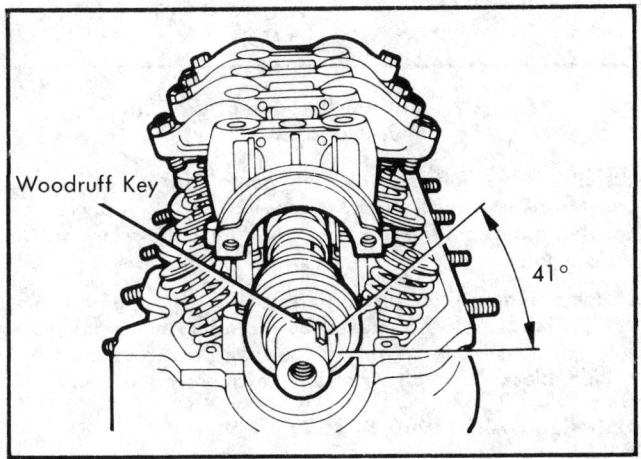

Fig. 4   Camshaft Woodruff Key Position for Installation (1600 cc Engine)

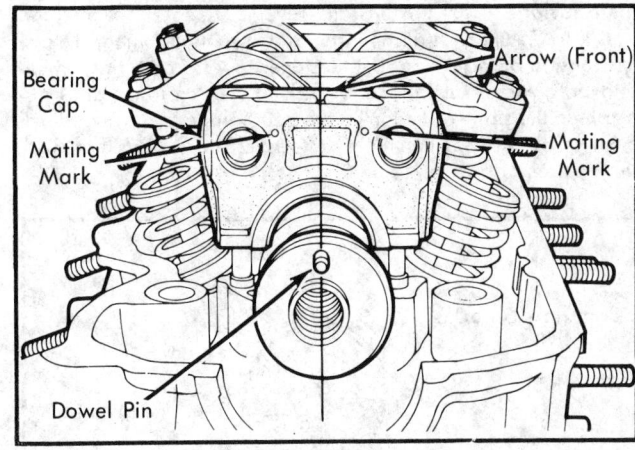

Fig. 5   Camshaft Installation Position and Bearing Cap/Rocker Arm Shaft Mating Marks (2000 and 2600 cc Engines)

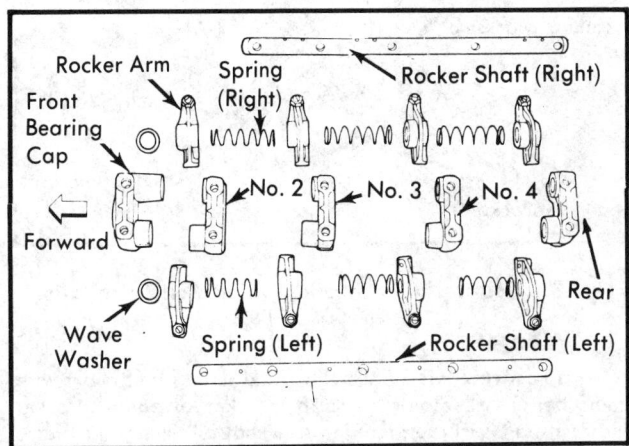

Fig. 6   Exploded View of Rocker Assembly

COUNTERBALANCE SHAFTS & TIMING BELT (1600 cc)

NOTE — Timing belt drives camshaft, oil pump and left counterbalance shaft. A separate belt drives counterbalance shaft on right side.

Removal — 1) With engine removed and timing belt marked. Remove crankshaft pulley, upper and lower timing belt front covers. Loosen belt tensioner mounting nut and bolt. Remove timing belt. Remove camshaft sprocket, crankshaft sprocket and flange, remove timing belt tensioner.

2) Remove plug at bottom of left side of cylinder block and insert a screwdriver, to keep left counterbalance shaft in position. Remove crankshaft sprocket and counterbalance shaft sprocket from right side. Remove timing belt covers from right side. Remove water pump and cylinder head assembly. Remove oil pan and oil pick-up screen. Remove oil pump cover.

3) With screwdriver through plug hole in cylinder block to hold counterbalance shaft, loosen oil pump driven gear bolt. Remove front case with left counterbalance shaft attached. Remove right counterbalance shaft from cylinder block.

1400, 1600, 2000 & 2600 cc 4 CYLINDER (Cont.)

Installation – **1)** To install, reverse removal procedure. Check to ensure that all timing marks are in alignment. To adjust tension on right side. Lift tensioner toward belt; tighten nut and bolt. Make sure that the shaft of the tensioner does not rotate in the same direction as the bolt tightens. Correct adjustment is obtained when belt deflects .20-.27" (5-7 mm) with finger pressure.

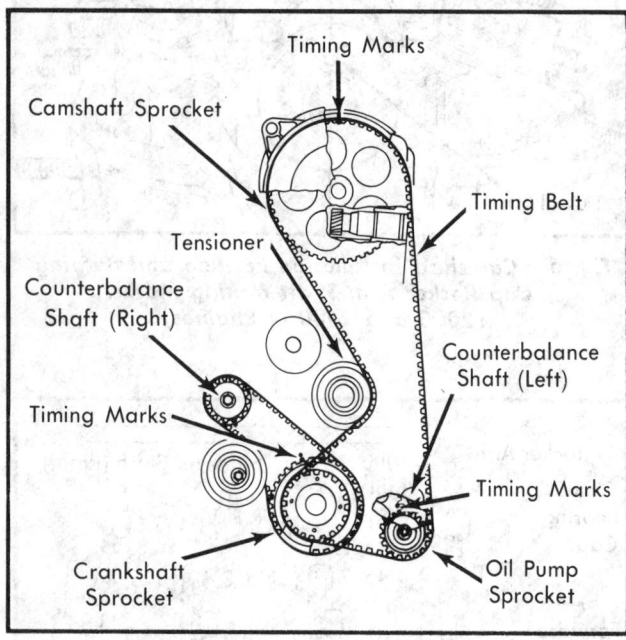

Fig. 7   Counterbalance and Timing Belt Installation (1600 cc)

2) To adjust counterbalance shaft and timing belt, start with timing belt installed on crankshaft sprocket, oil pump sprocket and camshaft sprocket, making sure that all timing marks are in alignment. With tensioner installed, lightly push up toward mounting nut, to make sure that timing belt comes into complete mesh with camshaft sprocket. Tighten mounting nut and bolt (tighten nut first).

3) Turn crankshaft through a complete rotation in normal direction. (Make sure that crankshaft is turned smoothly and in the correct direction.) Loosen tensioner mounting nut and bolt. At this time, the loose side of the belt will be given tension. Tighten nut and bolt (nut first).

COUNTERBALANCE DRIVE CHAIN (2000 & 2600 cc)

Removal – Remove crankshaft pulley and timing chain case. Remove chain guides A, B and C, sprocket B locking bolts and crankshaft sprocket (B). Remove both countershaft sprockets (B) and Drive Chain. See *Figs. 8* and *9*.

Installation – Refer to *Figs. 8* and *9* for component location and reverse removal procedure. Ensure that mating marks on sprockets align with plated links on counterbalance chain. Adjust tension by installing guides A and C, then shake counterbalance shaft sprockets to take slack from chain. Adjust guide B so that there will be .040-.140" (1.0-3.5 mm) clearance between guide and chain at point P. Tighten guide mounting bolts and complete assembly.

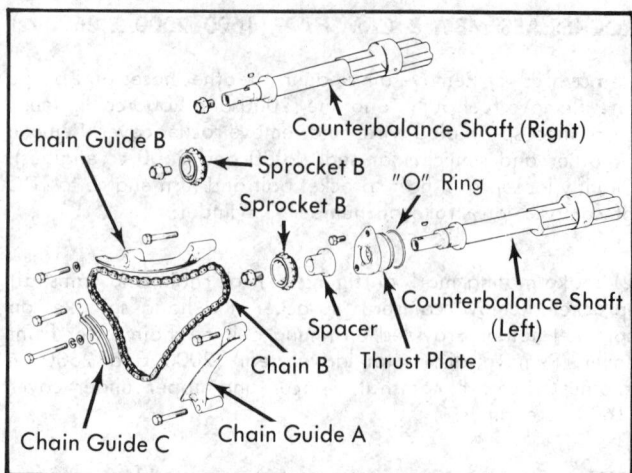

Fig. 8 Exploded View of Counterbalance Shafts and Drive Chain (2000 and 2600 cc)

COUNTERBALANCE SHAFTS (2000 & 2600 cc)

Removal & Installation – **1)** With counterbalance drive chain removed, remove oil pump mounting bolts. Remove bolt holding oil pump driven gear and counterbalance shaft together, then remove oil pump mounting bolts. Remove oil pump, then withdraw counterbalance shaft.

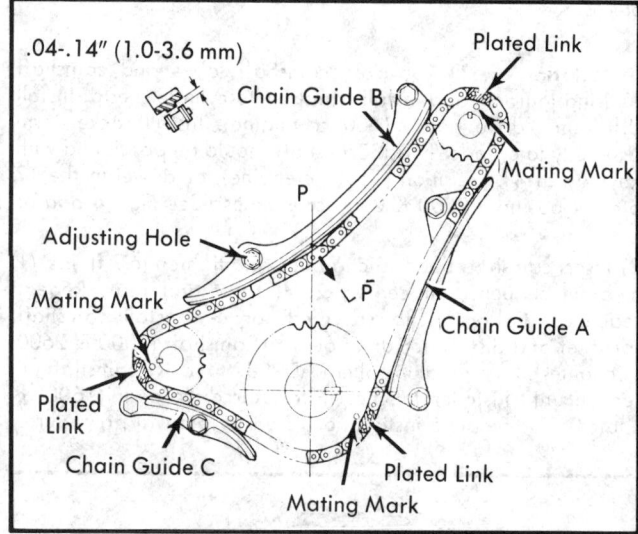

Fig. 9   Counterbalance Drive Chain (2000 and 2600 cc)

NOTE – *If bolt locking oil pump driven gear and counterbalance shaft is hard to loosen, remove oil pump and counterbalance shaft as an assembly. Then remove lock bolt to disassemble.*

2) Remove thrust plate supporting front of left counterbalance shaft. (Thrust plate is removed by threading bolts into plate holes at same time). Withdraw counterbalance shaft from cylinder block. To install, reverse removal procedure.

TIMING CHAIN (2000 & 2600 cc)

Removal & Installation – With counterbalance drive chain removed, take off chain tensioner and right and left chain guides. Remove camshaft sprocket and timing chain. To install,

1400, 1600, 2000 & 2600 cc 4 CYLINDER (Cont.)

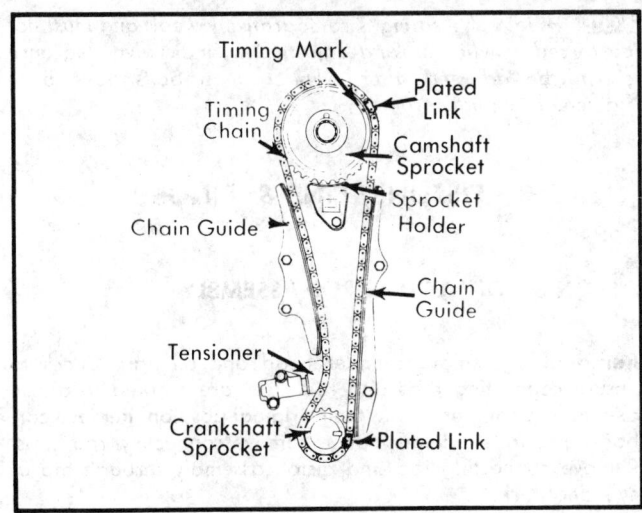

Fig. 10 Camshaft Sprocket Alignment and Installation (2000 & 2600 cc)

rotate crankshaft until number 1 piston is at TDC on compression stroke, align mating marks on sprockets and chain, then install chain on camshaft and crankshaft with keys and keyways aligned. Inspect chain tensioner and complete installation in reverse order of removal.

VALVES

VALVE ARRANGEMENT

Intake — Left side.
Exhaust — Right side.
Jet Valve — Left side.

JET VALVES

Using special Jet Valve Socket Wrench (MD998310), remove jet valves. Disassemble valve using spring pliers (MD998309) to compress spring and remove retainer lock. Check valve head and seat for damage and make sure jet valve slides smooth in body without play.

CAUTION — *Make certain that jet valve socket wrench is not tilted with respect to center of valve when used. If tool is tilted, stem may be bent resulting in defective valve operation and a broken wrench. Do not disturb jet valve and body combination. If defective, jet valve and body should be replaced as an assembly.*

VALVE SPRINGS

With camshaft and rocker arm assembly removed, use valve lifter and remove retainer locks (keepers). Remove all retainers, springs, spring seats and valves, keeping in proper order for reassembly. Check valve spring free length and pressure. Standard spring squareness should be 1.5° or less. If beyond 3°, replace spring.

VALVE GUIDE SERVICING

1) Check valve stem-to-guide clearance, and if clearance exceeds service limits as listed in table, replace valve guide with next oversize component. Guides are available in the following oversizes:

Valve Guide Oversizes		
Size Mark	Guide Size In. (mm)	Cyl. Head Bore In. (mm)
1400 cc		
5	.002 (.05)	.4766-.4770 (12.105-12.115)
25	.010 (.25)	.4844-.4848 (12.304-12.314)
50	.020 (.50)	.4943-.4947 (12.555-12.565)
1600, 2000 & 2600 cc		
5	.002 (.05)	.5138-.5145 (13.05-13.07)
25	.010 (.25)	.5216-.5224 (13.25-13.27)
50	.020 (.50)	.5315-.5323 (13.50-13.52)

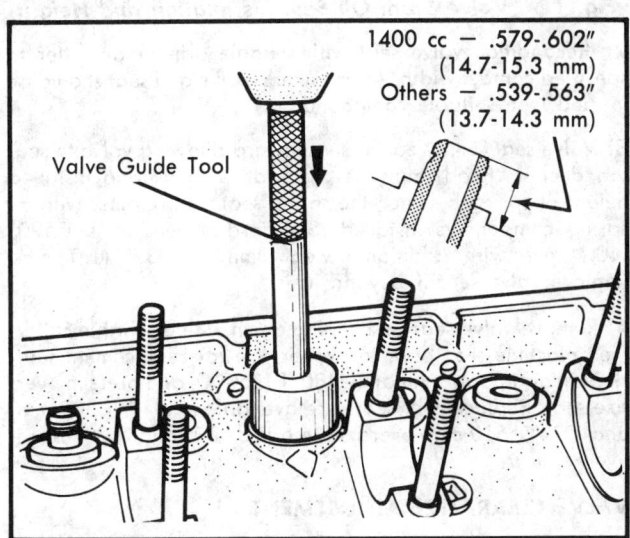

Fig. 11 Valve Guide Installation and Height

2) Heat cylinder head to approximately 480°F (249°C), and then use a suitable valve guide tool to drive out each guide toward the combustion chamber. Ream guide bore in cylinder head to specified size (after head has cooled to room temperature).

3) To install new guides, reheat head to same temperature, quickly insert and drive guides into head. Guide should protrude .579-.602" (14.7-15.3 mm) for 1400 cc or .539-.563" (13.7-14.3 mm) for other engines above head surface when properly installed. Check guide I.D. and ream as necessary.

VALVE STEM OIL SEALS

After installing valve spring seat, place stem seal on guide. Use installer to lightly hammer seal into correct position as tool bottoms on head. Do NOT use old seals and do NOT twist seals when installing.

VALVE SEAT SERVICING

1) Check valve seat for damage or wear. Replace or rework seat, as necessary. If reworking seat, check valve guide first. Make proper replacement, if required, then check seat for necessary corrections.

1400, 1600, 2000 & 2600 cc 4 CYLINDER (Cont.)

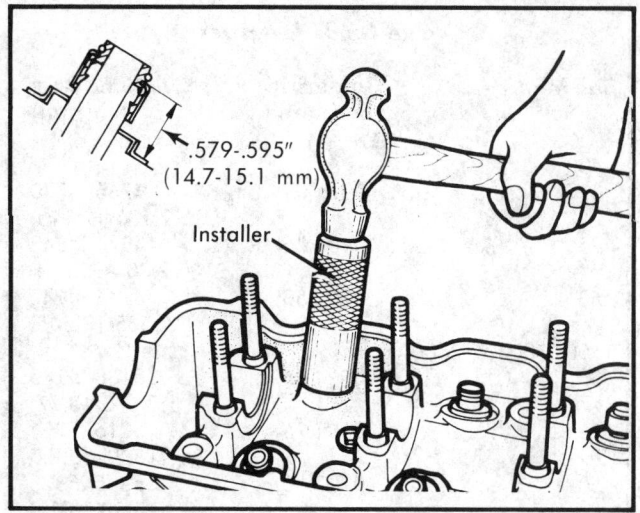

Fig. 12   Valve Stem Oil Seal Installation and Height

2) Recondition valve seat with suitable grinder or cutter to specified contact width. After rework, valve and seat should be lapped with suitable compound.

3) Valve seat sink (wear of seat inward allowing valve to seat too deep in head) must be checked by measuring installed height of spring between the spring seat and retainer with all spring components installed. Standard dimension is 1.590" (40.4 mm) with additional wear limit of .039" (1.0 mm). Replace valve seat if beyond limit.

4) Remove valve seat by thinning down with a suitable cutter, then machine seat bore to proper size for replacement seat. Heat head to approximately 480°F (250°C) and press in oversize seat. Replacement seats are available in .012" (.305 mm) and .024" (.610 mm) oversizes, marked "30" and "60" respectively.

VALVE CLEARANCE ADJUSTMENT

1) Ensure timing marks on camshaft sprocket and chain are aligned. With head assembly installed, temporarily adjust valves (sequence for adjustment; 1-3-4-2), according to following procedure: At compression stroke TDC, for cylinder being adjusted, loosen rocker arm nuts; then, turning adjusting screw, adjust valve clearance to specifications.

2) Complete engine assembly and temporarily install rocker cover. Warm engine until coolant temperature is 170 to 180°F. With piston at TDC on compression stroke, back intake valve adjusting screw off 2 or more turns. Adjust jet valve clearance, then adjust intake valve clearance. Adjust exhaust valve clearance and assure that all adjusting screw lock nuts are tightened securely.

Valve Clearance		
Application	Cold In. (mm)	Hot In. (mm)
Intake	.003 (.07)	.006 (.15)
Exhaust	.007 (.17)	.010 (.25)
Jet Valve	.003 (.07)	.006 (.15)

NOTE — *Jet valve spring is comparatively weak and must not be forced in when making adjustment. Final valve clearance should be adjusted after cylinder head bolts have been tightened to final torque.*

PISTONS, PINS & RINGS

PISTON & CONNECTING ROD ASSEMBLY

Removal — Remove cylinder head and oil pan. Check to ensure connecting rods and rod caps are marked to aid in assembling components to their original position. Remove carbon ridge from cylinder bores. Remove connecting rod caps. Remove connecting rod and piston assembly through top of cylinder block.

Installation — To reinstall, lubricate all internal surfaces with engine oil before installation. Make sure front mark on piston head faces front of engine. Use a ring compressor to compress rings (without changing their position) and install piston and connecting rod assembly in to cylinder block in their original position. Tap lightly on piston dome with wooden handle tool while guiding connecting rod onto crankshaft. Install rod cap onto proper piston and connecting rod assembly. Tighten attaching bolts. Install cylinder head and oil pan.

FITTING PISTONS

1) After checking block for distortion, cracks, scratches or other abnormalities, measure bores at 3 levels. If any distortion exceeds .001" (.02 mm) from standard bore size, block must be rebored and oversize pistons installed.

NOTE — *Pistons for all 4 engine sizes are available in standard, .010" (.25 mm), .020" (.50 mm), .030" (.75 mm) and .039" (1.0 mm) oversizes. Oversize pistons are stamped on crown to indicate oversize amount.*

2) Check outside diameter of piston by measuring at a point .079" (2 mm) from bottom of skirt and at 90° to pin bore. Determine amount of cylinder reboring required to meet specified clearance.

NOTE — *Pin-to-Rod fit at normal temperature for 1400 and 1600 cc engines will press in at 1,100-3,300 lbs.; for 2000 and 2600 cc engines, 1,654-3,859 lbs.*

PISTON PINS

Check piston pin-to-bore fit; pin should press in smoothly by hand (at room temperature). When assembling, apply engine oil to outside of pin and to piston pin bore, position rod to piston ("FRONT" mark upward), align pin with pressing tool, and press pin into piston and rod.

PISTON RINGS

Measure piston ring side and end clearance for all pistons and replace rings as necessary. When replacing a ring without correcting the cylinder bore, check ring end gap at lower part of

1400, 1600, 2000 & 2600 cc 4 CYLINDER (Cont.)

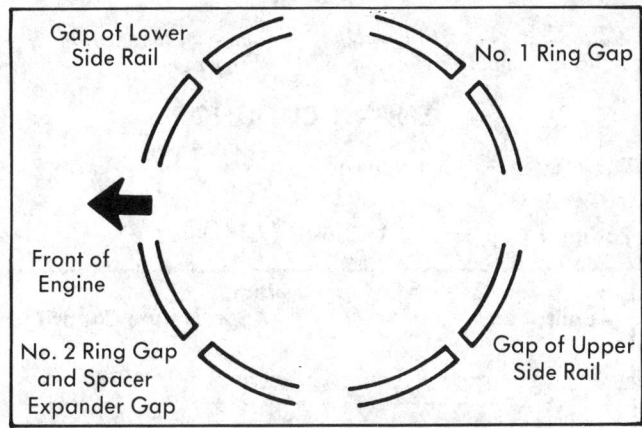

Fig. 13 Piston Ring Gap Positions

cylinder that is less worn. When replacing a ring, be sure to use one of the same size. Install rings on piston with end gaps staggered at 120° intervals, but make sure no ring gap is in line with thrust face of pin bore. Also be sure the manufacturer's marks are facing upward when rings are installed.

CAUTION — *Install oil ring first WITHOUT using a ring expander. Spacer expander gap should be installed more than 45° from side rail gaps, and rails should turn smoothly when installed.*

Piston Ring Sizes	
Ring Size	**Size Mark**
1400, 1600, 2000 & 2600 cc	
Standard	No Mark
.010" (.25 mm) OS	25
.020" (.50 mm) OS	50
.030" (.75 mm) OS	75
.039" (1.00 mm) OS	100

CRANKSHAFT MAIN & CONNECTING ROD BEARINGS

MAIN & CONNECTING ROD BEARINGS

1) Inspect each bearing for peeling, melting, seizure or improper contact. Replace defective bearings. Measure outside diameter of crankshaft and connecting rod journals to determine if out-of-round or tapered.

2) Cut Plastigage to same length as width of bearing. Place it parallel with journal (not over oil holes). Install crankshaft bearings and caps, tightening to specifications. Always install caps with arrow facing forward.

NOTE — *Do not turn crankshaft with Plastigage installed.*

3) Remove main bearing cap from crankshaft and measure Plastigage at widest part (using scale on Plastigage package). Repeat procedure for connecting rod bearings. If clearance exceeds limits, bearing should be replaced or undersize bearing installed. Undersize bearings are available in .010" (.25 mm), .020" (.50 mm), and .030" (.75 mm) undersizes.

THRUST BEARING

With crankshaft bearing caps installed, check thrust clearance (end play) by inserting feeler gauge between center main bearing and crankshaft thrust face. If clearance exceeds specified limits, replace center main bearing.

ENGINE OILING

ENGINE OILING SYSTEM

All engines use force-feed type lubrication system. 1400 cc engine uses gear-crescent type pump, 1600 cc WITHOUT silent shaft uses a trochoid type pump, and all other engines use gear type pump. Driven gear of oil pump also drives counterbalance shaft on silent shaft engines.

Crankcase Capacity (Includes Filter)	
Application	**Approximate Quantity**
1400 cc	3.7 quarts
1600 cc	4.2 quarts
2000 cc	4.5 quarts
2600 cc	4.5 quarts

Oil Pressure — 50-64 psi @ 2000 RPM.

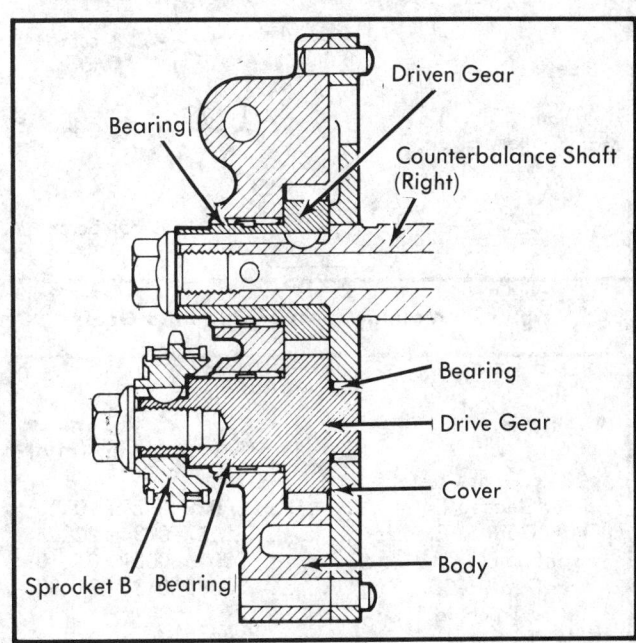

Fig. 14 Cutaway View of Gear Type Oil Pump

OIL PUMP

1400 cc — Gear-crescent type pump is mounted on front of engine assembly and driven directly by the crankshaft. Oil pan, oil screen and timing belt must be removed prior to removing front cover-oil pump assembly. Remove 7 mounting bolts and remove pump assembly. Inspect gears, case and seal for wear or damage. Ensure that gears are assembled in same direction as originally installed. Use new gaskets and install pump and pan. Use suitable sealer at joint faces and seams.

1600 cc (Without Silent Shaft) — Mounted at lower left of engine, driven by camshaft drive belt. Cover and rotor assembly may be removed after removing drive sprocket by taking out cover bolts and lifting assembly out. May also be removed with engine front case as an assembly.

1400, 1600, 2000 & 2600 cc 4 CYLINDER (Cont.)

1600 cc (With Silent Shaft) — Gear type pump mounted at lower left front of engine. To remove, first insert screwdriver in plug hole at bottom left of block to prevent counterbalance from turning, then remove drive sprocket. Remove pump cover and bolt holding driven gear to counterbalance. Pump gears and left counterbalance shaft may be removed along with front case. Inspect and replace worn gears or cover. To install, assure that timing marks on pump are aligned, insert left counterbalance shaft in driven gear, and temporarily tighten bolt. Install left counterbalance shaft with front case and oil pump as an assembly.

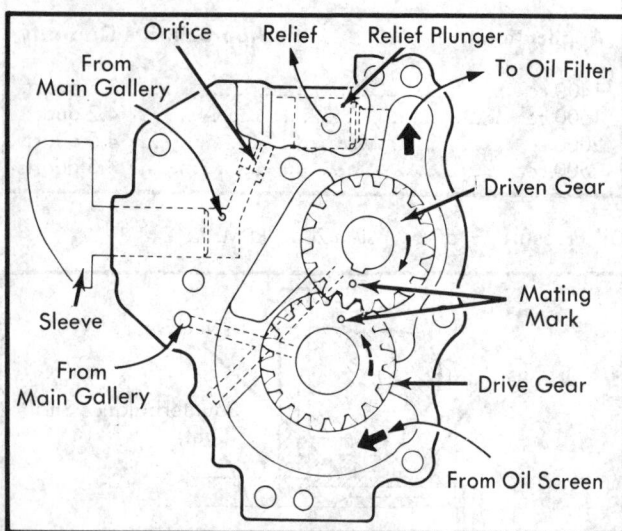

Fig. 15　Mating Marks of Oil Pump Gears

Oil Pump Specifications

Application	Clearance In. (mm)
1400 cc Gear-Crescent Type	
Outer Gear-to-Case	.0039-.0079 (.10-.20)
Outer Gear-to-Crescent	.0087-.0134 (.22-.34)
Gear End Play	.0016-.0039 (.04-.10)
Inner Gear-to-Crescent	.0083-.0126 (.21-.32)
1600 cc Trochoid Type	
Side Clearance	.0024-.0047 (.06-.12)
Tip Clearance	.0016-.0047 (.04-.12)
Body Clearance	.0039-.0063 (.10-.16)
Drive Shaft-to-Cover Clearance	.0008-.0020 (.02-.05)
1600 cc Gear Type	
Gear End Play	.0024-.0047 (.06-.12)
Gear Shaft-to-Pump Cover	.0008-.0019 (.02-.05)
Gear Tip-to-Body Clearance	.0039-.0276 (.1-.7)
Tip Clearance Between Gears	.0079-.0276 (.2-.7)
2000 & 2600 cc Gear Type	
Gear Tip-to-Body Clearance	.0043-.0059 (.11-.15)
Gear End Play	.0024-.0047 (.06-.12)
Drive Gear-to-Bearing	.0008-.0018 (.02-.046)
Drive Gear-to-Rear Bearing	.0016-.0028 (.04-.07)

2000 & 2600 cc — Pump is mounted at lower right side of engine block, and driven by countershaft drive chain. For removal, see *COUNTERBALANCE SHAFTS, 2000 & 2600 cc.* To install, reverse removal procedure, assuring that oil pump gear mating marks are aligned and that woodruff key on counterbalance shaft fits in keyway of driven gear.

CAUTION — *Prior to installing oil pump (all models), fill with sufficient amount of engine oil to prime pump.*

ENGINE COOLING

Thermostat — 180°F (82°C)

Radiator Cap — 11.3-14.2 psi (.79-1.0 kg/cm²)

	Cooling System	
Application		**Approximate Capacity**
1400 cc		4.7 quarts
1600 cc		4.7 quarts
2000 cc		9.5 quarts
2600 cc		9.7 quarts

WATER PUMP

Removal & Installation (1400 & 1600 cc) — Drain cooling system and disconnect battery. Remove drive belt, fan, pulley, and lower radiator hose to pump. Ensure that number 1 piston is at TDC on compression stroke, then remove camshaft pulley, timing belt covers, timing belt, camshaft sprocket, upper inner cover and timing belt tensioner. Remove mounting bolts and remove pump from engine. To install, use new gasket and reverse removal procedure.

Removal & Installation (2000 & 2600 cc) — Drain cooling system and disconnect battery. Remove fan shroud if so equipped and remove lower radiator hose. Remove drive belt, cooling fan, fan clutch and pulley. Remove water pump. To install, reverse removal procedure using new gasket.

TIGHTENING SPECIFICATIONS

Application	Ft. Lbs. (mkg)
Camshaft Bearing Cap	
1600 cc	14-15 (1.9-2.0)
2000 & 2600 cc	13-14 (1.8-1.9)
Camshaft Sprocket	
1400 cc	47-54 (6.4-7.3)
1600 cc	44-57 (6.0-8.0)
2000 & 2600 cc	37-43 (5.1-5.9)
Cylinder Head Bolts (Cold)	
1400 & 1600 cc	51-54 (7.0-7.5)
2000 & 2600 cc	65-72 (9.0-9.9)
Main Bearing Caps	
1400 & 1600 cc	37-39 (5.1-5.4)
2000 & 2600 cc	55-61 (7.6-8.4)
Connecting Rod Caps	
1400 & 1600 cc	24-25 (3.3-3.4)
2000 & 2600 cc	33-34 (4.6-4.7)
Crank Pulley	
1400 & 1600 cc	7.5-8.5 (1.0-1.2)
2000 & 2600 cc	80-94 (11.0-13.0)
Crankshaft Sprocket Bolt	
1400 cc	37-43 (4.9-5.8)
1600 cc	44-50 (6.0-6.9)
Flywheel-to-Crankshaft	94-101 (13.0-13.9)
Drive Plate-to-Crankshaft	
(Auto. Trans.)	94-101 (13.0-13.9)
Oil Pump/Cover	
1600 cc	11-13 (1.5-1.8)
1400, 2000 & 2600 cc	6-7 (.8-1.0)
Jet Valve	13-15 (1.8-2.0)

1400, 1600, 2000 & 2600 cc 4 CYLINDER (Cont.)
ENGINE SPECIFICATIONS

GENERAL SPECIFICATIONS

| Year | Displ. | | Carburetor | HP at RPM | Torque (Ft. Lbs. at RPM) | Compr. Ratio | Bore | | Stroke | |
	cu. ins.	cc					in.	mm	in.	mm
1980	86.0	1400	2-Bbl.	.....	.....	9.0:1	2.91	74.0	3.23	82.0
	97.5	1600	2-Bbl.	.....	.....	8.5:1	3.03	76.9	3.39	·86.0
	121.7	2000	2-Bbl.	93@5200	108@3000	8.5:1	3.31	84.0	3.54	90.0
	155.9	2600	2-Bbl.	105@5000	139@2500	8.2:1	3.59	91.1	3.86	98.0

VALVES

Engine & Valve	Head Diam.① In. (mm)	Face Angle	Seat Angle	Seat Width In. (mm)	Stem Diameter In. (mm)	Stem Clearance In. (mm)	Valve Lift In. (mm)
1400cc							
Intake	1.34 (34)	45°	45°	.035-.051 (.9-1.3)	.315 (8.0)	.001-.002 (.03-.06)	.346 (8.8)
Exhaust	1.18 (30)	45°	45°	.035-.051 (.9-1.3)	.315 (8.0)	.0020-.0035 (.05-.09)	.346 (8.8)
1600cc							
Intake	1.50 (38)	45°	45°	.035-.051 (.9-1.3)	.315 (8.0)	.0012-.0024 (.03-.06)	.362 (9.2)
Exhaust	1.22 (31)	45°	45°	.035-.051 (.9-1.3)	.315 (8.0)	.0020-.0035 (.05-.09)	.362 (9.2)
2000 & 2600cc							
Intake	1.7 (43)	45°	45°	.035-.051 (.9-1.3)	.315 (8.0)	.0012-.0024 (.03-.06)	.393② (10.0)
Exhaust	1.38 (35)	45°	45°	.035-.051 (.9-1.3)	.315 (8.0)	.0020-.0035 (.05-.09)	.393 (10.0)

① — Jet valve and body not individually serviceable. Replace as an assembly when defective.
② — 2600cc valve lift: .413" (10.5 mm).

PISTONS, PINS, RINGS

| Engine | PISTONS | PINS | | RINGS | | |
	Clearance In. (mm)	Piston Fit In. (mm)	Rod Fit In. (mm)	Rings	End Gap In. (mm)	Side Clearance In. (mm)
1400 & 1600 cc	.0008-.0016 (.02-.04)	①	Locked in Rod ②	No. 1	.008-.016 (.2-.4)	.0012-.0028 (.03-.07)
				No. 2	.008-.016 (.2-.4)	.0008-.0024 (.02-.06)
				Oil	.008-.020 (.2-.5)	....
2000 & 2600 cc	.0008-.0016 (.02-.04)	①	Locked in Rod ③	No. 1	.010-.018 (.25-.45)	.0024-.0039 (.06-.10)
				No. 2	.010-.018 (.25-.45)	.0008-.0024 (.02-.06)
				Oil	.008-.035 (.2-.9)	....

① — Thumb press fit without rod installed
② — Press in at 1100-3300 lbs. at room temp.
③ — Press in at 1654-3854 lbs. at room temp.

1400, 1600, 2000 & 2600 cc 4 CYLINDER (Cont.)

ENGINE SPECIFICATIONS (Cont.)

CRANKSHAFT MAIN & CONNECTING ROD BEARINGS							
	MAIN BEARINGS				CONNECTING ROD BEARINGS		
Engine	Journal Diam. In. (mm)	Clearance In. (mm)	Thrust Bearing	Crankshaft End Play In. (mm)	Journal Diam. In. (mm)	Clearance In. (mm)	Side Play In. (mm)
1400 cc	1.890 (48)	.0008-.0028 (.02-07)	No. 3	.002-007 (.05-.18)	1.653 (42)	.0004-.0024 (.01-.06)	.004-.01 (.10-.25)
1600 cc	2.244 (57)	.0008-.0028 (.02-.07)	No. 3	.002-.007 (.05-.18)	1.772 (45)	.0004-.0024 (.01-.06)	.004-.01 (.10-.25)
2000 & 2600 cc	2.362 (60)	.0008-.0028 (.02-.07)	No. 3	.002-.007 (.05-.18)	2.087 (53)	.0008-.0028 (.02-.06)	.004-.01 (.10-.25)

CAMSHAFT			
Engine	Cam Lobe Height In. (mm)	End Play In. (mm)	Lobe Lift In. (mm)
1400cc Intake	1.500 (38.1)	.002-.008 (.05-.20)	.....
Exhaust	1.504 (38.2)	.002-.008 (.05-.20)	.....
1600cc Int. & Exh	1.433 (36.4)	.002-.006 (.05-.15)	.359 (9.2)
2000 & 2600cc Int. & Exh	1.661 (42.2)	.004-.008 (.10-.20)	.393 (10.0)

VALVE SPRINGS			
Engine	Free Length In. (mm)	PRESSURE Lbs. @ In. (kg @ mm)	
		Valve Closed	Valve Open
1400 cc	1.697 (43.1)	69@1.417 (31.1@36)	.....
1600 cc	1.823 (46.3)	62@1.469 (27.9@37.3)	.....
2000 & 2600 cc	1.869 (47.5)	61@1.59 (27.6@40.4)	.....

① — Maximum wear limit is .020" (.5 mm)

2000 cc 4 CYLINDER

ENGINE CODING

ENGINE IDENTIFICATION

Vehicle engine information is stamped on a plate riveted to body at right rear of engine compartment.

Engine Identification	
Application	Code
2000 cc	C

ENGINE, CYLINDER HEAD & MANIFOLDS

ENGINE

Removal & Installation — 1) Remove hood and disconnect battery. Drain cooling system and remove radiator hoses. Disconnect hoses from air cleaner body and remove air cleaner assembly. Unbolt and remove radiator.

2) Disconnect accelerator linkage and fuel line at carburetor. Disconnect linkage from intake manifold, cable at air by-pass valve, choke cable, battery cables, coil wires at distributor and coil lead wires.

3) Remove fan, loosen alternator retaining bolts and remove alternator belt. If equipped with Thermactor (air pump), remove mounting bolts and pump drive belt. Remove alternator bracket and adjusting arm bolts and position alternator out of the way. Pull Thermactor hoses off pump, remove bracket and position pump aside. Disconnect heater hoses from intake manifold and Thermactor air hose from by-pass valve. Disconnect all vacuum lines running between engine and engine compartment components.

4) Disconnect lead wire and boot from oil pressure sending unit, battery cable from block and wires from starter solenoid. Raise vehicle and drain oil. Remove splash shield and separate exhaust pipe from manifold. Remove clutch housing and bottom starter bolts.

5) Lower vehicle, remove upper starter bolts and withdraw starter. Place a floor stand under transmission. Connect a lifting sling to engine hanger brackets. Disconnect engine mounts and pull engine forward until clear of transmission shaft. Lift engine from vehicle. To install, reverse removal procedures.

INTAKE MANIFOLD

Removal — 1) Disconnect and drain cooling system. Remove air cleaner assembly and accelerator linkage. Disconnect choke cable and fuel line at carburetor. Index mark and disconnect vacuum lines and electrical leads from intake manifold.

2) Disconnect Thermactor hoses (if equipped), crankcase ventilation hose, heater return hose and by-pass hose. Remove attaching nuts and lift manifold, with carburetor, off studs.

Installation — To install, reverse removal procedure while noting the following: Clean all gasket surfaces and install a new gasket. Install intake manifold and tighten attaching bolts working from the center of manifold towards each end. Fill cooling system when all components are installed.

EXHAUST MANIFOLD

Removal — 1) Remove hot air ducting. Remove spark plug wires. Remove air injection from exhaust manifold. Remove upper and lower heat insulators.

2) Disconnect EGR line. Raise vehicle. Remove exhaust pipe hanger from bracket on transmission. Disconnect exhaust pipe at manifold. Remove manifold nuts and manifold.

Installation — To install, reverse removal procedure using new gaskets and applying a light coat of graphite grease on exhaust manifold mating surfaces.

CYLINDER HEAD

Removal — 1) Drain cooling system. Remove air cleaner assembly. Remove exhaust manifold. Disconnect throttle and choke. Disconnect fuel lines.

2) From cylinder head, disconnect the following:
- Carburetor solenoid.
- Heater hoses.
- By-pass hose.
- Thermac air hoses.
- Vacuum lines.
- EGR valve.
- Electrical leads.

3) Remove water pump. Disconnect lead wire and vacuum line from distributor. Rotate crankshaft until No. 1 piston is TDC.

4) Remove valve cover. Remove distributor with plug wires. Remove timing chain tensioner cover and release chain tension. See Fig. 3. Refer to Timing Chain Tension in this article.

5) Remove nut, washer and distributor gear from crankshaft. Remove nut and washer from camshaft sprocket. Remove lower front head bolt located below camshaft sprocket on boss.

6) Remove cylinder head bolts. Remove rocker arm assembly. Separate camshaft and sprocket. Place camshaft sprocket and chain on top of chain guide strip and vibration damper. Make sure sprocket and chain are not moved. Remove cylinder head.

NOTE — *After removing cylinder head, release all tension from timing chain.*

Installation — To install, reverse removal procedure while noting the following: Clean all gasket surfaces and use new gaskets upon installation. Install cylinder head and tighten bolts to specifications in sequence as shown in illustration.

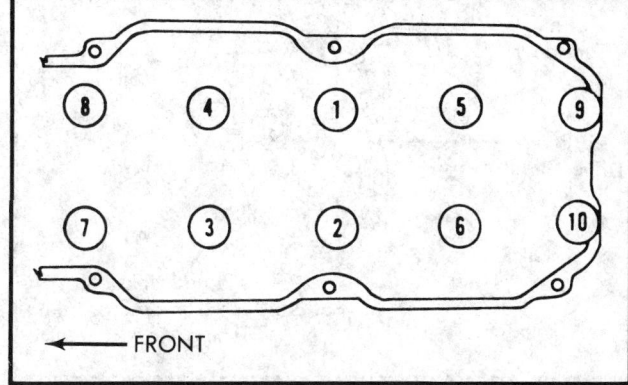

Fig. 1 Cylinder Head Tightening Sequence

2000 cc 4 CYLINDER (Cont.)

ENGINE FRONT COVER

Removal — 1) Remove hood and drain cooling system. Disconnect upper radiator hose at engine and lower hose at radiator. Remove radiator, drive belts, crankshaft pulley, and water pump. Remove cylinder head to front cover bolt. Raise vehicle and remove front splash shield.

2) Disconnect emission line from oil pan. Remove oil pan. Lower vehicle, remove alternator bracket to block bolts and position alternator to one side. Remove thermactor pump to block bolts and position to one side. Remove steel tube bolts and tube from front of engine. Remove attaching bolts for front cover and remove front cover.

Installation — To install engine front cover, reverse removal procedure.

CAMSHAFT

TIMING CHAIN

Removal — 1) Remove cylinder head and front cover. Remove oil pump gear attaching nut, oil pump-to-block attaching bolts and loosen gear on the pump. Remove oil pump, gear and oil pump chain.

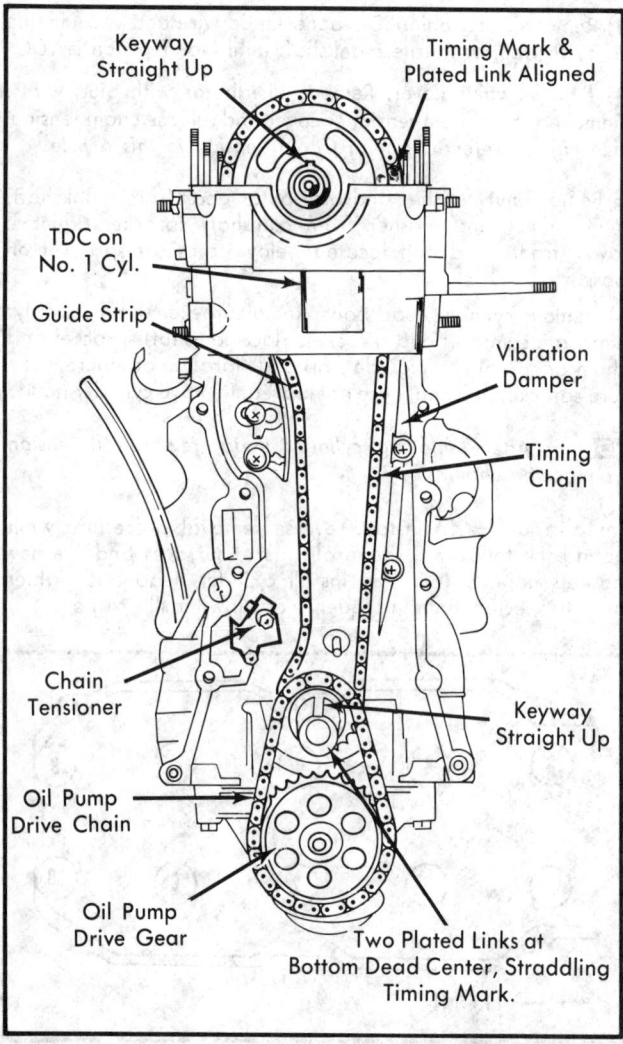

Keyway Straight Up

Timing Mark & Plated Link Aligned

TDC on No. 1 Cyl.

Guide Strip

Vibration Damper

Timing Chain

Chain Tensioner

Keyway Straight Up

Oil Pump Drive Chain

Oil Pump Drive Gear

Two Plated Links at Bottom Dead Center, Straddling Timing Mark.

Fig. 2   Timing Chain & Sprocket Alignment

2) Remove timing chain tensioner and loosen timing chain guide strip screws. Remove oil slinger. Remove outer gear (for oil pump chain) from crankshaft. Remove timing chain and crankshaft gear.

Installation — 1) Position crankshaft inner sprocket into timing chain, then install sprocket and chain onto crankshaft. Install oil pump with gear onto cylinder block. Install oil pump chain and outer sprocket to crankshaft while positioning chain onto oil pump gear. Install timing chain tensioner. See *Timing Chain Tensioner*. Do not release snubber spring tension. Install cylinder head and camshaft to cylinder block.

NOTE — *Do not install rocker arm assembly at this time.*

2) Obtain correct timing chain alignment referring to *Timing Chain Alignment* illustration and using the following procedure: Rotate crankshaft to TDC of compression stroke on number one cylinder. This will place crankshaft with keyway facing straight up. Position camshaft with keyway facing straight up. Timing chain must now be positioned on camshaft sprocket so single plated link is aligned with timing mark on right-hand side of camshaft sprocket at rocker arm cover joint face, while facing engine. The two plate links on timing chain must straddle timing mark on BDC of crankshaft sprocket.

3) Install rocker arm shaft assembly, cylinder head bolts, and tighten all bolts to specifications. Adjust timing chain tension. See *Timing Chain Tension*. Release tensioner snubber and install front cover. Install remaining components in reverse of removal procedure and adjust valve clearance.

TIMING CHAIN TENSION

1) Remove crankshaft pulley and water pump. Remove cover from tensioner. Rotate crankshaft slightly in direction of engine rotation. Lift release on tensioner and compress snubber spring fully. Install wedge in tensioner so it will not release.

2) Remove two access plugs and aluminum washers from holes in timing chain cover and side of head. Loosen guide strip attaching screws. Press top of strip with lever inserted through access hole in head.

3) Tighten guide strip attaching screws with screwdriver inserted through hole in cover. Remove wedge from tensioner, allowing snubber to take up chain slack.

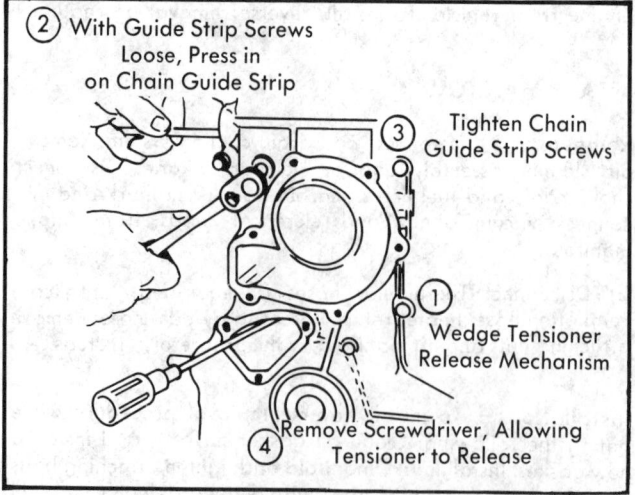

② With Guide Strip Screws Loose, Press in on Chain Guide Strip

③ Tighten Chain Guide Strip Screws

① Wedge Tensioner Release Mechanism

④ Remove Screwdriver, Allowing Tensioner to Release

Fig. 3   Adjusting Timing Chain Tension

2000 cc 4 CYLINDER (Cont.)

4) Install access plugs and aluminum washers to their respective holes. Replace chain tensioner cover and gasket. Install water pump and crankshaft pulley. Tighten bolts and adjust belt tension.

OIL PUMP CHAIN

Check oil pump chain for excessive deflection as shown in illustration. If deflection is more than .157" (3.97 mm), install adjusting shims between cylinder block and oil pump body.

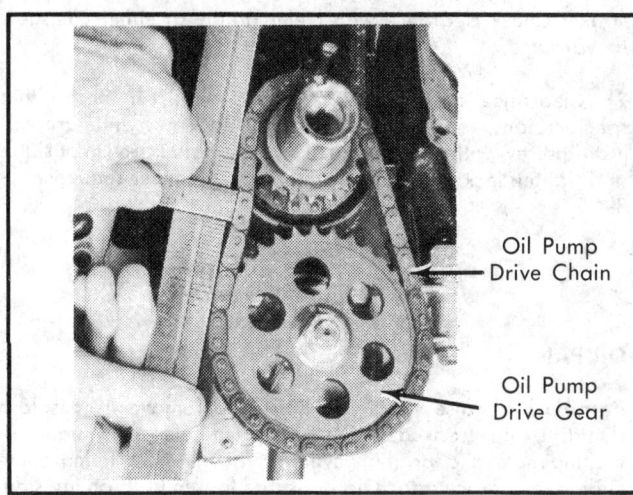

Oil Pump Drive Chain

Oil Pump Drive Gear

Fig. 4   Measuring Oil Pump Chain Deflection

CAMSHAFT

Removal — 1) Remove hood and water pump. Disconnect vacuum line and lead wire from distributor. Rotate crankshaft to position number one cylinder on TDC of compression stroke. Remove plug wires and distributor cap as an assembly, then remove distributor from engine. Remove rocker arm cover.

2) Remove crankshaft pulley, then remove cover from timing chain tensioner. Lift release on tensioner and compress snubber spring fully. Wedge a screwdriver in the tensioner to keep spring compressed. Remove cylinder head bolts and rocker arm assembly.

3) Remove nut, washer, and distributor gear from camshaft. Remove camshaft gear attaching nut and washer. Carefully remove camshaft from gear and engine block.

NOTE — *Do not remove camshaft gear from timing chain. Ensure that gear teeth-to-chain relationship is not disturbed.*

Installation — To install, reverse removal procedure while noting the following: When installing camshaft to gear take care not to disturb gear-to-chain relationship. Adjust timing chain tension. Check camshaft end play. Adjust valve clearance.

CAMSHAFT BEARINGS

Remove camshaft and inspect bearings for wear or damage. Use Plastigage method to determine clearance. Replace bearings which do not meet specifications.

CAMSHAFT END THRUST

Check camshaft end play with a feeler gauge inserted between thrust plate and camshaft flange. End play should be checked at time of overhaul, before gear and sprocket are replaced.

CAM LOBE LIFT

Remove rocker arm cover. Measure distance between major and minor diameters (see illustration) of each lobe with a Vernier caliper. Difference between diameters of each cam is lobe lift. If lobe lift loss exceeds .008" (.20 mm), replace camshaft. Check lift of each lobe in consecutive order and note each reading.

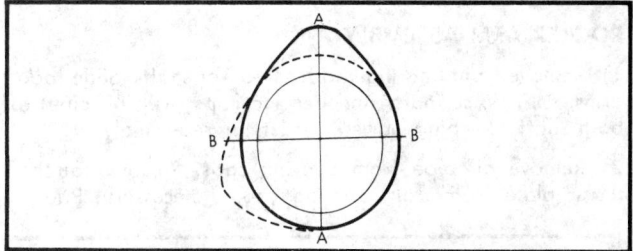

Fig. 5   Measuring Camshaft Base Circle and Lobe Lift

VALVE TIMING

Rotate crankshaft and camshaft until keyways are straight up. Place timing chain on camshaft sprocket so single plated link is aligned with timing mark on right-hand side of camshaft sprocket at rocker arm cover joint face, while facing engine. The two plate links on timing chain must straddle timing mark on BDC of crankshaft sprocket. Crankshaft in this position will be TDC of number one cylinder.

VALVES

VALVE ARRANGEMENT

Intake — Left side.
Exhaust — Right side.

VALVE GUIDE SERVICING

Check guides for wear or damage, replace as necessary. With valves removed, using suitable tool (T72J-6510), drive valve guides out top of cylinder head. Install new guides, making sure exhaust and intake guides are in proper locations. Drive guide in until ring around guide touches head.

VALVE STEM OIL SEALS

With valves and springs removed, pull oil seals off valve guides using suitable tools (T72J-6571 and T59L-100-B). Install new seals on valve guides with large diameter hole facing cylinder head.

VALVE SPRINGS

Removal — With cylinder head removed from engine proceed as follows: Compress valve springs and remove retainer locks. Release springs and remove spring retainers, springs, and valves.

NOTE — *Identify all valve components for installation in original positions. Exhaust and intake retainers must be installed in original positions to prevent premature valve failure.*

2000 cc 4 CYLINDER (Cont.)

Inspection — Check valve spring pressure at specified height, replace if not within specifications. Measure free length of spring, if not within 3% of specified value, replace spring. Using a square, check that springs are not more than $\frac{1}{16}$" (1.58 mm) out-of-square.

Installation — Lubricate valves, valve stems and valve guide with engine oil. Apply Lubriplate to valve tips. Install new valve oil seals on valve guides and install valves in guide from which it was removed. Install valve springs and retainer. Compress springs and install retainer locks. Release springs and install cylinder head.

ROCKER ARM ASSEMBLY

1) Remove front bearing cap from rocker shafts. Slide rocker arms, springs, supports and bearing caps (with oil pipe) off both shafts, keeping parts in order for reassembly.

2) Remove oil pipe from bearing caps. Remove camshaft thrust plate from front bearing cap, if necessary. Prior to reassembly, lubricate arms and shafts with heavy (MS) motor oil. When installing shafts in intake side, ensure ends with longer length between oil hole and tip are turned inward, toward each other. Make sure "O" ring on oil pipe is centered in middle bearing cap passage.

VALVE CLEARANCE ADJUSTMENT

1) With engine at normal operating temperature, rotate crankshaft until number one piston is at TDC of compression stroke. Check clearance with feeler gauge at either camshaft or valve.

2) Clearance must be .012" (.305 mm). If not within specifications, loosen adjusting screw lock nut and turn adjusting screw with feeler gauge in place. Hold screw in position and tighten lock nut. Adjust valves in firing order sequence; 1-3-4-2.

PISTONS, PINS & RINGS

OIL PAN

Removal — Raise vehicle on hoist and remove front splash shield. Drain crankcase, remove clutch release cylinder attaching nuts and position cylinder to one side. Remove the engine rear brace attaching bolts and loosen bolts on left side. Remove oil pan attaching nuts and bolts, and lower oil pan onto crossmember. Remove oil pump pick-up tube. Remove oil pan from vehicle.

Installation — To install, reverse removal procedure while noting the following: Clean all gasket surfaces and use new gaskets upon installation. Ensure that oil pump pick-up tube and screen are clean before installing.

PISTON & ROD ASSEMBLY

Removal — 1) With cylinder head and oil pan removed, remove oil pump. Rotate crankshaft until piston to be removed is at bottom of travel. Place a cloth on piston to collect cuttings, then using a ridge reamer, remove any ridge or deposits from upper end of cylinder.

NOTE — Do not cut into ring travel area in excess of $\frac{1}{32}$" (.79 mm).

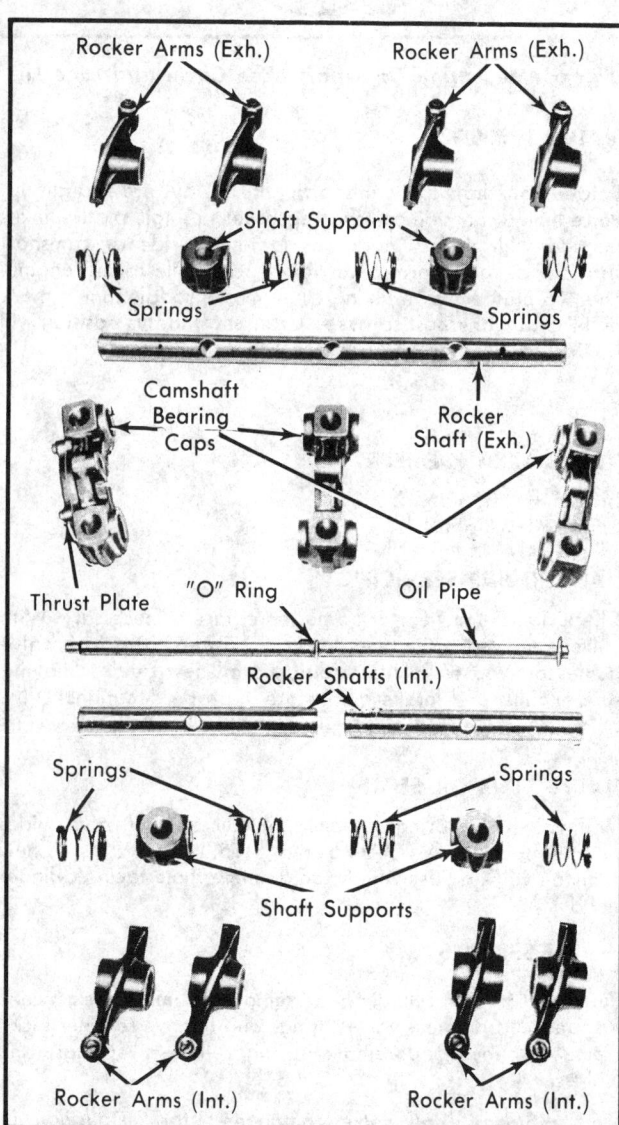

Fig. 6 Exploded View of Rocker Arm & Shaft Assembly

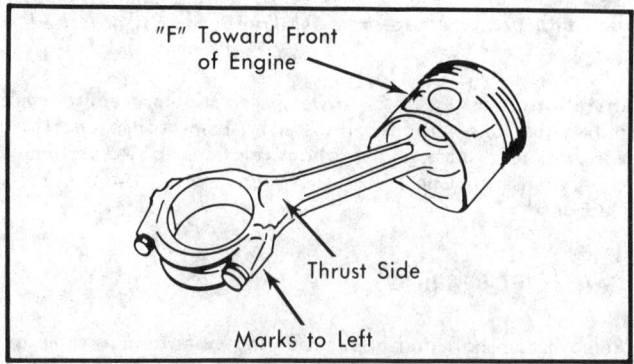

Fig. 7 Piston & Rod Assembly Installation Features

2000 cc 4 CYLINDER (Cont.)

2) Make sure connecting rod caps are marked so they may be replaced in their original positions, then remove rod caps. Push piston and rod assembly out top of cylinder. Take care not to damage bearing journal.

Installation — Oil piston rings, pistons and cylinder walls with engine oil. With rings properly spaced, install ring compressor onto piston. Install piston and rod assembly into its original bore. Make sure connecting rod marks are facing left side of engine and "F" mark on piston is facing forward (see illustration). Install rod caps and tighten rod bolts.

FITTING PISTONS

1) Determine piston-to-cylinder bore clearance. Check cylinder for out-of-round or taper. Fit new pistons if necessary. Pistons are available in .010", .020", .030" and .040" oversizes.

2) Place rings in cylinder near bottom of bore and measure end gaps. Place rings on piston and measure side clearance. If high steps have developed on lower back side of ring lands replace piston.

3) Place rings on piston with end gaps 120° apart so that no gap is located on thrust face or piston pin bore. Using suitable ring compressor, install piston in proper bore with "F" marking facing forward.

PISTON PINS

Piston pins are removed using an arbor press, pilots and driver. Measure pin and connecting rod diameters to ensure proper fit.

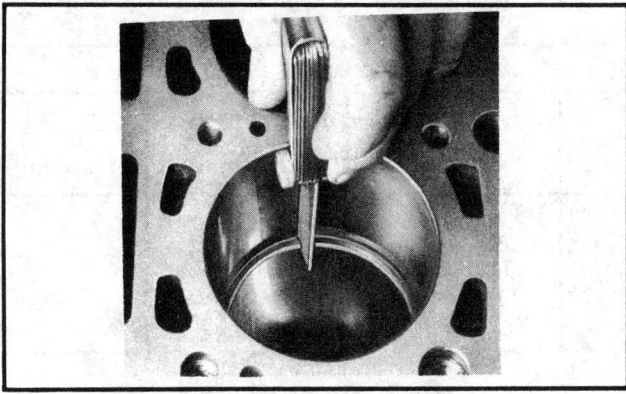

Fig. 8 Measuring Piston Ring Gap

CRANKSHAFT MAIN & CONNECTING ROD BEARINGS

MAIN & CONNECTING ROD BEARINGS

1) Inspect each bearing for scored, chipped or worn surface and replace if condition exists. If copper base is visible through bearing overlay, replacement is not necessary, if within specifications.

2) When installing new bearings, fit bearings to minimum specified clearance. Use Plastigage method to determine bearing clearances. Inserts are available in .010", .020" and .030" undersizes.

THRUST BEARING ALIGNMENT

Push crankshaft to one side to take up end play. Insert a feeler gauge between thrust washers and crankshaft. Replace thrust washers if measurement is not within specifications. Install new thrust washers with oil groove facing crankshaft thrust side.

REAR MAIN BEARING OIL SEAL

NOTE — *If rear main bearing seal replacement is only operation being performed, it can be done in vehicle; however if it is being replaced in conjunction with rear main bearing, engine must be removed.*

Remove transmission and clutch assembly. Using an awl, punch two holes in seal and install sheet metal screws. Using a pair of levers, pry out old seal. Press in new seal, reinstall clutch and transmission.

FRONT COVER OIL SEAL

Drain cooling system, disconnect radiator hoses and remove radiator. Loosen alternator and Thermactor attaching bolts (if equipped). Remove drive belts. Remove crankshaft pulley, then pull seal from shaft, using suitable tool (T72J-6700). Install new seal using suitable tool (T72J-6700-A). Reverse removal procedures for remaining components.

ENGINE OILING

Crankcase Capacity — 4 qts. (Add 1 qt. with filter change).
Oil Filter — Disposable type.
Oil Pressure — 50-64 psi (3.5-4.5 kg/cm²) at 3000 RPM; minimum 4.3 psi (.30 kg/cm²) at idle.

ENGINE OIL SYSTEM

Rotor type oil pump is chain driven by crankshaft. Timing chain is lubricated by oil jet in cylinder block and oil holes in slipper head of adjuster. Oil holes in large end of connecting rods align with oil holes in crankshaft to lubricate pistons and components.

OIL PUMP

1) Remove oil inlet tube from pump. Remove and discard gaskets. Remove cover, withdraw inner rotor and shaft assembly. Remove outer race. Remove cotter pin from body, pull cap out of chamber, and take out spring and plunger.

2) Assemble in reverse order. Rotor, shaft and outer race are serviced as an assembly. If one component is damaged, replace all three. Install new cotter pin and gasket. Prime pump with oil before installing unit in block.

2000 cc 4 CYLINDER (Cont.)

Oil Pump Specifications

Application	Clearance In. (mm)
Lobe-to-Lobe	.002-.006 (.051-.152)
Rotor End Clearance	.002-.004 (.051-.102)
Outer Rotor-to-Housing	.006-.010 (.152-.254)

ENGINE COOLING

Thermostat — Begins to open at 180°F (82°C); fully open at 203°F (95°C).

Cooling System Capacity — 7.6 qts.

Radiator Cap — 13 psi (.90 kg/cm²).

WATER PUMP

Remove hood and drain cooling system. Remove lower hose from water pump, disconnect upper radiator hose at engine and lower hose at radiator. Remove radiator from vehicle. Loosen alternator and Thermactor pump (if equipped). Remove drive belt(s), fan, and pulley. Remove crankshaft pulley. Remove water pump. To install, reverse removal procedure.

ENGINE SPECIFICATIONS

GENERAL SPECIFICATIONS

Year	Displ. cu. ins.	cc	Carburetor	HP at RPM	Torque (Ft. Lbs. at RPM)	Compr. Ratio	Bore in.	mm	Stroke in.	mm
1980	120.2	1970	2-Bbl.	.....	.....	8.6:1	3.15	80	3.86	96.5

VALVES

Engine & Valve	Head Diam. In. (mm)	Face Angle	Seat Angle	Seat Width In. (mm)	Stem Diameter In. (mm)	Stem Clearance In. (mm)	Valve Lift In. (mm)
1970 cc Intake	1.6496-1.6575 (41.90-42.10)	45°	45°	.055 (1.397)	.3161-.3167 (8.029-8.044)	.0007-.0021 (.017-.053)	.....
Exhaust	1.2953-1.3031 (32.90-33.09)	45°	45°	.055 (1.397)	.3159-.3167 (8.024-8.044)	.0007-.0023 (.017-.058)	.....

VALVE SPRINGS

Engine	Free Length In. (mm)	PRESSURE Lbs. @ In. (kg @ mm) Valve Closed	Valve Open
1970 cc Inner	1.438 (36.52)	20.9@1.260 (9.5@32)	.....
Outer	1.469 (37.31)	31.4@1.339 14.2@34	.....

VALVE TIMING

Engine	INTAKE Open (BTDC)	Close (ABDC)	EXHAUST Open (BBDC)	Close (ATDC)
1970 cc	14°	53°	58°	9°

Courier Engines

2000 cc 4 CYLINDER (Cont.)
ENGINE SPECIFICATIONS (Cont.)

PISTONS, PINS, RINGS

Engine	PISTONS	PINS		RINGS		
	Clearance In. (mm)	Piston Fit In. (mm)	Rod Fit In. (mm)	Rings	End Gap In. (mm)	Side Clearance In. (mm)
1970 cc	.0014-.0030 (.036-.076)	.0003-.0009 (.008-.023)	.....	1 & 2 Oil	.008-.016 (.20-.40) .012-.035 (.30-.89)	.0011-.0027 (.028-.069) .....

CRANKSHAFT MAIN & CONNECTING ROD BEARINGS

Engine	MAIN BEARINGS				CONNECTING ROD BEARINGS		
	Journal Diam. In. (mm)	Clearance In. (mm)	Thrust Bearing	Crankshaft End Play In. (mm)	Journal Diam. In. (mm)	Clearance In. (mm)	Side Play In. (mm)
1970 cc	2.4780-2.4786 (62.94-62.95)	.0005-.0024 (.013-.061)	5	.003-.009 (.076-.228)	2.0842-2.0848 (52.938-52.954)	.001-.003 (.025-.076)	.004-.008 (.102-.203)

CAMSHAFT

Engine	Journal Diam. In. (mm)	Clearance In. (mm) ①	Lobe Lift In. (mm)
1970 cc Front	1.7695-1.7701 (44.945-44.960)	.0007-.0027 (.018-.069)	②
Center	1.7691-1.7697 (44.935-44.950)	.0011-.0031 (.028-.079)	②
Rear	1.7695-1.7701 (44.945-44.960)	.0007-.0027 (.018-.069)	②

① — End play is .001-.007" (.025-.178 mm).
② — See Cam Lobe Lift procedure.

TIGHTENING SPECIFICATIONS

Application	Ft. Lbs.(mkg)
Main Bearing Caps	61-65 (8.4-9.0)
Connecting Rod Caps	36-40 (5.0-5.5)
Cylinder Head	
Cold	59-64 (8.1-8.9)
Hot	69-72 (9.5-9.9)
Oil Pan	5-9 (.7-1.2)
Flywheel	112-118 (15.5-16.3)
Distributor Drive Gear	51-58 (7.0-8.0)
Oil Pump-to-Block	13-20 (1.8-2.8)
Camshaft Sprocket	51-58 (7.0-8.0)
Rocker Arm Cover	1-2 (.1-.3)
Oil Pump Sprocket	22-26 (3.0-3.6)
Intake Manifold	14-20 (1.9-2.8)
Exhaust Manifold	16-21 (2.2-2.9)

2300 cc 4 CYLINDER

ENGINE CODING

ENGINE IDENTIFICATION

Vehicle identification and engine information is stamped on the model plate which is attached to the body at the right rear corner of the engine compartment. The fourth character of the vehicle identification number indicates engine model. 2.3 liter engine code is "B".

Engine Identification	
Application	**Code**
2300 cc	B

ENGINE, CYLINDER HEAD & MANIFOLDS

ENGINE

Removal & Installation — **1)** Mark location of hinges and remove hood. Disconnect battery and drain cooling system. Remove air cleaner and heat stove assembly. Disconnect radiator hoses and remove radiator and shroud. Disconnect thermactor hoses at pump. Disconnect heater hoses, choke cable and accelerator linkage. Disconnect brake vacuum booster hose and vacuum amplifier.

2) Disconnect all primary and secondary ignition connections as well as sensor, emission control and electrical power connections between chassis and engine. Disconnect fuel line from carburetor and vacuum hoses from engine-chassis connections. Raise vehicle and drain engine oil. Disconnect exhaust pipe from manifold and hanger on transmission.

3) Remove starting motor and bolts holding transmission to engine. Lower vehicle and support transmission with a suitable jack. Attach engine hoisting sling and remove motor mount nuts and bolts. Pull engine forward until it clears transmission shaft and lift engine from vehicle. To install, reverse removal procedure.

INTAKE MANIFOLD

Removal & Installation — Remove air cleaner and disconnect fuel line from carburetor. Disconnect distributor and crankcase ventilation hoses at intake manifold. Disconnect carburetor linkage from carburetor. Remove nuts and bolts, then remove intake manifold and carburetor as an assembly from engine. To install, reverse removal procedure while noting the following: Use a new gasket upon installation. Tighten manifold nuts and bolts, in two steps, using sequence as shown in illustration.

EXHAUST MANIFOLD

Removal & Installation — Remove air cleaner and two attaching nuts from top of exhaust manifold shroud. Remove attaching nuts from muffler inlet pipe and manifold, then remove exhaust manifold. To install, apply a light film of graphite grease on exhaust manifold and install manifold. Tighten manifold bolts to specifications in 2 progressive steps in the sequence shown.

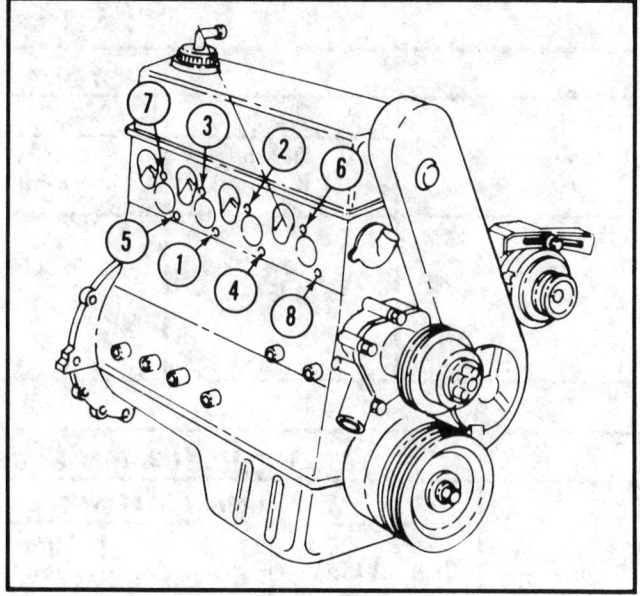

Fig. 1   Exhaust Manifold Tightening Sequence (Use Same Sequence for Tightening Intake Manifold)

CYLINDER HEAD

Removal — Drain cooling system, remove air cleaner and rocker arm cover. Remove exhaust manifold. Remove intake manifold and carburetor as an assembly. Disconnect spark plug wires from plugs. Remove all drive belts, fan, and pulley. Remove crankshaft pulley attaching bolt and crankshaft pulley. Remove camshaft drive belt cover, loosen drive belt tensioner and remove belt. Remove water outlet elbow from cylinder head. Remove timing belt inner cover-to-cylinder head attaching bolt. Remove cylinder head bolts, then remove cylinder head and camshaft as an assembly.

Installation — Clean gasket material from cylinder head and block. Install new gasket on block. Place cylinder head assembly on block and install head bolts. Tighten bolts, in two steps, using sequence shown in illustration. Reverse removal procedure for remaining components and adjust timing belt tension.

NOTE — *When installing cylinder head, ensure that locating pin at the front of the camshaft is in the 5:30 position. Valves may protrude and cause damage in any other position.*

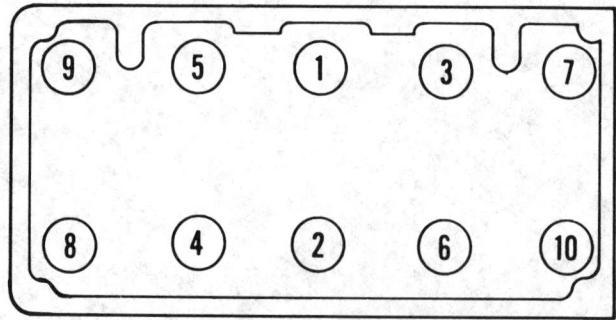

Fig. 2   Cylinder Head Tightening Sequence (Loosen in Reverse Order)

2300 cc 4 CYLINDER (Cont.)

CAMSHAFT

CAMSHAFT DRIVE BELT

Removal & Installation — *See Camshaft Timing.*

CAMSHAFT

Removal — With cylinder head removed from engine, remove rocker arms, keeping them in order for installation in original positions. Remove camshaft sprocket attaching bolt. Slide sprocket and belt guide plate from camshaft. Remove camshaft thrust plate from rear of cylinder head and carefully slide camshaft out rear of cylinder block.

Installation — Oil camshaft with engine oil and apply Lubriplate to valve stem tips. Oil rocker arms and carefully install camshaft in cylinder head. Install thrust plate, bolts and tighten. Check camshaft endplay and replace thrust plate if endplay is not within specifications.

NOTE — *Use new camshaft attaching bolt or use Teflon tape on threads of old bolt.*

CAMSHAFT BEARINGS

Removal & Installation — Use suitable tool (71P-6250A) to remove and install bearings.

NOTE — *Oil hole in bearing must be aligned with oil hole in journal.*

CAMSHAFT LOBE LIFT

Measure distance between major and minor diameters of each cam lobe with a micrometer. Difference in readings is lobe lift. If readings vary or do not meet specifications, replace camshaft.

CAMSHAFT END PLAY

With camshaft drive belt cover removed, push camshaft toward rear of engine. Install dial indicator so indicator point is on camshaft sprocket attaching screw or gear hub and zero dial indicator. Using a large screwdriver between camshaft sprocket or gear and cylinder head, pull the camshaft forward and release it. Read dial indicator and if endplay is not within specifications, replace thrust plate at rear of cylinder head.

CAMSHAFT TIMING

Checking Timing — **1)** Remove access plug from belt cover and position crankshaft to TDC by aligning pointer on cover with "O" mark on crankshaft damper.

CAUTION — *Turn engine in normal rotation direction only.*

2) Look through access hole and check that timing mark on camshaft drive sprocket is aligned with pointer on inner belt cover. Remove distributor cap and check that rotor is facing number 1 position on cap.

Adjusting Timing — **1)** If timing is incorrect or it is necessary to remove belt, remove timing belt outer cover and loosen belt tensioner adjustment screw. Position tension adjusting tool on tension spring roll pin and release belt tensioner. Tighten adjustment screw to hold tensioner in released position. Remove crankshaft damper, belt guide and drive belt.

2) Position crankshaft sprocket and camshaft sprocket as shown in illustration. Remove distributor cap and set rotor to No. 1 firing position by turning auxiliary shaft. Install drive belt over crankshaft sprocket and then counterclockwise over auxiliary and camshaft sprockets. Align belt fore and aft on sprockets.

3) Loosen tensioner adjustment screw and allow tensioner to move against drive belt. Remove spark plugs and rotate crankshaft two complete turns in direction of normal rotation to remove slack from belt. Tighten tensioner adjustment and pivot bolts. Recheck timing mark alignment.

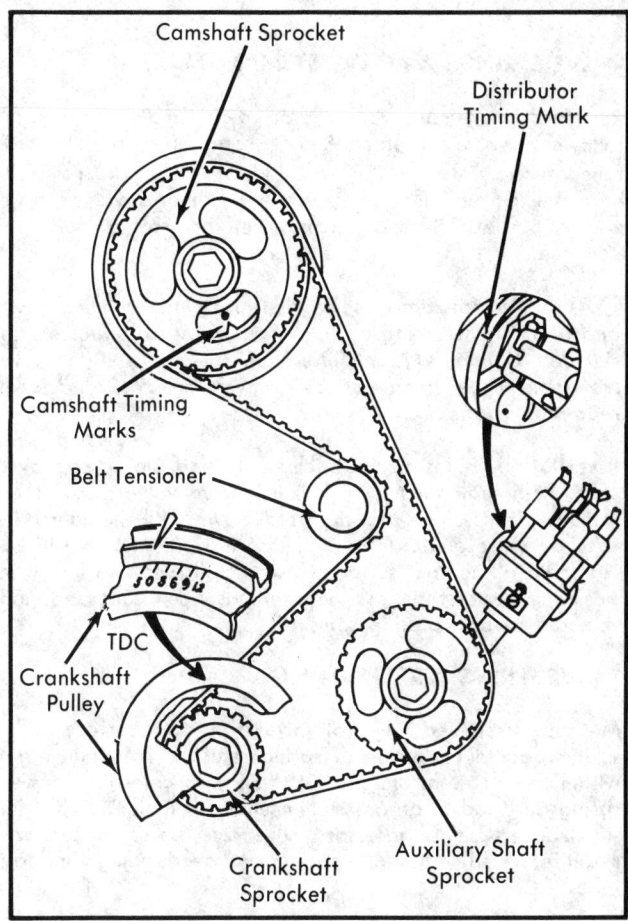

Fig. 3   Location of Timing Marks

AUXILIARY SHAFT

Removal — Remove drive belt cover, drive belt and auxiliary sprocket retaining bolt and washer. Slide sprocket from auxiliary shaft. Remove distributor and auxiliary shaft cover. Remove thrust plate and carefully remove shaft from cylinder block. Remove shaft bearing if worn or damaged.

Installation — **1)** If bearing was removed, align oil holes in bearing with those in block and drive bearing into place. Oil shaft and slide into cylinder block.

CAUTION — *Do not allow shaft gear and eccentric to touch bearing surfaces during installation.*

2) Install thrust plate, gasket and shaft cover, distributor and sprocket. Install and adjust drive belt. Install drive belt cover.

2300 cc 4 CYLINDER (Cont.)

VALVES

VALVE ARRANGEMENT

E-I-E-I-E-I-E-I (front to rear).

VALVE GUIDES

If valve guides become worn they may be reamed to install a new valve with oversize stem. When going from a standard size stem to oversize, always use reamers in sequence to obtain final desired bore. The valve seat must be refaced after a guide has been reamed, and a suitable tool used to break sharp corner (ID) of guide.

VALVE SPRINGS & VALVE STEM OIL SEALS

Removal — Remove rocker arm cover, and remove cam follower of valve concerned. Remove spark plug from affected cylinder and install air line and adapter. Use 140 psi (9.8 kg/cm²) line pressure to hold valve shut. Compress valve spring and remove locks (keepers). Remove retainer, spring and valve stem seals.

NOTE — *Air pressure must be kept on cylinder while springs and retainers are removed to prevent valve from falling into cylinder. If unable to maintain air pressure due to valve leakage, cylinder head must be removed and damaged valve repaired.*

Installation — Install new stem seal using plastic cap over stem. Push seal down until jacket touches valve guide, then remove plastic cover and push seal down until shoulder bottoms on valve guide. Install valve spring, retainer and locks. Lubricate all contact surfaces of cam follower and install in position. Ensure that lash adjuster has been collapsed and released before rotating camshaft.

VALVE SPRING INSTALLED HEIGHT

Measure assembled height of valve spring from surface of the spring pad to underside of spring retainer. If height is not within specifications, install .030" (.76 mm) spacer(s) between spring and pad to obtain recommended height. DO NOT install spacers unless necessary, as excess use of spacers will result in overstressing valve springs and overloading camshaft lobe.

Spring Height Specifications

Engine	Installed Height
2300 cc	1.531-1.594" (39.0-40.5 mm)

HYDRAULIC LASH ADJUSTER ASSEMBLY

Removal & Installation — With rocker arm cover removed, rotate camshaft so that cam lobe of applicable valve faces away from follower. Using suitable tool (T74P-6565-B), collapse adjuster or depress valve and slide follower out over adjuster. Lift adjuster out and inspect or clean as necessary. Replace entire assembly if plunger is not free in body. To install, reverse removal procedures.

CAUTION — *For any operation that requires removal of the rocker arm (follower), each affected lash adjuster must be collapsed after re-installation and released prior to rotating camshaft.*

HYDRAULIC LASH ADJUSTMENT

Position camshaft with lobe of valve to be checked pointing away from follower. Slowly apply pressure to follower with tool (T74P-6565-B) until adjuster is completely collapsed. Hold in this position and check clearance between follower and cam with feeler gauge. If not within specifications, check cam follower, cam, valve for sticking, and valve spring installed height.

Hydraulic Lash Adjustment

Application	①Clearance
Base of Lobe-to-Rocker Arm	
Desired	.040-.050" (1.0-1.3 mm)
Allowable	.035-.055" (.9-1.4 mm)

① — Leak down rate is 2-8 seconds.

PISTONS, PINS & RINGS

OIL PAN

Removal & Installation — Raise vehicle on hoist and remove front lower engine shield. Drain oil and remove clutch release cylinder, leaving the cylinder hanging. Remove engine rear brace attaching bolts and loosen bolts on left side. Remove oil pan bolts and lower pan from vehicle. To install, reverse removal procedure using guide pins to align pan in position. Tighten pan bolts to specifications in clockwise order, beginning with right-rear bolt.

PISTON & ROD ASSEMBLY

Removal — Remove cylinder head, oil pan and oil pump. Remove ridge at top of cylinder bores prior to removing pistons. Ensure that connecting rods and caps are marked for position and remove bearing caps. Push piston-rod assembly out of block from bottom, using caution not to nick crankshaft journals. Install rod caps on mating rods.

Installation — Oil piston rings and cylinder walls with engine oil. Install ring compressor and insert piston-rod assembly into corresponding cylinder. Notch on piston head must be toward front of engine. Tap piston into position using a wooden handle and carefully guide rod over crankshaft journal. Install rod bearing cap and tighten to specifications.

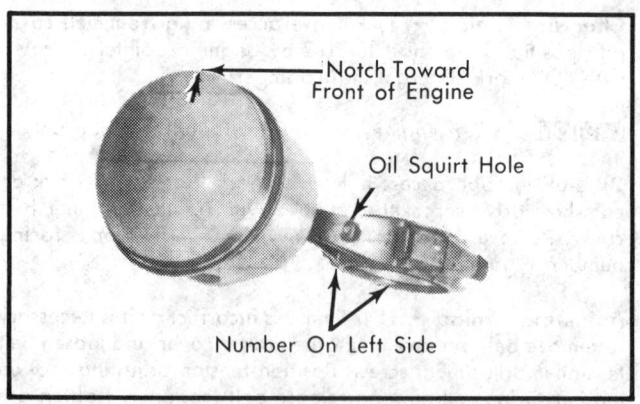

Fig. 4 Piston & Rod Assembly Identification

2300 cc 4 CYLINDER (Cont.)

FITTING PISTONS

1) Check piston to cylinder bore clearance by measuring the piston and cylinder bore diameters. Measure outer diameter of piston at centerline of piston pin bore and at 90° to pin bore axis. Measure the diameter of each cylinder bore at the top, middle and bottom, with the gauge placed at right angles and parallel to the centerline of the engine.

2) Standard size pistons are color coded; red, blue or have .003" OS stamped on the dome. Select the piston to assure the proper clearance. When the bore diameter is in the lower one third of specified range, a red piston should be used. When the bore diameter is in the middle one third a blue piston should be used. When the bore diameter is in the upper one third, the .003" OS piston should be used.

3) If no piston can be fitted, refinish the cylinder to provide proper clearance. When a piston has been fitted, mark it for assembly in the cylinder to which it has been fitted.

Piston Code	Diameter In. (mm)
Red	3.7780-3.7786 (95.961-95.976)
Blue	3.7792-3.7798 (95.991-96.006)
.003" O.S.	3.7804-3.7810 (96.022-96.037)

PISTON PINS

Removal — Remove bearing inserts from connecting rod and cap. Mark pistons and pins to assure assembly with same rod. Press piston pin from piston and connecting rod.

Installation — Apply light coat of engine oil to all parts. Assemble piston to connecting rod with oil squirt hole (in connecting rod) and notch (on piston head) positioned as shown in illustration. Start piston pin in piston and connecting rod, then press pin through piston and connecting rod until pin is centered in piston.

CRANKSHAFT MAIN & CONNECTING ROD BEARINGS

MAIN & CONNECTING ROD BEARINGS

NOTE — Following procedures are with oil pan and oil pump removed. If bearing replacement is required, both halves must be replaced. Do not use a new bearing in combination with a used bearing.

Connecting Rod Bearings — After ensuring rod caps are marked for cylinder identification, remove rod caps. Use Plastigage method to check for proper bearing clearance. If not within specifications, new bearings must be installed. New bearings are available in .001" (.025 mm) and .002" (.051 mm) undersizes. Selective fitting is required on each connecting rod. A standard bearing may be used in combination with either undersize bearing. Coat bearing surfaces with oil, install bearing and cap and tighten nuts to specifications.

Main Bearings — 1) Position jack under counterweight adjoining bearing being checked so weight of crankshaft will not compress Plastigage and provide an erroneous reading. With all bearing caps (other than one being checked) tight, check clearances using Plastigage method.

2) If clearances are excessive, a .001" (.025 mm) or .002" (.051 mm) undersize bearing may be used in combination with a standard bearing. If .002" (.051 mm) undersize bearings are used on more than one journal, they must be positioned in cylinder block rather than bearing cap. If standard and undersize bearings do not bring clearance within specified limits, crankshaft will have to be refinished and fitted with undersize bearings.

3) Remove all upper main bearings by inserting suitable tool in oil hole of crankshaft journal and rotating crankshaft clockwise to roll bearing from engine. Oil new upper bearing and insert plain (unnotched) end between crankshaft and indented (or notched) side of block. Rotate bearing into place. Install all main bearing caps with arrows pointing to front of engine.

REAR MAIN BEARING OIL SEAL

Removal & Installation — 1) Split lip type seal is provided for service replacement. Remove oil pan and oil pump. Loosen all main bearing cap bolts, allowing crankshaft to drop (not more than 1/32") and remove rear main bearing cap. Remove oil seal from cap and clean oil seal groove. Remove upper seal half from block using seal removal tool or small metal screw in end of seal.

CAUTION — Extreme care should be taken not to scratch or mar crankshaft seal surface.

2) Dip new split lip type seal halves in clean engine oil. Carefully install upper seal into its groove with undercut side of seal toward front of engine, by rotating it on seal journal of crankshaft until ends of seal are flush with block. Ensure that no rubber has been shaved from outside of seal.

3) Install lower seal in rear bearing cap with locating tab to rear. Seal ends should be flush with bearing cap. Apply 1/16" bead of suitable sealer to bearing cap mating surfaces, using care that sealer does NOT contact seals. Install bearing cap and tighten bolts to specifications.

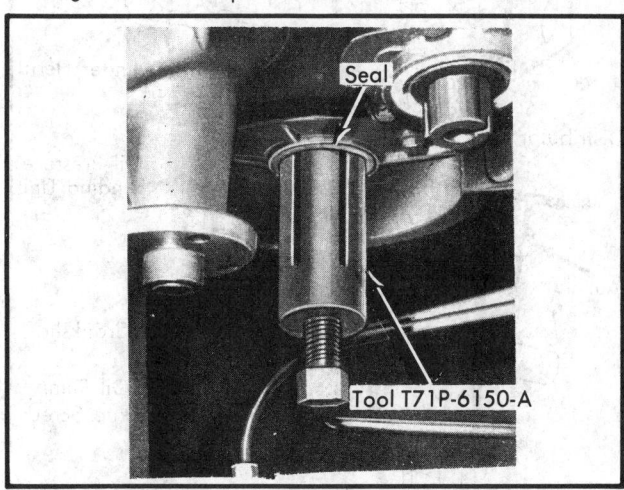

Fig. 5 Replacing Crankshaft Front Oil Seal

CRANKSHAFT FRONT OIL SEAL REPLACEMENT

Removal & Installation — Remove alternator drive belt and crankshaft pulley. Remove camshaft drive belt. See *Camshaft Drive Belt Replacement*. Slide camshaft drive belt sprocket and

2300 cc 4 CYLINDER (Cont.)

belt off crankshaft, using puller if necessary. Fit a suitable puller over end of crankshaft and remove seal. To install, use tool (T74P-6150-A) and reverse removal procedure.

NOTE — *Cylinder front cover and auxiliary shaft seals are replaced using procedure outlined above.*

ENGINE OILING

ENGINE OILING SYSTEM

Oiling system is force feed type using a full flow oil filter. Oil enters main oil gallery from oil filter and flows to main bearings and camshaft bearings. Connecting rod bearings are supplied from front and rear main bearings via inclined passages. A squirt hole in each rod bearing supplies oil to piston thrust side of cylinder. Auxiliary shaft is connected with main oil gallery. Distributor shaft receives oil from passage drilled in auxiliary shaft. Cams and cam follower arms are supplied from camshaft. Valve lash adjusters receive oil from drilled oil passages in cylinder head.

Crankcase Capacity — 4 qts. (5 qts. including filter.)

Oil Filter — Full flow, spin-on type.

Normal Oil Pressure (Hot) — 40-60 psi (2.8-4.2 kg/cm²) at 2000 RPM.

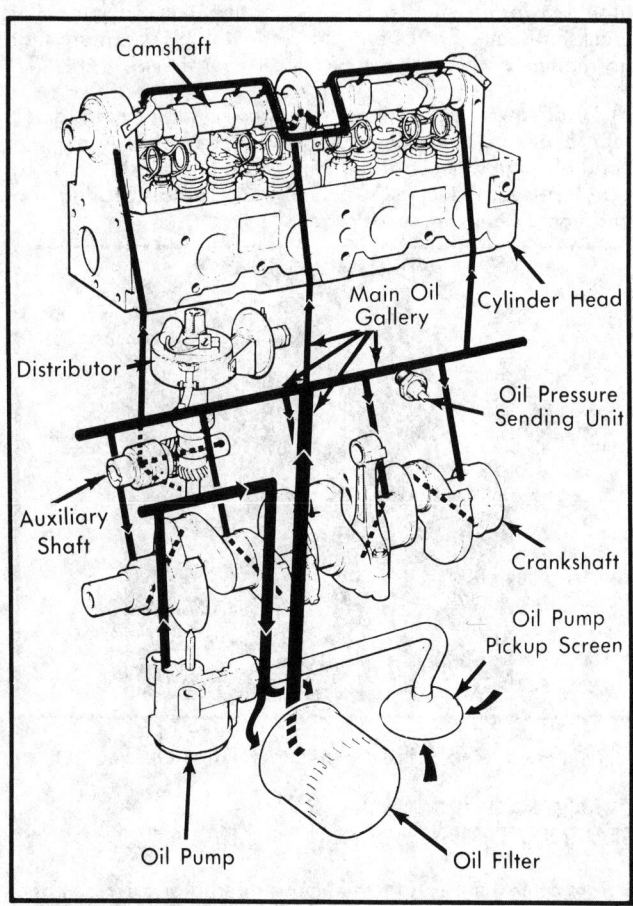

Fig. 6 Engine Oiling System

Pressure Relief Valve — Internal, non-adjustable.

OIL PUMP

Removal & Installation — With oil pan removed, remove oil pump mounting screws. Remove pump and take out oil inlet tube screws. Remove tube and gasket. Remove cover attaching screws and cover, inner rotor and shaft assembly, and pump outer race. If pump clearances are beyond limits, replace race, rotor and shaft as an assembly. To install, reverse removal procedures. Use new gaskets, prime pump with engine oil.

Oil Pump Specifications	
Application	**Clearance In. (mm)**
Drive Shaft-to-Housing	.0015-.0029 (.04-.08)
Rotor Assembly End Clearance	.001-.004 (.02-.10)
Outer Rotor-to-Housing	.001-.013 (.02-.33)
Relief Valve Spring Tension	15.2-17.2 lbs. @ 1.20″ (6.9-7.8 kg @ 30.4 mm)

ENGINE COOLING

Thermostat — Opens at 185-192°F (85-89°C). Full Open at 210-216°F (99-102°C).

Cooling System Capacity — 8.8 quarts.

Radiator Cap — 13 psi (.90 kg/cm²).

TIGHTENING SPECIFICATIONS	
Application	**Ft. Lbs. (mkg)**
Auxiliary Shaft Gear	28-40(3.9-5.5)
Auxiliary Shaft Thrust Plate	6-9(.8-1.2)
Belt Tensioner Pivot	28-40(3.9-5.5)
Belt Tensioner Adjuster	14-21(1.9-2.9)
Camshaft Sprocket	80-90(11.1-12.4)
Camshaft Thrust Plate	6-9(.8-1.2)
Connecting Rod	
Step 1	25-30(3.5-4.1)
Step 2	30-36(4.1-5.0)
Crankshaft Pulley	100-120 (13.8-16.6)
Cylinder Head	
Step 1	60(8.3)
Step 2	80-90(11.1-12.4)
Exhaust Manifold-to-Cylinder Head	16-23(2.2-3.2)
Flywheel-to-Crankshaft	54-64(7.5-8.8)
Front Cover	6-9(.8-1.2)
Intake Manifold-to-Cylinder Head	14-21(1.9-2.9)
Main Bearing Cap	
Step 1	60(8.3)
Step 2	80-90(11.1-12.4)
Oil Pan-to-Block	
M6 Bolts	7-9(1.0-1.2)
M8 Bolts	11-13(1.5-1.8)
Rocker Arm Cover	4-7(.6-1.0)
Timing Belt Cover	6-9(.8-1.2)
Water Pump-to-Cylinder Block	14-21(1.9-2.9)

2300 cc 4 CYLINDER (Cont.)
ENGINE SPECIFICATIONS

	GENERAL SPECIFICATIONS									
Year	Displ.		Carburetor	HP at RPM	Torque (Ft. Lbs. at RPM)	Compr. Ratio	Bore		Stroke	
	cu. ins.	cc					in.	mm	in.	mm
1980	140	2300	2-Bbl.	.....	.....	8.4:1	3.78	96.01	3.126	79.40

	VALVE SPRINGS			
Engine	Free Length In. (mm)	PRESSURE Lbs. @ In. (kg @ mm)		
		Valve Closed	Valve Open	
2300 cc	1.824 (46.3)	71-79@1.56 (32-36@39.6)	180-198@1.16 (82-90@29.5)	

	CAMSHAFT		
Engine	Journal Diam. In. (mm)	Clearance In. (mm)	Lobe Lift In. (mm)
2300 cc	1.7713-1.7720 (44.991-45.009)	① (.001-.003) (.025-.076)	.2437 (6.19)

① — End play is .001-.007" (.025-.178 mm).

	VALVES						
Engine & Valve	Head Diam. In. (mm)	Face Angle	Seat Angle	Seat Width In. (mm)	Stem Diameter In. (mm)	Stem Clearance In. (mm)	Valve Lift In. (mm)
2300 cc Intake	1.728-1.744 (43.89-44.30)	44°	45°	.060-.080 (1.52-2.03)	.3416-.3423 (8.68-8.69)	.0010-.0027 (.025-.069)	.3997 (10.15)
Exhaust	1.492-1.508 (37.90-38.30)	44°	45°	.070-.090 (1.78-2.29)	.3411-.3418 (8.66-8.68)	.0015-.0032 (.038-.081)	.3997 (10.15)

	PISTONS, PINS, RINGS					
	PISTONS	PINS		RINGS		
Engine	Clearance In. (mm)	Piston Fit In. (mm)	Rod Fit In. (mm)	Rings	End Gap In. (mm)	Side Clearance In. (mm)
2300 cc	.0014-.0022 (.035-.056)	.0002-.0004 (.005-.010)	①	Comp.	.010-.020 (.25-.51)	.002-.004 (.051-.102)
				Oil	.015-.055 (.38-1.40)	Snug

① — Interference Fit.

	CRANKSHAFT MAIN & CONNECTING ROD BEARINGS						
	MAIN BEARINGS				CONNECTING ROD BEARINGS		
Engine	Journal Diam. In. (mm)	Clearance In. (mm)	Thrust Bearing	Crankshaft End Play In. (mm)	Journal Diam. In. (mm)	Clearance In. (mm)	Side Play In. (mm)
2300 cc	.2.3982-2.3990 (60.91-60.93)	.0008-.0015 (.020-.038)	No. 3	.004-.008 (.10-.20)	2.0464-2.0472 (51.979-51.999)	.0008-.0015 (.020-.038)	.0035-.0105 (.089-.267)

Datsun Engines

210 & 310 4 CYLINDER

ENGINE CODING

ENGINE IDENTIFICATION

Engine serial and code number is stamped on right rear side of cylinder block, below mating surface of cylinder head and cylinder block. First 3 or 4 digits are engine code.

Engine Identification	
Application	**Code**
210 (1237 cc)	A12A
210 & 310 (1397 cc)	A14
210 (1488 cc)	A15

ENGINE, CYLINDER HEAD & MANIFOLDS

ENGINE

NOTE – *Manufacturer recommends that engine and transmission be removed as an assembly.*

Removal (210) – **1)** Disconnect battery ground and fusible links. Mark hood location and remove hood. Remove engine protective undercover. Drain coolant and engine oil.

2) Remove radiator. Disconnect electrical wires and other lines attached to air cleaner, then remove air cleaner assembly. Disconnect accelerator cable from carburetor. Disconnect the following components:
- Automatic choke wire.
- Throttle solenoid or throttle switch.
- Fuel cut solenoid.
- Vacuum switching valve.
- Coil and distributor.
- Thermal transmitter.
- Alternator and oil pressure switch.
- Engine ground and coil at engine wiring harness.
- Fuel pump and necessary emission control hoses.
- Water temperature switch.
- Vacuum switch.
- Battery cable to starter.

3) On models equipped with air conditioning, loosen compressor and lay out of the way without disconnecting any hoses. On models with manual transmissions, remove clutch slave cylinder. On all models, disconnect speedometer cable from extension housing. Remove shift linkage.

4) On manual transmission models, remove gear shift lever. On models with automatic transmissions, disconnect selector lever. On all models, disconnect exhaust at manifold and exhaust mounting bracket from transmission and hang up with wire.

5) Index mark and remove propeller shaft. Plug opening in rear of extension housing. Support transmission with a jack. Remove rear crossmember mounting bolts. Attach hoist to engine and raise slightly to support engine weight. Remove front engine mounts and remove engine and transmission as a unit.

Installation – To install, reverse removal procedure.

Removal (310) – **1)** Remove hood and battery and drain coolant. Disconnect ducting and tubes to air cleaner and remove air cleaner assembly. Disconnect accelerator cable. Remove radiator grille.

2) Disconnect following components so they are free when engine and transmission assembly is lifted out:
- Coil and distributor wires.
- Coil wires at block connector.
- Fusible links.
- Engine wiring harness.
- Fuel pump.
- Radiator and heater hoses.
- Master-Vac vacuum line.
- Air pump and carbon canister.
- Battery cables.
- Bonding wire (near strut mounting).

3) Remove carbon canister, auxiliary fan and washer tank. Remove radiator together with auxiliary fan motor. Remove clutch slave cylinder and disconnect speedometer cable. Remove buffer (damper) rods.

4) On models equipped with air conditioning, loosen air conditioning equipment and lay components out of way. Do not discharge system. Disconnect shift linkage. Attach hoist to engine.

5) Disconnect exhaust system at manifold, rear engine mount and "U" clamp. Disconnect both axle drive shafts at transaxle case. Lower out shift linkage. Disconnect engine mounts and lift out engine.

Installation – Install in reverse order of removal, ensuring that buffer (damper) rods are adjusted so that rubber will not be deformed.

INTAKE & EXHAUST MANIFOLDS

Removal & Installation – **1)** Remove air cleaner and disconnect accelerator cable and choke cable. Disconnect and plug fuel line at carburetor. Disconnect exhaust pipe at exhaust manifold.

2) Remove nuts retaining intake and exhaust manifold to cylinder head and remove intake and exhaust manifold as an assembly. Remove gasket and thoroughly clean mating surfaces. Remove bolts and separate intake and exhaust manifold. To install, reverse removal procedure and use new gasket. Tighten nuts and bolts to specifications.

CYLINDER HEAD

Removal – Remove manifold assembly and take off rocker arm cover. Loosen valve adjusting screws to take tension off push rods. Remove rocker shaft assembly and withdraw push rods, keeping them in order for installation. Loosen head bolts gradually in reverse of tightening sequence and remove cylinder head. See Fig. 1.

Installation – Thoroughly clean mating surfaces. Use new gasket with no sealer and install cylinder head. Install cylinder head retaining bolts and tighten in 2 or 3 steps to specifications. *Follow sequence shown in Fig. 1.* Reverse removal procedure to install remaining components. Adjust valve clearance.

NOTE – *One cylinder head bolt is smaller diameter and has a hollow head. Install this bolt on right side center of cylinder head.*

210 & 310 4 CYLINDER (Cont.)

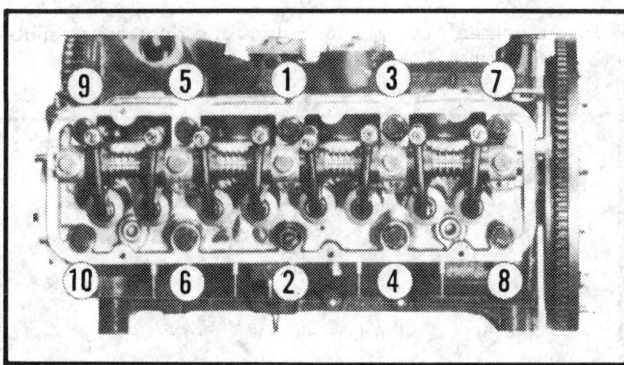

Fig. 1   Tightening Sequence for Cylinder Head
(Loosen in Reverse Sequence)

VALVES

VALVE ARRANGEMENT

E-I-I-E-E-I-I-E (front to rear).

VALVE GUIDE SERVICING

Check valve stem-to-guide clearance. If clearance is more than .0039" (.1 mm) and valve stem is not worn, valve guide must be replaced. Replace valve guide using the following procedure:

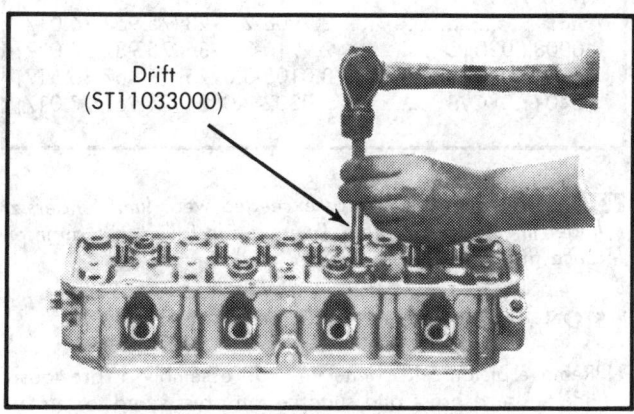

Fig. 2   Valve Guide Removal

1) Heat cylinder head to 302-392°F (150-200°C) to ease removal and installation and use suitable drift (ST11033000) to drive old guides out toward combustion chamber. Ream guide hole to .480" (12.2 mm) with head at room temperature.

2) With head heated, press new guide in position. Use suitable reamer (ST110320000) to finish stem bore to .31" (8.0 mm) and reface valve seat surface.

VALVE STEM OIL SEALS

Valve stem lip seals are used on all guides. Valve spring seat must be in position, then place seal on guide. Tap installer tool (KV10104800) with plastic hammer to ensure proper position of seal on guide.

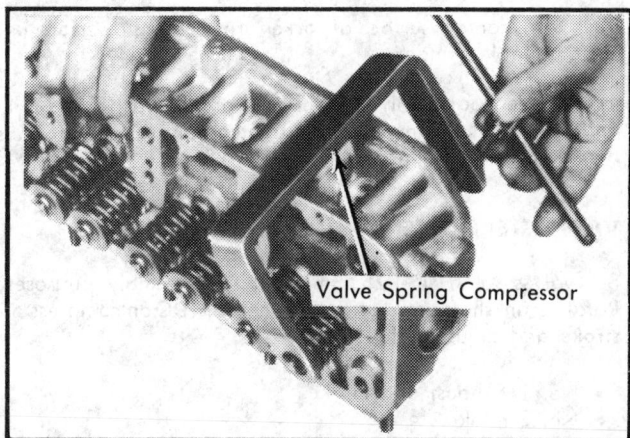

Fig. 3   Valve Spring Removal & Replacement

VALVE SPRINGS

Removal – With cylinder head removed, compress valve spring using a suitable valve spring compressor (ST12070000) and remove valve keepers. Release spring compressor and remove spring retainer and spring.

Installation – Install spring seat and oil seal, then insert valve in guide carefully to avoid damaging lip of seal. Install spring with close coiled end (painted white) toward head. Install retainer and keepers, ensuring that keepers are in proper position by tapping with plastic hammer.

VALVE SPRING INSTALLED HEIGHT

Valve spring must be square within $\frac{1}{16}$". Valve spring installed height is 1.52" (38.7 mm). Check valve spring by applying specified load and measuring spring height. If spring height and pressure, or squareness does not meet specifications, replace spring.

ROCKER ARM & SHAFT ASSEMBLY

1) Remove valve cover and loosen valve adjusting screws to remove tension. Loosen rocker arm assembly mounting bolts evenly and remove rocker arm and shaft assembly.

2) Slide off support stands, rocker arms and springs. Thoroughly clean and inspect all components for signs of wear or seizure. Measure rocker arm-to-shaft clearance by measuring diameter of rocker arm bore and shaft. Standard clearance is .0008-.0021" (.020-.054 mm). Replace as necessary.

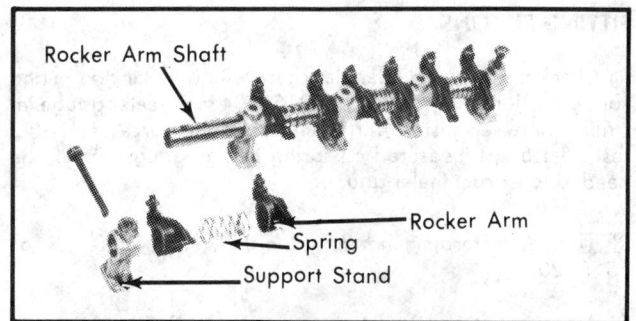

Fig. 4   Rocker Arm and Shaft Assembly

210 & 310 4 CYLINDER (Cont.)

3) If valve contact surface of rocker arm is worn, resurface using a suitable grinder.

4) Reverse disassembly and removal procedures to assemble and install rocker arm assembly. Tighten bolts to specifications and adjust valve clearance.

VALVE CLEARANCE

Set valves to .010" (.25 mm) cold for assembly purposes. Rotate crankshaft until No. 1 cylinder is at TDC on compression stroke and adjust as follows:

- No. 1 Exhaust and Intake.
- No. 2 Intake.
- No. 3 Exhaust.

Rotate crankshaft and bring No. 4 cylinder to TDC on compression stroke and adjust remaining valves.

- No. 2 Exhaust.
- No. 3 Intake.
- No. 4 Intake and Exhuast.

Warm engine to normal operating temperature and repeat adjustment procedure. Set clearance to .014" (.35 mm).

PISTONS, PINS & RINGS

PISTON & ROD ASSEMBLY

1) Remove cylinder head and oil pan. Remove nuts from connecting rod and remove connecting rod cap with bearing half. Push piston and connecting rod assembly with bearing half up and out through top of cylinder block.

2) To install piston and connecting rod assembly, thoroughly oil rings, piston and cylinder wall. Make sure ring gaps are situated approximately 180° apart and not on thrust side of piston. See Fig. 5. Make sure bearing halves are properly seated in connecting rod and cap.

3) Install a ring compressor and compress rings. Install piston in cylinder with number on top of piston toward front of engine. With piston installed in cylinder, and connecting rod and bearings seated against crankshaft journal, install rod cap with numbers on the same side as connecting rod. Tighten nuts to specification.

4) Install cylinder head and oil pan as previously outlined.

FITTING PISTONS

1) Check piston-to-cylinder clearance with a feeler gauge and spring tension gauge. With a .0016" (.04 mm) feeler gauge installed between piston and cylinder wall, a force of 1.1-3.3 lbs. (.5-1.5 kg) measured on spring tension gauge, should be needed to extract feeler gauge.

NOTE — It is recommended that piston and cylinder be at 68°F (20°C).

2) Measure piston diameter at top of skirt 90° to piston pin axis. Measure cylinder bore halfway down cylinder and

90° to crankshaft center line. Pistons and rings are available in standard and 3 oversizes.

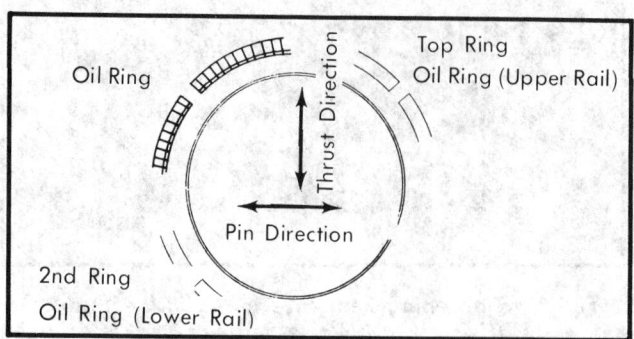

Fig. 5 Piston Ring Gap Positioning

Piston Specifications	
Application In. (mm)	Piston Size In. (mm)
A12A	
Std.	2.9515-2.9534 (74.967-75.017)
.0008 (.020) O/S	2.9522-2.9542 (74.987-75.037)
.020 (.50) O/S	2.9715-2.9734 (75.467-75.517)
.040 (1.0) O/S	2.9909-2.9928 (75.967-76.017)
A14 & A15	
Std.	2.9908-2.9928 (75.967-76.017)
.0008 (.020) O/S	2.9916-2.9936 (75.987-76.037)
.020 (.50) O/S	3.0105-3.0125 (76.467-76.517)
.040 (1.0) O/S	3.0302-3.0322 (76.967-77.017)

NOTE — If cylinder bore has exceeded wear limit, undersize cylinder liners are available. Liners are installed with an interference fit .0031-.0035" (.08-.09 mm).

PISTON PIN REPLACEMENT

1) Remove piston and connecting rod assembly as previously outlined. Use a press and suitable pin press stand to remove and install pin in piston/rod assembly.

2) Check piston-to-pin clearance by measuring pin and hole diameters. If clearance is not within specifications, replace both piston and piston pin. Piston pin should push fit by hand through piston with both piston and pin at room temperature.

3) Piston pin should be press fit into connecting rod. If interference fit is not within specifications, replace connecting rod or piston pin as necessary. If connecting rod is replaced, ensure weight difference between rods is within .176 ounces (5 grams).

4) To assemble piston and connecting rod assembly, use same mandral and driver used for disassembly. Thoroughly oil pin, piston and connecting rod. Install piston on connecting rod so that number on top of piston is pointing toward front of engine and oil squirt hole on connecting rod is toward right side of crankcase.

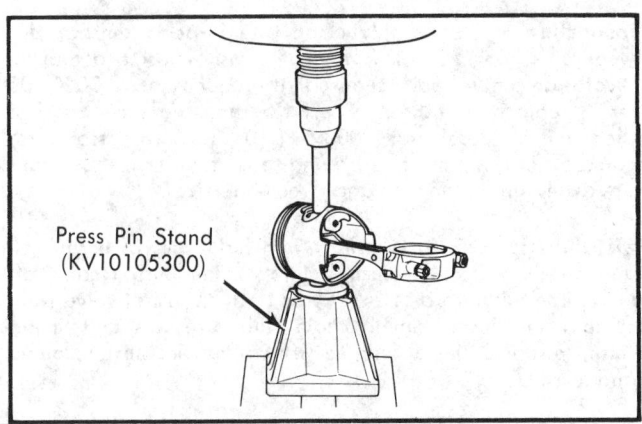

Fig. 6 Removing and Installing Piston Pin

Press Pin Stand
(KV10105300)

CRANKSHAFT MAIN & CONNECTING ROD BEARINGS

MAIN & CONNECTING ROD BEARINGS

Removal — With engine removed from vehicle, remove cylinder head, oil pan, and piston and connecting rod assemblies. Remove alternator and engine mounting bracket from left side. Remove water pump, crankshaft pulley, and timing chain cover. Remove oil thrower and chain tensioner. Remove camshaft sprocket bolt, and remove both sprockets and timing chain as an assembly. Remove clutch and flywheel. Loosen main bearing cap bolts in two or three steps, then remove caps. Remove rear oil seal and carefully lift out crankshaft.

Inspection — 1) Thoroughly clean and inspect crankshaft. Blow out oil passages with compressed air. Check crankshaft for runout on center main bearing journal. If runout is more than .002″ (.05 mm), crankshaft is bent and must be replaced.

2) Check all main and connecting rod bearings using Plastigage method. Check main and connecting rod journals for out-of-round or taper. If more than .0012″ (.03 mm), crankshaft must be ground to next undersize. Main and connecting rod journals may be ground to the undersizes indicated in tables.

Main Bearing Journals

Application In. (mm)	Diameter In. (mm)
Std.	1.9663-1.9671 (49.943-49.964)
.01 (.25) U/S	1.9567-1.9572 (49.701-49.714)
.02 (.50) U/S	1.9469-1.9474 (49.451-49.464)
.03 (.75) U/S	1.9378-1.9376 (49.201-49.214)

Installation — 1) Install main bearing halves to engine block ensuring that all bearings are on correct journal. Bearings for journal No. 1 and No. 5 are the same. Bearings for journals No. 2 and No. 4 are the same. Journal No. 3 requires the thrust bearing. Upper and lower bearings are not interchangeable except for journals No. 2 and No. 4.

Connecting Rod Journals

Application In. (mm)	Diameter In. (mm)
Std.	1.7698-1.7706 (44.958-44.974)
.003 (.08) U/S	1.760-1.7675 (44.881-44.894)
.01 (.25) U/S	1.7603-1.7608 (44.711-44.724)
.02 (.50) U/S	1.7504-1.7509 (44.461-44.474)
.03 (.75) U/S	1.7406-1.7411 (44.211-44.224)

2) Apply oil to main bearing surface and install crankshaft. Install main bearing caps with arrow pointing toward front of engine. Tighten main bearing caps in 2 or 3 steps, starting at center bearing and working outward. Ensure crankshaft rotates smoothly.

NOTE — *Apply sealer to rear main bearing cap at point where cap contacts cylinder block.*

3) Check crankshaft end play. See *Thrust Bearing Alignment.* Install timing chain in correct position with crankshaft and camshaft sprockets. Install rear oil seal. Install clutch and flywheel. Install oil thrower and chain tensioner. Install timing chain cover, crankshaft pulley, and water pump. Install alternator and engine mounting bracket. Install piston and connecting rod assemblies, oil pan, and cylinder head.

THRUST BEARING ALIGNMENT

Thrust bearing is installed on No. 3 main bearing journal. Check crankshaft end play by inserting a feeler gauge between flange of thrust bearing and crankshaft. End play should be .002-.006″ (.05-.15 mm). Service limit is .012″ (.30 mm).

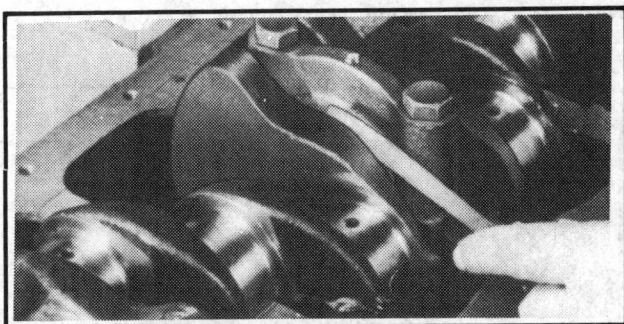

Fig. 7 Checking Crankshaft End Play

REAR MAIN BEARING OIL SEAL

Apply sealer to corners of crankcase at rear main bearing cap contact points and install cap. Lubricate seal lips and drive seal into position with suitable installer.

ENGINE FRONT COVER & OIL SEAL

Removal & Installation — Remove drive belt, fan, and water pump pulley. Remove water pump and crankshaft pulley. Remove oil pan and front cover. Replace seal in front cover whenever cover is removed. Thoroughly clean mating surfaces and apply sealer to both sides of gasket. Install gasket and cover. Tighten bolts and nuts to specifications. Reverse removal procedure to install remaining components.

CAMSHAFT

TIMING CHAIN

Removal — Remove engine front cover as previously outlined. Remove timing chain tensioner and bolt securing camshaft sprocket to camshaft. Pull off sprocket with timing chain.

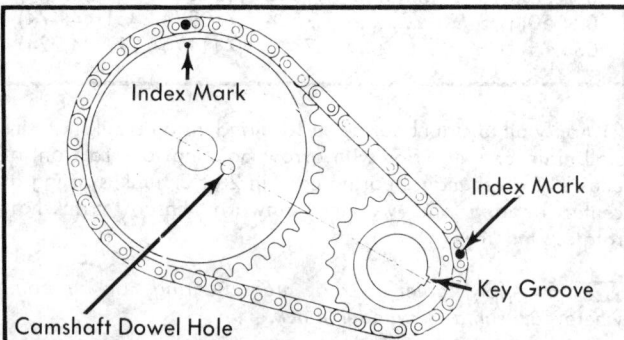

Fig. 8   Timing Chain Alignment Marks for Installation

Installation — **1)** Insert crank sprocket keys in keyways of crankshaft. Install camshaft and crankshaft sprockets temporarily for adjustment of tooth height by using adjusting washers. Adjust height difference so it is less than .020" (0.5 mm).

2) Install timing chain and camshaft sprocket with markings on chain and sprockets correctly aligned. See Fig. 8. Oil sprocket teeth and chain with engine oil. Install and tighten camshaft sprocket bolt. Install chain tensioner and tighten attaching bolts. Check dimension "L" of tensioner and if over .591" (15 mm), replace chain. See Fig. 9. Install oil thrower in front of camshaft sprocket. Install timing chain cover.

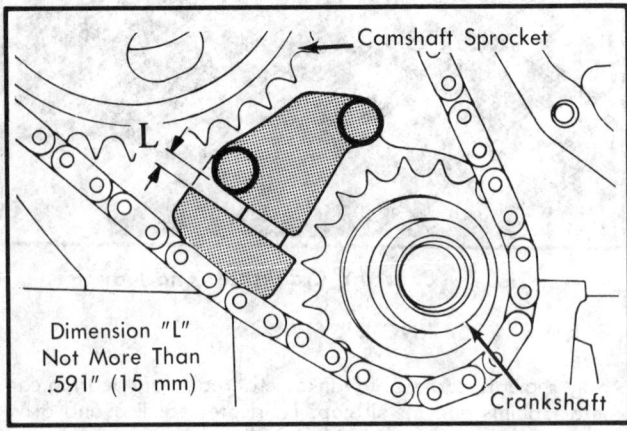

Fig. 9   Checking Timing Chain Tensioner Projection

CAMSHAFT

Removal — Remove engine front cover, and valve train components as previously outlined. Remove fuel pump and oil pump with filter. Remove timing chain tensioner and remove timing chain with sprockets. Remove two bolts from camshaft lock plate and carefully pull camshaft from engine block.

Inspection — Thoroughly clean and inspect camshaft for wear or scoring. Check runout of camshaft using a dial indicator on center bearing journal. If runout exceeds .002" (.05 mm), replace camshaft. Check journal diameter, and if diameter is more than .0039" (.10 mm) from standard, camshaft journals must be ground to next undersize. Bearings are available in standard and three undersizes.

Installation — Coat camshaft with light coat of engine oil and carefully install camshaft into engine. Install camshaft lock plate with word "LOWER" at bottom. Install valve train components. Install timing chain with sprockets and timing chain tensioner. Install engine front cover. Install fuel pump and oil pump.

CAMSHAFT END THRUST

Check camshaft end thrust with camshaft, lock plate, and camshaft sprocket in position by using a dial indicator on camshaft sprocket bolt. If end play exceeds .0039" (.10 mm), replace lock plate.

CAMSHAFT BEARING REPLACEMENT

1) With camshaft removed, check journal diameter and bearing inside diameter. If journal measurement is within tolerance and clearance between camshaft journals and bearings exceeds .0059" (.15 mm), bearings must be replaced.

2) Remove and install appropriate bearings in crankcase using a suitable driver (ST16110000). Make sure oil holes in bearings align with oil holes in crankcase. Bearings must be line bored after installation. Install taper plug in crankcase using sealer. Install camshaft as previously outlined.

ENGINE OILING

Crankcase Capacity (With Filter)	
Application	**Quantity**
A12A (1237 cc)	$3\frac{3}{8}$ quarts
A14 (1397 cc)	$3\frac{3}{8}$ quarts
A15 (1488 cc)	$3\frac{1}{4}$ quarts

Oil Filter — Full-flow, replaceable element.

Oil Pressure — More than 11 psi (.8 kg/cm²) at idle; 54-74 psi (3.8-5.2 kg/cm²) at 3000 RPM.

Pressure Relief Valve — Nonadjustable, located in oil pump cover.

ENGINE OILING SYSTEM

Oil is circulated through engine by pressure provided by a trochoid rotor type pump. Oil pump is mounted on side of crankcase and driven by camshaft. Oil is drawn from oil pan by oil pump and into full flow oil filter mounted under oil pump. Oil is then pumped into main oil gallery of crankcase where it is distributed to crankshaft journals, timing chain tensioner and squirter that lubricates timing chain. Oil is circulated from crankshaft main bearing journals to camshaft journals and from center camshaft journal to rocker arm shaft

210 & 310 4 CYLINDER (Cont.)

to lubricate rocker arms and valves. Cylinder walls and piston pins are lubricated by oil squirted from squirt hole in connecting rod.

OIL PUMP

Removal & Installation — Place suitable drain pan under oil pump/filter assembly and remove oil filter with oil filter wrench. Remove 3 pump mounting bolts. Take out bolt securing cover to body and check all clearances with a feeler gauge. If beyond wear limit replace entire pump assembly. To install, reverse removal procedure.

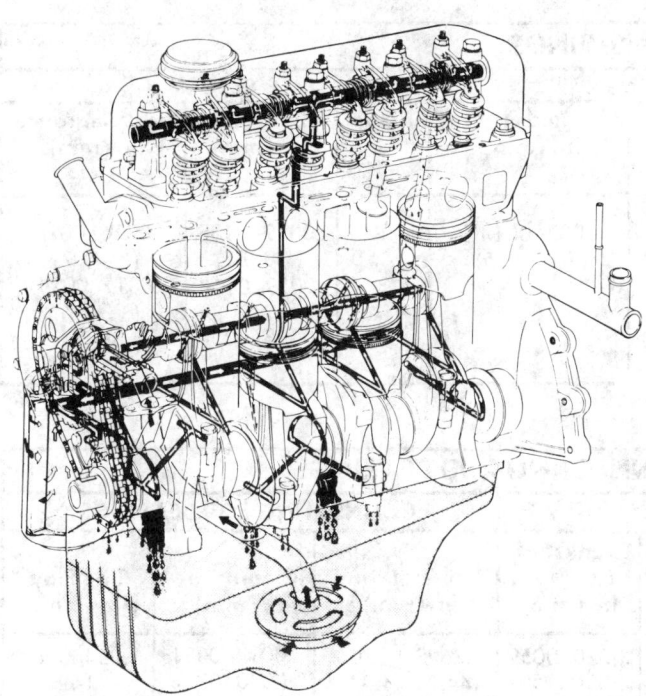

Fig. 10 Engine Oiling System

Oil Pump Specifications	
Application	**Wear Limit In. (mm)**
Rotor-to-Rotor Side Clearance	.0024 (.06)
Rotor-to-Tip Clearance	.0079 (.20)
Rotor-to-Pump Body	.0197 (.50)
Regulator Valve Spring	
Free Length	1.71 (43.49)
Length at 8.09 lbs. (3.67 kg)	1.19 (30.3)

ENGINE COOLING

WATER PUMP

Removal & Installation — Drain coolant. On 310, loosen belt and remove fan and pulley. On 210, loosen bolts retaining shroud to radiator and remove shroud. On air conditioned 210 models, remove fan blade from torque coupling and remove torque coupling and pulley from hub. On all models, remove water pump and gasket from front cover. To install, use new gasket and reverse removal procedure. Be sure to clean gasket contact surfaces.

Thermostat — Opens at 180°F (82°C).

Cooling System Capacity	
Application	**Quantity**
210 With Heater	
Auto. Trans.	6 quarts
Man. Trans.	6¼ quarts
210 Without Heater	
Auto. Trans.	5¼ quarts
Man. Trans.	6½ quarts
310	
With Heater	6¼ quarts
Without Heater	5⅝ quarts

ENGINE SPECIFICATIONS

GENERAL SPECIFICATIONS

Year	Displ.		Carburetor	HP at RPM	Torque (Ft. Lbs. at RPM)	Compr. Ratio	Bore		Stroke	
	cu. ins.	cc					in.	mm	in.	mm
1980										
A12A	75.5	1237	1 x 2-Bbl.	.....	.....	8.5:1	2.76	70	2.95	75
A14	85.2	1397	1 x 2-Bbl.	.....	.....	8.9:1	2.99	76	3.03	77
A15	90.9	1488	1 x 2-Bbl.	.....	.....	8.9:1	2.99	76	3.23	82

VALVES

Engine & Valve	Head Diam. In. (mm)	Face Angle	Seat Angle	Seat Width In. (mm)	Stem Diameter In. (mm)	Stem Clearance In. (mm)	Valve Lift In. (mm)
All							
Int.	1.46 (37)	45.5°	45.5°	.059 (1.5)	.3138-.3144 (7.970-7.985)	.0006-.0018 (.015-.045)	.3114 (7.91)
Exh.	1.18 (30)	45.5°	45.5°	.075 (1.9)	.3128-.3134 (7.945-7.960)	.0016-.0028 (.040-.070)	.3236 (8.22)

Datsun Engines

210 & 310 4 CYLINDER (Cont.)

ENGINE SPECIFICATIONS (Cont.)

VALVE SPRINGS

Engine	Free Length In. (mm)	PRESSURE Lbs. @ In. (kg @ mm)	
		Valve Closed	Valve Open
All	1.831 (46.5)	....	56.4@1.189 25.6@30.2

VALVE TIMING

Engine	INTAKE		EXHAUST	
	Open (BTDC)	Close (ABDC)	Open (BBDC)	Close (ATDC)
A12A	14°	54°	56°	12°
A14 & A15	14°	54°	56°	20°

PISTONS, PINS, RINGS

Engine	PISTONS	PINS		RINGS		
	Clearance In. (mm)	Piston Fit In. (mm)	Rod Fit In. (mm)	Rings	End Gap In. (mm)	Side Clearance In. (mm)
All	.0010-.0018 (.025-.045)	.0003-.0005 (.008-.012)	.0007-.0014① (.017-.035)	1	.0079-.0138 (.20-.35)	.0016-.0028 (.04-.07)
				2	.0059-.0118 (.15-.30)	.0012-.0024 (.03-.06)
				Oil	.0118-.0354 (.30-.90)	snug

① — Interference fit.

CRANKSHAFT MAIN & CONNECTING ROD BEARINGS

Engine	MAIN BEARINGS				CONNECTING ROD BEARINGS		
	Journal Diam. In. (mm)	Clearance In. (mm)	Thrust Bearing	Crankshaft End Play In. (mm)	Journal Diam. In. (mm)	Clearance In. (mm)	Side Play In. (mm)
All	1.9663-1.9671 (49.94-49.96)	.0010-.0035 (.026-.090)	No. 3	.0020-.0059 (.050-.150)	1.7698-1.7706 (44.95-44.97)	.0012-.0031 (.030-.079)	.004-.008 (.1-.2)

CAMSHAFT

Engine	Journal Diam. In. (mm)	Clearance In. (mm)	Lobe Lift In. (mm)
All No. 1	1.7237-1.7242 (43.78-43.80)	.0015-.0024 (.037-.060)	Int. .222 (5.65)
2	1.7041-1.7046 (43.28-43.30)	.0011-.0020 (.027-.050)	Exh. .233 (5.92)
3	1.6844-1.6849 (42.78-42.80)	.0016-.0025 (.040-.063)	
4	1.6647-1.6652 (42.28-42.30)	.0011-.0020 (.029-.050)	
5	1.6224-1.6229 (41.21-41.22)	.0015-.0024 (.037-.060)	

TIGHTENING SPECIFICATIONS

Application	Ft. Lbs. (mkg)
Cylinder Head	51-54 (7.0-7.5)
Connecting Rod	23-27 (3.2-3.8)
Main Bearing Caps	36-43 (5.0-6.0)
Camshaft Sprocket	29-35 (4.0-4.8)
Camshaft Lock Plate	3.6-5.8 (.5-.8)
Timing Chain Tensioner	4.3-5.8 (0.6-0.8)
Front Cover	3.6-5.1 (.5-.7)
Oil Pan	2.9-4.3 (.4-.6)
Oil Pump	6.5-10.1 (.9-1.4)
Rocker Arm Shaft	14-18 (2.0-2.5)
Manifolds	11-14 (1.5-2.0)
Crankshaft Pulley	108-145 (15-20)
Flywheel	58-65 (8.0-9.0)
Oil Strainer	6.5-10 (.9-1.4)
Engine Mounts	14-18 (1.9-2.5)
Water Pump	6.5-10.0 (.9-1.4)

200SX, 510 & PICKUP 4 CYLINDER

ENGINE CODING

ENGINE IDENTIFICATION

Engine number is stamped on right side of cylinder block on 510 and Pickup models and left side of block on 200SX model.

Engine Identification	
Application	**Code**
200SX	Z20E
510	Z20S
Pickup	L20B

ENGINE & CYLINDER HEAD

ENGINE

NOTE — *It is recommended that engine and transmission be removed as a unit. Engine can then be separated from transmission.*

Removal (200SX) — **1)** Reduce fuel pressure by disconnecting harness connector at upper-right fuel pump relay while engine is running. After stalling occurs, crank engine 2 or 3 times. Turn ignition to "OFF" and reconnect harness connector.

2) Mark hood and hinges for alignment on reassembly, then remove hood. Disconnect battery ground cable. Drain cooling system, transmission and crankcase. Disconnect all engine-to-chassis cables, hoses and wires.

3) On models with air conditioning, dismount compressor by removing mounting bolts and moving compressor aside toward fender. DO NOT discharge gas from compressor or system or separate refrigerant lines. Hold compressor out of way with wire to prevent interference with engine removal.

4) On models with power steering, dismount steering pump by removing belt and mounting bolts. Move aside toward fender and secure with wire to prevent interference with engine removal. DO NOT allow oil to drain from pump.

5) On manual transmission models, detach rubber boot, remove nut from shift lever and remove shift lever. On automatic transmission models, disconnect joint between control lever and selector rod. Remove oil cooler lines. On all models, remove radiator hoses, shroud and radiator.

6) Disconnect speedometer cable, downshift solenoid and inhibitor switch wires. On manual transmission models, remove clutch operating cylinder. On automatic transmission models, disconnect vacuum hose. On all models, mark for reassembly and remove propeller shaft. Remove front exhaust pipe.

7) Plug end of transmission. Attach a lifting hoist to engine and raise enough to take weight off engine mounts. Remove front and rear engine mounting bolts. Pull engine forward and carefully remove engine and transmission as an assembly.

Removal (510) — **1)** Disconnect battery ground cable. Drain cooling system, transmission and crankcase. Mark hood and hinges for alignment on reassembly, then remove hood. Remove grille.

2) Remove radiator hoses. Disconnect oil cooler lines and remove splash board on models with automatic transmission.

Disconnect inhibitor switch, downshift solenoid and engine ground cable wire connections.

3) Remove radiator and shroud. Remove all hoses and tubes to air cleaner, then remove air cleaner. Disconnect all engine-to-chassis cables, hoses and wires.

4) On models with air conditioning, dismount compressor by removing mounting bolts and moving compressor aside toward fender. DO NOT discharge gas from compressor or system or separate refrigerant lines. Hold compressor out of way with wire to prevent interference with engine removal.

5) Disconnect speedometer cable. On manual transmission models, detach rubber boot, remove nut from shift lever and remove shift lever. Remove clutch operating cylinder. On automatic transmission models, disconnect joint between control lever and selector rod.

6) Remove front exhaust pipe. Mark for reassembly and remove propeller shaft. Plug end of transmission. Attach a lifting hoist to engine and raise enough to take weight off engine mounts. Remove front and rear engine mounting bolts. Pull engine forward and carefully remove engine and transmission as an assembly.

Removal (Pickup) — **1)** Disconnect battery ground cable. Drain cooling system, transmission and crankcase. Mark hood and hinges for reassembly, then remove hood. Remove all hoses and tubes to air cleaner, then remove air cleaner. Disconnect all engine-to-chassis cables, hoses and wires.

2) On models with air conditioning, dismount compressor by removing mounting bolts and moving compressor aside toward fender. DO NOT discharge gas from compressor or system or separate refrigerant lines. Hold compressor out of way with wire to prevent interference with engine removal.

3) On manual transmission models, detach rubber boot, remove nut from shift lever and remove shift lever. Remove clutch operating cylinder. On automatic transmission models, disconnect joint between control lever and selector rod. Remove oil cooler lines.

4) Remove radiator hoses, shroud and radiator. Disconnect speedometer cable and all switch wires on transmission case. Remove parking brake cable. Disconnect vacuum hose and oil pipes on automatic transmission models.

5) Mark for reassembly and remove propeller shaft. Remove front exhaust pipe. Plug end of transmission. Attach a lifting hoist to engine and raise enough to take weight off engine mounts. Remove front and rear engine mounting bolts.

6) Remove steering idler arm mounting bolts and push down cross rod. Pull engine forward and carefully remove engine and transmission as an assembly.

Installation (All Models) — Replace any rubber engine mounts showing signs of deterioration or separation. Ensure proper placement of all engine mountings. Reverse removal procedures to complete installation.

CYLINDER HEAD

Removal (200SX) — **1)** Reduce fuel pump pressure. See *ENGINE REMOVAL.* Disconnect battery ground cable. Drain cooling system. Disconnect spark plug wires from spark plugs. Remove radiator and heater hoses.

Datsun Engines

200SX, 510 & PICKUP 4 CYLINDER (Cont.)

2) Disconnect drive belts, alternator bracket and adjusting bar. Move alternator aside. Remove fan, pulley and water pump. If equipped with air conditioning and/or power steering, remove necessary components. *See Step(s)* **3)** and/or **4)** in ENGINE REMOVAL.

3) Disconnect throttle linkage and air cleaner intake hoses. Disconnect all cables, hoses and wires running from cylinder head to chassis or engine. Disconnect all hoses and vacuum lines from intake manifold to cylinder head or engine block. Remove intake manifold.

4) Disconnect E.G.R. tube and front exhaust pipe. Remove exhaust manifold. Remove rocker cover. Turn crankshaft so No. 1 piston is at TDC on compression stroke. Paint alignment marks on timing chain and camshaft sprocket to aid in installation.

5) Remove camshaft sprocket and use retainer tool (KV10105800) to support timing chain as shown in *Fig. 1*. Remove cylinder head attaching bolts in reverse of sequence shown in *Fig. 2*. Remove cylinder head.

Removal (510) — **1)** Disconnect battery ground cable. Drain cooling system. Disconnect spark plug wires from spark plugs. Remove radiator and heater hoses. Disconnect drive belts, alternator bracket and adjusting bar. Move alternator aside.

2) Remove fan, pulley and water pump. If equipped with air conditioning, dismount compressor without disconnecting hoses and support out of way with wire. Disconnect throttle linkage. Remove air cleaner. Disconnect fuel and vacuum lines and electrical connectors to carburetor and intake manifold. Remove fuel pump, carburetor and intake manifold.

3) Remove E.G.R. and exhaust air induction tubes. Remove front exhaust pipe, exhaust manifold and rocker cover. Turn crankshaft so No. 1 piston is at TDC on compression stroke. Paint aligning marks on timing chain and camshaft sprocket to aid in installation.

4) Remove camshaft sprocket and use retainer tool (KV10105800) to support timing chain as shown in *Fig. 1*. Remove cylinder head attaching bolts in reverse of sequence shown in *Fig. 2*. Remove cylinder head.

Removal (Pickup) — **1)** Disconnect battery ground cable. Drain cooling system. Remove all hoses and ducts from air cleaner, then remove air cleaner. Disconnect spark plug wires from spark plugs. Remove rocker cover. Remove alternator.

2) Disconnect fuel hose from carburetor and remove fuel pump. Remove PCV hose and anti-backfire valve-to-EGR passage hose. Disconnect vacuum hoses and linkage to carburetor, then remove carburetor.

3) If equipped with air conditioning, dismount compressor without disconnecting hoses and support out of way with wire. Remove drive belts, fan and water pump. Disconnect all hoses and vacuum lines from intake manifold to cylinder head or block. Remove intake and exhaust manifolds as an assembly. Remove fuel pump drive cam.

4) Turn crankshaft so No. 1 piston is at TDC on compression stroke. Paint alignment marks on timing chain and camshaft sprocket to aid in installation. Remove camshaft sprocket and use retainer tool (KV10105800) to support timing chain as shown in *Fig. 1*. Remove cylinder head attaching bolts in reverse of sequence shown in *Fig. 2*. Remove cylinder head.

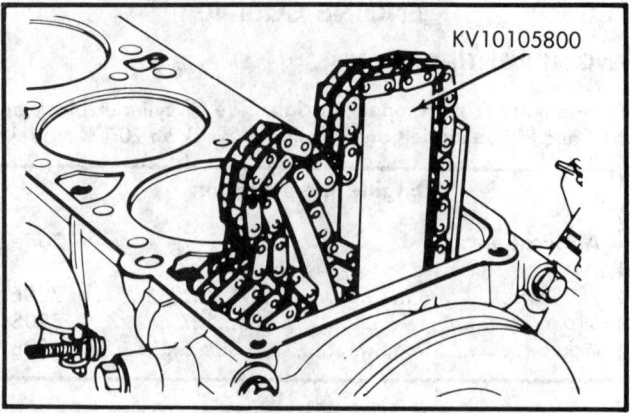

Fig. 1   Holding Timing Chain with Special Support Tool

Installation (All Models) — **1)** Ensure that mating surfaces of cylinder head and block are clean, then install cylinder head and gasket without sealer. Number 1 piston should be at TDC on compression stroke and camshaft sprocket location notch and plate oblong groove aligned.

2) Insert head bolts and tighten ① and ② to 14 ft. lbs. (2.0 mkg). Install and align sprockets and timing chain. Install remaining components in reverse order of removal, using new seals, gaskets and sealant where required.

3) Tighten head bolts in several steps in the sequence illustrated in *Fig. 2* to final specified torque. Recheck torque after engine has been running for several minutes.

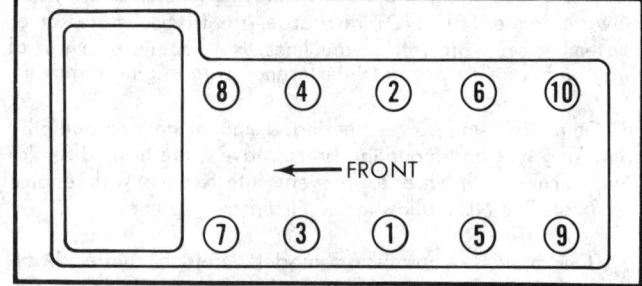

Fig. 2   Cylinder Head Tightening Sequence

CAMSHAFT

CAMSHAFT

Removal (200SX & 510) — With cylinder head removed, evenly loosen rocker arm bolts from outside in sequence. DO NOT remove bolts from each end of rocker arm shaft or assembly will spring apart. Remove rocker arm assembly. Carefully remove camshaft.

Installation — Install camshaft on cylinder head with front camshaft dowel pin facing up. Install rocker arm assembly aligning to dowel pin on cylinder head. Place cylinder head on wooden blocks to allow for valve space. Tighten rocker arm bolts in 2 or 3 steps in outward sequence from center bracket.

Removal (Pickup) — With cylinder head removed, remove valve rocker springs. Loosen valve rocker pivot lock nuts and remove rocker arms by pressing down on spring. Use care not to lose valve rocker guide. Remove locating plate. Carefully remove camshaft.

200SX, 510 & PICKUP 4 CYLINDER (Cont.)

Installation — Install camshaft into cylinder head, taking care not to damage bearings. Install camshaft locating plate with oblong groove on plate facing towards front of engine. Install remaining components in reverse of removal procedure and tighten all nuts and bolts.

CAMSHAFT BEARINGS

Measure inner diameter of camshaft bearing and outer diameter of camshaft journal. If wear or damage is excessive, replace cylinder head assembly.

ENGINE FRONT COVER

Removal — With engine removed from vehicle and mounted on engine stand, remove oil pump and drive spindle. Remove front cover attaching bolts and front cover.

Installation — Apply sealant at mating corners of oil pan, cylinder head and front cover. Oil seal should be coated with engine oil before installation in cover and before cover is installed. Use new gasket and install cover.

NOTE — Check height difference between cylinder block and front cover upper face. Difference must not exceed .006" (.15 mm).

TIMING CHAIN & GEARS

Removal — Remove valve cover. On Pickup and 510, remove fuel pump and fuel pump drive cam. Remove camshaft drive sprocket and engine front cover. Remove timing chain tensioner and guides. Remove timing chain, oil thrower, crankshaft worm gear and chain drive sprocket.

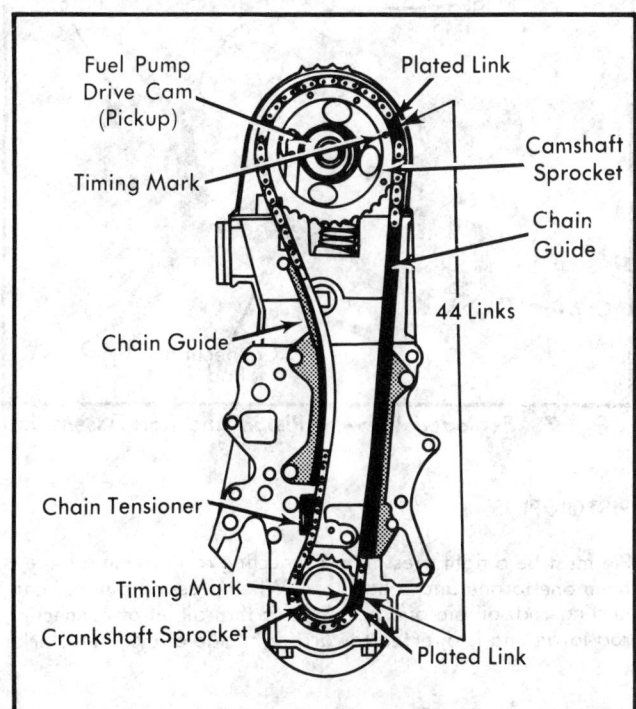

Fig. 3   Timing Chain and Sprocket Alignment

Installation — Ensure that crankshaft and camshaft keys point upward. Set timing chain so that mating marks align with crankshaft and camshaft sprockets. There are 44 chain links between the 2 timing marks. Complete installation in reverse order of removal.

VALVES

VALVE ARRANGEMENT

200SX & 510
Right Side — All Intake.
Left Side— All Exhaust.
Pickup — E-I-I-E-E-I-I-E (Front to Rear)

NOTE — Camshaft MUST be removed to take out valves. See Camshaft Removal & Installation in this Section.

VALVES

Removal — With camshaft removed, remove valves using valve spring compressor (ST12070000). Keep disassembled parts in order. Check each valve for worn, damaged or deformed heads or stems.

Installation — Install valve spring seat and oil seal on valve guide. Place springs in position with close-coiled (painted) end toward cylinder head. Use compressor and install valve collets and keepers. Install rocker guides.

VALVE GUIDE SERVICE

1) Measure clearance between valve stem and valve guide, with aid of micrometer and hole gauge. Check diameter of valve stem in three places: top, center, and bottom.

2) Insert hole gauge in valve guide bore and measure at center. Subtract highest reading of valve stem diameter from valve guide bore to obtain clearance.

NOTE — As a quick check, a valve may be inserted into valve guide and moved either left or right, (parallel with rocker arm). If tip moves .0079" (.2 mm) or more, clearance is beyond maximum limit of .0039" (.1 mm).

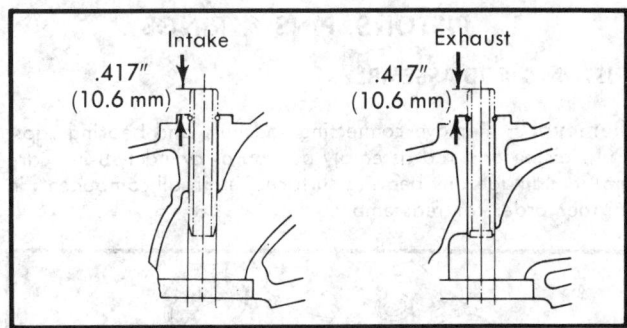

Fig. 4   Intake and Exhaust Valve Guides

VALVE SEAT INSERTS

1) Check valve seats for pitting at valve contact surface. Valve seat inserts of .0197" (.5 mm) oversize are available if necessary. To remove old inserts, machine should be set so that boring cannot continue beyond bottom face of insert recess in cylinder head.

2) Machine cylinder head recess diameter in concentric circles to valve guide center so that insert will have correct fit. Heat cylinder head to 302-392°F (150-200°C) and install insert, making sure that it seats on bottom face of recess.

3) Valve seats should be cut or ground to correct face angle and seat width and to head diameter of valve to be installed.

200SX, 510 & PICKUP 4 CYLINDER (Cont.)

VALVE SPRING INSTALLED HEIGHT

With valves closed, inner spring should have a height of 1.378" (35.0 mm) and outer spring should have a height of 1.575" (40.0 mm). See specification for pressure with valves opened or closed.

VALVE ADJUSTMENT

NOTE — *Valves should be adjusted with engine at normal operating temperature. Cold specifications are provided for initial settings after assembly.*

200SX & 510 — Turn engine until high point on No. 1 cam lobe points down. Adjust intake valve of No. 1 and 2, exhaust valve of No. 3 and 4. Turn engine until high point on No. 1 cam lobe points up. Adjust intake valve of No. 3 and 4, exhaust valve of No. 1 and 2.

Pickup — Turn engine until high point on No. 1 cam lobe points up. Adjust intake valve of No. 2 and 4, exhaust valve of No. 1 and 3. Turn engine until high point on No. 1 cam lobe points down. Adjust intake valve of No. 1 and 3, exhaust valve of No. 2 and 4.

Valve Adjustment Specifications		
Valve	**Hot**	**①Cold**
200SX & 510		
Intake	.012" (.30 mm)	.008" (.21 mm)
Exhaust	.012" (.30 mm)	.009" (.23 mm)
Pickup		
Intake	.010" (.25 mm)	.007" (.17 mm)
Exhaust	.012" (.30 mm)	.009" (.24 mm)
① — Use for initial settings only.		

PISTONS, PINS & RINGS

PISTON & ROD ASSEMBLY

Removal — Remove connecting rod nuts and bearing caps. Push piston and rod assembly out top of cylinder, using care not to damage any bearing surface. Retain all components in proper order for reassembly.

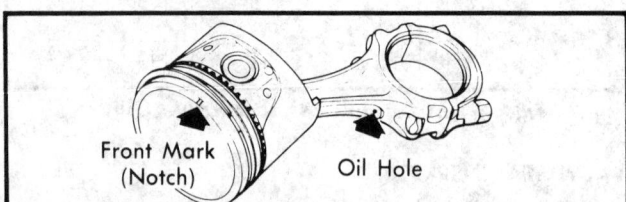
Fig. 5   Piston and Rod Assembly Installation Features

Installation — Reassemble piston and rod so that oil hole in connecting rod is facing right side of engine and notch on top of piston is facing forward. Install connecting rod on original journal with rod and cap marks on same side. Tighten connecting rod nuts and check rod side play.

FITTING PISTONS

1) Measure cylinder bores for wear or taper at top, bottom and middle on thrust face and at 90° to thrust face. If ex-

cessive wear is found rebore cylinder and install oversize pistons. Oversize pistons are available as shown in table.

2) When boring cylinders, use cylinder order of 2-4-1-3 to prevent heat distortion. After honing cylinder to final fit, check piston fit using spring tension pull scale. A force of .44-3.31 lbs. (.2-1.5 kg.) should be obtained extracting a .0016" (.04 mm) feeler gauge.

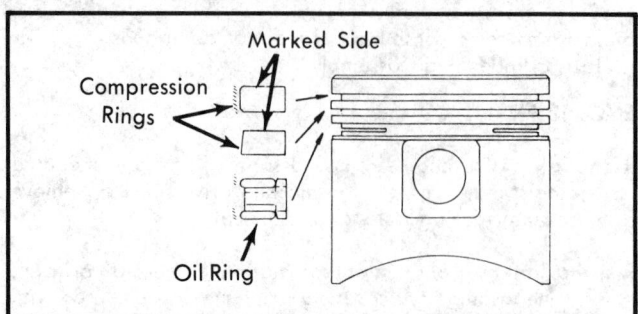
Fig. 6   Installation Order of Piston Rings

3) Measure piston ring end gap and side clearance and replace as necessary. Install rings on pistons with end gaps 180° apart and so no end gap is in line with thrust face. Install rings with top mark facing upward.

NOTE — *If only piston ring is to be replaced, measure gap at bottom of bore. Oversize rings are available in .020" (.50 mm) and .040" (1.00 mm).*

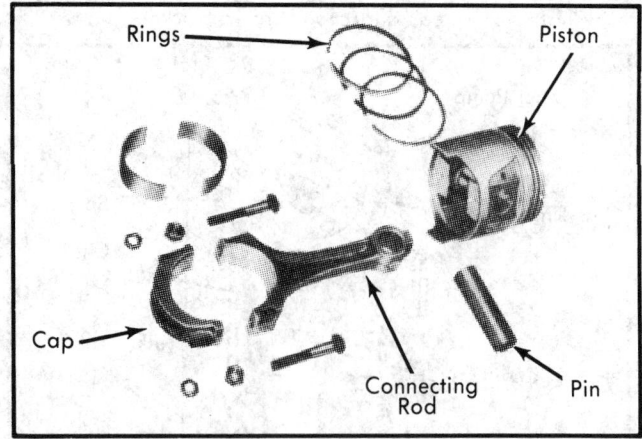
Fig. 7   Exploded View of Piston and Rod Assembly

PISTON PINS

Pin must be a tight press fit in connecting rod, pressing force is from one to one and a half tons. When pressing pin into connecting rod, oil pin and press pin so that oil jet of connecting rod large end is directed toward right side of cylinder block.

Piston Specifications	
Application	**Piston Size**
In. (mm)	**In. (mm)**
Standard	3.3459-3.3478 (84.985-85.035)
.020 (.50) OS	3.3648-3.3667 (85.465-85.515)
.040 (1.00) OS	3.3844-3.3864 (85.965-86.015)

200SX, 510 & PICKUP 4 CYLINDER (Cont.)

CRANKSHAFT MAIN & CONNECTING ROD BEARINGS

CRANKSHAFT

Removal — With engine removed from vehicle, remove cylinder head and oil pan. Remove flywheel and rear plate. Remove oil strainer, oil pump and drive spindle. Remove front cover, chain tensioner, chain slack side guide, and timing chain. Remove oil thrower, crankcase worm gear, and timing drive sprocket. Remove piston and rod assemblies. Remove main bearing caps using suitable puller (KV101041SO) to remove center and rear main bearing caps.

NOTE — *Keep all main bearing caps in order to aid in reassembly. Remove rear oil seal, remove crankshaft.*

Inspection — Check all crankshaft journals for scoring, wear or cracks. Taper and out-of-round on all journals must not exceed .001" (.025 mm). Check crankshaft for bend using dial indicator at center journal of crankshaft. If bend exceeds .002" (.05 mm), which is ½ of indicator reading, replace crankshaft. Check main driveshaft pilot bearing at rear of crankshaft for wear or damage and replace if necessary.

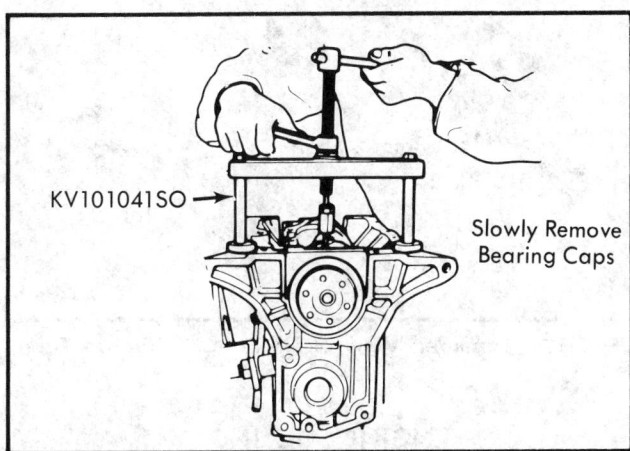

KV101041SO

Slowly Remove Bearing Caps

Fig. 8   Rear Main Bearing Cap Removal

Installation — 1) Install main bearing halves to engine block ensuring that all bearings are on correct journal. Journal No. 3 requires a thrust bearing. Bearing for No. 1 is the same as for No. 5 and bearing for No. 2 is the same as for No. 4. Upper and lower bearings are not interchangeable. Upper bearings have an oil groove.

2) Apply oil to main bearing surface and install crankshaft. Install main bearing caps with arrow pointing toward front of engine. Shift crankshaft toward front of engine, tighten main bearing caps, in two or three steps, starting at center bearing and working outwards. Ensure crankshaft rotates smoothly.

NOTE — *Apply sealer to rear main bearing cap at point where cap contacts cylinder block.*

3) Check crankshaft end play, and if not within specifications replace center thrust bearing. Install side seals in rear main bearing cap, after applying sealer to seals. Install rear oil seal. Install rear end plate and flywheel. Install piston and rod assemblies. Install remaining components in reverse of removal procedure

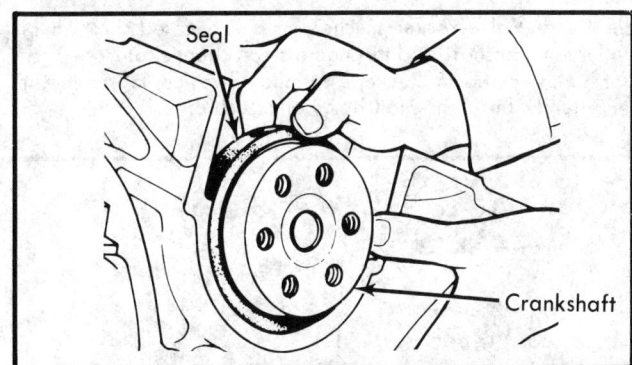

Seal

Crankshaft

Fig. 9   Rear Oil Seal Removal

MAIN BEARINGS

1) Check all bearings for scoring or wear and replace if damage is found. Clean oil from crankshaft and place a strip of Plastigage on crankshaft journal. Install main bearing cap, with bearing installed, and tighten to 33-40 ft.lbs. (4.5-5.5 mkg).

NOTE — *Plastigage should run parallel with crankshaft and not block oil hole. Do not turn crankshaft while Plastigage is inserted.*

2) Remove cap and measure width of Plastigage at widest point using gauge provided. If clearance is not to specifications, replace bearings. Bearings are available in undersizes of .01" (.25 mm), .02" (.50 mm), .03" (.75 mm) and .04" (1.00 mm).

CONNECTING ROD BEARINGS

Check connecting rod bearings in same manner as main bearings using Plastigage. Tighten connecting rod caps to 33-40 ft. lbs. (4.5-5.5 mkg). Bearings are available in undersizes of .01" (.25 mm), .02" (.50 mm) and .03" (.75 mm). Check for clearance of .001-.002" (.025-.055 mm) when installing new bearings. Maximum wear limit for old bearings is .005" (.12 mm).

ENGINE OILING

Crankcase Capacity (With Filter)	
Application	**Capacity**
200SX	4.4 qts.
510	4.6 qts.
Pickup	4.5 qts.

Oil Filter — Full-flow, disposable cartridge.

Oil Pressure — 50-60 psi. (3.5-4.2 kg/cm²) at 3000 rpm.

ENGINE OILING SYSTEM

Oil drawn from pan passes through screen to oil pump and is delivered to oil filter and to main oil gallery. Main oil gallery supplies oil to crankshaft main bearings and drilled passages in crankshaft. Oil sprayed from jet holes on connecting rods lubricates cylinders and piston pins. Oil from main gallery lubricates chain tensioner and timing chain. Center hole in crankshaft, center bearing feeds camshaft bearings on cylin-

200SX, 510 & PICKUP 4 CYLINDER (Cont.)

der head. Valve rocker mechanism is lubricated through oil gallery in camshaft and through a small channel at base circle portion of each cam. Rocker arms and valves are lubricated intermittently through small holes or oil pipe.

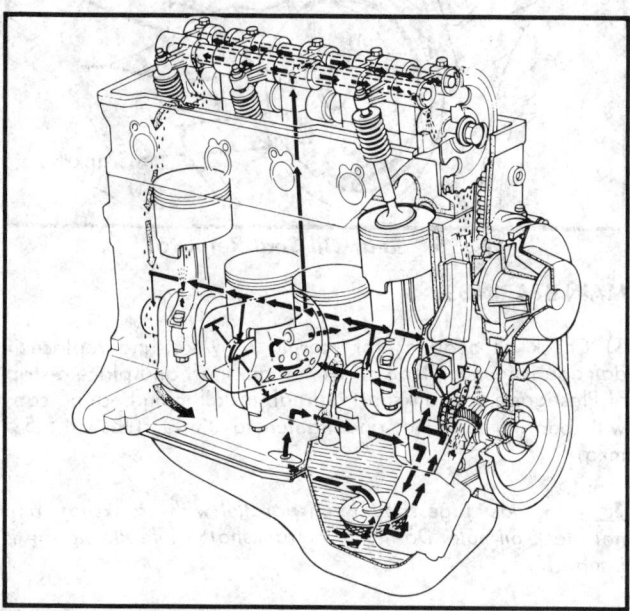

Fig. 10 Cutaway View of Engine Oiling System (200SX & 510 Shown; Pickup Similar)

OIL PUMP

Removal — Pump assembly is installed at bottom right of front cover and held in place by four bolts. Pump is driven by helical gear on crankshaft and in turn drives distributor shaft. Turn engine over until distributor rotor faces toward the rear of engine on Pickup and Calif. 200SX and 510 models. Rotor must face toward front of engine on Federal 200SX and 510 models. Timing mark on crankshaft pulley must be lined up on all models. Remove oil pump and drive spindle assembly.

Inspection — Remove cover from oil pump body, remove gears. Wash parts with cleaning solvent, inspect for wear or damage. Make sure clearances are to specification. Pump is serviced as an assembly only. Replace pump if any part is worn or damaged.

Installation — Make sure that distributor rotor is in same position as it was before removal. Fill pump housing with oil and align punch mark on drive spindle with hole in pump. See *Fig.*

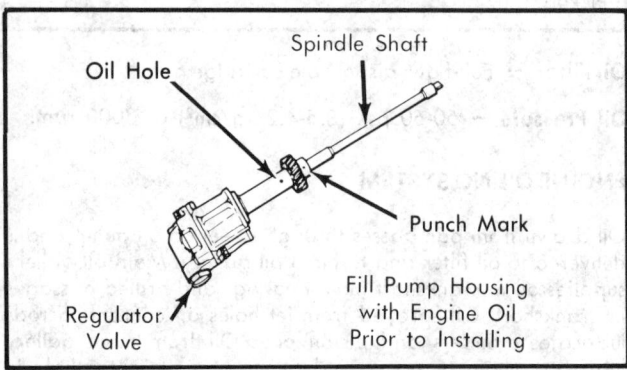

Fig. 11 Aligning Oil Pump Timing Marks

11. Using a new gasket, install oil pump and drive spindle assembly. Make sure that drive spindle tip securely fits distributor fitting hole. Tighten all bolts.

Oil Pump Specifications	
Application	①Clearance In. (mm)
Rotor Side Clearance (Rotor to Bottom Cover)	0.20 (0.0079)
Rotor Tip Clearance	0.20 (0.0079)
Outer Rotor to Body	0.5 (0.0197)

① — Wear limit specifications given.

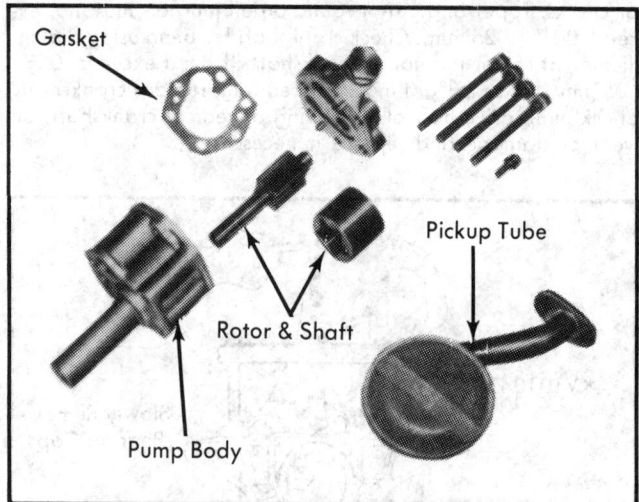

Fig. 12 Exploded View of Oil Pump & Pickup Tube

ENGINE COOLING

Thermostat — Opens at 180° F (82° C). Full open at 203° F (95° C).

Radiator Cap — 13 psi (.9 kg/cm²).

Cooling System Capacity	
Application	Capacity
200SX	10 qts.
510 & Pickup	9.25 qts.

WATER PUMP

Centrifugal type pump with aluminum body. To remove drain cooling system and remove upper and lower radiator hoses, shroud, fan, belts and pulley. Remove pump attaching bolts and remove water pump.

200SX, 510 & PICKUP 4 CYLINDER (Cont.)

ENGINE SPECIFICATIONS

GENERAL SPECIFICATIONS

Year	Displ.		Carburetor	HP at RPM	Torque (Ft. Lbs. at RPM)	Compr. Ratio	Bore		Stroke	
	cu. ins.	cc					in.	mm	in.	mm
1980										
Pickup	119.1	1952	2-Bbl.	.....	.....	8.5-1	3.35	85	3.39	86
200SX	119.1	1952	Fuel Inj.①	.....	.....	8.5-1	3.35	85	3.39	86
510	119.1	1952	2-Bbl.	.....	.....	8.5-1	3.35	85	3.39	86

① — Electronic Fuel Injection

CRANKSHAFT MAIN & CONNECTING ROD BEARINGS

Engine	MAIN BEARINGS				CONNECTING ROD BEARINGS		
	Journal Diam. In. (mm)	Clearance In. (mm)	Thrust Bearing	Crankshaft End Play In. (mm)	Journal Diam. In. (mm)	Clearance In. (mm)	Side Play In. (mm)
1952 cc	2.1631-2.1636 (54.942-54.955)	.0008-.0024 (.020-.062)	No. 3	.002-.007 (.05-.18)	1.9670-1.9675 (49.961-49.974)	.001-.002 (.025-.055)	.0079-.0118 (.20-.30)

VALVES

Engine & Valve	Head Diam. In. (mm)	Face Angle	Seat Angle	Seat Width In. (mm)	Stem Diameter In. (mm)	Stem Clearance In. (mm)	Valve Lift In. (mm)
1952 cc Pickup							
Intake	1.654-1.661 (42.0-42.2)	45°	45°	.047-.071 (1.2-1.8)	.3136-.3142 (7.965-7.980)	.0008.0021 (.020-.053)	.....
Exhaust	1.378-1.386 (35.0-35.2)	45°	45°	.063-.079 (1.6-2.0)	.3128-.3134 (7.945-7.960)	.0016-.0029 (.040-.073)	.....
200SX & 510							
Intake	1.654-1.661 (42.0-42.2)	45°	45°	.047-.071 (1.2-18)	.3136-.3142 (7.965-7.980)	.0008-.0021 (.020-.053)	.....
Exhaust	1.496-1.504 (38.0-38.2)	45°	45°	.059-.075 (1.5-1.9)	.3128-.3134 (7.945-7.960)	.0016.0029 (.040-.073)	.....

PISTONS, PINS, RINGS

Engine	PISTONS	PINS		RINGS		
	Clearance In. (mm)	Piston Fit In. (mm)	①Rod Fit In. (mm)	Rings	End Gap In. (mm)	Side Clearance In. (mm)
1952 cc	.0010-0018 (.025-.045)	.0002-.0005 (.006-.013)	.0006-.0014 (.015-.035)	No. 1	.010-.016 (.25-.40)	.0016-.0029 (.040-.073)
				No. 2	.006-.012 (.15-.30)	.0012-.0025 (.030-.063)
				Oil	.012-.035 (.30-.90)	.....

① — Interference fit.

200SX, 510 & PICKUP 4 CYLINDER (Cont.)

ENGINE SPECIFICATIONS (Cont.)

VALVE SPRINGS

Engine	Free Length In. (mm)	PRESSURE Lbs. @ In. (kg @ mm)	
		Valve Closed	Valve Open
1952 cc Pickup Inner	1.766 (44.85)	27.1@1.378 (12.3@35)	56.2@.965 (25.5@24.5)
Outer	1.968 (49.98)	47@1.575 (21.3@40)	108@1.161 (49@29.5)
200SX & 510 Inner	1.736 (44.10)	24.3@1.378 (11.0@35.0)	.....
Outer	1.959 (49.77)	50.7@1.575 (23@40.0)	.....

CAMSHAFT

Engine	Journal Diam. In. (mm)	Clearance In. (mm)	Lobe Lift In. (mm)
1952 cc Pickup	1.8878-1.8883 (47.949-47.963)	.0015-.0026 (.038-.067)	.008" (0.2)
200SX & 510	1.2967-1.2974 (32.935-32.955)	.0018-.0035 (.045-.090)	.008" (0.2)

TIGHTENING SPECIFICATIONS

Application	Ft. Lbs. (mkg)
Cylinder Head	
L20B	51-61 (7.0-8.5)
Z20E & Z20S	51-58 (7.0-8.0)
Front Cover	
6 mm Bolts	2.9-7.2 (.4-1.0)
8 mm Bolts	7-12 (1.0-1.6)
Connecting Rods	33-40 (4.5-5.5)
Flywheel	101-116 (14-16)
Main Bearings	33-40 (4.5-5.5)
Camshaft Sprocket	87-116 (12-16)
Oil Pan	4.3-7.2 (.6-1.0)
Crankshaft Pulley	87-116 (12-16)
Manifolds	
L20B	9-12 (1.2-1.6)
Z20E & Z20S	12-15 (1.6-2.1)
Rocker Pivot Lock Nuts (L20B)	36-43 (5.0-6.0)
Rocker Arm Nuts (Z20E & Z20S)	12-16 (1.6-2.2)

280ZX & 810 6 CYLINDER

ENGINE CODING

ENGINE IDENTIFICATION

Engine serial number is stamped on right rear side of cylinder block below mating surface with head.

Engine Identification		
Application	Engine Size	Code
280ZX	2753 cc	L28
810	2393 cc	L24

ENGINE, CYLINDER HEAD & MANIFOLDS

ENGINE

NOTE — *It is recommended that engine and transmission be removed as a unit. Engine can then be separated from transmission assembly.*

Removal — **1)** Remove hood. Bleed off fuel pressure as follows: Start engine. Disconnect fuel pump relay harness connector with engine running. After engine stalls crank engine 2 or 3 times. Turn ignition switch off. Disconnect battery ground cable.

NOTE — *On models equipped with power steering and/or air conditioner, remove power steering pump and/or air conditioner compressor from engine but DO NOT disconnect lines. Suspend pump and/or compressor with wire to prevent damage to hoses.*

2) Drain cooling system and engine crankcase. Remove radiator hoses. Remove air flow meter and air duct clamps and hoses. Remove air cleaner and disconnect hoses from canister, then remove canister. Disconnect transmission oil cooler lines (automatic transmission models), and remove radiator and shroud.

3) Disconnect accelerator linkage. Disconnect wiring to starter, alternator, oil pressure switch, neutral switch, back-up light switch, EGR solenoid valve, electronic fuel injection harness and connector, throttle valve switch, cold start valve, air regulator, vacuum cutting solenoid (manual transmission models), auxiliary cooling fan (if equipped), distributor and all wiring to thermostat housing. Remove canister hoses.

4) Disconnect wiring to boost controlled deceleration solenoid valve. Disconnect engine ground cable to engine, and high tension cable between coil and distributor. Disconnect wire for block terminal. Disconnect fuel return hose and fuel charge hose, heater hoses, and all vacuum hoses. On models with automatic transmission, disconnect wire to inhibitor switch and downshift solenoid.

5) Remove clutch operating cylinder on models with manual transmission. Disconnect speedometer cable from rear extension housing. Remove center console, "C" ring, and control lever pin from transmission striking rod guide, then remove control lever on models with manual transmission. On models with automatic transmission, disconnect shift control lever.

6) Disconnect exhaust pipe from exhaust manifold. Disconnect exhaust pipe bracket from rear extension housing and tie exhaust pipe out of the way. Mark propeller shaft and pinion flange to aid in reassembly, then remove propeller shaft from vehicle. Plug rear of extension housing to prevent oil leakage.

Support transmission with a jack and remove rear engine mount. Use a hoist to raise engine and remove front engine mount attaching bolts. Raise engine and transmission and remove from vehicle as a unit.

Installation — To install, reverse removal procedures noting that rear engine mount is attached to car first. Ensure proper routing and attachment of all electrical harnesses, vacuum and liquid tubes. Refill all fluids to specified level before starting engine.

MANIFOLDS

Removal & Installation — **1)** Disconnect battery ground cable and drain cooling system. Disconnect hose connecting rocker cover to throttle chamber at rocker cover. Disconnect tube connecting heater housing to water inlet at water inlet. Remove bolt securing water and fuel tubes to cylinder head.

2) Bleed off fuel pressure as described in step 1) under *Engine Removal*. Remove tube connecting heater housing to thermostat housing. Disconnect fuel line and remove intake manifold mounting bolts. Remove intake manifold as an assembly of fuel line, injector, air regulator, etc.

3) Disconnect exhaust pipe from exhaust manifold flange. Remove PCV valve hose, sub-heat shield plate and EGR tube. Remove exhaust manifold mounting bolts and take off manifold. To install, use new gasket and reverse removal procedure.

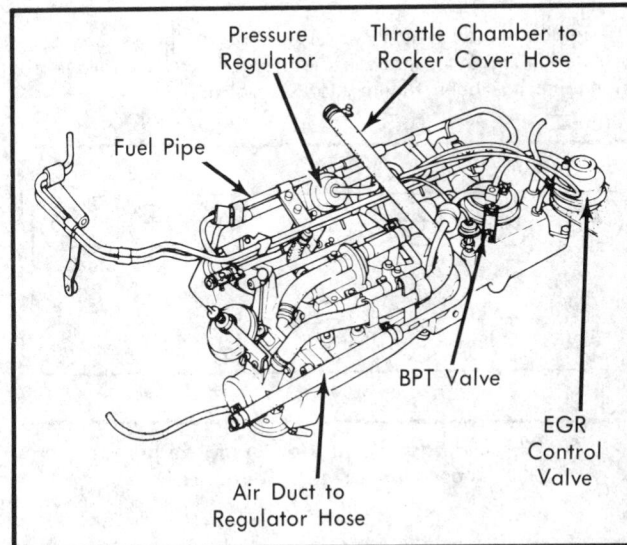

Fig. 1 Intake Manifold Assembly

CYLINDER HEAD

Removal — **1)** Drain cooling system and disconnect upper radiator hose and heater hoses. Dissipate fuel hose pressure to zero. *See step 1) under Engine Removal.* Remove air regulator and all connecting hoses as an assembly. Remove spark plug wires at plug end. Remove EGR control valve, vacuum switching valve and hoses as an assembly. Remove throttle chamber with dash pot and boost controlled deceleration device.

280ZX & 810 6 CYLINDER (Cont.)

2) Remove fuel lines, vacuum hoses, and canister purge hose pressure regulator. Remove thermostat housing and all attached switches as an assembly. Remove PCV valve hose, sub-heat shield plate, and EGR tube.

NOTE — *Remove clip attaching fuel inlet hose to injector and take care not to twist or bend hose during removal.*

3) Remove intake manifold and heat shield plate. Remove exhaust manifold. Remove all drive belts. Remove camshaft sprocket attaching bolt and remove sprocket from timing chain. Remove oil pipe. Remove cylinder head attaching bolts working outward from center of cylinder head. Remove bolts securing cylinder head to timing cover. Remove cylinder head from engine block.

NOTE — *Use special tool (ST1742001) to support timing chain so timing marks on crankshaft sprocket and timing chain will remain unchanged. This will simplify timing mark alignment during reassembly.*

Installation — 1) Ensure that mating surfaces of cylinder head and block are clean, then install cylinder head and gasket without sealer. Number 1 piston should be at TDC on compression stroke and camshaft sprocket location notch and plate oblong groove aligned.

CAUTION — *Do not rotate crankshaft and camshaft separately or valves may hit head of pistons.*

2) Insert head bolts and tighten first 2 in tightening sequence to 14 ft. lbs. (2 mkg). Install and align sprockets and timing chain. Install remaining components in reverse order of removal, using new seals, gaskets and sealant where required.

3) Tighten head bolts in several steps in the sequence illustrated in *Fig. 2* to final specified torque. Recheck torque after engine has been running for several minutes.

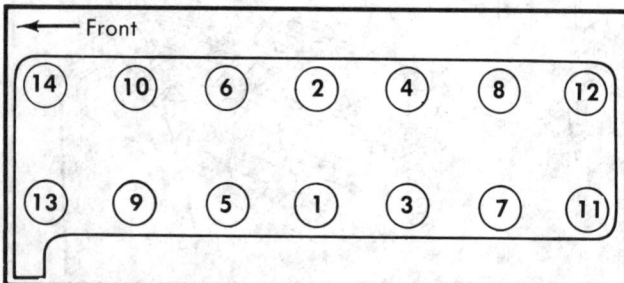

Fig. 2 Cylinder Head Tightening Sequence (Loosen in Reverse Sequence)

CAMSHAFT

CAMSHAFT

Removal — Remove cylinder head. Remove valve rocker springs. Loosen valve rocker pivot lock nuts and remove rocker arms by pressing down on spring. Use care not to lose valve rocker guide. Carefully remove camshaft from front of cylinder head.

Installation — Carefully install camshaft into cylinder head taking care not to damage bearings. Install camshaft locating plate with oblong groove of plate facing front of cylinder

head. Install camshaft sprocket and tighten attaching bolt. Install remaining components in reverse of removal procedure, and tighten all nuts and bolts.

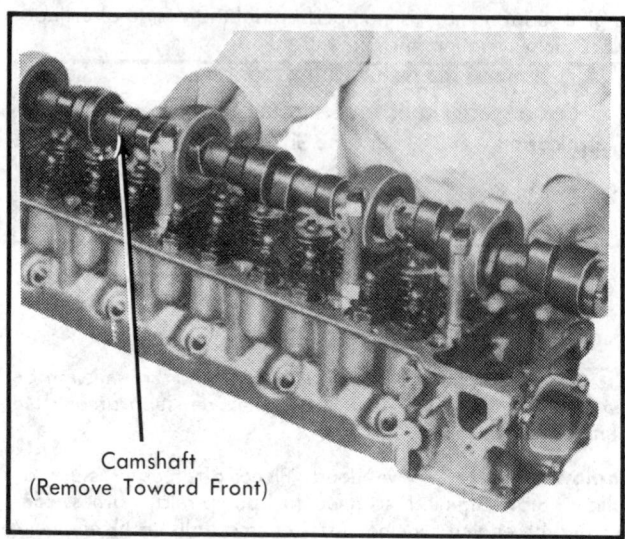

Camshaft
(Remove Toward Front)

Fig. 3 Removing Camshaft from Cylinder Head

CAMSHAFT BEARINGS

NOTE — *Do not remove camshaft bearings. If bearings are removed, bearing centers will be out of alignment and proper reassembly will be difficult without center boring.*

Measure inner diameter of camshaft bearings and outer diameter of camshaft journals. If excessively worn or damaged, replace camshaft and/or cylinder head assembly. In event of excess end play, replace locating plate.

ENGINE FRONT COVER

Removal — Drain cooling system, disconnect hoses and remove radiator. Remove all drive belts, fan blade and pulley. Disconnect all wiring and connections to thermostat housing and remove housing. Remove crankshaft pulley and water pump. Remove spark plug wires from plugs, mark position of distributor base to engine and position of rotor to distributor. Disconnect distributor wires from coil and remove distributor. Remove oil pump with its drive spindle. Remove front cover attaching bolts and front cover.

Installation — Apply sealant to front cover gasket, front of cylinder block, and top of front cover. Install front cover on cylinder block. Tighten front cover-to-cylinder block bolts and cylinder head-to-front cover bolts. Install oil pump with drive spindle. Install distributor while aligning index marks. Reconnect spark plug wires and all distributor connections. Install thermostat housing and reconnect all wiring. Install fan and pulley. Install drive belts, radiator, hoses, and fill cooling system and oil pan.

TIMING CHAIN

Removal — Remove engine front cover. Remove camshaft drive sprocket, timing chain, tensioner and chain guide. Remove oil thrower, crankshaft worm gear and crankshaft sprocket.

280ZX & 810 6 CYLINDER (Cont.)

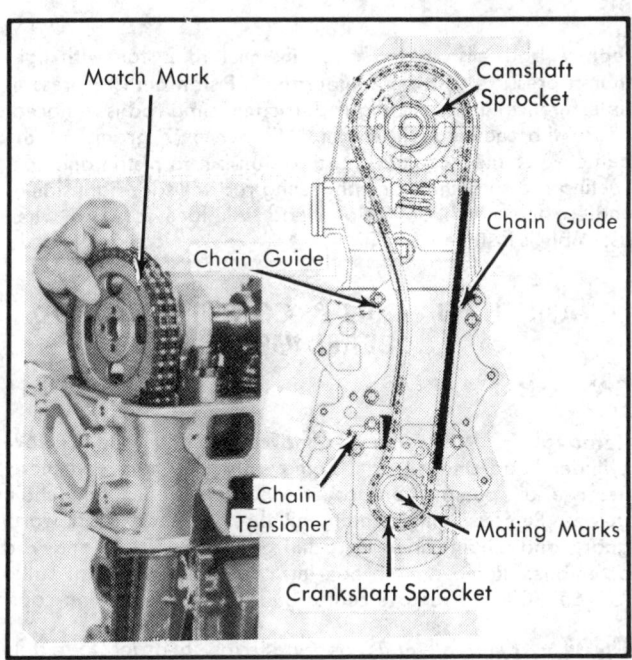

Fig. 4 Timing Chain and Sprocket Installation

Installation — Install components in reverse of removal procedure while noting the following: When installing timing chain, camshaft sprocket or crankshaft sprocket, make sure camshaft and crankshaft keys point upward. Set timing chain so that its mating marks match marks on crankshaft and camshaft sprockets on right-hand side. Factory setting of camshaft sprocket is number 1 hole. If chain is excessively stretched, use number 2 or 3 hole to achieve correct valve timing.

VALVES

VALVE ARRANGEMENT

E-I-I-E-I-E-E-I-E-I-I-E (front to rear).

VALVE GUIDES CHECKING

1) Measure clearance between valve stem and valve guide with aid of micrometer and hole gauge. Check diameter of valve stem in three places: top, center and bottom.

2) Insert hole gauge in valve guide bore and measure at center. Subtract highest reading of valve stem diameter from valve guide bore to obtain clearance.

NOTE — *As a quick check, a valve may be inserted into valve guide and moved either left or right (parallel with rocker arm). If its tip moves .0079" (.2 mm) or more, clearance is beyond maximum limit of .0039" (.1 mm).*

VALVE GUIDE REPLACEMENT

1) Using a press and drift pin, force worn guide from cylinder head working from combustion chamber side. Although this procedure may be carried out at room temperature, higher temperatures will aid removal.

2) Ream cylinder head side guide hole to provide interference fit of .0011-.0019" (.027-.049 mm). Press new valve guide into cylinder head so that it will fit smoothly when cylinder head is heated to 302-392°F (150-200°C).

3) Ream bore of valve guides to .3150-.3157" (8.000-8.018 mm). Correct valve seat surface using new valve guide as axis.

VALVE SEAT INSERTS

Check valve seats for pitting at valve contact surface. Valve seat inserts of .020" (.5 mm) oversize are available if necessary.

VALVE STEM OIL SEALS

An oil seal is installed on all intake and exhaust valve stems inside of valve spring.

VALVE SPRINGS

Removal — With cylinder head removed, loosen pivot lock nut and remove rocker arm by pressing valve spring down, taking care not to lose valve rocker guide. Remove camshaft taking care not to damage camshaft bearings and cam lobes. Compress valves and remove valve keepers. Remove compressing tool, then remove spring retainer, inner and outer springs, oil seal and valve spring seat.

Installation — Install spring seat and fit oil seal onto valve guide. Install inner and outer valve springs, spring retainer, valve keepers and rocker guide. **NOTE** — *Outer spring must be installed with painted side toward cylinder head.* Install camshaft to cylinder head. Press valve springs down using a screwdriver and install rocker arms. Install valve rocker springs.

VALVE SPRING INSTALLED HEIGHT

Outer valve spring must be less than .087" (2.2 mm) and inner spring must be less than .047" (1.2 mm) out of square. Valve spring installed height is 1.38" (35 mm) for inner spring and 1.57" (40 mm) for outer spring. If spring height, pressure or squareness do not meet specifications, replace spring.

VALVE ADJUSTMENT

Valves can not be adjusted while engine is in operation. Cold settings are shown to provide initial clearance after assembly. Warm engine to operating temperature and remove valve cover. Rotate crankshaft so No. 1 exhaust cam lobe points up and adjust exhaust valve clearance on No. 1, 4 and 5 cylinder. Adjust intake valves on No. 2, 4 and 6 cylinder. Rotate crankshaft 360° so that lobe of No. 1 exhaust valve points down. Adjust exhaust valve clearance on No. 2, 3 and 6, and intake clearance on No. 1, 3 and 5 cylinder.

Valve Adjustment Clearances		
Valve	**Hot**	**Cold**
Intake	.010" (.25 mm)	.007" (.17 mm)
Exhaust	.012" (.30 mm)	.009" (.24 mm)

PISTONS, PINS & RINGS

PISTON & ROD ASSEMBLY

Removal & Installation — 1) With cylinder head and oil pan removed, remove connecting rod nuts. Remove rod cap with bearing half. Push piston/rod assembly with bearing half up and out through top of engine. Rod caps must be kept with their respective piston and rod assembly as caps are not interchangeable.

280ZX & 810 6 CYLINDER (Cont.)

2) To install piston and connecting rod assembly, thoroughly oil rings, piston and cylinder wall. Make sure ring gaps are situated approximately 180° apart and not on thrust side of piston or in line with piston pin. Make sure bearing halves are properly seated in connecting rod and cap.

3) Install a ring compressor and compress rings. Install piston in cylinder with notch mark on piston head toward front of engine. With piston installed in cylinder, and connecting rod and bearings seated against crankshaft journal, install rod caps to their respective piston and rod assembly. Oil jet of connecting rod should face right side of cylinder block. Install cylinder head and oil pan.

FITTING PISTONS

1) Visually inspect cylinder block for cracks or flaws. Using a bore gauge, measure cylinder for out-of-round or excessive taper. If cylinder bore out-of-round or taper exceeds .0008" (.02 mm), refinish cylinder bore. When any one cylinder is bored, all cylinders must be bored.

2) Determine piston oversize according to amount of wear in cylinder (see specifications). By measuring piston at thrust face and adding mean of piston-to-cylinder clearance, finish hone of cylinder may be determined.

3) After honing cylinder to final fit, measure piston-to-cylinder clearance using pull scale and feeler gauge. Extracting force to pull scale should be .44-3.31 lbs. (.2-1.5 kg) using a .0016" (.04 mm) feeler gauge. If cylinder bores are worn beyond limits, undersize cylinder liners are available. Liners should have an interference fit of .0031-.0035" (.08-.09 mm) in cylinder block.

Piston Specifications	
Piston Size In. (mm)	Piston Diameter In. (mm)
280ZX	
Standard	3.3852-3.3872 (85.985-86.035)
.020 (.50) O/S	3.4014-3.4061 (86.465-86.515)
.040 (1.0) O/S	3.4238-3.4258 (86.965-87.015)
810	
Standard	3.2671-3.2691 (82.985-83.035)
.020 (.50) O/S	3.2860-3.2880 (83.465-83.515)
.040 (1.0) O/S	3.3057-3.3077 (83.965-84.015)

PISTON PINS

Using suitable press and related adaptors, remove piston pin from piston and connecting rod. Measure pin bore diameter in piston and connecting rod. If wear exceeds specifications,

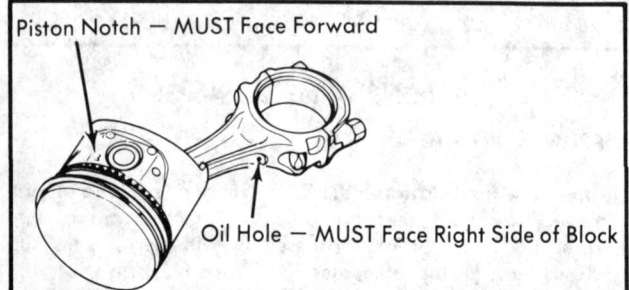

Piston Notch — MUST Face Forward

Oil Hole — MUST Face Right Side of Block

Fig. 5 Piston and Connecting Rod Alignment

replace both piston and pin. Pin must fit piston with light thumb pressure at room temperature. Piston pin is a press fit (interference) in connecting rod. If connecting rod is replaced, insure that new rod is within .247 ounce (7 grams) of the defective connecting rod. Install piston pin to piston and connecting rod so oil hole on connecting rod will face right side of engine and notch on piston head will face forward when assembly is installed.

CRANKSHAFT MAIN & CONNECTING ROD BEARINGS

CRANKSHAFT

Removal — With engine removed from vehicle, remove cylinder head and oil pan. Remove flywheel and end plate. Remove oil pump, front cover, chain tensioner and chain guides. Remove timing chain, oil thrower, crankshaft worm gear, and chain drive sprocket. Remove piston and rod assemblies. Remove main bearing caps using a special puller (ST1651S000) to remove center and rear main bearing caps.

NOTE — *Keep all main bearing caps in order to aid in reassembly.* Remove rear oil seal, then remove crankshaft.

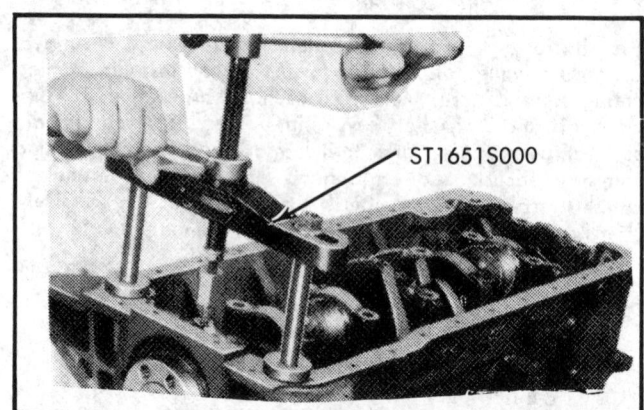

ST1651S000

Fig. 6 Rear Main Bearing Cap Removal

Inspection — Check shaft journals and crankpins for scoring, wear, or cracks. Taper and out-of-round of journals and crankpins must not exceed .0012" (.03 mm). Check crankshaft for bend using a dial indicator at center journal of crankshaft. If bend exceeds .004" (.10 mm), which is one-half of indicator reading, replace crankshaft. Check main drive shaft pilot bearing at rear of crankshaft for wear or damage and replace if necessary.

Installation — 1) Install main bearing halves to engine block ensuring that all bearings are on correct journal. Journal No. 4 requires a thrust bearing. Bearing for journal No. 1 is the same as for journal No. 7. Upper bearing halves have an oil groove and are not interchangeable with lower bearing halves.

2) Apply oil to main bearing surface and install crankshaft. Apply sealant to each side of rear main bearing cap and corners of cylinder block contact point. Install bearing caps so arrow faces front of engine. Shift crankshaft toward front of engine, then tighten main bearing caps in 2 or 3 steps, starting at center bearing and working outward. Ensure crankshaft rotates smoothly.

280ZX & 810 6 CYLINDER (Cont.)

3) Check crankshaft end play, and if not within specifications, replace center thrust bearing. Install side seals in rear main bearing cap after applying sealer to seals. Install rear oil seal. Install rear end plate and flywheel. Install piston and rod assemblies. Install cylinder head, crankshaft sprocket, worm gear, chain drive sprocket, oil thrower, and timing chain. Install chain guides and tensioner, front cover, oil pump and oil pan. Install remaining components in reverse of removal procedure.

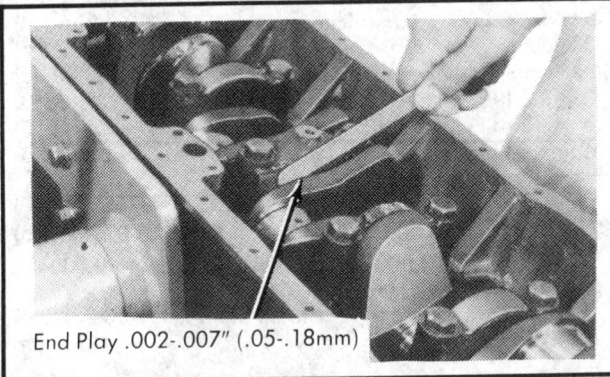

End Play .002-.007" (.05-.18mm)

Fig. 7   Measuring End Play at No. 4 Main Bearing

MAIN BEARING CLEARANCE

1) Check all bearings for scoring or wear and replace if damage is found. Clean oil from crankshaft and place a strip of Plastigage on crankshaft journal. Install main bearing cap, with bearing installed, and tighten to 33-40 ft. lbs. (4.5-5.5 mkg).

NOTE — *Plastigage should run parallel with crankshaft and journal and should not block oil hole. Do not turn crankshaft while Plastigage is inserted.*

2) Remove cap and measure width of Plastigage at widest point using gauge provided with Plastigage. If clearance is not to specifications, replace bearings. Bearings are available in undersizes of .01" (.25 mm), .02" (.50 mm), .03" (.75 mm), and .04" (1.0 mm).

CONNECTING ROD BEARING CLEARANCE

Check connecting rod bearing clearance in same manner as main bearing clearance using Plastigage. Tighten connecting rod caps to 33-40 ft. lbs. (4.5-5.5 mkg). Bearings are available in undersizes of .0024" (.06 mm), .005" (.12 mm), .01" (.25 mm), .02" (.50 mm), .03" (.75 mm), and .04" (1.0 mm).

ENGINE OILING

ENGINE OILING SYSTEM

Oil drawn from oil pan passes through a screen to oil pump. Oil is delivered to full flow oil filter and to main oil gallery. Main oil gallery supplies oil to crankshaft main bearings and drilled passages in crankshaft. Oil sprayed from jet holes on connecting rods lubricates cylinders and piston pins. Oil from main gallery lubricates chain tensioner and timing chain. A center oil hole in the crankshaft center bearing feeds camshaft bearings on cylinder head. Valve rocker mechanism is lubricated through oil gallery in camshaft and through a small channel at base circle portion of each cam. Rocker arms and valves are lubricated intermittently through small holes or oil pipe.

Crankcase Capacity (with Filter)

Application	Quantity
280ZX	4¾ quarts
810	5⅞ quarts

Oil Filter — Full-flow, with disposable cartridge.

Oil Pressure — 50-57 psi (3.5-4.0 kg/cm²) @ 2000 RPM.

OIL PUMP

Oil pump assembly is installed to bottom of front cover by four bolts. Pump is driven by oil pump drive spindle assembly which is in turn driven by gear on crankshaft. To remove oil pump, first remove distributor. Drain engine oil and remove oil pump body together with drive spindle. To disassemble, proceed as follows:

1) Remove pump cover and gasket. Slide pump rotors from pump body. Remove regulator cap, valve and spring. Clean all components with cleaning solvent, and inspect for wear or damage. Check the clearances indicated in the following table and ensure clearances are to specifications. If components are not to specifications, replace entire pump assembly.

2) Assemble pump in reverse order of disassembly while aligning hole in oil pump with punch mark on drive spindle. Fill pump housing with oil before installing to front cover.

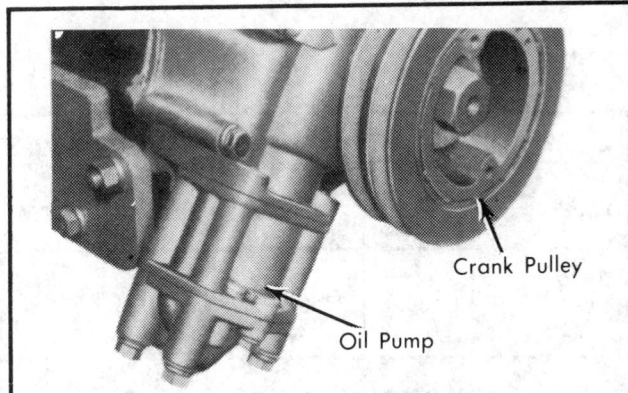

Crank Pulley

Oil Pump

Fig. 8   Location of Oil Pump Assembly

Oil Pump Specifications	
Application	Clearance In. (mm)
Rotor Tip Clearance	Less Than .0079 (.20)
Outer Rotor-to-Body	Less Than .0197 (.50)
Rotor-to-Cover	Less Than .0024 (.06)
Rotor Side Clearance	Less Than .0012 (.03)

ENGINE COOLING

WATER PUMP

Centrifugal type pump with aluminum body. To remove, drain cooling system and remove fan shroud. Remove fan belts, fan, and pulley. Remove pump attaching bolts and remove water pump from front cover.

Datsun Engines

280ZX & 810 6 CYLINDER (Cont.)

Thermostat — Opens at 180°F (82°C).

Cooling System Capacity — 11 qts.

Radiator Cap — 13 psi.

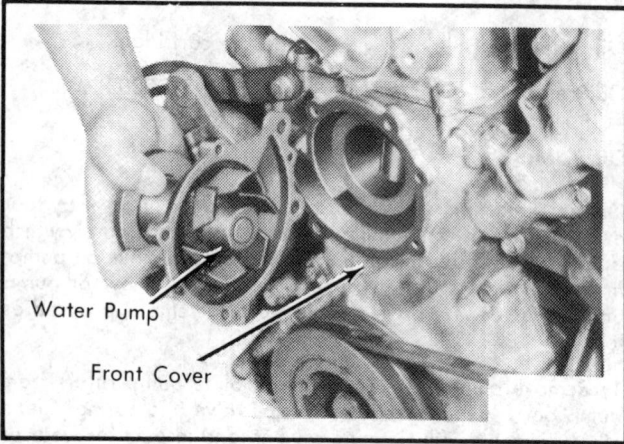

Fig. 9 Installing Water Pump to Front Cover

TIGHTENING SPECIFICATIONS

Application	Ft. Lbs.(mkg)
Cylinder Head	51-61 (7.0-8.5)
Connecting Rod	33-40(4.5-5.5)
Flywheel	94-108(13-15)
Camshaft Gear	94-108(13-15)
Oil Pan	4.3-7.2 (.6-1.0)
Oil Pump-to-Front Cover	8-11 (1.1-1.5)
Oil Pump Cover	4.3-7.2 (.6-1.0)
Camshaft Lock Plate	4.3-7.2 (.6-1.0)
Crankshaft Pulley	94-108(13-15)
Main Bearing Cap	33-40(4.5-5.5)
Front Cover	
6M Bolt	2.9-7.2 (.4-1.0)
8M Bolt	7.2-11.6(1.0-1.6)
Rocker Pivot Lock Nuts	36-43(5-6)
Intake & Exhaust Manifolds	
8M Bolts	11-13 (1.5-2.0)
10M Bolts	25-33 (3.5-4.5)

ENGINE SPECIFICATIONS

GENERAL SPECIFICATIONS

Year	Displ. cu. ins.	Displ. cc	Carburetor	HP at RPM	Torque (Ft. Lbs. at RPM)	Compr. Ratio	Bore in.	Bore mm	Stroke in.	Stroke mm
1980										
L28	168.0	2753	Fuel Inj.	.....	.....	8.6:1	3.39	86	3.110	79
L24	146.0	2393	Fuel Inj.	.....	.....	8.9:1①	3.27	83	2.90	73.7

① — 8.6:1 for California models.

VALVES

Engine & Valve	Head Diam. In. (mm)	Face Angle	Seat Angle	Seat Width In. (mm)	Stem Diameter In. (mm)	Stem Clearance In. (mm)	Valve Lift In. (mm)
2753 cc							
Int.	1.73 (44.0)	45.5°	45.5°	.055-.063 (1.4-1.6)	.3136-.3142 (7.965-7.980)	.0008-.0021 (.020-.053)	.433 (11)
Exh.	1.38 (35.0)	45.5°	45.5°	.071-.087 (1.8-2.2)	.3128-.3134 (7.945-7.960)	.0016-.0029 (.040-.073)	.433 (11)
2393 cc							
Int.	1.64 (42.0)	45.5°	45.5°	.055-.063 (1.4-1.6)	.3136-.3142 (7.965-7.980)	.0008-.0021 (.020-.053)	.394 (10)
Exh.	1.38 (35.0)	45.5°	45.5°	.071-.087 (1.8-2.2)	.3128-.3134 (7.945-7.960)	.0016-.0029 (.040-.073)	.413 (10.5)

280ZX & 810 6 CYLINDER (Cont.)

ENGINE SPECIFICATIONS (Cont.)

VALVE SPRINGS

Engine	Free Length In. (mm)	PRESSURE Lbs. @ In. (kg @ mm)	
		Valve Closed	Valve Open
2753 cc Inner	1.766 (44.85)	27.1@1.378 (12.3@35)	56.2@.965 (25.5@24.5)
Outer	1.968 (49.98)	47@1.575 (21.3@40)	108@1.161 (49@29.5)
2393 cc Inner	1.766 (44.85)	27@1.378 (12.3@35)	56.2@.965 (25.5@24.5)
Outer	1.968 (49.98)	47@1.575 (21.3@40)	108@1.161 (49@29.5)

VALVE TIMING

Engine	INTAKE		EXHAUST	
	Open (BTDC)	Close (ABDC)	Open (BBDC)	Close (ATDC)
2393 cc	12°	48°	54°	14°
2753 cc	16°	52°	54°	14°

CAMSHAFT

Engine	Journal Diam. In. (mm)	Clearance In. (mm)	Lobe Lift In. (mm)
2753 cc	1.8878-1.8883 (47.949-47.962)	.0015-.0026 (.038-.067)	In.&Exh. .275 (7.00)
2393 cc	1.8878-1.8883 (47.949-47.962)	.0015-.0026 (.038-.067)	In. .261 (6.65) Exh. .275 (7.00)

PISTONS, PINS, RINGS

Engine	PISTONS	PINS		RINGS		
	①Clearance In. (mm)	Piston Fit In. (mm)	Rod Fit In. (mm)	Rings	End Gap In. (mm)	Side Clearance In. (mm)
2753 cc	.0010-.0018 (.025-.045)	.0002-.0005 (.006-.013)	①.0006-.0013 (.015-.033)	No. 1	.0098-.0157 (.25-.40)	.0016-.0029 (.040-.073)
				No. 2	.0118-.0197 (.30-.50)	.0012-.0025 (.030-.066)
				Oil	.0118-.0354 (.30-.90)	Snug
2393 cc	.0010-.0018 (.025-.045)	.0002-.0005 (.006-.013)	①.0006-.0013 (.015-.033)	No. 1	.0098-.0157 (.25-.40)	.0016-.0029 (.040-.073)
				No. 2	.0059-.0118 (.15-.30)	.0012-.0025 (.030-.066)
				Oil	.012-.035 (.30-.90)	Snug

① — Interference fit.

CRANKSHAFT MAIN & CONNECTING ROD BEARINGS

Engine	MAIN BEARINGS				CONNECTING ROD BEARINGS		
	Journal Diam. In. (mm)	Clearance In. (mm)	Thrust Bearing	Crankshaft End Play In. (mm)	Journal Diam. In. (mm)	Clearance In. (mm)	Side Play In. (mm)
2753 cc & 2393 cc	2.1631-2.1636 (54.942-54.955)	.0008-.0026 (.020-.066)	Center	.002-.007 (.05-.18)	1.9670-1.9675 (49.961-49.974)	.0009-.0026 (.024-.066)	.0079-.0118 (.20-.30)

BRAVA & SPIDER 2000 4 CYLINDER

ENGINE CODING

ENGINE IDENTIFICATION

Engine identification number is stamped in pad above oil filter mount on left side of engine.

Engine Identification		
Application	Code	
	Carbureted	Fuel Injected
1995 cc	132 C3.040	132 C3.031

ENGINE & CYLINDER HEAD

ENGINE

Removal — 1) Remove hood and air cleaner. Loosen fuel tank cap to relieve pressure. Disconnect battery. Mark for identification and disconnect vacuum and fuel lines and electrical leads. Disconnect accelerator and remove linkage.

NOTE — *On A/C equipped cars, it will be necessary to discharge system and remove condenser and fan assembly prior to removal of engine. When installing, system will require evacuation and charging.*

2) Drain cooling system and disconnect hoses. Disconnect automatic transmission cooling lines (if equipped). Remove radiator and cooling fan assembly.

3) Disconnect remaining hoses and wires from chassis-to-engine at engine. Disconnect exhaust pipe at manifold. Remove automatic transmission dipstick from support bracket (if so equipped).

4) From underneath vehicle, remove oil filter, engine splash pans and any remaining electrical connections. Remove starter by passing through oil filter opening. (On A/C equipped vehicles, pull starter from mounted position and tie to engine until engine is removed.) Remove speedometer cable support bracket from engine mount.

5) On carbureted models, remove fuel inlet line from fuel pump. On all models, remove nuts and washers holding engine mount isolators to crossmembers. Remove ground strap to engine mount. Install transmission support and remove bolts securing transmission to engine. On automatic transmission models, remove bolts attaching flywheel to torque converter.

6) Attach engine sling and hoist engine until mount clears cross members. Move engine forward until clear and lift from engine compartment.

Installation — To install, reverse removal procedure. Ensure that pilot shaft engages clutch properly (manual transmission).

CYLINDER HEAD

Removal — 1) Drain cooling system. Remove air cleaner and heated air tube. Disconnect battery ground cable. Loosen and remove top radiator hose from thermostat housing. Remove union with hoses from attachment point at cylinder head. Remove timing belt cover.

2) Manually turn crankshaft so that holes in camshaft sprocket align with timing pointers. Block flywheel to prevent further turning and remove crankshaft pulley. Remove lower timing cover and take off oil dipstick tube. Loosen belt tensioner and remove timing belt.

NOTE — *Mark belt as "NOT USABLE". A new belt must be installed any time tension is removed from timing belt. See Timing Belt Replacement.*

3) Remove rear timing belt covers. From left side of engine, mark for identification and remove all fuel, vacuum, air and water hoses. Disconnect accelerator and remove linkage. At engine right side, remove coil wires from distributor and white lead wire from electronic control module.

4) Mark for identification and remove all remaining wires, hoses and tubes. Disconnect exhaust pipe from manifold and automatic transmission fluid dipstick (if equipped) from support bracket. Remove cylinder head bolts and lift off head assembly with gasket.

Installation — 1) Position camshafts so that reference marks on sprockets are aligned with fixed pointers on front of head. Ensure that crankshaft is positioned so that No. 1 and No. 4 pistons are at TDC. Install guide stud at front and rear of block.

2) Place new head gasket in position and guide head over studs, ensuring that camshafts are NOT moved from reference position. Install a few head bolts finger tight, then remove guide studs. Install remaining bolts and tighten in sequence shown to 29 ft. lbs. (4 mkg), then to final torque of 61 ft. lbs. (7.5 mkg). To complete installation, reverse removal procedure.

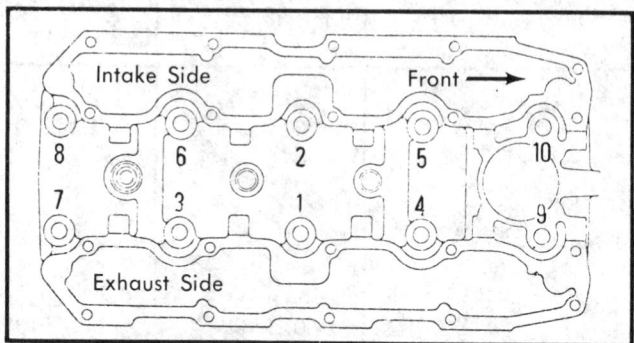

Fig. 1   Cylinder Head Tightening Sequence

CAMSHAFTS

CAMSHAFTS

Removal — 1) With cylinder head removed from engine, remove distributor and manifolds. Install pulley holder (A.60446) at front of cam housing and remove bolt, washer and pulley from camshaft.

2) Remove attaching bolts and lift off cam housing with camshaft. Remove cap from rear of housing and pull out camshaft. Repeat for other camshaft.

Installation — To install, reverse removal procedure, noting that distributor drive gear is on exhaust camshaft.

AUXILIARY SHAFT

Auxiliary shaft is driven by timing belt and drives oil pump and fuel pump. With engine out of vehicle and front crankshaft pulley removed, take off auxiliary drive pulley. Remove aux-

BRAVA & SPIDER 2000 4 CYLINDER (Cont.)

iliary shaft cover and gasket. Remove spacer and gasket. Rotate auxiliary shaft to raise oil pump gear and lift gear out with long nose pliers. Remove bolts holding retainer at front of block and pull out shaft along with retainer. To install, reverse removal procedure.

TIMING BELT REPLACEMENT

NOTE — *Timing belts must not be reused once tension is relieved. Crankshaft and/or camshafts must not be turned with belt removed due to resultant valve and/or piston damage.*

Removal — 1) Disconnect battery ground cable and drain cooling system. Remove spark plugs and set engine to fire (TDC) on No. 4 cylinder. Crankshaft and camshaft timing marks must be aligned with indicators. Remove upper radiator hose from "T" union, then unbolt and remove union from cylinder head.

2) Remove hot air hose from exhaust manifold to air intake. Remove all drive belts from crankshaft pulley. Remove water pump pulley bolts and take off pulley. Remove outer timing belt cover.

3) Lock crankshaft to prevent turning and remove crankshaft pulley. Remove lower timing cover. Loosen belt tensioner and lock in belt-slack position. Remove and discard timing belt.

Installation — Turn auxiliary sprocket to align hole in sprocket with sprocket bolt and spring retaining bolt. Install belt and adjust tensioner, then turn crankshaft 2 full turns and recheck tension and timing. To complete installation, reverse removal procedures.

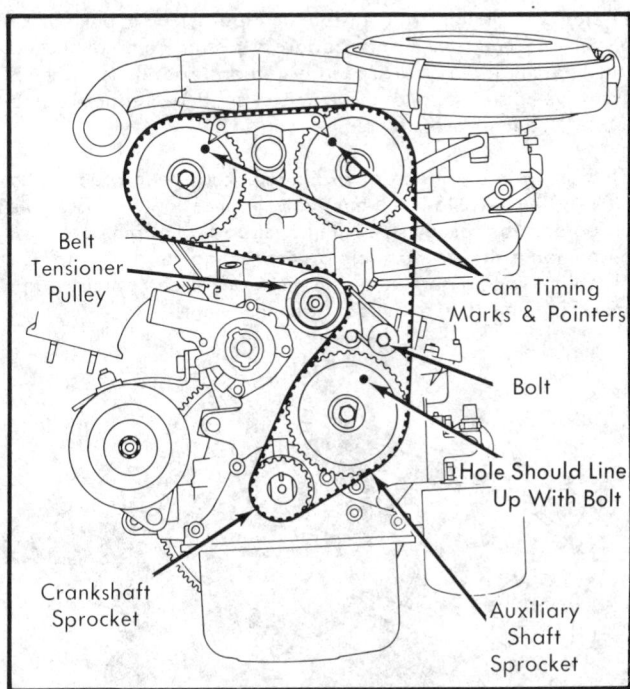

Fig. 2 Sprocket Alignment for Timing Belt Installation

VALVES

VALVE ARRANGEMENT

Left Side — All Intake
Right Side — All Exhaust

VALVE GUIDE SERVICING

1) Measure clearance of valve stem in guide with a dial indicator. If clearance exceeds specifications, valve guide must be replaced.

2) With driver (A.60153/60395), remove defective guides from head, driving from combustion chamber side. Press new guide in place from camshaft side with drift (A.60462). Guides are prefinished to size, however minor faults caused during replacement may be hand reamed if necessary.

VALVE SPRINGS

Removal & Installation — With cylinder head removed, remove camshaft carriers and camshafts. Compress valve spring with a suitable compressor and remove keepers. Release spring compressor and remove upper spring retainer, inner and outer springs and lower spring retainer. To install, reverse removal procedure.

VALVE CLEARANCE ADJUSTMENT

1) Valve clearance is checked and/or adjusted with engine cold. Remove camshaft covers from head and rotate crankshaft until camshaft lobe of valve being checked is pointing up and at right angle to valve. Using a feeler gauge, check clearance between camshaft lobe and valve tappet plate.

Valve Clearance Specifications		
Application	**Intake Valve** **In. (mm)**	**Exhaust Valve** **In. (mm)**
All Models	.016-.019 (41-48)....	.018-.021 (46-53)

2) Tappet plates are available in service thicknesses of .128" (3.25 mm) and increments of .004" (.10 mm) from .130" to .185" (3.30 mm to 4.70 mm). To replace tappet plate, rotate camshaft down to depress tappet. Install clamping tool (A.60594) over cam lobe of valve being adjusted.

3) Rotate crankshaft/camshaft and remove tappet plate by means of a scribe through notch in tappet. As an alternate method, tappet may be pried down using tool (A 60443) and tappet plate removed with a scribe. Insert proper thickness tappet plate and remove tool.

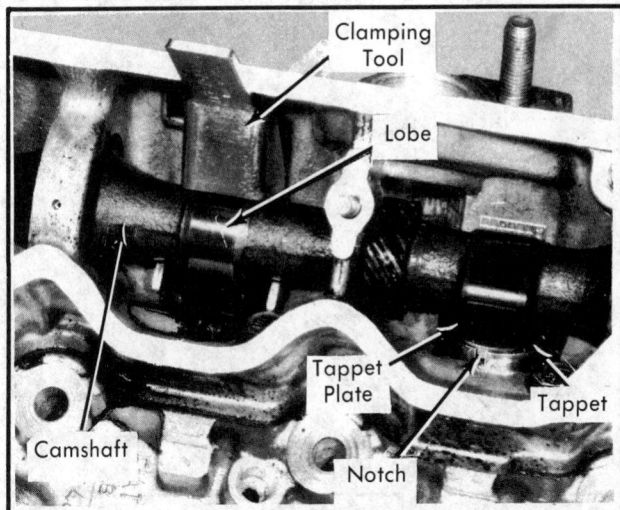

Fig. 3 Checking and Adjusting Valve Clearance

Fiat Engines

BRAVA & SPIDER 2000 4 CYLINDER (Cont.)

PISTONS, PINS & RINGS

OIL PAN

Removal — 1) Drain crankcase. Remove engine splash shields. Remove nuts from engine mounts at crossrails. Raise engine about 6" (152 mm).

2) Remove flywheel cover and oil pan bolts. Strike pan firmly with rubber mallet to free from block assembly.

Installation — To install, clean all mating surfaces and install gasket with sealer applied to BOTH sides. Reverse removal procedure and tighten bolts evenly.

PISTON & ROD ASSEMBLY

Lubricate cylinder bores, wrist pins and bearing journals with light engine oil. Ensure that piston ring gaps are staggered approximately 120° apart and that pistons and rings are coated lightly with engine oil. Use suitable compressor and install assembly so that numbers on connecting rod and cap are facing away from auxiliary shaft.

FITTING PISTONS

1) Standard pistons are manufactured in 3 size classes, and cylinder bores are machined according to piston class. Class of piston and bore is designated by a letter code.

2) Class code of piston is stamped on bottom of piston pin boss. Class of cylinder bore is stamped next to appropriate cylinder on oil pan flange at bottom of cylinder block.

3) Measure Piston size at right angles to piston pin and 1.181" (30 mm) from piston skirt. If piston is replaced for any reason, one of the same class must be installed.

NOTE — *Refer to class designation letter on bottom of piston pin boss and mating surface of crankcase. See Fig. 4 and 5.*

Std. Piston Class Designation & Size

Class	In. (mm)
A	3.3051-3.3055 (83.95-83.96)
C	3.3059-3.3063 (83.97-83.98)
E	3.3066-3.3070 (83.99-84.00)

4) Measure cylinder bore lengthwise and crosswise near top, center and bottom of bore. Check piston fit in bore at right angles to pin 1.876" (47.65 mm) below piston head using a feeler gauge. If clearance exceeds .0059" (.15 mm), cylinders must be rebored and oversized pistons installed.

Oversize Pistons

Application	Amt. of Oversize In. (mm)
1st Oversize	.0079 (0.2)
2nd Oversize	.0157 (0.4)
3rd Oversize	.0236 (0.6)

NOTE — *If replacement pistons are used, ensure that the 4 pistons are the same weight within ±.18 oz. (±5 g).*

5) Check ring side clearance in piston grooves prior to intallation on piston. Push rings squarely into cylinder bores and check ring gaps with feeler gauge. Install rings on pistons with gaps 120° apart.

PISTON PIN REPLACEMENT

1) Remove circlips from piston and push piston pin out of piston and connecting rod. Separate piston from connecting rod and check pin clearance in piston and rod. If clearance is excessive, piston and connecting rod must be rebored for a .0079" (.2 mm) oversize pin.

2) Bushing in small end of rod is replaceable and requires a .0017-.0040" (.043-.102 mm) interference fit. To assemble piston and rod, piston side with offset portion of pin bore must be on same side as numbers on connecting rod and cap. Oil piston pin and insert in piston and rod. Install circlips and check alignment and freedom of movement.

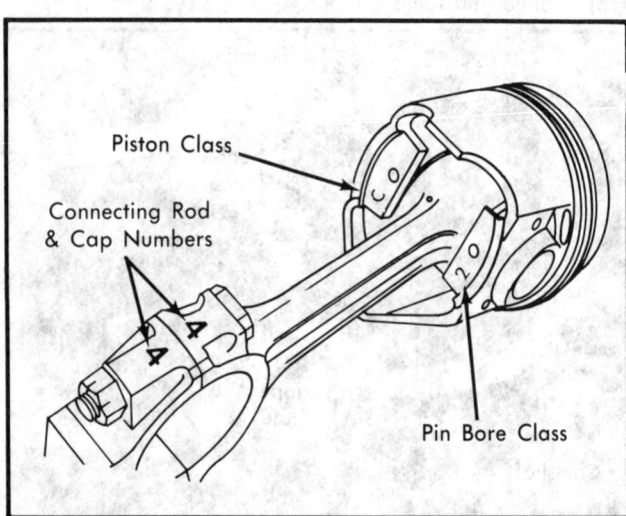

Fig. 4 Piston and Rod Assembly Markings

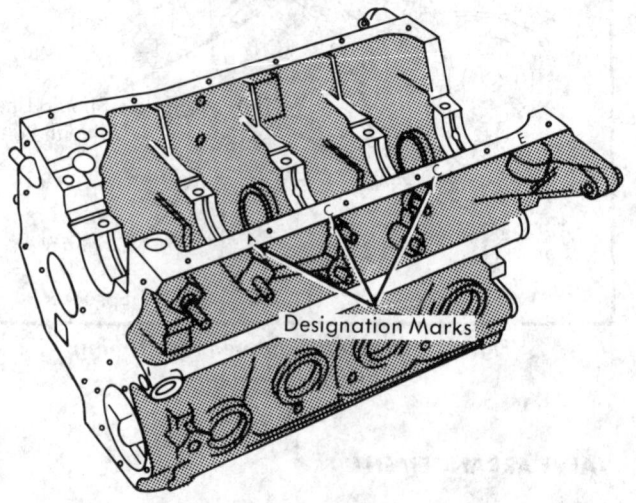

Fig. 5 Piston Bore Class Designation Marks

BRAVA & SPIDER 2000 4 CYLINDER (Cont.)

CRANKSHAFT MAIN & CONNECTING ROD BEARINGS

MAIN & CONNECTING ROD BEARINGS

1) With crankshaft removed, thoroughly clean and inspect for cracks or scoring on journals. Check all journals for out-of-round condition, using a micrometer. If journal is out-of-round or tapers more than .0002" (.005 mm), crankshaft must be reground for undersize bearings.

2) Bearing-to-journal clearance is checked using the Plastigage method. If clearance exceeds specifications, crankshaft must be ground for undersize bearings. Main and connecting rod bearings are available in .010" (.25 mm), .020" (.51 mm), .030" (.76 mm), and .040 (1.02 mm) undersizes.

NOTE — *Main bearing caps are stamped with a number that must correspond to the number stamped on crankcase near flywheel. Notches on caps face auxiliary shaft side and coincide with position. Front main bearing cap has no notch, however 2nd, center 4th and rear caps have 1, 2, 3, and 4 notches respectively.*

CRANKSHAFT END PLAY

Check crankshaft end play using a dial indicator mounted at front of engine. Pry crankshaft back and forth to read clearance. If beyond specifications, install new thrust washers to bring end play within limits.

ENGINE FRONT COVER & OIL SEAL

Engine front cover oil seal should be replaced whenever front cover is removed. Make sure new seal is squarely seated in cover. Lubricate seal contact lip before installing cover.

ENGINE OILING

Crankcase Capacity — Total capacity of entire system is 5.2 quarts. Normal drain and refill capacity (with filter) is 4 quarts.

Oil Filter — Full-flow, cartridge type.

Normal Oil Pressure — 50-71 psi (3.5-5.0 kg/cm^2) at idle.

Pressure Regulator Valve — Installed in pump cover.

NOTE — *On air conditioned models, oil filter support mounts A/C compressor. Filter screws on from side rather than from bottom.*

ENGINE OILING SYSTEM

Engine oiling system is full pressure lubrication utilizing a gear type oil pump driven by the auxiliary shaft. A full-flow filter and a pressure regulator valve is also used.

OIL PUMP

Removal — **1)** Drain crankcase and remove oil pan. See *Oil Pan.* Remove 2 bolts and washers holding oil pump to engine and remove pump and gasket. Visually inspect all parts for wear or damage.

2) Check gears for tooth-to-housing clearance. Clearance should be .004-.007" (.11-.18 mm). Place straightedge across pump body and measure gear end play. End play should be .0010-.0051" (.026-.131 mm). Check relief valve spring for pressure of at least 12.7 lbs. (5.8 kg) at .886" (22.5 mm).

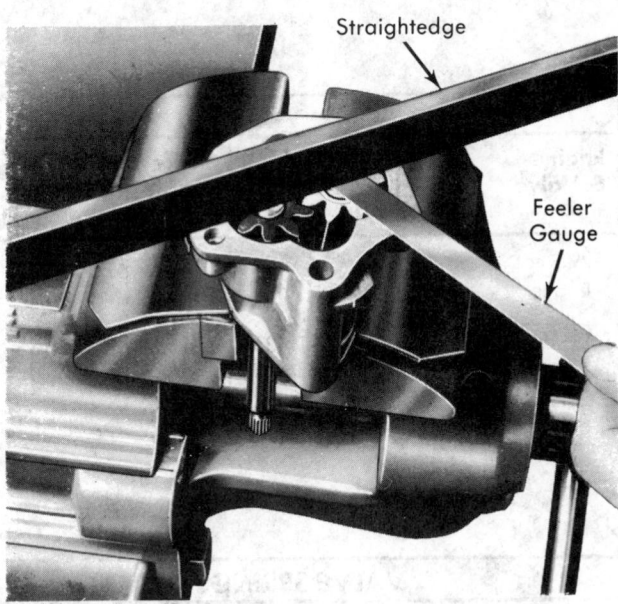

Straightedge

Feeler Gauge

Fig. 6   Checking Oil Pump Gear End Play

Installation — To install, reverse removal procedure and mount pump using a new gasket. Make sure pump is seated before tightening mounting bolts.

ENGINE COOLING

Thermostat — Opens at 172-180°F (78-82°C).

Thermoswitch — Operates at 194-201°F (90-94°C).

Cooling System Capacity	
Application	**Capacity**
Brava	8.5 quarts
Spider 2000	8.0 quarts

Radiator Cap — 11 psi.

WATER PUMP

Removal — Drain cooling system. Remove 3 water pump pulley bolts. Remove drive belt and water pump pulley. Remove radiator hose from water pump. Remove 4 mounting bolts, then remove pump.

Installation — To install, ensure that mating surfaces are clean. Install new gasket and reverse removal procedure.

Fiat Engines

BRAVA & SPIDER 2000 4 CYLINDER (Cont.)
ENGINE SPECIFICATIONS

GENERAL SPECIFICATIONS

Year	Displ.		Carburetor	HP @ RPM	Torque (Ft. Lbs. at RPM)	Compr. Ratio	Bore		Stroke	
	cu. ins.	cc					in.	mm	in.	mm
1980 Carb.	121.7	1995	1x2-Bbl.	80@5000	100@3000	8.1.1	3.31	84	3.54	90
Fuel Inj.	121.7	1995	Fuel Inj.	102@5500	110@3000	8.1.1	3.31	84	3.54	90

VALVES

Engine & Valve	Head Diam. In. (mm)	Face Angle	Seat Angle	Seat Width In. (mm)	Stem Diameter In. (mm)	Stem Clearance In. (mm)	Valve Lift In. (mm)
1995 cc Intake	1.638-1.654 (41.6-42.0)	45.5°	45°	.079 (2.0)	.3139-.3146 (7.974-7.992)	.0012-.0026 (.030-.066)	.3765 (9.564)
Exhaust	1.412-1.435 (35.85-36.45)	45.5°	45°	.079 (2.0)	.3139-.3146 (7.974-7.992)	.0012-.0026 (.030-.066)	.3765 (9.564)

VALVE SPRINGS

Engine	Free Length In. (mm)	PRESSURE Lbs. @ In. (kg @ mm)	
		Valve Closed	Valve Open
1995 cc Inner Spring	1.646 (41.8)	33@1.220 (14.9@31)	62@.846 (28.1@21.5)
Outer Spring	2.122 (53.9)	86@1.417 (38.9@36)	141@1.043 (59.5@26.5)

VALVE TIMING

Engine	INTAKE		EXHAUST	
	Open (BTDC)	Close (ABDC)	Open (BBDC)	Close (ATDC)
1995 cc	5°	53°	53°	5°

PISTONS, PINS, RINGS

Engine	PISTONS Clearance In. (mm)	PINS		RINGS		
		Piston Fit In. (mm)	Rod Fit In. (mm)	Rings	End Gap In. (mm)	Side Clearance In. (mm)
1995 cc	.0016-.0024 (.040-.060)	.0001-.0003 (.002-.008)	.0004-.0006 (.010-.016)	No. 1	.0118-.0177 (.30-.45)	.0018-.0030 (.045-.077)
				No. 2	.0118-.0177 (.30-.45)	.0011-.0027 (.030-.070)
				Oil	.0098-.0157 (.25-.40)	.0011-.0024 (.030-.062)

BRAVA & SPIDER 2000 4 CYLINDER (Cont.)

ENGINE SPECIFICATIONS (Cont.)

CRANKSHAFT MAIN & CONNECTING ROD BEARINGS							
	MAIN BEARINGS				CONNECTING ROD BEARINGS		
Engine	Journal Diam. In. (mm)	Clearance In. (mm)	Thrust Bearing	Crankshaft End Play In. (mm)	Journal Diam. In. (mm) ①	Clearance In. (mm) ②	Side Play In. (mm)
1995 cc	2.086-2.087 (52.99-53.00)	.001-.003 (.03-.07)	No. 5	.002-.012 (.05-.30)	1.9997-2.0001 (50.79-50.80)	.001-.003 (.03-.07)	.....

① — Journal diameter is machined in two sizes designated by class codes. Specification given is class "A". Class "B" is smaller by .0004" (.010 mm).

② — Clearance varies according to class of connecting rod journal. Specification given is class "A". Class "B" clearance is larger by .0001" (.002 mm).

CAMSHAFT			
Engine	Journal Diam. In. (mm)	Clearance In. (mm)	Lobe Lift In. (mm)
1995 cc			
Front	1.1788-1.1795 (29.94-29.96)	.0019-.0035 (.049-.090)	.3765 (9.56)
Middle	1.8013-1.8020 (45.75-45.77)	.0011-.0027 (.029-.070)	.3765 (9.56)
Rear	1.8171-1.8178 (46.15-46.17)	.0011-.0027 (.029-.070)	.3765 (9.56)

TIGHTENING SPECIFICATIONS

Application	Ft. Lbs. (mkg)
Cylinder Head Bolts①	61 (8.5)
Main Bearing Cap Bolts	
Front	59 (8.2)
Center & Rear	83 (11.5)
Intake & Exhaust Manifold Nuts	18 (2.5)
Intake Manifold Bolts	18 (2.5)
Connecting Rod Nuts	54 (7.5)
Flywheel-to-Crankshaft Bolt	105 (14.5)
Camshaft Sprocket Bolt	87 (12)
Oil Pump Mounting Bolt	14 (2.0)
Timing Belt Tensioner Nut	33 (4.5)

① — Tighten when cold only. Recheck after 700-1000 miles.

STRADA & X1/9 4-CYLINDER

ENGINE CODING

ENGINE IDENTIFICATION

Engine identification and serial numbers are stamped on crankcase on flywheel side of engine next to union for radiator hoses. Engine code is stamped above serial number.

Engine Identification		
	Code	
Application	Carbureted	Fuel Injected
1498 cc		
Strada	138 B2.040	138 B2.031
X1/9	138 BS.040	138 BS.031

ENGINE, CYLINDER HEAD & MANIFOLDS

ENGINE

NOTE — *Engine and transmission are removed as an assembly.*

Removal (Strada) — 1) Raise hood, mark hood hinge position, and remove hinge retaining bolts and hood. Remove spare tire and tools. Disconnect both battery cables. Drain cooling system. Remove radiator and heater hoses. On air conditioned models, slowly drain freon and remove compressor hoses.

2) On carbureted models, remove air cleaner cover, cartridge, hoses and housing. On fuel injected models, remove hose from air flow sensor to intake manifold. On all models, remove from engine all fuel lines, throttle control cables, vacuum hoses, wiring harnesses and electrical connectors.

3) Raise vehicle on lift. Remove front wheels and lower protective shields. Remove left side reaction rod bracket, reaction rod and hub support brackets. Remove left and right strut assemblies. Using suitable tool (A.47038), disconnect tie rod ball joints from hub carriers.

4) Remove axle shafts and control arms. Remove front section of exhaust system. Disconnect speedometer cable from transmission. On manual transmission models, mark gear control rod in relation to bracket and remove. On automatic transmission models, move gear selector to position "1". Disconnect shift cable from transmission lever and lay aside.

5) Attach a lifting fixture (A.60592) to engine and engine hoist. Lift engine slightly to remove weight from engine mounting points. Place a jack under center engine mount. Remove engine-to-body mounting bolts and engine support crossmember.

6) Remove mounting brackets and on automatic transmission models, the stabilizer bar. Remove engine and transmission from beneath vehicle. Separate transmission from engine once assembly is removed.

Removal (X1/9) — 1) Disconnect battery cables. Drain cooling system. Remove radiator and heater hoses. Remove cooling system expansion tank and disconnect hoses from thermostat.

2) On carbureted models, remove air cleaner assembly with fresh air duct. On fuel injected models, remove hose from air flow sensor to intake manifold. On all models, remove from engine all fuel lines, throttle control cables, vacuum hoses, wiring harnesses and electrical connectors.

3) Remove bolts holding louvered protection panel below carbon trap in rear firewall. Raise and support vehicle with safety stands. Remove remaining bolt attaching louvered panel in rear firewall, then remove panel. Remove alternator heat shield, engine panels and wheel panels.

4) Drain transmission and differential assembly. Disconnect back-up light and seat belt interlock connectors, then remove clamps to allow wires to come with engine. Disconnect speedometer cable and gearshift linkage from transmission.

5) Disconnect ground strap at engine, then remove muffler and muffler upper bracket. Remove axle boot retaining bolts and slide boots away from differential.

6) Remove nuts securing hand brake cable brackets to control arms. Remove bolts attaching control arms to body and swing arms down out of brackets. Move control arms away from differential until axles are free of differential.

7) Remove lower crossmember attaching bolts and remove crossmember. From above engine, disconnect reaction arm from bracket on engine, then remove front engine mount through bolt. Remove engine and transmission assembly from beneath vehicle. Separate transmission and differential from engine.

NOTE — *Record number of shims at control arm mounting points for installation purposes. Also note sizes of shims. If shims are worn or damaged, rear end alignment should be checked and adjusted, if necessary, after engine and transmission are reinstalled.*

Installation (All Models) — To install, reverse removal procedure. Upon completion of installation, refill cooling system and inspect all lines and hoses for tightness.

INTAKE & EXHAUST MANIFOLD

NOTE — *The following procedure refers to carbureted models only. Information is not available from manufacturer on fuel injected models.*

Removal — 1) Drain cooling system. Remove spare tire from engine compartment. Remove air cleaner and cartridge from carburetor. Remove carburetor pre-heating water hoses.

2) Remove carburetor with guard and gaskets. Remove shroud from intake and exhaust manifold. Remove intake and exhaust manifold from engine.

Installation — To install, reverse removal procedure and use new gaskets.

STRADA & X1/9 4-CYLINDER (Cont.)

CYLINDER HEAD

NOTE — *The following procedure refers to carbureted models only. Information is not available from manufacturer on fuel injected models.*

Removal — 1) Disconnect positive battery cable. Drain engine cooling system. Remove spare tire from engine compartment. Remove air cleaner housing and cartridge. Disconnect spark plug wires at spark plugs.

2) Disconnect accelerator linkage and choke cable at carburetor. Disconnect fuel line at carburetor. Disconnect wire from temperature sending unit.

3) Disconnect heater hose at cylinder head. Disconnect all water hoses at union on left side of engine. Disconnect exhaust pipe from exhaust manifold.

4) Disconnect reaction rod from engine bracket and hose from exhaust shroud. Remove timing cover, then remove alternator and water pump drive belt. Remove air pump drive belt, then loosen nut on tensioner pulley and remove timing belt. Remove cylinder head nuts and bolts, then remove head and manifolds as an assembly.

Installation — 1) Thoroughly clean all gasket surfaces on cylinder head and block. Use new gasket with word "ALTO" facing up when installing head.

2) Tighten bolts and nuts in sequence shown in *Fig. 1* in two steps; first to about 29 ft. lbs. (4.0 mkg), and then to final torque of 69 ft. lbs. (9.5 mkg). Complete installation in reverse order of removal. See *Timing Belt Replacement*.

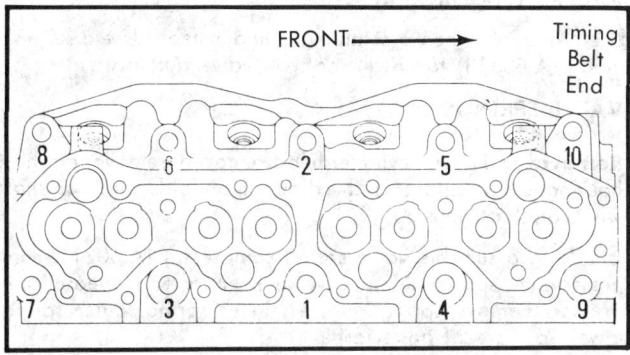

Fig. 1   Cylinder Head Tightening Sequence

CAMSHAFT

TIMING BELT REPLACEMENT

NOTE — *If timing belt is loosened or removed to perform repair work, install new belt.*

Removal (Strada) — 1) Remove right guard and loosen timing belt cover retaining screws. Remove timing belt cover. Check timing by aligning index marks on top and bottom of camshaft sprocket with index marks on engine mounting and upper case. Index marks on crankshaft sprocket and crankshaft seal case should be in alignment.

2) Put vehicle in low gear and apply hand brake to prevent crankshaft from turning. Remove fan belt, loosen tensioner pulley retaining nut and relieve tension. Remove timing belt.

Installation — Install new belt, making sure belt and sprocket teeth engage correctly. Tighten pulley support nut. Recheck timing. Install remaining components.

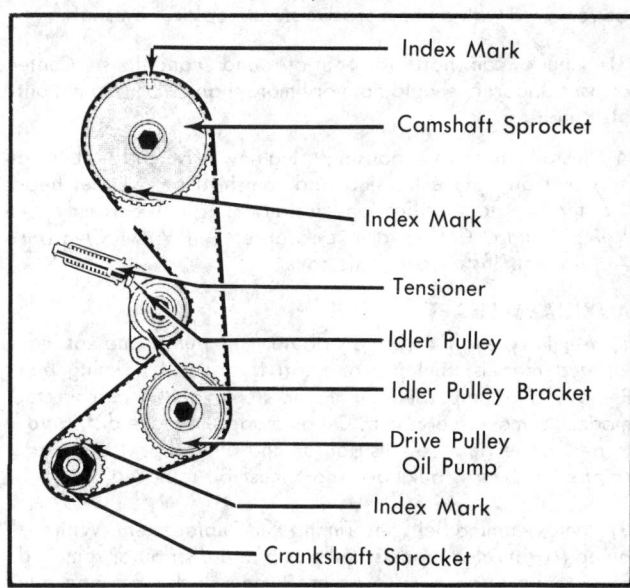

Fig. 2   Front View of Engine Showing Timing Belt Installed

Removal (X1/9) — 1) Rotate crankshaft to position No. 4 piston at TDC of compression stroke. Place gear selector in 4th gear position and set parking brake.

CAUTION — *DO NOT turn camshaft independently of crankshaft. This could cause valve to come in contact with pistons and damage engine.*

2) Remove right guard from under engine. Remove timing bolts and cover. Loosen alternator and remove alternator/water pump drive belt. Loosen air pump and remove drive belt.

3) Remove valve cover and check that camshaft lobes of No. 4 cylinder are pointing up. Remove distributor. Loosen idler pulley lock nut. Remove timing belt starting at idler pulley.

Installation — 1) Install timing belt making sure that teeth are properly engaged in sprockets. Start installation of timing belt at crankshaft pulley. Release idler pulley lock nut and retighten after tension is on belt.

CAUTION — *Never allow crankshaft to rotate counterclockwise. This could slacken belt, causing it to jump timing.*

2) Rotate engine one-half turn. Loosen idler pulley lock nut to ensure all slack is removed. Retighten lock nut. Rotate engine until No. 4 cylinder is in firing position (cam lobe up). Install remaining components in reverse of removal order.

CAMSHAFT

Removal & Installation — 1) Remove timing belt protective cover and loosen belt tensioner. Remove timing belt from camshaft sprocket and remove sprocket from camshaft. Remove camshaft cover, camshaft and housing. Remove camshaft from housing and thoroughly clean and inspect both camshaft and housing.

STRADA & X1/9 4-CYLINDER (Cont.)

2) If camshaft housing bores show signs of wear or scoring and are out of round, replace housing. Check camshaft for signs of seizure or scoring. If scoring or seizure marks cannot be removed with a fine abrasive stone, replace camshaft.

3) Check camshaft for out-of-round conditions. Center camshaft journal should not vary more than .008" (.2 mm) out-of-round.

4) Install camshaft in housing using new drive end seal. Install sprocket and place housing and camshaft on cylinder head. Tighten nuts to specifications. Install timing belt correctly. See *Valve Timing*. Check valve clearance. See *Valve Clearance Adjustment*. Install camshaft cover.

AUXILIARY SHAFT

1) Auxiliary shaft drives distributor, oil pump and, on carbureted models, fuel pump. Shaft is driven by timing belt. Remove oil pump. See *Oil Pump Removal*. On carbureted models, remove fuel pump. On all models, remove distributor. Inspect drive gears of distributor and oil pump. If gears are chipped or worn, auxiliary shaft must be replaced.

2) Remove timing belt. See *Timing Belt Replacement*. With fuel pump (carbureted models), oil pump and distributor removed, remove auxiliary shaft sprocket. Remove lock plate and auxiliary shaft. Throughly clean and inspect shaft.

3) Check inner and outer journals of shaft. If journal size is less than specified, replace shaft. Check inside diameter of inner and outer bushings, if more than specified, replace bushings.

4) To replace bushings, drive out of crankcase using a suitable driver (A.60372/1/2 outer journal and A.660372/1 inner journal). Install new bushings using same drivers as used for removal. Make sure oil holes in bushings align with oil holes in crankcase. Ream bushings to specified clearance with shaft using a suitable reamer (A.90365).

5) Install auxiliary shaft and lock plate. Install sprocket and secure with lock plate and screw. Install remaining components as previously outlined or in reverse of removal order.

Auxiliary Shaft Specifications

Application	Size
Auxiliary Shaft	
Outer Journal	1.4013-1.4023" (35.59-35.62mm)
Inner Journal	1.2575-1.2583" (31.94-31.96mm)
Bushings (Reamed)	
Outer Journal	1.4041-1.4049" (35.66-35.68mm)
Inner Journal	1.2598-1.2606" (32.00-32.02mm)
Clearance	
Outer Journal	.0018-.0036" (.046-.091mm)
Inner Journal	.0016-.0031" (.04-.08mm)

VALVE TIMING

1) With timing belt removed, rotate camshaft sprocket until marks on sprocket are in alignment with index marks on engine.

2) Rotate crankshaft sprocket until mark on sprocket aligns with index on end plate. Install timing belt as previously outlined, making sure camshaft or crankshaft are not rotated.

VALVES

VALVE ARRANGEMENT

E-I-I-E-E-I-I-E

VALVE GUIDE SERVICING

With cylinder head removed and disassembled, check clearance between valve stem and valve guide. If clearance is more than .006" (.15 mm) and valve stem is not worn, valve guide must be replaced. Use a suitable driver to remove and install valve guides.

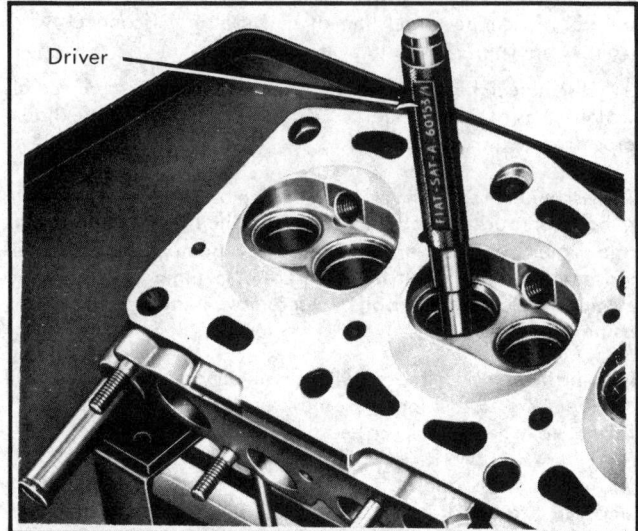

Driver

Fig. 3 *Using Special Driver to Remove Valve Guide*

VALVE STEM OIL SEALS

Use new seals when assembling cylinder head. Use a suitable guide (A.60313) to install seals on valve guides.

VALVE SPRINGS

Removal — 1) With cylinder head removed, remove camshaft housing cover, intake and exhaust manifolds and camshaft with camshaft housing.

2) Using a suitable valve spring compressor (A.60311) compress valve spring. Remove valve keepers and release compressor. Remove spring retainer, inner spring, outer spring, lower spring seat and washer.

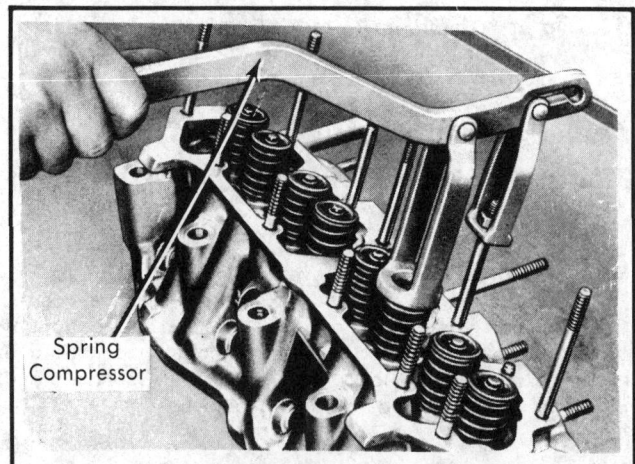

Spring Compressor

Fig. 4 *Using Special Valve Spring Compressor to Remove Valve Springs*

STRADA & X1/9 4-CYLINDER (Cont.)

3) Inspect valve springs for wear or cracking. Using a suitable spring tester (AP.5049) check inner and outer springs against specifications with specified load applied.

Installation — To install valve springs, reverse removal procedure. Install cylinder head as previously outlined.

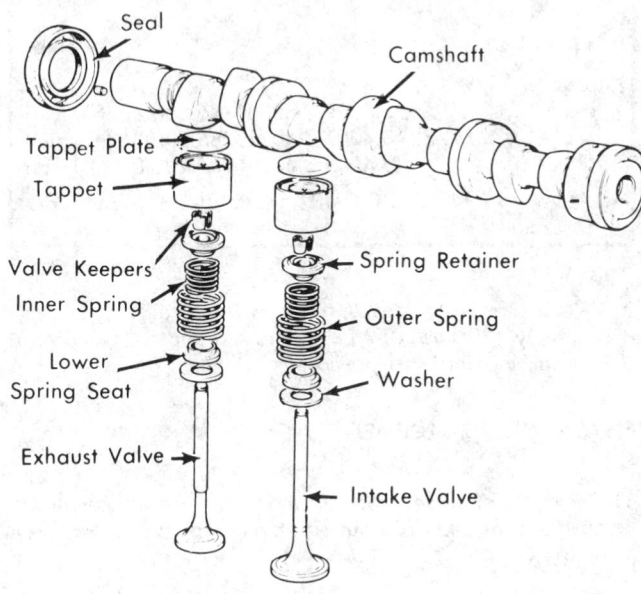

Fig. 5 Expanded View of Valve Train Components

VALVE CLEARANCE ADJUSTMENT

NOTE — *Check and adjust valve clearance with engine cold.*

1) Remove camshaft cover. Rotate engine until lobe on camshaft of valve being checked is pointing straight up. Using a feeler gauge, check clearance between camshaft lobe and valve tappet plate.

Fig. 6 Showing Where to Make Valve Clearance Check

2) If clearance is not as specified, insert a suitable spring compressor (A.60421) under camshaft to release spring tension against camshaft lobe. Remove tappet plate with a suitable removing tool (A.8700I). With plate removed, measure thickness to determine size of plate to be installed.

Valve Clearance Specifications		
Application	Intake Valve	Exhaust Valve
All .... .012" (.3 mm) .... .016" (.4 mm)		

3) Valve tappet plates are available in various thicknesses: .1457-.1850" (3.70-4.70 mm) in increments of .002" (.05 mm). Plate size is shown on face. Install side with plate size toward tappet. Use same procedure on both intake and exhaust valves. Recheck clearance and install camshaft cover.

Fig. 7 Using Special Tool to Remove Valve Tappet Plate

PISTONS, PINS & RINGS

OIL PAN

1) Attach a suitable engine support to top of engine. Remove protective shields and engine crossmember.

2) Drain oil. Remove oil pan retaining bolts and oil pan. To install, clean all gasket surfaces, use new gasket and reverse removal procedure.

PISTON & ROD ASSEMBLY

Removal — Remove oil pan and cylinder head as previously outlined. Remove oil pump. See *Oil Pump.* Remove nuts from connecting rods and remove rod caps. Push piston and rod assembly up and out through top.

STRADA & X1/9 4-CYLINDER (Cont.)

Installation — To install, compress piston rings with a ring compressor. Pistons must be installed with number stamped on connecting rod and rod cap facing away from auxiliary shaft. Tighten rod nuts. Install remaining components in reverse of removal procedure.

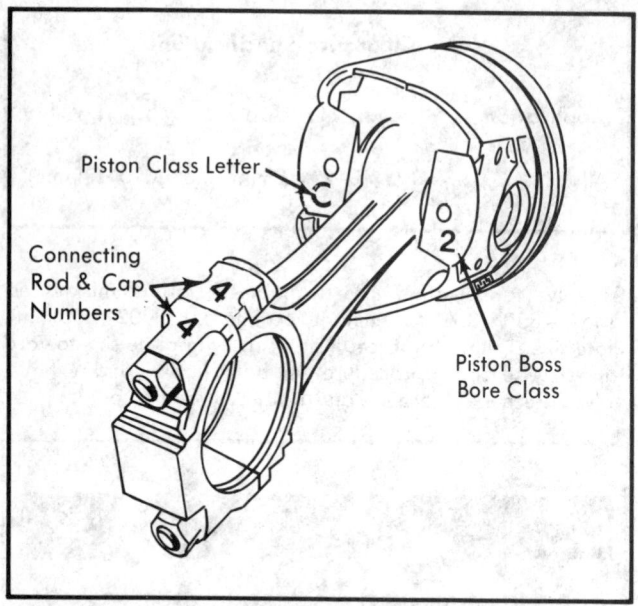

Fig. 8   Piston & Connecting Rod Assembly Showing Identification Class Numbers

FITTING PISTONS

1) With piston and rod assembly removed and disassembled as previously outlined, thoroughly clean piston. Check ring side clearance, side clearance should be no more than .006" (.15mm). Check ring end gap in cylinder against specifications.

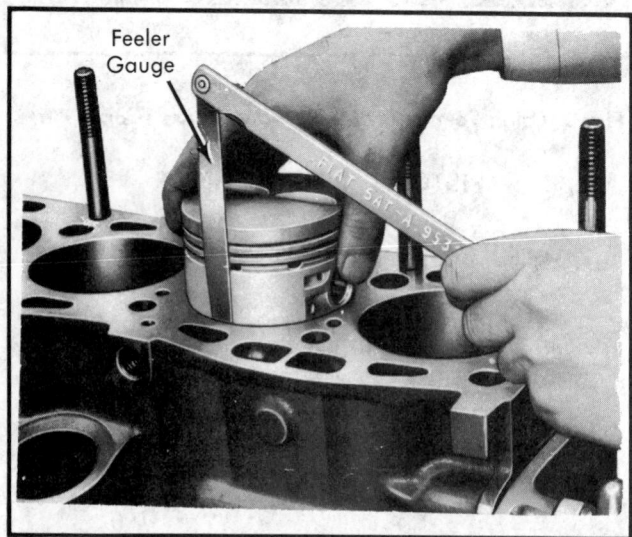

Fig. 9   Using a Feeler Gauge to Check Piston-to-Cylinder Wall Clearance

2) Check fit of piston in cylinders with rings removed. There should be no more than .006" (.15mm) clearance. Pistons are available in .0079" (.2mm), .0157" (.4mm) and .0236" (.6mm)

oversizes. There are three classes of standard size pistons. If piston is replaced, one of the same class must be installed. Class of piston is stamped on bottom of piston.

Piston Class Specification	
Application	**①Size**
Strada & X1/9	
Class A	3.3999-3.4003" (86.360-86.370 mm)
Class B	3.4007-3.4011" (86.380-86.390 mm)
Class C	3.4015-3.4019" (86.400-86.410 mm)
① — Measured at 1.08" (27.5 mm) from piston skirt edge.	

3) When installing rings, make sure gaps are spaced approximately 120° apart. Assemble piston and connecting rod and install in vehicle as previously outlined.

PISTON PIN REPLACEMENT

1) Remove piston and rod assembly as previously outlined. Remove circlips and drive out piston pin using a suitable driver (A.60251).

2) Check fit of pin in piston. Pin should be push fit in piston and should not fall through under its own weight. There are two classes of piston pin and piston bore sizes. If piston pin is replaced it must be replaced with a pin of the same class. Class of piston is stamped on bottom and class of pin is stamped on face of pin.

Piston Pin & Bore Class Specifications	
Application	**Size**
Piston Pin	
Class 1......................	.8658-.8659" (21.991-21.994mm)
Class 2......................	.8659-.8660" (21.994-21.996mm)
Piston Pin Bore	
Class 1......................	.8660-.8661" (21.996-21.999mm)
Class 2......................	.8661-.8662" (21.999-22.002mm)

3) Check piston pin clearance in connecting rod. If clearance is more than specified, drive bushing from connecting rod using a suitable driver (A.60054). Install a new bushing with same driver and ream to size with a new piston pin.

4) Piston pin bore in piston is offset .08" (2 mm). Install connecting rod with numbered side on same side as pin offset.

5) Lubricate piston and secure connecting rod big end in a vise. Place piston in proper position on connecting rod and push in piston pin using a suitable driver (A.60251). Install circlips.

6) Install piston and connecting rod assembly as previously outlined.

STRADA & X1/9 4-CYLINDER (Cont.)

CRANKSHAFT MAIN & CONNECTING ROD BEARINGS

MAIN & CONNECTING ROD BEARING SERVICE

1) Remove engine as previously outlined. Remove cylinder head, oil pan, clutch and flywheel as previously outlined. Remove oil pump. See *Oil Pump*. Remove all sprockets and timing belt. See *Timing Belt Replacement*.

2) Remove cover plates and seals from both ends of engine. Remove all piston and connecting rod assemblies. Remove main bearing caps with lower bearing halves.

3) Remove crankshaft and upper bearing halves. Remove thrust bearings from flywheel end main bearing saddle. Thoroughly clean and inspect crankshaft and crankcase.

4) Check crankshaft journals for out-of-round. If more than .0002" (.005 mm) out-of-round, crankshaft must be ground to next undersize. Bearings for undersize crankshafts are available in .010" (.25 mm), .020" (.50 mm), .030" (.76 mm) and .040" (1 mm) undersizes.

5) Use the Plastigage method to check main bearing clearances. Install upper bearing halves in crankcase and install crankshaft. Place a piece of Plastigage on journal and install main bearing cap with bearing. Tighten bolts to specifications and then remove main bearing cap.

6) With cap removed, check flattened Plastigage against scale on back of package to determine if clearance is as specified. Check connecting rod bearing clearance using same procedure. If clearance is incorrect, crankshaft must be ground to next undersize and bearings of corresponding undersize installed.

7) With correct clearance obtained, install upper bearing halves in crankcase. Lubricate bearings and install crankshaft. Install main bearing caps with bearings and tighten bolts to specifications. Rotate crankshaft to check for freedom of movement.

8) Check crankshaft endplay. See *Thrust Bearing Alignment*. Install remaining components in reverse of removal order or as previously outlined. Install engine as previously outlined.

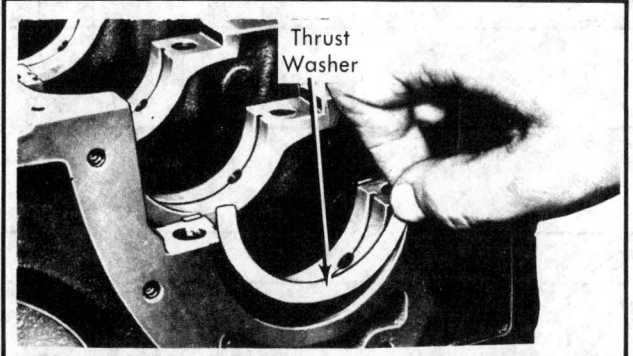

Fig. 10 Fitting Crankshaft Thrust Washer to Block

THRUST BEARING ALIGNMENT

1) With crankshaft installed and main bearing caps tightened, attach a dial indicator to crankcase with arm against flywheel

end of crankshaft. Pry crankshaft back and forth to measure end play.

2) If end play is more than .0137" (.35 mm), remove flywheel end main bearing cap and install oversize thrust rings. Thrust rings are available in .005" (.13 mm) oversize. Install thrust rings with grooves facing crankshaft shoulder.

FRONT & REAR MAIN BEARING OIL SEAL SERVICE

1) Front and rear main bearing oil seals are secured in end plates mounted to both ends of crankcase. Both seals should be replaced when crankshaft has been removed.

2) Drive seals from end plates and install new ones. Lubricate sealing lip of seal and use new gaskets when installing end plates.

ENGINE OILING

Crankcase Capacity — Total capacity of entire system is 5.3 quarts. Normal drain and refill capacity (with filter) is 4.5 quarts.

Oil Filter — Full flow, mounted on front side of engine.

Normal Oil Pressure — 50-71 psi. (3.5-5.0 kg/cm²) with engine @ 212°F.

Pressure Relief Valve — Mounted in oil pump. See *Oil Pump*.

ENGINE OILING SYSTEM

Oil is circulated through engine by pressure provided by a gear type oil pump. Pump is mounted on bottom of crankcase and driven by the auxiliary shaft. Oil is drawn from oil pan by oil pump and circulated through a full flow oil filter. Oil is then pumped into main oil gallery of crankcase where it is distributed to crankshaft and camshaft. Oil flows through crankshaft to lubricate main and connecting rod bearings. Cylinders, pistons and piston pins are lubricated by oil squirted from hole in connecting rod. Oil flows through camshaft to journals. Oil is squirted from number two and four journal to lubricate valve tappets and valves. Auxiliary shaft is lubricated by oil from main oil gallery. Excess oil flows back into oil pan.

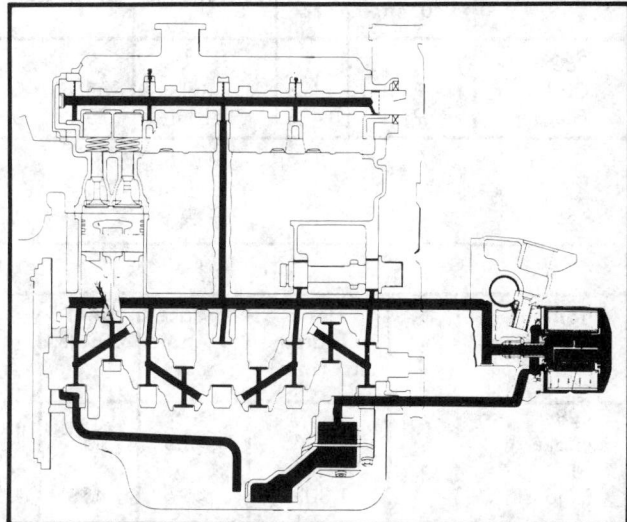

Fig. 11 Diagram Showing Engine Lubrication Flow

STRADA & X1/9 4-CYLINDER (Cont.)

OIL PUMP

Removal & Installation — 1) Remove oil pan as previously outlined. Remove retaining screws and slide out oil pump with suction tube.

2) Clamp pump housing in a vise and remove suction pipe with filter screen and relief valve. Remove pump cover and gears. Thoroughly clean all components.

3) Check both gears for excessive wear and replace as necessary. Check clearance between gears. If more than .010" (.25 mm), replace both gears. Check gear-to-pump housing clearance. If more than .010" (.25 mm), replace gears or housing as necessary.

4) Check gear end play by placing a straightedge on mating surface of pump and inserting a feeler gauge between straightedge and gears. If clearance is more than .006" (.15 mm), replace gears or housing as necessary. Check clearance between drive gear shaft and housing. If more than .004" (.10 mm), replace gear or housing as necessary.

5) Inspect pressure relief spring for cracking or wear. Inspect valve for wear or scoring.

6) Assemble oil pump in reverse order of disassembly. To install, reverse removal procedure.

Oil Pump Specifications	
Application	**Clearance**
Gear-to-Gear	.006" (.15mm)
Gear-to-Housing	.004-.007" (.11-.18mm)
Gear Endplay	.0008-.0041" (.02-.11mm)

ENGINE COOLING

Thermostat — Starts to open at 172-183°F (78-84°C) and is fully open at 194-201°F (90-94°C).

Thermoswitch — Operates at 189-198°F (87-92°C).

Cooling System Capacity	
Application	**Capacity**
Strada	7.5 quarts
X1/9	12.2 quarts

WATER PUMP

Removal — 1) Remove protective panels from bottom of engine and drain cooling system. Remove alternator and drive belt. On models with air conditioning, remove compressor and mount. On models with air pump, remove top half of timing belt cover, air pump and drive belt.

2) Disconnect hoses from water pump, then remove nuts attaching water pipe to pump and disconnect pipe. Remove bolts holding water pump to engine and remove pump.

Installation — Clean all gasket surfaces and install new gasket. Reverse removal procedure and refill cooling system. Run engine and check for leaks.

ENGINE SPECIFICATIONS

GENERAL SPECIFICATIONS										
	Displ.		**Carburetor**	**HP at RPM**	**Torque (Ft. Lbs. at RPM)**	**Compr. Ratio**	**Bore**		**Stroke**	
Year	**cu. ins.**	**cc**					**in.**	**mm**	**in.**	**mm**
1980 Carb.	91.4	1498	2-Bbl.	65@5100	.....	8.5:1	3.40	86.4	2.52	63.9
Fuel Inj.	91.4	1498	Fuel Inj.	75@5500	.....	8.5:1	3.40	86.4	2.52	63.9

VALVES							
Engine & Valve	**Head Diam. In. (mm)**	**Face Angle**	**Seat Angle**	**Seat Width In. (mm)**	**Stem Diameter In. (mm)**	**Stem Clearance In. (mm)**	**Valve Lift In. (mm)**
1498cc Intake	1.4173 (36)	45.5°	45°	.0787 (2)	.3139-.3146 (7.974-7.992)	.0012-.0026 (.030-.066)	.3622 (9.20)
Exhaust	1.3031 (33.1)	45.5°	45°	.0787 (2)	.3139-.3146 (7.974-7.992)	.0012-.0026 (.030-.066)	.3641 (9.25)

STRADA & X1/9 4-CYLINDER (Cont.)

ENGINE SPECIFICATIONS (Cont.)

VALVE SPRINGS			
Engine	Free Length In. (mm)	PRESSURE Lbs. @ In. (kg @ mm)	
		Valve Closed	Valve Open
1498 cc Inner	.....	32.8@1.220 (14.9@31.00)	.....
Outer	.....	85.7@1.417 (38.9@36.00)	.....

VALVE TIMING				
	INTAKE		EXHAUST	
Engine	Open (BTDC)	Close (ABDC)	Open (BBDC)	Close (ATDC)
1498 cc	12°	52°	52°	12°

PISTONS, PINS, RINGS						
	PISTONS	PINS		RINGS		
Engine	Clearance In. (mm)	Piston Fit In. (mm)	Rod Fit In. (mm)	Rings	End Gap In. (mm)	Side Clearance In. (mm)
1498cc	.0011-.0019 (.03-.05)	.0001-.0003 (.002-.008)	.0004-.0006 (.010-.016)	No. 1	.0118-.0177 (.30-.45)	.0018-.0030 (.045-.077)
				No. 2	.0118-.0177 (.30-.45)	.0016-.0028 (.040-.072)
				No. 3	.0098-.0157 (.25-.40)	.0012-.0024 (.030-.062)

CRANKSHAFT MAIN & CONNECTING ROD BEARINGS							
	MAIN BEARINGS				CONNECTING ROD BEARINGS		
Engine	Journal Diam. In. (mm)	Clearance In. (mm)	Thrust Bearing	Crankshaft End Play In. (mm)	Journal Diam. In. (mm)	Clearance In. (mm)	Side Play In. (mm)
1498cc	1.9990-1.9997 (50.775-50.795)	.0019-.0037 (.050-.095)	①	.0021-.0104 (.055-.265)	1.7913-1.7920 (45.498-45.518)	.0014-.0034 (.036-.086)	.....

① — Thrust ring is installed at flywheel end main bearing cap.

CAMSHAFT			
Engine	Journal Diam. In. (mm)	Clearance In. (mm)	Lobe Lift In. (mm)
1498 cc No. 1	1.1789-1.1795 (29.944-29.960)	.0011-.0028 (.029-.070)	....
No. 2	1.8872-1.8878 (47.935-47.950)	.0012-.0028 (.030-.070)	....
No. 3	1.8951-1.8957 (48.135-48.150)	.0012-.0028 (.030-.070)	....
No. 4	1.9030-1.9035 (48.335-48.350)	.0012-.0028 (.030-.070)	....
No. 5	1.9108-1.9114 (48.535-48.550)	.0012-.0028 (.030-.070)	....

TIGHTENING SPECIFICATIONS

Application	Ft. Lbs. (mkg)
Cylinder Head Bolts	69 (9.5)
Cylinder Head Nuts	69 (9.5)
Main Bearing Cap Bolts	58 (8.0)
Connecting Rod Cap Bolts	38 (5.2)
Intake and Exhaust Manifold Nuts	20 (2.8)
Camshaft Sprocket Bolt	61 (8.5)
Timing Belt Tensioner Pulley Nut	33 (4.5)
Crankshaft Pulley and Sprocket Nut	101 (14.0)
Flywheel-to-Crankshaft Bolts	61 (8.5)

1600 cc 4 CYLINDER

ENGINE CODING

ENGINE IDENTIFICATION

Push-rod operated overhead valve, 4-cylinder in-line engine is transversely mounted at front of car. Engine identification is stamped on number plate attached to panel under hood just above right headlight.

Engine Identification	
Application	**Code**
1600 cc	L4

ENGINE, CYLINDER HEAD & MANIFOLDS

ENGINE

NOTE — *Engine and transmission assembly are removed from vehicle as a unit. Removal and installation of assembly is accomplished with transmission in 4th gear to aid in subsequent installation adjustment.*

Removal — 1) Disconnect and remove battery. Drain coolant by removing radiator and heater hoses. (No petcock radiator drain is provided.) Remove air cleaner and breather hose.

2) Disconnect and remove accelerator cable and bracket from carburetor and intake manifold. Remove fuel line from pump to carburetor. Disconnect carburetor fuel vent hoses, and remove emission and servo vacuum hoses.

3) Disconnect the following electrical leads: temperature sending unit, oil pressure switch, distributor and coil wires, choke wire, fan switch, air pump ground wire and engine grounding strap. Disconnect speedometer cable at drive fitting. Unhook clutch cable. Remove exhaust manifold heat stove and inlet pipe from exhaust manifold.

4) Raise vehicle on hoist. Loosen clamp bolt and remove gear selector rod. Unhook spring between selector rod and longitudinal member. Back off mounting nuts on stabilizer rubber insulators and engine mounts. Loosen stud locknut and remove stud from transmission with an Allen wrench. Disconnect mounting rubbers and remove complete exhaust assembly.

5) Remove 4 bolts holding shift tower to floor pan, then remove shift tower. Rotate gear selector rod with stabilizer halfway around and hang from wire. Disconnect alternator and starter leads. Remove 6 Allen head bolts from right and left driveshaft couplings and disconnect couplings.

6) Support engine and transmission assembly on suitable jack. Remove engine mountings as follows: right front upper engine mounting rubber insulator, engine-to-body bracket in engine compartment, left engine mounting bolt, and bottom engine mounting strap. Raise hoist to lift vehicle away from transmission-engine assembly, then lower jack to remove assembly from beneath vehicle.

Installation — 1) Reverse removal procedure, using caution that front engine insulator stud engages right apron bracket. Front engine mount rubber insulators must be parallel to front of engine. Do NOT distort when nut is tightened.

2) Lower and remove jack. Assure that shift shaft is in 4th gear to position and slide selector rod onto shaft. Adjust as follows: pull gear selector rod and shift lever downward, lock shift lever in 4th gear position with suitable .16" (4 mm) arbor, insert 2.76" (70 mm) spacer between floor pan and selector rod,

turn shift shaft CLOCKWISE against stop using arbor, then tighten selector rod locating bolt. Remove spacer and arbor.

3) Complete installation noting that accelerator cable must be routed OVER air cleaner snorkel to prevent damage to cable from EGR pipe and to avoid interference with ignition system. Adjust cable so that clearance between throttle stop and pedal lever does not exceed .015" (.38 mm) with throttle fully open. Refill all fluids and check for leaks.

INTAKE MANIFOLD

Removal & Installation — 1) Partially drain cooling system, remove air cleaner and thermostat housing. Disconnect accelerator cable from throttle lever, fuel and vacuum lines from carburetor, and water outlet hose and crankcase ventilation hose from intake manifold.

2) Disconnect decel valve-to-carburetor pipe (if equipped) and fan switch. Remove attaching bolts and nuts and lift out manifold with old gasket. To install, reverse removal procedure, noting that if installing a new manifold, decel valve must be placed over adapter and installed with special tool.

EXHAUST MANIFOLD

Removal & Installation — Remove exhaust pipe flange nuts and separate the joint. (If necessary, remove air pump and mounting bracket before removing pipe.) Disconnect hot air pipe from air cleaner at exhaust manifold. Remove attaching bolts and nuts and lift off manifold. To install, reverse removal procedure using new gaskets.

CYLINDER HEAD

Removal — 1) Drain engine coolant, remove air cleaner assembly and fuel line from fuel pump to carburetor. Disconnect wires from spark plugs and tie out of way.

2) Disconnect the following: radiator fan switch, heater and vacuum hoses at intake manifold, hoses at choke housing, temperature sending unit wire, exhaust pipe, throttle linkage, and distributor vacuum advance hose from carburetor.

3) Remove thermostat and housing, rocker arm cover and gasket, rocker arm shaft assembly, and push rods. Remove head bolts and lift off cylinder head.

CAUTION — *Maintain push rods in order removed for installation in original location. Do not lay head flat as spark plugs or gasket surface may be damaged.*

Installation — To install, reverse removal procedure and tighten head bolts in increments in sequence shown in *Fig 1.* Adjust valve clearance to specifications.

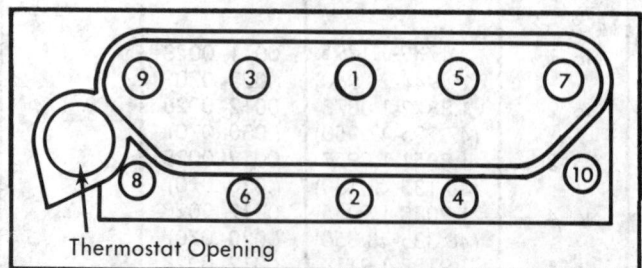

Fig. 1   Cylinder Head Bolt Tightening Sequence

1600 cc 4 CYLINDER (Cont.)

VALVES

VALVE ARRANGEMENT

E-I-I-E-E-I-I-E

VALVE GUIDES

If valve guides become worn they may be reamed to install valves with .015" (.39 mm) oversize stems.

VALVE STEM OIL SEALS

Valve stem oil seals should be replaced any time cylinder head is disassembled. Install new stem seal over valve stem with open end toward head. Replace spring and retainer.

VALVE SPRINGS

Use suitable spring compressor tool to remove locks and retainers. Spring may be removed with head installed on engine if rocker arms and push rods are removed. It will be necessary to hold the valves closed with compressed air during the operation.

VALVE SPRING INSTALLED HEIGHT

Measure spring installed height from surface of spring pad to bottom of retainer. If height is greater than specified, install .030" (.76 mm) spacers between spring pad and valve spring to bring within limits. Do NOT install spacers unless necessary due to excess strain on valve train.

ROCKER ARM ASSEMBLY OVERHAUL

Disassembly — With rocker arm assembly removed from head, remove cotter pin from one end of rocker shaft and slip flat washers and crimped washer from shaft. Remove shaft supports, rocker arms and springs, keeping them in proper order for reassembly. Remove plugs from rocker arm shafts in order to clean hollow of shaft.

Assembly — Drive new plugs in ends of rocker shaft. Assemble rocker arm shaft so that bolt hole in rocker arm shaft support is on same side as rocker arm adjusting screw. Rocker arms are right-hand and left-hand, with pads inclined toward support. Install washers and cotter pins.

VALVE CLEARANCE ADJUSTMENT

Adjust valves with engine cold. With valve cover off, rotate crankshaft until valves No. 1 and No. 6 are fully open. Check clearance on valves No. 3 and No. 8. Use feeler gauge inserted from front to rear (parallel to crankshaft centerline). Check remaining valves by rotating crankshaft until sequence shown in following table is completed.

Valves Fully Open:	1 & 6	2 & 4	3 & 8	5 & 7
Check Clearance on :	3 & 8	5 & 7	1 & 6	2 & 4

NOTE — When adjusting valves DO NOT use a go, no-go feeler gauge and DO NOT insert gauge perpendicular to crankshaft centerline.

Valve Clearance Specifications

Application	①Clearance
Intake	.010" (.25 mm)
Exhaust	.021" (.53 mm)

① — Adjust with engine cold.

PISTONS, PINS & RINGS

OIL PAN

Removal — Drain crankcase, remove oil dipstick and remove battery. Disconnect throttle linkage from carburetor and steering cable from rack and pinion. Disconnect rack and pinion from crossmember and move forward to provide clearance for removing pan. Remove starter motor and lower rear cover. Disassemble engine rear plate from rear plate assembly. Remove oil pan bolts, oil pan and oil pump inlet tube

Installation — Use new gaskets with sealer on engine block side and place on block. Place pan in position and tighten bolts evenly to specifications. Follow *Alphabetical* and then *Numerical* sequence shown in *Fig. 2.* Continue installation in reverse order of removal and replenish crankcase oil supply.

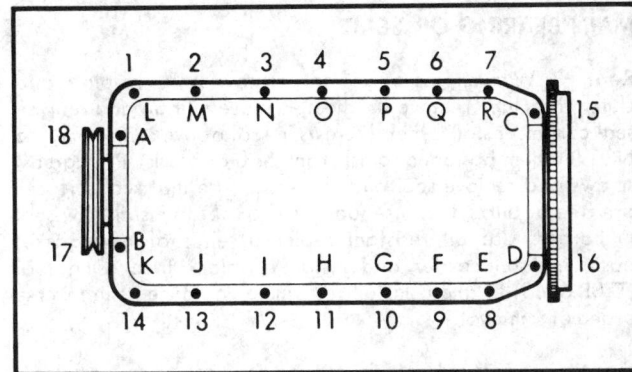

Fig. 2 Oil Pan Bolt Tightening Sequence

PISTON & ROD ASSEMBLY

Removal — With cylinder head and pan removed, partially loosen bearing cap bolts several turns, then tap them to release the cap. Completely remove bolts and bearing caps, keeping them in order so they can be installed in original positions. Push piston and connecting rod out of bore from bottom.

Installation — Place bearing liners in connecting rods and caps. Turn crankshaft to fit each rod to crankpin and install previously fitted bearing and cap. If bearings have not been previously fitted, use Plastigage method, then tighten caps to specified torque.

FITTING PISTONS

Determine piston-to-cylinder bore clearance by measuring bore at a point 2.344" (59.53 mm) from top, across axis of crankshaft. Then, measure piston diameter at a point 2.25" (57 mm) below dome and 90° to pin bore. If clearance is excessive, pistons are available in .0025" (.064 mm), .015" (.381 mm) and .030" (.762 mm) oversizes.

PISTON PIN REPLACEMENT

Full floating wrist pins are retained by snap rings in piston pin bore. Pin may be pushed from assembly after removing retainers. Pistons are only supplied in service complete with pin to ensure correct fit and pins must not be interchanged. When assembling, make sure that FRONT marking on connecting rod is on same side of the assembly as the arrow in the piston crown. Heat piston in oil or water prior to inserting pin and retain with snap rings.

1600 cc 4 CYLINDER (Cont.)

CRANKSHAFT MAIN & CONNECTING ROD BEARINGS

Connecting Rod Bearings — Bearing inserts are fitted in rod and cap in conventional manner, using Plastigage method to determine clearance. When installing, ensure that arrow on piston points to front of engine and that number on connecting rod and cap is on camshaft side.

Main Bearings — Conventional replaceable inserts are used in all 5 main bearings. Number 3 (center) main bearing controls end play by means of half-circle thrust bearings inserted between thrust faces of crankshaft and block. Bearing caps are marked in order F, R2, C, R4 and R for proper installation. Use Plastigage method to determine clearance and select undersize bearings as required. Check end play with feeler gauge and install thrust bearings of correct thickness to establish specified end play.

MAIN BEARING OIL SEALS

Rear — With engine out of car, remove pressure plate and clutch disc, then remove flywheel. Remove oil pan and rear oil seal carrier. Install 2 metal screws in seal above center line (do NOT let them bottom against crankshaft or block). Pry against screws and remove seal and carrier. Ensure that seal surfaces are free of burrs, then use tool (T70P-6165) to install new seal in carrier. Use oil resistant sealer at ends of new gasket positioned on carrier and install on block face using tool (T70P-6165) to align. Install remaining components in reverse order of removal.

Front — Front oil seal is pressed in front cover and seals against pulley hub. With cover off engine, support around oil seal and drive seal out from rear using installation/removal tool (T70P-6150). To install, turn cover over and support from rear. Use tool to drive new seal in position.

CAMSHAFT

Timing Chain — With front cover off, remove crankshaft oil slinger. Remove camshaft sprocket retainer and bolts, then remove chain tensioner and bolts. Remove camshaft sprocket and timing chain. To install, place timing chain over sprockets so that timing marks on camshaft gear and crankshaft gear are aligned. Install remaining components, then bend up locking tabs after bolts have been tightened to specifications.

Camshaft — Proceed as in *Timing Chain*, then remove oil pump and fuel pump. Remove rocker arm cover, rocker arm assembly, distributor, and push rods. Remove camshaft thrust plate and pull out camshaft. Valve lifters may be removed if desired. To install, reverse removal procedures assuring that timing marks are aligned when installing timing chain.

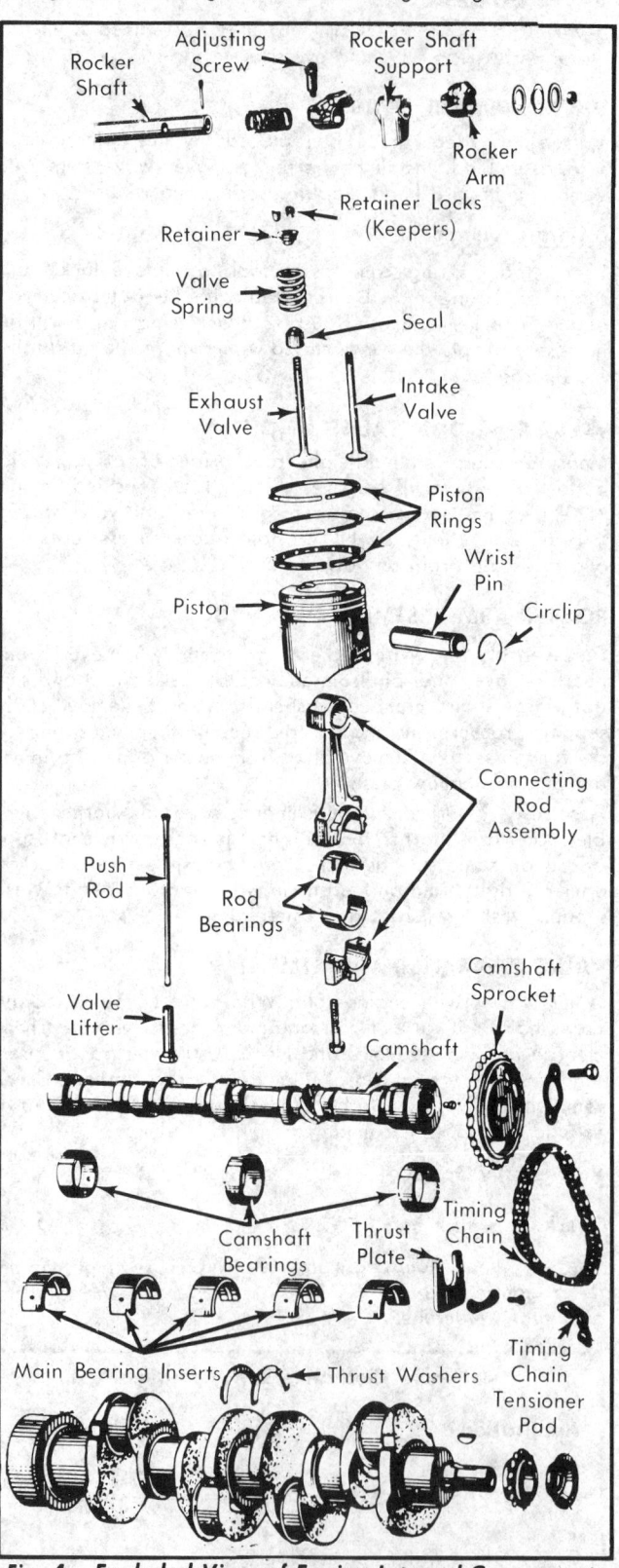

Fig. 4   Exploded View of Engine Internal Components

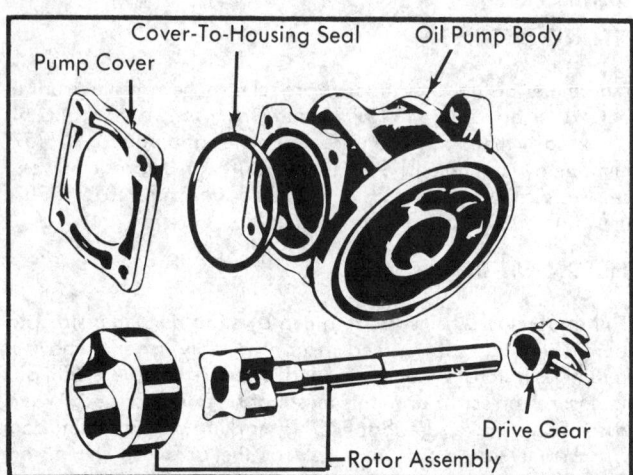

Fig. 3   Exploded View of Fiesta Oil Pump Assembly

1600 cc 4 CYLINDER (Cont.)

ENGINE OILING

OIL PUMP

Oil pump and filter assembly is bolted to right side of cylinder block. Assembly is removable with engine in place. Pump is driven by a gear on the engine camshaft. The full flow element type filter is bolted to a mounting flange integral with the oil pump body.

Engine Oiling System Specifications	
Application	**Specification**
Oil Pressure @ 2000 RPM① ...	24-45 psi (1.7-3.2 kg/cm²)
Oil Filter Type	Full Flow Element
Inner-to-Outer Rotor Clearance	.005" (.127 mm)
Outer Rotor-to-Housing Clearance	.010" (.254 mm)
Housing-to-Rotor Face Clearance	.0025" (.064 mm)
Relief Valve Spring Tension	7.5-8.5 lbs. @ 1.04"
	(3.4-3.9 kg @ 26.4 mm)
Relief Valve Clearance	.001-.003" (.025-.076 mm)
① — Engine hot.	

Crankcase Capacity — 3.5 qts. including filter.

Oil Filter — Disposable spin-on type.

ENGINE COOLING

Thermostat — Begins to open at 199°F (93°C); fully open at 222°F (106°C).

Cooling System Capacity — 6.6 qts. (includes heater).

Radiator Cap — 14.5 psi (1.0 kg/cm²).

Radiator — Cross-flow with electric cooling fan.

WATER PUMP

Disconnect battery and drain radiator. Loosen pump pulley bolts, then remove air pump and alternator drive belts. Remove lower radiator hose from pump. Remove pump pulley bolts and take pulley off shaft. Remove pump retaining bolts and lift pump from engine. To install, position pump on connecting hose and reverse removal procedures.

ENGINE SPECIFICATIONS

GENERAL SPECIFICATIONS										
Year	Displ.		Carburetor	HP at RPM	Torque (Ft. Lbs. at RPM)	Compr. Ratio	Bore		Stroke	
	cu. ins.	cc					in.	mm	in.	mm
1980	94	1600	2-Bbl.	.....	.....	8.6:1	3.188	80.97	3.056	77.62

VALVES							
Engine & Valve	Head Diam. In. (mm)	Face Angle	Seat Angle	Seat Width In. (mm)	Stem Diameter In. (mm)	Stem Clearance In. (mm)	Valve Lift In. (mm)
1600 cc Intake	1.410 (35.8)	45°	45°	.050-.065 (1.27-1.65)	.3098-.3105① (7.868-7.886)	.0008-.0027② (.020-.069)	.3536③ (8.98)
Exhaust	1.239 (31.47)	45°	45°	.070-.085 (1.78-2.16)	.3089-.3096① (7.846-7.863)	.0017-.0036② (.043-.091)	.3553③ (9.02)

① — .015" (.381 mm) oversize limits are:
  Intake — .3248-.3255" (8.25-8.26 mm).
  Exhaust — .3239-.3246" (8.22-8.24 mm).

② — Wear limit — .0055" (.139 mm).
③ — At ZERO valve lash.

VALVE SPRINGS			
Engine	Free Length In. (mm)	PRESSURE Lbs. @ In. (kg @ mm)	
		Valve Closed	Valve Open
1600 cc	1.48 (37.6)	47.5-52.5@1.263① (3.34-3.69@32)	122.5@.953② (8.61@24.2)

① — Wear Limit — 42 lbs.@1.263"
  (2.95 kg/cm²@32.08 mm).
② — Wear Limit — 104 lbs.@.953"
  (7.31 kg/cm²@24.2 mm).

CAMSHAFT			
Engine	Journal Diam. In. (mm)	Clearance① In. (mm)	Lobe Lift In. (mm)
1600 cc	1.5597-1.5605 (39.62-39.64)	.0010-.0023 (.025-.058)	.2309② (5.865) .2320③ (5.893)

① — End play is .0025-.0075" (.064-.191 mm).
② — Intake lobe.
③ — Exhaust lobe.

Fiesta Engines

1600 cc 4 CYLINDER (Cont.)
ENGINE SPECIFICATIONS (Cont.)

Engine	CRANKSHAFT MAIN & CONNECTING ROD BEARINGS						
	MAIN BEARINGS				CONNECTING ROD BEARINGS		
	Journal Diam. In. (mm)	Clearance In. (mm)	Thrust Bearing	Crankshaft End Play In. (mm)	Journal Diam. In. (mm)	Clearance In. (mm)	Side Play In. (mm)
1600 cc	2.1253-2.1261① (53.98-54.00)	.0005-.0015 (.013-.038)	No. 3②	.003-.011 (.076-.279)	1.9368-1.9376① (49.19-49.22)	.0004-.0015③ (.010-.038)	.004-.010④ (.102-.254)

① — Maximum out of round — .0004" (.010 mm).
② — Thrust washers.
③ — Allowable limit — .0004-.0024" (.010-.061 mm).
④ — Maximum limit — .014" (.356 mm).

Engine	PISTONS, PINS, RINGS					
	PISTONS	PINS		RINGS		
	Clearance In. (mm)	Piston Fit In. (mm)	Rod Fit In. (mm)	Rings	End Gap In. (mm)	Side Clearance In. (mm)
1600 cc	.0009-.0017 (.023-.431)	.0001-.0003① (.002-.008)	.0001-.0004② (.002-.010)	Comp.	.009-.014 (.228-.356)	.0016-.0036 (.041-.091)
				Oil	.009-.014 (.228-.356)	.0018-.0038 (.046-.097)

① — Tight.
② — Loose.

TIGHTENING SPECIFICATIONS

Application	Ft. Lbs. (mkg)
Cam Sprocket-to-Cam Bolt	12-15 (1.7-2.1)
Cam Thrust Plate Bolts	25-35 (3.5-4.8)
Connecting Rod Bolts	30-35 (4.1-4.8)
Cylinder Head Bolts	
1st Increment	5 (.7)
2nd Increment	20-30 (2.8-4.1)
3rd Increment	50-55 (6.9-7.6)
Final Torque	65-70 (9.0-9.7)
Crankshaft Pulley Bolt	24-28 (3.3-3.9)
Cylinder Front Cover	5-7 (.7-1.0)
Clutch Pressure Plate	
To Flywheel	12-15 (1.7-2.1)
Carburetor Nuts	12-15 (1.7-2.1)
Exhaust Manifold-to-Head Studs	9-12 (1.2-1.7)
Exhaust Manifold-to-Head Nuts	15-18 (2.1-2.5)
Pulley-to-Hub	
Metal	5-7 (.7-1.0)
Plastic	7-9 (1.0-1.2)
Flywheel-to-Crankshaft Bolts	50-55 (6.9-7.6)
Intake Manifold-to-Head Bolts	12-15 (1.7-2.1)
Intake Manifold-to-Head Nuts	12-15 (1.7-2.1)
Intake Manifold-to-Head Studs	9-12 (1.2-1.7)
Main Bearing Cap Bolts	55-60 (7.6-8.3)
Oil Pump-to-Block	12-15 (1.7-2.1)
Oil Drain Plug	20-25 (2.8-3.5)
Oil Pan Bolts	
Step 1	Finger Tight Corner Bolts
Step 2	Snug All Bolts
Step 3	6.8 (.94)
Rear Oil Seal Retainer-to-Block	12-15 (1.7-2.1)
Rocker Shaft Support Bolt	25-30 (3.46-4.15)
Spark Plug	10-15 (1.38 -2.1)
Water Pump-to-Block	
¼" Bolts	5-7 (.7-1.0)
5/16" Bolt	12-15 (1.7-2.1)

Honda Engines

ACCORD, CIVIC, & PRELUDE 4 CYLINDER

ENGINE CODING

ENGINE IDENTIFICATION

Engine serial number is stamped on firewall side of engine block, near the transaxle. Serial number is proceeded by engine model number.

Application	Code
Civic	
1335 cc	EJ1
1487 cc	EM1
Accord (1751 cc)	EK1
Prelude (1751 cc)	EK1

ENGINE, CYLINDER HEAD, & MANIFOLDS

ENGINE

Removal — 1) Remove battery cables, battery, and mounting tray. Remove headlight trim, front bumper apron, and grille to gain access to hood brackets. Remove hood. Drain coolant, engine oil, and transmission fluid. Remove air cleaner and attached ducting. Disconnect brake booster hose at elbow and all electrical connections and wires to engine. Disconnect fuel lines and throttle cable. Remove radiator hoses and heater hoses. If equipped, detach EGR control box and let hang next to engine. Remove alternator.

2) If equipped, remove air conditioner hoses and compressor (Accord). On other models, remove compressor with hoses attached and wire out of way. On manual transmission models, remove clutch slave cylinder with hydraulic line attached. On automatic transmission models, remove oil cooling lines. On all models, disconnect speedometer cable. If equipped, remove power steering pump and bracket.

3) Place front of vehicle on jack stands and remove front wheels. On Prelude, remove engine guards and stabilizer bars. On all models, disconnect right and left lower arm ball joints and tie rod ends. Remove right and left axles. On vehicles with automatic transmissions, remove shift console, indicator, shift cables, and housing. On manual transmission models, disconnect shift rod clevis and torque rod. On all models, disconnect exhaust pipes.

4) Attach suitable lifting device, and raise engine enough to off-load engine mounts. Remove engine support bolts, and push left engine support into shock mount bracket. Remove front and rear engine mounts and torque rods. Carefully lift engine/transaxle assembly out of vehicle, ensuring all wires and hoses are detached.

Installation — Install engine in reverse order of removal. When replacing axles, insert shaft until spring clip "clicks" into groove in differential side gear. Make sure all control cables are adjusted properly.

CYLINDER HEAD

NOTE — *To avoid damage, do not remove cylinder head until engine has been allowed to cool.*

Removal — 1) Disconnect battery, drain cooling system, and remove air cleaner and related hoses. Disconnect all electrical wires and connections to cylinder head. Disconnect fuel line, throttle cable, and emission hoses from carburetor, and remove carburetor.

2) Remove radiator and heater hoses. Disconnect hot air ducts and remove header pipe from exhaust manifold. On vehicles with air conditioning, remove alternator and bracket. On vehicles without air conditioning, remove bolt securing alternator bracket to cylinder head, and loosen alternator adjusting bolt. Remove valve cover and timing belt upper cover.

3) Bring No. 1 piston to TDC. Loosen timing belt pivot and adjusting bolts, and slip timing belt off camshaft pulley. Remove oil pump gear cover and pull oil pump shaft out of cylinder head. Remove cylinder head bolts in reverse of tightening sequence by turning 30° at a time until loose. Remove cylinder head.

NOTE — *Do not crimp or bend timing belt more than 90°, or less than 1" (25 mm) in diameter.*

4) Measure cylinder head warpage along the edge and 3 ways across center. If under .002" (.05 mm), resurfacing is not required. If clearance is .002-.008" (.05-.20 mm), resurfacing is necessary.

Installation — Ensure that all mating surfaces are clean and free of cracks. Using a new head gasket, place head in position, making sure dowel pins line up. On 1751 cc engines, "Up" mark on camshaft gear should be on top. On 1335 and 1487 cc engines, cutout in camshaft gear should be at top. On all models, tighten head bolts as shown in *Fig. 1*, and complete installation in reverse order of removal.

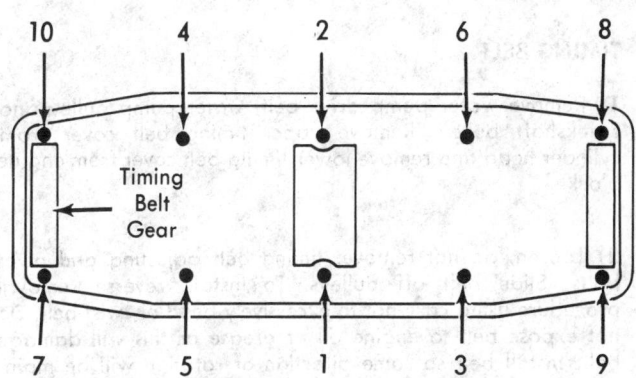

Fig. 1 Cylinder Head Tightening Sequence (Loosen in Reverse Sequence)

MANIFOLDS

Removal — Loosen 4 intake-to-exhaust manifold bolts, then remove special manifold-to-head mounting nuts in reverse of tightening sequence. See *Figs. 2 and 3*. Remove and disassemble manifolds.

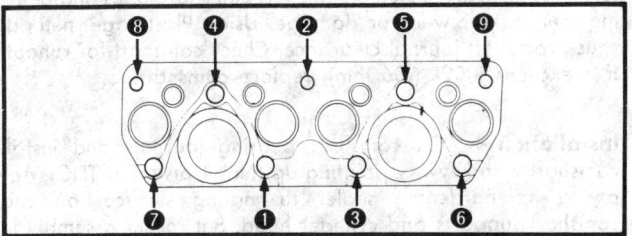

Fig. 2 Manifold Tightening Sequence (All Exc. Calif. Auto. Trans.)

ACCORD, CIVIC, & PRELUDE 4 CYLINDER (Cont.)

Installation — Use new gaskets between manifolds and heat shield and tighten 4 bolts holding manifolds together FINGER TIGHT. Place manifolds and new gasket in position on cylinder head and tighten special mounting bolts to final torque as shown in *Fig. 2*. Tighten intake-to-exhaust manifold bolts to final torque. On California vehicles with automatic transmissions, a different gasket is used. Follow same procedure, using tightening sequence shown in *Fig. 3*.

NOTE — *Spring washers under special nuts must be mounted with dished surface facing in.*

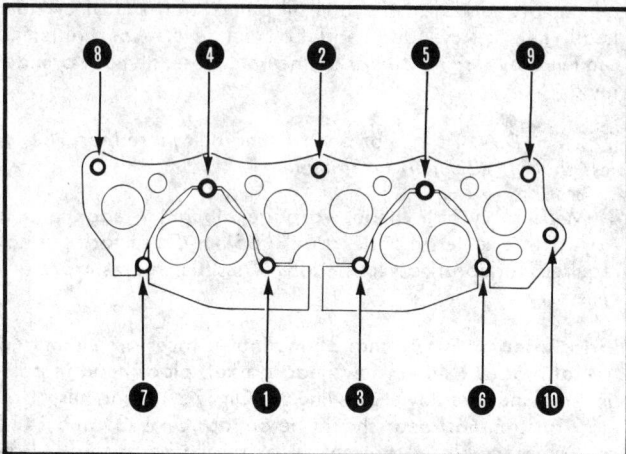

Fig. 3 Manifold Tightening Sequence (California Auto. Trans. Only)

TIMING BELT

1) Remove water pump drive belt, water pump pulley and crankshaft pulley. Remove upper timing belt cover from cylinder head and remove lower timing belt cover from engine block.

2) Loosen, do not remove, timing belt adjusting and pivot bolts. Slide belt off pulleys. To install, reverse removal procedure using care not to excessively bend or twist belt. Do not expose belt to engine oil or grease as this will damage belt. Install belt so same direction of rotation will be maintained to prevent excessive belt wear.

CAMSHAFT

Removal — Check camshaft end play before removing any valve components. Reading should be .002-.006" (.05-.15 mm). Replace camshaft if wear limit of .02" (.5 mm) is exceeded. Remove rocker assembly from head, taking care to remove rocker arm bolts 2 turns at a time to prevent damage to valves or rocker assembly. Inspect camshaft lobes and bearing journals for wear or damage. Using Plastigage method, check camshaft journal clearance. Check camshaft for runout. If it exceeds .002" (.06 mm), replace camshaft.

Installation — Oil camshaft bearing journals and install camshaft with keyway pointing up (No. 1 piston at TDC). Apply a non-hardening sealer to mating surfaces on end camshaft supports and cylinder head. Set rocker assembly in place and tighten bolts from the center out, two turns at a time until proper torque is reached.

CAMSHAFT

Camshaft Lobe Height

Application	In. (mm)
1335 cc	
Intake	1.4930-1.5025 (37.92-38.16)
Exhaust	1.4942-1.5037 (37.95-38.19)
Auxiliary	1.7316-1.7442 (43.98-44.30)
1487 cc	
Intake	1.4807-1.4901 (37.61-37.85)
Exhaust	1.4819-1.4913 (37.64-37.88)
Auxiliary	1.3214-1.3336 (33.56-33.87)
1751 cc (Exc. Calif. Auto. Trans.)	
Auto. Trans.	
Intake	1.4782-1.4876 (37.55-37.79)
Exhaust	1.4814-1.4909 (37.63-37.87)
Auxiliary	1.7219-1.7345 (43.74-44.06)
Manual Trans.	
Intake	1.4930-1.5025 (37.92-38.16)
Exhaust	1.4962-1.5057 (38.01-38.24)
Auxiliary	1.7219-1.7345 (43.74-44.06)
1751 cc (Calif. Auto. Trans.)	
Intake	1.4930-1.5025 (37.92-38.16)
Exhaust	1.4962-1.5057 (38.01-38.24)
Auxiliary	1.3121-1.3247 (33.33-33.65)

VALVE TIMING

1) Rotate crankshaft until TDC mark on flywheel or driveplate is aligned with index mark. On 1751 cc engines, "UP" mark on camshaft gear should be at 11 o'clock position and timing mark aligned with arrow on cylinder head. See *Fig. 4*.

2) On 1335 cc engines, cutaway in camshaft gear should be at top, and timing marks aligned with valve cover surface. On 1487 cc engines, cutaway should be at top and timing mark aligned with arrow on cylinder head. See *Fig. 5*. Slide timing belt on without disturbing pulley positions and adjust belt tension.

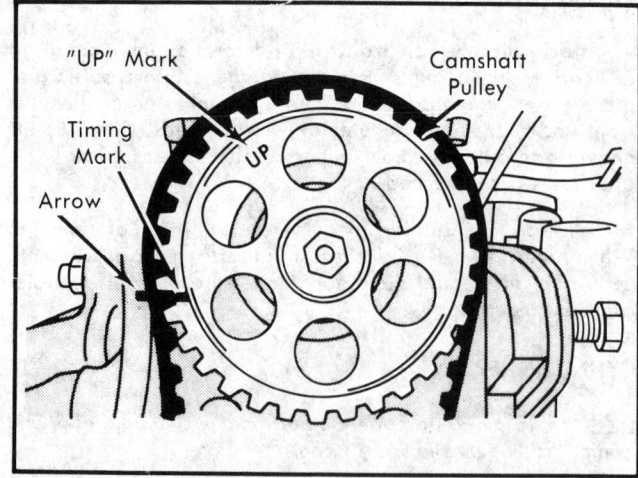

Fig. 4 Camshaft Alignment Marks in Position for Installing Camshaft Belt (1751 cc Engine)

ACCORD, CIVIC, & PRELUDE 4 CYLINDER (Cont.)

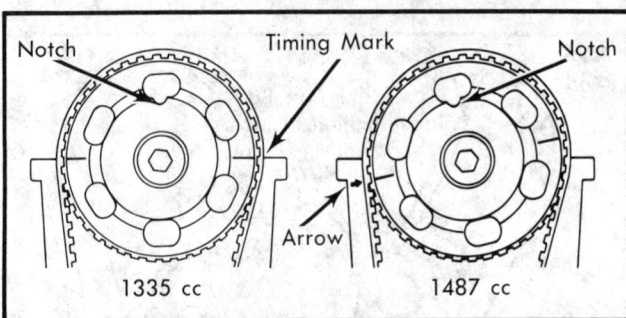

Fig. 5 Camshaft Alignment Marks (1335 & 1487 cc Engines)

TIMING BELT TENSION

Tension is spring loaded to apply proper tension to timing belt automatically after making the following adjustment: Loosen timing belt pivot bolt (upper) and adjusting bolt (lower). Rotate crankshaft approximately ¼ turn counterclockwise to create tension on timing belt. Tighten adjusting bolt, then tighten pivot bolt. Tighten bolts to 32 ft. lbs. (4.3 mkg).

VALVES

VALVE ARRANGEMENT

Rear Side — I-E-E-I-I-E-E-I (left to right).
Front Side — All Auxiliary.

ROCKER ARM ASSEMBLY

Removal — Loosen rocker arm shaft support bolts in criss-cross pattern starting with end supports. Pull out roll pins from both end shaft supports and remove supports, rocker collars, rocker arms and springs. Retain components in proper order for reassembly.

Installation — Measure all rocker arms for arm-to-shaft clearance. If clearance exceeds .0035" (.08 mm), replace rocker shaft and/or arms. Assemble in reverse of disassembly and install rocker arm assembly on engine. Tighten support bolts in a criss-cross pattern starting with center support.

VALVE SPRINGS

Intake & Exhaust Valves — Using valve spring compressor, remove valve keepers, collars and springs. Check valve springs for squareness, free length and tension. Install in reverse of removal procedure, making sure closely wound coils are nearest cylinder head.

AUXILIARY VALVES

1) Remove auxiliary valve holder nut using special "T" wrench (07907-657001) and pull valve holder assembly out of head. Auxiliary chamber collar may be removed with a slide hammer type puller.

2) Compress spring and remove keepers. Disassemble and inspect valve assembly. Valve seat may be reconditioned, however entire assembly should be replaced if any component exceeds service limit.

3) Install chamber collar in each auxiliary valve hole with 2 new gaskets. Use alignment tool (07944-6590000) inserted in round hole toward spark plug opening with oval hole of collar towards combustion chamber. Leave alignment tool in place and insert auxiliary valve with new "O" ring, torquing to final specification with same tool used for removal.

VALVE GUIDE SERVICING

NOTE — *For best results, heat cylinder head to 300°F (150°C) to remove or replace valve guides.*

Using suitable driver, drive valve guides out of cylinder head from port side. Install new guides from top of head with driver and attachment. Drive guide in until attachment bottoms on head. Ream valve guides to provide proper clearance.

VALVE CLEARANCE ADJUSTMENT

Remove valve cover and rotate crankshaft so that No. 1 piston is at TDC on firing stroke. Adjust valve clearance on No. 1 cylinder. Rotate crankshaft 180° COUNTERCLOCKWISE so that No. 3 piston is at TDC, and adjust it's valves. Rotate crankshaft an additional 180°, and adjust valves on cylinder No. 4. Finally, rotate crankshaft an additional 180°, and adjust valves on cylinder No. 2.

Valve Clearance Specifications	
Application	**In. (mm)**
1335 cc and 1487 cc	
Intake and Aux.	.005-.007 (.12-.17)
Exhaust	.007-.009 (.17-.22)
1751 cc	
Intake and Aux.	.005-.007 (.12-.17)
Exhaust	.010-.012 (.25-.30)

PISTONS, PINS & RINGS

PISTON & ROD ASSEMBLY

1) With oil pan and cylinder head removed, ream any ridge from top of cylinders. Mark piston and rod assemblies for proper reinstallation. Remove rod caps and push piston and rod assemblies out top of cylinder with a hammer handle.

2) Assemble piston and connecting rod with piston front mark and connecting rod oil jet hole on same side and facing intake manifold. Using a ring compressor, install piston and rod assemblies in proper cylinder.

NOTE — *Do NOT confuse reference number stamped across bearing cap and connecting rod with number indicating position of assembly in engine. This number indicates rod bore diameter only.*

FITTING PISTONS

1) Measure cylinder bore for taper and out-of-round. If taper exceeds .004" (.1 mm) or out-of-round exceeds .002" (.05 mm), rebore cylinder for oversize pistons. Determine piston-to-cylinder clearance. If not within specifications reboring is necessary. Oversize pistons are available with diameters of 2.84" (72.23 mm) or 1335 cc engines, 2.927 (74.22 mm) for 1487 cc engines, and 3.04" (72.22 mm) for 1751 cc engines.

2) Install 3 piece oil ring on piston with end gaps of rails and spacer staggered about 15°. Install top ring gap approx-

ACCORD, CIVIC, & PRELUDE 4 CYLINDER (Cont.)

imately 90° from oil spacer and second ring gap 180° from spacer. Make sure no end gaps are in line with piston pin or thrust face of piston. Install all rings with markings facing upward.

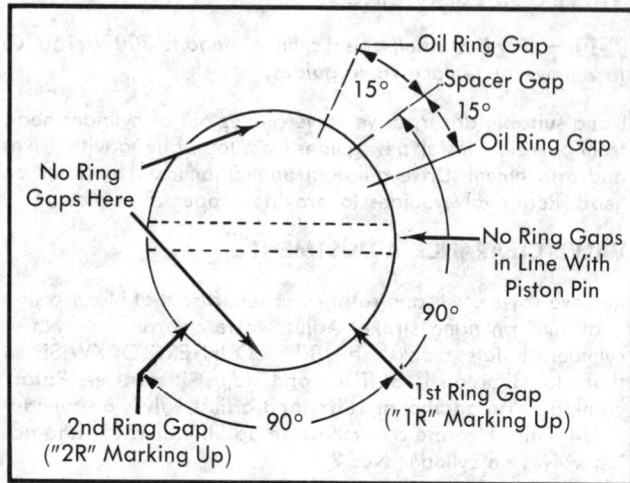

Fig. 6   Piston Ring Installation

PISTON PINS

Using a hydraulic press, remove piston pin from piston and connecting rod. Be sure recessed flat portion aligns with lips on collar. Install new pin by lightly oiling pin and pressing it into connecting rod until centered. Make sure piston is installed with mark on crown on same side as oil hole in connecting rod.

CRANKSHAFT MAIN & CONNECTING ROD BEARINGS

MAIN & CONNECTING ROD BEARINGS

1) Prior to disassembly, mark main and connecting rod bearings caps for reassembly in their original positions and check crankshaft endplay and connecting rod side play. Remove piston and connecting rod assemblies, remove main bearing caps and remove crankshaft.

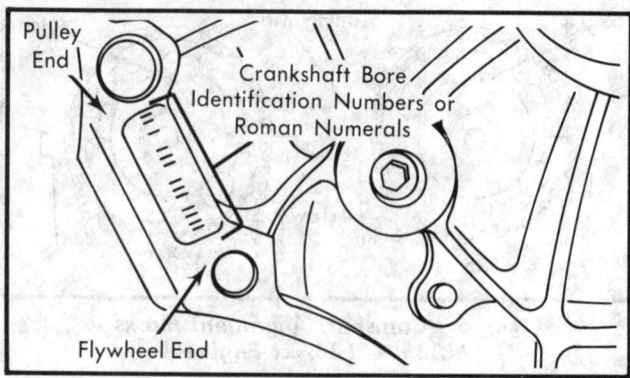

Fig. 7   Crankshaft Identification Locations
(1751 cc and 1487 cc Engines)

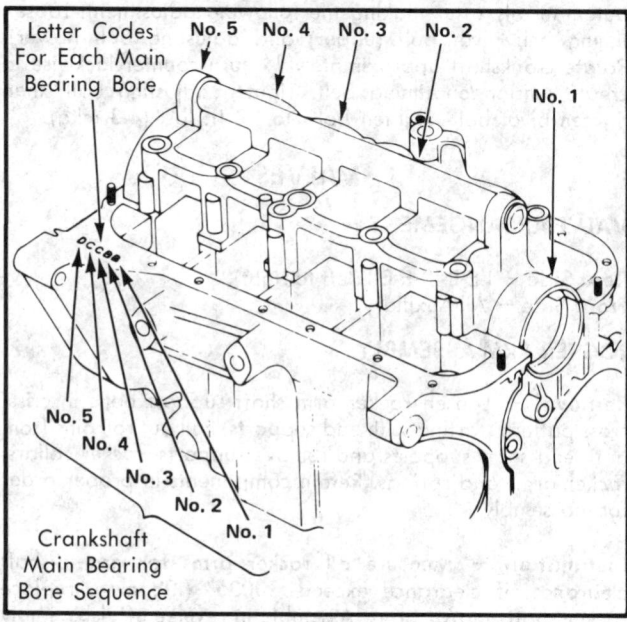

Fig. 8   Crankshaft Identification Locations
(1335 cc Engine)

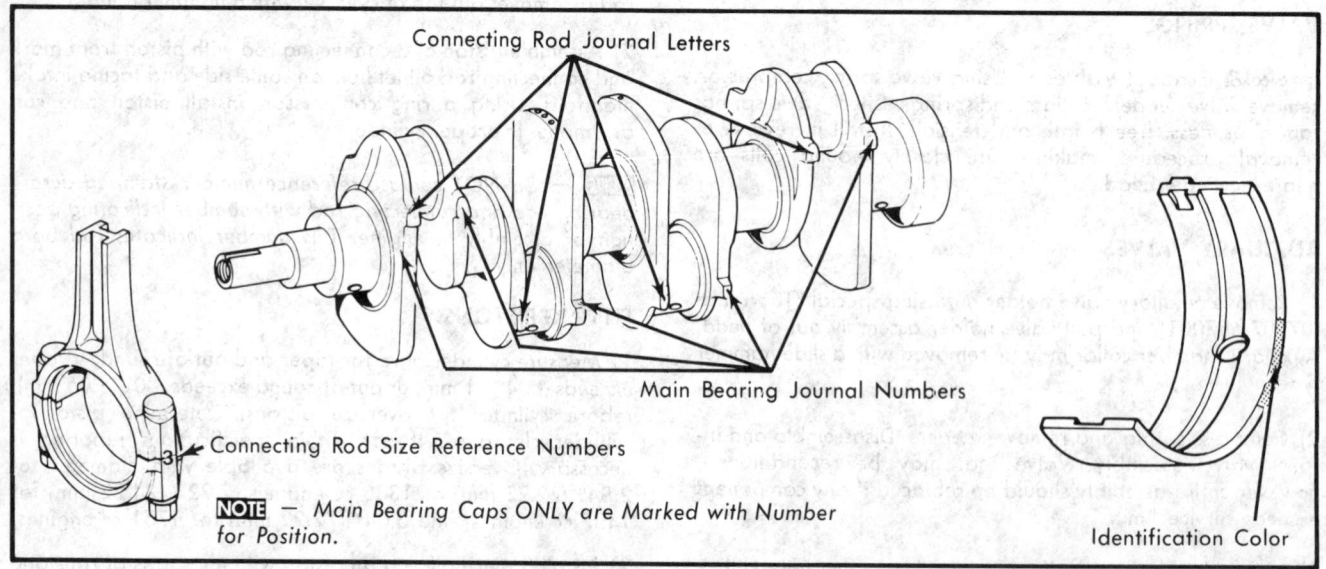

NOTE – Main Bearing Caps ONLY are Marked with Number for Position.

Fig. 9   Connecting Rod Bearing & Cylinder Block Identification Locations

ACCORD, CIVIC, & PRELUDE 4 CYLINDER (Cont.)

2) Measure crankshaft for bend, out-of-round and taper *(See Specifications)*. If any measurement exceeds specifications, crankshaft must be replaced. Do not attempt to regrind crankshaft as bearing journals are specifically heat-treated.

3) Using Plastigage method, determine bearing clearances. If bearing replacement is necessary, use following procedure to determine bearing size to use.

Crankshaft Wear Specifications

Application	Standard In. (mm)	Service Limit In. (mm)
Runout	.0012 (.03)	.0024 (.06)
Taper	.0002 (.005)	.0004 (.010)
Out-Of-Round	.0002 (.005)	.0004 (.010)

4) Referring to *Figs.* 7 and 9, note that all letters stamped on crankshaft counterweight pads apply to nearest connecting rod journal. All numbers stamped on crankshaft counterweight apply to nearest main bearing journal. Connecting rod caps have numbers stamped on cap.

5) The 1751 cc engine has Roman numerals stamped on a pad at flywheel end of engine block indicating each crankshaft bore dimension. The 1487 cc engine has the letters "A", "B", "C", or "D" stamped on a pad at flywheel end of engine block, also indicating each crankshaft bore dimension. The 1335 cc engine block has letters stamped on pads near contact surfaces of block, indicating each main bearing bore dimension. See *Fig. 8.*

6) To determine proper size (color) bearing insert, match crankshaft bore identification numerals or letters with main

CIVIC (1335 cc) MAIN BEARING JOURNALS In. (mm)

Journal Dia. 1.97 (50) \ Crankcase Bore Dia. 2.13 (54)	A ①0 to +.0002 (0 to +.006) ②-.0004 to -.0002 (-.010 to -.004)	B ①+.0002 to +.0005 (+.006 to +.012) ②-.0002 to +.0001 (-.004 to +.002)	C ①+.0005 to +.0007 (+.012 to +.018) ②+.0001 to +.0003 (+.002 to +.008)	D ①+.0007 to +.0009 (+.018 to +.024) ②+.0003 to +.0006 (+.008 to +.014)
1 -.0002 to 0 (-.006 to 0)	Red -.0001 to -.0002 (-.002 to -.005)	Pink -.0001 to +.00004 (-.002 to +.001)	Yellow +.00004 to +.0002 (+.001 to +.005)	Green +0002 to +.0003 (+.004 to +.007)
2 -.0005 to -.0002 (-.012 to -.006)	Pink -.0001 to +.00004 (-.002 to +.001)	Yellow +.00004 to +.0002 (+.001 to +.004)	Green +.0002 to +.0003 (+.005 to +.007)	Brown +.00004 to +.0003 (+.001 to +.007)
3 -.0007 to -.0005 (-.018 to -.012)	Yellow +.00004 to +.0002 (+.001 to +.005)	Green +.0002 to +.0003 (+.005 to +.007)	Brown +.00004 to +.0003 (+.001 to +.007)	Black +.0004 to +.0005 (+.010 to +.013)
4 -.0009 to -.0007 (-.024 to -.018)	Green +.0002 to +.0003 (+.005 to +.007)	Brown +.00004 to +.0003 (+.001 to +.007)	Black +.0004 to +.0005 (+.010 to +.013)	Blue +.0005 to +.0006 (+.013 to +.016)

① — Bore dia. tolerance for No. 1, 2, 4 or 5.
② — Bore dia. tolerance for No. 3 only.

CIVIC (1476 cc) MAIN BEARING JOURNALS In. (mm)

Journal Dia. 1.97 (50) \ Crankcase Bore Dia. 2.13 (54)	A +.0016 to +.0018 (+.040 to +.046)	B +.0018 to +.0020 (+.046 to +.052)	C +.0020 to +.0023 (+.052 to +.058)	D +.0023 to +.0025 (+.058 to +.064)
1 +.0009 to +.0012 (+.024 to +.030)	Red -.0001 to -.0002 (-.002 to -.005)	Pink -.0001 to +.00004 (-.002 to +.001)	Yellow +.00004 to +.0002 (+.001 to +.005)	Green +0002 to +.0003 (+.004 to +.007)
2 +.0007 to +.0009 (+.018 to +.024)	Pink -.0001 to +.00004 (-.002 to +.001)	Yellow +.00004 to +.0002 (+.001 to +.004)	Green +.0002 to +.0003 (+.005 to +.007)	Brown +.00004 to +.0003 (+.001 to +.007)
3 +.0005 to +.0007 (+.012 to +.018)	Yellow +.00004 to +.0002 (+.001 to +.005)	Green +.0002 to +.0003 (+.005 to +.007)	Brown +.00004 to +.0003 (+.001 to +.007)	Black +.0004 to +.0005 (+.010 to +.013)
4 +.0002 to +.0005 (+.006 to +.012)	Green +.0002 to +.0003 (+.005 to +.007)	Brown +.00004 to +.0003 (+.001 to +.007)	Black +.0004 to +.0005 (+.010 to +.013)	Blue +.0005 to +.0006 (+.013 to +.016)

Honda Engines

ACCORD, CIVIC, & PRELUDE 4 CYLINDER (Cont.)

journal identification numbers in the following tables. Where the column and row intersect, find proper bearing insert. Example: For a main bearing, use "Main Bearing Journals" table. If number stamped on crankshaft is "2", and Roman numeral or letter stamped on block for corresponding journal is "III" or "C" respectively, use a "green" insert.

THRUST BEARINGS

Measure crankshaft end play. If found to be excessive, inspect thrust washers and thrust surface of crankshaft. Replace parts if necessary. Do not change thrust washer thickness by either grinding or shimming.

ACCORD & PRELUDE (1751 cc) MAIN BEARING JOURNALS In. (mm)

Journal Dia. 1.97 (50) / Crankcase Bore Dia. 2.13 (54)	I	II	III	IIII
	+.0016 to +.0018 (+.041 to +.046)	+.0018 to +.0020 (+.046 to +.051)	+.0020 to +.0023 (+.051 to +.058)	+.0023 to +.0025 (+.058 to +.064)
1 +.0009 to +.0012 (+.023 to +.030)	Red −.0001 to −.0002 (−.002 to −.005)	Pink −.0001 to +.00004 (−.002 to +.001)	Yellow +.0002 to +.00004 (+.005 to +.001)	Green +.0002 to +.0003 (+.005 to +.007)
2 +.0007 to +.0009 (+.018 to +.023)	Pink −.0001 to +.00004 (−.002 to +.001)	Yellow +.0002 to +.00004 (+.005 to +.001)	Green +.0002 to +.0003 (+.005 to +.007)	Brown +.00004 to +.0003 (+.001 to +.007)
3 +.0005 to +.0007 (+.013 to +.018)	Yellow +.0002 to +.00004 (+.005 to +.001)	Green +.0002 to +.0003 (+.005 to +.007)	Brown +.00004 to +.0003 (+.001 to +.007)	Black +.0004 to +.0005 (+.010 to +.013)
4 +.0002 to +.0005 (+.005 to +.013)	Green +.0002 to +.0003 (+.005 to +.007)	Brown +.00004 to +.0003 (+.001 to +.007)	Black +.0004 to +.0005 (+.010 to +.013)	Blue +.0005 to +.0006 (+.013 to +.015)

CONNECTING ROD BEARING JOURNALS In. (mm)

Journal Dia. 1.654 (42) 1.57 (40)① / Connecting Rod Dia. 1.77 (45) ①1.69 (43)	1	2	3	4
	0 to +.0002 (0 to +.006)	+.0002 to +.0005 (+.006 to +.012)	+.0005 to +.0007 (+.012 to +.018)	+.0007 to +.0009 (+.018 to +.024)
A 0 to −.0002 (0 to −.006)	Red −.0002 to −.0003 (−.005 to −.008)	Pink −.0001 to −.0002 (−.002 to −.005)	Yellow −.0001 to +.00004 (−.002 to +.001)	Green +.00004 to +.0002 (+.001 to +.004)
B −.0002 to −.0005 (−.006 to −.012)	Pink −.0001 to −.0002 (−.002 to −.005)	Yellow −.0001 to +.00004 (−.002 to +.001)	Green +.00004 to +.0002 (+.001 to +.004)	Brown +.0002 to +.0003 (+.004 to +.007)
C −.0005 to −.0007 (−.012 to −.018)	Yellow −.0001 to +.00004 (−.002 to +.001)	Green +.00004 to +.0002 (+.001 to +.004)	Brown +.0002 to +.0003 (+.004 to +.007)	Black +.0003 to +.0004 (+.007 to +.010)
D −.0007 to −.0009 (−.018 to −.024)	Green +.00004 to +.0002 (+.001 to +.004)	Brown +.0002 to +.0003 (+.004 to +.007)	Black +.0003 to +.0004 (+.007 to +.010)	Blue +.0004 to +.0005 (+.010 to +.013)

① — 1335 cc Engine.

ACCORD, CIVIC, & PRELUDE 4 CYLINDER (Cont.)

ENGINE OILING

ENGINE OILING SYSTEM

A rotor type oil pump draws oil from oil pan and delivers it under pressure through main bearing cradle to main and connecting rod bearings. Oil passes through rods to an oil jet which lubricates pistons and cylinder walls. An oil passage carries oil to camshaft bearings and rocker arms. Oil mist lubricates valve stems.

OIL PUMP

1) Remove oil pan, then oil pump assembly may be removed by removing four long bolts (one bolt under strainer). Pull out relief valve cotter pin and remove seat, spring and valve.

2) Remove two pump body bolts and disassemble pump. Inspect pump for wear or damage. Measure pump operating clearances and relief valve spring free length. Reassemble pump making sure marks on rotors face outward and are adjacent to each other. Place oil pickup in container of oil and operate pump with screwdriver to ensure that it is operating. Place finger over outlet hole and check the pressure is created as pump is turned.

Oil Pump Specifications

Application	Standard In. (mm)	Service Limit In. (mm)
Inner-to-Outer Rotor	.002-.006 (.04-.14)	.008 (.20)
Rotor-to-Body	.0039-.0071 (.10-.18)	.008 (.20)
Rotor End Clearance	.0012-.0039 (.03-.10)	.006 (.15)

Crankcase Capacity (with Filter)

Application	Capacity
Civic (1335 and 1487 cc)	3.2 quarts
Accord & Prelude (1751 cc)	3.7 quarts

NOTE — If oil pump driven gear is to be replaced, camshaft must also be replaced.

Oil Filter — Disposable with built-in by-pass valve

Pressure Regulator Valve — Non-adjustable

Normal Oil Pressure — 1335 cc & 1487 cc engines, at operating temperature, minimum of 20 psi (1.41 kg/cm²) at idle and 48-60 psi (3.37-4.22 kg/cm²) at 3000 RPM. For 1751 cc engine, at operating temperature, minimum of 21 psi (1.48 kg/cm²) at idle and 54-60 (3.80-4.22 kg/cm²) at 3000 RPM.

ENGINE COOLING

Thermostat — Starts to open at 176-183°F (80-84°C) and is fully open at 203°F (95°C).

Thermoswitch — Operates at 191-197°F (88.5-91.5°C).

Cooling System Capacity

Application	Capacity (Qts.)
Civic	
1335 cc	5.2
1487 cc	6.4
Accord & Prelude (1751 cc)	6.4

WATER PUMP

Removal — Drain radiator and loosen alternator adjusting bolts. Push alternator toward engine and remove drive belt. Remove water pump and "O" ring seal.

Installation — 1) Reinstall water pump. Loosen cooling system bleed valve located on thermostat housing. Fill radiator with coolant. When air bubbles no longer appear in coolant draining from bleed valve, close valve.

2) Start engine and place heater temperature control lever in high position. Run engine about ten minutes. Again open bleed valve and bleed system until there are no air bubbles in coolant draining from bleed valve. Refill radiator.

ENGINE SPECIFICATIONS

GENERAL SPECIFICATIONS

Year	Displ.		Carburetor	HP at RPM	Torque (Ft. Lbs. at RPM)	Compr. Ratio	Bore		Stroke	
	cu. ins.	cc					in.	mm	in.	mm
1980 Civic	81	1335	1 x 3-Bbl.	.....	.....	7.9:1	2.83	72.0	3.23	82.0
	91	1487	1 x 3-Bbl.	.....	.....	9.0:1	2.91	74.0	3.41	86.5
Accord & Prelude	107	1751	1 x 3-Bbl.	.....	.....	8.0:1	3.03	77.0	3.70	94.0

Honda Engines

ACCORD, CIVIC, & PRELUDE 4 CYLINDER (Cont.)

ENGINE SPECIFICATIONS (Cont.)

VALVES							
Engine & Valve	Head Diam. In. (mm)	Face Angle	Seat Angle	Seat Width In. (mm)	Stem Diameter In. (mm)	Stem Clearance In. (mm)	Valve Lift In. (mm)
1335 cc							
Intake	1.374-1.382 (34.9-35.1)	45°	45°	.055-.061 (1.4-1.55)	.2591-.2594 (6.58-6.59)	.0008-.0020 (.02-.05)	.....
Exhaust	1.098-1.106 (27.9-28.1)	45°	45°	.055-.061 (1.4-1.55)	.2574-.2578 (6.537-6.547)	.0025-.0037 (.063-.093)	.....
Auxiliary	.469-.476 (11.9-12.1)	45°	45°	.0139-.0194 (.353-.494)	.215-.216 (5.472-5.487)	.0009-.0023 (.023-.058)	.....
1487 cc							
Intake	1.374-1.382 (34.9-35.1)	45°	45°	.055-.061 (1.4-1.55)	.2591-.2594 (6.58-6.59)	.0008-.0020 (.02-.05)	.....
Exhaust	1.098-1.106 (27.9-28.1)	45°	45°	.055-.061 (1.4-1.55)	.2574-2578 (6.537-6.547)	.0025-.0037 (.063-.093)	.....
Auxiliary	.469-.476 (11.9-12.1)	45°	45°	.0139-.0194 (.353-.494)	.2580-.2593 (6.572-6.587)	.0009-.0023 (.023-.058)	.....
1751 cc							
Intake	1.335-1.343① (33.9-34.1)	45°	45°	.049-.061 (1.25-1.55)	.2748-.2751 (6.98-6.99)	.0008-.0020 (.02-.05)	.....
Exhaust	1.098-1.106 (27.9-28.1)	45°	45°	.049-.061 (1.25-1.55)	.273-.274 (6.94-6.95)	.0024-.0035 (.06-.09)	.....
Auxiliary	.469-.476 (11.9-12.1)	45°	45°	.008-.020 (.20-.50)	.2580-.2593 6.572-6.587	.0009-.0023 (.023-.058)	.....

① — Calif. automatic — 1.37-1.38" (34.9-35.1 mm)

PISTONS, PINS, RINGS						
	PISTONS	PINS		RINGS		
Engine	Clearance In. (mm)	Piston Fit In. (mm)	Rod Fit In. (mm)	Rings	End Gap In. (mm)	Side Clearance In. (mm)
1335 cc	.0004-.0020 (.01-.05)	.0004-.0009 (.010-.022)	.0006-.0015 (.016-.039)	No. 1	.006-.014 (.15-.35)	.0008-.0018 (.020-.045)
				No. 2	.006-.014 (.15-.35)	.0008-.0018 (.020-.045)
				Oil	.012-.035 (.3-.9)	.....
1487 cc	.0004-.0024 (.01-.06)	.0004-.0009 (.010-.022)	.0006-.0016 (.014-.040)	No 1	.006-.014 (.15-.35)	.0008-.0018 (.020-.045)
				No. 2	.006-.014 (.15-.35)	.0008-.0018 (.020-.045)
				Oil	.012-.035 (.3-.9)	.....
1751 cc	.0008-.0028 (.02-.07)	.0004-.0009 (.010-.022)	.0006-.0016 (.014-.040)	No. 1 & 2	.006-.014 (.15-.35)	.0008-.0018 (.020-.045)
				Oil	.012-.035 (.3-.9)	.....

ACCORD, CIVIC, & PRELUDE 4 CYLINDER (Cont.)
ENGINE SPECIFICATIONS (Cont.)

CRANKSHAFT MAIN & CONNECTING ROD BEARINGS

| Engine | MAIN BEARINGS | | | | CONNECTING ROD BEARINGS | | |
	Journal Diam. In. (mm)	Clearance In. (mm)	Thrust Bearing	Crankshaft End Play In. (mm)	Journal Diam. In. (mm)	Clearance In. (mm)	Side Play In. (mm)
1335 cc	1.9687-1.9697 (50.006-50.030)	.0009-.0017 (.024-.042)	No. 4	.004-.014 (.10-.35)	1.69 (43)	.0008-0015 (.020-.038)	.006-.012 (.15-.30)
1487 cc	1.9687-1.9697 (50.006-50.030)	.0010-.0022 (.026-.055)	No. 4	.004-.014 (.10-.35)	1.77 (45)	.0008-.0015 (.020-.038)	.006-.012 (.15-.30)
1751 cc	1.9687-1.9697 (50.006-50.030)	.0010-.0017 (.026-.044)	No. 4	.004-.014 (.10-.35)	1.77 (45)	.0008-.0015 (.020-.038)	.006-.012 (.15-.30)

VALVE SPRINGS

| Engine | Free Length In. (mm) | PRESSURE Lbs. @ In. (kg @ mm) | |
		Valve Closed	Valve Open
1335 cc & 1487 cc Intake			
Inner	1.858 (47.2)	18@1.402 (8@35.6)	40@1.008 (18@25.6)
Outer	.200 (50.8)	50@1.488 (22@37.8)	100@1.094 (45@27.8)
Exhaust			
Inner	1.858 (47.2)	18@1.402 (8@35.6)	40@1.008 (18@25.6)
Outer	.200 (50.8)	50@1.488 (22@37.8)	100@1.094 (45@27.8)
Auxiliary			
1335 cc	1.146 (29.1)	16@.906 (7@23.0)	23@.787 (10@20.0)
1487 cc	1.122 (28.5)	15@.984 (7@25.0)	29@.866 (13@22.0)
1751 cc Intake			
Inner	1.665 (42.3)	9@1.402 (4@35.6)	31@1.008 (14@25.6)
Outer	1.665 (42.3)	28@1.488 (13@37.8)	108@1.094 (49@27.8)
Exhaust			
Inner	1.665 (42.3)	9@1.402 (4@35.6)	31@1.008 (14@25.6)
Outer	1.665 (42.3)	28@1.488 (13@37.8)	108@1.094 (49@27.8)
Auxiliary Calif. A/T	1.17 (29.7)	15@.984 (7@25.0)	33@.87 (15@22.0)
Others	1.122 (28.5)	15@.984 (7@25.0)	29@.866 (13@22.0)

CAMSHAFT

Engine	Journal Diam. In. (mm)	Clearance In. (mm)	Lobe Lift In. (mm)
1335 cc, 1487 cc & 1751 cc	.....	.002-.004 (.05-.098)	.002-.006 (.05-.15)

TIGHTENING SPECIFICATIONS

Application	Ft. Lbs. (mkg)
Connecting Rod Bolts	23 (3.2)
Main Bearing Bolts	48 (6.6)
Cylinder Head Bolts	43 (6.0)
Camshaft Sprocket Bolt	22 (3.0)
Intake-to-Exhaust Manifold Bolts	18 (2.5)
Manifold Nuts	16 (2.2)
Rocker Arm Support	
6 mm Bolts	9 (1.2)
8 mm Bolts	16 (2.2)
Tie Rod Ends	32 (4.4)
Stabilizer Bar Ends	32 (4.4)
Stabilizer Bar Brackets	28 (3.9)
Lower Arm Ball Joints	
Civic	25 (3.5)
Accord and Prelude	33 (4.5)

XJ6 6 CYLINDER

ENGINE CODING

ENGINE IDENTIFICATION

Engine can be identified by the number stamped on top of cylinder block at rear of engine and on identification plate in engine compartment.

ENGINE & CYLINDER HEAD

ENGINE

NOTE — *Engine and transmission are removed as an assembly.*

Removal — **1)** Remove hood and disconnect battery. Discharge air conditioning system. Disconnect and cap refrigerant lines. Remove fuel lines from fuel cooler and plug fuel inlet line. Remove fuel cooler mounting screws and secure cooler, receiver-drier, refrigerant lines and fuel lines away from engine.

2) Remove fender brace rods. Remove air cleaner. Detach and remove radiator. Disconnect coolant hoses to expansion tank. Remove both engine mount-to-bracket nuts. Drain power steering fluid. Disconnect power steering lines. Slacken pump mounting bolts and push pump as close as possible to engine.

3) Pull connectors from alternator. Separate connector plug from engine harness. Disconnect brake vacuum pipe at manifold, and secure pipe out of way. Release pipe clip and pull heater-A/C operating vacuum pipe from non-return valves; secure away from engine. Remove exhaust manifolds.

4) Remove starter cable and solenoid cable. Disconnect heater hoses at firewall connectors. From fuel injection system, disconnect the following: Thermotime switch, cold start injector, throttle switch, oxygen sensor, auxiliary air valve, water temperature sensor and throttle linkage. Disconnect hoses from charcoal canister.

5) Position suitable lifting device and attach to rear lifting eye on engine. Remove nut at center of rear transmission mounting. Unscrew nuts securing bracket on transmission. Remove heat shield. Position jack to support mounting plate of transmission and unscrew mounting bolts. Lower jack and remove mounting plate along with spring washers and rubber rings.

6) Remove special nuts securing propeller shaft to output flange. From transmission unit selector lever, remove nut to release ball peg on inner selector cable. Remove setscrew and spring washer securing outer selector cable clamp. Disconnect speedometer cable from transmission.

7) From front of vehicle, position jack to support transmission assembly below oil sump. Support engine on lifting assembly. Lift front of engine while lowering rear and withdraw engine/transmission assembly forward and upward.

CAUTION — *Use extreme care when withdrawing engine to prevent damage to air conditioning expansion valve.*

Installation — Fit insulating material across transmission and reverse removal procedure to complete installation. Ensure that all fluid levels are to specifications. Evacuate and charge air conditioning system.

CYLINDER HEAD

Removal — **1)** Disconnect battery and drain cooling system. Remove both wing valance stays (firewall-to-fender support rods), removing pressure line from support rod. Remove air cleaner. Detach throttle linkage and disconnect thermotime switch, cold start injector, throttle switch, oxygen sensor, auxiliary air valve and water temperature sensor.

2) Disconnect and plug fuel lines at fuel cooler (heat exchanger) and move cooler to side of engine compartment. Remove heat shield from exhaust manifold. Remove steering pump drive belt and swing pump away from engine. Remove top radiator hose and pull remote header and radiator bleed lines from header tank. Disconnect coolant hose from water pump.

3) Disconnect any remaining lines or wires from intake manifold, noting position for assembly. Detach exhaust manifolds from head. Remove distributor cap, spark plugs and plug wires. Disconnect 2 camshaft oil lines from rear of head and remove camshaft covers. Detach breather housing from front of head.

4) Remove camshaft sprocket retaining bolts from both camshafts and slide sprockets up support brackets. Mark aligning holes in adjuster plates. Working from center outward, remove cylinder head bolts. Carefully lift cylinder head assembly from engine.

CAUTION — *Crankshaft must NOT be rotated after camshaft sprockets are disconnected and head is still in place. When head is removed, it must not rest on a flat surface. Support head with wooden blocks at each end to protect open valves which protrude.*

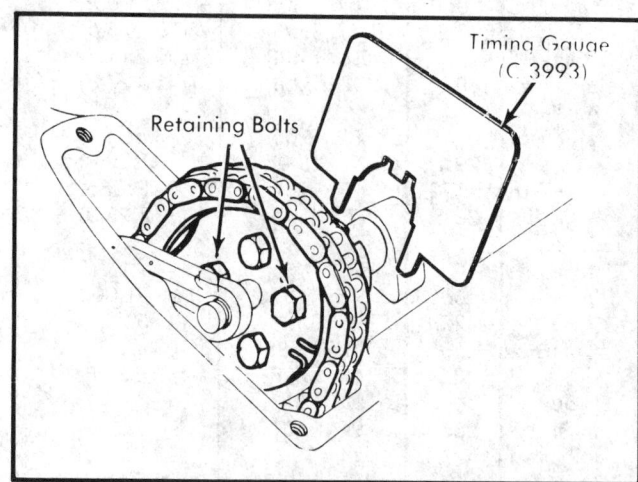

Fig. 1   Retaining Bolts Installed to Hold Camshaft During Cylinder Head Installation

Installation — **1)** Install new head gasket (ensuring "TOP" mark is upward). Rotate crankshaft until No. 6 cylinder (front) is at TDC, with rotor pointing approximately forward along engine.

2) Rotate camshafts until suitable timing gauge (C.3993) can be located in front flange slots. See Fig. 1. Lower cylinder head into position, attach spark plug wire brackets and lifting brackets to appropriate head studs, then place washers and

XJ6 6 CYLINDER (Cont.)

14 large domed nuts on stud. Affix nuts and washers at forward end of head, then tighten all nuts. See Fig. 2.

3) Locate sprockets on camshaft flanges and ensure both holes in each flange are positioned with aligning holes marked during removal. If necessary, remove circlip and reposition adjuster plate. Make sure engine is not rotated until camshaft sprockets are fully seated and chain installed.

4) Secure each adjuster plate to camshaft, then rotate engine until remaining attachment holes are accessible. Install bolts and bend up lock plate tabs. Set timing chain tension using a suitable adjusting tool (JD2B). Tighten lock nut.

5) Ensure No. 6 (front) cylinder is at TDC and recheck position of camshafts using timing gauge (C.3993). Complete installation by reversing remainder of removal procedures. Recheck ignition timing and perform exhaust emission check.

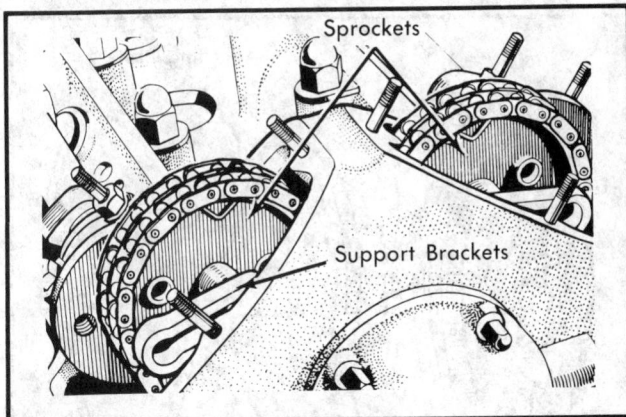

Fig. 3 Camshaft Sprockets in Disconnected Position

ENGINE FRONT COVER & OIL SEAL

Removal — 1) Remove radiator and fan belt. Mark position of vibration damper for reassembly. Remove pulley. Using a pair of levers, pry damper off of split cone. Remove split cone from crankshaft.

2) Remove oil pan and water pump. Unscrew screws attaching timing cover and slide timing cover and oil seal off of crankshaft.

Installation — 1) Place new seal in groove in timing cover. Using a new gasket and sealing compound, intall timing cover and seal. Reinstall oil pan with a new gasket. Install short screw in front right hand corner of oil pan.

2) Reinstall split cone on crankshaft. Position crankshaft damper to mark, install pulley and torque attaching bolts to specifications. Reinstall remaining components in reverse of removal procedures.

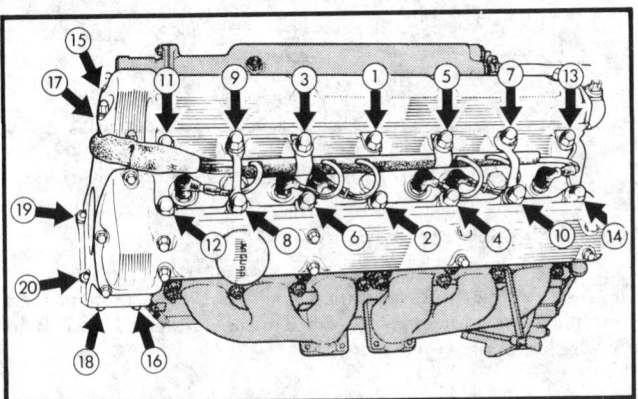

Fig. 2 Jaguar XJ6 Cylinder Head Tightening Sequence

CAMSHAFTS

CAMSHAFTS

Removal — 1) Remove camshaft covers and detach breather housing from front of head. Using suitable tool (JD.2B), slacken timing chain by rotating tool clockwise. Remove camshaft sprocket retaining bolts from each sprocket, rotating crankshaft as necessary to gain access to remaining bolts.

2) Rotate crankshaft further until timing gauge (C.3993) can be installed. Draw sprockets off camshaft and slide up support brackets. Mark attachment holes in adjuster plate for assembly reference. Remove camshaft bearing caps and withdraw camshaft.

CAUTION — Crankshaft MUST NOT be rotated after camshaft sprockets are removed.

Installation — To install, reverse removal procedure, ensuring that all components are replaced in original position.

NOTE — If preceding instructions have not been followed, it will be necessary to ensure that valve timing is still correct. See Valve Timing.

VALVE TIMING

1) Rotate engine so that No. 6 (front) piston is at TDC on compression stroke and distributor rotor arm points to No. 6 segment. Check that timing chains are properly adjusted. See Timing Chain Replacement.

2) Remove lock wire from camshaft sprocket screws. Rotate crankshaft until inaccessible screws can be removed. Return engine to TDC of No. 6 piston and remove retaining screws. Tap camshaft sprockets off camshaft flanges.

3) Position camshafts accurately with valve timing gauge, and check that TDC marks are in exact alignment. See Fig. 1. Withdraw clips from camshaft sprockets and press adjusting plates forward until serrations disengage. See Fig. 4.

4) Replace sprockets on flanges of camshaft and align two holes in adjuster plate with holes in flanges. Engage serrations of adjuster plates with serrations in sprocket.

NOTE — Screw holes must be in exact alignment. If difficulty is experienced in aligning holes turn adjuster plates 180° and realign holes.

5) Replace circlips in camshaft sprockets. Replace camshaft sprocket screws and lock wire. Recheck valve timing.

XJ6 6 CYLINDER (Cont.)

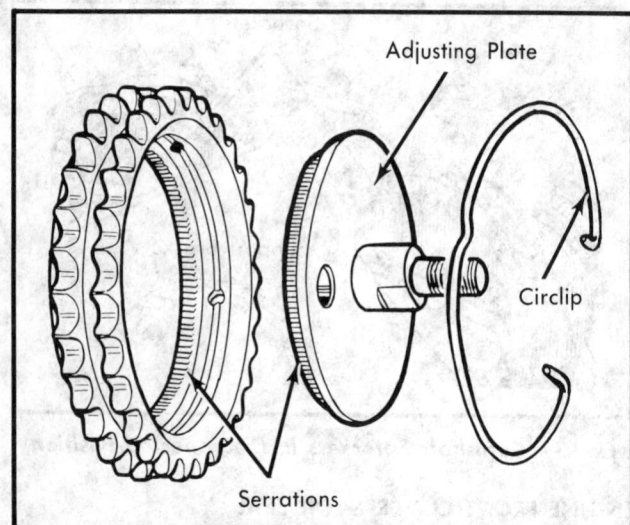

Fig. 4   Expanded View of Camshaft Sprocket Assembly

VALVES

VALVE ARRANGEMENT

Left Side — All exhaust.
Right Side — All intake.

VALVE GUIDE SERVICING

Check valve guide for wear and proper guide-to-valve stem clearance. If guide is worn beyond specifications, replace guide by heating head in boiling water for approximately 30 minutes (or by other suitable method), then drive guide(s) out of head from combustion chamber end. Coat new guide with graphite grease and refit circlip. Reheat head and drive new guide in from top until circlip is seated in groove.

NOTE — *When installing oversize replacement guides, check O.D. of guide to be used. If necessary, ream cylinder head bore to obtain proper interference fit.*

Replacement Valve Guides

Application	Size Mark	Dimension In. (mm)
Standard	No Mark	.501-.502 (12.73-12.75)
1st Oversize	1 Groove	.503-.504 (12.78-12.80)
2nd Oversize	2 Grooves	.506-.507 (12.85-12.87)
3rd Oversize	3 Grooves	.511-.512 (12.98-13.00)

VALVE SPRING SERVICING

CAUTION — *Support ends of cylinder head with wooden blocks to prevent damage to valves. Opened valves protrude below face of cylinder head.*

1) Remove camshaft bearing caps, note markings for reassembly. Remove camshaft, tappets and adjusting pads. Retain tappets and pads in proper order for reassembly.

2) Install suitable spring compressor (Churchill No. JD.6118C) and a block of wood between valve and work table. Compress springs and remove valve keepers. Compare old spring with new spring or with specification table. Replace springs as necessary. To install, reverse procedure.

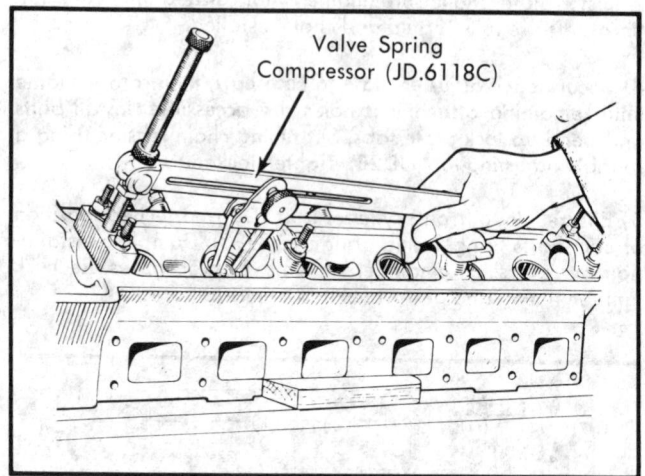

Fig. 5   Valve Spring Compressor Tool Installation

VALVE TAPPET SERVICE

NOTE — *Valves and operating mechanisms are numbered and must be kept in order when disassembled. No. 1 is at flywheel end of engine.*

1) Remove tappets and adjusting pads and inspect guides, tappets and pads for wear. If tappet guide is to be replaced, bore out old guide until it collapses, using care not to damage head bore. Ensure head is at room temperature and measure head bore of tappet guide.

2) Grind replacement guide to obtain a .003" (.076 mm) interference fit in head. Grind same amount from "lead-in" at bottom end of guide. Heat head and install tappet guide, ensuring that lip at top guide seats evenly in head recess. Allow to cool and ream guide bore to 1.375" (34.93 mm). Replace other parts as necessary.

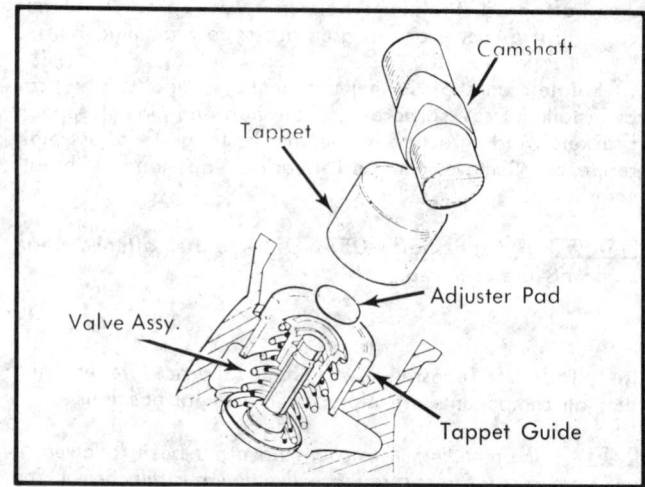

Fig. 6   Valve Tappet and Guide Assembly

XJ6 6 CYLINDER (Cont.)

VALVE TAPPET CLEARANCE

NOTE — *If checking valve clearances with cylinder head removed, the camshafts must be installed and checked one at a time. It is imperative that this be followed, as position fouling is likely if camshafts are rotated independently while both are installed.*

1) If not already done, remove camshaft covers. Rotate camshaft and record clearance between heel of each cam and its respective tappet. If head is installed, and adjustment is to be made, rotate camshaft and install valve timing gauge (C.3993) before removing final camshaft retaining bolt. If required, disconnect sprockets from camshafts. See *Valve Timing.*

2) Remove camshaft bearing caps and lift off camshaft. Remove each tappet that requires adjustment and note its location for assembly in original position. Remove adjusting pad and measure thickness.

3) Use measured pad thickness and difference between measured valve clearance and specified clearance to calculate required thickness of new adjusting pad. Adjusting pads are available in increments of .001" (.03 mm) from .085" (2.16 mm) to .110" (2.79 mm) and are marked with letters from "A" to "Z" respectively.

4) Insert correct adjusting pads and install tappets. Attach camshafts (using timing gauge). Torque camshaft bearing cap nuts to 9 ft. lbs. (1.2 mkg), connect camshaft sprockets, and install camshaft covers.

PISTONS, PINS & RINGS

OIL PAN

NOTE — *Oil pan removal is best accomplished with engine out of vehicle. Following procedures may be used with engine installed.*

Removal & Installation — Remove front suspension components to gain access and suitable clearance. Drain engine oil. Remove oil return pipe nuts and transmission oil cooler line clips. Remove screws and nuts holding pan to engine and remove pan. To install, ensure that all mating surfaces are clean. Lightly grease seals and gaskets and install pan. Reverse removal procedure to complete installation.

NOTE — *Do NOT trim seal ends. Press into groove until flush. Oil return pipe must have new "O" ring and fit in sump properly. Ensure that short screw is replaced in right front corner of pan.*

PISTON & ROD ASSEMBLY

NOTE — *Piston/connecting rod assemblies are numbered to their corresponding position in engine. No. 1 cylinder is at rear of engine.*

Removal — With cylinder head and oil pan (sump) removed, unscrew nuts from connecting rods and remove bearing caps. Remove bolts from connecting rods and push piston/rod assembly out top of cylinder.

Installation — Use suitable ring compressor and insert piston/rod assembly so that "FRONT" stamp on piston is toward front of engine. If installing new parts, stamp-mark with numbers "1" through "6" corresponding to the bore in

which they are installed. Liberally coat bearing shells and journals with oil and complete installation in reverse order of removal.

PISTON RINGS

After checking ring end gap and side play, install compression rings in top two grooves and oil ring in bottom groove. Both compression rings have tapered peripheries and are marked with "TOP" to ensure correct installation. The top ring is also chrome-plated and cargraph (red) coated; the red coating must NOT be removed. When fitting oil ring, ensure expander ends do not overlap.

PISTON PINS

When removing and replacing piston pins, immerse assembly in hot oil bath (or use other suitable method) to bring piston end of assembly to approximately 230°F (110°C). When installing pins, always use new pin circlips. Note that pins are color coded for grading purposes. Always select proper color pin for replacement.

FITTING PISTONS

Check piston and cylinder bore to determine if proper clearance exists. If necessary to rebore cylinder for installation of oversize piston, note that reboring is not to exceed .030" (.76 mm). Oversize pistons are available in .010", .020", and .030" (.25 mm, .51 mm, and .76 mm) oversizes. If replacing pistons with standard sizes (no reboring), note the following list of piston grades and select replacement piston of same grade. Piston grade is stamped in piston crown and on top face of block adjacent to cylinder.

Standard Piston Grading

Stamp Mark	Cylinder Diameter In. (mm)
F	3.6250-3.6253 (92.075-92.083)
G	3.6254-3.6257 (92.085-92.093)
H	3.6258-3.6261 (92.095-92.103)
J	3.6262-3.6265 (92.106-92.113)
K	3.6266-3.6269 (92.116-92.123)

CYLINDER LINERS

1) Should piston-to-cylinder clearance be excessive and reboring requires more than .030" (.76 mm) to clean up cylinders, new cylinder liners must be installed.

2) Press out the worn liners from below, using a suitable block. Lightly coat outer top half of new liner with a jointing compound, then press in new liner until flush with top of block. Smear more jointing compound around area of liner-to-block mating surface.

3) Bore out liner to correspond with grade of piston to be installed. Following reboring process, the blanking plugs in the main oil gallery should be removed and cylinder block oilways

XJ6 6 CYLINDER (Cont.)

thoroughly cleaned. When dry, coat interior of crankcase with an oil and heat resistant paint.

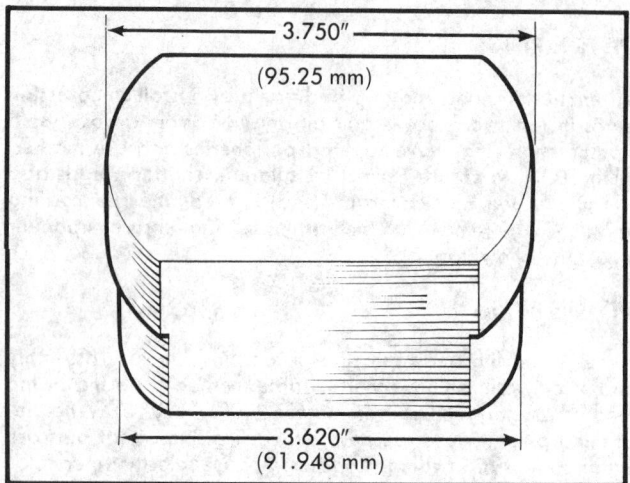

Fig. 7   Cylinder Liner Removing and Installing Block

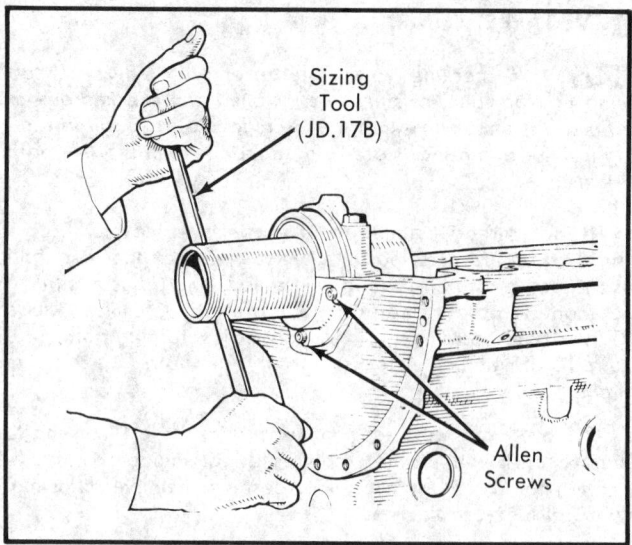

Fig. 8   Sizing Rear Oil Seal

CRANKSHAFT MAIN & CONNECTING ROD BEARINGS

THRUST BEARING ALIGNMENT

Thrust bearing washers are used on center main bearing caps to adjust endplay. If beyond specifications, bearings .004″ (.10 mm) oversize as well as standard are available. Install with white metal side (with groove) outwards.

MAIN BEARING SERVICE

Remove connecting rod and main bearing caps, retaining all parts in exact order for reassembly. Note that all caps are numbered for reassembly reference. When wear or out-of-roundness exceeds .003″ (.08 mm), regrind crankshaft and install undersize bearings. Bearings are available in .010″, .020″, .030″, and .040″ (.25 mm, .51 mm, .76 mm, and 1.02 mm) undersizes. If regrinding must exceed .040″ (1.02 mm), replace crankshaft.

REAR MAIN BEARING OIL SEAL

NOTE − *The following procedure must be performed before crankshaft is reinstalled.*

1) Carefully tap new rear oil seal halves into position, then roll seal into housing (with a hammer handle) until ends do not protrude. **NOTE** − *DO NOT cut seal ends.* When both halves are properly in place, secure them with Allen screws.

2) Attach rear main bearing cap without bearings and torque to 72 ft. lbs. (10 mkg). Assemble rear oil seal housing to cylinder block, using three Allen screws. Lightly coat inside surface of oil seal with graphite grease and insert a suitable sizing tool (JD.17B) as shown in illustration. Press tool inward and turn until it is fully seated; this should properly size the oil seal. Remove sizing tool by pulling and twisting in opposite direction. Remove oil seal housing and install crankshaft.

TIMING CHAIN

TIMING CHAIN REPLACEMENT

Removal − 1) Remove cylinder head, oil pan, water pump, crankcase breather, vibration damper (including cone and Woodruff key), and timing gear cover. Withdraw timing pointer, distance piece, and front oil seal.

2) Remove oil slinger from crankshaft. Unscrew two bottom timing chain tensioner and chain guides retaining screws. Withdraw conical filter behind tensioner. Slacken four setscrews securing top timing chain assembly (do not remove setscrews at this point).

3) Withdraw crankshaft timing sprocket and chain assembly. Be sure to remove spacers, top timing chain damper, and top timing chain retainer. Disengage camshaft sprockets from top chain. Remove nut and serrated washer from idler shaft and withdraw serrated plate, plunger, and spring.

4) Remove nuts retaining front mounting bracket to rear mounting bracket. Remove timing chains from intermediate and idler sprockets. Draw idler shaft, idler sprocket, and bushing from rear mounting bracket. Remove circlip and press intermediate shaft from rear mounting bracket. Note location of bushing and shim under intermediate sprocket.

Installation − 1) Position eccentric idler shaft to hole in front mounting bracket. Position spring and plunger in bracket and locate serrated plate on shaft. Loosely secure plate using washer and nut.

2) Attach idler sprocket (21 teeth) to idler shaft. Replace intermediate sprocket (large gear forward) onto intermediate shaft, placing shim in position. Install shaft assembly in rear mounting bracket, ensuring roll pin engages in slot; retain with circlip.

3) Locate top timing chain (longer) on small intermediate sprocket, and lower timing chain on large sprocket. Loop top chain beneath idler sprocket and secure top mounting bracket to rear bracket.

XJ6 6 CYLINDER (Cont.)

4) Install four long setscrews and spring washers to front mounting bracket and attach dampers, chain support plate, and spacers to setscrews. Equalize loops of top timing chain and locate camshaft sprockets in loops. Rotate eccentric idler shaft to lift idler sprocket to its highest position between camshaft sprockets.

5) Ensure Woodruff key is positioned in crankshaft. Locate crankshaft sprocket, but do not fully seat at this time. Loop bottom timing chain beneath crankshaft sprocket, then tap sprocket until it is fully seated. Position and secure crankshaft sprocket assembly.

6) Install, but do not tighten, bottom timing chain guides. Insert conical filter into its hole in cylinder block. Screw slipper into tensioner until .125″ (3.17 mm) exists between slipper and body. Locate tensioner on shims as necessary to ensure slipper runs central on chain, and secure using two setscrews and lock plate.

7) Place slip gauge or spacer card supplied with new tensioner between slipper and body of tensioner to maintain dimension set earlier, then adjust intermediate damper to touch chain. Tighten setscrews and bend up tabs of lock plate. Remove slip gauge and top chain or tensioner slipper to release ratchet. Position oil slinger on crankshaft. Replace timing cover.

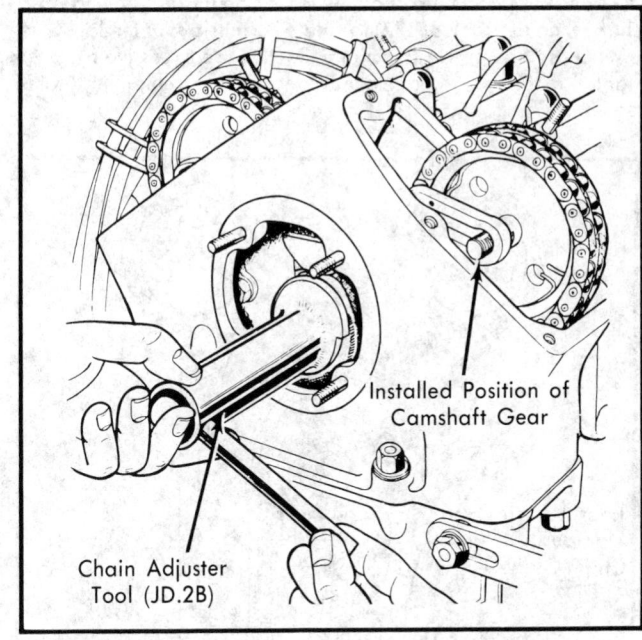

Fig. 10 Adjusting Upper Timing Chain

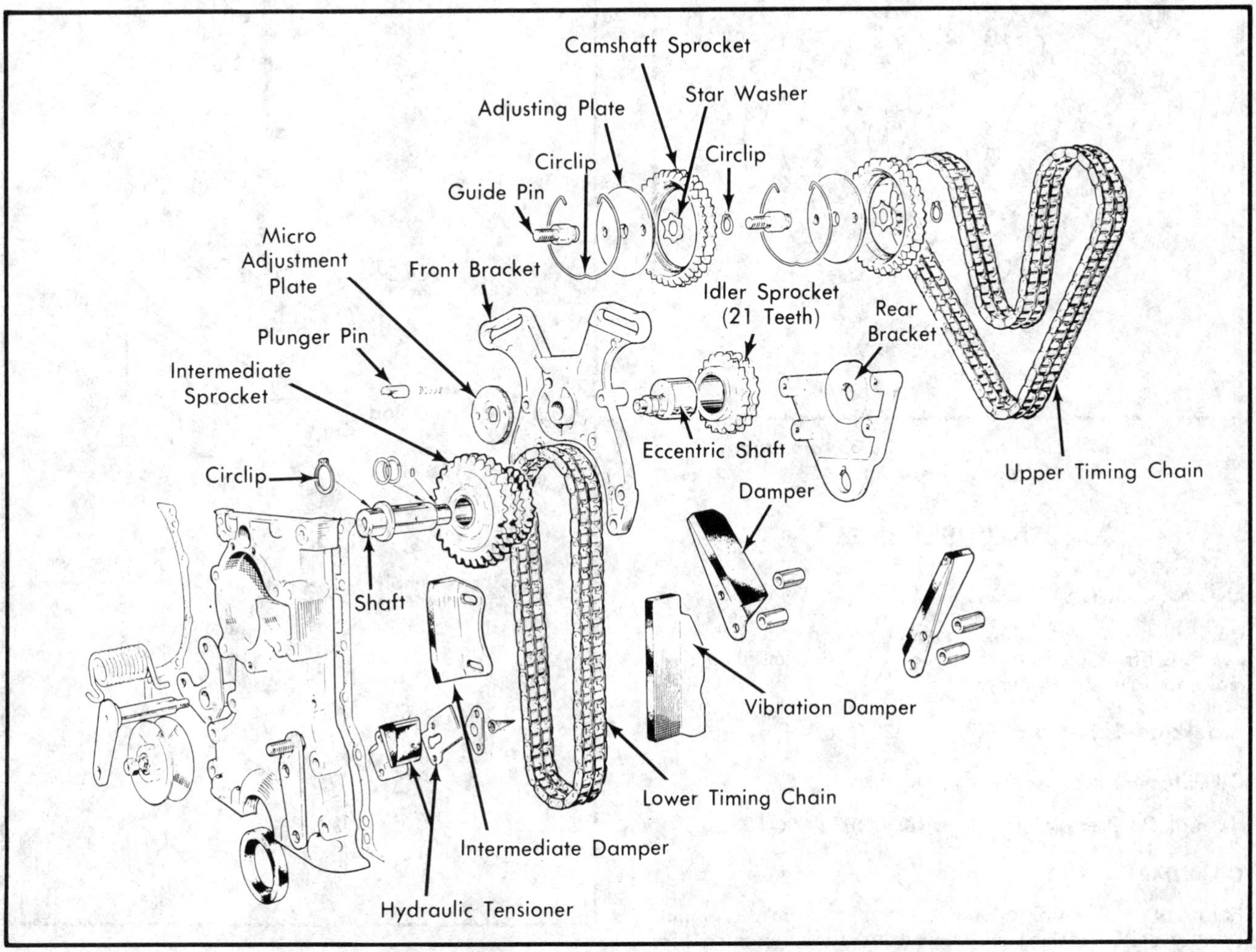

Fig. 9   Exploded View of Timing Gear and Chain Assembly

XJ6 6 CYLINDER (Cont.)

8) Adjust upper timing chain by loosening locknut on eccentric shaft, then use tool (JD.2B) to rotate eccentric counterclockwise until chain has proper tension. DO NOT use excessive force to tighten chain. Tighten lcoknut and install remaining components.

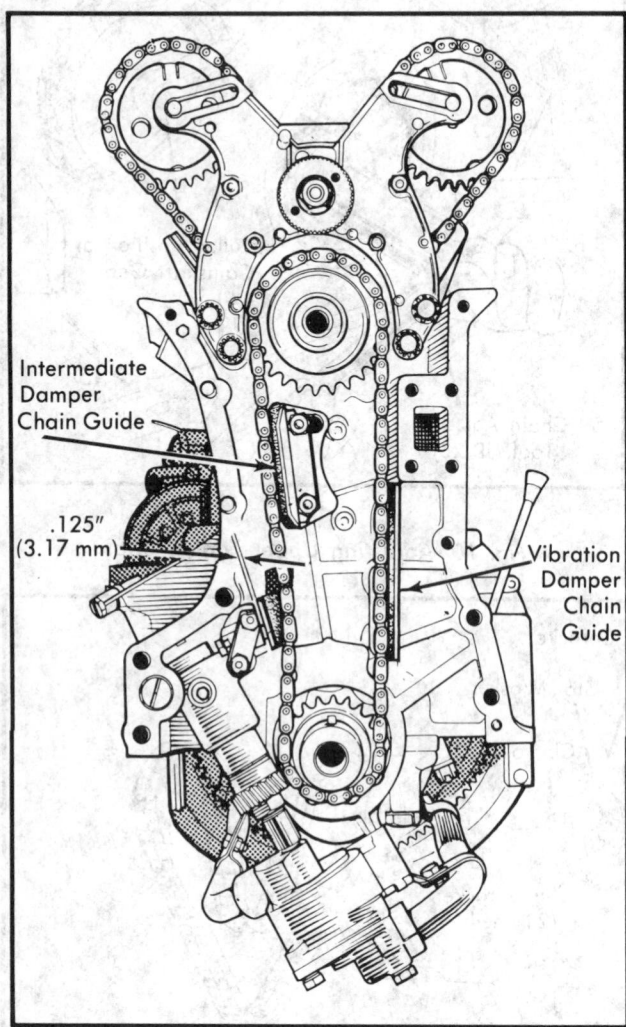

Fig. 11 Lower Timing Chain Adjustment Measuring Point

ENGINE OILING

ENGINE OILING SYSTEM

Lubrication is provided by a gear driven eccentric rotor type pump. Oil from pump goes through a full-flow oil filter to all moving engine components.

Crankcase Capacity — 8.7 quarts.

Oil Filter — Replace every 3,000 miles.

Normal Oil Pressure (Hot) — 40 psi @ 3,000 RPM.

OIL PUMP

Removal — Remove oil pan, suction and delivery pipes. Remove bolts attaching oil pump to front main bearing cap. Withdraw pump and coupling sleeve at top of drive shaft.

Disassembly — 1) Remove bolts and take off bottom cover. Remove inner and outer rotors. Inner rotor is pinned to drive shaft and cannot be disassembled.

2) Check clearances of inner and outer rotor lobes, outer rotor-to-body and rotor-to-cover plate. Place drive shaft in a soft jawed vise and check that rotor is tight on pin.

NOTE — *Drive shaft, inner and outer rotors are supplied as an assembly only.*

Reassembly — Reassemble in reverse order of disassembly. Install outer rotor to pump body with chamfered end forward. Use new "O" rings on suction and delivery pipes. To install, reverse removal procedures.

Oil Pump Specifications

Application	Clearance In. (mm)
Inner-to-Outer Rotor	.006 (.15)
Outer Rotor-to-Body	.010 (.25)
Rotor-to-Cover (End Play)	.0025 (.06)

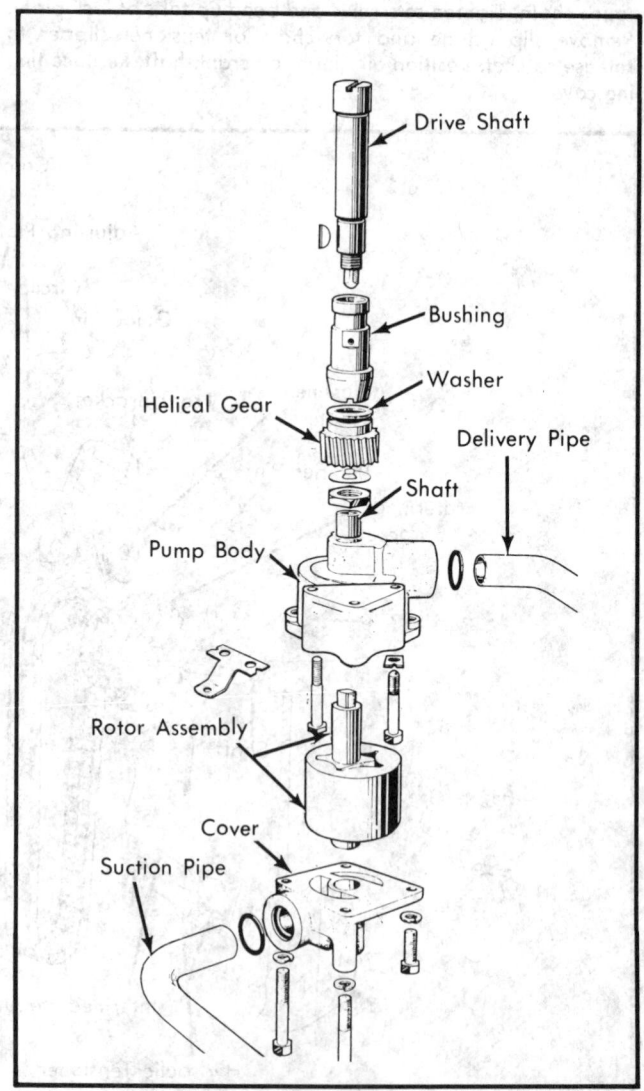

Fig. 12 Exploded View of Jaguar Oil Pump

XJ6 6 CYLINDER (Cont.)

ENGINE COOLING

WATER PUMP

Disassembly — 1) Remove water pump and gasket from timing cover. Pull fan hub from shaft with a puller. Loosen lock nut and remove Allen locating screw.

2) Using an arbor press and a tube measuring 1.094" (27.79 mm) O.D. and .969" (24.60 mm) I.D., press shaft and impeller assembly out of pump body.

3) Press shaft from impeller and remove seal and rubber thrower. Spindle and bearing assembly cannot be further disassembled.

4) Clean and inspect all parts for wear or damage. Bearing is sealed and lubricated, therefore do not wash in solvents.

Reassembly — 1) Install shaft and bearing assembly into pump body from rear. Align and install locating screw and lock nut. Place rubber thrower in its groove on shaft in front of seal.

2) Coat outside of brass seal housing with suitable water resistant sealer and install into recess in pump housing. Push seal into its housing with carbon face towards rear of pump.

3) Press impeller onto shaft until rear face of impeller is flush with end of shaft. Press fan hub onto shaft until it is flush with end of shaft.

Cooling System Capacity — 19.5 quarts.

TIGHTENING SPECIFICATIONS

Application	Ft. Lbs. (mkg)
Cylinder Head Nuts	54 (7.5)
Main Bearing Caps	72 (10)
Connecting Rod Caps	41 (5.7)
Flywheel	67 (9.2)
Camshaft Cap	9 (1.2)
Torque Converter	35 (4.8)
Camshaft Cover	5-6 (.7-.8)
Rear Engine Mount-to-Body	
5/16" Bolt	14-18 (1.9-2.5)
3/8" Bolt	27-32 (3.7-4.4)
Front Engine Bracket-to-Beam	14-18 (1.9-2.5)

ENGINE SPECIFICATIONS

GENERAL SPECIFICATIONS

Year	Displ.		Carburetor	HP at RPM	Torque (Ft. Lbs. at RPM)	Compr. Ratio	Bore		Stroke	
	cu. ins.	cc					in.	mm	in.	mm
1980	258.4	4235	Fuel Inj.	.....	.....	8.1:1	3.625	92.07	4.173	106

VALVES

Engine & Valve	Head Diam. In. (mm)	Face Angle	Seat Angle	Seat Width In. (mm)	Stem Diameter In. (mm)	Stem Clearance In. (mm)	Valve Lift In. (mm)
4235 cc Intake	1.75 (44.45)	45°	45°	.....	.310-.3125 (7.87-7.94)	.001-.004 (.025-.10)	.375 (9.525)
Exhaust	1.625 (41.28)	45°	45°	.....	.310-.3125 (7.87-7.94)	.001-.004 (.025-.10)	.375 (9.525)

CAMSHAFT

Engine	Journal Diam. In. (mm)	Clearance In. (mm)	Lobe Lift In. (mm)
4235 cc	.9990-.9995 (25.375-25.387)	.0005-.002 (.013-.05)	.....

VALVE TIMING

Engine	INTAKE		EXHAUST	
	Open (BTDC)	Close (ABDC)	Open (BBDC)	Close (ATDC)
4235cc	15°	57°	57°	15°

Jaguar Engines

XJ6 6 CYLINDER (Cont.)

ENGINE SPECIFICATIONS (Cont.)

PISTONS, PINS, RINGS						
	PISTONS	PINS		RINGS		
Engine	Clearance In. (mm)	Piston Fit In. (mm)	Rod Fit In. (mm)	Rings	End Gap In. (mm)	Side Clearance In. (mm)
4235 cc	.0007-.0013 (.018-.033)	① Press Fit	② Push Fit	No. 1	.015-.020 (.38-.51)	.0015-.0035 (.038-.089)
				No. 2	.009-.014 (.23-.35)	.0015-.0035 (.038-.089)
				Oil	.015-.045 (.38-1.14)	③

① — When heated to 230°F (110°C).   ② — At room temperature, without piston.   ③ — Self-expanding.

CRANKSHAFT MAIN & CONNECTING ROD BEARINGS							
	MAIN BEARINGS				CONNECTING ROD BEARINGS		
Engine	Journal Diam. In. (mm)	Clearance In. (mm)	Thrust Bearing	Crankshaft End Play In. (mm)	Journal Diam. In. (mm)	Clearance In. (mm)	Side Play In. (mm)
4235 cc	2.749-2.750 (69.85-69.86)	.0008-.0025 (.020-.063)	Center	.004-.006 (.10-.15)	2.086-2.0866 (52.98-53.00)	.001-.0027 (.025-.069)	.0058-.0087 (.147-.221)

VALVE SPRINGS			
Engine	Free Length In. (mm)	PRESSURE Lbs. @ In. (kg @ mm)	
		Valve Closed	Valve Open
4235 cc Inner	1.734 (44.04)	.....	.....
Outer	2.103 (53.42)	.....	.....

LUV PICKUP 4 CYLINDER

ENGINE CODING

ENGINE IDENTIFICATION

Engine number is located at upper right of cylinder block near distributor.

Engine Identification	
Application	Code
Pickup (1816 cc)	N

ENGINE, CYLINDER HEAD & MANIFOLDS

ENGINE

Removal — 1) Disconnect battery cables, drain crankcase and cooling system. Disconnect carburetor linkage, all necessary water and fuel hoses. Disconnect all necessary vacuum lines and electrical leads. Disconnect exhaust pipe at manifold flange. Remove radiator and cooling fan.

2) Disconnect drive shaft, slave cylinder and speedometer-cable. Remove starter. Remove flywheel inspection cover and bell housing bolts. Support transmission. Attach hoist and take up vehicle weight. Remove front and rear engine mount nuts. Pull engine forward and lift out of vehicle.

Installation — To install engine, reverse removal procedure.

INTAKE MANIFOLD

Removal & Installation — 1) Disconnect battery ground cable and drain cooling system. Remove air cleaner assembly. Remove EGR pipe clamp bolt at rear of cylinder head. From underneath vehicle, remove EGR pipe from manifolds, and remove EGR valve and bracket assembly from bottom of intake manifold.

2) Disconnect upper radiator hose at water outlet and heater hose at top of manifold. Disconnect fuel line, accelerator linkage, vacuum lines and electrical connections at carburetor. Remove manifold mounting nuts and pull assembly off studs. To install, reverse removal procedure and tighten nuts in several steps, beginning with inner nuts and working outward.

NOTE — *PCV hose must be on upper left side, hot idle compensator hose on upper right, and air vacuum hose on lower side. Incorrect installation could cause poor engine operation.*

EXHAUST MANIFOLD

Removal & Installation — 1) Disconnect battery ground cable and remove EGR pipe clamp bolt at rear of cylinder head. Working under vehicle, remove EGR pipe from manifolds and attachments from exhaust pipe to bell housing and manifold. Separate exhaust pipe from manifold.

2) Remove manifold shield bolts and shield. Disconnect heat stove hose at air cleaner and remove heat stove. Remove mounting nuts and take off manifold. To install, reverse removal procedure, ensuring that mounting nuts are tightened in steps from center outward.

CYLINDER HEAD

Removal & Installation — 1) Drain cooling system and disconnect exhaust pipe from manifold. Disconnect all necessary water hoses, vacuum lines, carburetor linkages, and electrical leads. Remove valve cover and air cleaner assembly. Rotate crankshaft so number 4 cylinder is in firing position. Lock timing chain adjuster by depressing and turning automatic adjuster slide 90° clockwise.

NOTE — *Do not remove timing chain from camshaft sprocket.*

2) Remove timing chain sprocket from camshaft. Remove front cover. Using suitable tool (J-24239), remove cylinder head bolts in progressional sequence starting with outer bolts. Remove cylinder head, intake and exhaust manifolds as an assembly. To install, reverse removal procedure.

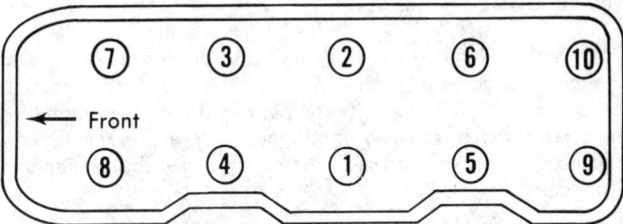

Fig. 1 Cylinder Head Tightening Sequence

CAMSHAFT

CAMSHAFT

Removal & Installation — 1) Remove valve cover and position No. 4 cylinder in firing position. Remove distributor cap and mark rotor position. Lock timing chain adjuster by depressing and turning automatic adjuster slide pin 90° in a clockwise direction. Ensure that chain is slack after locking adjuster.

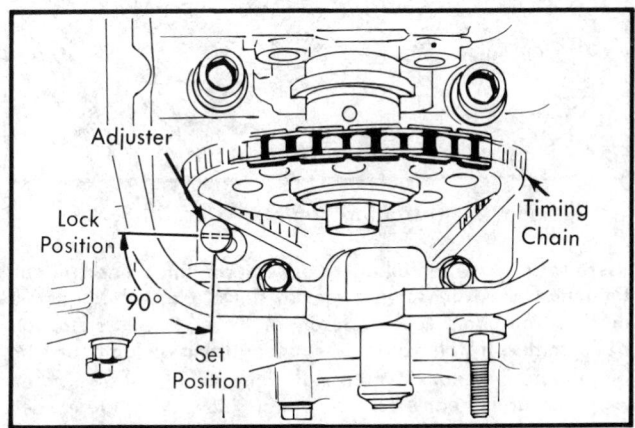

Fig. 2 Locking Timing Chain Adjuster

2) Remove timing sprocket from camshaft, keeping sprocket on chain damper and tensioner without removing sprocket from chain. Remove rocker arm shaft and bracket assembly. Remove camshaft.

3) Check camshaft journals and cams for wear or damage. Measure height of cams with a micrometer, and replace

LUV PICKUP 4 CYLINDER (Cont.)

camshaft if height is less than 1.4311" (36.3 mm). If working faces of cams have slight scores or steps, eliminate them by honing. Measure outside diameter of camshaft journals, replace camshaft if diameter is less than 1.3307" (33.8 mm). To install, reverse removal procedure.

CAMSHAFT END PLAY

Measure camshaft end play with thrust plate installed in thrust groove. Replace thrust plate if end play is found to exceed .0078" (.198 mm). Standard end play is .002-.006" (.05-.15 mm).

CAMSHAFT BEARING REPLACEMENT

Camshaft bearings are not replaceable. Camshaft rides in a carrier. If clearance is beyond limits, replace camshaft carrier.

FRONT COVER & OIL SEAL

Removal — Remove cylinder head and oil pan as previously outlined. Remove oil pump pickup tube. Remove harmonic balancer and AIR belt. If equipped with air conditioning, remove compressor and mounting brackets. Remove distributor cap (wires attached), then remove distributor. Remove front cover.

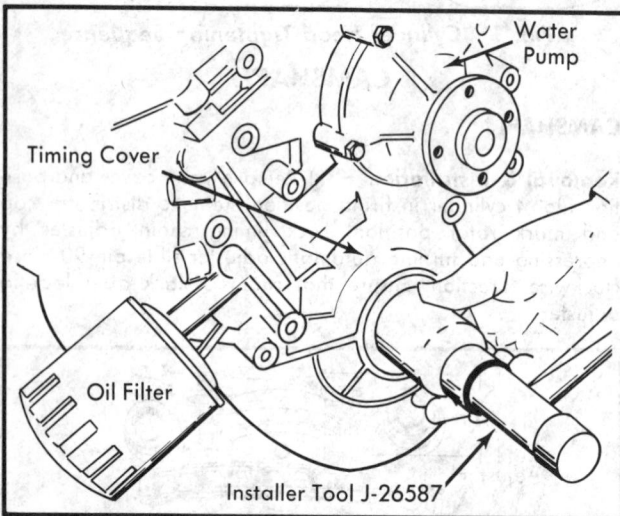

Fig. 3   Installing Timing Cover Oil Seal

Installation — Align oil pump drive gear punch mark with oil filter side of cover. Align center of dowel pin with alignment mark on oil pump case. Rotate No. 1 and 4 cylinders to top dead center. Install front cover by engaging pinion gear with oil pump drive gear on crankshaft. Ensure that punch mark on oil pump drive gear is turned to rear side as viewed between front cover and cylinder block. Slit at end of oil pump shaft must be offset forward and parallel with front face of cylinder block. Install front cover and reverse removal procedure.

TIMING CHAIN

Removal & Installation — 1) Remove front cover as outlined previously. Remove timing chain from crankshaft sprocket. Inspect sprockets, timing chain, adjuster and guide for wear and replace as required. Ensure that oil jet in chain guide mounting is not plugged.

2) Install timing sprocket and pinion gear, groove side toward front cover. Align key grooves with key on crankshaft, then drive into position with suitable installing tool (J-26587). Turn crankshaft so that key is turned toward cylinder head side and No. 1 and 4 cylinders are at top dead center.

NOTE — *Keep timing chain in position on camshaft until sprocket is installed on camshaft.*

3) Align mark plate on timing chain with mark on crankshaft timing sprocket. Side of chain with mark plate is on front side, and side of chain with most links between mark plates is on chain guide side. Camshaft timing sprocket marked side, faces forward and marks align with timing chain mark plate. Install front cover.

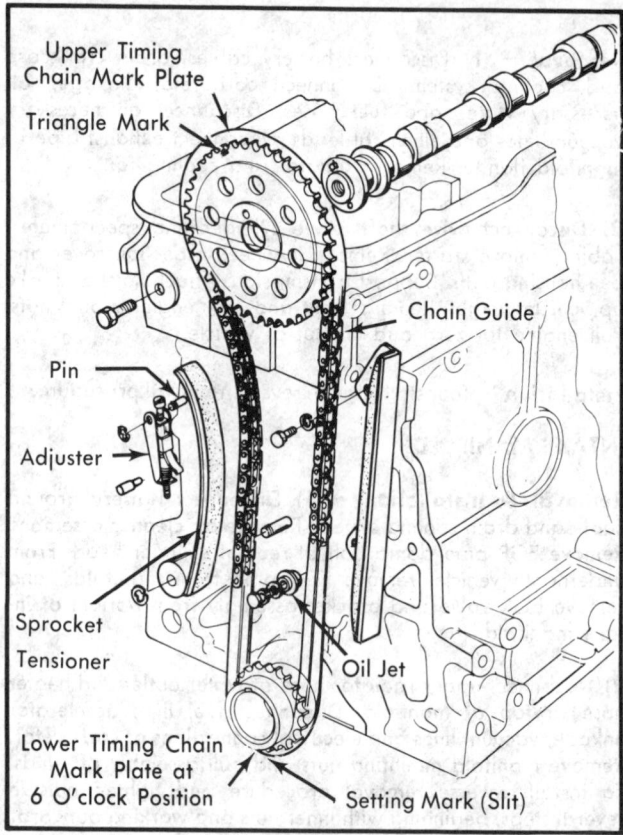

Fig. 4   Camshaft, Timing Chain and Components

VALVES

VALVE ARRANGEMENT

Right Side — Intake.

Left Side — Exhaust.

VALVE GUIDES

Removal & Installation — 1) Inspect inside diameter of valve guide for grooves or uneven wear. Measure inside diameter of valve guides with caliper gauge. Measure diameter of valve stem and compare measured values to determine clearance. If clearance is excessive, replace both valve and valve guide.

LUV PICKUP 4 CYLINDER (Cont.)

2) Use valve guide removal tool (J-26512) and drive old guide out from combustion chamber side. Remove lower spring seat. To install, oil outside of new guide and place in position in cylinder head. Use installer (J-26512-1&2) and drive guide in until tool bottoms on cylinder head.

VALVE SPRINGS & VALVE STEM OIL SEALS

Removal — With rocker arm shaft assembly removed, use compressed air method to hold valve in closed position. Use suitable spring compressor (J-26513) and remove valve spring retainers (keepers). Remove spring and cap. Remove valve stem oil seal and spring lower seat.

Installation — Lubricate valve stem and spring lower seat. Place seat in position, then slide new seal over valve stem and onto guide, ensuring that ridge in oil seal fits in groove in valve guide. Install springs and retainers.

VALVE SPRING INSTALLED HEIGHT

Visually check valve springs for damage and replace as necessary. Measure free length of valve springs using suitable calipers and replace if measured value is beyond limit. With a valve spring tester check valve spring tension and compare it with values in chart, replace as necessary.

ROCKER ARM ASSEMBLY

Removal & Installation — **1)** Loosen rocker shaft brackets in sequence, working from ends toward center. Remove spring from shaft, then remove brackets and rocker arms, keeping parts in order for reassembly.

2) Inspect rocker arm shaft for wear damage or excessive runout. If runout is greater than .0156" (.396 mm), replace shaft. Diameter of shaft is .8071" (20.5 mm). Replace shaft if diameter is less than .8012" (20.35 mm).

3) To install, apply engine oil to rocker arm shaft, rocker arms, and valve stems. Install longer shaft on exhaust side and shorter shaft on intake side. Aligning marks on shafts are turned to front side.

4) Assemble brackets and arms to shafts, so cylinder number (on upper face of bracket) is pointed to front of engine. Align No. 1 shaft bracket with mark on the intake and exhaust valve side rocker arm shafts. Place springs between shaft bracket and rocker arm. Punch mark on rocker arm shafts must be turned upward. Tighten shaft bracket nuts.

NOTE — *Hold rocker arm springs with a wrench while tightening nuts to prevent damaging springs.*

VALVE CLEARANCE

With No. 1 or No. 4 cylinder piston at top dead center, loosen lock nut and adjust intake valves to .006" (.15 mm), and exhaust valves to .010" (.25 mm). When valves are correctly adjusted reset lock nut.

Valve Adjustment Sequence

Application	Intake/Cylinder	Exhaust/Cylinder
No. 1 @ TDC	1,2	1,3
No. 4 @ TDC	3,4	2,4

PISTONS, PINS & RINGS

OIL PAN

Removal & Installation — Disconnect battery ground cable and drain engine oil. Remove front splash shield and front crossmember. Disconnect and lower relay rod at idler arm. Remove left hand bell-housing brace and disconnect vacuum line at oil pan. Remove oil pan bolts and lower pan from engine. To install, reverse removal procedure.

NOTE — *To remove pan on 4-wheel drive models, engine must be removed from vehicle.*

PISTON & ROD ASSEMBLY

Removal & Installation — **1)** With cylinder head and pan removed, mark piston, connecting rods and bearing caps on starter side for assembly order. Scrape carbon deposits from upper part of cylinder wall.

2) Remove connecting rod bearing cap nuts and bearing cap. Using a wood rod, push piston, together with connecting rod, upward. Removal sequence is 1, 4, 2, & 3.

NOTE — *Ensure piston and connecting rod are pulled parallel to cylinder wall.*

3) To install piston and rod assembly, position piston so notch mark on crown of piston is facing front of engine. Align cylinder number marks on connecting rods so they will be on right-hand side of front mark on piston.

PISTON PIN

Removal — Using a press and piston pin removal tool set (J-25270), press piston pin out of piston and connecting rod assembly.

Installation — Install new pin by placing pilot through piston and connecting rod. Lightly oil piston pin and place piston, rod, pin, and ram on press base. Press in pin until its centered in connecting rod.

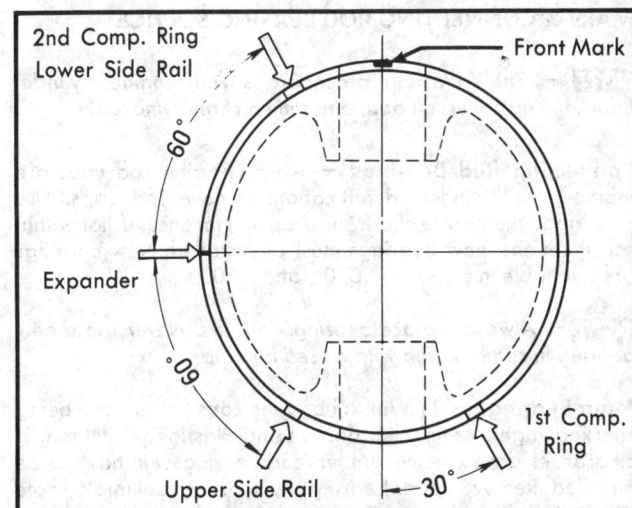

Fig. 5 Piston Ring Gap Arrangement

LUV PICKUP 4 CYLINDER (Cont.)

PISTON RINGS

1) Assemble piston rings to piston with a piston ring expander. When replacing piston rings, position compression rings so that "NPR" or "TOP" mark is turned up. The expander ring and side rail is not marked.

2) Install oil control ring in this order; expander ring, lower side rail, and upper side rail. After installing all rings, apply clean engine oil to the entire rings. Check that rings turn smoothly in their ring grooves.

FITTING PISTONS

1) Measure piston at right angles to piston pin, 1.575" (40 mm) below piston head. Measure bore diameter at lower section, where least wear occurs. If clearance exceeds specifications, pistons must be replaced.

2) Measure weight of assembled piston-rod assembly. Variance between assemblies must not exceed .42 oz. (.01 kg). If correction is necessary, arched portions of connecting rod bearing caps may be ground to reduce weight.

Piston Class

Piston Size	Piston Grade	Piston Diameter In. (mm)
Standard	A	3.3049-3.3053 (83.944-83.955)
Standard	B	3.3053-3.3057 (83.955-83.965)
Standard	C	3.3057-3.3061 (83.965-83.975)
Standard	D	3.3061-3.3065 (83.975-83.985)

NOTE – Pistons are available in .020" (0.5 mm) and .040" (1.0 mm) oversize.

CRANKSHAFT MAIN & CONNECTING ROD BEARINGS

MAIN & CONNECTING ROD BEARING SERVICE

NOTE – The following procedure is with engine, cylinder head, timing cover, oil pan, and timing chain removed.

Connecting Rod Bearings – After ensuring rod caps are marked for cylinder identification, remove rod caps. Use Plastigage method to check for proper clearance. If not within specifications, new bearings must be installed. New bearings are available in standard, .010", and .020".

NOTE – Always replace bearings in pairs. Never use a new bearing in combination with a used bearing.

Main Bearings – 1) With all bearing caps (except one being checked) tight, check clearances using Plastigage method. If clearances are excessive, undersized bearings will have to be installed. Remove upper bearings by inserting tool into oil hole of crankshaft and rotating crankshaft clockwise to roll bearing from engine.

2) To check crankshaft out of round place crankshaft on two "V" shaped blocks at No. 1 and No. 5 journals. Hold dial indicator in contact with No. 3 journal and slowly turn crankshaft, recording highest point on journal. Replace crankshaft if bend exceeds .0038" (.097 mm). Standard assembly value is .0012" (.030 mm) or less.

3) To check crankshaft end play, place bearings and crankshaft in crankcase. Install thrust bearing on both sides of No. 3 crankshaft journal. Shift crankshaft endwise and measure clearance between thrust bearing and journal side face. If clearance is greater than .0117" (.297 mm), install oversize thrust bearings. Standard value is .0024-.0094" (.061-.239 mm).

4) Install bearing caps so that arrow mark on rear face of each bearing cap is turned to front of engine. Bearings should be well lubricated prior to installation. Tighten in 2 steps in sequence of 3, 4, 2, 5 and 1.

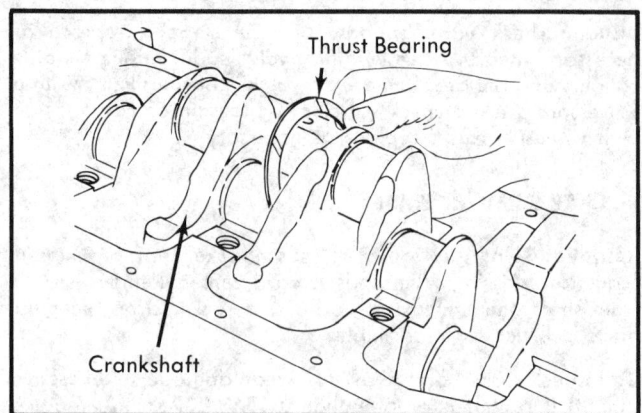

Fig. 6 Installing Crankshaft Thrust Bearing

REAR MAIN OIL SEAL

Removal – Remove oil pan and transmission. Remove clutch (if equipped). Remove starter and flywheel assembly. Remove seal retainer bolts and pry seal out of retainer.

Installation – To install, reverse removal procedure noting the following: Fill clearance between lips of seal with grease, and coat lips of seal with engine oil. Place retainer on flat surface and drive seal into place using suitable seal installer tool (J-22354).

ENGINE OILING

ENGINE OILING SYSTEM

Trochoid type oil pump is designed to deliver 3.7 gallons of oil per minute through the engine at a pump speed of 1400 RPM. Lubricating system is designed to deliver oil at a rate of 57 psi.

Crankcase Capacity – 4.2 qts. with filter.

Oil Filter – Full-flow disposable canister type.

Normal Oil Pressure – 57-71 psi (4-5 kg/cm²) at 2800 RPM.

Relief Valve – Located on side of cylinder block near oil filter. Opening pressure is 57-71 psi (4-5 kg/cm²).

LUV PICKUP 4 CYLINDER (Cont.)

OIL PUMP

NOTE — *Oil pump can be serviced with engine in or out of vehicle. Procedure given is with engine in vehicle.*

Removal — Remove front cover, distributor, and oil pan as outlined previously. Remove oil pickup tube. Remove oil pump mounting bolts and remove pump assembly.

Inspection — 1) Measure tip clearance with a feeler gauge, between drive rotor and driven rotor. Replace entire pump assembly if clearance is greater than .0079" (.2 mm).

2) Measure clearance between driven rotor and inner wall of pump body. Replace entire pump assembly if clearance is greater than .0098" (.249 mm).

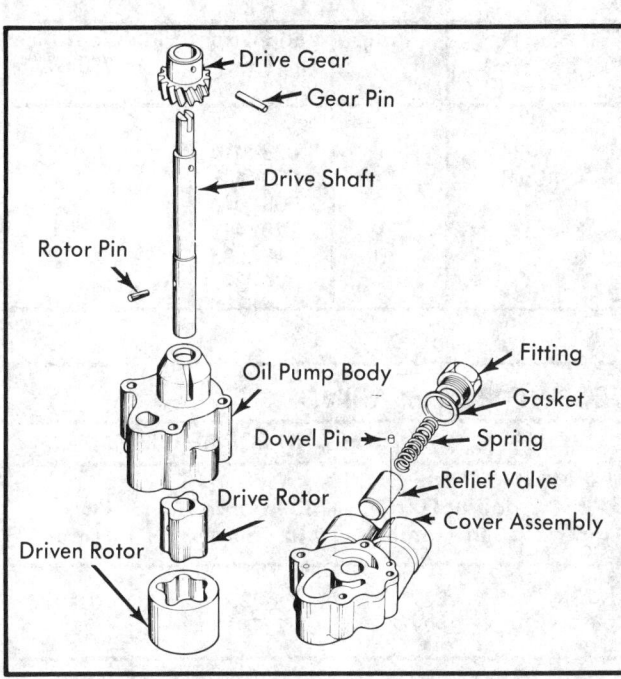

Fig. 7   Exploded View of Oil Pump Assembly

3) Using a square and a feeler gauge, measure clearance between drive rotor, driven rotor, and oil pump cover. Replace entire pump assembly if clearance is greater than .0079" (.2 mm). Inspect all parts wear or damage.

Installation — 1) Align mark on camshaft with mark on No. 1 rocker arm shaft bracket. Align notch on crankshaft pulley with "O" mark on front cover. When the two sets of marks are aligned, No. 4 cylinder is at top dead center on compression stroke.

2) Install driven rotor so that alignment mark aligns with mark on the drive rotor. Engage drive gear with pinion gear on crankshaft so alignment mark is turned rearward and is away from crankshaft by approximately 20° in clockwise rotation See Fig. 8.

3) When oil pump is installed, make sure mark on drive gear is turned to rear side as viewed from the clearance between front cover and cylinder block. Slit at end of shaft must be parallel with front face of cylinder block, and is offset as viewed through distributor fitting hole.

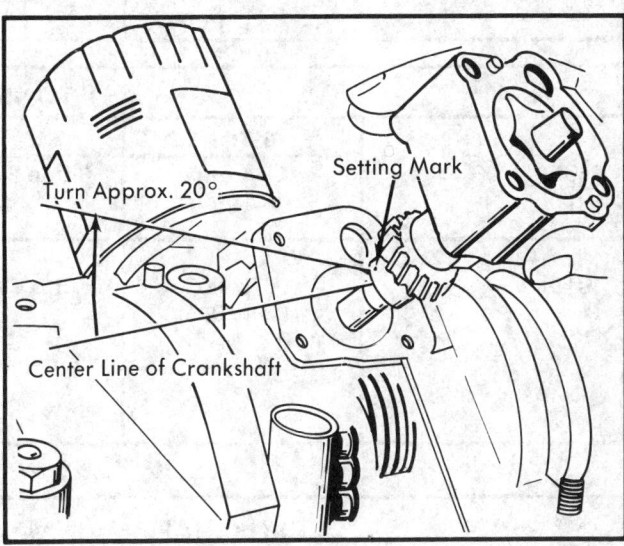

Fig. 8   Installing Oil Pump

4) Install pump cover by fitting it to the dowel pins, then install mounting bolts. Install relief valve assembly and rubber hose on cover. Reverse removal procedure.

ENGINE COOLING

WATER PUMP

Disconnect negative battery cable. Remove lower cover. Drain cooling system. If equipped with air conditioning, remove fan and air pump drive belt. Remove fan, fan pulley, and air pump drive pulley. Remove set plate and pulley. On all other models remove fan nuts and fan. On all models, remove attaching bolts and water pump from vehicle.

Thermostat — Opens at about 180°F (82°C).

Cooling System Capacity — 6.4 qts.

Pressure Cap — 15 psi (1.1 kg/cm²).

ENGINE SPECIFICATIONS

GENERAL SPECIFICATIONS

Year	Displ.		Carburetor	HP at RPM	Torque (Ft. Lbs. at RPM)	Compr. Ratio	Bore		Stroke	
	cu. ins.	cc					in.	mm	in.	mm
1980	110.8	1816	1x2-Bbl.	80 @4800	95 @3000	8.5:1	3.31	84	3.23	82

LUV PICKUP 4 CYLINDER (Cont.)

ENGINE SPECIFICATIONS (Cont.)

VALVES

Engine & Valve	Head Diam. In. (mm)	Face Angle	Seat Angle	Seat Width In. (mm)	Min. Stem Diameter In. (mm)	Stem Clearance In. (mm)	Valve Lift In. (mm)
1816 cc Int.	1.67 (42.4)	45°	45°	.047-.063 (1.19-1.60)	.3102 (7.88)	.0009-.0022 (.023-.056)	.....
Exh.	1.34 (34.0)	45°	45°	.047-.063 (1.19-1.60)	.3091 (7.85)	.0015-.0031 (.038-.079)	.....

PISTONS, PINS, RINGS

Engine	PISTONS	PINS		RINGS		
	Clearance In. (mm)	Piston Fit In. (mm)	Rod Fit In. (mm)	Rings	End Gap In. (mm)	Side Clearance In. (mm)
1816 cc	.0018-.0026 (.046-.066)	Press Fit	.0024 (.061)	1	.008-.016 (.20-.41)	.....
				2	.008-.016 (.20-.41)	.....
				Oil	.008-.035 (.20-.89)	.....

CRANKSHAFT MAIN & CONNECTING ROD BEARINGS

Engine	MAIN BEARINGS				CONNECTING ROD BEARINGS		
	Journal Diam. In. (mm)	Clearance In. (mm)	Thrust Bearing	Crankshaft End Play In. (mm)	Journal Diam. In. (mm)	Clearance In. (mm)	Side Play In. (mm)
1816 cc	2.205 (56.01)	.0016 (.041)	No. 3	.0118 (.3)	1.929 (48.99)	.0020 (.051)	.011 (.28)

CAMSHAFT

Engine	Journal Diam. In. (mm)	Clearance In. (mm)	Lobe Lift In. (mm)
1816 cc	1.3362-1.3370 (33.94-33.96)	.0024 ① (.061)	.....

① — End Play .002-.006" (.05-.15 mm)

VALVE TIMING

Engine	INTAKE		EXHAUST	
	Open (BTDC)	Close (ABDC)	Open (BBDC)	Close (ATDC)
1816 cc	21°	65°	55°	20°

VALVE SPRINGS

Engine	Free Length In. (mm)	PRESSURE Lbs. @ In. (kg @ mm)	
		Valve Closed	Valve Open
1816 cc Inner	1.78 (45.2)	21.5 @ 1.52 (9.7 @ 38.6)	.....
Outer	1.85 (47.0)	37.0 @ 1.61 (16.8 @ 40.9)	.....

TIGHTENING SPECIFICATIONS

Application	Ft. Lbs. (mkg)
Cylinder Head	
Step 1	61 (8.43)
Step 2	72 (9.95)
Main Bearings	72 (9.95)
Connecting Rod Bearings	43 (5.95)
Flywheel	69 (9.54)
Camshaft Sprocket	58 (8.02)
Rocker Arm Shaft Bracket Nuts	16 (2.21)

GLC, B2000 & 626 4 CYLINDER

ENGINE CODING

ENGINE IDENTIFICATION

Engine number is located on right front side of engine block.

ENGINE & CYLINDER HEAD

ENGINE

Removal — 1) Remove hood after marking hinge location. Drain cooling system and crankcase. On GLC, remove cooling fan. On all models, remove battery and air cleaner. Disconnect accelerator cable and choke heater wire from carburetor. Disconnect fuel lines at fuel pump and carburetor. On automatic transmission models, disconnect and plug transmission cooler lines at radiator. On all models, remove radiator hose and radiator. Disconnect all engine vacuum hoses.

2) Disconnect wires from temperature sending unit, oil pressure switch, alternator, distributor, back-up light switch and starter. Disconnect exhaust pipe from manifold. On manual transmission models, remove cover plate from clutch housing and clutch release cylinder. On automatic transmission models, remove torque converter and drive plate support bolts. On all models, support transmission with a jack and remove nuts and bolts attaching transmission to engine.

3) Remove starter. On manual transmission models, remove clutch slave cylinder. On all models, remove engine mount attaching nuts and bolts. Install a lifting sling to engine lifting brackets, attach a lifting hoist and raise slightly. Pull engine forward until clear of transmission. Lift engine from vehicle.

Installation — To install, reverse removal procedure.

CYLINDER HEAD

NOTE — *Before removal, check timing chain for excessive stretch. To check, readjust the chain tension as explained in TIMING CHAIN installation procedure. If gap between slipper head and chain tensioner body exceeds .51" (13 mm), replace the chain.*

Removal — 1) Remove engine lifting brackets from cylinder head. Remove exhaust manifold along with port liners and gaskets. Disconnect ignition wires and vacuum lines at distributor. Remove lock nut, then remove distributor from cylinder head.

2) Disconnect hoses and remove air pump with bracket. Remove water pump fan and pulley. Disconnect hose from PCV valve at intake manifold. On manual transmission models, disconnect anti-afterburn valve. On all models, remove attaching bolts, then remove intake manifold and carburetor as an assembly.

3) Remove rocker arm cover, gasket and oil seals. Install ring gear brake tool (49 0118 271A or equivalent) on flywheel to prevent flywheel from rotating. Remove lock nut and washer, then slide distributor drive gear from camshaft. Remove camshaft sprocket lock nut. Remove cylinder head-to-front cover attaching bolt.

4) Loosen cylinder head bolts gradually, in the reverse order of the tightening sequence, and remove bolts. Remove rocker arm assembly. Carefully pull camshaft to rear and remove from sprocket and cylinder head. Remove camshaft sprocket.

CAUTION — *Timing chain should be lifted upwards to prevent chain tensioner slipper head from disengaging and dropping down inside front cover. Installation of chain adjuster guide (49-3953-260 for 1415 cc, 49-0660-260 for 1970 cc engines) through front cover inspection hole prior to sprocket removal will prevent disengagement.*

5) Remove camshaft bearings from cylinder head, noting their respective locations. Remove the cylinder head and gasket.

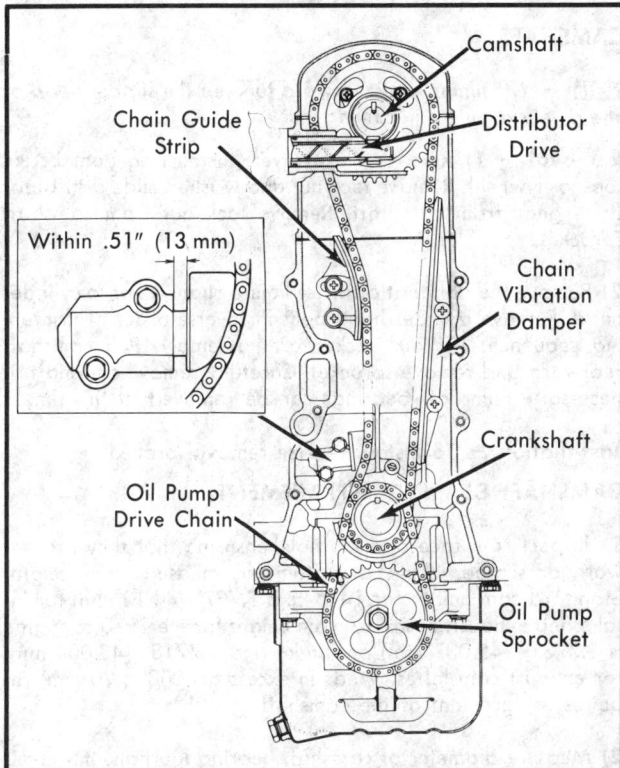

Fig. 1   Engine Cross-Section with Detail of Timing Chain Tensioner

Installation — 1) Install camshaft sprocket in timing chain and position on top of chain guide strip and chain vibration damper, ensuring that matching marks on chain and sprocket are aligned. Install new head gasket. Place cylinder head on aligning dowels.

2) Install camshaft bearings in cylinder head and bearing caps. Lubricate bearings with engine oil. Install camshaft in cylinder head. Install bearing caps. Carefully install camshaft on sprocket while aligning keyway. Position rocker arm assembly on cylinder head.

CAUTION — *Ensure that the flat surface of the ball on each rocker arm is facing down.*

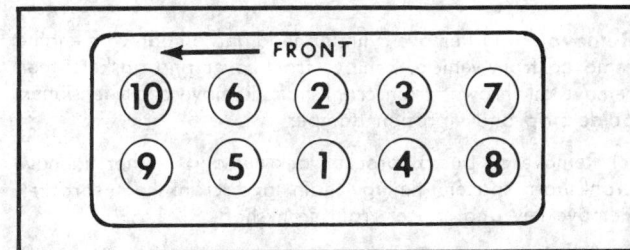

Fig. 2   Tightening Sequence for Cylinder Head

GLC, B2000 & 626 4 CYLINDER (Cont.)

3) Install cylinder head bolts and tighten, in steps, according to sequence shown in *Fig.* 2. Install cylinder head-to-front cover bolt. Install distributor drive gear, tighten nut and bend lock washer.

4) Adjust timing chain tension by carefully pressing top of chain guide strip, using a lever, through opening of cylinder head. Tighten guide strip attaching screws. Remove chain adjuster guide tool and tensioner will be properly set. Install remaining components in reverse order of removal procedure.

CAMSHAFT

CAMSHAFT

NOTE — *Lift timing chain upward to keep the slipper head of chain tensioner from coming out.*

Removal — 1) Remove valve cover. Install ring gear brake tool to flywheel. Remove lock nut and washer, slide distributor drive gear from camshaft. Remove lock nut from camshaft sprocket.

2) Remove the bolt that attaches timing chain cover to cylinder head. Remove cylinder head bolts in reverse order of tightening sequence. Lift out rocker arm assembly. Pull camshaft rearward and remove sprocket. Carefully remove camshaft. If necessary, camshaft bearings can be removed at this time.

Installation — To install, reverse removal procedure.

CAMSHAFT BEARING REPLACEMENT

1) Inspect cam face and journals, ensuring that they are not worn or scored. Using a micrometer, measure cam height. Standard cam height for 1415 cc is 1.737" (44.12 mm) for intake and exhaust. Standard cam height for the 1970 cc engine is 1.7731" (45.037 mm) on intake and 1.7718" (45.004 mm) for exhaust cam lobes. Wear in excess of .008" (.20 mm) requires replacement of the camshaft.

2) Measure diameter of camshaft bearing journals. If wear is more than .002" (.051 mm) below minimum standard diameter, camshaft must be ground to accept .010" (.25 mm), .020" (.50 mm) or .030" (.75 mm) undersize bearings.

3) Inspect camshaft bearing clearances using Plastigage method. If standard clearances are exceeded, replace bearings. If new bearings are properly fitted, correct clearance can be obtained without filing, shimming or scraping.

4) Using a dial indicator, check camshaft out-of-round. Camshaft must not exceed .0012" (.030 mm) out-of-round.

5) Check camshaft end play using a feeler gauge. Standard clearance is .001-.007" (.025-.178 mm). If wear limit of .008" (.20 mm) is exceeded, replace the thrust plate.

TIMING CHAIN

Removal — 1) Remove cylinder head and oil pan with engine removed from vehicle. Remove front cover and gaskets, then remove oil thrower from crankshaft. Remove chain tensioner, guide strip and vibration damper.

2) Remove oil pump sprocket lock nut and washer. Remove crankshaft spacer, timing chain and crankshaft sprocket. Remove key and spacer from crankshaft.

Installation — 1) On 1415 cc engines, install timing chain guide strip but do not tighten attaching screws. Install timing

chain vibration damper. On all engines, install spacer and key onto crankshaft. Place timing chain on crankshaft and camshaft sprockets with index marks aligned.

2) Align crankshaft and its sprocket keyway, then fit sprocket onto crankshaft. Install crankshaft spacer. Fit key on oil pump shaft. Install oil pump drive chain onto oil pump and crankshaft sprockets, align keyway and install assembly onto crankshaft and oil pump shafts. On 1415 cc models, install chain adjuster guide (49-3953-260) on adjuster. Install adjuster on cylinder block.

3) On 1415 cc engines, tighten oil pump sprocket nut and bend lock washer tab. Install oil baffle plate and spacer onto crankshaft. On all engines, check oil pump drive chain slack. Chain slack should not exceed .157" (4 mm). Excessive slack on 1970 cc engines can be reduced by installing adjusting shims between cylinder block and oil pump body. On 1415 cc engines, chain must be replaced. Tighten oil pump sprocket nut and bend lock washer tab.

4) On 1970 cc engines, install chain adjuster guide (49-0660-260) on adjuster with spring completely compressed. Install adjuster and chain vibration damper on cylinder block. Install chain guide strip but do not tighten screws. On all engines, adjust timing chain by slightly rotating engine in direction of engine revolution. Press top of chain guide strip with a lever through opening in top of cylinder head and tighten guide strip attaching screws with a screwdriver. Remove chain adjuster guide.

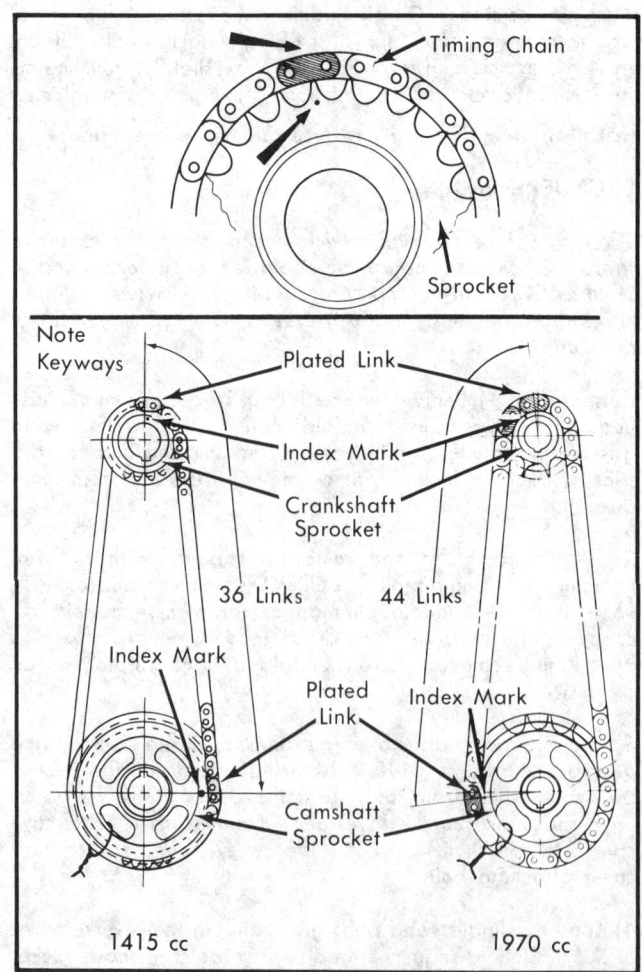

Fig. 3 Alignment Marks of Timing Chain & Sprockets

Mazda Engines

GLC, B2000 & 626 4 CYLINDER (Cont.)

VALVES

VALVE ARRANGEMENT

Right Side — All Intake
Left Side — All Exhaust

VALVE GUIDE SERVICING

Remove worn valve guide, using valve guide removal/installation tool (49-0221-251A) and hammer. Drive new guide in until ring of guide just touches cylinder head. Install new valve seal on valve guide using a seal pusher tool (49-0223-160D or equivalent).

NOTE — *The valve keepers for intake and exhaust valves are not interchangeable. Care must be taken to keep them properly identified.*

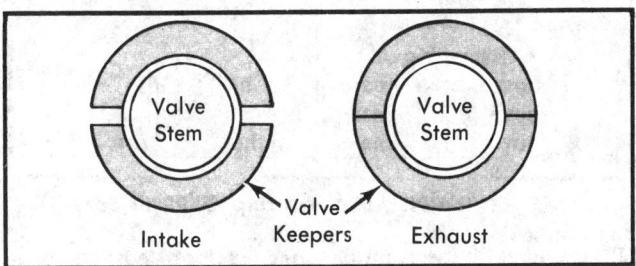

Fig. 4   Intake & Exhaust Valve Keeper Difference

VALVE SPRINGS

1) Remove all carbon from inside of combustion chamber. Using a suitable valve spring compressor, collapse springs and remove stem keepers, retainers, valve springs and seats. Valves can now be removed.

2) With valve springs removed, inspect for corrosion or obvious damage. Use a valve spring tester to determine valve spring condition under a load. Measure valve spring free length and compare findings with specifications.

ROCKER ARM ASSEMBLY

1) With rocker arm assembly removed and disassembled, inspect all components for wear or damage. The standard clearance between rocker arm bore and shaft on 1415 cc is .0008-.0029" (.020-.074 mm) and on 1970 cc is .0011-.0032" (.027-.081 mm). If measured clearance is more than .004" (.010 mm), replace rocker arm or shaft.

2) Reassemble and install rocker shaft while noting the following: Intake and rocker arm supports are interchangeable. Intake side uses 2 rocker shafts. On intake side, end of shaft with longer distance between oil hole and shaft end face each other. Center bearing cap oil hole faces toward intake side.

3) When installing the oil distribution pipe, make sure the oil holes face camshaft. After pipe is installed, press "O" ring into hole for pipe on center bearing cap. When installing rocker

arm assembly, make sure flat surface on ball of each rocker arm faces downward. Align dowels and install assembly on cylinder head. Before tightening cylinder head bolts, offset each of the rocker arms .040" (1 mm) from valve stem center by shifting the rocker shaft support stands slightly.

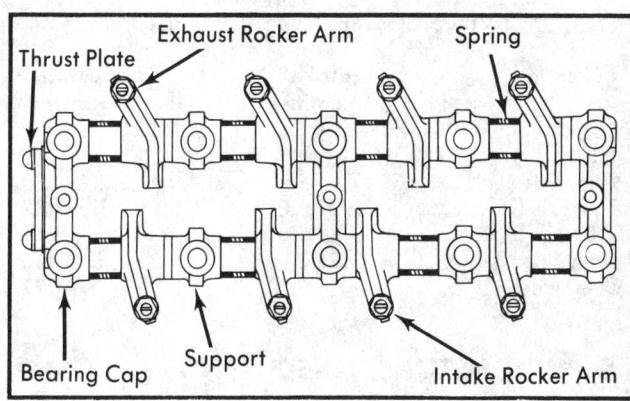

Fig. 5   1415 cc Rocker Arm Assembly

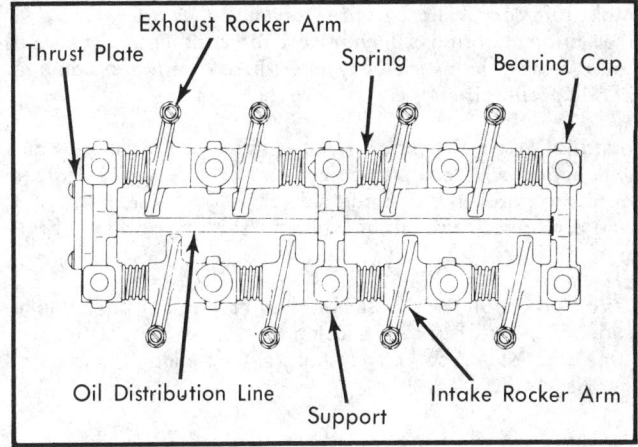

Fig. 6   1970 cc Rocker Arm Assembly

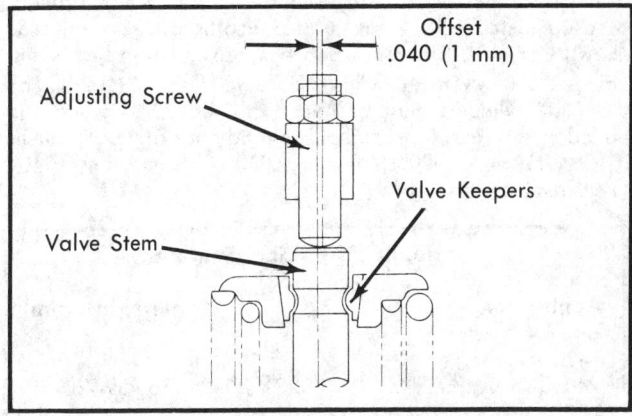

Fig. 7   Rocker Arm Offset

VALVE CLEARANCE

With engine warmed to operating temperature, having torqued the cylinder head bolts to specifications, adjust valves.

GLC, B2000 & 626 4 CYLINDER (Cont.)

Loosen lock nut and insert feeler gauge between rocker and valve stem. Turn adjusting screw until proper clearance is obtained.

NOTE — *Before adusting, ensure flat surface of ball on rocker arm is facing downward.*

Valve Clearance Specifications

Application	Intake In.(mm)	Exhaust In.(mm)
1415 cc		
Valve side	.010 (.25)	.012 (.30)
Cam side	.007 (.18)	.009 (.22)
1970 cc		
Valve side	.012 (.30)	.012 (.30)
Cam side	.009 (.22)	.009 (.22)

PISTONS, PINS & RINGS

PISTON & ROD ASSEMBLY

Removal — Remove oil pan, cylinder head, and oil pump. Make sure connecting rods are marked so they are replaced in their original positions, then remove rod caps. Push piston and rod assembly out of top of cylinder. Take care not to damage bearing journal.

Installation — Oil piston rings, pistons, and cylinder walls with engine oil. Place piston rings approximately 120 degrees apart, so gap is not on thrust side or piston pin side. Install a ring compressor onto piston without disturbing position of rings.

Install piston and rod assembly into its original bore. Make sure "F" mark of piston is facing front of engine. Install rod caps and tighten rod bolts. Install oil pump, oil pan, and cylinder head.

FITTING PISTONS

1) Cylinder bore can be measured using a cylinder gauge. Measurement must be taken at 3 depths and 2 angles as shown in *Fig. 8*. Difference between maximum and minimum values is actual wear. If cylinder bore wear is .006 (.15 mm) or more, all cylinders must be honed or rebored. If cylinder is honed or rebored, oversized pistons and rings are available in .010" (.25 mm), .020" (.50 mm), .030" (.75 mm) and .040" (1.00 mm) oversizes.

Standard Piston Specifications

Application	Diameter In. (mm)
1415 cc①	
A	3.0291-3.0299 (76.939-76.959)
1970 cc	
A	3.1474-3.1482 (79.944-79.964)
B	3.1489 (79.980)
C	3.1319 (79.550)

① — "B" and "C" diameters not available.

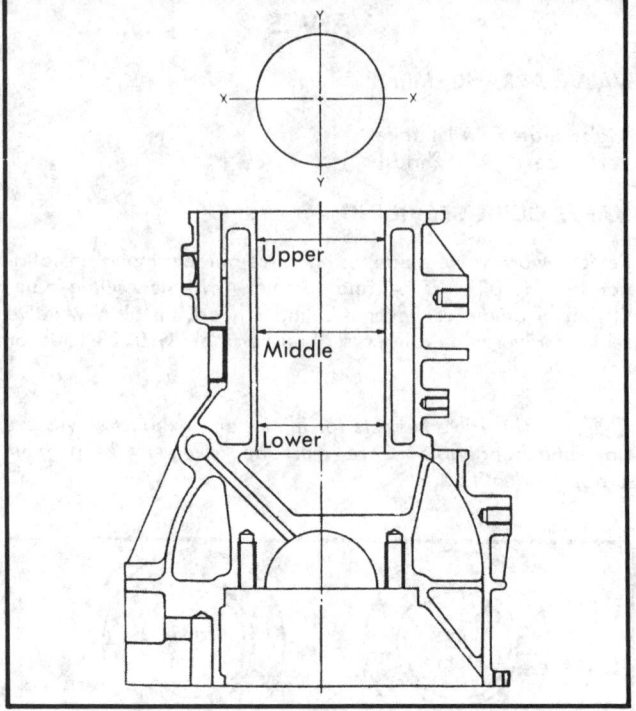

Fig. 8 Points for Measuring Cylinder Bore

2) Carefully inspect pistons and replace those severely damaged due to scoring, scratching or burning. Measure pistons at points A, B and C as shown in *Fig. 9*, using a micrometer. If piston is not within specifications, replace piston and rebore cylinder.

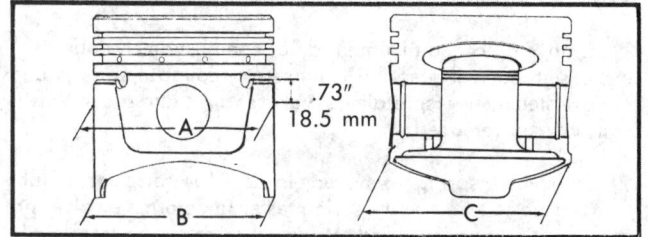

Fig. 9 Points for Measuring Piston

PISTON PIN REPLACEMENT

1) Piston pin is press fit in connecting rod. Use special tool set (49 8134 040 or equivalent) for removal and installation. For installation, a press load of 1102-3307 lbs. (500-1500 kg) is required. If the press load is not within the load range, replace the pin or connecting rod. Ensure that the piston pin offset is correct. The connecting rod big end oil hole and "F" mark on piston should correspond.

CRANKSHAFT MAIN & CONNECTING ROD BEARINGS

MAIN & CONNECTING ROD BEARINGS

Removal — Remove engine and oil pan. Remove rod and main bearing caps. Check rod and main bearing clearances using Plastigage method. If measured value exceeds correct clearance, bearings must be replaced.

GLC, B2000 & 626 4 CYLINDER (Cont.)

Inspection — 1) Using a micrometer, measure diameter of connecting rod and main journals. If wear is more than .002" (.051 mm) at any journal, crankshaft must be ground to fit .010" (.25 mm), .020" (.50 mm) or .030" (.75 mm) undersize bearings.

2) Using a dial indicator, check crankshaft for out-of-round. Maximum allowable out-of-round is .0012" (.030 mm).

Installation — 1) Fit 5 upper main bearings to cylinder block with oil grooved surface facing crankshaft thrust side. Fit new oil seal at rear of crankshaft. Insert side seals on both sides of rear bearing cap. Install main bearing caps. No. 1 through No. 4 bearing caps are marked for correct installation. No. 5 may or may not be indexed.

2) Insert connecting rod assembly into cylinder as previously described. Fit upper bearing to rod and over crankshaft. Fit lower bearing to rod cap and install cap. Tighten all bolts to specifications.

NOTE — *Ensure engine is free to turn.*

3) End play is compensated for by thrust washers placed at No. 5 main bearing. Check crankshaft end play using a dial indicator. End play must not exceed .012" (.305 mm). If specification is exceeded, thrust washers must be replaced. Thrust washers are available in .010" (.25 mm), .020" (.50 mm) and .030" (.75 mm) oversizes.

4) Compress camshaft tensioner slipper fully into tensioner body. Install tool (49 1975 260 for 1415 cc and 49 0660 260 for 1970 cc engines) to retain slipper and install tensioner assembly to cylinder block. On 1970 cc engines, install chain vibration damper and tighten screws. Install chain guide strip, but do not tighten screws at this time. Install oil deflector and seal in front cover. Install oil thrower on crankshaft with the edge facing forward.

5) On all engines, fill oil seal lip with grease and install front cover. Install oil pan and gasket. Position camshaft sprocket and chain on top of the chain guide strip and chain vibration damper. Install gasket and cylinder head on block.

NOTE — *Ensure matching marks of chain and sprockets are aligned.*

6) Install camshaft and bearings in cylinder head. Install rocker arm assembly. Position rocker arms .040" (1 mm) off center of valve stems and tighten cylinder head bolts. Turn crankshaft slightly in the direction of rotation. Press top of chain guide strip with a lever through opening in cylinder head, then tighten guide attaching screws through holes in front cover. Remove tool from tensioner and tension will be properly set. Install remaining components in reverse order of removal procedure.

ENGINE OILING

ENGINE OILING SYSTEM

Oil is circulated by a rotor-type pump. The pump is mounted inside the oil pan and is driven by the crankshaft.

Crankcase Capacity — 3.2 qts. for 1415 cc engines and 4.1 qts. for 1970 cc engines.

Oil Pressure — 50-64 psi (3.5-4.5 kg/cm²) at 3000 RPM.

Oil Filter — Full flow cartridge.

Pressure Regulator Valve — Non-adjustable

OIL PUMP

1) Check clearance between lobes of rotor with a feeler gauge. If clearance exceeds .010" (.25 mm), replace both rotors.

2) Inspect clearance between outer rotor and pump body, using a feeler gauge. Maximum clearance is .012" (.30 mm)

3) To check rotor ends, place a straightedge across pump body and measure clearance rotor and straightedge, using a feeler gauge. Then place straightedge across cover and measure clearance between straightedge and cover.

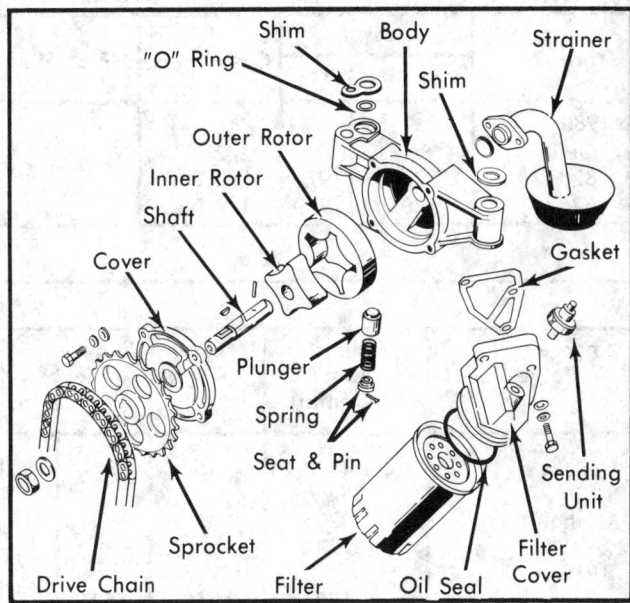

Fig. 10   1970 cc Oil Pump Assembly

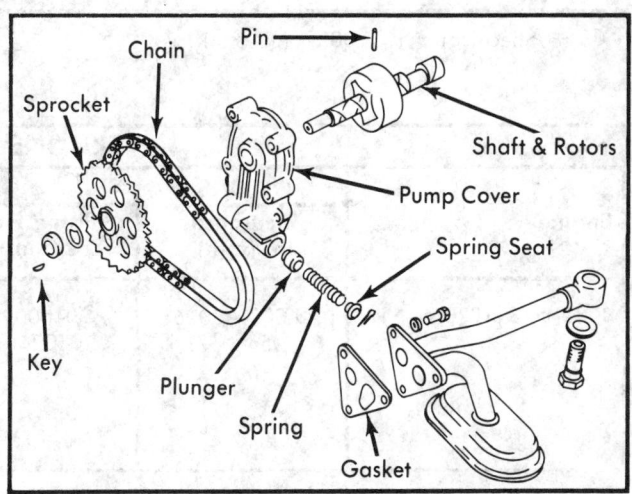

Fig. 11   1415 cc Oil Pump Assembly

Mazda Engines

GLC, B2000 & 626 4 CYLINDER (Cont.)

Oil Pump Specifications

Application	Clearance In. (mm)
Rotor-to-Rotor	.002-.006 (.051-.052)
Rotor-to-Body	.006-.010 (.152-.254)
End play	.002-.004 (.051-.102)

ENGINE COOLING

WATER PUMP

NOTE — *It may be necessary to remove radiator to facilitate water pump removal.*

Removal — Remove bolts mounting fan and pulley to water pump. Remove nuts and bolts holding water pump to timing chain cover. Remove alternator bracket and water pump.

Installation — Using a new gasket, install by reversing removal procedure.

Cooling System Capacity — 5.8 qts. for 1415 cc engines and 7.6 qts. for 1970 cc engines.

Thermostat — Begins to open at 190°F. (88°C) and is fully open at 212°F (100°C) for 1415 cc and begins to open 180°F (82°C) and is fully open at 203°F (95°C) for 1970 cc engines.

Radiator Cap — 13 psi

ENGINE SPECIFICATIONS

GENERAL SPECIFICATIONS										
Year	Displ.		Carburetor	HP at RPM	Torque (Ft. Lbs. at RPM)	Compr. Ratio	Bore		Stroke	
	cu. ins.	cc					in.	mm	in.	mm
1980										
GLC	86.4	415	1x2 Bbl	.....	.....	9.0:1	3.03	77	2.99	76
B2000	120.2	1970	1x2 Bbl	.....	.....	8.6:1	3.15	80	3.86	98
626	120.2	1970	1x2 Bbl	.....	.....	8.6:1	3.15	80	3.86	98

VALVES							
Engine & Valve	Head Diam.① In. (mm)	Face Angle	Seat Angle	Seat Width In. (mm)	Stem Diameter In. (mm)	Stem Clearance In. (mm)	Valve Lift In. (mm)
1415 cc							
Intake	1.4173 (35.99)	45°	45°	.055 (1.4)	.3162-.3168 (8.03-8.05)	.0007-.0021 (.018-.053)	.....
Exhaust	1.2205 (31.00)	45°	45°	.055 (1.4)	.3160-.3168 (8.025-8.05)	.0007-.0023 (.018-.058)	.....
1970 cc							
Intake	1.6536 (42.00)	45°	45°	.055 (1.4)	.3162-.3168 (8.03-8.05)	.0007-.0021 (.018-.053)	.....
Exhaust	1.2992 (32.99)	45°	45°	.055 (1.4)	.3160-.3168 (8.025-8.05)	.0007-.0023 (.018-.058)	.....

① — Specification is ±.0039″ (.01 mm).

PISTONS, PINS, RINGS						
	PISTONS	PINS		RINGS		
Engine	Clearance In. (mm)	Piston Fit In. (mm)	Rod Fit In. (mm)	Rings	End Gap In. (mm)	Side Clearance In. (mm)
1415 cc & 1970 cc	①.0021-.0026 (.054-.067)	②0-.0009 (0-.024)	.....	No. 1	.008-.016 (.20-.41)	③.0012-.0025 (.030-.064)
				No. 2	.008-.016 (.20-.41)	④.0012-.0025 (.030-.064)
				Oil	.012-.035 (.31-.89)	.....

① — 1970 cc should be .0014-.0030″ (.036-.075 mm).
② — Interference fit.
③ — 1970 cc should be .0012-.0028″ (.030-.070 mm).
④ — 1970 cc should be .0012-.0025″ (.030-.065 mm).

Mazda Engines

GLC, B2000 & 626 4 CYLINDER (Cont.)

ENGINE SPECIFICATIONS (Cont.)

CRANKSHAFT MAIN & CONNECTING ROD BEARINGS In. (mm)							
	MAIN BEARINGS				CONNECTING ROD BEARINGS		
Engine	Journal Diam.	Clearance	Thrust Bearing	Crankshaft End Play	Journal Diam.	Clearance	Side Play
1415 cc	1.9703-1.9709 (50.045-50.065)	.0009-.0017 (.024-.042)	No. 5	.004-.006 (.10-.15)	1.5766-1.5772 (40.045-40.060)	.0009-.0019 (.024-.048)	.004-.008 (.11-.21)
1970 cc	2.4822-2.4828 (63.045-63.060)	.0012-.0020 (.031-.050)	No. 5	.003-.009 (.08-.24)	2.0884-2.0890 (53.045-53.060)	.0011-.0030 (.027-.077)	.004-.008 (.11-.21)

VALVE SPRINGS			
Engine	Free Length In. (mm)	PRESSURE Lbs. @ In. (kg @ mm)	
		Valve Closed	Valve Open
1415 cc			
Inner	1.449 (36.8)	20.9 @ 1.26 (9.5 @ 32.0)	.....
Outer	1.587 (40.3)	43.7 @ 1.319 (19.8 @ 33.5)	.....
1970 cc			
Inner	1.449 (36.8)	20.9 @ 1.26 (9.5 @ 32.0)	.....
Outer	1.469 (37.3)	31.4 @ 1.339 (14.25 @ 34.0)	.....

VALVE TIMING				
	INTAKE		EXHAUST	
Engine	Open (BTDC)	Close (ABDC)	Open (BBDC)	Close (ATDC)
1415 cc 1970 cc	15°	55°	58°	12°
B2000	14°	53°	58°	9°
626	10°	57°	54°	13°

CAMSHAFT			
Engine	Journal Diam. In. (mm)	Clearance In. (mm)	Lobe Lift In. (mm)
1415 cc			
Front	1.6550-1.6558 (42.035-42.051)	.0014-.0030 (.035-.076)	.....
Center	1.6562-1.6568 (42.065-42.081)	.0026-.0042 (.065-.106)	.....
Rear	1.6550-1.6558 (42.035-42.051)	.0014-.0030 (.035-.076)	.....
1970 cc			
Front	1.7733-1.7739 (45.040-45.055)	.0007-.0027 (.019-.069)	.....
Center	1.7737-1.7743 (45.050-45.065)	.0011-.0031 (.029-.079)	.....
Rear	1.7733-1.7739 (45.040-45.055)	.0007-.0027 (.019-.069)	.....

TIGHTENING SPECIFICATIONS	
Application	Ft. Lbs. (mkg)
1415 cc	
Cylinder Head	
Cold	47-51 (6.5-7.0)
Hot	51-54 (7.0-7.5)
Main Bearing Cap	43-47 (6.0-6.5)
Connecting Rod Cap	22-25 (3.0-3.5)
Oil Pump Sprocket	22-25 (3.0-3.5)
Camshaft Sprocket	51-58 (7.0-8.0)
Crankshaft Pulley	80-87 (11.0-12.0)
Distributor Drive Gear	51-58 (7.0-8.0)
Intake Manifold	14-19 (1.9-2.6)
Exhaust Manifold	14-19 (1.9-2.6)
1970 cc	
Cylinder Head	
Cold	59-64 (8.2-8.8)
Hot	69-72 (9.5-10.0)
Main Bearing Cap	61-65 (8.4-9.0)
Connecting Rod Cap	30-33 (4.1-4.6)
Oil Pump Sprocket	22-25 (3.0-3.5)
Camshaft Sprocket	51-58 (7.0-8.0)
Crankshaft Pulley	101-108 (14.0-14.9)
Distributor Drive Gear	51-58 (7.0-8.0)
Intake Manifold	14-19 (1.9-2.6)
Exhaust Manifold	16-21 (2.2-2.9)

Mazda Engines

RX7 ROTARY ENGINE

ENGINE CODING

ENGINE IDENTIFICATION

Engine identification number is stamped on front engine housing behind the distributor.

Engine Identification	
Application	**Code**
RX7	12A

ENGINE REMOVAL & INSTALLATION

Removal − 1) Remove hood and disconnect battery ground cable. Drain engine oil and coolant. Remove engine under cover. Disconnect following electrical wires: Primary and secondary ignition wires at coils, pick-up coil wiring connections, condensor lead, oil level sensor lead, temperature sensor and oil thermo sensor (except California vehicles).

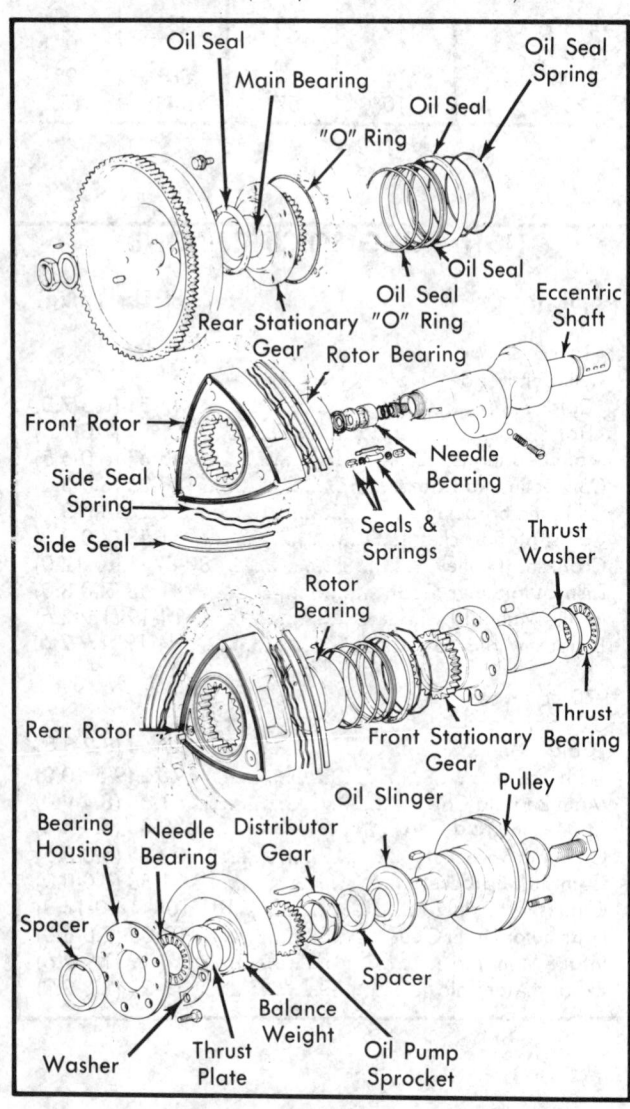

Fig. 1 Exploded View of Rotors & Eccentric Shaft Assembly

2) Remove air cleaner assembly. Disconnect the following tubes and hoses: Oil hoses at cooler, radiator hoses, automatic transmission cooler lines (if equipped), heater hoses, fuel supply and return hoses, vacuum and evaporative hoses, and heat exchanger pipe from rear of intake manifold.

3) Remove cooling fan and drive assembly, radiator, and radiator shroud assembly. Disconnect coupler and "B" terminal from alternator. Disconnect coupler from idle switch and coasting richer connector on manual transmission models. On all models, disconnect power valve solenoid.

NOTE − *If equipped with air conditioning, dismount compressor and condenser and tie out of way. DO NOT disconnect refrigerant lines.*

4) Disconnect choke heater and anti-afterburn valve solenoid couplers. Remove engine-to-transmission bolts and thermal reactor rear cover. Disconnect accelerator, choke and hot start assist cables. Disconnect any remaining wires, tubes or linkages remaining between engine and chassis at top of engine.

5) Raise and support vehicle and remove starter. Remove lower engine-to-transmission bolts. Disconnect air duct from thermal reactor and remove air pipe from lower side of reactor. Disconnect air duct hanger, air duct and heat exchanger pipe from pre-silencer.

6) Support front of transmission with suitable jack and remove left and right engine mount nuts. Attach sling to engine and take up slack. Pull engine forward to clear clutch shaft, then lift engine from vehicle.

Installation − To install engine, reverse removal procedure ensuring that linkages, tubes and electrical connections are restored in original position. Refill all fluids to specified levels, warm up engine and check for leaks.

ENGINE DISASSEMBLY

NOTE − *To ease engine disassembly, manufacturer recommends use of special engine stand (49 0107 680A) and hanger (49 1114 005).*

1) Loosen drive belts and remove air pump and alternator. Disconnect metering oil pump connecting rod and hoses at metering oil pump outlets. Disconnect air outlet pipe and vacuum sensing tube. Remove thermal reactor cover and take off manifold and carburetor assembly.

2) Remove thermal reactor (exhaust manifold), distributor, engine mounts, oil filter and cover, water pump and front drive pulley for A/C compressor. Turn engine over and remove oil pan and strainer. Install flywheel brake (49 1881 060) on manual transmission models or stopper (49 1881 055) on automatic transmission models.

3) Remove eccentric shaft pulley. Take off front cover with gasket and slide distributor gear off shaft. Remove "O" ring from oil passage. Remove oil pump sprocket nut and slide oil pump sprocket, eccentric shaft sprocket and drive chain off together. Remove oil pump.

RX7 ROTARY ENGINE (Cont.)

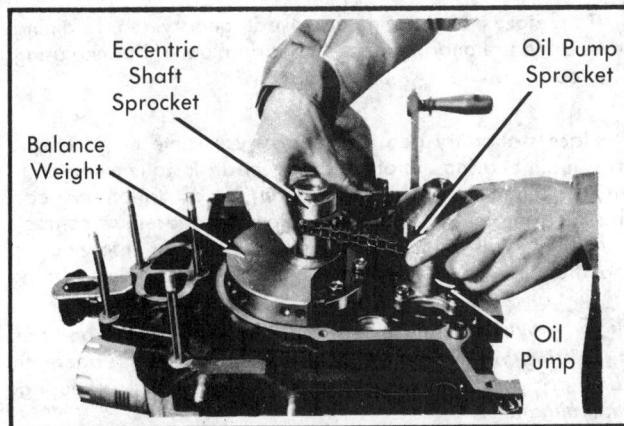

Fig. 2 Oil Pump Drive and Sprocket Removal

Balance Weight

Eccentric Shaft Sprocket

Oil Pump Sprocket

Oil Pump

4) Remove balance weight and following parts in order: Thrust washer, needle bearing, bearing housing, needle bearing, spacer and thrust plate. On manual transmission models, remove clutch assembly, then use puller to remove flywheel. On automatic transmission models, remove drive plate, then use puller to remove counterweight.

5) Remove tension bolts on rear housing in sequence shown in *Fig. 3* by loosening in 2 or 3 steps. Lift rear housing off shaft and remove any seals stuck to rotor sliding surface, placing them back in original positions. Remove seals and "O" rings from rear side of rear rotor housing.

6) Attach dowel puller (49 0813 215A) and pull tubular dowels off rear rotor housing. Hold rotor housing by hand to keep it from moving up and remove rear rotor housing. Use caution to avoid dropping apex seals and side pieces of rear rotor. Remove seals and "O" ring from front side of rear rotor housing.

Fig. 3 Loosening Sequence of Tension Bolts

7) Remove side pieces, apex seals and springs from rear rotor and store in order for reassembly. Remove all corner seals, corner seal springs, side seals and side seal springs and store in

order for reassembly. Remove rear rotor and place on clean pad with internal gear side down.

8) Remove seals and springs on remaining side of rotor and store in order for reassembly. Place suitable protector on seal inner lip and remove outer seal with remover (49 0813 225), then remove inner seal. Remove seals and springs and store in order for reassembly. Mark rear rotor with felt tip pen for assembly identification.

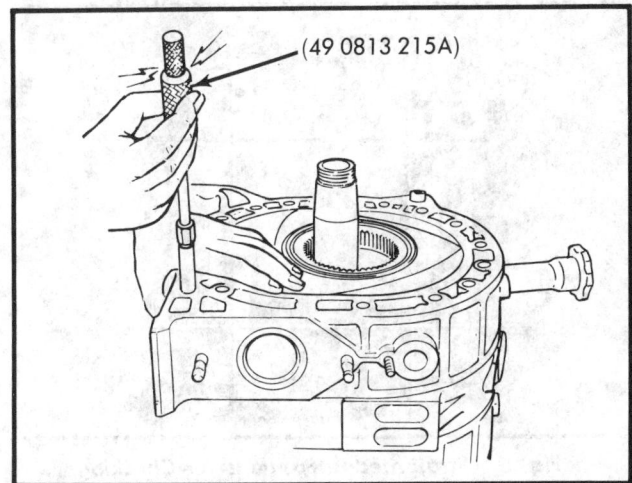

(49 0813 215A)

Fig. 4 Extracting Tubular Dowels from Engine

9) Attach puller and pull tubular dowels off intermediate housing while holding housing down. Remove intermediate housing by sliding beyond rear rotor journal on eccentric shaft. Lift out eccentric shaft carefully to avoid damage to rotor bearing and main bearing. Repeat steps **6)** through **8)** to remove front rotor housing and rotor assembly.

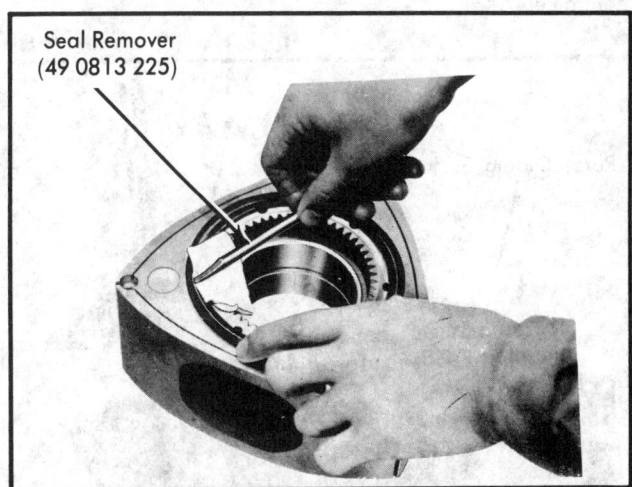

Seal Remover (49 0813 225)

Fig. 5 Prying Oil Seal from Rotor

INSPECTION & OVERHAUL

FRONT, INTERMEDIATE & REAR HOUSINGS

1) To clean front housing, use extra fine emery paper to remove carbon deposits from rotor running surface. Use ketone or thinner to remove sealing agent.

MAZDA Engines

RX7 ROTARY ENGINE (Cont.)

2) Inspect housing for signs of water or gas leakage. Check for wear or damage to rotor running surface or stationary gear. Check main bearings for signs of scoring or flaking.

3) Place a straightedge across housing surface in positions shown in illustration. Using a feeler gauge, measure distortion of front housing. Replace or reface housing if distortion limit of .0016" (.04 mm) is exceeded. (See Fig. 6).

Fig. 6   Straightedge Positions for Checking Housing Distortions

4) Check for wear on rotor sliding surfaces of housing and joint surfaces with rotor housing. Measurements are made using a dial indicator, *Fig. 7*. If wear exceeds .0039" (.10 mm), reface or replace housing.

NOTE – *Side housings (front, intermediate and rear housings) can be reused by grinding them, if the required finish can be maintained.*

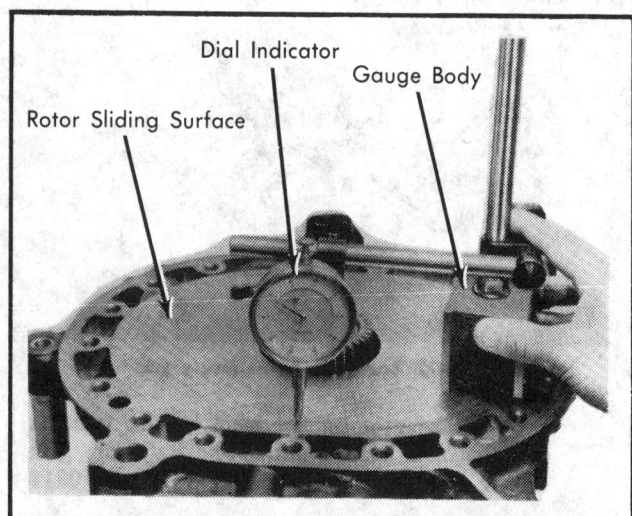

Fig. 7   Measuring Housing Wear with Dial Indicator

5) Measure inner diameter of main bearing and outer diameter of bearing journal on eccentric shaft. Standard clearance is .0016-.0028" (.04-.07 mm). If clearance exceeds .0039" (.10 mm), replace bearing or eccentric shaft.

6) To replace main bearing, remove stationary gear retaining bolts. Drive stationary gear, with bearing, out of housing using a suitable mandrel (49 0813 235).

7) Place stationary gear in a press, use same mandrel and press main bearing out of stationary gear. Install new bearing while aligning tang of bearing with slot of stationary gear. Press bearing into gear until adapter of mandrel just contacts stationary gear flange. Drive stationary gear into housing gear flange, *(Fig. 8)*. Tighten stationary gear retaining bolts.

NOTE – *When installing rear main bearing, check condition of "O" ring and replace if necessary. Apply sealing agent on stationary gear flange prior to installing it on rear housing. Align pin and slot.*

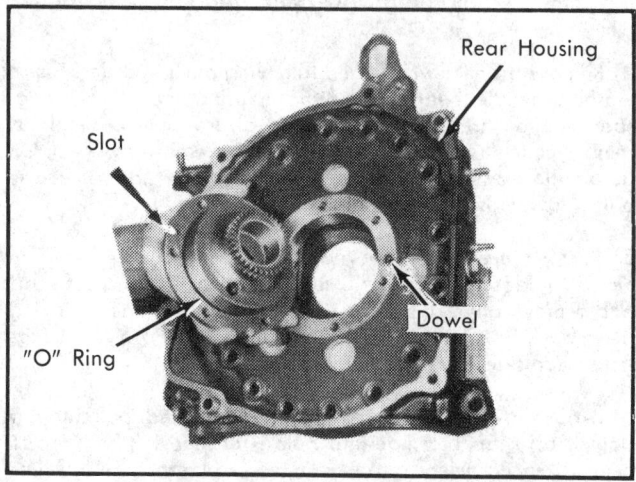

Fig. 8   Stationary Gear Slot & Dowel Alignment

ROTOR HOUSINGS

1) To clean housing, wipe off sealing agent or carbon in rotor running surface with a rag and ketone or thinner. Remove rust deposits in water cooling passages.

2) Inspect for cracks or damage to chromium plated surface. Check for signs of gas or water leakage. Housing must be replaced if any of these conditions exist.

Fig. 9   Measuring Rotor Housing for Distortion

RX7 ROTARY ENGINE (Cont.)

3) Place a straightedge across sealing surface of rotor housing and check for distortion, using a feeler gauge. If distortion exceeds .0016" (.04 mm), replace housing. See Fig. 9.

4) Check rotor housing thickness at points A, B, C, and D in Fig. 10. If micrometer readings vary between point A and minimum value for B, C, and D by more than .0024" (.06 mm), replace rotor housing.

NOTE – This excessive clearance would indicate a possibility of gas or water leakage.

ROTORS

1) Inspect rotor for wear or damage and check internal gear for chips, cracks or scoring. Measure rotor width at 3 points and subtract maximum width from width of rotor housing at point "A". Difference should be between .0047" (.12 mm) and .0071" (.18 mm). If clearance is excessive or rotor is damaged, replace rotor assembly.

2) If clearance is less than specified, internal gear may have come out. Strike internal gear lightly with plastic hammer and remeasure. Measure inner diameter of rotor bearing and outside diameter of rotor bearing journal on eccentric shaft. Replace rotor bearing if clearance exceeds .0039" (.10 mm) or any damage is shown. See Rotor Bearing Replacement.

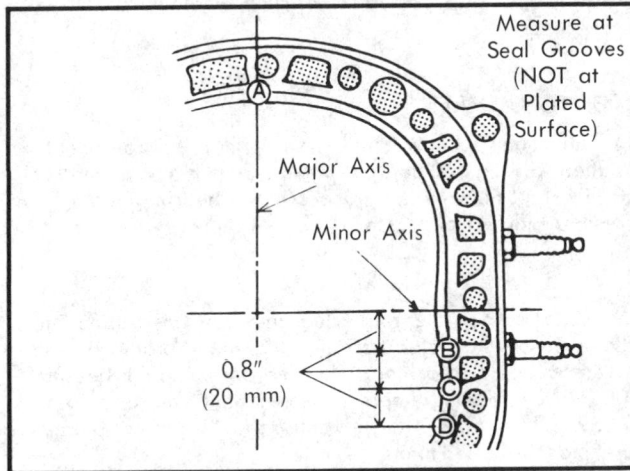

Fig. 10 **Rotor Housing Thickness Check Points**

ROTOR OIL SEAL

With oil seal installed in rotor, measure contact lip width of seal. Seal must be replaced if contact width exceeds .020" (0.5

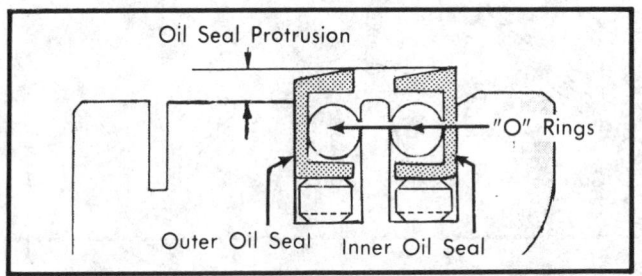

Fig. 11 **Measuring Point of Oil Seal Protrusion**

mm). Measure seal protrusion and replace seal spring if protrusion is less than .020" (0.5 mm). See Fig. 11.

ROTOR BEARING REPLACEMENT

Place rotor bearing on support so internal gear is facing downward. Using rotor bearing replacer (49 0813 240) without adapter ring, press bearing out of rotor, (Fig. 12). Clean bearing bore with emery paper if necessary. Place rotor on support with internal gear upward. Place a new rotor bearing so slot in rotor bore is in line with bearing lug. Press new bearing (using tool without adaptor), until bearing is flush with rotor boss.

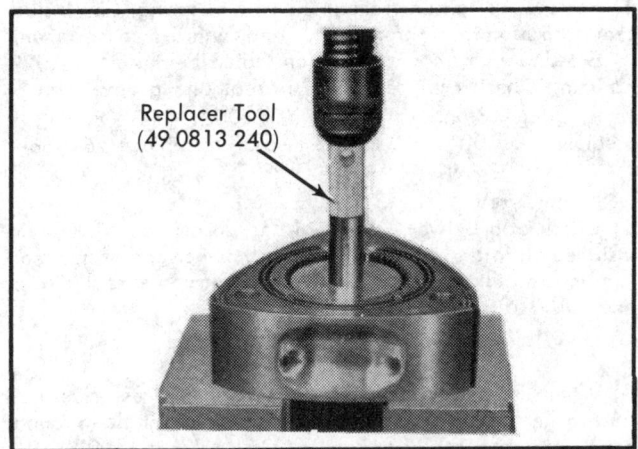

Fig. 12 **Pressing Rotor Bearing from Rotor**

APEX SEAL

1) Clean all carbon from apex seal and spring with a cleaning solution (not emery paper). Measure height of apex seal with a micrometer (see illustration). Replace seal if height is less than .275" (7.0 mm).

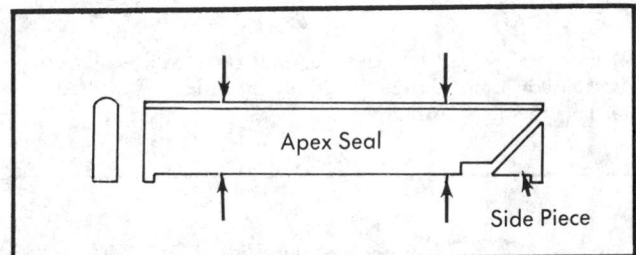

Fig. 13 **Measuring Apex Seal Height**

2) Check gap between apex seal and groove. To check gap, place apex seal in its respective groove on rotor and measure gap between apex seal and groove with a feeler gauge. Feeler gauge should be inserted until tip of gauge reaches bottom of groove. Standard clearance is .0020-.0035" (.05-.09 mm). If gap exceeeds wear limit of .0059" (.15 mm), replace apex seal.

3) When installing new apex seal, check gap between seal and side housing. Measure length of seal with micrometer and subtract length from rotor housing width at point A, (Fig. 10). Clearance should be .0051-.0075" (.13-.19 mm). If seal length is excessive, correct with emery paper. Check seal spring height at least .22" (5.5 mm).

Mazda Engines

RX7 ROTARY ENGINE (Cont.)

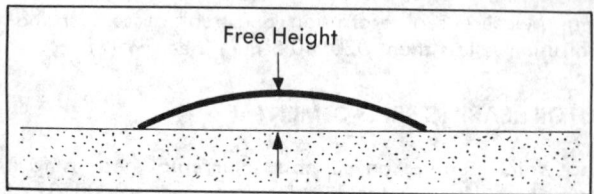

Fig. 14 *Measuring Free Height of Apex Seal Spring*

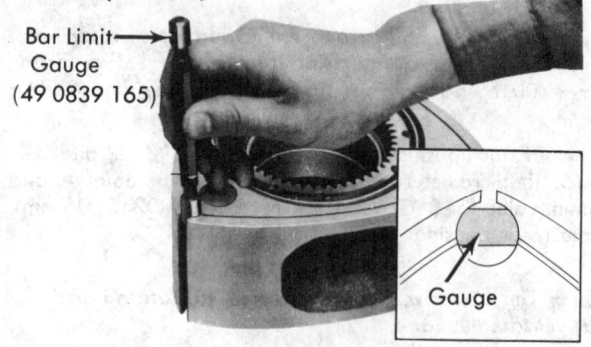

Fig. 16 *Checking Corner Seal Groove Measurement*

SIDE SEAL

1) Remove all carbon from side seal and spring. Check side seal protrusion from rotor surface, and confirm free movement by pressing with finger. Protrusion should be more than .02" (.5 mm). Check gap between side seal and groove with a feeler gauge. Standard gap is .0012-.0031" (.03-.08 mm). If wear limit of .004" (.10 mm) is measured, replace side seal.

2) Check gap between side seal and corner seal with seals installed on rotor. Insert feeler gauge between end of side seal (against rotating direction of rotor) and the corner seal. If gap exceeds .016" (.4 mm), replace side seal.

3) When side seal is replaced, adjust gap between side seal and corner seal by grinding one end of side seal along round shape of corner seal, using a fine file. Make gap .002-.006" (.05-.15 mm).

CORNER SEAL

1) Clean carbon from corner seal. Check corner seal protrusion from rotor surface, and check free movement by pressing with finger. Protrusion should be more than .02" (.5 mm).

2) Extent of corner seal groove wear is determined by using special Bar Limit Gauge (490839165), and is classified according to the following:

Neither End of Gauge Goes Into Groove — Indicates that gap conforms to specifications.

"Go" End of Gauge Goes Into Groove — Indicates that gap is more than standard, but less than wear limit. In this case replace corner seal, (Fig. 16).

Both Ends of Gauge ("Go" and "No Go") Fit in Groove — Indicates that gap exceeds wear limit. Replace rotor.

ECCENTRIC SHAFT

1) Thoroughly clean eccentric shaft in a suitable cleaning solution and blow out oil passages with compressed air. Inspect shaft for scratching or scoring of bearing journals and possible blocked oil passages.

2) Check rotor bearing clearance by measuring inner diameter of the rotor bearing and outer diameter of the eccentric shaft rotor journal. Clearance should be .0016-.0031" (.04-.08 mm). Replace the bearing if clearance exceeds .0039" (.10 mm). Replace eccentric shaft if journal diameters are under specified limits.

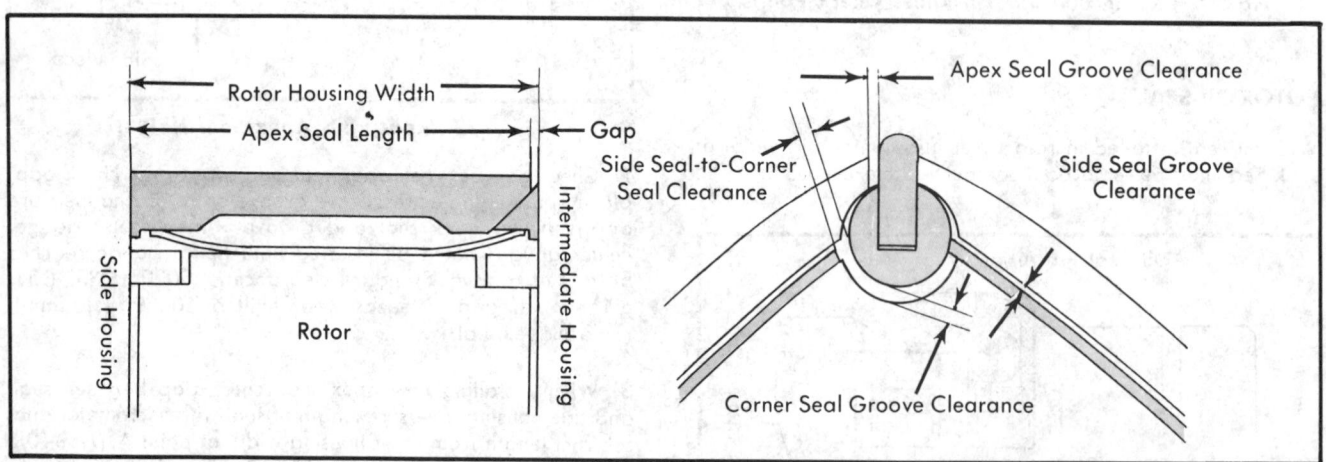

Fig. 15 *Measuring Clearance of Apex, Side & Corner Seals*

RX7 ROTARY ENGINE (Cont.)

3) Place eccentric shaft in two "V" blocks. Mount a dial indicator and check runout of both ends by rotating shaft slowly. If runout exceeds .0024" (.06 mm), replace shaft.

4) Oil passages in eccentric shaft are sealed by a blind plug in rear of shaft. Inspect plug for possible oil leakage. If leakage is detected, remove plug with an Allen wrench and install new "O" ring. Tighten plug.

5) Inspect needle bearings in end of shaft for wear or damage. Check for spring weakness, stuck, or damaged steel ball at the oil jets. Inspect front needle bearing, bearing housing, and thrust plate for wear or damage. Inspect front and rear oil seals for leaks, replace as necessary.

ENGINE REASSEMBLY

OIL SEALS

1) Place rotor on rubber pad or cloth. Install oil seal springs in their respective grooves on rotors, with each edge of spring fitted in stopper hole. Ensure oil seal springs have been painted in cream or blue color: cream colored springs must be placed on front faces of both rotors and blue springs on rear faces of rotors. When installing, painted side of spring must face oil seal (upward), *Fig. 17.*

2) Insert new "O" ring in each oil seal. Install inner oil seal to each side of rotor as follows: Position oil seal to groove so square edge of spring fits in stopper notch of oil seal. Press into position by using a used inner oil seal so lip of inner oil seal sinks into position approximately .016" (.4 mm) below surface of rotor.

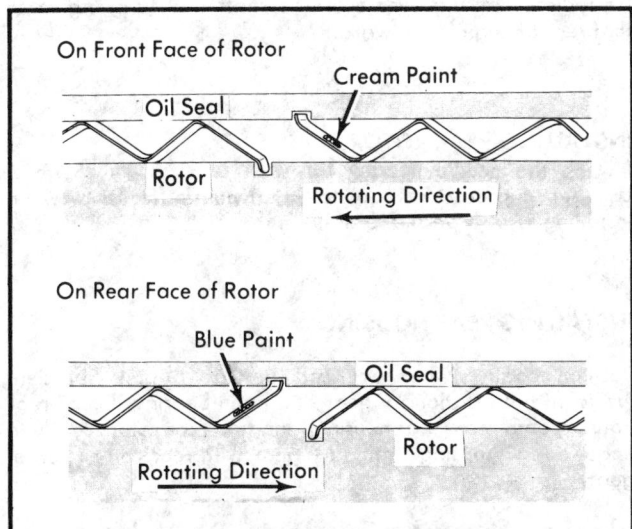

Fig. 17 Installing Oil Seal Spring on Rotor

3) Install outer oil seal so square edge of spring fits in stopper notch of oil seal. Push head of oil seal in position slowly with fingers. Apply sufficient lubricant to each oil seal and groove and confirm smooth movement of each seal by pressing head of seals. Check oil seal protrusion. *See Rotor Oil Seal Replacement.*

NOTE — *Take care not to deform lip of oil seal.*

APEX, CORNER & SIDE SEALS

NOTE — *Before installing apex seal, cut the assist piece with a knife to a length of .08-.10" (2.0-2.5 mm). Peel off paper and install assist piece on apex seal, Fig. 18.*

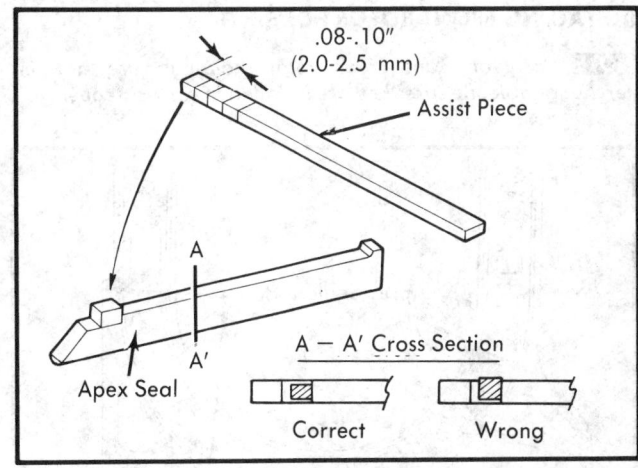

Fig. 18 Installing Assist Piece on Apex Seal

1) Position apex seals, without springs, and side pieces into their respective grooves so that each side piece rests on rear side of each rotor. Place corner seals and springs into their respective grooves, then position side seals and springs in proper grooves.

2) Apply engine lubricant to each spring. Ensure smooth movement of each spring. Check seal protusion, as described previously. Invert rotor and install seals on other side of rotor.

INSTALLING FRONT ROTOR

Mount front housing on engine stand and place front rotor assembly on housing. Use care not to drop seals into port. Mesh internal and stationary gear so that one rotor apex is set to one of 4 positions shown in *Fig. 19.*

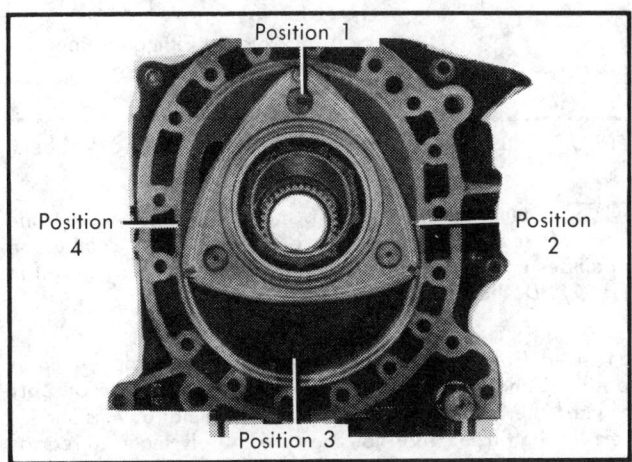

Fig. 19 Positioning Rotor Apex for Reassembly

RX7 ROTARY ENGINE (Cont.)

INSTALLING ECCENTRIC SHAFT

Lubricate front rotor journal and main journal on shaft with engine lubricant. Insert eccentric shaft being careful not to damage rotor bearing and main bearing.

INSTALLING FRONT ROTOR HOUSING

NOTE — *Front and rear rotor housings are not interchangeable. Be sure they are installed in correct sequence.*

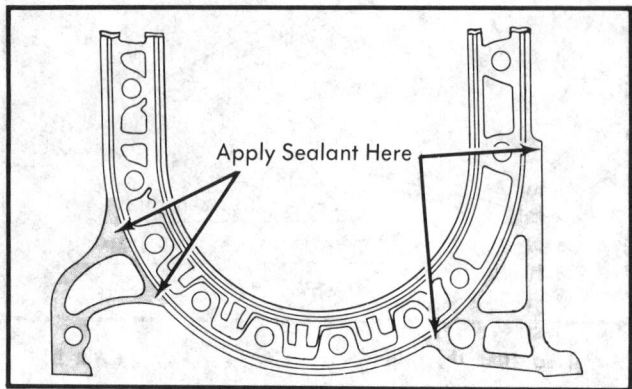

Fig. 20   Applying Sealing Agent to Rotor Assembly

1) Apply sealing agent to front side of rotor housing as shown in *Fig. 20.* To provide greater durability to sealing rubbers, install a protector behind each inner sealing rubber *(Fig. 21).* Install new "O" ring, sealing rubbers and protector in front side of engine housing. Apply light coat of petroleum jelly to hold seals in place.

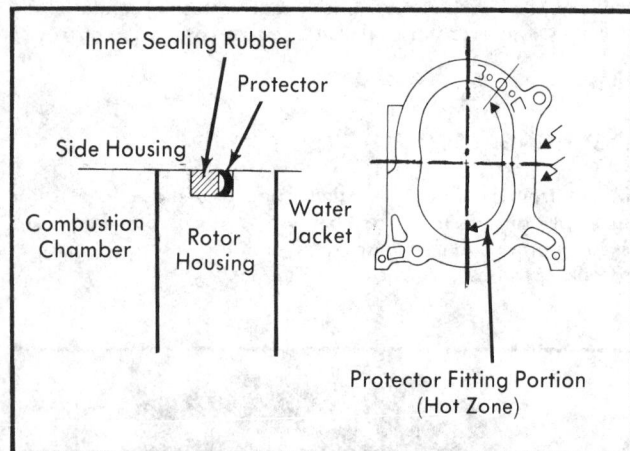

Fig. 21   Installing Protectors for Inner Sealing Rubbers

NOTE — *Inner sealing rubber is square type. The wider white line of sealing rubber should face toward combustion chamber and seam of rubber should be placed as shown in Fig. 22. Do not stretch sealing rubbers.*

2) Invert front rotor housing using care that seals remain in position, and install on front housing with air injection port toward intermediate housing. Lubricate tubular dowels and insert through front rotor housing holes. Apply sealer to rear of front rotor housing and place new "O" rings, sealing rubbers and protector on rear side of housing.

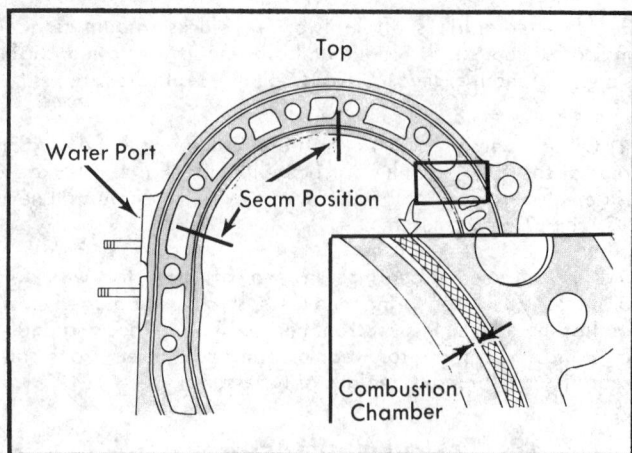

Fig. 22   Positioning Inner Sealing Rubber

3) Insert apex seal springs, confirming spring direction *(Fig. 15).* Install corner seal springs and corner seals in their respective grooves. Install side seal springs and side seals. Fit side pieces to original positions and lubricate with engine oil. Apply sealant to rear side of front rotor housing in areas shown in *Fig. 20.* Apply engine oil to sliding surfaces of front rotor housing.

INSTALLING INTERMEDIATE HOUSING

Turn front housing and rotor assembly so that top of housing is upward. Pull eccentric shaft outward approximately 1.0" (25 mm), but not more than 1.5" (38 mm). Rotate eccentric shaft until eccentric portion points to 2 o'clock position. Install intermediate housing over eccentric shaft and turn engine so that rear of engine is upward.

INSTALLING REAR ROTOR

Use same procedures up to *Intermediate Housing* when installing rear rotor and rotor housing.

INSTALLING REAR HOUSING

Position engine with rear end upward. Apply sufficient lubricant onto stationary gear and main bearing. Install rear housing onto rear rotor housing, and turn rear rotor slightly to engage rear housing stationary gear with rear rotor internal gear.

TIGHTENING TENSION BOLTS

Place a new sealing washer on each tension bolt and oil threads of each bolt. Refer to illustration and tighten bolts in sequence shown in *Fig. 23.* Tighten bolts in steps until final torque setting of 23-27 ft. lbs. (3.2-3.8 mkg) is reached. After tightening, turn eccentric shaft and make sure rotation is light and smooth.

RX7 ROTARY ENGINE (Cont.)

Fig. 23 *Tightening Sequence of Tension Bolts*

FLYWHEEL COUNTERWEIGHT INSTALLATION

With Man. Trans. — **1)** Apply lubricant to oil seal in rear housing. Mount flywheel to rear end of eccentric shaft so that key fits into flywheel keyway. Apply sealing agent to both sides of flywheel lock washer, and place washer in position. Fit lock nut by fingers. Hold flywheel with suitable ring gear brake tool (49 1881 060) and tighten lock nut to 289-362 ft. lbs. (40-50 mkg). Bend up lock tabs on washer.

2) Hold clutch disc in position with clutch disc centering tool (49 0813 310). Mount clutch cover and pressure plate assembly on flywheel and align the "0" marks of clutch cover and flywheel. Install 4 standard and 2 reamer bolts finger tight. To avoid distortion of pressure plate cover, tighten bolts in steps, a few turns at a time, until all are tight. Torque bolts to 13-20 ft. lbs. (1.8-2.7 mkg).

With Auto. Trans. — Fit key, lock washer and lock nut on eccentric shaft as described for Man. Trans. vehicles. Hold counterweight with suitable tool (49 1881 055) and tighten lock nut to 289-362 ft. lbs. (40-50 mkg). Bend tab of lock washer and attach drive plate on counterweight.

ECCENTRIC SHAFT END-THRUST ADJUSTMENT

1) Turn engine so front is up. Install thrust plate with chamfer downward, and slide spacer and needle bearing on eccentric shaft. Lubricate shaft and bearings and install bearing housing.

NOTE — *If bearing housing has not been removed, use care that center of needle bearing in bearing housing comes to center of eccentric shaft and that spacer is seated to thrust plate.*

2) Lubricate and install needle bearing, thrust washer, and balance weight on shaft. Install keys in oil pump and eccentric shaft keyways. Place oil pump drive chain on oil pump sprocket and eccentric shaft sprocket, and install sprockets on shafts.

3) Install key in eccentric shaft. Install distributor drive gear, with "F" mark on gear, facing front of engine. Install eccentric

shaft pulley on shaft. Use new washer and tighten pulley bolt to 72-87 ft. lbs. (10-12 mkg).

Fig. 24 *Measuring Eccentric Shaft End Play with Dial Indicator*

4) Turn engine so top is upward. Attach a dial indicator on the flywheel or counterweight so it contacts rear housing. Move flywheel or counterweight back and forth. Standard end play is .0016-.0028" (.04-.07 mm). If end play is more than .0035" (.09 mm) grind spacer on surface plate with emery paper or install thinner spacer. If end play is less than .0016" (.04 mm), install thicker spacer.

5) Oversize spacers are available in four oversizes from .3181" to .3150" (8.08 mm to 8.00 mm) and are identified by stamped letter "X", "Y", "V", and "Z" respectively. When spacer has been installed, recheck end play.

NOTE — *If end play is below specified amount, spacer thickness is too small; if end play is beyond specifications, spacer is too thick.*

INSTALLING FRONT COVER & ECCENTRIC SHAFT PULLEY

1) Turn engine so front is upward. Remove eccentric shaft pulley. Tighten oil pump sprocket nut and bend tab of lock washer.

2) Check oil pump drive chain slack by pressing finger against chain. See *Fig. 26.* Chain slack measurement should not exceed .47" (12 mm). If the slack exceeds the limit, replace drive chain.

3) Install new "O" ring on front housing oil passage. Install front cover and gasket on front housing. Lubricate oil seal in front cover. Install eccentric shaft pulley on shaft. Use new washer and tighten pulley bolt to 72-87 ft. lbs. (10-20 mkg).

RX7 ROTARY ENGINE (Cont.)

INSTALLING OIL STRAINER & OIL PAN

Invert engine so bottom of engine is up. Install oil strainer gasket and strainer on front housing. Cut off excess gaskets along mounting surface of oil pan. Apply sealant to joints of each housing. Place gasket and oil pan in position and torque bolts to 6-8 ft. lbs. (0.8-1.1 mkg).

INSTALLING WATER PUMP

Turn engine upright, position gasket and water pump on front housing and tighten attaching bolts. **NOTE** – *For further information on cooling system components, see Cooling System in this article.*

INSTALLING DISTRIBUTOR

Rotate eccentric shaft until yellow mark (leading timing mark) on pulley aligns with indicator pin on front cover. Align notch on distributor housing with punch mark on driven gear. Insert distributor and lock nut. Turn distributor housing until a trigger wheel blade aligns with pick-up coil. Tighten lock nut.

INSTALLING EXTERNAL COMPONENTS

Install thermal reactor, inlet manifold with carburetor, alternator and drive belt, air pump and drive belt, oil filter assembly and all other external components. Before removing engine from stand, install engine hanger bracket to front cover.

ENGINE OILING

Crankcase Capacity – 5.5 quarts.

Oil Filter – Full-flow, disposable cartridge-type filter mounted on rear housing.

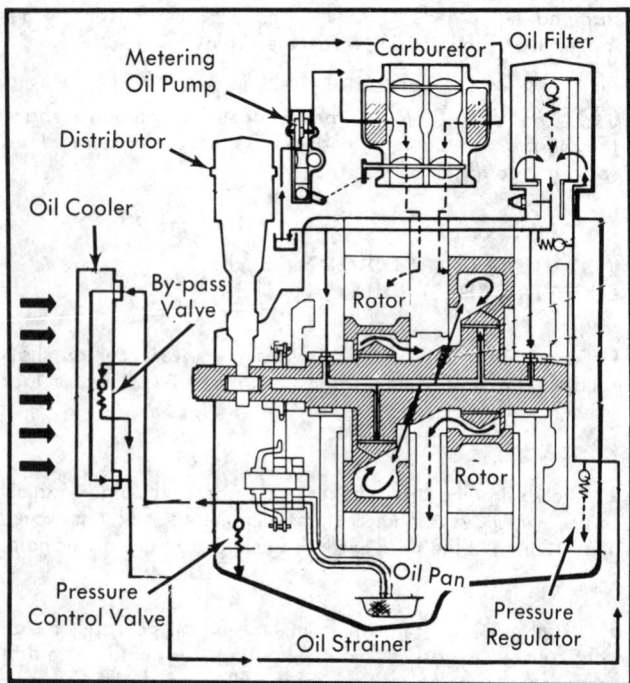

Fig. 25 Cutaway View of Engine Oiling System

Normal Oil Pressure – 13-38 psi (0.9-2.7 kg/cm²) at idle speed; 64-79 psi (4.5-5.5 kg/cm²) at 3000 RPM.

Pressure Regulator Valve – Mounted in rear housing, valve regulates oil pressure at high RPM. Valve opens to release oil pressure. If oil pressure is less than normal, check regulator valve piston for wear and ensure that spring free length is 2.874" (73 mm).

ENGINE OILING SYSTEM

Engine oiling system is forced circulation utilizing a two rotor type oil pump. Oil pump is mounted on front housing and is chain driven through eccentric shaft. A full-flow oil filter is mounted on rear housing. An oil metering pump, pressure regulator valve and an oil cooler in radiator are also employed.

OIL PUMP

NOTE – *Oil pump is mounted on front engine housing and must be checked or overhauled with front engine cover removed.*

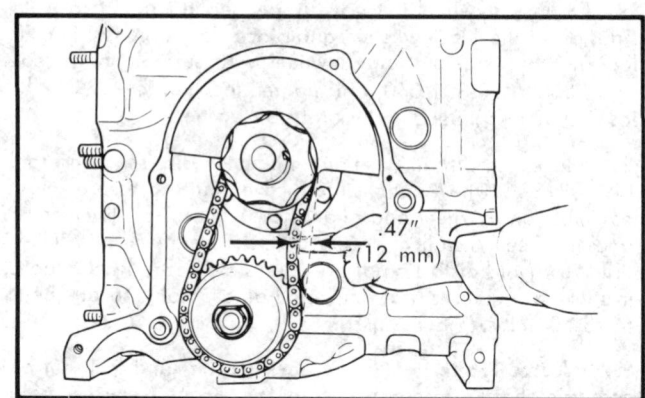

Fig. 26 Measuring Oil Pump Drive Chain Slack

1) With front engine cover removed, check oil pump drive chain slack by pressing finger against chain and measuring slack. If measurement exceeds .47" (12 mm), replace drive chain. *See Fig. 26.*

2) With oil pump removed, disassemble in following order: Remove snap ring, rear outer rotor, rear inner rotor, key and

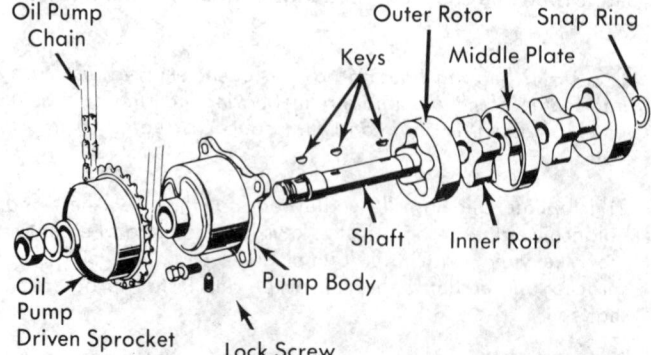

Fig. 27 Exploded View of Oil Pump Assembly

RX7 ROTARY ENGINE (Cont.)

middle plate; remove front inner rotor, key, shaft, spring pin and front outer rotor.

3) Insert a feeler gauge between lobes of inner and outer rotors and check clearance. If beyond .006"(.15 mm), replace both rotors.

4) Check clearance between outer rotor and pump housing with a feeler gauge. If clearance exceeds .012" (.30 mm), replace rotors or housing.

5) Place a straightedge across pump mounting surface and check rotor end play with a feeler gauge. If beyond .006" (.15 mm), correct pump body or replace rotors.

6) To assemble oil pump, reverse disassembly procedure. Install oil pump and tighten bolts. Install sprockets and chain as previously outlined. *See Eccentric Shaft Endthrust Adjustment.*

METERING OIL PUMP

Metering oil pump regulates amount of oil pumped to float chamber of carburetor. The oil enters combustion chamber with air/fuel mixture to lubricate seals within chamber. Amount of oil increases as engine RPM increases and the control lever on metering pump is actuated by a rod connected to throttle lever. To check amount of oil discharge proceed as follows:

1) Disconnect connecting rod, then disconnect oil lines at carburetor. Start engine and adjust idle to 2000 RPM. Once oil flow from hoses becomes steady, measure volume discharged. Pump should discharge 2.0-2.5 cc in six minutes.

NOTE — *As carburetor will not be receiving oil during test, add a small amount of clean oil to carburetor to provide proper lubrication during testing.*

2) To adjust oil metering pump, turn the adjusting screw clockwise to increase flow or counterclockwise to decrease flow. One complete turn will change oil discharge flow by 0.2-0.3 cc for six minutes of operation. Make sure lock nut of adjustment screw is locked, then recheck metering oil pump discharge rate.

OIL COOLER

1) Inspect oil cooler for damage, cracks and leakage. Any defects found are repaired by aluminum welding or replacement.

2) Drain engine oil and remove engine under cover. Remove cap nut at bottom of oil cooler and pull out by-pass valve.

3) Check by-pass valve after removing it from bottom of oil cooler. Heat and soak by-pass valve in oil gradually to 158°F (70°C) and check if protrusion of valve exceeds 0.2" (5 mm). If less, replace by-pass valve.

4) Install by-pass valve in reverse of removal procedure and fill engine with oil.

ENGINE COOLING

Thermostat — Wax pellet type, opens at 180° F (82° C).

Pressure Cap — 13 psi (0.9 kg/cm²)

WATER PUMP

1) Drain cooling system and remove air cleaner. Disconnect coupler from water temperature switch. Remove attaching bolts and drive fan. Loosen water pump pulley bolts. Remove air pump and drive belts.

2) Remove alternator and drive belt. Remove water pump pulley bolts and pulley. Remove water pump attaching nuts and bolts, then remove water pump. To install, reverse removal procedure.

ENGINE SPECIFICATIONS

GENERAL SPECIFICATIONS								
Year	cu. ins.	cc	Carburetor	HP at RPM	Torque (Ft. Lbs. at RPM)	Compr. Ratio	Rotor Housing Width	
							in.	mm
1980	70	1146	4-Bbl.	.....	.....	9.4:1	2.756	70

ROTOR HOUSING, INTERMEDIATE HOUSING & ROTOR							
	ROTOR HOUSING		INTERMEDIATE HOUSING		ROTOR		
Engine	Width In. (mm)	Distortion Limit In. (mm)	Width In. (mm)	Distortion Limit In. (mm)	Inside Diameter In.(mm)	Housing-to-Rotor Clearance In. mm)	Land Protrusion In. (mm)
1146 cc Rotary	2.756 (70)	.0024 (.06)	1.969 (50)	.0016 (.04)	.....	.0047-.0071 (.12-.18)	.....

Mazda Engines

RX7 ROTARY ENGINE (Cont.)
ENGINE SPECIFICATIONS (Cont.)

① APEX SEAL

Engine	Length	Seal Width	Height	Seal-to-Housing		Seal-to-Rotor	
				Clearance	Wear Limit	Groove Clearance	Wear Limit
1146 cc Rotary	2.750 (69.85)	.118 (3.0)	.335 (8.5)	.0051-.0075 (.13-.19)	.....	.0020-.0035 (.051-.089)	.006 (.15)

① — In. (mm)

SIDE SEAL

Engine	Thickness In. (mm)	Width In. (mm)	Seal-to-Groove		Side Seal-to-Corner Seal	
			Clearance In. (mm)	Limit In. (mm)	Clearance In. (mm)	Limit In. (mm)
1146 cc Rotary	.039 (1.0)	.138 (3.5)	.0012-.0031 (.03-.08)	.004 (.10)	.0020-.0059 (.05-.15)	.016 (.40)

CORNER SEAL

Engine	Diameter In. (mm)	Height In. (mm)	Seal-to-Groove		Side Seal-to-Corner Seal	
			Clearance In. (mm)	Limit In. (mm)	Clearance In. (mm)	Limit In. (mm)
1146 cc Rotary	.433 (11.0)	.276 (7.0)	.....	.....	.0020-.0059 (.05-.15)	.016 (.40)

ECCENTRIC SHAFT MAIN & ROTOR BEARINGS

Engine	MAIN BEARINGS			ROTOR BEARINGS	
	Journal Diameter In. (mm)	Clearance In. (mm)	Eccentric Shaft Endplay In. (mm)	Journal Diameter In. (mm)	Clearance In. (mm)
1146 cc Rotary	1.6929 (43)	.0016-.0031 (.04-.08)	.0016-.0028 (.04-.07)	2.9134 (74)	.0016-.0028 (.04-.07)

OIL SEAL

Height In. (mm)	Seal Lip Contact Width	
	Standard In. (mm)	Limit In. (mm)
.220 (5.6)	.020 (.5)	.....

PORT TIMING

Engine	INTAKE		EXHAUST	
	Open (ATDC)	Close (ABDC)	Open (BBDC)	Close (ATDC)
1146 cc Rotary	32°	40°	75°	38°

TIGHTENING SPECIFICATIONS

Application	Ft. Lbs. (mkg)
Oil Pump Sprocket	22-25 (3.0-3.5)
Oil Pan	6-8 (0.8-1.1)
Eccentric Shaft Pulley	72-87 (10-12)
Intake Manifold	14-19 (1.9-2.6)
Thermal Reactor	33-40 (4.5-5.5)
Flywheel Lock Nut	289-362 (40-50)
Crankshaft Pulley	72-87 (10-12)
Water Pump	13-20 (1.8-2.7)
Clutch Cover	13-20 (1.8-2.7)

4 & 5 CYLINDER DIESEL

ENGINE CODING

ENGINE IDENTIFICATION

Engine identification number is stamped on left side of cylinder block. First six digits of this number are used for engine identification purposes.

Engine Identification		
Application	**Chassis Type**	**Engine Code**
240D (4-Cyl.)	123.123	616.912
300D (5-Cyl.)	123.130	617.912
300CD (5-Cyl.)	123.150	617.912
300SD (5-Cyl. Turbo) .	116.120	617.950
300TD (5-Cyl.)	123.190	617.912

ENGINE & CYLINDER HEAD

ENGINE

Removal — 1) Drain cooling system from plug on side of crankcase. Remove engine hood, radiator and fan shroud. (On some models, hood may be raised 90° to allow engine removal.) Remove air filter with intake duct. Draw oil from power steering pump reservoir and disconnect hoses. If equipped with air conditioning, dismount and set compressor aside but DO NOT disconnect refrigerant hoses.

2) Remove control linkage with shaft and place aside. Disconnect all coolant, vacuum, oil, fuel and electrical lines which lead to engine. On turbocharged models, loosen oil filter cover and raise slightly, and disconnect exhaust system at turbocharger. On all other models, disconnect exhaust pipe at exhaust manifold. On all models, remove lateral support for exhaust pipe at transmission.

3) If equipped with level control, remove pump and set aside, leaving lines connected. Disconnect engine shock absorbers at chassis. Remove drive shaft shield and disconnect drive shaft at transmission. Disconnect shift lever and all connections at transmission. Unscrew front and rear engine mountings. Attach suitable sling to lifting eyes and hoist engine/transmission assembly out at an angle of approximately 45°.

Installation — Ensure that oil cooler, lines and filter housing have been flushed if installing new engine as a result of bearing failure. Lower engine/transmission assembly into position and complete installation in reverse order of removal.

NOTE — *DO NOT use oil or grease on engine stops or mounts.*

TURBOCHARGER (Turbo Diesel Only)

Removal — 1) Remove air filter assembly and all ducting. Disconnect wire from temperature switch and remove vacuum line and crankcase breather pipe. Disconnect engine oil supply line to turbocharger.

2) Remove air filter mounting bracket and disconnect exhaust flange. Remove exhaust bracket on automatic transmission and press exhaust pipe to rear. Remove intermediate flange mounting bracket. Remove 4 mounting nuts holding turbocharger to manifold and remove turbocharger. Cover oil return pipe.

Installation — Install new flange gasket so that reinforcing bead is towards exhaust manifold. Ensure that center housing is filled with approximately $\frac{1}{4}$ pint of oil. Install intermediate flange and oil return pipe and install turbocharger. Complete installation in reverse order of removal.

CYLINDER HEAD

NOTE — *Remove head only after engine has cooled down.*

Removal — 1) Drain cooling system and disconnect all water hoses attached to cylinder head. Remove air cleaner and ducting. If equipped with level control, remove pump and set aside, leaving lines connected. If equipped with power steering, remove pump with bracket and fuel filter and set aside. On turbocharged models, loosen and pull up oil filter cover slightly, and remove turbocharger.

2) Detach all remaining electrical connections, water, fuel and vacuum lines from cylinder head and intake manifold. Unbolt dipstick guide tube of automatic transmission from intake manifold. Disconnect exhaust pipe from manifold or turbocharger and at transmission support. Remove throttle control linkage and place aside. Remove injection lines and cover all connections.

3) Unbolt exhaust manifold support at manifold. Remove cylinder head cover and loosen, but do not remove camshaft sprocket bolt. Position camshaft to free rocker arms of tension and remove rocker arm assemblies. Rotate crankshaft by using socket tool on crankshaft pulley so that No. 1 cylinder is at TDC on firing stroke.

4) Mark camshaft sprocket and timing chain for proper assembly. Uscrew chain tensioner plug and remove compression spring. Remove guide rail from cylinder head and pull out guide rail bolt with an impact puller. Remove camshaft sprocket. Loosen and remove head bolts in reverse of tightening sequence. Injection nozzles must be removed prior to removing the 5 bolts next to nozzles.

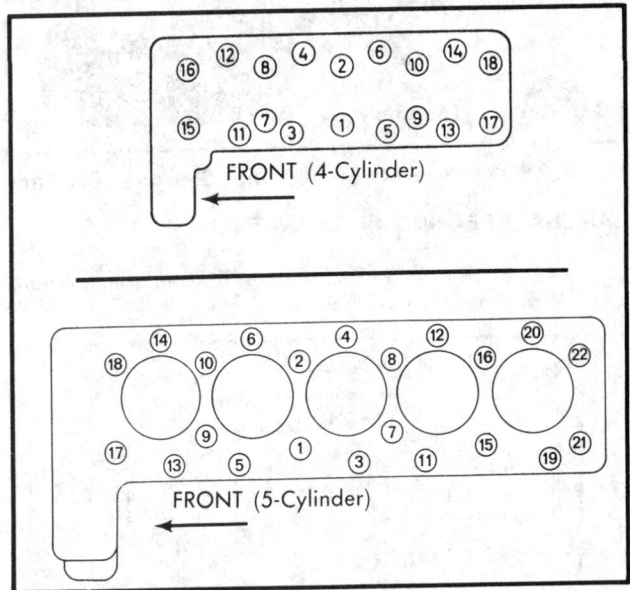

Fig. 1   Cylinder Head Tightening Sequence (Loosen in Reverse Order)

4 & 5 CYLINDER DIESEL (Cont.)

5) Attach sling to lifting eyes on head and lift head from engine. Thoroughly clean all mating surfaces of head and cylinder block.

Installation — 1) Ensure that No. 1 cylinder is still at TDC. Place new head gasket into position, ensuring that locating dowels are in correct position. Place head on block and insert oiled bolts of proper length. Tighten bolts to 51 ft. lbs. (7 mkg) in order shown, then to 72 ft. lbs. (10 mkg) in same order.

2) Complete installation in reverse order of removal and adjust valve clearance. Use new seals and gaskets when installing all components. Run engine to approximately 176°F (80°C), then loosen each head bolt ¼ turn and tighten to 72 ft. lbs. (10 mkg) in sequence shown.

CAMSHAFT

CAMSHAFT

Removal & Installation — Remove cylinder head cover and camshaft sprocket. (See CYLINDER HEAD in this article.) Remove shim from camshaft at front bearing support. Remove bearing support bolts and lift off camshaft together with bearings and oil pipe. To install, reverse removal procedure ensuring that camshaft supports and dowel pins are aligned.

Fig. 2 Rocker Arm Assemblies and Camshaft Bearings

CAMSHAFT BEARING REPLACEMENT

1) Inspect camshaft bearings for wear. If worn, grind bearing journals and fit undersize bearings.

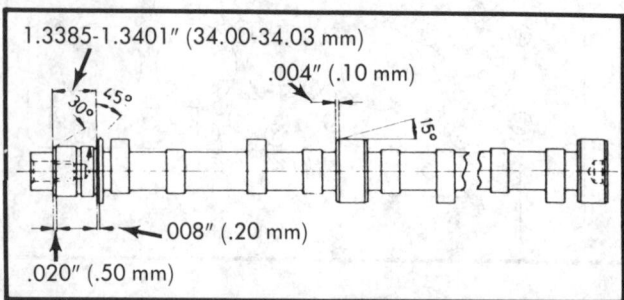

Fig. 3 Detailed View of Camshaft

2) Bearing on No. 1 journal controls camshaft end play. Width of journal is 1.3385-1.3401" (34.0-34.03 mm). Place bearing on camshaft and install retaining ring. Using a feeler gauge, measure clearance between camshaft flange and bearing (see illustation). Lap bearing to proper fit. The following table lists camshaft bearing journal diameters for standard and undersize bearings:

Camshaft Journal Diameters		
Application	**Front** In. (mm)	**Center & Rear** In. (mm)
Standard	1.375 (34.94)	1.926 (48.94)
Intermediate (Grey)	1.371 (34.84)	1.920 (48.76)
1st Undersize (Red)	1.365 (34.69)	1.916 (48.69)

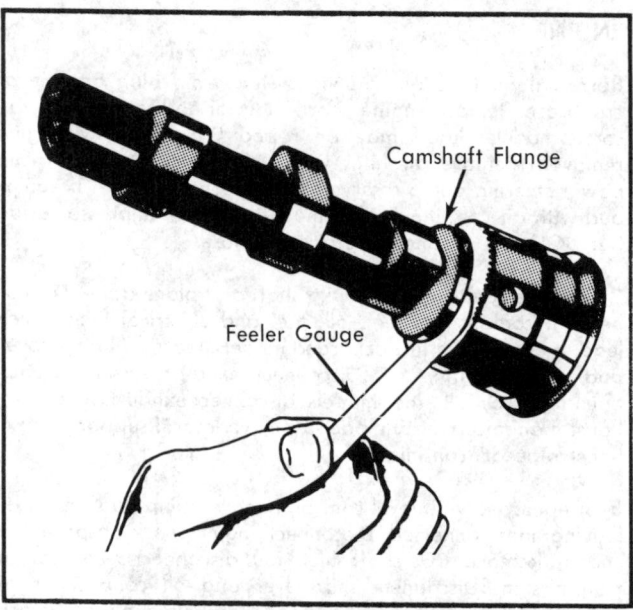

Fig. 4 Measuring Camshaft End Play

TIMING CHAIN

Removal & Installation — 1) A split link timing chain is available for repairs without dismantling engine. Remove glow plugs and cylinder head cover. Remove air cleaner adapter. Cover chain guard with cloth and grind open both pins of a link in the timing chain.

2) Remove old link and insert new split link with new chain attached. Turn crankshaft slowly in normal direction while feeding new chain in and old chain out. Ensure that chain does not slip on sprockets and install master (split) link from rear so that retainer will be at front.

3) Install spring lock with closed end facing direction of rotation. Rotate crankshaft through one complete revolution and check that all timing marks still agree. To complete installation, reverse removal procedures.

4 & 5 CYLINDER DIESEL (Cont.)

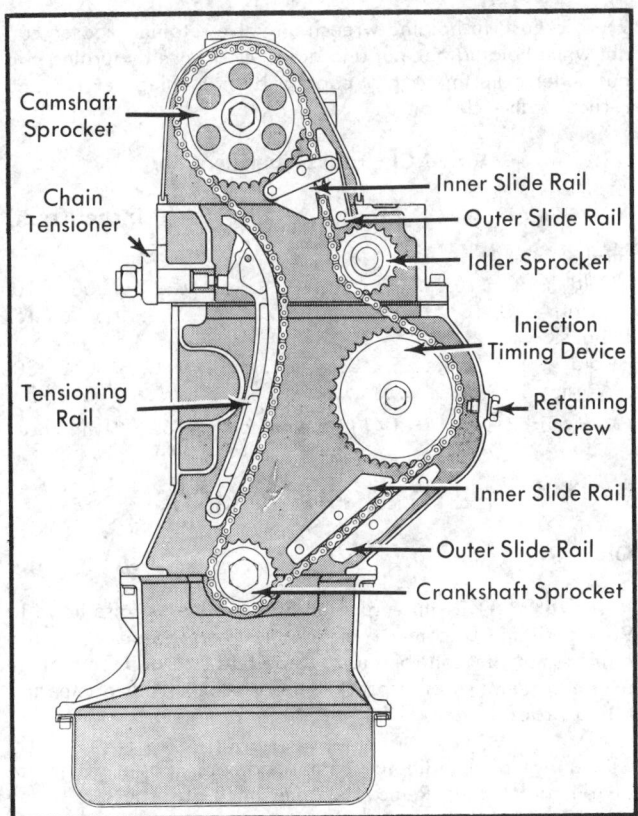

Fig. 5 Timing Chain and Related Components

VALVE TIMING

1) Rotate No. 1 piston to TDC of compression stroke. Align camshaft timing mark with mark on No. 1 camshaft bearing support bracket (see illustration). Install camshaft sprocket.

2) If correct valve timing is not achieved when camshaft sprocket is installed, offset Woodruff keys are available to make timing corrections, see following table:

Offset Woodruff Keys

Offset	Crankshaft Correction
.0275" (.7 mm)	4°
.0354" (.9 mm)	6 1/2°
.0433" (1.1 mm)	8°
.0511" (1.3 mm)	10°

Fig. 6 Camshaft Timing Mark Locations

INJECTION PUMP TIMING

1) To check injection pump timing (start of delivery), turn crankshaft in normal direction until 24° BTDC mark is under pointer with No. 1 piston on compression stroke. Remove first pumping element pipe connection and valve ports and install overflow pipe in their place.

2) Set control lever to full throttle position. Attach auxiliary fuel container to pump inlet fitting. Turn engine until fuel stream stops from overflow pipe and drips are at least 10-15 seconds apart. Delivery should occur when pipe stops dripping and crankshaft on 24° BTDC mark.

3) Turn crankshaft 2 more full turns and check that fuel stops dripping at end of second full turn if pump timing is correct. If adjustment is required, loosen pump mounting nuts and turn pump TOWARD engine to advance delivery and AWAY FROM engine to retard start of delivery.

4) When timing is correct, tighten mounting nuts and recheck start of delivery. Disconnect auxiliary fuel container and overflow pipe. Connect normal fuel line and install first pumping element with fittings.

VALVES

VALVE ARRANGEMENT

4 Cylinder — E-I-I-E-E-I-I-E

5 Cylinder — E-I-I-E-E-I-I-E-E-I (front to rear).

VALVE GUIDE SERVICING

1) Check valve guide bores and ensure they are not less than .3937" (10.00 mm) or larger than .3947" (10.025 mm). Remove all carbon before measuring guides.

2) Using a suitable drift, drive intake guide out toward top of head and exhaust guide toward combustion chamber.

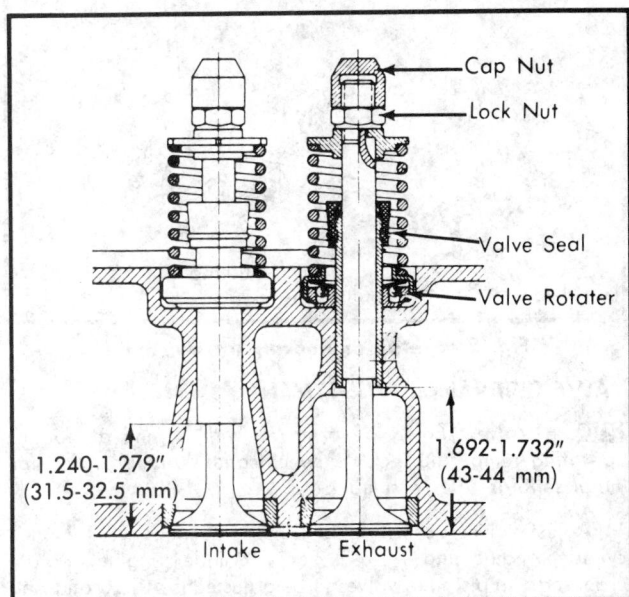

Fig. 7 Installed View of Valve Assemblies

Mercedes-Benz Engines

4 & 5 CYLINDER DIESEL (Cont.)

3) Press in new guides from combustion side until specified distance is achieved. *See Fig. 7.* Check guide bores and ream for proper clearance as required.

4) Valve guides are available in standard and one oversize (color red). An interference fit of .0004-.0015" (.010-.040 mm) is used. If guide does not meet specifications, replace. Note that intake guides are 2.362" (60 mm) long and exhaust guides are 1.909" (48.5 mm) long.

Valve Guide Specification

Application	Guide O.D. In. (mm)	Cyl. Head Bore In. (mm)
Standard	.5522-.5527 (14.03-14.04)	.5511-.5518 (14.00-14.02)
Oversize (Red)	.5601-.5605 (14.23-14.24)	.5590-.5597 (14.20-14.22)

VALVE STEM OIL SEALS

Removal — With rocker arms and brackets removed from head, use suitable compressor and unscrew adjusting cap and lock nut from valve stem. Remove collar and valve spring. Old seal may be pried off with screwdriver or pulled off with pliers.

Installation — Note that intake seals are color coded black and exhaust seals are green. Position assembly sleeve over valve stem and press new seal onto guide with suitable tool (617 589 00 43 00). Replace valve spring, collar, lock nut and adjusting cap.

ROCKER ARM ASSEMBLIES

Removal & Installation — Remove air cleaner and cylinder head cover. Loosen rocker arm bracket bolts and rotate camshaft so there is no load on rocker arms being removed. Remove front assembly (serving 2 front cylinders), then rotate camshaft so that rear assembly can be removed without tension. Disassemble and replace parts as required. To install, reverse removal procedures.

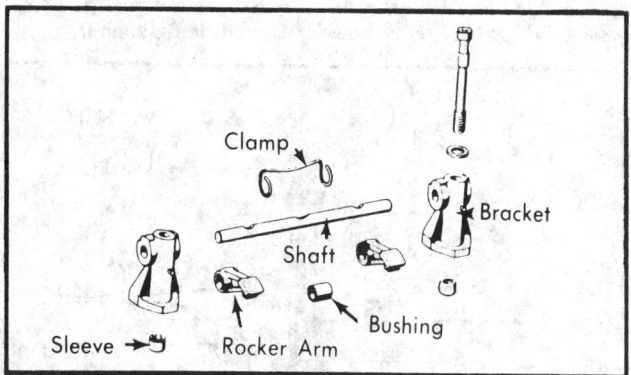

Fig. 8   Detail of Rocker Arm Assembly

VALVE CLEARANCE ADJUSTMENT

NOTE — *Valves should be adjusted with engine at normal operating temperature. Cold specifications are provided for initial settings after assembly.*

1) Adjust valves according to firing sequence (1-3-4-2 on 4 cylinder engine and 1-2-4-5-3 on 5 cylinder engine). Rotate crankshaft so piston of valves to be adjusted is at TDC on firing stroke. Measure clearance between slide surface of camshaft and rocker arm.

2) To adjust, fit holding wrench on valve retainer. Loosen cap nut while holding hex nut and adjust clearance by turning cap nut. After adjustment, lock cap nut by tightening hex nut and recheck valve clearance.

Valve Clearance Specifications

Valve	Inches (mm)
Intake	
Cold	.004 (.10)
Warm	.006 (.15)
Exhaust	
Cold	①.012 (.30)
Warm	①.014 (.35)

① — Turbo Diesel — .04" (.35 mm) cold, .016" (.40 mm) hot.

PISTONS, PINS & RINGS

OIL PAN

Removal — 1) Drain engine oil and remove or raise hood to 90° position. Disconnect air cleaner corrugated duct and remove throttle control shaft. Unbolt fan shroud and place over fan. Remove oil dipstick tube bracket at power steering pump bracket.

2) Remove air conditioner compressor and loosen clamp for air/oil cooler lines. Remove engine shock absorbers at frame crossmember. Loosen exhaust system lateral support at transmission. Remove engine mounting bolts from below. Unbolt oil cooler lines for automatic transmission at transmission, intermediate flange and upper section of pan.

3) Remove 4 lower bolts on intermediate flange and remove intermediate flange shield. Unbolt and remove LOWER oil pan. Use suitable drift and drive oil dipstick guide tube out as far as it will go. Remove strainer extension with strainer from oil pump. Remove upper oil pan bolts.

4) Attach engine sling and hoist to front of engine and raise enough to remove pan upper section. Pull out oil dipstick guide tube. Turn crankshaft until counterweights and connecting rods clear pan and lower pan from block.

Installation — 1) Install new radial seal in groove at rear of pan. Ensure that mating surfaces are clean and coat upper pan section with gasket compound. Place upper pan in position and insert dipstick guide tube. On turbocharged engine, insert oil return line from turbocharger.

2) Bolt upper section of pan to engine. Mount strainer extension and strainer to oil pump. Use new gasket and bolt lower pan to upper pan. To complete installation, reverse removal procedure.

PISTON & ROD ASSEMBLY

Removal — With cylinder head and oil pan removed, unscrew connecting rod nuts. Tap bolts with plastic mallet to loosen rod on crankshaft and push piston/rod assembly out of top of cylinder block. To remove piston from rod, remove piston pin circlips. Heat piston to 104-140°F (40-60°C) and press out piston pins.

4 & 5 CYLINDER DIESEL (Cont.)

NOTE — *On Turbo Diesel, oil spray nozzles in crankcase must be removed prior to removal and installation of pistons. Nozzles must be replaced in orginal location after piston/rod assemblies are installed.*

Installation — 1) Heat piston and install piston pin and circlips. Arrow on piston crown must face forward and bearing shell retaining notches on rod and cap must be on left side. Measure rod bolt shank to determine bolt stress. Replace if shank is less than .2834" (7.2 mm). New bolt shank diameter is .3307" (8.4 mm).

NOTE — *First tightening of NEW bolts is 50.6 ft. lbs. (7.0 mkg). Subsequent tightening should be to 36 ft. lbs. (5.0 mkg).*

2) Stagger ring gaps and fit ring compressor on piston. Insert piston/rod assembly so that arrow on piston crown faces front of engine and numbers on rod and cap are at left side of engine. Tighten rod cap to specifications and check for normal crankshaft rotation.

3) Measure piston protrusion above top of cylinder block with piston at TDC. Piston should project at least .020" (.50 mm), but not more than .035" (.90 mm) above block.

FITTING PISTONS

Measure piston and cylinder diameters to determine running clearance. Piston diameter is measured at 90° to piston pin bore near bottom of piston skirt. There are two compression rings and one oil ring. Install compression rings with markings "top" or "F" and oil ring with marking "GOE" or "F" facing upward.

CRANKSHAFT MAIN & CONNECTING ROD BEARINGS

MAIN BEARING SERVICE

Measure main bearing and connecting rod journals for out-of-round and taper. Out-of-round must not exceed .0002-.0004" (.005-.010 mm) and taper must not exceed .0004-.0006" (.010-.015 mm). Select proper undersize, if required, and grind crankshaft to following diameters:

Crankshaft Journal Diameters

Application	Main In. (mm)	Con. Rod In. (mm)
Standard	2.7541-2.7545 (69.95-69.96)	2.0454-2.0458 (51.95-51.96)
1st Undersize	2.7442-2.7446 (69.70-69.71)	2.0356-2.0360 (51.70-51.71)
2nd Undersize	2.7344-2.7348 (69.45-69.46)	2.0257-2.0261 (51.45-51.46)
3rd Undersize	2.7246-2.7249 (69.20-69.21)	2.0159-2.0163 (51.20-51.21)
4th Undersize	2.7147-2.7151 (68.95-68.96)	2.0060-2.0064 (50.95-50.96)

THRUST BEARING ALIGNMENT

Third main bearing is equipped with separate shells and thrust washers in place of 2 one piece bearing inserts. Two identical thrust washers are inserted in crankcase and 2 remaining halves are fitted in bearing cap. Bottom halves have 2 tabs to prevent turning and avoid incorrect installation. Following size thrust washers are available to adjust crankshaft end play: .085" (2.15 mm), .087" (2.20 mm), .089" (2.25 mm), .092" (2.35 mm) and .094" (2.40 mm).

CRANKSHAFT REAR OIL SEAL

Removal & Installation — With oil pan and crankshaft removed, pull old seal from groove in crankcase and oil pan. Insert new radial seal in groove and press into place using an oiled hammer handle. To provide overlap, cut seal off .040" (1 mm) above separation surface. Coat seal halves with engine oil.

FRONT OIL SEAL

Removal — With radiator and shroud removed, take off front pulley and vibration dampener. Pry old oil seal from engine with screwdriver. If fitted with original seal, remove spacer washer with puller (616 589 00 33 00).

NOTE — *On some engines, chrome plated spacer ring will not be required. Replacement seals for Turbo Diesel are of green Viton inside and black acrylic outside. Other seals are black outside and white inside.*

Installation — Install new spacer ring (if required) and lubricate seal lips with engine oil. Ensure that seal cavity is clean and free of nicks and scratches. Place seal SQUARELY in recess and use installation sleeve to press seal into proper position.

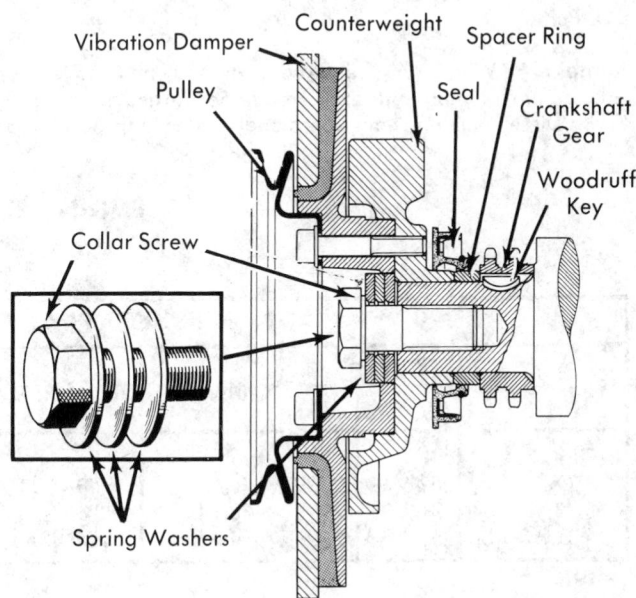

Fig. 9 Sectional View of Crankshaft Front Oil Seal

ENGINE OILING

ENGINE OILING SYSTEM

Engine lubrication is provided by a gear type oil pump, which force feeds oil through an oil filter to oil gallery. From oil gallery, oil flows to main and connecting rod bearings. Pistons, wrist pins and connecting rod bushings are splash lubricated. A vertical oil passage from oil gallery has a transverse passage which supplies oil to intermediate sprocket shaft and

Mercedes-Benz Engines

4 & 5 CYLINDER DIESEL (Cont.)

bearings. Another oil passage supplies oil to oil pump drive shaft and helical gear. Vertical passage also supplies oil to No. 1 camshaft bearing. An external oil tube attached to No. 1 camshaft bearing support lubricates other camshaft bearings and rocker arms.

NOTE — *Turbo Diesel models also have an external line feeding oil to the turbocharger with a gravity feed back to the crankcase. Additionally, the main oil gallery feeds spray nozzles for cooling of the pistons.*

Crankcase Capacities (With Filter)	
Application	**Capacity**
4 & 5 Cylinder	7.0 qts.
5 Cylinder Turbo	7.9 qts.

Normal Oil Pressure — 7.1 psi. (.5 kg/cm²) at 700-780 RPM idle speed; 42 psi. (3 kg/cm²) at 3000 RPM.

Oil Filter — Oil filter is vertically mounted and contains a single cartridge composed of a main and by-pass section.

Pressure Regulator Valve — Non-adjustable.

OIL PUMP

Removal — With oil pan removed, pump may be removed by taking out mounting bolts except on turbocharged engine. On Turbo Diesel, pump is chain driven and must have sprocket and chain removed prior to pump removal. Remove 5 mounting bolts and take off pump. Remove connecting pipe from engine block.

Installation — On Turbo Diesel, use new "O" ring and insert connecting pipe. Ensure that sprocket is mounted in duplex chain properly and install oil pump. Mount sprocket on pump drive shaft and install tensioning rail and spring. On all other models, install pump and tighten mounting screw on crankcase and bearing cap.

ENGINE COOLING

Thermostat — Opens at 172-180°F (78-82°C).

Cooling System Capacity	
Application	**Capacity**
4 Cylinder	10.6 qts.
5 Cylinder	11.6 qts.
5 Cylinder Turbo	12.7 qts.

WATER PUMP

Removal — Drain cooling system and loosen "V" belts. Remove fan and drive pulley. Remove or loosen hoses from pump and take out mounting bolts. Remove pump.

Installation — Coat new gasket with suitable sealer and mount with pump on engine. Install fan and hub and adjust belts. Fill radiator and expansion tank to mark and run engine. After temperature reaches approximately 140°F (60°C), install radiator cap and check for leaks.

ENGINE SPECIFICATIONS

GENERAL SPECIFICATIONS

Year	Displ.		Carburetor	HP at RPM	Torque (Ft. Lbs. at RPM)	Compr. Ratio	Bore		Stroke	
	cu. ins.	cc					in.	mm	in.	mm
1980										
4 Cyl.	146.4	2399	Fuel Inj.	67@4000	97@2400	21.0:1	3.57	90.9	3.64	92.4
5 Cyl.	183.0	2998	Fuel Inj.	83@4200	120@2400	21.0:1	3.57	90.9	3.64	92.4
5 Cyl. Turbo	183.0	2998	Fuel Inj.	120@4350	170@2400	21.5:1	3.57	90.9	3.64	92.4

VALVES

Engine & Valve	Head Diam. In. (mm)	Face Angle	Seat Angle	Seat Width In. (mm)	Stem Diameter In. (mm)	Stem Clearance In. (mm)	Valve Lift In. (mm)
All							
Intake	1.563-1.571 (39.70-39.90)	30°	30°	.051-.063 (1.3-1.6)	.3906-.3913 (9.92-9.94)	.0030 (.075)	.....
Exhaust	1.343-1.350 (34.10-34.30)	30°	30°	.098-.114 (2.5-2.9)	.3906-.3913 (9.92-9.94)	.0030 (.075)	.....

4 & 5 CYLINDER DIESEL (Cont.)
ENGINE SPECIFICATIONS (Cont.)

PISTONS, PINS, RINGS						
	PISTONS	PINS		RINGS		
Engine	Clearance In. (mm)	Piston Fit In. (mm)	Rod Fit In. (mm)	Rings	End Gap In. (mm)	Side Clearance In. (mm)
All	.0007-.0015 (.018-.038)	①	Push Fit	No. 1	.0079-.0138 (.20-.35)	.004-.005 (.100-.132)
				No. 2	.0079-.0138 (.20-.35)	.003-.004 (.070-.102)
				No. 3	.0098-.0157 (.25-.40)	.001-.002 (.030-.062)

① — Interference fit. *See Piston & Rod Assembly in this article.*

CRANKSHAFT MAIN & CONNECTING ROD BEARINGS							
	MAIN BEARINGS				CONNECTING ROD BEARINGS		
Engine	Journal Diam. In. (mm)	Clearance In. (mm)	Thrust Bearing	Crankshaft End Play In. (mm)	Journal Diam. In. (mm)	Clearance In. (mm)	Side Play In. (mm)
All	2.7541-2.7545 (69.95-69.96)	.0012-.0027 (.031-.068)	Center	.0039-.0090 (.10-.22)	2.0454-2.0458 (51.95-51.96)	.0012-.0027 (.031-.068)	.005-.010 (.12-.26)

VALVE SPRINGS			
	Free Length In. (mm)	PRESSURE Lbs. @ In. (kg @ mm)	
Engine		Valve Closed	Valve Open
All	2.015 (51.2)	.....	130.1@1.102 (59.0@28.0)

VALVE TIMING				
	INTAKE		EXHAUST	
Engine	Open (ATDC)	Close (ABDC)	Open (BBDC)	Close (BTDC)
All	13.5°	15.5°	19°	17°

CAMSHAFT			
Engine	Journal Diam. In. (mm)	Clearance In. (mm)	Lobe Lift In. (mm)
All No. 1	1.375 (34.94)	.0010-.0026 (.025-.066)	.003-.006 (.070-.149)
No. 2, 3 & 4	1.926 (48.94)	.0010-.0026 (.025-.066)	.....

TIGHTENING SPECIFICATIONS

Application	Ft. Lbs. (mkg)
Cylinder Head	
Step 1	51 (7)
Step 2	72 (10)
Step 3①	72 (10)
Rocker Arm Support Bolts	29 (4)
Prechamber in Cyl. Head	108-130 (15-18)
Nozzle Holder in Prechamber	51-58 (7-8)
Glow Plugs	36 (5)
Connecting Rod Caps	36 (5)
Main Bearing Caps	65 (9)
Crankshaft Front Hex Bolt	195-239 (27-33)
Oil Pan Bolts	7 (1)
Camshaft Sprocket Bolt	58 (8)
Cylinder Head Cover	10 (1.5)

① — Loosen head bolts ¼ turn and tighten in sequence to final torque after engine reaches approximately 176°F (80°C).

280 6 CYLINDER

ENGINE CODING

ENGINE IDENTIFICATION

Engine number is stamped on front left side of cylinder block. Engine is a six cylinder double overhead cam type referred to as an M110.

Engine Identification		
Application	**Chassis Type**	**Engine Coding**
280E	123.033	110.984
280CE	123.053	110.984
280SE	116.024	110.985

ENGINE, CYLINDER HEAD & MANIFOLDS

ENGINE

NOTE — *Engine and transmission must be removed as a unit. On 123 series vehicles, engine hood does not have to be removed. The hood can be opened to a 90° position and held in place by a locking mechanism on the left hinge.*

Removal & Installation — **1)** Remove radiator and fan. On vehicles with level control, remove pump from engine and set aside with hoses connected. On vehicles with air conditioning, remove compressor and set aside without disconnecting refrigerant hoses.

2) Drain oil supply tank and disconnect power steering hoses from pump. Remove retaining ring from longitudinal accelerator shaft and push toward firewall to remove.

3) Disconnect all water, vacuum, oil and electrical lines leading to engine. Disconnect exhaust pipes from manifold and strut on transmission. Attach suitable lifting sling and remove engine mounting hardware. Lift engine from vehicle at a 45° angle. To install, reverse removal procedures.

INTAKE MANIFOLD

Removal — Partially drain radiator and remove air cleaner. Disconnect electrical wires, water hoses and vacuum lines. Disconnect cold start valve and remove linkage. Remove attaching screws and remove intake manifold.

Installation — To install, reverse removal procedure, using a new gasket.

CYLINDER HEAD

NOTE — *Cylinder head may only be removed after engine has cooled down. Head is removed complete with manifolds and camshaft housing.*

Removal — **1)** Drain cooling system. Remove A/C compressor (leave lines connected) and level control oil pump for models so equipped. Remove both camshaft housing front covers.

2) Remove cover and vacuum pump from front of camshaft housing. Disconnect all electrical leads, water hoses and vacuum lines from cylinder head and manifold.

3) Remove longitudinal regulating linkage and EGR line. Disconnect oil return line at cylinder head. Loosen hose between water pump and thermostat housing. Disconnect bypass line at water pump.

4) Loosen dipstick guide tube at cylinder head and bend slightly to the side. Disconnect exhaust pipes at manifold and transmission. Remove preheater scoop. Using a screwdriver, force out rocker arm tension springs. Using suitable tool (110 589 04 61 00), remove all rocker arms.

5) Rotate crankshaft until both camshaft timing marks are correctly aligned with crankshaft at TDC on firing stroke. Using suitable holding wrench (116 589 01 01 00), remove both camshaft sprocket bolts.

6) Remove upper slide rail and pull out bearing bolts with suitable extractor (116 589 20 33 00). Remove chain tensioner. Push both camshafts to rear and remove sprockets.

7) Using suitable extractor, pull out bearing pins and remove idler pulley. Extract guide rail bearing pins and remove guide rail.

8) Loosen head bolts in reverse of tightening order. Remove two 8mm bolts in chain box with a magnet, do not drop washers into timing cover. Pull up timing chain and force tension rail toward center of engine. Using two men, lift cylinder head vertically from cylinder block.

Installation — **1)** Place head gasket on cylinder block. Lay two pieces of wood, ½"x1¾"x9½" long, upright between cylinders one and two and flat between cylinders five and six. Mount cylinder head at an inclined position, so that timing chain and tensioner rail can be installed.

2) Lift cylinder head and carefully remove wooden pieces. Lower head carefully, ensuring that front and rear dowels are properly engaged. Insert lubricated head bolts and tighten in 2 stages according to sequence shown in *Fig. 1*. Insert and tighten 8 mm bolts in chain box with Allen wrench.

NOTE — *After tightening all head bolts, camshaft should be free to turn by hand.*

3) Install lower slide rail and idler sprocket. Place spacer on intake camshaft journal. With engine at TDC, install camshaft sprockets with timing marks aligned.

NOTE — *TDC mark on vibration damper is next to dowel pin.*

4) Place spacers in front camshaft bearing of both camshafts. Install camshaft sprockets bolts, but do not tighten. Install upper slide rail and rigid chain tensioner. Using suitable holder tool (116 589 01 01 00), tighten expansion bolts.

5) Rotate engine two revolutions and recheck camshaft timing marks. Install swing lever and tensioner springs. Install chain tensioner and adjust valve clearances. Retighten head bolts after engine has been warmed to 176°F (water temperature). Tighten by first loosening head bolts a ¼ of a turn, one at a time and tighten in tightening order. Retighten 8mm bolts in chain box.

NOTE — *Further tightening of head bolts after 300-500 miles is no longer required. It is not necessary to recheck valve clearances after final tightening of head bolts.*

280 6 CYLINDER (Cont.)

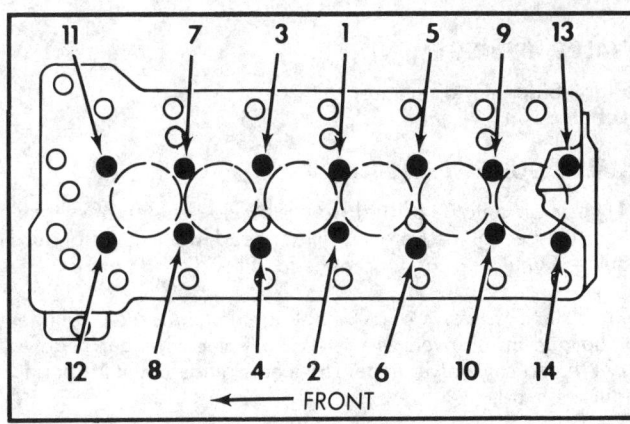

*Fig. 1   Cylinder Head Tightening Sequence
(Remove in Reverse Sequence)*

CAMSHAFT

TIMING CHAIN

1) Remove spark plugs and cylinder head cover. Remove rocker arms of right hand (exhaust) camshaft. Remove chain tensioner and install rigid chain tensioner (110 589 03 31 00).

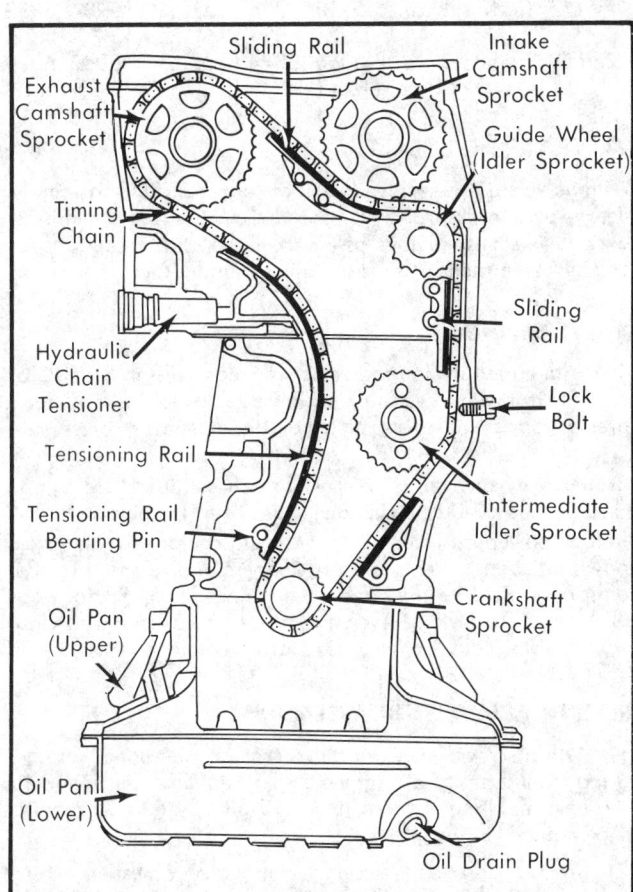

Fig. 2   Front View of Timing Chain and Sprockets

2) Cover chain box with a rag, using a chain breaker, separate chain. Join ends of new and old chains together with a master link. Rotate crankshaft in direction of rotation and pull old chain out of engine. Use care that chain does not jump a tooth on sprockets.

CAUTION – *Do not turn engine by camshaft bolts. Do not rotate crankshaft in reverse.*

3) Join ends of new chain. Rotate crankshaft and check timing marks. Replace rigid chain tensioner with normal chain tensioner. Install rocker arms and adjust exhaust valve clearance. Install camshaft cover and spark plugs.

CAMSHAFT & CAMSHAFT HOUSING

Removal – 1) Remove battery and A.I.R. pump. Disconnect air conditioning compressor and set aside with hoses connected. Drain radiator and remove hose between radiator and engine. Remove camshaft cover.

2) Remove camshaft sprocket covers from front of housing. Pry all rocker arm tension springs from rocker arms. Using a suitable tool (110 589 04 61 00), remove all rocker arms.

3) Using suitable holding tool (116 589 01 01 00), remove right-hand camshaft sprocket bolt. Set number one piston to TDC on firing stroke with both camshaft timing marks aligned. Remove chain tensioner.

4) Remove slide rail in camshaft housing, using suitable puller (115 589 19 33 00). Remove rear right-hand camshaft cover. Push camshaft to the rear, using suitable tool (110 589 03 33 00), while holding camshaft sprocket in place. Remove sprocket and slide camshaft back in place.

5) Remove head bolts, shown in illustration, in reverse of tightening sequence. Do not remove bolts marked with an "x" in illustration. Remove camshaft housing and camshafts.

NOTE – *Camshaft housing may only be removed after engine has cooled down.*

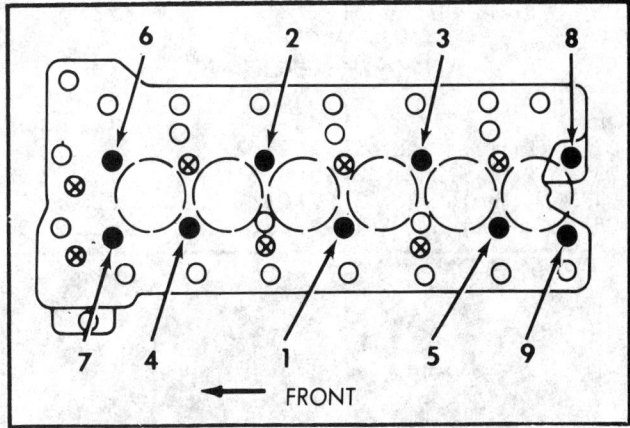

*Fig. 3   Camshaft Housing Tightening Sequence
(Remove ONLY Numbered Bolts in Reverse Sequence*

6) Remove left-hand camshaft sprocket in same manner as right-hand sprocket. Remove spacer ring at intake camshaft and slide both camshafts out rear of housing.

Mercedes-Benz Engines

280 6 CYLINDER (Cont.)

Installation — Install steel gasket on cylinder head without sealing compound. Place camshaft housing on head. Oil head bolts and tighten to 29 ft. lbs. (4.0 mkg), then to 51 ft. lbs. (7.0 mkg). Loosen 5 deeper head bolts slightly, then tighten all head bolts to final torque in sequence shown in *Fig. 1*. Tighten the 8 mm bolts to 18 ft. lbs. (2.5 mkg) working from center outward.

CAMSHAFT BEARINGS

If camshaft bearing journals are worn, damaged or have excessive clearance in camshaft housing bearings, camshaft journals may be ground undersize and a repair housing installed.

Front bearing journal is not ground and remains standard. See "a" in *Fig. 4*. Journal should be fitted with a spacer sleeve. Camshafts do not have to be ground or replaced because of rough surfaces or bearings.

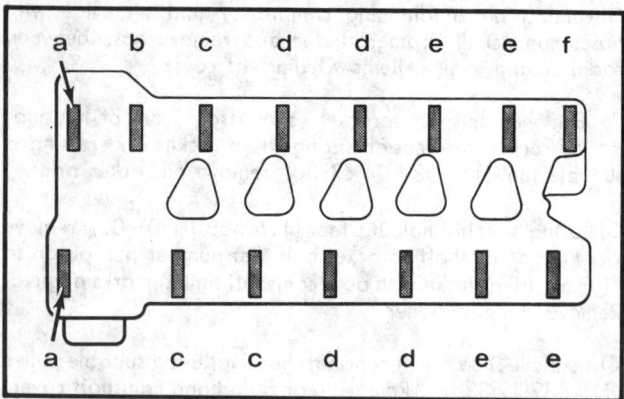

Fig. 4   Camshaft Housing Bearing Identification

VALVE TIMING

Rotate crankshaft until number one piston is at TDC on firing stroke. Both camshaft timing marks should be aligned with marks on camshaft housing. Offset woodruff keys are available to make corrections to timing. Remember that camshaft sprockets rotate in opposite directions, they rotate toward each other.

NOTE — *Some balance discs have two "O" degree marks. TDC is next to a dowel pin.*

Offset Woodruff Keys

Offset	Part No.	Correction
.0275" (.7 mm)	621 991 04 67	4°
.0354" (.9 mm)	621 991 02 67	6.5°
.0433" (1.1 mm)	621 991 01 67	8°
.0511" (1.3 mm)	621 991 00 67	10°

Fig. 5   Camshaft Timing Marks with No. 1 Piston at TDC on Firing Stroke

VALVES

VALVE ARRANGEMENT

Right Side — All exhaust.
Left Side — All intake.

VALVE GUIDE SERVICING

1) Using a suitable drift, drive valve guide out top of cylinder head. Inspect guide bore in cylinder head, drive new standard guide in until lock ring touches head, if head condition permits.

2) If standard valve guide is not tight in head, ream cylinder head and install oversize valve guide. Heat cylinder head to 194°F and chill valve guide. Drive new guide in until lock ring touches head.

Valve Guide Specifications

Application	Guide O.D. In. (mm)	Head I.D. In. (mm)
Intake		
Std.	.5523-.5331	.5519-.5527
	(14.03-14.05)	(14.02-14.04)
1st O.S. (red)	.5594-.5602	.5590-.5598
	(14.21-14.23)	(14.20-14.22)
2nd O.S. (white)	.5673-.5681	.5669-.5677
	(14.41-14.43)	(14.40-14.42)
Exhaust		
Std.	.5917-.5925	.5913-.5921
	(15.03-15.05)	(15.02-15.04)
1st O.S. (red)	.5988-.5996	.5984-.5992
	(15.21-15.23)	(15.20-15.22)
2nd O.S. (white)	.6066-.6074	.6062-.6070
	(15.41-15.43)	(15.40-15.42)

VALVE STEM OIL SEALS

With valve springs removed, pull off old seal. Place assembly sleeves over intake valve stems and slide new valve stem seal over valve stems. Remove assembly sleeve and force seal over end of valve guide with installation mandrel.

VALVE SPRINGS

1) With camshaft housing removed, place piston on TDC of cylinder from which springs are to be removed. Install a compressed air line to spark plug hole to pressurize valves.

2) Remove valve thrust pieces. Attach suitable holding rail (110 589 06 62 00) to cylinder head. Lightly tap valve collars to loosen keepers. Install suitable spring compressor and press down on springs. Remove valve keepers and release pressure on springs. Remove inner and outer springs and check for wear or fatigue. To install, reverse removal procedures with close wound coils (color coding) next to cylinder head.

ROCKER ARM & STUD ASSEMBLY

1) With a screwdriver, pry out rocker arm tensioner springs. Using crankshaft, rotate engine until heel of cam lobe is next to rocker arm. Using suitable tool (110 589 04 61 00), remove rocker arm.

2) Unscrew threaded bushing with valve adjusting screw. Lubricate threads of adjusting screw with tallow and check that screw has at least 14.5 ft. lbs. of turning torque in bushing.

280 6 CYLINDER (Cont.)

3) Install threaded bushing and adjusting screw in cylinder head. Lubricate rocker arm and pivot. Using suitable tool (110 589 04 61 00), install rocker arms and tensioner springs. Readjust valve clearances.

CAUTION — *Do not rotate engine by camshaft sprocket bolts. Do not rotate engine in reverse as camshaft sprocket may jump time.*

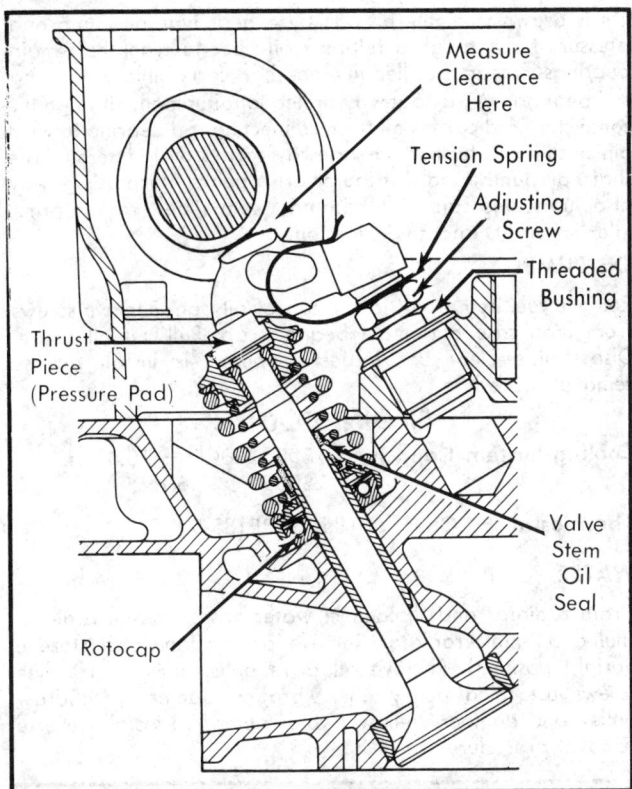

Fig. 6 Sectional View of Rocker Arm and Valve Assembly

VALVE CLEARANCE ADJUSTMENT

Rotate crankshaft until heel of camshaft lobe is next to rocker arm. Insert a feeler gauge between camshaft and rocker arm. Turn adjusting screw until proper clearance is achieved.

NOTE — *Valves should be adjusted with engine at normal operating temperature. Cold specifications are provided for initial settings after assembly.*

Valve Clearance

Application	In. (mm)
Intake	
Hot	①.006 (.15)
Cold	①.004 (.10)
Exhaust	
Hot	.012 (.30)
Cold	.010 (.25)

① — Winter Clearance, add .002" (.05mm).

PISTONS, PINS & RINGS

OIL PAN

NOTE — *A 2 piece oil pan is used. Due to complexity of operation, engine assembly must be removed to remove complete oil pan.*

Removal & Installation — To remove lower oil pan, drain engine oil, remove mounting bolts and separate lower pan from upper section. To install, use sealant on clean mating surface, use new gasket and reverse removal procedure.

PISTON & ROD ASSEMBLY

Removal — With oil pan and cylinder head removed, remove rod caps and push piston and rod assembly out top of cylinder. Remove wrist pin locks and push out wrist pins. Clean and inspect all parts.

Installation — 1) Place piston on connecting rod so that arrow faces forward and recess for bearing insert is facing rear of engine. Install piston and rod assembly in cylinder. Install rod cap with code numbers facing rod numbers.

2) Rod bolts should be checked for minimum diameter with a pair of sharp edged calipers. If diameter is less than .283", replace rod bolts. Tighten rod bolts to 36 ft. lbs. and then tighten an additional 100° rotation.

FITTING PISTONS

Measure cylinder bores near top, bottom, and center in at least 2 directions. If greater than .004" (.10 mm) from standard, cylinders must be bored and new pistons fitted.

Cylinder Bore Specifications

Application	In. (mm)
Standard	3.3858-3.3866 (86.0-86.02)
1st Oversize	3.4055-3.4063 (86.50-86.52)
2nd Oversize	3.4252-3.4260 (87.0-87.02)

PISTON PINS

Piston pins are retained with circlips in pistons. To remove pins, remove circlips and press out piston pins. To install, ensure that arrow on piston crown faces front (timing chain end) and that bearing retaining notch in connecting rod faces left (intake manifold) side of engine. Lubricate pin and press into piston/rod assembly by hand.

NOTE — *Do NOT heat piston to install piston pin.*

CRANKSHAFT MAIN & CONNECTING ROD BEARINGS

MAIN & CONNECTING ROD BEARINGS

1) Remove connecting rod and main bearing caps. Check all bearing journals for wear, taper or out-of-round. The following table gives maximum dimensions which are permissible without repair or new bearings.

Crankshaft Specifications

Application	In. (mm)
Out-of Round	.0002 (.005)
Journal Taper	.0004 (.010)
Journal Flatness	.0006 (.015)
Bearing Bore Out-of-Round	.0004 (.010)
Bearing Bore Taper	.0004 (.010)

2) Bearing inserts for both main and connecting rod journals are color coded. Main bearing inserts with no color are thicker than ones which are blue. Connecting rod inserts with red color are thicker than ones with blue color. Select inserts which will give the mean of clearance range.

280 6 CYLINDER (Cont.)

Crankshaft Journal Diameters

Application	Main Bearing In. (mm)	Connecting Rod In. (mm)
Std.	2.3602-2.3606 (59.95-59.96)	1.8878-1.8882 (47.95-47.96)
1st U.S.	2.3504-2.3508 (58.70-59.71)	1.8779-1.8783 (47.70-47.71)
2nd U.S.	2.3405-2.3409 (59.45-59.46)	1.8681-1.8685 (47.45-47.46)
3rd U.S.	2.3307-2.3311 (59.20-59.21)	1.8583-1.8587 (47.20-47.21)
4th U.S.	2.3209-2.3213 (58.95-58.96)	1.8484-1.8488 (46.95-46.96)

Bearing Insert Wall Thickness

Application	Main Bearing In. (mm)	Connecting Rod In. (mm)
Std.	.1378 (3.50)	.0713 (1.81)
1st U.S.	.1429 (3.63)	.0764 (1.94)
2nd U.S.	.1476 (3.75)	.0811 (2.06)
3rd U.S.	.1528 (3.88)	.0858 (2.18)
4th U.S.	.1575 (4.00)	.0909 (2.31)

THRUST BEARING ALIGNMENT

Install number three main bearing and measure clearance between bearing and crankshaft sides. If clearance is excessive, install new bearing. New bearings are supplied in oversize widths and must be lapped on non-thrust side to achieve proper clearance. Lap only side away from flywheel.

REAR MAIN BEARING OIL SEAL

Press pieces of seal into cylinder block and oil pan with a wooden hammer handle. Cut ends of seal so they protrude .020" (.5 mm) above parting surfaces. Oil seal halves liberally and install crankshaft and oil pan. Check for easy rotation of crankshaft and reassemble engine.

FRONT COVER OIL SEAL

1) Remove radiator and fan, pulley and vibration damper. Mark balance disc and crankshaft with punch for assembly purposes. Use suitable puller and remove balance disc.

2) Pry old seal out with screwdriver, using caution not to damage seal bore or crankshaft journal. Clean and inspect seal bore and apply oil to new seal (do NOT use sealing compound). Press seal into position with installing tool (110 589 07 61 00).

3) Install new spacing ring or turn used ring around so that worn groove is at rear. Install remaining components in reverse order of assembly.

ENGINE OILING

Crankcase Capacity — 6.3 qts. (including filter).

Oil Filter — Full flow type.

Normal Oil Pressure — 7.1 psi (.5 kg/cm²) at 800-900 RPM; 42 psi (3 kg/cm²) at 3000 RPM.

Pressure Regulator Valve — Nonadjustable.

ENGINE OILING SYSTEM

Oil is drawn from the oil pan by a gear type oil pump and pressure fed through a full-flow oil filter to crankshaft main bearings. Passages drilled in crankshaft carry oil to connecting rod bearings. A passageway drilled longitudinally through the connecting rod carries oil from connecting rod bearing to wrist pin bushing. A further passageway carries oil to intermediate shaft, oil pump, and distributor drive gears. This passageway also lubricates camshaft bearings, cam lobes, rocker arms, idler sprocket, and chain tensioner.

OIL PUMP

Remove fuel pump and lower half of oil pan. Remove screws from crankcase and main bearing cap. Pull out oil pump. Disassemble, clean and inspect oil pump. To install, reverse removal procedure.

ENGINE COOLING

Cooling System Capacity — 280E, 280CE — 10.6 qts.
280SE — 11.6 qts.

Thermostat — Opens at 185-193°F (85-89°C).

WATER PUMP

Drain radiator and disconnect water hoses. Loosen radiator shell and remove radiator. Remove fan and fan clutch (store in upright position). Remove all drive belts. Remove six Allen screws attaching pulley and vibration damper. Withdraw pulley and damper. Remove water pump. To install, reverse removal procedure.

TIGHTENING SPECIFICATIONS

Application	Ft. Lbs. (mkg)
Main Bearings	58 (8.0)
Connecting Rods	①36 (5.0)
Crankshaft Bolt	289-325 (40-45)
Camshaft Cover	4 (.5)
Cylinder Head Bolts	
Stage 1	51 (7.0)
Stage 2	72 (10)
Stage 3②	72 (10)
Camshaft Bolt	72 (10)
Oil Pump	21 (3.0)
Chain Tensioner Nut	36 (5.0)

① — Tighten bolts to 36 ft. lbs. (5 mkg) and then turn bolts an additional 100° of rotation.

② — With engine warm (176°F or 80°C), loosen all head bolts ¼ turn in tightening sequence, then tighten to final torque.

ENGINE SPECIFICATIONS

GENERAL SPECIFICATIONS

Year	Displ. cu. ins.	Displ. cc	Carburetor	HP at RPM	Torque (Ft. Lbs. at RPM)	Compr. Ratio	Bore in.	Bore mm	Stroke in.	Stroke mm
1980	167.6	2746	Fuel Inj.	140@5500	145@4500	8.0-1	3.39	86	3.10	78.8

280 6 CYLINDER (Cont.)
ENGINE SPECIFICATIONS (Cont.)

VALVES

Engine & Valve	Head Diam. In. (mm)	Face Angle	Seat Angle	Seat Width In. (mm)	Stem Diameter In. (mm)	Stem Clearance In. (mm)	Valve Lift In. (mm)
2746 cc Intake	1.775-1.783 (45.1-45.3)	45°	45°	.071-.098 (1.8-2.5)	.3524-.3531 (8.95-8.97)	.0019 (.05)	.....
Exhaust	1.5315-1.5354 (38.9-39.0)	45°	45°	.059-.079 (1.5-2.0)	.3520-.3528 (8.94-8.96)	.0023 (.06)	.....

PISTONS, PINS, RINGS

Engine	PISTONS Clearance In. (mm)	PINS Piston Fit In. (mm)	PINS Rod Fit In. (mm)	Rings	RINGS End Gap In. (mm)	RINGS Side Clearance In. (mm)
2746 cc	.0010-.0014 (.025-.035) Limit .003 (.08)	.00008-.0004 (.002-.011)	.0003-.0007 (.007-.017)	No. 1	.012-.018 (.30-.45)	.0019-.0032 (.050-.082)
				No. 2	.012-.018 (.30-.45)	.0011-.0024 (.030-.062)
				No. 3	.010-.016 (.25-.40)	.0004-.0016 (.010-.042)

CRANKSHAFT MAIN & CONNECTING ROD BEARINGS

Engine	MAIN BEARINGS Journal Diam. In. (mm)	Clearance In. (mm)	Thrust Bearing	Crankshaft End Play In. (mm)	CONNECTING ROD BEARINGS Journal Diam. In. (mm)	Clearance In. (mm)	Side Play In. (mm)
2746 cc	2.3602-2.3606 (59.95-59.96)	.001-.002 (.03-.05)	No. 3	.004-.009 (.10-.24)	1.8878-1.8882 (47.95-47.96)	.0005-.0020 (.013-.050)	.004-.009 (.10-.24)

VALVE SPRINGS

Engine	Free Length In. (mm)	PRESSURE Lbs. @ In. (kg @ mm) Valve Closed	PRESSURE Lbs. @ In. (kg @ mm) Valve Open
2746 cc Inner	1.772 (45)	26.01@1.299 (11.8@33)	50.7@.846 (23@21.5)
Outer	1.949 (49.5)	67.24@1.6535 (30.5@42)	194@1.20 (88@30.5)

VALVE TIMING

Engine	INTAKE Open (ATDC)	INTAKE Close (ABDC)	EXHAUST Open (BBDC)	EXHAUST Close (BTDC)
2746 cc	7°	21°	30°	12°

CAMSHAFT ①

Engine	Journal Diam. In. (mm)	Clearance In. (mm)	Lobe Lift In. (mm)
2746 cc a	.9441-.9445 (23.98-23.99)	.002-.005 (.06-.12)	.....
b	1.9654-1.9661 (49.92-49.94)	.003-.006 (.10-.14)	.....
c	1.9657-1.9665 (49.93-49.95)	.002-.004 (.06-.09)	.....
d	2.0244-2.0252 (51.42-51.44)	.002-.004 (.06-.10)	.....
e	2.0835-2.0842 (52.92-52.94)	.002-.004 (.06-.10)	.....
f	2.1228-2.1236 (53.92-53.94)	.002-.004 (.06-.10)	.....

① — Journal diameters vary, with steps from smaller to larger going from front to rear. See Fig. 4. End play is .002-.005" (.050-.128 mm).

Mercedes-Benz Engines

4.5 LITER V8

ENGINE CODING

ENGINE IDENTIFICATION

Identification number is located on tag attached to engine crankcase. First six digits of code are used to identify engine, as follows:

Engine Identification		
Application	Chassis Type	Engine Code
450SEL	116.033	117.986
450SL	107.044	117.985
450SLC	107.024	117.985

ENGINE, CYLINDER HEAD & MANIFOLD

ENGINE

Removal — 1) Remove head and drain cooling system. Note that there are both left and right engine block drains. Disconnect and remove battery and remove battery frame. Evacuate air conditioning system and remove pipe set at compressor. Disconnect and remove all water, vacuum, oil, fuel and electric lines leading to engine.

2) On 450 SEL, disconnect exhaust system and remove right drag link end from ball head. On 450 SL and 450 SLC, completely remove exhaust system. On all models, drain power steering reservoir and disconnect hoses. Unscrew TDC test socket and remove cable for TDC transmitter.

3) Remove left and right engine shock absorbers. Attach engine sling and hoist to engine and remove engine mount bolts. Remove rear engine carrier with engine mount. Loosen and disconnect driveshaft from transmission. Remove linkages connecting transmission to chassis and lift engine out (with transmission attached) at a 45° angle.

Installation — Ensure that oil cooler and all hoses have been flushed and are free from contamination. Renew engine mounts and components as required and reverse removal procedure. Evacuate and charge air conditioning system and check entire installation for leaks.

INTAKE MANIFOLD

Drain cooling system and remove air cleaner. Disconnect fuel injection linkage and fuel lines on pressure regulator. Disconnect fuel start valve. Remove ignition valves. Extract intake manifold bolts and lift manifold off in rearward direction. To install, reverse removal procedure.

CYLINDER HEAD

NOTE — *Cylinder head removal should not be attempted until engine has cooled down. Several specially shaped Allen wrenches are required for cylinder head bolt removal and replacement.*

Removal — 1) Remove left and right drain plugs and drain cooling system. Remove air cleaner and battery. Remove fuel line and injection valves. Disconnect fuel injection linkage.

2) Disconnect and remove intake pipe (manifold). Remove A/T fluid filler pipe from attachment to cylinder head. Remove alternator and mounting bracket. Remove distributor and power steering pump with mounting bracket.

3) Disconnect exhaust pipe from manifold and exhaust gas return line at 90° fitting. Remove chain tensioner and slide rails. Mark camshaft sprocket and timing chain position for assembly reference. Remove sprocket from camshaft. Using specially shaped Allen wrenches, remove head bolts and lift off head.

Installation — 1) Ensure that all mating surfaces are clean and install new cylinder head gasket. Tighten cylinder head bolts in sequence shown to 22 ft. lbs. (3 mkg), and then to 43 ft. lbs. (6 mkg). Tighten 8 mm bolts to 18 ft. lbs. (2.5 mkg).

2) Complete assembly in reverse order of removal and run engine until normal operating temperature is reached. Slightly loosen head bolts individually, then retighten in sequence shown to final warm torque of 43 ft. lbs. (6 mkg).

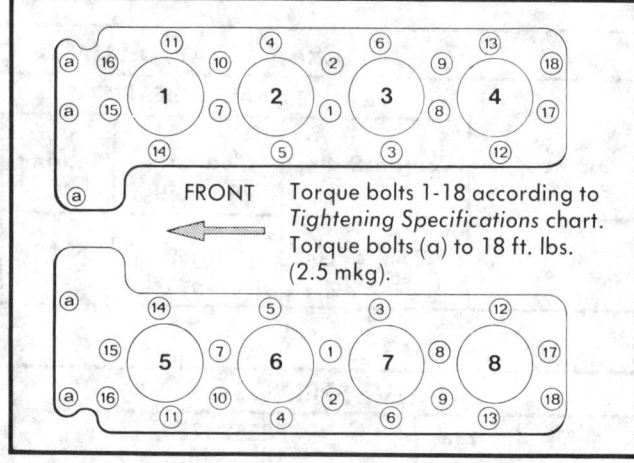

**Fig. 1 Cylinder Head Tightening Sequence
(Loosen in Reverse Order)**

CAMSHAFT

Removal — With cylinder head covers removed, set No. 1 piston at TDC firing position and remove rocker arms. Mark sprockets and timing chain for reassembly. Remove camshaft sprockets. Unbolt and remove camshaft bearings, oil tube and camshaft as an assembly.

Installation — 1) Assemble bearings on camshaft. Note that smooth bearing journals must fit in bearings with an oil groove, and camshaft journals with an oil groove fit only in bearings WITHOUT an oil groove.

2) Place camshaft and bearing assembly on head. Note that outer screw of left camshaft rear bearing must be inserted in bearing prior to mounting due to interference from brake unit.

4.5 LITER V8 (Cont.)

Oil pipe connections on bearings must be renewed to ensure proper oil pressure.

3) Tighten camshaft bearing mounting screws and check that camshaft rotates freely. Mount compensating washer so that both inner and outer notches align with Woodruff key in camshaft. Assmble sprockets to camshaft so that white color faces camshaft and timing marks are aligned.

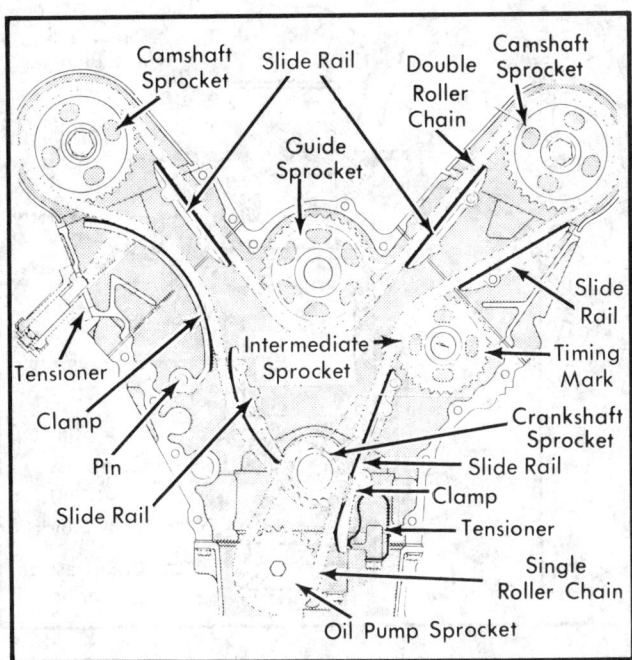

Fig. 2   Timing Chains and Sprockets

4) Install rocker arms and check basic clearance of lifters. Complete assembly in reverse order of removal.

NOTE — *Whenever it is necessary to install either new rocker arms or camshaft, both rocker arms and camshaft must be replaced. Camshaft journals may be reground and undersize bearings installed.*

DISTRIBUTOR DRIVE GEAR

1) With timing and crankshaft chains exposed, disconnect all chain dampers (slide rails) and timing chain tensioner. Remove chain from intermediate sprocket and pull sprocket from engine.

2) Use suitable puller to extract bushing from crankcase and cover. Press new bushings in position so that lubricating groove is at bottom. Lubricate bushings and install intermediate sprocket. Note that mark on sprocket must align with mark on crankcase with engine at TDC position. Continue assembly in reverse order of removal.

CHAIN TENSIONER

NOTE — *In all instances chain tensioner is lubricated and connected to oiling circuit.*

1) Remove air injector pipe and 3 screws fastening tensioner. Remove chain tensioner.

2) To check tensioner, place in container of oil vertically so that oil covers flange. Actuate plunger to fill tensioner with oil. After filling and venting, plunger should allow compression very slowly and evenly, and with considerable force.

3) To install, use new gasket and tighten screws evenly. Pressure pin of tensioner must press against lug of tensioning rail.

VALVE TIMING

1) Measure timing periods on inlet valves of cylinder 1 and 6. Remove hydraulic valve lifters and replace with adjusting screws (116 050 11 20). Adjust each screw so rocker arm just touches the base circle of the cam.

2) Attach dial indicator so that pointer rests vertically on valve spring retainer. Pin should have .118" (3 mm) preload and dial should be set to zero.

3) Turn engine in direction of normal rotation until pointer moves .0787" (2 mm), leaving a preload of .039" (1 mm). Readings should be in accordance with valve timing chart. Repeat for No. 6 intake valve.

4) If timing requires correction, install an offset Woodruff Key or new chain. Keys are available in four offsets providing corrections of 4°, 6½°, 8°, and 10°.

5) After checking and adjusting valve timing, reinstall hydraulic lifters and adjust for proper base setting. See *ADJUSTING LIFTERS TO BASE SETTING.*

VALVES

VALVE ARRANGEMENT

Right Bank — E-I-E-I-E-I-I-E (front to rear).
Left Bank — E-I-I-E-I-E-I-E (front to rear).

HYDRAULIC VALVE LIFTERS

1) Hydraulic valve lifters eliminate the need to adjust valve clearance. Constant contact of rocker arms with camshaft, valves and lifters not only reduces noise, but also compensates for wear or temperature changes.

2) Oil pressure to operate the lifters is supplied by the oil pump through a lateral passage in the cylinder head (with connecting bores to each lifter) and an oil passage in the fifth camshaft bearing. The spherical head plunger contains an oil reservoir, which is separated from the pressure chamber by a ball valve.

3) When engine is stopped and cam lobe exerts pressure on the valve lifter, the plunger can be completely depressed. Oil from pressure chamber flows to reservoir. Turning cam lobe away from rocker arm releases plunger and compression spring pushes it upward until rocker arm rests against cam. Upward plunger movement causes a suction in the pressure chamber, causing oil to flow from reservoir to chamber.

4.5 LITER V8 (Cont.)

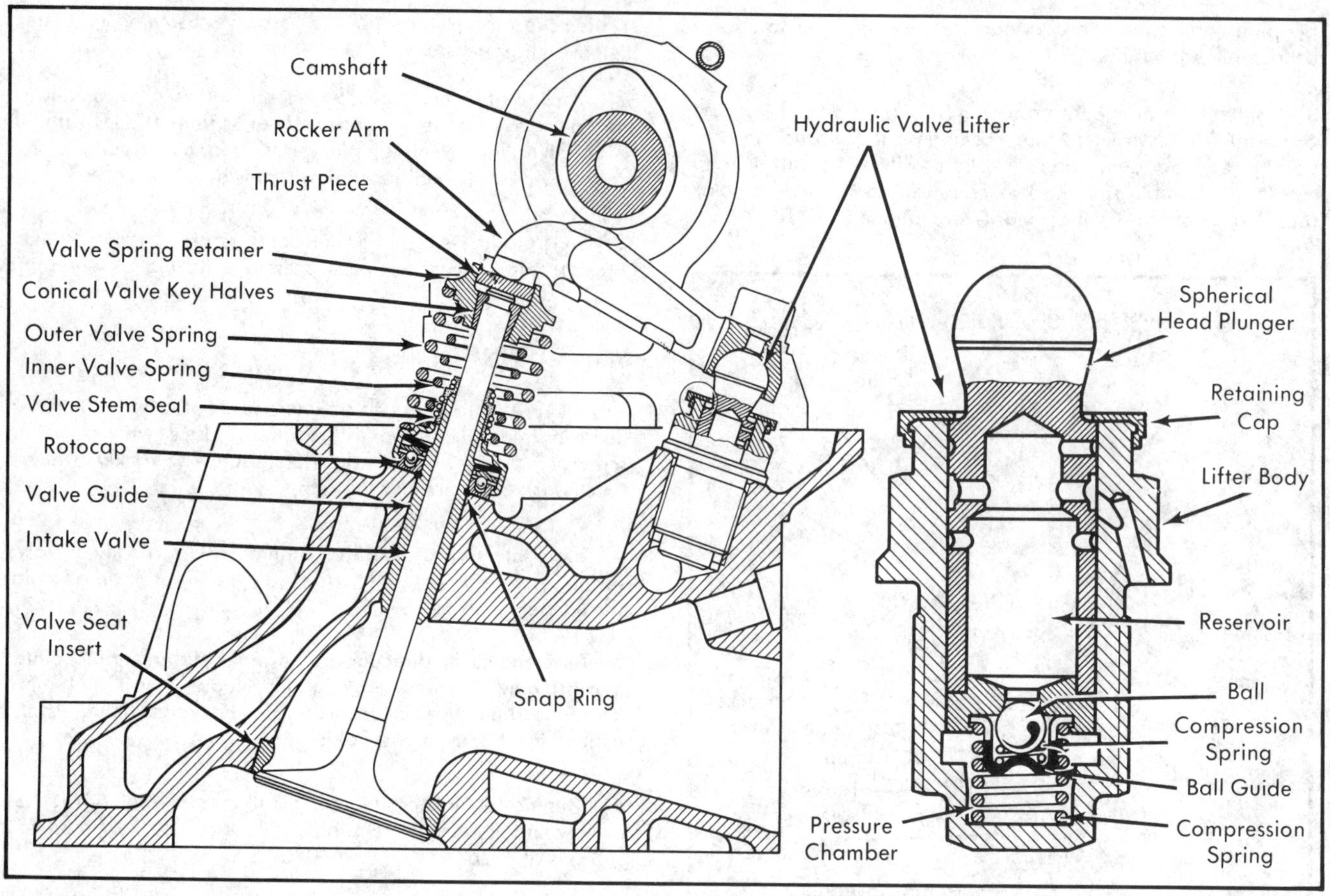

Camshaft

Rocker Arm

Thrust Piece

Valve Spring Retainer

Conical Valve Key Halves

Outer Valve Spring

Inner Valve Spring

Valve Stem Seal

Rotocap

Valve Guide

Intake Valve

Valve Seat Insert

Snap Ring

Hydraulic Valve Lifter

Spherical Head Plunger

Retaining Cap

Lifter Body

Reservoir

Ball

Compression Spring

Ball Guide

Pressure Chamber

Compression Spring

Fig. 3   Cutaway View of Valve System and Lifter

4) The ball valve closes when the cam lobe exerts pressure on rocker arm. Trapped oil in pressure chamber forms a solid hydraulic connection which prevents the plunger from moving fully downward. Leak-off vents permit air and excess oil to escape.

5) To check hydraulic compensating element (lifter) performance, press on rocker arm at lifter end with valve in closed position. If pressure bleeds off too rapidly in comparison with other elements, replacement is required. If lifters are removed, they should be stored in an upright position and reinstalled in original location.

VALVE GUIDE SERVICING

1) With cylinder head removed and suitably supported, clean bores of valve guides. Hard oil carbon deposits can be eliminated with a honing needle.

2) Using a suitable plug gauge, inspect valve guides. Inner diameter of new inlet guides should be .354-.355" (9.000-9.015 mm); exhaust guides should be .433-.434" (11.000-11.018 mm). If guide is beyond this tolerance, replace with new guide.

3) With suitable reamer/installer mandrel, drive worn guide from its bore. Inspect valve guide bore in cylinder head and ream to accept next oversize guide.

NOTE — *Replacement Inlet valve guides are available in overlapping sizes, ranging from .552-.568" (14.014-14.431 mm) outside diameter. Exhaust valve guides are available with outside diameters of .591-.608" (15.014-15.431 mm).*

4) Heat cylinder head to approximately 194° F (90° C) and cool valve guides (if possible). Coat guide bore with oil and, using remover/installer mandrel, seat new guide in bore.

NOTE — *Be sure snap ring is properly installed. Recheck valve guide clearance and that valve moves freely in guide.*

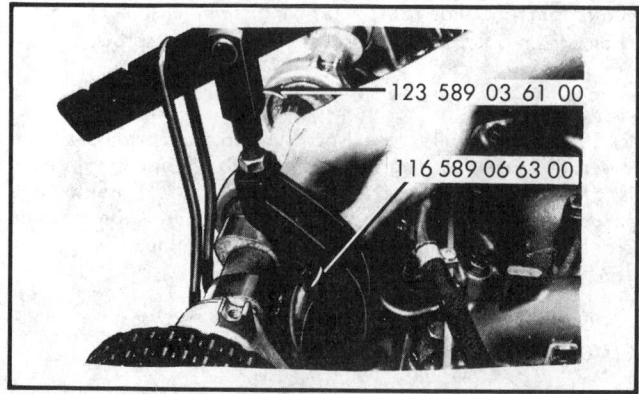

123 589 03 61 00

116 589 06 63 00

Fig. 4   Removing Conical Valve Key Halves (Keepers)

4.5 LITER V8 (Cont.)

VALVE STEM SEALS

Removal — Using spring compressor (116 589 00 61 00), remove rocker arms. See Fig. 3. Lift out thrust plate, and using special magnet (116 589 06 63 00), remove conical valve key halves (keepers). Remove spring retainer, inner and outer valve springs, valve stem seals and rotocaps.

Installation — Replacement valve stem seals are supplied in a kit which includes assembly sleeves. Place sleeve over stem and install lubricated seal with installing tool. See Fig. 4. Install remaining components in reverse order of removal.

116 589 00 43 00

Fig. 5 Installing Valve Stem Seal

VALVE SEAT RING

1) Check valve guide prior to removing seat ring. See Valve Guide Servicing. If seat ring is worn, carefully remove it by machining with a valve seat ring turning tool.

2) Thoroughly clean the receiving bore and check its diameter. If diameter is within specifications, install a new valve seat ring of the same size. If diameter is not within specification, 1.811-1.812" (46.0-46.02 mm) for intake or 1.575-1.576" (40.0-40.01 mm), machine bore to next oversize.

3) To install, heat cylinder head in water to approximately 140° F (60° C). Place pre-cooled seat ring into bore. To position seat ring, lightly tap ring, using a suitable mandrel and hammer. Machine valve seat to correct width and correct for runout. Do NOT machine rounded bead on lower part of valve seat. Valve seat runout should not exceed .0016" (.04 mm).

ROCKER ARMS

1) Rocker arms are individually-mounted on the 16 valves, without use of a shaft. They are in constant contact with the camshaft, thrust plates above the valve stems, and hydraulic valve lifters. To remove, compress spring on each valve using compressor (123 589 03 61 00). Mark each arm for installation in original position.

2) Rocker arms have a chamfer behind ball socket (lifter end). This prevents rocker arm from striking retaining cap of lifters in extreme cases. Do not use rocker arms unless they have this chamfer.

3) Whenever camshaft is replaced, new rocker arms must also be installed. Likewise, when new rocker arms are installed, replace the camshaft, as well. When making replacements, check base setting of hydraulic valve lifters using test gauge (100 589 04 23 00). Correct, as required, using new thrust piece. Thrust pieces are available in steps of .0014" (.35 mm) from .147" (3.7 mm) to .228" (5.8 mm). See Adjusting Lifters to Base Setting.

ADJUSTING LIFTERS TO BASE SETTING

NOTE — Always keep hydraulic valve lifters in an upright position. Rocker arms and valve lifters should always be reinstalled in original locations. When checking and adjusting lifter settings, crank engine for 30 seconds with starter contact switch.

1) When replacing compensating element (hydraulic lifters) or camshaft and rocker arms, basic position of compensating element must be checked. Rotate engine so that cam lobe of element to be checked is in the upright position and install test gauge (100 589 04 23 00).

2) Set measuring pin of gauge through rocker arm hole so that it rests on ball pin of lifter. Basic position is correct when red groove of pin is aligned with measuring edge of tool. If groove is below measuring edge, a plus (+) deviation is indicated, requiring a thinner thrust piece. Entire groove showing above measuring edge indicates a minus (−) deviation and requires a thicker thrust piece.

3) To correct setting, remove rocker arm and thrust piece. Install thinner or thicker thrust piece as required and reinstall rocker arm. Repeat measuring procedure. Position is correct when center of measuring groove aligns with edge of gauge.

PISTONS, PINS & RINGS

OIL PAN

450 SL and 450 SLC — 1) Remove radiator shell and shroud. Remove front axle assembly. Remove A/C compressor and mounting bracket. Remove supporting angle bracket between pan and transmission.

2) Remove oil pan bolts and lower oil pan along with dip stick guide tube from engine. To install, apply grease to clean mating surfaces and install new gasket. Place pan in position and reverse removal procedure.

450 SEL — 1) Remove A/C compressor and mounting bracket from engine. Remove drive belt tensioning pulley. Unbolt and remove oil pan lower half. Remove oil pump drive sprocket and mounting bolts. Remove oil pump.

2) Remove cooling fan pulley and thermostat housing cover. Knock oil pan dip stick guide tube from pan and disconnect transmission oil lines. Remove supporting angle bracket on transmission. Remove oil pan bolts and rotate crankshaft so that oil pan can be removed in a down and forward direction.

3) To install, ensure that all mating surfaces are clean and apply thin layer of grease. Use new gasket and install oil pan upper half. Continue assembly in reverse order of removal.

4.5 LITER V8 (Cont.)

PISTON & ROD ASSEMBLY

Removal — 1) With cylinder head and oil pan removed, remove connecting rod nuts and bearing caps. Push piston and rod assembly out top of cylinder. Use care not to damage any bearing surface.

2) Remove piston pin snap ring and press out piston pin. Retain all components in proper order for reassembly.

Installation — 1) Check rings for gap and end clearance. Replace if not within specifications. Lubricate piston pins and connecting rod bushings. Push in piston pin (do NOT heat piston) and insert snap rings.

2) Stagger ring gaps on piston and fit ring compressor. Install piston and rod assembly with arrow on piston facing toward front of engine.

3) Install rod caps, matching code numbers to and facing rod numbers. Tighten rod cap nuts and check all clearances.

FITTING PISTONS

Measure cylinder bores near top, bottom and center in at least 2 directions. If greater than .004" (.10 mm) from standard, cylinders must be bored and new pistons fitted.

Cylinder Bore Specifications	
Application	**In. (mm)**
Standard	3.6220-3.6228 (92.0-92.02)
1st Oversize	3.6417-3.6425 (92.50-92.52)
2nd Oversize	3.6614-3.6622 (93.0-93.02)

PISTON PINS

Piston pins are retained with circlips in pistons. To remove pins, remove circlips and press out piston pins. To install, ensure that arrow on piston crown faces front (timing chain end) and that bearing retaining notch in connecting rod faces toward outer side of engine. Lubricate pin and press into piston and rod assembly by hand.

NOTE — *Do NOT heat piston to install piston pin.*

CRANKSHAFT MAIN & CONNECTING BEARINGS

MAIN & CONNECTING ROD BEARINGS

1) Mount main bearing cap to cylinder block without bearings in place. Measure inside diameter at 3 locations as illustrated. Be sure cap is properly positioned when taking reading. Offset bearing caps can be moved into center position by lightly tapping them with a plastic hammer.

2) All three measurements should agree. If basic bores exceed specifications and the required overlap of bearing shell halves is not assured, remove .008" (.02 mm) from contact surfaces, using a surface plate.

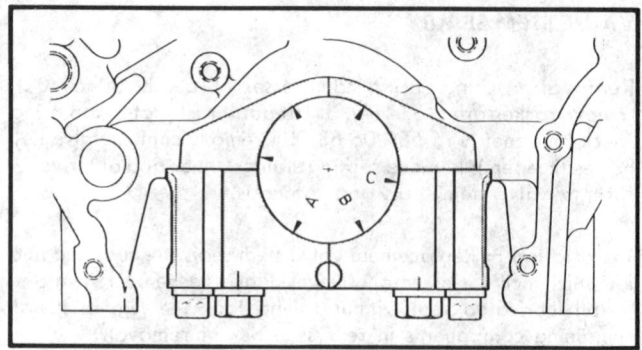

Fig. 6   Location for Measuring Main Bearing Bore Diameter

3) Measure main bearing and connecting rod bearings at front and rear to check for taper. If beyond .0006" (.015 mm), remove excess material from one side of bearing cap, using surface plate.

4 Use proper bearing shells to match measurements obtained. Several overlapping bearing sizes are available. Fit bearing halves into bearing bore and tighten bolts to proper torque. Measure inner diameter of bearings and outer diameter of journals. Difference in measurements should be within bearing clearance specifications. If not, change bearing shell halves.

5) When proper clearance is calculated, clean and oil all parts and install crankshaft. Torque to specifications according to sequence.

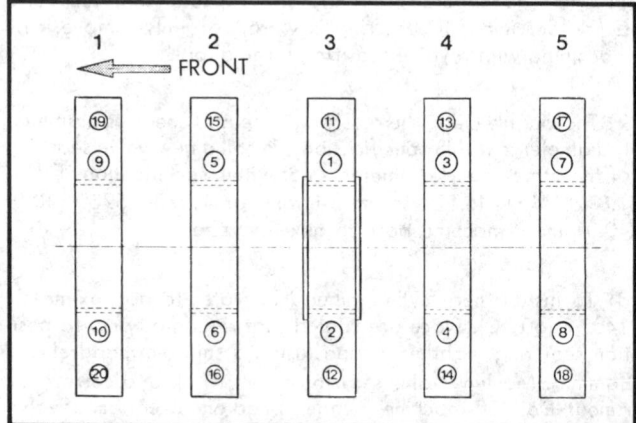

Fig. 7   Crankshaft Main Bearing Tightening Sequence

6) With crankshaft properly installed, check for free rotation and for proper end play. Install connecting rods.

REAR CRANKSHAFT SEALING RING

1) With engine removed from vehicle, unbolt and remove rear cover. Force out old sealing ring. Clean cover and sealing surfaces.

2) Check crankshaft running surface for scoring. Sealing ring with sealing lip offset inward is available in case of scored crankshaft. Press new seal into cover with suitable tool.

4.5 LITER V8 (Cont.)

Fig. 8   Removing Rear Cover and Seal

3) Lubricate lip of seal and coat cover with sealing compound. Place conical sleeve (116 589 03 43 00) over crankshaft end and place cover in position. Use care so that pan gasket is not damaged. Tighten cover bolts evenly and install drive plate.

NOTE — *Drive plate (flywheel) can only be mounted in one position due to offset of 1 of the 8 fastening bolts.*

Fig. 9   Installing Rear Cover and Seal

FRONT CRANKSHAFT SEALING RING

Removal — With engine removed from vehicle. Remove all V-belts, mark hub and crankshaft with paint or chalk. Remove vibration damper, pulley and hub. Remove sealing ring, making sure that crankshaft and receiving bore are not damaged.

Installation — Deburr edge of receiving bore before installing new seal. Lubricate receiving bore and seal lip with oil. Install sealing ring with installation sleeve (110 589 07 61 00). Reassemble remaining components in reverse of removal procedure.

ENGINE OILING

ENGINE OILING SYSTEM

Lubrication is provided by a gear type oil pump directly driven by crankshaft. Oil is picked up through a strainer from lower portion of oil pan and forced to oil filter through a duct in timing casing. After passing through filter, oil flows to center main duct, to crankshaft and through rod bearings up rods to piston pin bushing. Oil galleries run to cylinder head, valve assemblies and to camshafts. Circuit also includes chain tensioner, ignition and, if applicable, air compressor.

Oil Filter — Disposable cartridge type. Located near front of engine.

Normal Oil Pressure — 7.1 psi@idle; 42.6 psi@3000 RPM.

Over Flow Valve — Valve is located in crankcase and enters into main oil gallery. When filter becomes severely contaminated valve will open and oil will enter in an unfiltered state.

Crankcase Capacity — 8.4 quarts with filter.

ENGINE COOLING

WATER PUMP

Disconnect all necessary water hoses and any remaining components from water pump housing. Remove distributor and all mounting bolts. Remove pump from vehicle. To install, reverse removal procedure.

Thermostat — Located in water pump housing, as shown in illustration. To remove drain cooling system, remove air cleaner, disconnect battery and alternator. Remove housing and thermostat. When installing ensure ball valve is mounted at highest point.

Cooling System Capacity — 15.8 quarts.

Thermostat — Opens at 162-169° F (72-76° C).

Radiator Cap — 13-15 psi.

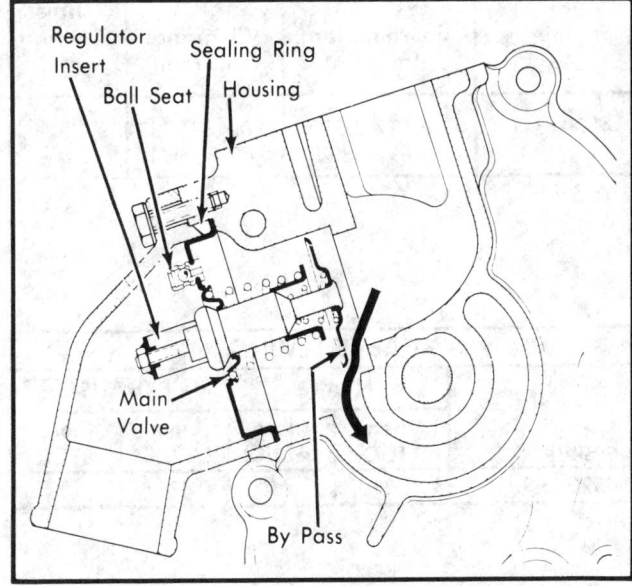

Fig. 10   Thermostat Installation

Mercedes-Benz Engines

4.5 LITER V8 (Cont.)
ENGINE SPECIFICATIONS

GENERAL SPECIFICATIONS

Year	Displ.		Carburetor	HP at RPM	Torque (Ft. Lbs. at RPM)	Compr. Ratio	Bore		Stroke	
	cu. ins.	cc					in.	mm	in.	mm
1980	275.8	4520	Fuel Inj.	160@4200	230@2500	8.0:1	3.62	92	3.35	85

VALVES

Engine & Valve	Head Diam. In. (mm)	Face Angle	Seat Angle	Seat Width In. (mm)	Stem Diameter In. (mm)	Stem Clearance In. (mm)	Valve Lift In. (mm)
4520 cc Int.	1.7362-1.7440 (44.10-44.30)	45°	45°	.051-.078 (1.3-2.0)	.3523-.3531 (8.95-8.97)	Limit .003 (.075)	.....
Exh.	1.4547-1.4665 (36.95-37.25)	45°	45°	.059-.079 (1.5-2.0)	.4303-.4311 (10.93-10.95)		.....

PISTONS, PINS, RINGS

Engine	PISTONS	PINS		RINGS		
	Clearance In. (mm)	Piston Fit In. (mm)	Rod Fit In. (mm)	Rings	End Gap In. (mm)	Side Clearance In. (mm)
4520 cc	.0005-.0015 (.012-.037)	.....	.0002-.0007 (.005-.018)	No. 1	.014-.022 (.35-.55)	.002-.0036 (.050-.092)
				No. 2	.014-.022 (.35-.55)	.0016-.0030 (.040-.082)
				Oil	.010-.016 (.25-.40)	.0012-.0030 (.030-.072)

CRANKSHAFT MAIN & CONNECTING ROD BEARINGS

Engine	MAIN BEARINGS				CONNECTING ROD BEARINGS		
	Journal Diam. In. (mm)	Clearance In. (mm)	Thrust Bearing	Crankshaft End Play In. (mm)	Journal Diam. In. (mm)	Clearance In. (mm)	Side Play In. (mm)
4520 cc	2.517-2.519 (63.93-63.98)	.0018-.0033 (.045-.084)	.....	.004-.009 (.10-.23)	2.044-2.047 (51.93-52.00)	.0008-.0027 (021-.068)	.009-.015 (.23-.39)

VALVE TIMING

Engine	INTAKE		EXHAUST	
	Open ATDC	Close (ABDC)	Open (ABDC)	Close BTDC
4520 cc	22°	6°	2°	14°

CAMSHAFT ①

Engine	Journal Diam. In. (mm)	Clearance In. (mm)	Lobe Lift In. (mm)
4520 cc No. 1	1.376-1.377 (34.96-34.98)	.0004-.0023 (.02-.06)	.....
No. 2 & 3	1.935-1.936 (49.16-49.18)	.011-.027 (.03-.07)	
No. 4 & 5	1.943-1.944 (49.36-49.38)	.0011-.0027 (.03-.07)	

① End play should be .003-.006" (.07-.14 mm).

4.5 LITER V8 (Cont.)
ENGINE SPECIFICATIONS (Cont.)

VALVE SPRINGS

Engine	Free Length In. (mm)	PRESSURE Lbs. @ In. (kg @ mm)	
		Valve Closed	Valve Open
4520 cc Inner	1.77 (45)	24.7@1.3 (11.2@33)	50.7@.846 (23@21.5)
Outer	1.95 (49.5)	67.24@1.65 30.5@42)	194@1.2 (88@30.5)

TIGHTENING SPECIFICATIONS

Application	Ft. Lbs. (mkg)
Cylinder Head Bolts	
Cold, First Stage	22 (3)
Cold, Second Stage	43 (6)
Warm, Third Stage	43 (6)
Rocker Cover Bolts	4 (.5)
Camshaft Bearing Bracket Bolts	36 (5)
Camshaft Sprocket Bolts	72 (10)
Injection Nozzle-to-Injection Valve	7 (1)
Connecting Rod Bolts	①33 (4.5)
Main Bearing Caps	
Large Bolt	72 (10)
Small Bolt	47 (6.5)
Crankshaft Bolt	195-239 (27-33)
Oil Pan	8 (1.1)
Oil Filter-to-Case	29 (4)
Oil Drain Plug	22 (3)
Oil Pressure Relief Valve	29 (4)
Flywheel or Driven Plate	①25 (3.5)
Hydraulic Valve Lifters	36 (5)
Chain Tensioner Nut	80 (11)
Spark Plugs	22 (3)

① — After torque values are achieved, torque an additional 90-100°.

MGB 4 CYLINDER

ENGINE CODING

ENGINE IDENTIFICATION

Engine identification and serial number are stamped on a plate secured to right side of engine just below spark plugs. Engine can also be identified by the second digit of the VIN code. Second digit should be an H.

Engine Identification	
Application	**Code**
All Models	18V

ENGINE, CYLINDER HEAD & MANIFOLDS

ENGINE

NOTE — *Remove engine and transmission as an assembly.*

Removal — 1) Disconnect battery. Remove hood. Drain engine oil and cooling system. Disconnect oil pressure line at block. Disconnect oil cooler lines from engine at filter. Disconnect all coolant hoses and remove radiator.

2) Disconnect alternator and distributor wires, then remove distributor cap. Place heater valve out of way. Disconnect preheater and temperature sender wires. Remove air cleaner.

3) Disconnect throttle cable and fuel inlet line at carburetor. Take off purge hose at rocker cover. Disconnect fuel evaporation canister lines. Disconnect both power brake vacuum and anti-diesel vacuum lines. Remove shifter lever.

4) Disconnect back-up lights, overdrive, and starter wiring. Remove wiring from clips. Separate clutch slave cylinder from clutch housing. Disconnect speedometer cable. Disconnect exhaust at manifold. Remove propeller shaft. Remove engine restraint rod.

5) Remove 4 bolts holding rear mounting crossmember to chassis and allow transmission to drop to fixed crossmember. Remove bolts mounting bracket (in middle of crossmember) to crossmember. Remove nuts holding rear mounts to crossmember; then remove crossmember. Take up weight of vehicle, free front motor mounts, and lift out engine/transmission assembly.

Installation — To install engine/transmission assembly, reverse removal procedure.

INTAKE & EXHAUST MANIFOLDS

Removal — 1) Drain cooling system. Remove air cleaner. Disconnect fuel evaporation hose at carburetor. Disconnect heater line from bottom radiator hose. Disconnect wire from preheater.

2) Remove carburetor (4 nuts) with pre-heater components. Disconnect brake unit vacuum hose, anti-diesel valve hose, and gulp valve hose. Remove gulp valve and swing out of way.

3) Remove hot air shroud. Separate exhaust pipe from bracket at front mount. Separate pipe at manifold. Remove manifold mounting nuts and bolts and lift off manifold assembly.

Installation — To install, reverse removal procedure and note: Attach exhaust pipe to manifold before tightening to mounting bracket.

CYLINDER HEAD

Removal — 1) Drain cooling system. Disconnect radiator hose at thermostat housing. Disconnect carburetor vent line and anti-diesel line. Remove hose secured to thermostat housing. Disconnect purge hose at rocker cover.

2) Free automatic choke water hose. Disconnect gulp valve, air pump, and check valve hoses. Remove necessary air pump bolts. Disconnect spark plug, temperature sender, and pre-heater wires.

3) Place heater valve out of way. Remove hose from water pump. Remove air cleaner assembly. Free hot air shroud. Slide shroud back and remove manifold.

4) Remove rocker shaft and withdraw push rods. Remove AIR manifold rail. Do not remove check valve. Remove cylinder head nuts making note of nut mounting AIR manifold. Lift off head.

Installation — To install, reverse removal procedure and note: New gasket is marked "TOP" and "FRONT". Top must face up and front must face water pump.

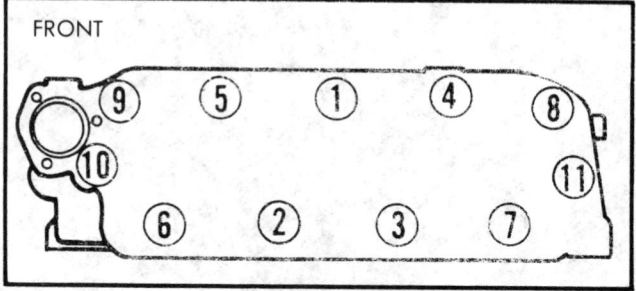

Fig. 1   MGB Cylinder Head Tightening Sequence

VALVES

VALVE ARRANGEMENT

E-I-I-E-E-I-I-E (front to rear)

VALVE GUIDE SERVICING

1) Remove cylinder head and valves. Rest cylinder head with machined face downward on a clean surface. Drive valve guide downwards into combustion chamber space with a suitable drift. When installing new guides, they must be driven in from top of cylinder head.

2) Guides must be inserted with end having largest chamfer at top. Guides should be driven into combustion chamber until exhaust valve guides are $5/8$" and intake valve guides are $3/4$" above machined surface of valve spring seating.

MGB 4 CYLINDER (Cont.)

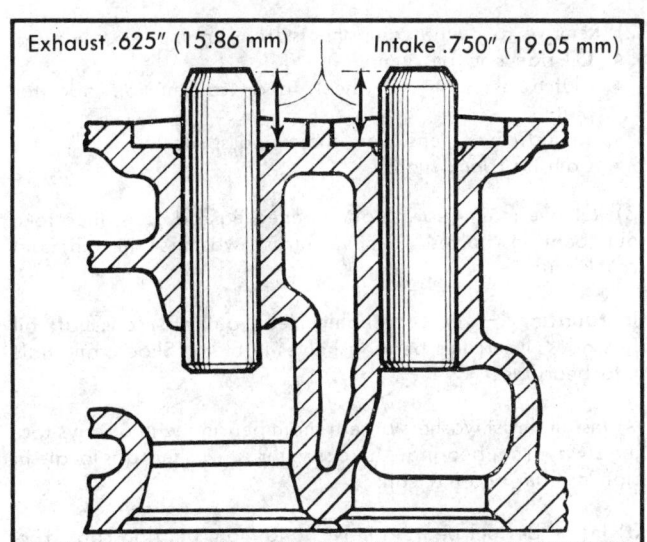

Fig. 2   Cross Sectional View of Installed Valve Guide

Exhaust .625" (15.86 mm)   Intake .750" (19.05 mm)

VALVE SPRINGS

Removal — Remove cylinder head and rocker arm assembly. Compress springs using suitable tool (18G45). Remove two valve keepers. Release valve springs and remove compressor. Take out valve spring retainer, spring, and bottom retainer. Remove "O" ring seal from groove and remove valve from guide.

Installation — Reverse removal procedure using new valve "O" ring seals. Soak rings in clean engine oil for a short time before use to ease installation.

ROCKER ARM ASSEMBLY

Removal — 1) Drain cooling system and disconnect breather pipe from rocker cover. Remove throttle cable, remove two rocker cover attaching nuts and lift off rocker cover. Take care not to damage cork gasket or lose washers or rubber seals.

2) Notice that under the right rear rocker stud nut there is a locking plate. Unscrew eight rocker shaft bracket nuts and external cylinder head nuts gradually, one turn at a time, until all load is released.

NOTE — *It is important that external cylinder head nuts are loosened at same time to avoid possibility of head distortion and water entering cylinders.*

3) Remove all rocker shaft bracket nuts and remove rocker assembly, complete with brackets and rockers. Remove push rods, arranging them so they may be replaced in same positions.

Disassembly 1) — Remove set screw locating rocker shaft in rear rocker mounting bracket, then remove cotter pins, flat washers and spring washers. Slide rockers, brackets, and springs off shaft. Make sure to note how components come off so they can be reassembled accurately.

2) Using suitable tool (18G226), place rocker on anvil and drive out worn bushing. Place new bushing on driver and position bushing with butt joint at top of rocker bore and oil groove in bushing at bottom of rocker bore.

3) It is necessary to drill oil holes in bushing to coincide with oilways in rocker. Holes may be drilled either before or after installation.

4) If holes are drilled after installation, remove adjuster screw and use .093" (2.36 mm) drill to extract end plug and to continue oilway through bushing.

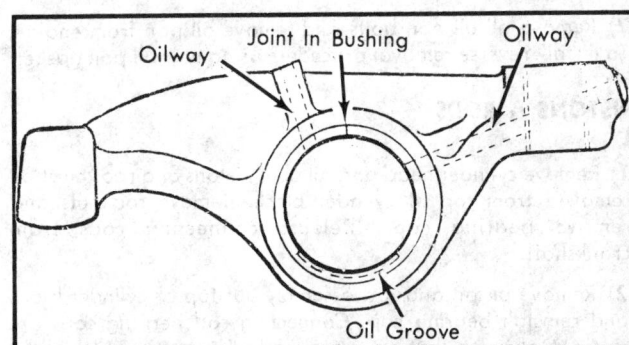

Fig. 3   Rocker Arm Bushing with Detail of Oil Holes

Oilway   Joint In Bushing   Oilway

Oil Groove

5) Replug end after operation using a rivet and weld rivet into position. Oil hole in top of rocker barrel must continue through the bushing with a No. 47 drill. Finally, burnish ream bushing to .6255-.6260" (15.89-15.90 mm).

Reassembly — Reverse disassembly procedure. Remember to replace rocker shaft locating screw lock plate.

Installation — To install rocker assembly on cylinder head, reverse removal procedure. Make sure cylinder head bolts are retorqued before installing rocker cover.

VALVE TAPPETS

Removal — Remove manifolds. Remove rocker shaft. Withdraw push rods and keep in order. Loosen clamp and separate hose from neck attached to tappet cover. Remove side covers and gaskets. Take out tappets keeping them in order.

Installation — To install valve tappets, reverse removal procedure and note: Tappets should seat without forcing.

VALVE CLEARANCE ADJUSTMENT

Remove valve cover and observe operation of valves. To check clearances, turn crankshaft until valves in the first column of table are fully open. Then, valves in second column may be checked and adjust to .013" (.33 mm). Set clearance with engine warm.

Valve Adjustment Sequence

Valves Open	Valves to Adjust
1	8
3	6
5	4
2	7
8	1
6	3
4	5
7	2

MGB 4 CYLINDER (Cont.)

PISTONS, PINS & RINGS

OIL PAN

1) Drain engine oil and drain coolant. Disconnect radiator hoses and remove engine front mounting bolts. Lift engine enough to gain access to front oil pan bolts.

2) Remove all oil pan bolts and remove oil pan from engine. To install, reverse removal procedure using new oil pan gasket.

PISTONS & RODS

1) Remove cylinder head and oil pan. Pistons and rods must be removed from top of cylinder block. Remove rod nuts and remove bearing caps. Release connecting rods from crankshaft.

2) Remove piston and rod assembly out top of cylinder block and reinstall bearing cap. Connecting rod bearing caps are offset. Make sure that parts are marked so reassembly will be in original position.

PISTON RINGS

1) Place rings in top of cylinder bore. Check ring gaps. Check oil ring to groove clearance. Fit oil control expander. Make sure ends of expander are butting, but not overlapping. Set gaps of rails and expander 90° to each other.

2) Fit stepped compression rings into SECOND groove with face marked "TOP" up. Fit top ring. Place ring gaps 90° to each other away from thrust side of piston.

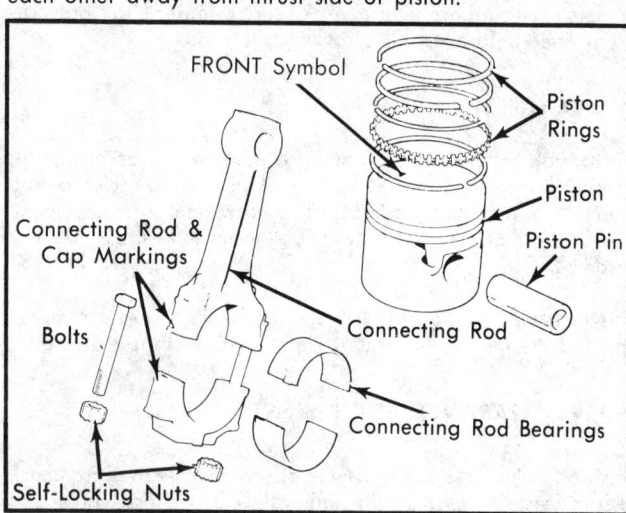

Fig. 4 Exploded View of Piston and Rod Assembly

PISTON PINS

Piston pins are press fit. Use suitable tool or press to remove or install pins.

CRANKSHAFT MAIN & CONNECTING ROD BEARINGS

CRANKSHAFT

Removal — 1) Drain cooling system. Remove engine as previously outlined. Separate transmission from engine.

2) Remove following components from engine:
- Oil pan and oil pump.
- Clutch assembly, flywheel, and transmission adaptor plate.
- Timing cover, tensioner, chain and sprockets.
- Camshaft lock plate.

3) Remove main bearing and connecting rod caps, then take out bearing halves. Remove thrust washers and lift out crankshaft.

Installation — 1) Thoroughly clean out all crankshaft oil passages. Insert top bearing halves in block. Slide crankshaft into bearings.

2) Install thrust washers at rear main bearing with oilways facing away from bearing. Make sure thrust washer tabs locate in slot in main bearing cap.

3) Install bottom bearing halves and main bearing caps. Torque cap bolts.

4) Check crankshaft end play and adjust if necessary with selective fit washers. End play should be as specified in table.

5) Install remaining components in reverse of removal procedure.

CONNECTING ROD BEARINGS

To remove bearings, bend down locking strips so that bolts may be removed. Remove connecting rod caps and extract bearings. No scraping of bearings is required as bearings are machined to give correct clearance of .001-.0027" (.03-.07 mm).

MAIN BEARINGS

1) Remove engine from car and remove flywheel and clutch, timing chain, oil pan and oil strainer. Remove rear engine mounting plate. Remove two bolts and locking plate holding front main bearing cap to engine front plate. Remove main bearing cap retaining nuts and remove caps and bearings.

2) Bearings are machined to give correct clearance of .001-.0027". When replacing bearings that have been used but are not damaged or worn, make sure that bearing and all surfaces are thoroughly cleaned. Rear main bearing cap horizontal joint surface should be lightly covered with Hylomar Jointing Compound or equivalent before cap is fitted to cylinder block. Tighten bearing cap nuts.

THRUST BEARINGS

A thrust washer is fitted on each side of center main bearing to take crankshaft end thrust. Washers each consist of two semicircular halves, one having a lug located in recess in removable half of bearing and other one being plain.

CAMSHAFT

FRONT COVER & OIL SEAL

Removal — Drain cooling system. Remove radiator. Remove alternator belt and A.I.R. pump belt. Remove fan and pulley from crankshaft. Remove front cover bolts and remove from vehicle. Pry or drive out crankshaft oil seal.

MGB 4 CYLINDER (Cont.)

Installation — Dip new oil seal in engine oil. Use installing tool 18G 134 and adapter 18G 134BD to fit seal. Be sure lip of seal is facing inward. Position oil thrower with "F" mark showing. Smear sealing compound on cover and seal. Tighten bolts evenly. Lubricate crankshaft hub and slide pulley on to crankshaft, engaging keyway. Put on new lock nut and tighten bolt.

TIMING CHAIN & TENSIONER

Removal — Remove front cover as previously outlined. Remove oil thrower. Bend back tensioner lock tabs. Remove tensioner bolts. Pry tensioner mechanism out of front plate. Slipper head (piece that rides against chain) is under spring tension. Remove all tensioner components and disassemble any that are not apart. Unlock and remove camshaft nut. Pull off camshaft and crankshaft sprockets.

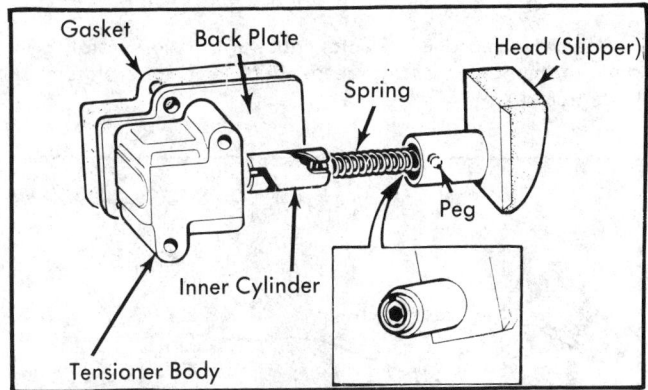

Fig. 5 Exploded View of Timing Chain Tensioner

NOTE — Use care not to lose sprocket packing washers behind crankshaft sprocket. Make sure to replace the same number of washers as removed. To determine correct thickness of washers to be used if new camshaft or crankshaft components have been installed, place straightedge across sides of crankshaft sprocket and measure gap between straightedge and crankshaft sprocket. Select and fit washers as required.

Installation — 1) When replacing timing chain and sprockets, set crankshaft keyway at TDC and camshaft keyway at 2 o'clock position. Assemble sprockets to timing chain with index marks in sprockets (if equipped) opposite each other.

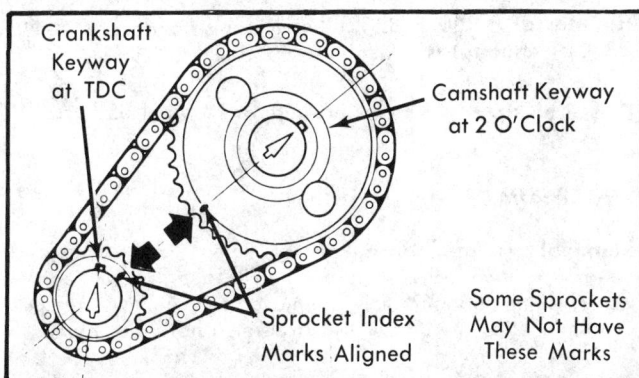

Fig. 6 Camshaft and Crankshaft Sprocket Alignment

2) Keep sprockets in this position and engage crankshaft sprocket keyway with key on crankshaft and rotate camshaft until camshaft sprocket keyway and key are aligned. Push sprockets onto shafts as far as possible and tighten with lock washer and nut.

3) Refit chain tensioner inner cylinder and spring into cylinder of slipper head. Make sure serrated seat in inner cylinder engages peg in slipper cylinder. Turn inner cylinder clockwise against tension until cover serrations in seat engage peg and retains inner cylinder in slipper cylinder. Refit tensioner with mounting bolts. Fit oil thrower with face marked "F" to front. Reverse removal procedure to install remaining components.

CAMSHAFT

Removal & Installation — 1) Disconnect battery and remove intake and exhaust manifolds (if necessary). Remove push rods and tappets. Remove timing cover, timing chain and timing sprockets.

2) Disconnect distributor vacuum line at distributor and remove 2 bolts with flat washers which hold distributor to housing. Do not loosen clamping plate bolt or ignition timing will be disturbed. Remove distributor assembly.

3) Remove oil pan, oil pump, and oil pump drive shaft. Remove 3 set screws and lock washers holding camshaft locating plate to cylinder block. Remove camshaft.

4) Before reassembly, fix camshaft thrust plate and sprocket to camshaft, then check end play. Specifications should not exceed .003-.007" (.076-.178 mm). Make measurement between retaining plate and thrust face of camshaft front journal.

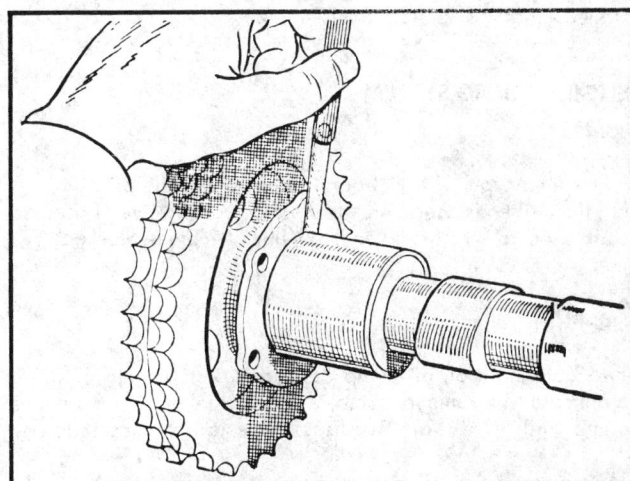

Fig. 7 Using a Feeler Gauge to Measure Camshaft End Play

CAMSHAFT BEARINGS

NOTE — Follow manufacturers instructions for proper adapter and washer use on each bearing for removal and installation.

MG Engines

MGB 4 CYLINDER (Cont.)

Removal — Use bearing removal/installation tool 18G 124A and adapters to remove camshaft front bearing. Remove rear bearing in same manner as front bearing, then index tool through front bearing bore to remove center bearing.

NOTE — *Be sure oil holes in new bearings are aligned with lubrication ports in block. The holes must not move once they have been located.*

Installation — Fit new bearings into bore in reverse order of removal. After bearings have been installed, use camshaft bearing bore tool 18G 123A to line bore new bearings.

NOTE — *Cutting edge of boring tool must be kept dry and free of cuttings at all times.*

VALVE TIMING

1) Set No. 1 cylinder intake valve clearance to .055" with engine cold. Turn crankshaft until valve is about to open. Indicator groove in flange of crankshaft pulley should be opposite longest pointer on indicator bracket beneath crankshaft pulley, indicating TDC.

2) After timing has been checked, valve clearance should be reset. See *Valve Clearance Adjustment.*

ENGINE OILING

Crankcase Capacity — 3.6 quarts with filter change.

Oil Filter — Full flow type with disposable cartridge.

Oil Pressure — 10-25 psi (.7-1.7 kg/cm²) @ idle; 50-80 psi (3.5-5.6 kg/cm²) @ 2000 RPM.

Oil Pump Relief Valve — Free length is 3" (76.2 mm). Installed length is 2.156" (54.77 mm).

ENGINE OILING SYSTEM

Force feed type with Hobourn-Eaton rotor type oil pump. A full-flow filter is used. An oil pressure relief valve is used to enable oil to by-pass filter if oil filter becomes blocked.

OIL PUMP

Two bolts hold on oil pump cover and 3 studs hold pump to crankcase. To remove pump, remove stud nuts and remove pump and drive shaft. To disassemble, proceed as follows:

1) Remove cover, located at base of oil pump by 2 dowels. Remove outer rotor complete with oil pump shaft. Clean all parts in kerosene and inspect for wear.

2) Rotor end play should be checked as follows: Install rotors in pump body and place straightedge across joint face of pump body. Measure clearance between top face of rotors and underside of straightedge. Clearance should not exceed .005" (.13 mm). If clearance is excessive, remove two cover locating dowels and tap the joint face of pump body.

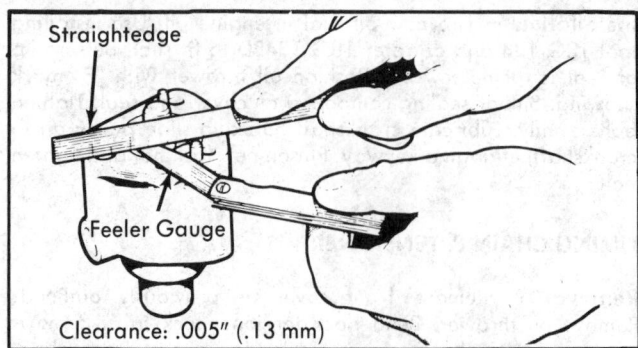

Fig. 8 Measuring Oil Pump Rotor End Play

3) Check clearance between outer rotor and rotor pocket in pump body. If clearance exceeds .010" (.25 mm), pump rotor, pump body, or complete pump assembly should be replaced.

4) Measure clearance of rotor lobes with rotors installed in pump body. If clearance exceeds .006" (.15 mm), rotors must be replaced.

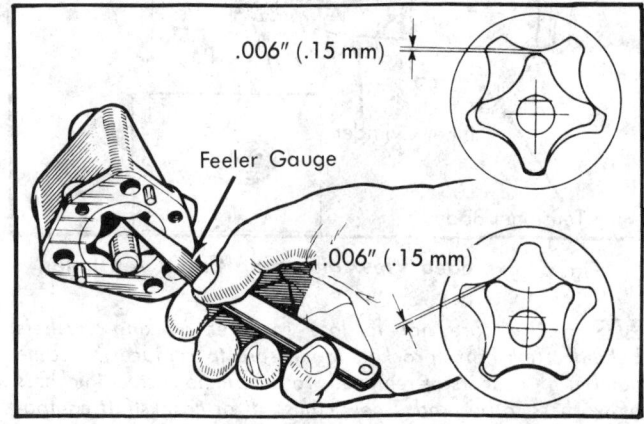

Fig. 9 Measuring Oil Pump Rotor Lobe Clearance

5) Reassemble pump and lubricate all parts with clean engine oil. Make sure outer rotor is installed in pump body with chamfered end at drive end of rotor pocket in pump body.

ENGINE COOLING

Cooling System Capacity — 7.2 quarts with heater.

Thermostat — 180°F (82°C) thermostat is standard. A 190°F (88°C) thermostat is available for use in cold climates.

Pressure Cap — Maintains pressure at 15 psi (1.05 kg/cm³).

WATER PUMP

Removal — Drain cooling system. Remove AIR pump and alternator drive belts, then pivot units out-of-way. Remove water pump bottom hose. Remove belt pulleys. Remove mounting bolts. Withdraw AIR brackets and water pump.

Installation — To install, reverse removal procedure and adjust both belts.

MGB 4 CYLINDER (Cont.)

ENGINE SPECIFICATIONS

GENERAL SPECIFICATIONS

Year	Displ.		Carburetor	HP at RPM	Torque (Ft. Lbs. at RPM)	Compr. Ratio	Bore		Stroke	
	cu. ins.	cc					in.	mm	in.	mm
1980	110	1798	1x1-Bbl.	.....	.....	8.0:1	3.16	80.26	3.50	88.90

VALVES

Engine & Valve	Head Diam. In. (mm)	Face Angle	Seat Angle	Seat Width In. (mm)	Stem Diameter In. (mm)	Stem Clearance In. (mm)	Valve Lift In. (mm)
1798 cc Int.	1.562-1.567 (39.67-39.80)	45°	45.5°	...	.3429-.3434 (8.70-8.72)	.0007-.0019 (.02-.05)	.3645 (9.25)
Exh.	1.343-1.348 (34.11-34.23)	45°	45.5°	...	.3423-.3428 (8.69-8.70)	.0013-.0025 (.03-.06)	.3645 (9.25)

PISTONS, PINS, RINGS

Engine	PISTONS	PINS		RINGS		
	Clearance In. (mm)	Piston Fit In. (mm)	Rod Fit In. (mm)	Rings	End Gap In. (mm)	Side Clearance In. (mm)
1798 cc	① .0021-.0033 (.053-.084) ② .0006-.0012 (.015-.030)	③	Press Fit	No. 1	.012-.022 (.30-.56)	.0015-.0035 (.038-.088)
				No. 2	.012-.022 (.30-.56)	.0015-.0035 (.038-.088)
				Oil	.015-.045 (.38-1.14)	.0016-.0036 (.04-.09)

① — Top.
② — Bottom.
③ — Hand Push Fit at 60°F (15.6°C).

CRANKSHAFT MAIN & CONNECTING ROD BEARINGS

Engine	MAIN BEARINGS				CONNECTING ROD BEARINGS		
	Journal Diam. In. (mm)	Clearance In. (mm)	Thrust Bearing	Crankshaft End Play In. (mm)	Journal Diam. In. (mm)	Clearance In. (mm)	Side Play In. (mm)
1798 cc	2.1262-2.1270 (54.01-54.02)	.001-.0027 (.03-.07)	Center	.004-.005 (.10-.13)	1.8759-1.8764 (47.64-47.66)	.001-.0027 (.03-.07)	.....

CAMSHAFT

Engine	Journal Diam. In. (mm)	Clearance In. (mm)	Lobe Lift In. (mm)
1798 cc Front	1.7888-1.7893 (45.42-45.44)	.001-.002 (.025-.051)	.250 (6.35)
Center	1.7288-1.7293 (43.91-43.92)		
Rear	1.6228-1.6233 (41.22-41.23)		

MG Engines

MGB 4 CYLINDER (Cont.)

ENGINE SPECIFICATIONS (Cont.)

VALVE SPRINGS

Engine	Free Length In. (mm)	PRESSURE Lbs. @ In. (kg @ mm)	
		Valve Closed	Valve Open
1798 cc	1.92 (48.8)	.....	.....

VALVE TIMING

Engine	INTAKE		EXHAUST	
	Open (BTDC)	Close (ABDC)	Open (BBDC)	Close (ATDC)
1798 cc	8°	42°	54°	18°

TIGHTENING SPECIFICATIONS

Application	Ft. Lbs. (mkg)
Main Bearing Nuts	70 (9.7)
Flywheel Set Screws	40 (5.5)
Connecting Rod Bolts	31-35 (4.2)
Rocker Bracket Nuts	25 (3.5)
Oil Pump-to-Crankcase	14 (.8)
Oil Pan Bolts	6 (.8)
Side Covers	3-4 (.4-.5)
Timing Cover	
¼" Screws	6 (.8)
⁵⁄₁₆" Screws	14 (1.9)
Rear Plate	
⁵⁄₁₆" Screws	20 (2.8)
⅜" Screws	30 (4.1)
Water Pump	17 (2.3)
Thermostat Housing	8 (1.1)
Rocker Cover Nuts	4 (.56)
Manifold Nuts	16 (2.2)
Clutch-to-Flywheel	25-30 (3.5-4.1)
Carburetor Stud Nuts	15 (2.1)
Cylinder Head	45-50 (6.2-6.9)

505 GASOLINE 4 CYLINDER

ENGINE CODING

ENGINE IDENTIFICATION

Engine serial number is stamped on left side engine mounting face and is also located on identification plate attached to top panel, above center of grille.

Engine identification number is stamped on camshaft tunnel on left side of block, near the starter. The letters at the beginning and end of the number are used for identification as follows:

Engine Identification Codes		
Application	Transmission	Engine Codes
XN6 Engine	Manual	BVM
XN6 Engine	Automatic	BVA

ENGINE & CYLINDER HEAD

ENGINE

Removal — 1) Remove hood, battery and fan shroud. Drain radiator and remove upper and lower hoses. Remove electrical lead from cooling fan switch, and remove radiator lower mounting bolts. Remove rubber duct hose at mixture regulator throttle plate housing.

2) Remove fuel supply and return hoses and hose from cold start injector. Remove PCV hose and electrical connectors from cold start injector and fuel distributor. Remove fuel hoses and electrical connector from control pressure regulator.

3) Remove fuel injectors, mixture regulator and air filter. If equipped, remove air conditioning compressor and freon hose clamp near alternator. Disconnect accelerator cable and electrical harness near brake master cylinder.

4) Remove diagnostic plug for TDC sensor, located near ignition coil. Separate 2 connectors. Remove high tension lead from coil. Remove vacuum hoses from charcoal canister.

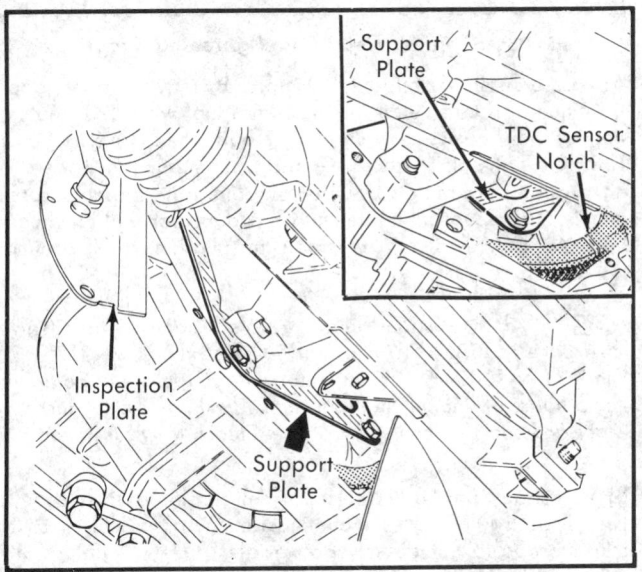

Fig. 1 Positioning Support Plate for Torque Converter

5) Remove heater hose near charcoal canister and fan. Remove oxygen sensor (Lambda) wire near vacuum switches, and disconnect air injection hose to catalytic converter. Remove vacuum switches support and 3-wire electrical connector nearby. Install engine sling assembly (8.0102-X).

6) Remove starter, clutch housing bolts, and left engine mount. Remove right engine mount. Remove 3 power steering pump bolts and set pump aside. Remove exhaust header pipe.

7) Remove inspection plates and clutch housing. On vehicles with automatic transmission, remove inspection plate without altering TDC sensor adjustment. To do so, position torque converter support plate as shown in *Fig. 1*. Mark TDC sensor notch in reference to support plate. Support torque converter with special clamp (8.0315-A).

8) Remove air conditioning condenser and set to left side, keeping hoses connected. Remove and set receiver-drier to one side. Lift engine with 8.0102-X engine sling assembly until top of bell housing contacts lower firewall. See *Fig. 2*.

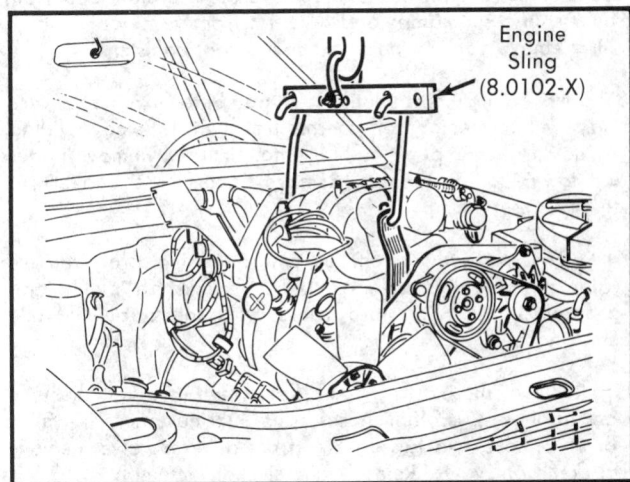

Fig. 2 Removing Engine from Vehicle

9) Install transmission supporting brace (8.0125). Disengage engine from transmission and lift engine carefully out of engine compartment. Check for electrical leads, cables, hoses or pipes which have not been detached from engine.

Installation — 1) To install engine, reverse removal procedures, noting the following precautions. On vehicles with automatic transmissions, lubricate torque converter centering nipple generously with Calysol grease (F 3015 or equivalent). Position TDC sensor notch, and align reference marks made during removal. Coat 4 torque converter bolts with normal-holding Loctite and tighten to 22 ft. lbs. (3 mkg). Use ring gear locking pawl (8.0110-J) when tightening bolts.

2) On vehicles with manual transmissions, lightly lubricate splines, front mainshaft and pilot bushing with Molykote 321 or equivalent. Place shift lever in gear. Torque engine mount-to-crossmember bolts to 22 ft. lbs. (3 mkg). Torque engine-to-clutch housing bolts to 40 ft. lbs. (5.5 mkg).

3) Adjust TDC sensor, if new, by bringing 3 nipples in contact. If reusing TDC sensor, deburr 3 nipples so gap of .067" (1.7 mm) exists between sensor and ring gear.

4) Refill radiator, cooling system, engine crankcase and automatic transmission. Check power steering fluid reservoir level.

505 GASOLINE 4 CYLINDER (Cont.)

5) To adjust accelerator cable, depress accelerator pedal against its stop, placing a .20" (5 mm) spacer between pedal and stop (full throttle position). Connect cable to throttle drum. Rotate drum to full throttle position. Exert slight pull on cable housing stop to place control under slight load. Install clip to obtain minimum gap between clip and common manifold.

6) To adjust kick-down cable, place throttle plate in idle position. Extend cable to obtain a maximum play of .02" (.5 mm) between cable housing stop and cable travel limiter. Tighten cable on drum.

CYLINDER HEAD

Removal — 1) Drain cooling system, including cylinder block. Disconnect battery. Remove exhaust header pipe and oxygen sensor. Remove mounting brackets for common manifold and intake manifold.

2) Pull common manifold off pipes. Remove distributor cap, injectors, and diagnostic plug bracket. Disconnect electrical connector near ignition coil and remove high tension lead from coil. Remove all clamps and wire ties from vicinity of ignition coil. Remove vacuum hoses from charcoal canister.

3) Remove air pump outlet hose at pump. Remove upper wire and lower connector from thermo-time switch. Remove sliding lug bolt from air pump-to-alternator bracket. Remove upper and lower radiator hoses. Remove heater hose and power steering reservoir.

4) Remove radiator fan shroud and fan. Using a rag, remove water pump belt from pulley. Use crankshaft pulley bolt sprocket (8.0118-PZ) to turn crankshaft counterclockwise while removing belt.

5) Remove thermostatic air slide valve bracket. Remove vacuum hoses, coolant hoses, and thermostatic wire from valve. Remove two large hoses from diverter valve. Remove bracket from valve. Remove air injection assembly.

6) Remove heater hose near dipstick and remove auxiliary air device. Remove remaining electrical connectors from switches or sensors mounted in cylinder head. Remove rocker arm oil feed pipe. Disconnect all vacuum hoses remaining on common manifold side of engine, including hose at diverter valve.

7) Remove spark plug wire brackets and wires at spark plug. Remove valve cover. Remove cooling fan brush holder. Remove sealing rings from spark plug tubes. Remove rocker arm assembly and push rods.

8) Use pivoting handles (0.0149) to break cylinder head loose. Install cylinder liner retainers (8.0132) to prevent liners from moving.

Inspection — 1) Plug passages in cylinder block for valve lifters and oil return. Clean and scrape cylinder block gasket surface, and run a tap in cylinder block bolt holes.

2) Check liner protrusion above block (.0028-.0055" or .07-.14 mm) at engine centerline. No liner should protrude more than .0015" (.04 mm) above adjacent liner. If not to specifications, replace liner gaskets.

3) Using a plastic or wooden scraper, clean cylinder head gasket surface. Clean cylinder head bolts. Check for cylinder head warpage (maximum allowable is .004" or .10 mm). Check

cylinder head thickness. Original thickness is 3.636-3.648" (92.35-92.65 mm), with minimum permissable thickness being 3.616" (91.85 mm). If cylinder head must be planed, check thickness before and after planing to be sure thickness is within tolerances.

4) Clean and check valve lifters, using caution not to mix them. DO NOT scrape carbon off piston tops, as liner damage could result.

Installation — 1) Install cylinder head in reverse of removal sequence, noting the following. When installing cylinder head, use 2 locating guides (8.0115-BZ). Install new gasket with word, "DESSUS", "ALTO" or "TOP" facing up (toward cylinder head).

2) Install cylinder head and rocker arm assembly. Lightly tighten cylinder head bolts (with flat washers), using a drop of engine oil on threads. Lightly tighten rocker shaft nuts. Remove 2 head guides, using removal tools (8.0115-A). Install last 2 head bolts.

NOTE — *Do not get oil in cylinder head bolt holes, as this could cause hydraulic blockage and prevent proper tightening.*

3) Using tightening sequence shown in *Fig. 3*, tighten head bolts to 36 ft. lbs. (5.0 mkg) and rocker shaft nuts to 11 ft. lbs. (1.5 mkg). Place angular head torquing tool (8.0129) on 2 center bolts (1 and 2). Completely loosen No. 1 bolt and retorque it to 14 ft. lbs. (2.0 mkg). Keep tool in place and maintain tension on torque wrench.

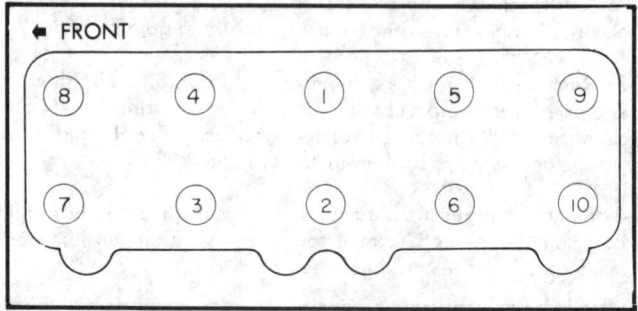

Fig. 3 Cylinder Head Bolt Tightening Sequence

4) Position pointer on tool at "0" notch by moving spring loop. Continue torquing until pointer lines up with "90" notch. Repeat entire procedure with No. 2 bolt. Then move tool and complete tightening procedure in proper sequence. If there is any doubt concerning torque of any one bolt, loosen it completely and repeat all tightening procedures for that one head bolt. Adjust valves, and complete installation. Refill cooling system.

NOTE — *After cylinder head removal, adjust intake valve clearance to .006" (.15 mm) and exhaust valves to .012" (.30 mm). After 1000-1500 miles, retorque cylinder head bolts (after 6 hours of engine cooling), and adjust valve clearances to standard specifications. See Valve Clearance Adjustment.*

5) Adjust air pump and alternator belt tension at idler pulley. Loosen both idler pulley mounting bolts. Apply 36 ft. lbs. (5 mkg) torque to nut directly above idler pulley. Tighten both mounting bolts. Turn engine one full turn to align belt on idler pulley. Loosen both mounting bolts and retorque to 58 ft. lbs. (8 mkg). Retighten both mounting bolts.

505 GASOLINE 4 CYLINDER (Cont.)

SPARK PLUG TUBE REPLACEMENT

Removal — With cylinder head supported, screw in plugs without springs to prevent dirt from falling into cylinder. Remove tubes using mallet or suitable extractor.

NOTE — *If tubes are removed, new tubes MUST be inserted.*

Installation — To install tubes, coat with suitable sealing compound and insert so plug caps are facing as shown in illustration. When tube is fully seated, it will protrude 2.835" (72 mm) upward from cylinder head.

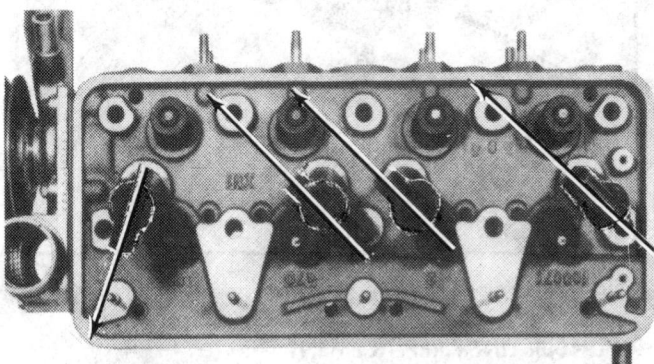

Fig. 4   Position of Spark Plug Tubes for Installation

VALVES

VALVE ARRANGEMENT
Left Side — Intake valves.
Right Side — Exhaust valves.

NOTE — *Cylinders and valves are numbered with number one at flywheel end.*

VALVE SPRING REPLACEMENT
Intake Valve — Turn crankshaft in direction of engine rotation and position where exhaust valve just begins to open. Slide rocker arm off intake valve then bring piston to TDC of compression stroke. Using suitable spring compressor, compress spring and remove keepers, spring retainer and spring.

Exhaust Valve — 1) Remove spark plug from cylinder requiring attention. Rotate crankshaft in direction of engine rotation and bring intake valve to fully closed position. Slide rocker arm off exhaust valve.

2) Insert suitable hinged tool (0 0136) into spark plug hole and bring piston to TDC without forcing as tool is between piston and valve. Using suitable spring compressor, compress spring and remove keepers, spring retainer and spring.

VALVE CLEARANCE ADJUSTMENT

NOTE — *Engine must be allowed to cool at least 6 hours before adjusting valves. Adjust valves in firing order sequence (1-3-4-2). No. 1 cylinder is on flywheel end.*

Rotate engine until exhaust valve number one is fully opened, then adjust intake valve number three and exhaust valve number four. Rotate engine one half turn until next number valve is fully opened and adjust corresponding valves. See table. Continue until all valves have been adjusted.

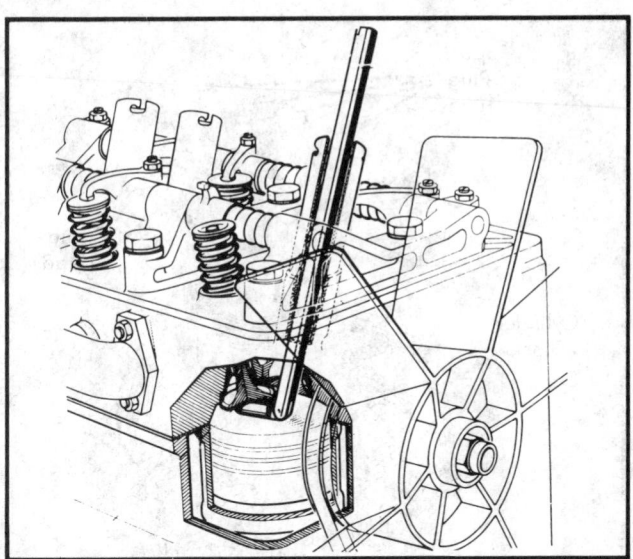

Fig. 5   Removing Valve Spring with Valve Held in Place

Valve Adjustment Sequence	
Valve Open	**Adjust Valves**
E 1	I 3 & E 4
E 3	I 4 & E 2
E 4	I 2 & E 1
E 2	I 1 & E 3

Valve Clearance Adjustment①

Application	Intake② In. (mm)	Exhaust③ In. (mm)
All Models	.004 (.10)	.010 (.25)

① — Tolerance range of +0 to +.002" (+0 to +.05 mm).

② — Adjust to .006" (.15 mm) after installing cylinder head. Retorque to above specifications after 1000-1500 miles.

③ — Adjust to .012" (.30 mm) after installing cylinder head. Retorque to above specifications after 1000-1500 miles.

PISTONS, PINS & RINGS

PISTON & ROD ASSEMBLY

NOTE — *Engine must be removed to replace liners and pistons.*

Removal — 1) Drain crankcase. With engine mounted on suitable engine stand, remove intake and exhaust manifolds. Remove all auxiliary equipment, including alternator, air pump and fuel pump plunger. See Fig. 6.

2) Remove cylinder head. See Cylinder Head Removal in this article. Remove camshaft hydraulic lifters, keeping them in original order. Remove distributor support drive shaft.

3) Remove oil pan and oil pump. Remove timing cover. Remove bearing caps, keeping them in original order. Remove pistons and connecting rods. Attach connecting rods to matching cap, mark rod assemblies 1-4.

505 GASOLINE 4 CYLINDER (Cont.)

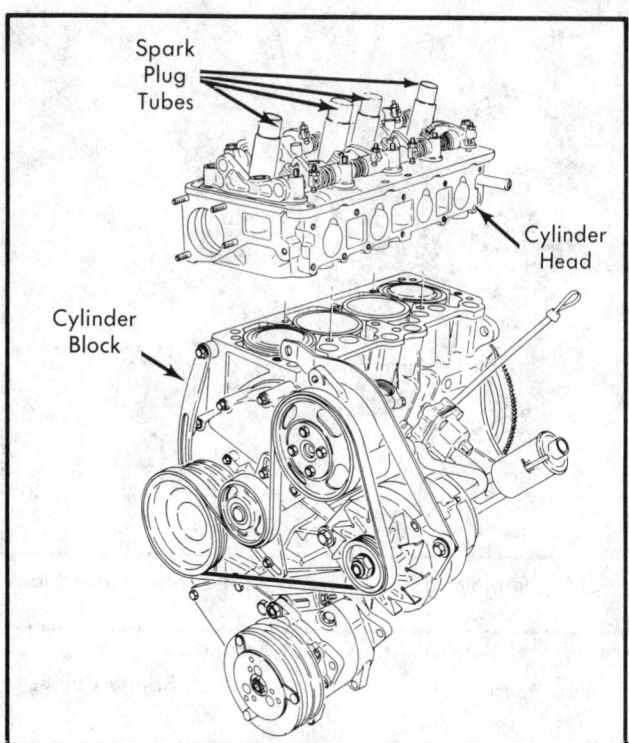

Fig. 6 Cylinder Block and Cylinder Head Assembly

Installation — 1) To install, fit piston ring clamp on piston. Insert piston and rod assembly, without twisting it. Index arrow must face front of engine.

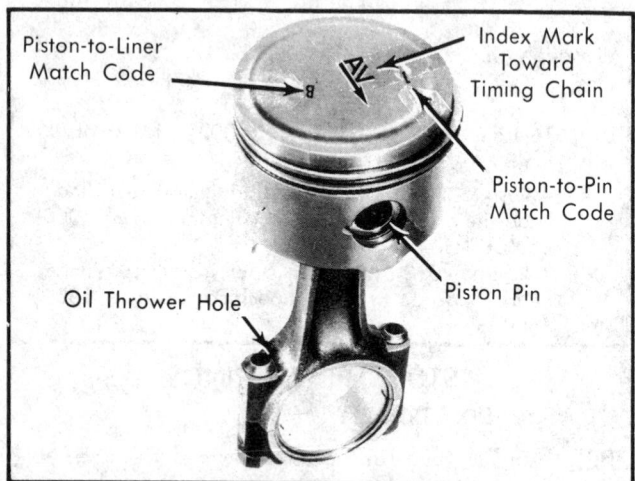

Fig. 7 Piston and Rod Assembly with Index Marks and Codes

2) Push piston down cylinder and guide connecting rod with bearing over crankshaft journal. Install bearing cap and tighten.

NOTE — Marks on rods and caps must be on same side.

PISTON PIN REPLACEMENT

Remove snap rings and piston pin. Fit piston to rod with index mark "AV" at right angle to oil thrower, so that it will face front of engine. If necessary heat piston in boiling water and insert pin. Install snap rings.

NOTE — "AV" mark on piston top must face front of engine. Pistons and liners must be matched by letter code. Number on top of piston refers to piston pin code (1 — Blue, 2 — White, and 3 — Red).

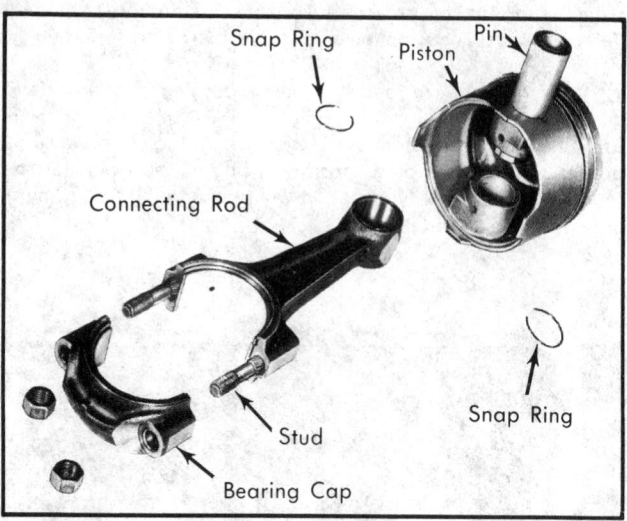

Fig. 8 Exploded View of Piston and Connecting Rod

CYLINDER LINER REPLACEMENT

1) Remove cylinder liners, using suitable extractor if required. Before installing liners, clean and inspect for burrs and dirt. Insert liners, without base gaskets, with flats on shoulder of liners 1-2 and 3-4 parallel.

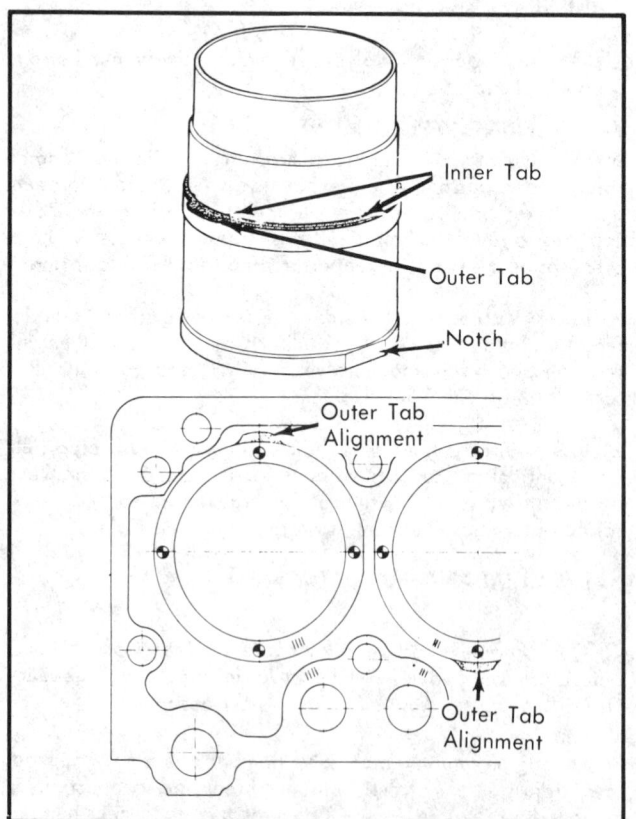

Fig. 9 Cylinder Liner Gasket Installation

505 GASOLINE 4 CYLINDER (Cont.)

NOTE — *Do not alter piston/liner pairings.*

2) Place a suitable dial gauge and support on block face. Synchronize dial at 0 and 5. Check each liner at 4 different points, noting the highest reading. Maximum allowable difference between 2 opposite points must be less than .003" (.07 mm). If specification is exceeded, it may be necessary to change position of liners.

NOTE — *Liners must be identified by position.*

3) Select a base gasket for each liner which will give a protusion of approximately .005" (.12 mm). Gaskets are available in 4 different sizes. Use only 1 gasket on each liner.

4) Fit gasket on liner. Engage gasket inner tabs in liner grooves. *See Fig. 9.* Position tab with reference mark at right angles to flat. Position liners with outer tabs in position. Install suitable liner compressor tools to block. Seat liners and ensure protrusion is correct. Remove compressor tools and install liner locks.

NOTE — *Difference in protrusion of adjoining cylinders must not exceed .0015" (.04 mm).*

CRANKSHAFT MAIN & CONNECTING ROD BEARINGS

THRUST BEARING WASHERS

After installing crankshaft, check end play. Play must not exceed .008" (.20 mm). If specification is exceeded, oversize thrust washers are available in .094" (2.40 mm), .096" (2.45 mm), and .098" (2.50 mm) sizes.

CAMSHAFT

TIMING CHAIN

Removal — 1) Remove radiator, fan belt and spark plugs. Remove crankshaft pulley and timing chain cover. Disengage chain tensioner by removing plug and turning 3 mm Allen wrench clockwise. It is possible to further disassemble chain tensioners.

NOTE — *Position camshaft as shown in Fig. 11 to avoid any possible contact of valves and pistons when rotating crankshaft with timing chain removed.*

2) Remove camshaft sprocket, timing chain, crankshaft sprocket and Woodruff key.

Installation — 1) Hold crankshaft in original position and install Woodruff key and sprocket. Position camshaft and then crankshaft as shown in *Fig. 12*.

2) Install timing chain first on camshaft sprocket, then on crankshaft sprocket. Ensure timing marks are in correct alignment. Fit camshaft with a new washer and tighten bolts. Bend up tabs.

3) Engage chain tensioner by adjusting Allen wrench in a clockwise manner. Install a new tab washer on plug and bend tab. Withdraw tool after installing tensioner.

4) Install thrust washers (if required) and timing chain cover. Install timing chain cover on 2 centering pins, protecting seal with suitable tool. Install crankshaft pulley after cover bolts are tightened.

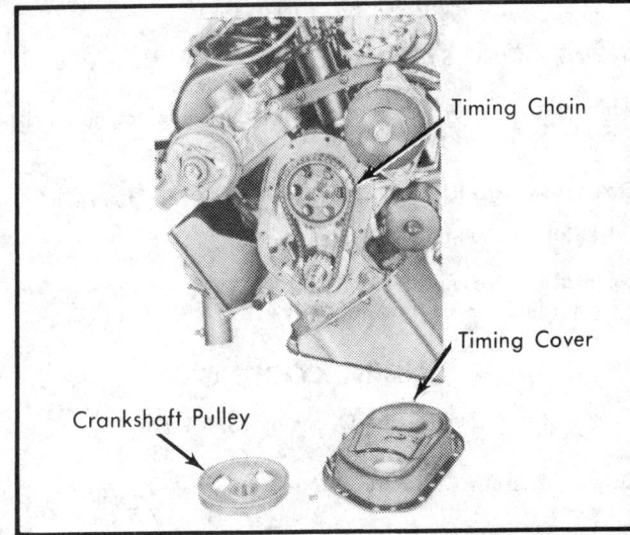

Fig. 10   Timing Cover Removed with Related Components

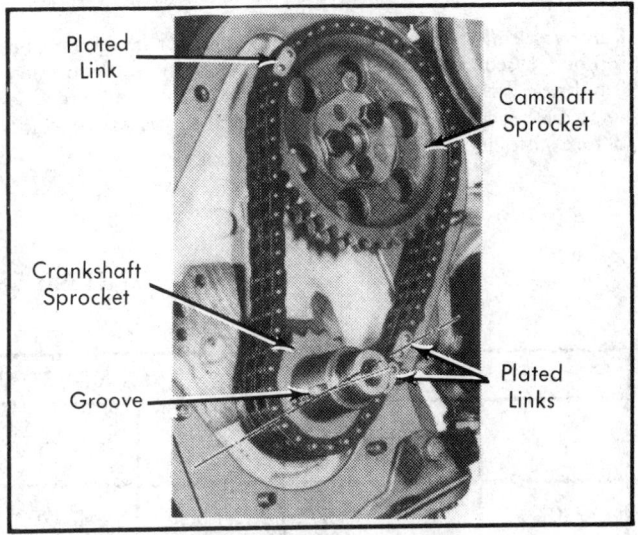

Fig. 11   Proper Alignment of Camshaft and Crankshaft for Removing Timing Chain

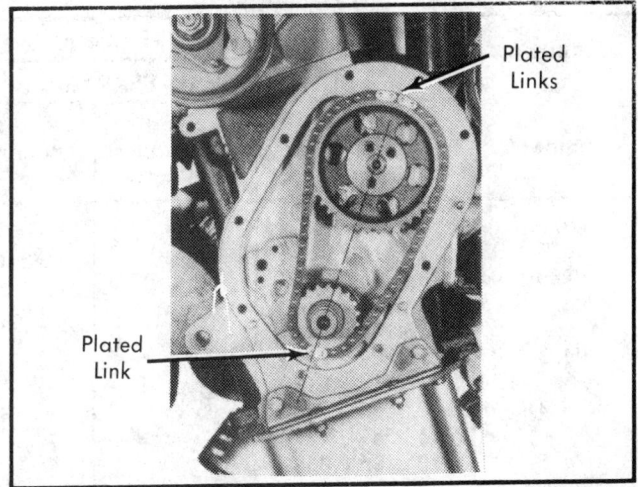

Fig. 12   Proper Alignment of Camshaft and Crankshaft

Peugeot Engines

505 GASOLINE 4 CYLINDER (Cont.)

ENGINE OILING

ENGINE OILING SYSTEM

A high output, gear type oil pump is mounted to engine block lower surface and is operated by camshaft.

Crankcase Capacity — Approximately 4.2 qts. for refill.

Oil Filter — Full-flow cartridge type.

Normal Oil Pressure — 28-51 psi (2-3.6 kg/cm²) at idle; 44-67 psi (3-4.7 kg/cm²) at 4000 RPM.

ENGINE COOLING

Thermostat — Summer — Opens at 167° F (75° C).
Winter — Opens at 190° F (88° C).

Cooling System Capacity — Auto. Trans. — 7.7 qts.
Man. Trans. — 7.5 qts.

Radiator Cap — 14.5 psi (1.02 kg/cm²).

WATER PUMP

Removal & Installation — Remove radiator, top hose and fan belt. Disconnect heater hose from pump and self-engaging fan brush holder. Remove water pump. To install, reverse removal procedure and ensure contact surfaces are clean before installing new gasket.

SELF-DISENGAGING FAN

Driven by water pump shaft and controlled by a thermal contact-breaker. Fan engages at approximately 190° F (88° C) and disengages at 174° F (79° C).

TIGHTENING SPECIFICATIONS	
Application	Ft. Lbs. (mkg)
Cylinder Head	See Text
Crankshaft Main Bearing Bolts	54 (7.5)
Connecting Rod Nuts	29 (4.0)
Camshaft Retaining Plate Bolts	12 (1.7)
Camshaft Sprocket Bolts	16 (2.25)
Crankshaft Pulley Bolt	123 (17)
Oil Pan Bolts	7 (1.0)
Flywheel-to-Crankshaft Bolts	49 (6.75)
Engine-to-Clutch Housing	16 (2.25)
Oil Pump Mounting Bolts	7 (1.0)
Engine-to-Converter Housing	22 (3.04)
Engine-to-Clutch Housing	40 (5.53)
Engine Mounts-to-Crossmembers	22 (3.04)
Oil Pump Mounting Bolts	7 (1.0)
Rocker Arm Support Nuts	11 (1.5)
Belt Tensioning Nut	①58 (8.0)

① — First step, tighten to 36 ft. lbs. (5 mkg), turn engine one full turn, and retighten to 58 ft. lbs. (8 mkg).

ENGINE SPECIFICATIONS

GENERAL SPECIFICATIONS										
Year	Displ.		Fuel Inj.	HP at RPM	Torque (Ft. Lbs. at RPM)	Compr. Ratio	Bore		Stroke	
	cu. ins.	cc					in.	mm	in.	mm
1980	120.3	1971	K-Jetronic	96@4900	116@3300	8.35:1	3.465	88	3.189	81

CRANKSHAFT MAIN & CONNECTING ROD BEARINGS							
	MAIN BEARINGS				CONNECTING ROD BEARINGS		
Engine	Journal Diam. In. (mm)	Clearance In. (mm)	Thrust Bearing	Crankshaft End Play In. (mm)	Journal Diam. In. (mm)	Clearance In. (mm)	Side Play In. (mm)
1970 cc No. 1 (Rear)	2.1616-2.1646 (54.905-54.980)	...	Rear	.003-.008 (.08-.20)	2.1123-2.1131 (53.652-53.673)	.0006-.003 (.016-.076)	.....
No. 2	2.2102-2.2112 (56.140-56.165)						
No. 3	2.2509-2.2515 (57.174-57.189)						
No. 4	2.3050-2.3060 (58.548-58.573)						
No. 5 (Front)	2.3386-2.3392 (59.401-59.416)						

504 & 505 4 CYLINDER DIESEL

ENGINE CODING

ENGINE IDENTIFICATION

Engine identification number is stamped on front left side of engine block just below cylinder head. Engine identification number corresponds with Vehicle Identification Number, and runs from number 1340000 upward.

Engine Identification	
Application	**Code**
504 & 505 Diesel	
Federal	XD2
Calif.	XD2C

ENGINE & CYLINDER HEAD

ENGINE

Removal — 1) Remove hood, battery and battery tray. Remove radiator expansion tank, air filter and intake pipe on vacuum pump. Disconnect upper and lower radiator hoses and upper and lower radiator mountings. Disconnect fan wiring and remove fan and radiator.

2) Disconnect injector pump controls, fuel inlet and fuel outlet lines. Remove heater hose return line. Disconnect starter, oil pressure switch, pre-heat circuit and thermistor wiring. Remove starter.

3) Disconnect alternator wiring and air conditioner hose from cylinder head. Disconnect exhaust pipe at manifold and remove right engine support nut. From left side of engine; disconnect clutch housing sealing plates, upper clutch housing-to-block bolt and left engine support nut.

4) Disconnect exhaust pipe support bracket from transmission. Remove right clutch housing cover plate. Install suitable engine lifting device and raise engine until transmission contacts tunnel. Support transmission.

5) Remove two lower clutch housing-to-block bolts. Carefully move engine forward to clear transmission shaft and lift up to remove from vehicle.

Installation — To install, reverse removal procedure and note: Coat splines of main shaft with Molykote 321 (or equivalent). Install and tighten all clutch housing-to-block bolts before removing transmission support.

CYLINDER HEAD

CAUTION — Cylinder head bolts must not be loosened while engine is warm.

Removal — 1) Drain cooling system. Remove air filter, hose to expansion tank and upper radiator hose. Remove vacuum hose, vacuum pump and belt, idler puller, and water pump belt.

2) Disconnect air conditioner line, and rocker shaft oil line union (located over center intake manifold port). Disconnect exhaust pipe at manifold. Disconnect injector feed lines and remove return lines. Disconnect pre-heat electrical connections at cylinder head.

CAUTION — Do not lose washer (seal) at oil inlet-to-cylinder head connection.

3) Remove rocker arm cover and rocker arm assembly. Remove push rods, taking care not to disturb tappets, and set aside in original order for proper installation.

4) Remove one bolt at each end of cylinder head and replace with suitable guide stands. Remove injection holders and injectors. Remove remaining head bolts and remove cylinder head.

Installation — 1) Measure amount of piston protrusion and select appropriate gasket. Install new dry gasket with large crimped side facing cylinder block. Place cylinder head over guides and install bolts. Note that 8 short bolts are installed on injector side, 7 medium length bolts on manifold side and 6 long bolts in center. Special ground bolt is installed in No. 16 position.

2) Tighten cylinder head bolts in first step to 33 ft. lbs. (4.5 mkg) in sequence shown in *Fig. 1.* In second step, tighten in sequence to 47 ft. lbs. (6.5 mkg). Third step consists of loosening each bolt one at a time ¼ turn in sequence, and then retightening to 47 ft. lbs. (6.5 mkg). Install injector holders (with new seals), injector shields and washers. Install push rods in original position and install rocker arm assembly. See *ROCKER ARM ASSEMBLY* in this article.

NOTE — Do not forget washer (seal) at oil inlet-to-cylinder head connection.

3) Adjust valves to .010″ (.25 mm) for intake and .014″ (.35 mm) for exhaust. See *Valve Clearance Adjustment.* After 600 miles, adjust valves to standard clearances.

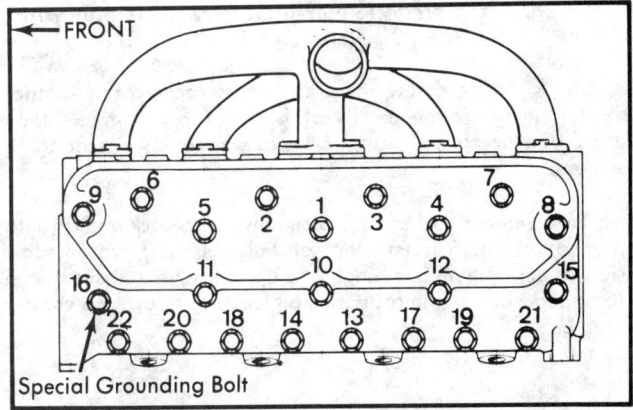

Fig. 1   Cylinder Head Bolt Tightening Sequence

NOTE — Cylinder head bolts MUST be retightened after 30 miles and again after 600 miles. Engine must be allowed to cool for 6 hours before retightening bolts. To retighten bolts, loosen bolts in sequence ¼ turn, then retighten to 47 ft. lbs. (6.5 mkg). Operation must be performed 2 times.

VALVES

VALVE ARRANGEMENT

I-E-E-I-I-E-E-I (Front to Rear).

NOTE — Cylinders and valves are numbered with number one at flywheel end.

504 & 505 4 CYLINDER DIESEL (Cont.)

VALVE DEPTH

After cylinder head has been resurfaced or valve seats ground or replaced, depth of valve face beneath cylinder head surface must be checked. Measure depth with dial gauge. Depth must be .030-.045" (.75-1.15 mm). If too shallow, regrind valve seats. If too deep, replace valves and/or valve seats.

ROCKER ARM ASSEMBLY

1) To remove rocker arm assembly, remove rocker arm cover and remove rocker shaft support bolts. Lift rocker arm assembly noting oil line union sealing washer.

2) To disassemble rocker arm assembly, remove end shaft supports and remove rocker arms, supports, springs and washers. Remove locating screw on lubrication fitting, then remove shaft.

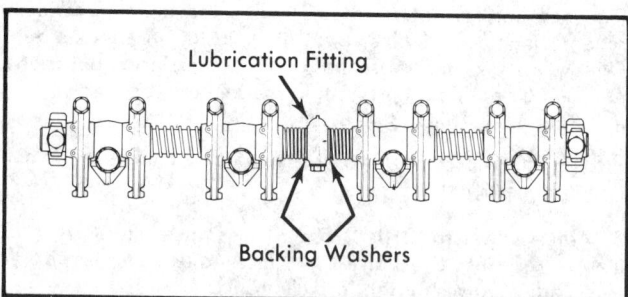

Fig. 2   Assembled View of Rocker Arm Assembly with Oil Holes Detailed

3) Check shaft diameter at areas where rocker arms contact shaft. Minimum diameter of shaft is .746" (18.95 mm). Replace shaft and/or rocker arms if excessive wear or scoring is evident.

4) To assemble rocker arm assembly, slide rocker shaft into lubrication fitting noting that oil holes in shaft are on same side as screw hole in fitting. Line up screw hole in shaft with threaded hole in fitting and install locating screw and copper washer.

Fig. 3   Installing Rocker Arm Assembly to Cylinder Head

5) Lubricate rocker shaft and install washers, springs, rocker arms and rocker supports. Install shims .004" (.10 mm) thick between outer rocker arms and end supports, then install oil union washer (seal).

6) Install rocker shaft assembly on cylinder head and tighten shaft support bolts. After all bolts are tightened, remove shims and check that all rocker arms operate smoothly.

VALVE CLEARANCE ADJUSTMENT

NOTE — *Engine must be allowed to cool at least six hours before adjusting valves.*

Rotate engine until exhaust valve number one is fully opened, then adjust intake valve number three and exhaust number four. Rotate engine one half turn until next number valve is fully opened and adjust corresponding valves. See table. Continue until all valves have been adjusted.

Valve Adjusting Sequence	
Valve Open	**Adjust Valves**
E1	I3 & E4
E3	I4 & E2
E4	I2 & E1
E2	I1 & E3

Valve Clearance Adjustment		
Application①	**Intake** In. (mm)	**Exhaust** In. (mm)
New Head Gasket	.014 (.35)	.014 (.35)
Standard Adjustment	.010 (.25)	.010 (.25)

① — Adjust valves to standard adjustment 600 miles after installing new head gasket and retightening cylinder head bolts.

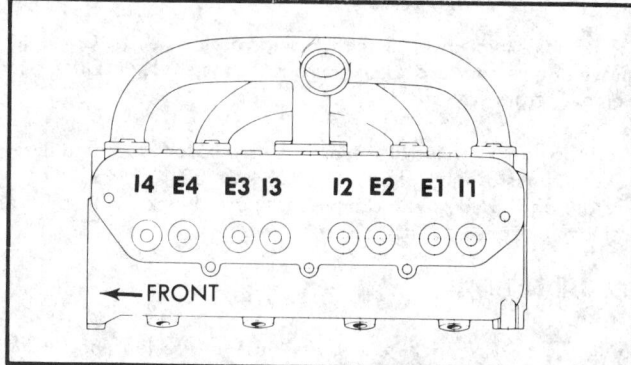

Fig. 4   View of Intake and Exhaust Valve Arrangement

COMBUSTION (SWIRL) CHAMBERS

Removal — Remove cylinder head from vehicle and remove injectors, injector studs, rocker arms, rocker arm mounting studs, manifolds and glow plugs. Using suitable drift (see illustration) carefully drive swirl chambers down and out of cylinder head. Tap drift LIGHTLY so as not to damage inner face of chamber.

504 & 505 4 CYLINDER DIESEL (Cont.)

CAUTION — *If the swirl chamber twists and/or sticks in its bore, turn head over, tap chamber back into place with soft mallet, and start over again.*

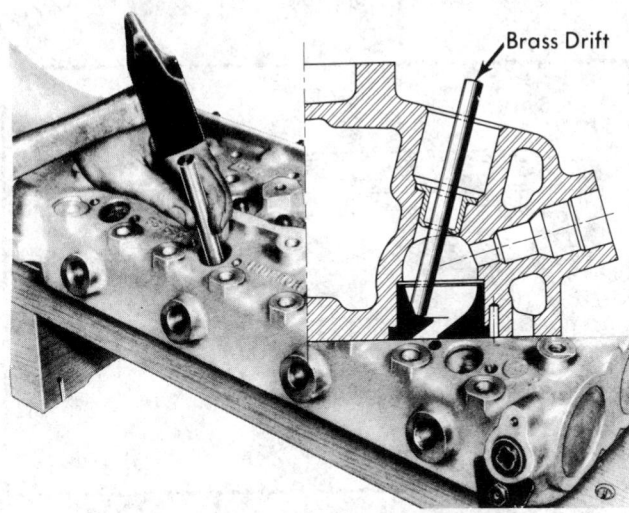

Fig. 5 **Removing Combustion Chamber with Hammer and Drift**

Inspection — **1)** Inspect swirl chambers for distortion and cracks. Small cracks around the gas outlet are acceptable and do not effect engine operation. Replace all doubtful chambers. Measure thickness of shoulder and overall height of chamber.

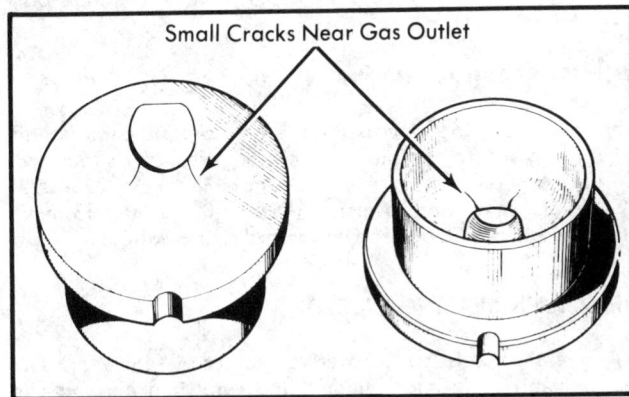

Fig. 6 **View Showing Acceptable Cracks in Combustion Chamber**

2) Place suitable truing punch (0.0139) over chamber bore in cylinder head, making sure dowel pin in punch is correctly located in head. Tap truing punch to make sure shoulder surface of bore is parallel with cylinder head. Slightly chamfer the edges of the chamber bore.

3) Measure depth of bore and depth to shoulder. Swirl chamber should protrude from cylinder head surface .000-.001" (.00-.03 mm) and clearance from swirl chamber to bottom of chamber bore should be .004-.020" (.10-.50 mm). To adjust clearances, chamber may be machined on shoulder surface and on bottom surface. Never machine face of chamber.

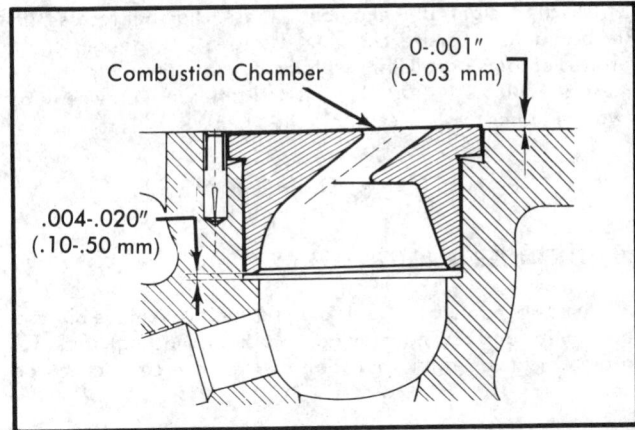

Fig. 7 **Cross-Sectional View Showing Combustion Chamber Clearance and Protrusion**

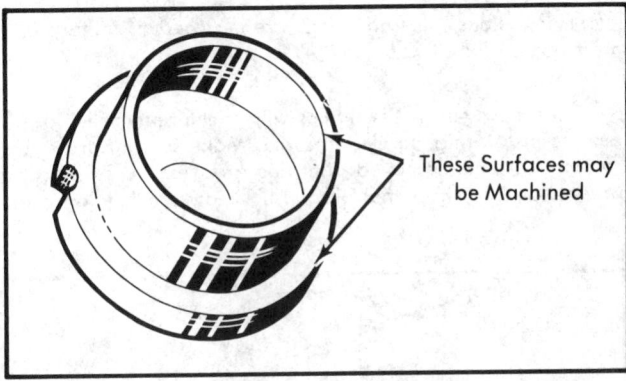

Fig. 8 **Combustion (Swirl) Chamber with Detail of Machinable Surfaces**

Installation — **1)** Insert new wedge pins into the cylinder head and using chamfered drift, drive pins .028" (.7 mm) below cylinder head surface. Carefully insert the swirl chambers in the original bores and lightly tap into place with soft mallet.

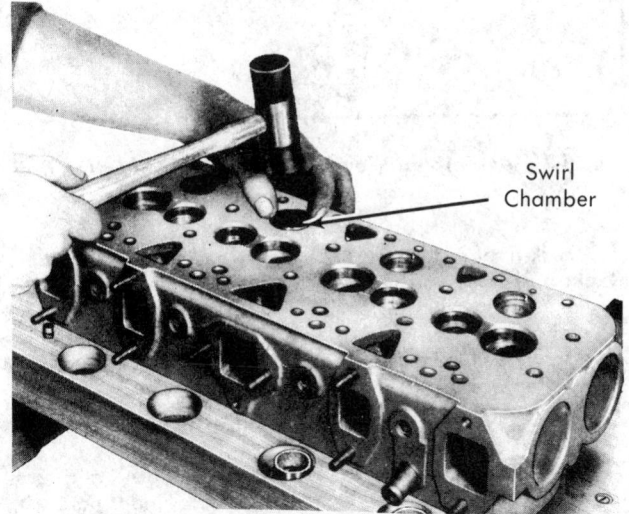

Fig. 9 **Installing Combustion (Swirl) Chambers**

504 & 505 4 CYLINDER DIESEL (Cont.)

2) Check for tight fit. If chamber is loose, chamber recess must be bored for oversize chamber. Using a dial gauge, check protrusion and parallelism with the cylinder head. Protrusion must be .000-.001" (.00-.03 mm) and difference between any two points must not exceed .001" (.03 mm).

PISTONS, PINS & RINGS

PISTON, LINER & ROD ASSEMBLY

1) Remove engine from vehicle and drain oil. Remove oil pan, oil pump and cylinder head. Mark connecting rods for replacement in original location and remove connecting rod caps.

2) Push pistons up through top of cylinder block and replace connecting rod caps so they do not become mixed. Remove piston pin circlip and remove piston pin.

NOTE — *Pistons, pins and rings are matched at factory and must not be intermixed.*

3) Clean new piston assemblies with trichlorethylene. Do not remove piston rings to clean pistons. Make sure all protective coating has been removed from ring grooves. Blow with compressed air and check that piston rings move freely in grooves.

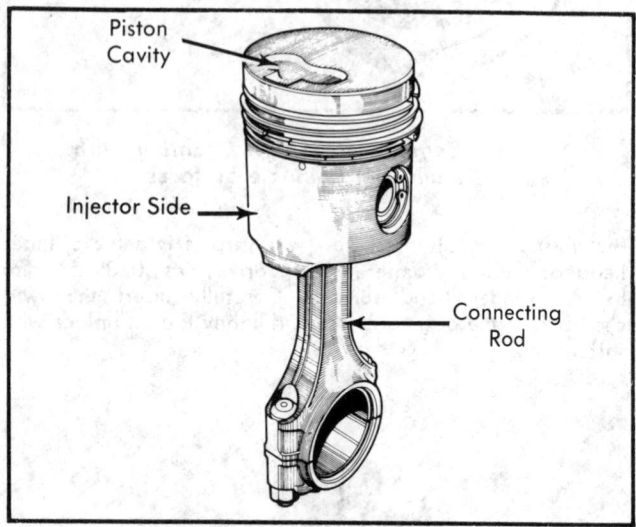

Fig. 10   Assembled View of Piston and Connecting Rod

4) Check fit of piston pin in connecting rod small end bushing. Ream bushing if too tight and replace bushing if too loose. Remove circlip from piston and partially remove piston pin. Position piston and rod so cavity on piston and reference marks on rod are on same side. Lubricate pin and install in piston. Replace circlip.

5) Lubricate pistons and bearings. Using suitable ring compressor, install each piston in its respective cylinder bore with cavity in piston facing injector side of engine. Install new rod cap nuts and bolts.

NOTE — *Standard-size pistons have an "A" or "B" stamped on top surface. Match pistons to cylinder bores, which have an "A" or "B" stamped on side of cylinder block adjacent to each bore. See Fig. 11. Oversize pistons are stamped with either a "C" or "D", depending upon size class.*

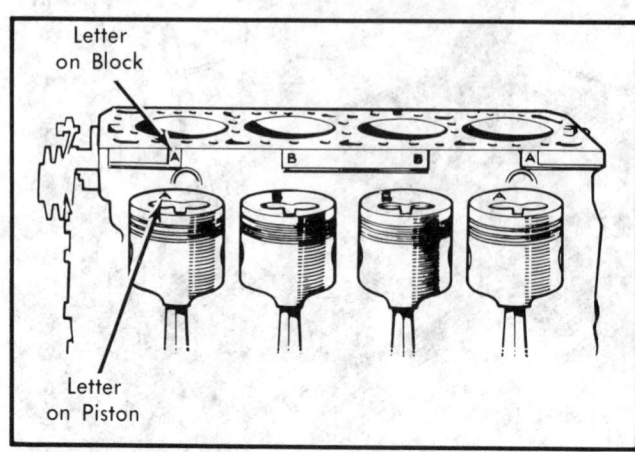

Fig. 11   Matching Pistons to Cylinder Bores

CRANKSHAFT MAIN & CONNECTING ROD BEARINGS

MAIN BEARINGS

Bearing caps are installed with the reference mark on injector side. Main bearing cap number two (as numbered from flywheel end) and number four are nearly identical. Bearing cap number two can be identified by letter after the part number.

THRUST BEARING ALIGNMENT

Thrust washers are located on both sides of center main bearing. Measure end play and replace washers as required. Thrust washers are available in standard thickness .091-.092" (2.30-2.33 mm) and oversize .098-.100" (2.50-2.53 mm). Install washers with oil grooves toward crankshaft.

REAR MAIN BEARING OIL SEAL

1) Crankshaft must be removed to replace oil seal. Work seal packing manually into cylinder block and into bearing cap grooves. Place seal forming mandrel (8.0110) onto packing and form packing into groove by tapping mandrel with a hammer.

2) Make sure packing is correctly seated in its groove without being crushed (see illustration). Cut seal packing clean flush with mating surface and follow same procedure for bearing cap.

3) Place side seals in grooves of bearing cap and hold seals into place with suitable shim tool (8.0110 CZ & 8.0110 BZ). Lubricate shims and bring into place in cylinder block, tapping down with hammer handle. Install and tighten bearing cap bolts and check that bearing cap has seated properly. Trim side seals with knife so that they protrude .002" (.05 mm) above lower crankcase mating surface.

504 & 505 4 CYLINDER DIESEL (Cont.)

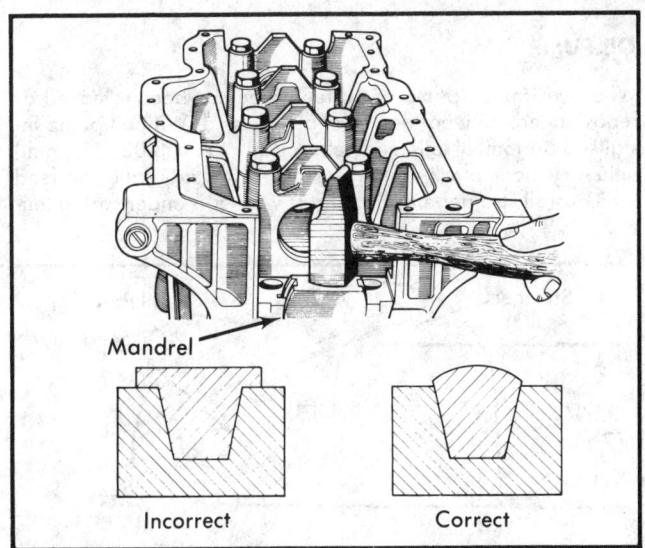

Fig. 12   Using a Mandrel and Mallet to Install Upper Rear Main Oil Seal

CAMSHAFT

TIMING CHAIN

Removal — With engine removed, remove oil pan and front engine cover. Remove plug from timing chain tensioner and release chain tensioner by inserting 3 mm Allen wrench, turning clockwise. Loosen idler gear fastening nut and move idler gear to slack position by turning eccentric. Remove bolts from injection pump gear and remove gear and timing chain.

Installation — 1) Check end play of injection pump support bearing. End play should be .002-.037" (.06-.94 mm). If engine front plate has been removed, lock countersunk screw with two punch marks. Position crankshaft gear timing mark down and camshaft gear mark at 11 o'clock postion. See Fig. 13.

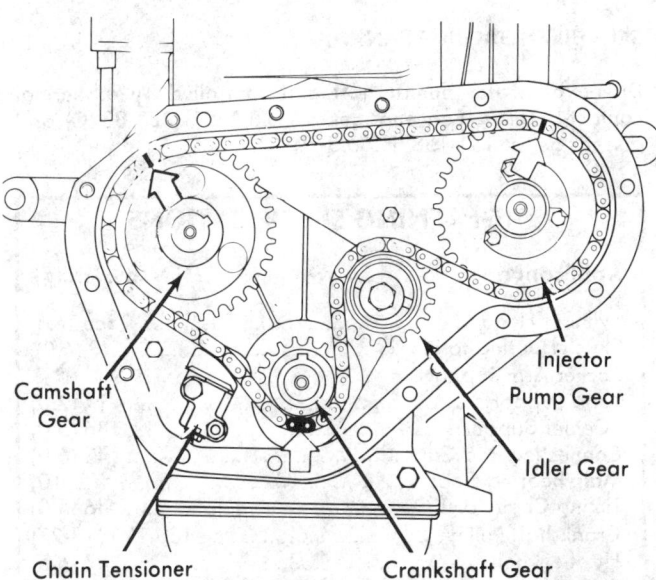

Camshaft Gear

Chain Tensioner

Crankshaft Gear

Idler Gear

Injector Pump Gear

Fig. 13   Timing Chain Installed to Illustrate Timing Mark Alignments

2) Install chain on injection pump gear aligning line on link with mark on gear. Install chain with pump gear onto camshaft and crankshaft sprockets, taking care to align copper link on chain with timing mark on crankshaft gear and link marked with line aligned with the line on camshaft gear. Install locating dowel in injection pump gear.

NOTE — *Crankshaft timing gears are available in 3 types. If any component part of timing gear has been replaced, crankshaft timing gear must be replaced with a 3-dot gear. ONLY gears with 1 or 3 reference dots can be used for repair.*

3) Adjust the idler gear eccentric by rotating eccentric counterclockwise until clearance between tensioner head and body is .020-.040" (.50-1.00 mm). Tighten idler gear fastening nut, then adjust tensioner by turning Allen wrench to right until tensioner head is pushing on chain. Install and lock tensioner plug.

CAMSHAFT

Removal — With timing chain removed, remove camshaft thrust plate bolts, gaining access through holes in camshaft gear. Carefully pull camshaft from cylinder block.

Installation — If gear was removed from camshaft, heat camshaft gear in well heated oil. Install thrust plate on camshaft, then install shaft key and press gear into place, leaving clearance of .002-.006" (.05-.15 mm) between thrust plate and gear hub. Install camshaft in block and tighten thrust plate bolts. Check camshaft end play, a specification of .002-.006" (.05-.015 mm) should be obtained.

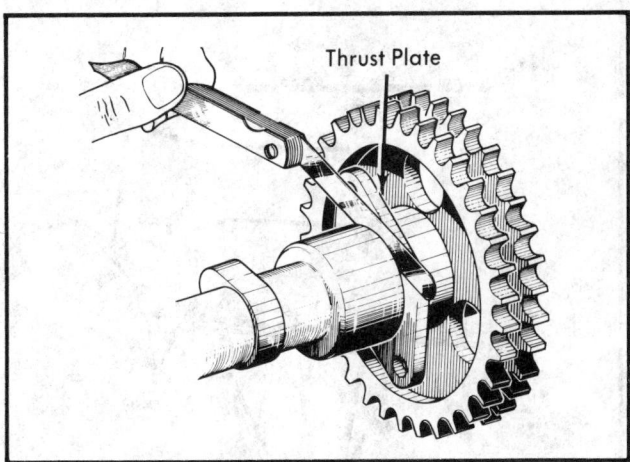

Thrust Plate

Fig. 14   Measuring Camshaft Thrust Plate Clearance

VALVE TIMING

1) With all valve components assembled and cylinder head installed, remove injectors or glow plugs to relieve compression. Adjust valves to correct clearance. See *Valve Clearance Adjustment.*

504 & 505 4 CYLINDER DIESEL (Cont.)

2) Place a .016" (.40 mm) feeler gauge between rocker arm and intake valve stem of each cylinder in succession. Rotate engine by hand to determine if there is contact between valve and piston at beginning of intake valve opening. If contact is felt, replace crankshaft timing gear with a gear having one timing reference mark.

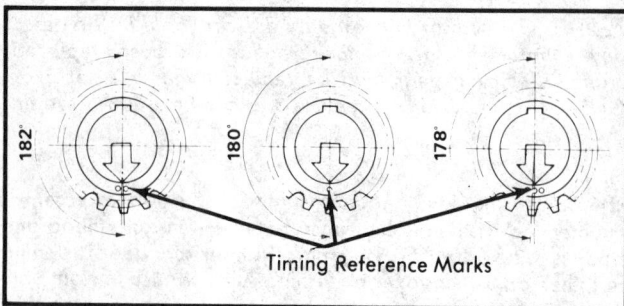

Fig. 15 Crankshaft Timing Gears Available

ENGINE OILING

Crankcase Capacity — 5.29 qt.
Oil Filter — Full flow cartridge type.
Pressure Regulator Valve — Located in oil pump.
Normal Oil Pressure — Minimum at idle, 22 psi (1.6 kg/cm²); at 4000 RPM, 42-58 psi (3-4.1 kg/cm²).

ENGINE OILING SYSTEM

A high output, gear type oil pump, driven by camshaft, is mounted in oil pan.

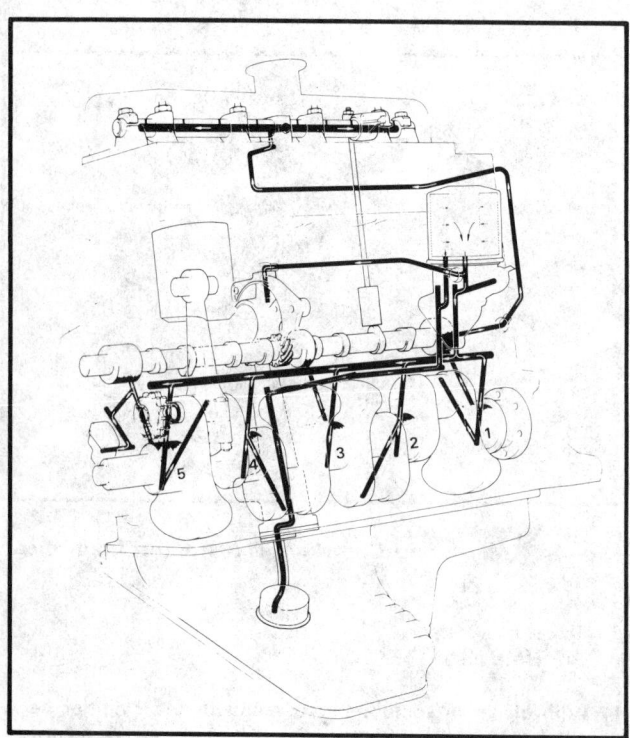

Fig. 16 Sectional View of Diesel Engine Oiling Circuit

OIL PUMP

Whenever the oil pump or oil feed tube has been removed or repositioned, oil feed tube must be adjusted. With oil pump installed, bottom of oil feed tube must extend 3.03" (77 mm) below cylinder block mating surface. After adjusting, oil feed tube, install strainer ensuring thrust washer is under spring tension.

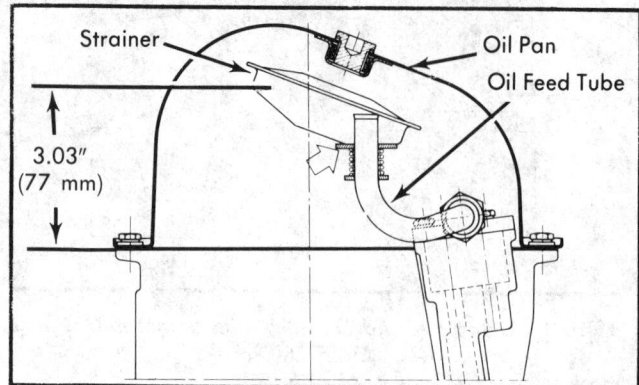

Fig. 17 Oil Pump Feed Tube Installation (Pan Inverted)

ENGINE COOLING

Thermostat — Begins opening at 162°F (72°C), fully open at 184°F (84°C).
Cooling System Capacity — 10.57 qt.

WATER PUMP

1) Remove radiator, top hose, and fan belt. Disconnect heater hose from pump and the self-disengaging fan brush holder. Remove water pump.

2) To install, reverse removal procedures, noting the following: clean contact surfaces before installing new gasket.

SELF-DISENGAGING FAN

Driven by water pump shaft and controlled by a thermal contact-breaker. Fan engages at 178-182°F (81-83°C) and disengages at 151-158°F (66.5-70°C).

TIGHTENING SPECIFICATIONS

Application	Ft. Lbs. (mkg)
Cylinder Head	See Text
Clutch Housing-to-Block	43 (6.0)
Rocker Arm Supports	
End Supports	14 (2.0)
Center Supports	36 (5.0)
Connecting Rod Caps	42 (6.0)
Main Bearing Caps	72 (10)
Timing Chain Idler Gear	36 (5.0)
Crankshaft Pulley	130-195 (18-27)
Flywheel Bolts	47 (6.5)
Glow Plugs	33 (4.5)
Manifolds	11 (1.5)
Injector Flanges	11 (1.5)

Peugeot Engines

504 & 505 4 CYLINDER DIESEL (Cont.)

ENGINE SPECIFICATIONS

GENERAL SPECIFICATIONS										
Year	Displ.		Carburetor	HP at RPM	Torque (Ft. Lbs. at RPM)	Compr. Ratio	Bore		Stroke	
	cu. ins.	cc					in.	mm	in.	mm
1980	140.6	2304	Fuel Inj.	71@4500	99@2500	23:1	3.700	94	3.267	83

VALVES							
Engine & Valve	Head Diam. In. (mm)	Face Angle	Seat Angle	Seat Width In. (mm)	Stem Diameter In. (mm)	Stem Clearance In. (mm)	Valve Lift In. (mm)
2304 cc Intake	1.594 (40.5)	30°	30°	.....	.3336-.3344 (8.473-8.495)	.0018 (.047)	.243 (6.173)
Exhaust	1.319 (33.5)	45°	45°	.....	.3328-.3337 (8.453-8.475)	.0026 (.067)	.243 (6.173)

PISTONS, PINS, RINGS						
	PISTONS	PINS		RINGS		
Engine	Clearance In. (mm)	Piston Fit In. (mm)	Rod Fit In. (mm)	Rings	End Gap In. (mm)	Side Clearance In. (mm)
2304 cc	.005-.006 (.13-.16)	Press Fit	.....	No. 1	.014-.024 (.35-.60)	.....
				No. 2	.014-.024 (.35-.60)	.....
				Oil	.006-.012 (.16-.30)	.....

CRANKSHAFT MAIN & CONNECTING ROD BEARINGS						
	MAIN BEARINGS				CONNECTING ROD BEARINGS	
Engine	Journal Diam. In. (mm)	Clearance In. (mm)	Thrust Bearing	Crankshaft End Play In. (mm)	Journal Diam. In. (mm)	Clearance In. (mm)	Side Play In. (mm)
2304 cc	2.1651-2.1661 (54.994-55.021)	.002-.004 (.05-.10)	Center	.003-.011 (.08-.29)	1.9678-1.9689 (49.984-50.011)	.002-.004 (.05-.10)	.....

VALVE TIMING				
	INTAKE		EXHAUST	
Engine	Open (BTDC)	Close (ABDC)	Open (BBDC)	Close (ATDC)
2304 cc	40°	28°	43°	1°

604 V6

ENGINE CODING

ENGINE IDENTIFICATION

Engine serial number is stamped on 2 plates fastened to the left side of engine block in front of oil filter. The first plate is stamped with the engine type (151.9). Second is stamped with engine serial number. Last two letters of serial number are decoded as follows:

Engine Identification	
Application	**Code**
604 (2849 cc)	
Man. Trans.	ZM
Auto. Trans.	ZA

ENGINE & CYLINDER HEADS

ENGINE

Removal — 1) Remove hood, carburetor air cleaner and ducting. Drain automatic transmission (if equipped) and cooling system. Disconnect and remove battery.

2) Disconnect electrical leads to air conditioning system and electric fan. Disconnect radiator hoses, heater hoses, and on automatic transmission vehicles only, coolant hoses. On all

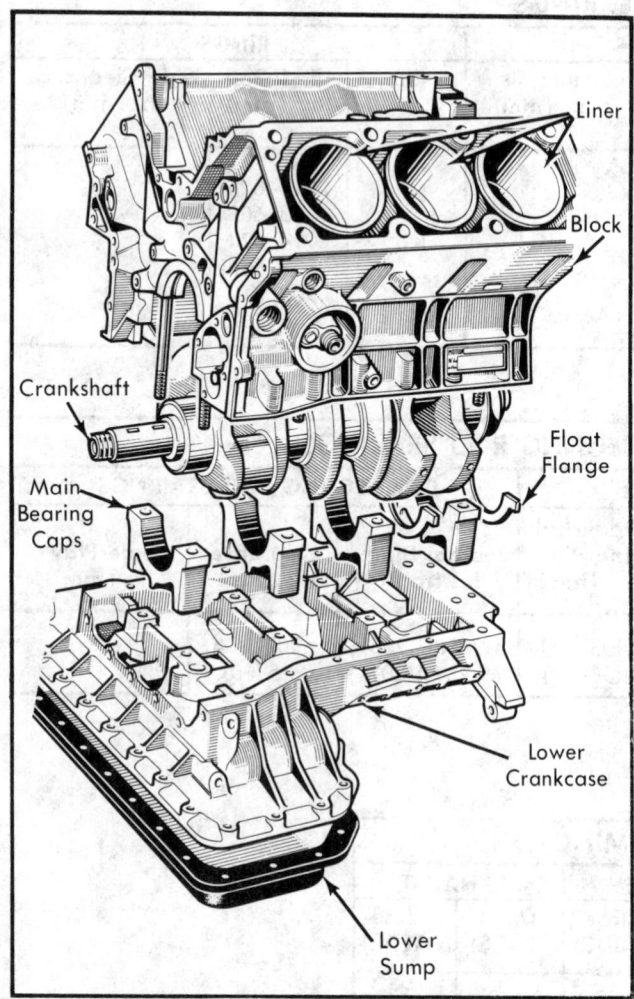

Fig. 1 Exploded View of Peugeot V6 Engine

vehicles, remove fan shroud and radiator. Remove air conditioning condenser and compressor mounting bolts and swing these units clear to the right side.

NOTE — *Do NOT disconnect any air conditioning system hoses or pressure connections.*

3) Disconnect rear heater hose, fuel lines, vacuum lines, throttle linkage and electrical connections. Remove upper bolts from clutch housing or torque converter. On automatic transmission models, remove filler pipe. Remove front exhaust pipe connections and engine mounting bolts.

NOTE — *After removing automatic transmission filler pipe, retighten upper lifting bracket bolt.*

4) Remove muffler and exhaust pipe brackets and heat deflector. Remove starter mounting bolts and clutch housing or converter cover plates. Remove power steering mounting bolts but do NOT disconnect lines. With suitable sling (8.0135) and hoist, lift engine until transmission touches tunnel, then lower about ⅜" (10 mm). Remove steering pump and hang to one side.

5) Fit propeller shaft tube support between muffler and body and tighten to support tube slightly. Remove steering coupling clamp bolt and replace rear steering rack bolts with slightly longer bolts. Remove front crossmember securing bolts and loosen rear bolts about 1" (25 mm) to lower crossmember.

6) On automatic transmission models, disconnect starter ring gear flange plate from torque converter. On all models, remove two lower housing securing bolts. Remove engine towards front. Use caution to avoid damaging power steering and automatic transmission cooling tubes. On automatic transmission models, hold torque converter in position.

Installation — To install, reverse removal procedure and note: Ensure clearance between steering wheel and column casing is ⁵⁄₆₄" (2 mm) and throttle controls are adjusted.

CYLINDER HEADS

NOTE — *Cylinder head removal may be performed with engine in vehicle.*

Removal — 1) Drain cooling system and remove engine hood. Remove air cleaner and ducts. Remove battery. Remove intake manifold and plug intake ports in cylinder heads. Remove insulating plate and hose connecting water pump to cylinder heads. Remove hose connecting heads.

2) To remove left head, lower the crossmember and remove fuel pump. Loosen positive battery lead and remove ground cable. To remove right head, remove distributor, coil and filler well for automatic transmission (if equipped). For either head, loosen front muffler mounting and remove exhaust pipe clamp under manifold. For left head, remove bolt from flexible steering coupler, then lower crossmember by ⅛" (3 mm).

3) Remove rocker arm cover and camshaft rear cover plate. Remove camshaft sprocket bolt access plug and position sprocket with drive stud or timing mark at top. Lock crankshaft in this position and loosen camshaft sprocket bolt. Place

604 V6 (Cont.)

camshaft sprocket support (8.0134 M) on front of timing gear casing and tighten mounting bolts finger tight. Attach sprocket to support through one of the holes in the sprocket web by means of bolt and nut tightened to no more than 11 ft. lbs. (1.5 mkg).

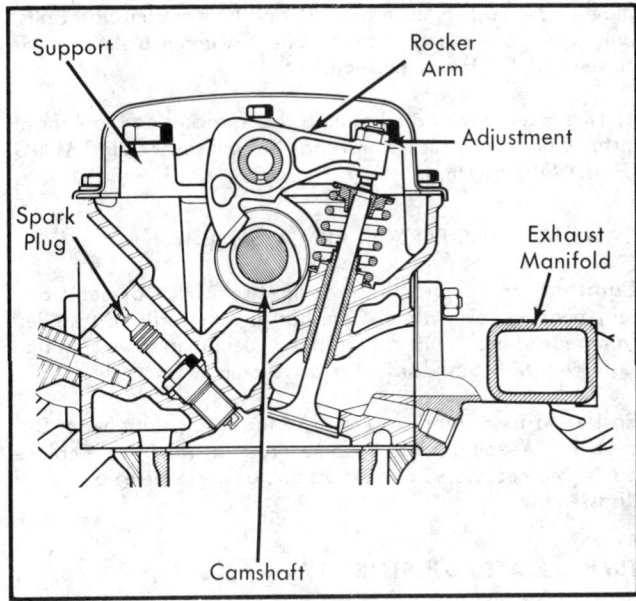

Fig. 2   Sectional View of Cylinder Head

4) Remove all 8 cylinder head bolts. On left head, brake booster prevents full removal of 2 rearmost bolts. Lift these as far as possible and fasten together with a rubber band. Loosen camshaft thrust flange retaining bolt and slide it along elongated hole until free. On each head, remove 4 bolts securing timing gear casing. Remove heads by inserting 2 "L" shaped rods into cylinder head bolt holes and jiggling until free. Lift off cylinder head/rocker arm assembly.

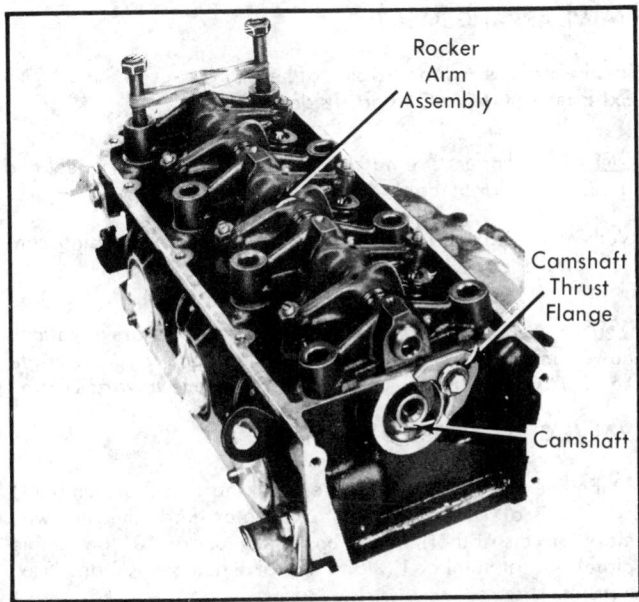

Fig. 3   Left Cylinder Head with Rear Bolts

NOTE — *Timing chain tension must not be released. If accidently released, timing cover must be removed in order to reposi-*

tion chain tensioner. Retaining bars should be installed to prevent cylinder liner movement.

Installation — **1)** Insert a pin punch in each of the holes under the locating dowels and insert new dowels. Remove liner retaining bars and fit a new head gasket (dry) on block. Place cylinder head/rocker arm assembly into position carefully and hand tighten 4 timing gear case bolts. The 2 rearmost bolts must be installed prior to positioning assembly on block.

2) Carefully align keyways and insert camshaft into sprocket. Raise rocker arms and turn sprocket bolt until camshaft has entered sprocket fully, then tighten lightly. Install but do not tighten oiled cylinder head bolts in position. Remove camshaft sprocket support. Install camshaft thrust flange into camshaft flange and tighten bolts.

3) Hold crankshaft and tighten camshaft sprocket bolt. Initially tighten cylinder head bolts in order shown to 43 ft. lbs. (6 mkg), then loosen individually and retighten 14 ft. lbs. (2 (mkg). Use angle socket (8.0134 B2) to tighten each bolt in sequence an additional 90° to final position. Tighten timing gear case bolts.

NOTE — *Due to the position of the brake servo, the two rear bolts on the left head (inserted in head prior to installation) will require special attention. If in doubt about proper tension on any bolt, it must be fully loosened and the tightening procedures repeated.*

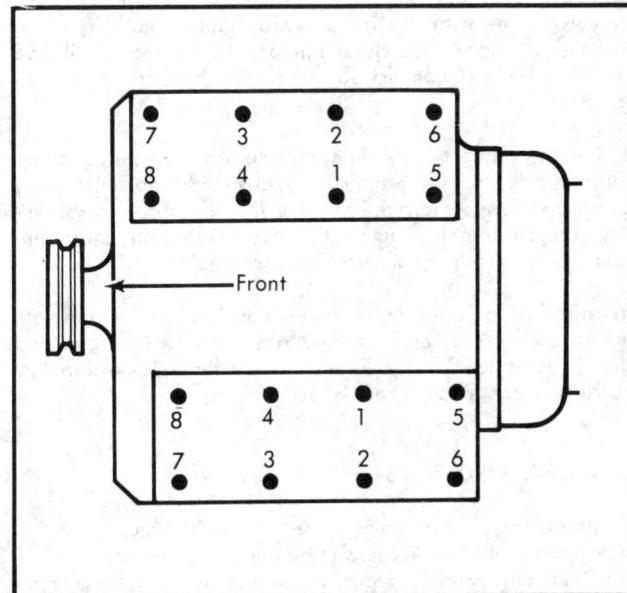

Fig. 4   Cylinder Head Tightening Sequence

4) Tighten access plug, gear case and rear bearing cover plate bolts. Rotate crankshaft to bring No. 5 (center, right bank) piston to Top Dead Center and align notch in crankshaft pulley under "10" mark on timing plate. With vacuum advance diaphragm to rear and unmarked rotor arm to front of engine, install distributor. Align rotor arm marks and distributor body at 4 o'clock position. Snug securing clamp. See Fig. 5.

604 V6 (Cont.)

Fig. 5   Installing Distributor

Labels on figure: Unmarked Rotor Arm; Marked Rotor Arm; Mark on Housing; Vacuum Advance Diaphragm

CAMSHAFT

TIMING GEAR COVER

NOTE — *Timing gear and cover repair work may be accomplished with engine installed or removed from vehicle.*

Removal — 1) Rotate crankshaft so that notch in pulley is absolutely in line with the 10° mark on timing plate and lock flywheel in place with clamping tool. Drain engine oil and cooling system. Disconnect battery and all hose connections to radiator.

2) Remove and set aside the following: Air filter and ducting, radiator and struts, fan and casing, drive belts, power steering pump and support, crankshaft pulley, rocker arm covers, timing gear cover bolts and timing cover. Oil pump, chain tensioners and timing gears are now accessible.

Installation — To install, reverse removal procedure and note the following: Gasket faces and gaskets must be clean and dry. Timing plate 10° mark must be directly in line with pulley notch. Adhere to all torque specifications.

CHAINS & SPROCKETS

Removal — With timing case cover off, plug ports to crankcase unless crankcase is to be removed. Remove oil pump sprockets, drive chain, spacer, key and oil pump. Release chain tensioners. Mark position of camshaft drive chains if they are to be reused. Remove right camshaft sprocket and chain first, then left side. Remove chain tensioners and drive sprocket.

Installation — 1) Reinstall filters in front of block. Lock chain tensioner plungers in retracted position, then install tensioners. Install tensioner strips and fixed pads.

2) With keyway at top of crankshaft, insert key and install sprocket with position mark visible from outside. Turn crankshaft so that keyway is aligned to left cylinder bank and camshaft centerline. Place chain over left camshaft sprocket

with mark on sprocket between marks on chain. Fit chain over drive sprocket with mark on link in line with position mark on sprocket.

3) Rotate crankshaft clockwise to bring mark on drive sprocket in line with bottom oil pump mounting hole. Align marks on chain and sprockets as in Step **2)** and tighten camshaft bolts. Unlock tensioners and allow to extend without assisting their movement. Tighten in position.

4) Fit spacer, key and oil pump drive sprocket on crankshaft. Install oil pump, sprocket and chain. Install cover as in *TIMING GEAR COVER* section.

CAMSHAFT AND ROCKER ARM ASSEMBLIES

Camshaft — Remove thrust flange from front of head and rear bearing cover plate. Camshaft is removed and installed from rear of head. Left camshaft has fuel pump drive cam and right camshaft has distributor drive pinion.

Rocker Arms — Mark rocker arms for left or right head. Disassemble, keeping parts in same order as removed. Replace parts as necessary and reassemble in reverse order of disassembly.

TIMING PLATE ADJUSTMENT

With intake manifold removed, rotate engine so that number 1 piston is approaching TDC on the firing stroke. Remove hex head plug near front of left bank of engine. Insert gauge rod to rest against crankshaft counterbalance weight. Turn crankshaft SLOWLY until rod enters slot and locks crankshaft. Check that notch in pulley is aligned with "0" on timing plate. If not, readjust plate and tighten in position.

VALVES

VALVE ARRANGEMENT

Intake Valves — Inboard side of heads.
Exhaust Valves — Outboard side of heads.

NOTE — *Cylinders are numbered from left bank flywheel end 1, 2 and 3; right bank 4, 5 and 6.*

Valves are removed and refitted in the usual way using conventional tools.

NOTE — *Left and right rocker arm assemblies are identical, however, circlip end is at front of left head and to rear on right head. Flat end of boss on support must face toward circlip.*

VALVE CLEARANCE ADJUSTMENT

1) Engine must be cold. Rotate crankshaft so that number 1 cylinder is at TDC on firing stroke (rotor mark lined up with mark on distributor; notch on pulley under "0" on timing plate). Adjust number 1, 2 and 4 intake; number 1, 3 and 6 exhaust clearance.

2) Rotate crankshaft one full revolution so that mark on rotor arm is 180° from mark on distributor housing and notch in pulley is again under "0" mark on timing plate. Adjust number 3, 5 and 6 intake; number 2, 4 and 5 exhaust clearance.

604 V6 (Cont.)

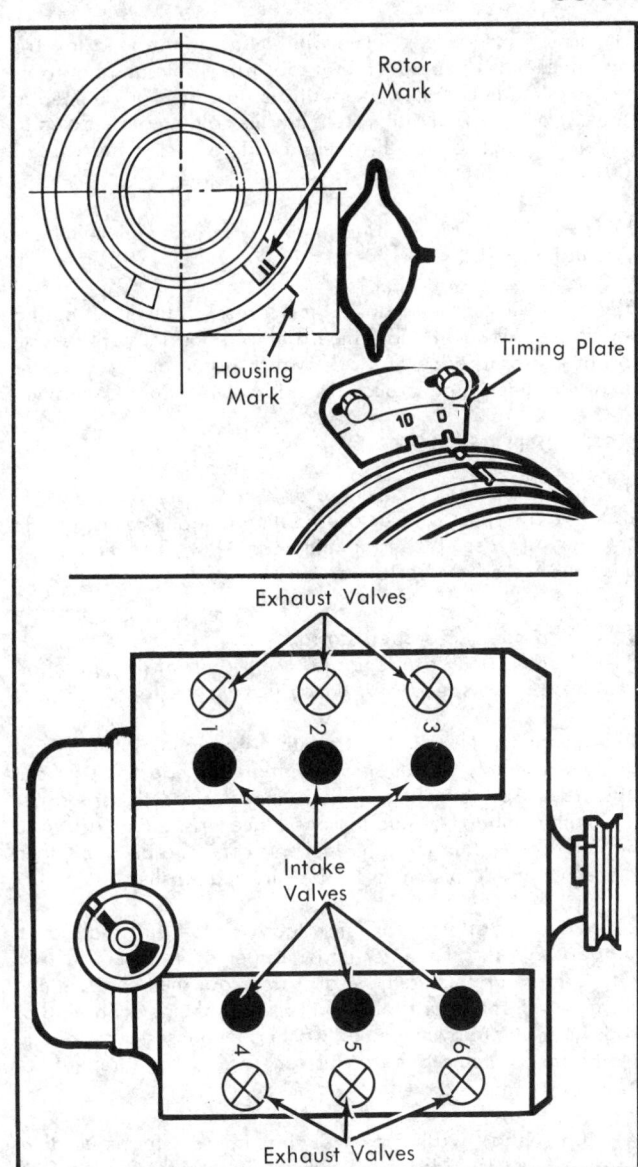

Fig. 6   First Adjusting Position for Setting Valves

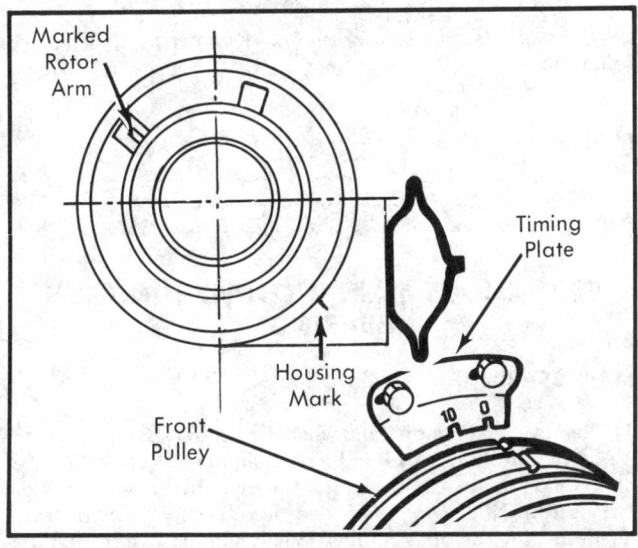

Fig. 7   Second Adjusting Position for Setting Valves

Valve Clearance Adjustment

Valve	In. (mm)
Intake	.004 (.10)
Exhaust	.010 (.25)

PISTONS, PINS & RINGS

PISTON & ROD ASSEMBLY

NOTE — *To accomplish further engine repairs, engine must be removed from car and placed on suitable stand.*

1) Remove cylinder heads, sump and lower crank case. Mark positions of components to ensure proper placement for reassembly. Remove connecting rod cap nuts and bearing caps. Slide protective tubing over rod bolts and remove piston and liner assembly individually.

NOTE — *Piston/rod assemblies must be kept with their respective liners. If piston is removed from rod, it will be necessary to install both a new liner and a new piston.*

2) Match piston and liner. Mount piston and rod assembly with bearing end in soft jawed vise. Arrow on piston top should point away from installer so that when liner is installed, arrow will be in 12 o'clock and notches on liner will be in 3 o'clock positions. Lubricate piston/ring assembly and apply suitable ring compressor. Push liner down over piston assembly without turning until ring compressor is free.

3) Slide protective tubing over connecting rod bolts, then insert piston/liner assemblies in block starting with number one. Finger tighten connecting rod nuts until all assemblies are installed, then tighten to specifications. See *Fitting Cylinder Liners.*

FITTING CYLINDER LINERS

1) Prior to fitting or installing liners, block and liners must be absolutely clean to assure proper fit. Liners will have one, two or three machined marks on top of outboard edge corresponding to "A", "B" or "C" marked on top of piston. For final assembly, liners must project above cylinder block gasket face by .006-.009" (.16-.23 mm).

NOTE — *Liner/piston assemblies must all be of the same category (I-A, II-B or III-C) when installed in any given engine. Do not attempt to install liners with different markings in the same engine.*

2) Place liner in position without its seal and place measuring plate (8.0132) over liner with smooth side up. Place dial indicator in support on plate and take a reading at four points around top of liner. Difference should not exceed .0008" (.02 mm).

3) Measure liner projection through the three elongated holes in plate by placing plunger against block. Difference should not exceed .002" (.05 mm). To determine lower liner seal thickness, subtract largest of readings from .0091" (.23 mm).

Example:

First reading	.0039" (.10 mm)
Second reading	.0032" (.08 mm)
Third reading	.0035" (.09 mm)

604 V6 (Cont.)

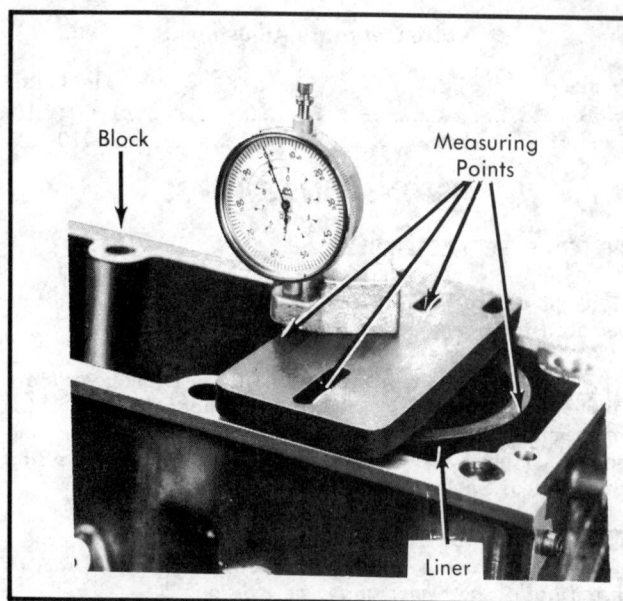

Fig. 8   Measuring Liner Projection

Subtract largest reading .0039" (.10 mm) from .0091" (.23 mm). Result .0052" (.13 mm) indicates thickness of lower liner seal.

Liner Seal Thickness

Tab Color	Thickness In. (mm)
Blue	.0034 (.087)
White	.0040 (.102)
Red	.0048 (.122)
Yellow	.0057 (.147)

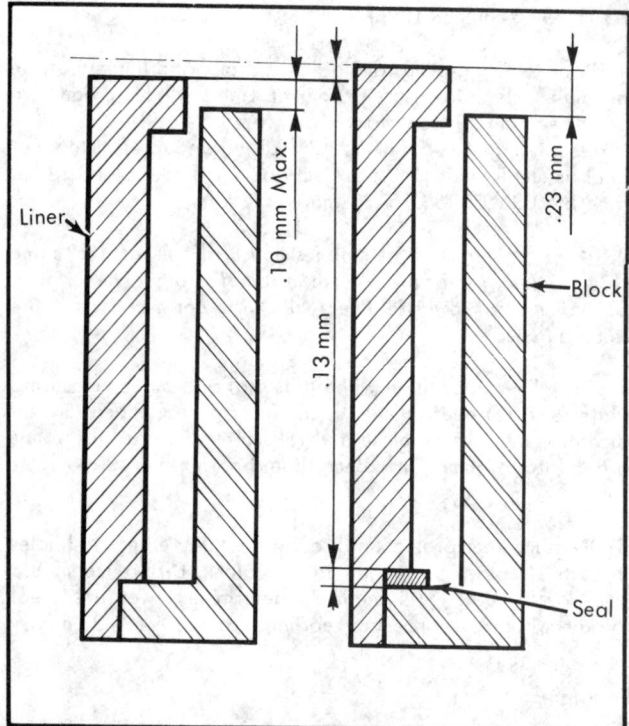

Fig. 9   Cylinder Liner and Seal Specifications

4) Fit identical seals to liners with color tab marking toward top. Place liners in block so that tabs are visible and not trapped under adjacent liner. Repeat measurement as outlined in steps **2)** and **3)** with seal installed while holding plate down to flatten out seal. Check that height differences do not exceed .0016" (.04 mm).

NOTE — *It is possible to adjust height differences on new liners by rotating them.*

5) In case liner or liners project too far, select thinner seal and repeat measurement. Mark the order and positions of liners on top of liner and edge of block. Match piston and rod assemblies with liners and proceed as in *Piston & Rod Assembly.*

PISTON PIN REPLACEMENT

1) Remove old wrist pin using a drift and a press. Discard old piston and inspect rod for overheating or galling. In order to satisfactorily assemble piston, pin and rod, wrist pin end of rod must be heated on hot plate.

NOTE — *In order to properly install wrist pins, special tool sets 8.0134 and 8.0139 are required. The success of the operation depends on the speed with which it is carried out.*

2) Arrange left (1, 2 & 3) rods with pistons and matched wrist pins for assembly. Install pistons with arrow head and DT mark upward in special tool and fit connecting rod thrust washer (F4) with number 1-2-3 up on tool. Place wrist pin on drift and tighten cone end finger tight. Immerse cone and pin in oil, then place rod inside piston to locate pin and washer.

3) With pin, drift and cone inserted in piston and rod, adjust support with thrust washer under center of large end of rod and tighten support. Remove drift and rod, then heat pin end of rods until resin core solder will melt on them. Collar end of rods must point downward on washer, then insert pin by hand until cone contacts base. Wait ten seconds and repeat for other rods.

4) Turn support washer over so that figure 4-5-6 is up, then arrange RIGHT side rods with collar pointing UPWARD. Repeat procedures used in Steps **2)** & **3)**. Mark all assemblies for installation with felt tip pen.

NOTE — *Pistons and pins are marked for wrist pin size. See following table:*

Mark on Piston	Wrist Pin Color
①	Blue
②	White
③	Red

CRANKSHAFT MAIN & CONNECTING ROD BEARINGS

MAIN BEARINGS

1) Remove crankshaft and measure main bearing shells. Measure journals for size and maximum run out of .0012" (.03 mm). Clean out all oil passages, keyways and screw threads on crankshaft. Oil bearing shells and place in block with oil holes lined up with passages in block. Shells with groove go in block while those without are placed in bearing caps.

604 V6 (Cont.)

2) Place copper-plated faces of lower end float flanges against shoulders on crankshaft rear bearing area. Fit both front and rear bearing caps so that raised boss is on timing gear side.

3) Place spacers (part of tool set 8.0134) on front and rear bearing caps and tighten nuts to 22 ft. lbs. (3 mkg). Loosen nuts and check crankshaft end play with dial indicator. Play should be .003-.011″ (.07-.27 mm). If not within specifications, replace float flanges. Float flanges are available in the following sizes: .0905″, .0945″, .0965″ and .0985″ (2.3, 2.4, 2.45 and 2.5 mm).

4) Use same procedures to fit connecting rod bearings as for main bearings. See *PISTON & ROD ASSEMBLY.*

FITTING LOWER CRANKCASE

Remove main bearing spacers from caps. Assure that boss on main bearing caps is on timing gear (front) side. Locating sleeve and new "O" ring must be in position on oil pump. Coat joint face of block with sealing compound and install lower crankcase, all fastenings finger tight. Tighten all main bearing caps to 22 ft. lbs. (3 mkg) in order illustrated. Further angle Tighten caps an additional 70° using angle socket (97030.60). Tighten lower crankcase peripheral bolts to 13 ft. lbs. (1.75 mkg). Install anti-emulsion plate, strainer and sump with new cork gasket.

Peripheral Bolts

Fig. 10   Main Bearing Tightening Sequence

ENGINE OILING

ENGINE OILING SYSTEM

Positive displacement gear type pump is located at lower left side of engine under timimg case cover. Pump is chain-driven from crankshaft. Oil is picked up through a screen and tube in lower sump, filtered through a 10 to 15 micron type filter and pressure fed through the oil gallery and passages to main and connecting rod bearings.

NOTE — *A 5 to 8 micron filter with red inscriptions is fitted to new or service exchange engines. It is also furnished with piston and liner sets. This filter must be replaced with a Purflux LS 410 (10-15 micron) at the 1,000 mile (1500 km) inspection.*

Crankcase Capacity — 6.3 qts.

Normal Oil Pressure — 29 psi (2 kg/cm²) @900 RPM; 64-81 psi (4.5-5.7 kg/cm²) @4,000 RPM.

ENGINE COOLING

ENGINE COOLING SYSTEM

Pressurized system uses viscus drive type fan. An additional electric fan is used on vehicles equipped with automatic transmission.

Cooling System Capacity — 11 qts.

WATER PUMP

1) Remove intake manifold as in *CYLINDER HEADS* and disconnect hoses at pump. Remove water pump-alternator drive belt and water pump securing bolts. Remove bolts securing water casings to block and remove water pump-casing assembly.

2) Install new "O" rings using sealing compound at water casing connections. Reinstall water pump and casing, then continue assembly in reverse order of disassembly.

ENGINE SPECIFICATIONS

GENERAL SPECIFICATIONS										
Year	Displ.		Carburetor	HP at RPM	Torque (Ft. Lbs. at RPM)	Compr. Ratio	Bore		Stroke	
	cu. ins.	cc					in.	mm	in.	mm
1980	174	2849	①	133@5250	163@3000	8.2:1	3.59	91	2.87	73

① — Solex 34 TBIA Single-barrel Primary; Solex 35 CEEI Two-barrel Secondary.

Peugeot Engines

604 V6 (Cont.)
ENGINE SPECIFICATIONS (Cont.)

VALVES							
Engine & Valve	Head Diam. In. (mm)	Face Angle	Seat Angle	Seat Width In. (mm)	Stem Diameter In. (mm)	Stem Clearance In. (mm)	Valve Lift In. (mm)
2849 cc Intake	1.73 (44)	30°	30°	.....	.315 (8)	.....	.....
Exhaust	1.46 (37)	45°	45°	.....	.315 (8)	.....	.....

CRANKSHAFT MAIN & CONNECTING ROD BEARINGS							
	MAIN BEARINGS				CONNECTING ROD BEARINGS		
Engine	Journal Diam. In. (mm)	Clearance In. (mm)	Thrust Bearing	Crankshaft End Play In. (mm)	Journal Diam. In. (mm)	Clearance In. (mm)	Side Play In. (mm)
2849 cc	2.7576-2.7583 (70.043-70.062)	.....	Rear	.0028-.0106 (.07-.27)	2.0589 (52.296)	.....	.....

TIGHTENING SPECIFICATIONS

Application	Ft. Lbs. (mkg)
Cylinder Head Bolts	①14 Plus 90°
Main Bearing Caps	22 (3.0) Plus 70°
Connecting Rod Nuts	34 (4.75)
Crankcase Peripheral Bolts	13 (1.75)
Lower Sump	9 (1.3)
Baffle Plate & Strainer	9 (1.3)
Flywheel Bolts	33 (4.5)
Camshaft Thrust Flange	9 (1.3)
Exhaust Manifold Nuts	13 (1.75)
Intake Manifold Bolts	9 (1.3)
Oil Pump Mounting Bolts	9 (1.3)
Oil Pump Sprocket Bolts	5 (.6)
Timing Cover Bolts	9 (1.3)
Crankshaft Pulley	123 (17)
Water Pump Mounting Bolts	13 (1.75)
Water Casing Bolts	9 (1.3)
Bell Housing Bolts	29 (4)

① — First tighten to 43 ft. lbs. (6.0 mkg), loosen, and retighten to specified value.

924 4 CYLINDER

ENGINE CODING

ENGINE IDENTIFICATION

Engine number is located on left side of crankcase next to the clutch housing. Engine number is coded as follows:

Engine Identification	
Application	**Code**
924	VC
924 Turbo	31/02

ENGINE, CYLINDER HEAD

ENGINE

NOTE — *Manufacturer does not provide specific instructions for 924 Turbo.*

Removal — 1) Disconnect battery cable and remove engine protection plate. Scribe hood at hinges and remove hood. Drain cooling system, remove hoses and expansion tank. Remove fan motors with shroud and alternator cooling hose.

NOTE — *Remove A/C compressor without disconnecting hoses and lay aside.*

2) Disconnect all wiring, hoses, lines, linkage and brackets from engine. On 924 Turbo, disconnect necessary parts of turbocharger and oiling system. On all models, disconnect exhaust pipe at manifold. Support drive line at front brace with wooden block. *See Fig. 1.*

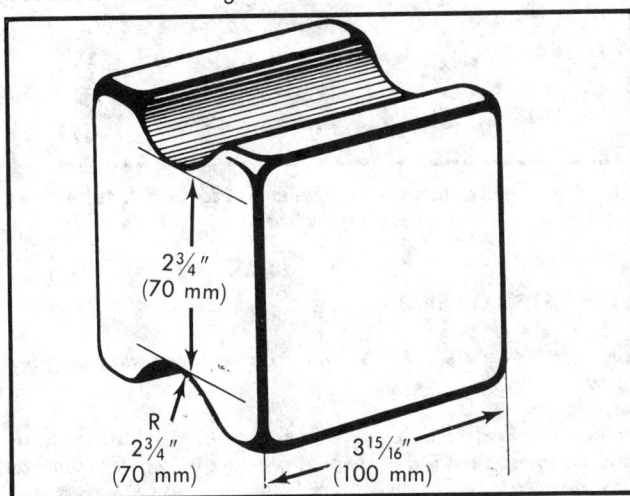

Fig. 1   Drive Line Support Block

3) Disconnect universal joint at steering rack. Disconnect stabilizer bar at frame on both sides and remove crossmember. Attach hoist and lift engine slightly. Remove bellhousing bolts and engine mounts. On vehicles equipped with automatic transmissions, remove bolts from metal/rubber damper. Lift engine carefully and turn at same time.

Installation — To install engine, reverse removal procedure.

CYLINDER HEAD

Removal & Installation — 1) Disconnect battery ground strap and drain cooling system. Remove hoses and wiring con-

nected to cylinder head. Remove exhaust pipe at manifold and remove camshaft timing belt and "V" belt.

2) Remove cylinder head cover and head bolts in sequence. To install, coat threads of cylinder head bolts with a light coat of oil and tighten in sequence as described below.

3) On 924, (with polygon head bolts), tighten to specifications, then mark position of bolts. Turn cylinder head bolts ½ turn (180°) further in specified sequence.

4) On 924 Turbo, tighten cylinder head bolts in sequence and in steps to specifications. After 1 hour, loosen bolts ¼ turn and retighten. After test drive, let engine cool, loosen bolts ¼ turn again and retighten.

NOTE — *Early 1980 normally aspirated engines may have hexagon head cylinder head bolts. These bolts must be tightened in the old manner: Tighten to 72 ft. lbs. (10 mkg) cold, 86 ft. lbs. (12 mkg) warm, in sequence. After 1000 miles of driving loosen bolts in sequence ¼ turn and retighten. Polygon cylinder head bolts do not require retighteinging.*

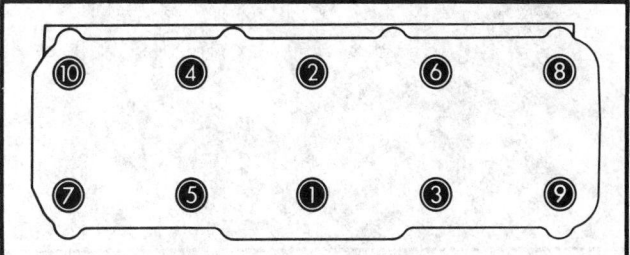

Fig. 2   Cylinder Head Tightening Sequence (Loosen in Reverse Order)

CAMSHAFT

FRONT MAIN BEARING OIL SEAL

Remove pulley bolt and using oil seal removing tool 10-221 (or equivalent), pry oil seal out of oil pump. Use installing tool 2033 to install new seal.

TIMING BELT

Remove belt cover and loosen drive belt tensioner. Remove crankshaft pulley and drive belt pulley. Remove drive belt. To install, reverse removal procedure.

NOTE — *Belt must be tightened until belt can be turned 90° with thumb and index finger at a point midway between crankshaft and camshaft.*

CAMSHAFT

1) Remove cylinder head cover and timing belt cover. Rotate crankshaft so marks on crankshaft pulley and camshaft sprocket are in No. 1 TDC position. Remove camshaft sprocket, distributor and distributor drive housing.

2) Remove camshaft lubrication tube, then replace nuts (hand tight) on bearing caps 2 and 4. Remove bearing caps 5, 1 and 3. Loosen bearing caps 2 and 4 evenly in a crosswise pattern and lift out camshaft.

NOTE — *Ensure that bearing caps are replaced in original position. Note the correct off-center position of bearing caps.*

924 4 CYLINDER (Cont.)

3) To install camshaft, reverse removal procedure and note the following: Place camshaft into position and install caps 2 and 4, tighten nuts in a crosswise pattern. Install caps 1, 3 and 5 and tighten all nuts to specifications. Loosen nuts 2 and 4 to install lubrication tube. Press in new camshaft oil seal.

VALVE TIMING

Using either TDC mark on flywheel and casting in bell housing, or crankshaft pulley TDC mark, rotate crankshaft to TDC position. Mark on rear of camshaft sprocket and indicator on cylinder head cover must be in line. Ensure that Woodruff key is installed and camshaft sprocket bolt is tightened properly. Install timing belt and adjust tension.

Fig. 3   Camshaft Sprocket Alignment

VALVES

VALVE ARRANGEMENT

I-E-I-E-I-E-I-E (Front to rear).

VALVE GUIDE SERVICING

1) With dial indicator, measure amount of clearance between valve and guide with end of stem flush with guide. If wear exceeds limits of .032" (0.8 mm) for intake, or .039" (1.0 mm) for exhaust, replace valve guides.

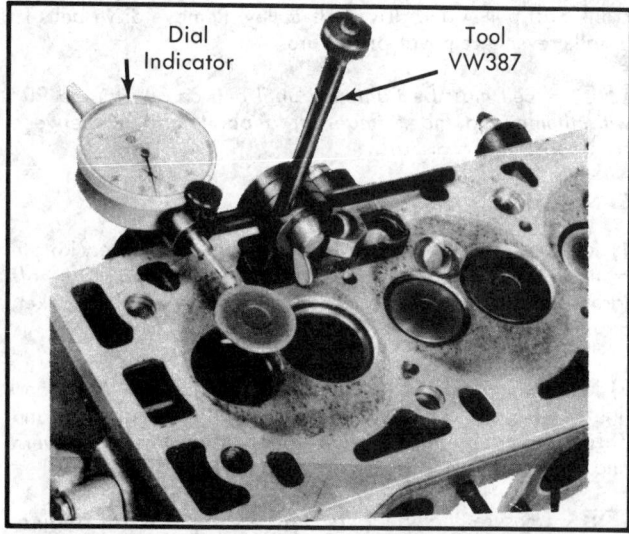

Fig. 4   Measuring Valve Guide Clearance

2) Press worn guide out from combustion chamber side. Place circlip into groove of replacement guide and press new guide in from camshaft side. Production guides do not have circlips and may be smooth or have one groove. Replacement guides have a circlip in addition to 1 or 2 grooves on camshaft end.

3) Ream replacement guide by hand with dry reamer for proper clearance. Change valve spring retainer resting on head to replacement type with groove.

Valve Guides

Identification	Circlip	Outside Diameter In. (mm)
Original Smooth	W/O Circlip	.548 (14.06)
Original 1 Groove	W/O Circlip	.556 (14.26)
Replacement 1 Groove	With Circlip	.556 (14.26)
Replacement 2 Groove	With Circlip	.564 (14.46)

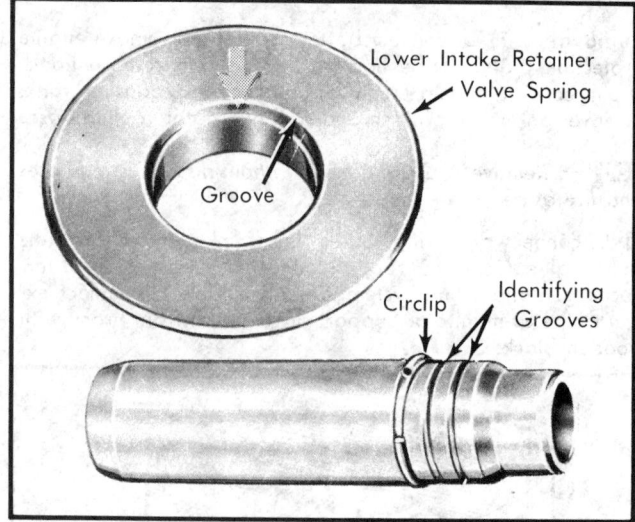

Fig. 5   Replacement Valve Guide and Intake Spring Retainer

VALVE STEM OIL SEALS

NOTE — *Valve stem oil seal may be replaced with cylinder head installed.*

Remove spark plug on cylinder being serviced, install air hose and adapter to maintain constant pressure in cylinder. Remove camshaft, tappets, valve stem keepers and valve spring. Remove oil seal and discard. To install, reverse removal procedures while noting the following; Be sure plastic sleeve is installed prior to seal installation. Place sleeve on valve stem, lubricate seal and install onto valve stem.

MECHANICAL VALVE LIFTERS

With camshaft removed, lift out tappet and inspect for wear or damage. Oil tappets lightly and replace in original position.

VALVE CLEARANCE ADJUSTMENT

1) Remove cylinder head cover and turn crankshaft until cam lobes of cylinder to be adjusted are pointing upward. Check valve clearance with feeler gauge between tappet and lobe.

924 4 CYLINDER (Cont.)

Fig. 6 Checking and Adjusting Valve Clearance (Note Cam Lobes Pointing Upward)

2) Basic valve clearance with engine cold (when reconditioning engine) is .004" (.10 mm) for intake valve and .016" (.40 mm) for exhaust valve. Valve clearance should be checked with engine warmed to 176°F (80°C) oil temperature. Intake valve clearance is .008" (.20 mm) and exhaust clearance is .018" (.45 mm).

3) Adjust clearance by turning screw mounted in tappet with adjusting tool US 8005. Adjustment must be in complete turns only. One turn of screw changes clearance by .002" (.05 mm). After adjusting valve, be sure edge of tappet is in line with green area of tool.

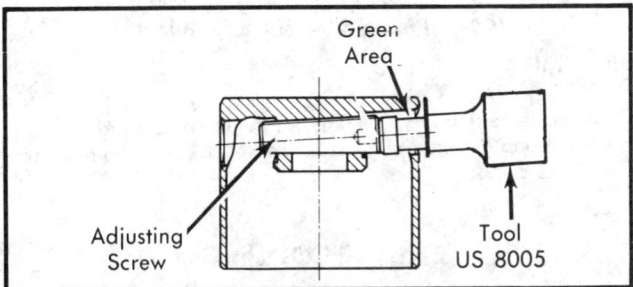

Fig. 7 Valve Lifter (Tappet) with Adjusting Screw and Tool

PISTONS, PINS & RINGS

OIL PAN

Drain engine oil and loosen left engine mount slightly. Disconnect steering at crossmember and remove crossmember. Remove oil pan bolts and lower oil pan. To install, reverse removal procedure and tighten pan bolts.

PISTONS & ROD ASSEMBLY

1) Before removing connecting rods, mark rod and cap for installation in original position. Remove rod caps and carefully push piston and rod assembly out top of block.

2) On reassembly of piston and rod assembly, cast bosses on rod and cap must face pulley end of engine. Code numbers must be on same side. Using a suitable ring compressor, install piston and rod assembly with arrow on crown of piston facing front of engine.

FITTING PISTONS

1) Measure cylinder bore .39" (9.9 mm) down from top and up same distance from bottom, also in the center. Take two measurements, one in line with crankshaft and again 90° to crankshaft.

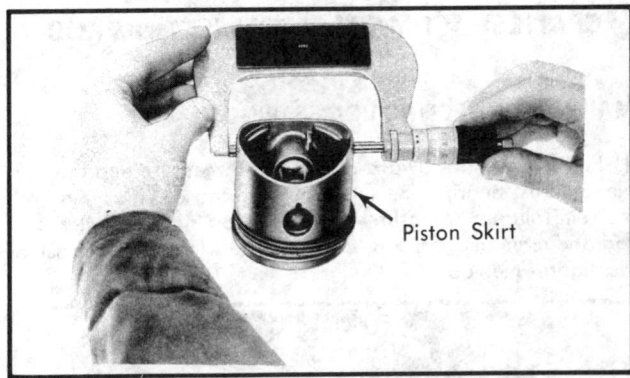

Fig. 8 Measuring Piston Diameter at Skirt

2) Measure piston .63" (16 mm) from bottom of skirt, 90° to pin bore. Combine measurements with those taken from cylinder bore. If piston-to-cylinder measurement exceeds .0016" (.04 mm), oversized pistons must be installed.

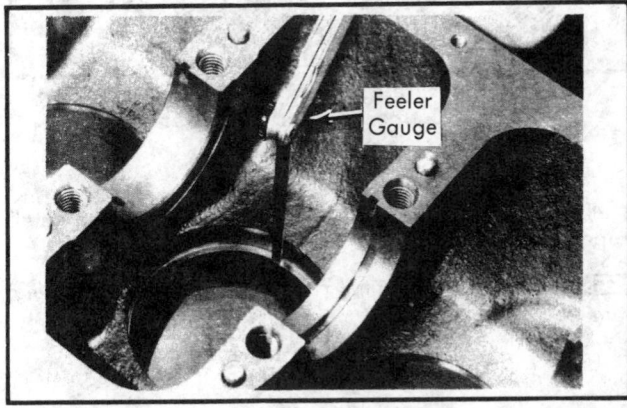

Fig. 9 Measuring Ring Gap in Cylinder Bore

3) Place piston rings squarely in bottom of cylinder bore approximately .59" (15 mm) from surface and measure ring gap. Wear limit is .039" (1.0 mm). Measure ring side clearance in piston. Wear limit is .004" (0.1 mm). Install rings with "TOP" mark facing piston crown and gaps offset 120° from each other.

PISTON PINS

Remove circlip and using piston pin remover VW 207c, remove pins. To install, reverse removal procedure.

NOTE — *If pin is hard to install, heat piston to approximately 140°F (60°C).*

924 4 CYLINDER (Cont.)

Fig. 10   Piston Pin Removal and Installation

CRANKSHAFT MAIN & CONNECTING ROD BEARINGS

MAIN & CONNECTING ROD BEARINGS

1) Push crankshaft toward one end and measure end play at No. 3 thrust bearing. Be sure main bearing caps are marked for reinstallation. Measure connecting rod side play. Remove rod and main bearing caps and check bearing clearance using Plastigage method.

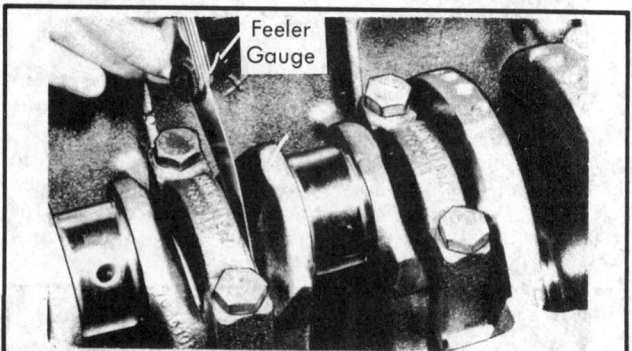

Fig. 11   Measure Crankshaft End Play as Shown (Check Connecting Rod Side Clearance Using Same Method)

2) Install plain bearing shell into bearing cap. Place grooved shell in block. Do not mix shells. Lubricate bearings and install caps.

NOTE — *On No. 5. bearing, coat mating surface of bearing with sealing compound.*

ENGINE OILING

Crankcase Capacity (Includes Filter) — 5.3 quarts for 924, 5.8 quarts for 924 Turbo.

Oil Filter — Spin-on type. Change at first oil change and every other one thereafter.

Oil Pressure — 73-101@5000 RPM.

ENGINE OILING SYSTEM

The engine oiling system is full pressure with rotary (sickle) type pump. Oil is picked up by pump through strainer and suction tube. Oil passes through pump and pressure control valve to oil filter and main oil channels. It is then distributed to main bearings, connecting rods and crankshaft. Camshaft lubrication is provided by spray tube at No. 1 cam bearing. Oil pressure switch is located at end of camshaft lubrication passage. A temperature sensor is located in oil pan. Lubrication system for 924 Turbo includes the following additional componets: an oil cooler in front of engine, oil filter flange with thermostat for the oil cooler, and delivery and return lines for the turbocharger.

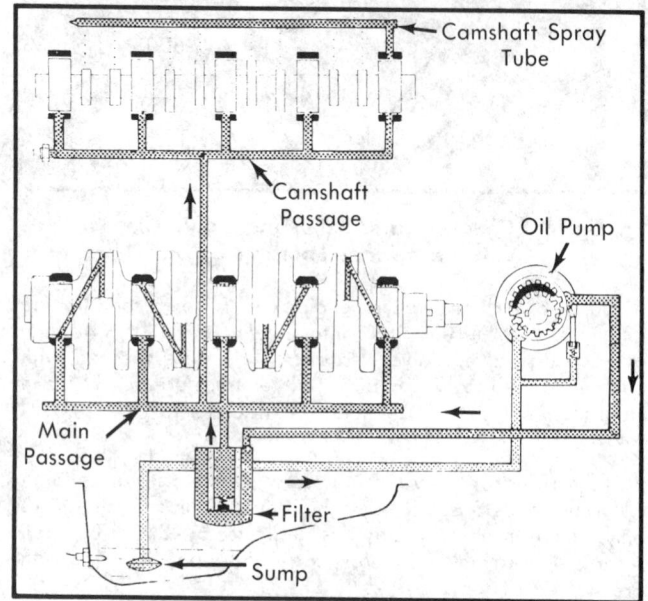

Fig. 12   Engine Oiling System (924 Shown, 924 Turbo Similar)

OIL PUMP

Oil pump is gear driven sickle type. Pump is mounted at front of engine and driven directly by crankshaft. Gear replacement is in pairs only.

ENGINE COOLING

Cooling System Capacity — 8.4 quarts with heater.

Thermostat — Opens at approximately 180°F.

Radiator Cap — 12.8-16.4 psi.

Cooling Fan — Comes on at 198°F, goes off at 189°F.

ENGINE SPECIFICATIONS

GENERAL SPECIFICATIONS										
Year	Displ.		Carburetor	HP at RPM	Torque (Ft. Lbs. at RPM)	Compr. Ratio	Bore		Stroke	
	cu. ins.	cc					in.	mm	in.	mm
1980 924 924 Turbo	121 121	1984 1984	Fuel Inj. Fuel Inj.	110@5750 147@5500	111@3500 147@3000	8.5:1 7.5:1	3.41 3.41	86.5 86.5	3.32 3.32	84.4 84.4

924 4 CYLINDER (Cont.)
ENGINE SPECIFICATIONS (Cont.)

VALVES

Engine & Valve	Head Diam. In. (mm)	Face Angle	Seat Angle	Seat ① Width In. (mm)	Stem Diameter In. (mm)	Stem Clearance In. (mm)	Valve Lift In. (mm)
1984 cc Int.	1.575 (40)	45°	45°	.087-.118 (2.2-3.0)	.3532 (8.97)	.0157 (0.4)	⋯⋯
Exh.	1.299② (33)	45°	45°	.087-.118 (2.2-3.0)	.3524 (8.95)	.020 (0.5)	⋯⋯

① — Maximum seat width .138" (3.5 mm).　　② — 924 Turbo 1.417" (36 mm) diameter.

PISTONS, PINS, RINGS

Engine	PISTONS	PINS			RINGS		
	Clearance In. (mm)	Piston Fit In. (mm)	Rod Fit In. (mm)	Rings	End Gap In. (mm)	Side Clearance In. (mm)	
1984 cc	.0012 (.03)	⋯⋯	.0004-.0008 (.01-.02)	⋯⋯	.012-.020 (.3-.5)	.0016-.0028 (.04-.07)	

CRANKSHAFT MAIN & CONNECTING ROD BEARINGS

Engine	MAIN BEARINGS				CONNECTING ROD BEARINGS		
	Journal Diam. In. (mm)	Clearance In. (mm)	Thrust Bearing	Crankshaft End Play In. (mm)	Journal Diam. In. (mm)	Clearance In. (mm)	Side Play In. (mm)
1984 cc	2.518-2.519 (63.95-63.97)	.0008-.0031 (.02-.08)	3	.004-.007 (.10-.18)	1.888-1.889 (47.95-47.97)	.0008-.0027 (.02-.07)	.002-.003 (.05-.08)

VALVE TIMING

Engine	INTAKE		EXHAUST	
	Open (BTDC)	Close (ABDC)	Open (BBDC)	Close (ATDC)
1984 cc①	6°	42°	47°	2°

① — With .039" (1 mm) valve clearance.

CAMSHAFT

Engine	Journal Diam. In. (mm)	Clearance In. (mm)	Lobe Lift In. (mm)
1984 cc	1.0213-1.0220 (25.94-25.96)	.0015-.0032 (.040-.081)	⋯⋯

TIGHTENING SPECIFICATIONS

Application	Ft. Lbs. (mkg)
Hexagon Cylinder Head Bolts	
Cold	72 (10)
Warm	86 (12)
Polygon Cylinder Head Bolts	
924	47 (6.5) Plus ½ Turn
924 Turbo	
Step 1	29.5 (4.1)
Step 2	59 (8.2)
Step 3	①81 (11.2)
Main Bearing Caps	58 (8)
No. 5 Allen Head Bolt	47 (6.5)
Connecting Rod Nuts	43 (6)
Flywheel	65 (9)
Crankshaft Pulley	180 (25)
Exhaust Manifold	18 (2.5)
Intake Manifold	17 (2.4)
Camshaft Bearing Cap Nuts	12-15 (1.6-2.1)
Camshaft Bearing Cap Bolts	7 (1)
Camshaft Sprocket Bolt	58 (8)

① — Retighten after 1 hour and again after test drive (with cool engine). Retighten by loosening ¼ turn and then retightening.

Porsche Engines

911SC 6 CYLINDER

ENGINE CODING

ENGINE IDENTIFICATION

Engine identification number is die stamped on blower fan support near oil temperature sensor. Second digit of number identifies engines as follows:

Engine Identification	
Application	Code
911SC (2994 cc)	4

ENGINE & CYLINDER HEADS

ENGINE

Removal — 1) Place vehicle on jack stands. Disconnect negative battery cable. Remove air cleaner. Detach air conditioning compressor from brackets, but leave hoses attached.

2) Disconnect all electrical wires running between engine and engine compartment. Remove fuel lines at filter and return line. Disconnect accelerator linkage.

3) Remove rear center tunnel cover in passenger compartment. Remove rubber boot in tunnel by pulling forward over the selector rod. Loosen shift rod coupling and pull coupling off of transmission inner shift rod.

4) Disconnect speedometer sensor wires in tunnel. Remove rubber plug with wire plug. Drain crankcase and plug hoses on engine and oil tank. Remove heater hoses at exchangers. Remove rear stabilizer.

5) Disconnect ground strap at body and battery wires at starter. Disconnect accelerator linkage from pedal and clutch cable from transmission. Loosen drive shaft flange socket head screws at transmission.

6) Place a suitable jack under engine/transmission assembly and apply a little upward pressure to relieve tension on motor mounts. Remove transmission and engine mount bolts. Lower engine/transmission assembly out of vehicle.

CAUTION — *Do not move vehicle unless drive shafts are suspended horizontally.*

Installation — Reverse removal procedure and note the following: Do not clamp heater hoses, slide them onto the exchangers just before the engine/transmission assembly is in final installation position.

CYLINDER HEADS

Removal — 1) With fuel injection system removed, take off distributor cap and spark plug wires. Remove cooling air ducts, cover shrouds, ducts connecting air blower outlets and heat exchanger inlets with cover shrouds.

2) Remove rear engine mount from holder. Remove exhaust system, engine mounting bracket, blower pulley and drive belt. Loosen both screws of band strap which attaches alternator to blower housing and pull housing rearward. Disconnect alternator cables and remove blower housing along with alternator.

3) Remove heat exchanger using suitable wrenches (P 205 & P 217). Disconnect camshaft oil lines between crankcase and chain housing covers. Remove covers. Remove chain tensioner, pivot lever and chain sprocket as an assembly.

4) Remove camshaft sprocket nuts using suitable tools (P 202 & P 203). Withdraw sprocket dowel pin with tool (P 212). Use a screwdriver to lift spring retainers from groove and remove chain guides. Remove camshaft sprockets and flanges. Pry Woodruff keys from camshafts.

NOTE — *Each cylinder has a separate head. If camshaft housing is removed, any single head may be removed. If camshaft housing is left attached to cylinder heads, cylinder heads and camshaft housing may be removed as an assembly.*

5) To remove a single head, rotate camshaft to take load off of rocker arm shaft to be removed. Loosen and remove rocker arm shafts and remove camshaft housing. With suitable tool (P 119), remove cylinder head nuts and lift off cylinder head.

NOTE — *Mark cylinder heads, cylinders and camshaft housings for reassembly in original positions.*

6) To remove all 3 cylinder heads and camshaft housing as an assembly, evenly loosen and unscrew cylinder head nuts with suitable tool (P 119).

Installation — 1) Place cylinder head gaskets on cylinders with perforated side of steel insert facing cylinder. Install cylinder heads and oil return tubes at same time. Coat oil return tubes with engine oil for easier installation. Lightly tighten cylinder head nuts.

NOTE — *Split (2 piece) oil return pipes may be installed without removing and disassembling the engine. If using this type, all "O" rings and seals must be lightly oiled and pipe telescoped. Extend pipe until end seals are seated and place retaining ring in its groove. Short pipe must be installed in crankshaft housing.*

2) Install cool air shrouds and attach with clamps. Thinly coat camshaft housing gasket with gasket compound. Slide camshaft housing onto mounting studs. Tighten camshaft housing nuts down a few turns to ensure gasket seal. Install Allen screws in proper location and tighten camshaft housing in a crosswise pattern.

NOTE — *Camshaft housings are interchangeable, but camshafts are not. Camshafts must be positioned on their proper side. See Fig. 4.*

3) Tighten cylinder head nuts in a crosswise pattern, checking that camshaft does not bind in housing. If camshaft binds, loosen cylinder head nuts and tighten in a different sequence. With cylinder head nuts tight, camshaft must be free to rotate.

4) Install rocker arms and shafts so grooves in shafts are recessed approximately .060" (1.52 mm) into bores. See Fig. 1. Tighten Allen bolts to 13 ft. lbs. (1.8 mkg) using suitable tools (P 210 & P 211).

911SC 6 CYLINDER (Cont.)

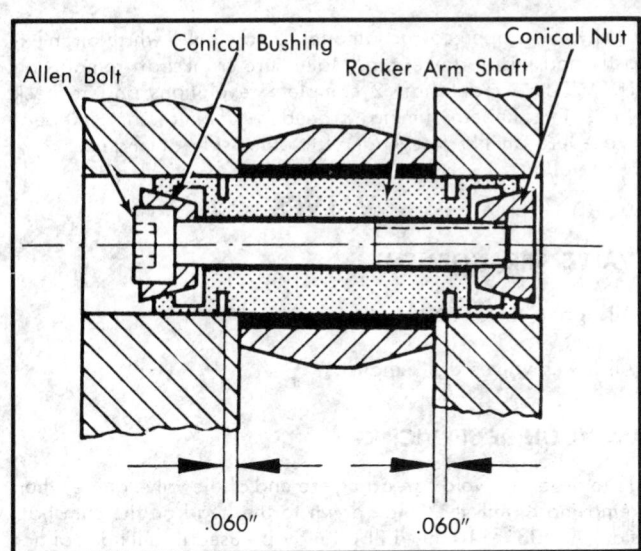

Fig. 1 Cross Section of Rocker Arm Shaft Assembly

5) Install gasket, "O" ring, sealing flange, thrust plate, spacer, Woodruff key and camshaft sprocket flange as shown in *Fig. 2*. No provision is made to adjust camshaft end play. If sealing flange is worn, replace it.

6) Install camshaft sprockets and check chain alignment. See *Fig. 5*. Install heat exchanger, then chain tensioner. Slide chain guides on mounting studs. Lift retaining spring with screwdriver and slide chain guide into place. Install chain tension pivot lever and sprocket. Ensure that oil holes in pivot stud face upward.

7) Fill and bleed chain tensioners. Depress and install tensioners. Left tensioner may be positioned in only far enough to let camshaft nut be installed after valve timing. *See Valve Timing*. Install chain housing covers and camshaft oil lines. To complete installation, reverse removal procedures.

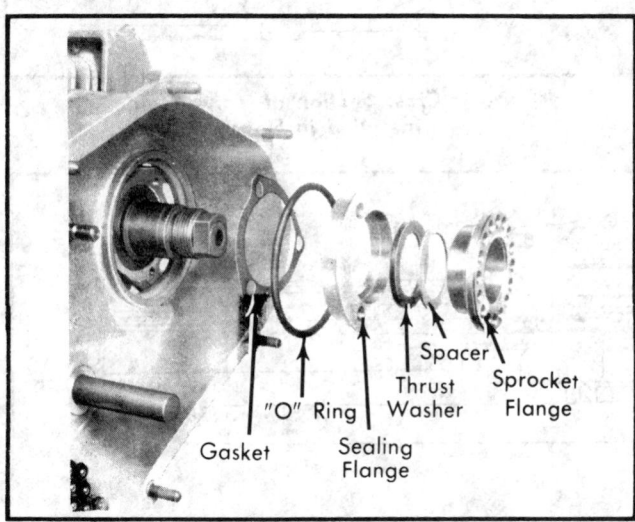

Fig. 2 Assembling Components to Install Camshaft Sprocket Flange and Sprocket

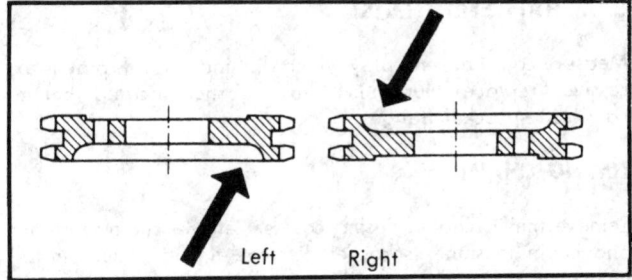

Fig. 3 Camshaft Sprocket Position (Viewed from Blower End of Engine)

CAMSHAFTS

CAMSHAFTS

Removal — 1) With engine out of vehicle, remove rocker covers and rocker arm assemblies. Remove muffler, oil hose from crankcase to chain housing cover, chain tensioner and chain tensioner sprocket.

2) Remove belt pulley from left camshaft. Remove bearing and chain housing covers. Remove ball bearing from camshaft with a puller.

3) Unscrew nuts attaching camshaft sprocket with suitable tools (P 202 & P 203). Remove dowel pin from camshaft sprocket with tool (P 212). Pull sprocket and sprocket flange from camshaft. Remove 3 attaching screws and sealing flange with "O" ring, and withdraw camshaft rearward. See *Fig. 2*.

NOTE — *Camshafts are not symetrical and must be replaced on side they were removed from during disassembly.*

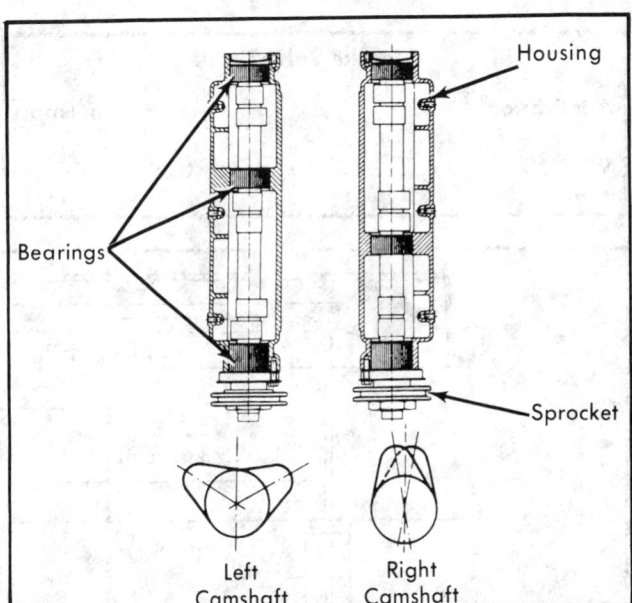

Fig. 4 Camshaft and Housing Viewed from Blower End of Engine

911SC 6 CYLINDER (Cont.)

CAMSHAFT END THRUST

Measure camshaft end play with a dial indicator. If play is excessive, replace aluminum thrust washer located behind camshaft sprocket flange.

TIMING CHAIN

Remove timing chain housing covers. Remove chain tensioner and chain tensioner sprocket. Remove timing chains. Install in reverse order of removal, ensuring that valve timing and chain alignment are as specified. See Figs. 5 and 7.

VALVE TIMING

1) Rotate crankshaft until mark "Z 1" on crankshaft pulley aligns with mark on crankcase. Use suitable tool (P 202) to rotate camshaft until dot on end of shaft is on top of camshaft vertical centerline. See Fig. 7. Find hole in camshaft sprocket which exactly lines up with camshaft flange and insert dowel pin. Install lock washer and nut.

CAUTION — Use care when rotating crankshaft or camshafts so that valve and piston do not collide. If resistance is felt, back off a little and rotate camshaft until you are free to continue.

2) Adjust cylinder No. 1 intake valve clearance to .004" (.10 mm). Install a dial indicator with pressure foot resting squarely on valve spring collar. Preload indicator to .4" (10 mm) to provide for valve movement. Depress chain tensioner with screwdriver on side to be measured and block it with a piece of metal.

3) Rotate crankshaft 360° until "Z 1" (TDC) mark is aligned with mark on crankcase. Read dial indicator and compare with measurement given in Intake Valve Lift Table.

4) If correct valve opening measurement is not achieved, loosen camshaft nut, remove dowel pin and rotate camshaft

Intake Valve Lift	
Application	In. (mm)
911SC	.055-.067 (1.4-1.7)

until valve is open correct amount. Locate holes which align exactly and install dowel pin. Make sure crankshaft remains on TDC. Rotate crankshaft 2 complete revolutions and recheck valve lift. Repeat timing procedure if necessary. Repeat procedure on No. 4 cylinder for other side of engine.

VALVES

VALVE ARRANGEMENT

All upper valves are intake.

All lower valves are exhaust.

VALVE GUIDE SERVICING

1) In order to avoid spreading the end of the valve guide when removing it, mill the guide down to the head on the camshaft side. A .433" (11 mm) drill bit may be used if milling tool not available. Drive valve guide out into combustion chamber.

2) Using a hole gauge, measure bore in cylinder head. Turn oversize guide down in a lathe so that O.D. gives an interference fit of .0024-.0035" (.060-.090 mm).

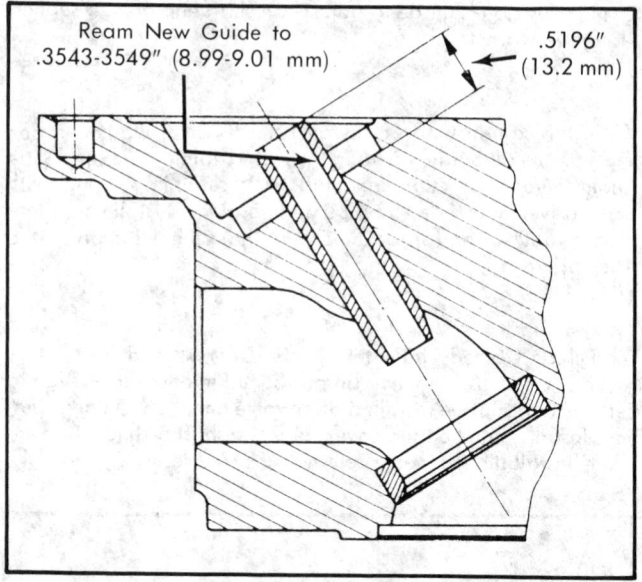

Fig. 6   Cross Section of Valve Guide Installed in Head

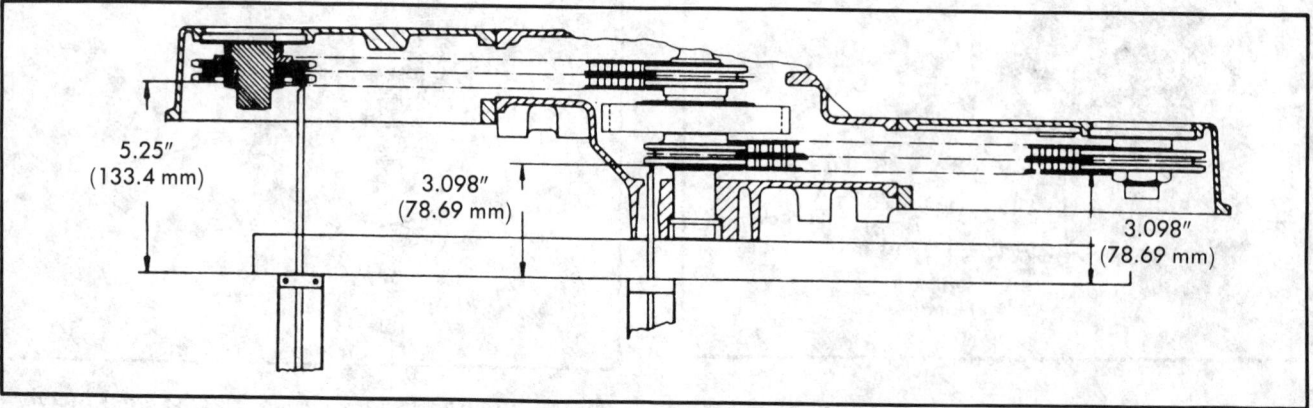

Fig. 5   Top View Showing Timing Chain Alignment

911SC 6 CYLINDER (Cont.)

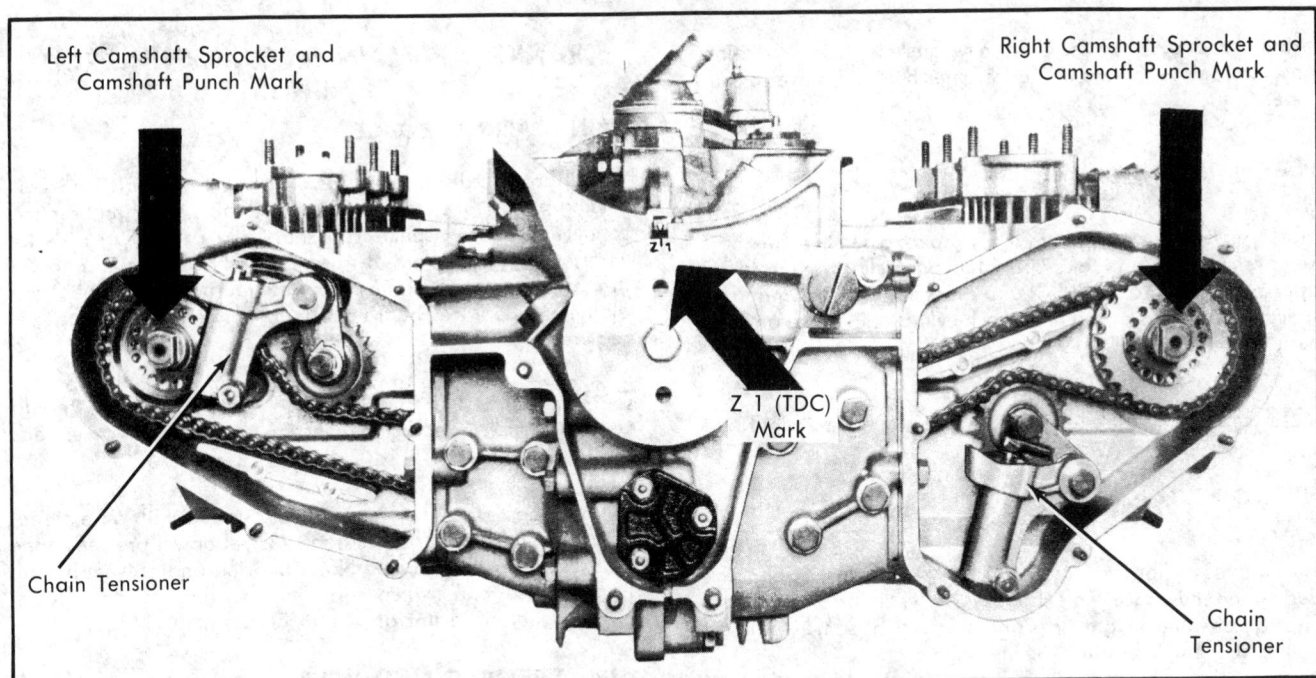

Left Camshaft Sprocket and Camshaft Punch Mark

Right Camshaft Sprocket and Camshaft Punch Mark

Z 1 (TDC) Mark

Chain Tensioner

Chain Tensioner

Fig. 7   View of Engine from Blower End (Rear of Car) Showing Valve Timing Marks

3) Press valve guide into head from camshaft side until a measurement of .5196" (13.2 mm) is reached. See *Fig. 6*. Use suitable grease as a lubricant when pressing in valve guides. Bore or ream valve guide I.D. to .3543-.3549" (8.99-9.01 mm).

VALVE STEM OIL SEALS

Removal & Installation — Using a suitable spring compressor, remove valve keepers and take off valve springs with collar. Remove valve stem oil seal from end of valve guide. Install new seal over stem, using caution to avoid damage to seal as it passes over keeper grooves. Force seal over end of valve guide evenly and install remaining components in reverse order of removal.

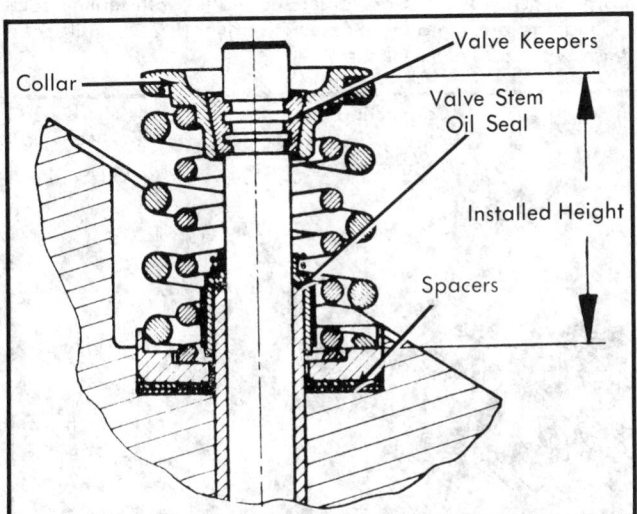

Valve Keepers

Collar

Valve Stem Oil Seal

Installed Height

Spacers

Fig. 8   Measurement of Valve Spring Installed Height

VALVE SPRING SERVICING

Remove valve springs as previously described and check for wear or fatigue. Replace as necessary and install with closely wound coils next to cylinder head. Check installed height with special tool (P 10) and add or remove spacers under the valve spring to attain specified installed height.

ROCKER ARMS

Using an Allen wrench, loosen rocker arm shaft bolt. Slide rocker shaft out of cylinder head and remove arm. Check rocker arm shaft and bushing for wear and replace as required. Install rocker arm shaft with Allen bolt facing either No. 2 or No. 5 cylinder. Center shaft in housing and tighten Allen bolt. See *Fig. 1*.

Rocker Arm Specifications (In.)

Application	Diameter	Wear Limit
Rocker Arm Bushing ...	.7090-.7094	.7106
Rocker Arm Shaft	.7080-.7084	.7074
Rocker Arm Width	1.015-1.019	1.011
Housing Width	1.023-1.029	1.033

VALVE CLEARANCE ADJUSTMENT

1) Valve clearance should be set to .004" (.10 mm) with engine cold. If valves or seats have been reground, set clearances to .010" (.25 mm), run engine for one-half hour, then reset valves to original cold clearance.

2) Adjust valves in firing order sequence: 1,6,2,4,3 and 5. Rotate to TDC of firing stroke on No. 1 cylinder and adjust clearance. Rotate crankshaft 120° for each cylinder to be adjusted until complete.

NOTE — *Cylinders are numbered from pulley end on left side, 1, 2, and 3, with 4, 5 and 6 on right side, 6 at flywheel end.*

PISTONS, PINS & RINGS

OIL PAN

Remove nuts attaching oil pan (strainer cover plate) and remove strainer plate gaskets and strainer. Clean and inspect

911SC 6 CYLINDER (Cont.)

strainer and cover plate. Using new gaskets, replace strainer and cover plate. Ensure that oil strainer hole slides over pickup tube.

PISTON ASSEMBLY

Mark piston and cylinder for proper assembly location. Remove cylinders and take out piston pin circlip. Heat piston to approximately 176°F (80°C) and press out pin. Clean and inspect piston, rings and pin for each cylinder. Replace parts as necessary.

NOTE – *See measurement procedures in Fitting Pistons.*

FITTING PISTONS

The 911SC piston has a depressed dome shape, and this depression must face the exhaust valve when installed. Pistons must be of same weight class and cylinders of same size in order to prevent unbalance of the engine.

1) Measure cylinder for wear and out-of-round. Cylinders and pistons are marked according to size. "0" indicates standard, while "1" or "2" indicates first or second oversize. Measure cylinder diameter 1.18" (30 mm) below top edge of cylinder.

2) Take one measurement in line with thrust face and another at 90° to this measurement. Cylinder is worn if diameter measurement is more than .004" (0.1 mm) beyond diameter specification. If difference in the two measurements is more than .0016" (.04 mm), then cylinder has exceeded its ovality limit.

3) Position piston rings in bottom of cylinder and measure ring gap. Check side clearance in piston ring grooves. Install rings on piston with marking "TOP" facing upward.

CRANKSHAFT MAIN & CONNECTING ROD BEARINGS

MAIN BEARING SERVICE

1) Separate crankcase halves. Lift out crankshaft and connecting rods. Place crankshaft on a suitable stand and remove connecting rods. Inspect crankshaft and connecting rods for wear, damage or out-of-true. Crankshaft main journals 1 through 7 and all connecting rod journals have the same diameter. Replace bearings or fit undersize bearings as required.

NOTE – *Connecting rod bolts are stretch bolts and should never be reused. Replace connecting rod bolts whenever rods are disassembled.*

2) Main bearing No. 8 is a special bearing with an external "O" ring and an internal oil seal. A steel dowel pressed in the crankcase is used to locate No. 8 bearing and prevent it from turning. Use care when installing bearing so that dowel engages hole and not groove in bearing.

THRUST BEARING ALIGNMENT

Check end play at No. 1 main bearing. Width of No. 1 bearing is 1.1024-1.1044" (28.0-28.05 mm). Maximum wear limit is .011" (.28 mm) beyond specifications. Replace main bearing or crankshaft if excessive wear is present.

MAIN BEARING OIL SEALS (BLOWER END)

Remove belt pulley. Using a screwdriver, pry out old seal. Coat new seal with oil and press in place with suitable tool (P 216).

MAIN BEARING OIL SEAL SERVICE (FLYWHEEL END)

Remove flywheel. Displace oil seal with a chisel or drift and pry out with screwdriver. Coat outer seal edges with sealing compound and press into crankcase with driver (P 215) until seal is flush with face of crankcase.

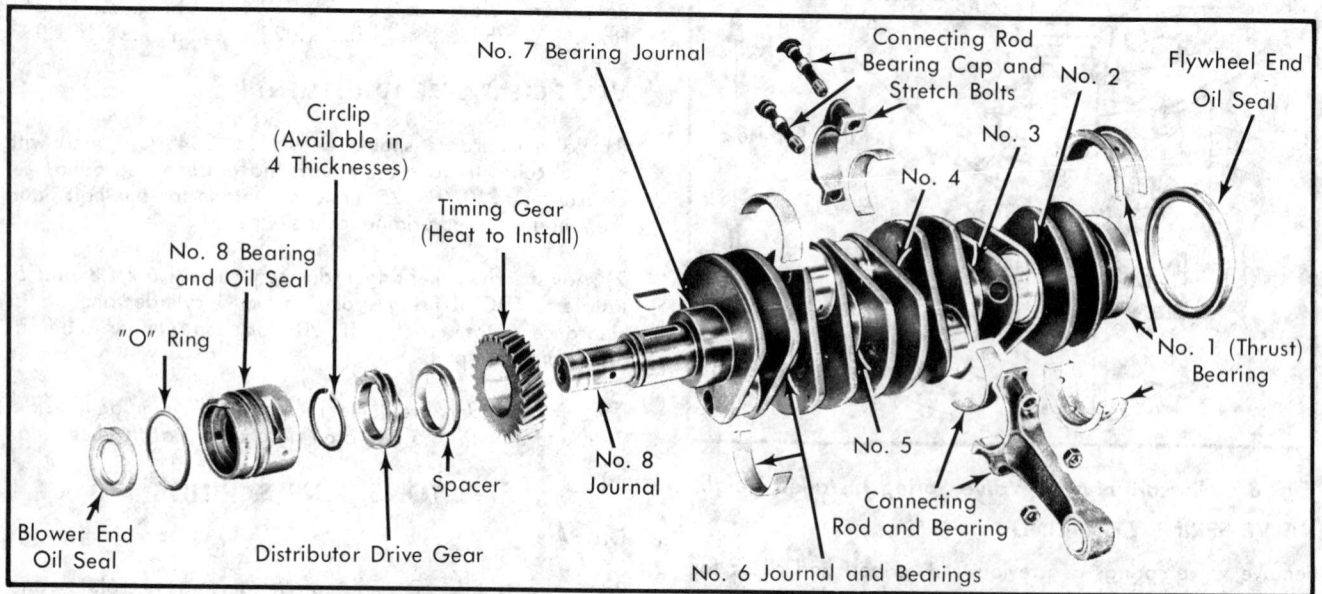

Fig. 9 Crankshaft Assembly with Component Locations

911SC 6 CYLINDER (Cont.)

INTERMEDIATE SHAFT BEARING SERVICE

With crankcase halves separated, lift out intermediate shaft and bearings. Inspect shaft and bearings for wear or damage and replace as necessary. Undersize bearings are NOT available.

ENGINE OILING

Oil Capacity — 13.7 qts. total; 10.6 qts for oil change.

Oil Filter — Disposable spin-on type.

Normal Oil Pressure — 65 psi (4.6 kg/cm) at 5000 RPM with an oil temperature of 194°F (90°C).

Pressure Relief and Safety Valves — Identically constructed coil spring operated valves. Safety valve is set to operate at a higher pressure than relief valve.

ENGINE OILING SYSTEM

Lubrication is dry sump type. Two independent oil pumps provide for pressure and suction in system. Pressure pump takes oil from an externally mounted oil tank and forces oil to individual oil passages for all main bearings. From main bearings, a drilled passage in crankshaft carries oil to connecting rod bearings. Another passage leads to front bearing of intermediate shaft. A passage in intermediate shaft takes oil to rear bearing of shaft.

Camshaft oiling is accomplished by external oil lines leading to camshaft housings. Camshaft housings contain aluminum tubes with holes; three holes of .12" (3.0 mm) diameter carry oil to lubricate camshaft. Six holes of .04" (1.0 mm) diameter splash oil on camshaft lobes. Remaining three holes allow oil to splash against intake valve cover in such a manner that it will drip on rocker arms and valve stems.

Suction pump takes oil from engine sump through a strainer and forces it through oil filter to oil tank. Oil collected in lower part of camshaft housing is returned to crankcase by oil return pipes. Suction pump then returns oil to oil tank. A tube in oil tank carries oil to base of oil tank and filter. The turbo charger is lubricated from a branch off of oil pressure indicator or oil temperature indicator.

Oil pressure regulation is controlled by means of four separate valves. A thermostatically controlled valve directs oil directly to engine when temperature is below 176°F. When temperature is above 176°F, oil flows through oil cooler and then to main bearings. A pressure relief and safety valve located in right crankcase half opens if oil pressure rises above 76.9-99.6 psi and oil is passed directly into crankcase. A safety valve is mounted in left crankcase half immediately after oil pump. It operates in event of a defective pressure relief valve to prevent damage to oil cooler or oil lines. As a safety measure, by-pass valves are built into filter base and filter body. If oil pressure exceeds 28.4 psi, oil by-passes oil filter and flows directly into oil tank.

OIL PUMP

Oil pump may be removed when crankcase halves are separated. No repair of pump is possible, replace if defective.

ENGINE COOLING

Cooling is accomplished by means of a blower, consisting of an impeller and blower housing. Center of blower housing holds support for alternator. Impeller and belt pulley are attached to alternator shaft. Blower delivers air required for cooling engine, oil cooler, alternator as well as fresh air for heating system. Cooling air flows through upper molded plastic air guides to cylinders and heads. Baffle plates provide uniform distribution of air. A duct incorporated into upper air guide leads air flow directly to oil cooler. Ducting for air delivery to heat exchangers is on both sides of blower housing. Adjustment of blower drive belt is done by adding or removing spacers between impeller housing and pulley half. This will cause belt to ride higher of lower on pulley, thereby loosening or tightening drive belt.

ENGINE SPECIFICATIONS

GENERAL SPECIFICATIONS

Year	Displ. cu. ins.	Displ. cc	Carburetor	HP at RPM	Torque (Ft. Lbs. at RPM)	Compr. Ratio	Bore in.	Bore mm	Stroke in.	Stroke mm
1980	182.7	2994	Fuel Inj.	172@5500	175@4200	9.3:1	3.74	95	2.77	70.4

VALVES

Engine & Valve	Head Diam. In. (mm)	Face Angle	Seat Angle	Seat Width In. (mm)	Stem Diameter In. (mm)	Stem Clearance In. (mm)	Valve Lift In. (mm)
2994 cc Intake	.....	45°	45°	.....	.....	.....	.....
Exhaust	.....	45°	45°	.....	.....	.....	.....

Porsche Engines

911SC 6 CYLINDER (Cont.)
ENGINE SPECIFICATIONS (Cont.)

CRANKSHAFT MAIN & CONNECTING ROD BEARINGS

Engine	MAIN BEARINGS				CONNECTING ROD BEARINGS		
	Journal Diam. In. (mm)	Clearance In. (mm)	Thrust Bearing	Crankshaft End Play In. (mm)	Journal Diam. In. (mm)	Clearance In. (mm)	Side Play In. (mm)
2994 cc Jrnls 1-7	2.362 (60)	.0003-.0028 (.008-.07)	No. 1	.0043-.0076 (.11-.19)	2.085 (53)	.0011-.0034 (.028-.086)	.....
Jrnl 8	1.220 (31)	.004 (.10)					

PISTONS, PINS, RINGS

Engine	PISTONS	PINS		RINGS		
	Clearance In. (mm)	Piston Fit In. (mm)	Rod Fit In. (mm)	Rings	End Gap In. (mm)	Side Clearance In. (mm)
2994 cc	.001-.002 (.025-.052)	Press Fit	.0007-.0015 (.018-.038)	No. 1	.004-.008 (.10-.20)	.003-.004 (.07-.10)
				No. 2	.004-.008 (.10-.20)	.001-.003 (.04-.07)
				Oil	.006-.012 (.15-.30)	.0008-.002 (.02-.05)

① — Limit .006" (.15 mm).

VALVE SPRINGS

Engine	Free Length In. (mm)	PRESSURE ① Lbs. @ In. (kg @ mm)	
		Valve Closed	Valve Open
2994 cc Intake	.....	1.358 (34.5)	.....
Exhaust	.....	1.358 (34.5)	.....

① — Measurement given is spring height; no pressure specification is provided. *See Valve Spring Servicing.*

VALVE TIMING

Engine	INTAKE		EXHAUST	
	Open (BTDC)	Close (ABDC)	Open (BBDC)	Close (ATDC)
2994 cc	1°	53°	43°	3°

TIGHTENING SPECIFICATIONS

Application	Ft. Lbs. (mkg)
Crankcase Joining Bolts	25 (3.5)
Camshaft Housing	18 (2.5)
Main Bearing Caps	25 (3.5)
Flywheel (9 Bolt)	65 (90)
Connecting Rod Caps	36 (5.0)
Cylinder Head	22 (3.3)
Crankshaft Pulley	58 (8.0)
Camshaft Nut	101 (14)
Rocker Arm Shafts	13 (1.8)

928 V8

ENGINE CODING

ENGINE IDENTIFICATION

Engine code and identification number is stamped on the front reinforcing rib in the top half of the crankcase.

Engine Identification	
Application	**Code**
928 (4474 cc)	M 28

ENGINE & CYLINDER HEADS

ENGINE

Removal — 1) With car standing on all 4 wheels, loosen engine compartment cross braces. Disconnect battery ground cable at spare wheel well. Detach windshield washer hoses and engine compartment light wires. Remove engine hood. Remove cap from coolant expansion tank. Remove air intake hoses and entire air cleaner assembly.

2) Raise car on hoist at specified pick up points. Place wooden block between central tube and rear tunnel brace. Detach splash shield at bottom and drain radiator. Remove left and right water drain plugs from crankcase. Drain engine oil and remove lower body brace. Disconnect exhaust pipes at manifolds and remove left and right heat shields. Detach ground cable at body. Install and tighten drain plugs.

3) Unscrew clutch slave cylinder at clutch housing and remove with line connected. Remove mounting strap for pressure line to slave cylinder. Disconnect wires at starter and remove clutch housing with starter.

4) Disconnect clutch lever by pressing down in direction of clutch. Release starter wire from clamps on steering cross member. Remove socket head bolts and push drive shaft coupling back on drive shaft. Unscrew throwout bearing sleeve mounting bolts and push sleeve toward flywheel.

5) Detach left and right engine shock absorbers at control arms, then at upper mountings. Disconnect air conditioner temperature switch wires on radiator and compressor clutch at connector plug. Loosen compressor and remove from console but do not disconnect hoses. Suspend compressor with wire.

6) Remove air pump filter housing and alternator cooling hose. Remove lower fan shroud. Disconnect all coolant hoses and bottom oil hose at radiator. Remove engine mounts separately by lifting with hydraulic jack and wooden block on oil pan. Lower engine to front cross member carefully. Move jack and pad to second side and remove mount in same manner.

7) Remove clutch/engine mounting bolts and lower car. Remove remaining coolant/heater hoses between engine and radiator/chassis. Disconnect upper oil hose at radiator. Remove radiator mounting bolts and lift out radiator. Disconnect engine wire harness and distributor wire transmitter plugs. Disconnect B+ wire and remove control unit. Detach and place ignition coil aside.

8) Disconnect fuel feed and return lines. Detach power steering pump lines at pump and supply tank. Drain oil and remove tank. Disconnect brake booster vacuum hose at manifold. Disconnect accelerator and cruise control cable, remove holder and clamp and place cables outside. Cover A/C condenser with a thin board to prevent damage when removing engine.

9) With engine adapter (9137) in eyelets provided, lift until snug with car resting on its wheels. Remove upper engine block/clutch housing mounting bolts. Pull engine forward carefully and remove short drive shaft with guide tube. Lift engine out of car.

Installation — To install, reverse removal procedures noting that heater lever should be in "warm" position when filling cooling system. Coolant level must reach center of expansion tank with engine warm.

CYLINDER HEADS

NOTE — *Manufacturer does not furnish removal and replacement procedures for cylinder heads. Heads may be removed with engine in vehicle. Following items must be noted when performing cylinder head operations:*

1) Allow engine to cool prior to draining coolant. Heads must not be removed while engine is still hot. Remove camshaft housing, then loosen cylinder head nuts in reverse of tightening sequence.

2) Left and right cylinder head gaskets are different. Arrow must face forward and word "TOP/OBEN" must face up. Tighten head in 3 steps according to the sequence shown in *Fig.1.* Tighten to final torque and allow to stand at least 30 minutes. Loosen nuts by ¼ turn, then tighten to final torque of 61 ft. lbs. (8.5 mkg).

NOTE — *Washers must not turn while tightening cylinder head nuts. Control by making paint marks if necessary.*

3) Flat gasket between cylinder head and camshaft housing must be placed properly to ensure that oil supply bore to camshaft is not blocked. Camshaft housing must be completely assembled prior to installation. Housing is located on heads with 2 dowel pins and mounted with Allen head bolts.

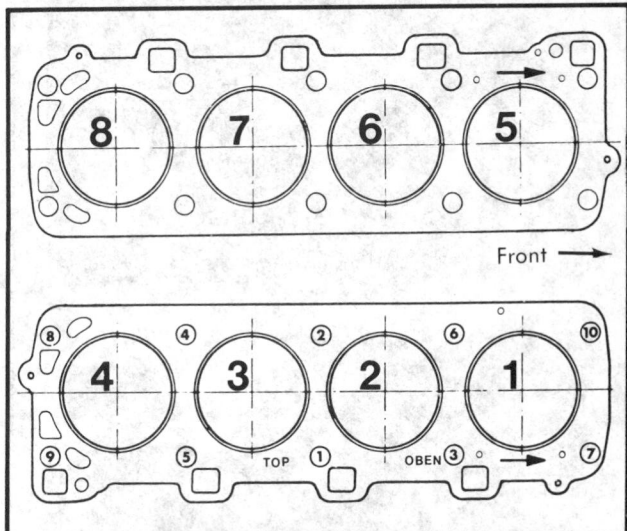

Fig. 1   Cylinder Head Tightening Sequence
(Loosen in Reverse Order)

CAMSHAFT

TIMING BELT

Toothed timing belt drives camshafts, distributor, oil pump and water pump. As the engine assembly heats and cools, belt ten-

928 V8 (Cont.)

sion varies, so a multiple disc belt tensioner is installed to compensate for these changes. To adjust tension, remove right hand camshaft drive belt upper cover. Turn engine in normal direction through two revolutions and check belt for damage or wear. Continue turning until TDC mark on crankshaft and camshaft align with markers. Using tester (9138), check belt tightness between tension roller and camshaft sprocket. Set adjustment screw on tensioner as required and recheck tension.

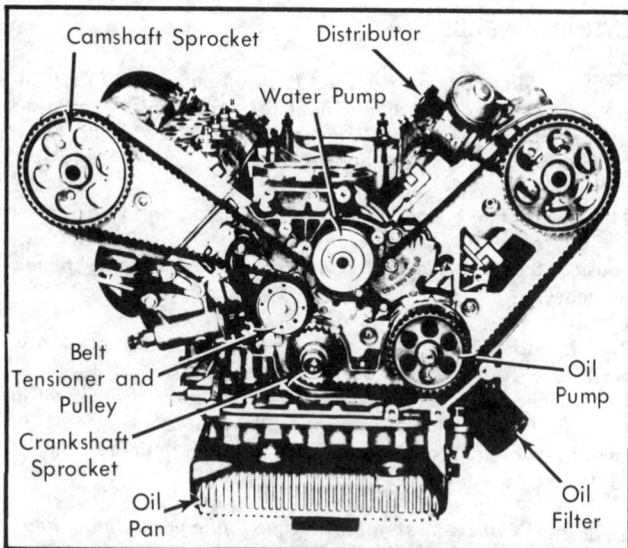

Fig. 2   Front View of Engine with Belt Covers Removed

Fig. 3   View of Left Camshaft Sprocket and Front Pulley with Timing Marks Aligned

CAMSHAFT TIMING ADJUSTMENT

With timing belt and tensioner removed, turn both camshafts until notches in drive sprockets align with marks on camshaft housings. Rotate crankshaft so that TDC mark on vibration damper aligns with indicator. Install belt and tensioner. Rotate crankshaft and recheck tension as in previous step.

DRIVE BELT TENSIONER

Tensioner consists of 8 packets of 5 bimetal discs stacked alternately. If service is required, remove housing from engine and disassemble, noting that housing contains transmission fluid. Clean and reassemble, ensuring that packs of 5 discs are installed alternately. Fill housing $\frac{1}{3}$ full with SAE 90 transmission fluid. Slide in piston assembly and install circlip. Add transmission oil, if necessary, until oil level reaches circlip. Replace dust cover, clamp and pressure rod. Install on engine.

CAMSHAFTS

Camshafts run in 5 bearings without shells in camshaft housing. Housing cover plates must be removed in order to remove rubber plugs covering top row of bolts. Camshaft housing assembly must be completely assembled before installation. Housing is located on heads with 2 dowel pins and mounted with Allen head bolts.

VALVES

VALVE ARRANGEMENT

Valves are arranged in-line with the larger, intake valve at the front of each cylinder.

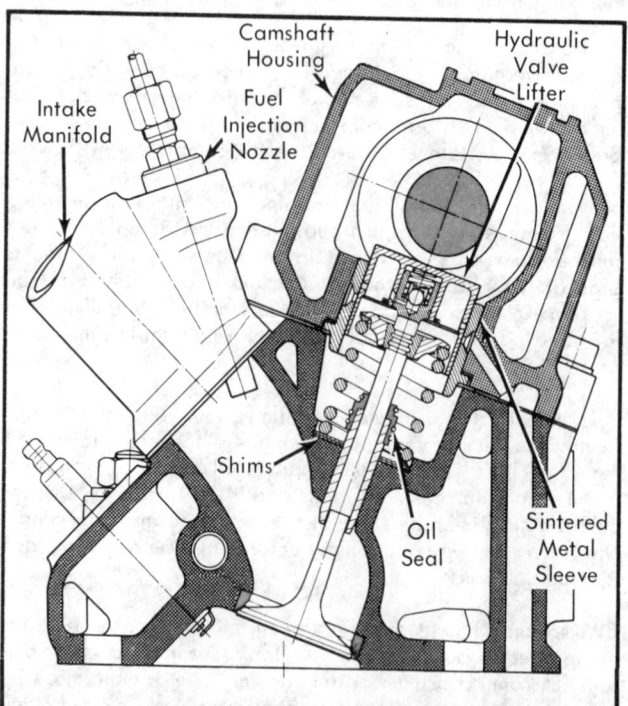

Fig. 4   Cross Sectional View of Cylinder Head with Valve Lifter and Camshaft

928 V8 (Cont.)

HYDRAULIC VALVE LIFTERS

Bucket type hydraulic lifters operate in sintered metal sleeves. Cam lobes depress the lifters which are filled with engine oil under pressure through internal passages. With hydraulic lifters, no further valve clearance adjustment is necessary.

NOTE — *Use caution that lifters and sleeves are installed in original positions. Do NOT mix up lifters and sleeves.*

VALVE SPRINGS

Valve springs may be removed using conventional overhead valve type compressor. Remove keepers and lift off retainer and spring. To install, reverse removal procedures.

CAUTION — *Note number of shims between valve spring and cylinder head and replace in same position.*

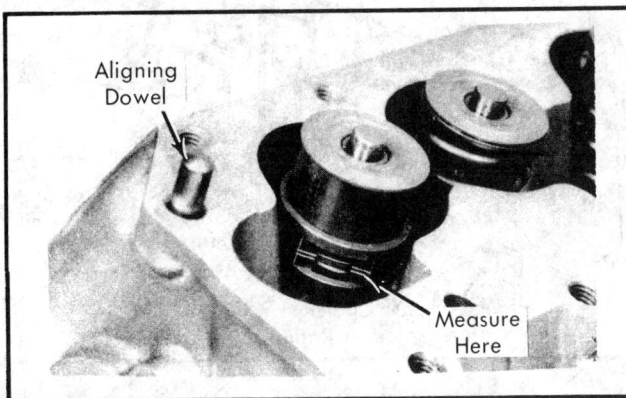

Fig. 5 Measuring Installed Valve Spring Length

VALVE SPRING INSTALLED LENGTH

To check valve spring installed length, install tool (9138) with shims for applicable valve, spring retainer and keepers. Read distance from tool and correct, if required, by adding or removing shims. Correct intake spring length is 1.544+ .020" (39.6+.5 mm) and exhaust length should be 1.505+.020" (38.6+.5 mm).

VALVE STEM OIL SEALS

With valve springs removed, pry off old seal using caution to prevent marring guide. Place plastic sleeve on valve stem, lubricate seal and push into place using "mushroom" type installing tool.

PISTONS, PINS & RINGS

OIL PAN

Oil pan is of cast aluminum design with ribs for reinforcing and cooling. Pan attaches to lower crankcase section with gasket and cap screws. Manufacturer does not provide specific removal and replacement instructions.

PISTONS

Pistons and bore diameters come in 3 tolerance groups. Piston crown is stamped "0", "1" or "2" to correspond with similar marking stamped on cylinder block.

Piston-Bore Tolerance Groups

Tolerance Group	Cylinder Bore In. (mm)	Piston Diameter① In. (mm)
0	3.7050 (95.000)	3.7036 (94.964)
1	3.7054 (95.010)	3.7040 (94.974)
2	3.7058 (95.020)	3.7044 (94.984)

① — ±.0003" (.007 mm).

Piston pin bore is offset from center of piston by .0058" (1.5 mm). Depressions for valves are cast into piston crown at an angle of 20°. Piston and rod must be properly assembled and installed with valve pockets facing EXHAUST manifold.

CRANKSHAFT MAIN & CONNECTING ROD BEARINGS

CRANKCASE LOWER SECTION

Crankcase lower section provides saddles for main bearings. When replacing, it is not necessary to remove old sealant. Clean grease from surfaces and apply Loctite 573 (green) with a short-pile roller. Install lower section and tighten mounting bolts by hand. Install oil pump, then tighten lower section mounting nuts to final torque in sequence illustrated.

MAIN & CONNECTING ROD BEARINGS

Use Plastigage method to determine main and connecting rod bearing clearance. Check crankshaft end play using dial indicator. Main bearing radial wear limit is .0062" (.16 mm) and end play limit is .0156" (.40 mm). Connecting rod bearing wear limit is .0039" (.10 mm). Ensure that connecting rods are installed to piston correctly. With piston indentations facing away from centerline (down), small chamfer on rod faces rod on same journal. Larger chamfer faces web of crankshaft.

Fig. 6 Crankcase Lower Section Tightening Sequence

CRANKSHAFT OIL SEALS

Crankshaft oil seals are installed with crankcase lower half removed. Use tool (9126) to align flywheel end seal, and tool (9125) to install pulley end oil seal.

928 V8 (Cont.)

ENGINE OILING

ENGINE OILING SYSTEM

Engine utilizes a wet sump with an oil cooler integrated in the car radiator as a heat exchanger. Sickle type oil pump is located in a separate cast iron housing bolted to the left front of the engine. Pump is driven by toothed belt. Full pressure system pumps oil to pressure relief valve, thermostat, main oil passage, filter, crankcase upper section, cylinder heads and camshaft housings. All main oil passages are cast into the mating surface of the crankcase lower section.

Oil Filter — Full-flow spin-on type oil filter is easily changed from beneath left side of car.

Normal Oil Pressure — 72 psi (5.06 kg/cm²) at 5000 RPM, 178°F (80°C).

Crankcase Capacity — Approximately 8.5 quarts, with filter change.

ENGINE COOLING

928 utilizes an aluminum radiator and a mechanically driven visco-fan. Water pump is driven by the back side of the toothed timing belt. An expansion tank with filler opening and water level sending unit is mounted at the right rear of the engine compartment. Water level is indicated on the instrument cluster.

Cooling System Capacity — 17 quarts.

Thermostat — Begins to open at 180°F (83°C).

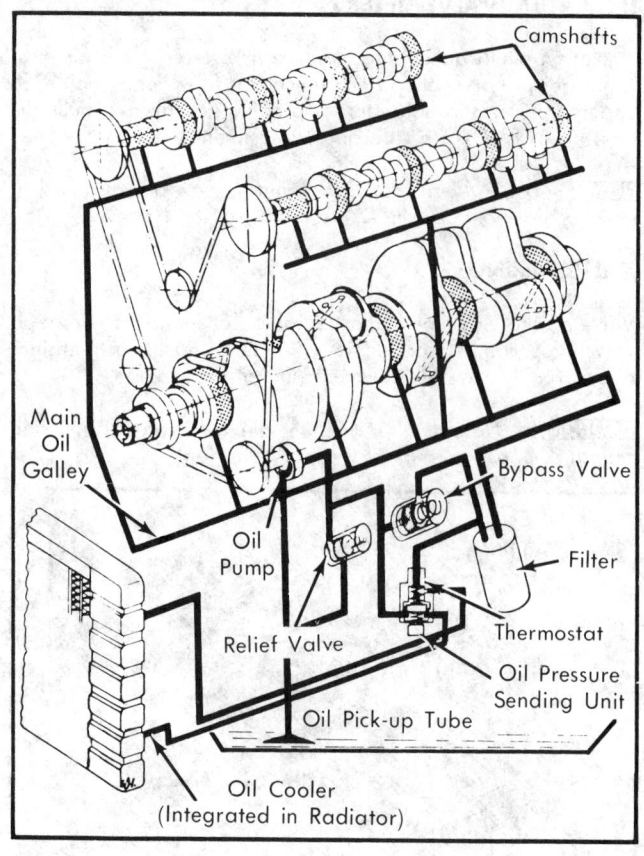

Fig. 7   Porsche 928 Engine Lubrication System

ENGINE SPECIFICATIONS

GENERAL SPECIFICATIONS										
Year	Displ.		Carburetor	HP at RPM	Torque (Ft. Lbs. at RPM)	Compr. Ratio	Bore		Stroke	
	cu. ins.	cc					in.	mm	in.	mm
1980	273	4474	Fuel Inj.	220@5500	265@4000	9:1	3.74	95.0	3.11	78.9

VALVES							
Engine & Valve	Head Diam. In. (mm)	Face Angle	Seat Angle	Seat Width In. (mm)	Stem Diameter In. (mm)	Stem Clearance In. (mm)	Valve Lift In. (mm)
4474 cc Intake	1.692 (43)	45°	45°	.067 (1.7)	.3498 (8.97)	.0003-.0018 (.008-.045)	.....
Exhaust	1.496 (38)	45°	45°	.078 (2.0)	.3490 (8.95)	.0014-.0026 (.036-.065)	....

928 V8 (Cont.)
ENGINE SPECIFICATIONS (Cont.)

PISTONS, PINS, RINGS

Engine	PISTONS Clearance In. (mm)①	PINS Piston Fit In. (mm)	Rod Fit In. (mm)	RINGS Rings	End Gap In. (mm)	Side Clearance In. (mm)②
4474 cc	.001-.002 (.024-.050)	Interference	.0007-.0012 (.019-.032)	1	.008-.015 (.20-.40)	.002-.003 (.050-.082)
				2	.008-.015 (.20-.40)	.002-.003 (.050-.082)
				3	.015-.055 (.40-1.4)	.0009-.005 (.023-.127)

① — Wear limit .003" (.080 mm).

② — For KS piston rings. For Mahle piston rings, No. 1 clearance is .002-.004" (.050-.102 mm), No. 2 clearance is .002-.003" (.050-.076 mm), and No. 3 clearance is .0005-.005" (.013-.127 mm). Piston manufacturer must match ring manufacturer.

CRANKSHAFT MAIN & CONNECTING ROD BEARINGS

Engine	MAIN BEARINGS Journal Diam. In. (mm)	Clearance In. (mm)	Thrust Bearing	Crankshaft End Play In. (mm)	CONNECTING ROD BEARINGS Journal Diam. In. (mm)	Clearance In. (mm)	Side Play In. (mm)
4474 cc	2.754-2.755 (69.97-69.99)	.0008-.0038 (.020-.098)	No. 3	.0039-.0157 (.100-.400)	2.046-2.047 (51.97-51.99)	.001-.004 (.034-.092)	.004-.016 (.10-.40)

VALVE TIMING

Engine	INTAKE Open (ATDC)	Close (ABDC)	EXHAUST Open (BBDC)	Close (BTDC)
4474 cc	8°	55°	38°	2°

TIGHTENING SPECIFICATIONS

Application	Ft. Lbs. (mkg)
Cylinder Head Bolts	
Step 1	14 (2.0)
Step 2	36 (5.0)
Step 3①	61 (8.5)
Main Bearing Carrier	
10 mm Bolt	
Step 1	14 (2.0)
Step 2	29-33 (4.0-4.5)
12 mm Bolt	
Step 1	14 (2.0)
Step 2	29 (4.0)
Step 3	43-46 (5.9-6.3)
Connecting Rod Nuts	42-46 (5.8-6.3)
Camshaft Housing	33 (4.5)
Flywheel	69-73 (9.5-10.0)
Front Pulley	181-188 (25.0-26.0)
Camshaft Pulley	29-33 (4.0-4.5)
Oil Pump	
Step 1	11 (1.5)
Step 2	14-16 (2.0-2.2)
Spark Plugs	18-25 (2.5-3.5)

① — Allow to stand for 30 min. after setting Step 3 torque, then loosen ¼ turn each. Retighten to 61 ft. lbs. (8.5 mkg).

Renault Engines

LE CAR 4 CYLINDER

ENGINE CODING

ENGINE IDENTIFICATION

Type of vehicle and engine number is marked on a number plate riveted to the left rear side of the engine block. Plate is located just below cylinder head mating surface. First five digits indicate engine type.

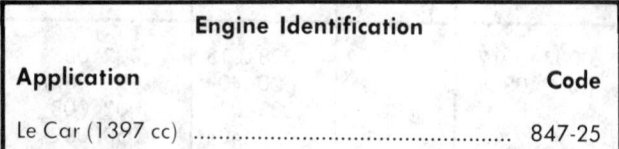

Engine Identification	
Application	Code
Le Car (1397 cc)	847-25

ENGINE, CYLINDER HEAD & MANIFOLDS

ENGINE

NOTE — *Engine and transaxle are removed as an assembly.*

Removal — 1) Remove battery. Drain coolant from engine and radiator. Drain oil. Take out grille. Remove hood and inner fender support. Remove air cleaner.

2) Disconnect all electrical leads, control cables, vacuum lines and coolant hoses that might interfere with engine removal. Mark each item as it is disconnected. Remove transaxle cover.

3) Remove exhaust pipe flange. Remove radiator mounting nuts. Lift out radiator, cooling fan, and expansion tank. Disconnect steering shaft at flexible coupling. Do not lose rubber bushing.

4) Remove front wheels. Remove brake calipers without disconnecting hoses and support out of way. Disconnect tie rods at rack. Use suitable tool and separate upper ball joints. Remove steering gear box. Be sure to index steering box shims.

5) Remove air pump complete with bracket. Remove top transaxle bolts on bell housing. Attach hydraulic hoist to engine. Remove nuts from engine mounts. Remove shift rod support bolts.

6) Disconnect clutch cable. Remove front transaxle mounting bracket. Slide transaxle to left, then right to free axle drive shafts. Remove engine assembly from vehicle.

Installation — To install, reverse removal procedure and note: Grease transaxle input shaft and axle drive shafts. Do not damage oil seals on axle drive shafts. Make sure axle drive shafts fully seat. Adjust clutch. Refit steering rubber bushing. Bleed cooling system.

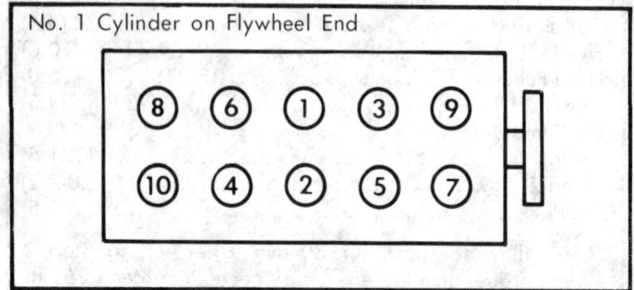

Fig. 1 Cylinder Head Tightening Sequence

INTAKE/EXHAUST MANIFOLD

Removal — Disconnect battery. Remove air filter hose. Disconnect and plug carburetor heating hose. Disconnect choke, accelerator, fuel lines and vacuum lines. Take off carburetor. Separate exhaust pipe. Remove manifold nuts and starter heat shield. Pull manifold from engine.

NOTE — *It may be necessary to remove nut on left engine mount and tilt engine to right to gain enough clearance for removal.*

Installation — To install, reverse removal procedure and replace all gaskets.

CYLINDER HEAD

Removal — 1) Disconnect battery. Drain cooling system. Remove air cleaner. Disconnect all hoses, vacuum lines, wires, and cables from cylinder head. Loosen air pump and take off belt. Disconnect exhaust pipe at manifold.

2) Disconnect hood lock control cable, place out of way. Take off valve cover. Remove cylinder head bolts; only loosen bolt next to distributor $\frac{1}{2}$ turn. Tap head until free. Remove bolt and head.

Installation — To install cylinder head, reverse removal procedure and note: Make sure new head gasket is installed with "HAUT-TOP" facing up.

VALVES

VALVE ARRANGEMENT

E-I-I-E-E-I-I-E

VALVE GUIDE SERVICING

1) Measure O.D. of worn guide and replace with nearest oversize. Standard valve guide O.D. is .433" (11 mm). First oversize is .437" (11.10 mm) and is identified by 1 groove mark. Second oversize is .443" (11.25 mm) and is identified by 2 groove marks.

2) Ream valve guide hole in head to accept new guide. Size of reamer must be equal to outside diameter of new valve guide. To install new guide, lightly lubricate with oil. Fit guide to press with chamfer facing out. Seat guide completely in head. Finish ream valve guide bore to accept valve.

VALVE SPRINGS

Removal, Cylinder Head Installed — Remove valve cover. Remove spark plug of cylinder requiring work. Loosen rocker arm as far as possible and remove push rod. Fit valve retaining tool in spark plug hole. Compress valve spring. Remove keepers, top cup, spring, and base washer. Check spring at free length and under a load.

Installation — Reverse removal procedure and note: Make sure valve spring is installed with closest coil spacing toward cylinder head.

LE CAR 4 CYLINDER (Cont.)

ROCKER SHAFT

After cleaning rocker shaft components, remove clips and take off springs, rocker arms, and support bearings. End plugs are press fit and cannot be removed. For correct reassembly sequence refer to *Fig. 2.*

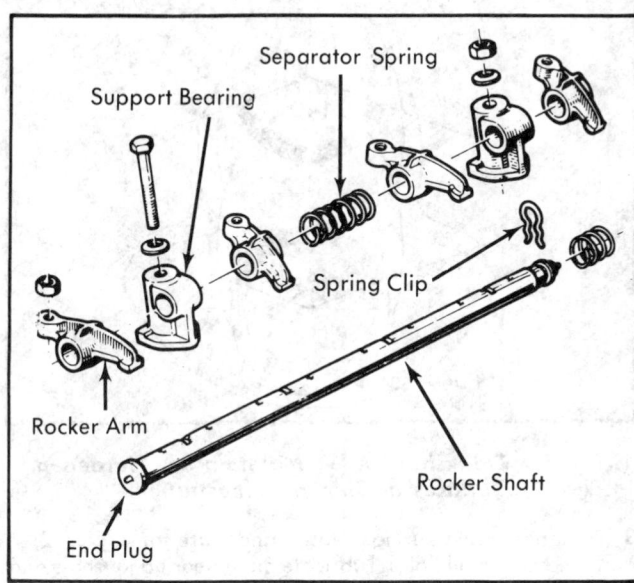

Fig. 2   Exploded View of Rocker Arm & Shaft Assembly

VALVE CLEARANCE

Set intake valve clearance to .006" (.15 mm) cold or .007" (.18 mm) hot. Set exhaust valve clearance to .008" (.20 mm) cold or .010" (.25 mm) hot. Hot refers to an engine that has been operated at normal engine temperature and allowed to cool for 50 minutes.

Valve Adjusting Sequence	
Valve Open	**Valve to Adjust**
No. 1 Exhaust..................	No. 3 Int. & No. 4 Exh.
No. 3 Exhaust..................	No. 4 Int. & No. 2 Exh.
No. 4 Exhaust..................	No. 2 Int. & No. 1 Exh.
No. 2 Exhaust..................	No. 1 Int. & No. 3 Exh.

PISTONS, PINS & RINGS

OIL PAN

Removal — 1) Drain oil. Remove sway bar "U" brackets and pull bar down. Remove lower transaxle metal cover. Remove transaxle bolts that mount through gear shift bracket. Clutch protective cover must be removed.

2) Place a jack under front of transaxle to support it. Remove front pad. Raise transaxle front. Remove mounting bolts and tilt pan toward back of vehicle. Rotate crankshaft to provide clearance. Clean gasket surfaces.

Installation — To install, reverse removal procedure and note: Apply gasket sealer to rubber gaskets. Make sure pan side gaskets overlap bearing gaskets.

CYLINDER LINERS

Removal — 1) Disconnect battery. Drain cooling system and oil pan. Remove air cleaner, cylinder head, oil pan, and oil pump. Fit liner clamp on head.

2) Index connecting rods and bearing caps. Remove connecting rod caps and bearings. Remove liner clamp and liner-piston-rod assembly.

Installation — 1) Check cylinder liner protrusion WITHOUT sealing "O" ring installed on liner base. Install dial indicator (Mot. 251) and measuring block (Mot. 252) as shown in *Fig. 3.* Protrusion must be .001-.004" (.02-.09 mm). If protrusion is incorrect, substitute a new set of liners to determine if defect is in liners or cylinder block.

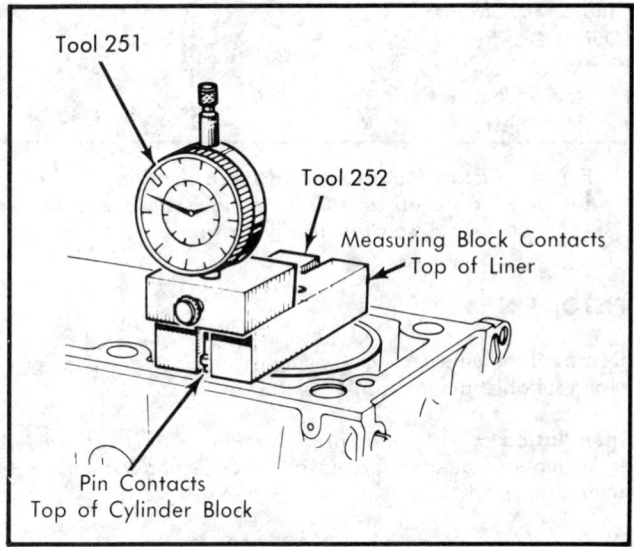

Fig. 3   Checking Cylinder Liner Protrusion

2) Remove liners from cylinder block and install "O" rings on base of liners. Install piston assemblies in liners.

3) Lubricate rod bearings and install liner-piston-connecting rod assemblies into block. Make sure No. 1 is at clutch end. Number on connecting rod bearing end is on opposite side of camshaft. Arrow on piston must face flywheel. Install connecting rod caps. Reverse removal procedure for remaining components.

PISTON & ROD ASSEMBLY

Removal — Remove piston and rod assembly from block with cylinder liners. *See Cylinder Liners.* Remove piston out bottom of liner. Take off rings, piston pin, and connecting rod. *See Piston Pins.*

LE CAR 4 CYLINDER (Cont.)

Installation — Fit piston pin. Fit rings. Piston rings are pregapped. Assemble with "O" mark or "TOP" facing up. Lubricate connecting rod assemblies with oil and fit to liner. Make sure machined side of connecting rod bearing is parallel with flat edge on liner top.

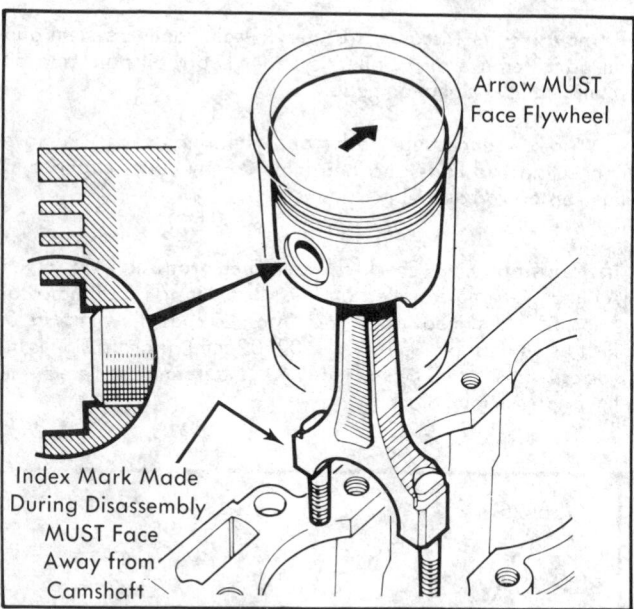

Arrow MUST Face Flywheel

Index Mark Made During Disassembly MUST Face Away from Camshaft

Fig. 4   Piston Mounting and Identification Marks. Reassemble Piston and Connecting Rod Assemblies According to Illustration

PISTON PIN

Removal — Remove piston assembly from liner. Remove rings. Using suitable tool (Mot. 574), extract piston pin.

Installation — 1) Position piston with arrow facing flywheel. Index mark made during removal on connecting rod must face away from camshaft.

2) Heat connecting rod to 482° F (250° C). Slide new piston over installing mandrel and screw in locating plug (part of tool kit Mot. 574). Lightly oil piston pin. Push mandrel, pin guide, and pin assembly through piston by hand, until piston pin makes contact with rod. This procedure will automatically center and correctly space pin.

CRANKSHAFT MAIN & CONNECTING ROD BEARINGS

MAIN BEARING SERVICE

1) Remove cylinder head and oil pan. Invert engine. Remove connecting rod bearing caps. Mark position of main bearing to block. Remove main bearing caps. Remove crankshaft, upper main bearings, and thrust washers.

2) Use a micrometer and measure crankshaft journals. If any main bearing journal is worn beyond 2.147" (54.55 mm) or any connecting rod journal is worn beyond 1.722" (43.73 mm), crankshaft must be reground and fitted with new bearings.

NOTE — *Connecting rod journals are roll hardened. Make sure roll hardening remains intact over a 140° section facing rotational centerline of crankshaft.*

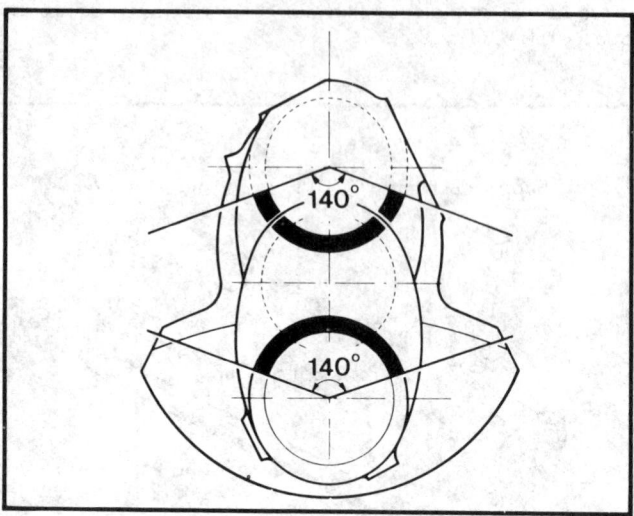

Fig. 5   Crankshaft MUST Maintain Roll Hardened Surfaces as Shown in Illustration

3) Fit upper main bearings. Nos. 1 and 3 are same. Nos. 2, 4, and 5 have two oil holes. Lubricate main bearing journals and fit crankshaft into position. Fit thrust washers, white metal toward crankshaft. Fit bearing to main bearing caps (those with no oil holes). Fit caps being sure to align with previously made reference marks.

4) Fit upper connecting rod bearings and slide over crankshaft. Fit lower half of bearing in cap, then tighten cap. Make sure crankshaft is free to turn.

5) Use a dial indicator and check crankshaft end play. Crankshaft should not have more than .002-.009" (.05-.23 mm) end play. Replace thrust washers if end play is beyond specification.

REAR MAIN BEARING OIL SEAL

With New Crankshaft — Fit new seal to tool Mot. 259-01 (or equivalent). Lubricate outer seal lip. Install seal in original position, seating it until tool lip just contacts cylinder block.

With Original Crankshaft — Offset new seal approximately ⅛" (3 mm) to position seal so it does not rest in same place original seal did. Drive seal into place with tool Mot 259-01 (or equivalent). Seal is seated when tool edge just touches block. Remove tool, insert ⅛" thick spacer, and repeat seating process. This will correctly seat seal into position.

CAMSHAFT

TIMING CHAIN

Removal — With engine removed and suitably supported, remove timing cover. Wire tensioner shoe away from chain. *See Fig. 7.* Remove camshaft sprocket lock bolt. Use a puller to remove camshaft sprocket with timing chain. Chain will come off without disturbing crankshaft sprocket.

LE CAR 4 CYLINDER (Cont.)

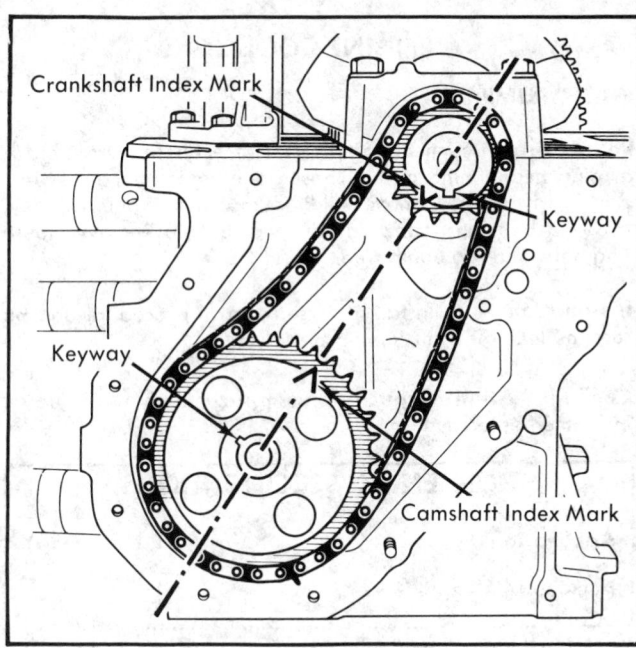

Fig. 6   Index Mark and Keyway Positions for Timing Chain Installation (Engine Inverted)

Installation — 1) Position chain on camshaft sprocket. Align camshaft reference mark with one on crankshaft. Note position of of camshaft and crankshaft keyway shown in *Fig. 6.* Using a small Allen wrench, activate tensioner mechanism.

2) Refit chain tensioner with thrust plate. Tighten mounting bolts and release load on automatic wear compensator tensioner. Release load by pressing down on bottom of tensioner body. Install new timing chain tensioner.

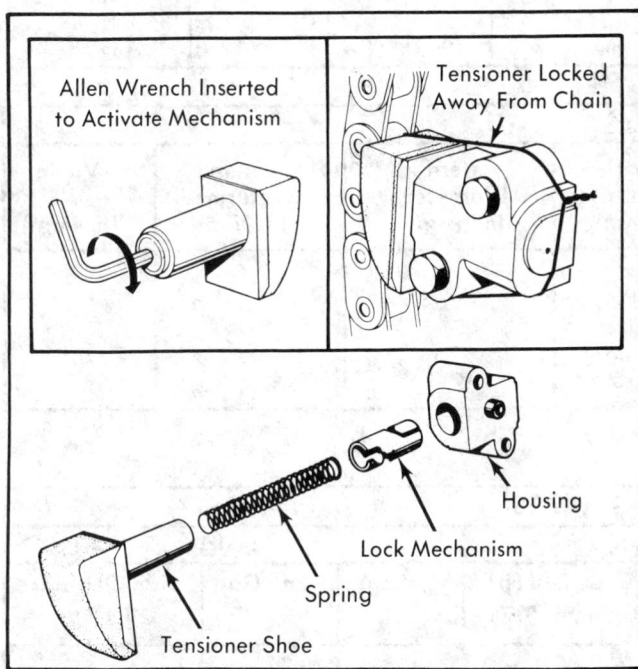

Fig. 7   Views of Timing Chain Tensioner

CAMSHAFT

Removal — Remove engine and suitably support on stand. Remove cylinder head, distributor drive gear, oil pan, timing chain cover, and timing chain. Work through access slots in camshaft sprocket and remove two flange bolts. Carefully slide camshaft from engine.

Installation — Check clearance between camshaft sprocket and flange. Clearance must not exceed .002-.005" (.05-.12 mm). Lubricate camshaft journals and lobes, then refit camshaft. Install flange and tighten. Refit sprocket and tighten mounting bolt. Make sure all camshaft and crankshaft alignment marks are matched. See *Fig. 6.* Reverse removal procedure for remaining components.

CAMSHAFT OIL SEAL

NOTE — *Camshaft oil seal can be changed without removing engine.*

Removal — Remove air cleaner, air pump, pump support, and drive belt. Remove serrated pulley from camshaft. Insert tool Mot. 500-01 (or equivalent) until lip of oil seal slips over shoulder of tool. Push tool sleeve in. Tighten tool bolt clockwise until seal is removed.

Installation — Slip sleeve of tool over end of camshaft to spread lip of seal. Lubricate seal and slide over sleeve. Using oil seal inserting tool (part of tool Mot. 500-01), press seal inward until it just touches block. Remove sleeve. Screw threaded rod into camshaft with nut and washer at rod end. Tighten nut until tool just meets clutch housing. Replace remaining components in reverse of removal procedure.

ENGINE OILING

Crankcase Capacity — 3.4 quarts with filter change.

Oil Filter — Disposable canister type.

Normal Oil Pressure — 10 psi (.7 kg/cm^2) at idle speed. 50 psi (3.5 kg/cm^2) at 4000 RPM.

OIL PUMP

Removal — Drain oil. Remove oil pan. Take out three bolts mounting oil pump and remove pump.

Disassembly — Remove four pump cover bolts. Remove cover slowly; relief valve is under spring tension. Remove driven gear, drive gear, and drive gear shaft.

Inspection — Examine splines on drive shaft. Check ball seat for damage. Check pressure relief spring for fatigue. Check clearance between gears and body. Replace gears if clearance exceeds .008" (.2 mm).

Reassembly — Reverse disassembly procedure.

Installation — Install pump, do not use gasket between oil pump and block. Tighten mounting bolts.

Renault Engines

LE CAR 4 CYLINDER (Cont.)

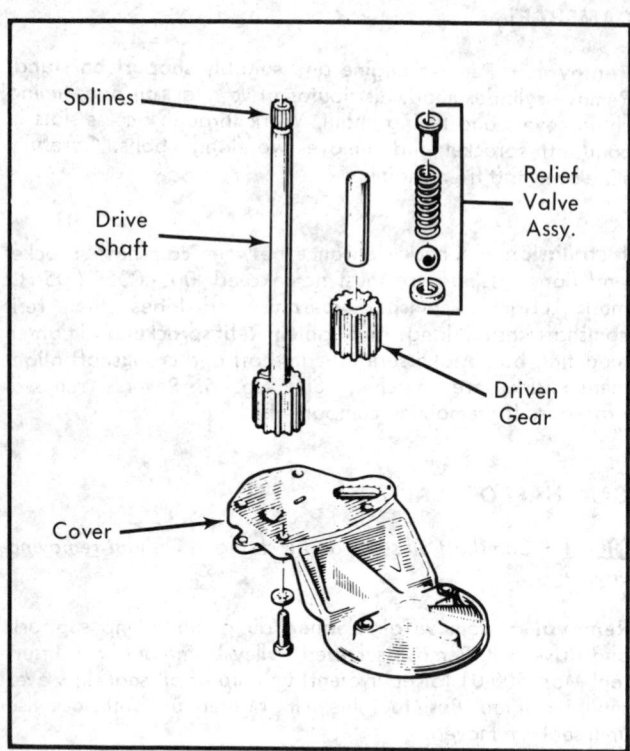

Fig. 8 Exploded View of Oil Pump Assembly

(Labels: Splines, Drive Shaft, Cover, Relief Valve Assy., Driven Gear)

ENGINE COOLING

WATER PUMP

Removal — Disconnect battery. Disconnect hoses. Drain block at plug near timing cover. Loosen alternator. Remove water pump drive belt. Remove A.I.R. pump, water pump pulley, grooved belt, and temperature sending unit. Remove mounting bolts and tap pump free.

Installation — To install, reverse removal procedure and be sure to bleed air from cooling system.

Cooling System Capacity — Approximately 6.5 quarts, including heater.

TIGHTENING SPECIFICATIONS

Application	Ft. Lbs. (mkg)
Cylinder Head Bolts	
Cold	40 (5.5)
Hot (After cooling 50 minutes)	45 (6.2)
Connecting Rods	35 (4.8)
Main Bearings	40-50 (5.5-6.9)
Manifolds	10 (1.4)
Rocker Arm Shaft	10-15 (1.4-2.1)
Timing Sprocket-to-Camshaft	20 (2.8)

ENGINE SPECIFICATIONS

GENERAL SPECIFICATIONS

Year	Displ. cu. ins.	Displ. cc	Carburetor	HP at RPM	Torque (Ft. Lbs. at RPM)	Compr. Ratio	Bore in.	Bore mm	Stroke in.	Stroke mm
1980	85.4	1397	1x2-Bbl.	.....	.....	8.8:1	2.99	76	3.03	77

VALVES

Engine & Valve	Head Diam. In. (mm)	Face Angle	Seat Angle	Seat Width In. (mm)	Stem Diameter In. (mm)	Stem Clearance In. (mm)	Valve Lift In. (mm)
1397 cc							
Int.	1.346 (34.2)	60°	60°	.043-.055 (1.1-1.4)	.276 (7)	.....	.....
Exh.	1.141 (29.0)	45°	45°	.055-.067 (1.4-1.7)	.276 (7)	.....	.....

PISTONS, PINS, RINGS

Engine	PISTONS Clearance In. (mm)	PINS Piston Fit In. (mm)	PINS Rod Fit In. (mm)	RINGS Rings	RINGS End Gap In. (mm)	RINGS Side Clearance In. (mm)
1397 cc	.....	Free Fit	Press Fit	.....	①	.....

① — Pre-set gap; do not alter.

LE CAR 4 CYLINDER (Cont.)

ENGINE SPECIFICATIONS (Cont.)

CRANKSHAFT MAIN & CONNECTING ROD BEARINGS							
	MAIN BEARINGS				CONNECTING ROD BEARINGS		
Engine	Journal Diam. In. (mm)	Clearance In. (mm)	Thrust Bearing	Crankshaft End Play In. (mm)	Journal Diam. In. (mm)	Clearance In. (mm)	Side Play In. (mm)
1397 cc	2.157 (54.80)	.....	No. 3	.002-.009 (.05-.23)	1.731 (43.97)	.....	.012-.022 (.30-.56)

CAMSHAFT			
Engine	Journal Diam. In. (mm)	Clearance In. (mm)	Lobe Lift In. (mm)
1397 cc	.....	①	.....

① — End play .002-.005" (.05-.12 mm).

VALVE TIMING				
	INTAKE		EXHAUST	
Engine	Open (BTDC)	Close (ABDC)	Open (BBDC)	Close (ATDC)
1397 cc	22°	62°	65°	25°

VALVE SPRINGS			
Engine	Free Length In. (mm)	PRESSURE Lbs. @ In. (kg @ mm)	
		Valve Closed	Valve Open
1397 cc	1.65 (42)	.....	80@1.0 (36@25)

99 & 900 4 CYLINDER

ENGINE CODING

ENGINE IDENTIFICATION

Engine number is stamped on block and is located near the summer setting on air cleaner.

Engine Identification	
Application	**Code**
99	BI 20 P04
900	
Man. Trans.	BI 20 P11
Auto. Trans.	BI 20 P12
Turbo	BSI 20 P02

ENGINE & CYLINDER HEAD

ENGINE

NOTE — *Engine and transaxle assembly are removed as a unit. Transaxle housing is engine lower crankcase (pan).*

Removal — 1) Remove hood and drain cooling system. Disconnect and remove battery. Disconnect ground strap between engine and chassis and disconnect positive cable from starter motor. Disconnect servo vacuum hose at manifold and remove bellows between air flow sensor and intake manifold.

2) Clean area around fuel distributor lines and detach at connectors. Cover openings and plug fuel line ends. Remove air cleaner assembly along with mixture control unit. Disconnect EGR system (if equipped). Disconnect upper and lower radiator hoses and heater hoses.

3) Disconnect the following: Ignition coil, temperature sender, cooling fan, thermostat contact, oil pressure sender, fuel injection warm-up regulator, auxiliary air valve, and throttle control wire. On model 99, disconnect headlights and remove grille. Remove retaining screws and take out entire front sheet consisting of headlights, radiator, cooling fan and supports.

4) On manual transmission models, disconnect clutch line from slave cylinder. Cap hose and slave cylinder opening, put gear lever in neutral, and drive front taper pin from shift rod joint. Separate joint from gear shift rod.

5) On automatic transmission models, remove protective cover from exhaust manifold (if equipped), and place gear selector in "P" position. Remove selector cable retaining screw, push back spring loaded sleeve on shift rod, and disconnect cable.

6) On all models, disconnect exhaust pipe at manifold. Loosen clamps and remove bellows from inner universal joints at transaxle. On model 900, place spacer tool (83 93 209) between upper control arm and body so front suspension will be unloaded when car is raised.

7) On all models, raise and support vehicle, then remove lower end piece from right side control arm. Remove rear engine mounting bolts and loosen front engine mounting nut so mount can be lifted from bracket. Turn steering wheel to left and raise engine slightly with hoisting sling.

8) Move engine to right and remove left universal joint, then move engine to left and withdraw right universal joint. Ensure that all cables and lines are free from engine and remove entire power unit from vehicle.

Installation — Ensure that universal joints are packed with grease. Lower engine assembly with flywheel end slightly low and assemble right side universal joint. Lower assembly to within 1" (20-30 mm) above engine mounts and insert left side universal joint. To complete installation, reverse removal procedure.

CYLINDER HEAD

Removal — 1) Disconnect battery leads and drain cooling system. Remove bellows between air flow meter and throttle valve housing. Disconnect throttle cable. Disconnect temperature sender wire and detach vacuum hose to servo cylinder from manifold. Disconnect and plug all fuel lines to injection valves.

2) Disconnect all coolant hoses from head and manifold. Disconnect exhaust pipe from manifold. Remove distributor cap and wires. Remove valve cover and bolt the mounting plate to center of camshaft sprocket using one of the retaining screws.

NOTE — *Tighten screw securely so chain and sprocket cannot shift to new position.*

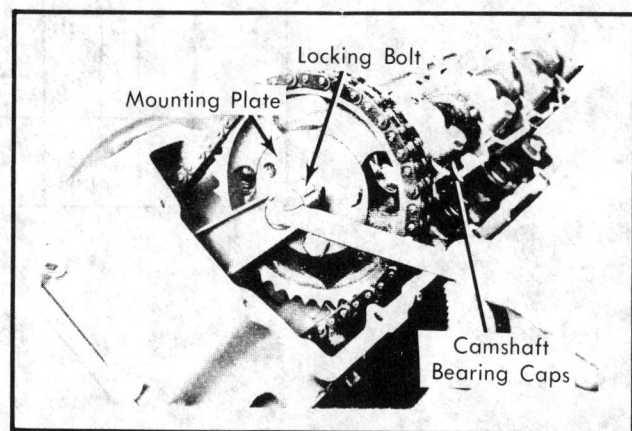

Fig. 1 Locking Camshaft Sprocket and Chain to Mounting Plate

3) Remove remaining screws from camshaft sprocket and separate sprocket from camshaft. Remove cylinder head bolts and insert 2 guide studs in 2 of the head bolt holes. Remove screws at transmission cover and lift off cylinder head.

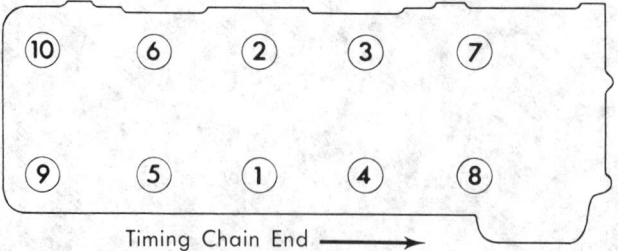

Fig. 2 Cylinder Head Tightening Sequence (Loosen in Reverse Order)

Saab Engines

99 & 900 4 CYLINDER (Cont.)

Installation — To install reverse removal procedures and note the following: Make sure camshaft and bearing cap index marks are aligned. Align flywheel mark with mark on cylinder block. Set ignition with No. 1 piston at TDC. Retorque head bolts after engine has run and allowed to cool.

CAMSHAFT

CAMSHAFT

Removal — Remove cylinder head cover and lock camshaft as previously described. Separate sprocket from camshaft. Remove camshaft bearing caps and lift out camshaft.

Installation — Install camshaft and bearing assembly so that feeler gauge openings are at top. Ensure that crankshaft is still at TDC for No. 1 cylinder and reverse removal procedure.

Fig. 3   Camshaft Timing Marks

VALVE TIMING & CHAIN REPLACEMENT

Removal — Remove chain and sprocket from camshaft as previously described. Remove drive belt pulley and timing chain cover. Remove, but do not disassemble, chain tensioner. Remove chain guides, mounting plate with sprocket and timing chain.

Installation — 1) Ensure that camshaft and crankshaft are still at firing position for No. 1 cylinder. Idler shaft mounting plate hole and bulge in hole of sprocket web must be aligned. Lower timing chain and mounting plate past camshaft flange until center stud of sprocket is lined up with camshaft.

2) Rotate camshaft sprocket until screw holes match threaded holes in camshaft flange. Fit chain over other sprockets so that it hangs straight from camshaft sprocket to crankshaft. Guide center stud of camshaft sprocket into camshaft and fit attaching screws.

3) Mount chain guide and mounting plate with 2 screws so that chain is slightly stretched. Install chain tensioner. Rotate crankshaft one complete turn in normal direction and check that there is at least .020" (.5 mm) but not more than .060" (1.5 mm) between housing and tensioner neck.

4) Remove screw from center of camshaft sprocket and install remaining components in reverse order of removal.

CHAIN TENSIONER MECHANISM

If chain tensioner mechanism has been dismantled or came apart, assemble as follows before fitting to engine:

- Place lock washer with ratchet sleeve into tensioner housing, large diameter end first.
- Fit spring against ratchet sleeve.
- Push neck of tensioner and spring into housing, simultaneously pressing and turning tensioner neck until seated.

NOTE — Tensioner neck must be kept depressed while tensioner mechanism is being fitted.

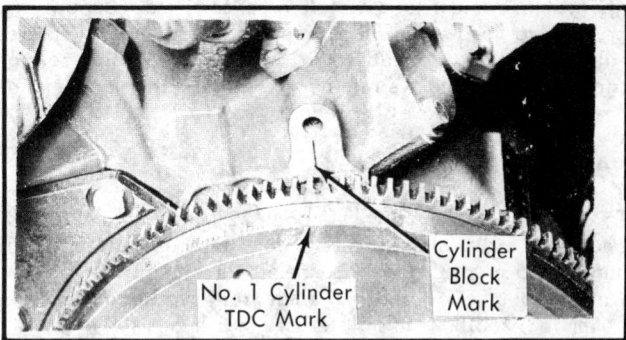

Fig. 4   Flywheel and Cylinder Block Markings

IDLER SHAFT

Removal — Ensure that crankshaft is at firing position for No. 1 cylinder. Counterhold idler shaft sprocket and remove retaining bolt. Remove sprocket and take out distributor. Unscrew idler shaft keeper plate and carefully withdraw idler shaft.

Fig. 5   Idler Shaft Index Marks. Bow in Cutout on Idler Shaft Sprocket Must Line Up with Small Hole in Mounting Plate.

Installation — Ensure that engine is at TDC for No. 1 and install idler shaft and lock plate. Bulge in hole of idler shaft sprocket must line up with small hole in lock plate. Install and adjust timing chain as previously described.

99 & 900 4 CYLINDER (Cont.)

VALVES

VALVE ARRANGEMENT

E-I-I-E-E-I-I-E

VALVE SPRINGS

NOTE — *Valve spring replacement is possible without removing cylinder head from engine.*

Removal & Installation — Remove camshaft as previously described. With cylinder head installed, take out spark plug of applicable cylinder and fit air hose connector. Supply air pressure to keep valve from dropping into cylinder. Remove valve depressors and adjusting pallets. Use suitable spring compressor and remove retainers (keepers) with a magnet. To install, reverse removal procedure.

VALVE GUIDE SERVICING

To check for wear, pull valve about .12" (3 mm) from its seat and check radial play at valve head. If play exceeds .020" (.5 mm), replace valve and/or guide. To replace guide, run hot water through head and pull guide from head using suitable puller (8392632). To install, ensure that head is warm as in removal. Use guide tool (8392632) and press new guide in from top.

VALVE CLEARANCE ADJUSTMENT

1) Check clearance with valve cover removed by rotating crankshaft so that cam lobe of valve to be measured points away from valve. Measure clearance with feeler gauge between heel of cam and follower. Clearance should be between .006-.012" (.15-.30 mm) for intake and .014-.020" (.35-.50 mm) for exhaust. Turbo exhaust valve clearance is .016-.020" (.40-.50 mm).

2) If any valve clearance is beyond limits, direct measurement of all valve clearance is required. Use tool (8391450) and a dial indicator to measure actual clearance. Record clearance readings on all valves. Adjust intake clearances if beyond .008-.010" (.20-.25 mm) and exhaust clearances if beyond .016-.018" (.40-.45 mm). Turbo exhaust clearance should be adjusted if beyond .018-.020" (.45-.50 mm).

3) Remove camshaft, followers and adjusting pallets of any valve requiring adjustment. Measure pallet thickness and add noted valve clearance to determine total clearance. Subtract proper valve clearance to find needed pallet thickness. Install new pallets. Install followers and camshaft and recheck valve clearance.

PISTONS, PINS & RINGS

PISTON & ROD ASSEMBLY

Removal — With cylinder head and pan removed, note that rods and rod caps are numbered. Remove carbon or wear ridge from top of cylinders. Remove bearing caps and place plastic sleeves over rod bolts. Push piston/rod assembly out of cylinder.

Installation — Ensure that ring gaps are staggered and fit suitable ring compressor. Notch on piston top must face transmission end. Remove protectors from rod bolts and install bearing and cap.

PISTON PIN REPLACEMENT

Pistons are retained by circlips. Remove circlips and press out piston pins. Check pins and bearings for wear or damage and replace as required.

FITTING PISTONS

1) To fit pistons to cylinder bores, use a feeler gauge .500" (12.7 mm) wide and .0005-.0016" (.014-.040 mm) thick. Oil cylinder lightly and insert piston without rings.

2) Attach feeler gauge to a spring scale. Insert feeler gauge between piston and cylinder wall at right angles to piston pin. When feeler gauge can be pulled out of cylinder with a force of 1.8-2.6 lbs. (.816-1.18 kg), piston clearance has been determined.

3) Repeat test at several different depths in cylinder bore. Graded standard and non-graded oversize pistons are available.

Piston Specifications

Application	Diameter In. (mm)
Std. (AB)	3.5425-3.5427 (89.980-89.986)
Std. (C)	3.5433-3.5437 (89.999-90.010)
1st Oversize	3.5619-3.5625 (90.472-90.487)
2nd Oversize	3.5816-3.5822 (90.972-90.987)

4) Check piston rings for end gap and side clearance, using an inverted piston to position ring in bore. On worn bores, measure at lower end of bore.

5) Install rings on piston, making sure gaps of compression rings are 180° apart with lower compression ring mark "TOP" facing up. On three piece oil ring make sure ends are staggered.

CRANKSHAFT MAIN & CONNECTING ROD BEARINGS

BEARING SERVICE

1) Remove connecting rods and main bearing caps. Measure journals with a micrometer. Out-of-round should not exceed .002" (.051 mm). If crankshaft is near or over stated limit of wear, regrind journals and fit undersize bearings.

2) Using "V" blocks and a dial indicator check crankshaft for bend. If bend exceeds .002" (.051 mm), replace or repair crankshaft.

99 & 900 4 CYLINDER (Cont.)

3) Using Plastigage method, check main bearing and connecting rod bearing journals. If clearance is found excessive, combine suitable undersize bearings to correct clearance. Undersize bearings are available in various thicknesses.

THRUST BEARING ALIGNMENT

Center main bearing is thrust bearing. Check crankshaft endplay. If beyond specifications, replace thrust washers with oil grooves facing crankshaft.

ENGINE OILING

Crankcase Capacity — 4.0 quarts with filter. (4.5 quarts for turbocharged engine.)

Oil Filter — Full-flow type.

Normal Oil Pressure — 43 psi (3.0 kg/cm²) @2000 RPM.

Pressure Regulator Valve — Non-adjustable; opens at 57-71 psi (4.0-5.0 kg/cm²).

ENGINE OILING SYSTEM

Oil pressure is generated by a dual-rotor pump mounted on the outside of the engine and driven by an idler shaft. Oil is forced through a full-flow filter and oil channels to crankshaft main and connecting rod bearings.

OIL PUMP

Removal — 1) Remove 4 screws attaching pump to engine and withdraw pump and "O" ring. Remove 2 screws attaching pump cover to housing. Remove rotors and "O" ring from housing.

2) Pull cotter pin from cover and remove plug, "O" ring, spring and pressure relief valve piston. Using a straightedge and feeler gauge, measure clearance between rotors and housing face. If clearance exceeds .002-.0035" (.05-.09 mm), use fine emery paper to resurface housing or sides of rotors.

Installation — 1) Clean and oil all parts. Install outer rotor with chamfered edge inward facing toward drive shaft. Install valve piston, spring plug, "O" ring and cotter pin in pump cover.

2) Place "O" ring in pump housing groove. Install cover and tighten screws. Rotate pump up until drive shaft engages in engine. Slide pump up against engine and install four attaching bolts.

ENGINE COOLING

Cooling System Capacity — Model 99, 8.5 quarts. Model 900, 10.5 quarts.

Thermostat — Thermostat begins to open at approximately 190°F (88°C).

Radiator Cap — Radiator pressure cap opens at approximately 14.2 psi.

WATER PUMP

Removal — 1) Drain coolant. Disconnect battery. Remove intake manifold. Remove alternator. Remove bolt mounting bracket to pump cover. Unbolt rear engine mounts. Raise rear of engine. Remove bolt mounting alternator bracket to transmission cover. Loosen lower bolt and twist bracket away from engine. Remove last two bolts from cover and remove.

2) Use extractor (8362649) or equivalent and pull pump from engine. Do NOT use slide hammer or similar tool to remove pump from engine. If bearing housing remains in cylinder block, it may be necessary to use slide hammer for removal of bearing.

Installation — To install, reverse removal procedure and note: It may be necessary to use sleeve 8392490 (or equivalent) to seat bearing housing.

TIGHTENING SPECIFICATIONS	
Application	**Ft. Lbs. (mkg)**
Main Bearings	79 (10.9)
Rod Bearings	40 (5.5)
Camshaft Bearing Caps	13 (1.8)
Camshaft Cover	1 (.14)
Crankshaft Pulley	137 (19.00)
Cylinder Head	
Step One	43 (6.0)
Step Two	69 (9.5)
Flywheel	43 (6.0)
Oil Pump	13 (1.8)
Idler Sprocket	18 (2.5)
Camshaft Sprocket	14 (1.9)
Intake Manifold	13 (1.8)
Exhaust Manifold	14 (1.9)

ENGINE SPECIFICATIONS

GENERAL SPECIFICATIONS										
	Displ.		Carburetor	HP at RPM	Torque (Ft. Lbs. at RPM)	Compr. Ratio	Bore		Stroke	
Year	cu. ins.	cc					in.	mm	in.	mm
1980 99 & 900										
Federal	121	1985	Fuel Inj.	115@5500	123@3500	9.25:1	3.54	90	3.07	78
Calif.	121	1985	Fuel Inj.	110@5500	119@3500	8.7:1	3.54	90	3.07	78
Turbo	121	1985	Fuel Inj.	135@5000	160@3500	7.2:1	3.54	90	3.07	78

Saab Engines

99 & 900 4 CYLINDER (Cont.)
ENGINE SPECIFICATIONS (Cont.)

CAMSHAFT

Engine	Journal Diam. In. (mm)	Clearance In. (mm) ①	Lobe Lift In. (mm) ②
1985 cc	1.139 (28.94)	.....	Int. .421 (10.7) Exh. .433 (11.0)

① — End play is .003-.010" (.08-.25 mm).

② — Turbo lobe lift is .358" (9.1 mm) for intake, .413" (10.5 mm) for exhaust.

VALVE TIMING

Engine	INTAKE① Open (BTDC)	INTAKE① Close (ABDC)	EXHAUST② Open (BBDC)	EXHAUST② Close (ATDC)
1985 cc 99 & 900	10°	54°	46°	18°
Turbo	12°	40°	62°	2°

① — With .014" (.35 mm) valve clearance.
② — With .022 (.55 mm) valve clearance.

VALVE SPRINGS

Engine	Free Length In. (mm)	PRESSURE Lbs. @ In. (kg @ mm) Valve Closed	PRESSURE Lbs. @ In. (kg @ mm) Valve Open
1985 cc	1.700 (43.1)	.....	170-183@1.161 (77-83@29.5)

VALVES

Engine & Valve	Head Diam. In. (mm)	Face Angle	Seat Angle	Seat Width In. (mm)	Stem Diameter In. (mm)	Stem Clearance In. (mm)	Valve Lift In. (mm)
1985 cc Int.	1.654 (42.0)	44.5°	45°	.004-.008 (1-2)	.313-.314 (7.950-7.976)	0.02 (0.5)	.....
Exh.	1.398 (35.5)	44.5°	45°	.004-.008 (1-2)	.313-.314 (7.950-7.976)	0.02 (0.5)	.....

PISTONS, PINS, RINGS

Engine	PISTONS Clearance In. (mm)	PINS Piston Fit In. (mm)	PINS Rod Fit In. (mm)	RINGS Rings	RINGS End Gap In. (mm)	RINGS Side Clearance In. (mm)
1985 cc	.0006-.0016 (.014-.040)	.0002-.0006 (.005-.014)	①	No. 1	.014-.021 (.35-.55)	.002-.003 (.050-.082)
				No. 2	.012-.018 (.30-.45)	.0016-.003 (.040-.072)
				Oil	.015-.055 (.38-1.40)	.....

① — Interference fit.

CRANKSHAFT MAIN & CONNECTING ROD BEARINGS

Engine	MAIN BEARINGS Journal Diam. In. (mm)	MAIN BEARINGS Clearance In. (mm)	MAIN BEARINGS Thrust Bearing	MAIN BEARINGS Crankshaft End Play In. (mm)	CONNECTING ROD BEARINGS Journal Diam. In. (mm)	CONNECTING ROD BEARINGS Clearance In. (mm)	CONNECTING ROD BEARINGS Side Play In. (mm)
1985 cc	2.283-2.284 (57.981-58.000)	.001-.002 (.026-.062)	Center	.003-.011 (0.08-0.28)	2.046-2.047 (51.981-52.000)	.001-.002 (.026-.062)	.....

Subaru Engines

1600 & 1800 4 CYLINDER

ENGINE CODING

ENGINE IDENTIFICATION

Engine number is stamped on a machined pad near distributor. See table below for engine codes.

Engine Identification	
Application	**Code**
2-WD	
Federal	
Man. Trans.	E71AA3, E71GA3A
Auto. Trans.	E81TA
Calif.	
Man. Trans.	E71AC3
Auto. Trans	E81TC
4-WD	
Federal	E71WA3, E71WA4
Calif.	E71WC3, E71WC4

ENGINE

ENGINE

NOTE — *It is possible to remove engine with transmission fitted. Removal procedure given is with transmission remaining in vehicle.*

REMOVAL & INSTALLATION

Removal — **1)** Disconnect battery cable. Remove spare wheel from engine compartment. Remove air cleaner assembly.

2) Disconnect fuel line from fuel pump intake, allow fuel to drain into a suitable container. Drain radiator and engine block. Disconnect radiator hoses at engine.

3) Disconnect all wiring to engine and accessories. On 4-WD models remove engine fan from pulley. On Automatic Transmission models disconnect oil cooler pipes.

4) Remove two upper radiator bolts and lift out radiator. Remove nuts on each end of engine-to-firewall strut and remove strut by moving to rear to clear engine hanger.

5) Remove all control cables and vacuum hoses from engine. On automatic transmission models, disconnect torque converter from engine by rotating crankshaft to allow removal of 4 bolts through timing hole. Use care that bolts do not fall into housing. On manual transmission models, remove clutch return spring. Remove nuts from brackets on engine and firewall, and remove engine stabilizer.

6) Remove engine-to-transmission bolts and nuts and disconnect exhaust pipe. Remove bolts securing front engine mounts-to-engine. Slightly hoist engine with chain hoist attached to front to rear hangers and separate engine from transmission.

7) When separating engine from transmission, ensure that torque converter remains with transmission (Automatic Transmission only). Also, it may be helpful to slightly jack up transmission during removal procedure. Remove engine completely and place on engine stand.

Installation — To install, reverse removal procedure and tighten all bolts and nuts. Adjust all controls and fill engine with suitable coolant.

ENGINE DISASSEMBLY & REASSEMBLY

NOTE — *Remove engine, place on engine stand (399814300X2 or equivalent). Remove starter and proceed as follows:*

Disassembly — **1)** Separate engine from transmission if necessary. Ensure that converter remains attached to automatic transmission (if equipped). Drain oil and coolant. Make sure that liquid does not run over clutch cover. On manual transmission models, remove clutch cover and disc.

2) Disconnect ignition wiring from engine. Remove distributor and distributor plate. Remove bolts securing alternator to alternator bracket and remove alternator. Remove EGR pipe and cover. Disconnect wiring harness leads for oil pressure gauge or switch. Remove clamp securing air suction manifold. Remove connecting hoses from valve covers. Unclamp heater hoses. Disconnect 2 water by-pass hoses from intake manifold. Remove intake manifold assembly. Remove alternator brackets and air suction system.

3) Remove oil filter duct. 4WD models have a bracket. Use a puller and remove crankshaft pulley. Remove oil pump and filter as an assembly. Remove water pump with hoses and tubes attached.

4) Turn engine over on stand and remove oil pan, crankcase, gasket and transmission cover (if necessary). Remove oil strainer and brackets. Remove either flywheel or converter drive plate. Take off flywheel housing.

5) Remove spark plugs and valve cover. Remove rocker assembly and push rods. Remove cylinder head bolts in sequence *See Fig. 1*. Remove cylinder head and gasket. Use Allen wrench and remove crankcase plug.

6) Position pistons at bottom dead center and remove circlip with long nosed pliers. Access to No. 1 and No. 2 pins is through front crankcase plug holes. Access to No. 3 and No. 4 pins is through rear service holes. Remove pins and pistons, marking for reassembly.

7) Work through hole in camshaft gear and straighten lockwasher, then remove nut. Remove nuts and washers and separate cases. Use valve lifter clips (899804100 or equivalent), to prevent upper crankcase lifters from falling off.

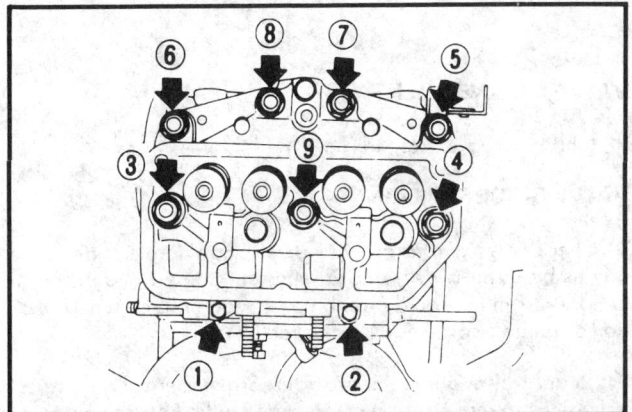

Fig. 1 Cylinder Head Nut Loosening Sequence

Subaru Engines

1600 & 1800 4 CYLINDER (Cont.)

NOTE — *Pull camshaft to rear for crankcase clearance.*

8) Remove oil seal. Lift out crankshaft, distributor gear, and connecting rods. Keep crankshaft bearings in order for reassembly. Remove camshaft and gear. Remove oil pressure switch and valve lifters.

Reassembly — Lubricate all friction surfaces with engine oil prior to reassembly. Install crankshaft and camshaft with bearings in left half (No. 2 & 4 Cyl.) of crankcase. Apply liquid gasket to mating surfaces of crankcase and continue in reverse order of disassembly. Tighten crankcase halves and cylinder heads in sequence shown.

NOTE — *Use spacers (899848600) in place of rocker arm supports when tightening head nuts.*

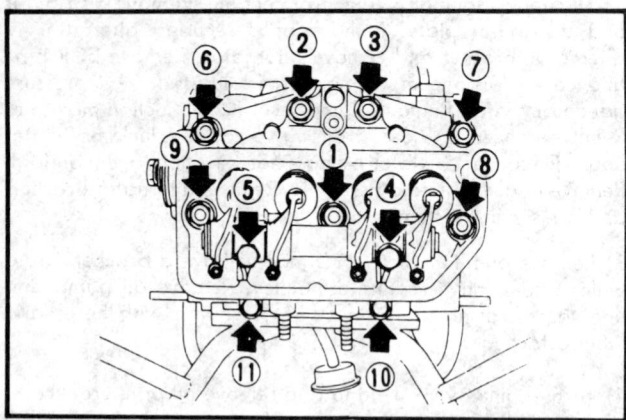

Fig. 2   Cylinder Head Tightening Sequence

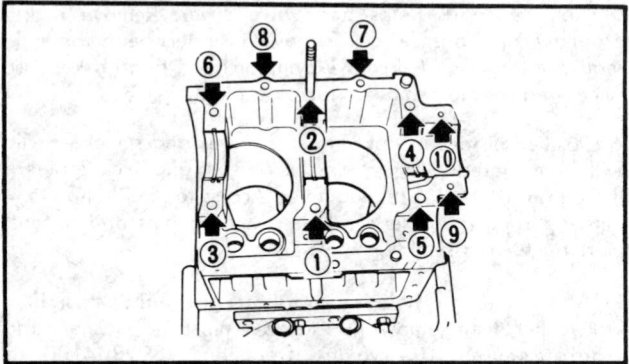

Fig. 3   Tightening Sequence for Crankcase

VALVES

VALVE ARRANGEMENT

I-E-E-I (both banks, front to rear).

VALVE GUIDE SERVICING

1) Check valve guide for wear or damage. Replace defective guides by using a drift and driving out guide through top of head. Press in new guide from top of head until correct projection of guide above head is achieved.

2) Ream valve guide to provide correct clearance. Inspect valve seat to make sure it is true with guide. Reface valve seat if necessary.

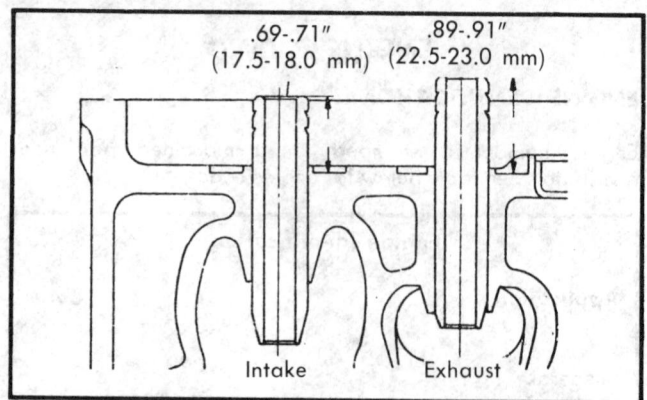

Fig. 4   Correct Projection of Valve Guides

VALVE STEM OIL SEALS

Valve stem oil seals are found only on intake valves. Slide seal off of valve guide and replace with a new seal. Use care when inserting valve stem not to damage seal.

VALVE SPRING

Use a spring compressor, remove "O" ring, valve keepers and spring retainer. Check spring under pressure and at free length. Replace if necessary. Install spring with wide spaced coils (paint mark) facing valve spring retainer.

ROCKER ARM ASSEMBLY

Check rocker shaft, rocker arm and bushing for wear or damage. Replace any worn parts. Press in new bushing and ream until a clearance of .0006-.002" (.016-.052 mm) is achieved between bushing and shaft.

VALVE TAPPET SERVICE

Remove lifters from crankcase. Inspect tappet for wear or clogged oil hole. Replace lifter if lifter-to-crankcase clearance exceeds .004" (.100 mm). Standard lifter clearance is .0012-.0028" (.030-.072 mm).

VALVE CLEARANCE ADJUSTMENT

With engine cold, rotate engine to TDC of firing stroke. Insert feeler gauge between rocker arm and valve stem. Clearances should be as follows:

Valve Clearance		
Application	**Intake** In. (mm)	**Exhaust** In. (mm)
1600 cc & 1800 cc	.009-.011 (.23-.27)	.013-.015 (.33-.37)

PISTONS, PINS & RINGS

FITTING PISTONS

1) Measure piston bore .028" (7 mm) from top of cylinder in line with crankshaft and again 90° from centerline of crankshaft. Make same measurements 1.48" (37 mm), and then 2.64" (67 mm) from top of cylinder bore. If cylinder inner diameter exceeds .0197" (0.5 mm) after boring and honing, replace crankcase.

1600 & 1800 4 CYLINDER (Cont.)

2) Measure piston 1.04" (26.3 mm) from bottom of skirt, 90° from piston pin hole.

NOTE – *Measurement of both pistons and cylinder bores should be performed at 68°F (20°C).*

3) Check piston ring end gap and side clearance. Check gap at bottom of cylinder bore. Fit piston rings with "R" or "N" facing up.

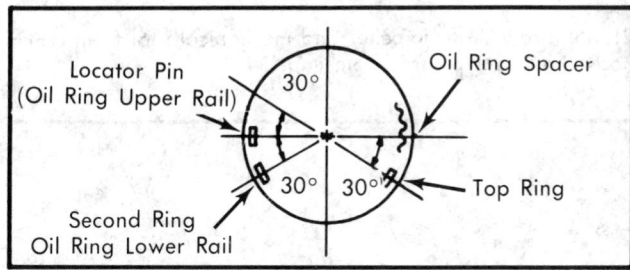

Fig. 5 Piston Ring Gap Position

PISTON PIN

Check piston pin for damage, cracks, wear or distortion. Check connecting rod bushing for wear. If pin or bushing are worn beyond specification, replace bushing in connecting rod and ream to fit standard pin. Piston pin is a thumb push fit at 68°F.

CRANKSHAFT MAIN & CONNECTING ROD BEARINGS

MAIN & CONNECTING ROD BEARINGS

1) Check connecting rod side play with a feeler gauge. If side play exceeds specifications, replace connecting rod.

2) Use Plastigage method to measure both main and connecting rod bearing clearances. Main bearing inserts are available in standard, .001" (.03 mm), .002" (.05 mm) and .010" (.25 mm) undersize. Connecting rod bearing inserts are available in standard, .002" (.05 mm) and .010" (.25 mm) undersize.

3) Check crankshaft for bend by placing front and rear main journals on "V" blocks and fitting a dial indicator on center journal. Correct or replace crankshaft if bend exceeds .0014" (.035 mm).

REAR MAIN BEARING OIL SEAL SERVICE

Seal is replaced when crankcase halves are split. After crankcase halves have been reassembled, install new seal.

CAMSHAFT

ENGINE FRONT COVER OIL SEAL

With front cover removed, drive out old seal. Install new seal using installer tool (49067000), with or without front cover on engine.

CAMSHAFT

1) Camshaft may be removed when crankcase has been split. Check for wear or damage, replace camshaft if necessary. Using a dial indicator, check that bend does not exceed .002" (.051 mm).

2) Measure thrust clearance between camshaft and camshaft plate. Standard clearance is .0008–.0035" (.02–.09 mm). If clearance exceeds limit of .008" (.20 mm), replace camshaft plate. Measure camshaft lobe height. If less than 1.276" (32.42 mm) overall, replace camshaft.

NOTE – *If camshaft is replaced, all valve lifters should also be replaced. Check identification marks. 1600 cc engine uses camshaft marked "51", while 1800 cc engine uses camshaft "72".*

3) Measure camshaft gear runout with dial indicator. Replace camshaft if runout exceeds .010" (.25 mm). Measure backlash between camshaft gear and crankshaft gear. If backlash exceeds .0039" (.10 mm), replace camshaft gear. Standard value of backlash is .0004–.0020" (.01–.05 mm).

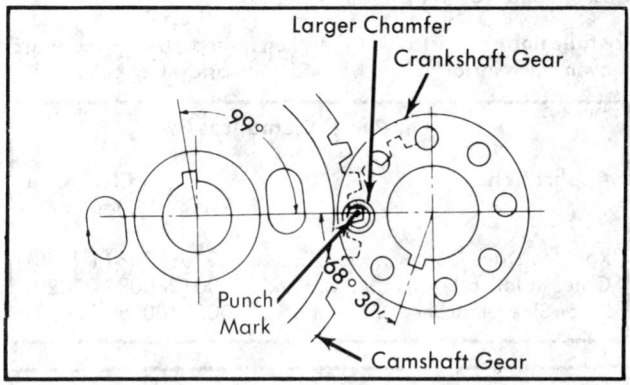

Fig. 6 Align Camshaft with Crankshaft as Shown

VALVE TIMING

With crankcase halves split, install crankshaft and camshaft so punch mark on camshaft gear is visible through chamfered hole in crankshaft gear.

ENGINE OILING

Crankcase Capacity – 1600 cc engine: 3.7 quarts. 1800 cc engine: 4.2 quarts.

Oil Filter – Full-flow.

Normal Oil Pressure – 1600 cc engine: 35 psi (2.5 kg/cm²) @ 500 RPM, 57 psi (4.0 kg/cm²) @ 2500 RPM. 1800 cc engine: 50 psi (3.5 kg/cm²) @ 500 RPM, 57 psi (4.0 kg/cm²) @ 2500 RPM.

Pressure Regulator Valve – Non-adjustable, opens at 57–64 psi (4.0–4.5 kg/cm²).

ENGINE OILING SYSTEM

Oil is pressure fed by a camshaft driven trochoid type oil pump. Pump incorporates an oil relief and by-pass valve in its body. Oil pump is located externally on engine. Oil from pump passes from main oil gallery to journals of camshaft and crankshaft. From there, oil goes to main bearings, pistons pin bearings and cylinder walls. Oil passes through valve lifters and push rods to oil rocker arms.

OIL PUMP

Removal – Remove four attaching bolts and pull pump and filter forward. Remove oil filter from pump.

Subaru Engines

1600 & 1800 4 CYLINDER (Cont.)

Disassembly — 1) Remove screws, lift cover and rotor from pump body. Remove "O" ring. Remove by-pass spring and ball. Unscrew plug and remove washers, spring and pressure relief valve.

2) Measure rotor-to-drive gear and rotor-to-body clearance. Measure rotor side clearance and measure diameters of rotor and drive gear. Replace any component that exceeds wear limits.

3) Inspect relief valve spring, valve and pump body for wear or damage.

NOTE — *Make sure oil pump shaft is aligned with slot in camshaft when reassembling.*

Reassembly — Reassemble in reverse order, using all new gaskets and "O" rings.

Installation — Install oil filter on pump. Using rearward movement reinstall oil pump and four attaching bolts.

Oil Pump Clearances

Application	Clearance In. (mm)
Rotor-to-Drive Gear	.0008-.008 (.02-.20)
Outer Rotor-to-Body	.0012-.008 (.03-.20)
Rotor Side Clearance	.0059-.0098 (.15-.25)

Oil Pump Dimensions

Application	Dimension In. (mm)
Drive Gear O.D.	1.1693-1.1709 (29.70-29.74)
Rotor O.D.	1.5957-1.5968 (40.53-40.56)
Relief Valve Spring Free Length	1.851 (47.10)

ENGINE COOLING

THERMOSTAT

Thermostat — On Federal Sedan, Hatchback and Hardtop models with automatic transmission, thermostat begins to open at 182-188°F (83.5-86.5°C) and fully opens at 208°F (98°C). On all other models, thermostat begins to open at 188-193°F (86.5-89.5°C) and fully opens at 212°F (100°C).

Coolant Capacity — 5.6-5.8 quarts.

WATER PUMP

Removal — Drain coolant and disconnect main radiator outlet hose. Remove drive belt and attaching bolts, remove water pump.

Disassembly — 1) Remove four screws attaching cover plate and gasket. Remove pulley and locking clip.

2) Withdraw shaft, impeller and mechanical seal from pump body. Press pump shaft from impeller.

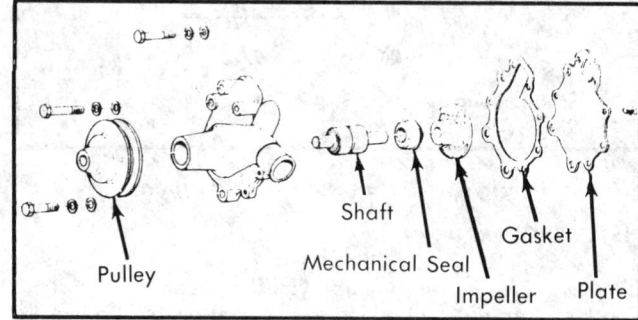

Pulley • Shaft • Mechanical Seal • Impeller • Gasket • Plate

Fig. 7   Exploded View of Water Pump

Reassembly — 1) Using an arbor press, press pump shaft into pump body until locking clip may be installed. Apply sealing compound to edge of mechanical seal and in housing with carbon ring facing toward impeller.

2) Press impeller onto shaft until impeller-to-body clearance is .020-.028" (0.5-0.7 mm). Press on bearing outer race, not shaft. Support impeller side of pump shaft and press on pulley until distance between center of pulley groove and rear face of pump housing is 2.406-2.429" (61.1-61.7 mm) for 1800 cc engine or 2.524-2.547" (64.1-64.7 mm) for 1600 cc engine.

Installation — Install water pump together with slotted clip, water pipe, and water by-pass pipe as a unit. Gradually tighten bolts alternately and evenly in several steps to prevent leakage. The clamps for the water hose should be positioned low to prevent interference with the EGR pipe.

ELECTRIC COOLING FAN

All models are equipped with an electric cooling fan motor. 4-WD models use a combination of electric fan, engine drive fan and forced cooling (water cooling). All other models utilize electric fan and forced cooling (water cooling).

ENGINE SPECIFICATIONS

GENERAL SPECIFICATIONS

Year	Displ.		Carburetor	HP at RPM	Torque (Ft. Lbs. at RPM)	Compr. Ratio	Bore		Stroke	
	cu. ins.	cc					in.	mm	in.	mm
1980										
1600 cc	97	1595	2-Bbl.	67@5200	81@2400	8.5:1①	3.62	92	2.36	60
1800 cc	109	1781	2-Bbl.	71@4400	94@2400	8.7:1	3.62	92	2.64	67

① — Federal Hatchback, Sedan DL, and Hardtop DL models 9.0:1.

1600 & 1800 4 CYLINDER (Cont.)

ENGINE SPECIFICATIONS (Cont.)

VALVES							
Engine & Valve	Head Diam. In. (mm)	Face Angle	Seat Angle	Seat Width In. (mm)	Stem Diameter In. (mm)	Stem Clearance In. (mm)	Valve Lift In. (mm)
1600 cc & 1800 cc Int.	.....	45°	45°	.028-.051 (.7-1.3)	.3130-.3136 (7.950-7.965)	.0014-.0026 (.035-.065)	.....
Exh.	.....	45°	45°	.039-.071 (1.0-1.8)	.3128-.3134 (7.945-7.960)	.0016-.0028 (.040-.070)	.....

PISTONS, PINS, RINGS						
	PISTONS	PINS		RINGS		
Engine	Clearance In. (mm)	Piston Fit In. (mm)	Rod Fit In. (mm)	Rings	End Gap In. (mm)	Side Clearance In. (mm)
1600 cc & 1800 cc	.0004-.0016 (.010-.040)	.00004-.00067 (.001-.017)	.0002-.0016 (.005-.040)	No. 1	.0079-.0138① (.20-.35)	.0016-.0031③ (.04-.08)
				No. 2	.0079-.0138① (.20-.35)	.0012-.0028③ (.03-.07)
				No. 3	.0079-.0354② (.20-.90)	.....

① — Limit .0591" (1.5 mm).
② — Limit .07987" (2.0 mm).
③ — Limit .0059" (.15 mm).

CRANKSHAFT MAIN & CONNECTING ROD BEARINGS							
	MAIN BEARINGS				CONNECTING ROD BEARINGS		
Engine	Journal Diam. In (mm)	Clearance① In. (mm)	Thrust Bearing	Crankshaft End Play② In. (mm)	Journal Diam. In. (mm)	Clearance③ In. (mm)	Side Play④ In. (mm)
1600 cc Front & Rear	1.9668-1.9673 (49.957-49.970)	.0004-.0014 (.010-.035)	Center	.0016-.0054 (.040-.137)	1.7715-1.7720 (44.995-45.010)	.0008-.0028 (.020-.070)	.0028-.013 (.07-.33)
Center	1.9673-1.9678 (49.970-49.982)	.0004-.0012 (.010-.030)					
1800 cc Front & Rear	2.1636-2.1642 (54.995-54.970)	.0004-.0012 (.010-.030)	Center	.0016-.0054 (.040-.137)	1.7715-1.7720 (44.995-45.010)	.0008-.0028 (.020-.070)	.0028-.013 (.07-.33)
Center	2.1636-2.1642 (54.995-54.970)	.0004-.0010 (.010-.025)					

① — Limit front and rear .0022" (.055 mm);
   Limit center .0018" (.045 mm).
② — Limit .0118" (.30 mm).
③ — Limit .0039" (.10 mm).
④ — Limit .016" (.40 mm).

Subaru Engines

1600 & 1800 4 CYLINDER (Cont.)
ENGINE SPECIFICATIONS (Cont.)

CAMSHAFT			
Engine	Journal Diam. In. (mm)	Clearance In. (mm)①	Lobe Lift In. (mm)
1600 cc Front & Center	1.0236-1.0243 (26.00-26.018)	.0010-.0023 (.025-.059)	.2262 (5.745)
1800 cc Front & Center	1.2598-1.2605 (32.000-32.018)	.0010-.0023 (.025-.059)	.2262 (5.745)
1600 cc & 1800 cc Rear	1.4173-1.4180 (36.000-36.018)	.0010-.0023 (.025-.059)	.2262 (5.745)

① — Limit — .0039" (.1 mm).

VALVE SPRINGS			
Engine	Free Length In. (mm)	PRESSURE Lbs. @ In. (kg @ mm)	
		Valve Closed	Valve Open
1600 cc & 1800 cc Inner	1.921 (48.8)	19.0-22.1@1.476 (8.6-10.0@37.5)	41.7-48.3@1.122 (18.9-21.9@28.5)
1600 cc & 1800 cc Outer	1.783 (45.3)	32.9-38.1@1.555 (14.9-17.3@39.5)	112.5-127.9@1.201 (51.0-58.0@30.5)

TIGHTENING SPECIFICATIONS

Application	Ft. Lbs. (mkg)
Cylinder Head	
Step 1	22 (3.0)
Step 2	43 (6.0)
Step 3	47 (6.5)
Connecting Rod Nuts	29-31 (4.0-4.3)
Crankshaft Pulley	39-42 (5.4-5.8)
Flywheel Housing	14-20 (2.0-2.8)
Crankcase Plug	46-56 (6.3-7.7)
Crankcase Halves 10 mm Bolts	29-35 (4.0-4.8)
8 mm Bolts	17-20 (2.3-2.7)
6 mm Bolts	3.3-4 (.45-.55)
Intake Manifold	13-16 (1.8-2.2)
Rocker Arm Cover	2.2-2.9 (.30-.40)
Flywheel	30-33 (.42-4.6)
Rocker Arm	47 (6.5)
Oil Pan	3.3-4.0 (.45-.55)

1A-C 4-CYLINDER

ENGINE CODING

ENGINE IDENTIFICATION

Engine serial number and code are stamped on left side of block.

Engine Identification	
Application	**Code**
Tercel (1452 cc)	1A-C

ENGINE, CYLINDER HEAD & MANIFOLDS

ENGINE

Removal — 1) Disconnect negative battery cable. Remove hood, air cleaner and, on models with automatic transmission, grille. Wrap drive shaft boots with shop towels.

2) Drain cooling system and remove hoses and oil cooler lines (if so equipped). Loosen fan shroud and remove radiator. Remove exhaust pipe and bracket, differential plate bolts and oil cooler pipe (if so equipped).

3) Disconnect ignition coil cable and all engine-to-chassis electrical connections at engine. Disconnect carburetor linkage, fuel lines and heater hoses.

4) On models with manual transmission, remove starter cable and windshield washer tank. On models with automatic transmission, remove starter and torque converter cover. On all models, support transmission with a floor jack and remove engine mounts.

5) Attach hoist to engine hangers and, with hoist supporting engine, remove transaxle bolts. On models with manual transmission, remove engine. On models with automatic transmission, remove 4 bolts to torque converter. Pull engine about 2" (50 mm) forward, disconnect torque converter and remove engine. On all models, suspend clutch or converter housing.

Installation — To install, reverse removal procedure, assuring that all adjustments and fluid levels are checked prior to starting engine.

MANIFOLDS

NOTE — *Intake and exhaust manifolds are removed and installed as an assembly.*

Removal — Remove air cleaner. Disconnect fuel and vacuum lines at carburetor. Disconnect choke and throttle linkage at carburetor. Remove heat insulator, PCV valve and PCV hose. Disconnect exhaust pipe at manifold. Remove manifold retaining nuts and bolts; remove manifold.

Installation — To install, reverse removal procedure, ensuring that mating surfaces are clean and new gaskets are used. Tighten 2 center bolts first, then tighten the remainder in a front-rear, top-bottom star pattern.

CYLINDER HEAD

Removal — 1) Drain cooling system and remove upper radiator hose. Remove manifold and carburetor assembly. Disconnect heater hose at rear of head. Remove rocker arm cover.

2) Remove spark plug wires, distributor and fuel pump. Position crankshaft to TDC by aligning mark on pulley to "O" mark on lower timing belt cover. Remove drive belt, water pump pulley and alternator.

3) Using a puller, remove crankshaft pulley. Remove timing belt covers and water pump. Mark position of camshaft timing sprocket and timing belt. Remove timing belt.

4) Loosen rocker arm support bolts in 3 or 4 steps and in sequence shown in *Fig. 1*. Remove rocker arm assembly and camshaft timing sprocket. Remove camshaft bearing caps in same general sequence as rocker arm supports and arrange in order.

5) Remove camshaft and distributor drive gear. Loosen cylinder head bolts in 2 or 3 steps and in sequence shown in *Fig. 2*. Lift head from engine.

Installation — 1) Ensure that mating surfaces are clean, then install new gasket and head. Tighten head bolts gradually in 2 or 3 steps as shown in *Fig. 2*.

2) Install distributor drive gear on camshaft. Install camshaft on head making sure that arrows on bearing caps face front. Apply grease to and install front oil seal.

3) Install front bearing cap and tighten all bearing cap bolts gradually in 3 or 4 steps. Check camshaft thrust clearance and adjust to specifications. Continue installation in reverse order of removal.

Fig. 1 Rocker Arm Tightening Sequence
(Loosen in Reverse Sequence)

Fig. 2 Cylinder Head Tightening Sequence
(Loosen in Reverse Sequence)

1A-C 4-CYLINDER (Cont.)

CAMSHAFT

TIMING BELT

Removal — 1) Remove water pump drive belt and pulley. Position crankshaft to TDC by aligning mark on pulley to "O" mark on lower timing belt cover.

2) Using a puller, remove crankshaft pulley. Remove upper and lower timing belt covers. Mark position of camshaft timing sprocket and timing belt. Remove timing belt.

Inspection — 1) If belt is severed, check timing gear gasket for damage or improper installation. If belt teeth are cracked or damaged, check to see if camshaft is locked.

2) If there is noticeable wear or cracks on belt face, check for nicks on idler pulley lock. If there is damage or wear on only one edge of belt, check belt guide and alignment of each pulley.

Installation — 1) Loosen timing belt idler pulley and move toward the left as far as possible. Using care not to excessively bend or twist timing belt, install timing belt.

2) Turn crankshaft 2 revolutions and align timing mark. Measure timing belt tension as shown in *Fig. 3* and adjust with timing belt idler pulley. Complete installation by reversing removal procedure.

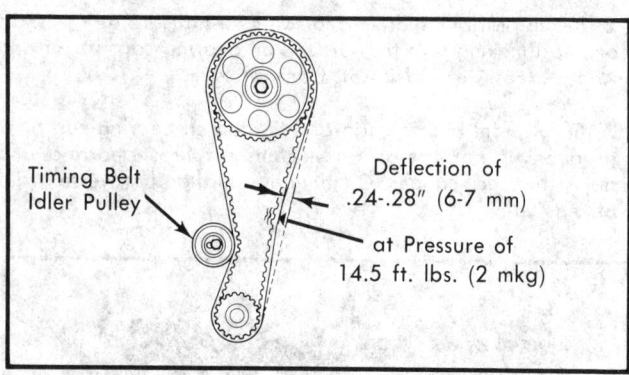

Fig. 3   Measuring Timing Belt Tension

CAMSHAFT

Removal — 1) Remove air cleaner and rocker arm cover. Remove front cover assembly and timing belt. See *TIMING BELT.* Loosen rocker arm support bolts in 3 to 4 steps and in sequence shown in *Fig. 1.* Remove rocker arm assembly.

2) Remove camshaft timing sprocket. Remove camshaft bearing caps in same general sequence as rocker arm supports and arrange in order.

3) Remove camshaft and distributor drive gear. Check cam lobe height. Check camshaft for maximum runout of .0024" (.06 mm).

NOTE — *Rotate camshaft one turn clockwise and divide maximum gauge difference by 2.*

Installation — 1) Using plastigage, adjust bearing caps to clearance specifications. Make sure arrows on bearing caps face front. Apply grease to and install front oil seal.

2) Install front bearing cap and tighten all bearing cap bolts gradually in 3 or 4 steps. Check camshaft thrust clearance and adjust to specifications. Continue installation in reverse order of removal.

VALVES

VALVE ARRANGEMENT

E-I-I-E-E-I-I-E

ROCKER ARM ASSEMBLY

Removal — 1) Remove air cleaner and rocker arm cover. Loosen rocker arm support bolts in 3 to 4 step and in sequence shown in *Fig. 1.* Remove rocker arm assembly.

2) Check arm-to-shaft clearance by twisting on shaft. Little or no movement should be felt. If worn excessively, disassemble and check. If clearance exceeds .0024" (.06 mm), replace rocker arm and/or shaft.

NOTE — *Disassemble and mark all parts for reassembly in proper order. Loosen adjusting screws and nuts prior to installation of assembly.*

Installation — To install, reverse removal procedure. Tighten rocker arm support bolts in 3 to 4 steps and in sequence shown in *Fig. 1.*

VALVES & VALVE SPRINGS

1) Mark each valve and, using valve spring compressor, remove valves, valve retainers, retainer locks, springs and valve stem oil seals.

2) Using inside micrometer, measure inside diameter of valve guide at several places (use maximum wear point for calculation). Measure valve stem diameter and subtract difference from valve guide inside diameter. If valve stem clearance exceeds specifications, replace valve and guide.

3) Using a caliper type ruler, measure valve spring free length and check for squareness within .079" (2.0 mm). Using a spring tester, measure tension of each spring at specified height. Replace springs that do not meet specifications.

VALVE GUIDE SERVICING

1) Break off valve guide bushing at snap ring and remove snap ring. Heat cylinder head to approximately 176-212°F (80-100°C) and drive out bushing toward combustion chamber.

2) Re-heat cylinder head and install new guides from top of head. Drive guide in until snap ring makes contact. Using a .28" (7.0 mm) reamer, ream valve guides to provide proper clearance.

VALVE CLEARANCE ADJUSTMENT

1) With No. 1 piston at TDC of compression stroke, adjust intake valves 2 and 4, and exhaust valves 3 and 4 to specified clearance.

2) Rotate crankshaft one turn (360°) clockwise to timing mark and adjust intake valves 1 and 3, and exhaust valves 1 and 2.

1A-C 4-CYLINDER (Cont.)

NOTE — *Valves should be adjusted with engine at normal operating temperature. Cold specifications are provided for initial settings after assembly.*

Valve Clearance Specifications		
Valve	**Hot** In. (mm)	**Cold** In. (mm)
Intake	.008 (.20)	.007 (.18)
Exhaust	.011 (.28)	.012 (.30)

PISTONS, PINS & RINGS

PISTON & ROD ASSEMBLY

Removal — With cylinder head and oil pan removed, machine ring ridge from top of cylinder. Mark rods and caps for correct assembly, then remove rod caps. Cover rod bolts with short lengths of hose to prevent crankshaft damage, then push piston/rod assembly out of block.

Installation — Lubricate piston, cylinder and journal with clean engine oil. Position rings on piston as illustrated in *Fig. 4* and apply ring compressor. Install piston/rod assembly in proper position with notch on connecting rod facing forward. Align rod and cap marks and tighten rod caps to specification.

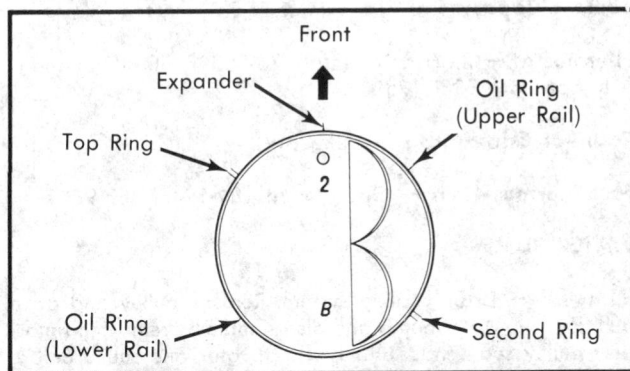

Fig. 4   Correct Piston Ring Gap Arrangement

FITTING PISTONS

Measure piston diameter at right angle to piston pin center line and at room temperature. Normal piston diameter is 3.047" (77.4 mm). Measure cylinder bore at top and bottom of wear

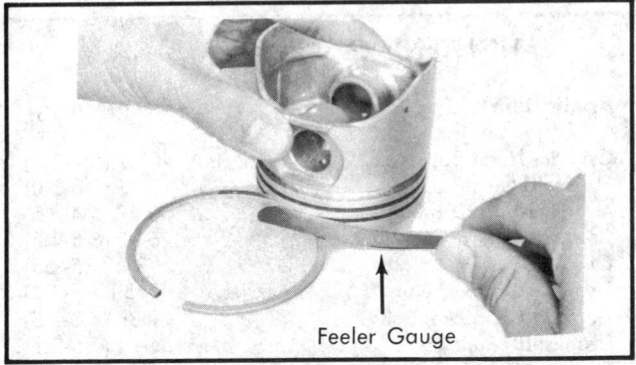

Fig. 5   Measuring Ring Groove Clearance

area and center of bore, in line with and at 90° to crankshaft. Standard bore is 3.053" (77.5 mm) with a wear limit of .008" (.2 mm). Maximum taper and out of round is .001" (.02 mm). If not within specifications, rebore and/or replace pistons. Measure ring end gap at bottom of ring travel. Check clearance of ring in ring groove. *See Fig. 5.*

PISTON PINS

Using a press and piston pin removal tool set, press piston pin out of piston and connecting rod. Lightly coat piston pin and pin hole with engine oil. Press in pin until centered in connecting rod.

CRANKSHAFT MAIN & CONNECTING ROD BEARINGS

MAIN & CONNECTING ROD BEARINGS

1) Prior to disassembly, mark main and connecting rod bearing caps for reassembly in their original positions and check crankshaft end play and connecting rod side play. Remove piston and connecting rod assemblies. Remove main bearing caps and remove crankshaft.

2) Measure crankshaft main and rod journal diameter. Check crankshaft for maximum runout of .0024" (.06 mm). If any measurement exceeds specifications, crankshaft must be replaced. Using Plastigage method, determine all bearing clearances. Replace any bearing not meeting specifications.

3) Install crankshaft and main bearing caps with arrows on caps facing front. Tighten bolts to tightening specifications and in sequence shown in *Fig. 6*. Measure crankshaft thrust clearance. If clearance exceeds .012" (.3 mm) replace thrust washers to achieve standard clearance of .0008-.0073" (.02-.18 mm).

4) Install piston and rod assemblies. Measure connecting rod thrust clearance. Standard clearance is .006-.010" (.15-.25 mm) and should not exceed specified limit of .012" (.3 mm).

Fig. 6   Main Bearing Tightening Sequence (Loosen in Reverse Order)

CRANKSHAFT FRONT OIL SEAL

Drive out oil seal from engine front cover. Using oil seal replacer, drive in new seal taking care not to install slantwise. Lightly coat seal lip with MP grease.

Toyota Engines

1A-C 4-CYLINDER (Cont.)

REAR MAIN BEARING OIL SEAL

Remove oil seal from oil seal case by driving out with a screwdriver. Using seal replacer (09218-56010) drive in new seal taking care not to bend or twist seal. Lightly coat seal lip with MP grease.

ENGINE OILING

Crankcase Capacity (Drain and Refill) — 3.7 qts. (Includes filter).

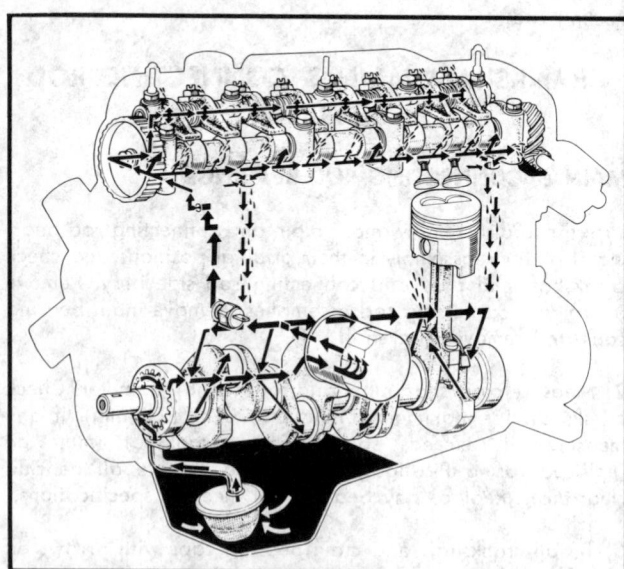

Fig. 7   Engine Oiling System

OIL PUMP

Removal — Remove timing covers and timing belt. See *TIMING BELT*. Remove oil pan and strainer. Remove oil pump and disassemble by removing (in order) cover, drive gear, driven gear, oil seal and relief valve. See Fig. 8.

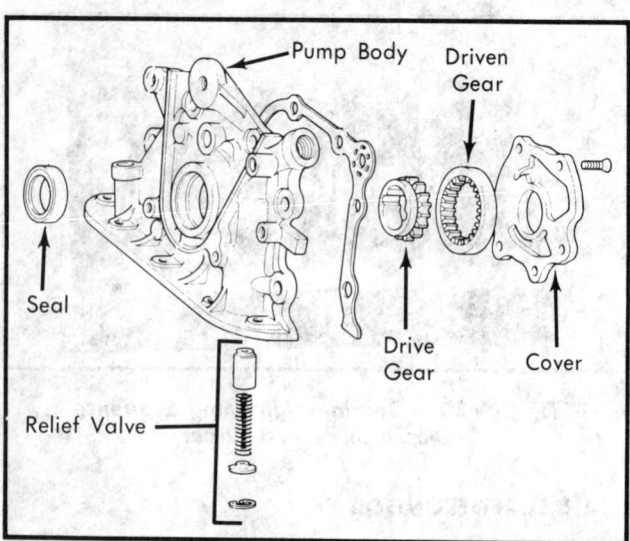

Fig. 8   Exploded View of Oil Pump and Pressure Relief Valve Assembly

Inspection — Check gears for wear or damage. Install new oil seal using oil seal replacer tool. Measure clearances between gear tips, gears and cover and drive gear to pump body. If any clearance exceeds specifications replace necessary part(s). Check relief valve for wear or damage.

Installation — To install, ensure that mating surfaces are clean and use new gasket. Reverse removal procedures to complete installation.

Oil Pump Specifications	
Application	**In. (mm)**
Gear Tip Clearance	
Drive Gear	.004-.010" (.102-.253 mm)
	Limit .013" (.35 mm)
Driven Gear	.002-.012" (.058-.310 mm)
	Limit .013" (.35 mm)
Gear Side Clearance	.001-.003" (.035-.085 mm)
	Limit .004" (.10 mm)
Gear-to-Body Clearance	.004-.007" (.100-.191 mm)
	Limit .008" (.20 mm)

ENGINE COOLING

Coolant Capacity — Approximately 5.5 quarts.

Thermostat — Starts to open at 176-183°F (80-84°C) and is fully open at 203°F (95°C).

Radiator Cap — 13 psi (.9 kg/cm²).

Fan Thermoswitch — Operates at 181-194°F (83-90°C).

WATER PUMP

Removal — Drain cooling system. Remove pulley and drive belt. Remove water pump and disassemble by removing (in order) pulley seat, shaft and bearing, rotor and seals. Before pressing out shaft and rotor, heat water pump body to about 167-185°F (75-85°C).

Inspection — Check all parts for cracks, damage or excessive wear and replace if necessary.

Installation — To install, use new gasket on clean mating surfaces and reverse removal procedures.

TIGHTENING SPECIFICATIONS	
Application	**Ft. Lbs. (mkg)**
Cylinder Head Bolts	40-47 (5.4-6.6)
Manifold Nuts	15-21 (2.0-3.0)
Main Bearing Cap Bolts	40-47 (5.4-6.6)
Connecting Rod Cap Nuts	26-32 (3.5-4.5)
Oil Pan Bolts	3-4 (.35-.55)
Timing Belt Cover Bolts	5-8 (.7-1.1)
Camshaft Sprocket Bolt	29-39 (4.0-5.5)
Crankshaft Pulley Bolt	55-61 (7.5-8.5)
Flywheel Bolts	55-61 (7.5-8.5)

Toyota Engines

1A-C 4-CYLINDER (Cont.)

ENGINE SPECIFICATIONS

GENERAL SPECIFICATIONS

Year	Displ. cu. ins.	Displ. cc	Carburetor	HP at RPM	Torque (Ft. Lbs. at RPM)	Compr. Ratio	Bore in.	Bore mm	Stroke in.	Stroke mm
1980	88.6	1452	1x2-Bbl	60@4800	72@2800	8.7:1	3.05	77.5	3.03	77.0

VALVES

Engine & Valve	Head Diam. In. (mm)	Face Angle	Seat Angle	Seat Width In. (mm)	Stem Diameter In. (mm)	Stem Clearance In. (mm)	Valve Lift In. (mm)
1452 cc Intake	.....	44.5°	45°	.055 (1.4)	.2744-.2750 (6.97-6.99)	.0010-.0024 (.025-.060)	.....
Exhaust	.....	44.5°	45°	.055 (1.4)	.2742-.2748 (6.96-6.98)	.0012-.0026 (.030-.065)	.....

PISTONS, PINS, RINGS

Engine	PISTONS Clearance In. (mm)	PINS Piston Fit In. (mm)	PINS Rod Fit In. (mm)	RINGS Rings	RINGS End Gap In. (mm)	RINGS Side Clearance In. (mm)
1452 cc	.004-.005 (.10-.12)	Press Fit	Press Fit	No. 1 No. 2 Oil	.008-.015 (.20-.40) .006-.013 (.15-.35) .004-.024① (.10-.60)	.0016-.0031 (.04-.08) .0012-.0028 (.03-.07) .....

① — For TP type rings; Riken type — .012-.035" (.30-.90 mm).

CRANKSHAFT MAIN & CONNECTING ROD BEARINGS

Engine	MAIN BEARINGS Journal Diam. In. (mm)	MAIN BEARINGS Clearance In. (mm)	Thrust Bearing	Crankshaft End Play In. (mm)	CONNECTING ROD BEARINGS Journal Diam. In. (mm)	CONNECTING ROD BEARINGS Clearance In. (mm)	Side Play In. (mm)
1452 cc	1.889-1.890 (47.985-48.000)	.0005-.0019 (.012-.049)	Center	.001-.007 (.025-.178)	1.5742-1.5748 (39.985-40.000)	.0008-.0020 (.020-.051)	.006-.010 (.15-.25)

VALVE SPRINGS

Engine	Free Length In. (mm)	PRESSURE Lbs. @ In. (kg @ mm) Valve Closed	PRESSURE Lbs. @ In. (kg @ mm) Valve Open
1452 cc	1.756 (44.6)	52.0@1.520 (23.6@38.6)	.....

CAMSHAFT

Engine	Journal Diam. In. (mm)	Clearance In. (mm)	Lobe Lift In. (mm)
1452 cc	1.101-1.102 (27.97-27.99)	.0015-.0029 (.037-.073)	1.553 (39.45)

3TC 4 CYLINDER

ENGINE CODING

ENGINE IDENTIFICATION

Engine can be identified by first group of numbers and letters in engine serial number. Engine serial number is located on left side of cylinder block behind dipstick.

Engine Identification	
Application	**Code**
Corolla (1770 cc)	3TC

ENGINE, CYLINDER HEAD & MANIFOLD

ENGINE

NOTE — *Following general procedures may not apply to all vehicles equipped with 3TC engine.*

Removal — **1)** Disconnect and remove battery. Drain cooling system and disconnect hoses and tubes at radiator. Hood may be removed to provide greater access to engine and increased clearance when removing engine. Remove radiator. Remove air cleaner and disconnect accelerator torque rod, bond cable and clutch hose bracket.

2) Disconnect heater hoses and coolant temperature gauge wiring from engine. Disconnect all engine-to-chassis electrical connections at engine. Disconnect fuel line at pump and exhaust pipe at manifold flange. Remove starter. If equipped with automatic transmission, remove 6 torque converter mounting bolts through service holes at front side of drive plate and ring gear.

3) Attach suitable sling to engine and take up slack. Remove engine-to-transmission mounting bolts and left and right engine mount nuts. Lift engine from vehicle. Use caution to avoid damage to clutch and brake fluid reservoirs.

Installation — Screw alignment dowel in rear of engine to ease alignment. If equipped with automatic transmission, screw alignment dowel in one of the lower torque converter mounting holes. Lower engine into position, replace mounting bolts and nuts, and reverse removal procedure.

INTAKE MANIFOLD

Removal — Remove air cleaner and brackets. Disconnect fuel line and throttle controls at carburetor. Disconnect all remaining tubes and lines from carburetor and manifold. Beginning at ends and working toward center, loosen manifold bolts and nuts in several steps. Remove intake manifold assembly with carburetor attached.

Installation — Install new gasket on clean mating surfaces and install manifold. Tighten bolts and nuts in several steps, beginning at lower center and working toward ends in a criss-cross pattern.

EXHAUST MANIFOLD

Removal — Remove air cleaner and intake heat tube. Disconnect exhaust pipe at manifold flange. Loosen bolts and nuts in several steps, beginning at ends of manifold. Remove manifold.

Installation — Install manifold with new gasket to clean mating surfaces. Beginning in center and working outward, tighten nuts and bolts in several steps to specified torque.

CYLINDER HEAD

Removal — Drain cooling system and remove manifolds as previously described. Set No. 1 cylinder at TDC on compression stroke. Remove spark plug wires by pulling on rubber boots. Remove rocker arm cover and loosen cylinder head bolts in several steps in reverse of tightening sequence. Lift off rocker arm assembly and take out push rods, keeping them in order for installation. Remove head.

Installation — Ensure that mating surfaces are clean and install new head gasket. Place push rods in proper positions. Loosen rocker arm adjusting screw lock nuts and install rocker arm assembly. Tighten head bolts in several steps in the sequence shown and continue installation in reverse order of removal.

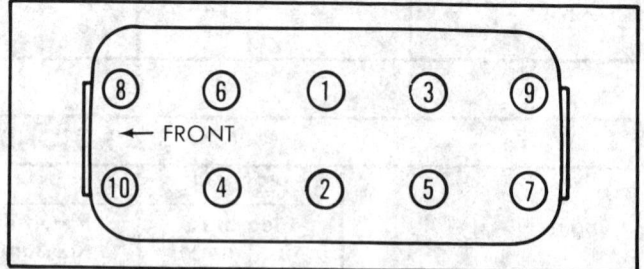

Fig. 1   Cylinder Head Tightening Sequence (Loosen in Reverse Order)

VALVES

VALVE ARRANGEMENT

Right Side — All intake.
Left Side — All exhaust.

VALVE GUIDE SERVICING

NOTE — *Manufacturer recommends using new valve guides whenever valves are replaced.*

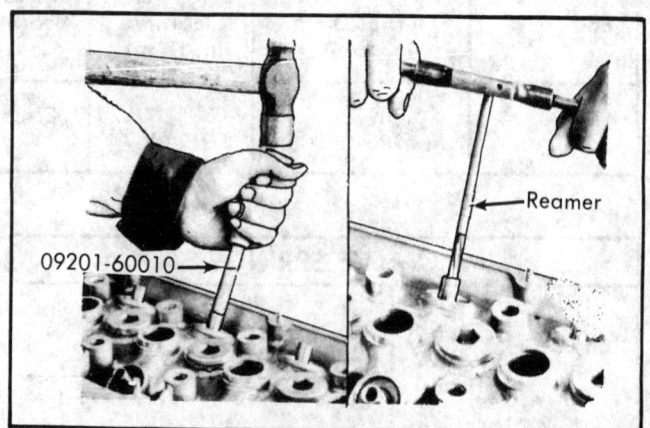

Fig. 2   Removing Valve Guide Bushing and Reaming to Proper Clearance

3TC 4 CYLINDER (Cont.)

1) Measure clearance between valve stem and valve guide bushing. If clearance is greater than .003" (.08 mm) for intake or .004" (.10 mm) for exhaust, replace valve and/or guide bushing.

2) Break off upper half of valve guide and heat cylinder head to 176-212°F (80-100°C). Using guide replacement tool (09201-60011), drive out guide bushing toward combustion chamber.

3) Apply thin coat of oil to guide and guide hole. Drive guide in until snap ring contacts head. Ream guide to achieve proper clearance.

VALVE STEM OIL SEALS

Cup type oil seals are used on all valves. Do not use old seals when valves have been removed. To install, lubricate valve stem and insert in cylinder head. Again lubricate valve stem and carefully push oil seal over valve guide.

NOTE — *Do not push down on top of seal; use pressure on seal sides only.*

VALVE SPRING FREE LENGTH & INSTALLED HEIGHT

Check all valve springs for correct free length, load length and squareness. Spring squareness should be within .075" (1.9 mm). When installed, valve spring height should be 1.484" (37.7 mm).

ROCKER ARM ASSEMBLY

1) Remove cylinder head. Remove rocker arm assembly. To disassemble, remove 4 retainer springs at each corner, both end supports, compression springs and 2 end rocker arms.

2) Remove remaining middle 3 supports, 4 rocker arms, and springs off rocker support shafts. Clearance between rocker arms and shaft should be .001-.002" (.02-.04 mm).

NOTE — *Mark all parts to reassemble in order. Place washer between rocker arm and support number three (center).*

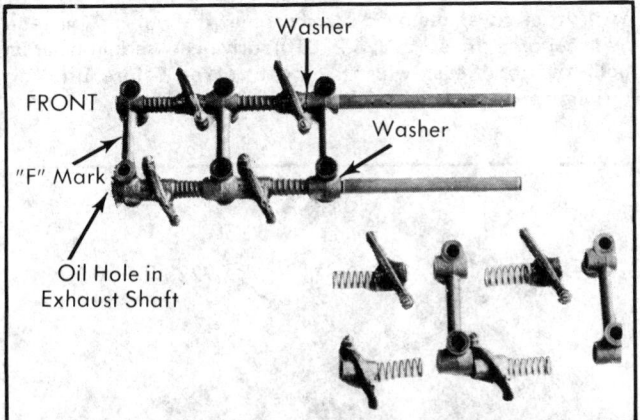

Fig. 3 Partially Disassembled View of Rocker Arm Assembly

VALVE LIFTERS

Inspect lifters and check clearance in bore. If clearance exceeds .004" (.10 mm), select oversize lifter and ream lifter bore to obtain clearance of .001-.002" (.02-.05 mm).

VALVE CLEARANCE ADJUSTMENT

Set number 1 cylinder to TDC on compression stroke. Adjust intake valves on number 1 and 2 cylinders, exhaust valves on number 1 and 3 cylinders. Turn crankshaft one revolution (360°) and adjust intake valves on number 3 and 4, exhaust valves on number 2 and 4 cylinders.

Valve Clearance Adjustment

Valve	Cold In. (mm)	Hot In. (mm)
Intake	.007 (.18)	.008 (.20)
Exhaust	.012 (.30)	.013 (.33)

PISTONS, PINS & RINGS

OIL PAN

Removal — 1) Disconnect left and right engine front mounts. Jack up vehicle and support on stands. Remove engine front undercover and right side stiffener plate. Remove stabilzer bar and oil pan bolts.

2) Place jack under clutch housing and raise slightly, taking care not to pull lower radiator hose. Lower oil pan and remove oil pump bolts. Pull oil pan and pump forward and outward.

Installation — Apply liquid sealer to 4 corners of oil pan gasket. To complete installation, reverse removal procedure.

PISTON & ROD ASSEMBLY

Removal — With oil pan and cylinder head removed, mark connecting rod and cap for correct assembly and take off bearing cap nuts. Tap studs lightly to loosen caps and remove bearing caps. Push piston/rod assembly out through top of cylinder block.

NOTE — *Cover rod bolts with short pieces of hose to prevent damage to crankshaft.*

Installation — Install piston rings on piston with ring gaps spaced as shown in *Fig. 4.* Code letter and number on ring should face UP. Lubricate piston, crankshaft and cylinder walls. Using suitable ring compressor, insert pistons in cylinders, making sure that notch in piston top is toward front of engine. Use hose pieces on studs to protect crankshaft. Install rod caps and tighten to specifications.

NOTE — *After tightening each cap, check rotation condition of crankshaft.*

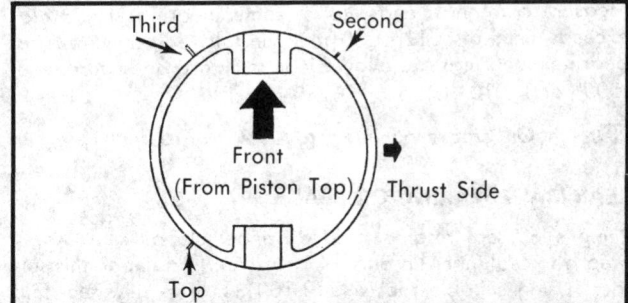

Fig. 4 Installed Position of Piston Rings

3TC 4 CYLINDER (Cont.)

FITTING PISTONS

1) Measure piston at right angle to pin center line, .40" (11 mm) below bottom ring. Standard piston diameter is 3.344-3.346" (84.94-84.99 mm). Oversize pistons are available .020", .030" and .040" (.50, .75 and 1.0 mm) over standard.

2) Measure cylinders at top, center and bottom of bore in two directions. If wear exceeds .008" (.20 mm) on any one cylinder, rebore all cylinders for oversize pistons.

3) Insert piston rings into cylinders and measure end gap at lower part of cylinder where wear is smallest. Measure clearance between ring and ring groove.

PISTON PIN REPLACEMENT

Check pin fit by trying to rock piston at right angle to pin. If any movement is felt, piston and pin must be replaced. Use suitable press and adapter (09221-25013) to press out piston pin. Install piston and pin to connecting rod so that notch in piston top is on same side of rod as trademark on rod center.

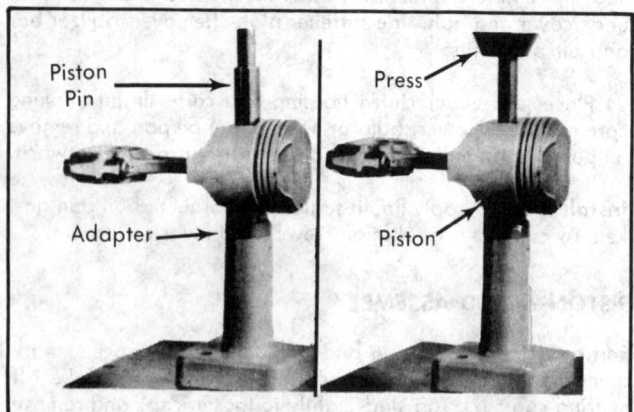

Fig. 5 Piston Pin Removal and Installation with Press and Adapter

CRANKSHAFT MAIN & CONNECTING ROD BEARINGS

MAIN & CONNECTING ROD BEARINGS

Use Plastigage method to measure bearing clearance. Clearance limit is .003" (.07 mm). Crankshaft bend limit is .002" (.06 mm). Taper and out-of-round limit is .0004" (.01 mm). If limits are exceeded, crankshaft must be ground for undersize bearings. Bearings are available .002", .010" and .020" (.05, .25 and .50 mm) undersizes.

THRUST BEARING ALIGNMENT

Measure crankshaft end play at center bearing. If end play exceeds limit of .012" (.30 mm), install replacement thrust bearings. Bearings are available in standard and oversizes of .005" and .010" (.125 and .250 mm).

NOTE — *Oil groove on bearing faces toward center.*

REAR MAIN BEARING OIL SEAL

Remove oil seal retainer and drive out old oil seal. Apply grease to seal inner lip and take care not to damage this surface. Using suitable tool (09250-10011), drive new seal into place. Replace oil seal retainer with new gasket.

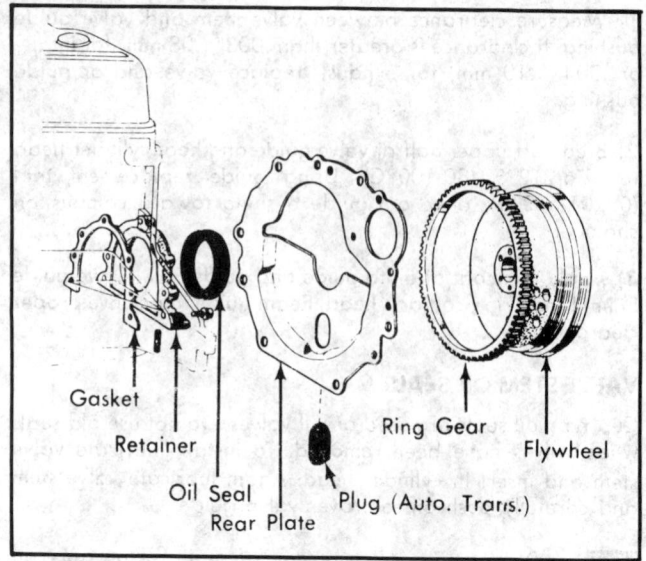

Fig. 6 Rear Oil Seal and Retainer with Related Components

ENGINE FRONT COVER

Removal — Remove water pump and fan assembly. Set No. 1 cylinder to TDC on compression stroke so key in crankshaft will be at top. Remove crankshaft pulley with suitable puller (09213-31021). Remove bolts from pan into cover and cover into block, then carefully remove cover from engine.

Installation — Ensure that mating surfaces are clean and install new gasket between cover and block. Use new section of pan gasket if old gasket at bottom has been damaged. Apply suitable sealer at corners and place cover in position. Install cover bolts and drive pulley into position with suitable tool (09214-60010). Complete assembly in reverse of removal procedure.

FRONT COVER OIL SEAL

With front cover removed from engine, pry out old oil seal. With suitable driver (09223-22010), drive new seal in position until it is about even with timing gear cover. Before installing on engine, coat seal lip with multi-purpose grease.

Fig. 7 Installing Front Cover Oil Seal

3TC 4 CYLINDER (Cont.)

CAMSHAFT

TIMING CHAIN & GEAR

Removal — With front cover off, remove camshaft gear retaining bolt. Remove camshaft gear, timing chain and crankshaft gear by pulling out evenly. Maximum elongation of chain is 11.47" (291.4 mm) with 11 lbs. (5 kg) tension.

Installation — Chain tensioner and plunger should be removed before installing timing chain and gears. Ensure that crankshaft and camshaft keys are pointing UP. Assemble chain and gears with marks aligned as illustrated and install as an assembly. Tighten camshaft timing gear bolt and install chain tensioner. Install remaining components in reverse order of removal.

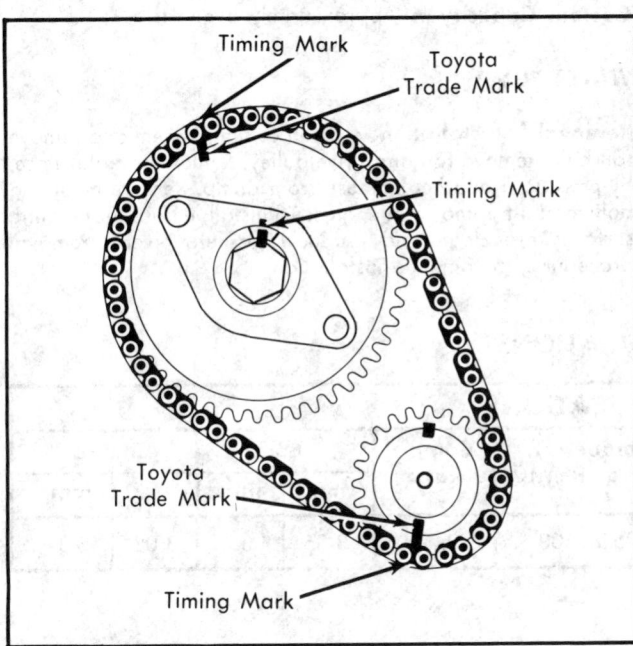

Timing Mark
Toyota Trade Mark
Timing Mark
Toyota Trade Mark
Timing Mark

Fig. 8 Timing Chain and Sprocket Alignment Marks

TIMING CHAIN TENSIONER & DAMPER

1) Inspect surfaces of tensioner plunger and bore of tensioner body. To test clearance, lubricate plunger and insert it into plunger body. Cover two oil passages with fingers and pull plunger. Vacuum strong enough to return plunger should be felt.

2) Measure thickness of tensioner head and chain damper wall. Head should be minimum .492" (12.5 mm) and chain damper should be minimum .20" (5.0 mm).

3) Install chain tensioner, then install damper. Clearance between chain and damper should be .020" (.5 mm) when properly installed.

NOTE — Chain tensioner must be filled with oil after replacing tensioner or timing chain.

CAMSHAFT

Removal — With cylinder head, timing chain cover and timing chain assembly removed, remove distributor and fuel pump. Lift out tappets and mark position for installation. Remove camshaft thrust plate. Insert timing gear retaining bolt and pull out camshaft slowly while turning.

Installation — Lubricate all bearing journals and insert camshaft. Place camshaft thrust plate in position with marked side outward. Install thrust plate retaining bolts. Install remaining components in reverse order of removal, ensuring that all timing marks are aligned.

CAMSHAFT BEARINGS

1) Using suitable bearing remover tool (09215-25010), pull out bearings 1, 2 and 5 toward front and bearings 3 and 4 toward rear. Using same tool, install new bearings in the following order: No. 4 using No. 1 as a guide, No. 2 using No. 1 as a guide and No. 3 using No. 5 as a guide.

2) Install No. 1 bearing using No. 2 as a guide and No. 5 bearing using No.1 and No. 4 as guides. Ensure that oil holes in bearings are aligned with oil holes in block. Bearings are available .005" and .010" (.125 and .250 mm) undersize.

NOTE — Apply liquid sealer to plug at rear of block.

CAMSHAFT END THRUST

To measure end thrust, install thrust plate and timing gear. Tighten timing gear bolt and check clearance with feeler gauge. Standard clearance is .003-.006" (.07-.15 mm) undersize. If maximum is exceeded, replace thrust plate.

ENGINE OILING

Crankcase Capacity — 4.0 qts. (including filter).

Oil Filter — Full flow type with integral relief valve.

Normal Oil Pressure — 28 psi (2 kg/cm²) at idle; 43 psi (3 kg/cm²) running (minimum values).

Oil Pressure Regulator Valve — Begins to open at 51-63 psi (3.6-4.4 kg/cm²).

OIL PUMP

Oil pump is driven by bottom of distributor shaft. With oil pan off, remove mounting bolt and pull pump from engine. Remove cover and strainer, and check clearances. Inspect relief valve for scoring or wear and replace as necessary. Drive rotor and driven rotor have punch marks on cover side for assembly identification. Assemble pump and check operation by submerging suction end in clean engine oil and turning shaft clockwise with a screwdriver. Oil should come out discharge hole. Close hole with thumb and turn shaft as before. Shaft should be difficult to turn.

Oil Pump Specifications	
Application	**In. (mm)**
Rotor Tip Clearance	.002-.006 (.04-.16)
	Limit .010 (.25)
Rotor Side Clearance	.001-.004 (.03-.09)
	Limit .006 (.15)
Rotor-to-Body Clearance	.004-.006 (.10-.16)
	Limit .010 (.25)

Toyota Engines

3TC 4 CYLINDER (Cont.)

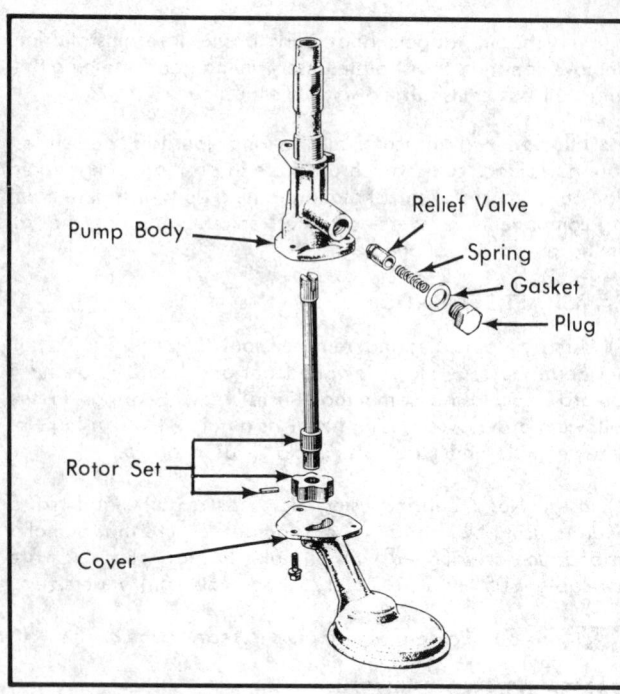

Fig. 9 Exploded View of Oil Pump and Pressure Relief Valve Assembly

ENGINE COOLING

Thermostat — Wax pellet type thermostat with opening temperature of 187-194°F (86-90°C). Fully opened at 212°F (100°C).

COOLANT DRAINING

Engine must be cool, then remove radiator cap. Loosen drain plugs at bottom of radiator and left side of engine block and drain coolant. To refill, make sure both drains are closed and fill radiator wth coolant. Start and run engine until warm, then top off radiator with coolant. Fill reservoir half full, then install radiator and reservoir caps.

Coolant Capacity — Approximately 8 quarts.

WATER PUMP

Removal & Installation — Drain cooling system and remove fan belt. Remove fan and drive pulley. Remove radiator hose, by-pass hose and heater hose from pump. Remove mounting bolts and lift pump from engine. To install, ensure that mating surfaces are clean and use new gasket. Reverse removal procedures to complete installation.

ENGINE SPECIFICATIONS

GENERAL SPECIFICATIONS

| Year | Displ. | | Carburetor | HP at RPM① | Torque (Ft. Lbs. at RPM)② | Compr. Ratio | Bore | | Stroke | |
	cu. ins.	cc					in.	mm	in.	mm
1980	108	1770	1x2-Bbl.	75@5000	95@2600	9.0:1	3.35	85	3.08	78

① — California: 73@5000.
② — California: 90@2600.

VALVES

Engine & Valve	Head Diam. In. (mm)	Face Angle	Seat Angle	Seat Width In. (mm)	Stem Diameter In. (mm)	Stem Clearance In. (mm)	Valve Lift In. (mm)
1770 cc Intake	.....	44.5°	45°	.047-.063 (1.2-1.6)	.3136-.3142 (7.97-7.98)	.0010-.0024 (.025-.061)	.....
Exhaust	.....	44.5°	45°	.047-.063 (1.2-1.6)	.3136-.3142 (7.97-7.98)	.0012-.0026 (.030-.066)	.....

PISTONS, PINS, RINGS

| Engine | PISTONS | PINS | | RINGS | | |
	Clearance In. (mm)	Piston Fit In. (mm)	Rod Fit In. (mm)	Rings	End Gap In. (mm)	Side Clearance In. (mm)
1770 cc	.002-.003 (.05-.07)	Press Fit	Press Fit	No. 1	.004-.010 (.10-.25)	.0008-.0024 (.02-.06)
				No. 2	.006-.012 (.15-.30)	.0006-.0022 (.015-.055)
				Oil	.008-.028 (.20-.70)	.....

Toyota Engines

3TC 4 CYLINDER (Cont.)
ENGINE SPECIFICATIONS (Cont.)

CRANKSHAFT MAIN & CONNECTING ROD BEARINGS

| Engine | MAIN BEARINGS | | | | CONNECTING ROD BEARINGS | | |
	Journal Diam. In. (mm)	Clearance In. (mm)	Thrust Bearing	Crankshaft End Play In. (mm)	Journal Diam. In. (mm)	Clearance In. (mm)	Side Play In. (mm)
1770 cc	2.282-2.284 (57.976-58.000)	.0009-.0019 (.024-.048)	Center	.0008-.009 (.02-.22)	1.8888-1.8898 (47.976-48.000)	.0009-.0019 (.024-.048)	.006-.010 (.16-.26)

CAMSHAFT

Engine	Journal Diam. In. (mm)	Clearance In. (mm)	Lobe Lift In. (mm)
1770 cc		.0010-.0026 (.025-.066)	.....
No.1	1.829-1.830 (46.46-46.48)		
No. 2	1.819-1.820 (46.21-46.23)		
No. 3	1.809-1.810 (45.96-45.98)		
No. 4	1.800-1.801 (45.71-45.73)		
No. 5	1.790-1.791 (45.46-45.48)		

TIGHTENING SPECIFICATIONS

Application	Ft. Lbs. (mkg)
Cylinder Head Bolts	62-68 (8.5-9.5)
Intake Manifold	14-18 (1.8-2.5)
Exhaust Manifold	22-32 (3.0-4.5)
Main Bearing Caps	53-63 (7.2-8.8)
Connecting Rod Caps	29-36 (4.0-5.0)
Crankshaft Pulley	47-61 (6.5-8.5)
Flywheel	42-47 (5.8-6.6)
Camshaft Sprocket	51-79 (7.0-11.0)
Camshaft Thrust Plate	8-11 (1.0-1.6)
Oil Pan	4-5 (.5-.8)
Exhaust Pipe to Manifold	29-36 (4.0-5.0)

VALVE SPRINGS

| Engine | Free Length In. (mm) | PRESSURE (LBS.) Lbs. @ In. (kg @ mm) | |
		Valve Closed	Valve Open
1770 cc	1.657 (42.1)	57.9@1.484 (26.3@37.7)	.....

Toyota Engines

20R 4 CYLINDER

ENGINE CODING

ENGINE IDENTIFICATION

Engine serial number is stamped on left side of cylinder block, behind the alternator. Last group of numerals and letters designates engine type.

Engine Identification	
Application	Code
Celica, Corona & Pickup (2189 cc)	20R

ENGINE & CYLINDER HEAD

ENGINE

Removal — 1) Remove hood and disconnect cable from negative battery terminal. With engine cool, drain cooling system. Remove air cleaner and cover carburetor. Remove radiator, shroud, hoses and upper bracket. If equipped with air conditioning, remove compressor and condenser but DO NOT disconnect refrigerant hoses.

2) Disconnect following hoses: Fuel hose from carburetor, water by-pass hose from carburetor coil housing, brake booster hose from intake manifold, heater hoses from engine, air injection tube at rear of engine and emission control hoses from carburetor and intake manifold.

NOTE — *Label all emission control hoses to ease installation.*

3) Disconnect accelerator linkage from carburetor. If equipped with automatic transmission, disconnect automatic transmission throttle cable. Raise vehicle and drain engine oil. Remove starter and disconnect exhaust pipe at manifold. Disconnect wires from oil pressure switch and sending unit.

4) Remove 2 transmission stiffener plates and engine undercover. Place block of wood on jack and put jack under transmission. If equipped with automatic transmission, disconnect cooler lines from engine and remove 6 torque converter mounting bolts through service holes at rear of engine. On all models, remove transmission housing mounting bolts.

5) Remove motor mount bolts (above crossmember). Disconnect wiring from coil, alternator, and water temperature sending unit. If equipped with power steering, remove pump and move to one side. Disconnect hoses from air pump. Attach sling to engine and lift carefully from vehicle. If equipped with automatic transmission, ensure that converter remains with transmission.

Installation — 1) Lower engine into position ensuring that engine is aligned with transmission and motor mount supports. On manual transmission models, install motor mount and transmission housing mounting bolts.

2) On automatic transmission models, install guide pin in the torque converter and align with one of the drive plate holes. Align upper starter stud with hole in starter housing on engine. Align sleeves on block with converter housing. Install motor mount bolts and remove hoisting sling. Install 2 longest bolts in upper converter housing. Install 6 torque converter bolts finger tight, then to final torque.

3) To complete installation on all models, reverse removal procedure and check for leaks.

CYLINDER HEAD

Removal — 1) Disconnect battery and drain cooling system. Disconnect exhaust pipe at manifold flange. Remove air cleaner and cover carburetor. Remove all hoses and linkages to intake manifold, carburetor and cylinder head. Remove distributor with cap and wires. Remove fuel pump. Remove cylinder head cover and set No. 1 piston to TDC on compression stroke.

2) Paint mating marks on camshaft sprocket and timing chain. Remove rubber half circle seal and cam sprocket retaining bolt. Pull distributor drive gear and fuel pump drive cam off of sprocket. Remove sprocket from camshaft, allowing sprocket and chain to rest in cylinder head. Remove chain cover bolt, then remove cylinder head bolts in reverse of tightening sequence. See *Fig. 1*.

3) Pry equally at front and rear of rocker arm assembly to clear locating dowels. Lift head carefully to clear locating dowels but *DO NOT PRY BETWEEN HEAD AND BLOCK*. Drain engine oil due to coolant which will run into pan during head removal.

Installation — Apply liquid sealer at 2 front corners of block and position head gasket over locating dowels. Place head in position and turn camshaft so dowel is at top. Install rocker arm assembly over locating dowels and tighten head bolts in 3 steps in the sequence shown in *Fig. 1*. Continue installation in reverse of removal sequence, ensuring that valve and ignition timing is properly set.

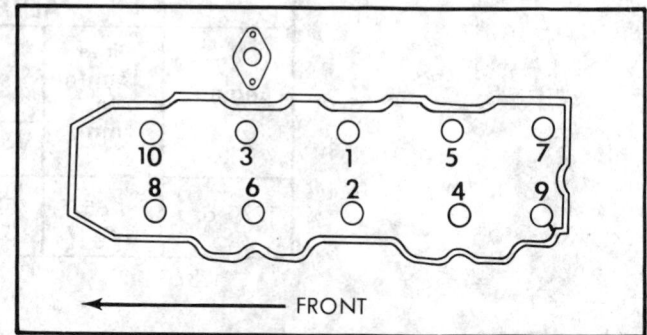

Fig. 1 Cylinder Head Tightening Sequence (Remove in Reverse Sequence)

CAMSHAFT

TIMING CHAIN

Removal — 1) Remove cylinder head and oil pan. Remove radiator, drive belts, air pump and alternator bracket. Remove crankshaft pulley and timing chain cover assembly.

2) Remove chain from damper sprocket and remove cam sprocket and chain. Using puller (09213-36010), remove both oil pump drive and chain sprocket. Check chain, sprockets, tensioner and chain dampers for wear and replace as necessary. With chain stretched tight by hand, maximum distance between 17 links should be 5.79" (147.0 mm).

Installation — 1) Turn crankshaft until shaft key is at TDC. Position chain with chromed link over sprocket in line with sprocket mark as illustrated. Chain must be positioned between the 2 dampers.

20R 4 CYLINDER (Cont.)

Fig. 2 Aligning Crankshaft Sprocket and Timing Chain

2) Install cam sprocket in chain so that timing mark on sprocket is located between 2 chromed links. Slide oil pump drive spline over crankshaft key. Install cover assembly with new gasket over dowels and pump spline.

Fig. 3 Aligning Camshaft Sprocket and Timing Chain

3) Continue installation in reverse of removal procedure and set camshaft timing as follows: With No. 1 cylinder at TDC on compression stroke, position camshaft so that dowel on sprocket flange is at 12 o'clock position. Complete assembly procedure.

CAMSHAFT

With cylinder head and rocker arm assembly removed, remove camshaft bearing caps and lift out camshaft. Camshaft bearing clearance may be checked using Plastigage method. If clearance exceeds specifications, replace cylinder head and/or camshaft. To install, reverse removal procedure. Install bearing caps in numbered order with arrows pointing toward the front. Adjust valve timing.

VALVE TIMING

Valve timing is determined by the relationship between the camshaft and the crankshaft. Turn crankshaft to position No. 1 piston at TDC (align mark on crankshaft with pointer on chain cover). Turn camshaft to locate dowel pin and stamped mark on camshaft at 12 o'clock position. Install timing gear and chain on camshaft. A locating pin may be needed to stretch chain and a hammer may be needed to drive on gear. Tighten timing gear bolts to specifications.

VALVES

VALVE ARRANGEMENT

Left Side – All exhaust.

Right Side – All intake.

VALVE GUIDE SERVICING

1) Measure clearance between valve stem and guide. If clearance exceeds specifications, valve guides must be replaced. If valve guide being replaced has a snap ring installed, break guide using brass punch and hammer. Using driver tool (09201-60011), drive old guide down through combustion chamber.

NOTE – *Only replacement valve guides have snap rings.*

2) Drive in new valve guide from top of head until snap ring contacts cylinder head. Guide should have .75" (19 mm) protrusion above cylinder head. Ream new valve guide to provide proper stem clearance.

VALVE STEM OIL SEALS

1) Using a suitable spring compressor, remove valve keepers. Withdraw spring retainer and springs. Remove valve stem oil seal from end of valve guide.

2) Slide a new oil seal over valve stem, using care not to damage seal as it passes over keeper grooves. Force seal over end of valve guide. Reverse removal procedure for remaining components.

VALVE SPRINGS

Check valve spring free length and squareness. If less than 1.8" (45.8 mm) long or out of square more than .07" (1.9 mm), replace spring. Use a spring tester and measure tension at installed height. Replace spring if less than specified.

ROCKER ARM ASSEMBLY

If rocker arms appear loose, disassemble rocker arm assembly and measure rocker arm-to-shaft clearance. Clearance should be .0004-.0020" (.01-.05 mm), with a maximum limit of .0031" (.08 mm). If clearance exceeds maximum limit, replace rocker arms and/or shafts. Reassemble in reverse of disassembly, noting that all rocker arms are identical, but that all rocker stands are different.

20R 4 CYLINDER (Cont.)

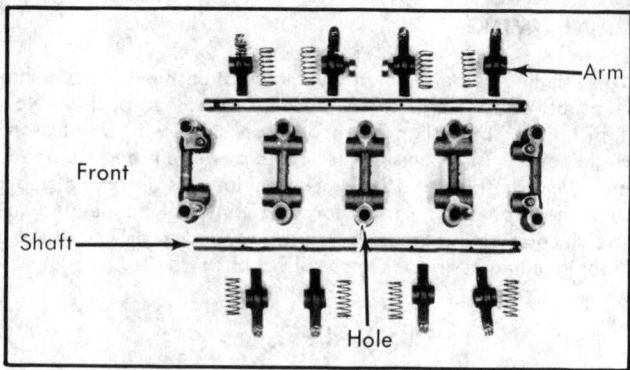

Fig. 4 Disassembled View of Rocker Arm Assembly

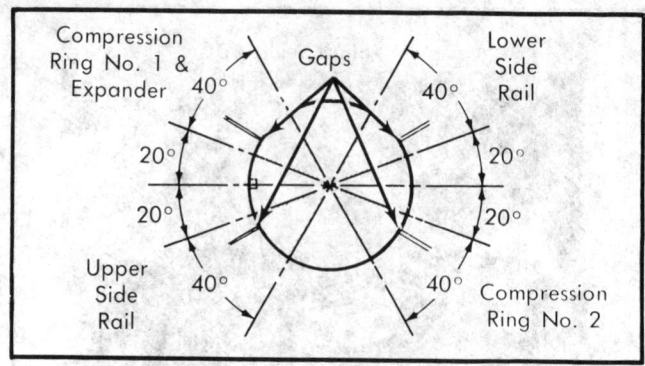

Fig. 5 Correct Piston Ring Gap Arrangement

VALVE CLEARANCE ADJUSTMENT

Engine should be at normal operating temperature. Remove valve cover and set No. 1 piston to TDC on compression stroke. Measure clearance between rocker arm and valve stem. Adjust intake valves 1 and 2 to .008" (.2 mm) and exhaust valves 1 and 3 to .012" (.3 mm). Rotate crankshaft one complete revolution and align timing mark at TDC. Adjust intake valves 3 and 4 to .008" (.2 mm) and exhaust valves 2 and 4 to .012" (.3 mm).

PISTONS, PINS & RINGS

OIL PAN

Removal — Drain engine oil, then remove engine undercover and detach steering idler arm bracket. On all Pickups except 4-WD, remove pitman arm and front crossmember. On Celica and Corona, remove engine shock absorber (if so equipped) and engine mount bolts. Jack engine up about 1" (25 mm). On all models, remove pan bolts and nuts, then take off pan and gasket.

Installation — Place gasket on pan and apply sealer to 4 corners where front cover and rear seal retainer join cylinder block. Install pan. To complete installation, reverse removal procedure.

PISTON & ROD ASSEMBLY

Removal — With cylinder head and pan removed, machine ring ridge from top of cylinder. Mark rods and caps for correct assembly, then remove rod caps. Cover rod bolts with short length of hose to prevent crankshaft damage, then push piston/rod assembly out of block.

Installation — Lubricate piston, cylinder and journal with clean engine oil. Position rings as illustrated and apply ring compressor. Stamped mark on ring must face upward. Install piston/rod assembly in proper position with notch on piston top facing forward.

PISTONS & RINGS

Measure cylinder bore at top and bottom of wear area and center of bore, in line with and at 90° to crankshaft. Standard bore is 3.484-3.485" (88.50-88.53 mm) with a wear limit of .008" (.2 mm). Maximum taper and out of round is .001" (.02 mm). Measure piston at right angle to and 1.02" (26 mm) below center line of pin. If not within specifications, rebore and/or replace pistons. Measure ring end gap at bottom of ring travel. Check clearance of ring in ring groove.

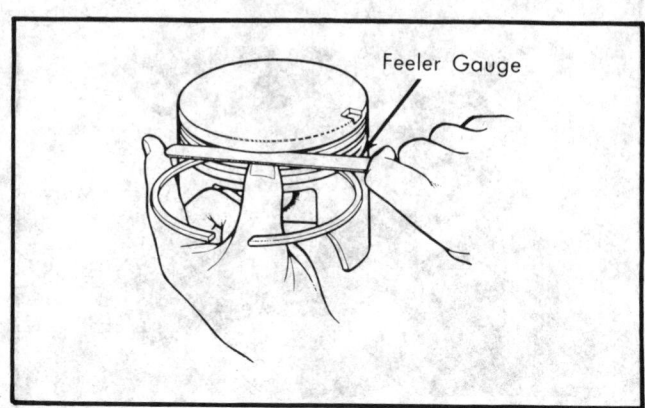

Fig. 6 Measuring Ring Groove Clearance

PISTON PINS

Removal — Heat piston to 176°F (80°C) and push piston pin out of piston and connecting rod. Piston pin should push through connecting rod with thumb pressure when rod is at 68°F (20°C). If pin is too loose in rod, press out bushing from connecting rod using press tool (09222-30010). Install and hone new bushing.

NOTE — *Piston and pin are a matched set.*

Installation — Heat piston to 176°F (80°C) and position piston and connecting rod so mark on rod and indent on piston crown face same direction. Push piston pin into piston and rod assembly.

20R 4 CYLINDER (Cont.)

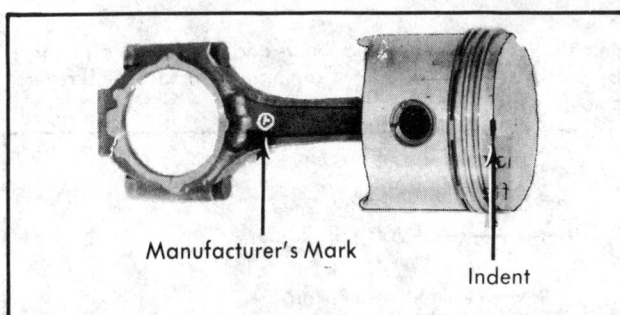

Fig. 7   Correct Alignment of Piston and Rod Assembly

CRANKSHAFT MAIN & CONNECTING ROD BEARINGS

MAIN & CONNECTING ROD BEARINGS

1) Measure crankshaft runout at center bearing journal. If runout exceeds .004" (.1 mm), replace crankshaft. Inspect all journals for wear or scoring. Check for out-of-round or taper. If crankshaft is worn excessively, grind journals for undersize bearings.

2) Measure bearing clearances using Plastigage method. If clearance exceeds specifications, grind journals for undersize bearings. Both main and connecting rod bearings are available .010" (.25 mm) undersize.

THRUST BEARING ALIGNMENT

Check crankshaft thrust clearance at thrust bearing using a feeler gauge. If end play exceeds limit of .012" (.3 mm), replace thrust washers. Thrust washers are available in two oversizes, .005" (.13 mm) and .010" (.25 mm).

REAR MAIN BEARING OIL SEAL

With rear main bearing oil seal retainer removed, pry out old seal. Using suitable tool (09223-41010) drive oil seal in place. After installing new seal, coat seal lip lightly with multi-purpose grease.

Fig. 8   Installed View of Rear Seal and Retainer

ENGINE FRONT COVER OIL SEAL

Seal is a press fit in oil pump body at front of crankshaft. Remove by prying out with screwdriver. Drive new seal in position using suitable tool (09223-50010). Lubricate seal lip lightly with multi-purpose grease after installation.

ENGINE OILING

Crankcase Capacity — 4.0 qts; 4.9 qts. including filter.

Pressure Relief Valve — 64 psi (4.5 kg/cm²) operating pressure.

Oil Filter — Full-flow type with paper elements. Located at right side of engine.

ENGINE OILING SYSTEM

Forced feed oiling system utilizing a gear and crescent type oil pump driven from front of crankshaft. Oil from oil pan is pumped through a full flow oil filter and then to oil galleries in cylinder block. Oil is fed to crankshaft bearings, timing chain assembly, camshaft and rocker arm assembly.

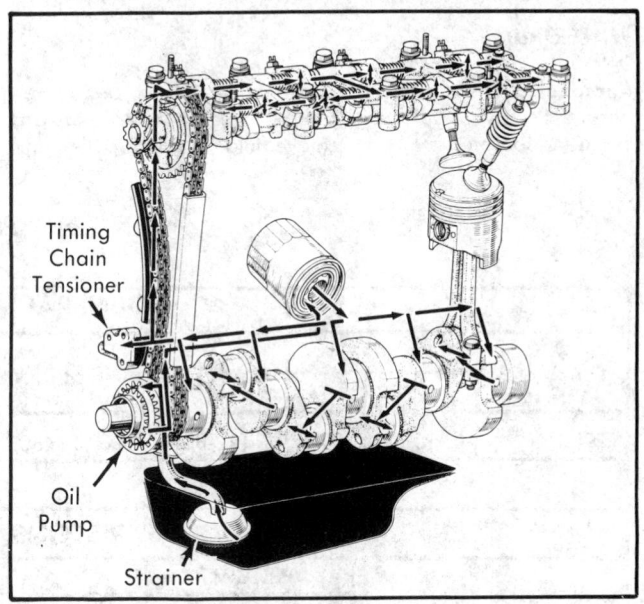

Fig. 9   Engine Oiling System

OIL PUMP

Oil Pump Specifications	
Application	**Clearance In. (mm)**
Drive Gear-to-Crescent	
Standard	.0087-.0098 (.22-.25)
Wear Limit	.012 (.30)
Driven Gear-to-Crescent	
Standard	.0059-.0083 (.15-.21)
Wear Limit	.012 (.30)
Driven Gear-to-Body	
Standard	.0035-.0059 (.09-.15)
Wear Limit	.008 (.20)
Gear Faces-to-Body	
Standard	.0012-.0035 (.03-.09)
Wear Limit	.0059 (.15)

Toyota Engines

20R 4 CYLINDER (Cont.)

Removal — Remove oil pan and strainer. Remove drive belts and crankshaft pulley. Remove 5 bolts and oil pump assembly. Remove oil pump drive spline from crankshaft and "O" ring from engine block. Remove relief valve plug, spring and piston from pump body. Remove driven and drive gear from pump body.

Installation — Reassemble pump and lubricate seal lip. Install new "O" ring in block and apply sealer to upper bolt. Install and tighten pump. Complete installation in reverse of removal procedure.

ENGINE COOLING

Thermostat — On Federal models except Cab and Chassis Pickup, starts to open at 190°F (88°C) and is fully open at 212°F (100°C). On Calif. models and all Cab and Chassis Pickups, starts to open at 180°F (82°C) and is fully open at 203°F (95°C).

Cooling System Capacity — 8.9 qts.

Radiator Cap — 13 psi (.9 kg/cm²).

WATER PUMP

Removal & Installation — Drain cooling system and loosen alternator pivot adjusting bolts. Pivot alternator toward engine to loosen drive belt. Remove fluid coupling, pulley and fan belt. Remove 7 bolts and 2 nuts and take pump off engine. To install, use new gasket on clean mating surfaces and reverse removal procedure.

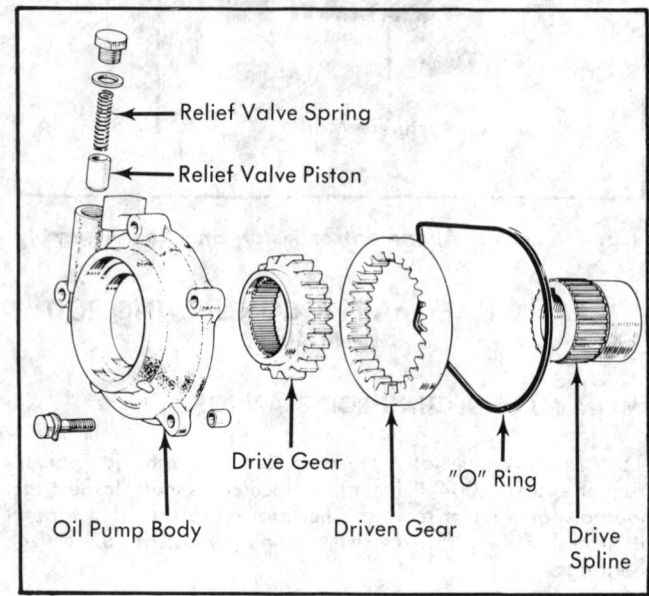

Fig. 10   Exploded View of Oil Pump

ENGINE SPECIFICATIONS

GENERAL SPECIFICATIONS

Year	Displ.		Carburetor	HP at RPM	Torque (Ft. Lbs. at RPM)	Compr. Ratio	Bore		Stroke	
	cu. ins.	cc					in.	mm	in.	mm
1980	133.6	2189	1x2-Bbl.	90 @ 4800	122@2400	8.4:1	3.48	88.5	3.50	89.0

PISTONS, PINS, RINGS

Engine	PISTONS	PINS		RINGS		
	Clearance In. (mm)	Piston Fit In. (mm)	Rod Fit In. (mm)	Rings	End Gap In. (mm)	Side Clearance In. (mm)
2189 cc	.0012-.0020 (.03-.05)	Press Fit ①	.0002-.0004 (.005-.011) ②	No. 1	.004-.012 (.10-.30)	.008 (.2)
				No. 2	.004-.12 (.10-.30)	.008 (.2)
				Oil	.....	.....

① — Push fit with piston heated to 176°F (80°C). ② — Push fit with piston at room temperature.

CRANKSHAFT MAIN & CONNECTING ROD BEARINGS

Engine	MAIN BEARINGS				CONNECTING ROD BEARINGS		
	Journal Diam. In. (mm)	Clearance In. (mm)	Thrust Bearing	Crankshaft End Play In. (mm)	Journal Diam. In. (mm)	Clearance In. (mm)	Side Play In. (mm)
2189 cc	2.3614-2.3622 (59.98-60.00)	.0010-.0022 (.025-.055)	Center	.0008-.0079 (.02-.20)	2.0862-2.0866 (52.99-53.00)	.0010-.0022 (.025-.055)	.0063-.0102 (.16-.26)

Toyota Engines

20R 4 CYLINDER (Cont.)
ENGINE SPECIFICATIONS (Cont.)

VALVES							
Engine & Valve	Head Diam. In. (mm)	Face Angle	Seat Angle	Seat Width In. (mm)	Stem Diameter In. (mm)	Stem Clearance In. (mm)	Valve Lift In. (mm)
2189 cc Intake	.....	44.5°	45°	.047-.063 (1.2-1.6)	.3138-.3146 (7.97-7.99)	.0008-.0024 (.02-.06)	.....
Exhaust	.....	44.5°	45°	.047-.063 (1.2-1.6)	.3136-.3142 (7.96-7.98)	.0012-.0028 (.03-.07)	.....

VALVE SPRINGS			
Engine	Free Length In. (mm)	PRESSURE Lbs. @ In. (kg @ mm)	
		Valve Closed	Valve Open
2189 cc	1.80 (45.7)	55 @ 1.59 (25 @ 40.5)	.....

CAMSHAFT			
Engine	Journal Diam. In. (mm)	Clearance In. (mm)	①Lobe Lift In. (mm)
2189 cc	1.2984-1.2992 (32.98-33.0)	②.0004-.0020 (.01-.05)	Int. 1.680 (42.68) Exh. 1.682 (42.74)

① — Total Lobe Height.
② — End play is .0031-.0071" (.08-.18 mm)

TIGHTENING SPECIFICATIONS	
Application	Ft. Lbs. (mkg)
Cylinder Head Bolts	52-64 (7.2-8.8)
Main Bearing Cap Bolts	69-83 (9.5-11.5)
Connecting Rod Cap Bolts	39-48 (5.4-6.6)
Camshaft Bearing Cap Bolts	12-17 (1.7-2.3)
Timing Chain Cover	7-12 (1.0-1.6)
Crankshaft Pulley Bolt	102-130 (14-18)
Flywheel Bolts	73-86 (10-12)
Camshaft Sprocket Bolt	51-65 (7.0-9.0)
Intake Manifold	11-15 (1.5-2.1)
Exhaust Manifold	29-36 (4.0-5.0)
Oil Pan	2-3 (.3-.4)

Toyota Engines

2F 6 CYLINDER

ENGINE CODING

ENGINE IDENTIFICATION

Engine number is stamped on right side of cylinder block above starter motor. First two digits indicate engine type.

Engine Identification	
Application	Code
Land Cruiser (4230 cc)	2F

ENGINE, CYLINDER HEAD & MANIFOLDS

ENGINE

Removal — 1) Drain crankcase and cooling system and remove battery. Remove hood and tip grill forward. Disconnect radiator and heater hoses and remove radiator. Remove air cleaner and ducting and cover carburetor. Disconnect throttle and choke controls to carburetor. If equipped with air conditioning, dismount compressor and condenser but DO NOT disconnect hoses.

2) Disconnect alternator and ignition wiring between engine and chassis. Tag all vacuum and emission control hoses for identification and disconnect from engine. If equipped with power steering, remove pump and reservoir from engine and tie out of way, but do not disconnect hoses.

3) Remove engine and transmission undercovers. Remove front propeller shaft and winch drive shaft. Place jack or suitable supporting device under transmission and transfer case. Remove bolts attaching transmission and transfer case to engine bell housing. Disconnect exhaust pipe from manifold and fuel line at pump.

4) Attach suitable hoist and sling to engine and remove engine mount bolts and nuts. Move engine forward and up very carefully to avoid damage to engine compartment components.

Installation — Use guide dowels in transmission bolt holes and lower into position. Use care when aligning clutch assembly over transmission pilot shaft. Continue installation in reverse sequence of removal.

INTAKE & EXHAUST MANIFOLDS

Removal — 1) Disconnect battery and remove air cleaner. Disconnect throttle rod, choke rod, accelerator wire, vacuum line, and fuel line from carburetor.

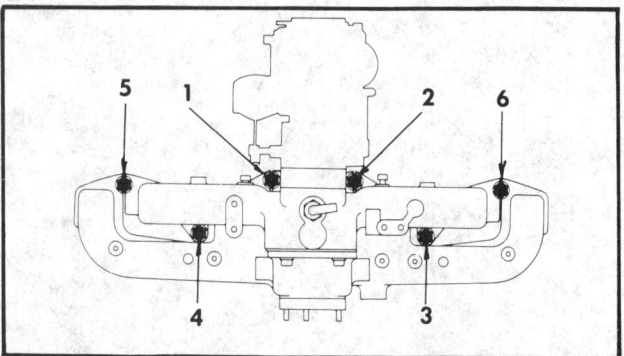

Fig. 1   Manifold Tightening Sequence

2) Disconnect magnetic valve wire from ignition coil terminal and remove carburetor assembly. Disconnect exhaust pipe from exhaust manifold. Remove manifold nuts, manifolds and gaskets.

Installation — Thoroughly clean all gasket surfaces and install new gaskets. Install manifold assembly and gradually tighten bolts working from center out. Install remaining components in reverse of removal procedure.

CYLINDER HEAD

Removal — Drain cooling system and remove intake and exhaust manifold as previously described. Disconnect spark plug wires and remove cylinder head cover. Remove rocker arm assembly and take out push rods, keeping them in order for installation. Loosen head bolts in 2 or 3 steps in reverse of tightening sequence and remove head.

Installation — Ensure that all mating surfaces are clean and place new head gasket on cylinder block. Ensure that mating oil hole on push rod side is between No. 4 and 5 cylinder. Install cylinder head and tighten bolts in 2 or 3 steps in the sequence illustrated. Complete installation in reverse sequence of removal.

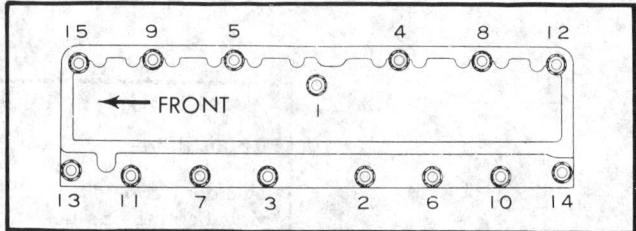

Fig. 2   Cylinder Head Tightening Sequence (Loosen in Reverse Order)

VALVES

VALVE ARRANGEMENT

E-I-I-E-E-I-I-E-E-I-I-E

VALVE GUIDE SERVICING

1) Check clearance between valve stems and valve guides. If clearance exceeds .004" (.10 mm) for intake or .005" (.12 mm) for exhaust, replace valve and/or valve guide.

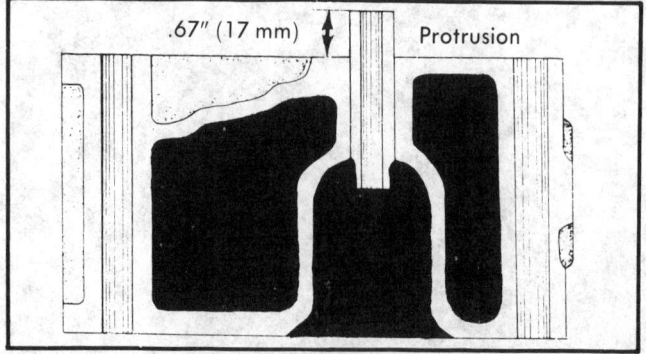

Fig. 3   Valve Guide Installation

2F 6 CYLINDER (Cont.)

2) To replace valve guide, drive toward combustion chamber with suitable tool (09201-60011). Use same tool to drive new guide in from top of cylinder head. When properly installed, guide should extend .67" (17 mm) from top of cylinder head. Intake valve guide length is 2.13" (54 mm) and exhaust guide is 2.32" (59 mm) long. After installing, ream guide for proper clearance.

VALVE SPRINGS

Removal — Using suitable compressor, compress valve spring and remove retainer locks (keepers). Release compressor and remove spring retainer, spring, valve stem oil seal and spring seat. Remove valves and keep in order. Check spring squareness, free height and tension at installed height. Spring should be square within .079" (2 mm).

Installation — Insert valve into valve stem guide, and install valve spring seat, valve spring, valve stem oil seal and valve spring retainer onto valve stem. Compress valve spring using suitable valve spring compressor and install valve spring retainer locks. Make sure retainer locks seat properly in valve stem groove.

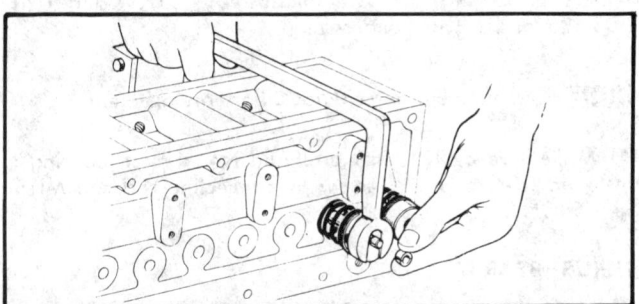

Fig. 4 Removing and Installing Valve Springs

ROCKER ARM ASSEMBLY

1) Check rocker arms and shaft for damage or wear. If clearance is excessive, replace bushing and ream to provide a clearance of .0007-.0015" (.017-.037 mm). When replacing bushing make sure oil hole in bushing lines up with oil hole in rocker arm.

2) Install rocker arms, springs and rocker shaft supports onto valve rocker shaft, then install valve rocker shaft lock springs.

NOTE — *There are two types of rocker arms and two types of rocker supports. Rocker support with oil hole is installed in the fourth position. Boss of rocker supports should face forward.*

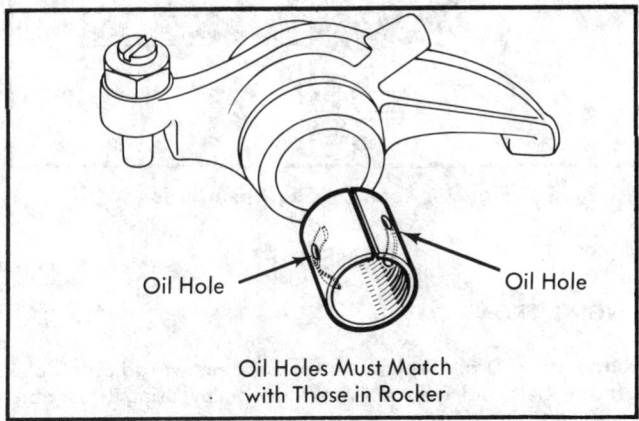

Oil Hole   Oil Hole

Oil Holes Must Match
with Those in Rocker

Fig. 5 Rocker Shaft Bushing Alignment

VALVE CLEARANCE ADJUSTMENT

1) Set No. 1 piston at TDC of compression stroke and align timing mark with pointer. Adjust valves 1,2,3,5,7 and 9 (as numbered from front).

2) Rotate crankshaft one complete turn and again align timing mark with pointer. Adjust remaining valves 4,6,8,10,11 and 12.

Valve Clearance Specifications

Valve	Clearance (Hot) In. (mm)
Intake	.008 (.20)
Exhaust	.014 (.35)

PISTONS, PINS & RINGS

OIL PAN

Removal — Remove engine undercovers, and remove flywheel side and undercover. Remove front propeller shaft. Drain oil, remove oil pan attaching bolts and oil pan.

Installation — Thoroughly clean all gasket mating surfaces. Apply liquid sealer onto both oil pan gasket surfaces, install oil pan and tighten bolts. Reverse removal procedure for remaining components.

PISTON & ROD ASSEMBLY

Removal — With cylinder head and oil pan removed, remove connecting rod caps and remove bearings. Push piston and rod assembly up through cylinder block. Mark all components with cylinder numbers for correct reassembly.

NOTE — *Cover rod bolts with a short piece of hose during removal and installation to prevent damage to crankshaft.*

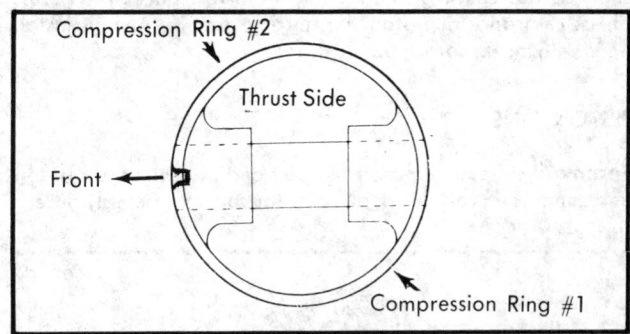

Fig. 6 Piston Ring Gap Spacing

Installation — Lubricate piston and rings and position ring gaps as illustrated. Use a ring compressor and install piston/rod assembly in proper position. Notch on piston must face FRONT and Toyota trademark on rod should face REAR. Oil hole in rod will face right (camshaft) side. Install bearings and caps.

NOTE — *Check for smooth rotation of crankshaft after tightening each bearing cap.*

FITTING PISTONS

1) Measure cylinder bores and pistons to be fitted. Measure piston with micrometer at bottom of skirt at right angles to piston pin. If clearance exceeds specifications, replace piston.

2F 6 CYLINDER (Cont.)

2) If cylinder bore is worn or tapered beyond specifications, cylinder must be bored and oversize pistons installed. Oversize pistons are available in .020" .040" and .060" (.50, 1.00 and 1.50 mm).

Cylinder Bore Specifications

Application	Wear Limits
Standard Bore	3.7008-3.7027" (94.00-94.05 mm)
Bore Wear Limit.................................	.008" (.2 mm)
Taper	.0008" (.02 mm)
Difference Between Cylinders	.002" (.05 mm)

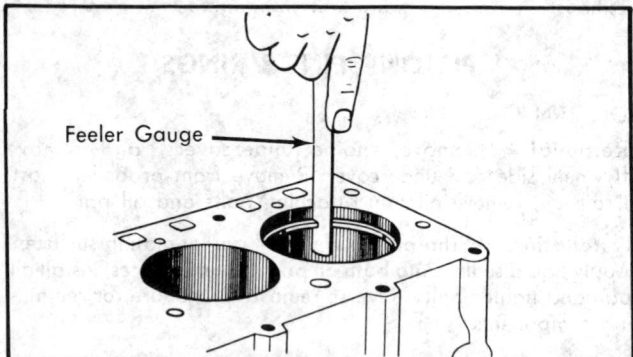

Fig. 7   Measuring Ring End Gap

3) Use .001-.002" (.03-.05 mm) feeler gauge with pull scale to check clearance of oversize pistons. Force of 2.2-5.5 lbs. (1.0-2.5 kg) must not be exceeded when pulling feeler gauge from cylinder.

4) Measure piston ring gaps in cylinder. If cylinder has not been bored, check gap with ring in lowest part of cylinder. Check clearance of piston ring in ring groove. Always install rings with marks facing upward.

PISTON PINS

Removal — Remove piston pin bolt and push pin from piston and connecting rod. Mark all parts for correct assembly order.

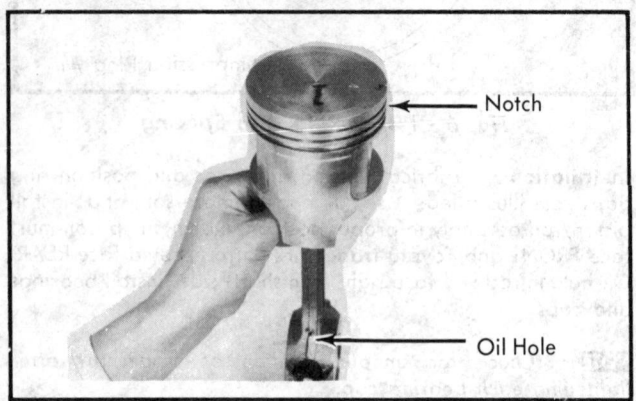

Fig. 8   Piston and Rod Assembled Properly

Installation — Position piston and connecting rod so that when notch on top of piston faces forward, oil hole in connecting rod faces camshaft side. Push pin into assembly and

center pin in piston. Center connecting rod between piston pin bosses and tighten piston pin bolt.

CRANKSHAFT MAIN & CONNECTING ROD BEARING

MAIN & CONNECTING ROD BEARINGS

1) Thoroughly clean crankshaft and blow out oil passages with compressed air. Check crankshaft for runout with a dial indicator on second or third main bearing journal. If runout exceeds .004" (.10 mm), straighten or replace crankshaft.

2) Check main and connecting rod bearing journals for taper or out-of-round. If taper or out-of-round exceeds .0004" (.01 mm), crankshaft must be ground to next undersize.

3) Main and connecting rod bearing clearance is checked by the Plastigage method. If clearance exceeds specifications, replace bearings. If crankshaft wear is excessive and clearance cannot be brought to specifications by use of new standard size bearings, crankshaft must be reground to next undersize. Bearings are available in .002", .010", and .020" (.05, .25, and .50 mm) undersize.

NOTE — *All main bearing configurations are different.*

4) Make sure oil hole in No. 1 and No. 4 main bearing is installed toward block. Arrow on connecting rod cap MUST face FRONT.

THRUST BEARING

Check crankshaft end play at No. 3 main bearing. If clearance exceeds .012" (.3 mm), replace crankshaft bearings.

REAR MAIN BEARING OIL SEAL

To install oil seal without disassembling engine, pry out oil seal with a screwdriver. Use crankshaft rear oil seal replacer tool (09223-60010) to drive new seal into place.

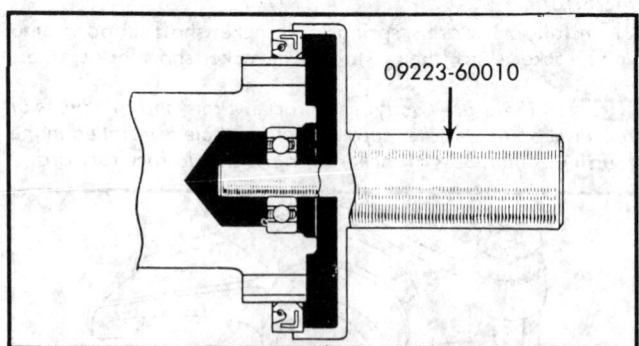

Fig. 9   Rear Oil Seal Installation

CAMSHAFT

ENGINE FRONT COVER

Removal — Drain cooling system and remove radiator. Take off fan belt and remove crankshaft pulley using a suitable puller (09213-60015). Remove timing gear cover bolts and take off cover.

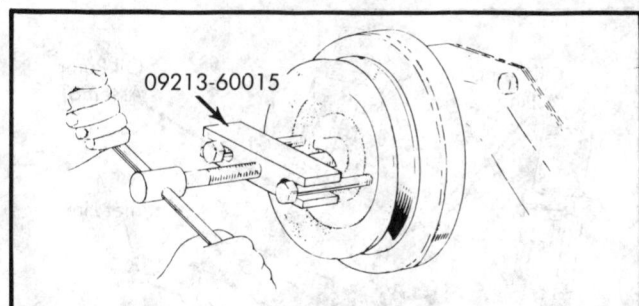

Fig. 10   Crankshaft Pulley Removal

Installation — Install cover and gasket. Ensure that bolts of proper length are used and screw in finger tight. Use liquid sealer on threads of lower 2 bolts. Drive pulley into position with suitable tool (09214-60010) to locate cover properly. Tighten cover bolts.

FRONT COVER OIL SEAL

Pry old oil seal out using screwdriver. Install new oil seal so that open end of seal is toward inside of timing gear cover. Drive seal in place with suitable tool (09515-35010).

Fig. 11   Front Oil Seal Installation

CAMSHAFT

Removal & Installation — Remove timing gear cover and slide oil slinger out from crankshaft. Remove 2 bolts retaining camshaft thrust plate to cylinder block by working through holes in camshaft timing gear. Remove camshaft by pulling out through front of block. Use care not to damage camshaft bearings or journals. To install, reverse removal procedure and set valve timing.

NOTE — *Ensure timing gear oil nozzle is positioned to direct oil onto timing gears. Stake into place with a punch.*

CAM LOBE HEIGHT

Measure height of cam lobe. If wear exceeds specification limit, replace camshaft. Intake lobe limit, 1.496" (38 mm); Exhaust lobe limit, 1.492" (37.9 mm).

CAMSHAFT BEARING

1) Inspect camshaft for runout. If runout exceeds .0059" (.15 mm), replace camshaft. Inspect camshaft journals and bearings for wear or damage. If clearance exceeds

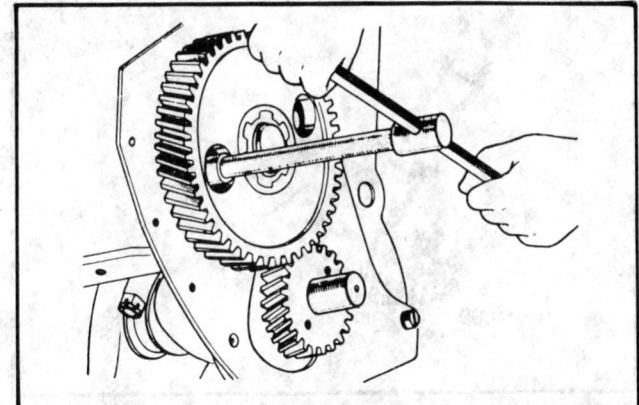

Fig. 12   Removing Crankshaft Thrust Plate Bolts

specifications, replace camshaft bearings and/or regrind camshaft. Bearings are available in standard .010" and .020" (.25 and .50 mm) oversizes.

2) Drive out camshaft rear expansion plug from cylinder block. Remove front and No. 2 bearing using Camshaft Bearing Remover (Tool 09215-60010). Place front and second bearing adapters against rear of respective bearing and place tool against front part of cylinder block.

3) Insert replacer shaft into the 3 parts and screw retainer nut onto replacer shaft. Hold slotted part of shaft with wrench to prevent shaft from turning. Front and No. 1 bearings will be pulled out to front by screwing in retainer nut with another wrench.

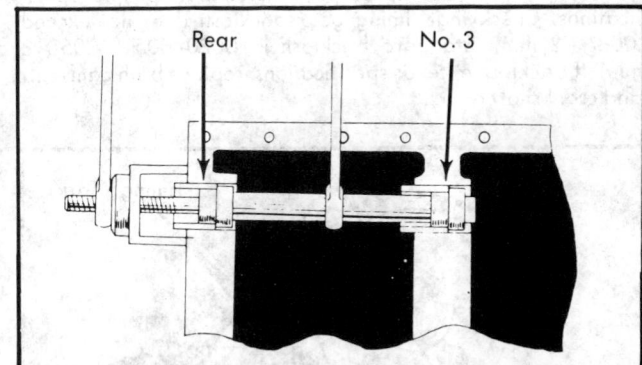

Fig. 13   Typical Camshaft Bearing Removal Procedure (No. 3 and Rear Bearings Shown)

4) Remove No. 3 and rear bearing toward rear of block using tool in same manner as for front and No. 1 bearing. When installing new bearings, ensure that oil holes of bearing match up with oil holes in cylinder block.

5) When new bearings have been installed, measure to obtain proper clearance. Only a very light cut is required to ream bearings to proper size. Coat rear expansion plug with sealer and reinstall plug in block.

CAMSHAFT END THRUST

Measure end thrust with feeler gauge. Thrust should be .0035-.0059" (.09-.15 mm). If thrust exceeds .008" (.2 mm), replace camshaft thrust plate.

Toyota Engines

2F 6 CYLINDER (Cont.)

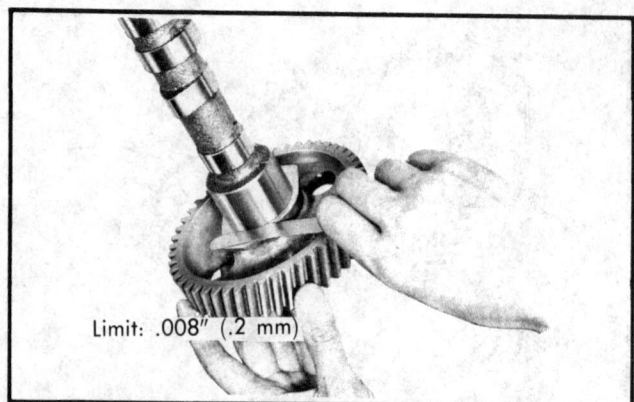

Fig. 14   Measuring Camshaft End Thrust

CRANKSHAFT TIMING GEAR

Remove pulley key from crankshaft. Using suitable puller (09213-60015), pull off crankshaft gear. To reinstall, drive on gear using suitable driver (09214-60010). Make sure timing mark on gear faces outward.

VALVE TIMING

1) With crankshaft timing gear installed, oil camshaft journals and bearings and insert camshaft. Align mating mark on camshaft timing gear with mark on crankshaft timing gear and push camshaft into position. No. 6 cylinder should be at TDC on compression stroke. If oil nozzle was removed, refit with oil hole facing down (toward gears).

2) Tighten camshaft thrust plate retaining bolts to specifications. Check that timing gear backlash does not exceed .008" (.2 mm). Standard backlash is .0020-.0051" (.05-.13 mm). If backlash exceeds specifications, replace both camshaft and crankshaft gears.

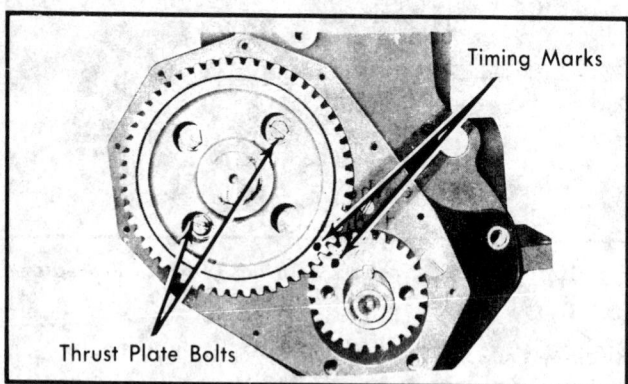

Fig. 15   Timing Mark Alignment

ENGINE OILING

Crankcase Capacity — 7.4 quarts (8.2 quarts with filter).

Oil Filter — Full flow cartridge type with integral relief valve.

Normal Oil Pressure — Pressure maintained at 50-64 psi (3.5-4.5 kg/cm²) by safety valve in oil pressure regulator.

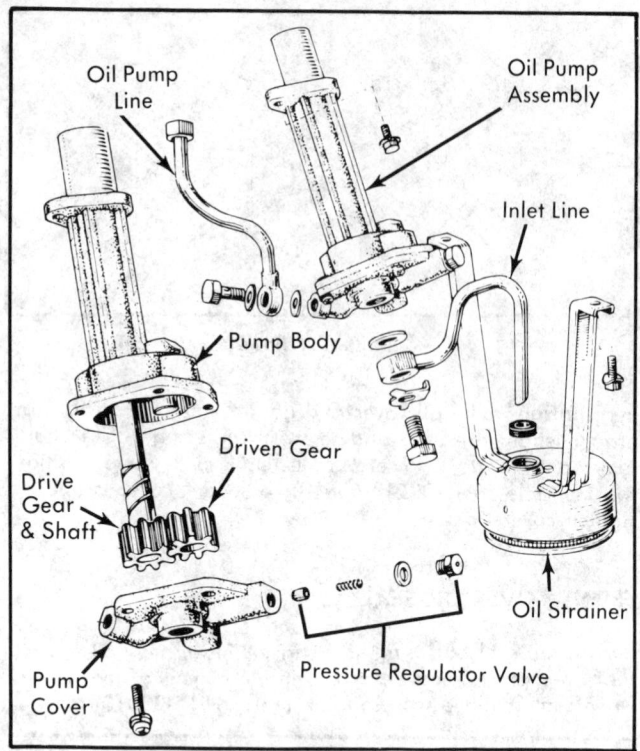

Fig. 16   Exploded View of Oil Pump Assembly

Pressure Regulator — Located in oil pump, non-adjustable.

ENGINE OILING SYSTEM

Force-feed system ensures positive lubrication through oil holes and galleries in engine block.

OIL PUMP

Removal — With oil pan removed, remove bolts attaching oil strainer to crankcase. Remove oil pump mounting bolt and oil pump line. Remove pump from engine. Remove cover and inspect gears and housing for proper clearances. Replace worn or damaged components.

Installation — Prior to installing assembled pump, check operation by submerging inlet line in fresh engine oil. Turn shaft clockwise with a screwdriver and check for oil flow from discharge hole. Cover discharge hole with thumb and turn as before. Turning resistance should be felt. Install pump on engine, noting that lower end of distributor drive shaft aligns with oil pump shaft. To complete installation, reverse removal procedure.

Oil Pump Specifications

Application	Standard In. (mm)	Wear Limit In. (mm)
Gear-to-Housing Clearance	.0012-.0043 (.03-.11)	.008 (.2)
Gear Backlash	.0020-.0028 (.05-.07)	.0374 (.95)
Gear Side Clearance	.0012-.0035 (.03-.09)	.0059 (.15)
Cover Wear		.0059 (.15)

Toyota Engines

2F 6 CYLINDER (Cont.)

ENGINE COOLING

Thermostat — Wax pellet type. Begins to open at 180°F (82°C) and is fully opened at 203°F (95°C).

Coolant capacity — Approximately 4.25 gallons.

WATER PUMP

Removal — Drain cooling system and loosen alternator adjusting bar. Remove fan, fan pulley and fan belt. Remove lower radiator hose and heater hose from pump. Remove water pump retaining bolts, pump and gasket.

Installation — Ensure that mating surfaces are clean and free from pitting or damage. Install pump with new gasket and tighten mounting bolts. Complete installation in reverse sequence of removal and adjust belt tension.

ENGINE SPECIFICATIONS

GENERAL SPECIFICATIONS

Year	Displ. cu. ins.	cc	Carburetor	HP at RPM	Torque (Ft. Lbs. at RPM)	Compr. Ratio	Bore in.	mm	Stroke in.	mm
1980	257.9	4230	1x2-Bbl.	125@3600	200@1800	7.8:1	3.70	94	4.00	101.6

VALVES

Engine & Valve	Head Diam. In. (mm)	Face Angle	Seat Angle	Seat Width In. (mm)	Stem Diameter In. (mm)	Stem Clearance In. (mm) ①	Valve Lift In. (mm)
4230 cc Intake	1.81 (46.0)	45°	45°	.055 (1.4)	.3138-.3144 (7.970-7.985)	.0012-.0024 (.03-.06)	.....
Exhaust	1.48 (37.5)	45°	45°	.067 (1.7)	.3134-.3140 (7.960-7.975)	.0016-.0028 (.04-.07)	.....

① — Wear limits: Intake — .004" (.10 mm), exhaust — .005" (.12 mm).

PISTONS, PINS, RINGS

	PISTONS	PINS		RINGS		
Engine	Clearance In. (mm)	Piston Fit In. (mm)	Rod Fit In. (mm)	Rings	End Gap In. (mm)	Side Clearance In. (mm)
4230 cc	.0012-.0020 (.03-.05)	.0003-.0005 (.008-.012)	Locked in Rod	No. 1	.008-.016 (.20-.40)	.0012-.0024 (.03-.06)
				No. 2	.008-.016 (.20-.40)	.0008-.0024 (.02-.06)
				Oil	.....	.....

CRANKSHAFT MAIN & CONNECTING ROD BEARINGS

	MAIN BEARINGS				CONNECTING ROD BEARINGS		
Engine	Journal Diam. In. (mm)	Clearance In. (mm)	Thrust Bearing	Crankshaft End Play In. (mm)	Journal Diam. In. (mm)	Clearance In. (mm)	Side Play In. (mm)
4230 cc No. 1	2.6367-2.6376 (66.972-66.996)	.0008-.0017 (.020-.044)	No. 3	.002-.006 (.06-.16)	2.1252-2.1260 (53.98-54.00)	.0008-.0024 (.020-.060)	.004-.009 (.11-.23)
No. 2	2.6957-2.6967 (68.472-68.496)						
No. 3	2.7548-2.7557 (69.972-69.996)						
No. 4	2.8139-2.8148 (71.472-71.496)						

Toyota Engines

2F 6 CYLINDER (Cont.)

ENGINE SPECIFICATIONS (Cont.)

		VALVE SPRINGS	
Engine	Free Length In. (mm)	PRESSURE (LBS.) Lbs. @ In. (kg @ mm)	
		Valve Closed	Valve Open
4230 cc	2.028 (51.5)	71.7@1.693 (32.5@43.0)	.....

	CAMSHAFT		
Engine	Journal Diam. In. (mm)	Clearance In. (mm)	Lobe Lift In. (mm)
4230 cc No. 1	1.8880-1.8888 (47.955-47.975)	.001-.003 (.025-.075)	.....
No. 2	1.8289-1.8297 (46.455-46.475)		
No. 3	1.7699-1.7707 (44.955-44.975)		
No. 4	1.7108-1.7116 (43.455-43.475)		

TIGHTENING SPECIFICATIONS

Application	Ft. Lbs. (mkg)
Cylinder Head	83-98 (11.5-13.5)
Piston Pin Bolt	39-51 (5.4-7.0)
Connecting Rod Bearing Caps	35-55 (4.8-7.6)
Crankshaft Main Bearing Caps	
Front, No. 2 & No. 3	90-108 (12.5-15)
Rear	76-94 (10.5-13)
Camshaft Thrust Plate Bolts	7-12 (1.0-1.6)
Manifold Nuts	
Federal	28-37 (3.5-5.1)
California	36-51 (5.0-7.0)
Flywheel Bolts	59-62 (8.1-8.5)
Crankshaft Pulley	116-145 (16-20)

4M-E 6 CYLINDER

ENGINE CODING

ENGINE IDENTIFICATION

Engine number is stamped on a machined pad on the right side of engine block. Engine code is also printed on a sticker attached to cylinder head cover.

Engine Identification	
Application	**Code**
Cressida & Supra (2563 cc)	4M-E

ENGINE, CYLINDER HEAD & MANIFOLDS

ENGINE

Removal — 1) Disconnect battery and drain cooling system. Remove hood and fan shroud. Remove radiator hoses, radiator, heater hoses and all oil cooler hoses. Remove oil pressure sending wire and alternator wiring.

2) Remove air cleaner and air intake ducting. Disconnect brake booster vacuum hose. Disconnect distributor primary wiring and coil secondary wiring. Label and disconnect all fuel lines, vacuum hoses and electrical wiring running between engine and engine compartment.

3) Disconnect starter wiring and accelerator connecting rod. If equipped with manual transmission, disconnect clutch flexible hose from master cylinder tube and cap hose end to prevent fluid leakage. On all models, disconnect power steering feed hose.

4) Raise front and rear of vehicle with jack and support on stands. Disconnect exhaust pipe from manifold and remove exhaust pipe supports and insulator. Disconnect speedometer drive cable and back-up light wiring.

5) On manual transmission models, remove console box and gear shift lever. On automatic transmission models, remove connecting rod swivel nut and disconnect control rod from shift lever.

6) On all models, remove propeller shaft and plug rear of transmission to prevent oil leakage. Take off rear engine undercover and remove front engine mounts. Support transmission with jack and remove rear engine mount and crossmember.

7) Lower jack supporting transmission and remove stands. Using an engine hoist, remove engine and transmission assembly from vehicle.

Installation — To install, reverse removal procedure and note the following: Check all fluid levels and linkage adjustments prior to starting engine.

INTAKE MANIFOLD

Removal — 1) Disconnect battery and drain coolant. Remove air cleaner and distributor cap. Remove radiator inlet hose and heater hoses. Disconnect temperature gauge sending wire and fuel line.

2) It is necessary to remove air intake chamber with throttle body prior to intake manifold removal. Mark all vacuum, coolant and fuel hoses for identification and disconnect from air chamber. Disconnect intake connector, cold start injector, throttle link and throttle wire for automatic transmission. Remove mounting bolts and lift air chamber off of manifold.

3) Disconnect fuel injection wiring connectors and remove wiring clamps. Remove 4 bolts and pull out fuel delivery pipe with injectors. Remove pressure regulator at center of manifold, EGR valve, and disconnect remaining hoses. Remove mounting bolts and lift off manifold.

CAUTION — *When disconnecting delivery pipe and injectors, use container to catch the large amount of gasoline which will be expelled.*

Installation — Thoroughly clean all gasket surfaces and install new gaskets. Install manifold assembly and gradually tighten bolts working from center out. Install remaining components in reverse of removal procedure.

NOTE — *When installing injectors, lubricate "O" rings and insulators with gasoline.*

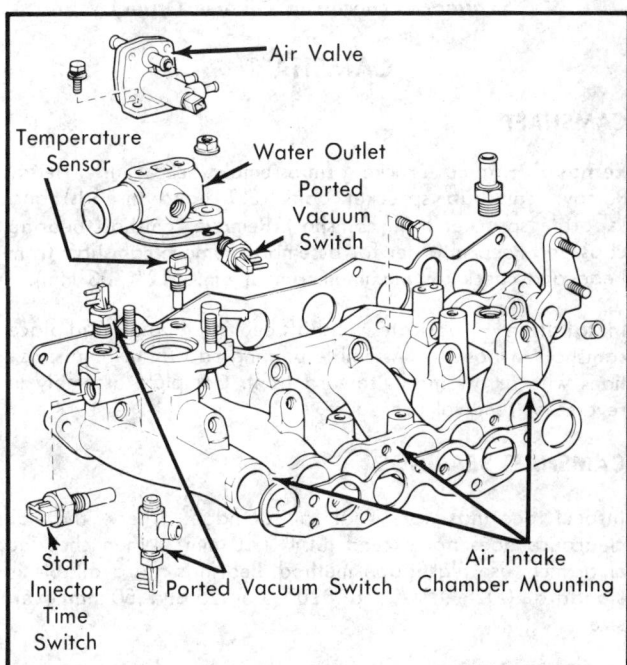

Fig. 1 Toyota 4M-E Intake Manifold Assembly

CYLINDER HEAD & ROCKER ARMS

Removal — 1) Remove intake and exhaust manifolds. Remove heater and by-pass hoses attached to head. Remove spark plugs and cylinder head cover. Turn crankshaft so that number 1 piston is at TDC on firing stroke and note that mating marks are aligned on timing gear and timing chain.

4M-E 6 CYLINDER (Cont.)

2) Remove chain tensioner, then remove timing gear bolt noting that bolt has *LEFT* hand threads. Loosen head/rocker shaft bolts a little at a time in reverse of tightening sequence illustrated. Lift off rocker arm assembly, then lift head straight up from block.

Installation — Clean all gasket surfaces and apply sealer to cylinder head, around oil holes in the block, and in area of timing chain cover and block. Install new gasket. Clean all foreign matter from bolt holes and place cylinder head on block. Make sure valve adjusting screws have been loosened and install rocker shaft assembly. Install bolts and tighten in several steps according to the sequence illustrated. Align timing marks and reverse removal procedure to complete assembly.

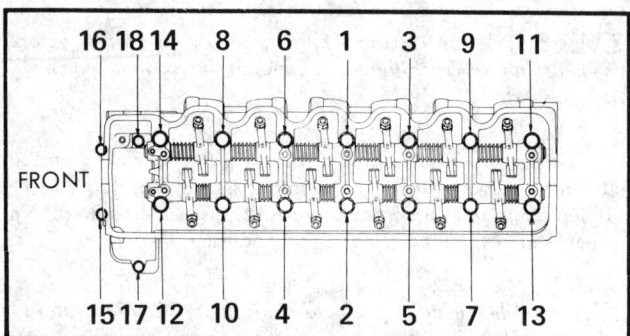

Fig. 2   Cylinder Head/Rocker Arm Bolt Tightening Sequence (Loosen in Reverse Order)

CAMSHAFT

CAMSHAFT

Removal — Remove rocker arm assembly. See *Cylinder Head*. Remove camshaft sprocket bolt (LEFT hand threads) and separate sprocket from camshaft. Remove camshaft bearing caps and keep in order for assembly. Remove camshaft from head and check for maximum runout of .0012" (.03 mm).

Installation — Lubricate camshaft bearing journals and place camshaft in position. Assemble bearing caps in original positions with arrow marks toward front. Complete assembly in reverse of removal procedure.

CAMSHAFT BEARINGS

Inspect bearings for wear or damage. Check that oil clearance does not exceed .004" (.10 mm). When checking clearance, use Plastigage method. Bearings are available in standard, .002", .010" and .020" (.05, .25 and .50 mm) oversizes.

CAMSHAFT END THRUST

Install camshaft in cylinder head and tighten all bearing caps. Attach dial indicator and check end thrust at flange end. Maximum clearance is .012" (.3 mm). Specified standard clearance is .003-.007" (.08-.18 mm).

CAM HEIGHT

Measure cam height. Minimum for intake is 1.696" (43.08 mm). Minimum for exhaust is 1.699" (43.15 mm). If height is less than specified, replace camshaft.

ENGINE FRONT COVER

Remove crankshaft damper attaching bolt and remove damper using suitable puller (09213-41013). Remove oil pan and remove front cover bolts and front cover. Use liquid sealer on front cover gaskets when assembling.

ENGINE FRONT COVER OIL SEAL

Inspect oil seal lip and replace if worn or damaged. Pry old seal out without damaging cover or retainer. Install seal using replacer tool (09223-50010). Apply multipurpose lubricant to seal lip.

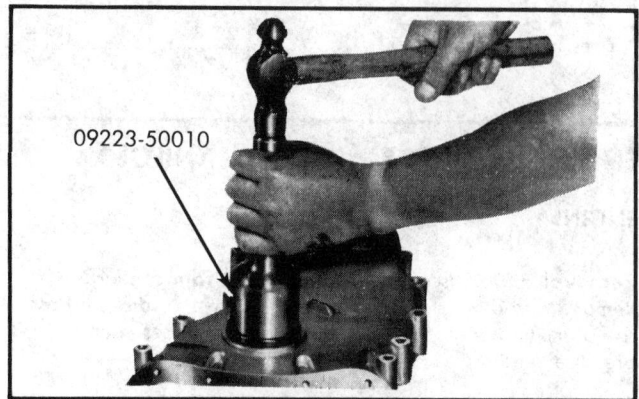

Fig. 3   Using Special Seal Installing Tool to Drive in Front Oil Seal

TIMING CHAIN

Removal — See *Valve Timing*. Remove cylinder head cover, rocker arm shafts and camshaft. Remove cylinder head. Remove crankshaft damper attaching bolt and remove damper using suitable puller (09213-41013). Remove oil pan, timing chain cover and timing chain.

Installation — **1)** Inspect chain, sprockets and tensioner. Position crankshaft sprocket so that key is pointed straight toward cylinder head and Toyota mark is in line with pump sprocket shaft. Install timing chain with white links aligned with punch marks on crankshaft gear and pump gear. See *Fig. 5*.

NOTE — *Do NOT confuse index marks. Plated or white links align with punch marks on gears. Toyota symbol marks align with each other.*

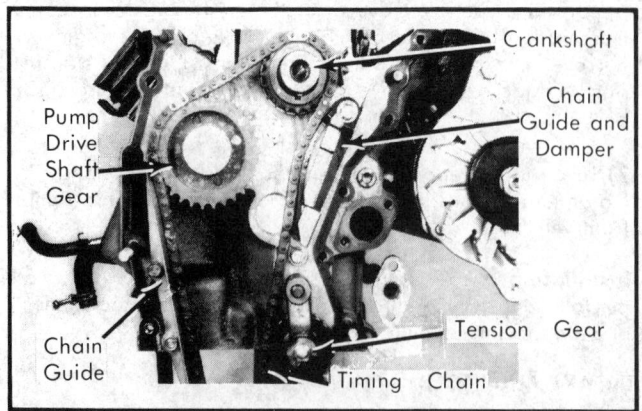

Fig. 4   Front View of Timing Chain and Gears

4M-E 6 CYLINDER (Cont.)

2) Insert bolt in collar and install both chain vibration dampers and guide. With head and camshaft in position, assure that camshaft flange pin is aligned with embossed mark on rocker support number 1. Align mating link on chain with punch mark on camshaft drive gear and install drive gear on camshaft. Note that attaching bolt has LEFT hand threads.

3) Adjust timing chain tension by first rotating engine in normal direction (clockwise) until chain is at most slack position. Loosen tensioner locknut, then turn adjusting screw clockwise until resistance is felt. Loosen screw 2 full turns and tighten lock nut. If chain is noisy after starting engine, loosen adjusting screw ½ turn more. See *Valve Timing*.

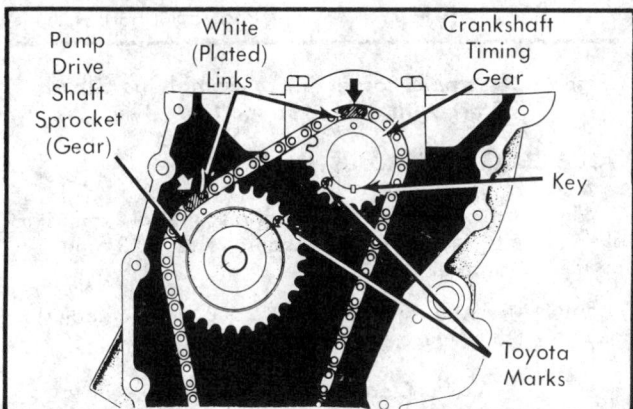

Fig. 5   Timing Chain with Pump Sprocket and Crankshaft Marks Aligned

OIL PUMP SHAFT

1) With front cover and timing chain removed, use puller (09213-36010) to remove pump shaft sprocket. Remove thrust plate bolt and pull pump shaft from cylinder block. Replace and tighten sprocket on shaft, then check end play between gear and plate with feeler gauge. If beyond limits, replace thrust plate.

2) Check bearing bore diameter with inside micrometer and journal diameter with outside micrometer. Standard clearance is .0010-.0026" (.025-.066 mm). If clearance exceeds .0031" (.08 mm), replace bearings with special tool (09233-41010).

Oil Pump Shaft Specifications	
Application	**In. (mm)**
Out-of-Round & Taper Limit	.0004 (.01)
Thrust Clearance	
Standard	.002-.005 (.05-.13)
Wear Limit	.012 (.30)
Bearing Clearance	
Standard	.0010-.0026 (.025-.066)
Wear Limit	.003 (.08)

VALVE TIMING

1) Rotate crankshaft in normal direction (clockwise) so that number 1 piston is at TDC on compression stroke. Check that camshaft flange timing pin is aligned with embossed mark on rocker support. (Timing chain cover graduation should indicate 0°mark aligned with notch in pulley.)

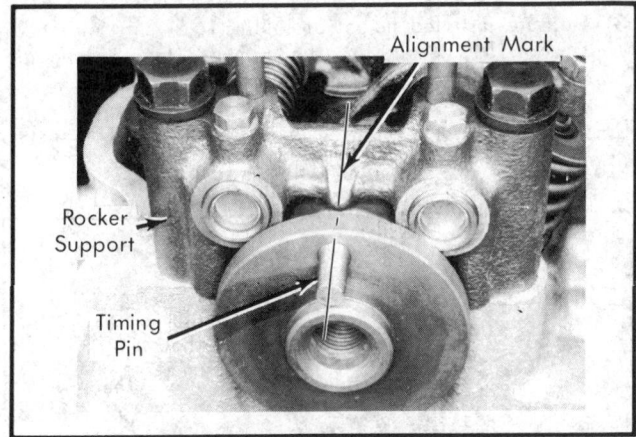

Fig. 6   Camshaft Flange Straight Pin Aligned with Support For Installation of Camshaft Gear

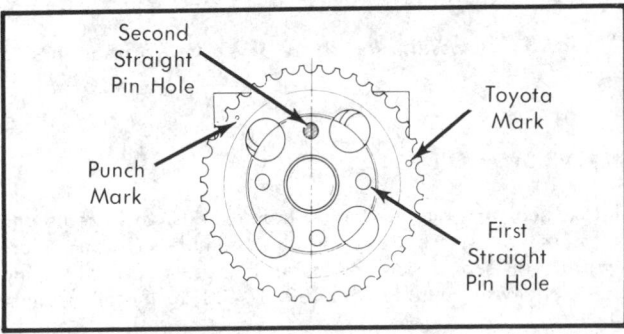

Fig. 7   Front View of Camshaft Gear with Alignment Marks and Straight Pin Holes

2) If marks are not as described, turn crankshaft until timing pin is in line with embossed mark and note timing cover graduation. Remove chain tensioner and timing gear set bolt. If timing was retarded 3 to 9 degrees, remove gear and install to second straight pin hole with piston at TDC. Install and adjust chain tensioner and recheck valve timing.

NOTE — *Movement of straight pin to No. 2 hole and No. 3 hole advances valve timing in steps of 6° each.*

VALVES

VALVE ARRANGEMENT

Left Side — All Intake.

Right Side — All Exhaust.

VALVE GUIDE SERVICING

1) Break off valve guide bushing at snap ring and remove snap ring. Heat cylinder head to approximately 176-212°F (80-100°C) and drive out bushing toward combustion chamber.

2) Allow head to cool and measure cylinder head bushing bore. If bore exceeds .5125" (13.018 mm), machine bore to .514" (13.054 mm) and insert .002" (.05 mm) oversize bushing. Head should be heated to 176-212°F (80-100°C) and bushing driven in with drift (09201-60011) until snap ring contacts head.

4M-E 6 CYLINDER (Cont.)

3) Measure installed height of .650" (16.5 mm) for intake guide and .551 (14 mm) for exhaust guide. Hand ream guide bore to provide specified stem clearance.

NOTE — *Valve guide replacement is recommended whenever new valves are installed.*

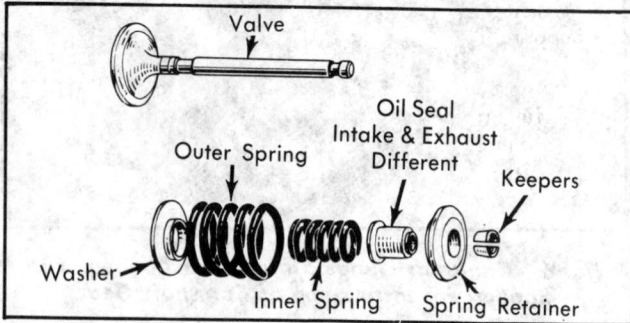

Fig. 8   Disassembled View of Valve Components

VALVE STEM OIL SEALS

Intake seals are slightly longer than exhaust valve seals and must not be switched. To install, assemble in order: plate washer, oil seal, inner and outer springs, and valve spring retainer. With suitable tool (09202-43011), install retainer locks.

VALVE & VALVE SPRING

Mark each valve and using valve spring compressor, remove valves, valve retainers, retainer locks, springs and valve stem oil seals. When replacing valve springs, closed coil ends face toward cylinder head.

VALVE SPRING HEIGHT

Measure valve spring free length with caliper type ruler and check for squareness within .063" (1.6 mm). Using a spring tester, check load when spring is compressed to installed height. Check installed height with valve in closed position by measuring distance from upper edge of washer to lower edge of spring retainer.

ROCKER ARM ASSEMBLY

Check arm-to-shaft clearance by twisting on shaft. Little or no movement should be felt. If movement is felt, disassemble and inspect. Bushings may be replaced and finished to give standard clearance of .0005-.0013" (.012-.033 mm) using pin hole grinder. Assemble rocker arm assembly, starting with rocker support number 1. Install on head and tighten bolts in sequence shown in *Fig. 2.*

NOTE — *Disassemble and mark all parts for reassembly in proper order. Loosen adjusting screws and nuts prior to installing rocker arm assembly.*

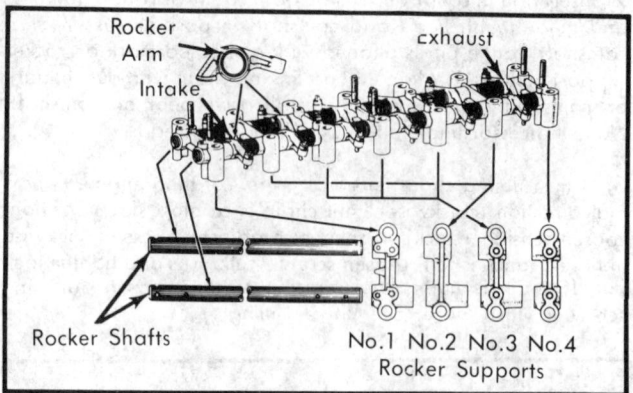

Fig. 9   Assemble Rocker Arm Assembly as Shown (Start with Rocker Support No. 1)

VALVE CLEARANCE ADJUSTMENT

1) With No. 1 piston at TDC of compression stroke, adjust intake valves 1, 2, and 4, and exhaust valves 1, 3, and 5 to specified clearance.

2) Rotate crankshaft one turn (360°) clockwise and adjust intake valves 3,5 and 6, and exhaust valves 2,4 and 6.

Valve Clearance Specifications

Valve	Hot In. (mm)	Cold In. (mm)
Intake	.011 (.28)	.010 (.25)
Exhaust	.014 (.35)	.013 (.33)

PISTONS, PINS & RINGS

PISTON & ROD ASSEMBLY

Removal — With cylinder head and oil pan removed, remove connecting rod caps and remove bearings. Push piston and rod assembly up through cylinder head side. Mark all components with cylinder numbers for correct reassembly.

Installation — **1)** Apply oil to piston and piston rings. Install rings with mark on side of ring facing upwards. Position piston ring gaps shown in illustration. Using suitable ring compressor, install piston and rod assembly in cylinder block. Make sure mark on piston faces front.

2) Replace connecting rod caps with mating marks aligned. Tighten nuts evenly in 2 or 3 steps and check connecting rod side play.

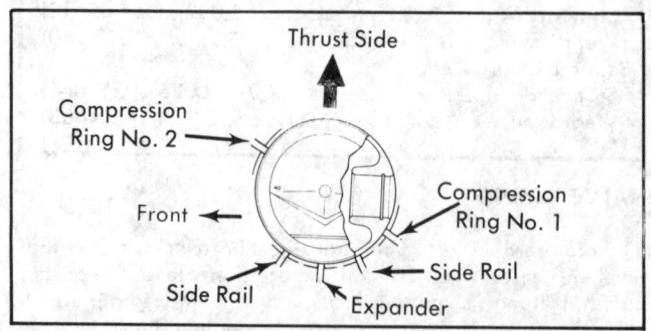

Fig. 10   Position Ring Gaps as Shown for Installation

4M-E 6 CYLINDER (Cont.)

FITTING PISTONS

Measure top, center and bottom of cylinder bore with dial indicator. If wear exceeds .008" (.2 mm) or taper and out-of-round exceeds .0008" (.02 mm), cylinders must be rebored. Bore in sequence number 1, 3, 6, 4, 2 and 5 cylinders. Last cut of boring bar should not remove more than .0020" (.05 mm). Finish to final dimension by honing the last .0008" (.02 mm).

Piston Diameter Table	
Application	**Piston O.D. In. (mm)**
Standard	3.146-3.148 (79.93-79.98)
.020" (.50 mm) Oversize	3.166-3.168 (80.43-80.48)
.030" (.75 mm) Oversize	3.176-3.178 (80.68-80.73)
.039" (1.0 mm) Oversize	3.186-3.188 (80.93-80.98)

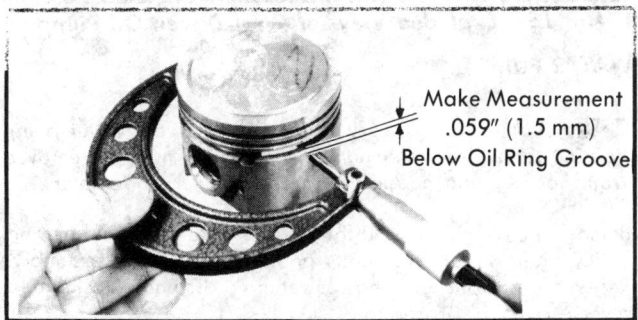

Make Measurement .059" (1.5 mm) Below Oil Ring Groove

Fig. 11   Measure Piston as Shown at 68°F (20°C)

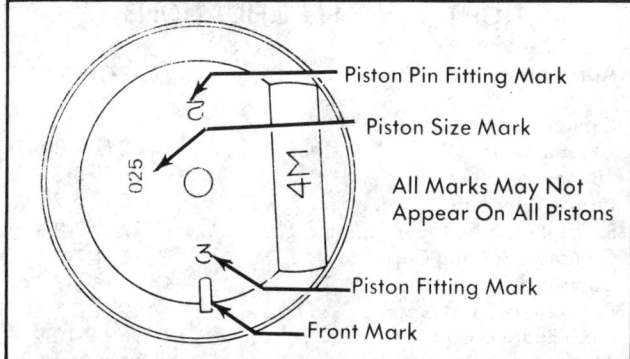

Piston Pin Fitting Mark

Piston Size Mark

All Marks May Not Appear On All Pistons

Piston Fitting Mark

Front Mark

Fig. 12   Typical Reference Marks on Piston Head

NOTE — Allow bore to cool after boring and honing to avoid erroneous readings while measuring. Cool measurement of piston and bore should provide .0020-.0028" (.05-.07 mm) for proper clearance.

Removal — Remove circlips in piston pin hole with needle nose pliers. Heat piston to about 140°F (60°C) and remove pin by tapping lightly with plastic hammer. Keep piston, pin and rod together as a set.

PISTON PINS

Installation — Install one circlip in piston and heat to about 140°F (60°C). Align piston notch with rod mark and push pin in with thumb. Install remaining circlip.

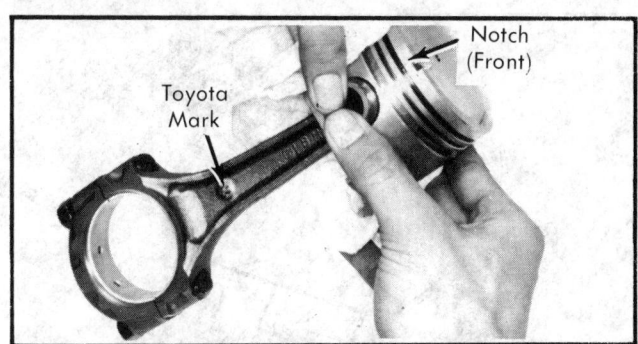

Notch (Front)

Toyota Mark

Fig. 13   Notch on Piston and Mark on Rod Must Face Same Direction When Installing Piston Pin

MAIN & CONNECTING ROD BEARINGS

1) Measure connecting rod side play with dial indicator. If greater than .012" (.3 mm), rod must be replaced. Wipe off bearing and journal, then check clearance with Plastigage. If clearance exceeds .003" (.08 mm) and cannot be corrected with .002" (.05 mm) undersize bearings, or if taper or out-of-round exceeds .0008" (.02 mm), crankshaft must be ground to next undersize.

2) Check crankshaft runout with dial indicator. If runout exceeds .0012" (.03 mm), correct or replace crankshaft. Check main bearing journal for taper and out-of-round. Check main bearing clearance using Plastigage. If required, crankshaft may be reground for undersize bearings. Undersize bearings for main and connecting rods are available in .002" (.05 mm), .010" (.25 mm) and .020" (.50 mm) as well as standard.

THRUST BEARING

Measure crankshaft end play with center (number 4) main bearing and cap installed. If clearance exceeds .012" (.3 mm), replace thrust washers to achieve standard clearance of .002-.010" (.05-.25 mm). Standard thickness of thrust washer is .115" (2.92 mm) with .005" (.13 mm) and .010" (.25 mm) oversizes available.

NOTE — Install thrust washers with oil grooves facing outward

REAR MAIN OIL SEAL

Inspect oil seal lip and replace if worn or damaged. Pry old seal out without damaging cover or retainer. Install seal using replacer tool (09223-41010). Apply multipurpose lubricant to seal lip.

ENGINE OILING

Pressure Relief Valves — There are 3 relief valves in the engine oiling system. The pressure relief valve in the oil pump opens at 71-85 psi (5.0-6.0 kg/cm²), the oil regulator valve-to-cooler opens at 38-50 psi (2.7-3.5 kg/cm²), and the relief valve in the filter opens with a pressure difference of 1-17 psi (.8-1.2 kg/cm²).

Oil Filter — Full flow spin-on type.

Crankcase Capacity — 4.9 qts. with filter, 4.3 qts. without filter.

Toyota Engines

4M-E 6 CYLINDER (Cont.)

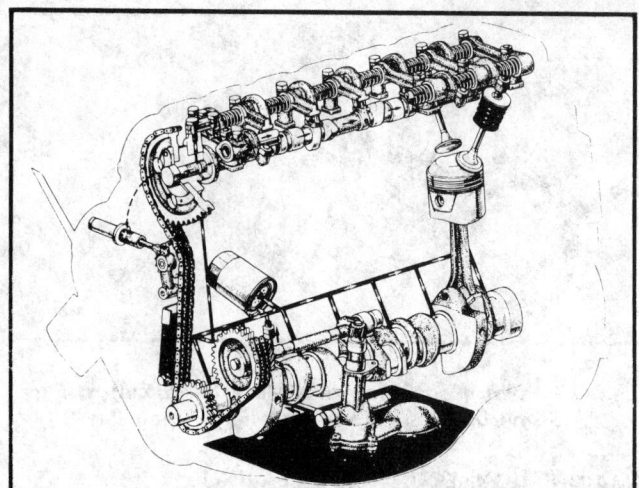

Fig. 14 *Diagram of Engine Lubrication System (Oil Cooler Not Shown)*

ENGINE OILING SYSTEM

System is force feed with full-flow filtering unit. Pressure is delivered by a gear-driven oil pump. From filter oil travels through cylinder block passages by which internal components are lubricated. An external oil cooler is mounted at the upper left front of the radiator. It receives oil from the regulator mounted on the block, cools and returns the oil to the pan.

OIL PUMP

With pan off engine, remove oil pump mounting bolts and take out oil pump. Disassemble pump by removing (in order) snap ring, spacer, driveshaft gear, Woodruff key, pump cover, pump shaft sub-assembly, driven gear, relief valve plug, gasket, spring and relief valve. Check side clearance between gear and cover for maximum of .006" (.15 mm). Check clearance between gear teeth and body for not more than .008" (.2 mm). Measure backlash between gear teeth with feeler gauge for no more than .035" (.9 mm). Clean and inspect components and reverse disassembly procedure. Pump may be checked for operation by immersing screen in oil and turning shaft clockwise. Oil should discharge from pump outlet.

ENGINE COOLING

Thermostat — Wax pellet type, begins to open at 176-183°F (80-84°C) and should open to more than .32" (8 mm) at 203°F.

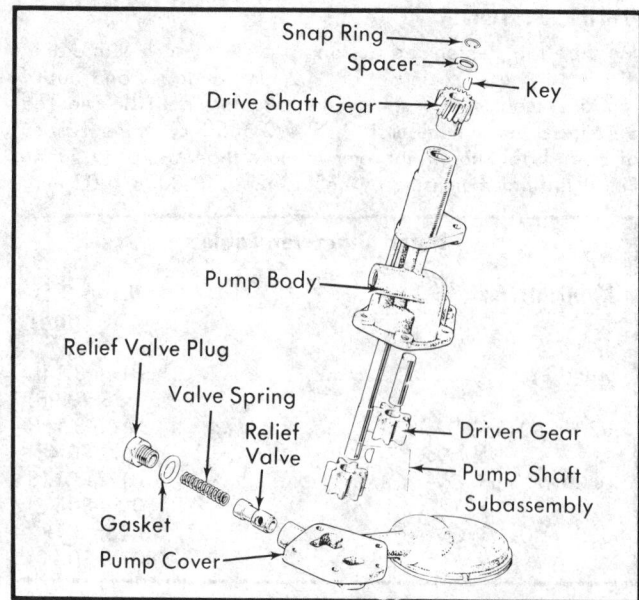

Fig. 15 *Exploded View of Gear Driven Oil Pump*

WATER PUMP

NOTE — *It is not necessary to remove complete water pump housing to service water pump. Pump cover may be removed from housing and housing may be left on cylinder block.*

Remove fluid coupling and fan assembly. Remove fan belt and pulley. Remove 5 cover bolts and take off cover assembly. Replaces seals and bearings as required. Use new gasket and reverse removal procedure.

TIGHTENING SPECIFICATIONS

Application	Ft.Lbs. (mkg)
Cylinder Head	
12 mm bolts	54-62 (7.5-8.5)
8 mm bolts	11-16 (1.5-2.2)
Intake Manifold	11-15 (1.5-2.1)
Exhaust Manifold	12-17 (1.7-2.3)
Camshaft Bearing Cap	12-17 (1.7-2.3)
Camshaft Timing Gear (L.H. Thread)	47-54 (6.5-7.5)
Pump Drive Shaft Gear	7-12 (1.0-1.6)
Main Bearing Caps	72-79 (9.9-10.9)
Connecting Rod Cap	30-35 (4.2-4.8)
Oil Pan	5-7 (.65-.95)
Crankshaft Pulley	98-119 (13.5-16.5)
Flywheel	51-58 (7.0-8.0)
Chain Tensioner	22-29 (3.0-4.0)

ENGINE SPECIFICATIONS

GENERAL SPECIFICATIONS

Year	Displ.		Carburetor	HP at RPM	Torque (Ft. Lbs. at RPM)	Compr. Ratio	Bore		Stroke	
	cu. ins.	cc					in.	mm	in.	mm
1980	156.4	2563	Fuel Inj.	110 @ 4800	136 @ 2400	8.5:1	3.15	80	3.35	85

4M-E 6 CYLINDER (Cont.)

ENGINE SPECIFICATIONS (Cont.)

VALVES							
Engine & Valve	Head Diam. In. (mm)	Face Angle	Seat Angle	Seat Width In. (mm)	Stem Diameter① In. (mm)	Stem Clearance In. (mm)	Valve Lift In. (mm)
2563 cc Intake	.....	44.5	45°	.047-.063 (1.2-1.6)	.3138-.3144 (7.970-7.985)	.0010-.0024 (.025-.060)	.....
Exhaust	.....	44.5	45°	.047-.063 (1.2-1.6)	.3134-.3140 (7.960-7.975)	.0014-.0028 (.035-.070)	.....

① — Wear limit for intake — .004" (.10 mm), exhaust — .005" (.13 mm).

VALVE SPRINGS			
Engine	Free Length In. (mm)	PRESSURE Lbs. @ In. (kg @ mm)	
		Valve Closed	Valve Open
2563 cc Inner	1.77 (44.9)	14.1-17.2@1.49 (6.4-7.8@37.9)	.....
Outer	1.84 (46.9)	37.3-46.5@1.63 (17.1-21.1@41.4)	.....

CAMSHAFT			
Engine	Journal Diam. In. (mm)	Clearance In. (mm)	Runout In. (mm)
2563 cc	1.3378-1.3384 (33.979-33.995)	.0007-.0022 (.017-.057)	.0024 (.06)

① — If valve spring is out of square more than .063" (1.6 mm), replace spring.

PISTONS, PINS, RINGS						
	PISTONS	PINS		RINGS		
Engine	Clearance In. (mm)	Piston Fit In. (mm)	Rod Fit In. (mm)	Rings	End Gap In. (mm)	Side Clearance In. (mm)
2563 cc	.0019-.0027 (.05-07)	.....	.0002-.0004 (.005-.011) Limit .0006 (.015)	No. 1	.0039-.0110 (.10-.28)	.0012-.0028 (.03-.07)
				No. 2	.0039-.0110 (.10-.28)	.0008-.0024 (.02-.09)
				Oil	.0079-.0200 (.20-.50)	

CRANKSHAFT MAIN & CONNECTING ROD BEARINGS							
	MAIN BEARINGS				CONNECTING ROD BEARINGS		
Engine	Journal Diam. In. (mm)	Clearance In. (mm)	Thrust Bearing	Crankshaft End Play In. (mm)	Journal Diam. In. (mm)	Clearance In. (mm)	Side Play In. (mm)
2563 cc	2.3617-2.3627 (59.988-60.012)	.0013-.0023 (.034-.058)	No. 4	.002-.010 (.05-.25)	2.0463-2.0472 (51.976-52.000)	.0008-.0021 (.021-.053)	.006-.012 (.16-.30)

SPITFIRE 4 CYLINDER

ENGINE CODING

ENGINE IDENTIFICATION

Engine number is stamped on a machined flange on left side of cylinder block.

Engine Identification	
Application	**Code**
All Models	FM XXXXXX UE

ENGINE, CYLINDER HEAD & MANIFOLD

ENGINE

Removal — 1) Disconnect battery. Drain coolant and engine oil. Remove hood. Remove air cleaner and disconnect emission control lines. From exhaust manifold, separate converter or pipe.

2) Disconnect all necessary water hoses, carburetor throttle linkage, and engine electrical leads. Disconnect and plug fuel lines.

3) Raise vehicle and place on safety stands. Separate exhaust pipe from bracket at transmission, then pull pipe downward past chassis. Take off engine restraint cable located near lower edge of bell housing. Remove lower bell housing nuts and bolts. Place a jack under bell housing.

4) Lower vehicle to ground. Attach hoist to engine. Remove remaining bell housing bolts, then take out starter. Remove motor mount bolts. Remove engine with hoist.

Installation — Reverse removal procedures to install engine.

INTAKE MANIFOLD

1) Remove air cleaner and disconnect fuel line. Disconnect hose to rocker cover. Unhook throttle return spring. Disconnect and remove throttle cable. Disconnect choke cable, ignition vacuum line and water hoses.

2) Unscrew manifold bolts connecting intake to exhaust manifold. Remove manifold-to-engine bolts and lift out manifold assembly.

CYLINDER HEAD

Removal — 1) Disconnect battery. Drain coolant. Disconnect emission control hoses and vacuum lines; mark for reinstallation. Loosen alternator belt. Disconnect heater hoses. On Federal vehicles, disconnect mixture cable attached at back carburetor. Disconnect fuel evaporation hoses. Separate throttle linkage from carburetors. Remove valve cover. Disconnect heater return line.

2) Remove heat shield from between carburetor and air cleaner. Disconnect exhaust (CAT, if equipped) at manifold flange. Remove water pump. Remove rocker arm assembly. Take out push rods. Disconnect fuel line and remove cylinder head.

NOTE — *It may be necessary to remove intake and exhaust manifolds.*

Installation — To install, reverse removal procedure and note the following: Make sure "TOP" tag on rear of gasket faces up. Tighten cylinder head bolts in sequence shown in *Fig. 1.*

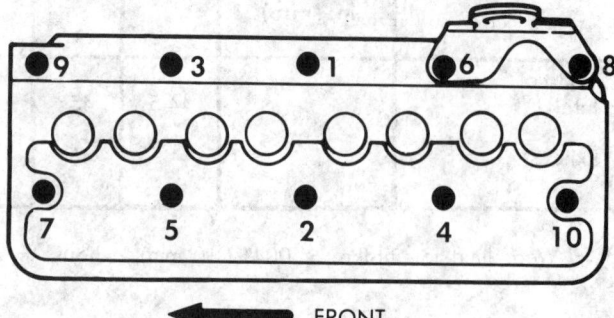

Fig. 1 Cylinder Head Tightening Sequence

VALVES

VALVE ARRANGEMENT

E-I-I-E-E-I-I-E (front to rear)

VALVE GUIDE SERVICING

1) Inspect valve guide wear by inserting a new valve, lifting it slightly off its seat, and rocking sideways. Movement of valve head across seat should not exceed .020" (.51 mm).

2) If replacement is required, use valve guide removal tool 60A and adapters to remove and replace valve guide. Guide protrusion above top face of cylinder head must be between .749-.751" (19.02-19.08 mm).

VALVE SPRINGS

Using suitable valve spring compressor, remove valve retainers. Withdraw collars and valves. Check valve springs for cracks, distortion and load length. When any one spring is defective, it is advisable to replace all springs.

NOTE — *Valve springs can be removed with cylinder head installed in vehicle. Apply air pressure to spark plug hole of spring (valve) to be removed. Air pressure will prevent valve from dropping.*

ROCKER ARM ASSEMBLY

Remove rocker arm cover. Progressively and evenly remove rocker arm pedestal nuts. Lift off rocker arm assembly. Pull cotter pin from front end of rocker shaft. Slide rockers, pedestals, springs and spacers from shaft, noting order for reassembly. Remove screw locating rear pedestal to shaft. Inspect and replace excessively worn parts. To install, reverse removal procedure making sure rear pedestal screw correctly engages rocker shaft.

VALVE TAPPETS

Check valve tappets for chips, score marks, ridges or excessive wear. Replace as necessary and ensure tappets are free to slide and rotate.

SPITFIRE 4 CYLINDER (Cont.)

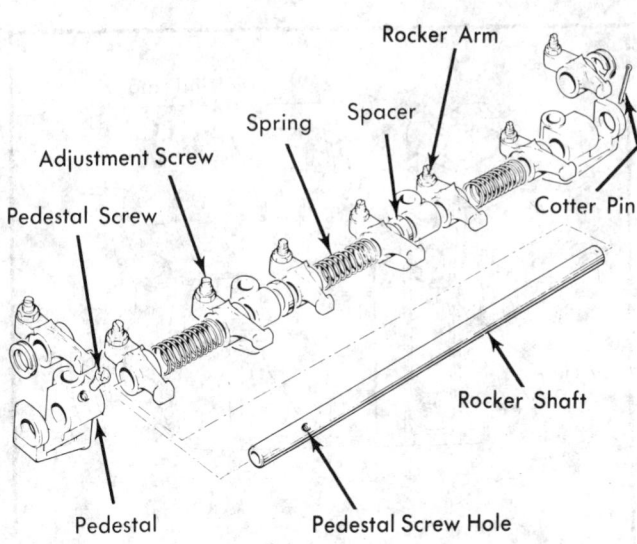

Fig. 2 Detailed View of Rocker Arm Assembly

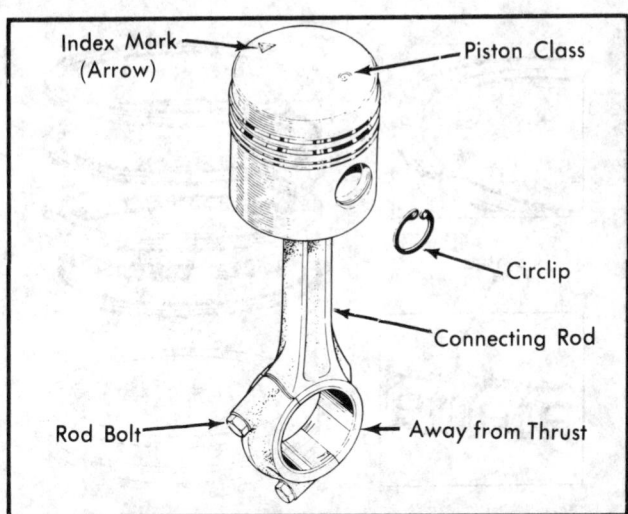

Fig. 3 Assembled View of Piston and Connecting Rod

VALVE CLEARANCE ADJUSTMENT

Disconnect battery, then remove rocker cover and spark plugs. Make necessary adjustment in sequence as indicated in chart below. Turning adjustment screw clockwise will decrease clearance, and turning screw counterclockwise will increase clearance. Proper clearance for intake and exhaust valves is .010" (.25 mm).

Valves Open①	Valves to Adjust
No. 8 & 6	No. 1 & 3
No. 4 & 7	No. 5 & 2
No. 1 & 3	No. 8 & 6
No. 5 & 2	No. 4 & 7

① — Counting from front.

PISTONS, PINS & RINGS

OIL PAN

Removal — Drain oil pan (Calif. models have a bolt with a banjo and two washers instead of the regular sump plug). Remove the 16 bolts mounting oil pan to engine. Drop out oil pan and remove gasket.

Installation — Clean mating surfaces. Lightly coat both sides of gasket with grease or sealer. Refit pan. Make sure longer bolts are fitted to rear of pan.

PISTON & ROD ASSEMBLY

1) Disconnect battery ground cable and drain engine oil. Remove oil pan and cylinder head as previously described.

2) Remove pickup strainer and bring No. 1 & No. 4 connecting rods to accessible position. Index bearing caps and connecting rods.

3) Remove connecting rod bolts and withdraw bearing caps. Push pistons and connecting rods upward, withdrawing them out top of cylinder. Attach bearing cap to respective connecting rod.

4) To install, position No. 1 and No. 4 connecting rods at bottom dead center. Lube journals and connecting rod assemblies with engine oil. Insert connecting rod assembly into cylinder. Make sure arrow on piston head faces engine FRONT. Stagger piston rings away from thrust side of piston. Make sure connecting rod bearing is away from thrust side of cylinder bore.

5) Fit upper bearing and pull connecting rod over crankshaft. Install lower bearing cap and torque bolts to specifications.

PISTON PIN REPLACEMENT

1) Remove circlips from pistons and extract piston pin. Separate piston from connecting rod. Inspect connecting rod bushing for wear and replace if necessary.

2) Using suitable press, remove worn bushing and install replacement. Ensure oil hole in new bushing is aligned with hole in connecting rod. Ream bushing to fit piston pin. Piston pin diameter is .8123-.8125" (20.63-20.64 mm) and is a thumb push fit at 68°F (20°C).

FITTING PISTONS

1) Measure piston across skirt. Check piston for scoring or cracks. Measure cylinder bore and determine if clearance is excessive.

2) Two grades of standard pistons are used: F and G. Identification mark is on piston head and cylinder block. Standard replacement pistons of .001" (.025 mm) oversize are available, but cylinder bores must be honed to provide specified piston clearance. Pistons are also available in .010" (.25 mm), .020" (.51 mm) and .030" (.76 mm) oversizes.

3) Install expanding ring in bottom groove of piston with end butting, but not overlapping. Work from bottom of piston and fit bottom rail. Fit top rail into position going over head of piston. Install middle ring with "TOP" facing up. Put on upper compression ring. Stagger rings.

SPITFIRE 4 CYLINDER (Cont.)

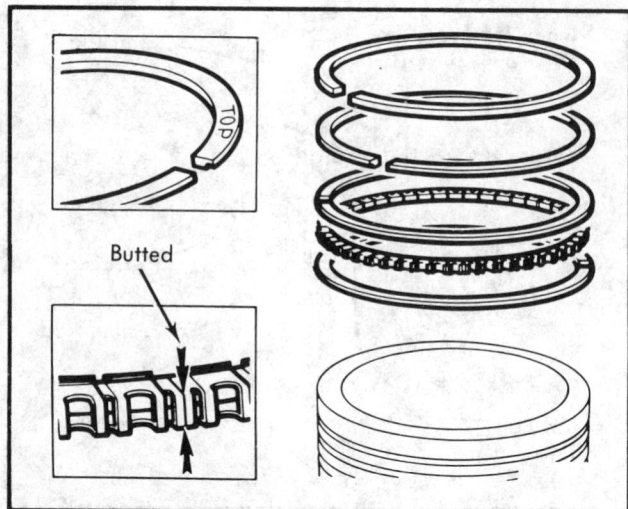

Fig. 4   Order and Detail of Piston Ring Installation

CRANKSHAFT MAIN & CONNECTING ROD BEARINGS

MAIN & CONNECTING ROD BEARINGS

1) Remove engine, cylinder head and oil pan. Remove main and rod bearing caps. Slightly push up connecting rod assembly but do not dislodge it from cylinder. Remove upper connecting rod bearings.

2) Remove crankshaft and upper main bearings. Remove thrust washers from rear main bearing. Examine all bearing journals and determine if regrinding is necessary.

3) Examine each bearing and replace as required. Bearings are available in .010", .020", and .030" (.25, .51, and .76 mm) undersizes. Any undersize crankshaft which is installed or has been installed in service should have a size marking stamped in which corresponds to similar marking on bearings.

4) To install main and connecting rod bearings, reverse removal procedure, noting the following: bend over locking tabs, if equipped.

CRANKSHAFT END PLAY

NOTE — End play can be adjusted with engine installed in vehicle. Procedure given is with engine removed. Difference occurs as to where dial indicator is mounted.

Use a dial indicator and set it up as shown in *Fig. 5*. Measure end play by prying against crankshaft and reading dial indicator. Obtained value must lie within specifications. If end play is exceeded, fit oversize thrust washers to rear main bearing.

REAR MAIN BEARING OIL SEAL

1) Remove rear transmission adaptor plate. Remove two bolts attaching oil pan to seal housing and seven bolts attaching seal housing to crankcase. Remove seal housing and press out old seal.

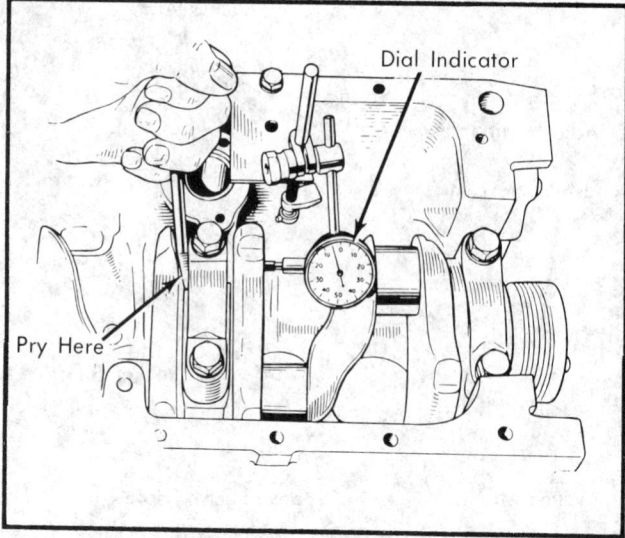

Fig. 5   Using Dial Indicator to Check Crankshaft End Play

2) Coat O.D. of seal with grease and press seal into housing with lip facing crankshaft. Install a new gasket coated with sealing compound. Carefully install seal housing with a plain copper washer on top bolt.

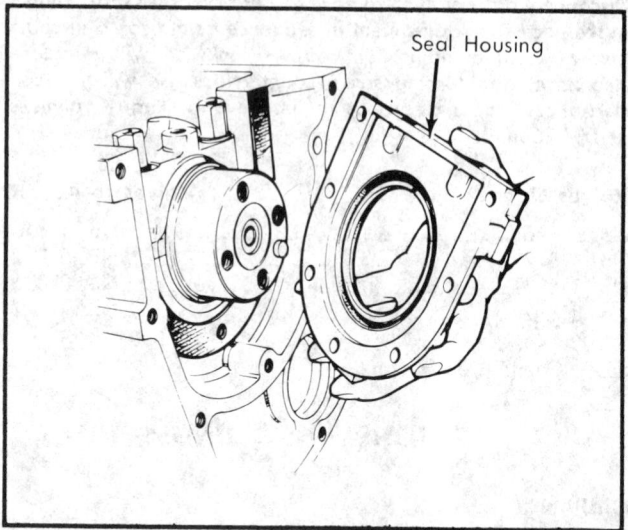

Fig. 6   Fitting Rear Main Bearing Seal Housing into Place

CAMSHAFT

ENGINE FRONT COVER & OIL SEAL

Removal — Remove radiator. Remove left side inner fender panel. Remove air pump, alternator, fan, and crankshaft pulley. Remove air pump/alternator brackets, adjusting links and spacer. Take out timing cover mounting hardware. Loosen and remove cover. Press out old seal. Refit new seal with open side facing engine.

Installation — Note for installation that chain tensioner is inside cover. To facilitate cover installation, use a short piece of welding rod bent 90° to hold tensioner off chain.

SPITFIRE 4 CYLINDER (Cont.)

CAMSHAFT

Removal — 1) Disconnect battery. Remove radiator. Remove cylinder head. Remove water pump and fan. Remove alternator, air pump, crankshaft pulley, timing cover and chain.

2) Remove two bolts mounting camshaft keeper plate, then withdraw plate. Remove cam followers and index mark for reinstallation. Take out distributor drive shaft and gear. Remove fuel pump. Withdraw camshaft.

Installation — To install, reverse removal procedure and note the following: Lube camshaft bearing journals. Fit keeper plate with two bolts. Check camshaft end play. Pull camshaft against keeper plate and insert feeler gauge between camshaft and plate. End play must not exceed .004-.008" (.110-.216 mm). Oversize thrust plates are available to bring end play within specifications.

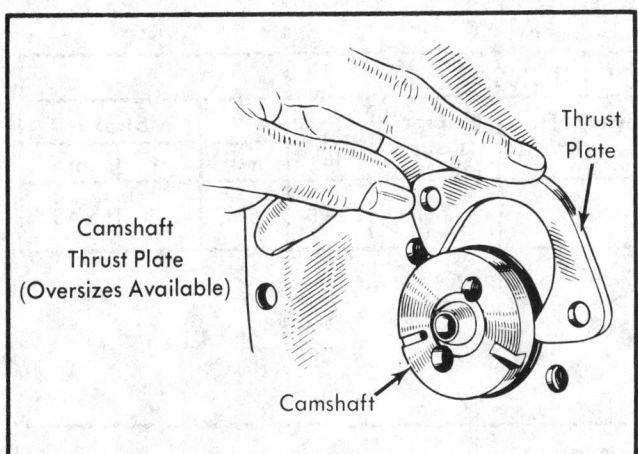

Fig. 7   Positioning Camshaft Thrust Plate

TIMING CHAIN

Removal — 1) Disconnect battery. Remove timing chain cover. Take off oil thrower. Rotate crankshaft until index marks on crankshaft and camshaft sprockets align. Make sure crankshaft keyway is at 12 o'clock and that camshaft punch marks are aligned.

2) Bend back camshaft nut lock tabs and remove bolts mounting camshaft sprocket to camshaft. Remove camshaft sprocket and timing chain.

NOTE — *DO NOT rotate camshaft or crankshaft while chain is off sprockets.*

Installation — 1) Remove crankshaft key. Refit both sprockets. Check alignment with straightedge. Install selective fit shims to crankshaft if misalignment occurs. Install key.

2) Fit chain to sprockets. Install sprocket, keep index marks aligned. Slightly secure camshaft sprocket. Measure chain deflection along slack run of chain. 3/8" (9.53 mm) slack should not be exceeded. Reverse removal procedure for remaining components.

VALVE TIMING

1) Remove valve cover. Adjust No. 7 and No. 8 valves to .080" (2.03 mm) clearance. Turn crankshaft until No. 1 piston is at TDC, compression stroke (pulley "V" aligned with zero line on timing cover scale).

2) Insert feeler gauge between valve tip and rocker pad to make sure No. 1 and No. 2 valves are fully closed. Make sure No. 7 and No. 8 valve clearances are unchanged (use two feeler gauges). Move crankshaft as necessary to maintain equality.

3) Readjust No. 7 and No. 8 valves to and all other valves to .010" (.25 mm). Replace rocker cover.

NOTE — *If chain or sprockets were removed, make sure timing marks are aligned when sprockets are reinstalled. See Timing Chain Removal and Installation.*

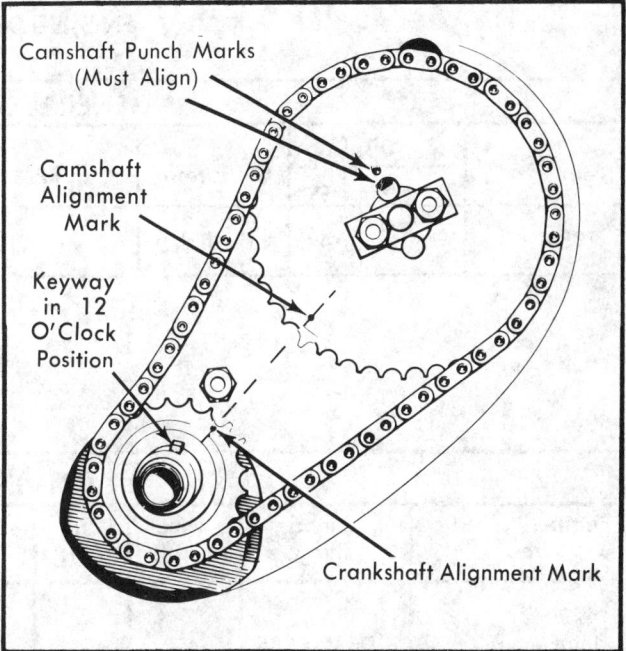

Fig. 8   Camshaft and Crankshaft Alignment

ENGINE OILING

ENGINE OILING SYSTEM

Oil is drawn from engine by a rotor type pump which discharges via a nonadjustable relief valve to a full-flow filter. Cylinder bores, pistons and piston pins are splash lubricated all other components are oiled through drilled passages.

Crankcase Capacity (Drain and Refill) — 4.2 quarts.

Oil Filter — Full-flow type. Disposable cannister.

Oil Pressure Relief Valve — Located in cylinder block beneath oil filter. Check relief valve spring free length; it should be 1.53" (38.8 mm).

SPITFIRE 4 CYLINDER (Cont.)

OIL PUMP

1) Remove oil pan previously described. Remove three bolts securing oil pump to crankcase. Lift from vehicle and place in a vise.

2) Place a straightedge across pump body, then use a feeler gauge to check clearance between rotor face and straight edge; it should be .004" (.10 mm).

3) Check clearance between inner rotor and outer rotor. Clearance must not exceed .010" (.25 mm).

4) Check clearance between outer rotor and body; it must not exceed .008" (.20 mm).

5) Check cover plate for scoring, and test on a surface plate for distortion. Examine pump spindle bearing surface in body for excessive wear.

6) Reassembly oil pump installing any new parts as necessary to satisfy specifications. To install oil pump, reverse removal procedure.

ENGINE COOLING

Cooling System Capacity — 5.6 quarts.

WATER PUMP

Drain cooling system. Remove radiator hoses, then unbolt and remove radiator. Detach fan belt. Unscrew three nuts securing water pump flange to thermostat and pump housing. Withdraw water pump. Remove fan. To install, reverse procedure.

ENGINE SPECIFICATIONS

GENERAL SPECIFICATIONS										
Year	Displ.		Carburetor	HP at RPM	Torque (Ft. Lbs. at RPM)	Compr. Ratio	Bore		Stroke	
	cu. ins.	cc					in.	mm	in.	mm
1980	91	1493	1x1-Bbl.	....	....	7.5:1	2.90	73.7	3.44	87.5

VALVES In. (mm)							
Engine & Valve	Head Diam.	Face Angle	Seat Angle	Seat Width	Stem Diameter	Stem Clearance	Valve Lift
1493 cc Intake	1.375-1.385 (34.97-35.01)	45°	45°	.....	.3107-.3113 (8.05-8.12)	.0008-.0023 (.020-.060)	...
Exhaust	1.168-1.172 (29.66-29.76)	45°	45°	.....	.3100-.3106 (7.874-7.887)	.0015-.0030 (.038-.076)	...

PISTONS, PINS, RINGS In. (mm)						
Engine	PISTONS	PINS		RINGS		
	Clearance	Piston Fit	Rod Fit	Rings	End Gap	Side Clearance
1493 cc	.002-.003 (.05-.07)	Push Fit	Push Fit	No. 1 & 2	.012-.022 (.30-.55)	.002-.0025 (.051-.063)
				Oil	①	.0025-.0035 (.063-.088)

① — Ends butt.

SPITFIRE 4 CYLINDER (Cont.)
ENGINE SPECIFICATIONS (Cont.)

CRANKSHAFT MAIN & CONNECTING ROD BEARINGS

| Engine | MAIN BEARINGS | | | | CONNECTING ROD BEARINGS | | |
	Journal Diam. In. (mm)	Clearance In. (mm)	Thrust Bearing	Crankshaft End Play In. (mm)	Journal Diam. In. (mm)	Clearance In. (mm)	Side Play In. (mm)
1493 cc	2.3115-2.3120 (58.713-58.725)	...	Rear	.004-.008 (.10-.20)	1.8750-1.8755 (47.625-47.638)	....	....

VALVE SPRINGS

| Engine | Free Length In. (mm) | PRESSURE Lbs. @ In. (kg @ mm) | |
		Valve Closed	Valve Open
1493 cc	1.52 (38.6)	.....	.....

VALVE TIMING

| Engine | INTAKE | | EXHAUST | |
	Open (BTDC)	Close (ABDC)	Open (BBDC)	Close (ATDC)
1493 cc	18°	58°	58°	18°

CAMSHAFT In. (mm)

Engine	Journal Diam.	Clearance	Lobe Lift
1493 cc	1.9659-1.9664① (49.934-49.947)	②	...

① — Intermediate Journal 1.9649-1.9654" (49.908-49.921).
② — End play should be .004-.008" (.11-.21 mm).

TIGHTENING SPECIFICATIONS

Application	Ft. Lbs. (mkg)
Connecting Rod Bolts	
Color Dyed	45 (6.2)
Phosphated	46 (6.4)
Sprocket-to-Camshaft	24 (3.3)
Crankshaft Pulley Nut	150 (20.7)
Cylinder Head Bolts	46 (6.4)
Flywheel-to-Crankshaft	
Cadmium Plated Bolt	40 (5.5)
Parkarised Bolt	45 (6.2)
Intake-to-Exhaust Manifold	14 (1.9)
Manifold-to-Head	25 (3.5)
Main Bearing Cap Bolts	65 (9.0)
Oil Pan Bolts	20 (2.8)
Oil Seal Block Screw	14 (1.9)
Rocker Cover-to-Head	2 (0.3)
Rocker Shaft-to-Head	34 (4.7)
Rear Crankshaft Seal	20 (2.8)
Spark Plugs	20 (2.8)
Timing Cover-to-Front Plate	
3/8" Screw	10 (1.4)
7/8" Screw	20 (2.8)
Stud	16 (2.2)
Bolt	20 (2.8)
Water Pump-to-Head	20 (2.8)

Triumph Engines

TR7 4 CYLINDER

ENGINE CODING

ENGINE IDENTIFICATION

Engine number is stamped on cylinder head and may be seen by looking down between intake manifold branches. Number can be broken down as shown in the following example:

CK12345UCA

1st and 2nd Digits — "CV" denotes carbureted models. "CK" denotes fuel injected models.

3rd through 7th Digits — Serial number.
Suffixes — "U" denotes Federal.
"UC" denotes California.
"A" denotes automatic transmission.

ENGINE, CYLINDER HEAD & MANIFOLD

ENGINE

Removal — 1) Disconnect battery and bottom radiator hose, allowing coolant to drain. Remove hood, radiator, air cleaner duct and air cleaner hot air hose. Disconnect heater hoses at firewall and brake booster vacuum hose at intake manifold. Disconnect vapor canister hoses from canister, cooling system expansion hose from thermostat housing and anti-run-on valve hose from intake manifold.

2) Disconnect all electrical leads, fuel lines, cables, and linkages from engine. Remove shift boot, release bayonet cap securing lever to transmission extension, and remove gearshift lever. Raise front and rear of vehicle and place on stands. Disconnect propeller shaft from transmission.

3) Disconnect wiring from transmission and remove exhaust downpipe from manifold. Disconnect speedometer cable and remove clutch slave cylinder. Remove nut securing the left-hand engine mount to the subframe. Remove complete engine torque strap assembly (if equipped), and disconnect wiring from starter. Release wiring harness from clutch housing clips. Remove clutch housing bolts necessary to remove clips, and release clutch hydraulic line.

4) Remove engine ground strap and hood lock from firewall. Relieve pressure from air conditioning system (if equipped) and disconnect hoses from compressor. Using a lifting sling with a 23" (58.4 cm) leg to rear lift eye and a 18" (45.7 cm) leg to front eye, raise hoist to remove weight of engine.

5) Disconnect right side engine mount and remove five bolts securing rear crossmember to body. Raise rear of vehicle. Hoist engine and remove left side engine mount. Continue raising engine and work it away from vehicle.

Installation — To install, reverse removal procedure.

INTAKE MANIFOLD

Removal — Disconnect battery and drain cooling system, including cylinder block. Remove ducts and air cleaner. Disconnect all hoses, wiring and control cables from manifold and carburetors. Remove distributor cap and 6 manifold bolts. Lift out manifold complete with carburetors or fuel rail (if fuel injected).

Installation — To install manifold, reverse removal procedure.

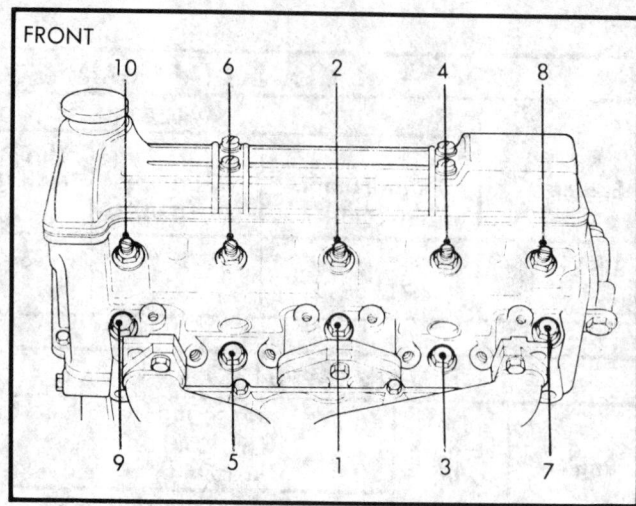

Fig. 1   Cylinder Head Tightening Sequence

CYLINDER HEAD

Removal — 1) Remove intake manifold. Then, remove camshaft cover and semi-circular grommet to gain access to camshaft sprocket nut. Crank engine until camshaft sprocket bottom bolt is accessible and remove bottom bolt. Anchor camshaft sprocket to support bracket. Crank engine so that timing mark on camshaft flange is in line with groove in camshaft front bearing cap and distributor rotor points to manifold rear attachment bolt hole in cylinder head.

2) Unlock and remove top sprocket retaining bolt. Disconnect air hose from air injection check valve and disconnect water pipe from thermostat housing. Disconnect exhaust pipe from manifold. Remove the two cylinder head to timing cover nuts and bolts. Loosen cylinder head nuts and bolts in reverse order of tightening sequence. See *Fig. 1*. Remove cylinder head complete with exhaust manifold.

Installation — To install, reverse removal procedure and tighten bolts to specification in sequence shown in *Fig. 1*.

CAMSHAFT

ENGINE FRONT COVER & OIL SEAL

1) Disconnect battery and remove crankshaft pulleys after first loosening drive belts and removing cooling fan. Remove alternator and mounting brackets. If equipped, remove air pump, diverter valve, brackets, and air conditioning compressor strut.

2) Remove two bolts and nuts securing front cover to cylinder head. Remove four bolts securing compressor to engine and three compressor adjusting bolts (if equipped). Remove two front oil pan bolts. Remove front cover center attachment bolt and bottom left side bolt. Remove front cover and gaskets and pry out old seal.

3) Dip new seal in engine oil and with lip facing inward, tap in squarely into front cover until flush with cover. Install front cover on engine in reverse of removal procedure using new gaskets.

TR7 4 CYLINDER (Cont.)

NOTE — *Front oil seal may be replaced with front cover installed by first removing crankshaft pulleys and prying out old seal.*

CAMSHAFT

1) Disconnect battery and remove camshaft cover. Crank engine until camshaft timing mark is 180° from groove in camshaft front bearing cap. Unlock and remove exposed camshaft sprocket retaining bolt. Crank engine so that timing mark on camshaft flange is exactly in line with groove in camshaft front bearing cap. Secure sprocket to support bracket with a suitable nut.

2) Unlock and remove remaining sprocket retaining bolt. Evenly loosen camshaft bearing cap nuts and remove bolts and washers. Check that bearing caps are numbered for identification and remove caps. Remove camshaft. To install, reverse removal procedure making sure timing marks are correctly aligned.

INTERMEDIATE SHAFT

1) Disconnect battery and remove fresh air duct, radiator, air conditioning condenser (if equipped), engine front cover, intake manifold, water pump cover and impeller, fuel pump, and camshaft cover. Crank engine so that timing mark on camshaft flange is in line with groove on front bearing cap. *See Fig. 3*. Remove distributor cap, and check that rotor points to last intake manifold bolt hole in cylinder head, indicating No. 1 piston is at TDC.

2) Remove the distributor, hydraulic chain tensioner and adjustable timing chain guide. Remove two Allen head screws and withdraw intermediate shaft keeper plate. Lift timing chain clear of sprocket and pull out intermediate shaft (complete with sprocket). Clamp intermediate shaft in a vise and remove sprocket retaining bolt, tab washer and sprocket. To install, reverse removal procedure, making sure valve timing is set correctly and adjusting timing chain tension.

TIMING CHAIN

1) Remove engine front cover, camshaft cover and distributor cap. Disconnect camshaft sprocket as described under *Camshaft Removal*. Make sure that camshaft timing marks are aligned when engine is TDC, No. 1 cylinder compression stroke. Remove hydraulic chain tensioner and guide plate.

2) Remove locking bolt from adjustable chain guide and common bolt securing adjustable guide and camshaft sprocket support bracket. Remove adjustable guide. Remove bolt securing camshaft support bracket and fixed guide while holding camshaft sprocket. Remove fixed guide and release chain from intermediate shaft and camshaft sprockets. Remove (upward) camshaft sprocket and bracket along with timing chain. To install, reverse removal procedure and check valve and intermediate shaft timing.

3) Set chain tension as follows: Insert a .100" (2.54 mm) feeler gauge between chain slipper and tensioner body. *See Fig. 2*. Loosen three chain guide retainer bolts and press down on timing chain guide between camshaft and intermediate shaft sprockets until feeler gauge is a sliding fit. Hold guide in this

position and tighten adjustable guide bolt first, then two remaining bolts. Remove feeler gauge and continue reassembly.

VALVE TIMING

Crank engine until timing mark on crankshaft pulley coincides with zero mark on front cover scale. At this time, distributor rotor should point to rear bolt securing intake manifold to cylinder head and timing mark on camshaft flange is in line with groove in camshaft front bearing cap. To adjust timing it is necessary to remove timing chain. *See Fig. 3*.

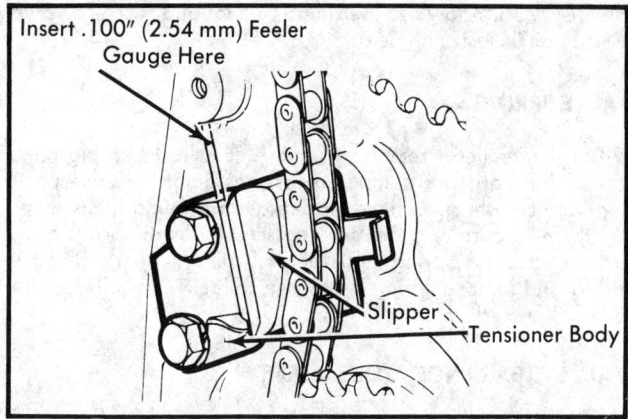

Fig. 2   Adjusting Timing Chain Tension

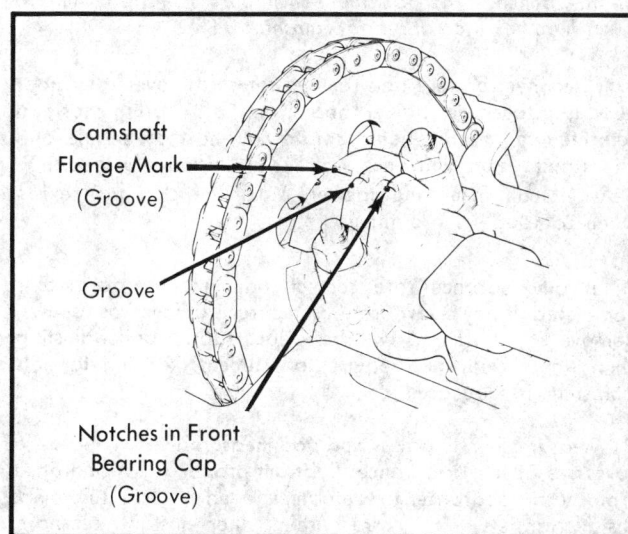

Fig. 3   Camshaft Timing Mark Alignment

VALVES

VALVE ARRANGEMENT

E-I-I-E-E-I-I-E (front to rear).

VALVE GUIDE SERVICING

1) Inspect valve guide wear by inserting a new valve, lifting it slightly from its seat, and rocking sideways. Movement of valve head across seat should not exceed .020" (.508 mm).

2) If replacement is required, use valve guide removal and installation tool S-60A and adapters to remove and replace valve guide. After guides are installed, ream out guide using a .3130" (7.95 mm) reamer.

Triumph Engines

TR7 4 CYLINDER (Cont.)

VALVE SEAT INSERT SERVICING

1) If valve seat inserts are too badly damaged to be refaced, replace inserts as follows: Machine-out existing inserts taking care not to damage insert bores in cylinder head. Machine intake valve seat bore to a diameter of 1.665-1.666" (42.29-42.32 mm) or exhaust valve seat bore to a diameter of 1.329-1.330" (33.75-33.78 mm).

2) Heat cylinder head uniformly to a temperature of 356°F (180°C) and immediately install new valve seats squarely into cylinder head. Allow cylinder head to cool and machine valve seats to an inclusive angle of 89°.

VALVE SPRINGS

With cylinder head removed, remove camshaft bearing caps (check that caps are numbered for reassembly in same position) and camshaft. Remove tappets and adjusting shims keeping them in correct order for reassembly. With spring compressor, depress spring and remove valve keepers. Release spring and remove spring and valve collar. To install, reverse removal procedure.

VALVE CLEARANCE ADJUSTMENT

NOTE — *This operation may be performed with cylinder head on the bench. When on the bench, turn camshaft using a wrench on hexagon at rear of camshaft.*

1) Disconnect battery and remove camshaft cover if cylinder head is installed on engine. Loosen camshaft bearing caps and retighten to specifications. Rotate camshaft or engine and check and record clearance of each valve using a feeler gauge between cam heel and tappet. Maximum clearance exists when cam lobe is straight up.

2) If all clearances are correct, adjustment procedure is completed. If any clearances are incorrect, proceed as follows: Remove camshaft and withdraw each tappet and adjusting shim where clearance requires adjustment, keeping tappets and shims in sequence.

3) Measure shim thickness and add measured valve clearance to arrive at total clearance. Subtract proper valve clearance from total clearance to determine needed shim thickness. Install tappets with correct shims then install camshaft. Recheck valve clearance and install camshaft cover.

Application	Valve Clearance
Intake	.008" (.2 mm)
Exhaust	.018" (.5 mm)

PISTONS, PINS & RINGS

OIL PAN

1) Disconnect battery and remove fresh air duct and fan shroud. Raise vehicle and drain engine oil. Remove two bolts securing coupling plate on bottom of oil pan to clutch housing. Remove engine torque strap assembly. Support front of engine using hoist or jack.

NOTE — *A bracket, made of angle iron, may be fabricated to bolt into lower timing cover bolt holes. Engine may then be supported by a jack via the fabricated bracket.*

2) Remove two engine right side mounting bolts, then remove left side engine mounting to sub-frame nut. Remove oil pan nuts and bolts. Raise engine sufficiently to enable oil pan, complete with left side engine mounting and cross-member to be removed. To install, reverse removal procedure.

PISTON & ROD ASSEMBLY

Connecting rods and rod caps are numbered. Note positioning and location before disassembly.

Removal — With oil pan and cylinder head removed, unscrew rod nuts and withdraw bearing caps. Place protective sleeves over rod bolts and push out rod and piston. Rotate crankshaft as necessary to gain access to piston and rod assemblies.

Installation — 1) Stagger piston ring gaps, lubricate pistons and rings and, using a ring compressor, place piston in cylinder bore, ensuring that raised flat portion of piston crown is toward right side of engine (viewed from driver's seat).

NOTE — *Some pistons may have arrows stamped on both sides of skirt, on the piston pin bore side, to indicate direction of pin off-set. Ensure that these arrows point to right side of engine also. Alternatively some pistons may have an arrow on the crown. These piston assemblies must be installed with arrow pointing to front of engine.*

2) Install bearing halves in connecting rod and cap and pull connecting rod onto crankpins. Install bearing caps to their respective numbered connecting rod making sure the bearing keeper recesses in connecting rods and caps are on the same side. Install new nuts and tighten.

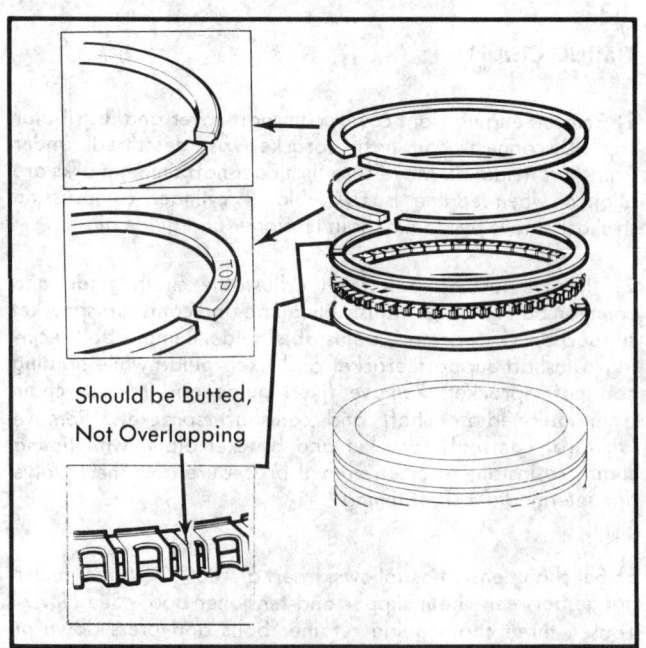

Fig. 4   View Showing Correct Piston Ring Installation

TR7 4 CYLINDER (Cont.)

PISTON PIN REPLACEMENT

1) Remove circlips from pistons and extract piston pin. Separate piston from connecting rod. Inspect connecting rod bushing for wear and replace if necessary.

2) Using a press, remove worn bushing and install replacement. Ensure oil hole in new bushing is aligned with hole in connecting rod. Ream bushing to .9377-.9380" (23.818-23.825 mm).

FITTING PISTONS

Inspect and measure cylinder for wear or taper. Measure piston diameter and determine if clearance is correct. Install expanding ring in bottom groove of piston with ends butting but not overlapping. From bottom of piston install bottom rail and from top, upper rail. Install middle ring with word "TOP" facing upward. See Fig. 4. Install upper compression ring and stagger ring gaps.

NOTE — *Oversize rings are available in .010 and .020" (.254 and .508 mm) oversizes.*

CRANKSHAFT MAIN & CONNECTING ROD BEARINGS

MAIN & CONNECTING ROD BEARINGS

1) Remove engine and separate engine and transmission. Remove clutch, flywheel, engine rear adapter plate, oil pan and dipstick. Remove rear main bearing oil seal, timing chain cover, oil pickup screen and oil slinger. Remove crankshaft sprocket, drive key and shims.

2) Remove connecting rod bearing caps and slightly push up connecting rod assembly but do not dislodge it from cylinder. Remove upper and lower connecting rod bearings and install protectors over connecting rod bolts. Remove timing chain and main bearing caps. Lift out crankshaft. Remove pilot bushing, upper and lower main bearing inserts and thrust washers.

3) Examine all bearing journals and determine if regrinding is necessary. When regrinding crankshaft, do not grind journal diameter to less than specified minimum diameter. Examine each bearing half and replace any damaged bearings. Bearings are available in various oversizes. To install, reverse removal procedure making sure that grooves in thrust washers face outward.

Minimum Crankshaft Regrind Diameters

Application	In. (mm)
Main Journal	2.0860-2.0865 (52.984-52.997)
Connecting Rod	1.7100-1.7105 (43.434-43.447)

CRANKSHAFT END PLAY

Using a feeler gauge or dial indicator, measure crankshaft end play by levering crankshaft back and forth. Value must be within specifications. If not, thrust washers are available in various oversizes.

REAR MAIN BEARING OIL SEAL

1) Disconnect battery and remove transmission, clutch and flywheel. Remove two rear oil pan bolts, loosen two right side rear and one left side rear oil pan bolts. Remove six bolts securing rear main bearing oil seal housing to crankcase. Press oil seal out of housing.

2) Lubricate outer diameter of new seal and press it squarely into housing with lip facing crankshaft. Clean gasket area and install new gasket using sealing compound. Lubricate crankshaft and carefully ease seal housing into position on two dowels. Install six retaining bolts noting that two lower bolts are longer. Evenly tighten bolts then install two pan bolts removed previously. Tighten all oil pan bolts and continue assembly in reverse of disassembly.

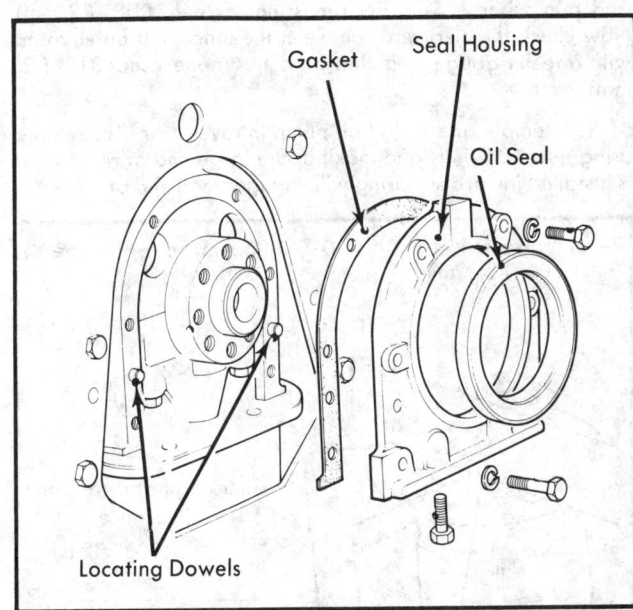

Fig. 5   Exploded View of Rear Main Bearing Oil Seal

ENGINE OILING

ENGINE OILING SYSTEM

Oil is drawn from engine by a rotor type pump which discharges via a nonadjustable relief valve to a full-flow filter. Cylinder bores, pistons and piston pins are splash lubricated. All other components are oiled through drilled passages.

Crankcase Capacity — 9.5 pts. (including filter).

Oil Filter — Full-flow, paper element type filter.

Oil Pressure Relief Valve — Nonadjustable.

OIL PUMP

NOTE — *Use care when removing slave cylinder that clutch release mechanism doesn't become dislodged. If mechanism does dislodge, transmission will have to be removed to repair it.*

1) Disconnect battery and raise vehicle. Remove 2 bolts securing clutch slave cylinder to clutch housing. Leave hydraulic line attached and wire slave cylinder out of way.

TR7 4 CYLINDER (Cont.)

2) Remove clutch housing nut and bolt, then remove four oil pump retaining bolts and washers. Remove pump from engine complete with hexagonal drive shaft. Remove "O" ring. To disassemble pump, first remove drive shaft. Remove two screws and lift off pump cover from body. Remove pump rotors and "O" ring. Remove cotter pin from pump body and pull out relief valve plug, spring and valve. Remove "O" ring from relief valve plug.

3) Clean all components and install rotors in pump body, ensuring that chamfered edge of outer rotor is at driving end of rotor pocket. Place a straight edge across pump body and with a feeler gauge check clearance between rotor and straight edge. This clearance should be .004" (.1 mm)

4) With a feeler gauge, check clearance between outer rotor and pump body. Clearance must not exceed .008" (.2 mm). Now check the clearance between the inner and outer rotors with a feeler gauge. This clearance must not exceed .010" (.25 mm).

5) Reassemble and install oil pump in reverse of disassembly, using new "O" rings and making sure large end of relief valve is installed inward so spring will engage small end of valve.

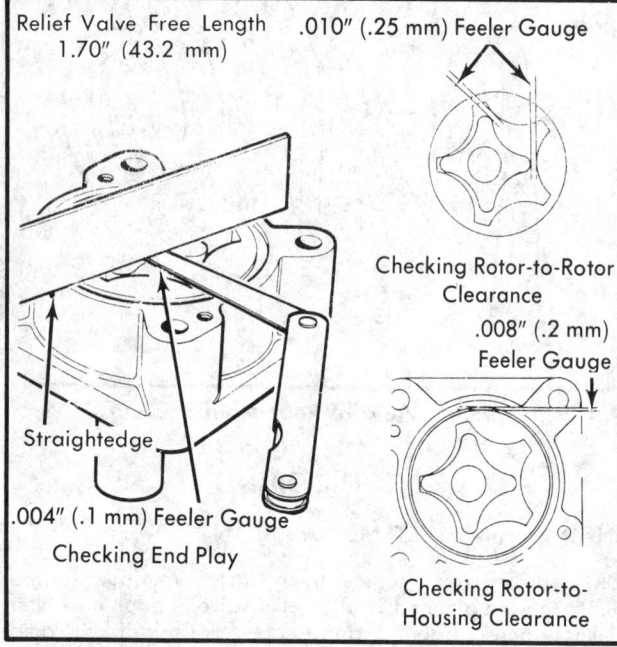

Fig. 6   View Showing Oil Pump Checking Points

ENGINE COOLING

WATER PUMP

1) Disconnect battery and remove intake manifold. Disconnect hoses from water pump cover and remove three bolts securing pump cover to engine. Lift off cover and gaskets. Turn impeller center bolt clockwise until either water pump is released from intermediate shaft drive gear and can be removed, or center bolt is removed. If center bolt comes out, use impact tool (4235A) and adapter (S4235A/10) to remove pump.

2) To overhaul pump, remove center bolt if not previously removed. Use a drift and support tool to remove impeller from shaft. Invert pump assembly (drive gear up) and drift shaft from housing. Remove "O" ring, graphite seal, water slinger, oil seal and circlip from pump shaft. Again invert shaft and drift shaft from bearing. Remove oil slinger. Remove "O" rings from housing.

3) To assemble, reverse disassembly procedure using new seals and "O" rings and noting the following: Make sure oil slinger dish is towards gear. Flat face of oil seal should face bearing. Dish of water slinger should be towards bearing. Install graphite seal with flat face towards bearing.

4) Place pump in housing. Make sure that pump and intermediate shaft gear mesh correctly and pump is seated properly. Clean gasket surfaces thoroughly, and temporarily install pump cover. Using feeler gauges, check that gap between pump cover and engine is equal. Equalize gap by adjusting bolts.

CAUTION — *Use of force or impact to seat pump will damage the pump and graphite seal.*

5) Select water pump cover gaskets to equal the gap noted in step 4) plus .010-.020" (.25-.5 mm) to provide running clearance. Remove pump cover, install selected gaskets, reinstall cover and tighten bolts to specifications. Complete installation in reverse of removal procedure.

Thermostat — Begins to open at about 190°F (88°C).

Cooling System Capacity — 15.5 pts. (including heater).

Radiator Cap — 15 psi (1.05 kg/cm²).

TIGHTENING SPECIFICATIONS

Application	Ft. Lbs. (mkg)
Main Bearing Caps	65 (9.0)
Camshaft Sprocket Bolt	10 (1.4)
Camshaft Bearing Caps	14 (1.9)
Connecting Rod Bolts	45 (6.2)
Crankshaft Pulley Bolt	120 (16.5)
Cylinder Head Bolts (Nuts)	55 (7.6)
Idler Shaft Sprocket Bolt	38 (5.3)
Timing Chain Tensioner-to-Block	7 (.9)
Timing Chain Support Brackets & Guides	20 (2.8)
Flywheel-to-Crankshaft	45 (6.2)
Intake Manifold	20 (2.7)

ENGINE SPECIFICATIONS

GENERAL SPECIFICATIONS

Year	Displ.		Carburetor	HP at RPM	Torque (Ft. Lbs. at RPM)	Compr. Ratio	Bore		Stroke	
	cu. ins.	cc					in.	mm	in.	mm
1980 Carbureted	122	1998	2x1-Bbl.	88.5@5200	100@2500	8.1:1	3.56	90.3	3.07	78.0
Fuel Injected	122	1998	Fuel Inj.	88.6@5000	105@4000	8.1:1	3.56	90.3	3.07	78.0

Triumph Engines

TR7 4 CYLINDER (Cont.)

ENGINE SPECIFICATIONS (Cont.)

Engine & Valve	Head Diam. In. (mm)	Face Angle	Seat Angle	Seat Width In. (mm)	Stem Diameter In. (mm)	Stem Clearance In. (mm)	Valve Lift In. (mm)
VALVES							
1998 cc							
Intake	1.560 (39.62)	45°	42.5°	.....	.3103-.3113 (7.881-7.907)	.0017-.0023 (.043-.058)	.....
Exhaust	1.280 (32.51)	45°	42.5°	.....	.3098-.3106 (7.87-7.89)	.0014-.0030 (.035-.076)	.....

PISTONS, PINS, RINGS

Engine	PISTONS Clearance In. (mm)	PINS Piston Fit In. (mm)	PINS Rod Fit In. (mm)	RINGS Rings	RINGS End Gap In. (mm)	RINGS Side Clearance In. (mm)
1998 cc	.0005-.0015 (.013-.038)	0-.0004 (0-.010)	.0001-.0006 (.003-.015)	No. 1	.015-.025 (.39-.64)	.0019-.0039 (.048-.082)
				No. 2	.015-.025 (.39-.64)	.0015-.0025 (.038-.064)
				Oil	.015-.055 (.39-1.40)	Ends Butted

CRANKSHAFT MAIN & CONNECTING ROD BEARINGS

Engine	MAIN BEARINGS Journal Diam. In. (mm)	MAIN BEARINGS Clearance In. (mm)	MAIN BEARINGS Thrust Bearing	MAIN BEARINGS Crankshaft End Play In. (mm)	CONNECTING ROD BEARINGS Journal Diam. In. (mm)	CONNECTING ROD BEARINGS Clearance In. (mm)	CONNECTING ROD BEARINGS Side Play In. (mm)
1998 cc	2.1260-2.1265 (54.000-54.013)	.0012-.0022 (.030-.055)	No. 3	.003-.011 (.08-.28)	1.7500-1.7505 (44.450-44.463)	.0008-.0023 (.020-.058)	.006-.013 (.15-.33)

VALVE SPRINGS

Engine	Free Length In. (mm)	PRESSURE Lbs. @ In. (kg @ mm) Valve Closed	PRESSURE Lbs. @ In. (kg @ mm) Valve Open
1998 cc	1.60 (40.40)	.....	.....

VALVE TIMING

Engine	INTAKE Open (BTDC)	INTAKE Close (ABDC)	EXHAUST Open (BBDC)	EXHAUST Close (ATDC)
1998 cc	16°	56°	56°	16°

TR8 V8

ENGINE CODING

ENGINE IDENTIFICATION

Engine number is stamped on cylinder head on left side of engine and may be viewed by looking down between intake manifold branches. Codes are as follows:

Engine Identification Codes	
Application	**Engine Code**
Carbureted	
Federal	
Man. Trans.	10E00001A
Auto. Trans.	11E00001A
Calif.	
Man. Trans.	12E00001A
Auto. Trans.	13E00001A
Fuel Injection	
Man. Trans.	14E00001A
Auto. Trans.	15E00001A

ENGINE, CYLINDER HEAD & MANIFOLDS

ENGINE

NOTE — *Remove engine and transmission as an assembly.*

Removal — 1) Disconnect battery, drain coolant from radiator and engine block, and remove hood. Remove fresh air duct, alternator belt and alternator. If equipped, remove air conditioning compressor, leaving hoses attached. Tie compressor to one side.

2) Remove gear shift lever boot and flange assembly. On fuel-injected engines, remove airflow meter, disconnecting pipe at plenum chamber.

3) On carbureted engines, remove cold air inlet hose from temperature control valves. Remove valves. Remove hot air hoses from air boxes.

4) On all models, disconnect heater hoses at firewall. Disconnect throttle cable from throttle linkage. Disconnect brake servo hose at intake manifold plenum chamber. Release clips securing hose to air boxes.

5) On carbureted engines, disconnect float-chamber vent pipe and engine breather pipe from charcoal canister. Remove rubber cover from starter motor lead and remove lead from terminal.

6) Disconnect starter motor and alternator harness multi-plug, located near radiator expansion tank. Disconnect cooling system hoses from thermostat housing. Disconnect all electrical leads from ignition coil.

7) On carbureted engines, disconnect fuel inlet pipe at filter. On fuel injected engines, depressurize fuel system and disconnect inlet pipe from fuel rail.

8) Remove connector from cooling fan switch. Raise front of vehicle until bottom of radiator is approximately 3 ft. (.9 m) above floor. Support body on stands. Raise rear of car and support on stands. Drain engine oil.

9) Disconnect back-up light wires at multi-plug connector. Loosen muffler front joint and balance pipe clamps. Remove rear rubber "O" rings from brackets, and remove muffler and tailpipe assembly front down pipes.

10) Mark propeller shaft and transmission flange position. Remove 4 bolts and nuts securing propeller shaft drive flange to transmission drive flange. Remove speedometer cable clamp bolt and cable. Disconnect clutch slave cylinder hydraulic pipe from hose.

11) Remove clutch hose bracket from clutch housing. Remove intermediate steering shaft lower 2 bolts. Loosen lock nuts holding brake hoses to front suspension struts. Remove steering arm front bolt and both rear steering arm lower caliper bolts. Remove remaining caliper bolts and calipers.

12) Remove 6 nuts securing damper and spring assemblies to inner wing valances. Remove power steering pipe bracket from subframe. Drain power steering fluid, and seal all pipes and housing ports.

13) Lower rear of vehicle. Place jack under subframe and raise to take the weight. Fit an engine lifting harness to engine and raise with mobile hoist to support weight of engine.

14) Remove engine mounting bolts and nuts. Remove subframe nuts, lower rubber bushings and spacers. Lower the subframe and suspension assemblies and remove from vehicle. Remove steering intermediate shaft.

15) Place jack under transmission, supporting weight, and remove engine rear mounting crossmember from body. Lower engine and transmission assembly, and remove from beneath vehicle.

Installation — To install engine and transmission assembly, reverse removal procedure. Be sure to refill and bleed power steering system and to refill cooling system and crankcase.

CARBURETED INTAKE MANIFOLD

Removal — 1) Drain cooling system and remove fresh air duct. Disconnect top hose and expansion hose from thermostat housing.

2) Disconnect hose from diverter valve and brake servo hose from manifold nipple, releasing it from clips. Remove plug from cooling fan switch. Remove distributor vacuum pipe from left-hand carburetor and remove bolt and clip. Disconnect hose from back of distributor capsule.

3) Disconnect vacuum hose from right-hand carburetor (to EGR valve). Disconnect air cleaner interconnecting pipe from left-hand air cleaner box. Remove asbestos-wrapped EGR valve pipe completely. Disconnect engine breather hose from right-hand valve cover flame trap.

4) Disconnect float-chamber vent hose from canister and left-hand carburetor. Unclip spark plug leads from air cleaners.

TR8 V8 (Cont.)

Disconnect air temperature control valve from both air cleaners. Disconnect throttle cable from carburetor linkage, and remove kickdown cable bracket (vehicles with automatic transmissions).

5) Disconnect heater hoses from front and rear of manifold. Disconnect coolant temperature sensor lead. Disconnect purge air filter line from left-hand valve cover and remove filter from clip. Disconnect main fuel line filter and release front clip.

6) Disconnect carburetor countershaft link rod from left-hand carburetor by moving sleeves outward. Remove 12 intake manifold bolts and lift off manifold complete with carburetors and air cleaners.

7) Clean outside of manifold gasket, making sure all coolant is removed. Remove front and rear gasket clamps, and lift off and discard gasket and gasket seals. Clean threads of manifold bolts.

Installation — 1) Apply silicon grease to each side of new gasket seals. Install seals in position, with ends engaged in notches formed between cylinder heads and block.

2) Apply Hylomar PL 32M sealing compound (or equivalent) to 4 corners of new gasket, on cylinder head side around area of water passage joints. Fit gasket with word, "FRONT" towards front of engine. Fit gasket clamps in place, but do not fully tighten clamp bolts.

3) Apply sealing compound to manifold side of gasket as in step **2)**. Locate intake manifold in position on cylinder heads. Coat intake manifold bolt threads with thread lubricant-sealant (3M EC 776 or equivalent). Install bolts, tightening evenly, beginning at the center and working outward. Tighten gasket clamp bolts.

4) Reverse remaining removal procedures to complete installation.

FUEL INJECTION INTAKE MANIFOLD

Removal — 1) Drain cooling system and remove fresh air duct. Disconnect top hose and expansion hose from thermostat housing. Remove plenum chamber, airflow meter and extra air valve.

2) Disconnect pipes and filters from manifold, placing them to one side. Disconnect temperature switches, sensors and thermotime switch. Remove injectors.

3) Remove 12 intake manifold bolts and lift off manifold. Clean outside of manifold gasket, making sure any accumulation of coolant is removed. Remove 2 bolts and front and rear gasket clamps. Lift off clamps and discard gasket. Remove and discard gasket seals and clean threads of manifold bolts.

Installation — To install intake manifold and gasket, follow installation instructions for carbureted intake manifold.

CYLINDER HEAD

Removal — 1) Remove intake manifold and gasket. Remove spark plug leads from valve cover clamp. On carbureted models, move check valve aside and remove air temperature

control valve and hoses. Also remove heat chamber from exhaust manifold.

2) Remove dipstick tube bracket from left-hand valve cover. Remove dipstick and tube. Remove valve cover screws and lift off valve cover. Remove right-hand valve cover. Remove 4 bolts to remove each rocker shaft assembly. Remove push rods. Mark and disconnect leads from spark plugs.

3) Remove 3 bolts attaching air conditioning compressor to left-hand cylinder head and bolts attaching air pump and alternator mounting bracket to right-hand cylinder head. On left-hand head removals, remove exhaust manifold bolts to gain access to head bolts. On right-hand head removals, disconnect exhaust front pipe from manifold.

4) Loosen and remove 14 cylinder head bolts, reversing the tightening sequence. *See Fig. 1.* Lift off cylinder head (also exhaust manifold on right-hand head removal). Remove and discard gasket.

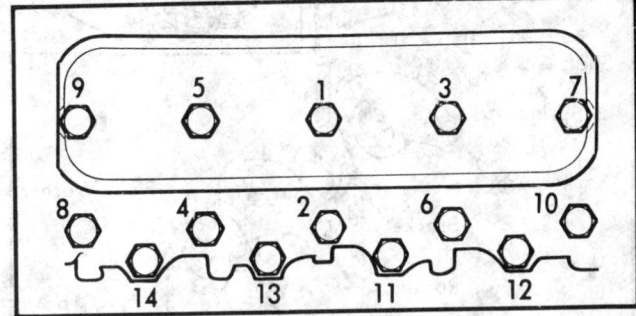

Fig. 1 Cylinder Head Bolt Tightening Sequence (Loosen in Reverse Order Shown)

5) Wash and wire brush cylinder head bolts in solvent (3M No. 2 or equivalent) to completely remove sealant. Examine bolts and replace any with signs of thread damage or elongation. Never install bolts more than 4 times.

Installation — 1) Clean cylinder head and block mating surfaces. Install a new gasket with word, "TOP", up. DO NOT use sealant on gasket surfaces.

2) Position cylinder head over dowel pins in block. Coat threads of cylinder head bolts with lubricant-sealant (3M EC 776 or equivalent). Use various length bolts in proper locations, as follows:

Cylinder Head Bolt Locations	
Application	**Bolt Numbers**
Long bolts	Nos. 1, 3 and 5
Medium bolts	Nos. 2, 4, 6, 7, 8, 9 and 10
Short bolts	Nos. 11, 12, 13, and 14

3) Tighten bolts evenly, a little at a time, in sequence shown in *Fig. 1.* Tighten bolts No. 1-10 to 65-70 ft. lbs. (9.0-9.7 mkg) and bolts No. 11-14 to 40-45 ft. lbs. (5.5-6.2 mkg).

TR8 V8 (Cont.)

VALVES

VALVE ARRANGEMENT

E-I-E-I-I-E-I-E (both banks front to rear).

ROCKER ARM ASSEMBLY

Disassembly — Remove cotter pin from end of shaft and remove plain washer, wave washer, rocker arms, brackets and springs. *See Fig. 2.* Store components in correct sequence for reassembly.

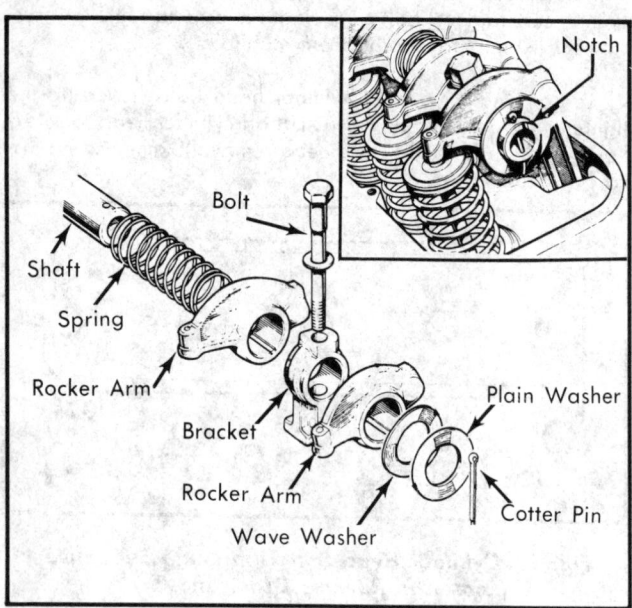

**Fig. 2   Rocker Shaft Assembly Sequence
(Inset Shows Notch on Shaft End)**

Reassembly — **1)** If new rocker arms are being installed, be sure to remove protective coating from each oil feed hole and push rod seat. Assemble plain washer against cotter pin in end of shaft. Install wave washer against plain washer.

NOTE — *Two different rocker arms are used and must be installed so that valve ends of arms slope away from brackets.*

2) Assemble rocker arms, brackets and springs in sets on rocker shaft. Compress springs and other components and install wave washer, plain washer and cotter pin in end of shaft.

3) Each rocker shaft is notched at one end and on one side only. The notch must be at top of shaft and toward front of the engine on right-hand side and toward rear of engine on left-hand side. *See Fig. 2.*

VALVE GUIDE SERVICING

1) Using a valve guide remover (274401), drive old guides out from combustion chamber side. Install specified spacer for valve guide drift (605774) on valve spring seat in top of cylinder head. *See Fig. 3.*

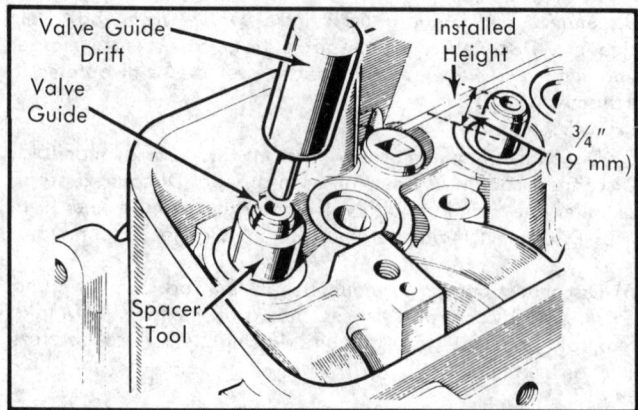

Fig. 3   Installing New Valve Guides

2) Lubricate new valve guide and insert into spacer. Using valve guide drift (600959), drive guide into cylinder head until drift bottoms against spacer. Installed guide should be ¾" (19 mm) above step surrounding valve guide boss.

NOTE — *Valve guides for service have an outside diameter .001" (.02 mm) larger than bore to provide an interference fit.*

VALVE SEAT INSERTS

1) Remove old seats, if necessary, by grinding them until thin enough to be cracked and pried out. Heat cylinder head evenly to approximately 150°F (65°C). Press new insert into recess in cylinder head.

NOTE — *Outside diameter of standard intake valve seat inserts is 1.6825-1.6838" (42.735-42.768 mm). Exhaust valve inserts are 1.4350-1.4545" (36.918-36.994 mm). Inserts for service are available in 2 oversizes, having .010" (.25 mm) and .020" (.50 mm) larger outside diameters.*

VALVE SERVICING

Removal — With cylinder heads removed, use valve spring compressor (276102 or equivalent) to remove valve locks. Keep components in proper order for later installation. Clean combustion chambers with a soft wire bush. Clean valves and valve guide bores. Regrind or install new valves, as necessary. If valves must be ground to a knife-edge to obtain a true seat, install new valves.

Installation — Lubricate valve stems and guides with engine oil. Insert each valve into its guide. Position valve springs on cylinder head (install new springs if compression tests prove springs are weak). Locate cap over top of spring. Compress spring with spring compressor (276102) and install valve lock. Install cylinder heads after rocker arm assembly and valves have been checked for proper assembly and ease of operation.

HYDRAULIC TAPPET SERVICING

1) Drain cooling system and remove fresh air duct. Remove intake manifold and valve covers. Remove rocker shaft assemblies. Remove push rods and keep in sequence for later installation. Remove tappets and store them with their respective push rods.

TR8 V8 (Cont.)

NOTE — *If tappets cannot be removed from bore, remove camshaft and remove tappet from bottom of bore.*

2) Inspect hydraulic tappets for blow holes or scoring. Replace if badly scored or grooved, or if blow hole would permit oil leakage from lower chamber. Some wear is permitted just above lower end of tappet body. This results from side thrust of cam against tappet body as tappet moves vertically in its guide.

3) Inspect cam contact surface of tappets. A round wear pattern is normal, as tappets rotate. A non-rotating tappet will have a square wear pattern, requiring tappet replacement. Be sure new tappets rotate freely in cylinder block before completing reassembly.

4) Install new tappets also if area of push rod contact is rough or otherwise damaged. Replace any push rods having a rough or damaged ball end seat.

NOTE — *Tappet noise is normal after an overhaul, due to oil drainage from tappet assemblies. If noise is excessive, run engine at 2500 RPM for a few minutes to eliminate noise.*

PISTONS, PINS & RINGS

OIL PAN

Removal — 1) Disconnect battery. Remove both cylinder heads and gaskets. Attach engine lifting brackets to second inboard cylinder head stud holes on each bank of block. Support engine weight (MS 53/3 supporting tool), so that 4 engine mounting nuts and bolts can be removed from subframe.

2) Raise engine about 1½" (38 mm). Raise vehicle and drain engine oil. Remove oil pan coupling plate bolts, oil pan bolts and oil pan. Remove oil pick-up strainer and oil pan baffle plate.

Installation — To install oil pan, reverse removal procedure.

PISTON & CONNECTING ROD ASSEMBLIES

NOTE — *Connecting rods and caps are not marked for reassembly reference. Be sure to mark caps for later reassembly to their respective rods. Also piston and rod assemblies must be marked for later assembly in their respective bores.*

Removal — Remove connecting rod caps. Screw guide bolts (605351) on to connecting rod bolts. Push connecting rod and piston assembly upward and remove from top of cylinder bore. Remove guide bolts.

Installation — 1) Position applicable crankshaft journal at BDC. Place upper bearing shell in connecting rod. Retain by screwing guide bolt (605351) on connecting rod.

2) Insert connecting rod and piston assembly into its respective bore. Dome-shaped bosses on connecting rods must face toward front of engine for right-hand bank of cylinders and toward rear of engine for left-hand bank. *See Fig. 4.* When connecting rods are installed, dome-shaped bosses will face each other.

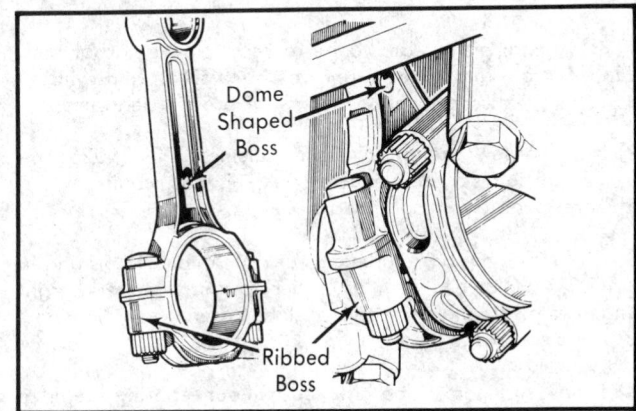

Fig. 4   Connecting Rod Positioning Marks

3) Position oil control piston rings so gaps are all on one side, between piston pin and thrust face. *See Fig. 5.* Ring rail gaps should be 1" (25 mm) to each side of expander ring gap.

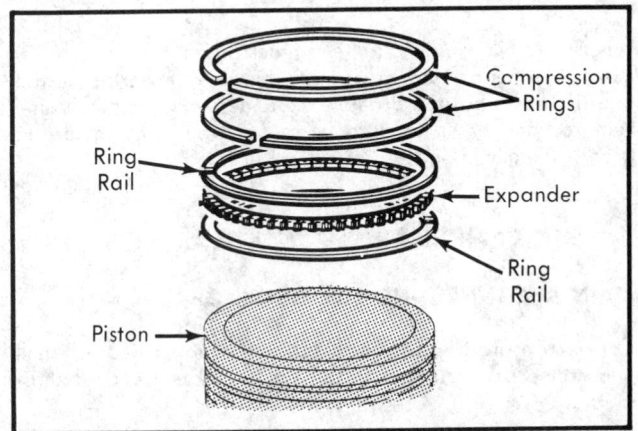

Fig. 5   Positioning Piston Rings

4) Position compression rings so their gaps are on opposite sides of piston, between piston pin and thrust face. Using a ring compressor, install piston and rod into its bore.

5) Install bearing lower shell into its connecting rod cap. Position cap and shell on its respective connecting rod, making sure ribbed edge of cap is toward front of engine on right-hand bank of cylinders and toward rear of engine on left-hand bank. *See Fig. 4.* Tighten connecting rod cap. Check for proper end play and free movement on crankshaft.

PISTON PINS

Removal & Installation — 1) Install piston and connecting rod on pressing tool (605350). Using a drift from tool set, press pin from piston and rod.

2) Locate piston pin guide on pressing tool (605350). Position piston and connecting rod on tool. Insert piston pin into piston and over guide. Position drift on piston pin and press pin in until it strikes shoulder of guide.

3) Make sure piston moves freely on piston pin and that no damage occurred during pressing. Install assemblies in their respective bores.

Triumph Engines

TR8 V8 (Cont.)

FITTING PISTONS

1) If original pistons are to be reused, remove carbon and deposits from ring grooves and compare piston and cylinder diameters with specifications to assure proper clearances.

2) If new pistons are to be installed, a single .001" (.025 mm) oversize piston is available for service. This may require honing of bore to obtain proper clearances.

3) Check cylinder bore diameters at right angles to piston pin 3.5-4.0" (90-100 mm) from top. Check piston diameter at right angles to piston pin at bottom of skirt. Difference in diameters is piston clearance.

4) If new rings are to be installed without reboring, deglaze cylinder walls in a cross-hatch pattern so as not to increase bore diameter. Install compression rings in cylinder bore to check end gaps. Also install compression rings in their respective grooves (chrome ring in top groove, stepped ring in second groove), and check clearance in grooves.

PISTON RINGS

When installing rings, install expander ring in bottom groove, making sure ends touch each other, but do not overlap. Install one ring rail above and below expander ring. Install chrome compression ring in top groove and stepped ring in second groove, with marking "T" or "TOP" upward.

CRANKSHAFT & ROD BEARINGS

MAIN & CONNECTING ROD BEARINGS

Connecting Rod Bearings — 1) Position upper bearing shell into connecting rod and install on its respective crankshaft journal.

NOTE — *Make sure rod is correctly installed as outlined in steps* **2)** *and* **5)** *of PISTON & CONNECTING ROD ASSEMBLIES.*

2) Install Plastigage (605238) across center of lower half of crankshaft journal. Install bearing on connecting rod cap and install cap to rod. Do not rotate crankshaft while Plastigage is installed.

3) Compare Plastigage reading with specified bearing clearance. If wear limit is exceeded, install new bearings.

Crankshaft Main Bearings — 1) With oil pan removed, remove bolts retaining main bearing caps 2, 3 and 4 complete with upper and lower bearing shells. Inspect caps, bearing shells and crankshaft journals for damage.

NOTE — *Do not remove all 5 main bearing caps at once, since weight of crankshaft would distort front and rear oil seals. Only caps 2, 3 and 4 are identified by number. Keep upper and lower bearing shells together as matched sets.*

2) Using Plastigage method, check main bearing clearances and replace bearings as necessary. Check crankshaft journals for out-of-round. If more than .0015" (.038 mm), grind crankshaft to next undersize or replace crankshaft.

3) Install upper bearing shell 3 (thrust bearing) to cylinder block. Upper shells have central oil hole and must be lubricated prior to installation. *See Fig. 6.* Install with locking slot end trailing. Then, install upper shells 2 and 4 in same manner.

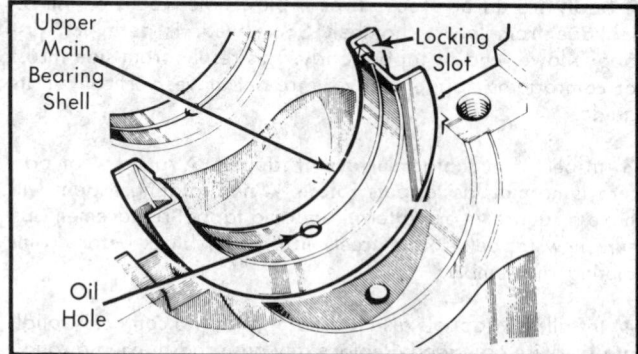

Fig. 6   Installing Upper Main Bearing Shell

4) Assemble lower shells to bearing caps, lubricate and install. Be sure all locking slots are together on right-hand side of engine. Tighten main bearing caps 2, 3 and 4 to specifications.

5) After main bearings 2, 3 and 4 have been checked and either reinstalled or replaced, remove main bearing caps 1 and 5 complete with lower bearing shells. Remove upper bearing shells. Discard main bearing side seals.

NOTE — *Main bearings 1 and 5 should be checked for proper clearance, using Plastigage method. Check crankshaft journals for damage and out-of-round in same manner as for bearings 2, 3 and 4.*

6) Install front upper bearing shell (with central oil hole) and place lower bearing shell in main bearing cap 1. Install to cylinder block. Be sure locking slots are together on right-hand side of engine. Tighten to specifications.

REAR MAIN BEARING & OIL SEAL

NOTE — *Oil seal is replaced with engine-transmission assembly removed, permitting removal of crankshaft. Seal may also be replaced with engine installed, by removing transmission, clutch and flywheel.*

1) With other 4 main bearing caps installed, install upper bearing shell in cylinder block. Install new side seals to rear main bearing cap. *See Fig. 7.* Do not cut seals to length, but permit them to extend 5/8" (1.5 mm) above bearing cap face.

2) Apply Hylomar PL 32M sealing compound (or equivalent) to rearmost half of rear main bearing cap or its cylinder block mating surface. Lubricate bearing half and side seals with clean engine oil.

3) Install rear main bearing cap snugly, but not completely, making sure it is squarely seated on cylinder block. Back off each main bearing cap bolt 1 turn.

4) Position seal guide (RO 1014) on crankshaft flange. Be sure oil seal guide and crankshaft journal are completely clean. Coat seal guide and oil seal journal with clean engine oil.

TR8 V8 (Cont.)

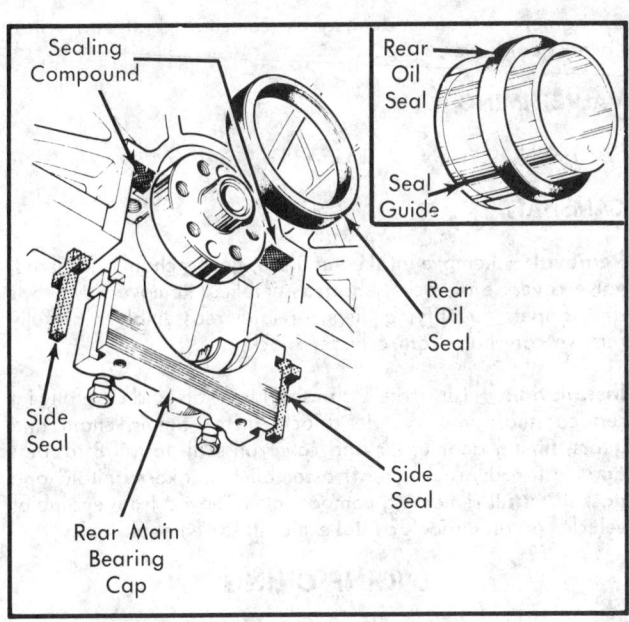

**Fig. 7   Installing Rear Main Bearing Cap
With Oil Seals**

NOTE — *Be sure lubricant covers entire outer surface of oil seal guide, preventing lip from turning back during assembly. Do not handle oil seal lip at any time.*

5) Place oil seal on seal guide with lipped surface toward engine. By hand, push oil seal fully and squarely into recess formed in bearing cap and cylinder block, until it is seated against machined step in recess. Remove seal guide.

6) Tighten rear main bearing cap to specifications and check crankshaft end play. Complete reassembly or installation of engine-transmission assembly.

CAMSHAFT

TIMING GEAR COVER

NOTE — *If not equipped with air conditioning, disregard references to such components.*

Removal — 1) Disconnect battery, drain cooling system and turn crankshaft so No. 1 cylinder is at TDC. Remove crankshaft pulleys, alternator drive belt tension strap and radiator bottom hose (from water pump). Remove air intake left-hand hose on carbureted engines to gain access to power steering bolts. Remove power steering pump.

2) Disconnect electrical lead from oil pressure switch. On carbureted models, loosen air pump belt tension and remove air pump and belt. Disconnect heater inlet hose from water pump and outlet hose from rear of timing gear cover. Remove water pump.

3) Remove electrical leads from distributor, ballast resistor and coil. Remove distributor cap and set it aside. Disconnect vacuum pipe from distributor capsule. Remove top radiator hose from thermostat housing.

4) Remove timing gear cover bolts and single nut and washer. Remove 2 bolts securing oil pan to cover. Loosen 2 adjacent oil

pan bolts. Remove timing gear cover, complete with distributor, oil pump and filter. *See Fig. 8.* Remove gasket. Clean bolt threads with solvent (3M No. 2).

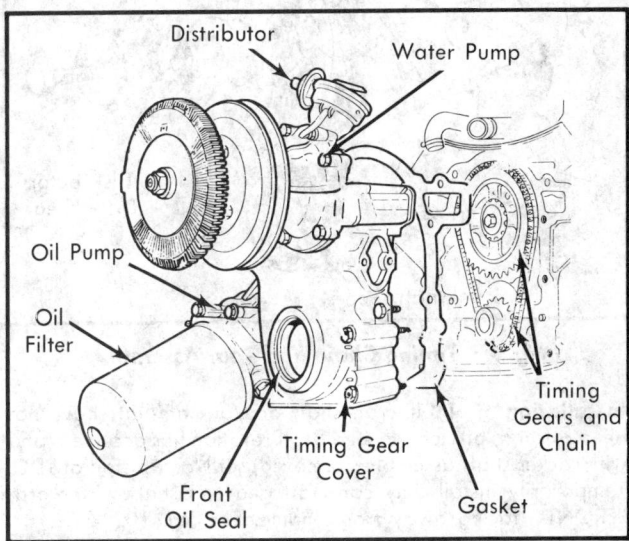

Fig. 8   Removing Timing Gear Cover Assembly

Installation — 1) To install, reverse the removal procedure. Be sure cylinder block and cover mating surfaces are clean. Coat both sides of new gasket with Hylomar PL 32M (or equivalent) and position on block or cover. Apply lubricant-sealer (3M EC 776 or equivalent) to threads of timing gear cover bolts.

2) Set distributor rotor arm to approximately 30° BTDC and install cover on cylinder block. Tighten bolts and nut with washer to specifications. Complete reversal of removal procedure.

TIMING GEAR COVER OIL SEAL

Removal — 1) Remove crankshaft pulleys. Remove fan and viscous coupling on non-air conditioned models. Screw extractor tool (18G 1328) into seal.

2) Turn center bolt clockwise to remove seal. Remove seal from extractor and discard seal.

Installation — 1) Clean seal housing in cover. Lubricate outside diameter of seal with clean engine oil. Using care not to damage seal, start seal into cover.

2) Fit adapter (18G 1291/5) to main tool (18G 1291/4) and screw bolt into crankshaft. Turn lock nut clockwise, drawing seal in until flush with cover. Remove tool and adapter. Lubricate seal lip with engine oil and install crankshaft pulleys.

TIMING CHAIN AND GEARS

Removal — With timing cover removed and No. 1 piston at TDC, remove distributor drive gear. *See Fig. 9.* Remove spacer and both gears with chain, keeping components assembled.

CAUTION — *Do not rotate engine shafts if rocker shafts are installed, as damage could result.*

Triumph Engines

TR8 V8 (Cont.)

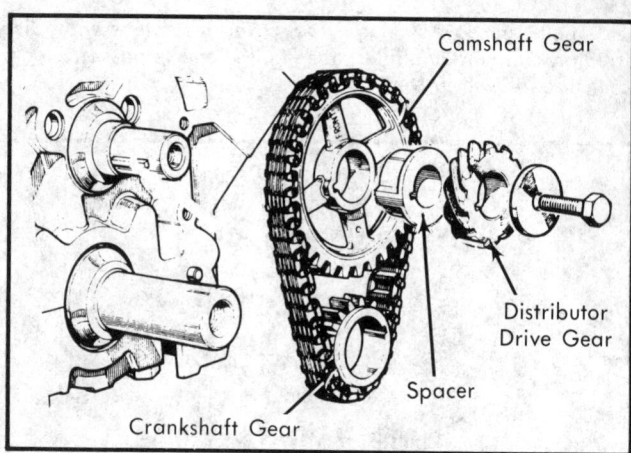

Fig. 9   Timing Chain and Gear Assembly

Installation — 1) If crankshaft and/or camshaft have not been rotated, proceed to step **3).** If rotation has occurred (and with rocker shaft assemblies removed) set No. 1 piston at TDC. Temporarily install only camshaft gear on shaft with word, "FRONT", facing away from engine. See Fig. 10.

2) Turn camshaft until timing mark on gear is at lower 6 o'clock position. See Fig. 10. Remove camshaft gear without disturbing camshaft. Place camshaft and crankshaft gears in chain so their timing marks align.

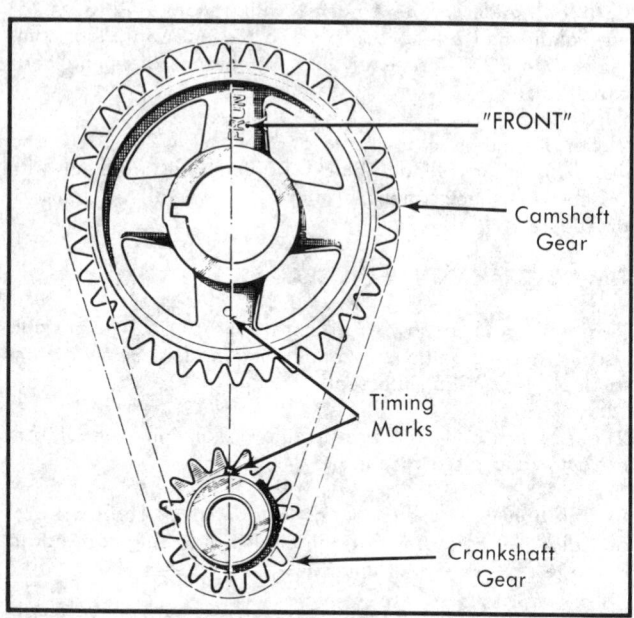

Fig. 10   Setting Valve Timing

3) Engage chain and gear assembly on camshaft and crankshaft key locations. Check that camshaft key is parallel to shaft axis for proper lubrication of distributor drive gear. Diameter of shaft including key should not exceed 1.187" (30.15 mm).

4) Again, check timing marks for proper alignment. Install spacer with flange toward front. Install distributor drive gear, making sure annular grooved side is to the rear (toward spacer).

5) Tighten distributor drive gear (camshaft) bolt and install timing gear cover.

VALVE TIMING

See TIMING CHAIN AND GEARS

CAMSHAFT

Removal — Remove intake manifold, timing chain and gears, valve covers and rocker shaft assemblies. Remove push rods and tappets, identifying them for later reassembly. Carefully remove camshaft from cylinder block.

Installation — Lubricate 5 camshaft journals and carefully insert camshaft into cylinder block. Install timing chain and gears, timing gear cover and cover oil seal. Install 8 tappets and push rods, rocker shaft assemblies, intake manifold and gasket. Install remaining components removed from engine or vehicle, as required for intake manifold removal.

ENGINE OILING

Crankcase Capacity — 5.4 quarts with filter. Normal drain and refill, 4.7 quarts.

Oil Filter — Disposable, full-flow type.

Pressure Relief Valve — Non-adjustable. Located in oil pump.

Normal Oil Pressure — 35 psi (2.46 kg/cm²) at 2400 RPM.

Oil Pump

A high capacity gear-type pump, driven by distributor shaft, which is geared to distributor drive gear on camshaft. Pump takes oil from pan, through a strainer and pumps it through oil filter to lubricate engine components.

Removal — Remove oil filter. Disconnect electrical lead from oil pressure switch. Remove bolts attaching oil pump cover assembly to timing gear cover. See Fig. 11. Lift off cover and gasket and slide out oil pump gears.

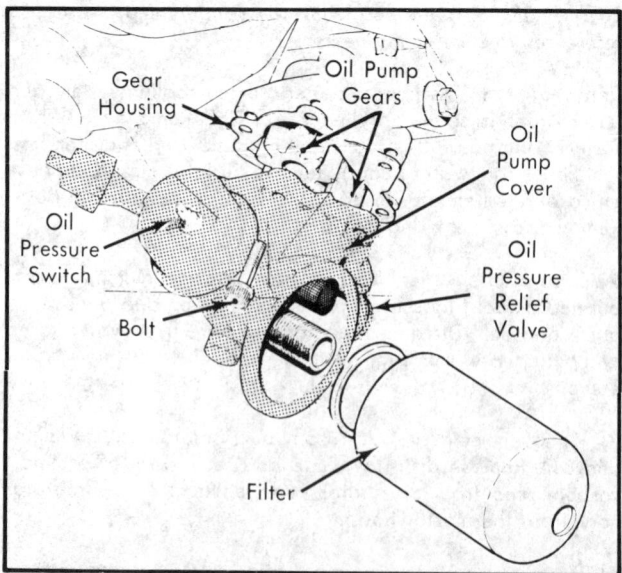

Fig. 11   Removing Oil Pump Cover from Housing

TR8 V8 (Cont.)

Inspection — Clean gears and inspect for wear or scoring. Replace worn gears. Remove oil pressure relief valve and inspect parts for wear. Replace spring if sides of spring are worn. Be sure valve moves freely in its bore, but has no side movement.

NOTE — *To check pump gears and housing for wear, install gears and shaft into timing gear cover. Place straightedge across face of gears and insert feeler gauge between straightedge and cover. If clearance is less than .0018" (.05 mm), check timing gear cover gear housing for wear.*

Installation — **1)** Lubricate and install pressure relief valve assembly. Fully pack oil pump gear housing with petroleum jelly (no other grease is suitable). Install oil pump gears, so petroleum jelly is forced into every cavity between teeth of gears.

CAUTION — *Unless pump is fully packed as indicated, pump may not prime itself upon reassembly and engine start-up. Use care when removing oil filter to replace filter immediately. If not replaced quickly, oil can drain from pump requiring pump removal and priming.*

2) Place a new gasket on oil pump cover and position cover on timing gear cover. Install and tighten bolts evenly and alternately. Connect electrical lead to oil pressure switch and install new oil filter. Check oil level in crankcase and bring to proper level.

ENGINE COOLING

Thermostat — Opens at 190°F (88°C).

Cooling System Capacity — 11.5 quarts with header tank; 10.5 quarts with expansion tank.

Radiator Cap — 15 psi (1.05 kg/cm²).

WATER PUMP

Removal — **1)** Disconnect battery and drain cooling system. Remove left-hand top hose from thermostat housing and other hoses from water pump.

2) Remove 4 bolts common to water pump and timing gear cover. Remove remaining 6 water pump bolts. Move air pump drive belt adjusting strap aside. Lift off water pump and gasket.

Installation — **1)** Clean water pump and timing gear cover mating surfaces. Grease gasket lightly and position on timing gear cover. Clean threads of mounting bolts and smear them with lubricant-sealant (3M EC 776).

2) Be sure 2 dowels are free of burrs. Install water pump over dowels and install bolts. Tighten evenly. Replace all hoses previously removed, install coolant and connect battery cables.

THERMOSTAT

Removal — Disconnect battery. Drain only radiator by disconnecting bottom hose. Remove top hose from thermostat housing. Remove 2 bolts and lift thermostat housing cover from intake manifold. See Fig. 12. Remove thermostat and gasket.

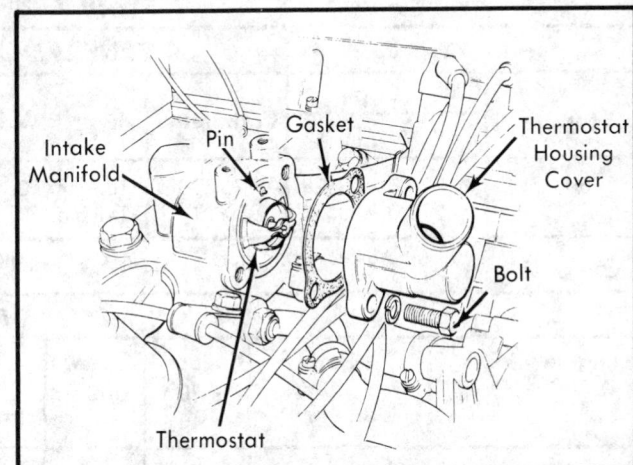

Fig. 12 Removing Thermostat and Gasket

Inspection — Note number stamped on thermostat, indicating temperature at which thermostat should be fully open. Place thermostat and a thermometer in water and heat, noting temperature at which thermostat opens. Install or replace, as necessary.

Installation — Clean gasket mating surfaces, and install thermostat with pin at 12 o'clock position. See Fig. 12. Install new gasket and position thermostat housing cover. Install and tighten bolts evenly. Connect hoses and battery.

TIGHTENING SPECIFICATIONS

Application	Ft. Lbs. (mkg)
Camshaft Sprocket	40-45 (5.5-6.2)
Vibration Damper	190-210 (26.3-29.0)
Intake Manifold	25-30 (3.5-4.2)
Intake Manifold Clamp	10-15 (1.4-2.1)
Exhaust Manifold	10-16 (1.4-2.2)
Cylinder Head	
Bolts 1 through 10	65-70 (9.0-9.7)
Bolts 11 through 14	40-45 (5.5-6.2)
Rocker Shaft Bracket	25-30 (3.5-4.2)
Connecting Rod Cap	35-40 (4.8-5.5)
Rear Main Bearing	65-70 (9.0-9.7)
Other Main Bearings	50-55 (6.9-7.6)
Flexible Plate-to-Crankshaft	50-60 (6.9-8.3)
Flywheel-to-Crankshaft	55-60 (7.6-8.3)
Oil Pan	
Rear	17-18 (2.3-2.5)
Others	8-9 (1.1-1.2)
Oil Pump	9-10 (1.2-1.4)
Pressure Relief Valve	30-35 (4.2-4.8)
Starter Motor	30-35 (4.2-4.8)
Timing Gear Cover	20-25 (2.8-3.5)
Power Steering Pump	20-25 (2.8-3.5)
Water Pump and Timing Gear Cover	20-25 (2.8-3.5)
Alternator-to-Cylinder Head	
3/8" Bolt	23-25 (3.2-3.5)
5/16" Bolt	17-18 (2.4-2.5)
A/C Compressor Bracket-to-Head	19-20 (2.6-2.8)
A/C Compressor-to-Bracket	
3/8" Set Screw	28-30 (3.9-4.2)
3/8" Stud	23-24 (3.2-3.4)

Triumph Engines

TR8 V8 (Cont.)
ENGINE SPECIFICATIONS

GENERAL SPECIFICATIONS

| Year | Displ. | | Carburetor | HP at RPM | Torque (Ft. Lbs. at RPM) | Compr. Ratio | Bore | | Stroke | |
	cu. ins.	cc					in.	mm	in.	mm
1980	215.0	3528	①175CDSET	133@4750	.....	8.15:1	3.50	88.9	2.80	71.1
	215.0	3528	②Fuel Inj.	148@4750	.....	8.15:1	3.50	88.9	2.80	71.1

① — Twin 1-Bbl. side-draft carburetors.   ② — Lucas digital electronic.

VALVES

Engine & Valve	Head Diam. In. (mm)	Face Angle	①Seat Angle	②Seat Width In. (mm)	③Stem Diameter In. (mm)	④Stem Clearance In. (mm)	Valve Lift In. (mm)
3528 cc							
Intake	1.565-1.575 (39.8-40.0)	45°	46°	.060 (1.575)	.3402-.3412 (8.6-8.7)	.0010-.0030 (.02-.07)	.39 (9.9)
Exhaust	1.348-1.358 (34.2-34.5)	45°	46°	.060 (1.575)	.3397-.3407 (8.6-8.7)	.0020-.0004 (.05-.10)	.39 (9.9)

① — Plus ¼ degree.   ② — Wear Limit .078″ (2.0 mm).
③ — Measured at valve head. Diameter increases .0005″ (.012 mm) away from head.
④ — Measured at top of guide. Subtract .0005″ (.012 mm) for bottom of guide clearance.

VALVE TIMING

| Engine | INTAKE | | EXHAUST | |
	Open (ATDC)	Close (ABDC)	Open (BBDC)	Close (ATDC)
3528 cc	30°	75°	68°	37°

VALVE SPRINGS

| Engine | Free Length | PRESSURE (LBS.) | |
		Valve Closed	Valve Open
3528 cc	.....	66.5-73.5 @ 1.577″	.....
	.....	123.5-136.5 @ 1.350″	.....
	.....	168.5-183.5 @ 1.187″	.....

PISTONS, PINS, RINGS

| Engine | PISTONS | PINS | | RINGS | | |
	Clearance In. (mm)	Piston Fit In. (mm)	Rod Fit In. (mm)	Rings	End Gap In. (mm)	Side Clearance In. (mm)
3528 cc	①.0007-.0013 (.018-.033)	.0001-.0003 (.002-.007)	Press Fit	No. 1	.017-.022 (.44-.57)	.003-.005 (.08-.13)
	②.0016-.0028 (.04-.08)			No. 2	.017-.022 (.44-.57)	.003-.005 (.08-.13)
	③.0296-.0350 (.73-.88)			Oil	.015-.055 (.38-1.40)	....

① — At bottom of skirt.   ② — At top of skirt.   ③ — At top land.

CRANKSHAFT MAIN & CONNECTING ROD BEARINGS

| Engine | MAIN BEARINGS | | | | CONNECTING ROD BEARINGS | | |
	Journal Diam. In. (mm)	①Clearance In. (mm)	Thrust Bearing	Crankshaft End Play In. (mm)	Journal Diam. In. (mm)	①Clearance In. (mm)	Side Play In. (mm)
3528 cc	2.2992-2.2997 (58.39-58.41)	.0009-.0024 (.023-.061)	No. 3	.004-.008 (.10-.20)	2.0000-2.0005 (50.80-50.81)	.0006-.0022 (.015-.055)	.006-.014 (.15-.37)

① — Wear limit .003″ (.08 mm).

DASHER, JETTA, RABBIT, RABBIT PICKUP, & SCIROCCO

ENGINE CODING

ENGINE IDENTIFICATION

Engine identification number is stamped on left side of engine block near ignition distributor.

Engine Identification	
Application	**Code**
Dasher	
Man. Trans.	YG
Auto Trans.	YH, YK
Jetta, Rabbit Pickup, & Scirocco	EJ
Rabbit	
Carbureted	FX
Fuel Injected	EJ

ENGINE, CYLINDER HEAD & MANIFOLDS

ENGINE

NOTE — *On Jetta, Rabbit, and Scirocco models, engine and transmission must be LOWERED out of vehicle as an assembly.*

Removal (Jetta, Rabbit, & Scirocco) — 1) Disconnect battery cables at battery. Loosen fuel filler cap to relieve tank pressure. Drain coolant by removing hose from thermostat flange and disconnect radiator fan motor and thermoswitch. Remove radiator with fan and ducts.

2) On air conditioned vehicles, remove air conditioner compressor and tie aside without disconnecting hoses. On all models, disconnect the following electrical connectors: Alternator, thermoswitch, oil pressure switch, warm-up regulator, coolant temperature sensor, coil and condenser wires, cold start valve and starter solenoid harness.

3) On carburetor equipped models, remove fuel hose. On fuel injection models, remove injectors. Remove fuel lines for cold start valve and warm-up regulator. On all models disconnect remaining fuel, coolant, emission control and vacuum lines and position out of way. Disconnect and remove accelerator linkage from engine.

NOTE — *When disconnecting fuel lines or components, have container available to catch leaking fuel in case system is still under pressure.*

4) Disconnect speedometer cable and ground cable from transmission. Detach selector cable and bracket on automatic transmission models. Detach clutch cable and relay shaft lever on manual transmission models. Disconnect starter wires and back up light switch on all models.

5) Remove exhaust flex-pipe nuts or spring clip. Remove starter. Disconnect both drive shafts from drive flanges. Remove horn and place out of way. Remove engine front mount. Remove axle nuts and disconnect lower ball joints from bearing housings, then remove drive shaft while holding strut assembly away from vehicle.

6) Reconnect ball joints so vehicle may be lowered onto wheels. Remove complete rear mount. Remove right front wheel. Attach suitable sling (US 1105) to engine and lift slightly. On manual transmission models, remove relay shaft and gearshift lever rods. On all models, remove bolts holding side mounts to body and lower engine/transmission assembly to dolly. Raise vehicle to clear and remove assembly from beneath car.

Installation — To install, reverse removal procedures using caution to observe all tightening specifications.

NOTE — *Mounts must be properly aligned and free of tension before tightening.*

Removal (Dasher) — 1) Remove battery and drain crankcase. Remove air cleaner and ducting. Disconnect and plug fuel inlet hose. On manual transmission models, disconnect clutch operating lever, then disengage cable housing from bracket on engine mount.

2) Remove fuse block mounting screws and bend open wiring harness clip. Tie fuel hose, clutch cable and fuse block out of way. Disconnect heater control cable. Remove front engine mount and mount support.

3) Disconnect coil and any electrical components that might interfere with engine removal. If equipped with A/C, remove condensers and compressor and set out of way without disconnecting hoses. Drain coolant then remove radiator and expansion tank.

4) Working under vehicle, remove starter and disconnect exhaust pipe at manifold. On automatic transmission models, remove converter bolts through hole left by starter removal. On all models, remove engine mount nuts and lower engine/transmission bolts.

5) Install support bar under transmission and attach engine hoist. Raise engine until assembly hits steering rack housing and remove upper engine/transmission bolts. Pry engine loose from transmission and remove intermediate plate. Lift and turn engine to left and remove from vehicle. Secure torque converter with strap on automatic transmission models.

Installation — To install, reverse removal procedures, ensuring that aligning dowels between engine/transmission are tight. Torque converter on automatic transmission models must be fully seated with front of pilot approximately $1^{3}/_{16}$" (30 mm) below bell housing flange. Check that all mounts are free of strain before tightening.

CYLINDER HEAD & MANIFOLDS

Removal — 1) On cars with carburetors, remove air cleaner and ducting. On fuel injection models, disconnect duct connecting throttle valve housing with mixture control unit. On all models, remove camshaft drive belt and drain engine coolant. If equipped with A.I.R. (California models), disconnect air lines from connections on exhaust manifold.

CAUTION — *Never drain coolant while engine is hot. Doing so could cause engine block or cylinder head to warp.*

DASHER, JETTA, RABBIT, RABBIT PICKUP, & SCIROCCO (Cont.)

2) Disconnect exhaust pipe. Remove nuts and bolts that hold exhaust manifold and intake manifold (air intake distributor) to head. Remove manifolds. Remove upper alternator bolt and adjusting bracket. Disconnect all coolant hoses and temperature gauge wire. Remove spark plugs.

3) Remove valve cover. Remove head bolts in reverse order of tightening sequence. If head is stuck, insert a block of wood in each outboard exhaust port and pry free.

Installation — To install, reverse removal procedure and note the following: Make sure head gasket is positioned with "OBEN" mark facing up. Tighten head bolts in sequence and steps shown.

Cylinder Head Tightening Steps	
Application	**Ft. Lbs. (mkg)**
Step One	29 (4.0)
Step Two	43 (6.0)
Step Three	54 (7.5) Plus ¼ Turn

NOTE — *Polygon (12 point) socket head bolts are set to final torque while cold and do not need to be retorqued when hot. Tighten in sequence to 54 ft. lbs. (7.5 mkg) plus an additional ¼ turn.*

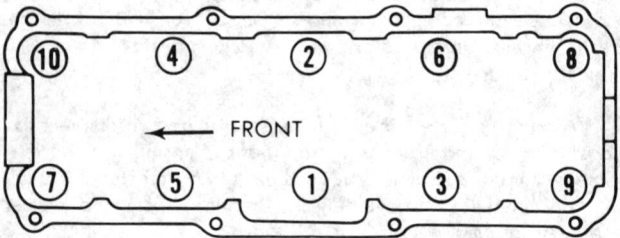

Fig. 1   Cylinder Head Tightening Sequence
(Loosen in Reverse Order)

CAMSHAFT

TIMING BELT

NOTE — *Sprockets DO NOT have to be removed to replace camshaft drive belt.*

Removal — On cars with carburetors, remove air cleaner and related ducting. Remove alternator belt, water pump pulley, and upper and lower drive belt covers. If equipped, remove air conditioning compressor drive belt and air injection pump belt. Loosen belt tensioner, and work belt off sprockets toward front of engine.

Installation — 1) Rotate camshaft sprocket until index punch mark on camshaft sprocket is lined up with top surface of valve cover mounting flange on spark plug side of head. Rotate crankshaft and intermediate shaft until index punch mark on intermediate shaft sprocket aligns with "V" notch on crankshaft pulley.

2) Use care not to move any sprocket. Fit belt on bottom first and then at top so there is no slack between sprockets. Tighten tensioner so belt can just be twisted 90° halfway between camshaft and intermediate sprockets. Tighten adjuster locknut and reverse removal procedure for remaining components.

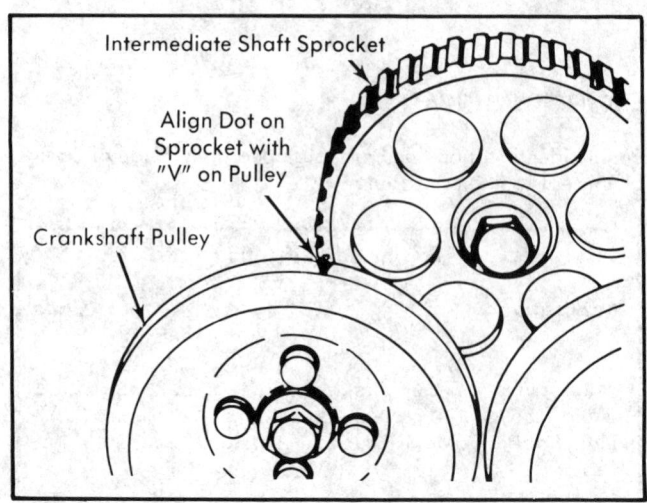

Fig. 2   Crankshaft and Intermediate Shaft Index Marks
Aligned with Notch on Crankshaft Pulley

CAMSHAFT

Removal — 1) Remove camshaft cover. Loosen and remove bearing caps in following sequence: 5, 1, and 3, then loosen bearing caps 2 and 4 diagonally. Bearing caps are numbered front to rear.

2) Check camshaft end play. Remove camshaft and lift out cam followers. Install camshaft using only bearing caps 1 and 5. Fit dial indicator so tip of gauge touches front of camshaft. Pry camshaft back and forth. Reading should not exceed .006" (.15 mm). If end play is beyond limits, replace either camshaft or cylinder head.

3) Check camshaft runout. Fit dial indicator so gauge pin is against camshaft center journal. Turn camshaft and record runout range. Runout must not exceed .0004" (.01 mm). Replace camshaft as necessary.

4) Inspect camshaft lobes for wear. Worn lobes usually indicate lack of lubrication. Check engine oiling passages to make sure they are not restricted. Replace worn camshafts and worn discs.

5) Inspect cam followers for signs of seizure or lack of lubrication. If any aluminum particles from head are found on cam followers, replace followers. Cylinder head must be replaced if any follower bores are worn or excessively rough.

Installation — Lightly lube cam follower bores, then fit followers in their original bores. Install adjusting discs. Place camshaft on cylinder head. Loosely attach No. 2 and No. 4 bearing caps. Gradually tighten caps. Fit No. 5 and No. 3 bearing caps. Install new oil seal in front of camshaft. Install No. 1 bearing cap. Make sure all caps are torqued to proper specifications.

VALVE TIMING

With timing belt removed as previously described, rotate crankshaft and intermediate shaft until index mark (punch mark) on intermediate shaft is positioned in "V" notch on

DASHER, JETTA, RABBIT, RABBIT PICKUP, & SCIROCCO (Cont.)

crankshaft pulley. See *Fig. 2.* This is firing point of No. 1 cylinder. Next, turn camshaft until timing mark on rear of camshaft sprocket is in line with top of cylinder head cover flange. See *Fig. 3.* Replace timing belt.

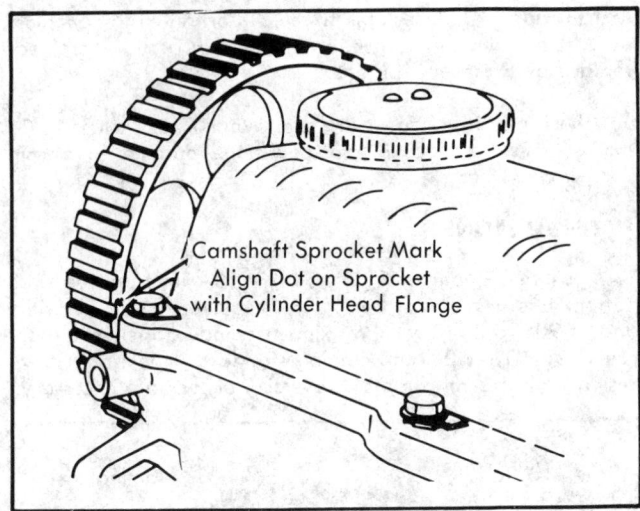

Camshaft Sprocket Mark
Align Dot on Sprocket
with Cylinder Head Flange

Fig 3   Index Mark on Camshaft Sprocket Aligned with Cylinder Head Flange

VALVES

VALVE ARRANGEMENT

E-I-E-I-I-E-I-E (front to rear).

VALVE GUIDE SERVICING

1) Clean valve guides before making measurements. To measure guide, attach a suitable mounting device with a dial gauge (VW689/1) to mounting surface of cylinder head. Insert a new valve until end of stem is flush with end of valve guide.

2) Rock valve head against dial indicator and check amount of rock recorded. Maximum allowable rock is .039" (1 mm) for intake valves and .051" (1.3 mm) for exhaust valves. Proper valve guide diameter is .315"-.316" (8.01-8.04 mm).

3) Use a press and suitable adaptor (10-206) to remove and install valve guides. To remove guides, press out from combustion chamber side of head.

4) Coat new valve guides with engine oil. Press new guides into cold head from camshaft side. Make sure shoulder of guide meets firmly with top of cylinder head. Ream guides to uniform inside diameter.

CAUTION — *Do not use more than 1 ton pressure once guide shoulder is seated or shoulder may break.*

VALVE SPRINGS

NOTE — *Although normal maintenance on valve system is performed with head removed, it is possible to replace stem seals, keepers, retainers or broken springs with cylinder head installed.*

Removal (Head Installed) — With camshaft and tappets removed, turn crankshaft until piston of cylinder you are working on is at BDC. Apply steady air pressure of at least 85 psi through spark plug hole adapter to keep valves seated. Compress spring with suitable tool (VW 541) and remove valve keepers. Remove and replace damaged or worn parts.

Removal (Head Removed) — With camshaft and tappets removed, use suitable compressor (VW 541) to depress retainer and remove keepers. Take out retainer and springs.

Installation — Check springs on spring tester and inspect for cracks or distortion. Reverse removal procedure and note the following: Lower edge of valve spring retainer should be chamfered to prevent valve stem scoring. If necessary, grind a chamfer using stone or other suitable tool. When installing the springs, make sure closely spaced coils of outer springs are against spring seats.

VALVE STEM OIL SEALS

With tappet, adjuster pad, keepers, springs, and spring seats removed, extract valve stem oil seal. When installing new seal, first position protective plastic sleeve on valve stem, lubricate seal, and use a suitable mandrel (10-204) to push seal onto valve guide.

VALVE CLEARANCE ADJUSTMENT

1) Adjust valves with engine at normal operating temperature. Clearance adjustments are to be checked and made according to firing order. Using a wrench on the crankshaft pulley bolt, turn clockwise to bring No. 1 piston to TDC (cam lobes pointing up). Determine valve clearance by inserting a feeler gauge between cam lobe heel and adjusting disc.

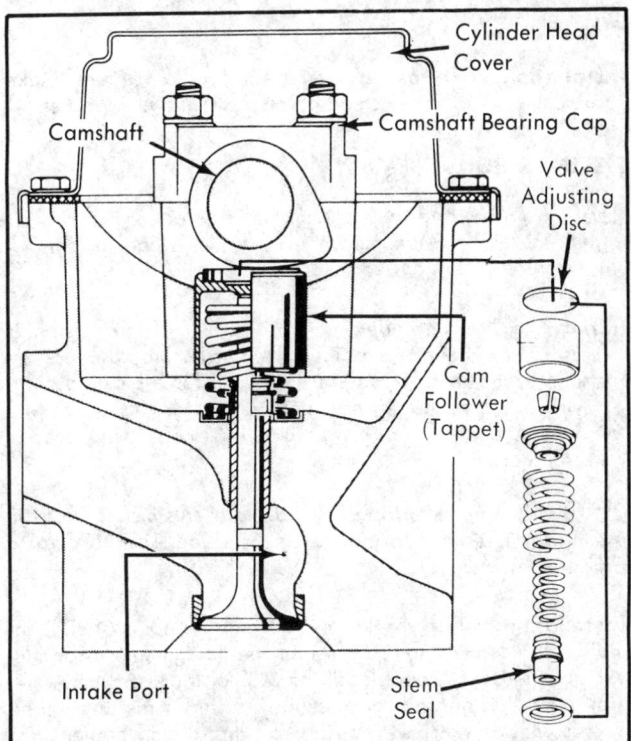

Fig. 4   Assembled View of Valve and Camshaft

DASHER, JETTA, RABBIT, RABBIT PICKUP, & SCIROCCO (Cont.)

2) Rotate crankshaft pulley 180° at a time, and check cylinders No. 3, No. 4 and No. 2, consecutively. If necessary, adjust to specifications by installing thicker or thinner adjusting discs. Discs are available in 26 different thicknesses in increments of .0019" (.05 mm). Disc thickness is stamped on the bottom, and ranges from .1181" (3.0 mm) to .1673" (4.25 mm). To install, press cam follower down with follower depressing tool (VW 546). Remove old disc with special pliers (VW 208), and insert new disc with stamped thickness marking toward cam follower.

Valve Clearance Specifications	
Application	**In. (mm)**
Intake	
Hot	.008-.012 (.20-.30)
Cold	.006-.010 (.15-.25)
Exhaust	
Hot	.016-.020 (.40-.50)
Cold	.014-.018 (.35-.45)

NOTE — *Cold settings are given for reference, as initial settings to be used during cylinder head rework. Final adjustments are made at normal operating temperature, and should be rechecked after approximately 1000 miles of operation.*

PISTONS, PINS & RINGS

OIL PAN

Removal — On Rabbit and Scirocco, drain oil, remove bolts and remove oil pan. On Dasher, support engine from above with support bar and threaded rod. Remove nuts holding engine mounts on subframe and bolts holding subframe to body. Pull subframe downward to separate engine mounts and body. Drain oil, remove mounting bolts and remove oil pan.

Installation — To install, reverse removal procedure. Make sure gasket surfaces are clean before installing new gaskets.

PISTON & ROD ASSEMBLY

NOTE — *Piston and rod assemblies can be removed with engine in vehicle. Manufacturer recommends engine removal for extensive overhaul work.*

Removal — Mark cylinder number on crown of each piston. If necessary, mark arrows pointing toward front of block on piston crowns. Remove rod cap bolts and force piston out top of cylinder. Use wooden hammer handle for this operation. Mark connecting rods and bearing caps for proper reinstallation.

NOTE — *If a ridge at top of cylinder prevents piston removal, use a ridge reamer to cut down the ridge. DO NOT force piston out of cylinder.*

Installation — Turn crankshaft so No. 1 journal is at BDC. Install piston connecting rod assembly until ring compressor contacts block. Use a wood handle to push piston into cylinder. Install No. 4 Piston and rod assembly. Ensure tabs on bearing halves engage notch in rod and cap. Install and tighten caps on rods 1 and 4. Turn crankshaft 180° and install No. 2 and 3 rod assemblies and rod caps.

PISTON PINS

Removal — Use needle-nosed pliers to remove pin circlips. Press out pin and remove piston from rod. For installation purposes, note direction piston is fitted to rod.

Installation — **1)** Check pin fit in each piston. Piston pin must be a thumb-push fit in piston. If correct fit is not obtained, replace both pin and piston.

2) Check pin fit in connecting rod. Wear limit is .0015" (.04 mm). Rebush connecting rod and hone bushing to obtain correct clearance.

FITTING PISTONS

1) Measure cylinder at 3 points: ⅜" (10 mm) from top and bottom, and at center of bore. Take measurements in line with, and at 90° to thrust face. Maximum cylinder taper or out-of-round is .0016" (.04 mm) beyond standard dimensions. If excessive, cylinder reboring and oversize pistons are necessary.

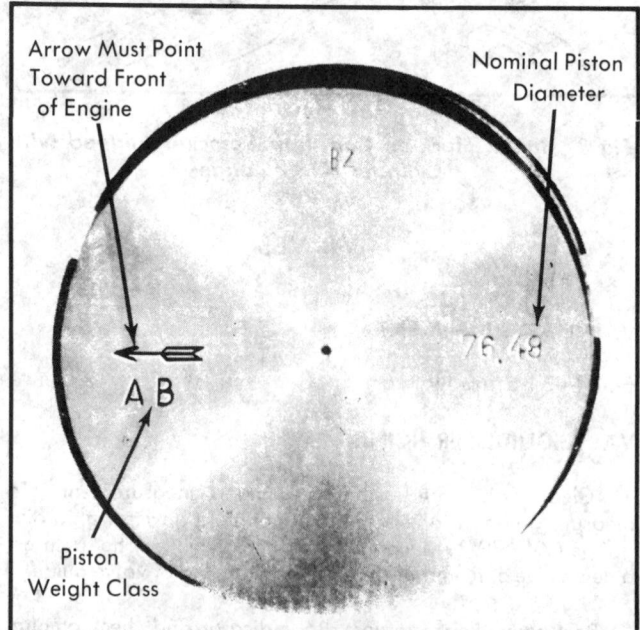

Fig. 5   Codes Stamped on Piston Head

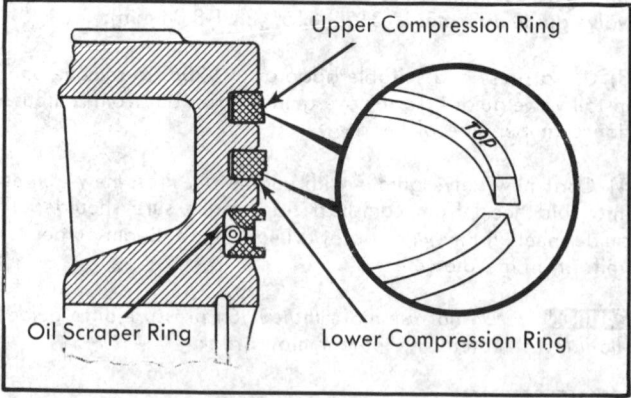

Fig. 6   Piston Ring Installation — Word TOP Must Face Piston Crown

2) Measure pistons at .63" (16 mm) from bottom of piston skirt (measuring 90° to pin bore). Combining this measure-

DASHER, JETTA, RABBIT, RABBIT PICKUP, & SCIROCCO (Cont.)

ment with measurement of corresponding cylinder bore, note piston-to-cylinder clearance. If this exceeds .0028" (.07 mm), oversize pistons must be installed.

3) Place piston rings squarely in top of cylinder bore (above ring ridge) and measure end gap. Measure ring side clearance. Install rings on piston with end gaps 120° offset to each other (start with oil ring gap directly to the rear). Ensure stamp mark "TOP" on rings is facing upward.

CRANKSHAFT MAIN & CONNECTING ROD BEARINGS

MAIN & CONNECTING ROD BEARINGS

1) Push crankshaft toward one end and measure crankshaft end play at No. 3 (thrust) bearing. Main bearing caps are stamped "1" to "5" (front to rear), and must be returned to original positions upon reassembly. Measure end play (side play) of connecting rods. Remove all bearing caps and check bearing clearance using Plastigage method.

2) Measure crankshaft journals with a micrometer to determine journal out-of-round and taper. The maximum allowable wear is .0012" (.03 mm). Install main bearing inserts with oil groove in the engine block, making sure anti-rotation tabs engage in saddle notches. Lubricate new bearings, place crankshaft in block, and install lower main shells and caps in proper order.

Crankshaft Journal Diameters		
Size	**Main Bearing In. (mm)**	**Rod Bearing In. (mm)**
Standard	2.124 (53.95)	1.809 (45.95)
1st US	2.114 (53.70)	1.799 (45.70)
2nd US	2.104 (53.45)	1.789 (45.45)
3rd US	2.094 (53.20)	1.779 (45.20)

REAR MAIN BEARING OIL SEAL

NOTE — *Rear main bearing oil seal may be replaced with engine in vehicle. Transmission and flywheel must be removed.*

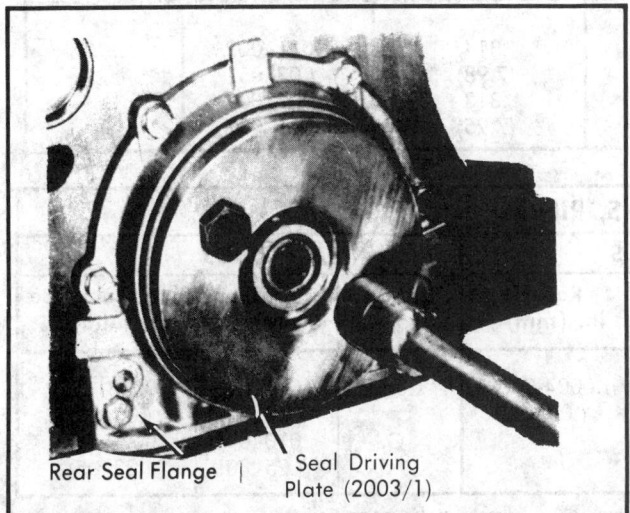

Rear Seal Flange | Seal Driving Plate (2003/1)

Fig. 7 Using Special Tool to Install Rear Main Oil Seal

Insert a large screwdriver between crankshaft flywheel flange and inside lip of oil seal. Pry out old seal. Install seal guide sleeve (2003/2A or equivalent) over crankshaft flange. Start new seal over guide sleeve, and into recess in seal carrier. Remove guide sleeve and bolt seal driving plate (2003/1 or equivalent) to flywheel mounting flange. Tighten bolts evenly to bring seal flush with carrier.

FRONT MAIN BEARING OIL SEAL AND INTERMEDIATE SHAFT OIL SEAL

Remove camshaft belt. Remove crankshaft sprocket. Pry seal from seal carrier, being careful not to damage carrier. Use removing tool (10-219 or equivalent) to remove seal. *See Fig. 8.* Using installing tool (10-203 or equivalent), press in new seal until flush with seal carrier. If tool 10-203 was used, remove it and using aluminum part of tool, press seal in until recessed .080" (2.0 mm) in seal carrier.

NOTE — *Same procedure applies to intermediate shaft oil seal except: Remove intermediate shaft sprocket. Only press new seal in until flush with seal carrier.*

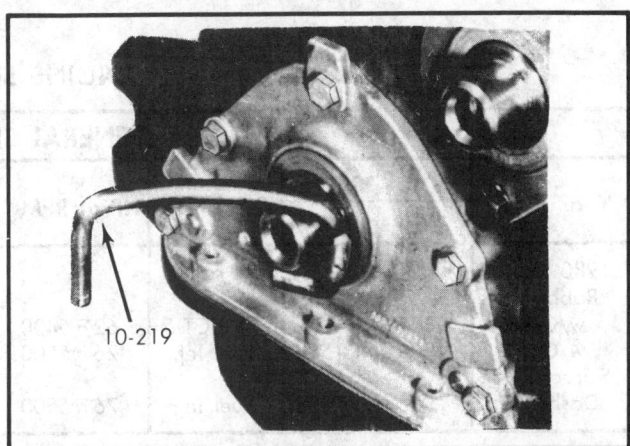

10-219

Fig. 8 Using Special Tool to Remove Front Oil Seal

ENGINE OILING

Crankcase Capacity — On Rabbit and Scirocco models, 3.7 quarts with filter change. On Dasher models, 3.2 quarts with filter change.

Oil Filter — Replaceable spin-on type.

Normal Oil Pressure — Minimum of 28 psi (1.97 kg/cm²) with engine at normal operating temperature.

ENGINE OILING SYSTEM

Oiling system is a pressure feed type. A gear oil pump lifts oil from pan and pressure feeds it to crankshaft journals, camshaft bearings, and intermediate shaft. Other parts of system receive oil mist or splash for lubrication.

OIL PUMP

Removal — 1) With oil pan removed (see *OIL PAN* in this article), remove pump mounting bolts. Remove oil pump, leaving pickup tube attached.

2) Separate pickup tube from pump. Check oil pump gear backlash. Clearance should be between .002-.008" (.05-.20 mm). If specification is exceeded, replace gears or pump.

Volkswagen Engines

DASHER, JETTA, RABBIT, RABBIT PICKUP, & SCIROCCO (Cont.)

3) Measure oil pump gear end play. If end play exceeds .006" (.15 mm), replace pump.

Installation — To install, reverse removal procedure. Make sure all mating surfaces are clean before installing gaskets. Oil pump drive shaft must align with distributor drive gear.

ENGINE COOLING

Cooling System Capacity	
Application	**Capacity (Qts.)**
Jetta, Rabbit, Rabbit Pickup & Scirocco	4.9
Dasher	
With Expansion Tank	6.9
Without Expansion Tank	6.4

Thermostat — Begins to open at 185°F (85°C), and is fully open at 221°F (105°C).

WATER PUMP

NOTE — *The front portion of water pump (shaft, seals, bearing, and housing) can be replaced separately. To do this camshaft drive belt and sprockets must be removed. To avoid removing drive belt, remove water pump as an assembly.*

Removal — Drain coolant with engine cool. Remove alternator belt and alternator. Remove air injection pump belt (if equipped). Disconnect hoses from water pump and remove bolt holding camshaft drive belt cover to water pump. Remove water pump bolts and pump assembly.

Installation — To install, reverse removal procedure and make sure to use new "O" ring in recess in pump mounting flange.

NOTE — *Do not use sealer between water pump mounting flange and engine block.*

ENGINE SPECIFICATIONS

GENERAL SPECIFICATIONS

Year	Displ.		Carburetor	HP at RPM①	Torque (Ft. Lbs. at RPM)	Compr. Ratio	Bore		Stroke	
	cu. ins.	cc					in.	mm	in.	mm
1980 Rabbit										
w/Carb.	88.9	1457	34 PICT-5	62@5400	76.6@3000	8.0:1	3.13	79.5	2.89	73.4
w/CIS①	97.0	1588	Fuel Inj.	76@5500	82.7@3200	8.2:1	3.13	79.5	3.15	80.0
Scirocco & Dasher	97.0	1588	Fuel Inj.	76@5500	82.7@3200	8.2:1	3.13	79.5	3.15	80.0

① — Includes Jetta & Rabbit Pickup.

VALVES

Engine & Valve	Head Diam. In. (mm)	Face Angle	Seat Angle	Seat Width In. (mm)	Stem Diameter In. (mm)	Stem Clearance In. (mm)	Valve Lift In. (mm)
1457 cc & 1588 cc							
Intake	1.338 (33.9)	45°	45°	.079 (2.0)	.314 (7.98)	.001-.002 (.03-.05)	....
Exhaust	1.220 (31.0)	45°	45°	.095 (2.4)	.313 (7.95)	.002-.003 (.05-.07)	....

PISTONS, PINS, RINGS

Engine	PISTONS	PINS		RINGS		
	Clearance In. (mm)①	Piston Fit In. (mm)	Rod Fit In. (mm)②	Rings	End Gap In. (mm)③	Side Clearance In. (mm)④
1457 cc & 1588 cc	.0012 (.03)	Push Fit	.0004-.0008 (.01-.02)	Comp.	.012-.018 (.30-.45)	.0008-.002 (.02-.05)
				Oil	.010-.016 (.25-.40)	.0008-.002 (.02-.05)

① — Wear limit .027" (.07 mm). ② — Wear limit .010" (.25 mm). ③ — Wear limit .039" (1 mm).
④ — Wear limit .006" (.15 mm).

DASHER, JETTA, RABBIT, RABBIT PICKUP, & SCIROCCO (Cont.)
ENGINE SPECIFICATIONS (Cont.)

CRANKSHAFT MAIN & CONNECTING ROD BEARINGS

| Engine | MAIN BEARINGS | | | | CONNECTING ROD BEARINGS | | |
	Journal Diam. In. (mm)	Clearance In. (mm)①	Thrust Bearing	Crankshaft End Play In. (mm)②	Journal Diam. In. (mm)	Clearance In. (mm)③	Side Play In. (mm)④
1457 cc & 1588 cc	2.124 (53.95)	.001-.003 (.025-.076)	No. 3	.003-.007 (.07-.17)	1.809 (45.95)	.0011-.0033 (.028-.088)	.010 (.25)

① — Wear limit .007″ (.17 mm). ② — Wear limit .015″ (.37 mm). ③ — Wear limit .0047″ (.12 mm).
④ — Wear limit indicated.

CAMSHAFT

Engine	Journal Diam. In. (mm)	Clearance In. (mm)①	Lobe Lift In. (mm)
1457 cc & 1588 cc	.....	.0008-.002 (.02-.05)	.....

① — End play .006″ (.15 mm)

VALVE SPRINGS

| Engine | Free Length In. (mm) | PRESSURE Lbs. @ In. (kg @ mm) | |
		Valve Closed	Valve Open
1457 cc & 1588 cc Inner	....	46-51@.719 (21-23@18.3)	....
Outer	....	96-106@.916 (43.5-48@22.3)	....

TIGHTENING SPECIFICATIONS

Application	Ft. Lbs. (mkg)
Timing Belt Tensioner Lock Nut	33 (4.5)
Intermediate Sprocket Bolt	58 (8.0)
Crankshaft Sprocket Bolt	58 (8.0)
Water Pump Pulley Bolts	14 (2.0)
Crankshaft Pulley Bolts	14 (2.0)
Main Bearing Cap Bolts	47 (6.5)
Drive Plate-to-Crankshaft Bolts	54 (7.5)
Connecting Rod Cap Bolts	33 (4.5)
Camshaft Sprocket Bolt	58 (8.0)
Camshaft Bearing Cap Bolts	14 (2.0)
Cylinder Head Bolts	54 (7.5) plus ¼ turn
Ball Joints	36 (5.0)
Axle Nuts	174 (24.0)
Manifolds-to-Cylinder Head Bolts	18 (2.5)
Water Pump Bolts	14 (2.0)
Oil Pan Bolts	14 (2.0)

Volkswagen Engines

DASHER, RABBIT, & RABBIT PICKUP 4 CYLINDER DIESEL

ENGINE CODING

ENGINE IDENTIFICATION

Engine coding for Volkswagen Diesel engines is CK. Engine identification is stamped on left side of block on machined pad near number three cylinder.

ENGINE, CYLINDER HEAD & MANIFOLDS

ENGINE

NOTE — *Manufacturer recommends that engine/transmission assembly be LOWERED out of Rabbit models as a unit.*

Removal (Rabbit) — 1) Disconnect ground strap at battery and open coolant expansion tank. Open heater valve and drain all coolant from system at thermostat flange. Remove radiator with fan. Remove alternator and detach fuel filter from body.

2) Disconnect wires for fuel shut-off solenoid, glow plugs, oil pressure switch and coolant temperature sensor. Disconnect hoses for heater and expansion tank. Remove fuel supply and return lines and disconnect accelerator cable with bracket from injection pump. Disconnect cold start cable.

3) On air conditioned vehicles, remove air conditioner compressor and mounting brackets and set out of way without disconnecting hoses. On all models, disconnect wires from starter and back-up light switch and ground from transmission mount. On manual transmission models, detach clutch cable and remove relay shaft lever.

4) Remove exhaust flex pipe nuts or spring clips. Disconnect drive shafts from drive flanges. Remove starter, horn, oil filter and front engine mount. Remove axle nuts and disconnect lower ball joints from bearing housings, then remove drive shaft while holding strut assembly away from vehicle.

5) Reconnect ball joints so vehicle may be lowered onto wheels. Remove complete rear mount. Remove right front wheel. Attach suitable sling (US 1105) to engine and lift slightly. On manual transmission models, remove relay shaft and gearshift lever rods.

6) On all models, remove bolts holding side mounts to body and lower engine/transmission assembly to dolly. Raise vehicle to clear and remove assembly from beneath car.

Installation — To install, reverse removal procedures noting that fuel supply and return union screws are not interchanged. Fuel return pipe union screw is marked "OUT" on hex. head.

Removal (Dasher) — 1) Disconnect battery ground strap and open heater valve. Drain cooling system by removing thermostat and remove thermoswitch connector. Remove radiator with fan and shroud. Disconnect fuel supply and return lines at injection pump.

2) Detach accelerator cable and bracket from pump body. Disconnect cold start cable. Disconnect wires for fuel shut off solenoid, coolant temperature sensor, oil pressure switch, and glow plugs. Disconnect coolant and vacuum hoses. Disconnect clutch cable from bracket and lever on manual transmission models.

3) Loosen right engine mount at top and bottom. Remove alternator. Remove entire front engine mount and loosen left engine mount at top. Remove exhaust pipe from manifold and bracket from transmission. Remove starter. Remove engine/transmission bolts and flywheel cover plate bolts.

4) Install support bar under transmission and attach suitable engine sling (US 1105). Raise engine until assembly hits steering rack housing and remove left engine mount. Detach engine from transmission. Lift from vehicle while at the same time turning to clear body.

Installation — Ensure that dowel bushings fit block properly and install intermediate plate on bushings. (Use grease to stick plate to block.) Place starter on engine carrier before installing engine. Complete installation in reverse sequence of removal. Ensure that all mounts, cables and pipes are aligned and tightened without tension.

CYLINDER HEAD & MANIFOLDS

NOTE — *Cylinder head may be removed and installed with engine in car.*

Removal — 1) Remove air cleaner and ducting, then drain cooling system. Remove camshaft drive belt. Unbolt thermostat housing from water pump. Disconnect battery ground strap.

2) Disconnect accelerator cable from injection pump. Detach fuel lines at injectors by unscrewing unions. Disconnect wire from glow plug bus, temperature sending wire and any other wires which could interfere with removal of cylinder head.

3) Remove nuts holding exhaust pipe to manifold and unbolt exhaust pipe support from engine/transaxle assembly. From underneath car, remove bolts and nuts holding exhaust manifold to cylinder head, then remove manifold from head. Disconnect coolant hoses from head and remove any other hoses which may interfere with head removal.

4) Remove cylinder head cover bolts and retaining plates. Carefully lift off cover and gasket. Loosen head bolts beginning at outer ends and work toward center. Lift off head and remove injectors and glow plugs to prevent damage while working on head.

5) Remove combustion chamber inserts by placing drift through injector hole and tapping out with hammer. Prior to installation, pre-chamber inserts must be reinstalled. When replacing injectors, new heat shields must be used between each injector and cylinder head. Remove old heat shield and place new shield in position with recess upward, towards injector. Tighten injector to 50 ft. lbs. (7.0 mkg).

NOTE — *Combustion chamber inserts are NOT supplied as spare parts on latest models. If inserts are damaged it will be necessary to replace cylinder head.*

Installation — 1) Clean gasket surface and ensure that cylinder head and block are not warped. Maximum distortion of .004" (.010 mm) is allowed. If installing on original piston and block assembly select a new head gasket that has the same marks as the original.

DASHER, RABBIT, & RABBIT PICKUP 4 CYLINDER DIESEL (Cont.)

2) To determine proper gasket, measure projection of piston above block when at TDC. Select proper gasket from following table:

Available Cylinder Head Gaskets

Piston Projection in Inches (mm)	Gasket Thickness in Inches (mm)	Identification Notches
.017-.025 (.43-.63)	.051 (1.30)	2
.025-.032 (.63-.82)	.055 (1.40)	3
.032-.036 (.82-.92)	.059 (1.50)	4
.036-.040 (.92-1.02)	.063 (1.60)	5

Gasket must be installed with word "OBEN" facing up.

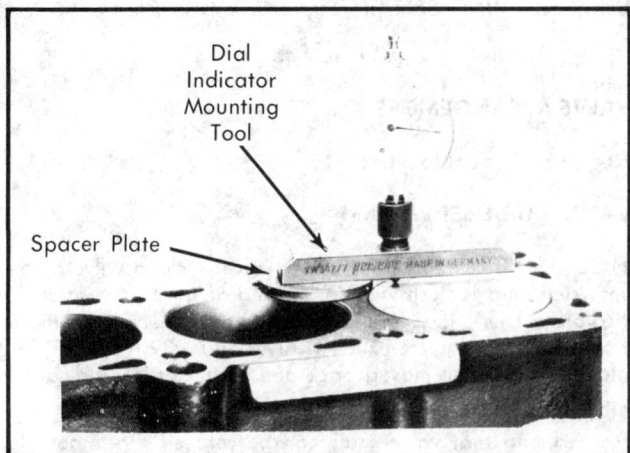

Fig. 1   Measuring Piston Projection

CAUTION — *Due to the aluminum construction of the head, do not use metal brushes or scrapers to clean gasket sealing surface or combustion chambers. Use solvent and wooden or plastic scrapers to remove foreign material. Do not mar piston tops when cleaning cylinder block. Ensure that all bolt holes and cylinder bores are absolutely free of debris prior to installing head or bolts.*

3) Lower head carefully onto gasket using 2 of the outermost bolts and washers to keep gasket and head aligned with block. Tighten head bolts in the sequence shown, first to 35 ft. lbs. (5.0 mkg), then to 50 ft. lbs. (7.0 mkg) and finally to 65 ft. lbs. (9.0 mkg). Complete installation in reverse order of removal.

NOTE — *After approximately 1000 miles, retorque cylinder head bolts. Loosen them 30° in proper sequence, one at a time, and then retighten to 65 ft. lbs. (9.0 mkg).*

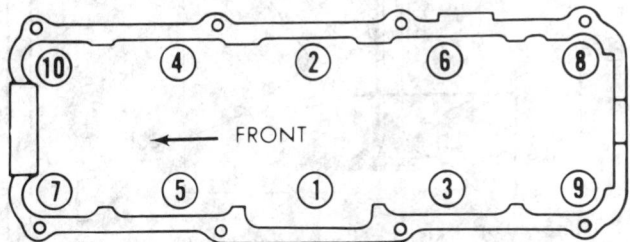

Fig. 2   Cylinder Head Tightening Sequence (Loosen in Reverse Order)

CAMSHAFT

TIMING BELT

NOTE — *Sprockets do not have to be removed to replace drive belt.*

Removal — Loosen alternator and remove V-belt and crankshaft V-belt pulley. Remove air cleaner and ducting, drive belt cover, and cylinder head cover. Remove timing plug on top of bell housing. Rotate engine to bring No. 1 piston to TDC. Check that TDC mark on flywheel is aligned with reference mark. See Fig. 3. Using locking tool (2065 or equivalent), lock camshaft in place from rear of engine. Lock injection pump in TDC position with special pin (2064). Loosen drive belt tensioner and remove belt.

CAUTION — *Do not turn camshaft or crankshaft with drive belt removed.*

Installation — 1) Make sure that flywheel is still aligned with TDC mark. With camshaft and injection pump still locked in position, loosen camshaft sprocket bolt ½ turn and lightly tap camshaft drive gear loose from camshaft. Install drive belt.

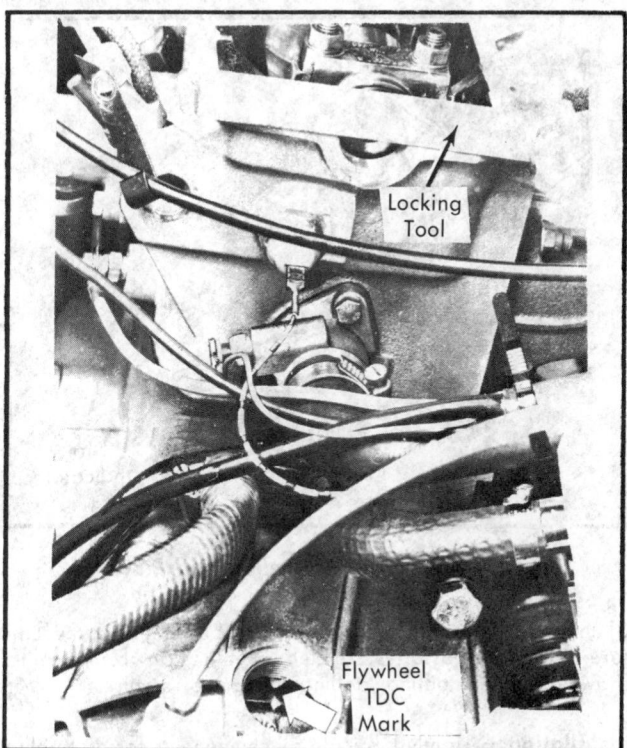

Fig. 3   Flywheel TDC Mark and Camshaft Locking Tool

2) Adjust belt tension by turning tensioner to right until scale reads 12-13 on VW 210 tool. Tighten camshaft sprocket bolt to 33 ft. lbs. (4.5 mkg). Remove locks from injection pump and camshaft. Turn crankshaft 2 revolutions in direction of engine rotation (clockwise). Using a rubber hammer, strike belt once between camshaft sprocket and injection pump sprocket. Recheck belt tension and install remaining components in reverse of removal procedure.

Volkswagen Engines

DASHER, RABBIT, & RABBIT PICKUP 4 CYLINDER DIESEL (Cont.)

NOTE — *Belt tension may also be checked by grasping belt between camshaft sprocket and pump, and twisting 90°. Belt is too loose if it will twist more than 90°; too tight if it will not twist 90°.*

CAMSHAFT

Removal — Remove timing belt. Loosen bearing caps in following sequence: 5, 1, and 3, then loosen caps 2 and 4 diagonally. Bearing caps are numbered front (sprocket end) to rear (flywheel end).

Inspection — **1)** Number and remove cam followers, then reinstall camshaft using only end (1 and 5) bearing caps. Check axial play of camshaft with dial indicator. If play exceeds .006" (.15 mm), either head or camshaft is worn and must be replaced.

2) To measure camshaft bearing clearance, install caps one at a time and check with either a dial indicator or Plastigage. Check camshaft runout by installing shaft between centers and applying dial indicator at center bearing journal. Runout must not exceed .0004" (.01 mm) when camshaft is rotated.

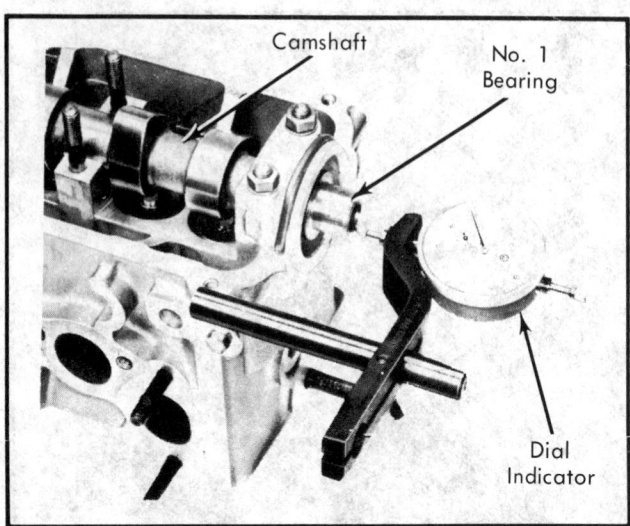

Fig. 4 Measuring Camshaft End Play

3) Inspect cam lobes, followers, and all bearing surfaces. Ensure that all oil passages are clean. Replace any components showing signs of pitting, galling or signs of seizure.

Installation — Lightly lubricate all components for assembly. Install cam followers in original bores with matching adjusting discs. Place camshaft and number 2 and 4 bearing caps in position with cam lobes of No. 1 cylinder pointing upward. Gradually tighten all 4 bearing cap nuts until camshaft is fully seated; then install caps 5, 3, and 1. Use seal installer (10-203 or equivalent) to install front oil seal and complete installation in reverse order of removal.

VALVE TIMING

See *TIMING BELT* procedures in this article.

INJECTION PUMP TIMING

1) To check injection pump timing, remove valve cover and timing belt cover. Set engine to TDC on No. 1 cylinder with TDC mark on flywheel in line with boss on bell housing. Attach setting bar (VW 2065) to camshaft and turn until one end rests on head.

2) Measure clearance at opposite end of bar with a feeler gauge, then take 2 feeler gauges ½ of this thickness and insert under each end of bar. Check that pin (VW 2064) fits in holes in pump sprocket and mounting plate.

3) If pin does NOT fit in holes, remove drive belt and turn sprocket until marks on sprocket and mounting plate are in line. Lock pump sprocket with pin (VW 2064) and install drive belt. See *TIMING BELT* procedures in this article.

VALVES

VALVE ARRANGEMENT

E-I-E-I-I-E-I-E (front to rear).

VALVE GUIDE SERVICING

1) To check for wear, insert NEW valve in clean valve guide until stem end is flush with spring end of guide. Use dial indicator to check that lateral (rocking) movement is no more than .051" (1.3 mm) for exhaust valves and .039" (1.0 mm) for intake valves when moved back and forth against indicator.

2) Prior to replacing worn guides, check that head is not cracked and that valve seats can be refaced. Press out old guides and coat new guides with oil. Press new guides in up to shoulder but do not use more than one ton of pressure once shoulder is seated. Hand ream guides to proper uniform diameter of .315-.316" (8.013-8.035 mm).

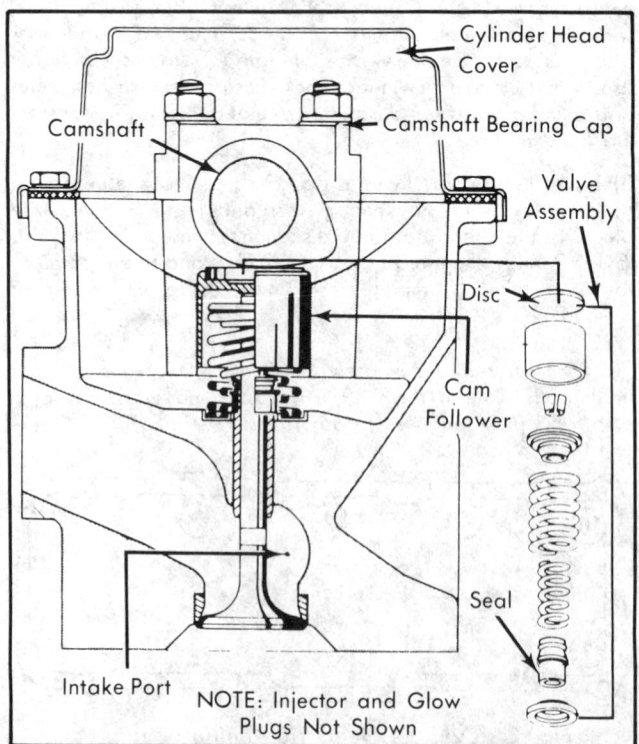

Fig. 5 End View of Camshaft and Valve Assembly

DASHER, RABBIT, & RABBIT PICKUP 4 CYLINDER DIESEL (Cont.)

VALVE STEM SEALS AND SPRINGS

NOTE — *It is possible to replace valve springs and seals with head installed provided camshaft and tappets are removed. Piston of cylinder concerned must be at top dead center position.*

Use suitable spring compressor to depress spring and retainer. Remove keepers, then remove retainer and springs. Remove stem seal. Use protective sleeve over valve stem and install new seal. Complete assembly in reverse order of disassembly.

VALVE CLEARANCE ADJUSTMENT

1) Engine should be near operating temperature (coolant at about 95°F (35°C). Rotate crankshaft so that cam lobes for No. 1 cylinder (curb side) point upward. Check intake and exhaust clearance between heel of cam lobe and follower.

2) Use crankshaft pulley to rotate crankshaft 180° at a time and check No. 3, No. 4, and No. 2 clearance. If clearances are not within specifications, use thinner or thicker adjusting discs to increase or decrease clearance.

CAUTION — *Do not turn engine by camshaft pulley as this will stretch drive belt. Use a wrench to turn crankshaft or push vehicle in 4th gear to move crankshaft/valve train.*

3) Twenty-six different thicknesses of discs are available in increments of .0019" (.05 mm) from .1181" (3.0 mm) to .1673" (4.25 mm). To install, turn crankshaft about ¼ turn past TDC and press cam follower down with suitable tool (VW 546). Remove old disc with special pliers (VW 10-208) and insert new disc with etched thickness marking toward cam follower.

Valve Clearance Specifications

Application	In. (mm)
Intake	
Hot	.008-.012 (.20-.30)
Cold	.006-.010 (.15-.25)
Exhaust	
Hot	.016-.020 (.40-.50)
Cold	.014-.018 (.35-.45)

NOTE — *Cold settings are given for reference as initial settings to be used during cylinder head rework. Final adjustments are made at normal operating temperatures and should be checked after 1000 miles of operation.*

PISTONS, PINS & RINGS

OIL PAN

Due to transverse suspension of engine ahead of front suspension, oil pan may be removed simply by removing mounting bolts. Oil pump may inspected or removed and replaced with pan off. It is recommended that any further repairs be accomplished with engine removed from car.

PISTON & ROD ASSEMBLY

Removal — Mark cylinder number on crown of each piston. If necessary, mark arrows pointing toward front of block on piston crowns. Remove rod cap bolts and force piston out top of cylinder using wooden hammer handle. Mark rods and bearing caps for proper installation.

NOTE — *If ridge at top of cylinder prevents piston removal, use ridge reamer prior to further disassembly. DO NOT force piston out of cylinder.*

Installation — Turn crankshaft so No. 1 journal is at BDC. Install piston/rod assembly until ring compressor contacts block. Guide rod over journal and use wooden handle of hammer to push piston into cylinder. Repeat with No. 4 piston and rod assembly ensuring that tabs on bearing halves engage notches in respective rod and cap. Tighten caps on rods 1 and 4, then rotate crankshaft 180° and install No. 2 and No. 3 piston/rod assemblies.

PISTON PINS

Removal — Use needle-nose pliers to remove circlips. Press out pin and remove piston, noting direction piston is fitted to rod. If pin is too tight, heat piston to approximately 140°F (60°C) and then press out.

Installation — Check piston/pin fit for thumb push fit. Connecting rod/pin wear limit is .0015" (.04 mm). Connecting rod may be rebushed and honed to proper size if required. If pin is too loose in piston, replace both pin and piston.

FITTING PISTONS

Measure cylinder at 3 points: ⅜" (10 mm) from top and bottom, and at center of bore. Measure in line with and at 90° to thrust face. Cylinder wear limit is .0015" (.04 mm) out of round. If limit is exceeded, cylinders must be honed and new pistons fitted.

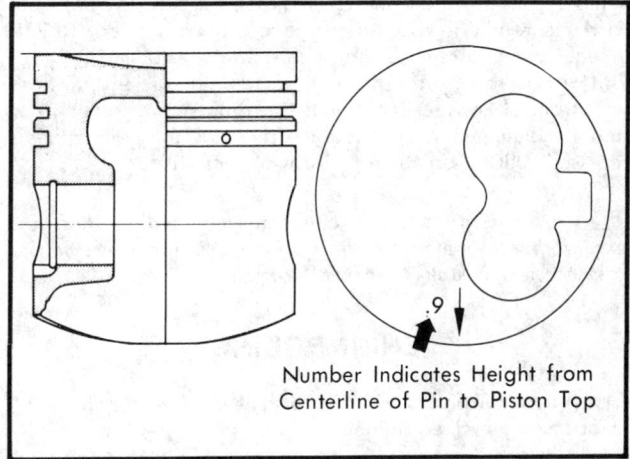

Fig. 6   Side and Top View of Diesel Piston

CRANKSHAFT MAIN & CONNECTING ROD BEARINGS

MAIN & CONNECTING ROD BEARINGS

1) Push crankshaft toward one end and measure end play at No. 3 (thrust) bearing. Main bearing caps are numbered "1"

DASHER, RABBIT, & RABBIT PICKUP 4 CYLINDER DIESEL (Cont.)

to "5" with "1" at drive belt end and "5" at flywheel end. Measure connecting rod end play (side play). Check all bearing clearances by the Plastigage method.

2) Measure crankshaft journals to determine size and any out-of-round. Maximum allowable out of round is .0012" (.03 mm). Install main inserts with bearing half having oil groove into block. Lubricate bearings and install caps in original positions.

Crankshaft Journal Diameters

Size	Main Bearing In. (mm)	Rod Bearing In. (mm)
Standard	2.124 (53.95)	1.809 (45.95)
1st US	2.114 (53.70)	1.799 (45.70)
2nd US	2.104 (53.45)	1.789 (45.45)
3rd US	2.094 (53.20)	1.779 (45.20)

REAR MAIN BEARING OIL SEAL

NOTE — *Rear main bearing oil seal may be replaced with engine in vehicle. Transmission and flywheel must be removed.*

Insert screwdriver between crankshaft flywheel flange and inside lip of oil seal. Pry oil seal out. Install guide sleeve tool 2003/2A (or equivalent) over crankshaft flange. Start new oil seal into recess in carrier. Remove guide sleeve then fit drive plate 2003/1 (or equivalent) and seat seal by tightening flywheel bolts in plate.

FRONT MAIN BEARING OIL SEAL AND INTERMEDIATE SHAFT OIL SEAL

NOTE — *Diesel engine intermediate shaft rotates counterclockwise and utilizes a different seal than the gas engine. Arrow pointing counterclockwise on seal indicates correct application for Diesel model.*

Remove camshaft belt and crankshaft sprocket. Pry seal from carrier carefully to avoid damage to carrier. Use tool 10-219 or equivalent to remove seal. Use suitable installing tool (10-203 or equivalent) and press new seal into carrier until flush with front of carrier. Remove steel driving sleeve from carrier and use aluminum part of tool to drive seal further in until it is recessed .080" (2 mm) from front of seal carrier.

NOTE — *Same procedures are used for intermediate shaft seal except that intermediate shaft sprocket is removed. Seal is pressed in only until flush with carrier.*

ENGINE OILING

Crankcase Capacity — 3.7 quarts with filter change; 3.2 quarts without filter change.

Oil Filter — Replaceable spin-on type.

Normal Oil Pressure — Minimum of 28 psi@2000 RPM and at normal operating temperature.

ENGINE OILING SYSTEM

Gear type oil pump provides oil for pressure feed to crankshaft journals, camshaft bearings, and intermediate shaft. A larger, heavy-duty oil filter and revised oil pump drive

are used in the Diesel. Other lubrication characteristics are similar to the spark ignition engines.

OIL PUMP

Removal — Drain oil and remove oil pan. Remove pump mounting bolts and pump along with pick-up tube. Install in vise and remove pick-up tube.

Inspection — Check oil pump gear backlash with feeler gauge. Clearance should be between .002-.008" (.05-.20 mm). Measure pump gear end play using machinist's square and feeler gauge for .006" (.15 mm) clearance or less. If specifications are exceeded, replace gears or pump.

Installation — To install, assure that all mating surfaces are clean, install gaskets and reverse removal procedure.

ENGINE COOLING

Cooling System Capacity — 7.3 quarts.

Thermostat — Begins to open at 190°F (87°C) and is fully open at 215°F (102°C). Radiator fan thermoswitch starts fan running at approximately 204°F (95°C), and shuts it off when coolant temperature drops to 195°F (91°C) or below. Radiator relief pressure should be 17-19 psi.

CAUTION — *Never drain the coolant while the engine is hot. Cylinder head or engine block could warp if not allowed to cool prior to draining.*

WATER PUMP

Removal — Drain cooling system. Disconnect battery ground strap and unplug alternator wires. Remove alternator. Disconnect thermostat housing and hoses from water pump. Remove bolts holding pump to engine block and remove pump.

Installation — To install, reverse removal procedure and use new "O" ring in recess in pump mounting flange.

NOTE — *Do NOT use sealer between water pump mounting flange and engine block.*

TIGHTENING SPECIFICATIONS

Application	Ft. Lbs. (mkg)
Timing Belt Tensioner Lock Nut	32 (4.5)
Intermediate Sprocket Bolt	32 (4.5)
Crankshaft Sprocket Bolt	58 (8.0)
Water Pump Pulley Bolts	14 (2.0)
Crankshaft Pulley Bolts	14 (2.0)
Main Bearing Cap Bolts	47 (6.5)
Flywheel-to-Crankshaft Bolts	54 (7.5)
Connecting Rod Cap Bolts	32 (4.5)
Camshaft Sprocket Bolt	32 (4.5)
Camshaft Bearing Cap Nuts	14 (2.0)
Cylinder Head Bolts	65 (9.0)
Manifolds-to-Cylinder Head	18 (2.5)
Axle Nuts	174 (24)
Ball Joints	36 (5.0)

Volkswagen Engines

DASHER, RABBIT, & RABBIT PICKUP 4 CYLINDER DIESEL (Cont.)
ENGINE SPECIFICATIONS

GENERAL SPECIFICATIONS

| Year | Displ. | | Carburetor | HP at RPM | Torque (Ft. Lbs. at RPM) | Compr. Ratio | Bore | | Stroke | |
	cu. ins.	cc					in.	mm	in.	mm
1980 Diesel	90.0	1471	Fuel Inj.	48@5000	56.5@3000	23:1	3.012	76.5	3.150	80.00

VALVES

Engine & Valve	Head Diam. In. (mm)	Face Angle	Seat Angle	Seat Width In. (mm)	Stem Diameter In. (mm)	Stem Clearance In. (mm)	Valve Lift In. (mm)
1471 cc Diesel Intake	1.338 (33.9)	45°	45°	.079 (2.0)	.314 (7.98)	.039 (1.0)	.....
Exhaust	1.220 (31.0)	45°	45°	.095 (2.4)	.313 (7.95)	.051 (1.30)	.....

PISTONS, PINS, RINGS

| Engine | PISTONS | PINS | | RINGS | | |
	Clearance In. (mm)①	Piston Fit In. (mm)	Rod Fit In. (mm)	Rings	End Gap In. (mm)②	Side Clearance In. (mm)
1471 cc Diesel	.001 (.03)	Push Fit	.0004-.0008 (.01-.02)	Comp.	.012-.020 (.30-.50)	.002-.004③ (.06-.09)
				Oil	.010-.016 (.25-.40)	.001-.002④ (.03-.06)

① — Wear Limit .027" (.07 mm). ② — Wear Limit .039" (1.0 mm). ③ — Wear Limit .008" (.20 mm). ④ — Wear Limit .006" (.15 mm)

CRANKSHAFT MAIN & CONNECTING ROD BEARINGS

| Engine | MAIN BEARINGS | | | | CONNECTING ROD BEARINGS | | |
	Journal Diam. In. (mm)	Clearance In. (mm)①	Thrust Bearing	Crankshaft End Play In. (mm)②	Journal Diam. In. (mm)	Clearance In. (mm)③	Side Play In. (mm)
1471 cc Diesel	2.126 (54)	.001-.003 (.03-.08)	No. 3	.003-.007 (.07-.17)	1.81 (46)	.0011-.0035 (.028-.088)	.014 (.37)

① — Wear Limit .007" (.17 mm). ② — Wear Limit .015" (.37 mm). ③ — Wear Limit .0047" (.12 mm).

VALVE SPRINGS

| Engine | Free Length In. (mm) | PRESSURE Lbs. @ In. (kg @ mm) | |
		Valve Closed	Valve Open
1471 cc Diesel Inner	.....	46-51@.719 (21-23@18.3)	.....
Outer	.....	96-106 @ .875 43.5-48@22.3	.....

CAMSHAFT

Engine	Journal Diam. In. (mm)	Clearance In. (mm)①	Lobe Lift In. (mm)
1471 cc Diesel	.....	.0008-.002 (.02-.05)	.....

① — End play .006" (.1 mm)

VANAGON 4 CYLINDER

ENGINE CODING

ENGINE IDENTIFICATION

Engine code number is stamped on crankcase below breather, near coil. First two digits of cast number are engine code.

Engine Identification	
Application	**Engine Code**
Vanagon (1970 cc)	CV

ENGINE, CYLINDER HEAD & MANIFOLD

ENGINE

Removal — **1)** Disconnect battery. Remove air cleaner with air flow sensor and air intake duct. Remove rubber boot to heater booster. Disconnect electrical wiring from the following components: alternator, distributor and oil pressure sending unit. Disconnect plug at control unit. Pull oil dipstick. Disconnect vacuum hose from brake booster. Disconnect all remaining vacuum hoses and electrical wiring leads running between engine and engine compartment.

2) Remove nuts of upper engine mounting bolts and disconnect accelerator cable. On automatic transaxle models, remove plug on top of transaxle housing, pull ATF dipstick and remove ATF filler tube grommet. Remove three 8 mm bolts of torque converter through hole on top off transaxle housing.

NOTE — *To gain access to bolts of torque converter, engine must be rotated until each bolt appears in hole on top of transmission housing. Use adapter (3052) to turn engine crankshaft.*

3) On all models, remove heater flap housing bolt; clamp fuel line and detach. Also clamp fuel line from pressure regulator and detach. Disconnect wiring from starter. On manual transaxle models, loosen transaxle mount bolt at front of transaxle. On automatic transaxle models, loosen accelerator cable at selector lever and detach. Loosen transaxle mount bolt at front of transaxle.

4) On all models, place a support (VW785/1) under transaxle. Place a floor jack under engine. Raise jack until engine is just supported. Remove nuts from lower engine mounting bolts. Remove bolts from engine carrier. Lower engine/transaxle assembly until transaxle rests on support (VW785/1). Slide engine assembly slightly to rear until it clears input shaft. Remove engine from transaxle and lower engine with floor jack.

Installation — To install, reverse removal procedure and note the following: Replace all self-locking nuts. On manual transaxle models, check clutch release bearing for wear; lubricate splines on main drive shaft, contact points of clutch release bearing and clutch release lever. Adjust accelerator cable at full throttle position. On automatic transaxle models, adjust accelerator cable.

INTAKE MANIFOLD

Removal — **1)** Fuel injection manifold can be removed with engine in vehicle. Remove air cleaner, hoses, and pressure switch.

2) Disconnect wires on fuel injectors and remove two screws. Pull injectors off with plate and retainer. Make sure locating bushings are removed from manifold. Disconnect hoses on injectors and remove.

3) Remove intake manifold cover plate. Remove nuts and washers securing manifold to cylinder heads. Lift up on manifold and pull from tubes on air distributor.

Installation — To install manifold, reverse removal procedure and note the following: Use new gaskets and tighten intake manifold mounting nuts uniformly. Make sure gray protective cap on injector is to rear and cap is to front.

CYLINDER HEAD

NOTE — *Engine must be removed from vehicle and manifolds removed, before removing cylinder heads. If cylinders are not to be removed, use retaining device to keep cylinders from pulling free.*

Removal — **1)** Remove rocker arm cover and gasket. Remove rocker arm shaft retaining nuts, loosening gradually one at a time to relieve spring tension evenly. Remove rocker arm assemblies.

2) Remove push rods, keeping in order for reassembly. Loosen cylinder head nuts gradually working in sequence from outside toward center.

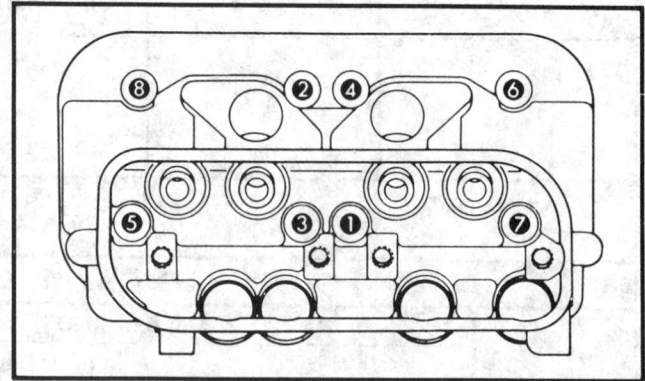

Fig. 1 Cylinder Head Bolt Tightening Sequence

Installation — **1)** Remove metal gasket rings from combustion chambers and inspect head. Place new metal gasket rings in peripheries of combustion chambers and install head over cylinder studs. Tighten head to specifications in 2 steps according to sequence shown in *Fig. 1.*

2) Install push rod through top of cylinder head with black sealing ring at bottom and white ring at top. Install remaining components in reverse order of removal. Ensure that push rod tube retaining wires bear against ends of tubes and engage slots in rocker arm supports before installing cylinder head cover.

VALVES

VALVE ARRANGEMENT

E-I-I-E (both banks)

VANAGON 4 CYLINDER (Cont.)

VALVE GUIDE SERVICING

Place new valve in guide with stem flush with end of guide. With dial indicator, measure valve rock at valve head. If rock exceeds .047" (1.2 mm), replace valve and/or guide. Guides must be removed and replaced using a press with adapters. Ream to proper clearance after installation.

CAUTION — *DO NOT use a hammer and drift to replace guides due to the danger of damage to the cylinder head.*

VALVE SPRINGS

NOTE — *Valve spring may be removed with cylinder head installed. Apply constant air pressure (minimum 85 psi) to cylinder through spark plug hole to hold valve in place while compressing spring.*

Removal — Remove cylinder head cover and rocker arm shaft. Install suitable valve spring compressor tool (VW311s with cylinder head removed, VW653/2 with cylinder head installed). Compress spring retainer and spring and remove valve keepers. Release compressor and remove spring retainer and spring.

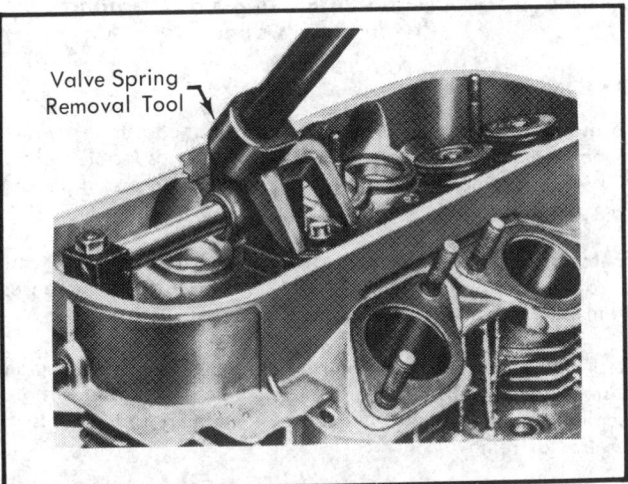

**Fig. 2   Using Special Tool VW311s
to Remove Valve Spring**

Installation — Install valve, valve spring, and valve spring retainer. **NOTE** — *Install spring with closely spaced coils against cylinder head.* Compress spring with suitable compressor and install valve keepers.

ROCKER ARM ASSEMBLY

Removal — Disengage wire valve cover clip. Remove valve cover. Remove 4 rocker shaft retaining nuts. Each side has two separate shafts. Make sure mounting nuts are gradually and evenly loosened until spring tension is relieved.

Inspection — Check rocker arms and shafts for wear. If inside diameter of rocker arm is worn more than .789" (20.0 mm),

replace rocker arm. If diameter of rocker shaft is worn to less than .783" (19.9 mm), replace rocker shaft.

Installation — To install, reverse removal procedure and note: Make sure push rod tube retaining wire is reinstalled. Adjust valve clearance.

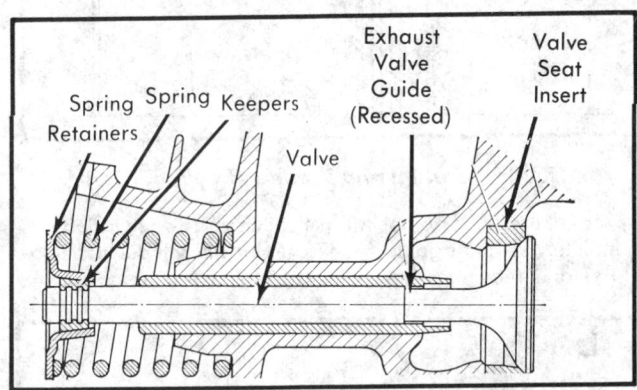

Fig. 3   Sectional View of Valve with Related Parts

HYDRAULIC VALVE LIFTERS

NOTE — *Valve lifters may be removed and installed without removing or disassembling engine.*

Removal — Valve covers, rocker arms, push rods and push rod covers must be off of engine. Remove lifters by withdrawing with a magnetic tool. Mark all lifters for installation in original position.

Installation — Ensure that lifters are filled with oil and reverse removal procedure. Back off adjusting screws in rocker arms until threaded part is flush with bottom of rocker arm. Proceed as in *Valve Clearance Adjustment.*

VALVE CLEARANCE ADJUSTMENT

Loosen all adjusting screws until flush with bottom of rocker arm. Hand turn crankshaft until number 1 cylinder is in firing position (number 1 firing mark on distributor body and rotor aligned). Turn adjusting screws for both rocker arms of number 1 cylinder until tips just touch valve stems (zero clearance). Tighten screws 2 additional turns and tighten locknuts. Turn crankshaft so rotor moves counterclockwise in 90° increments and repeat adjustment for number 2, 3 and 4 cylinders.

PISTONS, PINS & RINGS

CYLINDERS

Removal — Remove engine and remove cylinder head. **NOTE** — *Mark cylinders to insure they are reinstalled in original position.* Remove deflector plates from bottom of cylinders and pull cylinders from pistons.

Installation — 1) Check seating surfaces of cylinders on both ends. Make sure seating areas are perfectly clean and true before installing cylinders. Stagger ring gaps 120° apart so that oil ring gap faces upward when cylinder is installed.

2) Apply oil to cylinder, piston, rings and piston pin. Compress rings with suitable ring compressor (VW123). Install new sealing gasket on crankcase side and slide cylinder over piston.

VANAGON 4 CYLINDER (Cont.)

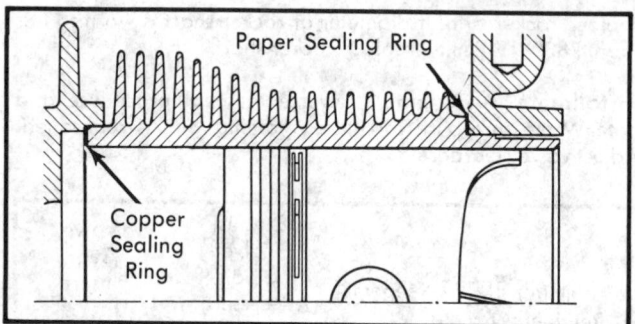

Fig. 4   Location and Seating of Cylinder Seal

3) Make sure studs do not contact cooling fins when cylinder is completely seated against crankcase. Install cylinder deflector plates and remaining components in reverse of removal.

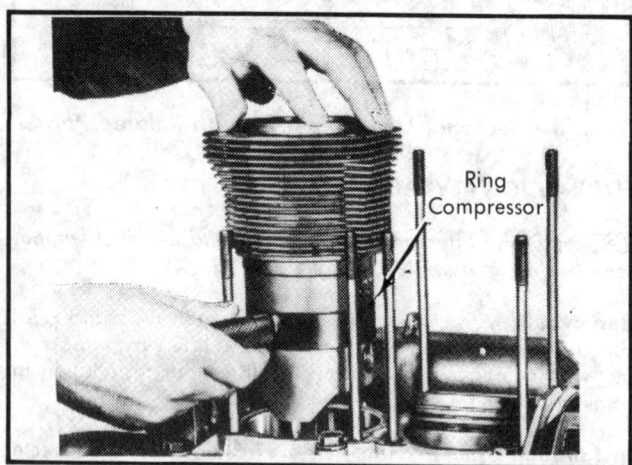

Fig. 5   Installing Cylinder Assembly into Case

FITTING PISTONS

1) With piston and cylinder removed, measure clearance between piston and cylinder. Check piston size at bottom of skirt and 90° to piston pin. Check cylinder size at several points throughout cylinder, using largest reading to determine clearance.

2) If clearance exceeds .008" (.20 mm), replace piston and cylinder as a set. New piston must be of same weight grade as original or within 10 g of original piston weight. Piston size, weight and installation position are marked on top of piston

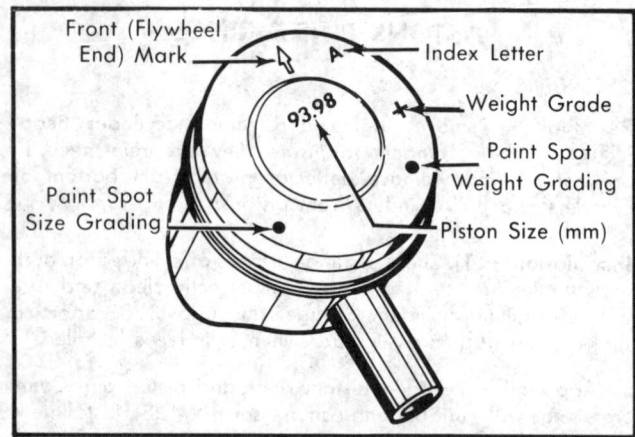

Fig. 6   Top View of Piston with Detail of Piston Markings

See *Fig. 6.* Pistons and cylinders are available in 2 oversizes: .020" (.508 mm) and .040" (1.016 mm).

NOTE – *Piston alone may be replaced with one of matching size. Only pistons of same size and weight grade should be installed in same engine.*

3) New piston rings are size graded to match piston/cylinder sets. Measure ring gap with ring installed approximately 3/16" in cylinder. If ring end gap exceeds .035" (.90 mm) for compression rings or .037" (.95 mm) for oil scraper, replace.

4) Install rings on piston and measure ring side clearance using feeler gauge. If clearance exceeds .005" (.12 mm) on upper and middle rings or .004" (.10 mm) on oil scraper ring, piston must be replaced.

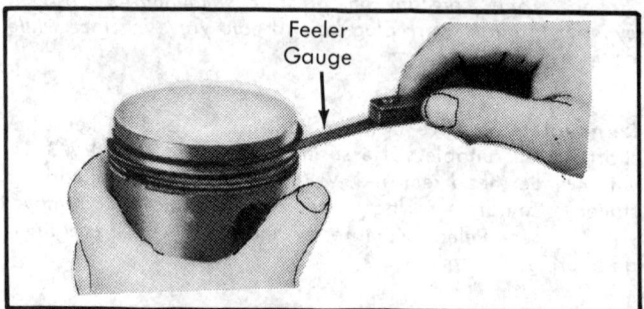

Fig. 7   Measuring Piston Ring Side Clearance with Feeler Gauge

PISTON PINS

Removal – Remove cylinders and mark pistons before removing for proper installation. Using suitable pliers (VW122b), remove piston pin circlips and push piston pin out of piston.

Installation – **1)** Check fit of pin in piston. At room temperature piston pin should be light push fit. If pin is too loose, both pin and piston must be replaced.

2) Install one circlip in piston on side facing flywheel. Position piston on connecting rod and push piston pin through piston. Replace remaining circlip. Replace remaining components in reverse of removal.

NOTE – *Piston may be heated to ease pin installation.*

CRANKSHAFT MAIN & CONNECTING ROD BEARINGS

CRANKCASE

Crankcase must be taken apart to replace connecting rods, connecting rod bearings and main bearings. It is also necessary to disassemble crankcase to remove crankshaft, camshaft, and camshaft bearings.

Disassembly – **1)** Remove engine from vehicle and remove cylinder heads, cylinders, and pistons. Remove flywheel or drive plate, and crankshaft pulley. Remove distributor, distributor drive shaft and fuel pump.

2) Remove oil cooler, oil filter and bracket, and oil pump assembly. *See Oil Pump Removal.* Remove rear engine carrier crossmember, bonded rubber mountings, and fan hub. Remove oil pan and oil filler pipe mounting bracket bolt.

VANAGON 4 CYLINDER (Cont.)

3) Remove six 10 mm main bearing nuts and bolts and five 8 mm nuts and bolts from crankcase flange. Using spring clips, clamp tappets in right half of crankcase and lift off right hand crankcase half.

CAUTION — *Never insert tools between crankcase flanges to separate halves. If stuck together, use rubber hammer to loosen right hand half from left.*

Reassembly — 1) Thoroughly clean and inspect both crankcase halves. Remove old sealing compound from mating surfaces and from all bolts, studs and washers. Blow out oil passages with compressed air. Check studs for tightness and check oil suction pipe for tightness.

2) Install crankshaft with connecting rods, in left side crankcase half, making sure dowel pins are properly seated in bearings. Install camshaft. *See Camshaft Installation.* Install camshaft plug using liquid sealer all around plug. Spread liquid sealer over mating surfaces of crankcase halves.

3) Using spring clips, clamp tappets in right hand half of crankcase to join crankcase halves. Coat main bearing bolt heads (10 mm) with sealer and install in crankcase.

NOTE — *Install plastic dampers (part No. 021 101 107) on shank of main bearing bolts whether or not originally equipped.*

4) Coat the sealing nuts for main bearing bolts with sealer and install nuts with sealing rings outward. Tighten main bearing nuts and bolts and hand turn crankshaft to check for free movement. Coat bolt heads and nuts of 8 mm bolts with sealer, then install and tighten.

5) Check crankshaft end play. *See Thrust Bearing Alignment.* Install new crankshaft oil seals. *See Front Crankshaft Oil Seal Replacement and Rear Crankshaft Oil Seal Replacement.* Install remaining components in reverse of removal procedure.

MAIN & CONNECTING ROD BEARING SERVICE

1) With crankshaft and connecting rod assembly removed, remove snap ring securing distributor drive gear and crankshaft gear to crankshaft. Remove distributor drive gear and crankshaft gear by pressing or using suitable mandrel (VW457). Remove number 3 bearing. Remove connecting rods.

2) Thoroughly clean and inspect crankshaft. Blow out oil passages with compressed air. Check runout of crankshaft. If runout exceeds .0008" (.020 mm), regrind crankshaft to next undersize.

3) Check crankshaft journals for wear, if journals are worn more than .0012" (.030 mm), regrind crankshaft to next undersize. Main and connecting rod bearings are available in .010", .020" and .030" undersize.

4) Lubricate and install number 3 bearing. Heat crankshaft gear to approximately 176° F in an oil bath and install on crankshaft over Woodruff key. Chamfer on gear bore must face number 3 main bearing journal. Install spacer, distributor drive gear and lock ring (circlip).

5) Using Plastigage method, check main and connecting rod bearings. If main bearing clearance on Nos. 1 and 3 exceeds .007" (.18 mm), .0067" (.17 mm) on No. 2, or .0075" (.19 mm) on No. 3; replace bearing. If clearance on any connecting rod bearing exceeds .007" (.15 mm), replace bearing.

6) Install numbers 1, 3 and 4 main bearings on crankshaft. *See Step 4)* for number 3 main bearing installation. Install lower bearing half of number 2 in crankcase, ensuring that dowel in

crankcase engages hole in bearing half. Turn bearings on crankshaft to properly position oil holes and dowel holes. Install bearing halves in cap and rod so that tangs in shells engage notches in rod bore. Fit to crankshaft with numbers on rod and cap on same side. Forged mark on rod must face UP when crankshaft is installed.

7) Check connecting rod side play with feeler gauge. If side play exceeds .0275" (.70 mm), replace connecting rod. Install crankshaft and connecting rod assembly as previously outlined. Check crankshaft end play. *See Thrust Bearing Alignment.*

Fig. 8   Using a Feeler Gauge to Check Connecting Rod Side Clearance

CRANKSHAFT END PLAY

NOTE — *Crankshaft end play is checked with engine assembled.*

1) Install flywheel with 2 shims, but do not install "O" ring and crankshaft oil seal. Attach dial indicator to crankcase and measure back and forth movement of crankshaft.

Fig. 9   Using a Dial Indicator to Check Crankshaft End Play

VANAGON 4 CYLINDER (Cont.)

2) Calculate necessary thickness of third shim. Install third shim and recheck end play. Thickness of shim is etched on face of shim, always use three shims to obtain correct end play.

Thrust Bearing Shims

MM Markings on Shim	Inch Equivalent
.24 mm	.0095"
.30 mm	.0118"
.32 mm	.0126"
.34 mm	.0134"
.36 mm	.0142"
.38 mm	.0150"

3) With correct shim thickness determined, install crankshaft oil seal. See Front Crankshaft Oil Seal. Install flywheel, tighten bolts as required, and recheck crankshaft end play.

CRANKSHAFT REAR OIL SEAL

Removal & Installation — Remove blower impeller and pull impeller hub off crankshaft with suitable tool (VW185). Pry old seal out, using caution to avoid scratching shaft or crankcase. Clean recess and chamfer edges of seal seat, if necessary. Coat outside of seal lightly with sealer and start into position by hand. Press into final position with tool (VW190) and lightly lubricate fan hub before completing installation.

CRANKSHAFT FRONT OIL SEAL

Removal & Installation — Remove flywheel and carefully pry out old seal. Clean seat and chamfer edges if necessary. Apply thin film of sealer to outside edges and start seal into recess by hand. Seal lip must point toward crankcase. Complete installation with tool (VW191). Lubricate contact surface on flywheel and install flywheel.

DISTRIBUTOR DRIVE INSTALLATION

When crankcase has been assembled, and remaining components installed, distributor drive must be installed. Rotate crankshaft until No. 1 piston is at TDC, compression stroke. Align timing mark on pulley with 0° mark on ignition timing scale. Insert distributor drive with slot at a 12° angle to center line of engine. Small segment of slot must face toward outside of vehicle (See Fig. 10).

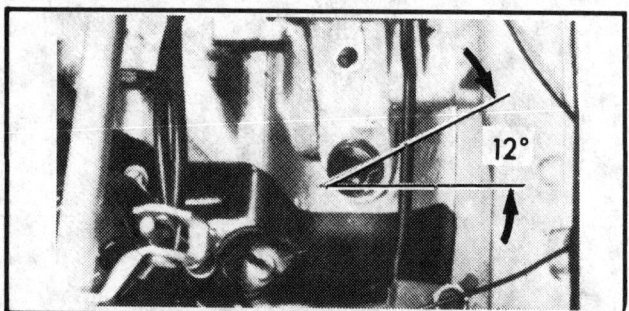

Fig. 10   Engine Distributor Drive Installation Position

CAMSHAFT

CAMSHAFT INSTALLATION

1) With camshaft removed, check riveting of camshaft gear to camshaft. Check camshaft for maximum runout of .0016" (.041 mm). If beyond limit, replace camshaft.

2) Check gear backlash with camshaft and crankshaft installed in crankcase half. Correct backlash is .002" (.05 mm). Gears have correct fit when crankshaft is rotated backwards and camshaft does not try to lift out of bearings.

Fig. 11   Position of Camshaft Timing Gear

3) If camshaft rises out of bearings, teeth on camshaft gear have the wrong pitch radius for crankshaft gear. Camshafts with gears that have various pitch radii are available. Pitch radius is stamped on back of gear facing number three bearing journal of camshaft.

4) Install camshaft with "O" stamped in tooth on outside of camshaft gear between 2 teeth with punch marks on crankshaft gear. Assemble crankcase halves as previously outlined. See Fig. 11.

CAMSHAFT END PLAY

Camshaft end play is checked with camshaft installed in crankcase half. Measure back and forth movement of camshaft with a dial indicator. If end play exceeds .006" (.16 mm), replace camshaft and/or bearings.

Fig. 12   Measuring Camshaft End Play with a Dial Indicator

VANAGON 4 CYLINDER (Cont.)

VALVE TIMING

Install camshaft with "O" stamped in tooth on outside of camshaft gear between 2 teeth with punch marks on crankshaft gear. *See Fig. 11.*

ENGINE OILING

Oil Capacity — 3.2 qts. Add .5 qt. with filter change.
Oil Pressure — 29 psi (2.04 kg/cm²) at 2000 RPM with engine at 176°F (80°C).
Oil Filter — Full-flow, throw-away type oil filter.

Pressure Regulator Valves — Oil pressure relief valve, used to protect oil cooler from excessive pressure, is located in crankcase under oil filter. Oil pressure control valve, used to control oil pressure to bearings, is located in crankcase below oil breather. Oil pressure relief spring should have length of 1.54" (39 mm) at 15-19 lbs. (6.8-8.8 kg) load. Oil pressure control valve spring should have a length of 1.02" (26 mm) at 3¾-4⅜ lbs. (1.7-2.0 kg) load.

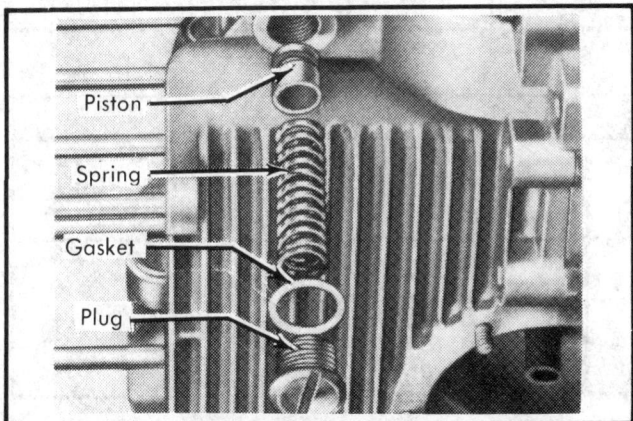

Fig. 13   *Expanded View of Relief Valve Components*

ENGINE OILING SYSTEM

Full pressure lubrication system utilizing a gear-type oil pump and installed in rear of engine and driven by camshaft. Oil is pumped through oil filter, oil cooler and into main oil

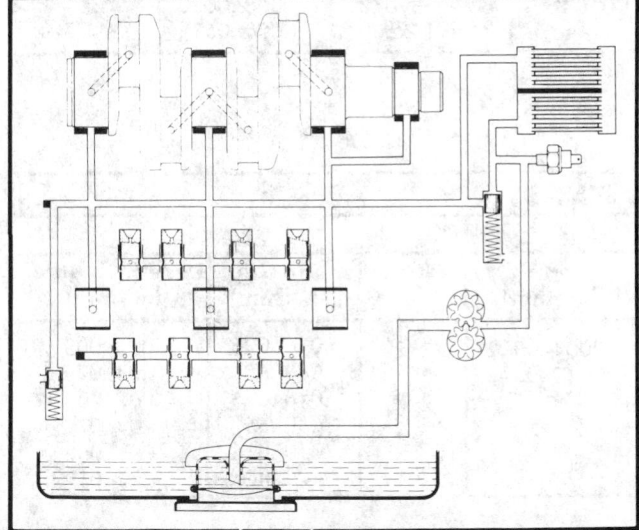

Fig. 14   *Distribution of Oil for Engine Lubrication*

passages in crankcase. Crankshaft main and connecting rod journals are oiled through cross-drilled oil passages in the crankcase. Oil is pumped to camshaft through oil passages that also lubricate valve tappets. Oil flows through push rods to lubricate rocker arms and shafts. Valve stems are lubricated by splash oil from rocker arms. Excess oil flows back into crankcase through push rod tubes. Cylinder walls and piston pins are lubricated by splash oil.

OIL COOLER

To remove oil cooler, remove cooling air fan housing, three 6 mm nuts with washers attaching oil cooler to rear of crankcase, and bolts attaching oil cooler support strap. Remove support strap and oil cooler as unit. Always use new rubber seals when installing oil cooler.

OIL PUMP

Removal — Remove engine. Remove 4 nuts holding oil pump. Using 2 levers, pry oil pump out of crankcase. *See Fig. 15.*

Inspection — Check housing for excessive wear, mainly in gear seating portions. Measure gear backlash for wear. Backlash must not exceed .008" (.20 mm). Replace bearing plate if scored.

Installation — Hand turn oil pump drive shaft until fully engaged in camshaft. Rotate crankshaft two revolutions. Pump plate should now be aligned with camshaft. Refit new gasket and reverse removal procedure for remaining components.

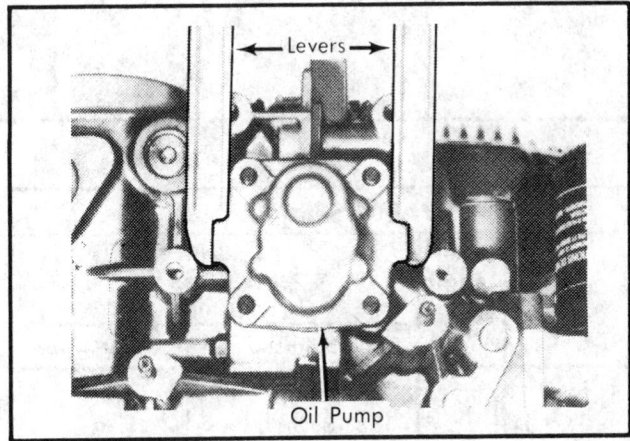

Fig. 15   *Using Levers to Remove Oil Pump*

ENGINE COOLING

Thermostat — At 185-194°F (85-90°C), thermostat length should be at least 1¹³⁄₁₆" (46 mm) measured from shoulders on bellows shaft.

COOLING SYSTEM

Engine is cooled by a radial blower mounted to rear end of crankshaft. Blower draws air through opening in blower shroud at rear of engine. Blower shroud is two-piece unit, mounted around blower and attached to crankcase. As air is drawn in, it is directed over finned cylinders and cylinder heads by deflector plates. As engine warms up, thermostat opens flaps completely to allow total flow of air.

Volkswagen Engines

VANAGON 4 CYLINDER (Cont.)

BLOWER SHROUD REMOVAL

1) Remove engine as previously outlined. Remove ignition timing scale, fan with crankshaft pulley and alternator belt.

2) Disconnect cooling air control cable from control flap shaft. Remove four nuts attaching blower shroud to crankcase and pull assembly to rear and off engine. To install, reverse removal procedure. Adjust air flap control cable by pushing flaps into closed position and tighten cable.

3) Disconnect flap actuating cable from control shaft. Remove nuts securing shroud to crankcase and remove both halves of blower shroud.

4) To install, reverse removal procedure. Adjust air flap control by pushing flaps into closed position and tighten cable control.

5) Install drive belt and tighten alternator into proper belt tensioning position. Belt should have a maximum 0.6" (15.2 mm) deflection. Install cover plates and engine.

ENGINE SPECIFICATIONS

GENERAL SPECIFICATIONS										
Year	Displ.		Carburetor	HP at RPM	Torque (Ft. Lbs. at RPM)	Compr. Ratio	Bore		Stroke	
	cu. ins.	cc					in.	mm	in.	mm
1980	120	1970	Fuel Injection	67@4200	101@3000	7.3:1	3.70	94	2.795	71

VALVES							
Engine & Valve	Head Diam. In. (mm)	Face Angle	Seat Angle	Seat Width In. (mm)	Stem Diameter In. (mm)	Stem Clearance In. (mm)	Valve Lift In. (mm)
1970 cc Int.	1.547 (39.3)	29.5	30°	.071-.087 (1.80-2.21)	.3125-.3129 (7.936-7.948)	.018 (.46)	.....
Exh.	1.299 (33.0)	45°	45°	.079-.098 (2.01-2.49)	.3508-.3512 (8.910-8.920)	.014 (.35)	.....

VALVE SPRINGS			
Engine	Free Length In. (mm)	PRESSURE Lbs. @ In. (kg @ mm)	
		Valve Closed	Valve Open
1970 cc Int. & Exh.	.....	168-186@1.14 (76.20-84.37@28.96)	.....

CAMSHAFT			
Engine	Journal Diam. In. (mm)	Clearance In. (mm)	Lobe Lift In. (mm)
1970 cc	.9839-.9843 (24.991-25.001)	.0008-.0020 (.020-.051)	.....

PISTONS, PINS, RINGS						
	PISTONS	PINS		RINGS		
Engine	Clearance In. (mm)	Piston Fit In. (mm)	Rod Fit In. (mm)	Rings	End Gap In. (mm)	Side Clearance In. (mm)
1970 cc	.001-.002 (.02-.05)	①	.0004-.0012 (.010-.030)	1	.016-.026 (.40-.65)	.002-.003 (.04-.07)
				2	.016-.026 (.40-.65)	.002-.003 (.04-.07)
				3	.010-.016 (.25-.40)	.001-.002 (.02-.05)

① — Push fit with light thumb pressure at room temperature.

VANAGON 4 CYLINDER (Cont.)
ENGINE SPECIFICATIONS (Cont.)

	CRANKSHAFT MAIN & CONNECTING ROD BEARINGS						
	MAIN BEARINGS				CONNECTING ROD BEARINGS		
Engine	Journal Diam. In. (mm)	Clearance In. (mm)	Thrust Bearing	Crankshaft End Play In. (mm)	Journal Diam. In. (mm)	Clearance In. (mm)	Side Play In. (mm)
1970 cc No. 1	2.3609-2.3617 (59.967-59.987)	.0016-.0039 (.041-.099)	No. 1	.0027-.0050 (.069-.127)	1.9677-1.9685 (49.98-50.00)	.0008-.0027 (.020-.069)	.004-.016 (.10-.41)
2	2.3609-2.3617 (59.967-59.987)	.0012-.0035 (.030-.089)					
3	2.3609-2.3617 (59.967-59.987)	.0016-.0039 (.041-.099)					
4	1.5739-1.5748 (39.977-40.025)	.0020-.0039 (.051-.099)					

TIGHTENING SPECIFICATIONS

Application	Ft. Lbs. (mkg)
Connecting Rod Nut	25 (3.45)
Crankcase Half Nuts (8 mm)	14 (1.94)
Crankcase Half Sealing Nuts (10 mm)	25 (3.46)
Cylinder Head Nuts	22 (3.04)
Rocker Shaft-to-Cylinder Head Nuts	11 (1.52)
Heat Exchanger-to-Cylinder Head	16 (2.21)
Oil Pan-to-Crankcase Nuts	9 (1.24)
Drive Plate-to-Crankshaft	65 (8.99)
Hub-to-Crankshaft Bolt	23 (3.18)
Fan-to-Hub	14 (1.94)
Engine-to-Transmission	22 (3.04)
Oil Pump-to-Crankcase	18 (2.48)
Oil Cooler-to-Crankcase	14 (1.94)
Flywheel-to-Crankshaft	80 (11.06)
Clutch-to-Flywheel	18 (2.5)
Torque Converter-to-Drive Plate	18 (2.48)

Volvo Engines

B21F 4-CYLINDER

ENGINE CODING

ENGINE IDENTIFICATION

Engine identification number is located on camshaft timing belt cover. Last 3 digits identify engine.

Engine Identification	
Application	**Code**
DL, GL, GT (2130 cc)	
Man. Trans.	498 848
Auto. Trans.	498 849

ENGINE, CYLINDER HEAD & MANIFOLDS

ENGINE

Removal — 1) Remove battery. Disconnect windshield washer hose and engine compartment lamp. Remove hood. Remove rubber boot and snap ring at base of gearshift lever (manual transmission only).

2) Remove cap from expansion tank. Open radiator drain cock and drain coolant. Disconnect lower radiator hose at radiator, crankcase ventilation hose at cylinder head, and upper radiator hose at engine. Detach expansion tank hoses from radiator. Disconnect oil cooler pipes for automatic transmission at radiator. Remove fan shroud screws, disconnect radiator, and lift radiator and fan shroud from car.

3) Remove air cleaner and hose assembly. Loosen tensioner nut and remove belt from air pump. Disconnect hoses at pump and remove pump and bracket assembly. Remove vacuum pump after disconnecting hoses, including hose to brake power cylinder. Remove tensioner bar bolts, drive belt and power steering pump.

4) If equipped with air conditioning, remove crankshaft pulley and A/C drive belt. Reinstall pulley loosely. Disconnect and remove compressor and bracket.

5) Mark and disconnect four vacuum hoses at engine and two carbon filter hoses. Remove wire or connector from distributor, high tension lead from coil, and starter motor cables and clutch cable clamp from starter.

6) Detach wiring harness from voltage regulator. Disconnect throttle cable at pulley and A/C wire at solenoid on intake manifold.

7) Remove fuel cap to relieve pressure, and remove fuel hoses from filter and return pipe. Remove guard plate for ballast resistor, and disconnect two wire connectors from intake manifold micro switch, four in wiring harness, and two at ballast resistor.

8) Disconnect heater hoses at firewall and drain oil from engine. Remove exhaust pipe flange nuts and gasket. Remove front engine mounting bolts and front exhaust pipe mounting bracket. Disconnect gearshift control rod (automatic transmission) or clutch cable (manual transmission).

9) Disconnect speedometer cable, propeller shaft U-joint, and gearshift selector from control rod. If manual transmission has overdrive, disconnect wire to gearshift selector. Using a wooden block, place jack under transmission. Remove transmission support member.

10) Attach lifting yoke assembly (5035) to three engine lifting eyes, and adjust lifting beam (2810) to its rearmost position. Hoist slightly to release front engine mount dowels. Check for wires or hoses, and disconnect as necessary. Adjust lifting beam to forward position and lift engine from car.

Installation — To install, reverse removal procedure and check for proper installation of all lines, hoses and electrical leads.

INTAKE & EXHAUST MANIFOLDS

Removal — 1) Disconnect battery ground cable, then remove air bellows from CI unit to intake manifold. Disconnect PCV hoses at intake manifold and flame arrester. Disconnect vacuum pump hose at intake manifold. Disconnect diverter valve hoses. Disconnect air pump with tensioner and position to one side.

2) Disconnect the following fuel lines: control pressure regulator (one hose), cold start injector (one hose), distributor pipe to engine (two hoses) front fuel filter to engine (two hoses), and injector hoses (four hoses). Disconnect wiring at control pressure regulator, cold start injector, and auxiliary air valve.

3) Remove air injection pipe. Disconnect throttle cable from intake manifold. Disconnect charcoal canister hoses and EGR valve hose from intake manifold. Remove intake manifold brace, attaching nuts, and intake manifold. Disconnect transmission fill pipe from flywheel housing (automatic transmissions only). Remove attaching nuts and exhaust manifold.

Installation — To install, reverse removal procedure and use new manifold gaskets. Tighten nuts and bolts to specifications.

CYLINDER HEAD

Removal — 1) Drain cooling system at radiator and cylinder block. Disconnect battery ground cable. Disconnect upper radiator hose at engine. Disconnect air bellows between CI unit and air cleaner. Remove PCV hoses from intake manifold and oil trap on block. Disconnect vacuum pump hose at intake manifold.

2) Disconnect diverter valve hoses. Remove air pump and bracket. Disconnect the following fuel lines: control pressure regulator (one hose), cold start injector (one hose), distributor pipe to engine (two hoses), front fuel filter to engine (two hoses), and injector hoses (four hoses).

3) Disconnect wires at following components: control pressure regulator, cold start injector, auxiliary air valve, and temperature sender. Disconnect throttle cable from intake manifold. Disconnect charcoal canister hoses and EGR valve hose from intake manifold. Disconnect transmission fill pipe from transmission housing (automatic transmissions only).

4) Remove water pipe rear clamp from manifold. Remove exhaust manifold to exhaust pipe attaching nuts. Remove intake manifold brace. Disconnect spark plug cables at plugs, then disconnect upper water hose at firewall. Remove timing belt cover, slacken drive belt tensioner and remove drive belt.

Volvo Engines

B21F 4-CYLINDER (Cont.)

Remove valve cover and cylinder head bolts. Lift cylinder head from engine.

Installation — 1) Install new head gasket with "TOP" mark upward. Be sure all contact surfaces are clean. Position cylinder head over gasket.

2) Dip head bolts and washers in engine oil before installation. Install and tighten bolts in sequence shown in *Fig. 1*.

3) Adjust valves. Reverse remainder of removal procedure and make final valve adjustment after running engine for 10 minutes. See *Valve Clearance Adjustment*. Retorque cylinder head bolts.

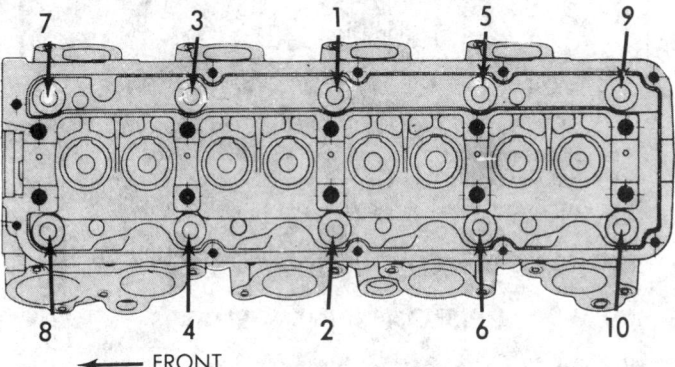

Fig. 1   Cylinder Head Tightening Sequence

CAMSHAFT

Removal — 1) Remove valve cover and gasket. Check and note markings on camshaft bearing caps. Remove center bearing cap and install holder tool (5021) to hold camshaft in place while removing remaining bearing caps.

2) Remove timing belt cover and slacken drive belt tensioner. Pull off drive belt and remove camshaft sprocket. Remove remaining bearing caps and take out front camshaft oil seal. Release screw on holder tool and lift out camshaft.

Installation — Ensure that dowel for sprocket is UP (12 o'clock position) and lubricate all bearing and friction surfaces. To complete installation, reverse removal procedure.

DRIVE BELT INSTALLATION

1) Install belt tensioner if previously removed. Align notch in crankshaft belt guide with timing mark on front cover. Rotate intermediate shaft so timing mark on sprocket aligns with mark on belt guard. Align marks on camshaft belt guide with timing mark on valve cover.

2) New drive belts have yellow markings. Two lines should fit toward crankshaft marks and next mark toward intermediate shaft mark. Place belt over crankshaft sprocket first, then intermediate shaft. Stretch belt on tension side and fit over camshaft sprocket. Slide back of belt inside tension roller.

3) Loosen nut on belt tensioner to permit spring tension to act against drive belt. Recheck timing marks for proper location and tighten tensioner nut. Attach pulley to front hub on crankshaft.

VALVES

VALVE ARRANGEMENT

E-I-E-I-E-I-E-I — Front to Rear.

VALVE GUIDE SERVICING

Removal & Installation — Heat cylinder head to 140° F (60° C) and press old guides out with drift (2818). To install, use intake guide drift (5027) and exhaust guide drift (5028) to press in new guides. Press in until drift contacts cylinder head to give proper height above cylinder head. Installed height for intake guide is .610"±.004" (15.5±.1 mm) and .709"±.004" (18.0±.1 mm) for exhaust guide.

NOTE — *Ensure that replacement guide is same size as old guide. At least 2000 lbs. (907 kg) force should be required to press in new guide; if not, head must be fitted with oversize guide.*

VALVE SPRINGS

Removal & Installation — With cylinder head removed, compress valve springs using suitable valve spring compression tool, and remove valve retainers. Disassemble valve spring components and place valves in order in suitable valve rack. To install, place valves in position, fit valve guide seal, valve spring, upper washer and retainer.

CRANKSHAFT MARKS   INTERMEDIATE SHAFT MARKS   CAMSHAFT MARKS

Fig. 2   Timing Marks for Crankshaft, Intermediate Shaft and Camshaft

Volvo Engines

B21F 4-CYLINDER (Cont.)

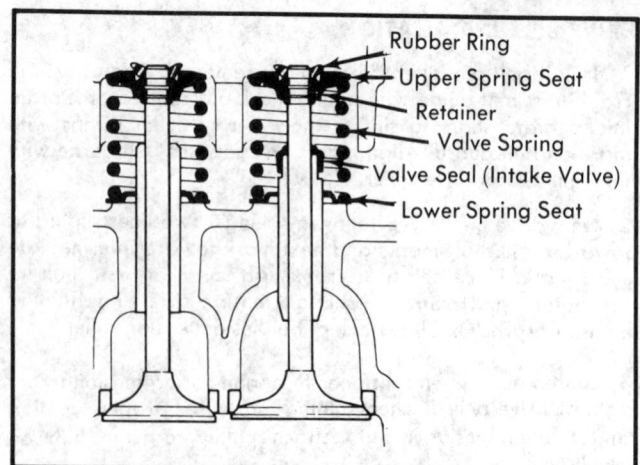

Fig. 3   Valve and Guide Assembly

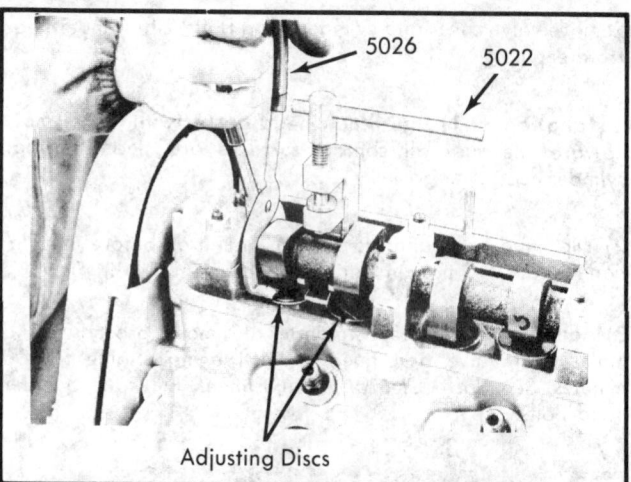

Fig. 4   Removing Valve Adjusting Discs

VALVE SPRING INSTALLED HEIGHT

Valve spring ends must be square. Installed height of valve spring cannot exceed specifications. Measure spring height from base of spring pad on cylinder head to underside of spring retainer.

VALVE CLEARANCE ADJUSTMENT

1) Valve clearance is adjusted with engine off, and may be done either warm or cold. Remove valve cover. Turn crankshaft center bolt until camshaft is in position for firing No. 1 cylinder. Both cam lobes should point up at equally large angles. Pulley timing mark should be on 0°.

2) Using feeler gauge, check valve clearance of No. 1 cylinder, measuring between camshaft lobe and discs. Intake and exhaust valves should have same clearances:

Valve Clearances

When Checking	In. (mm)
Cold engine	.012-.018" (.30-.45 mm)

When Setting	In. (mm)
Cold Engine	.014-.016" (.35-.40 mm)
Hot Engine	.016-.018" (.40-.45 mm)

3) If clearance is incorrect, line up notches in valve depressors, so they are at right angles to engine center line. Install valve adjustment tool (5022) and turn handle downward until depressor groove is just above edge of cylinder head. Remove adjusting disc with special pliers (5026).

4) Using micrometer, measure thickness of disc. Then determine proper thickness required of new disc to bring clearance within specifications. For example: Measure existing clearance and subtract correct clearance. Difference should be added to thickness of old disc to determine thickness of new disc required. Discs are available in thicknesses ranging from .130" (3.30 mm) to .177" (4.50 mm) in increments of .002" (.05 mm).

5) Discs should be oiled and installed with marks down. Remove valve adjustment tool (5022), rotate crankshaft to cor-

rect firing position for No. 3 cylinder and repeat procedure. Then adjust valve clearance for No. 4 and No. 2 cylinders. When all four cylinders have been adjusted, turn camshaft a few turns and recheck valve clearance at all cylinders.

6) Position gasket on cylinder head and install valve cover.

PISTONS, PINS & RINGS

OIL PAN

Removal — 1) Raise and support front of vehicle. Remove splash guard. Remove engine mount nuts from underside of crossmember. Disconnect steering shaft at steering gear. Remove steering "U" joint lower bolt, loosen upper bolt and slide "U" joint up on shaft.

2) Position lifting tools (5006, 5033 and 5115) and lift engine slightly. See Fig. 5. Take out crossmember bolts. Lower crossmember. Remove left engine mount. Remove support bracket (located between rear of oil pan and clutch housing). Remove oil pan bolts. Turn and lower oil pan.

Fig. 5   Lifting Tools Installed for Oil Pan Removal

Installation — To install oil pan, reverse removal procedure.

PISTON & ROD ASSEMBLY

Removal — Remove cylinder head, oil pan and oil pump. Be sure connecting rods and caps are properly marked, so they

B21F 4-CYLINDER (Cont.)

may be reinstalled in original location. Remove carbon ridge from cylinder bores. Remove rod cap, and using wooden hammer handle, push piston out top of cylinder bore. Reinstall rod cap on piston and rod from which removed.

Installation — 1) Remove rod cap from connecting rod. Secure piston pin with retaining rings. Be sure "TOP" mark on rings is facing top of piston and end gaps are 120 degrees from each other and rings are properly installed. Install bearings in connecting rods and caps. Lubricate cylinder bores, pistons and bearings.

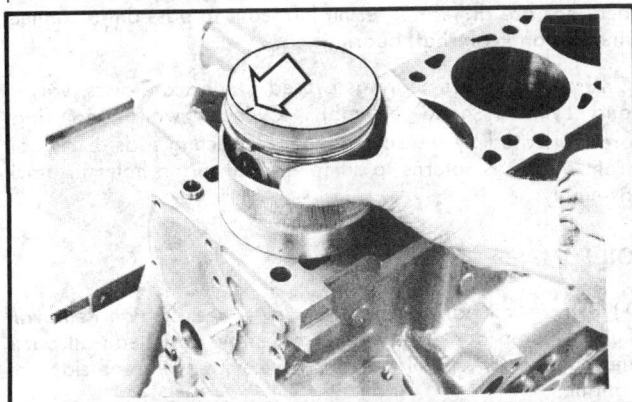

Fig. 6 Installation of Piston in Cylinder Block

2) Using piston ring compressor (5031), insert rod and piston into bore, with mark on top of piston and on connecting rod toward front of engine.

3) Using wooden hammer handle, tap lightly on top of piston. Align marks and tighten end caps. Install oil pump, oil pan and cylinder head.

FITTING PISTONS

Measure piston diameter at right angle to piston pin bore and .25" (7 mm) from lower edge. Measure cylinder bore at

Fig. 7 Thumb Pressure Piston Fit

several positions. If difference exceeds clearance specifications, oversize pistons are available.

PISTON PINS

Piston pins are available in .002" (.05 mm) oversize from standard diameter. If replacement oversize pins are needed, piston pin hole should be reamed out to correct measurement using suitable reaming tool. Use reamer fitted with pilot guide, take only small cuts at a time. Pin fit is correct when pin can be pushed through connecting rod hole by hand, with only light resistance.

CRANKSHAFT MAIN & CONNECTING ROD BEARINGS

MAIN & CONNECTING ROD BEARINGS

Removal & Installation — 1) Remove oil pan and related parts. *See Oil Pan Removal.* Identify and mark connecting rod caps and main bearing caps to ensure correct replacement.

2) Remove connecting rod caps and push pistons towards top of cylinders. Remove main bearing caps (one at a time) and thoroughly clean all bearing surfaces.

3) Measure all journals, using a micrometer. Out-of-roundness on connecting rod bearings should not exceed .003" (.07 mm) and on main bearings, it should not exceed .002" (.05 mm). If values obtained are close to, or in excess of wear limits, crankshaft must be reground to next suitable undersize.

4) If all journals check out to standard size, refit with replacement bearings. Reinstall main bearing caps, refit connecting rods to crankshaft and tighten all nuts and bolts to specifications. Reassemble engine in reverse order of removal.

REAR MAIN BEARING OIL SEAL

Removal & Installation — 1) Remove transmission, clutch, and flywheel from engine. Remove two bolts from oil pan (into rear flange). Slacken two bolts on each side of flange, and remove flange. Use a suitable drift (2817) to remove oil seal.

2) Clean flange area thoroughly and inspect seal mating surface of crankshaft. Install new seal to flange using drift (2817).

NOTE — *If a new crankshaft has been installed, screw center bolt of tool in fully and install seal at outer position of flange. If crankshaft has not been replaced, install seal with center bolt of tool screwed out a couple of turns.*

3) Oil new seal and install flange with new gasket to cylinder block. Install attaching bolts and tighten. Install oil pan attaching bolts and tighten. Install flywheel, clutch, and transmission.

ENGINE FRONT COVER OIL SEAL

Removal — 1) Remove fan shroud, fan belt and fan pulley. Remove water pump pulley and camshaft drive belt cover. Remove crankshaft hub, sprocket and belt guide. Remove sprocket from intermediate shaft. Detach wiring harness across front of engine. Remove two oil pan bolts from base of

B21F 4-CYLINDER (Cont.)

front cover and loosen two on each side of them. Remove drive belt guard plate and front cover.

2) Using suitable tool (5025) press out intermediate shaft seal from front cover. Using similar tool (5024) press out crankshaft seal. Use same tools to install new seals.

Installation — 1) Using new gasket, install front cover. Install oil pan, drive belt guard plate, and wiring harness.

2) Using tool (5024), install crankshaft seal. Using similar tool (5025), install intermediate shaft seal in front cover. Install inner belt guide on camshaft (collar facing away from belt). Install camshaft sprocket, aligning notch with dowel on camshaft. Install outer belt guide, washer and center bolt. Hold sprocket with holder tool (5034) and tighten bolt.

3) Install sprocket on intermediate shaft, aligning notch with dowel on shaft. Use tool (5034) to hold shaft while tightening center bolt.

4) Install belt guide and sprocket on crankshaft. Install front hub and tighten bolt. Install drive belt and complete installation of previously removed parts.

ENGINE OILING

Crankcase Capacity — 4 qts. including filter.

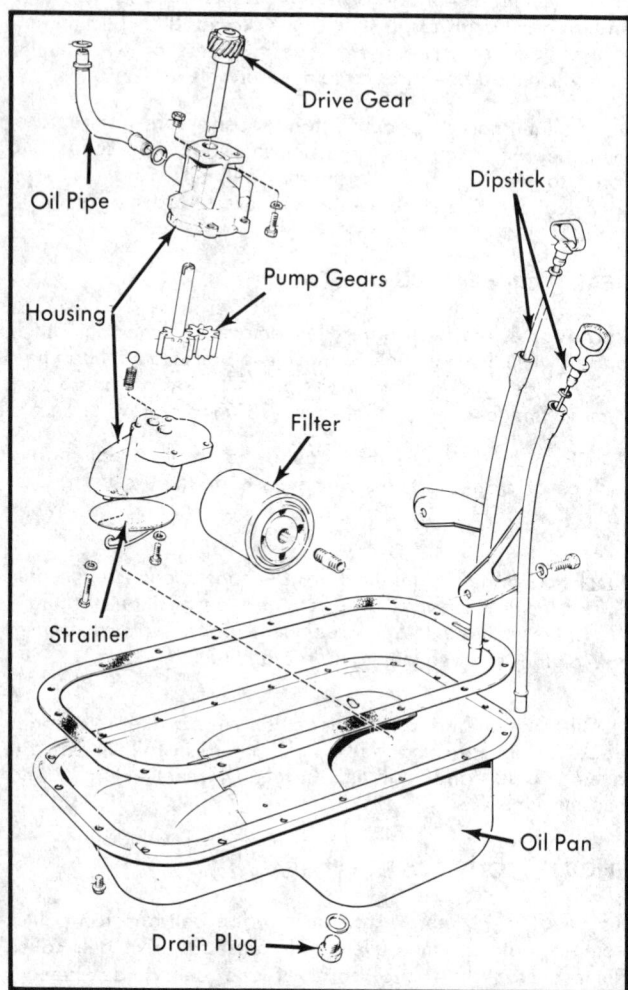

Fig. 8   Oiling System Components

Oil Filter — Full-flow canister, disposable type.

Normal Oil Pressure — 35-85 psi (2.6-6.0 kg/cm²) at 2000 RPM with engine at normal operating temperature.

ENGINE OILING SYSTEM

Engine utilizes a force-feed lubricating system. Oil circulates through oil pump to oil filter on outside of engine block assembly. From filter, oil is forced to drilled gallery in center of block, where it moves under pressure to main bearings. Main bearings are drilled to permit lubricant to pass on to connecting rod and camshaft bearings.

Oil from camshaft bearings is used to lubricate discs, valves, and cylinder head assembly. Cylinder walls and rings are lubricated by the splash from connecting rods. Excess oil from all areas returns to sump through drain holes in block assembly.

OIL PUMP

1) Remove oil pan and related parts. *See Oil Pan Removal.* Pull oil pump out of engine, disassemble and clean all parts thoroughly. Check all parts for excessive wear or signs of fatigue.

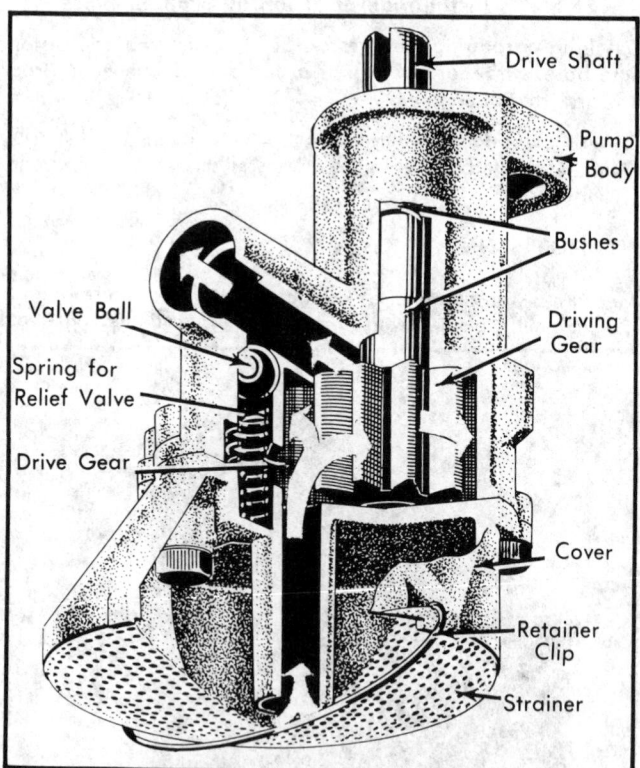

Fig. 9   Cutaway & Operational View of Oil Pump Assembly

2) Measure backlash (clearance) between pump gears. It should be .006-.014" (.15-.35 mm). Also measure end play of gears. Allowable end play is .0008-.0048" (.02-.12 mm). If any parts show excessive wear or play, replace necessary components. Drive shaft and gear are matched set and must be replaced as an assembly.

B21F 4-CYLINDER (Cont.)

3) Reinstall oil pump, making sure that sealing rings on oil delivery pipe are securely in place. Be sure oil pump properly engages pump drive shaft. Replace oil pan and related components.

ENGINE COOLING

WATER PUMP

Removal & Installation — 1) Remove expansion tank cap, open engine block drain cock, and disconnect lower radiator hose at radiator. Remove fan shroud and fan. Loosen alternator and air pump and remove drive belts.

2) Remove water pump pulley, timing gear cover, and lower radiator hose. Remove retaining bolt and slide coolant pipe rearward. Remove pump.

3) Clean all surfaces. Place new sealing ring on coolant pipe. Install new gasket when mounting pump. Install other components previously removed. Fill with coolant.

Thermostat — Standard wax type (marked 87°) opens at 189°F (87°C); fully open at 207°F (97°C).

Cooling System Capacity — 10 qts.

ENGINE SPECIFICATIONS

GENERAL SPECIFICATIONS										
Year	Displ.		Carburetor	HP at RPM	Torque (Ft. Lbs. at RPM)	Compr. Ratio	Bore		Stroke	
	cu. ins.	cc					in.	mm	in.	mm
1980 B21F	130.0	2130	Fuel Inj.	107@5250	114@2500	9.3:1	3.623	92	3.150	80

VALVES							
Engine & Valve	Head Diam. In. (mm)	Face Angle	Seat Angle	Seat Width In. (mm)	Stem Diameter In. (mm)	Stem Clearance In. (mm)	Valve Lift In. (mm)
2130 cc Intake	1.732 (44)	45.5°	44.75°	.068-.092 (1.7-2.3)	.3134-.3138 (7.96-7.97)	.0012-.0024 (.030-.060)	.44 (11.2)
Exhaust	1.278 (35)	45.5°	44.75°	.068-.092 (1.7-2.3)	.3122-.3126 (7.93-7.94)	.0024-.0035 (.060-.090)	.44 (11.2)

PISTONS, PINS, RINGS						
	PISTONS	PINS		RINGS		
Engine	Clearance In. (mm)	Piston Fit In. (mm)	Rod Fit In. (mm)	Rings	End Gap In. (mm)	Side Clearance In. (mm)
2130 cc	.0004-.0012 (.010-.030)	Push Fit	Push Fit	2 Comp.	.0138-.0217 (.35-.55)	.0016-.0028 (.040-.072)
				Oil	.010-.016 (.25-.40)	.0012-.0024 (.030-.062)

CRANKSHAFT MAIN & CONNECTING ROD BEARINGS						
	MAIN BEARINGS				CONNECTING ROD BEARINGS	
Engine	Journal Diam. In. (mm)	Clearance In. (mm)	Thrust Bearing	Crankshaft End Play In. (mm)	Journal Diam. In. (mm)	Clearance In. (mm)	Side Play In. (mm)
2130 cc	2.4981-2.4986 (63.451-63.464)	.0011-.0033 (.028-.083)	.....	.0015-.0058 (.037-.147)	2.1255-2.1260 (53.987-54.000)	.0009-.0028 (.024-.070)	.006-.014 (.15-.35)

Volvo Engines

B21F 4-CYLINDER (Cont.)

ENGINE SPECIFICATIONS (Cont.)

VALVE SPRINGS

Engine	Free Length In. (mm)	PRESSURE Lbs. @ In. (kg @ mm)	
		Valve Closed	Valve Open
2130 cc	1.77 (45)	63-72@1.50 (29-33@38)	160-178@1.06 (73-81@27)

CAMSHAFT

Engine	Journal Diam. In. (mm)	Clearance In. (mm)	Lobe Lift In. (mm)
2130 cc	1.1437-1.1445 (29.050-29.070)	.0012-.0028 (.030-.071)	.....

TIGHTENING SPECIFICATIONS

Application	Ft. Lbs (mkg)
Cylinder Head Bolts	
Step 1	37 (5.1)
Step 2	52 (7.2)
Step 3	①66 (9.1)
Main Bearing Caps	85-91 (11.8-12.6)
Connecting Rod Caps	43-48 (6.0-6.6)
Camshaft Bearing Caps	13-16 (1.8-2.2)
Exhaust & Intake Manifold Bolts	15 (2.0)
Flywheel Bolts	47-54 (6.5-7.5)
Engine Mount Bolts	15 (2.0)
Spark Plugs	25-29 (3.5-4.0)
Sprockets	
Camshaft	37 (5.1)
Intermediate Shaft	37 (5.1)
Crankshaft	122 (16.9)
Fan Bolt	33 (4.6)
Drive Belt Tensioner Nut	37 (5.1)
Oil Pan Bolts	8 (1.1)

① — After tightening to this specification, run engine until it reaches normal operating temperature and retorque to this specification. Retorque after 600-1200 miles.

D24 6 CYLINDER DIESEL

NOTE — *Complete specifications and procedures for this engine were not available.*

ENGINE CODING

Engine Identification — Code for Volvo 6 cylinder diesel is D24. Engine serial number is located under vacuum pump on left side of engine block.

Engine Identification	
Application	**Code**
D24 Auto. Trans.	498705
D24 Man. Trans.	498704

ENGINE & CYLINDER HEAD

ENGINE

Removal — **1)** Disconnect battery. Disconnect windshield washer hoses and remove hood. Remove lower radiator hose, drain coolant, and remove coolant hoses attached to engine. Remove radiator, expansion tank, and any attached hoses. Disconnect accelerator cable and vacuum lines.

2) Disconnect wires at main terminal, glow plug relay, and voltage regulator and hang out of way. Remove power steering belt and pump with brackets, and hang out of the way with hoses attached. Remove and plug fuel lines at filter and injection pump

3) Remove cooling fan and spacer, pulleys, and drive belts. Disconnect exhaust pipes at front and rear manifolds and remove air cleaner and ducting. Drain engine oil. Disconnect driveshafts, speedometer cable, and gear lever from transmission. On vehicles with manual transmission, disconnect clutch cable and pull out from clutch lever and housing. Position jack under transmission, raise slightly, and remove transmission crossmember. Detach engine mounts.

4) Attach lift 2810, and hooks 5185 and 5186, or a suitable lifting device to engine. Move hoist to rear position on beam 2810, and hoist engine enough to off-load left engine mount. Remove jack from under transmission. Move hoist to front position and carefully lift out engine, ensuring all wires and hoses clear assembly.

Installation — To install engine, reverse removal procedures.

CYLINDER HEAD

Removal — **1)** Remove splash guard, expansion tank cap, and lower radiator hose. Drain radiator and disconnect battery. Remove radiator, fan, spacer, pulleys and fan belt. Remove drive belt for power steering. Remove valve cover and front and rear timing belt covers. Disconnect all wires to cylinder head.

2) Remove air cleaner and attached hoses. Disconnect vacuum pump and move to wheel housing. Remove vacuum pump plunger from cylinder head. Remove and plug fuel delivery pipes and disconnect cold start device. Set No. 1 piston to TDC, (timing mark on flywheel at "0"). Loosen water pump retaining bolts to relieve tension on timing gear belt, and remove belt.

3) Use wrench 5199 to hold camshaft drive gear in place, and remove center retaining bolt. Camshaft MUST NOT rotate, or damage to valves and pistons could result. Tap gear loose from camshaft tapered end. Remove injection pump drive belt by loosening retaining bracket bolts. Use wrench 5199 to hold rear camshaft sprocket, and remove center retaining bolt. Tap gear loose from camshaft.

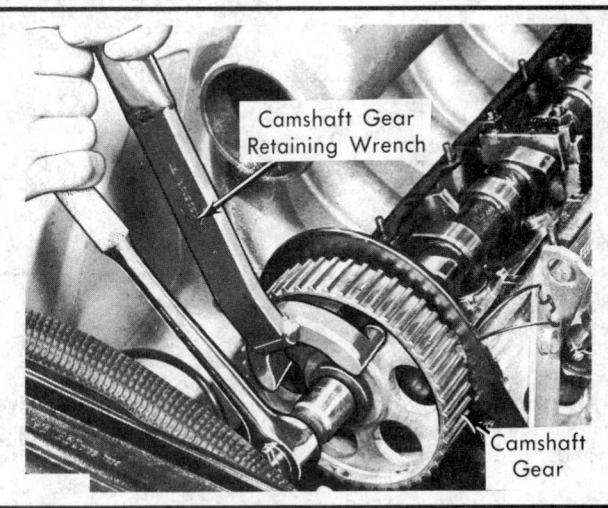

Fig. 1 Using Camshaft Gear Retaining Wrench

4) Loosen cylinder head bolts in reverse order of tightening sequence. Carefully lift cylinder head from engine, making sure rear glow plug clears injection pump bracket, and valves do not touch cylinder walls. Set cylinder head on wooden blocks so it does not rest on the valves.

Installation — **1)** Clean all mating surfaces and check that cylinder head is not warped. Maximum allowable distortion is .02" (.5 mm) diagonally, and .008" (.2 mm) crosswise.

NOTE — *Cracks between valve seats not wider than .02" (.5 mm) do not warrent replacement of cylinder head, as they do not impair engine function.*

2) Select a head gasket with the same number of notches as previous gasket, unless pistons, rods, or crankshaft were disassembled or repaired. Then piston projection above engine block must be measured. Use a dial indicator to measure each piston while at TDC, and select proper gasket from the following table:

Available Cylinder Head Gaskets		
Piston Projection In. (mm)	**Notches**	**Gasket Thickness**
.026-.031 (.67-.80) 1		.055" (1.4 mm)
.032-.035 (.81-.90) 2		.059" (1.5 mm)
.036-.040 (.91-1.02) 3		.063" (1.6 mm)

3) Set No. 1 piston at TDC. Set camshaft for injection on cylinder No. 1 (both cam lobes of No. 1 cylinder should point up at equally large angles). Use stop tool 5190 to lock camshaft in place. Install aligning dowels 5189 in outer bolt holes. Remove rear glow plug to protect it from hitting injection pump. Carefully set cylinder head into place. Install the head bolts

Volvo Engines

D24 6 CYLINDER DIESEL (Cont.)

with new washers with coned side facing up. Torque cylinder head bolts in 3 stages:

Stage 1 .... 37 ft. lbs. (5.1 mkg)
Stage 2 .... 52 ft. lbs. (7.2 mkg)
Stage 3 .... 66 ft. lbs. (9.1 mkg)

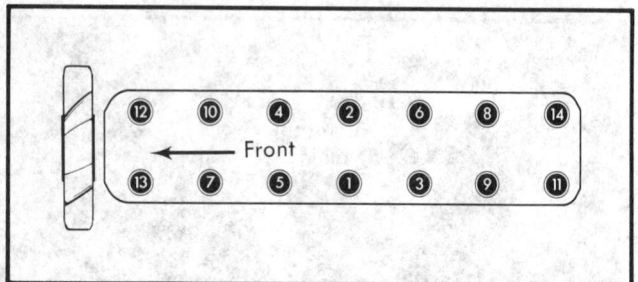

**Fig. 2   Cylinder Head Tightening Sequence
(Loosen in Reverse Order)**

4) Complete installation by reversing removal procedure. Run engine until it reaches operating temperature, and retorque cylinder head bolts in proper sequence to 66 ft. lbs. (9.1 mkg).

NOTE — *After 600 - 1200 miles, cylinder head bolts must be retorqued. Vacuum pump and plunger must be removed to gain access to cylinder head bolt. With the engine cool, slacken each bolt individually by 30°, and then tighten to 66 ft. lbs. (9.1 mkg).*

CAMSHAFT

TIMING BELT

Removal – 1) Disconnect battery. Disconnect lower radiator hose and drain coolant. Remove coolant hoses attached to head. Remove coolant hoses attached to head. Remove radiator, expansion tank cap, and engine splash guard. Remove fan, spacers, pulleys and fan belt. Remove drive belt for power steering. Remove valve cover, and front and rear timing belt covers. Disconnect all wires to cylinder head.

2) Using a 1¹⁄₁₆" (27 mm) wrench on crankshaft pulley bolt, bring No. 1 cylinder to TDC. Remove vibration damper center bolt using wrench 5187 to hold damper from turning. Remove Allen screws and pull off vibration damper. Remove lower belt shield. Loosen water pump bolts and remove gear belt.

NOTE — *Idler pulley must be replaced when replacing timing gear belt. Use puller 5202 or equivalent to remove pulley.*

3) Using holding tool 5199 to keep camshaft from moving, remove center bolt on camshaft rear gear and tap gear off camshaft. Install camshaft locking gauge 5190 in groove on rear of camshaft. Position a .008" (.2 mm) feeler gauge under left (injection pump) side of locking gauge. Remove camshaft front gear using holding tool 5199 to keep camshaft from turning while removing center bolt.

Installation – 1) Making sure gear belt is fitted securely to all gears, install gear belt and camshaft front gear together. Install center bolt finger tight so gear can rotate. Camshaft must not rotate. Install lower belt shield and vibration damper using sealing agent 277961-9 (or equivalent) on damper center bolt.

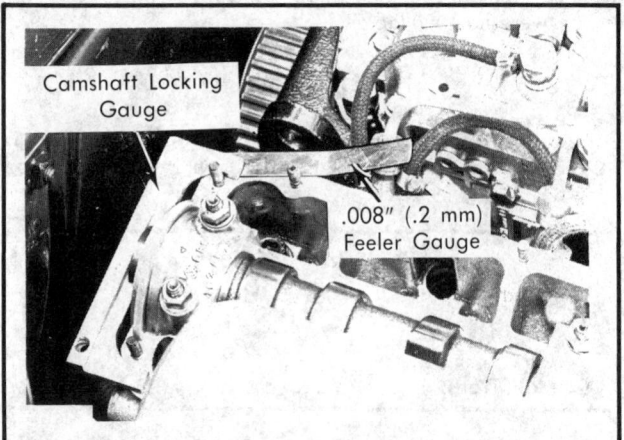

**Fig. 3   Using Camshaft Locking Gauge
to Set Engine Timing**

2) Check that No. 1 piston is at TDC and timing mark on flywheel is on "0". Adjust gear belt tension to 12-13 on tension gauge 5197 using the water pump for adjustment. Strike the belt heavily by hand and recheck tension.

3) Using wrench 5199 to hold gear, tighten camshaft front gear center bolt. Remove gauge 5190 and install rear camshaft gear without moving camshaft. Install injection pump drive belt and adjust belt tension to 12-13 on tension gauge 5197. Reverse removal procedure to complete installation.

CAMSHAFT

Removal — With camshaft drive sprockets and vacuum pump removed, and engine at TDC, remove bearing caps 1 and 4. Alternately loosen cap nuts on caps 2 and 3. Lift out camshaft and remove seals.

Installation – 1) Lightly lubricate bearings and contact surfaces. Install gauge 5190 on camshaft rear and position camshaft on cylinder head. Cam lobes for cylinder No. 1 should point up at equally large angles. Install bearing caps 2 and 3 and tighten cap nuts alternately. Use gauge 5190 to guide rear end when tightening. Remove gauge.

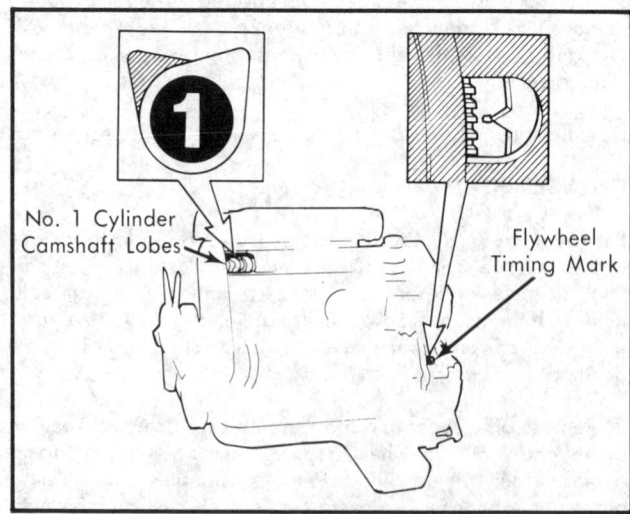

**Fig. 4   No. 1 Cylinder, Top Dead Center
Reference Mark**

D24 6 CYLINDER DIESEL (Cont.)

2) Install new oil seals on camshaft, but do not press them to bottom. Make sure seals are not cocked. Install bearing caps 1 and 4. Use adaptor 5200 and press seals into final position. Reverse removal procedure to complete installation.

INJECTION PUMP

Removal — 1) Pinch off hoses to cold start device and disconnect. Disconnect accelerator cable and automatic transmission kickdown cable (if equipped). Remove rear timing gear cover, vacuum pump, and fuel delivery pipes. Plug all fuel lines and connections to prevent contamination of fuel system. Disconnect wire at stop valve. Turn crankshaft pulley to bring No. 1 piston to TDC. Loosen injection pump bracket bolts to relieve belt tension and remove drive belt. Tighten one bolt to retain pump in an upright position.

2) Loosen camshaft rear gear center bolt enough to allow gear to rotate on camshaft without letting camshaft rotate. Lock injection pump gear with stop 5193, and remove gear nut. Using puller 5204, remove injection pump gear. Remove bolts retaining front injection pump bracket to engine. Bracket comes out with pump. Remove Allen screws retaining injection pump, and remove pump.

Installation — To install, reverse removal procedure, noting that mark on injection pump and bracket coincide, and shaft key is correctly installed before replacing gear.

Pump Timing — 1) To check pump timing, remove rear timing belt cover and set No. 1 piston to TDC. Disconnect cold shart device by loosening the screw nearest the lever, and pushing lever forward. Rotate sleeve 90° and push lever back against stop. DO NOT loosen clamp screw at end of cable.

2) Install a dial indicator with adaptor 5194 in place of plug at injector pump distributor. Set dial indicator with .08" (2 mm) preload between plunger and pump shaft. Turn crankshaft counterclockwise until dial indicator is at minimum reading. Set dial indicator to zero and turn crankshaft to bring No. 1 piston back to TDC. Dial indicator reading should now be .028" (.70 mm).

3) If necessary, loosen injection pump retaining screws and turn pump to obtain proper setting. Tighten screws and rotate crankshaft 2 complete turns, bringing No. 1 piston back to TDC. Dial indicator should still read .028" (.07 mm). Readjust and recheck as necessary to obtain proper setting. Remove dial indicator, and install timing gear cover and cold start device.

VALVES

VALVE ARRANGEMENT

E-I-E-I-E-I-I-E-I-E-I-E   (front to rear)

VALVE CLEARANCE ADJUSTMENT

1) Remove valve cover and rotate crankshaft so that No. 1 piston is at TDC, and cab lobes point up. Flywheel mark should be at "0". Check intake and exhaust clearance between heel of cam lobe and cam follower. Check remaining cylinders in firing order sequence.

2) If adjustment is required, turn the crankshaft ¼ turn clockwise from piston TDC, as there is no room to depress valves. Using depressor tool (5196), press down valve depressor and remove disc with special pliers (5195).

3) Calculate thickness of disc required to reach proper setting. Discs are available in thicknesses of .130-.167" (3.30-4.25 mm) in increments of .002" (.05 mm). Lubricate and position new disc with stamped marking down. Rotate crankshaft several times and recheck all settings. Install valve cover.

Valve Clearance Specifications	
Application	**In. (mm)**
Intake	
Hot	.008-.012 (.20-.30)
Cold	.006-.010 (.15-.25)
Exhaust	
Hot	.016-.020 (.40-.50)
Cold	.014-.018 (.35-.45)

VALVE GUIDE SERVICING

1) With cylinder head removed from engine, and camshaft and lifters removed, attach a valve spring compressor to valve. Compress valve spring and remove retaining lock, upper valve spring washer, valve springs, and valve. Remove valve guide seals and lower valve spring washers.

2) Using a dial indicator, measure valve guide clearance by placing a new valve in guide bore with a valve stem end edge to edge with valve guide. Use proper intake or exhaust valve for bores as stem diameters are different.

3) Rock valve back and forth and observe dial indicator reading. Clearance must not exceed .051" (1.3 mm). If clearance is excessive, replace valve guides. Press out old guides from combustion chamber side of cylinder head using a drift (5218 or equivalent).

4) Oil replacement valve guide and press in place from camshaft side of cylinder head until guide flange bottoms in cylinder head. Do not use more than 1 ton force, or flange may break off of guide. Ream guides using hand reamer (5224 or equivalent).

NOTE — *Valves and seats must be reground if valve guides are replaced.*

5) Replace valve components, camshaft, and cylinder head in reverse order of removal.

PISTONS, PINS, & RINGS

PISTON & ROD ASSEMBLY

Removal — 1) With oil pan and cylinder head removed, mark each piston assembly for proper installation. Ream any ridge from cylinder bores using a ridge reamer. Place a rag on top of piston to collect cuttings.

2) Remove connecting rod cap and bearing shells, and push piston assembly out through top of cylinder bore.

D24 6 CYLINDER DIESEL (Cont.)

Installation — 1) Fit bearing shells in connection rod and rod caps. Lubricate cylinder bores, pistons, and bearing shells. Turn crakshaft so that journal for piston being serviced is at bottom of stroke.

2) Using a ring compressor, fit piston to bore noting that arrow on piston crown faces forward. Push piston down, and locate connecting rod to crankshaft. Fit rod cap to connecting rod and tighten new nuts. Install all pistons and check that crankshaft rotates freely.

FITTING PISTONS

1) Using a bore indicator, measure each cylinder bore at 3 points, both parallel and at right angles to crankshaft. Measure .393" (10 mm) from top, bottom, and at center of cylinder bore. The cylinder bore reading must not deviate by more than .002" (.04 mm) from basic value.

2) Measure piston diameter at right angle to piston pin .590" (15 mm) from lower edge. Subtract reading from that taken of cylinder bore. If specification is exceeded reboring or oversize pistons must be used.

NOTE — *Pistons with rounded edges on pressure side may not be used again. Round edges are caused by faulty injectors, which must be serviced before installation.*

3) Place each piston ring squarely into bottom of cylinder bore and measure ring gap. Place ring approximately .59" (15 mm) from lower edge of cylinder.

PISTON PINS

Removal & Installation — 1) Remove circlips retaining piston pin. Push out pin with a drift. If pin moves stiffly, heat piston to approximatley 140°F (60°C). Assemble in reverse order.

2) If piston pin bushing warrants replacement, press bushing out using drift (5017 or equivalent). Press in new bushing until edges are flush with connecting rod. Drill out lubricating hole in bushing and ream bushing with a reamer. Piston pin must be loose, but still able to slide through hole with slight resistance.

PISTON RINGS

Removal — Using ring pliers, remove rings from piston. Remove any carbon deposits from ring lands and piston.

Installation — Fit expander ring in lowest groove of piston. Fit oil ring so ring gap is opposite spring opening. Install lower compression ring with "Top" marking upward. Install upper compression ring. Turn compression rings so all gaps are 120° apart. Do not turn oil control ring.

CRANKSHAFT MAIN & CONNECTING ROD BEARINGS

MAIN & CONNECTING ROD BEARINGS

Removal — Check markings on main and connecting rod bearings and remark if necessary. Using Plastigage method

check main and connecting rod bearing clearance. If clearance is excessive, replace bearings. Do not mix old and new bearings. Replace in sets only.

Installation — Fit main bearing shells in engine block and main bearing caps. Install bearing shells with oil hole to engine block. Lubricate bearings and place crankshaft in position. Fit main bearing caps with No. 1 toward vibration damper and No. 7 toward flywheel. See *Piston and Rod Assembly* for connecting rod installation procedure.

Crankshaft Front Seal — With vibration damper removed, pull old seal from housing using puller 5205 (or equivalent). Grease seal lips, and press into place by hand. Use adapter 5200, a thick washer and camshaft center bolt to press seal into housing until seated.

Crankshaft Rear Seal — With flywheel removed, pry out old seal with a screwdriver. Coat seal contact surfaces and lips with oil and hand start into position. Tap seal into housing until it bottoms, using drift 5208 (or equivalent).

ENGINE OILING

Crankcase Capacity — 7.4 quarts with filter change, and 6.6 quarts without filter change.

Oil Filter — Replaceable spin-on type.

Normal Oil Pressure — Minimum of 28 psi@2000 RPM with engine at normal operating temperature.

ENGINE OILING SYSTEM — Gear-type oil pump pressure lubricates pistons, piston pins, and crankshaft. Three nozzles in the head distribute oil to cam lobes, valve depressors and vacuum pump piston.

OIL PUMP — The oil pump cannot be removed without removing the engine, therefore no repairs can be made in the vehicle. The oil pump must be replaced as an assembly as there are no separate replaceable parts.

ENGINE COOLING

Cooling System Capacity — 10 quarts

Thermostat — Begins to open at 186°F (87°C), and is fully open at 236°F (102°C).

WATER PUMP

Removal — Remove timing belt as described in *TIMING BELT* in this article, making sure to mark belt position on belt, camshaft and crankshaft gears. Also, mark belt as to which parts face upward and forward. Remove protective plate and pump retaining bolts, and remove water pump.

Installation — Making sure all gasket surfaces are clean, lightly grease a new "O" ring and fit it to the pump. DO NOT use any other sealing agent. Install the pump with the longest retaining bolt in the upper hole. Reverse removal procedure to complete installation.

Volvo Engines

D24 6 CYLINDER DIESEL (Cont.)
ENGINE SPECIFICATIONS

GENERAL SPECIFICATIONS

Year	Displ.		Carburetor	HP at RPM	Torque (Ft. Lbs. at RPM)	Compr. Ratio	Bore		Stroke	
	cu. ins.	cc					in.	mm	in.	mm
1980 D24	145	2383	Fuel Inj.	82@4800	105.5@2800	23.5:1	3.01	76.5	3.40	86.4

PISTONS, PINS, RINGS

Engine	PISTONS	PINS		RINGS		
	Clearance In. (mm)①	Piston Fit In. (mm)	Rod Fit In. (mm)	Rings	End Gap In. (mm)②	Side Clearance In. (mm)
2383 cc	.0012-.0019 (.03-.05)	Push Fit	Close Running Fit	Comp 1	.012-.020 (.30-.50)	.0023-.0035③ (.06-.09)
				Comp 2	.012-.020 (.30-.50)	.0019-.0031③ (.05-.08)
				Oil	.010-.016 (.25-.40)	.0011-.0023④ (.03-.06)

① — Wear limit .0051" (.13 mm)　② — Wear limit .040" (1.0 mm)
③ — Wear limit .0078" (.2 mm)　④ — Wear limit .0059" (.15 mm)

CRANKSHAFT MAIN & CONNECTING ROD BEARINGS

Engine	MAIN BEARINGS				CONNECTING ROD BEARINGS		
	Journal Diam. In. (mm)	Clearance In. (mm)①	Thrust Bearing	Crankshaft End Play In. (mm)②	Journal Diam. In. (mm)	Clearance In. (mm)③	Side Play In. (mm)
2383 cc	2.283 (58.0)	.0006-.0029 (.016-.075)	No. 4	.003-.007 (.07-.18)	1.88 (47.8)	.0006-.0024 (.015-.062)	.0157 (.40)

① — Wear Limit .0063" (.16mm)　② — Wear limit .010" (.25 mm)　③ — Wear limit .0047" (.12 mm)

VALVES

Engine & Valve	Head Diam. In. (mm)	Face Angle	Seat Angle	Seat Width In. (mm)	Stem Diameter In. (mm)	Stem Clearance In. (mm)①	Valve Lift In. (mm)
2383 cc Intake	1.417 (36.0)	44.5°	45°	.079 (2.0)	.314 (7.97)	.0118 (.30)	.335 (8.5)
Exhaust	1.221 (31.0)	45°	45°	.094 (2.4)	.313 (7.95)	.0118 (.30)	.354 (9.0)

① — Wear limit .05" (1.3 mm)

CAMSHAFT

Engine	Journal Diam. In. (mm)	Clearance In. (mm)①	Lobe Lift In. (mm)
2383 cc Front	1.257-1.258 (31.92-31.95)	.002-.004 (.05-.10)	.....
Others	1.786-1.795 (29.94-29.96)		

① — End play .006" (.15 mm)

VALVE SPRINGS

Engine	Free Length In. (mm)	PRESSURE Lbs. @ In. (kg @ mm)	
		Valve Closed	Valve Open
2383 cc Inner	1.33 (33.9)	16.2 @ 1.13 (.72 @ 28.6)	49.4 @ .72 (2.2 @ 18.3)
Outer	1.58 (40.2)	40.0 @ 1.28 (1.8 @ 32.6)	102.5 @ .89 (4.5 @ 22.3)

Volvo Engines

B28F V6

ENGINE CODING

ENGINE IDENTIFICATION

Engine identification number is located on the front left side of engine block, below the exhaust manifold, and above the power steering pump bracket.

Engine Identification Numbers		
Application	Man. Trans.	Auto. Trans.
GLE & Coupe (2849 cc)		
Federal	498628	498629
California	498630	498631

ENGINE, CYLINDER HEADS, & MANIFOLDS

ENGINE

Removal — **1)** Remove gearshift lever (manual) or place lever in "P" (automatic). Remove battery, hood, air cleaner, and engine splash guard.

2) Drain cooling system (each side of block), and disconnect all coolant hoses. Disconnect automatic transmission oil cooler pipes at radiator. Remove radiator and fan shroud. Disconnect heater hose at intake pipe, power brake hose at intake manifold, and vacuum pump hose at pump. Remove vacuum pump.

3) Disconnect fuel hoses at filter and return pipe. Disconnect wiring harness and relay connectors. Remove high tension lead from distributor and heater hoses at fire wall. Disconnect carbon filter hose at filter, and hose from EGR valve. Remove connector at voltage regulator and wire clamp. Disconnect connector for distributor, throttle cable, vacuum amplifier hose at T-pipe, and wax thermostat hoses.

4) Remove hose from air pump to backfire valve and wires from solenoid valve and micro switch. Remove nuts from both exhaust manifold flanges. Remove A/C compressor and drive belt without disconnecting hoses. Drain engine oil. Remove power steering pump and belt.

5) Remove nuts from front engine mounts. Remove exhaust pipe clamps (front exhaust pipe with catalytic converter). Disconnect shift control lever at automatic transmission.

6) Disconnect slave cylinder from clutch (manual transmission) and detach speedometer cable. Disconnect propeller shaft. Put stands under front of car, and using wooden block, place jack under oil pan. Remove transmission attachment member.

7) Using suitable sling and hoist, lift engine/transmission assembly from car.

NOTE — *When removing engine, check for hoses and wires not previously removed.*

Installation — To install, reverse removal procedures.

CYLINDER HEAD & MANIFOLDS (ENGINE IN VEHICLE)

Removal — **1)** Disconnect battery ground cable. Remove air cleaner and disconnect throttle cable. Disconnect kick-down cable (automatic transmission) and remove pipe from EGR valve and intake manifold. Disconnect vacuum hose at EGR valve. Remove oil filler cap and stuff rag in filler hole. Disconnect crankcase ventilation pipe from intake manifold and remove intake manifold front, gaskets, and rubber rings.

2) Disconnect fuel line and connector from cold start injector. Disconnect vacuum hose, connector and two fuel lines from control pressure regulator. Disconnect hoses, pipes and electrical connectors, and remove auxiliary air valve. Remove connector at fuel distributor and wiring harness. Disconnect high tension leads from spark plugs and injectors from holders in both banks.

3) Disconnect vacuum hose at distributor, and remove vacuum, carbon filter, diverter valve, power brake, and heater hoses at intake manifold. Disconnect wires at throttle micro switch and solenoid valve, and fuel lines from filter and return pipe. Remove fuel distributor.

4) Disconnect EGR valve hose from throttle housing. Remove cold start injector and pipe. Remove intake manifold and rubber rings. Remove splash guard under engine and drain coolant from both sides of block. Remove air pump, vacuum pump and vacuum hoses at thermostat. Disconnect upper radiator hose and remove A/C compressor (do not remove hoses).

5) Remove distributor and EGR valve and bracket. Disconnect relay connectors and remove rear A/C bracket. Remove lower radiator hose at water pump and hoses from pump to cylinder heads. Disconnect supply hose from cylinder heads, and separate air manifold at rear of engine. Remove backfire valve and air hose. Remove valve covers.

6) On left side, remove four upper timing gear cover bolts and Allen head screw (not camshaft center bolt). On right side, remove four upper timing gear cover bolts and cover plate. Remove exhaust pipe clamps from under vehicle, and remove oil dipstick tube. Remove exhaust pipe flange nuts and exhaust manifold. Remove cover plates at rear of cylinder heads.

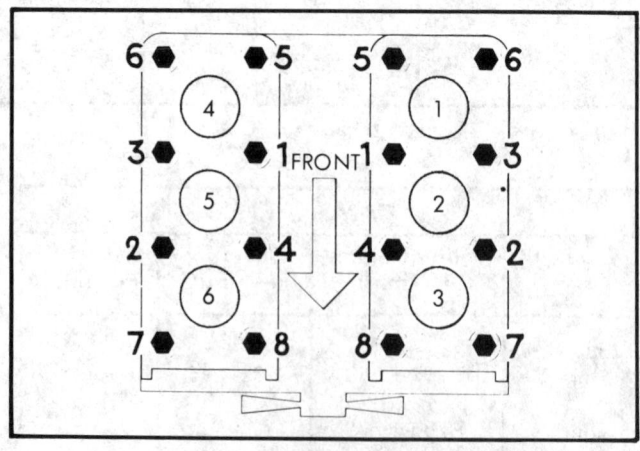

Fig. 1   Sequence for Removing and Installing Cylinder Head Bolts

B28F V6 (Cont.)

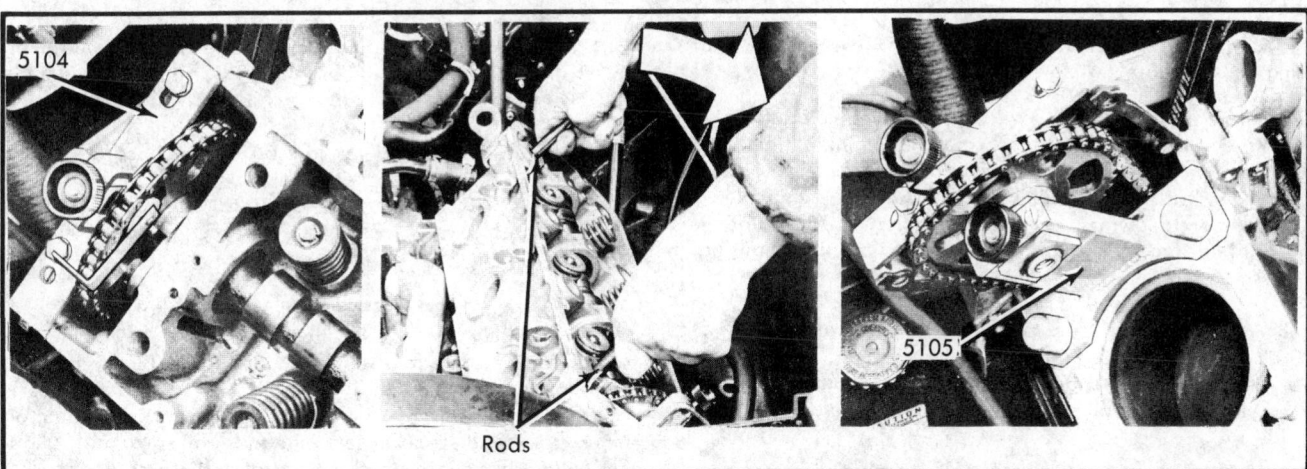

Fig. 2   Special Tools for Removing Cylinder Heads

7) Rotate each camshaft until large hole in sprocket aligns with rocker arm shaft. Remove rocker arm and shaft assembly by removing bolts in sequence shown in *Fig. 1*. Loosen bolt and push camshaft lock fork to one side.

8) Install tool to hold camshaft sprocket in place (5104). With tool installed, remove camshaft center bolt and slide camshaft to rear. Be sure camshaft stud is free from sprocket.

NOTE — *If tool is not used, camshaft chain will slacken and be held by chain tensioner. Sprocket then cannot be pulled upward when installing camshaft. If this should occur, timing gear cover must be removed for access to chain tensioner.*

9) Insert two 12" long rods into cylinder head bolt holes, *Fig. 2*, and push downward to loosen cylinder head from block. Do not attempt to remove cylinder head by lifting straight upward. If liners are not to be removed, be sure they do not separate from their seals in lower liner seat. If seals are damaged, coolant will enter crankcase. Lift out cylinder head carefully.

10) Tap guide sleeves flush with block face and remove gasket. Install liner holders (5093) to secure liners against seat seals. Clean gasket surfaces and install camshaft retaining tool (5105). After tool is securely in place, remove fixing bolt from previously installed tool (5l04). *See Fig. 2.*

NOTE — *Sprocket retaining tool (5105) should be kept securely in place while cylinder heads are removed. This prevents camshaft chains from slackening, yet permits turning of crankshaft.*

Installation — **1)** Insert fixing bolt into camshaft sprocket retainer (5104) and remove other retainer (5105) from cylinder block face. Pull up on guide sleeves and insert a ⅛" drill bit under each sleeve. Remove liner holders (5093) and position cylinder head gasket on block face (left and right gaskets differ). Install cylinder head with one bolt and push camshaft into camshaft sprocket. Install camshaft center bolt, but do not torque. Remove drill bits from under guide sleeves

2) Position rocker arm and shaft assembly and install cylinder head bolts. Tighten all bolts in sequence shown in *Fig. 1* in three stages:

Cylinder Head Tightening Specifications	
Sequence	**Ft. Lbs. (mkg)**
Step One	7 (1.0)
Step Two	22 (3.0)
Step Three	①44 (6.1)
① — After 10-15 minutes retorque with protractor (5098).	

3) Torque camshaft center bolt and remove sprocket retainer (5104). Center lock fork over camshaft and tighten. Back off all cylinder head bolts in sequence, *Fig. 1*. Tighten to 11-14 ft. lbs. Using protractor (5098) on standard socket, torque head bolts as follows:

1. Use rocker arm and shaft as a guide line for protractor.
2. Fit socket over bolt 1 and take up slack of tool. Rotate protractor so that "0" mark aligns with rocker arm and shaft assembly.
3. Tighten bolt until protractor angle of 116-120° aligns with rocker arm guide line.
4. Repeat procedure in proper tightening sequence for other head bolts.
5. After engine is assembled, run at operating temperature for 15 minutes and cool for 30 minutes. Back off head bolts once more and torque to 11-14 ft. lbs. Then use protractor to torque bolts in sequence shown (*Fig. 3*) to 113-117°.

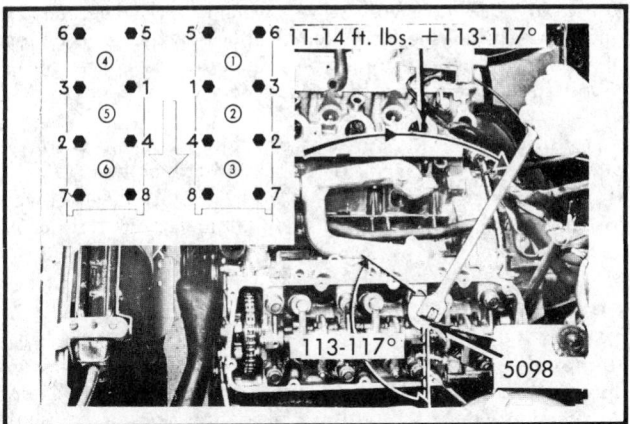

Fig. 3   *Final Torquing of Cylinder Head Bolts After Running and Cooling Engine*

Volvo Engines

B28F V6 (Cont.)

4) Install remainder of components in reverse order of removal procedure, noting the following:

1. Before installing valve cover, adjust valves (cold setting).
2. When installing distributor, rotor should initially point to clamp clockwise from mark on distributor housing. Crankshaft should still be in position for firing No. 1 cylinder following valve adjustment. When distributor is pushed into place, rotor will point to mark on housing. *Fig. 4 and 5.*
3. Use new gaskets and rubber sealing rings.
4. When installing spark plug wires, firing order is 1-6-3-5-2-4.
5. Be sure to fill engine with oil and coolant. Retorque cylinder head bolts after assembly is completed.

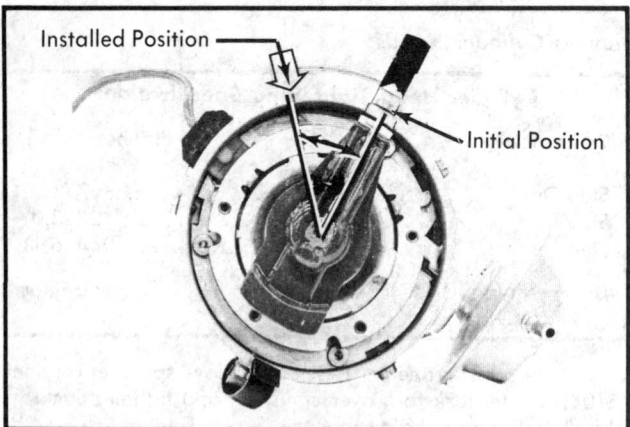

Fig. 4   Distributor Rotor Position Prior to Final Positioning

CAMSHAFT

CAMSHAFT

Removal & Installation — With cylinder head removed, remove lock fork and rear cover plate. Pull camshaft out from rear of head. To install, place camshaft in from rear of cylinder head. Note that camshaft for right bank has distributor drive gear at rear end. Install lock fork at front and cover plate at rear of head.

TIMING GEAR COVER

Removal — Remove both valve covers, lock flywheel (5112), and remove crankshaft nut. Remove pulley while key is on top of shaft (prevents dropping key in crankcase). Use puller (5069) to remove crankshaft seal. Remove timing gear cover.

Installation — Clean surfaces and place gaskets on block and timing gear cover. Install cover and tighten bolts to 7-11 ft. lbs. Install crankshaft seal (drift 5103). Block flywheel with locking tool (5112), install pulley and tighten crankshaft nut to 118-132 ft. lbs.

CHAINS & SPROCKETS

Removal — **1)** Remove timing gear cover, oil pump chain, sprocket, oil pump and gears. Turn each tensioner lock ¼ turn counterclockwise and push in piston to slacken camshaft chains. Remove both tensioners, strainers, and curved and straight dampers. Remove camshaft sprockets and chains.

2) Stuff rag in holes near crankcase to keep key from falling in crankcase. Remove outer sprocket and inner double sprocket from crankshaft (either by hand or with puller).

Installation — **1)** Place key in crankshaft. Oil sprocket and shaft. Install double sprocket (drift 4028) with mark outward. Install spacer ring and outer key. Install oil pump sprocket, strainers and chain tensioners, and curved and straight dampers.

2) Rotate crankshaft so key aligns with camshaft in left bank (No. 1 cylinder at TDC). Position camshaft so key points upward (rocker arms for No. 1 cylinder rock). Place chain on camshaft sprocket so that link between two white lines is centered over camshaft sprocket timing mark. Place chain on inner crankshaft sprocket so timing mark on sprocket is aligned with white mark on chain. Install left camshaft sprocket onto camshaft so that pin on sprocket slips into recess in camshaft. Chain should be stretched on tension side. Use screwdriver to hold sprocket and tighten center bolt to 51-59 ft. lbs.

Fig. 5   Adjusting Crankshaft to Firing Position for No. 1 Cylinder

3) Rotate crankshaft clockwise 150° so that key points straight downward. Set right camshaft so keyway is in position shown in *Fig. 6*. Place chain on sprocket so link between

Fig. 6   Right Camshaft Keyway and Timing Marks

B28F V6 (Cont.)

white lines on chain aligns with sprocket timing mark. Place chain on crankshaft center sprocket so that chain and sprocket timing marks align. Fit sprocket on camshaft with chain stretched on tension side. Pin on sprocket should slip into camshaft recess. Use screwdriver to hold sprocket and torque center bolt to 51-59 ft. lbs.

4) Turn lock on each chain tensioner ¼ turn clockwise. Tension chains by rotating crankshaft 2 full turns in direction of rotation (clockwise). Remove crankshaft nut. Markings on chains and sprockets will no longer align. Reassemble oil pump, install chain and chain sprocket. Install timing gear cover after removing rag from crankcase holes.

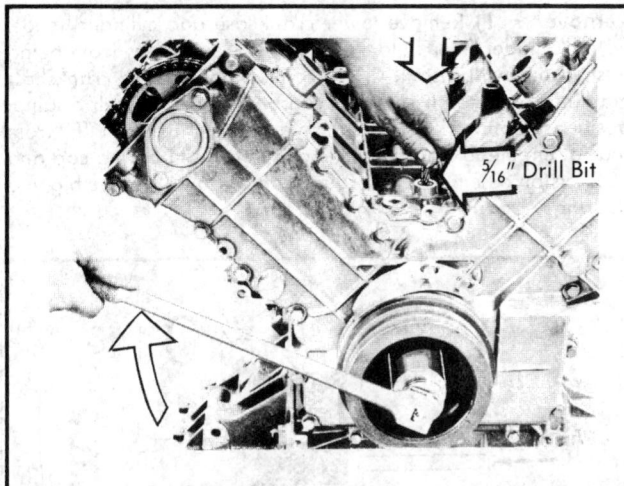

Fig. 7   Locating Top Dead Center for No. 1 Cylinder

IGNITION TIMING PLATE

1) Rotate crankshaft so that mark No. 1 is at 20° mark on ignition timing plate. See Fig. 5. Remove plug and insert ⁵⁄₁₆" drill bit or similar rod into hole and against crankshaft counterweight. See Fig. 7. Rotate crankshaft in direction of normal rotation until drill bit can be pressed into recess in counterweight (TDC for No. 1 cylinder).

NOTE – Do not drop drill bit into engine. Use drill or pin up to 10" long.

2) Loosen two bolts and adjust ignition timing plate so that "0" mark is aligned with pulley mark. Tighten two bolts, remove drill bit or rod and install plug. Check camshaft setting. Valve clearance should be .028" (.7 mm). Intake valves for cylinders No. 1 and 6 should open between 6 and 12 degrees on crankshaft vibration damper.

ROCKER ARM ASSEMBLY

Removal – Mark rocker assemblies as to which head they belong. Remove lock ring from end of shaft, and remove rocker arms, shaft supports, spacer sleeves, and springs. Keep all parts in order for correct assembly. Remove the lock bolt and rocker shaft support from rocker shaft. Check shaft-to-arm clearance. New part clearance is .0005-.0021" (.012-.054 mm). New shaft diameter is .7858-.7866" (19.96-19.98 mm). Replace worn parts as necessary.

Installation – Install rocker shaft support on rocker shaft with lubricating holes pointing downward. The flat top surface should face toward lock ring groove in other end of shaft. Tighten lock bolt. Install thick spacer, exhaust rocker arm, thin spacer, intake rocker arm, spring, and rocker shaft support, in order. After installing 2 more such sets, install lock ring in rocker shaft groove.

VALVES

VALVE ARRANGEMENT

Right Bank	E-I-E-I-E-I (Front-to-Rear)
Left Bank	I-E-I-E-I-E (Front-to-Rear)

VALVE STEM OIL SEALS AND VALVE SPRINGS

With cylinder head removed from engine, remove spark plugs, injectors, rear cover plate, lock fork and camshaft. Using valve spring compressor, remove valve collets, spring retainer, spring, lower spring seat and valve. Remove valve guide seal from guide. Place valves in order in suitable rack.

VALVE GUIDE SERVICING

1) Check valve guides for wear. If replacement is necessary, press out old guide using drift (2818). Ream hole in cylinder head to oversize class 1 or 2:

Valve Guide Specifications

Application	Diameter In. (mm)
Cylinder Head Hole, Class 1	.5193-.5209 (13.19-13.23)
Cylinder Head Hole, Class 2	.5311-.5327 (13.49-13.53)
Valve Guide, Class 1	①.5228-.5232 (13.28-13.29)
Valve Guide Class 2	①.5346-.5350 (13.58-13.59)

① — Oversize Valve Guides Shown

2) Using drifts (5108 for intake; 5109 for exhaust), press in new guides. Ream guides to .3150-.3158" (8.00-8.02 mm). Check for burrs and be sure valves move freely in guides.

RECONDITIONING VALVES

After inspection, grind valves, mill or grind valve seats, and lap valves with grinding paste, as necessary. Check valve springs for proper length and tension. Install seals, valves, spring seats, spring, and spring retainers. Compress spring and install collets. Remove tool, and reinstall all parts previously removed from cylinder head.

VALVE CLEARANCE ADJUSTMENT

1) Rotate crankshaft with 1⁷⁄₁₆" (36 mm) wrench to bring No. 1 piston to TDC. See Fig. 5. In this position, both rocker arms for No. 1 cylinder should have clearance and not rock. Check and adjust the following cylinders for clearance: Intake valves on cylinders 1, 2, and 4; exhaust valves on cylinders 1, 3, and 6 (White valves in Fig. 8).

Volvo Engines

B28F V6 (Cont.)

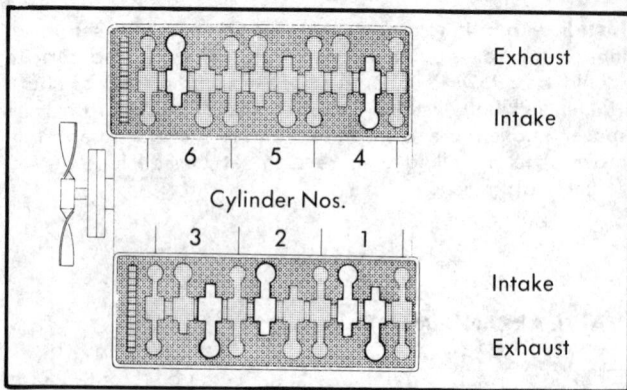

Fig. 8   Valve Clearance Adjustment Sequence

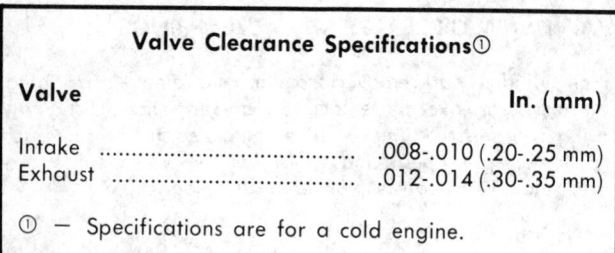

Valve Clearance Specifications①	
Valve	**In. (mm)**
Intake	.008-.010 (.20-.25 mm)
Exhaust	.012-.014 (.30-.35 mm)

① — Specifications are for a cold engine.

2) Rotate crankshaft one full turn so marking is again opposite 0° mark. Rocker arms for No. 1 cylinder will now rock. Check and adjust the following cylinders for clearance: Intake valves on cylinders 3, 5, and 6; exhaust valves on cylinders 2, 4, and 5 (Grey valves in *Fig. 8*).

PISTONS, PINS & RINGS

LOWER CRANKCASE

Removal — Remove oil pan and gasket, oil strainer and baffle plate. Remove 14 crankcase bolts and 8 main bearing nuts. Lift off lower crankcase. Install main bearing cap retainers (5096) on two outer bearings.

Installation — 1) Install rubber ring for oil channel. Clean and apply sealing compound to crankcase and block surfaces. Remove main bearing cap retainers and install lower crankcase.

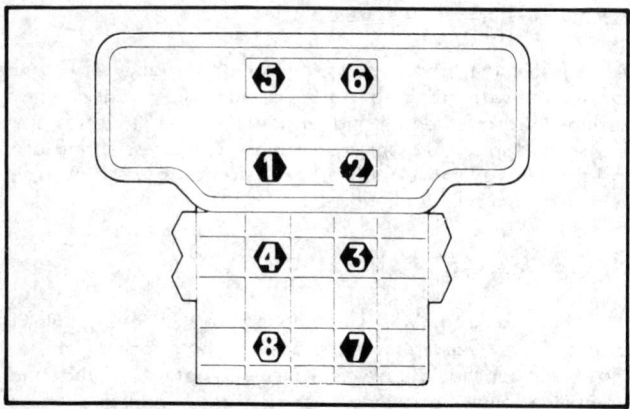

Fig. 9   Tightening Sequence for Main Bearing Nuts

2) Be sure crankcase and block are flush at rear end and tighten main bearing nuts to 22 ft. lbs. (3.1 mkg) torque. Use sequence shown in *Fig. 9*, then back off No. 1 nut and retorque to 22-25 ft. lbs. (3.1-3.5 mkg). Using protractor tool (5098), tighten nut an additional 73-77°. Continue in sequence, backing off each nut, torque tightening, and then angle tightening to specifications.

3) Tighten 14 lower crankcase bolts to 11-15 ft. lbs. Install baffle plate, oil strainer, gasket and oil pan.

PISTON & ROD ASSEMBLIES

Removal — 1) Remove lower crankcase and cylinder heads. Install cylinder liner holders (5093) to keep liners from being pushed out with piston. Check connecting rod and crankshaft markings so piston assemblies can be installed in their original positions. Connecting rods are marked "A" through "F" from rear of engine to front. Remove cap nuts and bearing cap and push piston assembly out through top of bore. Remove big end bearing.

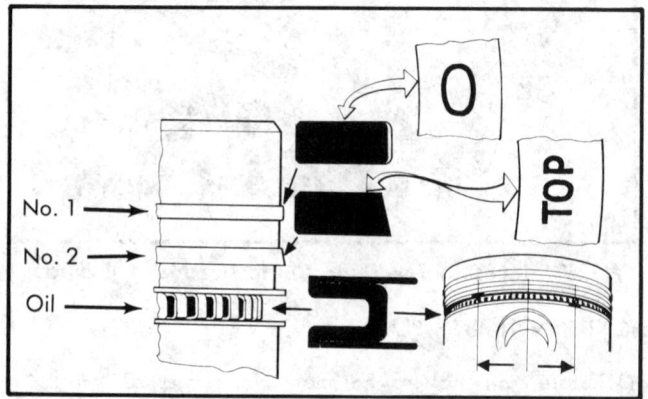

Fig. 10   Piston Ring Location and Markings

2) Remove piston rings and clean ring grooves and piston of any carbon deposits. Measure the side clearance and end gap of piston rings with a feeler gauge. Replace any components not within specifications.

Installation — 1) Install piston rings with end gaps at 120° angles from each other. Offset the gaps on the oil control rings. Note position marking on compression rings, and install with markings pointing up. See *Fig. 10*.

2) Lightly lubricate rings, and, using installation tool (5106) press piston into proper bore. Make sure that stamped arrow on top of piston is pointing toward the front of engine. This will introduce a clearance between the big end bearing and the crankshaft journal. This clearance should be positioned behind for cylinders 1, 2, and 3, and in front for cylinders 4, 5, and 6. Install bearing cap, and tighten to 33-37 ft. lbs. (4.6-5.1 mm).

PISTONS & LINERS

1) Pistons and liners are available only as matched sets. Pistons are classified by diameter in 3 catagories. Marking on piston top is either A, B, or C, and corresponds to liners marked 1, 2, or 3 respectively. The liners are marked in the recesses at the top of the liner. Pistons and piston pins are also

Volvo Engines

B28F V6 (Cont.)

classified by diameters, with blue, red, and white markings being used instead of numbers for proper matching.

Piston and Liner Diameters	
Piston Designation	**Diameter In. (mm)**
"Mahle" A	3.5815-3.5819 (90.97-90.98)
"Mahle" B	3.5819-3.5823 (90.98-90.99)
"Mahle" C	3.5823-3.5827 (90.99-91.00)
Liner Designation	**Diameter In. (mm)**
"1" (for piston A)	3.5827-3.5831 (91.00-91.01)
"2" (for piston B)	3.5831-3.5835 (91.01-91.02)
"3" (for piston C)	3.5835-3.5839 (91.02-91.03)

2) Measure piston diameter at right angles to pin bore. Take measurements .236" (6.0 mm) above lower edge. With an inside dial indicator, check cylinder liner taper, wear, and out-of-round. Take measurement for maximum wear immediately below top dead center, and at a right angle to engine center line. Take measurement for minimum wear at bottom dead center of piston stroke.

3) To determine piston-to-cylinder clearance, subtract piston diameter from maximum and minimum bore diameters. Do not remove pistons from connecting rods, unless piston and liner replacement is necessary.

4) If liner is to be removed for cleaning or inspection, mark liner and block with colored pen. Do not damage gasket surface. Remove liner holders and pull up liners. When installing liners, be sure contact surfaces on block and liner are clean and without defect. Install No. 1 liner first (without shims) using previous pen markings for alignment. Tighten liner by hand, using two liner holders (5093). Using dial indicator, measure liner height above block at three points. Largest measurement should not exceed smallest measurement by more than .002" (.05 mm). Liner should be as close to .0091" (.23 mm) above block face as possible. Use correct shims to achieve dimension:

Liner Shim Thicknesses①	
Color	**Thickness — In. (mm)**
Blue	.0028-.0041 (.070-.105)
White	.0033-.0047 (.085-.120)
Red	.0041-.0055 (.105-.140)
Yellow	.0051-.0065 (.130-.165)
① — Use same thickness shims for all liners.	

5) Install shims with color marking up and positioned as shown in *Fig. 11*. Inner tabs on shims should be in liner groove.

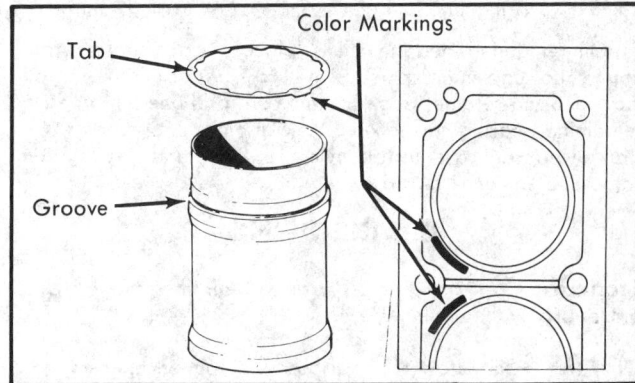

Fig. 11   Positioning Shims on Liners

6) After shimming, install four liner holders (5093) for each bank. Again measure each liner at three points. Largest and smallest dimensions should be within .002" (.05 mm). Measure three liners at points shown in *Fig. 12*. Difference in measurements between points "1" and "2" and between "3" and "4" should not exceed .0016" (.04 mm). If height difference is excessive, change shims.

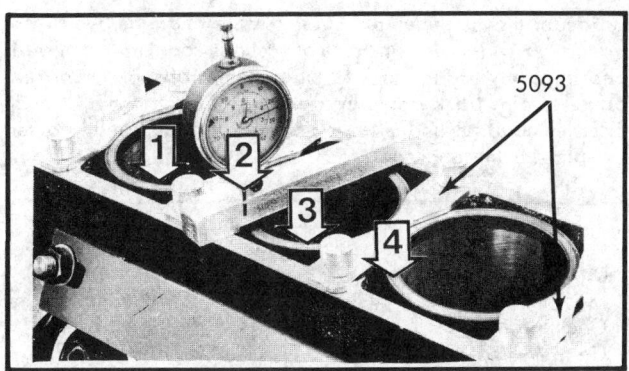

Fig. 12   Checking Liner Height Above Block Face

CRANKSHAFT MAIN & CONNECTING ROD BEARINGS

CRANKSHAFT

Removal — 1) Remove oil pan, lower crankcase, cylinder heads, clutch, drive plate or flywheel, spacer (automatic transmission) and input shaft pilot bearing (manual transmission). Remove seal holder and use drift (5107) to press out seal. Press new seal in flush with retainer.

2) Check main bearing cap markings (marked 1 through 4, from rear-to-front). Remove main bearing retainers and caps. Remove upper and lower thrust bearings and lift out crankshaft. Remove main bearings from block and caps.

Installation — 1) After inspecting crankshaft and measuring journals for wear, position oiled main bearings with oil holes to the engine block. Carefully set crankshaft into place. Oil and install thrust bearings with notched ends in the engine block groove. Oil and install unnotched thrust bearings on the crankshaft.

2) Noting that cap identification number faces front of engine, lubricate bearing shell and position in bearing cap. Install bearing cap and bearing retainers (5096). Using a dial in-

Volvo Engines

B28F V6 (Cont.)

dicator, measure crankshaft end play and install thrust washers to bring end play to .0028-.0106" (.07-.27 mm).

3) Oil remaining bearing shells, place in caps, and install, noting that cap number points toward front of engine. Install main bearing retainer on rear main cap, and one nut on each remaining bearing cap to keep them in place until ready to install lower crankcase. Install lower crankcase and torque main caps. See *Lower Crankcase.*

ENGINE OILING

Crankcase Capacity — 6.8 quarts with oil filter change, and 6.3 quarts without filter change.

Oil Filter — Full-flow type, disposable, spin-on element.

Oil Pressure — With engine warm and a new filter installed, minimum 26 psi@900 RPM, and 58 psi@3000 RPM.

ENGINE OILING SYSTEM

Engine utilizes a force-feed lubrication system. Oil moves from oil pan through strainer to oil pump and full-flow oil filter mounted outside of engine block assembly. Oil is pressure fed from filter to drilled galleries in block.

Lubricant moves under pressure to main bearings, which are drilled to pass oil on to connecting rod and camshaft bearings, upward in block to rocker arm shafts. Excess or run-off oil drains back down into oil pan through drain holes in cylinder head. Cylinder walls and piston rings are lubricated by splash from connecting rods.

Dimension Application	In. (mm)
Gear Width, Class I	1.2167-1.2175 (30.95-30.925)
Gear Width, Class II	1.2175-1.2183 (30.925-30.945)
Housing Width, Class I	1.2185-1.2195 (30.950-30.975)
Housing Width, Class II	1.2195-1.2209 (30.97531.010)
End Play	.0010-.0033 (.025-.033)
Clearance (Tooth-to-Housing) ...	①.0043-.0073 (.11-.185)
Backlash	①.0067-.0106 (.17-.27)
Bearing Clearance, Driving Shaft	.0006-.0021 (.015-.053)
Bearing Clearance, Trailing Shaft	.006-.0020 (.015-.051)
Relief Valve Spring Length, No Load	3.52 (89.5)

① — Excluding bearing clearance.

OIL PUMP

The oil pump is stocked as a complete unit (housing cover with impeller, and relief valve). Inspect housing, cover, and gears for damage and wear. Replace if necessary.

Removal — Remove both valve covers, crankshaft pulley, and timing gear cover. Remove oil pump drive sprocket and chain. Loosen the 4 retaining bolts, and lift out oil pump and gears.

Installation — Place gears on shaft, and oil the housing, gears and shaft. Install pump assembly, ensuring pump gears and shafts are centered in housing before tightening bolts. Install pump drive sprocket and chain. Install remaining components in reverse of removal order.

ENGINE COOLING

Thermostat — Wax-type. Begins to open at 176-181° F (80-83° C); fully open at 194-201° F (90-94° C). Marking, 180° F (82° C).

Cooling System Capacity — All models, 11.5 quarts.

Radiator Cap — 9-12 psi.

WATER PUMP

1) Drain coolant from both sides of block. Remove intake manifold, two expansion tank hoses from radiator, upper radiator hose and automatic transmission oil cooler pipes. Remove fan shroud, radiator and fan.

2) Remove hoses from pump to block. Remove fan belts, water pump pulley, and remaining hose clamps. Remove senders from water pump, and pump from block. Remove cover and thermostat and cover from body. Install in reverse order.

TIGHTENING SPECIFICATIONS

Application	Ft. Lbs. (mkg)
Cylinder Head Bolts	
Step 1	7 (1.0)
Step 2	22 (3.1)
Step 3	44 (6.1)
Main Bearing Cap Nuts	22-25 (3.1-3.5) Plus 75°
Connecting Rod Cap Nuts	33-37 (4.6-5.1)
Flywheel Bolts	33-37 (4.6-5.1)
Camshaft Gear Center Bolt	51-59 (7.1-8.2)
Crankshaft Pulley Nut	118-132 (16.0-18.0)
Transmission-to-Engine	30-36 (4.2-5.0)
Intake Manifold Bolts	7-11 (4.2-5.0)
Exhaust Manifold Bolts	7-11 (4.2-5.0)
Lower Crankcase Bolts	11-15 (1.5-2.0)

ENGINE SPECIFICATIONS

GENERAL SPECIFICATIONS

Year	Displ.		Carburetor	HP at RPM	Torque (Ft. Lbs. at RPM)	Compr. Ratio	Bore		Stroke	
	cu. ins.	cc					in.	mm	in.	mm
1980 B28F	174	2849	Fuel Inj.	130@5500	153@2750	8.8:1	3.58	91.0	2.87	73

Volvo Engines

B28F V6 (Cont.)

ENGINE SPECIFICATIONS (Cont.)

VALVES							
Engine & Valve	Head Diam. In. (mm)	Face Angle	Seat Angle	Seat Width In. (mm)	① Stem Diameter In. (mm)	① Stem Clearance In. (mm)	Valve Lift In. (mm)
2849 cc Intake	1.73 (44)	30°	30°	.067-.083 (1.7-2.1)	.3140-.3146 (7.97-7.99)	.0004-.0018 (.010-.046)	.2364 (6.004)
Exhaust	1.46 (37)	30°	30°	.079-.094 (2.0-2.4)	.3136-.3142 (7.96-7.98)	.0008-.0022 (.020-.056)	.2364 (6.004)

① — Stem diameter gets larger from disc toward collet end of valve, where measurement above is taken.

PISTONS, PINS, RINGS						
	PISTONS	PINS		RINGS		
Engine	Clearance In. (mm)	Piston Fit In. (mm)	Rod Fit In. (mm)	Rings	End Gap In. (mm)	Side Clearance In. (mm)
2849 cc	Mahle .0008-.0016 (.020-.040)	Push Fit .0004-.0006 (.010-.015)	Press Fit .0008-.0016 (.020-.041)	Comp. 1	.016-.022 (.40-55)	.0018-.0029 (.045-.074)
				Comp. 2	.016-.022 (.40-.55)	.0010-.0021 (.025-.054)
				Oil	.015-.055 (.38-1.4)	.0004.0092 (.009-.233)

CRANKSHAFT MAIN & CONNECTING ROD BEARINGS						
	MAIN BEARINGS				CONNECTING ROD BEARINGS	
Engine	Journal Diam. In. (mm)	Clearance In. (mm)	Thrust Bearing	Crankshaft End Play In. (mm)	Journal Diam. In. (mm)	Clearance In. (mm)	Side Play In. (mm)
2849 cc	2.7576-2.7583 (70.043-70.062)	.0015-.0035 (.038-.088)	.....	.0028-.0106 (.070-.270)	2.0578-2.0585 (52.267-52.286)	.0012-.0031 (.030-.080)	.008-.015 (.20-.38)

CAMSHAFT			
Engine	Journal Diam. In. (mm)	Clearance In. (mm)	Lobe Lift In. (mm)
2849 cc Front	1.5921-1.5931 (40.440-40.465)	①.0014-.0033 (.035-.085)	.....
2nd	1.6157-1.6173 (41.040-41.065)		
3rd	1.6394-1.6404 (41.640-41.665)		
4th	1.6630-1.6640 (42.240-42.265)		

VALVE SPRINGS			
Engine	Free Length In. (mm)	PRESSURE Lbs. @ In. (kg @ mm)	
		Valve Closed	Valve Open
2849 cc	1.854 (47.1)	52-60@1.57 (24-27@40)	135-152@1.181 (61.3-68.9@30.0)

① — End play should be .0028-.0057" (.070-.144 mm).

Contents

Section 6
CLUTCHES

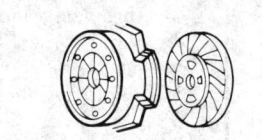

Clutches

CLUTCH TROUBLE SHOOTING

CONDITION	POSSIBLE CAUSE	CORRECTION
▶ Chattering or Grabbing	1) Incorrect Lever Adjustment	1) Adjust Clutch
	2) Oil or Grease on Facings	2) Check for Oil Leaks
	3) Loose "U" Joint Flange	3) Check "U" Joint Flange and Tighten
	4) Worn Input Shaft Spline	4) Replace Shaft
	5) Binding Pressure Plate	5) Check for Binding, Replace as Necessary
	6) Binding Release Lever	6) Free Binding Levers or Replace
	7) Binding Disc Hub	7) Replace Disc and Adjust Clutch
	8) Glazed Facings	8) Replace Disc After Checking Pressure Plate and Flywheel for Scoring. Replace as Necessary
	9) Unequal Pressure Plate Contact	9) Check Release Lever Clearance, Disc Thickness, and Pressure Plate for Paralleism with Flywheel
	10) Bent Clutch Disc	10) Replace Clutch Disc
	11) Uneven Spring Pressure	11) Adjust Spring Tension
	12) Incorrect Transmission Alignment.	12) Check Clutch Housing Alignment
	13) Loose Facings	13) Replace Clutch Disc
	14) Scored Pressure Plate	14) Replace Pressure Plate if Warped More Than .015"
	15) Worn Pressure Plate, Disc or Flywheel	15) Replace When There are Signs of Excessive Wear, Heat Checking or Scoring
	16) Clutch Disc Hub Sticking on Shaft	16) Check Shaft for Excessive Wear or Burrs, Check Shaft for Distortion and Replace as Necessary
	17) Worn or Binding Release Levers	17) Replace Levers and Release Bearing
	18) Broken or Weak Pressure Springs	18) Replace Springs
	19) Sticking Clutch Pedal	19) Check for Worn or Misaligned Components
	20) Incorrect Disc Facing	20) Replace Clutch Disc
	21) Engine Loose in Chassis	21) Check Motor Mounts and Replace or Tighten
▶ Spinning	1) Dry or Worn Bushings	1) Replace Bushings
	2) Misaligned Clutch Housing	2) Check Clutch Housing Alignment
	3) Bent or Distorted Clutch Disc.	3) Replace Clutch Disc
	4) Warped Pressure Plate	4) Replace Pressure Plate
	5) Excessive Pedal Free Play	5) Readjust Pedal Free Play

Clutches

CLUTCH TROUBLE SHOOTING

CONDITION	POSSIBLE CAUSE	CORRECTION
▶ **Dragging**	1) Oil or Grease on Facings	1) Free Release Levers
	2) Incorrect Lever Adjustment	2) Check for Damage and Readjust Lever
	3) Incorrect Pedal Adjustment	3) Adjust Pedal
	4) Dust or Dirt on Clutch	4) Disassemble Clutch and Clean Throughly
	5) Worn or Broken Facings	5) Replace Clutch Disc
	6) Bent Clutch Disc	6) Replace Clutch Disc, Check for Cause
	7) Clutch Disc Hub Binding on Shaft	7) Check Shaft for Burrs or Gummed Splines
	8) Binding Pilot Bushing	8) Replace Pilot Bushing
	9) Sticking Release Bearing Sleeve	9) Free Sleeve, Check for Scoring or Rough Spots
	10) Warped Pressure Plate	10) Replace Pressure Plate if Worn More Than .015"
▶ **Rattling**	1) Weak or Broken Release Lever Spring	1) Replace Spring
	2) Damaged Pressure Plate	2) Replace Pressure Plate and Adjust Clutch
	3) Broken Clutch Return Spring	3) Replace Return Spring
	4) Worn Splines in Clutch Disc Hub or Transmission Input Shaft	4) Replace Clutch Disc or Transmission Input Shaft
	5) Worn Clutch Release Bearings	5) Replace Release Bearing, Check Tips of Release Levers for Wear, Replace as Necessary
	6) Dry or Worn Pilot Bushing	6) Lubricate or Replace Pilot Bushing
	7) Unequal Release Lever Contact	7) Readjust Release Levers
	8) Incorrect Pedal Freeplay	8) Adjust Pedal Free Play
	9) Warped Clutch Disc	9) Replace Clutch Disc, Check Pressure Plate for Wear and Replace as Necessary
▶ **Slipping**	1) Pressure Springs Worn or Broken	1) Replace Springs
	2) Worn Facing	2) Replace Clutch Disc
	3) Incorrect Clutch Alignment	3) Adjust Clutch
	4) Oil or Grease on Facings	4) Replace Clutch Disc, Fix Oil Leaks
	5) Warped Clutch Disc	5) Replace Clutch Disc
	6) Warped or Scored Pressure Plate	6) Replace Pressure Plate if Scored, Heat Checked, or Warped More Than .015", Test Spring Tension and Replace Clutch Disc
	7) Binding Release Levers	7) Free Release Lever
	8) Binding Clutch Pedal	8) Check for Worn or Misaligned Parts

Clutches

CLUTCH TROUBLE SHOOTING

CONDITION	POSSIBLE CAUSE	CORRECTION
► Squeaking	1) No Lubrication in Release Bearing	1) Lubricate
	2) Worn Release Bearing	2) Replace Release Bearing
	3) Dry or Worn Pilot Bushing	3) Lubricate or Replace Pilot Bushing
	4) Pilot Bearing Turning in Crankshaft	4) Replace Pilot Bearing
	5) Worn Input Shaft Bearing	5) Replace Input Shaft Bearing
	6) Incorrect Transmission Alignment	6) Check Clutch Housing Alignment
	7) No Lubrication Between Clutch Fork and Pivot	7) Lubricate
	8) No Lubrication in Torque Shaft	8) Lubricate
► Heavy, Stiff Pedal	1) Dry or Binding Linkage Components	1) Lubricate Linkage Components
	2) Sticking Release Bearing Sleeve	2) Check Release Bearing Sleeve for Wear, Burrs or Roughness on Mating Surface
	3) Dry or Binding Pedal Hub	3) Replace Bushing or Bearings in Pedal Hub and Lubricate
	4) Pedal Interference With Floorboard or Mat	4) Check for Pedal Interference
	5) Rough, Dry or Binding Pivot Ball, or Fork Pivots	5) Lubricate All Moving Points
► Grinding	1) Dry Release Bearing	1) Replace Release Bearing
	2) Worn or Dry Pilot Bearing	2) Lubricate or Replace Pilot Bearing
	3) Worn Input Shaft Bearing	3) Replace Input Shaft Bearing
► Whirring	1) Incorrect Pedal Free Play	1) Adjust Pedal Free Play
	2) Incorrect Transmission Alignment	2) Check Clutch Housing Alignment

AUDI 4000

DESCRIPTION

Clutch is single plate dry disc type, using a diaphragm type pressure plate and a pre-lubricated clutch release bearing. Clutch is cable actuated.

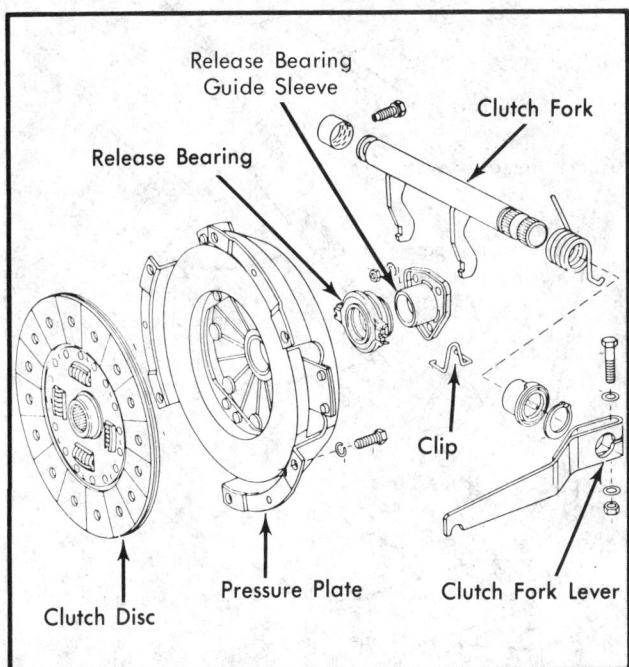

Fig. 1 Exploded View of Clutch Assembly

REMOVAL & INSTALLATION

CLUTCH ASSEMBLY

Removal — 1) Disconnect negative battery cable. Disconnect exhaust header pipe at manifold and bracket on transmission.

2) Remove bolt mounting shift assembly coupling to rear of transmission shifting shaft and separate assemblies. Unhook clutch cable at release lever. Disconnect speedometer.

3) Disconnect axle drive shafts at inner drive flanges. Remove starter. Take out front clutch housing cover plate. Remove transmission-to-engine mounting bolts.

4) Suitably support transmission with jack. Remove transmission rear mounts and brackets. Pry transmission away from engine and slide it out of vehicle.

5) Install holding tool (10-201) to flywheel and index (mark) pressure plate and flywheel. Loosen pressure plate bolts ¼ turn at a time in a diagonal pattern. Slide pressure plate off flywheel dowels and separate clutch disc.

Installation — To install, reverse removal procedure and note: Use clutch alignment tool to fit pressure plate and clutch. Make sure alignment marks are observed.

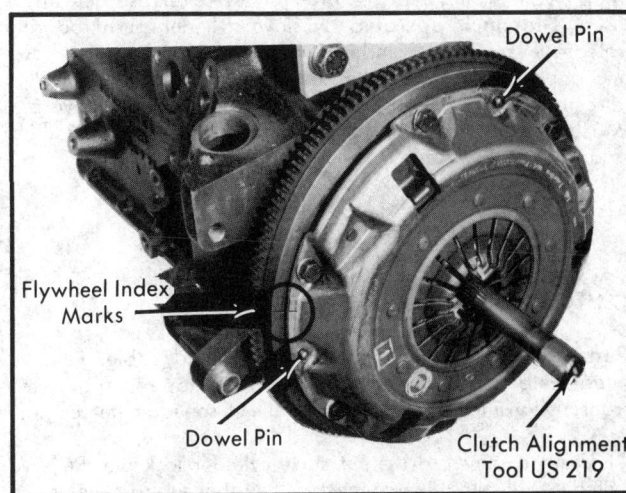

Fig. 2 Aligning Clutch Assembly Reference Marks for Reinstallation

CLUTCH RELEASE BEARING

1) With transmission separated from engine, remove spring clips securing release bearing to clutch fork. Bearing is pre-lubricated; do not wash in any cleaning solution.

2) Rotate bearing and check for roughness or noise, replace as necessary. Apply Molykote paste to bearing contact points on clutch fork. To install, reverse removal procedure.

PILOT BEARING

Lock flywheel to prevent rotation. Install suitable remover (10-202) and remove pilot bearing. Install bearing with suitable installer (VW207C) and seat bearing until distance from flywheel recess to bushing edge is ¹⁄₁₆" (1.5 mm). Lubricate bearing.

ADJUSTMENT

CLUTCH PEDAL FREE PLAY

Adjust clutch pedal free play by loosening and adjusting both counternuts at clutch cable. Pedal will have .59" (15 mm) free play when properly adjusted.

TIGHTENING SPECIFICATIONS

Application	Ft. Lbs. (mkg)
Clutch Assembly-to-Flywheel	18 (2.5)
Transmission-to-Engine	40 (5.5)

Clutches

AUDI 5000

DESCRIPTION

Clutch is a single plate, dry disc type. Pressure plate is a diaphragm spring type. A pre-lubricated release bearing is used. Bearing is operated by slave cylinder push rod and release lever. Slave cylinder is mounted to top of clutch housing and extends to inside of housing. Clutch pedal is hooked directly to clutch master cylinder push rod fork via a clevis pin. Master cylinder is secured to clutch/brake pedal mounting brace.

REMOVAL & INSTALLATION

CLUTCH ASSEMBLY

Removal — 1) Disconnect battery ground cable. Remove windshield washer bottle. Remove upper engine-to-transmission mounting bolts. Disconnect speedometer cable.

2) Using a punch, drive out slave cylinder lock pin. Remove cylinder with fluid line connected. Suitably support weight of engine. Remove exhaust heat shield. Disconnect exhaust pipe at manifold.

3) Disconnect axle drive shafts at transaxle and hang out of way. Disconnect back-up light wire. Pry off both shifting and adjusting rods. Remove lower engine-to-transmission mounting bolts.

4) Take out starter. Remove subframe cover shield. Slightly raise transmission. Remove transmission support bolts and bushings from both sides of subframe, then loosen both rear subframe mounting bolts. Remove right side transmission bracket. Remove transmission off dowels and take out of vehicle.

5) Index mark position of pressure plate in relation to flywheel. Insert flywheel retainer tool. Loosen pressure plate mounting bolt evenly in a diagonal pattern until pressure is relieved. Remove pressure plate and clutch disc.

Installation — To install, reverse removal procedure and note following: Clutch disc spring cage must face pressure plate. Clutch disc must slide freely with no radial play on input shaft. Lubricate input shaft splines with appropriate grease. Align pressure plate index marks. Use clutch disc alignment tool to center disc.

RELEASE BEARING & LEVER

Removal — Remove transmission. Remove cap bolt (attaching 2 retainer pieces) at lower edge of release lever. Slide release lever and bearing out of slave cylinder push rod and off guide sleeve. Disengage circlip and retainer clips keeping release bearing to lever. Separate bearing from lever. If necessary, guide sleeve can also be removed.

Inspection — Check clutch release bearing for wear or unusual noise. Do not wash bearing in solvent. If bearing is excessively noisy, replace.

Installation — To install, reverse removal procedure and note: Lubricate ball cap located in clutch housing with appropriate grease. Make sure clutch release lever locates directly into slave cylinder push rod tip. Push rod tip should be lubricated.

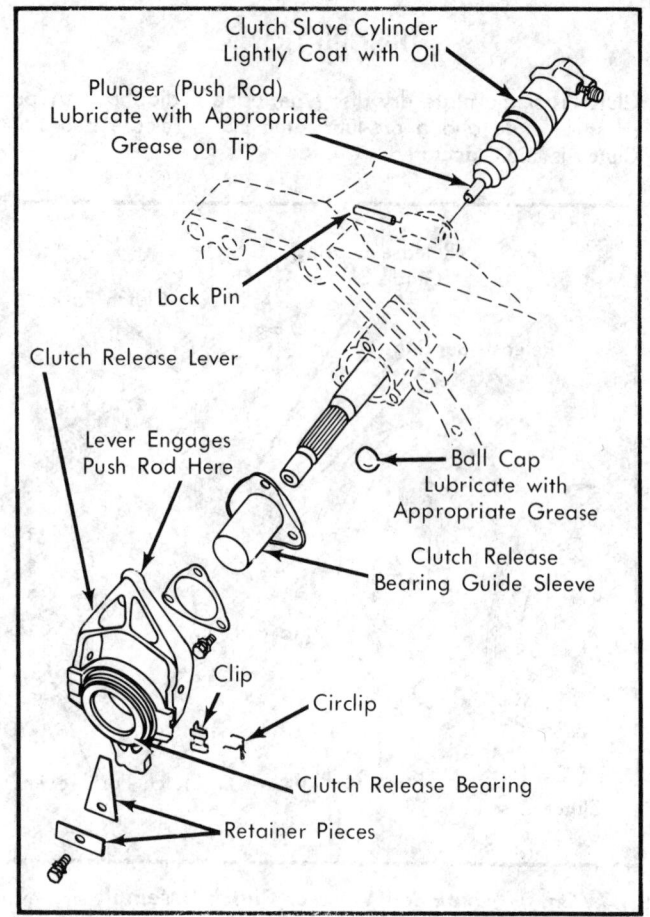

Fig. 1 Clutch Release Bearing with Related Components

MASTER CYLINDER

Removal — Disconnect and plug fluid lines. Separate cylinder from clutch pedal by removing clevis pin. Remove 2 bolts mounting master cylinder to pedal bracket and take out cylinder.

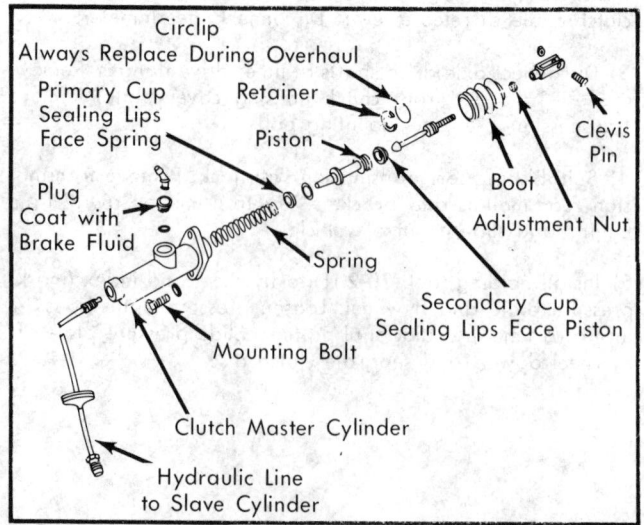

Fig. 2 Exploded View of Master Cylinder

Clutches

AUDI 5000 (Cont.)

Installation — Reverse removal procedure and bleed air from fluid line.

SLAVE CYLINDER

Removal — Working from under vehicle, drive out slave cylinder lock pin located on top of transmission. Slide cylinder back until push rod clears, then maneuver cylinder until fluid line can be disconnected and plugged.

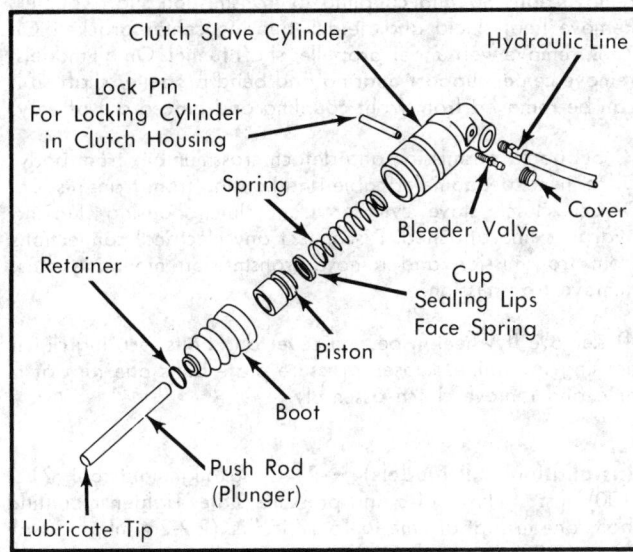

Fig. 3   Exploded View of Slave Cylinder

Installation — To install, reverse removal procedure. Coat outer surface of cylinder with oil before inserting into place. Bleed air from fluid line.

ADJUSTMENTS

CLUTCH PEDAL

Adjust master cylinder push rod so that in the rest position clutch pedal stands ⅜″ (10 mm) above brake pedal.

NOTE — *If clutch pedal is correctly adjusted but fails to properly return, check hydraulic system for air, a tight pedal bushing or jammed return spring.*

HYDRAULIC SYSTEM BLEEDING

Use only pressure bleeding equipment to bleed system. Follow manufacturer's instructions.

TIGHTENING SPECIFICATIONS

Application	Ft. Lbs. (mkg)
Pressure Plate Bolts	18 (2.5)
Drive Flange Bolt	18 (2.5)
Drive Shaft-to-Transaxle Bolts	32 (4.5)

Clutches

BMW

320i
528i
633CSi
733i

DESCRIPTION

Clutch is dry single disc type using a diaphragm spring pressure plate. System is hydraulically operated by a clutch housing mounted slave cylinder and a firewall mounted master cylinder. Slave cylinder automatically adjusts for disc wear.

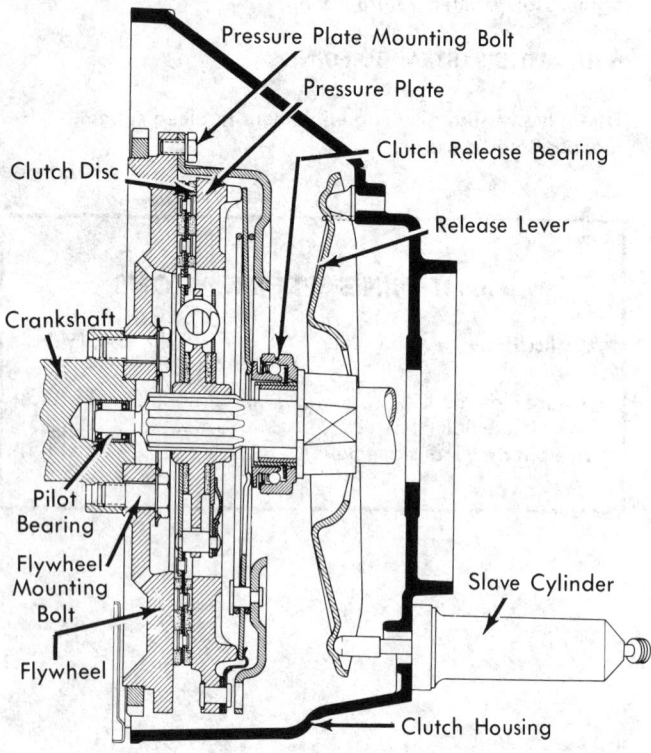

Pressure Plate Mounting Bolt
Pressure Plate
Clutch Disc
Clutch Release Bearing
Release Lever
Crankshaft
Pilot Bearing
Flywheel Mounting Bolt
Flywheel
Slave Cylinder
Clutch Housing

Fig. 1 Typical BMW Clutch Assembly

REMOVAL & INSTALLATION

CLUTCH ASSEMBLY

Removal (320i) — 1) Remove console and lift off circlip and washer from selector with transmission in reverse gear. Lift off selector rod, leaving gearshift lever attached to vehicle. Disconnect speedometer cable and housing from rear of transmission. Disconnect back-up light switch wires.

2) Remove exhaust pipe support bracket and disconnect exhaust pipe from manifold. Fit clamp tool (26 1 012) to propeller shaft coupling and remove bolts mounting propeller shaft to transmission. Remove heat shield and detach center support bearing. Bend propeller shaft down and pull it from centering journal. Place shaft out of way.

3) Detach clutch slave cylinder and hydraulic line bracket from clutch housing. Remove flywheel inspection cover and bolts securing transmission to engine. Support transmission with jack and remove crossmember-to-body bolts. Slide transmission

rearward and lower clear of engine. Loosen pressure plate bolts one turn at a time and remove clutch assembly.

Removal (Except 320i) — 1) Detach selector rod from gearshift lever. From inside vehicle, lift shift lever dust boot and remove circlip holding lever in position. Remove shift lever. Detach any exhaust system components which may interfere with transmission removal.

2) Fit clamp tool (26 1 011) to propeller shaft coupling and remove bolts holding coupling to transmission shaft coupler. Remove heat shield and detach bearing center bracket. On 733i, remove web under propeller shaft tunnel. On all models, remove center support bearing and bend propeller shaft so it can be removed from front coupling and placed out of way.

3) Support transmission and detach crossmember from body. Disconnect speedometer cable and housing from transmission. Detach clutch slave cylinder from clutch housing, leaving hydraulic line attached. Disconnect any electrical connections from transmission and remove transmission mounting nuts. Remove transmission.

4) Remove flywheel inspection cover and bolts securing clutch housing to engine. Loosen pressure plate bolts one turn at a time and remove clutch assembly.

Installation (All Models) — 1) Using alignment tool (21 2 100), install clutch disc and pressure plate. Tighten mounting bolts one turn at at time to 16-17 ft. lbs. (2.2-2.4 mkg). On all except 320i, install clutch housing. On all models, apply light film of grease to all friction surfaces and install transmission.

2) Install slave cylinder so that bleeder screw is at bottom. Install propeller shaft and preload center bearing by moving bracket .078" (2.0 mm) forward in slots provided. Install and tighten NEW nuts to 72 ft. lbs. (10.3 mkg) while holding bolts in front propeller shaft coupling.

RELEASE BEARING & LEVER

Removal & Installation — With transmission and clutch housing removed from engine, remove spring from pivot end of release arm and slide off arm and bearing assembly. Separate release bearing from arm and measure for overall length of 1.95±.02" (49.5±.4 mm). Replace as required. To install, pack lubricating groove with suitable lubricant and reverse removal procedure.

CLUTCH MASTER CYLINDER

Removal — Remove trim under left side of instrument panel and remove bolt attaching master cylinder push rod to clutch pedal. Siphon off most of fluid from master cylinder reservoir and detach hydraulic lines from cylinder. On 733i only, remove windshield washer tank. On all models, remove mounting bolts at firewall and remove cylinder from vehicle.

Installation — To install, reverse removal procedures and bleed hydraulic system. On 633CSi and 733i, ensure that pedal over center spring is engaged in pedal guide before attaching push rod.

Clutches

BMW (Cont.)

CLUTCH SLAVE CYLINDER

Removal & Installation – Siphon fluid from reservoir and detach slave cylinder from housing. Disconnect hydraulic line and remove cylinder. To install, reverse removal procedure ensuring that cylinder is mounted with bleeder screw at bottom. Fill reservoir and bleed system.

OVERHAUL

CLUTCH MASTER CYLINDER

Slide dust boot off and remove circlip holding push rod. Remove piston assembly and clean master cylinder and parts with alcohol. Inspect cylinder bore for corrosion or scoring; replace if required. Lubricate internal parts with brake fluid and reassemble. Adjust push rod length to approximately 5.5" (140 mm). *See Fig. 2.*

NOTE – *Coat friction surfaces of external controls lightly with Molykote 2 (or equivalent) prior to assembly.*

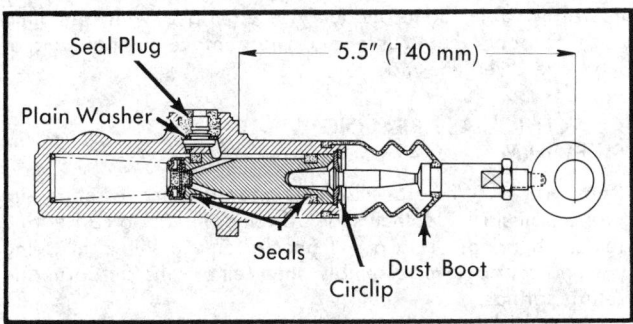

Fig. 2   Sectional View of Clutch Master Cylinder

CLUTCH SLAVE CYLINDER

Remove retaining ring and take out push rod and boot. Remove piston and clean all internal parts with alcohol. Inspect bore for scoring and corrosion; replace if necessary. Lubricate all internal parts with brake fluid and reassemble.

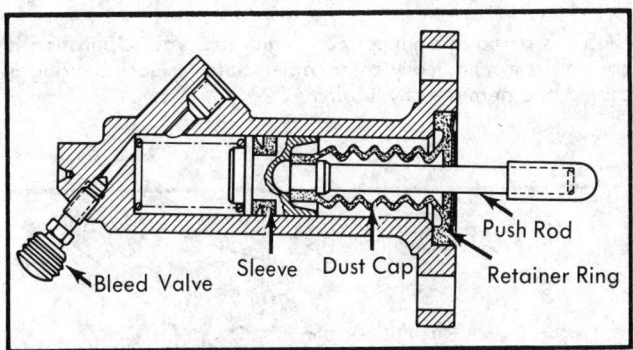

Fig. 3   Sectional View of Clutch Slave Cylinder

ADJUSTMENT

NOTE – *Clutch free play is automatically adjusted for disc wear.*

HYDRAULIC BLEEDING

Ensure that fluid reservoir is full and attach bleeder hose to bleed screw on slave cylinder. Submerge end of hose in partly filled container of brake fluid and pump clutch pedal about 10 times. Hold pedal down on last stroke and loosen bleeder screw to allow air to escape. Close bleeder screw and repeat until air is bled from system.

NOTE – *Coat friction surfaces of bearing points lightly with Molykote 2 (or equivalent) prior to assembly.*

CHRYSLER CORP. IMPORTS — EXC. FRONT-WHEEL-DRIVE MODELS

Arrow	Colt Wagon
Arrow Pickup	D50 Pickup
Challenger	Sapporo

DESCRIPTION

Clutch is a diaphragm spring, single disc type. Operation is controlled mechanically by a cable. Clutch release bearing is sealed and permanently lubricated.

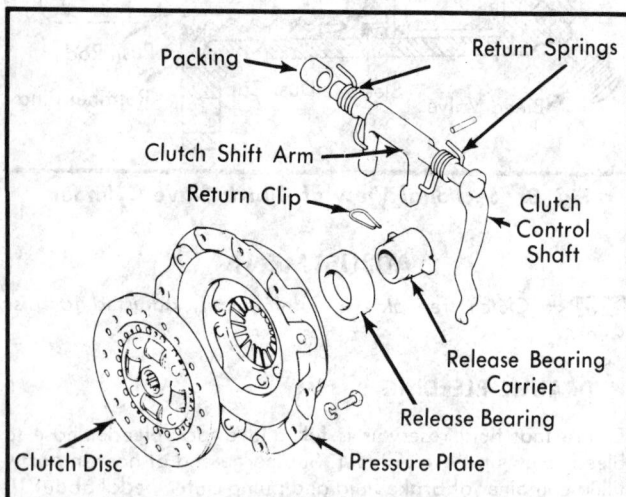

Fig. 1   Exploded View of Clutch Assembly

REMOVAL & INSTALLATION

CLUTCH ASSEMBLY

1) Disconnect battery ground cable. Remove air cleaner and starter. Remove bell housing-to-transmission mounting bolts.

2) From inside vehicle, remove console box (if equipped); remove back bone carpet. Remove dust cover retaining plate. Remove extension housing attaching bolts and control lever assembly.

NOTE — *Lever should be in 2nd gear on 4-speed transmissions and in 1st gear on 5-speed transmissions.*

3) Raise and support vehicle on jack stands; drain transmission fluid. Disconnect propeller shaft-to-differential pinion flange bolts and remove propeller shaft from transmission. Disconnect speedometer and backup light connector from transmission. Disconnect exhaust pipe and clutch cable from transmission and exhaust manifold. Support rear of engine on safety stands. With a service jack placed under transmission, remove rear engine support bracket.

NOTE — *Place jack under transmission oil pan, with the support area as wide as possible.*

4) Remove bell housing cover and remaining transmission-to-bell housing mounting bolts. Pull transmission assembly rearward from engine and remove from vehicle.

NOTE — *Use care not to twist front end of main drive gear.*

5) Insert clutch centering tool (MD998017) into clutch center hole to prevent dropping clutch disc. Alternately loosen clutch attaching bolts diagonally and evenly and remove clutch cover assembly. Separate pressure plate and clutch disc.

6) To install, reverse removal procedure and note the following: Use clutch centering tool (MD998017) to center clutch disc on flywheel. Adjust clutch cable and clutch pedal.

NOTE — *Clutch disc must be installed with stamped manufacturer's mark on pressure plate side.*

CLUTCH CABLE

Removal — Loosen cable adjusting wheel inside engine compartment, then loosen clutch pedal lock nut. Remove clutch cable from pedal lever, then remove cable from clutch shift lever and remove.

Installation — To install clutch cable, reverse the removal procedure and note following: Apply engine oil as necessary to install cable. Some models are equipped with insulating pads. Fit pads where cable routes near intake manifold and at rear side of engine mount.

CLUTCH RELEASE BEARING & SHIFT ARM

Removal — With transmission removed, remove return clip on transmission side, then slide off release bearing carrier and release bearing. Using a 3/16" punch, remove shift arm spring pin and control lever assembly, then remove the shift arm and return springs.

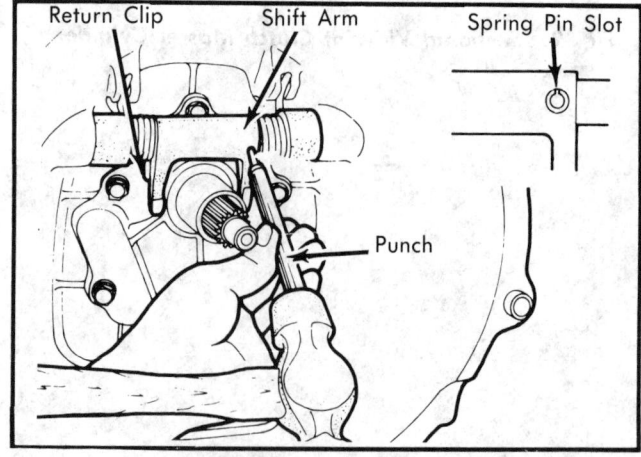

Fig. 2   Installing Shift Arm Spring Pins

Installation — 1) Insert lever and shaft into transmission case from left side. Place shift arm, felt packings and return springs on shaft assembly.

2) Apply grease to inside of bushing and oil seal lips. Apply engine oil to felt packings. Align shift arm pin holes and control shaft pin holes. Drive spring pins into position. See Fig. 2.

NOTE — *Spring pin slot direction must be at right angle to control shaft centerline.*

Clutches

CHRYSLER CORP. IMPORTS — EXC. FRONT-WHEEL-DRIVE MODELS (Cont.)

ADJUSTMENTS

PEDAL HEIGHT ADJUSTMENT

Rotate clutch pedal adjusting bolt (at top of clutch pedal) so that height is as indicated in table. Height is measured between toe board and top of clutch pedal pad.

	Clutch Pedal Height and Travel	
	Height	**Travel**
Application	In. (mm)	In. (mm)
Pickup Trucks		
2000 cc Engine	6.5 (166)	5.5 (140)
2600 cc Engine	6.9 (176)	5.9 (150)
All Others		
1600 cc	6.8 (175)	5.5 (140)
2600 cc	7.2 (185)	5.9 (150)

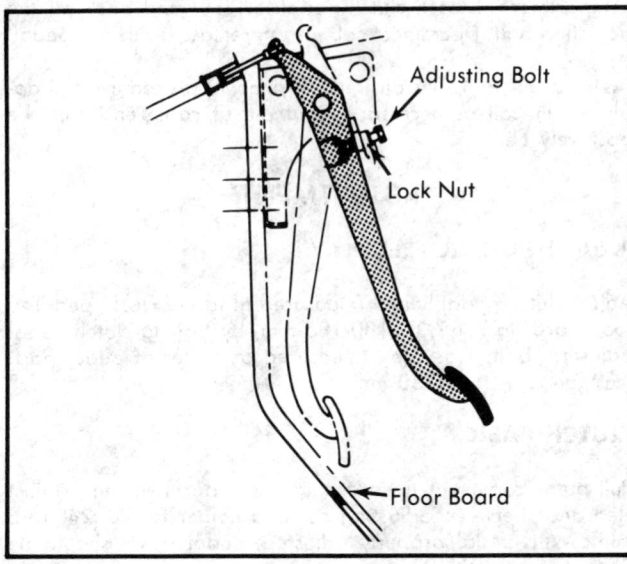

Fig. 3   Clutch Pedal Adjustment Procedure

CLUTCH CABLE

Pull clutch outer cable toward engine compartment. Rotate cable adjusting nut until .12-.16" (3-4 mm) clearance is obtained between adjusting nut and holder. Clutch pedal free play should be .8-1.2" (20-30 mm) for Arrow passenger cars, .8-1.4" (20-35 mm) for Arrow and D50 Pickups, and .6-.8" (15-20 mm) for all other models.

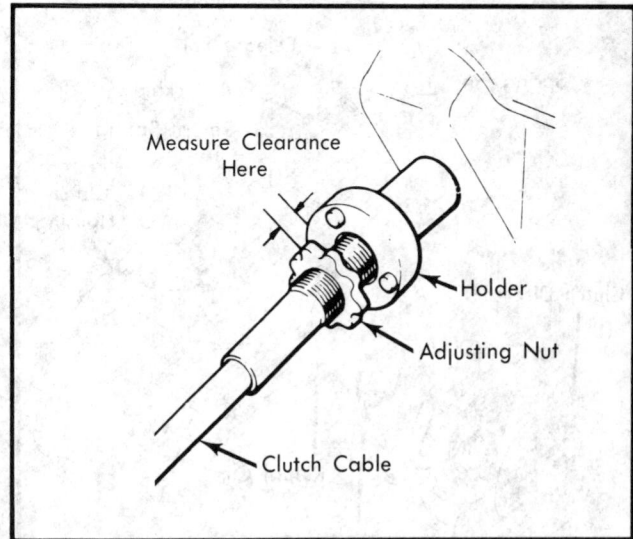

Fig. 4   Clutch Cable Adjustment Point

TIGHTENING SPECIFICATIONS	
Application	Ft. Lbs. (mkg)
Transmission-to-Engine Bolts	22-30 (3.0-4.2)
Transmission-to-Engine Flange Bolts	32-39 (4.4-5.4)
Starter Bolts	16-23 (2.2-3.2)

CHRYSLER CORP. IMPORTS — FRONT-WHEEL-DRIVE MODELS

Champ
Colt Hatchback

DESCRIPTION

Clutch is a diaphragm spring, single disc type. Operation is controlled mechanically by a cable. Clutch release bearing is sealed and permanently lubricated.

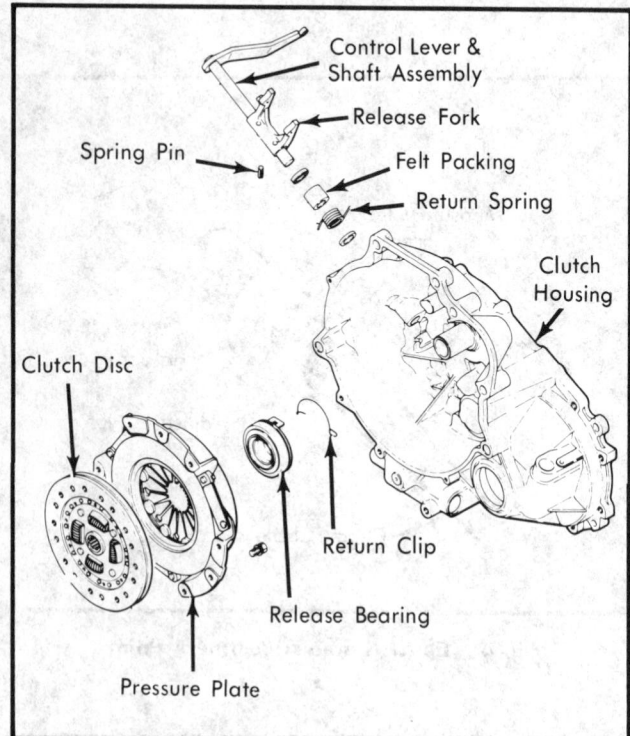

Fig. 1   Exploded View of Champ & Colt Clutch Assembly

REMOVAL & INSTALLATION

CLUTCH ASSEMBLY

Removal — 1) From inside engine compartment, disconnect negative cable from battery. Remove the following from transaxle:

- Clutch cable
- Speedometer cable
- Backup light switch harness
- Starter motor
- Front roll rod
- Four top engine-to-transaxle bolts

2) Raise vehicle and remove front tires. Remove under cover and remove shift rod from extension. Drain transaxle fluid. Disconnect drive shafts from transaxle.

CAUTION — *Drive shaft retaining rings should be replaced with new ones on reassembly. Also, use care not to damage drive shaft boots.*

3) Disconnect range selector cable. Remove engine rear cover. Remove coupling bolt at each end of front roll bar, and at the same time, loosen engine side roll rod bracket.

4) Support engine with a suitable lifting device, then remove engine-to-transaxle mounting bolts. Remove transaxle mount insulator-to-transaxle mount bracket nuts, and at the same time, loosen transaxle mount bracket. Remove and lower transaxle assembly from vehicle.

5) Insert clutch disc guide tool (MD998017) in clutch center hole, loosen pressure plate attaching bolts diagonally one by one and remove pressure plate assembly. Remove clutch disc.

Installation — To install, reverse removal procedure and note the following: Use clutch disc guide tool (MD998017) to center clutch disc on flywheel. Adjust clutch cable and clutch pedal.

NOTE — *Clutch disc must be installed with stamped manufacturer's mark on pressure plate side.*

CLUTCH CABLE

Removal — Loosen the cable adjusting wheel inside engine compartment. Loosen clutch pedal lock nut and back off the adjusting bolt. Disconnect cable from release lever and pedal.

Installation — To install, reverse removal procedure and apply engine oil as necessary. Split pin at cable end must be positively bent.

ADJUSTMENTS

PEDAL HEIGHT & FREE PLAY

Adjust clutch pedal height (measured at top of clutch pedal to toe board) to 7.1-7.3" (180-185 mm) by turning clutch pedal adjusting bolt. Free play (measured at center of pedal pad) must be .8-1.2" (20-30 mm).

CLUTCH CABLE

Pull outer cable out toward engine compartment and adjust clearance between adjusting nut and holder to .20-.24" (5-6 mm). With pedal properly adjusted, pedal travel should be 5.7" (145 mm).

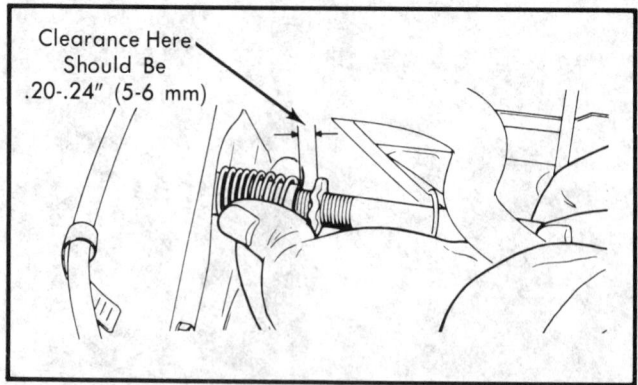

Fig. 2   Clutch Cable Adjustment

Clutches

COURIER

Pickup

DESCRIPTION

Clutch is of single dry disc type. Clutch assembly consists of clutch disc, clutch cover and pressure plate assembly, and clutch release mechanism. Clutch housing also acts as the transmission input shaft bearing retainer, and contains the input shaft bearing oil seal and a selective fit thrust washer for controlling input shaft end play. Clutch release mechanism is hydraulic, consisting of a firewall mounted master cylinder and a slave cylinder mounted on flywheel housing. To control clutch engagement, a one-way valve is mounted on clutch master cylinder to control the flow of return fluid when pressure on clutch pedal is released (2300 cc engine).

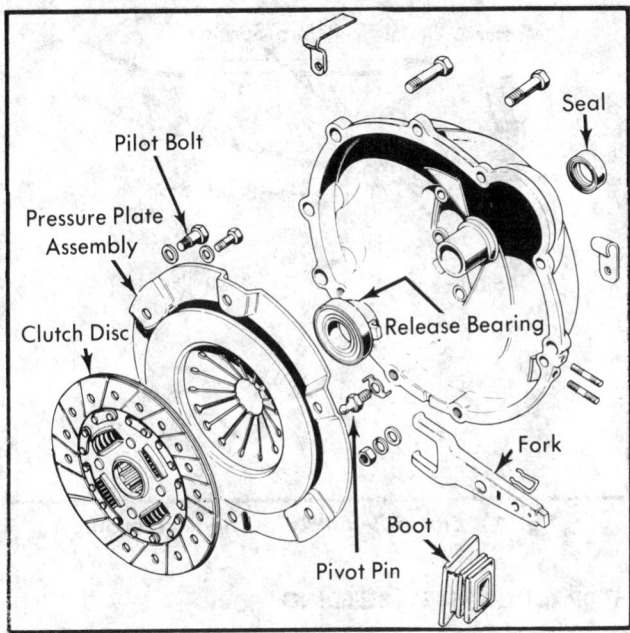

Fig. 1   Exploded View of Clutch Assembly with Detail of Internal Components

REMOVAL & INSTALLATION

CLUTCH ASSEMBLY

Removal — **1)** Disconnect negative battery cable. Place transmission in neutral and remove shift lever, tower and boots as an assembly; cover hole. Raise vehicle. Disconnect drive shaft and remove from transmission.

2) Disconnect exhaust pipe brackets from transmission case and clutch housing. Remove exhaust pipe and catalytic assembly. Disconnect clutch release lever return spring. Remove clutch slave cylinder and secure to one side.

3) Remove speedometer cable from extension housing and disconnect wiring from starter and transmission. Using a suitable jack, support engine and remove starter. Support transmission and remove transmission-to-engine rear plate attaching bolts.

4) Remove crossmember attaching bolts at transmission and frame side rails, and remove crossmember. Lower jack supporting engine and remove transmission by sliding rearward and downward. Mark location of two pilot bolt holes on flywheel and pressure plate and remove clutch attaching bolts and clutch assembly.

NOTE — *Transmissions have aluminum cases. Install flat washer between case and attaching bolt or nut.*

Installation — To install, reverse removal procedure and note: Align clutch disc and flywheel with centering tool. Install pressure plate and bolts finger tight, then tighten bolts a few turns at a time in a criss-cross pattern. Bleed hydraulic system and adjust clutch pedal free play.

RELEASE LEVER & BEARING

Removal — With transmission removed, disconnect release collar spring and slide out release lever, boot and bearing. Inspect all parts for wear or damage.

Installation — To install, apply lubricant to input shaft bearing retainer of clutch housing and pivot bolt. Seat release lever on pivot. Apply lubricant to bearing contact surface of lever. Install release bearing and hook release collar spring. Lubricate face of release bearing. Lever and bearing must operate freely.

CLUTCH MASTER CYLINDER

Removal — Disconnect and plug hydraulic lines. Remove master cylinder attaching nuts. Remove master cylinder.

Installation — To install, start pedal push rod into cylinder, then position cylinder against firewall. Install and tighten attaching nuts. Connect hydraulic line. Bleed hydraulic system and check pedal free play.

CLUTCH SLAVE CYLINDER

Removal — **1)** Disconnect brake fluid inlet hose at slave cylinder.

2) Unhook release lever from push rod.

3) Remove nuts attaching slave cylinder to clutch housing. Remove cylinder.

Installation — **1)** Locate cylinder on studs in housing. Tighten nuts.

2) Connect fluid inlet hose.

3) Fill master cylinder. Bleed hydraulic system.

4) Hook clutch release lever into slave cylinder push rod.

OVERHAUL

CLUTCH MASTER CYLINDER

1) Clean outside of cylinder, drain fluid and remove dust boot. Using a screwdriver, remove piston stop ring and washer. Remove piston, piston cup and return spring from cylinder.

2) Wash all parts in clean alcohol or brake fluid. Check all rubber components and replace if damaged, worn, softened or swollen. Check cylinder bore for wear or damage, and check clearance between cylinder bore and piston. Replace cylinder or piston if clearance is more than .004" (.102 mm).

3) To assemble, dip all parts in clean brake fluid and reverse disassembly procedure. When assembled, fill reservoir with fluid and operate piston with a screwdriver until fluid is ejected at outlet fitting.

COURIER (Cont.)

CLUTCH MASTER CYLINDER ONE-WAY VALVE

Disassembly — Remove cap from side of clutch master cylinder. See Fig. 2. Slide out washer, one-way valve and spring.

Reassembly — Position spring along with one-way valve into cylinder housing. Fit cap and washer.

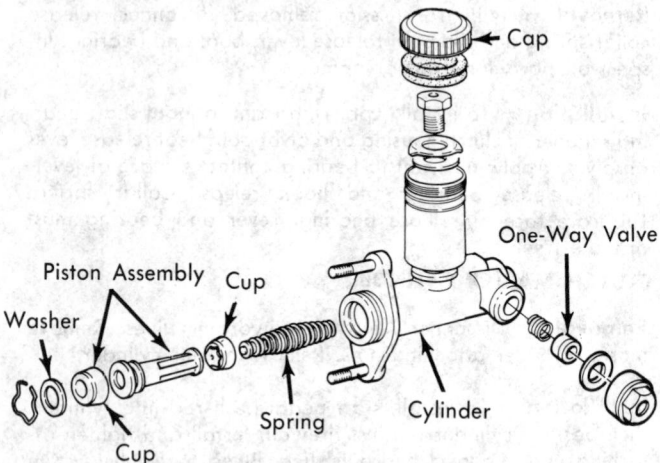

Fig. 2   **Exploded View of Clutch Master Cylinder Assembly with Detail of One-Way Valve Used on Models Equipped with 2300 cc Engine**

SLAVE CYLINDER

Disassembly — 1) Clean outside of housing. Remove dust boot and clutch release rod.

2) Remove piston assembly and return spring. Remove bleeder screw cap, bleeder screw and steel ball.

Inspection — Check cylinder bore and piston for roughness, wear or scoring. Clearance between cylinder bore and piston should be .004" (.102 mm). Replace piston or cylinder if specification is exceeded.

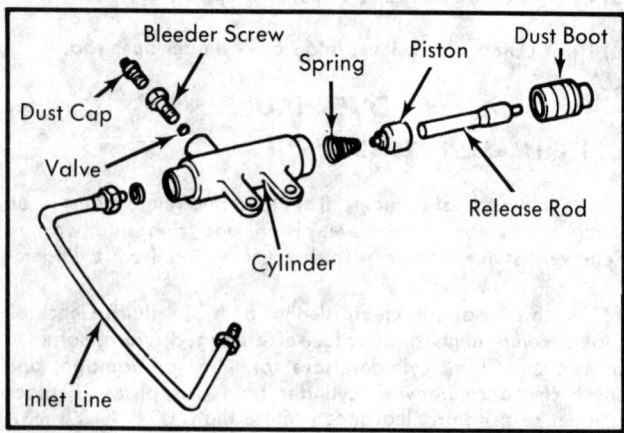

Fig. 3   **Exploded View of Courier Slave Cylinder**

Reassembly — 1) Lightly coat piston and cups with brake fluid. Fit cups to piston. Install piston into cylinder.

2) Install release rod and boot. Place steel ball into cylinder. Screw in bleeder and fit dust cap.

ADJUSTMENTS

CLUTCH PEDAL

Pedal free play is adjusted by loosening lock nut on push rod and rotating rod until .025-.121" (.64-3.07 mm) free travel is obtained at pedal pad. See Fig. 4. Tighten lock nut when adjustment is completed.

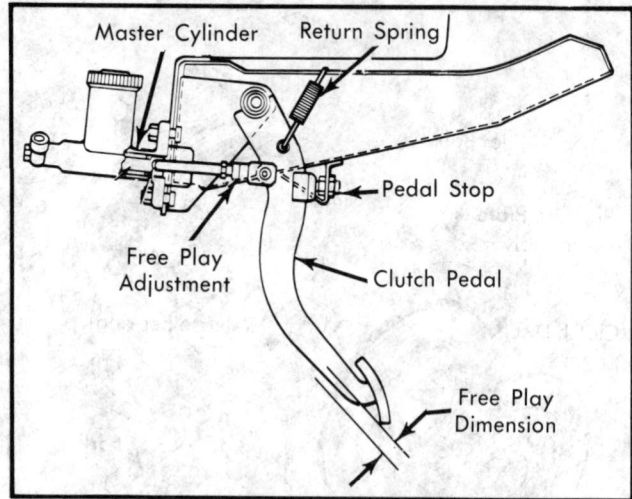

Fig. 4   **Clutch Pedal Adjustment Procedure**

HYDRAULIC SYSTEM BLEEDING

Remove rubber cap from bleeder valve and attach a bleeder tube and fixture to bleeder screw. Place other end of tube in a glass jar of brake fluid and open bleeder screw. Depress clutch pedal and allow to return slowly. Continue pumping action until air bubbles cease to appear in glass jar, then close bleeder screw. Install rubber cap on bleeder screw and fill master cylinder.

NOTE — During bleeding, master cylinder must be kept ¾ full of brake fluid.

TIGHTENING SPECIFICATIONS

Application	Ft. Lbs. (mkg)
Clutch Housing-to-Engine	
2000 cc Engine	34-45 (4.7-6.2)
2300 cc Engine	28-40 (3.9-5.5)
Pressure Plate-to-Flywheel	13-20 (1.8-2.8)
Slave Cylinder-to-Clutch Housing	12-17 (1.7-2.4)
Pivot Pin	23-34 (3.2-4.7)
Master Cylinder Attaching Bolts	13-18 (1.8-2.4)

DATSUN — EXCEPT 310

DESCRIPTION

Clutch is dry, single disc type. All models use a diaphragm spring type pressure plate and pre-lubricated clutch release bearing. Clutch is operated by a firewall mounted master cylinder and a clutch housing mounted slave cylinder. All models except 210 with 5-speed transmissions have non-adjustable slave cylinder assembly.

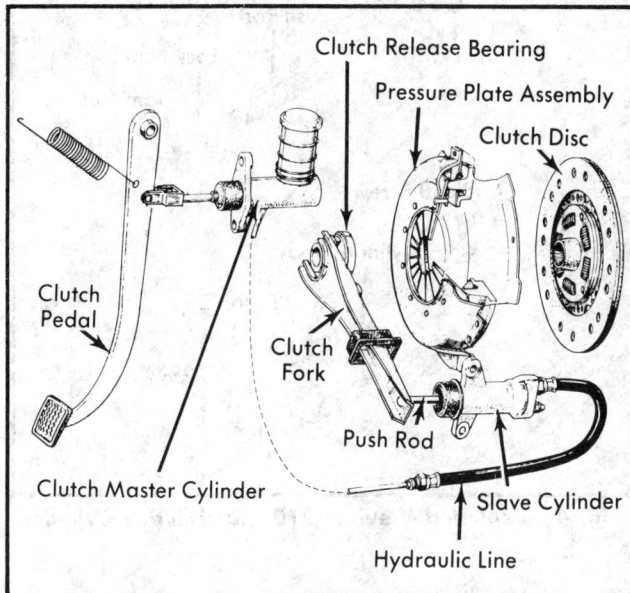

Fig. 1 Typical Datsun Hydraulically Operated Clutch System

REMOVAL & INSTALLATION

CLUTCH ASSEMBLY

NOTE — *Removal procedure is general. Not all steps apply to each model.*

Removal — 1) Disconnect negative battery cable and accelerator linkage. Remove console box and place transmission shift lever in neutral. Remove control lever boots, snap ring (nut, if required), and shift lever pin. Remove shift control lever.

2) Raise and support vehicle on safety stands and disconnect exhaust pipe from manifold. If required, remove bolts mounting exhaust pipe bracket to extension housing or rear engine crossmember. Remove exhaust pipe insulator (if equipped) and lay over exhaust pipe.

3) Disconnect back-up light, neutral, overdrive and transmission controlled spark connectors (if equipped). Disconnect speedometer cable on all except 4-WD models. On 4-WD models, remove primary and front propeller shafts, and front differential carrier crossmember.

NOTE — *Index mark propeller shafts and companion flanges prior to removal.*

4) Remove slave cylinder. On all except 4-WD, separate center support bearing (if equipped) from crossmember and remove

propeller shaft. On all models, plug rear extension of transmission after removing propeller shaft to prevent loss of transmission fluid.

5) Support engine on suitable jack. Support transmission with transmission jack, then loosen rear engine mount attaching bolt and remove rear engine mounting bracket. Remove starter. Remove engine-to-transmission bolts. With engine supported and transmission mounted on transmission jack, slide transmission rearward and remove from vehicle.

6) Install clutch aligning tool and loosen pressure plate mounting bolts one turn at a time. Use a criss-cross pattern to loosen bolts until spring pressure is relieved. Remove clutch disc and pressure plate assembly.

Installation — To install, reverse removal procedure and note the following:

- Lubricate clutch disc splines with small amount of multipurpose grease.
- Slip clutch assembly over guide dowels.
- Use clutch aligning tool to center disc and pressure plate.
- Tighten bolts one turn at a time in a criss-cross pattern.
- Adjust linkage and pedal.
- Check and refill transmission lubricant.
- Bleed clutch hydraulic system and replenish fluid.

CLUTCH MASTER CYLINDER

Removal & Installation — Disconnect master cylinder push rod at clevis. Disconnect hydraulic line to slave cylinder. Remove cylinder attaching bolts and remove cylinder. Remove master cylinder dust cover if equipped. On 280ZX models only, remove windshield washer tank and clear fuel injection resistor before removing master cylinder. To install, reverse removal procedure and bleed hydraulic system.

CLUTCH SLAVE CYLINDER

Removal & Installation — Remove clutch fork return spring (if equipped). Disconnect hydraulic line from cylinder, remove bolts attaching cylinder to clutch housing, and remove slave cylinder. To install, reverse removal procedure and bleed hydraulic system.

CLUTCH RELEASE BEARING & LEVER

Removal — With transmission removed from vehicle, remove dust boot from clutch housing. Disconnect release lever retaining spring or return spring, as required, and retaining clips holding release bearing to lever. Remove bearing and lever through front of clutch housing. Remove bearing from collar using a puller.

Installation — To install, reverse removal procedure and note the following: Apply multi-purpose grease to inside surface of bearing collar, release bearing contact points, release bearing, ball pin in clutch housing, and ball contact points on release lever.

DATSUN — EXCEPT 310 (Cont.)

OVERHAUL

NOTE — *Master cylinders and slave cylinders may be supplied by more than one manufacturer. Parts are not interchangeable. Ensure that overhaul kit matches cylinder.*

CLUTCH MASTER CYLINDER

1) With master cylinder removed, remove filler cap and drain fluid. Remove dust cover and snap ring. Remove push rod and stopper. Remove supply valve stopper, then take out piston, spring seat and return spring.

2) Clean all parts in clean brake fluid and inspect for wear or damage. If cylinder-to-piston clearance exceeds .006" (.15 mm) replace defective part. Replace piston cup and dust cover during overhaul. To assemble, coat all parts with brake fluid and reverse disassembly procedure. Bleed hydraulic system and adjust pedal height.

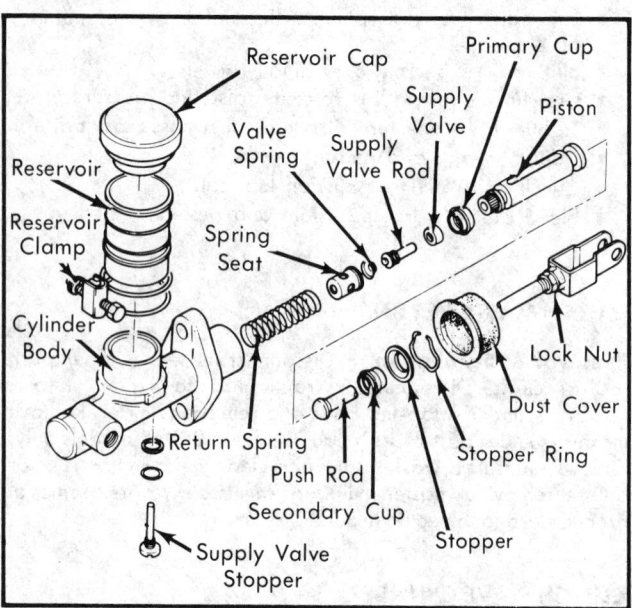

Fig. 2   Exploded View of Clutch Master Cylinder

CLUTCH SLAVE CYLINDER

1) With slave cylinder removed, remove push rod and dust cover. Remove piston and piston cup as an assembly. Remove bleeder screw.

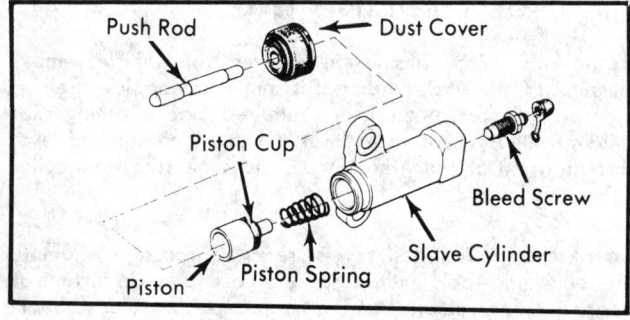

Fig. 3   Exploded View of Clutch Slave Cylinder Assembly (Except 210)

2) Clean all parts in clean brake fluid and inspect for wear or damage. If cylinder-to-piston clearance exceeds .006" (.15 mm), replace defective part. Replace piston cup and dust cover during overhaul. To assemble, coat all parts with brake fluid and reverse disassembly procedure. Ensure piston cup is installed properly and bleed hydraulic system.

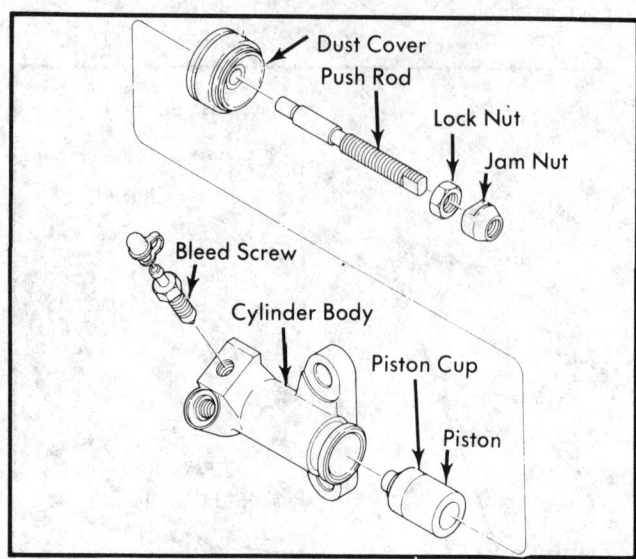

Fig. 4   Exploded View of 210 Clutch Slave Cylinder

ADJUSTMENT

PEDAL HEIGHT & FREE PLAY

Adjust clutch pedal height to specification with adjusting rod on 280ZX or by turning pedal stopper adjusting nut on other models. Adjust pedal free play to .04-.20" (1-5 mm) by turning clutch master cylinder push rod in or out.

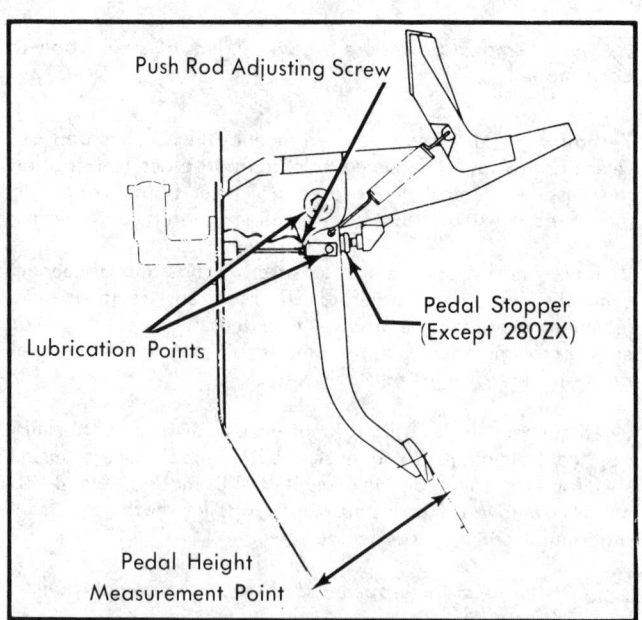

Fig. 5   Clutch Pedal Height Measurement and Free Play Adjustment Locations

DATSUN – EXCEPT 310 (Cont.)

Pedal Height Specifications	
Application	**In. (mm)**
200SX	6.61-6.85 (168-174)
210	5.63-5.87 (143-149)
280ZX	7.99 (203)
510	6.34-6.57 (161-167)
810	6.91 (176)
Pickup	6.73-6.97 (171-177)

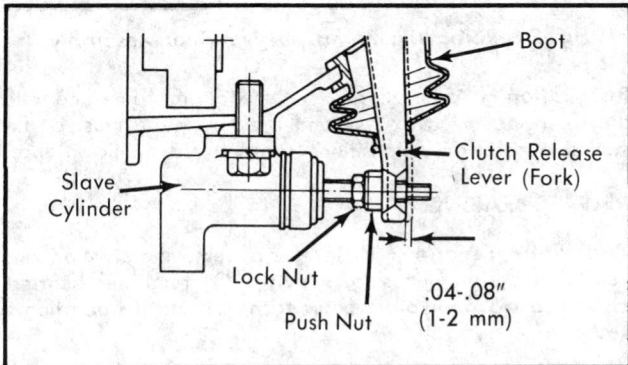

Fig. 6   Clutch Fork Free Play Adjustment Location for Datsun 210

CLUTCH FORK FREE PLAY (310)

Loosen lock nut and push rod nut and turn push rod until release bearing lightly touches clutch diaphragm spring. Turn rod back (in opposite direction) about 1¼ turn and tighten lock nut. This provides about .04-.08" (1-2 mm) clearance between push nut and lever. Work clutch pedal several times and recheck pedal play.

HYDRAULIC SYSTEM BLEEDING

1) Remove dust cap from slave cylinder bleed plug. Check fluid level in master cylinder, fill as necessary. Open bleed plug approximately ¾ turn.

2) Attach a tube to slave cylinder bleed plug, and place opposite end of tube in a container half-full of brake fluid. Push clutch pedal to bottom of travel.

3) With pedal down, tighten bleed plug. Continue operation until air bubbles are no longer seen in container. Close bleed plug on a downward stroke of pedal. Install dust cap and adjust fluid level in master cylinder.

TIGHTENING SPECIFICATIONS	
Application	**Ft. Lbs. (mkg)**
Clutch-to-Flywheel	12-15 (1.6-2.1)
Engine-to-Transmission	
210	12-16 (1.6-2.2)
All Others	32-43 (4.4-5.9)

DATSUN 310

DESCRIPTION

Clutch is a single, dry disc, diaphragm spring type. Main components consist of: clutch cover, pressure plate, and diaphragm spring. Clutch plates are riveted together. A release bearing and fork control clutch engagement and disengagement. Clutch is hydraulic type with a firewall mounted master cylinder and clutch housing mounted slave cylinder.

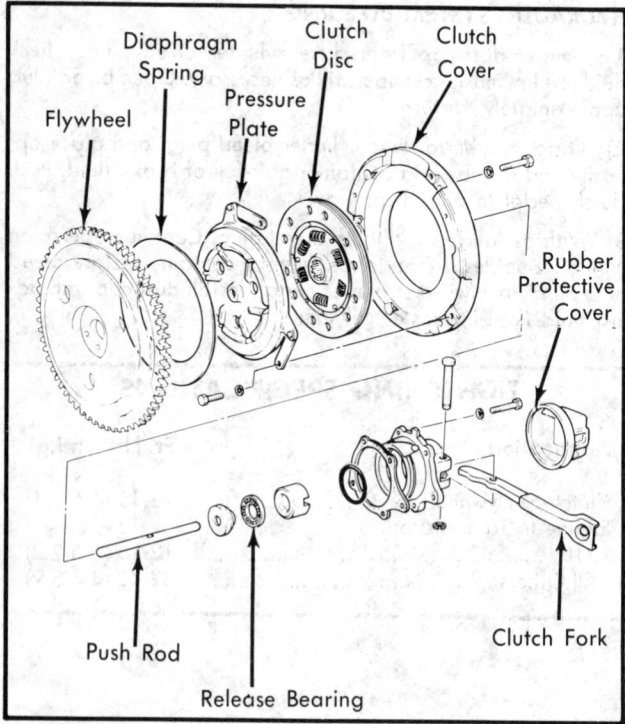

Fig. 1   Exploded View of Clutch Components

REMOVAL & INSTALLATION

CLUTCH ASSEMBLY

NOTE — *Clutch assembly can be serviced, removed, or overhauled while transmission and engine remain in vehicle. Also, transmission cannot be removed without removing engine.*

Removal — 1) Disconnect battery ground cable, fresh air duct and high tension cable between coil and distributor. Remove fuel filter from bracket. Remove clutch slave cylinder. Remove access hole cover from right wheel well and detach dust cover. Remove clutch release fork retaining clip and pin and remove release fork through access hole.

2) Remove bearing housing attaching bolts and remove primary drive gear assembly through access hole. See Fig. 2. Remove upper clutch housing inspection cover. Rotate ring gear with suitable tool and loosen clutch cover attaching bolts evenly. Lift out clutch cover and disc through inspection cover opening. Remove strap securing pressure plate to clutch cover and remove disc.

NOTE — *Keep strap in relative position. It is part of clutch cover dynamic balance.*

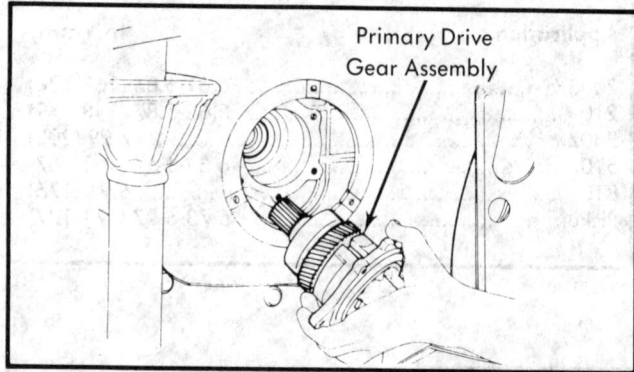

Fig. 2   Removing Primary Drive Gear Assembly

Installation — To install, reverse removal procedure and note the following: Clutch cover and pressure plate must be installed in their original positions to maintain dynamic balance.

RELEASE BEARING

Removal — Separate release lever by removing pivot pin and removing bearing housing. Remove "O" ring and bearing. Hold bearing and rotate outer race, replace if operation is rough or noisy.

Installation — To install, reverse removal procedure and apply multi-purpose grease to sliding parts of release lever.

CLUTCH MASTER CYLINDER

Removal & Installation — Disconnect master cylinder push rod at clevis. Disconnect hydraulic line to slave cylinder. Remove cylinder attaching bolts and remove cylinder. To install, reverse removal procedure and bleed hydraulic system.

SLAVE CYLINDER

Removal & Installation — Disconnect clutch hose from slave cylinder. Remove slave cylinder attaching bolts and remove cylinder. To install, reverse removal procedure and bleed hydraulic system.

OVERHAUL

MASTER CYLINDER

Disassembly — Remove filler cap and drain fluid. Remove dust cover and snap ring. Remove push rod and stopper. Remove supply valve stopper, then take out piston, spring seat and return spring.

Cleaning & Inspection — Clean all parts in clean brake fluid and inspect for wear or damage. If cylinder-to-piston clearance exceeds .006" (.15 mm), replace defective part. Replace piston cup and dust cover during overhaul.

Reassembly — To assemble, coat all parts with brake fluid and reverse disassembly procedure. Bleed system and adjust pedal height.

DATSUN 310 (Cont.)

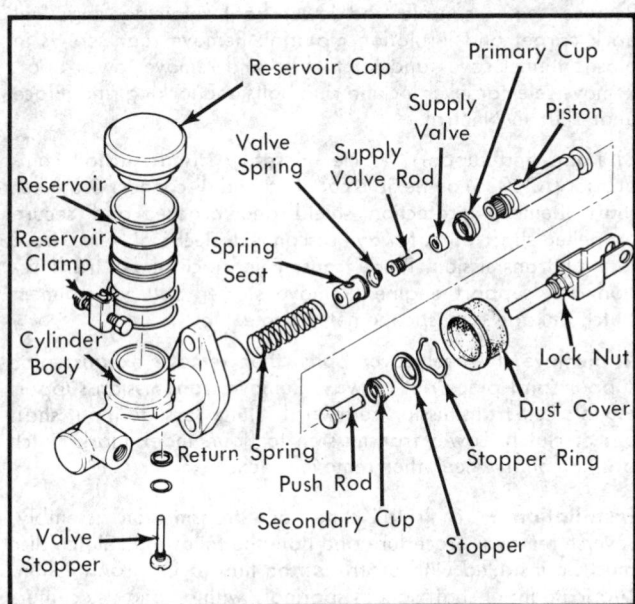

Fig. 3   *Exploded View of Master Cylinder*

NOTE — *When pressure plate and clutch disc are replaced, or if any components of release mechanism is replaced, a new push rod may have to be installed.*

ADJUSTMENTS

CLUTCH PEDAL HEIGHT & FREE PLAY

Adjust clutch pedal height by turning master cylinder push rod. Correct height is 7.05-7.28" (179-185 mm). Tighten lock nut. Adjust stopper nut so pedal free play is .04-.20" (1-5 mm). Tighten lock nut. See *Fig. 5*.

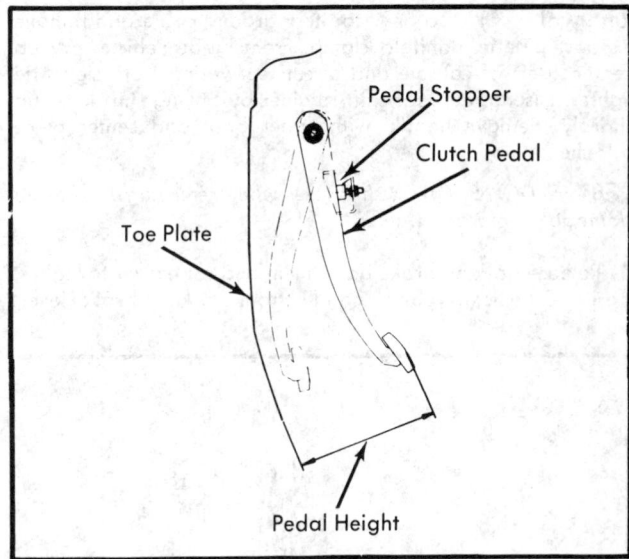

Fig. 5   *Pedal Height and Free Play Adjustment*

SLAVE CYLINDER

Disassembly — Remove push rod and dust cover. Remove piston and piston cup as an assembly. Remove bleeder screw.

Cleaning & Inspection — Clean all parts in clean brake fluid and inspect for wear or damage. If cylinder-to-piston clearance exceeds .006" (.15 mm), replace defective part. Replace piston cup and dust cover during overhaul.

Reassembly — To assemble, coat all parts with brake fluid and reverse disassembly procedure. Ensure piston cup is properly installed and bleed system.

HYDRAULIC SYSTEM BLEEDING

Fit bleeder hose to bleeder valve. Place opposite end into a clear container partially filled with brake fluid. Pump clutch pedal two or three times and hold to floor. Break bleeder valve loose and allow air to vent. Close bleeder screw and allow pedal to return. Repeat procedure until no air bubbles are present in discharged fluid.

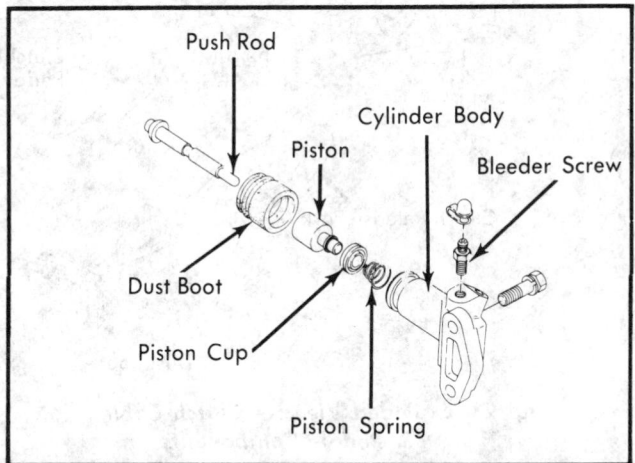

Fig. 4   *Exploded View of Clutch Slave Cylinder*

TIGHTENING SPECIFICATIONS	
Application	**Ft. Lbs. (mkg)**
Clutch Cover Assy.-to-Flywheel Bolt	5-7 (.7-1.0)
Pressure Plate Strap Bolt	7-9 (1.0-1.3)

Clutches

FIAT BRAVA

DESCRIPTION

Clutch is a dry, single disc type using a diaphragm spring pressure plate. Clutch disc is a conventional friction lining kind. Clutch operation is accomplished by a control cable attached at upper end directly to clutch pedal and lower end to clutch release fork.

REMOVAL & INSTALLATION

CLUTCH ASSEMBLY

Removal — 1) Disconnect battery ground cable and remove exhaust pipe-to-manifold clamp. From inside vehicle, pry up center insert of console and disconnect wiring from cigarette lighter. Disengage gear shift retainer by pulling shift lever up sharply. Remove handle with upper boot and center piece attached.

NOTE — *DO NOT twist shift lever while removing to prevent damage to plastic retainer.*

2) Release parking brake adjustment and raise lever to highest position. Remove rubber handle from parking brake lever.

Remove center console and lower boot retaining ring. Pull back carpet and insulation material. Remove rear screws in plastic tunnel cover and lift to free and remove lower boot. Remove selector lever locking ring bolts and locking ring. Place gear shift in Neutral.

3) Raise and support vehicle on safety stands. Install compressor (A70025) on flexible coupling and disconnect propeller shaft. Remove protection shield and bracket and secure propeller shaft out of way. Disconnect electrical wires from rear of transmission. Place transmission jack under transmission and support engine. Remove starter bolts. Disconnect clutch linkage and speedometer cable.

4) Remove flywheel cover bolts, then remove exhaust pipe support and place out of way. Remove transmission support mount. Pull transmission rearward, tilting to slide input shaft out of clutch. Lower transmission to floor. Index mark clutch position on flywheel, then remove clutch.

Installation — To install clutch and transmission assembly, reverse removal procedure and note the following: Clutch disc must be installed with protrusion on hub facing transmission. Lubricate input shaft splines sparingly with oil and use centering tool to align clutch disc.

ADJUSTMENT

CLUTCH PEDAL HEIGHT

Clutch pedal height is adjusted by loosening lock nut (near firewall) and rotating adjustment nut until pedal height is adjusted.

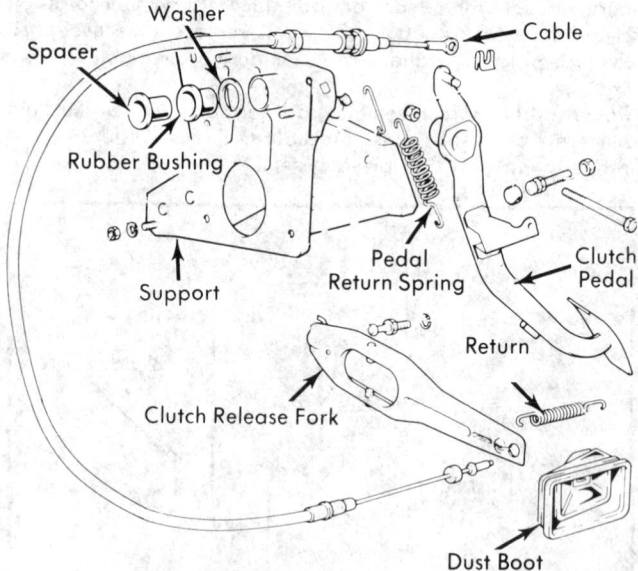

Fig. 2 **Exploded View of Clutch Cable & Pedal Components**

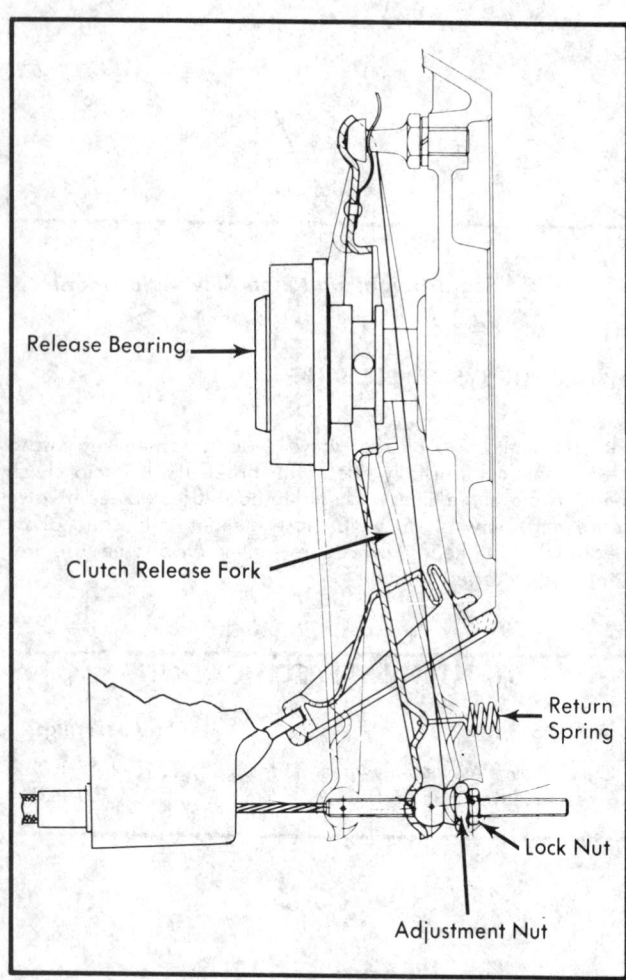

Fig. 1 **Clutch Actuating Components**

TIGHTENING SPECIFICATIONS

Application	Ft. Lbs. (mkg)
Clutch-to-Flywheel	22 (3.0)

Clutches

FIAT SPIDER 2000

DESCRIPTION

Clutch is a dry, single-disc, diaphragm spring type. Clutch is engaged or disengaged through a cable which is actuated by the clutch pedal. Mechanism is self-adjusting to compensate for wear and there is no pedal free play.

REMOVAL & INSTALLATION

CLUTCH ASSEMBLY

Removal — 1) Raise and support vehicle. From inside driver's compartment, press down on gearshift lever and pry out retaining ring with screwdriver. Remove transmission cover.

2) From under vehicle, disconnect propeller shaft from transmission and remove safety cross strap. Remove propeller shaft center pillow block. Disconnect speedometer drive from transmission. Disconnect all electrical leads from transmission case. Disconnect clutch fork return spring and remove adjusting rod.

3) Remove inspection cover from bottom of clutch housing. Disconnect exhaust pipe support bracket from rear of transmission and remove starter from clutch housing. Position a suitable transmission holding fixture (A. 70509) to a floor jack and position under transmission.

4) Remove bolts securing transmission to engine and remove rear crossmember. With transmission supported by jack, pull to rear until input shaft clears release bearing. Lower jack when transmission is clear and remove from under vehicle. Remove clutch assembly from flywheel after marking their relationship for reinstallation.

Installation — To install transmission and clutch assembly, reverse removal procedure and note the following: Use centering tool to align clutch and flywheel. Lubricate transmission input shaft splines sparingly.

ADJUSTMENT

CLUTCH PEDAL HEIGHT

Loosen lock nut and rotate adjustment nut until clutch pedal height reaches desired level.

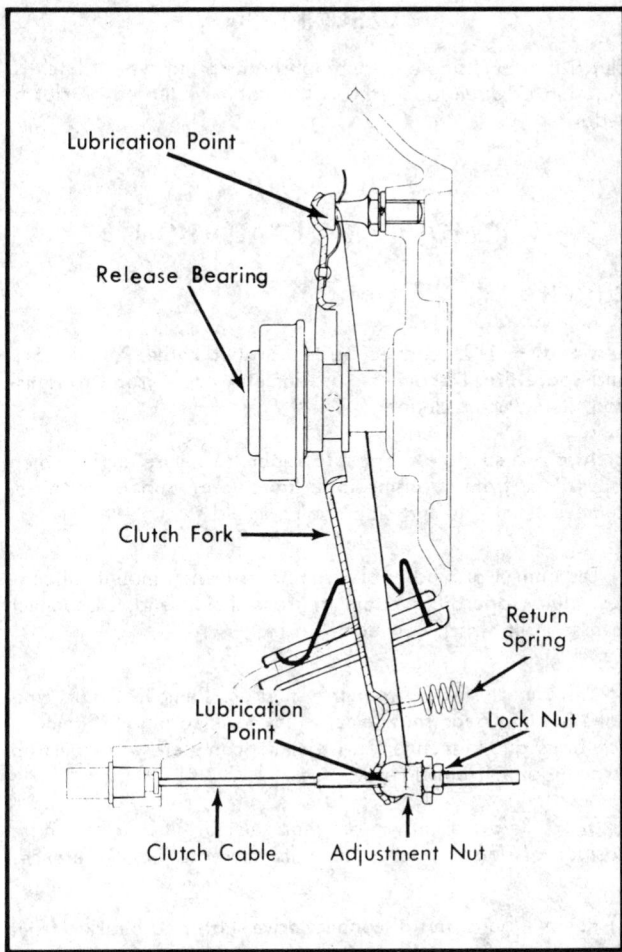

Fig. 1 Clutch Actuating Components Showing Cable Adjustment Point

TIGHTENING SPECIFICATIONS

Application	Ft. Lbs. (mkg)
Clutch-to-Flywheel	22 (3.0)
Transmission Case-to-Bell Housing Bolts	36 (5.0)
Transmission Case-to-Bell Housing Nut	18 (2.5)
Bell Housing-to-Engine Mounts	61 (8.4)

FIAT STRADA

DESCRIPTION

Clutch is a dry, single disc, diaphragm spring type. Clutch is engaged or disengaged through a cable, actuated by clutch pedal.

REMOVAL & INSTALLATION

CLUTCH

Removal – 1) Disconnect battery ground cable. Remove jack and spare tire. Disconnect speedometer cable from transmission. Remove air cleaner.

2) Attach a suitable support to engine to secure engine when separated from transmission. Raise and support vehicle. Remove front and left side engine shields.

3) Disconnect ground cable from transmission mount. Disconnect clutch operating cable at transmission end. Disconnect reverse light switch connector.

4) Disconnect starter from transmission. Remove 2 nuts and bolts holding gear shift selector link to linkage joint. Remove hex bolts and disconnect drive shaft (complete with constant velocity joint) from flange.

NOTE – *Before removal of gear selector link, index mark position of slots in relation to bolts for reassembly reference.*

5) Remove bolts and disconnect drive shaft and bearing from transmission. Support transmission and remove center mount bolt. Remove transmission bracket and flywheel guard.

6) Remove remaining nuts and bolts attaching transmission to engine. Disconnect left side rubber mount and bracket, and lower transmission out of vehicle. Index mark clutch cover and flywheel, and loosen attaching bolts alternately and evenly. Remove clutch assembly.

Installation – With protruding portion of clutch assembly facing away from flywheel, loosely assemble clutch assembly to flywheel. Use clutch aligning tool (70210) to center clutch disc. Tighten clutch cover bolts alternately and evenly. To complete installation, reverse removal procedure.

CLUTCH CABLE

Removal – Remove spring clip from pin on clutch pedal. Remove cable eyelet from pin. At transmission end of cable, remove lock nut, adjusting nut and block. Remove threaded cable end from lever and remove bushing. Remove bolts at cable housing flange and remove cable.

Installation – Grease inside diameter of cable eyelet. Install in reverse order of removal. Adjust pedal height if necessary.

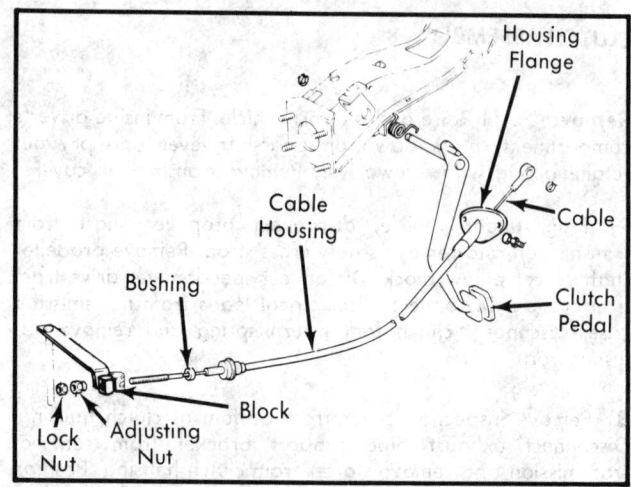

Fig. 1 Clutch Cable Components

ADJUSTMENT

CLUTCH PEDAL HEIGHT (STRADA)

Clutch pedal height should be 1.18" (30 mm) lower than brake pedal. If height is not to specification, loosen adjustment lock nut and rotate adjusting nut until pedal height is as specified.

TIGHTENING SPECIFICATIONS	
Application	**Ft. Lbs. (mkg)**
Clutch Cover-to-Flywheel	28 (3.9)
Transmission-to-Clutch Housing	18 (2.5)
Clutch Housing-to-Engine	58 (8.0)
Axle Shaft-to-Hub	159 (22)
Starter-to-Clutch Housing	18 (2.5)

FIAT X1/9

DESCRIPTION

Clutch is a dry, single plate, diaphragm spring type. Clutch actuation is hydraulic, using a firewall mounted master cylinder and a clutch housing mounted slave cylinder. A prelubricated clutch release bearing is also used.

REMOVAL & INSTALLATION

CLUTCH ASSEMBLY

Removal — 1) Disconnect positive battery cable. Remove air cleaner and carburetor duct cooling. From inside engine compartment, separate slave cylinder from transmission case. Install engine support. Remove upper transmission-to-cranckcase mounting bolts.

2) Working from under the vehicle, disconnect and swing out-of-way shifting flexible link. Disconnect back-up lights and seat belt warning system wire. Remove starter. Disconnect and remove exhaust pipe.

3) Remove nuts from the hub end of half shaft. Remove attaching hardware mounting suspension control arm to supports. Free half shaft from hub end and fix other end to transmission to prevent premature disconnection.

4) Remove the following items: Flywheel cover, engine cross-member support, and lower engine-to-transmission bolts. Remove transmission/differential from below vehicle. Mark clutch position on flywheel and remove clutch.

Installation — To install, reverse removal procedure using suitable tool (A. 70210) to center clutch assembly.

CLUTCH MASTER CYLINDER

Removal — Steering column must be removed to gain access to clutch master cylinder. Disconnect and cap master cylinder hydraulic line. Remove two bolts attaching cylinder to support plate. Withdraw cylinder from actuating rod and remove from vehicle.

Installation — To install, reverse removal procedure and bleed hydraulic system.

CLUTCH SLAVE CYLINDER

Removal — Remove slave cylinder hydraulic hose and union. Disconnect cylinder push rod from clutch release bearing fork. Slightly compress return spring and remove two mounting bolts; slowly withdraw cylinder from support plate.

Installation — To install, reverse removal procedure ensuring slave cylinder snugly fits against support and that hydraulic system is bled.

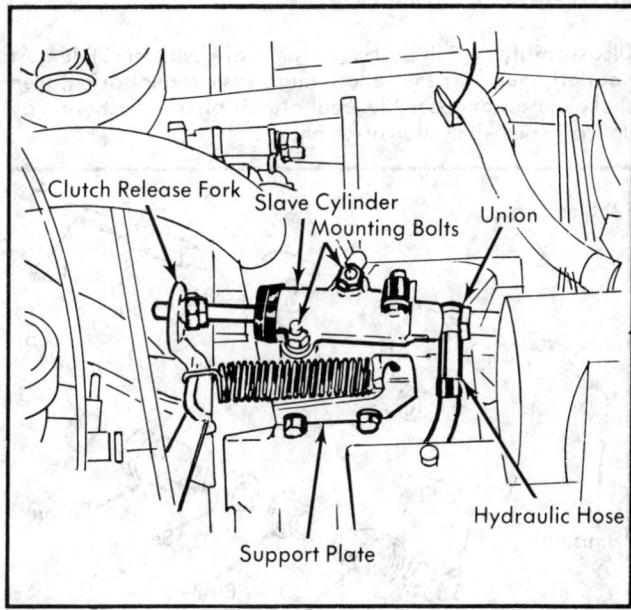

Fig. 1   Clutch Slave Cylinder Location

ADJUSTMENT

NOTE — Clutch mechanism automatically adjusts to compensate for wear and there is no pedal free play.

OVERHAUL

CLUTCH MASTER CYLINDER

Disassembly — Ease rubber dust boot back and remove snap ring, using long nosed pliers. Remove seal and complete plunger assembly. Pull out remaining gasket, seal and spring.

Reassembly — Lightly coat all components with brake fluid. Insert spring and seal into position. Fit piston assembly and seal, then install snap ring. Slip boot over cylinder housing.

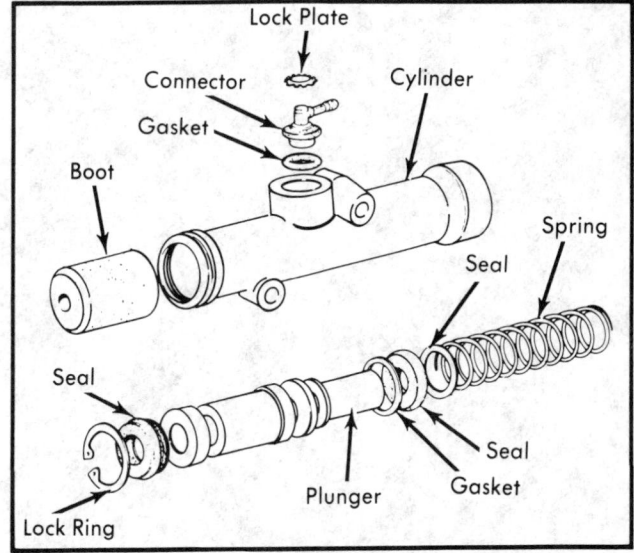

Fig. 2   Exploded View of Clutch Master Cylinder

FIAT X1/9 (Cont.)

CLUTCH SLAVE CYLINDER

Disassembly — Pull push rod from slave cylinder. Slide dust boot off housing. Remove lock ring, washer, and spring, then shake out piston assembly. Seal at rear of cylinder bore may not come out with piston assembly.

Reassembly — Lightly coat all components with brake fluid before reassembly. Insert rear seal, and piston assembly. Refit spring, washer, and lock ring. Install dust boot and push rod.

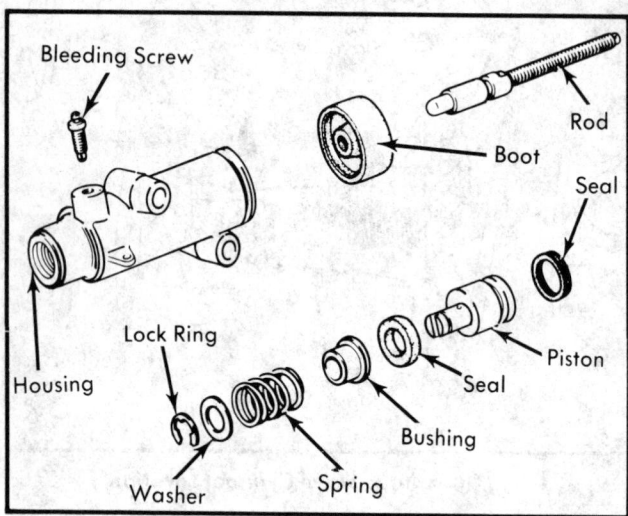

Bleeding Screw

Rod

Boot

Seal

Housing

Lock Ring

Piston

Seal

Bushing

Washer

Spring

Fig. 3 Exploded View of Clutch Slave Cylinder

TIGHTENING SPECIFICATIONS

Application	Ft. Lbs. (mkg)
Clutch Flywheel Bolts	11 (1.5)
Clutch Release Fork Bolt	18 (2.5)
Slave Cylinder Piston Adjusting Nut	18 (2.5)
Slave Cylinder Support Plate-to-Transmission Case	18 (2.5)
Support Plate-to-Transmission Case Stud Nut	18 (2.5)

FIESTA

Hatchback

DESCRIPTION

The Fiesta clutch consists of a single dry plate clutch disc and a diaphragm spring pressure plate. The disc has 4 torsion springs. The clutch assembly is operated by an automatic self-adjusting device with a release shaft and thrust bearing inside the clutch housing. Fiesta uses two types of gearshift mechanisms, one with a boot on the selector rod, and one with a cranked shifter rod.

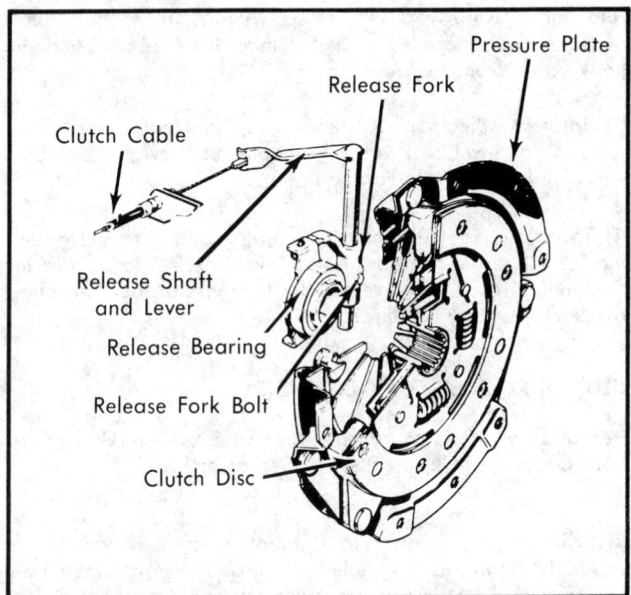

Fig. 1   Clutch Components

REMOVAL & INSTALLATION

CLUTCH ASSEMBLY

Removal — 1) Engage transmission in 4th gear position to ensure correct adjustment after installation. Disconnect battery ground cable. Install suitable engine support bar and clamp. Engine must be supported when transmission is removed.

2) Unscrew speedometer driven gear. Unhook clutch cable from release lever by pulling cable through between lever and support. Remove 4 upper transmission flange bolts. Raise vehicle and drain transmission fluid.

NOTE — *Remove plunger retainer and drain fluid out through plunger retainer hole.*

3) Remove selector rod spring from selector rod. Loosen selector rod locating bolt. Withdraw selector rod from shift shaft. Remove stabilizer shift assembly from transmission.

4) Unscrew and reposition 2 inner nuts on rubber coupling and engine support. Loosen lock nut on stud and remove stud from transmission housing with Allen wrench.

NOTE — *Allow stabilizer and screw to hang on engine support bar.*

5) Remove left drive shaft by removing 6 Allen bolts at coupling of inner constant velocity joint and stub shaft. Remove starter and transmission breather tube. Remove 2 lower flange bolts from transmission.

6) Remove 3 bolts from engine mounting. Withdraw transmission to free input shaft from clutch spline. Lower transmission on suitable jack and remove. Remove screws from pressure plate evenly (one turn at a time) and remove clutch assembly from flywheel.

Installation — 1) Apply light coating of grease to splines of drive shaft and differential gear, input shaft splines and thrust bearing carrier bore.

2) Ensure engine adapter plate is properly seated on engine guide bushings. Install transmission. Insert 2 flange bolts and snug. Align engine adapter plate and secure with 2 pins.

3) Mount transmission and clutch adapter plate to engine mounting using 3 new self-locking bolts. Lower engine and tighten bolts. Tighten 2 flange bolts at this time. Install control shaft plunger with spring and retainer.

NOTE — *Lightly coat retainer threads with "Omnifit" type lubricant.*

4) Install starter and connect cable. Install breather tube so it is suspended freely through hole in side member. Install stabilizer gear to transmission, gently turning Allen screw in as far as stop in transmission housing.

5) Lock screw with nut on rubber coupling of stabilizer. Bring inner nuts on engine mount into contact, and torque outer engine mount nuts.

6) On models with selector rod with boot, place shift shaft and lever in 4th gear position. Pull selector rod down onto shaft and align hole in selector housing with shift lever. Lock in place with a .16" (4 mm) pin.

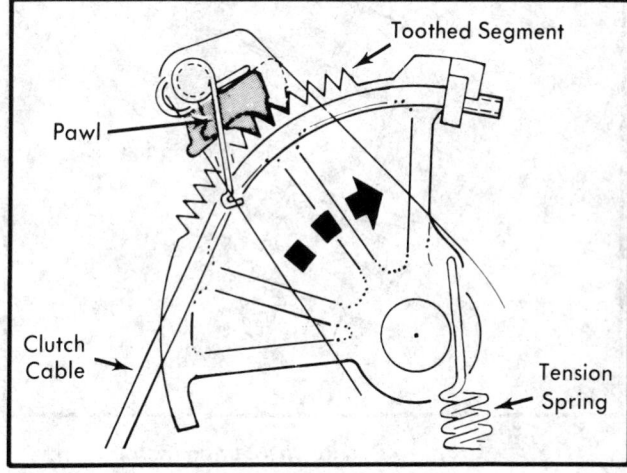

Fig. 2   Automatic Clutch Cable Adjuster

7) Insert suitable spacer between floor pan and selector rod. *See Fig. 4 for spacer dimensions.* Using a suitable arbor, turn shift shaft clockwise to stop. Tighten selector rod locating bolt.

8) Fit selector rod spring into position on selector rod and frame member. Check operation of shift lever.

FIESTA (Cont.)

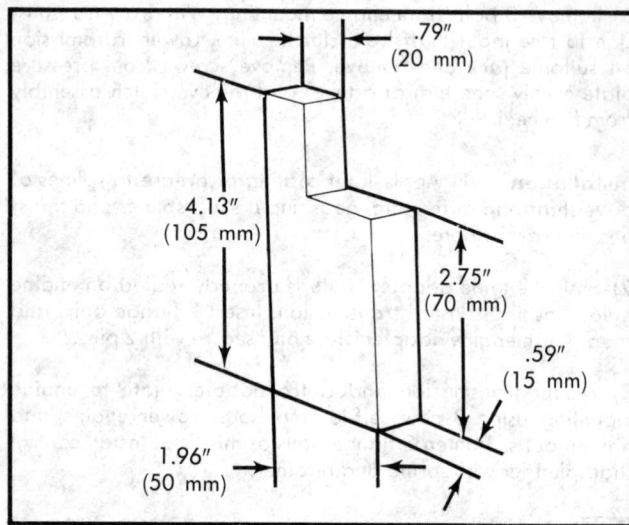

Fig. 3   Selector Rod Spacer Dimensions

9) On models with cranked rod gear shift mechanism place shift shaft and lever in 4th gear position. Loosen selector rod locating bolt and pull shift lever down. Align lever with hole in selector housing and lock with a .16" (4 mm) pin.

10) Using a suitable arbor, rotate shaft clockwise to stop. Tighten selector rod locating bolt. Remove arbor and check shift operation.

NOTE — After installation of the new cranked rod gear shift mechanism, and before any adjustment is made, the retract spring must be installed.

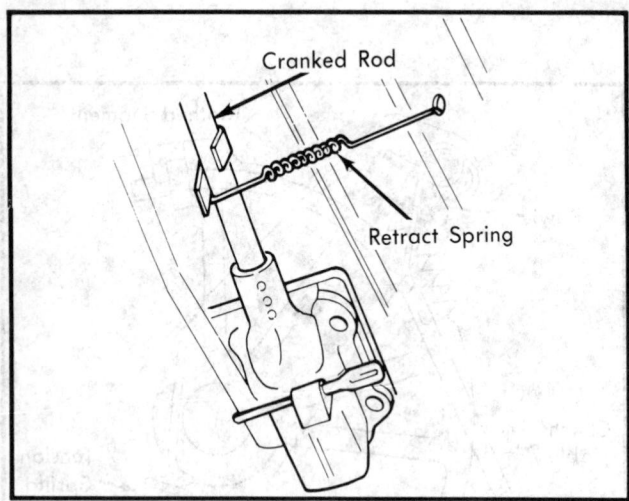

Fig. 4   Cranked Rod Retract Spring Installation

AUTOMATIC CLUTCH CABLE ADJUSTER

Fiesta is equipped with an automatic clutch cable adjuster, and no manual adjustment is required. Automatic adjuster is located at upper end of clutch pedal. Cable tension is set whenever clutch pedal is depressed as pawl engages with nearest adjusting segment.

CLUTCH CABLE

Removal & Installation — 1) Push cable between lever and support; release and unhook cable from release lever with suitable pliers.

2) Remove lower insulating panel on left side of dash. Bend retaining tabs upward; remove screws and lift off. Pull clutch pedal rearward to release pawl from toothed segment and unhook cable from pedal.

3) Rotate toothed segment forward, unhook cable and allow segment to swivel backward. Pull cable out through recess between pedal and automatic adjuster.

4) To install, reverse removal procedure and note the following: Clutch cable must be routed under pedal stop. After installation, press pedal several times to ensure proper operation of clutch automatic adjuster.

CLUTCH RELEASE FORK & LEVER

Removal — With transmission removed, remove release fork bolt. Separate fork, shaft and lever assembly.

Installation — 1) Prior to installation of shaft and lever assembly, align fork bolt hole in shaft and lever assembly and ensure that the hole is not misaligned with counterbore.

2) Thread fork bolt into position until bolt shank is fully seated in counterbore. If bolt fails to seat in counterbore by hand, replace shaft and lever assembly. Reverse removal procedure and tighten release fork bolt.

TIGHTENING SPECIFICATIONS

Application	Ft. Lbs. (mkg)
Gearbox-to-Engine Flange Bolts	30 (4.1)
Gearbox-to-Engine Brace	
Self-Locking Bolts	65 (9.0)
Small Housing-to-Large Housing	18 (2.5)
Gearshift Lock Cap Nut-to-Housing	22 (3.0)
Gear/Differential Housing	
10.9 Grade Bolt	59 (8.1)
12.9 Grade Bolt	70 (9.6)
Shift Housing-to-Floor Pan	12 (1.7)
Cover-to-Housing	
Sheet Metal Bolt	7.5 (1.0)
Die Cast Bolt	9 (1.2)
Pressure Plate-to-Flywheel	13 (1.8)
Selector Rod Mechanism-to-	
Stabilizer Allen Screw	40 (5.5)

Clutches

HONDA ACCORD & PRELUDE

DESCRIPTION

Clutch is a single plate, dry disc type. Clutch assembly consists of clutch disc, clutch cover and pressure plate assembly, and clutch release mechanism. Clutch release mechanism is hydraulic, consisting of a firewall mounted master cylinder and a slave cylinder mounted to clutch housing. Clutch release fork free play is adjustable.

REMOVAL & INSTALLATION

CLUTCH

Removal — 1) Disconnect battery ground at transmission. Put gear shift in Neutral. Disconnect following electrical wiring.

- Positive battery cable at starter.
- Black/White wire from starter solenoid.
- Yellow/Green wire from water temperature sending unit.
- Black/Yellow and yellow wires from ignition timing thermosensor.
- Green/Black and yellow wires from back-up light switch.
- Red/Blue wires (Accord) or Pink/Blue wires (Prelude) from distributor.

2) On Prelude, remove speedometer cable clip and cable without disassembling gear holder. On all models, remove clutch slave cylinder with hydraulic line attached. Remove transmission side starter mount bolt and upper transmission mounting bolts.

3) Raise and suitably support vehicle; drain transmission fluid. Remove front wheels and engine shields. Support transmission with transmission jack. Remove stabilizer bar retaining nuts. On Prelude, remove both mounting brackets and then stabilizer bar.

4) On Accord, remove bolt securing speedometer drive holder and pull assembly out of transmission. Remove subframe center beam and transmission stopper bracket from front of clutch housing. Disconnect lower torque rod at transmission and remove shift rod yoke attaching bolt.

5) On all models, disconnect both lower arm ball joints and tie rod end ball joints with suitable remover. Turn right steering knuckle to outer most position with screwdriver against inboard constant velocity (CV) joint. Pry right axle out of transmission housing ¼" (forcing axle spring clip out of groove inside differential gear splines). Pull axle out of housing. Repeat operation on left axle.

6) On Prelude, disconnect shift lever torque rod from clutch housing; remove shift rod clevis bolt and engine torque rods and brackets. On Accord, remove clutch cover.

7) On all models, remove remaining starter mounting bolt and remove starter. Remove remaining transmission mounting bolts. On Accord, remove engine-to-transmission mounting bolts.

8) On Prelude, remove upper engine damper bracket bolt. On all models, pull transmission away from engine to clear dowel pins (remove both lower damper bracket bolts at same time on Prelude). Lower transmission and remove from vehicle.

9) Check diaphragm for wear at release bearing contact area by inserting alignment tool (07974-6890100). Measure clearance between tool and fingers of spring with feeler gauge. Maximum limit is .04" (1.0 mm). Install holding device on ring gear and loosen pressure plate bolts 2 turns at a time in a criss-cross pattern. Remove pressure plate and separate clutch disc.

Installation — To install, reverse removal procedure and note: Make sure flywheel dowels align with pressure plate dowel holes. Use suitable clutch disc alignment tool and torque pressure plate bolts in criss-cross pattern. Refill transmission with SAE 10W-40 oil.

CLUTCH MASTER CYLINDER

Removal — Separate clutch pedal operating rod from master cylinder push rod by removing through pin at clevis. Disconnect and plug hydraulic lines. Remove nuts mounting master cylinder to firewall. Make sure brake fluid does not spill on painted surfaces.

Installation — To install, reverse removal procedure and bleed hydraulic system.

CLUTCH SLAVE CYLINDER

Removal — Disconnect hydraulic line from slave cylinder. Unhook return spring. Separate threaded rod from end of slave cylinder. Remove slave cylinder mounting bolts and take cylinder off clutch housing.

Installation — To install, reverse removal procedure and bleed hydraulic system.

CLUTCH RELEASE FORK AND BEARING

Removal — With transmission removed, separate slave cylinder push rod from release fork. Remove boot and carefully remove fork retainer clip. Pull fork through clutch housing from inside. Remove bearing retainer clip and pull bearing assembly from sleeve. If worn, bearing may be driven from holder and a new bearing installed. Radius side of bearing must go on holder first.

Installation — Coat all contact areas lightly with grease. Attach bearing and holder to fork with retainer clips. Install fork and sliding bearing assembly onto sleeve. Ensure that fork snaps onto pivot bolt and install boot. Move release fork back and forth to check for freedom of movement.

OVERHAUL

MASTER CYLINDER

NOTE — *The master cylinders used on Accord and Prelude differ in external appearance. Overhaul procedures are similar.*

Disassembly & Reassembly — 1) Remove boot and take off snap ring. Cover open end of cylinder with a shop rag and force piston out with compressed air. Bend spring retainer tabs and separate piston, cups, retainer, return spring and valve assembly.

2) Clean all parts with brake fluid and check for wear or damage. If cylinder bore-to-piston clearance exceeds .006" (.15 mm), replace defective part. Replace all rubber parts during overhaul. Reassemble by reversing disassembly procedure: Rotate piston during installation.

HONDA ACCORD & PRELUDE (Cont.)

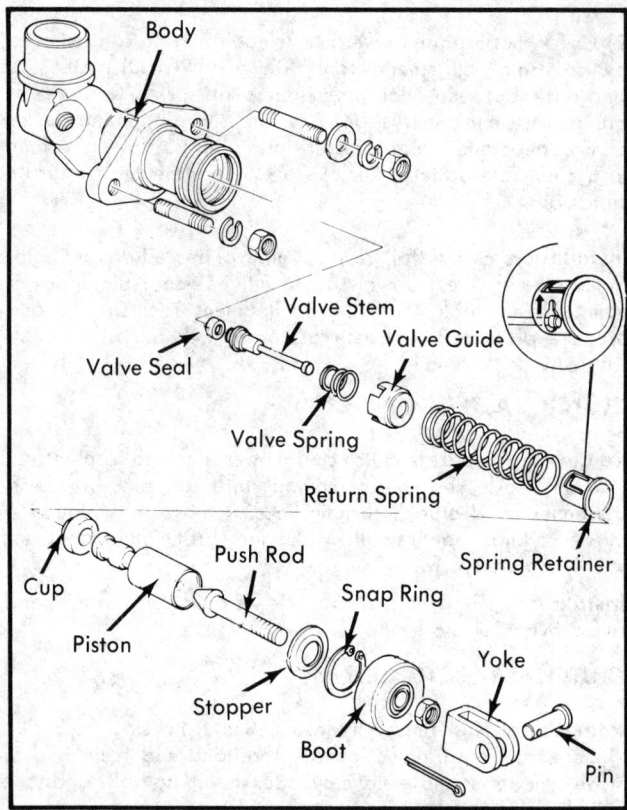

Fig. 1 Exploded View of Accord Master Cylinder. Prelude Cylinder is Similar Except Fluid Reservoir Is Separate From Cylinder Body

CLUTCH SLAVE CYLINDER

Disassembly & Reassembly — 1) Remove push rod and dust boot. Cover open end of cylinder with a shop rag and force piston out with compressed air. Remove piston cup and bleed screw.

2) Clean all parts in brake fluid and check for wear or damage. If cylinder bore-to-piston clearance exceeds .006" (.15 mm), replace defective part. Replace all rubber parts dur-

ing overhaul and coat all parts with brake fluid prior to reassembly. To reassemble, reverse disassembly procedure and insert piston with rotating motion.

ADJUSTMENT

CLUTCH PEDAL HEIGHT AND FREE PLAY

Adjust clutch pedal height to 7.24" (184 mm) by rotating pedal stop bolt in direction necessary to achieve specified height. Adjust pedal free play clearance (between clutch pedal push rod and master cylinder) to .05-.13" (1-3 mm) by loosening lock nut on push rod and rotating push rod.

CLUTCH RELEASE FORK FREE PLAY

Release fork free play should be .08-.10" (2.0-2.6 mm). To adjust, loosen lock nut and hold push rod end nut stationary while rotating push rod with screwdriver. Turn clockwise to decrease free play; counterclockwise to increase free play.

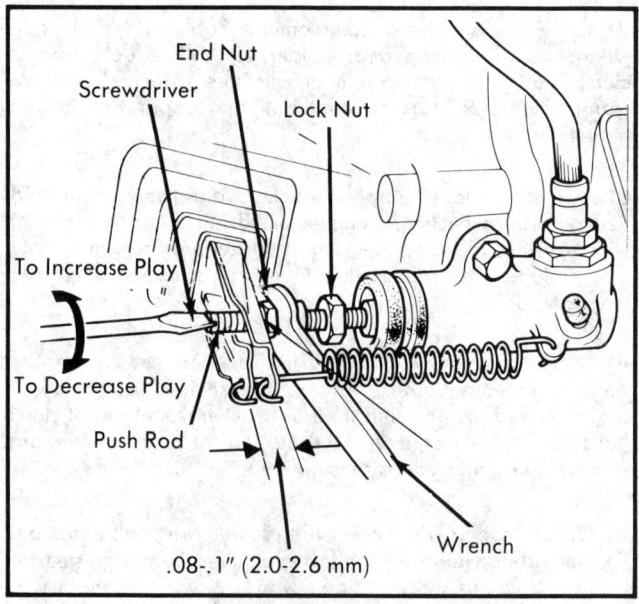

Fig. 3 Clutch Release Fork Adjustment Locations

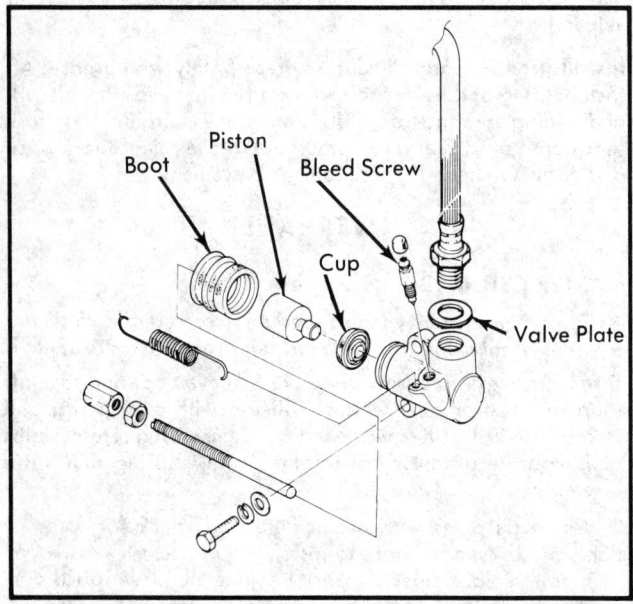

Fig. 2 Exploded View of Slave Cylinder

TIGHTENING SPECIFICATIONS

Application	Ft. Lbs. (mkg)
Flywheel-to-Crankshaft Bolts	
Accord	49-53 (6.8-7.3)
Prelude	51 (7.1)
Pressure Plate-to-Flywheel	
Accord	7-10 (1.0-1.4)
Prelude	19 (2.6)
Front and Rear Torque Rod Bolts	54 (7.5)

HONDA CIVIC

DESCRIPTION

Clutch is single plate dry disc type, using a diaphragm spring to engage pressure plate. Clutch has a mechanical release system consisting of clutch pedal, cable, clutch release lever, and release bearing.

REMOVAL & INSTALLATION

CLUTCH

Removal — 1) Disconnect battery ground at transmission. Release steering lock and put gear shift lever in neutral. Disconnect following engine compartment wiring:

* Positive battery cable at starter.
* Black/White wire from starter solenoid.
* Yellow/Green wire from water temperature sending unit.
* Black/Yellow and yellow wires from ignition timing thermosensor.
* Green/Black and yellow wires from back-up light switch.

2) Remove speedometer cable clip and cable but do not disassemble speedometer gear holder. Disconnect clutch cable at release arm and remove transmission side starter mounting bolt. Remove top transmission mounting bolt and forward bolt for rear torque arm bracket.

3) Raise and support vehicle and drain transmission oil. Remove front wheels and stabilizer bar mounting brackets. Disconnect lower support arms at ball joints OR at pivot bolts. Disconnect tie rod end ball joints.

4) Turn right side steering knuckle outward as far as it will go and pry inboard constant velocity (CV) joint out of transmission housing approximately ½" to force spring clip out of differential gear splines. Pull axle out the rest of the way and repeat for left side. Disconnect shift lever torque rod from clutch housing. Slide pin retainer back and drive spring pin out with punch, then disconnect shift rod.

5) Place a jack under engine with a wooden block between jack pad and engine, then raise engine enough to take weight off mounts. Remove both front and rear torque rods and rear torque rod brackets. Remove engine damper bracket from transmission and remove rear engine mount with its bracket.

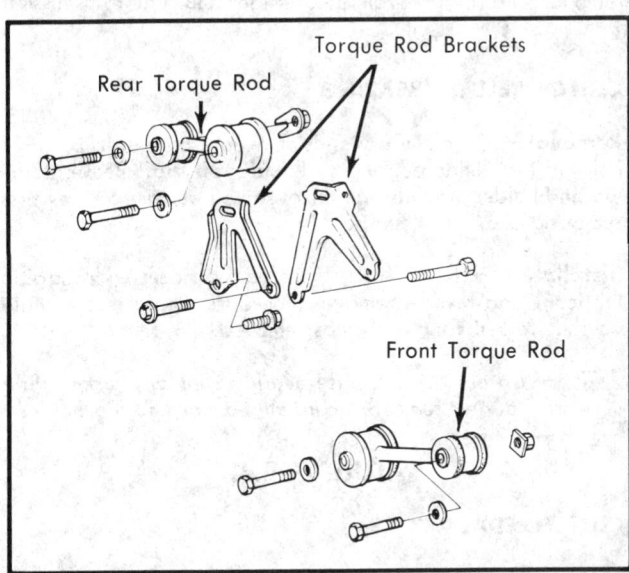

Fig. 2   Torque Rod and Bracket Components

6) Place a 1" x 2" x 4" block of wood between center beam and oil pan, then lower jack so that engine rests on center beam. Remove engine side starter mounting bolt, then remove starter and lower through chassis. Remove 2 remaining transmission mounting bolts. Raise transmission enough with transmission jack to take weight off engine and pull away from engine. Lower transmission clear of engine.

7) Install ring gear holder to keep flywheel from turning. Loosen pressure plate mounting bolts 2-turns at a time in a criss-cross pattern to prevent warping. Remove pressure plate and clutch disc.

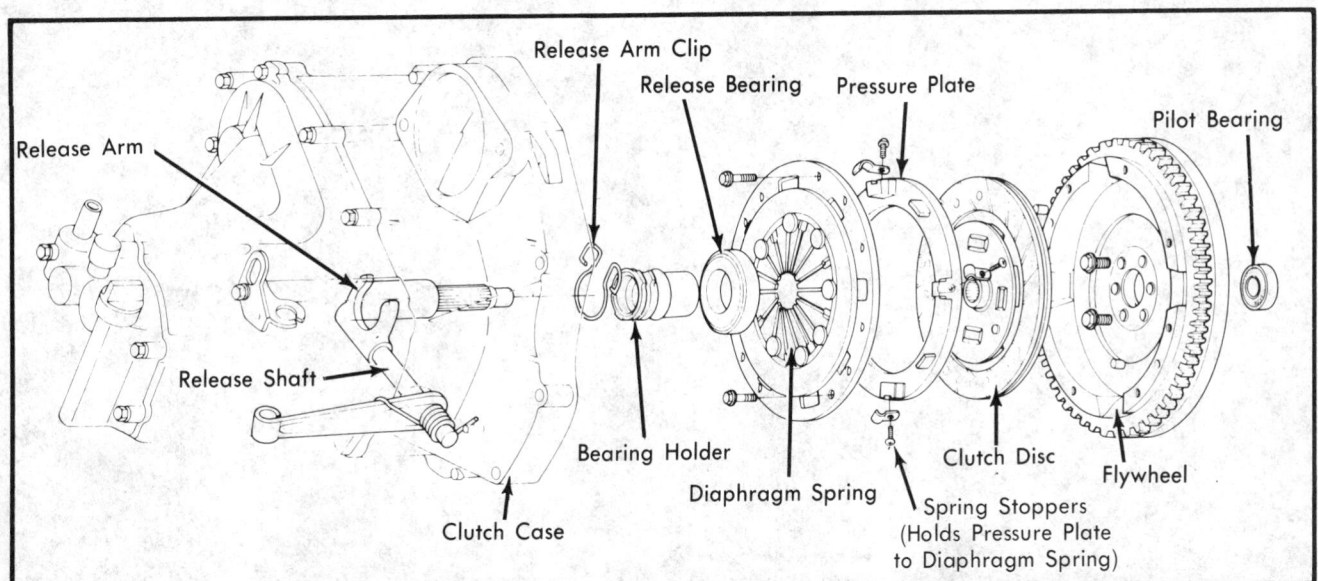

Fig. 1   Exploded View of Clutch Assembly with Bell Housing

HONDA CIVIC (Cont.)

Installation – Use a suitable alignment tool and install disc and pressure plate. Tighten bolts 2-turns at a time in a criss-cross pattern. Ensure that the 2 dowel pins are installed in clutch housing and complete installation in reverse order of removal. Ensure that drain plug is tight and refill transmission with SAE 10W-40 oil.

CLUTCH RELEASE BEARING

Removal – Carefully pry ends of release bearing clip out of holes in fork. Slide bearing and holder off shaft sleeve. Bearing and holder may also be removed with release fork by first removing clutch fork shaft.

Installation – Lightly coat all contact surfaces with suitable lubricant and reverse removal procedure. Replace lock plate on shift fork if fork shaft was removed.

NOTE – *Do not bend release bearing clips any further than necessary during removal or installation of bearing holder.*

ADJUSTMENT

CLUTCH PEDAL

Ensure that pedal return spring holds clutch pedal against stop-pad. Turn adjusting nut in or out to give 1/8 - 5/32" (3-4 mm) free play at release arm. Free play at pedal should be 3/8 - 1 3/16" (10-30 mm) and disengagement height should be at least 1 3/16" (30 mm) from floor. If free play and/or pedal disengagement height exceed these specifications, clutch components may require replacement.

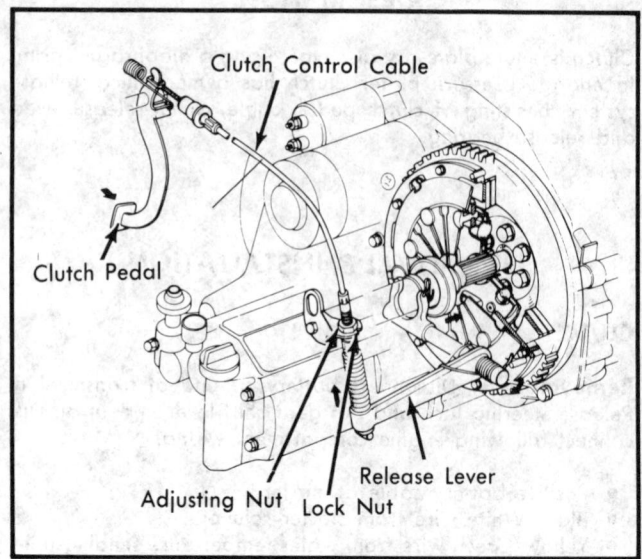

Fig. 3   Clutch Adjustment Point for Civic

TIGHTENING SPECIFICATIONS

Application	Ft. Lbs (mkg)
Clutch-to-Flywheel	9 (1.2)
Flywheel-to-Crankshaft	50 (7.0)
Front and Rear Torque Rod Bolts	54 (7.5)

LUV

Pickup

DESCRIPTION

Clutch assembly is a single dry disc type using a diaphragm spring pressure plate with a pre-lubricated release bearing. Clutch release lever is cable actuated. Cable is hooked to release lever and clutch pedal.

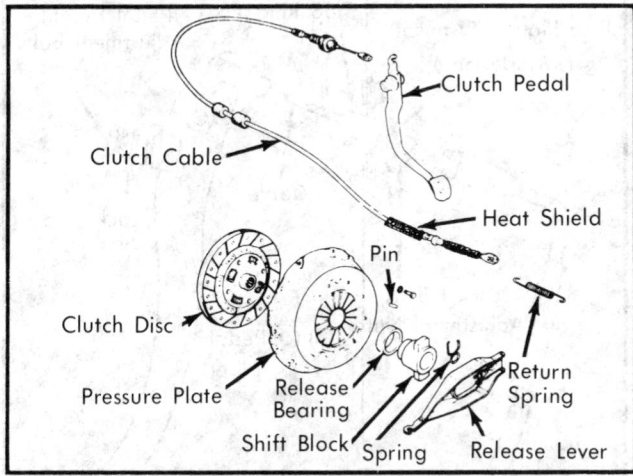

Fig. 1 Exploded View of LUV Clutch Assembly

REMOVAL & INSTALLATION

CLUTCH ASSEMBLY

NOTE — *Transfer case is removed with transmission on 4-WD models. Disconnect additional components as required during transmission removal.*

Removal — 1) Disconnect negative battery cable. Slide gearshift lever boot upward on lever, remove gearshift lever attaching bolts and remove lever assembly. Remove starter attaching bolts and lay starter aside.

2) Raise vehicle on hoist and disconnect exhaust pipe hanger at transmission. Disconnect speedometer cable at transmission. Remove propeller shaft.

3) Remove clutch release lever return spring. Remove flywheel inspection cover. Remove 3 bolts mounting frame bracket to rear mount. Using a jack slightly raise transmission and remove 4 crossmember-to-frame bracket bolts. Remove 2 bolts mounting transmission extension housing. Lower engine/transmission assembly and support rear of engine.

4) Disconnect electrical leads at transmission. Remove transmission to engine attaching bolts and remove transmission.

5) Mark pressure plate and flywheel for reassembly reference. Loosen clutch to flywheel attaching bolts one turn at a time until spring pressure is released. Support clutch assembly with a suitable clutch aligning tool, remove bolts, and remove clutch.

Installation — Apply a thin coat of Lubriplate or equivalent to clutch disc splines. Install clutch assembly to flywheel, matching alignment marks made at disassembly. Use a suitable clutch alignment tool to center assembly on flywheel, then install and tighten attaching nuts. To complete installation, reverse removal procedures.

RELEASE BEARING, SHIFT BLOCK & RELEASE LEVER

Removal — Remove release lever from transmission case. Disengage release bearing to lever retaining springs. Slide out release bearing with shift block. Remove release lever from transmission ball stud.

Inspection — 1) Check release bearing for noise or lubricant loss by spinning bearing. Replace bearing if either condition exists.

2) Inspect release lever ball socket and lever contact surface for signs of excessive wear. Also, check retaining spring for signs of weakening. Make sure spring will hold lever tightly to ball stud.

Installation — Install release lever ball stud in cover. Lube shift block inner groove, ball seat and release bearing contact surface. Install release lever and bearing assembly. Attach release bearing spring to lever and spring clip to ball stud.

PILOT BEARING

Check pilot bearing for seizing, sticking, abnormal noise or wear. If replacement is required, use a suitable tool (J-23907) to remove bearing.

CLUTCH CABLE

Removal — 1) Loosen clutch cable lock nut and adjusting nut. Free cable from various routing clips in engine compartment. Working under vehicle, disengage return spring from release lever.

2) Disconnect cable from release lever and pull cable forward through bracket. Separate cable from clutch pedal and pull cable into engine compartment. Remove cable out of engine compartment. Make sure boots are not damaged.

Installation — To install, reverse removal procedure and note: Make sure cable is not kinked or bent sharply.

ADJUSTMENT

CLUTCH CABLE

Pull cable into engine compartment. Rotate adjuster nut until washer damper assembly is brought back into contact with firewall. Work clutch pedal several times. Pull cable out again and fully tighten nut. Back adjusting nut off until there is about .196" (5 mm) between adjusting nut and boot. See *Fig. 2*. Tighten lock nut.

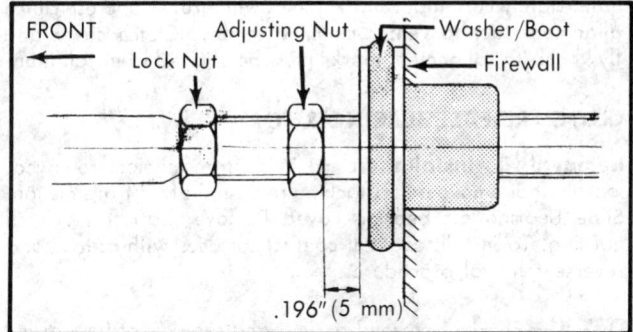

Fig. 2 Clutch Cable Adjustment Gap

MAZDA GLC

DESCRIPTION

Clutch is a dry, single disc, diaphragm type, and cable actuated. A prelubricated clutch release bearing is used and is located in the transmission housing.

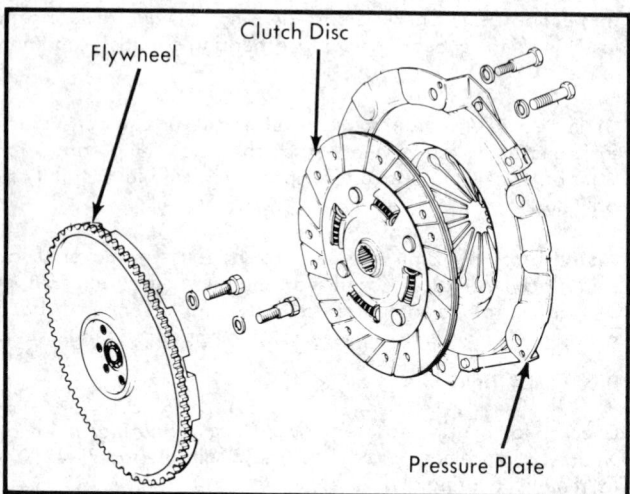

Fig. 1   Exploded View of Clutch Assembly

REMOVAL & INSTALLATION

CLUTCH ASSEMBLY

Removal — 1) Disconnect battery ground cable. Place gear shift lever in neutral; remove lever and hardware. Raise and support vehicle; drain transmission. Disconnect and remove propeller shaft. Disconnect speedometer cable, back-up light switch and exhaust pipe hanger on clutch housing.

2) Remove exhaust pipe support bracket from clutch housing and disconnect clutch cable from release lever. Remove clutch housing splash guard. Remove starter. Disconnect exhaust pipe hanger from extension housing. Place jack under rear of engine, protecting oil pan with a block of wood.

3) Disconnect transmission support member. Remove engine-to-transmission attaching bolts and carefully slide transmission back until it can be lowered from the vehicle. Install flywheel holding tool and loosen pressure plate mounting bolts evenly until assembly can be removed. Separate clutch disc and pressure plate.

Installation — To Install, reverse removal procedures and note: Lightly coat input shaft splines with grease and use clutch alignment tool to center clutch assembly. Clutch cover and flywheel "O" alignment marks must be aligned at installation.

CLUTCH RELEASE BEARING & FORK

Removal & Installation — With transmission removed, loosen and remove bolt attaching release shaft to transmission. Slide bearing off bearing cover. Remove shaft from clutch housing. To install, coat all contact surfaces with grease and reverse removal procedures.

NOTE — *Bearing is prelubricated and should not be washed in any solvent or cleaning solution.*

CLUTCH CABLE

Removal & Installation — Loosen cable lock nut and adjustment nut. Pull cable toward clutch pedal and disconnect from pedal. Push cable through stop ring into engine compartment and disconnect cable at clutch lever. Remove retainer ring at bracket, separate cable housing at bracket and remove cable. See *Fig. 2.* To install, reverse removal procedure.

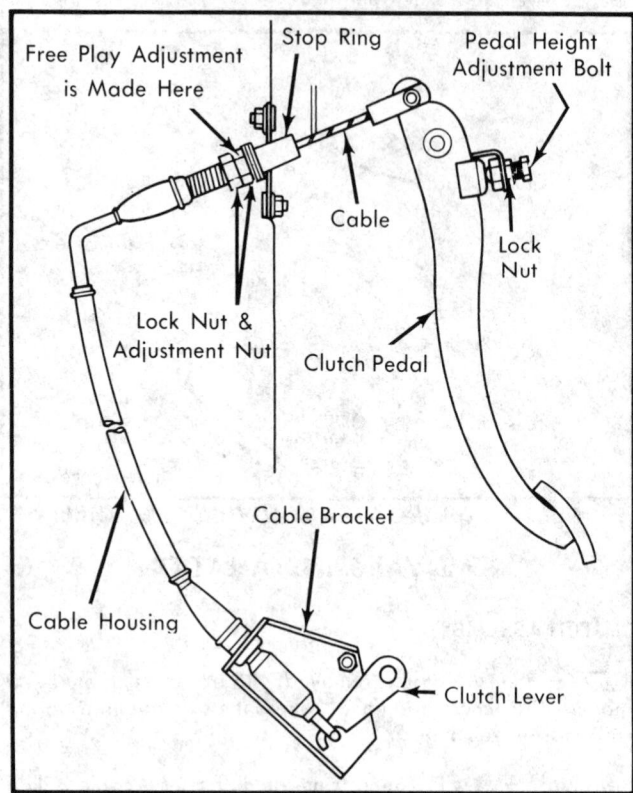

Fig. 2   Installed View of Clutch Cable with Detail of Items to Disconnect for Cable Removal. Illustration Also Shows Pedal Height Location.

PILOT BEARING

Removal & Installation — Pilot bearing is pressed into flywheel. Remove by using suitable puller. To install, lubricate bearing and install using suitable driver.

ADJUSTMENTS

CLUTCH PEDAL HEIGHT & FREE PLAY

Pedal Height — Adjust pedal height to 7.5-7.7" (190-195 mm) by loosening lock nut and rotating adjusting bolt until correct height is obtained. Tighten lock nut. See *Fig. 2.*

Free Play — Clutch pedal free play should be .39-.59" (10-15 mm) and is adjusted by setting release cable clearance at engine compartment side of firewall. Loosen lock nut, pull outer cable and turn adjusting nut until clearance is .06-.09" (1.5-2.3 mm). Tighten lock nut and check pedal free play. See *Fig. 2.*

TIGHTENING SPECIFICATIONS

Application	Ft. Lbs. (mkg)
Flywheel-to-Crankshaft	60-65 (8.3-8.9)
Pressure Plate Assembly-to-Flywheel	13-20 (1.8-2.7)

MAZDA 626, RX7 & B2000 PICKUP

DESCRIPTION

Clutch is a dry, single disc, diaphragm spring type. Clutch system is hydraulic using a firewall mounted master cylinder and a slave cylinder attached to clutch housing. Release bearing is pre-lubricated and sealed.

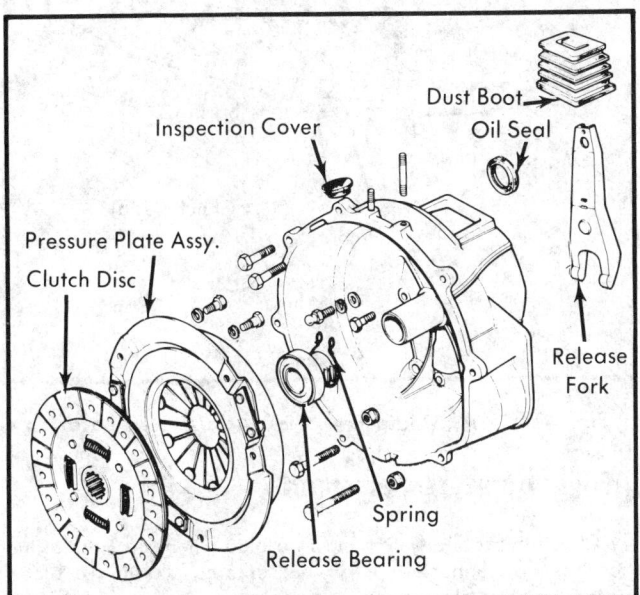

Fig. 1   Exploded View of Mazda Clutch Assembly

REMOVAL & INSTALLATION

CLUTCH ASSEMBLY

Removal — 1) Disconnect negative battery cable. Place gearshift lever in neutral and remove gear shift knob. Remove console box or insert (if equipped). Remove gearshift lever dust boot, retainer (if equipped) and gearshift lever. B2000 gearshift lever components include wave washer, shim and bushing.

2) Raise and support vehicle; drain transmission. Disconnect and remove propeller shaft. Disconnect and/or remove exhaust and emission control components as required. Remove clutch release cylinder and place out of way without disconnecting fluid line. Disconnect and remove starter, speedometer cable, back-up lights and other electrical connections.

3) Place jack under rear end of engine, protecting oil pan with wooden block. Position transmission jack under transmission and remove transmission-to-engine mounting bolts. If equipped, remove transmission-to-crossmember bolts, crossmember-to-frame bolts and crossmember.

4) Slide transmission back until input shaft is cleared and remove from vehicle. Install flywheel holding tool and loosen pressure plate mounting bolts evenly until assembly can be removed. Separate clutch disc and pressure plate. Remove release bearing and fork.

Installation — To install, reverse removal procedure and note: Lightly coat input shaft splines with grease and use clutch alignment tool to center clutch assembly. Clutch cover and flywheel "O" alignment marks must be aligned at installation.

CLUTCH MASTER CYLINDER

Removal & Installation — Disconnect hydraulic line from master cylinder. Remove nuts mounting cylinder to firewall. Unhook clutch pedal from cylinder push rod. Remove cylinder. To install, reverse removal procedure and bleed hydraulic system.

CLUTCH SLAVE CYLINDER

Removal & Installation — Raise vehicle and support. Disconnect fluid hose. Remove nuts mounting slave cylinder to clutch housing and slide off cylinder. To install, reverse removal procedure and bleed clutch.

PILOT BEARING

Rotary Engine Models — Remove nut mounting flywheel to eccentric shaft. Free flywheel from shaft. It may be necessary to use puller to remove flywheel. Use a slide hammer (49 1285 071) to remove bearing and seals. Use installer tool 49 0823 72A (or equivalent) to seat new bearing into place. Install seal.

Piston Engine Models — Pilot bearing is pressed into flywheel. If replacement is required, remove using a suitable puller. To install lubricate bearing with grease and install into flywheel using a driver.

OVERHAUL

CLUTCH MASTER CYLINDER

NOTE — Master cylinder used on B2000 has different external appearance. Disassembly procedure is identical.

Disassembly — 1) Clean outer portion of cylinder. Remove reservoir cap assembly and drain brake fluid. Remove reservoir connector link and reservoir. Remove piston stop ring, washer and piston assembly. Separate piston, cups and return spring.

2) Clean all parts in alcohol or brake fluid and blow dry with compressed air. Check all parts for wear, damage or deforma-

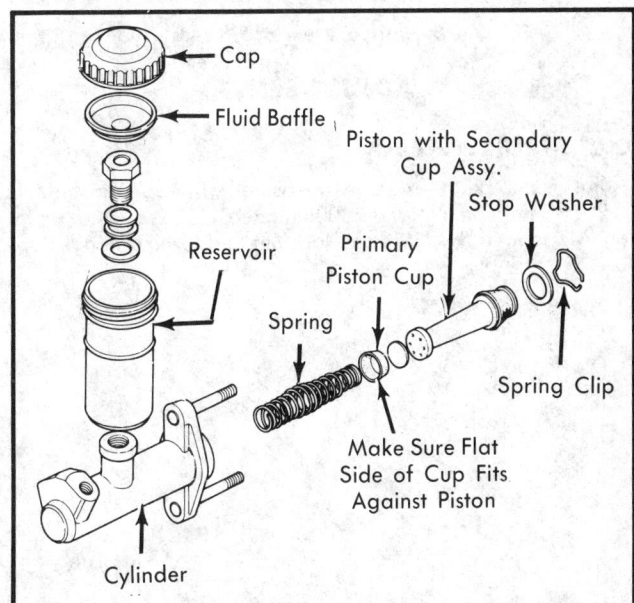

Fig. 2   Exploded View of Clutch Master Cylinder

MAZDA 626, RX7 & B2000 PICKUP (Cont.)

tion. If cylinder bore-to-piston clearance exceeds .006" (.15 mm), replace defective part. Replace parts as required and coat all components with brake fluid before assembly.

Reassembly — Reverse disassembly procedure and note: Install primary cup with flat side of cup against piston and ensure compensating port is open. After assembly, fill reservoir with clean brake fluid and operate piston with screwdriver until fluid is ejected at outlet port.

CLUTCH SLAVE CYLINDER

1) Clean outside of cylinder. Remove dust boot and release rod. Remove piston and cup assembly from cylinder, using compressed air if required. Remove spring, bleeder screw and valve. Clean all parts in brake fluid or alcohol and dry with compressed air.

2) Check all parts for wear or damage. If cylinder bore-to-piston clearance exceeds .006" (.15 mm), replace piston or cylinder. To reassemble, reverse disassembly procedure.

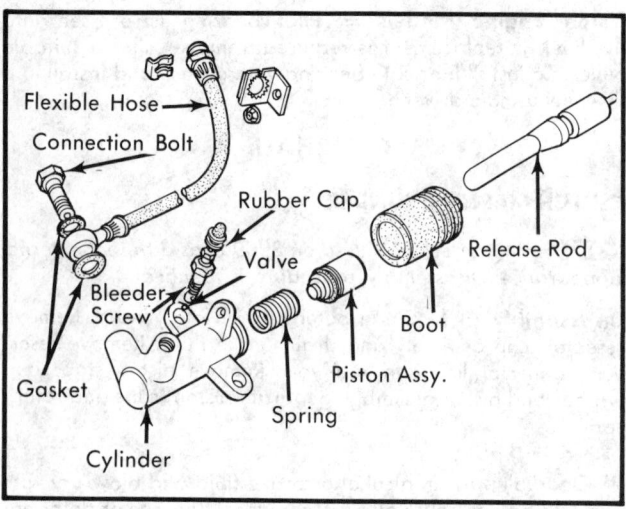

Fig. 3   Exploded View of Slave Cylinder

ADJUSTMENTS

CLUTCH PEDAL FREE PLAY

Adjust clutch pedal free play (measured at pedal pad) to .04-.12" (1-3 mm) on 626 and B2000 models, or .02-.12" (.5-3 mm) on RX7 models, by loosening lock nut and turning pedal stop-per bolt to correct specifications. Tighten lock nut. When free play is correct, pedal height should be 7.5-7.7" (190-195 mm) on RX7; 7.6-7.8" (193-198 mm) on 626 and 8.5-8.7" (215-220 mm) on B2000 models.

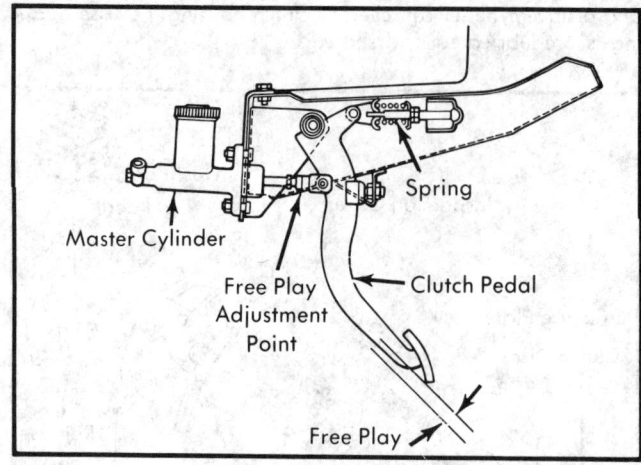

Fig. 4   Clutch Pedal Free Play Adjustment Location

HYDRAULIC SYSTEM BLEEDING

1) Clutch hydraulic system must be bled whenever a fluid line has been disconnected or air has entered system. To bleed system, remove bleed screw cap at slave cylinder and attach a hose. Place opposite end in a jar partially filled with brake fluid. Check master cylinder fluid reservoir often during bleeding process and maintain level at ¾ full.

2) Open bleed screw, depress clutch pedal and allow pedal to return slowly. Continue operation until no air bubbles are seen in discharged fluid. Close bleeder screw, remove hose and attach dust cap to bleed screw.

TIGHTENING SPECIFICATIONS

Application	Ft. Lbs. (mkg)
Flywheel-to-Crankshaft (Piston Engines)	112-118 (15.5-16.3)
Flywheel-to-Eccentric Shaft (Rotary Engines)	289-362 (40-50)
Clutch-to-Flywheel	13-20 (1.8-2.7)

MERCEDES-BENZ

240D

DESCRIPTION

Dry single disc type clutch uses a diaphragm spring type pressure plate. Clutch actuation is hydraulic, using a clutch pedal mounted master cylinder and a clutch housing mounted slave cylinder. A pedal mounted over-center spring assists in clutch pedal actuation. A sealed prelubricated clutch release bearing is also used.

REMOVAL & INSTALLATION

Removal — 1) Disconnect battery ground cable, support transmission with suitable jack, then remove rear crossmember, exhaust support bracket, exhaust pipe and clamp. Loosen, DO NOT remove, propeller shaft center bearing, remove propeller shaft-to-transmission bolts, and ensuring that companion plate remains attached to propeller shaft, push propeller shaft towards rear.

2) Remove tachometer drive from rear of transmission. Remove clutch slave cylinder and pull towards the rear with lines connected, until rod is released from clutch housing. Remove shift linkage from transmission shift levers. Remove starter.

3) Remove transmission-to-intermediate flange attaching bolts (removing two upper bolts last). Pull transmission out horizontally, until input shaft is clear of clutch. Then remove in a downward direction.

4) Loosen pressure plate attaching bolts 1 to 1½ turns at a time until tension is released, then remove all bolts, pressure plate and clutch disc.

Installation — 1) To install, place slave cylinder and line above transmission, then, using an aligning tool, center clutch disc on flywheel and install pressure plate. Tighten bolts 1 to 1½ turns at a time until tight.

NOTE — *When installing propeller shaft to transmission, raise engine and transmission with suitable jack. Tighten propeller shaft center bearing clamp nut to 22-29 ft. lbs. (3-4 mkg).*

CAUTION — *During installation, make sure that clutch is fully pulled into recess in flywheel.*

2) To complete installation, reverse removal procedure. Bleed slave cylinder and check hydraulic fluid level. Check clutch adjustment and shift linkage adjustment.

RELEASE BEARING & LEVER

Removal — Remove release bearing from bearing tube on front transmission cover. Move release lever down and to the left, then pull from ball pin on clutch housing.

Installation — To install, apply suitable lubricant to all bearing and lever contact surfaces, and reverse removal procedure.

CLUTCH MASTER CYLINDER

Removal — 1) Remove floor mats and lining from driver compartment, then remove cover under instrument panel. Siphon fluid from reservoir to below minimum mark and loosen input line by pulling elbow out of rubber clamping ring on master cylinder.

2) Disconnect pressure line from master cylinder and unscrew master cylinder from pedal assembly. Remove master cylinder and connecting hose, leaving push rod on clutch pedal.

Installation — To install, reverse removal procedure, adjust fluid level in reservoir, adjust master cylinder push rod length to a clearance of .008" (.2 mm) by loosening hex nut of eccentric adjusting screw and turning screw. Bleed hydraulic system.

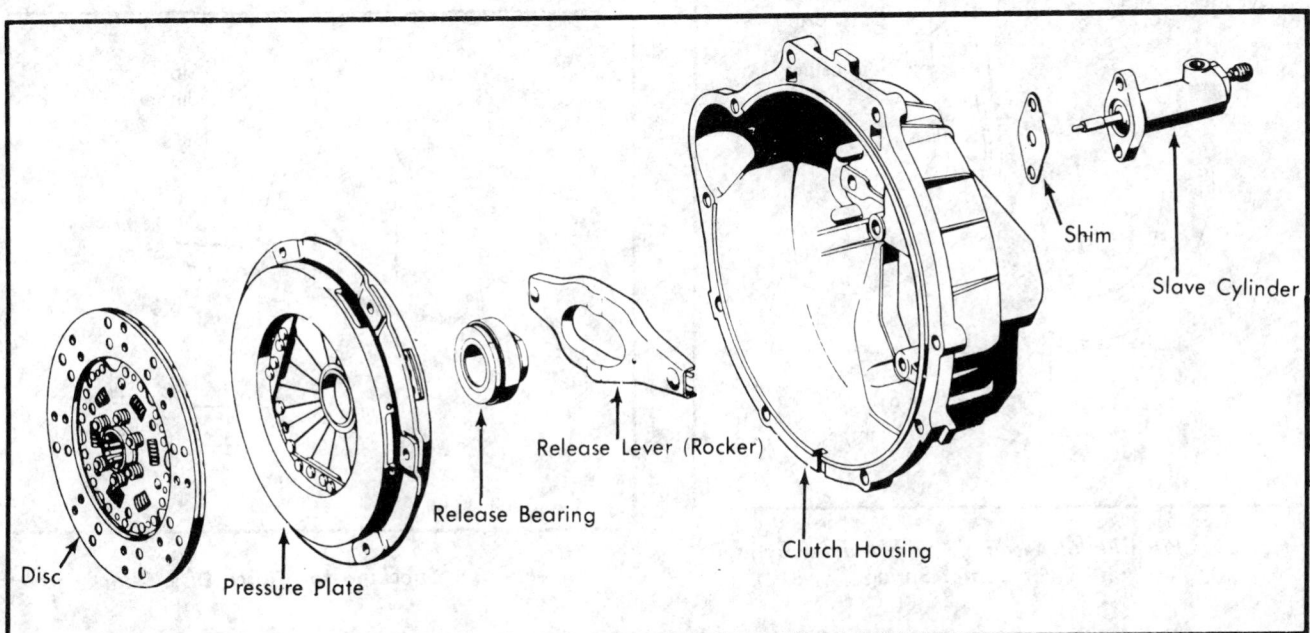

Fig. 1 Mercedes 240D Clutch Components

MERCEDES-BENZ (Cont.)

CLUTCH SLAVE CYLINDER

Removal — Disconnect hydraulic line from slave cylinder, then plug line with a rubber cap to prevent loss of fluid. Remove bolts attaching cylinder to clutch housing, then remove slave cylinder and push rod from housing as an assembly.

NOTE — *Take care not to lose plastic shim installed between cylinder and housing. Shim is recessed to accommodate inspection gauge.*

Installation — To install, place shim with grooved end against clutch housing and hold in position. Insert slave cylinder with push rod into clutch housing, and install and tighten mounting bolts. Connect hydraulic line to cylinder and bleed hydraulic system.

NOTE — *Wear on clutch disc may only be checked using special inspection gauge inserted in groove of plastic shim. Disc is serviceable if notches on gauge disappear in flange. If notches remain visible, wear limit is exceeded and disc must be replaced. See illustration.*

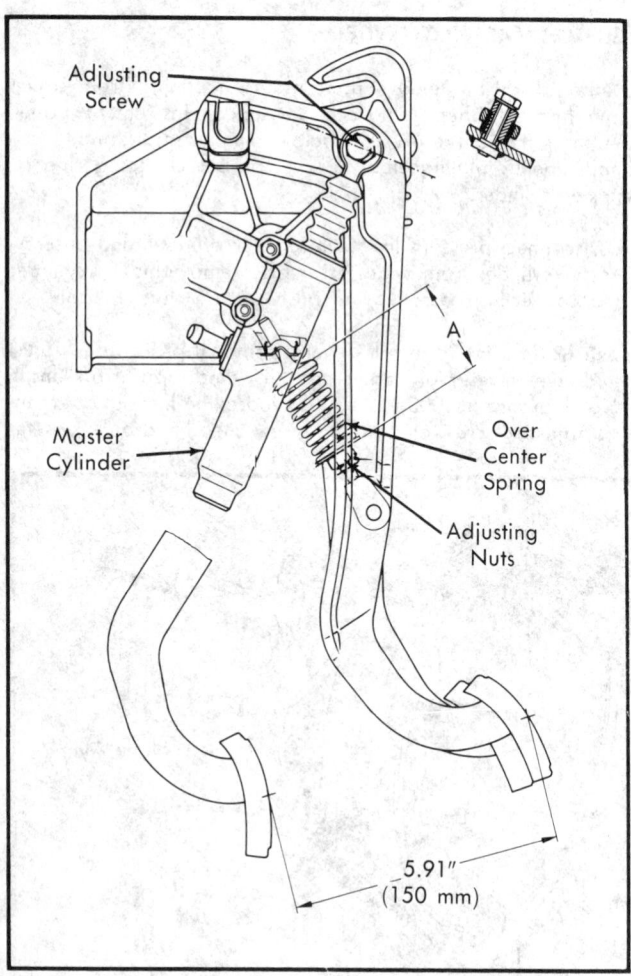

Fig. 2   Clutch Pedal Assembly with Master Cylinder and Over Center Spring

ADJUSTMENT

OVER CENTER SPRING

Adjust nuts at bottom of over center spring so that spring length measured across retainers is 2.05" (52.5 mm). Improper adjustment will result in failure of pedal to return when released or excessive pressure required to depress pedal.

HYDRAULIC SYSTEM BLEEDING

With Pressure Bleeder — 1) Connect pressure line of bleeder to opened bleeder screw of slave cylinder. Fluid reservoir of vehicle should be almost empty so brake fluid can flow from bottom upward through system, allowing air to escape in upward direction.

2) Make sure bleeder is set at lowest possible pressure, and watch reservoir to prevent overflow of fluid. When fluid approaches maximum level in reservoir, remove bleeder and close bleeder screw. Adjust fluid level in reservoir, if necessary, to maximum level in reservoir.

With Assistance of Brake System — 1) Check fluid level in reservoir and make sure it is at maximum level. Place a hose on bleeder screw of right front brake caliper and open screw. Press down on brake pedal until hose is filled with brake fluid and no more air bubbles are showing.

2) Place opposite end of hose on clutch slave cylinder bleeder screw, and open screw. Keep pressure on brake pedal. Close bleeder screw on caliper and release brake pedal. Repeat operation until no more air bubbles appear at fluid reservoir.

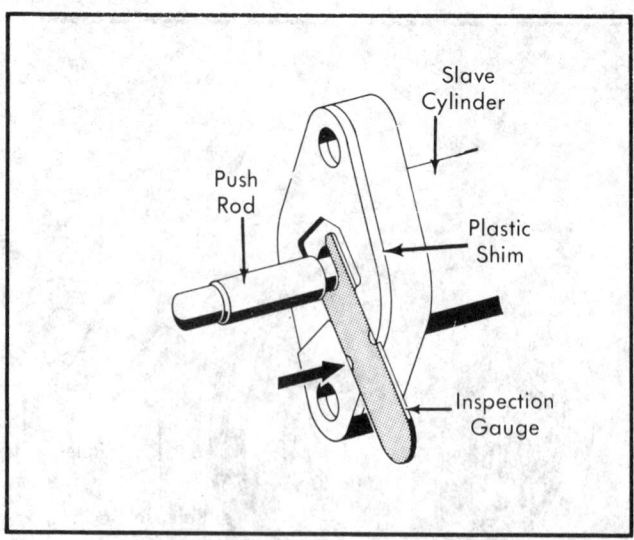

Fig. 3   Checking for Clutch Disc Wear

MGB

DESCRIPTION

Clutch is single dry disc type, using a diaphragm spring type pressure plate. Clutch actuation is hydraulic, using a firewall mounted master cylinder and a bell housing mounted slave cylinder. Release bearing is graphite type, and is mounted in a cup which fits into fork of clutch release lever.

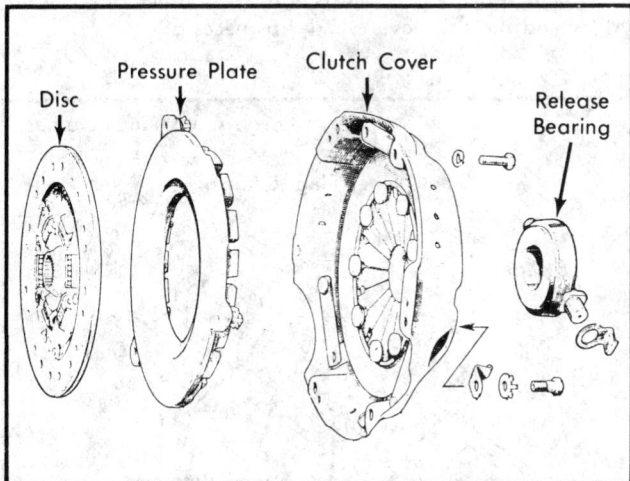

Fig. 1   Exploded View of Clutch Assembly

REMOVAL & INSTALLATION

CLUTCH ASSEMBLY

Removal — 1) Disconnect battery, remove hood, and drain oil and coolant. Disconnect oil cooler lines at filter and oil pressure line at block. Remove all coolant hoses and radiator.

2) Remove air cleaner, heater valve, and distributor cap. Disconnect all electrical wiring, vacuum hoses and throttle linkage. Remove shift lever. Disconnect wires from transmission and remove from retaining clips. Separate clutch slave cylinder from housing and wire out of way.

3) Disconnect speedometer cable, exhaust pipe at manifold, and drive shaft. Remove engine restraint rod. Remove 4 bolts holding rear mounting crossmember to chassis, and lower transmission to fixed crossmember.

4) Remove bolts holding bracket to crossmember, then remove nuts holding rear mounts to crossmember. Remove crossmember. Attach hoist and lift engine slightly, free front engine mounts, and lift out engine/transmission assembly.

5) Remove bolts securing transmission to engine. Separate engine from transmission, then loosen the clutch bolts evenly to remove plate from flywheel. Flywheel side of clutch disc is marked.

Installation — Use aligning tool to center clutch disc and install disc with "Flywheel Side" marking toward flywheel. Place pressure plate in position with marks on flywheel and pressure plate aligned. Tighten mounting bolts gradually to 25-30 ft. lbs. (3.5-4.1 mkg). To complete installation, reverse removal procedure.

CLUTCH MASTER CYLINDER

Removal — 1) Drain fluid from master cylinder through slave cylinder bleeder. Remove facia panel below left side of steering wheel, then remove rubber plug in bulkhead. See *Fig. 2*.

2) Remove 8 screws holding cover plate and seal to pedal box. Separate push rod from clutch pedal at clevis pin. Disconnect hydraulic outlet line and remove master cylinder.

NOTE — *Access to lower bolt is achieved inside car through hole in bulkhead.*

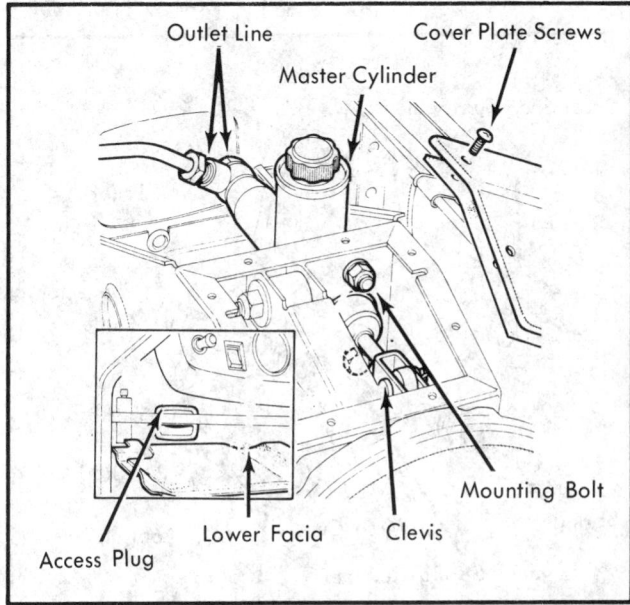

Fig. 2   Items to Take Off in Order to Free Master Cylinder for Removal

Installation — Reverse removal procedure and bleed hydraulic system.

CLUTCH SLAVE CYLINDER

Removal — Remove bolts and washers holding slave cylinder. Slide cylinder from push rod. Remove fluid hose from cylinder being careful not to lose copper sealing washer. Plug open end of hose.

Installation — Reverse removal procedure and bleed hydraulic system.

CLUTCH RELEASE BEARING

Removal & Installation — With transmission separated from engine, release clips holding release bearing to fork by rotating clips forward. Slide bearing from fork. To install, reverse removal procedure, ensuring that spring arms on clips are on transmission side of clutch fork.

MGB (Cont.)

OVERHAUL

CLUTCH MASTER CYLINDER

Disassembly — **1)** Drain fluid and pull dust boot back. Remove circlip from push rod, then withdraw rod, washer, clip, and boot.

2) Remove piston with secondary cup seal. Remove piston washer, main cup, seal spring retainer, and spring. Remove secondary cup seal from piston by stretching over end of piston.

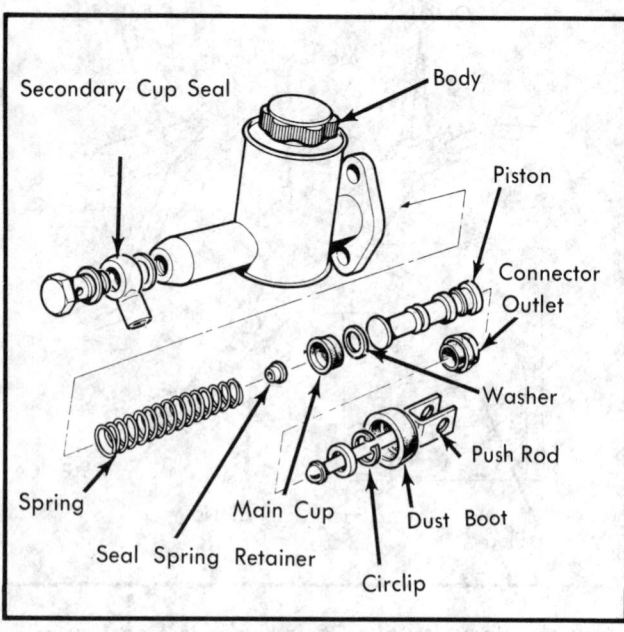

Fig. 3   Exploded View of MGB Clutch Master Cylinder

Inspection — Wash cylinder body in alcohol and clean internal parts with brake fluid. If bore is free of ridges, scores or grooves, new seals may be used. If not, replace master cylinder body.

Reassembly — Coat all components with brake fluid. reverse removal procedure and note the following: Be sure secondary cup seal lip faces toward rear of piston. Insert spring into cylinder bore, large end first. Install circlip, then dust boot.

CLUTCH SLAVE CYLINDER

Disassembly — Remove retaining ring, pull back dust cover and remove small internal retaining ring. Apply air pressure to fluid port and remove piston, cup, spring retainer, and spring. Remove bleeder screw.

Inspection — Wash cylinder in alcohol and clean internal parts with brake fluid. Check bore for scoring, grooves or ridges and replace slave cylinder as necessary.

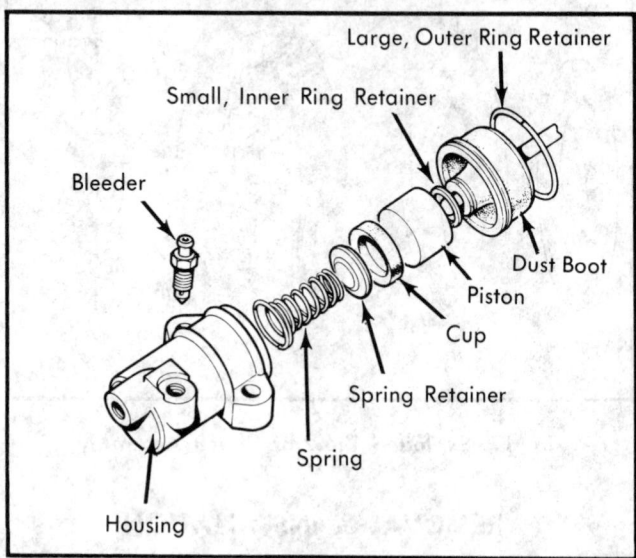

Fig. 4   Exploded View of MGB Clutch Slave Cylinder

Reassembly — Reverse removal procedure, noting the following: Install bleeder screw last, after checking that orifice is not blocked. Use a new cup seal.

ADJUSTMENT

HYDRAULIC BLEEDING

1) Fill master cylinder. Attach bleed tube to bleed valve on slave cylinder. Submerge free end of tube in container of brake fluid.

2) Slowly depress pedal to force air out. Close bleed valve and let pedal rise unassisted. Check that fluid level does not drop too low, and repeat until no more bubbles of air are visible.

PEUGEOT

504
505
604

DESCRIPTION

Clutch is a dry, single disc, diaphragm spring type. Clutch actuation is hydraulic, using a firewall mounted master cylinder and a bell housing mounted slave cylinder. A pre-lubricated clutch release bearing is also used. Due to hydraulic system design, no adjustments, with the exception of bleeding hydraulic system, is necessary.

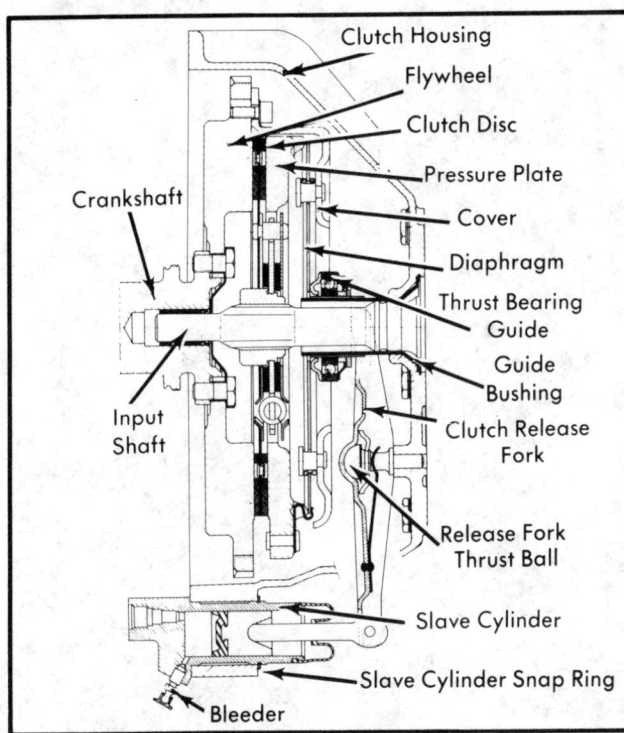

Fig. 1 Sectional View of Clutch Assembly

REMOVAL & INSTALLATION

CLUTCH ASSEMBLY

NOTE — *Engine and transmission must be removed as an assembly.*

Removal — 1) Remove hood, battery with tray, ignition coil, starter, radiator, expansion tank, and windshield washer bottle. Disconnect heater hoses, fuel lines, throttle controls, vacuum lines, and all chassis-to-engine electrical wires. Remove air cleaner and ducting to fuel injection or carburetion system.

2) On models equipped with air conditioning, it will be necessary to remove and set aside under hood components of the air conditioning system. DO NOT disconnect hoses or pressure connections. Disconnect electrical leads to compressor, pressure switch, thermostat, and electric cooling fan. Free receiver-drier, condenser and compressor from their mountings and move to right side of vehicle.

3) If equipped with power steering, remove power steering pump and set aside without disconnecting hoses. On all models, remove upper clutch housing-to-engine mounting bolts and inspection plates. Disconnect exhaust pipe from manifold and remove muffler and exhaust pipe supporting brackets with heat deflector.

4) Attach suitable hoisting sling and raise engine until transmission contacts tunnel. On 604 models, fit propeller shaft tube support between muffler and body and tighten to support tube slightly. Remove steering coupling clamp bolts and replace with slightly longer bolts. Lower front cross member about 1.2" (30 mm) with steering rack attached.

5) On 504 and 505, attach transmission support tool (8.0125) and tighten to support transmission. On all models, remove lower clutch housing-to-engine bolts. Pull engine slightly forward and carefully lift from vehicle. Attach engine to suitable workstand and mark pressure plate and flywheel for reassembly reference. Remove pressure plate mounting bolts evenly and remove clutch assembly.

NOTE — *Clutch slave cylinder and release assembly remains with housing.*

Installation — Lubricate transmission input splines and clutch release bearing guide with Molykote (or equivalent). Use centering tool to align clutch assembly on flywheel and tighten pressure plate bolts evenly to 11 ft. lbs. (1.5 mkg). To complete installation, reverse removal procedure, ensuring that all reference marks are aligned.

NOTE — *Clutch disc must be installed with flexible hub toward transmission. Replace pressure plate mounting bolt washers during installation.*

CLUTCH RELEASE BEARING & FORK

Removal — Remove slave cylinder from clutch housing. Remove release bearing from fork by turning it counter-clockwise. Remove clutch fork by pulling it outward until backing spring is disengaged from ball stud.

Installation — Pack rubber cup on ball stud with grease. To install clutch fork, slide fork from inside toward outside of clutch housing. Lift fork backing spring with a screwdriver and engage fork on ball stud with spring seated against rubber cup. Install release bearing by sliding onto shaft and engaging fork with clockwise rotation.

NOTE — *Bushing is self-lubricated. DO NOT wash in any cleaning solution. Lubricate with motor oil when installing.*

PILOT BUSHING

Bushing is press fit in rear of crankshaft. Bushing must be replaced if excessive clearance with transmission input shaft is evident. Remove and install bushing using suitable pullers and drivers.

CLUTCH MASTER CYLINDER

Removal & Installation — Disconnect and plug master cylinder hydraulic lines from fluid reservoir and to slave cylinder. Remove bolts securing master cylinder to pedal assembly and

PEUGEOT (Cont.)

remove master cylinder. To install, reverse removal procedure and bleed hydraulic system.

CLUTCH SLAVE CYLINDER

Removal & Installation — Disconnect hydraulic line at slave cylinder. Remove snap ring securing cylinder in clutch housing, then slide slave cylinder from clutch housing mounting. To install, reverse removal procedure and bleed hydraulic system.

NOTE — *Overhaul procedures for clutch slave cylinder and master cylinder not provided by manufacturer.*

ADJUSTMENT

HYDRAULIC SYSTEM BLEEDING

Fabricate bleed tube using suitable rubber hose, clamps and adaptor from suitable bleeder kit (ARC 50). Attach hose to slave cylinder bleeder and pressure bleeder (ARC 50 or equivalent) to bleed tube. Adjust bleed pressure to 25.6 psi (1.8 kg/cm²). Open bleed screw and observe fluid level in master cylinder. Close bleed screw when fluid reaches specified level.

PORSCHE

911SC
924
928

DESCRIPTION

The 928 model uses a dual disc dry clutch and a diaphragm spring type pressure plate. All other models use a single disc dry clutch with the diaphragm spring type pressure plate. The 924 Turbo and 928 clutches are hydraulically operated and self adjusting, while the 911SC and 924 models are mechanically operated through an adjustable cable.

REMOVAL & INSTALLATION

CLUTCH ASSEMBLY

Removal (911SC) — 1) Raise and support vehicle. Disconnect negative battery cable and remove air cleaner. Loosen engine block vent hose at engine and plug vent cover hole. If equipped with air conditioning, detach compressor and place out of way but DO NOT disconnect hoses.

2) Remove relay plate cover and disconnect the engine wires at relay plate, adapter plug, relay plate socket, and ignition control unit. Remove fuel hoses at filter and return line. Disconnect accelerator linkage.

3) Remove rear center tunnel cover in passenger compartment. Slide boot forward over shift selector rod and disconnect coupling from inner shift rod. Disconnect speedometer sensor wires in tunnel. Drain engine oil and plug hoses on engine and oil tank.

4) Remove heater hoses at exchangers. Remove rear stabilizer. Disconnect ground strap at body and battery wires at starter. Disconnect accelerator linkage from pedal and clutch cable at transmission. Remove axle shafts from flanges at transmission.

5) Place suitable jack under engine/transmission assembly and lift slightly, using caution to prevent damage to secondary air injection pipes. Loosen transmission and engine mounting bolts and carefully lower assembly from vehicle.

6) Remove circlip from clutch release lever shaft and pull off lever and rubber ring. Remove mounting bolts and pull transmission from engine. Mark pressure plate and flywheel for reassembly and insert alignment tool. Loosen bolts 1 or 2 turns at a time in a diagonal pattern and separate clutch assembly from engine.

Removal (924 and 924 Turbo) — 1) Support front of engine and disconnect battery ground cable. Loosen and remove clutch cable at holder, then remove holder nut. Remove bottom engine cover and clutch bell housing inspection cover. Disconnect oil temperature sensor wire at rear of oil pan.

2) Loosen clutch pressure plate mounting bolts evenly, about 2 turns at a time until all are removed. Turn engine with crankshaft pulley bolt. Place a block of wood between drive shaft tube and crossmember, then remove engine to bell housing bolts.

3) Remove exhaust system from primary muffler to rear of vehicle. Disconnect plug for backup light switch and remove

wires from clip on transmission. Remove back-up light switch. Working inside vehicle, pull up shift lever boot and remove circlip, selector rod and wave washer from shift lever pin.

4) Remove axle shafts from transmission. Suspend with wire in a horizontal position to prevent damage to axle shaft boots. Carefully lift transmission slightly, and remove mounts. Move transmission and central tube back about 3.35" (85 mm). Remove clutch disc, pressure plate and release bearing.

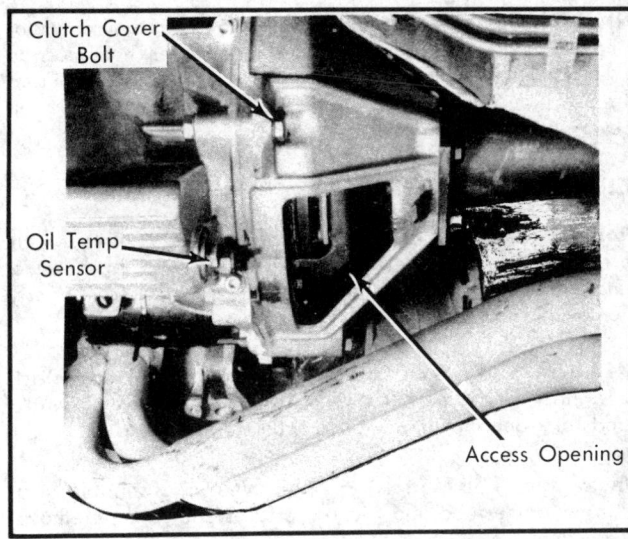

Fig. 1   924 Clutch Housing Access

Removal (928) — 1) Remove lower body brace. Remove slave cylinder, leaving line connected. Remove lower clutch housing with starter attached and suspend from stabilizer bar. Remove coupling screws and push coupling back onto drive shaft.

2) Remove release bearing sleeve mounting bolts and push sleeve toward flywheel. Mark pressure plate, intermediate ring and flywheel for reassembly alignment since they are a balanced unit. Loosen pressure plate mounting bolts evenly 1 or 2 turns at a time until free. Disconnect release lever at ball stud and remove pressure plate, intermediate plate, clutch discs, release bearing, release bearing sleeve, and short drive shaft as an assembly.

Inspection — 1) Check pressure plate and disc for wear, cracks, burning or loose rivets. Replace any part found defective. Check ends of diaphragm spring for wear marks from release bearing.

2) Lay a straightedge across pressure plate face and check for distortion; up to .011" (.3 mm) is permissible. Place clutch disc on input shaft and see that it moves freely on splines. Check disc for maximum allowable runout of .24" (.6 mm).

3) Check clutch release bearing for noise or rough operation. Do not wash bearing in any cleaning solution; clean with a lint free cloth only. Replace bearing if contaminated or loud. Check pilot bearing in crankshaft for rough operation, replace as necessary.

Installation (All Models) — 1) On 928, assemble and install clutch as a unit, noting that rigid disc is against flywheel and

PORSCHE (Cont.)

spring center disc is between pressure plate and intermediate plate. Use short drive shaft to ensure alignment. On 911SC and 924 models, use alignment tool and install clutch assembly.

2) On all models, ensure that marks on flywheel and clutch assembly are aligned and tighten pressure plate bolts one turn at a time in a diagonal pattern. If installing new clutch, balancing marks on clutch and flywheel should be offset 180°.

3) On 911SC models, pull release lever in opposite direction of engine when transmission is installed on engine. There must be at least .78" (20.0 mm) clearance between release lever and transmission housing. On all models, complete installation in reverse order of removal.

CLUTCH RELEASE BEARING

Removal (911SC & 928) — Bearing is removed with pressure plate. Remove by laying pressure plate on bearing and removing snap ring on flywheel side of clutch fingers. Remove bearing along with washers.

Removal (924 & 924 Turbo) — With clutch removed, detach bearing spring clips from release lever. Move lever forward and take bearing off of guide tube.

Installation (All Models) — Apply thin coat of suitable lubricant to guide tube and friction surfaces and reverse removal procedures.

ADJUSTMENT

CLUTCH ADJUSTMENT

911SC — Clutch free play must be checked at transmission adjusting lever due to auxiliary clutch spring. With cable snug, adjust play at lever to .040" (1.0 mm). Clutch pedal travel may be adjusted at stop on floor plate. Release travel should be .965-1.004" (24.5-25.5 mm) when measured at cable end.

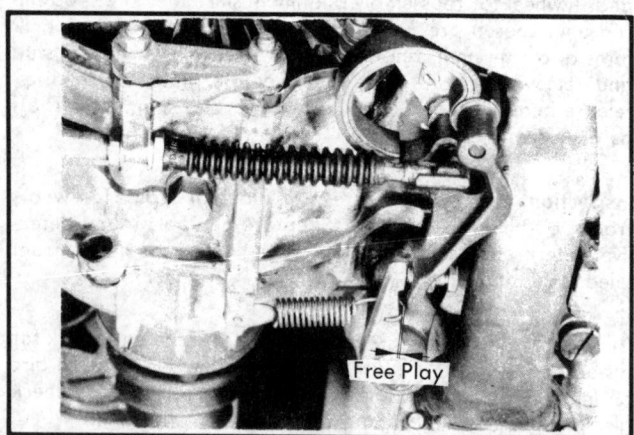

Fig. 2   View of 911SC Clutch Adjusting Mechanism

924 — With release bearing against diaphragm spring, lower end of cable should be 5.36-5.52" (136.0-140.0 mm) when measured from lower edge of cable holder to pin at release lever. To adjust, turn outboard release lever on shaft and tighten in position. Adjust cable with counternuts on holder to give .8-1.0" (20.0-25.0 mm) free play at clutch pedal.

924 Turbo & 928 — No adjustment is necessary due to automatic adjustment by slave cylinder. There must be .02" (.5 mm) play between end of push rod and master cylinder piston. This gives approximately .12" (3.0 mm) free play at pedal pad. If necessary, correct play by adjusting push rod.

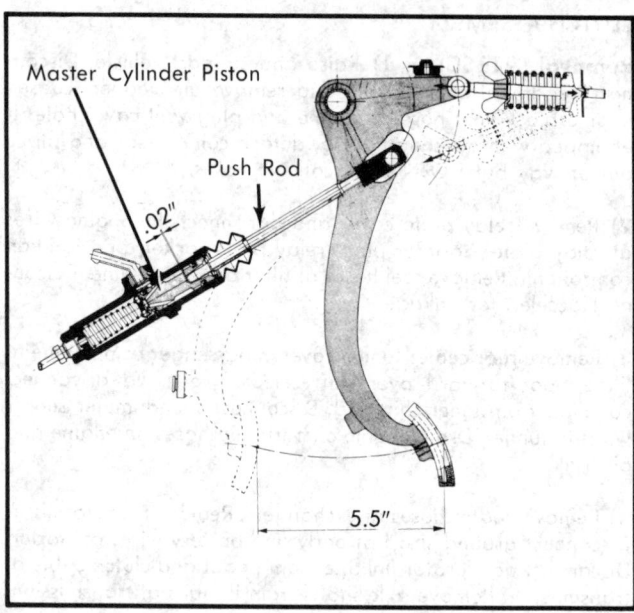

Fig. 3   924 Turbo and 928 Clutch Push Rod Adjustment

PEDAL ADJUSTMENT

911SC & 924 — 1) With engine running and warm, reverse gear must be able to be engaged silently when clutch pedal is fully depressed. Release lever should move .6" (15.0 mm) to completely disengage clutch. If cable housing rests on bottom of guide clamp when clutch pedal is fully depressed, inner cable must be adjusted at yoke end.

2) Measure from threaded cable end of yoke to outer edge of lock nut. Adjust if not within .7-.9 (17.0-22.0 mm). If arc of cable is too large and allows cable to come out of guide clamp when pedal is released, inner cable must be shortened at yoke end.

Clutches

RENAULT

Le Car

DESCRIPTION

Clutch system is single disc dry plate type. Main components are: Disc, diaphragm spring operated pressure plate, ball bearing type clutch release bearing, release fork, and pilot bearing. Clutch operation is mechanical through cable actuation.

REMOVAL & INSTALLATION

CLUTCH ASSEMBLY

Removal — 1) Disconnnect battery. Separate speedometer. Remove water pump belt, camshaft belt, and air injection components. Remove both upper starter bolts (it may be necessary to use special wrench Ele. 565).

2) Remove clutch housing mounting bolts. Take off calipers and support out of way. Disconnect tie rods at steering rack end. Disconnect upper ball joints. Separate axle drive shafts by pulling stub axle out and down.

NOTE — *Be careful not to damage oil seal lips on differential adjusting ring nuts.*

3) Remove bolts from support tab on underside of transaxle. Disconnect and free clutch cable lever. Remove tubular crossmember bolts and slide crossmember out rearward. Use a jack and support front of transaxle. Remove front mount. Remove lower starter bolt. Remove clutch cover and any side reinforcement bolts. Remove transaxle from vehicle. Mark pressure plate assembly for installation reference and remove entire clutch assembly.

Installation — To install, reverse removal procedure and note following: Larger end of clutch disc hub should face engine. Use centering tool to align pressure plate and disc. Lightly grease input shaft and axle drive shaft splines. Make sure axle drive shafts fully seat into side gears.

CLUTCH CABLE

Removal — Disconnect cable from lever on transaxle. Free transaxle end of cable from sleeve stop. From inside vehicle, remove clutch pedal retaining clip and cable-to-pedal clevis pin. Slide pedal off of pivot rod, free cable from sleeve stop on pedal bracket, and remove cable.

Installation — To install, reverse removal procedure and note the following: Lubricate pedal bores and retaining pins with Molykote BR 2 lubricant. Adjust clutch free play.

CLUTCH RELEASE BEARING & FORK

Removal — With transaxle removed, disconnect the return spring from release bearing and fork, and slide bearing off transmission input shaft. Using a suitable tool (Emb. 384), extract fork retaining roll pins. Remove fork shaft, fork, and return spring.

Installation — 1) Lubricate fork shaft with Molykote BR 2 grease. Slide shaft into transaxle housing (fitted with rubber seal) and through release fork and return spring.

2) Align holes in shaft with those in fork and install roll pins, making sure that pins protrude $\frac{1}{32}$" on forward side of fork. Lubricate bearing sleeve and fork fingers with Molykote BR 2 grease, and slide bearing onto transmission input shaft.

3) Install return spring, placing ends in holes of release bearing support and in fork. Lubricate bearing face and portion of clutch diaphragm spring which bearing contacts with Molykote BR 2 grease. Install transmission and adjust clutch free play.

PILOT BEARING

Removal — Remove transaxle, clutch assembly and flywheel. Using a suitable tool (Mot. 11), extract bearing from crankshaft.

Installation — Using a suitable driver, install pilot bearing into crankshaft. Install flywheel, clutch assembly and transaxle. Adjust clutch free play.

OIL SEAL

Removal — Remove transaxle from vehicle. Remove the clutch housing attaching bolts and separate clutch housing from transmission. Using a suitable tool, remove oil seal from clutch housing.

Installation — Fit oil seal into place over special tool B. Vi. 526 or 488. Coat paper gasket with sealer. Place tool inside clutch release bearing guide to spread seal lip. Refit clutch housing on transaxle and slide tool along clutch shaft, then remove tool. Tighten clutch housing nuts.

ADJUSTMENT

CLUTCH FREE PLAY

Loosen lock nut. Turn adjusting nut to obtain free travel at end of release lever of $\frac{1}{8}$-$\frac{5}{32}$" (3-4 mm).

TIGHTENING SPECIFICATIONS

Application	Ft. Lbs. (mkg)
Flywheel-to-Crankshaft	35 (4.8)
Clutch Housing-to-Transmission	
8 mm Bolts	15 (2.0)
10 mm Bolts	30 (4.1)

SAAB

99
900

DESCRIPTION

Clutch is dry, single plate, diaphragm spring type. Primary components are: Disc, pressure plate assembly, and release bearing. Release bearing is a special design ball bearing with elongated outer ring which presses directly against diaphragm when clutch pedal is let out. Clutch operation is hydraulic. Clutch pedal operates on a master cylinder which is connected to slave cylinder. Slave cylinder is located inside clutch cover around input shaft. Slave cylinder acts directly on release bearing. Clutch adjustment is automatic.

REMOVAL & INSTALLATION

CLUTCH ASSEMBLY

Removal — 1) On 99 models, drain coolant, remove hood and disconnect negative battery cable. Disconnect wiring harness from fan housing and the following electrical leads: ignition coil, oil pressure switch, temperature switch, headlight wiper motor and thermal fan switch on radiator.

2) Disconnect radiator hoses. Remove grille and radiator. On all models, remove clutch housing cover, and install suitable spacer (8390023) between cover and diaphragm spring.

NOTE — Clutch pedal must be depressed to fit spacer.

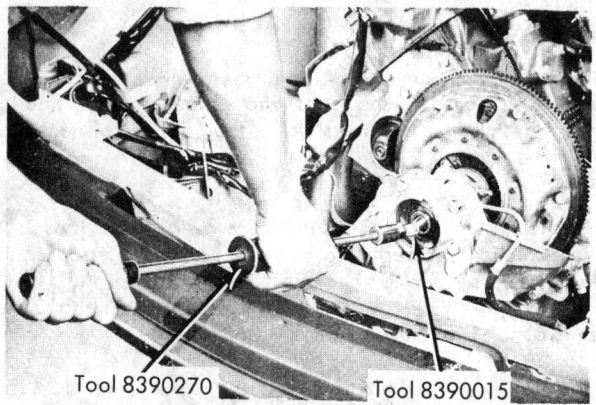

Fig. 1   Pulling Input Shaft Using Special Tools

3) Remove retaining ring and seal cap from input shaft. Remove plastic propeller from input shaft. On 99 models, pull out input shaft using slide hammer (8390270) and universal adapter (8390015). On 900 models, insert an M8 bolt into clutch shaft and install tool 8393175. Withdraw the shaft as far as possible.

4) Remove slave cylinder retaining bolts. Remove pressure plate mounting bolts and remove pressure plate, clutch disc, slave cylinder (hydraulic line attached) and release bearing as an assembly.

NOTE — Make sure diaphragm spring does not damage slave cylinder sleeve.

Fig. 2   Lifting Out Clutch Assembly — Illustration Shows Relationship of Clutch Assembly to Surrounding Engine Components

NOTE — Before beginning clutch installation make sure input shaft seal is in good condition. Seal is located inside slave cylinder in primary gear case. Seal forms a direct bond with sealing surface of input shaft.

CAUTION — Make sure diaphragm spring does not damage slave cylinder sleeve during installation.

Installation — 1) Reassemble clutch assembly and loosely install two pressure plate retaining bolts.

NOTE — Hardened side of release bearing faces diaphragm spring.

2) Bolt slave cylinder guide sleeve to primary gear casing. Install input shaft and make sure it engages clutch disc splines and bearing. Install plastic propeller, seal cap and retaining ring to input shaft.

3) Tighten clutch assembly (pressure plate) to flywheel. Depress clutch pedal and remove spacer. With pedal depressed, install sliding lock ring toward slave cylinder. Complete installation by reversing removal procedure.

NOTE — DO NOT depress clutch pedal farther than necessary. Seal lip may be pressed too far, causing a hydraulic leak and seal damage.

CLUTCH MASTER CYLINDER

Removal & Installation — Remove hydraulic line at rear of cylinder. From under instrument panel in vehicle, remove access cover on left side. Remove push rod pin at clutch pedal. Remove master cylinder retaining nuts from firewall. From engine compartment, remove fluid supply line from top of cylinder and position so fluid does not leak. Remove master cylinder. To install, reverse removal procedure and bleed system.

CLUTCH SLAVE CYLINDER

NOTE — Slave cylinder removal is accomplished during clutch assembly removal. See Clutch Assembly Removal in this article.

SAAB (Cont.)

OVERHAUL

CLUTCH MASTER CYLINDER

Disassembly — Pull back sealing bellows and remove retaining ring. Remove push rod and washer. Remove piston, convex washer, piston seal, and spring. Inspect cylinder bore for wear or damage. Replace complete assembly if cylinder is worn or damaged. Replace seal if worn or swollen.

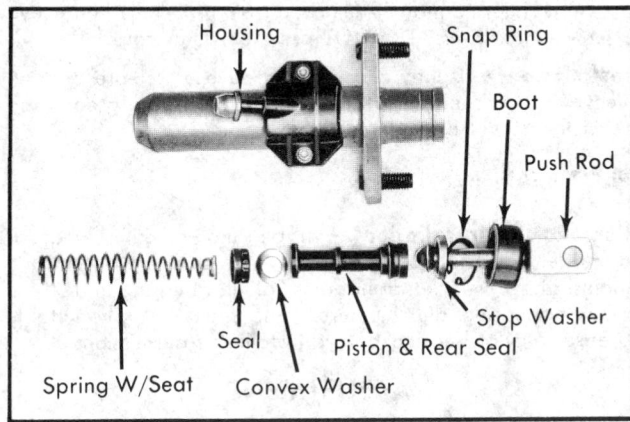

Fig. 3   Exploded View of Clutch Master Cylinder

Reassembly — Install return spring and spring retainer. Lubricate piston and seals with Girling Rubber Grease No. 3 . Install seals, convex washer and piston. Install push rod followed by washer and retaining ring. Install sealing bellows.

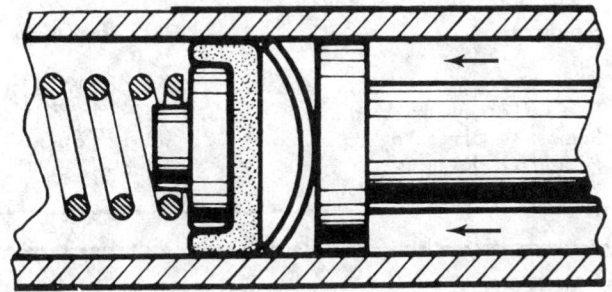

Fig. 4   Cut-Away View of Clutch Master Cylinder Bore Showing Convex Washer Correctly Installed. Convex Side MUST Face Master Cylinder Piston

CLUTCH SLAVE CYLINDER

Disassembly — 1) Remove clutch release bearing from slave cylinder.

2) Set slave cylinder with release bearing end facing up. Press cylinder sleeve out.

3) Remove "O" ring from sleeve.

4) Remove piston and lip seal.

NOTE — *Before beginning reassembly, lightly coat lip seal and piston (not "O" ring) with Caster Rubber Grease (or equivalent).*

Reassembly — 1) Fit "O" ring to sleeve flange.

2) Slide seal lip on sleeve.

3) Coat sleeve flange with brake fluid. Insert sleeve into cylinder. Push seal lip part way into cylinder.

4) Guide sleeve and cylinder together by pushing on piston until lock rings and "O" ring are fitted.

5) Place slave cylinder on support and seat sleeve into cylinder.

6) Fit release bearing to piston.

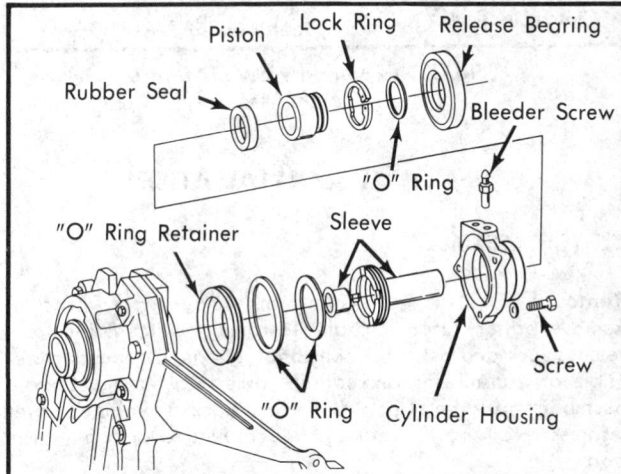

Fig. 5   Exploded View of Clutch Slave Cylinder

ADJUSTMENT

HYDRAULIC SYSTEM BLEEDING

1) Connect a ¼ " hose to slave cylinder bleeder screw, and place opposite end in a container partially filled with hydraulic fluid. Fill master cylinder reservoir with hydraulic fluid. Open bleeder screw on slave cylinder ½ turn.

2) Place a coolant system tester over filler opening of master cylinder. Pump tester until all air has been removed from system. Close slave cylinder bleeder screw and check to see that all air has been expelled by depressing clutch pedal.

SUBARU

1600

DESCRIPTION

Clutch is a single dry disc type with a diaphragm spring pressure plate. Actuation is mechanical through a cable. Sealed release bearing requires no lubrication.

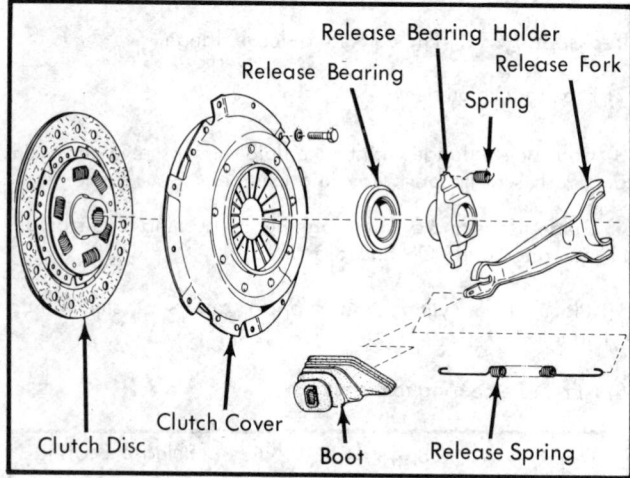

Fig. 1 *Exploded View of Subaru Clutch Assembly*

REMOVAL & INSTALLATION

CLUTCH ASSEMBLY

Removal — 1) Remove spare tire and support bracket. Remove battery ground cable. Disconnect clutch cable from release fork and detach rubber boot. Disconnect speedometer cable at transmission and loosen cable retainer clip. Disconnect back-up lamp switch connector, black and white starter harness (NOT battery cable), and ground cable on vehicle body.

2) Remove starter with battery cable attached. Remove upper engine-to-transmission bolts and loosen lower nuts. Loosen transmission side torque rod stopper nut by about .4" (10 mm) and tighten engine side nut by the same amount. On 4-WD models, separate both the gear selector and 4-WD selector system from the transmission.

3) On all models, raise and support front end of vehicle and remove front exhaust pipe assembly. On 4-WD models, remove transmission cover and rear drive shaft. Plug rear of transmission to prevent oil from running out. Remove exhaust cover and gearshift system from all except 4-WD models.

4) On all models, remove stabilizer, then lower both left and right transverse links. Drive spring pins from inner ends of axle shafts and push wheels out until axles separate from driving splines. Remove clamp on left side of hand brake cable. Remove nuts from transmission mounting pads.

5) Support transmission with a jack and remove crossmember. Remove nuts securing transmission to engine and move transmission away from engine. Ensure that mainshaft clears engine and lower transmission from vehicle. Remove pressure plate mounting bolts and take off clutch assembly.

Installation — Using alignment tool, place clutch disc and pressure plate in position on flywheel. Ensure that there is a gap of 120° between "O" marks on flywheel and pressure plate. Tighten bolts to 12 ft. lbs. (1.6 mkg) gradually in a criss-cross pattern. Reverse removal procedure to complete installation.

CLUTCH RELEASE BEARING

Removal — With transmission separated from engine, disconnect return springs from transmission and remove bearing assembly. Bearing may be removed from or installed on sleeve using suitable press. DO NOT press on outer race.

Installation — Lightly coat inner groove of release bearing sleeve and all contact surfaces with multi-purpose grease and reverse removal procedures.

PILOT BEARING

Removal & Installation — If bearing indicates wear or damage, extract bearing and oil seal. Inspect transmission mainshaft for wear or damage. Install new bearing and seal in crankshaft using aluminum rod and mallet. Apply suitable grease to pilot bearing before installing transmission.

ADJUSTMENT

CLUTCH FREE PLAY

Remove fork return and adjust spherical nut so that there is .08-.12" (2.0-3.0 mm) play at fork end. Use care not to twist cable during adjustment. Attach return spring and ensure that cable is routed without kinks or sharp bends.

Clutch Adjustment Specifications	
Application	**In. (mm)**
Clutch Pedal Stroke	5.1-5.4 (129-137)
Release Fork Stroke	.67-.71 (17-18)
Release Fork Free Play	.08-.12 (2.0-3.0)
Pedal Free Play	.50-.80 (1.3-2.0)

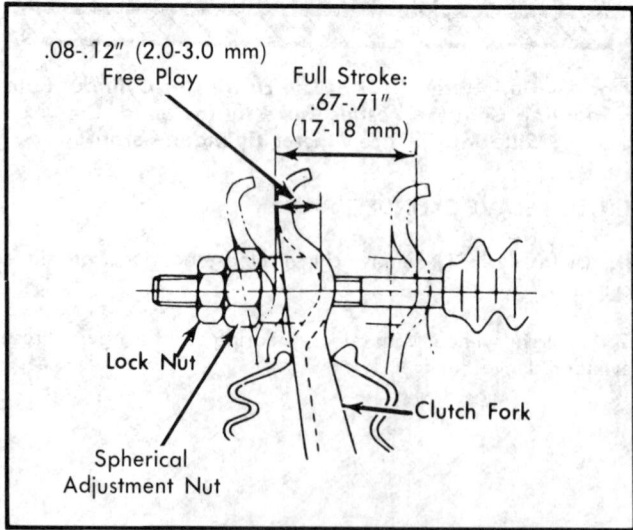

Fig. 2 *Clutch Cable Adjustment Locations and Specifications*

TOYOTA CELICA, COROLLA, CORONA, PICKUP & SUPRA

DESCRIPTION

Clutch is a dry, single plate, diaphragm spring type which is hydraulically operated by a firewall mounted master cylinder and clutch housing mounted slave cylinder. The slave cylinder used on 4-WD Pickup is adjustable; all others are non-adjustable and clearance is automatically compensated for by internal design of cylinder.

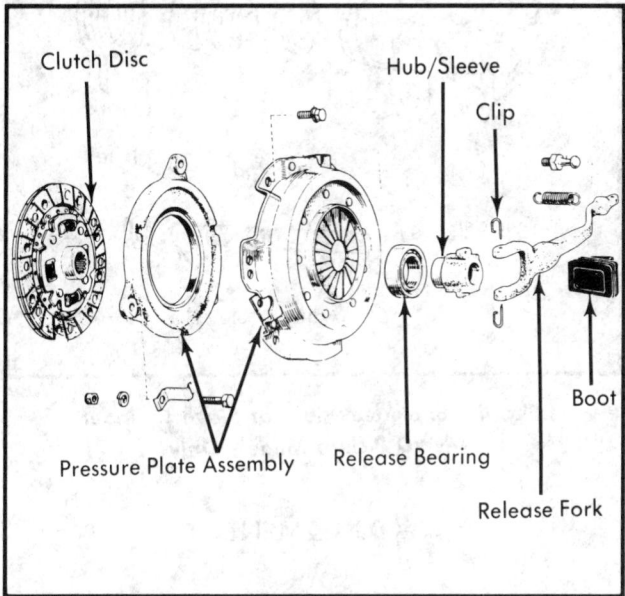

Fig. 1 Exploded View of Typical Clutch Arrangement. Pressure Plate Assembly and Hub/Sleeve Retainer Springs May Vary Between Models.

REMOVAL & INSTALLATION

CLUTCH ASSEMBLY

NOTE — Clutch removal procedures are of a general nature written to cover all Toyota models.

Removal — 1) Disconnect battery cable. Remove air cleaner and drain cooling system, then disconnect top radiator hose. Disconnect accelerator control rod linkage. Remove shift lever boot and shifter assembly. Remove starter.

2) Raise vehicle and support at front and rear with jack stands. If equipped, remove protective cover from under engine.

3) Remove clutch slave cylinder, but only disconnect hydraulic line if necessary. Disconnect exhaust pipe support bracket from mounting and separate exhaust pipe from manifold. Disconnect speedometer cable and electrical leads from transmission.

4) Scribe index marks on drive shaft and coupling for reinstallation reference, then remove drive shaft. Insert suitable plug into extension housing to prevent oil spillage.

5) Support engine with suitable jack, using a wooden block to protect oil pan. Support transmission with transmission jack and remove rear support crossmember. Lower transmission jack slightly and remove transmission-to-engine bolts. Pull transmission to rear; lower and remove from vehicle.

6) Index mark clutch assembly and flywheel for reassembly reference. Loosen bolts securing clutch assembly, alternately and evenly until pressure plate is released. Separate clutch disc and pressure plate.

Installation — To install, reverse removal procedure and note the following: Use a suitable aligning tool to center clutch disc on flywheel. Tighten clutch pressure plate attaching bolts alternately and evenly in a diagonal progression. With transmission installed, adjust clutch.

CLUTCH MASTER CYLINDER

Removal & Installation — Disconnect master cylinder push rod at clutch pedal by removing cotter pin and clevis. Disconnect hydraulic line at cylinder. Remove cylinder attaching nuts and remove cylinder from firewall. To install, reverse removal procedure and adjust pedal height, free play and bleed hydraulic system.

CLUTCH SLAVE CYLINDER

Removal & Installation — Raise and support vehicle on safety stands. Disconnect hydraulic line and clip. Remove slave cylinder attaching nuts and remove slave cylinder. To install, reverse removal procedure and bleed hydraulic system.

CLUTCH RELEASE BEARING

Removal — With transmission removed, check release bearing for freedom of rotation with bearing still installed on hub. To remove, disconnect spring clips from bearing collar and slide bearing off transmission input shaft. Use a press to remove and install bearing on sleeve.

Installation — Slide bearing and collar over transmission input shaft and secure to release lever with new retaining clips. Apply grease to diaphragm spring contact points before installing transmission.

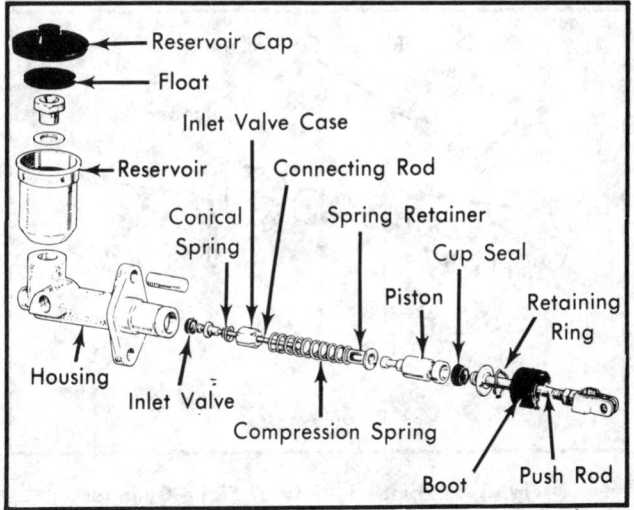

Fig. 2 Exploded View of Clutch Master Cylinder

TOYOTA CELICA, COROLLA, CORONA, PICKUP & SUPRA (Cont.)

OVERHAUL

CLUTCH MASTER CYLINDER

Disassembly — 1) With cylinder removed from vehicle, clamp it into a soft jawed vise. Remove reservoir, snap ring, and push rod. Pull out piston, cup, and remaining internal components. Further disassemble piston by prying up spring retainer and separating retainer from piston.

Cleaning & Inspection — Wash all parts in clean brake fluid and dry with compressed air. Master cylinder bore-to-piston clearance should not exceed .006" (.15 mm). Check compression spring for distortion or weakening and reservoir for damage. Ensure reservoir vent hole is open. Replace defective parts as required.

Reassembly — Dip cylinder cups into clean brake fluid or coat with rubber grease before assembly. Assemble piston components in reverse order of disassembly. Install piston assembly, push rod and reservoir into master cylinder.

CLUTCH SLAVE CYLINDER

Disassembly — Remove rubber boot and push rod. Remove piston assembly and spring from bore. If necessary, remove bleeder screw.

Cleaning & Inspection — Wash all parts in clean brake fluid and dry with compressed air. Slave cylinder bore-to-piston clearance should not exceed .006" (.15 mm). Replace defective parts. Replace piston cups during overhaul.

Reassembly — Install piston cups on piston and coat with brake grease. Install spring and piston assembly into cylinder bore and install rubber boot (protruded part down). Install push rod and bleeder screw.

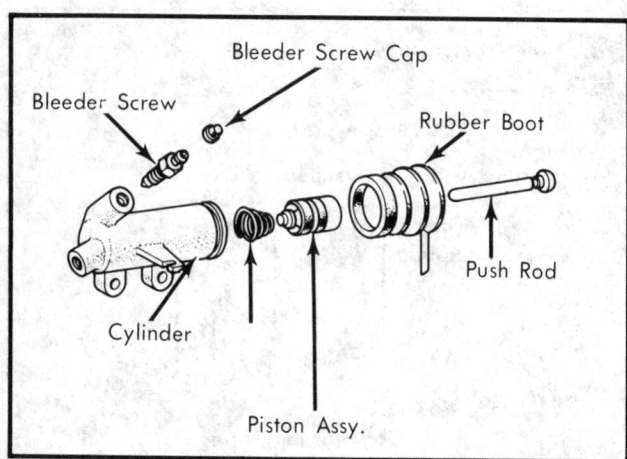

Fig. 3　Exploded View of Slave Cylinder (External Design Differs Among Models)

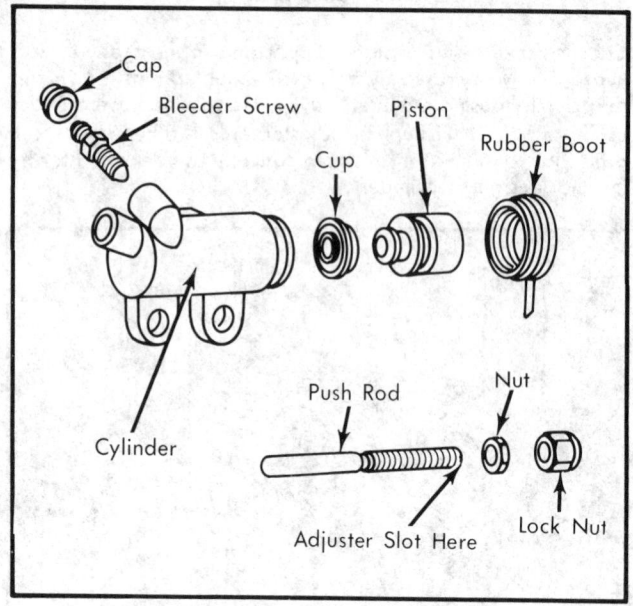

Fig. 4　Exploded View of Slave Cylinder (4-WD Pickup Models Only)

ADJUSTMENT

PEDAL HEIGHT

Adjust pedal stop bolt at top of pedal assembly until specified pedal height is obtained. Height is measured from floor mat to top of pedal pad.

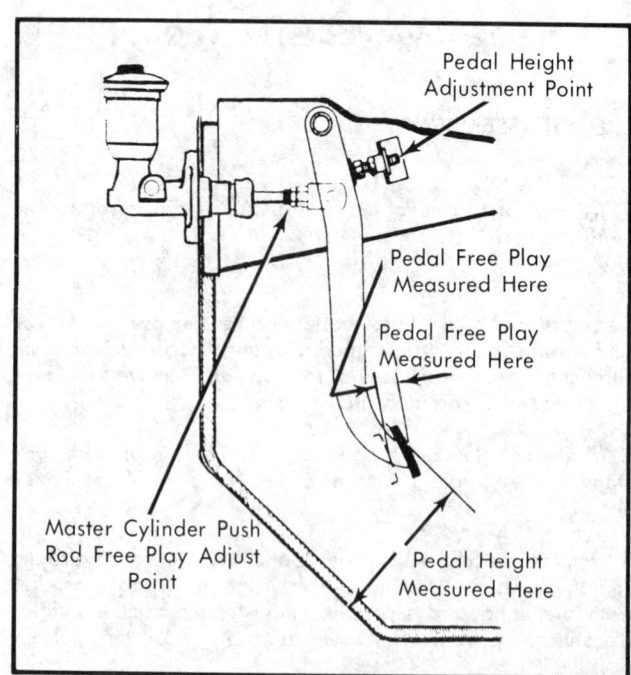

Fig. 5　Pedal Height and Free Play Measuring Points

TOYOTA CELICA, COROLLA, CORONA, PICKUP & SUPRA (Cont.)

Pedal Height Specifications

Application	Height In. (mm)
Celica & Supra	6.3-6.7 (159.5-169.5)
Corolla	6.9-7.3 (175-185)
Corona	6.5-6.9 (166-176)
Pickup	6.0-6.4 (152-162)

Pedal Free Play

Application	In. (mm)
Celica, Corolla & Corona	.5-.9 (13-23)
2-WD Pickup & Supra	.2-.6 (5-15)
4-WD Pickup	1.0-1.8 (25-45)

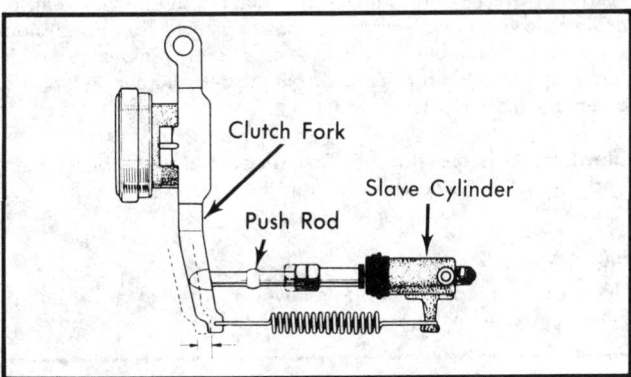

Fig. 6 Clutch Fork Free Play Adjustment (4-WD Pickup Models Only)

PEDAL FREE PLAY

Except 4-WD Pickup — To adjust free play (measured at pedal pad), loosen lock nut on master cylinder push rod and turn push rod in or out until free play is within specifications. Tighten lock nut.

4-WD Pickup — Prior to adjusting pedal free play as described for other models, adjust clutch fork free play. To adjust fork free play, loosen lock nut on slave cylinder push rod and screw push rod in or out to obtain .08-.12" (2-3 mm) free play at clutch fork. Tighten lock nut and adjust pedal free play to 1.0-1.8" (25-45 mm).

HYDRAULIC SYSTEM BLEEDING

1) Raise and support vehicle on safety stands. Check master cylinder reservoir often during bleeding operation; add fluid as required. Remove slave cylinder bleeder screw cap and connect flexible hose to bleeder and immerse opposite end of tube in jar partially filled with brake fluid.

2) Pump clutch pedal several times. With pedal depressed, loosen screw ½ turn, exhaust air and close before pressure is depleted. Repeat operation until no air bubbles are seen in discharged fluid. Close bleeder screw on down stroke of pedal. Check system for leaks and fill master cylinder reservoir.

TIGHTENING SPECIFICATIONS

Application	Ft. Lbs. (mkg)
Pressure Plate-to-Flywheel	11-15 (1.5-2.0)
Clutch Housing-to-Engine	
Supra	22-23 (3.0-4.5)
All Others	36-58 (5.0-8.0)

Clutches

TOYOTA LAND CRUISER

DESCRIPTION

Clutch is a dry single disc type using a diaphragm type pressure plate. Clutch is hydraulically operated by a firewall mounted master cylinder and a clutch housing mounted slave cylinder. A prelubricated sealed release bearing is used.

REMOVAL & INSTALLATION

CLUTCH ASSEMBLY

Removal — 1) Drain transmission oil, transfer case oil, and fuel tank. Remove transmission undercover and disconnect front and rear driveshafts, power take-off shaft, speedometer cable and parking brake cable. Remove front seat with frames and console box. Remove rear heater tube clamp and shift lever knobs.

2) Remove fuel tank cover and fuel tank. Remove shift lever dust boots and transmission cover. Disconnect front drive indicator wire harness, transfer switch wire harness, and vacuum hoses (if equipped). Disconnect back-up light switch harness.

3) Using suitable tool (09305-60010), remove shift lever hold down nut and lift out shift lever. Support transmission assembly with rope and floor jack. Remove bolts attaching transmission to engine and lower assembly from vehicle.

4) Disconnect clutch fork return spring and remove slave cylinder, but do not disconnect hydraulic line unless necessary. Remove release bearing retaining clips, and release bearing with collar. Remove clutch lever assembly.

5) Mark pressure plate and flywheel for reassembly reference. Loosen clutch attaching bolts one turn at a time until spring pressure is released, then remove bolts and clutch assembly

Installation — To install, reverse removal procedure and note the following: Use suitable aligning tool to center disc on flywheel. Tighten clutch attaching bolts alternately and evenly. After reinstallation, adjust clutch fork free play and bleed hydraulic system if necessary.

CLUTCH MASTER CYLINDER

Removal — Remove clevis pin connecting master cylinder push rod to clutch pedal. Disconnect hydraulic line from cylinder body and plug opening. Remove cylinder attaching bolts at firewall and remove master cylinder. **CAUTION** — *Do not allow fluid to spill on painted surfaces.*

Installation — To install, reverse removal procedure, adjust pedal height and clutch pedal free play, and bleed hydraulic system. Check hydraulic system for leaks.

CLUTCH SLAVE CYLINDER

Removal — Plug master cylinder reservoir cap. Disconnect clutch return spring from hanger. Disconnect flexible hose from metal line and remove clip. Remove slave cylinder retaining bolts and remove slave cylinder.

Installation — To install, reverse removal procedure, adjust clutch fork free play and bleed hydraulic system.

CLUTCH RELEASE BEARING

Removal & Installation — With clutch assembly removed, remove release bearing from hub with suitable bearing remover/installer (0931500021). To install bearing, lubricate with multi-purpose grease and seat bearing with the remover/installer.

PILOT BEARING

Removal & Installation — With clutch assembly removed, check pilot bearing in end of crankshaft for roughness or noise during rotation. If defective, remove using a suitable puller (09303-55010). To install, lubricate bearing with multi-purpose grease and insert into crankshaft using driver (09304-47010).

OVERHAUL

CLUTCH MASTER CYLINDER

Disassembly — With master cylinder rer oved from vehicle, drain fluid from reservoir and remove push rod, boot and snap ring as an assembly. Using a deep socket, remove reservoir retaining nut and lift reservoir from master cylinder. Pull piston assembly from master cylinder.

Cleaning & Inspection — Wash all parts in clean brake fluid and inspect for wear or damage. Replace master cylinder if scored or worn excessively.

Reassembly — Use cylinder overhaul kit and soak all parts in clean brake fluid. Assemble in reverse order of disassembly. Fill reservoir with fluid and bleed cylinder.

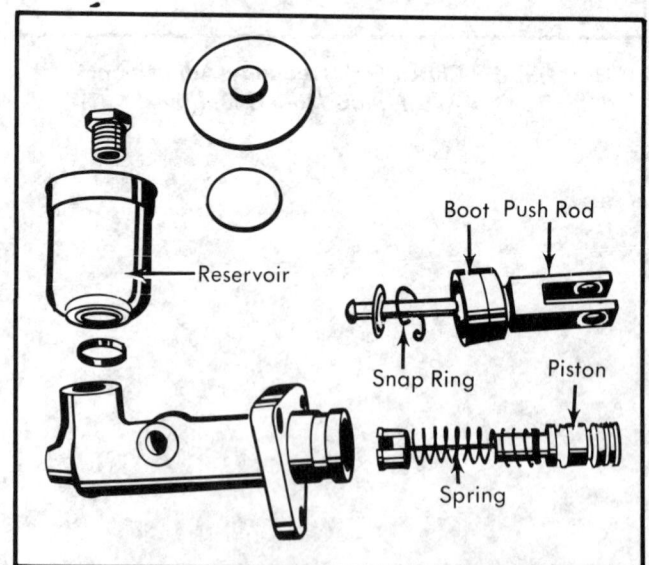

Fig. 1 Exploded View of Clutch Master Cylinder

CLUTCH SLAVE CYLINDER

Disassembly — Remove push rod assembly and rubber boot from cylinder body. Withdraw cylinder piston and cup seal. Loosen and remove bleeder screw.

TOYOTA LAND CRUISER (Cont.)

Cleaning & Inspection — Wash all parts in clean brake fluid and inspect for wear or damage. If slave cylinder bore-to-piston clearance exceeds .006" (.15 mm), replace defective part. Replace piston cups during overhaul.

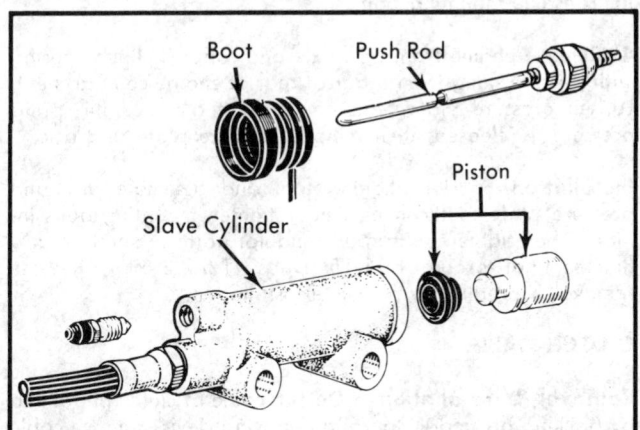

Fig. 2 Exploded View of Clutch Slave Cylinder

Reassembly — Soak all parts in clean brake fluid before reassembly. Reverse disassembly procedure and install boot with protruded part down.

ADJUSTMENTS

PEDAL HEIGHT

Pedal height is measured from floor to top of pedal pad. To adjust, loosen lock nut and turn stop bolt to give pedal height of 8.5" (215 mm) on vehicles equipped with power brake unit, or 7.8" (198 mm) on vehicles without power brakes.

PEDAL FREE PLAY

Clutch pedal free play is that distance of free movement before master cylinder push rod contacts piston. To adjust, loosen lock nut and turn push rod to obtain .02-.12" (.5-3.0 mm) free play. Tighten lock nut.

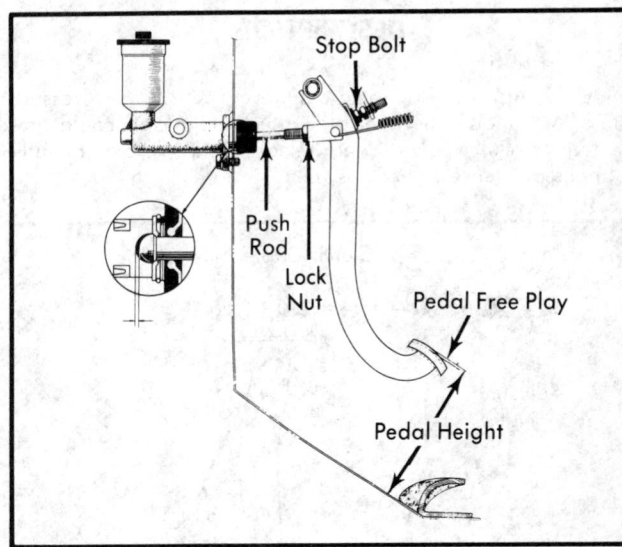

Fig. 3 Pedal Height Measuring and Adjustment Points

CLUTCH FORK FREE PLAY

To adjust clutch fork free play, loosen lock nut at slave cylinder and turn push rod tip while holding push rod nut with suitable wrench. Free play should be .12-.16" (3-4 mm). Tighten lock nut and check clutch pedal free play.

HYDRAULIC SYSTEM BLEEDING

1) Connect a flexible tube to slave cylinder bleeder screw, and place opposite end in a container partially filled with brake fluid.

2) Pump clutch pedal several times. With pedal depressed, loosen bleeder screw one-third to one-half turn and allow air to bleed out. Tighten bleeder screw.

3) Continue operation until air bubbles are no longer seen in fluid being discharged into container. Tighten bleeder screw securely and install cap. Check fluid level in master cylinder reservoir, and check system for leaks.

TOYOTA TERCEL

DESCRIPTION

Clutch is single dry disc using diaphragm spring type pressure plate. Actuation is mechanical, using an adjustable cable connected to clutch pedal and release fork. A permanently lubricated release bearing is used.

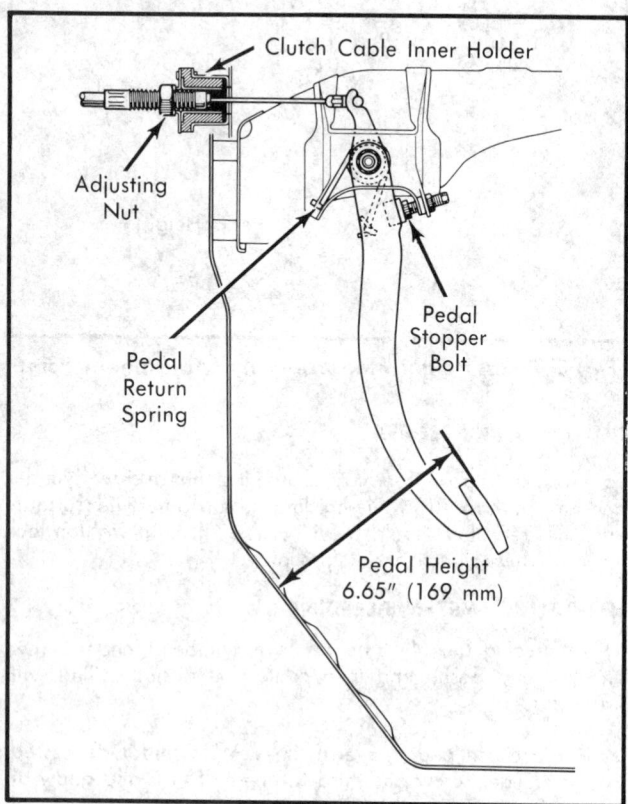

Fig. 1 Pedal Height and Free Play Adjustment

REMOVAL & INSTALLATION

CLUTCH ASSEMBLY

NOTE — *Engine must be removed to replace clutch assembly.*

Removal — 1) Remove engine hood, air cleaner case and battery negative terminal. Drain cooling system and wrap drive shaft boots with shop towels. Disconnect solenoid valve, water temperature switch and electric cooling fan connectors. Remove differential side plate stiffener bolts and exhaust pipe.

2) Remove radiator and windshield washer tank. Disconnect heater, fuel and brake booster hoses. Disconnect accelerator, choke and clutch release cables. Disconnect high tension wire from coil, alternator "B" terminal and connector from alternator and starter cable at starter.

3) Ensure that no bonding wires are connected from engine to chassis and disconnect engine mounts and engine shock absorber at lower right front of engine. Attach engine hoisting sling to engine and support differential with a jack. Remove engine to transaxle mounting bolts.

4) Remove engine from transaxle and support clutch housing with a cable slung from a bar at rear of engine compartment. Loosen pressure plate bolts one turn at a time until spring pressure is released, then remove pressure plate and disc.

Installation — Use aligning tool and assemble disc and pressure plate to flywheel. Finger tighten mounting bolts initially, then tighten bolts in a triangular pattern, one turn at a time to final torque of 11-15 ft. lbs. (1.5-2.2 mkg). Reverse removal procedure to complete installation.

CLUTCH CABLE

Removal & Installation — Detach cable at clutch pedal end by backing off pedal stop and removing clevis. Remove cable from release fork and free from engine compartment. To install, lubricate clevis attachment points with multipurpose grease and reverse removal procedure. Adjust pedal stop.

CLUTCH RELEASE BEARING

Removal & Installation — With engine removed from vehicle, remove retaining clips from bearing collar and clutch fork. Slide assembly from transmission. If bearing does not rotate smoothly, press off collar with driver (09315-00010). Use press and driver (09315-00021) to install new bearing on sleeve. Lightly grease inner groove of bearing collar and all contact surfaces and reverse removal procedures.

PILOT BEARING

Removal & Installation — If pilot bearing is worn or damaged, pull from crankshaft with puller (09303-35010). Coat new bearing with multipurpose grease and drive into crankshaft with installer (090304-12012).

ADJUSTMENTS

PEDAL HEIGHT

Measure distance from floor panel to upper surface of clutch pedal. Adjust pedal stopper bolt to give 6.65" (169 mm) pedal height.

CLUTCH PEDAL FREE PLAY

With release bearing contacting pressure plate, pedal play should be .8-1.4" (20-35 mm). To adjust, pull slightly on release cable and turn adjusting nut. Ensure that adjusting nut protrusion and cable holder inner notch are aligned, then depress pedal several times and recheck pedal play.

TRIUMPH

Spitfire
TR7
TR8

DESCRIPTION

Clutch is dry, single plate, diaphragm spring type. Clutch actuation is hydraulic, using a firewall mounted master cylinder and a clutch housing-mounted slave cylinder. Due to self-adjusting feature of clutch assembly, no adjustment, with the exception of bleeding hydraulic system, is necessary.

REMOVAL & INSTALLATION

CLUTCH ASSEMBLY

Removal (Spitfire) — **1)** Disconnect battery. Remove gear shift lever. On models equipped with overdrive, pry off knob cap and disconnect wires. Remove knob.

2) Remove transmission tunnel cover and propeller shaft cover. Disconnect propeller shaft and speedometer cable. Remove clutch slave cylinder, raise vehicle, and drain transmission.

3) Support engine. Disconnect exhaust pipe bracket and remove rear mounting nuts from transmission. Remove cable from clutch housing, remove lower housing bolts, and lower vehicle.

4) Remove starter bolts. Disconnect wires from transmission. Remove upper clutch housing bolts and remove transmission. Separate transmission and clutch housing.

Removal (TR7) — **1)** Raise and support vehicle. Disconnect battery ground cable. Remove gear shift lever assembly. Index mark and separate propeller shaft from transmission. Disconnect exhaust pipe at intake manifold (pipe may have to be completely removed).

2) Disconnect speedometer cable and all electrical wires attached to transmission. Remove starter heat shroud. Place a jack (with wood block) under oil pan. Remove slave cylinder without disconnecting fluid line. Hang cylinder out of way.

3) Remove 2 bolts holding oil pan plate to clutch housing. Remove 4 nuts keeping transmission rear crossmember to body. Slightly lower engine. Remove starter.

4) Remove nuts and bolts mounting clutch housing to engine. Support transmission with appropriate jack. Slide back transmission/clutch housing assembly and remove from vehicle.

5) Index mark pressure plate with flywheel. Loosen 6 pressure plate mounting bolts evenly (a few turns at a time). Slide out pressure plate with clutch disc.

Removal (TR8) — **1)** Disconnect battery. Remove gear shift lever assembly. Raise and support vehicle. Remove exhaust system, leaving tail pipes loosely in place. Disconnect oxygen sensors (if so equipped). Index mark and separate propeller shaft from transmission. Place a jack (with wood block) under oil pan. Raise engine.

2) Remove 2 bolts holding oil pan plate to clutch housing and bolt holding clutch pipe to rear engine plate. Remove heat shield and slave cylinder without disconnecting fluid line. Sup-

port cylinder out of way. Remove nuts attaching transmission rear crossmember to body. Lower engine.

3) Disconnect and remove speedometer cable. Disconnect wiring harness plug. Remove all but 3 clutch housing bolts. Remove 4 bolts holding flywheel cover to clutch housing. Support transmission with appropriate jack and remove 3 remaining clutch housing bolts. Slide back transmission/clutch housing assembly and remove from vehicle.

4) Index mark pressure plate with flywheel. Loosen 6 pressure plate mounting bolts evenly (a few turns at a time). Slide out pressure plate with clutch disc.

Installation (All Models) — Reverse removal procedure and note the following: Ensure index marks on pressure plate align with those on flywheel. Use clutch aligning tool to center clutch disc. Tighten clutch bolts evenly and gradually.

CLUTCH MASTER CYLINDER

Removal — **1)** Disconnect hydraulic line and drain fluid. Plug open port and line.

2) Disconnect clevis mounting push rod to clutch pedal.

3) Remove 2 bolts (Spitfire) or 2 nuts (TR7 and TR8) mounting master cylinder to bracket (Spitfire) or bulkhead (TR7 and TR8).

Installation — Reverse removal procedure and bleed hydraulic system.

CLUTCH SLAVE CYLINDER

Removal — Raise and support vehicle. Disconnect and plug hydraulic line and remove slave cylinder.

NOTE — *On TR7 and TR8 models, do not move operating rod in a forward direction. Forward movement may cause release lever to dislodge. Transmission removal would then become necessary for installation of release lever.*

Installation — Reverse removal procedure and note:
- On Spitfire models, centralize push rod in housing before sliding slave cylinder in position.
- On TR7 and TR8 models, slave cylinder must be mounted with bleed screw ABOVE fluid pipe.
- Bleed hydraulic line.

CLUTCH RELEASE BEARING

Removal (Spitfire) — With transmission assembly removed, remove clutch fork pivot pin and remove fork and bearing assembly. Drive pins from fork and remove bearing and sleeve. Using a suitable press, remove bearing from sleeve.

Installation — Reverse removal procedure. Lubricate all bearing contact points with multi-purpose grease.

Removal (TR7 and TR8) — With transmission assembly removed, use crow's foot wrench (ST 1136) and unscrew clutch release lever pivot bolt from clutch housing. Remove release lever, complete with pivot bolt and release bearing.

TRIUMPH (Cont.)

Installation — Reverse removal procedure, making sure fork and collar engage evenly.

OVERHAUL

CLUTCH MASTER CYLINDER

Disassembly (Spitfire) — 1) Drain fluid and remove master cylinder. Pull back rubber boot and release circlip, then pull out push rod and washer.

2) Apply compressed air to fluid inlet to remove piston and spring assembly. Remove thimble and spring from piston assembly, then disengage valve stem from slot in thimble. Remove seal spacer from valve stem and seals from valve and piston.

Reassembly — Reverse removal procedure, using new rubber seals and lubricating parts with brake fluid.

Disassembly (TR7 & TR8) — 1) Remove master cylinder. Pull up rubber boot and remove snap ring. Slide out push rod and washer.

2) Pull out piston, spring, and seal as an assembly. It may be necessary to use air pressure to force out assembly.

3) Straighten spring thimble prong, then remove thimble and spring from piston. Disengage valve stem from slot in thimble. Slip spacer off valve stem. Remove valve seal.

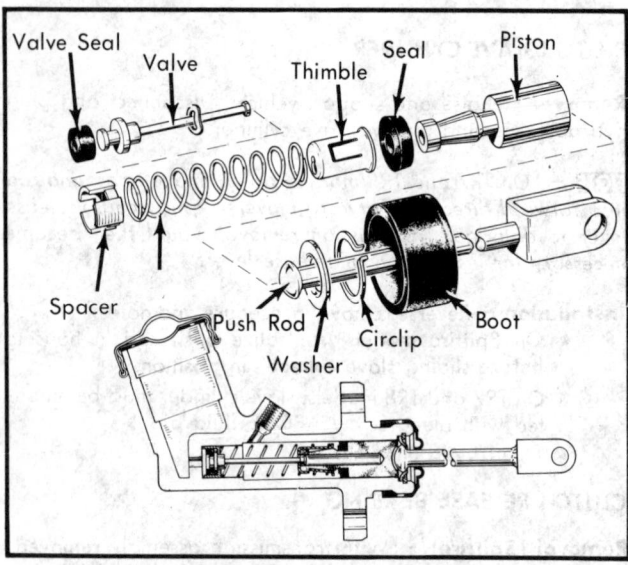

Fig. 1   Exploded View of Master Cylinder (TR7 and TR8 Shown; Spitfire Similar)

Reassembly — 1) Fit spacer, spring and thimble to valve stem. Fit new seal to piston with lip facing spring. Put spring thimble on piston and depress thimble prong.

2) Lubricate master cylinder bore with brake fluid and slide seal assembly, spring and piston into place. Reverse disassembly procedure to assemble remaining components.

CLUTCH SLAVE CYLINDER

Disassembly — Remove slave cylinder and pull off dust cover. Remove circlip, then take out piston, seal and spring.

Inspection — Look at cylinder bore and piston for signs of damage. Replace either or both parts if wear is excessive.

Reassembly — Reverse removal procedure, lubricating parts with brake fluid and fitting small end of spring to piston.

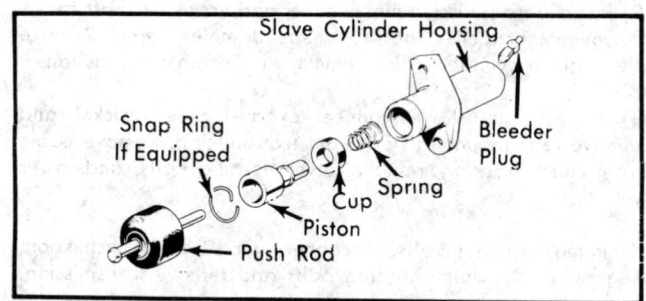

Fig. 2   Exploded View of Slave Cylinder (TR7 and TR8 Shown; Spitfire Similar)

ADJUSTMENT

HYDRAULIC SYSTEM BLEEDING

1) Fill master cylinder. Attach bleed tube to bleed valve on slave cylinder. Submerge free end of tube in container of brake fluid.

2) Slowly depress pedal to force air out. Close bleed valve and let pedal rise unassisted. Check that fluid level does not drop too low, and repeat until no more air bubbles are visible.

TIGHTENING SPECIFICATIONS

Application	Ft. Lbs. (mkg)
Clutch Assembly-to-Flywheel	22 (3.0)
Clutch Housing-to-Transmission	32 (4.4)
Slave Cylinder-to-Clutch Housing	21 (2.9)

VOLKSWAGEN DASHER

DESCRIPTION

Clutch is single plate dry disc type, using a diaphragm type pressure plate and a pre-lubricated clutch release bearing. Clutch is cable actuated.

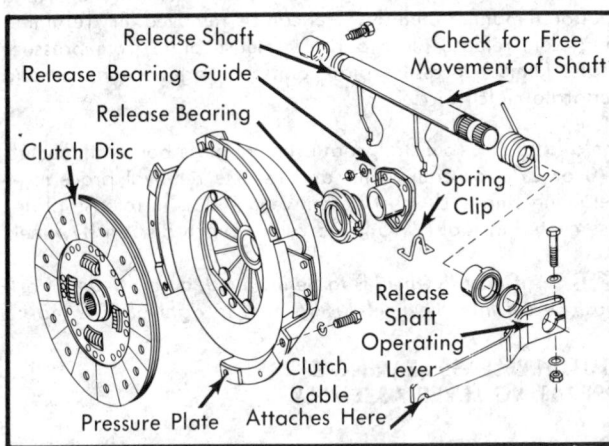

Fig. 1 Exploded View of Clutch Assembly

REMOVAL & INSTALLATION

TRANSAXLE & CLUTCH ASSEMBLIES

Removal — 1) Disconnect battery ground cable from battery. Disconnect exhaust pipe at manifold. Disconnect exhaust pipe bracket from rear of transaxle.

2) Disconnect gear shift lever and shift linkage. Disconnect back-up light wires. On some models there is a bolt mounting gear shift linkage to transaxle that must be removed.

3) Loosen clutch cable adjustment nut and disengage clutch housing from left side engine mount. Separate clutch cable from operating lever. Disconnect speedometer cable.

4) Disconnect front wheel axle drive shafts at transaxle. Suspend drive shafts with wire out of way. Remove starter.

5) Remove clutch housing front cover plate. Remove bolts mounting transaxle-to-engine. Place a jack under transaxle for support. Unbolt transaxle carrier from body. Slide transaxle to rear until input shaft is clear of clutch assembly. Lower out transaxle.

6) Lock flywheel to prevent rotation and index mark pressure plate and flywheel. Loosen pressure plate bolts ¼ turn at a time, working in a diagonal pattern. Slide pressure plate off dowels on flywheel.

Installation — 1) Using a clutch alignment tool, fit pressure plate with clutch. Make sure alignment marks are observed. Loosely attach assembly with 6 bolts.

NOTE — *If replacement pressure plate has white paint spot, it is a balance mark and should be 180° from countersunk hole or 180° from white paint mark on flywheel.*

2) Tighten pressure plate bolts in criss-cross pattern about 2 turns at a time.

3) Position transaxle to engine. Loosely fit bolts holding transaxle carrier to body. Reverse removal procedure to install remaining components.

Fig. 2 View Showing Clutch Assembly Alignment on Flywheel

CLUTCH RELEASE BEARING

Removal & Installation — With transaxle removed, remove spring clips without removing bearing from release shaft. Slide bearing off bearing guide. To install, roughen plastic guide sleeve with emery cloth, but do not lubricate. Lubricate metal guide sleeve with molybdenum disulphide paste. Coat pivoting points between bearing and operating shaft with multi-purpose grease. Position bearing to shaft and install spring clips.

NOTE — *Bearing is pre-lubricated, DO NOT wash in solvent.*

CLUTCH CABLE

Removal & Installation — Loosen cable adjusting nuts and free clutch cable housing from support bracket. Separate cable from clutch operating lever (mounted on side of clutch housing). Disconnect cable at pedal and force cable and housing into passenger compartment and remove. To install new cable, reverse removal procedure and adjust pedal free play.

NOTE — *If new clutch cable has been installed, make sure to recheck clutch pedal free play after 300 miles.*

PILOT BEARING

Removal & Installation — Lock flywheel to prevent rotation. Install suitable remover (10-202) and remove pilot bearing. Install bearing with suitable installer (VW207C) and seat bearing until distance from flywheel recess to bushing edge is ¹⁄₁₆″ (1.5 mm). Lubricate bearing.

ADJUSTMENT

CLUTCH PEDAL FREE PLAY

Clutch pedal free play (measured at pedal pad) should be ⅝″ (16 mm). To increase measurement, loosen top adjusting nut until specification is obtained. Tighten bottom nut until locked against bracket. To decrease measurement, loosen bottom adjusting nut until specification is obtained. Tighten top nut until locked against bracket.

TIGHTENING SPECIFICATIONS

Application	Ft. Lbs. (mkg)
Clutch Assembly-to-Flywheel	18 (2.5)
Transmission-to-Engine	40 (5.5)
Clutch Lever-to-Transmission	18 (2.5)
Drive Shaft-to-Transmission	33 (4.5)

VOLKSWAGEN JETTA, RABBIT, RABBIT PICKUP & SCIROCCO

DESCRIPTION

Clutch is a single plate dry disc type, using a diaphragm type pressure plate and a transmission mounted clutch release bearing. Clutch is cable operated.

REMOVAL & INSTALLATION

TRANSAXLE & CLUTCH ASSEMBLY

Removal — 1) Disconnect battery ground strap and attach an engine support assembly. Remove left transaxle mount bolts and mount. Disconnect back-up light wires, speedometer drive cable (plug hole) and clutch cable.

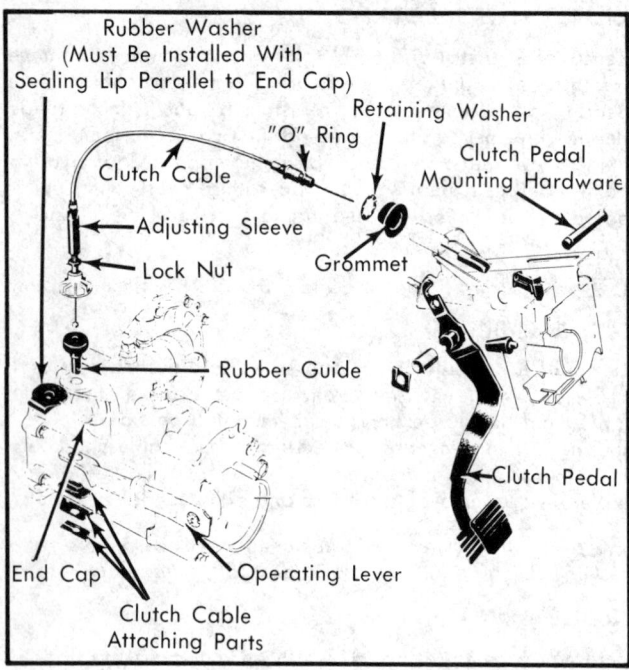

Fig. 1   Clutch Cable Routing & Adjusting Location

2) Remove upper clutch housing-to-transaxle bolts. Remove starter. Align flywheel lug with boss on bell housing (models equipped with flywheel which has cutouts). Disconnect shift linkage at rod lever and relay lever and remove front selector rod.

NOTE — *Vehicles with cutouts in flywheel can be identified by a stud/nut at right engine-to-transaxle mounting position. Flywheel on this type vehicle MUST be aligned before separating engine/transaxle.*

3) Remove exhaust pipe bracket. Remove transaxle rear mount and support transaxle on suitable jack. Disconnect left and right drive shafts at transaxle and wire up out of way. Remove large plate cover bolts (plate remains on engine). Remove small cover bolts and cover.

4) Remove right engine-to-transaxle bolt (stud/nut). Vehicles with cutouts in flywheel, pull transaxle away from engine to clear dowels and lower and remove transaxle. On all other vehicles, pull transaxle away from engine; cocking engine so

right side drive flange clears flywheel. Lower and remove transaxle.

5) With transaxle removed from engine, install holding tool (VW558) to ring gear or pressure plate. Remove bolts in a diagonal manner until flywheel can be removed. Pry retaining ring from release plate and lift release plate from pressure plate. Remove pressure plate bolts in diagonal manner and separate clutch disc.

Installation — To install, coat pressure plate bolts with Loctite 270 or 271 (or equivalent) and reverse removal procedure. Retaining ring ends must be between 2 slots in release plate. Use centering tool (VW547) to center clutch disc on flywheel.

NOTE — *If new flywheel is to be installed, a new timing mark must be cut into flywheel ¼" (6 mm) to right of TDC mark.*

CLUTCH RELEASE BEARING & OPERATING LEVER ASSEMBLY

Removal — 1) Remove 4 bolts and washers mounting clutch release cover to the far left end of transaxle case. Cover is waffle patterned. Remove 2 circlips located at each side of clutch lever.

2) Pull operating lever and release shaft assembly out of case. Lift return spring along with clutch lever out of transaxle case. Take out release bearing, guide sleeve and push rod. Check all seals and bearing; replace defective parts.

Installation — 1) Coat ends of push rod with multi-purpose grease and insert back into position. Grease sliding surface of bearing and guide sleeve.

2) Position return spring and clutch lever inside transaxle case. Return spring center hook should fit on top of clutch lever lug. Spring end hooks must point down to hold clutch lever away from release bearing.

3) Lightly coat release shaft with multipurpose grease. Fit shaft. Work operating lever until splines on release shaft mesh with those in clutch lever.

4) Install circlips. Make sure when operating lever is in normal position that return spring has tension. Fit gasket and cover.

ADJUSTMENT

CLUTCH PEDAL FREE PLAY

Clutch pedal free play should be ⁹⁄₁₆-1" (15-25 mm) at clutch pedal and ¼" (6 mm) at operating lever. To adjust, loosen clutch cable lock nut in engine compartment. Turn adjusting sleeve until correct measurement is obtained and tighten lock nut. Operate clutch pedal several times and check free play.

TIGHTENING SPECIFICATIONS	
Application	**Ft. Lbs. (mkg)**
Transmission-to-Engine	47 (5.5)
Drive Shaft-to-Transmission	32 (4.5)
Pressure Plate Bolts	54 (7.5)
Flywheel Bolts	14 (2.0)
Cover Plate	11 (1.5)

Clutches

VOLKSWAGEN VANAGON

DESCRIPTION

Clutch is dry, single disc, diaphragm spring type which is hydraulically operated by a firewall mounted master cylinder and a clutch housing mounted slave cylinder. Slave cylinder is non-adjustable and clearance is automatically compensated for by internal design of cylinder.

REMOVAL & INSTALLATION

CLUTCH ASSEMBLY

Removal – 1) Disconnect battery ground strap. Remove right upper engine/transmission bolt.

2) Remove hydraulic clutch line bracket from transmission but do not disconnect line. Remove slave cylinder from mounting bracket and suspend with wire.

3) Remove left upper engine/transmission bolt. Remove left lower engine/transmission nut. Remove left drive shaft hex bolts and remove drive shaft from transmission and suspend with wire.

4) Disconnect starter cables, remove right drive shaft hex bolts and suspend drive shaft with wire. Remove right side lower engine/transmission nut.

5) Support engine with chain or engine support (VW 785/1). Disconnect ground strap from near transmission mount. Remove front transmission mount from body.

6) Support transmission using jack (US 618 & US 618/5) and lower front of transmission by loosening engine support (loosen spindle on VW 785/1) until there is enough room to remove transmission. Separate transmission from engine and remove from vehicle.

7) Lock flywheel with VW 215C (or equivalent). Index mark pressure plate and flywheel for reassembly reference. Loosen pressure plate-to-flywheel bolts evenly in a diagonal fashion and remove clutch assembly.

Installation – Apply molybdenum disulphide grease to release bearing. Lubricate transmission input shaft with molybdenum disulphide powder. Position clutch disc against flywheel and align using a centering tool. Install pressure plate and tighten bolts evenly in a diagonal fashion. Replace transmission, reversing removal procedure and noting the following:

- Insert rear bolt for slave cylinder before installing.
- Position air deflector plates correctly.

CLUTCH RELEASE BEARING

Removal – Remove transmission as outlined in Clutch Assembly in this article. Pry off clip retainers from bearing and disengage spring clips. Remove release bearing by sliding off guide tube.

NOTE – *Do not wash bearing in solvent or cleaning solution. Wipe with dry cloth to clean.*

Installation – Lubricate release shaft and release bearing pivot points with molybdenum disulphide grease. Position bearing to shaft and install spring clips and retainers. Make sure clips are correctly positioned.

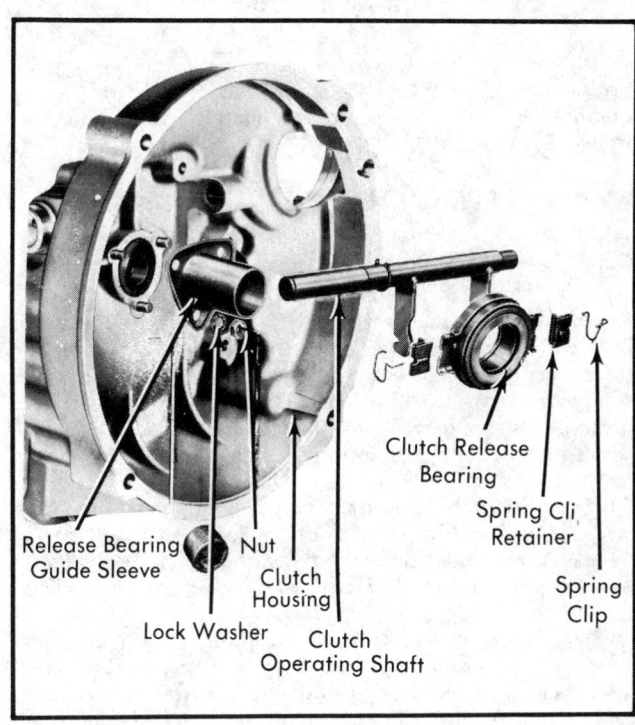

Fig. 1 Clutch Release Bearing Assembly

CLUTCH MASTER CYLINDER

Removal & Installation – Disconnect master cylinder push rod at clutch pedal by removing cotter pin and clevis. Disconnect hydraulic line at cylinder. Remove cylinder attaching bolts and remove cylinder from firewall. To install, reverse removal procedure and pressure bleed the system following bleeder manufacturer's instructions.

CLUTCH SLAVE CYLINDER

Removal – Disconnect hydraulic line from slave cylinder. Disconnect slave cylinder push rod from clutch lever ball. Remove mounting bolts and remove cylinder.

Installation – Grease clutch lever ball lightly. Insert rear bolt to slave cylinder and install on vehicle. Install front bolt, attach hydraulic line and clutch lever. Pressure bleed system following bleeder manufacturer's instructions.

TIGHTENING SPECIFICATIONS

Application	Ft. Lbs. (mkg)
Engine-to-Transmission Nuts & Bolts	22 (3.0)
Drive Shaft-to-Transmission Bolts	33 (4.5)
Pressure Plate-to-Flywheel Bolts	18 (2.5)

VOLVO

DL	GLE
GL	Coupe
GT	Diesel

DESCRIPTION

Clutch is single dry disc type using a diaphragm spring type pressure plate. GLE and Coupe models use a hydraulically operated 9" clutch, while all other models use a cable controlled 8¼" clutch.

REMOVAL & INSTALLATION

CLUTCH ASSEMBLY

Removal — 1) Disconnect battery ground cable and back-up light wiring harness connector. Working from under vehicle, disconnect gear shift lever from gear shift rod. On GLE and Coupe, unbolt clutch slave cylinder from housing and disconnect from release arm. On all other models, unhook clutch fork spring and separate cable from housing.

2) Separate shift boot from carpet. Using a 4 mm Allen wrench, remove reverse gear detent fork. Remove lock ring with snap ring pliers and lift out gearshift lever. Remove front exhaust pipe bracket and position a support under engine.

3) Remove crossmember at rear of transmission. Index mark propeller shaft and disconnect from transmission. Disconnect speedometer cable from transmission. Lower rear end of engine and remove all except top right clutch housing bolts. Remove front starter bracket and free starter from clutch housing.

4) Install transmission jack and remove last clutch housing bolt. Pull transmission to rear and turn to clear propeller shaft tunnel. Lower transmission clear of vehicle. Loosen pressure plate bolts gradually in a diagonal pattern and remove clutch assembly.

Installation — To install transmission and clutch assembly, reverse removal procedure and note the following: Install clutch disc with long side of hub to rear using alignment tool 999 5111 (or equivalent). Install pressure plate and tighten bolts gradually in a criss-cross pattern. Adjust clutch pedal play on all except GLE and Coupe.

NOTE — *GLE and Coupe pressure plates have raised fingers and use a 1⁷⁄₁₆" (36.5 mm) long release bearing. Remaining model pressure plate fingers are straight and require the use of a 1¹¹⁄₁₆" (43.0 mm) long release bearing. Pressure plates and bearings must never be mixed.*

CLUTCH CABLE

Removal — Remove return spring and disconnect clutch cable at clutch fork; extract cable. Remove cover panel under instrument cluster. Remove clevis pin at upper end of cable. Separate clutch fork adjustment mechanism from clutch housing, if necessary. Force cable out of rubber grommet located in firewall.

Installation — Insert new cable into rubber grommet, feed it through cable guide and attach at upper end with clevis pin. Position adjustment mechanism into clutch housing. Attach cable to clutch fork, then refit return spring.

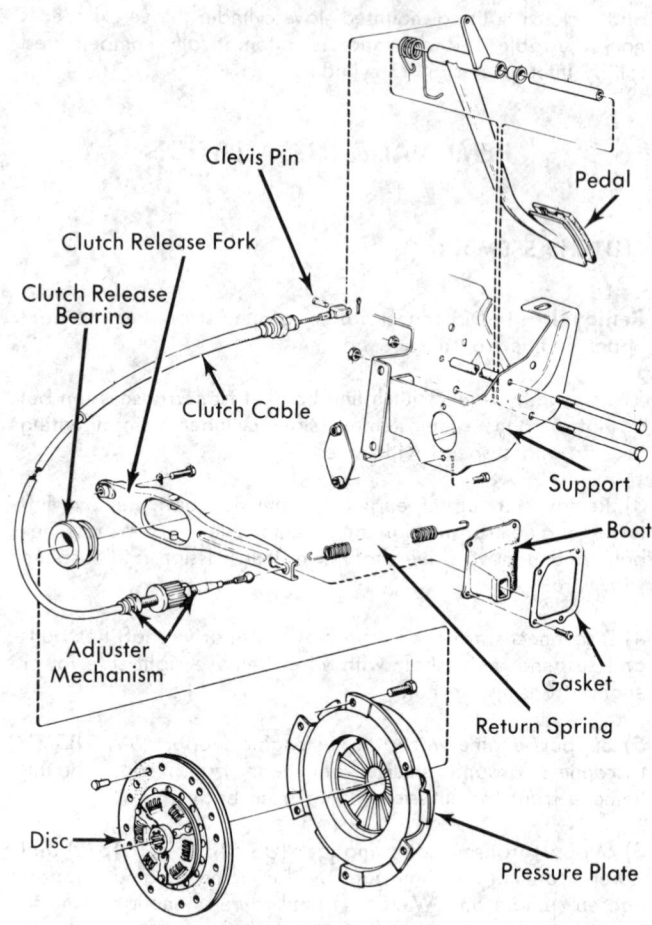

Fig. 1 Volvo Mechanical Linkage Clutch System

HYDRAULIC CLUTCH ACTUATION

Manufacturer does not provide maintenance instructions for hydraulically operated clutch linkage. There should be no free play in this type linkage.

PILOT BEARING

Remove retaining clip and remove bearing using puller (SVO 4090). Pack bearing with heat resistant grease and install into crankshaft using a driver. Install retaining clip.

ADJUSTMENT

CLUTCH FREE PLAY (EXCEPT GLE & COUPE)

Using adjustment mechanism attached to clutch housing, set free play. Adjustment is correct when approximately ⅛" (3-5 mm) clutch fork free play is obtained.

Section 7
BRAKES

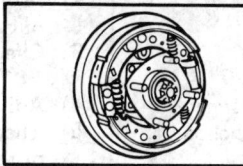

Contents

NOTE — ALSO SEE GENERAL INDEX.

Brakes

BRAKE SYSTEM TROUBLE SHOOTING

NOTE — *This is a general trouble shooting guide. Not all steps will apply to all brake systems. When using this guide, locate the condition in column one that corresponds to your problem and determine the possible causes in column two. Match the number of the possible causes with the same number in column three.*

CONDITION	POSSIBLE CAUSE	CORRECTION
▶ Brake chatter, squeal, squeak	1) Dust on drums/rotors, oil stained linings 2) Weak shoe return spring 3) Drum out of round 4) Excessively worn pads or shoes 5) Uneven rotor surface 6) Excessive lateral rotor runout 7) Excessive wheel bearing play	1) Remove drum/rotor, clean 2) Check, replace springs 3) Turn drum on lathe 4) Replace pads or shoes 5) Check rotor surface in various locations with micrometer 6) Check runout with dial indicator, resurface or replace rotor 7) Readjust or replace bearings
▶ Excessive pedal travel	1) Excessive rotor runout 2) Brake fluid boil 3) Warped or excessively worn pads or shoes 4) Rear brakes out of adjustment 5) Power brake unit malfunction	1) Check rotor with dial gauge, resurface or replace 2) Drain system, refill with fluid of correct specification 3) Check and replace pads or shoes 4) Adjust shoe to drum clearance 5) Check and either overhaul or replace unit
▶ Poor brake operation	1) Too long brake lever stroke 2) Brake cable sticking 3) Excessive shoe to drum clearance	1) Readjust brake pedal lever 2) Check brake cable routing and lubricate 3) Check self-adjuster mechanism; readjust or replace components
▶ Shock when pedal applied	1) Brake drum cracked or distorted 2) Uneven brake drum wear 3) Broken return spring	1) Replace drum 2) Resurface drum or replace 3) Replace springs
▶ Leaks in caliper piston cylinder	1) Damaged or excessively worn caliper piston seal 2) Deep scores or corrosion on surface of cylinder bore	1) Overhaul caliper and install new seals 2) Overhaul caliper and hone (unless not recommended by manufacturer); install new seals
▶ Rattling in front brakes	1) Pad anti-rattle spring clip broken or missing 2) Excessive clearance between pads and caliper	1) Install new part or reposition existing one 2) Fit caliper with new pads
▶ Pull when brake applied	1) Incorrect tire pressure 2) Front end out of alignment 3) Unmatched tires 4) Restricted brake lines or hoses	1) Inflate tires evenly as indicated in owners manual 2) Check and align front end 3) Make sure all tires have approximately equal amounts of tread and pressure 4) Inspect for soft hoses or damaged lines. Replace with new hoses or brake tubing

BRAKE SYSTEM TROUBLE SHOOTING (Cont.)

CONDITION	POSSIBLE CAUSE	CORRECTION
▶ Excessive pedal pressure required	1) Linings coated with brake fluid, oil or grease 2) Entire pad not contacting rotor 3) Scored brake rotors 4) Incorrect pads 5) Seized piston 6) Power brake failing	1) Fit new pads or shoes 2) Replace pads 3) Resurface rotor according to specs. 4) Check pads 5) Overhaul caliper, check piston 6) Check power unit and replace
▶ Low pedal effect	1) Air in hydraulic system, brakes not properly bled 2) Hydraulic fluid leaking past primary cup in master cylinder 3) Bleeder screw not tight	1) Check for air leaks and bleed hydraulic system 2) Overhaul master cylinder making sure to replace cups 3) Tighten bleeder screw
▶ Uneven braking	1) Linings contaminated 2) Unmatched disc pads 3) One or more seized pistons 4) Incorrect tire pressure 5) Front wheel out of alignment 6) Brake hose or line clogged 7) Caliper alignment improper	1) Clean or refit with new pads/shoes 2) Ensure all pads on any axle are same quality 3) Overhaul caliper to free piston 4) Inflate tires according to manufacturer's recommendations 5) Align front wheels 6) Free restriction 7) Remove and realign caliper
▶ Brake pedal pulsation	1) Excessive rotor lateral runout 2) Rotor not parallel 3) Wheel bearings out of adjustment 4) Rear drums out of round	1) Check rotor runout with dial gauge 2) Check rotor and replace 3) Adjust 4) Check drums and turn or replace
▶ Spongy pedal	1) Air in brake system 2) Swollen brake hose(s) 3) Brake fluid boiling point too low 4) Filler cap vent hole plugged	1) Bleed system 2) Replace hose and bleed system 3) Drain, flush and refill with fluid of proper specifications 4) Clean, then bleed system
▶ Pedal yield under slight pressure	1) Deteriorated check valve 2) External brake fluid leaks 3) Internal leak in master cylinder	1) Replace valve, bleed system 2) Check master cylinder, lines, and wheel cylinders; replace 3) Overhaul master cylinder
▶ Brake failure or heavy pedal	1) Power unit diaphragm damaged 2) Check valve malfunctioning 3) Defective vacuum hose 4) Twisted air valve and valve rod plunger	1) Check and/or replace diaphragm 2) Replace valve 3) Replace hose 4) Disassemble and repair
▶ Brakes react slowly	1) Check valve malfunction 2) Vacuum hose blocked or broke 3) Air cleaner clogged or restricted	1) Clean or replace check valve 2) Replace hose 3) Clean or replace air cleaner
▶ Brake drag or slow return	1) Push rod out of alignment 2) Operating rod out of adjustment 3) Air valve and push rod plunger twisted	1) Disassemble and repair 2) Adjust 3) Adjust

Brake Servicing

HYDRAULIC BRAKE BLEEDING

DESCRIPTION

Hydraulic system bleeding is necessary any time air has been introduced into system. Bleed brakes at all 4 wheels if master cylinder lines have been disconnected or master cylinder has run dry. Bleeding may be done either by using pressure bleeding equipment or by manually pumping brake pedal and using bleeder tubes.

MANUAL BLEEDING

Fill master cylinder, then install bleeder hose to first bleeder valve to be serviced. See *Bleeding Sequence*. Place other end of hose in clean glass jar, partially filled with clean brake fluid, so end of hose is submerged in fluid. Open bleeder valve ¾-1 turn. Depress brake pedal slowly through its full travel (except as noted in Bleeding Sequence chart). Close bleeder valve, then release pedal. Repeat procedure until flow of fluid shows no signs of air bubbles.

NOTE — *Check fluid level in master cylinder frequently during bleeding sequence to ensure air does not enter system.*

PRESSURE TANK BLEEDING

Clean master cylinder cap and surrounding area, then remove cap. With pressure tank at least ⅓ full, connect master cylinder using suitable adapters. Attach bleeder hose to first bleeder valve to be serviced. See *Bleeding Sequence*. Place other end of hose in clean glass jar, partially filled with clean brake fluid, so end of hose is submerged in fluid. Open release valve on pressure bleeder. Unscrew valve ¾-1 turn, noting fluid flow. When fluid flow from bleeder valve into container is free of bubbles, close bleeder valve securely. Bleed remaining cylinders in correct sequence and in same manner. Remove pressure tank from master cylinder and check fluid level of master cylinder reservoir.

Bleeding Pressures①	
Application	**psi (kg/cm²)**
BMW	
733i	56 (3.9)
All Others	28 (2.0)
Porsche	32 (2.3)
Renault	30 (2.1)
Volvo	50-60 (3.5-4.2)

① — For models not listed, refer to pressure tank manufacturer's specifications.

BLEEDING SEQUENCE

Before bleeding system, exhaust all vacuum from power unit by depressing brake pedal several times. Bleed hyraulic system in the following sequence:

Bleeding Sequence	
Application	**Sequence**
Audi & Volkswagen①	RR, LR, RF, LF
BMW②	Longest Line First
Chrysler Corp. Imports	
Champ & Colt Hatchback	LR, RF, RR, LF
All Others③	RR, LR, RF, LF
Courier④	Longest Line First
Datsun	
310	Master Cyl., LR, RF, RR, LF
810	Longest Line First
Pickup .... Master Cyl., Comb. Valve, Longest Line First	
All Others	Master Cyl., Longest Line First
Fiat	Longest Line First
Fiesta⑤	RF, LR, LF, RR
Honda	LF, RR, RF, LR
Jaguar⑥	LR, RR, Front
LUV	Shortest Line First
Mazda⑦	Longest Line First
Mercedes-Benz	Longest Line First
MG⑧	Shortest Line First
Peugeot⑨	Longest Line First
Porsche⑩	LR, RR, RF, LF
Renault	Longest Line First
Saab	LR, RF, RR, LF
Subaru	Master Cyl., LR, RF, RR, LF
Toyota	Longest Line First
Triumph	
Spitfire⑪	RR, LR, RF, LF
TR7 & TR8⑫	RF, LF, RR, LR
Volvo⑬	LF, RF, RR, LR

① — Before bleeding rear brakes, push brake pressure regulator in direction of rear axle.

② — The 528i and 633Csi have 3 bleed valves on each front caliper. Bleed lower inboard valve first, then other 2 at same time.

③ — Arrow with rear drum brakes does not require bleeding of RR.

④ — Front and rear circuits are independent. Bleed each circuit separately.

⑤ — Container must be 12" (300 mm) higher than bleed valve. Before bleeding each rear wheel, apply parking brake; release after bleeding each rear wheel.

⑥ — Engine running at idle speed.

⑦ — GLC has independent front and rear circuits. Bleed each circuit separately.

⑧ — Before bleeding, disconnect and unscrew brake failure switch 3½ turns. Tighten and reconnect after bleeding.

⑨ — If pressure tank is used, bleed all wheels at same time.

⑩ — If equipped with inner and outer caliper bleed valves, bleed outer valve first, then inner.

⑪ — Use light pedal pressure. DO NOT use full pedal travel.

⑫ — Remove pressure differential switch before bleeding.

⑬ — Rear wheels must be higher than front wheels. Front calipers are each equipped with 3 bleed valves. Bleed all 3 valves at same time.

AUDI

4000
5000

DESCRIPTION

NOTE — *In this article, non-turbocharged Audi 5000 models are referred to as "5000"; turbocharged models are referred to as "Turbo".*

Brake system is hydraulically operated using a tandem master cylinder and power brake unit. Front brakes are sliding caliper disc on 4000 and Turbo; sliding yoke, fixed caliper on 5000. Rear brakes on Turbo are sliding caliper disc; all other models use leading/trailing shoe drum brakes. A wear indicator is mounted in the outboard brake pad and signals the need for pad replacement via a dashboard light on 5000. Brake hydraulic system incorporates a brake pressure regulator to prevent premature lock-up of rear wheels. All service brake systems are self-adjusting. Parking brake is cable actuated on rear brake system.

ADJUSTMENT

STOP LIGHT SWITCH

Loosen lock nut and turn stop light switch until distance between plunger tip and switch body is .087-.098" (2.2-2.5 mm). Tighten lock nut and check operation of switch.

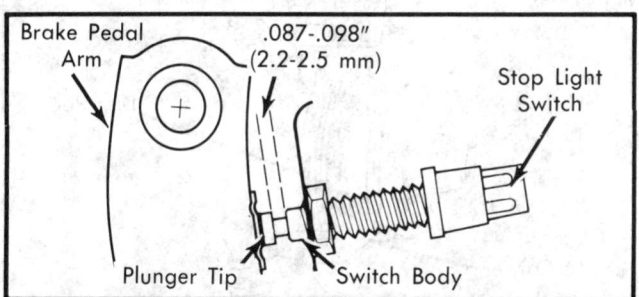

Fig. 1   Adjusting Stop Light Switch

PARKING BRAKE

NOTE — *Parking brake adjustment on Turbo is required only if rear calipers or parking brake parts are replaced.*

Turbo — Raise and support vehicle. Release parking brake lever and ensure parking brake levers at each rear wheel are resting on caliper stops (loosen parking brake cable adjustment if necessary). Depress brake pedal 40 times, then pull parking brake lever up to 3rd notch. Tighten adjusting nut at equalizer until both wheels can just be turned by hand. Release parking brake lever and check that wheels rotate freely and levers on calipers return to stops. See Fig. 2.

Except Turbo — Raise and support vehicle. Firmly depress brake pedal once. Set parking brake lever at 3rd notch (2nd on 4000) from fully released position. Tighten adjusting nut at equalizer until both wheels can just be turned by hand. Release parking brake lever and ensure both wheels rotate freely.

BRAKE WARNING LIGHT

A dual warning light is mounted on dash. Light should glow when parking brake lever is pulled 1 notch and go off when lever is fully released (ignition on). To check circuit warning sensor, release parking brake (ignition on) and ensure light is off. Open bleeder screw on 1 wheel and depress brake pedal; light should glow.

BRAKE PRESSURE REGULATOR

Checking & Adjusting — 1) Regulator is located on rear frame. Empty vehicle, fill fuel tank and load driver's seat to 165 lbs. (74.8 kg). Bounce rear of car several times and allow vehicle to settle normally. Firmly depress brake pedal and release quickly; regulator should have moved.

2) Measure distance from top of tire rim to lower edge of fender lip (both sides). Install left spring tensioner. Raise vehicle on hoist and insert right spring tensioner (upper end only). Lower vehicle and bounce rear of car several times. Allow car to settle normally and attach right spring tensioner to axle.

NOTE — *Spring tensioners and measurement are not required if drive-on type hoist is used to support vehicle.*

3) Raise vehicle and check measurement; adjust if necessary. Connect 1500 psi (110 kg/cm²) gauge to left front caliper and another to right rear wheel cylinder (caliper). Bleed gauges and depress brake pedal firmly several times. Depress brake pedal until front gauge reaches specification listed in table. Check rear gauge reading.

Brake Pressure Regulator Pressures		
Application	**Front Gauge** psi (kg/cm²)	**Rear Gauge** psi (kg/cm²)
4000		
1st Reading	725 (51)	457-566 (32-40)
2nd Reading	1450 (102)	725-914 (51-64)
5000 & Turbo		
1st Reading	725 (51)	493-566 (35-40)
2nd Reading	1450 (102)	827-899 (58-63)

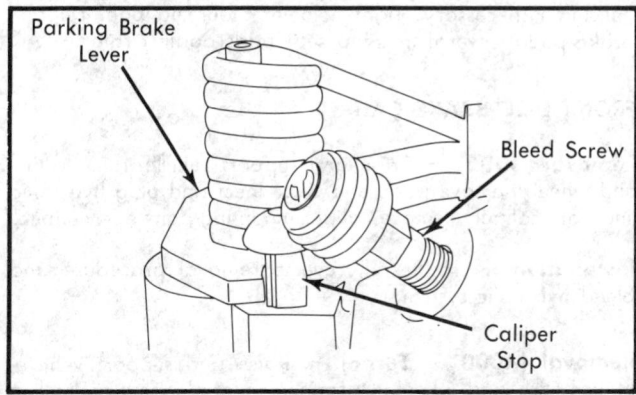

Fig. 2   Turbo Rear Disc Brake Caliper Parking Brake Lever Resting Position

4) If pressures are consistently high at rear gauge, loosen regulator clamp bolt and REDUCE spring tension. If pressures were consistently low, INCREASE spring tension. If pressures cannot be obtained after adjustment, replace regulator.

Brakes

AUDI (Cont.)

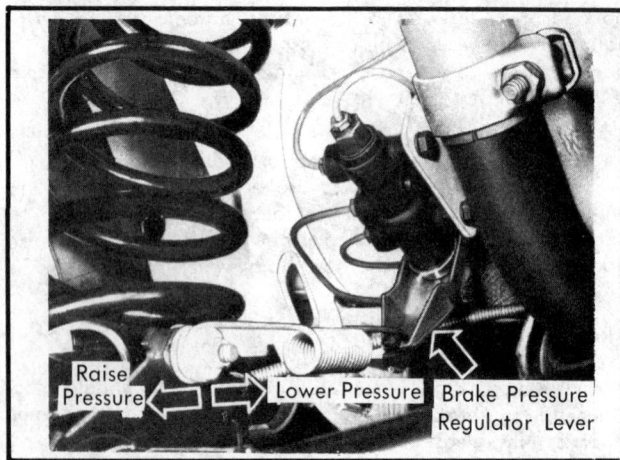

Fig. 3 Brake Pressure Regulator Adjustment (Audi 4000 Regulator is Mounted in Reverse Direction)

REMOVAL & INSTALLATION

FRONT DISC BRAKE PADS

NOTE – *During removal or installation of brake pads or calipers, siphon small amount of brake fluid from master cylinder reservoir BEFORE pushing caliper piston into cylinder bore to prevent overflowing.*

Removal (5000) – 1) Raise and support vehicle; remove tire and wheel. Detach wear indicator wire at connector. Remove retaining clip and drive out pad retaining pins.

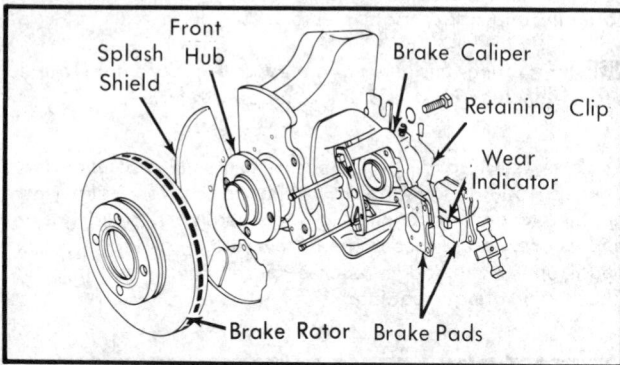

Fig. 4 Exploded View of Audi 5000 Front Disc Brake Assembly

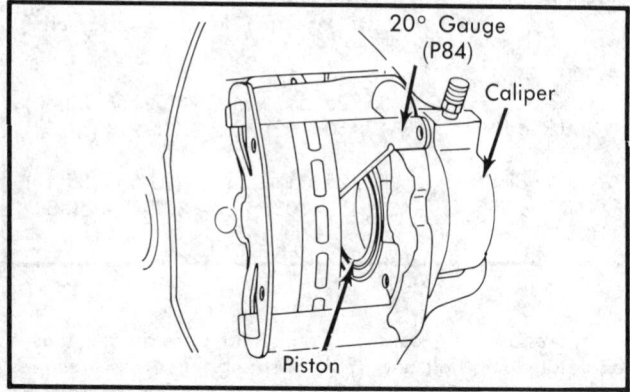

Fig. 5 Positioning Piston in Audi 5000 Caliper

2) Pull out inner brake pad. Press floating frame and cylinder outward and remove outer brake pad. Remove wear indicator from hole in pad.

Installation – 1) Press piston into caliper bore and position piston using 20° gauge (P84). Insert brake wear indicator in outboard pad and install pads.

2) Slide in pad retaining pins and install clip. Connect wear indicator wire at connector. Pump brake pedal several times to seat pads. Bleed hydraulic system if necessary.

Removal (4000 & Turbo) – 1) Raise and support vehicle; remove tire and wheel. Using hand pressure, force caliper to slide outward (toward outer wheel bearing) to seat piston in caliper bore.

2) Hold guide pin head with open end wrench while removing lower mounting bolt. Rotate caliper assembly upward. See *Fig. 6*. Remove disc pads from carrier.

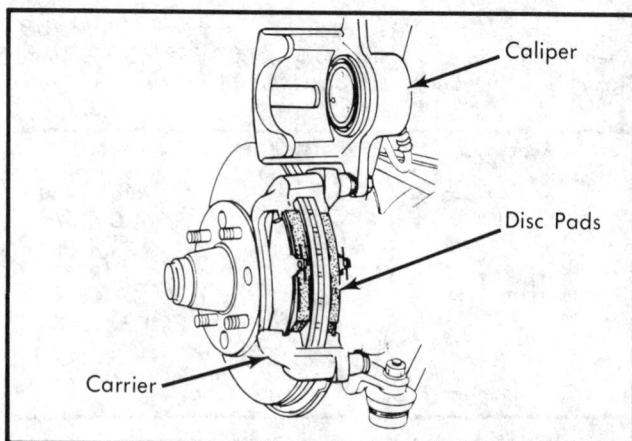

Fig. 6 Audi 4000 and Turbo Front Disc Pad Removal

Installation – 1) Clean area where pads rest. Make sure grommets on guide pins are not damaged. Guide pins must slide smoothly in housing. Install brake pads. Swing caliper housing down.

NOTE – *When replacing disc pads on Turbo, install heat shield (furnished with repair kit) on piston side of inner pad.*

2) Make sure pads do not hit piston; force piston deeper into housing if necessary. Tighten lower mounting bolt. Depress brake pedal several times to seat pads against rotor.

FRONT DISC BRAKE CALIPER

Removal (5000) – Raise and support vehicle; remove tire and wheel. Remove pads and disconnect and plug hydraulic line from caliper. Remove caliper mounting bolts and caliper.

Installation – To install, reverse removal procedure and bleed hydraulic system.

Removal (4000 & Turbo) – Raise and support vehicle; remove tire and wheel. Disconnect and plug hydraulic line from caliper. Bend back locking tabs (if equipped) on mounting bolts. Hold guide pin head with open end wrench

AUDI (Cont.)

and remove mounting bolts and caliper. Remove brake pad carrier mounting bolts and carrier.

Installation — To install, reverse removal procedure and bleed hydraulic system.

FRONT DISC BRAKE ROTOR

Removal — Raise and support vehicle; remove tire and wheel. Remove caliper as previously described and hang from vehicle frame with wire. DO NOT disconnect hydraulic line unless necessary. Remove screw securing rotor to spindle (4000) and pull rotor from spindle.

Installation — To install rotor assembly, reverse removal procedure. Bleed hydraulic system if necessary.

REAR DISC BRAKE PADS

Removal — Raise and support vehicle; remove tire and wheel. Hold guide pin head with open end wrench while removing mounting bolts. Remove caliper and hang from vehicle frame with wire. DO NOT disconnect or damage hydraulic line. Remove disc pads from carrier.

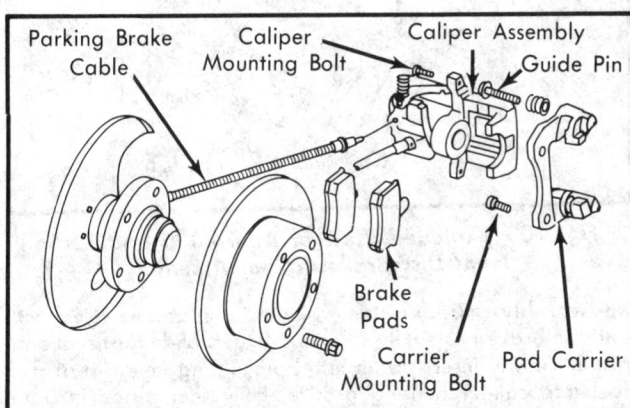

Fig. 7 Exploded View of Audi Turbo Rear Disc Brake Assembly

Installation — Using an Allen wrench, turn piston in clockwise rotation while pushing into caliper bore. Install brake pads in carrier. Install caliper assembly and tighten mounting bolts. Pump brake pedal 40 times to seat pads. Check parking brake adjustment and bleed hydraulic system if necessary.

REAR DISC BRAKE CALIPER

Removal — Raise and support vehicle; remove tire and wheel. Disconnect parking brake cable from caliper assembly. Disconnect and plug hydraulic line from caliper. Remove caliper mounting bolts while holding guide pin head with open end wrench and remove caliper. Remove pad carrier mounting bolts and carrier.

Installation — 1) Fill caliper cylinder with brake fluid and pre-bleed caliper. Install brake pad carrier, then install caliper assembly. Tighten mounting bolts.

2) Reconnect hydraulic line and parking brake cable to caliper. Pump brake pedal 40 times to seat pads. Check parking brake adjustment and bleed hydraulic system.

REAR DISC BRAKE ROTOR

Removal — Raise and support vehicle; remove tire and wheel. Remove caliper as previously described and hang from frame with wire. DO NOT disconnect hydraulic line. Remove rotor from spindle.

Installation — To install, reverse removal procedure.

REAR BRAKE DRUM

Removal — Raise and support vehicle. Remove tire. Before removing right drum, release spring pressure on pressure regulator. Remove 1 wheel bolt. Using a screwdriver inserted through wheel bolt hole, push adjusting wedge upward. Reinstall wheel bolt. Remove wheel bearing hardware. Remove drum assembly without dropping thrust washer or outer bearing.

Installation — To install, reverse removal procedure and adjust wheel bearings. See *Wheel Bearing Adjustment in WHEEL ALIGNMENT Section.* Depress brake pedal firmly to set self-adjusting mechanism.

REAR BRAKE SHOES

Removal — 1) Remove brake drum. Remove hold-down springs and pins. Remove brake shoes from anchor pins and remove return springs.

2) Disconnect parking brake cable from lever. Disconnect adjusting wedge spring and upper return spring. Remove brake shoes. Place adjuster strut and shoe in vise; remove tension spring. Separate shoe and components.

Installation — To install, reverse removal procedure and note the following: Lug on adjusting wedge faces backing plate. Adjust wheel bearings. See *Wheel Bearing Adjustment in WHEEL ALIGNMENT Section.* After installing drum, depress brake pedal firmly to set adjuster mechanism.

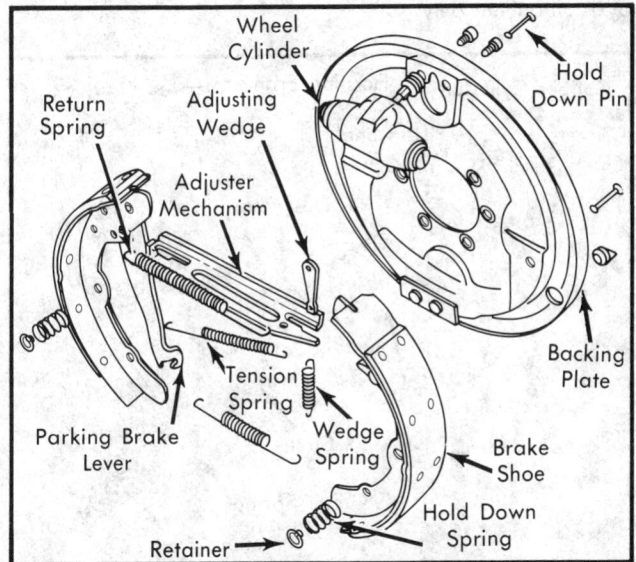

Fig. 8 Exploded View of Rear Drum Brake Assembly (Audi 4000 and 5000 Models)

Brakes

AUDI (Cont.)

MASTER CYLINDER

Removal — Siphon brake fluid from reservoir and remove hydraulic lines from master cylinder. Disconnect warning light electrical lead. Remove mounting bolts and separate master cylinder from power brake unit.

Installation — Replace "O" ring between master cylinder and power brake unit. Reverse removal procedure and bleed hydraulic system.

POWER BRAKE UNIT

Removal — Remove master cylinder from power brake unit. Remove pin at brake pedal and disconnect operating rod. Remove mounting nuts from firewall. Disconnect vacuum line and remove power unit.

Installation — To install, reverse removal procedure and note the following: Replace filter at operating rod end.

NOTE — *Clevis and brake lever each have 2 holes. Install clevis pin only in holes nearest front of vehicle.*

Check Valve — Large diameter side fits into power unit. To test, remove vacuum line and check valve. Blow into large diameter hole; valve should open. In the other direction, valve should close. Replace if defective.

OVERHAUL

FRONT DISC BRAKE CALIPER

Disassembly (5000) — Remove pads and wear indicator. Push caliper mounting frame off floating frame. Insert wooden block in floating frame, then use brass drift to drive cylinder from frame. Support piston on wooden block and force out with compressed air. Remove piston seal without damaging bore.

Cleaning & Inspection — Clean all parts in alcohol only. Check cylinder bore and piston for damage. Parts are serviced by replacement only.

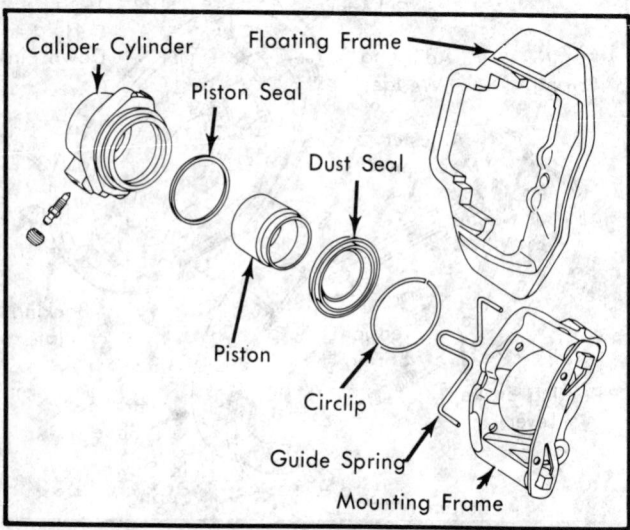

Fig. 9   Exploded View of Audi 5000 Front Disc Brake Caliper Assembly

Reassembly — Coat all parts with ATE brake cylinder paste (or equivalent), reverse disassembly procedure and note the following: Use new seals, dust boots and retaining rings when reassembling. Make sure machined surface of piston face makes a 20° angle to wall of caliper bore. Install disc pads after caliper has been installed on vehicle.

Disassembly (4000 & Turbo) — Remove caliper and clean outside surfaces. Remove mounting bolts. Place a block of wood between piston and housing. Force piston out with compressed air and remove piston. Remove dust seal circlip and seal. Carefully remove piston seal without damaging bore or groove.

Cleaning & Inspection — Clean all parts in alcohol only. Check cylinder bore and piston for wear or damage. Parts are serviced by replacement only. Boots, guide pins and other minor parts are only available with new pad carrier.

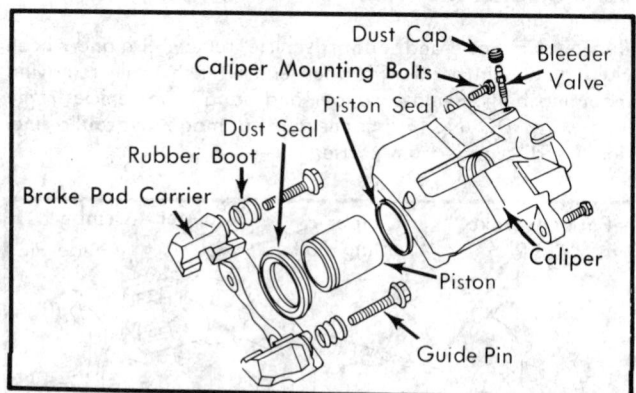

Fig. 10   Exploded View of Audi 4000 and Turbo Front Disc Brake Caliper Assembly

Reassembly — Coat piston, cylinder bore, and new seal with suitable brake paste. Fit seal into cylinder. Slide dust seal onto piston. Slowly insert piston into bore, fitting inner lip of dust seal into caliper housing groove. Fully seat piston in bore. Engage outer lip of dust seal into piston groove.

REAR DISC BRAKE CALIPER

Disassembly — 1) Remove caliper and clean outside surfaces. Remove parking brake lever housing bolts and housing. Remove guide pin and sleeve, then remove return spring and lever from housing. Remove and discard seal and "O" ring.

2) Using hand pressure, push piston out rear of caliper assembly. Remove push rod from rear of piston, then "O" ring, seals and spacer. Carefully remove piston seal without damaging bore or groove.

Cleaning & Inspection — Clean all parts in alcohol only. Check all parts for wear or damage. Guide pins, dust boots, seals, "O" rings and pad carrier are the only serviceable parts. Any damage to other parts requires replacement of caliper assembly.

Installation — 1) Coat piston, piston seal and parking brake guide pin with suitable brake paste. Fit seal into cylinder groove. Slide dust seal onto piston, then install spacer, "O" ring and seal onto piston push rod. Fit push rod to piston. Push piston into caliper bore from rear.

AUDI (Cont.)

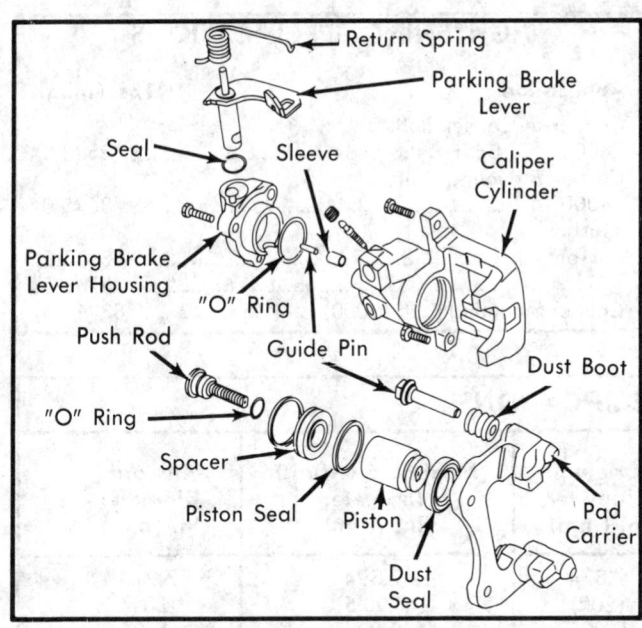

Fig. 11 *Exploded View of Rear Disc Brake Assembly*

2) Replace seals on parking brake lever assembly, then install return spring and brake lever into housing. Install guide pin and sleeve in housing. Fit parking brake lever housing to rear of caliper and ensure push rod pin aligns with housing. Install and tighten bolts. Pre-bleed caliper assembly.

REAR WHEEL CYLINDER

Disassembly — Thoroughly clean outside of cylinder. Remove boots, piston assemblies, cups and spring. Remove dust cap and bleeder screw.

Cleaning & Inspection — Clean all parts in alcohol only. Check all parts for rust, corrosion or wear. If necessary, replace complete cylinder.

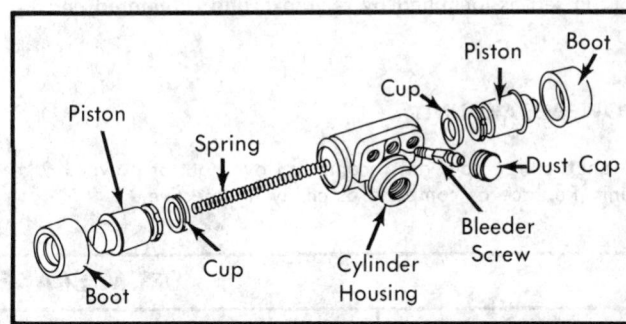

Fig. 12 *Exploded View of Rear Wheel Cylinder*

Reassembly — Reverse disassembly procedure and note the following: Refer to *Fig. 12* for correct installation position of wheel cylinder pistons.

MASTER CYLINDER

Disassembly — Remove "O" ring from master cylinder housing. Remove retaining ring and loosen piston stop screw, then remove both pistons from housing. Remove pressure valves and reservoir from master cylinder housing. Disassemble piston assemblies as necessary.

Cleaning & Inspection — Clean all parts in alcohol and check for rust, corrosion, or other damage; replace parts as necessary. Make sure compensating and filler holes are not plugged.

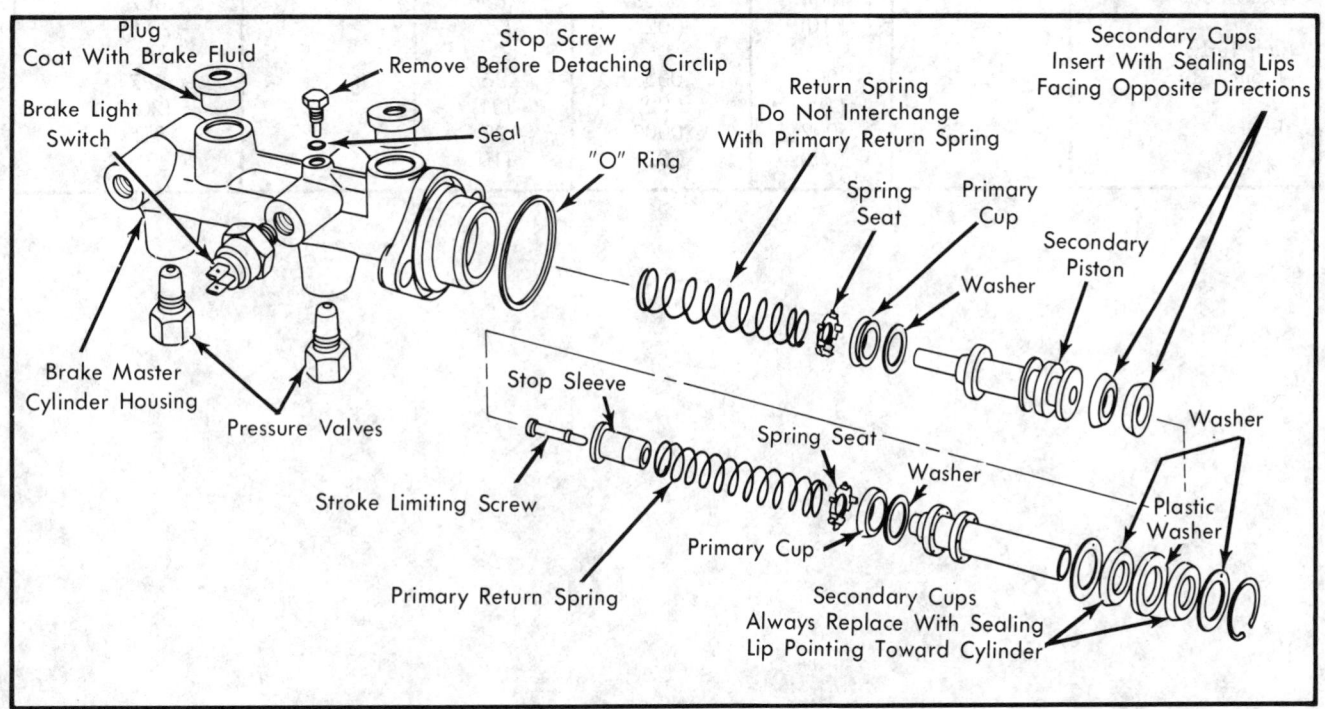

Fig. 13 *Master Cylinder Component Relationship*
(Audi 4000 Housing External Design Differs — Internal Parts Are Identical)

Brakes

AUDI (Cont.)

Reassembly — Reverse disassembly procedure and note the following: Lubricate primary piston shaft with silicone grease and all other parts with brake cylinder paste. Replace all rubber parts. DO NOT interchange primary cup and piston seal; piston seal is identified by a groove and chamfered end.

POWER BRAKE UNIT

Manufacturer does not recommend overhaul of power brake unit. Replace as complete assembly if defective.

TIGHTENING SPECIFICATIONS

Application	Ft. Lbs. (mkg)
Caliper-to-Carrier Bolts	
4000 & Turbo (Front & Rear) 25 (3.5)	
Carrier Mounting Bolts	
4000 .... 36 (5.0)	
Turbo	
Front 83 (11.5)	
Rear 47 (6.5)	
Caliper Mounting Bolts (5000) 83 (11.5)	

DRUM BRAKE SPECIFICATIONS

Application	Wheel Cyl. Bore Diameter In. (mm)	Drum Diameter In. (mm)	Original Diameter In. (mm)	Maximum Refinish Diameter In. (mm)	Discard Diameter In. (mm)
Audi 4000	.....	7.874 (200)	7.874 (200)	7.894 (200.5)	7.913 (201)
Audi 5000	.....	9.005 (230)	9.005 (230)	9.094 (231)	9.135 (232)

DISC BRAKE SPECIFICATIONS

Application	Caliper Bore Diameter In. (mm)	Lateral Runout In. (mm)	Parallelism In. (mm)	Original Thickness In. (mm)	Minimum Refinish Thickness In. (mm)	Discard Thickness In. (mm)
Audi 4000	.....	.002 (.05)	.....	.472 (12)	.....	.394 (10)
Audi 5000	.....	.004 (.10)	.0008 (.02)	.866 (22)	.....	.807 (20.5)
Audi Turbo						
Front	.....	.002 (.05)	.0008 (.02)	.866 (22)	.....	.787 (20)
Rear	.....	.002 (.05)	.0008 (.02)	.394 (10)	.....	.315 (8)

BMW

320i
528i
633CSi
733i

DESCRIPTION

Brake system is hydraulically operated using a tandem master cylinder and power brake unit. All models except 320i are equipped with 4 piston, ATE front disc brake calipers and 2 piston, ATE rear disc brake calipers. The 320i is equipped with 2 piston, ATE front disc brake calipers and rear drum brakes. Disc pad wear indicator lights are mounted on the instrument panel of 320i and 528i to indicate need for pad replacement. On 633CSi and 733i models, pad wear indicator lamp is component of "Check Control" system. An optional brake pressure regulator may be installed to reduce fluid pressure to rear brakes. Parking brake is cable actuated on service brake of 320i and internally mounted parking brake shoes on all rear disc brake systems.

ADJUSTMENT

REAR DRUM BRAKE SHOES

320i — Raise and support vehicle; release parking brake. While rotating tire, tighten brake adjusters (turn left adjuster counterclockwise; right adjuster clockwise) until brake shoes lock drum. Loosen each adjuster $\frac{1}{8}$ turn or until wheel rotates without drag.

BRAKE PEDAL HEIGHT

Brake pedal height (measured from firewall to pedal pad center) should be 9.4-9.8" (239-249 mm) on 320i; 9.1-9.5" (230-241 mm) on 528i and 633CSi and 9.9-10.2" (251-260 mm) on 733i. To adjust pedal height, loosen stop light switch lock nut and position stop light switch out of way. Loosen brake operating rod lock nut and turn operating rod until correct pedal height is obtained. Tighten lock nut, reposition and adjust stop light switch and tighten stop light switch lock nut.

STOP LIGHT SWITCH

Stop light switch is located under instrument panel in front of brake pedal arm. To adjust stop light switch, loosen lock nut and turn adjusting nut so contact plunger just touches pedal arm and extended length of plunger is .20-.24" (5-6 mm). Tighten lock nut.

PARKING BRAKE

NOTE — *Before adjusting parking brake (except 320i), pull parking brake lever until resistance is felt, then 1 additional notch. With parking brake lever engaged as described, drive vehicle maximum of 1300 ft. (400 m).*

Except 320i — 1) Raise and support vehicle; remove tire and wheel and release parking brake. Insert a screwdriver into rotor inspection hole. Turn adjuster until parking brake shoes lock rotor, then back off adjuster 4-6 notches.

2) Working inside driver compartment, tighten adjustment nuts on lever until parking brake holds vehicle securely before fifth ratchet stop is reached.

320i — 1) Raise and support rear of vehicle. Fully release parking brake. Tighten brake shoes until wheel is locked. Back off adjusters about $\frac{1}{8}$ turn or until wheel can just barely turn.

2) Work inside passenger compartment and tighten nuts on lever until parking brake holds vehicle securely before fifth ratchet stop is reached.

BRAKE WARNING LIGHT

A dual warning light is mounted on instrument panel. Light should glow when parking brake lever is pulled 1 notch (ignition on) and go off when lever is fully released. To check circuit warning sensor, fully release parking brake and ensure light is off (ignition on). Raise master cylinder filler cap; warning lamp should glow. If not, check bulb or circuit connections.

REMOVAL & INSTALLATION

DISC PADS

Removal — Raise and support vehicle. Remove wheels. Disconnect pad wear sensors. Drive out retaining pin toward inside of vehicle. Remove cross spring. Using an extractor tool, remove disc pads from caliper. If disc pad thickness has worn to .080" (2 mm), replace pads. Only replace pads in matched sets.

Installation — 1) Using a cylinder brush, clean guide surface and support surface in caliper. Siphon sufficient fluid from master cylinder reservoir to prevent overflowing, then press pistons to bottom of bores.

2) On rear calipers and 320i front calipers, ensure machined position of piston face makes a 20° angle with caliper wall. *See Fig. 1.* (Rotate piston with tool 341050 if necessary). Install disc pads, shims (if required), cross spring and retaining pins. After installation, depress brake pedal several times to seat disc pads.

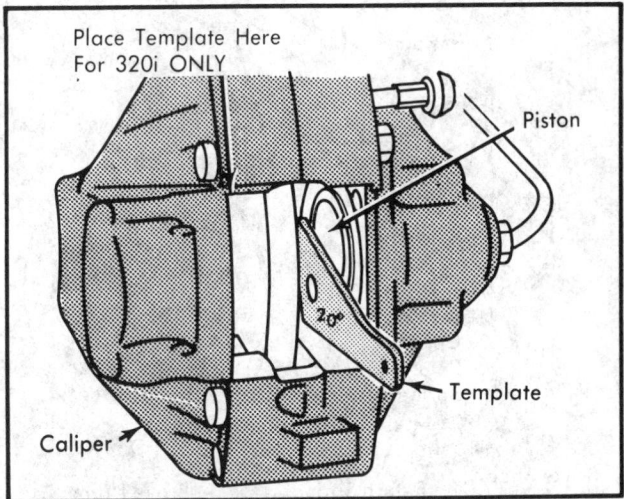

Fig. 1   Piston Alignment for Dual Piston Calipers

CALIPER ASSEMBLY

Removal — Drain brake fluid from master cylinder reservoir. Remove caliper mounting bolts. Disconnect disc pad wear in-

BMW (Cont.)

dicator electrical lead. Disconnect brake fluid inlet lines. Lift caliper off rotor.

Installation — Reverse removal procedure and bleed hydraulic system.

ROTOR

Removal — Raise and support vehicle; remove tire and wheel. On front calipers, separate bracket from strut. On all models, remove caliper and hang from frame with wire; DO NOT disconnect hydraulic line. On rear calipers, slip hydraulic line out of holding clamp. Remove rotor mounting bolt and remove brake rotor.

NOTE — *Front brake rotors are balanced; DO NOT remove or reposition balance clips. If any rotor must be replaced, replace rotors in axle sets.*

Installation — To install, reverse removal procedure.

PARKING BRAKE SHOES

Removal — With rear caliper and rotor removed, disconnect lower return spring using brake spring pliers. Turn retaining springs 90° using removal tool, then set spring aside. Pull brake shoes apart at bottom and lift upward.

Installation — To install, reverse removal procedure, adjust parking brake shoes and check operation.

BRAKE DRUM

Removal & Installation — Loosen brake adjuster cams. Remove countersunk Allen bolt and slide off brake drum. To install, reverse removal procedure and note: If one brake drum is reground, drum on other side must also be reground.

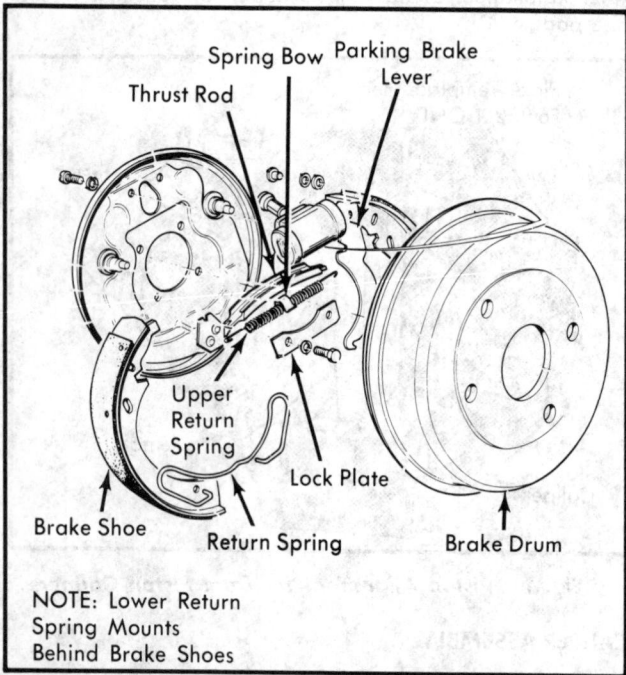

NOTE: Lower Return Spring Mounts Behind Brake Shoes

Fig. 2 Exploded View of Rear Drum Brake Assembly

BRAKE SHOES

Removal — Remove brake drum. Disengage mounting spring, retainer and pin from each shoe. Disconnect bottom return spring. Pull shoes apart and out of wheel cylinder. Disconnect parking brake cable and remove brake shoes. If brake shoe lining has worn to .118″ (3.0 mm) or less, replace brake shoes.

Installation — Reverse removal procedure and note: Connect long end of spring between parking brake lever and brake shoe.

MASTER CYLINDER

NOTE — *On 320i models only, mixture control unit must be removed to take off master cylinder.*

Removal — 1) Siphon off brake fluid from reservoir. On 320i, disconnect clutch hose connection. On 633CSi, remove air cleaner. On 528i and 633CSi, remove relay holder attaching bracket with all components still attached and position out of way.

2) Disconnect all hydraulic lines from master cylinder. Remove nuts mounting master cylinder to power booster. On 320i models, remove nuts mounting master cylinder support to inner fender panel. Remove support and master cylinder.

Installation — To install, reverse removal procedure and note: Make sure "O" ring on master cylinder is not damaged. An imperfect fit will not allow correct vacuum build-up.

POWER BRAKE UNIT

NOTE — *Power brake unit must be removed with master cylinder attached. On 320i, mixture control unit must be removed prior to removal of power brake unit.*

Removal — 1) Siphon brake fluid from master cylinder reservoir. On all models except 320i, remove left portion of lower dash panel. On all models, remove operating rod clevis pin from brake pedal arm. On 633CSi, remove air cleaner. On 528i and 633CSi, remove relay holder as previously described.

2) Disconnect and plug hydraulic lines at master cylinder, including clutch hose. Disconnect vacuum hose from power brake unit (hydraulic lines on 733i). Remove power brake unit mounting bolts. On 320i only, separate master cylinder support from inner fender panel. Remove power unit/master cylinder assembly from vehicle. Separate master cylinder from power brake unit.

NOTE — *On 733i models only, power steering pump also supplies hydraulic pressure through hydraulic accumulator to the power brake unit. If power steering fails, there will be sufficient pressure in the hydraulic accumulator to provide a few brake applications with full power.*

Installation — To install, mount master cylinder to power brake unit and reverse removal procedure. Bleed hydraulic system after installation.

Check Valve Replacement (Exc. 733i) — Check valve is located in vacuum line between power unit and intake manifold. To remove, loosen hose clamps, remove vacuum lines

BMW (Cont.)

and remove valve. To install, reverse removal procedure. Make sure arrow or black portion of valve faces intake manifold.

Filter Replacement (Exc. 733i) — With power brake unit removed from vehicle, pull back rubber dust boot. Remove retaining ring. Remove silencer and filter. To install, reverse removal procedure.

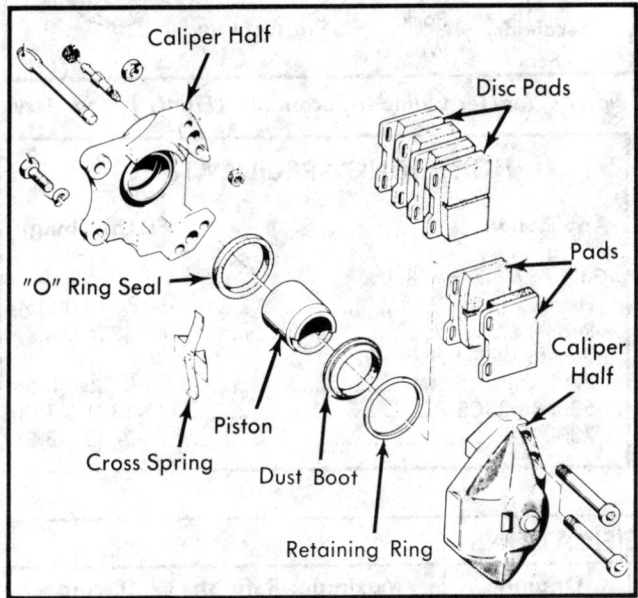

Fig. 3   Disassembled View of Dual Piston Caliper Used as Rear Caliper on 528i, 633CSi and 733i Models and Front Caliper on 320i Models Only

OVERHAUL

BRAKE CALIPER

NOTE — *DO NOT disassemble 4 piston caliper halves.*

Disassembly — With pads removed from caliper, remove retaining ring and dust boot. Using suitable clamp, hold one piston in position, insert wooden block in caliper cavity, then apply compressed air to fluid inlet to force out opposite piston. Repeat procedure for each piston. Remove piston seals without damaging caliper bore.

Cleaning & Inspection — Clean components in clean brake fluid and blow dry. Inspect caliper bore and pistons for wear or damage. Replace caliper assembly if corroded or worn; DO NOT hone. Replace piston seals and dust boots at each overhaul.

Reassembly — Coat pistons and caliper bores with ATE brake cylinder paste. Install piston seals, then install pistons. Make sure pistons are not tilted when inserting. On 2 piston calipers ensure 20° piston angle position is preset. Install dust boots and retaining rings.

REAR WHEEL CYLINDER

Disassembly — Remove dust boots and force out pistons and return spring. Separate and discard cylinder cups from pistons.

Cleaning & Inspection — Clean all parts in clean brake fluid. Check cylinder bore and dust boot retaining grooves for

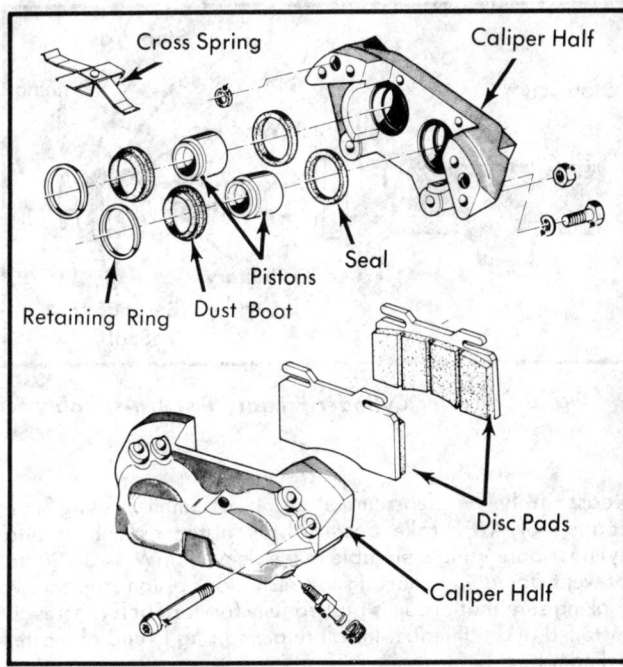

Fig. 4   Disassembled View of 4 Piston Caliper Used as Front Caliper on 528i, 633CSi and 733i

rust and corrosion. Replace wheel cylinder assembly if defective; DO NOT hone. Replace all rubber parts during overhaul.

Reassembly — Coat all parts with ATE brake cylinder paste. Reassemble wheel cylinder by reversing disassembly procedure.

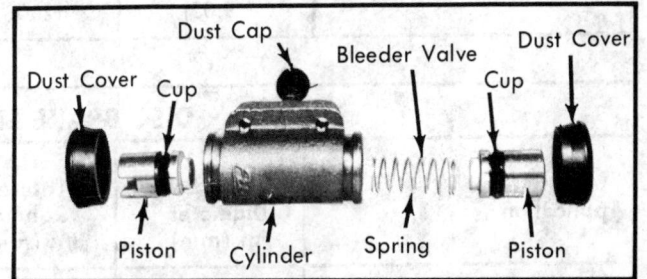

Fig. 5   Exploded View of 320i Rear Wheel Cylinder

MASTER CYLINDER

NOTE — *All master cylinders are similar, procedures outlined are general.*

Disassembly — Push in on primary piston and remove secondary piston stop screw. Remove snap ring from end of cylinder and remove primary and secondary piston assemblies and return spring. Disassemble piston assemblies noting number and position of parts used.

Cleaning & Inspection — Clean all parts in alcohol and inspect for wear or damage. Master cylinder bore diameter is .812" (20.64 mm) on 320i, .938" (23.81 mm) on 528i and 633CSi and .875" (22.23 mm) on 733i.

NOTE — *Cylinders with surface defects in bores must be replaced; do not overhaul.*

BMW (Cont.)

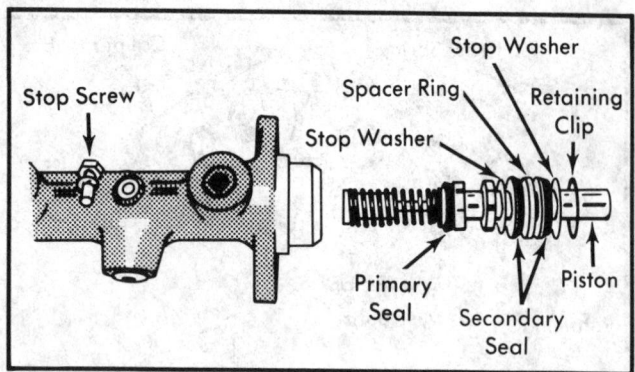

Fig. 6   Master Cylinder Primary Piston Assembly

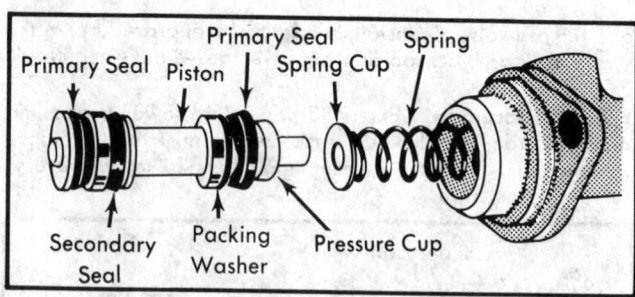

Fig. 7   Master Cylinder Secondary (Front) Piston Assy.

Reassembly — Reassemble piston assemblies using thin coating of ATE brake paste. Install piston assemblies into cylinder bore using a suitable guide sleeve (BMW 34 3 000) to prevent damaging seals. Install secondary piston stop screw, making sure that piston is pushed fully forward before screw is installed and tightened. Install retaining ring in end of master cylinder bore.

TIGHTENING SPECIFICATIONS

Application	Ft. Lbs. (mkg)
Caliper Mounting Bolts	
Front	58-69 (8.0-9.5)
Rear	43-48 (6.0-6.7)
Rotor-to-Wheel Hub	
320i	3.0-3.5 (.4-.5)
528i & 633CSi	11-13 (1.5-1.8)
733i	23-24 (3.2-3.3)

DRUM BRAKE SPECIFICATIONS

Application	Wheel Cyl. Bore Diameter In. (mm)	Drum Diameter In. (mm)	Original Diameter In. (mm)	Maximum Refinish Diameter In. (mm)	Discard Diameter In. (mm)
320i					
Rear	.750 (19.05)	9.84 (250)	9.84 (250)	9.88 (251)	.....

DISC BRAKE SPECIFICATIONS

Application	Caliper Bore Diameter In. (mm)	Lateral Runout In. (mm)	Parallelism In. (mm)	Original Thickness In. (mm)	Minimum Refinish Thickness In. (mm)	Discard Thickness In. (mm)
320i						
Front	1.89 (48)	.008① (.2)	.0008 (.02)	.866 (22)	②	.827 (21)
528i						
Front	1.57 (40)	.008① (.2)	.0008 (.02)	.866 (22)	②	.827 (21)
Rear	1.65 (42)	.008① (.2)	.0008 (.02)	.374 (9.5)	②	.334 (8.5)
633CSi						
Front	1.57 (40)	.008① (.2)	.0008 (.02)	.866 (22)	②	.827 (21)
Rear	1.65 (42)	.008① (.2)	.0008 (.02)	.748 (19)	②	.709 (18)
733i						
Front	1.57 (40)	.006① (.15)	.0008 (.02)	.866 (22)	②	.827 (21)
Rear	1.30 (33)	.006① (.15)	.0008 (.02)	.394 (10)	②	.354 (9)

① — Installed on vehicle.
② — Machining of each braking surface is .020″ (.5 mm). Minimum rotor thickness must be observed.

CHRYSLER CORP. IMPORTS

Arrow
Arrow Pickup
Challenger
Champ

Colt
D50 Pickup
Sapporo

DESCRIPTION

Brake system is hydraulically operated using tandem master cylinder, proportioning valve to control braking action and vacuum power brake unit. Arrow, Champ and Colt Hatchback models are equipped with pin caliper type front disc brakes, all other models are equipped with sliding caliper front disc brakes. Rear brakes are duo-servo drum on Arrow and D50 pickups and leading/trailing drum on all other models except Arrow with 2600 cc engine. Arrow with 2600 cc engine rear brakes are sliding caliper disc (optional on Challenger and Sapporo). All service brake systems are self-adjusting. Parking brake is cable actuated to rear brake system on all models.

ADJUSTMENT

PEDAL HEIGHT & FREE PLAY

Back off stop light switch. Adjust pedal height (distance from top of pedal to floor board) to specification by loosening lock nut and rotating master cylinder push rod (yoke, if equipped). DO NOT depress push rod. Tighten lock nut and ensure brake pedal free play is .4-.6" (10-15 mm) on all models.

STOP LIGHT SWITCH

On Champ and Colt Hatchback models, loosen lock nut and adjust switch-to-pedal arm clearance to .01-.04" (.5-1 mm). Tighten lock nut. On all other models, adjust stop light switch until it just contacts brake pedal lever. DO NOT depress master cylinder push rod during stop light switch adjustment.

Pedal Height Specifications	
Application	**Pedal Height In. (mm)**
Arrow	
Man. Trans.	6.4 (163)
Auto. Trans.	6.5 (165)
Challenger, Sapporo &	
Colt Station Wagon	6.9 (175)
Champ & Colt Hatchback	7.1-7.3 (180-185)
Arrow & D50 Pickup	6.5 (165)

PARKING BRAKE

Arrow (Exc. Rear Disc) — Remove parking brake lever cover and fully release brake lever. Adjust nut (underside of lever) until lever-to-stop clearance is .008-.08" (.2-2 mm) and stroke is 5-7 notches at 44 lbs. force.

Challenger, Sapporo (Exc. Rear Disc) & Colt Sta. Wgn. — 1) Release parking brake lever and ensure that rubber hanger-to-bracket clearance (at rear axle) is .2-.6" (5-15 mm). Then loosen cable attaching bolt and adjusting nut for left wheel. Move cable lever to the right and adjust clearance between extension lever and stopper on left wheel to .1" (2.5 mm) or less.

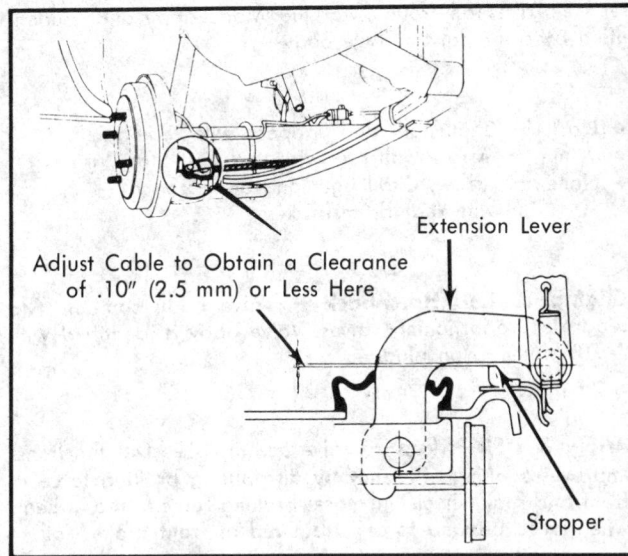

Adjust Cable to Obtain a Clearance of .10" (2.5 mm) or Less Here

Extension Lever

Stopper

Fig. 1 Adjusting Parking Brake on Challenger, Sapporo and Colt St. Wgn.

2) With left cable adjusted, turn adjusting nut until the same clearance is obtained on right wheel extension lever. With parking brake properly adjusted, lever stroke should be 4-6 notches at 44 lbs. force.

Arrow, Challenger & Sapporo (W/Rear Disc) — Fully release parking brake lever and depress brake pedal twice. Loosen adjusting nut at center of rear axle housing (brake lever on Arrow). Adjust cable so rear wheel drag is 23 lbs. (10 kg) or less after brake pedal is depressed, measured with spring pull scale. Parking brake lever stroke should be 5-7 notches at 44 lbs. force.

Champ & Colt Hatchback — Remove parking brake lever cover and release brake lever. Adjust both cables to equal lengths, allowing enough slack in cables to prevent brake shoe drag. Properly adjusted parking brake lever stroke should be 6-7 notches at 44 lbs. force.

Arrow & D50 Pickups — Service brake adjustment must be accurate before making parking brake adjustment. Fully release parking brake and allow slack in rear cable to prevent brake shoe drag. Set balancer-to-crossmember clearance to 8" (203 mm) by adjusting turnbuckle. Balancer must be parallel with center line of vehicle. Brake lever stroke should be 16-17 notches at 66 lbs. force.

NOTE — *If parking brake lever stroke is larger than specified after adjustment for all models, automatic adjuster is malfunctioning.*

PROPORTIONING VALVES

Different types of proportioning valves are used between models. However, pressure testing is similar on all models. The following are special descriptions that apply by model:

Arrow, Challenger, Colt Sta. Wgn. & Sapporo — Valve accomplishes three functions: Pressure control of rear service brakes; deactivating rear brake pressure control when front

Brakes

CHRYSLER CORP. IMPORTS (Cont.)

service brakes fail; trouble warning. Model application is identified by color dot on valve body:

- Black — Challenger and Sapporo with rear disc.
- White — Arrow with rear disc and Colt Sta. Wgn.
- None — Arrow, Challenger and Sapporo with rear drum brakes.

Champ & Colt Hatchback — Valve body contains two separate proportioning valves. Valve body is identified with "A70" stamped on plug.

Arrow & D50 Pickup — Valve accomplishes two functions: Improves braking efficiency by distributing braking force to front and rear wheels; increases braking force to rear wheels when large braking force is required or front brakes fail.

Pressure Test — Performed using two pressure gauges that measure at least 1500 psi. Hook one gauge to master cylinder rear side and one to rear wheel cylinder. Pressure readings should be as shown in chart. Replace defective part as required. DO NOT disassemble proportioning valve.

NOTE — The proportioning valve on Champ and Colt Hatchback models contains two valves; each must be tested separately.

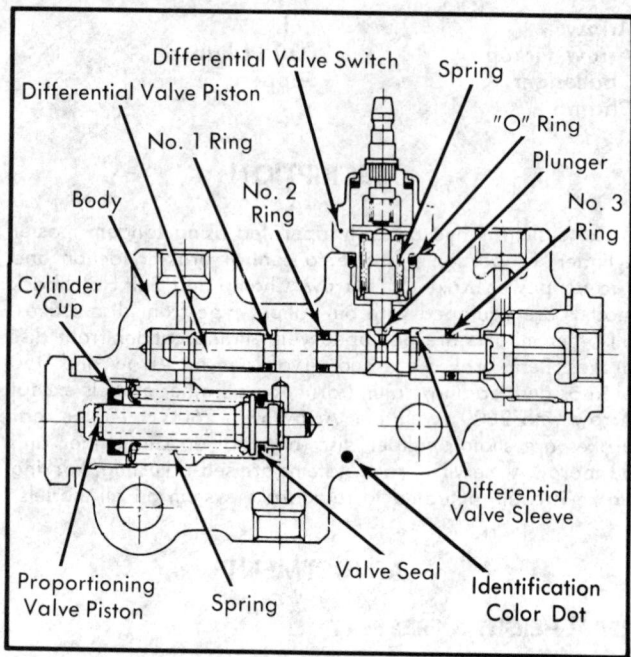

Fig. 2   Sectional View of Proportioning Valve Arrow, Challenger, Sapporo & Colt Sta. Wgn.

Brake Hydraulic Pressure Chart (psi)		
Application	**Wheel Cyl. Pressure**	**Master Cyl. Pressure**
Challenger & Sapporo W/Rear Disc	674	853
Arrow W/Rear Disc & Colt Sta. Wgn.	531	711
Arrow, Challenger & Sapporo W/Rear Drum	460	640
Champ & Colt Hatchback	496-525	853
Pickups	437-493	711

Warning Light Test — To test warning light (if equipped), loosen bleeder screw of one wheel cylinder and depress brake pedal; warning light should come on. If not, check switch and wire connector.

Proportioning Valve Reset (Exc. Champ, Colt Hatchback & Pickups) — After repairs on brake system, bleed brake lines. With all lines bled and bleeder valves secured, depress brake pedal hard. This will center valve and warning light should go out.

REMOVAL & INSTALLATION

FRONT DISC BRAKE PADS

Removal (Arrow, Champ & Colt Hatchback) — Raise and support vehicle. Remove front wheel. Remove protector by prying up edge of clip at center of protector. Hold center of "M" clip, detach "M" clip from pad and its ends from retaining pins; remove clip. Remove retaining pins from caliper and remove "K" spring. Remove pads and anti-squeal springs from caliper by grasping backing plate area of pads with pliers.

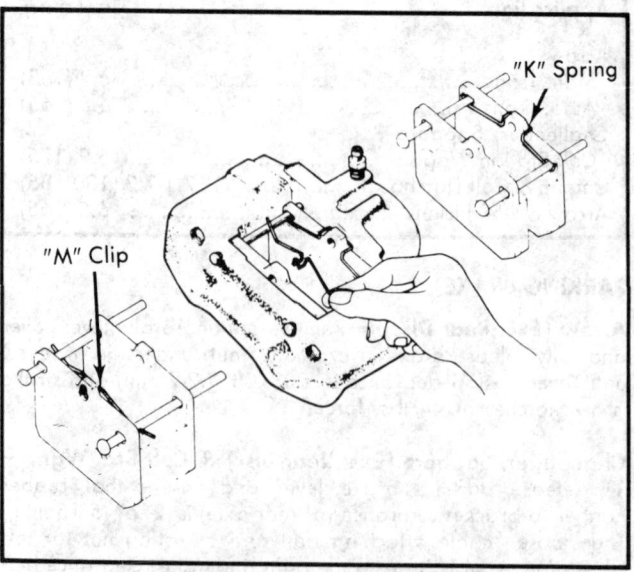

Fig. 3   Installing Spring and Clip on Brake Pads (Arrow, Champ and Colt Hatchback)

Brakes

CHRYSLER CORP. IMPORTS (Cont.)

NOTE — *Replace all pads (left and right side) at same time.*

Installation — Press piston to bottom of bore using a suitable tool, install disc pads and retaining pins. Install "K" spring and "M" clip, making sure positions are not reversed. *See Fig. 3.* Install pad protector with retaining clips on inner side of caliper (Champ and Colt) and on outer side of caliper (Arrow).

Removal (All Others) — Raise and support vehicle. Remove front wheel. Remove retaining clip and pull out stopper plug. Loosen caliper assembly mounting bolts. Pull caliper assembly up and down in a diagonal manner and remove from mounting bracket. Remove inner and outer pad clips, then pull pads and anti-squeal shims from caliper support.

Installation — To install, reverse removal procedure and note the following: Press piston to bottom of caliper bore prior to pad installation. Ensure pad retaining clips are installed as shown in *Fig. 4.*

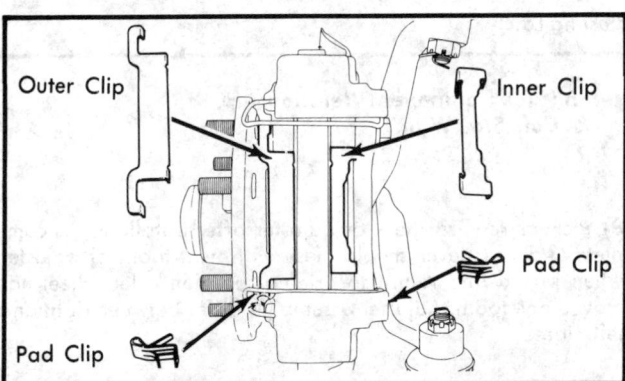

Fig. 4 Installing Pad Retaining Clips on Front Disc Brakes of Challenger, Sapporo, Colt Sta. Wgn. & Pickups

FRONT DISC BRAKE CALIPER

Removal (Arrow, Champ & Colt Hatchback) — Remove disc pads. Disconnect hydraulic line and remove bolts attaching caliper assembly to steering knuckle. Remove caliper assembly.

Installation — Reverse removal procedure, tighten caliper mounting bolts evenly and bleed hydraulic system.

Removal (All Others) — Remove disc pads. Pull out hose clip from strut area, then disconnect brake hose from caliper. Remove caliper.

Installation — To install, reverse removal procedure, tighten caliper mounting bolts evenly and bleed brake system.

FRONT DISC BRAKE ROTOR

Removal — With caliper assembly removed, remove hub dust cap, cotter pin, locknut (if used) and adjusting nut. On Champ and Colt Hatchback, remove drive shaft from hub with suitable puller. On all models, pull hub and rotor assembly from spindle using care not to drop outer wheel bearing. Remove hub-to-rotor attaching bolts and separate rotor from hub.

Installation — To install, reverse removal procedures and tighten hub-to-rotor bolts evenly. Bleed hydraulic system if necessary and adjust wheel bearings. *See Wheel Bearing Adjustment in WHEEL ALIGNMENT Section.*

REAR DISC BRAKE PADS

Removal — 1) Raise and support vehicle. Remove rear wheels. Remove caliper assembly dust cover. Disconnect parking brake cable from caliper.

2) Remove retaining pin and pull out stopper plug. Remove caliper assembly from rotor. Pull pads from caliper support.

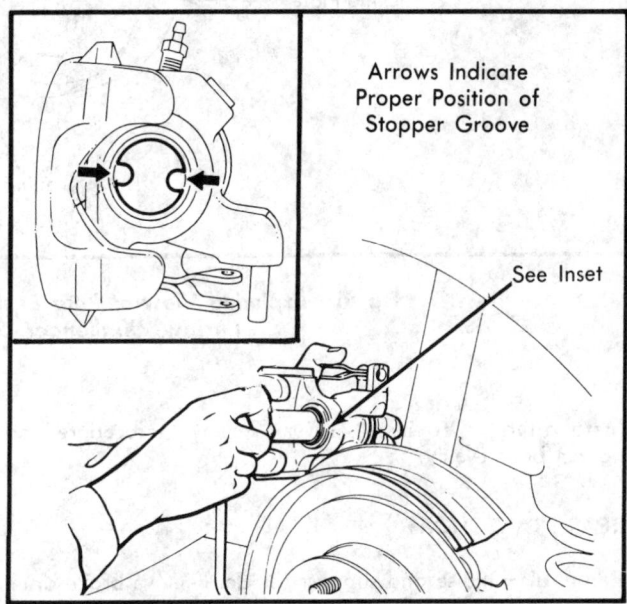

Arrows Indicate Proper Position of Stopper Groove

See Inset

Fig. 5 Positioning of Piston Stopper Groove on Rear Disc Brakes

Installation — To install, reverse removal procedure and note the following: Press the piston into its original position with clockwise rotation using a suitable driver. Ensure piston stopper groove is positioned as shown in *Fig. 5* so projection on back of pad will securely fit groove. Pad clips must be installed properly.

NOTE — *DO NOT use screwdriver to push piston into original position.*

REAR DISC BRAKE CALIPER

Removal — Remove disc pads. Pull out hose clip from axle housing and disconnect brake hose from caliper assembly. Remove clevis pin connecting lever assembly to parking brake cable. Remove caliper assembly.

Installation — To install, reverse removal procedure and bleed brake system.

REAR DISC BRAKE ROTOR

Removal — Remove disc pads. Remove caliper support-to-axle housing bolts. Remove caliper support. Remove rotor from axle shaft.

CHRYSLER CORP. IMPORTS (Cont.)

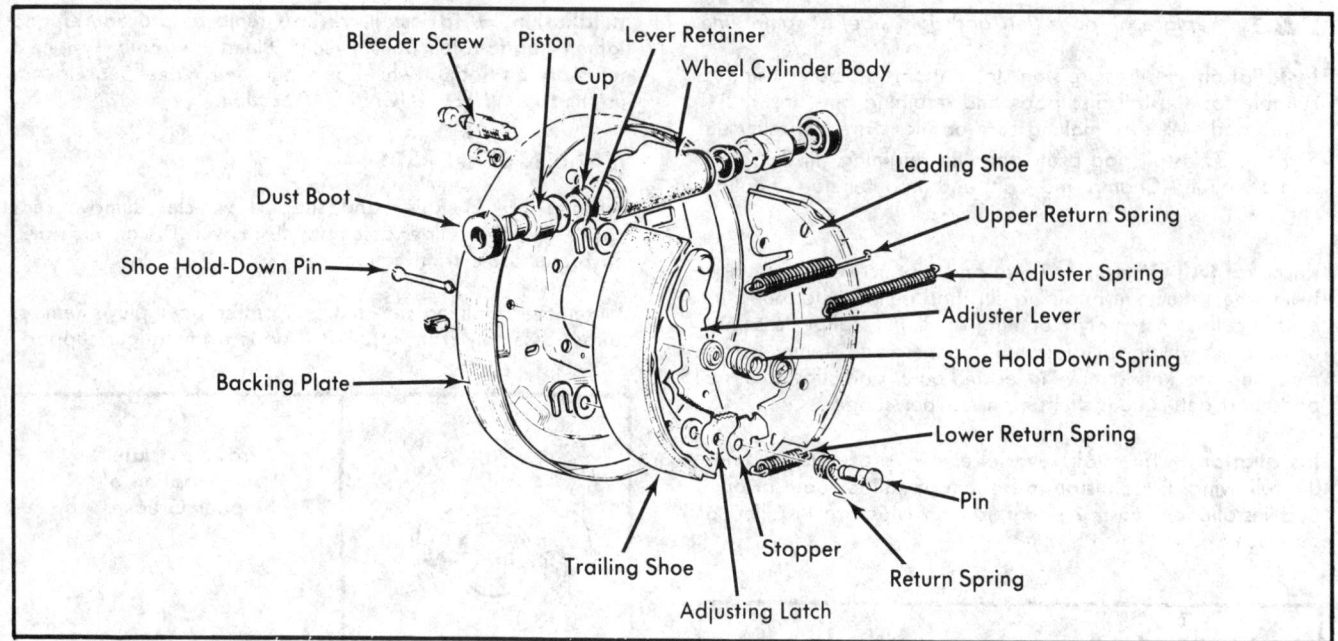

Fig. 6 *Exploded View of Rear Brake Assembly for Component Relationship (Arrow, Challenger, Sapporo & Colt Sta. Wgn.)*

Installation — To install, reverse removal procedure and tighten bolts evenly.

REAR BRAKE SHOES

Removal — Raise and support vehicle. Remove brake drum and complete the following by model:

- Champ & Colt Hatchback — Remove clip spring, shoe return spring and hold down spring. Remove shoes and adjuster as an assembly and separate. Remove parking brake cable from lever.

- Pickups — Remove return springs, adjusting spring and lever. Remove shoes and adjuster as an assembly and separate. Remove parking brake cable from lever.

- All Other Models — Remove hold down springs. Disconnect strut-to-shoe spring and upper shoe return spring end from trailing shoe. Remove trailing shoe and lower return spring. Hold adjuster latch down, pull adjusting lever toward center of brake and remove leading shoe assembly. Remove upper shoe return spring and strut-to-shoe spring.

Installation — 1) Reverse removal procedure and note the following: Apply brake grease to all shoe contact points, adjuster assembly, wheel cylinder and parking brake lever pin. Adjust amount of engagement of adjusting lever with strut, only after pulling lever fully toward center of brake. Note that adjusting lever and latch spring differ between right and left sides.

2) Champ and Colt Hatchback models require check of parking brake cable to ensure it will not advance brake lever when released. Adjuster will malfunction if lever advances.

3) Pickups require check of adjuster after installation is complete. Adjuster lever should mesh with next tooth of adjuster when pulled and return to original position after wheel has moved one tooth. Adjuster assemblies differ between right and left sides.

MASTER CYLINDER

Removal — Remove sensor connector (if equipped). Disconnect brake lines from master cylinder. Slowly depress brake pedal several times to drain fluid from cylinder housing. Remove master cylinder from booster unit and separate reservoirs from housing.

Installation — Reverse removal procedure, check and adjust clearance between back of master cylinder piston and power brake push rod prior to installation. Clearance should be 0-.03" (0-.75 mm) on all models. Check and adjust pedal height and bleed hydraulic system after installation.

POWER BRAKE UNIT
CHECK VALVE REPLACEMENT

NOTE — *Before removal, test check valve. Pull off vacuum hose, place finger over check valve and crank engine; vacuum should be created.*

Removal — Remove hose clamps from both ends of check valve. Remove check valve clamp and remove check valve.

Installation — Coat both ends of check valve with sealer and install valve with arrow (identification mark) pointing toward intake manifold side. Install check valve clamp, vacuum hoses and secure hose clamps.

CHRYSLER CORP. IMPORTS (Cont.)

OVERHAUL

FRONT DISC BRAKE CALIPER

Disassembly (Arrow, Champ & Colt Hatchback) — Remove caliper attaching bridge bolts. Separate inner and outer caliper halves and remove torque plate. Remove retaining ring and dust seal. Apply compressed air to fluid inlet to remove piston. Remove piston seal without damaging caliper bore or seal groove.

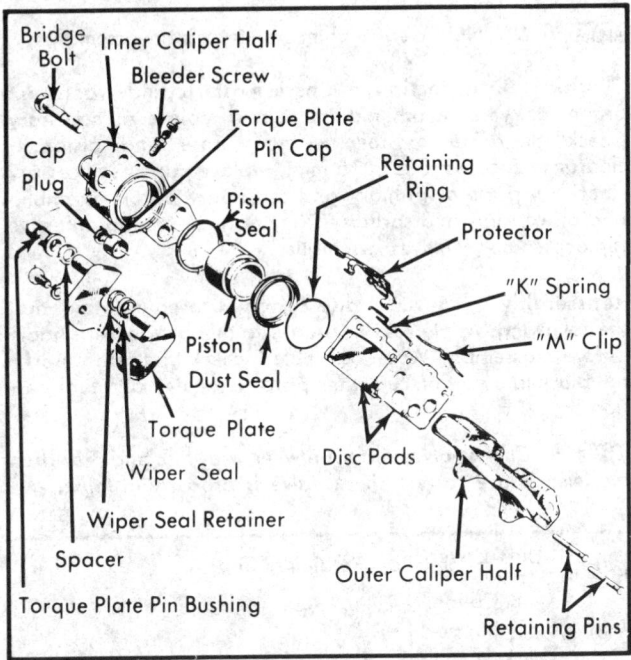

Fig. 7   Disassembled View of Disc Brake Caliper (Arrow, Champ & Colt Hatchback)

Cleaning & Inspection — Clean all metal parts in trichloro-ethylene, alcohol or brake fluid; clean piston seal in brake fluid or alcohol; clean dust seal and other rubber parts in alcohol only. Inspect caliper bore and piston for wear, damage or rust; replace parts as necessary. Always replace piston seal and dust seal.

NOTE — *Repair kits contain proper lubricants to be used during reassembly.*

Reassembly — Reverse disassembly procedure and note the following: Apply rubber grease to piston seal and brake fluid to piston when reassembling. If torque plate was removed from inner caliper half, clean torque plate shaft and shaft bore in caliper, then apply special rubber grease to rubber bushing, wiper seal inner surface, and torque plate shaft before reassembly. Tighten bridge bolts of caliper halves evenly.

NOTE — *Possible cause of increased pedal stroke is: Insufficient fit between piston and piston seal. Correct by manually levering piston to seat several times. This will create a better fit between piston and seal. Make sure brake pad is removed during this procedure.*

Disassembly (All Others) — Remove dust boot. Apply compressed air to fluid inlet to remove piston. Remove piston seal without damaging caliper bore or seal grooove.

Cleaning & Inspection — Clean all metal parts in trichloro-ethylene, alcohol or brake fluid; clean piston seal in alcohol or brake fluid; clean dust boot and other rubber parts in alcohol only. Inspect caliper bore and piston for wear, damage or rust; replace parts as necessary. Always replace piston seal and dust boot.

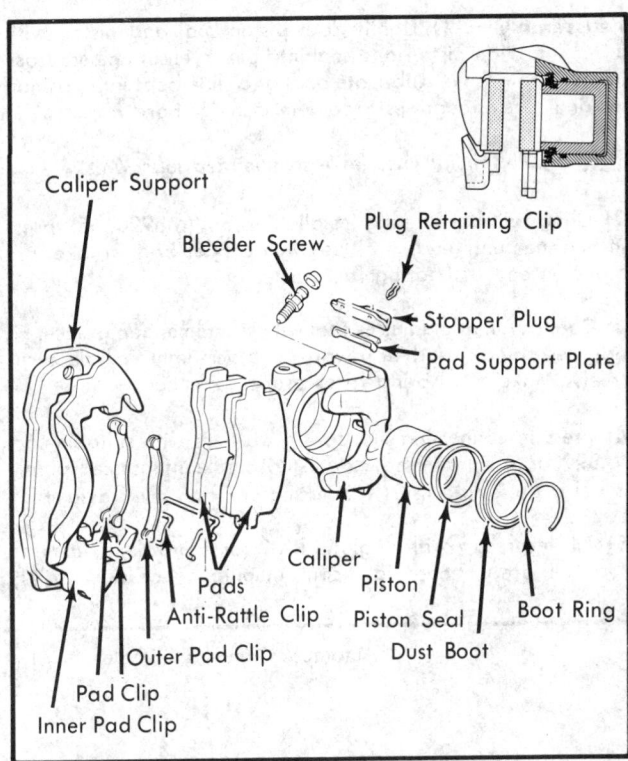

Fig. 8   Exploded View of Front Disc Brake Caliper (Challenger, Sapporo, Colt Sta. Wgn. & Pickups)

Reassembly — Coat piston seal with suitable rubber grease. Slide seal into groove in cylinder bore. Slip piston into bore making sure seal is not twisted. Lightly coat dust seal groove with recommended rubber grease. Fit dust boot into place. Refit cylinder to caliper.

REAR DISC BRAKE CALIPER

Disassembly — 1) Remove cap ring and take off lever cap. See *Fig. 9.* Remove retaining ring and spring, then pull out lever assembly. Slightly rotate automatic adjuster spindle, using pliers if necessary, and pull out assembly.

2) Using suitable bearing remover tool (MB990665), pull bearings from caliper. Take off piston boot. Working through vacant area created by adjuster spindle removal, force piston out of caliper. Use a blunt tool to push out piston. Remove piston seal without damaging caliper bore or seal groove.

Cleaning & Inspection — 1) Clean all metal parts in tri-chloroethylene, alcohol or brake fluid; clean piston seal and adjuster seal in alcohol or brake fluid; clean piston boot and other rubber parts in alcohol only. Check cylinder and piston for wear, damage or rust; replace worn parts as necessary. Always replace piston seal, adjuster seal and piston boot.

Brakes

CHRYSLER CORP. IMPORTS (Cont.)

2) Check bearings, connecting link, springs, adjuster spindle and lever assembly for wear, damage or rust. Check lever assembly for excessive play between shaft and bearing. Check staking of piston inner sleeve stopper plate. Ensure piston-to-automatic adjuster spindle clearance is .013-.017" (.33-.43 mm).

Reassembly — 1) Lightly coat piston seal and piston with lubricant. Slide piston and seal into place, ensuring seal does not twist in groove. Lubricate boot and slide boot into position making sure it engages groove in cylinder bore.

NOTE — *Repair kit includes recommended lubricants.*

2) Using suitable bearing installation tool (MB990665), press in bearings until ends are flush with caliper body. Make sure mark on end of bearing faces out.

3) Coat automatic adjuster seal with recommended grease. Fit adjuster spindle and hardware in place until spindle turns freely. Make sure spring faces proper direction.

4) Press in connecting link spring washers with suitable tool (MB990666). Fit automatic adjuster spindle into place (spindle is not a press fit). Insert connecting link and lever assembly.

5) Fill lever cap with Niglube RX-2 (or equivalent), making sure all areas have significant amount of grease. Lightly grease stopper plug and caliper sliding surface. Assembly is ready for installation.

MASTER CYLINDER

Disassembly — Remove dust boot, retaining ring, stop washer and piston stop bolt. Withdraw primary piston assembly, secondary piston assembly and secondary return spring from master cylinder. Remove check valve caps, tube seats, check valves and check valve springs. Champ and Colt Hatchback master cylinders are equipped with two identical check valves.

NOTE — *DO NOT disassemble primary piston assembly.*

Cleaning & Inspection — Check master cylinder bore and piston for wear or other damage and replace as necessary. Check clearance between cylinder bore and piston; if clearance exceeds .006" (.15 mm), replace parts as necessary. Check all parts of primary and secondary piston assemblies and piston cups and springs; if any parts are found defective, replace components as assemblies.

Reassembly — Reverse disassembly procedure and note the following: Apply rubber grease to all parts (except boots) before reassembly. When assembled, check that return port is not blocked by piston cup when piston is located at return position.

NOTE — *Check valves differ between rear disc and rear drum models. Ensure correct check valve is properly installed.*

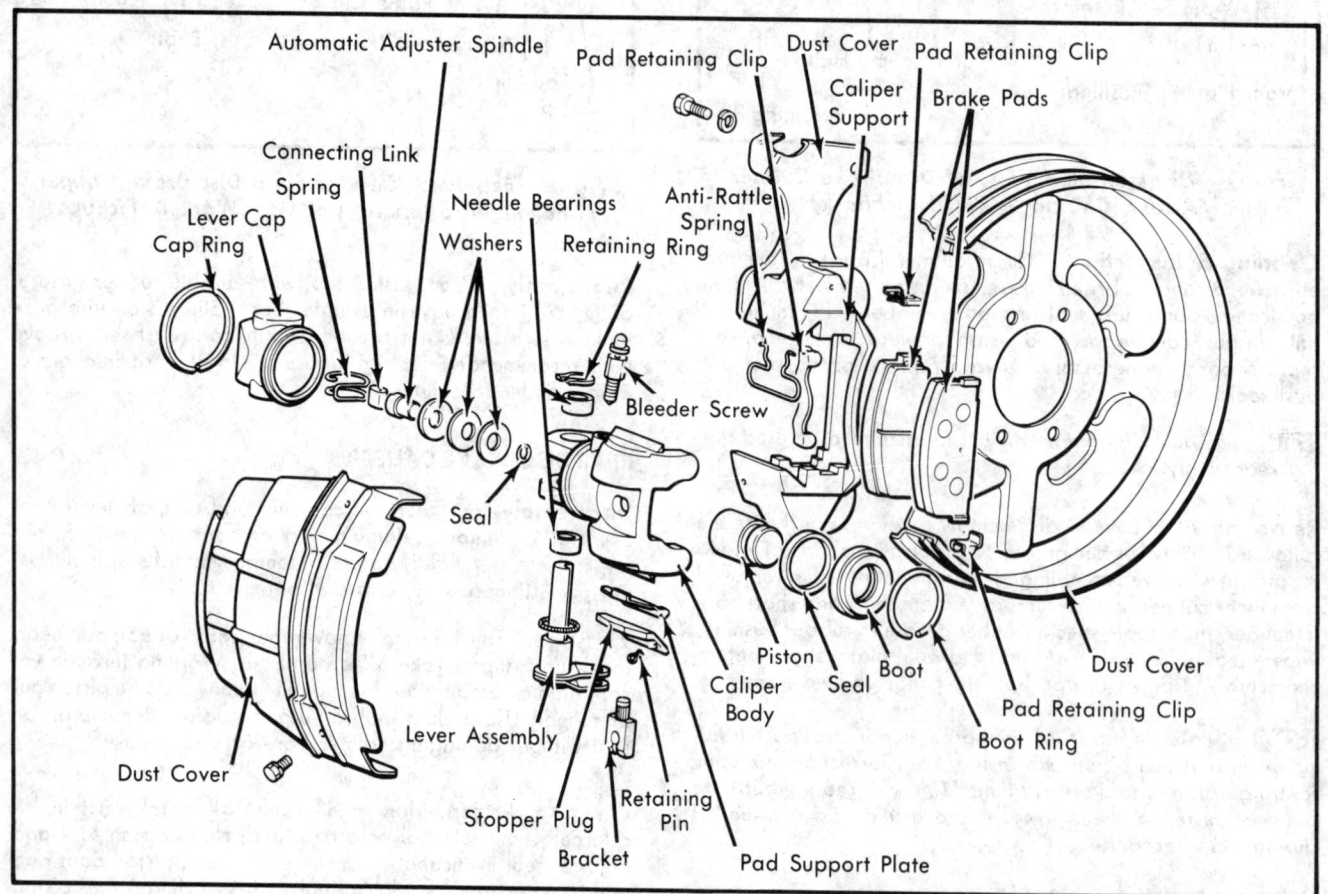

Fig. 9 Exploded View of Rear Disc Brake Caliper Assembly

Brakes

CHRYSLER CORP. IMPORTS (Cont.)

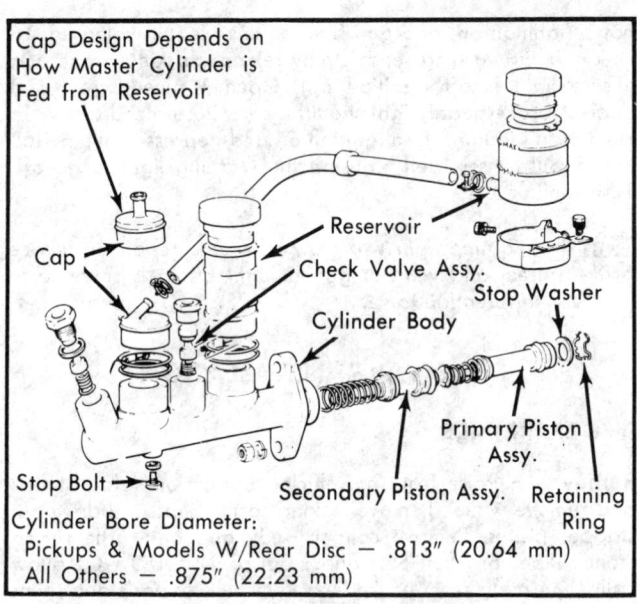

Cap Design Depends on How Master Cylinder is Fed from Reservoir

Cap

Stop Bolt

Reservoir

Check Valve Assy.

Stop Washer

Cylinder Body

Primary Piston Assy.

Secondary Piston Assy.

Retaining Ring

Cylinder Bore Diameter:
Pickups & Models W/Rear Disc — .813" (20.64 mm)
All Others — .875" (22.23 mm)

Fig. 10 Disassembled View of Master Cylinder

TIGHTENING SPECIFICATIONS

Application	Ft. Lbs (mkg)
Rotor-to-Hub Bolts	
Champ & Colt Hatchback	29-36 (4.0-5.0)
Pickups	34-38 (4.5-5.0)
All Others	25-29 (3.5-4.0)
Caliper	
Adapter (Front)	
Challenger, Sapporo & Colt Sta. Wgn.	29-36 (4.0-5.0)
Torque Plate (Front)	
All Except Arrow,	
Champ & Colt Hatchback	51-65 (7.0-9.0)
Bridge Bolts (Front)	
Arrow, Champ & Colt Hatchback	58-69 (8.0-9.5)
Caliper Assembly	
Front	
Champ & Colt Hatchback	43-58 (6.0-8.0)
All Others	51-65
Rear (Support)	29-36 (4.0-5.0)

DRUM BRAKE SPECIFICATIONS

Application	Wheel Cyl. Bore Diameter In. (mm)	Drum Diameter In. (mm)	Original Diameter In. (mm)	Maximum Refinish Diameter In. (mm)	Discard Diameter In. (mm)
Arrow (With Rear Drum)	.750 (19.05)	9.00 (229.0)	9.00 (229.0)	.....	9.08 (230.6)
Champ & Colt Hatchback	.750 (19.05)	7.10 (180.3)	7.10 (180.3)	....	7.20 (182.0)
Pickups	.750 (19.05)	9.50 (241.3)	9.50 (241.3)	.....	9.58 (243.3)
All Others	.813 (20.7)	9.00 (229.0)	9.00 (229.0)	.....	9.08 (230.6)

DISC BRAKE SPECIFICATIONS

Application	Caliper Bore Diameter In. (mm)	Lateral Runout In. (mm)	Parallelism In. (mm)	Original Thickness In. (mm)	Minimum Refinish Thickness In. (mm)	Discard Thickness In. (mm)
Arrow (With Rear Drum)	.....	.006 (.15)	.....	.51 (13.0)	.....	.45 (11.4)
Champ & Colt Hatchback	2.01 (51.1)	.006 (.15)	.....	.51 (13.0)	.....	.45 (11.4)
Pickups	1.18 (30.0)	.006 (.15)	.....	.79 (20.1)	.....	.72 (18.4)
All With Rear Disc Front	.....	.006 (.15)	.....	.49 (12.5)	.....	.43 (11.0)
Rear	.....	.006 (.15)	.....	.39 (10.0)	.....	.33 (8.4)

COURIER

Pickup

DESCRIPTION

Brake system is hydraulically operated using a tandem master cylinder and vacuum power brake unit. Front brakes are sliding caliper disc; rear are leading/trailing drum. Brake system is protected by a pressure differential combination valve and warning light. If a leak occurs in front or rear brake system, or uneven fluid pressure develops, piston is moved off center, activating the warning light. Light will remain on until problem is corrected. Service brake systems are self-adjusting. Parking brake is cable actuated on rear wheels.

ADJUSTMENT

DRUM BRAKES

CAUTION — *Shoe-to-drum clearance must be made with brake drums at normal room temperature.*

1) Rear brakes are self-adjusting and require manual adjustment only after brake shoes have been replaced or adjusting rod length has been changed. To adjust, raise rear of vehicle and support on safety stands. Release parking brake and remove adjusting hole plugs from rear of backing plate.

2) Insert screwdriver through hole, rotate star wheel in direction of arrow stamped on backing plate until wheel locks. Insert a pointed tool through hole and push adjusting lever off star wheel. Back off star wheel 3 or 4 notches until wheel rotates freely without drag. Test drive vehicle after adjustment to ensure equal brake action.

NOTE — *Adjustment must be equal on both wheels.*

PEDAL FREE PLAY

Loosen lock nut on master cylinder push rod at clevis. Turn push rod in or out to obtain .33-.39" (8.5-10.0 mm) free play, measured at pedal pad. When clearance is correct, tighten lock nut.

STOP LIGHT SWITCH

Loosen lock nut and adjust stop light switch until it just contacts brake pedal stopper. DO NOT depress master cylinder push rod during stop light switch adjustment.

PARKING BRAKE

Adjust length of cable at equalizer so rear brakes are locked when parking brake lever is pulled out 5 to 10 ratchet clicks (1⅝-3⅛"; 40-80 mm). After adjustment, operate parking brake several times to ensure wheels rotate freely when parking brake is released.

NOTE — *Service brakes must be properly adjusted prior to adjusting parking brake.*

BRAKE WARNING LIGHT

A dual warning light is mounted on instrument panel. Parking brake light should glow when parking brake lever is pulled 1 notch (ignition on) and go off when lever is fully released. To check circuit warning sensor, fully release parking brake and ensure light is off (ignition on). Open 1 bleed screw and depress brake pedal; light should glow. Close bleed screw. To reset warning light; turn ignition on and depress brake pedal. Piston will center itself, causing the warning light to go off. Turn ignition off.

NOTE — *Warning light will glow after any repair on service brake system and will not go out until piston is centered in pressure differential valve.*

REMOVAL & INSTALLATION

DISC BRAKE PADS

Removal — Raise front of vehicle, support on safety stands and remove wheel. Remove locking spring clips and drive out stopper plates. Remove caliper body and anti-rattle spring from caliper bracket. Set caliper out of way; DO NOT allow caliper to hang from brake line. Remove disc pads and shims (if equipped). Note position of shims.

NOTE — *All pads must be replaced at same time.*

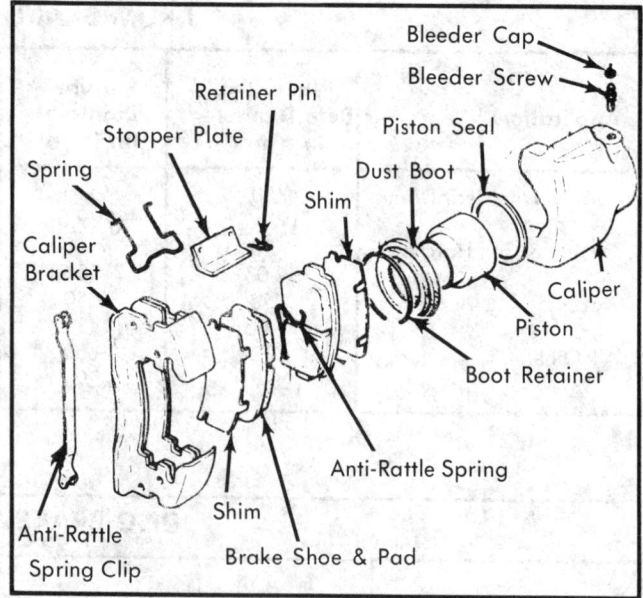

Fig. 1 Exploded View of Front Disc Brake

Installation — 1) Pull bleeder cap off caliper and attach a tube to bleed screw. Open bleed screw and seat piston in bore with "C" clamp. Tighten bleed screw and remove clamp.

2) Install new pads and shims (if required) when pad thickness has worn to .276" (7 mm). Install anti-rattle spring and caliper body. Apply light coat of grease to stopper plates. Install plates and spring clips. Install wheel. Check brake fluid level and test brakes for proper operation.

FRONT DISC BRAKE CALIPER

Removal — Raise and support vehicle on safety stands; remove wheel. Remove clip at connection of flexible hose and

COURIER (Cont.)

brake line; separate and plug openings. Remove caliper bracket mounting bolts and remove entire assembly.

Installation — Reverse removal procedure, bleed brake system and centralize differential valve.

BRAKE ROTOR

Removal — With caliper assembly removed, remove dust cap, cotter pin, adjusting cap, adjusting nut, thrust washer and outer bearing. Remove hub and rotor assembly from spindle. Remove hub-to-rotor bolts and separate hub from rotor.

Installation — Reverse removal procedure, tighten hub-to-rotor bolts securely and adjust wheel bearings. *See Wheel Bearing Adjustment in WHEEL ALIGNMENT Section.*

BRAKE DRUM

Removal — Raise and support vehicle on safety stands; remove tire and wheel. Remove brake drum attaching screws and install them in tapered holes in brake drum. Turn screws in evenly to force drum away from wheel hub. Remove drum.

Installation — Align attaching screw holes with ones in wheel hub. Transfer screws to retaining position and tighten evenly. Install tire and wheel.

BRAKE SHOES

Removal — With brake drum removed, remove brake shoe return springs, retaining springs and guide pins. Disconnect hand brake cable from lever. Remove brake shoes as an assembly and separate components.

Installation — 1) Apply brake grease to adjusting screw threads, contact surfaces of brake shoes and backing plate ledges. Attach parking brake lever to rear shoe with retaining clip. Hold shoe close to backing plate and install parking brake cable to lever.

2) Position both shoes on backing plate, insert adjuster assembly between shoes; ensure shoe slots are engaged in wheel cylinder pistons and adjuster assembly. Install guide pins, retaining springs and return springs. Install drum and adjust brakes.

MASTER CYLINDER

Removal — Disconnect brake hydraulic lines and reservoir lines; plug all openings. Remove master cylinder-to-brake booster mounting nuts. Lift master cylinder outward and upward away from booster and push rod.

Installation — Reverse removal procedure and carefully guide push rod into master cylinder piston. Bleed brake system and check pedal free play.

PRESSURE DIFFERENTIAL VALVE

Removal — Disconnect warning light wire and hydraulic lines from combination valve. Remove mounting bolt and differential valve.

Installation — To install, reverse removal procedure and note the following: Bleed hydraulic system and center pressure differential valve.

POWER BRAKE BOOSTER

Removal — With master cylinder removed, disconnect vacuum line from booster. From inside vehicle, remove cotter pin attaching operating rod clevis to brake pedal, then remove mounting nuts from dash panel. Remove brake booster from engine compartment.

Installation — To install, reverse removal procedure and note the following: Install master cylinder, bleed hydraulic system, check pedal free play, center pressure differential valve and ensure proper brake operation.

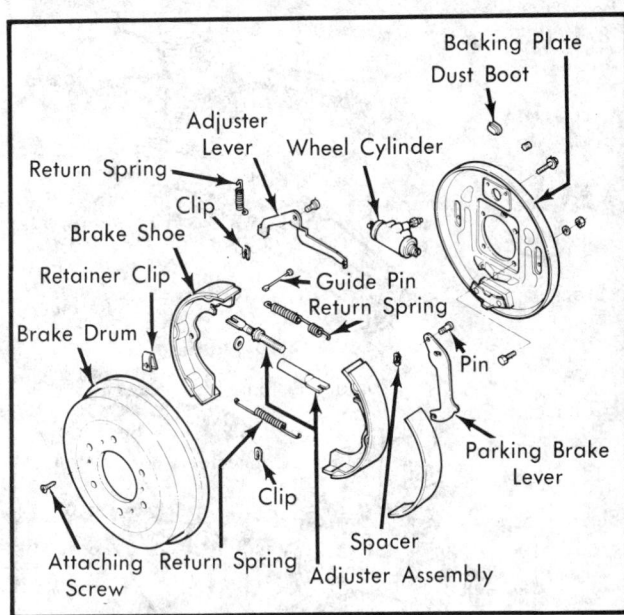

Fig. 2   Exploded View of Rear Brake Assembly

OVERHAUL

FRONT DISC BRAKE CALIPER

Disassembly — 1) Clean outside of caliper. Separate cylinder from bracket. Remove boot retainer and slide off dust boot. Force compressed air into brake line hole to remove piston from caliper.

2) It may be necessary to tap outside of piston housing with plastic hammer while applying air pressure to unseat piston. Dig out piston seal from inside caliper bore.

Cleaning and Inspection — Wash all disassembled parts in clean brake fluid and completely dry with compressed air. Inspect caliper bore and piston for scratches, grooves or rust. Minor imperfections can be eliminated with crocus cloth. Piston seal and dust boot must be replaced during each overhaul.

Reassembly — Lightly coat piston seal with brake fluid and insert into groove in caliper bore. Make sure seal is not twisted in groove. Lubricate piston and bore with brake fluid, then slide piston into place. Fit dust boot with flange seated in inner groove of caliper. Fit dust boot retainer.

COURIER (Cont.)

MASTER CYLINDER

Disassembly — 1) Drain brake fluid from reservoir and separate reservoir from master cylinder inlet ports. Remove primary piston snap ring and stop washer. Slide out primary piston, return spring and cup from bore.

2) Loosen secondary piston stop screw. Push secondary piston into cylinder bore with a screwdriver and remove stop screw and "O" ring. Insert fabricated guide pin *(See Fig. 4)* into stop screw hole and release pressure on secondary piston. Remove secondary piston return spring and cup (using low pressure air if required). Remove brake line fittings, gaskets, check valves and springs.

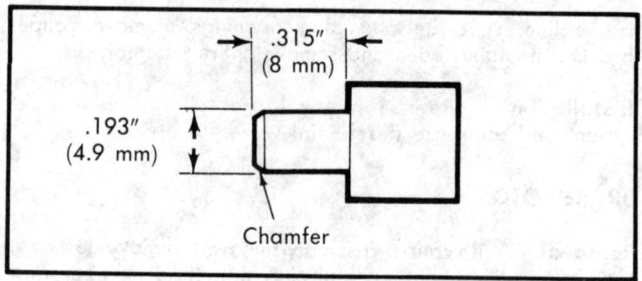

Fig. 4 *Dimensions for Fabricating Guide Pin*

2) Install secondary and primary cups to secondary piston. Insert fabricated guide pin into stop screw hole. Slide piston assembly and spring into cylinder; seat piston with screwdriver, remove guide pin and install stop screw and "O" ring. Release pressure on secondary piston.

3) Install cups to primary piston and insert piston assembly and spring into cylinder. Install washer and snap ring. Install reservoir and hoses to master cylinder.

POWER BRAKE BOOSTER

Disassembly — 1) Fit booster in vise with rod facing up and scribe index mark on both shells. Remove lock nut, clevis and dust boot. Rotate shell clockwise, unlocking it from front shell. Lift off shell complete with:

- Diaphragm
- Power Piston Assembly
- Valve Rod
- Plunger Assembly

2) Remove spring from front shell. From inside rear shell remove:

- Diaphragm
- Power Piston Assembly
- Valve Rod
- Plunger Assembly

3) Remove rear seal, with punch, from rear shell only if seal needs replacing. Take out air silencer retainer and air filter from power piston. DO NOT damage piston.

4) Press in valve rod and remove retainer key. Take valve rod and plunger assembly off power piston. Press out reaction disc. Slide push rod out of front shell.

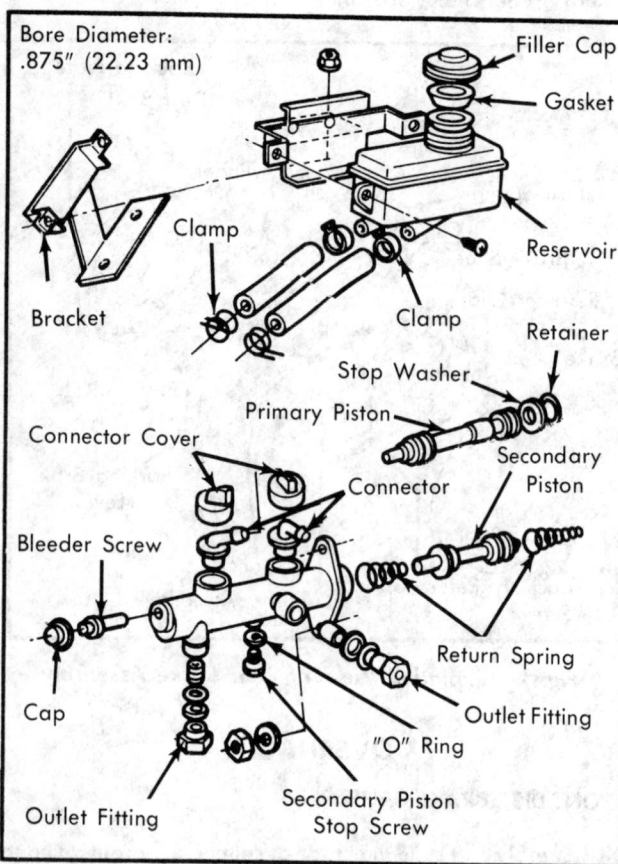

Fig. 3 *Exploded View of Master Cylinder and Related Components*

Cleaning & Inspection — Clean all parts in isopropyl alcohol and dry with compressed air. Check cups for wear, cracks or deformation. Check cylinder bore and pistons for wear, roughness or scoring. Replace defective parts. Check cylinder bore-to-piston clearance; if greater than .006" (.15 mm), replace pistons.

Reassembly — 1) Apply brake fluid to pistons and cups. Install check valves and springs, gaskets and brake line fittings in outlet holes.

NOTE — *Check valve with hole must be installed in outlet hole on side of master cylinder.*

Cleaning & Inspection — Wipe parts clean and inspect rubber parts for cuts, nicks or deformation. Inspect power piston for cracks, chipping, distortion and damaged seats. Inspect reaction disc, valve rod and plunger assembly and shells for nicks, dents or other damage. Inspect diaphragm for cuts. Replace defective parts.

Reassembly — 1) Apply brake fluid to inside of power piston bore and to surface of valve rod and plunger assembly. Insert valve rod and plunger assembly into power piston. Press in valve rod and align plunger groove with slot in power piston. Insert retainer key.

COURIER (Cont.)

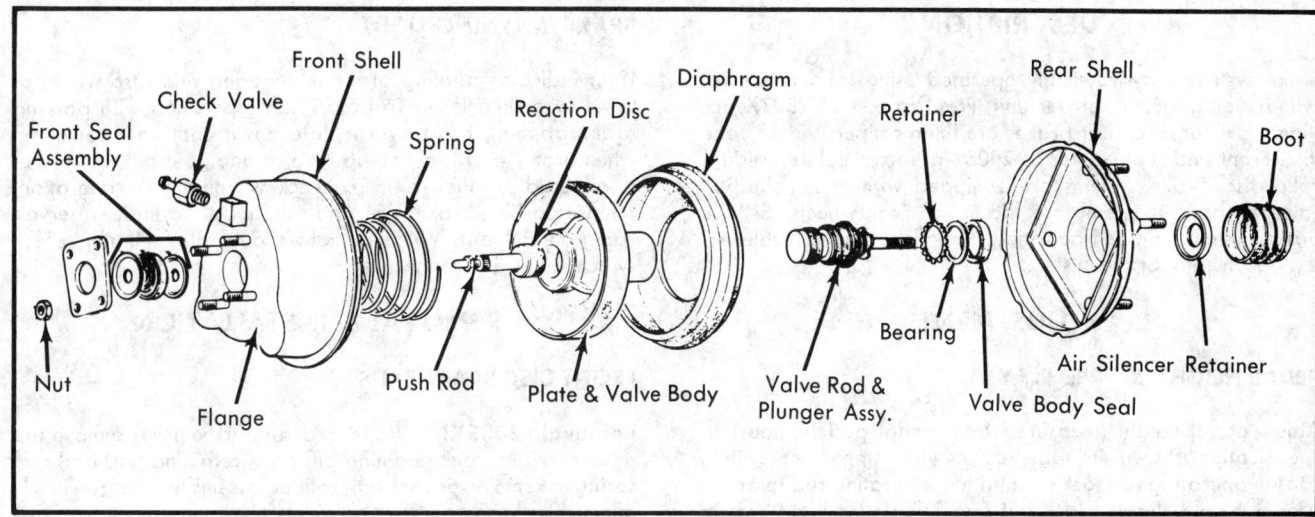

Fig. 5   Exploded View of Power Brake Booster

2) Install diaphragm on power piston; diaphragm must be seated in piston groove. Install air silencer and filter over valve rod and insert in power piston. Coat reaction disc surface with brake fluid and install in power piston.

3) Coat outer edge of diaphragm and rear shell seal with brake fluid. Carefully guide tube end of power piston through rear shell seal. Install push rod to front of power piston. Install return spring in front shell. Position rear shell over front shell, press down and rotate counterclockwise until scribe marks align.

4) Install dust boot, clevis and lock nut. Check push rod clearance with fabricated gauge (See Fig. 6). Clearance should be .004-.020" (.10-.51 mm).

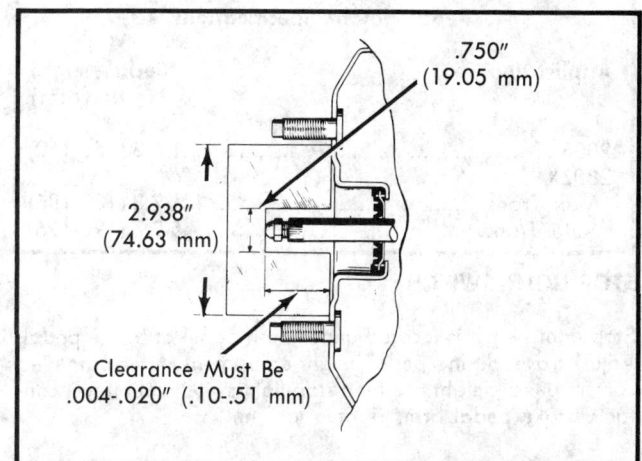

Fig. 6   Adjusting Push Rod Clearance (Dimensions Shown for Making Gauge)

DRUM BRAKE SPECIFICATIONS

Application	Wheel Cyl. Bore Diameter In. (mm)	Drum Diameter In. (mm)	Original Diameter In. (mm)	Maximum Refinish Diameter In. (mm)	Discard Diameter In. (mm)
Pickup	.875 (22.23)	10.236 (260)	10.236 (260)	10.276 (261)	.....

DISC BRAKE SPECIFICATIONS

Application	Caliper Bore Diameter In. (mm)	Lateral Runout In. (mm)	Parallelism In. (mm)	Original Thickness In. (mm)	Minimum Refinish Thickness In. (mm)	Discard Thickness In. (mm)
Pickup	2.125 (53.98)	.004 (.10)	.....	.472 (12)	.433 (11)	.....

Brakes

DATSUN 200SX & 280ZX

DESCRIPTION

Brake system is hydraulically operated using tandem master cylinder and vacuum power unit. Front brakes of 280ZX are sliding caliper disc; rear brakes are fixed caliper, sliding yoke disc. Front and rear brakes of 200SX are fixed caliper, sliding yoke disc. Brake systems are equipped with a combination valve to prevent premature lockup of rear wheels. Service brake systems are self-adjusting. Parking brake is cable actuated on rear brake systems.

ADJUSTMENT

PEDAL HEIGHT & FREE PLAY

Adjust pedal height (measured from pedal pad to floor) to specification shown in table by moving stop light switch. Loosen operating rod lock nut and turn operating rod to attain proper height, tighten lock nut and adjust stop light switch. Pedal free play should be .04-.20" (1-5 mm). If specification is exceeded, adjust push rod length.

Pedal Height Specifications	
Application	**Pedal Height In. (mm)**
200SX	6.1-6.3 (155-160)
280ZX	
Man. Trans.	7.1-7.3 (181-186)
Auto. Trans.	7.5-7.7 (190-196)

STOP LIGHT SWITCH

Stop light switch is located under dash panel at brake pedal. Adjust travel during pedal height adjustment. After obtaining correct pedal height, position stop light switch until it just contacts brake pedal arm. Tighten lock nut.

PARKING BRAKE

200SX — Adjust parking brake by rotating turnbuckle. Rear wheels should lock when brake lever is pulled 7-8 notches with 44 lbs. (20 kg) force. After releasing lever, ensure rear wheels rotate freely, rear cables are not slack and that rear brake toggle levers are in original positions.

280ZX — Adjust front cable adjusting nut so when parking brake lever is pulled with 60 lbs. (27 kg) force, lever stroke is 4-6 notches and rear wheels are locked. After releasing lever, ensure rear wheels rotate freely, rear cables are not slack and that rear brake toggle levers are in original positions.

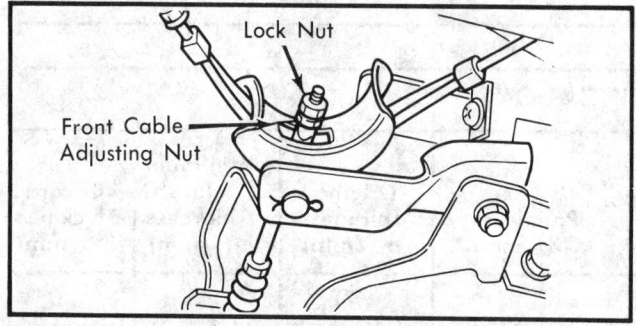

Fig. 1   Location for Adjusting 280ZX Parking Brake

BRAKE WARNING LIGHT

Light indicates parking brake is engaged and also warns of low brake fluid level. To adjust light operation with parking brake applied, bend switch plate down until light comes on when brake lever is pulled up 1 notch and goes out when lever is released (ignition on). To check warning light operation, release parking brake lever and raise master cylinder reservoir cap (ignition on). Warning light should glow. If not, check switch and wire connector.

REMOVAL & INSTALLATION

FRONT DISC BRAKE PADS

Removal (200SX) — Raise and support vehicle; remove tire and wheel. Remove retaining pin clips, retaining pins and pad springs. Remove pads from caliper assembly, using suitable pliers if necessary.

CAUTION — *DO NOT force piston groove inside piston seal. Piston seal could be damaged and caliper will have to be disassembled.*

Installation — 1) Clean and apply P.B.C. grease to cylinder body yoke guide groove, yoke sliding contact points and piston end surface. Loosen bleeder screw and push outer piston into cylinder until piston end surface coincides with boot retaining ring end surface. Tighten bleeder screw and install inner brake pad.

2) Push inner piston into cylinder by pulling on yoke, then install outer pad. Install pad springs, retaining pins and clips. Depress brake pedal several times to seat pads and bleed hydraulic system if necessary.

Removal (280ZX) — Raise and support vehicle; remove tire and wheel. Remove lower pin bolt and rotate caliper body upward. Remove pad retainers, shims and brake pads.

NOTE — *Do not pull caliper body away from rotor; use upper pin bolt as center of rotation.*

Installation — 1) Clean piston and area around pin bolts with brake fluid. Install inner pad and seat piston by placing lever through opening in caliper body and pushing piston into bore. Apply brake grease to pad retainer points on caliper assembly and install outer pad and both shims.

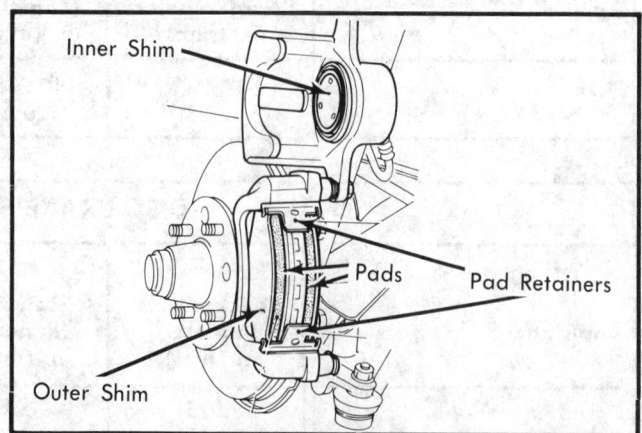

Fig. 2   Front Disc Brake Pad Retainer Location on 280ZX

DATSUN 200SX & 280ZX (Cont.)

2) Install pad retainers. Rotate caliper body down into original position and install lower pin bolt. Tighten pin bolt and depress brake pedal several times to seat pads.

FRONT DISC BRAKE CALIPER

Removal — Raise and support vehicle; remove tire and wheel. Remove brake pads (200SX only) and disconnect and plug hydraulic line from caliper. Remove caliper mounting bolts and remove caliper assembly. On 280ZX only, remove carrier mounting bolts and carrier.

Installation — To install, reverse removal procedure, tighten caliper bolts securely and bleed hydraulic system.

FRONT DISC BRAKE ROTOR

Removal — Remove caliper assembly as previously described and hang from frame with wire; DO NOT disconnect hydraulic line. Remove hub dust cap, "O" ring, cotter pin, adjusting cap and lock nut. Remove hub and rotor assembly from spindle without dropping outer bearing and washer. Remove outer bearing, washer and hub-to-rotor bolts. Separate rotor from hub.

NOTE — *Avoid damage to hub dust cap "O" ring during removal of dust cap.*

Installation — Reverse removal procedure and adjust front wheel bearings. *See Wheel Bearing Adjustment in WHEEL ALIGNMENT Section.*

REAR DISC BRAKE PADS

Removal — Raise and support vehicle; remove tire and wheel. Remove pin clip, then remove pad pins while holding anti-squeal springs with fingers. Remove disc pads and shims (200SX).

Installation — **1)** Apply brake grease to caliper body-to-pad clearance, yoke-to-pad clearance, pin-to-pad clearance, pin-to-bracket clearance and both sides of shims (200SX). Preset piston before installing pads by pushing and turning outer piston clockwise until it retracts into caliper body. Preset yoke clearance by placing a lever between rotor and yoke; move yoke until clearance is equal to piston clearance.

NOTE — *Avoid damaging dust seal while turning outer piston.*

2) Align outer piston so cut out portion is level and install inner pad with protrusion of pad seated in piston cut out. Install shims on 200SX. Install outer pad, anti-squeal springs, pad pins and pin clip. Depress brake pedal several times to adjust pad-to-rotor clearance; clearance is correct when pedal stroke is constant. Add brake fluid and bleed hydraulic system.

REAR DISC BRAKE CALIPER

Removal — Disconnect hydraulic line from caliper and plug openings. Disconnect parking brake cable. Remove mounting bolts and remove caliper.

Installation — Reverse removal procedure and bleed hydraulic system if necessary. Depress brake pedal several times; when pedal stroke is constant, brake pad-to-rotor clearance is properly adjusted. Turn rotor to make sure no excessive drag is present.

REAR DISC BRAKE ROTOR

Removal — With caliper removed, pull rotor from axle stub.

Installation — Install rotor and caliper assembly. After installation, depress pedal until pedal stroke is constant to adjust pad-to-rotor clearance.

MASTER CYLINDER

Removal — Remove heat shield plate (if equipped). Disconnect brake fluid level gauge wiring and hydraulic lines from master cylinder. Remove master cylinder-to-power unit mounting nuts and remove master cylinder from power brake unit.

Installation — Reverse removal procedure, check pedal height and bleed hydraulic system.

POWER BRAKE UNIT

NOTE — *Before removal, test check valve. Using suitable brake booster tester, apply 19.7 in. Hg to brake unit side of 200SX check valve; 7.9 in. Hg to brake unit side of 280ZX check valve. If pressure drops more than .39 in. Hg in 15 seconds, replace check valve. Also, if valve does not open when pressure is applied to brake unit side of check valve, replace check valve. If check valve is not defective, check brake system and vacuum lines for leaks; replace booster as an assembly.*

Removal — Disconnect power unit push rod from brake pedal by removing clevis pin. Disconnect hydraulic lines from master cylinder, vacuum line from power unit, remove master cylinder mounting nuts, and remove master cylinder. Remove nuts attaching power unit to firewall, and remove power unit from engine compartment.

Installation — Reverse removal procedure and check push rod length, operating rod length and pedal height. Push rod length should be .38-.39" (9.75-10 mm) on 200SX and .37-.41" (9.5-10.5 mm) on 280ZX. Push rod length on 200SX can NOT be adjusted; if not to specification, replace power unit. Adjust push rod length on 280ZX by turning tip of push rod.

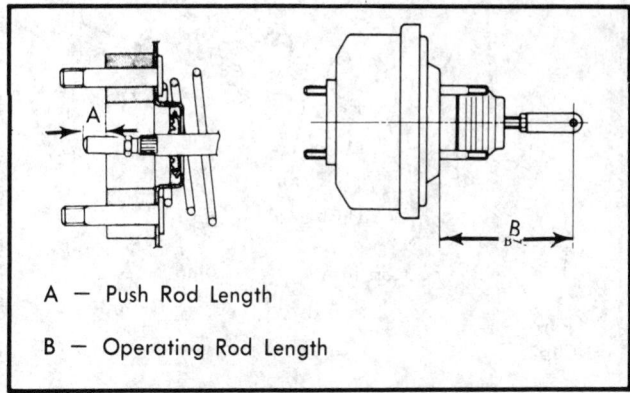

A — Push Rod Length

B — Operating Rod Length

Fig. 3 Location for Measuring Push Rod and Operating Rod Lengths

DATSUN 200SX & 280ZX (Cont.)

2) Operating rod length should be 5.12" (130 mm) on 200SX and 5.63" (143 mm) on 280ZX. Adjust operating rod length by loosening lock nut and turning operating rod to attain proper length. Tighten lock nut and clevis. Bleed hydraulic system.

Check Valve Replacement — Check valve is located in vacuum line between intake manifold and power unit on firewall. To remove, disconnect retaining clip from firewall, remove hose clamps, separate hoses from valve, and remove check valve. To install, reverse removal procedure.

OVERHAUL

FRONT DISC BRAKE CALIPER

Disassembly (200SX) — With caliper and pads removed, drain any remaining fluid from cylinder. Remove gripper pin attaching bolts. Separate yoke and cylinder body. Remove yoke holder from piston. Remove retaining rings and dust seals from pistons. Push both pistons out in one direction. Remove piston seals. Remove gripper, if necessary.

Cleaning & Inspection — Clean all parts with brake fluid and check all components for wear or damage. If minor corrosion cannot be removed from cylinder bore with fine emery cloth, cylinder must be replaced. Replace all seals during overhaul.

NOTE — Piston surfaces are plated and must be replaced if corroded or worn. DO NOT polish with emery cloth.

Reassembly — 1) Install piston seals without damaging seals. Coat cylinder bore and pistons with brake fluid. Push outer piston into cylinder until piston end surface coincides with boot retaining ring end surface. DO NOT force piston groove inside piston seal. Push inner piston into cylinder bore by holding cylinder body and align piston yoke groove with cylinder yoke groove.

2) Apply brake grease to sealing surface of dust seal and install dust seal; clamping securely with retaining ring. Install yoke holder to inner piston. Install gripper to yoke. Apply 1%

soap solution to inner gripper wall and drive gripper pin into position. Install yoke to yoke holder by supporting outer piston end and pressing yoke into yoke holder with 44-66 lb. (20-30 kg) force. No clearance should be present between piston and yoke.

Disassembly (280ZX) — Drain brake fluid from caliper body and clean exterior of caliper assembly. Remove pin bolts, separate caliper body from pad carrier and remove pad retainers and pads. Force piston and dust seal out of bore by applying compressed air to brake inlet. Remove piston seal without damaging seal and bore. Remove sub pin, main pin, sub pin bushing and seals.

Cleaning & Inspection — Clean all parts in brake fluid only. Check caliper bore for wear, rust, corrosion or other damage; minor deposits or scratches can be removed with fine emery cloth. Check pad carrier for wear, cracks or other damage; replace if defective. Check piston for rust, wear or damage; replace if defective. Check main pin and sub pin for wear, cracks or other damage; replace if defective. Replace piston seal and dust seals during overhaul.

Reassembly — 1) Apply brake fluid to sliding portions of piston and caliper bore. Apply rubber grease to inside of dust seals. Install piston seal in bore; install dust seal on piston and slide piston into caliper bore. Secure dust seal in piston groove and caliper groove.

2) Apply multi-purpose grease to sub pin rubber bushing, main pin and sub pin. Install seals, sub pin rubber bushing, sub pin and main pin. Apply brake grease to disc pad-to-carrier contact portions and mount pad carrier to caliper body. Install upper pin bolt, install disc pads, shims and rotate caliper down into position and install lower pin bolt. When caliper assembly is mounted on vehicle, turn rotor to ensure there is not excessive drag.

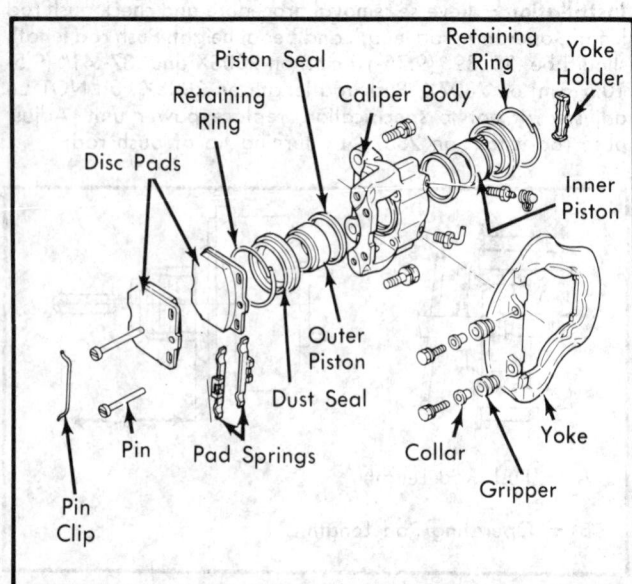

Fig. 4 Exploded View of 200SX Front Disc Brake Caliper

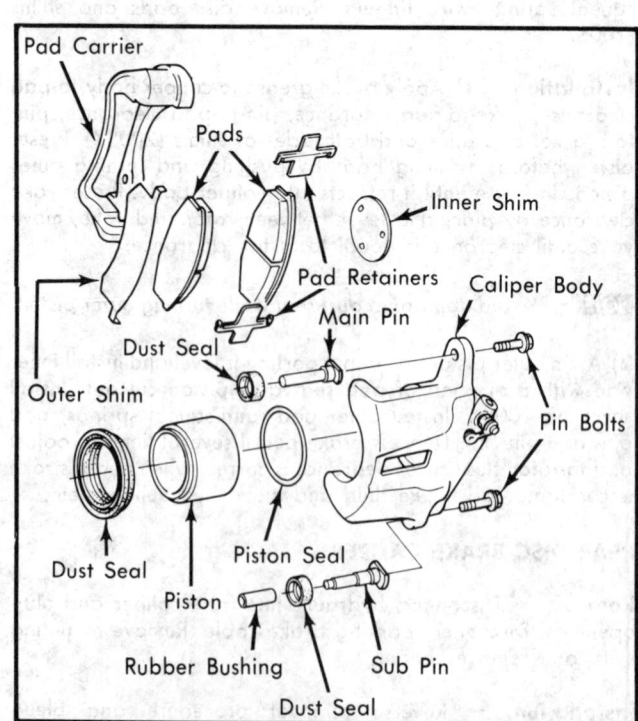

Fig. 5 Exploded View of 280ZX Front Disc Brake Caliper

DATSUN 200SX & 280ZX (Cont.)

REAR DISC BRAKE CALIPER

Disassembly — 1) Drain brake fluid from caliper body and clean exterior of caliper. Remove pads. Place caliper assembly on a work bench with yoke down; push in caliper body and separate caliper and yoke. Remove retaining rings and dust seals from piston ends. Push outer piston to remove piston assembly from caliper bore. Remove piston seals without damaging caliper bore.

2) Disengage piston assembly by turning inner and outer pistons counterclockwise. Disassemble outer piston by removing outer piston snap ring. Remove spacers, wave washer, bearing, adjusting nut and oil seal. To disassemble inner piston, remove inner piston snap ring. Remove spring cover, spring and spring seat. Remove push rod retaining ring, key plate, push rod, "O" ring and strut. Place parking brake lever in vise and remove nut, washer, return spring, lever, dust seal and cam.

Cleaning & Inspection — Clean all parts in brake fluid only. Check caliper bore for wear, rust, corrosion or other damage; minor deposits or scratches can be removed with fine emery cloth. Check yoke for wear, cracks or other damage; replace if defective. Check pistons for rust, wear or damage; replace if defective. Replace piston seals, dust seals, oil seal and push rod "O" ring during overhaul.

NOTE — *DO NOT use abrasives on piston plated surfaces.*

Reassembly — 1) Apply suitable grease to push rod groove, "O" ring, strut ends, oil seal, piston seals and inside dust seals. Install new oil seal on adjusting nut. *See Fig. 7.* Slide adjusting nut and seal into outer piston, then install bearing, spacer, wave washer, second spacer and secure components in position with outer piston snap ring.

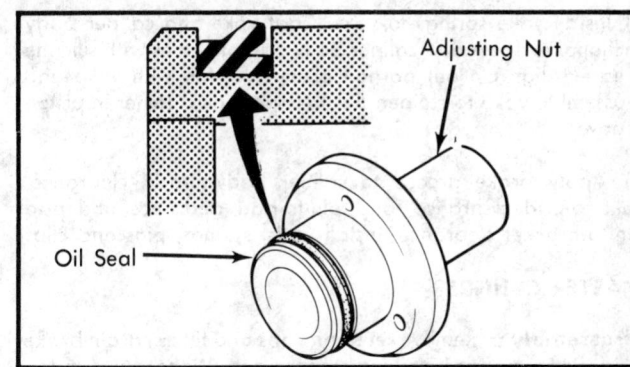

Fig. 7   Installation of Oil Seal on Rear Caliper Adjusting Nut

2) Place cam inside inner piston and securely fit strut in cam hole. Install "O" ring on push rod without twisting "O" ring. Align square hole in key plate with push rod and slide assembly into inner piston bore; rounded portion of plate must seat in piston. Install push rod retaining ring. Position spring seat, spring and spring cover in position. Hold spring and spring cover in position with suitable drift and install inner piston snap ring.

NOTE — *Do not use excessive force on spring cover; cover will require replacement if deformed.*

3) Install toggle lever dust seal on cam (cam must face direction of parking brake operation) and align square hole in toggle lever on cam. Install return spring, lock washer and tighten nut. Reassemble piston assembly by turning clockwise. Coat sliding portions of piston assembly and caliper bore with brake fluid. Slide piston assembly into bore (outside piston first) from rear of caliper assembly. Install new dust seals and secure in position with retainer rings.

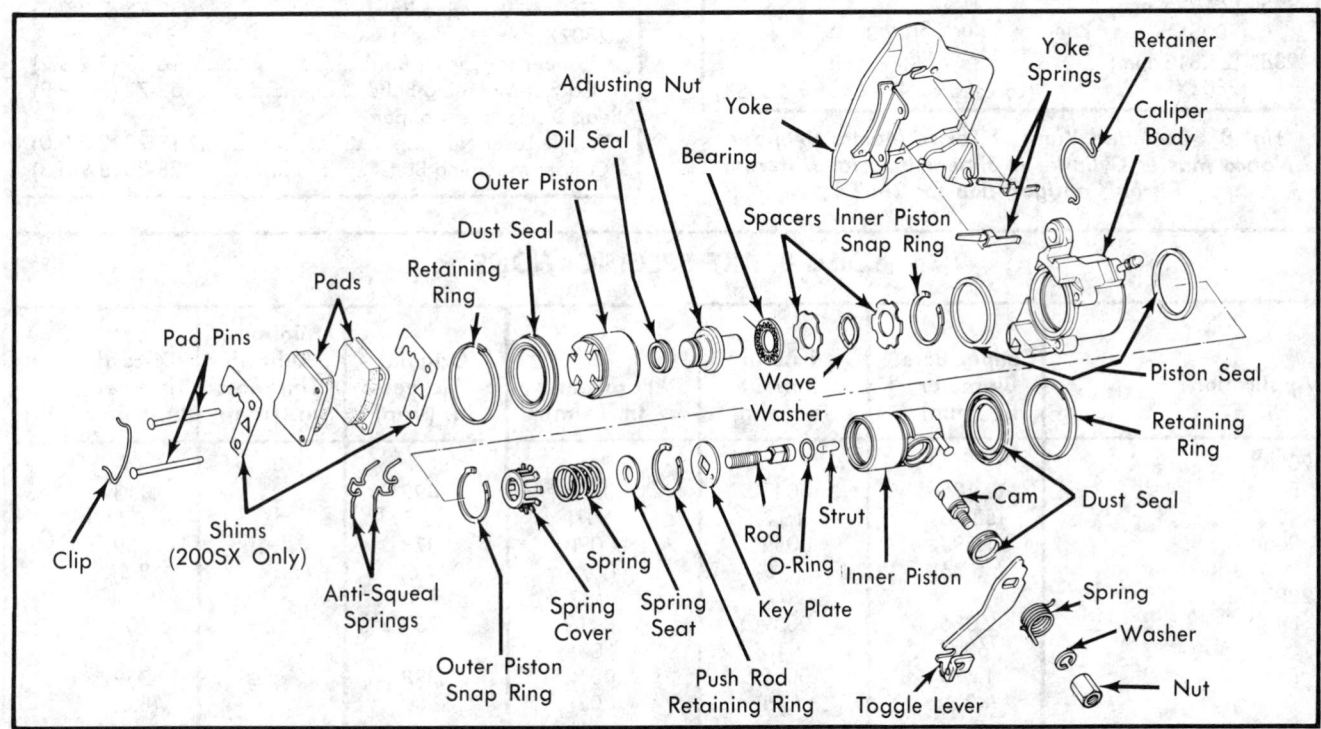

Fig. 6   Exploded View of Rear Disc Brake Caliper

DATSUN 200SX & 280ZX (Cont.)

4) Install yoke springs to yoke. Coat yoke and caliper body frictional surfaces and caliper body pad pin holes with silicone grease. Align cut out portion of inner piston with yoke and reassemble yoke to caliper. Securely position retainer in piston groove.

5) Apply brake grease to caliper body-to-pad clearance, yoke-to-pad clearance, pad pin-to-pad clearance and pad pin-to-bracket clearance. Install pads, springs, pins and clip.

MASTER CYLINDER

Disassembly — Remove reservoir caps and filters; drain brake fluid. Remove snap ring and stopper bolt. Withdraw stopper, primary piston assembly, secondary piston assembly and springs. Remove check valve plugs and withdraw check valve assemblies.

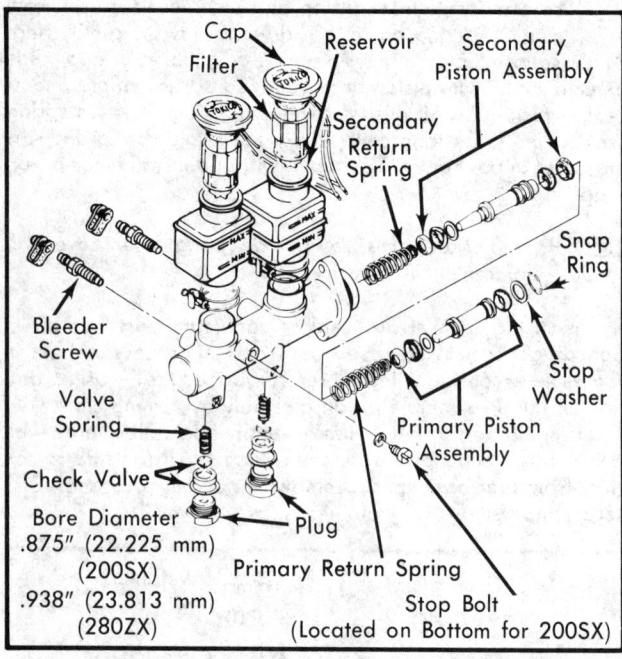

NOTE — *Do not remove reservoir tanks. If tanks are removed for any reason, discard and install new tanks. Also, do not remove or disassemble brake fluid level gauge.*

Cleaning & Inspection — Clean all parts in brake fluid and check components for excessive wear or damage. If piston-to-cylinder clearance exceeds .006" (.15 mm) replace defective part. Caps, gaskets, packing and valves must be replaced during overhaul.

NOTE — *Master cylinders are produced by two companies and parts are not interchangeable. Ensure repair kit matches master cylinder. Only "Tokico" master cylinder is used on 200SX.*

Reassembly — Reverse disassembly procedure and note the following: Apply rubber grease to all rubber parts and brake fluid to remaining parts when assembling to prevent damage.

POWER BRAKE UNIT

NOTE — *Manufacturer does not recommend disassembly of this unit. If a problem is determined to be in power brake unit, complete assembly must be replaced. Do not disassemble power brake unit.*

Fig. 8 Exploded View of Tokico Master Cylinder Nabco Master Cylinder is Similar But Has Different Piston Configuration for 280ZX

TIGHTENING SPECIFICATIONS

Application	Ft. Lbs. (mkg)
Hub-to-Rotor Bolts	
200SX (Front)	28-38 (3.9-5.3)
280ZX (Front)	40-54 (5.5-7.5)
Front Disc Brake Caliper	
200SX	
Yoke-to-Caliper Bolts	12-15 (1.5-2.0)
Caliper Mounting Bolts	53-72 (7.3-9.9)
280ZX	
Caliper-to-Carrier Bolts	16-23 (2.2-3.2)
Carrier Mounting Bolts	53-72 (7.3-9.9)
Rear Disc Brake Caliper	
Toggle Lever Nut	18-22 (2.5-3.0)
Caliper Mounting Bolts	28-38 (3.9-5.3)

DISC BRAKE SPECIFICATIONS

Application	Caliper Bore Diameter In. (mm)	Lateral Runout In. (mm)	Parallelism In. (mm)	Original Thickness In. (mm)	Minimum Refinish Thickness In. (mm)	Discard Thickness In. (mm)
200SX						
Front	2.125 (53.98)	.0047① (.12)	.0028 .(.07)	.492 (12.5)	.....	.413 (10.5)
Rear	1.593 (40.46)	.0059① (.15)	.0028 (.07)	.378 (9.6)	.....	.339 (8.6)
280ZX						
Front	2.386 (60.6)	.0039① (.10)	.0012 (.03)	.787 (20)	.....	.709 (18)
Rear	1.685 (42.8)	.0059① (.15)	.0012 (.03)	.378 (9.6)	.....	.339 (8.6)

① — Maximum allowable at center of pad contact area.

Brakes

DATSUN 210, 310, 510, 810 & PICKUPS

DESCRIPTION

Brake system is hydraulically operated using tandem master cylinder and vacuum power unit. All models are equipped with single cylinder, dual piston, fixed caliper, sliding yoke type front disc brakes. Rear brake systems are duo-servo drum on pickups and leading/trailing drum on all other models. All models are equipped with combination valves to prevent premature rear wheel lock-up. The combination valve on pickup models is mounted at a 10° incline on frame to change braking power of rear wheels in response to changes in load and brake fluid pressures. Parking brake systems are cable operated at rear wheels.

ADJUSTMENT

DRUM BRAKES

Pickups — Raise and support vehicle. Release parking brake and remove dust boot from backing plate. Lightly tap adjuster housing and move it forward. Rotate adjuster down with a screwdriver until drum locks. Back off adjuster 12 notches for correct shoe-to-drum clearance. Rotate brake drum by hand and ensure no excessive drag is present. Readjust clearance if necessary. Reinstall rubber boot and lower vehicle.

Except Pickups — Drum brakes are self-adjusting and no adjustment in service is required.

PEDAL HEIGHT & FREE PLAY

Adjust pedal height (measured from pedal pad to floor) to specification shown in table by moving stop light switch. Loosen operating rod lock nut and turn operating rod to attain proper height, tighten lock nut and adjust stop light switch. Pedal free play should be .04-.20" (1-5 mm). If specification is exceeded, adjust push rod length.

Pedal Height Specifications	
Application	Pedal Height In. (mm)
210	5.6-5.9 (142-150)
310	7.0-7.3 (178-186)
510	6.1-6.3 (155-160)
810	7.1 (180)
Pickups	6.6-6.9 (168-175)

STOP LIGHT SWITCH

Stop light switch is located under dash panel at brake pedal. Adjust travel during pedal height adjustment. After obtaining correct pedal height, position stop light switch until it just contacts brake pedal arm. Tighten lock nut.

PARKING BRAKE

810 Station Wagon & Pickups — Adjust parking brake by applying parking brake with 44 lbs. (20 kg) force to obtain lever stroke of 6 notches on 810 and 6-10 notches on pickups. Adjust equalizer link with adjusting nut until rear wheels are locked. Release parking brake and ensure rear wheels turn freely. After adjustment, parking brake should operate smoothly without noise or drag.

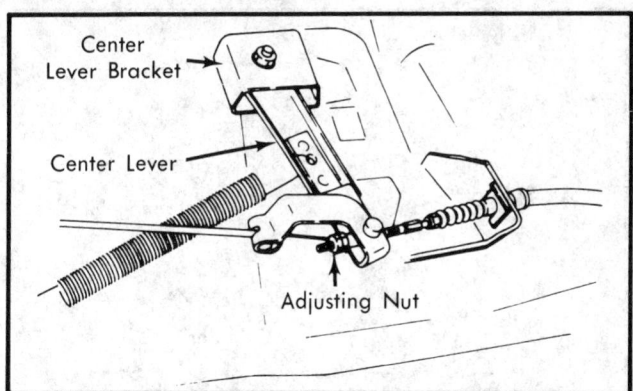

Fig. 1   Parking Brake Adjustment Location 810 Station Wagon Shown — Pickups Similar

Except 810 Station Wagon & Pickups — Adjust parking brake by rotating turnbuckle until rear brakes are locked when brake lever is pulled 5-6 notches on 810 and 7-8 notches on all other models with 44 lbs. (20 kg) force. Release parking brake and ensure rear wheels turn freely. After adjustment, ensure cables are slack and all parts are in original positions.

BRAKE WARNING LIGHT

Light indicates parking brake is engaged. To adjust light operation, bend switch plate until light comes on when brake lever is pulled 1 notch and goes out when lever is released (ignition on). On all models except pickups, light also indicates low fluid level when parking brake is released. To check warning light operation, release parking brake and raise master cylinder reservoir cap. Warning light should glow; if not, check switch and wire connector.

REMOVAL & INSTALLATION

FRONT DISC BRAKE PADS

Removal — Raise and support vehicle; remove tire and wheel. Remove retaining clip and then remove pad pins while holding anti-squeal springs. Remove disc brake pads, using suitable pliers if necessary. Remove pad spring (210 and 310) and shims (310) with brake pads.

CAUTION — *DO NOT force piston groove inside piston seal. Piston seal could be damaged and caliper will have to be disassembled.*

Installation — 1) Clean and apply P.B.C. grease or equivalent to cylinder body yoke guide groove, yoke sliding contact points and piston end surface. Loosen bleeder screw and push outer piston into cylinder until piston end surface coincides with boot retaining ring end surface. Tighten bleeder screw and install inner brake pad.

NOTE — *Make sure arrow mark on pad shims of 310 are installed in forward rotating direction.*

2) Push inner piston into cylinder by pulling on yoke, then install outer pad. Install anti-squeal springs, coil springs (210 and 310), retaining pins and clip. Depress brake pedal several times to seat pads, and bleed hydraulic system if necessary.

DATSUN 210, 310, 510, 810 & PICKUPS (Cont.)

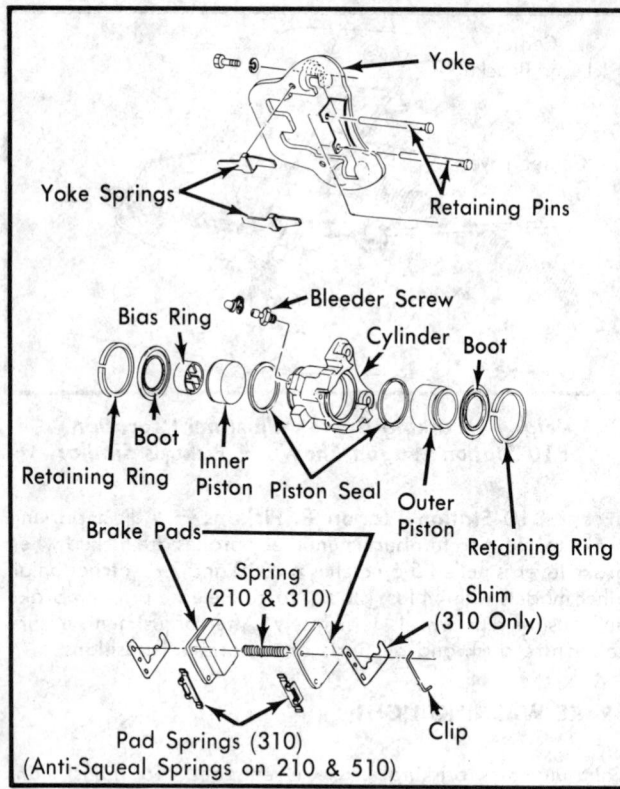

**Fig. 2   Exploded View of Front Disc Brake
(210, 310 and 510 Models)**

FRONT DISC BRAKE CALIPER

Removal — Raise and support vehicle; remove tire and wheel. Disconnect hydraulic line from caliper and plug all openings. On 310 models, remove strut assembly and knuckle arm mounting bolt. On all models, remove caliper mounting bolts and remove caliper.

Installation — To install, reverse removal procedure and bleed hydraulic system.

FRONT DISC BRAKE ROTOR

Removal (4-WD Pickup) — Raise and support vehicle; remove tire and wheel. Remove caliper assembly as previously described and hang caliper from frame with wire. DO NOT disconnect hydraulic lines. Set locking hub to "Lock" position and remove cover assembly bolts and cover.

2) Remove snap ring and remove clutch assembly by turning clockwise. Ensure lock pin is retained without damage. Remove drive shaft. Remove knuckle arm-to-knuckle bolt. Loosen but do not remove upper and lower ball joint nuts. Using ball joint tool (ST29020001), separate ball joints from spindle. Raise lower link with a jack and remove ball joint nuts. Remove knuckle assembly.

3) Straighten wheel lock washer and remove lock washer. Using lock nut remover (KV40102500), remove lock nut, lock washer and bearing washer. Push bearing support out of wheel hub. Using suitable puller, remove knuckle from hub. Remove hub-to-rotor bolts and remove rotor.

Installation — 1) Install hub-to-rotor bolts and tighten. Press knuckle onto hub, then install bearing support, bearing washer, lock washer and lock nut. Rotate hub several times to seat bearings and check bearing preload. Bend lock washer lip up into a lock nut groove.

2) Install spindle assembly and tighten suspension components. After installing drive shaft, check that axle shaft end play is .004-.012" (.1-.3 mm). Adjust axle shaft end play with proper thickness of snap ring. Mount caliper and tighten; bleed hydraulic system if necessary.

Removal (310) — With caliper removed, remove cotter pin. Remove hub nut from drive shaft end while holding hub with suitable tool. Using a puller, remove hub and rotor assembly. Remove hub-to-rotor bolts. With rotor supported on wooden blocks, remove hub from rotor with suitable press and drift.

Installation — Reverse removal procedure, tighten hub-to-rotor bolts evenly and adjust wheel bearings. See *Wheel Bearing Adjustment* in *WHEEL ALIGNMENT* Section. Bleed hydraulic system.

Removal (All Other Models) — With caliper removed, remove hub dust cap, "O" ring, cotter pin, adjusting cap and lock nut. Remove hub and rotor assembly from spindle without dropping outer bearing and washer. Remove outer bearing and washer and hub-to-rotor bolts. Separate hub and rotor.

NOTE — *Avoid damaging dust cap "O" ring while removing hub dust cap.*

Installation — Reverse removal procedure, tighten hub-to-rotor bolts evenly and adjust wheel bearings. See *Wheel Bearing Adjustment* in *WHEEL ALIGNMENT* Section. Bleed hydraulic system.

REAR BRAKE SHOES

Removal (810 Sedan) — 1) Raise and support vehicle on safety stands; remove tire and brake drum. Apply hand brake, lightly tap stopper head and remove stopper and fastener as an assembly. Release parking brake.

2) Remove retainers, anti-rattle springs and pins and spring seats. Remove return springs and brake shoes with adjuster assembly. Remove parking brake cable from lever. Pry off snap ring and remove lever from brake shoe.

CAUTION — *Left hand thread adjuster must be installed on RIGHT wheel and right hand thread adjuster must be installed on LEFT wheel.*

Installation — To install, reverse removal procedure and apply brake grease to all contact points and mating surfaces. Make sure adjuster operates properly, readjust shoe-to-drum clearance and bleed hydraulic system, if necessary.

Removal (Pickups) — 1) Raise and support vehicle on safety stands; remove tire and wheel. Loosen parking brake and remove brake drum. Remove retainers, anti-rattle springs, spring seats and anti-rattle pins.

DATSUN 210, 310, 510, 810 & PICKUPS (Cont.)

2) Remove strut and return springs. Remove primary shoe. Before removing secondary shoe, remove clip and washer from rear of toggle lever and withdraw toggle pin. Remove secondary shoe. Disconnect toggle lever from parking brake cable. Remove adjuster boot and lock assembly; remove adjuster assembly from backing plate.

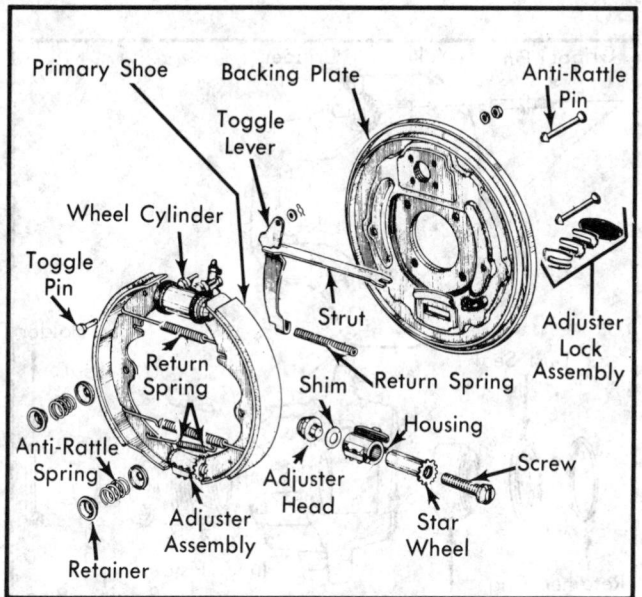

Fig. 3   Exploded View of Pickup Rear Brake Assembly

Installation — To install, reverse removal procedure and note the following: Apply brake grease to moving parts of adjuster assembly and all metal contact surfaces of brake shoes. Adjuster sliding resistance (measured with spring scale) should be 11-26 lbs. (5-12 kg); if not, install new adjuster shim.

Removal (Except Pickups & 810 Sedan) — **1)** Raise and support vehicle on safety stands; remove tire and wheel. Apply parking brake and remove stopper pin, then remove stopper from lever. Release parking brake and remove brake drum. Remove parking brake cable from backing plate (except 810 Station Wagon).

2) On 810 Station Wagon, remove hand brake return spring, cross rod cotter pin, then dust cover and lever with adjuster assembly. On all models, remove retainers, anti-rattle springs, pins and spring seats. Remove return springs and brake shoes.

CAUTION — *Right hand thread adjuster must be installed on RIGHT wheel and left hand thread adjuster must be installed on LEFT wheel.*

Installation — Apply brake grease to all contact points and mating surfaces; reverse removal procedure to install brake shoes and note the following: Make sure adjuster operates properly, readjust shoe-to-drum clearance and bleed hydraulic system, if necessary.

MASTER CYLINDER

Removal — Disconnect electrical wiring at cylinder reservoir (if equipped). Disconnect and plug hydraulic lines at master cylinder and drain cylinder. Remove cylinder mounting nuts and remove master cylinder.

Installation — To install master cylinder, reverse removal procedure and note the following: Bleed hydraulic system and check pedal height.

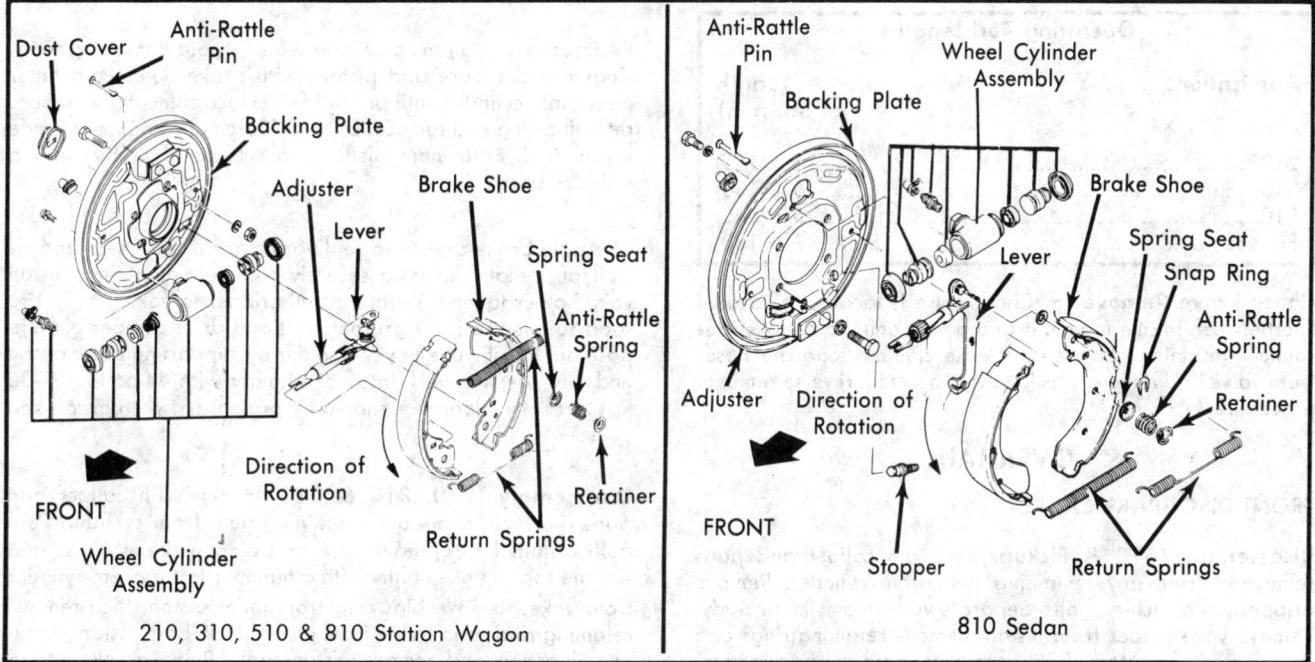

210, 310, 510 & 810 Station Wagon

810 Sedan

Fig. 4   Exploded View of Rear Brake Assembly (Except Pickups)

DATSUN 210, 310, 510, 810 & PICKUPS (Cont.)

POWER BRAKE UNIT

NOTE — *Before removal, test check valve. Using a brake booster tester, apply 19.7" Hg to brake unit side of check valve. If pressure drops more than .39" Hg in 15 seconds, replace check valve. Also, if valve does not open when pressure is applied to brake unit side of check valve, replace check valve. If check valve is not defective, check brake system and vacuum lines for leaks; replace booster as an assembly.*

Removal — With master cylinder removed, disconnect vacuum line from power unit. From inside vehicle, disconnect pedal return spring, push rod from brake pedal, and power unit mounting nuts. Remove power unit from engine compartment.

Installation — Reverse removal procedure and adjust push rod length to .38-.39" (9.75-10.0 mm) by turning tip of push rod. Check pedal height and free play and bleed hydraulic system.

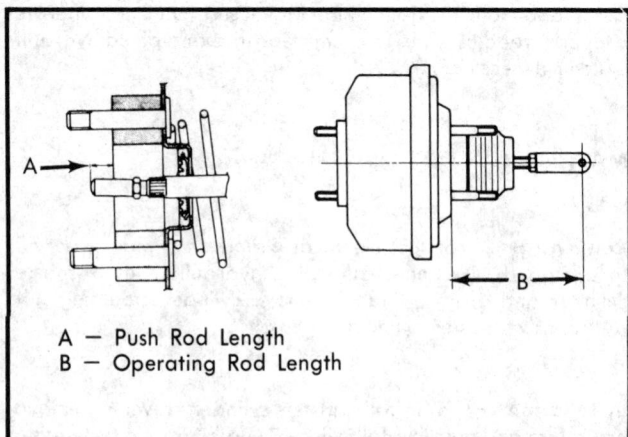

A — Push Rod Length
B — Operating Rod Length

Fig. 5 Location for Measuring Push Rod and Operating Rod Lengths

Operating Rod Lengths	
Application	**Length In. (mm)**
210 & 510	5.3 (135)
310	5.1 (130)
810	5.7 (145)
Pickups	7.1 (180)

Check Valve Removal — Check valve is located in vacuum line between intake manifold and power unit. To remove, disconnect retaining clip, remove hose clamps, separate hoses from valve and remove check valve. To install, reverse removal procedure.

OVERHAUL

FRONT DISC BRAKE CALIPER

Disassembly (810 & Pickups) — With caliper and pads removed, drain any remaining fluid from cylinder. Remove gripper pin attaching bolts. Separate yoke and cylinder body. Remove yoke holder from piston. Remove retaining rings and dust seals from pistons. Push both pistons out in one direction. Remove piston seals. Remove gripper, if necessary.

Cleaning & Inspection — Clean all parts with brake fluid and check all components for wear or damage. If minor corrosion can not be removed from cylinder bore with emery cloth, cylinder must be replaced. All seals must be replaced during overhaul.

NOTE — *Piston surfaces are plated and must be replaced if corroded or worn. DO NOT polish with emery cloth.*

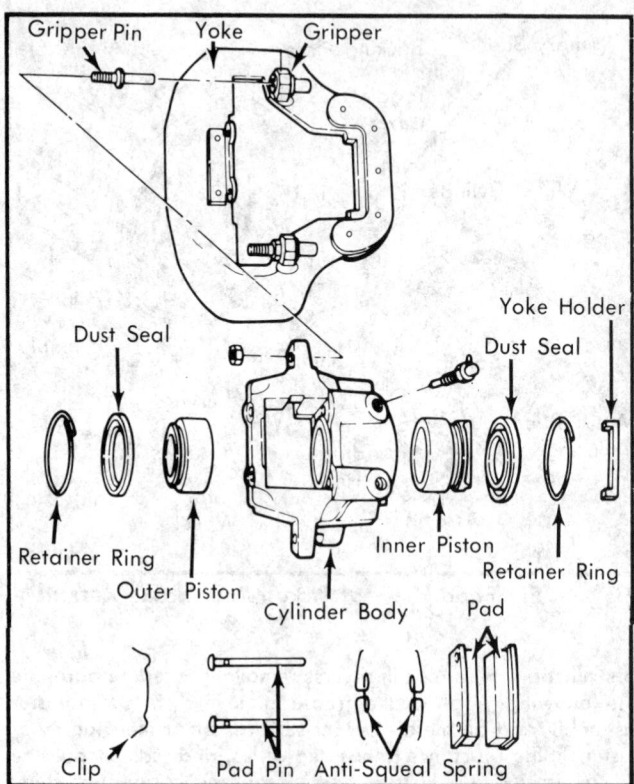

Fig. 6 Exploded View of Front Disc Brake Caliper (810 and Pickups)

Reassembly — **1)** Install piston seals without damaging seals. Coat cylinder bore and pistons with brake fluid. Push outer piston into cylinder until piston end surface coincides with boot retaining ring end surface. DO NOT force piston groove inside piston seal. Push inner piston into cylinder bore by holding cylinder body.

2) Apply brake grease to sealing surface of dust seal and install dust seal; clamping securely with retaining ring. Install yoke holder to inner piston. Install gripper to yoke. Apply 1% soap solution to inner gripper wall and drive gripper pin into position. Install yoke to yoke holder by supporting outer piston end and pressing yoke into yoke holder with 44-66 lb. (20-30 kg) force. No clearance should be present between piston and yoke.

Disassembly (210, 310 & 510) — **1)** With caliper and pads removed, drain any remaining fluid from cylinder. Push both pistons into cylinder bore and place yoke in a vise and tap the top of yoke lightly with a hammer to separate cylinder from yoke. Remove bias ring from inner piston, then remove retaining rings and boots from piston. Push both pistons out in one direction and remove piston seals. Remove yoke spring from yoke.

DATSUN 210, 310, 510, 810 & PICKUPS (Cont.)

Cleaning & Inspection — Clean all parts with brake fluid and check all components for wear or damage. If minor corrosion cannot be removed from cylinder bore with emery cloth, cylinder must be replaced. Piston seals, dust covers and bias ring must be replaced during overhaul.

NOTE — *Piston surfaces are plated and must be replaced if corroded or worn. DO NOT polish with emery cloth.*

Reassembly — **1)** Apply brake fluid to cylinder bore and install piston seal. Insert bias ring into inner piston with rounded end in bottom of piston bore.

NOTE — *Bias ring must be installed in inner piston. Inner piston is identified with a recession on inside bottom surface.*

2) Lightly coat piston with brake fluid and insert inner piston until yoke groove of bias ring aligns with cylinder yoke groove. DO NOT force piston groove inside piston seal. Push outer piston into cylinder bore by holding cylinder body. Install dust boots and retaining rings. Install yoke springs on yoke and bias spring to yoke. Align bias ring groove so it coincides with yoke. With yoke springs lightly inserted in cylinder groove, assemble cylinder body and yoke by tapping yoke lightly.

REAR WHEEL CYLINDER

Disassembly — With rear wheel cylinder removed, remove dust covers and remove components.

Cleaning & Inspection — Clean all parts in brake fluid and check cylinder bore and pistons for excessive wear or damage. If piston-to-cylinder clearance is greater than .006″ (.15 mm), replace necessary parts. Replace any torn or damaged rubber parts.

NOTE — *Wheel cylinders are produced by two companies and parts are not interchangeable. Ensure repair kit matches wheel cylinder.*

Reassembly — Apply brake fluid to cylinder bore, pistons and piston cups. Reverse disassembly procedure and install parts.

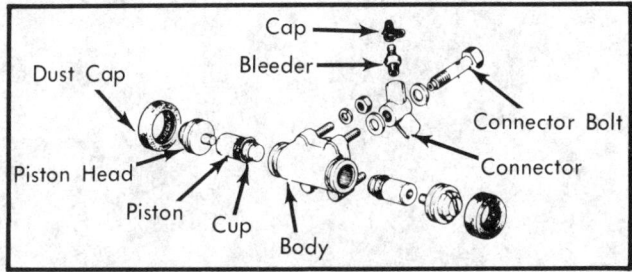

Fig. 7 Exploded View of Pickup Wheel Cylinder

MASTER CYLINDER

NOTE — *Do not remove reservoir tanks. If tanks are removed for any reason, discard and install new tanks.*

Disassembly — Remove master cylinder reservoir caps and filters and drain brake fluid. Using a screwdriver, pry off stopper ring. Remove stopper screw and pull out primary piston assembly, spring and secondary piston assembly. Remove plugs and pull out front and rear check valves.

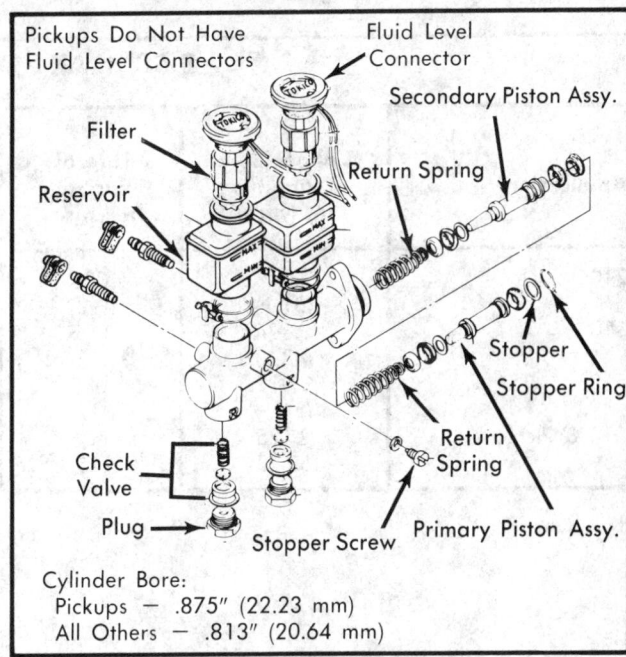

Fig. 8 Exploded View of Tokico Master Cylinder Nabco Master Cylinder is Similar But Has Different Piston Configuration

Cleaning & Inspection — Clean all parts in brake fluid and check components for excessive wear or damage. If piston-to-cylinder clearance is greater than .006″ (.15 mm), replace necessary part. Caps, gaskets and valves must be replaced during overhaul.

NOTE — *Master cylinders are produced by two companies and parts are not interchangeable. Ensure repair kit matches master cylinder.*

Reassembly — Reverse disassembly procedure and note the following: Coat all parts with brake fluid (rubber parts with brake grease) when assembling.

POWER BRAKE UNIT

NOTE — *Manufacturer does not recommend disassembly of this unit. If a problem is determined to be in booster unit, complete assembly must be replaced. Do not disassemble booster unit.*

TIGHTENING SPECIFICATIONS

Application	Ft. Lbs. (mkg)
Hub-to-Rotor Bolts	
310	18-25 (2.5-3.5)
All Others	28-38 (3.9-5.3)
Caliper Mounting Bolts	
310	40-47 (5.5-6.5)
All Others	53-72 (7.3-10)
4-WD ONLY	
Locking Hub	18-25 (2.5-3.5)
Drive Shaft-to-Carrier	20-27 (2.8-3.7)
Spindle Nut	87-108 (12-15)

Brakes

DATSUN 210, 310, 510, 810 & PICKUPS (Cont.)

DISC BRAKE SPECIFICATIONS						
Application	Caliper Bore Diameter In. (mm)	Lateral Runout In. (mm)	Parallelism In. (mm)	Original Thickness In. (mm)	Minimum Refinish Thickness In. (mm)	Discard Thickness In. (mm)
210	2.012 (51.1)	.005 (.12)	.001 (.03)	.394 (10)	.....	.331 (8.4)
310	1.894 (48.1)	.005 (.12)	.001 (.03)	.378 (9.6)	.....	.339 (8.6)
510	2.012 (51.1)	.005 (.12)	.003 (.07)	.394 (10)	.....	.331 (8.4)
810 & Pickups	2.125 (53.98)	.006 (.15)	.003 (.07)	.492 (12.5)	.....	.413 (10.5)

DRUM BRAKE SPECIFICATIONS					
Application	Wheel Cyl. Bore Diameter In. (mm)	Drum Diameter In. (mm)	Original Diameter In. (mm)	Maximum Refinish Diameter In. (mm)	Discard Diameter In. (mm)
210	.813 (20.64)	8.00 (203)	8.00 (203)	.....	8.05 (204.5)
310	.687 (17.46)	8.00 (203)	8.00 (203)	.....	8.05 (204.5)
510 & 810	.813 (20.64)	9.00 (228.6)	9.00 (228.6)	.....	9.06 (230)
Pickups	.625 (15.88)	10.00 (254)	10.00 (254)	.....	10.06 (255.5)

FIAT

Brava
Spider 2000
Strada
X1/9

DESCRIPTION

Brake system is hydraulically operated, using a tandem master cylinder and vacuum power brake unit. Spider 2000 and X1/9 models use single piston, sliding caliper, 4-wheel disc brakes. All other models are equipped with single piston, floating caliper front disc and leading/trailing rear drum brakes. All front and rear brake applications are self-adjusting. All models except X1/9 use pressure differential valves in rear brake circuits. All parking brakes are cable actuated and operate on rear brake application.

ADJUSTMENT

PARKING BRAKE

Pump service brakes several times to seat pistons, then fully release parking brake lever. Pull parking brake lever up 3-4 notches (3 notches on Brava and Strada). On Spider 2000 and X1/9 models, tighten nut on equalizer until rear wheels lock. X1/9 models have an opening provided in floor pan under body for access to equalizer. On Brava and Strada models, loosen lock nut located under parking brake handle and tighten adjusting nut until rear wheels lock. On all models, release parking brake and ensure rear wheels rotate freely. Repeat adjustment procedure if rear wheels drag.

BRAKE WARNING LIGHT

A dual warning light is mounted on dash. Light should glow when parking brake lever is pulled 1 notch and go off when lever is fully released (ignition on). To check circuit warning, release parking brake (ignition on) and ensure light is off. Lift master cylinder reservoir cover until level indicator is above fluid level; light should glow.

BRAKE PRESSURE REGULATOR

Brava — Install regulator and leave mounting bolts loose. Bring torsion bar (7) to dimension shown in *Fig. 1* from base of buffer end (11). Remove rubber boot (3) from regulator, then rotate regulator until piston (6) is just touching torsion bar (1). Tighten mounting bolts.

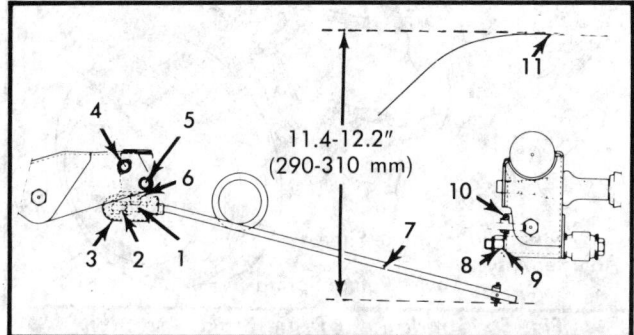

Fig. 1 Brake Pressure Regulator Measurement and Adjustment Points for Brava Models

Spider 2000 — 1) Bring end of torsion bar (E) to distance shown in *Fig. 2* from buffer resting surface. Use a jack to raise body to gain appropriate height, or place weight in passenger seat before tightening.

2) Lift dust boot (C) and check contact of regulator piston (D) with torsion bar end (E).

3) Pivot regulator body on screw (A) until piston (D) is just touching torsion bar end (E).

4) First, tighten screw (B) and then screw (A) in all the way. Connect link (G) to torsion bar eye end (E) with screw and nut while inserting rubber bushings and spacer.

NOTE — *Fluid inlet from master cylinder must be connected to lower union (R) and fluid line to rear brakes must be connected to upper union (S).*

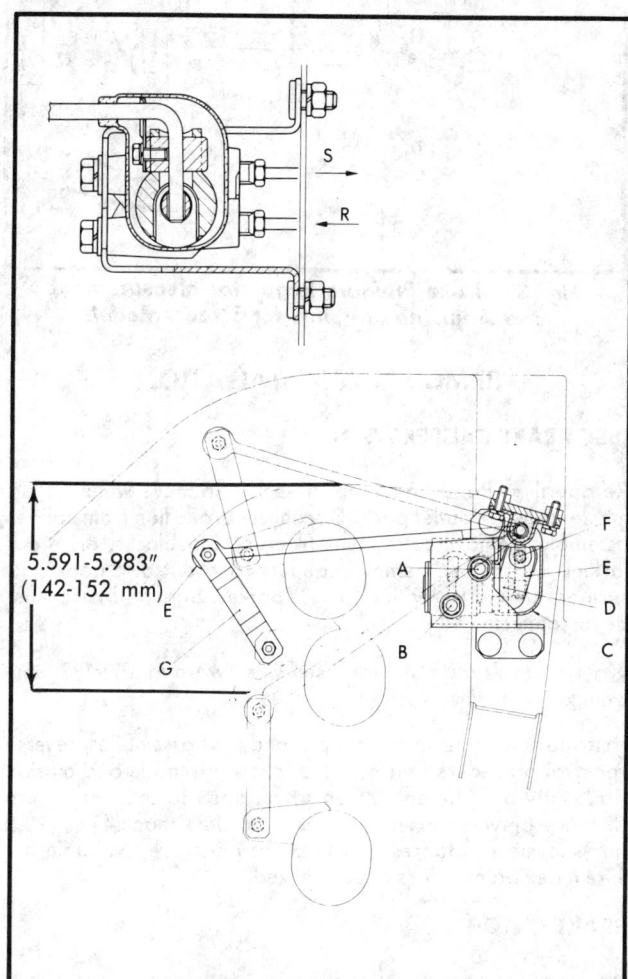

Fig. 2 Brake Pressure Regulator Measurement and Adjustment Points for Spider 2000

Strada — Raise and support vehicle. Loosen compensator (1) attaching bolts (7). Unclip plastic clamp and slide dust boot (9) from compensator. Disconnect torsion bar (3) from connecting link (4). Distance between center of suspension rubber buffer seat (2) and torsion bar end (3b) must be as shown in *Fig. 3*. Once specification is obtained, rotate compensator until piston (8) is just touching torsion bar (3a). Tighten bolts, connect torsion bar to connecting link. Slide dust boot onto compensator and secure with plastic clamp.

NOTE — *Vehicle must not be loaded if drive-on type lift is used to support vehicle.*

FIAT (Cont.)

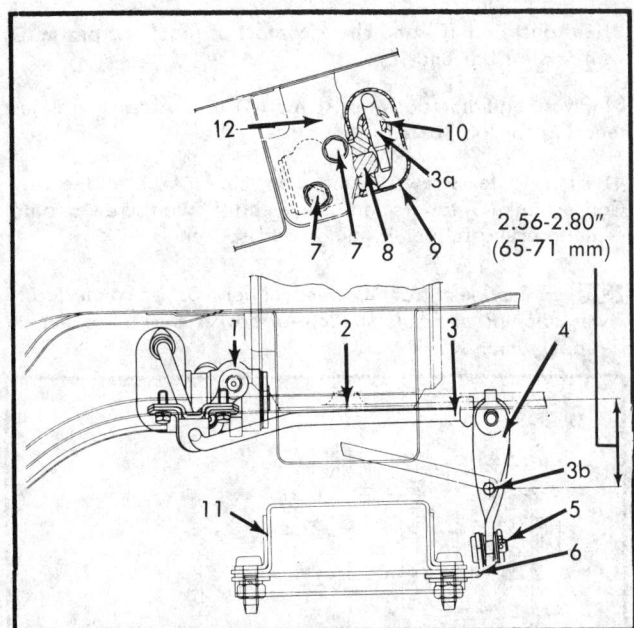

Fig. 3   Brake Pressure Regulator Measurement and Adjustment Points for Strada Models

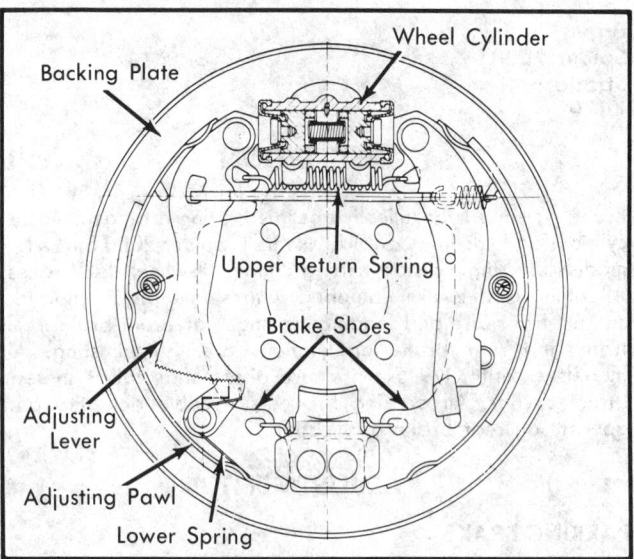

Fig. 4   Brava Rear Drum Brake Assembly

REMOVAL & INSTALLATION

DISC BRAKE CALIPERS & PADS

Removal — Raise and support vehicle; remove wheels. Plug master cylinder outlet ports. Disconnect brake line from caliper assembly. Remove cotter pins from locking blocks, drive out locking blocks and remove caliper. Take out disc pads and springs. On models with rear disc brakes, parking brake must be disconnected.

NOTE — *Pads MUST be replaced when worn to .079" (2 mm) from original thickness.*

Installation — To install caliper and pad assemblies, reverse removal procedure and note the following: Inside and outside pads may be different. When fitting pads to calipers, ensure distance between inner surfaces is not less than .413" (10.5 mm). In most instances two kinds of pads are available, be sure index paint stripes are not mixed.

BRAKE ROTOR

Removal — Remove caliper as previously outlined. Mount a dial indicator so plunger is .08" (2 mm) from outer edge of rotor and record runout. Remove caliper support bracket from support plate (front) or from axle housing (rear). Remove bolts mounting rotor to hub. Remove hub plate (if equipped), then using a puller or drift, remove rotor from hub.

Installation — Fit rotor onto wheel hub, install attaching bolts and tighten evenly.

REAR BRAKE DRUM

Removal — Raise and support vehicle; remove tire and wheel. Remove locating pin and attaching bolt. Remove brake drum, releasing shoe adjustment, if required.

Installation — To install, reverse removal procedure.

REAR BRAKE SHOES

Removal — 1) Raise and support vehicle; remove tire and wheel. Remove brake drum. Retain wheel cylinder pistons in position with a clamp. Remove upper and lower return springs, shoe guide pins, springs and cups.

2) Disconnect parking brake cable from brake shoe link and remove brake shoes. Place brake shoes on work bench and remove self-adjusting lever by removing retaining clip on back of brake shoe. Remove adjusting pawl by removing spring retainer and spring, then remove adjusting pawl.

Installation — To install, reverse removal procedure and note the following: Longer return spring is upper return spring. Install brake shoes with ends correctly positioned in wheel cylinder pistons.

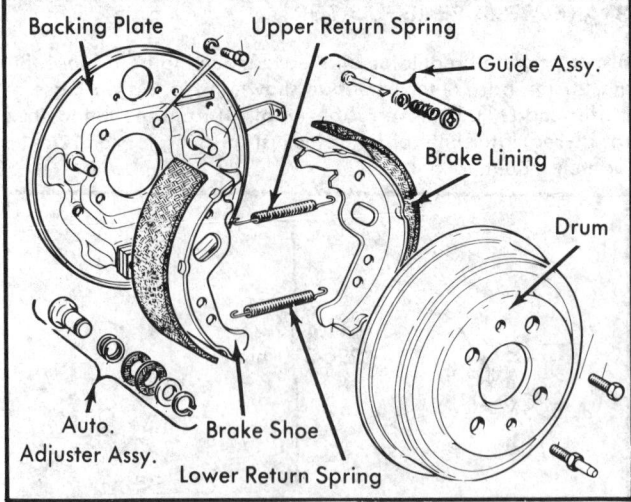

Fig. 5   Strada Rear Drum Brake Assembly

MASTER CYLINDER

Removal (X1/9) — Remove steering column. *See Steering Column Removal in STEERING Section.* Disconnect hydraulic lines from reservoir. Remove mounting nuts and slide unit off supports. Disconnect outlet lines from master cylinder.

FIAT (Cont.)

Installation — To install, reverse removal procedure and bleed hydraulic system.

Removal (All Others) — Remove jack and spare tire from engine compartment (if equipped), then remove spare tire support. While holding brake fluid level sensor, unscrew reservoir cover and remove assembly. Siphon fluid from reservoir. Gently rock reservoir from side to side and remove. Disconnect and plug hydraulic lines. Remove mounting nuts and remove master cylinder from power brake unit.

Installation — To install, reverse removal procedure and bleed hydraulic system.

POWER BRAKE UNIT

Removal — Remove master cylinder as previously outlined. Loosen vacuum hose clamp and remove vacuum hose from power brake unit. Remove cotter pin, lock nut and washer from operating rod clevis at brake pedal. Remove brake unit mounting nuts and remove power brake unit.

Installation — To install, reverse removal procedure and note the following: After installing master cylinder, bleed hydraulic system.

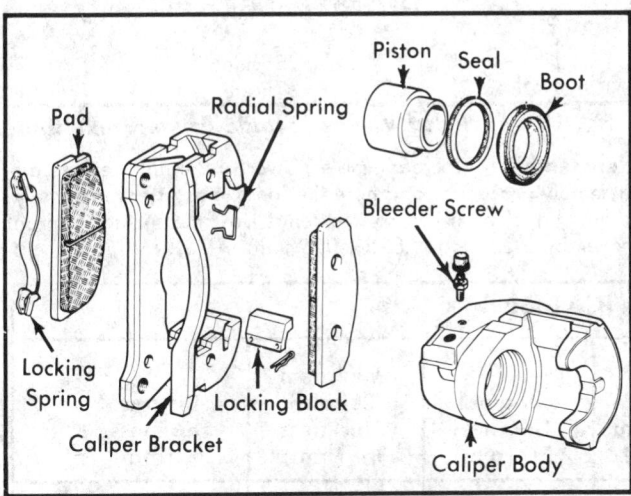

Fig. 6   Exploded View of Front Brake Caliper for All Models Except X1/9

OVERHAUL

BRAKE CALIPERS

Disassembly (Front) — With caliper assembly on bench, remove dust boot. Apply light air pressure to brake fluid inlet union and gently force piston from caliper. Remove piston seal from groove in cylinder bore.

NOTE — *Be sure bore is not scratched during removal process.*

Cleaning & Inspection — Clean all components in suitable solvent (Fiat LDC). Inspect each part for damage or excessive wear. Replace all piston seals and dust boots.

Reassembly — Fit piston seal in caliper. Insert piston to bottom end of cylinder bore. Position dust boot on caliper body. Fit caliper body into caliper bracket and reinstall on vehicle.

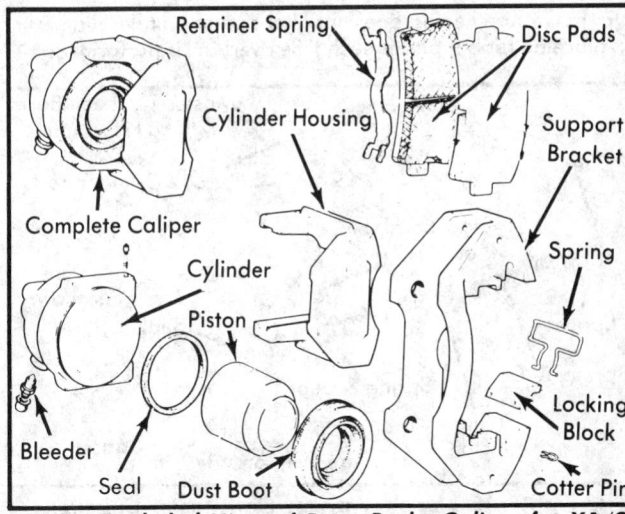

Fig. 7   Exploded View of Front Brake Caliper for X1/9

Disassembly (Rear) — With caliper assembly on bench, remove dust boot. With a screwdriver, separate piston from plunger. Remove piston seal from groove in piston cylinder bore. Remove cam lever, pivot pin, and lever. Lift out self-adjusting plunger, plunger seal, disc spring, and spring thrust washer.

Cleaning & Inspection — Clean all components in suitable solvent (Fiat LDC). Inspect each part for damage or excessive wear. Replace all piston seals and dust boots.

Reassembly — Fit self-adjusting plunger complete with seal, disc springs, and thrust washer. Fit parking brake cam lever complete with pivot pin. Fit pivot pin bushing and snap ring. Fit piston sealing ring into caliper cylinder. Screw piston into cylinder until fully seated. Align piston slot so it is opposite bleed connection. Refit dust boot.

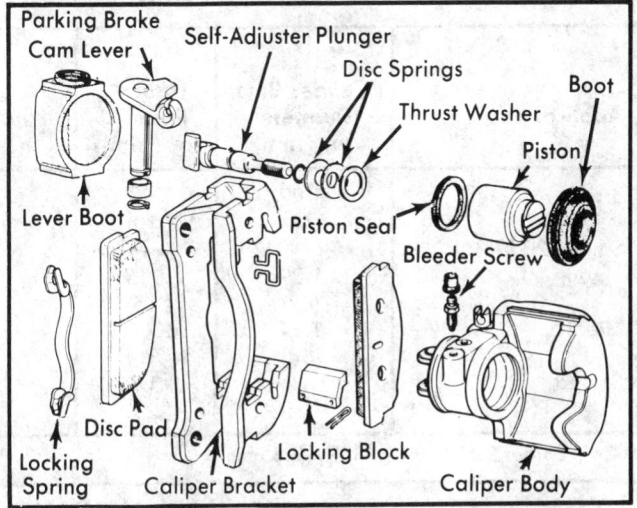

Fig. 8   Exploded View of Rear Brake Caliper Spider 2000 Shown — X1/9 Similar

MASTER CYLINDER

Disassembly — Remove connector(s) and cylinder bore dust boot. Remove stop bolt(s) and seal(s). Remove set screws and end plug (if equipped). Remove piston assemblies, return springs, cups, seals and spacers.

Inspection — Clean and thoroughly dry all parts, then inspect for wear or damage. Light scoring may be removed by hon-

FIAT (Cont.)

ing, make sure honing does not alter size of cylinder diameter. Replace all rubber pieces each time overhaul is performed.

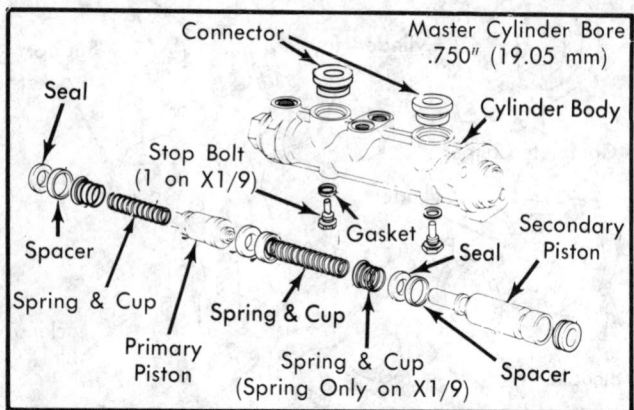

Fig. 9   Exploded View of Fiat Master Cylinder

Reassembly — To reassemble, reverse disassembly procedure and lightly coat all components with brake fluid before reassembly.

POWER BRAKE UNIT

NOTE — *The following procedure is for Strada models; all other models may require variations from the procedure outlined.*

Disassembly — **1)** Remove check valve and grommet from front shell. Place wooden blocks on both master cylinder mounting studs and 4 power brake mounting studs, then place unit in a vise. Slowly tighten vise until rear shell can be rotated clear of front shell locking tabs.

2) Separate front and rear shells. Slowly release vise until spring pressure is released, then remove power brake unit. Remove dust boot from rear shell. Remove filter assembly. Remove key to remove plunger and valve. Separate diaphragm from rear shell. Remove rear seal assembly.

3) Remove guide bushing front seal, vacuum piston, piston rod, backing plate and spring from front shell. DO NOT disturb adjustment of piston rod.

Inspection — Manufacturer recommends replacing the following parts during overhaul: Backing plate, front seal, filter assembly and rear seal assembly. Inspect all other parts for wear or damage and replace as required.

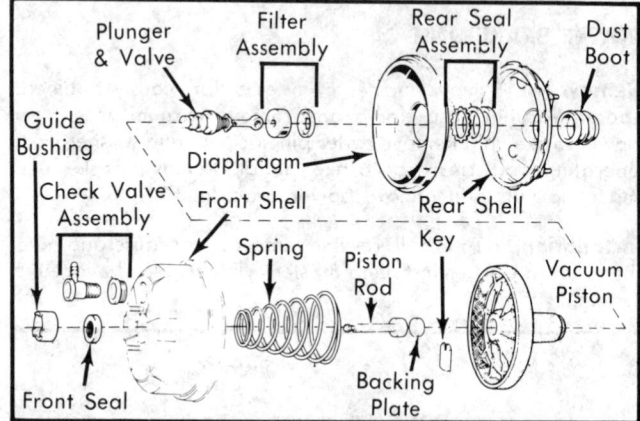

Fig. 10   Exploded View of Strada Power Brake Unit

Reassembly — To reassemble power brake unit, reverse disassembly procedure and note the following: After reassembly, adjust tip of push rod so it extends past the surface of front cover by .032-.040" (.825-1.025 mm). Adjust by turning nut.

DISC BRAKE SPECIFICATIONS

Application	Caliper Bore Diameter In. (mm)	Lateral Runout In. (mm)	Parallelism In. (mm)	Original Thickness In. (mm)	Minimum Refinish Thickness In. (mm)	Discard Thickness In. (mm)
Brava	1.89 (48)	.004 (.10)	.....	.425 (10.8)	.....	.386 (9.8)
Spider 2000 & X1/9						
Front	1.89 (48)	.006 (.15)	.....	.392-.400 (9.95-10.20)	.368 (9.35)	.354 (9.0)
Rear	1.34 (34)	.006 (.15)	.....	.392-.400 (9.95-10.20)	.368① (9.35)	.354 (9.0)
Strada	.....	.10 (.25)	.....	.421-.429 (10.7-10.9)	.368 (9.35)	.354 (9.0)

① — Spider 2000 rear is .372" (9.45 mm).

DRUM BRAKE SPECIFICATIONS

Application	Wheel Cyl. Bore Diameter In. (mm)	Drum Diameter In. (mm)	Original Diameter In. (mm)	Maximum Refinish Diameter In. (mm)	Discard Diameter In. (mm)
Brava	.875 (22.2)	9.00 (228.6)	9.00 (228.6)	9.03 (229.4)	9.055 (230)
Strada	.687 (17.46)	7.30 (185.4)	7.30 (185.4)	7.335 (186.3)	7.355 (186.8)

FIESTA

Hatchback

DESCRIPTION

Fiesta brake system is hydraulically operated using a tandem master cylinder and optional vacuum brake booster. Front brakes are single piston, sliding caliper disc; rear brakes are drum. Parking brake is cable actuated and operates on rear wheels.

Primary chamber of master cylinder provides fluid for right front/left rear brake system. Secondary chamber provides fluid for left front/right rear brake system. A warning light is installed on master cylinder reservoir to warn of low fluid level.

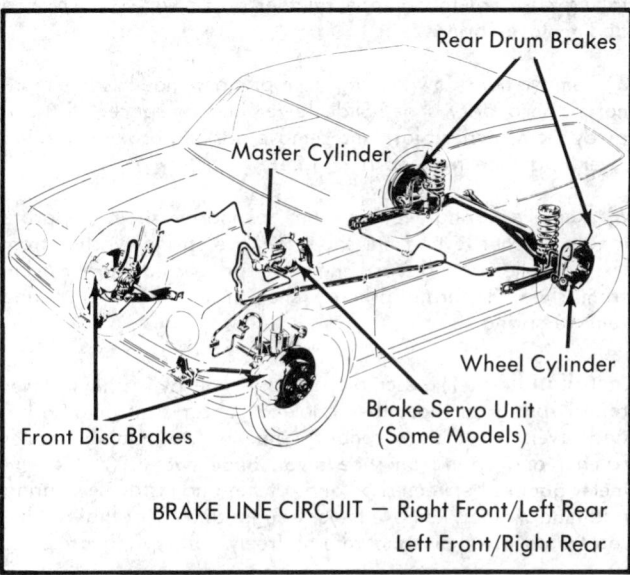

Fig. 1   Fiesta Brake System — Overall View

ADJUSTMENTS

REAR BRAKE SHOES

Rear brakes are self-adjusting during operation of brake pedal.

STOP LIGHT SWITCH

Stop light switch is located under dash, above brake pedal. To adjust, loosen lock nut and adjust switch so stop lights glow when pedal travel (measured at center line of pad) is .2-.8" (5-20 mm). Tighten lock nut.

PARKING BRAKE

CAUTION — *Raise and support rear of vehicle first when lifting vehicle.*

Raise and support vehicle on safety stands; release parking brake. Loosen adjuster nut "A" and rotate cable adjuster "B" until cable is slack. See *Fig. 2*. Ensure parking brake is OFF, then turn adjuster until slack is out of cable. After brake levers have just begun to move, turn adjuster 3 complete turns and tighten lock nut.

NOTE — *When adjustment is completed, machined groove "C" must not protrude past lock nut "A".*

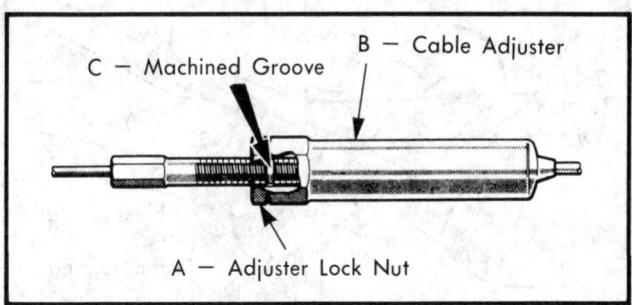

Fig. 2   Fiesta Parking Brake Adjuster

BRAKE WARNING LIGHT

A dual warning light is mounted on dash. Light should glow when parking brake lever is pulled 1 notch and go off when lever is fully released (ignition on). To check circuit warning sensor, release parking brake (ignition on) and ensure light is off. Depress test switch on top of master cylinder reservoir; light should glow. If not, check light and cap assembly.

REMOVAL & INSTALLATION

FRONT DISC BRAKE PADS

NOTE — *Disc brake pads must be installed in sets and must match vehicle.*

Removal — 1) Raise and support vehicle; remove tire and wheel. Remove and discard caliper retaining pins. Lightly press piston housing against caliper tension spring; slide out and discard keys.

2) Remove caliper from rotor and support out of way. DO NOT let caliper hang from hydraulic line. Remove and discard brake pads and anti-rattle clips from pad housing.

Installation — 1) Carefully apply pressure to face of piston and seat piston in bore. Do not damage piston face. Install new anti-rattle clips to top of brake pads. Install new pads in housing.

2) Install piston housing above caliper tension springs. Lightly press piston housing against caliper tension springs and slide in new keys. Align retaining pin holes, insert new pins from disc side and secure. Pump brake pedal several times to adjust pad-to-rotor clearance. Install tire and wheel; lower vehicle.

FRONT DISC BRAKE CALIPER

Removal — With tire and wheel removed; disconnect flexible hydraulic line from caliper and plug openings. Remove caliper retaining bolts and remove caliper.

Installation — Reverse removal procedure and bleed hydraulic system.

NOTE — *Retaining bolts are identified by the number 10.9 stamped on bolt head and nylon locking patch on threads.*

FIESTA (Cont.)

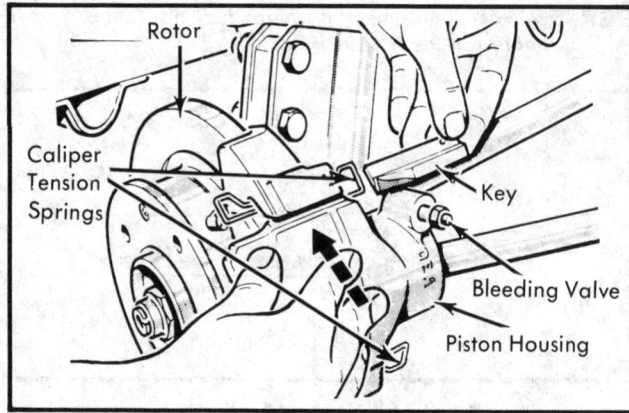

Fig. 3   *Removing Disc Brake Caliper*

FRONT DISC BRAKE ROTOR

Removal — With caliper removed, remove rotor retaining screw and remove rotor from hub.

Installation — Make sure all parts are clean and reverse removal procedure to install rotor.

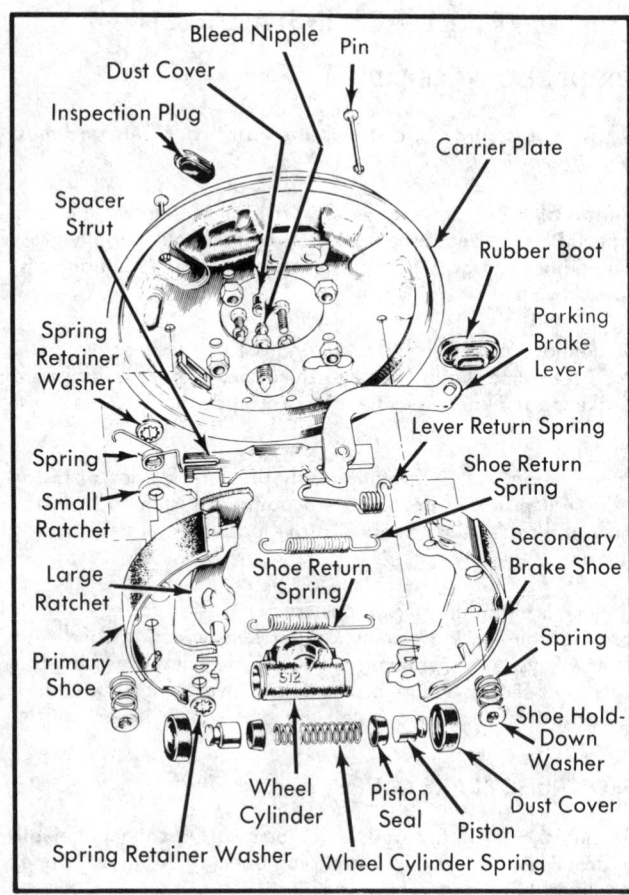

Fig. 4   *Exploded View of Fiesta Rear Brake Assembly*

REAR BRAKE SHOES

NOTE — *Replace brake shoes in sets of four.*

Removal — 1) Raise and support vehicle on safety stands; remove tire and wheel. Release parking brake. Disconnect parking brake cable from brake assembly by removing spring clip and clevis pin. Remove hand brake lever and rubber dust boot from carrier plate.

2) Remove dust cap, cotter pin, adjusting nut retainer, adjusting nut, washer, and outer bearing. Slide hub and drum assembly off spindle.

3) Remove hold down spring from secondary shoe by depressing and turning washer 90°. Remove spring and washer and remove pin from carrier plate.

4) Twist secondary shoe out and up away from carrier plate, taking care not to damage cylinder dust cover. Detach shoe and remove springs.

5) Remove hold down spring from primary shoe in same manner as secondary shoe. Slide lower end of spacer strut out away from carrier plate and remove parking brake actuating lever and shoe from carrier plate.

6) Remove spring washer from secondary shoe. Separate longer ratchet lever from shoe. Remove spring washer from short ratchet and discard. Remove spring and short ratchet from shoe. Separate primary shoe from spacer strut and remove spring.

Installation — 1) Assemble primary shoe by installing lever return spring on shoe, then hooking spacer strut onto spring and lever. Assemble secondary shoe by positioning smaller ratchet and spring on shoe pivot. Slide two .008″ (.2 mm) feeler gauges between shoe and ratchet and install new spring retaining washer. Remove feeler gauges and check that ratchet rotates on pivot pin and returns freely with spring pressure.

NOTE — *Be sure parking brake lever rotates freely relative to spacer strut. Pin should be tightly riveted to lever and rotate in strut hole.*

2) Mount large ratchet on brake shoe with new spring clip. Seat clip fully (ratchet should rotate freely). Align ratchets with an overlap. Reverse removal procedure and install stronger return spring between pivot end of shoes (opposite wheel cylinder). Weak spring mounts between shoes at wheel cylinder.

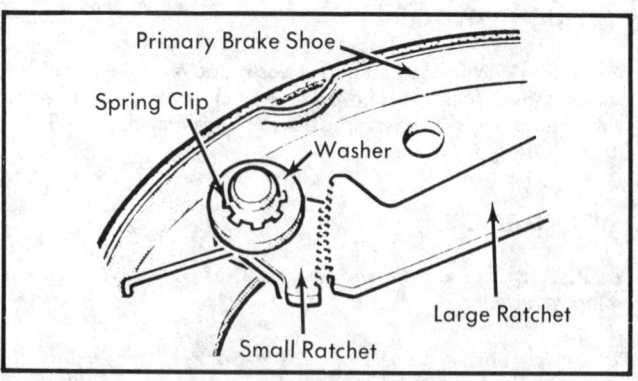

Fig. 5   *Assembling Ratchets on Brake Shoe*

3) Adjust outer wheel bearing by tightening nut to 15-18 ft. lbs. (2.0-2.4 mkg) while rotating drum counterclockwise.

FIESTA (Cont.)

Loosen nut ½ turn; retorque nut to 3.6-7.2 INCH Lbs. (4.15-8.30 cmkg) and install nut retainer. Install new cotter pin and put on dust cap. Pump brake pedal several times to adjust shoe-to-drum clearance. Road test for proper brake operation.

MASTER CYLINDER

NOTE — *If brake fluid contacts any painted surfaces, wash immediately with cold water.*

Removal — 1) Disconnect battery. Draw fluid from reservoir. Remove hydraulic lines and plug openings. Disconnect electrical connection from differential valve switch (if equipped).

2) From inside vehicle, disconnect push rod (booster linkage) from brake pedal. Remove master cylinder retaining nuts and remove master cylinder.

Installation — Reverse removal procedure, bleed hydraulic system and road test vehicle.

POWER BRAKE UNIT

Removal — With master cylinder removed; remove operating rod from brake pedal. Disconnect vacuum line from booster. Remove booster mounting nuts and remove booster.

Installation — Reverse removal procedure and bleed hydraulic system.

OVERHAUL

FRONT DISC BRAKE CALIPER

Disassembly — Remove piston rubber bellows. To remove piston, force air pressure or low hydraulic pressure into piston via brake fluid inlet port. Remove piston seal with pointed tool.

Cleaning & Inpsection — Clean piston and caliper bore with alcohol or brake fluid. Check piston and bore for wear, scoring, scratches or other damage. Replace defective parts.

Reassembly — Fit piston seal in piston housing groove. Lightly coat piston with brake fluid. Push piston into bore until fully seated. Make sure piston seal is not damaged as piston is seated. Fit piston rubber bellows between piston housing and piston seal.

WHEEL CYLINDER

Disassembly — Remove dust covers. Force out piston assemblies from cylinder bore. Separate piston seals from spring and flat side of piston. Remove bleed screw, if necessary.

Cleaning & Inspection — Clean cylinder bore and pistons in alcohol or brake fluid. Check pistons and cylinder bore for scratches or scoring. Replace defective parts.

Reassembly — Install dust covers on pistons. Install one piston and dust cover in position. From opposite end, slide in piston seal (flat side first), spring, piston seal (flat side out), piston and dust cover. Install bleeder screw.

MASTER CYLINDER

Disassembly — 1) Separate reservoir from master cylinder and remove rubber seals. Support cylinder in a soft-jaw vise. Depress push rod to relieve piston stop pin pressure and remove stop pin.

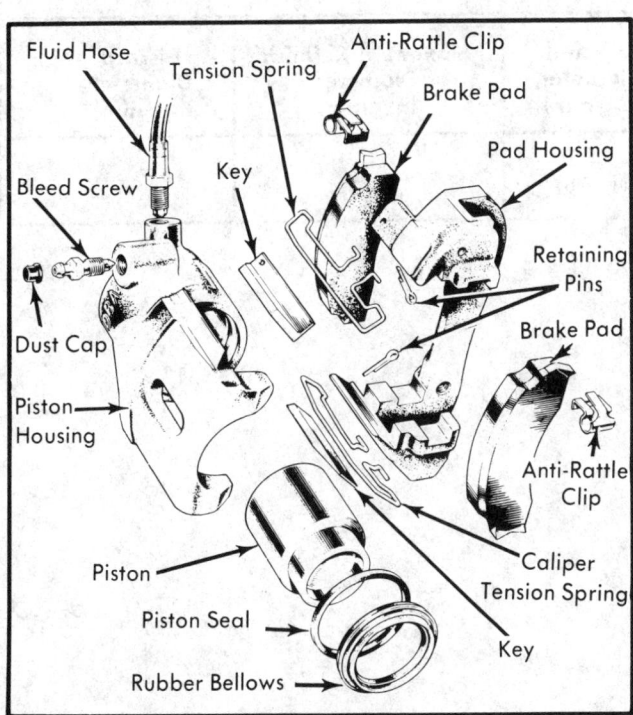

Fig. 6   Exploded View of Front Disc Brake Caliper

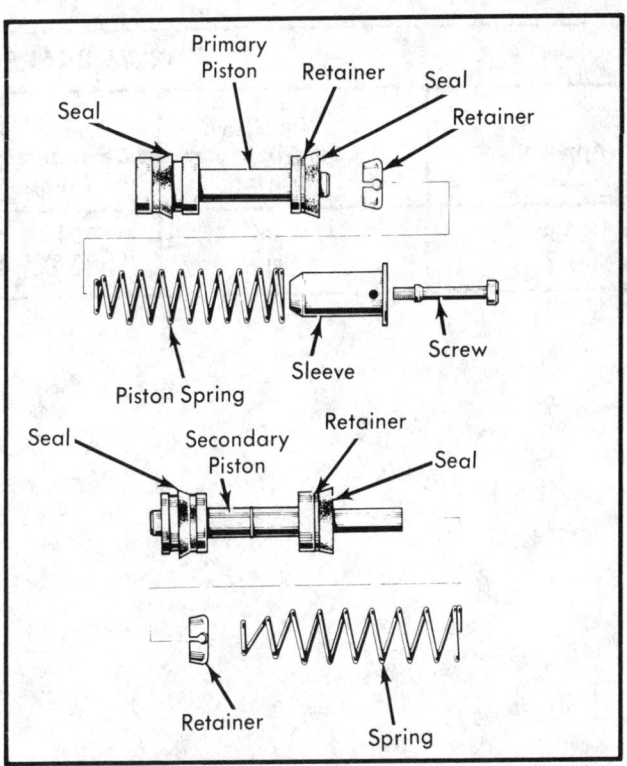

Fig. 7   Exploded View of Master Cylinder Piston Assemblies

FIESTA (Cont.)

2) Peel back dust boot and remove retaining clip. Remove push rod, boot and washer. Separate components. Remove primary piston assembly. Tap master cylinder in palm of hand to jar out secondary piston. Remove screw in primary piston and disassemble piston assemblies.

Cleaning & Inspection — Clean all parts in alcohol or brake fluid. Check cylinder bore and pistons for wear, scratches and corrosion. Replace defective parts. Replace all rubber parts during overhaul.

Reassembly — 1) Correctly install new secondary piston seals and secure with retainer. Lightly coat secondary piston assembly with brake fluid, slide spring and piston assembly into cylinder bore. Install new primary piston seals and secure with retainer, spring, sleeve and screw.

2) Lightly coat primary piston assembly with brake fluid and insert in cylinder bore (spring first). Install new rubber boot on push rod and install washer. Install rod in master cylinder and secure with new retaining clip. Mount rubber boot on master cylinder. Depress push rod and insert piston stop pin in secondary inlet port. Install reservoir and rubber seals.

TIGHTENING SPECIFICATIONS

Application	Ft. Lbs. (mkg)
Caliper-to-Front Suspension Unit	38-45 (5.3-6.2)
Carrier Plate-to-Axle Housing	15-18 (2.1-2.5)

DISC BRAKE SPECIFICATIONS

Application	Caliper Bore Diameter In. (mm)	Lateral Runout In. (mm)	Parallelism In. (mm)	Original Thickness In. (mm)	Minimum Refinish Thickness In. (mm)	Discard Thickness In. (mm)
Hatchback	1.89 (48)	.006 (.15)	.....	.39 (10)	.....	.37 (8.7)

DRUM BRAKE SPECIFICATIONS

Application	Wheel Cyl. Bore Diameter In. (mm)	Drum Diameter In. (mm)	Original Diameter In. (mm)	Maximum Refinish Diameter In. (mm)	Discard Diameter In. (mm)
Hatchback	.59 (15)	7.00 (177.8)	7.00 (177.8)	.....	.....

HONDA

Accord
Civic
Prelude

DESCRIPTION

Brake system is hydraulically operated using a tandem master cylinder and vacuum brake unit. All models are equipped with single piston, floating caliper, front disc brakes and leading/trailing rear drum brakes. All models use dual valve combination valves to prevent premature rear wheel lock-up. A brake warning light is mounted on the dash to indicate loss of brake fluid, uneven fluid pressure between brake systems and parking brake engagement. Parking brake is cable actuated at rear wheels.

ADJUSTMENT

REAR DRUM BRAKE SHOES

Accord — Raise and support rear of vehicle. Release parking brake and make 2-3 brake applications. Turn brake adjuster on backing plate clockwise until wheel locks. Back off adjuster 2 clicks, rotate wheel; if brakes drag, back off 1 additional click.

Except Accord — Rear brake shoes are self-adjusted by brake pedal action. No adjustment in-service is required.

PEDAL HEIGHT

Pedal height is measured from center of pedal pad to floor-board (without carpet). To adjust, loosen stop light switch lock nut and position switch out of way. Loosen power unit push rod lock nut and rotate push rod until pedal height is 7.25" (184 mm). Tighten lock nut, reposition and adjust stop light switch.

STOP LIGHT SWITCH

Stop light switch is located under dash, above brake pedal. To adjust, turn switch until plunger is fully depressed (threaded end touching pedal arm pad). Back off switch ½ turn and tighten lock nuts. Check that brake lights go off when pedal is released.

PARKING BRAKE

With rear brakes adjusted, raise and support rear of vehicle on safety stands. Loosen equalizer nut (located between rear lower control arms) and pull brake lever up 1 notch. Tighten adjusting nut until rear wheels drag slightly. Release brake lever; rear wheels should rotate freely. Rear wheels should lock when lever is pulled 4-8 notches on Civic and 3-7 notches on Accord and Prelude.

BRAKE WARNING LIGHT

Light indicates parking brake is engaged and also warns of low brake fluid level. To adjust light operation with parking brake applied, bend switch plate down until light comes on when brake lever is pulled 1 notch and goes out when lever is released (ignition on). To check warning light operation, release parking brake lever and raise master cylinder reservoir cap (ignition on). Warning light should glow; if not, check switch and wire connector.

REMOVAL & INSTALLATION

FRONT DISC BRAKE PADS

Removal (Civic Hatchback & Prelude) — Raise and support vehicle; remove tire and wheel. Remove lower caliper guide pin and pivot caliper body up out of way. Remove pads, pad shim and anti-rattle springs.

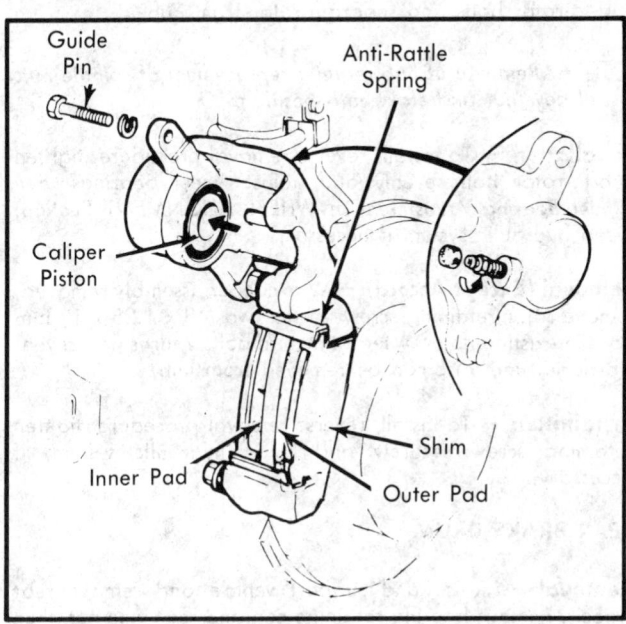

Fig. 1   Replacing Front Disc Brake Pads (Civic Hatchback and Prelude)

Installation — Install anti-rattle springs and pads. Install shim against outer pad. Loosen bleed screw, seat piston in caliper bore and tighten bleed screw. Rotate caliper body down and tighten lower caliper guide pin. Depress brake pedal several times to seat brake pads.

Removal (Except Civic Hatchback & Prelude) — Raise and support vehicle; remove tire and wheel. Remove spring clips and guide plates. Remove caliper body and hang from frame with wire; DO NOT disconnect hydraulic line or allow caliper to hang by hydraulic line. Remove anti-rattle clips, pads and shim(s).

NOTE — *Shims for Accord must have high temperature grease (Dow Corning DC# 5 or equivalent) applied to red sides. Install red coated side against brake pad backing plate.*

Installation — Install anti-rattle clips and pads. Install shim(s); shim on Civic Station Wagon is installed at outer pad. Loosen bleed screw, seat piston in caliper bore and tighten bleed screw. Install caliper, guide plates and spring clips. Depress brake pedal several times to seat brake pads.

FRONT DISC BRAKE CALIPER

Removal — Raise and support vehicle; remove tire and wheel. Disconnect and plug hydraulic line at caliper. On Civic Hatchback and Prelude, remove caliper guide pins and remove caliper. On Civic Station Wagon and Accord, remove spring pins and guide plates, then remove caliper. Remove disc pads as previously described and remove caliper mounting bracket.

Brakes

HONDA (Cont.)

Installation — To install, reverse removal procedure and bleed hydraulic system.

DISC BRAKE ROTOR

Removal (Accord) — With caliper assembly removed, remove cotter pin and spindle nut. Using a slide hammer with hub puller attachment, remove hub and rotor assembly. Remove hub-to-rotor bolts and separate rotor from hub.

NOTE — *Removal of hub requires replacement of spindle nut. Install new nut and stake into position.*

Installation — To install, reverse removal procedure, tighten hub-to-rotor bolts evenly and adjust wheel bearings. *See Wheel Bearing Adjustment in WHEEL ALIGNMENT Section.* Bleed hydraulic system if necessary.

Removal (Except Accord) — With caliper assembly removed, remove rotor retaining screw. Install two M8 x 1.25 x 12 mm bolts in existing holes. Alternately turn bolts 2 turns (to prevent warpage) until disc can be removed from hub.

Installation — To install, reverse removal procedure, tighten retaining screw securely and bleed hydraulic system, if necessary.

REAR BRAKE DRUM

Removal — Raise and support vehicle and remove rear wheels. Remove bearing retaining cap and rear axle nut, then remove brake drum.

NOTE — *If drum is difficult to remove, use slide hammer with hub puller attachment.*

Installation — To install, reverse removal procedure and tighten axle nut.

REAR BRAKE SHOES

NOTE — *All models use same basic brake design. Some minor variations may exist between systems.*

Removal — With brake drum removed, remove retaining clips and pins and return springs (note original position of return springs). Disconnect brake shoes from parking brake lever assembly and remove brake shoes.

NOTE — *Upper and lower return springs are not interchangeable.*

Installation — Apply light coat of grease to adjuster assembly, sliding surfaces of brake shoes and metal contact areas of backing plate. To install, reverse removal procedure, observing the precautions listed below for each model. Adjust and bleed brakes.

- Accord — Upper return spring has small loops and is installed between shoes with coils facing outward. Lower spring has larger loops and is installed with coils facing inward.

- Civic & Prelude — Upper return spring is identified by single coil. Before installing brake drum, release brake adjuster ratchet with screwdriver. Mark engaged teeth. Install drum and spindle nut. Depress brake pedal, remove drum and ensure ratchet has moved and brakes have self-adjusted.

MASTER CYLINDER

Removal — Disconnect hydraulic lines at master cylinder, remove retaining nuts, and remove master cylinder from power brake unit.

Installation — To install, reverse removal procedure and bleed hydraulic system.

POWER BRAKE UNIT

Removal — Disconnect vacuum hose at power brake unit, and hydraulic lines at master cylinder. Remove clevis pin retaining power brake unit push rod to brake pedal, and bolts attaching power unit to firewall, then remove power brake unit and master cylinder as an assembly.

Installation — To install, reverse removal procedure, tighten all bolts and bleed hydraulic system.

Check Valve Replacement — Check valve is located in vacuum line between brake unit and intake manifold. Before removal, test check valve. Disconnect valve from vacuum hose by removing clamps. Blow air through manifold side of valve; valve should not open. Repeat procedure on booster side of valve; valve should open. Replace defective valve and secure clamps.

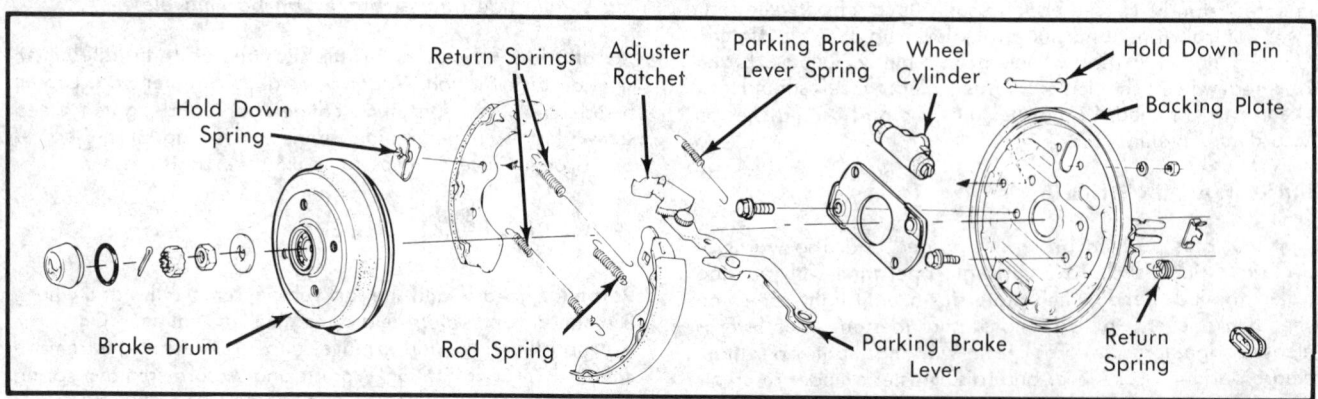

Fig. 2 Exploded View of Civic and Prelude Rear Brake

HONDA (Cont.)

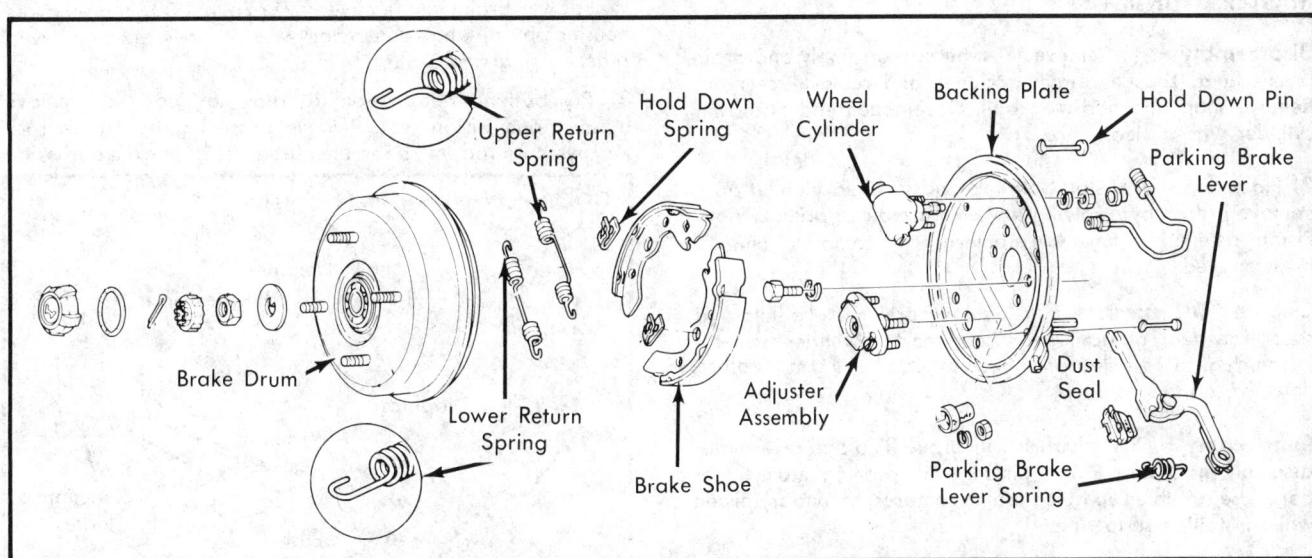

Fig. 3 Exploded View of Accord Rear Brake Assembly

OVERHAUL

DISC BRAKE CALIPER

Disassembly — Remove retaining ring (if equipped), then remove piston boot. Place rags in front of piston and force piston out of caliper bore by applying light (30 psi) air pressure to brake fluid inlet port. Remove piston seal without damaging cylinder bore.

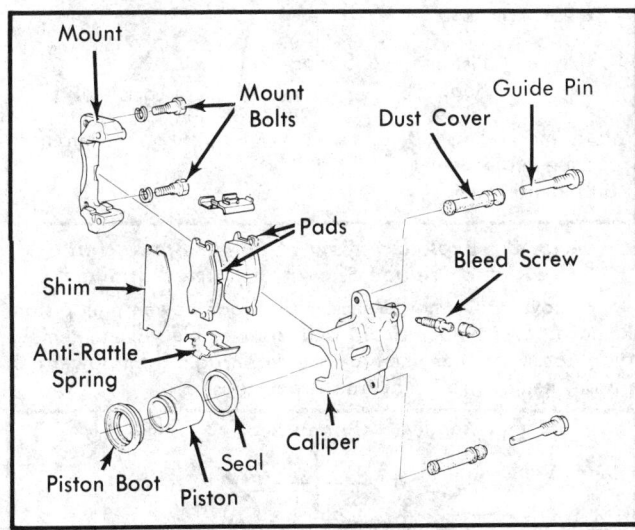

Fig. 4 Exploded View of Front Disc Brake Caliper (Civic Hatchback and Prelude)

Cleaning & Inspection — Clean all parts in brake fluid and check for wear or damage. Check cylinder bore and pistons; replace if scratched or scored. Replace all rubber components during overhaul.

Reassembly — Apply brake fluid to caliper bore, piston surface and piston seal. Reverse disassembly procedure and make sure seals and boots are properly installed.

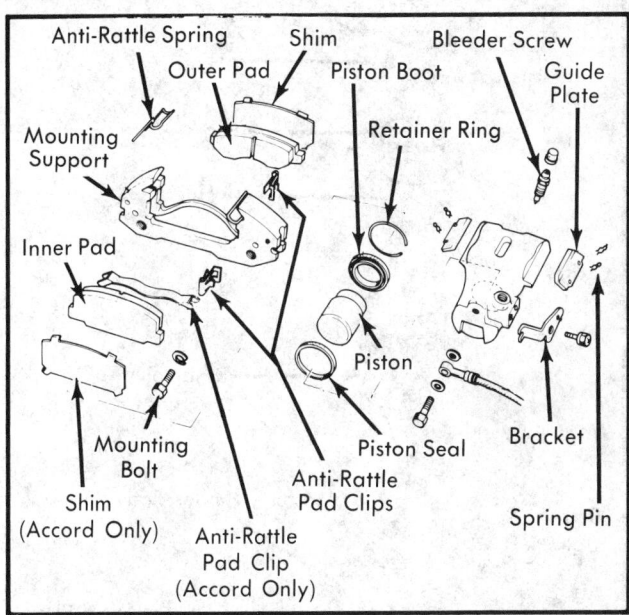

Fig. 5 Exploded View of Front Disc Brake Caliper (Accord Shown — Civic Station Wagon Similar)

REAR WHEEL CYLINDER

Disassembly — Remove dust seals and pistons. Remove cylinder cups from pistons. If necessary, remove bleeder screw.

Cleaning & Inspection — Clean all parts in brake fluid and check for wear or damage, replace parts. Check cylinder bore-to-piston clearance; if clearance exceeds .005" (.13 mm) on Accord or .004" (.10 mm) on all other models, replace defective part.

Reassembly — Coat cylinder bore, pistons and cups with brake fluid. Reverse disassembly procedure and install parts in cylinder bore. Install dust covers securely in cylinder body grooves.

NOTE — *Lips of piston cups must face center of cylinder.*

HONDA (Cont.)

MASTER CYLINDER

Disassembly — 1) Remove reservoir cap assembly and drain brake fluid. Loosen retaining clamp and remove reservoir. Remove snap ring and stop bolt. Cover open end of master cylinder with a clean rag.

2) Place finger over stop bolt hole and secondary outlet port. Remove pistons by applying low pressure air to primary port. Piston assemblies must be replaced as complete units if disassembled.

Cleaning & Inspection — Clean all parts in brake fluid and check for wear or damage. Check master cylinder bore-to-piston clearance. If clearance exceeds .006″ (.15 mm), replace defective part.

Reassembly — Coat all parts with brake fluid and reverse disassembly procedure. Rotate pistons while pushing into cylinder bore. Use suitable cup guide tool to compress secondary piston when installing snap ring.

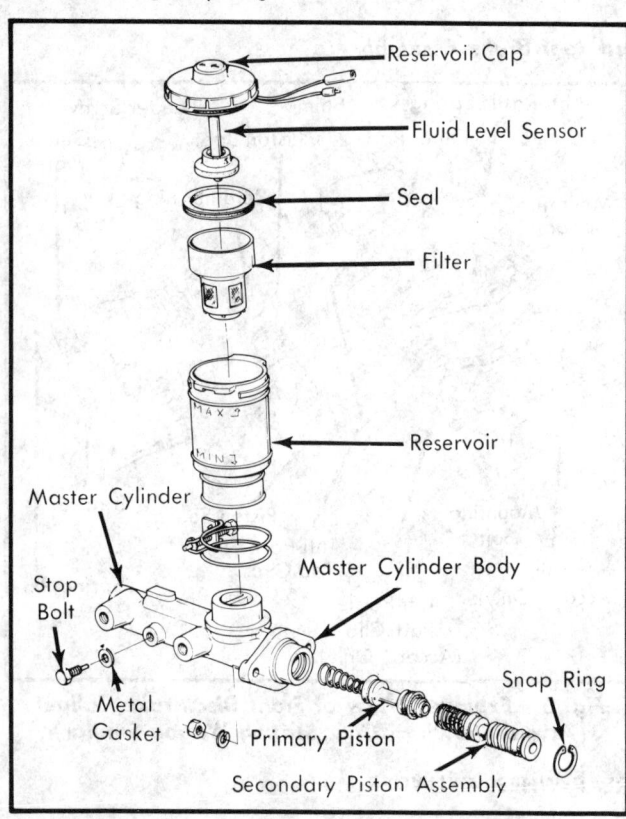

Fig. 6   Exploded View of Master Cylinder

POWER BRAKE UNIT

NOTE — *Power brake units vary among models; overhaul procedures are the same for all models.*

Disassembly — 1) Remove master cylinder, but leave retaining plate attached to front housing. Remove spring clip and retaining tab (except Accord), then remove push rod from master cylinder.

CAUTION — *Housing assemblies are spring loaded.*

2) Place power brake unit in vise with rear housing upward. Index housing shells. Remove retaining bolts (Accord only). In-

stall power brake unit remover (079676340000) and separate housings by turning counterclockwise. Remove reaction cover, reaction ring and plates.

3) Pry bushing retainer out of rear housing, then remove bushing and piston seal. Remove snap ring from push rod. Remove push rod and boot, then separate boot from push rod.

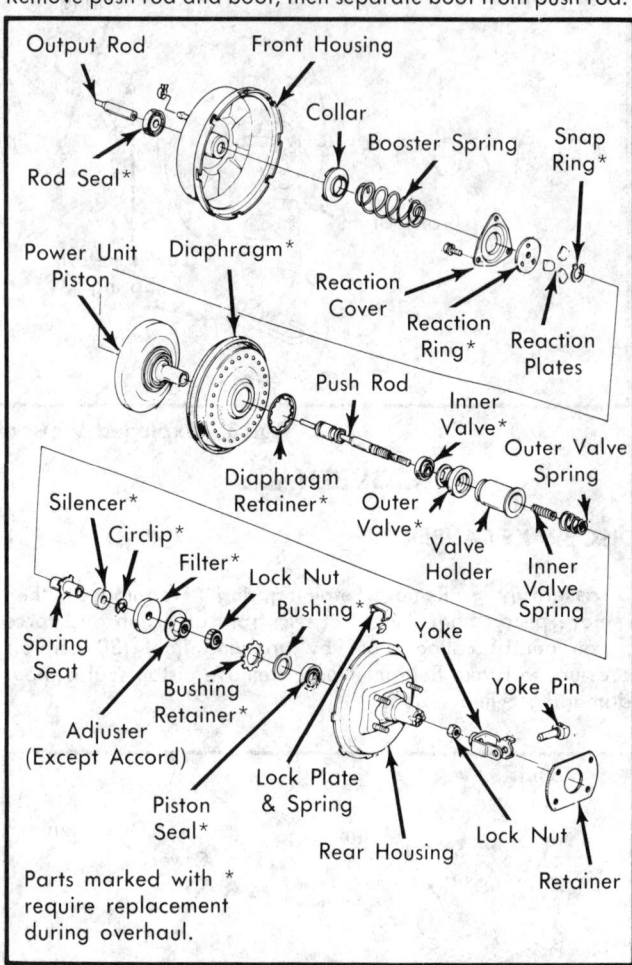

Parts marked with * require replacement during overhaul.

Fig. 7   Exploded View of Power Brake Unit (Civic and Prelude Shown — Accord Similar)

4) Remove valve holder assembly from power unit piston. Remove valve holder circlip and disassemble valves. Remove diaphragm retainer, then remove diaphragm from power unit piston. Remove rod seal from front housing.

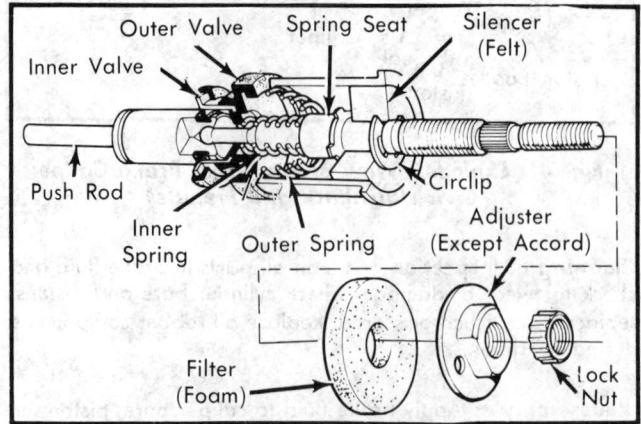

Fig. 8   Exploded View of Power Brake Valve Holder Assembly

HONDA (Cont.)

Cleaning & Inspection — Clean all parts in alcohol and dry with compressed air. Check all parts for wear or damage. Check booster piston for cracks or deformation. Replace all parts as indicated in illustration during overhaul.

Reassembly — 1) Apply silicone grease to rod seal lip and piston. Reverse disassembly and note the following: Ensure rod seal is fully seated and "O" ring is not twisted. Install reaction plate with curved sides up. Ensure diaphragm is properly seated.

2) Before installing valve assembly, coat inner valve with silicone grease. Assemble valve assembly as shown in *Fig. 8*. Install new diaphragm and retainer. Apply silicone grease to inner and outer surfaces of piston tube, then press valve holder assembly into piston tube.

3) Before installing master cylinder to power brake unit, check master cylinder-to-push rod clearance. Place rod bolt adjustment gauge (*Fig. 9*) on master cylinder open end with knurled knob up.

4) Turn screw until it just contacts piston. Remove gauge from master cylinder and place on power brake unit with knurled knob down. Without moving adjusting screw position, measure clearance between adjusting screw end and booster push rod. Clearance should be .004-.020" (.1-.6 mm) on Accord and 0-.016" (0-.4 mm) on all other models. If not, remove adjusting bolt, loosen lock nut and turn adjusting bolt to correct specification (Accord). On Civic and Prelude, set clearance by loosening star lock nut and turning adjuster.

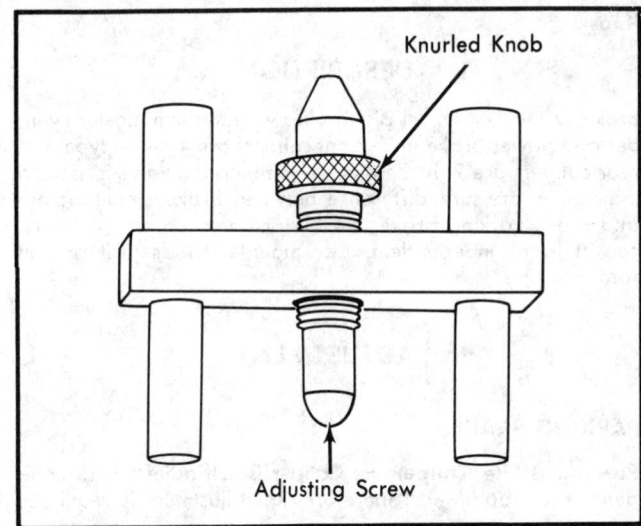

Fig. 9   Push Rod Adjustment Gauge

TIGHTENING SPECIFICATIONS

Application	Ft. Lbs. (mkg)
Hub-to-Rotor Bolts (Accord)	40 (5.5)
Caliper Mounting Bracket (All)	56 (7.7)
Caliper Guide Pin Bolts	
Civic Hatchback	20 (2.8)
Prelude	13 (1.8)

DISC BRAKE SPECIFICATIONS

Application	Caliper Bore Diameter In. (mm)	Lateral Runout In. (mm)	Parallelism In. (mm)	Original Thickness In. (mm)	Minimum Refinish Thickness In. (mm)	Discard Thickness In. (mm)
Accord & Prelude	.....	.006 (.15)	.0006 (.015)	47 (12)	.....	.39 (10)
Civic						
Hatchback	.....	.006 (.15)	.0006 (.015)	.43 (11)	.....	.35 (9)
Station Wagon	.....	.006 (.15)	.0006 (.015)	.47 (12)	.....	.39 (10)

DRUM BRAKE SPECIFICATIONS

Application	Wheel Cyl. Bore Diameter In. (mm)	Drum Diameter In. (mm)	Original Diameter In. (mm)	Maximum Refinish Diameter In. (mm)	Discard Diameter In. (mm)
Accord & Prelude	.....	7.09 (180)	7.09 (180)	7.13① (181)	.....
Civic					
Hatchback	.....	7.09 (180)	7.09 (180)	7.13① (181)	.....
Station Wagon	.....	7.87 (200)	7.87 (200)	7.91① (201)	.....

① — If maximum refinish diameter disagrees with specification stamped on drum; use stamped specification.

JAGUAR

XJ6

DESCRIPTION

Brake system is 4-wheel disc brakes with tandem master cylinder and power brake unit. Front calipers are 4 piston type and rear calipers are 2 piston type. A combination valve is used to indicate a pressure difference between brake circuits (front and rear). Parking brake is cable actuated on rear calipers, consisting of independent, disc mounted pads that act on rotor.

ADJUSTMENT

PARKING BRAKE

Parking Brake Caliper — Caliper is self-adjusting to compensate for pad wear, therefore, no adjustment is required.

Parking Brake Cable — Fully release parking brake lever. Loosen lock nut on front yoke and disconnect yoke from bell crank lever at clevis pin. Rotate yoke on adjusting rod so that when yoke is reconnected, there is a slight amount of slack in cable. Reconnect yoke and tighten lock nut.

BRAKE WARNING LIGHT

A dual warning light is mounted on instrument panel. Parking brake light should glow when parking brake lever is pulled one notch (ignition on) and go off when lever is fully released. To check circuit warning sensor, fully release parking brake and ensure light is off (ignition on). Open any bleed screw and light should glow. Close bleed screw, then release and reapply brake pedal; warning light should go out.

REMOVAL & INSTALLATION

DISC PADS (SERVICE BRAKES)

Removal — Raise vehicle and remove wheels. Remove pin clips, pad retaining pins, anti-chatter springs (if equipped) and lining pads.

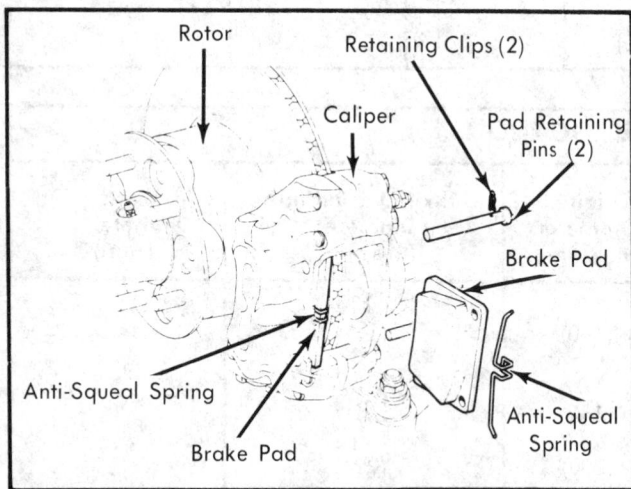

Fig. 1   Removing Front Disc Brake Pads

Installation — Draw out about half the brake fluid from reservoir(s). This will enable caliper pistons to be pushed back into cylinders without overflowing fluid. Lever pistons back, insert new pads, springs and replace retaining pins and clips. Check pads for freedom of movement within caliper. Check reservoirs for correct fluid level.

DISC PADS (PARKING BRAKE)

Removal & Installation — Parking brake calipers must be removed to replace disc pads. See *Parking Brake Caliper Removal & Installation.*

PARKING BRAKE CALIPER

Removal — **1)** Raise and support vehicle. Remove nuts and bolts attaching rear suspension mounting plate to rear suspension unit and remove plate from vehicle. Disconnect parking brake cable and return spring from caliper.

2) Remove caliper mounting bolts and release lever, then slide caliper around rotor and remove through hole left by suspension plate. To remove disc pads, remove nut and spring washer securing pads to pad carriers.

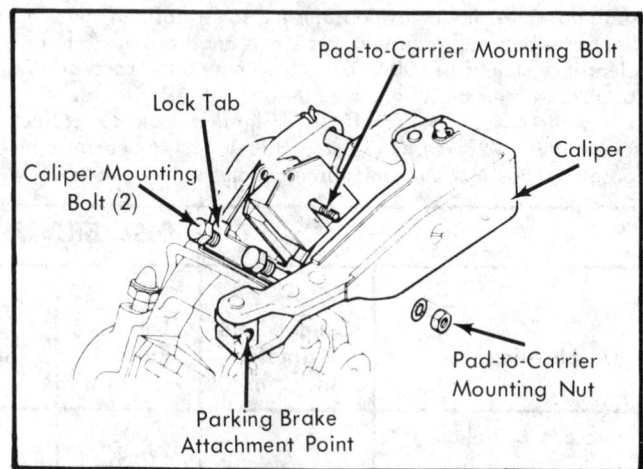

Fig. 2   Detail of Parking Brake Caliper

Installation — To install, reverse removal procedure and note the following: Adjust caliper if new pads have been installed or if caliper has been overhauled. Adjust by holding one pad carrier stationary and turning remaining carrier until there is a clearance of .75" (19 mm) between disc pad surfaces. Operate caliper actuating lever until adjuster ratchet stops clicking. Install remaining components and check operation of brakes.

SERVICE BRAKE CALIPER

NOTE — *Do not separate caliper halves for repair. If a leak exists between halves, replace caliper*

Removal (Front) — Raise vehicle and remove wheels. Disconnect caliper fluid line and plug. Discard locking wire from mounting bolts. Remove caliper.

NOTE — *Check position and number of shims between steering arm and caliper; replace shims in order.*

JAGUAR (Cont.)

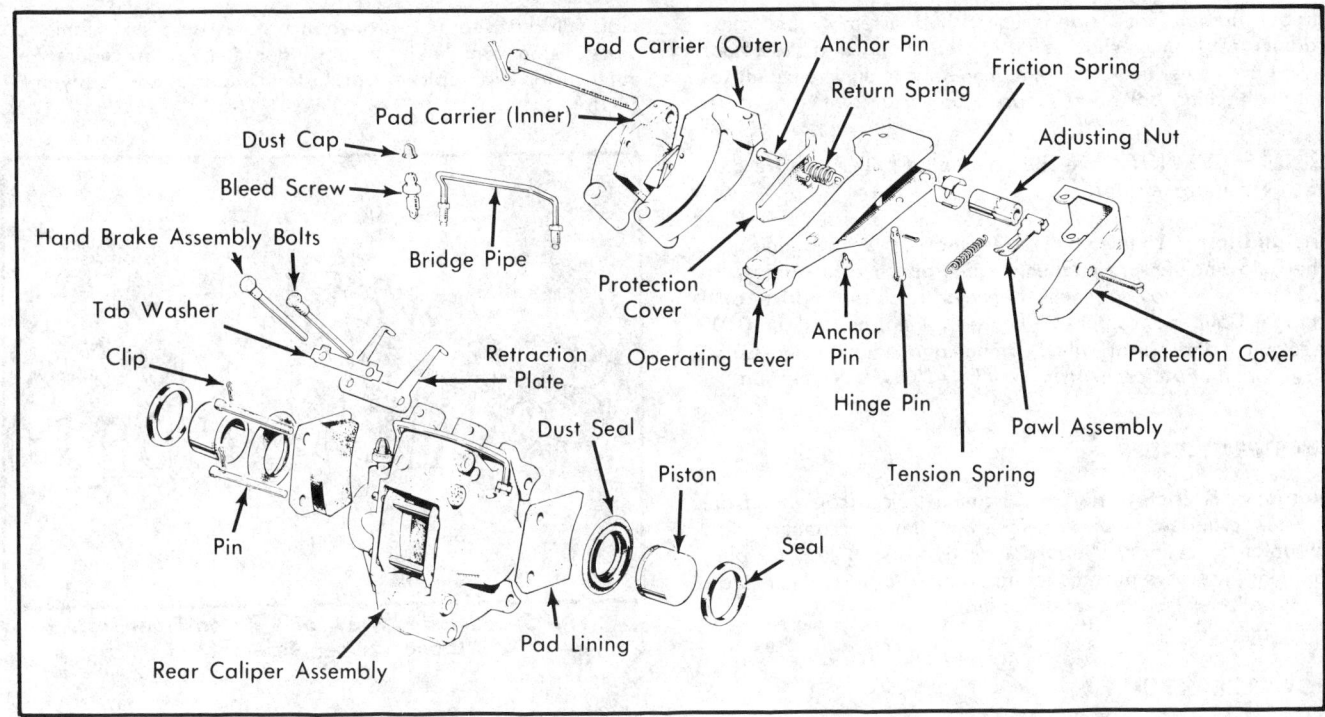

Fig. 3 Exploded View of Rear Brake Caliper with Detail of Parking Brake Assembly

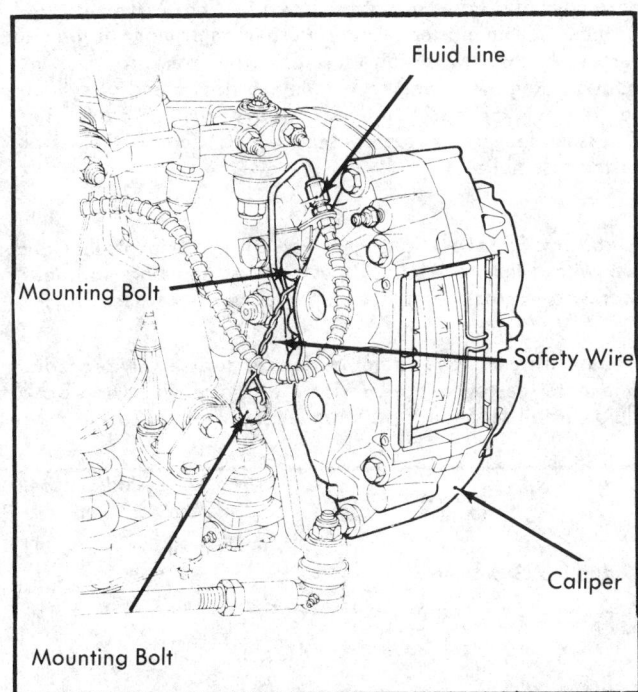

Fig. 4 Components to Remove to Allow Removal of Front Disc Brake Caliper

Installation — 1) Place caliper in position. If original caliper is being reinstalled, refit shims. Install mounting bolts and safety wire. Bleed brakes.

2) If new caliper is being used, check gap between caliper abutment and rotor face. Gap should be no more than .010" (.25 mm). Gap on upper and lower abutment on SAME SIDE must be equal. If rotor is not centered, remove one caliper

mounting bolt and add or subtract shims as necessary. Repeat procedure on other bolt.

Removal (Rear) — Remove parking brake caliper as previously outlined. Disconnect and plug hydraulic line from caliper mounting bolts and lock wire. Slide caliper around brake rotor and out hole left by suspension plate.

Installation — Place caliper in position, install shims (if equipped) and secure bolts. Check rotor for centering between caliper. If necessary, adjust shims between drive flange and rotor. If shim adjustment is performed, rear wheel camber must be checked. See *Jaguar Rear Wheel Camber Adjustment in WHEEL ALIGNMENT Section.* Complete installation by reversing removal procedure.

BRAKE ROTOR

Removal (Front) — 1) Remove brake caliper as previously outlined. Remove hub-to-rotor attaching bolts and washers. Remove hub dust cap, then remove cotter pin, axle nut and washer from axle stub and remove hub.

2) Insert a punch through access hole in splash shield and lightly tap on it to free water deflector. Remove rotor assembly by sliding it from caliper jaws and over axle stub.

Installation — To install, reverse removal procedure and note the following: Pack hub and wheel bearings with suitable grease and adjust wheel bearing end play. See *Wheel Bearing Adjustment in WHEEL ALIGNMENT Section.*

Removal (Rear) — Remove brake caliper as previously outlined. Disconnect shock absorber from lower mount and remove radius arm locking bolt and lower control arm outer

JAGUAR (Cont.)

grease fitting. Place stands under hub assembly and slide radius arm from anchor point. Loosen clamp and slide boot away from inner universal joint, then remove universal joint-to-rotor attaching bolts and separate universal joint from rotor.

NOTE — *DO NOT move shims mounted between drive axle flange and brake rotor.*

Installation — To install, reverse removal procedure and note the following: Ensure caliper is centered on rotor; adjust by adding or removing shims between rotor and drive axle flange. Caliper is centered when gap is not more than .010" (.25 mm). Check rear wheel camber and adjust if necessary. See *Camber Adjustment* in WHEEL ALIGNMENT Section.

MASTER CYLINDER

Removal & Installation — Disconnect electrical wires from master cylinder reservoir. Remove filter. Disconnect clips mounted to cylinder. Separate all hydraulic lines and plug openings. Remove nuts mounting cylinder to power unit studs. To install, reverse removal procedure.

POWER BRAKE UNIT

Removal — **1)** Disconnect battery. Disconnect and plug master cylinder lines. Pry vacuum hose from power unit. Remove fluid reservoir.

2) Remove bolt securing upper pedal box. Remove reservoir mounting bracket and stop light switch. Remove 6 bolts attaching pedal box. Remove brake pedal pad. Withdraw pedal box, master cylinder and power brake unit as an assembly, then separate.

Installation — To install, reverse removal procedure and bleed hydraulic system.

OVERHAUL

BRAKE CALIPER

NOTE — *DO NOT separate caliper halves for service; pistons and seals may be changed without splitting caliper. If a leak is detected between caliper halves, replace caliper as a unit.*

Disassembly — With disc pads removed, install a suitable piston clamp to retain outboard piston(s), then apply compressed air to fluid inlet port and remove inboard piston(s). Pull dust seal from piston(s) and caliper grooves. Carefully remove piston seal from cylinder.

NOTE — *Inboard piston(s) must be installed before outboard piston(s) can be removed.*

Cleaning & Inspection — Clean all parts in alcohol and inspect for wear or damage. Check cylinder bore and pistons for scratches, rust or corrosion; replace all damaged parts.

Reassembly — Coat cylinder, piston and seal with brake fluid before installing. Place piston seal in bore. Install dust seal over cylinder groove and carefully insert piston through dust

seal. Pull dust seal into groove in piston. Use piston clamp to press piston completely into cylinder. Repeat procedure for outer piston seal replacement. Install caliper as previously outlined.

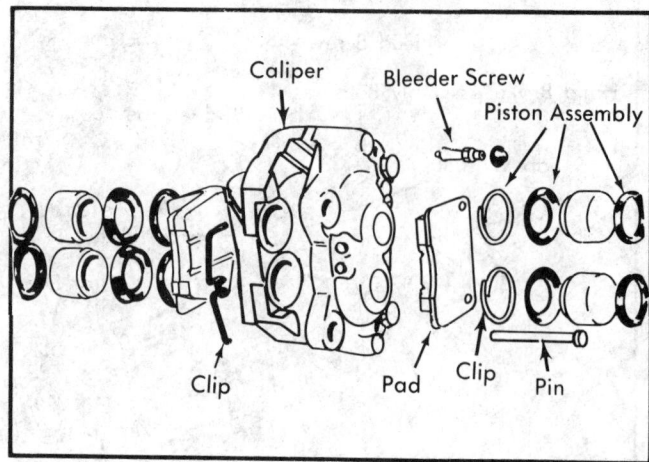

Fig. 5   Exploded View of 4 Piston Front Disc Brake Caliper Assembly

MASTER CYLINDER

Disassembly — With master cylinder removed from vehicle, carefully pry hose adapters from sealing grommets and grommets from master cylinder. Push in on primary piston and remove secondary piston stop pin from forward grommet housing. Remove spring lock, then tap flange end of cylinder to remove primary and secondary piston assemblies. Disassemble springs, spring seats, seals and washers from piston assemblies.

Cleaning & Inspection — Clean all parts in alcohol and dry with a lint-free cloth. Inspect pistons and bore for wear, scores, or corrosion; replace damaged parts as necessary.

Reassembly — To reassemble, reverse disassembly procedure and note the following: Lubricate all parts with clean brake fluid. Install secondary piston inner seal with lip facing away

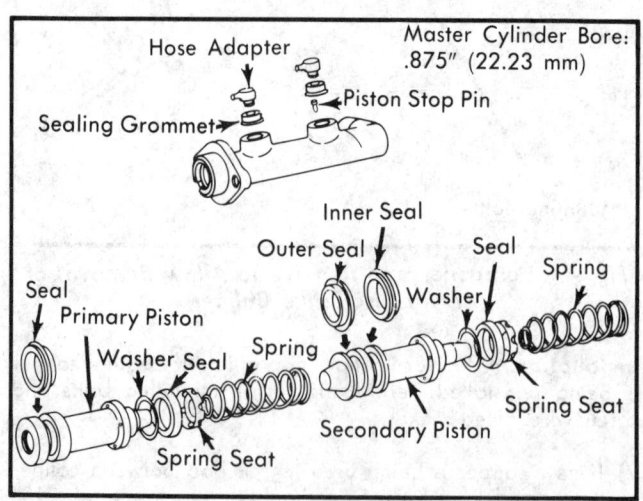

Fig. 6   Exploded View of Master Cylinder Assembly

Brakes

JAGUAR (Cont.)

from primary piston and install outer seal with lip facing primary piston. Install primary piston seal with lip facing away from spring lock. Install master cylinder and bleed brake system.

POWER BRAKE UNIT

NOTE — *Power brake unit CANNOT be overhauled; if determined defective, replace entire unit.*

TIGHTENING SPECIFICATIONS

Application	Ft. Lbs. (mkg)
Caliper Mounting Bolts	
Front	50-60 (7.0-8.3)
Rear	49-55 (6.7-7.6)

DISC BRAKE SPECIFICATIONS

Application	Caliper Bore Diameter In. (mm)	Lateral Runout In. (mm)	Parallelism In. (mm)	Original Thickness In. (mm)	Minimum Refinish Thickness In. (mm)	Discard Thickness In. (mm)
XJ6						
Front	.....	.004 (.1)	.....	.950 (24.1)	.....	.....
Rear	.....	.004 (.1)	.....	.500 (12.7)	.....	.....

LUV

Pickup

DESCRIPTION

Brake system is hydraulically operated using a tandem master cylinder and vacuum power brake unit. Front brakes are single piston, floating disc; rear brakes are duo-servo drum. A combination valve is used in all brake systems and is equipped with a fail indicator switch. If hydraulic pressure varies between front and rear systems; warning light on instrument panel will light. Warning light will glow until defect has been repaired. Parking brake is cable actuated on rear drums.

ADJUSTMENT

REAR DRUM BRAKE SHOES

Rear brakes self-adjust on reverse brake applications. No in-service adjustment is required. Initial adjustment must be made after changing brake linings or adjuster setting has been changed. To adjust, place vehicle on safety stands and follow one of the below methods:

Preferred Method — Remove brake drum. Measure drum diameter with drum-to-brake shoe gauge (J-21177); transfer gauge to brake shoes. Adjust star wheel until gauge just slides over linings. Install drum; lower car. Make final adjustment by making alternate forward and reverse brake applications until pedal height remains constant.

Alternate Method — Remove adjuster access plugs. Rotate star wheel until drum rotates with slight drag. Back off star wheel 1¼ turns; install access plugs. Lower vehicle and make final adjustment by making alternate forward and reverse brake applications until pedal height is constant.

PEDAL HEIGHT

Pedal height (measured from pedal pad center to floorboard) should be 5.9-6.3" (150-160 mm). To adjust, disconnect negative battery cable and stop light switch electrical lead. Remove stop light switch from bracket. Rotate push rod to obtain correct pedal height. Install and adjust stop light switch. Install electrical leads.

STOP LIGHT SWITCH

Stop light switch is located under dash, above brake pedal. To adjust, loosen lock nut and adjust clearance at switch housing (not actuating pin) and brake pedal tab to .02-.04" (.5-1 mm). Tighten lock nut.

PARKING BRAKE

NOTE — *Service brake must be properly adjusted prior to parking brake adjustment.*

Apply parking brake 2 notches from fully released position. Loosen equalizer check nut and adjust front jam nut until a light to moderate drag is felt when rear wheels are rotated forward. Tighten nuts securely, release parking brake and ensure no drag is present.

BRAKE WARNING LIGHT

A dual warning light is mounted on dash. Light should glow when parking brake lever is pulled 1 notch and go off when

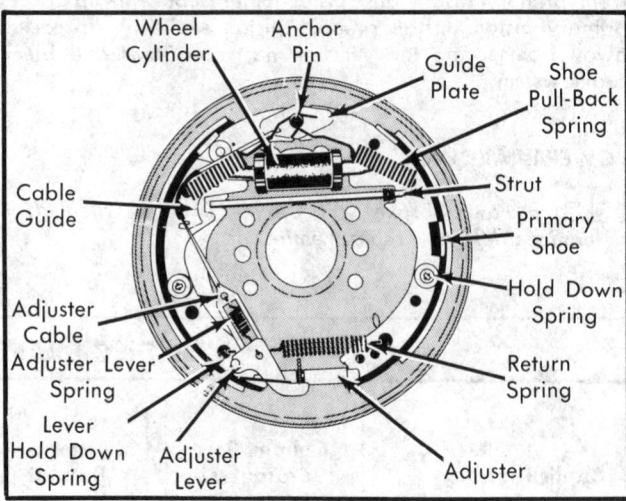

Fig. 1   Rear Brake Drum Assembly

lever is fully released (ignition on). To check circuit warning sensor, release parking brake (ignition on) and ensure light is off. Open bleed screw on 1 wheel and depress brake pedal; light should glow.

REMOVAL & INSTALLATION

FRONT DISC BRAKE PADS

Removal — **1)** Raise and support vehicle on safety stands; remove tire and wheel. Remove caliper stop spring pins and stops. Remove caliper from support and remove stop plates from caliper. Suspend caliper from frame with wire. DO NOT damage flex hose.

2) Remove pads and shims (mark pads if they are to be reused). Remove anti-rattle springs from support. Replace pads if they have less than .039" (1 mm) of lining left. Always replace pads in axle sets.

Installation — Reverse removal procedure and note the following: Original pads must be installed in original position. Install pads to supports with wear indicators facing LOWER SIDE. Apply brake lubricant to shims, stop plates and caliper sliding surfaces.

NOTE — *Manufacturer recommends replacing stop plates and pins.*

FRONT DISC BRAKE CALIPER

Removal — Raise and support vehicle on safety stands; remove tire and wheel. Remove caliper stop spring pins and stops. Disconnect hydraulic flex hose from brake line and plug openings. Remove caliper from support. Remove stop plates from caliper. Remove support mounting bolts and support assembly.

Installation — Reverse removal procedure and note the following: Apply brake grease to stop plates and caliper sliding surfaces. Flex hose identification stripe must follow a straight line with no binding. Install new stop plates and pins. Bleed hydraulic system.

LUV (Cont.)

FRONT DISC BRAKE ROTOR

Removal — With caliper removed, remove caliper support bolts and support. Remove grease cap, cotter pin, spindle nut retainer and nut. Remove hub and rotor assembly without dropping wheel bearings. Separate only if replacing either component.

Installation — Reverse removal procedure and adjust wheel bearings. *See Wheel Bearing Adjustment in WHEEL ALIGNMENT Section.* Tighten caliper support bolts evenly and bleed hydraulic system if necessary.

REAR BRAKE DRUM

Removal — Raise and support vehicle on safety stands; remove tire and wheel. Remove retaining screws and brake drum (neutralize shoes if required). Mark drum for reassembly reference.

Installation — To install drums, reverse removal procedures. Install drums in original position. Adjust brakes.

REAR BRAKE SHOES

Removal — **1)** With drum removed, remove shoe pull-back springs, hold down springs, pins and retainers. Remove adjuster lever spring, adjuster cable and guide plate.

2) Remove adjuster lever and lever hold down spring. Remove brake shoes as an assembly. Separate primary and secondary shoes, adjuster, return spring and strut.

3) Separate parking brake lever and rear cable. Remove clip and washer and separate brake lever from secondary shoe.

Installation — Install parking brake lever to secondary shoe and rear cable to lever. Connect brake shoes together with return spring, and place adjuster screw into position, making sure star wheel is nearest secondary shoe. Install parking brake strut with spring on primary shoe end, then fit shoes to wheel cylinder push rods. Install hold down springs, self-adjuster assembly and return springs. Install drum and adjust and bleed hydraulic system.

MASTER CYLINDER

Removal — Disconnect battery ground cable. Disconnect hydraulic lines at master cylinder and cover ends to prevent entry of dirt. Remove bracket bolt at front end of cylinder, and nuts retaining cylinder to power unit, then remove master cylinder and gasket from power unit.

Installation — Reverse removal procedure, bleed hydraulic system and adjust pedal height if necessary.

POWER BRAKE UNIT

Removal — Disconnect battery ground cable. Disconnect hydraulic lines at master cylinder and cover ends to prevent entry of dirt. Remove bolts attaching bracket to master cylinder and fender and remove bracket. Disconnect vacuum line at power unit and place out of way. Disconnect brake pedal return spring and push rod. Remove nuts attaching power unit to firewall, and remove power unit and master cylinder as an assembly.

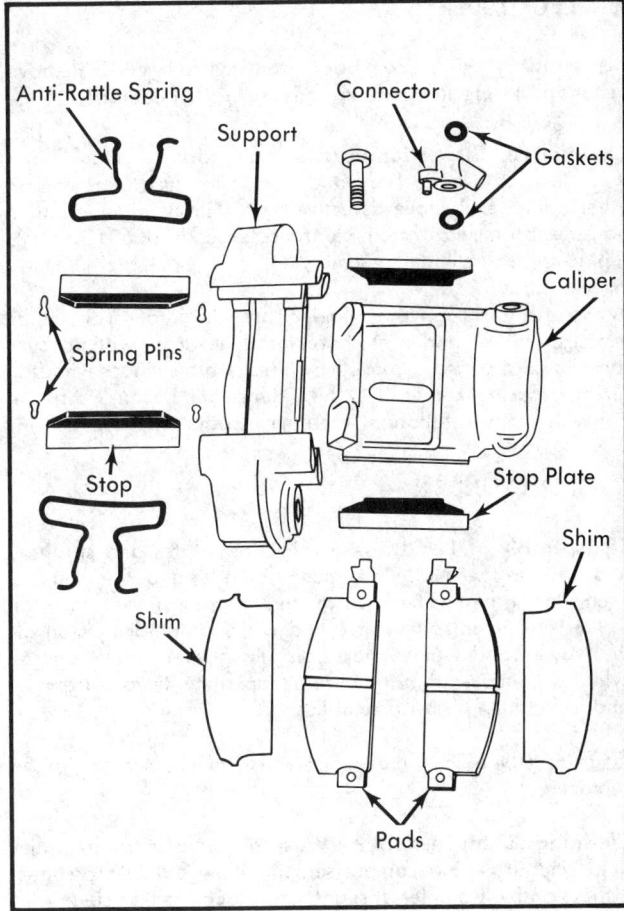

Fig. 2   Exploded View of Front Disc Brake Assy.

Installation — Reverse removal procedure, bleed hydraulic system and adjust pedal height if necessary.

OVERHAUL

FRONT DISC BRAKE CALIPER

Disassembly — Remove flex hose from caliper. Using pointed, but blunt instrument, remove seal from caliper. Place a block of wood between piston and caliper cavity wall, then apply enough compressed air pressure to force piston from cylinder. Remove and discard piston ring seal.

Cleaning & Inspection — Clean all parts in clean brake fluid and dry with filtered, dry, compressed air. Check cylinder bore and piston for wear, scuffing or corrosion. Replace if defective. Minor imperfections can be removed from caliper bore with crocus cloth. Replace dust seal and piston seal during overhaul.

NOTE — *DO NOT polish piston outer surfaces with abrasive.*

Reassembly — Lubricate piston seal and insert into caliper bore. Carefully insert piston into caliper assembly. Install dust seal on piston and caliper. Fit seal ring into dust seal.

LUV (Cont.)

WHEEL CYLINDER

Disassembly — Remove boots from cylinder ends. Remove pistons and cups. Remove expander springs, if equipped.

Cleaning & Inspection — Clean all parts in clean brake fluid. Inspect cylinder bore and pistons for rust, corrosion or other damage. Replace defective parts. Check wheel cylinder bore-to-piston clearance. If clearance exceeds .006" (.15 mm), replace wheel cylinder assembly.

Reassembly — Lubricate cylinder bore with clean brake fluid. Install spring expander into bore. Install new cups with flat surfaces toward outside. Install new pistons into cylinder with flat surfaces facing center. DO NOT lubricate pistons, cups or boots prior to installation. Press new boots onto cylinder.

MASTER CYLINDER

Disassembly — Remove reservoir caps, plates and strainers and drain brake fluid. Place master cylinder in a vise. Remove connector, gasket, check valve and return spring from rear system side (front outlet of cylinder). Push primary piston all the way in and remove stop bolt and gasket on left side of cylinder. Remove primary piston snap ring. Remove primary and secondary piston assemblies.

NOTE — *DO NOT remove reservoirs unless they are to be replaced.*

Cleaning & Inspection — Wash all parts in clean brake fluid and dry using compressed air. Blow out all passages, orifices and valve holes. If slight rust is found, polish clean with crocus cloth or emery paper. Inspect cylinder bore for scoring, pitting or other damage. Check cylinder bore-to-piston clearance; if clearance exceeds .006" (.15 mm), replace master cylinder. Replace all rubber parts and gaskets during overhaul.

Reassembly — Lubricate cylinder bore and all parts with clean brake fluid, reverse disassembly procedure, and note the following: Use all new gaskets and seals when reassembling. When reassembly is complete, bench bleed master cylinder as follows: Install plugs in all outlet ports of cylinder, fill reservoirs with clean brake fluid, and press in and out on primary piston until air bubbles are no longer seen in fluid.

POWER BRAKE UNIT

Disassembly — 1) Remove master cylinder reservoir and drain remaining brake fluid from cylinder. Scribe alignment marks on front and rear shells to assure reassembly in original position. Clamp flange of master cylinder in a vise with power unit up. Loosen push rod clevis lock nut and remove clevis and lock nut, then remove push rod boot.

2) Place suitable wrench (J-9504) over rear shell mounting studs. Press down on wrench while rotating counterclockwise and remove rear shell, piston rod, power piston, return spring and spring retainer. Remove nuts and lock washers and separate master cylinder and power unit front shell, then remove and discard gasket.

NOTE — *Power brake unit removal tool (J-9504) must be modified to fit brake unit.*

NOTE — *DO NOT disassemble push rod assembly; if defective, replace complete assembly.*

3) Pry retainer off power piston and remove air silencer and filter, then remove rubber diaphragm from piston. Rotate power piston until push rod retainer slot is down, then press in on rod, allowing retainer to fall out of power piston. Remove push rod assembly and reaction disc.

4) If rear shell is defective, pry out seal retainer and remove spacer and seal assembly. If front seal is defective, pry out retainer and remove seal. If vacuum check valve is defective, remove using a twisting motion, then remove grommet.

NOTE — *Do not clean parts with a mineral based solvent.*

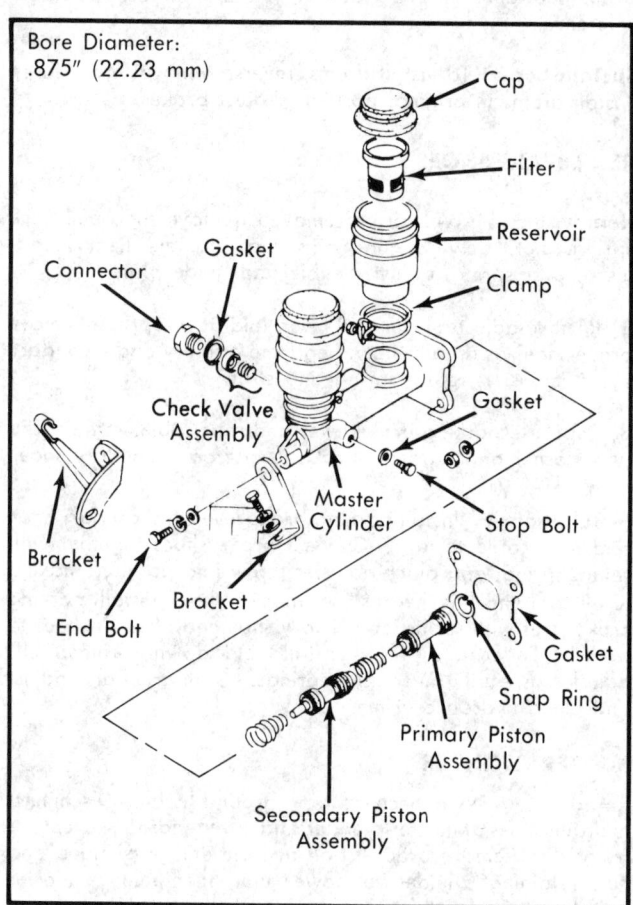

Bore Diameter: .875" (22.23 mm)

Fig. 3   Master Cylinder Assembly

Cleaning & Inspection — Clean all parts in denatured alcohol and blow dry with compressed air. Inspect inner surface of both shells for wear or damage; slight rust can be removed with fine emery cloth or crocus cloth. Inspect all parts for cracks, nicks, distortion or other damage; replace parts as necessary.

Reassembly — Reverse disassembly procedure and note the following: Apply a coat of silicone grease to parts before in-

LUV (Cont.)

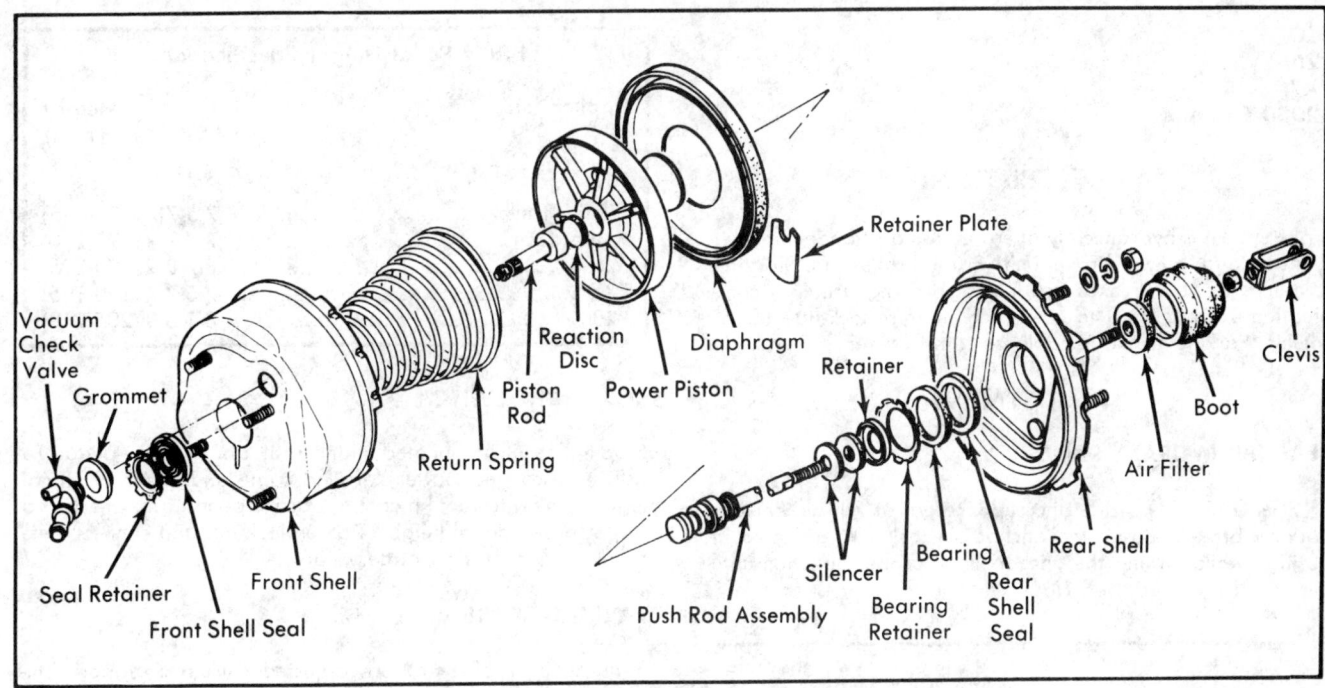

Vacuum Check Valve
Grommet
Seal Retainer
Front Shell Seal
Front Shell
Return Spring
Piston Rod
Reaction Disc
Power Piston
Diaphragm
Retainer Plate
Retainer
Silencer
Push Rod Assembly
Bearing Retainer
Bearing
Rear Shell Seal
Rear Shell
Air Filter
Boot
Clevis

Fig. 4 Exploded View of Power Brake Assembly

stallation. When assembling front shell to rear shell, ensure marks made at disassembly are aligned. When reassembly is completed, remove master cylinder from power unit. Place suitable gauge (J-24568) over piston rod so that legs rest on master cylinder mounting surface. Piston rod should touch cut-out portion of gauge. If rod must be adjusted, hold rod at serrated portion and turn threaded end.

NOTE — *Push rod must be bottomed in power unit before making adjustment.*

TIGHTENING SPECIFICATIONS

Application	Ft. Lbs. (mkg)
Rotor-to-Hub	36 (5.0)
Adapter-to-Knuckle	
Large Bolt	55 (7.6)
Small Bolt	35 (4.8)
Support-to-Adapter	64 (9.0)

DISC BRAKE SPECIFICATIONS

Application	Caliper Bore Diameter In. (mm)	Lateral Runout In. (mm)	Parallelism In. (mm)	Original Thickness In. (mm)	Minimum Refinish Thickness In. (mm)	Discard Thickness In. (mm)
Pickup	1.06 (26.9)	.005① (.13)	.0005 (.013)	.709 (18)	.668 (16.97)	.653 (16.6)

① — Max. rate of change must not exceed .001" (.03 mm) in 30°.

DRUM BRAKE SPECIFICATIONS

Application	Wheel Cyl. Bore Diameter In. (mm)	Drum Diameter In. (mm)	Original Diameter In. (mm)	Maximum Refinish Diameter In. (mm)	Discard Diameter In. (mm)
Pickup	.750 (19)	10.0 (254)	10.0 (254)	10.059 (255.5)	10.079 (255.6)

Brakes

MAZDA

GLC
626
RX7
B2000 Pickup

DESCRIPTION

Brake system is hydraulically operated using a tandem master cylinder and power brake unit. Front brakes are floating caliper disc; rear brakes are leading/trailing drum. A combination valve is used to prevent premature lock-up of rear wheels. Parking brake is cable actuated on rear wheels.

ADJUSTMENT

REAR DRUM BRAKE SHOES

RX7 & GLC — 1) Raise and support rear of vehicle. Release parking brake. Loosen the anchor pin lock nut and hold in position while turning the anchor pin in proper direction until the wheel is locked. See *Fig 1.*

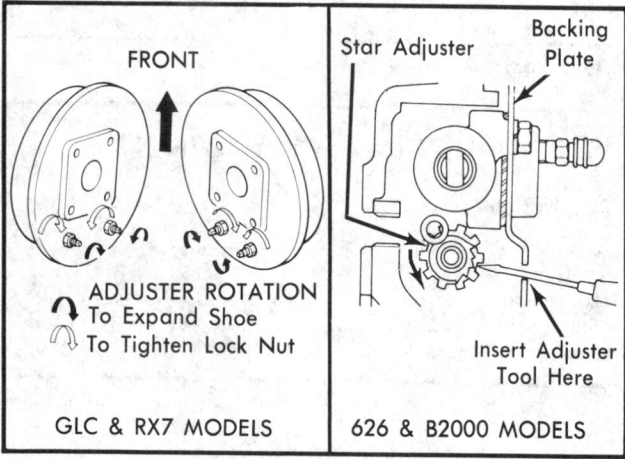

Fig. 1 Rear Brake Shoe-to-Drum Adjustment

2) Back off anchor pin until wheel just turns freely. Hold the anchor in position and tighten lock nut. Repeat the procedure for each shoe and ensure adjustment is equal on both wheels.

Except RX7 & GLC — Raise and support rear of vehicle. Release parking brake. Remove adjusting hole plugs from backing plate. Using a brake adjusting tool, rotate star wheel adjuster (direction marked on backing plate) until wheel locks. Back off adjuster 3-4 notches, until wheel rotates freely. Install adjusting hole plugs.

PEDAL HEIGHT & FREE PLAY

1) Pedal height (measured from fire wall to pedal pad center) should be as shown in chart. To adjust, disconnect negative battery cable and stop light switch connector. Loosen stop light switch lock nut and turn switch until correct pedal height is obtained. Tighten lock nut and connect electrical leads.

2) Pedal free play should be .28-.35" (7-9 mm). To adjust, loosen push rod lock nut and turn push rod until correct free play is obtained. Tighten lock nut.

Brake Pedal Height Specifications	
Application	Height In. (mm)
GLC	
Man. Trans.	7.5-7.7 (190-195)
Auto. Trans.	7.7-7.9 (195-200)
626	8.7-8.9 (220-225)
RX7	7.5-7.7 (190-195)
B2000	8.1-8.3 (205-210)

STOP LIGHT SWITCH

Stop light switch is located under dash, above brake pedal. To adjust, disconnect battery ground cable and switch electrical lead. Turn switch until it contacts brake pedal arm. Check and adjust brake pedal height. Tighten lock nut and connect electrical connection and battery cable.

PARKING BRAKE

With service brakes properly adjusted, raise and support vehicle. On all models except B2000, remove parking brake lever boot and turn lever adjusting screw so rear wheels are locked when lever is pulled 3-7 notches (5-7 on 626). Replace brake lever boot. On B2000, turn adjusting nut at equalizer (underside of vehicle) so rear wheels are locked when brake lever is pulled 5-10 notches. On all models, apply and release parking brake several times and ensure rear wheels rotate freely.

BRAKE WARNING LIGHT

B2000 — Light indicates parking brake is engaged and warns of brake system malfunction. To adjust light operation with parking brake applied, bend switch plate down until light comes on when brake lever is pulled 1 notch and goes out when lever is released (ignition on). To check warning light operation, release parking brake and ensure light is off (ignition on). Open bleeder screw on wheel and depress brake pedal; light should glow. Close bleeder screw and replenish brake fluid in master cylinder reservoir. With ignition on, depress brake pedal firmly to center combination valve piston. Light should go off; turn ignition off.

NOTE — *Brake warning light on B2000 will glow whenever any repairs are made to service brake system. Combination valve piston must be centered using this procedure.*

Except B2000 — Light indicates parking brake is engaged and also warns of low fluid level. Light should glow when parking brake lever is pulled 1 notch and go off when lever is fully released (ignition on). To check warning light operation, release parking brake lever and ensure light is off. Raise master cylinder reservoir cap and light should glow (ignition on). If not, check switch and wire connector.

REMOVAL & INSTALLATION

FRONT DISC BRAKE PADS

Removal — Raise and support vehicle; remove tire and wheel. Disconnect pad wear indicator (if equipped). On 626 and RX7, remove lower caliper guide pin and pivot caliper body up out of way. On GLC and B2000, remove spring clips and guide

MAZDA (Cont.)

plates. Remove caliper body and hang from frame with wire; DO NOT disconnect hydraulic line. On all models, remove anti-rattle springs (clips), pads and shims (if equipped).

Installation — To install, reverse removal procedure and note the following: Before mounting caliper, loosen bleed screw and seat piston. Tighten bleed screw. After pad installation, depress brake pedal several times to seat pads and bleed hydraulic system, if required.

FRONT DISC BRAKE CALIPER

Removal — Raise and support vehicle; remove tire and wheel. Disconnect and plug hydraulic line at caliper. On 626 and RX7, remove caliper guide pins and remove caliper. On GLC and B2000, remove spring clips and guide plates, then remove caliper. Remove disc pads as previously described and remove caliper mounting bracket.

Installation — To install, reverse removal procedure and bleed hydraulic system.

FRONT DISC BRAKE ROTOR

Removal — With caliper assembly removed, remove wheel hub grease cap, cotter pin, nut lock, and bearing adjusting nut. Remove thrust washer and outer bearing from hub, then slide hub and rotor assembly from spindle. On B2000, remove hub-to-rotor bolts and separate rotor from hub.

Installation — To install, reverse removal procedure and tighten hub-to-rotor bolts evenly (B2000). Adjust wheel bearings. See *Wheel Bearing Adjustment in WHEEL ALIGN-MENT Section.*

REAR BRAKE DRUM

Removal — Raise and support vehicle; remove tire and wheel. Remove brake drum retaining screws and insert into tapped holes of brake drum. Turn screws evenly and force brake drum off flange.

Installation — To install, reverse removal procedure and tighten retaining screws securely.

REAR BRAKE SHOES

Removal — With brake drum removed, remove brake shoe return springs, retaining springs and guide pins. Remove brake shoes. Remove parking brake strut and disconnect parking brake cable from operating lever of secondary shoe.

Installation — 1) Lubricate adjusting screw threads and contact surfaces of shoes and backing plate with brake grease. Install parking brake operating lever to secondary shoe and secure with clip. Engage lever in parking brake cable.

2) Position operating strut between slots of shoes. Mount assembly to backing plate so slots in shoes are toward adjusting screws. Install return springs and retainer springs.

MASTER CYLINDER

Removal — Disconnect hydraulic lines at master cylinder and plug openings to prevent entry of dirt and loss of fluid. Remove nuts attaching cylinder to firewall or power brake unit and remove master cylinder from vehicle.

Installation — To install reverse removal procedure and bleed hydraulic system.

POWER BRAKE UNIT

Removal — Disconnect hydraulic lines at master cylinder, and vacuum line at power brake unit. From inside vehicle, remove cotter pin and clevis pin retaining push rod to brake pedal, and separate. Remove nuts retaining power unit to firewall, then remove power brake unit and master cylinder as an assembly. Separate master cylinder from power brake unit.

Installation — To install, reverse removal procedure and bleed hydraulic system.

OVERHAUL

DISC BRAKE CALIPER

Disassembly — Thoroughly clean exterior of caliper and remove retainer and dust boot. Place a piece of wood in front

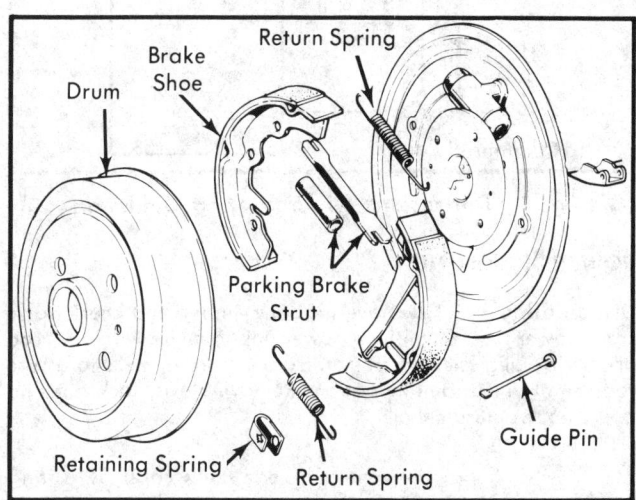

**Fig. 2 Disassembled View of GLC Rear Brakes
Other Models Similar**

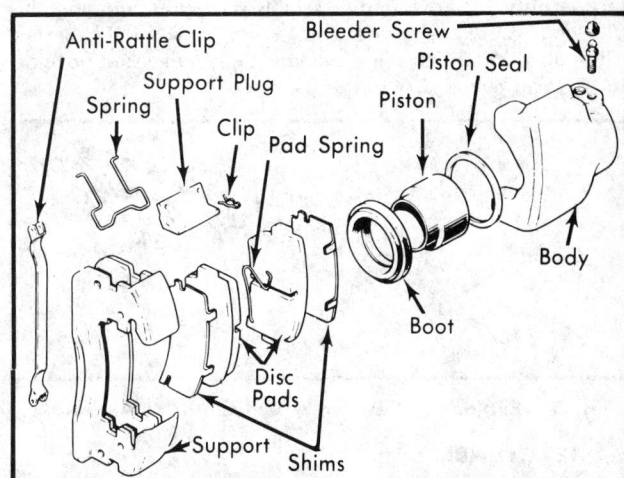

**Fig. 3 Exploded View of GLC and B2000
Front Disc Brake Caliper Assembly**

Brakes

MAZDA (Cont.)

of piston, apply compressed air to fluid inlet and remove piston (tapping caliper with plastic hammer, if required). Remove piston seal without damaging caliper bore.

Cleaning & Inspection — Wash all parts in alcohol or brake fluid and air dry. Inspect cylinder bore and piston for scoring, scratches or rust. Replace defective parts. Minor damage may be removed with crocus cloth. Always replace dust boot and piston seal when caliper is disassembled.

Reassembly — Apply clean brake fluid to cylinder bore, piston and piston seal, then seat piston seal in caliper bore. Install piston carefully into cylinder bore and install dust boot and retainer.

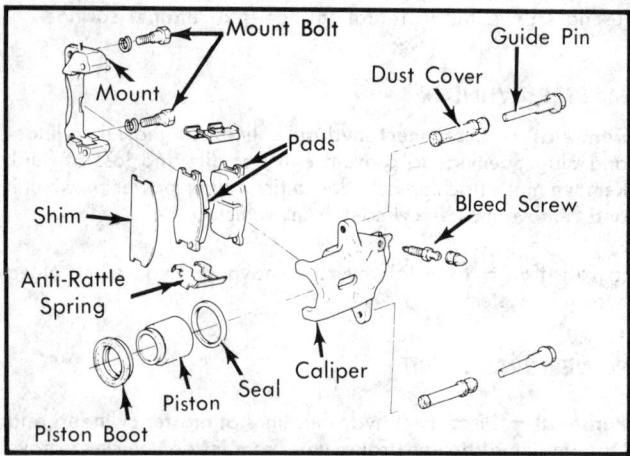

Fig. 4 Exploded View of 626 and RX7 Front Disc Brake Caliper Assembly

WHEEL CYLINDERS

Disassembly — Remove dust boots. Remove pistons with adjuster assemblies. Press on 1 cylinder cup to force out filling blocks and return spring.

Cleaning & Inspection — Clean all parts in alcohol or brake fluid. Check cylinder bore and pistons for scores, roughness or wear. Check clearance between cylinder bore and pistons; replace if clearance exceeds .006" (.15 mm). Check cups for deformation; replace as necessary.

Reassembly — Reverse disassembly procedure and note the following: Coat all parts with clean brake fluid before reassembly. When installing cylinder cups, make sure flat side of cup faces outward.

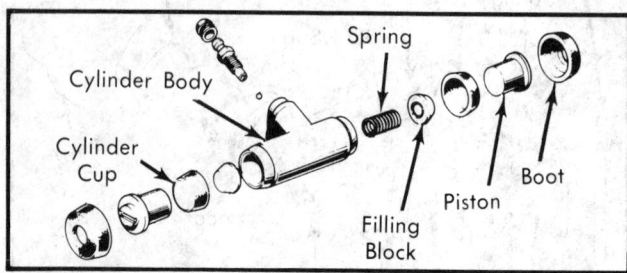

Fig. 5 Exploded View of Wheel Cylinder Assembly

MASTER CYLINDER

Disassembly — Thoroughly clean exterior of cylinder and pour out any remaining brake fluid. If equipped, remove reser-

voir and dust boot. Depress primary piston assembly, remove retaining ring from rear of cylinder bore, and remove washer, primary piston assembly, and return spring. Depress secondary piston, remove secondary piston stop bolt and insert guide pin. Carefully withdraw secondary piston assembly and return spring. Remove fluid fittings, check valves and springs.

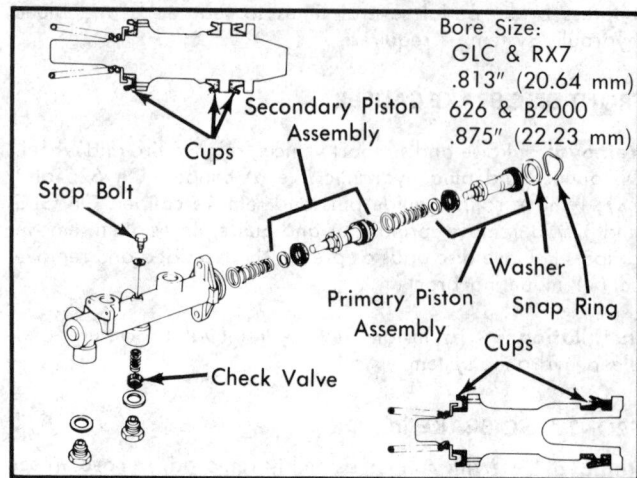

Fig. 6 Exploded View of Master Cylinder Assembly

Cleaning & Inspection — Clean all parts in alcohol or brake fluid. Check all parts for scoring, roughness or wear. Check piston-to-cylinder clearance. If clearance exceeds .006" (.15 mm), replace parts as necessary. Remove all foreign matter from internal passages and recesses with compressed air. Check cylinder cups for deformation and replace as required.

Reassembly — Reverse disassembly procedure and note the following: Coat all parts with clean brake fluid before reassembly. Use new gaskets at all hydraulic unions. When assembled, make sure piston cups do not cover compensating ports. Make sure valve with hole in center faces front side outlet hole.

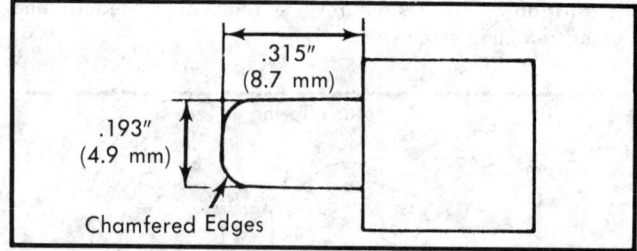

Fig. 7 Dimensions for Fabricating Guide Pin

POWER BRAKE UNIT

Disassembly — 1) Remove master cylinder and check valve from power unit, then place power unit in a vise with push rod up. Scribe alignment marks on front and rear shells to assure reassembly in original position. Remove clevis, lock nut and dust boot from rear shell.

CAUTION — *Separate front and rear shells carefully; spring tension may cause rear shell to release quickly.*

2) Attach removal tool to rear shell mounting studs, then press down on tool while rotating clockwise to unlock rear shell. Lift

MAZDA (Cont.)

rear shell assembly from power unit, then separate diaphragm and power piston assembly, valve rod and plunger assembly from rear shell. Remove return spring from power unit.

3) Remove diaphragm from power piston, then lift air silencer and filter from piston. Press in on valve rod and remove retainer key, then remove valve rod and plunger assembly. Press reaction disc from power piston. Remove push rod from front shell and if necessary, remove front seal.

Cleaning & Inspection — Clean all parts and blow dry with compressed air. Inspect all rubber parts for cuts, nicks, deterioration or other damage. Check power piston for cracks, distortion, chipping and damaged seats. Inspect front and rear shells for scratches, scores, pits, dents or other damage. Replace any defective parts.

Reassembly — Reverse disassembly procedure and note the following: Apply clean brake fluid to parts before reassembly. When assembling rear shell assembly to front shell, ensure marks made during disassembly are aligned. Before installing master cylinder to power unit, measure clearance between master cylinder primary piston and power unit push rod. Clearance should be .004-.020" (.1-.5 mm). If clearance is not within specifications, correct by adjusting push rod length.

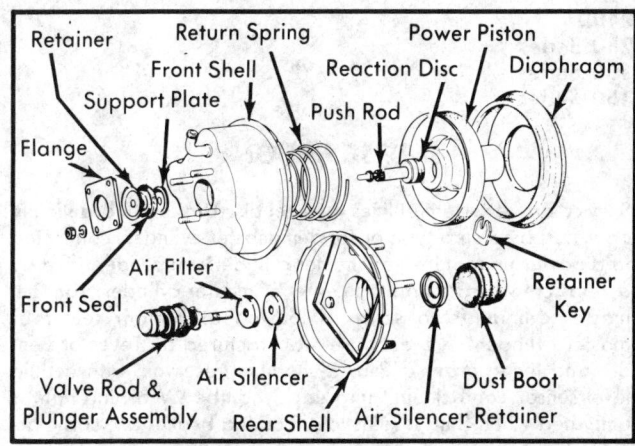

Fig. 8 Exploded View of Power Brake Unit

TIGHTENING SPECIFICATIONS

Application	Ft.Lbs. (mkg)
Caliper Mounting Bracket (B2000)	40-47 (5.5-6.5)
Caliper Guide Pin (626)	33-40 (4.5-5.5)
Wheel Nut	
B2000	58-65 (8.0-9.0)
All Others	65-80 (9.0-11.0)

DISC BRAKE SPECIFICATIONS

Application	Caliper Bore Diameter In. (mm)	Lateral Runout In. (mm)	Parallelism In. (mm)	Original Thickness In. (mm)	Minimum Refinish Thickness In. (mm)	Discard Thickness In. (mm)
GLC	2.0 (50.8)	.002 (.06)	.....	.512 (13)	.....	.472 (12)
626	2.125 (54)	.004 (.10)	.....	.512 (13)	.....	.472 (12)
RX7	2.0 (50.8)	.004 (.10)	.....	.709 (18)	.....	.669 (17)
B2000	2.125 (54)	.004 (.10)	.....	.472 (12)	.....	.433 (11)

DRUM BRAKE SPECIFICATIONS

Application	Wheel Cyl. Bore Diameter In. (mm)	Drum Diameter In. (mm)	Original Diameter In. (mm)	Maximum Refinish Diameter In. (mm)	Discard Diameter In. (mm)
GLC	.750 (19.05)	7.87 (200)	7.87 (200)	.....	7.91 (201)
626	.813 (20.64)	7.87 (200)	7.87 (200)	.....	7.91 (201)
RX7	.750 (19.05)	7.87 (200)	7.87 (200)	.....	7.91 (201)
B2000	.875 (22.23)	10.24 (260)	10.24 (260)	.....	10.28 (261)

MERCEDES-BENZ

240D
280 Series
300 Series
450 Series

DESCRIPTION

Service brake system utilizes 4-wheel disc brakes, hydraulically operated by a step-type or tandem master cylinder, connected to a power unit. Step-type master cylinder can be identified by a stop screw located on top center of master cylinder. Tandem master cylinder stop screw is located at bottom center of master cylinder. Cylinders are manufactured by Teves or Bendix and incorporate a 2 or 3-chamber reservoir with a fluid level sensor contact built into each chamber. Warning light is activated when fluid level is low. Parking brakes are cable actuated, internal expanding shoe-type, housed in rear brake rotors.

ADJUSTMENT

PEDAL HEIGHT & FREE PLAY

Pedal height (measured from pedal pad to pedal stop) should be 5.9" (150 mm). To adjust pedal height, loosen lock nuts and turn stop light switch until correct height is obtained. Tighten lock nuts. Pedal free play should be .2-.6" (5-15 mm).

STOP LIGHT SWITCH

Stop light switch is located under dash, above brake pedal. To adjust, loosen lock nuts and adjust switch so that contact button extends .24-.32" (6-8 mm). Tighten lock nuts.

PARKING BRAKE

Remove one wheel lug bolt at each rear wheel. Raise and support vehicle, and rotate wheels until lug bolt hole is positioned over parking brake adjuster (approximately 45° in upward and forward direction from wheel center). Using a screwdriver inserted through lug bolt hole, turn adjuster until wheel cannot be turned by hand. Back off adjuster until wheel can be turned by hand without restriction.

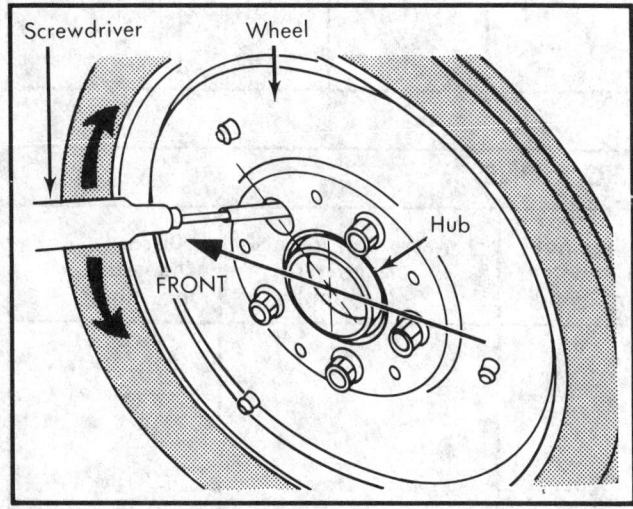

Fig. 1   Fitting Parking Brake Adjuster Tool Into Adjusting Mechanism

BRAKE WARNING LIGHT

A dual warning light is mounted on dash. Light should glow when parking brake lever is pulled 1 notch and go off when lever is fully released (ignition on). To check circuit warning sensor, release parking brake (ignition on) and ensure light is off. Open bleed screw on 1 wheel and depress brake pedal; light should glow. Close bleed screw, replenish brake fluid and bleed hydraulic system.

REMOVAL & INSTALLATION

DISC PADS

Removal — Raise vehicle, support with safety stands and remove wheels. If equipped, remove shaft cover plate from caliper and disconnect wear indicator wires. Drive out retaining pins toward inside of vehicle (on Bendix brakes, retaining pins have locking keys in pins) and remove cross spring. Loosen bleed fitting using suitable extractor tool, remove disc pads from caliper assembly.

NOTE — *All bolts are self-locking hex-head and should be used once only.*

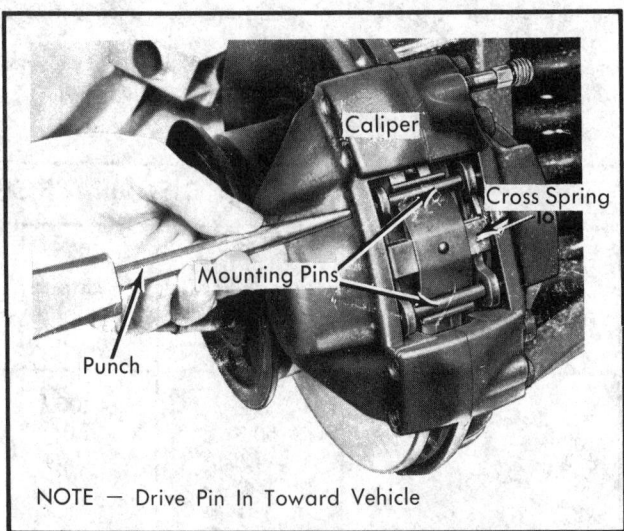

NOTE — Drive Pin In Toward Vehicle

Fig. 2   Knocking Out Disc Pad Mounting Pins On Teves Model Brakes

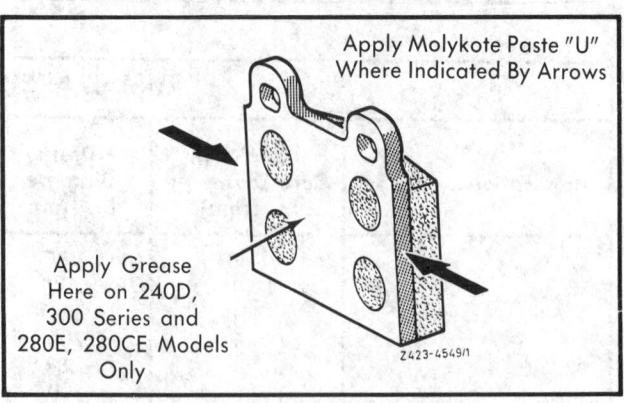

Fig. 3   Typical Mercedes-Benz Disc Brake Pad Illustration Shows Molykote Application Points

MERCEDES-BENZ (Cont.)

Installation — Using a cylinder brush, clean disc pad guide surface in caliper. Siphon sufficient fluid from master cylinder reservoir to prevent overflowing, then press pistons to bottom of bores. Install disc pads, cross spring and retaining pins. If equipped, install cover plate, retaining pin locking keys and wear sensor wires.

BRAKE CALIPER

Removal — Raise and support vehicle, and remove wheel. Disconnect brake lines at caliper assembly, and plug lines to prevent entry of foreign matter. Remove caliper attaching bolts, and remove caliper assembly from vehicle.

Installation — Reverse removal procedure ensuring that calipers are replaced in matched pairs from either manufacturer. Tighten all nuts and bolts and bleed hydraulic system.

BRAKE ROTOR

Removal & Installation (Front) — With caliper assembly removed, remove hub grease cap. Remove contact spring for radio shielding, loosen socket screw on clamping nut on wheel spindle, remove clamping nut and washer, then remove wheel hub and rotor assembly. Remove Allen head bolts securing rotor to hub and remove rotor. To install, reverse removal procedure, tighten all bolts and fittings evenly, and bleed hydraulic system if necessary. Adjust front wheel bearing. See *Wheel Bearing Adjustment in WHEEL ALIGNMENT Section.*

Removal & Installation (Rear) — Remove rear wheel and caliper assembly, then pull rotor out from axle shaft flange. To install, reverse removal procedure, tighten all bolts and fittings evenly, and bleed hydraulic system if necessary.

Fig. 4   Assembled View of Rear Hub and Caliper

MASTER CYLINDER

Removal — Drain master cylinder brake fluid. Disconnect and plug brake lines, disconnect electrical wires. Remove bolts securing master cylinder to power booster and remove master cylinder.

Installation — Reverse removal procedure and note the following: Always replace rubber "O" ring seal between master cylinder and power unit. Bleed hydraulic system and check complete system for fluid leaks.

POWER BRAKE UNIT

Removal — Drain master cylinder and remove master cylinder from vehicle. Disconnect vacuum line at power brake unit and disconnect push rod at brake pedal. Remove power brake unit attaching hardware and remove assembly from vehicle.

Installation — To install, reverse removal procedure, tighten all nuts and bolts, and bleed hydraulic system.

OVERHAUL

BRAKE CALIPER

Disassembly — With caliper removed from vehicle and disc pads removed from caliper, remove dust cap from piston housing. Hold one piston in place using a suitable clamp, then apply compressed air to fluid inlet and remove opposite piston. Remove piston seal from groove of cylinder bore. Remove remaining piston and seal in same manner.

NOTE — *DO NOT separate caliper halves.*

CAUTION — *DO NOT polish chrome plated surfaces of pistons.*

Cleaning & Inspection — Remove deposits on pistons with a soft brass wire brush. Check cylinder bore of caliper for wear or damage. Small rust deposits may be removed with polishing cloth. Heavier deposits in front of piston seal groove may be removed with fine emery cloth.

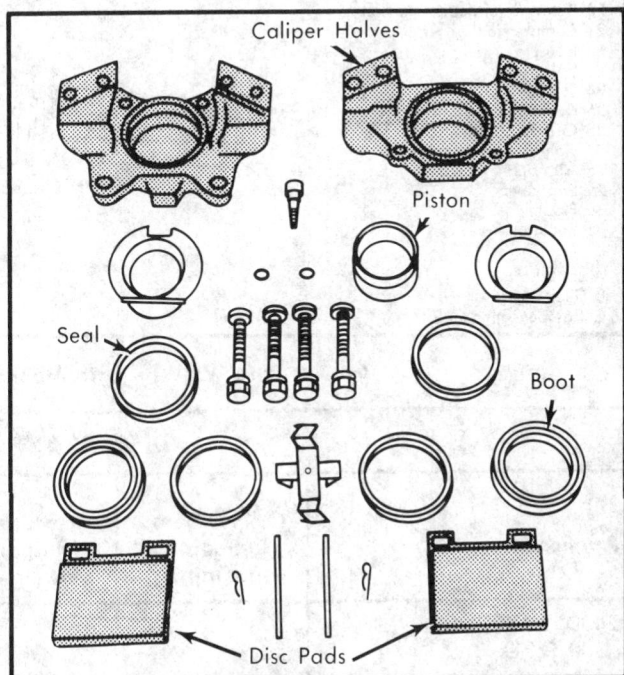

Fig. 5   Disassembled View of Typical Mercedes-Benz Brake Caliper

Reassembly — Coat piston and caliper bore with ATE brake cylinder paste (or equivalent), install piston seal into caliper bore and install piston. Install dust cap, then install heat shield into piston with recess in shield fitting into elevation of piston.

NOTE — *Elevation on piston MUST face downward and project at least .004" (.1 mm) above shield.*

MERCEDES-BENZ (Cont.)

MASTER CYLINDER

CAUTION — *Bendix master cylinder, spray painted blue, cannot be repaired.*

Disassembly (Tandem and Step Tandem) — Remove reservoir, push piston in with screwdriver, then remove stop screw and "O" ring. Remove lock ring from housing, then remove piston, stop washer, 2 vacuum seals and intermediate ring. Remove intermediate piston by rapping lightly with a wooden board.

NOTE — *Teves reservoir only, remove cap, end covers, strainer, splash guard, "O" rings and contact inserts. Bendix model, remove strainer from cover. DO NOT remove contact inserts. All models, master cylinder diameter should be .937" (23.81 mm).*

Inspection — Clean all parts with alcohol or brake fluid. Check bore in housing and piston for scoring and rust. Small rust spots in housing may be removed with polishing cloth. Scored or badly rusted parts cannot be repaired, replace complete master cylinder.

Reassembly — Reverse disassembly procedure and bleed hydraulic system.

TIGHTENING SPECIFICATIONS

Application	Ft. Lbs. (mkg)
Caliper Mounting Bolts	
Front	83 (11.5)
Rear	65 (9.0)
Hub-to-Rotor Bolts	83 (11.5)

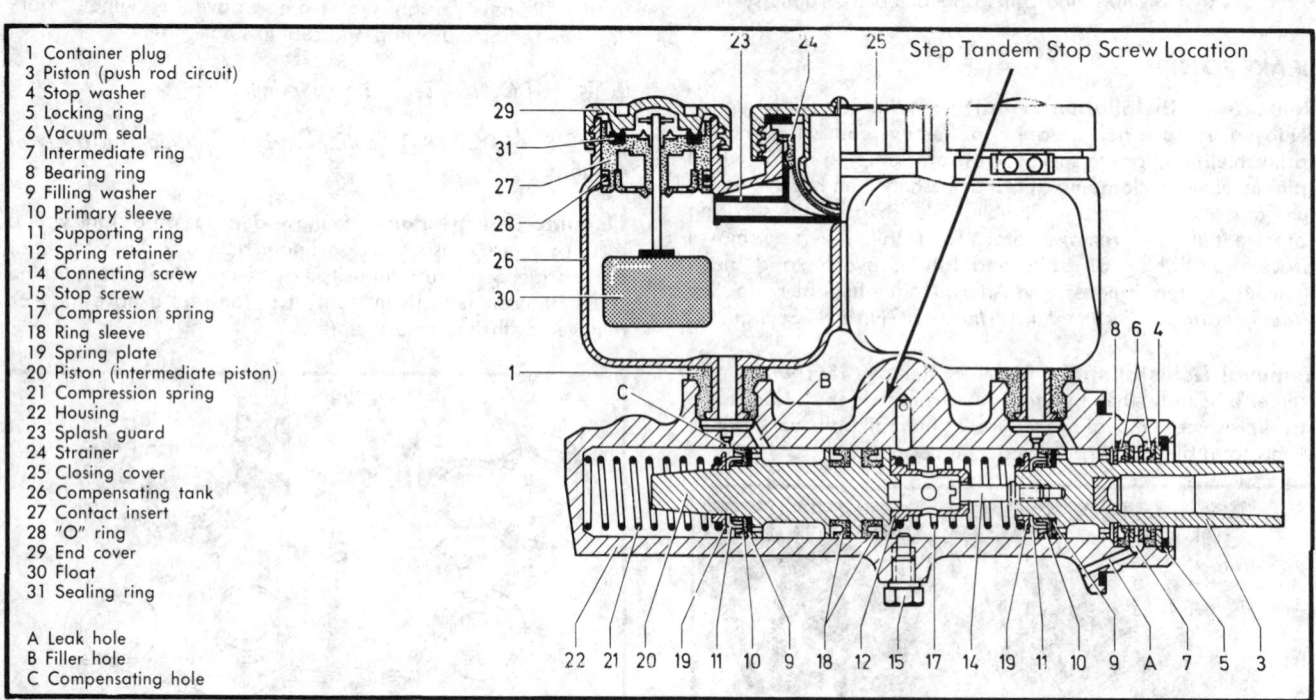

1 Container plug
3 Piston (push rod circuit)
4 Stop washer
5 Locking ring
6 Vacuum seal
7 Intermediate ring
8 Bearing ring
9 Filling washer
10 Primary sleeve
11 Supporting ring
12 Spring retainer
14 Connecting screw
15 Stop screw
17 Compression spring
18 Ring sleeve
19 Spring plate
20 Piston (intermediate piston)
21 Compression spring
22 Housing
23 Splash guard
24 Strainer
25 Closing cover
26 Compensating tank
27 Contact insert
28 "O" ring
29 End cover
30 Float
31 Sealing ring

A Leak hole
B Filler hole
C Compensating hole

Step Tandem Stop Screw Location

Fig. 6 Sectional View of Late Model Mercedes-Benz Tandem Master Cylinder

DISC BRAKE SPECIFICATIONS

Application	Caliper Bore Diameter In. (mm)	Lateral Runout In. (mm)	Parallelism In. (mm)	Original Thickness In. (mm)	Minimum Refinish Thickness In. (mm)	Discard Thickness In. (mm)
240D, 280E, 280CE, 300 Series						
Front	2.36 (60)	.005 (.12)	.0008 (.02)	.496 (12.6)	.....	.417 (10.6)
Rear	1.50① (38)	.005 (.12)	.0008 (.02)	.394 (10)	.....	.327 (8.3)
280SE & 450 Series						
Front	2.36 (60)	.005 (.12)	.0008 (.02)	.866 (22)	.....	.787 (20)
Rear	1.50 (38)	.005 (.12)	.0008 (.02)	.394 (10)	.....	.327 (8.3)

① — 300TD Caliper bore diameter — 1.65" (.42 mm).

Brakes

MGB

DESCRIPTION

Brake system is hydraulically operated using tandem master cylinder (with pressure differential) and power brake unit. Front brakes are self-adjusting disc type; rear brakes are leading/trailing drum type. A brake pressure warning switch is mounted to master cylinder and connected to dual warning light on instrument panel. Parking brake is cable actuated on rear wheels.

ADJUSTMENT

REAR DRUM BRAKE SHOES

Raise and support rear of vehicle and fully release parking brake. Turn shoe adjuster clockwise until wheel is locked. Back off adjuster until wheel is free to rotate without binding.

NOTE — *Adjustment on drum brakes also tightens up parking brake.*

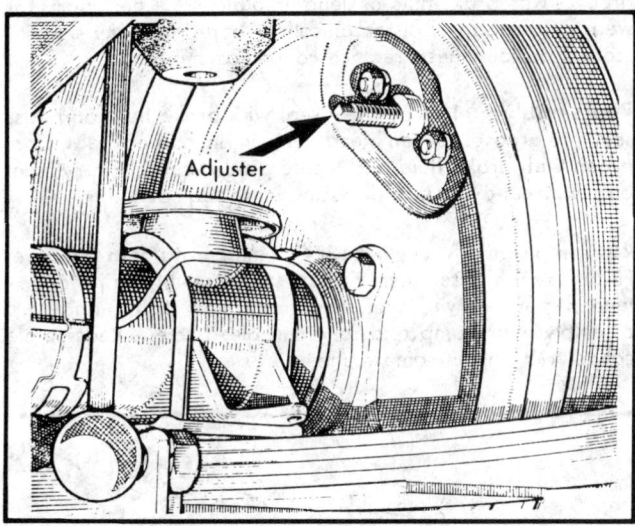

Fig. 1   Rear Drum Brake Shoe Adjuster Location

PEDAL FREE PLAY

Pedal free play (measured at center of pedal pad) should be .125″ (3.18 mm). To adjust free play, disconnect stop light switch, loosen lock nut and turn switch clockwise to DECREASE free play, counterclockwise to INCREASE free play. Tighten lock nut and reconnect stop light switch.

STOP LIGHT SWITCH

Stop light switch is located under instrument panel above brake pedal. To adjust, disconnect electrical connection and loosen lock nut. Adjust switch until it just contacts pedal arm. Tighten lock nut and reconnect electrical connection.

PARKING BRAKE

Raise and support vehicle. With rear brake shoes properly adjusted, pull parking brake lever up to 3rd notch from fully released position. Rear wheels should just be able to be rotated with considerable drag. If not, hold cable nut and turn adjusting nut until cables are not slack and rear wheels are partially locked when parking brake lever is pulled 3 notches.

BRAKE WARNING LIGHT

A dual warning light is mounted on instrument panel. Light should glow when parking brake lever is pulled 1 notch and go off when lever is fully released (ignition on). To check circuit warning sensor, release parking brake (ignition on) and ensure light is off. Open bleed screw on one wheel and depress brake pedal; light should glow. Close bleed screw, replenish brake fluid and bleed hydraulic system.

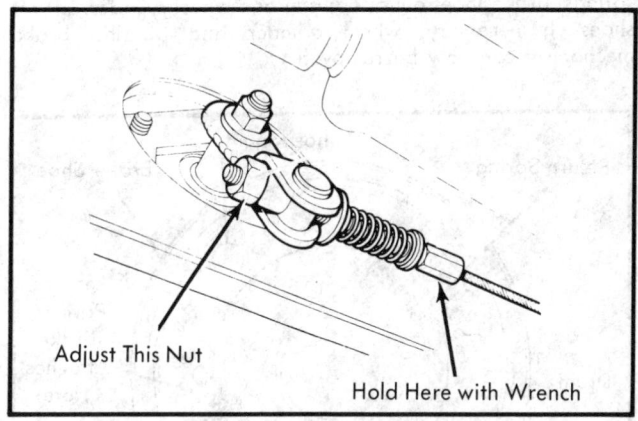

Adjust This Nut

Hold Here with Wrench

Fig. 2   Parking Brake Cable Adjustment Location

REMOVAL & INSTALLATION

FRONT DISC BRAKE PADS

Removal — Raise and support vehicle; remove tire and wheel. Depress pad retaining springs and remove cotter pins with retaining springs. Carefully lift out and remove pads.

Installation — Before inserting disc pads, clean piston head and caliper cavity. Seat piston in cylinder bore with suitable clamp. Machined portion of piston face must be seated at inner end of caliper. Insert pads, retaining springs and cotter pins. Filing of high spots from pads is acceptable to provide some movement of pads in caliper. Pump brake pedal several times to set pad-to-rotor clearance.

FRONT DISC CALIPER

Removal — Raise and support vehicle; remove tire and wheel. Disconnect and plug hydraulic line at caliper. Remove caliper mounting bolts and remove caliper assembly.

Installation — To install, reverse removal procedure and bleed hydraulic system.

FRONT DISC ROTOR

Removal — Raise and support vehicle; remove tire and wheel. Remove caliper assembly as previously described and hang from frame with wire; DO NOT disconnect hydraulic line. Remove hub grease cap, cotter pin and spindle nut. Using puller, remove hub and rotor assembly from spindle without dropping outer wheel bearing. Remove hub-to-rotor bolts and remove rotor.

Installation — To install, reverse removal procedure and tighten hub-to-rotor bolts evenly. Adjust wheel bearings. *See Wheel Bearing Adjustment in WHEEL ALIGNMENT Section.*

MGB (Cont.)

REAR BRAKE SHOES

Removal — 1) Raise and support rear of vehicle. Remove wheel. Release parking brake. Loosen brake shoe adjuster. Remove screws and pull off brake drum.

2) Make note of how springs at wheel cylinder end attach. Separate parking brake lever spring. Remove each brake shoe mounting pin, retainer, and spring. Pry (by spreading return springs) brake shoes out of adjuster and wheel cylinder. Lift off shoes. If necessary, wheel cylinder and parking brake mechanism can now be removed.

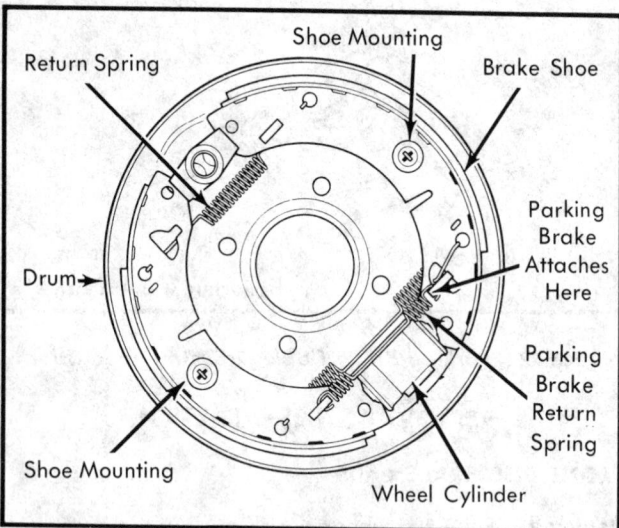

Fig. 3   Installed View of Rear Brake Drum Assembly

Installation — To install, reverse removal procedure and note: Apply suitable brake grease to shoe contact points. Adjust brake shoes.

MASTER CYLINDER

Removal — Remove pedal box cover and drain master cylinder reservoir. Disconnect hydraulic lines from master cylinder. Disconnect electrical connections. Remove master cylinder mounting nuts and remove master cylinder.

Installation — To install, reverse removal procedure. Start hydraulic lines before tightening master cylinder. Bleed hydraulic system and adjust brakes, if necessary.

POWER BRAKE UNIT

Removal — Disconnect throttle return spring from air cleaner, then remove air cleaner from vehicle. Remove pedal box cover. Disconnect hydraulic lines from mounting clips. Separate master cylinder from power brake unit and support cylinder out of way. Disconnect vacuum source and pedal return spring, then remove pin securing pedal to push rod. Remove nuts and spring washers mounting power brake unit to pedal box and lift out unit.

Installation — To install, reverse removal procedure and bleed hydraulic system.

OVERHAUL

FRONT CALIPER

Disassembly — 1) Remove brake caliper, leaving inlet hose connected. Clamp piston in mounting half of caliper and gently apply service brakes. This procedure will force rim half piston out enough to be removed by hand.

2) Using a blunt instrument, remove fluid seal, taking care not to damage bore or retaining groove. To remove dust seal, insert a screwdriver between retainer and seal, and gently pry retainer from mouth of caliper bore. Disassembly procedure is same for mounting half.

NOTE — *Caliper rim half must be reassembled before disassembling mounting half.*

Cleaning & Inspection — Clean piston, caliper bore and grooves with brake fluid or denatured alcohol. Check parts for wear or damage. If piston or caliper bore show any signs of scoring or roughness, replace caliper assembly.

Reassembly — 1) Coat new seal with brake fluid and ease seal into groove. Loosen bleed screw in rim half one turn. Coat piston with brake fluid and locate piston squarely in cylinder bore with cut-away portion facing inner edge of caliper.

2) Press piston down until .313″ (7.9 mm) protrudes from bore. Fit dust seal into retainer. Position seal assembly on piston extended portion with seal innermost. Seat piston and seal assembly with clamp and retighten bleed screw. Reassemble caliper rim half in same manner.

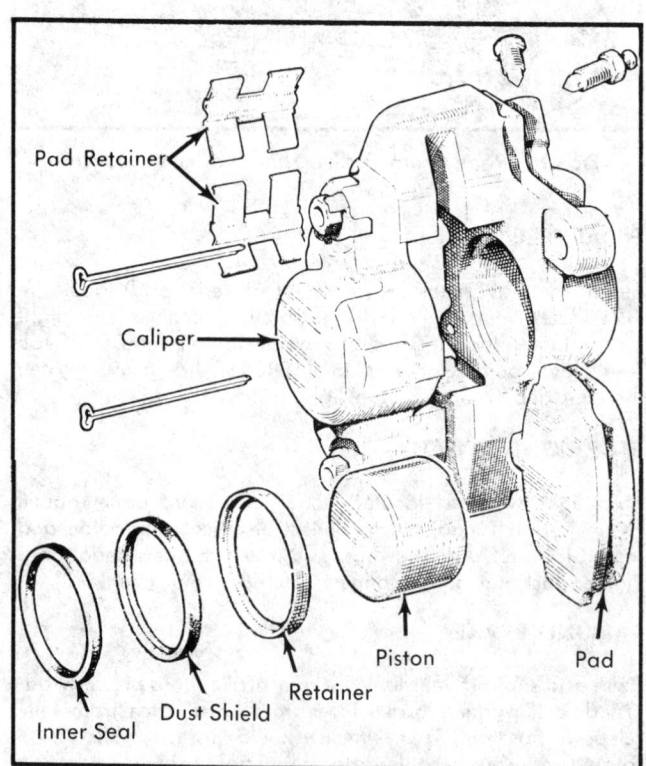

Fig. 4   Exploded View of Front Brake Caliper Assembly

MGB (Cont.)

REAR WHEEL CYLINDER

Disassembly — Pry off dust seals from each end of wheel cylinder. Slide pistons out. Remove seals taking care not to damage the seal groove.

Cleaning & Inspection — Clean all components in alcohol and allow to dry. If cylinder bore shows any signs of scoring or roughness, replace wheel cylinder assembly.

Reassembly — Lightly coat all internal components with brake fluid. Slide in each seal with flat surface toward slotted end of piston. Push piston into bore. Pull seal over end of assembly.

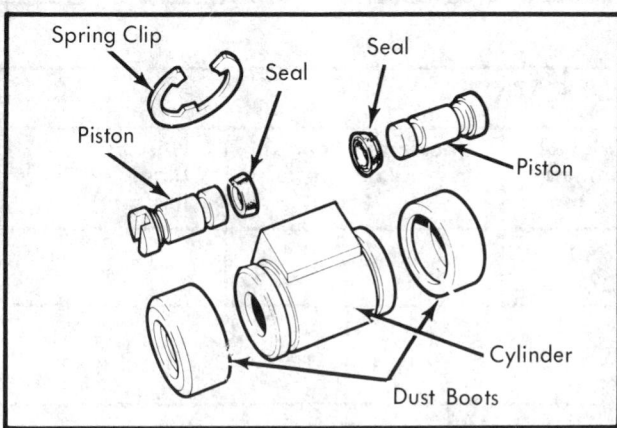

Fig. 5 Exploded View of Rear Wheel Cylinder

MASTER CYLINDER

Disassembly — 1) Remove brake pressure failure switch. Place cylinder in vise and remove reservoir. Take out seal and adapter assembly from primary feed port, then remove secondary port seal. Extract spring clip from cylinder bore and take out primary piston, return spring and cup.

2) Insert a rod into bore and depress secondary piston, take out stop plug from secondary feed port and withdraw secondary piston assembly. Remove pressure differential piston assembly. Pull rubber seals from pistons.

Cleaning & Inspection — Clean all components in brake fluid. Check cylinder bore for scoring or ridges, replace components as required.

Reassembly — 1) Lubricate all components with brake fluid. Fit "O" ring seals to pressure warning piston. Place a shim on primary and secondary pistons. Install seal to both pistons, lip facing away from shim. Fit the thinner of remaining seals to secondary piston with lips toward primary seat. Fit the secondary seal to primary piston with lip toward first seal. Fit return spring and cup to secondary piston and insert assembly.

2) Depress secondary piston and insert stop plug when piston head has passed feed port. Fit return spring and cup to primary piston and insert assembly. Refit spring clip.

3) Reinstall pressure differential valve and fit end plug. Fit "O" ring and seal to primary feed port adapter and install into port recess. Install secondary feed port seal, round edge first. Reposition reservoir and brake pressure switch.

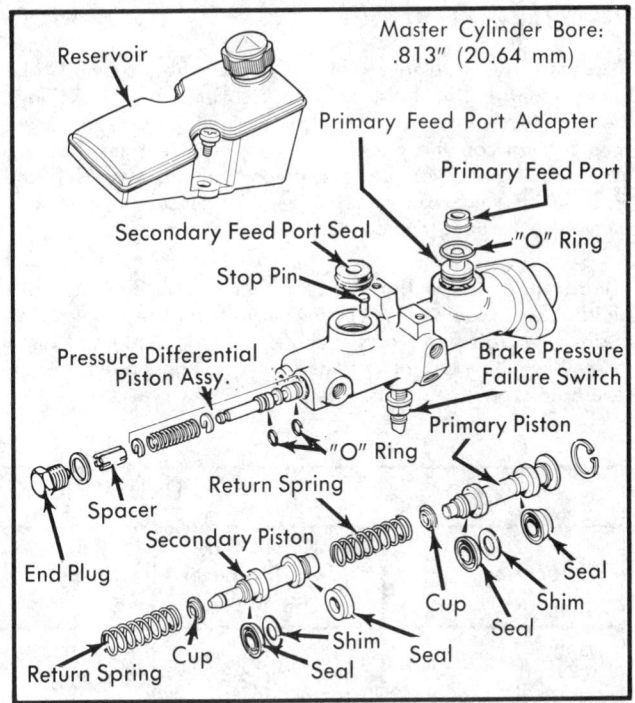

Fig. 6 Exploded View of Master Cylinder Assembly

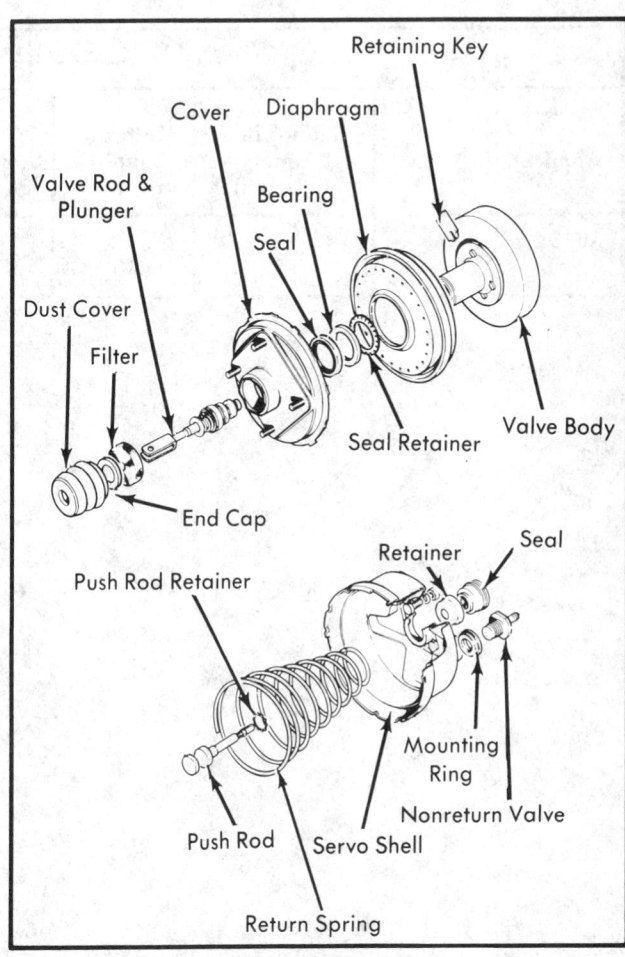

Fig. 7 Exploded View of Power Brake Unit

Brakes

MGB (Cont.)

POWER BRAKE UNIT

Disassembly — Remove seal and retainer from power brake unit. Mount unit in a vise and mark cover and shell. Remove dust cover and pull out filter. Remove cover by pressing down and turning counterclockwise. Remove seal retainer, bearing and seal from cover. Remove diaphragm from valve body. Push in on valve rod and plunger to release retaining key. Remove remaining components.

Cleaning & Inspection — Clean all components in brake fluid. Check components for wear or damage, replace as necessary. Valve rod and plunger must be replaced as an assembly. Replace all retainers and rubber parts during overhaul.

Reassembly — Coat all rubber components with brake fluid. To reassemble, reverse disassembly procedure and note: Push rod must extend .40″ (10.16 mm) from brake unit. Adjust by turning adjuster.

TIGHTENING SPECIFICATIONS

Application	Ft. Lbs. (mkg)
Caliper Mounting Bolts	43 (6.0)
Hub-to-Rotor Bolts	43 (6.0)

DRUM BRAKE SPECIFICATIONS

Application	Wheel Cyl. Bore Diameter In. (mm)	Drum Diameter In. (mm)	Original Diameter In. (mm)	Maximum Refinish Diameter In. (mm)	Discard Diameter In. (mm)
MGB	.80 (20.3)	10 (254)	10 (254)	.....	.....

DISC BRAKE SPECIFICATIONS

Application	Caliper Bore Diameter In. (mm)	Lateral Runout In. (mm)	Parallelism In. (mm)	Original Thickness In. (mm)	Minimum Refinish Thickness In. (mm)	Discard Thickness In. (mm)
MGB	.....	.006 (.15)	.001 (.025)	.34-.35 (8.6-8.9)	.....	.30-.31 (7.6-7.9)

PEUGEOT

504
505
604

DESCRIPTION

Brake system is hydraulically operated using a tandem master cylinder and power brake unit. The 504 is equipped with sliding yoke front disc brakes and rear drum brakes. All other models are equipped with 4-wheel sliding yoke disc brakes. All models are equipped with a load actuated compensator to provide equal fluid distribution to front and rear brakes. Parking brake is cable operated at rear wheels.

ADJUSTMENT

REAR DRUM BRAKE SHOES

Raise and support rear of vehicle. To adjust, rotate front adjustment eccentric clockwise until wheel locks, then back off until wheel just turns freely. Repeat procedure for rear adjustment eccentric, but rotate the eccentric counterclockwise.

NOTE — *Do not alter the adjustment of brake pedal.*

PARKING BRAKE

504 — Remove center console and raise and support vehicle. Fully release parking brake lever. Loosen lock nut at lever and tighten adjusting screw until wheels are locked with 4-7 notches of lever travel. Tighten lock nut and ensure wheels rotate freely with parking brake fully released.

Except 504 — Parking brake is self-adjusting and requires no in-service adjustment. Normal lever travel should be 7-13 notches.

BRAKE WARNING LIGHT

A triple warning light is mounted on instrument panel. Light will glow to indicate disc pad replacement, parking brake is engaged and brake fluid is low or malfunction exists in brake system. Light should glow when parking brake lever is pulled 1 notch and go off when lever is fully released (ignition on). To check circuit warning sensor, release parking brake (ignition on) and ensure light is off. Open bleed screw on 1 wheel and depress brake pedal; light should glow. Close bleed screw, replenish brake fluid and bleed hydraulic system.

REMOVAL & INSTALLATION

DISC BRAKE PADS

CAUTION — *Peugeot uses brake calipers from various manufacturers. Removal and Overhaul procedures may vary slightly. Disc pads and calipers MUST match for each axle application.*

Removal — Raise and support vehicle under frame; remove tire and wheel. Disconnect pad wear indicator electrical lead. Remove retaining spring and pins, then remove damper spring and brake pads.

NOTE — *Manufacturer recommends applying Permatex "High Tack" adhesive to back portion of pads prior to installation.*

Installation — 1) Remove small amount of brake fluid from master cylinder reservoir. Using suitable tool, press piston into cylinder bore. On rear calipers, rotate piston clockwise 1/8 turn before pressing into cylinder. After piston is seated in bore of rear caliper, return piston to original position by rotating counterclockwise 1/8 turn.

2) On all calipers, install pads and damper spring. Damper spring of rear caliper MUST be installed with arrow (or hole) at top. On all brake calipers, reconnect pad wear indicator. Bleed hydraulic system.

DISC BRAKE CALIPER

Removal — Raise and support vehicle; remove tire and wheel. Remove disc pads as previously described. Remove and plug hydraulic line from caliper. On rear caliper, disconnect parking brake cable and casing from operating lever. On all calipers, remove mounting bolts and remove caliper assembly.

Installation — Mount caliper and install mounting bolts with new lock washers coated with Loctite (or equivalent). Complete installation by reversing removal procedure and ensure hydraulic hose is not twisted. Bleed hydraulic system.

FRONT DISC BRAKE ROTOR

Removal — Remove caliper mounting bolts and support out of way without disconnecting hydraulic line. Remove hub grease cap, adjusting nut, washer and outer wheel bearing. Remove hub and rotor assembly from spindle. Separate hub and rotor by removing attaching bolts and washers from rear of hub.

Installation — Apply Loctite (or equivalent) to new lock washers and tighten hub-to-rotor bolts. Complete installation by reversing removal procedure and adjust wheel bearings. *See Wheel Bearing Adjustment in WHEEL ALIGNMENT Section.*

REAR DISC BRAKE ROTOR

Removal — 1) Disconnect hydraulic line retaining clip on control arm. Remove pad electrical lead and disc pads. Remove caliper mounting bolts and support caliper out of way without disconnecting hydraulic line. Remove axle shaft nut. Align bearing housing access hole and remove bearing housing bolts.

2) Remove shaft, hub and rotor as an assembly. Remove drive shaft from hub assembly with suitable puller. Mount hub assembly in a padded vise and install suitable extractor and remove bearing housing nut with a 35 mm socket. Install suitable extractor and thrust pad and remove bearing housing. Remove hub-to-rotor bolts and separate assembly.

Installation — 1) Apply Loctite (or equivalent) to new lock washers and tighten hub-to-rotor bolts. Install bearing housing nut to bearing housing and tighten nut. Mount hub and rotor assembly on bearing housing. Coat drive shaft splines with Molykote 321 (or equivalent) and install drive shaft in hub.

2) Mount shaft, hub and rotor assembly on vehicle. Install new washers coated with Loctite (or equivalent) on bearing housing bolts and tighten bolts. Install axle nut and tighten. Mount caliper and install new washers coated with Loctite (or equivalent) on mounting bolts. Install brake pads.

REAR BRAKE DRUM

Removal — Raise and support vehicle; remove tire and wheel. Slide brake drum off brake assembly. It may be necessary to neutralize brakes by removing backing plate plug and pushing parking brake lever off the seat.

Brakes

PEUGEOT (Cont.)

Installation — To install, reverse removal procedure.

REAR BRAKE SHOES

Removal — With brake drum removed, remove and discard hold down springs. Remove return springs, separate parking brake linkage from brake shoe and remove parking brake cable from operating lever. Remove brake shoes. Remove parking brake lever and strut from shoes.

Installation — To install, reverse removal procedure and note: Replace hold down springs during installation and ensure proper operation of parking brake.

MASTER CYLINDER

Removal & Installation — Using a siphon, drain brake fluid from master cylinder. Disconnect all hydraulic lines from master cylinder. Remove master cylinder-to-power brake unit attaching nuts and lift off master cylinder. To install, reverse removal procedure, fill master cylinder with new brake fluid and bleed hydraulic system.

OVERHAUL

FRONT DISC BRAKE CALIPER

Disassembly — Clamp caliper assembly in a soft-jawed vise and remove disc brake pads. Seat pistons in cylinder bore and remove thrust spring and yoke. Remove protector retaining clips and protectors. Force both pistons from cylinder bore and remove nylon spacer on yoke piston. Remove and discard piston seals.

Cleaning & Inspection — Clean all parts in denatured alcohol and check cylinder bore and pistons for wear, damage or scoring. If any defects are found, defective parts must be replaced. Replace piston seals during overhaul.

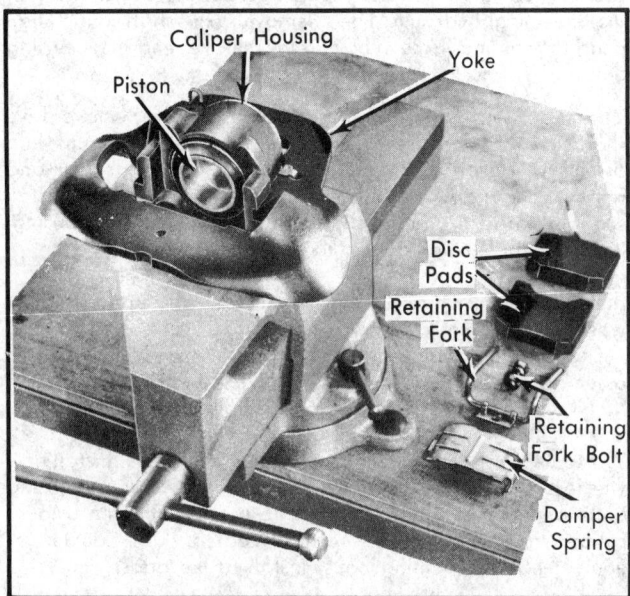

Fig. 1 Disassembling Front Disc Brake Caliper

Reassembly — Lubricate pistons and seals with suitable lubricant and install seals. Insert pistons in cylinder bore with nylon spacer seated against yoke piston. Install protectors and

retaining clips (thin clip on rotor side). Coat yoke and caliper sliding parts with Molykote 321 (or equivalent) and install yoke and thrust spring. Seat pistons in cylinder bore and install disc pads.

REAR DISC BRAKE CALIPER

Disassembly — 1) Clamp caliper assembly in a soft-jawed vise and remove disc pads. Rotate piston clockwise 1/8 turn and seat piston assembly in cylinder bore. Remove thrust spring and yoke.

2) Remove parking brake lever return spring. Lift lever and remove nylon spacer. Remove protector retaining clips and protectors. Force piston assembly from cylinder bore. Remove and discard piston seals.

Cleaning & Inspection — Clean all parts in denatured alcohol and check cylinder bore and piston assembly for wear or damage. If any defects are found, replace defective part. Separate piston assembly and inspect wear compensation assembly. Replace piston seals during overhaul.

Reassembly — 1) Lubricate piston assembly and seals with suitable lubricant and install seals. Insert piston assembly from rear of cylinder assembly without damaging piston seals. Install protectors and retaining clips (thin clip on rotor side). Raise parking brake lever and install nylon spacer. Install return spring.

2) Coat yoke and caliper sliding parts with Molykote 321 (or equivalent) and install yoke and thrust spring. Seat piston assembly in caliper bore, then rotate piston assembly counter-clockwise to original position. Install disc pads.

MASTER CYLINDER

Disassembly — 1) Mount master cylinder in a soft jaw vise. On Lockheed master cylinders, remove reservoir attaching screw from inside each reservoir and separate each reservoir from master cylinder. On Teves master cylinders, separate reservoir from master cylinder by pulling it from sealing grommets, then remove grommets.

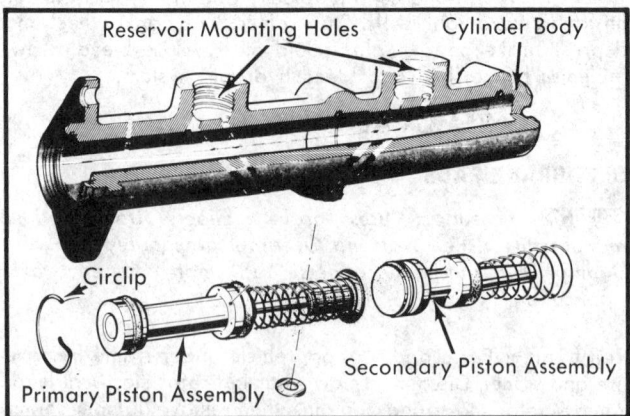

Fig. 2 Sectional View of Master Cylinder Assembly

2) On all master cylinders, remove piston stop screw. Remove piston circlip and stop washer, then extract primary piston assembly. Using compressed air, force out secondary piston assembly.

NOTE — *DO NOT disassemble piston assemblies; if piston or seals are damaged or worn, replace both piston assemblies.*

PEUGEOT (Cont.)

Cleaning & Inspection — Wash all parts in denatured alcohol and dry with compressed air. Inspect all parts for wear, scoring, burrs or corrosion and replace as necessary.

NOTE — *DO NOT polish cylinder bore with emery cloth.*

Reassembly — Reverse disassembly procedure and note the following: Coat all parts with clean brake fluid prior to reassembly. After reassembly is completed, push in primary piston several times and ensure it returns fully and smoothly to its stop each time.

POWER BRAKE UNIT

NOTE — *Power brake unit is serviced as an assembly only. Do not attempt to overhaul.*

TIGHTENING SPECIFICATIONS

Application	Ft. Lbs. (mkg)
Caliper Mounting Bolts	
Front	51 (7)
Rear	31 (4.3)
Retaining Fork Bolt	13 (1.8)
Hub-to-Rotor Bolts	36 (5)
Bearing Housing Nut	181 (25)
Bearing Housing Mounting Bolts	31 (4.3)
Rear Axle Shaft Nut	181 (25)

DRUM BRAKE SPECIFICATIONS

Application	Wheel Cyl. Bore Diameter In. (mm)	Drum Diameter In. (mm)	Original Diameter In. (mm)	Maximum Refinish Diameter In. (mm)	Discard Diameter In. (mm)
504 Rear	.....	11.00 (280)	11.00 (280)	11.06 (281)	11.08 (281.5)

DISC BRAKE SPECIFICATIONS

Application	Caliper Bore Diameter In. (mm)	Lateral Runout In. (mm)	Parallelism In. (mm)	Original Thickness In. (mm)	Minimum Refinish Thickness In. (mm)	Discard Thickness In. (mm)
504 Front	.....	.003 (.07)	.0008 (.02)	.502 (12.75)	.443 (11.25)	.423 10.75
505 Front	.....	.003 (.07)	.0008 (.02)	.502 (12.75)	.443 (11.25)	.423 (10.75)
Rear	.....	.003 (.07)	.0008 (.02)	.472 (12.0)	.433 (11.0)	.413 (10.5)
604 Front	.....	.003 (.07)	.0008 (.02)	.787 (20.0)	.748 (19.0)	.709 (18.0)
Rear	.....	.003 (.07)	.0008 (.02)	.472 (12.0)	.433 (11.0)	.413 (10.5)

Brakes

PORSCHE

911SC
924
928

DESCRIPTION

Brake system is hydraulically operated using a tandem master cylinder and power brake unit. The 911SC and 928 models are equipped with 4-wheel disc brakes. All other models are equipped with front disc brakes/rear drum brakes (optional 4-wheel disc brakes). All models utilize a dual brake warning light to detect pressure drop in either brake circuit. Warning light will not go out until problem is corrected. Parking brake is cable actuated on rear wheels of all models.

ADJUSTMENT

REAR DRUM BRAKE SHOES

Raise and support vehicle. Release parking brake. Turn adjuster until a slight drag is felt when rotating brake drum. Back off adjuster until drum is just free to rotate.

BRAKE PEDAL TRAVEL & FREE PLAY

Brake Pedal Travel — Pedal travel (measured from pedal pad center to point of brake application) should be 1.19-1.56" (30-40 mm). To adjust pedal travel, loosen operating rod lock nut and rotate rod until correct pedal travel is obtained. Tighten operating rod lock nut.

Free Play — Pedal free play (measured from pedal pad center to floorboard) should be about 3/8" (10 mm). To adjust pedal free play, loosen operating rod lock nut and set free play to specification. Check pedal travel and tighten operating rod lock nut.

PARKING BRAKE

Except 924 Models — Raise and support vehicle; remove tire and wheel. Release parking brake lever and push caliper pistons and pads into caliper to allow rotor to turn freely. Loosen parking brake cable lock nuts until cable is slack. Working through access hole in parking brake drum, turn star wheel adjuster until rotor cannot be turned by hand. Adjust parking brake cable at rear cable end until it just begins to pull and tighten lock nuts. Back off star wheel adjuster until rotor turns freely without drag. Repeat operation on opposite wheel and check parking brake operation.

924 Models — Raise and support vehicle; ensure service brakes are properly adjusted. From inside vehicle, pull parking brake lever up 2 notches and turn adjuster nut at base of brake lever until both wheels can just be turned by hand.

BRAKE WARNING LIGHT

NOTE — *Warning light will glow after any repair on service brake system and will not go out until manually reset.*

A dual warning light is mounted on instrument panel. Parking brake light should glow when parking brake lever is pulled 1 notch (ignition on) and go off when lever is fully released. To check circuit warning sensor, fully release parking brake and ensure light is off (ignition on). Open 1 bleed screw and depress brake pedal; light should glow. To reset warning light, bleed hydraulic system and test service brakes. Disconnect and reconnect negative battery cable; warning lamp should go out.

REMOVAL & INSTALLATION

DISC PADS

NOTE — *Mark pads and calipers before removal. If pads are to be reused, they must be installed in original position. If only 1 pad (front or rear) needs replacing, all pads on same axle must be replaced.*

Removal — Raise and support vehicle; remove tire and wheel. Disconnect pad wear indicator electrical connection, if equipped. Remove retaining pin clip and retaining pins. On 911SC, squeeze spreader spring and remove disc pads. On all other models, remove inside brake pad with pad remover. Outside disc pad is guided by a tab on sliding caliper frame; remove outer pad by pushing frame out away from rotor and removing pad.

CAUTION — *If fluid level is too high in reservoir, overflow will result when pistons (during installation) are pushed back into calipers.*

Installation — Push piston back into caliper using suitable tool (P83), or wooden block. Remove anti-rotation locks (if equipped) and clean all parts with alcohol. Inspect all parts for damage or wear. Ensure piston 20° position is correct using suitable gauge (P84). Install remaining parts in reverse order of removal, replace parts as necessary.

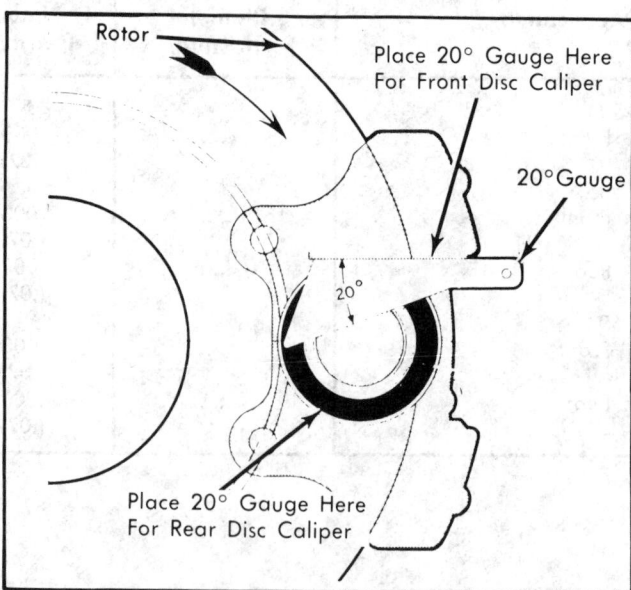

Fig. 1 Positioning Caliper Piston Using 20° Gauge

BRAKE CALIPER

CAUTION — *When any fluid fitting is disconnected, fluid will drain from reservoir through master cylinder and out open fitting. To avoid this, depress brake pedal far enough so piston cup will pass the compensating (resupply) port.*

PORSCHE (Cont.)

Removal — Raise and support vehicle; remove tire and wheel. Remove brake pads as previously described and remove splash shield (if equipped). Disconnect and plug hydraulic line, remove caliper mounting bolts and remove caliper.

Installation — To install, reverse removal procedure and bleed hydraulic system.

BRAKE ROTOR

Removal — Raise and support vehicle; remove tire and wheel. Remove caliper as previously described and hang from frame with wire; DO NOT disconnect hydraulic line. On front brake rotors, remove dust cap, loosen clamp lock screw, then remove clamp nut and thrust washer. Remove rotor and wheel bearings as an assembly and separate. On rear brake rotors, remove rotor attaching bolts and remove rotor. Mark rotor and hub for reassembly reference, remove hub-to-rotor bolts (if equipped) and separate hub from rotor.

NOTE — *If rear rotor cannot be removed by hand, insert two 8 mm bolts into attaching screw holes and alternately tighten bolts to press rotor from hub.*

Installation — To install, reverse removal procedure, bleed hydraulic system and adjust front wheel bearings. *See Wheel Bearing Adjustment in WHEEL ALIGNMENT Section.*

NOTE — *Rotors must be installed in original position due to cooling holes and internal ventilation channels. These holes and channels are different for right and left sides.*

REAR BRAKE SHOES

Removal — Raise and support vehicle and remove wheels. Using suitable puller (40-107) remove brake drum. Remove shoe hold down springs. Remove upper and lower return springs and pressure rod. Remove parking brake rod from brake shoe. stalling parking brake rod.

Installation — Reverse removal procedures and note the following: Lubricate adjusting screws and sliding surfaces of brake shoes lightly. Use new bearing pin and clip when installing parking brake lever.

PARKING BRAKE SHOES
(REAR DISC BRAKE ONLY)

Removal — Raise and support vehicle; remove tire and wheel. Remove parking brake drum retaining screws and remove parking brake drum. Remove parking brake cable from shoes. Remove expander, shoe retaining springs and pins, then raise upper shoe and remove adjuster and spring. Remove lower shoe retainer and remove parking brake shoes.

Installation — To install, reverse removal procedure.

MASTER CYLINDER

Removal — On 911SC, raise and support vehicle and drain fluid from reservoir. Pull back on accelerator pedal to detach pedal from pad. Remove floor mat and floor board and withdraw boot from master cylinder. Remove underpanel covering front axle. On all models, remove hydraulic lines, electrical connections and reservoir tubes (if equipped). Remove mounting nuts and remove master cylinder.

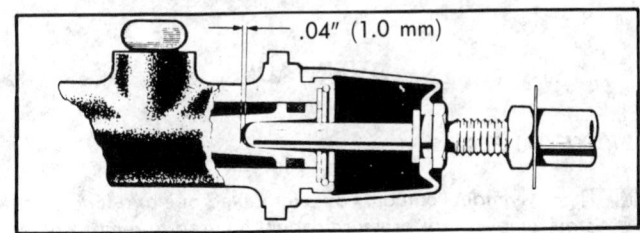

Fig. 3   Illustrating Push Rod-to-Master Cylinder Piston Clearance on 911SC Models

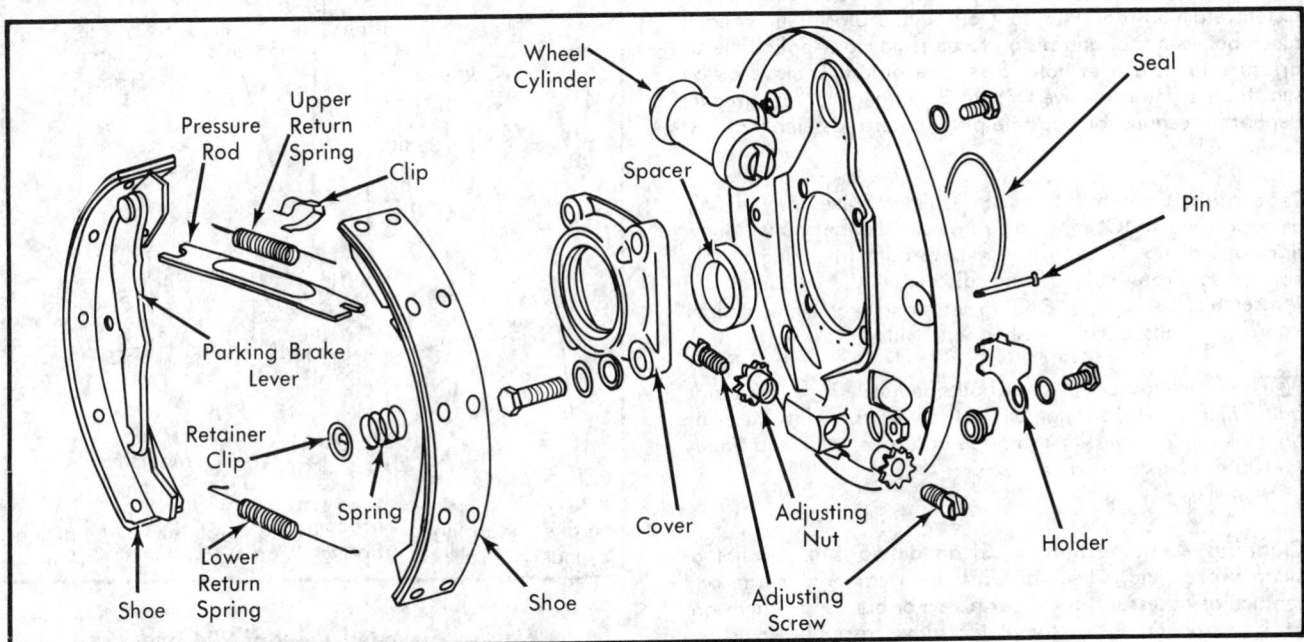

Fig. 2   Exploded View of 924 Rear Brake Assembly

PORSCHE (Cont.)

Installation — To install, reverse removal procedure and note the following: On 911SC, be sure push rod is correctly installed and that clearance between push rod and piston is about .04" (1.0 mm). Use a sealing material on cylinder flange to prevent water leakage into driver's compartment. Bleed hydraulic system.

POWER BRAKE UNIT

NOTE — *Before removal, test check valve and power brake unit for operation. To check valve, pull off vacuum hose, place finger over check valve and crank engine; vacuum should be created. To check power brake unit, push on brake pedal several times with engine stopped, hold pedal down and start engine. If power brake unit is operating properly, brake pedal will drop slightly.*

Removal — With master cylinder removed, disconnect vacuum hose from power brake unit. Remove pin connecting power brake unit operating rod to brake pedal assembly, remove nuts and remove power brake unit from vehicle.

Installation — Reverse removal procedures and note the following: Apply suitable sealer to power brake unit mounting surface and vacuum line connections. Adjust pedal height and bleed hydraulic system.

OVERHAUL

BRAKE CALIPER

NOTE — *Cylinders can only be overhauled one at a time. With 1 piston removed, air pressure cannot be used to remove other piston.*

Disassembly (911SC) — Clamp caliper (by mounting flange) in vise. Remove dust boot retaining ring and dust boot. Install piston retaining tool (P83) to 1 piston and place thin wooden block between tool and piston to be removed. Apply light air pressure to fluid inlet hole to remove piston. Remove piston seal from cylinder groove without damaging bore or groove. Repeat procedure for opposite piston after reassembly of first piston.

Separating Caliper Halves — Caliper halves should only be separated if "O" ring seals between caliper halves show signs of leaking. To separate, remove bolts attaching caliper halves, separate caliper and discard "O" ring seals. To reassemble, install new "O" ring seals and reassemble caliper using new bolts, spring washers and nuts.

NOTE — *Install shorter bolts in outside holes. Tighten 2 inside bolts first and then tighten outside bolts. Bolts must be tightened in 2 stages; first to 50% of torque value and finally to 100% of torque value.*

Cleaning & Inspection — Clean all parts in alcohol or clean brake fluid. Check all parts for wear or damage and replace as necessary. If caliper piston or bore show any signs of wear or damage, complete caliper assembly must be replaced.

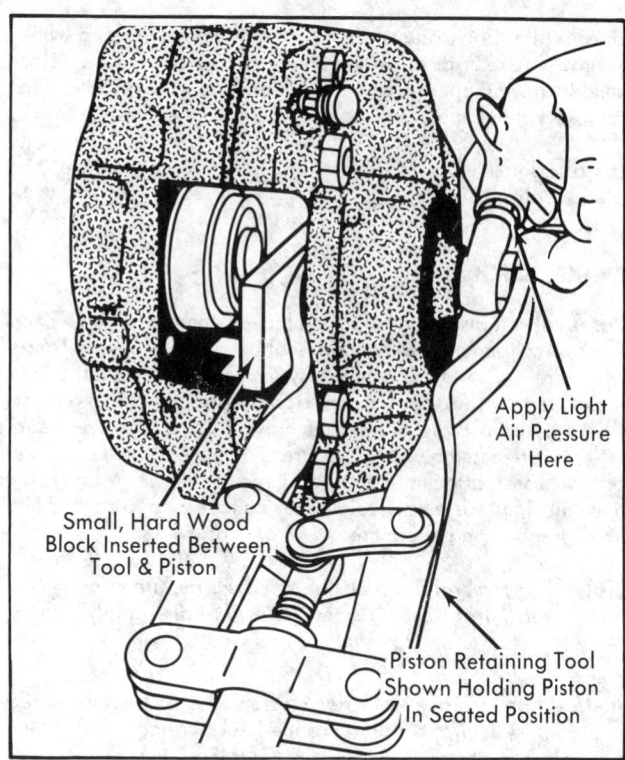

Fig. 4 Using Air Pressure to Remove 911SC Caliper Piston

Reassembly — Reverse disassembly procedure and note the following: Use new rubber components, dust cover retaining ring and pad retaining plates. Apply brake cylinder paste to piston and cylinder seal. Assure piston is straight with cylinder by using a suitable piston installing clamp. Check 20° position of piston with suitable gauge and correct using piston rotating pliers (if needed). Replace fluid inlet bolt and adapter seals.

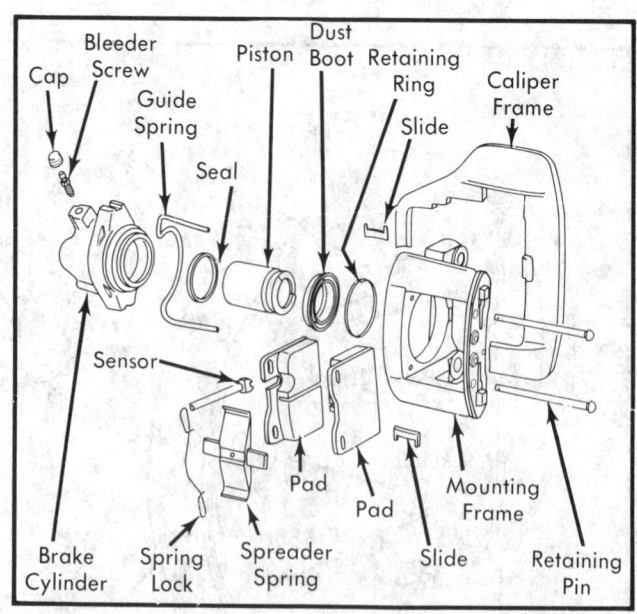

Fig. 5 Exploded View of 924 and 928 Brake Caliper Assembly

Brakes

PORSCHE (Cont.)

Disassembly (Except 911SC) — With disc pads removed, press caliper frame off mounting frame. Insert wooden block in caliper frame and force cylinder assembly off caliper frame with plastic hammer. Remove dust boot retaining ring and dust boot. Force piston out of caliper bore with light air pressure. Remove piston seal from cylinder groove without damaging groove or bore.

Cleaning & Inspection — Clean all parts in alcohol or clean brake fluid. Check all parts for wear or damage and replace as necessary. If caliper piston or bore show any signs of wear or damage, complete caliper assembly must be replaced.

Reassembly — To reassemble, reverse disassembly procedure and note the following: Use new rubber components, dust cover retaining ring and pad retaining plates. Apply brake cylinder paste to piston and cylinder seal. Assure piston is straight with cylinder by using piston installing clamp. Check 20° position.

MASTER CYLINDER

Disassembly — Push in on primary piston to remove lock ring, then remove stop plate and primary piston assembly. Remove piston stop screw and, using compressed air, remove secondary piston. Remove secondary piston support washer, spring seat and return spring. To remove hydraulic warning system assembly, remove sending unit and retaining bolt from master cylinder, and using compressed air, remove pistons and springs.

Cleaning & Inspection — Clean all parts with alcohol. Check all pistons and cylinders for out-of-round, corrosion or damage. Inspect all other parts for scoring, excessive wear, corrosion or other damage.

Reassembly — To reassemble, reverse disassembly procedure and note the following: Lightly coat all parts with brake cylinder paste before installation. Use new "O" ring seals on warning system sending unit and retaining bolt. Tighten all hydraulic lines and fittings. Bleed hydraulic system.

POWER BRAKE UNIT

Manufacturer does not recommend overhaul of power brake unit. Replace as complete assembly if defective.

TIGHTENING SPECIFICATIONS

Application	Ft. Lbs.
Caliper Mounting Bolts	
911SC	50 (7.0)
924	60 (8.3)
928	61 (8.4)
Caliper Housing Bolts (911SC, Front)	43 (6.0)
Rotor-to-Hub Bolts	17 (2.4)

DRUM BRAKE SPECIFICATIONS

Application	Wheel Cyl. Bore Diameter In. (mm)	Drum Diameter In. (mm)	Original Diameter In. (mm)	Maximum Refinish Diameter In. (mm)	Discard Diameter In. (mm)
924 Rear	.750 (19.05)	9.05 (230)	9.05 (230)	9.09 (231)	9.11 (231.5)

DISC BRAKE SPECIFICATIONS

Application	Caliper Bore Diameter In. (mm)	Lateral Runout In. (mm)	Parallelism In. (mm)	Original Thickness In. (mm)	Minimum Refinish Thickness In. (mm)	Discard Thickness In. (mm)
911SC Front	.....	.008 (.2)	.0012 (.03)	1.26 (32)	1.20 (30.6)	1.18 (30)
Rear	.....	.008 (.2)	.0012 (.03)	1.10 (28)	1.05 (26.6)	1.02 (26)
924 Front	1.89 (48)	.....	.....	.512 (13)	.472 (12)	.453 (11.5)
928 Front	2.126 (54)	.004 (.1)	.0012 (.03)	.787 (20)	.732 (18.6)	.709 (18)
Rear	1.417 (36)	.004 (.1)	.0012 (.03)	.787 (20)	.732 (18.6)	.709 (18)

RENAULT

Le Car

DESCRIPTION

Brake system is hydraulically operated using a tandem master cylinder and optional power brake unit. All models are equipped with front disc brakes and rear drum brakes. A pressure limiter valve is installed in rear brake circuit to prevent premature rear wheel lock-up. Parking brake is cable actuated on rear wheels.

ADJUSTMENT

REAR DRUM BRAKE SHOES

Two adjusting lugs are located on backing plate. Using a wrench, turn front lug counterclockwise and rear lug clockwise until shoes just contact drum. Then, back off adjustment until drum rotates freely.

BRAKE PEDAL FREE PLAY

Brake pedal free play (measured at pedal pad center) should be .203" (5 mm). To adjust free play, loosen operating rod lock nut and rotate operating rod until specified free play is obtained. Tighten lock nut.

PARKING BRAKE

Adjust service brakes, then fully release parking brake. Loosen lock nut on adjustment rod. Tighten adjustment nut until lining just meets drum. At this point, parking brake lever travel should be about 6 notches. Tighten lock nut. Check operation.

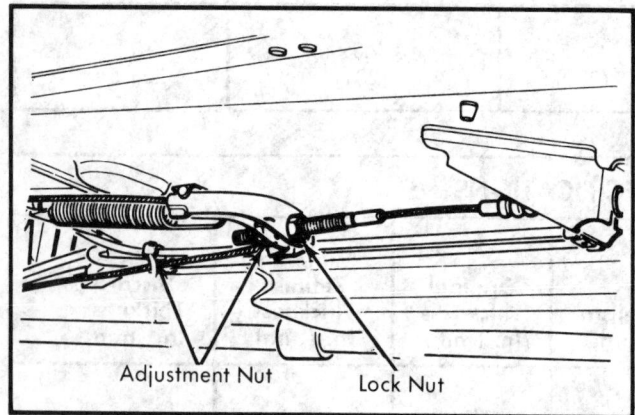

Fig. 1   Parking Brake Adjustment Points

BRAKE WARNING LIGHT

A dual warning light is mounted on instrument panel. Light should glow when parking brake lever is pulled 1 notch and go off when lever is fully released (ignition on). To check circuit warning sensor, release parking brake (ignition on) and ensure light is off. Raise master cylinder reservoir cap; light should glow. If not, check bulb or circuit connections.

REAR BRAKE PRESSURE LIMITER

NOTE — Limiter must always be checked and adjusted with vehicle on level ground, fuel tank full, trunk empty and driver's seat occupied.

1) To check limiter, remove 1 rear wheel cylinder bleeder screw and connect a pressure gauge (Fre. 214-02) into vacant hole. Bleed brake system. Depress brake pedal and check pressure obtained at wheel cylinder. Pressure should be 405-465 psi (28.5-32.5 kg/cm²).

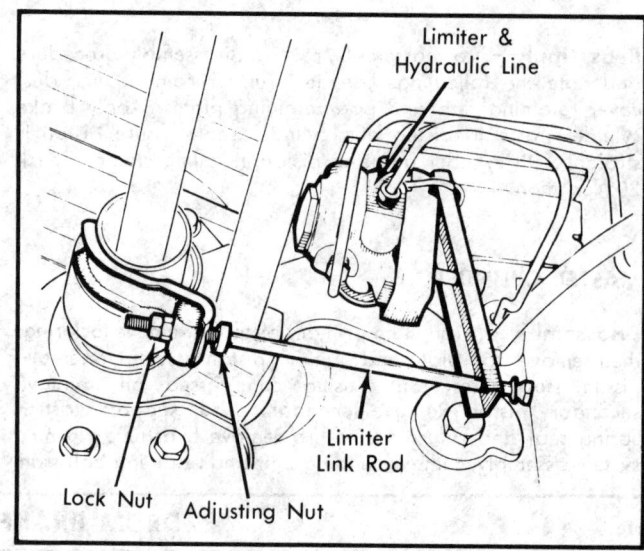

Fig. 2   Pressure Limiter Adjustment Points

2) To adjust limiter, release lock nut and tighten adjustment nut to **increase** pressure or loosen it to **reduce** pressure.

3) Apply brake pedal several times and recheck adjustment. Remove pressure gauge and bleed brake system.

REMOVAL & INSTALLATION

FRONT DISC PADS

Removal & Installation — Caliper must be removed to replace disc pads. See Disc Brake Caliper Removal & Installation.

FRONT DISC CALIPER

Removal — Raise and support vehicle and remove front wheels. Remove spring clips and slide keys out of caliper and mounting bracket. Disconnect brake line fitting from flexible hose and remove hose retaining clip from body. Remove caliper from mounting bracket and disconnect flexible hose from caliper. Remove brake pads and pad spring from caliper.

Installation — To install, reverse removal procedure and note the following: Install longest pad spring on outside of caliper. Tighten all fittings and bleed hydraulic system.

RENAULT (Cont.)

FRONT DISC ROTOR

Removal — Remove caliper as previously described and remove caliper mounting bracket. Attach holding tool (Rou. 604 or Rou. 436-01) to wheel studs and remove axle shaft nut. Attach slide hammer to hub and remove hub and rotor assembly. Remove hub-to-rotor bolts and remove rotor from hub.

Installation — To install, reverse removal procedure and tighten hub-to-rotor bolts evenly. Bleed hydraulic system if required.

REAR BRAKE DRUM

Removal — Remove hub grease cap, cotter pin, nut and washer. Back off brake shoe adjusters. Attach slide hammer and remove drum.

Installation — To install reverse removal procedure and note the following: Apply a suitable grease to wheel bearings. After installing drum assembly, adjust wheel bearings. *See Wheel Bearing Adjustment in WHEEL ALIGNMENT Section.* Apply brake pedal several times to adjust brake shoes.

REAR BRAKE SHOES

Removal & Installation — Remove wheel and brake drum from vehicle. Install wheel cylinder clamp, then remove upper brake shoe return spring. Disconnect parking brake cable from actuator lever. Remove parking brake actuator link and lower return spring. Unhook shoe hold-down springs and remove brake shoes. To install, reverse removal procedure.

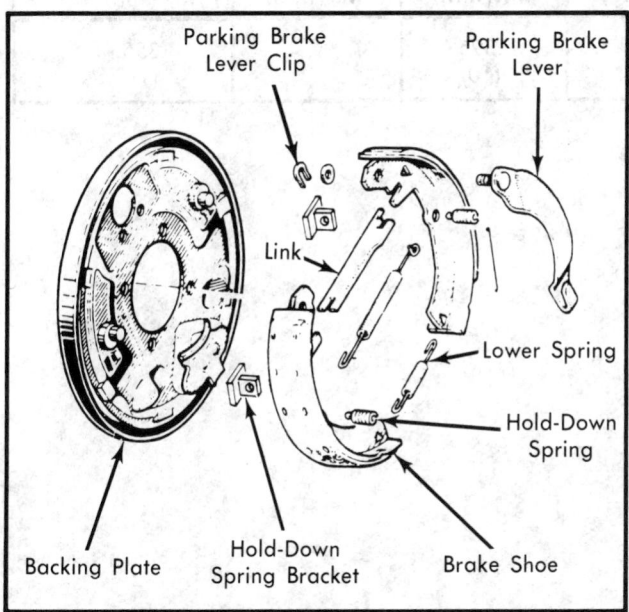

Fig. 3 Exploded View of Brake Shoe Assembly

MASTER CYLINDER

Removal — Drain fluid from master cylinder reservoir and disconnect and plug hydraulic lines. Remove pressure loss indicator bolt (if equipped). Disconnect push rod from brake pedal (without power brake unit). Remove mounting hardware and remove master cylinder.

Installation — To install, reverse removal procedure and adjust brake pedal free play. Bleed and adjust hydraulic system.

POWER BRAKE UNIT

NOTE — *Power brake unit is not serviceable, only the air filter and check valve can be serviced.*

Removal — Disconnect battery, and remove fluid from master cylinder. Remove engine air filter (if necessary). Disconnect hydraulic lines at master cylinder, and remove pressure loss indicator valve bolt (if equipped). Disconnect vacuum hose, and remove clevis from brake pedal. Remove power brake unit attaching nuts from pedal side of firewall, and remove master cylinder and power brake unit as an assembly. Separate master cylinder from power brake unit.

Installation — To install, reverse removal procedure and adjust push rod-to-master cylinder clearance to .36" (9.13 mm) by turning push rod nut. Bleed hydraulic system.

Check Valve Replacement — Check valve is located on power brake unit. To replace, remove vacuum input line and pull and turn check valve out of power unit. Install new check valve by pushing and turning to seat valve. Reconnect vacuum line.

OVERHAUL

NOTE — *Master Cylinder, Power Brake Unit, and Brake Pressure Limiter cannot be Overhauled.*

FRONT CALIPER

Disassembly — Remove caliper assembly from vehicle, and remove piston dust cover. Using compressed air, introduced at caliper fluid port, carefully remove piston from caliper assembly. Remove piston seal from cylinder. Using a wedge, spread legs of caliper piston bracket a small amount. Remove caliper stop peg from piston bracket. Slide cylinder assembly from bracket.

Cleaning & Inspection — Clean all parts in denatured alcohol and inspect for piston and cylinder wear. Replace worn parts as required. Replace all rubber seals during overhaul.

Reassembly — Lubricate cylinder bore, piston, and seals with brake fluid prior to reassembly. To reassemble, reverse disassembly procedure.

RENAULT (Cont.)

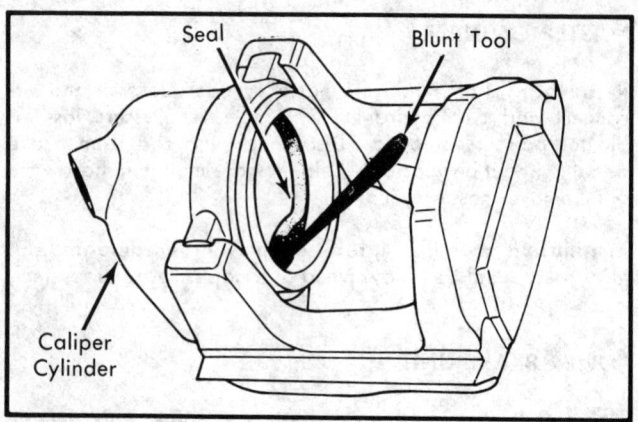

Fig. 4 Prying Out Seal from Caliper Cylinder Bore

WHEEL CYLINDER

Disassembly & Reassembly — Remove dust boots, pistons, cups and spring. Examine components for damage or excessive wear. Replace worn parts as required. Before reassembly, dip pistons and cups in clean brake fluid.

TIGHTENING SPECIFICATIONS

Application	Ft. Lbs. (mkg)
Caliper Bracket Bolts	50 (6.9)
Rotor-to-Hub	20 (2.8)
Stub Axle Nut	90 (12.5)

DRUM BRAKE SPECIFICATIONS

Application	Wheel Cyl. Bore Diameter In. (mm)	Drum Diameter In. (mm)	Original Diameter In. (mm)	Maximum Refinish Diameter In. (mm)	Discard Diameter In. (mm)
Le Car	.866 (22)	7.10 (180)	7.10 (180)	7.136 (181)	.....

DISC BRAKE SPECIFICATIONS

Application	Caliper Bore Diameter In. (mm)	Lateral Runout In. (mm)	Parallelism In. (mm)	Original Thickness In. (mm)	Minimum Refinish Thickness In. (mm)	Discard Thickness In. (mm)
Le Car	1.772 (45)	.004 (.10)	.....	.395 (10)	①	.355 (9)

① — Rotor cannot be machined; it must be replaced.

SAAB

99
900

DESCRIPTION

Service brake system is hydraulically operated by a tandem master cylinder and vacuum power brake unit acting on four-wheel disc brakes. Front calipers are sliding yoke Girling calipers; rear brakes are fixed yoke ATE calipers. Master cylinder contains level sensor which illuminates a warning lamp on instrument panel if fluid level becomes low. Brake circuit is double diagonal system (right front, left rear/left front, right rear). Parking brake is mechanically operated on FRONT brake caliper assemblies.

ADJUSTMENT

PARKING BRAKE

Before adjusting cable, apply brake lever several times to stretch cables. Rotate cable adjusting nuts located at rear of parking brake lever under plastic cover until distance between lever on front caliper and yoke is .016-.022" (.41-.56 mm). Check distance with parking brake fully released.

NOTE — *Parking brake cables are crossed, so to adjust left parking brake mechanism (cable), right adjusting nut must be rotated and vice versa.*

BRAKE WARNING LIGHT

A dual warning light (individual lights on 900) is mounted on instrument panel. Parking brake light should glow when parking brake lever is pulled 1 notch (ignition on) and go off when lever is fully released. To check circuit warning sensor, fully release parking brake and ensure light is off (99 only). Open engine compartment and raise master cylinder filler cap; warning lamp should glow. If not, check bulb or circuit connections.

REMOVAL & INSTALLATION

DISC BRAKE PADS

Removal — Raise and support vehicle on safety stands; remove wheel. Rotate brake rotor until recess in edge of rotor is aligned with brake pads. On Girling calipers, remove damper spring, pin retaining clips and retaining pins. On ATE calipers, remove cover plate, mounting pins and retaining spring. Remove brake pads; use extractor tool (8995771) if required.

Installation — Open bleeder screw and seat piston into cylinder bore; close bleeder screw. On Girling calipers, rotate piston while pressing into cylinder bore. On ATE calipers, check piston position with template (8995342). Install brake pads. On Girling calipers, install retaining pins, clips and damper spring. On ATE calipers, install spring, lock pins and cover plate. Pump brake pedal several times to set pad-to-rotor clearance.

NOTE — *Girling caliper brake pads are not interchangeable. Outer pads are identified by "V" notch.*

DISC BRAKE CALIPER

Removal — Raise and support vehicle and remove wheels. On front wheel calipers, disconnect parking brake cable from lever on caliper. On all wheels, disconnect hydraulic line from hose, then plug lines to prevent entry of dirt and loss of fluid. Remove caliper attaching bolts and lift off caliper.

Installation — To install, reverse removal procedure and note the following: Tighten all attaching bolts, bleed hydraulic system and adjust parking brake cables.

DISC BRAKE ROTOR

Removal — Remove caliper assembly (hydraulic line attached) and support out of way. DO NOT allow caliper to hang by hydraulic line. On front disc, apply parking brake, remove rotor and hub attaching nut from spindle and release parking brake. Remove rotor and hub assembly from spindle with a puller, remove hub-to-rotor bolts and separate rotor. On rear disc, remove rotor attaching bolts and rotor.

Installation — To install, reverse removal procedure. Tighten all nuts and bolts and adjust parking brake if necessary.

MASTER CYLINDER

Removal — Disconnect electrical lead to warning switch on master cylinder. Disconnect clutch master cylinder hose from fluid reservoir, then plug reservoir nipple to prevent loss of fluid. Disconnect hydraulic lines from master cylinder. Remove master cylinder-to-power brake unit attaching nuts and lift off master cylinder.

Installation — To install, reverse removal procedure and bleed hydraulic system.

POWER BRAKE BOOSTER

NOTE — *Before power brake unit can be removed on 900 Series, ash tray and lower portion of instrument panel must be removed.*

Removal — From inside engine compartment, remove upper circlip from brake pedal push rod. Disconnect all electrical leads, hydraulic and vacuum lines from master cylinder and power brake unit. Remove 4 attaching nuts and lift off master cylinder and power unit as an assembly. Separate master cylinder from power unit.

NOTE — *Three power unit attaching nuts are removed from inside vehicle while fourth is removed from engine compartment, 99 Series only. All attaching nuts are removed from inside vehicle on 900 Series.*

Installation — To install, reverse removal procedure and bleed hydraulic system.

Check Valve Replacement — Remove vacuum hose clamps at check valve and remove check valve from power unit. To install, reverse removal procedure.

Filter Replacement — Remove power brake unit from vehicle. Remove rubber dust boot and filter retainer. Withdraw silencer and filter from end of booster. To install, cut a slit in filter and slip over push rod. Reverse removal procedure and ensure slots in filter and silencer are 180° apart.

SAAB (Cont.)

OVERHAUL

CALIPER ASSEMBLY

Disassembly (Girling Type) — 1) With caliper removed from vehicle, mount assembly in a soft jawed vise. Remove parking brake return spring. Separate yoke from caliper assembly. Remove spring and parking brake lever from yoke.

2) Remove retaining ring and dust boot, then using compressed air, force out indirect piston assembly from caliper. Press direct piston push rod and remove piston from caliper. Remove "O" rings and seal rings from caliper bore and pistons.

Cleaning & Inspection — Wash all parts, except indirect piston assembly, in clean brake fluid and dry with a lint-free cloth. Inspect all parts for corrosion, damage or wear; replace defective parts. Replace all rubber parts during overhaul.

NOTE — *Indirect piston assembly must be wiped clean only. DO NOT use any type of solvent or brake fluid.*

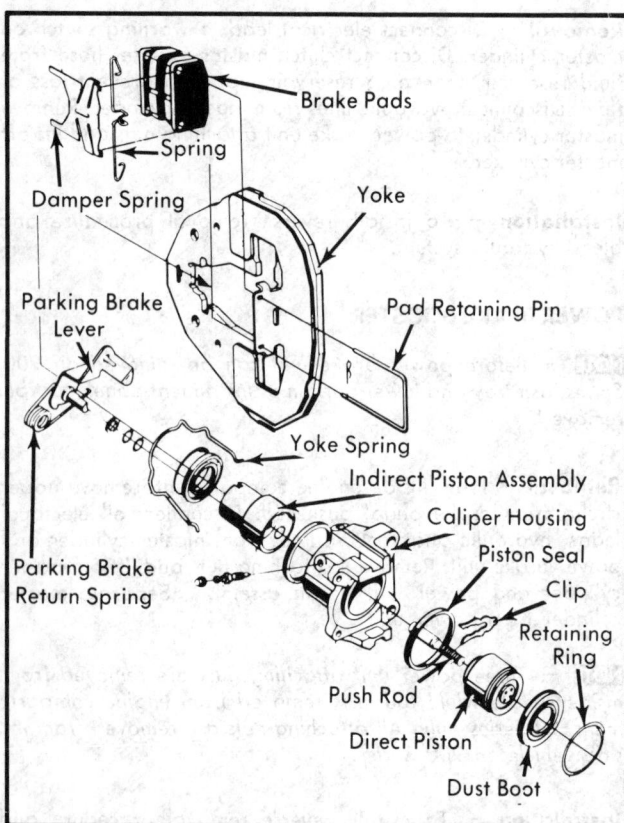

Fig. 1   Exploded View of Girling Caliper

Reassembly — 1) Lubricate pistons and caliper bore with clean brake fluid, then install new "O" rings and seal rings to pistons and caliper bore. Install indirect piston into caliper with recess for yoke aligned with groove in caliper housing, then install direct piston in the same manner. Press in indirect piston and screw in direct piston until edges of dust boot grooves are flush with caliper housing.

2) Install dust boots and retaining rings. Fit yoke spring and parking brake lever to yoke, then align yoke guide edges with groove on caliper housing and install yoke. Lift parking brake

lever and install axle pin into hole in indirect piston. Install parking brake return spring. Check yoke-to-caliper housing clearance; no clearance is permissible on bleeder screw side, opposite side clearance must be .006-.012" (.15-.30 mm). See Fig. 2.

NOTE — *Yoke must seat in indirect piston recess.*

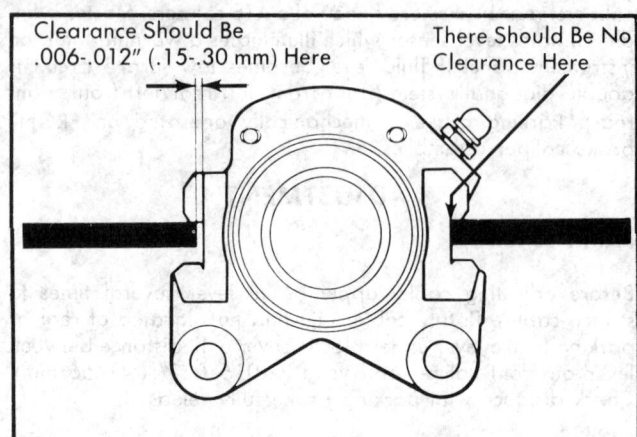

Fig. 2   Girling Caliper Clearance Measuring Points

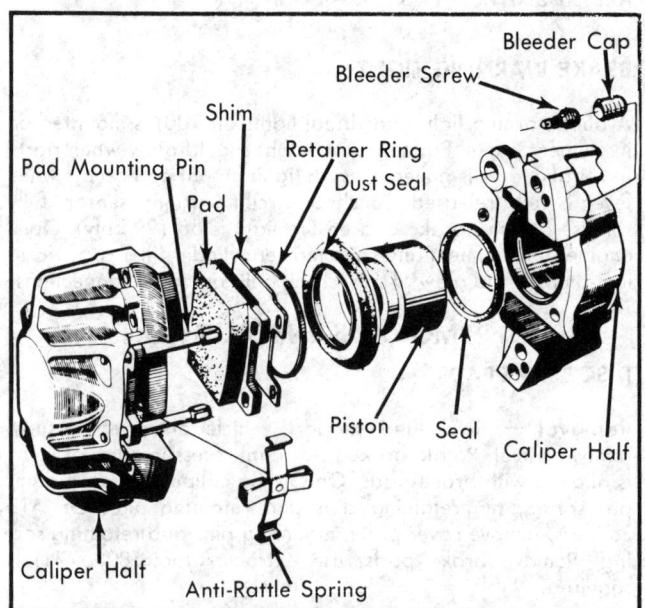

Fig. 3   Exploded View of ATE Caliper

Disassembly (ATE Type) — With caliper and pads removed, clean outer portion of caliper. Remove dust covers and retaining rings. Insert wooden block between pistons and carefully apply compressed air to fluid inlet port to force pistons out of cylinder bores. Remove piston seals from cylinder bores without damaging bores. Remove bleeder screw.

NOTE — *DO NOT separate caliper halves.*

Cleaning & Inspection — Wash all parts in clean brake fluid. Inspect cylinder bores and pistons for corrosion, damage or wear; replace defective parts. Replace all rubber parts during overhaul.

Reassembly — Coat all parts with clean brake fluid and install new piston seals in cylinder bores. Carefully install pistons

SAAB (Cont.)

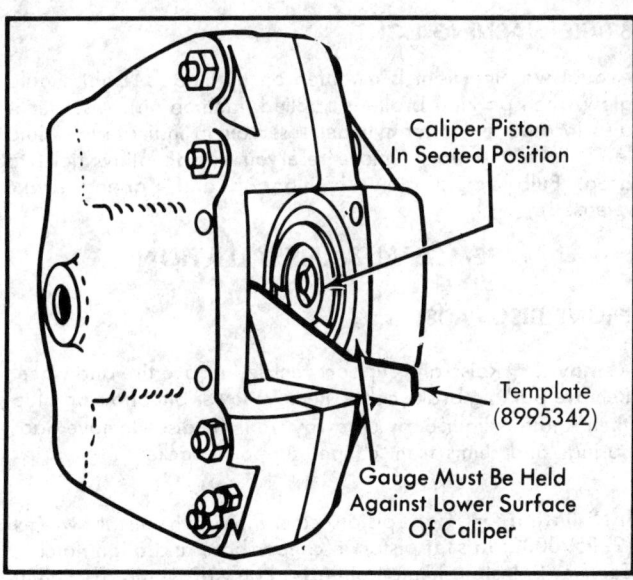

Fig. 4   Checking ATE Caliper Piston Position

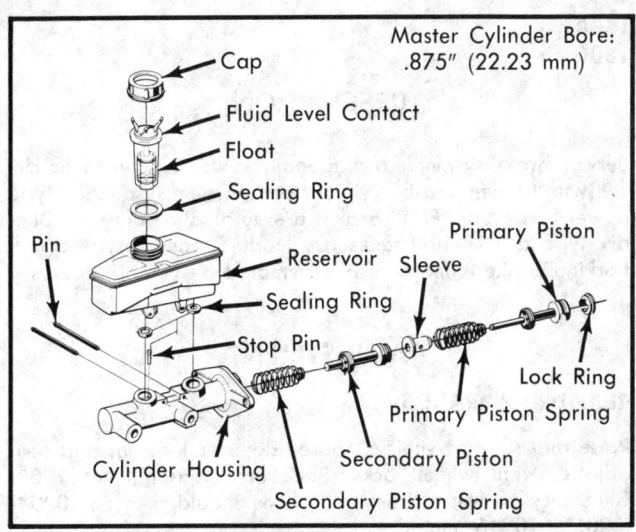

Fig. 5   Exploded View of Master Cylinder

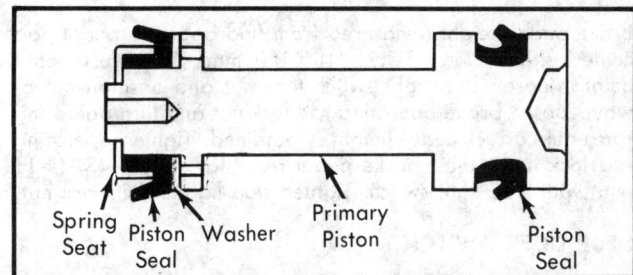

Fig. 6   Primary Piston Seal Installation

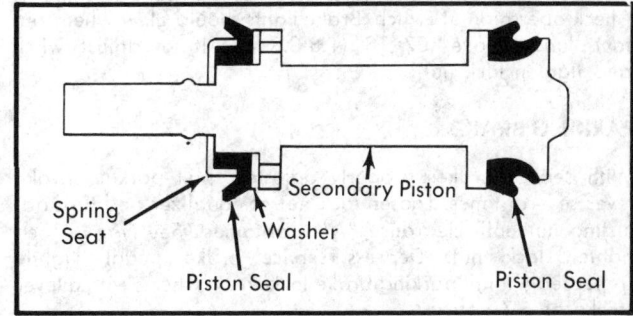

Fig. 7   Secondary Piston Seal Installation

MASTER CYLINDER

Disassembly — 1) With master cylinder removed from vehicle, drain brake fluid from reservoir. Mount cylinder in a soft jaw vise. Remove retaining pins and separate reservoir from master cylinder (pins may have to be driven out). Remove rubber seals from reservoir mounting holes in cylinder.

2) Push in on primary piston and pull secondary piston stop pin from forward reservoir mounting hole. Remove circlip and take out primary piston assembly and spring. Remove cylinder from vise and carefully knock it against a block of wood to remove secondary piston assembly and spring. Remove brake warning switch from master cylinder, then remove end plug and lift out warning valve assembly.

Cleaning & Inspection — Wash all parts in clean brake fluid and dry with a clean, lint-free cloth. Inspect all parts for corrosion, damage or wear; replace defective parts. Replace rubber parts during overhaul.

Reassembly — Reverse disassembly procedure. Coat all parts with clean brake fluid and use care not to damage seals during installation of pistons.

DISC BRAKE SPECIFICATIONS						
Application	Caliper Bore Diameter In. (mm)	Lateral Runout In. (mm)	Parallelism In. (mm)	Original Thickness In. (mm)	Minimum Refinish Thickness In. (mm)	Discard Thickness In. (mm)
99 & 900 Front	2.126 (54)	.004 (.10)	.0006 (.015)	.500 (12.7)	.461 (11.7)	.460 (11.6)
Rear	1.181 (30)	.004 (.10)	.0006 (.015)	.413 (10.5)	.374 (9.5)	.373 (9.4)

SUBARU

1600
1800

DESCRIPTION

Service brake system is a diagonally split, dual hydraulic circuit with tandem master cylinder and vacuum suspended type power brake unit. Front brakes are automatic adjusting, Bendix type disc. Rear brakes are leading/trailing type drum. Parking brake is mechanically actuated on FRONT brakes.

ADJUSTMENT

REAR DRUM BRAKE SHOES

Raise and support vehicle. Loosen adjuster lock nut and turn adjuster until wheel locks. Back off adjusting nut 180°. Clearance between drum and shoes should then be .0004-.0006" (.10-.15 mm).

PEDAL HEIGHT & FREE PLAY

Brake pedal height (measured from floorboard to pedal pad center) should be 5.3-5.9" (135-150 mm). To adjust pedal height, loosen stop light switch lock nut and position out of way. Loosen brake operating rod lock nut and turn operating rod until correct pedal height is obtained. Tighten operating rod lock nut. Adjust brake pedal free play to .20-.43" (5-11 mm) with stop light switch. Tighten stop light switch lock nut.

STOP LIGHT SWITCH

Stop light switch is located under instrument panel, above brake pedal. To adjust stop light switch, loosen lock nut and position switch so contact plunger touches pedal arm stopper. Check operation of switch. Brake lights should glow when contact plunger moves .07-.13" (1.8-3.3 mm). If not, adjust switch and tighten lock nut.

PARKING BRAKE

With service brakes properly adjusted, pull parking brake lever several times. Loosen lock nut at equalizer and turn adjusting nut until clearance "A" is obtained. See Fig. 1. Then tighten lock nut. Depress service brake pedal slightly (repeatedly) until parking brake locks front wheels with a lever stroke of 6-7 notches.

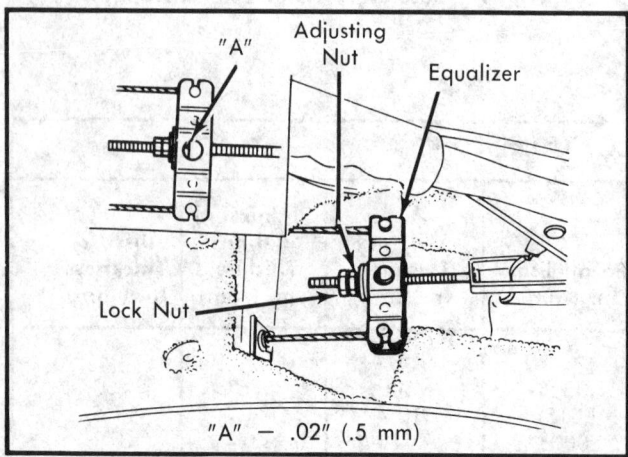

Fig. 1   Location for Adjusting Parking Brake

BRAKE WARNING LIGHT

A dual warning light is mounted on all models. Light should glow when parking brake is applied (ignition on). A sensor is also located in master cylinder reservoir to indicate low fluid level. To test sensor, remove reservoir cap to allow float to drop. Bulb should glow (ignition on and parking brake released).

REMOVAL & INSTALLATION

FRONT DISC PADS

Removal — Raise and support vehicle; remove tire and wheel. Remove parking brake cable. Remove lower pin and stop plug, then rotate caliper body up away from the disc. Remove pads, springs and shims from caliper support bracket.

Installation — Turn piston clockwise with piston wrench (925590000) to seat piston in caliper bore and align notches. See Fig. 2. Install shim on outer pad only (if required), then install pads and springs. Rotate caliper body down and install stop plug and pin. Reconnect parking brake cable. Depress brake pedal several times to set pad-to-rotor clearance.

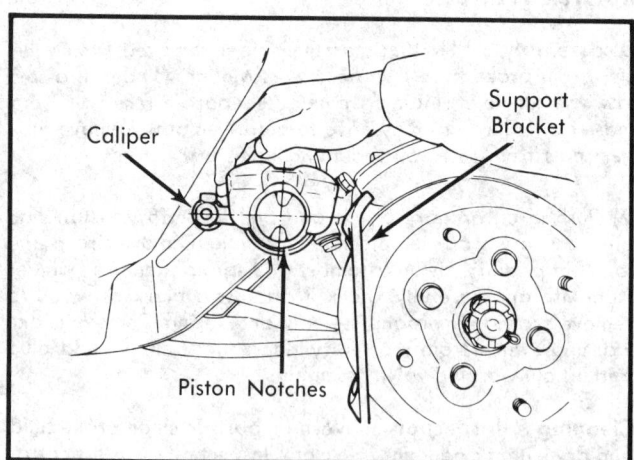

Fig. 2   Aligning Caliper Piston Notches for Replacing Disc Brake Pads

FRONT DISC CALIPER

Removal — Raise and support vehicle; remove tire and wheel. Remove pads as previously described. Disconnect and plug hydraulic line at caliper and remove parking brake cable. Remove caliper assembly. DO NOT remove support bracket unless rotor is being removed.

Installation — Apply silicone grease to lock pin and guide pin. Install caliper assembly, pads and parking brake cable. Install hydraulic line, then bleed hydraulic system.

FRONT DISC ROTOR

Removal — Raise and support vehicle; remove tire and wheel. Remove disc pads as previously described. Remove caliper assembly and hang from frame with wire; DO NOT disconnect hydraulic line. Remove caliper mounting bracket bolts and bracket. Using a puller, pull rotor and hub assembly from axle. Remove hub-to-rotor bolts and separate rotor from hub.

SUBARU (Cont.)

NOTE – *Replace mounting bracket when rotor is replaced.*

Installation – To install, reverse removal procedure and tighten hub-to-rotor bolts evenly. Depress brake pedal several times to seat pads.

REAR BRAKE DRUM

Removal – Raise and support vehicle; remove tire and wheel. Remove dust cap and wheel bearing components (2-wheel drive). Remove cotter pin and castle nut on 4-wheel drive. Remove brake drum. Loosen brake adjustment if necessary and use puller if required to pull off brake drum.

Installation – To install, reverse removal procedure and adjust wheel bearings. *See Wheel Bearing Adjustment in WHEEL ALIGNMENT Section.*

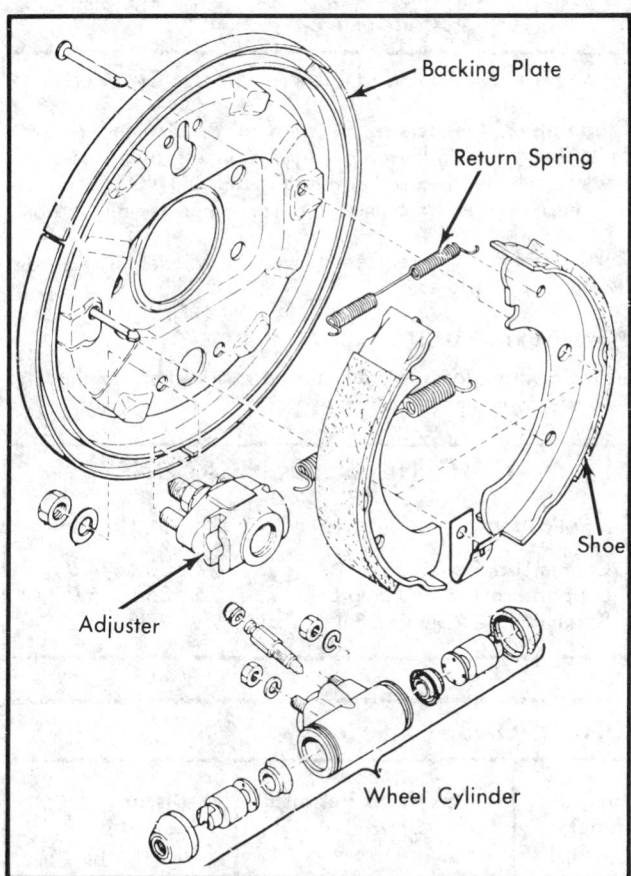

Fig. 3 Exploded View of Rear Drum Brake Assembly

REAR BRAKE SHOES

Removal – With brake drum removed, remove and plug hydraulic line from wheel cylinder. Remove backing plate bolts and remove complete assembly. Separate shoes from backing plate by removing hold down springs then disconnect lower end first and then remove upper end from wheel cylinder. Separate return springs from shoes.

Installation – To install, reverse removal procedure and note the following: Return springs are installed with coils on inside of shoe assemblies (next to backing plate). Return springs are not interchangeable; lower spring is thicker diameter. Adjust brakes and bleed hydraulic system.

MASTER CYLINDER

Removal & Installation – Siphon brake fluid from reservoir. Disconnect warning light electrical connection. Remove hydraulic lines. Remove retaining nuts and remove master cylinder from power brake unit. To install, reverse removal procedure and bleed hydraulic system.

POWER BRAKE UNIT

Removal & Installation – From inside vehicle, remove cotter pin and disconnect push rod from brake pedal. Remove power brake retaining nuts from firewall. In engine compartment, remove master cylinder retaining nuts. Disconnect vacuum hose at power brake unit and wiring harness from master cylinder. Position master cylinder to one side without damaging hydraulic lines. Remove power brake unit. To install, reverse removal procedure and bleed hydraulic system.

OVERHAUL

FRONT CALIPER

Disassembly – 1) Thoroughly clean exterior of caliper with clean brake fluid. Remove outer pad clip and bleed screw. Remove dust boot retainer and dust boot. Apply compressed air or liquid to fluid inlet and force piston out of caliper bore.

2) Carefully remove guide pin boot and piston seal. Remove parking brake lever cap ring and lever cap, then remove snap ring from lever and spindle assembly.

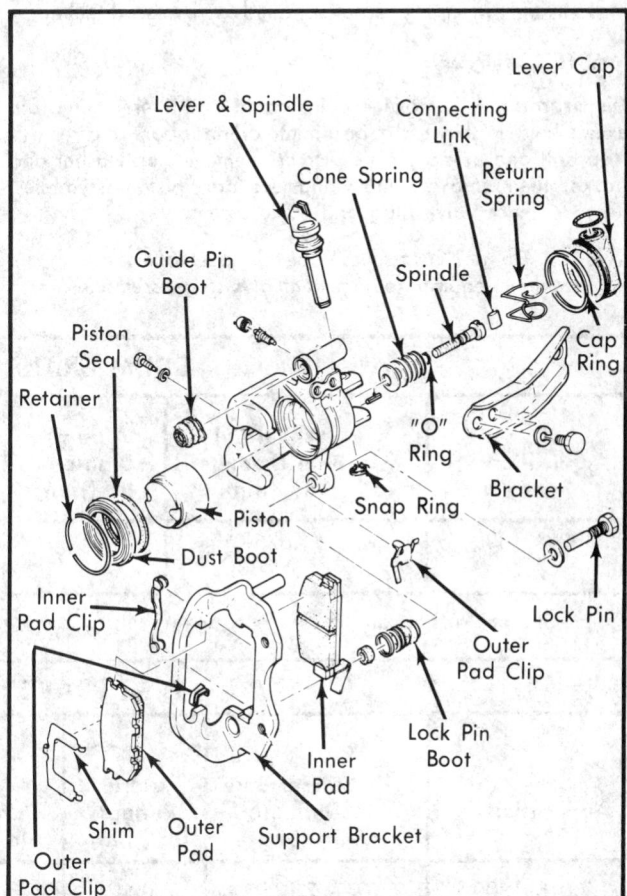

Fig. 4 Exploded View of Front Disc Caliper Assembly

SUBARU (Cont.)

3) Mount caliper assembly in soft-jaw vise and install puller (925471000) to release spring washer tension. With spring tension released, pull out lever and spindle. Remove puller and remove connecting link, return spring, spindle and cone spring.

Cleaning & Inspection — Clean all components with brake fluid and ensure that inner cylinder wall is not scratched or corroded. Replace any damaged parts.

Reassembly — **1)** Coat piston seal with silicone grease and insert into cylinder by hand. Coat piston, piston boots and cylinder wall with brake fluid; hand insert piston. Install boot and retainer.

2) Lightly coat spindle and "O" ring with silicone grease. Insert spindle and install spring washers with puller (925471000). Lubricate and install connecting link (thick side in slot.) Install parking brake lever assembly, snap ring, lever cap and retainer.

REAR WHEEL CYLINDER

Disassembly — Remove boot and take out piston with cup. DO NOT separate cup unless replacement is available.

Cleaning & Inspection — Clean all parts in brake fluid only. If cylinder is out of round or burred, replace as an assembly; DO NOT hone.

NOTE — *Removal of fluid reservoir requires installation of new reservoir.*

Reassembly — To reassemble, reverse disassembly procedure and ensure piston cup is not installed in reverse direction.

MASTER CYLINDER

Disassembly — Remove level indicators and filters, then drain excess fluid. Push primary piston into cylinder bore and remove stop bolt and primary piston circlip. Remove stop washer and gasket, then remove primary and secondary piston assemblies. Remove check valve plug and valve assembly.

NOTE — *Do not disassemble piston assemblies. Piston cup replacement requires replacement of piston assemblies.*

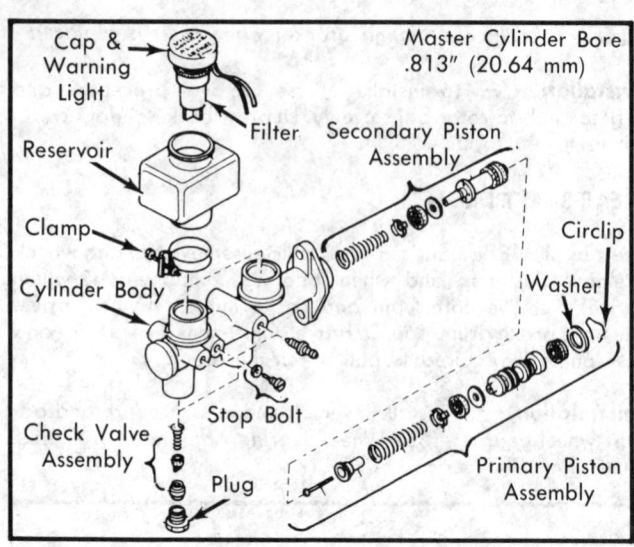

Fig. 5 Exploded View of Master Cylinder

Cleaning & Inspection — Clean all components in brake fluid. Inspect cylinder bore for smoothness and roundness. Replace cylinder if scored or out of round. DO NOT hone cylinder. Inspect piston-to-cylinder clearance and replace if worn.

Reassembly — To reassemble master cylinder, reverse disassembly procedure.

POWER BRAKE UNIT

Manufacturer does not recommend disassembly of this unit. Replace as complete assembly.

TIGHTENING SPECIFICATIONS

Application	Ft. Lbs. (mkg)
Caliper Lock Pin	33-54 (4.6-7.5)
Support Bracket Mounting Bolts	36-51 (5.0-7.0)
Backing Plate Mounting Bolts	23-32 (3.2-4.4)

DRUM BRAKE SPECIFICATIONS

Application	Wheel Cyl. Bore Diameter In. (mm)	Drum Diameter In. (mm)	Original Diameter In. (mm)	Maximum Refinish Diameter In. (mm)	Discard Diameter In. (mm)
1600 & 1800	.625① (15.88)	7.09 (180)	7.09 (180)	.....	7.17 (182)

① — Station Wagon and all 4-wheel drive vehicles have wheel cylinder bore of .687" (17.46 mm).

DISC BRAKE SPECIFICATIONS

Application	Caliper Bore Diameter In. (mm)	Lateral Runout In. (mm)	Parallelism In. (mm)	Original Thickness In. (mm)	Minimum Refinish Thickness In. (mm)	Discard Thickness In. (mm)
1600 & 1800	2.125 (53.97)	.004 (.10)	.....	.492 (12.5)	.....	.394 (10)

TOYOTA

Celica   Land Cruiser
Corolla   Pickup
Corona   Supra
Cressida   Tercel

DESCRIPTION

Brake systems are hydraulically actuated using a tandem master cylinder and vacuum power brake unit. Power assist units vary among models and Land Cruiser models use a separate vacuum pump to supply vacuum to power unit. Supra is equipped with 4-wheel disc brakes. All other models are equipped with front disc brakes and rear drum brakes. A load sensing proportioning valve is installed in rear circuit of all Pickup models (except ½ ton). Rear brakes on Pickup and Land Cruiser models require adjustment; all others are self-adjusting. All parking brakes are cable actuated and operate on rear discs of Supra; rear of transfer case on Land Cruiser and rear drum brakes of all other models.

NOTE – Brake caliper applications vary among models. Check and compare calipers with those shown in this article for correct service procedures.

ADJUSTMENTS

DRUM BRAKES

Pickup & Land Cruiser – Raise and support vehicle on safety stands. Release parking brake and ensure wheel rotates freely. Remove plug from adjusting hole. Turn adjusting screw with suitable adjusting tool until wheel can not be turned. Depress brake pedal and ensure drum is locked. On Land Cruiser, back off adjuster 4-5 notches or until wheel turns with slight drag. On Pickup models, back off adjuster 10-12 notches or until wheel turns freely.

BRAKE PEDAL HEIGHT

Brake pedal height is measured from center of brake pedal to asphalt sheet under carpet. To adjust clearance, loosen stop light switch and lock nut on brake pedal push rod. Adjust pedal height by turning push rod. After setting pedal height, tighten lock nut, adjust stop light switch and tighten stop light switch lock nut. See Fig. 1.

Brake Pedal Height	
Application	**Height In. (mm)**
Celica, Corona & Supra	6.5-6.9 (165-175)
Corolla	6.9-7.3 (175-185)
Cressida	6.1-6.5 (156-166)
Land Cruiser	8.5 (215)
Pickup	6.2-6.6 (157-167)
Tercel	6.4-6.5 (164-165)

BRAKE PEDAL FREE PLAY

Pedal free play is distance brake pedal travels before initial resistance of power brake push rod is contacted. To adjust pedal free play, stop engine and depress brake pedal several times to exhaust vacuum from power brake unit. Place a straightedge beside brake pedal, then press pedal down with fingers until initial resistance is felt. See Fig. 1. Free play should be .16-.28" (4-7 mm) for Tercel and .12-.24" (3-6 mm) for all others. If pedal travel is not as specified, adjust pedal height, start engine and confirm free play measurement. Check brake pedal height.

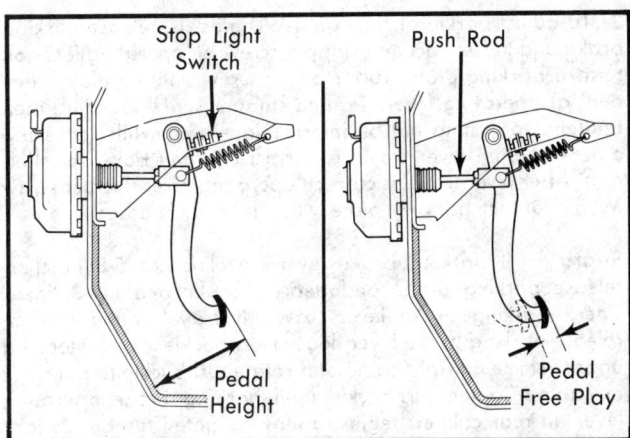

Fig. 1 Measuring Pedal Height and Free Play

PARKING BRAKE

NOTE – Before adjusting parking brake, release parking brake lever. Pull parking brake and count number of notches lever travels. If lever travel meets specifications, do not adjust parking brake. Pickup models require adjustment of service brakes before adjusting parking brake. On all other models, except Supra, if parking brake requires adjustment, first set brake shoe-to-drum clearance by depressing release knob on parking brake lever and operating lever several times. Recheck lever travel.

Celica & Corolla – If parking brake lever travel is not 3-6 notches, remove console (if equipped), release parking brake, loosen lock nut and turn adjusting screw on lever until lever travel is correct. Tighten lock nut and install console (if equipped). Wheels should be locked when parking brake is applied and rotate freely when lever is released.

Corona – If parking brake lever travel is not 3-7 notches; release parking brake, loosen lock nut on turnbuckle (under vehicle) and rotate turnbuckle until travel is correct. Tighten lock nut. Wheels should be locked when parking brake is applied and rotate freely when lever is released.

Cressida – If parking brake lever travel is not 5-7 notches; release parking brake and loosen lock nut on turnbuckle located under vehicle on right cable. Rotate turnbuckle until .39" (10 mm) of threaded cable end is inside turnbuckle. Tighten lock nut. Remove slack from rear cables by loosening lock nut on equalizer and turning adjusting nut. Tighten lock nut. Wheels should be locked when parking brake is applied and rotate freely when lever is released.

Land Cruiser – Fully release parking brake and turn adjusting cam on back of backing plate (at rear of transfer case) until brake shoes seat against drum. Back off adjusting cam 1 notch at a time until drum locks when parking brake is applied and spins freely when released. After adjusting brake shoes, adjust parking brake travel to 12 notches by turning cable adjusting nut or turnbuckle. Wheels should be locked when parking brake is applied and rotate freely when lever is released.

Brakes

TOYOTA (Cont.)

Pickup – 1) If parking brake lever travel is not 7-15 notches, adjust parking brake, AFTER adjusting service brakes. To adjust parking brake on 2-WD models, release parking brake and turn adjusting nut on intermediate lever (under vehicle) until lever travel is correct. Wheels should be locked when parking brake is applied and rotate freely when lever is released.

2) To adjust parking brake on 4-WD models, release parking brake and loosen lock nut stopper screw on operating lever on rear of backing plate. Turn stopper screw until no play is evident at operating lever. Tighten stopper screw lock nut, then tighten 1 adjusting nut on intermediate lever while loosening other nut until lever travel is correct. Tighten both adjusting nuts. After lever travel is correct, operating lever stopper screw MUST contact backing plate when lever is released.

Supra – If parking brake lever travel is not 5-8 notches; release parking brake and depress brake pedal 2-3 times. Check parking brake lever travel. If travel is not correct; release parking brake lever, loosen turnbuckle lock nut located under vehicle on right cable and rotate turnbuckle to put slack in cable. Tighten turnbuckle until parking brake operating lever on rear caliper begins to move. Tighten turnbuckle lock nut. Check parking brake operation.

NOTE – *With either operating lever pushed away from caliper, it should not move when opposite operating lever is pushed away from caliper. If it does, cable is too tight and parking brake must be readjusted.*

Tercel – If parking brake lever travel is not 2-5 notches; release parking brake and loosen lock nut on equalizer (under vehicle). Turn adjusting nut until lever travel is correct. Wheels should be locked when parking brake is applied and rotate freely when lever is released.

STOP LIGHT SWITCH

Stop light switch is located under dash, above brake pedal. To adjust, loosen lock nuts and adjust switch so contact button just touches brake pedal. Tighten lock nut and check pedal height.

BRAKE WARNING LIGHT

A dual warning light is mounted on dash of all vehicles except Pickups (single warning light). On all models, light should glow when parking brake lever is pulled 1 notch and go off when lever is fully released (ignition on). To check circuit warning on all models except Pickups, release parking brake (ignition on) and ensure light is off. Open bleed screw on 1 wheel and depress brake pedal; light should glow. Close bleed screw, replenish brake fluid and bleed hydraulic system.

LOAD SENSING PROPORTIONING VALVE (PICKUPS, EXCEPT ½ TON)

1) Set rear axle load (including vehicle weight) to 1433 lbs. (650 kg) on 4-WD pickup and to 1323 lbs. (600 kg) on all others. Install a load sensing proportioning gauge (09705-29017) to front caliper and another to rear wheel cylinder on same side of vehicle. Depress brake pedal and raise pressure on front gauge to 711 psi (50 kg/cm²).

NOTE – *DO NOT depress brake pedal more than 1 time and do not release pedal while setting front pressure reading.*

2) After 2 seconds, rear brake pressure reading should be 398-540 psi (28-38 kg/cm²). Depress brake pedal further and raise front brake pressure reading to 1138 psi (80 kg/cm²). Rear brake pressure reading should be 526-726 psi (37-51 kg/cm²). If pressure on rear gauge does not meet specifications outlined in steps **1)** and **2)**, adjust load sensing proportioning valve.

3) To adjust load sensing proportioning valve, adjust length of the lower shackle. See *Fig. 2*. If rear pressure was low, lengthen the distance "A" shown in *Fig. 2*. If rear pressure was high, shorten the distance. Repeat procedure and check pressure readings.

NOTE – *Turning the lower shackle 1 turn changes pressure reading 8.5 psi (.6 kg/cm²).*

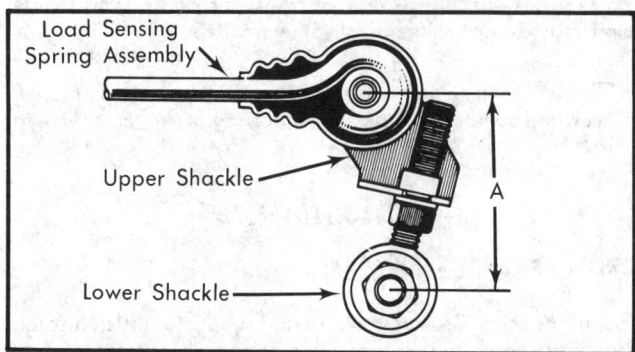

Fig. 2 Adjusting Load Sensing Proportioning Valve

4) If rear pressures do not conform to specifications shown in steps **1)** and **2)** after adjusting length of lower shackle, loosen valve body retaining nuts and reposition valve body. If rear pressure was low, lower valve body. If rear pressure was high, raise valve body. Tighten retaining nuts and adjust length of lower shackle to standard length. Standard length for 4-WD pickup should be 4.72" (120 mm) and 3.07" (78 mm) for all others. Repeat procedure and check brake pressure readings.

5) If pressures do not meet to those specified in step **1)** and **2)**, position valve body in upper most position and depress brake pedal to obtain readings shown in Load Sensing Proportional Valve Specifications table. If measured value does not meet specifications shown in table, replace valve assembly.

Load Sensing Proportioning Valve Specifications	
Front Reading psi (kg/cm²)	**Rear Reading** psi (kg/cm²)
71 (5) 71 (5)	
711 (50) 280-337 (19.7-23.7)	
1138 (80) 424-509 (29.8-35.8)	

REMOVAL & INSTALLATION

NOTE – *Front disc calipers used on Toyota vehicles may vary between manufacturer and model. Refer to appropriate illustrations to assist in identification of caliper.*

TOYOTA (Cont.)

FRONT DISC BRAKE PADS

Removal ("F" Type) — Raise and support vehicle; remove tire and wheel. Remove spring clips and guides. Remove cylinder and suspend out of way without disconnecting hydraulic line. Remove disc pads, shims (if equipped), guide plates, anti-rattle springs and pad support plates. See Fig. 3.

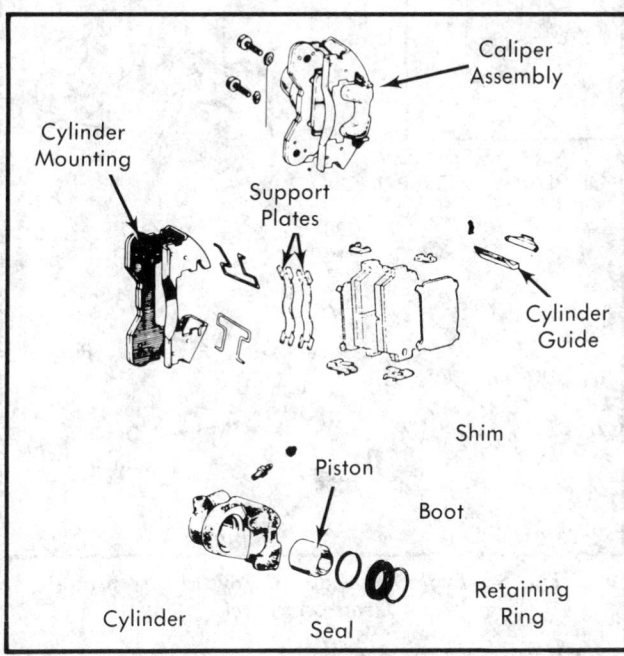

Fig. 3   Exploded View of "F" Type Disc Brake Used on Celica and Supra

Installation — Clean piston and cylinder assembly, then seat piston in cylinder bore, opening bleed screw if necessary. Install pad support plates, anti-rattle springs, guide plates, disc pads and shims (if equipped). Apply brake grease to cylinder guides. Install cylinder and retain with guides and spring clips.

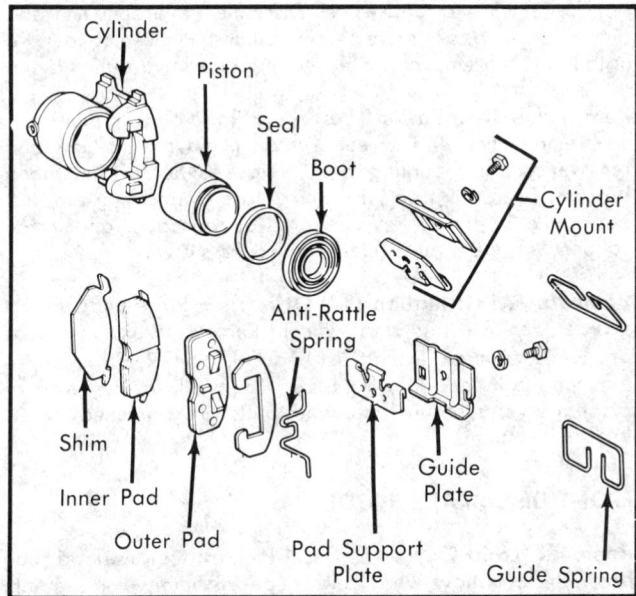

Fig. 4   Exploded View of "K" Type Disc Brake Used on Cab and Chassis Pickup

Removal ("K" Type) — Raise and support vehicle; remove tire and wheel. Remove guide plates, support springs and pad support plates. Remove cylinder with outer pad attached and suspend from frame without disconnecting hydraulic line. Remove outer pad anti-rattle spring. Remove outer pad and shim (if equipped). Remove inner pad and shim (if equipped) from cylinder mount. See Fig. 4.

Installation — Clean piston and cylinder assembly, then seat piston in cylinder bore, opening bleed screw if necessary. Install inner pad and shim (if equipped) to cylinder mount. Install outer pad, shim (if equipped) and anti-rattle spring on cylinder. Apply brake grease to cylinder guides. Install cylinder (with outer pad installed) over inner pad, then install pad support plates, support springs and guide plates.

NOTE — Larger side of support springs MUST face away from vehicle.

Removal (Girling) — Raise and support vehicle; remove tire and wheel. Remove clip, pins, anti-rattle spring, pads and shims.

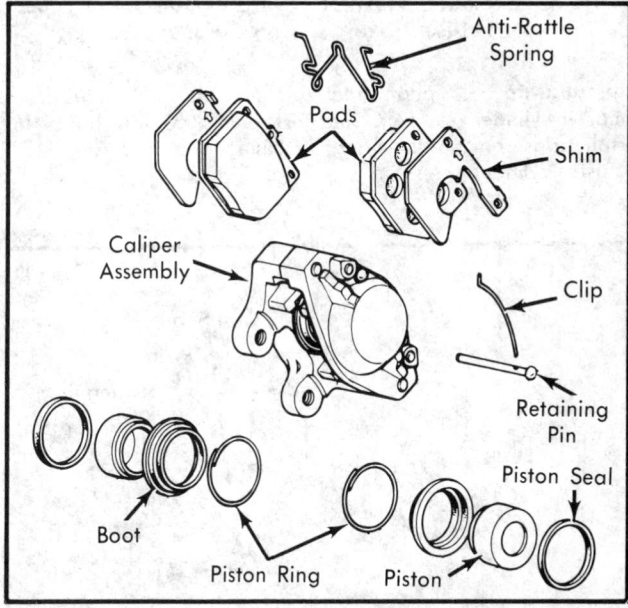

Fig. 5   Exploded View of Girling Type Disc Brake Used on Corona, Cressida and Standard Pickups

Installation — Coat both sides of shim with brake grease. Remove small amount of brake fluid from master cylinder reservoir. Push pistons into cylinder bore. Install shims with arrows pointing in forward rotation of disc. Install springs, pins and clips. Refill master cylinder reservoir.

Removal & Installation (Corolla) — Raise and support vehicle; remove tire and wheel. Remove pad protector, anti-rattle springs, spring pins, pad and shims (if equipped). Clean dirt from pin portion of torque plate. To install, clean piston assembly and seat piston in cylinder bore. Insert pads and shims (if equipped). Install retaining pins, anti-rattle springs and protector.

Removal (Land Cruiser & 4-WD Pickup) — Raise and support vehicle; remove tire and wheel. Remove clip, retaining pins and anti-rattle spring. Pull disc pads from caliper cavity.

Brakes

TOYOTA (Cont.)

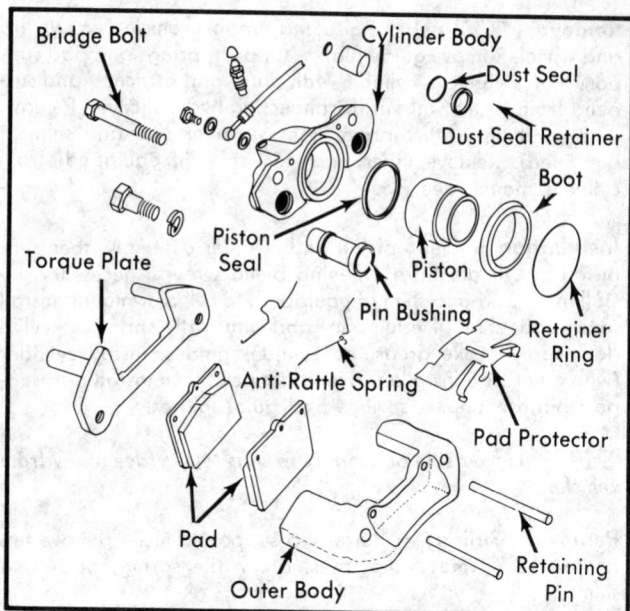

Fig. 6 Exploded View of Toyota or Sumitomo Type Disc Brake Used on Corolla

Installation — Siphon small amount of brake fluid from master cylinder reservoir. Seat pistons into cylinder bores. Install pads, anti-rattle spring, retaining pins and clip. Refill master cylinder reservoir.

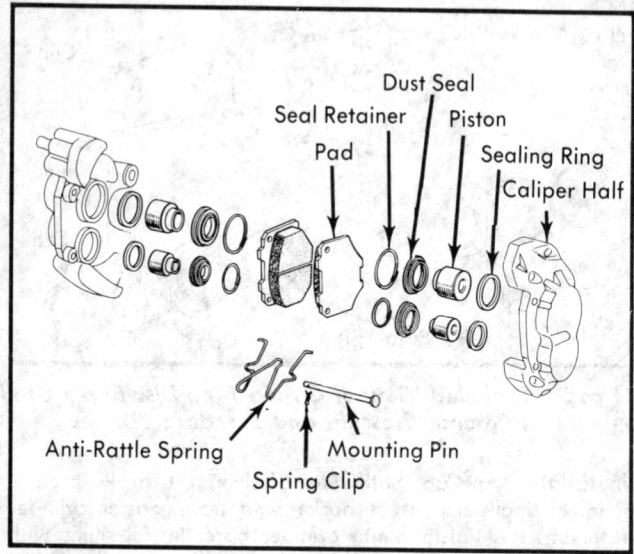

Fig. 7 Exploded View of Disc Brake Assembly Used on Land Cruiser and 4-WD Pickup

Removal (Tercel) — Raise and support vehicle; remove tire and wheel. Using 2 wrenches, remove cylinder mounting bolts and suspend cylinder from frame without disconnecting hydraulic line. Remove inner pad, then remove outer pad with shim attached. Remove anti-rattle springs, pad guide plates and support plates. Remove inner shim from piston and separate shim from outer pad.

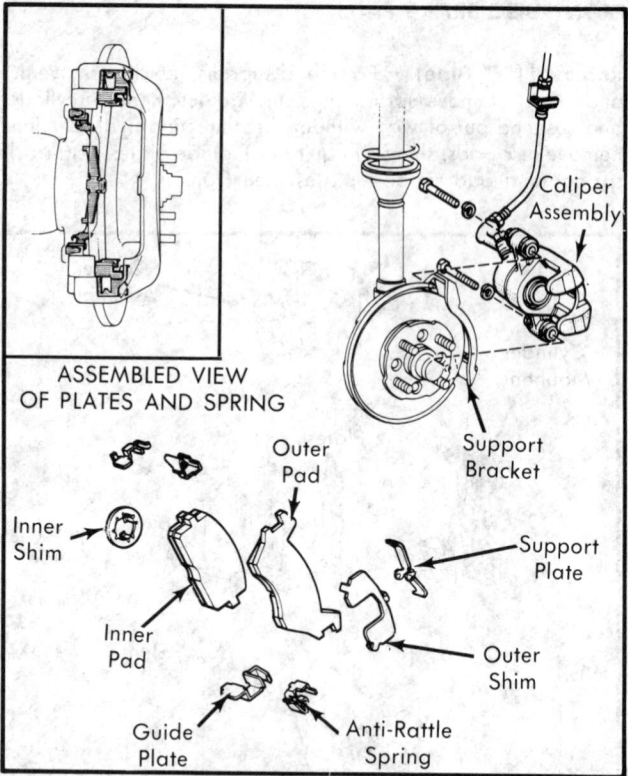

Fig. 8 Exploded View of Toyota Disc Brake Used on Tercel

FRONT DISC BRAKE CALIPER

Removal & Installation ("F" Type) — Raise and support vehicle; remove tire and wheel. Remove spring clips and guide plates. Disconnect hydraulic line and remove caliper. Remove brake pads as previously outlined. To install, apply brake grease to guides and reverse removal procedure. Bleed hydraulic system.

Removal & Installation ("K" Type) — Raise and support vehicle; remove tire and wheel. Disconnect hydraulic line and remove brake pads as previously outlined. Remove caliper. To install, reverse removal procedure and bleed hydraulic system.

Removal & Installation (Tercel) — Raise and support vehicle; remove tire and wheel. Disconnect hydraulic line and remove caliper mounting bolts. Slide caliper off mounting bracket. To install, apply rubber grease to retaining pin dust boots and bushings. Reverse removal procedure and install caliper with NEW pins. Bleed hydraulic system.

Removal & Installation (All Others) — Raise and support vehicle; remove tire and wheel. Remove brake pads as previously outlined. Disconnect hydraulic line. Remove caliper mounting bolts and lift off caliper. To install, reverse removal procedure and ensure mounting bolts are tightened. Bleed hydraulic system.

FRONT DISC BRAKE ROTOR

Removal (Land Cruiser & 4 x 4 Pickup) — Raise and support vehicle; remove wheel and caliper assembly. Remove hub grease cap, snap ring, flange and gasket. Remove free wheel hub (if equipped). Remove lock nut and adjusting nut with

TOYOTA (Cont.)

suitable socket (09607-60020). Remove rotor and hub as an assembly. Mark hub and rotor for reassembly reference and separate.

NOTE — *Free wheel hub control handle must be set to "FREE" position for removal.*

Installation — To install, reverse removal procedure and note the following: Adjust wheel bearings. *See Wheel Bearing Adjustment in WHEEL ALIGNMENT Section.*

Removal (Tercel) — 1) Raise and support vehicle; remove tire and wheel. Remove cotter pin and castellated cap. Depress brake pedal and loosen bearing lock nut. Remove caliper assembly as previously described and suspend from frame without disconnecting hydraulic line.

2) Disconnect tie rod end using remover (09610-20011). Using a jack, raise left lower arm assembly. Remove stabilizer bar and strut bar from lower arm. Remove bolt securing lower arm to crossmember and disconnect lower arm from crossmember.

3) Remove bearing lock nut and washer. Using puller (09950-20013), pull hub from drive axle shaft. Remove shock absorber-to-steering knuckle retaining bolt. Separate shock absorber from knuckle. Remove steering knuckle and hub assembly from vehicle with lower arm attached.

NOTE — *Before removing hub assembly, suspend drive axle shaft up so it does not fall or become damaged.*

4) Separate lower arm from steering knuckle. Remove inner dust shield and remove oil seal. Using hub remover (09608-16031), force hub out of steering knuckle. Place alignment marks on hub and rotor for reassembly reference. Remove hub-to-rotor bolts and separate hub from rotor.

Installation — 1) Install new outer bearing if removed and adjust bearing preload. *See Wheel Bearing Adjustment in Wheel Alignment Section.* Align marks made during removal and install hub to rotor. Tighten hub-to-rotor bolts evenly. Install spacer in steering knuckle, then install inner bearing and race.

2) Using installer (09636-20010), press steering knuckle onto hub with 2205 lbs. (1000 kg) of pressure. With pressure still applied, rotate steering knuckle to settle bearings. Using a spring pull scale, measure frictional force of steering knuckle with pressure still applied. Frictional force should be 13-26 ozs. (370-750 g).

3) Increase pressure to 7716 lbs. (3500 kg), rotate steering knuckle to settle bearings and measure frictional force. Force should be 13-40 ozs. (370-1120 g). If frictional force is not to specification, insert thinner spacer to raise force or thicker spacer to lower force.

4) Tap oil seal into steering knuckle until it is recessed .16" (4 mm) from end of steering knuckle. Install dust shield and coat oil seal lip with multi-purpose grease. Attach lower arm to steering knuckle. Place steering knuckle and lower arm into position and insert drive axle shaft into hub assembly. Attach steering knuckle to shock absorber. Loosely install bearing washer and lock nut.

5) Loosely install strut bar to lower arm. Align stopper on shock absorber with steering knuckle. Raise lower arm with a

jack until steering knuckle contacts shock absorber stopper. Attach lower arm to crossmember and loosely install retaining bolt. Insert bolt to retain steering knuckle to shock absorber and tighten.

6) Connect stabilizer bar to lower arm and tighten nut. Connect and tighten tie rod to steering knuckle. Install disc brake caliper, depress brake pedal and tighten axle nut. Bounce vehicle several times to settle suspension, then tighten lower arm-to-crossmember bolt and strut bar with vehicle weight resting on suspension system. Check front alignment. *See WHEEL ALIGNMENT Section.*

Removal (All Others) — Raise and support vehicle; remove tire and wheel. Remove caliper as previously outlined. Remove hub grease cap, cotter pin, washer and castellated nut. Carefully remove outer wheel bearing. Remove rotor and hub assembly and place alignment marks on rotor and hub for reassembly reference. Remove hub-to-rotor bolts and separate hub from rotor.

REAR DISC BRAKE PADS

Removal — Raise and support vehicle; remove wheel. Remove parking brake cable from brake lever. Remove cylinder guides and plates. Remove cylinder and hang out of way. DO NOT let cylinder hang by hydraulic line. Remove pad springs, shims and springs. Remove anti-rattle springs, pad guide plates and pad support plates.

Installation — Preset piston before installing pads by pushing and turning piston clockwise until it retracts into cylinder body. Install pad support plates, pad guide plates and anti-rattle springs. Install pads, shims and springs. Install cylinder, guides and plates. Install parking brake cable.

NOTE — *Piston stopper groove and inner pad protrusion must be aligned.*

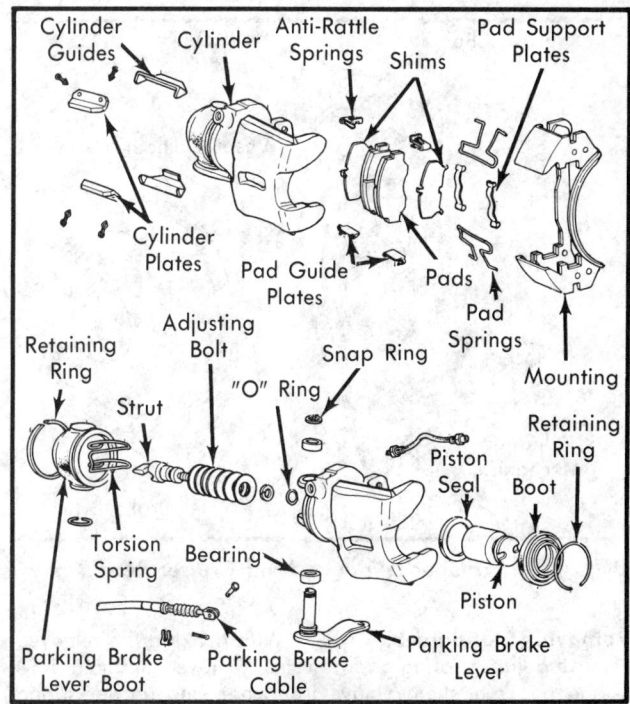

Fig. 9 Exploded View of Supra Rear Disc Brake

TOYOTA (Cont.)

REAR DISC BRAKE CALIPER

Removal & Installation — Raise and support vehicle; remove wheel. Remove parking brake cable from brake lever. Remove cylinder guides and plates. Remove and plug hydraulic line at cylinder. Remove cylinder and mount. To install, reverse removal procedure and bleed brake system.

REAR DISC BRAKE ROTOR

Removal & Installation — With wheel and caliper removed, slide rotor off axle flange. To install, reverse removal procedure and bleed brake system.

REAR BRAKE DRUM

Removal (All Models) — Raise and support vehicle; remove wheel. Remove set screws from brake drum (if equipped). Pull drum from axle flange. It may be necessary to loosen brake adjustment before removing drum.

Installation — On all models (except Land Cruiser) set brake shoe-to-drum clearance by measuring inside diameter of brake drum and diameter of brake shoes. Turn brake adjuster until difference between diameters is .02" (.6 mm). Install brake drum and adjust brakes if required.

BRAKE SHOES

Removal (Land Cruiser) — With brake drum removed, remove hold down pins and clips. Remove return springs and remove brake shoes.

Installation — Position brake shoes over wheel cylinders with front return spring hooked on inner side of shoe. Install rear return spring to outer side of shoe. Install hold down pins and clips. Adjust and bleed brakes.

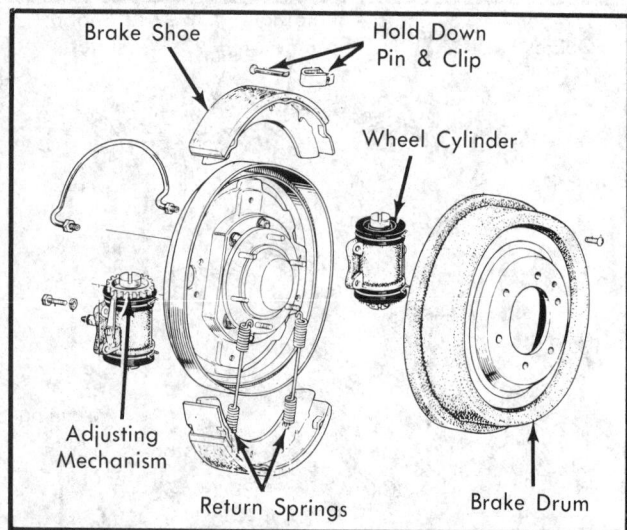

Fig. 10 Exploded View of Land Cruiser Rear Brake

Removal (Standard Pickup) — With brake drum removed, remove adjuster spring and adjuster. Remove front hold down spring and pin, then remove front shoe and anchor spring. Remove rear hold down spring and pin and remove rear shoe. Remove adjusting strut and spring from adjusting lever. Dis-

connect parking brake cable from lever. Using a screwdriver, remove "C" washers retaining parking brake lever and adjuster lever to rear shoe. Remove levers from shoe.

Installation — To install, reverse removal procedure and note the following: Install parking brake lever and adjuster lever to rear shoe with new "C" washers. After installation of brake assembly, move adjuster back and forth and ensure adjusting bolt moves. If not, check installation of brake assembly. Bleed hydraulic system.

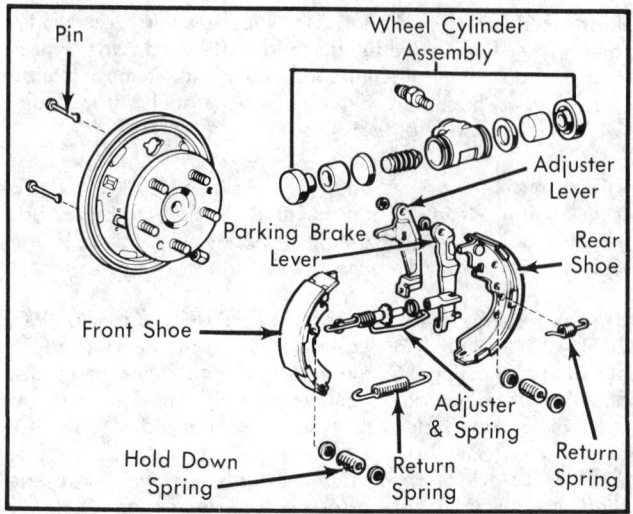

Fig. 11 Exploded View of Standard Pickup Rear Brake

Removal (Cab & Chassis Pickup and 4-WD Pickup) — With brake drum removed, remove upper return springs. Remove adjuster cable, cable guide, adjuster lever and anchor plate. Remove adjuster lever tension spring and strut. Remove hold down springs and pins. Pull brake shoes from backing plate and separate adjusting mechanism and return spring. Disconnect parking brake cable from lever. Mount rear shoe in a vise and remove "C" washer retaining parking brake lever to shoe. Remove parking brake lever.

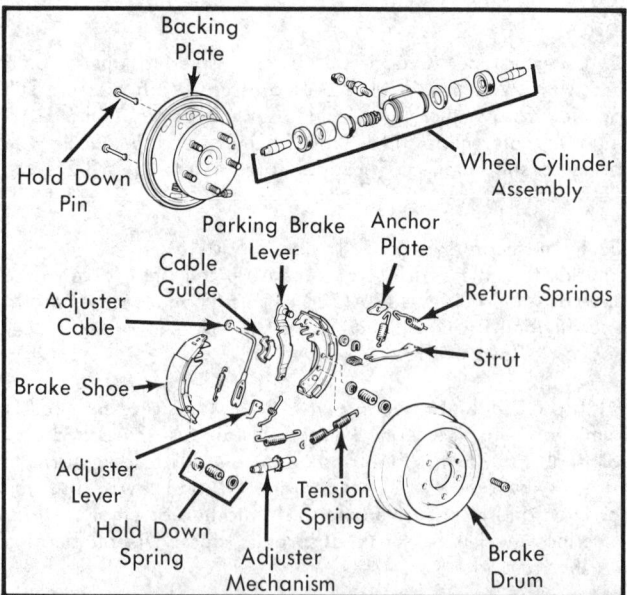

Fig. 12 Exploded View of Cab and Chassis Pickup and 4-WD Pickup Rear Brake

TOYOTA (Cont.)

Installation — To install, reverse removal procedure and note the following: Adjuster mechanisms are not interchangeable. Left-hand thread — right wheel; right-hand thread — left wheel. After installation of brake assembly, pull adjusting cable backward and release; adjusting bolt should move. If not, check installation of brake assembly. Install drum and adjust brakes.

Removal (Tercel) — With brake drum removed, remove return spring. Remove hold down springs and pins. Disconnect front shoe from parking brake strut and disconnect lower return spring. Remove front shoe. Disconnect parking brake lever return spring. Remove rear shoe from backing plate and disconnect parking brake cable from lever. Remove "C" washer retaining parking brake lever and adjusting lever to rear shoe, then remove levers from rear shoe. Remove "C" washer retaining parking brake lever on adjusting lever and separate levers.

Installation — 1) Install parking brake lever onto adjusting lever with NEW "C" washer. Install lever assembly on rear shoe and retain in position temporarily with NEW "C" washer. Measure clearance between adjusting lever and rear of shoe. Remove "C" washer and install correct shim(s) which will give a clearance of 0-.014" (0-.35 mm). Install and stake "C" washer and ensure lever moves.

2) Complete installation by reversing removal procedure and note the following: Adjuster mechanisms are not interchangeable. Left-hand thread — left wheel; right-hand thread — right wheel. Install drum and bleed hydraulic system.

NOTE — Shims are available in 6 sizes: .008" (.2 mm), .012" (.3 mm), .016" (.4 mm), .020" (.5 mm), .024" (.6 mm) and .035" (.9 mm). Shims may be installed in pairs to provide proper clearance.

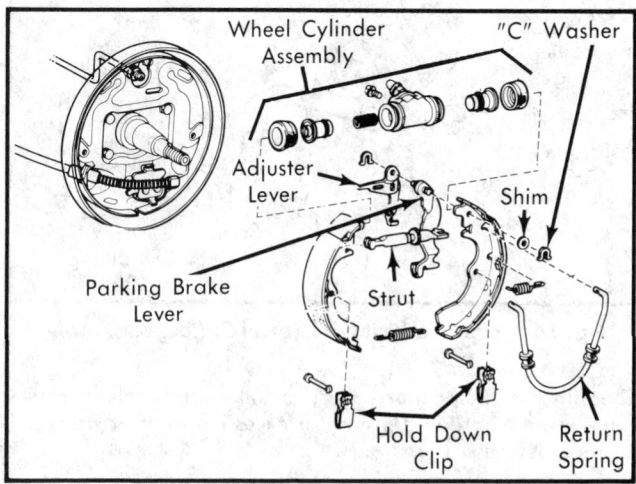

Fig. 13 Exploded View of Tercel Rear Brake

Removal (All Others) — With brake drum removed, remove hold down pins and clips. Remove anchor spring and return spring. Remove front shoe and adjuster strut. Remove parking brake cable from parking brake lever. Remove rear shoe, parking brake lever and adjusting lever as an assembly. Remove "C" washer retaining parking brake lever and adjusting lever to rear shoe and separate levers from shoe.

Installation — Install adjusting lever and parking brake lever to rear shoe with NEW "C" washer. Measure clearance between lever and shoe. Remove "C" washer and install correct shim(s) which will give a clearance of 0-.014" (0-.35 mm). Install and stake "C" washer and ensure lever moves. Complete installation by reversing removal procedure and note the following: Adjuster mechanisms are not interchangeable. Left-hand thread — right wheel; right-hand thread — left wheel. Install drum and bleed hydraulic system.

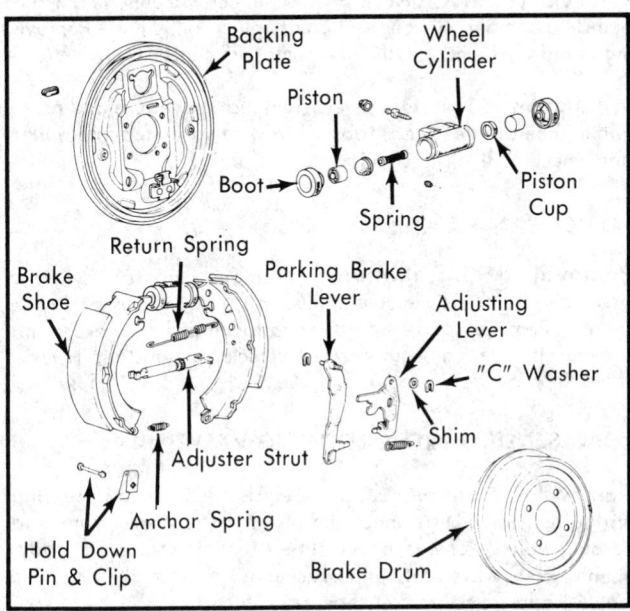

Fig. 14 Exploded View of Rear Brake Used on Celica, Corolla, Corona and Cressida

REAR BRAKE WHEEL CYLINDER

Removal (All Drum Brake Models) — With brake drum and shoes removed, disconnect hydraulic line from wheel cylinder. Remove mounting bolts and remove wheel cylinder.

Installation — To install, reverse removal procedure and note the following: Wheel cylinders and adjusting mechanisms on Land Cruiser are not interchangeable. Wheel cylinders are stamped "L" for left and "R" for right; left-hand thread adjuster mounts on right wheel cylinder and right-hand thread adjuster mounts on left wheel cylinder. Leading wheel cylinder must be installed with adjuster at top of cylinder; trailing wheel cylinder must be installed with adjuster at bottom of cylinder. Bleed brake cylinder.

PARKING BRAKE

Removal (Land Cruiser) — Drain oil from transfer case. Disconnect front of drive shaft and wire out-of-way. Remove drum mounting nut and slide drum off splines. Remove return springs and tension springs, then take off hold down springs and pins. Disconnect parking brake cable from shoes.

Installation — To install, reverse removal procedure and note: Make sure lower tension spring is installed so it lies between back plate and shoes. Refill transfer case with 1.8 quarts of SAE 90. Tighten drum mounting nut and adjust parking brake.

TOYOTA (Cont.)

MASTER CYLINDER

Removal & Installation — Disconnect electrical lead (if equipped). Disconnect and plug hydraulic lines. Remove master cylinder-to-power brake unit mounting nuts. Remove master cylinder. To install, reverse removal procedures and bleed brake system.

VACUUM PUMP

Removal (Land Cruiser) — Disconnect vacuum line from pump assembly. Disconnect and plug oil lines. Remove mounting nuts and gently pry pump off studs.

Installation — To install, reverse removal procedure and note: Run engine at idle speed. Loosen screw at vacuum pump outlet and check that oil is circulating.

POWER BRAKE UNIT

Removal & Installation — Remove master cylinder assembly from vehicle. Disconnect push rod clevis at brake pedal. Remove power booster attaching hardware, and remove booster assembly from vehicle. To install, reverse removal procedure.

LOAD SENSING PROPORTIONING VALVE

Removal — Raise and support vehicle. Remove load sensing spring assembly. Disconnect and plug hydraulic lines from load sensing valve. Remove brake tube bracket from valve body, then remove valve body and bracket as an assembly. Separate valve body from bracket. *See Fig. 15.*

NOTE — *DO NOT disassemble valve body.*

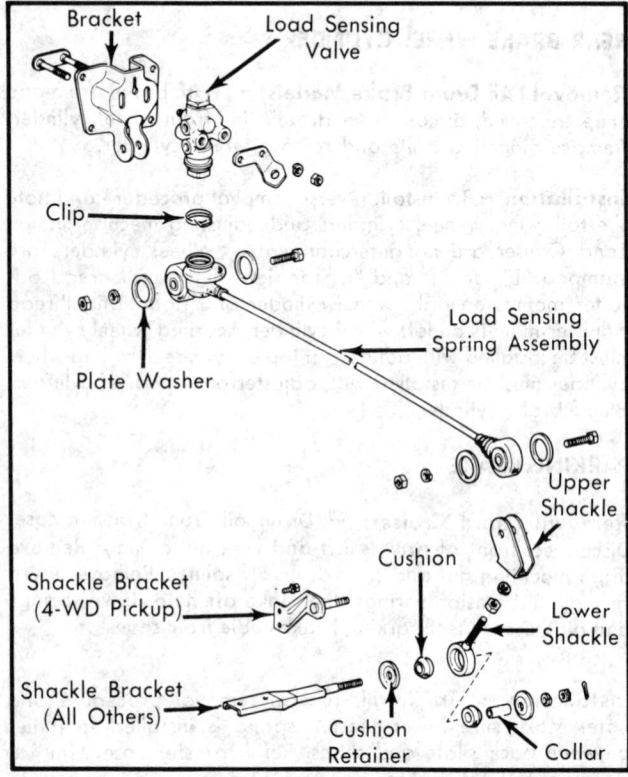

Fig. 15   Exploded View of Load Sensing Proportioning Valve

Installation — Wipe parts and inspect for rust or damage. Inspect valve piston pin and load sensing contact surface for wear (bottom of valve). Replace as an assembly if wear exceeds .028" (.7 mm). To install, reverse removal procedure and note the following: Apply rubber grease to all rubbing areas. Install new rubber plate on valve body side of spring. Adjust length of upper and lower shackle to original height. After installation, position valve body so valve piston lightly contacts load sensing spring. Bleed hydraulic system and check brake pressures.

NOTE — *DO NOT mistake valve side of load sensing spring for shackle side.*

OVERHAUL

NOTE — *When overhauling caliper, wheel cylinder, or master cylinder assemblies, all rubber components should be replaced. If cylinder bores in any part are pitted, or scored more than light honing will repair, entire assembly should be replaced.*

DISC BRAKE CALIPER

Disassembly ("F" & "K" Types and Tercel) — Remove retainer ring (if equipped) and boot. Apply light air pressure to fluid inlet port and expel piston from cylinder. Remove seal from cylinder without damaging bore. See Fig. 3, Fig. 4, Fig. 8 and Fig. 16.

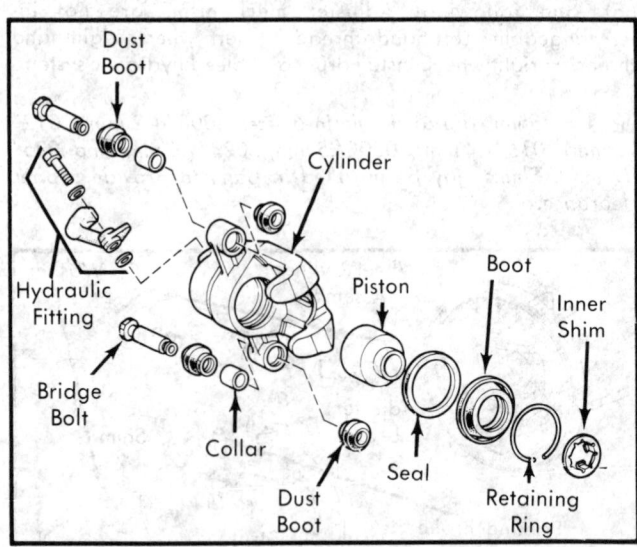

Fig. 16   Exploded View of Tercel Caliper Assembly

Cleaning & Inspection — Clean all parts in clean brake fluid. Inspect bore and piston for excessive wear or damage; replace defective parts.

Reassembly — Coat piston, seal and cylinder bore with rubber grease before reassembly. To reassemble, reverse disassembly procedure and note the following: On "K" type, install seal, fit boot to piston, then fit boot to cylinder and push piston into cylinder bore.

Disassembly (Corolla) — Loosen both bridge bolts (caliper half mounting bolts) and separate cylinder casting from outer body. Pull out torque plate. Remove retainer ring and boot. Force light air pressure through fluid inlet port and expel

TOYOTA (Cont.)

piston. From caliper, remove following: Piston seal, bushings, hole plug, retainers and dust seals. See *Fig. 6*.

Cleaning & Inspection — Clean all parts in alcohol or clean brake fluid. Inspect parts for excessive wear or damage; replace defective parts. If torque plate pins are excessively worn or if pin weld parts are abnormally corroded, caliper must be replaced.

Reassembly — 1) Ensure torque plate pins and bushing bores are clean and coat with grease furnished in repair kit. Coat piston seals and cylinder bore with rubber grease. Fit dust seal, retainers and bushings to cylinder.

2) Fit piston seal on cylinder and push piston in by hand. Install dust boot and ring. Reassemble torque plate pins in cylinder body. Make sure torque plate is free to slide smoothly. Install bridge bolts and tighten.

Disassembly (Land Cruiser & 4-WD Pickup) — Remove dust seal retainer ring and seal. Insert small block of wood into cylinder cavity. Apply light air pressure to one side of cylinder to expel pistons; repeat procedure on opposite side. Remove piston seals without damaging bores. See *Fig. 7*.

NOTE — *DO NOT separate caliper halves.*

Cleaning & Inspection — Clean all parts in clean brake fluid. Inspect pistons and cylinder bores for excessive wear, damage or corrosion; replace defective parts.

Reassembly — Lightly coat all parts with rubber grease Insert new piston seal, being careful that seals properly enter grooves. Fit piston and slide dust seal into position. With dust seal seated, fit retainer ring.

Disassembly (All Others) — Remove dust boot retainer ring and dust boot. Insert small wooden block between pistons and apply light air pressure to fluid inlet port to expel pistons. Remove seals without damaging bores. See *Fig. 5*.

NOTE — *DO NOT separate caliper halves.*

Cleaning & Inspection — Clean all parts in clean brake fluid. Inspect bores and pistons for excessive wear or damage; replace defective parts.

Reassembly — Coat piston seals, cylinder bores and pistons with brake grease. To reassemble, reverse disassembly procedure.

Disassembly (Supra Rear Caliper) — 1) Remove dust boot retaining ring and boot. Remove piston by turning it counterclockwise with suitable remover (09719-14010). Remove piston seal from cylinder groove without damage to cylinder bore. See *Fig. 6*.

2) Remove retaining ring from parking brake lever boot. Pull boot back over parking brake lever and remove shaft retaining ring. Using arbor press and suitable remover (09719-14010), remove parking brake lever; separate boot from lever.

3) Remove torsion spring and strut. Mount caliper assembly in padded vise and remove bearings. Separate components and arrange for reassembly reference.

Cleaning & Inspection — Wash all parts in clean brake fluid. Inspect all parts for excessive wear, damage or corrosion; replace defective parts.

Reassembly — 1) Coat all parts with rubber grease. Install bearings. Fit new "O" ring and spring washer on adjusting bolt. Ensure "O" ring and washer do not touch. Install adjusting bolt and strut into bore with strut against raised side of bolt. Strut must be angled toward torsion spring retaining pin. Install torsion spring with formed loop seated around retaining pin.

2) Fit rubber boot to parking brake lever. Install parking brake lever with arbor press and suitable tool (09719-14010). Install shaft retaining ring. Pull boot over lever assembly and install retaining ring.

3) Install piston seal into cylinder bore. Install piston into cylinder bore by turning it clockwise with suitable installer (09719-14010J). Align piston with piston stopper groove; install dust boot and retaining ring.

MASTER CYLINDER

Disassembly — Remove reservoir(s) and switches (if equipped) and mount cylinder in soft-jawed vise. Remove dust boot and check valve(s). Push pistons into cylinder bore and remove stop bolt. Remove snap ring and withdraw piston assemblies. Remove unions, outlet plugs, and other external components. Disassemble piston assemblies by removing springs, retainers and cups. See *Fig. 18*.

Cleaning & Inspection — Wash all parts in clean brake fluid and inspect for wear, damage or corrosion. Replace defective parts as required.

Reassembly — To reassemble, reverse disassembly procedure using all new rubber parts and lubricating all components with clean brake fluid.

VACUUM PUMP

Disassembly (Land Cruiser) — Drive dowel pins from end cover toward case. Separate end cover. Continue to drive dowels through case and stop with them flush with end frame. Remove end frame with pins still fitted. Remove both "O" rings and discard. Slide rotor and blades from case.

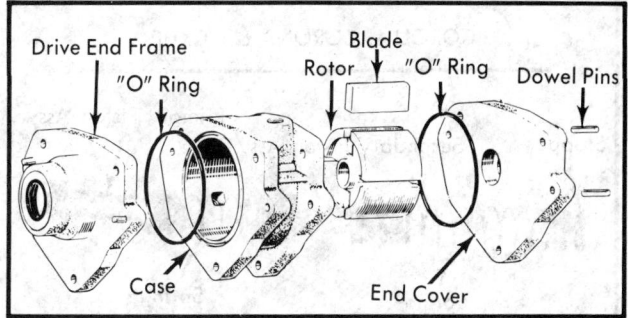

Fig. 17   Exploded View of Land Cruiser Vacuum Pump

Inspection — Inspect end cover and casing for damage or wear. Casing bore must not be worn beyond 2.29" (5.82 mm). Check rotor-to-alternator shaft spline play. Rotor wear must

Brakes

TOYOTA (Cont.)

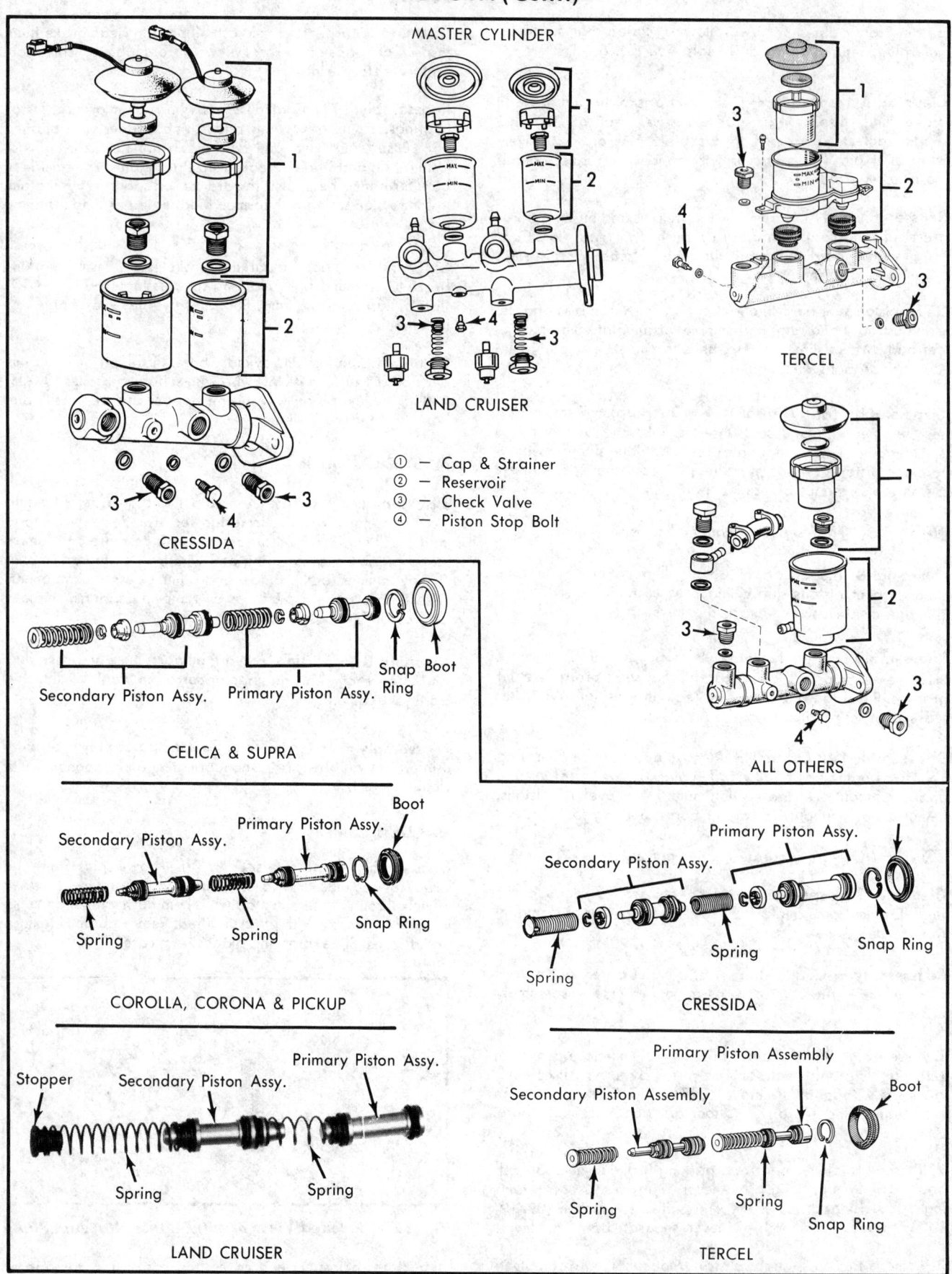

MASTER CYLINDER

LAND CRUISER

CRESSIDA

TERCEL

① — Cap & Strainer
② — Reservoir
③ — Check Valve
④ — Piston Stop Bolt

ALL OTHERS

Secondary Piston Assy.   Primary Piston Assy.   Snap Ring   Boot

CELICA & SUPRA

Secondary Piston Assy.   Primary Piston Assy.   Boot
Spring   Spring   Snap Ring

COROLLA, CORONA & PICKUP

Secondary Piston Assy.   Primary Piston Assy.
Spring   Snap Ring
Spring

CRESSIDA

Stopper   Secondary Piston Assy.   Primary Piston Assy.
Spring   Spring

LAND CRUISER

Secondary Piston Assembly   Primary Piston Assembly   Boot
Spring   Spring   Snap Ring

TERCEL

Fig. 18   Exploded View Of Master Cylinders With Detail of Each Model's Piston Assemblies Shown

TOYOTA (Cont.)

not exceed .095" (2.4 mm). Inspect rotor blades for following wear limits: Height .47" (12 mm); length 1.377" (34.98 mm); width .036" (.92 mm). Check end frame bushing and oil seal. Bushing bore must not exceed .635" (16.14 mm). Replace oil seal by prying out and pressing in new one.

Reassembly — Lightly coat new "O" rings and insert into grooves. Refit rotor and blades. Drive in dowel pins.

POWER BRAKE UNIT

NOTE — *Power brake units are produced by several manufacturers and may vary slightly between model application. The following overhaul procedures can be used with minor attention to detail of specific booster being repaired. Refer to Fig. 19, Fig. 20 and Fig. 21.*

Disassembly — **1)** Remove check valve and grommet from front of unit (except Corolla, Pickup and Tercel), then remove push rod (except Land Cruiser). From rear of unit, remove clevis, nut and dust boot. Using a screwdriver, pry off retainer and remove filter and silencer pack.

NOTE — *Check valve on Corolla, Pickup and Tercel is located in vacuum line and is mounted on firewall.*

2) Place an alignment mark on front and rear shells for reassembly reference. Mount unit in suitable support to prevent internal spring pressure from forcing shells apart. On units equipped with clamping band, remove bolt and nut. Remove band and separate front and rear shells. On all other units, rotate front shell counterclockwise and separate front and rear shells.

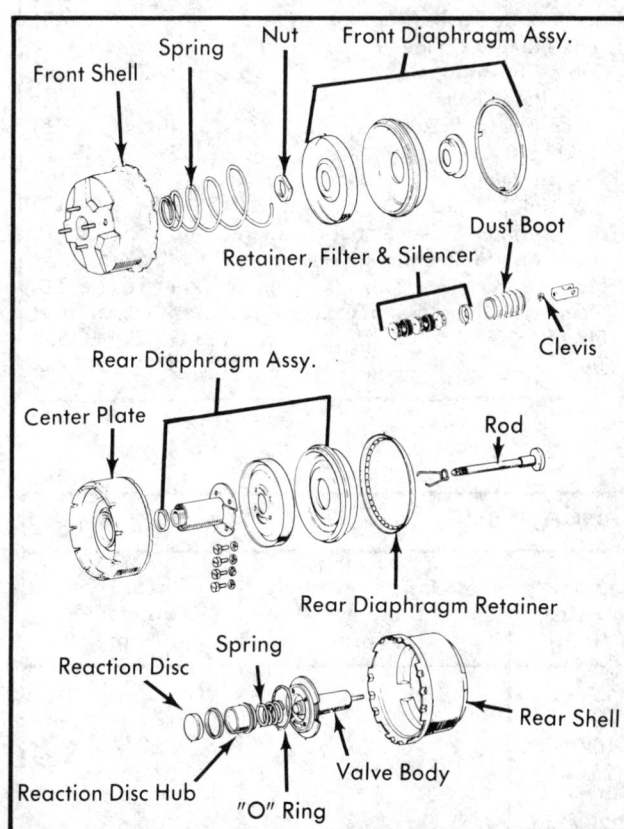

Fig. 19 Land Cruiser Power Brake Unit

3) On Land Cruiser, remove front diaphragm lock nut and separate front diaphragm assembly. Remove rear diaphragm retainer and center plate. Remove rear diaphragm lock nut and 4 hub bolts. Remove hub and separate rear diaphragm assembly. Remove push rod and spring, reaction disc, reaction disc hub and spring, valve body and "O" ring from rear shell.

4) On Aisin units, remove spring from front shell. Remove spring retainer, reaction plate and levers and "O" ring from diaphragm plate. Remove snap ring, then pull operating rod out through rear of diaphragm plate. Remove diaphragm retainer, then separate diaphragm and diaphragm plate. Remove star washer, seal and boot from rear shell.

5) On JKK units, remove push rod and spring from front shell. Remove diaphragm from diaphragm plate. Depress operating rod, remove stopper key, then pull out operating rod and reaction disc. Remove star washer, seal and bearing from rear shell.

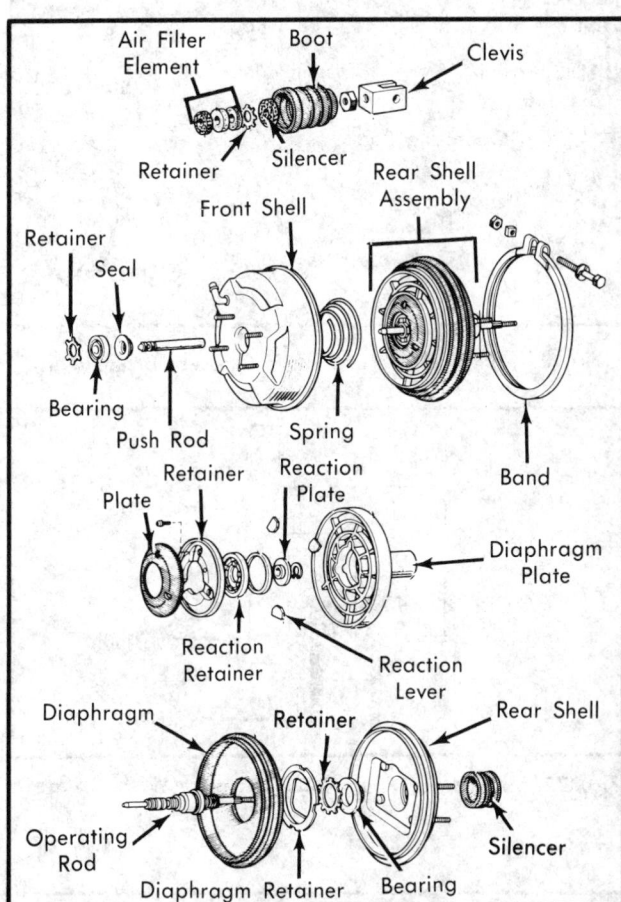

Fig. 20 Exploded View of Aisin Power Brake Unit

Cleaning & Inspection — Wash all parts in denatured alcohol. Inspect all components for wear or damage; replace defective parts. Replace all rubber parts during overhaul.

Reassembly — **1)** Apply silicone grease to front and rear shell seals and reaction disc. Coat diaphragm edge with light coat of oil before final tightening. Shell halves must align with index marks.

2) Reassemble power brake unit by reversing removal procedure and note the following: On Aisin units, secure

TOYOTA (Cont.)

diaphragm to diaphragm plate by turning retainer 45°. On JKK units, rear seal must be seated .40-.43" (10-11 mm) from rear shell body. On Land Cruiser, fit reaction disc with protrusion directed toward valve body and install center plate on hub with large groove facing front side.

3) After installation, adjust push rod length. Using depth gauge (09737-00010), place gauge on master cylinder (with gasket in place, if equipped) and turn pin until tip just touches piston. See Fig. 21. Without disturbing gauge setting, turn gauge upside down on power brake unit. Adjust length of push rod by turning nut until clearance between gauge and tip of push rod is obtained as shown in Push Rod Clearance Specifications table.

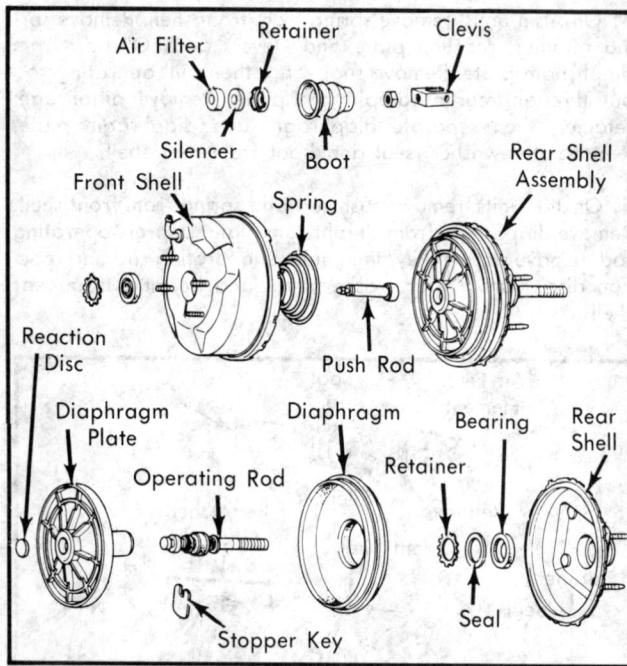

Fig. 21 Exploded View of JKK Power Brake Unit

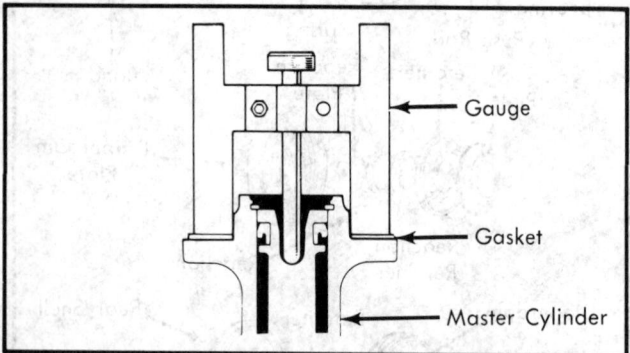

Fig. 22 Adjusting Push Rod Clearance With Gauge

Push Rod Clearance Specifications

Application	Clearance In. (mm)
Corolla	Zero
Corona, Cressida, Land Cruiser & Tercel	.024-.026 (.60-.66)
All Others	.004-.020 (.10-.51)

TIGHTENING SPECIFICATIONS

Application	Ft. Lbs. (mkg)
Caliper Mounting Bolts	
Celica, Corolla & Supra	40-54 (5.5-7.5)
Corona, Cressida & Pickup	68-86 (9.5-12.0)
Land Cruiser & 4-WD Pickup	54-76 (7.5-10.5)
Caliper Bracket-to-Steering Knuckle	
Cab & Chassis Pickup	80-126 (11.0-17.5)
Tercel	33-39 (4.5-5.4)
Caliper-to-Caliper Bracket (Tercel)	11-15 (1.5-2.0)
Caliper Bridge Bolts (Corolla)	58-68 (8.0-9.5)
Guide Plate-to-Caliper Bolts	
Cab & Chassis Pickup	29-39 (4.0-5.4)
Hub-to-Rotor Bolts	
Cab & Chassis Pickup	40-54 (5.5-7.5)
All Others	29-39 (4.0-5.4)
Tercel Suspension Components	
Axle Nut	73-108 (10.0-15.0)
Lower Arm-to-Crossmember	51-65 (7.1-9.0)
Lower Arm-to-Steering Knuckle	40-52 (5.5-7.2)
Stabilizer Bar	11-15 (1.5-2.0)
Steering Knuckle-to-Shock	40-52 (5.5-7.2)
Strut Bar	29-29 (4.0-5.4)
Tie Rod End	37-50 (5.1-7.0)

DRUM BRAKE SPECIFICATIONS

Application	Wheel Cyl. Bore Diameter In. (mm)	Drum Diameter In. (mm)	Original Diameter In. (mm)	Maximum Refinish Diameter In. (mm)	Discard Diameter In. (mm)
Land Cruiser	.....	.....	.....	.....	11.5 (292)
Pickups	.....	10.0 (254)	10.0 (254)	.....	10.079 (256)
All Others	.....	9.0 (228.6)	9.0 (228.6)	.....	9.079 (230.6)

TOYOTA (Cont.)

DISC BRAKE SPECIFICATIONS						
Application	Disc Diameter	Lateral Runout	Parallelism	Original Thickness	Minimum Refinish Thickness	Discard Thickness
Cab & Chassis Pickup	.....	.006 (.15)	.....	.787 (20)	.....	.748 (19)
Land Cruiser	.....	.005 (.12)	.....	.790 (20.1)	.....	.740 (18.8)
Supra Front	.....	.006 (.15)	.....	.492 (12.5)	.....	.453 (11.5)
Rear	.....	.006 (.15)	.....	.394 (10)	.....	.354 (9)
All Others	.....	.006 (.15)	.....	.492 (12.5)	.....	.453 (11.5)

TRIUMPH

Spitfire
TR7
TR8

DESCRIPTION

All models are equipped with front disc and rear drum brakes. A tandem master cylinder with 2 independent and complete hydraulic circuits is used on all models. A pressure differential valve is used on all models to detect low pressure in either front or rear brake circuit. When a pressure differential exists between the 2 circuits, the pressure differential valve will be positioned off-center and cause the brake failure warning lamp on instrument panel to glow. A vacuum servo unit is used on TR7 and TR8 models for power braking. Parking brake on all models is cable actuated on rear brakes.

ADJUSTMENT

DRUM BRAKES

Spitfire — Release parking brake and raise rear wheels off ground. Rotate square-ended adjuster on bottom center of backing plate clockwise until wheel locks. After wheel locks, rotate adjuster counterclockwise until wheel is just free to turn.

NOTE — *Rear brakes on TR7 and TR8 models are equipped with self-adjusting mechanism incorporated in parking brake linkage.*

PARKING BRAKE

NOTE — *Adjustment of rear brakes will normally provide satisfactory parking brake adjustment. If cables are stretched, further adjustment is performed as follows:*

Spitfire — **1)** Raise and support vehicle. Release parking brake and lock both rear wheels. Check that front cable-to-rear cable equalizer is at a 15° angle as shown in *Fig. 1.* Adjust front and rear cables as necessary to obtain this specification.

2) To adjust front cable, remove seats, carpet, and parking brake lever cover to expose lever. Loosen cable lock nut and rotate cable clockwise to tighten or counterclockwise to loosen. Tighten lock nut and replace parking brake lever cover, carpet, and seats.

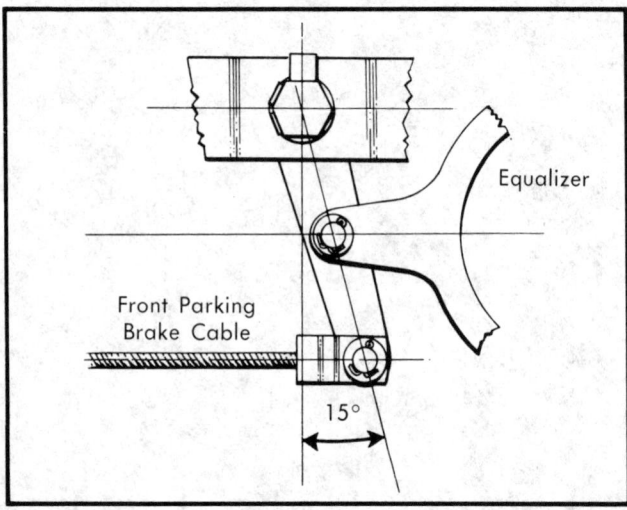

Fig. 1   Positioning Spitfire Front Parking Brake Cable and Equalizer for Parking Brake Adjustment

NOTE — *Before adjusting front cable, it may be necessary to release rear cables from rear backing plate operating levers.*

3) To adjust rear cables, disconnect parking brake cable clevis pins from operating levers on brake backing plates. Adjust each clevis equal amounts until clevis pin can be easily inserted into operating levers. Secure clevis pins and check operation.

TR7 & TR8 — **1)** Raise and support rear of vehicle; release parking brake lever. Disconnect parking brake cable clevis pins from operating levers on brake backing plates. With light finger pressure, push operating levers inward to ensure operating levers are in contact with brake shoes.

2) Align parking brake cable equalizer (located on right side of differential housing) ½" (12.5 mm) to left of vertical position. Adjust each clevis equal amounts until clevis pins can be easily inserted into operating levers. Secure clevis pins and check operation. Brakes should not drag. Parking brake lever travel should be 5-7 notches with 25 ft. lbs. (3.5 mkg) force applied to lever.

BRAKE WARNING LIGHT

NOTE — *Warning light will glow after any repair on service brake system and will not go out until manually reset by bleeding hydraulic circuit.*

A dual warning light is mounted on instrument panel. Parking brake light should glow when lever is pulled 1 notch (ignition on) and go off when lever is fully released. To check circuit warning sensor, fully release parking brake and ensure light is off (ignition on). Open 1 bleed screw and depress brake pedal; light should glow. To reset warning light, bleed hydraulic system and check operation of brakes. After bleeding brakes, turn ignition on; warning lamp should not glow. If warning lamp glows, center differential valve.

NOTE — *During bleeding process, use only short strokes to prevent differential valve from being forced off-center.*

REMOVAL & INSTALLATION

DISC BRAKE PADS

Removal — Raise and support vehicle; remove tire and wheel. Remove retaining pins and springs. Lift out brake pads, complete with damper shims.

Installation — Clean surfaces of pistons and caliper cavity. Ease caliper pistons into bores (with bleed screw slightly opened) to provide clearance. Insert new pads and shims. Arrow on Spitfire shim faces up; smaller cut-out on TR7 and TR8 faces up. Install retaining springs and pins.

DISC BRAKE CALIPER

Removal (Spitfire) — Raise and support vehicle; remove tire and wheel. Disconnect and plug hydraulic line-to-caliper flex hose. Remove nut securing flex hose to front suspension bracket and remove hose from bracket. Disconnect and plug hose at caliper. Remove 2 caliper mounting bolts and washers. Remove caliper and shield.

Installation — To install, reverse removal procedure and bleed hydraulic system.

Removal (TR7 & TR8) — Raise and support vehicle; remove tire and wheel. Disconnect and plug hydraulic line at caliper. Remove 2 bolts and washers retaining steering arm and lower

TRIUMPH (Cont.)

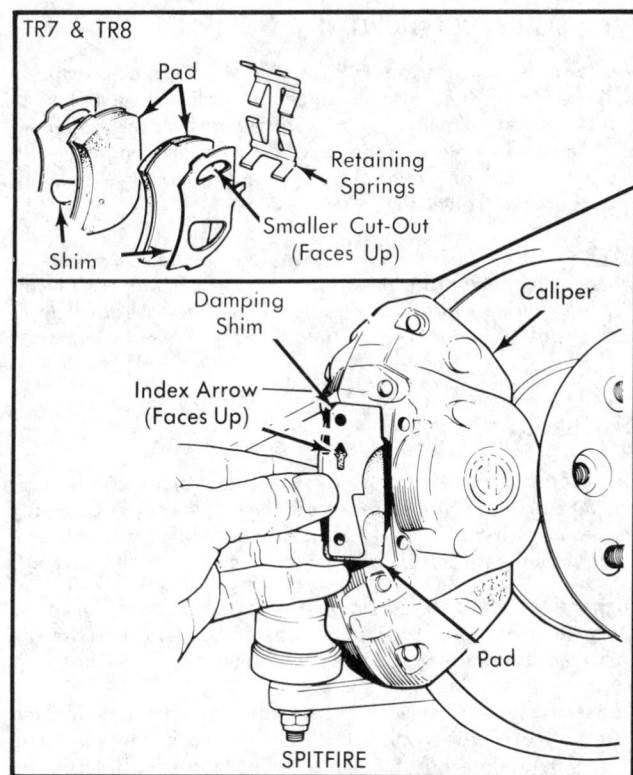

Fig. 2 Installing Disc Brake Pads

caliper mounting lug to stub axle. Push steering arm clear. Remove upper caliper mounting bolt and remove caliper.

Installation — To install, reverse removal procedure and bleed hydraulic system.

DISC BRAKE ROTOR

Removal — Raise and support vehicle; remove tire and wheel. Remove caliper without disconnecting hydraulic line and hang out of way. Remove grease cap, cotter pin, castellated nut and washer. Remove hub, complete with bearings and disc. Remove 4 hub-to-rotor bolts and separate hub from rotor.

Installation — To install, reverse removal procedure and note the following: On Spitfire, adjust hub end play to .003-.005" (.076-.127 mm). On TR7 and TR8, eliminate end play, but do not tighten hub more than 5 ft. lbs. (.70 mkg). On all models, adjust wheel bearings. *See Wheel Bearing Adjustment in WHEEL ALIGNMENT section.*

REAR BRAKE DRUM

Removal — Raise and support vehicle; remove tire and wheel. Remove 2 brake drum retaining screws. Release parking brake and remove brake drum. On TR7 and TR8, if drum is difficult to remove, release self-adjuster. To release adjuster, remove dust cover on rear of backing plate, insert small screwdriver and engage slotted hole in small adjusting lever. Press lever down to release adjuster.

Installation — To install, reverse removal procedure and note the following: On TR7 and TR8, if brake adjustment was released, neutralize brakes, install brake drum and depress brake pedal to set shoe-to-drum clearance. On all models, tighten retaining screws evenly.

REAR BRAKE SHOES

Removal (Spitfire) — **1)** Remove brake drum as previously outlined. Remove parking brake lever cotter pin, shoe anchor pins, springs and cups. Release lower end of rear shoe from adjuster, then release upper end from wheel cylinder.

2) Disconnect return springs and remove brake shoe. Release lower end of front shoe from adjuster, then release parking brake lever from top of shoe. Carefully remove front shoe from wheel cylinder, without pulling piston out of wheel cylinder. Remove brake adjuster retaining nuts and brake adjuster.

Installation — To install, reverse removal procedure and adjust brakes. Return springs are installed on inboard side of shoes.

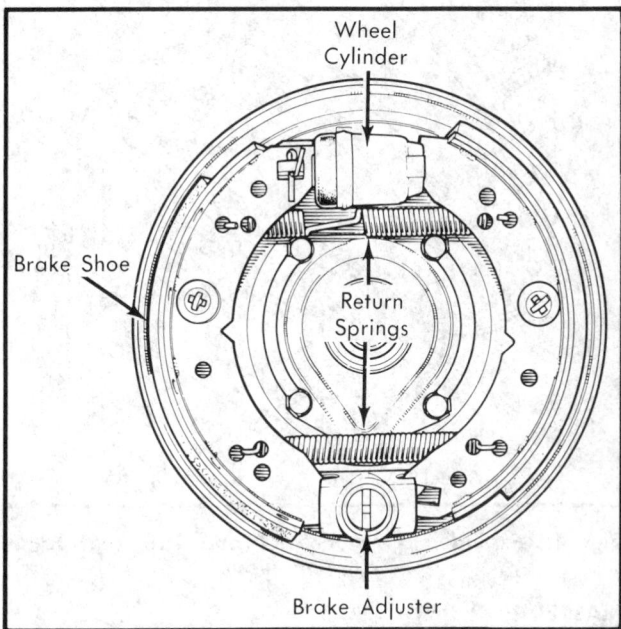

Fig. 3 Exploded View of Spitfire Rear Brake Assembly

CAUTION — *Upper and lower return springs are not interchangeable on TR7 and TR8 models. Note position of each spring prior to removal.*

Removal (TR7 & TR8) — **1)** Remove brake drum as previously outlined. Remove cotter pin from parking brake lever on rear of backing plate. Separate lever from parking brake lever. Remove rear shoe anchor pins, springs and cups. Disconnect and remove lower return spring.

2) On rear shoe, disconnect and remove parking brake lever return spring. Place a clamp on wheel cylinder to prevent pistons from popping out of wheel cylinder. Remove lower end from wheel cylinder without damaging cylinder boot. Disconnect upper return spring and remove rear shoe.

3) On front shoe, remove "E" clips from shoe retainers. Carefully withdraw lower end of shoe from wheel cylinder. Remove front shoe from backing plate with upper return spring and parking brake lever installed. Separate parking brake lever and strut from shoe. Remove upper return spring.

Installation — **1)** To install, reverse removal procedure and note the following: Upper return spring must be installed on inboard side of brake shoes. After installation, check operation

TRIUMPH (Cont.)

of adjusting mechanism by lightly applying brakes with drum removed. After shoes have expanded, adjusting ratchet should move.

2) Replace brake drum, depress brake pedal several times to set shoe-to-drum clearance. Bleed hydraulic system and road test vehicle. If parking brake and service brake operation is poor during road test, make 4 brake applications (moderate pedal effort) to decelerate vehicle from 20 to 0 MPH. This will ensure proper adjustment of rear brakes.

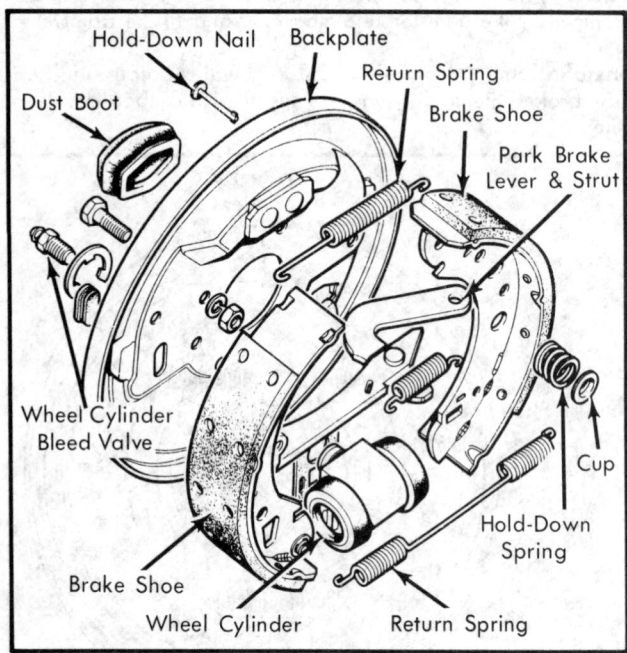

Fig. 4   Exploded View of TR7 and TR8 Rear Brake Assembly

MASTER CYLINDER

Removal — Disconnect all hydraulic lines and electrical connections (if equipped) from master cylinder. On models equipped with vacuum servo unit, remove mounting nuts and washers, then remove master cylinder. On models without vacuum servo unit, disconnect master cylinder push rod from brake pedal. Remove 4 mounting bolts securing master cylinder to firewall, then remove 2 bolts securing cylinder to front bracket. Remove master cylinder.

Installation — To install, reverse removal procedure and note the following: Bleed hydraulic system and check that pressure differential valve is centered.

VACUUM SERVO UNIT

Removal & Installation — Remove master cylinder as previously outlined. Disconnect vacuum hose from check valve. Remove clevis pin from servo operating rod and brake pedal lever. Remove 4 mounting nuts and washers, then remove servo. To install, reverse removal procedure.

PRESSURE DIFFERENTIAL VALVE

Removal & Installation — Disconnect electrical leads. Disconnect inlet and outlet lines and plug all ports to prevent loss of fluid and entry of dirt. Remove bolt securing valve and remove unit. To install, reverse removal procedure, bleed brakes and if necessary, center valve shuttle.

REAR BRAKE WHEEL CYLINDER

Removal & Installation — Remove brake shoes as previously outlined. Drain fluid and disconnect flexible hydraulic line at wheel cylinder. Remove wheel cylinder dust cover, retaining clip and spring plate. Remove wheel cylinder complete with parking brake operating lever. To install, reverse removal procedure and bleed hydraulic system.

NOTE — *TR7 and TR8 models have single bleed screw on right wheel cylinder and no bleed screw on left cylinder. Left cylinder has fluid line installed in place of screw to transfer fluid to right wheel cylinder. DO NOT interchange wheel cylinders.*

OVERHAUL

DISC BRAKE CALIPER

Disassembly — Using low air pressure, force pistons from caliper bores. If pistons are seized, the whole caliper assembly must be removed. Carefully pry dust seal retainer from groove, using a blunt instrument. Take out dust seal and then fluid seal.

Inspection — Clean caliper bores and inspect for deep scratches or pitting. Look at pistons and ensure they are not corroded or damaged. Replace components as necessary.

Reassembly — Fit new fluid seals into caliper bores, making sure they are properly located. Lightly coat bores with clean brake fluid. Insert pistons into caliper bores with approximately 5/16" (7.9 mm) of each piston protruding from mouth of each bore. Fit new dust seal into retainer, then slide assembly, seal first, into mouth of bore. Fully seat pistons, ensuring retainers are not distorted.

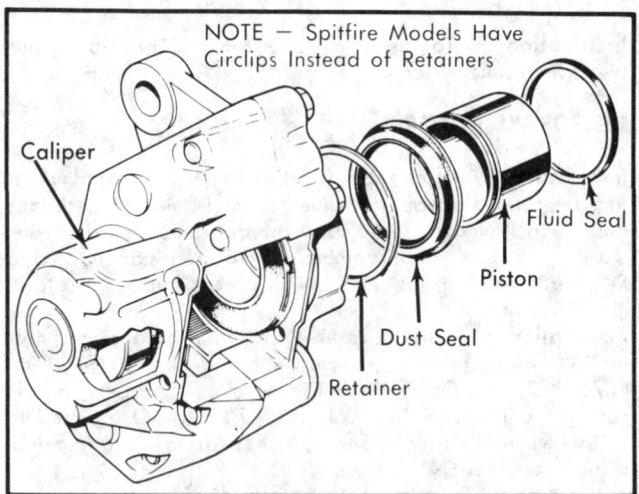

Fig. 5   Disassembled Front Disc Brake Caliper Spitfire Shown — Others Similar

REAR WHEEL CYLINDER

Disassembly — Remove wheel cylinder as previously outlined. Remove dust cover retaining ring (if equipped) and dust cover(s). On Spitfire, remove piston and separate seal from piston using fingers only. On TR7 and TR8, press on one piston to force pistons, seals and springs from cylinder.

Cleaning & Inspection — Clean all parts in alcohol or brake fluid and examine cylinder bore and piston for score marks, ridges or corrosion. If either bore or piston is damaged, replace entire cylinder assembly.

TRIUMPH (Cont.)

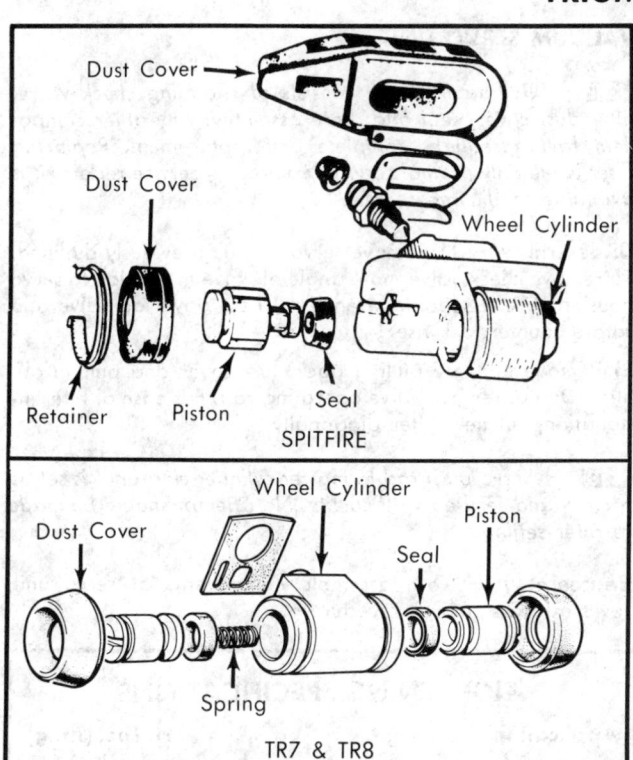

Fig. 6   Exploded View of Rear Wheel Cylinders

Reassembly — Install new seal(s) on piston(s). Lubricate seal(s), inside of cylinder and piston(s) with clean brake fluid. Reverse disassembly procedure to complete reassembly of wheel cylinder.

MASTER CYLINDER

Disassembly — **1)** Drain and discard hydraulic fluid from reservoir. Remove reservoir from master cylinder. Note size and location of reservoir seals, then remove seal from master cylinder.

2) On Spitfire, slide push rod dust boot off master cylinder to expose push rod circlip. Remove circlip, withdraw push rod and separate components. Withdraw primary piston assembly.

3) On TR7 and TR8, remove metal cap and rubber boot from end of master cylinder. Remove circlip, then withdraw primary piston assembly.

4) On all models, insert a rod into bore to depress secondary piston assembly. With piston assembly depressed, remove stop pin, then extract secondary piston assembly.

5) On TR7 and TR8, unscrew pressure failure switch from cylinder body. Remove end plug and copper washer, withdraw spacer, return spring and pressure differential piston as an assembly. Remove spring retainer, then separate spring and piston. Remove and discard "O" rings.

6) On all models, note size and position of all piston seals, washers and spring retainers. Remove seals using fingers only.

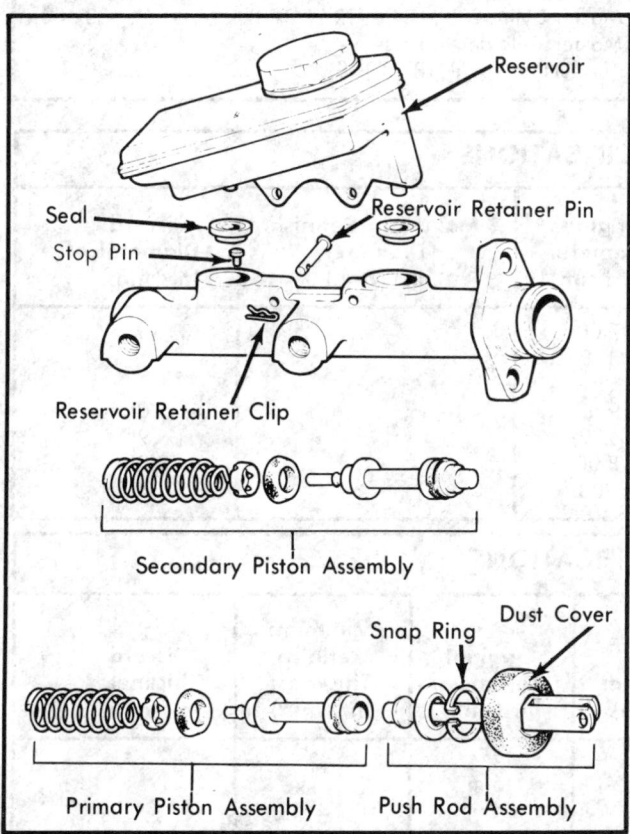

Fig. 7   Exploded View of Spitfire Master Cylinder

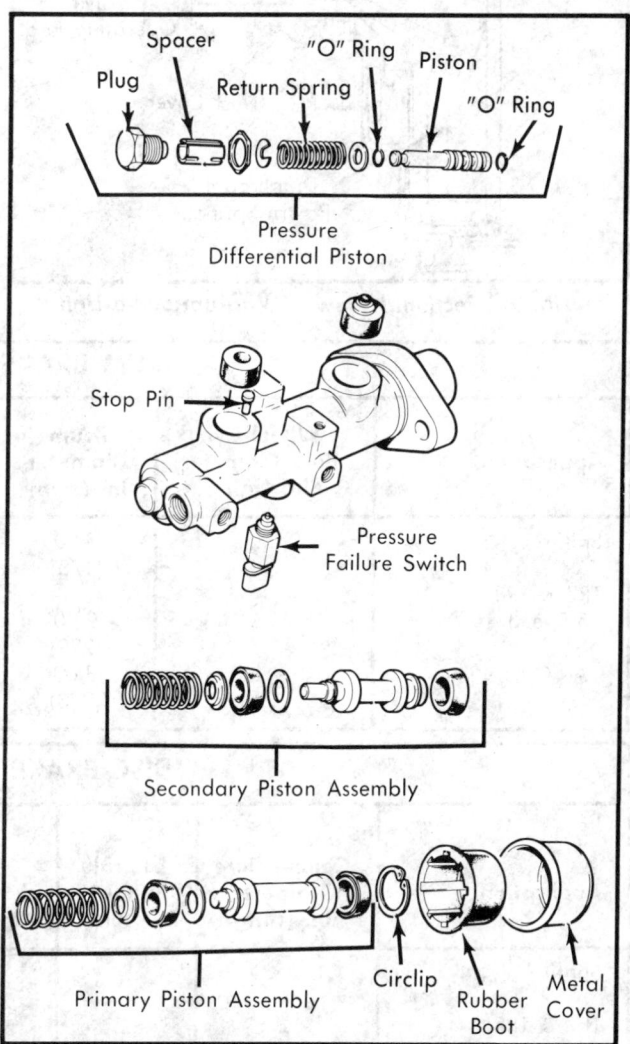

Fig. 8   Exploded View of TR7 and TR8 Master Cylinder

TRIUMPH (Cont.)

Reassembly — 1) Install seals on primary and secondary pistons, using fingers only. Ensure all seals, springs and washers are properly installed. To assemble, reverse disassembly procedure and note the following:

2) On TR7 and TR8, install new "O" rings, and assemble pressure differential piston assembly. Install pressure differential assembly using new copper washer and tighten end plug. Install reservoir with 2 new screws.

3) On all models, depress secondary piston assembly in cylinder bore and install stop pin. Install primary piston assembly and retain in position with new circlip.

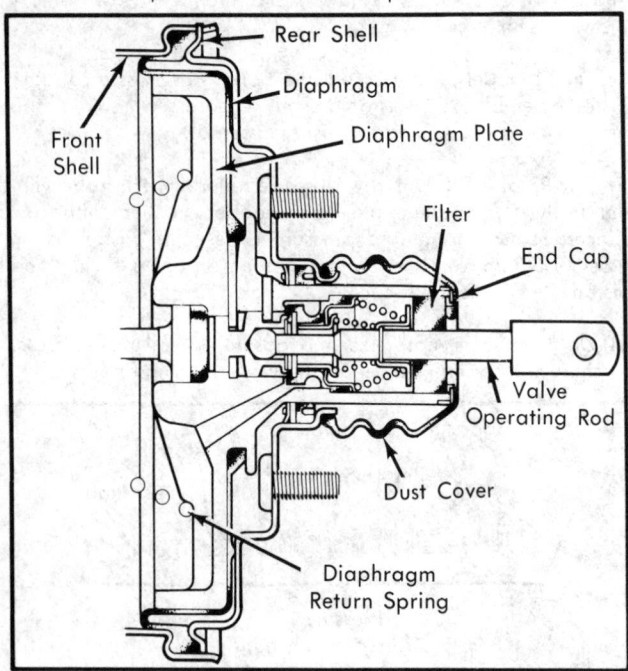

Fig. 9   Sectional View of Vacuum Servo Unit

VACUUM SERVO UNIT

NOTE — *Overhauling unit consists of changing check valve, filter dust cover, seal and plate assembly. Any other component failure requires complete unit replacement. Replacing filter is the only normal service required. A service repair kit is available for limited service.*

Disassembly — 1) Remove servo unit as previously outlined. To remove check valve, note angle of valve in relation to servo housing. Use a suitable wrench to press down on valve and rotate counterclockwise ⅓ turn.

2) Remove filter by pulling back dust cover and pulling out filter. Do not remove valve operating rod. For ease of filter installation, cut new filter diagonally.

NOTE — *Servo push rod to master cylinder clearance is set by factory and secured with Loctite. No attempt should be made to alter setting.*

Reassembly — To reassemble components of servo unit, reverse disasssembly procedure.

TIGHTENING SPECIFICATIONS

Application	Ft. Lbs. (mkg)
Rotor-to-Hub	
Spitfire	34 (4.7)
TR7 & TR8	32 (4.4)
Caliper Mounting Bolts	
Spitfire	65 (9.0)
TR7 & TR8	74 (10.2)
Reservoir-to-Master Cylinder (TR7 & TR8)	5 (.69)
Master Cylinder End Plug (TR7 & TR8)	33 (4.6)
Master Cylinder-to-Press.	
Reduction Valve (TR7 & TR8)	9 (1.2)

DRUM BRAKE SPECIFICATIONS

Application	Wheel Cyl. Bore Diameter In. (mm)	Drum Diameter In. (mm)	Original Diameter In. (mm)	Maximum Refinish Diameter In. (mm)	Discard Diameter In. (mm)
Spitfire	.....	7.00 (178)	7.00 (178)	.....	.....
TR7 & TR8					
5-Speed	.....	9.00 (229)	9.00 (229)	.....	9.05 (229.9)
All Others	.....	8.00 (203)	8.00 (203)	.....	8.05 (204.5)

DISC BRAKE SPECIFICATIONS

Application	Caliper Bore Diameter In. (mm)	Lateral Runout In. (mm)	Parallelism In. (mm)	Original Thickness In. (mm)	Minimum Refinish Thickness In. (mm)	Discard Thickness In. (mm)
Spitfire	.....	.....	.....	.375 (9.5)	.....	.....
TR7 & TR8	.....	.....	.....	.375 (9.5)	.....	.....

VOLKSWAGEN

Dasher   Rabbit Pickup
Jetta   Scirocco
Rabbit   Vanagon

DESCRIPTION

Brake systems are hydraulically actuated using a tandem master cylinder and optional power brake unit. All models are equipped with front disc brakes and self-adjusting rear drum brakes. Jetta, Rabbit and Rabbit Pickup models are equipped with a brake proportional valve and all other models are equipped with a pressure regulator in rear brake circuit to avoid rear wheel lock-up. All models are equipped with cable actuated parking brake which operates on rear brakes.

ADJUSTMENT

PEDAL HEIGHT

Dasher — Pedal height is measured from center of brake pedal pad to bottom of steering wheel. To adjust, loosen clevis lock nut and turn push rod until distance is 23.8" (605 mm). Tighten lock nut.

PEDAL FREE PLAY

NOTE — Pedal free play is adjusted at the power brake unit on all models except Dasher. Power brake unit (if equipped) must be removed to adjust free play.

STOP LIGHT SWITCH

Jetta, Rabbit & Rabbit Pickup — Stop light switch is located under dash, above brake pedal. To adjust, loosen lock nuts and adjust switch so distance between brake pedal arm and switch body is .20-.24" (5-6 mm). Tighten lock nuts. See Fig. 1.

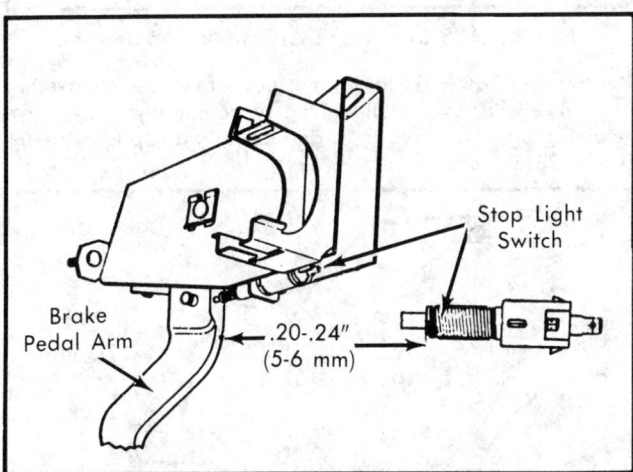

Fig. 1 Adjusting Stop Light Switch on Jetta, Rabbit and Rabbit Pickup Models

PARKING BRAKE

Dasher & Vanagon — Raise and support vehicle and ensure rear brakes are properly adjusted. From under vehicle, loosen parking brake cable lock nut(s). Pull parking brake handle up 2 notches (2-4 notches on Vanagon) and tighten cable adjusting nut(s) until rear wheels lock. Tighten lock nut(s) and ensure rear wheels rotate freely with parking brake fully released.

All Others — Raise and support vehicle and ensure rear brakes are properly adjusted. Pull back rubber (plastic) boot at base of parking brake handle and loosen parking brake cable lock nuts. Pull handle up 2 notches and tighten each adjusting nut until rear wheels lock. Tighten lock nuts and refit boot. Ensure rear wheels rotate freely with parking brake fully released.

BRAKE WARNING LIGHT

A dual warning light is mounted on dash. Light should glow when parking brake lever is pulled 1 notch and go off when lever is fully released (ignition on). To check circuit warning operation, release parking brake (ignition on) and ensure light is off. Open bleed screw on 1 wheel and depress brake pedal; light should glow. Close bleed screw, replenish brake fluid and bleed hydraulic system.

NOTE — Jetta, Rabbit and Rabbit Pickup models are equipped with warning sensor which is connected to brake proportioning valve. This sensor DOES NOT indicate fluid level in master cylinder. All other models are equipped with sensor which indicates fluid level in reservoir.

BRAKE PROPORTIONING VALVE

Jetta, Rabbit & Rabbit Pickup — 1) Valve is located below master cylinder. Connect a 1500 psi (110 kg/cm²) gauge to left front caliper and another gauge to right rear wheel cylinder. Bleed gauges and depress brake pedal several times.

2) Apply brake pedal until front gauge reads indicated pressure for first reading in Brake Pressure Chart. Record rear gauge reading. Increase pedal pressure until front gauge reads indicated pressure for second reading. Record rear gauge reading. Remove gauges and bleed hydraulic system. If pressures do not meet specifications, replace proportioning valve.

BRAKE PRESSURE REGULATOR

Dasher & Scirocco — 1) Regulator is located on right rear frame on Dasher and left rear frame on Scirocco. Empty vehicle, fill fuel tank and load driver's seat to 165 lbs. Bounce car several times and allow vehicle to settle normally.

2) Measure distance from top of tire rim to lower edge of fender lip (both sides). Attach spring tensioners to hold vehicle in settled position. See Fig. 2. Raise and support vehicle, check measurement and adjust tensioners if required. Connect a 1500 psi (110 kg/cm²) gauge to left front caliper and another gauge to right rear wheel cylinder. Bleed gauges.

3) Pump pedal several times. Depress brake pedal until front gauge reads indicated pressure for first reading in Brake Pressure Chart. Record rear gauge reading. Increase pedal pressure until front gauge reads indicated pressure for second reading. Record rear gauge reading.

4) If both pressures were high on rear wheel, loosen regulator clamp bolt and REDUCE spring tension. INCREASE spring tension if pressures were too low. Replace pressure regulator if spring adjustment does not correct pressures.

NOTE — Do NOT adjust spring tension with brake pedal depressed.

VOLKSWAGEN (Cont.)

NOTE: Tensioners will keep vehicle in a settled position.

Fig. 2   Tensioner Position on Scirocco (Dasher Tensioner is Mounted With Wing Nut on Top)

Vanagon — 1) Regulator is mounted on right rear frame. Raise and support vehicle and connect a 1500 psi (110 kg/cm²) gauge to left front caliper and another gauge to left rear wheel cylinder. Bleed gauges and depress brake pedal several times.

2) Remove regulator attaching nuts, then remove regulator from mounting studs. Depress brake pedal until front gauge reads indicated pressure for first reading in Brake Pressure Chart. Maintain pressure and tilt front of regulator down at a 30° angle. Increase pedal pressure until front gauge reads indicated pressure for second reading. Record rear gauge reading.

NOTE — *Do not damage brake lines when tilting regulator.*

3) If pressures are as specified in Brake Pressure Chart, return and secure regulator to proper position. Remove gauges and bleed hydraulic system. If pressures are not as specified, replace regulator.

Brake Pressure Chart

Application	Front Gauge psi (kg/cm²)	Rear Gauge psi (kg/cm²)
Dasher		
1st Reading	710 (50)	469-526 (33-37)
2nd Reading	1450 (102)	782-839 (55-59)
Jetta & Rabbit		
1st Reading	725 (51)	420-537 (30-38)
2nd Reading	1450 (102)	682-885 (48-62)
Rabbit Pickup		
1st Reading	725 (51)	479-595 (34-42)
2nd Reading	1450 (102)	740-885 (52-62)
Scirocco		
1st Reading	725 (51)	441-498 (31-35)
2nd Reading	1450 (102)	754-811 (53-57)
Vanagon		
1st Reading	725 (51)	725 (51)
2nd Reading	1450 (102)	798-943 (56-66)

REMOVAL & INSTALLATION

FRONT DISC BRAKE PADS

NOTE — *ATE, Girling or Kelsey-Hayes calipers may be used on front disc brakes. Dasher is equipped with new type Girling calipers. Disc pads are interchangeable between ATE and Girling calipers only.*

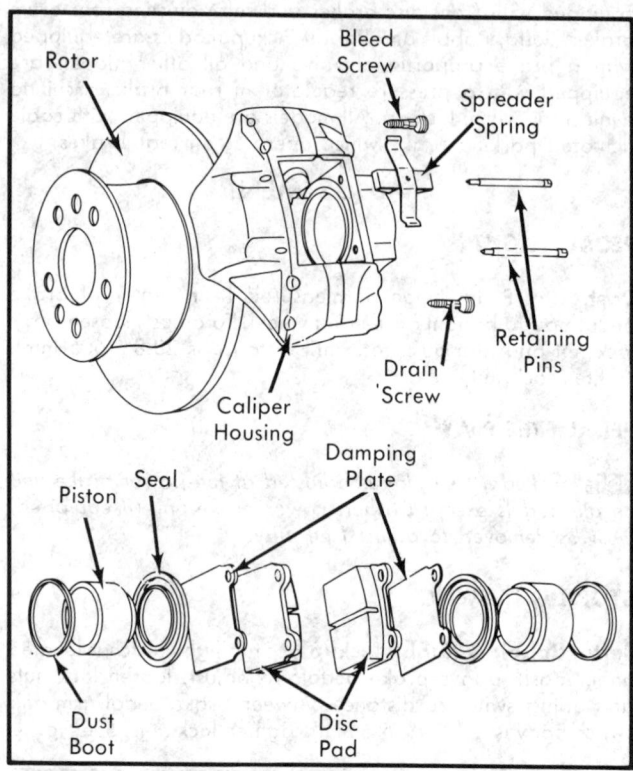

Fig. 3   ATE Disc Brake Assembly — Vanagon

Removal (ATE) — 1) Raise and support vehicle; remove tire and wheel. Remove retaining clip (if equipped) and remove retaining pins and spreader spring. Using a disc pad extractor (US 1023/3), remove inner brake pad.

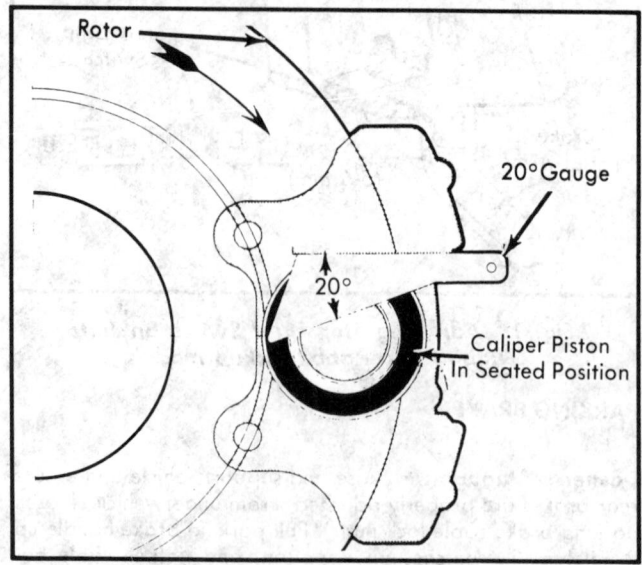

Fig. 4   Using a 20° Gauge to Position Piston in ATE Caliper Bore (Except Vanagon)

VOLKSWAGEN (Cont.)

2) Separate outer pad from notch in piston, then extract outer brake pad. Remove damping plates. Replace brake pads if thickness is less than .08" (2 mm) on Vanagon or .25" (6 mm) on all other models.

Installation — **1)** Siphon small amount of brake fluid from master cylinder reservoir. Seat piston in bore with compressor (US 1023/4). Check position of piston. On Vanagon, notches in piston must face bottom of caliper; rotate with pliers (US 1023/2) if required. On all others, use 20° gauge to position piston. *See Fig. 4.*

2) Install noise damping plates with lugs engaged in piston recesses. Install brake pads and new spreader spring. Install retaining pins and clips (if equipped). Depress brake pedal several times to set pad-to-rotor clearance.

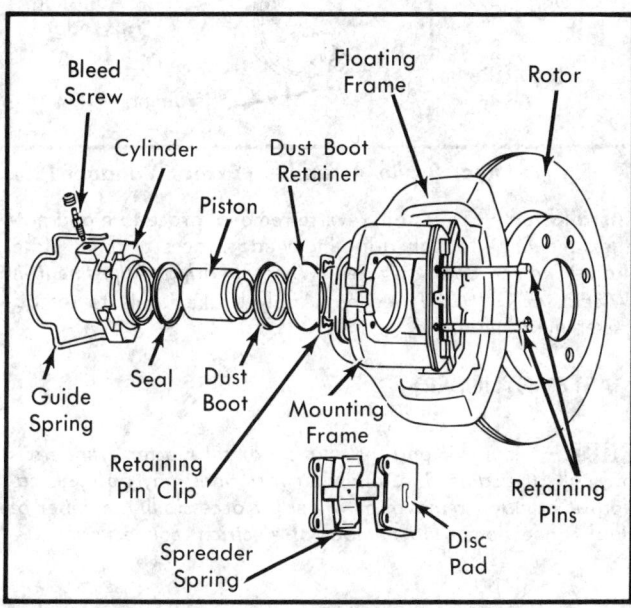

Fig. 5 ATE Disc Brake Assembly — Except Vanagon

Removal (Girling; Exc. Dasher) — **1)** Raise and support vehicle; remove tire and wheel. Remove spreader spring. Remove pin retaining bolt (pin clips) and remove pad pins.

2) Using extractor tool (US 1023/3), remove pads and damping plates (if equipped). Replace brake pads if thickness is less than .08" (2 mm) on Vanagon or .25" (6 mm) on all other models.

Installation — **1)** Remove small amount of brake fluid from reservoir. Seat pistons in caliper bore with suitable tool. Install pads and damping plates (if equipped). Damping plates must be installed with arrows pointing in forward wheel rotation.

2) Attach spreader spring (if stamped with an arrow, install with arrow pointing down). Install pad pins and pin retaining bolt (pin clips). Depress brake pedal several times to adjust pad-to-rotor clearance.

Removal (Girling; Dasher) — **1)** Raise and support vehicle on safety stands; remove tire and wheel. Remove small amount of brake fluid from reservoir. Using hand pressure, seat piston in housing by pushing caliper toward outer bearing.

2) Remove lower caliper mounting bolt while holding guide pin head with open end wrench. Rotate caliper body upward and remove pads. Replace pads if lining is less than .28" (7 mm).

Installation — To install, reverse removal procedure and install new lower mounting bolt. Depress brake pedal several times to adjust pad-to-rotor clearance.

Removal (Kelsey-Hayes) — Raise and support vehicle on safety stands; remove tire and wheel. Remove anti-rattle springs and guide pins. Remove and suspend caliper with wire. DO NOT allow caliper to hang from hydraulic line. Remove pads.

Installation — Insert pads in caliper support (inner pad is identified by chamfered ends). Remove brake fluid from reservoir and seat piston with suitable tool. Position caliper on support. Lube guide pins with silicone grease and install (long pin on top). Install anti-rattle springs. Depress brake pedal several times to adjust pad-to-rotor clearance.

DISC BRAKE CALIPER

Removal — Raise and support vehicle and remove wheel. Disconnect brake line from caliper and plug opening to prevent entry of dirt and foreign matter. Bend back locking tabs (if equipped) on mounting bolts. Remove caliper mounting bolts and take off caliper assembly.

Installation — To install, reverse removal procedure, using new lock plates and mounting bolts.

DISC BRAKE ROTOR

Removal — Remove grease cap (if equipped), cotter pin and loosen adjusting nut. Raise and support vehicle on safety stands; remove wheel and tire. Remove wheel bearing hardware. Pull hub and rotor from spindle without dropping outer bearing. Separate hub and rotor if necessary by removing Allen head bolts and using rubber hammer.

NOTE — *Vanagon rotor can not be separated from hub. Replace as complete assembly.*

Installation — To install hub and rotor assembly, reverse removal procedure and adjust wheel bearings. *See Wheel Bearing Adjustment in WHEEL ALIGNMENT Section.*

REAR BRAKE DRUM

CAUTION — *Loosen and tighten spindle nut only with wheels on the ground.*

Removal (Vanagon) — Remove dust cap, cotter pin and loosen castellated nut. Raise and support vehicle; remove tire and wheel. Release parking brake at equalizer and back off adjuster. Remove drum retaining screws. Install puller and remove drum.

NOTE — *Drum must rotate freely during removal.*

Installation — To install, reverse removal procedure and ensure drum retaining screws are tight. Adjust parking brake and depress brake pedal several times to set self-adjusting mechanism.

VOLKSWAGEN (Cont.)

Removal (All Others) — Raise and support vehicle. Remove 1 wheel bolt and push adjusting wedge upward with a screwdriver. Reinstall wheel bolt, remove wheel bearing hardware and remove drum assembly from spindle without dropping thrust washer or outer bearing.

Installation — To install, reverse removal procedure and adjust wheel bearings. *See Wheel Bearing Adjustment in WHEEL ALIGNMENT Section.* Apply brake pedal firmly to set self-adjusting mechanism.

BRAKE SHOES

Removal (Vanagon) — 1) With wheel and drum removed, remove hold down springs and pins. Disconnect parking brake cable from lever on brake shoe. Remove lower return spring and adjuster spring.

2) Move brake shoes out of lower support and remove return springs. Remove brake shoes as an assembly from backing plate without pulling pistons out of wheel cylinder. Separate brake shoes and disconnect parking brake lever from brake shoe. Remove lower support bolts and support.

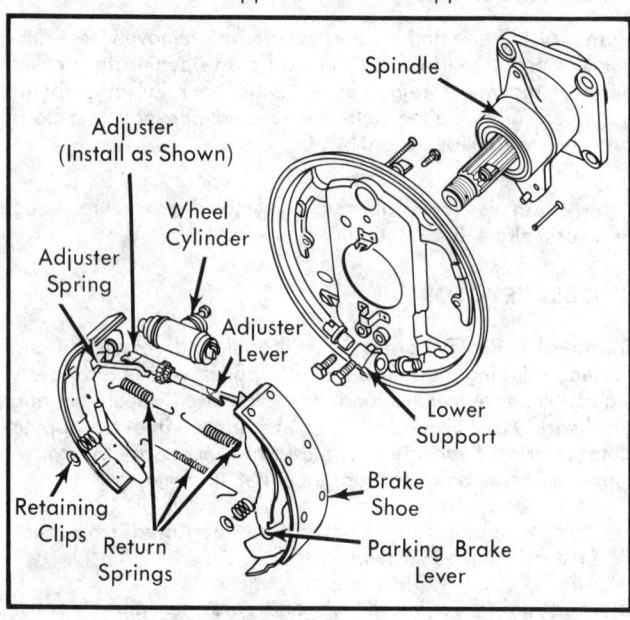

Fig. 6   Vanagon Rear Brake Assembly

Installation — 1) To install, reverse removal procedure and note the following: After installing brake shoes, adjust brake shoes by setting distance (measured from outer surface of each brake lining) to 9.87" (250.7 mm).

2) Adjust parking brake at equalizer (there must not be any free play between parking brake lever on brake shoe and adjusting rod). Install brake drum and depress brake pedal several times to set self-adjusting mechanism.

Removal (All Others) — 1) With drum removed, remove hold down springs and pins. Remove brake shoes from anchor pins and remove return spring.

2) Disconnect parking brake cable from lever. Disconnect adjusting wedge spring and upper return spring. Remove brake shoes. Place adjuster strut and shoe in vise; remove tension spring. Separate shoe and components.

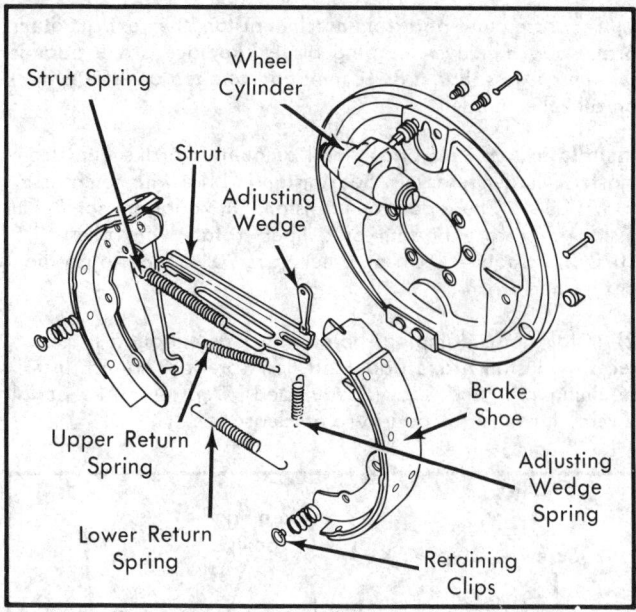

Fig. 7   Rear Brake Assembly (Except Vanagon)

Installation — To install, reverse removal procedure and note the following: Lug on adjusting wedge faces backing plate. Adjust wheel bearings. *See Wheel Bearing Adjustment in WHEEL ALIGNMENT Section.* Apply brake firmly to set adjuster mechanism.

MASTER CYLINDER

NOTE — *Removal and installation of all master cylinders is basically the same. The following variations may apply: Location of cylinder, removal of wheel for accessibility, number of fluid connections, and number of electrical connections.*

Removal (Vanagon) — 1) Remove instrument panel, then drain or siphon fluid from master cylinder reservoir. Disconnect fluid lines and electrical connections from master cylinder. Remove vacuum lines from power brake unit. Remove pedal and bracket assembly.

2) Disconnect brake push rod from brake pedal. Remove power brake unit and master cylinder assembly from pedal bracket. Remove master cylinder-to-power brake unit attaching bolts and remove master cylinder.

Installation — To install, reverse removal procedure and note the following: Install a new "O" ring between master cylinder and power brake unit. Adjust brake push rod length. See *POWER BRAKE UNIT.* Bleed hydraulic system.

Removal (All Others) — Drain or siphon fluid from reservoir. Raise and support vehicle and remove cover plate (if equipped). Disconnect fluid lines and electrical connections at master cylinder. On models without power unit, remove brake push rod from brake pedal. Remove master cylinder-to-power brake unit attaching bolts and remove master cylinder.

NOTE — *If spacers are used on attaching bolts, do not drop or lose spacers.*

VOLKSWAGEN (Cont.)

Installation — To install, reverse removal procedure and note the following: Install a new "O" ring between master cylinder and power brake unit. Adjust brake push rod length (brake pedal height on Dasher). *See POWER BRAKE UNIT for push rod length adjustment.* After installation, bleed hydraulic system.

POWER BRAKE UNIT

Function Test — Depress and release brake pedal several times (engine off) to exhaust vacuum. Depress and hold pedal; start engine. Pedal should fall slightly then hold. Replace booster assembly if check valve is operative and no defects or leaks are present in vacuum or hydraulic systems.

Removal (Vanagon) — Remove instrument panel and separate power brake unit from master cylinder as previously described.

Installation — **1)** To install, reverse removal procedure and note the following: Before installing brake push rod to brake pedal, adjust push rod length.

2) To adjust push rod length (measured from power unit flange to centerline of push rod clevis), loosen lock nut and turn push rod until distance is 4.39" (111.5 mm). Tighten lock nut. Complete installation and bleed hydraulic system.

Removal (All Others) — Remove master cylinder from power brake unit as previously described. Disconnect brake push rod from brake pedal. Disconnect vacuum lines from power brake unit. Remove mounting nuts from firewall and remove power brake unit.

Installation — **1)** To install, reverse removal procedure and note the following: Always replace damping ring, washer, filter and "O" ring. Slots in damping washer and filter must be offset 180°. Adjust push rod clearance.

2) To adjust push rod clearance (measured from power unit flange to centerline of push rod clevis), loosen lock nut and turn push rod until distance is 8.11" (206 mm). Tighten lock nut. Complete installation and bleed hydraulic system.

CHECK VALVE

Function Test — Check valve is located in vacuum line between power brake unit and intake manifold. Blowing into large diameter side must unseat valve; valve must seat when test is performed on opposite side. Replace defective valve.

VACUUM BOOSTER
(CIS FUEL INJECTED MODELS ONLY)

1) An adjustable or non-adjustable vacuum booster is installed to increase vacuum to power brake unit. To check booster, warm engine until oil reaches 140°F. Install "T" connector between distributor vacuum unit and intake manifold. Gauge should read 7.4" (188 mm) vacuum with engine idling. If not, check vacuum lines for leaks.

2) If vacuum is as specified in step **1)**, check booster as follows: Remove and plug hose from right side of booster. Loosen lock nut (if equipped) and install vacuum gauge and hose. Gauge should read 11.8" (300 mm) vacuum with engine idling. Adjust screw in or out to obtain correct reading (if equipped). Replace defective booster.

VACUUM PUMP
(DIESEL ONLY)

Removal & Installation — Remove vacuum lines from upper housing. Remove unit from engine block. To install, reverse removal procedure and replace "O" ring at mounting base.

OVERHAUL

DISC BRAKE CALIPER

Disassembly (ATE & Girling; Vanagon) — **1)** Remove disc pads and damping plates as previously described. Clamp mounting flange in a soft-jawed vise and remove dust boot retainer (if equipped) and dust boot.

2) Install piston retainer tool (US 1023/5) on 1 piston. Insert wooden block in caliper and remove piston with compressed air. Repeat procedure for opposite piston. Remove piston seals without damaging bore.

Cleaning & Inspection — Clean all parts in brake fluid. Check piston and caliper bore for wear or damage; replace as necessary. DO NOT split caliper housings; assembly must be replaced if split. Replace all parts included in repair kit.

Reassembly — Apply light coat of brake paste to piston and seal. Fit seal in groove, install piston in bore and press into bore using retainer (US 1023/5). Lightly coat inside of dust boot with brake paste and fit to piston. Using press clamp (VW 442), press dust cap onto bore groove and seat piston. Install dust boot retainer (if equipped). Install damping plates. Repeat procedure for other piston.

NOTE — *Ensure pistons are properly seated and piston damping plates are properly installed on ATE calipers.*

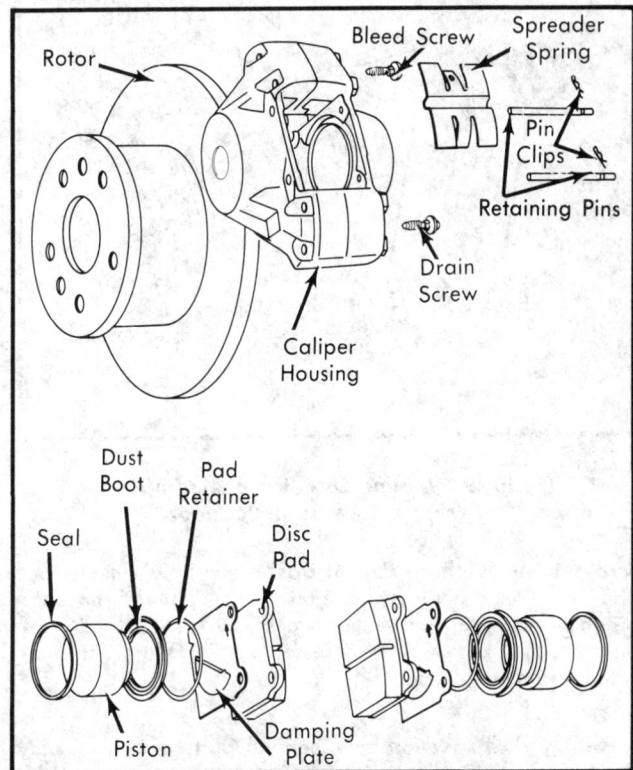

Fig. 8 Girling Disc Brake Assembly — Vanagon

VOLKSWAGEN (Cont.)

Disassembly (ATE; All Others) — 1) Remove disc pads as previously described. Press caliper frame off floating frame. Insert wooden block in floating frame and drive cylinder and guide spring off with brass drift.

2) Remove piston retaining ring and dust seal. Protect piston with wooden block and force piston out with compressed air. Remove piston seal without damaging bore.

Cleaning & Inspection — Clean all parts in brake fluid. Check piston and bore for wear or damage; replace as necessary. Replace all parts included in repair kit.

Reassembly — Reverse disassembly procedure and note the following: Coat piston with brake paste. Use a vise to seat piston. Use a brass drift to fit brake cylinder to floating frame. Make sure both grooves in mounting frame are pushed over ribs on floating frame. Make sure piston is properly positioned. See Fig. 4.

Reassembly — To reassemble, reverse disassembly procedure and note: Coat pistons and seals with brake paste before refitting.

Disassembly (Girling; Dasher) — Separate cylinder housing from pad carrier. Remove dust cap. Insert wooden block in housing and blow out piston with compressed air. Remove piston seal without damaging bore.

Cleaning & Inspection — Clean all parts in brake fluid. Check piston and bore; if corroded, pitted or scored, replace defective part. DO NOT use abrasives. Replace all parts included in repair kit.

Reassembly — Coat piston, cylinder bore and new seal with brake paste. Fit seal into cylinder. Slide dust seal onto piston, then slowly insert piston into cylinder, fitting inner lips of dust seal on housing groove. Fully seat piston into cylinder. Engage outer lip of dust seal on groove of piston.

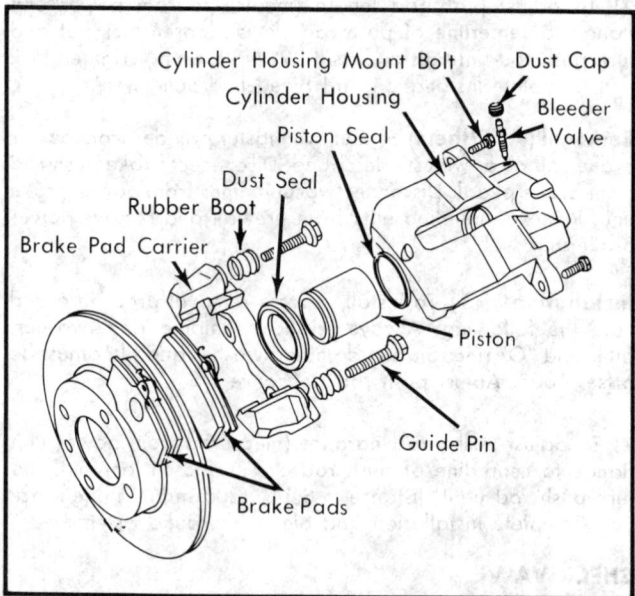

Fig. 10 *Girling Disc Assembly Used on Dasher Kelsey-Hayes Disc Assembly is Similar*

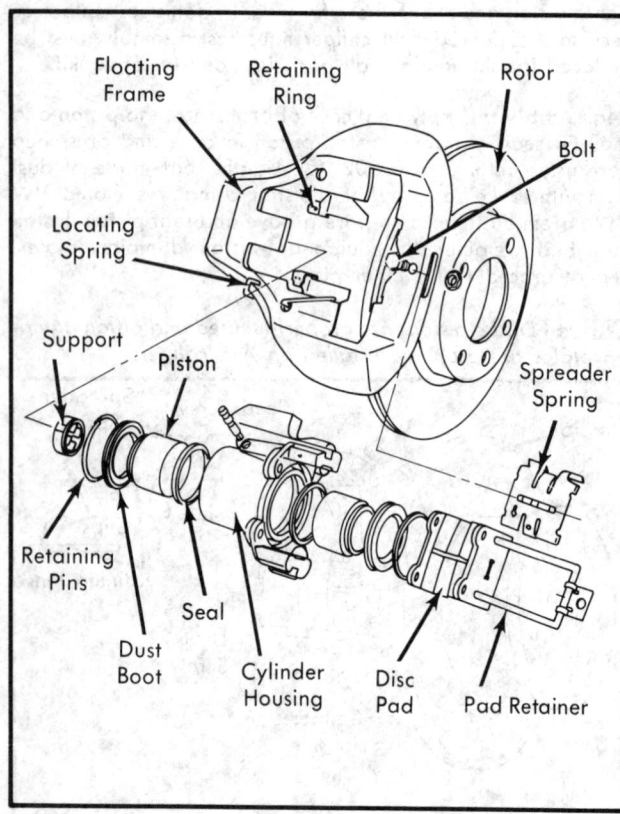

Fig. 9 *Girling Disc Brake Assembly (Except Dasher and Vanagon)*

Disassembly (Girling; Except Dasher) — Press cylinder out of frame. Remove dust boot and retaining ring from each piston. Hold piston between padded jaws of vise and blow pistons out of bore with compressed air. Remove piston seals without damaging bore.

Cleaning & Inspection — Clean all parts in brake fluid. Check piston and caliper bore for wear or damage; replace as necessary. Replace all parts included in repair kit.

Disassembly (Kelsey-Hayes) — Disconnect brake hose from caliper. Remove caliper from support assembly. Remove anti-rattle springs and guide pins. Remove support from spindle. Remove dust boot from piston. Place wooden block in caliper housing and blow piston out with compressed air. Remove piston seal without damaging bore. Remove guide pins and bushings, if required.

Cleaning & Inspection — Clean all parts in brake fluid. Check cylinder bore and piston for wear or corrosion; replace defective part. Replace all parts included in repair kit.

Reassembly — Coat seals, dust boot, cylinder bore and piston with brake paste. Coat guide pins with silicone grease. Reverse disassembly procedure and note the following: Seat dust boot with brass drift. Long guide pin is installed in top hole of caliper housing.

VOLKSWAGEN (Cont.)

MASTER CYLINDER

NOTE — *Master cylinders differ in external design and primary piston configuration between power assist and non-power assist models. Disassembly procedures are the same.*

Disassembly — Remove dust boot (if equipped) and piston stop screw. Remove circlip and washer. Tap open end of cylinder and remove piston assemblies. Remove all external mountings and hardware from cylinder.

Cleaning & Inspection — Clean all parts with brake fluid or denatured alcohol. Check cylinder bore and pistons for wear; replace as complete assembly if defective. Replace all rubber parts during overhaul and use all parts included in repair kit.

Reassembly — Reverse disassembly procedure and note the following: Coat primary piston shaft with lubricant supplied in repair kit. Coat pistons and cups with brake paste. DO NOT interchange return springs or piston cups. (ATE secondary cups are identified by chamfer and groove.)

POWER BRAKE UNIT
PRESSURE REGULATING VALVE
& PROPORTIONING VALVE

NOTE — *Manufacturer recommends replacing each unit as complete assembly. DO NOT disassemble.*

VACUUM PUMP
(DIESEL ONLY)

Disassembly — **1)** Remove cover from upper housing and separate components. Remove upper housing retaining screws and separate housings. Remove diaphragm retaining nut and separate diaphragm and plates.

2) Remove drive shaft cover and gasket. Remove retainer and washer from drive shaft. Push drive shaft back until push rod is free. Remove push rod.

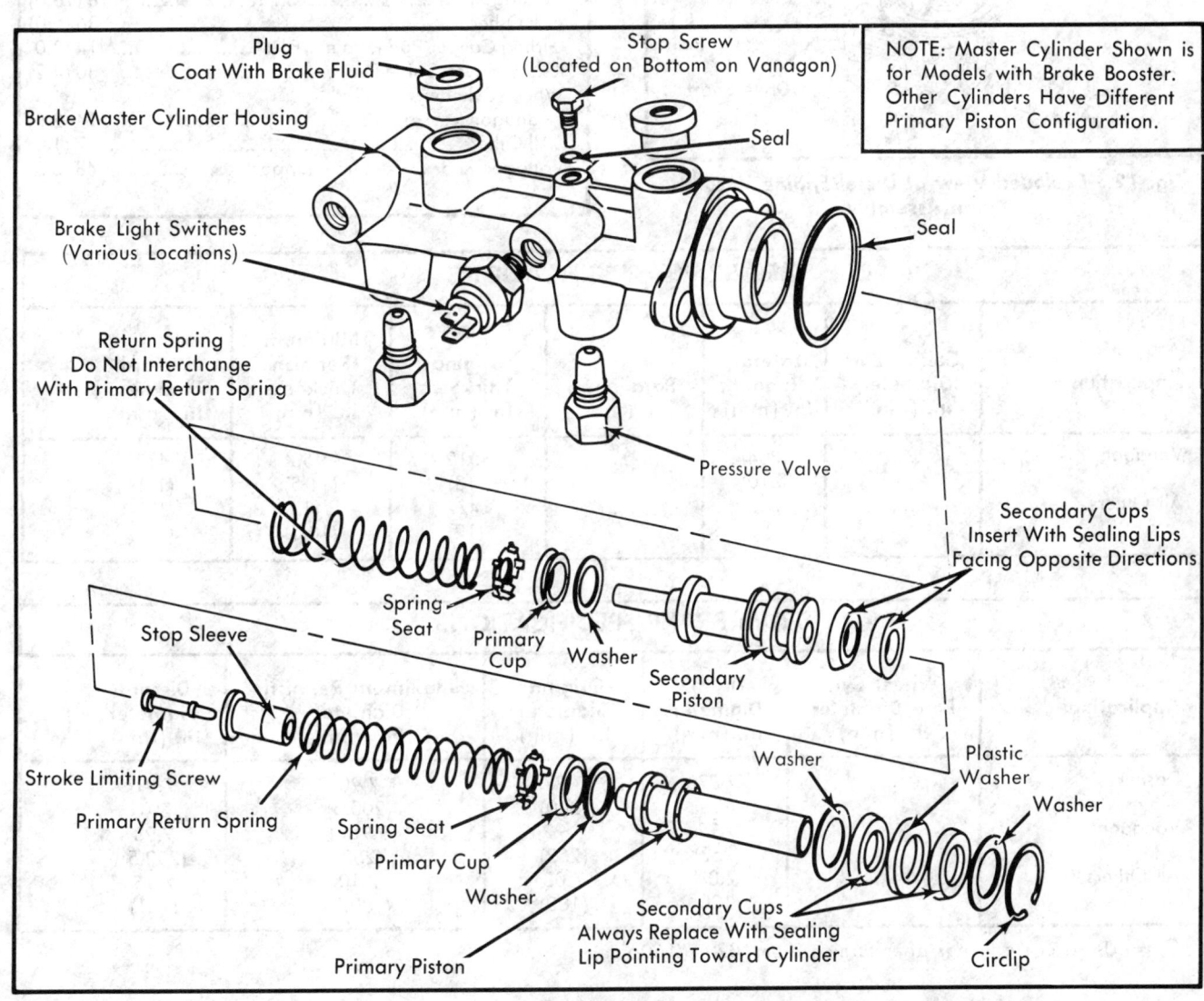

Fig. 11 Exploded View of Master Cylinder

VOLKSWAGEN (Cont.)

Cleaning & Inspection — Clean all parts in denatured alcohol and inspect body for cracks. Inspect diaphragm for cracks and deformation. Replace defective parts as required. Replace diaphragm retaining nut and all rubber parts during overhaul. Use all parts included in repair kit.

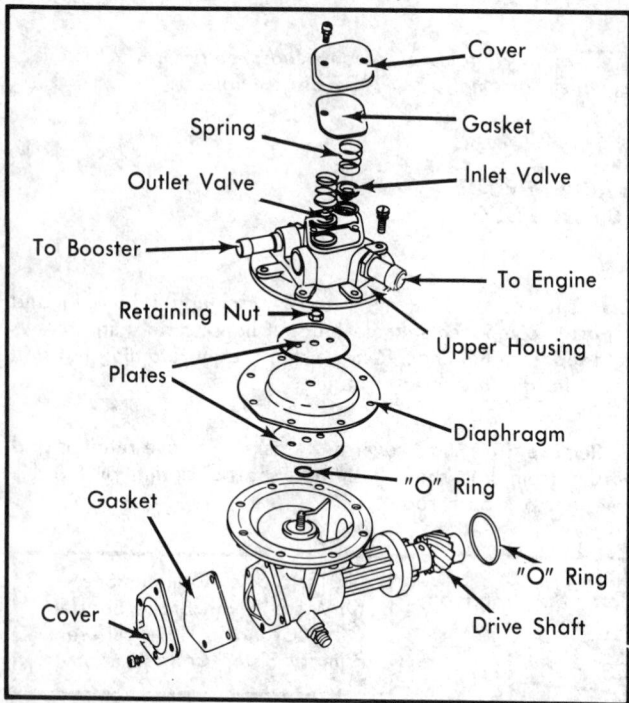

Fig. 12 Exploded View of Diesel Engine Vacuum Pump Assembly

Installation — **1)** Reassemble diaphragm assembly with diaphragm molded center facing up. Coat new retaining nut with sealing compound and tighten to 5 ft. lb. (0.7 mkg). Install upper housing plate with brake booster connection pointing straight up. Loosely install retaining screws.

2) Press and hold push rod into position. Tighten upper housing retaining screws. Push drive shaft into position and secure with washer and retainer. Replace spring sealing washers and install valves with spring seat toward housing. Replace gaskets and install covers.

TIGHTENING SPECIFICATIONS

Application	Ft. Lbs. (mkg)
Master Cylinder-to-Booster	
Vanagon	11 (1.5)
All Others	9 (1.3)
Caliper Mounting Bolts	
Dasher (Support Bolt)	43 (6.0)
Dasher (Caliper-to-Support Bolt)	25 (3.5)
Vanagon	118 (16.0)
All Others	36 (5.0)
Girling Caliper Pad Retainer Bolt	14 (2.0)
Kelsey-Hayes Guide Pins	30 (4.2)
Wheel Cylinder	
Vanagon	14 (2.0)
All Others	7 (1.0)
Vanagon Rear Brake Shoe Support	48 (6.5)

DISC BRAKE SPECIFICATIONS

Application	Caliper Bore Diameter In. (mm)	Lateral Runout In. (mm)	Parallelism In. (mm)	Original Thickness In. (mm)	Minimum Refinish Thickness In. (mm)	Discard Thickness In. (mm)
Vanagon	.....	.004 (0.10)	.....	.512 (13)	.453 (11:5)	.433 (11)
All Others	.....	.....	.....	.472 (12)	.413 (10.5)	.393 (10)

DRUM BRAKE SPECIFICATIONS

Application	Wheel Cyl. Bore Diameter In. (mm)	Drum Diameter In. (mm)	Original Diameter In. (mm)	Maximum Refinish Diameter In. (mm)	Discard Diameter In. (mm)
Dasher	.....	7.87 (200)	7.87 (200)	7.90 (200.5)	7.91 (201)
Vanagon	.....	9.92 (252)	9.92 (252)	9.96① (253)	9.98 (253.5)
All Others	.....	7.08 (180)	7.08 (180)	7.10 (180.5)	7.13 (181)

① — Use oversize linings after turning drum .020" (0.50 mm).

Brakes

VOLVO

DL   GLE
GL   Coupe
GT   Diesel

DESCRIPTION

Volvo models may be equipped with Girling calipers on all 4 wheels or Girling front calipers; ATE rear calipers. Service brakes are hydraulically operated by tandem master cylinder and vacuum power brake unit. Master cylinder distributes hydraulic pressure to distribution/warning valve. Distribution/warning valve equally distributes hydraulic pressure to each circuit. One circuit is lower front caliper pistons and right rear caliper; other circuit is upper front caliper pistons and left rear caliper. If hydraulic pressure differs between circuits, dash mounted light will glow. Each rear brake line has a pressure valve to prevent rear wheel lock-up. Parking brake is mechanically operated on rear wheel mounted, internal brake shoes.

ADJUSTMENT

PEDAL HEIGHT

Brake pedal height should be equal to clutch pedal. To adjust, loosen lock nut, remove cotter pin and turn push rod until height is equal. Replace cotter pin and tighten lock nut. Pedal travel should then be 5.7-6.5" (145-165 mm).

NOTE — *Pedal travel can only be measured during brake bleeding operation. See Hydraulic System Bleeding article in this section.*

STOP LIGHT SWITCH

Stop light switch is located under instrument panel, in front of brake pedal. To adjust, loosen retaining screws and position switch so contact plunger just contacts pedal arm. Measureable distance from switch body to pedal arm should be .08-.24" (2-6 mm). Tighten retaining screws.

PARKING BRAKE

NOTE — *Adjust parking brake when full application stroke of brake lever exceeds 3 or 4 notches.*

1) Remove center console rear ash tray, then working through ash tray hole, loosen parking brake cables adjusting screw until cables are slack. Raise and support rear of vehicle, then remove wheels. Align hole in parking brake drum with starwheel adjuster.

2) Tighten starwheel until drum can just be rotated by hand, then back off adjuster until drum just rotates freely. Install rear wheels. Tighten parking brake cable adjusting screw until parking brake is fully applied when lever is pulled 2 or 3 notches. Install ash tray and lower vehicle.

BRAKE WARNING LIGHTS

Brake Failure Light — This light will glow if pressure differential is exceeded or fluid level is low. Light will continue to glow until problem is corrected. Check calipers, hydraulic lines, master cylinder, power brake unit and vacuum pump for defects and repair as required.

Parking Brake Light — This light will glow when parking brake lever is pulled 1 notch and go out when fully released (ignition on).

REMOVAL & INSTALLATION

DISC PADS

Removal — 1) Raise and support vehicle; remove tire and wheel. On Girling calipers, remove lock clip then remove one lock pin while holding damper spring in place. Remove springs and other lock pin. On ATE calipers, drive out upper guide pin and remove tensioning spring. Drive out lower guide pin.

2) Pull disc pads from caliper with pad extractor tool (2917). Replace pads in sets if lining thickness is less than $\frac{1}{8}$" (3 mm). If pads are to be reinstalled, mark for reference.

Installation — 1) Siphon small amount of fluid from master cylinder reservoir. Seat pistons in caliper bore with piston tool (2809). On ATE rear calipers, check piston position by installing template (SV02919). Piston recess should incline 20° in relation to lower guide area on caliper. If distance from one recess to the other (*Measurement "A" in Fig. 1*) exceeds .04" (1 mm), adjust position.

2) Install new pads, install intermediate plates (if equipped) or damper washers (if equipped) in original positions. On Girling calipers, install one lock pin, then install damper springs and other lock pin. Install new locking clips on pins. On ATE calipers, tap one guide pin into position, install new tensioning spring and install other guide pin while holding tensioning spring in position.

NOTE — *Install damper washers with small contact face toward pad. DO NOT install intermediate plates in calipers equipped with damper washers.*

3) After installation, depress brake pedal several times to seat pads against rotor. Ensure proper operation of brakes, install wheel and lower vehicle.

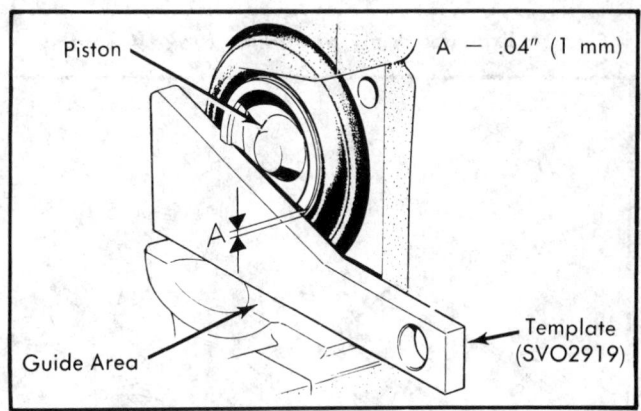

Fig. 1 Checking ATE Rear Caliper Piston Angle

CALIPER ASSEMBLY

Removal — Raise and support vehicle, and remove wheel. Disconnect brake line connections at caliper, and cap lines to prevent entry of foreign matter. Remove caliper mounting bolts and lift caliper from vehicle.

Brakes

VOLVO (Cont.)

Installation — Position caliper assembly on mounting bracket, and install attaching bolts. After installing bolts, check clearance between disc pads and rotor on both sides of rotor; maximum deviation between sides should not exceed .022″ (.01 mm) for front calipers or .010″ (.25 mm) for rear calipers. If clearance is not within specifications, correct by adding shims to caliper. Connect hydraulic lines and bleed hydraulic system.

DISC BRAKE ROTOR

Removal & Installation — With caliper assembly removed, mount a dial indicator and check rotor runout. Runout must not exceed .004″ (.10 mm). Measure rotor thickness through one revolution; thickness variance must not exceed .0008″ (.02 mm). Unscrew rotor lock bolts and pull rotor from hub. To install, reverse removal procedure.

PARKING BRAKE SHOES

Removal — Remove center console rear ash tray and loosen parking brake cable adjusting nut until cables are slack. Raise

and support rear of vehicle and remove wheels. Remove caliper (without disconnecting hydraulic line) and support out of way, then remove rotor. Remove brake shoe return springs and lift off shoes and adjuster.

Installation — Reverse removal procedure and note the following: Replace brake drum (rotor) if out-of-round more than .008″ (.2 mm). Apply a thin coat of heat resistant graphite grease to brake shoe sliding surfaces and to adjusting starwheel. After installation, adjust parking brake. See *Parking Brake*.

MASTER CYLINDER

Removal & Installation — Disconnect hydraulic lines at master cylinder and cap openings to prevent entry of foreign matter. Remove cylinder attaching hardware, and remove cylinder assembly from vehicle. To install, reverse removal procedure, and bleed hydraulic system.

POWER BRAKE UNIT

Removal & Installation — With master cylinder removed, disconnect vacuum hose at power unit. From inside vehicle, disconnect push rod link at brake pedal and remove clutch pedal stop bracket. Remove power unit attaching nuts at firewall. Tilt power unit slightly forward and remove lock nut and yoke. Remove power unit from engine compartment. To install, reverse removal procedure and note: Install new gasket between power unit and firewall; discarding sealing putty (if equipped). Install vacuum hose connector facing down. Bleed hydraulic system.

Check Valve Replacement — Remove vacuum hose clamps at check valve, and remove check valve from vehicle. When installing check valve into vacuum hose, install valve with arrow on valve housing pointing toward intake manifold.

Filter Replacement — Remove power brake unit from vehicle. Remove rubber dust boot, and filter retainer washer. Withdraw silencer and filter from end of booster. To install, reverse removal procedure, making sure slots in filter and silencer are 180° apart.

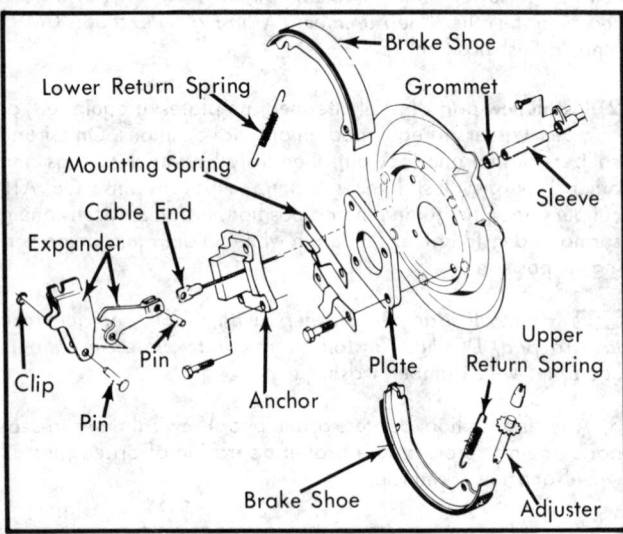

Fig. 2   Exploded View of Parking Brake Assembly

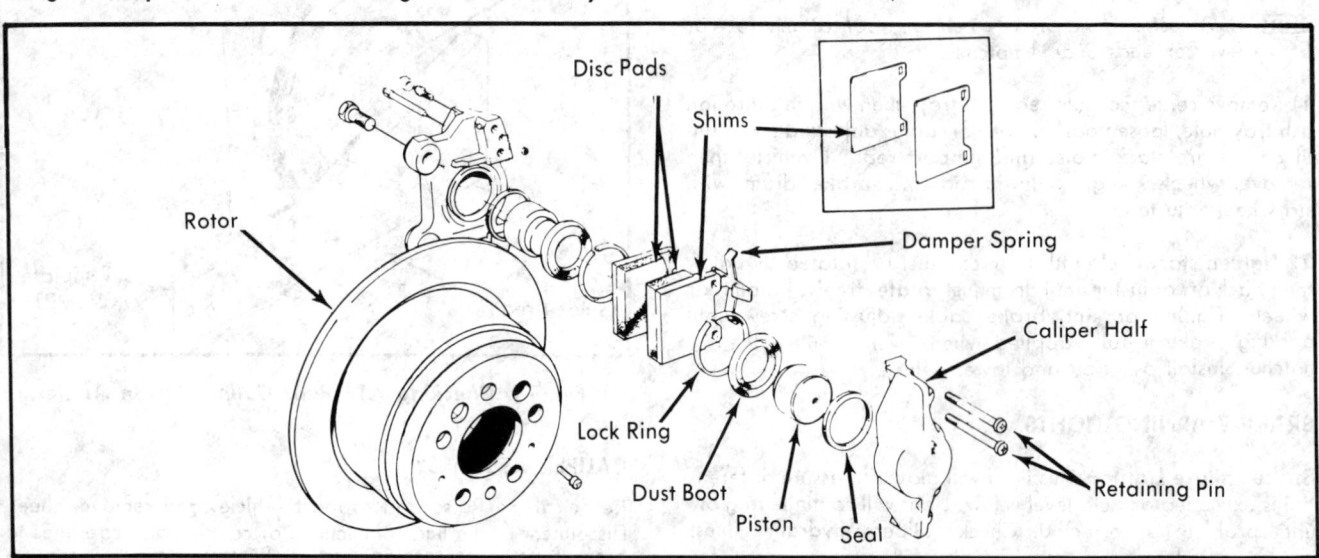

Fig. 3   ATE Rear Caliper Assembly

VOLVO (Cont.)

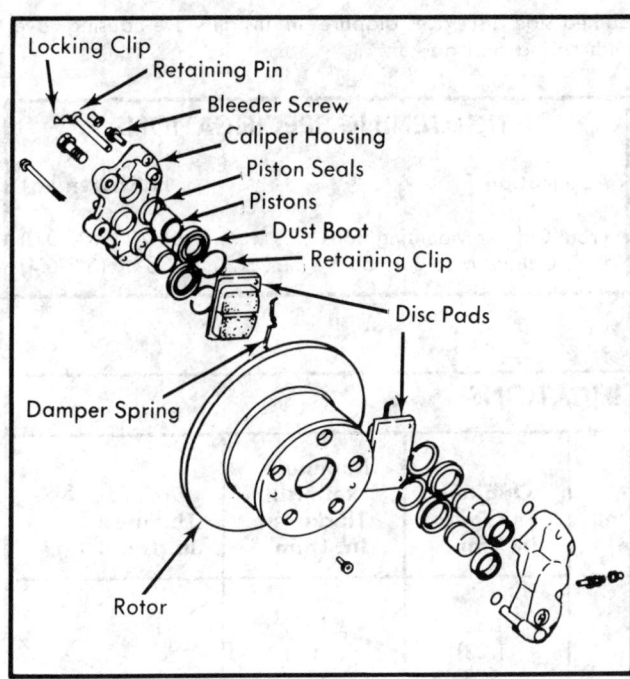

Fig. 4 Girling Front Caliper Assembly

VACUUM PUMP

Removal & Installation — Disconnect hoses at vacuum pump and remove mounting bolts and pump. Clean mating surfaces to remove gasket material, install new gasket and reverse removal procedure to complete installation.

OVERHAUL

BRAKE CALIPER

Disassembly — With caliper removed from vehicle, remove disc pads, piston dust covers and retaining clips. Insert wooden

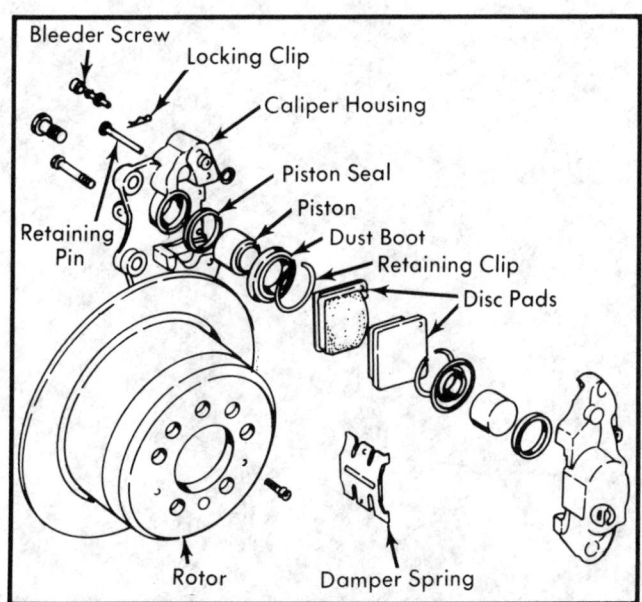

Fig. 5 Girling Rear Caliper Assembly

block into caliper housing and apply compressed air at fluid inlet ports to force pistons out of caliper. Remove piston seals from cylinder bore with blunt tool without damaging cylinder bore. Remove bleeder screw.

NOTE — *DO NOT separate caliper halves.*

Cleaning & Inspection — Clean all parts in brake fluid or alcohol. Inspect cylinder bores for scoring, rust or corrosion, replace if defective. Replace rubber seals and dust covers during overhaul.

Reassembly — Coat all parts with clean brake fluid and install new piston seals in cylinder bores. Carefully install pistons into cylinder bores. Check piston position on ATE rear brake calipers. Install rubber dust boots and retaining clips. Install bleeder screw and disc pads.

MASTER CYLINDER

Disassembly — Remove master cylinder from vehicle, and clamp mounting flange in a vise. Remove reservoir from cylinder, and remove rubber sealing rings. Remove piston stop screw, and remove retainer ring from end of cylinder bore. Remove pistons from cylinder bore.

Cleaning & Inspection — Wash all parts in clean brake fluid or alcohol and blow dry with compressed air. Inspect cylinder bore for scratches, rust or corrosion; replace if defective. Replace both pistons with connector sleeve as an assembly.

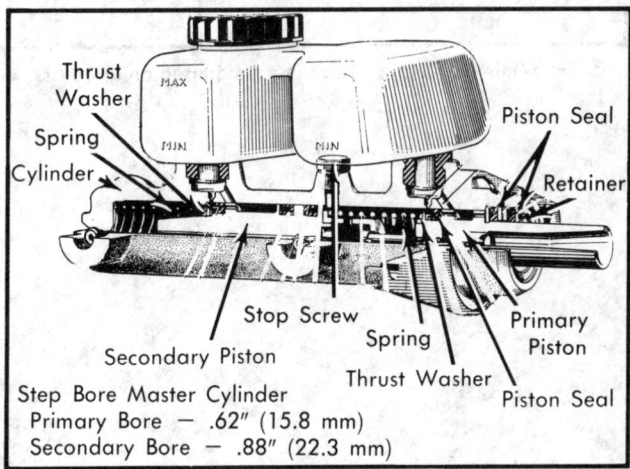

Fig. 6 Master Cylinder Assembly

Reassembly — Lubricate all parts with clean brake fluid prior to reassembly. Position washer, seal, and back-up ring on secondary piston. Install spring thrust washer on piston, and install piston assembly into cylinder bore. Install washer, seal, and back-up ring on primary piston. Install spring, with plate and sleeve on piston, then install piston assembly into cylinder bore. Push piston into cylinder bore, and install piston stop screw. Install reservoir sealing rings, and install reservoir.

VACUUM PUMP

Disassembly — 1) Place pump in soft jawed vise. Index mark valve housing with cover. Remove valve housing. Remove diaphragm, washers, and spring from pump.

Brakes

VOLVO (Cont.)

2) Turn pump over. Remove bottom cover. Remove actuating lever pin. Slide out pump lever, pump rod and nylon bushing.

Reassembly — 1) Place bushing on pump rod. Put rod in pump housing. Fit lever and pin. Install bottom cover and gasket.

2) Place washer and "O" ring on diaphragm screw. Remember to lightly coat end of screw with suitable thread locking compound. Install diaphragm assembly. Insert valve housing aligned with index marks. Fit valves and seals. Make sure

domed side disc faces diaphragm. Install valve housing cover with spring and gasket.

TIGHTENING SPECIFICATIONS

Application	Ft. Lbs. (mkg)
Front Caliper Mounting Bolts	65-72 (9.0-10.0)
Rear Caliper Mounting Bolts	38-46 (5.3-6.4)

DISC BRAKE SPECIFICATIONS

Application	Caliper Bore Diameter In. (mm)	Lateral Runout In. (mm)	Parallelism In. (mm)	Original Thickness In. (mm)	Minimum Refinish Thickness In. (mm)	Discard Thickness In. (mm)
DL & GL						
Front	.....	.004 (.10)	.0008 (.02)	.563 (14.3)	.557① (14.1)	.....
Rear	.....	.004 (.10)	.0008 (.02)	.378 (9.6)	.331 (8.4)	.....
GT, GLE, Coupe & Diesel						
Front	.....	.004 (.10)	.0008 (.02)	.945 (24.0)	.990① (22.8)	.....
Rear	.....	.004 (.10)	.0008 (.02)	.378 (9.6)	.331 (8.4)	.....

① — Minimum Refinish Thickness is stamped on all rotors. Adhere to stamped specifications.

Section 8

WHEEL ALIGNMENT

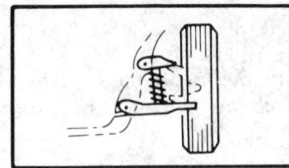

Contents

NOTE — ALSO SEE GENERAL INDEX.

Wheel Alignment

WHEEL ALIGNMENT TROUBLE SHOOTING

NOTE — *This is a general trouble shooting guide. When using this guide, locate the condition in column one that corresponds to your problem and determine the possible causes in column two. Match the number of the possible cause with the same number in column three, and you will have the suggested correction.*

CONDITION	POSSIBLE CAUSE	CORRECTION
► Tire wear	1) Tire pressure too low 2) Wheel alignment out of tolerance 3) Excessively worn wheel bearings 4) Improper or no tire rotation	1) Check manufacturer's recommended pressure and set to specifications. 2) Check alignment and set to specs or replace components 3) Check, adjust or replace bearings 4) Follow manufacturer's recommended procedures. Perform a 4 or 5-tire rotation
► Grating tire noise	1) Improper tire pressure 2) Wheel alignment out of tolerance 3) Damaged or defective spindle or suspension components	1) Check manufacturer's recommended pressure and set to specifications 2) Reset alignment or replace necessary suspension components 3) Inspect and replace components
► Uneven tire wear	1) Uneven tire pressure 2) Tire pressure too low (shoulders on tire worn) 3) Tire pressure too high (center of tread worn) 4) Bent rotor or wheel 5) One side of front tread worn 6) Inside of tread worn 7) Outside of tread worn 8) Excessive wheel bearing play 9) Brake operation on only one side	1) Check manufacturer's recommended pressure and set to specifications 2) See correction 1 3) See correction 1 4) Check and replace part 5) Inadequate camber 6) Inadequate toe-in 7) Excessive toe-in 8) Inspect and adjust bearings 9) Check and adjust brakes
► Road noise	1) Abnormal tire wear 2) Tire out of balance 3) Tire pressure too low	1) Replace tire 2) Rebalance tire 3) Check manufacturer's recommended pressure and set to specifications

WHEEL ALIGNMENT SPECIFICATIONS

Application	Caster (Degrees)	Camber (Degrees)	Toe-In (Inches)	Remarks
AUDI				
4000				① — Toe-in given in degrees.
Front	$\frac{1}{2}\pm\frac{1}{2}$	$-\frac{2}{3}\pm\frac{1}{2}$	$\frac{1}{6}\pm\frac{1}{6}$①	② — $1\frac{1}{6}\pm\frac{2}{3}$ for Turbo.
Rear	.....	$-1\pm\frac{1}{3}$	$\frac{1}{3}\pm\frac{1}{3}$①	
5000				
Front	$-\frac{1}{6}\pm\frac{2}{3}$②	$-\frac{1}{2}\pm\frac{1}{2}$	$\frac{1}{12}$ to $-\frac{1}{6}$①	
Rear		$-\frac{1}{2}\pm\frac{1}{2}$	$\frac{1}{6}$ to $\frac{5}{12}$①	
BMW				
320i				
Front	$8\frac{1}{3}\pm\frac{1}{2}$	$0\pm\frac{1}{2}$	$\frac{3}{64}$ to $\frac{3}{32}$	
Rear	.....	$-2\pm\frac{1}{2}$	0 to $\frac{5}{64}$	
528i				
Front	$7\frac{2}{3}\pm\frac{1}{2}$	$\frac{1}{2}\pm\frac{1}{2}$	$\frac{3}{64}$ to $\frac{3}{32}$	
Rear	.....	$-2\pm\frac{1}{2}$	0 to $\frac{5}{6}$	
633CSi & 733i				
Front	$9\pm\frac{1}{2}$	$0\pm\frac{1}{2}$	0 to $\frac{1}{16}$	
Rear	.....	$-1\pm\frac{1}{2}$	$\frac{5}{64}$ to $\frac{9}{64}$	
CHRYSLER CORP. IMPORTS				
Arrow	$2\frac{1}{12}\pm\frac{1}{2}$	$1\pm\frac{1}{2}$	$\frac{5}{64}$ to $\frac{15}{64}$	① — A toe-in to toe-out range.
Champ & Colt				
Hatchback	$\frac{5}{6}\pm\frac{1}{3}$	$\frac{1}{2}\pm\frac{1}{2}$	$\frac{5}{32}$ to $\frac{5}{64}$①	
Challenger & Sapporo	$2\frac{2}{3}\pm\frac{1}{2}$	$1\frac{1}{4}\pm\frac{1}{2}$	$\frac{5}{64}$ to $\frac{23}{64}$	
Colt Wagon	$2\frac{2}{3}\pm\frac{1}{2}$	$1\frac{1}{4}\pm\frac{1}{2}$	$\frac{5}{64}$ to $\frac{23}{64}$	
Arrow & D50 Pickups	$2\frac{1}{2}\pm1$	$1\pm\frac{1}{2}$	$\frac{5}{64}$ to $\frac{23}{64}$	
COURIER				
Pickup	$1\pm\frac{1}{4}$	$\frac{1}{2}$ to $1\frac{1}{4}$	0 to $\frac{1}{4}$	
DATSUN				
200SX	$2\frac{1}{2}\pm\frac{3}{4}$	$\frac{1}{12}\pm\frac{3}{4}$	0 to $\frac{5}{64}$	① — $2\frac{2}{3}\pm\frac{3}{4}$ for Wagon.
210	$2\frac{5}{12}\pm\frac{3}{4}$①	$\frac{3}{4}\pm\frac{3}{4}$	$\frac{3}{64}$ to $\frac{1}{8}$	
280ZX				② — $1\frac{2}{3}\pm\frac{3}{4}$ for Wagon.
Front	$4\frac{11}{12}\pm\frac{3}{4}$	$\frac{1}{6}\pm\frac{3}{4}$	$\frac{3}{64}$ to $\frac{1}{8}$	③ — $-\frac{5}{6}\pm\frac{3}{4}$ for Wagon.
Rear	.....	$\frac{2}{3}\pm\frac{3}{4}$	$\frac{5}{64}$ to $\frac{5}{32}$	
310				
Front	$1\frac{1}{6}\pm\frac{3}{4}$	$1\pm\frac{3}{4}$	0 to $\frac{5}{64}$	
Rear	.....	$\frac{3}{4}\pm1$	0	
510	$1\frac{5}{6}\pm\frac{3}{4}$②	$\frac{1}{2}\pm\frac{3}{4}$③	$\frac{3}{64}$ to $\frac{1}{8}$	
810				
Front	$1\frac{11}{12}\pm\frac{3}{4}$	$\frac{3}{4}\pm\frac{3}{4}$	0 to $\frac{5}{64}$	
Rear	.....	$1\frac{1}{6}\pm\frac{3}{4}$	$\frac{5}{32}$ to $\frac{35}{64}$	
Pickup	$1\frac{1}{3}\pm\frac{1}{2}$	$\frac{1}{2}\pm\frac{1}{2}$	$\frac{13}{64}$ to $\frac{9}{32}$	
FIAT				
Brava	$3\frac{1}{4}\pm\frac{1}{2}$	$1\pm\frac{1}{2}$	$\frac{5}{32}$ to $\frac{5}{16}$	① — Toe-out.
Spider 2000	$3\frac{1}{2}\pm\frac{1}{2}$	$\frac{1}{2}\pm\frac{1}{2}$	$\frac{3}{64}$ to $\frac{3}{16}$	
Strada				
Front	$2\pm\frac{1}{2}$	$1\frac{3}{4}\pm\frac{19}{32}$	$\frac{11}{64}$ to $\frac{7}{64}$①	
Rear	.....	$1\pm\frac{1}{2}$	0 to $\frac{5}{32}$	
X1/9				
Front	$6\frac{3}{4}\pm\frac{5}{64}$	$-\frac{1}{2}\pm\frac{1}{2}$	$\frac{3}{32}$ to $\frac{15}{64}$	
Rear	.....	$-1\frac{1}{4}\pm\frac{1}{2}$	$\frac{13}{64}$ to $\frac{11}{32}$	
FIESTA				
Hatchback	$\frac{1}{3}\pm\frac{5}{6}$	$2\frac{1}{4}\pm1$	$\frac{3}{64}$ to $\frac{9}{64}$	

Wheel Alignment

WHEEL ALIGNMENT SPECIFICATIONS (Cont.)

Application	Caster (Degrees)	Camber (Degrees)	Toe-In (Inches)	Remarks
HONDA				
Accord				
Front	$1\frac{1}{4}\pm\frac{1}{2}$	$\frac{1}{2}\pm\frac{1}{2}$	$\frac{3}{64}\pm\frac{1}{8}$ ①	① — Toe-out.
Rear	.....	$\frac{1}{4}\pm\frac{1}{2}$	$\frac{3}{64}\pm\frac{5}{64}$ ②	
Civic				② — Toe-in.
Front	$1\frac{3}{4}\pm1$ ③	0 ± 1	$0\pm\frac{1}{8}$ ①	③ — $\frac{1}{2}\pm\frac{1}{2}$ for Wagon.
Rear	.....	.....	$0\pm\frac{5}{32}$ ②	
Prelude				
Front	$1\frac{1}{2}\pm1$	0 ± 1	$0\pm\frac{1}{8}$ ①	
Rear	.....	0 ± 1	$\frac{1}{8}\pm\frac{5}{64}$ ②	
JAGUAR				
XJ6				
Front	$2\frac{1}{4}\pm\frac{1}{4}$	$\frac{1}{2}\pm\frac{1}{4}$	$\frac{1}{16}$ to $\frac{1}{8}$	
Rear	.....	$-\frac{3}{4}\pm\frac{1}{4}$	$0\pm\frac{1}{32}$	
LUV				
2-WD Pickup	$-\frac{1}{6}$	$\frac{1}{2}$	0	
4-WD Pickup	$\frac{1}{3}$	$\frac{7}{12}$	0	
MAZDA				
GLC	$1\frac{2}{3}\pm\frac{3}{4}$ ①	$\frac{3}{4}\pm\frac{1}{2}$ ②	0 to $\frac{15}{64}$	① — $1\frac{3}{4}\pm\frac{3}{4}$ for Wagon.
626	③	$1\frac{1}{4}\pm\frac{1}{2}$	0 to $\frac{15}{64}$	② — $1\pm\frac{1}{2}$ for Wagon.
RX7	④	$1\frac{1}{6}\pm\frac{1}{2}$	0 to $\frac{15}{64}$	③ — $3\frac{2}{3}\pm\frac{3}{4}$ for right side.
				$3\frac{1}{6}\pm\frac{3}{4}$ for left side.
B2000 Pickup	$1\pm\frac{1}{3}$	$\frac{3}{4}\pm\frac{1}{3}$	0 to $\frac{15}{64}$	④ — $4\frac{1}{2}\pm\frac{1}{2}$ for right side.
				$4\pm\frac{1}{2}$ for left side.
MERCEDES-BENZ				
280SE, 300SD & 450SEL	$10\pm\frac{1}{2}$	$-\frac{1}{6}\pm\frac{1}{6}$	$\frac{1}{8}\pm\frac{3}{64}$	
450SL & 450SLC	$3\frac{2}{3}\pm\frac{1}{3}$	$-\frac{1}{6}\pm\frac{1}{2}$	$\frac{5}{64}\pm\frac{3}{64}$	
All Others	$8\frac{3}{4}\pm\frac{1}{2}$	$0\pm\frac{1}{6}$	$\frac{1}{8}\pm\frac{3}{64}$	
MG				
MGB	$6\pm\frac{1}{8}$	$\frac{1}{2}\pm\frac{3}{4}$	$\frac{1}{16}$ to $\frac{3}{32}$	
PEUGEOT				
504	$2\frac{2}{3}\pm\frac{1}{2}$	$-\frac{2}{3}\pm\frac{1}{2}$	$\frac{5}{64}$ to $\frac{5}{32}$	
505	.....	$\frac{2}{3}\pm\frac{1}{2}$	$\frac{1}{8}$ to $\frac{5}{32}$	
604				
Front	$3\frac{1}{2}\pm\frac{1}{2}$	$\frac{1}{2}\pm\frac{3}{4}$	$\frac{5}{64}$ to $\frac{5}{32}$	
Rear	.....	$-1\frac{1}{2}\pm\frac{1}{2}$	$\frac{3}{64}$ to $\frac{5}{32}$	
PORSCHE				
911SC				
Front	$6\frac{1}{12}\pm\frac{1}{4}$	$\frac{1}{2}\pm\frac{1}{6}$	0 ①	
Rear	.....	$0\pm\frac{1}{6}$	$\frac{1}{6}\pm\frac{1}{6}$ ①	
924 & 924 Turbo				
Front	$2\frac{2}{3}\pm\frac{1}{2}$	$-\frac{1}{3}\pm\frac{1}{4}$	$-\frac{1}{12}\pm\frac{1}{6}$ ①	① — Toe-in given in degrees
Rear	.....	$-1\pm\frac{1}{2}$ ②	$0\pm\frac{1}{12}$ ①	
928				
Front	$3\frac{1}{2}\pm\frac{1}{2}$	$-\frac{1}{2}\pm\frac{1}{6}$	$0\pm\frac{1}{12}$ ①	② — $\frac{1}{4}\pm\frac{1}{2}$ for 924 Turbo
Rear	.....	$-\frac{2}{3}\pm\frac{1}{6}$	$\frac{1}{6}\pm\frac{1}{12}$ ①	"Sport".
RENAULT				
Le Car				
Front	$12\frac{1}{2}\pm\frac{1}{2}$	$\frac{1}{2}\pm\frac{1}{2}$	$\frac{3}{64}$ to $\frac{3}{16}$	
Rear	.....	$\frac{1}{2}\pm\frac{1}{2}$	$\frac{3}{64}$ to $\frac{1}{8}$	
SAAB				
99 & 900	$1\pm\frac{1}{2}$	$\frac{1}{2}\pm\frac{1}{2}$ ①	0 to $\frac{3}{64}$	① — $2\pm\frac{1}{2}$ with power steering.

WHEEL ALIGNMENT SPECIFICATIONS (Cont.)

Application	Caster (Degrees)	Camber (Degrees)	Toe-In (Inches)	Remarks
SUBARU				① — $-\frac{5}{6}$ to $\frac{2}{3}$ for Wagon.
Exc. 4-WD Wagon				
Front	$-1\frac{1}{6}$ to $\frac{1}{3}$①	$1\frac{1}{2}\pm\frac{3}{4}$②	$\frac{5}{64}$ to $\frac{5}{16}$	
Rear	.....	$0\pm\frac{3}{4}$	$0\pm\frac{3}{4}$	② — $1\frac{3}{4}\pm\frac{3}{4}$ for Wagon.
4-WD Wagon				
Front	$-1\frac{5}{12}$ to $\frac{1}{12}$	$1\frac{5}{6}$ to $3\frac{1}{3}$	$\frac{15}{64}$ to $\frac{15}{32}$	
Rear	.....	$-\frac{5}{16}$ to $1\frac{1}{12}$	$-\frac{1}{12}$ to $1\frac{1}{12}$	
BRAT				
Front	$-3\frac{1}{4}\pm1\frac{2}{3}$	$1\frac{1}{3}\pm\frac{3}{4}$	$\frac{5}{64}$ to $\frac{15}{64}$	
Rear	.....	$1\frac{1}{3}\pm\frac{3}{4}$	$\frac{5}{64}$ to $\frac{15}{64}$	
TOYOTA				① — $\frac{5}{32}\pm\frac{3}{64}$ with power steering.
Celica	$1\frac{2}{3}\pm\frac{1}{2}$	$1\pm\frac{1}{2}$	$\frac{3}{64}\pm\frac{3}{64}$①	
Corolla	$1\frac{3}{4}\pm\frac{1}{2}$②	$1\pm\frac{1}{2}$	$\frac{1}{8}\pm\frac{3}{64}$③	② — $1\frac{1}{2}\pm\frac{1}{2}$ for Wagon.
Corona	$1\frac{1}{2}\pm\frac{1}{2}$	$1\pm\frac{1}{2}$	$\frac{1}{8}\pm\frac{3}{64}$③	
Cressida	$1\pm\frac{1}{2}$	$1\pm\frac{1}{2}$	$\frac{3}{64}\pm\frac{3}{64}$④	③ — $\frac{3}{64}\pm\frac{3}{64}$ with radial tires.
Land Cruiser	1	1	$\frac{5}{32}\pm\frac{3}{64}$⑤	④ — $\frac{1}{8}\pm\frac{3}{64}$ with radial tires.
2-WD Pickup	$\frac{1}{2}\pm\frac{1}{2}$	$1\pm\frac{1}{2}$	$1\frac{3}{64}\pm\frac{3}{64}$⑥	
4-WD Pickup	$3\frac{1}{2}$	1	$\frac{5}{32}\pm\frac{3}{64}$③	⑤ — $0\pm\frac{3}{4}$ with radial tires.
Supra	$1\frac{3}{4}\pm\frac{1}{2}$	$1\pm\frac{1}{2}$	$0\pm\frac{3}{64}$	⑥ — $\frac{5}{64}$ with radial tires.
Tercel				
Front	$2\frac{1}{6}\pm\frac{1}{2}$	$\frac{1}{2}\pm\frac{1}{2}$	$\frac{5}{64}\pm\frac{3}{64}$	
Rear	.....	$0\pm\frac{1}{2}$	$0\pm\frac{3}{64}$	
TRIUMPH				
Spitfire				
Front	$4\frac{1}{2}\pm\frac{1}{2}$	$2\pm\frac{1}{2}$	0 to $\frac{1}{16}$	
Rear	.....	$-3\frac{1}{4}\pm\frac{1}{2}$	0 to $\frac{1}{16}$	
TR7 & TR8	$3\frac{1}{2}\pm1$	$-\frac{1}{4}\pm1$	0 to $\frac{1}{16}$	
VOLKSWAGEN				① — Toe-in given in degrees.
Dasher				
Front	$\frac{1}{2}\pm\frac{1}{2}$	$\frac{1}{2}\pm\frac{1}{2}$	$\frac{1}{6}\pm\frac{1}{4}$①	
Rear	.....	$-\frac{2}{3}\pm\frac{2}{3}$	$0\pm\frac{5}{6}$①	
Jetta, Rabbit & Scirocco				
Front	$1\frac{5}{6}\pm\frac{1}{2}$	$\frac{1}{3}\pm\frac{1}{2}$	$-\frac{1}{12}$ to $-\frac{1}{2}$①	
Rear	.....	$-1\frac{1}{4}\pm\frac{7}{12}$	$\frac{1}{3}\pm\frac{1}{3}$①	
Rabbit Pickup				
Front	$1\frac{5}{6}\pm\frac{1}{2}$	$\frac{1}{3}\pm\frac{1}{2}$	$-\frac{1}{2}$ to $\frac{1}{6}$①	
Rear	.....	0 ± 1	-1 to $1$①	
Vanagon				
Front	$7\frac{1}{4}\pm\frac{1}{4}$	$\frac{2}{3}\pm\frac{1}{2}$	$\frac{2}{3}\pm\frac{1}{3}$①	
Rear	.....	$-\frac{5}{6}\pm\frac{1}{2}$	$0\pm\frac{1}{6}$①	
VOLVO				① — $\frac{1}{2}\pm\frac{1}{4}$ for GT.
All Models				
Man. Steering	$2\frac{1}{2}\pm\frac{1}{2}$	$1\frac{1}{4}\pm\frac{1}{4}$①	$\frac{3}{16}\pm\frac{1}{16}$	
Pow. Steering	$3\frac{1}{2}\pm\frac{1}{2}$	$1\frac{1}{4}\pm\frac{1}{4}$①	$\frac{1}{8}\pm\frac{1}{16}$	

AUDI

ADJUSTMENT

TIRE INFLATION (COLD)

Before attempting to check and adjust wheel alignment, ensure tires are properly inflated. Tire sizes and pressures can be found on a sticker located on side panel of left door on all models.

CASTER

Caster angle is not adjustable. If caster is not within specifications, check suspension components for excessive wear or damage. Replace components as necessary to bring caster into specifications.

CAMBER

4000 — With vehicle loaded down or placed on blocks, measure camber angle. If not to specifications, loosen ball joint nuts and attach wedge (US 4490). Tighten wedge nut to break joint loose from control arm. See Fig. 1.

NOTE — When tool nut is loosened weight of vehicle will move wheel to negative camber. After adjustment retorque ball joint nuts to 47 ft. lbs. (6.5 mkg).

5000 — Work under hood and loosen the 3 upper strut mounting nuts. Place a socket over suspension strut nut. Move strut around in slots until camber is correct. Tighten nuts to 14 ft. lbs. (2.0 mkg). Recheck camber after tightening nuts.

Fig. 1   Camber Adjusting Tool for Audi 4000

TOE-IN

Loosen adjustable tie rod lock nuts (5000) or clamp and lock nut (4000). Rotate threaded collar (5000) or rod (4000) until toe-in is within specifications. Tighten locking components. If necessary, remove steering wheel and reposition so wheel spokes are horizontal when front wheels point straight-ahead.

BMW

ADJUSTMENT

TIRE INFLATION (COLD)

Before attempting to check and adjust wheel alignment, ensure tires are properly inflated. Tire sizes and pressures can be found in the owner's manual.

CASTER & CAMBER

Before checking caster and camber, vehicle must be in loaded condition. See Vehicle Loading Table. If caster or camber are not within specifications, check suspension components for damage.

Vehicle Loading Table	
Application	**①Lbs. (kg)**
Each Front Seat	150 (68)
Rear Seat	150 (68)
Luggage Compartment	46 (21)
① — Fuel tank full.	

TOE-IN

Before checking toe-in, vehicle must be in loaded condition. See Vehicle Loading Table. Check toe-in with front wheels in straight-ahead position. If not within specifications, loosen tie rod tubes until correct toe-in is obtained. Tighten clamping bolts.

CHRYSLER CORP. IMPORTS

ADJUSTMENT

TIRE INFLATION (COLD)

Before attempting to check and adjust wheel alignment, ensure tires are properly inflated. Tire sizes and pressures can be found in owner's manual.

CASTER

Pickups — To adjust caster, adjust by tightening upper arm shaft. A half turn of upper arm shaft will cause .049" (1.25 mm) front or rear movement of upper arm shaft, resulting in ¼° change in caster adjustment.

All Others — Caster, as a general rule, requires no adjustment. However, slight adjustment can be made by moving strut bar nut until specified caster angle is obtained.

CAMBER

Pickups — To adjust camber, hold upper arm shaft-to-crossmember bolt in position and remove nut from engine compartment side. Adjust number of shims between upper arm shaft and crossmember until correct camber specification is obtained.

All Others — Camber requires no adjustment. Steering knuckle is integral with strut assembly and camber is preset at

CHRYSLER CORP. IMPORTS (Cont.)

the factory. If camber is not within specifications, check suspension components for damage.

TOE-IN

Arrow, Champ & Colt Hatchbacks — Position wheels in straight-ahead position. If toe-in is not to specifications, loosen locking nuts on tie rod turnbuckles. Rotate buckles until toe-in is within specifications. Tighten lock nuts. Adjustment must be made equally to both sides of vehicle.

All Others — Position wheels in straight-ahead position. If toe-in is not to specifications, loosen locking nut on left tie rod turnbuckle. Rotate buckle until toe-in is within specifications. Tighten lock nut.

NOTE — *After adjusting toe-in, check difference in lengths of left and right tie rods. If difference exceeds .20" (5 mm), remove right tie rod and adjust length until difference is .20" (5 mm) or less.*

COURIER

ADJUSTMENT

TIRE INFLATION

Before attempting caster or camber adjustments, ensure tires are correctly inflated. Specifications are located on glove box door; especially consider radial tires, they require a different pressure than conventional tires.

NOTE — *Vehicle must be unloaded, except fuel, water, and oil should be at their proper levels.*

CASTER

To adjust caster, adjust shims between upper control arm and frame or turn control arm shaft until correct specifications are obtained.

CAMBER

To adjust camber, adjust shims between upper control arm and frame until correct specifications are obtained. Shims are available in the following sizes: .039" (1 mm), .063" (1.6 mm), .079" (2 mm) and .126" (3.2 mm).

TOE-IN

1) Raise vehicle until front wheels clear ground. Turn wheel by hand and scribe a line in center of each tire tread. Measure distance between marked lines in front of front wheel and at rear of front wheel. Both measurements must be taken at equal distances from ground.

2) If distance between wheels at rear is greater than that at front, but within specifications, adjustment is correct. If adjustment is wrong, loosen clamp bolts and adjust tie rod to specifications.

NOTE — *Tighten clamping bolts with bolts horizontal and below steering link to prevent interference with center steering link.*

DATSUN

ADJUSTMENT

TIRE INFLATION (COLD)

Before attempting to check or adjust wheel alignment, make sure that tires are properly inflated. Refer to manufacturer's specifications given in owner's manual.

CASTER

Pickup — Caster is adjusted by increasing or decreasing thickness of shims inserted between upper link spindle and upper link mounting bracket. Caster adjustment affects camber adjustment, if you change caster specification, camber specification is also changed.

NOTE — *Total thickness of shims must be within .236" (6.0 mm) and must not collectively total more than 3 individual shims. Difference of total thickness between front and rear must be within .079" (2.0 mm).*

All Others — Caster is preset at factory and cannot be adjusted. If not to specifications, check suspension for wear or damage and repair or replace components as necessary.

CAMBER

Pickup — Camber is adjusted by increasing or decreasing thickness of shims inserted between upper link spindle and upper link mounting bracket. If you change camber adjustment you also change caster adjustment.

NOTE — *Total thickness of shims must be within .236" (6 mm) and must not collectively total more than 3 individual shims. Difference of total thickness between front and rear shims must be within .079" (2 mm).*

All Others — Camber is preset at factory and cannot be adjusted. If not to specifications, check suspension for wear or damage and repair or replace components as necessary.

TOE-IN

810 — Place front wheel facing straight ahead. Ensure steering gear faces same direction. Adjust side rod (tie rod) so that steering gear side has a distance of 14.35" (364.5 mm) bet-

DATSUN (Cont.)

ween ball joints. Adjust idler arm side so distance between ball joints is 14.19" (360.5 mm). Tighten clamp bolts after adjustment.

All Others — Place wheels in straight-ahead position, then make sure steering wheel and steering gear are also in straight-ahead position. Adjust toe-in by varying the length of steering side rods (tie rods). Loosen lock nuts and rotate rods evenly until toe-in is within specifications.

Normal Toe-In Specifications①		
Application	Distance Between Lock Nuts	Distance Between Ball Joints
210	12.4" (315 mm)	....
280ZX		
Man. Steering	1.16" (29.5 mm)	....
Power Steering		14.42" (366.3 mm)
310	5.24" (133 mm)	....
510	5.0" (127 mm)	....
Pickup		13.07" (332 mm)

① — Basic adjustment specifications. For final adjustment specifications, see Wheel Alignment Specifications in this section

FIAT

ADJUSTMENT

TIRE INFLATION (COLD)

Before attempting to check or adjust wheel alignment, make sure tires are properly inflated. Refer to manufacturer's specifications given in owner's manual.

CASTER

Brava & Strada — If caster is not to specifications, raise and support front of vehicle. Remove stabilizer bar (strut rod) to control arm nut and disconnect control arm from body. Remove end of stabilizer bar (strut rod) from control arm. To adjust caster, additon of shims between end of stabilizer bar (strut rod) and rubber pad of control arm will decrease caster angle. Removal of shims will increase caster angle. Reverse removal procedure and recheck caster.

Spider 2000 — If caster is not within specifications, raise front of vehicle and remove wheel and shock absorber. Using suitable tool (A.74174), compress spring to relieve lower control arm and loosen nuts holding control arm pivot bar to crossmember. To adjust caster, remove shims from front stud and move to rear stud to increase caster. To decrease caster, remove shims from rear stud and move shims to front stud. Reverse removal procedure and check caster.

X1/9 — If caster is not to specifications, adjust by adding or removing shims located between stabilizer bar and stabilizer bar support.

CAMBER

Brava & Strada (Front) — Camber is preset at factory and cannot be adjusted. If not to specifications, check suspension for wear or damage and repair or replace components as necessary.

Strada (Rear) — If rear camber is not to specifications, raise rear of vehicle and compress one end of leaf spring (shifting it from flexible guide anchoring spring to control arm). Remove guide and slowly release spring. Remove nuts attaching pivot to body and loosen screw to free adjustment shims. To increase camber, add an equal number of shims on both screws attaching control arm to body. To decrease camber, remove equal number of shims from both screws. Reverse removal procedure and recheck camber.

Spider 2000 — If camber is not within specifications, adjust by changing amount of shims. Raise front of vehicle, remove wheel and shock absorber. Using suitable tool (A.74174), compress spring to relieve lower control arm and loosen nuts holding control arm pivot bar to crossmember. To increase camber, remove equal amount of shims from both studs. To decrease camber, add an equal amount of shims to both studs. Reverse removal procedure and check camber.

NOTE — Adding or removing equal amount of shims will not affect caster.

X1/9 (Front & Rear) — Camber is nonadjustable. If not within specifications, inspect suspension for damage and repair or replace parts as necessary.

TOE-IN

Brava, Strada & X1/9 (Front) — Place front wheels in straight-ahead position. If toe-in is not to specifications, loosen sleeve locking nut on tie rods. To adjust, rotate tie rod until correct toe-in specifications are obtained. Hold tie rod in position and lock nut against tie rod sleeve.

Spider 2000 — Place front wheels in straight-ahead position. If toe-in is not within specifications, loosen 4 clamps securing sleeves on tie rods. Rotate tie rods in opposite direction (by equal amounts) to set toe-in to specifications. Tighten clamp nuts.

NOTE — Expansion slot in sleeve must coincide with clamp joint when clamp is fully tightened.

Strada (Rear) — If rear toe-in is not to specifications, raise rear of vehicle and compress one end of leaf spring (shifting it from flexible guide anchoring spring to control arm). Remove guide and slowly release spring. Remove nuts attaching pivot to body and loosen screws to free adjustment shims. To increase toe-in, add shims to rear screw or remove shims from front screw. To decrease toe-in, add shims to front screw or remove shims from rear screw.

X1/9 (Rear) — If rear wheel toe-in is not within specifications, loosen clamps securing sleeves to reaction rods. Adjust toe-in by lengthening or shortening reaction rods. Tighten clamps and recheck toe-in.

FIESTA

ADJUSTMENT

TIRE INFLATION (COLD)

Before attempting to check and adjust wheel alignment, make sure tires are properly inflated. Refer to manufacturer's specifications given in owner's manual.

CASTER

Caster is not adjustable. If caster is not to specifications, inspect suspension system for wear or damage and repair or replace components as necessary.

CAMBER

Camber is not adjustable. If camber is not to specifications, inspect suspension system for wear or damage and repair or replace components as necessary.

TOE-IN

Loosen lock nuts on outer ends of tie rods. Lock nuts are located next to ball joints. Loosen clamps on outer ends of steering gear bellows. Adjust both tie rods equal amounts until toe-in is within specifications. Tighten lock nuts. Install new clips to outer ends of bellows.

HONDA

ADJUSTMENT

TIRE INFLATION (COLD)

Before checking or adjusting wheel alignment, make sure tires are correctly inflated. Refer to manufacturers specifications located in glove box.

RIDING HEIGHT

Make sure tires are properly inflated. Measure from top of wheel opening to ground. If front height measurement is not within specifications, check rear height before attempting to repair front suspension. See *Riding Height Specifications* table.

Riding Height Specifications		
	Front	**Rear**
Application	In. (mm)	In. (mm)
Accord		
LX	25.2 (639)	.... 23.7 (603)
Hatchback	25.6 (651)	.... 23.7 (603)
Sedan	25.4 (646)	.... 23.7 (603)
Civic		
Hatchback	24.9 (632)	.... 24.5 (623)
Station Wagon	25.0 (636)	.... 25.7 (653)
Prelude	24.4 (620)	.... 24.2 (615)

CASTER

Caster is nonadjustable. If alignment is not within specifications, inspect for damaged parts and replace as necessary.

CAMBER

Camber is nonadjustable. If alignment is not within specifications, inspect for damaged parts and replace as necessary.

TOE-OUT

Front — Loosen lock nuts at each end of tie rods. Turn tie rod until toe-out is within specifications. Use same procedure for both sides. To center steering wheel after toe has been adjusted, turn both tie rods in same direction until steering wheel (spokes) are centered. Tighten lock nuts.

TOE-IN

Rear — To adjust toe-in, loosen lock nuts on radius arm adjusting bolts. Rotate adjusting bolt until toe is within specifications, then tighten lock nuts. On Accord models, each notch on cam plate is equal to .20" (5 mm). On Civic models, each notch on cam plate is equal to .63" (16 mm). On Prelude models, each notch on cam plate is equal to .60" (15 mm).

NOTE — *Notches on cam plate are for reference only. Do not use notches to equalize adjustments on rear radius rods.*

JAGUAR

ADJUSTMENT

TIRE INFLATION (COLD)

Before attempting to check or adjust wheel alignment, make sure tires are properly inflated. Refer to owner's manual for manufacturer's specifications.

RIDING HEIGHT

XJ6 (Front) — Check that vehicle is full of fuel, oil and water, and that tires are properly inflated. Press down on front bumper and slowly release, then lift up on bumper and slowly release. This will settle front suspension. Measure distance between center of outer headlight and ground on both sides of vehicle. Height should be 24.6" (611 mm) minimum. To adjust height, install or remove spring spacers from front coil springs.

NOTE — *Spring spacers are ⅛" (3.2 mm) thick and will change riding height approximately 5/16" (7.9 mm).*

XJ6 (Rear) — Check that vehicle is full of fuel, oil and water, and that tires are properly inflated. Roll vehicle forward 3 car lengths to settle rear suspension system. Measure distance between lower surface of rear crossmember and ground on both sides of vehicle. Correct height should be 7.2-7.7" (183-195 mm). If height is not within specifications, replace all 4 rear springs.

PREPARATION FOR CASTER & CAMBER ADJUSTMENT

1) Ensure vehicle is on level ground and that tires are properly inflated. Before checking or adjusting caster or camber, fabricate 2 setting tools as shown in *Fig. 1*.

JAGUAR (Cont.)

2) Compress front suspension and insert tools under upper control arms, adjacent to control arm rubber stops and over brackets welded to bottom of control arms.

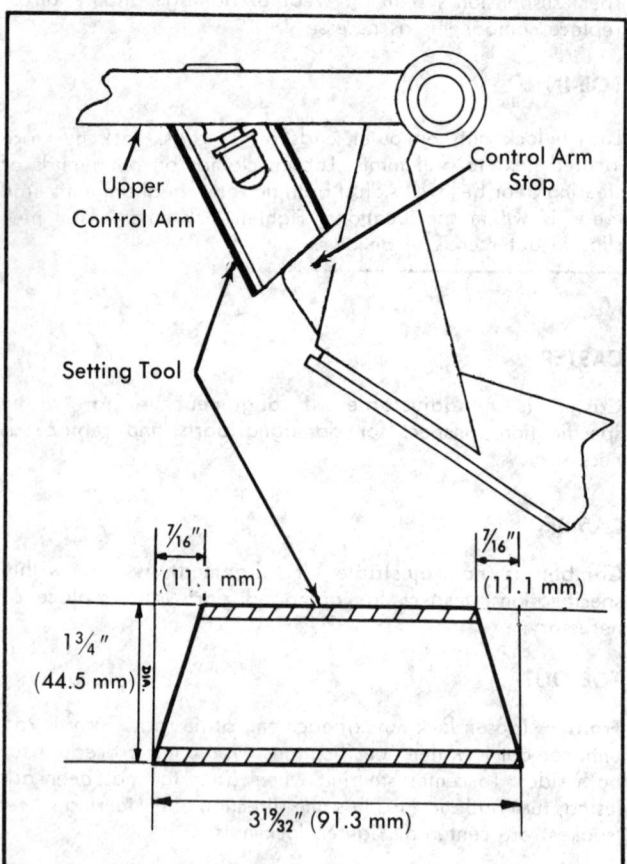

Fig. 1   Dimensions for Fabricating Setting Tools

3) Compress rear suspension and install setting links (J. 25) to lock rear suspension in place. See *Fig. 2*. Vehicle is now locked in half-loaded condition and caster and camber can be checked and adjusted.

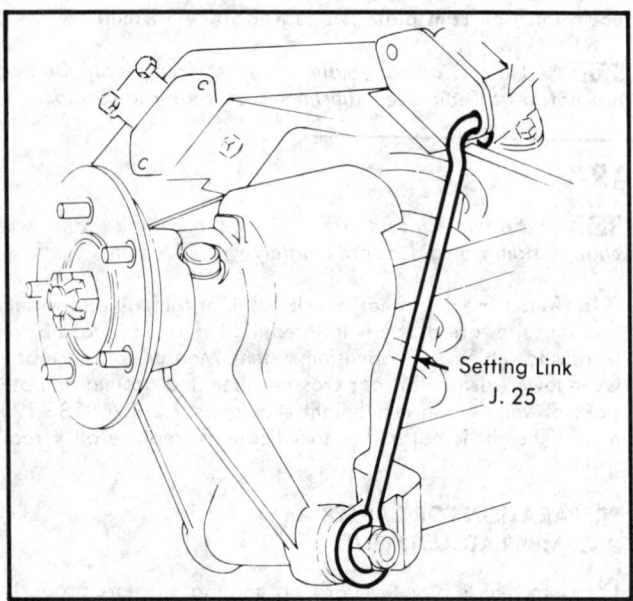

Fig. 2   Rear Suspension in Locked Position with Special Tool

CASTER

NOTE — *Before adjusting caster angle, make sure car is standing at normal riding height.*

XJ6 — If caster angle is not within specifications, adjust by moving shims on front and rear of upper control arm ball joint. To increase caster, loosen bolts securing upper ball joint and move shims from rear of ball joint to front of ball joint. To decrease caster, reverse procedure. Tighten ball joint attaching bolts and recheck caster angle.

CAMBER

NOTE — *Before attempting to check or adjust camber angle it will be necessary to make sure that vehicle is in half-loaded condition.*

XJ6 (Front) — Place wheels in straight-ahead position. Measure camber angle. Make sure front wheels are within $\frac{1}{4}°$ of each other. Adjustment is accomplished by adding or subtracting shims. See *Fig. 3*. Adding shims increases camber angle. Make sure same number of shims are used on each bolt.

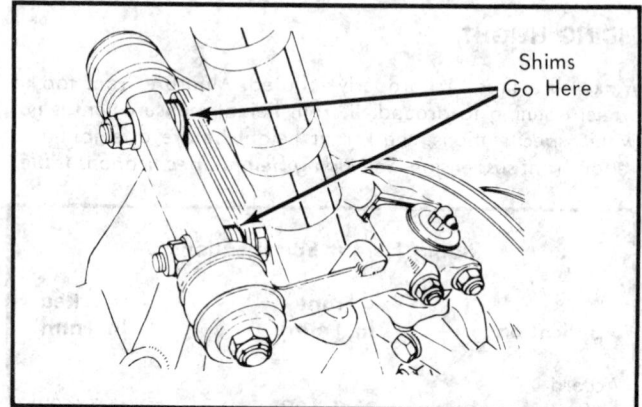

Fig. 3   Shim Placement for Front Camber Angle Adjustment

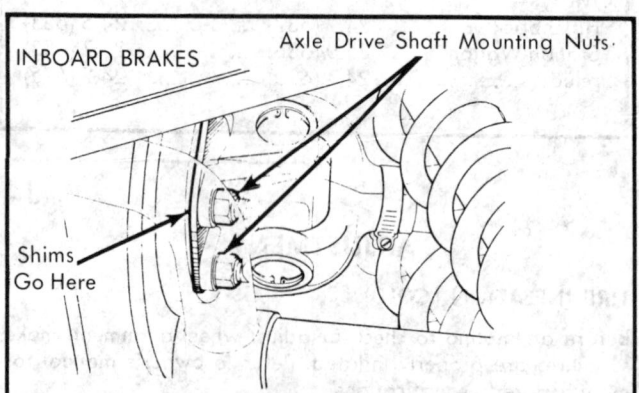

Fig. 4   Placement of Shims for Rear Camber Angle Adjustment

XJ6 (Rear) — Before checking rear wheel camber, rear suspension must be in the half-loaded position. See *Preparation for Caster & Camber Adjustment*. To adjust, remove suspension setting links (J. 25), raise and support rear of vehicle and remove wheels. Loosen nuts securing half-shaft to brake disc, then add or remove shims as required to bring camber angle within specifications.

JAGUAR (Cont.)

NOTE — *Addition of one .020" (.5 mm) shim will alter camber ¼ °.*

TOE-IN

XJ6 — Place wheels in straight-ahead position. Remove grease nipple from rack adjuster nut. Put centralizing tool (12279) into locating hole. Push tool onto back of rack bar. Slowly turn steering wheel until tool drops into back of rack bar. Measure toe-in. If toe-in is not within specifications, adjust by loosening steering link lock nuts and rotating adjuster sleeves equal amounts, as necessary. Tighten lock nuts and recheck toe-in.

LUV

ADJUSTMENT

TIRE INFLATION

Before checking or adjusting wheel alignment, ensure tires are correctly inflated. Refer to manufacturer's specifications located in glove box or on right door lock pillar.

RIDING HEIGHT

1) Place vehicle on smooth level surface. Bounce vehicle several times. Raise vehicle and allow to settle at normal height. Measure distance as shown in *Fig. 1 and 2*.

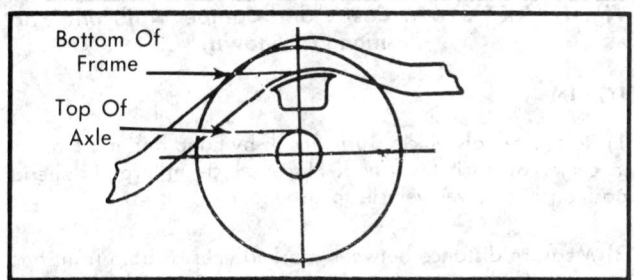

Fig. 1   Rear Suspension Riding Height Measuring Point

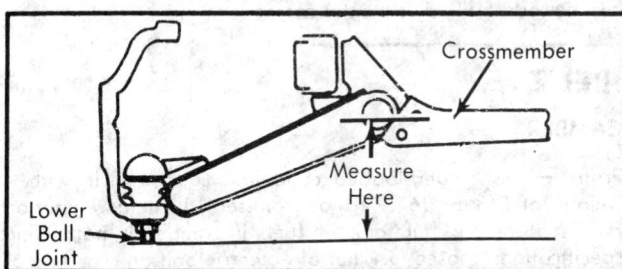

Fig. 2   Front Suspension Riding Height Measuring Point

NOTE — *Height check should be made with a full tank of gas, spare tire installed, and jack included. No passengers should be in vehicle.*

2) Difference between measurements of each side must not be more than ½" (12.7 mm). If an adjustment is necessary, it can be made at bolt on height control arm.

Riding Height Specifications			
	Front		**Rear**
Application	**In. (mm)**		**In. (mm)**
2-WD			
Standard	4.6 (116.8)		6.1 (155)
Long Wheelbase	4.6 (116.8)		7.5 (190)
4-WD	4.8 (122)		7.7 (195)

TORSION BAR SPRING HEIGHT

1) Park vehicle on level surface. Jounce vehicle several times and allow vehicle to return to settled position.

2) On 2-WD vehicles, measure buffer clearance (clearance between rubber bumper and lower control arm). Using bolt located on height control arm, adjust buffer clearance to about .866" (22 mm).

3) On all models, turn adjuster bolt on torsion bar until correct riding height specification is obtained.

NOTE — *Rotating bolt inward increases vehicle height.*

CAMBER & CASTER

Camber and caster adjustments may be made at same time with shims inserted between upper control arm pivot shaft and frame. Adding or subtracting equal number of shims at both front and rear pivot shaft bolts will decrease positive camber. Adding or subtracting shims from front to rear or rear to front pivot shaft bolts will change caster. Transfer of 1 shim from front to rear bolt will decrease positive caster.

TOE-IN

NOTE — *Toe-in must be adjusted after caster and camber adjustment.*

Toe-in can be adjusted by rotating the intermediate rod after loosening lock nuts. Rotate intermediate rod towards front of vehicle to reduce toe-in and towards rear of vehicle to increase toe-in until proper specification is obtained.

MAZDA

ADJUSTMENT

TIRE INFLATION (COLD)

Before attempting to check or adjust wheel alignment, make sure tires are properly inflated. Refer to manufacturer's specifications given in owner's manual.

CASTER

GLC — Caster is not adjustable. If caster is not to specifications, inspect suspension for excessive wear or damage. Replace components as necessary.

RX7 & 626 — Caster and camber angles are adjusted by changing position of shock absorber support. To adjust,

MAZDA (Cont.)

remove 4 nuts attaching shock absorber support to fender apron. Raise front of vehicle and support with jack stands, then remove wheel on side to be adjusted.

2) Press shock absorber downward and change position of support according to table and *Fig. 1*. Tighten shock absorber support mounting nuts. Install wheel, lower vehicle and recheck caster and camber.

Caster and Camber Adjustment			
Adjustment		Variation	
	Shock Absorber Support	Caster	Camber
A	0	0	0
B	90°	½ °	0
C	180°	½ °	½ °
D	270°	0	½ °

Pickup — To adjust, change shims between upper arm shaft and support bracket or turn upper arm shaft until specifications are obtained.

CAMBER

GLC — Camber is not adjustable. If caster is not to specifications, inspect suspension for excessive wear or damage. Replace components as necessary.

RX7 & 626 — *See procedure given under Caster adjustment.*

Pickup — To adjust, change shims between upper arm shaft and support bracket until specifications for camber are within limits.

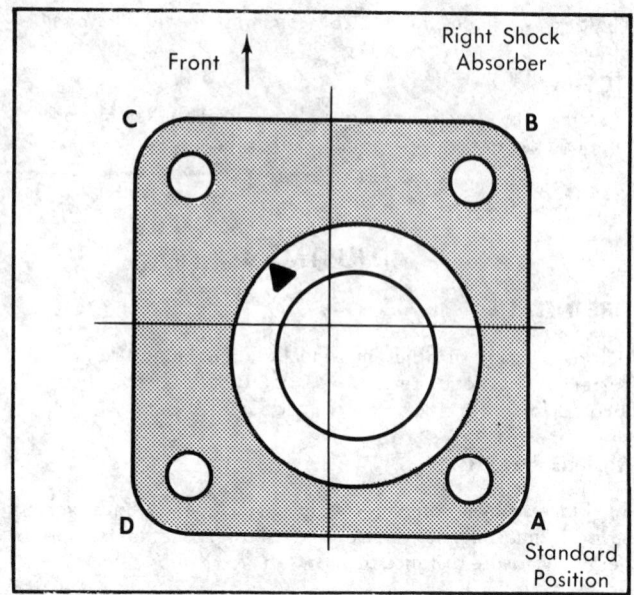

Fig. 1   RX7 & 626 Caster and Camber Adjusting Pad (Position "C" Shown)

TOE-IN

1) Raise front of vehicle. Turn wheels by hand and mark a line in center of each tire tread. Place vehicle in straight-ahead position and lower vehicle to ground.

2) Measure distance between marked lines at both front and rear of wheel. Make sure measurements are made equal distances from ground. Distance at rear of wheel should be .24" (6 mm) more than that at front wheels. Loosen lock nuts and turn tie rods until adjustment is correct.

MERCEDES-BENZ

ADJUSTMENT

TIRE INFLATION (COLD)

Before attempting to check or adjust wheel alignment, make sure tires are properly inflated. Refer to manufacturer's specifications given in owner's manual.

CASTER

Front — Test under loaded condition. Load vehicle with 2 weights of 143 lbs. (64.9 kg) on rear seat and a full tank of fuel. If caster is not to specifications, loosen lock nut on eccentric bolt on front side of lower control arm. To adjust, rotate eccentric bolt until caster angle is within specifications. Hold eccentric bolt in place and tighten lock nut.

CAMBER

Front — Test under loaded condition. Load vehicle with 2 weights of 143 lbs. (64.9 kg) on front seat, 1 similar weight on rear seat and a full tank of fuel. If camber is not within specifications, loosen lock nut of eccentric bolt on rear side of lower control arm. To adjust, rotate eccentric bolt until camber is within specifications. Hold eccentric bolt in place and tighten lock nut.

TOE-IN

Front — Place wheels in straight-ahead position. If toe-in is not within specifications, adjust by loosening lock nuts on outer steering links and rotating links to obtain specified toe-in. Make sure steering links are adjusted equally.

MG

ADJUSTMENT

TIRE INFLATION (COLD)

Before attempting to check or adjust wheel alignment, make sure tires are properly inflated. Refer to manufacturer's specifications given in owner's manual.

NOTE — *All checks must be made with vehicle unloaded, tires properly inflated and steering wheel in straight-ahead position. Before making checks, ensure suspension components are in good condition. If necessary, repair damaged components before making wheel alignment checks.*

CAMBER & CASTER

Camber and caster are not adjustable. If alignment is not within specifications, inspect for damaged suspension parts and repair or replace as necessary.

Wheel Alignment

MG (Cont.)

TOE-IN

Turn front wheels to straight-ahead position and check toe-in measurement. Move vehicle ahead so front wheels rotate 180° and take second reading. Average both readings to check toe-in. If not within specifications, loosen lock nut for each tie rod and loosen clips securing rubber boots to tie rods. To adjust, rotate both tie rods equally to obtain specified toe-in. Tighten lock nuts and clips on tie rods.

NOTE — *Tie rods must be equal lengths.*

PEUGEOT

ADJUSTMENT

TIRE INFLATION (COLD)

Before attempting to check or adjust wheel alignment, make sure tires are properly inflated. Refer to manufacturer's specifications given in owner's manual.

TOE-IN

Position wheels in straight-ahead position. If toe-in is not to specifications, loosen clamping bolts on the 2 steering links. To adjust, rotate 2 steering links simultaneously in either direction necessary to obtain specified toe-in. Tighten clamping bolt and recheck toe-in.

CAMBER & CASTER

Camber and caster are not adjustable. If alignment is not within specifications, inspect for damaged suspension parts and repair or replace as necessary.

PORSCHE

ADJUSTMENT

TIRE INFLATION (COLD)

Before attempting to check or adjust wheel alignment, make sure tires are properly inflated. Refer to manufacturer's specifications given in owner's manual.

RIDING HEIGHT

NOTE — *Riding height should be set with fuel tank full and spare tire included.*

911SC (Front) — 1) Checking or adjusting riding height can only be performed with vehicle on level surface. Mark center of front wheel hub cap (grease retainer cup). Bounce vehicle several times to settle suspension. Measure distance "A" shown in *Fig. 1*. Measure distance "B" shown in *Fig 1*. Difference between measurements (riding height) should be 3.7-4.1" (94-104 mm).

2) If necessary, loosen or tighten torsion bar adjusting bolt until correct height is obtained. Bounce vehicle several times and recheck height. Make sure difference between right and left side measurements does not exceed .20" (5 mm).

911SC (Rear) — Checking or adjusting riding height can only be performed with vehicle on level surface. Mark center of rear wheel. Bounce vehicle several times to settle suspension. Measure distance "a" shown in *Fig. 2*. Distance "a" plus 1.26-1.65" (32-42mm) equals "b"; however, distance "b" is difficult to measure because the torsion bar is mounted off center in its rubber bushing. Therefore it is necessary to measure distance "b1" and add .585" (14.8 mm), radius of bushing. This total should equal "b". After calculating "b", difference between "a" and "b" should be 1.26-1.65" (32-42 mm). Difference in height from left to right should not exceed .20" (5 mm). If values are not within specifications, check front height and rear torsion bar adjustment. Correct as required.

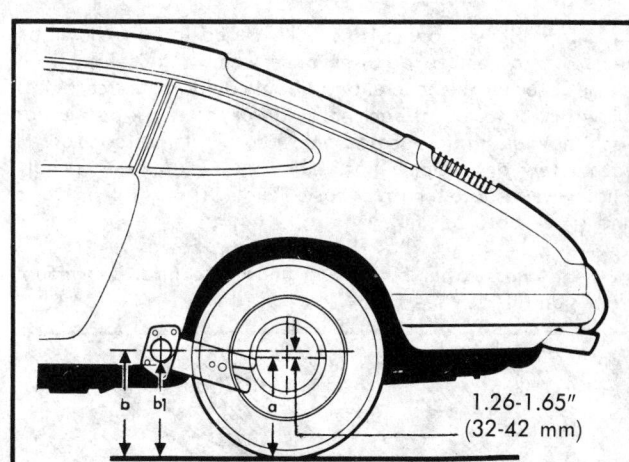

Fig. 2   Rear Suspension Riding Height Measuring Points for 911SC

924 (Rear) — Rear height is adjusted at 2-piece spring plate; spring plate removal is not required. Loosen mounting bolt and adjust vehicle height with eccentric bolt. *See Fig. 3.* Height should be .311-.319" (7.9-8.1 mm) when measured from torsion bar center to center of wheel.

NOTE — *If spring plate angle is 19° (with stabilizer bar) or 23° 40' (without stabilizer bar), vehicle height will be correct.*

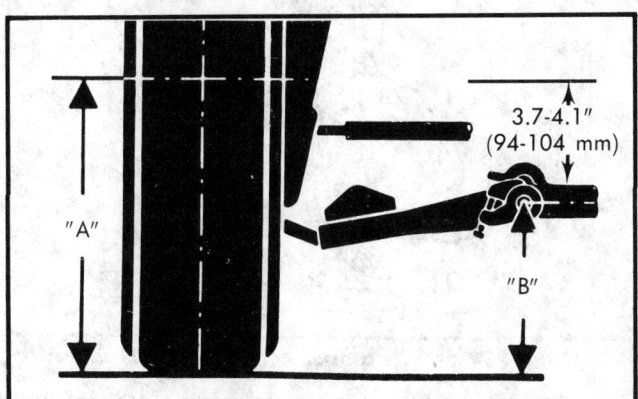

Fig. 1   Front Suspension Riding Height Measuring Points for 911SC

PORSCHE (Cont.)

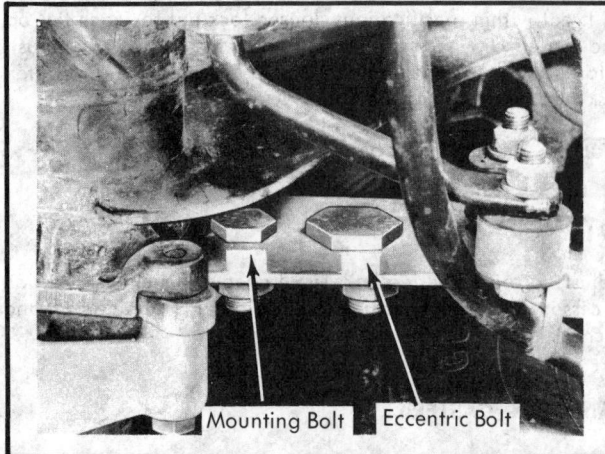

Fig. 3 Location of 924 Rear Riding Height Adjusting bolt

928 (Front) — Park vehicle on level ground. Place wheels in straight-ahead position. Measure distance from boss (on forward underside of lower control arm) to ground. Distance should be about 7.48" (190 mm). Height is determined by coil spring and is not adjustable at front axle.

928 (Rear) — Place vehicle on level surface. Place front wheels in straight-ahead position. Measure distance from lower edge of crossmember (below camber adjusting cam) to ground. Distance should be 6.81-7.20" (173-183 mm).

- To adjust vehicle upward turn coil spring adjusting nut (located at under side of lower spring retainer) clockwise.
- Rear height must be adjusted to match front height. EXAMPLE: If front height is .394" (10 mm) too high, rear height must be raised .394" (10 mm).

CASTER

911SC — If caster angle is not within specifications, it will be necessary to remove adjuster plate which attaches to front shock absorber. Remove enough front compartment carpet to allow access to top of each shock absorber. Mark position of each movable plate, located below each Allen screw. Loosen each screw and upper shock absorber nut. Move assembly lengthwise to obtain correct caster angle. Tighten all 3 screws and shock absorber nut.

924 — Adjust caster by moving the rear control arm mount from side-to-side. See Fig. 4.

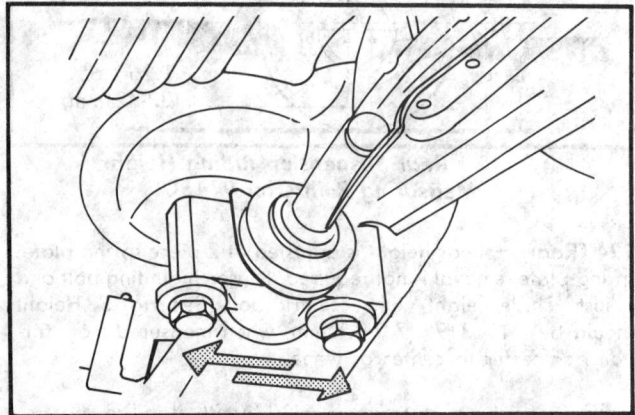

Fig. 4 924 Caster Adjustment Location

928 — Caster is adjusted at eccentric located on lower control arm. To adjust caster, use eccentric closest to brake disc.

CAMBER

911SC (Front) — If camber angle is not within specifications, it will be necessary to move adjuster plate which attaches to front shock absorber. Follow procedure outlined for adjusting caster and move assembly from side-to-side to obtain correct camber angle. Tighten all 3 screws and shock absorber nut.

911SC (Rear) — To obtain correct camber angle at rear wheels, it is necessary to adjust rear torsion bars first. See Torsion Bar Adjustment. Then, loosen nuts on retaining bolts and on eccentric bolt at rear axle flange. Turn camber eccentric until camber angle is within specifications. Tighten retaining nuts and eccentric bolt nuts.

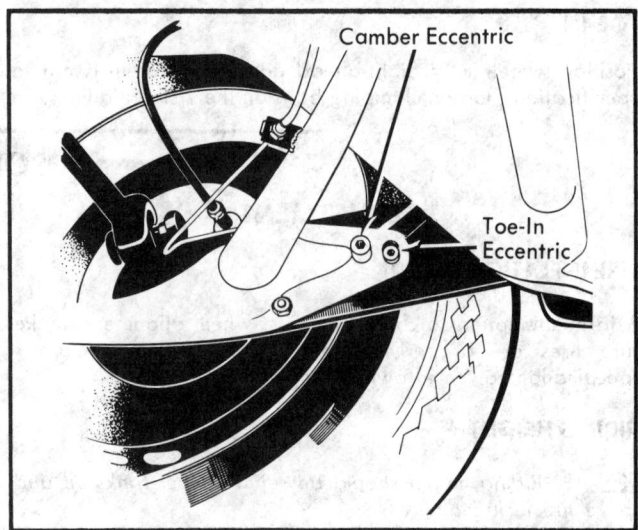

Fig. 5 911SC Rear Camber Adjustment Points

924 (Front) — Adjust camber by turning eccentric bolt shown in Fig. 6.

924 (Rear) — Loosen bolts between spring plate and diagonal arm flange. Bring camber to specification by turning eccentric.

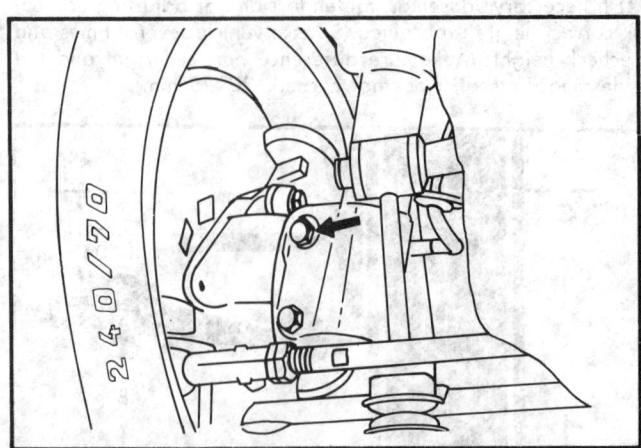

Fig. 6 924 Front Camber Eccentric Bolt Location

928 (Front) — Camber is adjusted at eccentric located on lower control arm. To adjust camber, use eccentric farthest away from brake disc.

PORSCHE (Cont.)

928 (Rear) — Make camber adjustments at eccentric bolt located on inner control arm bushing.

TOE-IN

All Models (Front) — Place front wheels in straight-ahead position. Adjust left and right steering links (tie rods) equally to obtain specified setting. Coat each steering link with anti-corrosive compound after adjustment.

911SC (Rear) — To adjust rear wheel toe-in, loosen nuts on retaining bolts and adjusting eccentrics at rear axle flange. Turn toe-in eccentric until toe-in is set to specifications. Hold eccentric stationary and tighten all lock nuts.

924 (Rear) — Adjust toe-in by repositioning control arm flange in slots of spring plate. Use of special tool 1979 is suggested.

928 (Rear) — Rear toe-in adjustments are made at eccentric bolt located on front control arm bushing.

TORSION BAR ADJUSTMENT

911SC (Rear) — Place torsion bar into transverse tube with inner end splines first. Slip radius arm onto outer end splines of torsion bar. Place leveling tool (VW 261) on lower edge of door opening and adjust level so bubble is in center of glass. Check adjustment (degrees) of free hanging radius arm with same leveling tool. If not to specifications, adjust by turning torsion bar and radius arm in opposite directions. Adjustment of both radius arms must each equal $36\frac{3}{4}° \pm \frac{1}{4}°$.

RENAULT

ADJUSTMENT

TIRE INFLATION (COLD)

Before attempting to check or adjust wheel alignment, make sure tires are properly inflated. Refer to manufacturer's specifications given in owner's manual.

RIDING HEIGHT

NOTE — *Riding height should be set with fuel tank full and without additional weight in vehicle.*

Front — Checking or adjusting riding height can only be performed with vehicle on level surface. To calculate front riding height, measure distance from ground to center of wheel ("H₁" in *Fig. 1*) and distance from ground to front side member ("H₂" in *Fig. 1*) in line with wheel centers. Then subtract the measurements. Difference should be $1\frac{7}{8}$-$2\frac{5}{8}$" (48-68 mm), with the variation between right and left sides not to exceed $\frac{3}{8}$" (10 mm). To adjust front riding height, mark position of torsion bar in bracket, then remove and rotate torsion bar until correct riding height is obtained.

Rear — Rear riding height is calculated by measuring from ground to center of wheel ("H₄" in *Fig. 1*) and to punched out hole in rear side member (H₅" in *Fig. 1*). The difference in the measurements should be $\frac{1}{16}$-$\frac{9}{16}$" (1.5-14 mm) with variation between right and left sides not to exceed $\frac{3}{8}$" (10 mm). Adjust rear riding height in same manner as front riding height.

CASTER

Vehicle riding height must be calculated before adjusting caster. Caster angle corresponds to the difference in front and rear riding heights between "H₂" and "H₅" as shown in *Fig. 1*. After calculating the difference, refer to Caster Angle table for correct caster angle. To adjust caster angle, loosen both lower control arm mounting bolts and add or remove shims to adjust caster to specifications. The addition or removal of 1 shim equals about 1° change in caster angle.

NOTE — *Never use more than 2 shims between bushing and side member. Always check steering box height after caster adjustment.*

Caster Angle Table	
Difference Between "H₂" & "H₅"	**Caster Angle**
$1\frac{9}{16}$" (40 mm)	$12\frac{1}{2}°$
$2\frac{3}{8}$" (60 mm)	$12°$
$3\frac{3}{16}$" (80 mm)	$11\frac{1}{2}°$
$3\frac{15}{16}$" (100 mm)	$11°$
$4\frac{3}{4}$" (120 mm)	$10\frac{1}{2}°$
$5\frac{1}{2}$" (140 mm)	$10°$

CAMBER

Camber angle is not adjustable. If not within specifications, inspect front suspension for wear or damage and repair or replace components as necessary.

TOE-IN

If toe-in is not to specifications, disconnect steering arm at rack end. Loosen lock nut on steering end fitting. To increase toe-in, unscrew end fitting. To decrease, screw in fitting. Tighten lock nut and connect steering arm. Recheck toe-in.

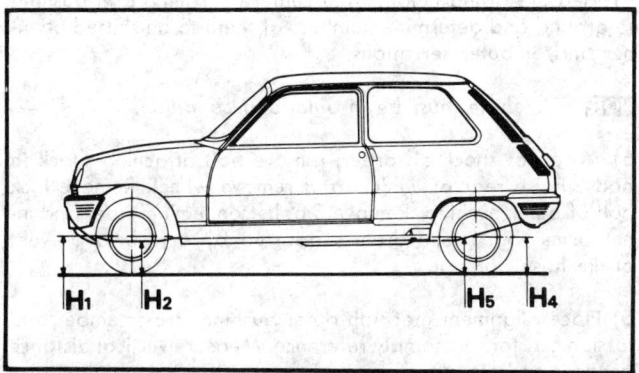

Fig. 1   Riding Height Measurement Points

Wheel Alignment

SAAB

ADJUSTMENT

TIRE INFLATION (COLD)

Before attempting to check or adjust wheel alignment, make sure tires are properly inflated. Refer to manufacturer's specifications given in owner's manual.

CASTER

To adjust caster, add or remove shims under upper control arm bushing brackets. Changing shims from front to rear bracket increases caster angle. Moving shims from rear to front decreases caster angle.

NOTE – *Same shim thicknesses removed from front must be placed under rear and vice versa. Change in caster also affects camber.*

CAMBER

To adjust camber, add or remove shims under upper control arm bushing brackets. Increasing shims under both brackets reduces camber angle and removing shims under both increases camber.

NOTE – *Always add or remove same thickness of shims at front and rear or caster angle will be affected.*

TOE-IN

With wheels in straight-ahead position, loosen steering link (tie rod) lock nut and turn adjustable sleeve until correct toe-in is obtained. Tighten lock nuts and recheck toe-in.

NOTE – *After adjustment of toe-in, measurement "A" (Fig. 1) of tie rod must not exceed 1.0" (25 mm) or 1.02" (26 mm) for power steering models. For tie rods opposite each other, the difference between measurements "A" must not exceed .08" (2 mm).*

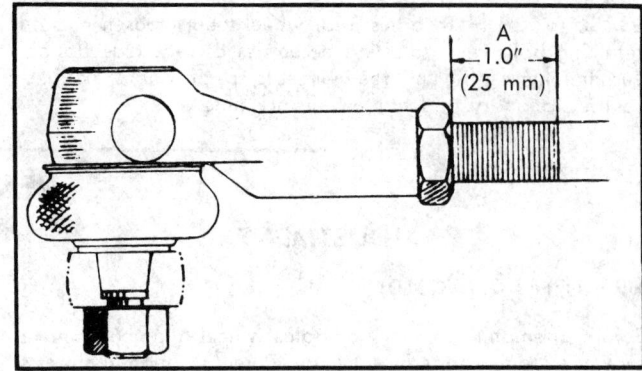

Fig. 1   View Showing Tie Rod Length Measurement

SUBARU

ADJUSTMENT

TIRE INFLATION (COLD)

Before attempting to check or adjust wheel alignment, make sure tires are properly inflated. Refer to manufacturer's specifications given in owner's manual.

RIDING HEIGHT

Front (All Models) – Place vehicle on level surface. Measure distance between ground and front end of transverse link attaching bolt. Adjust clearance by turning nuts (at same time) on strut until specified height is obtained. See *Riding Height Specifications* table.

Rear (4-WD) – Place vehicle on level surface. Measure the distance between ground and center of outer end face of torsion bar on BRAT and between ground and lowest point of crossmember pipe on all others. Adjust clearance by turning adjusting bolt clockwise to increase riding height and counterclockwise to decrease height. See *Riding Height Specifications chart.*

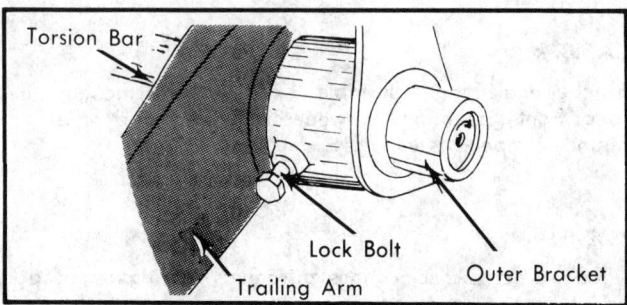

Fig. 1   Installed View of Torsion Bar Outer End Attachment

NOTE – *Adjusting bolt is accessible through service hole located in vehicle floor.*

Rear (2-WD) – **1)** Riding height is adjusted by changing the angle between trailing arm center line and markings on outer bracket. See *Fig. 1.* The trailing arm and outer bracket have full serrations around the torsion bar mounting hole, while torsion bar has 1 missing serration, thus allowing torsion bar to be inserted at any angle.

2) To increase riding height, turn outer end and inner end of torsion bar in direction opposite to cast-in arrow on outer end of bar. Height changes .20" (5 mm) with each shift in serration.

3) Initially set vehicle rear riding height by inserting torsion bar with its missing serrations aligned with markings on outer bracket surface and trailing arm inner surface. This should equal the approximate riding height. See *Riding Height Specifications chart.*

4) Measure riding height from center of trailing arm bushing to ground and determine numbers of teeth to be shifted on inner and/or outer serrations.

NOTE – *Vehicle must be in unloaded condition.*

5) At top of shock absorber, remove bolt attaching shock to body. Raise rear of vehicle and remove wheel. Remove lock bolt of outer bushing. Remove 3 bolts connecting outer and inner arms with brake drum supported by a jack to prevent brake hose damage.

6) Place alignment mark on outer bushing, crossmember and torsion bar for reassembly reference. Measure vertical distance between end of outer arm and vehicle body. Pull out outer arm and torsion bar until inner serration is completely disengaged.

SUBARU (Cont.)

Riding Height Specifications

Application	Front In. (mm)	Rear In. (mm)
1600 & 1800 (2-WD)		
Station Wagon	9.65-10.63 (245-270)	11.02-11.81 (280-300)
All Others	9.45-10.43 (240-265)	10.24-11.02 (260-280)
1600 & 1800 (4-WD)		
Hatchback	10.43-11.42 (265-290)	12.60-13.39 (320-340)
Station Wagon	10.63-11.61 (270-295)	13.19-13.98 (335-355)
BRAT	9.84-10.83 (250-275)	13.58-14.37 (345-365)

7) Rotate torsion bar and outer arm to shift matching of inner serration by appropriate pitches and engage inner serration with crossmember. Pull outer arm from torsion bar and rotate outer arm in opposite direction to shift matching of outer serration by appropriate pitches.

NOTE — *DO NOT disengage inner serration of torsion bar from crossmember.*

8) Install outer arm to torsion bar and crossmember, then measure vertical distance between end of outer arm and vehicle body. Change in this distance shows half of change in riding height clearance caused by adjustment.

9) Install 3 bolts connecting outer and inner arms. Repeat adjustment procedure on opposite wheel. Install wheels and lower vehicle. Install shock absorbers and outer bushing lock bolt. Check rear riding height adjustment. If correct, tighten lock bolt on outer bushing. If incorrect, repeat adjustment on each wheel.

CASTER

Caster angle is not adjustable. If angle is not to specifications, inspect suspension for wear or damage and repair or replace components as necessary.

CAMBER

Camber angle is not adjustable. If angle is not to specifications, inspect suspension for wear or damage. Repair or replace components as necessary.

TOE-IN

If toe-in is not within specifications, loosen both left and right tie rod lock nuts. Turn both tie rods an equal amount until specified toe-in is obtained.

TOYOTA

ADJUSTMENT

TIRE INFLATION (COLD)

Before attempting to check or adjust wheel alignment, make sure tires are properly inflated. Refer to manufacturer's specifications given in owner's manual.

CAMBER & CASTER

NOTE — *Caster and camber adjustments should always be made in one operation.*

Pickup (2-WD) — If camber or caster angles are not within specifications, adjust by adding or removing shims between upper control arm shaft and front suspension crossmember. To increase camber, remove shims from upper control arm shaft bolts in equal amounts. To decrease camber, add shims to upper control arm shaft bolts in equal amounts. To increase caster, add shims to rear side of upper control arm shaft bolt or remove shims from front side. To decrease caster, remove shims from rear side of upper control arm shaft bolt or add shims to front side.

Land Cruiser & Pickup (4-WD) — Camber and caster are not adjustable. If not within specifications, inspect and repair or replace front suspension components as necessary.

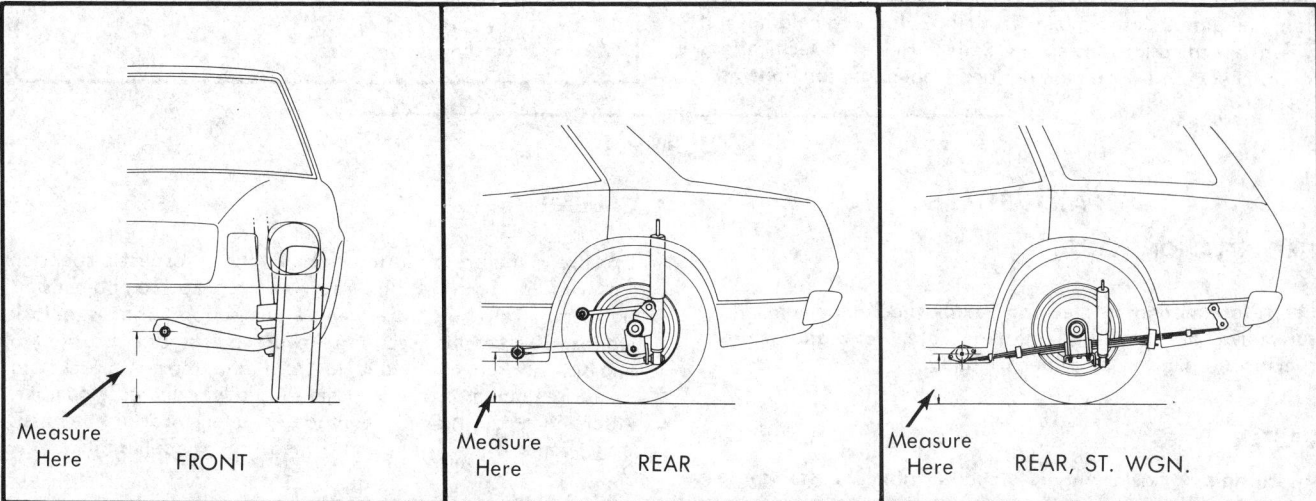

Fig. 1   Riding Height Measurement Points for All Models — Except Pickup & Land Cruiser

TOYOTA (Cont.)

All Other Models — If angles are not within specifications, adjust by turning nuts on lower arm. If caster angle is too large, increase distance between staked nut and lower arm. If caster angle is too small, decrease distance between staked nut and lower arm. If caster or camber cannot be adjusted to specifications, inspect and repair or replace front suspension components as necessary.

NOTE — *Always loosen strut bracket side nut first.*

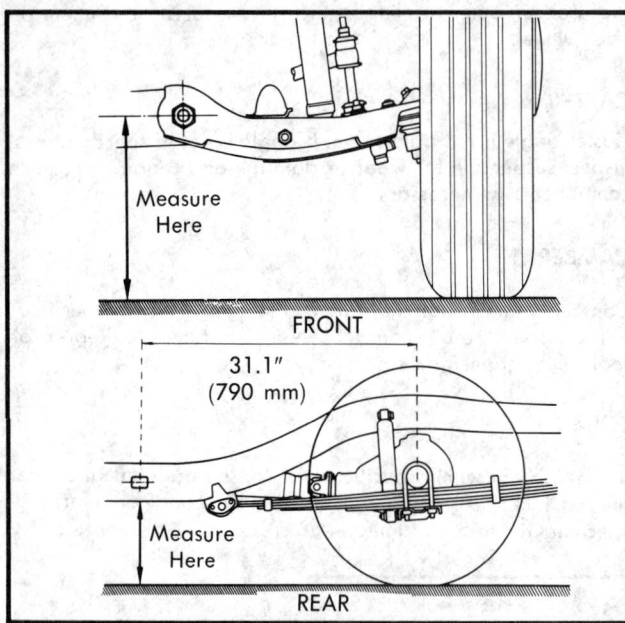

Fig. 2 Riding Height Measurement Points for 2-WD Pickup Models

TOE-IN

All Models — If toe-in is not within specifications, loosen steering link (tie-rod) clamping bolts and rotate adjusting sleeves an equal amount until correct toe-in is obtained. Position clamp bolts at right angles to slot in tie rod and tighten bolts.

RIDING HEIGHT

Before adjusting wheel alignment, check riding height. Riding height must be checked with vehicle on level surface. Bounce vehicle several times and allow suspension to settle. Check riding height as shown in *Fig. 1* or *Fig. 2*. If riding height is not within specifications listed in Riding Height Specifications table, check and repair or replace suspension components.

Riding Height Specifications①

Application	Front In. (mm)	Rear In. (mm)
Celica & Supra		
165SR14	9.21 (234)	9.25 (235)
175SR14	9.41 (239)	9.45 (240)
185/70 SR14	9.33 (237)	9.37 (238)
Corolla		
Station Wagon		
165SR13	9.13 (232)	9.13 (232)
All Others		
6.45-13	9.33 (237)	9.49 (241)
165SR13	9.06 (230)	9.21 (234)
185/70 SR13	9.13 (232)	9.29 (236)
185/70 HR13	9.13 (232)	9.29 (236)
Corona		
Station Wagon		
5.60-13	9.1 (231)	8.9 (225)
6.45-13	9.0 (229)	8.8 (223)
165SR13	8.8 (223)	8.54 (217)
165SR14	9.25 (235)	9.0 (229)
175SR14	9.49 (241)	9.25 (235)
All Others		
5.60-13	9.1 (231)	9.2 (233)
6.45-13	9.0 (229)	9.1 (231)
165SR13	8.8 (223)	8.9 (225)
165SR14	9.25 (235)	9.33 (237)
175SR14	9.49 (241)	9.6 (243)
Cressida		
Station Wagon		
(All Tires)	7.68 (195)	9.06 (230)
Pickup (2-WD)		
½ Ton		
7.00-14 6PR	10.29 (261.4)	11.35 (288.3)
185SR14 4PR	9.83 (249.6)	10.65 (270.4)
E78-14(B)	10.02 (254.4)	11.08 (281.3)
ER78-14(B)	9.87 (250.6)	10.67 (271.0)
¾ Ton		
7.50-14 6PR	10.96 (278.4)	12.02 (305.3)
Tercel		
155-13 &		
6.15-13 4PR	8.82 (224)	10.47 (266)
155SR12	8.19 (208)	9.84 (250)
165/70 SR13	8.54 (217)	10.20 (259)

① — According to tire size.

TRIUMPH

ADJUSTMENT

TIRE INFLATION (COLD)

Before attempting to check or adjust wheel alignment, make sure tires are properly inflated. Refer to manufacturer's specifications given in owner's manual.

CASTER

All Models — Caster angle is not adjustable. If caster angle is not to specifications, inspect suspension system for wear or damage and repair or replace components as necessary.

CAMBER

Spitfire — Before adjusting camber angle, inspect suspension for wear or damage and repair or replace components as necessary. To adjust, raise vehicle and support chassis on jack stands. Loosen nuts securing lower control arm bracket to chassis. Add shims equally to front and rear of bracket to decrease camber or remove shims equally to increase camber. After each adjustment is made, tighten bracket-to-chassis bolts, remove jack stands and measure camber angle.

TR7 & TR8 — Camber angle is not adjustable. If camber angle is not within specifications, inspect suspension system for

TRIUMPH (Cont.)

wear or damage and repair or replace components as necessary.

TOE-IN

All Models (Front) — Set front wheels in straight ahead position. If adjustment is necessary, loosen steering link (tie rod) lock nuts and gaiter clips. Rotate adjusting sleeves equal amounts until correct toe-in is obtained. Tighten lock nuts and recheck toe-in.

Spitfire (Rear) — If toe-in is not to specifications, loosen bolts holding strut front support. Adjust as necessary by adding to or removing from the shims fitted between support and body. Tighten bolts and recheck toe-in.

VOLKSWAGEN

ADJUSTMENT

TIRE INFLATION (COLD)

Before attempting to check or adjust wheel alignment, make sure tires are properly inflated. Refer to manufacturer's specifications given in owner's manual.

CASTER

Vanagon — If caster is not within specifications, adjust by changing length of strut bar at crossmember mount. After adjusting caster, check and adjust camber.

All Others — Caster angle is not adjustable. If not within specifications, inspect front suspension for wear or damage and repair or replace components as necessary.

CAMBER

Dasher (Front) — If camber is not within specifications, loosen nuts attaching ball joint to track control arm. To adjust, insert adjusting tool (40-200) in adjusting holes in control arm and pry ball joint sideways until camber is set to specifications. Tighten attaching nuts and recheck camber. Camber should not vary more than 1° between right and left sides.

NOTE — *Insert tool from front on right side and from rear on left side.*

Vanagon (Front) — If camber is not within specifications, loosen nut on upper control arm shaft and rotate shaft until camber angle is set to specifications. Tighten nut and recheck camber.

Vanagon (Rear) — If camber is not within specifications, loosen outer bolt on trailing arm and adjust camber by using a screwdriver to move trailing arm up or down. Tighten trailing arm bolt and recheck camber.

All Other Models (Front) — If camber is not within specifications, loosen nuts of suspension strut-to-wheel bearing housing mounting bolts. Turn eccentric bolt (upper mounting bolt) until specified camber angle is obtained. Tighten mounting bolt nuts and recheck camber.

All Other Models (Rear) — Rear camber is not adjustable. If camber angle is not within specifications, inspect rear suspension for wear or damage and repair or replace components as necessary.

TOE-IN

Vanagon (Front) — Place wheels in straight-ahead position and ensure lug on rubber washer of pinion shaft is aligned with notch in steering gear housing. Loosen lock nuts and rotate both tie rods equal amounts until toe-in specifications are obtained. Tighten lock nuts, ensure steering wheel is centered on steering shaft and that dust boots are not twisted.

Vanagon (Rear) — If toe-in is not to specifications, loosen inner bolt on trailing arm. Using a screwdriver, adjust toe-in by moving trailing arm forward or rearward until correct toe-in specification is obtained. Tighten trailing arm inner bolt.

All Other Models (Front) — Place wheels in straight-ahead position. Loosen lock nuts on adjustable tie rod end (if equipped). Hold axle boot to avoid twisting. Adjust tie rod until specified toe-in is obtained. Tighten lock nut and recheck toe-in.

All Other Models (Rear) — Toe-in is not adjustable. If toe-in is not within specifications, inspect rear suspension for wear or damage and repair or replace components as necessary.

VOLVO

ADJUSTMENT

TIRE INFLATION (COLD)

Before attempting to check or adjust wheel alignment, make sure tires are properly inflated. Refer to manufacturer's specifications given in owner's manual.

CASTER

Caster cannot be adjusted. If not within specifications, check front end components for damage.

CAMBER

If camber is not within specifications, loosen nuts at strut assembly upper attachment. Use special tool 5038 (or equivalent) at strut upper attachment to adjust camber. Tighten lock nuts. Recheck camber.

TOE-IN

Place wheels in straight-ahead position and loosen lock nut and rubber dust boot outer clamp. Turn tie rods until toe is within specifications. Make sure length of tie rods does not differ more than .08" (2 mm). Measure difference between groove in tie rod and lock nut.

AUDI

4000 (Front) — Adjustment not required. Torque spindle nut to 167 ft. lbs. (23 mkg).

4000 (Rear) — Remove grease cap, cotter pin and castle nut. Tighten spindle nut and loosen for adjustment. Adjust by lightly tightening spindle nut until plain washer (beneath spindle nut) can just be moved from side to side with a screwdriver.

5000 (Front) — Adjustment not required. Torque spindle nut to 203 ft. lbs. (28 mkg).

5000 (Rear) — Tighten adjustment nut firmly while rotating wheel. Make sure bearing is fully seated. Back off nut until thrust washer can be moved with screwdriver. Insert cotter key.

BMW

320i Models — While rotating wheel hub, tighten castle nut to 22-24 ft. lbs. (3.0-3.3 mkg), then rotate hub at least 2 more times. Loosen castle nut until bearing end play is noticed. Tighten castle nut to a maximum of about 2 ft. lbs. (.3 mkg), then loosen to nearest hole and install cotter pin.

NOTE — *After adjustment, slotted washer should move easily, without noticeable resistance.*

528i, 633CSi & 733i Models — Tighten castle nut to 22-24 ft. lbs. (3.0-3.3 mkg), while continuously rotating wheel. Loosen castle nut until there is visible axial bearing play. Again rotate wheel and tighten bearing, this time to 2 ft. lbs. (.3 mkg). Insert cotter pin. Thrust washer should have movement with only slight resistance after adjustment.

CHRYSLER CORP. IMPORTS

Champ & Colt Hatchback — **1)** To obtain correct bearing preload spacer, install spacer selection gauge (MB 990768) to hub and tighten to 14 ft. lbs. (1.9 mkg).

2) Rotate hub and special tool assembly to seat wheel bearings. Install dial indicator on special tool and load approximately .2" (5 mm) of travel on dial indicator. Zero dial indicator.

3) Measure travel by holding threaded stud of special tool with a wrench, then back off nut slowly until travel no longer registers on dial indicator. Note reading.

4) Repeat procedure to ensure accurate reading. Average the readings and select a spacer of the correct thickness. Install spacer, with chamfered side toward steering knuckle.

All Other Models — Tighten adjusting nut to 14.5 ft. lbs. (2.0 mkg) on Arrow, Challenger, Colt Station Wagon and Sapporo models or to 21.7 ft. lbs. (3.0 mkg) on pickup models. After seating bearing components, loosen nut to 0 torque reading. Tighten to 5.8 ft. lbs. (.8 mkg) for pickup models or to 3.6 ft. lbs. (.5 mkg) on all other models. Insert cotter pin.

NOTE — *Do not loosen adjusting nut more than 30° on pickup models or 15° on all other models.*

COURIER

All Models — While rotating wheel, hub and drum assembly, tighten adjusting nut to 17-25 ft. lbs. (2.4-3.5 mkg). Back adjusting nut off ¼ turn and retighten nut where castellations on lock nut are aligned with cotter pin hole in spindle. Install new cotter pin and check wheel rotation.

DATSUN

All Models (Except 310) — Tighten spindle nut to torque specifications in table. Spin wheel and retorque spindle nut. Loosen nut according to specifications in table and then tighten to align cotter pin hole. Insert cotter pin.

Wheel Bearing Adjustment

Application	Torque Ft. Lbs. (mkg)	Loosen
210, 510	22-25 (3.0-3.5)	90°
200SX, 810, 280ZX	18-22 (2.5-3.0)	60°
Pickup	25-29 (3.5-13)	45°

310 — **1)** With vehicle raised and supported, remove wheel and steering knuckle. Disassemble components. Determine required thickness of bearing spacer as follows: Place outer bearing on base (KV40100700-3) and place steering knuckle over it so bearing seats in outer race. Then slide inner bearing over dummy shaft (KV40100700-1) and place shaft bearing in knuckle with end of shaft in outer bearing and inner bearing in inner race.

2) Slide weight (KV40100700-2) over dummy shaft and down onto knuckle. Turn knuckle back and forth to seat bearing. Assemble suitable dial indicator with contact button resting on top of dummy shaft, and set indicator to zero. Pull upward on shaft until it reaches end of travel, rotate it 1 revolution and record maximum deflection of indicator needle.

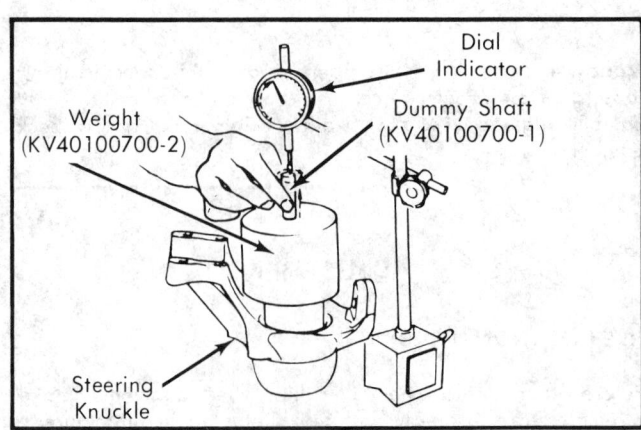

Fig. 1 *Determining Required Spacer Thickness (Datsun 310)*

3) To determine required spacer thickness, add recorded dial indicator reading to metric thickness dimension stamped on side of flange on end of dummy shaft.

EXAMPLE — *Determine required spacer thickness as follows:*

Dial Indicator Reading .... .094" (2.38 mm)
Thickness Stamped on Shaft .... .203" (5.16 mm)

EQUALS

Required Spacer Thickness .... .297" (7.54 mm)

4) Select required spacer. Spacers are available in 18 sizes, ranging from .291-.293" (7.38-7.44 mm) to .331-.333" (8.40-8.46 mm) in .002" (.05 mm) increments. For size identification, spacers are numbered "05" (smallest size) through "22" (largest size).

5) Pack grease seals and bearings with suitable bearing grease. Install outer grease seal and press outer bearing onto stub axle. Install rotor on stub axle. Place knuckle in position on stub axle, install spacer and press inner bearing onto stub axle and knuckle assembly until it just bottoms. Install inner seal, then reinstall knuckle and wheel to vehicle.

6) Tighten spindle nut to 29-33 ft. lbs. (4.0-4.6 mkg) and rotate wheel several times in both directions to settle bearings. Retorque spindle nut. Loosen nut 90° and tighten to align cotter pin. Insert cotter pin.

NOTE — *Spindle nut may be tightened as much as 15° to insert cotter pin.*

FIAT

Brava & Spider 2000 — While rotating hub, torque spindle nut to 14.5 ft. lbs. (2 mkg). Completely loosen nut and retighten to 5 ft. lbs. (.7 mkg). Loosen nut 30° and stake collar of spindle nut into machined slot on spindle. Attach dial indicator with magnetic base on brake drum and actuating foot on spindle. Hub end play should not exceed .004" (.1 mm).

NOTE — *Whenever spindle nut has been removed it must be replaced with a new nut.*

Strada — Tighten front and rear spindle nuts to 159 ft. lbs. (22 mkg), then stake collar of spindle nut to spindle.

X1/9 — Tighten front and rear spindle nuts to 112 ft. lbs. (15.5 mkg). When spindle nuts are properly tightened, stake collar of spindle nut into machined slot on spindle.

FIESTA

Front — No adjustment is required. Tighten front spindle nut to 150-175 ft. lbs.(21-24 mkg).

Rear — Adjust rear bearing by tightening nut to 15-18 ft. lbs. (2.1-2.5 mkg) while rotating drum. Loosen nut ½ turn and fit nut retainer with cotter pin.

HONDA

All Models (Front) — Front wheel bearings are not adjustable. Torque front spindle nut to 108 ft. lbs. (15.0 mkg).

All Models (Rear) — Tighten spindle nut to 14-22 ft. lbs. (2.0-3.0 mkg) and rotate drum several times. Loosen lock nut. Tighten spindle nut to 3 ft. lbs. (.4 mkg) on Civic and Prelude or 2-4 ft. lbs. (.3-.6 mkg) on Accord.

JAGUAR

All Models — While rotating hub, tighten nut until no end play is evident. Loosen nut 1 or 2 flats to line up cotter key and install cotter key. End play should be measured with a dial indicator and should be .002-.006". If not within specifications, adjust axle nut to correct end play.

LUV

On 4-WD models, place transfer case in "2H" and free wheeling hub in "FREE", then remove hub cover, snap ring, shims, free wheeling hub body and lock washer. On all models, rotate wheel or hub and tighten nut. On 4-WD, tighten nut until wheel locks. On 2-WD, torque nut to 22 ft. lbs. (3 mkg). Loosen nut until it can be turned by fingers, then tighten nut with fingers. No play should be felt at this point. Using an accurate spring tension gauge, adjust nut so starting force is 2.6-4 lbs. (1.2-1.8 kg) on 4-WD or 1.1-2.6 lbs. (.5-1.2 kg) on 2-WD models.

MAZDA

GLC — Tighten adjustment nut to 14-18 ft. lbs. (2.0-2.5 mkg). Rotate brake discs several times in both directions. Loosen adjustment nut. Using a spring pull scale, set bearing preload (using adjustment nut) to .33-1.32 lbs. (.15-.60 kg).

All Other Models — With vehicle raised and supported under lower control arms, remove wheel. On RX7 and pickup models, tighten nut until wheel locks. On all other models, torque wheel nut to 14-18 ft. lbs. (2-2.5 mkg). On all models, rotate hub to seat bearings. Loosen nut, then using spring tension gauge, tighten nut until correct starting force is obtained. Starting force should be .77-1.92 lbs. (.35-.87 kg) on 626, .99-1.43 lbs. (.45-.65 kg) on RX7, or 1.3-2.4 lbs. (.59-1.1 kg) on pickup.

MERCEDES-BENZ

All Models — While rotating hub, tighten clamping nut until hub can just be turned. Loosen clamping nut and release bearing tension by striking steering knuckle spindle with plastic hammer. Using a suitable dial indicator, check wheel bearing end play. End play should be .0004-.0008" (.01-.02 mm). Adjust clamping nut until end play is within limits. Tighten socket bolt of clamping nut. Washer between outer bearing and clamping nut should rotate with light pressure applied to it.

MG

MGB — Raise front of vehicle and remove front wheels. Using suitable dial indicator, measure hub end play. Correct end play is .002-.004" (.05-.10 mm). If not within specifications, remove spindle nut, washer, and outer bearing. Add or remove shims behind outer bearing until correct end play is obtain with spindle nut torqued to 40 ft. lbs. (5.5 mkg)

PEUGEOT

All Models — Raise and support front of vehicle. While rotating wheel or hub, tighten spindle nut to 29 ft. lbs. (4 mkg) on 604 models or to 22 ft. lbs. (3 mkg) on all other models. Loosen spindle nut and retighten to 7.2 ft. lbs. (1 mkg).

PORSCHE

All Models (Front) — Tighten adjusting nut while turning hub. Loosen adjusting nut until thrust washer can just be moved by exerting hand pressure with a screwdriver. Tighten socket head bolt (pinch bolt).

RENAULT

LeCar (Front) — Torque stub axle nut to 90 ft. lbs. (12.4 mkg).

LeCar (Rear) — Tighten stub axle nut to 25 ft. lbs. (3.5 mkg). Loosen nut about ¼ turn. Check bearing end play, it should be between .0004-.002″ (.01-.05 mm). Adjust stub axle as necessary. Fit lock plate and cotter pin. Refill hub dust cover cap with ⅓ oz. of grease.

SAAB

All Models (Front) — Front wheel bearings are not adjustable. Torque front spindle nut to 246-261 ft. lbs. (34-36 mkg).

All Models (Rear) — Install washer and lock nut. Tighten lock nut to 36 ft. lbs. (5 mkg) to seat bearings. Loosen lock nut completely, then tighten nut to 1.4-2.9 ft. lbs. (.2-.4 mkg) and lock nut in place by bending flange into slot of lock nut.

SUBARU

All Models (Front) — Front wheel bearing is not adjustable. Tighten spindle nut (axle shaft nut) to 145 ft. lbs. (20 mkg). If cotter pin hole is not aligned, tighten further a maximum of 30° to align hole.

4-WD (Rear) — No adjustment required. Tighten axle nut to 145 ft. lbs. (20 mkg). If cotter pin hole is not aligned, tighten further a maximum of 30° to align hole.

All Other Models (Rear) — While rotating brake drum, tighten nut to 36 ft. lbs. (5 mkg). Rotate drum several times then back nut off approximately ⅛ turn. Measure rotating force at a wheel stud. Force should be 1.9-3.2 lbs. (.85-1.45 kg).

TOYOTA

Land Cruiser (Front) — Tighten spindle shaft nut snugly using appropriate tool (SST 09607-60020). Back off nut approximately ⅛ turn then install outer lock nut and tighten to 11-16 ft. lbs. (1.5-2.2 mkg).

Land Cruiser (Rear) — Rotate drum and tighten adjustment nut to 43 ft. lbs. (6 mkg). This will seat bearings. Loosen adjust-ment nut about ⅛ turn. Install washer and lock nut, then tighten to 58-72 ft. lbs. (8-10 mkg).

Pickup (Exc. 4-WD) — Tighten spindle nut to 22 ft. lbs. (3 mkg) and rotate hub a couple times to ensure bearings are seated. Back off nut until nut can just be turned by hand. Install a socket (without handle) and tighten not as tight as possible by hand. Measure rotating torque with spring gauge. Torque should be 1.1-2.7 lbs. (.55-1.7 kg). Install cotter pin. If hole does not line up, tighten nut as little as possible until holes align.

Pickup (4-WD) — Tighten spindle nut to 43 ft. lbs. (6 mkg) and rotate hub a couple times to ensure bearings are seated. Loosen nut until it can just be turned by hand. Tighten nut to 2.9-5 ft. lbs. (.4-.7 mkg). Measure rotating torque. Torque should be 6.2-12.6 lbs. (2.8-5.7 kg). Lock nut in place by bending lock washer tab inward.

Tercel — **1)** Raise and support vehicle, remove wheel and steering knuckle. Disassemble components. Determine required thickness of bearing spacer as follows: Install outer race in steering knuckle. Assemble inner bearing on wheel bearing ad-justing tool (SST 09608-16040), insert original spacer and in-stall assembly into steering knuckle.

2) Coat bearings with oil and install outer bearing to ad-justing tool assembly. Tighten nut on adjusting tool to 90 ft. lbs. (12.5 mkg) and rotate adjusting tool in both directions to seat bearings. Using an INCH lb. torque wrench, measure preload while turning assembly in both directions. Preload should be 3.5-8.7 INCH lbs. (4-10 cmkg). Measure preload 3 or 4 times in each direction.

3) If preload is not within specifications, select and insert a thinner or thicker spacer. Spacers are available in 20 thicknesses, ranging from .32″ (8.03 mm) to .35″ (8.79 mm) in .002 (.04 mm) increments. Each spacer will change turning tor-que about 3-4 INCH lbs. (3-5 cmkg). Remove adjusting tool and wheel bearings.

4) Assemble hub and rotor assembly. Pack wheel bearings with grease and install outer bearing race, bearing and oil seal. Pack hub with grease. Insert selected spacer, inner wheel bearing and race into steering knuckle. Using press and arbor (SST 09636-20010), press steering knuckle into hub with a force of 2204.6 lbs. (1000 kg).

5) Turn steering knuckle to settle bearings. Measure fractional force at steering knuckle stopper with a spring tension gauge with pressure still applied. Frictional force should be .8-1.7 lbs. (.36-.77 kg). Increase pressure on steering knuckle to 7716 lbs. (3500 kg), turn steering knuckle to seat bearings and measure preload with spring tension gauge.

6) Preload at steering knuckle stopper (with force still applied) should be .8-2.5 lbs. (.36-1.13 kg). If not to specifications, replace spacer. If under specification, use a thinner spacer; if over, use a thicker spacer. Install oil seal so it is seated .157″ (4 mm) below outer edge of steering knuckle. Complete installa-tion of steering knuckle and tighten spindle nut to 73-108 ft. lbs. (10-15 mkg).

All Other Models — Tighten nut to 22 ft. lbs. on Celica, Cressida and Supra models or to 19-23 ft. lbs. for all other models while turning hub to seat bearings. Loosen nut until it can be turned with fingers. Tighten nut finger tight using a

Wheel Bearing Adjustment

socket without the handle. If not aligned for cotter pin installation, tighten until installation is possible. Preload at hub (while turning) should be within specifications listed in Bearing Preload Specifications table.

Bearing Preload Specifications

Application	Preload Lbs. (kg)
Celica, Corolla & Supra	.7-1.5 (.3-.7)
Corona	.8-1.9 (.35-.87)
Cressida	.9-2.2 (4.1)

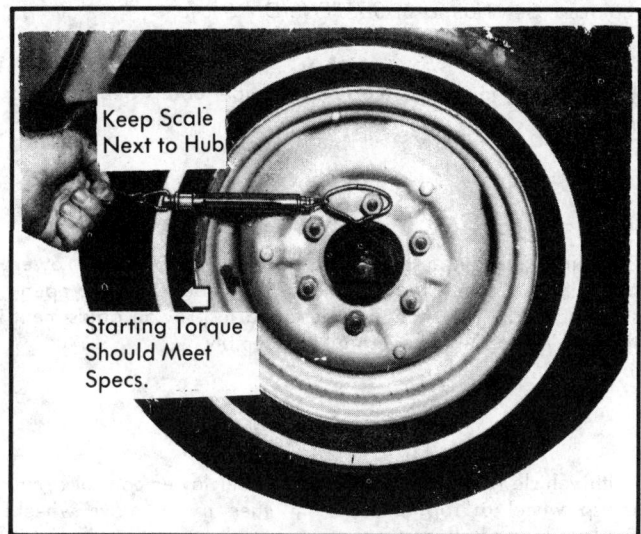

Fig. 2   Using a Pull Scale to Measure Toyota Wheel Bearing Starting Torque

TRIUMPH

Spitfire — Raise and support front of vehicle, then remove wheel and brake caliper. Attach a dial indicator and measure wheel bearing end play. If end play exceeds .003-.005" (.08-.13 mm), remove cotter key and loosen or tighten spindle nut until end play is within specifications. Install new cotter key.

NOTE — *Do not exceed 5 ft. lbs. (.7 mkg) when torquing spindle nut.*

TR7 & TR8 — Raise and support front of vehicle; remove tire and wheel. Check hub for excessive end play. If adjustment is necessary, remove grease cap and cotter pin. Tighten spindle nut to 5 ft. lbs. (.7 mkg), then back nut off 1 flat and install cotter pin.

VOLKSWAGEN

Vanagon (Front) — Tighten spindle nut firmly to seat bearings while turning hub. Back off nut. Wheel bearing is correctly adjusted when thrust washer can be moved slightly with a screwdriver and finger pressure. After adjustment, peen flange of spindle nut over spindle.

Vanagon (Rear) — No adjustment required. Tighten axle nut to 253 ft. lbs. (35 mkg) while rotating wheel to seat bearings. Always replace cotter pin.

All Others (Front) — Front wheel bearings are pressed into bearing housing and no adjustment is required. Tighten front axle nut on Dasher to 145 ft. lbs. (20 mkg) for M 18x1.5 nuts or 175 ft. lbs. (24 mkg) for M 20x1.5 nuts. For Rabbit and Scirocco models tighten nuts to 175 ft. lbs. (24 mkg).

All Others (Rear) — Wheel bearings are correctly adjusted if thrust washer can be moved slightly with a screwdriver. This will provide axial play of approximately .001-.003" (.025-.076 mm).

VOLVO

All Models — While rotating hub, torque nut to 50 ft. lbs. (6.9 mkg). Loosen nut 1/3 turn and check for hub rotating freely with no end play. If necessary to align cotter pin holes, loosen nut and install cotter pin.

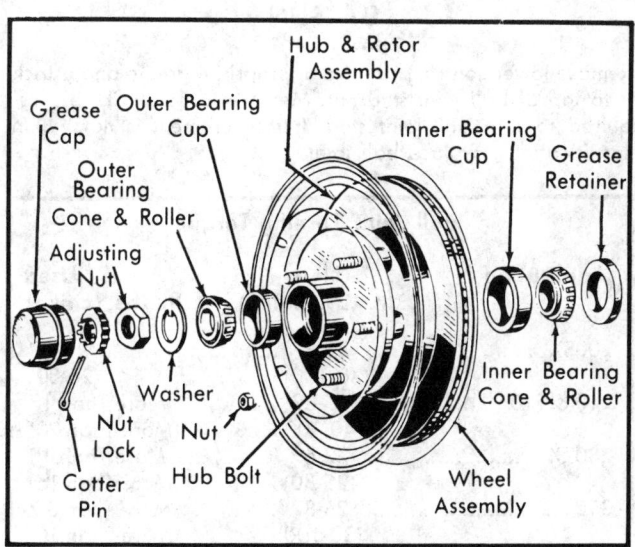

Fig. 3   Exploded View of Wheel Bearing Components With Disc Brakes

BMW

Axial movement of ball joint with pressure applied by leverage should be .055" (1.4 mm) or less. If play exceeds specifications, replace control arm assembly.

CHRYSLER CORP. IMPORTS

Pickup Models — With components removed from vehicle, check upper ball joint for starting torque and lower ball joint for axial play. Starting torque should be .6-2.5 ft. lbs. (.08-.35 mkg). Axial play should be .02" (.5 mm) or less. Replace components as necessary.

All Other Models — With components removed from control arm and ball joint still installed, check following: Axial and radial play should be 0" and rotating torque should be 2.2-4.3 ft. lbs. (.3-.6 mkg) on Champ and Colt hatchbacks. Starting torque should be 9 ft. lbs. (1.2 mkg) on Champ and Colt hatchbacks and 4-7 ft. lbs. (.55-.98 mkg) on all other models. If not to specifications, replace components.

COURIER

Check working surfaces of ball joints and studs for wear or damage. End play should not exceed .031" (.8 mm). If end play is excessive, replace ball joint. *See Courier in SUSPENSION Section.*

DATSUN

Remove lower control arm. Use appropriate gauge and attach it to top of ball joint stud nut. Measure force (INCH lbs.) required to turn ball joint stud. If measurement is not within specifications, replace ball joint.

Ball Joint Turning Torque		
Application	New In. Lbs. (cmkg)	Used In. Lbs. (cmkg)
200SX	35-87 (40-100)	17-69 (20-80)
210 & 510	35-87 (40-100)	More Than 17 (More Than 20)
280ZX	22-69 (25-80)	More Than 13 (More Than 15)
310	26-87 (30-100)	More Than 8.7 (More Than 10)
810	52-104 (60-120)	More Than 35 (More Than 40)
Pickup Upper	8.7-43.3 (10-50)	More Than 8.7 (More Than 10)
Lower	①	①

① — Axial play limits — .004-.039" (.1-1.0 mm).

FIAT

Strada — Raise and support vehicle on drive on-type hoist. Using a jack, raise lower control arm. Insert ball joint gauge (A.96505) over ball joint. Lower edge of gauge must not touch threaded portion of bolt. If not to specifications, replace ball joint and/or control arm. *See Fiat in SUSPENSION Section.*

All Other Models — With vehicle raised and supported under lower control arms, grasp wheel at top and bottom and try to shake wheel. If any movement is noted, control arm must be removed and further inspected. *See Fiat in SUSPENSION Section.*

HONDA

Raise and support front of vehicle. Attach dial indicator to lower control arm with indicator tip on steering knuckle near ball joint. Place pry bar between lower control arm and steering knuckle. Push on pry bar and observe movement on dial indicator. If movement exceeds .020" (.5 mm), ball joint must be replaced. *See Honda in SUSPENSION Section.*

NOTE — *Do not damage ball joint rubber boot when inserting pry bar.*

JAGUAR

Ball joints must be replaced if signs of wear are evident. Lower ball joint uses shims. These shims are not to be used to compensate for wear. The shims are designed to provide adjustment for ball joints during overhaul reassembly.

LUV

With vehicle raised and supported under lower control arms, grasp wheel at top and bottom, then try to move wheel. Replace lower ball joint or upper control arm with ball joint if movement exceeds .06" (1.52 mm).

MAZDA

RX7 — Check ball joint dust seal for wear or damage. If damage is evident, control arm with ball joint must be replaced. *See Mazda in SUSPENSION Section.*

All Other Models — Check ball joint dust seal for wear or damage and replace seal, if necessary. Ball joint end play must not exceed .039" (1 mm). If end play exceeds specifications, replace ball joints. *See Mazda in SUSPENSION Section.*

MERCEDES-BENZ

There should be no lateral movement of ball joint. Vertical movement is adjusted by adding or removing washers.

PORSCHE

924 — Measure distance between upper edge of control arm and lower edge of steering knuckle using a vernier caliper. Place a lever under ball joint and pry upward. Record any movement. New ball joints should have no play. Wear limit for other ball joints is about .078" (2 mm).

All Other Models — Check ball joint seal for signs of wear or damage. If any damage is noted, ball joints must be replaced. *See Porsche in SUSPENSION Section.*

Ball Joint Checking

RENAULT

Inspect ball joints for wear or excessive play. Replace ball joints as necessary. *See Renault in SUSPENSION Section.*

SAAB

Check ball joints for excessive play or looseness. Replace components as necessary.

SUBARU

Check ball joints for excessive play or looseness. Also check rubber boot for damage. Replace components as necessary.

TOYOTA

Celica, Corolla, 2-WD Pickup & Supra — Check vertical play of ball joints. If vertical play exceeds .091" (2.3 mm) on 2-WD Pickup, replace ball joints (upper and/or lower). If vertical play exceeds .098" (2.5 mm) on all other models, lower arm with ball joint must be replaced. *See Toyota in SUSPENSION Section.*

All Other Models (Exc. 4-WD Pickup & Land Cruiser) — Check ball joints for damaged rubber boot, excessive looseness or play. If damaged or excessively worn, replace lower control arm with ball joint. *See Toyota in SUSPENSION Section.*

TRIUMPH

Inspect ball joints for excessive wear or play. Replace ball joints as necesary. *See Triumph in SUSPENSION Section.*

VOLKSWAGEN

Vanagon — Inspect ball joints for wear or excessive play. Replace ball joints as necessary.

All Other Models — Raise and support front of vehicle and turn steering wheel to one side. Install suitable levering tool so that ball joint spring may be compressed. With spring compressed, position a vernier caliper with lower jaw on ball joint stud and upper jaw on top of clamping bolt for ball joint stud. Note reading. Slowly release tension from spring and note travel of caliper. This reading indicates ball joint play. If play exceeds .040" (1 mm) for new ball joints or .100" (2.5 mm) for used ball joints, replace ball joint. *See Volkswagen in SUSPENSION Section.*

VOLVO

Maximum permitted axial play for lower ball joint is .12" (3 mm). Check ball joint by prying back and forth with a bar. If specifications are exceeded, replace ball joints. *See Volvo in SUSPENSION Section.*

Jacking & Hoisting

ALL MANUFACTURERS

NOTE — *These illustrations are not intended to represent exact structure of each vehicle's frame, underbody or body outline. They are presented only to give the mechanic some point of reference.*

FRAME & UNDERBODY

The following illustrations indicate areas (parts) of the underbody and frame which may be used to raise and support the vehicle, using either floor jack or hoist. These points are indicated by shaded areas on the frame. See *sample illustration.*

OUTERBODY

Those points designated on the outline of the body were specifically designed to facilitate the use of the vehicle's own jack, but may also be used to raise and support the vehicle by means of a floor jack or hoist. These jacking points are indicated by circular dots on the outline of the body. See *sample illustration.* If floor jack or hoist is employed, extreme care should be exercised to avoid damaging the outer body shell.

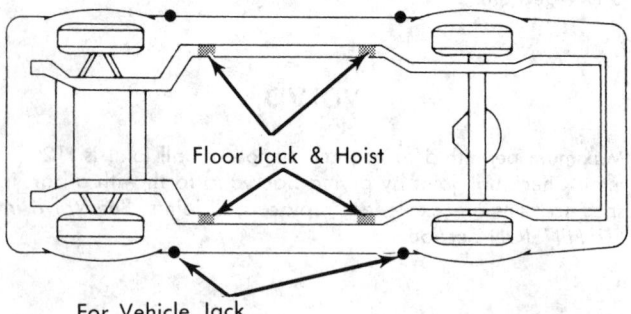

Fig. 1   Sample Jacking & Hoisting Points (Typical Illustration)

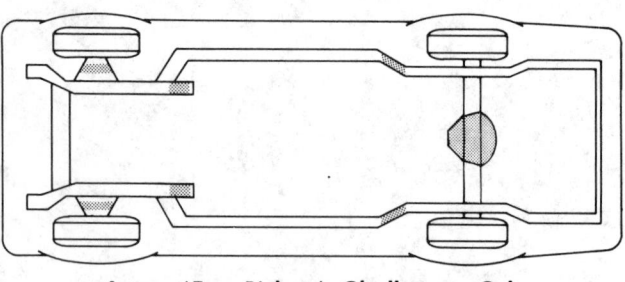

Arrow (Exc. Pickup), Challenger, Colt Station Wagon & Sapporo

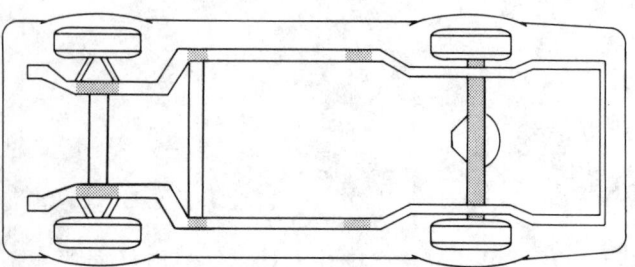

Arrow & D50 Pickups

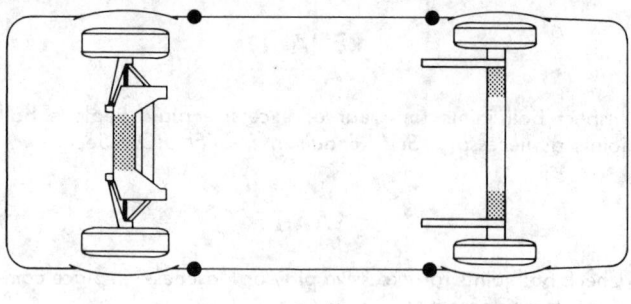

Audi

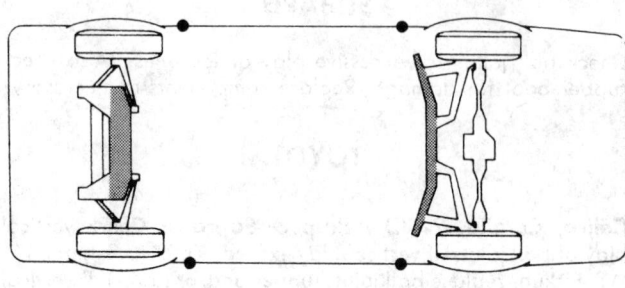

BMW

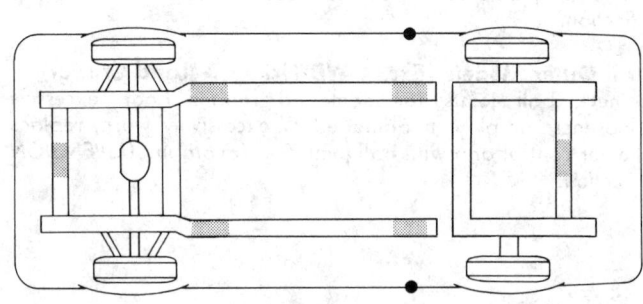

Champ & Colt Hatchbacks

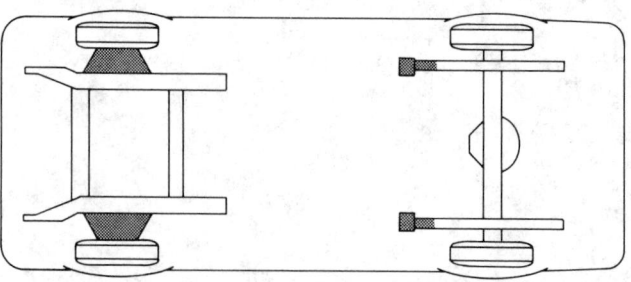

Courier

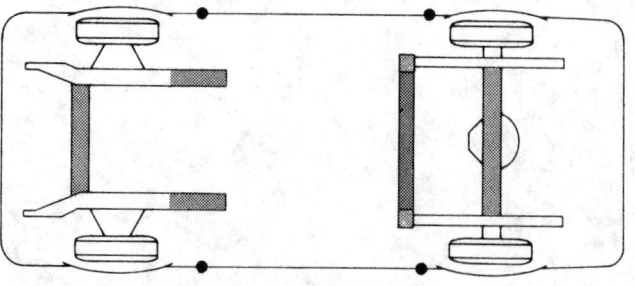

Datsun (Exc. Pickup & 310)

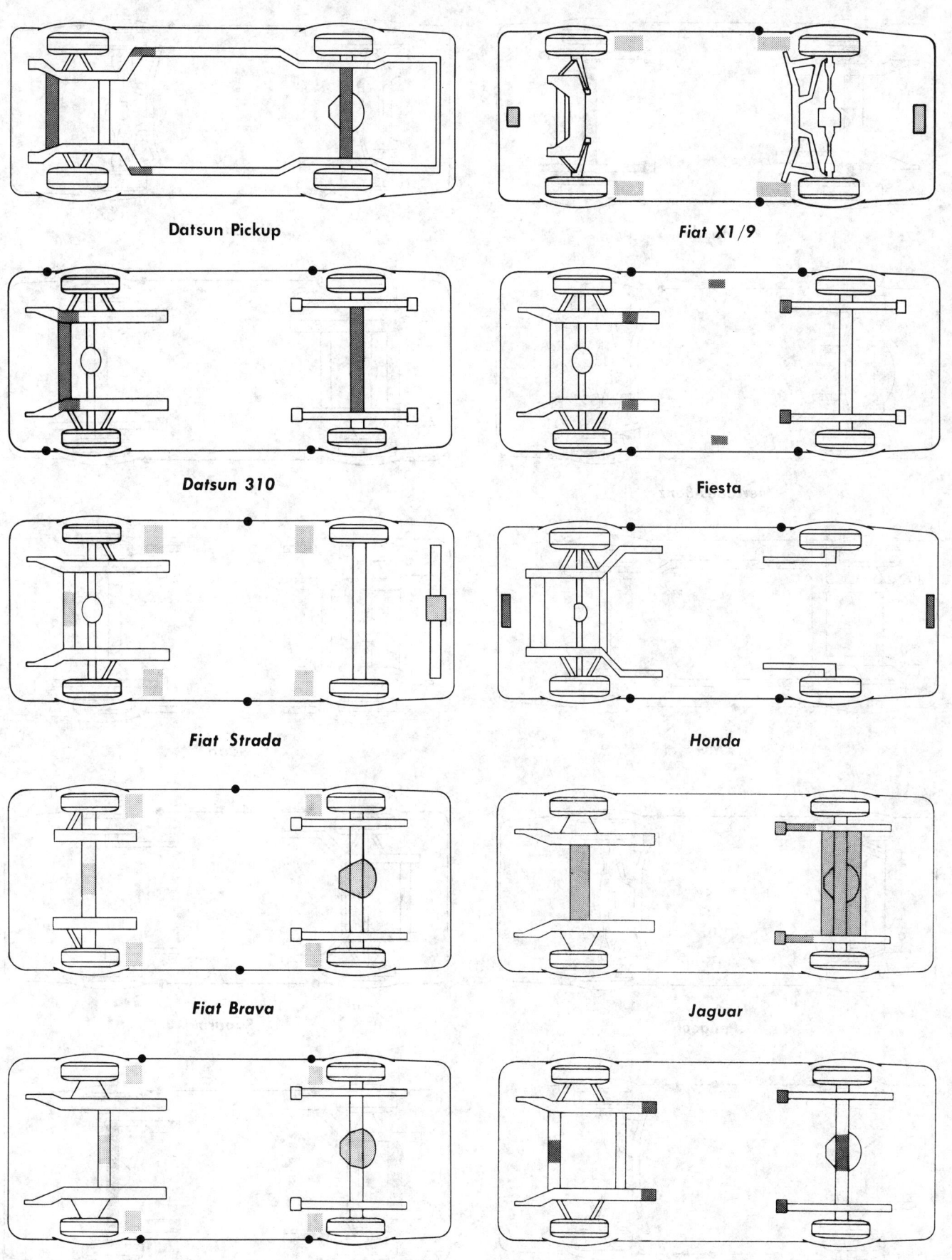

Datsun Pickup

Fiat X1/9

Datsun 310

Fiesta

Fiat Strada

Honda

Fiat Brava

Jaguar

Fiat Spider 2000

LUV

Jacking & Hoisting

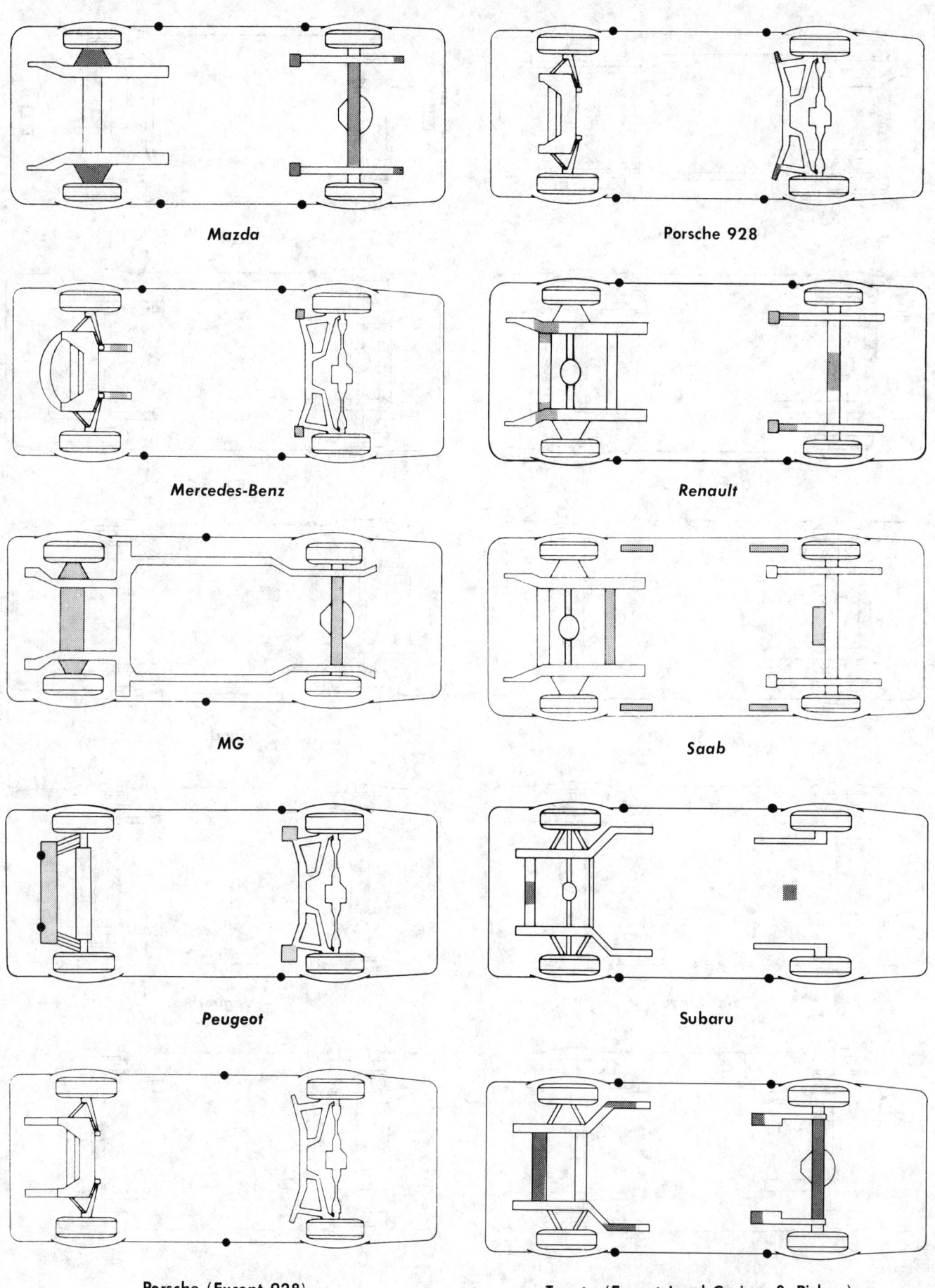

Mazda

Porsche 928

Mercedes-Benz

Renault

MG

Saab

Peugeot

Subaru

Porsche (Except 928)

Toyota (Except Land Cruiser & Pickup)

WHEEL ALIGNMENT

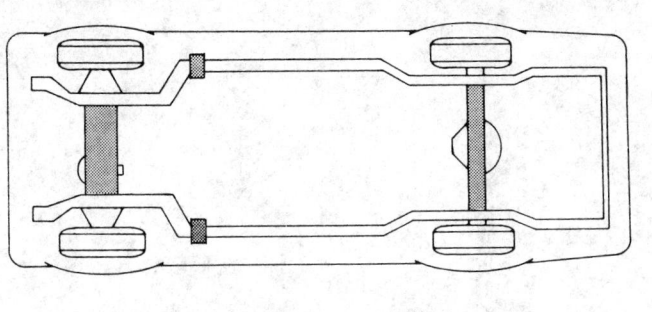

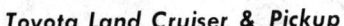

Toyota Land Cruiser & Pickup

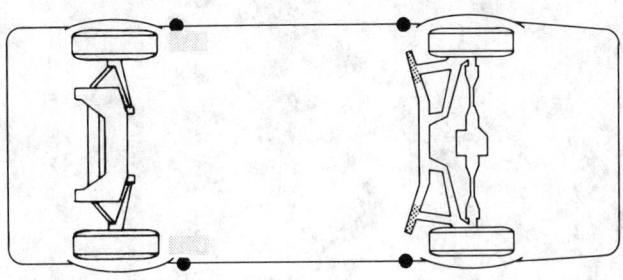

Volkswagen Pickup & Vanagon

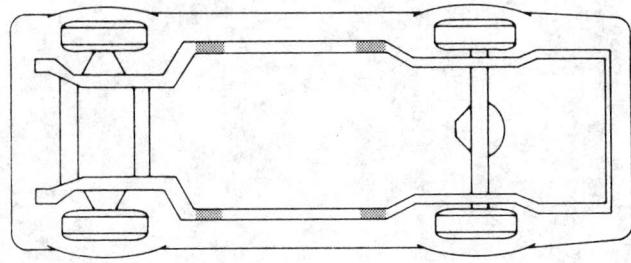

Triumph

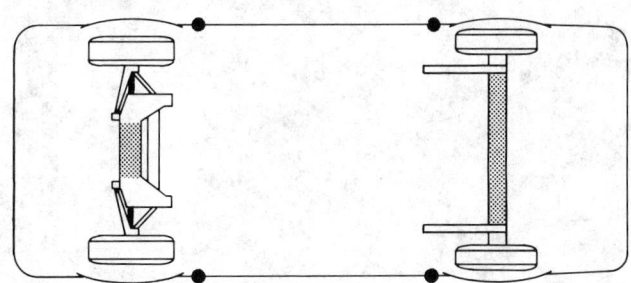

Volkswagen (Except Pickup & Vanagon)

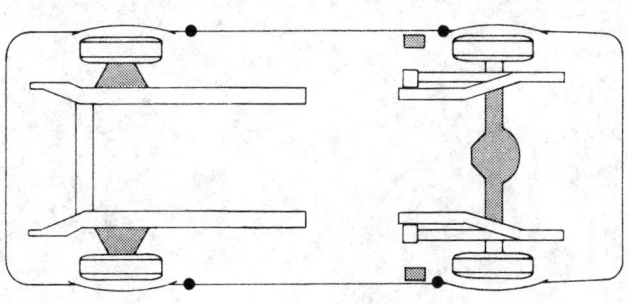

Volvo

Section 9
SUSPENSION

Contents

NOTE — ALSO SEE GENERAL INDEX.

Suspension

SUSPENSION TROUBLE SHOOTING

NOTE — *This is a general trouble shooting guide. When using this guide, locate the condition in column one that corresponds to your problem and determine the possible causes in column two. Match the number of possible cause with the same number in column three, and you will have the suggested correction.*

CONDITION	POSSIBLE CAUSE	CORRECTION
▶ Hard Steering	1) Tire pressure too low 2) Front wheels out of alignment 3) Lower control arm ball joint siezed	1) Check manufacturers recommended pressure and set to specifications 2) Check alignment and set to specifications or replace parts 3) Check specifications set or replace parts
▶ Pulls to one side	1) Crossmember broken, cracked or loose 2) Left and right side wheel base uneven 3) Loose or excessively worn wheel bearings 4) Loose wheel lug nuts	1) Replace crossmember 2) Check frame and repair 3) Adjust wheel bearings or replace 4) Tighten lug nuts
▶ Steering wheel wander	1) Excessive ball joint wear 2) Lower control arm and strut 3) Lower control arm pivot bolt (shaft) loose or sloppy 4) Lower control arm and strut damaged or worn	1) Replace ball joint or adjust if possible 2) Replace defective component bar(s) damaged 3) Tighten or replace parts 4) Inspect bushings and replace as required
▶ Body roll	1) Stabilizer broken or damaged 2) Shock absorbers worn out	1) Replace parts 2) Check and replace
▶ Noise	1) Coil spring broken 2) Bad shock absorber 3) Insufficient lubrication 4) Components loose or excessively worn 5) Damaged wheel bearing 6) Improper tire pressure	1) Replace, may be matched set 2) Check operation and replace 3) Grease fittings 4) Tighten or replace 5) Adjust or replace wheel bearings 6) Check inflation
▶ Steering hard to control	1) Broken front coil spring 2) Defective shock absorber 3) Loose control arm bushings 4) Strut assembly loose 5) Tire pressure 6) Wheel alignment out of tolerance 7) Damaged suspension links	1) Replace coil spring 2) Replace shock absorber 3) Replace bushings 4) Tighten or replace assembly 5) Check and set to specifications 6) Check and adjust or replace components 7) Replace parts

AUDI

4000
5000

DESCRIPTION

Suspension is independent type, having strut assembly, control arm and stabilizer bar. Strut assembly consists of shock absorber surrounded by a coil spring. It is attached to inner fender panel at top and is integral with steering knuckle at bottom. Lower control arm is connected by ball joint to steering knuckle and by bushing connection to frame (note configuration differences in *Fig. 1*). Stabilizer bar is connected by brackets to subframe and by bracket to control arm on 4000 and by bushing and bolt on 5000.

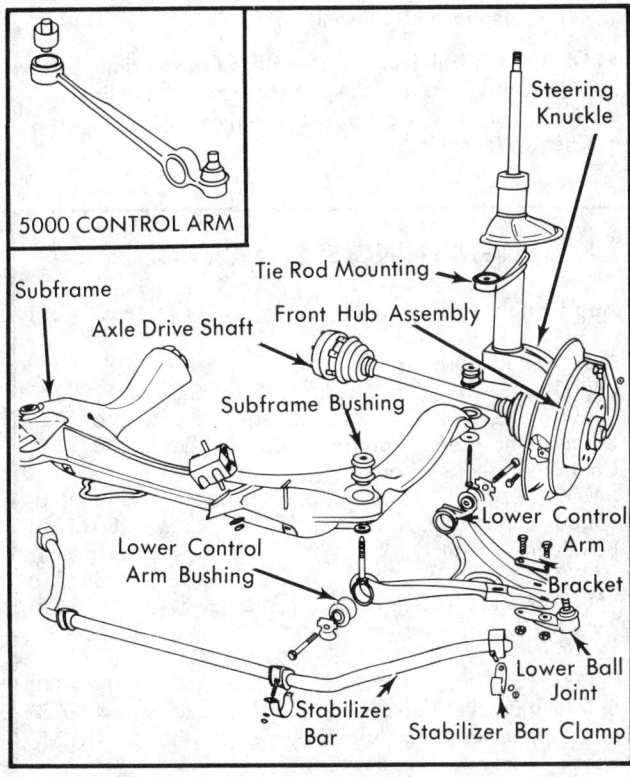

Fig. 1   Exploded View of Audi Front Suspension

ADJUSTMENTS

WHEEL ALIGNMENT SPECIFICATIONS & PROCEDURES

See Wheel Alignment Specifications and Procedures in WHEEL ALIGNMENT section.

WHEEL BEARING ADJUSTMENT

See Wheel Bearing Adjustment in WHEEL ALIGNMENT section.

BALL JOINT CHECKING

See Ball Joint Checking in WHEEL ALIGNMENT section.

REMOVAL & INSTALLATION

NOTE — *During any removal and installation procedure, if axle nut is removed or installed, do so with vehicle resting on ground at full curb weight.*

STRUT ASSEMBLY

NOTE — *When removing strut on 5000, install strut tool 2070 before removing. Mount tool retaining plate, tighten spindle and spindle nut until seated.*

Removal — 1) Loosen axle nut. Raise and support vehicle; remove wheel. Without detaching brake hose or line, unbolt caliper, remove brake hose bracket and suspend caliper out of way.

2) Detach stabilizer bar from sub-frame on 5000 and from lower control arm on 4000. Remove wheel bearing housing/ball joint clamp bolt on 4000.

3) Remove brake rotor and ball joint on 5000. On both models, use suitable tool and press off tie rod end. On 5000, remove ball joint from hub and using suitable puller attached to hub studs, press out drive shaft from hub.

4) On 4000, remove axle nut, push control arm down and pull drive shaft out of wheel bearing housing. On 5000, remove 3 nuts holding strut to body while holding strut from below. On 4000, loosen top nut on shock absorber while holding piston rod with hex wrench.

6) On 5000, pull hub off drive shaft. On both models, remove strut from vehicle.

Disassembly — 1) With strut assembly on bench, attach suitable spring compressor to coil spring and compress enough to remove upper piston rod retaining nut. Remove strut top plate.

2) Slowly release tension from coil spring and remove spring.

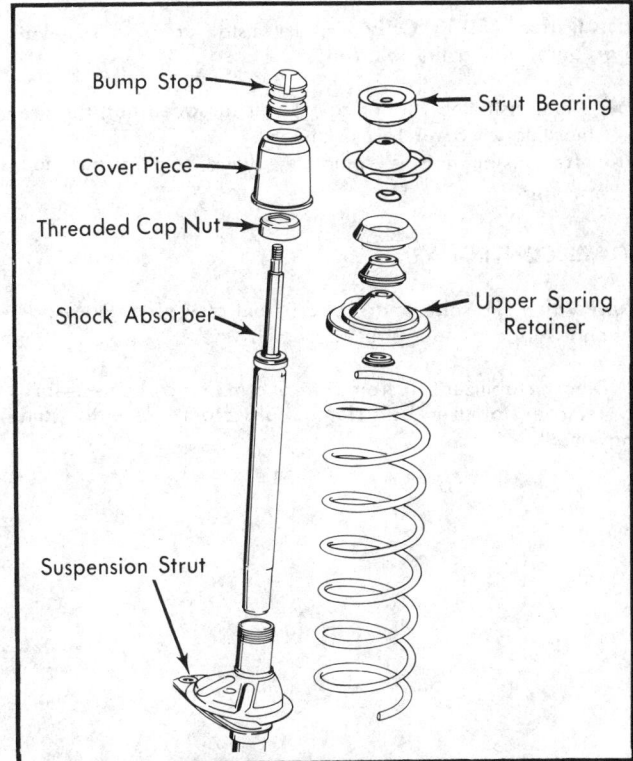

Fig. 2   Disassembled View of Strut Assembly
(4000 Shown; 5000 Similar)

AUDI (Cont.)

3) Use suitable tool (40-201A, 4000; 2069, 5000) to remove threaded cap from top of shock absorber. Remove shock absorber.

Reassembly & Installation — To reassemble and install, do so in reverse of disassembly and removal procedure, noting the following:

- On 5000 models, be sure damping ring locating tabs are mated with indentations on upper spring retainers.
- If nuts or bolts are covered with undercoat or grease, clean threads thoroughly before installation.
- Drive axle splines must be grease-free. Also, apply a narrow ring of suitable locking compound (D6) around outer end of drive shaft splines and allow 1 minute to dry before installing.
- Tighten drive axle nut with vehicle resting on ground.

SHOCK ABSORBER (ON-CAR)

Removal (5000 Only) — **1)** Leave vehicle sitting on ground at full curb weight. Remove top shock absorber nut.

2) Mark position of top retaining plate (camber adjustment) and remove 3 retaining nuts from plate and lift off plate.

3) Turn steering wheel so shock absorber rod can be aligned in center of upper spring retainer (insert piece of wood between spring and wheel housing to hold this position).

4) Remove washer, rubber bump stop, cover and threaded cap from shock absorber. Remove shock absorber.

NOTE — *Threaded cap removal may require use of special wrench 2069.*

Installation (5000 Only) — To install, reverse removal procedure, noting the following:

- When installing rubber cover over threaded nut, be sure marking on cover faces outward.
- After installation is complete, check camber and toe settings.

LOWER CONTROL ARM

Removal — **1)** Raise and support front of vehicle. Place additional support under strut assembly.

2) Detach stabilizer bar from control arm. It may be necessary to remove stabilizer bar clamp bolts from frame to gain movement.

3) Loosen control arm mounting bolts. Remove axle drive shaft if necessary.

4) On 4000, index mark ball joint nuts and bracket. Remove ball joint mounting nuts, bolts and bracket (4000) and separate ball joint from strut. Remove control arm.

Bushing Replacement — Using suitable support (VW 401) and driver (VW 409 for 4000; 2040 for 5000 inner side, VW 408a for 5000 outer side), remove old bushings from control arm. Using same tools, lubricate and replace bushings.

Installation — To install lower control arm, reverse removal procedure, noting the following:

- On 4000, if ball joint is not replaced at this time, be sure index marks made during removal are aligned.
- Tighten all nuts and bolts to specifications.
- Check alignment.

TIGHTENING SPECIFICATIONS

Application	Ft. Lbs. (mkg)
Stabilizer Bar Bracket	
4000	18 (2.5)
5000	76 (10.5)
Stabilizer Bar-to-Control Arm (5000)	80 (11.0)
Control Arm-to-Subframe	
4000	43 (6.0)
5000	80 (11.0)
Ball Joint-to-Strut Nut	
4000	36 (5.0)
5000	47 (6.5)
Axle Nut①	
4000	167 (23.1)
5000	203 (28.0)
Ball Joint Bracket Nuts (4000)	47 (6.5)
Strut Upper Retaining Nuts (5000)	18 (2.5)
Shock Absorber Threaded Cap	
4000	108 (15.0)
5000	130 (18.0)
Shock Piston Rod Nut	
4000	36 (5.0)
5000	43 (6.0)
Strut Upper Plate (5000)	18 (2.5)

① — Always replace.

BMW

320i
528i
633CSi
733i

DESCRIPTION

Strut type suspension consisting of a vertically mounted strut assembly. Strut assembly is mounted to chassis frame at top by means of a thrust bearing. Lower end of strut assembly is mounted to ball joint which is bolted to lower control arm. Strut assembly connects to ball joint by means of a steering knuckle which is bolted to strut assembly and ball joint. Strut assembly consists of a shock absorber built into strut tube. A coil spring is mounted on outside of strut assembly. A stabilizer bar is mounted to front of axle carrier (crossmember) and is connected at ends to lower control arms. On all models except 320i, a strut rod is connected to lower control arm and axle carrier.

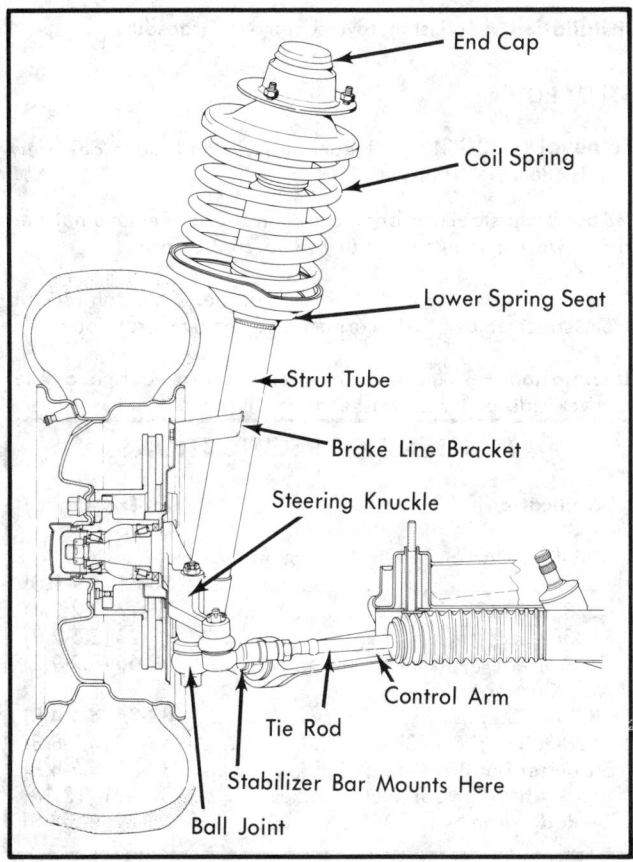

Fig. 1   BMW 320i Front Suspension Assembly

ADJUSTMENTS

WHEEL ALIGNMENT SPECIFICATIONS & PROCEDURES

See Wheel Alignment Specifications and Procedures in WHEEL ALIGNMENT Section.

WHEEL BEARINGS

See Wheel Bearing Adjustment in WHEEL ALIGNMENT Section.

BALL JOINT CHECKING

See Ball Joint Checking in WHEEL ALIGNMENT Section.

REMOVAL & INSTALLATION

Removal — 1) Raise and support vehicle. Remove front wheels. Detach brake line mounting brackets from strut tube. If equipped with brake wear sensor, unplug connector and remove ground wire at caliper. On all models, remove calipers and suspend out of way (with hydraulic lines connected). On 320i, disconnect stabilizer bar at frame.

2) Disconnect steering shaft pinch bolt at universal joint. Index mark shaft and separate from "U" joint. Drain power steering unit, detach power steering hoses and plug openings. Remove nuts from engine dampers, heat shields and engine mounts (as equipped). Remove clamps from automatic transmission cooling lines (if equipped).

3) Check along front axle for engine ground wire. If attached at this location, remove wire. Detach top strut-to-fender mountings. Using overhead hoist to support engine and a floor jack to support suspension, detach right end of front axle from frame member and lower suspension from vehicle.

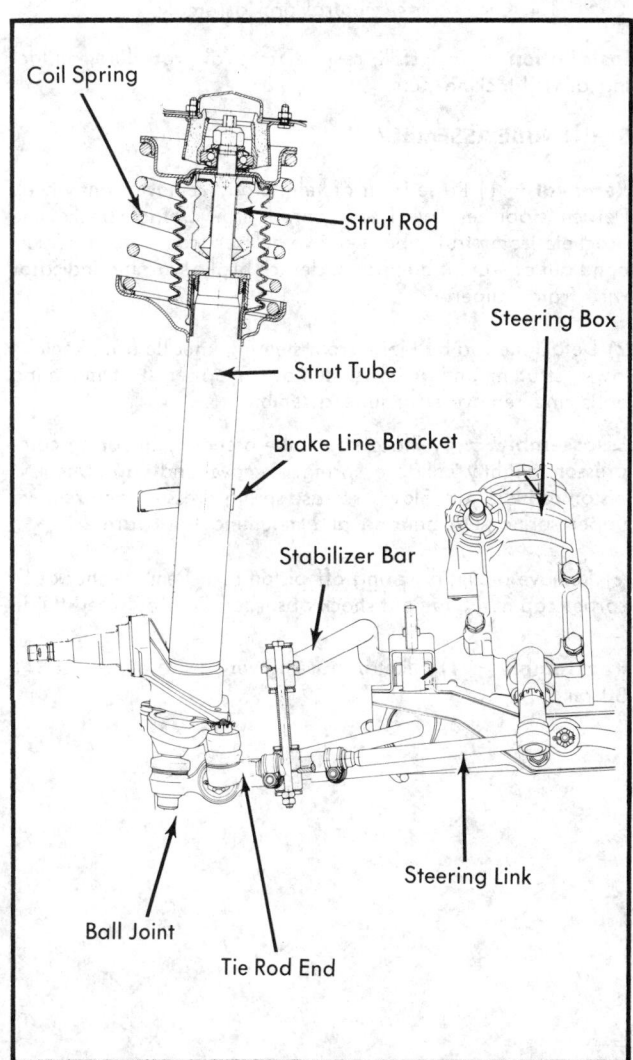

Fig. 2   BMW 528i, 633CSi and 733i Front Suspension

Front Suspension

BMW (Cont.)

Installation — To install reverse removal procedure and note the following: Make sure shoulder of engine mount engages properly in opening. Reconnect steering shaft while front wheels are pointing straight ahead. Ensure steering shaft index marks are aligned and that mounting screw engages safety groove. Check wheel alignment and bleed power steering unit, if equipped.

LOWER CONTROL ARM

Removal — **1)** Raise vehicle and remove front wheel. Disconnect stabilizer link or bar from control arm. If strut rod connects to control arm, remove from arm.

2) Detach inner end of control arm from axle carrier. On models held with castle nut only, remove castle nut and press control arm from steering knuckle. If held with safety wire, remove wire, then separate control arm and steering knuckle from shock absorber assembly.

3) Detach tie rod ball joint. Remove castle nut from steering knuckle arm (if not done so in previous step) and press control arm free.

Inspection — Check axial play of ball joint. If play exceeds .055" (1.4 mm), replace control arm assembly.

Installation — To install, reverse removal procedure, replacing all self-locking nuts.

STRUT TUBE ASSEMBLY

Removal — **1)** Raise front of vehicle and remove front wheel. Detach stabilizer bar from control arm. Detach brake line brackets from strut tube. Remove caliper from rotor and suspend out of way. If equipped, detach brake warning indicator wire from caliper.

2) Detach tie rod ball joint from steering knuckle arm. Remove lower strut mounting bolts. Remove 3 upper strut mounting bolts and remove strut tube assembly.

Disassembly — **1)** Place strut tube assembly in spring compressor. Slightly collapse spring. Remove end cap. Unscrew piston rod lock nut. Slowly release spring pressure and remove upper spring seat bearing and mounting hardware.

2) Remove auxiliary spring off piston rod. Remove shock absorber cap nut. Slide out shock absorber. Pour out used fluid.

Reassembly — **1)** Fill strut housing with 1-1.5 ounces of SAE 30 oil.

2) Fit shock absorber. Tighten cap nut. Slide auxiliary spring into place. Guide coil spring into lower spring seat. Set upper bearing mount (upper spring seat) on top of coil spring. Slide piston rod through opening, after extending rod as far as possible. Attach compressor and collapse spring enough to install upper mounting nut.

Installation — To install, reverse removal procedure and tighten all nuts and bolts.

STABILIZER BAR

Removal — Raise and support vehicle. Remove front wheels for easier access. Detach stabilizer link or bar from control arms. Remove stabilizer bar brackets and take stabilizer bar from vehicle.

NOTE — Before installation, inspect bushings for excessive wear and replace as necessary.

Installation — To install, reverse removal procedure.

STRUT ROD

Removal (633CSi) — **1)** Raise vehicle and place on safety stands. Remove front wheels.

2) Separate stabilizer bar from control arm. Remove nut and thrust washer mounting strut rod to control arm.

3) Remove opposite end strut rod nut. Separate control arm from crossmember (axle carrier) and remove strut rod.

Installation — To install, reverse removal procedure and note: Convex side of thrust washer faces nut.

TIGHTENING SPECIFICATIONS

Application	Ft. Lbs. (mkg)
Stabilizer Bar or Link-to-Control Arm	
320i	50-65 (6.9-9.0)
528i & 633CSi	16-17 (2.2-2.4)
733i	18-20 (2.5-2.8)
Control Arm-to-Axle Carrier	59-66 (8.2-9.2)
Axle Carrier-to-Body	
320i	32-35 (4.4-4.8)
528i, 633CSi & 733i	54-60 (7.5-8.3)
Stabilizer Bar Brackets	34-37 (4.3-4.8)
Shock Absorber Cap Nut	87-101 (12-14)
Tie Rod Castle Nut	25-29 (3.5-4.0)

CHRYSLER CORP. IMPORTS – EXCEPT PICKUPS

Arrow
Challenger
Champ
Colt
Sapporo

DESCRIPTION

Strut type suspension consisting of a vertically mounted strut assembly, lower control arm and stabilizer bar. Strut assembly is mounted to top of fender panel by a rubber insulator. On rear-wheel drive models, the strut assembly mounts at bottom to steering arm and pivots in ball joint. On front-wheel drive (FWD) models, the lower end of strut is bolted to a separate steering knuckle. On all models, a stabilizer bar and strut bars are attached to front chassis members and ends of lower control arms.

ADJUSTMENTS

WHEEL ALIGNMENT SPECIFICATIONS & PROCEDURES

See Wheel Alignment Specifications and Procedures in WHEEL ALIGNMENT Section.

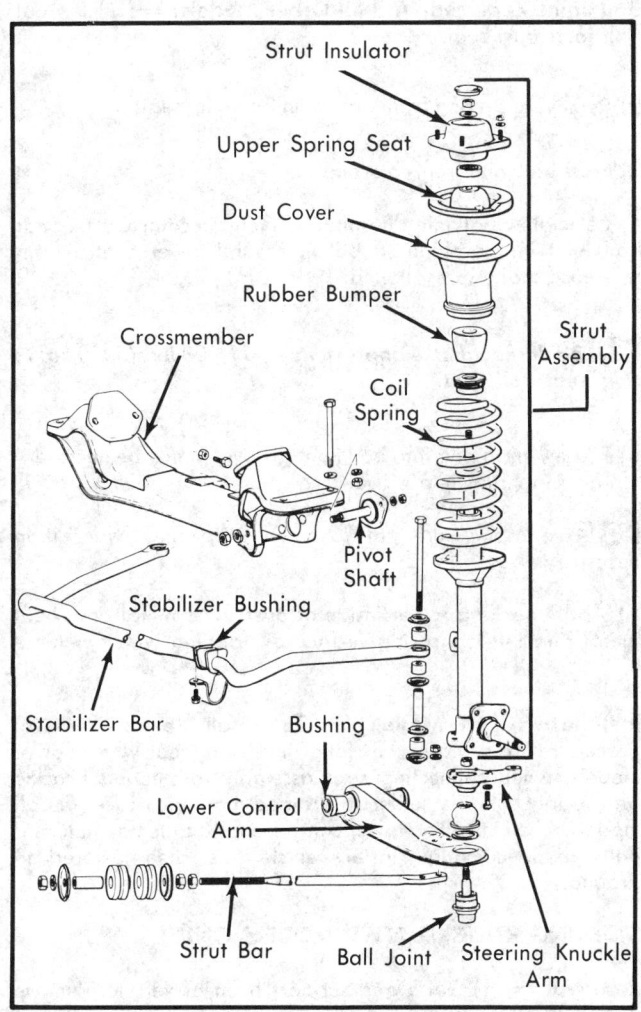

Fig. 1 Exploded View of Front Suspension (Rear-Wheel Drive Models)

WHEEL BEARING ADJUSTMENT

See Wheel Bearing Adjustment in WHEEL ALIGNMENT Section.

BALL JOINT CHECKING

See Ball Joint Checking in WHEEL ALIGNMENT Section.

REMOVAL & INSTALLATION

STRUT ASSEMBLY

Removal (FWD Models) — Raise and support front of vehicle. Remove wheel. Disconnect brake line from strut. Remove attaching nuts and bolts at ends of strut. Remove strut.

Removal (All Other Models) — 1) Raise and support front of vehicle, allowing suspension to hang free. Remove front wheel.

2) Remove caliper assembly and front hub assembly.

3) Disconnect stabilizer link and lower control arm. Remove strut assembly, knuckle arm and strut insulator retaining bolts. Remove strut assembly from vehicle.

Disassembly — 1) Clamp strut assembly in vise and use proper tool to compress coil spring. Remove dust cover. Remove nuts holding insulator to strut sub-assembly. Remove insulator and then coil spring.

NOTE — Steering knuckle is welded to strut sub-assembly and cannot be separated.

2) If oil loss is found, disassemble sub-assembly after thoroughly cleaning it. Place sub-assembly vertically in vise. Use special wrench (CT-1112) to remove seal assembly. Compress piston rod to lowest position during this procedure.

3) Drain fluid. Using small screwdriver, remove square-cut "O" ring from rod and draw out rod assembly and guide. Remove guide from piston rod.

Reassembly — 1) Clean and replace all components as required. Apply hydraulic fluid to sliding surfaces. Insert piston rod in cylinder. Compress piston ring with fingers as it slides into cylinder.

2) Assemble cylinder and piston assembly with strut outer casing. Fill unit with approximately 14 oz. of new hydraulic fluid.

3) With guide flange at top, insert piston rod until guide flange contacts shock absorber cylinder end. Install "O" ring between guide and strut outer cylinder (always use new "O" ring).

4) Cover piston rod end with seal guide (CT-1111B), slide in seal after applying oil to seal lip and tighten seal assembly until seal nut edge contacts strut outer cylinder.

NOTE — Be sure to replace seal assembly when shock absorber has been disassembled.

CHRYSLER CORP. IMPORTS — EXCEPT PICKUPS (Cont.)

5) Attach compressor to coil spring and place spring onto strut assembly. Pull shock absorber fully out and position bumper rubber and spacer.

6) Align "D" shaped hole in spring seat upper assembly with indentation on piston rod. Install insulator assembly. Install self-locking nut and tighten temporarily.

NOTE — *If replacing coil springs, be sure to use same color-code class as original.*

7) After seating upper and lower end of coil spring on grooves of spring seats, remove spring compressor. Using special tool (CT-1112) tighten spring seat and self-locking nut to specified torque.

Installation (All Models) — To install, reverse removal procedure, noting the following:

- Secure top of strut assembly to mounting bracket first. Apply sealant to lower end of assembly and connect it to knuckle arm, using dowel pins as locating guides.
- Pack strut upper bearing with grease and install dust cap. Install stabilizer, hub assembly and wheel.

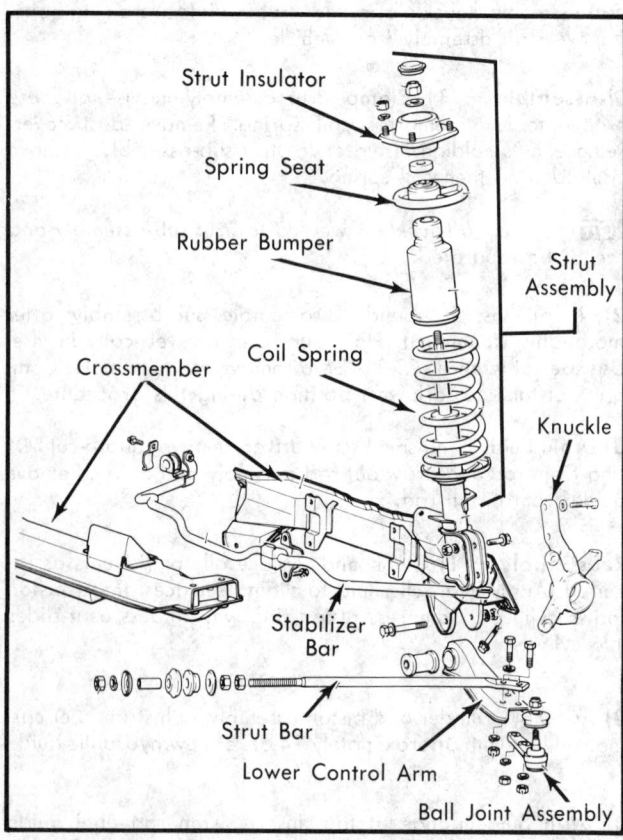

Fig. 2 Exploded View of Front Suspension (Front-Wheel Drive Models)

LOWER CONTROL ARM

Removal (FWD Models) — Raise and support front of vehicle. Disconnect ball joint and strut bar bolts from lower control arm. Remove lower control arm pivot bolt from crossmember. Remove arm assembly.

NOTE — *Do not remove the ball joint from steering knuckle unless ball joint is to be replaced.*

Removal (All Other Models) — 1) Raise and support front of vehicle. Remove front wheel(s).

2) Disconnect stabilizer bar and strut bar from lower control arm. Remove strut assembly.

3) Using suitable puller, detach tie rod ball joint from steering knuckle arm.

4) Remove bolt retaining strut assembly and steering knuckle arm. Separate them using a soft-faced hammer.

5) Turn steering wheel to gain clearance for removing lower control arm from crossmember. Using puller, disconnect knuckle arm from lower control arm ball joint.

Ball Joint Replacement (FWD Models) — Ball joint is bolted to lower control arm and steering knuckle and is replaceable as a unit.

Ball Joint Replacement (All Other Models) — 1) Pry out ball joint dust seal.

2) Remove snap ring from groove in ball joint seat.

3) Press ball joint from control arm.

4) Select new ball joint. Position ball joint in control arm. Seat ball joint into position so ball joint and lower control arm reference marks are aligned.

NOTE — *It should take approximately 11,000 lbs. (5000 kg) to fully seat ball joint.*

5) Fit new snap ring into ball joint groove. It may be necessary to tap snap ring into place.

NOTE — *Make sure not to open snap ring wider than necessary.*

6) Apply packing sealer inside of dust cover metal ring. Seat metal ring into snap ring surface by tapping with hammer.

Installation (All Models) — To install, reverse removal procedure and note the following: On rear-wheel drive models, when connecting strut assembly to steering knuckle arm, apply suitable sealer to flanged mating surface. On all models, when installing lower control arms, tighten all nuts and bolts to specifications after vehicle has been lowered to ground.

STEERING KNUCKLE (FWD MODELS ONLY)

Removal — 1) Raise and support front of vehicle. Remove wheel. Remove cotter pin, axle nut and washer. Remove underside cover. Remove strut bar and disconnect ball joint from lower control arm. Drain transaxle.

CHRYSLER CORP. IMPORTS — EXCEPT PICKUPS (Cont.)

2) Insert a pry bar between the transaxle case and the shoulder of the constant velocity joint of axle shaft. Do not insert pry bar more than .28" (7 mm) to avoid damaging inner seal. Pry axle shaft from transaxle and support.

3) Using an axle shaft puller (CT-1003 or equivalent), force axle shaft out of hub and remove from vehicle. Remove brake assembly.

4) Using a tie rod puller, remove tie rod end from knuckle. Disconnect the knuckle from strut and remove hub and knuckle as an assembly.

Installation — To install, reverse removal procedure, noting the following: Replace the constant velocity joint retainer ring each time the axle shaft is removed from transaxle case.

STABILIZER & STRUT BAR

Removal — Raise vehicle and support on safety stands. Disconnect stabilizer and strut bars from mountings on lower control arm. Remove strut bracket from body mounting position. Remove stabilizer bracket on each side and take off stabilizer. Next, lift off strut bar after noting position of all washers and bushings.

Installation — To install, reverse removal procedure and note the following: Make sure distance between strut bar end and inner lock nut is 3.1" (78.7 mm) on rear-wheel drive models or 2.6" (67 mm) on front-wheel drive models. Install strut bar bushing with convex surface to front side.

TIGHTENING SPECIFICATIONS

Application	Ft. Lbs. (mkg)
Rear-Wheel Drive Models	
Knuckle Arm-to-Ball Joint	29-43 (4.0-5.7)
Knuckle Arm-to-Tie Rod Ball Joint	29-36 (4.0-5.0)
Control Arm Flange Bolt	6-9 (0.8-1.2)
Control Arm Shaft Nut	43-51 (5.7-6.0)
Stabilizer-to-Control Arm	18-25 (2.5-3.5)
Strut Bar-to-Control Arm	36-43 (5.0-5.7)
Front-Wheel Drive Models	
Drive Axle Nut	87-130 (12.0-18.0)
Knuckle-to-Strut	54-65 (7.5-9.0)
Control Arm-to-Ball Joint	69-87 (9.5-12)
Control Arm-to-Strut Bar	69-87 (9.5-12)
Knuckle-to-Tie Rod	11-25 (1.5-3.5)
Stabilizer-to-Crossmember	18-25 (2.5-3.5)

CHRYSLER CORP. IMPORTS — PICKUPS

Arrow Pickup
D50 Pickup

DESCRIPTION

Independent front suspension with coil springs. Wheel is supported by steering knuckle mounted between upper and lower control arms by ball joints. Upper and lower control arms pivot on shafts connected to crossmember. The coil spring ends fit in pockets formed in crossmember and lower control arm. The shock absorber mounts between crossmember and lower control arm, inside the coil spring. A stabilizer bar and two strut bars mount to frame and connect to ends of lower control arms.

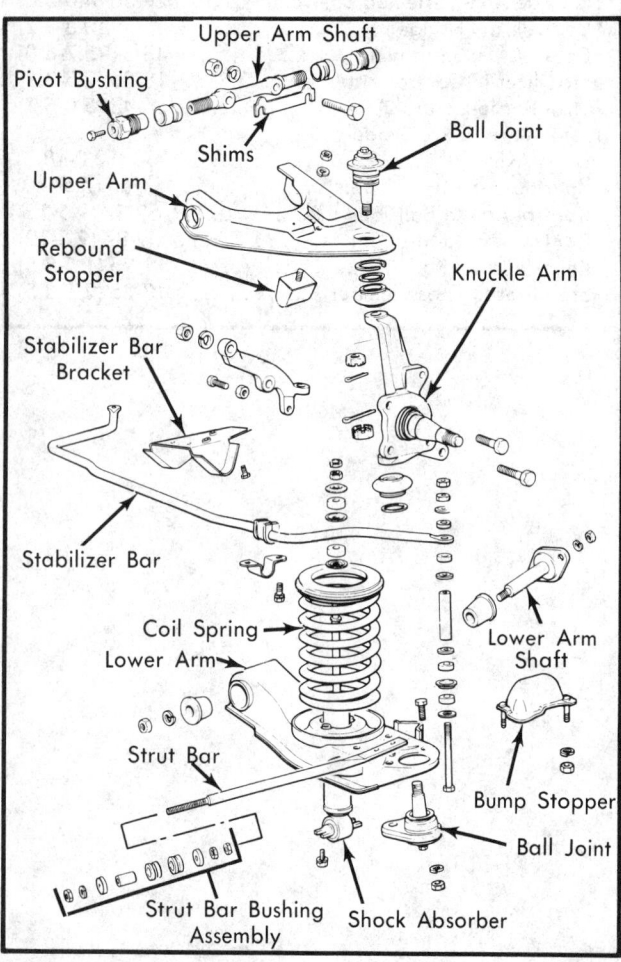

Fig. 1 Exploded View of Front Suspension Assembly

ADJUSTMENT

WHEEL ALIGNMENT SPECIFICATIONS & PROCEDURES

See Wheel Alignment Specifications & Procedures in WHEEL ALIGNMENT Section.

WHEEL BEARING ADJUSTMENT

See Wheel Bearing Adjustment in WHEEL ALIGNMENT Section.

BALL JOINT CHECKING

See Ball Joint Checking in WHEEL ALIGNMENT Section.

REMOVAL & INSTALLATION

SHOCK ABSORBERS

Removal — Raise and support front of vehicle. Remove upper shock mounting nuts and bushings. Remove lower shock mounting bolts and remove shock absorber.

Installation — To install, reverse removal procedure.

STEERING KNUCKLE

Removal — 1) Raise and support front of vehicle. Remove wheel, brake assembly and hub.

2) Loosen nuts at forward end of strut bar, then disconnect it from control arm. Disconnect stabilizer bar from control arm. Remove shock absorber.

3) Using spring compressor, compress coil spring. Remove cotter pins and nuts from upper and lower ball joint studs. Use ball joint removal tool to disconnect ball joints from knuckle.

4) Loosen spring compressor slowly, and remove knuckle and coil spring.

Installation — To install, reverse removal procedure.

LOWER CONTROL ARM, COIL SPRING & BALL JOINT

Removal — 1) Raise and support front of vehicle. Loosen nuts at forward end of strut bar. Disconnect stabilizer bar and strut bar from control arm. Remove shock absorber.

2) Use coil spring compressor to compress coil spring. Remove cotter pin and nut from lower arm ball joint stud.

3) Use ball joint tool to disconnect lower ball joint from knuckle. Loosen coil spring compressor and remove coil spring.

4) Remove lower arm pivot shaft and remove lower control arm.

Inspection — Inspect arm, bushings and ball joint for wear or damage. Replace defective parts as necessary.

Installation — To install, reverse removal procedure noting the following: Install pivot shaft to crossmember and tighten bolts, leaving shaft nut loose. Tighten shaft nut to specifications after vehicle has been lowered to the ground. The distance from the forward end of the strut bar to the face of the rear adjusting nut is 3.9" (100 mm).

UPPER CONTROL ARM & BALL JOINT

Removal — 1) Raise and support front of vehicle. Remove wheel and shock absorber. Use a coil spring compressor to compress the coil spring.

2) Remove cotter pin and nut from upper ball joint. Using a ball joint tool, disconnect ball joint from knuckle.

CHRYSLER CORP. IMPORTS — PICKUPS (Cont.)

3) Remove bolts attaching upper control arm shaft to crossmember. Remove upper control arm as an assembly.

Inspection — Inspect arm, bushings and ball joint for wear or damage. Replace parts as necessary.

Ball Joint Replacement — Ball joints are removed and installed with a press and suitable adapters. The ball joint requires a minimum press load 2200 lbs. (998 kg) for removal and an initial 1550 lbs. (703 kg) during installation. Final press load required to seat ball joint is 11,000 lbs. (4989 kg). Install a new snap ring and dust cover on ball joint.

Installation — To install, reverse removal procedure, noting the following: Reinstall camber shims in original location between upper arm shaft and crossmember. Check wheel alignment.

TIGHTENING SPECIFICATIONS

Application	Ft. Lbs. (mkg)
Shock Absorber Mount Bolts	6-9 (.83-1.24)
Shock Absorber Mount Nut	9-13 (.83-1.8)
Lower Arm Shaft Nut	40-54 (5.5-7.5)
Strut Bar Lock Nut	54-61 (7.5-8.4)
Ball Joint-to-Lower Arm	22-30 (3.0-4.1)
Upper Ball Joint-to-Knuckle	43-65 (5.9-9.0)
Lower Ball Joint-to-Knuckle	87-130 (12.0-18.0)
Upper Arm Pivot Bushing	181-253 (25.0-35.1)
Upper Arm Shaft-to-Crossmember	40-54 (5.5-7.5)
Strut Bar-to-Lower Arm	51-61 (7.0-8.4)

Pickup

DESCRIPTION

Independent type suspension, consisting of upper and lower control arms and wheel spindle mounted between upper and lower arms by means of ball joints. Upper control arm pivots on a shaft attached to frame. Lower control arm pivots on a shaft mounted to crossmember. A coil spring is mounted between lower control arm and frame. Shock absorber is hydraulic, double-action type mounted inside coil spring.

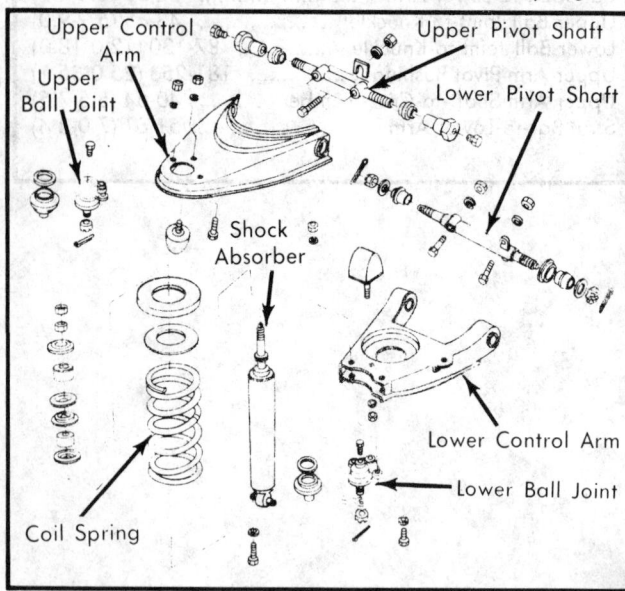

Fig. 1 Exploded View of Front Suspension Assembly

ADJUSTMENT

WHEEL ALIGNMENT SPECIFICATIONS & PROCEDURES

See Wheel Alignment Specifications and Procedures in WHEEL ALIGNMENT Section.

WHEEL BEARING ADJUSTMENT

See Wheel Bearing Adjustment in WHEEL ALIGNMENT Section.

BALL JOINT CHECKING

See Ball Joint Checking in WHEEL ALIGNMENT Section.

REMOVAL & INSTALLATION

SHOCK ABSORBERS

Removal — Remove nut, rubber bushing and washer attaching upper end of shock absorber to crossmember. Remove lower retaining bolts holding shock absorber to lower control arm. Remove shock absorber from vehicle.

Installation — To install, reverse removal procedure and tighten mounting bolts to specifications.

UPPER BALL JOINT & CONTROL ARM

Removal — 1) Raise and suitably support vehicle under lower control arm. Lower vehicle until arm is off rubber bumper stop.

Remove tire and wheel. Remove cotter pin and nut attaching upper ball joint to spindle.

2) Tap with a hammer to break ball joint loose and separate it from spindle. Remove 3 retaining nuts and bolts and remove ball joint from control arm. Open hood and remove 2 upper arm retaining bolts. Remove control arm from vehicle.

Installation — Position ball joint in upper arm and tighten bolts. Install control arm in vehicle and tighten bolts. Install spindle on ball joint, tighten nut and install cotter pin. Install tire and wheel, remove safety stands and lower vehicle. Check wheel alignment.

LOWER CONTROL ARM, BALL JOINT & COIL SPRING

Removal — 1) Raise vehicle and place safety stands under frame behind both lower control arms. Remove wheel and tire. Remove lower shock absorber bolts and collapse shock absorber up into spring. Remove retaining bolt attaching stabilizer bar to lower control arm.

2) Install a floor jack under spring area of lower arm and raise arm to relieve spring pressure. Remove cotter pin and nut attaching lower control arm to spindle, strike tapered fit with hammer and separate ball joint from spindle.

3) Remove three bolts and nuts retaining ball joint to lower control arm and remove ball joint. Release jack and lower arm enough to remove coil spring. Remove three bolts and nuts retaining lower control arm to crossmember and remove arm from vehicle.

Installation — 1) Place lower control arm in position, install three retaining bolts and nuts, DO NOT tighten. Place coil spring in position in lower arm and hold in place with a "C" clamp. Place upper end of spring in pocket in frame and raise lower control arm with a jack.

2) Position ball joint in lower arm and tighten bolts. Raise lower control arm with jack enough to install ball joint in spindle, refit nut.

3) Tighten three lower arm retaining bolts left loose. Pull shock absorber down and tighten retaining bolts. Install stabilizer bar as previously outlined. Install tire and wheel, remove safety stands and lower vehicle. Check caster, camber and toe-in.

TIGHTENING SPECIFICATIONS

Application	Ft. Lbs. (mkg)
Upper Ball Joint Stud	47(6.5)
Lower Ball Joint Stud	65(9.0)
Ball Joint-to-Upper Arm	17(2.4)
Ball Joint-to-Lower Arm	65(9.0)
Shock Absorber	
Lower Mount	14.5(2.0)
Upper Mount	①
Control Arm-to-Frame	
Lower	62(8.6)
Upper	69(9.5)
Lower Arm Shaft-to-Lower Arm	61.5(8.5)
Bumper-to-Lower Arm	65(9.0)
Bumper-to-Upper Arm	17(2.4)
① — Distance from top of lock nut to top of shock absorber stud should be .256" (6.5 mm).	

DATSUN 200SX, 210, 280ZX, 510 & 810

DESCRIPTION

Strut type suspension consisting of a vertically mounted strut assembly, lower control arm, stabilizer bar and compression rod. Strut assembly is mounted at top to chassis frame by a thrust bearing and at bottom to lower control arm by a ball joint. Strut assembly consists of a shock absorber built into outer strut tube, a coil spring mounted on outside of strut tube, and a wheel spindle integral with bottom of strut tube. Compression rod is mounted between lower control arm and chassis. Stabilizer bar is mounted to front chassis member and is connected at end of lower control arm.

ADJUSTMENTS

WHEEL ALIGNMENT SPECIFICATIONS & PROCEDURES

See Wheel Alignment Specifications & Procedures in WHEEL ALIGNMENT Section.

WHEEL BEARING ADJUSTMENT

See Wheel Bearing Adjustment in WHEEL ALIGNMENT Section.

BALL JOINT CHECKING

See Ball Joint Checking in WHEEL ALIGNMENT Section.

REMOVAL & INSTALLATION

SPRING & STRUT ASSEMBLY

Removal — 1) Raise and support front of vehicle. Remove front wheels. Detach brake hose from bracket on front strut (if required). Remove caliper assembly retaining bolts and remove caliper from axle.

2) Remove bolts holding strut to knuckle arm. Detach knuckle arm from bottom of strut by forcing off with suitable pry bar.

3) Place jack under strut to support it when nuts are removed. Remove 3 nuts holding strut to hood ledge and remove strut and spring as an assembly.

Disassembly — 1) Thoroughly clean strut assembly. Fix assembly in suitable holding tool (KV48100300) and clamp tool in vise.

2) With spring compressor, press spring down just far enough to permit turning of strut mounting insulator and remove self-locking nut.

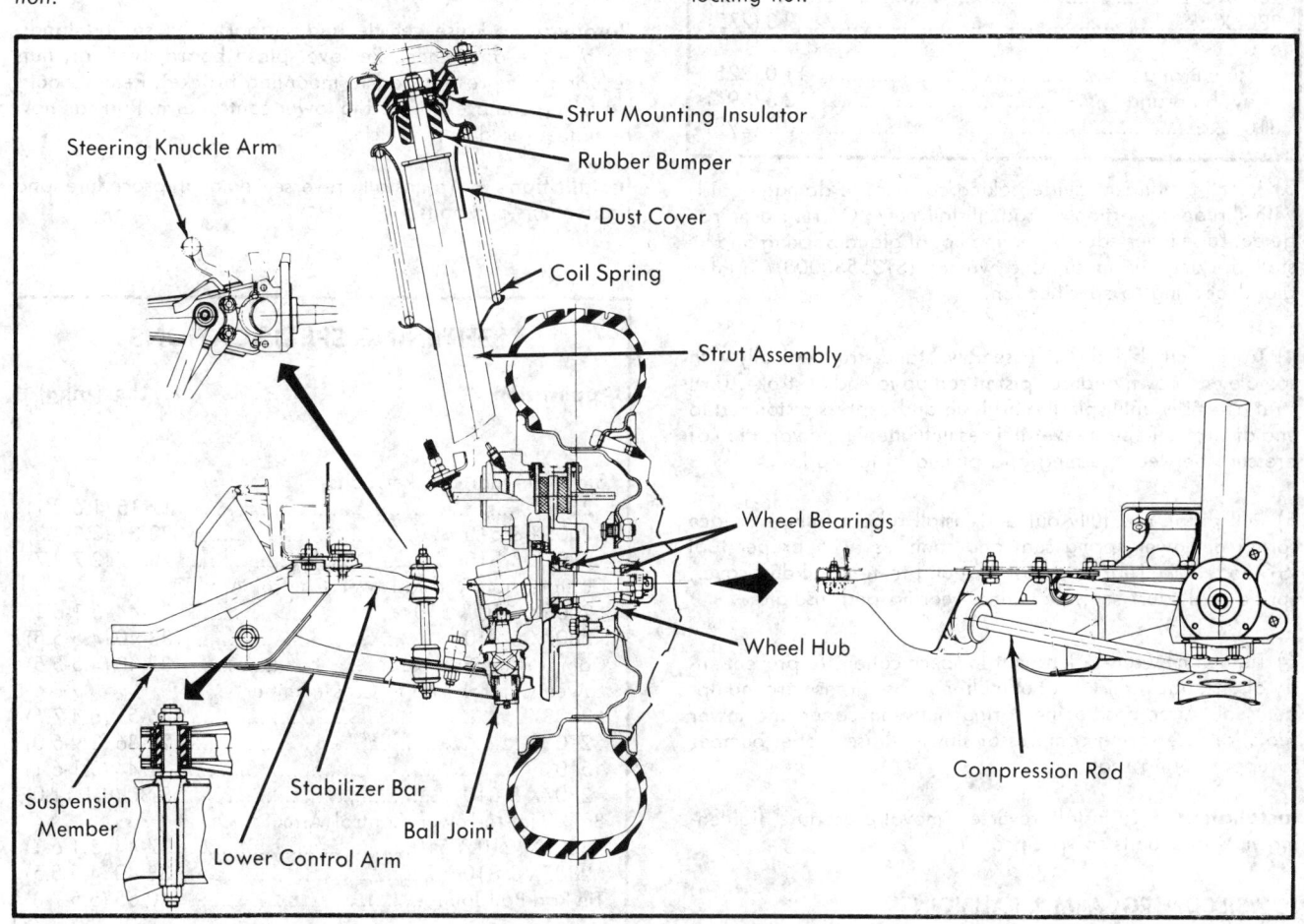

Fig. 1   Assembled View of 210 Front Suspension, with Some Items Shown in Detail (All Other Models Are Similar)

DATSUN 200SX, 210, 280ZX, 510 & 810 (Cont.)

NOTE — *Be sure spring tool evenly engages on at least 3 coils. Do not hit piston rod of strut with spring tool.*

3) Take out strut insulator, bearing, dust seal, upper spring seat, spring and rubber bumper.

4) Push piston rod down until it bottoms. Remove gland packing using suitable wrench (ST35500001). Remove "O" ring from top of piston rod guide and lift out piston rod and cylinder.

NOTE — *The piston rod, piston rod guide and cylinder are furnished as a matched set with precision mating surfaces.*

5) Drain fluid from inner and outer cylinder and discard. Wash all parts in solvent.

Reassembly — **1)** Install strut outer casing onto suitable holding tool (KV48100300). Install cylinder and piston rod assembly (shock absorber kit) in outer casing.

2) Remove piston rod guide from cylinder and pour in specified amount of new fluid (outer casing).

Strut Oil Replacement Amounts	
Application	**Oz. (cc)**
200SX & 210	11.0 (325)
280ZX	9.3 (275)
510	
Atsugi Brand	11.0 (325)
Kayaba Brand	13.3 (394)
810	10.1 (299)

3) Install piston rod guide, taking care not to damage guide with threaded portion of rod. Install new "O" ring over rod guide. Lube inner edge of sealing lips of gland packing and install packing, using suitable wrench (ST35530000). Tighten gland packing to specification.

4) To correctly bleed strut assembly, stand strut vertically with spindle end down and pull piston rod up to end of stroke. Turn strut assembly until spindle end is up and depress piston rod to end of stroke. Repeat several times until there is no variation of pressure between pushing and pulling piston rod.

5) Pull piston rod fully out and install rubber bumper. Place spring on lower spring seat and compress with proper tool (ST35651001). Lubricate dust seal and then install dust cover, spring seat, dust seal, mounting bearing and insulator.

6) Tighten new self-locking nut to specification. To prevent entry of dirt, apply thick coat of multi-purpose grease around upper seal. After positioning spring between upper and lower seats, release spring compressor slowly. Raise rubber bumper to upper spring seat.

Installation — To install, reverse removal procedure, tightening nuts and bolts to specification.

LOWER CONTROL ARM & BALL JOINT

Removal — **1)** Raise vehicle. Support with stands. Remove tire, wheel and splash guard (if equipped).

2) Detach tie rod at ball socket. Remove steering knuckle arm bolts and separate arm from bottom of strut. Separate compression rod and stabilizer bar from lower control arm. Remove bolt connecting lower control arm to crossmember. Remove lower control arm with ball joint and knuckle arm.

3) Place arm in vise, loosen control arm ball joint bolts and remove ball joint. Place steering knuckle arm in vise and remove cotter pin and nut. Remove knuckle from control arm.

4) With suitable tool (ST36720000), extract bushing, from lower control arm.

NOTE — *On 810 models, steering gear arm must be separated from sector shaft and steering linkage lowered to remove lower control arm from driver's side. On passenger side, idler arm assembly must be separated from frame and linkage lowered.*

Installation — Using suitable bushing replacement tool set (ST36700000) press bushing into control arm. To install lower control arm, reverse removal procedure. Do not tighten nuts and bolts to final torque until weight of vehicle is on front wheels.

COMPRESSION RODS

Removal — Raise vehicle and support with safety stands; remove tire and wheel. Remove splash board, back off nuts securing compression rod to mounting bracket. Remove bolts attaching compression rod to lower control arm. Rod can now be maneuvered from vehicle.

Installation — To install, reverse removal procedure and tighten nuts and bolts.

TIGHTENING SPECIFICATIONS	
Application	**Ft. Lbs. (mkg)**
Stabilizer Bar Bracket Bolts	
210	12-15 (1.6-2.1)
200SX & 510	23-31 (3.2-4.3)
280ZX & 810	20-27 (2.7-3.7)
Compression Rod-to-Lower Control Arm	
200SX, 210 & 510	37-44 (5.1-6.1)
280ZX & 810	33-40 (4.5-5.5)
Compression Rod Nut	33-40 (4.5-5.5)
Lower Control Arm-to-Crossmember	
200SX	46-55 (6.4-7.6)
210	28-36 (3.9-5.0)
510	37-44 (5.1-6.1)
280ZX & 810	58-80 (8.1-11.0)
Ball Joint-to-Lower Control Arm	
200SX, 210 & 510	37-44 (5.1-6.1)
280ZX & 810	33-40 (4.5-5.5)
Tie Rod Ball Joint	40-55 (5.5-7.6)

DATSUN 310

DESCRIPTION

All models use a strut type front suspension system. Shock absorbers are built into each strut. Upper end of strut is mounted to inner fender panel. Lower end is connected by a ball joint to lower control arm. Control arm mounts at two points on subframe. Steering knuckle is removable from strut. Knuckle bolts to strut with four bolts and has a hole for axle drive shafts to pass through.

ADJUSTMENTS

WHEEL ALIGNMENT SPECIFICATIONS & PROCEDURES

See Wheel Alignment Specifications and Procedures in WHEEL ALIGNMENT Section.

WHEEL BEARING ADJUSTMENT

See Wheel Bearing Adjustment in WHEEL ALIGNMENT Section.

BALL JOINT CHECKING

See Ball Joint Checking in WHEEL ALIGNMENT Section.

REMOVAL & INSTALLATION

CONTROL ARM

Removal — Raise and support vehicle with safety stands. Remove tire and wheel. Remove bolts securing lower control arm to ball joint. Take off nut mounting stabilizer bar to control arm. Disconnect control arm from subframe by removing two mounting bolts.

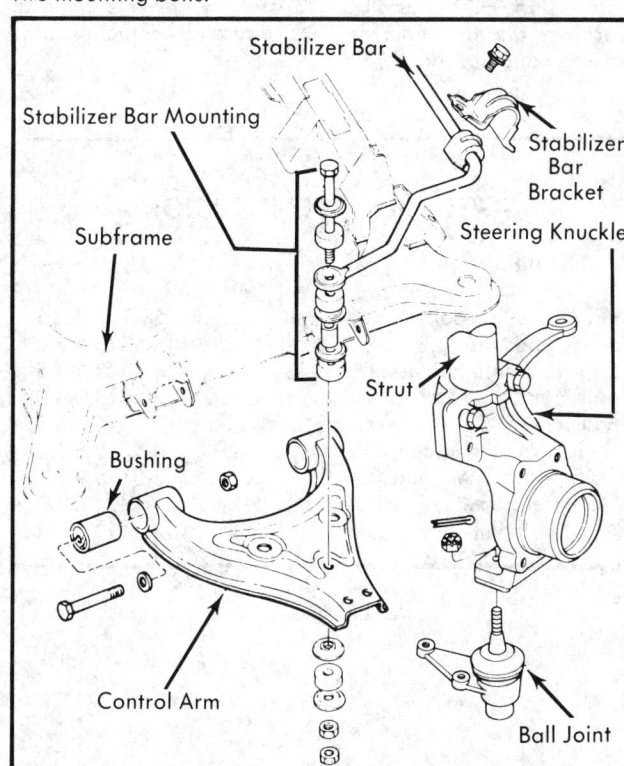

Fig. 1   Exploded View of Control Arm and Stabilizer Bar

Inspection — Inspect arm for distortion. Replace control arm bushings using a press. Make sure new bushings extend evenly on both sides of hole.

Installation — To install, reverse removal procedure and note: Control arm bolts must be tightened with weight of vehicle on ground.

STEERING KNUCKLE

Removal — Raise vehicle and place on safety stands. Remove tire and wheel. Detach and plug brake line and remove brake caliper. Remove axle nut. Using a puller, remove stub axle and brake rotor assembly from axle shaft. Disconnect ball joint and support control arm. Remove 4 bolts securing steering knuckle to strut.

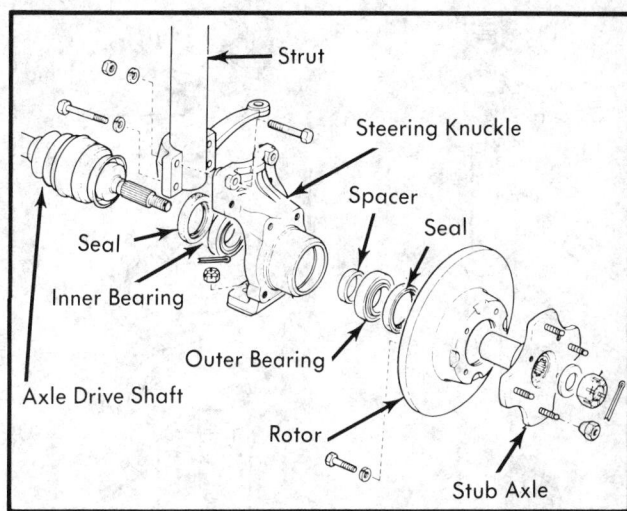

Fig. 2   Exploded View of Steering Knuckle and Strut

Installation — To install, reverse removal procedure and note: Adjust wheel bearings.

BALL JOINT

Removal — Raise vehicle and support on safety stands. Remove tire and wheel. Remove ball joint stud nut. Use ball joint driver and hammer to drive ball joint stud out of knuckle. Remove bolts securing ball joint to lower control arm.

NOTE — Take care not to damage ball joint dust cover.

Installation — To install ball joint, reverse removal procedure and make sure new cotter pin is installed. Replace ball joint dust cover if cracked.

STABILIZER BAR

Removal — **1)** Raise vehicle and support on safety stands. Support subframe with jack. Disconnect exhaust pipe from exhaust manifold and front body mount. Disconnect transmission control linkage and transmission support rod at transmission.

2) Remove stabilizer-to-control arm nuts. Loosen, but do not remove, subframe attaching bolts. Lower subframe just enough to allow removal of stabilizer bar clamp bolts from subframe. Remove stabilizer bar from vehicle.

Front Suspension

DATSUN 310 (Cont.)

Installation — To install, reverse removal procedure and replace any bushing that is worn or cracked.

STRUT ASSEMBLY

Removal — 1) Raise vehicle and suitably support with safety stands. Remove tire and wheel. Working from inside engine compartment, remove cap. Partially loosen lock nut mounting piston rod. Disconnect brake line and plug opening. Detach tie rod from steering knuckle.

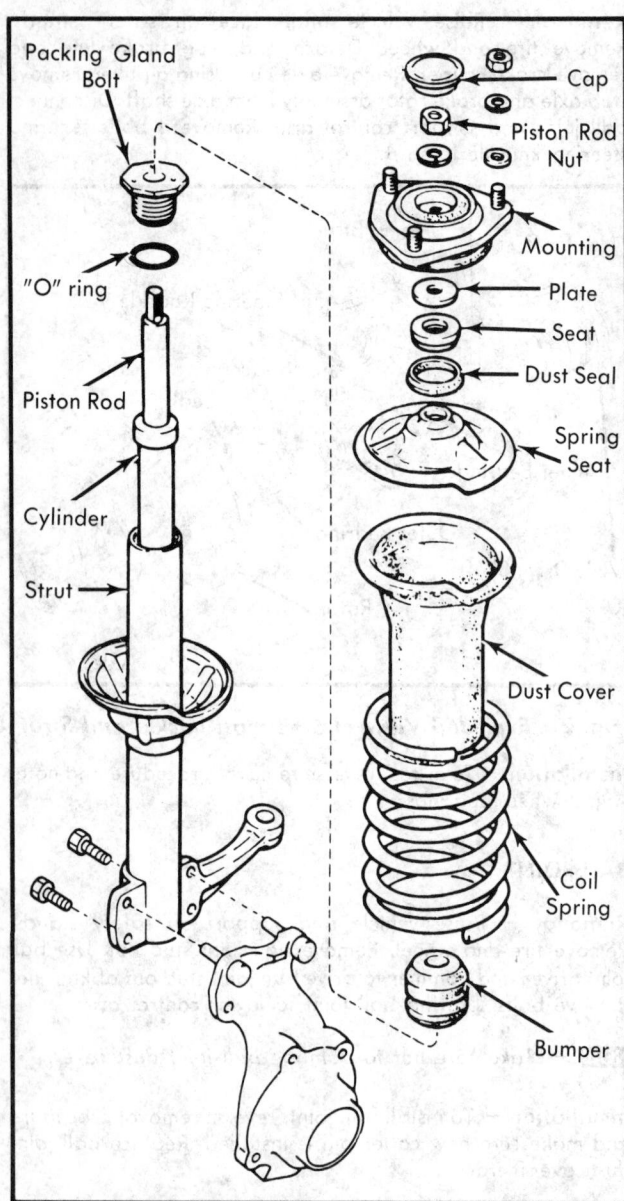

Fig. 3   Exploded View of Strut Assembly

Labels on figure:
Packing Gland Bolt
"O" ring
Piston Rod
Cylinder
Strut
Cap
Piston Rod Nut
Mounting
Plate
Seat
Dust Seal
Spring Seat
Dust Cover
Coil Spring
Bumper

2) Place safety stand under control arm for support. Remove four bolts mounting strut to steering knuckle. Remove three nuts keeping upper portion of strut to inner fender panel. Maneuver strut and coil spring assembly from vehicle.

Disassembly — 1) Place strut in a vise and use a spring compressor to slightly compress coil spring. Remove piston rod nut and all upper mounting hardware.

2) Push piston rod into cylinder until it bottoms. Remove packing gland bolt. Remove "O" ring, then slowly lift out piston rod and cylinder as a unit. Drain all fluid from inner cylinder and strut casing. Discard inner cylinder. Flush strut casing with solvent.

Inspection — Inspect all components for damage or excessive wear. Always replace packing gland and "O" ring.

Reassembly — 1) Install cylinder and piston rod in strut casing. Remove piston rod guide from cylinder. Add 7 oz. (210 cc) of strut oil to Atsugi struts or 7.4 oz. (220 cc) to K.Y.B. struts. Place piston rod guide in cylinder and install new "O" ring over rod guide. Install and tighten gland packing bolt.

NOTE — *Lubricate gland packing bolt sealing lips with multi-purpose grease.*

2) Bleed air from cylinder by pumping piston rod in and out until equal resistance is felt on inward and outward strokes. Refit coil spring on strut.

NOTE — *Install a new piston rod nut, but do not torque it until strut is installed in vehicle.*

Installation — To install strut assembly, reverse removal procedure and note following: Make sure all contact surfaces are clean and dirt free.

TIGHTENING SPECIFICATIONS

Application	Ft. Lbs. (mkg)
Packing Gland Bolt	58-116 (8-16)
Piston Rod Nut	46-53 (6.3-7.3)
Strut-to-Steering Knuckle	24-33 (3.3-4.5)
Ball Joint Stud Nut	2-29 (3.0-4.0)
Ball Joint-to-Control Arm	0-47 (5.5-6.5)
Caliper Mounting Bolt	0-47 (5.5-6.5)
Control Arm Mounting Nut	2-51 (5.8-7.0)
Stabilizer Bar	6-9 (.8-1.2)
Axle Shaft Nut	87-145 (12-20)

DATSUN PICKUP

DESCRIPTION

Front suspension is an independent type with upper and lower control arms which are connected by ball joints. This suspension also incorporates a torsion bar which connects to lower control arm inner end and to frame bracket, a strut rod which connects to lower control arm outer end and a stabilizer bar. A double-acting shock absorber is also used. See Fig. 1.

ADJUSTMENT

WHEEL ALIGNMENT SPECIFICATIONS & PROCEDURES

See Wheel Alignment Specifications & Procedures in WHEEL ALIGNMENT Section.

WHEEL BEARING ADJUSTMENT

See Wheel Bearing Adjustment in WHEEL ALIGNMENT Section.

BALL JOINT CHECKING

See Ball Joint Checking in WHEEL ALIGNMENT Section.

REMOVAL & INSTALLATION

SHOCK ABSORBER

Removal — Turn steering wheel to either side to provide access to shock absorber. Disconnect upper and lower fixing nuts. Remove shock absorber, noting positions of mounting hardware.

Installation — To install, reverse removal procedure and tighten nuts and bolts to specifications.

TORSION BAR

Removal — 1) Raise and support vehicle. Remove torsion bar anchor bolt. On 2-WD models, remove dust cover and detach snap ring from anchor arm.

2) On all models, pull anchor arm rearward. Withdraw torsion bar rearward. Remove torsion bar torque arm.

Installation — 1) Install torque arm to lower control arm. On 2-WD, set snap ring and dust cover to torsion bar. On all models, coat serrations on torsion bar with grease and install torsion bar to torque arm.

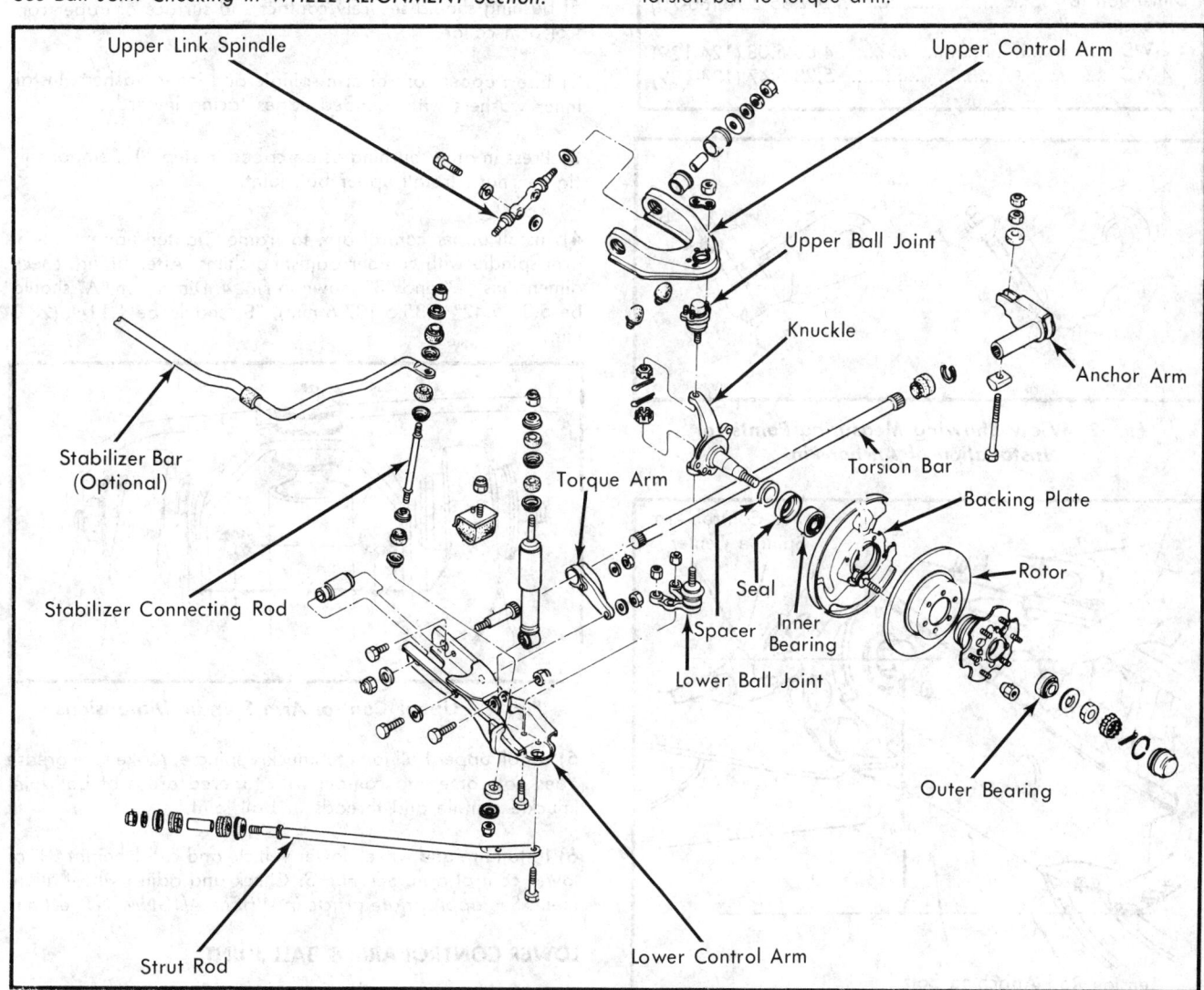

Fig. 1 Exploded View of Datsun Pickup Front Suspension
(2-WD Shown, 4-WD Similar)

DATSUN PICKUP (Cont.)

NOTE — *Torsion bars are identified for left and right installations with an "R" and "L" on end of bar.*

2) Install anchor arm to serrations on torsion bar. Install anchor arm adjusting bolt to anchor arm. On 2-WD, install snap ring and dust cover to anchor arm. On all models, tighten anchor arm adjusting bolt to obtain specified dimension "A" when bar is in contact with rubber bumper. *See Fig. 2.*

3) Temporarily adjust anchor arm adjusting bolt to obtain dimensions "B" and install lock nut. *See Fig. 2.* On 2-WD, install snap ring and dust cover to anchor arm.

4) On all models, lower vehicle and turn anchor arm adjusting nut to obtain specified "H" dimension with vehicle unladen. *See Fig. 3.*

Dimensions for Setting Torsion Bar	
Application	**In. (mm)**
Dimension "A"	.28-.67 (7-17)
Dimension "B"	2.36-2.76 (60-70)
Dimension "H"	
2-WD	4.88-5.08 (124-129)
4-WD	5.28-5.47 (134-139)

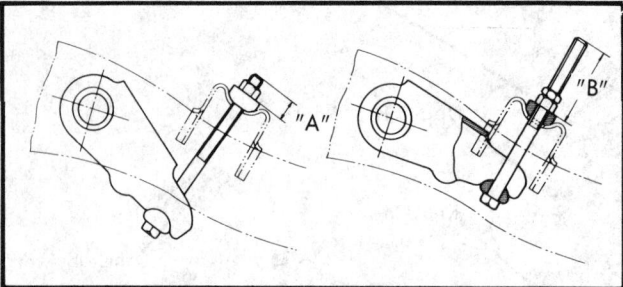

Fig. 2   View Showing Measuring Points for Installation of Anchor Pin

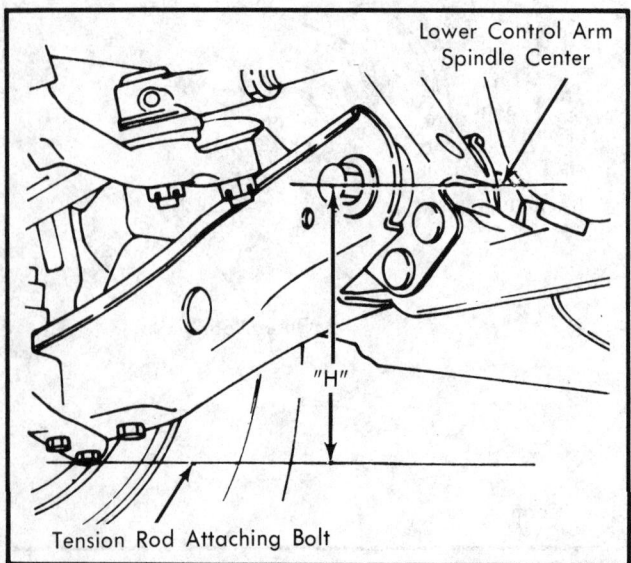

Lower Control Arm Spindle Center

"H"

Tension Rod Attaching Bolt

Fig. 3   View Showing Dimension "H" (Unladen Vehicle)

UPPER CONTROL ARM & BALL JOINT

Removal — 1) Raise and support front of vehicle and remove wheel and tire. Jack up lower control arm.

2) Remove cotter pin and nut from upper ball joint and separate ball joint from steering knuckle with suitable tool.

3) Loosen bolts holding upper ball joint to upper control arm and remove ball joint.

4) Remove bolts retaining upper link spindle and remove spindle and upper control arm from mounting, collecting all camber adjusting shims present.

5) Remove nuts and washers at both ends of upper link spindle. Place assembly on a vise and press upper link spindle from one end and remove rubber bushing. Press from other end and remove other bushing. Remove spindle from upper control arm.

Installation — 1) Apply soap suds to rubber bushings and press bushings into place from outside of control arm. Flange of bushing should securely contact end surface of upper control arm collar.

2) Insert upper control arm spindle and inner washers. Install inner washers with rounded edges facing inward.

3) Press in other bushing as described in step **1)**. Temporarily tighten nuts. Install upper ball joint.

4) Install upper control arm to frame. Tighten upper control arm spindle with camber adjusting shims. After fitting, check dimensions "A" and "B" shown in *Fig. 4*. Dimension "A" should be 5.34-5.42" (135.6-137.6 mm), "B" should be 1.114" (28.3 mm).

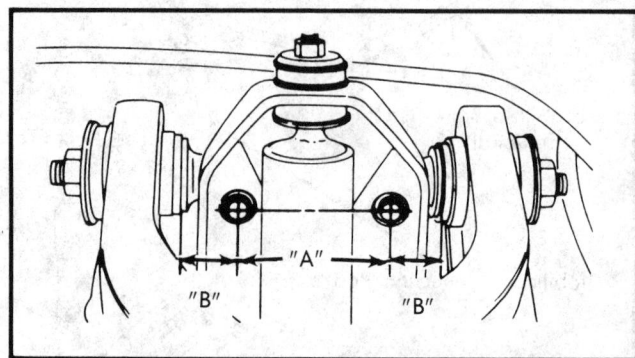

Fig. 4   Upper Control Arm Spindle Dimensions

5) Install upper ball joint to knuckle spindle. Make sure grease does not come into contact with tapered areas of ball joint knuckle spindle and threads of ball joint.

6) Install tire and wheel, lower vehicle and check height "H" of lower control arm. *See Fig. 3.* Check and adjust wheel alignment. See *appropriate article in WHEEL ALIGNMENT section.*

LOWER CONTROL ARM & BALL JOINT

Removal — 1) Raise and support front of vehicle. Remove wheel assembly. Remove torsion bar, and disconnect lower end of shock absorber from control arm.

DATSUN PICKUP (Cont.)

2) Press out lower ball joint from knuckle. Disconnect stabilizer bar connecting rod from control arm. Remove torque arm from lower control arm.

3) Remove lower control arm spindle from control arm and remove control arm from frame. Remove lower ball joint nuts and bolts and remove ball joint from control arm.

4) Using a suitable drift, (KV40102000), drive out lower control arm bushings. See *Fig. 5*.

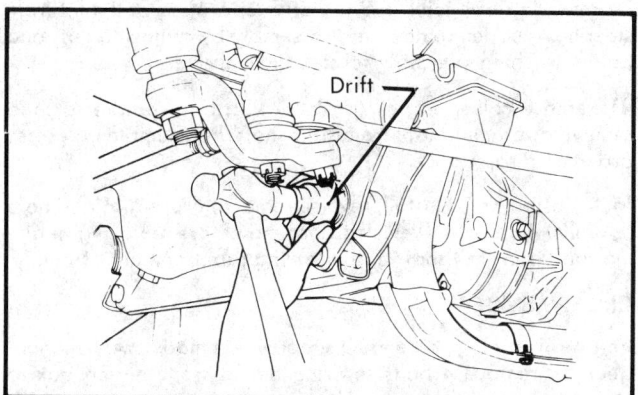

Fig. 5 *Removing Bushings from Lower Control Arm*

Installation — To install, reverse removal procedure, tightening nuts and bolts to specifications. Be sure grease does not contact tapered area of ball joint stud or knuckle hole and does not contact ball joint threads. Turn anchor bolt adjusting nut to obtain specified "H" dimension. See *Fig. 3*. Check and adjust wheel alignment. See *appropriate article in WHEEL ALIGNMENT section*.

STRUT ROD

Removal — Remove bolt holding strut rod to lower control arm and separate these parts. Remove nut attaching strut rod to bracket and remove rod with bushings, collar and washers.

Installation — To install, reverse removal procedure, noting the following: Swing strut rod a few times to settle bushings and washers; do not allow grease or oil to contact rubber bushings; tighten retaining nuts and bolts to specifications.

STABILIZER BAR

Removal — Remove nut holding stabilizer connecting rod to lower control arm. Remove bolt holding stabilizer mounting bracket to frame. Remove nut attaching stabilizer and connecting rod and remove these parts.

Installation — To install, reverse removal procedure and note the following; white mark painted on stabilizer bushing seat can be seen from both sides of vehicle when correctly installed.

TIGHTENING SPECIFICATIONS

Application	Ft. Lbs. (mkg)
Shock Absorber Upper Nut	12-16 (1.7-2.2)
Shock Absorber Lower Nut	22-30 (3.1-4.1)
Anchor Bolt Lock Nut	22-30 (3.1-4.1)
Upper Control Arm Spindle Nut	56-76 (7.7-10.5)
Upper Link Spindle-to-Frame	80-108 (11.1-15.0)
Upper Ball Joint-to-Control Arm	12-16 (1.7-2.2)
Upper Ball Joint-to-Knuckle	
4-WD	58-72 (8-10)
2-WD	36-65 (5-9)
Lower Ball Joint-to-Control Arm	
2-WD	28-38 (3.9-5.3)
4-WD	43-72 (6-10)
Torque Arm-to-Lower Control Arm	
Outer Nut	20-27 (2.7-3.7)
Inner Nut	26-33 (3.6-4.6)
Lower Control Arm Spindle Nut	80-108 (11.1-15.0)
Lower Ball Joint-to-Knuckle	
2-WD	87-123 (12-17)
WD	42-72 (6-10)
Strut Rod-to-Frame	87-116 (12-16)
Strut Rod-to-Lower Control Arm	28-38 (3.9-5.3)

Front Suspension

FIAT BRAVA

DESCRIPTION

Strut type front suspension consisting of a vertically mounted strut assembly. Strut assembly is mounted to body at the top by means of a rubber mount and lower end of strut is connected to steering knuckle. Strut assembly consists of hydraulic shock absorber with a coil spring mounted over outside. Lower control arm is connected to steering knuckle through ball joint and to front crossmember. A stabilizer bar is mounted to lower control arm and to frame.

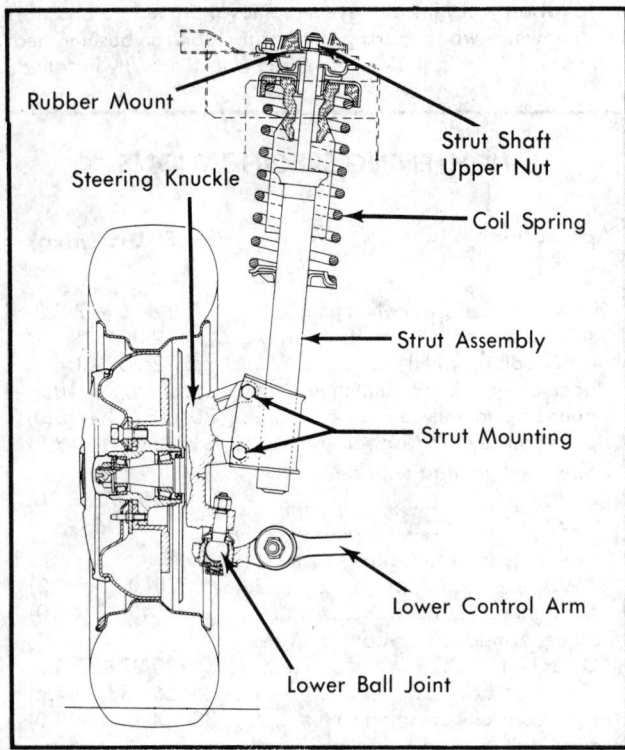

Rubber Mount
Steering Knuckle
Strut Shaft Upper Nut
Coil Spring
Strut Assembly
Strut Mounting
Lower Control Arm
Lower Ball Joint

Fig. 1   Fiat Brava Front Suspension Assembly

ADJUSTMENTS

WHEEL ALIGNMENT SPECIFICATIONS & PROCEDURES

See Wheel Alignment Specifications and Procedures in WHEEL ALIGNMENT Section.

WHEEL BEARING ADJUSTMENT

See Wheel Bearing Adjustment in WHEEL ALIGNMENT Section.

BALL JOINT CHECKING

See Ball Joint Checking in WHEEL ALIGNMENT Section.

REMOVAL & INSTALLATION

FRONT SUSPENSION ASSEMBLY

Removal — 1) With vehicle on ground, remove upper nut and washer from strut shaft. Remove the 3 rubber mount nuts and washers. Remove rubber mount assembly. Install and tighten retaining tool (A74375) on strut shaft. Remove the 2 nuts and washers retaining strut to body.

2) Jack up vehicle and remove wheel. Disconnect brake hose from tube at clip on fenderwell. Disconnect tie rod from steering knuckle.

3) Position a jack under suspension assembly. Remove nut, washer and rubber bushing from end of sway bar. Remove nut, washer and bolt from control arm at frame. Remove arm from bracket. Push arm to rear to remove from sway bar end. Carefully lower suspension from vehicle.

Disassembly and Reassembly — 1) Disconnect control arm by removing ball joint stud nut and separating ball joint from steering knuckle. Remove strut assembly by removing nuts and bolts attaching assembly to steering knuckle.

2) Remove coil spring by using a coil spring compressor and removing retaining tool from strut shaft. Reassemble in reverse order of disassembly.

Installation — To install, reverse removal procedure and note the following: Lower vehicle to ground before removing retaining tool from strut shaft and installing rubber mount assembly.

CROSSMEMBER

Removal — 1) Install engine support. On models with manual steering, remove 4 bolts securing mounts for steering box to crossmember. On models with power steering, remove bolt holding left steering box mount to crossmember. Remove 2 bolts holding right steering box mount to crossmember.

2) On all models, remove battery cable from clips on crossmember. On models with power steering, remove 2 screws holding hydraulic line to crossmember.

3) On all models, remove 2 nuts holding crossmember to engine mounts. Remove 2 nuts and bolts holding lower support arms to crossmember. Remove 4 bolts and washers holding crossmember to frame. Remove crossmember.

Installation — To install, reverse removal procedure.

STRUT ASSEMBLY

Removal — With vehicle on ground, remove upper nut and washer from strut shaft. Remove the 3 rubber mount nuts and washers. Remove the rubber mount assembly. Install and tighten retaining tool (A74375) on strut shaft. Remove the 2 nuts and washers retaining strut to body. Remove 2 strut-to-knuckle bolts and remove strut.

NOTE — To remove coil spring from strut, see Disassembly and Reassembly under Front Suspension Assembly.

Installation — To install, reverse removal procedure and note the following: Lower vehicle to ground before removing retaining tool from strut shaft and installing rubber mount assembly.

TIGHTENING SPECIFICATIONS

Application	Ft. Lbs. (mkg)
Ball Joint-to-Steering Knuckle	58 (8)
Control Arm-to-Crossmember	65 (9)
Strut Assembly-to-Knuckle	36 (5)
Strut Assembly-to-Upper Mount	43 (6)
Strut Upper Mount-to-Body	18 (2.5)
Stabilizer Bar-to-Crossmember	65 (9)
Stabilizer Bar-to-Control Arm	43 (6)
Crossmember-to-Body	65 (9)

FIAT SPIDER 2000

DESCRIPTION

Independent wishbone type suspension with coil springs and telescopic, hydraulic, double-acting shock absorbers. Shock absorbers are mounted inside coil springs between upper and lower control arms. Control arms are connected to steering knuckle with ball joints.

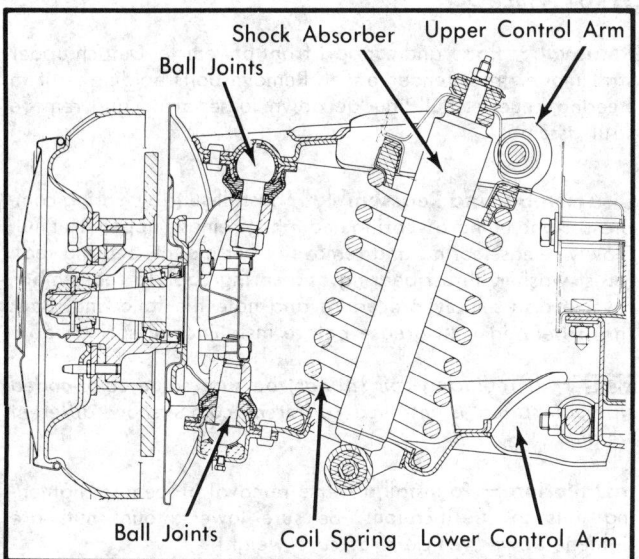

Fig. 1 Sectional View of Front Suspension Assembly

ADJUSTMENTS

WHEEL ALIGNMENT SPECIFICATIONS & PROCEDURES

See Wheel Alignment Specifications and Procedures in WHEEL ALIGNMENT Section.

WHEEL BEARING ADJUSTMENT

See Wheel Bearing Adjustment in WHEEL ALIGNMENT Section.

BALL JOINT CHECKING

See Ball Joint Checking in WHEEL ALIGNMENT Section.

REMOVAL & INSTALLATION

FRONT SUSPENSION ASSEMBLY

Removal — 1) Raise and support vehicle. Place cross support over engine compartment and attach to engine. Remove wheels and shock absorbers. Compress coil spring with spring compressor to relieve tension from lower control arm.

2) Disconnect and cap brake lines. Using a puller, disconnect tie rod from steering knuckle arm. Remove pivot bolt and detach upper control arm from body. Remove nuts and bolts securing lower control arm to crossmember and remove suspension.

Installation — To install, reverse removal procedure. Tighten all nuts and bolts, bleed brakes and check wheel alignment.

STEERING KNUCKLE

Removal — 1) Raise and support vehicle. Remove wheel, brake caliper, brake disc and plate. Using suitable puller, remove front grease cap. Remove hub using puller A.47015 (or equivalent). Remove inner race from inside hub bearing with a puller. Remove arm from steering knuckle.

2) Remove nut attaching lower control arm to steering knuckle and place suitable tool (A.47042) between control ball joints, then remove lower ball joint. Remove nut attaching upper ball joint to steering knuckle. Separate upper ball joint from steering knuckle.

Installation — Inspect all parts for signs of wear or damage. To install, reverse removal procedure and tighten all nuts and bolts.

COIL SPRINGS

Removal — Raise and support vehicle so suspension hangs freely. Remove wheels and shock absorbers. Disconnect stabilizer bar from lower control arm. Support lower control arm with a jack and disconnect lower ball joint stud from steering knuckle. Install suitable spring compressor and rotate lower control arm down carefully. Coil spring may now be removed.

Installation — To install, reverse removal procedure.

STABILIZER BAR

Removal — Remove front stabilizer bar by removing nuts and bolts securing bar to crossmember. Remove nuts and bolts attaching ends of stabilizer bar to lower control arms and remove stabilizer bar.

Installation — To install, reverse removal procedure.

TIGHTENING SPECIFICATIONS

Application	Ft. Lbs. (mkg)
Lower Control Arm Pin-to-Crossmember	43 (6.0)
Lower Control Arm-to-Crossmember	72 (10.0)
Upper Control Arm	65 (9.0)
Lower Shock Absorber	43 (6.0)
Steering Arm-to-Steering Knuckle	43 (6.0)
Brake Caliper	36 (5.0)
Crossmember-to-Side Member	69 (10.0)

FIAT STRADA

DESCRIPTION

Suspension is independent, strut type. Consists of double-action shock absorbers with surrounding coil springs . Strut assemblies are mounted to inner fender panel at top and to steering knuckle at bottom. Steering knuckle is also bearing carrier for drive axles. Lower control arm is connected to knuckle by ball joint. On models with manual transmission, a reaction strut is connected to chassis and lower control arm. On models with automatic transmission, a stabilizer bar is used in place of reaction struts.

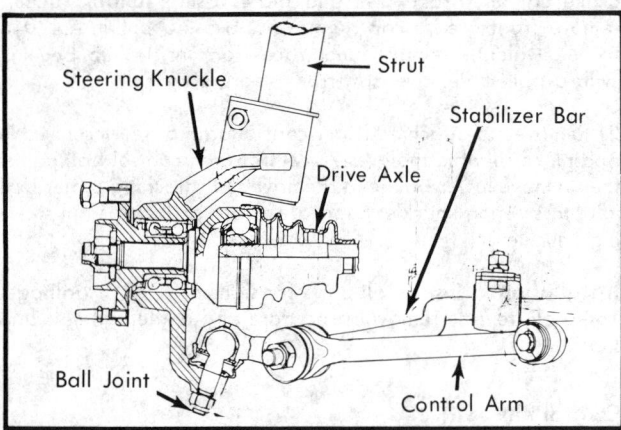

**Fig. 1 Strada Front Suspension
(Auto. Trans. Model Shown)**

ADJUSTMENTS

WHEEL ALIGNMENT SPECIFICATIONS & PROCEDURES

See Wheel Alignment Specifications and Procedures in WHEEL ALIGNMENT section.

REMOVAL & INSTALLATION

COMPLETE SUSPENSION ASSEMBLY

NOTE – *This procedure is for complete suspension assembly on one side only.*

Removal –1) Raise and support front of vehicle. Remove wheel. With brakes applied, remove hub nut and washer. Remove brake caliper, without detaching brake hose, and suspend out of way (be sure there is no strain on hose or line).

2) Remove nut from tie rod end stud and separate tie rod end from steering knuckle. Remove nut from reaction strut or stabilizer bar at control arm. Note any shims at this connection.

3) Remove control arm pivot bolt from chassis mount, and pull control arm away from reaction rod or sway bar. Note the number and location of shims. Remove nut securing control arm to steering knuckle. Remove bolts securing strut to steering knuckle.

4) Detach upper strut assembly mount from fender panel and remove strut assembly. Disconnect drive shaft rubber boot from steering knuckle. Separate steering knuckle/brake assembly from drive shaft, and remove suspension assembly.

Installation – To install, reverse removal procedure, tightening axle nut before lowering vehicle and tightening all other nuts and bolts with vehicle resting on ground. Be sure all shims are in proper position.

STRUT ASSEMBLY

Removal – Raise and support front of vehicle. Detach upper strut mount from fender panel. Remove bolts holding strut to steering knuckle. Pull knuckle down to separate and remove strut assembly.

Disassembly and Reassembly – Install suitable spring compressor and compress spring enough to remove upper strut nut. Slowly release spring and remove upper mount, bearing seat, thrust washer, thrust bearing and spring cap. To reassemble, reverse disassembly procedure and note the following: Pack thrust bearing with grease before installing on spring cap.

NOTE – *If replacing coil springs, be sure same color-coded class of spring is installed (different colors show different weights).*

Installation – To install, reverse removal procedure, tightening nuts to specifications. Be sure lower mount nuts are tightened after vehicle is at curb weight.

CONTROL ARM, BUSHINGS & BALL JOINTS

Removal – Remove complete suspension assembly as outlined. Remove ball joint stud nut and separate from steering knuckle.

Disassembly – To replace control arm bushings, drill out metal sleeve from inside rubber bushings and remove bushings. If ball joint is defective, replace entire control arm assembly.

Reassembly – Place outer washer, bushing and sleeve on centering pin of suitable bushing installation tool. Place control arm over bushing. Position inner bushing and washer on control arm. Place this assembly in a vise and press into place. Sleeve will bellow out over washers, securing bushings in control arm.

Installation – To install, reverse removal procedure.

TIGHTENING SPECIFICATIONS

Application	Ft. Lbs. (mkg)
Front Axle-to-Hub Nut	159 (22.0)
Control Arm Pivot Bolt	29 (4.0)
Stabilizer Bar-to-Control Arm	51 (7.0)
Stabilizer Bar-to-Chassis	36 (5.0)
Ball Joint Nut	40 (5.5)
Strut Assembly Mount	
Upper	25 (3.5)
Lower	43 (6.0)

FIAT X1/9

DESCRIPTION

Independent type front suspension consisting of lower control arms and hydraulic shock absorbers, surrounded by coil springs. Steering knuckle is attached to lower control arm at sealed ball joint. Shock absorber is attached to steering knuckle at bottom and to fender panel at top. Lower control arm pivots in rubber bushings attached to crossmember. Stabilizer bar is mounted to lower control arm and at front, to frame.

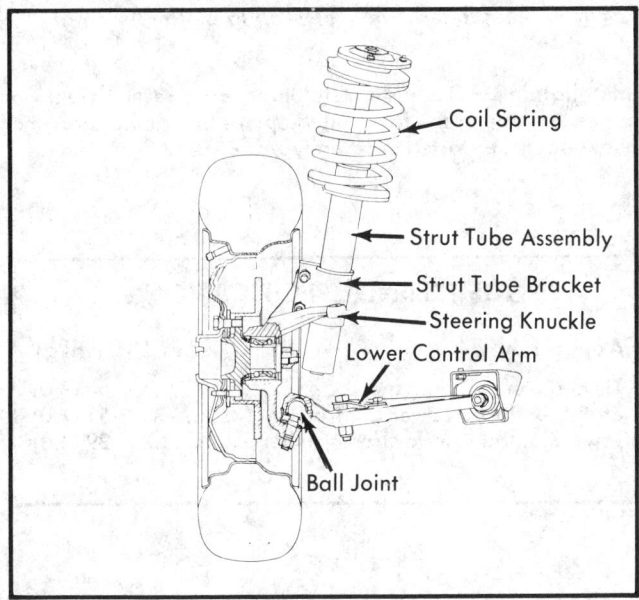

Coil Spring

Strut Tube Assembly

Strut Tube Bracket

Steering Knuckle

Lower Control Arm

Ball Joint

Fig. 1 Sectional View of Front Suspension Assembly

ADJUSTMENT

WHEEL ALIGNMENT SPECIFICATIONS & PROCEDURES

See Wheel Alignment Specifications and Procedures in WHEEL ALIGNMENT Section.

WHEEL BEARING ADJUSTMENT

See Wheel Bearing Adjustment in WHEEL ALIGNMENT Section.

BALL JOINT CHECKING

See Ball Joint Checking in WHEEL ALIGNMENT Section.

REMOVAL & INSTALLATION

FRONT SUSPENSION ASSEMBLY

Removal — Raise and support vehicle; remove tire and wheel. Remove front disc brake caliper assembly. *See appropriate article in BRAKE section.* Remove bolts and plate holding shock absorber tube to steering knuckle. Separate shock absorber at top by removing upper mounting nuts. Disconnect lower control arm from stabilizer bar bracket and ball joint. Remove tie rod nut and force tie rod from steering knuckle. Maneuver assembly from vehicle.

Inspection — Check rubber bushings in control arm and replace any that appear worn. Inspect ball joints for excessive play or damage; replace as necessary.

Installation — To install suspension assembly, reverse removal procedure ensuring all nuts and bolts are properly torqued.

STRUT ASSEMBLY

Removal — Raise and support vehicle under chassis. Disconnect upper strut assembly mount from inner fender panel. Remove bolts securing strut assembly to steering knuckle and carefully maneuver strut from vehicle.

Disassembly — 1) Install strut assembly in suitable spring compressor and collapse coil. Remove nut from center of upper mount. Release spring compressor and remove upper mount and coil spring.

2) Inspect springs for cracks or distortion. Springs are manufactured in two classes and identified by paint markings. Class A springs are marked with a yellow stripe on outside of center coils and class B springs are marked with a green stripe. If springs are replaced for any reason, use a spring of same class.

Reassembly — Using same spring compressor as previously outlined, reverse disassembly procedure to assemble strut assembly.

Installation — To install strut assembly, reverse removal procedure. Do not tighten strut assembly lower mount until weight of vehicle is on ground.

CONTROL ARM, BUSHINGS & BALL JOINTS

Removal — Remove complete front suspension assembly as previously outlined. Remove ball joint stud nut and separate ball joint from steering knuckle with a suitable puller.

Disassembly — Inspect ball joint for wear or distortion. If ball joint is defective, complete control arm must be replaced. Inspect bearings for wear or damage. If defective, drill out metal sleeve from inside rubber bushing and extract bushing.

Reassembly — Position outer washer, bushing and sleeve on centering pin of a suitable bushing installation tool. Place control arm over bushing and washer for opposite side. Place control arm, components and tool into a press. Position remaining tool components in sleeve and press into position with a pressure of approximately 2200-2645 lbs. (1000-1200 kg).

Installation — To install control arm, attach to steering knuckle, tighten ball joint stud nut and install suspension assembly as previously outlined.

Front Suspension

FIAT X1/9 (Cont.)

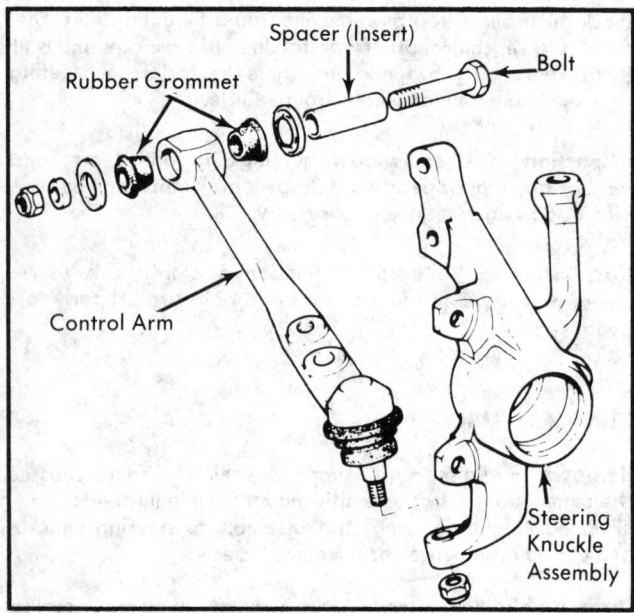

Fig. 2 Exploded View of Lower Control Arm Assembly

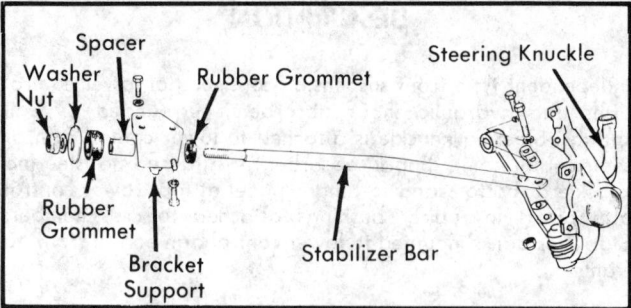

Fig. 3 Exploded View of Stabilizer Bar Assembly

Installation — To install stabilizer bar, reverse removal procedure noting the following: Replace any rubber grommet that appears distorted or severely worn.

STABILIZER BAR

Removal — Raise and support vehicle. Disconnect stabilizer mounting bolt from lower control arm. Remove stabilizer attaching hardware from front end of stabilizer and carefully maneuver bar from vehicle.

TIGHTENING SPECIFICATIONS

Application	Ft. Lbs. (mkg)
Tie Rod Nut	58 (8.0)
Stabilizer Bar-to-Lower Control Arm	51 (7.0)
Lower Control Arm-to-Crossmember	29 (4.0)

Front Suspension

FIESTA

Hatchback

DESCRIPTION

Front suspension is MacPherson strut type. A shock absorber is mounted to steering knuckle at bottom and to inner fender panel at top. It is surrounded by a coil spring. A tie rod ball joint connects steering knuckle arm to rack-and-pinion steering assembly. Lower ball joint connects underside of knuckle to lower control arm which attaches to frame member. A stabilizer bar attaches to same mounting as lower ball joint and connects to bushing mount at front of vehicle.

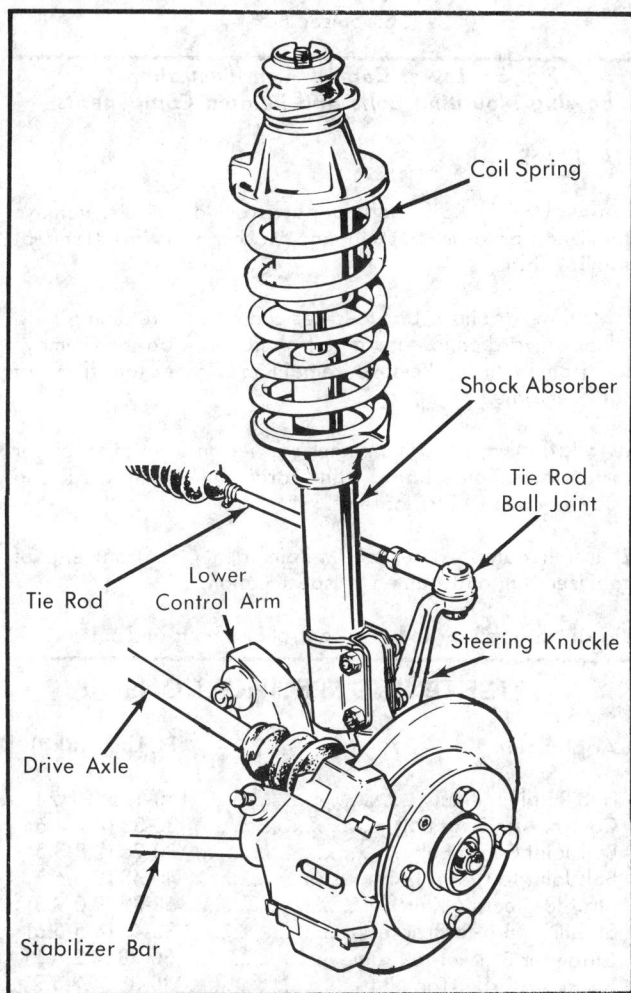

Fig. 1   Fiesta Front Suspension Assembly Components

ADJUSTMENTS

WHEEL ALIGNMENT SPECIFICATIONS & PROCEDURES

See Wheel Alignment Specifications and Procedures in WHEEL ALIGNMENT section.

WHEEL BEARING ADJUSTMENT

See Wheel Bearing Adjustment in WHEEL ALIGNMENT section.

BALL JOINT CHECKING

See Ball Joint Checking in WHEEL ALIGNMENT section.

REMOVAL & INSTALLATION

STEERING KNUCKLE & STRUT ASSEMBLY

Removal — 1) Loosen wheel bolts. Raise and support front of vehicle and remove front wheel. Apply foot brake and remove drive axle retaining nut.

2) Detach flexible brake hose at coupling on holding clip and plug hose to prevent fluid loss.

3) Remove 3 bolts retaining stabilizer bar bracket to frame.

4) Detach tie rod end ball joint from steering knuckle arm.

5) Remove lower control arm pivot bolt. Remove 2 upper strut-to-fender retaining bolts and withdraw suspension and knuckle assembly.

NOTE — *It may be necessary to use a puller to remove knuckle and strut assembly from drive shaft.*

Installation — To install, reverse removal procedure.

STRUT ASSEMBLY

Removal — 1) Loosen wheel bolts, raise and support front of vehicle. Remove front wheel.

2) Remove 2 bolts holding lower strut mounting to steering knuckle. Remove 2 upper strut-to-fender panel bolts and withdraw strut assembly from vehicle.

Disassembly — 1) Attach a suitable spring compressor to coil spring and compress enough to remove tension from top mount assembly.

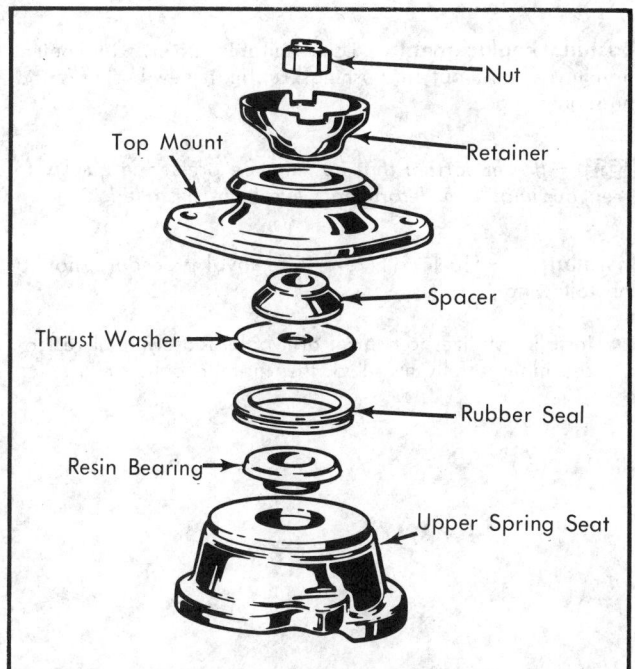

Fig. 2   Exploded View of Top Mount Components for Fiesta Strut Assembly

FIESTA (Cont.)

2) Remove top mount retaining nut by holding inner spindle with Allen wrench and turning nut off with box-end wrench.

NOTE — *Allen wrench must be used to keep shock absorber rod from turning while removing and installing top nut; otherwise, gland seal will be damaged and leakage will result.*

3) Remove top mount assembly components. Remove tension from coil spring compressor and lift off coil spring.

Reassembly & Installation — To reassemble and install strut assembly, reverse appropriate procedures and note the following:

- Strut assembly is retained to steering knuckle with special bolts which have double-knurled design. If not installed, manufacturer recommends that these bolts be used to assure proper alignment of strut-to-knuckle (part no. E800615-S72).
- Be sure to hold piston rod with Allen wrench while installing top retaining nut.
- Reset toe alignment if necessary.

LOWER CONTROL ARM

Removal — **1)** Raise and support front of vehicle. Remove lower control arm pivot bolt.

2) Remove clinch bolt from ball joint stud at lower steering knuckle connection. Separate ball joint from knuckle.

3) Remove 2 bolts holding stabilizer bar to lower control arm. Remove control arm from vehicle.

Bushing Replacement — Using suitable driver, with control arm in vise, push out old bushings. Lubricate new bushings and press into place.

NOTE — *It is important that bushings be pressed in quickly to keep bushing from deforming while being installed.*

Installation — To install, reverse removal procedure, noting the following:

- Install stabilizer-to-control arm bolts loosely until rest of assembly is fully installed, then tighten bolts fully.

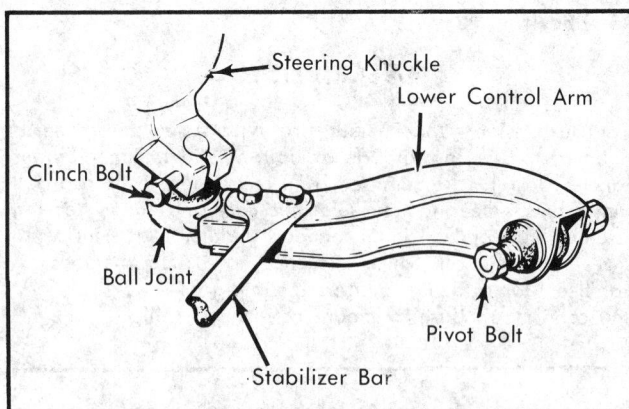

Fig. 3   Lower Control Arm Illustration Showing Mounting Bolts and Related Components

STABILIZER BAR

Removal — **1)** Raise and support front of vehicle. Remove stabilizer bar-to-bracket nut and washer from front end of stabilizer bar.

2) Remove stabilizer bar-to-lower control arm retaining nuts. Pull downward on lower arm to free stabilizer bar and remove bar from vehicle. Remove remaining washer on front of stabilizer bar.

Installation — **1)** Position inner washer on front of stabilizer bar on lower control arm (with "Ford" marking upward) and install retaining bolts loosely.

2) Install outer washer and retaining nut on front end of stabilizer bar and tighten to specification.

3) Tighten stabilizer-to-lower control arm bolts and nuts.

TIGHTENING SPECIFICATIONS

Application	Ft. Lbs. (mkg)
Hub Retaining Nut	150-175 (21-24)
Control Arm Pivot Bolt	30-33 (4.2-4.6)
Ball Joint Clinch Bolt	20-26 (2.8-3.5)
Ball Joint-to-Control Arm	40-48 (5.6-6.6)
Strut-to-Steering Knuckle	68-72 (9.0-9.5)
Stabilizer Bar-to-Bracket	32-40 (4.5-5.6)
Stabilizer Bracket-to-Frame	30-38 (4.2-5.2)
Shock Absorber Top Nut	30-38 (4.2-5.2)
Top Mount-to-Fender	15-18 (2.0-2.4)
CV Joint Allen Bolts	28-32 (3.8-4.5)

HONDA

Accord
Civic
Prelude

DESCRIPTION

Strut type front suspension consisting of a vertically mounted strut assembly. Strut assembly is mounted to body at the top by means of a thrust bearing. Lower end of strut is connected to steering knuckle, which is mounted to lower control arm by means of a ball joint. Strut assembly consists of a shock absorber built into strut outer tube and a coil spring mounted to outside upper portion of strut tube. On Accord, radius rods are attached to crossmember and lower control arms. A stabilizer bar is attached to lower control arms on Civic and Prelude models and is attached to radius rods on Accord.

ADJUSTMENT

WHEEL ALIGNMENT SPECIFICATIONS & PROCEDURES

See Wheel Alignment Specifications & Procedures in WHEEL ALIGNMENT Section.

WHEEL BEARING ADJUSTMENT

See Wheel Bearing Adjustment in WHEEL ALIGNMENT Section.

BALL JOINT CHECKING

See Ball Joint Checking in WHEEL ALIGNMENT Section.

REMOVAL & INSTALLATION

STEERING KNUCKLE

Removal — **1)** Raise and support vehicle and remove wheel. Remove spindle nut. Remove brake caliper without disconnecting hydraulic line and support out of way. On Civic and Prelude, screw 2 M8 x 1.25 x 12 mm bolts into threaded holes in brake rotor until rotor is pulled off hub.

2) On all models, install hub puller and slide hammer and remove hub (with brake rotor attached on Accord) from steering knuckle. Disconnect tie rod end from steering knuckle using suitable tool.

3) Taking care not to damage ball joint seals, detach lower control arm from ball joint at steering knuckle. Loosen lock bolt holding steering knuckle to strut assembly and slide steering knuckle off axle.

NOTE — Since removing hub assembly involves use of slide hammer and subjects wheel bearings to severe loads, both inner and outer wheel bearings must be replaced each time hub assembly is removed.

Installation — To install, reverse removal procedure and note. Wheel bearing and seal must be replaced. Press out old bearing, then insert new one using a press to fully seat bearing and seal.

STRUT ASSEMBLY

Removal — Raise and support vehicle, then remove wheel. Disconnect brake line at strut assembly and remove retaining clip. On Prelude and Civic, remove brake caliper without disconnecting hydraulic line and support out of way. On all models, loosen lock bolt securing strut to steering knuckle and separate knuckle from strut. Remove nuts retaining upper end of strut to body and remove strut.

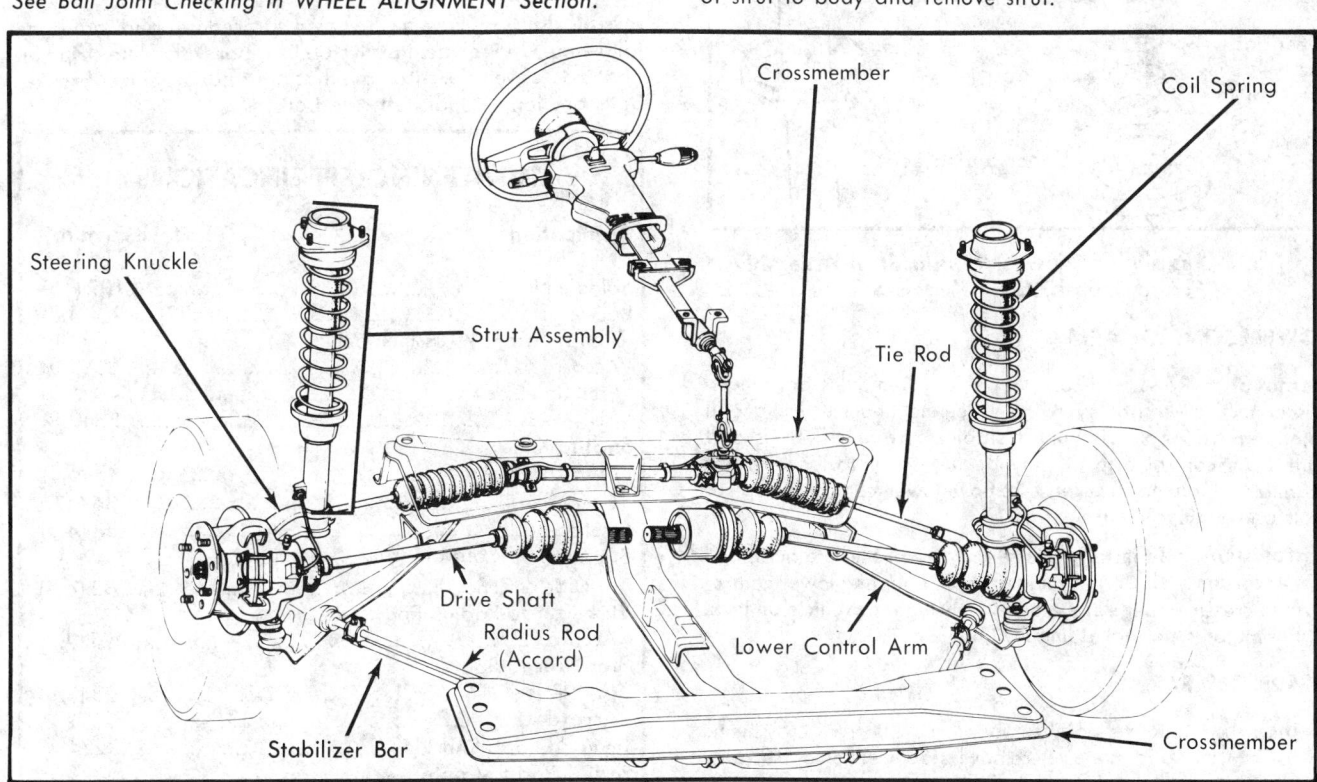

Fig. 1   Assembled View of Honda Front Suspension Showing Component Relationships

HONDA (Cont.)

Disassembly — Using suitable tool, compress coil spring to relieve tension from upper shock absorber retaining nut. Remove nut, seals, spacers, etc. (noting arrangement), beneath upper mounting plate. Slowly remove pressure from spring and lift spring off. Shock absorber may now be replaced, if necessary.

Reassembly — Reverse disassembly procedure using *Fig.* 2 as a guide. Also, make sure shock absorber components do not show any signs of leaking.

Installation — Reverse removal procedure and note: Make sure slot in steering knuckle is engaged in tab on shock (strut) housing before seating it into steering knuckle.

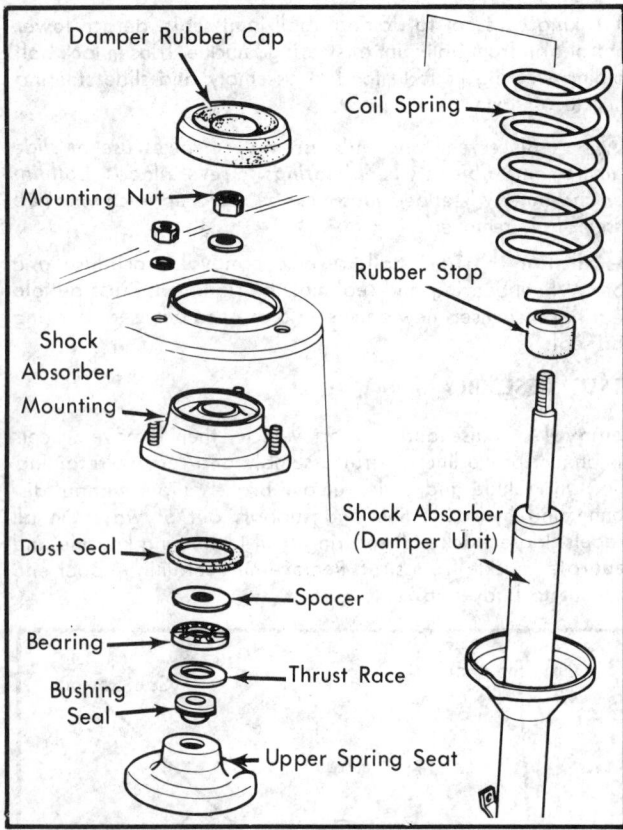

Fig. 2   Exploded View of Honda Strut Assembly (Accord Shown; Civic Models Similar)

LOWER CONTROL ARM

Removal — Raise and support vehicle. Remove front wheel. Disconnect lower ball joint from steering knuckle, using ball joint remover tool. Disconnect stabilizer retaining bolts and nuts from control arm (it may be necessary to loosen front stabilizer retaining brackets). Remove lower control arm pivot bolt and remove control arm.

Installation — To install, reverse removal procedure and note: On Accord models only, make sure bolt mounting lower control arm to crossmember is tightened with weight of vehicle on jack. This simulates normal riding height.

STABILIZER BAR

Removal — Remove stabilizer bar brackets from crossmember. On Civic and Prelude, remove stabilizer-to-control arm nuts and remove stabilizer bar. On Accord, remove stabilizer-to-radius rod bolts and remove stabilizer bar.

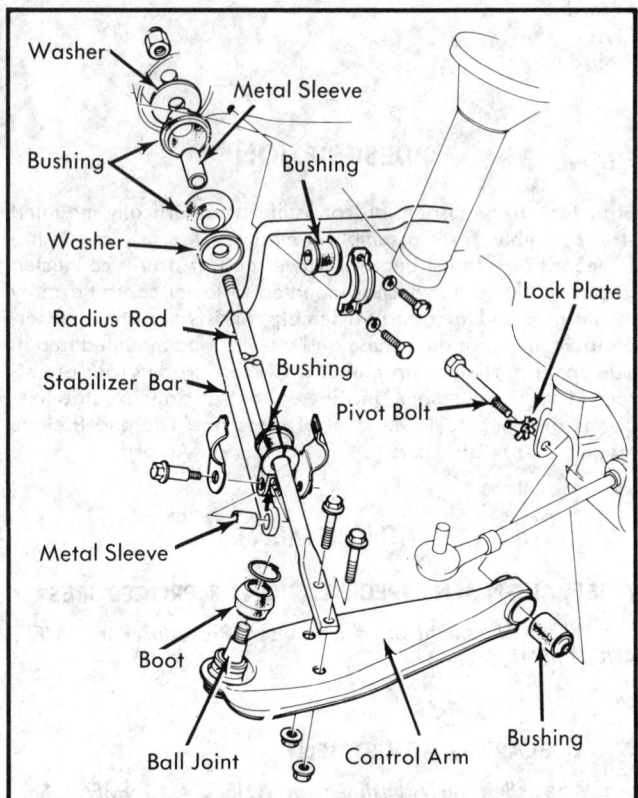

Fig. 3   Exploded View Showing Stabilizer Bar and Radius Rod (Accord Shown; Other Models Similar)

Inspection — Inspect all rubber bushings and metal sleeves for excessive wear or damage.

Installation — Reverse removal procedure and note the following: On Prelude, install stabilizer bar with white stripe on right side of vehicle. Also note that right side stabilizer bracket bolts are longer than left side bolts.

TIGHTENING SPECIFICATIONS

Application	Ft. Lbs. (mkg)
Spindle Nut	109 (15)
Ball Joint	32-33 (4.4-4.5)
Control Arm-to-Crossmember	
Accord	36 (5.0)
Prelude	40 (5.5)
Civic	28 (3.9)
Strut-to-Knuckle	
Accord & Prelude	47 (6.5)
Civic	36 (5.0)
Strut-to-Body	33 (4.5)
Stabilizer-to-Control Arm	
Prelude & Civic	32 (4.4)
Stabilizer-to-Radius Rod	
Accord	16 (2.2)
Stabilizer-to-Body	
Civic & Prelude	28 (3.9)
Accord	16 (2.2)
Tie Rod End-to-Knuckle	32 (4.4)
Radius Rod-to-Control Arm	
Accord	40 (5.5)

JAGUAR

XJ6

DESCRIPTION

Suspension consists of upper and lower control arms, double acting hydraulic shock absorbers, coil springs, stabilizer bar and steering knuckles. The upper control arms are mounted inboard to fulcrum shafts and are mounted outboard to steering knuckles by upper ball joints. Lower control arms are mounted inboard to crossmember and outboard to steering knuckles by lower ball joints. Coil springs are mounted between lower control arms and crossmember. Shock absorbers are attached at the bottom to lower control arms and at the top to body. Stabilizer bar is attached to lower control arms and crossmember.

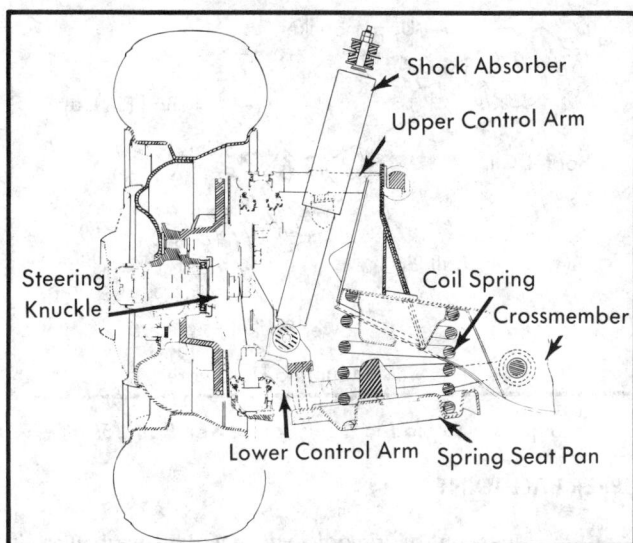

Fig. 1 Sectional View of Front Suspension Assembly

ADJUSTMENT

WHEEL ALIGNMENT SPECIFICATIONS & PROCEDURES

See Wheel Alignment Specifications and Procedures in WHEEL ALIGNMENT Section.

WHEEL BEARING ADJUSTMENT

See Wheel Bearing Adjustment in WHEEL ALIGNMENT Section.

BALL JOINT CHECKING

See Ball Joint Checking in WHEEL ALIGNMENT Section.

FRONT SUSPENSION ASSEMBLY

Removal — **1)** Disconnect battery and remove air cleaners. Disconnect the upper end of shock absorber. Drain and discard power steering fluid. Disconnect and plug power steering inlet and outlet hoses.

2) Remove nuts securing engine mounts to brackets on frame crossmember. Disconnect rear crossmember mountings, then separate stabilizer bar from link. Turn steering column until pinch bolt holding lower "U" joint to pinion shaft is accessible. Remove pinch bolt.

3) Return steering to straight-ahead position. Set ignition to "LOCK" and remove key. Separate lower steering column from upper "U" joint, then from pinion shaft.

4) Raise and support vehicle. Remove front wheels. Disconnect brake hoses and lines. Detach ground strap from engine. Remove suspension mounting bolts. Collect and note location of all washers, spacers and bushings. Remove suspension assembly from vehicle.

Installation — To install, reverse removal procedure and note the following:

- Be sure brake lines and hoses are properly routed without bends or kinks.
- It may be helpful to remove protective heat shield covering boot on rack and pinion steering prior to positioning suspension into place.
- Be sure power steering reservoir is full before starting engine after installation.
- If additional information is required on steering column installation, *see appropriate article in STEERING section of this manual.*
- Bleed brake system.

SHOCK ABSORBERS

Removal — Detach upper shock absorber mounting. Raise and support vehicle. Remove front wheel if necessary for access to lower mounting. Remove lower shock absorber mounting and remove from vehicle.

Installation — To install, reverse removal procedure.

COIL SPRINGS

Removal — Raise and support vehicle, then remove tire and wheel. Fit a spring compressor (JD-6D & adaptor JD-6D-1) and collapse spring coil enough to allow load on pan seat to be relieved. Remove hardware mounting spring pan to lower control arm. Slightly loosen spring compressor and remove assembly complete.

NOTE — *Be sure to note number and location of any packing shims.*

Installation — To install coil spring, reverse removal procedure noting the following: Floor jack can be placed under lower ball joint to aid in aligning spring pan bolt. A maximum of three packers may be placed in spring pan and no more than two can be fitted on crossmember.

LOWER CONTROL ARM

Removal — **1)** Remove complete suspension assembly as described in this article.

2) With assembly on bench, detach tie rod ball joints from steering knuckle, then detach and remove steering rack from crossmember. Use spring compressor to remove coil spring. Separate upper ball joint, noting location of all caster shims. Detach lower ball joint.

3) Remove stabilizer bar support bracket and shock absorber lower mounting. Remove cotter pin and pivot shaft nut. Drive pivot shaft from crossmember and collect spacers. Remove lower control arm.

Installation — To install, reverse removal procedure. Do not tighten pivot shaft nut until vehicle is resting on ground at full curb weight.

JAGUAR (Cont.)

UPPER CONTROL ARM

Removal — 1) Raise and support vehicle. Remove front wheel. Detach upper ball joint from control arm. Note number of all caster adjusting shims present.

2) Wire steering knuckle to coil spring and remove bolts holding upper control arm pivot shaft to vehicle. Note number and location of all camber adjusting shims. Remove control arm from vehicle.

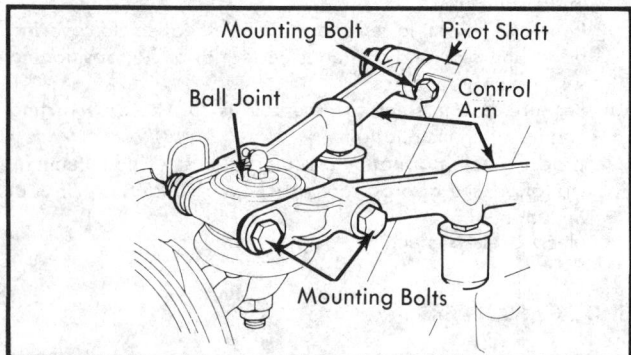

Fig. 2   Upper Control Arm Mounting Points

Installation — To install upper control arm, reverse removal procedure and tighten all nuts and bolts. Recheck wheel alignment.

STABILIZER BAR

Removal — Raise and support vehicle. Remove front wheels. Detach both ends of stabilizer bar from mounting links. Remove both mounting brackets from frame. Remove all mounting bushings from bar. Detach 1 tie rod end from steering knuckle and maneuver stabilizer from vehicle.

Installation — To install, reverse removal procedure, fully tightening stabilizer bar-to-link nuts after vehicle is resting on ground.

LOWER BALL JOINT

Removal — 1) Raise front of vehicle and place on safety stands. Remove wheel. Disconnect brake line from caliper and plug openings. Disconnect tie rod from steering arm. Twist stub axle carrier to gain access to bolts securing upper ball joint to control arm, then remove bolts. Note position and number of shims.

2) Remove nut mounting lower ball joint to control arm. Use tool JD 24 (or equivalent) to separate ball joint from control arm, then maneuver assembly from vehicle.

Disassembly & Reassembly — 1) Pry back tab washers and remove four screws keeping ball pin cap. Lift out ball pin. Release clip and remove upper socket from stub axle.

2) Clean all components and inspect for excessive wear or damage.

3) Install new upper socket to stub axle. Fit lip of boot clip in recess in socket. Lip MUST be near lower face of clip. Install new boot to clip and attach with plastic retaining ring. Grease new ball pin and put into position.

4) Put ball pin cap into vise and cut out lower socket. Clean shavings and fit new socket. Refit shims and replace ball cap.

Fit four setscrews with lock tabs and tighten, continually checking ball joint movement.

5) If ball pin is loose in socket, remove shims. If pin is excessively tight, add shims until movement is correct. Movement should be slightly stiff.

Installation — Insert ball joint in lower control arm and tighten lock nut. Align stub axle with upper control arm and insert bolts (bolt heads MUST face front). Make sure packing pieces and shims are properly installed. Reconnect tie rod. Attach brake lines and bleed brakes. Check camber and caster angles.

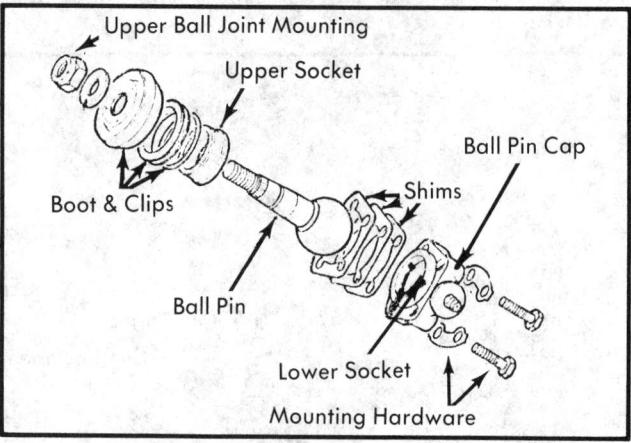

Fig. 3   Exploded View of Lower Ball Joint

UPPER BALL JOINT

NOTE — *Upper control arm ball joint cannot be overhauled. If ball joint is excessively worn, assembly must be replaced.*

Removal — 1) Raise vehicle and place on safety stands. Remove wheel. Twist steering to full lock position. Wire stub axle to crossmember to prevent tension on brake hose when ball joint is separated.

2) Remove bolt mounting upper ball joint to control arm. Note number of shims and position of packing pieces. Remove ball joint lock nut and separate ball joint from control arm. Maneuver assembly from vehicle. Withdraw ball joint from stub axle.

Installation — Apply grease to replacement ball joint and place in position in stub axle. Hold ball joint against taper fit washer and tighten retaining nut. Refit upper control arm mounting bolts (bolt heads must face forward) and caster shims. Check camber and caster angles.

TIGHTENING SPECIFICATIONS

Application	Ft. Lbs. (mkg)
Upper Pivot Shaft-to-Crossmember	49-55 (6.8-7.6)
Upper Ball Joint-to-Arm	26-32 (3.6-4.4)
Pivot Shaft-to-Upper Arm	45-55 (6.3-7.6)
Pivot Shaft-to-Lower Arm	32-50 (4.4-6.9)
Upper Shock Absorber	27-32 (3.8-4.4)
Lower Shock Absorber	32-36 (4.4-5.0)
Spring Pan	27-32 (3.8-4.4)
Stabilizer-to-Link	14-18 (2.0-2.5)
Tie Rod Nut	35-50 (4.8-6.9)

LUV

Pickup

DESCRIPTION

Independent type suspension, using torsion bars. Upper control arms are mounted to bracket which is part of shock tower. Lower control arm is mounted to crossmember. Ball joints attach both upper and lower control arms to steering knuckles, which are part of the front wheel spindle. Torsion bars are connected in front to lower control arm and at rear to frame crossmember. Back and forth movement of front suspension is regulated by a strut bar connecting lower control arm to frame, by means of a rubber bumper at frame end of strut. A stabilizer bar is attached to lower control arms and frame.

ADJUSTMENT

WHEEL ALIGNMENT SPECIFICATIONS & PROCEDURES

See Wheel Alignment Specifications & Procedures in WHEEL ALIGNMENT Section.

WHEEL BEARING ADJUSTMENT

See Wheel Bearing Adjustment in WHEEL ALIGNMENT Section.

BALL JOINT CHECKING

See Ball Joint Checking in WHEEL ALIGNMENT Section.

REMOVAL & INSTALLATION

UPPER CONTROL ARM & BALL JOINT

Removal — 1) Raise and support vehicle with safety stands under lower control arms. Remove tire and wheel. Remove shock absorber dust cover. Remove upper ball joint cotter pin and nut.

2) Separate ball joint from steering knuckle and wire the knuckle and brake caliper assembly out of way. Do not allow assembly to hang from brake hose. Note number and placement of shims at upper control arm bracket.

3) Remove 2 bolts from upper pivot shaft. Remove upper stem retaining nut, retainer and rubber grommet and depress shock absorber lever. Remove control arm from bracket.

4) If replacing pivot shaft and bushings, remove bolts from each side of pivot shaft, and remove lock washer and plate. Remove pivot shaft and bushings using suitable remover tool (J-29755).

Inspection — Check control arm and pivot shaft for cracks or distortion. Replace both pivot shaft and bushings if either is found defective. Replace ball joint and control arm as an assembly if either is defective.

Installation — 1) If pivot shaft and bushings have been removed, install pivot shaft and bushings on control arm using installer tool (J-29755). Install bolt with plate, washer and lock washer on each side of pivot shaft and tighten.

2) Install ball joint stud through knuckle. Install castle nut. Tighten to specifications, plus just enough more to install cotter pin. Mount control arm to chassis and install shims in equal thickness to those removed during disassembly.

3) Tighten bolt at thin shim pack first, then bolt at thicker shim pack. Install shock absorber dust cover, wheel and tire. Lower vehicle to ground.

4) Mount lower control arm to chassis and tighten. Install torsion bar, strut rod, and stabilizer bar as described in this article. Leave strut rod nut semi-tight until adjusting vehicle height.

5) Install wheel and tire, remove stands and lower vehicle to ground. Adjust vehicle height and tighten strut rod nuts. See *appropriate article in WHEEL ALIGNMENT Section.*

LOWER CONTROL ARM & BALL JOINT

Removal — 1) Raise front of vehicle and place safety stands under frame. Remove front wheel.

2) Remove strut bar, torsion bar and stabilizer bar as described in this article.

3) Detach lower end of shock absorber. Remove cotter pin and nut from lower ball joint stud. Remove lower control arm retaining nuts and bolts and remove lower control arm om vehicle.

Inspection — Check all parts for distortion, cracking or excessive wear. Replace all worn parts.

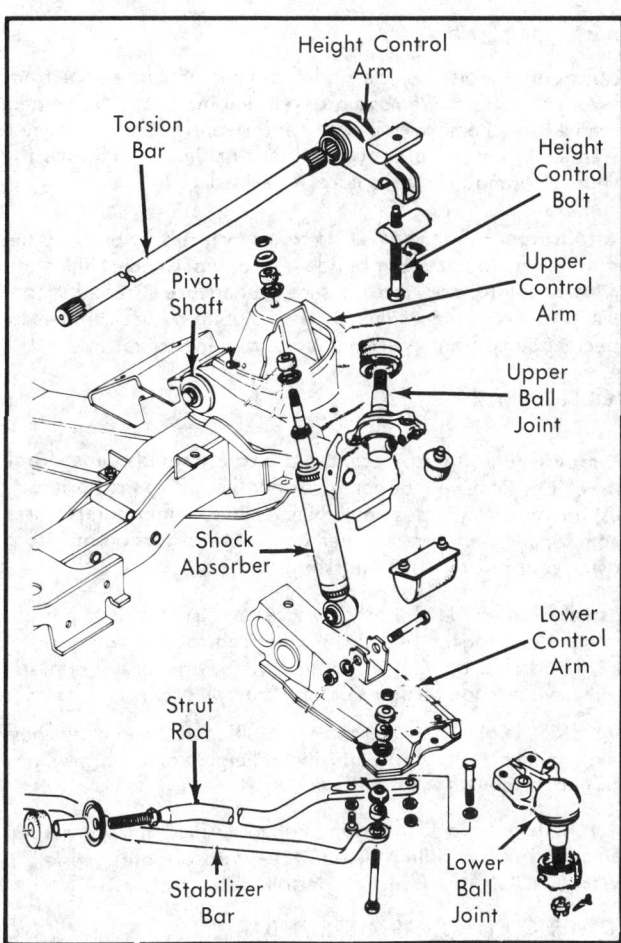

Fig. 1 Exploded View of Front Suspension (2-WD Shown, 4-WD Similar)

Front Suspension

LUV (Cont.)

Installation — 1) If ball joint was removed from lower control arm (it can be replaced separately), install new ball joint to control arm.

2) Place ball joint stud in steering knuckle spindle, tighten nut and install new cotter pin.

NOTE — *If cotter pin hole does not align after tightening ball joint nut to specification, tighten further to align hole; do not loosen nut.*

3) Install torsion bar, strut bar and stabilizer bar as described in this article. Install front wheel, remove stands and lower vehicle.

SHOCK ABSORBER

Removal — Raise vehicle and support on safety stands. Remove shock absorber dust cover. Hold shock absorber upper stem with a wrench and remove retaining nut, retainer and rubber grommet. Remove shock absorber lower pivot bolt from lower control arm and remove shock absorber.

Installation — Check shock absorber and replace if necessary. Fully extend shock absorber, place lower retainer and grommet on stem and slide shock absorber into position. Install upper grommet and retainer on stem and tighten nut to specification. Slide bolt thru lower shock absorber mount and shock absorber. Install shock absorber dust cover, tighten mounting bolt and lower vehicle.

STABILIZER BAR

Removal — Raise vehicle and disconnect stabilizer bar from lower control arm. Remove brackets holding bar to frame and remove bar. Remove link bolt, spacers and rubber grommets from lower control arm or stabilizer bar. Inspect all parts for wear or damage and replace if necessary.

Installation — Bolt brackets to frame over rubber bushings installed over stabilizer bar but do not tighten. Connect link bolts to lower control arm, making sure washers are installed in correct position. Connect link bolts to stabilizer, and tighten to specifications. Tighten bracket bolts to specifications.

TORSION BAR

Removal — Raise vehicle and place safety stands under front of vehicle. Remove stopper plate and height control arm adjusting bolt. Mark position, then remove height control arm from torsion bar and crossmember. Remover torsion bar from lower control arm after marking position.

Installation — 1) Thoroughly grease serrated portions at both ends of torsion bar. Raise lower control arm with jack to position rubber bumpers in contact with lower control arm. Install front end of torsion bar into control arm.

2) Install height control arm into position so its end reaches height control bolt (grease portion of height control arm which fits into frame).

3) Turn height control adjusting bolt to position marked during removal. Check riding height. *See appropriate article in WHEEL ALIGNMENT section.* Install stopper plate.

LOWER CONTROL ARM STRUT BAR

NOTE — *Correct caster angle can be maintained by marking positions of strut rod nuts for reassembly reference.*

Removal — Raise vehicle and remove double nuts, washers and rubber bushings from front side of strut bar. Remove two bolts holding strut bar to lower control arm and remove strut bar.

Installation — Place washer and bushing on strut bar and slide rod through frame bracket. Place second set of washers and bushings on end through bracket, then start on washer and one nut, but do not tighten. Bolt other end of strut to lower control arm and tighten to specifications. Lower vehicle and tighten bracket nut, install second nut and tighten to specifications.

STEERING KNUCKLE

Removal — 1) Raise vehicle and place safety stands under front of vehicle. Remove brake caliper assembly without disconnecting line and support out of way.

2) On 4-WD models, shift transfer case lever into "2H" position and set free wheeling hub knob to "FREE" position. Remove hub cover assembly, then remove snap ring and shims from spindle end. Remove hub body from hub assembly. Remove hub nut and lock washer using hub nut wrench.

3) On 2-WD models, remove grease cap, cotter pin, spindle nut retainer and spindle nut. On all models, remove hub and rotor assembly. Remove 4 bolts surrounding spindle, then remove brake backing plate assembly.

4) Remove cotter pins and attaching nuts for upper and lower ball joints. Disconnect knuckle from ball joints, then remove steering knuckle from vehicle.

Installation — To install, reverse removal procedures. Adjust wheel bearings. Tighten all bolts and nuts to specifications.

TIGHTENING SPECIFICATIONS	
Application	**Ft. Lbs. (mkg)**
Backing Plate-to-Knuckle	29 (4.1)
Ball Joint-to-Lower Control Arm	
2-WD	30 (4.2)
4-WD	45 (6.2)
Ball Joint Stud Nut	75 (10.4)
Upper Control Arm	
Pivot-to-Frame	74 (10.2)
Bushings	87 (12.0)
Lower Control Arm-to-Crossmember	
2-WD	90 (12.5)
4-WD	94 (13.0)
Shock Absorber	
Lower End	45 (6.2)
Upper End	14 (1.9)
Stabilizer Bar	
Frame Attachment	55 (7.6)
Control Arm Attachment	7 (1.0)
Strut Bar-to-Lower Control Arm	
2-WD	30 (4.2)
4-WD	45 (6.2)

MAZDA GLC, 626 & RX7

DESCRIPTION

Independent hydraulic strut type suspension with coil springs. Strut assemblies mount between lower control arms and upper fender panels. Strut assemblies consist of: hydraulic shock absorbers (built into strut tube), coil springs around outside of strut tube housing, and a steering knuckle that is connected to both lower control arm and strut. Lower control arms pivot at crossmember and are connected by ball joints to steering knuckle. A stabilizer bar is attached to chassis and at each end to lower control arm. On 626 and RX7 models, tension rods are installed to maintain alignment and stability.

ADJUSTMENT

WHEEL ALIGNMENT SPECIFICATIONS & PROCEDURES

See Wheel Alignment Specifications & Procedures in WHEEL ALIGNMENT Section.

WHEEL BEARING ADJUSTMENT

See Wheel Bearing Adjustment in WHEEL ALIGNMENT Section.

BALL JOINT CHECKING

See Ball Joint Checking in WHEEL ALIGNMENT Section.

REMOVAL & INSTALLATION

LOWER CONTROL ARM

Removal — 1) Raise vehicle. Support weight with safety stands. Remove tire and wheel.

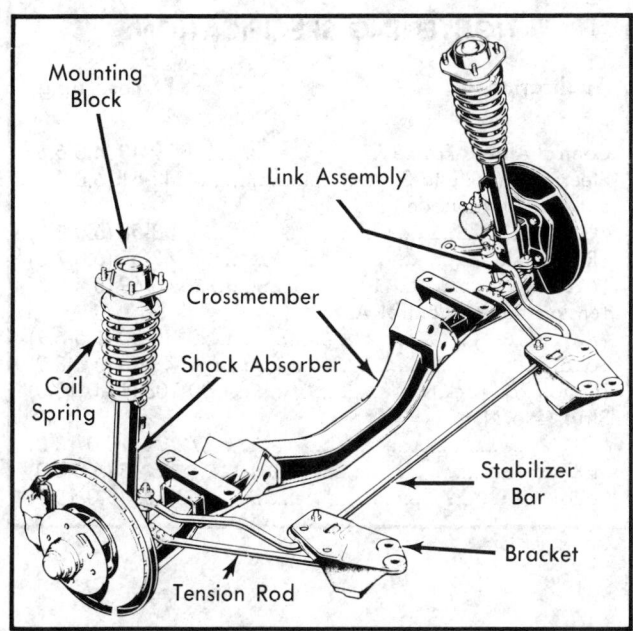

Fig. 1   626 & RX7 Front Suspension Assembly

Labels: Mounting Block, Link Assembly, Crossmember, Shock Absorber, Coil Spring, Stabilizer Bar, Bracket, Tension Rod

2) Remove cotter pin from tie rod nut. Remove nut. Separate tie rod ball joint using a puller.

3) Remove bolts mounting steering knuckle to strut tube. On GLC models, remove nut from front of stabilizer bar. Begin to separate stabilizer bar from control arm. On all other models, disconnect and remove stabilizer bar and tension rod.

4) Remove lower control arm pivot bolt mounting arm to crossmember. Pull strut outward and force control arm out of vehicle.

Ball Joint Replacement — Ball joint is not replaceable. Ball joint and lower control arm must be replaced as a unit.

Installation — To install, reverse removal procedure.

STRUT ASSEMBLY

Removal — 1) Raise and suitably support vehicle. Remove tire and wheel.

2) Remove nuts (3 or 4) retaining strut to upper fender panel. Nuts are accessible from inside engine compartment.

3) Remove clip mounting brake hydraulic line to strut housing (if equipped). Remove bolts attaching caliper (bracket) and pull caliper assembly off disc. Hang caliper out of way using a short wire.

4) Remove hub grease cap, cotter pin, nut lock and bearing from spindle. Remove thrust washer and outer bearing. Pull off hub and brake assembly. Remove inner bearing and grease seal.

5) Remove backing plate and bolts mounting strut to steering knuckle. Drop lower control arm down. Slide strut assembly with coil spring out of vehicle.

Disassembly — 1) Clamp strut in vise. Use spring compressor and collapse coil. Remove lock nut and washer from top of piston rod.

2) Remove shock absorber support, spring seat, thrust bearing, coil spring, dust boot and damper stopper.

NOTE — *Check hydraulic strut (shock absorber) by forcing piston rod in and out several times. If resistance is weak or there is a free travel spot somewhere in the stroke, strut must be replaced or repaired.*

3) Place strut in a soft jawed vise. Remove cap nut and seal. Pry "O" ring from guide rod. Pull piston rod and pressure tube assembly out of strut (reservoir tube).

4) Remove piston rod, guide, base valve and pressure tube assembly from reservoir tube. Take strut from vise and drain hydraulic fluid.

NOTE — *Piston rod, guide and base valve are serviced as an assembly only. Do not remove items listed in step 4) from pressure tube.*

Inspection — 1) Check reservoir tube for cracks or damage. Replace tube if necessary.

2) Check mounting rubbers, replace if deteriorated.

MAZDA GLC, 626 & RX7 (Cont.)

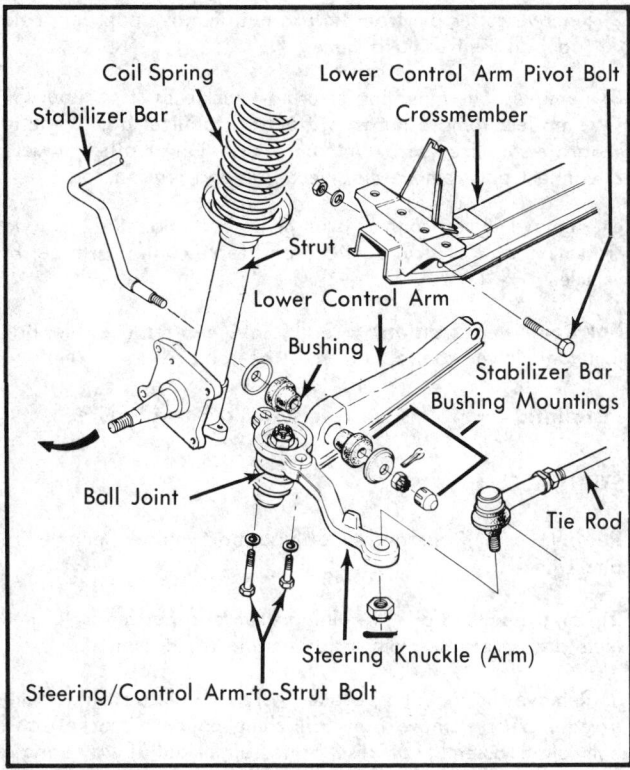

Fig. 2 Exploded View of GLC Front Suspension Assembly

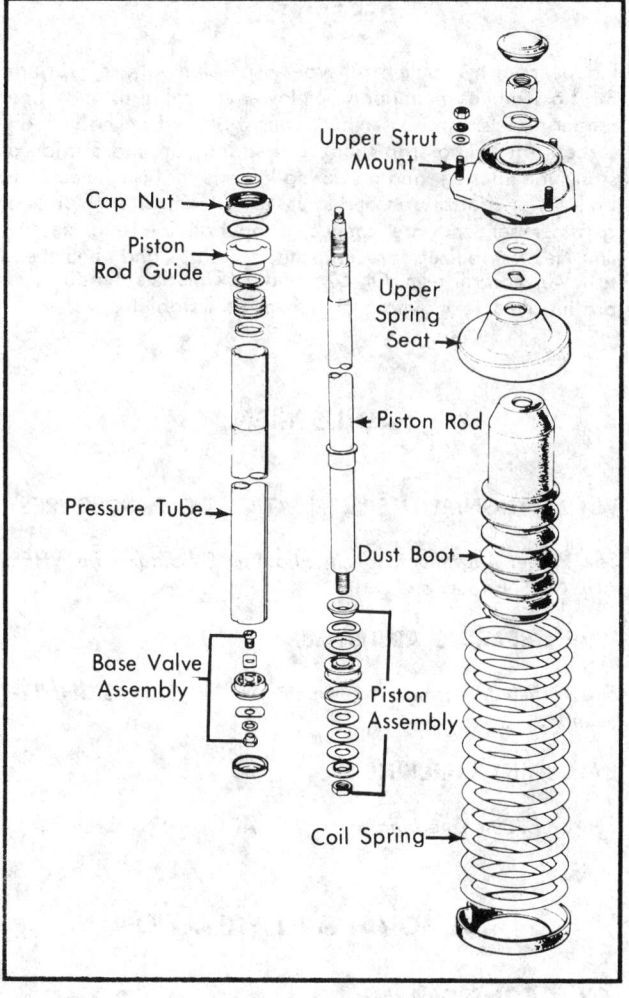

Fig. 3 Exploded View of Strut Assembly

3) Inspect coil spring for signs of fatigue, cracks or damage.

Reassembly — 1) Hold reservoir tube in a vice. Insert pressure tube, piston rod and base valve assembly into tube as a set. Pour appropriate amount of hydraulic fluid into reservoir.

2) Install piston rod guide into pressure tube. Fit new "O" ring between rod guide and reservoir tube.

3) Fit a pilot (49 0259 590) over threads of piston rod. Apply grease to lip of oil seal and insert cap nut through pilot onto piston rod.

4) Tighten cap nut and pull out piston rod. Seat piston and torque cap nut. Install coil spring and retaining components in reverse of removal procedure.

Installation — To install, reverse removal procedure.

Strut Reservoir Volume	
Application	**Ounces**
RX7	7.61
GLC	8.45
626	8.15

TIGHTENING SPECIFICATIONS

Application	Ft. Lbs. (mkg)
Control Arm-to-Frame	29-40 (4.0-5.6)
Steering Knuckle-to-Strut	43-51 (6.0-7.0)
Ball Joint-to-Knuckle	
GLC	43-58 (6.0-8.0)
RX7	43-51 (6.0-7.0)
626	46-69 (6.4-9.5)
Tension Rod-to-Control Arm	
RX7	40-50 (5.5-6.9)
626	48-58 (6.6-8.0)
Tension Rod Lock Nut	80-108 (11.0-15.0)
Strut Cap Nut	
GLC	72-94 (10.0-13.0)
RX7	36-43 (5.0-6.0)
626	58-105 (8.0-15.0)

Front Suspension

MAZDA B2000 PICKUP

DESCRIPTION

Independent type suspension, consisting of upper and lower control arms and wheel spindle mounted between upper and lower arms by means of ball joints. Upper control arm pivots on a shaft attached to frame; lower control arm pivots on a shaft mounted to crossmember. A coil spring is mounted between lower control arm and frame. Shock absorber is hydraulic, double-action type, mounted between lower control arm and frame inside coil spring. A stabilizer bar is also incorporated which connects to the lower control arm on each side by bushings and links.

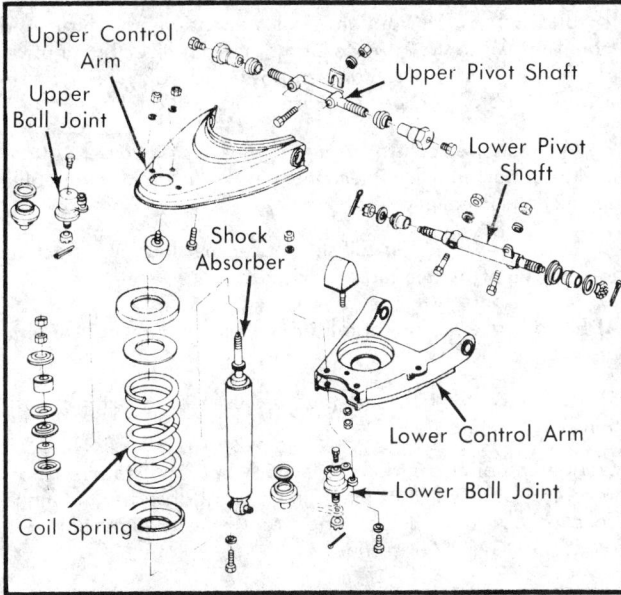

Fig. 1   Exploded View of Front Suspension Assembly for Component Identification

ADJUSTMENTS

WHEEL ALIGNMENT SPECIFICATIONS & PROCEDURES

See Wheel Alignment Specifications & Procedures in WHEEL ALIGNMENT section.

WHEEL BEARING ADJUSTMENT

See Wheel Bearing Adjustment in WHEEL ALIGNMENT section.

BALL JOINT CHECKING

See Ball Joint Checking in WHEEL ALIGNMENT section.

REMOVAL & INSTALLATION

SHOCK ABSORBERS

Removal — Remove nut, rubber bushing and washer attaching upper end of shock absorber to crossmember. Remove lower retaining bolts holding shock absorber to lower control arm, and remove shock absorber from vehicle.

Installation — Reverse removal procedure and tighten mounting bolts.

COMPLETE SUSPENSION ASSEMBLY

Removal — 1) Raise and support front of vehicle with safety stands placed just behind lower control arms. Remove front wheel. Remove shock absorber.

2) Detach upper ball joint from steering knuckle. From under hood, remove upper control arm retaining bolts and nuts, noting number and position of alignment shims. Remove upper control arm from vehicle.

3) Remove 3 nuts and bolts holding ball joint to upper control arm and remove ball joint.

4) Remove stabilizer bar retaining nut, washers and bushings. Detach stabilizer bar from lower control arm.

5) Position floor jack under lower control arm and raise arm to relieve pressure. Using suitable tool, compress coil spring, then detach lower ball joint from steering knuckle.

6) Lower floor jack under lower control arm and remove coil ring from vehicle. Remove 2 lower control arm retaining bolts and remove arm from vehicle. Remove ball joint from lower control arm.

Installation — To install, reverse removal procedure.

TIGHTENING SPECIFICATIONS

Application	Ft. Lbs. (mkg)
Ball Joint-to-Knuckle	51-65 (7.0-9.0)
Ball Joint-to-Lower Cont. Arm	60-70 (8.8-9.7)
Control Arm-to-Frame (Both)	54-69 (7.5-9.5)

MERCEDES-BENZ — EXCEPT 450SL & 450SLC

240D
280 Series
300 Series
450SEL

DESCRIPTION

Front suspension consists of upper and lower control arms, coil springs, shock absorbers, steering knuckles and a stabilizer bar.

ADJUSTMENTS

WHEEL ALIGNMENT SPECIFICATIONS & PROCEDURES

See Wheel Alignment Specifications and Procedures in WHEEL ALIGNMENT section.

WHEEL BEARING ADJUSTMENT

See Wheel Bearing Adjustment in WHEEL ALIGNMENT section.

BALL JOINT CHECKING

See Ball Joint Checking in WHEEL ALIGNMENT section.

REMOVAL & INSTALLATION

NOTE — Manufacturer requires that shock absorber mountings and stabilizer attachments not be loosened or tightened unless vehicle is resting on ground or axle is supported to simulate vehicle load.

SUSPENSION ASSEMBLY (ONE SIDE)

Removal — 1) Remove front shock absorber by detaching upper mounting first, then lower mounting. Raise front of vehicle, with jacks placed under outer edge of lower control arms. Remove front wheel.

2) Remove coil spring, as described in this article. Use suitable tool to separate tie rod ball joint from steering knuckle arm.

3) Detach flexible brake hose from brake line at connection on fender well. Loosen plug connection of brake lining wear indicator on caliper. Remove bolts holding brake support to frame.

4) Support front axle half. Mark position of lower control arm eccentric to crossmember for reinstallation purposes. Remove eccentric bolt.

5) Remove stabilizer bar support from upper control arm. Remove hex bolt holding upper control arm bushing to body. Remove front suspension assembly.

Installation — 1) Position front suspension in vehicle and mount upper control arm to body and stabilizer bar, but do not fully tighten bolts. Raise opposite side of vehicle as required to obtain proper stabilizer bar position.

2) Attach upper control arm to frame crossmember. Attach brake support to frame. Reconnect brake line to hose and plug connection of caliper wear indicator.

3) Install coil spring. Install shock absorber loosely. Attach tie rod ball joint to steering knuckle arm.

4) Bleed brake system. Install front wheel and lower vehicle to ground.

5) Place eccentric bolt of camber adjustment to original position and tighten.

6) Tighten upper control arm-to-body bolt and stabilizer bar-to-control arm support bolt. Tighten shock absorber mounting bolts. Check axle height and front wheel alignment. See WHEEL ALIGNMENT section.

UPPER CONTROL ARM

NOTE — Loosen hex nuts on ball joints with coil spring installed ONLY when supporting jacks are under lower control arm and not body. If jack cannot be so positioned, remove coil spring.

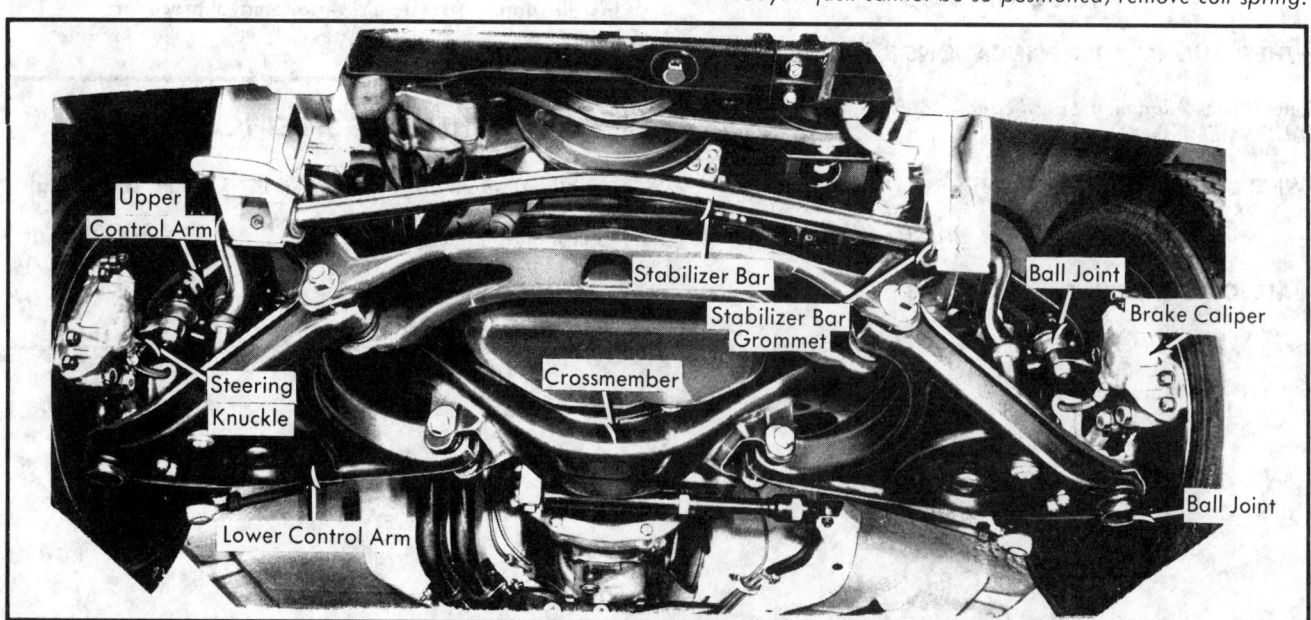

Fig. 1 Assembled View of Mercedes-Benz Front Suspension
(280 Series Shown; Others Similar with Major Difference in Stabilizer Bar Configuration and Mounting)

MERCEDES-BENZ — EXCEPT 450SL & 450SLC (Cont.)

Removal — 1) Raise front of vehicle, placing jacks under outer edges of control arms.

2) Remove upper ball joint nut. Using suitable tool, detach ball joint from steering knuckle arm. Wire steering knuckle to frame so it will not drop.

3) Remove upper control arm support from stabilizer bar and from body. Remove upper control arm.

Installation — 1) Position upper control arm in vehicle and install control arm-to-body bolt. Connect upper ball joint to steering knuckle.

2) Mount stabilizer bar support to upper control arm, attaching bolt loosely. Lower vehicle to ground and tighten all bolts to specifications. Check front end alignment.

LOWER CONTROL ARM

Removal — 1) Loosen top shock absorber mounting, then lower mounting. Remove shock absorber. Raise front of vehicle, with jacks placed under outer edge of control arm.

2) Remove front wheel. Remove coil spring as described in this article. Detach tie rod ball joint from steering knuckle arm.

3) Mark position of lower control arm eccentric bolt and bushing to crossmember for reassembly reference.

4) Remove bolts holding brake support to frame. Remove lower control arm eccentric bolt. Detach lower ball joint from control arm. Remove lower control arm with brake support.

Installation — 1) Mount lower control arm to ball joint. Position control arm bushing to frame.

2) Attach brake support to frame. Install coil spring. Install shock absorber, loosely. Mount front wheel and lower vehicle to ground.

3) Tighten shock absorber mountings. Position eccentric bolt to original position and tighten to specifications.

4) Attach tie rod ball joint to steering knuckle arm. Check wheel alignment.

COIL SPRING

Removal — 1) Release upper shock absorber mount. Raise front of vehicle with jack placed under lower control arm. Remove front wheel.

2) Attach suitable coil spring compressor. Tighten spring compressor while raising jack under lower control arm to assist compressing operation. Slowly lower jack and remove the coil spring and rubber mounting.

Installation — 1) Position rubber mount on coil spring. With spring compressed, position in vehicle. Slowly release spring, being sure it rests in mounting groove.

2) Mount front wheel and lower vehicle to ground. Attach upper shock absorber mount.

STABILIZER BAR

Removal — 1) Raise front of vehicle, with jacks placed under lower control arms. Remove front wheels.

2) Detach upper control arm support from stabilizer bar.

3) Remove master cylinder and booster. Remove heater hoses, air cleaner, regulator linkage, vacuum lines and electrical wiring as required to allow clearance for stabilizer bar removal.

4) Remove stabilizer bar mounting brackets and bushings. Remove end covers and remove stabilizer bar.

Installation — 1) Position stabilizer bar in vehicle and loosely attach bar support to upper control arm.

2) Position rubber bushings on stabilizer bar, with splits facing against frame. Install brackets loosely.

3) Attach left and right end covers and replace all hoses, linkage, wiring and brake components removed. Mount front wheels and lower vehicle to ground.

4) Tighten stabilizer bar-to-control arm support bolt. Tighten mounting brackets. Check Front wheel alignment.

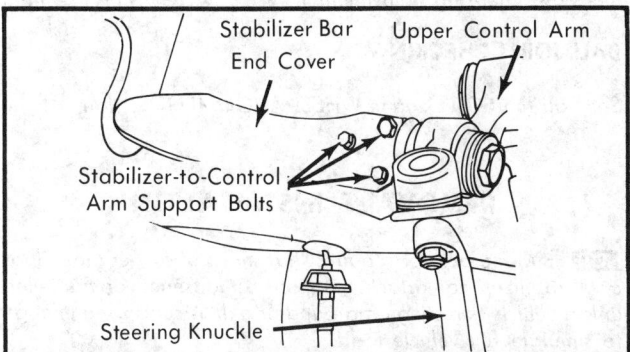

Fig. 2   Showing Attachment of Upper Control Arm and Stabilizer Bar

STEERING KNUCKLE

Removal — 1) Raise front of vehicle, with jacks placed under outer edge of lower control arm. Remove front wheels.

2) Detach steering knuckle arm from steering knuckle. Remove caliper from steering knuckle and suspend out of way with wire. Remove front wheel hub.

3) Loosen brake hose holder on backing plate. Remove nut from upper ball joint and separate from steering knuckle.

4) Remove nut from lower ball joint. Swivel upper end of steering knuckle slightly outward and use suitable tool to detach steering knuckle from lower ball joint. Remove knuckle from vehicle.

Installation — To install, reverse removal procedure.

TIGHTENING SPECIFICATIONS

Application	Ft. Lbs. (mkg)
Lower Shock Absorber Mount	18 (2.5)
Stabilizer Bar Bracket Bolts	18 (2.5)
Steering Linkage Bolts	25 (3.5)
Steering Knuckle Arm Bolts	58 (8.0)
Upper Control Arm Eccentric Bolts	43 (6.0)
Lower Control Arm Eccentric Bolts	87 (12.0)
Upper Ball Joint Nut	43 (6.0)
Lower Ball Joint Nut	58 (8.0)

Front Suspension

MERCEDES-BENZ 450SL & 450SLC

DESCRIPTION

Front suspension assembly is a coil spring type, having separately mounted coil springs and shock absorbers between upper and lower control arms. Other front suspension components include steering knuckle, tie rods and a stabilizer bar.

ADJUSTMENTS

WHEEL ALIGNMENT SPECIFICATIONS & PROCEDURES

See Wheel Alignment Specifications and Procedures in WHEEL ALIGNMENT section.

WHEEL BEARING ADJUSTMENT

See Wheel Bearing Adjustment in WHEEL ALIGNMENT section.

BALL JOINT CHECKING

See Ball Joint Checking in WHEEL ALIGNMENT section.

REMOVAL & INSTALLATION

NOTE — *Manufacturer requires that shock absorber mountings and stabilizer bar attachments not be loosened or tightened unless vehicle is resting on ground or axle is supported enough to simulate full vehicle load.*

SHOCK ABSORBERS

Removal — With vehicle on ground, detach upper and lower shock absorber mountings. Compress shock absorber to gain clearance and remove from vehicle.

Installation — To install, reverse removal procedure.

COIL SPRING

Removal — 1) Loosen lower shock absorber mounting and stabilizer bar connecting linkage. Raise front of vehicle. Remove front wheel.

2) Mark position of lower control arm eccentric bolts on inner end of arm for reinstallation reference. Attach and engage a suitable coil spring compressor. Remove eccentric bolts.

3) Place suitable cradle-type support beneath lower control arm directly below coil spring position. Slowly lower cradle, allowing inner end of control arm to drop down, and remove coil spring.

Installation — To install, reverse removal procedure, fully tightening stabilizer bar mountings and lower shock absorber mounting after vehicle is resting on ground.

STABILIZER BAR

Removal — Loosen stabilizer bar connecting linkage from both lower control arms. Remove stabilizer bar-to-frame mounting brackets and remove torsion bar.

Installation — To install, reverse removal procedure.

STEERING KNUCKLE

Removal — 1) Install coil spring compressor on spring. Raise and support front of vehicle. Remove front wheel.

2) Remove bolt holding steering knuckle arm to steering knuckle. Detach flexible brake hose from brake line and plug openings. Remove caliper.

NOTE — *On some models, it may be possible to remove caliper from rotor and suspend out of way without detaching brake hose. This will eliminate necessity of bleeding brake system after installation.*

3) Remove nuts from upper and lower ball joint studs. Detach both ball joints from steering knuckle. Remove steering knuckle.

Installation — To install, reverse removal procedure, bleed brakes and check front wheel alignment.

UPPER CONTROL ARM

Removal — 1) Attach suitable spring compressor to coil spring. Raise and support front of vehicle. Remove front wheel.

NOTE — *Shock absorber remains installed.*

2) Remove bolt holding steering knuckle to steering knuckle arm. Detach brake hose from brake line and plug openings.

3) Remove nuts from upper and lower ball joint studs. Using suitable tool, detach upper ball joint from steering knuckle.

4) Remove both upper control arm mounting nuts and remove arm.

Installation — To install, reverse removal procedure. Bleed brakes and check front wheel alignment.

LOWER CONTROL ARM

Removal — 1) Loosen and detach lower shock absorber mounting. Raise front of vehicle and remove front wheel.

2) Detach steering knuckle arm from steering knuckle. Separate brake hose from brake line and plug openings. Remove brake hose retaining clip.

3) Remove coil spring as described in this article.

4) Remove nuts from upper and lower ball joint studs. Detach lower control arm from lower ball joint. Remove control arm.

Installation — To install, reverse removal procedure, bleed brake system and tighten shock absorber mounting (after vehicle is resting on ground). Check front wheel alignment.

TIGHTENING SPECIFICATIONS

Application	Ft. Lbs. (mkg)
Lower Shock Absorber Mount	14 (2.0)
Upper Ball Joint Nut	29 (4.0)
Lower Ball Joint Nut	29 (4.0)
Tie Rod Ball Joint Nut	14 (2.0)
Lower Control Arm-to-Frame	130 (18.0)
Steering Arm-to-Steering Knuckle	57 (8.0)
Upper Control Arm Clamping Bolt	21 (3.0)
Upper Control Arm-to-Body	60 (8.0)

MGB

DESCRIPTION

Suspension consists of a lower control arm assembly, on which a coil spring is mounted. A kingpin connects lower control arm to steering knuckle. A shock absorber assembly is mounted on top of steering knuckle. A stabilizer bar is connected to lower control arm.

ADJUSTMENT

WHEEL ALIGNMENT SPECIFICATIONS & PROCEDURES

See *Wheel Alignment Specifications and Procedures* in *WHEEL ALIGNMENT* Section.

WHEEL BEARING ADJUSTMENT

See *Wheel Bearing Adjustment* in *WHEEL ALIGNMENT* Section.

REMOVAL & INSTALLATION

COIL SPRING

Removal — Raise and support vehicle on safety stands. Remove wheels. Remove stabilizer bar link from spring pans. Using spring compressor, compress spring and remove spring pan bolts from lower control arm. Release spring compressor. Remove spring pan and spring.

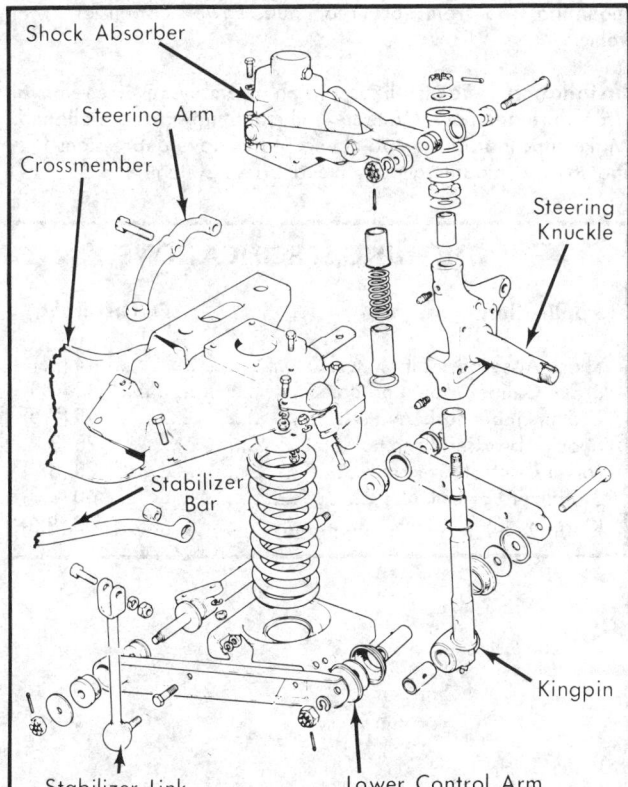

Fig. 1 Exploded View of MGB Front Suspension Assembly

Inspection — Before installing coil spring, make sure free length of coil spring is 10.2" (259 mm). Also, check that under a load of approximately 1030 lbs. (467 kg) spring height is 7.4" (190 mm).

Installation — To install, reverse removal procedure and note: Shortest spring pan screw must be fitted to rear hole closest to wheel.

SHOCK ABSORBERS

Removal — **1)** Raise and support front of vehicle. Place floor jack under spring pan and raise until shock absorber is clear of rebound bumper.

2) Remove cotter pin and remove castle nut from fulcrum bolt. Loosen clamp bolt and center bolt on shock absorber arm.

3) Drive out fulcrum pin. Pry shock absorber halves apart and swing trunnion out of way. Wire steering knuckle to crossmember in an upright position. Remove 4 bolts mounting shock absorber to crossmember and slide out shock.

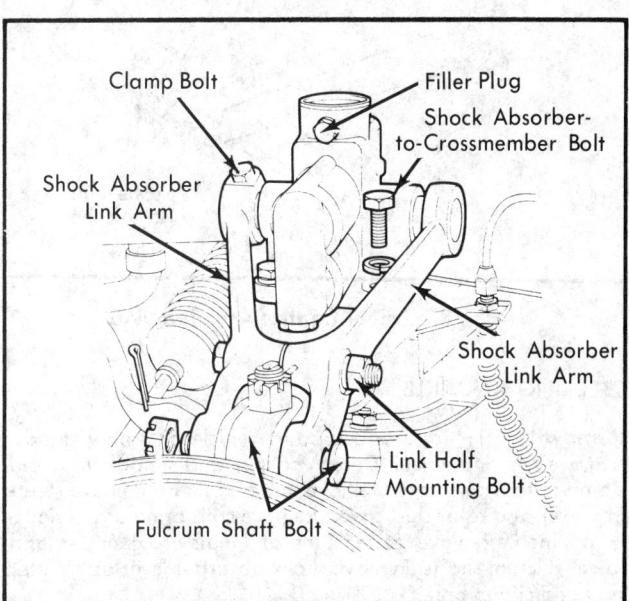

Fig. 2 Shock Absorber Removal

Inspection — **1)** Place shock absorber vertically in vise. Remove filler plug. Move shock absorber levers back and forth to ensure they are firm and also to bleed air from housing. Recheck fluid level, fill to plug opening.

2) Check trunnion bushings to make sure they are not deteriorated or severely worn. Replace bushings if necessary.

Installation — To install, reverse removal procedure and note: Grease kingpin.

LOWER CONTROL ARMS

Removal — **1)** Raise and support front of vehicle. Remove tire and wheel. Remove coil spring as previously outlined.

2) Remove cotter pin and castle nut mounting lower control arm link at kingpin. Remove cotter pin and castle nut mounting control arm link to pivot shaft.

Front Suspension

MGB (Cont.)

3) Support hub assembly. Pull off front control arm link. Pull out control arm link mounting bolt at kingpin and force off back control arm link.

Inspection — Replace any bushings that show signs of excessive wear.

Installation — To install, reverse removal procedure and note: Make sure thrust washers face bushing correctly. Tighten castle nuts with vehicle weight on ground. If cotter pin cannot be fitted, tighten nut to next opening. Grease kingpin.

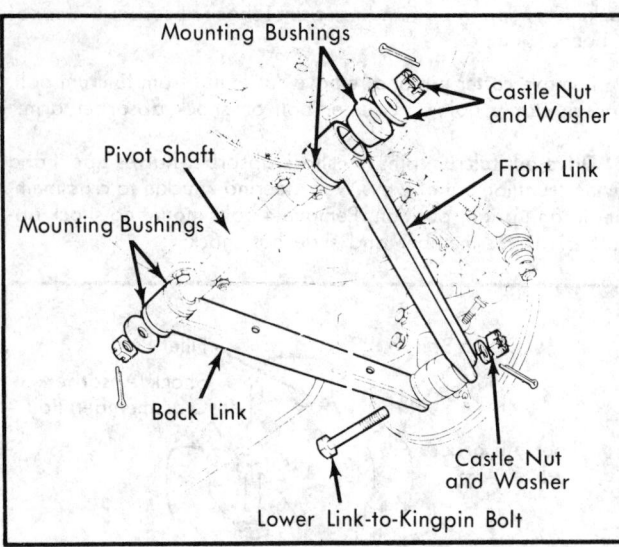

Fig. 3 Lower Control Arm Removal

STEERING KNUCKLE

Removal — **1)** Raise and support vehicle on safety stands. Remove tire and wheel. Detach caliper and support to avoid damage to brake hose. Remove hub and rotor. Remove steering lever and rotor dust cover. Remove coil spring as previously outlined. Remove cotter pins and nuts from upper and lower fulcrum shafts. Remove shock absorber lever arm center bolt and clamp bolt. Ease arm off.

2) Raise jack under spring pan. Loosen 2 bolts mounting lower arm link to the spring pan. Remove kingpin fulcrum bolt. Separate lower control links. Remove kingpin and spindle assembly. If necessary, kingpin can be separated from spindle assembly.

Installation — Check all parts for wear or damage. Check fulcrum shafts for out of round. Replace parts and shafts as necessary. To install, reverse removal procedure. Tighten nuts and bolts.

STABILIZER BAR

Removal — **1)** Raise and support front of vehicle. Disconnect stabilizer bars at lower control arm links.

2) Remove bolts mounting bushing clamps to body. Slide stabilizer bar from vehicle.

3) Pry mounting clamps away from bushings and slide bushings off stabilizer bar. Force link mounting bushings from each end of stabilizer bar. If bushings show signs of wear or severe deterioration, replace with new parts.

Installation — To install, reverse removal procedure. If bar is replaced, put old locaters 9⁵⁄₁₆" from center of stabilizer bar.

FRONT SUSPENSION ASSEMBLY

Removal — **1)** Raise and support vehicle. Remove tire and wheel. Disconnect tie rods from steering knuckle. Disconnect stabilizer bar at lower control arm connecting links.

2) Remove 4 bolts mounting steering rack to crossmember. Tie rack to stabilizer bar.

3) Disconnect brake hose at bracket. Plug openings. Place floor jack under crossmember.

4) Put rods through holes in crossmember to retain body to crossmember studs. Loosen both REAR stud lock nuts keeping crossmember to body.

5) Work inside of engine compartment and remove lock nuts and washers from both FRONT mounting studs. Remove mounting pad from each rear stud. Lower suspension from vehicle.

Installation — To install suspension assembly, reverse removal procedure and note: Make sure all mounting pads are aligned. Make sure that REAR stud clamp plates have depressions facing toward mounting pad. Bleed brake system.

TIGHTENING SPECIFICATIONS

Application	Ft. Lbs. (mkg)
Shock Absorber Bolts	44 (6.1)
Brake Caliper Mounting Bolts	43 (6.0)
Crossmember-to-Body	55 (7.6)
Shock Absorber Pinch Bolt	28 (3.9)
Lower Control Arm Nuts	28 (3.9)
Stabilizer Bar Link Nut	60 (8.3)
Kingpin Nut	60 (8.3)

PEUGEOT

504
505
604

DESCRIPTION

An independent, strut front suspension is used. Wheels are supported by steering knuckles that are attached to vertical strut assemblies. Lower control arms are attached to bottom of steering knuckles by ball joints. Inner ends of control arms pivot on front crossmember. Attached to lower control arms are strut rods that run forward to mounting points on front crossmember. Top of vertical strut assemblies are attached to inner fender panels. Coil springs fit into spring seats attached to strut assemblies. Hydraulic shock absorbers are built into strut assemblies. A stabilizer bar is mounted to frame and connected at ends to lower control arm.

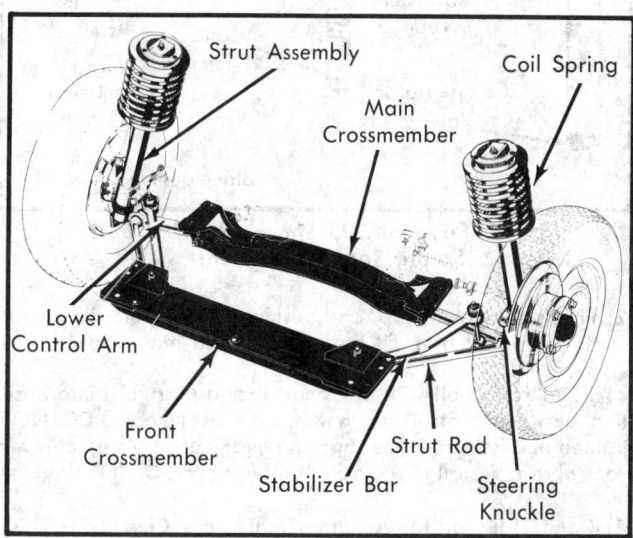

Fig. 1 Sectional View of Peugeot Front Suspension Assembly

ADJUSTMENTS

WHEEL ALIGNMENT SPECIFICATIONS & ADJUSTMENTS

See Wheel Alignment Specifications and Adjustments in WHEEL ALIGNMENT Section.

FRONT WHEEL BEARINGS

See Front Wheel Bearing Adjustment in WHEEL ALIGNMENT Section.

BALL JOINT CHECKING

See Ball Joint Checking in WHEEL ALIGNMENT Section.

REMOVAL & INSTALLATION

FRONT STRUT ASSEMBLY

Removal — 1) Raise vehicle and place safety stands under front crossmember. Remove wheel. Remove brake caliper and suspend with a wire from underbody. DO NOT disconnect hydraulic line.

2) Separate tie rod from rear arm. Disconnect stabilizer bar at mounting on lower control arm. Remove control arm pivot bolt nut and tap bolt out. Remove nut mounting strut rod to control arm.

3) Place a jack under steering knuckle and remove bolts mounting strut to inner fender panel. Hold spring by one coil and lower jack to remove strut assembly.

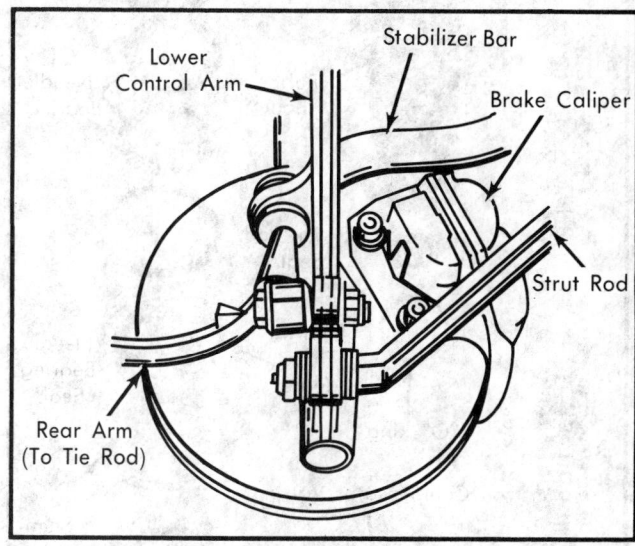

Fig. 2 Components That Must Be Disconnected Prior to Strut Assembly Removal

Disassembly — 1) Install suitable strut holder and spring compressor to strut assembly. Mount assembly horizontally in vise and compress spring enough to unseat it. Hold shock absorber piston rod and remove top nut and retainer. Slowly release tension on spring. Remove upper spring seat assembly, coil spring and rubber boot from shock absorber rod.

2) Suspend strut assembly vertically in vise. Remove shock absorber gland nut. Pull up slowly on piston rod and remove piston rod assembly. Remove support cup with rod seal, thrust washer, and upper spring and bushing "O" ring from piston rod.

3) Pry bumper and lower spring seat off strut housing. Take strut housing from vise and drain hydraulic fluid. Unscrew strut housing and remove compensator valve.

Cleaning & Inspection — Clean and inspect all parts for wear or damage; replace defective parts. All components indicated in *Figs. 3* and *4* must be replaced during overhaul.

Reassembly — 1) Mount strut vertically in vise. Install recoil bumper with lower spring seat. Install compensator valve to shock absorber tube by lightly tapping with rubber mallet. Blow off valve, shock absorber tube and shock absorber inner housing with compressed air.

PEUGEOT (Cont.)

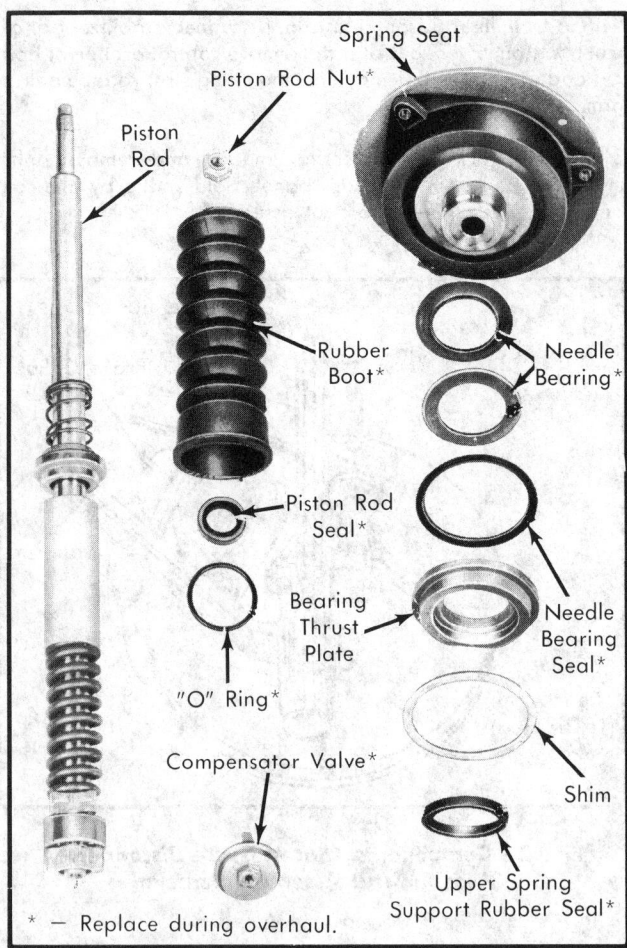

Fig. 3   Peugeot 504 and 604 Shock Absorber and Spring Seat Components

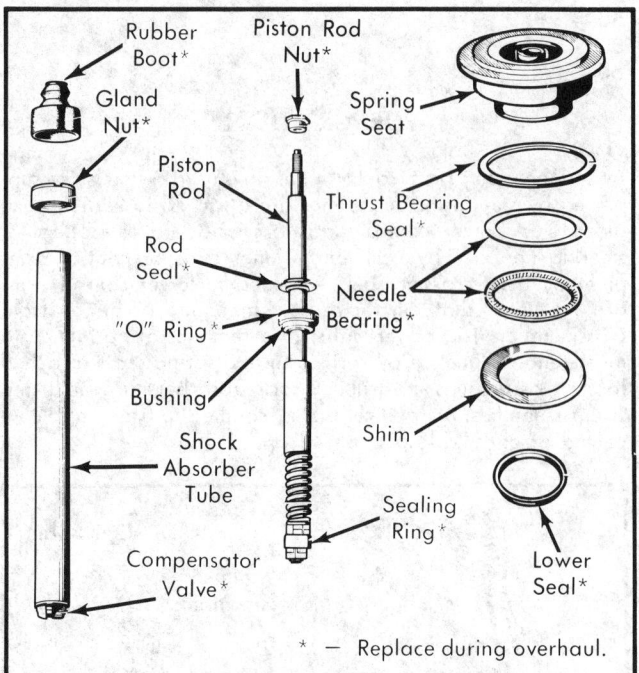

* — Replace during overhaul.

Fig. 4   Peugeot 505 Shock Absorber and Spring Seat Components

2) Fit shock absorber tube to strut housing. Fill shock absorber with 10 oz. (504 and 604) or 11 oz. (505) of Esso Oleofluid 40X (or equivalent). Slowly insert piston rod assembly into shock absorber tube. Clearance between upper shock absorber housing and upper bushing must be .12" (3 mm).

3) Install new "O" ring, then install upper spring and thrust washer (convex side up). Install new piston rod seal to cup. Position cup and seal over rod and force assembly down until thrust washer engages spring. Tighten gland nut. Check rod rotation and operation.

4) Install rubber dust boot. Fully extend piston rod and place holding clamp between bottom of dust boot and shock absorber cap nut. Place housing horizontally in vise. Fit new seal to bearing thrust plate. Reassemble upper spring seat components as shown in *Figs. 3 and 4*.

5) Install spring and upper spring seat. Install and tighten spring compressor until retainer and new locking nut can be installed. Tighten nut while holding rod.

Installation — 1) Mount assembled strut assembly and guide into position while raising steering knuckle with jack. Install upper mounting bolts. Retainer must be parallel with centerline of car.

2) Fit thrust washer, cup, and bushing to strut rod. Slide strut rod into control arm. Fit bushing cup and new stop nut.

3) Insert pivot bolt with bolt head facing rearward into position between control arm and front crossmember. DO NOT tighten nut. Refit stabilizer bar (nut end nearest front) to lower control arm. Install new washer and nut but DO NOT tighten.

4) Connect tie rod to rear arm. Tighten nut. Clean brake disc and refit brake caliper. Tighten mounting bolts after placing few drops of Loctite (or equivalent) on washers.

5) Refit wheel. Lower vehicle. Push in front suspension strut rod and tighten all nuts to final torque.

STABILIZER BAR

Removal — With vehicle on ground, remove 2 bolts mounting stabilizer bar near front crossmember. Disconnect both links mounting stabilizer bar at connecting links. Guide bar from vehicle.

Installation — Fit cup, spacer and bushing to control link. Install stabilizer mounting bolts and spacers.

TIGHTENING SPECIFICATIONS

Application	Ft. Lbs. (mkg)
Shock Absorber Piston Nut	33 (4.6)
Shock Absorber Housing Nut	58 (8.0)
Vertical Strut-to-Fender Bolts	7 (1.0)
Rear Arm-to-Control Arm Nut	33 (4.6)
Rear Arm-to-Tie Rod Nut	31 (4.3)
Strut Rod-to-Control Rod Nut	33 (4.6)
Stabilizer Bar-to-Control Arm	33 (4.6)
Control Arm Pivot Bolts	33 (4.6)

Front Suspension

PORSCHE 911SC

DESCRIPTION

Independent strut type suspension with torsion bars. Strut assemblies are mounted to inner fender panels at top by thrust bearings. Bottom of strut assemblies are mounted to control arms by ball joints. Steering knuckle and shock absorbers are integral with individual strut assembly. Control arms pivot in mounts connected to body at front and in mounts integral with suspension crossmember at rear. Torsion bars anchor to control arm at front and to suspension crossmember at rear. Suspension crossmember also serves as mount for steering gear and is removable.

ADJUSTMENT

WHEEL ALIGNMENT SPECIFICATIONS & PROCEDURES

See Wheel Alignment Specifications & Procedures in WHEEL ALIGNMENT Section.

WHEEL BEARING ADJUSTMENT

See Wheel Alignment Specifications & Procedures in WHEEL ALIGNMENT Section.

BALL JOINT CHECKING

See Ball Joint Checking in WHEEL ALIGNMENT Section.

REMOVAL & INSTALLATION

STRUT ASSEMBLY AND THRUST BEARING

Removal — 1) Raise vehicle and place safety stands under body. Remove wheel and tire. Remove brake rotor and brake caliper.

NOTE — If necessary, refer to appropriate article in BRAKE SYSTEMS section.

2) Remove tie rod end strut nut and separate tie rod end from steering arm. Unscrew adjusting screw from torsion bar adjusting lever and remove lever. Remove ball joint retaining bolt at bottom of strut assembly and push control arm down to separate strut assembly from ball joint.

3) Remove center nut from upper strut assembly mount from inside luggage compartment. Remove lock washer, tab washer and strut assembly. Mark position of pressure plates on fender panel and remove Allen head bolts and pressure plates. Remove thrust , bearing and support.

NOTE — Thrust bearing can be removed without completely removing strut assembly by disconnecting upper mount and pulling down on control arm to separate from thrust bearing.

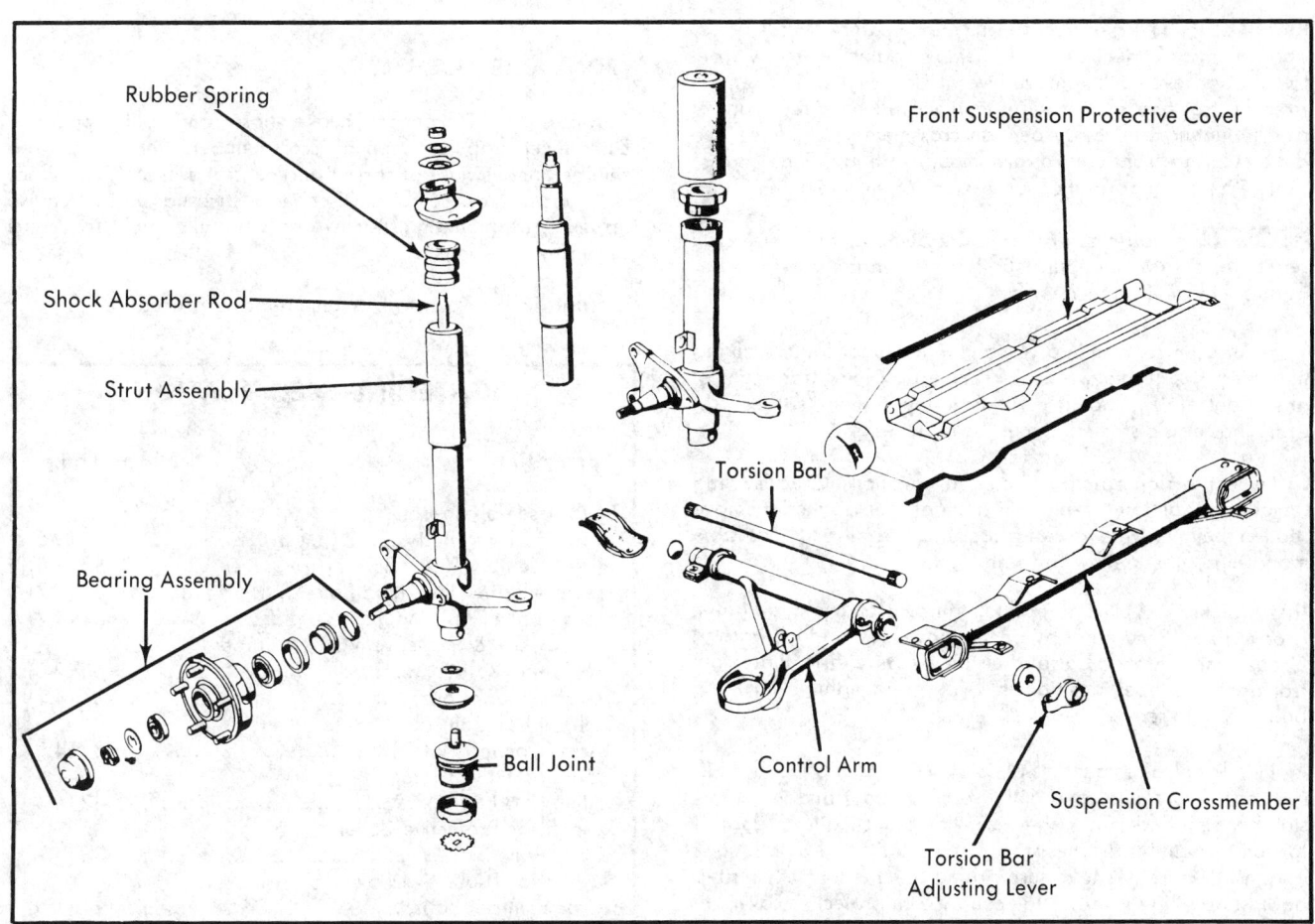

Fig. 1   Exploded View of Front Suspension Assembly

PORSCHE 911SC (Cont.)

Installation – 1) Install thrust bearing and support. Place pressure plates in proper position and tighten Allen head bolts. Inspect strut assembly for leaks, if leak is discovered, strut assembly must be replaced.

2) Push rod to bottom of stroke, if flange does not bottom out against strut tube, replace strut assembly. There should be no variation of pressure when pushing in or pulling out on rod.

3) Install strut assembly in proper position in vehicle. Install hollow rubber spring, new lock washer, and tighten nut. Fit strut assembly to ball joint and tighten nut.

NOTE – *Make sure steel washer is between ball joint and stud.*

4) Push control arm lever down to stop and install adjusting lever on torsion bar. Grease threads of adjusting screw with suitable grease and install screw. Make sure closing cover is correctly seated against adjusting lever.

5) Install tie rod and retighten nut. Install remaining components. *See appropriate article in BRAKE SYSTEM Section.* Tighten all nuts and bolts, bleed brake system, check wheel alignment and riding height.

CONTROL ARM & BALL JOINT

Removal – 1) Raise vehicle and place safety stands under body. Remove wheel and tire. Remove adjusting screw from torsion bar lever and remove lever. Disconnect strut assembly from control arm as previously outlined. Remove rear control arm mounting bolt at suspension crossmember. Remove two bolts securing front control arm mount to body. Slide control arm with torsion bar out of suspension crossmember.

CAUTION – *If both control arms are being removed, reinstall rear control arm mounting bolt in suspension crossmember before removing opposite side.*

2) Secure control arm in a vise and remove ball joint retaining nut using a suitable wrench. Remove ball joint from control arm. Control arm should pivot smoothly in mounts. If control arm binds or is distorted, it must be replaced.

3) Inspect torsion bars for damaged serrations. Check sealing bellows on ball joint, replace if damaged or cracked. Remove sealing bellows with a flat chisel and install using suitable mandrel to press bellows on with.

Installation – 1) Install ball joint in control arm and tighten grooved nut. Secure nut by bending over tab on lock washer. Grease entire torsion bar and install in control arm. Place control arm in proper position in vehicle and tighten mounting bolts (front to rear).

2) Install strut assembly on ball joint and tighten retaining bolt. Push down on control arm until it contacts stops and install torsion bar seal and adjusting lever. Slide adjusting lever against torsion bar until it reaches stop. Grease adjusting bolt threads and install in lever. Make sure closing cover is correctly seated against adjusting lever. Install control arm protective cover. Install wheel and tire, lower vehicle and check riding height and wheel alignment.

SUSPENSION CROSSMEMBER

Removal – Raise vehicle and place safety stands under vehicle. Remove front axle protective cover. Remove steering gear bolts from crossmember. Remove rear control arm mounting bolts as previously outlined and remove suspension crossmember. Place crossmember on level surface and check for distortion. Inspect for cracks or damage.

Installation – Place crossmember in proper position in vehicle and install control arm mounting bolts as previously outlined. Install steering gear bolts and tighten. Install front suspension protective cover. Lower vehicle and check riding height and wheel alignment.

FRONT AXLE STABILIZER

Removal – Remove stabilizer shackles. Unbolt stabilizer lever retaining nuts and extract lever. Remove stabilizer mounting cover hardware and gently pry cover from vehicle.

Installation – Check all rubber grommets for signs of wear and replace components as necessary. Coat rubber parts with suitable lubricant. Reinstall stabilizer mounting cover, center stabilizer, then tighten attaching bolts. Seat stabilizer lever in position so stabilizer protrudes approximately .118" (3 mm) beyond lever. Tighten retaining nuts and install shackles.

FRONT AXLE ASSEMBLY

Removal – Disconnect brake hose and plug opening. Disconnect stabilizer bar at crossmember. Remove tie rod shield. Remove bolts at carrier and control arm brackets. Place jack under crossmember. Disconnect steering shaft. Remove upper strut mounting hardware. Carefully pull front axle assembly from vehicle.

Installation – To install, reverse removal procedure.

TIGHTENING SPECIFICATIONS

Application	Ft. Lbs. (mkg)
Strut Assembly-to-Ball Joint Securing Bolt	47 (6.5)
Strut Assembly Thrust Bearing	58 (8.0)
Pressure Plate Allen Head Bolts	34 (4.7)
Front Control Arm Mount	34 (4.7)
Control Arm & Suspension Crossmember Mounting Bolt	65 (9.0)
Steering Gear Bolts	34 (4.7)
Ball Joint-to-Control Arm Grooved Nut	108 (14.9)
Front Protective Clamp Allen Head Bolt	32 (4.4)
Suspension Protective Cover-to-Body Bolts	34 (4.7)
Suspension Protective Cover-to-Crossmember Bolts	11 (1.5)
Tie Rod End Strut Nut	32 (4.4)

Front Suspension

PORSCHE 924

DESCRIPTION

Vehicle uses independent strut type front suspension. Lower control arms mount with a ball joint to steering knuckle. Back branch of control arm mounts to frame with "U" clamp around control arm pivot shaft. Front branch attaches to frame with bushings and pivot bolt. Strut assembly mounts at top to body with 3 nuts and at bottom to steering knuckle with 2 bolts. Tie rod mounts to steering knuckle with ball joint.

ADJUSTMENTS

WHEEL ALIGNMENT SPECIFICATIONS & PROCEDURES

See Wheel Alignment Specifications and Procedures in WHEEL ALIGNMENT Section.

WHEEL BEARING ADJUSTMENT

See Wheel Bearing Adjustment in WHEEL ALIGNMENT Section.

BALL JOINT CHECKING

See Ball Joint Checking in WHEEL ALIGNMENT Section.

REMOVAL & INSTALLATION

STRUT ASSEMBLY

Removal — 1) Raise vehicle so front suspension and front wheels are not supported.

2) Remove bolts mounting suspension strut to steering knuckle. Note that top bolt is one used to adjust front wheel camber.

3) Detach brake line from brake line bracket on strut. Remove brake caliper assembly and suspend out of way. Pry strut off of steering knuckle.

4) Support front suspension. Work inside engine compartment and remove strut upper mounting nuts. Guide assembly out of vehicle.

Disassembly — 1) Fit strut to spring compressor. Slightly collapse coil spring. Remove shock absorber piston rod nut. Take off the following:
- Stop
- Seal
- Bearing flange
- Bearing
- Spring seat

2) Slowly release spring pressure, remove coil spring. Lift off rubber buffer and protective sleeve. Hold shock absorber upright and work piston rod through entire stroke several different times. Equal pressure must be felt in both directions. Remove cap nut and take out shock absorber.

Reassembly — 1) Place shock absorber in strut tube and fit cap nut. Slide on protective sleeve and buffer. Position coil spring into lower seat.

NOTE — If new coil spring is being installed, ensure that paint stripe color code matches that of spring on opposite side.

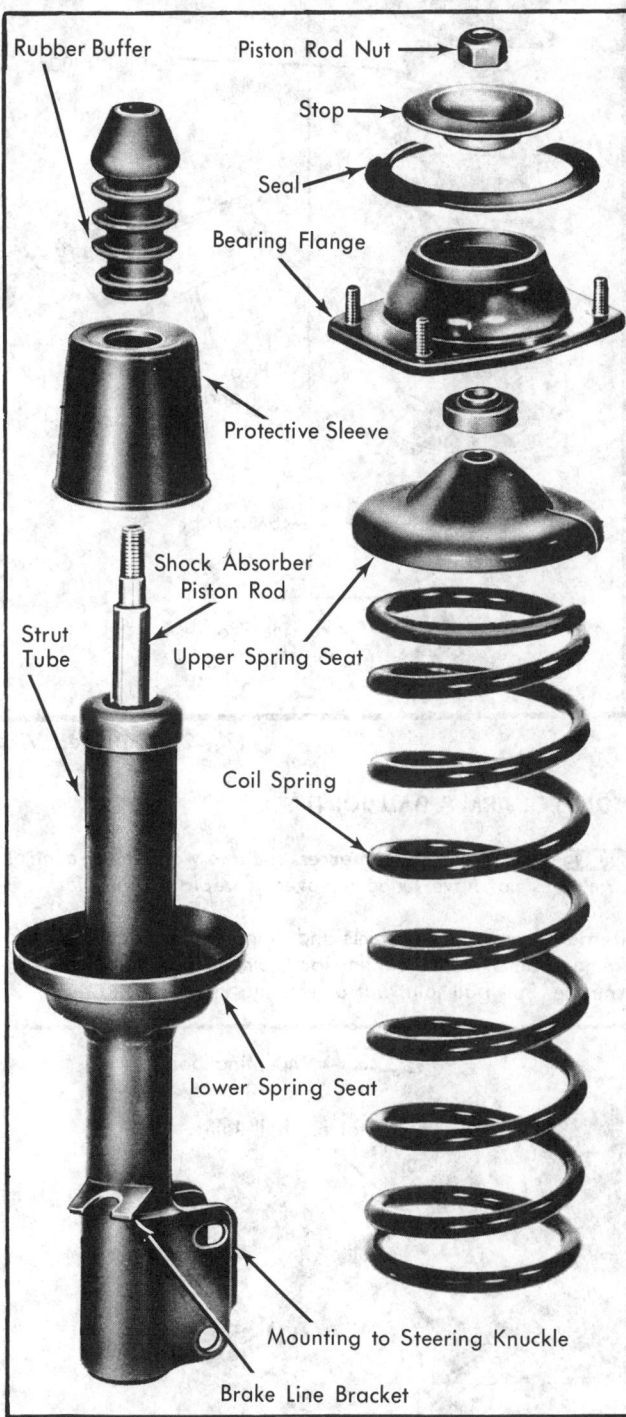

Fig. 1 Exploded View of Strut Assembly

2) Fit coil spring to compressor and collapse coil enough to allow piston rod threads to be exposed after upper mounting hardware is fitted. Tighten piston rod lock nut. Release spring pressure.

Installation — To install, reverse removal procedure and check front wheel alignment.

PORSCHE 924 (Cont.)

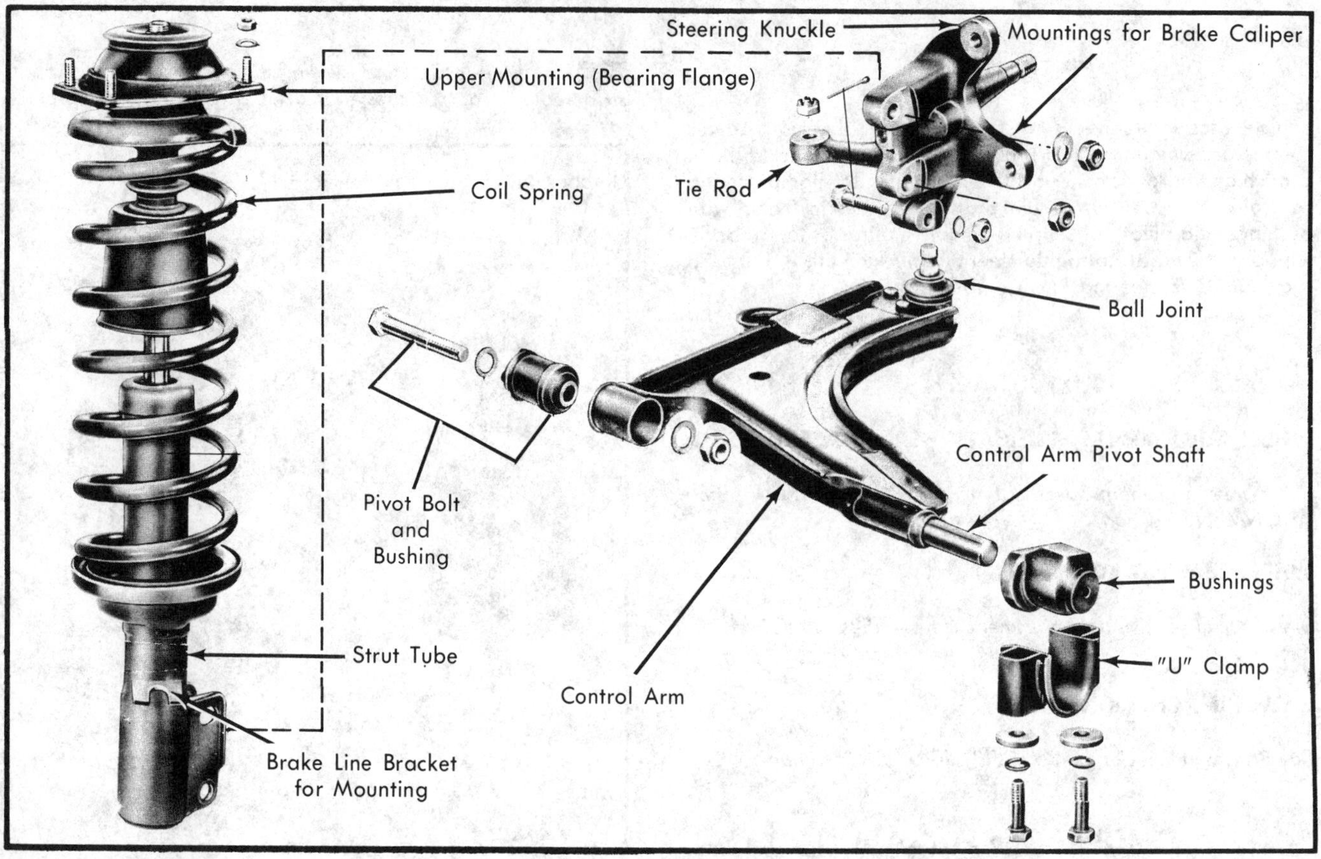

Steering Knuckle — Mountings for Brake Caliper

Upper Mounting (Bearing Flange)

Coil Spring

Tie Rod

Ball Joint

Pivot Bolt and Bushing

Control Arm Pivot Shaft

Strut Tube

Bushings

Control Arm

"U" Clamp

Brake Line Bracket for Mounting

Fig. 2   Exploded View of 924 Front Suspension

CONTROL ARM & BALL JOINT

NOTE — *If there is enough access room to work, lower control arm does not have to be removed to replace ball joint.*

Removal — **1)** Raise vehicle and support so suspension is free. Remove pinch bolt mounting ball joint in bottom of steering knuckle. Pull ball joint out of steering knuckle.

2) If control arm is not being removed, drill through ball joint rivets with about $^{15}/_{64}$" (6 mm) bit. Chisel off rivet heads. Fit new ball joint into slot on control arm and install bolts so heads are on top.

3) If control arm is being removed, take out mounting pivot bolt and "U" clamp housing inner pivot pin. Slide out control arm. For ball joint replacement, refer to step **2)**.

Inspection — Check control arm bushings. If bushings are bad they can be replaced. Press out worn bushings. Select new bushing and press into position. Make sure new bushings do not twist when seating into position.

Installation — To install, reverse removal procedure.

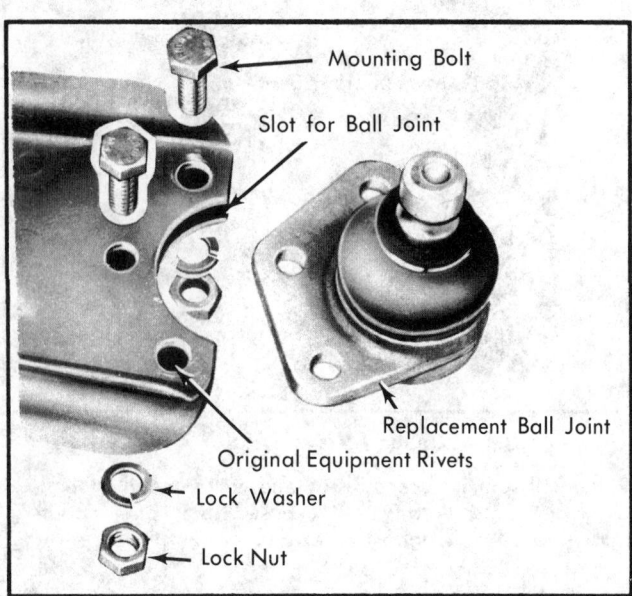

Mounting Bolt

Slot for Ball Joint

Replacement Ball Joint

Original Equipment Rivets

Lock Washer

Lock Nut

Fig. 3   Ball Joint Location in Control Arm

TIGHTENING SPECIFICATIONS

Application	Ft. Lbs. (mkg)
Control Arm-to-Crossmember	40-54 (5.5-7.5)
"U" Clamp Bolts	30 (4.2)
Tie Rod Castle Nut	22-36 (3.0-5.0)
Strut Piston Rod Nut	56-58 (7.7-8.0)
Strut-to-Steering Knuckle	51-72 (7.0-10.0)
Upper Strut Mount	15-21 (2.1-2.9)
Ball Joint-to-Control Arm (Replacement)	18 (2.5)
Ball Joint Pinch Bolt	36-43 (5.0-6.0)

PORSCHE 928

DESCRIPTION

Front suspension is an independent type strut suspension. It consists of a strut assembly, surrounded by a coil spring. This assembly is connected at top to inner fender panel and at bottom to lower control arm. Lower control arm connects at outer end to steering knuckle through a ball joint. At inner end of the "T" shaped control arm, 2 bushings connect arm to frame member. An upper control arm is attached by ball joint to steering knuckle and by pivot shaft to frame member. A stabilizer bar is connected via a link to lower mounting of strut assembly.

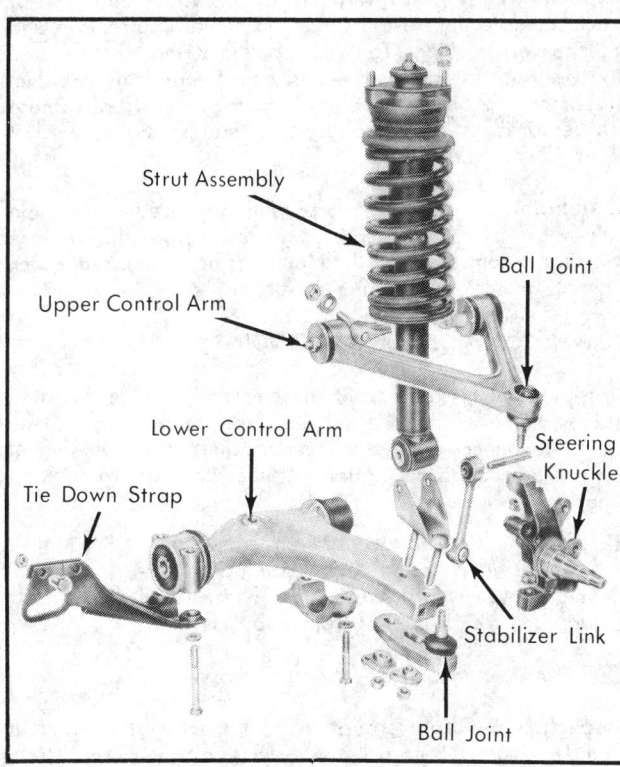

Fig. 1 Exploded View of Porsche 928 Front Suspension Assembly

ADJUSTMENTS

WHEEL BEARING ADJUSTMENT

See Wheel Bearing Adjustment in WHEEL ALIGNMENT section.

WHEEL ALIGNMENT SPECIFICATIONS & PROCEDURES

See Wheel Alignment Specifications and Procedures in WHEEL ALIGNMENT section.

BALL JOINT CHECKING

See Ball Joint Checking in WHEEL ALIGNMENT section.

REMOVAL & INSTALLATION

STRUT ASSEMBLY & UPPER CONTROL ARM

Removal — 1) Remove 3 self-locking nuts securing top of strut assembly to inner fender panel in engine compartment. Raise and support vehicle. Remove front wheel.

2) Unscrew flange locknut and use suitable tool to separate upper control arm ball joint from steering knuckle. Remove self-locking nuts holding upper control arm pivot shaft to body (access in engine compartment).

3) Remove strut lower mounting bolt and maneuver strut assembly and upper control arm out of vehicle.

Disassembly — 1) Place strut assembly in vise and attach coil spring compressor. Apply enough tension to coil spring to allow removal of top self-locking nut, washer and mounting plate.

2) Release spring compressor. Remove upper spring retainer, coil spring and components from piston rod.

3) Mark position of lower spring retainer to shock absorber for proper reassembly reference.

Reassembly — 1) Reassemble strut assembly components in reverse order of disassembly. If replacing coil spring, be sure proper weight class springs are used.

2) If replacing lower spring retainer, coil spring or shock absorber, position of spring retainer to shock absorber must be determined. Install assembly in vehicle by attaching upper retainers. Position upper end of spring against upper retainer stop. Position lower retainer and turn until against stop. Mark position.

3) Remove strut assembly back to vise and complete reassembly.

Installation — To install, reverse removal procedure.

TIGHTENING SPECIFICATIONS

Application	Ft. Lbs. (mkg)
Upper Control Arm-to-Body	101 (14)
Lower Control Arm-to-Body	
Front	61 (8.5)
Rear	87 (12)
Stabilizer Bar-to-Body	33 (4.6)
Stabilizer Link Nut	61 (8.5)
Ball Joints-to-Knuckle	61 (8.5)

RENAULT

Le Car

DESCRIPTION

Independent type suspension, consisting of upper and lower control arms with stub axles mounted between upper and lower control arms by ball joints. Upper control arm pivots on shaft attached to frame. Lower arm pivots on shaft secured to crossmember. Shock absorbers mount off body brackets at top and off purchases built into control arm on bottom.

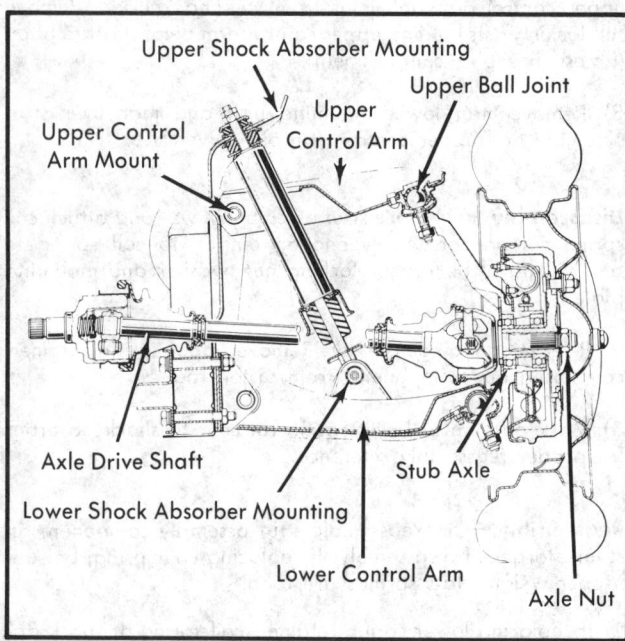

Fig. 1 Cut-Away View of Le Car Front Suspension

ADJUSTMENT

WHEEL ALIGNMENT SPECIFICATIONS & PROCEDURES

See Wheel Alignment Specifications & Procedures in WHEEL ALIGNMENT Section.

WHEEL BEARING ADJUSTMENT

See Wheel Bearing Adjustment in WHEEL ALIGNMENT Section.

BALL JOINT CHECKING

See Ball Joint Checking in WHEEL ALIGNMENT Section.

RIDING HEIGHT ADJUSTMENT

See Riding Height Adjustment in WHEEL ALIGNMENT Section.

REMOVAL & INSTALLATION

SHOCK ABSORBERS

Removal — Raise vehicle and suitably support vehicle with safety stands. Remove lock nut, mounting nut, and bushing attaching shock absorber to upper bracket. Remove lower

retaining bolt holding shock absorber to lower control arm. Maneuver shock absorber from vehicle.

Installation — To install, reverse removal procedure.

UPPER CONTROL ARM & BALL JOINT

Removal — Take out overflow tank and remove ignition coil. Using tool T. Av. 476 (or equivalent) disconnect upper ball joint. Remove nut from inboard edge of pivot shaft. Place a lock nut on outer end of pivot shaft and turn mounting nut to remove shaft. Pivot shaft will clear brake lines. Maneuver control arm from vehicle.

Inspection & Replacement — Inspect rubber bushings for cracks or distortion. Use a press and mandrel to remove and replace worn bushings. To replace ball joint, place control arm in a vise and drill out rivet heads. Fit new ball joint with shim placed on top of control arm. Tighten nuts and bolts (those that replaced rivets). Make sure bolt head is installed on dust cover side of joint.

Installation — To install, reverse removal procedure and note following: Apply a light coat of grease to pivot shaft before inserting in control arm. If ball joint has been replaced, check wheel alignment and steering box height.

LOWER CONTROL ARM & BALL JOINT

Removal — 1) Raise front of vehicle and place on safety stands. Remove stub axle nut. Disconnect and remove torsion bars. Disconnect sway bar from brackets and mounting on control arm. Separate bottom of shock absorber from mounting.

2) Remove lower control arm from crossmember. Put tool T. Av. 235 (or equivalent) in brake drum or hub. With a spacer located between thrust screw and axle drive shaft, force shaft inward and free ball joint from stub axle carrier.

NOTE — *Make sure axle drive shaft is not removed.*

Inspection & Replacement — 1) Inspect rubber bushings and sleeve inserts for cracks, excessive damage or wear. Use a mandrel and press to replace bushings. Make sure each bushing is centered and has adequate protrusion out each side of control arm.

2) Place control arm in suitable holding fixture (vise). Chisel or drill out rivet heads. Remove nuts, if necessary. Separate joint from control arm. Fit new ball joint into control arm. Make sure bolt heads face dust cover side.

Installation — To install, reverse removal procedure and note following: Make sure castor adjusting shims are under bushing. Check wheel alignment after reinstallation.

STUB AXLE

Removal — Raise vehicle and place on safety stands. Remove hub and disc assembly. Using tool T. Av. 476 (or equivalent) disconnect upper and lower ball joints, then separate steering arm ball joint. Use a slide hammer and withdraw drum/hub assembly. Make sure axle drive shaft does not drop.

Installation — Install stub axle into position while guiding ball joints into position. Pull drive shaft into carrier housing. Refit brake components. Tighten stub axle nut.

RENAULT (Cont.)

TORSION BAR

Removal — 1) Slide seat forward and tilt seat. Loosen lock nut and turn cam screw counterclockwise to zero. Raise vehicle and place on safety stands. Remove dust cover from adjusting lever. Fit special tool 545 (or equivalent) in adjusting lever. From inside vehicle, remove lever housing attachment bolts. Remove housing cover cam assembly from adjusting lever, then slowly release pressure on wrench.

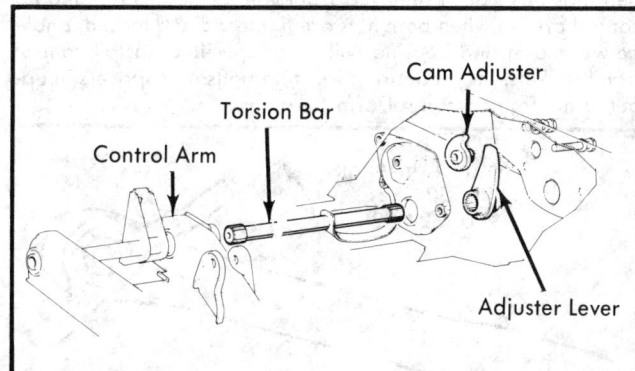

Fig. 2   Exploded View of Torsion Bar Assembly

2) Index mark position of adjusting lever with floor crossmember. Mark position of torsion bar on lower arm anchor sleeve. Disconnect stabilizer bar brackets. Remove bar from arm and check that mark made on lower arm anchor sleeve is aligned with punch mark on torsion bar. If punch marks do not align, count number of revolutions and spines displaced to align marks.

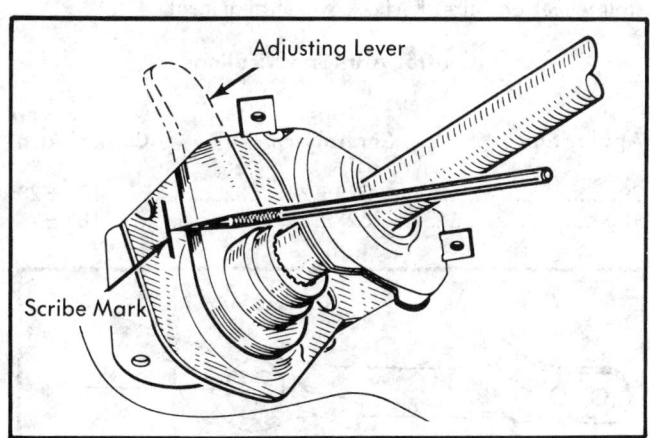

Fig. 3   Scribing Marks on Floor Crossmember

Installation — 1) Lightly grease torsion bar ends with grease. Reassemble cover seal, cam housing, and adjusting lever over torsion bar. Insert bar into lower control arm, aligning index mark made during removal. Fit adjusting lever on splines, aligning with mark on floor crossmember.

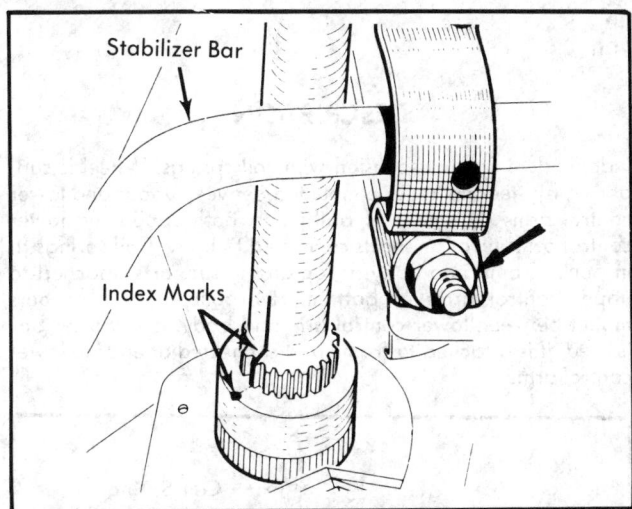

Fig. 4   Lower Arm Anchor Sleeve Scribe Mark

2) Place adjusting lever ⅜-¾" (10-20 mm) as shown in *Fig. 5*. Insert wrench 545 (or equivalent) and take up tension on bar. Center the cover by resetting cam. Hold assembly with vise grips and insert mounting bolts. Adjust under body height by turning adjusting cams.

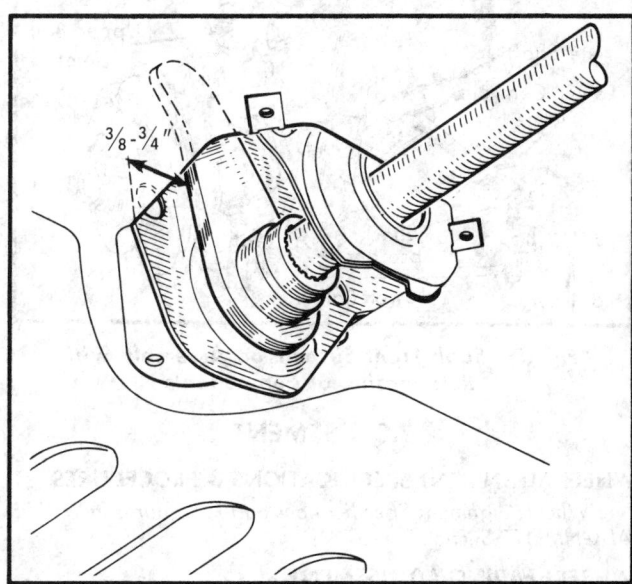

Fig. 5   Position of Adjusting Lever

TIGHTENING SPECIFICATIONS

Application	Ft. Lbs. (mkg)
Lower Shock Absorber Bolt	30 (4.2)
Lower Ball Joint	40 (5.5)
Upper Ball Joint	25 (3.5)
Lower Control Arm Nuts	75 (10.4)
Axle Nut	90 (12.4)

SAAB

99
900

DESCRIPTION

Independent front suspension with coil springs. Wheel is supported by steering knuckle mounted between upper and lower control arms by means of ball joints. Both upper and lower control arms pivot on shafts connected to body. Coil springs fit in pockets built into body at top and in supports attached to upper control arms at bottom. Hydraulic shock absorbers mount between lower control arm and body. If stabilizer bar is used, it is attached to frame and connected at ends to lower control arms.

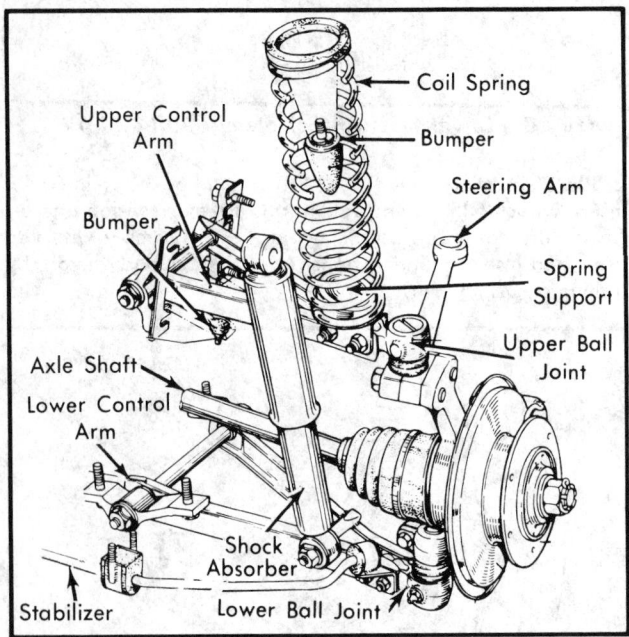

Fig. 1 Saab Front Suspension Assembly with Relationship of Components

ADJUSTMENT

WHEEL ALIGNMENT SPECIFICATIONS & PROCEDURES
See Wheel Alignment Specifications and Procedures in WHEEL ALIGNMENT Section.

WHEEL BEARING ADJUSTMENT
See Wheel Bearing Adjustment in WHEEL ALIGNMENT Section.

BALL JOINT CHECKING
See Ball Joint Checking in WHEEL ALIGNMENT Section.

REMOVAL & INSTALLATION

CONTROL ARMS

NOTE – *Engine must be removed prior to removing upper left control arm.*

Removal – 1) Remove upper shock absorber nut. Raise and support vehicle. Remove tire and wheel. If removing upper control arm, use a spring compressor (8995839) to remove coil spring. Remove ball joint-to-control arm retaining bolts, providing support under steering knuckle housing to prevent brake line damage.

NOTE – *Remove shock absorber prior to jacking up 900 series vehicles; or by supporting shock in position with a jack placed under outer end of lower control arm.*

2) Remove control arm attaching bolts and control arm. If control arm bushings are being replaced, press them out using proper adapter and driver. Note amount and location of upper control arm spacers for reassembly reference.

Installation – 1) Replace worn or damaged components. If bearings have been removed from control arm, position onto control arm so when both nuts are tightened and locked, angle between arm and bearing will be as specified. Install control arm brackets. Install bearing locating bolts and spacers in upper arm. Tighten control arm bearings.

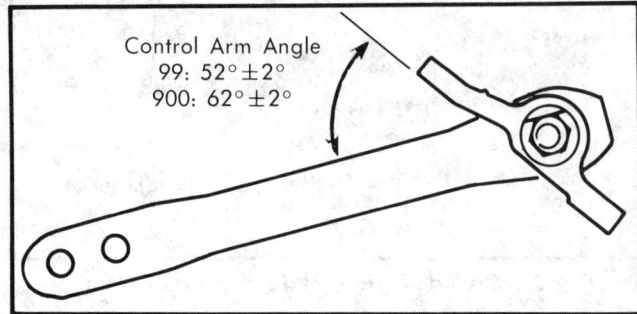

Fig. 2 Upper Control Arm-to-Bearing Angle

2) Install ball joint-to-control arm bolts. Correctly position upper spring spacer and support ring on upper control arm. Install compressed coil spring onto upper control arm with rubber buffer. Raise outer end of lower control arm slightly with a jack and install shock absorber. Tighten all mounting bolts. Install wheel and tire. Recheck wheel alignment.

Control Arm Specifications

Application	Upper Control Arm	Lower Control Arm
99	52°±2°	18°±2°
900	62°±2°	18°±2°

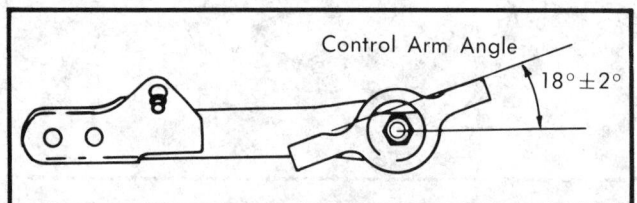

Fig. 3 Lower Control Arm-to-Bearing Angle

SHOCK ABSORBERS

NOTE – *Pneumatic shock absorbers require special handling to prevent personal injury. Drill a hole ³⁄₈-⁵⁄₈" (10-15 mm) from pressure chamber edge before discarding.*

Removal & Installation – Remove upper shock absorber nut before raising vehicle. Raise and support vehicle on safety stands; remove tire and wheel. Remove nuts securing shock absorber and remove shock. Save the washers and rubber parts for use in installation. To install, reverse removal procedure.

SAAB (Cont.)

BALL JOINTS

Removal — Raise and support vehicle; remove tire and wheel. Take weight off control arm travel stop (if equipped) and raise outer portion of lower control arm with a jack. Remove lower shock absorber mounting. Lower jack until drive shaft is aligned with body grommet. With jack under arm for support, remove caliper and hang out of way. Remove ball joint nut. Using suitable tool (8995409) separate ball joint from steering knuckle.

NOTE — *Maximum stroke of control arm is limited by shock absorber. Therefore, upper shock absorber nut must be removed before raising vehicle or support shock absorber with a jack under outer edge of lower control arm.*

Installation — Fit new ball joint to steering knuckle. Tighten nut. Insert ball joint mounting into control arm and tighten using new lock nuts. Reinstall brake caliper. Raise control arm and reinstall shock absorber.

TIGHTENING SPECIFICATIONS

Application	Ft. Lbs. (mkg)
Upper Control Arm Nuts	54-66 (7.5-9.0)
Lower Control Arm Nuts	70-77 (9.7-10.6)

SUBARU

1600
1800

DESCRIPTION

Suspension is strut type, utilizing a hydraulic shock absorber/coil spring assembly forming a strut. Strut is secured at top to body and at bottom to steering knuckle. Steering knuckle pivots on ball joint attached to lower control arm. Lower control arms are attached to front crossmember. Radius rods are bolted to lower control arms and attached to rear crossmember with rubber bushings, washers and nuts. A stabilizer bar is attached to rear crossmember and to radius rods with clamps and rubber bushings.

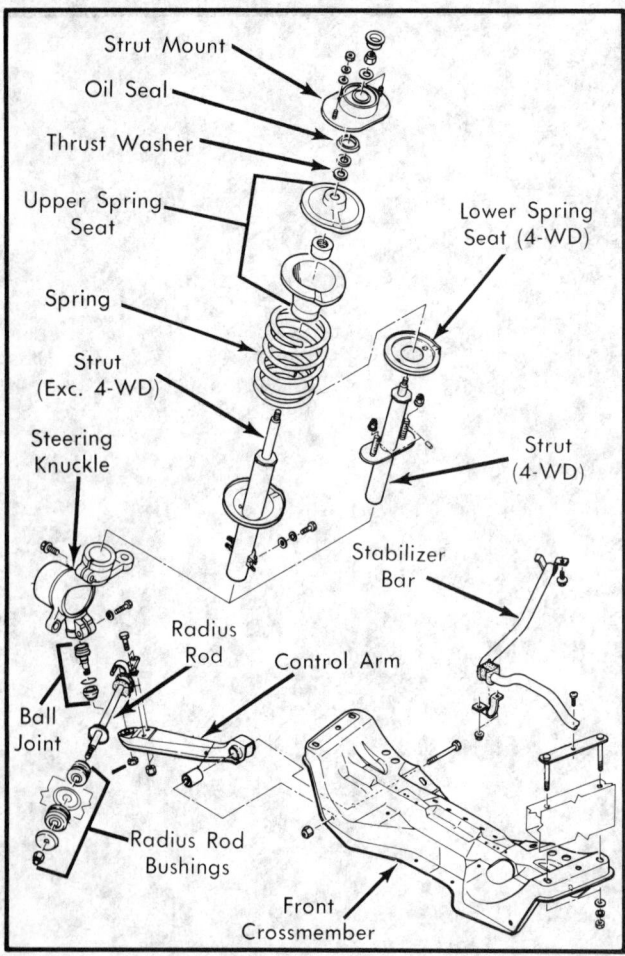

Fig. 1   Exploded View of Subaru Front Suspension

ADJUSTMENTS

WHEEL ALIGNMENT SPECIFICATIONS & PROCEDURES

See Wheel Alignment Specifications and Procedures in WHEEL ALIGNMENT Section.

WHEEL BEARING ADJUSTMENT

See Wheel Bearing Adjustment in WHEEL ALIGNMENT Section.

BALL JOINT CHECKING

See Ball Joint Checking in WHEEL ALIGNMENT Section.

REMOVAL & INSTALLATION

FRONT SUSPENSION

Removal — 1) Detach battery ground cable. Raise and support vehicle and remove front wheel(s).

2) Remove parking brake cable hanger from tie rod end, remove cable end from caliper lever, remove outer cable clip from caliper, remove cable bracket from housing and remove cable mounting bracket from lower control arm.

3) Disconnect brake hose from brake line and plug line. Drive out spring pins from inner ends of drive axles nearest transaxle housing.

4) Remove self-locking nut and bolt holding control arm to crossmember. Pull control arm downward from crossmember.

5) Use suitable tool to separate tie rod end from steering knuckle arm.

6) Detach radius rod from rear crossmember. Remove stabilizer bar brackets.

7) Remove upper strut assembly mounting nuts. Pull drive shaft from transaxle and remove suspension assembly from vehicle.

Installation — To install, reverse removal procedure, noting the following points:

- Be sure to align spring pin holes in drive axle before installing.
- When installing strut top mount, be sure stud marked "FRONT" is forward on Sedan, Hatchback and Hardtop models, and stud marked "VAN/4WD" is forward on Station Wagon and 4-WD models.
- When installing stabilizer, be sure slit in bushing is facing downward in clamp.
- Replace all self-locking nuts.
- Before installing radius rod bushing, soak it in soapy solution or rubber lubricant to assist installation.
- When installing castellated nuts on ball joints, tighten nut, as required, beyond specified torque setting to align cotter pin hole.
- Always use new spring pins for attaching inner end of drive shaft.
- Bleed brake system.

STRUT ASSEMBLY

Removal — 1) Detach battery ground cable. Raise and support vehicle. Remove front wheel. Disconnect brake hose from brake line, strut and brake caliper. Plug brake line.

2) Remove strut-to-knuckle bolts and pull strut out of knuckle. Remove upper strut mounting nuts. Remove strut from vehicle.

Disassembly — 1) Mount strut in spring compressor/holding fixture (925651000) and place in horizontal position. Compress spring until upper seat is separated from coil spring.

2) Use wrench portion of tool to hold upper mounting plate while removing self-locking nut from top end of strut. Remove thrust washer, oil seal and thrust bearing. Remove the upper spring seat from rod.

Front Suspension

SUBARU (Cont.)

3) Carefully remove tension from coil spring and remove tool and spring from strut.

Reassembly — To reassemble, reverse diassembly procedures, replacing self-locking nut with a new one. Place small amount of grease on thrust washer.

Installation — To install, reverse removal procedure, noting the following:

- Be sure upper strut mounting plate is facing in proper direction as described under "Front Suspension" installation procedure in this article.
- When reattaching brake line and hose, be sure to allow enough clearance from wheel apron.
- Bleed brake system.

STABILIZER BAR

Removal — Raise front of vehicle, and support with safety stands. Remove clamps securing stabilizer bar to radius rod. Remove clamps attaching stabilizer bar to rear crossmember.

Installation — Check all bushings for wear or damage and replace as necessary. Check stabilizer bar for possible cracking. To install, reverse removal procedure.

LOWER CONTROL ARM

Removal — Raise front of vehicle, support with safety stands, and remove wheel and tire. Disconnect brake cable bracket from control arm. Disconnect stabilizer bar from radius rod.

Disconnect radius rod from control arm. Remove control arm-to-front crossmember bolt. Remove ball joint-to-knuckle bolt and separate ball joint from knuckle. Remove control arm from vehicle. Remove ball joint castle nut and separate ball joint from control arm.

Installation — Check ball joint for wear or damage. Check pivot bushing for wear or damage. To install lower control arm, reverse removal procedure and note: Torque ball joint castle nut and continue tightening until cotter pin hole is aligned.

TIGHTENING SPECIFICATIONS

Application	Ft. Lbs. (mkg)
Stabilizer Bracket Nuts	13-16 (1.8-2.2)
Radius Rod-to-Rear Crossmember	51-62 (7.0-8.5)
Tie Rod End Ball Joint Nut	18-22 (2.5-3.0)
Wheel Nuts	58-72 (8.0-10.0)
Upper Strut Mounting Nuts	22-29 (3.0-4.0)
Strut-to-Piston Rod Nut	43-54 (6.0-7.5)
Lower Strut End-to-Knuckle	22-29 (3.0-4.0)
Control Arm-to-Crossmember	40-47 (5.5-6.5)
Ball Joint-to-Control Arm	29 (4.0)
Ball Joint-to-Knuckle	22-29 (3.0-4.0)

TOYOTA CELICA, COROLLA, CORONA, CRESSIDA & SUPRA

DESCRIPTION

Independent strut type suspension consisting of vertically mounted strut assemblies, lower control arms, strut rods and a stabilizer bar. Individual strut assembly is mounted at top to inner fender by a thrust bearing and at bottom to lower control arm by means of a ball joint. Strut assembly consists of a shock absorber built into strut outer tube, a coil spring mounted on outside of strut tube and a steering knuckle integral with bottom of strut tube. A strut rod is mounted between lower control arm and frame. A stabilizer bar is mounted to front frame members and connected at ends to lower control arms. The suspension crossmember that serves as support for all suspension components is removable.

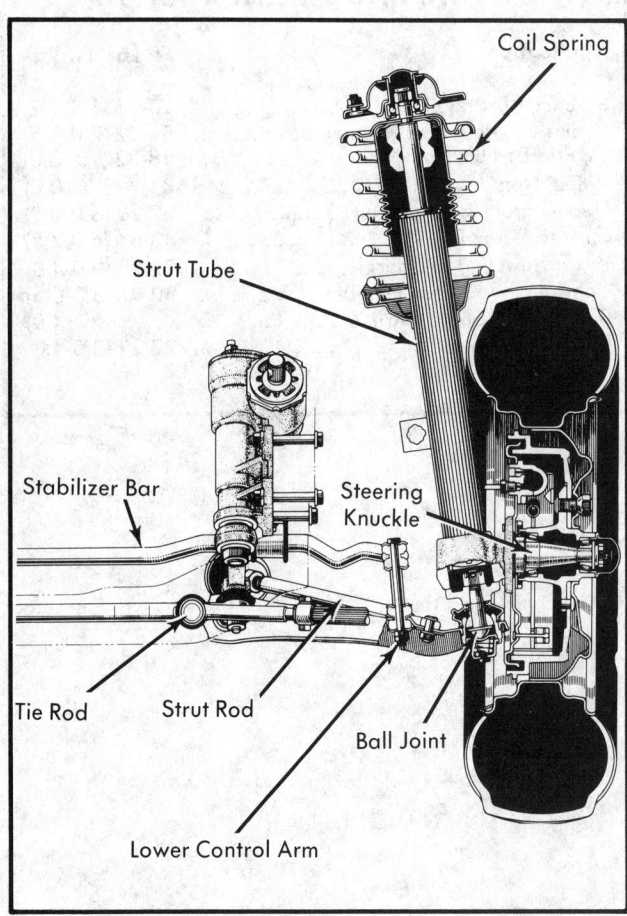

Fig. 1 Assembled View of Front Suspension Assembly (Corolla Shown; Other Models Similar)

ADJUSTMENT

WHEEL ALIGNMENT SPECIFICATIONS & PROCEDURES

See Wheel Alignment Specifications & Procedures in WHEEL ALIGNMENT Section.

WHEEL BEARING ADJUSTMENT

See Wheel Bearing Adjustment in WHEEL ALIGNMENT Section.

BALL JOINT CHECKING

See Ball Joint Checking in WHEEL ALIGNMENT Section.

REMOVAL & INSTALLATION

STRUT ASSEMBLY

Removal — 1) Raise and support vehicle. Remove front wheel. Disconnect brake tube and flexible hose.

2) Remove 3 nuts retaining top of strut assembly to vehicle. Remove bolts holding lower end of strut tube to steering knuckle.

3) Pull down on control arm to gain clearance and remove strut assembly (with brake and hub assembly attached) from vehicle.

Disassembly — 1) Install assembly in vise, clamping portion of strut tube below flange.

2) Use suitable spring compressor to collapse spring enough to remove strut rod top nut. Relieve pressure and remove spring.

3) Using ring nut removing tool, remove ring nut. Remove gasket by picking out with a needle. Remove piston rod, rod guide and rebound stopper.

4) Remove cylinder from shell, and using a brass rod, remove base valve from cylinder.

NOTE — Do not attempt to disassemble piston rod and valve.

Reassembly — Thoroughly clean and inspect all components. Replace any damaged parts. Install shock absorber components into cylinder in reverse of disassembly procedure, noting the following:

- After installing piston nut, stake it in place.
- When installing base valve onto cylinder, use a soft-face hammer to drive into place.
- Add specified amount of new shock absorber oil to cylinder.
- Install new oil seal to ring nut.
- Before fully tightening ring nut, pull piston rod out of cylinder about 3-4".
- Always use new self-locking nut on top of piston rod.

Shock Absorber Oil Amount	
Application	**Ounces (cc)**
Celica & Supra	11.0 (325)
Corolla	10.6 (315)
Corona	
13" (330 mm) Shock	10.6 (315)
14" (356 mm) Shock	11.0 (325)
Cressida	10.8 (320)

Installation — To install strut assembly in vehicle, reverse removal procedure, noting the following:

- After top end of strut is attached to mounting, fill bearing recess, which protrudes into engine compartment, with multi-purpose grease.

TOYOTA CELICA, COROLLA, CORONA, CRESSIDA & SUPRA (Cont.)

CONTROL ARM

Removal — 1) Raise and support vehicle. Remove wheel. On Cressida, remove engine under cover and detach strut bar and stabilizer bar from lower arm.

2) On all models, remove strut assembly-to-knuckle mounting bolts. Push lower arm down and disconnect strut from knuckle arm. On Corolla, separate stabilizer bar and strut bar from lower arm.

3) On Celica, Corolla, Corona and Supra, disconnect knuckle arm from ball joint. On Celica, Supra and Corona, disconnect stabilizer bar and strut bar from lower arm. On Cressida, detach tie rod end from knuckle arm.

4) On all models, remove bolt holding lower arm to crossmember and remove lower arm.

Disassembly — 1) On Cressida, place control arm in a vise and use suitable puller to remove knuckle arm from ball joint.

2) On all models, pry dust cover from ball joint and discard (also discard dust cover snap ring or retaining wire).

3) Press bushing out of control arm toward front side of arm, using suitable press and arbor.

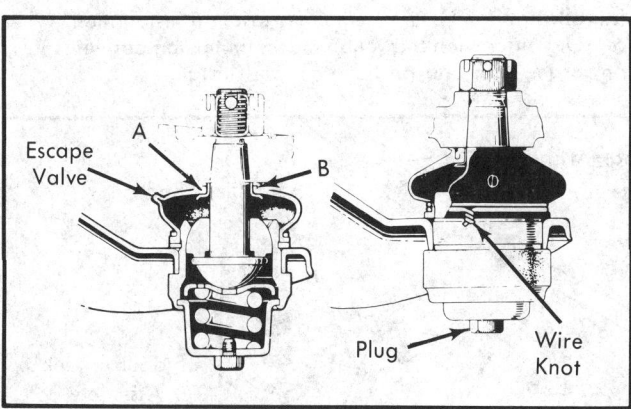

Fig. 2 Ball Joint and Dust Cover

Reassembly — 1) Use suitable support and press in new bushing. Apply ball joint grease to points "A" and "B" of new dust cover. *See Fig. 2.*

2) Install dust cover with escape valve facing rear of vehicle. Wind wire twice around dust cover and bend wire knot down, facing rear of ball joint.

3) Remove plug and install grease fitting. Fill ball joint with grease. Remove fitting and install plug.

Installation — To install, reverse removal procedure.

STABILIZER BAR

Removal — Remove strut rods from lower arms. Remove engine under cover, if so equipped. Disconnect stabilizer bar from lower arms. Remove bolts securing stabilizer brackets to chassis and remove stabilizer bar.

Installation — To install, reverse removal procedure. Make sure components connecting stabilizer bar to control arms are installed properly.

STRUT ROD

Removal — Raise vehicle and place safety stands under vehicle. Remove nut from front of strut rod and remove washer, retainer, and rubber grommet. Remove bolts connecting strut rod to control arm and remove rod from vehicle.

NOTE — *Do not attempt to loosen staked nut.*

Installation — 1) Check distance between staked nut and center of bolt hole. Celica, Corona and Supra should measure 14.92" (379 mm), Corolla 14.64" (372 mm) and Cressida 15.90" (405 mm). Place rod in vehicle and tighten mounting hardware.

CROSSMEMBER

Removal — 1) Remove engine under cover, if so equipped. Remove nuts holding both sides of crossmember to engine mounts. Raise and support vehicle on safety stands. Remove bolts holding lower arms to crossmember. On Corolla and Corona, remove engine shock absorber.

2) On all models, raise engine with chain or jack. On Cressida, disconnect stabilizer bar from lower arm. On all models, remove bolts securing crossmember to frame and remove crossmember.

Installation — To install, reverse removal procedure. Make sure components connecting stabilizer bar to control arms are installed in correct order.

TIGHTENING SPECIFICATIONS	
Application	**Ft. Lbs. (mkg)**
Control Arm-to-Crossmember①	
Cressida	65-94 (9.0-13.0)
All Other Models	51-65 (7.0-9.0)
Control Arm-to-Strut Rod	
Cressida	43-53 (6.0-7.0)
All Other Models	29-40 (4.0-5.5)
Control Arm-to-Stabilizer	11-15 (1.4-2.2)
Ball Joint-to-Knuckle Arm	51-65 (7.0-9.0)
Knuckle Arm-to-Strut Tube	
Corolla	51-65 (7.0-9.0)
All Other Models	58-86 (8.0-12.0)
Piston Rod-to-Mounting Plate	29-40 (4.0-5.5)
Piston Rod Ring Nut	73-108 (10.0-15.0)

① — With vehicle at full curb weight.

Front Suspension

TOYOTA PICKUP

DESCRIPTION

Independent front suspension with torsion bars. Wheel is supported by steering knuckle mounted between upper and lower control arms by ball joints. Upper and lower control arms pivot on shafts connected to frame. Torsion bars mount in anchor arms at frame and in torque arms mounted to lower control arms. Strut bars mount at frame and at lower control arm ends. Hydraulic shock absorbers mount between lower control arms and frame. A stabilizer bar is mounted to frame and connected at ends to lower control arms.

ADJUSTMENT

WHEEL ALIGNMENT SPECIFICATIONS & PROCEDURES

See Wheel Alignment Specifications & Procedures in WHEEL ALIGNMENT Section.

WHEEL BEARING ADJUSTMENT

See Wheel Bearing Adjustment in WHEEL ALIGNMENT Section.

BALL JOINT CHECKING

See Ball Joint Checking in WHEEL ALIGNMENT Section.

REMOVAL & INSTALLATION

SHOCK ABSORBERS

Removal — 1) Raise vehicle and place on jack stands under frame. Remove wheel and tire. Remove 2 nuts holding shock absorber to bracket. Remove washers and cushions from shaft of shock absorber.

2) Remove bolts securing shock absorber lower mount to control arm. Fully compress shock absorber, tilt forward and remove from vehicle.

Installation — To install, reverse removal procedure. Tighten all nuts and bolts.

TORSION BAR

Removal — 1) Raise and support front of vehicle. Remove wheel. Remove torsion bar boots at both ends and mark anchor arm and torque arm for correct spline alignment during reassembly.

2) Remove adjuster bolt lock nut. Measure distance from end of adjuster bolt to lower face of adjusting nut. Record distance for use during installation.

3) Place a jack under the anchor arm and raise slightly. Remove adjusting nut, lower jack slowly and remove the anchor arm and torsion bar.

Inspection — Inspect all parts for wear or damage. Check all splines carefully. Note that left and right torsion bars are not interchangeable.

Installation — 1) Grease splines prior to installation. When re-using old torsion bar, align marks on torsion bar with marks on torque arm and anchor arm and install.

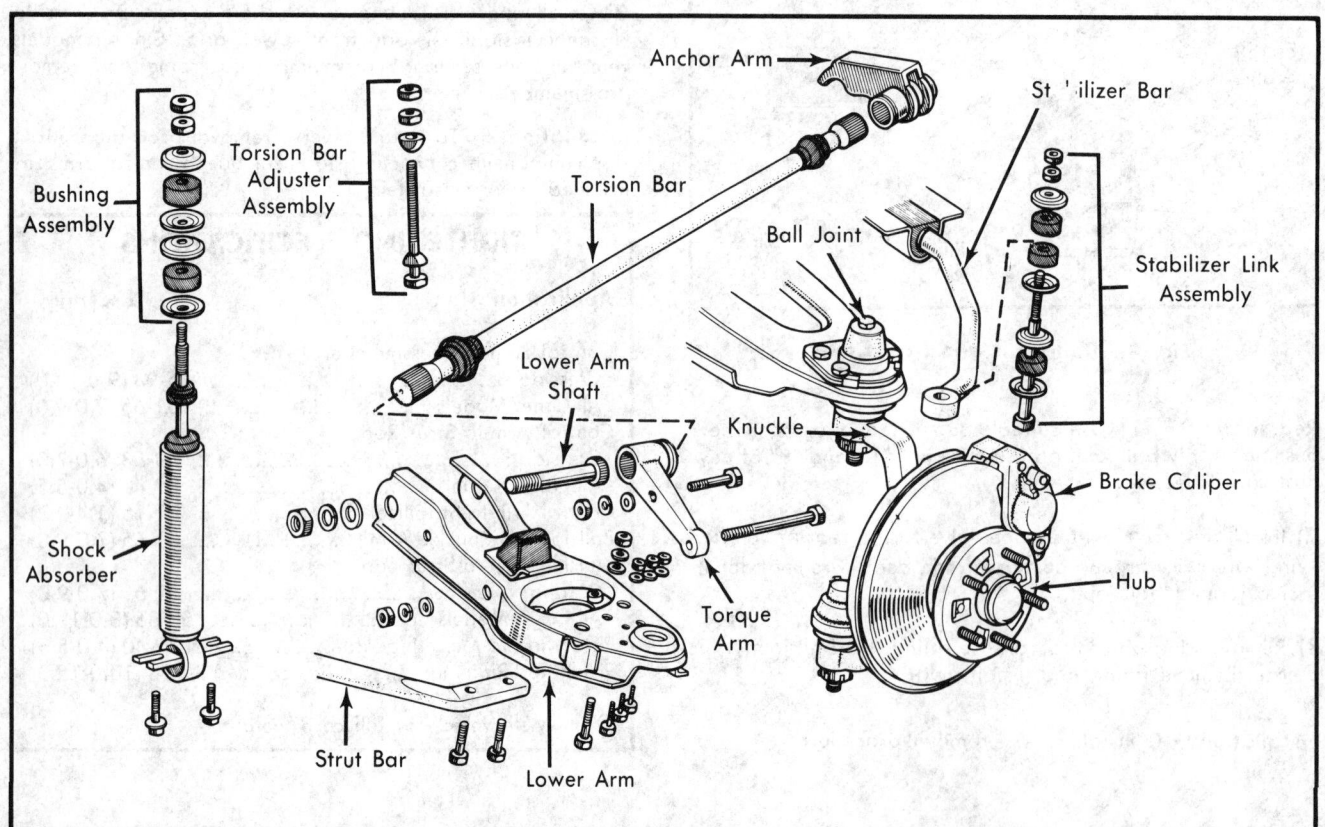

Fig. 1   Exploded View of Toyota Pickup Front Suspension

TOYOTA PICKUP (Cont.)

2) When using new torsion bar, jack up front of vehicle and block tire up to height of 7.09-7.87" (180-200 mm). Lower jack until clearance between spring bumper on lower arm and frame is .51" (13 mm).

NOTE — *Place stands under vehicle for safety.*

3) Install new torsion bar so adjusting bolt protrusion is .31-1.10" (7.87-27.94 mm) for ½ ton vehicles and .43-1.22" (11-31 mm) for ¾ ton vehicles. Remove block from under wheel and lower front of vehicle until it rests on stands. Tighten adjusting nut until bolt protrudes 2.72-3.50" (69-89 mm).

4) With either old or new torsion bar, grease boot lips and install boots to torque arm and anchor arm. Remove stands and bounce vehicle several times to settle suspension. Adjust vehicle to standard height with adjusting nut. *See Riding Height Specifications in Wheel Alignment Section.* Using 2 wrenches, tighten lock nut.

NOTE — *If bolt protrusion is not 2.72-3.50" (69-89 mm), change the position of anchor arm spline and reassemble.*

UPPER CONTROL ARM & BALL JOINT

Removal — **1)** Raise vehicle by placing jack under lower control arm. Place stands under frame and leave jack in place. Remove wheel. Remove cotter pin and nut from upper ball joint stud. Using a puller, separate ball joint from knuckle.

2) Remove bolts securing upper control arm shaft, noting size and number of shims between pivot shaft and frame. Remove control arm as an assembly. Remove bolts securing ball joint to control arm, and remove ball joint. Press off bushings using suitable adapters and remove shaft.

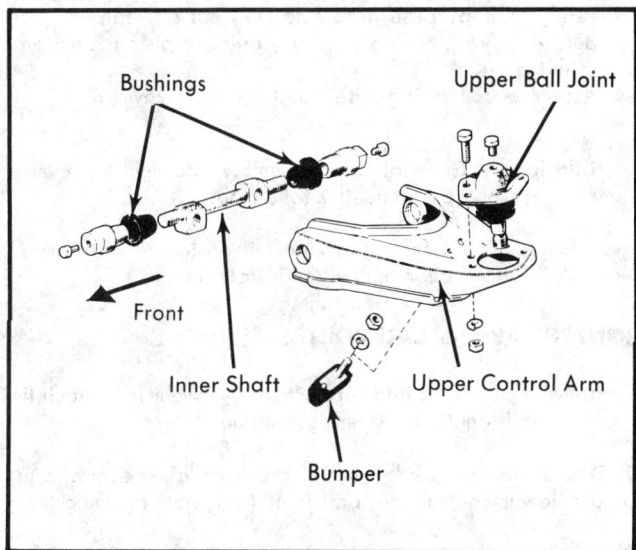

Fig. 2   Exploded View of Upper Control Arm Assembly

Installation — Inspect all components for wear or distortion. Install pivot shaft with offset mounting hole to front. Reverse removal procedure for installation, making sure wheel alignment shims are installed in correct position. Tighten all bolts and nuts to specifications. Check wheel alignment.

LOWER CONTROL ARM & BALL JOINT

Removal — **1)** Raise and support vehicle. Remove wheel. Remove torsion bar and shock absorber. Disconnect stabilizer bar and strut bar from control arm.

2) Remove cotter pin and nut from lower ball joint stud and, using a puller, separate ball joint from steering knuckle. Remove torque arm and pivot shaft from control arm. Remove control arm from vehicle. Remove bolts securing ball joint to control arm and remove ball joint. Remove bushings from frame, if necessary.

Installation — To install, reverse removal procedure, noting the following: Tighten lower arm mount nut to specifications after vehicle has been lowered to the ground. Check wheel alignment.

STEERING KNUCKLE

Removal — **1)** Raise and support vehicle. Remove wheel. Disconnect brake tube from brake caliper. Remove caliper from knuckle.

2) Remove cap, cotter pin, nut lock, nut and axle hub with rotor. Remove knuckle arm and dust cover. Suspend brake hose out of the way.

3) Remove cotter pins and nuts from ball joint studs. Use a puller and separate ball joints from steering knuckle. Remove knuckle.

Installation — To install, reverse removal procedure. Check wheel alignment.

TIGHTENING SPECIFICATIONS

Application	Ft. Lbs. (mkg)
Lower Ball Joint-to-Steering Knuckle	87-123 (12.0-17.0)
Upper Ball Joint-to-Steering Knuckle	66-94 (9.0-13.0)
Ball Joint-to-Lower Arm (8 mm)	15-21 (2.0-3.0)
Ball Joint-to-Lower Arm (10 mm)	29-39 (4.0-5.5)
Ball Joint-to-Upper Arm	15-21 (2.0-3.0)
Lower Arm-to-Frame	145-217 (20.0-30.0)
Upper Arm Shaft-to-Frame	51-65 (7.0-9.0)
Upper Arm-to-Shaft	62-79 (8.5-11.0)
Strut Bar-to-Lower Arm	55-75 (7.5-10.5)
Shock Absorber-to-Lower Arm	11-15 (1.5-2.2)
Shock Absorber-to-Bracket	14-22 (1.9-3.1)

Front Suspension

TOYOTA TERCEL

DESCRIPTION

Vehicles are equipped with front wheel drive and independent strut type suspension. Vertically mounted strut assemblies are surrounded by coil springs and mounted at inner fender at top and steering knuckle at bottom. Tie rod ends connect rack and pinion steering to steering knuckle. Lower ball joint connects knuckle to lower control arm which attaches to frame crossmember. Stabilizer bar attaches to lower control arm and crossmember in front of wheels and strut rod attaches to lower control arm and chassis to the rear of front wheels.

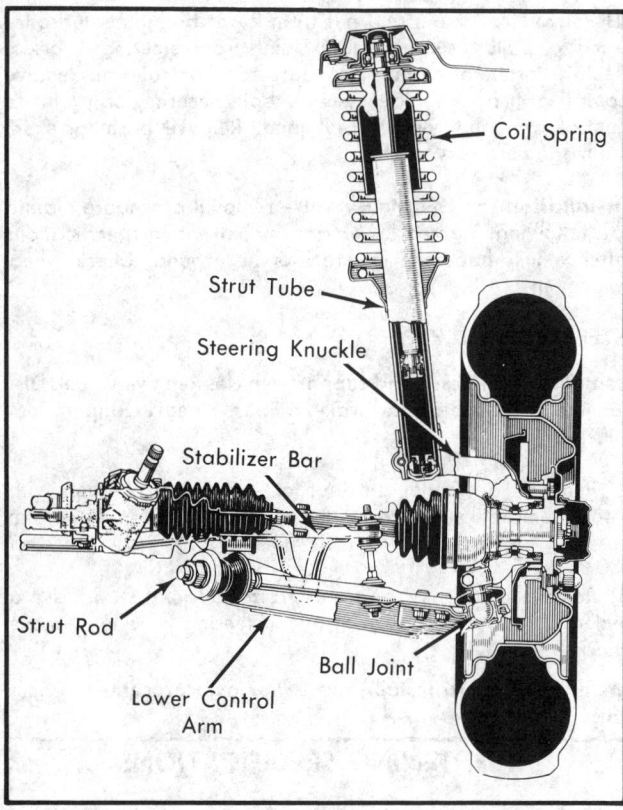

Coil Spring

Strut Tube

Steering Knuckle

Stabilizer Bar

Strut Rod

Lower Control Arm

Ball Joint

Fig. 1 Assembled View of Tercel Front Suspension

ADJUSTMENT

WHEEL ALIGNMENT SPECIFICATIONS & PROCEDURES

See Wheel Alignment Specifications & Procedures in WHEEL ALIGNMENT Section.

WHEEL BEARING ADJUSTMENT

See Wheel Bearing Adjustment in WHEEL ALIGNMENT Section.

BALL JOINT CHECKING

See Ball Joint Checking in WHEEL ALIGNMENT Section.

REMOVAL & INSTALLATION

STRUT ASSEMBLY

Removal — 1) Raise and support vehicle. Remove wheel and tire. Remove brake caliper and suspend with wire. Disconnect stabilizer bar end from lower control arm.

2) Remove bolt attaching strut assembly to steering knuckle. Tap on knuckle with a hammer to separate it from lower end of strut. Remove 3 nuts holding top of strut to fender and remove strut from vehicle.

Disassembly — 1) Install assembly in a vise, clamping portion of strut tube below flange or use holding fixture (09714-16010).

2) Use suitable spring compressor to collapse spring enough to remove strut rod top nut. Relieve pressure on spring and remove spring, and disassemble shock absorber top end retaining components.

3) Using ring nut removing tool, remove ring nut. Remove gasket by picking out with a needle.

4) Withdraw piston and rod guide from cylinder. Remove cylinder from shell, and using brass rod, remove base valve from cylinder.

NOTE — *Do not attempt to disassemble piston rod and valve.*

Reassembly — Thoroughly clean and inspect all components. Replace any damaged parts. Install shock absorber components into cylinder in reverse order of disassembly, noting the following:

- When installing base valve into cylinder, use a soft face hammer to drive it into place.
- Fill shock absorber with 7.8 ounces (230 cc) new shock absorber fluid.
- After assembling rod guide, install new gasket.
- Apply multi-purpose grease to ring nut oil seal.
- Before fully tightening ring nut, pull out piston rod from cylinder 3-4".
- Assemble coil spring with paint mark downward.

Installation — To install strut assembly into vehicle, reverse removal procedure, noting the following:

- Always use a new self-locking nut on top of piston rod.
- Check wheel alignment after installation.

CONTROL ARM & BALL JOINT

Removal — 1) Raise and support front of vehicle. Detach tie rod end ball joint from steering knuckle.

2) Detach strut rod and stabilizer bar from lower control arm. Detach lower control arm ball joint from steering knuckle.

3) Remove control arm pivot bolt and remove control arm from vehicle.

NOTE — *On left side, jack up control arm to remove bolt.*

Bushing Replacement — Use suitable press to remove and install bushing. When installing, there must be no oil or grease on bushing or arm boss. Press only on flange of outer tube.

NOTE — *Control arm and ball joint are servicable as a unit only. If damaged, replace entire assembly.*

TOYOTA TERCEL (Cont.)

Installation — To install, reverse removal procedure, noting the following:

- Tighten the lower arm with vehicle weight on suspension.
- Check front wheel alignment.

STABILIZER BAR

Removal and Installation — Remove engine under cover. Remove stabilizer bar ends from control arms, noting bushing positioning, then remove bolts securing mounting brackets to chassis. Remove stabilizer bar. To install, reverse removal procedure, ensuring components connecting bar to control arms are installed in correct order.

STRUT ROD

Removal — Raise and support front of vehicle. Jack up lower control arm, remove nut from front of strut rod and remove washer, retainer, and rubber grommet. Remove bolts connecting strut rod to control arm and remove rod from vehicle.

Installation — Set distance between outer side of staked nut (inside retaining nut) and inner mounting bolt to 13.0" (330.4 mm). Place rod in vehicle and tighten mounting hardware.

SUSPENSION CROSSMEMBER

Removal — **1)** Raise and support front of vehicle. Disconnect steering intermediate shaft pinch bolt. Remove engine under cover and detach tie rod end ball joints from steering knuckle.

2) Remove stabilizer bar. Remove lower control arm pivot bolt, and detach engine shock absorber from crossmember. Remove steering link housing brackets and remove steering assembly from vehicle.

3) Remove engine mounting nuts and prop up engine from below. Remove lower crossmember retaining bolts and remove crossmember.

Installation — To install, reverse removal procedure and note the following:

- For the left side, jack up lower control arm to install to crossmember.
- Lower and rock vehicle before tightening lower arm pivot bolts.
- Check front end alignment.
- Make sure components connecting stabilizer bar to control arms are installed in correct order.

TIGHTENING SPECIFICATIONS

Application	Ft. Lbs. (mkg)
Control Arm-to-Crossmember①	51-65 (7.0-9.0)
Control Arm-to-Strut	40-52 (5.5-7.2)
Control Arm-to-Stabilizer	11-15 (1.4-2.2)
Control Arm-to-Strut Rod	29-39 (4.0-5.5)
Ball Joint-to-Steering Knuckle	40-52 (5.5-7.2)
Tie Rod End-to-Steering Knuckle	37-50 (5.0-7.0)
Piston Rod Ring Nut	66-97 (9.0-13.5)
Piston Rod-to-Mounting Plate	29-39 (4.0-5.5)
Strut-to-Upper Mount	15-21 (2.0-3.0)
Crossmember Mounting Bolts	30-39 (4.1-5.5)
Engine Mounting Bolts	26-39 (3.5-5.5)
Steering Link Brackets	22-32 (3.0-4.5)
Stabilizer Bar Brackets	22-32 (3.0-4.5)
Caliper Mounting Bolts	33-39 (4.5-5.5)

① — With vehicle at full curb weight.

TRIUMPH SPITFIRE

DESCRIPTION

Independent type front suspension consisting of upper and lower control arms, coil spring and shock assemblies, and steering knuckles. Control arms pivot in mounts connected to chassis. Coil spring and shock assemblies are mounted between lower control arms and mounts integral with chassis. Steering knuckles are connected to upper control arms by means of trunnion joints. A stabilizer bar is attached to chassis and lower control arms.

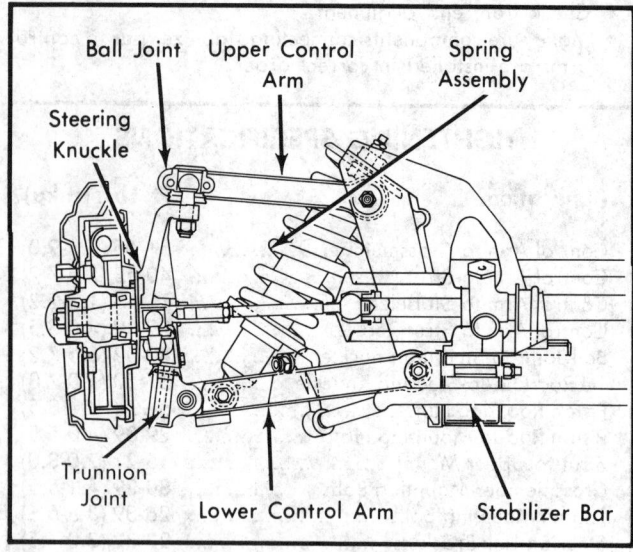

Fig. 1   Assembled View of Spitfire Front Suspension

ADJUSTMENTS

WHEEL ALIGNMENT SPECIFICATIONS & PROCEDURES

See Wheel Alignment Specifications and Procedures in WHEEL ALIGNMENT Section.

WHEEL BEARING ADJUSTMENT

See Wheel Bearing adjustment in WHEEL ALIGNMENT Section.

BALL JOINT CHECKING

See Ball Joint Checking in WHEEL ALIGNMENT Section.

REMOVAL & INSTALLATION

COIL SPRING & SHOCK ABSORBER

Removal — Raise and support vehicle. Place safety stands behind front wheels and remove wheel and tire. Loosen bolts securing lower control arm to trunnion joint. Remove bolts securing bottom spring assembly mount to control arm. Remove 3 nuts securing upper spring assembly mount to chassis, and remove spring and shock absorber as an assembly.

Disassembly — Using a spring compressor, compress coil spring until it is not contacting upper spring seat. Remove upper shock absorber nut and mounting hardware. Release spring compressor and remove coil spring.

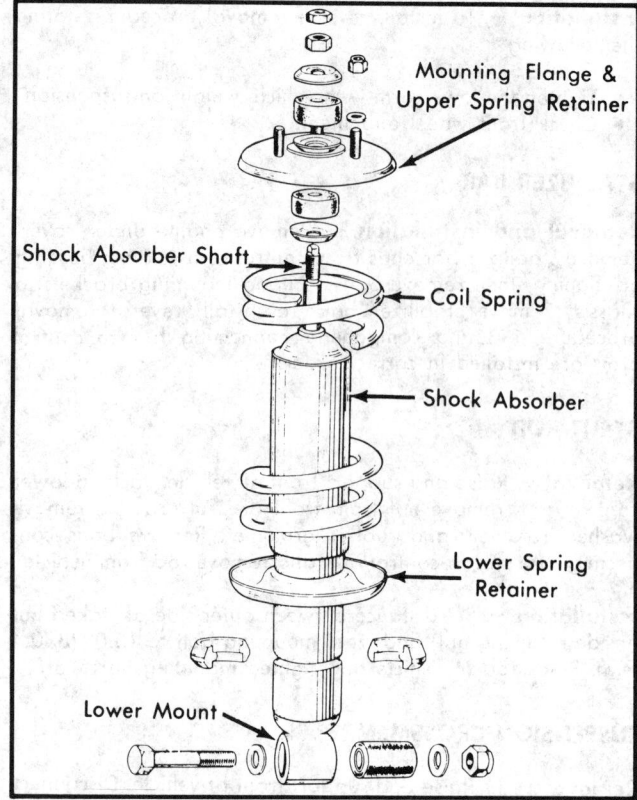

Fig. 2   Coil Spring and Shock Absorber Assembly

Reassembly — Push shock absorber shaft in and out a few times. Resistance should be constant and equal on either stroke. If little or no resistance is felt, or if shaft cannot be moved, replace shock absorber. To assemble coil spring and shock assembly, reverse disassembly procedure.

Installation — To install coil spring and shock absorber assembly, reverse removal procedure.

UPPER CONTROL ARM

Removal — Raise vehicle, position safety stands behind front wheels and remove wheel and tire. Remove coil spring and shock assembly as previously outlined. Remove bolts securing upper control arm to ball joint. Remove both upper control arm pivot bolts. Separate control arm from pivot mounts and ball joint.

Installation — To install upper control arm, reverse removal procedure and note the following: Do not tighten pivot bolts until weight of vehicle is on front wheels.

LOWER CONTROL ARM

Removal — Raise vehicle, position safety stands behind front wheels and remove wheel and tire. Disconnect stabilizer bar link from lower control arm. Disconnect bottom spring mount from control arm. Remove bolt securing control arm to trunnion joint. Remove inner pivot bolts and remove control arm.

Installation — To install lower control arm, reverse removal procedure and note the following: Do not tighten inner pivot bolts until weight of vehicle is on front wheels.

TRIUMPH SPITFIRE (Cont.)

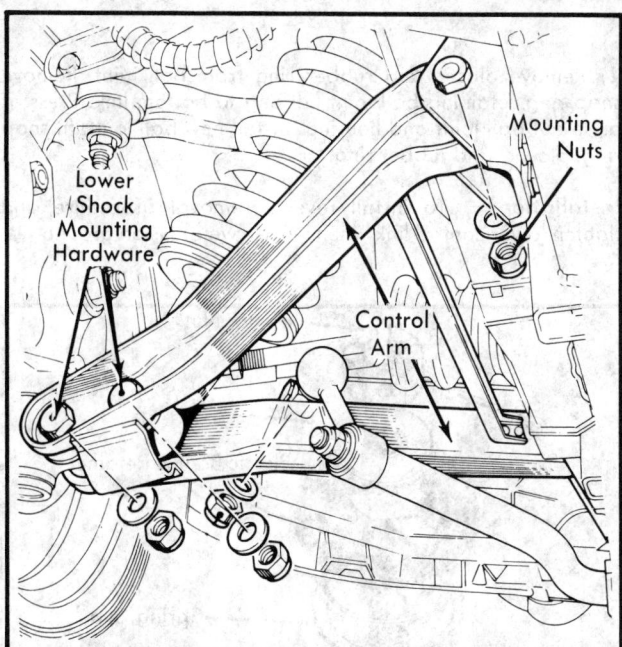

Fig. 3 Nuts and Bolts to Remove Before Taking Out Lower Control Arm

UPPER BALL JOINT

Removal — Raise vehicle and place on safety stands; remove tire and wheel. Remove ball joint stud nut and separate ball joint from steeing knuckle. Remove bolts securing ball joint to control arm and remove ball joint.

Installation — To install ball joint, reverse removal procedure.

LOWER TRUNNION JOINT

Removal — Raise vehicle, position safety stands behind front wheels and remove wheel and tire. Remove wheel hub and dust shield. Remove bolt securing trunnion joint to lower con-trol arm. Disconnect shock absorber mount from lower control arm. Pull trunnion and steering knuckle from lower control arm and unscrew trunnion from steering knuckle.

Disassembly — Pry loose 2 end washers. Slide out both dust seals. Lightly press out single spacer piece. Force out each of the nylon bearings and remove inner washers. Check all pieces for excessive wear and replace as necessary.

Reassembly — Reverse disassembly procedure after lightly greasing nylon bearings with suitable grease.

Installation — To install trunnion joint, screw trunnion on steering knuckle as far as possible and back off to first work-ing position. This will allow full turning radius. Reverse removal procedure to complete installation.

STEERING KNUCKLE

Removal — Raise vehicle, position safety stands behind front wheels and remove wheel and tire. Remove brake caliper, disc hub and dust shield from steering knuckle. Remove steering arm from knuckle. Remove ball joint stud nut and separate ball joint from steering knuckle. Disconnect shock absorber from lower control arm. Remove bolt securing trunnion joint to con-trol arm and remove steering knuckle. Remove trunnion from steering knuckle. If necessary, remove nut securing spindle to steering knuckle and press spindle from knuckle.

Installation — To install steering knuckle, reverse removal procedure.

STABILIZER BAR

Removal — Remove nuts securing stabilizer bar to lower control arm. Remove nuts and plain washers holding bushing brackets to chassis. Remove bushing and withdraw stabilizer bar from vehicle.

Installation — To install stabilizer bar, reverse removal procedure.

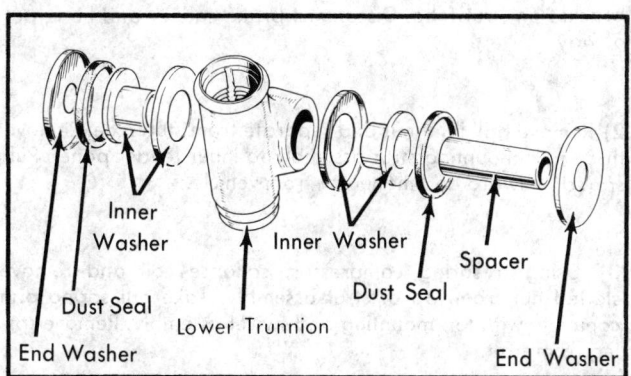

Fig. 4 Exploded View of Lower Trunnion Assembly

TIGHTENING SPECIFICATIONS

Application	Ft. Lbs. (mkg)
Stabilizer Bar Stud	14 (1.9)
Ball Joint-to-Upper Control Arm	20 (2.8)
Ball Joint Stud Nut	38 (5.2)
Tie Rod End Ball Joint	32 (4.4)
Trunnion-to-Lower Control Arm	45 (6.2)
Lower Control Arm-to-Frame	25 (3.5)

Front Suspension

TRIUMPH TR7 & TR8

DESCRIPTION

Suspension is strut type with a coil spring around strut tube. Strut is secured at top to inner fender and at bottom to control arm link. A stabilizer bar is connected to chassis and lower control link. Control arm links are mounted by a ball joint at stub axles and through bolts at chassis.

ADJUSTMENT

WHEEL ALIGNMENT SPECIFICATIONS & PROCEDURES

See Wheel Alignment Specifications and Procedures in WHEEL ALIGNMENT Section.

WHEEL BEARING ADJUSTMENT

See Wheel Bearing Adjustment in WHEEL ALIGNMENT Section.

BALL JOINT CHECKING

See Ball Joint Checking in WHEEL ALIGNMENT Section.

REMOVAL & INSTALLATION

LOWER CONTROL LINK

Removal — 1) Raise and support vehicle with safety stands. Remove tire and wheel. Remove mounting hardware from end of stabilizer bar. Remove bolts holding steering arm to stub axle and move out of way. Remove nut and separate ball joint. Remove bolt and nut securing lower control link to chassis, then take out link.

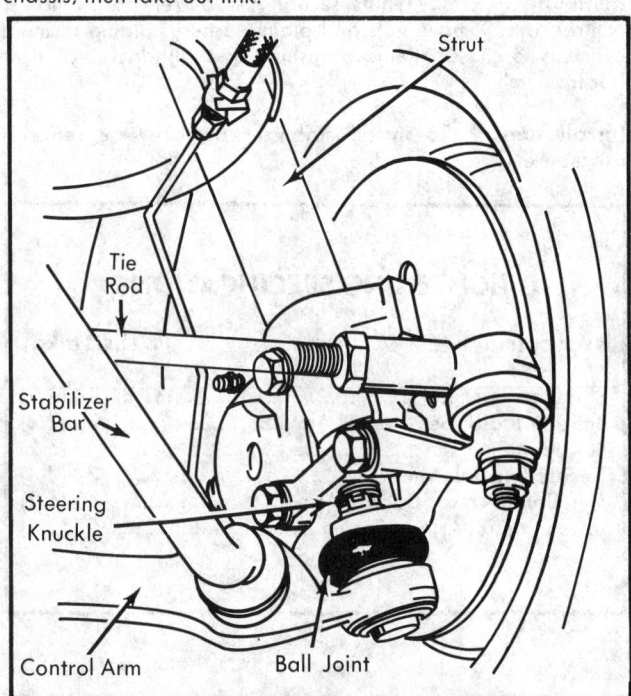

Fig. 1   Detail of Components to Remove in Order to Take Off Lower Control Link and Strut Assembly

2) Remove plastic and rubber ring from ball joint. Remove snap ring retaining ball joint housing to bottom link. Press or drive out ball joint and housing. Install new ball joint, fit snap ring, plastic, and rubber ring.

Installation — To install reverse removal procedure and tighten lower control link when vehicle weight is on ground.

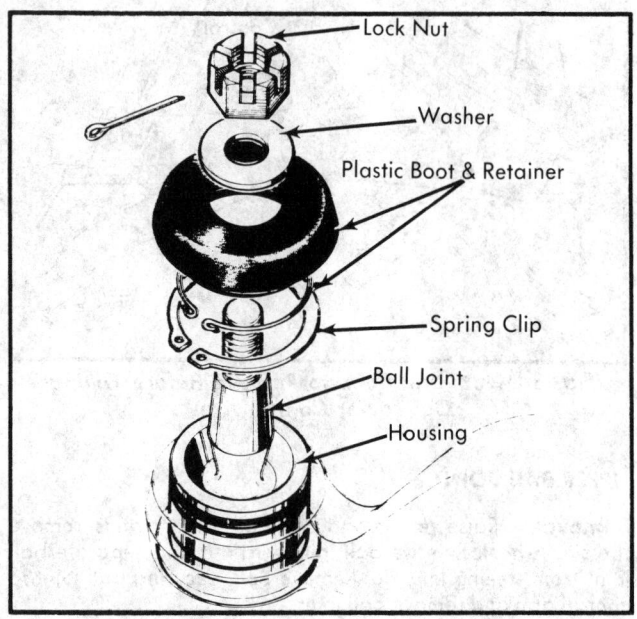

Fig. 2   Exploded View of Ball Joint Assembly

STRUT ASSEMBLY

Removal — 1) Raise vehicle and support with jack stands. Remove tire and wheel. Separate steering arm from stub axle assembly by removing two bolts. Disconnect brake hose from bracket on strut tube. Disconnect brake caliper and hang out of way.

2) Remove ball joint nut and separate from stub axle. Remove three nuts mounting strut assembly to inner fender panel. Pull strut downward and maneuver from vehicle.

3) Using a spring compressor, collapse coil and remove slotted nut from top of strut assembly. Take out spring pan complete with top mounting and swivel assembly. Remove spring from strut.

Disassembly — Using plug nut wrench (RTR359), remove plug nut. Slide shock absorber from strut tube.

Reassembly — Fit shock absorber to strut tube, then fit plug nut and tighten.

TRIUMPH TR7 & TR8 (Cont.)

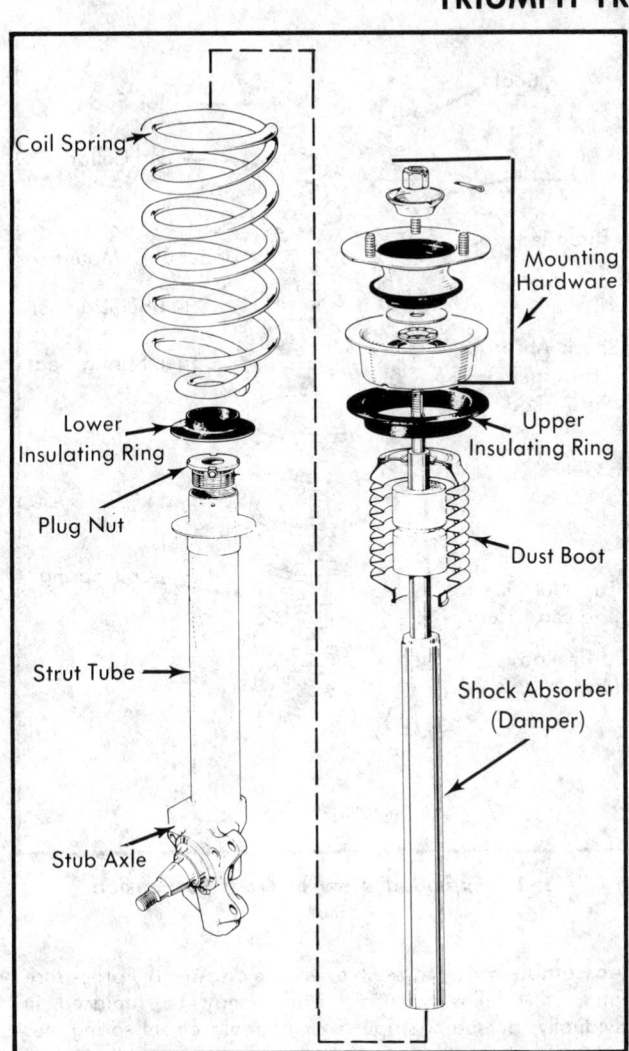

Fig. 3   Disassembled View of Strut

Coil Spring

Mounting Hardware

Lower Insulating Ring

Upper Insulating Ring

Plug Nut

Strut Tube

Dust Boot

Shock Absorber (Damper)

Stub Axle

Installation — 1) Compress coil spring and ensure bumper stop is correctly positioned. Fully extend strut rod and fit the following: lower insulating ring, rubber seal, spring, upper insulating ring, and spring pan. Fit seal to thrust collar and place on upper spring pan.

2) Install plain washer (smearing first with light coating of grease) with ground surface facing spring pan. Insert rubber mounting to strut and secure with dished washer and slotted nut. To complete installation, reverse removal procedure. Bleed brake system.

STABILIZER BAR

Removal — Raise vehicle and place on safety stands. Remove bolts and brackets mounting stabilizer bar to chassis. Remove mounting nut and rubber bushing securing stabilizer bar to lower control link. Pull out stabilizer, adjusting vehicle height as necessary. If necessary, inner bushing and mounting bushings can now be removed and replaced.

Installation — Refit inner dished washer with dish facing bushing, then install inner bushing on each end of stabilizer bar. Insert stabilizer bar and fit outer rubber bushings with dished washers. Reinstall mounting brackets and tighten all nuts and bolts.

TIGHTENING SPECIFICATIONS

Application	Ft. Lbs. (mkg)
Stabilizer Bar-to-Chassis	37 (5.1)
Stabilizer Bar-to-Lower Control Link	59 (8.1)
Strut Mounting-to-Body	21 (2.9)
Strut-to-Mounting	44 (6.0)
Tie Rod-to-Stub Axle	74 (10.2)
Strut Tube Plug Nut	74 (10.2)

VOLKSWAGEN DASHER

DESCRIPTION

Volkswagen Dasher is front wheel drive with independent strut type front suspension. Axles are supported by lower control arms, vertically mounted strut assemblies, and a stabilizer bar. Strut assemblies consist of double action shock absorbers with coil springs mounted over the outside. The top part of strut is attached to the inner fender panel and the lower portion is attached directly to steering knuckle. Tie rods are connected to supports under coil springs. Stabilizer bar is connected to lower control arms at each end and to crossmember below engine.

ADJUSTMENT

WHEEL ALIGNMENT SPECIFICATIONS & PROCEDURES

See *Wheel Alignment Specifications & Procedures* in *WHEEL ALIGNMENT* Section.

WHEEL BEARING ADJUSTMENT

See *Wheel Bearing Adjustment* in *WHEEL ALIGNMENT* Section.

BALL JOINT CHECKING

See *Ball Joint Checking* in *WHEEL ALIGNMENT* Section.

REMOVAL & INSTALLATION

STRUT & COIL SPRING ASSEMBLY

Removal — 1) Loosen axle nut and wheel lugs. Raise and support vehicle; remove wheel and tire. Remove brake hose clips, disconnect brake caliper and move out of way.

2) Loosen bolt holding suspension ball joint stud in bottom of strut assembly. Using suitable tool, remove tie rod end from mounting under coil spring seat. Disconnect stabilizer bar from lower control arm.

3) Force lower control arm down until ball joint stud is removed from suspension strut. Remove axle nut. Support axle drive shaft, then pull strut outward and off of axle drive shaft. Remove both upper mounting nuts. Guide strut from vehicle.

Disassembly — 1) Place strut in a vise and install coil spring compressor. Tighten compressor until pressure is taken off upper retainer. Remove upper collar mounting nut. Take off upper mounting hardware. Release spring compressor and remove coil spring.

2) Hold shock absorber cartridge center shaft with suitable tool. Loosen and remove threaded cap nut. If shock absorber cartridge will not easily pull front strut tube, thread a nut on center shaft and tap until corrosion breaks free.

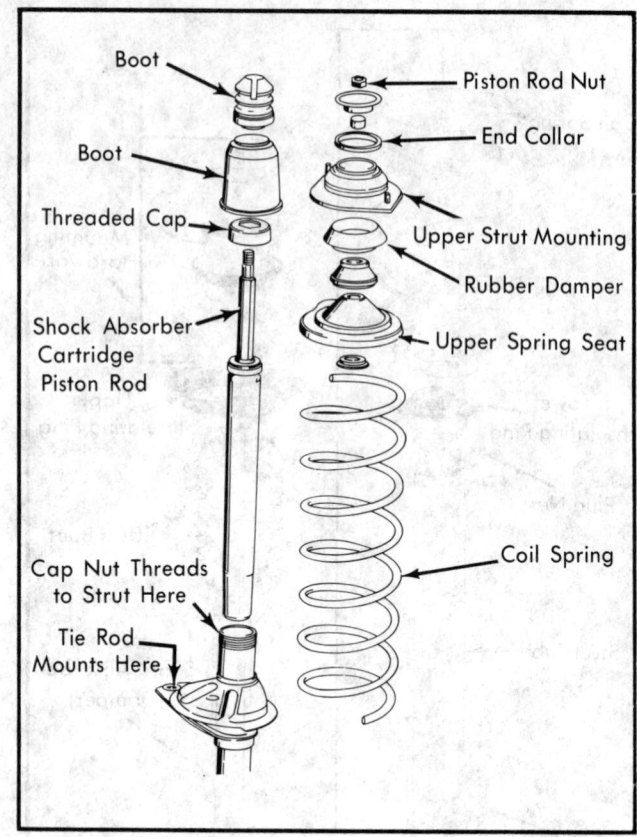

Fig. 1   Exploded View of Front Suspension Strut

Reassembly — To reassemble, reverse disassembly procedure, noting the following: Coil springs may be replaced individually, but paint stripe color of replacement spring must match stripe color of original spring.

Installation — To install, reverse removal procedure and note the following. When assembling ball joint to lower control arm always use a new bolt and nut. Face bolt head toward front of vehicle.

LOWER CONTROL ARM

Removal — 1) Raise vehicle so that front wheel and suspension are not supported.

2) Disconnect stabilizer bar at control arm and subframe. Slide stabilizer bar out of vehicle.

3) Loosen ball joint clamp bolt. Force lower control arm down until ball joint stud is removed from suspension strut. Remove bolts mounting control arm to subframe. Guide arm from vehicle.

Bushing Replacement — 1) Check bushing in control arm for signs of excessive wear or damage. If bushings are bad they can be replaced.

2) Support wide points on control arm. Press bushings from each side of control arm.

VOLKSWAGEN DASHER (Cont.)

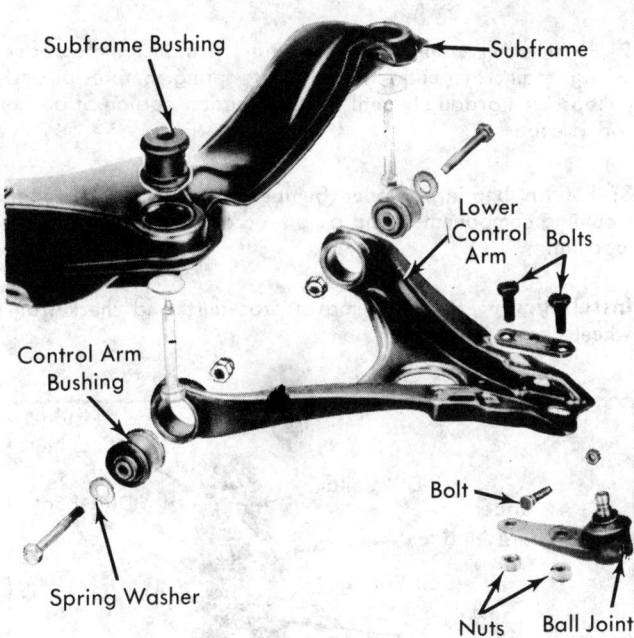

Subframe Bushing

Subframe

Lower Control Arm

Bolts

Control Arm Bushing

Spring Washer

Bolt

Nuts   Ball Joint

Fig. 2   Exploded View of Lower Control Arm

3) Select new bushings. Lightly coat each bushing with brake paste. Press bushing into position in control arm. Make sure bushing does not twist when pressing into place. Use bushing guide if necessary.

Installation — Reverse removal procedure and note: Use water pump pliers to compress clamps around bushing when trying to start bolts. Check front wheel alignment.

STABILIZER BAR

Removal — **1)** Raise vehicle and suitably support with safety stands. Remove brackets mounting stabilizer bar to lower control arm .

2) Loosen and remove "U" brackets mounting stabilizer bar to subframe. Guide stabilizer bar from vehicle. Inspect rubber bushings for damage or excessive wear and replace as necessay.

Installation — To install, reverse removal procedure. Install with end sections pointing down. Drive vehicle around the block before fully tightening clamp bolts.

TIGHTENING SPECIFICATIONS

Application	Ft. Lbs. (mkg)
Axle Nut	
18 mm Nut	145 (20.0)
20 mm Nut	175 (24)
Lower Control Arm-to-Subframe	50 (7.0)
Upper Strut Assembly-to-Body	18 (2.5)
Stabilizer Bar-to-Subframe	18 (2.5)
Piston Rod Nut	43 (6)
Shock Absorber Cap Nut	108 (15.0)
Stabilizer Bar-to-Lower Control Arm	7 (.9)
Ball Joint-to-Suspension Strut	36 (5.0)
Tie Rod Castle Nut	29 (4.0)
Ball Joint-to-Lower Control Arm	47 (6.5)

Front Suspension

VOLKSWAGEN JETTA, RABBIT, RABBIT PICKUP & SCIROCCO

DESCRIPTION

Vehicles are equipped with front wheel drive and independent strut type front suspension. Axles are supported by lower control arms, and vertically mounted strut assemblies. Strut assemblies consist of double action shock absorbers with coil springs mounted over the outside. The top portion of strut is attached to inner fender panel and lower portion is attached directly to steering knuckle. Tie rods are connected to steering knuckle.

ADJUSTMENT

WHEEL ALIGNMENT SPECIFICATIONS & PROCEDURES

See Wheel Alignment Specifications & Procedures in WHEEL ALIGNMENT Section.

WHEEL BEARING ADJUSTMENT

See Wheel Bearing Adjustment in WHEEL ALIGNMENT Section.

BALL JOINT CHECKING

See Ball Joint Checking in WHEEL ALIGNMENT Section.

REMOVAL & INSTALLATION

STRUT ASSEMBLY

NOTE – Suspension strut does not need to be removed to replace end collar. Only requirement is to leave vehicle on ground.

Removal – 1) Raise vehicle so front suspension and front wheels are not supported.

2) Remove bolts mounting suspension strut to steering knuckle. Note that top bolt is one used to adjust front wheel camber.

3) Remove brake caliper assembly and suspend out of way. Pry or force suspension strut out of steering knuckle.

4) Support front suspension by hand. Also, support lower control arm and related components. Work inside engine compartment and remove upper strut mounting nuts. Guide out strut assembly.

Disassembly – Fit strut to spring compressor. Slightly collapse coil spring. Remove shock absorber piston rod nut. Slowly release spring pressure. Take off upper mounting hardware and coil spring.

Reassembly – 1) Fit protective sleeve and buffer over piston rod.

NOTE – Both coil springs must be of same class. If set cannot be matched, both springs will have to be replaced. Springs are color coded.

2) Position coil spring into lower spring seat. Install the upper spring retainer. Fit entire assembly into spring compressor and collapse coil gradually until whole threaded portion of piston rod is exposed.

3) Put on bearing, rubber bumper and remaining upper mounting components. Hold piston rod and tighten piston rod lock nut.

Installation – Reverse removal procedure and check front wheel alignment.

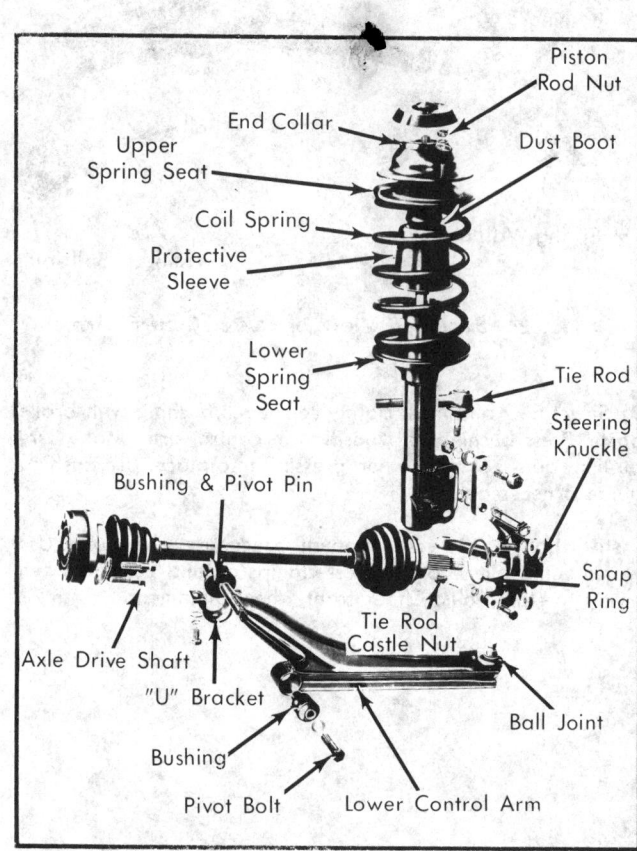

Fig. 1 Exploded View of Front Suspension Components

FRONT SUSPENSION ASSEMBLY

Removal – 1) Raise vehicle so front suspension and wheels are not supported. Disconnect brake line, leave flex line in place, and plug openings.

2) Remove tie rod castle nut. Press tie rod from steering knuckle. Remove bolts mounting inner portion of constant velocity joint to transaxle drive flange.

3) Remove lower control arm front pivot bolt. Remove 2 bolts mounting "U" shaped bracket holding control arm rear pivot.

NOTE – On vehicles equipped with automatic transmissions, engine may have to be slightly raised to gain access to pivot bolts.

VOLKSWAGEN JETTA, RABBIT, RABBIT PICKUP & SCIROCCO (Cont.)

4) Support suspension assembly. Remove upper strut mounting nuts located in engine compartment. Guide assembly from vehicle.

Installation – Reverse removal procedure and note: Make sure convex side of thrust washer faces pivot bolt head.

LOWER CONTROL ARM & BALL JOINT

NOTE – *Ball Joint can be replaced while control arm is in vehicle.*

Removal – 1) Raise vehicle and suitably support with front suspension free. Remove nut and clamp bolt mounting ball joint in bottom of steering knuckle. Force ball joint out of steering knuckle. Leave control arm hanging in mounts at subframe.

2) If control arm is not being removed, drill out 3 ball joint rivets with a $9/32''$ (7 mm) drill. After drilling it still may be necessary to chisel off rivet heads. Remove ball joint.

3) If control arm is being removed, take out pivot bolt and "U" bracket housing inner pivot pin. Slide out control arm.

NOTE – *On vehicles equipped with automatic transmissions, engine may have to be slightly raised to gain access to pivot bolts.*

Inspection – Check lower control arm bushings. If bushings are bad they can be replaced. Press out worn bushing. Select new bushing and press into position. Make sure bushing does not twist when seating into place.

Installation – Slide new ball joint into slot in control arm. Tighten ball joint mounting bolts. Refit lower control arm to subframe (chassis). Install ball joint into lower section of suspension strut.

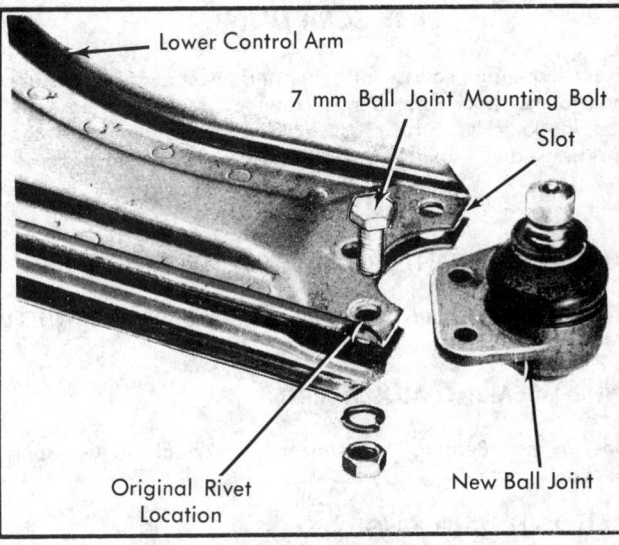

Fig. 2 New Ball Joint Installation Location in Lower Control Arm

TIGHTENING SPECIFICATIONS

Application	Ft. Lbs. (mkg)
Ball Joint Clamp Bolt-to-Steering Knuckle	36 (5.0)
Tie Rod Castle Nut	22 (3.0)
New Ball Joint-to-Control Arm	18 (2.5)
Suspension Strut-to-Inner Fender	14 (2.0)
Control Arm-to-Subframe (Chassis)	50 (6.9)
Pivot Pin "U" Bracket	32 (4.5)
Axle Drive Shaft-to-Transaxle	32 (4.5)
Suspension Strut-to-Steering Knuckle	58 (8.0)
Piston Rod Nut	58 (8.0)
Axle Shaft Nut	173 (24.0)

VOLKSWAGEN VANAGON

DESCRIPTION

Front suspension consists of upper and lower control arms and ball joints, shock absorbers surrounded by coil springs, and steering knuckles. Strut rods attach to chassis and lower control arms, and stabilizer bar attaches to chassis and strut rod.

ADJUSTMENT

WHEEL ALIGNMENT SPECIFICATIONS & PROCEDURES

See Wheel Alignment Specifications and Procedures in WHEEL ALIGNMENT Section.

WHEEL BEARING ADJUSTMENT

See Wheel Bearing Adjustment in WHEEL ALIGNMENT Section.

BALL JOINT CHECKING

See Ball Joint Checking in WHEEL ALIGNMENT Section.

REMOVAL & INSTALLATION

LOWER CONTROL ARM, STEERING KNUCKLE & COIL SPRING

Removal — 1) Raise and support front of vehicle. Remove tire and wheel. Detach stabilizer bar from strut rod.

2) Remove 3 nuts holding strut rod, steering knuckle, and lower control arm together. Remove brake caliper and brake hose bracket.

NOTE — Strut rod length determines caster angle. If setting at body mounting is changed, caster must be readjusted.

3) Hang caliper from body with wire hook. Using suitable pressing tool, detach tie rod end from steering knuckle.

4) Remove upper ball joint from upper control arm. Detach steering knuckle from upper and lower control arms.

5) Loosen shock absorber lower mounting on lower control arm. Support lower control arm with a jack, and pull out shock absorber bolt from lower control arm.

6) Lower jack slowly and remove coil spring. Remove lower control arm pivot bolt and remove control arm from vehicle.

Bushing Replacement — Using suitable press and adapters, press out old bushings and press in replacements.

Installation — 1) Install lower control arm to vehicle with pivot bolt. Position coil spring so straight end is at bottom.

2) Attach damping ring to spring with tape. Install spring in control arm spring depression.

3) Lift control arm with a jack and attach shock absorber lower mount. Attach steering knuckle to control arm.

4) Attach strut rod to steering knuckle and control arm lower connection. Install stabilizer bar, tie rod end, and brake caliper.

NOTE — When installing strut rod bolts, spring washers go under bolt heads. Always use new self-locking nuts.

5) Install wheel and tire. Lower vehicle. Turn wheel to full-lock position and check distance between wheel and brake hose. Bend bracket as necessary to adjust distance to 1" (25 mm).

SHOCK ABSORBER

Removal — 1) Raise and support front of vehicle. Loosen shock absorber lower mounting bolt.

2) Lower vehicle to ground and remove mounting bolt. Raise vehicle and remove shock absorber upper mounting hardware and remove shock absorber from vehicle.

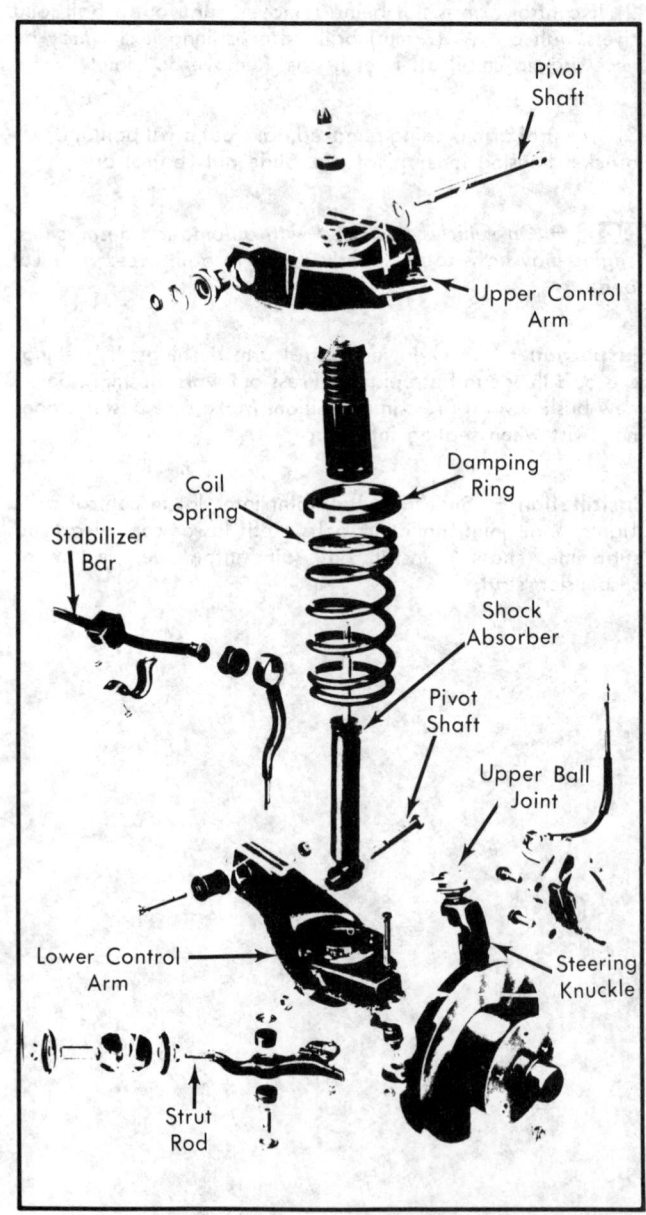

Fig. 1 Exploded View of Vanagon Front Suspension

VOLKSWAGEN VANAGON (Cont.)

Installation — With vehicle raised off ground, install shock absorber to upper mounting. Lower vehicle and attach shock absorber to lower control arm.

NOTE — *When lifting vehicle with shock absorber disconnected, avoid damaging upper ball joint.*

UPPER CONTROL ARM

Removal — 1) Raise and support vehicle. Remove tire and wheel. Remove bolts holding upper ball joint to upper control arm.

2) Swing steering knuckle carefully to one side. Note the position of upper control arm pivot shaft and remove from control arm. Remove control arm from vehicle.

Bushing Replacement — Note the position of and grind off spot welds holding in bushings. Using suitable press and adapters, press out old bushing and press in replacements. Secure bushing with spot welds in noted locations. Clean up welds and paint surface.

Installation — 1) Lubricate pivot shaft with multi-purpose grease. Install upper control arm to body and position pivot shaft as noted during disassembly. Install ball joint to upper control arm. Install tire and wheel and lower vehicle.

NOTE — *Flat on pivot shaft must be vertical and face center of vehicle. Larger side of eccentric washer faces down.*

STABILIZER BAR

Removal & Installation — Disconnect stabilizer bar from strut rod. Remove bolts holding mounting bracket to chassis and remove stabilizer bar. To install, reverse removal procedure.

STRUT ROD

Removal & Installation — Disconnect stabilizer bar from strut rod. Remove 3 nuts holding strut rod, steering knuckle and lower control arm together. Remove hardware mounting strut rod to chassis and remove strut rod from vehicle. To install, reverse removal procedure and adjust caster.

NOTE — *When attaching strut rod, steering knuckle, and lower control arm, spring washers are to be installed under bolt heads. Always use new self-locking nuts.*

BALL JOINTS

Removal — Remove steering knuckle from vehicle. Using ball joint adapter tool (VW 267a), remove ball joint adapter from lower ball joint. Remove nuts securing ball joints to steering knuckle and using same tool, press out upper ball joint. Remove circlip from lower ball joint and use suitable press to press ball joint from steering knuckle.

Installation — Press in ball joints with flat side of shoulder facing spindle. Attach adapter loosely to lower ball joint.

NOTE — *Do not tighten adapter fully. Adapter must be aligned with control arm when steering knuckle is installed or rubber boot will tear.*

2) Install steering knuckle to vehicle and tighten ball joints and adapter with new self-locking nuts.

TIGHTENING SPECIFICATIONS

Application	Ft. Lbs. (mkg)
Strut Rod-to-Lower Control Arm①	
1st Tightening	47 (6.5)
2nd Tightening	51 (7.0)
Strut Rod-to-Chassis	72 (10.0)
Stabilizer-to-Strut Rod	22 (3.0)
Stabilizer Bracket-to-Chassis	14 (1.9)
Tie Rod End-to-Steering Knuckle	22 (3.0)
Lower Control Arm Pivot Bolt	65 (9.0)
Brake Caliper-to-Mounting	115 (15.9)
Upper Ball Joint-to-Control Arm	43 (6.0)
Ball Joint Locking Nuts①	80 (11.1)
Upper Control Arm Pivot Bolt	54 (7.5)
Shock Absorber Top Nut	22 (3.0)

① — Always use new self locking nuts.

VOLVO

DL GLE
GL Coupe
GT Diesel

DESCRIPTION

Strut type suspension consisting of a vertically mounted strut assembly. Strut assembly is mounted to chassis frame at top by means of a thrust bearing. Lower end of strut assembly is mounted to a ball joint which is bolted to lower control arm. Steering knuckle is an integral part of strut assembly. Strut assembly consists of a shock absorber built into strut outer tube; a coil spring mounted on outside of strut assembly; and a spindle integral with bottom of strut. A stabilizer bar connects the control arms through rubber mounted links.

ADJUSTMENT

WHEEL ALIGNMENT SPECIFICATIONS & PROCEDURES

See Wheel Alignment Specifications & Procedures in WHEEL ALIGNMENT Section.

WHEEL BEARING ADJUSTMENT

See Wheel Bearing Adjustment in WHEEL ALIGNMENT Section.

BALL JOINT CHECKING

See Ball Joint Checking in WHEEL ALIGNMENT Section.

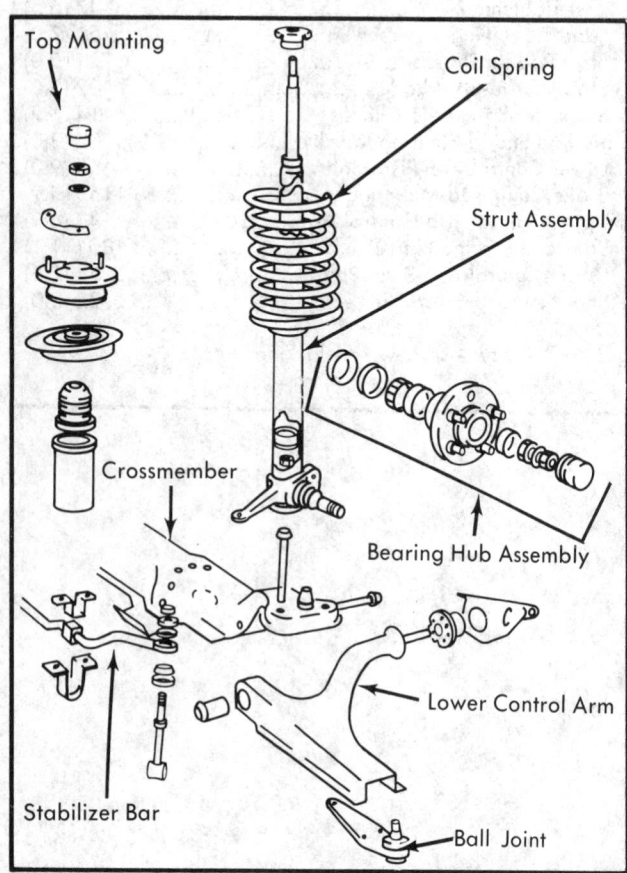

Fig. 1 Exploded View of Front Suspension Assembly

REMOVAL & INSTALLATION

CONTROL ARM

Removal — Raise vehicle and support on safety stands, then remove wheel and tire. Disconnect stabilizer bar-to-link assembly. Disconnect ball joint from control arm at three attaching bolts. Remove front attaching bolt for control arm. Remove bracket attaching rear of control arm to chassis, then remove control arm from vehicle. If control arm bushing is being replaced, press out using proper adapter (9995085) and driver (9995091).

Installation — Inspect all components for wear or damage. Use proper adapter (9995085) and driver (5555084) to install new bushings if necessary. If bushing in bracket is replaced, ensure that small slots on new bushing will point in a horizontal position when bracket is installed on vehicle. Install bracket, with control arm, to chassis but do not tighten bolts. Install front attaching bolt for control arm but do not tighten. Install ball joint to control arm and tighten bolts. Position a jack under control arm and raise so coil spring is compressed. Connect stabilizer bar to link. Tighten control arm attaching nuts and bolts. Install wheel and tire.

NOTE — Tighten rear bushing nut with vehicle weight resting on wheel.

SHOCK ABSORBER

Removal — **1)** Raise vehicle and support on safety stands, then remove wheel and tire. Position jack under control arm and raise slightly to provide support. Using a spring compressor, compress coil spring being sure to engage five coils with tool. Disconnect steering rod from steering arm and stabilizer bar from link at control arm. Remove bolt attaching brake line bracket. Remove cover on upper end of strut and spring assembly. Remove center nut using tool as indicated in Fig. 2.

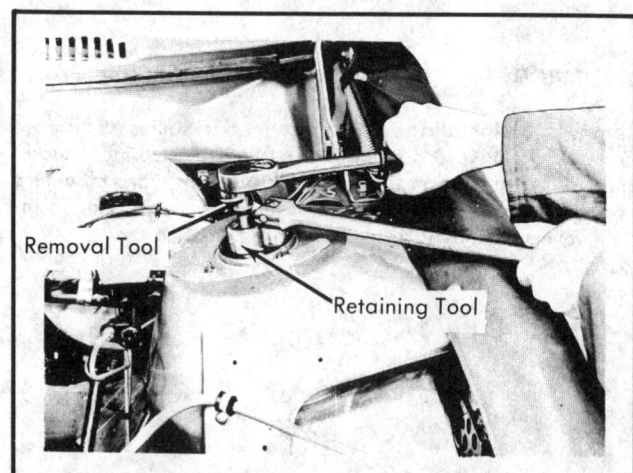

Fig. 2 View Showing Removal of Strut Assembly Center Nut

2) Lower jack supporting control arm while supporting strut assembly so brake lines and hoses are not damaged. Hook special tool (9995045) to strut assembly and stabilizer to support unit during remaining removal procedures. Remove the spring seat and rubber bumper. Remove coil spring with compressor tool attached. Remove shock absorber retaining nut while holding strut outer casing at the weld. Pull shock absorber from casing.

VOLVO (Cont.)

Installation — 1) Install new shock absorber and retaining nut while holding strut outer casing at the weld. Pull shock absorber spindle to fully extended position. Install coil spring onto strut assembly making sure spring end is properly aligned on strut bracket. Install rubber bumper and install spring seat on coil spring. Guide strut assembly into upper mount and shock absorber spindle through upper mount. Connect stabilizer bar to stabilizer link.

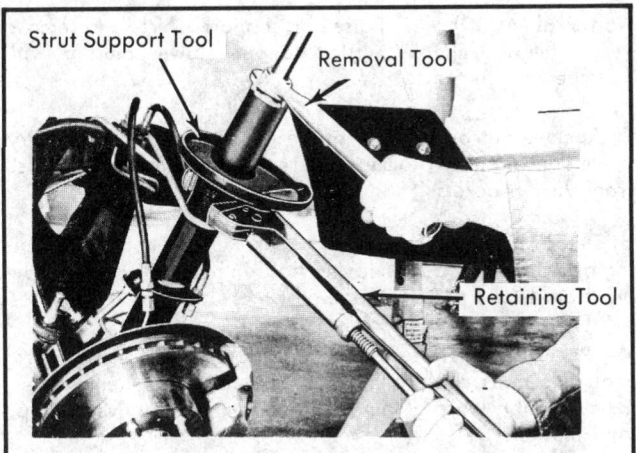

Fig. 3   View Showing Removal of Shock Absorber Nut

2) Position jack under control arm and raise slightly. Install and tighten washer and nut to shock absorber spindle while using proper retaining tool. Install cover, then connect brake line bracket to chassis. Connect steering arm to steering rod and remove coil spring compressor tool slowly. Install wheel and tire.

BALL JOINTS

Removal — Raise vehicle and support with safety stands. Loosen shock absorber nut. Remove 4 bolts attaching ball joint to strut assembly. Remove ball joint from control arm, then remove ball joint nut and separate from attachment.

Installation — Position new ball joint to attachment and tighten nut. Install ball joint assembly to strut assembly and to control arm. Tighten shock absorber retaining nut.

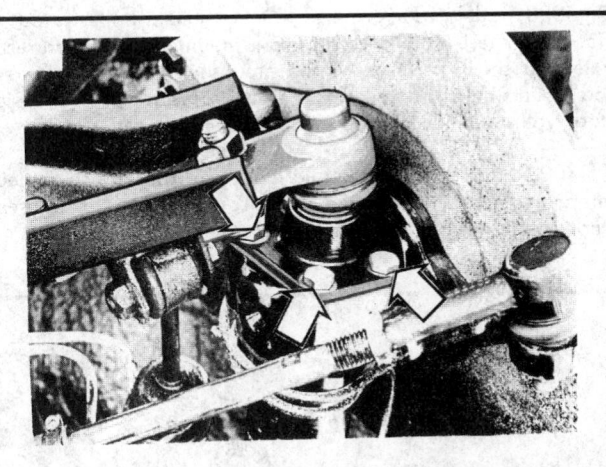

Fig. 4   View Showing Ball Joint Retaining Bolts

TIGHTENING SPECIFICATIONS

Application	Ft. Lbs.(mkg)
Ball Joint-to-Control Arm	70-95 (9.7-13.0)
Ball Joint Assembly-to-Strut	15-20 (2.0-2.5)
Ball Joint-to-Bracket	35-50 (5.0-7.0)
Control Arm Retaining Bolts	
Front	40-70 (5.5-9.7)
Rear	36-43 (5.0-6.0)
Control Arm Bracket-to-Frame	22-36 (3.0-5.0)

AUDI

4000
5000

DESCRIPTION

Suspension on all Audi models consists of coil springs, shock absorbers, transverse rod and trailing arms. Some design differences occur between models.

On 5000 models, rear suspension arrangement is illustrated in *Fig. 1*. On these models, coil spring is mounted directly on rear axle and shock absorber is mounted separately. Transverse rod mounts behind axle beam. Top end of shock absorber is a stud type mount incorporating a rubber damper assembly.

On 4000 models, coil spring and shock absorber are combined into a single, strut type assembly. A transverse rod is also used and mounts diagonally in front of axle beam. See *Fig. 2*.

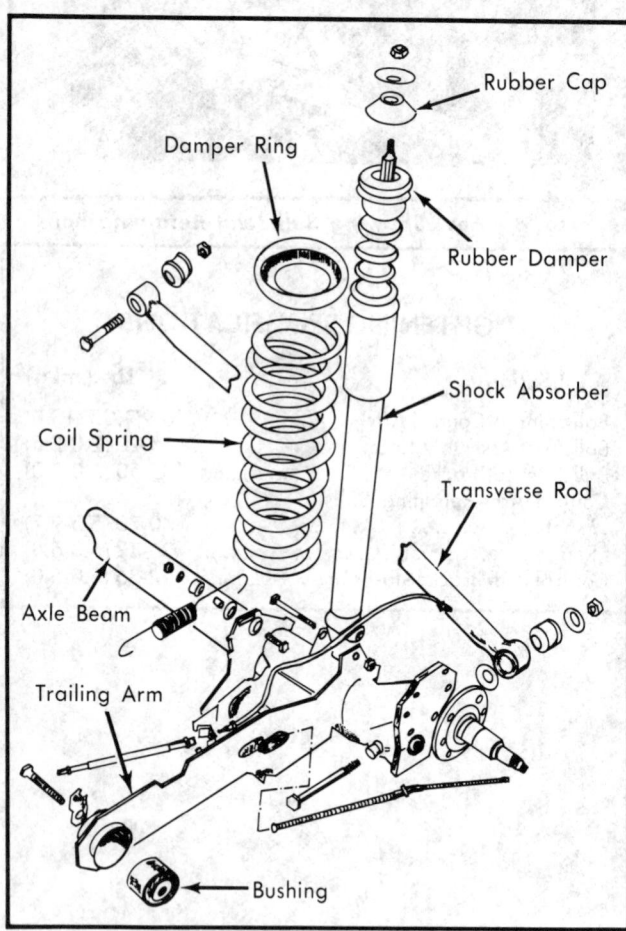

Fig. 1 Exploded View of Audi 5000 Rear Suspension

ADJUSTMENTS

WHEEL ALIGNMENT SPECIFICATIONS & PROCEDURES

See *Wheel Alignment Specifications and Procedures* in WHEEL ALIGNMENT Section.

WHEEL BEARING ADJUSTMENT

See *Wheel Bearing Adjustment* in WHEEL ALIGNMENT Section

REMOVAL & INSTALLATION

REAR AXLE ASSEMBLY

Removal (4000) – 1) Raise and support vehicle and remove rear wheels. Unhook muffler hangers, lower muffler with tailpipe and secure.

2) Remove nut on parking brake linkage equalizer bar. Pry cable sleeves out of brackets and remove parking brake cables from their brackets.

3) Detach brake hoses and plug lines. Remove nuts from trailing arm mounting bolts, leaving bolts in place. Disconnect spring from brake pressure regulator.

4) Remove transverse rod mounting bolt, suspension strut mounting bolts, and trailing arm mounting bolts. Remove rear axle assembly while guiding parking brake cable over tailpipe and muffler.

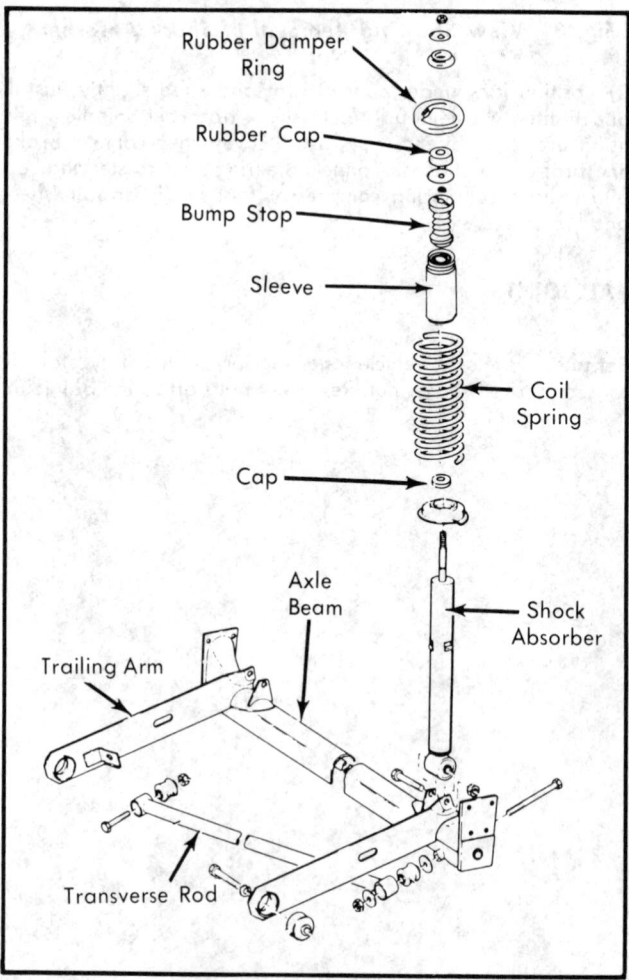

Fig. 2 Exploded View of Audi 4000 Rear Suspension

AUDI (Cont.)

Bushing Replacement (4000) — Place trailing arm in press and force bushing from arm. Reverse process to install new bushing. Make sure bushing slots are positioned horizontally in trailing arm.

Installation (4000) — 1) Raise and support vehicle. Place rear axle in position. Install both trailing arm bolts and hand tighten. Install rear wheels, lower vehicle and tighten trailing arm bolts with wheels on ground.

2) Install transverse rod, brake hoses, and spring for pressure regulator. Bleed brakes, attach parking brake cable and adjust.

Removal (5000) — 1) Loosen, but do not remove wheel bolts. Raise and support vehicle. Remove bolt from transverse rod at axle mounting. Detach right brake hose at coupling with steel tubing. Plug openings.

2) Detach brake pressure regulator spring (hooked to lower mounting bolt of shock absorber). Detach left brake hose at connection with tubing and plug openings.

3) Remove right fuel tank retaining strap. Remove parking brake cable from guide on fuel tank. Loosen left side parking brake cable bolt. Loosen parking brake adjusting nut and disconnect parking brake cable.

4) Remove rear mounting for exhaust system. Lower vehicle to ground. Remove both shock absorber top nuts. Using frame jack, raise vehicle slowly until coil spring can be removed from axle mountings. Remove rear wheels.

5) Remove trailing arm mounting bolts, with rear axle suitably supported on a jack. While slowly lowering axle assembly from vehicle, guide parking brake cable over exhaust pipe.

Bushing Replacement (5000) — Place trailing arm in press and force bushing from arm. Reverse process to install new bushing. Align cutouts with center axis.

Installation (5000) — 1) Raise vehicle and position rear axle in vehicle. Install and lightly tighten trailing arm mounting bolts. Install both rear wheels and lower vehicle to ground.

2) Position rubber damper rings on coil springs, jack up vehicle body, position springs and slowly lower body to hold springs (3 persons may be required to perform this step).

3) Tighten shock absorber top mounting nuts. Raise vehicle and check position of coil springs. If necessary, turn springs in mounting to correct their positions.

4) With vehicle resting on ground, tighten trailing arm bolts. Install transverse rod, brake hoses, spring for brake pressure regulator and fuel tank retaining strap.

5) Bleed brake system, attach and adjust parking brake cable.

TRANSVERSE ROD

Removal (All Models) — Raise and support vehicle. Remove nuts from transverse rod bolts and tap bolts out of holes. Inspect bushings and sleeves for wear and replace if necessary.

Installation (All Models) — To install, reverse removal procedure.

SHOCK ABSORBERS

NOTE — *Remove and install shock absorbers one at a time. Do not allow rear axle to hang from body mounts only.*

Removal (4000) — Loosen trunk sheet metal trim and remove shock absorber top protective cap. Remove upper mounting nut. Raise vehicle, remove lower mounting bolt and remove shock absorber.

Removal (5000) — Remove top shock absorber mounting. Remove lower mounting and shock.

Installation (All Models) — To install, reverse removal procedure. On 4000 models, be sure top protection cap is properly installed.

TIGHTENING SPECIFICATIONS

Application	Ft. Lbs. (mkg)
Shock Absorbers	
4000	
Upper	14 (2.0)
Lower	43 (6.0)
5000	
Upper	14 (2.0)
Lower	40 (5.5)
Transverse Rod	
4000	51 (7.0)
5000	65 (9.0)
Trailing Arm	
4000	72 (10.0)
5000	69 (9.5)

BMW

320i
528i
633CSi
733i

DESCRIPTION

Independent type rear suspension with rear struts. Semi-trailing control arms pivot on crossmember and are integral with axle shaft bearing housing. Shock absorber (strut assembly) mounts to purchase on top of control arm and to body. A stabilizer bar is attached to each trailing arm and at two points on crossmember.

ADJUSTMENTS

WHEEL ALIGNMENT SPECIFICATIONS & PROCEDURES

See Wheel Alignment Specifications and Procedures in WHEEL ALIGNMENT Section.

REMOVAL & INSTALLATION

STRUT ASSEMBLIES (SHOCK ABSORBERS)

Removal (Exc. 733i) — Raise vehicle and remove rear wheel. Place jack under control arm. Disconnect shock at lower mounting. Remove centering shell and mounting nuts from top of shock absorber. Remove assembly from vehicle.

Removal (733i) — Remove rear seat backrest. Raise and support vehicle under control arms. Detach lower mounting. Remove package shelf and detach centering shell at wheel housing. Remove shock absorber from vehicle.

Disassembly (All) — Using spring compressor, collapse spring and remove centering shell. Remove coil spring and boot. Pull retainer and auxiliary spring off shock absorber. Inspect and replace any defective parts.

Reassembly (All) — Reverse disassembly procedure, making sure coil spring is properly aligned before releasing spring compressor. Vent opening on spring faces inside retainer.

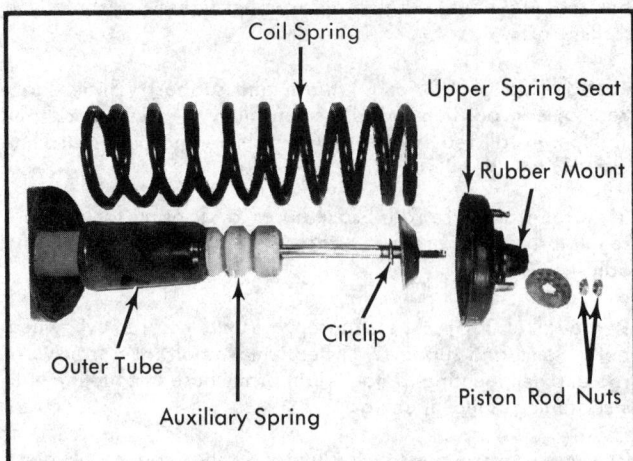

Fig. 2   Exploded View of BMW Rear Suspension Strut Assembly — 320i Shown

Installation (All) — To install, reverse removal procedure. Tighten bolts and nuts after vehicle is resting on ground.

SEMI-TRAILING CONTROL ARM

Removal (Exc. 733i) — **1)** Raise vehicle and remove rear wheels. Remove parking brake lever. Disconnect and plug brake line at union bracket. Detach brake pad wear sensor from right control arm (if equipped).

2) Remove stabilizer bar from control arm. Remove strut assembly (shock absorber) from vehicle. Disconnect axle drive shaft from bearing carrier. Place jack under control arm. Remove trailing arm pivot bolts at crossmember and lower arm to ground.

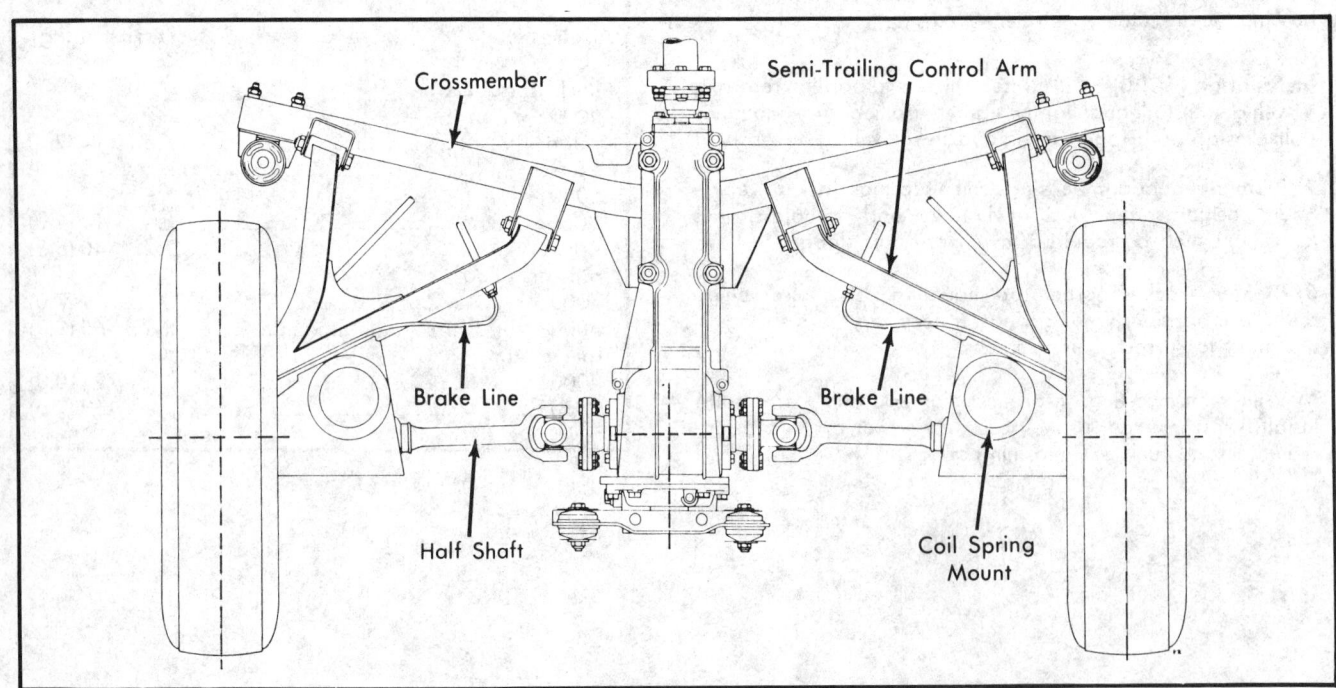

Fig. 1   Overhead View of BMW Rear Suspension

Rear Suspension

BMW (Cont.)

Removal (733i) — 1) Raise and support vehicle. Remove rear wheel. Pull up parking brake lever and detach output shaft at drive flange. Remove parking brake lever.

2) Using a syringe, draw off fluid from reservoir and detach and plug brake lines. Detach control arm from rear axle carrier. Detach shock absorber and remove control arm.

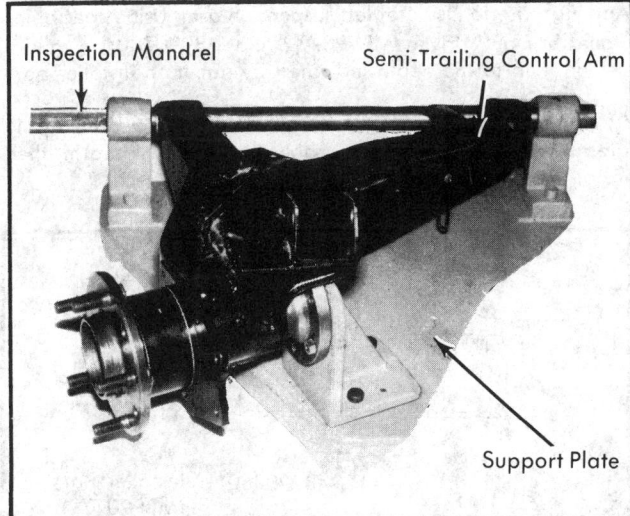

Inspection Mandrel   Semi-Trailing Control Arm

Support Plate

Fig. 3 Trailing Arm Fitted to Support Plate to Check Alignment

Inspection (All) — 1) Visually inspect bushings and replace as necessary. Before pressing out worn bushings, cut off collar. When pressing in new bushings, lubricate them with oil. Note that collared edge faces out.

2) Check trailing arm alignment. Place arm in support plate. *See Fig. 3.* Slide inspection mandrel through control arm to crossmember mounting bushings bores (bushings removed). If control arm is out of alignment it can be straightened if there is no other damage to arm.

Installation (All) — To install, reverse removal procedure and tighten nuts fully after vehicle is resting on ground. Bleed and adjust brakes.

TIGHTENING SPECIFICATIONS

Application	Ft. Lbs. (mkg)
Lower Shock Absorber Mount	
320i	36-39 (5.0-5.4)
528i, 633CSi & 733i	87-94 (12-13)
Upper Shock Absorber Mount	
All Models	18-20 (2.5-2.8)
Trailing Arm-to-Crossmember	
320i	58-65 (8.1-9.0)
528i, 633CSi & 733i	49-54 (6.7-7.5)

CHRYSLER CORP. IMPORTS – FRONT-WHEEL-DRIVE MODELS

Champ
Colt Hatchback

DESCRIPTION

Rear suspension is independent design and consists of left and right suspension arms, shock absorbers and coil springs. Suspension arms slide together on bushings. Suspension arms are attached to frame by shock absorbers and a clamp that utilizes bushings. Some models are equipped with a stabilizer bar which is attached to suspension arms near pivot points.

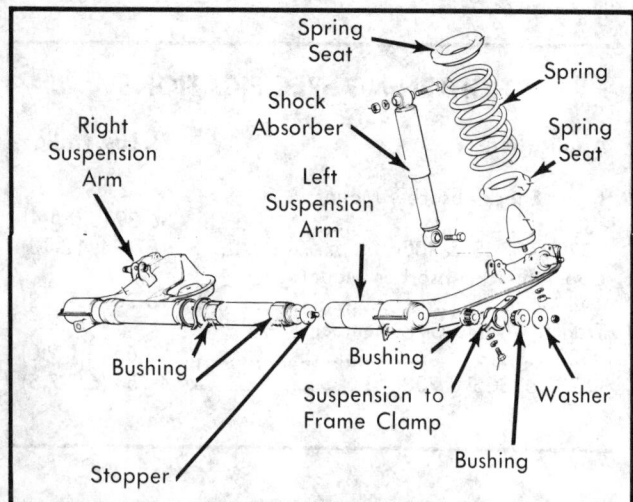

Fig. 1 Exploded View of Champ and Colt Hatchback Rear Suspension Assembly

ADJUSTMENT

WHEEL ALIGNMENT SPECIFICATIONS & PROCEDURES

See Wheel Alignment Specifications and Procedures in WHEEL ALIGNMENT Section.

WHEEL BEARING ADJUSTMENT

See Wheel Bearing Adjustment in WHEEL ALIGNMENT Section.

REMOVAL & INSTALLATION

REAR SUSPENSION ASSEMBLY

Removal — 1) Raise and support rear of vehicle with jacks under frame. Remove rear brake assembly. Remove muffler. Raise suspension slightly.

2) Remove shock absorber, then lower jack and remove coil spring, Temporarily install shock absorber to suspension arm. Disconnect and plug brake hose at suspension arm.

3) Remove shock absorber and suspension clamp bolts. Remove suspension assembly from vehicle.

Disassembly — 1) With suspension assembly removed from vehicle, loosen nuts at both ends of suspension arms. Remove clamps washer and bushings. Remove dust cover (clamp).

2) On models with stabilizer bar, make an index mark at each end of bar in alignment with punch marks on brackets. On all models, separate suspension arms. Remove rubber stopper from right arm. Pry first bushing out of left arm. Using a punch and hammer, drive inner bushing out of left arm.

Reassembly — 1) Replace any worn or damaged bushings. Apply grease to inside of left suspension arm. Using special installer bar and driver (MB990779 and MB990780), install inner bushing to the depth indicated by notch on installer bar.

2) Install new dust cover to the right suspension arm. Apply grease to the inside surface of the right suspension arm, then install rubber stopper.

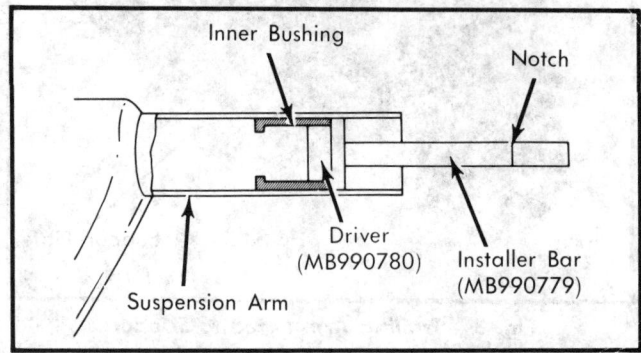

Fig. 2 Installing Inner Bushing to Suspension Arm

3) Slowly push right and left suspension arms together. Wipe off excess grease. On models with stabilizer bar, align index marks on bar ends with punch marks on brackets. On all models, install bushing, clamp and washer on suspension arms. Ensure that washer is installed with toothed side facing bushing.

4) Install nut on suspension arm. Pack dust cover with grease, then secure it to suspension arm with clamp.

Installation — 1) With suspension assembly in place, install clamp bolts. Install coil springs and shock absorbers. Temporarily tighten shock absorber bolts.

NOTE — Make sure that upper and lower spring seats are installed correctly.

2) Install rear brake assembly. Install wheels. Lower vehicle and tighten suspension arm end nuts and shock absorber bolts. Bleed and adjust brakes.

TIGHTENING SPECIFICATIONS

Application	Ft. Lbs (mkg)
Suspension Arm End Nuts	36-51 (3.7-5.2)
Suspension Clamp-to-Frame	36-51 (3.7-5.2)
Shock Absorber	47-58 (4.8-6.0)

Rear Suspension

DATSUN 200SX, 210 & 510

DESCRIPTION

Rear suspension is a coil spring and link type, consisting of coil springs, shock absorbers and 4 links which control axle movement.

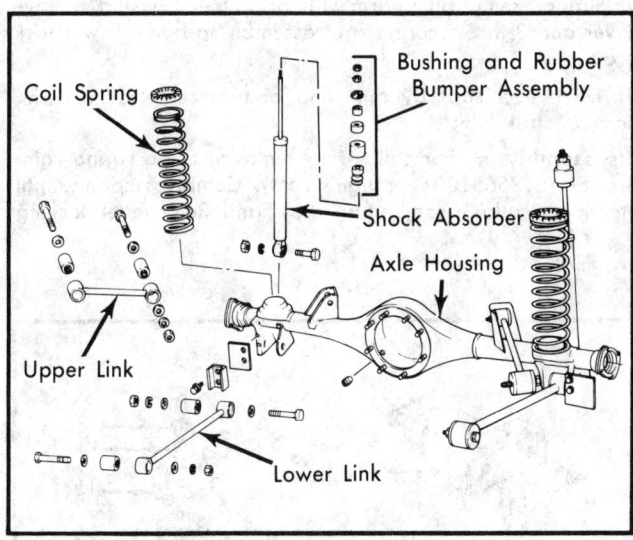

Fig. 1 Exploded View of Datsun 210 & 510 Rear Suspension

REMOVAL & INSTALLATION

SHOCK ABSORBERS

Removal — From inside vehicle, remove upper shock absorber nut. Remove lower shock absorber bolt from bracket. Remove shock absorber.

Installation — To install, reverse removal procedure.

COIL SPRINGS

Removal — 1) Block front wheels. Raise and support rear of vehicle. Support the center of the differential with a jack.

2) Remove rear wheels. Remove shock absorber mount bolts from axle assembly. Lower axle assembly slowly and remove coil springs as they are extended.

Installation — To install, reverse removal procedure.

REAR AXLE ASSEMBLY

Removal — 1) Block front wheels. Raise and support rear of vehicle. Support center of differential with a jack. Remove rear wheels.

2) Disconnect propeller shaft, brake hose and parking brake cable adjuster. Remove lower shock absorber mounting bolts.

3) Lower jack slowly and remove coil springs. Raise jack to original position. Remove bolts securing upper and lower links at axle housing. Lower jack slowly and remove axle assembly from under vehicle.

Installation — To install, reverse removal procedure.

LINK ASSEMBLY

NOTE — *Do not remove more than one link at a time without first removing rear axle assembly.*

Removal — Remove bolts from each end and remove link assembly.

Inspection — Inspect link bushings for wear or damage. Replace as necessary.

Installation — To install, reverse removal procedure.

TIGHTENING SPECIFICATIONS

Application	Ft. Lbs. (mkg)
Link Assembly Bolts	51-58 (7.0-8.0)
Shock Absorber Upper Nuts	11-14 (1.5-2.0)
Propeller Shaft Flange Bolts	17-24 (2.5-3.5)

Rear Suspension

DATSUN 280ZX & 810

DESCRIPTION

Rear suspension is of the semi-trailing arm, independent type. The rear wheel is supported by a spring and shock absorber strut assembly and the semi-trailing arm. The upper end of the strut is attached directly to the upper body. The lower end of the strut is attached to the end of the semi-trailing arm. The differential gear carrier is installed directly to the suspension subframe and a differential mounting bracket and insulator. The semi-trailing arm is installed on the subframe with rubber bushings and pivot bolts. The rear wheel bearing housing and lower strut mount bracket are welded to the end of the semi-trailing arm. 280ZX models have an additional rear stabilizer bar attached for added suspension control.

REMOVAL & INSTALLATION

STRUT & COIL SPRING

Removal — 1) Block front wheels. Raise rear of vehicle and support with stands.

2) Support semi-trailing arm with jack. Open trunk lid, remove cover and 3 nuts securing strut assembly to body. Lower jack gradually.

3) Disconnect strut by removing bolt at semi-trailing arm. Remove strut vehicle.

Disassembly — For coil spring removal, use a spring compressor (ST35651001 or equivalent). Compress spring until mounting insulator can be turned by hand. Remove self-locking

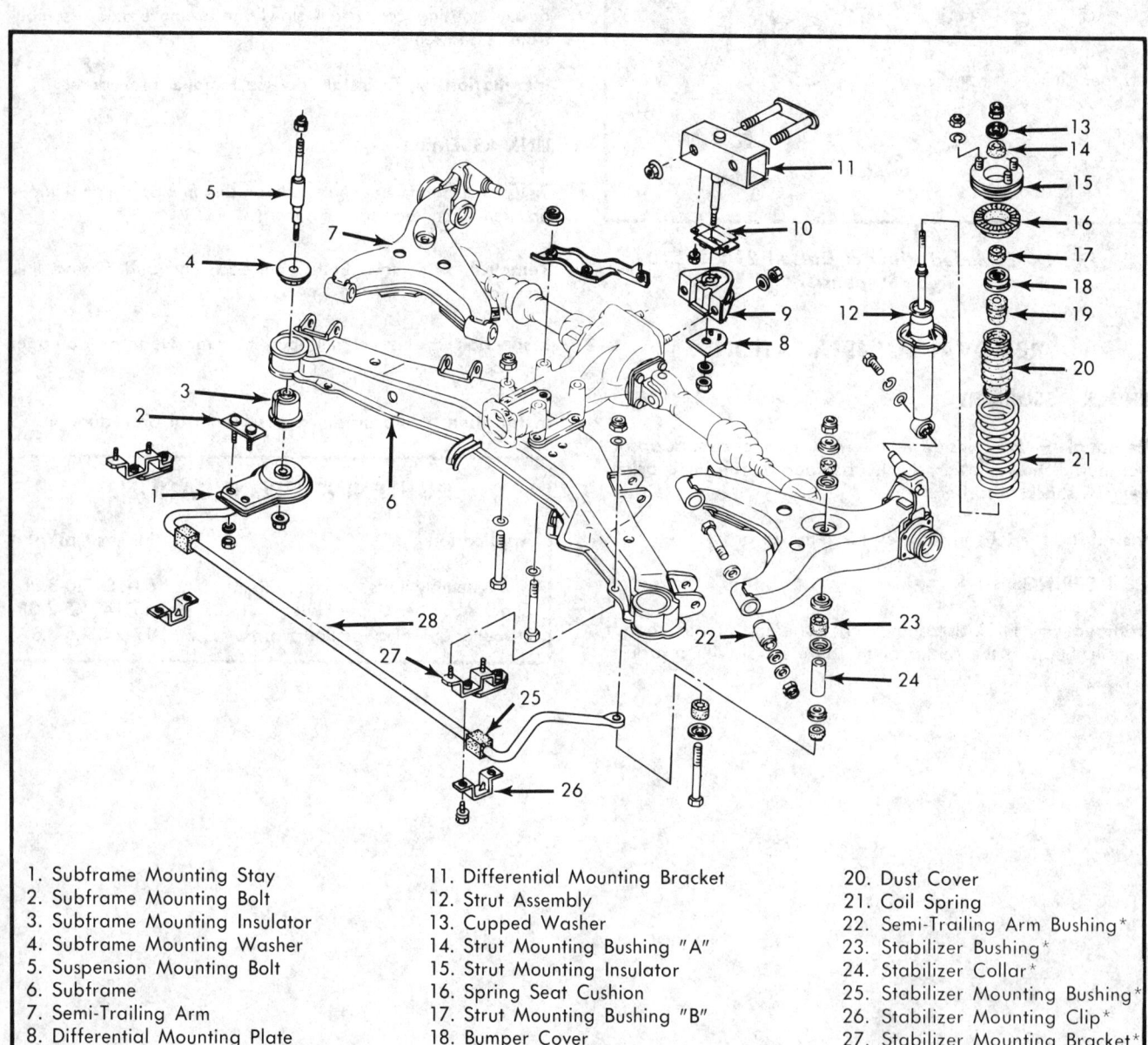

1. Subframe Mounting Stay
2. Subframe Mounting Bolt
3. Subframe Mounting Insulator
4. Subframe Mounting Washer
5. Suspension Mounting Bolt
6. Subframe
7. Semi-Trailing Arm
8. Differential Mounting Plate
9. Differential Mounting Insulator
10. Differential Mounting Adapter Plate*

11. Differential Mounting Bracket
12. Strut Assembly
13. Cupped Washer
14. Strut Mounting Bushing "A"
15. Strut Mounting Insulator
16. Spring Seat Cushion
17. Strut Mounting Bushing "B"
18. Bumper Cover
19. Rubber Bumper

20. Dust Cover
21. Coil Spring
22. Semi-Trailing Arm Bushing*
23. Stabilizer Bushing*
24. Stabilizer Collar*
25. Stabilizer Mounting Bushing*
26. Stabilizer Mounting Clip*
27. Stabilizer Mounting Bracket*
28. Stabilizer Bar*

* — 280ZX only.

Fig. 1   Exploded View of Datsun 280ZX & 810 Rear Suspension Assembly

Rear Suspension

DATSUN 280ZX & 810 (Cont.)

nut on strut shaft. Release spring compressor and remove coil spring.

Reassembly — Reverse disassembly procedure using a new self-locking nut on strut shaft.

Installation — Install strut assembly to upper body first, then connect lower end of strut to semi-trailing arm and tighten bolt to specifications.

SEMI-TRAILING ARM

Removal — **1)** Block front wheels, raise rear of vehicle and remove rear wheels. Disconnect brake line from hose at semi-trailing arm and brake assembly. Remove brake line. Disconnect axle shaft from stub shaft by removing the 4 flange bolts.

2) On 280ZX, remove stabilizer bar bolt and related hardware. On all models, disconnect strut from semi-trailing arm. Disconnect semi-trailing arm from subframe by removing pivot bolts. Remove semi-trailing arm from vehicle.

Installation — Reverse removal procedure, noting the following: Replace all self-locking nuts. Tighten semi-trailing arm-to-subframe bolts to specifications only after installing wheels and lowering vehicle to ground. Bleed and adjust brakes.

REAR SUSPENSION ASSEMBLY

Removal — **1)** Block front wheels. Raise and support rear of vehicle and remove rear wheels. Remove rear exhaust pipe and muffler. Mark flange of propeller shaft and companion flange, then remove propeller shaft.

2) Disconnect and plug rear brake hoses at semi-trailing arms. Place a jack under center of suspension and differential assembly. Disconnect hand brake cables and lower strut ends.

3) Remove subframe nuts at body. Remove differential mount lock nut. Lower rear suspension assembly and remove from under vehicle.

Disassembly — **1)** Disconnect axle shafts from differential and stub shafts. Remove differential assembly from subframe. Remove pivot bolts and semi-trailing arms.

2) Insulator bushings can be removed with removal/installation tool (ST38280000 or equivalent).

Reassembly & Installation — Assemble and install in reverse order of disassembly and removal, while noting the following: Final tightening of semi-trailing arm pivot lock nuts should be done after vehicle has been lowered to the ground.

TIGHTENING SPECIFICATIONS

Application	Ft. Lbs. (mkg)
Propeller Shaft-to-Flange	25-33 (3.5-4.5)
Strut Upper Mount Nut	19-29 (2.6-4.0)
Strut Lower Mount Bolt	43-58 (6.0-8.0)
Subframe-to-Body Nuts	58-72 (8.0-10.0)
Differential Mount Lock Nut	58-72 (8.0-10.0)
Semi-Trailing Arm Pivot Nuts	58-72 (8.0-10.0)

DATSUN 310

DESCRIPTION

Rear suspension is of the trailing arm, independent type and consists of a coil spring, shock absorber and trailing arm. The forward end of the trailing arm pivots at the body and is suspended by the coil spring. The shock absorber mounts adjacent to the spring and controls trailing arm movement.

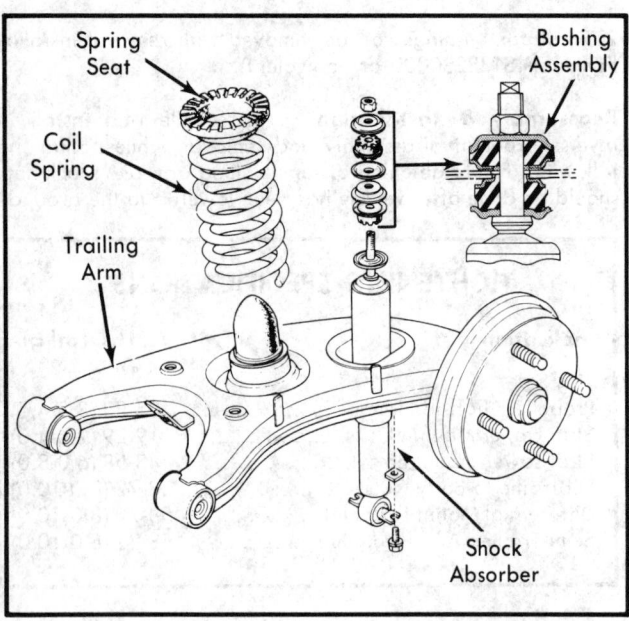

Fig. 1   Exploded View of Datsun 310 Rear Suspension

REMOVAL & INSTALLATION

SHOCK ABSORBER

Removal — Block front wheels. Raise and support rear of vehicle. Remove rear wheel. Support lower end of trailing arm securely with a jack. Remove nut and bolts from shock absorber ends. Lower jack slowly and remove shock absorber.

Installation — Install in reverse order of removal.

COIL SPRING

Removal — Block front wheels. Raise and support rear of vehicle. Remove rear wheel. Support lower end of trailing arm securely with jack. Remove shock absorber. Trailing arm can now be lowered completely and coil spring removed.

Installation — Install in reverse order of removal.

TRAILING ARM

Removal — 1) Block front wheels. Raise and support rear of vehicle. Place a jack under lower end of trailing arm. Remove rear wheel. Disconnect parking brake cable.

2) Remove hub cap, cotter pin and wheel bearing retaining nut. Remove brake drum with bearings. Disconnect and plug brake line. Remove brake assembly.

3) Remove shock absorber and coil spring. Remove pivot nuts and bolts. Remove trailing arm. Inspect pivot bushings and replace as necessary.

Installation — To install, reverse the removal procedure, noting the following: Final tightening of the pivot bolts should be performed after vehicle is lowered to ground. Bleed brake system.

TIGHTENING SPECIFICATIONS

Application	Ft. Lbs. (mkg)
Trailing Arm Pivot Bolt	40-48 (5.5-6.7)
Shock Absorber Lower Bolt	11-17 (1.5-2.4)
Shock Absorber Upper Nut	5.8-8.7 (.8-1.2)
Brake Backing Plate Bolt	18-25 (2.5-3.4)
Wheel Nut	58-65 (8.0-9.0)

Rear Suspension

FIAT BRAVA

DESCRIPTION

Rear suspension consists of upper and lower reaction struts, shock absorbers encased by coil springs and a track bar. Lower reaction struts mount near wheels under axle housing and at forward end to car body. Upper reaction struts mount off bracket on axle housing and at front end to bracket on body. A track bar is connected at one end to bracket mounted off frame and at opposite end to bracket below axle housing. Coil springs mount between axle assembly and frame. Hydraulic shock absorbers are used and are mounted between axle and body, inside of coil springs.

REMOVAL & INSTALLATION

REAR SUSPENSION ASSEMBLY

Removal — Raise vehicle, support with safety stands, and remove rear wheels. Disconnect propeller shaft from rear axle.

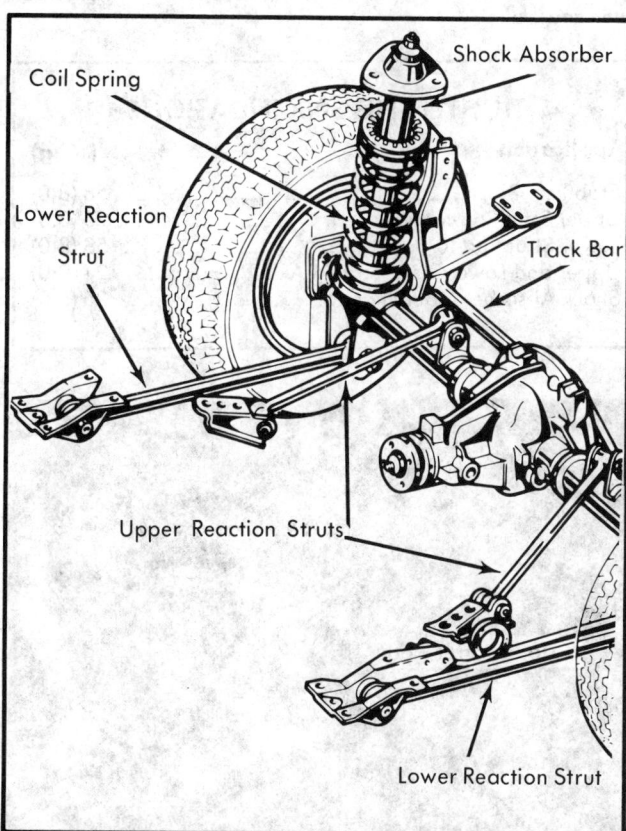

Coil Spring

Shock Absorber

Lower Reaction Strut

Track Bar

Upper Reaction Struts

Lower Reaction Strut

Fig. 1   Fiat Brava Rear Suspension Assembly

Disconnect parking brake cable from cable housing assembly. Disconnect track bar from frame. Position a jack under axle assembly and raise jack enough to support axle. Disconnect lower strut rods from frame bracket, then remove brake cable and brake regulator rod from bracket. Disconnect brake hose from "T" fitting on rear axle. Disconnect upper reaction struts from frame bracket. Disconnect shock absorber from upper mount and upper mount from body. Lower rear axle with suspension from vehicle.

Installation — To install rear axle, reverse removal procedure while noting the following: Tighten nuts and bolts to specifications with weight of vehicle on ground. Bleed brake system after installation.

SHOCK ABSORBERS

Removal — Remove rear suspension assembly. Take out lower shock absorber mounting bolt and remove shock absorber.

CAUTION — *Coil spring is under tension.*

Installation — To install, reverse removal procedure.

STRUT RODS

Removal (Lower) — Remove nut and bolt mounting strut in rear axle bracket. Disconnect parking brake cable from bracket on strut. Remove strut from front bracket and lift out.

Removal (Upper) — Remove hardware mounting strut in rear bracket, then separate strut from front bracket and remove.

Installation (Upper and Lower) — To install, reverse removal procedure.

TIGHTENING SPECIFICATIONS

Application	Ft. Lbs. (mkg)
Shock Absorber-to-Upper Mount	11 (1.5)
Upper Mount-to-Body	18 (2.5)
Shock Absorber Lower Mount	36 (5)
Reaction Strut Rods	
Upper	58 (8)
Lower	36 (5)
Track Bar-to-Rear Axle	72 (10)
Track Bar-to-Body	58 (8)

Rear Suspension

FIAT SPIDER 2000

DESCRIPTION

Link type rear suspension with coil springs. System uses upper and lower strut rods to attach rear axle to body. Brackets on rear axle and body support coil springs with hydraulic, double acting shock absorbers mounted inside coil spring. A stabilizer bar pivots on rear axle and body.

REMOVAL & INSTALLATION

UPPER & LOWER STRUT RODS

Removal — Raise and support vehicle. Place support under rear axle. Remove nuts and bolts attaching strut rods to axle and to body. Remove strut rods.

Installation — Before installing, inspect all parts for signs of damage or wear and replace as necessary. To install, reverse removal procedure.

SHOCK ABSORBERS

Removal — Remove shock absorber upper retaining nuts from inside luggage compartment. Remove nuts attaching shock absorber to spring seat plate and remove shock absorber.

Installation — To install, reverse removal procedure and tighten all nuts and bolts.

COIL SPRINGS

Removal — Raise rear of vehicle and support. Remove wheels and disconnect brake lines. Disconnect parking brake. Remove nuts attaching shock absorbers to body. Disconnect pressure regulator link from axle housing. Support axle with jack, disconnect upper and lower control arms and stabilizer bar. Lower suspension assembly and remove springs.

Installation — Before installing, inspect all parts for signs of excessive wear or damage and replace as necessary. To install, reverse removal procedure and tighten all nuts and bolts. Bleed and adjust brakes if necessary.

STABILIZER BAR

Removal — Remove nuts and bolts attaching stabilizer bar to rear axle and body and remove bar.

Installation — Inspect all parts for signs of distortion, wear or damage. To install, reverse removal procedure and tighten all nuts and bolts.

TIGHTENING SPECIFICATIONS

Application	Ft. Lbs. (mkg)
Stabilizer Bar	58 (8.0)
Upper Strut Rod-to-Body	25 (3.5)
Lower Strut Rod-to-Body	58 (8.0)
Upper and Lower Strut Rods-to-Axle	72 (10.0)
Shock Absorber Mountings	36 (5.0)

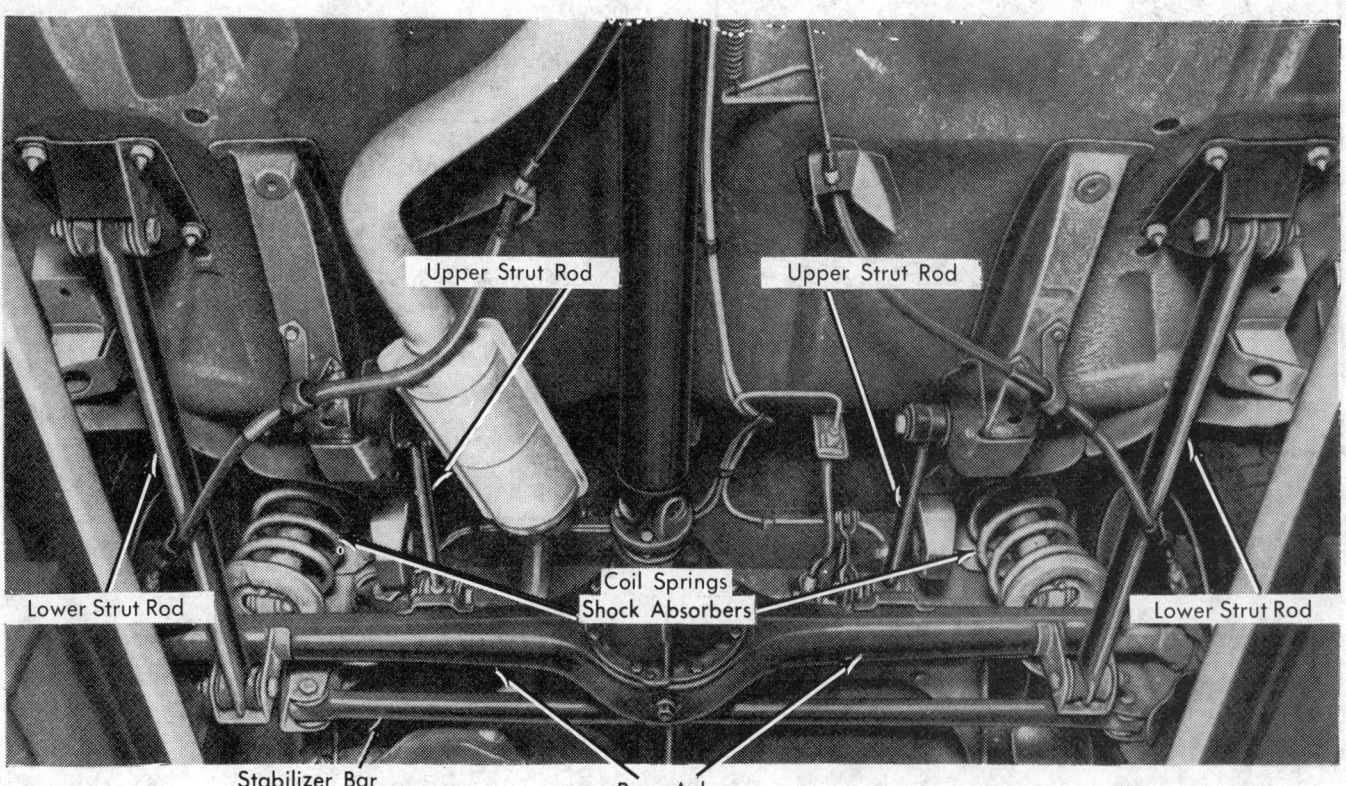

Fig. 1   Installed View of Fiat Spider 2000 Rear Suspension Assembly

Rear Suspension

FIAT STRADA

DESCRIPTION

Independent type rear suspension utilizing a transverse leaf spring. Wheel bearing carriers are supported by control arms connected to chassis and by hydraulic double action shock absorbers connected at top to inner fender panel. Transverse leaf spring is connected to chassis at center and to control arms at outside.

ADJUSTMENT

WHEEL ALIGMENT SPECIFICATIONS & PROCEDURES

See Wheel Alignment Specifications & Procedures in WHEEL ALIGNMENT Section.

WHEEL BEARING ADJUSTMENT

See Wheel Bearing Adjustment in WHEEL ALIGNMENT Section.

REMOVAL & INSTALLATION

SHOCK ABSORBER & CONTROL ARM

Removal — 1) Raise rear of vehicle, position safety stands under chassis and remove rear wheels. Disconnect and plug brake flex line. Disconnect retainer to remove torsion bar from connecting link. Disconnect parking brake cable from lever on back of backing plate.

2) Position a jack under control arm, raise slightly and disconnect upper shock absorber mount (accessible from inside luggage compartment). Lower control arm and repeat for the other side. Remove leaf spring rubber bumper. Remove 2 nuts to disconnect control arm pivot shaft from chassis and remove control arm from chassis, keeping track of shims as control arm is removed.

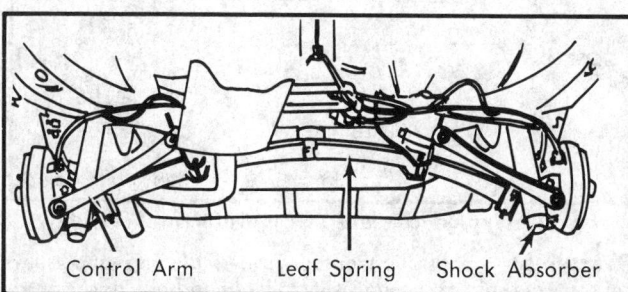

Control Arm   Leaf Spring   Shock Absorber

Fig. 1 Installed View of Rear Suspension Assembly

Installation — To install control arm and shock absorber, reverse removal procedure. Bleed brake hydraulic system. Tighten control arm pivot shaft nuts with weight of vehicle on rear wheels.

CONTROL ARM BUSHINGS

Removal — 1) Remove shock absorber and control arm as previously outlined. Remove pivot bolt securing control arm to bearing carrier and shock absorber mount.

2) Remove inner pivot shaft nuts at control arm. Using a press and suitable mandrel, press out on pivot shaft until bushing is partially removed. This allows for removing tool to properly center on opposite bushing.

3) Using same procedure, remove other bushing. Remove control arm from press and extract remaining bushing. Use a puller to remove bearing carrier bushings from control arm.

Installation — 1) Using same tools as used for removal in addition to a suitable spacer installed between inner legs of control arm, press bushings into control arm and onto pivot shaft. Use same tool used for removal to reinstall bearing carrier bushings into control arm.

2) Reinstall control arm, bearing carrier and shock absorber as previously outlined. Tighten control arm-to-bearing carrier pivot bolt with weight of vehicle on rear wheels.

TRANSVERSE LEAF SPRING

Removal — Raise rear of vehicle, position on safety stands and remove wheels. Place a jack under left end of spring and raise enough to release spring from rubber mounting pad on control arm. Remove cotter pin and disconnect rod linking spring to brake regulator (if equipped). Remove mount for rubber pad on bottom of control arm and lower jack to release spring. Repeat same procedure for opposite side. Remove two guides securing spring to chassis and remove spring.

Installation — Inspect spring making sure there are not any cracked or broken leaves. Inspect all rubber mounts and inter leaf shims for wear or damage. To install transverse leaf spring, reverse removal procedure.

TIGHTENING SPECIFICATIONS

Application	Ft. Lbs. (mkg)
Rear Wheel Hub Nut	159 (22.0)
Leaf Spring Mounting Pad-to-Control Arm	22 (3.0)
Control Arm-to-Bearing Carrier Pivot Bolt	58 (8.0)
Control Arm-to-Chassis Pivot Bolt	36 (5.0)
Control Arm Pin Nuts	30 (4.2)
Upper Shock Absorber Mount	18 (2.5)
Lower Shock Absorber Mount	43 (6.0)
Brake Backing Plate Assembly-to-Bearing Carrier	18 (2.5)

Rear Suspension

FIAT X1/9

DESCRIPTION

Fiat X1/9 is a rear engine mounted and rear wheel driven vehicle utilizing independent rear suspension. All rear suspensions consists of the following: Lower control arms, bearing housings and hydraulic, strut type, shock absorbers. Control arms are attached to chassis in rubber bushings and to bearing housing with a ball joint. Hydraulic strut assembly attaches to bearing housing just above axle shaft and mounts at top to inside of engine compartment. A reaction rod is also attached to bearing housing and is used to adjust rear wheel alignment.

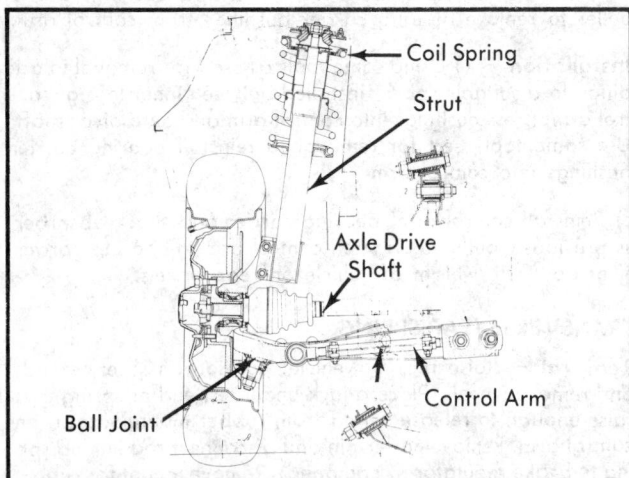

Fig. 1 Sectional View of Fiat X1/9 Rear Suspension Assembly

ADJUSTMENTS

WHEEL ALIGNMENT SPECIFICATIONS & PROCEDURES
See Wheel Alignment Specifications and Procedures in WHEEL ALIGNMENT Section.

WHEEL BEARING ADJUSTMENT
See Wheel Bearing Adjustment in WHEEL ALIGNMENT Section.

REMOVAL & INSTALLATION

SUSPENSION ASSEMBLY

Removal — Raise and support vehicle. Remove tire and wheel. Remove rear brake caliper and disconnect parking brake cable. *See appropriate article in the BRAKE section.* Remove exhaust pipe. Note number and position of shims on control arm. Separate front and rear ends of lower control arm from chassis; do not lose shims. Remove hub nut and washer. Remove nuts mounting strut assembly at top. Slide suspension off axle shaft and secure axle to prevent pulling out of differential.

Installation — To install suspension assembly, reverse removal procedure. Make sure axle nut is properly torqued before lowering vehicle. Tighten all remaining bolts with weight of vehicle on all four wheels. Ensure correct amount of shims are installed.

STRUT ASSEMBLY

Removal — Raise and support vehicle; remove tire and wheel. Disconnect upper strut assembly mounts from inside engine compartment. Remove bolts mounting strut to bearing housing and carefully maneuver strut assembly from vehicle.

Disassembly — 1) Using a suitable spring compressor, collapse spring coil. With spring compressed, remove nut from center of upper mount. Release spring compressor and remove upper mount and coil spring.

2) Inspect springs for cracks or distortion. Springs are manufactured in two classes and identified by paint marks. Class A springs are marked with a yellow stripe on outside of center coils and class B springs are marked with a green stripe. If springs are replaced, use one of same class.

Reassembly — Using same spring compressor as previously implemented, reverse disassembly procedure.

Installation — To install strut assembly, reverse removal procedure. Do not tighten strut assembly lower mount until weight of vehicle is on ground.

CONTROL ARM, BUSHINGS & BALL JOINTS

Removal — Remove complete front suspension assembly as previously outlined. Remove ball joint stud nut and separate ball joint from bearing housing using suitable puller.

Disassembly — Inspect ball joint for wear or excessive play. If ball joint is defective, replace complete control arm. Inspect bushings for wear or damage. If defective bushings are found, drill out bushing metal sleeve and force rubber from control arm.

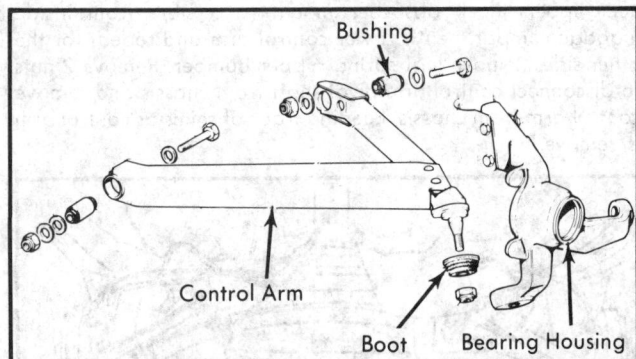

Fig. 2 Exploded View of Control Arm Assembly

Reassembly — Position outer washer, bushing and sleeve on centering pin of a suitable installer (mandrel). Place control arm over bushing and install bushing and washer for opposite side. Using suitable mandrel and necessary adaptors press in new bushing until properly seated. Repeat procedure for other side.

Installation — To install control arm, attach to bearing housing, tighten ball joint stud nut, and position suspension assembly as previously outlined.

TIGHTENING SPECIFICATIONS

Application	Ft. Lbs. (mkg)
Wheel Hub Nut	112 (15.5)
Reaction Rod-to-Control Arm	51 (7.0)
Ball Joint Nut	72 (10.0)
Control Arm Pivot Pin Nut	72 (10.0)
Strut-to-Bearing Housing Bolts	43 (6.0)
Brake Caliper-to-Bearing Housing	36 (5.0)
Wheel Bearing Nut	43 (6.0)

FIESTA

Hatchback

DESCRIPTION

Rear suspension assembly components mount on a tubular steel axle and consist of separately mounted coil springs, shock absorbers, transverse rod, trailing arms and a stabilizer bar (some applications).

ADJUSTMENTS

WHEEL BEARING ADJUSTMENT

See Wheel Bearing Adjustment in WHEEL ALIGNMENT section.

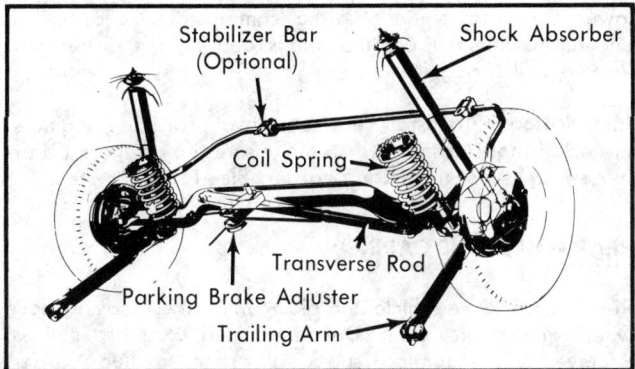

Fig. 1   Assembled View of Fiesta Rear Suspension

REMOVAL & INSTALLATION

REAR AXLE & SUSPENSION ASSEMBLY

Removal — **1)** Raise and support vehicle. Detach parking brake cable from adjuster. Remove bolts holding transverse rod to body and axle and remove transverse rod.

2) Detach flexible brake lines from axle connections and plug openings. Working from engine compartment, disconnect exhaust pipe from manifold, then from both rear supports. Remove pipe.

3) Place jack under center of rear axle. Remove bolts holding trailing arms to body. Remove stabilizer bar-to-body bolts.

4) Raise tailgate and package tray, remove plastic caps and remove shock absorber upper retaining nuts. Slowly lower jack (watching coil springs) and remove complete axle and suspension assembly.

Installation — **1)** Position axle assembly and, with coil springs in position, support with jack and attach trailing arm-to-body bolts.

2) Install and tighten shock absorber top mounts. Reposition stabilizer bar and tighten locknuts. Loosely install trailing arm-to-axle bolts. Remove jack.

3) Install transverse rod and secure both ends. Connect handbrake cable to adjuster and set to proper operating tension. Reconnect brake lines and bleed brake system. Install exhaust pipe.

4) Lower vehicle to ground and fully tighten trailing arm bolts and nuts.

COIL SPRINGS

Removal — **1)** Raise and support vehicle. Remove rear wheels. Positon a jack below center of rear axle.

2) From beneath package tray, remove shock absorber top mountings. Remove trailing arm-to-axle bolts. Detach 2 stabilizer bar-to-body nuts.

3) Slowly lower jack and remove coil springs and insulators.

Installation — To install, reverse removal procedure, but do not fully tighten trailing arm-to-axle bolts until vehicle is resting on ground.

TRAILING ARM

Removal — Raise and support vehicle. Remove trailing arm-to-body bolts. Remove trailing arm-to-axle bolts and remove arm.

Installation — To install, reverse removal procedure, noting the following:
- Be sure trailing arm flanges point toward centerline of vehicle.
- Do not fully tighten trailing arm-to-axle bolts until vehicle is resting on ground.

STABILIZER BAR

Removal — Remove nuts from body mounting brackets. Remove bolts at each end of stabilizer bar (same as lower shock absorber mounting). Remove stabilizer bar.

Installation — To install, reverse removal procedure.

NOTE — *Right end of stabilizer bar is stamped with an arrow and the word "TOP".*

SHOCK ABSORBERS

Removal — **1)** Raise and support vehicle. Remove rear wheels. Position a jack below rear axle and raise slightly. From beneath package tray, remove mounting pieces, noting position of upper insulators for reinstallation reference.

2) Remove nut and bolt from lower mounting. Use a lever and pry lower end of shock absorber from locating peg. Remove from vehicle.

Installation — To install, reverse removal procedure.

TIGHTENING SPECIFICATIONS

Application	Ft. Lbs. (mkg)
Transverse Rod Bolts	40-48 (5.4-6.4)
Trailing Arm Bolts	40-48 (5.4-6.4)
Shock Absorber	
Upper	18-22 (2.5-3.5)
Lower	40-48 (5.4-6.4)
Stabilizer Bar-to-Body	15-18 (2.1-2.5)

Rear Suspension

HONDA

Accord
Civic
  Except Wagon
Prelude

DESCRIPTION

Rear suspension system on all models is an independent type. Major components are: Control arm (lower), shock absorber with coil spring assembly, radius rod (Accord) or radius arm (Civic and Prelude) and rear hub carrier. Prelude models are equipped with a rear stabilizer bar.

REMOVAL & INSTALLATION

SHOCK ABSORBER

Removal — 1) Raise vehicle and suitably support on safety stands. Remove rear wheels. Disconnect brake line from bracket on shock absorber housing. Plug open ends and place lines out of way. Disconnect parking brake cable from lever on backing plate.

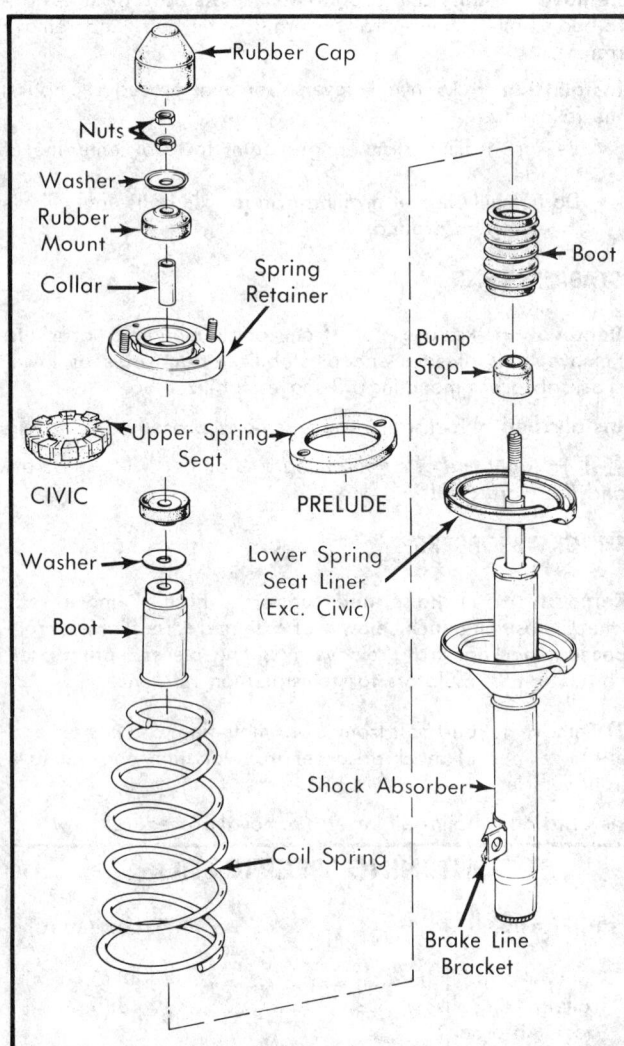

Fig. 1 Exploded View of Shock Absorber Assembly (Civic and Prelude Shown; Accord Similar)

2) On Prelude, remove nut from stabilizer bar connecting link. On Civic and Prelude, loosen control arm pivot bolt and front radius arm pivot bolt. On Accord, remove cotter pin and loosen outer control arm pivot bolt.

3) On all models, remove bolt mounting shock absorber to hub carrier. Remove 2 upper shock absorber retaining nuts. Lower shock absorber and coil spring from vehicle.

Disassembly — Fit spring compressor and slightly compress coils. Remove lock nut and piston rod center nut. Take off upper mounting hardware and coil spring.

Inspection — Check piston rod for smooth, even operation. Inspect for signs of oil leaks. Listen for noise or unusual binding during inspection.

Reassembly — Select new shock absorber. Fit coil spring to lower spring seat. Refit spring compressor. Collapse coil enough to insert upper mountings and tighten piston rod. Release coil spring.

Installation — To install, reverse removal procedure and note: Fit top of shock absorber first. Make sure tab on shock absorber engages slot in bearing carrier. Bleed brake system.

REAR WHEEL HUB CARRIER

Removal — Raise vehicle and place on safety stands. Remove wheel and brake drum. Disconnect and plug brake lines. Remove bolt mounting shock absorber to hub carrier. Disconnect control arm and radius rod or arm from hub carrier. Maneuver hub carrier from vehicle.

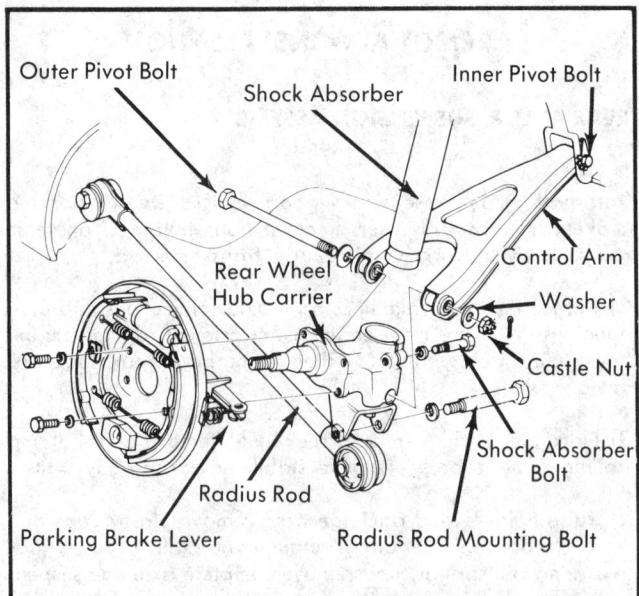

Fig. 2 Exploded View of Accord Rear Suspension

Installation — To install hub carrier, reverse removal procedure and note following: Bleed brake system and check rear wheel alignment.

HONDA (Cont.)

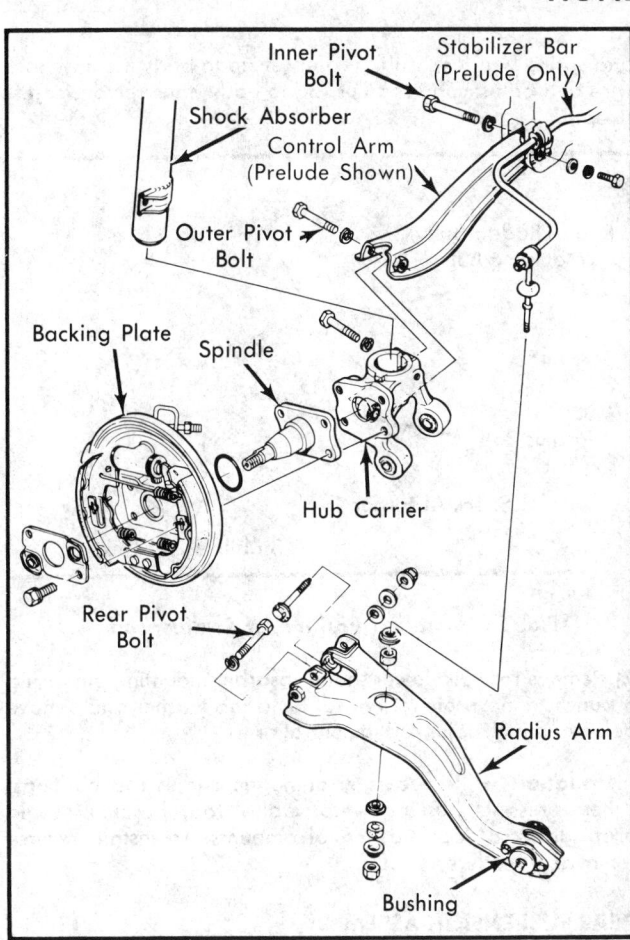

Fig. 3 Exploded View of Civic and Prelude Rear Suspension

RADIUS ROD OR ARM

Removal — Raise and support rear of vehicle. On Prelude, remove stabilizer bar-to-radius arm nuts. On all models, remove bolt(s) mounting radius rod or arm to hub carrier. Remove bolt mounting opposite end of radius rod or arm to body bracket.

Inspection — Inspect all bushings and grommets for damage or excessive wear. Replace defective parts. Make sure radius rod or arm adjusting bolt is not damaged.

Installation — To install, reverse removal procedure and note: Either lower vehicle to ground or raise rear of vehicle to simulate normal weight before tightening radius rod or arm pivot bolts. Check and adjust wheel alignment as required.

CONTROL ARM

Removal — Raise vehicle and place on safety stands. Remove wheel and brake drum. Remove brake hoses from shock absorber mounting, then plug openings. Remove brake backing plate. Remove bolt mounting shock absorber to hub carrier. Remove both inside and outside control arm pivot bolts. Pull out control arm.

Inspection — Inspect all control arm bushings for damage or excessive wear. Replace any parts found defective. Always replace bolt lock tabs.

Installation — To install, reverse removal procedure and note following: Bleed brake system and check rear wheel alignment.

STABILIZER BAR (PRELUDE ONLY)

Removal — Remove stabilizer bar-to-radius arm nuts. Remove bolts attaching stabilizer bar to body. Maneuver stabilizer bar out of vehicle.

Installation — To install, reverse removal procedure and note the following: Install bar so that outside edges of yellow paint stripes on bar align with outside edges of stabilizer bar bushings.

TIGHTENING SPECIFICATIONS

Application	Ft. Lbs. (mkg)
Outer Control Arm Pivot Bolt	
Accord	60 (8.3)
Civic	36 (5.0)
Prelude	40 (5.5)
Inner Control Arm Pivot Bolt	
Accord	35 (4.8)
Civic & Prelude	40 (5.5)
Lower Shock Absorber Bolt	40 (5.5)
Shock Absorber Piston Nut	24 (3.3)
Radius Rod-to-Hub Carrier	
Accord	50 (7.0)
Radius Rod-to-Body	
Accord	47 (6.5)
Radius Arm-to-Hub Carrier	
Civic & Prelude	
Outer Bolt	74 (10.2)
Inner Nut	40 (5.5)
Radius Arm-to-Body	
Civic & Prelude	61 (8.5)

JAGUAR

XJ6

DESCRIPTION

Independent, coil spring type suspension. Outer bearing carrier and hub assembly is supported by control arms at bottom and utilizes drive axles as upper support. Suspension is controlled by 2 coil spring/shock absorber assemblies mounted at each rear wheel. Movement of lower control arms is controlled by radius arms connected to control arms at rear and to chassis members at front.

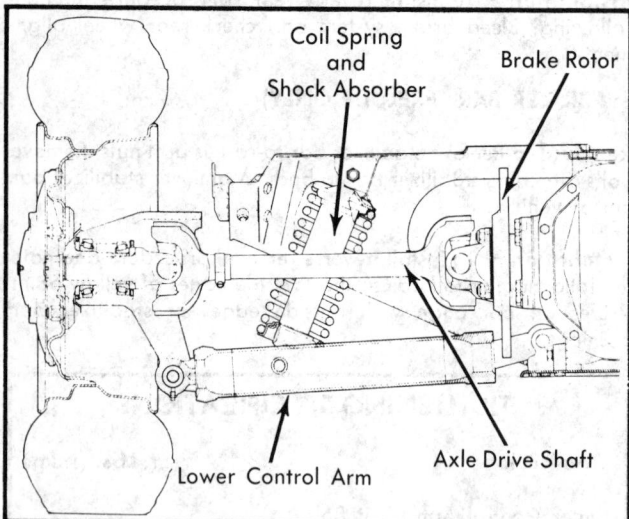

Fig. 1   Jaguar Rear Suspension Assembly

ADJUSTMENTS

WHEEL ALIGNMENT SPECIFICATIONS & PROCEDURES

See Wheel Alignment Specifications and Procedures in WHEEL ALIGNMENT Section.

REMOVAL & INSTALLATION

COIL SPRING & SHOCK ABSORBER

NOTE — *Rear springs can be removed with rear suspension installed in vehicle.*

Removal — Raise vehicle and support at lift points with jack stands. Position floor jack under control arm. Remove nut and bolt mounting top of shock absorbers to the suspension assembly crossmember. Remove washers and nuts securing shock absorbers to lower mounting. Using a drift, remove mounting piece. Withdraw shock absorber and coil spring assembly. Using a spring compressor, collapse spring until collets and spring seat can be removed. Release pressure and separate shock absorber from spring.

Installation — To install spring and shock absorber assembly, reverse removal procedure and tighten all nuts and bolts.

RADIUS ROD

Removal — 1) Raise and support vehicle on safety stands forward of radius rods. Remove tire and wheel. Remove bolt

and spring washer securing safety strap to body. Remove lock wire and bolt securing radius rod to body, then remove safety strap.

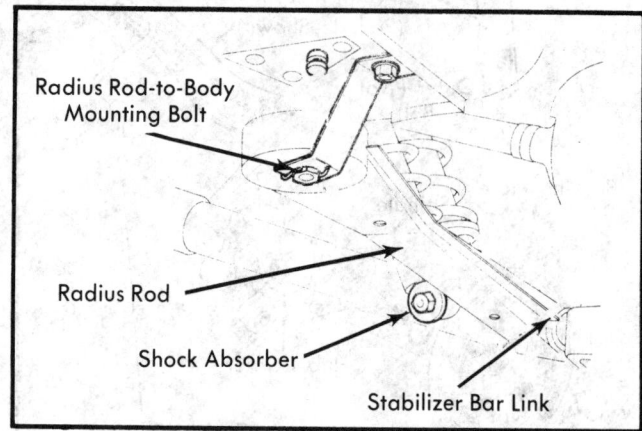

Fig. 2   Installed Position of Radius Rod

2) Remove forward lower shock absorber mounting pin. Using a punch, remove pin rearward. Bend tab washer and remove bolt mounting radius rod to control arm.

Installation — Replace any damaged radius rod bushings. When pressing bushings into radius rod, bushing should protrude from each side equal amounts. To install, reverse removal procedure.

REAR SUSPENSION ASSEMBLY

Removal — 1) Raise and support vehicle forward of radius rods. Remove tires and wheels. Place floor jack (with adaptor to hold suspension assembly) under rear suspension.

2) Disconnect intermediate exhaust pipes at both ends and remove from vehicle. Support rear mufflers out of way. Disconnect radius rod-to-body mounting hardware.

3) Separate brake line union from body bracket. Disconnect brake lines at flexible hoses and plug openings. Disconnect propeller shaft at differential and lower out of way.

4) Release parking brake. Disconnect parking brake cable from junction at rear suspension assembly. Remove suspension mounting bracket nuts. Lower suspension assembly to ground and slide from vehicle.

Installation — Reverse removal steps and bleed brake system.

LOWER CONTROL ARM

Removal — 1) Raise and support vehicle with stands placed ahead of radius rods. Remove tire and wheel.

2) Remove lock nut and drift out bearing carrier fulcrum shaft. Fit dummy shaft for support. Collect shims and oil seal retainers.

3) Lift bearing carrier up, clear of control arm. Keep carrier in postion with heavy wire attached to crossmember. Separate radius rod from body.

JAGUAR (Cont.)

4) Remove 14 bolts mounting support plate to crossmember and inner fulcrum brackets. Separate shock absorber at upper mount. Drift out pivot pin.

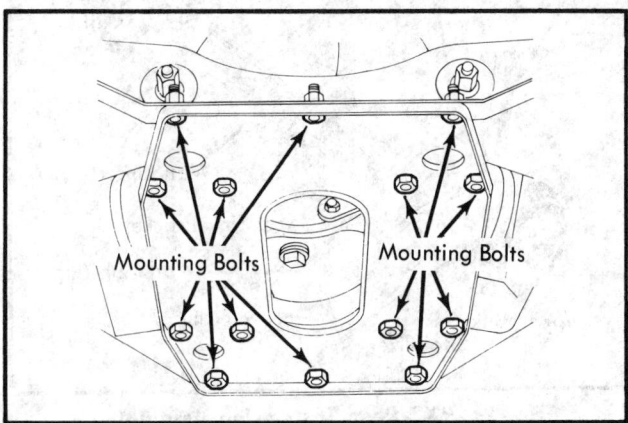

Fig. 3   Bolts and Setscrews Mounting Support Plate to Crossmember and Inner Fulcrum Brackets

5) Separate inner fulcrum from control arm. Guide out control arm and radius rod.

Installation — 1) Smear bearing cage with grease and force bearing into lower control arm. Marking cast on bearing faces out. Insert bearing tube for other end and force in opposite end bearing. Repeat procedure for other boss.

2) Assemble radius rod to control arm. Lightly coat thrust washers, new oil seals and oil seal retainers with grease. Fit assemblies into place on control arm.

3) Insert control arm to inner fulcrum mounting bracket. Make sure radius rod bracket faces toward front of suspension.

4) Insert dummy shaft from each end to keep bearings positioned then locate control arm in bracket. Slip in fulcrum shaft while pushing out dummy shaft. Install lock nut.

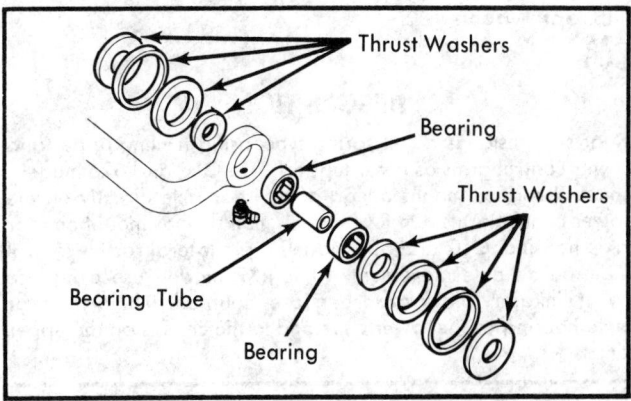

Fig. 4   Fulcrum Boss Assembly

5) To install remaining components, reverse removal procedure.

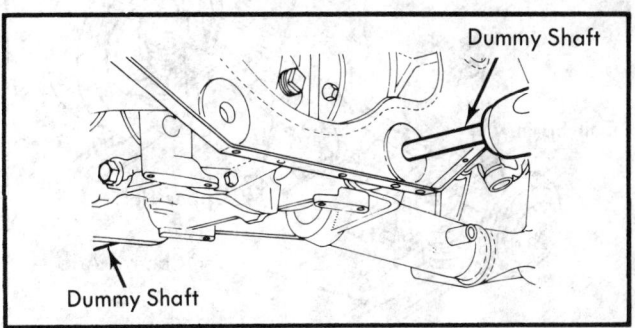

Fig. 5   Locating Control Arm in Mounting Bracket with Dummy Shafts

TIGHTENING SPECIFICATIONS

Application	Ft. Lbs. (mkg)
Radius Rod-to-Control Arm	60-70 (8.3-9.7)
Radius Rod-to-Body	40-45 (5.5-6.2)
Shock Absorbers	32-36 (4.4-5.0)
Support Plate-to-Crossmember and Inner Fulcrum Mounting	14-18 (1.9-2.5)
Inner Fulcrum Shaft	45-50 (6.2-6.9)
Stabilizer Bar Bracket-to-Body	14-18 (1.9-2.5)

Rear Suspension

MAZDA

GLC
  Except Wagon
626
RX7

DESCRIPTION

Rear suspension is a coil spring type, using trailing upper and lower control arms as pivot supports. On GLC and 626 models, the coil springs mount ahead of the rear axle directly on the lower control arms. On RX7 models, coil springs mount on rear axle housing. GLC and 626 models use a lateral rod to control side-to-side axle movement, while RX7 models use a 3-piece Watt linkage. Shock absorbers are mounted behind the rear axle housing at the lower ends and to the chassis on the upper ends.

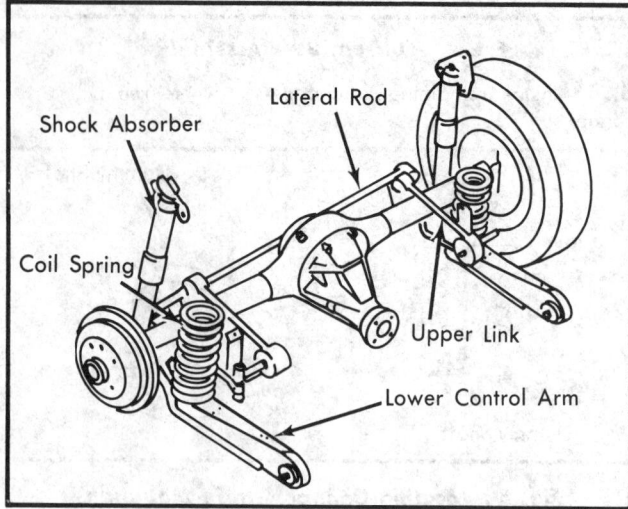

Fig. 1 GLC & 626 Rear Suspension Assembly

REMOVAL & INSTALLATION

SHOCK ABSORBERS

Removal — Raise and support rear of vehicle. Remove wheels. Disconnect upper shock absorber mounting. Remove lower shock absorber mount nuts. Remove shock absorber.

Installation — To install, reverse removal procedure and tighten nuts and bolts to specifications.

COIL SPRINGS

Removal (GLC) — Raise and support rear of vehicle. Remove rear wheels. Support rear axle housing with a jack. Remove shock absorber. Remove lower arm pivot bolt at axle housing and slowly lower axle. Remove spring.

Removal (626) — Disconnect shock absorber lower end. Disconnect lateral rod at axle housing. Disconnect upper and lower control pivot bolts at axle housing. Disconnect rear stabilizer bar (if equipped). Slowly lower axle and remove spring.

Removal (RX7) — Disconnect shock absorber lower end. Disconnect upper and lower control arm pivot bolts at axle housing. Disconnect Watt links at axle housing. Disconnect stabilizer bar (if equipped). Slowly lower axle and remove spring.

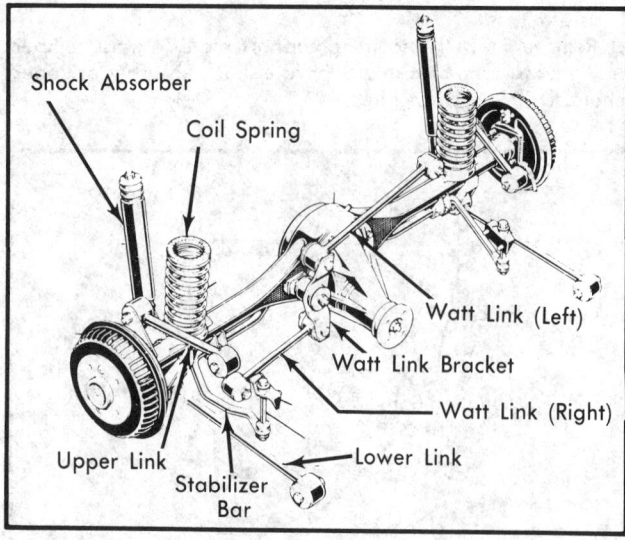

Fig. 2 RX7 Rear Suspension Assembly

Installation (All Models) — To install, reverse removal procedure and note the following: On 626 and RX7 models, install springs with painted marks facing toward rear axle housing. Tighten nuts and bolts after vehicle has been lowered to ground.

CONTROL ARMS, LINKS & RODS

Removal — Raise and support vehicle. Remove control arms, lateral rods or Watt links by removing attaching nuts and bolts, noting their proper installed locations.

Inspection — Inspect all components for wear or damage. Inspect and replace bushings as necessary.

Installation — To install, reverse removal procedure. Tighten all nuts and bolts to specifications after vehicle has been lowered to the ground.

STABILIZER BAR

Removal — Raise and support rear of vehicle. Remove attaching nuts and bolts. Remove stabilizer bar and hardware.

Inspection — Inspect all components for wear or damage. Replace parts as necessary.

Installation — Reverse removal procedure. Tighten nuts and bolts to specifications after vehicle has been lowered to the ground.

TIGHTENING SPECIFICATIONS

Application	Ft. Lbs. (mkg)
Upper & Lower Control Arm Bolts	
GLC	47-59 (6.5-8.2)
626 & RX7	56-76 (7.7-10.5)
Shock Absorber-to-Mount	47-59 (6.5-8.2)
Shock Absorber Bracket-to-Body	34 (4.7)
Lateral Rod-to-Mounts	
GLC	47-59 (6.5-8.2)
626	56-76 (7.7-10.5)
Watt Links-to-Mounts	47-59 (6.5-8.2)
Watt Link Bracket-to-Axle	56-76 (7.7-10.5)
Stabilizer Bar Mount-to-Body	27-38 (3.8-5.3)
Stabilizer Bar Mount-to-Axle	27-38 (3.8-5.3)

MERCEDES-BENZ

240D
280 Series
300 Series
450 Series

NOTE – *For 300TD components not covered in this article, see Automatic Level Control article in this section.*

DESCRIPTION

Rear suspension is independent with coil springs and semi-trailing arms. Rear axle carrier is mounted to body at three points and supports rear axle assembly. Axle shafts serve as upper control arms to rear wheels. Wheel hubs are supported by semi-trailing arms which run forward to pivot points on rear axle carrier and body. Shock absorbers are mounted inside of coil springs, attached to body on top and to semi-trailing arms on bottom. Stabilizer bar is mounted to body and to wheel hubs at ends.

ADJUSTMENT

WHEEL ALIGNMENT SPECIFICATIONS & ADJUSTMENTS

See Wheel Alignment Specifications & Adjustments in WHEEL ALIGNMENT Section.

REMOVAL & INSTALLATION

SHOCK ABSORBERS (EXC. 300TD)

NOTE – *Shock absorbers should be removed only when vehicle is on wheels or when semi-trailing arm is supported.*

Removal – On vehicles with coupe top, remove top and open flap. On all models, remove rear seat and backrest. Remove locking lever from top flap and unscrew lining. Remove nut and rubber ring of upper shock mount. Remove lower shock mount on semi-trailing arm. Remove shock absorber in a downward direction.

Installation – To install, reverse removal procedure.

COIL SPRINGS

Removal – Remove shock absorbers as previously outlined. Raise and support rear of vehicle on safety stands. Raise semi-trailing arm until approximately level. Using suitable spring compressor, compress spring. Carefully lower semi-trailing arm and remove spring with rubber mounting.

Installation – To install, reverse removal procedure.

REAR STABILIZER BAR

Removal – Raise and support rear of vehicle with safety stands. Remove wheels. Detach connecting rod from stabilizer on both sides of vehicle. Remove stabilizer bar holding brackets. Loosen exhaust pipe mounts (rubber rings) and lower slightly. Remove stabilizer bar in a downward direction.

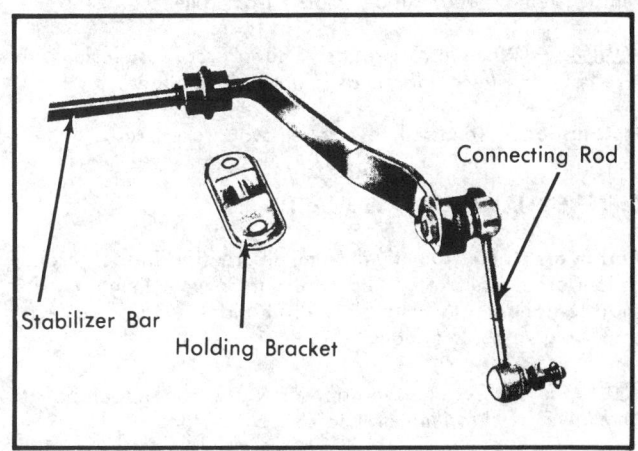

Connecting Rod

Stabilizer Bar

Holding Bracket

Fig. 2   Stabilizer Bar and Mounting Locations

Installation – To install, reverse removal procedure.

NOTE – *When installing rear stabilizer bar, ensure that bend of bar is pointing upward.*

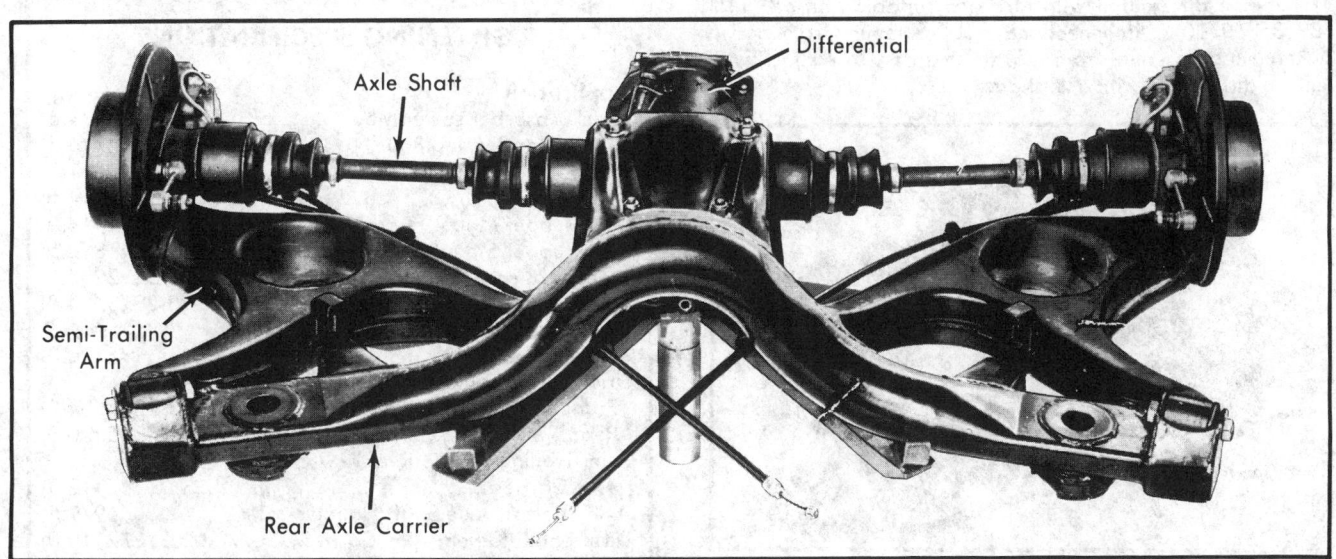

Axle Shaft

Differential

Semi-Trailing Arm

Rear Axle Carrier

Fig. 1   Typical Mercedes-Benz Rear Suspension

MERCEDES-BENZ (Cont.)

REAR SUSPENSION & AXLE

Removal — 1) Raise and support vehicle with safety stands. Remove wheels. Disconnect exhaust system. Detach parking brake control cables at frame and compensating lever.

2) Loosen clamp nut and disconnect drive shaft intermediate bearing from frame. Disconnect rear of drive shaft and slide forward, out of centering position.

NOTE — *On 3-piece drive shaft, loosen front clamp nut only.*

3) Remove shock absorber and coil spring. Detach and plug brake lines. Disconnect stabilizer bar holding clamps.

4) Place suitable support jack under rear suspension. Disconnect supporting plates and front and rear rubber mounts from frame. Carefully lower jack and remove rear suspension from vehicle. Remove rear rubber mount from axle.

CAUTION — *When lowering and removing rear suspension, be sure cover plates of disc brakes are not damaged.*

Installation — To install, reverse removal procedure.

DIFFERENTIAL WITH AXLE SHAFTS

Removal — 1) Drain fluid from differential. Detach brake caliper from right rotor and wire out of way. Remove axle shaft-to-flange attaching bolts (both sides) and force rear shafts out of shaft flanges.

NOTE — *If required, loosen right shock absorber upper mount and lower semi-trailing arm to deflection stop.*

2) If required, remove exhaust system. Loosen clamp nut and detach drive shaft intermediate bearing from frame. Remove drive shaft from differential and push from centering alignment.

NOTE — *On 3-piece drive shaft, loosen front clamp nut only.*

3) Support differential with jack and suitable support (115 589 35 63 00). Disconnect rear rubber mount from body. Disconnect differential from rear axle carrier. Lower jack and remove differential with axle shafts.

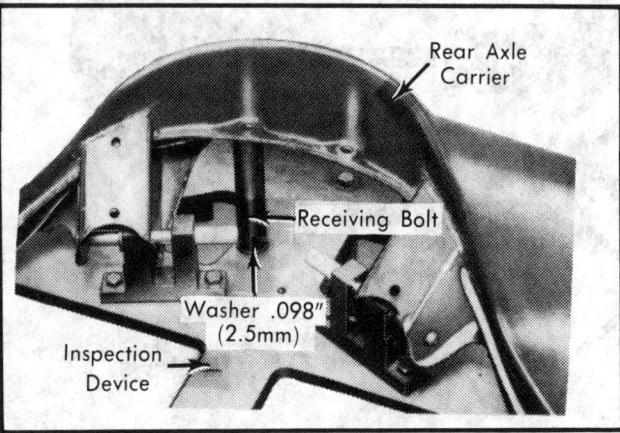

**Fig. 3 Proper Washer Placement for
Rear Axle Carriers without Spot Welds**

CAUTION — *When moving differential with axle shafts, make sure that axle shafts are supported and DO NOT drop down, as this might damage inner joints.*

Installation — Check all rubber parts and replace as necessary. To install differential with rear axle shafts, reverse removal procedure. Tighten down all nuts and bolts, except when connecting drive shaft to differential. These bolts must be torqued after vehicle has been rolled forward and backward to seat parts. Install exhaust system, if removed.

REAR AXLE CARRIER

Removal — Remove rear suspension, differential with rear axle shafts and semi-trailing arms as previously outlined.

Inspection — Using inspection tool (115-589 04 23 00), check rear axle carrier. See *Fig. 4.* When checking rear axle carriers without spot welded washers, place a .098" (2.5 mm) thick washer under receiving bolt. See *Fig. 3.*

Installation — To install rear axle, reverse removal procedure.

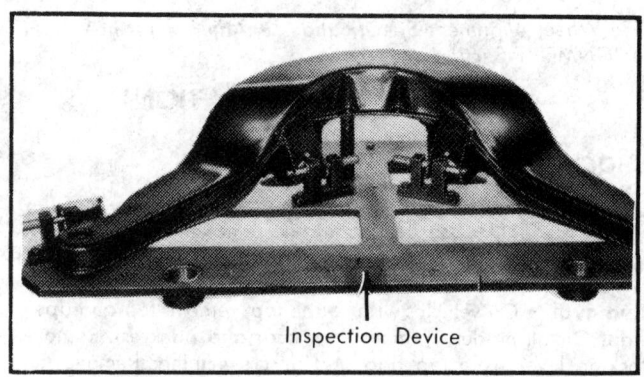

Fig. 4 Inspection Tool 115 589 04 23 00

TIGHTENING SPECIFICATIONS

Application	Ft. Lbs. (mkg)
Shock Absorber Lower Mount	33 (4.6)
Torsion Bar Bearing Bolts	47 (6.5)
Torsion Bar Connecting Rod Ball Joints	33 (4.6)
Rear Rubber Mount-to-End Cover	101 (14.0)
Rear Rubber Mount-to-Frame	18 (2.5)
Front Rubber Mounts-to-Frame	29 (4.0)
Supporting Plate-to-Frame	23-29 (3.2-4.0)
Drive Shaft Clamp Nut (Two Piece)	145 (20.0)
Drive Shaft Clamp Nut (Three Piece) Front	23-29 (3.2-4.0)
Rear	145 (20.0)
Semi-Trailing Arm-to-Rear Axle Carrier	87 (12.0)
Axle Shaft-to-Axle Shaft Flange	69 (9.5)
Differential-to-Rear Axle Carrier	72 (10.0)
Brake Caliper Bolts	23-29 (3.2-4.0)

PEUGEOT

505
604

DESCRIPTION

Independent rear suspension utilizing trailing arms and coil springs. Rear hub is supported by lower trailing arms which pivot at points on rear axle crossmember. Coil springs are mounted between suspension crossmember at top and trailing arm at bottom. Hydraulic shock absorbers also mount between suspension crossmember and trailing arm, and are located inside coil spring. A stabilizer bar is mounted to frame and connected at ends to trailing arms.

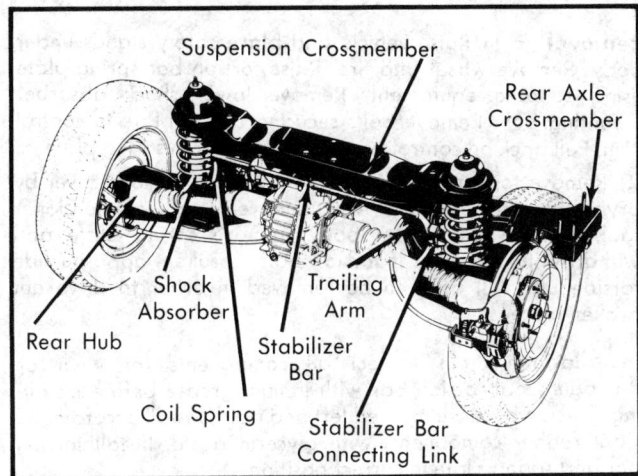

Fig. 1 Sectional View of Peugeot Rear Suspension

REMOVAL & INSTALLATION

SHOCK ABSORBERS

Removal — From inside luggage compartment, remove lock nut at top of shock absorber while holding shock to prevent rotation. On trailing arm, remove lower pivot bolt and remove shock absorber.

Installation — To install, reverse removal procedure using new rubber washers and lock nut. Tighten upper mounting to specification, then tighten lower.

TRAILING ARMS

Removal — 1) Raise and support vehicle on safety stands under rear crossmember; remove tire and wheel. Remove brake disc pads. Disconnect hydraulic line from trailing arm. Remove caliper mounting bolts and suspend caliper out of way. Use care not to bend or kink hydraulic lines.

2) Remove drive shaft nut. Remove bearing housing bolts and pull shaft, hub and disc assembly from arm. Raise the lower arm with a jack to compress spring; remove shock absorber. Disconnect parking brake cable from lower arm. Remove stabilizer connecting link nut at lower arm; remove metal cup and rubber mount and refit nut to prevent upper parts from falling inside arm.

3) Unscrew rear arm pivot nuts and carefully lower jack. Remove spring and upper rubber mount. Remove rear arm pivots and remove trailing arm.

Installation — To install, reverse removal procedure, replacing all lock nuts and lock washers. Torque all nuts and bolts to specifications, however, do not torque lower shock absorber nut and trailing arm pivot nuts until weight of vehicle, with two people in rear seat, is on suspension.

TIGHTENING SPECIFICATIONS

Application	Ft. Lbs. (mkg)
Upper Shock Absorber Nut	9 (1.2)
Lower Shock Absorber Nut	33 (4.6)
Trailing Arm Pivot Nuts	47 (6.5)
Rear Hub Nut	181 (25.0)
Stabilizer Bar Link Nut	9 (1.2)

Rear Suspension

PORSCHE 911SC

DESCRIPTION

Independent torsion bar type rear suspension. Torsion bars are mounted inside rear crossmember tube and anchored in center by a splined hub. Outer end of torsion bars mount into splined hubs integral with spring plates which connect at ends to control arms. Control arms pivot in mounts integral with body and also serve as rear wheel bearing carriers. Hydraulic shock absorbers mount between control arms and inner fender panel. A stabilizer bar is installed on some models.

ADJUSTMENT

WHEEL ALIGNMENT SPECIFICATIONS & PROCEDURES

See Wheel Alignment Specifications & Procedures in WHEEL ALIGNMENT Section.

REMOVAL & INSTALLATION

SHOCK ABSORBERS

Removal — 1) Raise vehicle and place safety stands in a position so weight of vehicle is still on rear wheels. Remove rubber cap from upper mount (accessible from inside engine compartment) and remove nut from shock absorber stem.

2) Remove bolt securing shock absorber to control arm and remove shock absorber. Remove rod cover and rubber buffer from shock absorber.

Installation — Inspect rubber buffer for wear or cracking and replace if necessary. Make sure that stop disc grooves face bottom of shock absorber when assembling. Install rubber buffer and cover and reverse removal procedure to install remaining components. Tighten upper and lower mounts.

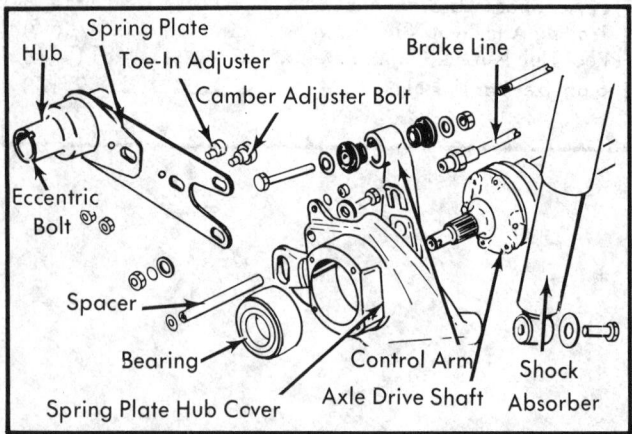

Fig. 1   Exploded View of Porsche Rear Suspension

CONTROL ARM

Removal — 1) Raise vehicle and place safety stands under body. Remove rear wheels. Detach brake system components from rear wheel hub. See Porsche in BRAKE Section. Remove axle hub cotter pin and nut. Remove Allen head bolts from axle shaft flanges and remove axle shaft.

2) Using a suitable driver, remove rear wheel hub from control arm. Remove cotter pin and nut from parking brake cable and pull cable out toward center of vehicle. Remove

bolts securing parking brake assembly to control arm and remove assembly.

3) Raise torsion bar spring plate to take tension from shock absorber with a suitable tool. Remove lower shock absorber mount. Remove bolts securing spring plate to control arm. Disconnect brake hose from bracket on control arm. Remove nut from control arm pivot bolt and drive bolt out with a punch. Remove control arm from vehicle.

Installation — Reverse removal procedure and note the following: Use new self-locking nuts and tighten all bolts and nuts. Check wheel alignment and bleed brake system.

TORSION BAR & SPRING PLATE

Removal — 1) Raise vehicle and place safety stands under body. Remove wheel and tire. Raise torsion bar spring plate using suitable equipment. Remove lower shock absorber mounting bolt. Remove bolts securing spring plate to control arm. Pull back on control arm to separate from spring plate.

2) Remove torsion bar hub cover bolts and remove cover by prying off with a screwdriver. Remove torsion bar tensioner tool. Remove plug from body, remove spring plate and withdraw torsion bar. If torsion bar is broken, opposite side torsion bar will have to be removed in order to drive out broken piece.

Installation — 1) Inspect all components for wear or damage. Coat torsion bar with lithium grease before installing. Torsion bars are marked left and right; install accordingly. Coat rubber components with glycerin paste. Install torsion bar and spring plate in correct position.

2) Adjust torsion bars as follows: using suitable protractor (VW261), place onto lower edge of door sill. Adjust protractor so that bubble in glass tube marked "Axle Housing/Angle" is in the center.

3) Reset glass tube carrier by value specified. Place protractor onto spring plate and adjust to .468±.20" (12±5 mm) by turning eccentric screw on spring plate.

NOTE — Difference between right and left measurement must not exceed .20" (5 mm).

4) Install hub cover and start three bolts that are accessible. Raise spring plate until remaining bolt can be installed. Reverse removal procedures for remaining components. Check rear wheel alignment.

TIGHTENING SPECIFICATIONS

Application	Ft. Lbs. (mkg)
Control Arm Pivot Bolt	87 (12.0)
Spring Plate-to-Control Arm Bolts	65 (9.0)
Camber Adjusting Bolt	43 (6.0)
Tracking Adjusting Bolt	36 (5.0)
Lower Shock Absorber Mount	54 (7.5)
Hub Nut	235 (32.5)
Axle Shaft Allen Head Bolts	
M10-8G	34 (4.7)
M8-12K	31 (4.3)
M10x55-12K	60 (8.3)
Torsion Bar Hub Cover Bolts	34 (4.7)

Rear Suspension

PORSCHE 924

DESCRIPTION

Independent torsion bar type rear suspension. Torsion bars mount in rear crossmember tube and anchor in center of tube by a splined hub. Outer ends of torsion bar mount into splined hubs integral with spring plates. Spring plates are bolted to control arm at a flange. Control arms pivot in mounts on crossmember tube and are integral with stub axle housing. Hydraulic shock absorbers mount on control arm and to upper body.

ADJUSTMENTS

WHEEL ALIGNMENT SPECIFICATIONS & PROCEDURES

See Wheel Alignment Specifications and Procedures in WHEEL ALIGNMENT Section.

REMOVAL & INSTALLATION

SHOCK ABSORBERS

Removal — Raise vehicle and place on safety stands. Remove wheel. Remove both bottom and top mounting nuts and bolts, then slide shock absorber from vehicle.

Installation — Inspect for hydraulic leaks and replace shock absorber if excessive leaking is apparent. Check shock absorber for smooth, even operation. To install, reverse removal procedure.

CONTROL ARM

Removal — 1) Remove cotter pin and loosen rear hub nut. Raise vehicle and place on safety stands. Remove wheel. Remove shock absorber.

2) Remove bolts mounting axle drive shaft to stub axle. Separate axle drive shaft from stub axle and wire out of way. Use protective cap to cover exposed end of axle drive shaft.

3) Remove drum and disconnect parking brake and hydraulic lines. Index mark spring plate in relation to a point on control arm. Remove control arm pivot bolt and remove arm from vehicle.

Installation — To install, reverse removal procedure. Tighten pivot bolt and lock in place by staking edge to metal shoulder on bracket. Align spring plate marks with those on control arm. Bleed brake system.

CROSSMEMBER TUBE

Removal — 1) Raise and support vehicle. Remove wheels. Disconnect parking brake cable from lever. Remove cable.

2) Disconnect and remove rear portion of exhaust system from catalytic converter. Remove transaxle mount nuts. Support transaxle with a chain by attaching ends to frame.

3) Disconnect shock absorbers from control arms. Support control arms with jacks or stands. Remove stabilizer bar links. Mark location of spring plate on control arm and remove camber eccentric and mounting bolts between spring plate and control arm flange.

4) Remove parking brake retainer straps from spring plates. Reattach shock absorbers temporarily. Remove control arm pivot bolts.

5) Disconnect parking brake cable from crossmember tube. Remove crossmember lower mount bolts. Remove torque strut bolts from upper mounts. Remove crossmemeber tube.

Installation — 1) Apply rubber lubricant to lower mount bushings. Install crossmember tube with lower mount bolts. Remove upper mounts from body and install on torque struts, but do not tighten bolts.

2) Install control arms with pivot bolts. Disconnect shock absorber from control arm. Install control arm to spring plate, but do not tighten bolts. Reinstall shock absorber to control arm.

3) Install upper mount bolts to body approximately 2-3 threads deep. Tighten torque strut-to-mount bolts first, then tighten all remaining mount bolts.

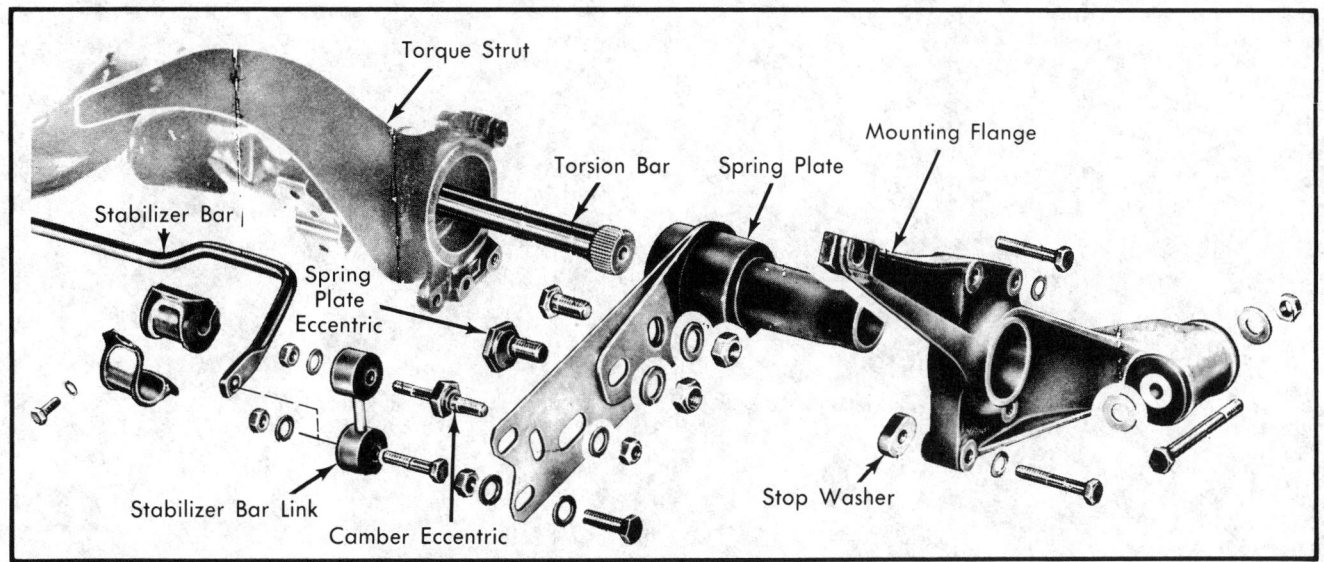

Fig. 1   Exploded View of 924 Rear Suspension

PORSCHE 924 (Cont.)

4) Lower transmission and remove support chain. Install and tighten transaxle mount nuts. Reinstall parking brake cables and retainers. Install wheels and lower vehicle.

5) Check and adjust rear axle alignment. After alignment, raise vehicle and remove rear wheels. Tighten all nuts and bolts to specifications. Install stabilizer bar links.

TORSION BARS & SPRING PLATES

Removal — With crossmember tube removed and placed in a vise, remove mounting flange bolts and flange. Pry off spring plate. Remove spring plate and withdraw torsion bars.

NOTE — *Left and right torsion bars are not interchangeable.*

Installation — **1)** Position crossmember tube so that flat surface of torque strut is horizontal. Using suitable protractor (VW 261) and a straightedge, measure any deviation from horizontal and record that figure. Add 23° 40' to recorded figure for setting spring plate angle.

2) Set protractor at indicated angle and turn spring plate or torsion bar until bubble in level is centered.

3) Install mounting flange, using rubber lubricant, with the 3 short bolts, until the long fourth bolt for stop washer can be inserted. Install mounting flange-to-torque strut bolt temporarily.

4) Compress spring plate with jack or compression tool (VW 655/3). Install spring plate stop washer and tighten bolt slightly. Remove tool, allowing spring plate to position stop washer. Tighten all flange bolts to specifications.

TIGHTENING SPECIFICATIONS

Application	Ft. Lbs. (mkg)
Mounting Flange-to-Crossmember	33 (4.6)
Mounting Flange-to-Body	51 (7.0)
Mounting Flange-to-Upper Mount	33 (4.6)
Upper Mount-to-Body	33 (4.6)
Torque Strut Mount-to-Body	33 (4.6)
Torque Strut Mount-to-Strut	17 (2.3)
Control Arm Camber Eccentric	65 (9.0)
Control Arm-to-Spring Plate	75 (10.3)
Spring Plate Height Eccentric	177 (24.5)
Stabilizer Bar Link	33 (4.6)
Shock Absorber-to-Body	44 (6.1)
Shock Absorber-to-Control Arm	44 (6.1)

PORSCHE 928

DESCRIPTION

Porsche 928 rear suspension is a strut type, consisting of a strut assembly (shock absorber and coil spring) which is mounted at bottom to the rear wheel hub and lower control arm and at top to vehicle body. An upper control arm is also incorporated. A stabilizer bar is connected by a link to the lower control arm.

ADJUSTMENTS

WHEEL ALIGNMENT SPECIFICATIONS & PROCEDURES

See Wheel Alignment Specifications and Procedures in WHEEL ALIGNMENT section.

REMOVAL & INSTALLATION

REAR SUSPENSION ASSEMBLY

Removal — 1) Raise and support vehicle. Detach axle shaft from differential by removing Allen-head bolts.

2) Detach caliper from rotor. Remove 2 countersunk screws and take off rotor. Remove parking brake shoes and spreader lever. Pull parking brake cable out of guide in hub assembly.

3) Remove hub assembly with upper control arm attached after removing control arm retaining bolt.

4) Remove lower control arm retaining nuts and bolts and remove control arm from vehicle. Remove stabilizer bar and link, if necessary.

Installation — To install, reverse removal procedure.

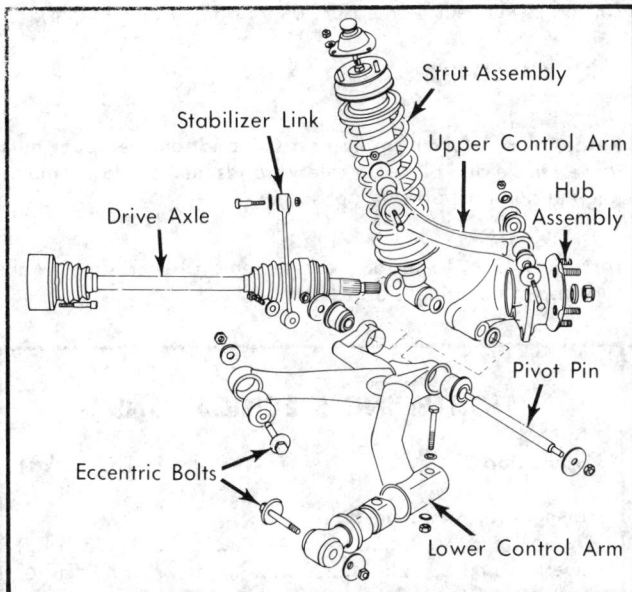

Fig. 1   Exploded View of 928 Rear Suspension

STRUT ASSEMBLY

Removal — 1) Working from luggage compartment, remove 3 self-locking nuts from upper strut mounting plate. Raise and support vehicle and remove rear wheel(s).

2) While holding rear nut, remove front nut from pivot pin of lower control arm (it may be necessary to double-nut the shaft end with another M14 x 1.5 nut). Remove pivot pin.

3) Remove stabilizer bar link from its attachment at lower control arm to gain additional clearance, then remove strut assembly from vehicle.

Disassembly — 1) Attach a suitable coil spring compressor to coil spring and compress enough to allow removal of top piston rod nut. Loosen spring compressor slowly, and remove coil spring.

2) Lift off cover pieces, unscrew adjusting nut and remove threaded sleeve.

Reassembly — Reassemble in reverse of disassembly procedure, using appropriate illustration as a guide. Fig. 2.

Installation — To install, reverse removal procedure.

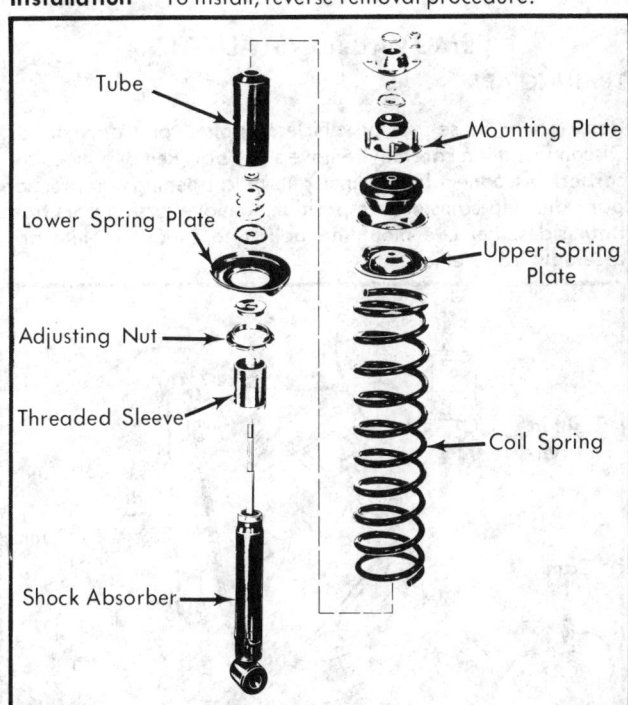

Fig. 2   Disassembled View of 928 Strut Assembly

TIGHTENING SPECIFICATIONS

Application	Ft. Lbs. (mkg)
Caliper-to-Hub Bolt	61 (8.5)
Lower Control Arm-to-Hub	101 (14.0)
Upper Control Arm-to-Crossmember	33 (4.6)
Upper Control Arm-to-Hub	33 (4.6)
Hub-to-Stub Axle	333 (46.0)
Wheel Nuts	93 (13.0)
Upper Strut Mount-to-Body Locknuts	33 (4.6)
Stabilizer Bar-to-Body	33 (4.6)
Stabilizer Bar-to-Link	33 (4.6)
Stabilizer Link-to-Control Arm	33 (4.6)
Lower Control Arm-to-Link Pin	61 (8.5)
Shock Absorber-to-Upper Strut Mount	42 (5.8)

RENAULT

Le Car

DESCRIPTION

System is torsion bar type with a trailing arm. Trailing arms are mounted off chassis and have torsion bars connected to in-board edge.

ADJUSTMENT

WHEEL ALIGNMENT SPECIFICATIONS & PROCEDURES

See Wheel Alignment Specifications and Procedures in WHEEL ALIGNMENT Section.

RIDING HEIGHT ADJUSTMENT

See Riding Height Adjustment in WHEEL ALIGNMENT Section.

REMOVAL & INSTALLATION

TRAILING ARM

Removal — Raise rear of vehicle and place on safety stands. Disconnect, then carefully remove sway bar. Remove shock absorber. Disconnect brake lines and plug openings. Put torsion bar adjusting cams in zero position. Remove torsion bars from both sides. Remove mounting bolts and slide complete arm assembly from vehicle.

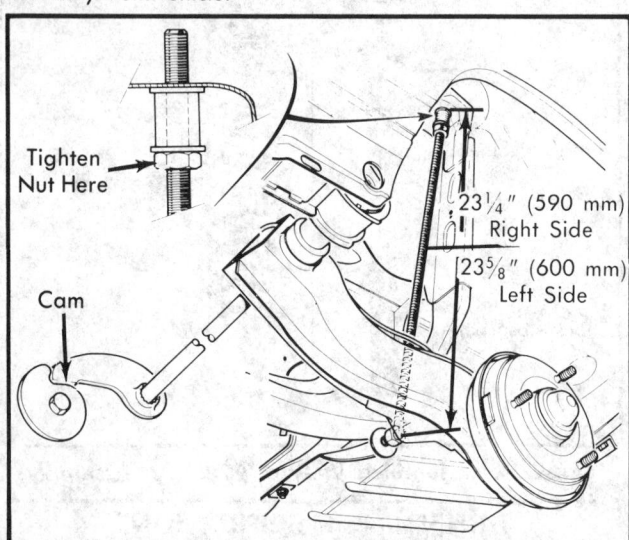

Fig. 1   Trailing Arm and Torsion Bar Assembly

Inspection — Check all bushings and spacers for obvious signs of wear or damage. Use suitable puller and/or mandrel (with press) to replace bushings.

Installation — To install, reverse removal procedure and note: Bleed brake system. Recheck brake pressure equalizer. Check rear wheel alignment.

TORSION BAR

Removal — Raise vehicle and place on safety stands. Loosen lock nut on cam and adjust until cam is zeroed. Remove shock absorber. Fit fabricated tool where shock absorber has been removed. Tighten nut until adjuster lever is raised from cam. Remove torsion bar.

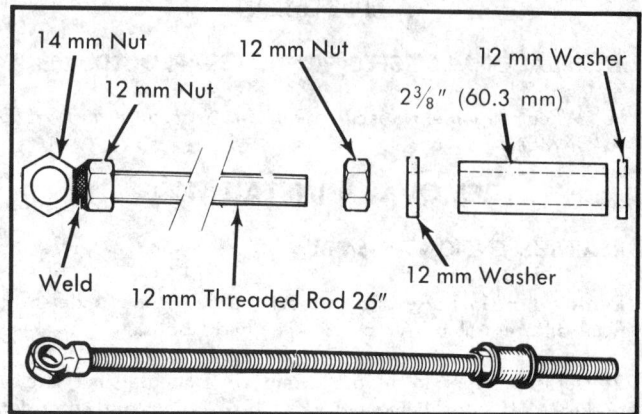

Fig. 2   Specifications for Tool Fabrication

NOTE — *Before installing torsion bar, adjust nut on tool to 23¼" (590 mm), right side and/or 23⅝" (600 mm), left side. This will allow torsion bar to be inserted.*

Installation — Put adjuster lever so it touches cam. Lightly coat torsion bar splines with grease, then insert into lever and arm. Tighten cam lock nut. Take off tool. Install shock absorber. Lower vehicle. Measure under body (riding height).

SHOCK ABSORBER

Removal — Work from inside trunk and remove upper nuts. Raise vehicle and place on safety stands. Remove lower mounting nut and take off shock absorber.

Installation — To install, reverse removal procedure. Make sure upper mounting is attached first.

TIGHTENING SPECIFICATIONS

Application	Ft. Lbs. (mkg)
Trailing Arm Mounting Bolts	
Outer	30 (4.2)
Inner	55 (7.6)
Shock Absorber Nuts	60 (8.3)

SAAB

99
900

DESCRIPTION

Tube type rear axle with coil springs. Rear axle is straight tube with stub axles press fitted into the ends. Axle is mounted to body by two lower control arms, which are connected at rear to the axle tube and to the body at front. Rear links are also used which mount rearward from stub axle assembly to body. A cross bar is mounted from right side of axle and attaches to body support in center. Coil springs are mounted between lower control arms and body. Telescopic shock absorbers are used which are attached between lower control arms and body.

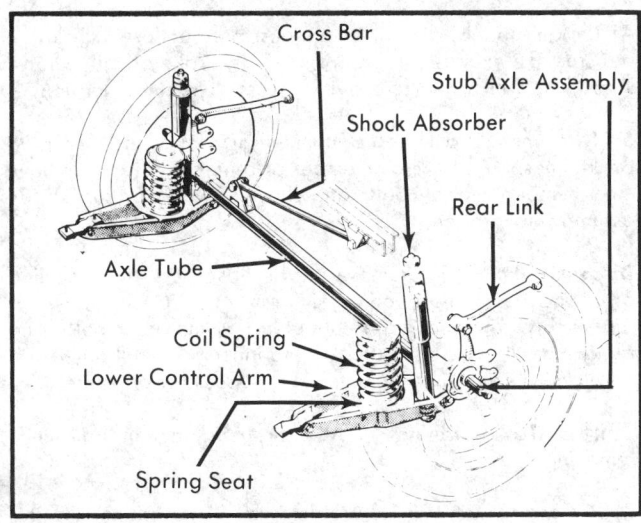

Fig. 1   Saab Rear Suspension Assembly

ADJUSTMENT

REAR WHEEL BEARINGS

See Wheel Bearing Adjustment in WHEEL ALIGNMENT Section.

REMOVAL & INSTALLATION

CAUTION — *DO NOT raise vehicle with jack under rear axle.*

COIL SPRINGS

Removal — **1)** Apply handbrake and loosen wheel lug nuts. Raise and support vehicle on safety stands; remove tire and wheel. Support control arm with jack. Slightly raise arm and disconnect lower end of shock absorber.

2) Disconnect control arm from body. Support rear axle with suitable stand to prevent sudden drop of axle. Lower control arm and remove spring, spring support and rubber spacer (if equipped). Check spring for wear or damage and free length.

Coil Spring Table

Application	Free Length
Coil with GREEN Stripe	12.1" (308 mm)
Coil with WHITE Stripe	12.4" (315 mm)
Coil with BLUE Stripe	12.7" (324 mm)

Installation — To install reverse removal procedure. Use new lock nuts to attach control arm to body.

REAR AXLE ASSEMBLY

CAUTION — *DO NOT raise vehicle with jack under rear axle.*

Removal — Raise rear of vehicle and support on safety stands. Remove wheels and tires. Disconnect rear brake hoses, lower shock absorber attachments, and cross bar. Position a jack under rear axle, lower axle and remove rear springs. Remove screws of spring link rear bushings and remove axle assembly from vehicle.

Installation — **1)** To install, reverse removal procedure and note: When repositioning axle tube, DO NOT place jack in center of axle tube. Either use two jacks (one at each end) or one jack and one safety stand.

2) DO NOT tighten bushings until car weight is on suspension to ensure bushings are aligned correctly. Cross bar-to-body mounting bolt must be installed with nut facing forward. Bleed brake system.

SHOCK ABSORBERS

CAUTION — *DO NOT raise vehicle with jack under rear axle.*

Removal & Installation (Standard Type) — Raise and support vehicle on safety stands; remove tire and wheel. Disconnect shock absorber from upper and lower mounting brackets. Remove shock. Bleed air from shock before installation by holding shock upright and work it through full cycle several times. Reverse removal procedure to install shock.

CAUTION — *Pneumatic shock absorbers require special handling to prevent personal injury. Drill a hole ⅜-⅝" (10-15 mm) from pressure chamber edge before discarding.*

Removal & Installation (Pneumatic Type) — Raise and support vehicle on safety stands; remove tire and wheel. Support rear axle with safety stand to prevent sudden drop of axle. Raise control arm with a jack placed near axle. Remove shock mounting nuts and control arm-to-rear axle mounting bolts. Lower control arm and remove shock. To install, reverse removal procedure.

Rear Suspension

SUBARU

1600
1800

DESCRIPTION

Rear suspension is of the independent type and utilizes semi-trailing arms and torsion bars. A crossmember, which contains the torsion bars, is attached to body. The semi-trailing arms attach to crossmember at inner pivot points and to torsion bar ends at outer pivot points. Double-acting shock absorbers are mounted between body and semi-trailing arms. Models with 4-WD have an arm mounted in center of crossmember which simplifies adjustment of riding height.

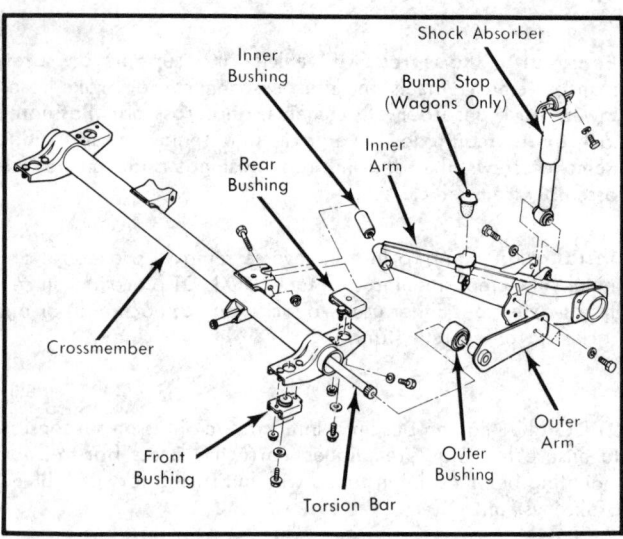

**Fig. 1 Subaru Rear Suspension Components
(2-Wheel Drive Shown; 4-Wheel Drive Similar)**

ADJUSTMENT

WHEEL ALIGNMENT SPECIFICATIONS & PROCEDURES

See Wheel Alignment Specifications and Procedures in WHEEL ALIGNMENT Section.

REMOVAL & INSTALLATION

REAR SUSPENSION ASSEMBLY

NOTE — *Rear suspension assembly must be removed to repair or replace any rear suspension components (except shock absorbers).*

Removal — 1) Remove shock absorber upper mounting bolts. Raise rear of vehicle and support with safety stands. Remove wheels.

2) On 4-WD models, disconnect rear drive system as follows: Drive spring pins out of axle drive shaft ends. Disconnect outer CV joint from spindle by pushing inner CV joint inward and brake drum downward. Pull drive shaft out of differential. Repeat for remaining drive shaft.

3) Continuing work on 4-WD models, disconnect propeller shaft from differential. Slowly pull propeller shaft out of transmission. Plug hole in transmission immediately to prevent oil spillage. Support differential with jack, remove differential-to-body bolts and remove differential from vehicle.

4) On all models, disconnect exhaust pipe at forward flange and remove exhaust system from vehicle. Take off all exhaust shrouding which interferes with access to rear suspension.

5) Disconnect brake hoses at inner arm brackets and plug brake lines. Support crossmember at center with jack. Remove crossmember-to-body bolts and slowly lower rear suspension assembly to ground.

Disassembly — 1) Remove shock absorbers from trailing arms. Scribe a mark on outer arm and crossmember for reassembly reference. Loosen outer bushing lock bolts and remove bolts attaching outer arm to inner arm. Pull outer arm and torsion bar out of crossmember. Repeat for opposite side.

NOTE — *Take care not to twist or bend torsion bar while removing.*

2) Remove torsion bar from outer arm. Remove inner arm-to-crossmember bolt and remove inner arm. If inner bushing is worn or damaged, press it out of inner arm.

Reassembly — To reassemble, reverse disassembly procedure and note the following: When installing torsion bar and outer arm, align scribe marks made during disassembly to achieve correct outer arm angle.

Installation — To install, reverse removal procedure and note the following: Tighten outer bushing lock bolts with vehicle on ground. Bleed brake system and check rear wheel alignment.

TIGHTENING SPECIFICATIONS

Application	Ft. Lbs. (mkg)
Outer-to-Inner Arm Bolts	87-101 (12.0-14.0)
Inner Arm-to-Crossmember Bolts	54-69 (7.5-9.5)
Crossmember-to-Body Bolts	87-108 (12.0-15.0)
Differential Mounting Nuts (4-WD)	51-58 (7.0-8.0)
Propeller Shaft Bolts (4-WD)	13-18 (1.8-2.5)
Outer Bushing Lock Bolts	23-29 (3.2-4.0)

TOYOTA CELICA, CRESSIDA & SUPRA

DESCRIPTION

Coil spring type suspension utilizing upper and lower control arms as pivot supports. Coil springs are mounted between axle and chassis member. Shock absorbers are connected to axle housing at bottom and to chassis members at top. A lateral control arm is mounted to rear side of axle and runs parallel with axle to mount at side of body. Celica and Supra models have stabilizer bar attached to chassis at ends and at axle with 2 brackets.

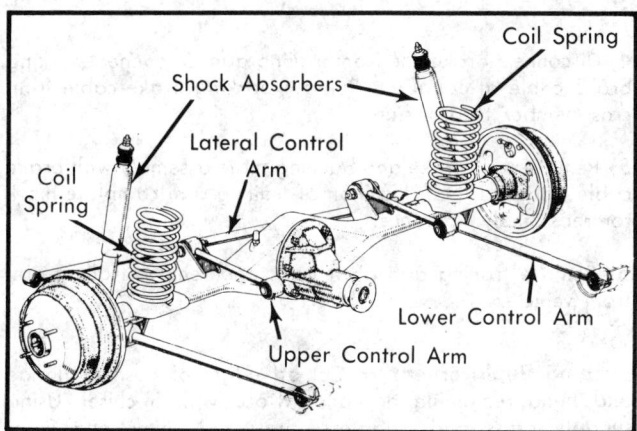

Fig. 1 Rear Suspension Arrangement of Toyota Cressida (Celica & Supra Similar)

REMOVAL & INSTALLATION

SHOCK ABSORBERS

Removal — Raise vehicle and place saftey stands under axle housing. Remove nut holding shock absorber to rear axle. Remove nut holding shock absorber to body, and remove shock absorber.

NOTE — *Use screwdriver to keep shaft from turning.*

Installation — Reverse removal procedure for installation. Tighten all nuts and bolts to specifications.

COIL SPRINGS

Removal — 1) Raise and support rear axle housing and support body with saftey stands. Leave a jack under rear axle. Remove nut holding shock absorber to rear axle and disconnect shock.

2) Disconnect rear stabilizer bar on Celica and Supra. On all models, remove nut holding lateral control rod to rear axle housing and disconnect lateral control rod. Slowly lower axle jack and remove coil springs and insulators.

NOTE — *Be careful of brake lines and parking brake cable while lowering axle.*

Installation — To install, reverse removal procedure.

CONTROL ARMS

Removal — 1) Raise and support vehicle at frame. Place an additional support jack under rear axle.

2) To remove upper control arm, remove bolt holding upper control arm to body and bolt holding control arm to axle housing. Remove upper control arm.

3) To remove lower control arm, remove arm-to-body bolt and arm-to-axle housing bolt. Remove control arm.

4) To remove lateral control arm, remove arm-to-body bolt and arm-to-axle bolt. Remove lateral arm.

Installation — To install, temporarily attach control arms, then raise axle jack until vehicle is lifted from body stands. Tighten control arm bolts to specifications. Lower vehicle to ground.

STABILIZER BAR

Removal — Raise vehicle at rear axle and place support stands beneath axle. Remove bolts from body and axle and remove stabilizer bar.

Installation — Attach stabilizer bar to body and axle mounts, leaving slightly loose. Lower vehicle to ground and jounce several times to settle stabilizer bar bushings. Torque stabilizer bar bolts to specifications.

TIGHTENING SPECIFICATIONS

Application	Ft. Lbs. (mkg)
Upper Control Arm-to-Axle	
Celica, Supra	73-108 (10.0-15.0)
Cressida	87-123 (12.0-17.0)
Upper Control Arm-to-Body	
Celica, Supra	87-123 (12.0-17.0)
Cressida	109-137 (15.0-19.0)
Lower Control Arm-to-Axle	
Celica, Supra	73-108 (10.0-15.0)
Cressida	87-123 (12.0-17.0)
Lower Control Arm-to-Body	87-123 (12.0-17.0)
Lateral Control Arm-to-Axle	
Celica, Supra	30-55 (4.1-7.7)
Cressida	54-80 (7.5-11.0)
Lateral Control Arm-to-Body	
Celica, Supra	51-65 (7.0-9.0)
Cressida	65-98 (9.0-13.5)
Shock Absorber-to-Body	16-24 (2.2-3.4)
Shock Absorber-to-Axle	22-32 (3.0-4.5)
Stabilizer Bar-to-Axle	22-32 (3.0-4.5)
Stabilizer Link-to-Bar	14-22 (1.9-3.1)
Stabilizer Bar-to-Body	55-75 (7.5-10.5)

TOYOTA TERCEL

DESCRIPTION

Rear suspension is independent, coil spring type. Trailing arms are mounted by 2 bushings and pivot bolts to suspension crossmember, and supported by coil springs and shock absorber. Stabilizer bar attaches to crossmember and trailing arm.

ADJUSTMENTS

WHEEL ALIGNMENT SPECIFICATIONS & PROCEDURES

See Wheel Alignment Specifications and Procedures in WHEEL ALIGNMENT Section.

WHEEL BEARING ADJUSTMENT

See Wheel Bearing Adjustment in WHEEL ALIGNMENT Section.

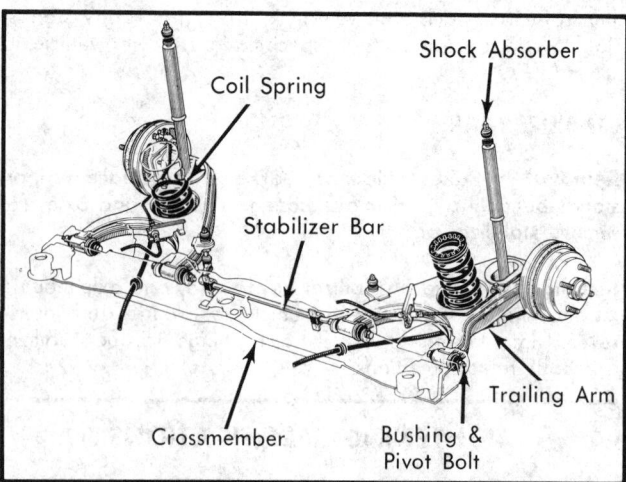

Fig. 1   Assembled View of Tercel Rear Suspension

REMOVAL & INSTALLATION

SHOCK ABSORBER & COIL SPRING

Removal — 1) Raise and support rear of vehicle. Remove tire and wheel. Support trailing arm with a jack.

2) Remove stabilizer bar end set bolt. Remove shock absorber upper mounting nut. Remove shock absorber lower mounting bolt and remove shock from vehicle.

3) Lower trailing arm with the jack. Remove coil spring and spring seat.

Installation — To install, reverse removal procedure and note the following:

- Align coil spring in hollow portion of trailing arm.
- Lower vehicle and bounce to stabilize bushings before tightening shock absorber and stabilizer mounting hardware.

TRAILING ARM

Removal — 1) Raise and support rear of vehicle. Remove stabilizer bar end set bolt.

2) Remove shock absorber and coil spring. Remove grease cap, cotter pin, adjusting cap, and claw nut from rear axle hub.

3) Remove claw washer, outer wheel bearing, brake drum, inner bearing and oil seal.

NOTE — It may be necessary to back off brake adjustment to remove brake drum. Raise automatic adjuster lever with a screwdriver and insert brake tool to adjust.

4) Disconnect brake line from trailing arm. Disconnect parking brake cable at equalizer. Pull out parking brake cable from crossmember to arm side.

5) Remove rear brake and backing plate assembly with brake cable attached. Note position of trailing arm camplate mark for reassembly reference.

6) Remove trailing arm pivot bolts and remove trailing arm from vehicle.

Bushing Replacement — Cut off edges of bushing flange and bend remaining portions inward with a chisel. Using suitable press and adapters, press out outer and inner bushings and press in replacements.

Installation — To install, reverse removal procedure and note the following:

- Align camplate mark on trailing arm camplate to same position as it was prior to removal.
- Lower vehicle and bounce before tightening suspension arm, shock absorber, and stabilizer bar end.
- Adjust wheel bearings and check wheel alignment. See appropriate article in WHEEL ALIGNMENT Section.

STABILIZER BAR

Removal & Installation — Remove stabilizer bar end set bolt. Remove bolts from stabilizer bar brackets and remove stabilizer bar from vehicle. To install, reverse removal procedure. Lower vehicle and bounce before tightening mounting hardware.

SUSPENSION CROSSMEMBER

Removal — 1) Raise and support rear of vehicle. Remove tires and wheels. Remove exhaust tailpipe and muffler assembly.

2) Remove stabilizer bar, shock absorber and coil springs. Remove trailing arm with parking brake cable and brake tube attached.

3) Remove suspension crossmember mounting bolts and remove crossmember from vehicle.

Bushing Replacement — Remove bushings with a plastic hammer. Install new bushings with notch aligned in the

TOYOTA TERCEL (Cont.)

forward/reverse direction, and tap in from underside of crossmember.

NOTE — *Do not tap on rubber portion of bushings.*

Installation — To install, reverse removal procedure and note the following:

- Align camplate mark on trailing arm camplate to the same position as it was prior to removal.
- Align coil spring in hollow portion of trailing arm.
- Lower vehicle and bounce before tightening trailing arm, shock absorber, and stabilizer bar end.
- Adjust wheel bearings and check alignment. *See appropriate article in WHEEL ALIGNMENT Section.*

TIGHTENING SPECIFICATIONS

Application	Ft. Lbs. (mkg)
Rear Brake Assembly	22-32 (3.0-4.5)
Shock Absorber	
Upper Mounting Nut	14-22 (1.9-3.0)
Lower Mounting Bolt	11-15 (1.5-2.2)
Stabilizer Bar	
Bracket	11-15 (1.5-2.2)
Bar End Set Bolt	10-15 (1.4-2.2)
Suspension Crossmember Bolts	58-72 (8.0-10.0)
Trailing Arm Pivot Bolts	73-97 (10.0-13.5)

TRIUMPH SPITFIRE

DESCRIPTION

Semi-trailing arm, independent type suspension utilizing a transverse leaf spring. Strut rods are connected at front to chassis and at rear to axle bearing carrier. Transverse leaf spring is mounted in center to differential and at ends to mounts connected to bearing carrier. Hydraulic shock absorbers are mounted between bearing carrier at bottom and chassis at top.

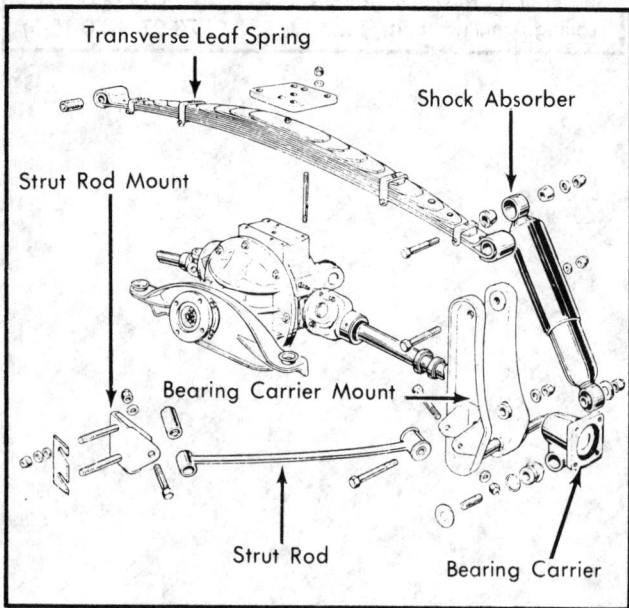

Fig. 1   Exploded View of Rear Suspension Assembly

ADJUSTMENT

WHEEL ALIGNMENT SPECIFICATIONS & PROCEDURES

See *Wheel Alignment Specifications and Procedures* in WHEEL ALIGNMENT Section.

REMOVAL & INSTALLATION

TRANSVERSE LEAF SPRING

Removal — Raise vehicle, position safety stands under chassis and remove both rear wheels. Remove bolts connecting transverse leaf spring to bearing carrier mount. Place a jack under lower shock absorber mount and disconnect lower shock absorber from mount on bearing carrier. From inside luggage compartment, remove plate covering spring mount on differential. Remove nuts and clamp plate from spring mount. Remove mounting studs from differential and pull spring out through side of fender well.

Installation — To install transverse leaf spring, reverse removal procedure. Spring is marked "FRONT" and must be installed correctly. Do not tighten spring-to-bearing carrier bolts until weight of vehicle is on rear wheels.

STRUT ROD

Removal — Raise vehicle, position safety stands under chassis, and remove wheels. Place a jack under lower shock absorber mount and raise jack until strut rod bolts can be removed easily. If shims are removed from strut rod mount on chassis, note number for installation reference.

Installation — To install strut rod, reverse removal procedure and note the following: Install same number of shims at front mount as removed and check rear wheel alignment.

BEARING CARRIER MOUNT

Removal — Raise vehicle, position safety stands under chassis and remove wheel and tire. Disconnect strut rod from bearing carrier mount. Remove pivot bolt securing mount to bearing carrier and remove mount.

Installation — To install bearing carrier mount, reverse removal procedure.

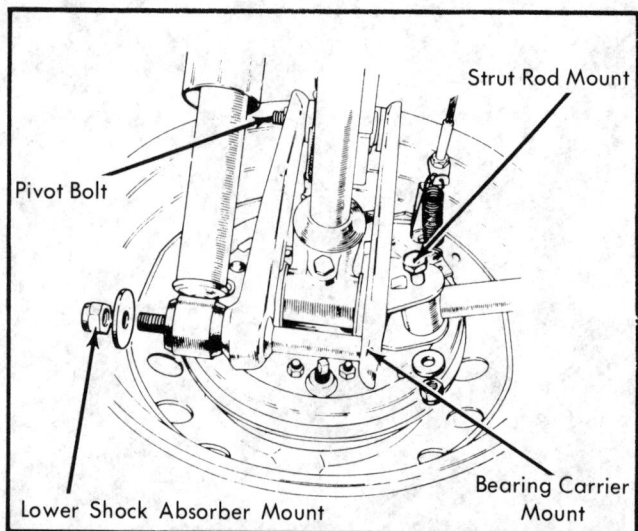

Fig. 2   Components to Remove to Take Out Bearing Carrier Mount

TIGHTENING SPECIFICATIONS

Application	Ft. Lbs. (mkg)
Lower Shock Absorber Mount	28-38 (3.9-5.3)
Upper Shock Absorber Mount	38-48 (5.3-6.6)
Strut Rod Pivot Bolts	24-32 (3.3-4.4)
Strut Rod Bracket-to-Chassis	24-32 (3.3-4.4)
Mounts-to-Bearing Carrier	38-48 (5.3-6.6)
Transverse Spring Pivot Bolts	38-48 (5.3-6.6)

TRIUMPH TR7 & TR8

DESCRIPTION

Rear suspension system consists of a control arm (trailing arm), radius rod, and a stabilizer bar. A coil spring is mounted between body and control arm. Shock absorbers mount off axle housing at bottom and at top to body.

ADJUSTMENT

WHEEL ALIGNMENT SPECIFICATIONS & PROCEDURES

See Wheel Alignment Specifications in WHEEL ALIGNMENT Section.

REMOVAL & INSTALLATION

COIL SPRING & CONTROL ARM

Removal — Raise vehicle and place on safety stands. Remove wheel. Place jack under suspension control arm and compress spring ensuring vehicle does not come off stands. Remove two nuts and bolts mounting stabilizer bar to control arm. Remove nut and bolt securing rear end of suspension arm to axle bracket. Lower jack and remove spring and insulating rubbers. Detach suspension control arm front mounting and remove arm.

SHOCK ABSORBERS

Removal — Jack up vehicle and place on safety stands; remove wheel. On right side, remove fuel filler assembly. On left side, remove upper access plate. On both sides, disconnect upper end of shock absorber and remove hardware. Disconnect and remove lower shock absorber mounting, then pull shock absorber from vehicle.

Installation — To install, reverse removal procedure and tighten nuts.

STABILIZER BAR

Removal & Installation — Raise vehicle and place on safety stands. Remove the four bolts mounting stabilizer bar to rear suspension arms. Remove stabilizer bar with shims, if equipped. To install, reverse removal procedure and ensure shims are refitted.

RADIUS ROD

Removal & Installation — Raise vehicle and place on safety stands. Disconnect radius rod from rear axle bracket and from bracket attached to body; then remove radius rod. If bushings are damaged, press out of rod and install new ones. To install, reverse removal procedure.

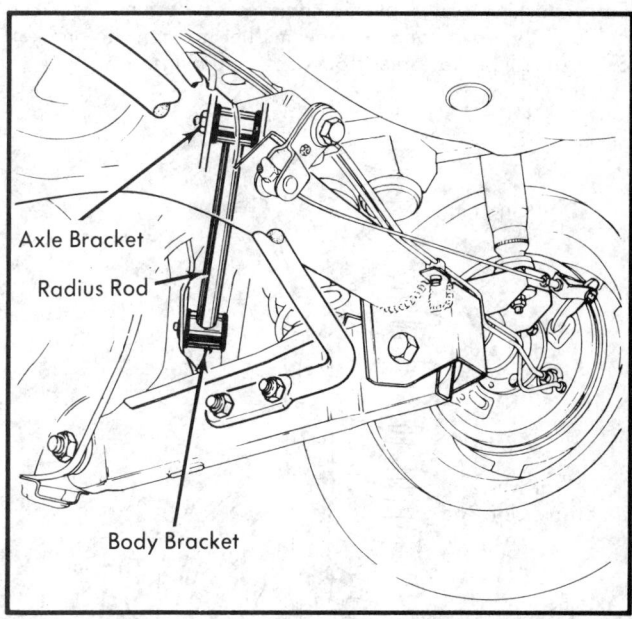

Fig. 2 Detailed View of Radius Rod Removal

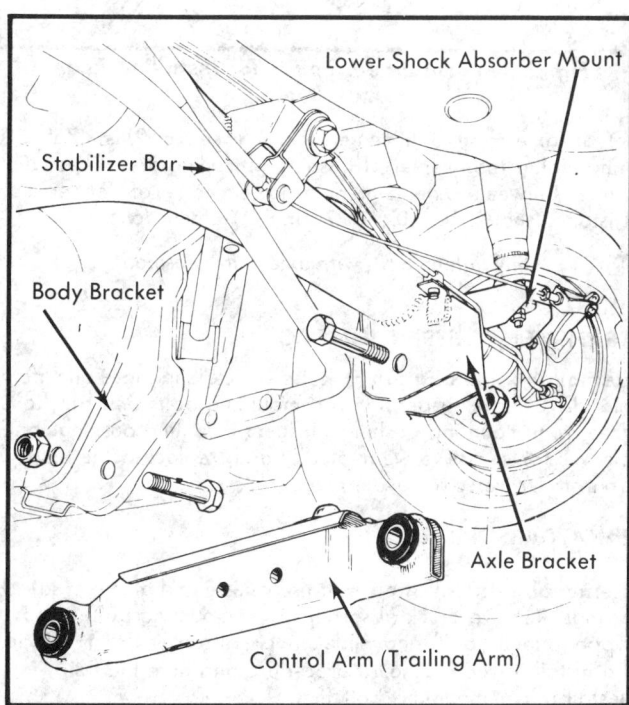

Fig. 1 Detailed View of Control Arm Removal

Installation — Ensure spring insulators are in correctly then fit spring. With jack positioned under control arm and front (body bracket end) of control arm installed, fit rear end of suspension control arm in axle bracket. Reconnect stabilizer bar to suspension arm and install wheel. Tighten suspension components with vehicle weight on ground.

TIGHTENING SPECIFICATIONS

Application	Ft. Lbs. (mkg)
Stabilizer Bar-to-Control Arm	30-37 (4.2-5.1)
Shock Absorber-to-Control Arm	10-14 (1.4-1.9)
Shock Absorber-to-Body	10-14 (1.4-1.9)
Suspension Arm-to-Axle Bracket	38-48 (5.3-6.6)
Suspension Control Arm-to-Body Bracket	38-48 (5.3-6.6)

Rear Suspension

VOLKSWAGEN DASHER

DESCRIPTION

Rear suspension is coil spring type utilizing a transverse mounted suspension rod and a trailing arm. Suspension rod is used to improve stability. Shock absorbers mount off bracket on axle beam and to upper body. Coil spring rides in spring seat welded to axle beam and wedges against damper ring at chassis/body.

ADJUSTMENTS

WHEEL ALIGNMENT SPECIFICATIONS & PROCEDURES

See Wheel Alignment Specifications and Procedures in WHEEL ALIGNMENT Section.

WHEEL BEARING ADJUSTMENT

See Wheel Bearing Adjustment in WHEEL ALIGNMENT Section

REMOVAL & INSTALLATION

REAR AXLE BEAM ASSEMBLY

Removal — 1) Raise vehicle and place safety stands under body. Take nuts off parking brake linkage equalizer bar. Force parking brake plastic cable guide bushing from clip holder. Pry down and unhook muffler from front bracket. Separate all brake cables from body mountings.

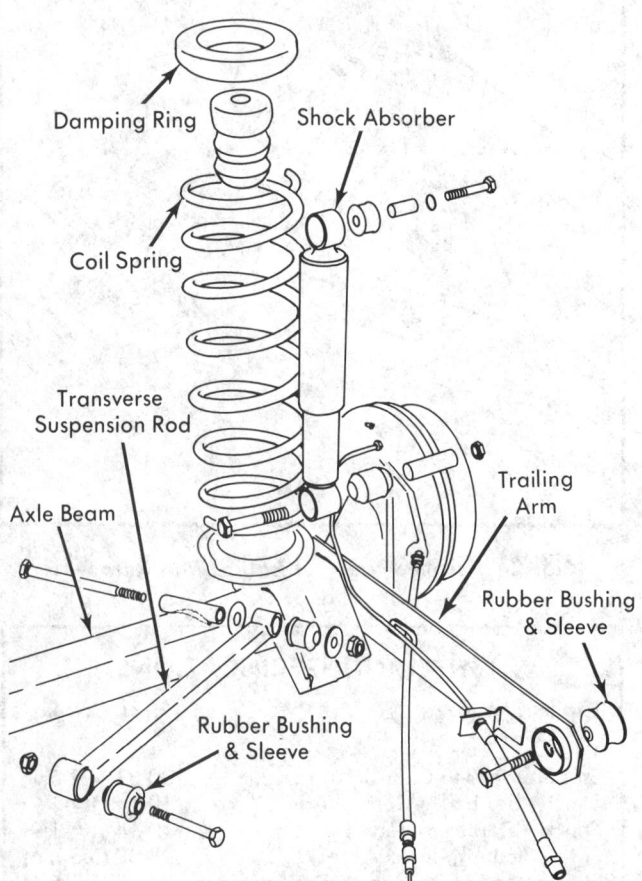

Damping Ring — Shock Absorber

Coil Spring

Transverse Suspension Rod

Axle Beam

Trailing Arm

Rubber Bushing & Sleeve

Rubber Bushing & Sleeve

Fig. 1   Exploded View of Dasher Rear Suspension

2) Disconnect brake lines and plug open ends. Remove trailing arm mounting bolts from body. Detach muffler from rear mounting. Remove suspension rod-to-axle mounting bolt. Detach lower end of shock absorber and guide rear axle assembly (on a jack) from vehicle.

Bushing Replacement — Place trailing arm in press and force bushing from arm. Make sure when installing new bushings that bushing slots are aligned horizontally in arm.

Installation — 1) To install rear axle assembly, reverse removal procedure and note the following: Make sure trailing arm bushings are free of tension. Before tightening trailing arm bolts ensure arms are in middle of moving range.

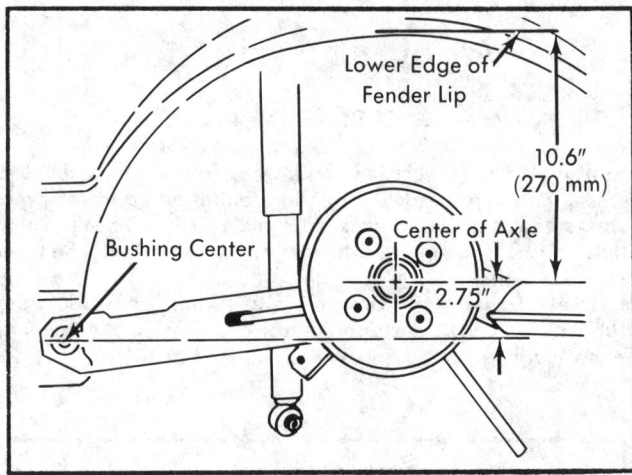

Lower Edge of Fender Lip

10.6"
(270 mm)

Bushing Center

Center of Axle

2.75"

Fig. 2   Measurement Points for Installing Rear Axle Beam

2) Lift axle beam until center of axle (See Fig. 2) is 2.75" (70 mm) higher than center of bushing in trailing arm. Check distance between axle center to lower edge of fender lip. Distance should be 10.6" (270 mm). Tighten bolts.

NOTE — Only tighten bolts with axle in this position.

TRANSVERSE SUSPENSION ROD

Removal & Installation — Raise vehicle and place on safety stands. Remove suspension rod mounting bolts and tap bolts free from mounting bushings. Inspect mounting bushings and sleeves for excessive wear or damage; replace as necessary. To install, reverse removal procedure.

SHOCK ABSORBER

Removal & Installation — Raise vehicle and place on safety stands. Remove shock absorber lower mounting bolt. Remove upper mount bolt and slide shock absorber from vehicle. To install, reverse removal procedure and note the following: Install upper mounting bolt first.

TIGHTENING SPECIFICATIONS	
Application	Ft. Lbs. (mkg)
Shock Absorber Mounting Bolts	43 (6.0)
Suspension Rod Mounting Bolts	50 (7.0)
Trailing Arm Bolt	43 (6.0)

VOLKSWAGEN JETTA, RABBIT & SCIROCCO

DESCRIPTION

Rear suspension is a link type with coil springs and using control arms and torsion beam for stabilization. Control arm and torsion beam are combined as one unit. Hydraulic shock absorbers are mounted inside coil springs and attached to control arm at the bottom and to vehicle body at the top.

REMOVAL & INSTALLATION

SUSPENSION STRUT & COIL SPRING

Removal — **1)** Leave vehicle on ground. Take off plastic cap covering rear strut upper mounting nuts. Remove nuts.

2) Slowly raise vehicle until weight is off spring. Remove bolt holding lower end of strut shock absorber to axle beam mount. Raise vehicle until strut can be removed.

NOTE — *It is not necessary to use spring compressor to disassemble strut.*

Disassembly — Set strut assembly in vise. Hold piston rod and remove strut mounting nut. Take off components down to slotted nut. Remove slotted nut. Take off spacer and coil spring.

Inspection — **1)** Hand check shock absorber for even resistance through entire piston stroke. Worn shock absorbers cannot be overhauled.

NOTE — *If a coil spring is being replaced, ensure that paint stripe color code on replacement spring matches original spring code.*

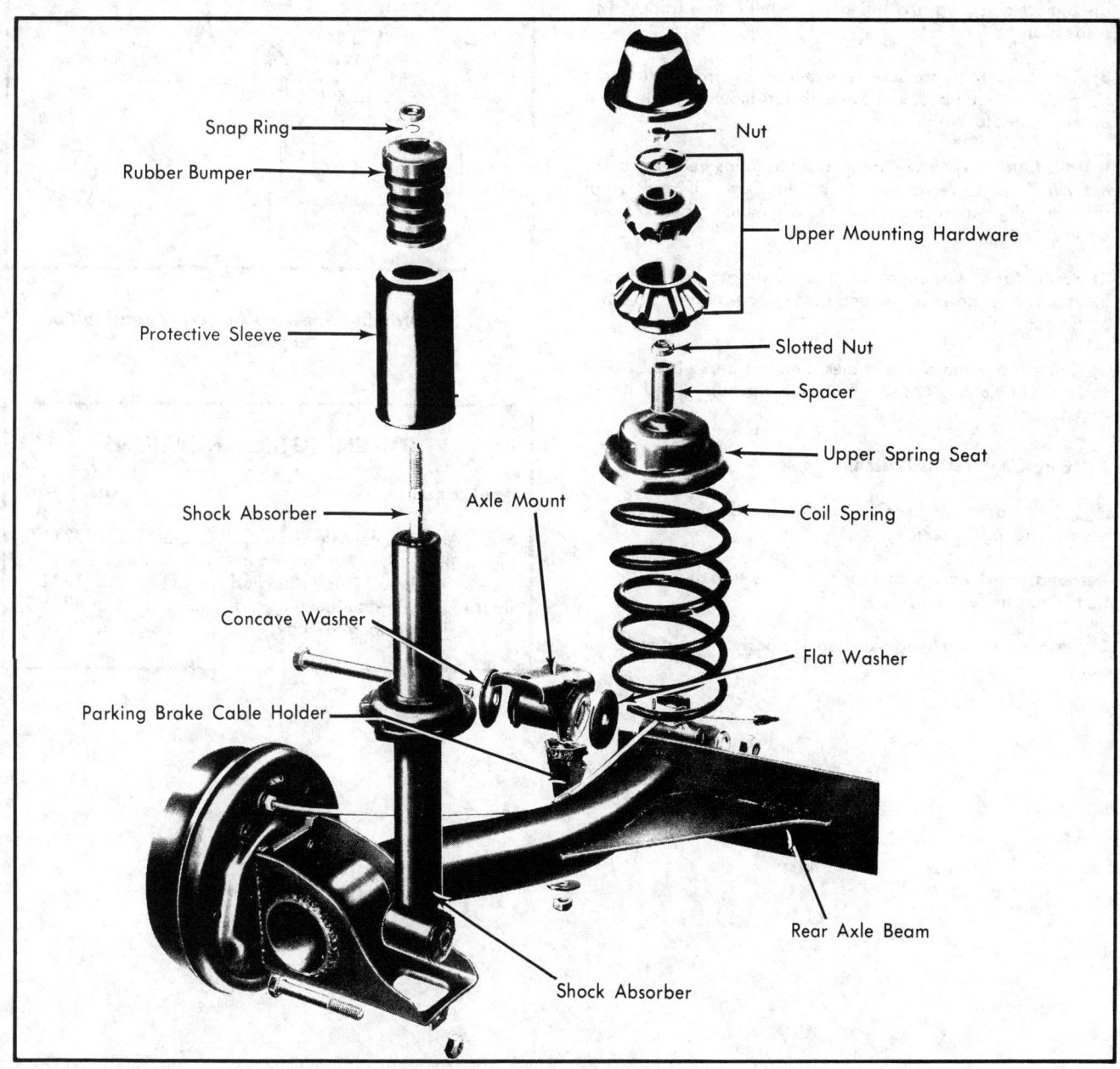

Fig. 1   Exploded View of Rear Suspension Components

Rear Suspension

VOLKSWAGEN JETTA, RABBIT & SCIROCCO (Cont.)

Reassembly — 1) Fit protective cap on shock absorber. Install rubber buffer, with small diameter end downward. Insert snap ring and washer.

2) Place spring into lower seat. Fit upper retainer with spacer sleeve. Tighten slotted nut holding piston rod. Put on remaining upper mounting hardware and tighten piston rod.

Installation — Reverse removal procedure.

SUSPENSION ASSEMBLY

Removal — 1) Leave vehicle on ground. Disconnect upper strut mounting at body. Raise vehicle and support at rear with jack stands.

2) Disconnect parking brake at holder near rear axle mount. Disconnect and plug brake lines. Leave flex hose attached to suspension.

3) Separate brake pressure regulator spring from axle beam on models so equipped. Remove both nuts mounting axle beam on each side to body.

Installation — 1) If axle beam mounting has been removed, use *Fig.* 2 to correctly adjust mounting pad. If pad is not correctly aligned, torsional preload of mounting bushings will be incorrect.

2) Position rear suspension on body. Refit nuts keeping axle beam to body. Raise wheel and guide upper end of strut into body mounting.

3) Connect parking brake cables. Connect brake lines. Lower vehicle and tighten upper strut mounting nuts. Bleed brake system.

AXLE BEAM PIVOT BUSHING

NOTE — *Procedure given is for replacing bushing with axle beam installed in vehicle.*

Removal — 1) Raise and support vehicle so axle beam pivot bolt is not under load.

2) Remove 2 nuts holding axle beam to body and tap out pivot bolt.

3) Press out bushing. Select new bushing and press bushing into place. Loosely install mounting on axle beam. Concave washer and bolt head must face toward outside of vehicle. Bolt head must recess into washer.

4) Align mount as shown in *Fig.* 2. Tighten pivot bolt nut. Lower vehicle.

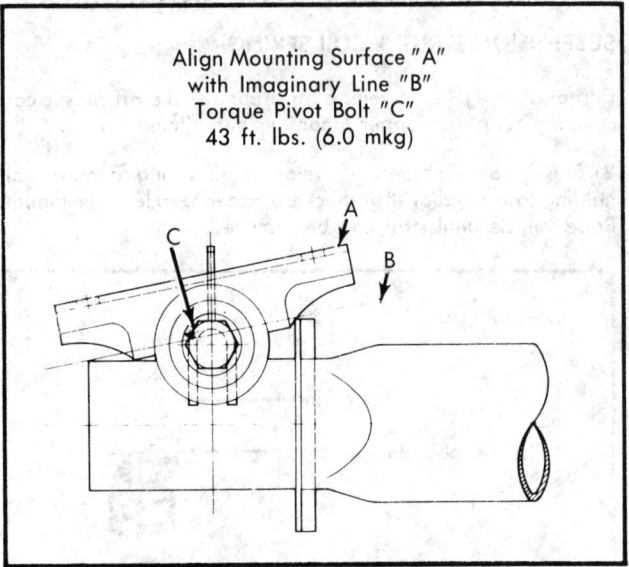

Align Mounting Surface "A"
with Imaginary Line "B"
Torque Pivot Bolt "C"
43 ft. lbs. (6.0 mkg)

Fig. 2   Drawing Showing Correct Mounting Pad Alignment

TIGHTENING SPECIFICATIONS

Application	Ft. Lbs. (mkg)
Shock Absorber-to-Axle Beam	32 (4.5)
Piston Shock Absorber Top Mounting	23 (3.2)
Coil Spring Retainer-to-Piston Rod	14 (2.0)
Rear Axle Beam-to-Mounting Pad	43 (6.0)
Rear Axle Mounting-to-Body	32 (4.5)

VOLKSWAGEN VANAGON

DESCRIPTION

Rear suspension is independent, coil spring type. Trailing arms mount in front to 2 pivot brackets having provision for caster and toe-in adjustment. Shock absorber mounts at top to chassis and at bottom to rear of trailing arm. Coil spring mounts to trailing arm and chassis in spring seats ahead of shock absorber. Drive shafts run through trailing arms and attach to inside of wheel hub.

ADJUSTMENT

WHEEL ALIGNMENT SPECIFICATIONS & PROCEDURES

See Wheel Alignment Specifications & Procedures in WHEEL ALIGNMENT Section.

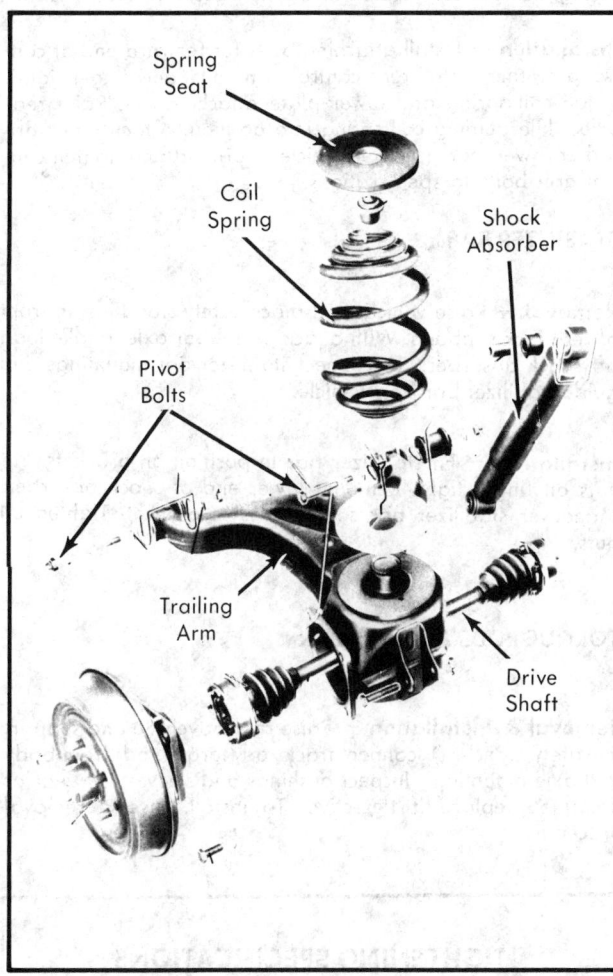

Fig. 1 Exploded View of Vanagon Rear Suspension

REMOVAL & INSTALLATION

TRAILING ARMS

Removal — **1)** Raise and support rear of vehicle. Remove tire and wheel. Support trailing arm with a jack.

2) Remove 4 nuts attaching brake drum and axle hub assembly to trailing arm. Using hex wrench, remove hex screws at drive shaft-to-transaxle joint.

3) Pull drive shaft and brake drum assembly through trailing arm and remove from vehicle. Remove shock absorber lower mounting bolt and slowly lower jack.

4) Remove coil spring and spring seats. Note relative position of trailing arm in mounting brackets and remove pivot bolts. Remove trailing arm from vehicle.

Bushing Removal — Using bushing remover and adapter (VW 442, 30-14), and threaded rod, pull bushing out of trailing arm.

NOTE — *Coat washer with oil and place between nut and tool.*

Bushing Installation — Coat hole in trailing arm, installation tool, and bushing with soap solution. Using bushing installation tool (3053), and threaded rod, pull bushing into trailing arm until sleeve contacts tool. Wait about 30 seconds and remove tool.

NOTE — *Bushing should seat itself. If necessary, press edge of bushing out.*

Installation — To install, reverse removal procedure and note the following:

- Depressions in spring seats must be aligned with ends of coil springs.
- Align depression in lower spring seat with depression in trailing arm.
- Install trailing arm in noted position in brackets.
- After installation, adjust toe-in and camber.

SHOCK ABSORBER & COIL SPRING

Removal — **1)** Raise and support rear of vehicle. Support trailing arm with a jack. Remove shock absorber mounting bolts and remove shock absorber.

NOTE — *If only coil spring is to be removed, remove only one shock absorber mounting.*

2) Slowly lower jack. Remove coil spring and spring seats.

Bushing Replacement — Using suitable press, press out bushings in shock absorber. File off any sharp edges on sleeve before installation. Coat parts with soap solution and press sleeve 1/2 way into bushing using vise. Using press, fully push bushing and sleeve into shock absorber.

Installation — To install, reverse removal procedure and note the following:

- End of coil spring must fit in spring seat depressions. Depression in lower spring seat should fit into depression in trailing arm.

TIGHTENING SPECIFICATIONS

Application	Ft. Lbs. (mkg)
Drive Shaft Hex Screws	33 (4.6)
Trailing Arm Pivot Bolts	76 (10.5)
Drum & Hub Assembly-to-Trailing Arm	101 (14.0)
Shock Absorber Lower Mounting Bolt	65 (9.0)

Rear Suspension

VOLVO

DL GLE
GL Coupe
GT Diesel

DESCRIPTION

Rear suspension consists of coil springs mounted between control arms and body rubber mounts, double-acting shock absorbers mounted on control arms and to body, a stabilizer bar attached at both ends to control arms, two torque rods running forward from axle brackets and a track bar attached nearly parallel to axle housing.

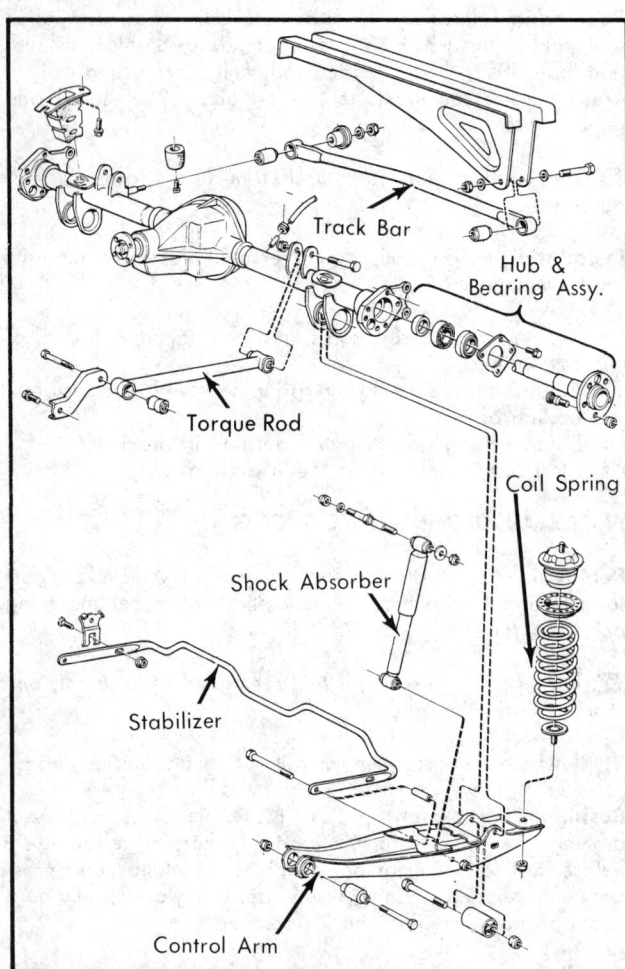

Fig. 1 Exploded View of Volvo Rear Suspension

REMOVAL & INSTALLATION

COIL SPRINGS

Removal — Raise vehicle and place on safety stands. Remove tires and wheels. Place jack under rear axle housing and jack up axle until spring compresses. Disconnect lower shock absorber mounting, then remove spring lower retaining nut. Lower jack and remove coil spring.

Installation — To install, reverse removal procedure and tighten all nuts and bolts. Make sure rubber spring support is in correct position.

SHOCK ABSORBER

Removal — Raise rear of vehicle and support on safety stands. Remove wheel and tire. Use jack to raise rear axle. Remove upper and lower attaching nuts, then remove shock absorber.

Installation — To install, reverse removal procedure and make sure spacer sleeve is in correct position.

CONTROL ARMS

Removal — Raise rear of vehicle and position on safety stands. Position jack under rear axle housing and jack up axle until spring compresses. Disconnect shock absorber from control arm. Remove coil spring lower retaining nut, then remove spring. Remove control arm attaching bolts, and control arm.

Installation — Install attaching bolts for forward end of control arm, then install rear control arm bolts (only finger tight). Install coil spring and lower plate attaching nut. Raise rear axle while guiding coil spring into position. Attach shock absorber lower mount. Lower vehicle to ground and tighten control arm bolts to specifications.

STABILIZER BAR

Removal — Raise vehicle and place safety stand just in front of rear jack supports. With a jack, raise rear axle to take load off shock absorbers. Disconnect stabilizer bar mountings and guide stabilizer bar from vehicle.

Installation — Fit stabilizer bar in position on brackets. Put nuts on finger tight. Remount lower end of shock absorber. Maneuver stabilizer bar so it settles in bracket. Tighten all nuts.

TORQUE RODS & TRACK BAR

Removal & Installation — Raise rear of vehicle and support on safety stands. Disconnect track rod (torque rod) from body and axle mountings. Inspect bushings and sleeves for wear or damage. Replace if defective. To install, reverse removal procedure.

TIGHTENING SPECIFICATIONS

Application	Ft. Lbs. (mkg)
Track Bar-to-Axle	43 (6.0)
Track Bar-to-Body	61 (8.5)
Shock Absorber Bolts	61 (8.5)
Stabilizer Bar	
M10 Thread Bolt	33 (4.5)
M12 Thread Bolt	61 (8.5)
Control Arm Bolts	94 (13.0)
Torque Rod Bolts	61 (8.5)

MERCEDES-BENZ 300TD

DESCRIPTION

The 300TD rear suspension uses an automatic leveling system. The system contains a hydraulic pump, reservoir, leveling valve, pressure reservoir and special combination shock absorber/suspension struts. The leveling valve lever, which is connected to the torsion bar, has 3 positions: neutral, filling and return flow. This positioning of the leveling valve lever, due to the load in vehicle, controls amount of fluid in the special shock absorber which raises or lowers rear of vehicle to maintain a level attitude.

OPERATION

As rear of vehicle is lowered due to added weight, the leveling valve lever raises to the filling position. This allows fluid to flow from pump to pressure reservoir then to special shock absorber, through check valves. This added fluid will raise the rear of the vehicle until the leveling valve lever is moved back to the neutral position. When the added weight is removed, rear of vehicle raises which moves the leveling lever to the return flow position. This allows the fluid in the special shock absorber to drain back into the reservoir until the leveling lever is back in the neutral position and the vehicle is level.

TESTING

HYDRAULIC OIL PUMP & LEVELING VALVE

NOTE — *These tests can only be performed on a ready-to-drive vehicle. Check leveling valve for leaks during test. In case of leaks on valve housing parting surface, install O-ring (006 997 69 45).*

NOTE — *Make sure hydraulic oil is not hot before starting test.*

1) Disconnect connecting bar at leveling valve lever. Tighten 4 leveling valve housing screws.

CAUTION — *Do not loosen clamping screw securing lever on valve control shaft.*

2) Attach an oil drain line to bleed screw and release pressure in system by opening bleed screw. Remove bleed screw and attach pressure tester (Mercedes-Benz No. 038a) directly to leveling valve via 3 or 4-way distribution fitting.

3) Push leveling valve lever up into filling position. Run engine at idle (800-1000 RPM) for a short time and observe pressure reading on tester. Pressure should read 1885 psi (132.5 kg/cm^2) minimum.

NOTE — *Perform this test quickly to avoid damage to components.*

4) Turn off engine. Move leveling valve lever down to return flow position and observe base pressure reading. After a stabilization period of 5 minutes, repeat test procedure. Leave pressure tester connected at least 4 hours and observe.

NOTE — *Base pressure must not drop after the stabilization period. This also applies to extended periods, such as overnight.*

5) Bleed base pressure at bleed screw, disconnect tester and install bleed screw. Fill level control system by running engine at medium RPM's and pushing leveling valve lever up into filling position for approximately 30 seconds.

6) Turn off engine. Reconnect connecting bar at leveling valve lever. Check reservoir oil level. Oil level should be between "Max." and "Min." for unloaded vehicle, "Min." for loaded vehicle.

PRESSURE RESERVOIR

NOTE — *This test can be performed only on a ready-to-drive vehicle.*

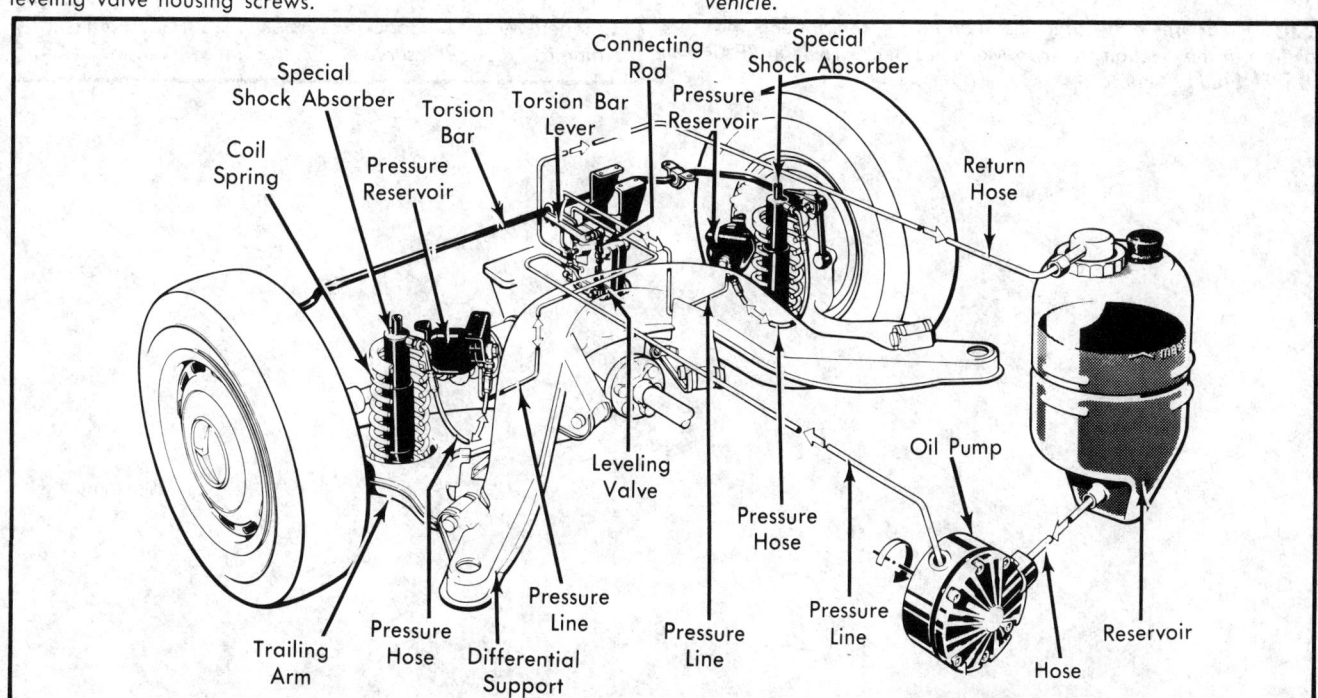

Fig. 1 Mercedes-Benz 300TD Level Control Rear Suspension System

MERCEDES-BENZ 300TD (Cont.)

1) Disconnect connecting bar at leveling valve. Push leveling valve lever down to return flow position. Release pressure in system by opening bleed screw, and remove bleed screw.

2) Connect pressure tester (Mercedes-Benz No. 038a) to leveling valve. Disconnect pressure line from leveling valve to pressure reservoir from left and right pressure reservoirs (near special shock absorbers).

3) Plug lines with couplings and bleed screws. Attach pressure hose from gauge to either right or left pressure reservoir.

4) Push leveling valve lever down to return flow position. Run engine at idle speed. Push leveling valve lever up to filling position and observe pressure gauge.

5) Gas pressure in reservoir is indicated at point where pressure gauge needle changes from indication of a gradual pressure increase to an indication of rapid increase. This increase is caused when oil pressure exceeds gas pressure.

6) Gas pressure should be 304-363 psi (21.4-25.5 kg/cm²) for new pressure reservoirs, and a minimum of 217 psi (15.2 kg/cm²) for used pressure reservoirs. Repeat this test for the other reservoir.

7) Disconnect pressure tester, install bleed screw and reconnect pressure lines to pressure reservoirs. Run engine at medium RPM and push leveling valve lever up to filling position for approximately 30 seconds to fill control system.

8) Turn off engine. Reconnect connecting bar at leveling valve lever. With engine off, check oil reservoir oil level. Oil level should be between "Max." and "Min." for unloaded vehicle, "Min." for loaded vehicle.

REMOVAL & INSTALLATION

NOTE — *For removal and installation of components not covered in this Section, refer to Mercedes-Benz article in REAR SUSPENSION Section.*

SHOCK ABSORBER

Removal — 1) Drain leveling control hydraulic system by opening the bleed screw. From inside storage area of vehicle, remove floor covering by turning "T" lever and lifting up. Fold down rear seat back rest. Remove screws and then covering to frame crossmember. Remove cover plate from frame crossmember.

2) Disconnect pressure hose at special shock absorber. Disconnect connection fitting from shock absorber. Cap pressure hose and plug hole in shock absorber.

3) Loosen bolt of upper mount and remove with rubber bushing. Remove bolts securing bottom of shock absorber. Remove shock absorber from bottom; then remove lower rubber bushing of upper mount.

Installation — 1) To install, reverse removal procedure and note the following: Install bottom rubber bushing onto top of special shock absorber before installing into vehicle.

2) Plugged hole in shock absorber must point toward frame crossmember and mounting pin must protrude through bore in frame crossmember.

3) Make sure all bolts and fittings are tight and reservoir is full; then fill leveling valve by starting engine and moving leveling lever up to filling position. Check leveling suspension system for proper operation.

TIGHTENING SPECIFICATIONS	
Application	**Ft. Lbs. (mkg)**
Upper Mount Bolt	22 (3.0)
Lower Mount Bolt	33 (4.6)
Pressure Hose-to-Shock Absorber Fitting	15 (2.0)
Pressure Hose-to-Fitting	15 (2.0)
Spherical Mount on Shock Absorber	48 (6.6)
Fitting at Pressure Reservoir	32 (4.4)

Section 10
STEERING

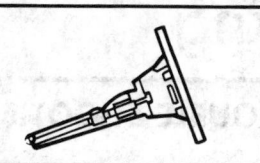

Contents

NOTE — ALSO SEE GENERAL INDEX.

Steering

MANUAL STEERING TROUBLE SHOOTING

CONDITION	POSSIBLE CAUSE	CORRECTION
▶ Hard steering	1) Incorrect tire pressure 2) Gear housing lubricant low 3) Insufficient lubrication or abnormal wear on steering linkage 4) Seized or damaged ball joints 5) Steering shaft too tight 6) Steering column incorrectly aligned	1) Inflate tires to correct pressure 2) Refill and check for leaks 3) Lubricate or replace components 4) Replace ball joints 5) Readjust 6) Realign column
▶ Drifting	1) Incorrect tire pressure 2) Loose lug nuts 3) Mismatched tires 4) Worn or loose wheel bearings 5) Brake drag 6) Faulty shock absorbers or coil springs 7) Pitman arm binding 8) Loose steering gear 9) Vehicle uneven riding height	1) Inflate tires to correct pressure 2) Tighten 3) Replace and match 4) Replace or tighten 5) Check and readjust brakes 6) Replace broken or faulty parts 7) Adjust or replace arm 8) Check for worn parts — replace and adjust 9) Adjust level
▶ Excessive steering wheel play	1) Steering wheel shaft loose or worn 2) Steering linkage loose or worn 3) Worn wheel bearings 4) Worn ball joints 5) Worm shaft bearing out of adjustment 6) Loose steering gear housing	1) Adjust shaft or replace 2) Adjust or replace 3) Replace bearings 4) Replace or adjust ball joints 5) Readjust 6) Tighten housing
▶ Steering wheel slides	1) Worm shaft or ball damaged 2) Sector shaft damaged	1) Replace components 2) Replace components
▶ Vibration or shimmy	1) Incorrect tire pressure 2) Tire out of balance 3) Worn shock absorbers or springs 4) Loose steering gear housing 5) Loose steering linkage	1) Inflate to correct pressure 2) Balance tire 3) Replace defective parts 4) Tighten 5) Adjust or replace linkage
▶ Noise	1) Incorrect tire pressure 2) Wheel bearings loose or worn 3) Hub caps or rims loose	1) Inflate tires to correct pressure 2) Repair or replace 3) Tighten or replace

POWER STEERING TROUBLE SHOOTING

CONDITION	POSSIBLE CAUSE	CORRECTION
▶ Hard Steering	1) Fluid level low 2) Control valve binding 3) Kinked or broken hoses 4) Fluid lines blocked 5) Air in system 6) Low pump pressure 7) Loose drive belt	1) Add fluid, check for leaks 2) Replace or repair control valve 3) Straighten or replace 4) Check, clean, or replace lines 5) Bleed, refill and check for leaks 6) Check pump for worn or damaged parts 7) Adjust or replace belt
▶ Noise	1) Loose drive belt 2) Low fluid 3) Faulty valves or pump wear	1) Check, tighten, or replace belt 2) Check and add fluid 3) Repair or replace
▶ Excessive steering wheel play	1) Control valve binding	1) Repair or replace valve
▶ Sticking steering wheel	1) Control valve binding	1) Repair or replace valve

AUDI

4000
5000

REMOVAL & INSTALLATION

STEERING WHEEL & HORN

Disconnect battery ground cable. Using hand pressure, pull off steering wheel center pad. Unscrew steering wheel nut and use wheel puller to remove steering wheel.

NOTE — *On 5000 models, make sure horn leads slide out of recess in steering wheel during removal of center pad.*

TURN SIGNAL, WIPER/WASHER, DIMMER

4000 — Disconnect battery ground cable. Remove steering wheel. Unscrew 3 steering column switch housing mounting screws and pull housing off column tube. Make sure electrical wires are disconnected before completely pulling switch housing off. Remove switch mounting screws and switches.

TURN SIGNAL, WIPER/WASHER HAZARD, DIMMER

5000 — Remove steering wheel. Working through hole in bottom of column shrouding, release mounting and take off shroud. Disconnect electrical wire connectors and undo switch mounting screws. Lift out switches.

STEERING COLUMN LOCK

Power Steering — Remove lower cover and switches. Remove lock washer and contact ring. With key inserted in ignition,

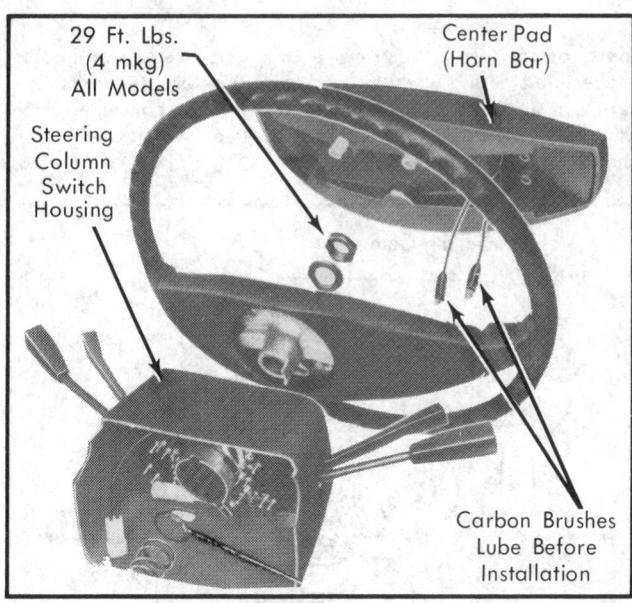

Fig. 1   Audi 5000 Steering Wheel Assembly

remove bolt and lock assembly. To install, reverse removal procedure and tighten bolt to 7 ft. lbs. (1 mkg).

All Others — Remove lower cover. Disconnect electrical wires from back of ignition switch. With key inserted in ignition, drill out shear bolts. Separate lock from column. To install, reverse removal procedure and make sure lugs on steering lock engage column tube. Tighten mounting bolts until heads shear off.

BMW

320i
528i
633CSi
733i

REMOVAL & INSTALLATION

STEERING WHEEL

Removal — Place wheels in straight-ahead position. Pry steering wheel cover off to expose wheel mounting nut. Index mark wheel and main shaft. Remove mounting nut and pull steering wheel off main shaft.

Installation — To install, reverse removal procedure and refer to reference marks made during removal.

HORN CONTROLS

Horn Button — Remove screw on back side of steering wheel spoke to free horn button.

Contact Spring — Pry off cover concealing contact spring. Replace spring if broken or if spring is unable to provide adequate contact. Make sure contact pins face inward when reinstalling existing spring or fitting new one.

Slip Ring — Disconnect electrical lead at each spoke. Remove 2 slip ring mounting screws and slide slip ring off steering wheel.

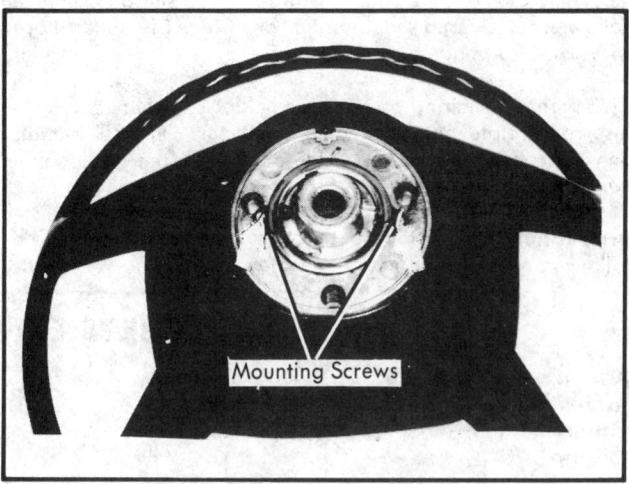

Fig. 1   Screws to Take Out for Slip Ring Removal

TURN SIGNAL & DIMMER SWITCH

Removal — Disconnect battery ground cable. Remove 3 mounting screws and pull down lower shroud. Remove steering wheel as previously outlined. Separate wiring from mounting straps on steering column. On 320i models, disconnect electrical plug under instrument panel. On other models, disconnect central fuse/relay plug. Remove 4 switch mounting screws and slide off switch with harness.

BMW (Cont.)

Installation — To install, reverse removal procedure and note: Make sure steering wheel is lined up with reference marks. Ensure turn signal assembly is centered. Finger on cancelling cam must face toward center. Distance between switch and finger should be about .118" (3 mm).

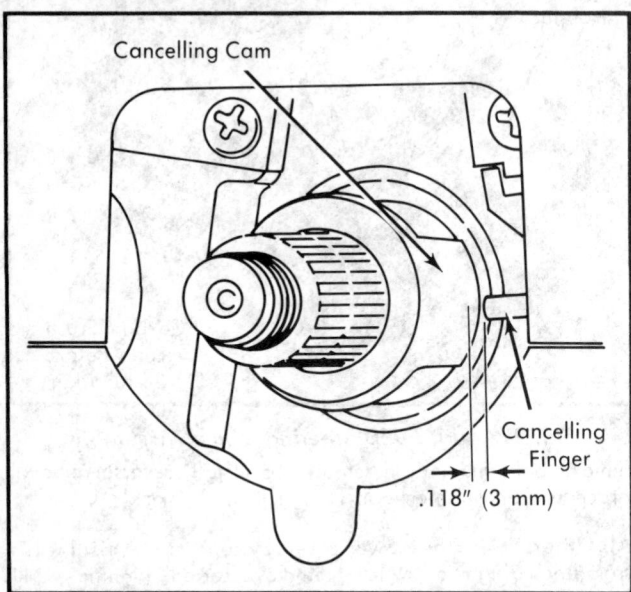

Fig. 2   Cancelling Cam and Finger with Clearance Shown

IGNITION SWITCH

Removal — 1) Disconnect battery ground cable. Remove mounting screws and pull off lower plastic shroud. Remove hollow set screw and slide out ignition switch. Disconnect horn wires on 320i models only.

2) Disconnect steering column wire holders. Disconnect central fuse/relay plate plug and plug connector. On 320i models only, disconnect central plug. On all models, remove ignition switch.

Installation — To install, reverse removal procedure and note following: Make sure to turn ignition key all the way back

before inserting. Set ignition switch at "O" position before installing. On 320i models only, marks on ignition switch must oppose each other.

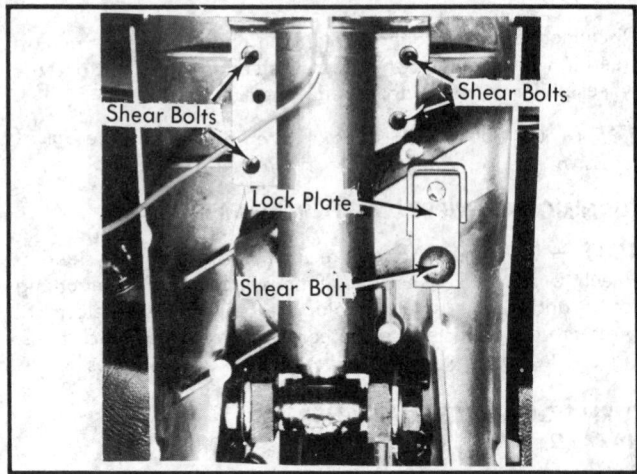

Fig. 3   Location of Shear Bolts. View Looking Up From Under Steering Column. All Models Except 320i

STEERING LOCK

Removal (Exc. 320i) — 1) Disconnect battery ground. Remove steering wheel. Remove 3 screws holding lower steering column shroud. Disconnect and remove turn signal and wiper/washer switch plate.

2) Remove shear bolts from switch plate with chisel. Remove set screw on outside of steering column tube. Pull out ignition switch. Remove steering lock plate shear bolt and pull out steering lock.

Installation — To install, reverse removal procedure.

Removal (320i) — Disconnect electrical wires from under instrument panel. Remove shroud. Remove shear bolt from lock plate and pull out steering lock.

Installation — To install, reverse removal procedure.

CHRYSLER CORP. IMPORTS

Arrow
Arrow Pickup
Challenger
Champ

Colt
D50 Pickup
Sapporo

REMOVAL & INSTALLATION

STEERING WHEEL & COMBINATION SWITCH

Removal — 1) Disconnect battery ground cable. Remove horn pad. Mark main shaft and steering wheel for reassembly reference. Remove steering wheel nut. Remove steering wheel with suitable puller (DT1001A).

NOTE — *If equipped with tilt steering, handle must be in lowest position before removing steering wheel.*

2) Remove column cover. Disconnect electrical connections at base of steering column. Remove retaining screws and pull combination switch out.

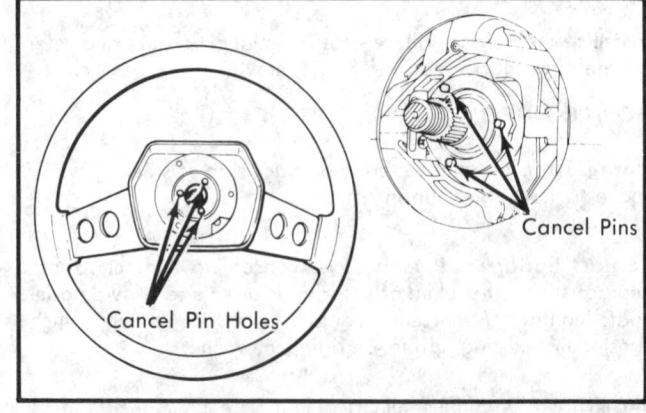

Fig. 1   Installation of Steering Wheel on Arrow, Challenger, Colt Station Wagon and Sapporo Models

CHRYSLER CORP. IMPORTS (Cont.)

Installation – **1)** Install combination switch and retaining screws. Connect electrical connections at base of column and route harness along center of tube.

2) To install steering wheel, place front wheels in straight-ahead position. On Arrow, Challenger, Colt Station Wagon and Sapporo models, align cancel pins of column switch with holes in bottom of steering wheel. On all models, refit steering wheel with index marks aligned. Tighten nut and install horn pad. Connect battery ground cable.

STEERING LOCK

Removal – With steering wheel removed, disconnect negative battery cable. Remove column levers and switches. Cut a slot in mounting head screws and bracket with a hack saw. Remove screws and remove steering wheel lock.

Installation – To install reverse removal procedure and install new bracket and screws.

COURIER

Courier

REMOVAL & INSTALLATION

STEERING WHEEL & COMBINATION SWITCH

Removal – **1)** Disconnect battery ground cable. Remove steering wheel nut cover. Index mark main shaft and steering wheel. Disconnect electrical leads. Pull steering wheel from shaft.

2) Remove plastic hazard light indicator and steering column shroud. Disconnect electrical wires at base of steering column. Remove headlight switch knob from shaft.

3) Remove snap ring retaining switch and force turn indicator cancelling cam off shaft. Take out single bolt, near bottom of switch, and pull out complete switch assembly.

Installation – **1)** Fit switch assembly on steering column then, refit one retaining bolt. Place turn indicator cancelling cam into position and install snap ring. Reconnect electrical plug at column base.

2) Insert and tighten headlight knob switch. Install column shroud and plastic hazard light indicator. Refit steering wheel with index marks aligned. Connect battery ground cable.

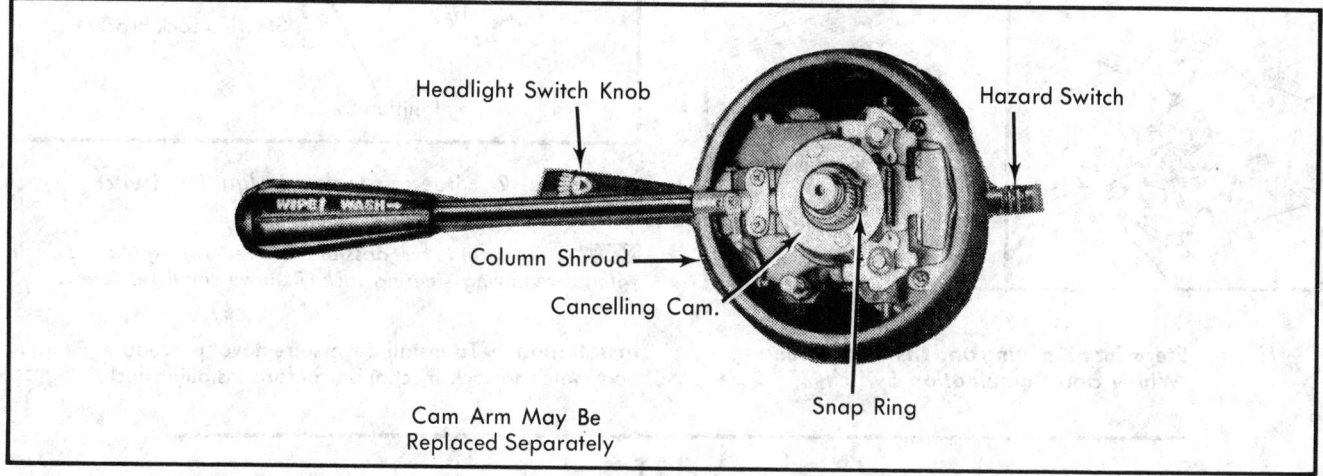

Headlight Switch Knob — Hazard Switch — Column Shroud — Cancelling Cam. — Snap Ring — Cam Arm May Be Replaced Separately

Fig. 1 Top View of Steering Column with Steering Wheel Removed to Expose Combination Switch

DATSUN

200SX	510
210	810
280ZX	Pickup
310	

REMOVAL & INSTALLATION

STEERING WHEEL & HORN PAD

Removal – **1)** Disconnect battery ground cable. Use the following procedures to remove horn pad for particular model:

- On 200SX and Pickup models, pull horn pad off steering wheel.

- On 210 models, remove 3-spoke horn pad by pulling off. Remove 2-spoke horn pad by removing bolts on back side of steering wheel, then pull off pad. Remove horn wire.
- On 280ZX and 310 models, pull horn pad off.
- On 510 and 810 models, remove bolts on back side of steering wheel and pull off pad. Remove horn wire.

2) Remove retaining nut. Using puller (27180001), remove steering wheel. Do not hammer on steering wheel. Pounding may cause damage to collapsible steering column.

Installation – On all models, reverse removal procedure. Grease any sliding components. Match index marks made during removal. Check operation.

DATSUN (Cont.)

COMBINATION SWITCH

Removal — Disconnect battery ground cable. Remove steering wheel. Remove steering column shrouds. Disconnect switch connector. Remove screws holding switch to column and lift switch out of shaft.

NOTE — *On Pickup models switch connector is near lower edge of instrument panel.*

Installation — To install, reverse removal procedure. Make sure switch tab locates in hole in column.

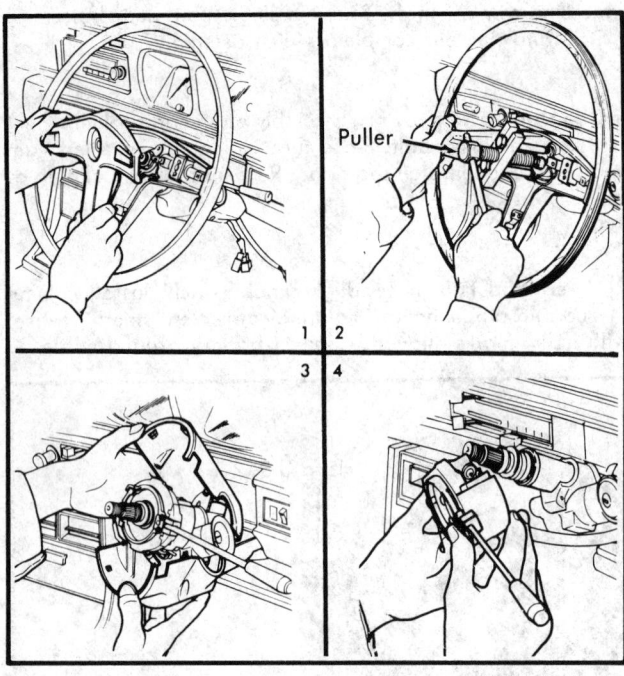

Fig. 1 Steps for Removing and Installing Steering Wheel and Combination Switch

HAZARD WARNING SWITCH

Removal — Disconnect battery ground cable. Remove mounting screws and steering column shrouds. Disconnect lead wires at connector. Remove retaining screws and take switch out of shroud.

Installation — To install, reverse removal procedure.

STEERING LOCK & IGNITION SWITCH

Removal — Disconnect battery ground cable. Remove steering column shroud. Drill out shear bolts. Separate steering lock from column shaft. If ignition switch is to be removed, separate electrical connector, then remove small set screw holding switch body. Remove switch.

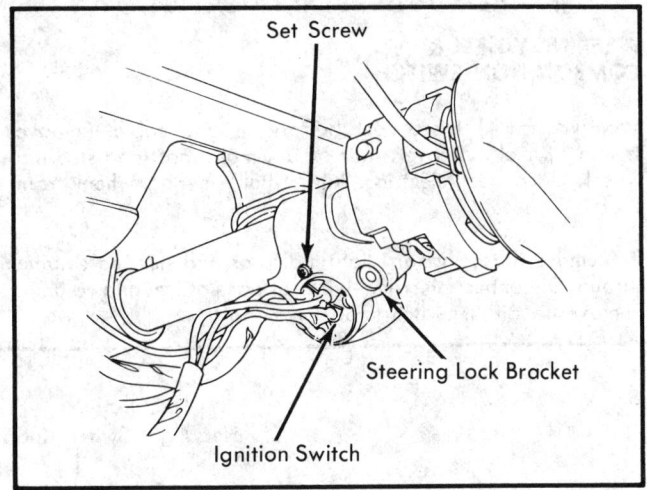

Fig. 2 Steering Lock and Ignition Switch

NOTE — *It should be possible to remove ignition switch without removing steering lock. Remove small set screw.*

Installation — To install, reverse removal procedure. Fit ignition switch to lock mechanism before installing lock.

FIAT

Brava
Spider 2000
Strada
X1/9

REMOVAL & INSTALLATION

HORN COVER & STEERING WHEEL

Removal (Brava & Strada) — Disconnect battery ground cable. Remove steering column shrouds. From behind steering wheel, pry 2 plastic locking tabs inward to remove horn button. Remove nut and washer and remove steering wheel.

Installation — To install, reverse removal procedure.

Removal (All Others) — Disconnect battery ground cable. Remove steering column cover (if equipped) and remove horn

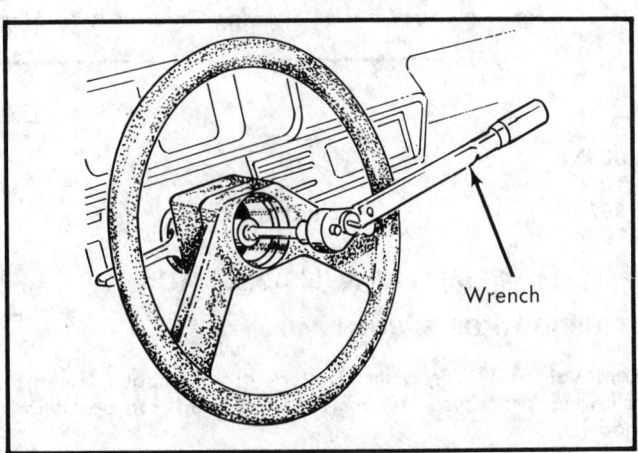

Fig. 1 Steering Wheel Removal (Brava & Strada Shown)

FIAT (Cont.)

cover. Disconnect horn wires (if required). Remove retaining nut and washer and remove steering wheel. On Spider 2000, remove 6 retaining screws and remove wheel.

Installation — To install, reverse removal procedure.

COMBINATION SWITCH

Removal — Remove steering wheel and column shrouding. Disconnect battery ground cable. Disconnect electrical connection. Remove retaining nut (screws) and remove switch from shaft.

Installation — To install, reverse removal procedure.

FIESTA

Fiesta
STEERING WHEEL

Disconnect battery ground. Pry out insert in center of steering wheel. Remove retaining nut. Pull off steering wheel along with turn signal indicator cam.

IGNITION SWITCH CYLINDER

Disconnect battery cables. Remove upper and lower column shrouds. Be careful when sliding lower shroud past choke control. Place key in accessories (I) position. Use a small screwdriver inserted through hole on under side of ignition housing to push up retaining spring clip. While clip is free pull out cylinder with key.

IGNITION SWITCH

Disconnect battery cables. Remove upper and lower steering column shrouds. Remove ignition switch retaining screws located on back side of switch near electrical plug. Disconnect wires. Remove switch from lock assembly.

IGNITION/STEERING COLUMN LOCK

Disconnect battery cables. Remove upper and lower steering column shrouds. Disconnect electrical wires. Drill out steering column/ignition lock shear bolts and remove lock mechanism.

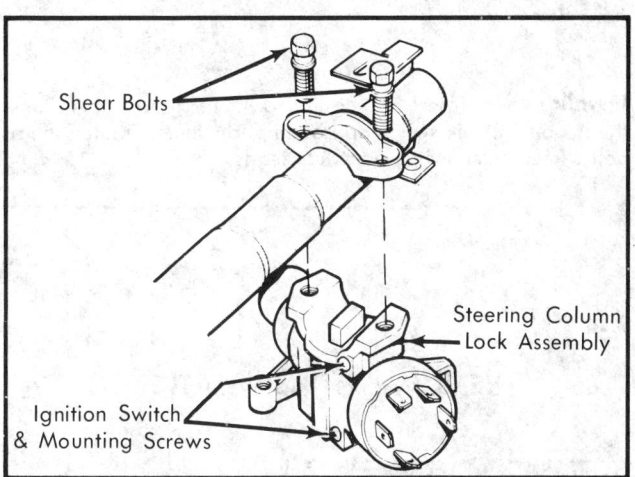

Fig. 1 Steering Column Lock Assembly and Ignition Switch

HONDA

Accord
Civic
Prelude

REMOVAL & INSTALLATION

HORN PAD & STEERING WHEEL

Removal — 1) Disconnect battery ground cable. Remove steering wheel horn pad. With wheels in straight ahead position, mark position of steering wheel to shaft. Remove retaining nut.
2) Remove steering wheel by using suitable puller or by hitting backside of wheel with hand. Steering wheel components can be disassembled and replaced if necessary.

CAUTION — *Do not apply heavy hitting force or shear pins within steering column may be damaged.*

Installation — To install, reverse removal procedure and ensure wheels are straight ahead and marks made at removal are aligned.

COMBINATION SWITCH

Removal — Remove steering pad. Remove column shrouding. Disconnect electrical connectors and remove steering wheel. Remove mounting screws and lift out combination switch. Washer/wiper switch can be separated from turn signal switch. Do not drop or lose turn signal cancel cam key when removing combination switch.

Installation — To install, reverse removal procedure and note: Insert lug on turn signal switch assembly into recess in steering column. Turn signal cancel key lugs must fit into recess in steering wheel. Horn switch spring terminal must touch contact ring.

HONDA (Cont.)

HAZARD SWITCH

Switch is located in the top column shrouding. Remove top shrouding, disconnect electrical wires and remove switch from mounted position.

NOTE — *Accord models also have an indicator light switch located in the upper column shrouding. The switch, when depressed, will allow all indicator lights to function. Procedures for Hazard switch apply.*

STEERING LOCK & IGNITION SWITCH

Removal — Remove steering column upper and lower shrouding. Disconnect ignition switch electrical wiring at lower end of steering column. Center punch shear bolts. Drill out shear head bolts and extract from lock bracket. Remove ignition switch.

Installation — Insert new ignition switch. Hand tighten new shear bolts. Check switch operation at this time. Tighten shear bolts. Reconnect switch electrical leads.

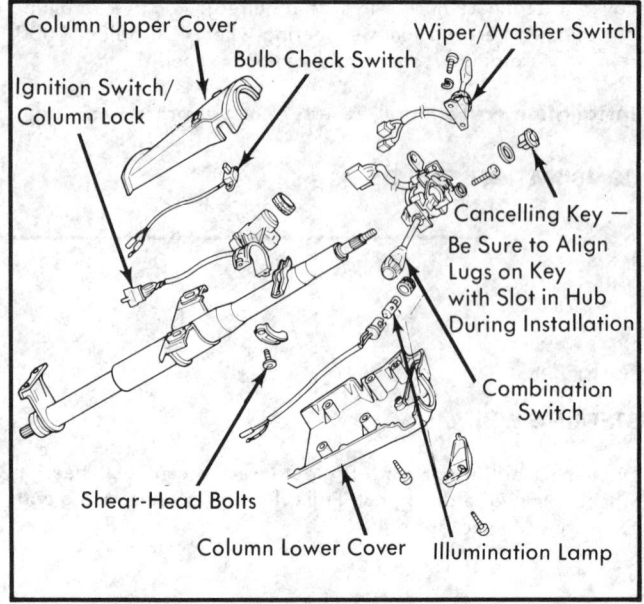

Fig. 1   Disassembled View of Upper Column Components — Accord Shown; Others Similar

---

JAGUAR

XJ6

REMOVAL & INSTALLATION

HORN PAD & STEERING WHEEL

Removal — 1) Set front wheels in straight-ahead position. Mark position on steering wheel and column. Remove 3 screws securing lower switch cover. Detach cover.

2) Working from below, remove clamp bolt securing split collet adapter to steering column. *See Fig. 1.* Loosen lock nut on set screw and loosen screw 2 turns. Remove steering wheel, complete with hand lock nut, impact rubber bumper, collet adapter and shaft.

Disassembly — 1) Remove 2 self-tapping screws from lower face of steering wheel boss and lift off padded horn contact. Unscrew nylon nut from top of steering wheel shaft and carefully remove it, taking out horn contact tube also.

2) Remove self-locking nut and plain washer which retain steering wheel. Carefully pull steering wheel from shaft, collecting both halves of split cone.

Reassembly — To reassemble, reverse disassembly procedure.

Installation — To install, reverse removal procedure and note the following: Be sure that front wheels are always kept in a straight-ahead position. When tightening collet clamp, tighten grub screw finger-tight, snug down its lock nut and torque clamp bolt to 10-12 ft. lbs. (1.4-1.6 mkg).

STEERING LOCK

Removal — Take off upper column shrouding. Using a center punch, make several dimples in shear bolt and rotate bolt out.

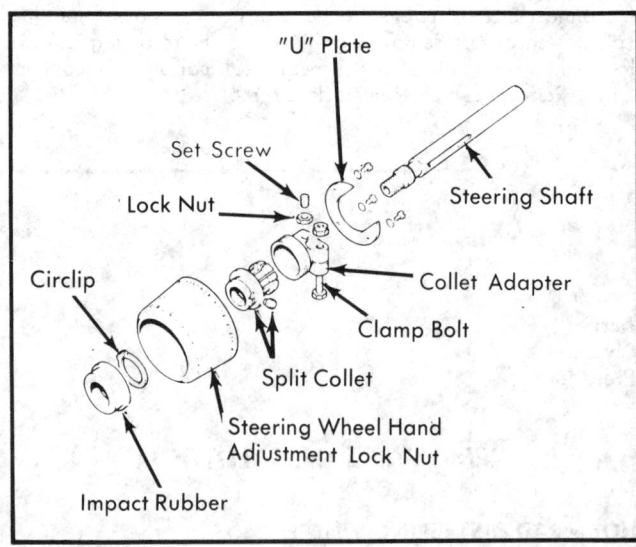

Fig. 1   Components Located Behind Steering Wheel

Installation — To install, reverse removal procedure.

IGNITION SWITCH

Disconnect battery ground cable. Separate column shrouding from switch side. Disengage retaining ring holding ignition

JAGUAR (Cont.)

switch in housing. Disconnect ignition switch wiring at multi-pin connector. Remove switch and harness. To install, reverse removal procedure.

COMBINATION SWITCH

Removal — 1) Disconnect battery ground cable. Take off steering column lower shroud. Remove steering wheel as previously outlined. Remove steering column upper shroud and cover from below instrument panel.

2) Loosen pinch bolt and pull combination switch assembly from steering column. Disconnect electrical wiring. Hazard flasher can now be separated by disconnecting wires, depressing tangs and pushing switch through mounting plate.

Installation — To install, reverse removal procedure.

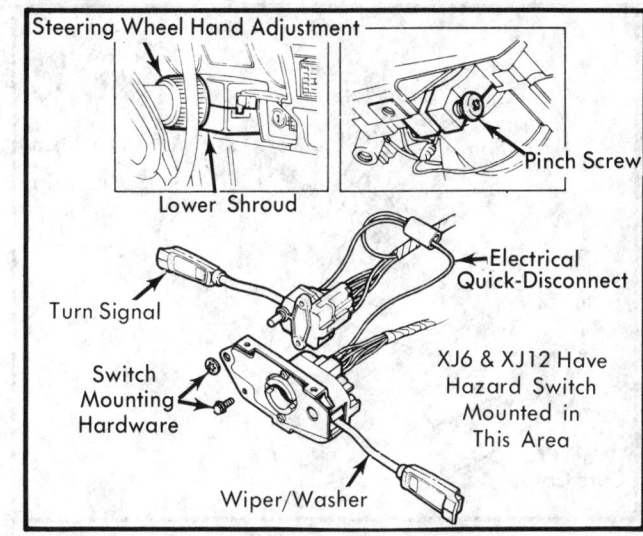

Fig. 2   Exploded View of Combination Switch

LUV

Pickup

CAUTION — *Steering shaft is an energy-absorbing unit. During any service operation, avoid jarring or leaning on any portion of column.*

REMOVAL & INSTALLATION

HORN BUTTON & STEERING WHEEL

Removal — 1) Disconnect battery. Remove horn pad and spring by pushing in on pad and turning counterclockwise.

2) Remove horn contact ring and wire. Unscrew steering wheel retaining nut. Mark position of steering wheel on column shaft. Remove steering column cowling (4 screws).

3) Using appropriate puller (J-24292 for standard wheel or J-2927/J-2927-10 for sport type wheel), remove steering wheel.

Installation — To install, reverse removal procedure.

COMBINATION SWITCH

Switch consists of turn signal and headlight dimmer assembly. Disconnect battery ground and remove steering column shrouds. Disconnect wires to switch harness. Remove switch by separating from clamp on mast jacket (2 screws). To install, reverse removal procedure.

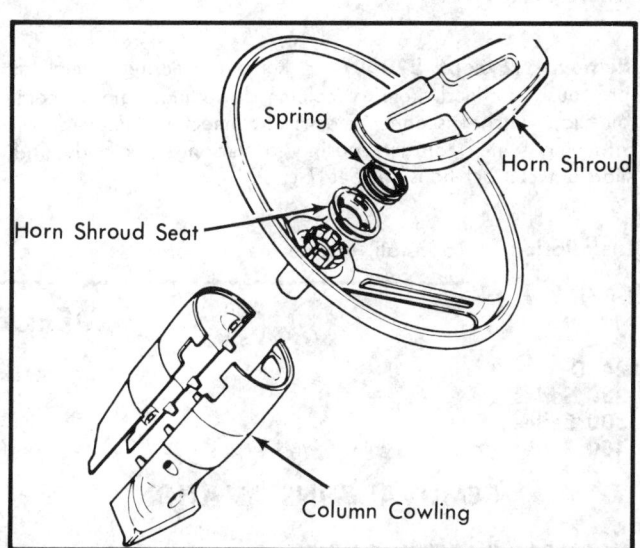

Fig. 1   LUV Steering Wheel Assembly

HAZARD WARNING SWITCH

Disconnect battery ground cable. Remove steering column shroud screws. Hazard warning switch is retained on upper half of shroud by 2 screws. Disconnect switch wiring harness at connector, remove mounting screws and withdraw switch. To install, reverse removal procedure.

MAZDA

GLC	B2000
626	RX7

REMOVAL & INSTALLATION

STEERING WHEEL & COMBINATION SWITCH

Removal — 1) Disconnect battery ground cable. Pull off horn cap. Place front wheels in straight-ahead position. Index mark column shaft and steering wheel.

2) Remove steering column shrouding. Disconnect electrical connectors. To disconnect electrical connections on RX7, remove air duct at base of steering column. Remove steering shaft stop ring, cancel cam and spring. Remove retaining screws and combination switch assembly.

NOTE — *Wiper switch can be removed with combination switch or separated from it.*

Installation — To install, reverse removal procedure.

MAZDA (Cont.)

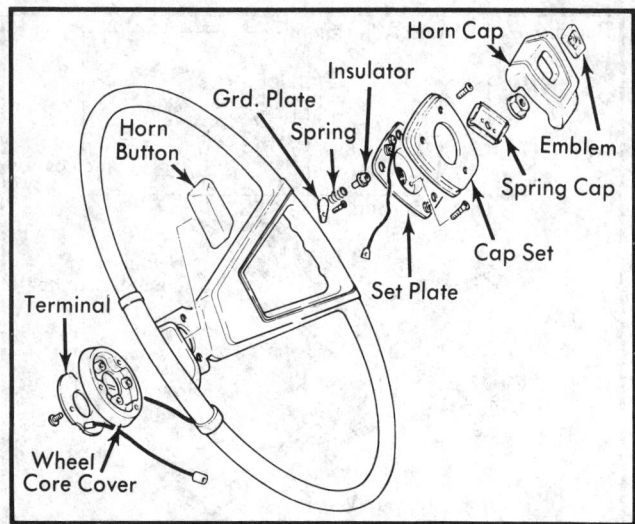

Fig. 1 *Typical Mazda Steering Wheel Assembly*

IGNITION SWITCH

Removal (Except B2000) — Remove steering wheel as previously outlined. Remove column shrouding. Remove combination switch. Disconnect electrical connector. Remove screw attaching switch contact housing to steering lock body and slide out contact housing. See *Fig. 2*.

Installation — To install, reverse removal procedure.

STEERING LOCK

Removal (Except B2000) — Remove steering wheel, column shrouding and combination switch. Put a groove in bolt attaching steering lock body to column shaft and remove bolt. Remove steering lock.

Installation — To install, reverse removal procedure and tighten new shear bolts until heads break.

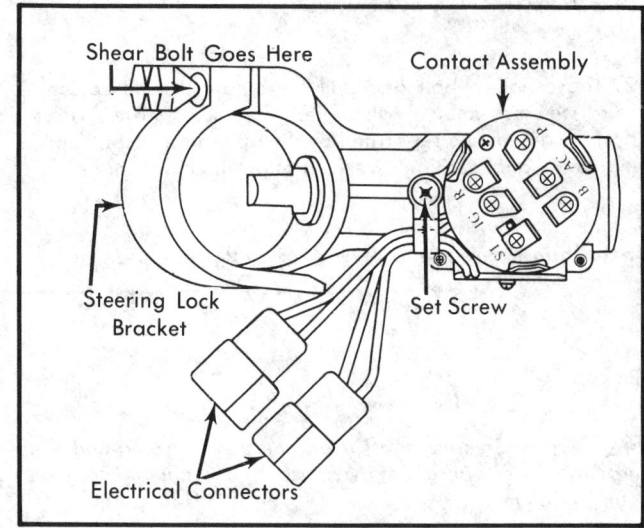

Fig. 2 *Exploded View of Ignition Switch Assembly (Except B2000)*

MERCEDES-BENZ

**240D
280 Series
300 Series
450 Series**

REMOVAL & INSTALLATION

HORN PAD & STEERING WHEEL

Polyurethane Wheel (Soft Rubber) — Place alignment marks on wheel and shaft. Grip horn pad near one corner and pull straight up until free. Pull up other corner. Remove pad from steering wheel. Unscrew retaining nut, remove spring washer and pull steering wheel from shaft. To install, reverse removal procedure and align marks made during removal. Spokes on wheel must be horizontal.

Rigid Plastic Wheel (Bealit) — 1) Remove vehicle emblem from horn pad. Unscrew steering wheel retaining nut and pull wheel from shaft with pad still attached. Unscrew hex nuts on backside of wheel and separate steering wheel from pad.

NOTE — *Horn wire is still attached to steering wheel, so care must be taken to avoid breaking it.*

2) Detach horn wire from contact ring and remove steering wheel. Remove countersunk screws from steering wheel hub

and centering pad of contact ring. Remove horn ring from steering wheel. Remove locking ring from hub of pad, then remove slip ring.

3) To install, reverse removal procedure and ensure wheels are kept in straight-ahead position and that steering wheel spokes are horizontal.

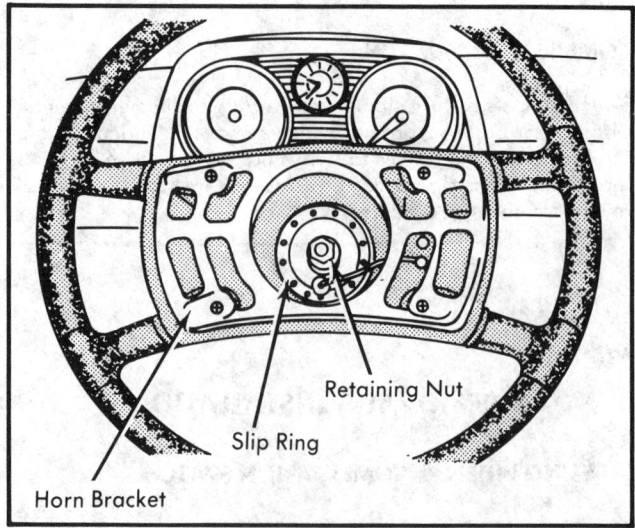

Fig. 1 *Mercedes-Benz Steering Wheel with Cover Removed*

MG

MGB

REMOVAL & INSTALLATION

STEERING WHEEL

Removal — Disconnect battery ground cable. Remove steering wheel pad. Remove mounting nut. Mark position of steering wheel and column. Use puller (18G 1317) to remove steering wheel from shaft.

Installation — Reverse removal procedure and note: Line up index marks. Make sure cancel cam has ridge facing indicator switch. Make sure steering wheel projections (tongues) slip into slots on cancel cam.

COMBINATION SWITCH

Removal — Disconnect battery ground cable. Remove steering wheel. Remove steering column shroud screws and remove shrouding. Disconnect electrical connections at base of column and remove retaining tape. Remove wiper switch retaining screws and loosen switch clamp screw. Remove combination switch from shaft.

Installation — To install, reverse removal procedure and note: Ensure locating tang of switch aligns with outer slot of steering column.

STEERING COLUMN LOCK & IGNITION SWITCH

Removal — Remove necessary shrouding to gain access to lock. Make sure steering lock is disengaged. Disconnect ignition switch multi-pin connector. Drill out and remove shear bolts from lock bracket. Remove steering screw holding switch in lock and remove switch.

Installation — Center locking mechanism on column. Hand tighten new shear bolts. Reconnect multi-pin connector. Check switch and lock operation. Tighten shear bolts until heads break.

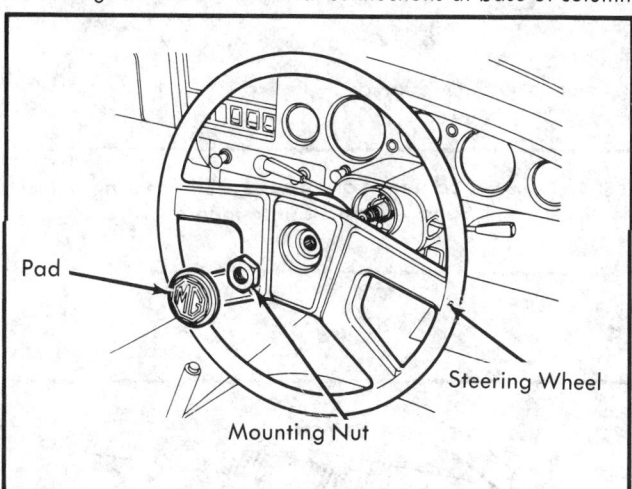

Fig. 1   Exploded View of Steering Wheel Assembly

(labels: Pad, Mounting Nut, Steering Wheel)

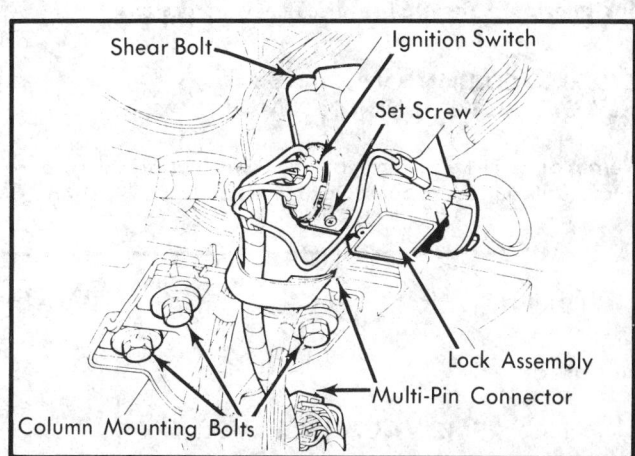

Fig. 2   Bottom View of Steering Column Showing Ignition Switch and Column Lock

(labels: Shear Bolt, Ignition Switch, Set Screw, Lock Assembly, Multi-Pin Connector, Column Mounting Bolts)

PORSCHE

911SC
924
928

REMOVAL & INSTALLATION

HORN PAD & STEERING WHEEL

NOTE — *On models equipped with a collapsable "can" behind the steering wheel, care must be taken in all service procedures. Do not apply excessive or striking forces to the steering wheel or steering column.*

Removal (911SC) — 1) Align front wheels in straight ahead position. Disconnect battery cable.

2) Grasp horn pad and rotate counterclockwise while pushing in. When horn pad is free, lift from steering wheel and disconnect horn contact finger.

3) Loosen steering wheel retaining nut. Mark position of steering wheel to steering shaft. Attach a suitable puller and remove the steering wheel.

Installation — To install steering wheel, reverse removal procedure and note the following: Lightly lubricate horn contact finger with electrical contact grease before reinstalling.

Removal & Installation (924) — Disconnect battery. Carefully pry off horn pad. Unscrew wheel retaining nut. Pull wheel upward and off shaft. To refit wheel, reverse removal procedure.

Removal (928) — Disconnect battery ground. Place wheels in straight-ahead position. Take off horn pad. Disconnect horn wires. Index mark steering wheel and column shaft. Unscrew mounting nut. Remove steering wheel.

Installation — Align index marks and replace steering wheel so spokes are horizontal. Install mounting nut. Fit horn wires into place in pad. Press horn pad onto retaining pins.

COMBINATION SWITCH

Removal (924) — 1) Disconnect battery ground. Using hand pressure, lift up steering pad. Remove steering wheel mounting nut. Pull steering wheel off shaft.

PORSCHE (Cont.)

2) Remove shroud from around switch housing. Pull up on switch plate and disconnect electrical wires. Remove entire switch assembly then, separate wiper/washer switch from turn signal switch by taking out screw that mounts them together.

Installation — Refit switches together with screw. Slide switch assemblies back into place refitting spacer at same time. Make sure spacer is driven in until there is a distance of 1.6" (41 mm) from face (top edge) of spacer to top edge of shaft. This distance will ensure there is .08-.15" (2-4 mm) between steering wheel and steering column switches. Reverse removal procedure to install remaining components.

Removal (928) — Disconnect battery ground. Remove steering wheel. Remove cover from under steering column switch. Remove steering column switch mounting screw. Remove instrument cover mounting screws. Maneuver instrument cover until electrical wires can be disconnected. Remove column switch.

Installation — To install, reverse removal procedure.

STEERING COLUMN LOCK, KEY CYLINDER & IGNITION SWITCH

Removal — **1)** Remove combination switch as previously outlined. Drill out shear bolts. Disconnect ignition switch wiring.

Disengage snap ring and slide out switch housing with bearing.

2) Using a pointed tool (scribe), push cylinder lock retainer in to release cylinder. With key inserted and retainer depressed, pull cylinder from housing. Remove ignition switch set screw and remove ignition switch back from housing.

Installation — To install, reverse removal procedure.

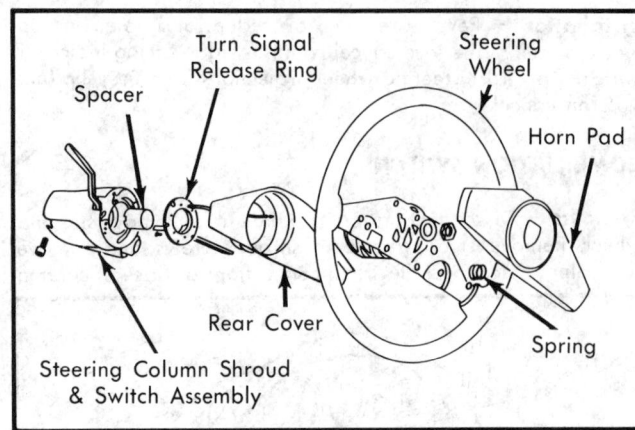

Fig. 1   Exploded View of Porsche 924 Steering Wheel and Related Components

RENAULT

Le Car

REMOVAL & INSTALLATION

HORN PAD & STEERING WHEEL

Disconnect battery ground cable. Remove horn pad. Unscrew steering wheel retaining nut. Using a puller (Dir. 21A or equivalent), remove steering wheel from shaft. To install, reverse removal procedure and note: Ensure wheels are in straight-ahead position and steering wheel spokes are in horizontal position.

TURN SIGNAL & LIGHTING SWITCH

NOTE — *For the following procedure, steering wheel does not have to be removed.*

Removal — Disconnect battery and remove horn pad. Remove steering wheel nut and use puller (Dir. 21A) to remove steering wheel.

Installation — To install, reverse removal procedure, ensuring wheels are straight ahead when wheel is installed.

IGNITION SWITCH/COLUMN LOCK

Removal — **1)** Disconnect battery ground cable. Remove shroud from around switch assembly. Disconnect electrical con-

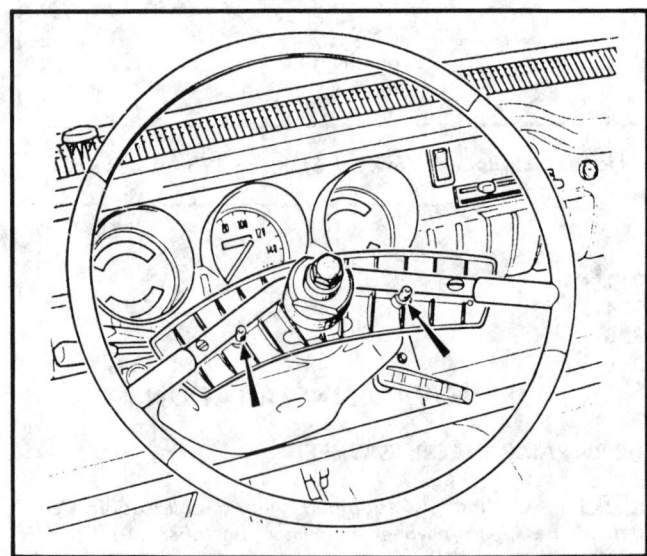

Fig. 1   Top View of Steering Wheel with Detail of Horn Pad Mounting Pins

nections. Turn ignition switch to "G" (Garage) and remove switch.

2) Remove set screw and press in retaining catch with a small punch. Push switch body from rear to release it. *See Fig. 3.*

Installation — To install, reverse removal procedure.

RENAULT (Cont.)

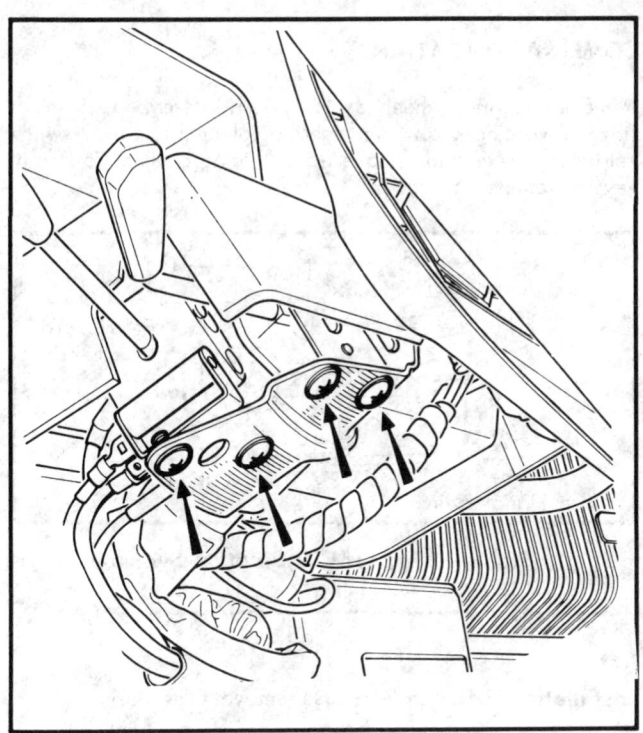

Fig. 2 Location of Switch Assembly Retaining Screws

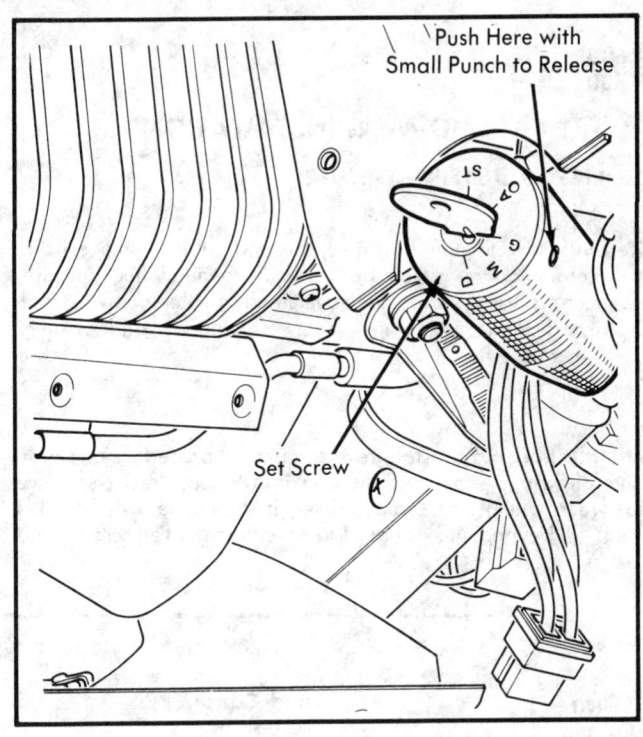

Fig. 3 Ignition Switch Removal

SAAB

99
900

REMOVAL & INSTALLATION

HORN CONTROL & STEERING WHEEL

Removal — Disconnect battery ground cable. Remove bottom cover retaining screws and cover. On standard steering wheel, remove retaining screws from behind steering wheel, then remove pad and horn contact. On 3-spoke wheel, lift pad from spokes, then reach under and disconnect horn leads while supporting pad.

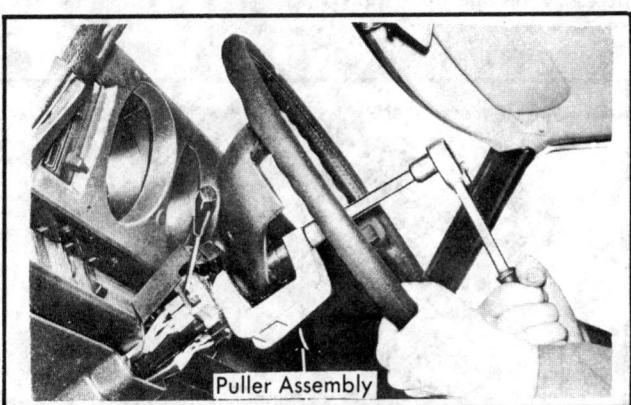

Fig. 1 Using a Universal Puller Tool to Remove Steering Assembly

2) Mark position of steering wheel to shaft and remove retaining nut and washer. Remove wheel from shaft with suitable wheel puller.

Installation — To install, reverse removal procedure.

COMBINATION SWITCH

Removal — Disconnect battery ground cable. Remove steering wheel shrouding and lower instrument panel shroud. Disconnect electrical connections at base of column. Remove retaining screws and direction/wiper switch assembly.

Installation — To install, reverse removal procedure and note: Directional signal must be properly aligned on column.

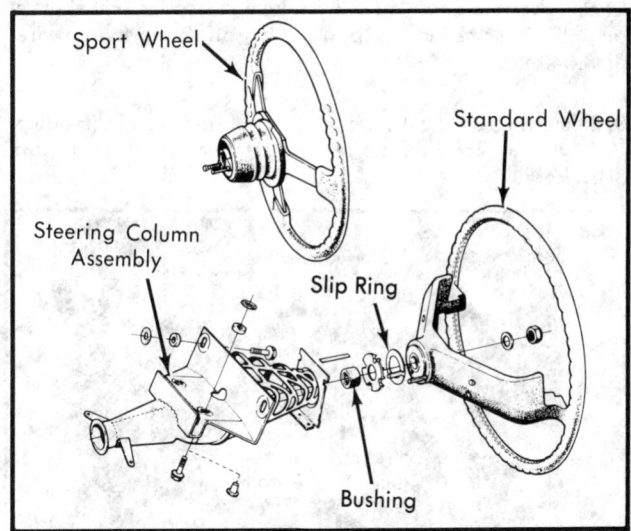

Fig. 2 Exploded View of Steering Wheel Assembly

SUBARU

1600
1800

REMOVAL & INSTALLATION

HORN PAD & STEERING WHEEL

Removal — Disconnect battery ground cable. Remove horn pad retaining screws from back side of steering wheel and disconnect electrical wiring. Remove steering column covers and horn pad. Remove steering wheel retaining nut and washer. Pull steering wheel from shaft.

Installation — To install, reverse removal procedure and note the following: After steering wheel is installed, check clearance between wheel and column cover; it should be .04-.12" (1-3 mm). If beyond this range, loosen column cover screws and adjust.

COMBINATION SWITCH

Remove steering wheel as previously described. Remove hazard warning knob from steering column. Remove 2 switch retaining screws and remove from steering column. To install, reverse removal procedure.

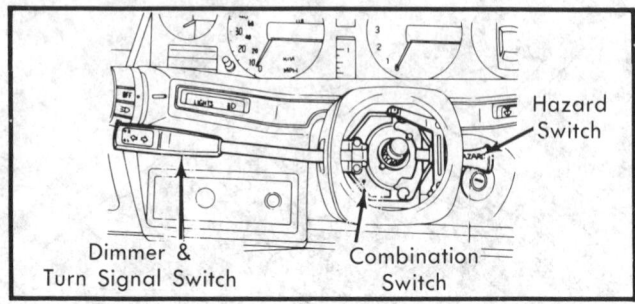

Fig. 1 View of Combination Switch

TOYOTA

Celica	Land Cruiser
Corolla	Pickup
Corona	Supra
Cressida	Tercel

REMOVAL & INSTALLATION

STEERING WHEEL

NOTE — Steering wheel removal procedure is a general one. It should be noted that all steps may not apply to every model.

CAUTION — Some models are equipped with collapsible type steering, DO NOT apply excessive pressure or impact to mainshaft.

Removal — 1) Disconnect battery ground. From lower portion of steering column, disconnect any electrical wiring for indicator lights, horn or dimmer switch.

2) Remove retaining screws from behind steering wheel (if required). On some models, pad will pry off. Remove horn wires (if required).

3) Remove steering wheel mounting nut and washer (if equipped), then using a puller, remove steering wheel from shaft. See Fig. 1.

Installation — To install, reverse removal procedure.

COMBINATION SWITCH

Removal — After removing steering wheel as previously outlined, combination switch may be removed by detaching steering column covers, removing retaining screws from face of switch assembly and unplugging necessary electrical connectors.

Installation — To install, reverse removal procedure and make sure all electrical connections are properly made. Check cancelling operation of turn signal switch.

COLUMN LOCK & IGNITION SWITCH

Removal — 1) Disconnect battery ground. Remove steering wheel as previously outlined.

NOTE — Steering wheel removal is optional if only the ignition switch portion is being removed. Removal of wheel makes access to this operation easier.

Fig. 1 Using Puller to Remove Steering Wheel

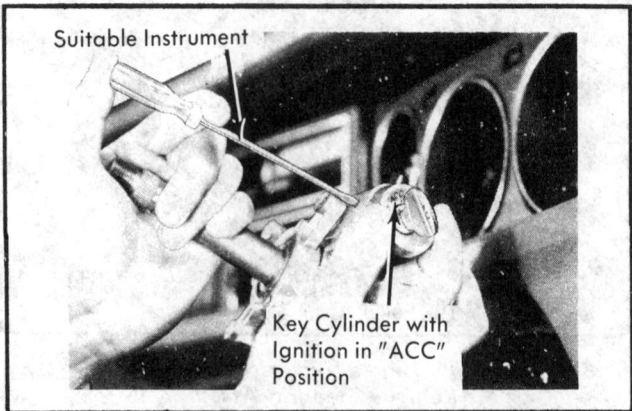

Fig. 2 Disengaging Key Cylinder from Position on Mainshaft

TOYOTA (Cont.)

2) Remove screws mounting upper and lower column covers and disconnect any electrical couplings not detached during steering wheel removal.

NOTE — *On some models, access to ignition switch for its removal is gained by removing lower cover only. It is easier to perform this operation, however, by removing both cover halves.*

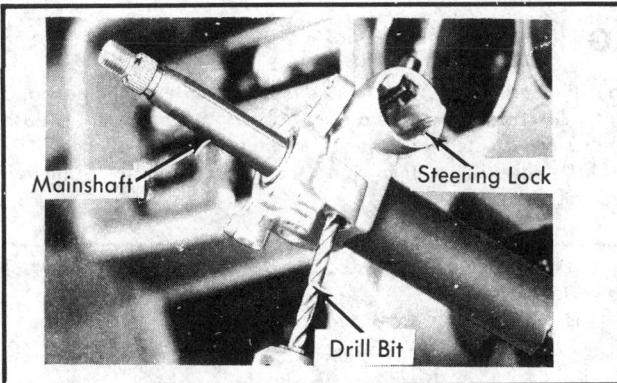

Mainshaft
Steering Lock
Drill Bit

Fig. 3 Drilling Out Shear Head Bolt to Remove Steering Lock from Shaft

3) Remove turn signal switch assembly (only if column lock assembly is being removed). Remove mainshaft bearing retainer and snap ring (if required). Insert key and turn ignition to "ACC" position. Using a small pointed tool to press down stop pin on side of cylinder, free mechanism and pull cylinder from housing. See Fig. 2.

4) On Celica and Supra models, drill out shear bolts holding lock mechanism to steering column. On all other models, lock is part of upper column bearing assembly. Remove bolts mounting upper bearing assembly and slide off column.

Installation — 1) To install column lock and switch assembly, reverse removal procedure. Tighten lock housing shear-head bolts (new) until the heads shear off.

2) Fit key cylinder so ignition switch and cylinder will be aligned in "ACC" position. Insert into housing and check for proper locking operation and key movement.

3) Replace all other components (combination switch assembly, bearing retainer, steering wheel) as removed. Check for proper turn signal switch cancelling operation and smoothness of steering wheel movement.

TRIUMPH

Spitfire
TR7
TR8

REMOVAL & INSTALLATION

STEERING WHEEL

Disconnect battery ground cable. Place wheels in straight-ahead position. Remove steering wheel pad and retaining nut. Mark position of steering wheel and shaft. Using a puller, remove steering wheel. To install, reverse removal procedure.

COMBINATION SWITCH

Removal — 1) Disconnect battery. Unscrew retaining screws for column cover halves and remove covers. Remove steering wheel as previously described.

2) Note location of all wiring harnesses. Remove wire harness clip securing switch harnesses. Disconnect 2 harness plugs. Loosen switch clamp screw and remove switch assembly.

3) Individual switches may be replaced at this time, but note that the 2 center cross-head screws are not to be removed. Switches are separated by drilling out 2 retaining rivets and removing 1 cross-head screw (right side of switch face).

Installation — To install, reverse removal procedure and note: Switch assembly must engage outer column assembly. Turn signal cancel collar must align in steering wheel.

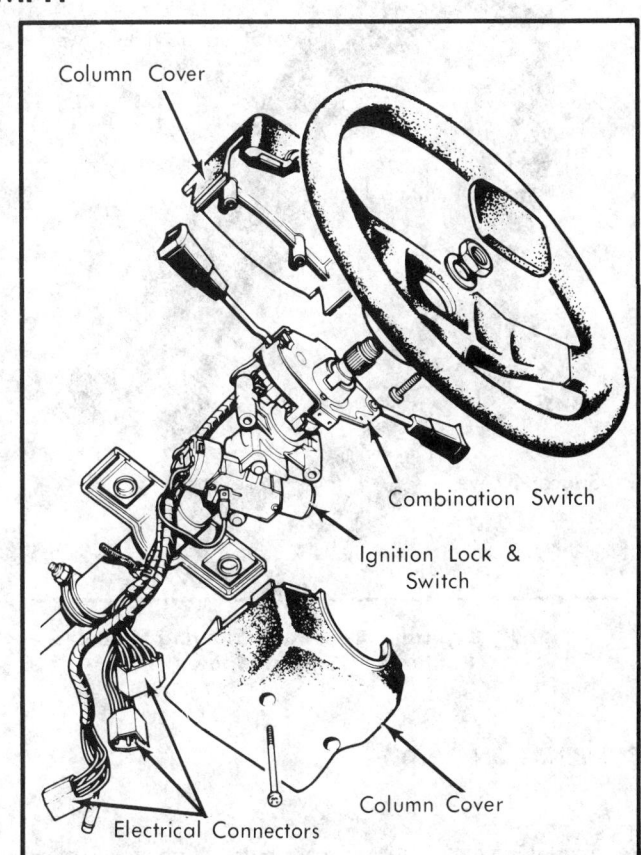

Column Cover
Combination Switch
Ignition Lock & Switch
Column Cover
Electrical Connectors

Fig. 1 TR7 and TR8 Steering Wheel and Column Switches

TRIUMPH (Cont.)

IGNITION SWITCH AND STEERING COLUMN LOCK

Removal — Disconnect battery ground cable. On Spitfire only, remove nuts and washers securing steering lock shroud and withdraw shroud and column support. On all models, center punch both shear bolts mounting steering lock to column. Using a small chisel (or equivalent), remove bolts. Disconnect electrical plug and remove steering lock.

NOTE — *It is possible to remove ignition switch without taking out column lock. There are 2 set screws mounting switch assembly in column lock housing.*

Installation — To install ignition switch and steering column lock, reverse removal procedure and note the following: Ensure dowel pin aligns in column drilling. Fit new shear head bolts and tighten evenly.

VOLKSWAGEN

Dasher	Rabbit Pickup
Jetta	Scirocco
Rabbit	Vanagon

REMOVAL & INSTALLATION

HORN PAD & STEERING WHEEL

Disconnect battery ground cable. Carefully pry off horn pad and disconnect electrical connectors. Remove steering wheel retaining nut and washer (if equipped). Pull wheel off shaft.

CAUTION — *Steering column has a collapsible section. Care must be used when working with steering assembly.*

Installation — To install, reverse removal procedures and note: Drive spacer sleeve on until upper end of spacer is flush with bevel on steering column. Make sure steering wheel is installed with lug for turn signal cancel mechanism facing left side of vehicle.

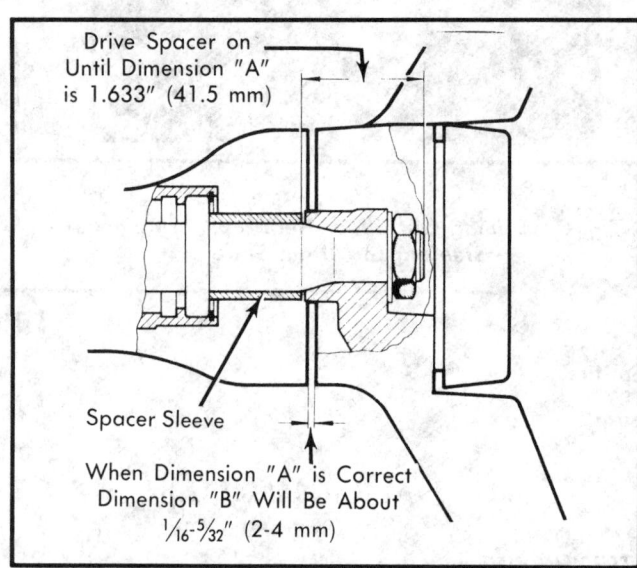

Fig. 2 *Dimensions for Installing Spacer Sleeve*

Removal (All Others) — Disconnect battery ground cable and remove steering wheel as previously outlined. Remove 3 screws securing switch assembly to steering lock mechanism. Force switch assembly toward instrument panel and remove spacer sleeve. Pull up on switch assembly and disconnect electrical wires. Remove switch and separate windshield wiper lever from dimmer/turn signal lever.

Installation — Refit switches together with screw and spacer sleeve. Slide switch assembly onto column and hook up wires. Spacer sleeve must be installed as shown in *Fig. 2.*

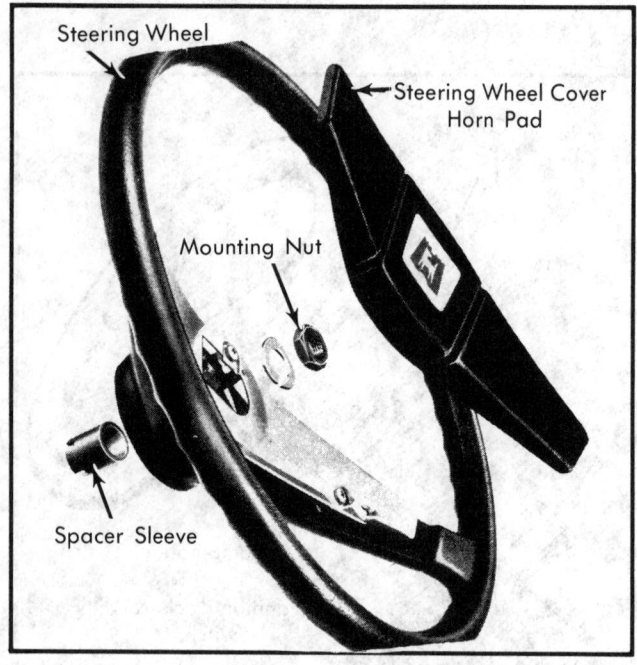

Fig. 1 *Typical Volkswagen Steering Wheel Rabbit and Scirocco Shown*

COMBINATION SWITCH

Removal (Dasher) — Disconnect battery ground. Remove steering wheel. Remove 2 screws mounting lower switch housing. Disconnect electrical wires. Remove 3 screws attaching turn signal and wiper switches to ignition switch mounting. Remove switches.

COLUMN LOCK & IGNITION SWITCH

Removal — 1) Disconnect battery ground cable and remove steering wheel and combination switch as previously outlined. If necessary, drill a 1/8" (3.18 mm) hole in cylinder to gain access to cylinder release pin. Refer to *Fig. 3* for location of access hole.

VOLKSWAGEN (Cont.)

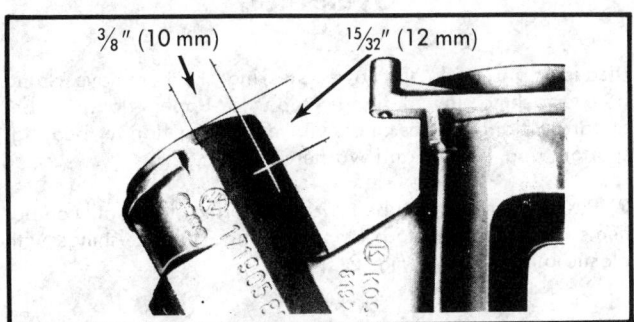

Fig. 3 Location for Drilling into Lock Cylinder

3/8" (10 mm) 15/32" (12 mm)

2) Insert a pin through hole and press down spring holding lock cylinder in housing. It may be necessary to insert key to pull out cylinder. To remove ignition switch, remove locking mechanism shear bolts and remove switch housing. Remove set screw on back side of switch, near wire connector. Remove ignition switch.

Installation — To install, reverse removal procedure and note: Before shearing bolt head, set clearance between steering wheel and switch to .08-.12" (2-3 mm).

VOLVO

Coupe	GL
Diesel	GLE
DL	GT

REMOVAL & INSTALLATION

HORN PAD & STEERING WHEEL

Removal — Disconnect battery cable. Remove horn pad by squeezing top and bottom towards center of pad and unfolding upper edge of pad. Disconnect electrical wires and remove steering wheel nut. Use puller (2263) to remove steering wheel.

Installation — To install, reverse removal procedure.

TURN SIGNAL & WIPER SWITCHES

NOTE — *Steering wheel does not have to be removed to remove combination switch; however, removal of switch is easier with steering wheel removed.*

Removal — Disconnect battery ground cable. Remove column covers from steering column. Disconnect electrical connectors from switches to be removed and remove switches.

Installation — To install, reverse removal procedure.

IGNITION SWITCH & STEERING LOCK

Removal — Disconnect battery ground. Remove steering wheel and column covers. Remove turn signal and wiper switches. Remove upper bearing spring and race. Drill out center of shear bolts and remove with suitable screw extractor. Remove lock assembly. Disconnect electrical connections and remove ignition switch.

Installation — To install, reverse removal procedure and note: Position front of lock assembly 3.81" (97 mm) from upper end of steering column.

Puller (2263)

Fig. 1 Using Puller to Remove Steering Wheel

Steering Column

AUDI 4000

DESCRIPTION

The Audi 4000 uses a 2 piece safety steering column with a slip joint flange connection. Steering column is supported by the column tube and steering lock assembly.

REMOVAL & INSTALLATION

STEERING COLUMN

Removal — 1) Disconnect battery ground strap. Remove steering wheel and column switches. See *Audi 4000 under STEERING WHEELS & COLUMN SWITCHES in this Section.*

2) From under hood, remove clamp bolt attaching steering shaft clamp to steering gear pinion shaft. Remove column cover bolts and then upper and lower steering column covers. See *Fig. 1.*

3) Pry lock washer off of steering shaft and remove spring. Remove contact ring, then remove steering lock assembly. Remove support ring from column tube. See *Fig. 1.* Center punch shear bolt attaching column tube to dash. Drill out shear bolt, then remove socket head screw attaching column tube to dash.

4) From inside vehicle, force dust boot out of floor boards. Remove steering column tube and shaft as an assembly.

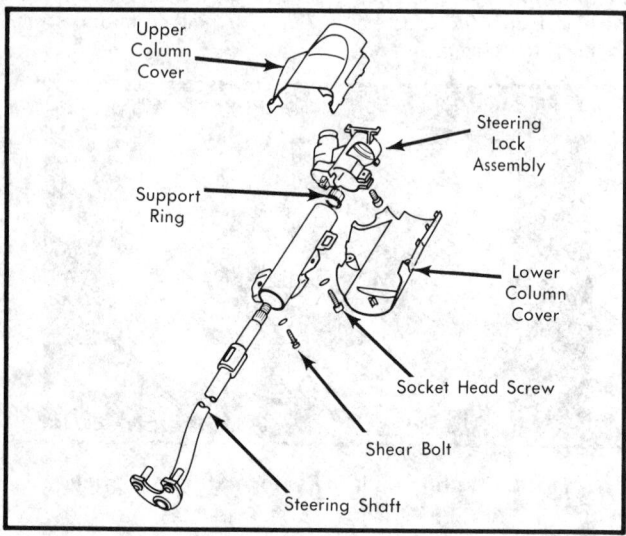

Fig. 1   Exploded View of Audi 4000 Upper Steering Column

Installation — 1) Install assembled steering column into vehicle. Install shear bolt and socket head bolt finger tight. Push dust boot into floor boards until seated. Place clamp onto steering gear pinion shaft. Place support ring into column tube.

2) Install steering lock assembly to steering column, then install contact ring, spring and a new lock washer. Tighten socket head screw. Tighten shear bolt until head snaps off.

3) Install upper and lower column covers, then install column switches and steering wheel. See *Audi 4000 under STEERING WHEELS & COLUMN SWITCHES in this Section.*

OVERHAUL

Disassembly — 1) On lower steering shaft, remove clamp bolt attaching lower flange tube to upper flange tube. Separate flange tubes and remove bearing flange, bearing, support ring, spring and washer. See *Fig. 2.*

2) Push upper flange tube towards steering shaft until components can be separated. Remove flange tube bushings with plastic bushings. See *Fig. 2.*

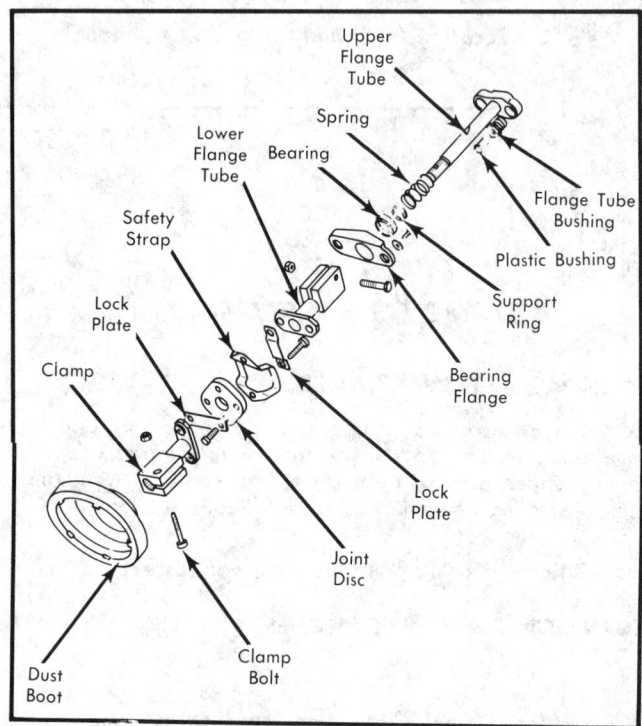

Fig. 2   Exploded View of Audi 4000 Lower Steering Column

3) Remove lower flange tube-to-clamp bolts; then separate lower flange tube from clamp. Inspect joint disc, safety strap and lock plates for damage or wear.

4) On steering shaft, slide column tube off of steering shaft. Inspect steering shaft, support ring and steering lock assembly for wear or damage. Replace components as necessary. See *Fig. 1.*

Reassembly — To reassemble steering column, reverse disassembly procedures. Press flange tube bushing and plastic bushing in by hand.

TIGHTENING SPECIFICATIONS

Application	Ft. Lbs. (mkg)
Steering Wheel Nut	29 (4.0)
Socket Head Screw	14 (1.9)
Clamp Bolt	22 (3.0)
Lower Flange Tube Bolt	22 (3.0)
Lock Plate Bolts	18 (2.5)

Steering Columns

AUDI 5000

DESCRIPTION

The Audi 5000 uses a two-piece steering column/shaft assembly. The steering shaft is designed with an offset slip joint that engages the flange tube. In a collision, the gear box and flange tube may be moved rearward, but the force will not be transmitted through the upper column shaft. An anti-theft locking device prevents the steering wheel from turning when the ignition key is removed.

REMOVAL & INSTALLATION

Removal — 1) Disconnect battery ground wire and loosen flange tube-to-pinion shaft clamp bolt. Pull off horn pad by hand and remove steering wheel with suitable puller.

2) Insert screwdriver through access hole at bottom of switch cover and loosen clamp. Remove switch assembly and disconnect ignition switch wiring. Place ignition switch in "ON" position.

3) Centerpunch shear bolts holding steering lock. Drill out shear bolts. Remove switch and unbolt mounting flange from under dash. Remove steering column and shaft as a unit.

Disassembly — Remove retaining ring, spring and support ring. Pull steering shaft out of column from the bottom. If necessary, press bearing race out of column.

Reassembly — Examine race and replace if excessively worn. Slide steering shaft back into column tube, then replace support ring, spring, and use a new retaining ring to lock in place.

Installation — 1) Place column assembly in vehicle. Install steering lock shear bolts finger tight and check operation of lock. Bolt mounting flange onto bracket.

2) Connect ignition wiring. Install flange tube over steering column pins and press on pinion shaft. Hold flange tube and shaft together with pliers and check length of shaft protruding from upper end of column. Adjust by moving flange tube on pinion shaft until distance is 2.56" (65 mm). See *Fig. 2*.

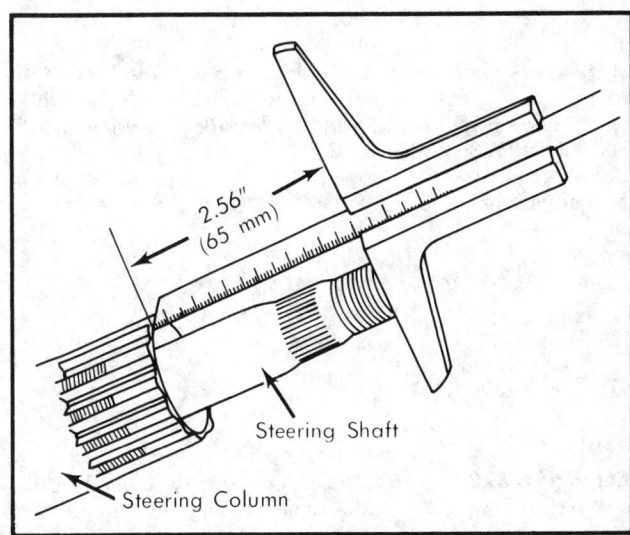

Fig. 2   Steering Shaft Installation Measurement

3) Tighten shear bolts until heads break. Install switch assembly flush with dashboard. With wheels in straight position, turn signal lever in middle position and cancelling lug to right, install steering wheel. Tighten steering wheel nut to 30 ft. lbs. (4.1 mkg). Gap between wheel and switch assembly should be 1/8" (3 mm). Adjust if necessary and tighten flange clamp bolt on pinion shaft.

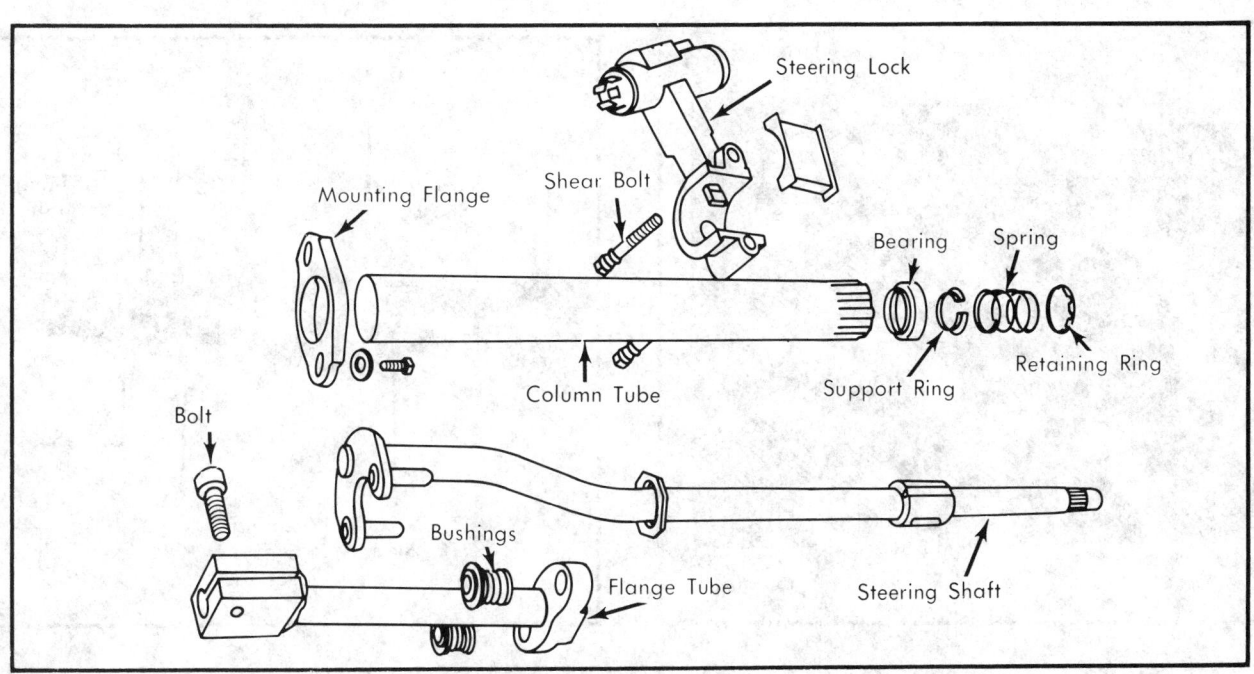

Fig. 1   Exploded View of Audi 5000 Steering Column

Steering Columns

BMW

320i
528i
633CSi
733i

DESCRIPTION

Steering column consists of a padded steering wheel with horn contact, turn signal/headlight dimmer switch, windshield wiper switch and an anti-theft steering column lock/ignition switch. Columns on 528i, 633CSi and 733i are telescoping, while the 320i column is fixed in position. Column is connected to steering gear by universal joints and flexible coupling.

REMOVAL & INSTALLATION

STEERING COLUMN

Removal (320i) – 1) Disconnect battery ground cable. Remove lower half of steering column casing. Lift off pad from center of steering wheel and remove steering wheel.

2) Remove windshield wiper and turn signal switches at switch plate. Remove flasher relay. Loosen set screw and pull out ignition switch.

3) Detach steering shaft at universal joint next to firewall in engine compartment. Loosen casing tube clamp at base of tube in driver's compartment. Drill or chisel off shear head bolts holding steering column to instrument panel. Remove steering column.

NOTE – *On 320i only, lower bearing may be replaced by driving shaft and bearing out from top. Remove snap ring, split ring and bearing. When reinstalling, stem of split ring must face bearing and snap ring must fit in locking groove.*

Installation – To install, reverse removal procedure and note the following: Upper column casing and tube must be aligned prior to tightening. When installing turn signal switch, wheels must point straight ahead with switch in center position. With dog pointing to center of cancelling cam, adjust switch so that dog is about .12" (3 mm) from cancelling cam.

Removal (528i & 633CSi) – 1) Disconnect battery ground cable and remove steering wheel. Detach lower half of housing below column, then remove turn and wiper switches.

2) Remove steering shaft holder at top of column. Loosen adjusting nut and mark position of upper and lower shafts. Carefully pry steering shaft bearing from top of column and pull shaft out from above.

3) To remove upper outer tube, disconnect horn wire at carbon brush. Drill or chisel off switch plate shear screws and disconnect wiring harnesses. Loosen clamp bolt and support screws, then slide down lower outer tube. Lift up outer casing and pull out outer tube.

Installation – To install, reverse removal procedures noting the following: Prior to tightening clamp bolt, assure that distance from centerline of clamp bolt to end of upper outer tube is between 1.65-1.77" (42-45 mm). Align upper and lower steering shaft marks and tighten adjusting nut.

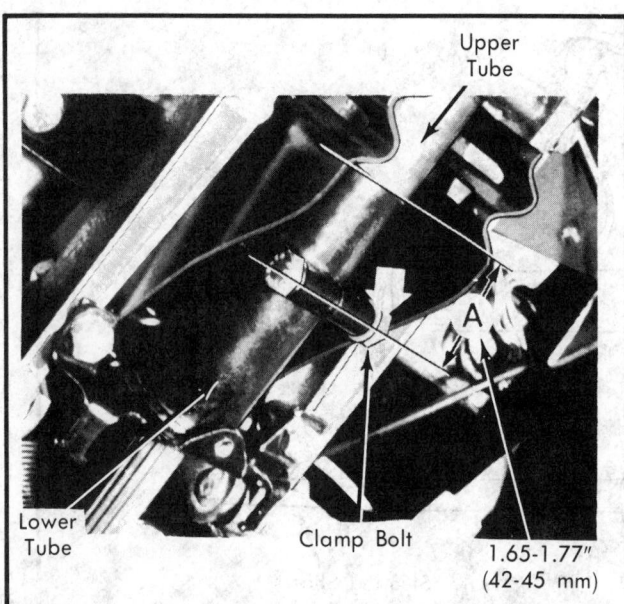

Fig. 1 Outer Tube and Clamp Bolt (528i & 633CSi)

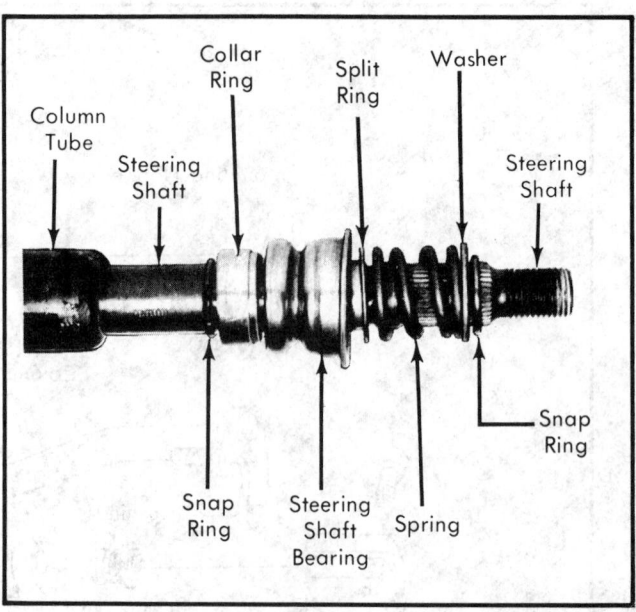

Fig. 2 Upper Steering Shaft and Bearing (All Models Except 733i)

BMW (Cont.)

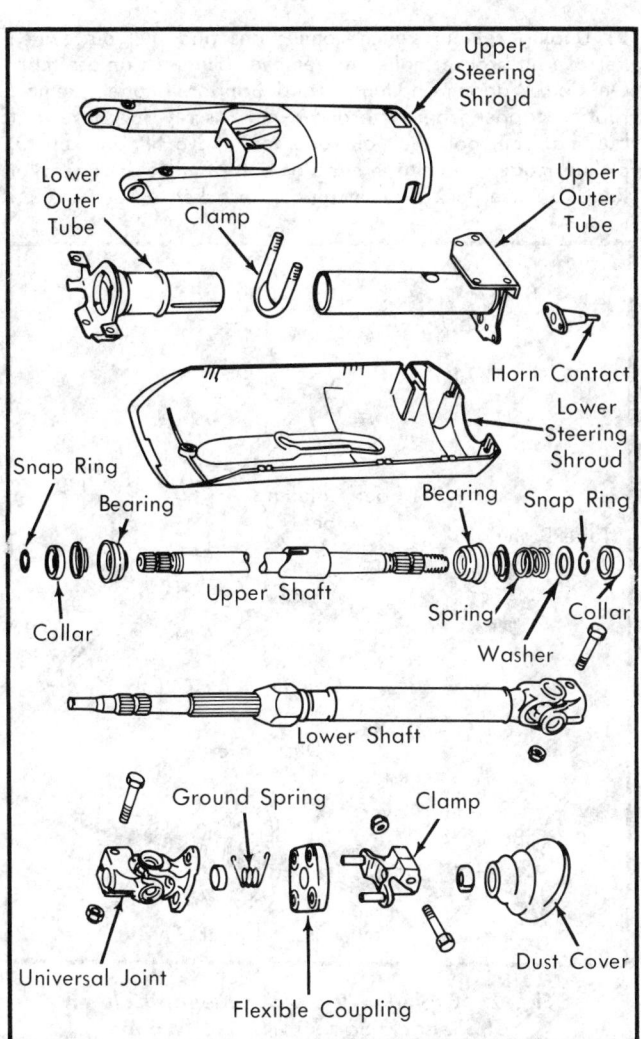

Fig. 3 Exploded View of Steering Column (733i)

Removal (733i) — 1) Disconnect ground lead at battery and remove steering wheel. Remove lower instrument panel cover and steering column housing. Disconnect switches and remove all wiring and ignition switch.

2) Remove clamp bolt and detach lower shaft. Remove 5 bolts holding column assembly to dash and pedal bracket. Remove upper shroud and shaft. Disconnect lower shaft from clamp in engine compartment and pull into passenger compartment.

3) Remove inner steering shaft by taking off collar, snap ring, washer, spring, and lock ring. Pry out upper bearing with screwdrivers. Pry out lower bearing and remove shaft. Remove snap ring, collar, ring and bearing.

Installation — To install, reverse removal procedure. Wheels must be in straight ahead position when shafts are connected. Ensure all washers and spacers are replaced. Ignition switch must be in "O" position when installed.

TIGHTENING SPECIFICATIONS

Application	Ft. Lbs. (mkg)
Steering Wheel Nut	62-69 (8.5-9.5)
Universal Joint-to-Steering Shaft	18-20 (2.5-2.8)
Casing Tube Clamp Bolt	
320i	12-14 (1.7-1.9)
528i & 633CSi	16-17 (2.2-2.4)
Column-to-Housing	10 (1.5)
Column Bracket-to-Dashboard	16 (2.2)
Lower-to-Upper Shaft Bolt (733i only)	18 (2.5)

CHRYSLER CORP. IMPORTS – EXC. FRONT-WHEEL-DRIVE MODELS

Arrow   **Colt Wagon**
Arrow Pickup   **D50 Pickup**
Challenger   **Sapporo**

DESCRIPTION

Collapsible steering column is comprised of a 2-piece column shaft, joined by a collapsible section. This section contracts under impact without affecting turning motion. The upper column cover incorporates slits that allow it to collapse under impact.

REMOVAL & INSTALLATION

STEERING COLUMN

NOTE – *During any service operations of collapsible columns or components avoid jarring or leaning on any portion of column.*

Removal – 1) Remove air cleaner and unbolt clamp connecting shaft to gear box. If vehicle is equipped with air conditioning, perform this step from underneath vehicle. Remove horn pad, steering wheel nut, and pull steering wheel off. Loosen tilt lock lever or knob and lower wheel. Remove column cover and floor dust cover.

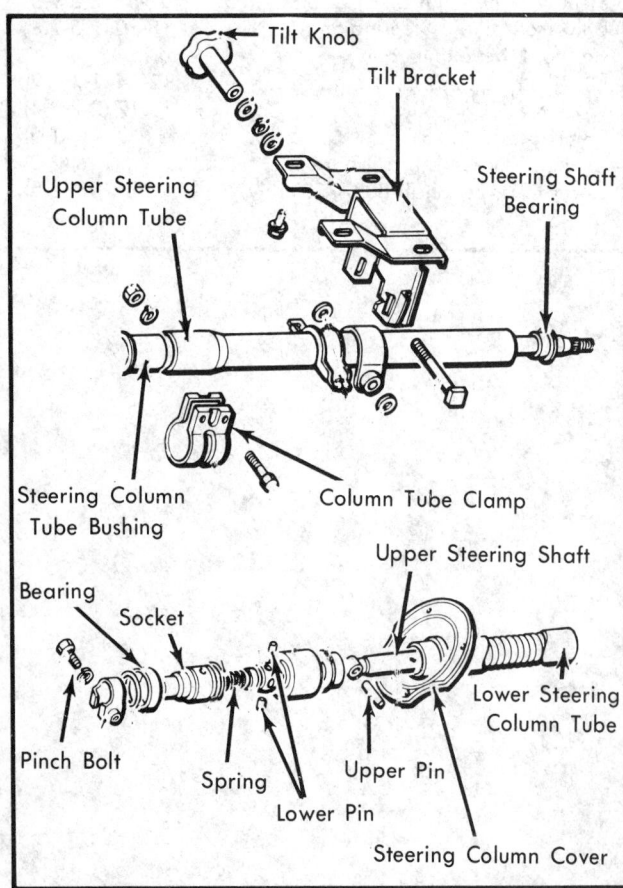

Fig. 1   Exploded View of Steering Column Arrow

2) Unplug column switch connections and pull out switch. Remove tilt bracket bolts and remove column as an assembly. On Colt Wagon, Challenger and Sapporo models, remove rubber stopper from tilt bracket and unscrew lock lever and bushing from bolt. Pull out bolt to remove tilt bracket. On pickup models, cut slot in head of bolt of wheel lock bracket. Remove wheel lock bracket and tilt bracket.

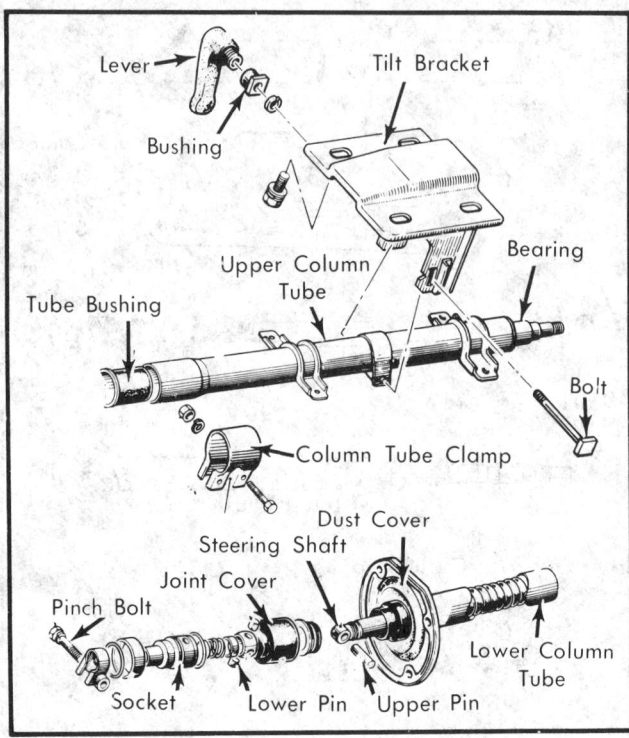

Fig. 2   Exploded View of Steering Column Challenger, Sapporo & Colt Wagon

Installation – 1) Be sure shaft can easily be turned within the column, insert column assembly, and position against instrument panel. Connect shaft to steering gear housing mainshaft with clamp bolt head upward. Position tilt bracket so upper end of steering shaft to upper column end measurement is 3.60-3.64" (91.5-92.5 mm). Note that this measurement is not used on pickup models. Tighten tilt bracket bolts and install dust cover, applying sealant to the bolt.

2) Install column switch, routing harness along center of column tube, then replace cover. With front wheels in straight ahead position, install steering wheel. On Challenger, Sapporo, and Colt Wagon, fit the 3 cancel pins on the column switch into bottom of steering wheel with a screwdriver. Tighten retaining nut and make sure free play at wheel rim does not exceed .04" (1.0 mm).

OVERHAUL

Disassembly – 1) On pickup models, remove snap ring, then remove steering shaft from column. Disconnect coupling from steering shaft. On all other models, pull the lower shaft bushing out of column and remove shaft. Remove cover from the steering shaft joint socket; remove stopper and joint pin retainer. With steering shaft held upright, press down on shaft and remove joint retaining pin with a magnet. Do not drive pin out. Remove joint socket.

CHRYSLER CORP. IMPORTS — EXC. FRONT-WHEEL-DRIVE MODELS (Cont.)

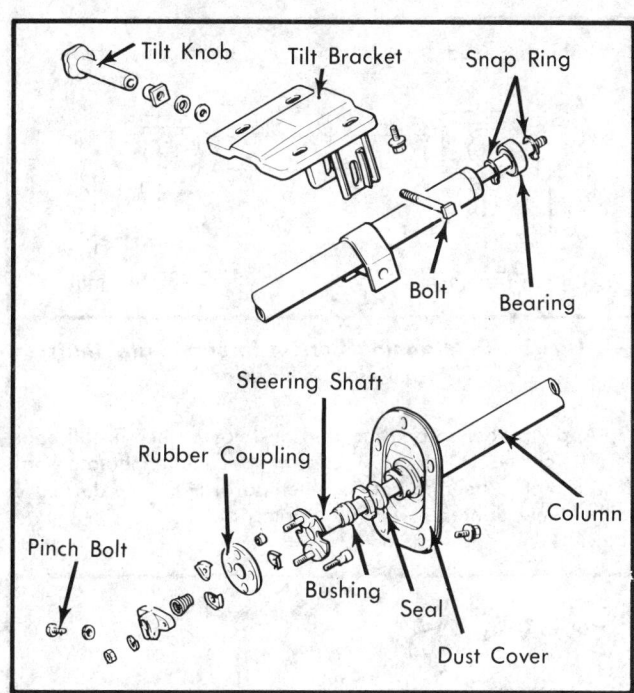

Fig. 3   Exploded View of Steering Column D50 & Arrow Pickup

2) Loosen column tube clamp, draw out column tube, and remove the column bushing. When removing the tilt bracket, cut a slot in head of retaining studs, then unscrew studs, and remove steering lock. Lightly tap the tilt bracket with a wooden hammer to drive the bracket assembly from the upper end of column tube.

Inspection — 1) Measure steering shaft length. On pickup models, length should be 31.5" (801.4 mm). Arrow models should be 28.15" (714.5 mm). Challenger, Sapporo and Colt Wagon models should be 28.62" (726.9 mm). On pickup models, check steering shaft-to-column bearing clearance. Clearance should be .0004-.002" (.01-.05 mm).

2) On all models except pickup, check clearance between upper coupling joint pin and bearing. Also check clearance between upper coupling joint pin and socket. Clearance should be .0006-.0022" (.016-.056 mm) for both measurements.

3) Check interference fit between lower coupling joint pin and shaft. Fit should be .0001-.0013" (.003-.034 mm). Check free play of lower joint pin and bearing. Free play should be .0006-.0022" (.016-.056 mm).

4) Check steering shaft bend. Distortion must not exceed .020" (.5 mm). Hold lower end of steering shaft and move upper shaft. Note any excessive movement. Replace components as necessary.

5) Check column tube bushing stop. Replace bushing if wear is excessive.

6) Inspect upper and lower steering column bearings. Replace if excessively worn. Clearance between shaft and bearings is .0001-.0045" (.003-.115 mm).

7) Check tilt bracket. Slots give and break through when driver impact hits steering wheel. Make sure slots are not damaged.

Reassembly — 1) On pickup models, reverse disassembly procedure. On all other models, install bearing on steering shaft lower end with flange facing upward, then insert pin. Make sure pin does not interfere with bearing operation.

2) Grease socket, dust cover and seat. Insert spring seat and spring into socket. Place steering shaft vertically and hold other portion of steering shaft down, fit lock pin. Make sure shaft and socket rotate freely.

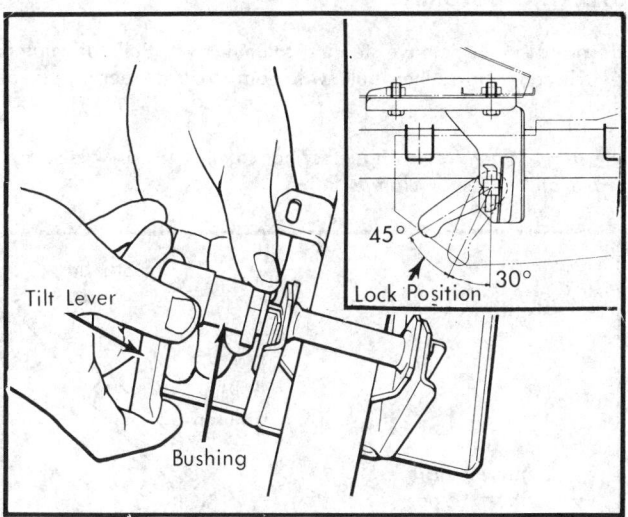

Fig. 4   Tilt Lever Installation Challenger, Colt Wagon and Sapporo

3) Fit spacer on shaft and install in steering column. Wipe grease off lower bearing retainer and inside of column. Apply a thin coat of adhesive to end of column.

4) On Arrow models, place tilt bracket on column, insert spacers, bolt, washers and tilt knob.

5) On Challenger, Sapporo, and Colt wagon, align tilt bracket with column tube and insert bolt. Tighten bushing on tilt lever until it stops, then back off ½ turn. Install tilt lever on bolt and adjust bushing until tilt lever locks column without hitting bracket.

6) Install shaft assembly in car. Fit column tube bushings onto upper and lower column tubes until stop touches column tube end. Tighten clamp bolt. Align column tube hole with steering wheel lock guide dowel. Insert ignition key and check operation.

TIGHTENING SPECIFICATIONS

Application	Ft. Lbs. (mkg)
Steering Shaft Clamp	
Pickup	11-15 (1.5-2.1)
All Others	15-18 (2.1-2.5)
Steering Wheel Nut	25-33 (3.5-4.6)

Steering Columns

CHRYSLER CORP. IMPORTS — FRONT-WHEEL-DRIVE MODELS

Champ
Colt Hatchback

DESCRIPTION

Collapsible steering system is comprised of a two-piece (upper and lower) column shaft, joined by a collapsible (bellows type) section. The bellows section contracts axially under impact without affecting turning motion.

REMOVAL & INSTALLATION

STEERING COLUMN

Removal — 1) Remove steering column cover. Pull out column switch connectors, then pull switch out toward steering wheel end.

NOTE — *When removing steering column as an assembly, leave all connector clamps intact.*

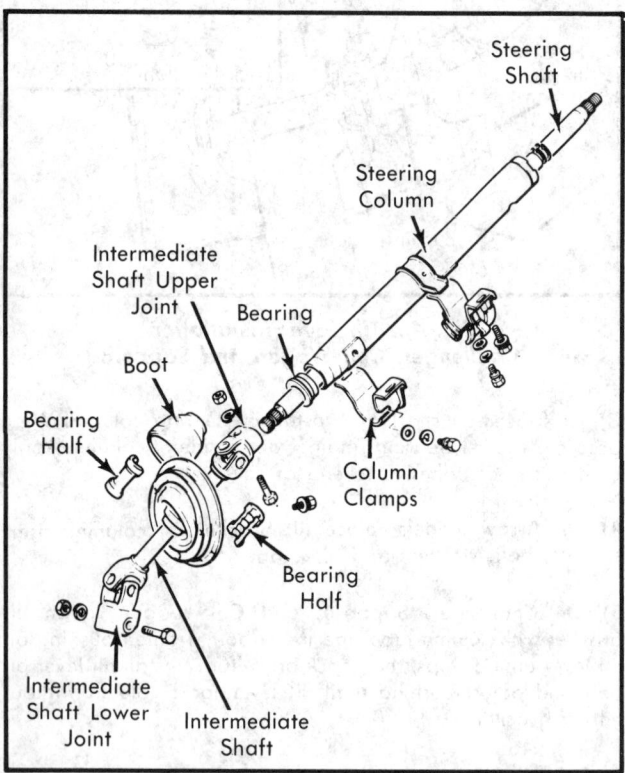

Fig. 1   Exploded View of Steering Column

2) Remove steering shaft upper coupling bolt. Remove bolts securing steering column brackets to frame. Disconnect steering shaft from coupling (inside vehicle) and remove steering column assembly.

3) Remove intermediate shaft lower coupling bolt (at steering gear). Remove dust cover mounting bolts. Remove intermediate shaft (with dust cover) toward inside of vehicle.

Installation — 1) Install dust cover to intermediate shaft. Make sure bearing side of cover faces steering shaft side of intermediate shaft. See Fig. 2 and 3.

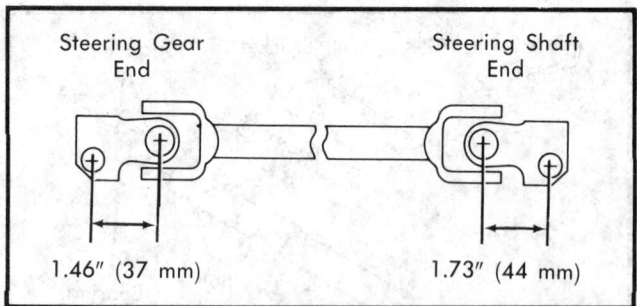

Fig. 2   Determining Correct Intermediate Shaft Installation Position

2) Apply grease to bearing and dust cover, then install bearing (two pieces) into dust cover. Attach intermediate shaft lower joint to steering gear and temporarily tighten dust cover bolts. Now tighten lower joint clamp bolt.

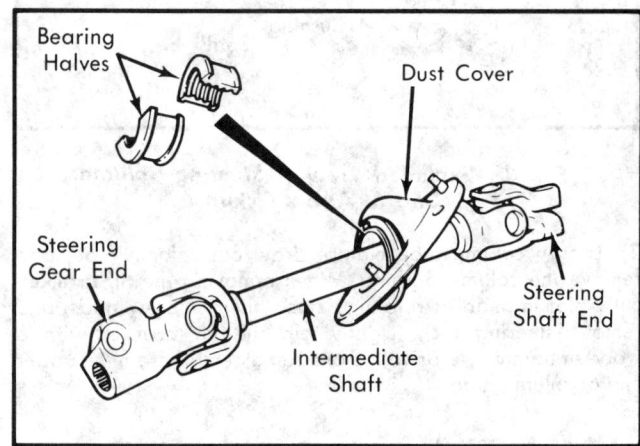

Fig. 3   Dust Cover and Bearing Installation

3) Connect intermediate shaft upper joint to steering shaft. Attach steering column brackets to dash. Tighten clamp bolt of intermediate shaft and column bracket bolts.

4) Loosen dust cover bolts and position dust cover so no clearance exists between joint and dust cover sliding surfaces. Tighten dust cover bolts. Adjust steering wheel position if necessary.

OVERHAUL

Disassembly — 1) Remove the two-piece bearing from dust cover of intermediate shaft. Remove dust cover from intermediate shaft.

2) Remove snap ring from steering shaft (steering wheel end). Unlock steering wheel lock (with ignition key), then remove steering shaft from column by lightly tapping shaft with soft (rubber or plastic) mallet.

3) If steering lock is to be removed, cut a slot in mounting screws with hacksaw. Use a flat blade screwdriver to remove screws then remove steering lock. Always use new screws and bracket when replacing steering lock.

CHRYSLER CORP. IMPORTS — FRONT-WHEEL-DRIVE MODELS (Cont.)

4) If steering column bracket is removed, cut a slot in mounting bolt with hacksaw. Remove bolts with flat blade screwdriver. Always use new bolts when installing bracket to steering column.

Inspection — Check steering shaft for runout and length. Runout should be .02" (.5 mm) or less, length should be 23.17" (588.5 mm). Check for a worn or damaged bearing. On intermediate shaft, check for play, noise or rough rotation in joints. Also check for a damaged dust cover. Replace components as required.

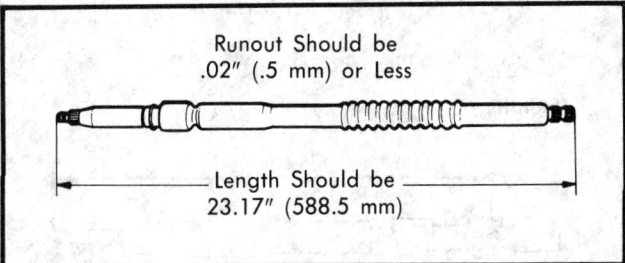

Runout Should be
.02" (.5 mm) or Less

Length Should be
23.17" (588.5 mm)

Fig. 4 Check Steering Shaft for Length and Damage

Reassembly — 1) Install steering shaft in steering column and install snap ring. Install and tighten column tube bracket bolt until bolt head snaps off.

NOTE — *Torque needed to snap bolt head off should be approximately 9 ft. lbs. (1.2 mkg).*

2) Fill bearing with grease and install in end of steering column. Make sure bearing is fully seated. Align steering lock with column boss. Make sure that steering lock is operational (by using ignition key to make lock function) before tightening lock securing screw.

NOTE — *Steering lock securing screws are special one way design.*

TIGHTENING SPECIFICATIONS	
Application	**Ft. Lbs. (mkg)**
Column Tube-to-Bracket Bolt	
Torque Required to Snap Head Off	9 (1.2)
Column Support Bracket Bolts	7 (1.0)
Clamp Joint Bolts	
Upper and Lower	11-14 (1.5-2.0)
Steering Wheel Nut	29-36 (3.9-4.9)

Steering Columns

DATSUN 200SX, 210, 310, 510 & 810

DESCRIPTION

Steering columns used on these Datsun vehicles are safety, collapsible type. These columns compress on impact. 310 model uses 2 universal joints between column and steering gear. These joints provide the most desirable steering wheel position and angle. On all other models, a flexible rubber coupling attaches column to steering gear assembly

REMOVAL & INSTALLATION

NOTE — *During any service procedure involving the steering assembly, do not hammer or exert extreme pressure on the steering column or damage to the collapsible section may result.*

Removal (310) — **1)** Disconnect lower column "U" joint from steering gear assembly. Remove steering wheel. *See Datsun under STEERING WHEEL & COLUMN SWITCHES in this Section.*

2) Remove steering column cover. Separate turn signal switch assembly and combination light switch from column.

3) Remove joint cover and bracket bolts. Remove column mounting bolts and remove steering column through passenger compartment.

Inspection — **1)** Check column bearings for smooth even operation. If necessary, grease bearings with suitable lubricant.

2) Check column tube for deformation or breaks. Replace components as required.

3) If vehicle has been involved in a collision, check steering column dimensions "A" and "B". *Fig. 1.* Dimension "A" should be 24.04-24.16" (610.7-613.7 mm). Dimension "B" should be 16.56-16.67" (420.5-423.5 mm). If either dimension is not within specifications, replace steering column assembly.

4) Check distance from lower "U" joint centerline to end of splined shaft. If distance is not 5.77-5.85" (146.5-148.5 mm), replace lower "U" joint.

Installation — **1)** Set steering gear in straight-ahead position. Connect lower joint to steering column. Slide steering assembly through hole in floor board.

2) Tighten column tube mounting bolts. Loosen splined shaft set screw and connect shaft to joint. Connect opposite end to steering gear. Tighten pinch bolt and set screw.

3) Make sure column tube hole seal is not twisted and that lower lip makes contact with joint shaft.

Removal (Except 310) — **1)** Remove steering shaft pinch bolt. Remove steering wheel. *See Datsun under STEERING WHEEL & COLUMN SWITCHES in this section.*

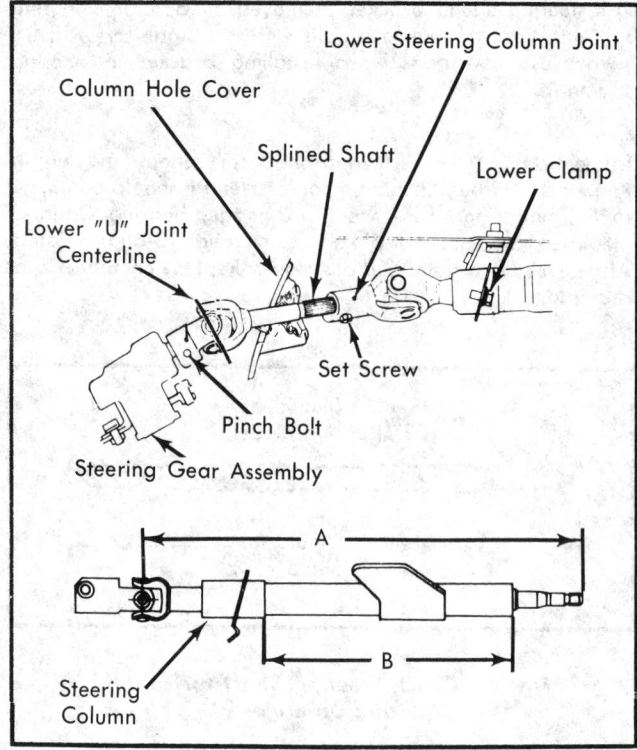

Fig. 1   Datsun 310 Steering Column Assembly

2) Remove upper and lower steering column shroud covers. Loosen screws and take off turn signal switch or combination switch assembly. Remove heater duct from dash panel side (this is necessary on 200SX models only).

3) Remove bolts mounting steering column tube cover to floorboard. From under instrument panel, remove bolts mounting column clamp and remove clamp. Pull steering assembly from vehicle by removing it through passenger compartment.

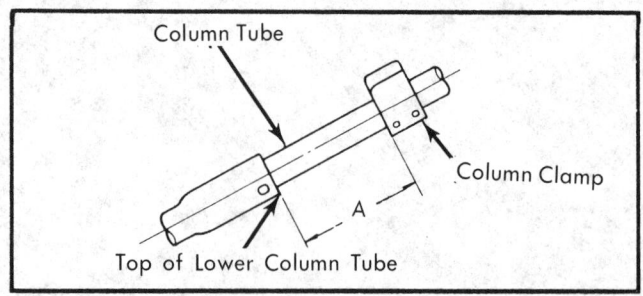

Fig. 2   Column Tube Measurement Specification

Inspection — **1)** Check column bearings for smooth even operation. If necessary, grease bearings with suitable lubricant.

2) Check column tube for deformation or breaks. Replace components if necessary.

DATSUN 200SX, 210, 310, 510 & 810 (Cont.)

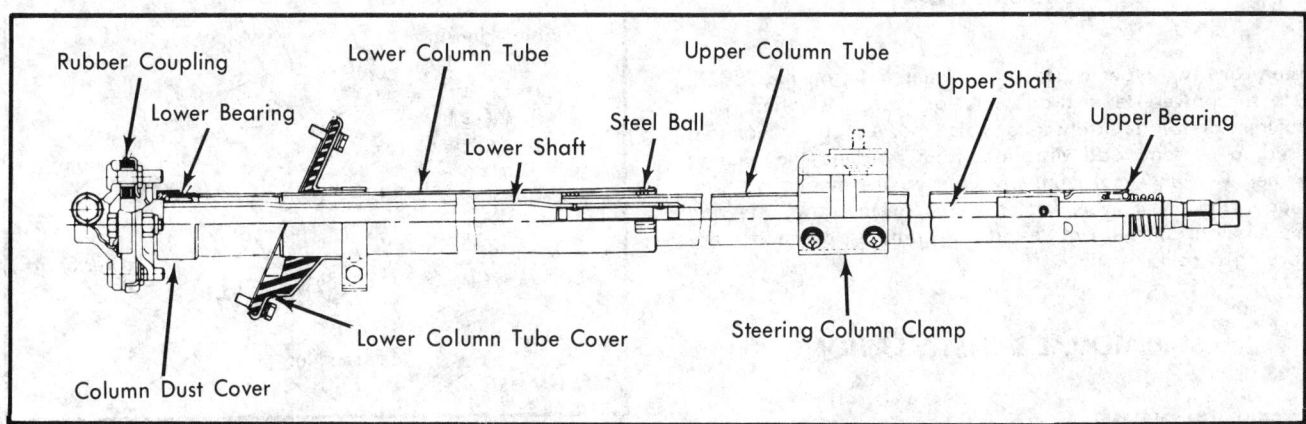

Fig. 3 *Sectional View of Datsun Collapsible Steering Column (All Except 310)*

3) Check column shaft spring and replace spring if it seems weak. Check for any space between the column tube bracket and the block (mounted in the bracket.) If there is any clearance between block and bracket, steering column has been damaged and must be replaced.

4) On all models except 810, measure distance between column clamp and top end of lower column tube. Distance should be 7.52" (191 mm) on 210 models or 7.24" (184 mm) on 510 models. Distance for 200SX manual steering should be 7.05" (179 mm) and 7.09" (180 mm) for power steering. See Fig. 2.

5) On 810 models, measure distance between top end of upper column tube and top end of lower column tube. Distance should be about 16.27" (413.5 mm).

Installation — **1)** Place steering gear so wheels point straight-ahead.

NOTE — *On 200SX models with power steering, a special steering column centering band is used. Centering band is installed to column in place of column band prior to column installation and then removed and replaced with column band after installation.*

2) Slide steering column into position through passenger compartment. Guide column over worm shaft. Make sure punch mark faces up, then tighten pinch bolt.

3) Fix column under instrument panel. Refit column tube cover at floor board. Reverse removal procedure for remaining components. Make sure steering wheel rotates freely.

OVERHAUL

NOTE — *200SX, 210, 510 and 810 models do not have an overhaul procedure; it is recommended that, should damage to the column occur, it be replaced as an assembly.*

Disassembly (310 Models Only) — On steering column shaft, remove snap ring. Remove washer and pull column shaft out of column tube, from the bottom of column tube. Remove "O" ring. Inspect column tube and shaft for excessive wear or damage. Replace as necessary.

Reassembly — Install new "O" ring, then slide column shaft into column tube, from bottom. Install washer, then install snap ring. Make sure column shaft rotates easily in column tube.

TIGHTENING SPECIFICATIONS

Application	Ft. Lbs. (mkg)
Steering Wheel Nut	
310	22-25 (3.0-3.5)
All Others	27-38 (3.7-5.3)
Steering Column Clamp Bolts	
310	6.5-10 (0.9-1.4)
All Others	9-13 (1.2-1.8)
Rubber Coupling-to-Worm Shaft	
Manual Steering	29-36 (4.0-5.0)
Power Steering	24-28 (3.3-3.9)
Joint Shaft-to-Column Bolt	
310 (Upper and Lower)	17-22 (2.4-3.0)

DATSUN 280ZX

DESCRIPTION

There are two types of steering columns used on the 280ZX, one for power steering and one for manual steering. Both columns are of the safety collapsible type. A rubber coupling is used to prevent road vibrations from reaching the steering wheel. Two universal joints are used on the manual steering model and one universal joint is used on the power steering model. Both columns are designed to compress on impact, absorbing a collision shock.

REMOVAL & INSTALLATION

STEERING COLUMN

NOTE – *During any service procedure involving the steering assembly, do not hammer or exert extreme pressure on the steering column or damage to the collapsible section may result.*

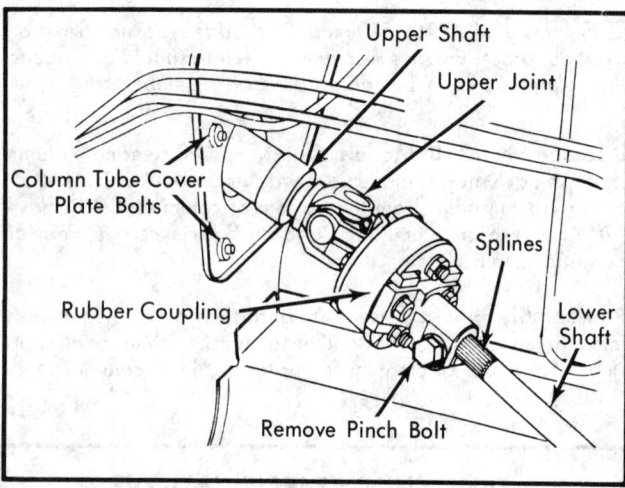

Fig. 1   Separating Upper and Lower Shafts on Manual Steering Models

Removal – On power steering, remove bolt securing stub shaft to rubber coupling. On manual steering, remove bolt securing lower joint to rubber coupling. On power and manual steering, remove steering wheel. *See Datsun under STEERING WHEEL & COLUMN SWITCHES in this section.* Remove column tube bracket and cover from dash panel. Remove column mounting bracket and draw out steering column assembly from passenger compartment side.

Inspection – Check for smoothness of rotation at all steering components. Inspect jacket tube for deformation or breakage (replace if necessary). Check column shaft spring for proper tension: free length, 1.075" (27.3 mm); loaded length, .059"@66 lbs. (15 mm@30 kg). Measure distance from upper end of tube collapsible section to first diameter change of tube (see *Fig. 3*). Measurement should be 15.73-15.77" (399.5-400.5 mm). If measurement is not correct, tube has been crushed and should be replaced. Also inspect inserts in column support clamp. If there is any space between inserts and bracket, damage to column may be suspected.

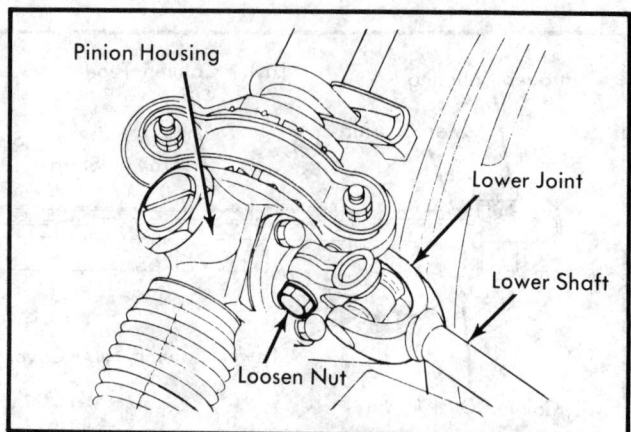

Fig. 2   Separating Lower Shaft from Pinion Gear on Manual Steering Models

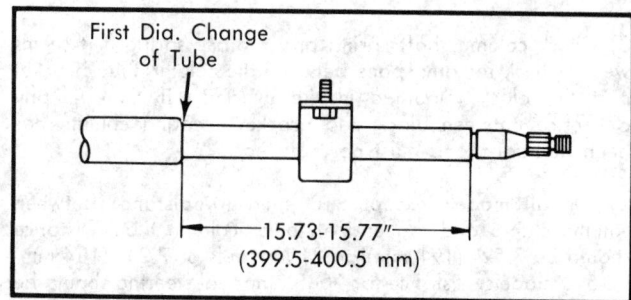

Fig. 3   Measurement for Damage of Collapsible Column on Power and Manual Steering Models

Installation – Install steering column onto stub shaft (power steering) or onto lower joint (manual steering) after installation of steering column through dash panel. Set front wheels in staight ahead position, line up slits of universal joints with punch mark on upper end of steering shaft (punch mark should be on top), then connect column and tighten bolts as required. After installation, ensure steering wheel rotates smoothly.

OVERHAUL

NOTE – *Refer to Inspection in this article for description of components which may be replaced; however, if damage to the collapsible section is suspected, steering column replacement is recommended.*

TIGHTENING SPECIFICATIONS

Application	Ft. Lbs. (mkg)
Steering Wheel Nut	29-36 (4.0-5.0)
Column Clamp Bolt	9-13 (1.3-1.8)
Coupling-to-Column Shaft	
Power Steering	11-16 (1.5-2.2)
Manual Steering	12-14 (1.7-2.0)
Manual Steering Only	
Lower Joint-to-Rubber Coupling	17-20 (2.3-2.7)
Lower Joint-to-Pinion Gear	29-36 (4.0-5.0)
Power Steering Only	
Stub Shaft-to-Coupling	24-28 (3.3-3.9)

DATSUN PICKUP

DESCRIPTION

Pickup steering columns are safety collapsible type. Columns are supported by a column bracket at the dash and attached to floor pan by a floor bracket. Steering shaft uses a universal joint and is attached to gearbox by a flexible rubber coupling.

REMOVAL & INSTALLATION

NOTE — *During any service procedure involving the steering assembly, do not hammer or exert extreme pressure on the steering column or damage to the collapsible section may result.*

Removal — 1) Remove rubber coupling to gearbox bolt. Remove steering wheel. See *Datsun* under *STEERING WHEEL & COLUMN SWITCHES* in this Section.

2) Remove steering column shell covers. Remove combination switch assembly. Remove heater duct from under dash (around steering column).

3) Remove column bracket and floor bracket. Remove steering column assembly through passenger compartment.

Installation — 1) Place wheels in straight ahead position. Install steering column assembly through passenger compartment. Attach rubber coupling to gear box, making sure punch mark on upper end of steering shaft faces up.

2) Install column bracket bolts, then install floor pan bracket bolts. With column and floor bracket bolts installed, tighten rubber coupling bolt. Tighten column bracket bolts and then floor pan bracket bolts. Complete installation in reverse order of removal. Make sure steering wheel turns smoothly.

OVERHAUL

Disassembly — 1) Remove rubber coupling assembly. On steering lock assembly, drill out shear type screws, install screw extractor, and then remove screws. Disconnect and remove steering lock.

2) Compress steering column spring and hold compressed with wire. Remove collar fixing wire, collar, snap ring, plain washer, column spring and spring seat. Pull column shaft out of column tube.

NOTE — *When removing steering shaft, be careful not to damage upper and lower bearings in column tube.*

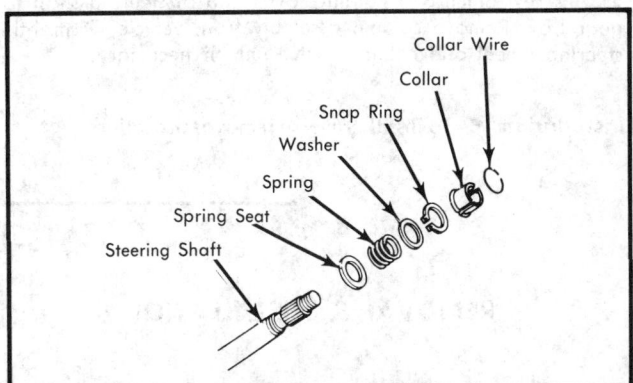

Fig. 2 *Exploded View of Upper End of Steering Shaft*

Inspection — Check column tube bearings for smooth operation and grease or replace. Check column tube for bending or breakage, replace if necessary. Check column spring for damage and replace if necessary.

Reassembly — Reassemble in reverse order of disassembly and note these points: Apply grease to column bearings, spring and other moving parts. Be careful not to damage remote control lever bracket. Always use new snap ring.

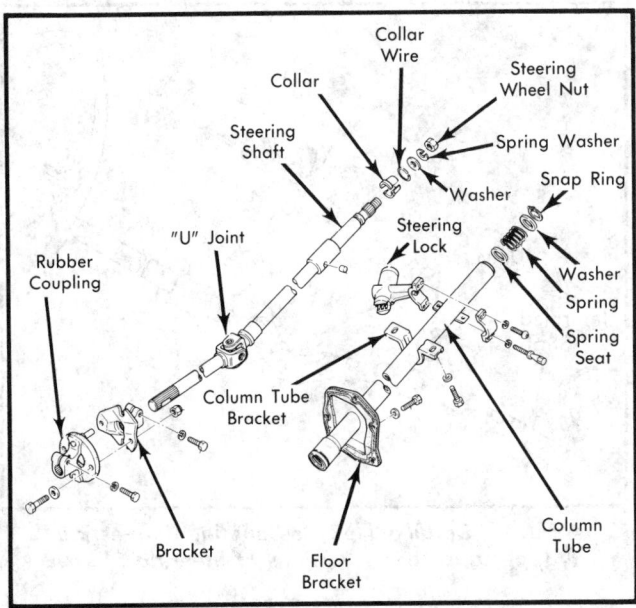

Fig. 1 *Exploded View of Steering Column Assembly*

TIGHTENING SPECIFICATIONS

Application	Ft. Lbs. (mkg)
Rubber Coupling Bolt	29-36 (4.0-5.0)
Steering Wheel Nut	29-36 (4.0-5.0)

Steering Columns

FIAT BRAVA, STRADA & X1/9

DESCRIPTION

The steering column is composed of 2 sections. The top section is mounted on 2 ball bearings, while the lower section is equipped with 2 universal joints. On Brava models, the upper section pivots to allow steering wheel height adjustment.

REMOVAL & INSTALLATION

STEERING COLUMN (ALL MODELS)

Removal — 1) Disconnect battery. Remove screws holding column cover halves. On Brava models, remove steering column tilt adjustment knob. On all models, detach electrical connectors at steering column. Remove nuts and washers retaining column at support bracket below instrument panel.

2) Unscrew pinch bolt holding lower end of steering shaft to gear box. Remove column assembly from vehicle. Dismantle steering wheel and column switch unit, if necessary.

Installation — To install, reverse removal procedure.

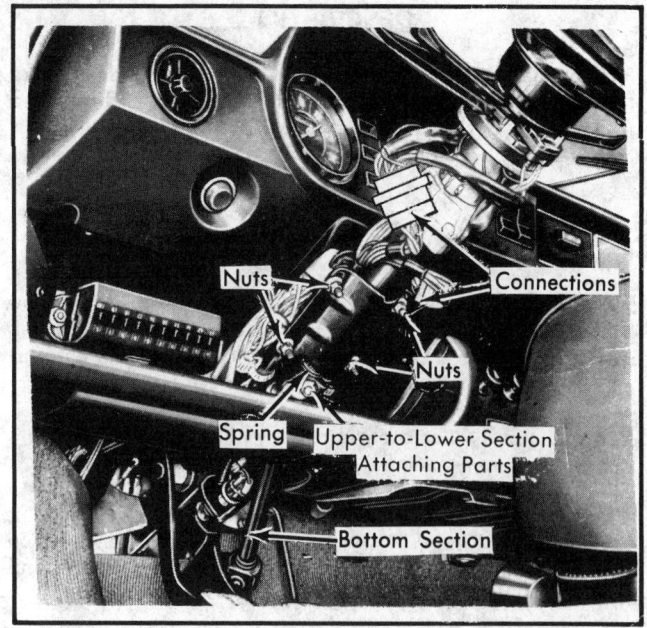

Fig. 1   Installed View of Typical Steering Column as Viewed from Under Instrument Panel

FIAT SPIDER 2000

REMOVAL & INSTALLATION

Removal — After removing steering wheel, horn button and column switch assembly, remove steering column bracket by disconnecting column from ignition switch and removing 4 column-to-instrument panel retaining screws. Unbolt clamp securing steering column to worm shaft and pull column up into passenger compartment.

Installation — 1) Insert column through opening in instrument panel. Fit worm shaft to steering column and lock with clamp. Replace column support bracket to steering column and connect with attaching screws (loosely).

2) Replace steering wheel temporarily and turn from side to side 2 or 3 times. Attach column switch assembly, then torque column bracket bolts to 11 ft. lbs. (1.5 mkg). Tighten steering wheel nut and connect switch wiring. Replace remaining components in reverse of removal procedure.

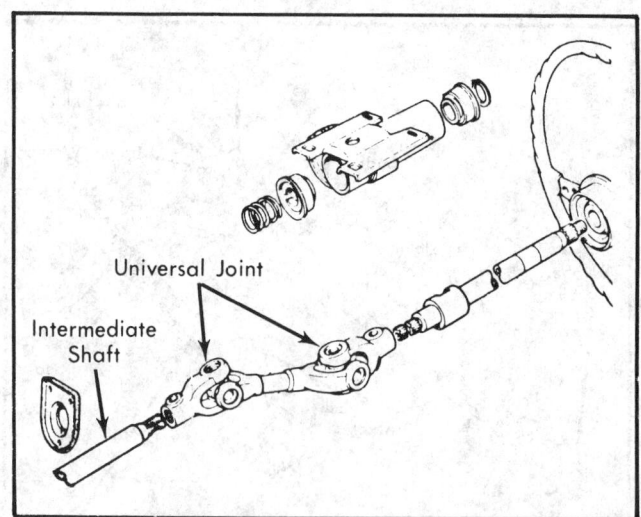

Fig. 1   Detail of Flexible Coupling Connecting Upper and Lower Portions of Steering Shaft

Hatchback

DESCRIPTION

Steering column is two-piece, with a slip joint that allows either part to move without transmitting force to the other end. A steering column jacket over the upper part of the steering shaft will also collapse under impact. No universal joints or flexible couplings are used between the shaft and steering gear.

REMOVAL & INSTALLATION

STEERING COLUMN

Removal — 1) Disconnect battery ground strap. Remove pinion-to-steering shaft clamp bolt. Inside vehicle, remove upper and lower steering column shrouds and lower dash insulation panel.

2) Loosen two screws retaining switch assembly to column and unplug wiring connectors. Remove column mounting bolts and nuts. Carefully remove column and shaft assembly from vehicle.

3) Remove steering wheel from assembly. Remove directional signals cam and bearing tolerance ring from shaft. Lift off

FIESTA

column tube, remove washers and spring, then disconnect halves of shaft.

Installation — 1) Assemble upper and lower shafts, replace washers and spring, then insert shaft into column. Position bearing tolerance ring and directional signals cam, then install steering wheel.

2) Place column assembly in vehicle, with lower shaft loosely over pinion shaft. Secure column in place with supporting nuts and bolts. Reconnect ignition and replace column switches and wiring.

3) Ensure pins on lower shaft are fully engaged in upper shaft bushings. Tighten clamp bolt after checking steering wheel position. Replace column shrouds and dash insulation cover. Reconnect battery. Column upper shroud-to-instrument panel clearance should be .28" (7.0 mm). Adjust as necessary.

TIGHTENING SPECIFICATIONS

Application	Ft. Lbs. (mkg)
Steering Wheel Nut	30-37 (4.1-5.1)
Column-to-Pinion Shaft Clamp Bolt	30-37 (4.1-5.1)

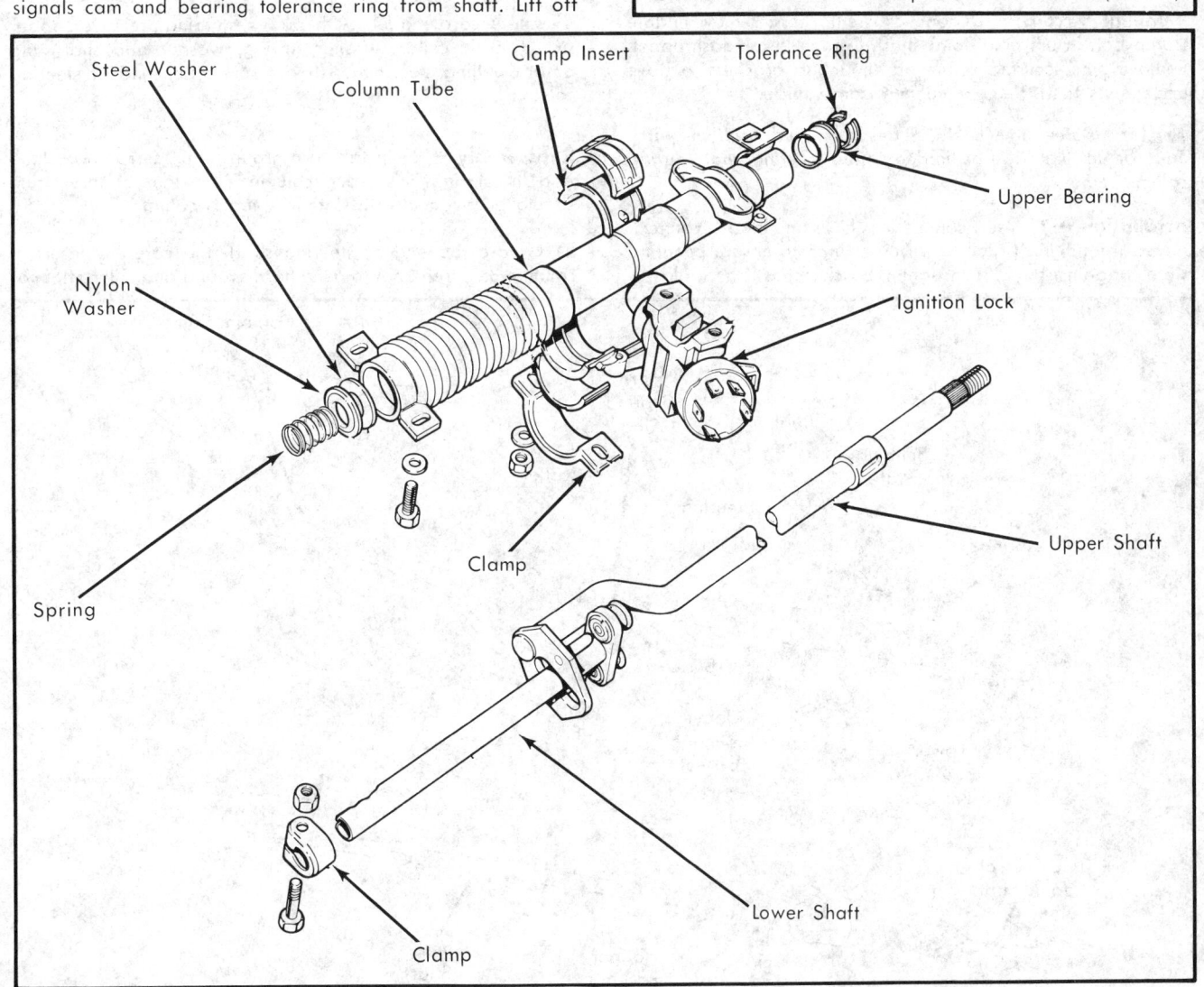

Fig. 1 Exploded View of Fiesta Steering Column Assembly

HONDA

Accord
Civic
Prelude

DESCRIPTION

Steering columns are mounted with an impact-absorbing plate on the upper bracket that deforms under pressure. A plastic bracket collar at the lower end of the column allows the assembly to slide, and double universal joints absorb impact without the need for a collapsing column.

REMOVAL & INSTALLATION

STEERING COLUMN

Removal (Civic & Prelude) — Disconnect steering joint at splines by removing clamp bolt. Remove wire connectors below column. Remove attaching bolts (upper bolts first) and take entire assembly out of vehicle.

Installation — To install, reverse removal procedure and ensure that front wheels are straight ahead when steering wheel is installed.

Removal (Accord) — Disconnect wire harness. Remove middle clamp bolt in universal joint shaft. Detach lower dash panel. Remove nuts securing column to mounting brackets (remove upper nuts first). Remove column from vehicle.

NOTE — *If steering wheel has been removed, ignition switch must be in "LOCK" position to retain steering shaft during column removal.*

Installation — 1) Insert column in vehicle and loosely connect universal joint shaft. Pull down on column to ensure bending plate is against hook, then tighten bracket nuts. Check plastic collar to ensure it is all the way on column, then install lower column bracket.

2) On models with manual steering, tighten universal joint clamp bolt. On power steering models, install special tool (07973-6710000) on top of steering shaft. Pull down on universal joint shaft until legs on special tool are seated against turn signal switch body, then tighten bolt.

OVERHAUL

Disassembly — 1) Remove steering wheel and column switches. *See Honda under STEERING WHEEL & COLUMN SWITCHES in this Section.*

2) Remove rubber bands, bending plate and upper mounting plate. On Civic and Prelude models, remove snap ring and steering shaft washer from upper end of steering shaft. Turn ignition switch to "I" position on Prelude or "ACC" position on Civic.

3) On all models, remove plastic collar, shaft bushing and column hanger bushing. Pull steering shaft out from bottom end of column. Remove thrust ring, bushing and horn ring from top end of column.

4) On Accord models with power steering, remove rubber stop, plastic collar, washer, spring, washer and snap ring before pulling steering shaft out of bottom end of steering column.

Reassembly — 1) Install horn ground ring, serrated bushing and thrust ring in steering column. Flat sides of thrust ring should be aligned with slots in steering column.

2) Grease top end of steering shaft and carefully insert in column. Be careful not to bend horn ground ring. Fill bottom of

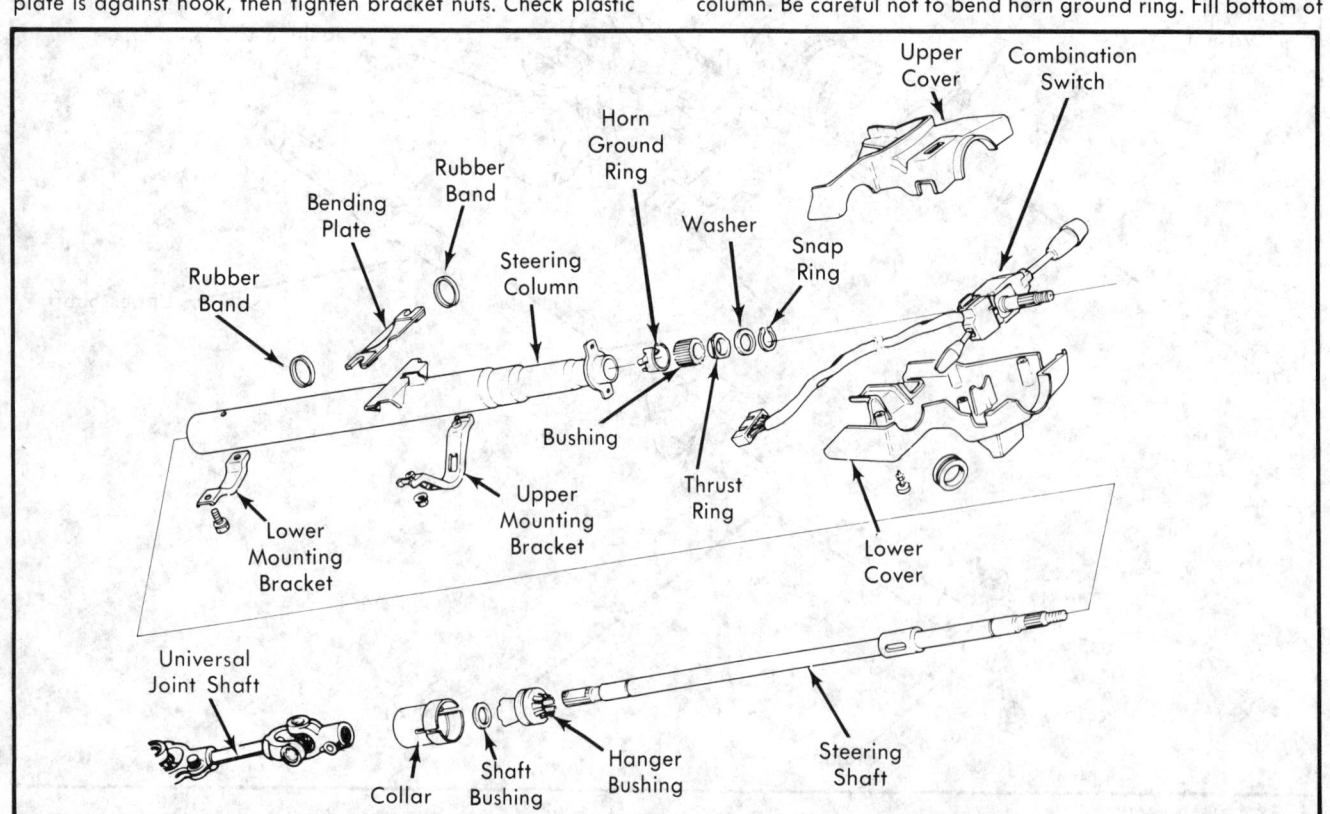

Fig. 1   Exploded View of Civic and Prelude Steering Column

HONDA (Cont.)

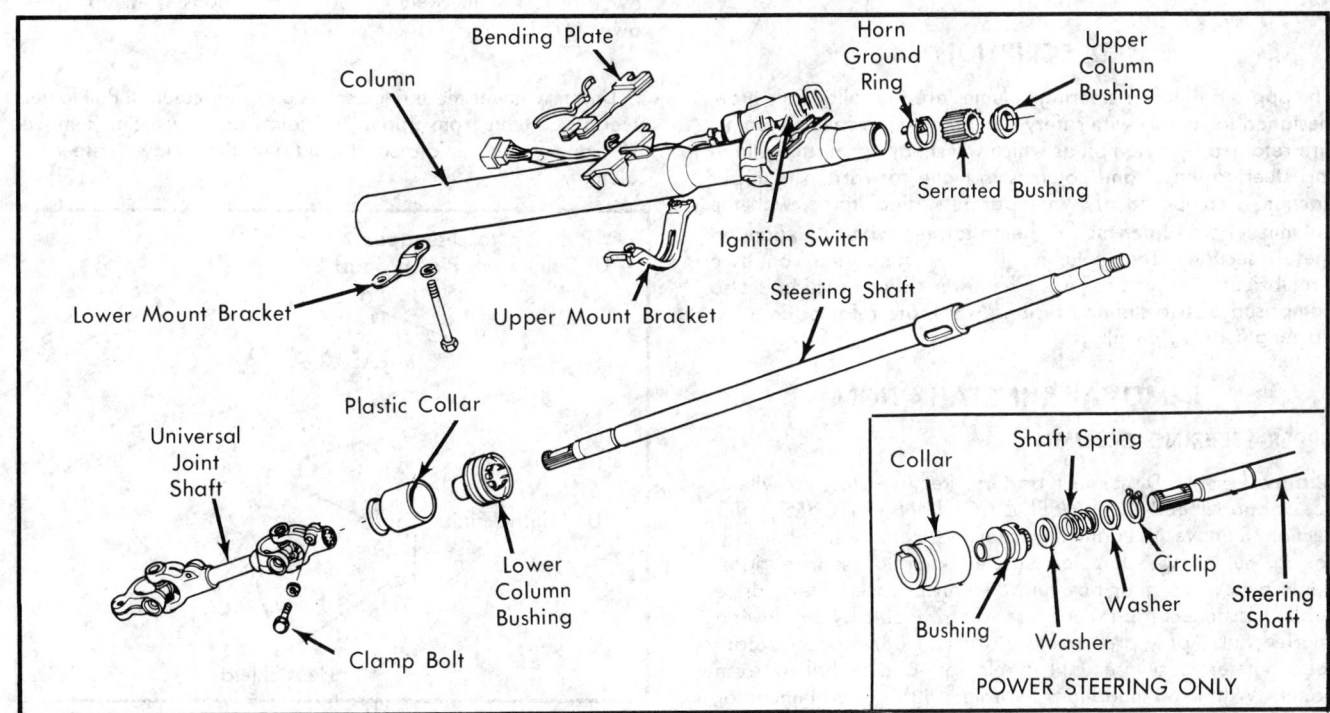

Fig. 2 Exploded View of Accord Steering Column

column with grease and install plastic hanger bushing. Align tab in column with cut-away in bushing. On Accord models with power steering, install snap ring, washer, spring and washer before installing plastic hanger bushing.

3) On all models, install plastic collar to bottom of column, align round projection on inside of collar with hole in column. On Accord models with power steering, install rubber stop. On Civic and Prelude models, install snap ring to top end of steering shaft. On Accord models, attach connector shaft universal joint to steering shaft so clamp bolt rests at bottom of machined flat of steering shaft. Tighten clamp bolt.

NOTE — *On Accord models, place ignition switch in the "O" position to prevent shaft from sliding out during installation.*

4) Install column switches. Use rubber bands to assemble upper bracket and bending plate to steering column. Bending plate should fit under hook on column with arrow mark facing out and pointing down. Install upper and lower covers.

TIGHTENING SPECIFICATIONS

Application	Ft. Lbs. (mkg)
Column Bracket Bolts	
Upper	9 (1.3)
Lower	16 (2.2)
Universal Clamp Bolts	22 (3.0)

JAGUAR

XJ6

DESCRIPTION

The upper and lower steering columns are the collapsible type, designed to comply with safety regulations. The collapse points are retained by nylon plugs which will shear on impact, allowing steering wheel and columns to move forward. The upper column is composed of two separate sliding shafts, with the column tube on later models being formed with an expanded metal section. The column shaft is supported on two prelubricated roller bearings. The lower column section is also comprised of two sliding portions, which are retained in a fixed length by nylon plugs.

REMOVAL & INSTALLATION

UPPER STEERING COLUMN

Removal — 1) Disconnect battery. Remove steering wheel. See Jaguar STEERING WHEEL & COLUMN SWITCHES in this Section. Remove speedometer as follows: Remove speedometer casing. Behind speedometer, unscrew knurled nut from right-angle bracket to gear box and disconnect speedometer drive cable. Disconnect trip record reset control cable by unscrewing knurled nut. Apply pressure to instrument panel bezel, rotate speedometer clockwise until it releases, and withdraw from panel. Withdraw headlight warning light and illuminator lights.

2) Remove tachometer as follows: Apply pressure to instrument bezel and rotate counterclockwise until tachometer releases. Disconnect electrical plug and socket. Remove ground lead. Withdraw illumination light holder.

3) Remove trim panel below the upper steering column. Disconnect electrical switch connections (three socket and plug connections). Detach horn contact at upper column. Unscrew self-locking nut and remove pinch bolt securing upper universal joint to lower steering column.

4) Loosen 2 set screws holding lower end of upper column. Reach through instrument openings and remove two nuts holding top of column. Collect washers, shims, and nuts, and support column. Remove 2 set screws previously loosened and carefully remove complete steering column assembly from vehicle.

CAUTION — Do not use excessive force when separating upper column from lower column.

Inspection — Examine column for straightness. Any wear, damage, or variation in length means the column should be replaced. Length from end to end (without "U" joint) should be between 21.56-21.70" (547.7-551.0 mm).

Installation — If universal joint and/or adjusting clamp have been removed, refit, then reverse removal procedure and note the following: Check that ⅜" (9.5 mm) clearance exists axially in lower universal joint; if necessary, move upper universal joint further along lower column to increase clearance. Ensure self-cancelling operation of turn signals functions properly and that steering wheel spokes are horizontal when straight-ahead position is set; if not adjust as necessary.

LOWER STEERING COLUMN

Removal — 1) Raise vehicle on hoist and remove pinch bolt securing lower "U" joint to pinion shaft. Lower vehicle. Detach lower parcel shelf. Remove both pinch bolts from upper-to-lower "U" joint.

2) Unscrew lower mounting screws of upper column. Pull lower steering column from upper "U" joint. Raise vehicle. Remove "U" joint from pinion shaft and withdraw lower steering column.

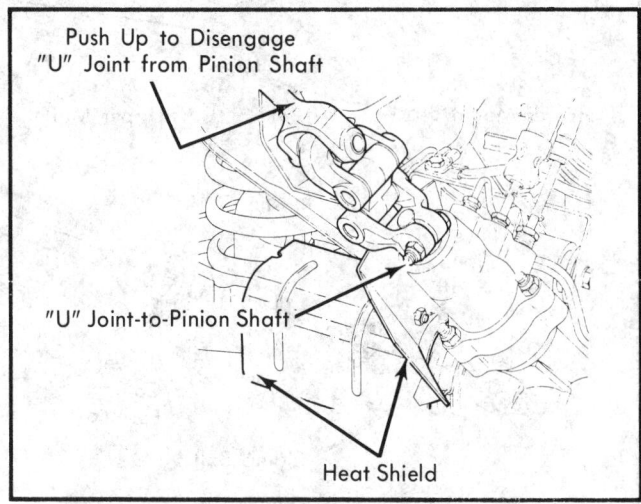

Fig. 1   Disconnecting Lower Steering Column from Pinion Shaft

Installation — To install, reverse removal procedure and ensure gap of ⅜" (9.5 mm) exists in universal joint.

NOTE — Front wheels should be kept in straight ahead position during this operation.

STEERING COLUMN ADJUSTING CLAMP

Removal — Remove steering wheel. Pull impact rubber from steering wheel shaft. Unscrew three small cheese-head screws from beneath adjusting clamp (lock nut) and withdraw retaining plate. Unscrew collet adaptor completely and remove from shaft. Remove circlip from within upper side of adjuster. Withdraw adjuster (lock nut) collecting stop button. Slide split collet off shaft.

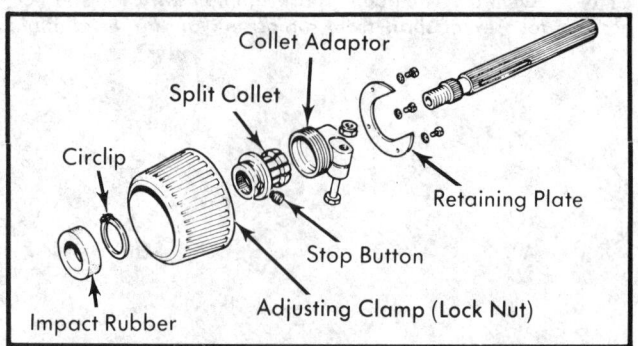

Fig. 2   Exploded View of Steering Column Adjusting Clamp

Installation — Clean parts thoroughly and remove any burrs with a file. Lightly lubricate all enclosed metal components. Install by reversing removal procedure.

JAGUAR (Cont.)

STEERING COLUMN LOWER SEAL

Removal — Remove upper steering column, as previously outlined. Loosen hose clip attaching upper sealing sleeve to lower column; remove clip and sleeve. Remove 3 screws securing seal retainer to instrument panel. Slide seal, retainer and sealing sleeve up and off lower column.

Installation — Fit assembly of sealing sleeve, seal, and retainer over end of lower column carefully. Insert and tighten three retaining set screws. Carefully slide second sealing sleeve, flanged end first, over lower column as far as first sealing sleeve; position hose clip, but do not tighten. Move second sealing sleeve approximately ¼" (6 mm) toward dash, to preload it against first sealing sleeve. Secure this position with hose clip. Replace upper column assembly.

OVERHAUL

UPPER & LOWER STEERING COLUMNS

NOTE — *No repairs, adjustments, or overhaul procedures are given by the manufacturer. If damage is evident or suspected, replacement of assemblies is necessary.*

TIGHTENING SPECIFICATIONS	
Application	**Ft. Lbs. (mkg)**
Universal Joint Bolts	14-18 (1.9-2.5)
Steering Wheel	25-30 (3.5-4.1)
Column-to-Brackets	14-18 (1.9-2.5)

Steering Columns

LUV

Pickup

DESCRIPTION

Column is fastened to steering gear through a flexible coupling. The energy-absorbing shaft will collapse during frontal impact under predetermined loads, by shearing plastic pins.

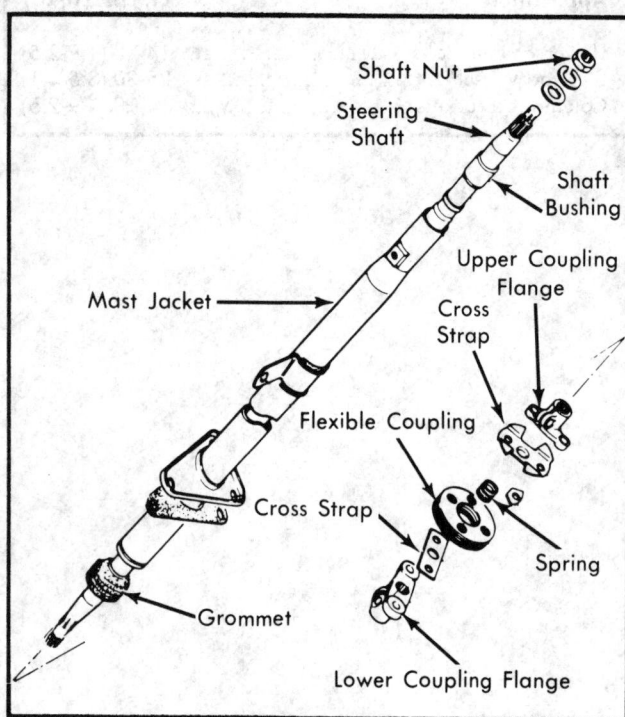

Fig. 1   Exploded View of Steering Column Assembly

REMOVAL & INSTALLATION

NOTE — *Before beginning removal and installation, inspect steering shaft shear pins. If steering shaft plastic pins have been sheared, shaft will rattle when struck lightly from side.*

STEERING COLUMN

Removal — **1)** Disconnect battery ground. Remove horn cover and spring. Remove steering column shrouding and hazard warning light switch. Remove combination switch. Remove steering wheel. See *LUV* under *STEERING WHEEL & COLUMN SWITCHES* in this Section.

NOTE — *Avoid impact to steering wheel at all times.*

2) Raise front of vehicle and support. Remove pinch bolt holding shaft to lower coupling flange. Remove 3 mast jacket to firewall bolts. Remove 2 steering column to instrument panel bolts.

3) Separate rubber coupling from steering shaft. Carefully slide steering shaft toward inside of passenger compartment and remove from vehicle.

Installation — To install, reverse removal procedure, noting the following: Leave column-to-panel bolts slightly loose until vehicle is lowered to ground.

FLEXIBLE COUPLING

Removal — **1)** Raise front of vehicle. Remove coupling through bolts (only two can be removed). Remove coupling assembly by loosening clamp bolts.

2) If necessary to remove clamps, steering column must be loosened. Remove column mounting screws at cowl. Remove instrument panel mount bolts and slide column rearward about 1" (25 mm), then remove steering column flexible coupling.

Installation — Replace clamps without pinch bolts. Position rubber coupling and tighten through-bolts as required. Install and tighten clamp pinch bolts. If column was loosened, lower vehicle to floor and slightly tighten column-to-instrument panel screws. Install column cowling, then completely tighten column support screws.

TIGHTENING SPECIFICATIONS

Application	Ft. Lbs. (mkg)
Steering Wheel Nut	25 (3.5)
Coupling Through-Bolts	18 (2.5)
Shaft Coupling Clamp	20 (2.8)
Coupling-to-Wormshaft Clamp	20 (2.8)
Column-to-Cowl	10 (1.4)

MERCEDES-BENZ

240D
280 Series
300 Series
450 Series

DESCRIPTION

Steering column assembly includes an impact absorbing steering wheel, upper and lower column shafts and flexible coupling. Lower shaft on 123 Series models is corrugated for additional impact protection.

CHASSIS IDENTIFICATION

Application	Chassis Type
240D, 280E, 280CE, 300D, 300CD, 300TD	123
450SL, 450SLC	107
280SE, 300SD, 450SEL	116

STEERING COLUMN

Removal — 1) On 123 Series, remove screws holding upper and lower cover on instrument panel and remove covers. On all models, disconnect battery and remove steering wheel. Remove instrument cluster by pulling outward as far as possible and loosening tachometer, temperature, and oil pressure connections.

2) On all models, remove steering lock. Disconnect wiring connectors. Remove Allen head screw of flexible coupling and all nuts and screws holding casing and column to dashboard. Remove steering column housing.

Installation — To install, reverse removal procedure and note the following: On chassis types 107 and 123, always use new steering wheel Allen screw when installing steering wheel. On 450 models, hold steering shaft in place with pin through hole in jacket tube. Check that lower tube on chassis type 123 is not bent or distorted. Use caution when installing jacket tube to prevent damage to this shaft.

STEERING COLUMN SHAFT

Removal, 123 Series (Lower) — 1) From engine compartment, remove both Allen head screws holding flexible coupling to worm shaft and steering shaft. Slide coupling down on worm shaft and off steering shaft.

2) From inside car, remove upper and lower cover from instrument panel/steering column. Remove Allen screws at upper coupling and slide coupling and lower shaft off of upper shaft.

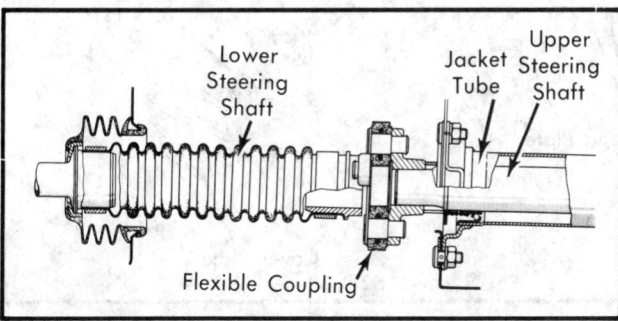

Fig. 1 Lower Steering Shaft (123 Models)

Installation — To install, lubricate inner lips of bellows seal at firewall and reverse removal procedures.

NOTE — *Wheels must be in straight ahead position and notch on upper shaft must point directly upward during installation.*

Removal, 123 Series (Upper) — 1) With column out of car, remove combination switch. Remove jacket tube casing, then remove spacing ring from steering shaft.

2) Remove gripper ring, compression spring, supporting ring and ball bearing from steering shaft. Knock steering shaft upward out of jacket tube with plastic hammer.

Installation — Inspect and replace bearings and races if required. Reverse removal procedure and reinstall upper steering shaft.

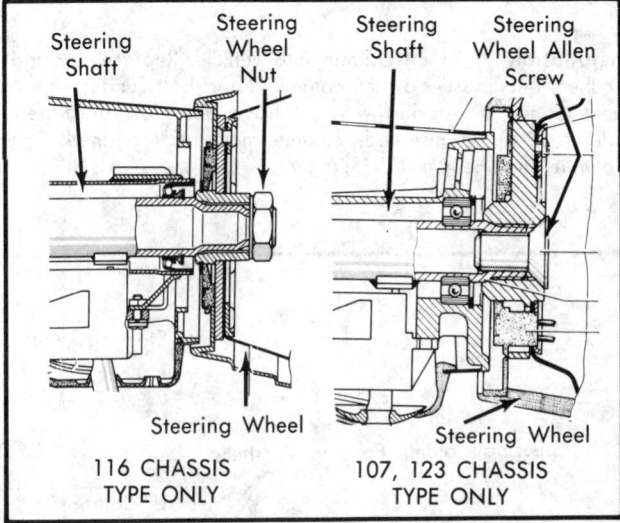

Fig. 2 Sectional View of Mercedes-Benz Steering Column and Steering Shaft

Removal, 107 and 116 Series — 1) Remove steering wheel and combination switch rubber cover. Loosen switch mounting screws on bearing body and pull switch out slightly. Loosen screws holding cable of contact carbon on combination switch.

2) Remove Allen screw from upper end of steering coupling. Remove screws from jacket tube and pull steering shaft with bearing body out of jacket tube.

Installation — Replace bearings and races as required and reverse removal procedure. Check shaft adjustment; pin inserted through hole in jacket casing should locate check bore of steering shaft. Mark on end of shaft should be up when installing.

NOTE — *Steering shaft length should be 31.7" (805 mm); tap gently with plastic mallet to adjust length before installation.*

TIGHTENING SPECIFICATIONS

Application	Ft. Lbs. (mkg)
Steering Wheel	
107, 123	59 (8.2)
116	37 (5.1)
Flexible Coupling (Allen)	18 (2.5)

Steering Columns

MGB

REMOVAL & INSTALLATION

STEERING COLUMN

Removal — Remove steering wheel. *See MGB under STEER-ING WHEEL & COLUMN SWITCHES in this section.* Remove pinch bolt clamping steering column to "U" joint. Disconnect column wiring at multi-wire connector. Remove column bracket mounting bolts and note position of packing washers. Remove column from vehicle.

Disassembly — Remove column covers, take off wiring and combination switch. Drill and use screw extractor to remove ignition switch bolts. Remove switch.

Reassembly — Reverse disassembly procedure.

Installation — **1)** Fit column into vehicle. Replace packing washers and loosely attach column clamp bolts under instrument panel. If packing washers have been lost or if new column is being installed, column must be realigned. See *Column Alignment in this Section.*

2) Connect wiring plug and set wheels straight ahead. Slide steering shaft into "U" joint, making sure grooves align with pinch bolt holes. Fit pinch bolt and tighten.

ADJUSTMENTS

STEERING COLUMN ALIGNMENT

1) Remove "U" joint. Fit alignment gauge shown in *Fig. 2*. Make sure setscrew seats in splined groove.

2) Fit 1 packing washer between each upper column mounting bracket. Tighten bolts until washers are just pinched. Tighten column plate bolts just enough to retain column in center of hole. Make sure rack has original amount of shims. Tighten bolts.

3) To correct horizontal misalignment, move end of column, then tighten column plate bolts.

4) To correct vertical misalignment, use shims placed between rack mounting brackets and bring left and right alignment into tolerance. Do not use more than 3 shims on either bracket. Refit rack and tighten mounting bolts.

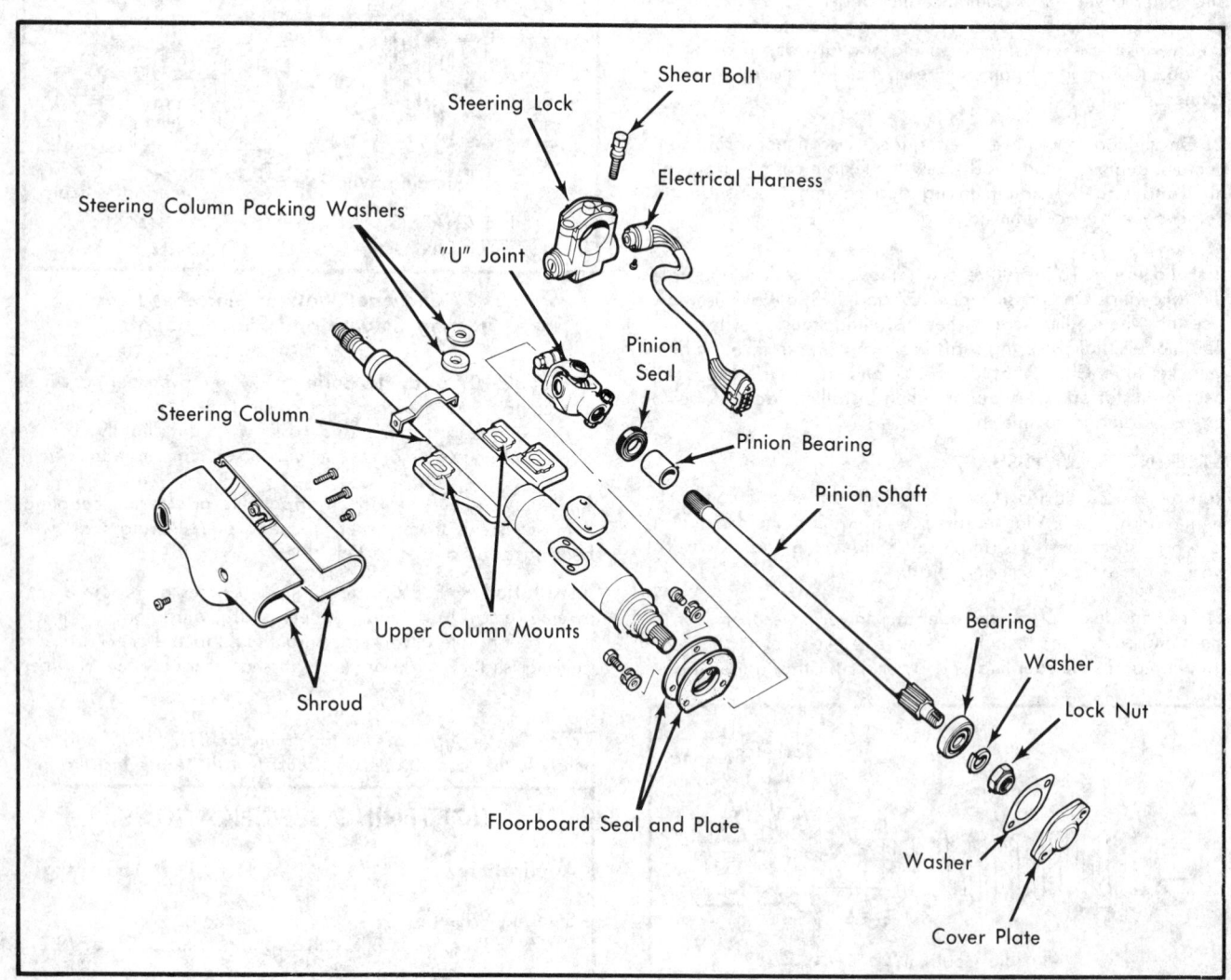

Fig. 1   Exploded View of Steering Column and Related Components

MGB (Cont.)

5) Check gauge alignment. Make sure pinion has clearance. If there is interference, adjust shims. If alignment is still not adequate, readjust upper shims (packing washers). Make sure not to exceed .235″ (6 mm) thickness with shims. Tighten top bolts. Take off gauge set.

6) Measure gap between column upper mounting flange and body bracket at third bolt position. Fit packing shims equal to gap. Tighten bolt. Make sure to rivet shims to rack mounting bracket before completing job.

TIGHTENING SPECIFICATIONS

Application	Ft. Lbs. (mkg)
Upper Column Mounting Bolts	12-17 (1.7-2.4)
Universal Clamp Bolts	20-22 (2.8-3.0)
Steering Wheel Nut	27-29 (3.7-4.0)

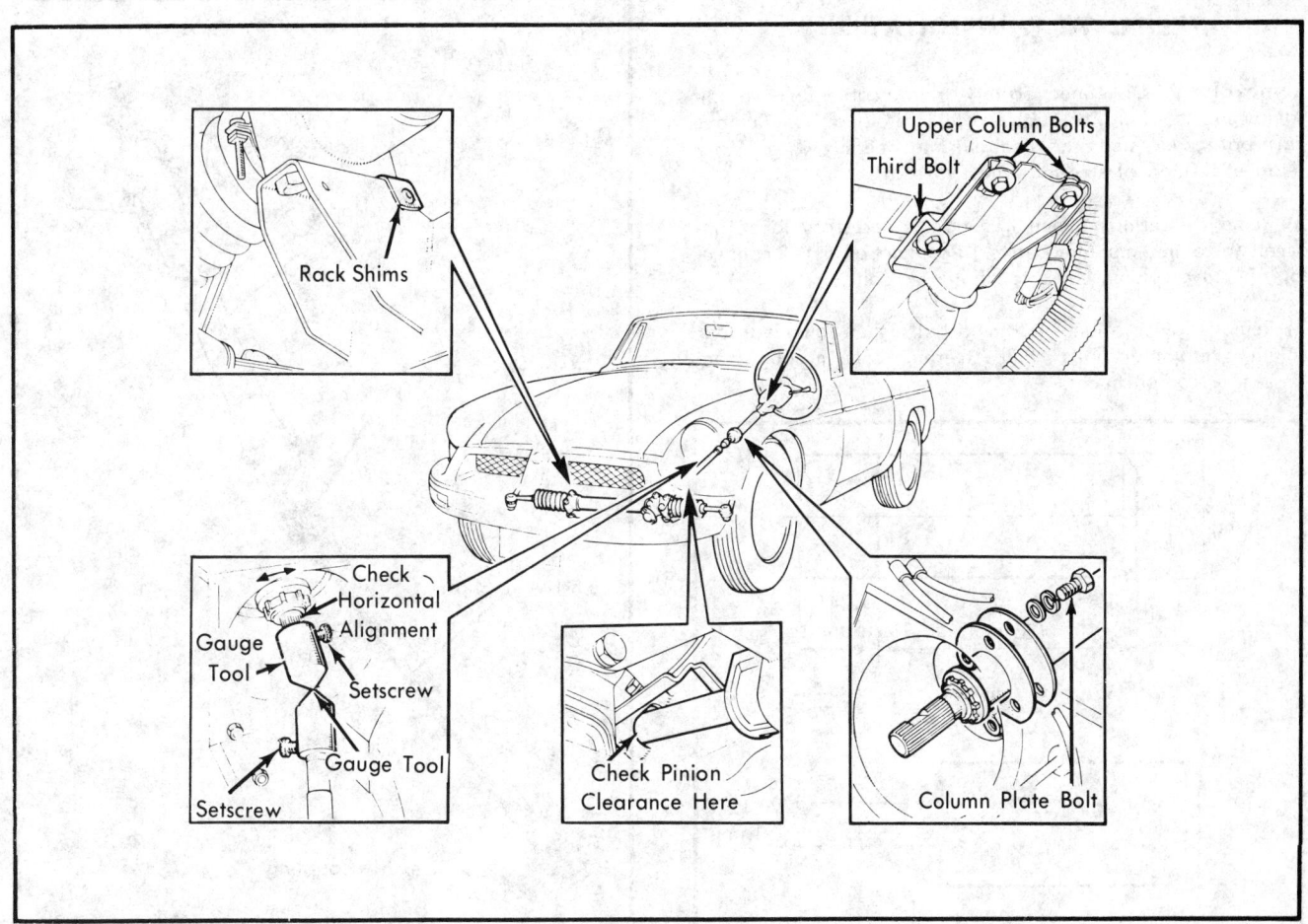

Fig. 2   Steering Column Alignment Steps

Steering Columns

PEUGEOT

504
505
604

DESCRIPTION

Steering column consists of an upper and lower steering shaft connected by a universal joint. Steering shaft utilizes a rubber flexible coupling at its lower end to help absorb road shocks. Steering column contains the steering lock, turn signal/horn switch, headlight dimmer/washer switch and on some models, the speed control switch.

REMOVAL & INSTALLATION

Removal — 1) Disconnect battery ground cable. Remove bolt connecting steering shaft rubber coupling to gear box. Remove horn pad cover, steering wheel nut and steering wheel. Mark relative position of steering wheel to shaft.

2) Remove steering column trim panels necessary to obtain access to column mounting bolts. Disconnect all switch connectors. Remove column cover to floor pan bolts.

3) Remove lower column retaining bolts, then remove upper column retaining bolts. Pull steering column out from passenger compartment.

Installation — 1) To install steering column, reverse removal procedures and note the following: Place front wheels in straight ahead position. Install column assembly, from passenger compartment, and align lower shaft with flexible coupling. Tighten column mounting bolts.

2) On 504 models, insert fabricated clearance gauge into recess at flexible coupling and tighten pinch bolt. Remove gauge. On all models, make sure all switches are installed, connected and operate properly. Install column trim covers and steering wheel.

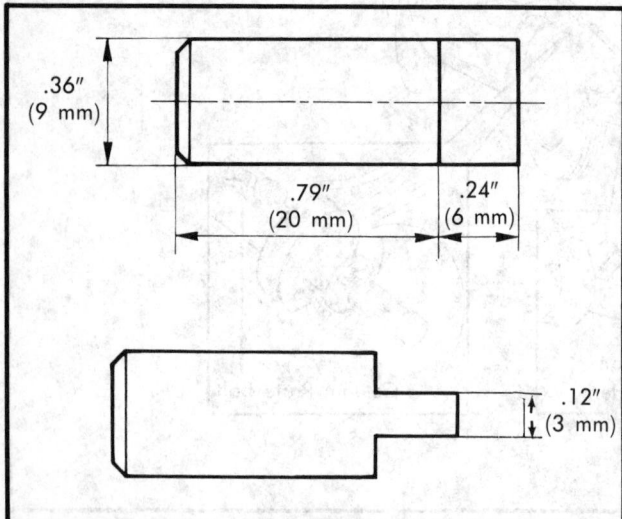

Fig. 1   Dimensions for Fabricating Clearance Gauge (504 Models Only)

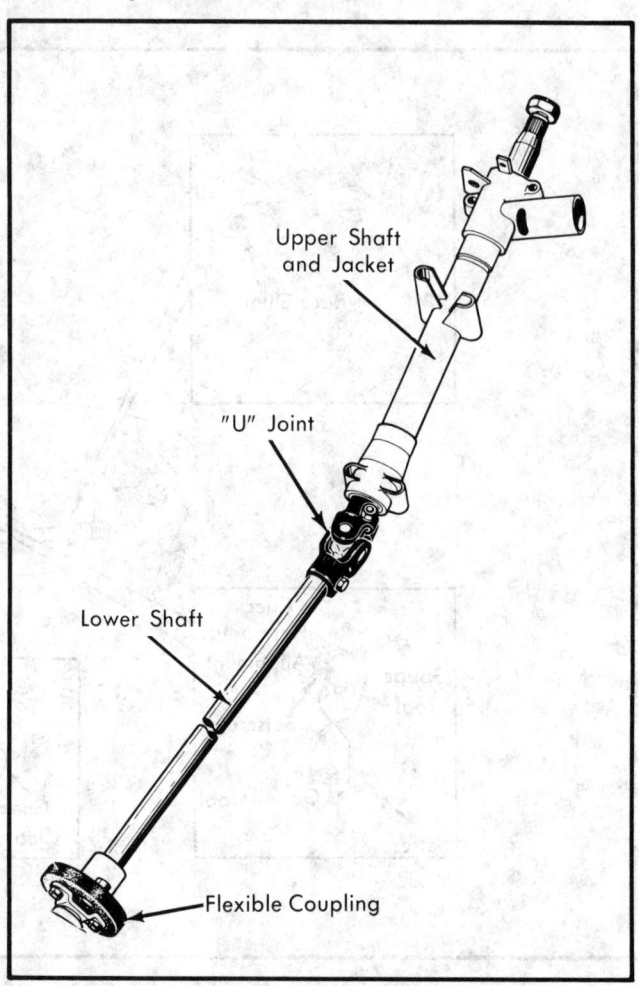

Fig. 2   Peugeot Steering Column Assembly (504 Shown, 505 and 604 Similar)

PORSCHE

911SC
924

NOTE — *Steering column removal and installation information for 928 is not available.*

DESCRIPTION

The steering column assemblies on all Porsche models are essentially the same, consisting of a three-piece, energy-absorbing unit, with the three pieces connected by two universal joints. The offset design of the steering shaft and the collapsible element in the steering column provide the energy-absorbing protection for the driver. An energy absorbing steering wheel with rebound chambers and padded hub cover provides additional protection.

REMOVAL & INSTALLATION

Removal (911SC) — **1)** Disconnect battery. From front compartment, remove blower, ducting and steering shaft cover. Remove universal joint retaining bolt.

2) From driver's compartment, remove knee strip, light switch and tachometer. Drill or grind off shear bolts holding ignition switch/steering lock in panel mounting.

3) Lift off hub cover and remove steering wheel. Detach wire connection and remove steering column switch assembly along with steering shaft and tube.

Installation — To install, reverse removal procedure and tighten attaching shear bolts until heads break off.

Removal (924) — **1)** Disconnect battery and lift off steering wheel pad. Remove steering wheel. Remove upper universal joint retaining bolt.

2) Disconnect wiring plugs from rear of switches. Drill out casing tube shear bolts holding column to instrument panel. Remove upper steering column and switches as an assembly.

Installation — To install, reverse removal procedure noting the following: Tighten shear bolts holding column to panel until heads break off. Steering must be centered and hub lubricated when installing steering wheel. Tighten to specified torque with spokes in horizontal position.

OVERHAUL

STEERING COLUMN ASSEMBLY

Disassembly (911SC) — **1)** With column out of vehicle and switches removed from column, drive steering shaft out of tube. Remove lower end circlip and lower ball bearing.

2) Press Seeger ring out of top end of steering shaft tube. Remove ball bearing and contact ring.

Reassembly — **1)** Install ball bearing against circlip at lower end of steering column and seat bottom circlip against bearing. Circlips must seat in recessed grooves. Place contact ring and upper bearing together on steering shaft.

2) With section of pipe, drive bearing into place on shaft. Pipe should contact inner race only. Complete assembly in reverse order of disassembly.

Disassembly (924) — Remove turn signal and windshield wiper switches. Remove circlip and upper ball bearing from housing.

Reassembly — **1)** Reverse disassembly procedures and note the following: Drive ball bearing in up to stop in housing. Switches must be in OFF position when installed.

2) Lubricate needle bearing at lower end with multi-purpose grease. Use light coat of silicone grease or talcum powder on rubber bearing.

3) Drive steering shaft spacer sleeve onto shaft so that top of sleeve is 1.614" (41 mm) below top of shaft. Cancelling tab of turn signal release ring must face to right.

TIGHTENING SPECIFICATIONS

Application	Ft. Lbs. (mkg)
Universal Joint Bolts	18-25 (2.5-3.5)
Steering Wheel Nut	
911SC	54 (7.5)
924	25-40 (3.5-5.5)
Steering Column Switch-to-Casing (Allen)	8-14 (1.0-2.0)

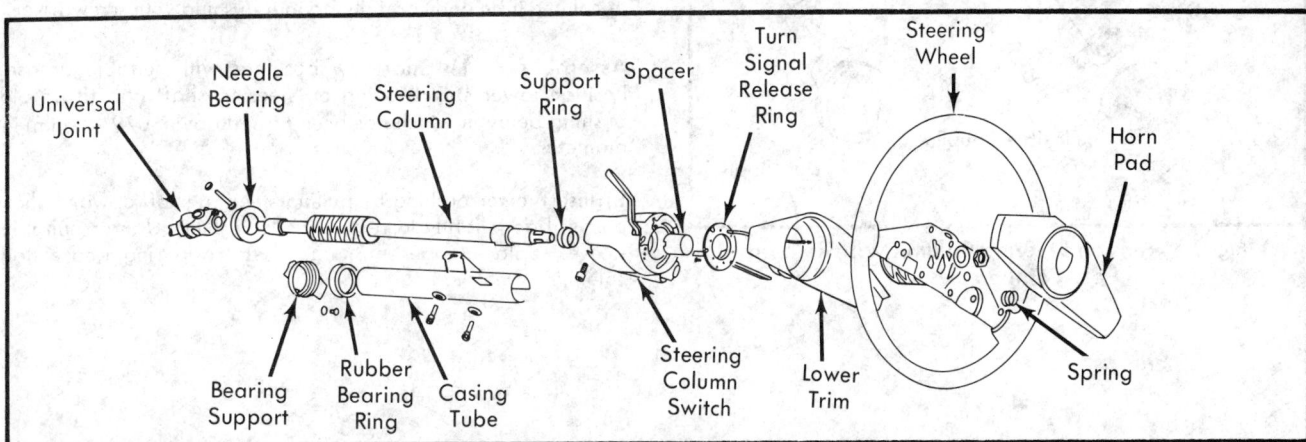

Fig. 1   Porsche 924 Steering Column

RENAULT

Le Car

DESCRIPTION

Vehicles are equipped with an energy-absorbing collapsible column. The steering column is designed in two separate sections, which are joined by a universal joint. The upper portion of the column is designed with a sliding section which compresses on vehicle impact. At the lower end of the bottom section, the steering column is connected to the pinion flange of the steering gear through a flexible rubber coupling.

REMOVAL & INSTALLATION

STEERING COLUMN

Removal — 1) Disconnect battery and unclip speedometer cable in engine compartment. Remove instrument cluster cowl. Pry clips on sides of cluster inward and pull cluster forward. Disconnect wiring and speedometer cable, then remove cluster.

2) Remove steering wheel pad and steering wheel. Detach lower column cover, remove screws and lift off combination switch from column. Disconnect wiring from switch. Remove fuse box screws and place box to one side. Disconnect universal joint.

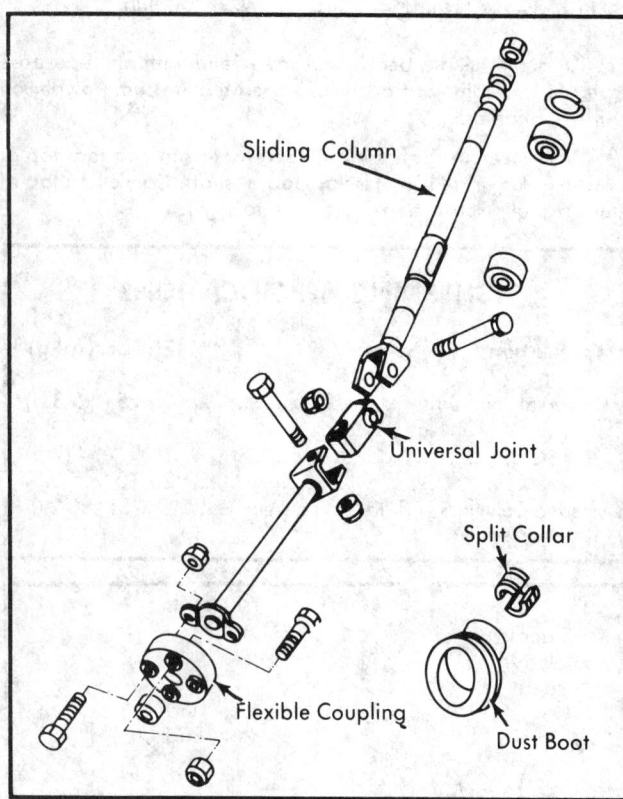

Fig. 1   Renault Steering Column with Related Components

3) Mark column clamp position, remove shaft flexible coupling at steering box, and remove clamps from column tube. Pull column assembly free from dashboard.

Installation — 1) To install, reverse removal procedures, noting the following: Tighten upper column clamp at the end of installation. Set gear at center position before connecting universal joint in the following manner:

2) Raise front end of vehicle. Set steering box at center point. Tighten bottom joint pin. Turn steering 1/4 turn to left or right, then tighten upper universal joint pin.

3) Reconnect all wiring, tighten bolts securely and check shaft for binding or rubbing.

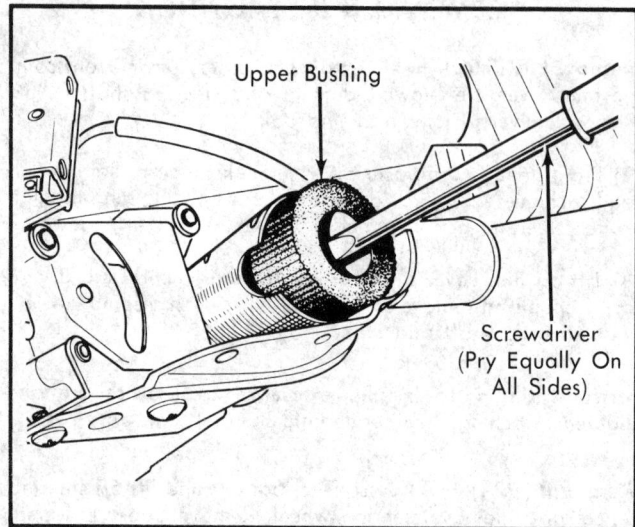

Fig. 2   Removing Upper Column Bushing

OVERHAUL

REPLACING COLUMN BUSHINGS

Disassembly — Tap upper end of steering shaft until lower bushing comes out of column tube. Remove snap ring from top of column tube and carefully pry out bushing with screwdriver.

Assembly — 1) Coat new bushings with suitable grease. Position lower split bushing on steering shaft and fit an old bushing below it which has been turned down .079" (2 mm) in diameter.

2) Insert lower bushing by pulling steering shaft upward, then push it back slightly to recover used bushing. Using a suitable sleeve, replace upper bushing. Insert snap ring and install column in vehicle.

SAAB

99
900

DESCRIPTION

Steering columns used on these models are safety, telescopic type. The lower portion of the steering shaft is designed to retract into the upper portion when frontal impact is experienced. On 99 models, the steering shaft is mounted in column tube by bushings. Column tube is mounted at one end to pedal bracket and at other end to body. On 900 models, steering shaft is mounted in column support by needle bearings. Column support is mounted to a cross member under dash. An intermediate shaft, with "U" joints at each end, transmits steering shaft movement to steering gear. On 99 models with power steering, double "U" joints are used.

REMOVAL & INSTALLATION

STEERING COLUMN

Removal (99) — Remove locking bolt at universal joint and lower retaining screws at pedal bracket. Remove upper column-to-instrument panel retaining screws. Detach quick-release wiring connection and lift out steering column assembly.

CAUTION — *On 99 models, steering wheel must be mounted on shaft before column is installed. Otherwise, tension on wheel and column may result.*

Installation (99) — Position steering column tube in place with steering shaft and wheel attached. Bolt steering shaft to "U" joint. Make sure mounting bolt is opposite groove in steering shaft. Tighten bolt. Mount steering column tube to pedal bracket and body. Connect electrical harness. Adjust steering wheel.

Removal (900) — Remove locking bolt at universal joint. Remove lower bearing cover and safety padding under instrument panel. Remove direction switch and wiper switch assembly. Remove rubber boot at dash and the four screws in steering column bearing support. Remove complete steering column assembly.

Installation (900) — Bolt steering shaft to "U" joint, making sure bolt engages groove in shaft. Install four steering column bearing support screws and tighten slightly. Position support so holes align with holes in dash. Tighten screws. Install rubber boot to dash, install electrical switches, safety padding and steering joint cover. Adjust steering wheel.

INTERMEDIATE SHAFT SEALING BELLOWS

Removal — Remove cover under instrument panel. Unscrew steering column-to-intermediate shaft retaining screw. Unbolt

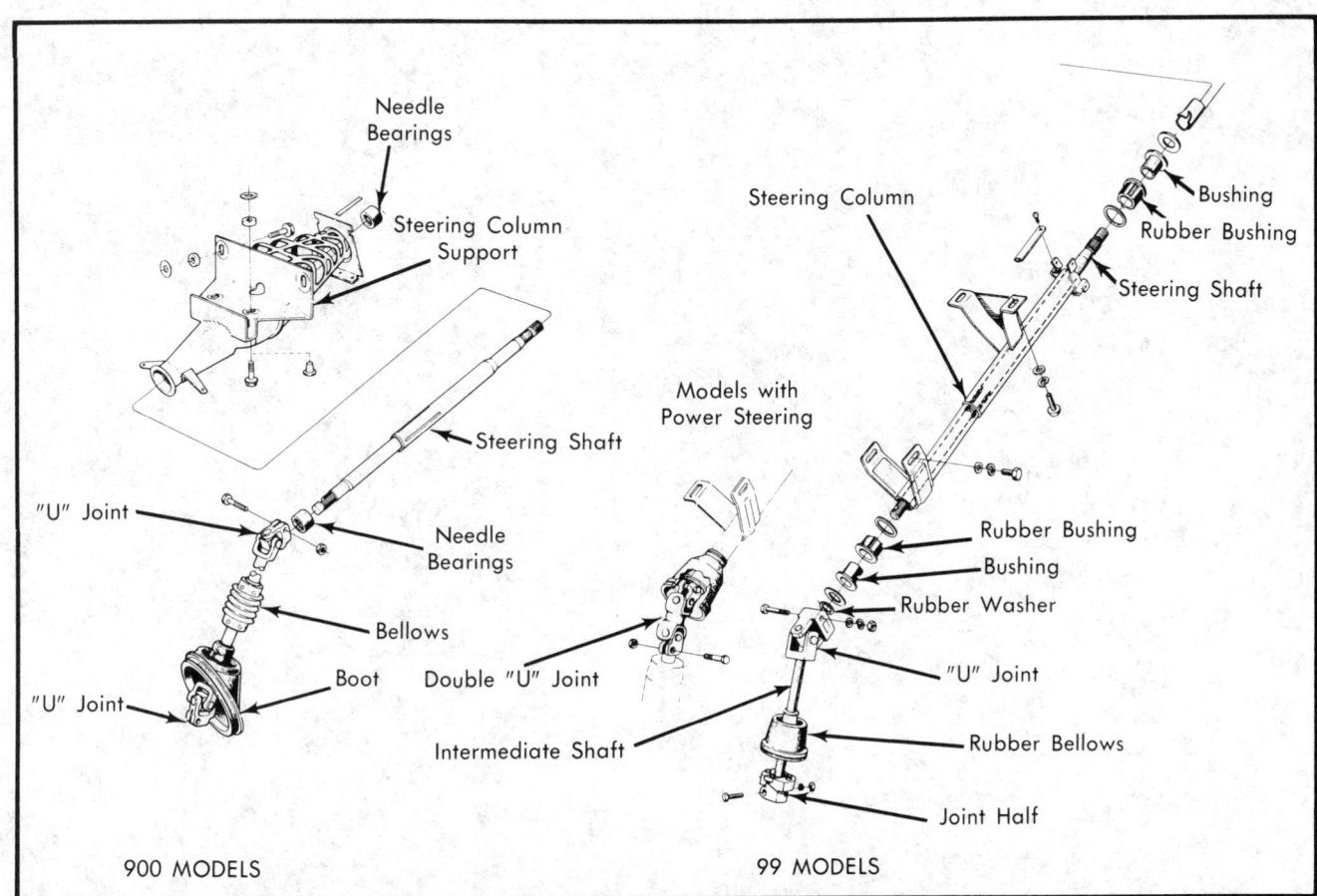

Fig. 1 Exploded View of Steering Column Assembly

SAAB (Cont.)

column tube from instrument panel. Pull steering column from intermediate shaft. Cut off old sealing bellows.

Installation — Lubricate suitable installation tool (8995813) with vaseline or soapy water. Place tool against intermediate shaft. Ease new bellows over tool and joint. Ensure bellows are not damaged in this process. Replace steering column into intermediate shaft. Make sure that shaft is pushed in so that screw is located directly opposite the groove. Tighten retaining screw. Attach steering column to instrument panel. Check position of steering wheel and adjust if necessary. Fit bellows in dash panel. Replace cover under dash.

OVERHAUL

STEERING COLUMN

NOTE — *The only overhaul procedure possible on 900 models is replacement of the two needle bearings.*

Disassembly — Remove three retaining screws and remove plastic cover under steering wheel. Pull steering wheel shaft out of tube. Withdraw two rubber bushings with steering wheel shaft bushings and washers.

Reassembly — To reassemble, reverse disassembly procedure. Replace required bushings.

SUBARU

1600
1800

DESCRIPTION

Steering column assembly consists of a steering wheel incorporating a horn control, a combination turn signal, hazard warning, and headlight dimmer switch assembly, and an energy absorbing steering shaft. The steering column is connected to the steering gear through a universal joint coupling. The energy absorbing steering shaft is designed to collapse during a front end collision. An anti-theft locking mechanism is used to prevent steering shaft from turning when key is removed.

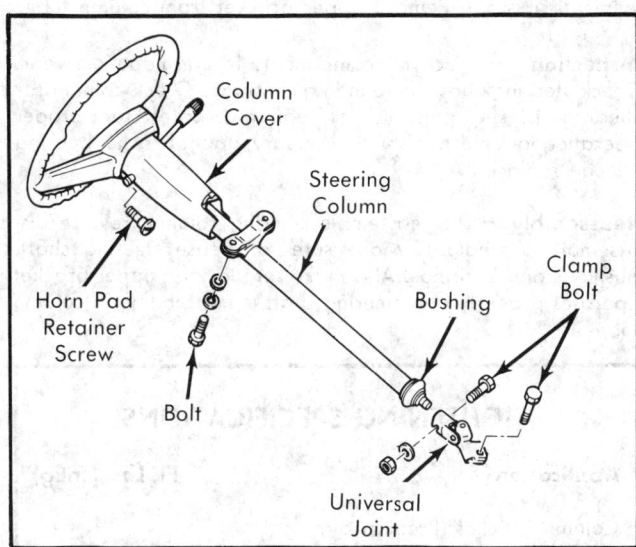

Fig. 1   Subaru Steering Column Assembly

REMOVAL & INSTALLATION

Removal — **1)** Disconnect battery ground strap. Loosen the universal joint clamp bolt and separate shaft from joint.

2) Remove trim panel and unplug all wiring connectors to steering column switches. Remove steering shaft bolt from instrument panel and pull steering column from floorboard.

Installation — Insert column through floorboard into universal joint. Install column bolt into dashboard and tighten. Connect all electrical connections. Tighten universal joint bolt.

OVERHAUL

Disassembly — **1)** Clamp steering column carefully in a vise. Remove single screw holding horn pad on 2 spoke steering wheels, or remove 4 horn pad retaining screws on 4 spoke steering wheels. Remove horn pad. Remove steering wheel nut then remove steering wheel. Remove column covers, combination switch and horn brush.

2) Remove screws retaining bearing to steering column. Pull out shaft from the bottom of cover and remove snap ring, washer, "O" ring and bearing.

Inspection — **1)** Universal joint should have no play in any direction. Replace if any play exists. Flex universal joint and check for binding. Replace if torque required to flex joint exceeds 0.43 ft. lbs. (0.06 mkg). Check plastic washer for damage, and serration for wear.

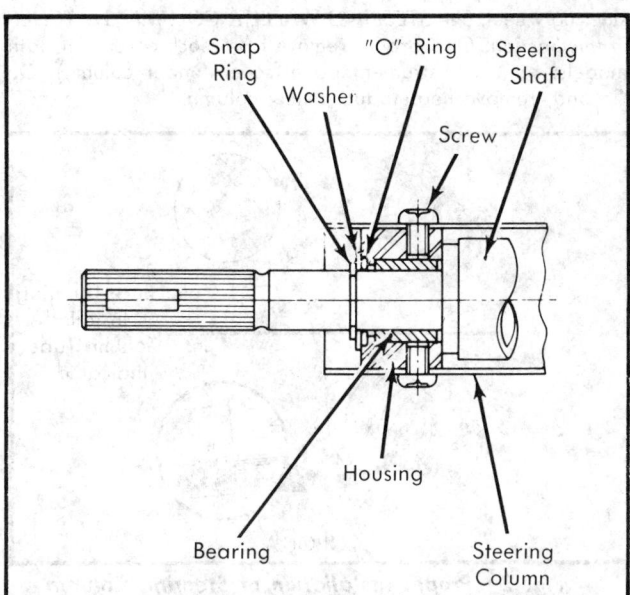

Fig. 2   View of Steering Shaft Lower Components

2) Check steering shaft for runout and length. Length should be 33.78" (857.9 mm). Runout for elliptical part of shaft should be less than 1.28" (32.6 mm). Runout for collar part of shaft should be less than .024" (.6 mm). Runout for upper end of shaft should be less than .047" (1.2 mm). Replace steering shaft if not to specifications. Check bearings for wear or damage, replace if necessary.

Reassembly — To reassemble, reverse disassembly procedure and note the following: With steering wheel in place, check clearance between wheel and cover. If clearance exceeds .04-.12" (1.0-3.0 mm), loosen column cover screws and adjust cover.

TIGHTENING SPECIFICATIONS

Application	Ft. Lbs. (mkg)
Steering Wheel Nut	22-29 (3.0-4.0)
Column Bracket Bolt	14-23 (2.0-3.2)
Universal Joint Bolt	16-19 (2.2-2.6)

TOYOTA COROLLA & CORONA

DESCRIPTION

Columns used on Corolla and Corona models are collapsible two-piece design. Columns use plastic shear pins to absorb collision impact. A flexible coupling connects steering shaft to steering gear.

REMOVAL & INSTALLATION

STEERING COLUMN

Removal — 1) Disconnect battery negative terminal. Remove steering wheel. *See STEERING WHEEL & COLUMN SWITCHES in this Section.* On Corona, remove fuse block cover. On both models, remove instrument panel cover (under column). On Corona, remove heater duct below column.

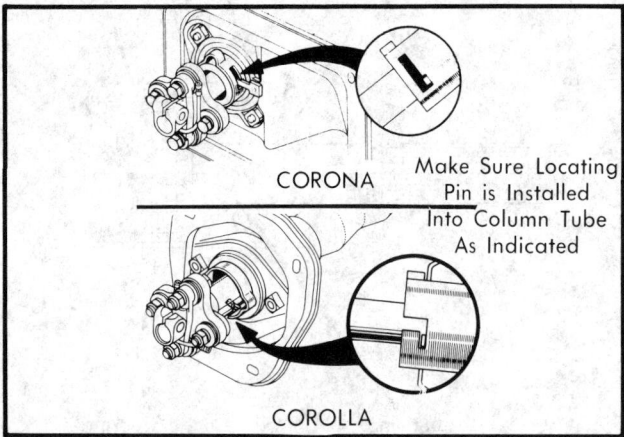

CORONA

Make Sure Locating Pin is Installed Into Column Tube As Indicated

COROLLA

Fig. 2   Proper Installation of Steering Column Locating Pin

2) Remove upper and lower column covers, then remove combination switch. Remove flexible coupling bolt connecting steering shaft with gear (mark flexible coupling-to-gear shaft before removing). Remove column bracket bolts and floor hole cover bolts. Remove steering column from inside vehicle.

Installation — To install steering column, reverse removal procedures and note the following: make sure marks on flexible coupling and gear shaft are aligned. Make sure steering wheel is in straight ahead position when wheels are straight ahead.

OVERHAUL

STEERING COLUMN

Disassembly — Remove retainer and snap ring from upper end of steering column. Remove flexible coupling from steering shaft. Remove hole cover, ring, plate and seal from lower end of steering shaft. Pull column tube off steering shaft from upper end of shaft. Remove upper bracket from column tube.

Inspection — Check all components for damage or wear. Check steering shaft for bending damage. Check column for sheared plastic pins. Check upper bracket for proper operating lock mechanism. If necessary, upper bracket bearing can be replaced.

Reassembly — To reassemble steering column, reverse disassembly procedures. Make sure to grease steering shaft, bushings and bearings. Also make sure lock on upper bracket operates properly and steering shaft is not binding in column tube.

TIGHTENING SPECIFICATIONS

Application	Ft. Lbs. (mkg)
Column Bracket (Breakaway)	
Corolla	22-33 (3.0-4.5)
Corona	14-22 (1.9-3.0)
Flexible Coupling Bolt	15-22 (2.0-3.0)
Steering Wheel	22-29 (3.0-4.0)

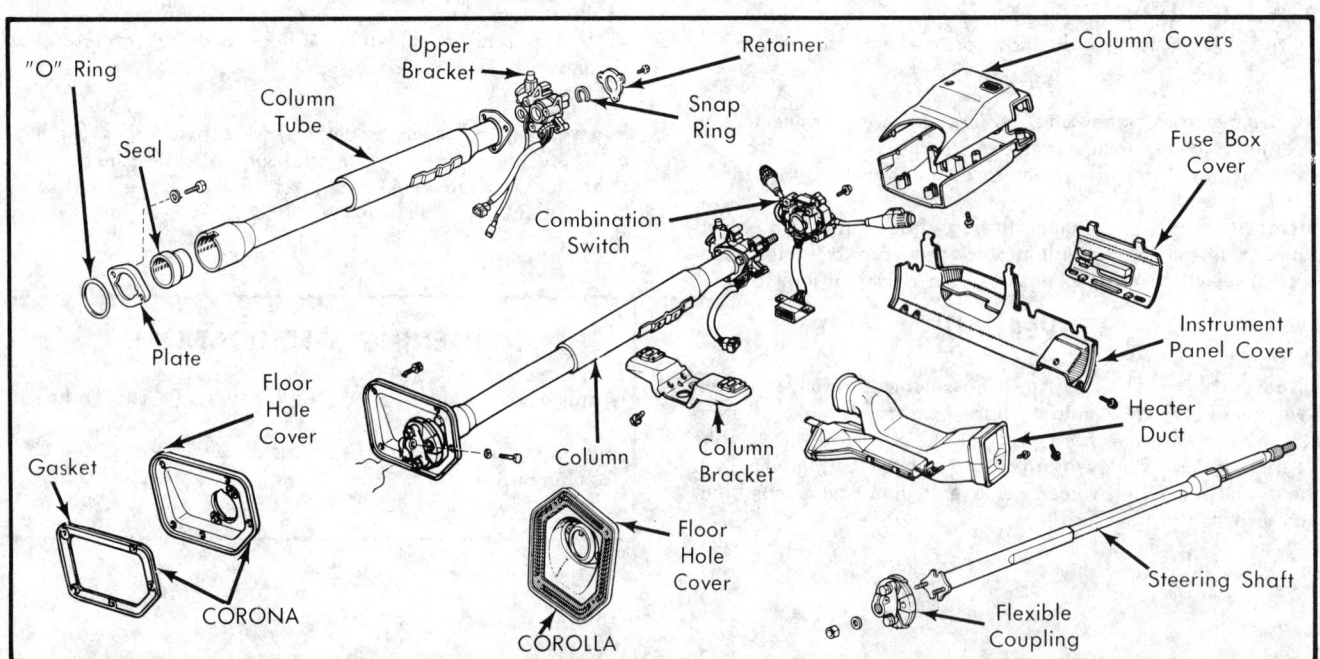

Fig. 1   Exploded View of Corolla and Corona Steering Column

TOYOTA CELICA, CRESSIDA, PICKUP & TERCEL

DESCRIPTION

Columns used on these models are of the collapsible two-piece design. Columns use shear pins to absorb collision impact. Steering shaft is connected directly to steering gear with flexible couplings on Celica and Cressida models. Tercel and pickup models use intermediate steering shafts. On Pickup 2-WD models, intermediate shaft is connected to steering gear by a flexible coupling. On Tercel and Pickup 4-WD models, intermediate shaft is connected to steering gear and to main steering shaft by universal joints.

NOTE – *For models with Tilt Wheel steering columns, see Tilt Wheel Steering Columns article in this section.*

REMOVAL & INSTALLATION

Removal – **1)** Disconnect cable from battery negative terminal. Remove steering wheel. On Cressida models, remove fuse box cover, lower instrument trim panel and heater duct (located under steering column). On all models, remove upper and lower steering column covers, then remove combination switch.

2) On Tercel and Pickup 4-WD models, mark position of "U" joints-to-shafts and remove intermediate steering shaft. On all other models, mark position of flexible coupling-to-steering gear and remove flexible coupling bolt. Remove floor pan cover bolts and column bracket bolts. Remove steering column toward inside of vehicle.

NOTE – *Remove steering column with intermediate shaft on Pickup 2-WD models.*

Installation – To install steering column, reverse removal procedures and note the following: Make sure "U" joint and flexible coupling alignment marks (made upon removal) are correctly aligned.

OVERHAUL

Disassembly – **1)** Remove bearing retainer and snap rings from upper end of column tube. On Tercel models, remove upper bracket from column tube. On all models, pull steering shaft out bottom of column tube. On Pickup 2-WD, mark main steering shaft-to-intermediate shaft, then remove snap ring and separate intermediate shaft from steering shaft. Be careful not to lose bearing blocks (located on intermediate shaft).

2) On Celica, Cressida and Pickup 2-WD models, remove flexible coupling from steering shaft. On all models, except Tercel, remove upper bracket from column tube. On Celica models, upper bracket bolts have to be drilled and removed with a screw extractor.

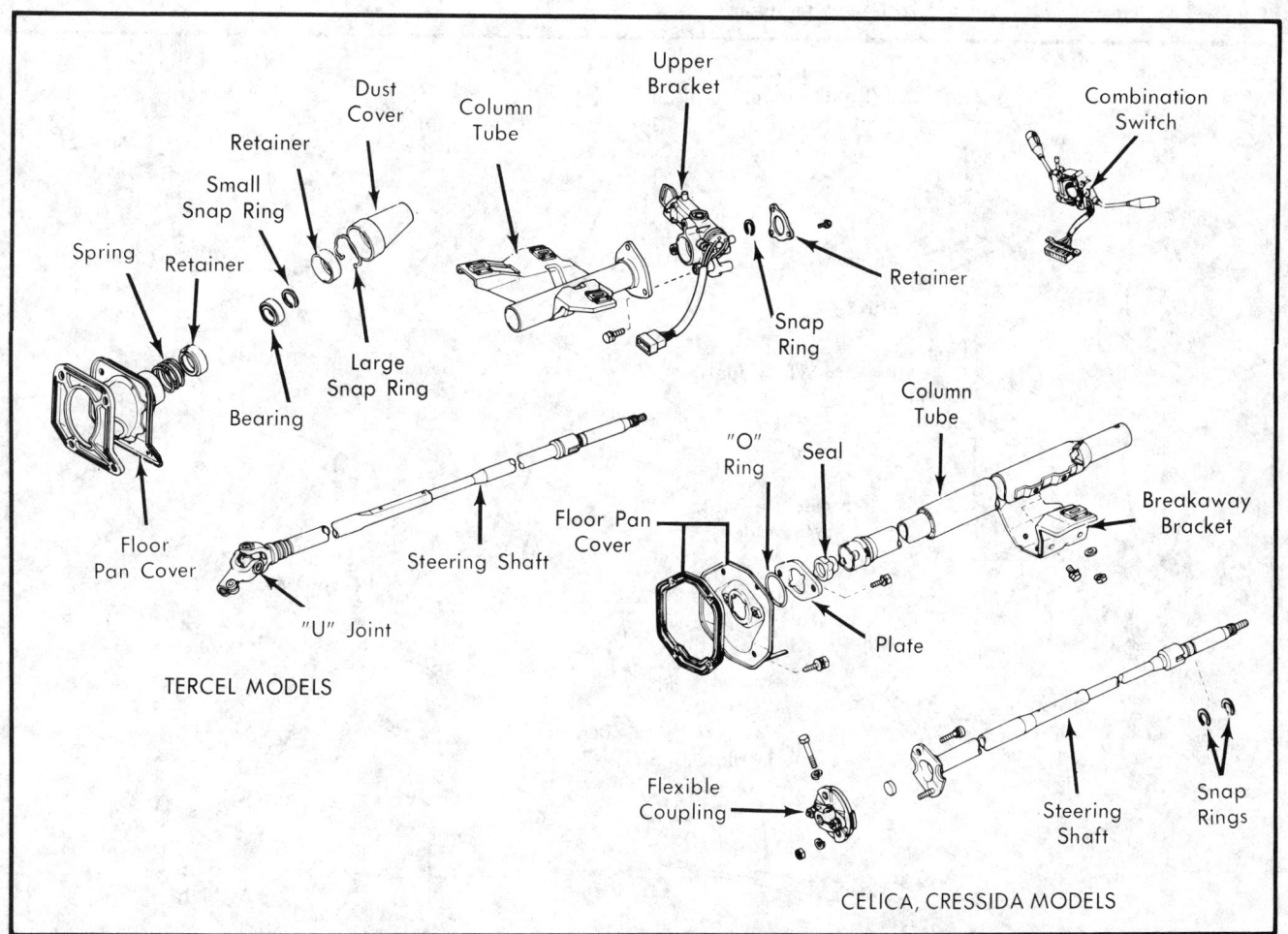

TERCEL MODELS

CELICA, CRESSIDA MODELS

Fig. 1 *Exploded View of Celica, Cressida and Tercel Steering Columns*

TOYOTA CELICA, CRESSIDA, PICKUP & TERCEL (Cont.)

3) On Tercel, remove dust cover; then compress shaft toward floor pan cover and remove large snap ring. Remove spring retainer, and again compress shaft to remove small snap ring. Remove bearing, spring retainer and spring. Remove floor pan cover from steering shaft. On all other models, separate floor pan cover from column tube plate and be careful not to damage "O" ring (dust seal on Pickup 4-WD models).

4) On Celica and Cressida, remove bracket from column tube. Remove plate and seal from bottom of column tube. On Pickup 2-WD, remove plate spring, bearing retainers and bearing from bottom of column tube.

5) On Pickup 4-WD, remove bolt from column support tube clamp. Remove column support tube from column tube. Remove snap ring and bearing from column support tube.

Inspection — **1)** Inspect all components for wear or damage. Check bearings for smooth operation. Check steering shafts for collision damage. Check steering lock mechanism (located in upper bracket) for proper operation. Replace components as necessary.

2) On Pickup 2-WD, temporarily assemble main steering shaft to intermediate shaft and measure amount of radial play between shafts. Allowable limit is .0024" (.06 mm). Replace pin and bearing blocks if necessary.

NOTE — *If replacing pin and bearing blocks, make sure new bearing blocks have the small anti-rattle rubber inserts in-* *stalled before assembling intermediate shaft to main steering shaft, otherwise steering shafts will rattle when installed in vehicle.*

3) On Tercel and Pickup 4-WD, check "U" joints for excessive axial play. Maximum play is .002" (.05 mm). Replace "U" joints if necessary.

Reassembly — To reassemble steering columns, reverse disassembly procedures and note the following:

- Grease main steering shaft and all bearings.
- When installing upper bracket on Celica models, use new shear bolts. Tighten bolts until head shears off.
- Make sure marks made to flexible couplings and to "U" joints are aligned.
- Make sure steering column and shafts do not bind after installation.

TIGHTENING SPECIFICATIONS

Application	Ft. Lbs. (mkg)
Column Bracket	15-22 (2.0-3.0)
Flexible Coupling	15-22 (2.0-3.0)
Steering Wheel	22-29 (3.0-4.0)
"U" Joint Clamp Bolts	22-33 (3.0-4.5)

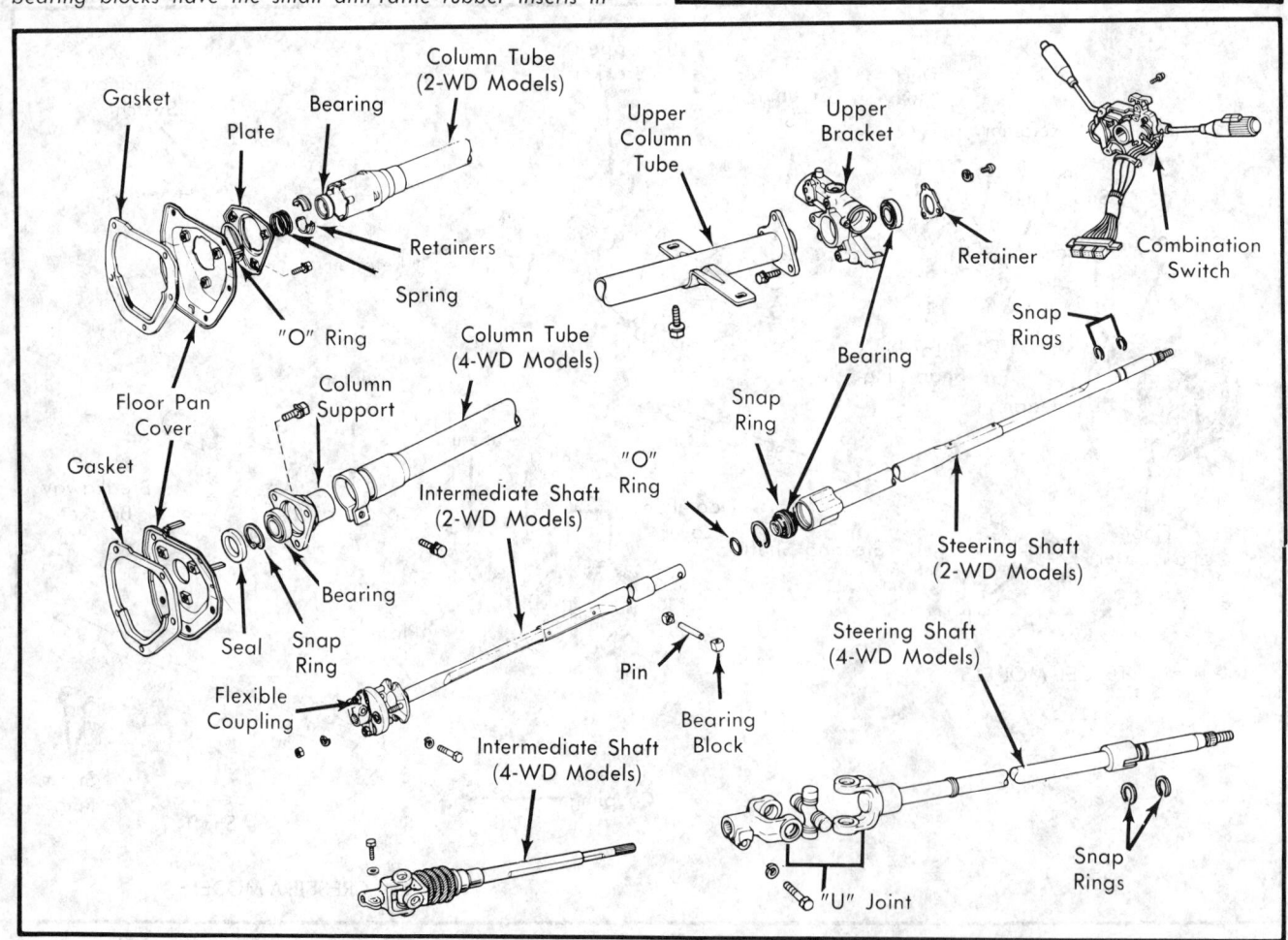

Fig. 2 Exploded View of Pickup Steering Columns

TOYOTA LAND CRUISER

DESCRIPTION

The steering shaft assembly consists of a one-piece steering shaft rotating inside a column tube. Steering shaft is connected to steering gear by a flexible coupling. Column tube is attached to instrument panel by a clamp and to floor pan by a floor cover.

REMOVAL & INSTALLATION

STEERING COLUMN

Removal — 1) Place index marks on steering shaft and flexible coupling, then remove flexible coupling clamp bolt. Remove horn pad, steering wheel and column covers.

2) Remove combination switch. Remove floor pan cover bolts and column clamp bolts. Remove steering column from inside vehicle.

Installation — To install steering column, reverse removal procedure. Make sure index marks on steering gear and flexible coupling are aligned during installation.

OVERHAUL

Disassembly — 1) Remove bearing retainer, snap rings and upper bracket from column tube. Remove steering shaft from column tube.

2) Separate flexible coupling from steering shaft. Remove floor pan cover-to-column tube bolts and remove floor pan cover. Remove column tube seal from lower end of column tube.

Inspection — Check all components for wear or damage. Check lock mechanism, located in upper bracket, for proper operation. Replace components as necessary.

Reassembly — To reassemble steering column, reverse disassembly procedure and note the following: Grease upper bearing, replace column tube seal and floor pan cover gasket if necessary. After reassembly, make sure steering shaft does not bind in column tube.

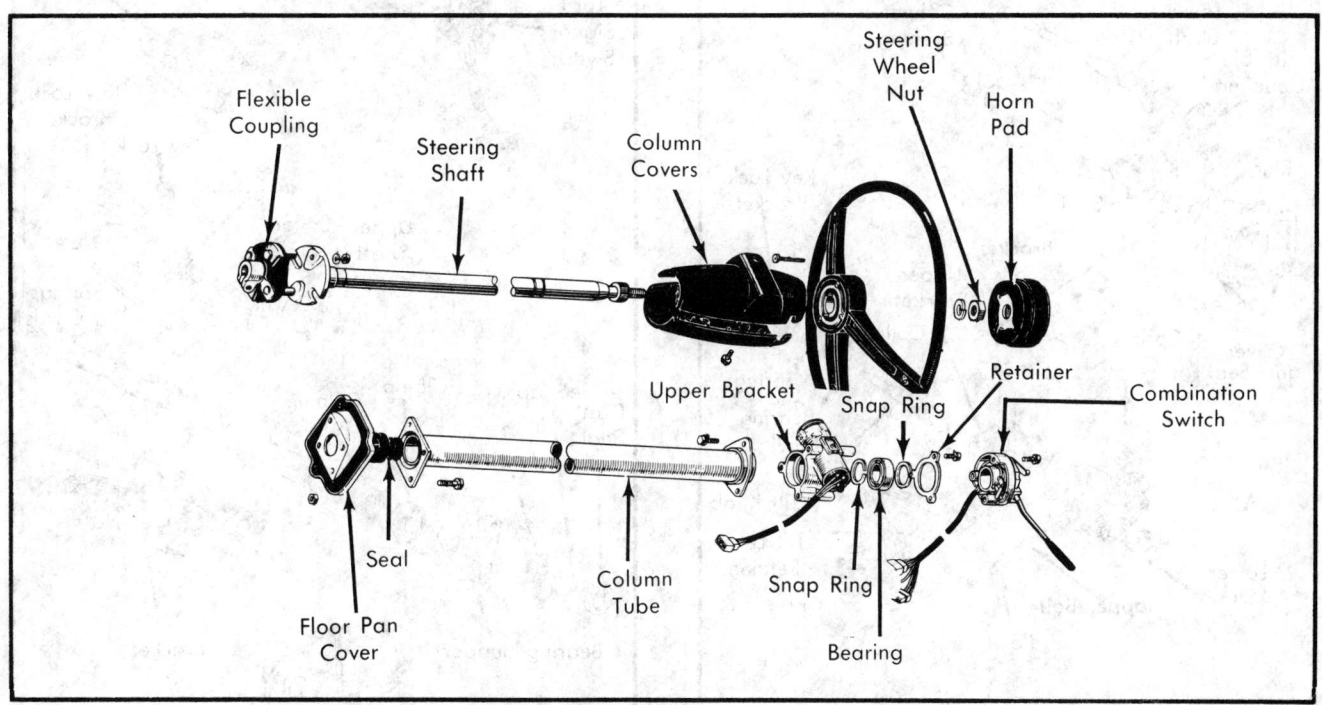

Fig. 1   Exploded View of Land Cruiser Steering Column

TOYOTA CELICA, CORONA, CRESSIDA, PICKUP & SUPRA — TILT WHEEL

DESCRIPTION

Tilt steering wheels incorporate an upper steering shaft attached, by a universal joint, with an intermediate steering shaft. These shafts are held in place by upper and lower brackets. Brackets are pinned together so that the upper bracket will move up or down. Upper bracket is locked in place by a pawl attached to a lever. Steering columns, on passenger vehicles, are of the collapsible type while the pickup steering column is non-collapsible.

REMOVAL & INSTALLATION

Removal — 1) Remove steering wheel pad. Mark steering shaft and wheel for installation. Remove steering wheel. Remove dash panels and pads, if necessary. On models with air conditioning, remove air duct under steering column.

2) Remove column bracket covers. Remove turn signal or combination switch. From under hood, disconnect steering shaft universal joint from steering gear (on passenger vehicles) or from lower steering shaft (on pickup models). Be sure to mark universal joint and shaft for installation.

3) Remove bolts from column hole cover. Remove column support bracket bolts, then remove steering column from vehicle.

Installation — 1) Install steering column in vehicle and tighten column bracket bolts finger tight. Install column hole cover bolts, then tighten column bracket bolts.

2) Make sure alignment marks are aligned on universal joints then tighten clamp bolts. Install turn signal or combination switch. Install bracket covers, dash panels and pads. Install air ducts (if equipped).

3) Install steering wheel and steering wheel pad. Make sure alignment marks on steering shaft and steering wheel are aligned.

Fig. 1 Exploded View of Passenger Car Tilt Steering Column

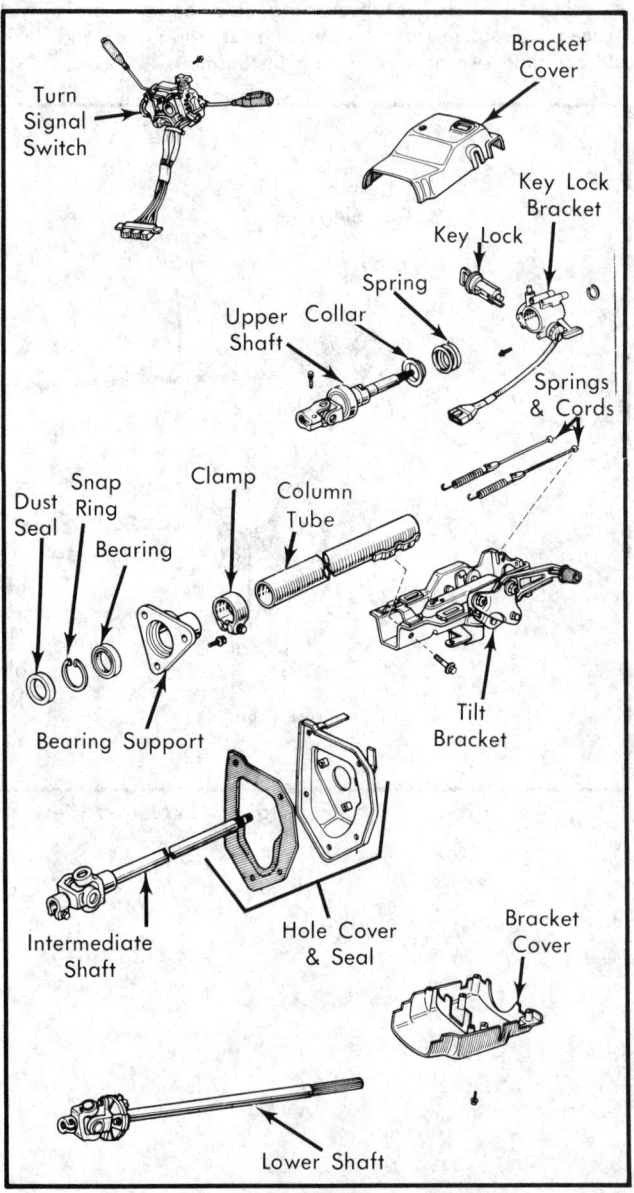

Fig. 2 Exploded View of Pickup Tilt Wheel Steering Column

TOYOTA CELICA, CORONA, CRESSIDA, PICKUP & SUPRA — TILT WHEEL (Cont.)

OVERHAUL

Disassembly — 1) On pickup models, remove ignition key cylinder. On all models, remove tension springs and cords. Mark universal joint and lower steering shaft. Remove clamp bolt, then lower steering shaft. Remove hole cover from column.

2) Remove snap ring from upper steering shaft. Remove reclining pawl release pin and steering pawl. Drive out serrated bolt with plastic hammer, then remove reclining pawl set bolt.

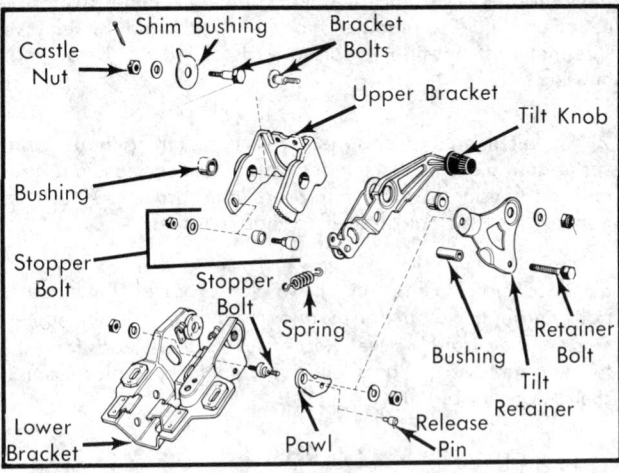

**Fig. 3   Exploded View of Tilt Wheel Bracket
(All Models Shown)**

Inspection — Check upper bracket for damage. Check upper bearing for rotating smoothness. Check steering shafts for bending, damaged splines or damaged universal joints. Check tilt bracket for worn bushings, damaged pawl, broken or damaged breakaway brackets. Check column tube for bending or other damage. Repair or replace components as necessary.

Reassembly — Reassemble in reverse order of disassembly procedure and note the following; make sure all bushings, bearings, shims and bolts are not damaged or worn.

TIGHTENING SPECIFICATIONS

Application	Ft. Lbs. (mkg)
Castle Nut	11-21 (1.5-3.0)
Flexible Coupling	15-21 (2.0-3.0)
Steering Wheel Nut	22-28 (3.0-4.0)
Support Bracket	
Pickup	11-15 (1.5-2.0)
All Others	14-22 (1.9-3.1)
Support Bracket-to-Column	11-15 (1.5-2.0)
Tilt Lever Retainer Bolt	11-15 (1.5-2.0)
Tilt Steering Support Stopper Bolt	6-8 (.8-1.2)
Universal Joint Clamp Bolt①	15-21 (2.0-3.0)

① — Tighten clamp bolt at steering gear on pickup models to 22-32 ft. lbs. (3.1-4.5 mkg).

TRIUMPH SPITFIRE

DESCRIPTION

Steering column is a telescoping, safety unit which is designed to compress on impact. The lower section of column will move into the steering column, absorbing impact shock. Column is connected to pinion gear through a flexible coupling and is mounted to the instrument panel on two column supports. A set screw is inserted through the lower support clamp and retains the lower telescoping portion in place.

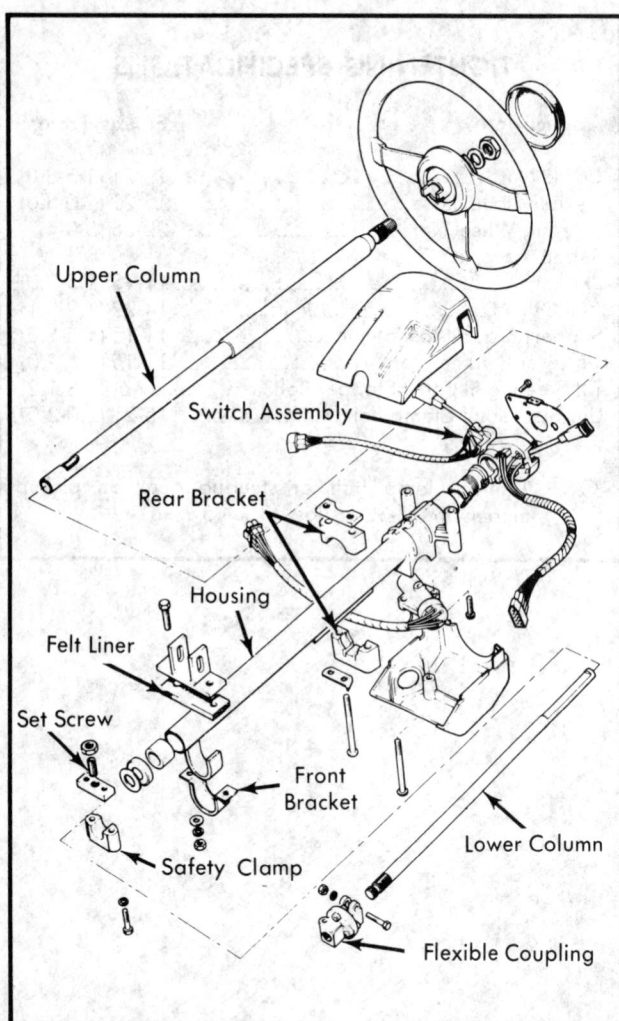

Fig. 1   Exploded View of Spitfire Steering Column Assembly

REMOVAL & INSTALLATION

Removal — 1) Disconnect battery. Remove driver's parcel shelf. Unscrew pinch bolts securing steering mast to flexible coupling at gear housing. Remove nuts and washers from two bolts securing steering column forward bracket. Withdraw forward support housing and felt liner.

2) Disconnect electrical couplings for horn, turn signal switch, lights, and column lock. Remove two cap screws securing steering column rear bracket, then withdraw both clamp halves and upper plate. Remove steering column assembly.

Installation — 1) Set front wheels in straight-ahead position. Hold steering wheel with center spoke straight down, then engage lower end of steering mast in splines of flexible coupling. Slide cardboard tube rearward and fit felt over steering mast housing, ensuring ends of felt are below mast housing.

2) Fit felt liner and engage forward mounting bolts, using spring and plain washers under nuts. Ensure spring clip is fitted on mast housing to align with rear clamp bracket. Attach upper and lower clamp halves to mast housing.

3) Place plate in bracket above clamp halves. Enter clamp bolts through clamp halves and mounting bracket. Tighten nuts securing front bracket. Reconnect electrical leads for horn, turn signal switch, lights and steering lock. Replace parcel shelf. Connect battery.

OVERHAUL

Disassembly — 1) Remove steering wheel. Detach column switches. Unlock steering column lock. Remove two set bolts and spring washers securing safety clamp, and remove safety clamp and thrust washer.

2) Withdraw lower steering mast. Pull cap from lower end of steering column tube and remove tubular cardboard spacer. Push column housing upward and withdraw turn signal cam. Pull housing toward lower end of column until it presses against column bushing. Depress rubber locating tabs on column lower bushing and withdraw steering mast and lower bushing. Pull bushing from mast. Remove upper bushing.

Reassembly — To reassemble steering column, reverse disassembly procedure, noting that rubber dots on bushings are facing bottom of tube.

TIGHTENING SPECIFICATIONS

Application	Ft. Lbs. (mkg)
Flexible Coupling Pinch Bolt	14 (2.0)
Safety Clamp Bolts	9 (1.2)
Safety Clamp Set Screw	20 (2.8)

TRIUMPH TR7 & TR8

DESCRIPTION

Steering column houses ignition switch, column lock, and light and wiper controls. The steering column is divided into upper and intermediate shafts which are coupled by universal joints.

REMOVAL AND INSTALLATION

STEERING COLUMN ASSEMBLY

Removal — 1) Disconnect battery ground. Take out pinch bolt securing upper universal to steering mast. Disconnect electrical harness from steering column and separate plug connectors (*Fig. 1*). Remove plastic cover from around steering column.

2) Center punch shear head bolts and use a small chisel to remove. With wheels facing in a straight ahead position, withdraw steering column, noting number and position of flat and concave washers.

Installation — 1) To install steering column assembly, reverse removal procedures, noting the following: Make sure front wheels are in straight ahead position and steering wheel is centered. Check for proper positioning of flat and concave washers.

2) Align steering column mounting holes, then install new bolts and tighten evenly until heads shear. Tighten upper universal pinch bolt to specification.

INTERMEDIATE SHAFT

Removal — Remove pinch bolt mounting intermediate shaft to upper universal coupling and pinch bolt securing universal joint to rack pinion. With front wheels in straight ahead position, slide intermediate shaft upward to remove it from pinion shaft universal joint, then pull shaft downward to disengage from upper universal joint.

Installation — To install intermediate shaft, reverse removal procedure, noting the following: Make sure steering wheel is in straight ahead position and splines on intermediate shaft and rack pinion are fully engaged. Tighten pinch bolts to specification.

OVERHAUL

STEERING COLUMN ASSEMBLY

Disassembly — With steering column assembly removed from vehicle, remove the steering wheel spoke pad. Remove steering wheel from column. Remove shear head bolts. Withdraw column housing from steering mast. Remove nut and bolt securing clamp to steering mast and remove clamp. With a drift, remove top and bottom bushings from steering column housing.

Reassembly — Align slots in bushings with lugs in column housing, then press in bushings. Install steering lock in column housing and secure with shear bolts. Refit all electrical connectors and indicator control cams and arms. Tighten steering hub and wheel into position, then refit spoke cover.

TIGHTENING SPECIFICATIONS

Application	Ft. Lbs. (mkg)
Steering Wheel Nut	30-37 (4-5)
Column Clamp-to-Column	6-9 (.8-1.2)
Universal Joint Pinch Bolts	16-21 (2.2-2.9)

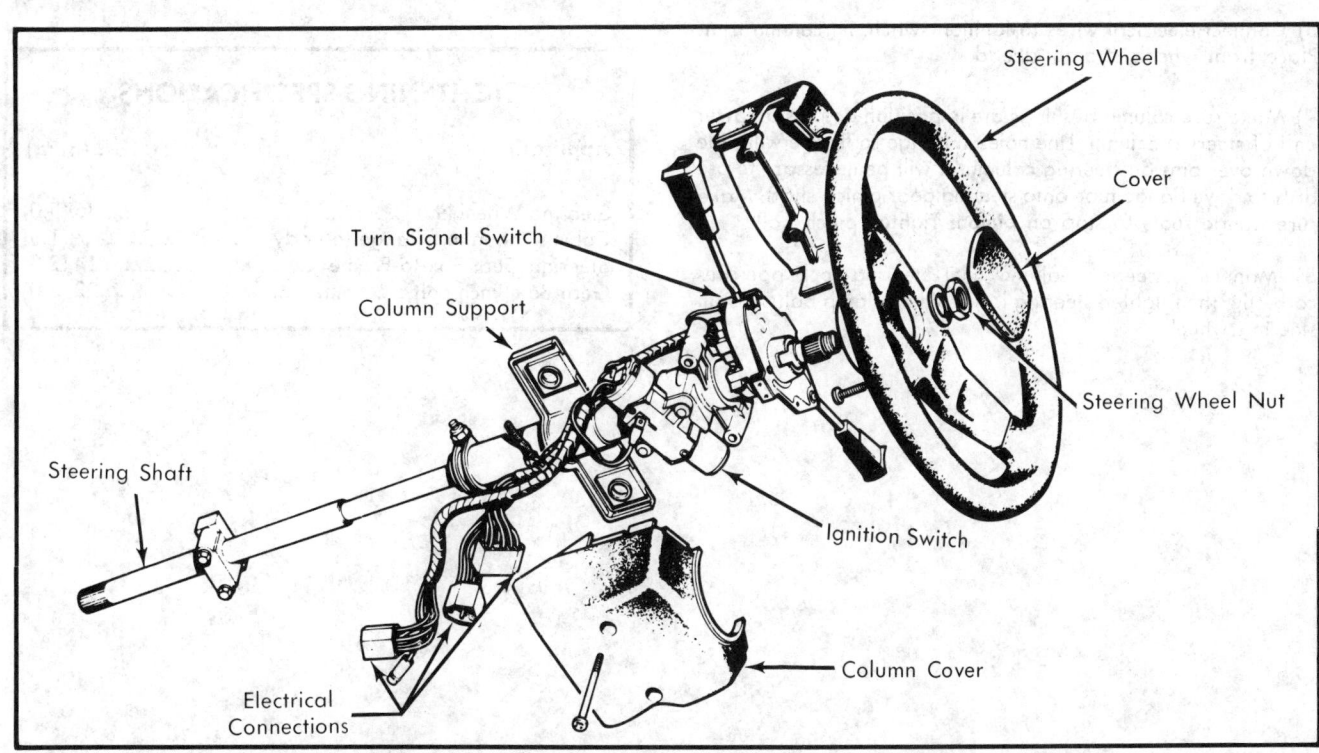

Fig. 1 Partially Disassembled View of TR7 & TR8 Upper Steering Column

VOLKSWAGEN DASHER

DESCRIPTION

The Volkswagen Dasher uses a two-piece safety steering column which incorporate a flange connection. A lattice metal column support is used under the instrument panel. This device is designed to absorb some of the impact shock which may otherwise be transmitted to the driver.

REMOVAL & INSTALLATION

STEERING COLUMN

Removal — 1) Disconnect battery ground strap. Remove steering wheel. See *Volkswagen under STEERING WHEELS & COLUMN SWITCHES in this Section.*

2) Remove all steering column switches.

3) From under hood, remove pinch bolt holding steering column flange to pinion shaft.

4) Work under brake pedal and unbolt mounting flange from bracket. Disconnect electrical wires from ignition switch. Put ignition switch in "ON" position.

5) Remove bolts from steering lock/column clamp. Remove steering column and shaft as a unit.

Installation — 1) Position column assembly back in vehicle. Install steering column lock. Make sure lock lug will snap into recess in steering column. Fit new shear bolts finger tight.

2) Bolt steering column mounting flange onto bracket so long side of flange faces right side of vehicle. Snug up flange bolts and steering lock/column clamp bolts.

3) Connect electrical wires to ignition switch. Fit column trim. Place front wheels straight-ahead.

4) Make sure column bushings are in position on pins at lower end of steering column. Line holes in flange so flange will slide down over pins on steering column. It will be necessary to use drift to drive flange tube onto steering gear pinion shaft. Make sure flange seats to stop on pinion. Tighten pinch bolt.

5) Maneuver steering column until steering lock operates correctly, then tighten steering lock/column clamp bolts. Install steering wheel.

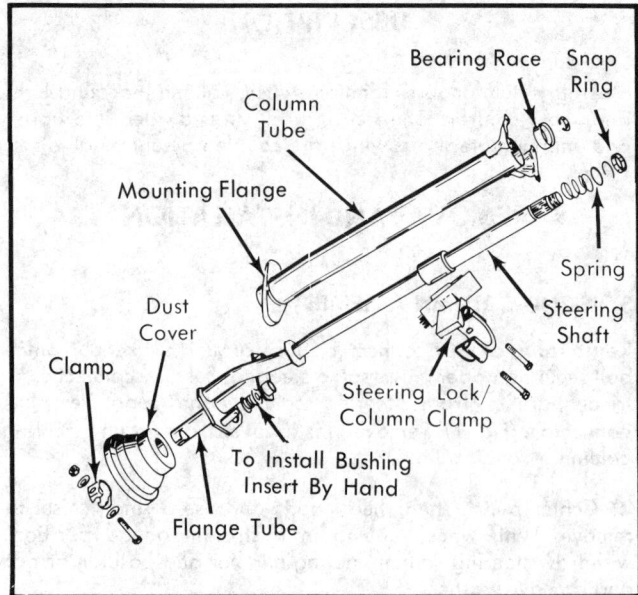

Fig. 1 Expanded View of Dasher Steering Column

OVERHAUL

Disassembly — Pull off steering wheel spacer ring and snap ring. Remove flat washer and spring. Pull steering shaft out through bottom of column. Press race out of column.

Reassembly — Examine race and replace if excessively worn. Slide steering shaft back into column then refit spring and snap ring.

TIGHTENING SPECIFICATIONS

Application	Ft. Lbs. (mkg)
Steering Wheel Nut	36 (5.0)
Column Mounting Flange-to-Body	7 (1.0)
Steering Gear Box-to-Frame	14 (2.0)
Gear Box Pinch Bolt	22 (3.0)

STEERING *(vertical, right margin)*

VOLKSWAGEN JETTA, RABBIT, PICKUP & SCIROCCO

DESCRIPTION

Volkswagen Jetta, Rabbit, Rabbit Pickup and Scirocco models use a swing-away type steering column. The column is held in place by a clamp and leaf spring. On impact, the lower angled portion of the column pushes upper column against leaf spring. The spring allows the column to disengage and swing to the side.

REMOVAL & INSTALLATION

STEERING COLUMN ASSEMBLY

NOTE — *Do not attempt to remove steering shaft from column without first removing entire assembly from the vehicle.*

Removal — **1)** Disconnect battery ground. Remove steering wheel. See *Volkswagen under STEERING WHEEL & COLUMN SWITCHES in this Section.*

2) Remove socket head bolt and Phillips head screw from switch housing recess. Tilt switch unit toward instrument panel. Pry off spacer sleeve on steering column. Pull switch unit up enough to disconnect wires. Remove switch unit from column.

3) Disconnect steering shaft from "U" joint shaft. Disconnect brake pedal push rod. Separate clutch pedal from actuating cable under instrument panel.

4) Push leaf spring retainer clip down with a screwdriver and disengage it from mounting slot. Remove bolts mounting column under instrument panel. Shear bolts will have to be centerpunched and drilled out. Pull entire column (with shaft) out of vehicle.

Bearing Replacement — Drive steering shaft from column. Remove bearings. Press in steering shaft and bearings. It should not take more than a force of 100-200 lbs. (45-90 kgs) to properly seat bearings into position.

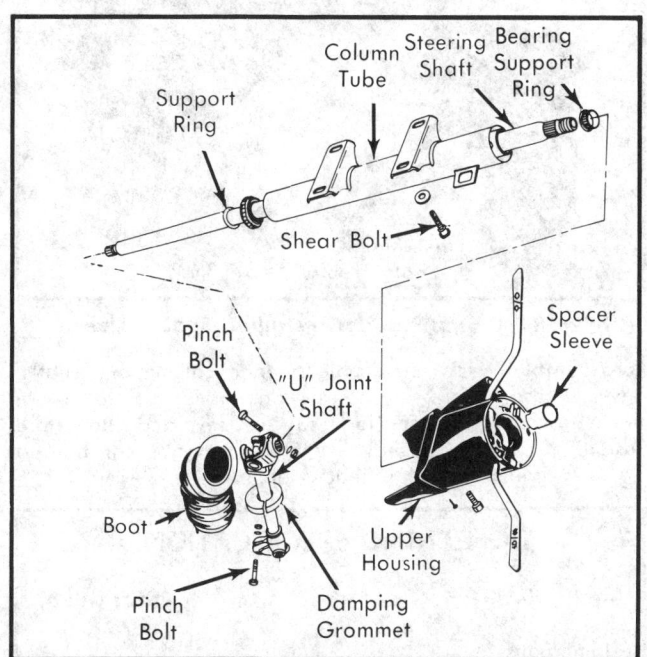

Fig. 1   Exploded View of Jetta, Rabbit, Rabbit Pickup and Scirocco Steering Column

Installation — To install, reverse removal procedure and note: Make sure front wheels point straight-ahead before tightening pinch bolt. Before fitting column switch unit, install spacer to dimensions shown in *Fig. 2*. Adjust both brake pedal and clutch pedal height.

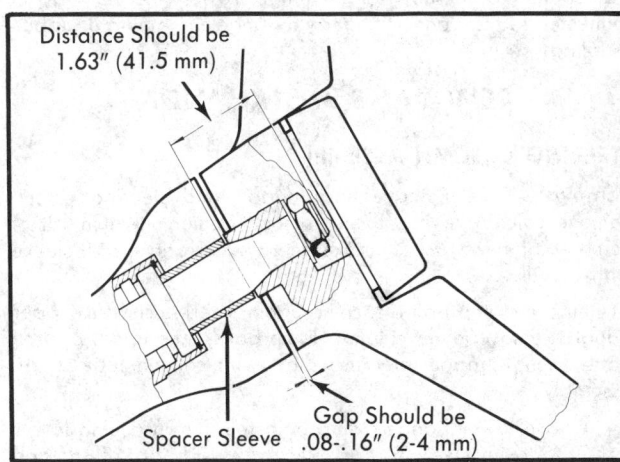

Fig. 2   Spacer Sleeve Adjustment Dimensions

"U" JOINT SHAFT

Removal — **1)** Separate manual gearshift linkage from steering box.

2) Remove pinch bolt connecting lower end of "U" joint shaft with steering gear pinion shaft.

3) Remove nuts mounting steering gear box to frame. Pull box down to separate from lower "U" joint. Remove rubber boot from lower "U" joint.

4) Remove pinch bolt connecting upper "U" joint to steering shaft. Pull down on joint and remove shaft with "U" joints from vehicle.

Installation — **1)** Fit "U" joint to steering shaft. Make sure notch in steering shaft aligns with slot in lower "U" joint.

2) Install boot and damping grommet. Fit steering gear box to frame while guiding pinion shaft into lower "U" joint. Finger tighten gear box nuts.

3) Place front wheels straight-ahead. Align pinion shaft and "U" joint. Tighten pinch bolt. Tighten gear box nuts. Connect manual gearshift linkage to gear box. Check linkage operation.

TIGHTENING SPECIFICATIONS

Application	Ft. Lbs. (mkg)
Steering Wheel Nut	36 (5.0)
Steering Column-to-Instrument Panel Mounting Bolt	14 (2.0)
Shear Bolts	①
Pinch Bolts	22 (3.0)

① — Until bolt head snaps.

VOLKSWAGEN VANAGON

DESCRIPTION

Volkswagen Vanagon models use an energy absorbing steering column. Column is attached to dash by brackets and to floor pan by a dust boot. Steering shaft is made up of an upper steering shaft and lower steering shaft. Shafts are connected together by a short upper flange. Lower steering shaft is connected to the transfer gear by a flange containing a rubber coupling.

REMOVAL & INSTALLATION

STEERING COLUMN ASSEMBLY

Removal — 1) Remove horn button and steering wheel. Remove column covers, then disconnect column switch wires. Remove column switch. Remove steering lock and spacer sleeve with a puller.

2) Remove clamp bolt attaching upper steering shaft to upper flange. Remove lower column clamp bolts, then upper column bolts. Remove upper steering shaft with column tube as an assembly.

3) Remove lower flange clamp bolt, the one attaching lower flange to lower steering shaft. Remove dust boot-to-floor pan bolts and remove lower steering shaft.

Installation — 1) To install steering column, reverse removal procedures and note the following: Install new gasket on dust boot. Install steering shaft and column tube as an assembly.

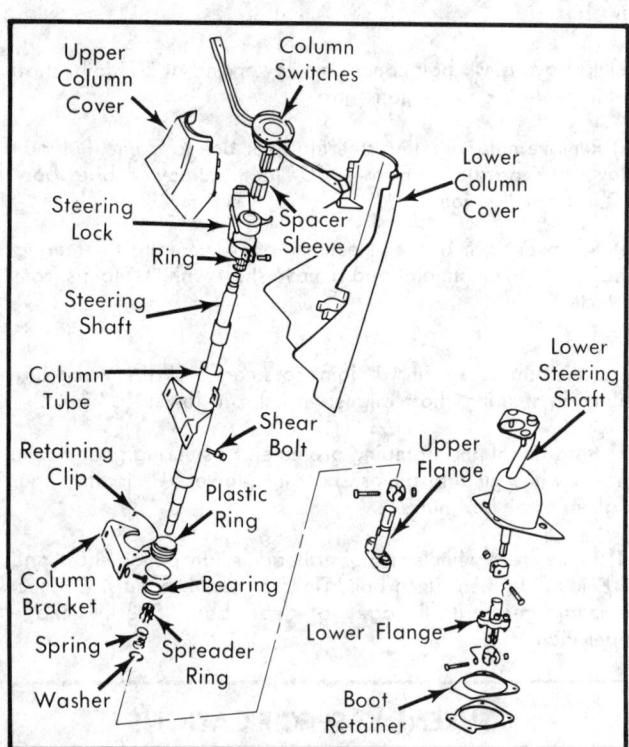

Fig. 1 Exploded View of Volkswagen Vanagon Steering Column Assembly

2) When installing steering lock and spacer sleeve, clamp lower steering shaft to upper flange with tool VW 267a. Make sure distance from top of column tube to top of upper steering shaft (with steering wheel and nut installed) is 1.634" (41.5 mm) and space between column switch and steering wheel is .079-157" (2-4 mm). See *Fig. 2.*

OVERHAUL

Disassembly — 1) On lower steering shaft, remove flange from steering shaft. Remove clamp from flange. Remove gasket and boot retainer from dust boot.

2) On upper steering shaft, remove washer, spring, spreader ring, bearing, column bracket and plastic ring from bottom end of shaft. Remove steering lock ring from upper end of steering shaft.

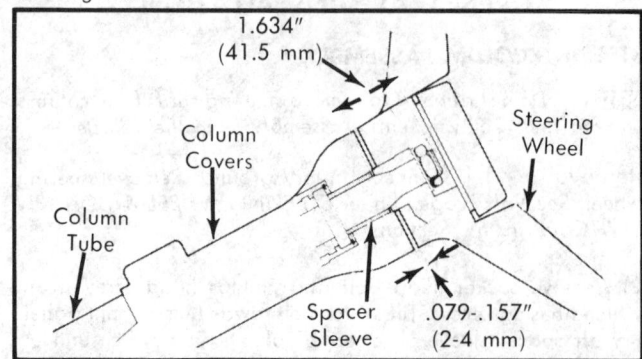

Fig. 2 Measurements for Installing Spacer Sleeve

3) On column tube, drill out and remove shear bolt. Remove column tube from steering shaft.

Inspection — Check all components for excessive wear, scoring or other damage. Check steering shafts for bending, cracks or other collision damage. Replace components as necessary.

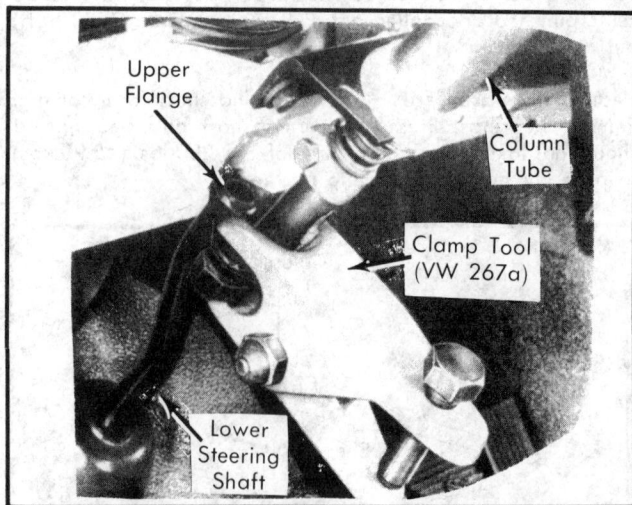

Fig. 3 Clamp Tool for Installing Spacer Sleeve

Reassembly — To reassemble steering column and shafts, reverse disassembly procedures and note the following: Always assemble steering lock, spacer sleeve and ring before installing to steering shaft. When installing shear bolt to column, tighten bolt until head snaps off.

TIGHTENING SPECIFICATIONS

Application	Ft.Lbs.(mkg)
Clamp Bolts	14 (1.9)
Lower Bracket Bolts	18 (2.5)
Steering Wheel Nut	36 (5.0)

VOLVO

DL
GL
GT

GLE
Coupe
Diesel

DESCRIPTION

Steering column is divided in two sections. Upper and lower sections are joined by means of a flange. A heavy frontal impact would cause flange to break from upper column. The upper portion of steering column would retain its position, eliminating possibility of its being forced toward driver. Upper part of column is carried in two ball bearings located in jacket tube. Lower end of steering column is connected to steering shaft by a flange.

REMOVAL & INSTALLATION

STEERING COLUMN

Removal — 1) Disconnect battery ground. Remove steering wheel. *See Volvo under STEERING WHEEL & COLUMN SWITCHES in this Section.*

2) Work inside engine compartment and disconnect clamp holding column shaft to lower shaft universal joint. Pry clamp apart with screwdriver, do not tap with hammer.

3) Remove column covers. Disconnect wiring and remove turn signal and wiper switches. Remove switch retainer, spring, and bearing race.

4) Drill steering column lock bolts and remove with a screw extractor.

5) Slide out steering column rubber grommet at firewall. Remove steering column lower mounting bolts. Force steering column through firewall until clear of lower portion of instrument panel. Pull column toward passenger compartment and remove from vehicle.

6) Place steering column assembly in a soft jawed vise and remove steering lock mechanism.

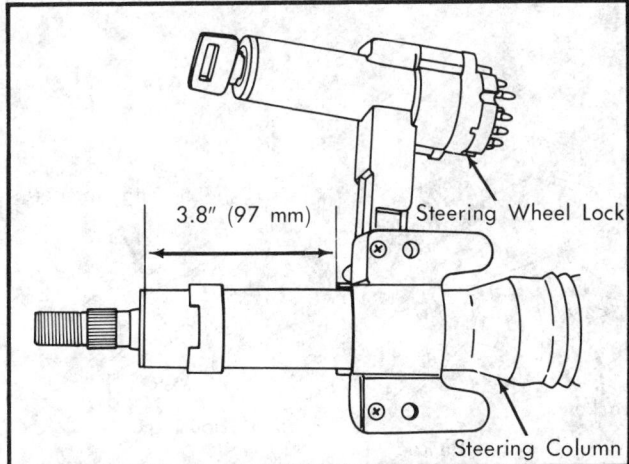

Fig. 1   Steering Wheel Lock Position

Installation — 1) Measure steering column to ensure length is 27.08-27.17" (688-690 mm). Position steering wheel lock on column so lock upper edge is 3.8" (97 mm) from upper edge of steering column. See Fig. 1.

2) Place rubber seal on column and insert column through firewall. Make sure both plastic guides are in position on the dashboard and install bolts loosely in upper and lower attachments.

3) Adjust column position. Steering wheel lock should protrude from dashboard .53-.65" (13.5-16.5 mm) when measured at key position "III" at the lock. Check for binding and rubbing, and adjust dashboard beam if necessary. Tighten lower bolts to 15-22 ft. lbs. (2-3 mkg).

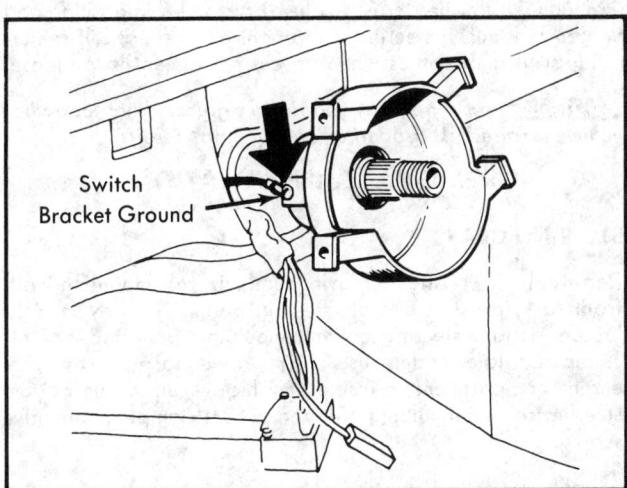

Fig. 2   Switch Bracket Ground on Steering Column

4) Install switch bracket. Make sure to use one of mounting screws as a ground. Install race and spring for upper race. Install turn signal, wiper switch and ignition switch. Connect horn wire lead.

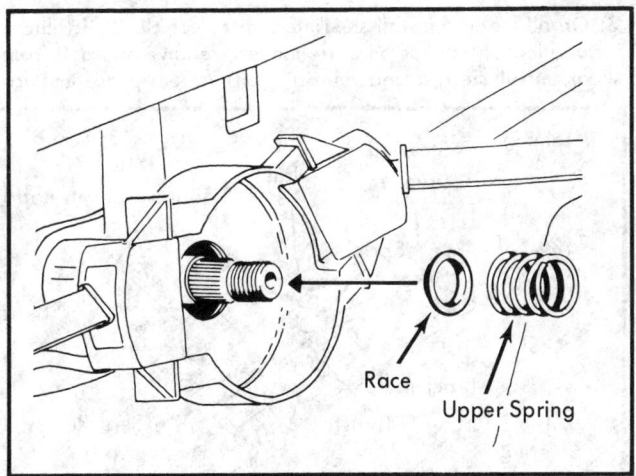

Fig. 3   Install Upper Bearing Race and Spring to Steering Column

5) Replace column covers after tightening upper bolts until the heads shear off. Install steering wheel and tighten nut to 33-55 ft. lbs. (4.6-7.6 mkg). Tighten lower column clamp bolt in engine compartment to 15-22 ft. lbs. (2-3 mkg).

NOTE — *Rattling in steering column can be corrected by placing 1 or 2 flat washers between steering wheel and upper bearing spring.*

AUDI 4000 RACK & PINION

DESCRIPTION

Steering system is a direct-acting rack and pinion gear mounted to crossmember and connected to tie rods by a bracket. Tie rods are connected to steering knuckle by ball joints.

ADJUSTMENT

RACK ADJUSTMENT

Loosen lock nut on steering gear cover. Hand tighten adjusting screw until it touches thrust washer. Hold screw in position and tighten lock nut. If steering is too tight or does not self center, readjust. If gear rattles when driven, adjustment is too loose.

CAUTION — *Do not turn gear hard against either lock when vehicle is raised off ground or damage may result.*

REMOVAL & INSTALLATION

STEERING GEAR

Removal — 1) After removing both tie rod mounting bolts from rack, pry tie rods off steering gear. On early models, loosen bottom steering column mounting bolt and pry off clamp. On late models, use a screwdriver to push cap from engine compartment to inside of vehicle, then loosen bottom steering column mounting bolt and pry off clamp. Also remove seal ring.

2) On all models, drive bottom of column off gear using a brass mandrel. Remove gear mounting bolts from body. Turn wheels to right lock and remove steering gear through opening in right wheel well.

Installation — 1) On early models, before installing steering gear in vehicle, install the slider (in which both sealing sleeves are welded into the cup, see *Fig. 2*).

2) On all models, install steering gear to vehicle. To facilitate installation of tie rods on early models, remove one bolt from slider, install tie rod and reinstall bolt. Repeat procedure for other tie rod. Install bracket. On late models, install tie rods to tie rod bracket, then install bracket to steering drive pawl. Install steering drive pawl to steering gear rack. Install seal ring. On all models, install clamp and attach column to steering gear. On late models, push cap from inside vehicle to steering gear.

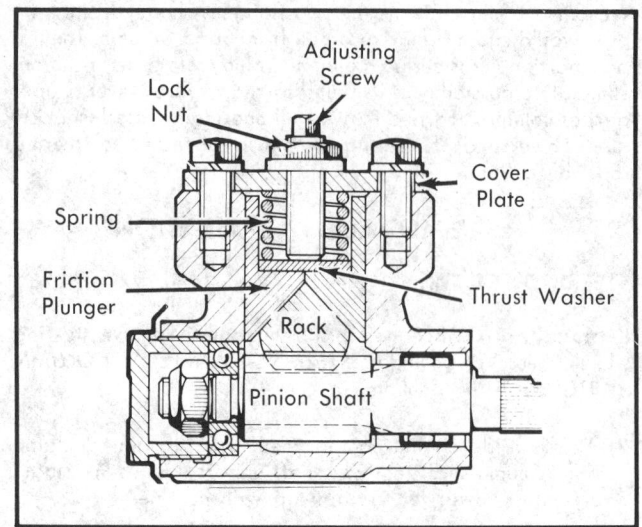

Fig. 1 Cross Sectional View of Pinion Shaft with Rack Adjustment

STEERING DAMPER

NOTE — *Replacement of steering damper is the only service procedure recommended. Do not attempt repairs on this unit.*

OVERHAUL

NOTE — *Manufacturer does not recommend overhaul of this rack and pinion steering unit. If unit is determined defective, replace as assembly.*

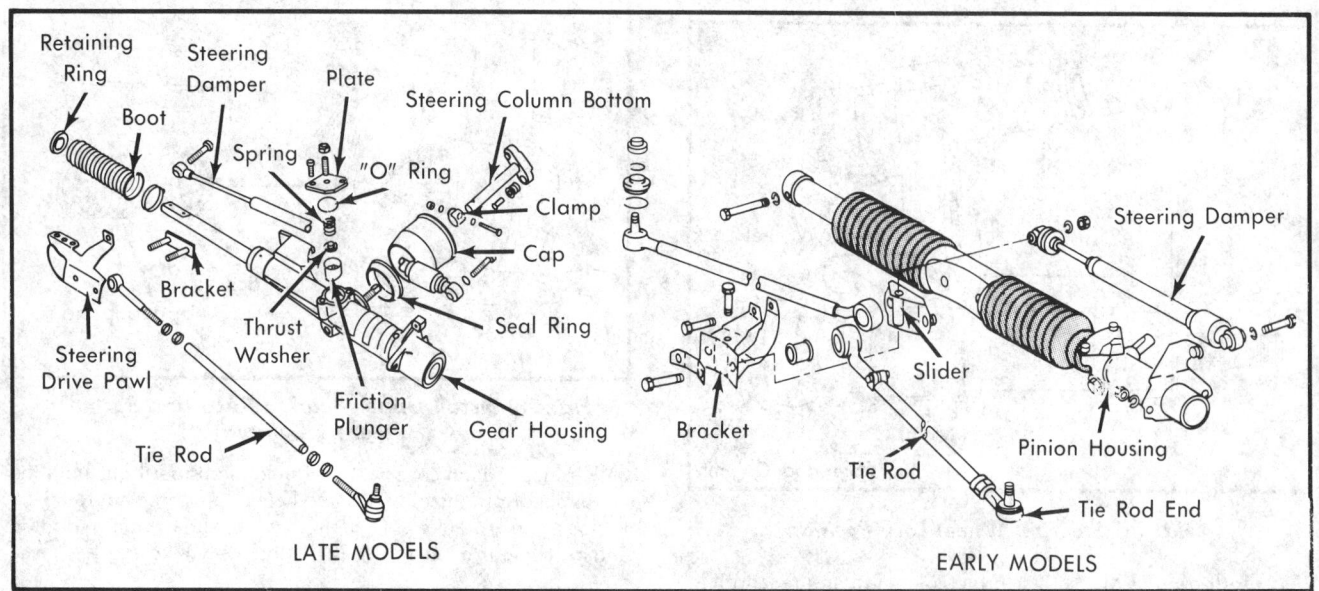

LATE MODELS

EARLY MODELS

Fig. 2 Exploded View of Audi 4000 Rack and Pinion Assembly (Early and Late Models)

BMW RACK & PINION

320i

DESCRIPTION

Direct-acting manual rack and pinion gear on resilient rubber mounts is of ZF design. Steering is dampened by a single tube-type hydraulic damper. Tie rods attached at outer end of central steering rack connect to steering knuckles.

ADJUSTMENT

Steering gear assembly should be removed for proper adjustment. See OVERHAUL procedures in this article.

REMOVAL & INSTALLATION

STEERING GEAR

Removal and Installation — Disconnect tie rods from steering knuckles with special tool (32 2 050). Detach steering gear mounting bolts at front axle support. Remove pinch bolt from steering shaft and pull steering gear loose from universal coupling. To install, reverse removal procedure noting that wheels must point straight ahead and raised mark on dust seal must align between raised marks on steering gear box.

OVERHAUL

Disassembly — 1) Mount gear in suitable holding fixture held in a vise. Bend open right lockplate and slide rack in up to stop. Detach damper at holder.

2) Using special tool (32 2 110), detach right tie rod at rack. Loosen bellows clamp and slide bellows off housing. Move rack in far enough to apply special tool (32 2 100) to left side of rack. Loosen clamp and slide back bellows onto rack. Bend open lockplate and detach left tie rod at rack.

3) Remove cap from pinion housing, then pull out cotter pin holding set screw. Unscrew set screw with special tool (32 1 040) and remove spring retainer and spring. Lift rack to remove pressure pad and "O" ring from housing.

4) Remove pinion shaft dust cover, "V" lock ring and notched ring. Remove pinion shaft set screw with special tool (32 1 040), then pull out "O" ring and washer.

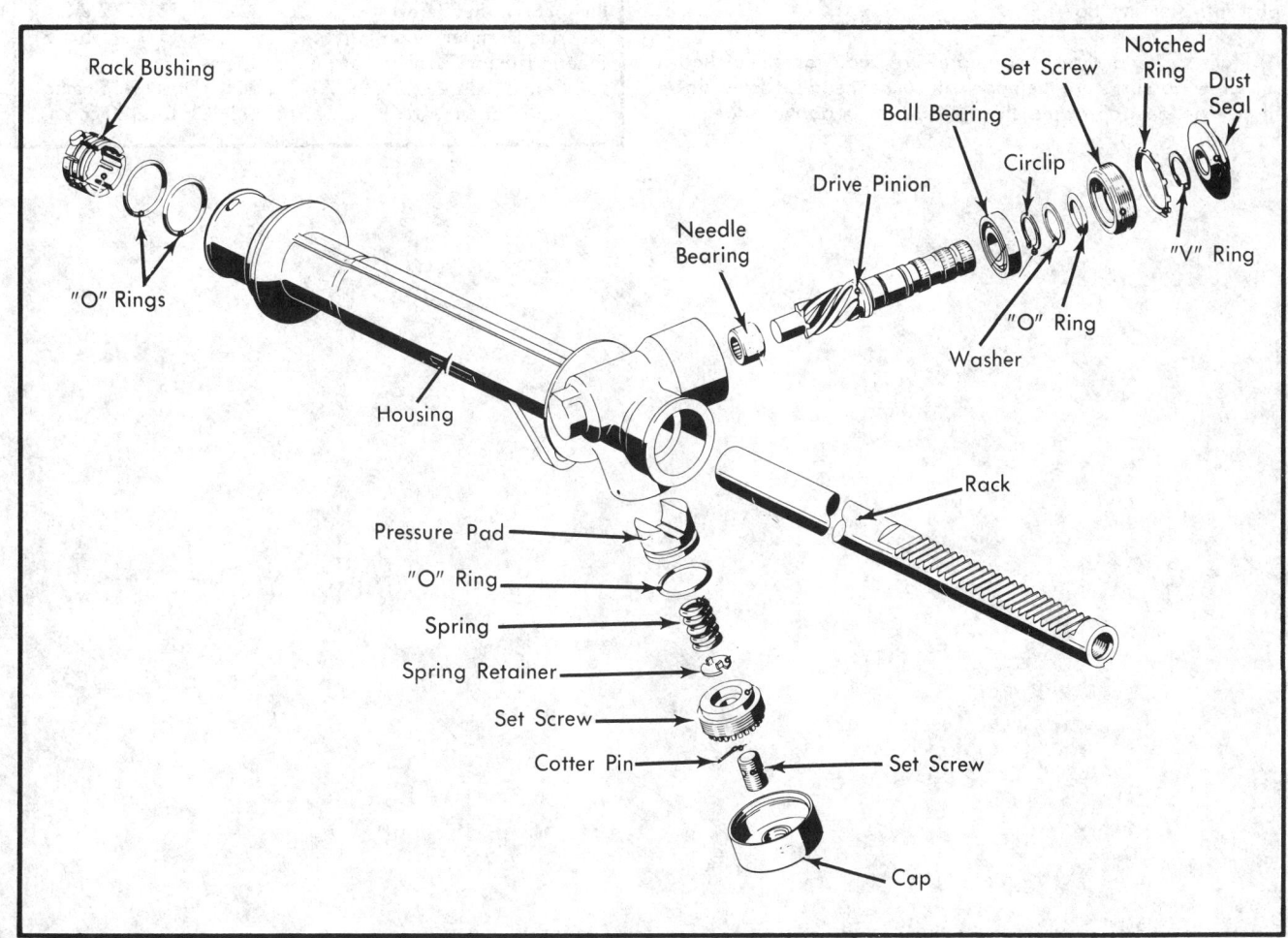

Fig. 1 Exploded View of BMW Rack & Pinion Steering Gear Assembly

BMW RACK & PINION (Cont.)

5) Clamp drive pinion spline in soft jawed vise and remove drive pinion from housing by tapping housing with plastic hammer. Remove circlip from pinion shaft and press ball bearing off of drive pinion shaft.

6) Needle bearing may be removed from housing with suitable screw type puller (Kukko 00 8 510). Remove rack bushings from housing by prying out with two screwdrivers.

Assembly — 1) Place new "O" rings on rack bushings and install bushings in steering box. Locking tabs must enage in housing lock holes. Drive needle bearing, flat side down, into box using suitable mandrel.

2) Press ball bearing onto drive pinion with closed end facing spline and install circlip. Apply thick coat of grease to spline surface of rack and thin coating to remainder of surface. Insert rack into box. Dip assembled pinion shaft in grease and install in box. Install plastic washer and "O" ring to pinion shaft.

3) Tighten set screw to specifications. Insert "V" ring up to groove and press notched ring up to stop. Center rack in housing. Right end of rack should extend 3.031" (77 mm) beyond housing. Place dust seal on shaft so mark on seal is between marks on housing. Place "O" ring into pressure pad and slide pad into steering box.

4) Place spring and retainer on pressure pad. Tighten notched set screw against stop, then back off socket head set screw until it extends approximately ½" (12 mm) above edge of housing.

Adjustment — 1) Tighten notched set screw to 4 ft. lbs. (.6 mkg), then back off by 1 full castle slot to cotter pin hole. Install adapter (32 1 000) and torque wrench (00 2 000) on pinion shaft. Turn rack over entire length to check for sticking or binding. Set screw may be backed off no more than one notch in event of sticking or binding.

2) Move rack to center position and determine turning torque. If not within specifications, self locking set screw may be turned right to increase or to left to decrease friction.

3) Use new seals and lock plates and complete assembly procedure in reverse order of disassembly.

NOTE — *Shoulder of lock plates must engage opening of rack when installing tie rods. If replacing rubber bushing supporting steering damper, short spacers must be in place prior to tightening cover plate.*

TIGHTENING SPECIFICATIONS	
Application	**Ft. Lbs. (mkg)**
Tie Rod to Rack	51-56 (7-8)
Tie Rod to Steering Knuckle	25-29 (3.5-4.0)
Steering Gear to Axle	35-39 (4.9-5.4)
Pinion Shaft Pinch Bolt	18-20 (2.5-2.8)
Pinion Shaft Set Screw	16-19 (2.2-2.6)
Steering Damper Mounting	11-13 (1.5-1.8)
Steering Gear Turning Torque	
At Center	7.8-11.2 INCH lbs. (9-13 cmkg)
Beyond Center (Max.)	17.4 INCH lbs. (20 cmkg)

CHRYSLER CORP. IMPORTS RACK & PINION

Champ
Colt Hatchback

DESCRIPTION

Rack and pinion type steering is mounted by rubber insulators to crossmember. Adjustment is provided for pinion gear preload. Pinion shaft is coupled to the steering shaft and tie rods connect end of rack to steering arms of front wheels.

ADJUSTMENT

NOTE — *Adjustments of pinion gear preload are performed during overhaul. See OVERHAUL procedure.*

REMOVAL & INSTALLATION

Removal — Raise and support front of vehicle. Remove wheels. Remove coupling bolt from pinion shaft joint. Using a puller, disconnect tie rod ends from knuckle arms. Remove mount bolts at crossmember and remove rack and pinion assembly.

Installation — Install in reverse order of removal. Check wheel alignment.

OVERHAUL

Disassembly — **1)** With rack and pinion assembly mounted in a soft-jawed vise, remove tie rod staking with a chisel. Then, use a wrench to remove tie rod assemblies.

2) Remove lock nut and using a special socket (MB990607 or equivalent), remove yoke adjusting screw. Remove yoke spring, rubber cushion and support yoke. Carefully pry out oil seal.

3) Remove snap ring and remove pinion and bearing. Remove snap ring retaining bearing to shaft and press off bearing.

4) Remove rack from left side of housing to avoid damage from rack teeth during removal.

Reassembly & Adjustment — **1)** Use grease on all friction surfaces during assembly. Install rack from left side. Install

bearing to pinion, then install pinion into housing. Install snap ring that eliminates axial play. See *Pinion Bearing Snap Ring chart*. Install new oil seal.

Pinion Bearing Snap Rings	
Snap Ring Color	**In. (mm)**
Blue	.063 (1.59)
White	.066 (1.67)
Yellow	.069 (1.74)

2) Grease and install support yoke, cushion, and spring with yoke adjusting screw. Using special socket, torque adjusting screw to 5-11 ft. lbs. (.69-1.52 mkg), then back off 30° to 60°. Install lock nut with sealer. Install tie rod assemblies and stake ends to rack keyways.

3) Measure rack starting force and pinion preload with a torque wrench and adapter at pinion shaft. Pinion preload should be 3.5-9.5 INCH lbs. (4-11 cmkg). Starting force should measure 11-66 ft. lbs. (1.52-9.13 mkg). If specifications are not obtained, replace yoke spring and rubber cushion and readjust.

4) Install rack and pinion assembly on crossmember. Connect tie rod ends to steering knuckles and pinion shaft to steering shaft coupler. Check wheel alignment.

TIGHTENING SPECIFICATIONS	
Application	**Ft. Lbs. (mkg)**
Pinion Gear-to-Steering Shaft	11-14 (1.5-1.9)
Housing-to-Crossmember	22-29 (3.0-4.0)
Yoke Screw Lock Nut	36-51 (5.0-7.0)
Ball Joint-to-Knuckle Arm	11-25 (1.5-3.5)
Tie Rod-to-Rack	58-72 (8.0-10.0)
Tie Rod Lock Nut	36-40 (5.0-5.5)

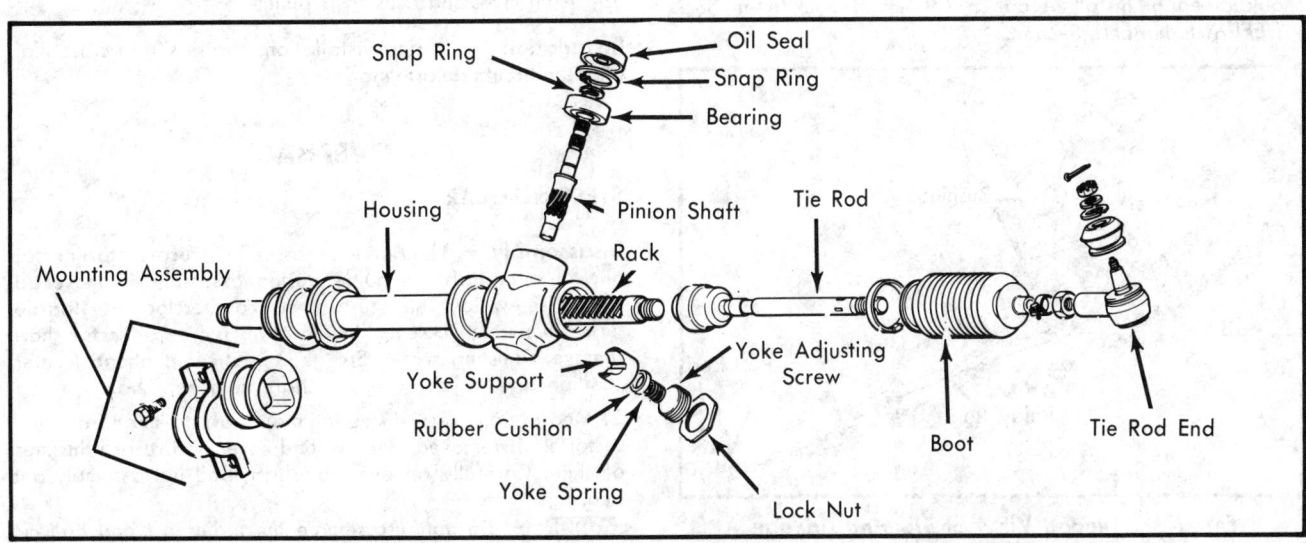

Fig. 1 Exploded View of Champ and Colt Hatchback Rack and Pinion Steering

CHRYSLER CORP. IMPORTS RECIRCULATING BALL

Arrow   Colt Wagon
Arrow Pickup   D50 Pickup
Challenger   Sapporo

DESCRIPTION

Steering system uses a recirculating ball gear of variable ratio. This type of gear minimizes gear ratio at the straight-ahead position, resulting in high stability at center; however, as the wheel is turned from center, gear ratio increases, allowing easy maneuvering.

Two sizes of steering box are used: a small box on models equipped with the 1600 cc engine, and a larger box for models equipped with the 2000 and 2600 cc engines. Both are serviced by the same procedures.

REMOVAL & INSTALLATION

STEERING GEAR

Disconnect steering shaft from gear box main shaft. Using suitable puller, separate relay rod from pitman arm. Remove gear box from frame. Pull pitman arm from cross shaft. To install, reverse removal procedure.

TIE ROD ASSEMBLY

Removal — Disconnect tie rod ends from steering knuckle, using puller. Unscrew tie rods ends from tie rod.

Installation — **1)** Grease tie rod end dust cover and coat lower edge of cup with packing sealer before installation. Temporarily install tie rod ends to tie rods.

2) Distance from center-to-center of tie rod ends should be 11.89" (302 mm) for Arrow; 12.36" (314 mm) for Challenger, Colt Wagon and Sapporo; 14.78" (375.5 mm) left tie rod and 14.84" (377 mm) right tie rod on Pickup models.

3) Amount of threads showing on each side of tie rod sleeve should be equal. Install tie rods to vehicle and check toe-in. See *WHEEL ALIGNMENT* Section.

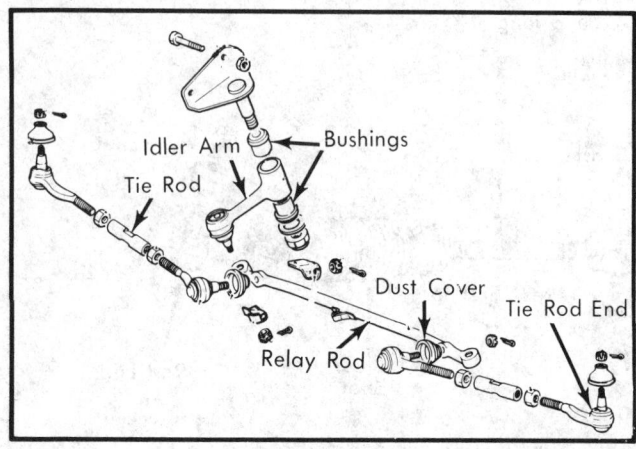

Fig. 1   *Exploded View of Steering Linkage (Arrow)*

RELAY ROD

Removal — Disconnect tie rod ends from steering knuckle arms using puller. Detach pitman arm and idler arm, using the same puller. Remove relay rod.

Installation — To install, reverse removal procedure, noting the following: Ensure dust covers are well greased and that lower edge of covers are coated with packing sealer.

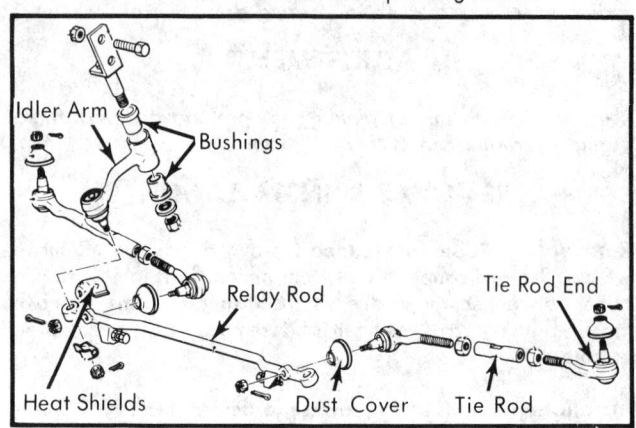

Fig. 2   *Exploded View of Steering Linkage (Challenger, Colt Wagon, Sapporo and Pickups)*

IDLER ARM

Removal — Disconnect idler arm from relay rod, using puller. Remove idler arm assembly from frame.

NOTE — *Do not disassemble idler arm and support unless absolutely necessary.*

Installation — Apply soapy water to bushings and idler arm. Push bushings into arm, using a vise if necessary. Grease bracket shaft and inner surface of bushing, then insert shaft into idler arm. Install washer with knurled side toward bushing and using a new self-locking nut, tighten to specification.

PITMAN ARM

Removal — After removing steering gear, disconnect pitman arm from cross shaft, using a puller.

Installation — During installation, ensure slit on cross shaft aligns with pitman arm mark.

OVERHAUL

STEERING GEAR

Disassembly — **1)** Prior to disassembly, record starting torque of mainshaft (as guide during assembly). Remove adjusting screw lock nut, turn screw counterclockwise (partial turn), then remove cover. When cover is free of sector shaft, remove adjusting screw. Set gear in straight ahead (center) position and withdraw sector shaft from gear box.

2) Measure and record steering mainshaft starting torque with sector shaft removed. Remove end cover and record thickness of shim. Carefully remove mainshaft, ball nut assembly and bearings.

CAUTION — *Do not disassemble the mainshaft and ball nut assembly.*

CHRYSLER CORP. IMPORTS RECIRCULATING BALL (Cont.)

Inspection — Check components for excess wear or free play. If rough rotation or excess play is found in mainshaft or ball nut, replace both as an assembly. Do not force ball nut to either end of mainshaft.

Reassembly & Adjustment — 1) Place gear box in vise with mainshaft in horizontal position. Replace end cover with shim (same as removed) and tighten. Measure mainshaft preload. If less or greater than 3.0-4.8 INCH lbs. (3.5-5.5 cmkg), reduce or increase shim size to obtain proper preload. *Refer to Mainshaft Shim Chart.*

Mainshaft Shims	
Shim No.	**Thickness In. (mm)**
1	.0020 (.05)
2	.0024 (.06)
3	.0030 (.07)
4	.0040 (.10)
5	.0080 (.20)
6	.0120 (.30)
7	.0200 (.50)

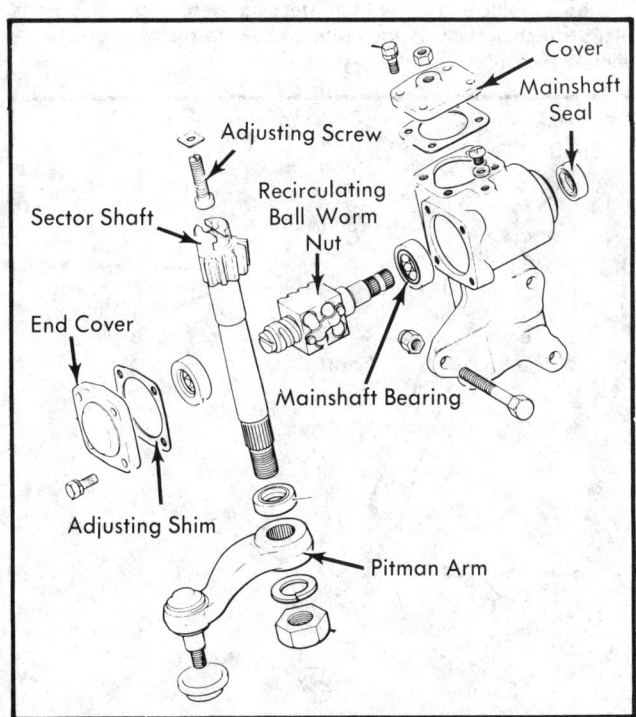

Fig. 3   Exploded View of Recirculating Ball & Nut Steering Gear — Small Gear Box

2) Install adjusting screw and proper shim in groove on sector shaft. Be sure axial play of shaft is no greater than .002" (.05 mm). If greater, change shim size. *Refer to Sector Shaft Shim chart.* Lubricate and install sector shaft in housing. Replace cover and cover bolts. Turn sector shaft several times from side to side, then turn adjusting screw in and out several times, to set proper gear mesh.

Sector Shaft Shims	
Shim No.	**Thickness In. (mm)**
1	.077 (1.95)
2	.079 (2.00)
3	.081 (2.05)
4	.083 (2.10)

3) Loosen adjusting screw until no play is noticed at main shaft when gear is in central position. Tighten lock nut. Recheck main shaft preload; it should now be 5.7-7.4 INCH lbs. (6.5-8.5 cmkg). Fill gear box with SAE 90 gear oil. Check oil level through lower right bolt hole. Proper level from hole is .8" (20 mm).

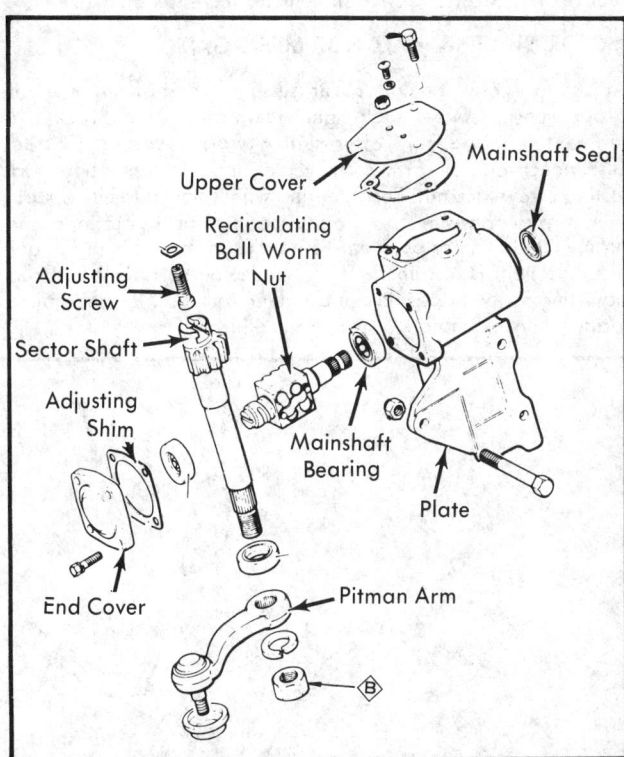

Fig. 4   Exploded View of Recirculating Ball & Nut Steering Gear — Large Gear Box

TIGHTENING SPECIFICATIONS

Application	Ft. Lbs. (mkg)
Gear Box-to-Frame	
Small Box	25-29 (3.5-4.0)
Large Box	32-36 (4.4-5.0)
Gear Box End Cover	11-14 (1.5-2.0)
Pitman Arm-to-Gear Box	94-108 (13-15)
Idler Arm Bracket-to-Frame	29-43 (4.0-6.0)
Tie Rod Stud Nuts	36-40 (5.0-5.5)
Tie Rod End Lock Nuts	36-40 (5.0-5.5)
Relay Rod-to-Pitman Arm	25-33 (3.5-4.5)
Relay Rod-to-Idler Arm	25-33 (3.5-4.5)

COURIER RECIRCULATING BALL

Pickup

DESCRIPTION

Steering gear is a recirculating ball and nut type. Two tubes carry the balls through worm channels, thus transmitting the turn action of the steering shaft. Worm bearing preload and ball-nut meshload have adjustments provided, to maintain smooth steering operation.

ADJUSTMENT

WORM BEARING PRELOAD

Drain gear box. Disconnect pitman arm from gear. Loosen sector adjusting screw lock nut and turn screw counterclockwise. Using torque wrench, rotate worm shaft. Preload should be 5.2-7.8 INCH lbs. (6.0-9.0 cmkg). If not within specification, remove end cover and shims. If preload is below minimum, reduce shim size. If above maximum, increase shim size.

SECTOR SHAFT & BALL-NUT MESHLOAD

Adjusting screw in side cover sets sector shaft to provide proper mesh between sector gear teeth and ball-nut rack. Adjustment is made only after setting worm bearing preload. Disconnect pitman arm from center link. Loosen sector adjusting screw lock nut. Turn steering wheel slowly to either stop, then turn to opposite stop. Count steering wheel rotations and turn wheel to center position. Turn adjusting screw in or out until adjustment is obtained. There should be no backlash. Hold adjusting screw in position and tighten lock nut. Recheck mesh load. Connect pitman arm to center link.

REMOVAL & INSTALLATION

STEERING GEAR

Removal — 1) Remove steering wheel and switches. See *Courier* in *STEERING WHEELS & COLUMN SWITCHES in this Section.* Remove support bracket, move floor mat away from column, and separate toe plate/boot from dash. Remove column jacket from shaft.

2) Take off air cleaner assembly. Disconnect heater hoses. Remove hydraulic lines from brake and clutch master cylinders, plug ports on both cylinders and remove from vehicle.

3) Raise vehicle on hoist. Disconnect pitman arm from sector shaft. Remove steering gear retaining bolts. Lower vehicle and remove gear and shaft assembly.

Installation — 1) Position gear to frame and install mounting bolts finger tight. Replace column jacket and dash panel boot and toe plate. Reposition floor covering. Install cancelling cam and snap ring on steering shaft, then connect directional signal/dimmer switch wires.

2) Install steering wheel (align marks made during removal). Replace spring and horn button. Install brake and clutch master cylinders and hydraulic lines. Reattach heater hoses and install air cleaner assembly.

3) Raise vehicle and tighten steering gear mounting bolts. Bleed clutch system. Attach pitman arm to sector shaft. Lower vehicle and bleed brake system.

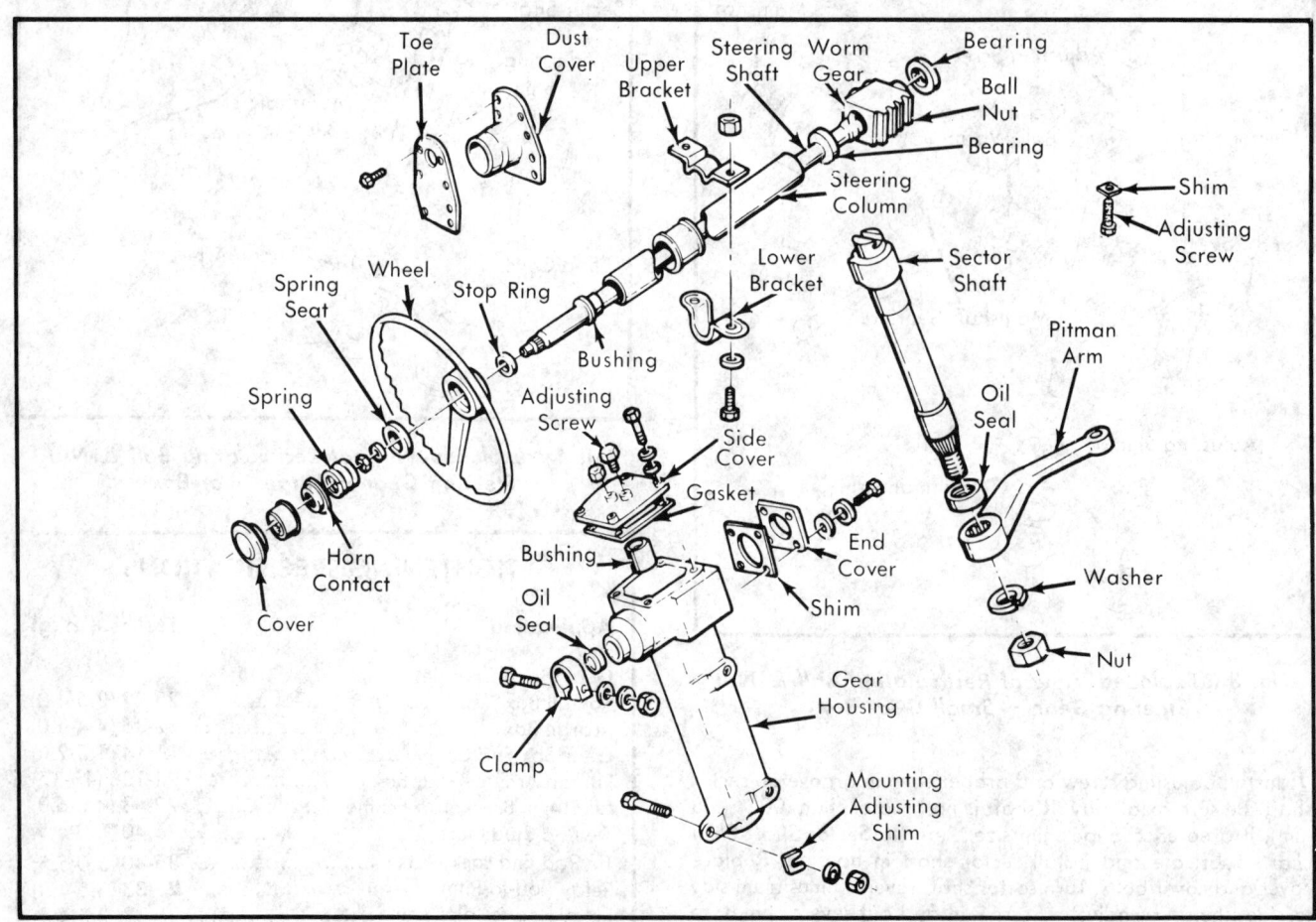

Fig. 1 Exploded View of Courier Recirculating Ball Steering Column and Gear

COURIER RECIRCULATING BALL (Cont.)

STEERING LINKAGE

Center link can be removed from both tie rods, pitman arm, and idler arm by removing ball joint nuts and using suitable puller. After center link removal, pitman arm can be removed from sector shaft. Tie rods can also be removed with puller. Toe-in must be reset when tie rods or ball joints are replaced.

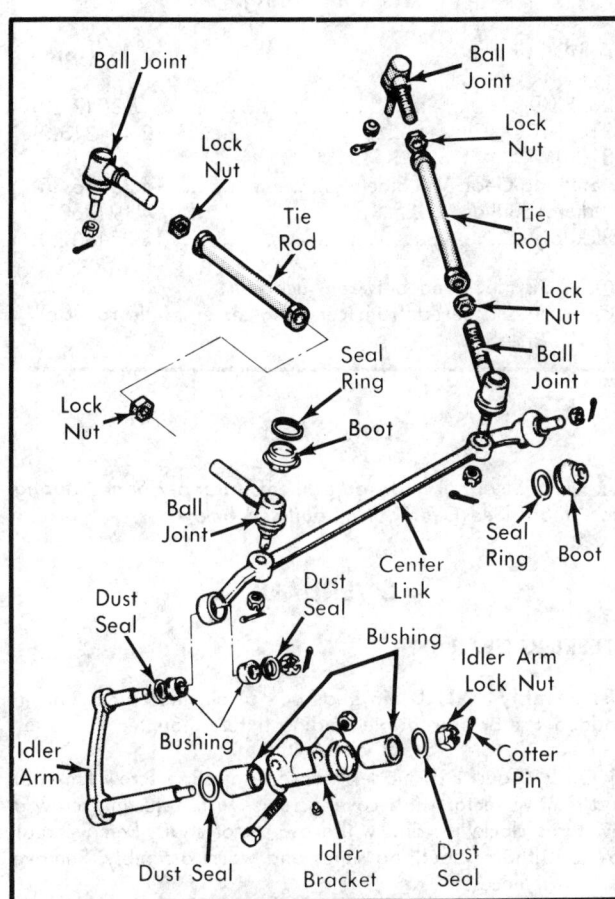

Fig. 2 Exploded View of Courier Steering Linkage

OVERHAUL

STEERING GEAR

Disassembly — With gear removed and drained, position gear in vise. Remove pitman arm from gear. Remove sector shaft adjusting screw lock nut. Take off side cover by removing bolts and turning adjusting screw clockwise. Remove adjusting screw and shim from sector shaft. Extract shaft from housing. Remove worm shaft and ball-nut assembly through bottom of housing after end cover and shims are removed.

Inspection — Check operation of ball-nut assembly on worm shaft. If travel is not smooth or any part is worn, replace entire assembly. Check and replace all other components as necessary.

Assembly & Adjustment — 1) Insert worm shaft and ball-nut assembly into gear housing. Install end cover and shims. Adjust bearing preload, as previously described. Place adjusting screw in slot of sector shaft and check end clearance with feeler gauge; adjust to 0-.004″ (0-.1 mm) by adding or subtracting shims.

2) Turn worm shaft and place rack in center position of worm. Insert sector shaft and adjusting screw into gear housing, being careful not to damage bushings or seal. Align center of sector gear with center of rack. Place side cover on adjusting screw, turn screw to position cover, then install cover retaining bolts.

3) Adjust sector gear and rack backlash, as previously described. Tighten adjusting screw lock nut. Install pitman arm to sector shaft and torque to specification.

TIGHTENING SPECIFICATIONS	
Application	**Ft. Lbs. (mkg)**
Gear-to-Frame	33-42 (4.56-5.81)
Side Cover Bolts	12-17 (1.66-2.35)
Steering Wheel Nut	22-29 (3.04-4.01)
Column Support Bracket	12-17 (1.66-2.35)
Pitman Arm-to-Gear	109-130 (15.1-18.0)
Column Jacket Clamp-to-Gear	7-9 (0.97-1.24)

Steering Gears & Linkage

DATSUN 200SX, 210, 510, 810 & PICKUP RECIRCULATING BALL

DESCRIPTION

The steering gear used on these vehicles is a recirculating ball type. The worm shaft is joined to the steering shaft by a rubber shock-absorbing coupling. The steering linkage is a relay design, with the steering gear attached by a pitman arm to one end of the center link (cross shaft), while the other end of the center link moves on the idler arm.

REMOVAL & INSTALLATION

STEERING GEAR

Removal — 1) On 210 models, remove clutch operating cylinder (if equipped). Do not remove clutch hose. Disconnect exhaust pipe from manifold (disconnect any brackets holding exhaust pipe in place). On all models, remove bolt holding worm shaft to rubber coupling.

2) Remove nut holding gear arm to sector shaft and remove steering gear arm from sector shaft. Remove bolts securing steering gear housing to body side member. Remove steering gear housing from vehicle.

Installation — To install, reverse removal procedure, aligning markings on pitman arm with markings on sector shaft.

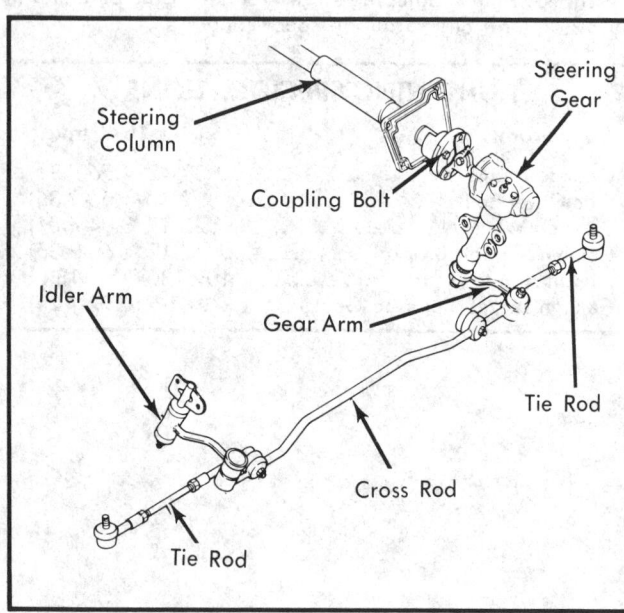

**Fig. 1 Datsun Steering Gear Linkage
(210 Shown, Others Similar)**

STEERING LINKAGE

Removal — Jack up front of vehicle and support with stands. Detach both outer tie rod ends from steering knuckles. Separate cross shaft from idler arm and pitman arm, then remove cross shaft and tie rods as an assembly. Idler assembly may be removed from side member, if necessary to replace bushing.

Installation — To install, reverse removal procedure, noting the following: Set tie rod end length to the prescribed setting, then check wheel alignment. See *Datsun* in *WHEEL ALIGNMENT* section.

Tie Rod Settings	
Application	**In. (mm)**
200SX①	2.80 (71.0)
210, 510②	12.40 (315.0)
810②	
Steering Gear Arm Side	14.35 (364.5)
Idler Arm Side	14.19 (360.5)
Pickup②	13.07 (332.0)
① — As measured between lock nuts.	
② — As measured from center-to-center of tie rod ball studs.	

ADJUSTMENT

NOTE — *Steering gear adjustments are performed during reassembly. See Overhaul as outlined below.*

OVERHAUL

STEERING GEAR

Disassembly — 1) Drain gear box of oil, then place unit in padded vise or on suitable holding fixture mounted in a vise.

2) On 210 and 810 models, loosen adjusting screw lock nut and remove sector shaft cover screws. Turn adjusting screw a few turns clockwise and withdraw sector shaft. Remove rear cover. Withdraw bearing shims and worm assembly. Remove oil seal if necessary.

3) On 200SX, 510 and Pickup models, place worm gear in straight ahead position and remove sector shaft cover with sector shaft. Separate cover from sector shaft and remove oil seal if necessary. Remove adjusting plug lock nut and adjusting plug. Withdraw worm assembly out of gear box. Remove oil seal from adjusting plug.

NOTE — *Do not remove sector shaft bearings or bushings from housing. If defective, replace housing assembly. Do not disassemble ball nut; replace, if necessary, with worm shaft assembly. Do not let ball nut bottom out on either end of worm shaft, or damage to ball guides will result.*

Inspection — Inspect gear teeth on sector shaft and ball nut for wear or damage; replace as necessary. Check bearings for wear or roughness during rotation. Ensure ball nut moves smoothly over its entire length of travel.

Reassembly and Adjustment — 1) On 210 and 810 models, lubricate bearings, gear, and other moving parts with gear oil. Apply suitable grease to oil seal lip and press seal into rear cover. Install worm assembly, with bearings, into housing. Install "O" ring (810 models only), shims (thicker shim to housing side) and rear cover. Standard shim thickness for 810 and 210

DATSUN 200SX, 210, 510, 810 & PICKUP RECIRCULATING BALL (Cont.)

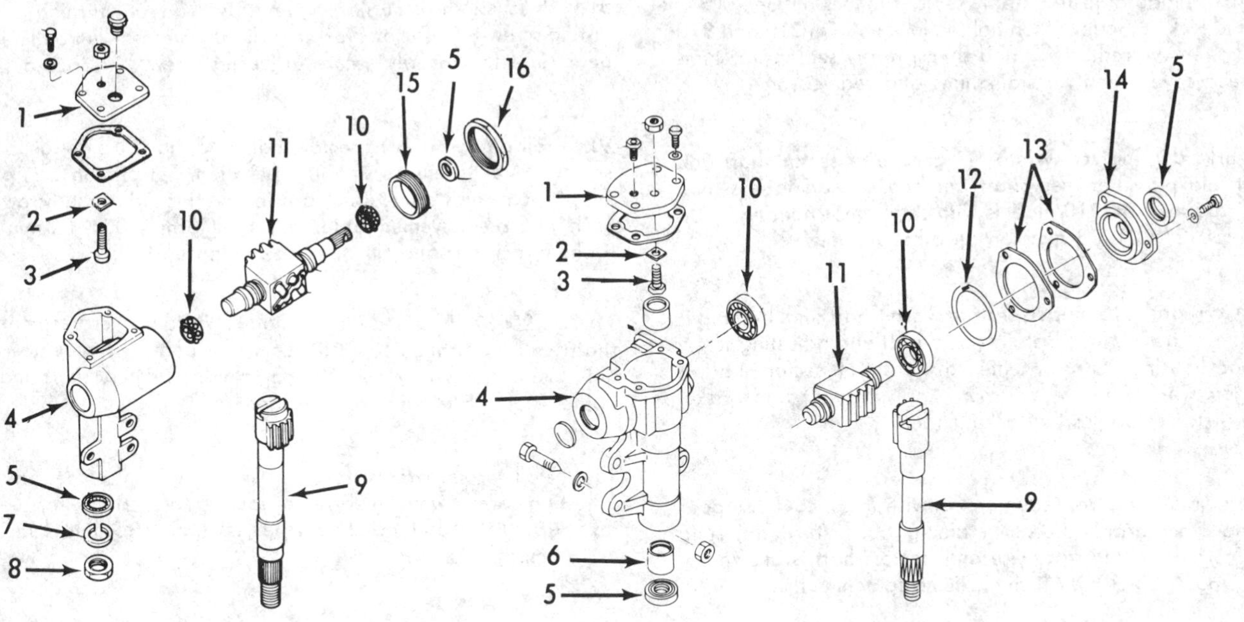

200SX, 510, PICKUP MODELS

810 MODELS (210 MODELS SIMILAR)

1 — Sector Shaft Cover	7 — Washer	12 — "O" Ring (810 Models)
2 — Shim	8 — Nut	13 — Shims
3 — Adjusting Screw	9 — Sector Shaft	14 — Rear Cover
4 — Housing	10 — Bearing	15 — Adjusting Plug
5 — Oil Seal	11 — Ball Nut & Worm Assembly	16 — Lock Nut
6 — Bushing		

Fig. 2   Exploded View of Datsun Recirculating Ball Steering Gear Assembly

(large housing) is .059" (1.5 mm); for 210 (small housing), .020" (.5 mm). *Refer to Worm Bearing Shim chart for available shims.*

bearing preload (initial turning torque). *See Worm Bearing Preload Chart for specifications.* Add or subtract shims on 210 and 810 models; or tighten adjusting plug on 200SX, 510 and Pickup models until bearing preload (initial turning torque) is to specifications.

Worm Bearing Shims

Shim No.	In. (mm)
810, 210 (Large Housing)	
1	.030 (.762)
2	.010 (.254)
3	.005 (.127)
4	.002 (.050)
210 (Small Housing)	
1	.0020 (.050)
2	.0027 (.070)
3	.0031 (.080)
4	.0040 (.100)
5	.0080 (.200)

Worm Bearing Preload Specifications

Application	INCH Lbs. (cmkg)
210	3.5-7.8 (4.0-9.0)
810	3.5-6.9 (4.0-8.0)
200SX, 510, Pickup	3.5-5.2 (4.0-6.0)

2) On 200SX, 510 and Pickup models, lubricate bearings, gear and all other moving parts with gear oil. Apply suitable grease to oil seal lip and press seal into adjusting plug.

3) On all models, rotate worm shaft a few times to settle assembly. Attach torque wrench to worm shaft and measure

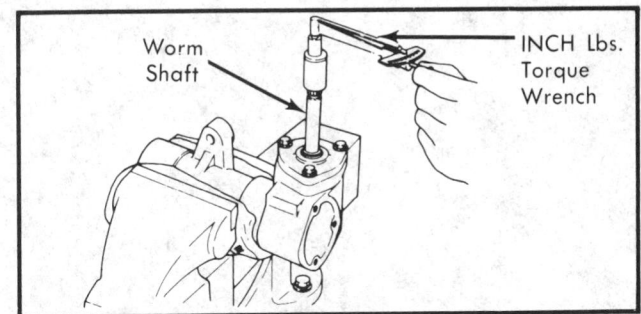

Fig. 3   Measuring Steering Gear Initial Turning Torque

DATSUN 200SX, 210, 510, 810 & PICKUP RECIRCULATING BALL (Cont.)

4) With preload adjusted, apply sealant to lock nut on 200SX, 510 and Pickup models, then tighten lock nut. On 210 and 810 models, remove rear cover and shims; apply sealant to shims and rear cover, then reinstall shims and rear cover.

5) Insert adjusting screw into "T" groove of sector shaft and adjust end play between shaft and screw head to less than .002" (.05 mm) on 210 models with small gear housing, or to .0004-.0012" (.01-.03 mm) on all other models.

6) On 210 and 810 models, rotate worm shaft until ball nut is in center of travel, then install sector shaft and adjusting screw in gear housing. Ensure center of tooth of sector shaft is engaged with center of ball nut. Apply sealant and gasket material to sector shaft attaching face.

7) Turn adjusting screw counterclockwise to set cover on gear housing. Temporarily install retaining bolts. Turn adjusting screw further counterclockwise until sector shaft is drawn upward about .08-.12" (2-3 mm). Fully tighten bolts.

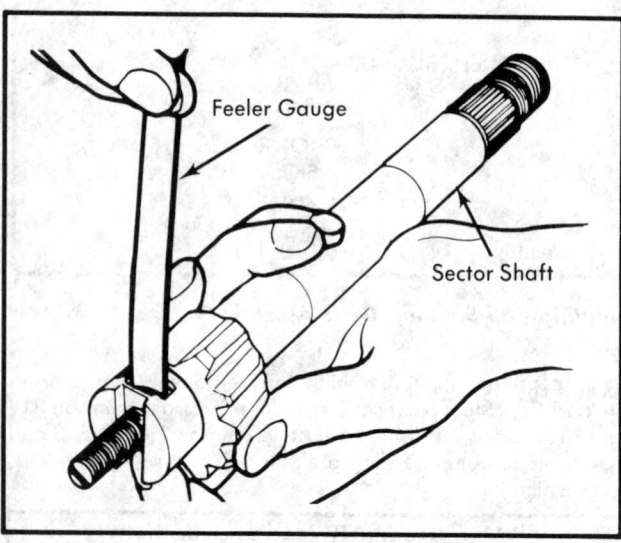

Fig. 4   Measuring Sector Shaft-to-Adjusting Screw End Play

8) Push sector shaft against ball nut by gradually turning adjusting screw until sector shaft gear lightly meshes with ball nut gear, and temporarily secure adjusting screw with lock nut.

9) Install pitman arm to sector shaft and move it side-to-side several times to ensure smooth operation. Set pitman arm at center point and adjust backlash (by turning adjusting screw) such that free movement at top of pitman arm is .004" (.1 mm). Tighten lock nut and fill gear box with gear oil.

10) On 200SX, 510 and Pickup models, install cover to sector shaft (with adjusting screw). Place worm gear in center position, then install sector gear to gear housing (with gasket) and tighten bolts. Fill gear box with gear oil.

11) Install torque wrench to worm shaft. Tighten sector shaft adjusting screw while measuring total gear turning torque (preload). Total preload should be less than 10.9 INCH lbs. (12.5 cmkg).

NOTE — *Always adjust preload by tightening adjusting screw, never by loosening.*

TIGHTENING SPECIFICATIONS

Application	Ft. Lbs. (mkg)
Adjusting Plug Lock Nut	
200SX, 510, Pickup	181-231 (25.0-32.0)
Ball Stud Nuts	
200SX, 210, 510	22-51 (3.0-7.0)
810, Pickup	40-72 (5.5-10.0)
Gear-to-Frame	
200SX, 810	38-46 (5.3-6.3)
210, 510	51-58 (7.0-8.0)
Pickup	33-38 (4.6-5.3)
Pitman Arm-to-Gear	94-108 (13.0-15.0)
Tie Rod Lock Nuts	
810, Pickup	8-12 (1.1-1.7)
200SX, 210, 510	58-72 (8.0-10.0)

DATSUN 280ZX & 310 RACK & PINION

DESCRIPTION

Steering assembly is a direct-acting rack and pinion system. Unit consists of a rack bar and toothed pinion, both working in the plain bearing of the rack housing. Backlash is held to zero by the retainer and retainer spring.

REMOVAL & INSTALLATION

Removal — 1) Raise and support front of vehicle. On 310 models, remove joint cover and loosen bolts attaching steering column to lower joint. On 280ZX models, loosen bolt attaching lower joint shaft to rubber coupling. On both models, remove bolt attaching lower joint to steering pinion gear and remove lower joint.

2) Disconnect tie rod ball joints from steering knuckles. Remove steering rack housing mounting clamp bolts, then remove complete steering gear assembly from vehicle.

NOTE — *Raise front engine mount approximately ½" (with jack) before trying to remove steering gear.*

Installation — Install in reverse order of removal procedure. Check wheel alignment. For wheel alignment procedures, see *Datsun* in *WHEEL ALIGNMENT section.*

ADJUSTMENT

NOTE — *Adjustments are performed during gear assembly process. See Overhaul as outlined.*

OVERHAUL

Disassembly — 1) Clamp steering gear and linkage in a padded vise. Remove both dust boot clamps. Loosen inner joint lock nut and remove tie rod from rack.

NOTE — *Do not disassemble inner joint assembly and tie rod socket assembly.*

2) Loosen adjuster lock nut and remove retainer adjust screw. Remove retainer spring and steering gear retainer out of steering gear housing. Remove oil seal and pry off snap ring from steering gear housing. Remove steering pinion assembly and rack from steering gear housing.

3) Pry off snap ring securing pinion bearing from pinion gear. Press bearing from pinion gear, then remove inner snap ring from pinion gear.

4) On 310 models, remove steering gear rubber mount bushing by striking with rubber mallet. Remove snap ring and bushing from gear housing.

Inspection — Check rack and pinion gear for wear or damage, replace if necessary. Inspect tie rod inner socket for smooth operation and for excessive looseness, replace if necessary. Replace all oil seals. On 310 models, check rack bushing (in gear housing) for wear by measuring amount of play of rack when moved up and down then sideways. Play for up and down movement should be less than .020" (.5 mm) and less than .028" (.7 mm) for sideways movement.

Reassembly and Adjustment — 1) Install inner snap ring to pinion gear and then press bearing onto pinion gear. Install outer snap ring onto pinion gear. Outer snap ring thickness should be selected so that bearing play is less than .004" (.1 mm).

2) On 310 models, install rubber mount bushing to housing and secure with snap ring. Install rubber mount with plate onto end of housing. Make sure cut out section of rubber mount is aligned with hole in housing and that ventilation hole is not clogged with grease.

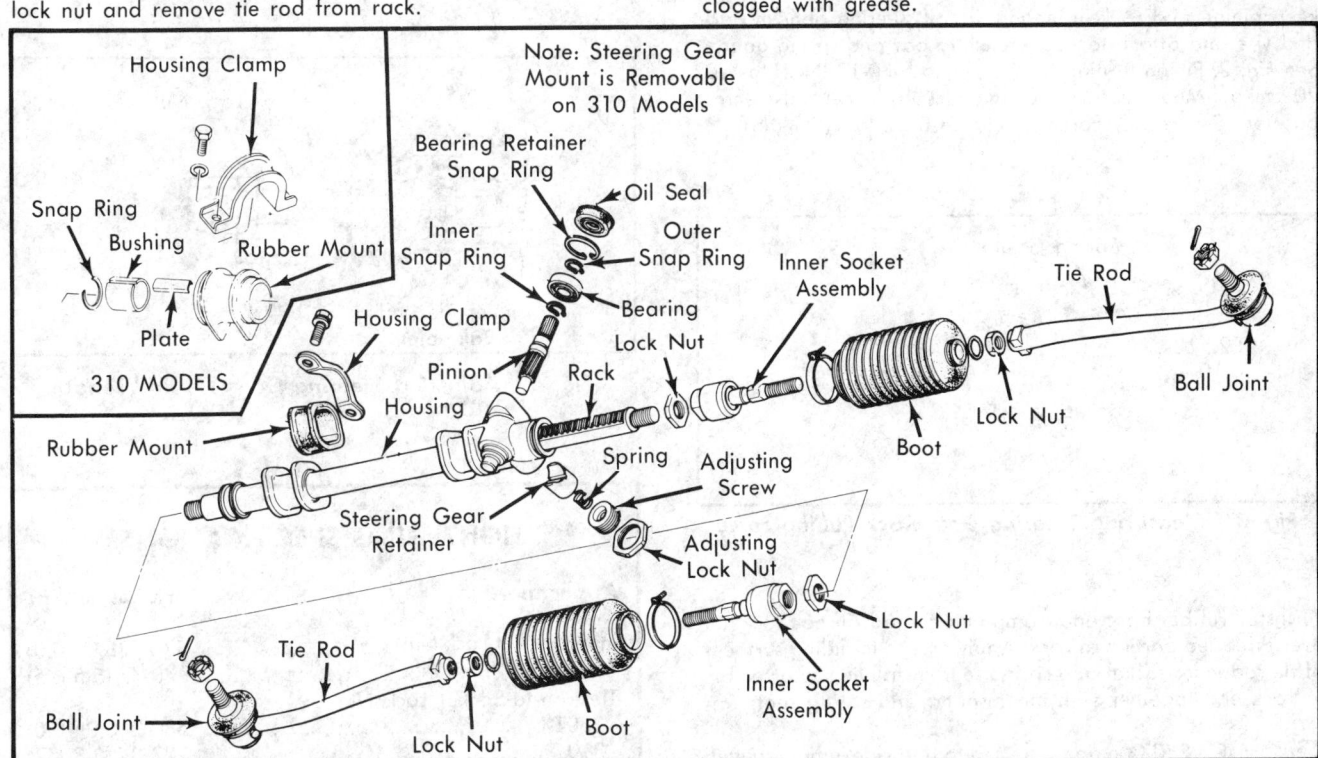

Fig. 1 Exploded View of Datsun Rack and Pinion Steering Gear Assembly

Steering Gears & Linkage

DATSUN 280ZX & 310 RACK & PINION (Cont.)

3) On all models, clamp steering gear in padded vise. Coat rack teeth and friction surfaces of rack with grease. Install rack into housing from pinion gear side and make sure rack teeth are facing correct direction. Install pinion gear (coated with grease), make sure pinion gear teeth and rack teeth mesh properly. Make sure rack protrudes same amount from each end of housing.

4) Install snap ring to steering gear housing (snap ring retains pinion bearing in place). Snap ring thickness should be selected so that pinion gear movement is less than .004" (.1 mm). Pack grease seal with grease and install. Make sure pinion assembly rotates smoothly.

5) Apply grease to steering gear retainer and insert gear retainer and retainer spring into housing. Turn adjusting screw in and install lock nut. Fully tighten adjusting screw then back off approximately 20-25°. Apply liquid sealant around lock nut and tighten lock nut.

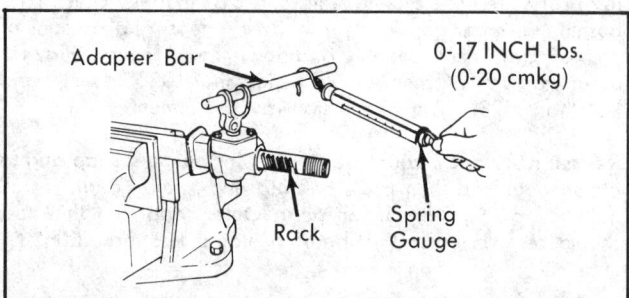

Fig. 2   Measuring Pinion Shaft Rotary Torque

6) With steering gear assembled, measure torque required to keep pinion and rack in motion. Install steering gear in padded vise and attach torque wrench to bar and spring gauge. See Fig. 2. Pinion turning torque should be 0-17 INCH lbs. (0-20 cmkg). Measure force to pull rack from neutral (center) position. See Fig. 3. Force should be 0-22 lbs. (0-10 kg).

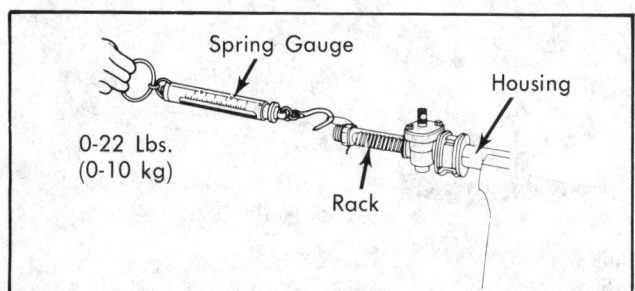

Fig. 3   Measuring Steering Gear Rack Pulling Force

7) Install rubber boot and clamp onto tie rod. Thread lock nut over threaded portion of rack. Apply grease to sliding surfaces of tie rod inner socket and spring seat. Install tie rod assembly to rack end together with inner spring and spring seat.

NOTE – On 280ZX models, tie rod for left side is marked with an "L". No mark is used for right side tie rod.

8) Screw inner socket portion until ball seat reaches rack end and then tighten lock nut. Upon completion of tie rod assembly, measure swinging torque and axial play of tie rod inner socket. Swinging torque (measured at outer end of tie rod) should be 0-43 INCH lbs. (0-50 cmkg) on 280ZX models and 13-61 INCH lbs. (15-70 cmkg) on 310 models. Axial play should not exceed .002" (.05 mm) on 280ZX models. 310 models should have no axial play.

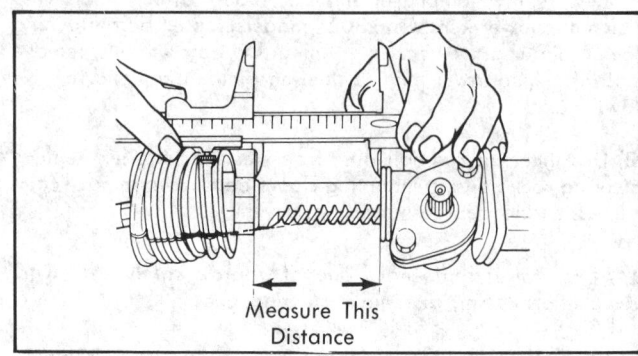

Fig. 4   Measuring Steering Gear Rack Protrusion

9) Measure rack protrusion on both sides of housing. 280ZX models should be 2.614" (66.4 mm) and 310 models should be 2.680" (68 mm). Attach boot and clamps, insert grease nipples at both ends of housing, and lubricate gear assembly (until a small amount of grease appears at boot outlet hole). Adjust tie rod length so that distance from outer side of lock nut to end of boot mounting groove is 1.161" (29.5 mm) on 280ZX models or 5.24" (133 mm) on 310 models.

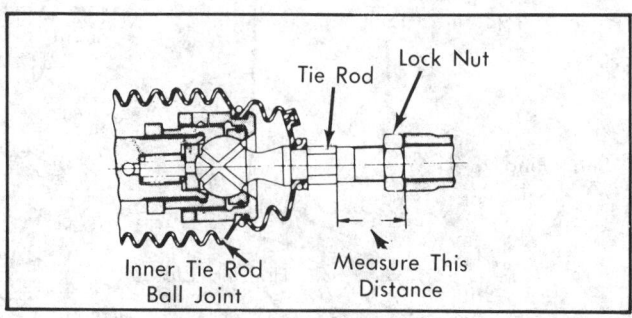

Fig. 5   Adjusting Steering Gear Tie Rod Length

TIGHTENING SPECIFICATIONS

Application	Ft. Lbs. (mkg)
Inner Socket Lock Nut	58-72 (8.0-10.0)
Tie Rod Ball Joint Nut	40-47 (5.5-6.5)
Tie Rod-to-Socket Lock Nut	
280ZX	58-72 (8.0-10.0)
310	27-34 (3.8-4.7)

FIAT SPIDER 2000 WORM & ROLLER

DESCRIPTION

The steering gear is a worm and roller type, having a gear ratio of 16.4:1. The steering gear box is mounted on the crossmember in front of the firewall.

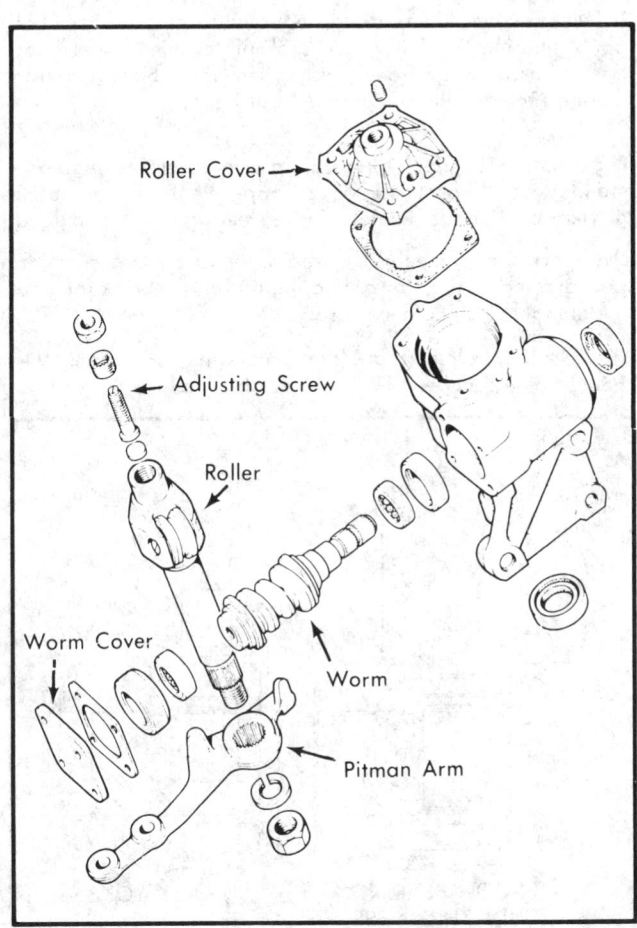

Roller Cover →

Adjusting Screw →

Roller

Worm Cover →

Worm

Pitman Arm

Fig. 1   Exploded View of Spider 2000 Steering Gear

ADJUSTMENT

NOTE — *Adjustments are performed as part of gear reassembly. See Overhaul in this article.*

REMOVAL & INSTALLATION

STEERING GEAR

Removal — Using suitable puller, remove tie rod and center link from Pitman arm. Loosen steering column clamp on worm shaft. Remove three bolts holding steering gear to body, noting number and position of shims. Remove steering box.

Installation — Bolt steering box to body, but do not tighten bolts. Clamp steering column on worm shaft and reconnect tie rod and center link. Turn steering wheel from side to side several times to align shaft and box, then tighten bolts to specification.

OVERHAUL

STEERING GEAR

Disassembly — **1)** Unscrew oil plug and drain gear oil, then mount assembly on suitable overhaul stand. Use a puller to detach pitman arm from roller shaft.

2) Remove nuts and washers attaching roller shaft cover to gear box, then take off cover with roller shaft adjusting screw, adjusting disc, lock washer, and lock nut. Extract roller shaft assembly from gear housing.

3) Remove worm shaft thrust cover and shims. Turn shaft and remove bearing. Using a suitable puller (A. 47004), remove worm shaft rear bearing. This will release shims located behind bearing. Remove roller shaft oil seal, and bearings if necessary with puller (A. 74105).

Assembly & Adjustment — **1)** If installing new roller shaft bearings, drive into place with drift. Ream to correct bore diameter, 1.1298-1.1306" (28.698-28.720 mm). Replace shims and rear worm shaft bearing.

NOTE — *If proper center mesh position was found during inspection, install same shims. If not, adjust shim pack.*

2) Fit worm bearing races and install worm into gear box. Drive front ball bearing race into gear box and replace thrust cover with shims. Check starting torque of worm shaft. It must not exceed 4.3 INCH lbs. (5.0 cmkg). If torque is higher, shimming must be increased; if lower than specified, reduce shimming.

3) Insert roller shaft oil seal, roller shaft, and cover plate with gasket and shims. Replace pitman arm temporarily to roller shaft. The roller shaft should be free to rotate through 30° on either side of center. Eliminate any clearance using adjusting screw. Turning torque after adjustment should be 7.8-10.4 INCH lbs. (9-12 cmkg).

4) When adjustment is complete, tighten pitman arm retaining nut to specification. Fill steering box with 7.25 oz. of SAE 90 EP lubricant.

TIGHTENING SPECIFICATIONS

Application	Ft. Lbs. (mkg)
Steering Column Bracket Bolts	11 (1.5)
Linkage-to-Pitman Arm	22 (3.0)
Steering Gear-to-Body	29 (4.0)
Steering Wheel Nut	36 (5.0)
Pitman Arm-to-Gear	174 (24.1)

FIAT STRADA & X1/9 RACK & PINION

DESCRIPTION

Rack and pinion steering gear is mounted in rubber insulators and attached to body. Gear is attached to steering shaft through universal joints. Adjustments are provided for pinion bearing play and rack yoke free play. At each end of steering rack, tie rods connect steering mechanism to front wheels.

ADJUSTMENT

NOTE — *Adjustments of the pinion bearing and rack yoke are performed during rebuilding. See Overhaul procedure.*

REMOVAL & INSTALLATION

STEERING GEAR

Removal — 1) Center steering wheel and front wheels. Raise and support front of vehicle and remove front wheels. On Strada models, it may be necessary to remove spare tire.

2) Disconnect drive pinion from lower steering column section by detaching universal joint inside vehicle. Using a suitable puller, remove tie rods from steering knuckles.

3) Remove stone shield if necessary. Unbolt and remove steering gear assembly by sliding out from right-hand side of vehicle.

Installation — Set wheels in straight-ahead position, then connect drive pinion to steering column and tighten pinch bolt to 19 ft. lbs. (2.6 mkg). Remount steering gear to body. Connect tie rods to steering knuckle and tighten to 25 ft. lbs. (3.5 mkg).

2) If steering gear has been disassembled, perform pinion and rack adjustments, and replace front wheels. Lower vehicle to ground and turn steering wheel fully to the right. Raise vehicle on left side and loosen clamp on left boot. Fill steering gear with 4.4 ounces lithium-base grease containing molybdenum disulphide.

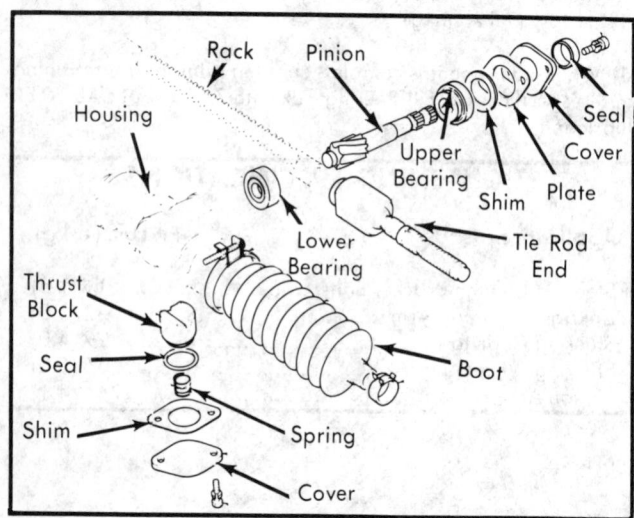

Fig. 1   Exploded View Steering Gear Components

OVERHAUL

Disassembly — 1) With steering gear removed from vehicle, remove rubber boots from steering gear. Disconnect tie rod end ball joints from rack (inner ends of tie rods).

2) Remove cover, shim, spring, seal and thrust block from bottom of housing. Remove cover, seal, plate, shim, upper bearing, and drive pinion from housing. See Fig. 1. Slide rack from housing. Remove lower bearing from housing.

Inspection — 1) Clean all metal parts in a suitable degreaser and blow dry. Inspect rack, pinion, upper bearing and housing for wear or damage. Replace entire steering box if damaged.

2) Inspect boots for tears or breaks. Replace if necessary. Inspect bushing, spring, lower bearing and thrust block for wear or damage. Replace if necessary.

3) Check that ball joints are free to move in all directions. They should not fall under their own weight. Replace if worn.

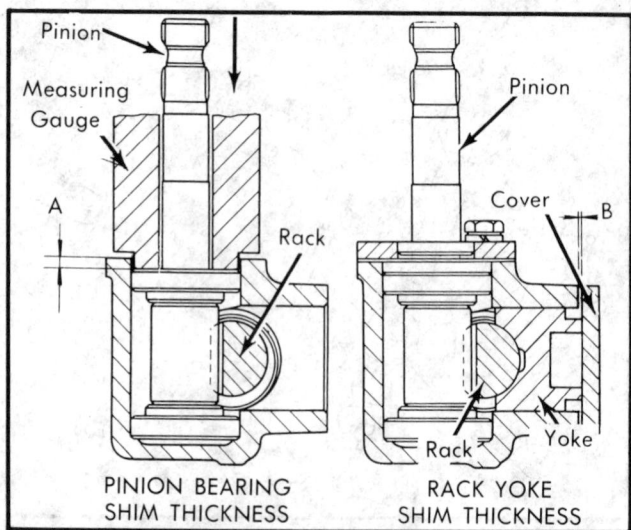

Fig. 2   Measurement of Rack Yoke Shim Thickness and Pinion Bearing Shim Thickness

Reassembly and Adjustment — 1) Coat all bearings and gear surfaces with molybdenum disulphide grease. Reassemble in reverse order of disassembly.

2) Remove cover, plate and seal from drive pinion side of rack housing. Using suitable driver, make sure upper bearing is firmly seated. Measure distance "A" from top of bearing to pinion cover facing. See Fig. 2. Add .003±.002" (.078±.053 mm) to dimension "A" and install shims centered on pinion to make up new dimension. Install plate, cover and seal.

3) Center rack in its travel. Remove cover, shims and spring to gain access to rack thrust block. While holding rack thrust block against rack, turn pinion through 180° in both directions. Measure dimension "B" from top of rack thrust block to cover facing. See Fig. 2. To "B" add .0035±.0015" (.09±.04 mm). Combine shims to make up new dimension. Install spring, shims and cover.

NOTE — *Lubricate dust boots with silicon spray and be sure they are not twisted after installation.*

FIESTA RACK & PINION

Hatchback

DESCRIPTION

Rack and pinion steering gear is mounted to firewall by rubber-insulated clamps. Pinion shaft is supported by a bushing and a ball bearing, eliminating the need for preload adjustment. Excessive rack play is prevented by a spring loaded slipper that bears against rack. Rubber boots seal ends of gear, and tie rods transfer turning motion to front wheels.

ADJUSTMENT

RACK

1) Mount rack in vise, with padded jaws, with rack slipper bearing cover up. Remove bolts and cover, shims and gasket. Using dial indicator, measure rack slipper deflection as rack is moved from end-to-end (full travel).

2) Assemble shim pack (including gasket) which is .002-.005" (.05-.125 mm) thicker than measurement obtained. Fit shims and gasket to housing and tighten cover bolts to 55-80 INCH lbs. (63.25-92.0 cmkg). Measure pinion turning torque to check adjustment. Torque should measure 5-18 INCH lbs. (5.8-20.8 cmkg).

REMOVAL & INSTALLATION

Removal — 1) Place front wheels in center position. Raise and support vehicle, then remove clamp bolt securing steering shaft to pinion shaft. Remove tie rod outer ball joints from steering arms.

2) Bend lock tabs and remove steering gear bolts and clamps. Remove steering gear from vehicle, then loosen lock nuts and detach tie rod ends from gear.

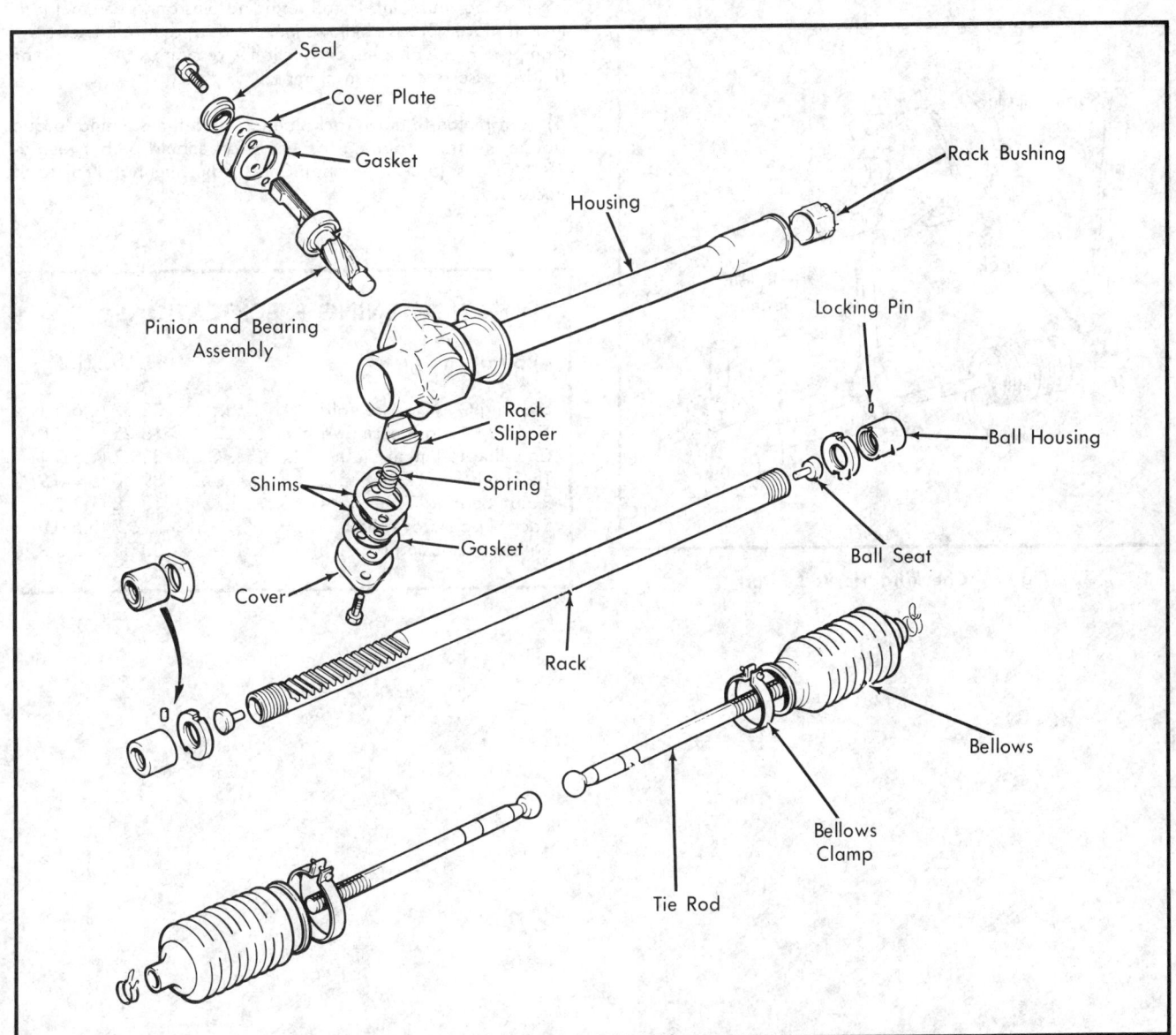

Fig. 1 Exploded View of Fiesta Rack & Pinion Steering Gear

FIESTA RACK & PINION (Cont.)

Installation — To install, reverse removal procedure and install new lock plates and cotter pins. Check wheel alignment and steering wheel position.

OVERHAUL

Disassembly — 1) Remove bellows and drain fluid lubricant from steering gear, then mount in padded vise. Drill out pins securing tie rod ball joint housings to rack, using 5/32" (4.0 mm) drill bit.

CAUTION — *Do not drill deeper than .4" (9.5 mm).*

2) Separate ball joint housing and lock ring, then remove housings, tie rods and ball seats. Remove rack slipper cover plate, shims, gasket, spring and slipper.

3) Remove pinion bearing cover plate, gasket, and seal. Remove pinion and bearing assembly. If necessary, use suitable tool (T77F-3504-F) and slide hammer to remove pinion bushing. Remove rack from housing.

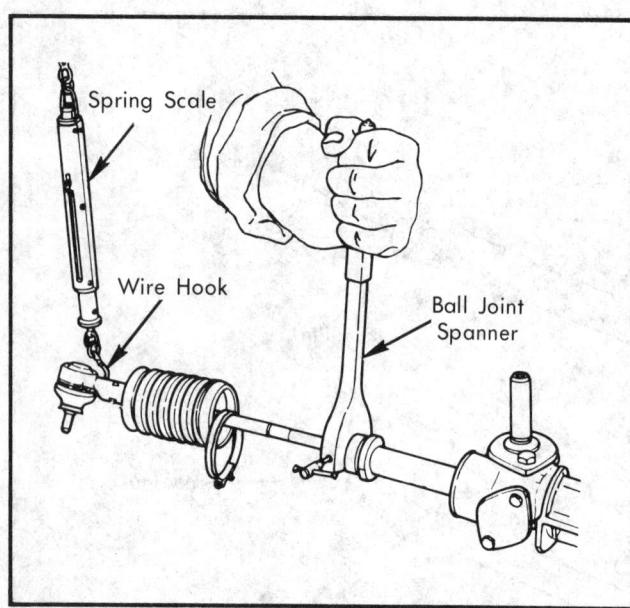

Fig. 2 Checking Tie Rod Effort

Spring Scale

Wire Hook

Ball Joint
Spanner

Inspection — Clean all parts and inspect for wear. Pinion shaft and bearing are serviced as an assembly and must be replaced if damaged. Rack support bushing at end of housing can be replaced separately if necessary.

Reassembly — 1) Position rack in housing. With rack centered, insert pinion and bearing assembly. Flat on pinion must face right hand side of vehicle and be at 90° to centerline of rack. Install pinion shaft gasket, cover and seal, applying sealer to bolts. Tighten to specification.

2) Install rack slipper, spring, shims, gasket and cover plate. Select shims as described in *Adjustment* in this article.

3) Grease tie rod ball and seat and assemble on end of rack. Tighten ball seat until effort required to move tie rod is 2.6-5.1 lbs. (1.2-2.3 kg) when measured 1/4" (6.0 mm) from end of rod. See *Fig. 2*.

4) Centerpunch and drill 5/32" hole .4" (9.5 mm) deep at housing and lock nut joint. Install retaining pins and peen metal to lock in place. Grease bellows inner ends and install. Use screw clamps in place of some production wire clamps. Add .2 pt. of fluid grease and tighten clamps.

5) Turn pinion to move rack side to side 5 times. Using torque gauge, measure rotating torque. Effort should be between 5-18 INCH lbs. (5.8-20.8 cmkg). Check adjustment and correct if necessary.

TIGHTENING SPECIFICATIONS

Application	Ft. Lbs. (mkg)
Steering Gear-to-Firewall	33-37 (4.6-5.1)
Tie Rod End-to-Steering Arm	18-22 (2.5-3.0)
Coupling-to-Pinion Clamp	33-37 (4.6-5.1)
Tie Rod End Lock Nut	39-50 (5.4-6.9)
Pinion Bearing Cover Bolts	13-18 (1.7-2.4)
Rack Slipper Cover Bolts	4.5-6.7 (0.6-0.9)
Ball Joint Housing Lock Nut	33-38 (4.6-5.3)

HONDA RACK & PINION

Accord
Civic
Prelude

DESCRIPTION

Rack and pinion type steering is mounted by rubber insulators to crossmember. Adjustment is provided for pinion gear preload. Pinion shaft is coupled to the steering shaft and tie rods connect end of rack to steering arms of front wheels.

ADJUSTMENT

NOTE – *Rack piston must be adjusted whenever steering gear assembly is removed and installed.*

STEERING WHEEL TURNING FORCE

Raise and support front of vehicle, so front wheels are off ground. Attach spring gauge to steering wheel spoke, near wheel rim. Turn wheel with spring gauge and note reading. If reading is more than 3.3 lbs. (1.5 kg), adjust rack piston adjusting screw until turning force is to specifications.

RACK PISTON ADJUSTMENT

Loosen rack screw lock nut. Tighten rack screw until lightly bottomed then back off screw 45° from bottomed position. Tighten lock nut and recheck steering wheel turning force.

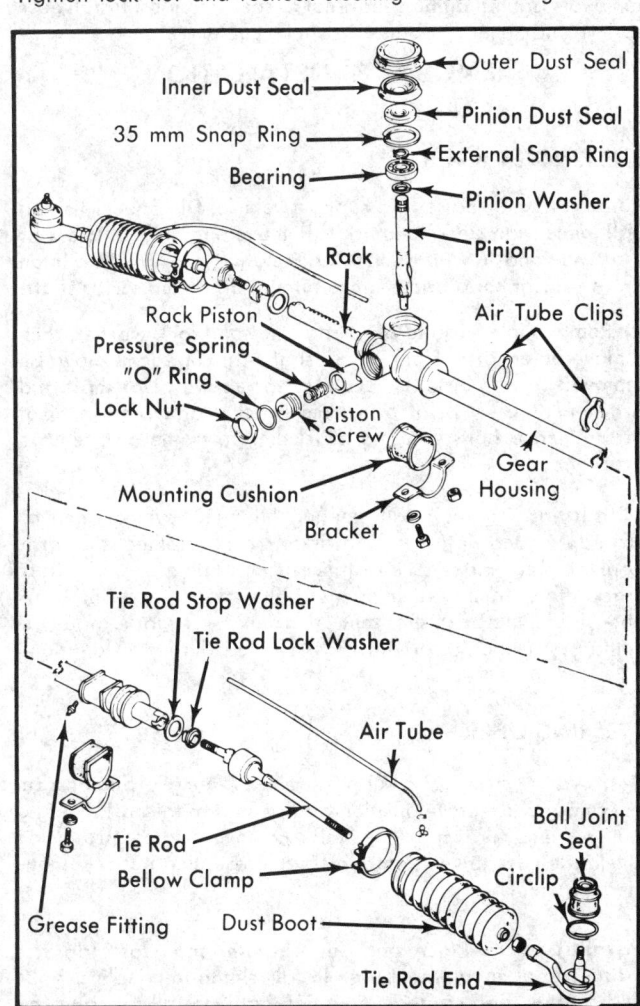

Fig. 1   Exploded View of Honda Rack & Pinion Steering Gear Assembly

REMOVAL & INSTALLATION

STEERING GEAR

Removal (Accord) – **1)** Raise and support front of vehicle. Remove front wheels. Disconnect tie rod ball joints from steering knuckles. Disconnect exhaust pipe at manifold.

2) Place Man. Trans. in 1st or 3rd and remove shift rod yoke bolt. Remove engine crossmember. Disconnect shift lever torque arm at transmission. On Auto. Trans. remove center engine mount and splash guard, then disconnect shift cable.

3) Turn steering wheel full left. Remove steering shaft connector bottom bolts, then steering gear brackets. Lower gear to disconnect steering shaft. Move gear right to clear subframe then move left to remove.

Installation – To install steering gear assembly, reverse removal procedures.

Removal (Civic & Prelude) – **1)** Raise and support front of vehicle. Remove wheels. Disconnect tie rods from steering knuckles. Remove bolt from steering shaft to pinion gear connector. Remove steering gear mounting bracket bolts.

2) Lower gear to disconnect steering shaft, rotate gear 180° forward and remove gear through left side of vehicle.

Installation – To install steering gear, reverse removal procedures. Check operation of steering gear for smoothness and binding after installation.

OVERHAUL

STEERING GEAR

Disassembly – **1)** Place steering gear in a vise. Disconnect air tube and dust boot clamps. Push dust boots out of way, bend up lock washer tabs and remove tie rods from rack.

2) Remove rack adjusting screw lock nut, adjusting screw, washer, spring and rack piston. Remove pinion gear grommets, dust seal and snap ring, then pull pinion gear out of steering housing. Remove rack and rack bushing.

Inspection – Check all components for wear or damage, replace as necessary. Measure rack piston adjustment spring length, replace if not to specifications. New spring length should be 1.028" (26.1 mm) for Accord, 1.126" (28.6 mm) for Civic, and .750" (19.04 mm) for Prelude. Service limit for springs should be .945" (24 mm) for Accord, 1.035" (26.3 mm) for Civic, and .689" (17.5 mm) for Prelude.

Reassembly – Coat sliding surfaces with grease, then reassemble in reverse order of disassembly. Use new lock washers on tie rods and adjust steering after installation in vehicle.

TIGHTENING SPECIFICATIONS

Application	Ft. Lbs. (mkg)
Adjusting Screw Lock Nut	18 (2.5)
Ball Joint Nuts	32 (4.4)
Tie Rod Lock Nut	32 (4.4)

LUV RECIRCULATING BALL

Pickup

DESCRIPTION

STEERING GEAR

Steering gear is a recirculating ball and nut type. A worm gear is incorporated on lower end of steering shaft and is engaged with ball nut through a number of recirculating balls. Adjustment is provided for backlash between sector gear and ball nut by a tapered sector gear in steering unit (adjustment screw is on sector shaft).

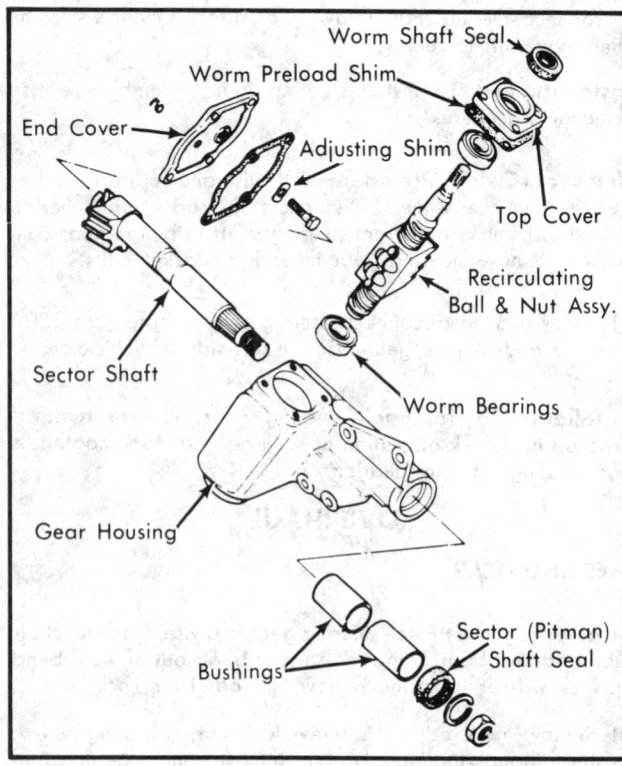

Fig. 1 Exploded View of Recirculating Ball Steering Gear Assembly

STEERING LINKAGE

Linkage consists of splined pitman arm connected to an adjustable center link on 2-WD models or non-adjustable center link on 4-WD models. Center link is attached to an idler arm and then to tie rods. Idler arm is attached to frame by a bracket. Tie rods are non-adjustable on 2-WD models. Tie rods are adjustable on 4-WD models.

ADJUSTMENT

PRELOAD & LASH

1) Disconnect battery ground cable, then raise and support front of vehicle. Remove pitman arm nut and mark position of arm-to-shaft. Remove arm using puller. Remove horn shroud and spring.

CAUTION — *Do not turn wheel hard against stops, as damage to ball guides may result.*

2) Turn steering wheel in one direction until stopped by gear, then turn back half way. Measure and record "bearing drag" by attaching torque wrench to steering wheel nut and rotating through a 90° arc.

NOTE — *Do not use a torque wrench having a maximum reading of more than 50 INCH lbs. (57.6 cmkg).*

3) Adjust sector lash by turning steering wheel from one stop to the other, turn wheel back exactly halfway (to obtain center position), then turn sector adjusting screw clockwise to eliminate backlash between ball-nut and sector gear. Tighten lock nut.

4) Check torque at steering wheel nut, taking highest reading as steering wheel turns through center. Torque should be 4.3-8.7 INCH lbs. (5.0-10.0 cmkg). If not, loosen lock nut and readjust sector screw. Tighten lock nut and recheck torque at steering wheel.

5) If maximum specification is exceeded, turn adjusting screw counterclockwise, then turn adjuster lock nut clockwise. Reassemble pitman arm to shaft, lining up marks made during removal. Tighten pitman shaft nut to specifications. Install horn spring and shroud. Connect battery cable.

REMOVAL & INSTALLATION

STEERING LINKAGE

Removal — **1)** Raise and support vehicle. Disconnect tie rod ball joints from steering knuckle. Remove pitman arm-to-sector shaft nut and lock washer. Mark relative position of pitman arm-to-sector shaft and remove pitman arm from sector shaft.

2) Remove idler arm-to-pivot shaft nut and lock washer, then remove idler arm from pivot shaft. Linkage can now be removed from vehicle. If necessary to remove pivot shaft and bracket, unscrew pivot arm from bracket and remove pivot arm. Remove bolts securing bracket from frame and remove bracket.

Installation — To install steering linkage, reverse removal procedures and note the following: When installing idler arm to pivot shaft, make sure distance from bottom of pivot shaft bracket to bottom of idler arm is 1.280-1.366" (32.5-34.7 mm) after tightening pivot shaft nut. Also make sure marks made on pitman arm and sector shaft are aligned during installation.

STEERING GEAR

Removal — Raise and support vehicle. Remove pitman arm nut and mark relative position of pitman arm-to-shaft. Using a puller, remove arm from shaft. Remove engine protection shield. Remove lower clamp-to-flexible coupling bolts. Remove steering gear.

Installation — Place gear in position and start (do not torque) gear mounting bolts. Install clamp-to-coupling bolts and torque. Tighten gear mounting bolts. Install pitman arm, aligning index marks and tighten nut. Install engine protection shield.

LUV RECIRCULATING BALL (Cont.)

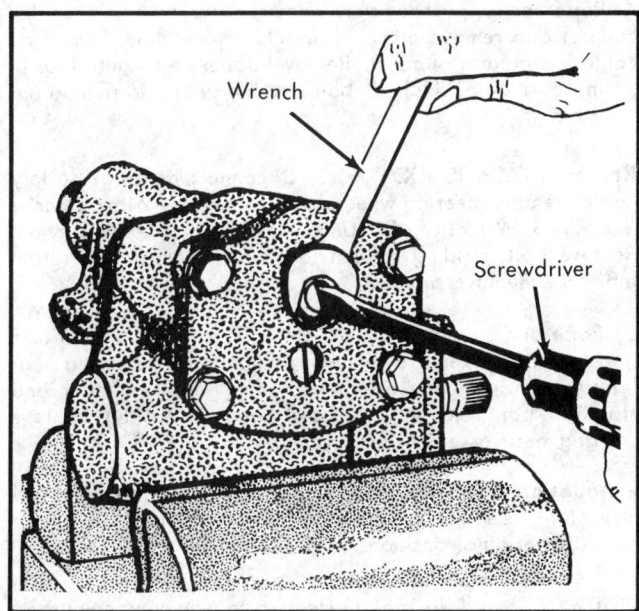

Fig. 2   Adjusting Sector Gear Lash

OVERHAUL

STEERING GEAR

NOTE — *Recirculating ball and nut assembly parts are selectively combined. Ball tube clamp plate is sealed with paint to prevent disassembly. Any worn part, therefore, necessitates entire assembly replacement.*

Disassembly — **1)** Remove steering gear as previously described. Disconnect flexible coupling from worm shaft. Drain gear box through filler plug hole. Place sector shaft in straight ahead (center) position.

2) Remove top cover bolts and adjusting screw lock nut. Separate top cover from gear box by turning adjusting screw clockwise. Hold sector shaft in straight-ahead position during removal and DO NOT drive shaft off gear box by impact.

3) Remove adjusting screw and sector shaft from gear case. Remove end cover bolts and shims. Pull worm gear and ball nut assembly from gear box and take out lower bearing.

CAUTION — *Keep assembly in horizontal position or ball nut will fall onto end of worm gear, damaging ball tubes.*

Inspection — Check all parts for wear or damage. Check sector shaft for bending or excessive wear. Standard size of sector shaft is 1.126" (28.6 mm). Replace shaft if wear is .001" (.025 mm) or more. Check worm and ball nut for wear, scoring, pitting and smooth, quiet operation. If any part fails to meet specifications, replace part, assembly or complete steering gear assembly.

Reassembly & Adjustment — **1)** Insert lower bearing into position in gear box. Install worm shaft assembly in box. Check lower end of worm shaft for proper fit in lower bearing.

2) Assemble upper bearing onto worm shaft and install adjusting shims between gear housing and end cover. Install and tighten bolts.

NOTE — *Apply liquid gasket to end cover during installation.*

3) At this point, measure starting torque of pinion shaft (see illustration). Reading should be 2.9-6.0 lbs. (1.3-2.7 kg) when coupling begins to rotate. If not within limits, add or remove shims as necessary.

4) Bring ball nut to center of worm and insert sector shaft into gear box. Engage center tooth of shaft with center tooth of worm. Insert adjusting screw in sector shaft slot. Screw should slide freely within the slot and have no more than .001" (.025 mm) clearance. If clearance is excessive, insert adjusting shim. Install sector cover while turning adjusting screw out. Tighten lock nut.

5) Check total gear preload (starting torque) using pull scale shown in illustration. If reading is between 4.9-11.7 lbs. (2.2-5.3 kg), no further adjustments are required. If correct specification is not obtained, turn adjusting screw until preload is within specifications. Tighten lock nut.

6) Connect sector shaft to pitman arm (align marks made during removal) and tighten pitman arm nut. Install and tighten pinch bolt. Fill gear assembly with .5 pts. of lubricant; do not overfill.

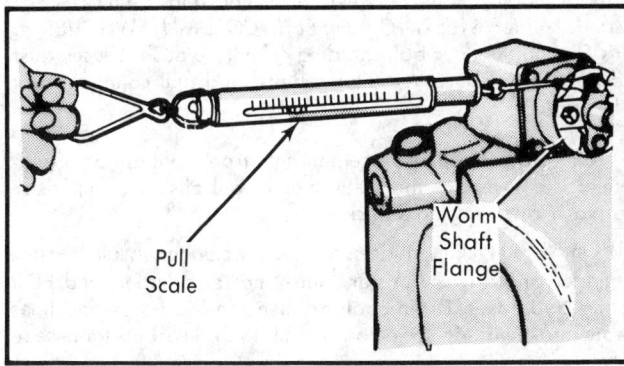

Fig. 3   Measuring Steering Gear Starting Torque

PITMAN SHAFT SEAL REPLACEMENT

NOTE — *If replacement has been determined as necessary, it may be done without removing the steering gear.*

1) Raise and support vehicle. Remove pitman arm as previously described. Clean area around seal. Pry out old seal, being careful not to damage housing bore.

CAUTION — *Check gear lubricant for contamination. If contamination of any kind is detected, gear overhaul is necessary.*

2) Coat new seal with gear lubricant and tap into position. Install pitman arm and nut. Lower vehicle and check lubricant level in gear assembly.

TIGHTENING SPECIFICATIONS

Application	Ft. Lbs. (mkg)
Ball Joint Nut	44 (6.1)
Center Link Lock Nut	89 (12.2)
Idler Arm Nut	89 (12.2)
Pitman Arm Nut	162 (22.4)

Steering Gears & Linkage

MAZDA RECIRCULATING BALL

GLC
626
RX7
B2000 Pickup

DESCRIPTION

Steering gear is a recirculating ball type with a variable ratio, depending on turning angle of sector shaft. The worm gear and steering shaft are an integral (non-separable) unit. Steering linkage is basically the same for all models, having a non-adjustable center link, 2 adjustable tie rods, an idler arm assembly, and pitman arm.

ADJUSTMENT

NOTE – *Adjustments are performed during assembly portion of overhaul. See Overhaul procedure in this article.*

REMOVAL & INSTALLATION

STEERING GEAR

Removal (GLC, B2000 Pickup) – 1) Disconnect negative battery cable. Remove steering wheel and switches. See *Mazda under STEERING WHEEL & COLUMN SWITCHES in this Section.* Remove bolts holding column to dash. Loosen dust cover screws, any other column bolts, and pull column jacket off shaft.

2) On GLC, disconnect center link from pitman arm with puller. Remove steering gear mounting bolts and pull gear forward after raising vehicle.

3) On B2000 Pickup models, remove air cleaner, brake master cylinder and power booster, clutch master cylinder, and EGR pipes and hoses. Drain coolant, then remove hoses and lines from intake manifold. Remove manifold and carburetor assembly.

4) Raise and support vehicle. Remove left front wheel, then disconnect and remove pitman arm. Place jack under lower left control arm and support. Remove upper left control arm, noting position of shims. Unbolt steering gear and pull up out of vehicle.

Removal (626 & RX7) – 1) Disconnect negative battery cable. Remove steering wheel and switches. See *Mazda under STEERING WHEEL & COLUMN SWITCHES in this Section.* Remove bolts holding column to dash. Tape holes to retain lubricant. Remove air duct.

2) Raise and support front of vehicle. Disconnect pitman arm and center link. Remove nuts and bolts retaining steering gear housing to body. Remove under cover, engine mount and stabilizer bar (626 only). Remove hood (RX7 only). Remove steering gear assembly from vehicle.

Installation (All Models) – To install, reverse removal procedure, ensuring any shims which were removed are installed in original positions.

NOTE – *To avoid damage to steering column components, do not apply bending or striking forces to steering shaft or column.*

STEERING LINKAGE

Steering linkage may be removed as an assembly or as individual components. Whenever tie rod setting is disturbed, toe-in must be reset. See *Mazda in WHEEL ALIGNMENT section.*

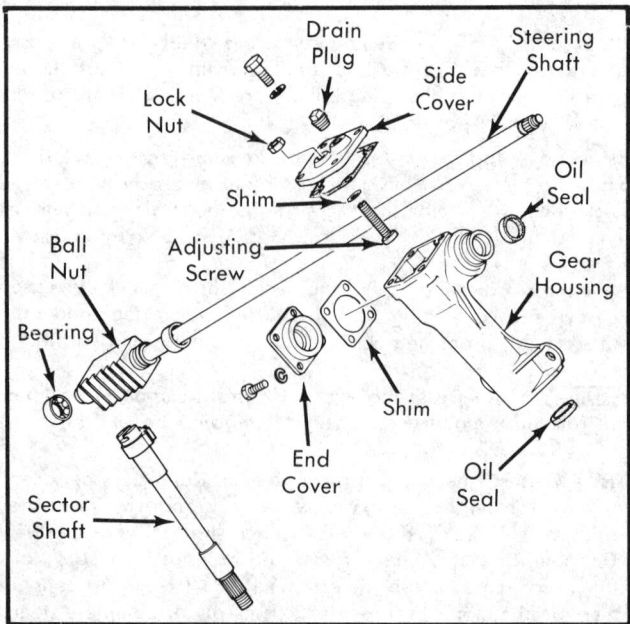

Fig. 2   Exploded View of Steering Gear Assembly (B2000 Models)

OVERHAUL

STEERING GEAR

Disassembly – 1) Drain gear oil from housing. Remove pitman arm from sector shaft, if not removed previously. Remove

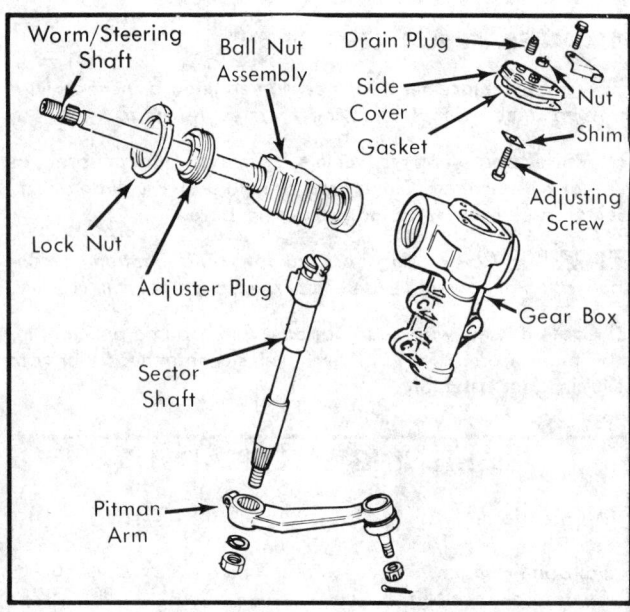

Fig. 1   Exploded View of Steering Gear Assembly (GLC, 626 and RX7 Models)

MAZDA RECIRCULATING BALL (Cont.)

sector shaft adjusting screw lock nut. Remove side cover attaching bolts and remove side cover by turning adjusting screw clockwise.

2) Remove sector shaft adjusting screw and shim from sector shaft. Remove sector shaft carefully to avoid damage to oil seal. On B2000 models, remove end cover bolts, cover and shim. Then carefully remove ball nut, worm gear and steering shaft assembly from gear housing.

3) On GLC, 626 and RX7 models, remove ball nut/worm gear adjusting plug lock nut. Then remove adjusting plug and withdraw ball nut, worm gear and steering shaft assembly from gear housing.

Inspection — Check ball nut rotation on worm gear. If movement is not smooth for full length of travel, replace worm and ball nut assembly. Ball nut is not to be serviced separately. Check worm bearings and cups, sector shaft gear surface, and oil seal. Check clearance between sector shaft and housing bore. Clearance should be .004" (.1 mm) or less. If any component is defective, replace it.

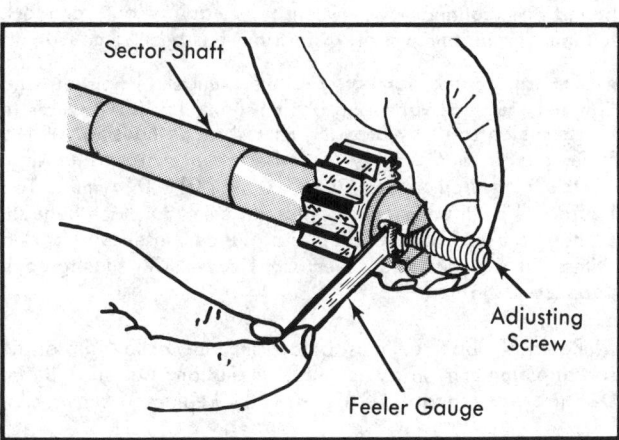

Fig. 3   Checking Sector Shaft Adjusting Screw End Clearance

Reassembly & Adjustment — **1)** Replace oil seals if necessary. Insert worm gear, ball nut and steering shaft assembly into gear housing. On B2000 models only, position end cover with bearing preload adjusting shims and install end cover and bolts. On GLC, 626 and RX7 models, install adjuster plug to gear housing.

2) On all models, attach an INCH lb. torque wrench to steering shaft and check preload. *See Initial Worm Bearing Preload chart.* On B2000 models, reduce shim thickness if preload is high or increase shim thickness if preload is low. On GLC, 626 and RX7 models, tighten or loosen adjusting plug if preload is not to specifications. Then install lock nut.

Initial Worm Bearing Preload	
Application	INCH Lbs. (cmkg)
All Models	1.7-4.3 (2.0-5.0)

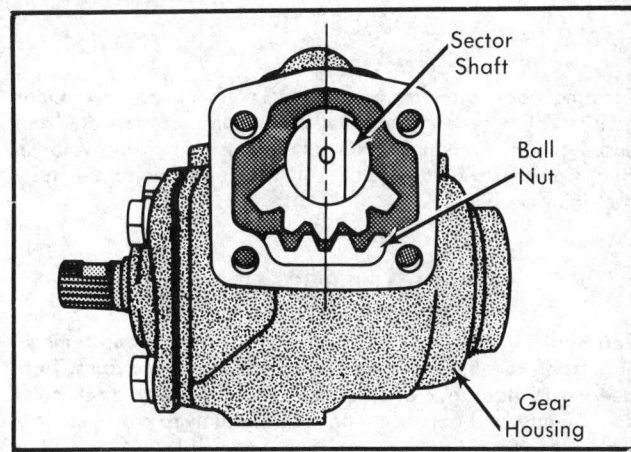

Fig. 4   Aligning Sector Shaft to Ball Nut

3) Check clearance between sector shaft adjusting screw and sector shaft. Insert shim so that final clearance will be .004" (.1 mm) or less. Insert sector shaft into gear housing, aligning center of sector shaft with ball nut. *See Fig. 4.* Insert adjusting screw and shim in sector shaft. Place side cover and gasket over adjusting screw and turn adjusting screw until cover is in place, then install cover bolts.

4) Install pitman arm to sector shaft. Install and tighten retaining nut. Measure pitman arm backlash. If necessary, turn sector adjusting screw until zero backlash is obtained. Tighten adjusting screw lock nut, taking care not to disturb backlash adjustment.

5) Check worm shaft rotating torque. Attach an INCH lb. torque wrench to steering shaft upper end. If not to specifications, adjust as necessary. *See Final Worm Bearing Preload chart.* Fill gear housing with lubricant (A.P.I. GL-4 SAE 90).

Final Worm Bearing Preload	
Application	INCH Lbs. (cmkg)
GLC, 626, RX7	5.2-10.4 (6.0-12.0)
B2000	5.2-7.8 (6.0-9.0)

TIGHTENING SPECIFICATIONS	
Application	Ft. Lbs. (mkg)
Pitman Arm-to-Sector Shaft	
B2000, RX7	108-130 (15.0-18.0)
GLC, 626	58-87 (8.0-12.0)
Worm Gear, Ball Nut & Steering Shaft	
Adjusting Plug (Exc. B2000)	166-188 (23.0-26.0)
Tie Rod Lock Nut	
B2000	80-87 (11.0-12.0)
GLC, 626, RX7	51-58 (7.0-8.0)

Steering Gears & Linkage

MGB RACK & PINION

DESCRIPTION

Steering gear is a direct-acting rack and pinion type. Gear consists of rack bar and toothed pinion mounted on front suspension crossmember. No adjustment for bearing wear in gear box is provided. Steering column is attached to pinion by "U" joint coupling.

REMOVAL & INSTALLATION

Removal — Raise and support front of vehicle and remove both front wheels. Detach tie rod ends from steering arms. Turn steering to right lock and remove "U" joint lower pinch bolt. Remove nuts and bolts securing rack assembly to crossmember, noting that front bolts are attached with self-locking nuts and that shims may be found between rack assembly and frame brackets. Withdraw rack assembly downward and remove from vehicle.

Installation — To install, reverse removal procedure after first setting steering gear and steering column in straight-ahead position.

NOTE — *If new rack is being installed, it must be aligned. See Alignment in MGB article under Steering Columns in this section.*

OVERHAUL

Disassembly — 1) Clamp rack in padded vise. Remove pinion end cover and joint washer, placing container beneath assembly to catch oil. Remove damper cover and shims. Extract yoke, damper pad, and spring, then withdraw pinion.

2) Unlock tie rod outer lock nuts and remove tie rod ends. Unclamp and remove both rubber bellows. Release bellows seal clips and withdraw seals. Pry up tab on locking rings, slacken rings, and unscrew housing to release tie rod, ball seat, and spring.

3) Pull rack out pinion end of housing. To remove rack housing bushing, unscrew self-tapping screw and carefully drive out bushing.

Inspection — Thoroughly clean all parts and examine for wear. Particularly, note condition of rubber bellows; if they show any sign of wear, replace them. Outer ball socket assembly cannot be disassembled; if worn, it must be replaced as assembly.

Assembly — 1) Insert rack bushing and carefully drive it in until flush with housing end. Drill outer housing of bushing through screw hole with a $\frac{7}{64}$" (2.78 mm) drill to a depth of .20" (5 mm) so that a new retaining screw may be inserted. Coat screw head with sealing compound before tightening.

2) Replace rack from pinion end. Position seat spring, ball seat, tie rod, and ball housings. Coat ball seats liberally with SAE 90 oil. Tighten ball housings until tie rods are held firmly, without free play. This tightening is correct when a force of 32-52 INCH lbs. (37-60 cmkg) is required to move the tie rods. Tighten new locking rings and bend tabs.

3) Insert pinion complete with ball races and locking nut into housing. Replace pinion end cover and seal, using sealing compound on mounting edges. Peen outer edge of ball race lock nut into slot in pinion shaft, if lock nut has been removed.

4) To adjust rack damper, replace plunger in housing and tighten cover, without spring or shims, until it is just possible to rotate pinion shaft by drawing rack through housing. With a feeler gauge, measure clearance between cover and housing. To this measurement add .0005-.003" (.013-.076 mm). This figure will be the correct thickness of shims to place beneath damper cover. Remove cover and plunger, insert spring and shims with plunger and cover. Coat cover with sealing compound and tighten.

5) Replace rubber bellows; before securing bellow clip on tie rod at pinion end, stand assembly on end and pour in 1/3 pint (.2 litre) of suitable SAE 90 oil. Replace bellow clip.

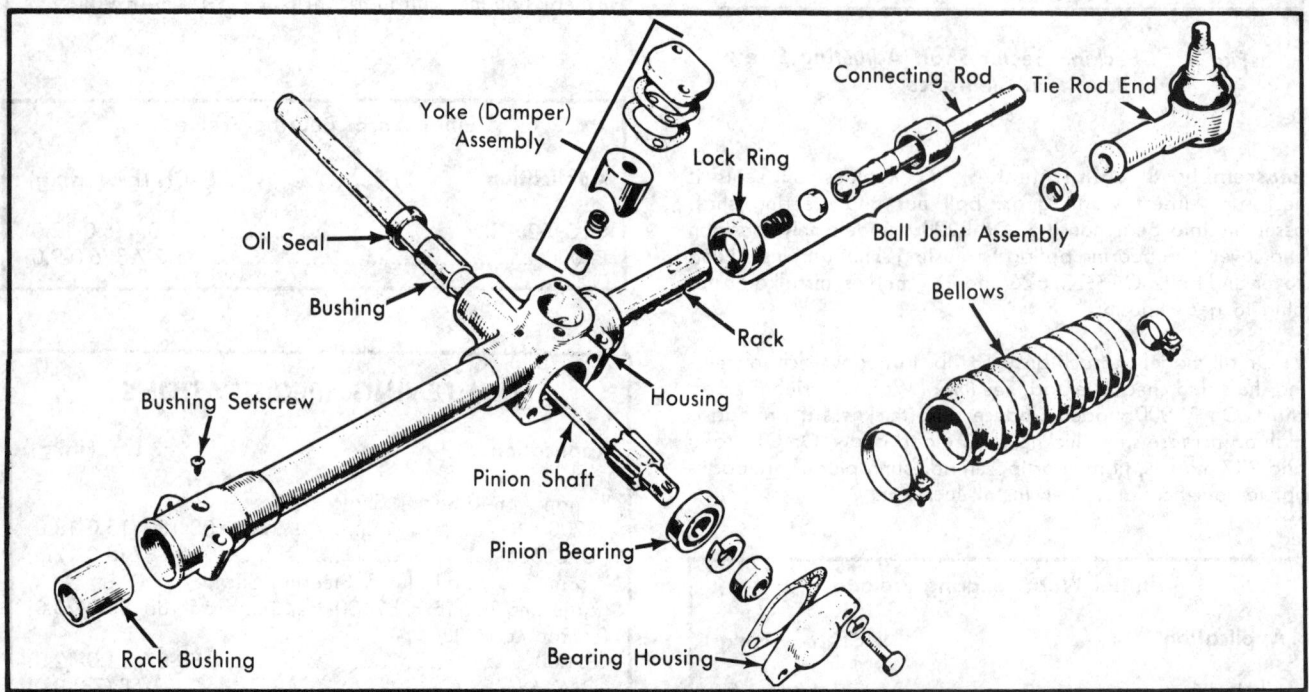

Fig. 1 Exploded View of MGB Rack and Pinion Assembly

PORSCHE RACK & PINION

911SC
924

DESCRIPTION

Porsche models use rack and pinion steering. Tie rods on 911SC attach to rack with yoke and eyebolts, while the 924 uses a ball swivel joint. Pinion on 924 is offset to the left of center. Pinion on 911SC is centered in rack housing. Pinion shafts on all models are supported by ball bearings.

ADJUSTMENT

STEERING GEAR

Steering gear adjusting methods vary according to type of steering rack pressure block: (1) Steel pressure block with plastic contact surface and external housing dust boot seat; (2) Plastic pressure block with no external housing dust boot seat; (3) Adjusting screw on 924 extends through cover to take play out of steering rack.

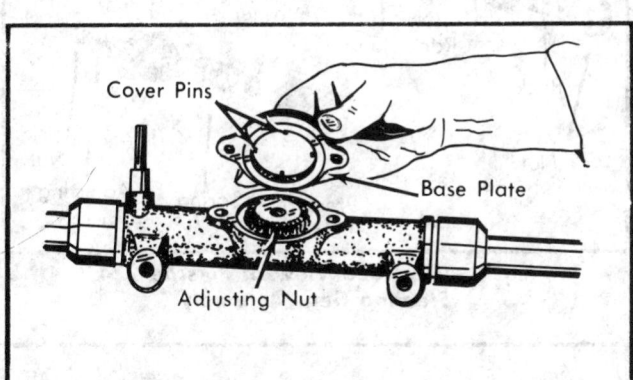

Fig. 1   Adjusting Nut with Cover

Steel Pressure Block Type — 1) With housing assembly in padded vise, detach base plate. Tighten adjusting nut seating contact. Back nut off contact by 3 teeth.

NOTE — *Base plate has integral pins which may be used as a wrench for this adjustment.*

2) Check steering gear drag at pinion flange, using an INCH-lb. torque wrench. A measurement of 6.94 INCH lbs. (8 cmkg) should be obtained. If beyond this measurement, loosen adjusting nut; however, if this measurement is not less than 3.47 INCH lbs. (4 cmkg), do not retighten adjusting nut. Install base plate with gasket.

NOTE — *When installing base plate, pin in plate must fit easily between teeth of adjusting nut. If necessary, move nut slightly.*

Plastic Pressure Block Type — Remove base plate and tighten adjusting nut until 6.94 INCH lbs. (8 cmkg) torque is obtained, using method as described above. Install base plate with gasket.

External Adjustment (924 Only) — With rack centered, loosen lock nut and tighten adjusting screw until it just touches thrust washer. Hold screw and tighten lock nut.

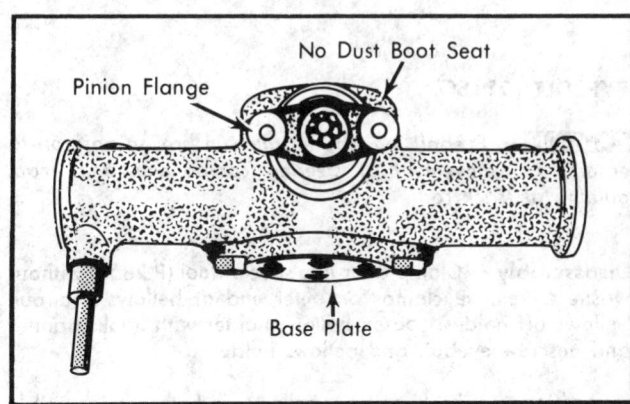

Fig. 2   Plastic Pressure Block Housing Assembly

REMOVAL & INSTALLATION

STEERING GEAR

Removal — 1) Remove bottom bolt attaching universal joint to pinion shaft. Remove nuts and detach tie rod ball joints from steering knuckles.

2) Remove steering housing retaining bolts and extract entire steering housing from right side of vehicle. Detach track rods from rack.

Installation — To install, reverse removal procedures noting that indentation in pinion shaft must line up with bolt hole in lower universal joint. On 924 only, insert special centering bolt (9116) to center gear during installation.

OVERHAUL

STEERING GEAR

Disassembly — 1) Mount steering housing in padded vise and remove base plate retaining bolts. Unscrew adjusting nut (base plate may be used as wrench). Remove pressure block and spring.

2) Move steering rack to either lock position and remove castellated nut. Using suitable puller (P 293), remove flange from pinion. Remove oil seal, lock ring and spacer. Using suitable puller (P 282), remove pinion from pinion carrier (ensure bearing does not bind against housing). Remove Woodruff key from pinion and press bearing off pinion.

3) Mark position of rack (for assembly), remove from housing, and withdraw pinion carrier. Press bearing out of pinion carrier. Remove rack bushing spring retainer from end of housing. Extract support ring and drive rack bushing out.

PORSCHE RACK & PINION (Cont.)

Reassembly – Reverse disassembly procedure, noting the following: Coat all components with suitable lubricant, then fill housing with gear lubricant using bolt hole opposite base plate. Use shims to adjust pinion axial play to zero.

EYEBOLT (911SC)

CAUTION – *Eyebolt must be installed in precise position to ensure free movement of steering components and exact guiding of track rod.*

Disassembly – Clamp gear into special tool (P 285b) without washers. Remove clamps on outer end of bellows and pull bellows off holder. Loosen bellows holder with hook spanner and unscrew eyebolt and bellows holder.

Inspection – Check eyebolt, bellows and clamps for visible wear. Replace as required.

Reassembly – Mount bellows on housing. Screw bellows holder on eyebolt. Coat eyebolt threads and rack face end with sealer. Install eyebolts. Attach steering gear, without

washers, to original holding tool (P 285b). Locating pins should slide easily into eyebolts, with flattened end resting against outer pin. Tighten bellows holder. Clamp bellows to gear assembly.

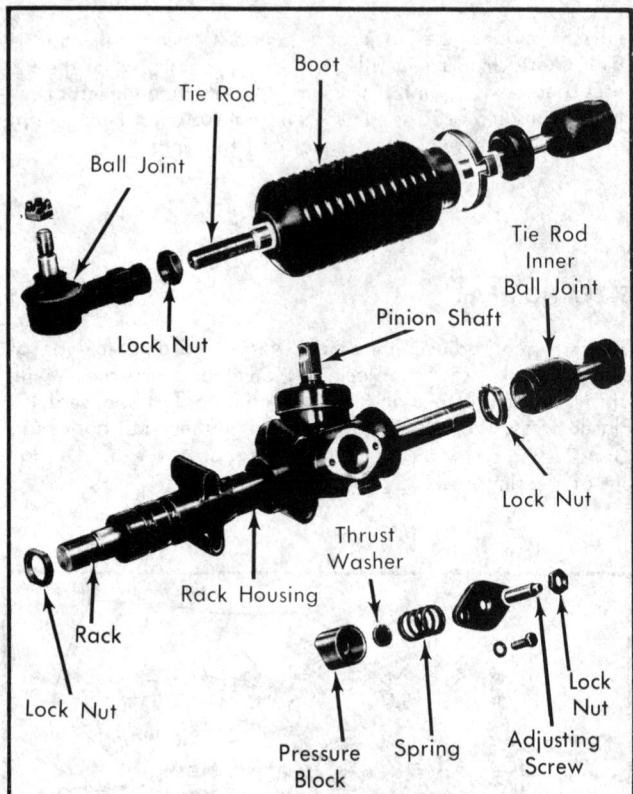

Fig. 4   Exploded View of Porsche 924 Steering Gear Assembly

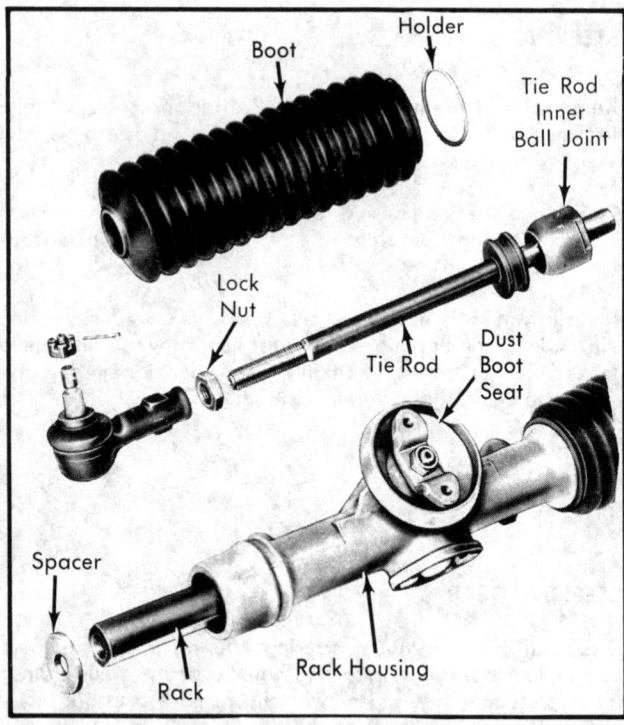

Fig. 3   Exploded View of 911SC Steering Gear Assembly

TIGHTENING SPECIFICATIONS

Application	Ft. Lbs. (mkg)
Housing-to-Crossmember	
911SC	34 (4.7)
924	14-17 (2.0-2.4)
Tie Rod-to-Steering Knuckle	
911SC	33 (4.5)
924	22-36 (3.0-5.0)
"U" Joint Coupling	23 (3.5)

RENAULT RACK & PINION

Le Car

DESCRIPTION

Vehicles are fitted with a rack and pinion steering gear, which has direct steering linkage (tie rods) to each front wheel. Steering housing is mounted to front crossmember and connected to steering column through a flexible coupling.

ADJUSTMENT

STEERING GEAR HEIGHT (TOE-OUT)

NOTE — *This adjustment must be performed whenever steering gear is removed or replaced.*

1) Place vehicle on lift, or alignment rack, with front wheels on radius gauges. Attach a brake press to pedal (to prevent rolling movement of wheels). Set steering at center point and lock in position with suitable holding tool (MS. 504) attached to steering wheel.

2) Load front of vehicle until measurement from centerline of front wheel to bottom of lower frame member (at front wheel) is $4^5/_{16}$" (110 mm). Mount scale boards (T. Av. 552) on side of body so distance from wheel center to board is $51^3/_{16}$" (1.30 m). See *Fig. 1*.

3) Mount measuring tools on both front wheels of vehicle so pointers are in line with crosses on scale boards. Remove load from vehicle (and raise with jack if necessary) so position is $3^1/_8$" (80 mm) higher than loaded position. Pointer should move to 6-7.75 on scale board. If not, steering gear must be adjusted.

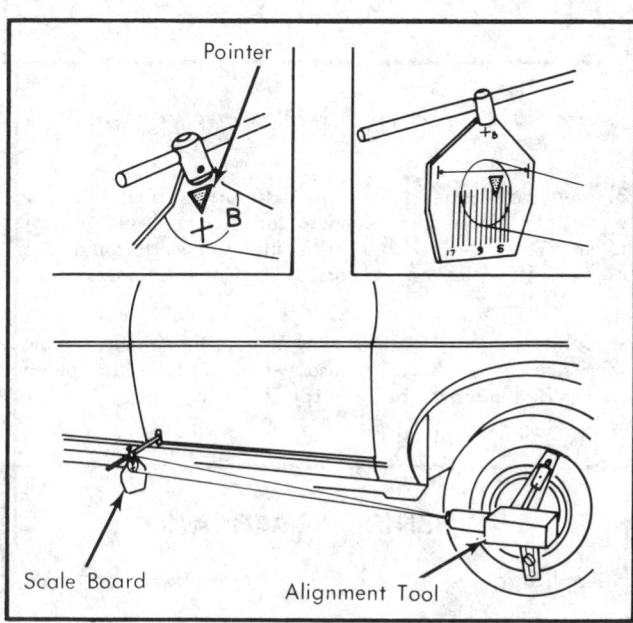

Fig. 1   Measurements for Steering Gear

4) Slotted shims are used to adjust steering gear. Position of slot in shim varies to move gear up and down. To replace or adjust shims, remove transaxle cover. Loosen steering gear bolts and remove adjusting shims. See *Fig. 2*.

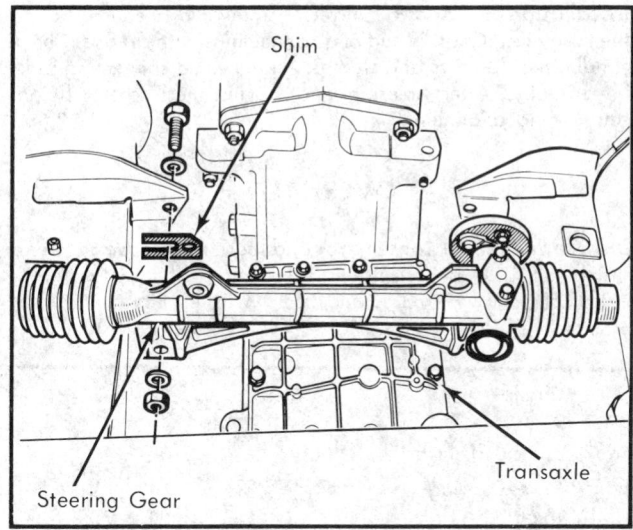

Fig. 2   Location of Adjustment Shim

SETTING STEERING CENTER POINT

To find center steering point, set center of rivet head on flexible coupling in line with index mark on pinion housing. This should result in a measurement of $2^{13}/_{16}$" (71.5 mm).

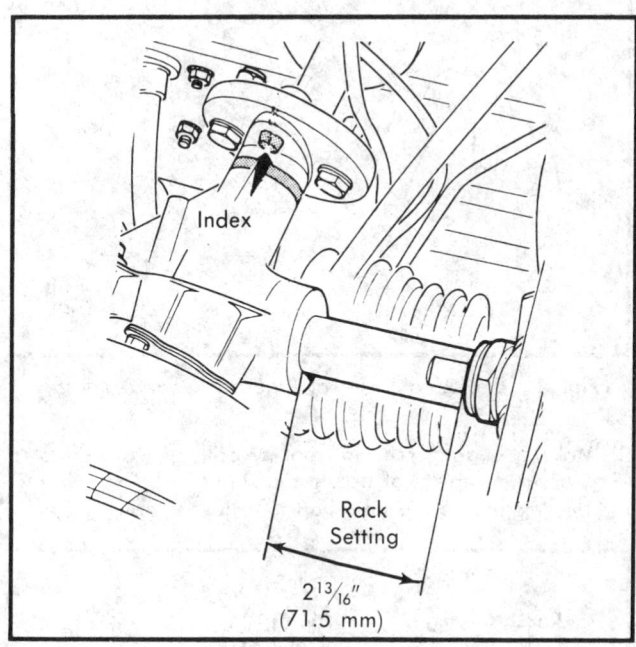

Fig. 3   Steering Center Measurement

REMOVAL & INSTALLATION

Removal — Remove spare tire and disconnect battery. Remove air cleaner and cooling fan relay, without disconnecting wiring. Remove governor, connector, valve, and air pump pipe. Remove air filter bracket bolts and place assembly on engine. Remove air pump filter. Remove steering shaft flexible coupling bolts and gear mounting bolts. Disconnect tie rod ends and remove steering gear. Mark shim location to reinstall in correct position.

RENAULT RACK & PINION (Cont.)

Installation — To install, reverse removal procedure, noting the following: Coat tie rod end connections with grease. Check condition of bellows and clamps. Align tie rod connecting bolts horizontally. After steering gear is installed, check height setting and alignment.

OVERHAUL

Disassembly — 1) Loosen rack and locknut. Remove rack end fitting, opposite pinion, noting the number of turns required. Take off bellows, circlip, and thrust washer. Pry out rubber washer.

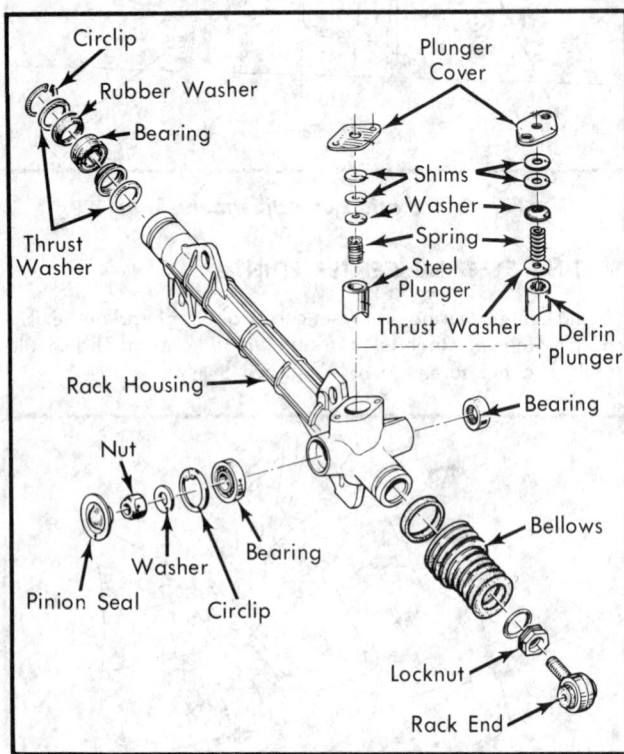

Fig. 4   Exploded View of Steering Gear Assembly

2) Make a bearing removal tool by drilling two $5/32$" holes $1\frac{1}{16}$" apart in a piece of steel strap. Turn two $1/8$" screws into old bearing and turn pinion shaft to remove bearing.

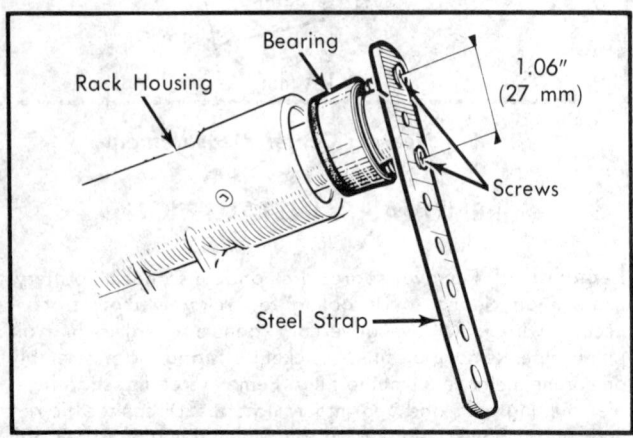

Fig. 5   Removal of Rack Bearing

3) Remove plunger cover, washers, spring and plunger. Pry out pinion seal plug, then remove pinion nut and washer. Pull out pinion and rack. Remove circlip and tap out bearings.

Inspection — Clean all parts with soft cloth and check for excessive wear or damage. Replace parts if necessary.

Reassembly & Adjustment — 1) Tap pinion bearings into place. Replace thrust washers, rubber rings and bushing in end of rack housing. Be sure slot is clear, and refit circlip. Spread Molykote grease over rack and pinion, then center rack in housing and install pinion. Replace washer, nut, and seal.

2) Grease plunger, spring and washers, and replace in housing. Fabricate a dial indicator bracket using a spare plunger cover. Drill a hole in the center and weld on a flange to hold indicator outer shaft. See *Fig. 6*.

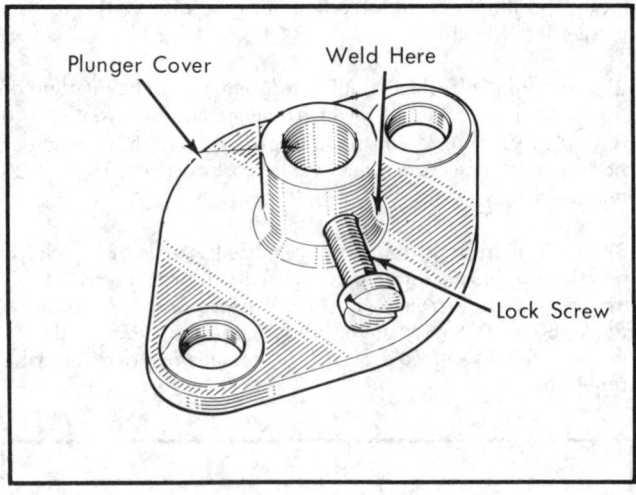

Fig. 6   Tool for Rack Play Measurement

3) Measure plunger movement while turning pinion. Set rack at position of greatest measurement, then reset dial indicator to zero. Pry rack back and forth without moving from position, and measure play on indicator.

4) Select a shim .0016" (.04 mm) smaller than measured play, then remove spare cover, insert shim, and replace plunger cover. Tighten cover bolts to specification.

TIGHTENING SPECIFICATIONS

Application	Ft. Lbs. (mkg)
Plunger Cover Bolts	7.5 (1.0)
Pinion Nut	7.5 (1.0)
Flexible Coupling Bolts	11 (1.5)
Tie Rod-to-Rack Bolts	25 (3.5)
Gear-to-Frame Bolts	25 (3.5)

SAAB RACK & PINION

99
900

DESCRIPTION

Steering gear is the rack and pinion type. Rack is protected from dirt by rubber bellows. The pinion bearing uses an adjustable spring-loaded plunger. The gear is oil-lubricated. The steering linkage is a direct link from the steering rack to the steering knuckles, consisting of tie rods and ball joints.

ADJUSTMENT

NOTE — See Overhaul procedure in this article.

REMOVAL & INSTALLATION

STEERING GEAR

Removal (99) — 1) From under instrument panel, loosen the rubber bellows for steering gear intermediate shaft. Raise vehicle and remove screw mounting "U" joint to steering gear pinion. Loosen steering column tube from body, then separate steering column "U" joint from pinion.

2) Suspend steering column, with wiring harness, out of way. Remove front wheels. Using a puller, remove tie rod ends. Take off the two steering gear clamps and move rack to right stop.

NOTE — Be sure bellows is not damaged against body.

3) Place steering gear far enough to the right to allow tie rod to be bent down into body opening. Pull rack maximum stroke to left and lift steering gear through body opening.

Removal (900) — 1) Remove steering gear to intermediate shaft clamp bolt. Raise and support vehicle. Remove front wheels. Separate tie rods from steering knuckles.

2) Remove steering gear clamp bolts. Separate steering column (intermediate shaft) joint from steering gear, lift steering gear to the side and remove by guiding it diagonally downwards through opening in engine compartment.

Installation (All Models) — To install, reverse removal procedures and check toe-in and wheel alignment.

OVERHAUL

STEERING GEAR

Disassembly — Remove tie rod ends and rubber bellows. Drill out lock pins from inner ball joints, using a 4 mm bit and drilling only ⅜" deep. Remove outer bearing cups and lock nuts. Remove rack adjustment screw, cap with gasket, shims, spring, and plunger. Remove pinion and cap with gasket shims, and upper bearing. Pull rack out from housing. Tap out lower pinion bearing.

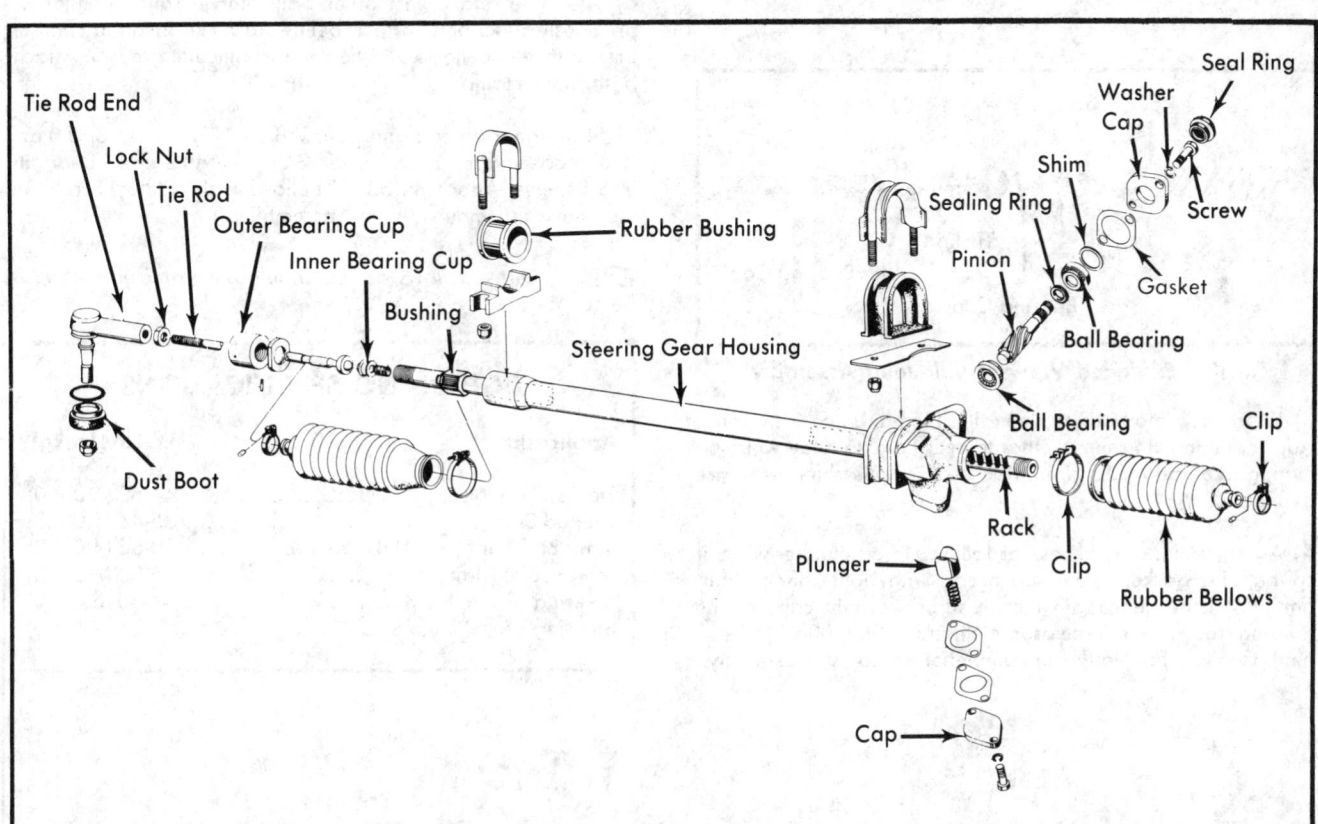

Fig. 1   Exploded View of Saab Rack & Pinion Steering Gear Assembly

SAAB RACK & PINION (Cont.)

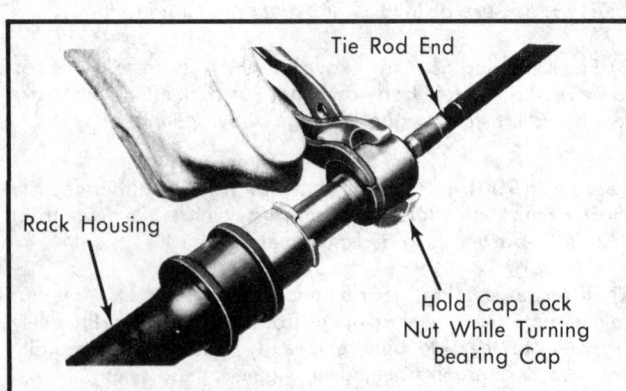

Fig. 2   Procedure for Removing Outer Bearing Cap Lock Nut

Reassembly — 1) Ensure all parts are thoroughly cleaned before proceeding with reassembly. Lubricate all parts during reassembly. Seat the lower pinion bearing.

NOTE — *Be sure extended parts of the inner bearing tracks are facing each other.*

2) Assemble inner ball joint on pinion end of rack as follows: Thread lock nut onto rack. Fit outer bearing cup on rack and fill with suitable gear oil. Insert spring and inner bearing cup. Tighten bearing cup so that there is no looseness in ball joint, but without tightness. If rack, with tie rod mounted, is held horizontally, the tie rod should be able to be placed in any position without falling under its own weight. Tighten lock nut against bearing cup and recheck ball joint tightness. Drill a new 4 mm hole ⅜" deep and insert and stake lock a new lock pin.

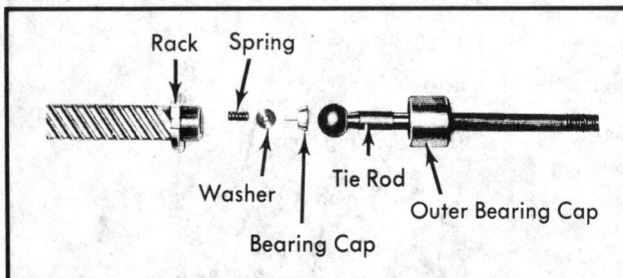

Fig. 3   Exploded View of Ball Joint Assembly

3) Insert rack into housing, then fit pinion and upper bearing. Adjust pinion with shims so that there is no axial play when pinion gasket and cap are attached. Various shim sizes are available.

4) Adjust radial play of rack as follows: Insert plunger without spring and gasket, then attach cap with bolts (finger tight only). Measure clearance which exists between the cap and the housing face. To this measurement add .002-.006" (.05-.15 mm), to allow for play after completion of adjuster assembly.

This total thickness will be the thickness of gasket and shims required. Measure shims and gasket together, then remove cap and install shims, gasket, and cap. Check rack for free movement by rotating pinion.

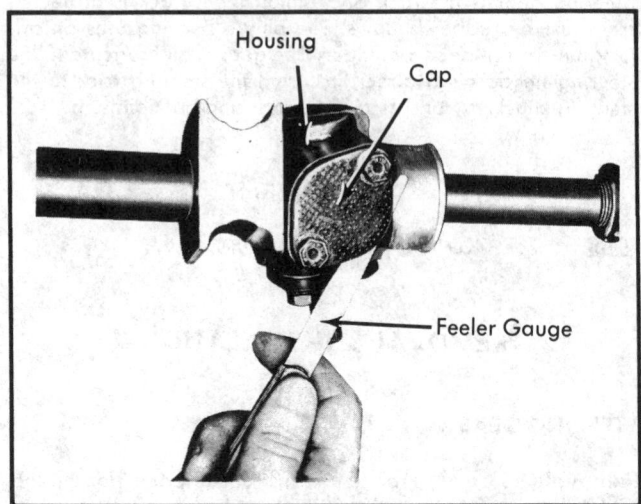

Fig. 4   Measuring Clearance Between Cap and Gear Housing

5) On 900 models, measure pinion rotating torque. Using a torque wrench and a 12 sided 18 mm socket, rotate pinion through full travel of rack. Pinion torque should be 7-24 ft. lbs. (1.0-3.3 mkg).

6) Assemble and adjust other ball joint in same manner as previously described. Attach bellows after lubricating contact area between bellows and tie rod (use silicone grease). Attach both inner clamps.

7) Stand gear on end and pour 7.8 oz. (99 models) or 5.0 oz. (900 models) of BP Energrease FGL (or suitable EP 90 gear oil) into bellows. Attach outboard bellows with clamps. Screw on lock nuts and mount tie rod assemblies.

NOTE — *Outer bellows clamps should be protected with rubber caps.*

TIGHTENING SPECIFICATIONS

Application	Ft. Lbs. (mkg)
Tie Rod Lock Nut	44-60 (6.0-8.0)
Tie Rod End	35-44 (5.0-6.0)
Inner Ball Joint Lock Nut	30-36 (4.0-5.0)
Lower Joint Clamp Bolt	26-30 (3.5-4.2)
Steering Gear Clamp Bolts	44-60 (6.0-8.0)
Steering Wheel Nut	22 (3.0)

SUBARU RACK & PINION

1600
1800

DESCRIPTION

Steering gear, mounted on crossmember, is a rack and pinion type, with backlash automatically adjusted. Pinion is connected to steering shaft by a flexible rubber coupling. Steering knuckle arms are connected to rack by tie rods which are threaded onto ball joint studs at each end of rack.

ADJUSTMENT

BACKLASH

Backlash is automatically held to a minimum by a spring-loaded rack plunger which bears against rack. Adjustment is not normally required. End play of rack plunger may be corrected if necessary by turning adjusting screw in until it contacts plate, then backing screw out $1/24$th ($15°$) of a turn. This will give a clearance of .0025″ (.063 mm) between adjusting screw and rack plunger. Hold adjusting screw from turning and tighten lock nut.

REMOVAL & INSTALLATION

Removal — 1) Disconnect battery negative terminal. Raise and support front of vehicle. Remove both front wheels. Disconnect ball joints from steering knuckles.

2) Disconnect flexible coupling from pinion gear. Remove hot air stove from exhaust manifold and air cleaner. Disconnect exhaust manifold and pull down out of way. Remove rubber boot protector.

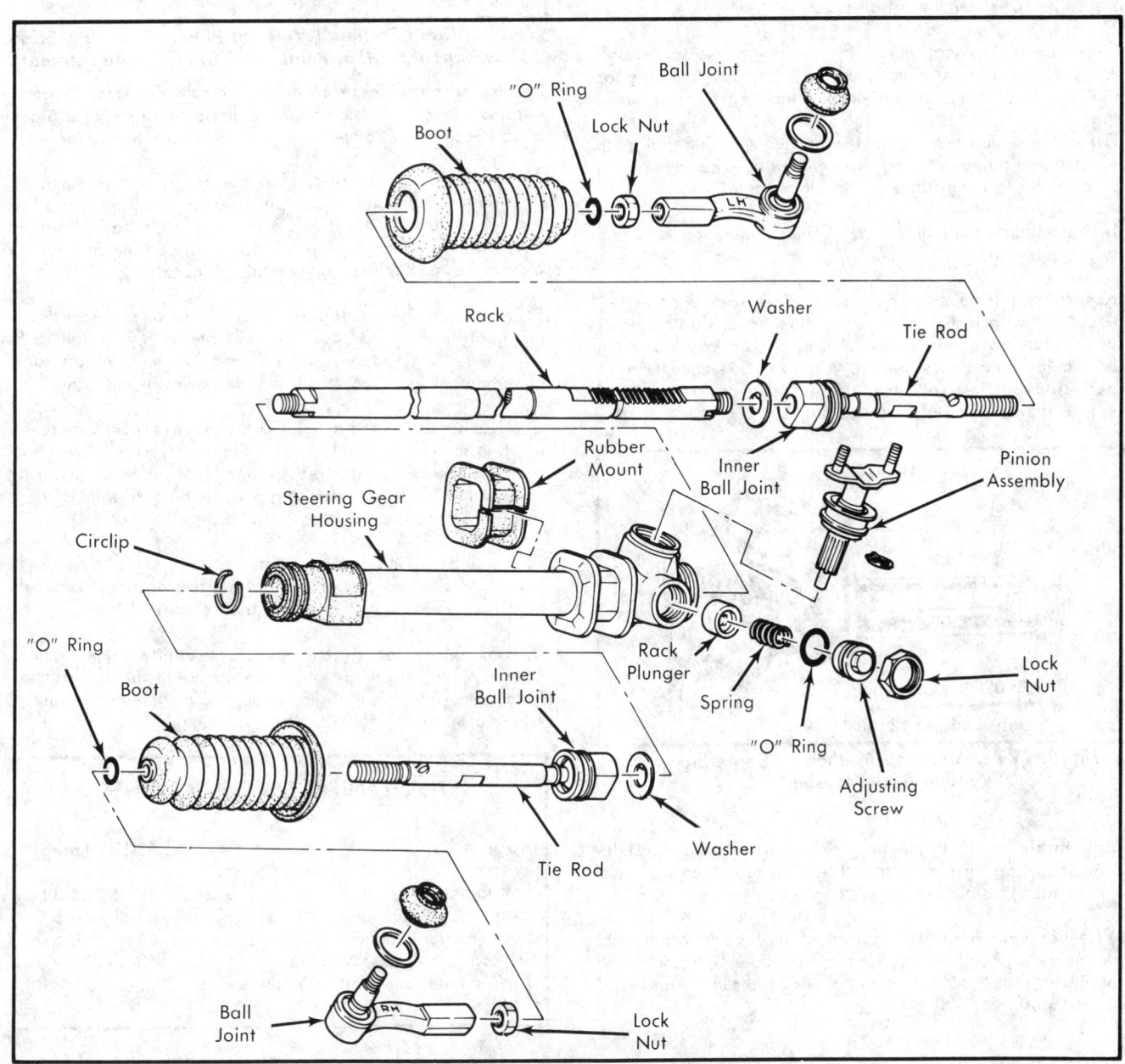

Fig. 1 Exploded View of Subaru Rack & Pinion Steering Gear Assembly

SUBARU RACK & PINION (Cont.)

3) Remove bolts attaching steering gear housing to crossmember. Lower gear housing until pinion gear is disconnected from flexible coupling. Rotate gear housing backwards and remove gear housing from left side.

Installation — To install steering gear assembly, reverse removal procedures and note the following: tighten left steering gear housing bracket first. Tighten ball joint nuts to specifications, then turn a maximum of $1/6$ turn to align cotter pin hole.

OVERHAUL

Disassembly — 1) Place steering gear housing in a padded vise. Loosen lock nuts and remove ball joints from rods. Remove "O" rings from outside of rubber boots, then remove rubber boots. Unbend tab on inner ball joint lock washer, then loosen lock nut and remove inner ball joint from rack. Repeat procedure for other inner ball joint.

2) Remove rack plunger lock nut, adjusting screw, spring and rack plunger. Remove pinion gear oil seal from steering gear housing. Remove pinion gear large snap ring from housing.

3) Remove pinion gear from steering gear housing. Pull rack out of steering gear housing, from pinion side. Remove pinion gear small snap ring (located on pinion gear).

4) Press bearing off pinion gear, then remove oil seal and large snap ring.

Inspection — Check for bent rack. Place rack ends in "V" blocks and attach dial indicator so plunger rests on center of rack. Rotate rack and note deflection of gauge. Maximum deflection should be less than .004" (.1 mm). Replace if not to specifications. Check all other steering gear components and replace if worn, scored or damaged.

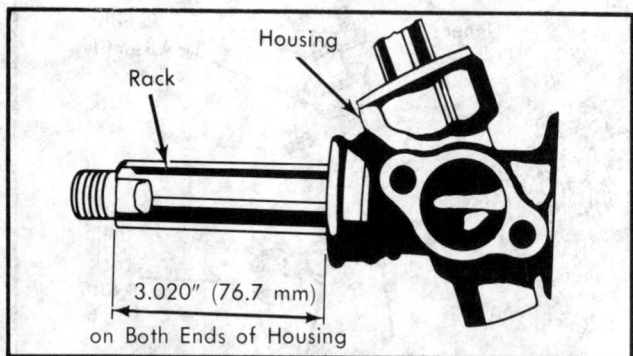

Fig. 2   View Showing Method of Centering Rack in Gear Housing

Reassembly — 1) If pinion gear was disassembled, slide large snap ring on pinion. Install new oil seal, then press on new bearing. Install small snap ring to pinion gear.

2) Grease toothed and sliding portions of rack and install rack into steering gear housing, from pinion side. Locate rack in housing so that 3.02" (76.7 mm) of rack protrudes from each end of housing.

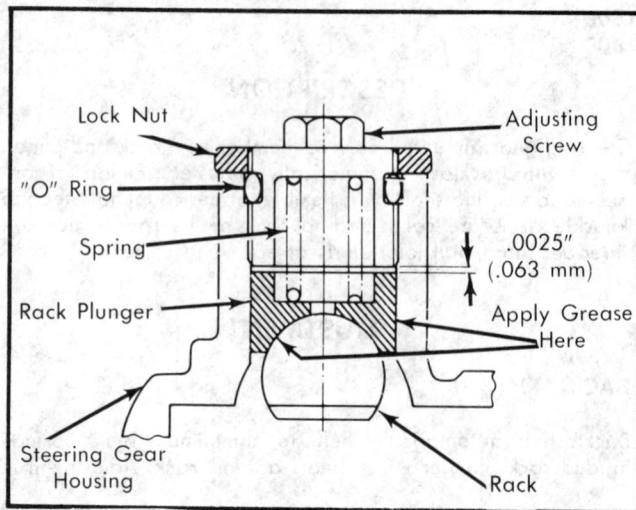

Fig. 3   Cross Sectional View of Pinion Gear and Rack Showing Lubrication Points and Backlash Adjustment

3) Grease pinion gear teeth and install into steering gear housing. Flange on pinion gear should be out of line of straight ahead position by 36° when meshed with rack teeth properly.

4) Install large snap ring, of pinion gear, to steering gear housing. Measure amount of pinion gear end play. End play should be less than .012" (.3 mm). If end play is not to specifications, check for worn snap rings, bearing or steering gear housing. Replace components as necessary.

5) With pinion gear end play correct, press oil seal into steering gear housing. Grease rack plunger cavity. Install rack plunger, spring, adjusting screw and lock nut. Adjust rack plunger backlash. See backlash adjustment in this article.

6) Install tie rod inner ball joint lock washer to rack. Grease inner ball joint and install to rack. Bend lock washer over flat area on inner ball joint. Grease inside lip of rubber boot (large end) and install boot to steering gear housing. Install "O" ring to boot outer end.

7) Install ball joints and lock nuts to tie rods. Make sure ball joints are installed on correct end of steering gear. Left ball joint is marked "LH", right ball joint is marked "RH".

8) Make sure steering gear operates properly and smoothly. Check pinion rotating torque in straight ahead position. Rotating torque should be .8 ft. lbs. (.11 mkg) with a maximum allowable torque of 1.1 ft. lbs. (.15 mkg).

TIGHTENING SPECIFICATIONS

Application	Ft. Lbs. (mkg)
Ball Joint Nut	18-25 (2.5-3.5)
Gear-to-Crossmember	33-40 (4.5-5.5)
Rack Plunger Lock Nut	29-43 (4.0-6.0)
Tie Rod-to-Ball Joint Lock Nut	58-65 (8.0-9.0)
Tie Rod Inner Ball Joint Lock Nut	58 (8.0)

TOYOTA (EXC. LAND CRUISER) RECIRCULATING BALL

Celica
Corolla
Corona
Cressida
Pickup

DESCRIPTION

STEERING GEAR

Steering gear is a variable ratio, recirculating ball type. Ball bearings circulate within grooves in worm and nut. As worm shaft turns, ball nut moves up or down, turning the sector shaft and pitman arm.

STEERING LINKAGE

Linkage consists of an idler arm, center relay rod, adjustable tie rods, and steering knuckles. Pickups also use a steering damper attached to center relay rod. The connection between each component is by ball joints. Linkage assembly is connected to steering gear by a pitman arm.

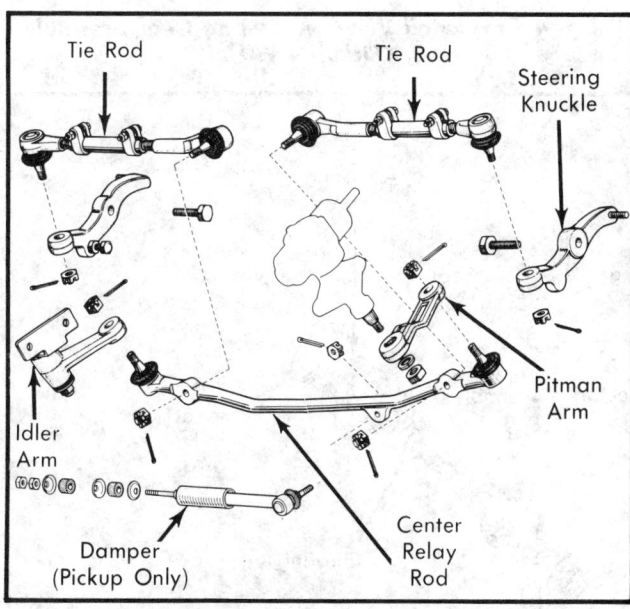

Fig. 1   Exploded View of Toyota Steering Linkage (Except Pickup 4-WD Models)

ADJUSTMENT

See *Overhaul* procedures in this article.

REMOVAL & INSTALLATION

STEERING GEAR

Removal — Mark steering gear shaft at flexible coupling or universal joint. Mark steering gear shaft at pitman arm. Disconnect pitman arm from steering gear. Remove steering gear bolts from frame and disconnect steering gear from steering shaft as gear is removed.

Installation — To install steering gear, reverse removal procedures and note the following: Make sure marks made upon removal are aligned upon installation.

STEERING LINKAGE

Removal — 1) On all models except Pickup 4-WD, mark pitman arm at sector shaft. Use a suitable puller to disconnect the following components: Pitman arm from sector shaft, and tie rod ball joints from steering knuckles. On Pickup 2-WD models, disconnect steering damper from crossmember. Remove idler arm bracket bolts, then remove steering linkage assembly from vehicle.

2) On Pickup 4-WD models, mark pitman arm at sector shaft and disconnect pitman arm. Disconnect steering damper from front axle. Remove steering knuckle-to-front axle bolts and remove steering linkage assembly from vehicle.

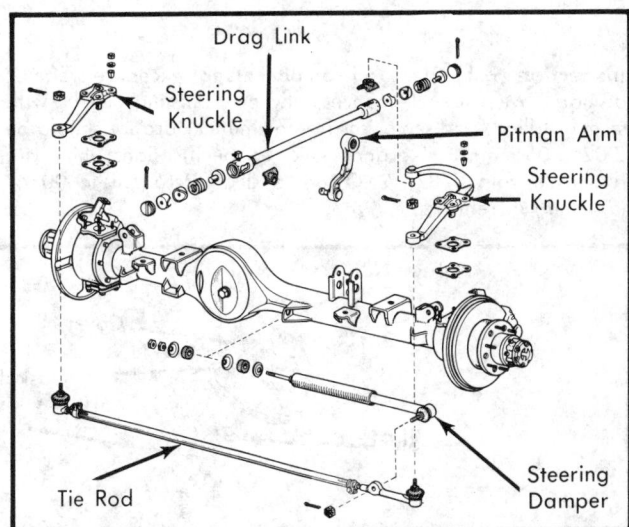

Fig. 2   Exploded View of Toyota Steering Linkage (Pickup 4-WD)

Installation — To install steering linkage, reverse removal procedure and note the following: Make sure pitman arm-to-sector shaft marks are aligned. To aid in toe-in adjustment, make sure tie rod lengths are to specifications. Measure tie rod lengths from center-to-center of ball joints. See *Tie Rod Length* chart.

Tie Rod Length	
Application	**In. (mm)**
Celica, Corona	12.60 (320)
Corolla	12.52 (318)
Cressida	①
Pickup	
2-WD	12.36 (314)
4-WD	47.24 (1200)
① — Both tie rods should be the same length.	

TOYOTA (EXC. LAND CRUISER) RECIRCULATING BALL (Cont.)

OVERHAUL

STEERING GEAR

Disassembly — 1) On all models except Pickup 4-WD, mark pitman arm at sector shaft and remove pitman arm. Remove sector shaft adjusting screw lock nut. Remove sector shaft cover, then sector shaft. Be careful not to lose adjusting screw and shim. Remove worm assembly lock nut, adjusting screw and oil seal. Remove worm assembly and bearings.

NOTE — *Do not disassemble ball nut from worm. If recirculating ball assembly has damaged or worn components, replace entire assembly.*

2) On Pickup 4-WD models, mark pitman arm at sector shaft and remove pitman arm. Remove sector shaft adjusting screw lock nut. Remove sector shaft cover and sector shaft. Remove worm assembly cover and shims. Remove worm assembly with bearings.

Inspection — 1) Check all components for excessive wear or damage. Measure clearance between adjusting screw (with shim installed) and sector shaft. Maximum clearance should be .002″ (.05 mm). If clearance is not to specifications, shims are available from .0787″ (2.00 mm) to .085″ (2.16 mm) in .0016″ (.04 mm) increments.

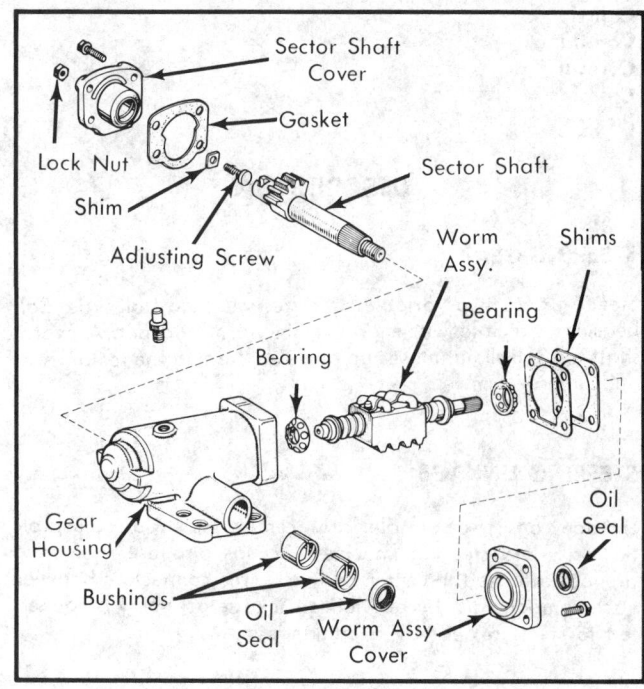

Fig. 4 *Exploded View of Steering Gear Assembly (Pickup 4-WD)*

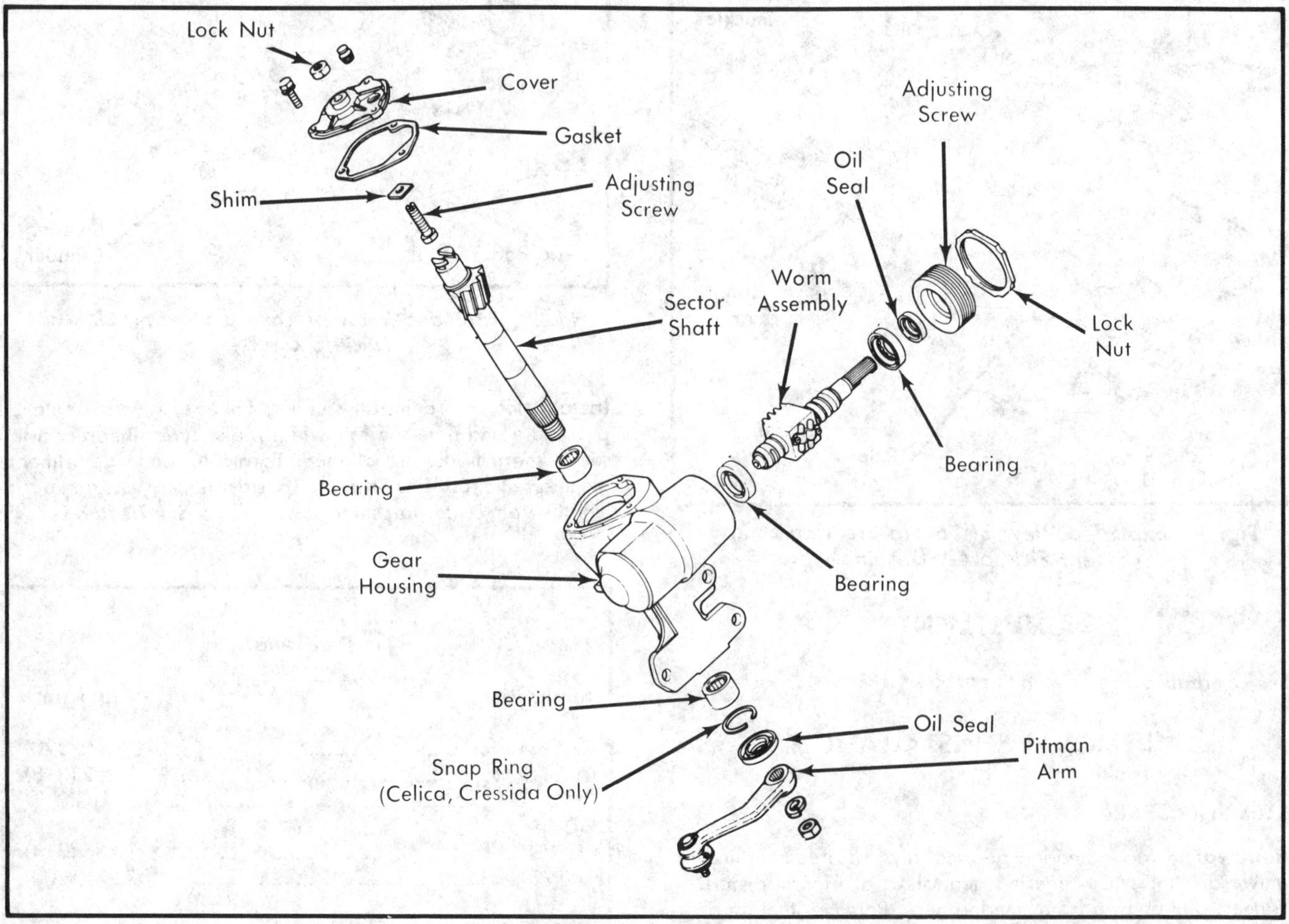

Fig. 3 *Exploded View of Steering Gear Assembly (Except Pickup 4-WD)*

TOYOTA (EXC. LAND CRUISER) RECIRCULATING BALL (Cont.)

2) On all models except Pickup 4-WD, check sector shaft bearings for pitting and smooth operation. Replace if necessary. On Pickup 4-WD, measure sector shaft diameter. Minimum diameter is 1.258" (31.95 mm). Measure sector shaft bushings (in gear housing) for clearance between sector shaft and bushings. Maximum clearance is .004" (.1 mm). If clearance exceeds specifications and sector shaft is not worn beyond limit, replace bushings in gear housing and hone bushings to obtain standard clearance of .0004-.0024" (.01-.06 mm).

CAUTION — *When checking worm gear and ball nut, do not let ball nut bottom out on either end of worm gear. If ball nut bottoms out, damage to worm assembly will occur.*

3) On all models, check worm assembly bearings; replace bearings if damaged or worn. Check worm gear and ball nut for damage. Hold worm assembly up at an angle so ball nut will travel down worm gear (full travel) and check for smooth operation. Replace worm assembly if any damage is found or operation is not smooth.

Reassembly & Adjustment — 1) Grease all bearings and sliding portions of gear assembly. Install bearings on worm assembly. Install worm assembly to gear housing.

2) On all models except Pickup 4-WD, install oil seal and adjusting nut. Tighten nut while rotating worm gear to seat bearings. Loosen adjusting nut, then tighten while measuring preload. *See Initial Worm Bearing Preload chart.* With preload to specification, hold adjusting nut, install and tighten lock nut.

3) On Pickup 4-WD, install oil seal to worm assembly cover. Install same shims as removed, then install end cover and tighten bolts. Measure preload of worm assembly. *See Initial Worm Bearing Preload chart.* If not to specifications, add or remove shims until preload is to specifications. Shims are available from .002-.004" (.05-.1 mm) in .0004" (.01 mm) increments, with 2 larger sizes available; .008" (.2 mm) and .020" (.5 mm).

Initial Worm Bearing Preload

Application	INCH Lbs. (cmkg)
Celica, Corona	2.3-3.0 (2.6-3.5)
Corolla	1.7-3.5 (2.0-4.0)
Cressida	2.6-3.5 (3.0-4.0)
Pickup	
2-WD	2.3-3.7 (2.6-4.3)
4-WD	3.0-5.6 (3.5-6.5)

4) Center ball nut on worm shaft and install sector shaft so center teeth of both are meshed together. Install shim (selected previously) to adjusting screw and install to sector shaft.

5) Install sector shaft end cover to gear housing and loosen adjusting nut as far as possible. Install cover bolts and tighten. Adjust final worm bearing streload by tightening adjusting screw. *See Final Worm Bearing Preload chart.* Install lock nut and tighten while holding adjusting nut from turning.

Final Worm Bearing Preload

Application	INCH Lbs. (cmkg)
Celica, Corona	4.3-5.2 (5.0-6.0)
Corolla, Cressida	2.6-3.5 (3.0-4.0)
Pickup	
2-WD	5.2-7.4 (6.0-8.5)
4-WD	6.9-9.5 (8.0-11.0)

6) Install pitman arm and nut (aligning mating marks). Attach dial indicator so plunger touches end of pitman arm. Sector shaft should have no backlash when measured at any point 100° on either side of centered position.

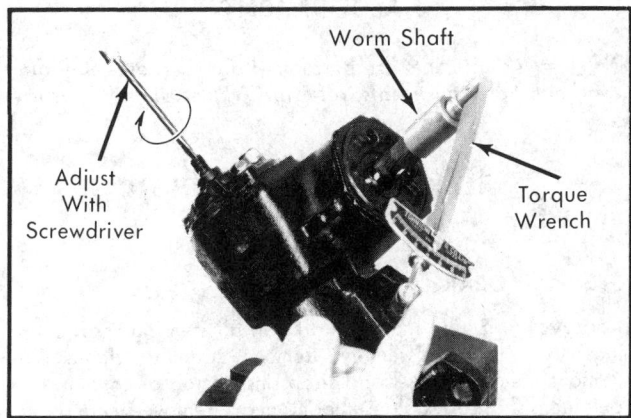

Fig. 5 Measuring Final Worm Bearing Preload

TIGHTENING SPECIFICATIONS

Application	Ft. Lbs. (mkg)
Ball Joint Nuts (All)	
Pickup	①54-80 (7.5-11.0)
All Other Models	36-51 (5.0-7.0)
Idler Arm Nut	
Pickup (2-WD Only)	58-87 (8.0-12.0)
All Other Models	51-65 (7.0-9.0)
Pitman Arm-to-Sector Shaft Nut	
Corolla	72-101 (10.0-14.0)
Pickup	
2-WD	80-90 (11.0-12.5)
4-WD	116-137 (16.0-19.0)
All Other Models	80-101 (11.0-14.0)
Sector Shaft Adjusting Screw Lock Nut	
Corona	15-25 (2.0-3.5)
Pickup	
2-WD	14-22 (1.9-3.1)
4-WD	25-36 (3.5-5.0)
All Other Models	14-22 (1.9-3.1)
Worm Assembly Adjusting Screw Lock Nut	
Corona	166-188 (23.0-26.0)
Pickup (2-WD Only)	166-188 (23.0-26.0)
All Other Models	94-123 (13.0-17.0)

① — Damper-to-relay rod should be 36-51 ft. lbs. (5.0-7.0 mkg).

Steering Gears & Linkage

TOYOTA LAND CRUISER RECIRCULATING BALL

DESCRIPTION

STEERING GEAR

Steering gear mechanism is of the recirculating ball type. Gear mounts off a bracket that is attached to frame. Adjustment screws are provided for backlash and preload. Initial preload is achieved with shims.

STEERING LINKAGE

Steering linkage consists of the following: pitman arm, relay rod, tie rod, damper, center arm and drag link. Tie rod and relay rod are adjustable to correct wheel alignment.

ADJUSTMENT

NOTE — *Adjustments are performed during reassembly after overhaul. For adjustments, refer to OVERHAUL in this article.*

REMOVAL & INSTALLATION

STEERING GEAR

Removal — Scribe mating marks on all steering shaft couplings to aid in reassembly. Remove coupling clamp bolt. Remove steering wheel and snap ring at top of column, then pull main shaft back from steering gear. Remove steering gear mounting bolts and pitman arm using suitable puller. Remove gear from frame.

Installation — To install, reverse removal procedure and tighten all mounting bolts.

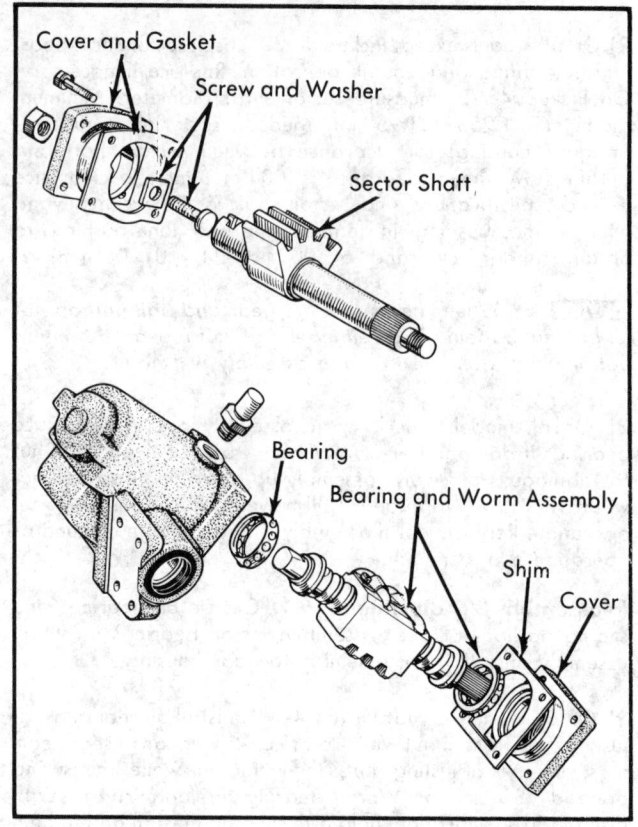

Fig. 1 Toyota Land Cruiser Steering Gear

STEERING LINKAGE

Removal — 1) — Raise and support front of vehicle, then remove front wheels. Index mark relative position of pitman arm to sector shaft and remove arm, using suitable puller. Disconnect steering drag link from steering center arm.

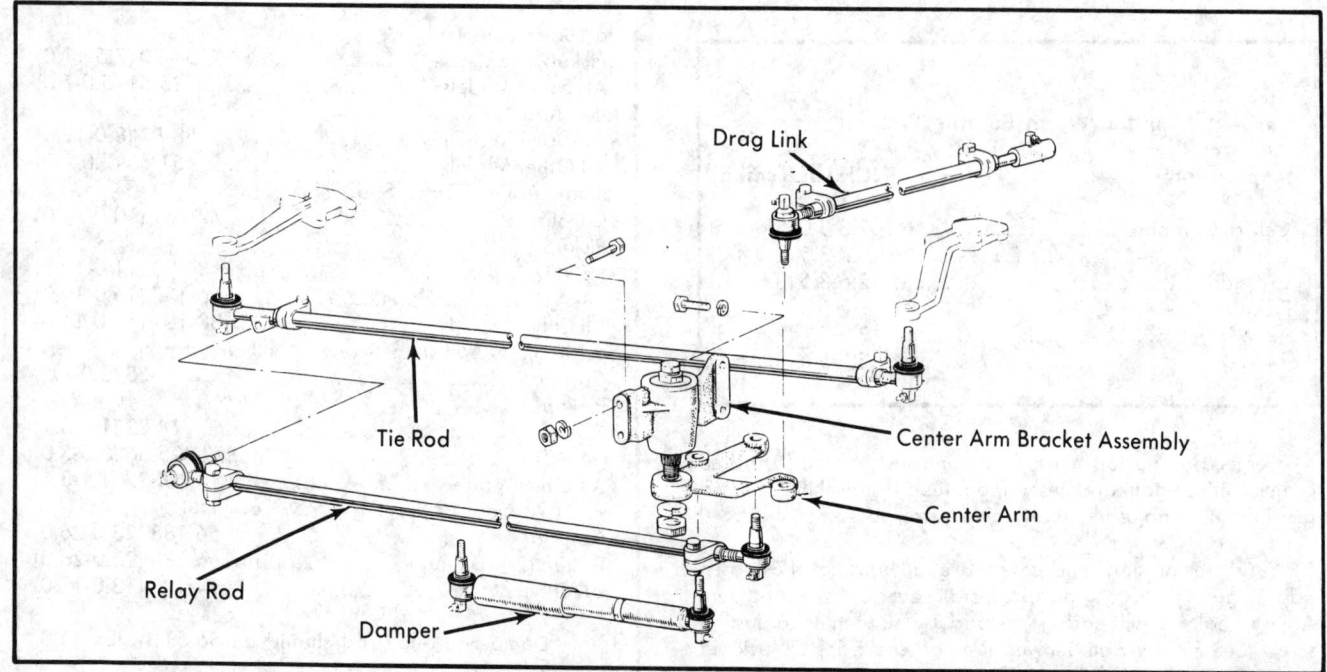

Fig. 2 Toyota Land Cruiser Front Steering Linkage

TOYOTA LAND CRUISER RECIRCULATING BALL (Cont.)

2) Disconnect tie rod ends from both sides. Disconnect relay rod from steering center arm, then remove tie rod assembly with relay arm assembly. Disconnect end of steering damper from bracket on crossmember. Loosen and remove center arm from bracket (with steering damper). Remove steering center arm bracket from frame.

Installation — To install, reverse removal procedure and note the following: Adjust tie rod, relay rod and drag link as shown in *Fig. 3*.

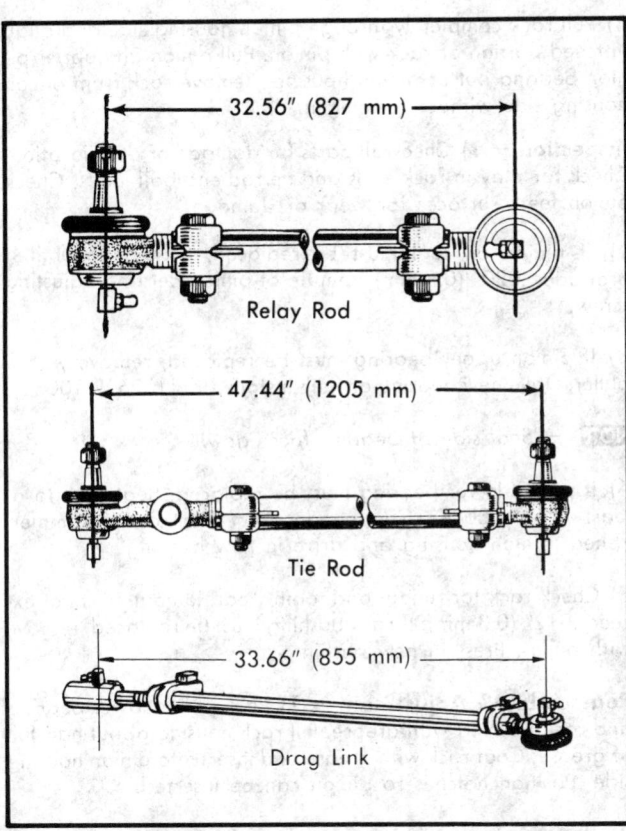

Fig. 3   Adjustment Lengths for Installation of Tie Rod, Relay Rod and Drag Link

OVERHAUL

Disassembly — Drain gear lubricant, then secure housing in a vise. Remove sector shaft end cover and gasket. With sector shaft positioned at rotational center, pull assembly out of gear housing. Note number and placement of shims as they are removed. Remove gear housing end cover and gasket. Take out worm assembly, keeping bearings in sequence. Do not attempt to disassemble worm assembly.

Inspection — Wash all disassembled parts and inspect for wear or damage; replace as necessary. If inner or outer races are scored or pitted, replace as required. Inspect sector shaft and bushings for wear. If replacement is necessary, use a press to remove and replace bushings. Hone bushings until clearance between bushing and sector shaft is .0004-.0024" (.009-.060 mm). Install new oil seal. Measure sector shaft thrust clearance, then select thrust washer that provides minimum clearance between sector shaft and adjustment screw: .004" (.1 mm).

Reassembly — **1)** Install cover with same number of shims that were removed, then tighten bolts.

NOTE — *When tightening cover bolts, keep checking worm to ensure that it will turn freely.*

2) Using a pull scale, measure initial (starting) worm bearing preload for 8.8-13.2 lbs (4-6 kg). If preload is not within specifications, correct by selecting proper thickness shim(s).

3) Position worm ball nut at center, then insert sector shaft ensuring ball nut and sector mesh together at center. Loosen ball adjusting bolt all the way and install cover.

4) Set worm shaft preload to 17.6-24.2 lbs. (8-11 kg) with adjusting bolt. Make sure measurement is made with meshing positioned at center.

5) Install pitman arm and check backlash. There should be zero backlash when worm is rotated within 45° to either side. Tighten adjustment screw lock nut and recheck preload.

TIGHTENING SPECIFICATIONS

Application	Ft. Lbs. (mkg)
Sector End Cover Bolts	22-32 (3.0-4.5)
Worm Bearing Cap	22-32 (3.0-4.5)
Gear Box Bracket	29-40 (4.0-5.5)
Pitman Arm Nut	119-141 (16.5-19.5)

Steering Gears & Linkage

TOYOTA TERCEL RACK & PINION

DESCRIPTION

Steering assembly is a direct-acting rack and pinion system. This unit consists of a rack bar and toothed pinion. Adjustment is provided for pinion gear preload. Rack is protected from dirt by rubber boots.

ADJUSTMENT

NOTE – *Adjustments are performed during gear reassembly. See overhaul as outlined.*

REMOVAL & INSTALLATION

Removal – **1)** Raise front of vehicle and support with safety stands. Position steering wheel so front wheels point straight ahead. Remove pinch bolts from intermediate shaft. Disconnecting pinion side first, remove intermediate shaft.

2) Remove cotter pins and nuts from tie rod ends. Use a puller to disconnect tie rod ends from steering knuckles. Remove 6 lower crossmember retaining bolts, then remove lower crossmember. Remove rack housing brackets, taking care not to damage rack boots. Remove steering gear.

Installation – To install, reverse removal procedure and note the following: Check toe-in. See *WHEEL ALIGNMENT* Section for specifications and procedures.

OVERHAUL

Disassembly – **1)** Place steering gear in a vice and mark rack end threaded areas for reassembly reference. Remove tie rods, spring clips, rack end dust seals and rack boot clamps. Remove rack boots.

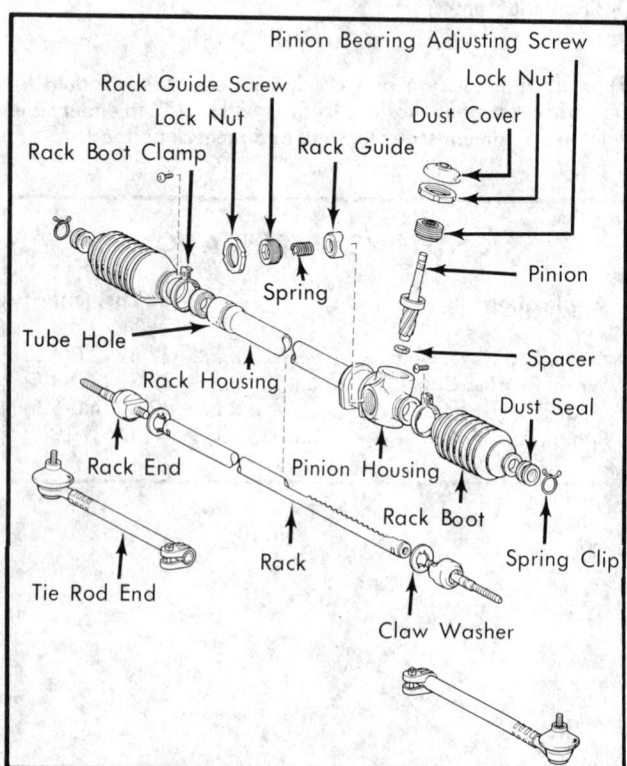

Fig. 1 Exploded View of Tercel Rack and Pinion Steering Gear Assembly

NOTE – *Left and right tie rod ends, rack boots and rack ends are different and should be marked accordingly.*

2) Unstake claw washers and remove rack ends. Using guide screw lock nut wrench (09617-10010), remove lock nut. Then, using rack guide screw wrench (09612-10020), remove guide screw and spring. Remove rack guide by pulling out with needle-nose pliers.

3) Remove pinion bearing adjusting screw lock nut with lock nut wrench (09617-10010) and pinion bearing adjusting screw with pin tool (09616-10091).

4) Pull rack completely through pinion housing side and align notched portion of rack with pinion. Pull pinion and upper pinion bearing out of pinion housing. Remove rack from pinion housing side without rotating it.

Inspection – **1)** Check all parts for damage or deterioration. Check for play in rack ends and tie rod end ball joints. Check pinion teeth surfaces for wear or damage.

2) If pinion oil seal must be replaced, drive it in until it protrudes .020" (0.5 mm) from tip of pinion bearing adjusting screw.

3) If pinion upper bearing must be replaced, remove with a puller. Drive new bearing on with installer tool (09612-10061).

NOTE – *Seal side of bearing faces down.*

4) If pinion lower bearing must be replaced, heat rack to at least 176°F (80°C). Tap bearing out with plastic hammer. Reheat pinion housing and drive in new bearing.

5) Check rack for runout and tooth wear. Runout must not exceed .012" (0.3 mm). If rack bushing must be replaced, remove with puller. Press in new bushing.

Reassembly & Adjustment – **1)** Pack pinion lower bearing and rack bushing with grease. Fill rack housing about half full of grease. Coat rack with grease and insert into pinion housing side. Position notches so pinion can be inserted.

2) Pack grease into pinion bearing. Coat pinion teeth with grease and insert spacer and pinion into pinion housing. Pinion end must be securely positioned in pinion lower bearing. Coat oil seal with grease and install pinion bearing adjusting screw. Place an INCH Lb. torque wrench and adapter (09616-10010) on end of pinion and tighten adjusting screw until pinion turning torque is 3.5 INCH Lbs. (4 cmkg). Then, loosen adjusting screw until pinion turning torque is 1.7-2.6 INCH Lbs. (2-3 cmkg).

3) Apply liquid sealer to adjusting screw lock nut and housing contact points. Tighten lock nut to 58-75 ft. lbs. (8.0-10.5 mkg). Check pinion turning torque. It should be 1.3-2.2 INCH Lbs. (1.5-2.2 cmkg).

NOTE – *Tightening lock nut decreases pinion turning torque by 0.4 INCH Lbs. (0.5 cmkg).*

4) Mesh rack and pinion. Coat rack guide with grease. Install rack guide, spring and rack guide screw. Using torque wrench and guide screw wrench, tighten guide screw to 18 ft. lbs. (2.5 mkg). Loosen screw about 30° from tightened position. Measure pinion turning torque and adjust by turning guide screw. Acceptable range is 4.3-11.3 INCH Lbs. (5-13 cmkg).

TOYOTA TERCEL RACK & PINION (Cont.)

5) Apply liquid sealer to lock nut and housing contact points, and, using torque wrench and lock nut wrench, tighten lock nut to 37-47 ft. lbs. (5.0-6.5 mkg). Recheck total preload with a full stroke of the rack. Apply grease to rack end ball joints. Align claw washer with rack groove and tighten rack end into housing. Stake claw washer.

6) Coat rack end dust seal with grease. Clear rack housing tube hole of any grease. Install rack boots. Spring clips must have bends facing outward. Rack boot clamp on pinion housing side should have a gap of .197-.236" (5-6 mm) but tube side clamp should have no gap.

7) Rotate pinion and check rack stroke. Rack stroke should be 4.88" (124 mm). There should be no contour change of rack boots during this operation. Install tie rod ends and position them according to marks made on threads during disassembly.

TIGHTENING SPECIFICATIONS

Application	Ft. Lbs. (mkg)
Intermediate Shaft Pinch Bolts	22-28 (3.0-4.0)
Pinion Bearing Adjusting Screw Lock Nut	73-94 (10.0-13.0)
Rack Guide Screw Lock Nut	44-57 (6.0-8.0)
Rack End-to-Rack	48-65 (6.5-9.0)
Rack Housing Bracket-to-Body	22-32 (3.0-4.5)
Tie Rod-to-Knuckle	37-50 (5.0-7.0)
Tie Rod-to-Rack End	11-14 (1.5-2.0)

Steering Gears & Linkage

TRIUMPH RACK & PINION

Spitfire
TR7

DESCRIPTION

Steering gear is a rack and pinion type with direct linkage (tie rods) to steering arms. Gear housings are mounted by bolts through frame on TR7; by "U" bolts on Spitfire models. A flexible coupling links the steering gears to steering shaft.

ADJUSTMENTS

Rack and pinion free play are adjusted through the use of shims on the rack damper and pinion shaft. These adjustments are performed as part of overhaul procedure. See Overhaul below.

REMOVAL & INSTALLATION

RACK AND PINION

Removal — 1) Raise vehicle and place on safety stands. Scribe an index mark on pinion shaft and lower steering coupling for installation purposes. Disconnect tie rod ends from steering knuckle.

2) Remove pinch bolt attaching lower steering coupling to rack pinion. On TR7 models only, withdraw bolts mounting pinion end of rack to chassis. On all other models, "U" bolts mount steering rack to chassis.

3) On TR7 only, remove remaining rack mounting hardware, disconnect lower pinion shaft coupling and take rack out driver's side. On all others, slide rack forward disengaging rack pinion splines from flexible coupling. Disconnect ground strap from rack plug and withdraw steering rack.

Installation — 1) If rack has been disassembled, it must be centralized before reinstallation: Remove center plug from thrust pad and, using a piece of welding rod, locate dimple in rack shaft. When dimple in rack shaft is aligned with plug hole rack is centralized.

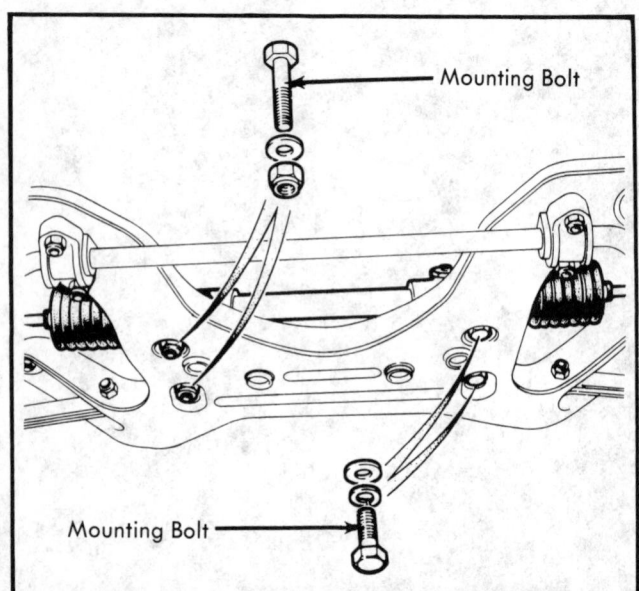

Fig. 1   Installed View of TR7 Rack Assembly

2) Carefully slide rack assembly into position but DO NOT disturb rack shaft. On TR7 models only, secure rack to chassis with mounting hardware, refit tie rod ends and tighten pinion coupling pinchbolt.

3) On all other models, hold steering wheel in straight-ahead position and engage rack pinion shaft splines in flexible coupling. Install and tighten pinch bolt. Keep rubber grommets correctly positioned on inboard side of rack flanges with lip under straight face of flange, then fit "U" bolts (Fig. 2). Refit tie rod outer ends to steering arms.

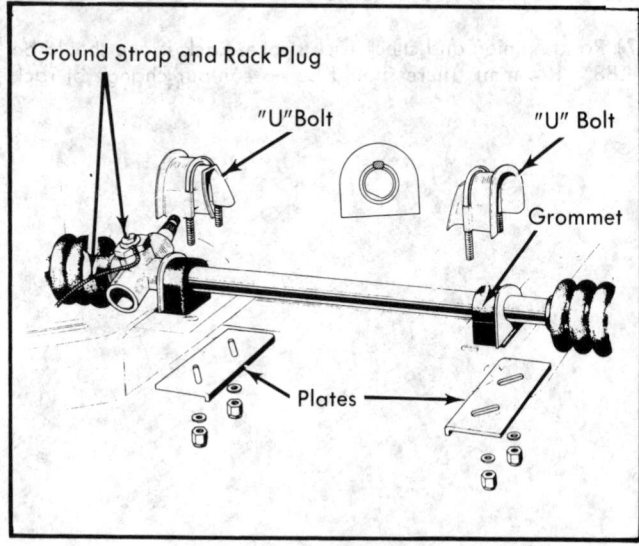

Fig. 2   Spitfire Rack with Rubber Grommets

4) Make sure all nuts and bolts are tightened and check front wheel alignment. See Triumph in WHEEL ALIGNMENT Section.

OVERHAUL

RACK AND PINION

Disassembly — 1) Release clip and slide bellows toward outer ball joint. Slacken inner lock nut and unscrew tie rod assembly from rack. Withdraw spring from rack end. Straighten tab washer, unscrew sleeve nut, and remove tab washer, shims, and cup.

2) Slacken outer lock nut and unscrew tie rod end from tie rod. Remove outer lock nut, bellows, and cup nut. Remove inner lock nut from rack. Repeat on other end.

3) Remove damper plug, spring, shims and damper. On Spitfire models, remove circlip from top of pinion and carefully pull out pinion, retainer, shims, bushing and thrust washer. Remove "O" ring from retainer. Be careful not to lose dowel pin. On TR7 models, remove rubber seal and pinion retaining plug then pull out pinion shaft and bearing. Remove circlip to slide bearing off pinion shaft.

4) Pull out rack and remove bushings from housing if necessary.

TRIUMPH RACK & PINION (Cont.)

Reassembly — 1) Install end cover and lower bushing in rack housing (if removed). Place rack shaft in housing with teeth toward pinion end. Install lock nuts, tie rods, springs and shims, then tighten. Pack inner joints with grease, then install bellows and clips.

2) Rotate rack shaft until teeth mesh with pinion. On Spitfire models, install pinion. Replace thrust washer, bushing, shims, and retaining ring with new "O" ring. Fit circlip and check to see that end play does not exceed .010" (.254 mm). Adjust shim pack if necessary. *See Fig. 3.*

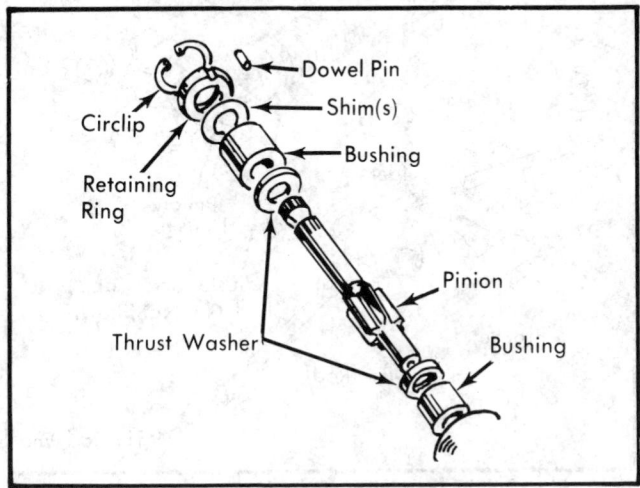

Fig. 3 Exploded View of Spitfire Pinion Assembly

3) On TR7 models, slide ball bearing on pinion and secure with circlip. Lubricate pinion shaft and insert into housing. Tighten end plug and replace rubber seal.

4) On all models, install rack damper, shims, spring and cap. Adjust rack side play by adding shims so movement does not exceed .004-.008' (.1-.2 mm) for Spitfire, or .001-.007 (.03-.18 mm) for TR7. Install rack in vehicle and reconnect ground strap (if removed).

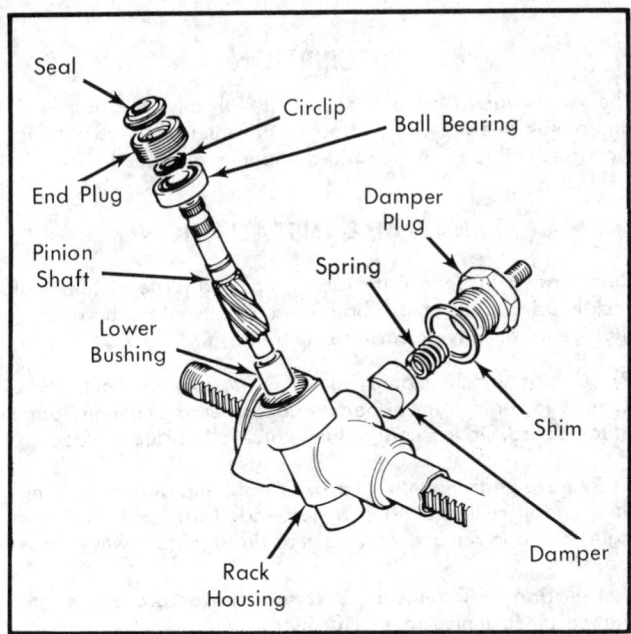

Fig. 4 Exploded View of TR7 Pinion and Damper

TIGHTENING SPECIFICATIONS

Application	Ft. Lbs. (mkg)
Steering Gear-to-Frame	
TR7	22-29 (3.0-4.0)
Spitfire	16 (2.2)
Tie Rod Lock Nuts	
TR7	30-37 (4.1-5.1)
Spitfire	38 (5.2)
Universal Joint Pinch Bolts	
TR7	16-21 (2.2-2.9)
Spitfire	14 (1.9)

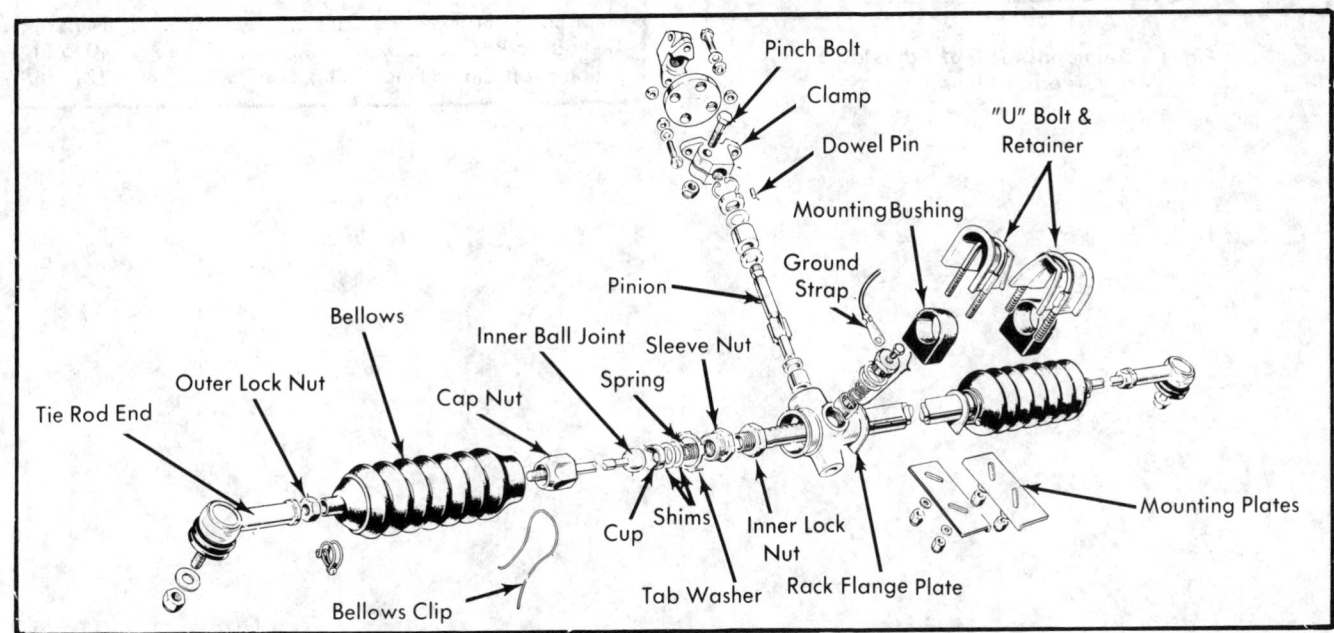

Fig. 5 Triumph Spitfire Rack and Pinion Steering

VOLKSWAGEN DASHER RACK & PINION

DESCRIPTION

The Volkswagen Dasher is equipped with an adjustable rack and pinion steering gear. Attached to center of the rack housing are 2 tie rods. A steering damper is also used.

REMOVAL & INSTALLATION

Removal — 1) Bend back tabs on locking plate at center of rack housing and remove both tie rod bolts. Move tie rods so that gear will have clearance for removal.

2) Unbolt pinch clamp at pinion-to-column connection. Remove lower instrument panel. Loosen steering column flange at toe board. Drive steering flange tube off of steering gear.

3) Remove gear mounting screw at right end of rack housing, then unbolt rack mounting at left end. Turn front wheels to right lock, and remove steering gear through right wheel housing.

Installation — To install, reverse removal procedure and tighten all fasteners to specifications.

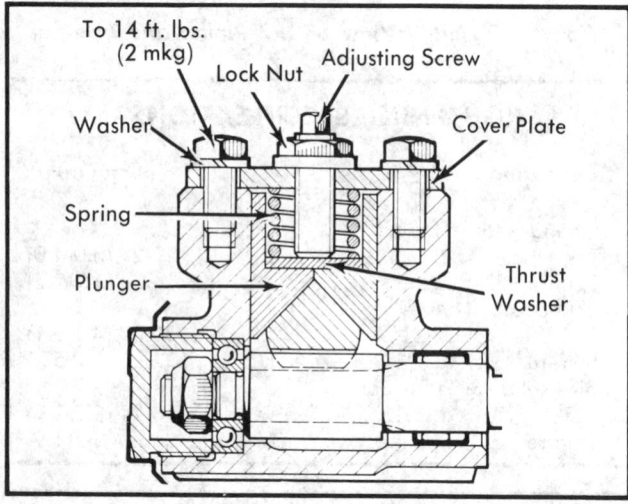

Fig. 1   Sectional View of Adjustable Steering Gear

ADJUSTMENT

With components installed on vehicle, tighten adjusting screw by hand until screw just contacts thrust washer. Hold adjusting screw in position and tighten lock nut *(Fig. 1)*.

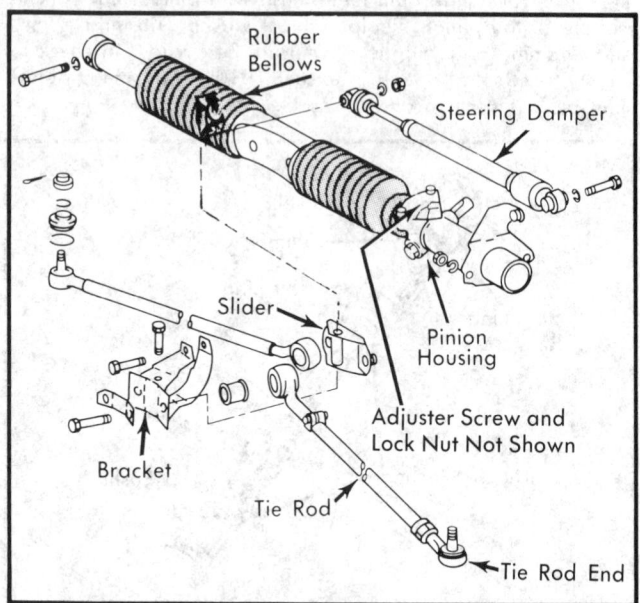

Fig. 2   Volkswagen Dasher Rack and Pinion Assembly

OVERHAUL

NOTE — *Manufacturer does not recommend overhaul of this unit. If it is determined to be defective, replace as an assembly.*

TIGHTENING SPECIFICATIONS

Application	Ft. Lbs. (mkg)
Gear Box-to-Brackets	14 (2.0)
Tie Rods-to-Rack	40 (5.5)
Pinion Shaft Clamp Pinch Bolt	22 (3.0)

VOLKSWAGEN JETTA, RABBIT, PICKUP & SCIROCCO RACK & PINION

DESCRIPTION

Steering gear is a rack and pinion type. Tie rods attach to ends of rack. Late production racks are mounted with "U" bolts and rubber bushings rather than welded mounting plates.

REMOVAL & INSTALLATION

Removal — Disconnect shift linkage bearing plate from rack housing. Loosen pinch bolts on steering shaft and remove shaft from pinion. Disconnect tie rod ends from steering linkage, using suitable puller. Remove mounting bolts and remove rack with tie rods attached.

Installation — When installing steering gear assembly, correctly align and insert pinion shaft with steering shaft lower universal joint before securing steering gear housing clamp bolts. Connect tie rod outer ends to steering linkage. Tighten upper and lower universal joint pinch bolts. Connect and adjust shift linkage bearing plate to gear housing.

ADJUSTMENT

RACK & TIE RODS

1) Center rack in housing so rack protrudes an equal amount from each end of housing.

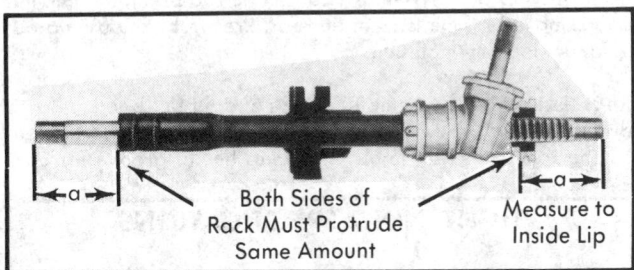

Fig. 1   Centering Rack in Steering Gear Housing

2) If replacing the non-adjustable left tie rod with adjustable type, adjust tie rod length "D" to 14.92" (379 mm).

3) Screw tie rods onto rack and adjust to specified dimensions without moving rack from center position. When adjustment is correct, secure tie rods with lock nuts and install rubber boots. See *Fig. 2.*

Tie Rod Specification		
Application	Dimension "B"	Dimension "C"
Man. Trans.	2.72" (69 mm)	2.72" (69 mm)
Auto. Trans.	2.64" (67 mm)	2.72" (69 mm)

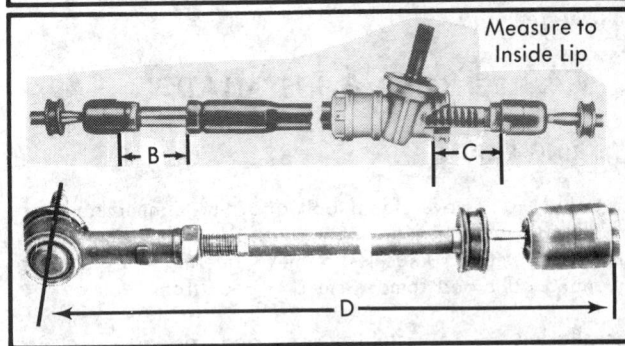

Fig. 2   Installation Adjustment of Tie Rods on Rack

4) Loosen pinion shaft adjusting screw lock nut, then turn adjusting bolt until it just contacts thrust washer. Tighten lock nut.

TIGHTENING SPECIFICATIONS

Application	Ft. Lbs. (mkg)
Tie Rod End to Steering Arm	22 (3.0)
Tie Rod End Lock Nut	29 (4.0)
Gear Box Rubber Mounting Bolts	22 (3.0)
Universal Joint Pinch Bolt	22 (3.0)

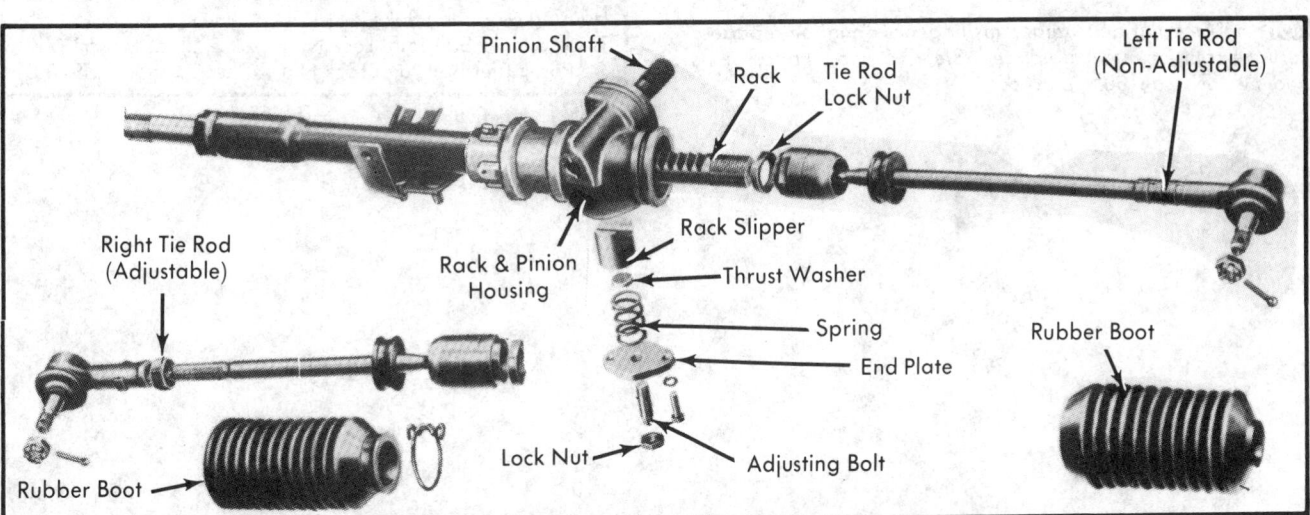

Fig. 3   Disassembled View of Rack & Pinion Steering Gear Assembly

VOLKSWAGEN VANAGON RACK & PINION

DESCRIPTION

Volkswagen Vanagon models use a rack and pinion steering gear. A transfer gear is used to connect steering shaft to steering gear. Tie rods are connected to rack and directly to steering knuckle, with ball joints. Both tie rods are adjustable for toe-in.

ADJUSTMENT

STEERING GEAR

NOTE — *Steering gear is not adjustable on these models. If gear is damaged or does not operate properly, complete unit must be replaced.*

REMOVAL & INSTALLATION

STEERING GEAR

Removal — Remove clamp bolt attaching connecting shaft coupling to steering gear pinion shaft. Disconnect tie rod ball joint from steering knuckles. Remove steering gear housing mounting bolts and remove steering gear from vehicle.

Installation — To install steering gear assembly, reverse removal procedure.

TRANSFER GEAR

Removal — Remove clamp bolt attaching connecting shaft coupling to transfer gear shaft. Remove clamp bolt attaching lower steering shaft flange to transfer gear shaft. Remove transfer gear attaching bolts and remove transfer gear.

Installation — To install transfer gear assembly, reverse removal procedure.

NOTE — *During installation of steering gear and/or transfer gear, always replace rubber couplings in connecting shaft and steering shaft lower flange.*

OVERHAUL

NOTE — *Steering gear and transfer gear cannot be repaired. Replace components if damaged. Steering gear rubber boots and tie rods can be replaced.*

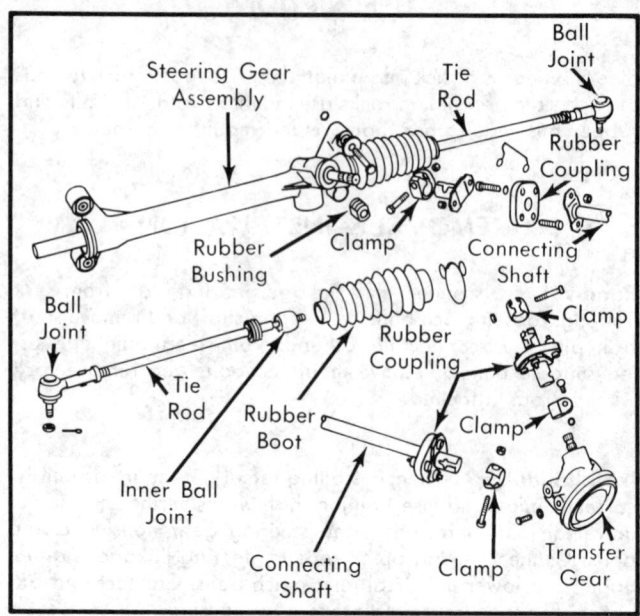

Fig. 1 Exploded View of Volkswagen Vanagon Steering Gear and Transfer Gear Assembly

TIE RODS AND RUBBER BOOTS

Disassembly — With steering gear assembly removed, remove clamps holding rubber boot to tie rod and steering gear housing. Using a punch, remove staking of tie rod inner ball joint washer to rack. Remove tie rods and rubber boots from steering gear assembly. Loosen tie rod ball joint lock nut and remove ball joints from tie rods. Press rubber bushing out of gear housing mounting.

Reassembly — To assemble tie rods and rubber boots, reverse disassembly procedure and note the following: After tightening tie rod inner ball joints, stake washer to groove in rack.

TIGHTENING SPECIFICATIONS	
Application	**Ft.Lbs. (mkg)**
Clamp Bolts	14 (1.9)
Housing Mounting Bolts	18 (2.5)
Tie Rod Inner Ball Joint Lock Nut	51 (7.0)
Tie Rod Outer Ball Joint Lock Nut	58 (8.0)

VOLVO RACK & PINION

DL

NOTE — *For models equipped with power steering, refer to appropriate article under Power Steering in this section.*

DESCRIPTION

Rack and pinion steering gear is mounted in rubber insulators to front crossmember. Movement of steering wheel is transmitted by steering shaft assembly to helical pinion. Rotation of pinion causes rack to move laterally where tie rods, attached to rack, transmit this movement to spindle arms, causing front wheels to change direction. Two types of steering gears are used by Volvo. The first is a Cam Gear unit which may be recognized by the two bolt rack damper cover. The second type is a ZF unit which has a plug type rack damper cover.

REMOVAL & INSTALLATION

STEERING GEAR

Removal — Push protective cover up out of way of lower joint. Remove lock bolt and nut from pinion flange. Bend flange apart slightly. Raise and support front of vehicle and remove wheels. Remove Tie rod nuts and disconnect ball studs from spindle using ball joint removal tool (9995043). Remove splash guard and bolts securing steering gear to crossmember. Disconnect gear from flange and remove gear.

Installation — To install, reverse removal procedure making sure that recess on pinion shaft is aligned towards lock bolt opening in flange.

TIE RODS

Removal — Raise vehicle and remove wheels. Remove tie rod nuts and disconnect ball studs from spindle using ball joint removal tool (9995043). Remove splash guard. Loosen inner clamps for both rubber bellows and drain oil, then re-attach clamp on side not being removed (if applicable). Bend up tie rod lock and disconnect rod from steering gear. Clamp ball stud in vise, loosen lock nut and unscrew rod, counting number of thread turns. Remove outer clamp for rubber bellows and remove bellows.

Installation — Install rubber bellows and outer clamp. Screw on lock nut same number of turns as when removed. Install ball stud and tighten lock nut. Attach tie rod to steering gear and punch ball stud edge into rack groove. Fill a suction gun with 6.75 oz. (200 cc) of 20W-50 engine oil and inject oil into steering gear through rubber bellows inner end. Install inner bellows clamp and tighten clamp and tighten clamp after turning tie rod so that ball stud is up. Connect tie rod to spindle making sure that both rods are the same length within .08" (2 mm).

ADJUSTMENT

NOTE — *Adjustments are performed during gear assembly process. See Overhaul as outlined.*

OVERHAUL

CAM GEAR

Disassembly — 1) Clean steering gear exterior and check inner ball joints for wear. Loosen pinion side rubber bellows and drain oil. Remove pinion side ball stud, lock nut and rubber bellows. Bend up locked portion of ball joint and unscrew pinion side tie rod. Repeat procedure on opposite side of gear.

2) Remove rack damper cover, spring, "O" ring and piston. Remove pinion cover and lift out pinion assembly. Pull out rack from pinion side of gear housing and remove rack bushing using a puller (4078). Use a puller (5047) to remove pinion lower bearing. Clean all parts and check for wear. Replace all seals, rack bushing and worn parts.

Assembly & Adjustment — 1) Oil all parts prior to assembly with 20W-50 engine oil. Install new rack bushing so that locks align with gear housing slots, using driver tool (2993). Install pinion lower bearing using driver tool (5048). Install pinion with upper bearing, but no shims, in housing. Install pinion spacer sleeve and cover with gasket but no seal. Use a dial indicator to measure pinion end play and record for later use. Remove pinion assembly.

2) Insert rack in gear housing from pinion side using care that rack teeth do not damage rack bushing. Apply a non-hardening gasket compound to pinion cover seal and install seal in cover using suitable driver (2734). Calculate required pinion shim thickness by adding .004-.010" (.10-.25 mm) to pinion end play previously measured. This will give correct amount of pinion preload. Install pinion, shims and spacer sleeve with shims between upper bearing and spacer sleeve. Install pinion cover with gasket and seal.

3) Place rack damper piston in housing without "O" ring or spring. Using straight edge and feeler gauge, measure end play between end of piston and housing (see *Fig. 1*). Measure thickness of gasket and calculate shim thickness required to obtain a total thickness, between gasket and shim, of .001-.006" (.02-.15 mm) greater than the measured piston end play to obtain correct preload. Install spring and "O" ring in piston, install shims, gasket and cover.

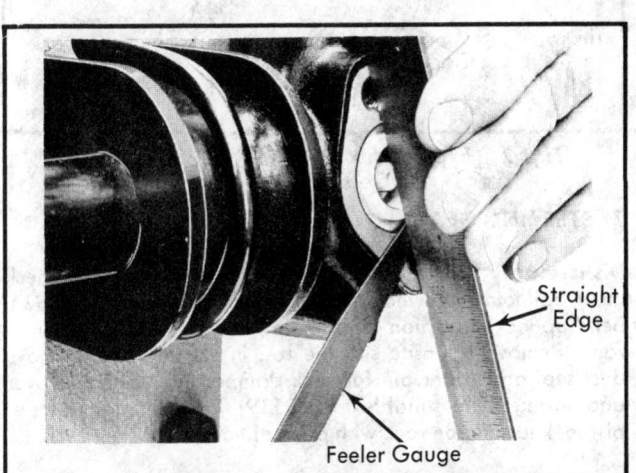

Straight Edge

Feeler Gauge

Fig. 1 Measuring Rack Damper Piston End Play (Cam Gear)

VOLVO RACK & PINION (Cont.)

4) Using suitable torque gauge (5053), crank rack back and forth from one end to the other. Torque reading should be 8-14 INCH lbs. (9-16 cmkg). Install pinion side tie rod and punch ball joint edge into rack groove.

NOTE — *When installing old tie rod, place a thin shim between ball joint and rack shoulder so unused portion of ball can be used for punch locking.*

5) Install pinion side rubber bellows with inner clamp only. Install lock nut and ball stud. Repeat procedure for other side of gear and adjust both rods to the same length within .08" (2 mm). Use a suction gun to inject 6.75 ozs. (200 cc) of 20W-50 engine oil through outer end of pinion side rubber bellows. Install outer clamps on bellows.

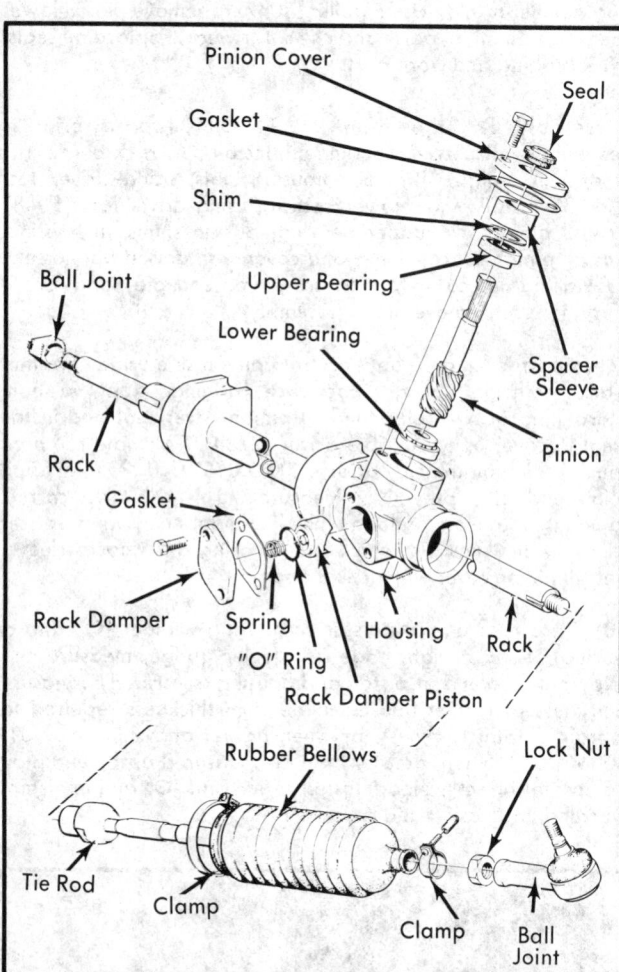

Fig. 2   Exploded View of Cam Gear Steering Gear Assembly

ZF STEERING GEAR

Disassembly — 1) Clean exterior of steering gear and check inner ball joints for wear. Remove pinion side rubber bellows. Bend up locked portion of ball joint and unscrew tie rod from rack. Remove opposite side tie rod in like manner. Remove dust seal and cotter pin for rack damper, then remove cover and spring using suitable tool (5119). Remove rack damper piston, knocking on rack with palm of hand to aid removal.

2) Remove pinion shaft dust seal. Unscrew the pinion shaft nut using suitable tool (5119). Clamp pinion shaft in a soft

jawed vise and tap lightly on housing with soft mallet to remove pinion. Remove rack from pinion side of housing and remove rack bushing by pressing in locking tabs and prying bearing out. Press pinion thrust washer and bearing from shaft. Clean all parts and check for wear. Replace all "O" rings and worn parts.

Assembly & Adjustment — 1) Press bearing onto pinion and install snap ring and thrust washer. Install new "O" rings on rack bushing and press bushing into housing making sure that tabs on bushing fit correctly into slots in housing. Grease rack with Calypsol D 4024-OK grease or equivalent. Insert rack into pinion side of housing using care not to damage rack bushing with rack teeth. Grease pinion using same grease as for rack and install pinion with bearing.

2) Install new "O" ring in pinion nut and install nut using suitable tool (5119). Torque to 18±1.5 ft. lbs. (2.5±.2 mkg). Install snap ring and press down against nut. Fill cavity on top of nut with grease and install dust seal. Install new "O" ring on rack damper piston, grease piston and install piston and spring. Install, but do not tighten rack damper cover (use tool 5119). Using torque gauge, crank rack back and forth between end positions. Torque should be 8-14 INCH lbs. (9-16 cmkg). To increase torque, screw in rack damper cover. Lock cover in correct position with cotter pin and install dust cover.

3) Crank out rack fully and fill rack tooth spaces with Calypsol D 4024-OK grease or equivalent. Crank rack in and then out again and repeat grease application. Approximately 1 oz. (25 g) of grease should be used. Install tie rods using new lock washers and bend washer to lock rod in place. Install rubber bellows.

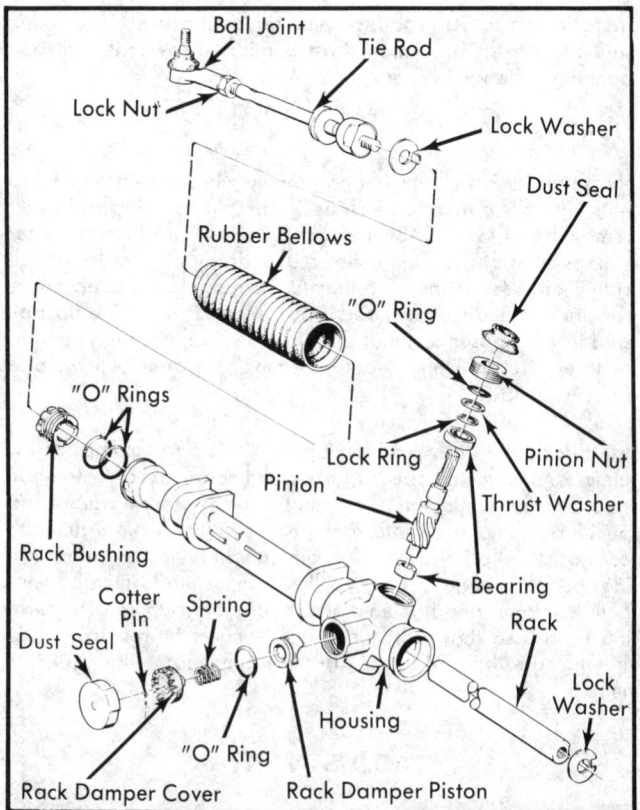

Fig. 3   Exploded View of ZF Steering Gear Assembly

AUDI 4000 POWER-ASSISTED RACK & PINION

DESCRIPTION

A power-assisted rack and pinion steering gear is only used on Audi 4000 models with a 5-cylinder engine and automatic transmission. The system consists of a vane pump, rotary piston pinion gear assembly and an oil reservoir. The vane pump draws fluid from the reservoir and supplies it to the flow control valve. The control valve supplies fluid to the proper side of the rack-piston as the steering wheel is turned. The pump is belt driven and mounted on the front of the engine. The reservoir is located near the firewall.

GENERAL SERVICE

Capacity — 1 qt.

Lubricant — ATF Dexron or Dexron II.

Oil Level Check — Remove reservoir cover, start engine and check fluid level. Fluid level should be at mark on upper inside of reservoir.

Hydraulic System Bleeding — Start engine and allow to idle. Check that fluid is at proper level. Turn steering wheel lock to lock several times quickly. Continue until fluid level remains at reservoir mark. Make sure that no bubbles appear in reservoir when steering wheel is turned. Shut off engine and check that oil level does not rise more than $\frac{3}{8}$" above mark.

Oil Filter Replacement — Remove outer cover, gasket and spring from reservoir. Remove inner filter cover and filter insert. Replace filter. Install new filter, replace old filter cover, spring, gasket and top cover. Check fluid level.

NOTE — *Oil filter insert must be replaced whenever repairs are made to power steering system.*

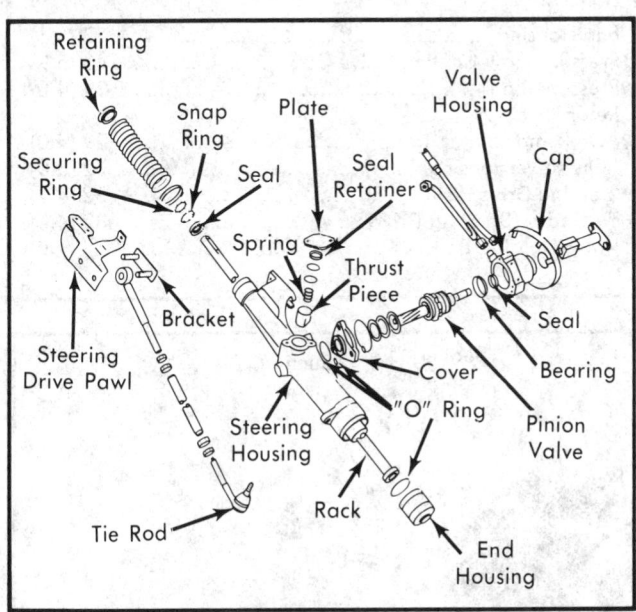

Fig. 1 Audi 4000 Power Steering Gear Exploded View

ADJUSTMENT

PUMP BELT

Remove belt from alternator and air conditioning compressor. Loosen 2 nuts on pump mounting bracket. Turn adjusting nut on bracket until belt deflection is $\frac{3}{8}$" (9.5 mm) at center of

belt. Tighten nuts. Reinstall alternator and air conditioning belts.

STEERING GEAR

Loosen lock nut on steering gear. Hand tighten adjusting screw until it just touches the thrust plate. Hold adjusting screw and tighten lock nut. Check adjustment with engine idling. No play should be felt. Readjust if necessary.

TESTING

SYSTEM PRESSURE TEST

Install pressure gauge (US1074/2) between pressure hose and pressure pipe of valve housing, with the pressure gauge valve open. Run engine at idle. Turn steering wheel lock to lock several times. Check pressure. Correct pressure is 967-1166 psi (68-82 kg/cm²). If pressure is not within limits, replace steering gear.

PUMP PRESSURE TEST

1) With pressure gauge installed, start engine and idle. Close valve (no longer than 5 seconds) and check pressure. Correct pressure is 967-1166 psi (68-82 kg/cm²). If pressure differs, check pressure/flow limiting valve. If valve is all right, replace power steering pump.

2) To check limiting valve, inspect bores in valve and piston for obstructions, and that piston moves freely in housing. Install new valve if necessary.

LEAKAGE TEST

With engine idling, turn steering wheel to full lock and hold in position. Inspect all connections and tighten if necessary. If leak shows at steering pinion, replace housing seal and both intermediate cover seals. If pinion shaft seal is leaking, fluid will have entered gear housing. Check for fluid by loosening outer clamp on right steering boot and pushing boot in. If seal is leaking, disassemble steering gear and replace all seals.

REMOVAL & INSTALLATION

STEERING GEAR

Removal — Drain fluid from system. Disconnect pressure and return pipes from valve housing. Disconnect lower steering shaft from pinion shaft. Move cap out of way. Remove steering drive pawl and tie rod bracket nuts, then disconnect tie rods from bracket. Remove bolts attaching gear housing to body then remove gear housing.

Installation — Reverse removal procedures. To facilitate tie rod installation, install one tie rod to steering gear and tighten before installing other tie rod.

VANE PUMP

Removal — Remove alternator and vane pump belts. Disconnect pressure and suction lines from pump and cover openings. Remove mounting bolts from bracket and lift pump from engine.

Installation — Reverse removal procedures noting the following: Adjust belt deflection to $\frac{3}{8}$" (9.5 mm) at center. After installation of pressure and suction lines, start engine and turn steering wheel to full lock and check for leaks in connections.

AUDI 4000 POWER-ASSISTED RACK & PINION (Cont.)

OVERHAUL

NOTE — *Before disassembling steering gear, check output and system pressure. Always use all parts in repair kit (811 498 020) and always use new self-locking nuts.*

PINION HOUSING SEALS

Disassembly — 1) Remove attaching bolts from valve housing and remove housing. Remove pinion gear and intermediate cover.

2) Remove "O" rings from intermediate cover (1 on each side) and, using suitable tool, drive out intermediate cover oil seal. Anchor housing in padded vise and drive out oil seal from the back.

3) Install new seals from the inside cover and housing. Make sure that seal lip on housing seal faces intermediate cover, and seal lip of cover seal faces valve housing. Replace both intermediate cover "O" rings.

Reassembly — Reverse removal procedure noting the following: Protect pinion teeth on shaft when replacing intermediate cover. Do not damage "O" rings during installation.

STEERING GEAR

Disassembly — 1) With steering gear assembly removed from vehicle, remove pinion valve housing and pinion valve assembly. Remove plate, seal retainer, spring and thrust piece from steering housing.

2) Remove retaining ring, clamp and boot from steering housing. Remove securing ring and snap ring from steering housing.

3) Remove end housing and "O" ring from steering housing. Pull rack out of steering housing. Using oil seal puller, remove oil seal from steering housing.

Reassembly — 1) To install new oil seal to steering housing, place oil seal on flat surface and push sleeve (available in repair kit 811 498 020) into oil seal. Slide rack into steering housing then slide oil seal with sleeve over rack and into steer-

ing housing using suitable tools (VW 426 and VW 4166). Remove sleeve. Install snap ring and securing ring.

2) Install end housing with new "O" ring. Install thrust piece, spring, "O" ring, seal retainer and plate. Install clamp, boot and retaining ring. Then install pinion valve assembly as previously described.

VANE PUMP OIL SEAL

Disassembly — 1) With pump removed from vehicle, remove pulley and Woodruff key from vane shaft. Disengage outer snap ring and screw pulley nut onto pinion shaft.

2) Anchor pulley nut and shaft in padded vise, strike pump housing with mallet to drive out vane shaft. Remove from vise and disengage inner snap ring.

3) Insert extractor into housing and tighten nut on extractor until jaws on extractor engage metal case of seal. Anchor nut of extractor in vise and strike pump housing with mallet to drive out seal.

Reassembly — Lubricate space between lips of new seal. Drive seal onto seat with seal lips facing interior of housing. Install inner snap ring. Carefully drive pump shaft onto seat with mallet, watching alignment of pump shaft and vane splines. Install outer snap ring, Woodruff key, pulley and nut.

TIGHTENING SPECIFICATIONS

Application	Ft. Lbs. (mkg)
End Housing	37 (5.1)
Pressure-Flow Limiting Valve Cap	43 (5.9)
Pressure Pipe	29 (4.0)
Return Pipe	
On Pump	29 (4.0)
On Valve Housing	22 (3.0)
Steering Drive Pawl	32 (4.4)
Tie Rod-to-Steering Drive Pawl	32 (4.4)
Valve Housing Bolts	14 (1.9)

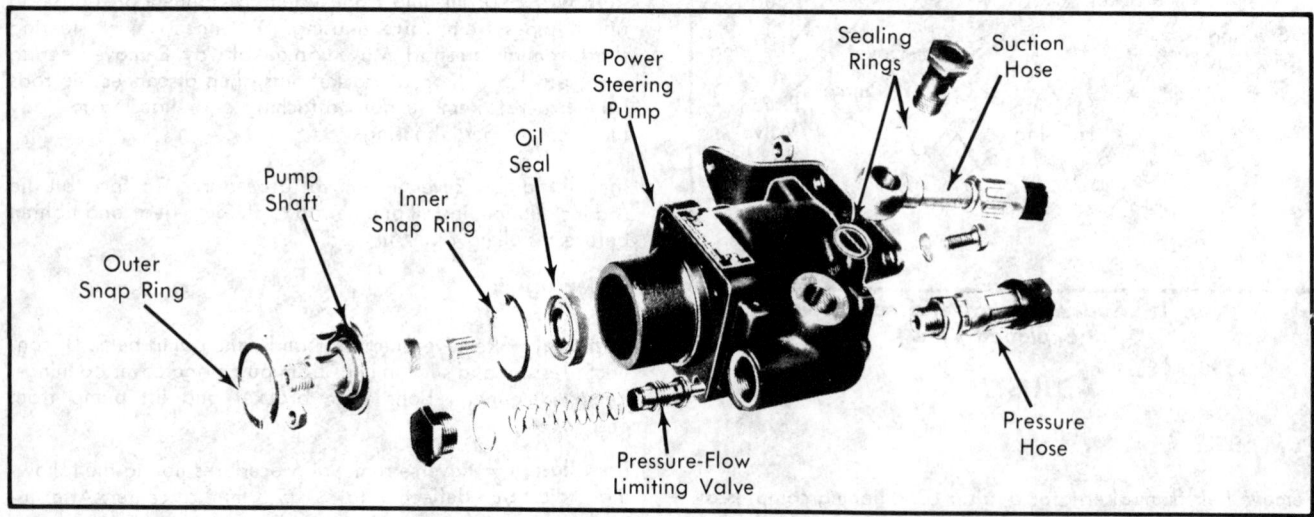

Fig. 2 Exploded View of Vane Pump Assembly

AUDI 5000 POWER-ASSISTED RACK & PINION

DESCRIPTION

A power-assisted rack and pinion steering gear is used on Audi 5000 models. The system consists of a vane pump, rotary piston pinion gear assembly and an oil reservoir. The vane pump draws fluid from the reservoir and supplies it to the flow control valve. The control valve supplies fluid to the proper side of the rack-piston as the steering wheel is turned. The pump is belt driven and mounted on the front of the engine. The reservoir is located near the firewall.

GENERAL SERVICE

Capacity — 1 qt.

Lubricant — ATF Dexron or Dexron II

Oil Level Check — Remove reservoir cover, start engine and check fluid level. Fluid level should be at mark on upper inside of reservoir.

Hydraulic System Bleeding — Start engine and allow to idle. Check that fluid is at proper level. Turn steering wheel lock to lock several times quickly. Continue until fluid level remains at reservoir mark. Make sure that no bubbles appear in reservoir when steering wheel is turned. Shut off engine and check that fluid level does not rise more than 3/8" (9.5 mm) above mark.

Oil Filter Replacement — Remove outer cover, gasket and spring from reservoir. Remove inner filter cover and filter insert. Replace filter. Install new filter, replace filter cover, spring, gasket and cover. Check fluid level.

NOTE — *Oil filter insert must be replaced whenever repairs are made to power steering system.*

ADJUSTMENT

PUMP BELT

Remove "V" belt from alternator and air conditioning compressor. Loosen 2 nuts on pump mounting bracket as shown in *Fig. 3*. Turn adjusting nut on bracket until belt deflection is 3/8" (9.5 mm) at center. Tighten nuts. Reinstall alternator "V" belts.

STEERING GEAR

Loosen lock nut on steering gear. Hand tighten adjusting screw until it touches the thrust plate. Hold adjusting screw and tighten lock nut. Check adjustment with engine idling. No play should be felt. Readjust if necessary.

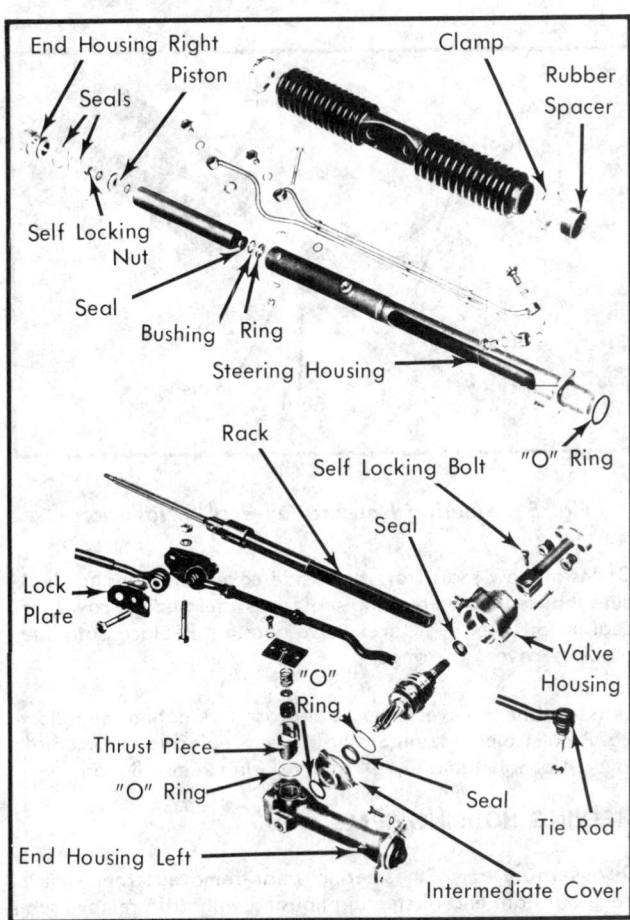

Fig. 1   Exploded View of Audi 5000 Steering Gear Assembly

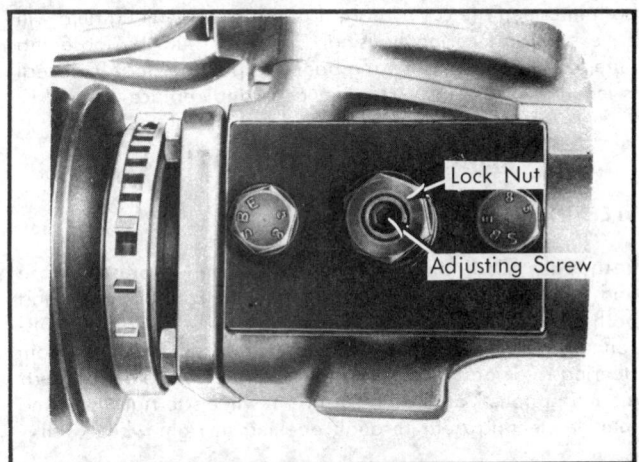

Fig. 2   Steering Gear Adjustment

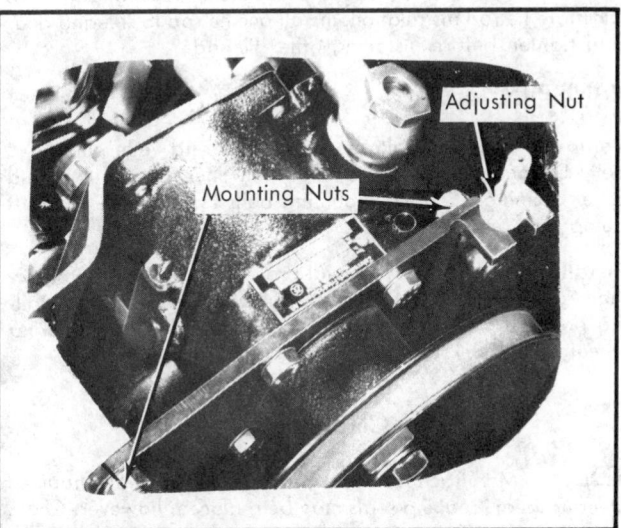

Fig. 3   Power Steering Belt Adjustment

AUDI 5000 POWER-ASSISTED RACK & PINION (Cont.)

TESTING

SYSTEM PRESSURE TEST

Install pressure gauge (US1074) between expansion hose and connecting pipe of valve housing, with valve open. Run engine at idle. Turn steering wheel lock to lock several times. Check pressure. Correct pressure is 967-1166 psi (68-82 kg/cm²). If pressure is not within limits, replace steering gear.

PUMP PRESSURE TEST

1) With pressure gauge installed, start engine and idle. Close valve (no longer than 5 seconds) and check pressure. Correct pressure is 967-1166 psi (68-82 kg/cm²). If pressure differs, check pressure/flow limiting valve. If valve is all right, replace power steering pump.

2) To check limiting valve, inspect bores in valve and piston for obstructions, and that piston moves freely in housing. Install new valve if necessary.

LEAKAGE TEST

With engine idling, turn steering wheel to full lock and hold in position. Inspect all connections and tighten if necessary. If leak shows at steering pinion, replace pinion housing seal and both intermediate cover seals. If piston rod is leaking fluid will have entered steering housing. Check for fluid by loosening outer clamp on right steering boot and pushing boot in. If seal is leaking, disassemble steering gear and replace all seals.

REMOVAL & INSTALLATION

STEERING GEAR

Removal — Drain fluid from system. Disconnect pressure hose and return line. Cap openings. Remove tie rod lock plate and both tie rod mounting bolts. Pry tie rods off steering gear. Disconnect steering damper. Disconnect flange tube clamp from steering gear and remove flange tube. Remove steering gear mounting bolts from body. Turn front wheels to right lock and remove steering gear through opening in right wheel well.

Installation — Reverse removal procedures, noting the following: Replace tie rod lock plate before reinstallation. To facilitate tie rod installation, install one tie rod to steering gear and tighten before installing other tie rod.

VANE PUMP

Removal — Remove alternator "V" belt and vane pump "V" belt. Disconnect pressure and suction lines from pump and cover openings. Remove mounting bolts from bracket and lift pump from engine.

Installation — Reverse removal procedures noting the following: Adjust "V" belt deflection to ³⁄₈" at center. After reinstalling pressure and suction lines, start engine and turn steering wheel to full lock and check for leaks in connections.

OVERHAUL

NOTE — *Manufacturer does not recommend overhaul of steering gear. Leaking seals may be replaced, however. Check output and system pressure before removing steering gear. Steering gear must be removed to replace seals.*

PINION HOUSING SEALS

Disassembly — 1) Remove attaching bolts from valve housing and remove housing. Remove pinion gear and intermediate cover.

2) Remove "O" rings from intermediate cover (one on each side) and, using suitable tool, drive out intermediate cover oil seal. Anchor housing in padded vise and drive out oil seal from the back.

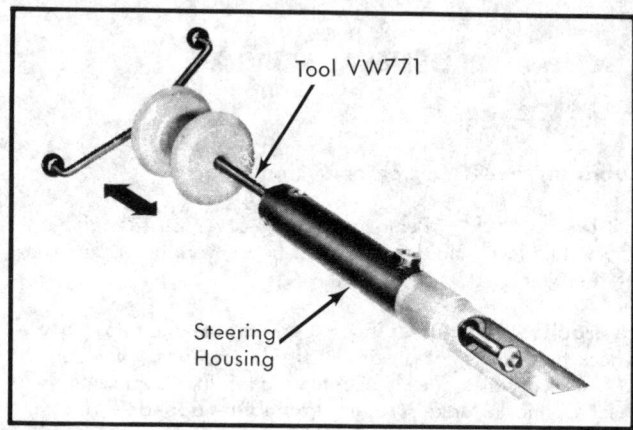

Fig. 4   Steering Housing Oil Seal Removing

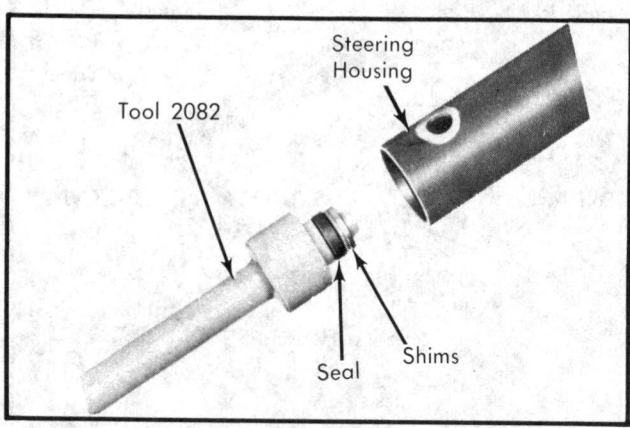

Fig. 5   Steering Housing Oil Seal Installation

3) Install new seals from the inside cover and housing. Make sure that seal lip on housing seal faces intermediate cover, and seal lip of cover seal faces valve housing. Replace both intermediate cover "O" rings.

Reassembly — Reverse removal procedure noting the following: Protect pinion teeth on shaft when replacing intermediate cover. Do not damage "O" rings during reinstallation.

STEERING HOUSING SEALS

Disassembly — With steering gear removed from vehicle, drive out right end of steering housing with drift, remove seals and "O" ring. Clamp rack in vise, remove self locking nut and piston. Insert special tool (VW771) into right steering housing and remove oil seal and shims.

AUDI 5000 POWER-ASSISTED RACK & PINION (Cont.)

Reassembly — Using special tool (2082), install shims and seal with thin shim behind seal, and seal lip facing piston. Replace piston and self locking nut. Tighten to specification. Replace seals, "O" ring, and end housing.

VANE PUMP OIL SEAL

Disassembly — 1) With pump removed from vehicle, remove pulley and woodruff key from pinion shaft. Disengage outer circlip with pliers and screw pulley nut onto pinion shaft.

2) Anchor pulley nut and shaft in padded vise, and strike pump housing with plastic mallet to drive out shaft. Remove from vise and disengage inner circlip with pliers. Insert extractor into housing. Tighten nut on extractor until two jaws on extractor engage on metal case of seal.

3) Anchor nut of extractor in vise and strike pump housing with plastic hammer to drive out seal.

Reassembly — Lubricate space between lips of new seal. Drive seal onto seat with lips facing interior of housing. Install inner circlip. Carefully drive pump shaft onto seat with plastic hammer, watching alignment of pump shaft and impeller splines. Install outer circlip, woodruff key and pulley.

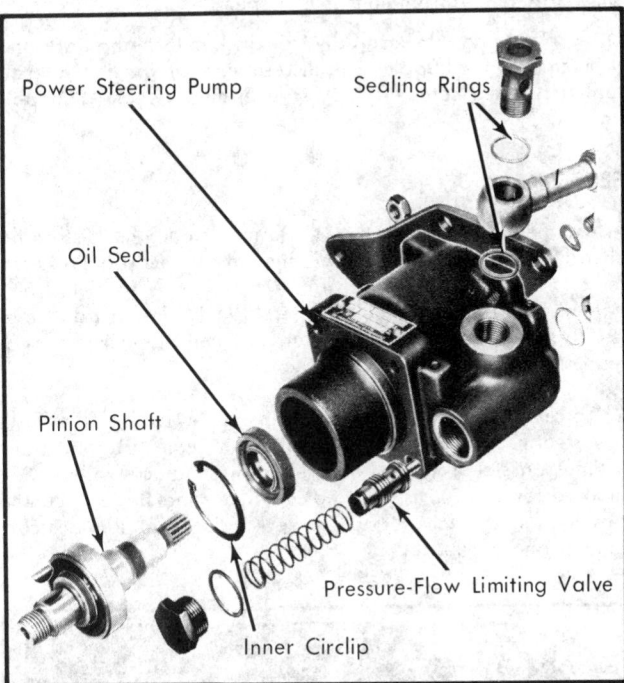

Fig. 6 Exploded View of Power Steering Pump Assembly

Power Steering Pump

Sealing Rings

Oil Seal

Pinion Shaft

Pressure-Flow Limiting Valve

Inner Circlip

TIGHTENING SPECIFICATIONS

Application	Ft. Lbs. (mkg)
Pulley to Pump Shaft	36 (6)
Pump Mounting Bolts	14 (2)
Pinion Shaft Nut	14 (2)
Steering Damper	29 (4)
Tie Rod to Steering Gear	43 (6)
Valve Housing Bolts	7 (1)
Tie Rod Locking Nut	43 (6)
Steering Housing Locking Nut	29 (4)
Expansion Hose	29 (4)
Suction Hose	29 (4)
Flange Tube to Steering Gear	22 (3)

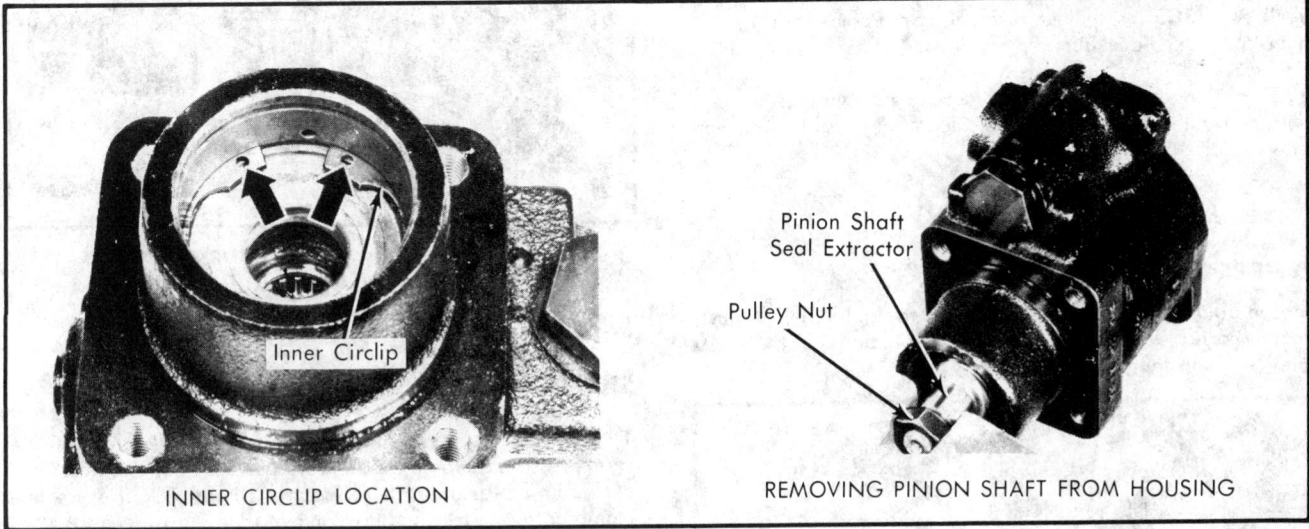

Inner Circlip

INNER CIRCLIP LOCATION

Pinion Shaft Seal Extractor

Pulley Nut

REMOVING PINION SHAFT FROM HOUSING

Fig. 7 Vane Pump Oil Seal Removal

Power Steering

BMW POWER-ASSISTED RECIRCULATING BALL

528i
633CSi
733i

DESCRIPTION

STEERING GEAR

Power steering gear consists of a gear housing containing a sector shaft with sector gear, a power piston with gear teeth in side of piston which is in constant mesh with sector shaft teeth, and a worm shaft connecting steering shaft to power piston through a universal joint coupling. Worm shaft is geared to piston through recirculating ball contact, and a steering valve is incorporated into upper end of worm gear assembly.

STEERING PUMP

Power steering pump is a high pressure, belt driven, vane type pump. A fluid reservoir incorporating a filter element supplies hydraulic fluid to pump. Pump maintains hydraulic pressure to power steering gear assembly.

LUBRICATION

CAPACITY

System Capacity — 528i & 633CSi: 2.5 pts.
733i: 3.8 pts.

LUBRICANT TYPE

Initial or Subsequent Filling — BMW recommends the use of ATF Dexron II (or equivalent) type of fluid.

FILTER REPLACEMENT

528i & 633CSi — Remove reservoir cap. Remove spring and filter cover. Replace filter.

733i — Remove reservoir cap. Remove nut, washer, spring, fine mesh filter screen and filters. Clean fine mesh filter screen and replace filters.

ADJUSTMENT

PUMP BELT

Loosen adjustment bolts and shift pump to tighten belt. Adjustment is correct when it is possible to press in belt 0.2-0.4" (5-10 mm) with the thumb.

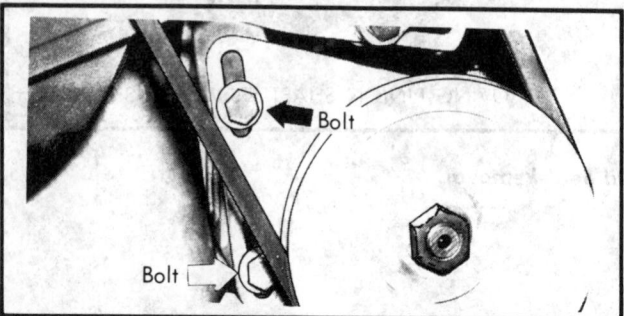

Fig. 1   Power Steering Belt Adjustment Locations

HYDRAULIC SYSTEM BLEEDING

1) Power steering must be bled whenever system is opened, or oil level falls so low that the vane type pump picks up air. Fill reservoir to upper mark with fluid. Turn engine over with starter and continue to add fluid. When oil level no longer falls, start and run engine at idle speed.

2) Turn steering wheel rapidly from lock to lock and back until no further air bubbles rise in reservoir. During this operation, and when completed, fluid level must remain at upper mark.

SECTOR SHAFT

Adjustment (In Vehicle) — 1) Position front wheels straight ahead. Remove cotter pin and castle nut from tie-rod. Press off center tie-rod from steering arm. Remove BMW emblem from steering wheel. Turn wheel counterclockwise 1 turn from center. Install torque wrench on nut, turn wheel clockwise and read frictional torque.

2) Torque should be 2.7-3.5 INCH lbs. (3.1-4 cmkg). To adjust, turn steering wheel counterclockwise from center 1 turn. Loosen locknut on steering gear and turn adjusting screw clockwise until correct torque is reached when passing through center position. Tighten locknut and recheck adjustment. Replace cotter pin and castle nut.

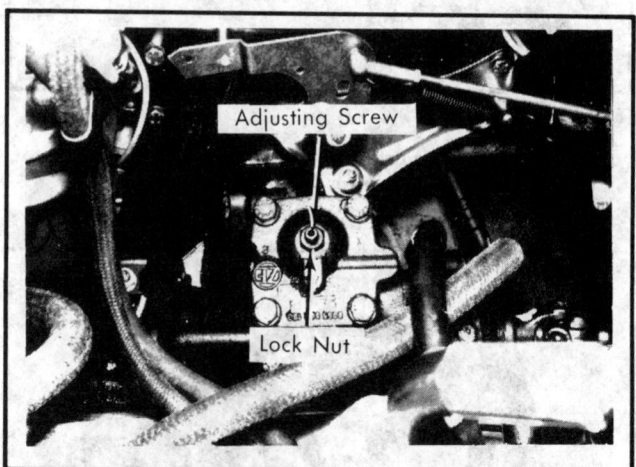

Fig. 2   Sector Shaft Adjusting Screws

TESTING

STEERING PUMP PRESSURE

1) Disconnect pressure line from pump. Install pressure line from pressure gauge 32-4-000 (or equivalent) in its place. Connect pump pressure line to gauge. Disconnect pressure line from control regulator and connect it to pressure gauge.

2) Shut cut-off valve on gauge. Open shut-off valve on pressure line (See Fig. 6), and bleed system with engine running at idle. After bleeding, close valve in pressure line for 10 seconds maximum and read pressure. On 528i and 633CSi, pressure should be 1400 ± 140 psi (98.5 ± 9.8 kg/cm^2). On 733i, pressure should be 1560 ± 156 psi (109.5 ± 11 kg/cm^2). If pressure is not within limits, check belt tightness. Repair or replace pump if belt adjustment does not remedy problem.

BMW POWER-ASSISTED RECIRCULATING BALL (Cont.)

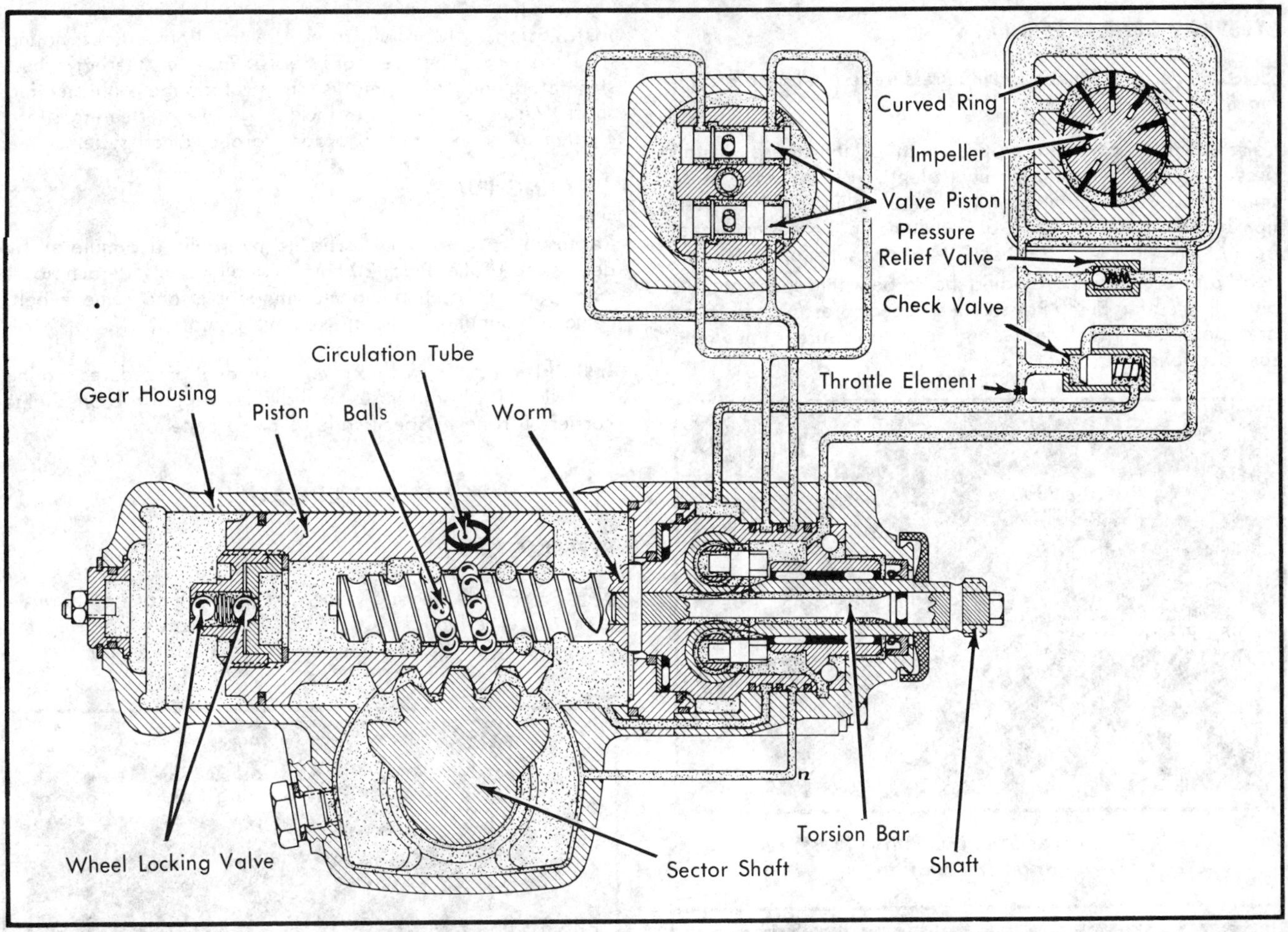

Curved Ring

Impeller

Valve Piston

Pressure Relief Valve

Check Valve

Throttle Element

Gear Housing

Piston

Balls

Circulation Tube

Worm

Wheel Locking Valve

Torsion Bar

Shaft

Sector Shaft

Fig. 3 Cross-Sectional View of Power Steering Gear Assembly

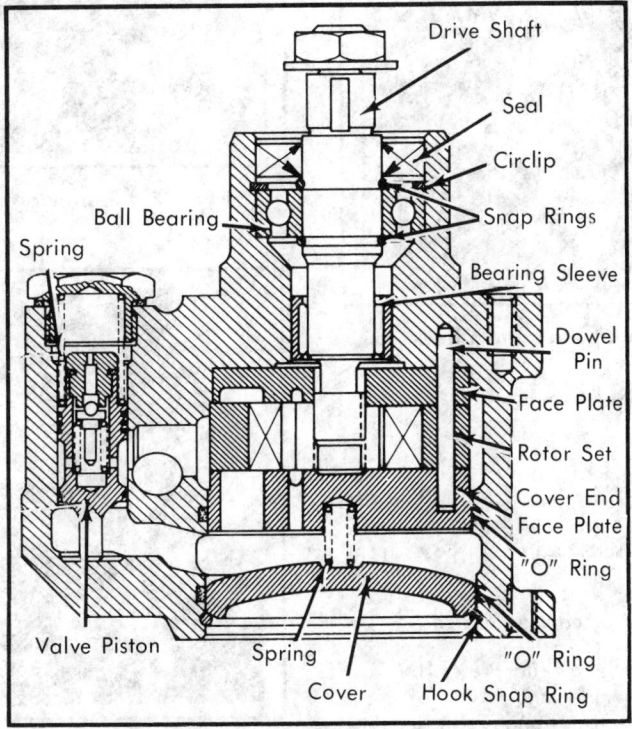

Drive Shaft

Seal

Circlip

Snap Rings

Bearing Sleeve

Dowel Pin

Face Plate

Rotor Set

Cover End Face Plate

"O" Ring

"O" Ring

Hook Snap Ring

Cover

Spring

Valve Piston

Spring

Ball Bearing

Fig. 4 Cross-Sectional View of Power Steering Pump

Power Steering

BMW POWER-ASSISTED RECIRCULATING BALL (Cont.)

STEERING GEAR PRESSURE

NOTE — *Perform Steering Pump Pressure test before performing this test.*

Raise front of car and support with safety stands. Install pressure tester 32-4-000 (or equivalent), in same position as pump pressure test. Limit steering from reaching full lock position by ½-¾ turn. With engine running, pull steering wheel against final lock with 22 lbs. (9.9 kg) pressure for 5 seconds. Read pressure. Pressure reading should be within specifications given in Steering Pump Pressure test. Check pressure with gear at opposite lock. Replace steering gear if pressure is not within specifications.

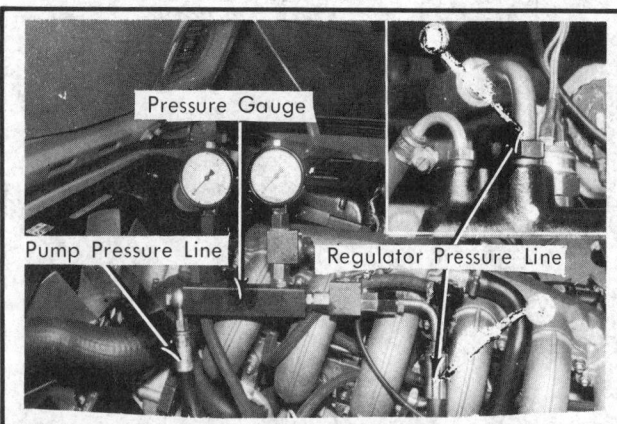

Fig. 5 *Power Steering Pump Pressure Gauge Installation*

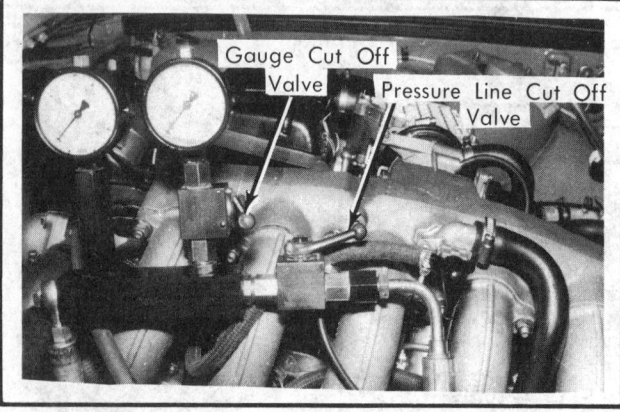

Fig. 6 *Power Steering Pump Pressure Check*

REMOVAL & INSTALLATION

STEERING GEAR

Removal — 1) Turn steering to full left lock. On 733i, discharge hydraulic accumulator by depressing brake pedal 20 times. On all models, detach pressure and return hoses from steering gear and cap openings.

CAUTION — *Do not reuse fluid drained from system.*

2) Remove cotter pin and nut from tie rod end. Press off tie rod from steering arm. Remove bolt from locking groove of steering shaft (See Fig. 7). Push up pivot flange with steering column. Detach steering gear from front axle carrier.

Installation — To install, reverse removal procedures, noting the following: Replace hose seals. Position steering wheel straight ahead. Align marks on pivot flange with steering shaft. Make sure bolt is in locking groove of steering shaft. Tighten all connections to proper torque. Bleed system.

STEERING PUMP

Removal — On 733i, discharge hydraulic accumulator by depressing brake pedal 20 times. On all models, detach hoses from pump. Loosen pump mounting bolts and remove belt. Remove mounting bolts and remove pump.

Installation — To install, reverse removal procedures, noting the following: Install hoses so that they do not rub on engine carrier. Torque to specifications. Bleed system.

OVERHAUL

STEERING GEAR

NOTE — *Power steering gear assembly cannot be repaired except in exceptional cases. BMW recommends replacing the entire unit if malfunctions occur in the steering gear.*

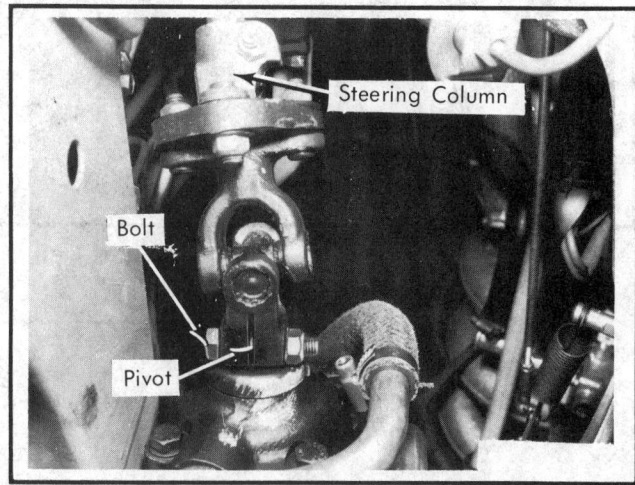

Fig. 7 *Removing Steering Shaft Flange*

Fig. 8 *Steering Gear-to-Front Axle Removal*

BMW POWER-ASSISTED RECIRCULATING BALL (Cont.)

POWER STEERING PUMP

NOTE — *Overhaul procedures are for 528i and 633CSi only. For 733i, BMW recommends replacing power steering pump if malfunctions occur.*

DISASSEMBLY

1) Press cover in slightly and remove retaining ring. Remove cover, coil spring and "O" ring. Remove end plate and "O" ring, noting location of pin in one of the small holes in end plate.

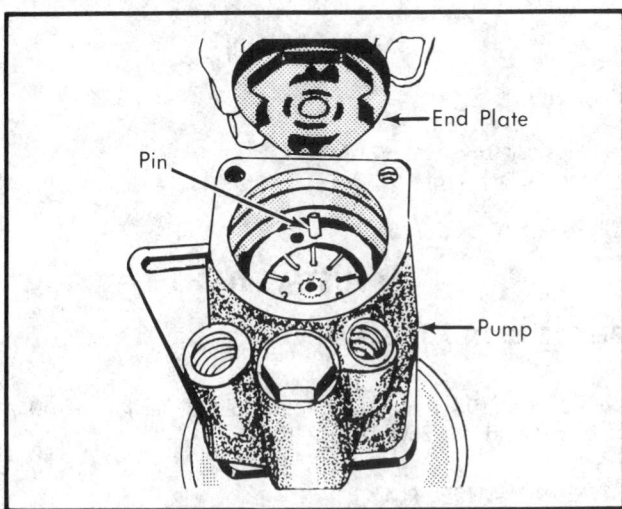

Fig. 9   Pin Location Inside of Pump Housing

2) Tilt housing and remove cam ring and rotor. Note that side of rotor with recessed hole faces drive shaft, the rounded off side of rotor faces cam ring, and the cast-in half arrow indicates direction of rotor rotation.

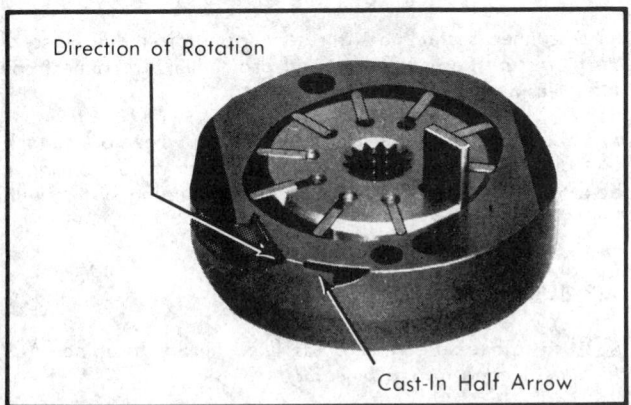

Fig. 10   Mark Showing Direction of Rotation

3) Remove drive end face plate and "O" ring. If it should be necessary to remove input shaft, proceed as follows: Remove pulley, shaft seal, and snap ring from housing. Remove circlip and press ball bearing off of shaft. Using a mandrel, press bearing sleeve out of housing.

4) Remove plug from pressure valve bore, then remove coil spring and valve piston. Note that threaded section on valve piston faces coil spring.

CAUTION — *Do not alter length of coil spring or thickness of plug sealing ring.*

5) The valve tolerance group (1 or 2) is stamped into housing adjacent to pressure valve bore and valve barrel should be scribed with one or two marks (lines) agreeing with group number stamped into housing.

CAUTION — *If valve must be replaced, install valve of same tolerance group.*

CAUTION — *When disassembling piston, do not clamp across sliding surfaces.*

7) A pressure valve is located inside valve piston (flow limit valve) and thickness of washers determines cut-in range of pressure valve. Maximum pump pressure should not be more than 10% below the value stated on plate attached to pump.

REASSEMBLY

To reassemble, reverse disassembly procedure, replacing all seals and worn components.

TIGHTENING SPECIFICATIONS

Application	Ft. Lbs. (mkg)
Steering Gear to Front Axle	32-35 (4.4-4.8)
Worm End Cover	25 (3.5)
Sector Shaft End Cover	23 (3.1)
Adjusting Screw Counternut	22 (3.0)
Adjusting Screw Lock Nut for Piston Movement	4 (.5)
Steering Pump Mounting	17 (2.4)
Hose Connections	33-37 (4.5-5.1)

CHRYSLER CORP. IMPORTS POWER-ASSISTED RECIRCULATING BALL

Arrow Pickup
Challenger
Colt Wagon
D50 Pickup
Sapporo

DESCRIPTION

POWER STEERING GEAR BOX

The power steering gear box displaces fluid to provide hydraulic pressure assist when turning. A torsion bar transmits road feel to the driver. A one piece rack-piston nut is geared to the sector shaft. An adjusting screw on the shaft maintains backlash between the shaft and the rack-piston. There are 2 sizes of gear boxes, small and large. The small gear boxes are only used with the 1.6L engine. The large gear boxes are used with the 2.0L and the 2.6L engines. Both gear boxes are serviced in the same manner.

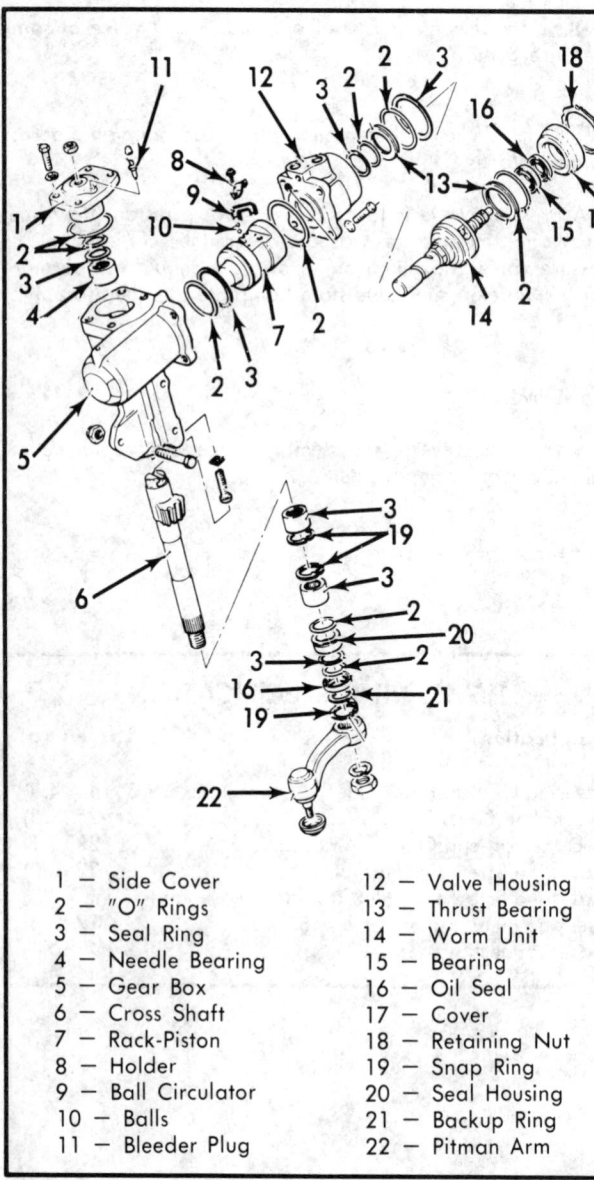

1 — Side Cover	12 — Valve Housing
2 — "O" Rings	13 — Thrust Bearing
3 — Seal Ring	14 — Worm Unit
4 — Needle Bearing	15 — Bearing
5 — Gear Box	16 — Oil Seal
6 — Cross Shaft	17 — Cover
7 — Rack-Piston	18 — Retaining Nut
8 — Holder	19 — Snap Ring
9 — Ball Circulator	20 — Seal Housing
10 — Balls	21 — Backup Ring
11 — Bleeder Plug	22 — Pitman Arm

Fig. 1 Exploded View of Chrysler Corp. Power Steering Gear (Large and Small Gear Box Same)

POWER STEERING PUMP

There are 3 different pumps used on these models: "A", "B" and "C". The "A" pump uses a retaining ring to hold pump end plate to pump housing and uses a separate reservoir. Pumps "B" and "C" use bolts to hold pump end plate to pump body. Pump "B" uses a separate reservoir while pump "C" uses an integral reservoir. Pump "A" can be used on all models. Pump "B" is only used on Challenger, Colt Wagon and Sapporo models. Pump "C" is only used on pickup models. All pumps are constant displacement vane type and are belt driven by the crankshaft.

LUBRICATION

Capacity

Pumps "A" and "B" — 1.1 qts.
Pump "C" — 1 qt.

Type — ATF Dexron II

ADJUSTMENT

BELT TENSION ADJUSTMENT

With 22 lbs. (10 kg) pressure applied, belt deflection at center of belt should be .250-.375" (7-10 mm).

STEERING WHEEL PLAY

Raise front of vehicle. Start engine and idle at 1000 RPM. With steering wheel in center position check that free play is within 1" (25 mm). If necessary, adjustment can be made at the steering gear housing adjusting bolt.

FLUID REPLACEMENT

1) Disconnect suction hose at reservoir and drain fluid. Disconnect pressure hose at pump and drain fluid. Disconnect coil high tension wire.

2) Raise and support vehicle. Turn steering wheel lock to lock several times while cranking engine to drain fluid from gear box. Reconnect all hoses and fill power steering system with fluid. Bleed system.

AIR BLEEDING

NOTE — *Make sure reservoir is filled before bleeding. Add fluid as needed during bleeding.*

1) Raise and support front of vehicle. Disconnect coil high tension wire. Turn steering wheel lock to lock, 5 or 6 times, while cranking engine.

2) Lower vehicle and install a 20" (500 mm) hose to bleeder screw of gear box. Place other end of hose in a container. Connect coil wire.

3) Start engine and idle. Turn steering wheel to left lock and loosen bleeder screw. Repeat this until no more bubbles appear in container (from hose). Remove hose and tighten

CHRYSLER CORP. IMPORTS POWER-ASSISTED RECIRCULATING BALL (Cont.)

bleeder screw. Check fluid level, add fluid if necessary. Turn steering wheel lock to lock and note that fluid level in reservoir does not change more than .12-.16" (3-4 mm).

CAUTION — *Abrupt rising of fluid level after engine is shut off signals incomplete bleeding. Repeat procedure as needed.*

FLUID PRESSURE TESTING

1) Remove pressure hose from oil pump and attach adapter for special pressure gauge (C3309E). Start engine and place thermometer in reservoir until fluid temperature reaches 122°F (50°C). Bleed system if necessary.

2) Start engine and let idle. Close and then fully open the shut-off valve of the pressure gauge and read fluid pressure. Valve closed pressure for the "A" type of pump should be 1066-1210 psi (75-85 kg/cm²) and 925-1066 psi (65-75 kg/cm²) for "B" and "C" type of pumps. Valve open pressure should be 142 psi (10 kg/cm²) for all pumps.

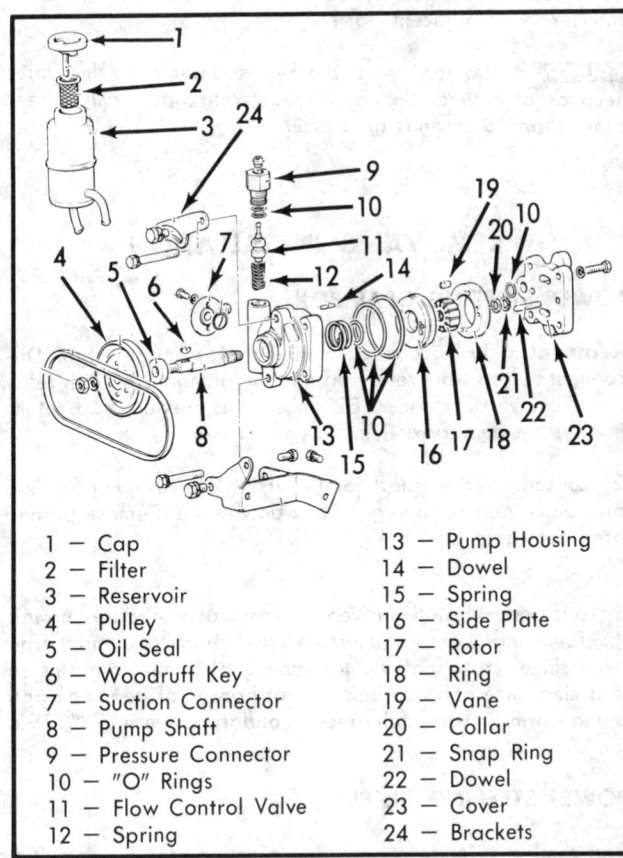

1 — Cap	13 — Pump Housing
2 — Filter	14 — Dowel
3 — Reservoir	15 — Spring
4 — Pulley	16 — Side Plate
5 — Oil Seal	17 — Rotor
6 — Woodruff Key	18 — Ring
7 — Suction Connector	19 — Vane
8 — Pump Shaft	20 — Collar
9 — Pressure Connector	21 — Snap Ring
10 — "O" Rings	22 — Dowel
11 — Flow Control Valve	23 — Cover
12 — Spring	24 — Brackets

Fig. 3 Exploded View of Power Steering Pump (Type "B")

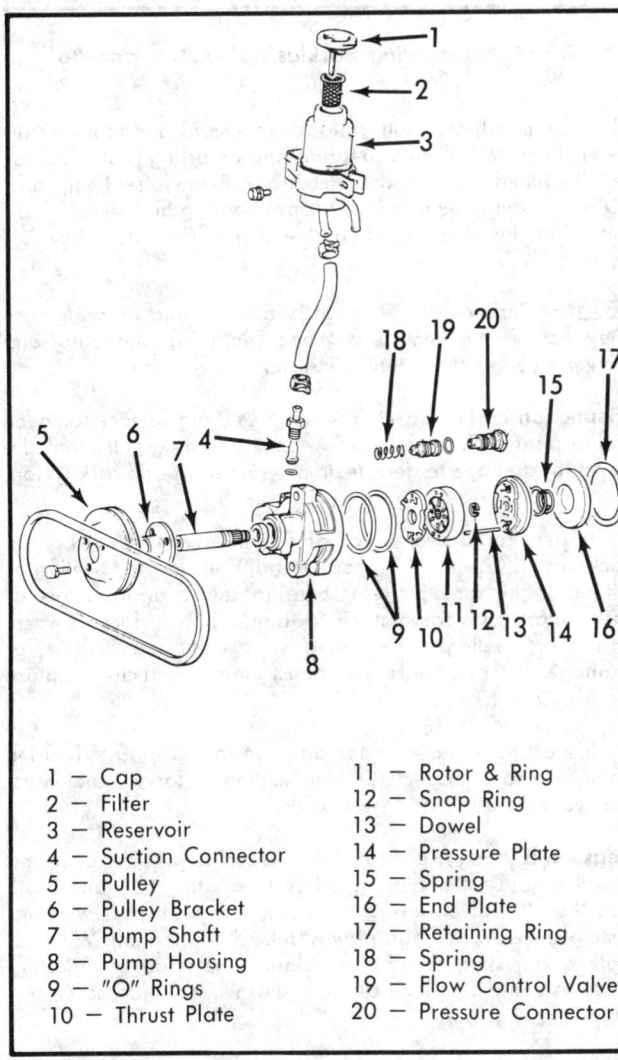

1 — Cap	11 — Rotor & Ring
2 — Filter	12 — Snap Ring
3 — Reservoir	13 — Dowel
4 — Suction Connector	14 — Pressure Plate
5 — Pulley	15 — Spring
6 — Pulley Bracket	16 — End Plate
7 — Pump Shaft	17 — Retaining Ring
8 — Pump Housing	18 — Spring
9 — "O" Rings	19 — Flow Control Valve
10 — Thrust Plate	20 — Pressure Connector

Fig. 2 Exploded View of Power Steering Pump (Type "A")

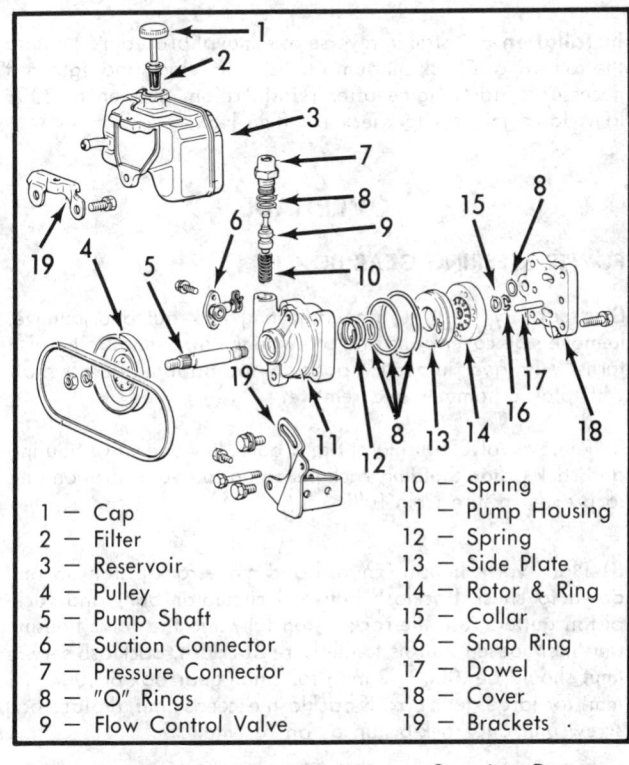

1 — Cap	10 — Spring
2 — Filter	11 — Pump Housing
3 — Reservoir	12 — Spring
4 — Pulley	13 — Side Plate
5 — Pump Shaft	14 — Rotor & Ring
6 — Suction Connector	15 — Collar
7 — Pressure Connector	16 — Snap Ring
8 — "O" Rings	17 — Dowel
9 — Flow Control Valve	18 — Cover
	19 — Brackets

Fig. 4 Exploded View of Power Steering Pump (Type "C")

CHRYSLER CORP. IMPORTS POWER-ASSISTED RECIRCULATING BALL (Cont.)

3) Reinstall pressure hose, taking care not to twist it or make it interfere with adjacent parts.

CAUTION — *Do not keep shut-off valve closed more than three seconds at a time. Do not keep steering wheel fully turned more than 10 seconds at a time.*

REMOVAL & INSTALLATION

POWER STEERING GEAR BOX

Removal — 1) Disconnect steering shaft from gear box. Disconnect tie rod from relay rod and the pitman arm from relay rod. Remove air cleaner. Disconnect the pressure and return hoses from gear box. Remove under-cover.

2) Loosen steering shaft joint bolt, kickdown linkage shield and bolts, and remove gear box downward. Remove pitman arm from gear box.

Installation — Install in reverse of removal procedures, noting the following: When connecting cross shaft to pitman arm, align slit of cross shaft tip to marking of pitman arm. Insure that clearance between bolt hole at bottom of gear box and pitman arm is within tolerance. Standard value is .77" (19.6 mm).

POWER STEERING OIL PUMP

Removal — On power steering pump types "B" and "C", loosen pulley nut before removing belt. On all pumps, remove pulley and belt. Disconnect pressure and suction hoses and cap openings. Remove oil pump attaching bolts and remove pump.

Installation — Install in reverse of removal procedures, noting the following: Check oil pump bracket for slack and tighten if necessary. Start engine after reinstallation and run at 2000 RPM for 5 minutes to check for fluid leaks.

OVERHAUL

POWER STEERING GEAR BOX

Disassembly — 1) Loosen adjusting lock nut and remove. Remove side cover bolts and screw in the adjusting bolt 2 or 3 turns. With gear in neutral position, tap bottom of cross shaft with plastic hammer and remove.

2) Remove valve housing nut and bolts. Remove valve housing and rack piston, holding rack-piston up to avoid rotation and to prevent piston from falling.

3) Place valve housing in vise and move rack-piston up and down to check backlash between circulator balls and rack-piston gutter. Turn the rack-piston fully into the valve housing and then loosen 2 turns to measure backlash. Backlash service limit should be .008" (.2 mm) for small gear box or .004" (.1 mm) for large gear box. If backlash exceeds limit, replace ball screw unit and rack-piston as an assembly.

4) Remove rack-piston by turning counterclockwise. Do not lose circulator balls. Remove top cover and "O" ring from

valve housing. Remove input worm unit from housing. Remove circulator, circulator holder, seal ring and "O" ring from the rack-piston. Remove bearings, plates and rings from input worm unit and valve housing.

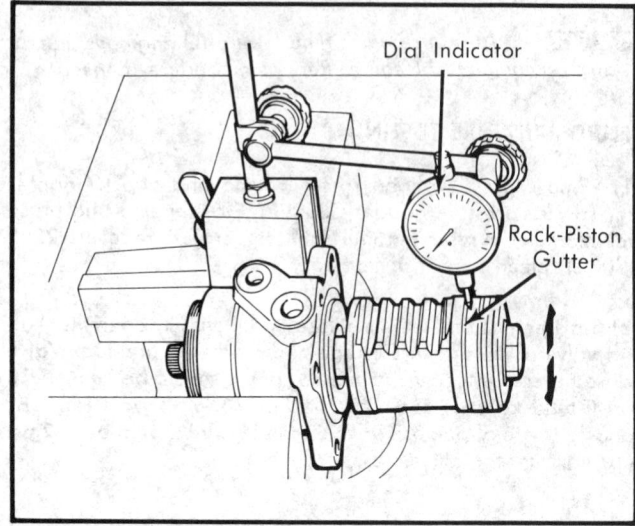

Fig. 5   Measuring Backlash of Gutter and Ball

5) Screw in adjuster bolt at tip of cross shaft and remove side cover. Remove "O" ring, bearing and adjusting plate. Do not remove bleeder plug unless necessary. Remove seal ring and "O" ring from valve housing. Remove bearing and oil seal from top cover. Remove oil seal and seal ring from gear box.

NOTE — *Replace all "O" rings, seal rings and oil seals once they have been removed. When replacing, lubricate with power steering fluid before insertion.*

Inspection — 1) Inspect cross shaft bearing surface for peeling or pitting. Check stepped wear of adjusting bolt shank. Inspect for damage to gear teeth on cross shaft and rack-piston.

2) Inspect for uneven wear of circulator rolling surface on rack-piston. Check for damage to balls. Inspect for peeling or pitting on thrust needle roller bearing, and bearing surface of thrust plate on worm unit. Check ball rolling surface of worm shaft for peeling and sealing surface of input shaft for damage. If thrust bearing or thrust plate is defective, replace both as a set.

3) Inspect valve housing for damage to seal ring-to-housing contact surface. Inspect "O" ring sealing surface of seal housing, valve housing and side cover.

Reassembly — 1) Lubricate bearing surface of side cover and install needle roller bearings. Insert adjusting bolt and plate into the" T" slot on top of cross shaft, and set play with adjusting shims. Cross shaft play is 0-.002" (0-0.5 mm). When installing adjusting shims place chamfered edge of adjusting plate to contact surface of cross shaft. Install side cover "O" ring. *See Fig. 6.*

2) Align cross shaft with side cover and tighten with adjusting bolt. Tighten lock nut temporarily. Install ball bearing and oil seal in top cover. Gently insert "O" ring and seal ring into seal housing and install housing in gear box with "O" ring side

CHRYSLER CORP. IMPORTS POWER-ASSISTED RECIRCULATING BALL (Cont.)

toward the main shaft. Install oil seal back-up ring and snap ring in gear box.

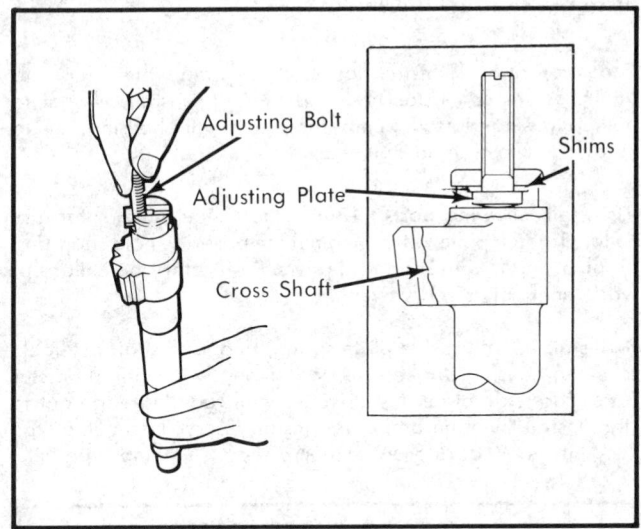

Fig. 6   Adjusting the Cross Shaft "T" Slot

3) Install "O" ring and seal ring to input worm shaft. Install thrust plates and needle bearings in input worm unit.

NOTE — *Install top cover side thrust plate with smaller outside diameter first.*

4) Install "O" ring and seal ring into valve housing. Fit 2 "O" rings in groove at end of valve housing. Install input worm unit in valve housing. Fit top cover "O" ring, and install top cover to valve housing. Tighten nut. Measure input worm unit preload. Torque should be 2.2-5.8 INCH lbs. (2.5-6.6 cmkg). Adjust, if necessary, by loosening valve housing nut and retightening.

5) Fit "O" ring and seal ring to rack-piston. Insert rack-piston into worm unit and turn worm unit to align ball sliding surfaces. Install 19 balls, into small gear box or 20 balls into large gear box, into rack-piston through the 2 openings.

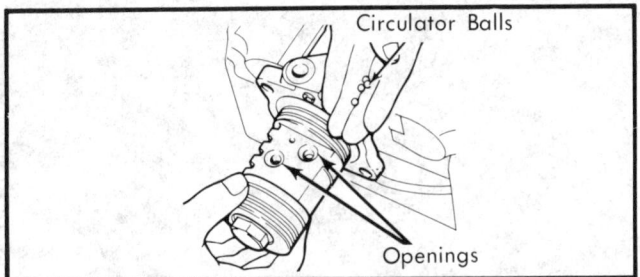

Fig. 7   Installing Circulator Balls to Rack-Piston

NOTE — *Do not move rack-piston when installing balls, as balls may fall into wrong groove.*

6) After installing specified number of balls, measure distance from rack-piston to the ball. If distance is more than .5" (13 mm) on small gear box or .08" (2 mm) on large gear box, this

indicates a ball has fallen into wrong groove. Remove balls then reinstall them, being sure all balls are installed correctly. Insert remaining 7 balls (on small gear box) or 6 balls (on large gear box) and install circulator holder.

7) Install rack-piston of the ball screw unit assembly to gear box and tighten. Install seal ring of rack-piston and place rack-piston in neutral (center) position. Install cross shaft and side cover and tighten.

8) Measure starting torque of input shaft and adjust to 4.3-7.8 INCH lbs. (5.1-9.2 cmkg) on large gear box or to 3.5-7.0 INCH lbs. (4.1-8.2 cmkg) on small gear box. Tighten valve housing nut. Measure preload after tightening. Connect cross shaft with pitman arm.

POWER STEERING PUMP

Disassembly (Pump Type "A") — 1) Remove pulley bracket with puller then remove suction connector. Remove pressure connector. Remove retaining ring using small punch inserted in hole of pump housing, opposite flow control valve hole, and then pry out ring with screwdriver.

2) Remove end plate and "O" ring. Remove flow control valve and spring. Tap on pump shaft with plastic hammer just enough to loosen pressure plate. Remove pressure plate, pump shaft, ring, vanes and rotor.

Inspection — Check flow control valve, rotor and ring, end plates and pump shaft for damage, scoring or excessive wear. Inspect pump housing for cracks or signs of visual damage. Check "O" ring seats for scratches or burrs. Inspect pump shaft bushing, in pump housing. If bushing is damaged, replace pump housing. Replace any parts necessary. If any internal pump parts are found to be damaged, flush steering gear or disassemble and clean gear.

NOTE — *Lubricate "O" rings and all internal pump components with ATF Dexron II fluid before reassembly.*

Reassembly — 1) Install new pump shaft seal in pump housing. Install new pressure plate "O" ring to 3rd groove from end of pump housing. Insert both dowel pins into pump housing. Install thrust plate and rotor to pump shaft, then install new snap ring to pump shaft. Make sure rotor is installed with countersunk side toward thrust plate.

2) Install pump shaft into pump housing, making sure thrust plate slides over dowel pins properly. Install ring into pump housing, over dowel pins and with arrow (on ring) toward rear of pump housing. Install vanes in rotor and make sure rounded edge of vanes face outward.

3) Install pressure plate into pump housing and over dowel pins. Make sure circular depression (for spring) is toward rear of housing. Install new "O" ring in 2nd groove from rear of pump housing. Place spring on pressure plate, then install end plate to pump housing. Depress end plate just enough to install retaining ring. Make sure retaining ring seats properly.

Disassembly (Pump Types "B" & "C") — 1) Remove Woodruff key from pump shaft on pump type "B" or the reservoir from pump type "C". On both types of pumps, place pump housing in vise, loosen and remove pump cover. Remove snap

CHRYSLER CORP. IMPORTS POWER-ASSISTED RECIRCULATING BALL (Cont.)

ring, then take out following parts from pump body: collar, ring, rotor, vanes, "O" rings, dowel, side plate and side plate spring.

2) Measure clearance between shaft and pump body. If clearance is more than .0035" (.09 mm), replace pump body as an assembly. Remove pump shaft by tapping it with a plastic hammer. Remove oil seal and suction connector. Remove pressure connector, flow control valve, spring and "O" rings.

Inspection — 1) Inspect pump shaft oil seal lip and bushing end for damage. Inspect groove of rotor vane and cam surface for stepped wear. Check vane for damage and ring and rotor sides for grooving. Replace entire assembly if any damage is seen.

2) Inspect side plate and pump cover for grooving. Check side plate spring. Minimum length should be .61" (15.5 mm) for

pump type "B" or .67" (17 mm) for pump type "C". Check flow control spring. Minimum length should be 1.95" (49.5 mm) for both types of pumps. Check sliding surfaces and ports of flow control valve for obstructions.

Reassembly — 1) Install flow control spring, valve, "O" ring and pressure connector to pump housing. Install oil seal to pump housing. Install pump shaft to pump housing, being careful not to damage oil seal.

2) Install following parts to pump shaft: side plate, rotor and collar. Tighten pulley attaching nut temporarily, hold snap ring on pump shaft with snap ring pliers. Push rotor and collar upward until collar seats over snap ring.

3) Install "O" ring, side plate spring, ring, and shaft assembly to pump housing. Make sure side of ring with small diameter bores face side plate. Install vanes with rounded edge out to ring. Install "O" ring and cover. Install reservoir on pump type "C". Install Woodruff key to pump shaft on pump type "B".

Fig. 8   Measuring Clearance Between Shaft and Pump Body

TIGHTENING SPECIFICATIONS

Application	Ft. Lbs. (mkg)
Gear Box-to-Frame	40-47 (5.5-6.5)
Oil Pump Cover	22-29 (3.0-4.0)
Pitman Arm-to-Cross Shaft	94-109 (13.0-15.1)
Pressure Connector	51-72 (7.1-10.0)
Side Cover	33-40 (4.6-5.5)
Valve Housing	33-40 (4.6-5.5)
Valve Housing Nut	130-166 (18.0-23.0)

DATSUN POWER-ASSISTED RECIRCULATING BALL

200SX
280ZX
810

DESCRIPTION

Power steering is composed of a power steering pump, steering gear and connecting hoses. The pump has an integral reservoir on 280ZX and 810 models or a separate reservoir on the 200SX models. Power steering gear is an integral unit consisting of a spool valve and power cylinder (worm shaft ball nut assembly) connected to the sector shaft. Power steering gear is pressure operated by the pump through the connecting lines.

GENERAL SERVICE

HYDRAULIC SYSTEM LUBRICANT

Capacity
200SX — 1.25 qt.
280ZX — .63 qt.
810 — 1.06 qt.

Type — ATF Type DEXRON

BELT TENSION ADJUSTMENT

Apply thumb pressure of 22 lbs. (10 kg) midway between idler pulley and power steering pump pulley. Deflection should be .31-.47" (8-12 mm).

HYDRAULIC SYSTEM PRESSURE CHECK

1) Disconnect pressure line at pump and connect pressure gauge and shut-off valve. Check fluid level, open shut-off valve and run engine for about five seconds. Check fluid level and restart engine.

2) Turn steering wheel from lock-to-lock several times to expel air from system and to allow fluid to reach normal operating temperature. Slowly close shut-off valve. Pressure at idle, should be 782 psi (55 kg/cm^2) for 200SX models or 953-1123 psi (67-79 kg/cm^2) for 280ZX and 810 models.

NOTE — *Do not close shut-off valve for more than 15 seconds, as this may result in undue pump wear and abnormally increased lubricant temperature.*

3) If pressure is below specifications, the pump is faulty. If pressure is above specifications, the pressure relief valve in pump is faulty. In either case, replace pump.

HYDRAULIC SYSTEM BLEEDING

Check fluid level in reservoir, raise and support front of vehicle. With engine not running, turn steering wheel from lock-to-lock several times. Check fluid level, start engine and turn steering wheel from lock-to-lock several times. If system is not bled, turn steering wheel to left lock and open bleeder screw to expel remaining air.

ADJUSTMENT

BACKLASH

On Car — 1) Place vehicle on level dry surface, inflate tires to specified pressure and run engine until power steering fluid is at normal operating temperature.

2) With steering wheel in straight ahead (centered) position, turn steering wheel 1 complete turn (360°). Attach spring gauge to outer rim of wheel and measure turning force. Turning force should be 6.6-7.7 lbs. (3.0-3.5 kg). If turning force is not to specifications, remove steering gear and check turning torque of steering gear.

Off Car — 1) With steering gear removed from car, mount gear to a plate that can be clamped in a vise or to special tool KV48100300. Attach a torque wrench to worm shaft splines (where steering shaft connects) and center steering gear.

NOTE — *Center position can be found by turning gear to full lock position then turning back 2⅛ turns.*

2) Measure turning torque of steering gear 360° from center position. Torque should be 10 INCH lbs. (12 cmkg). Then turn worm shaft back to center position and measure torque. Torque at this point should be .9-1.7 INCH lbs. (1-2 cmkg) more than torque measured at 360° from center position on 810 models, or .9-3.5 INCH lbs. (1-4 cmkg) more on 200SX and 280ZX models.

3) If turning torque is not to specifications, loosen adjusting bolt lock nut and turn (always tighten to adjust) adjusting bolt until correct turning torque specification is obtained. If the correct turning torque cannot be obtained, replace steering gear.

REMOVAL & INSTALLATION

STEERING GEAR

Removal — 1) Remove air cleaner, remove bolt from universal joint to worm shaft. Disconnect fluid lines and plug them to prevent fluid spillage. Remove nut and washer from sector shaft.

2) Remove pitman arm from sector shaft using a puller. Remove steering gear mounting bolts, then remove steering gear from vehicle.

Installation — To install, reverse removal procedure and note the following: Align groove in worm shaft with bolt hole in universal joint and pass bolt through undercut section of worm shaft.

STEERING PUMP

Removal — Disconnect fluid lines at pump and block off fittings. Remove pump mounting bolts and remove drive belt from pulley. Remove pump from vehicle.

Installation — To install, reverse removal procedure.

OVERHAUL

NOTE — *Overhaul of steering gear is limited to oil seal replacement. If any further repair is necessary, replace entire steering gear assembly. Always check turning torque before disassembly.*

ADJUSTING SCREW SEAL REPLACEMENT

Remove adjusting screw lock nut. Remove "O" ring from lock nut. Grease new "O" ring and insert in lock nut. Make sure "O" ring is installed correctly, then replace lock nut to adjusting screw. Adjust steering gear turning torque.

NOTE — *Always use new copper washer when adjusting screw lock nut is removed.*

DATSUN POWER-ASSISTED RECIRCULATING BALL (Cont.)

SECTOR SHAFT SEAL REPLACEMENT

Disassembly — 1) With steering gear assembly mounted in a vise, set sector shaft to center position. Remove sector shaft cover bolts. Using a mallet, tap sector shaft out approximately ¾" (.79 mm).

NOTE — *Wrap a piece of plastic film (stiff) around the sector shaft, approximately the same diameter as the sector shaft and approximately 8" (200 mm) long. This will prevent bearings from falling into gear housing.*

2) Pull sector shaft from gear housing, at same time pull plastic film into gear housing. Remove snap ring from gear housing and remove dust seal, special large washer, oil seal and special small washer. Remove "O" ring from sector shaft cover.

Reassembly — 1) Install new special small washer, oil seal, special large washer, dust seal and snap ring to gear housing. Be sure to grease oil seal and dust seal. Also make sure radius side of snap ring faces inside of gear housing.

2) Install new "O" ring to sector shaft cover. Make sure worm shaft and rack piston is in centered position. Wrap splined and threaded portions of sector shaft, with tape, to prevent damage to oil seal.

3) Slowly insert sector shaft into gear housing, pushing plastic film out and being careful not to damage oil seal. With sector shaft fully installed, plastic film removed and components operating smoothly, install and tighten sector shaft cover bolts. Check and adjust steering gear turning torque.

REAR HOUSING SEAL REPLACEMENT

Disassembly — 1) Install steering gear assembly to mounting plate and place in a vise. Loosen rear cover bolts approximately .20" (5 mm), do not remove bolts. Turn sector shaft clockwise slightly to raise rear cover through piston.

2) Place piston and worm shaft in center position and remove sector shaft. See *Sector Shaft Seal Replacement* for removal procedures. Remove rear housing bolts and pull out rear housing with intermediate cover and worm gear assembly.

NOTE — *When worm assembly is removed, piston may turn and come off under its own weight. Hold piston to prevent this. Do not damage Teflon ring at piston end when removing.*

3) Turn worm assembly upside down and lightly tap worm shaft against bench to remove rear housing. Remove rear housing oil seal. Remove large and small "O" rings from both sides of intermediate cover.

Reassembly — 1) Lubricate and install rear housing oil seal, sector shaft oil seal and intermediate cover "O" rings. Install worm assembly into rear housing then into gear housing.

CAUTION — *Be careful not to damage Teflon ring at rear of piston when installing.*

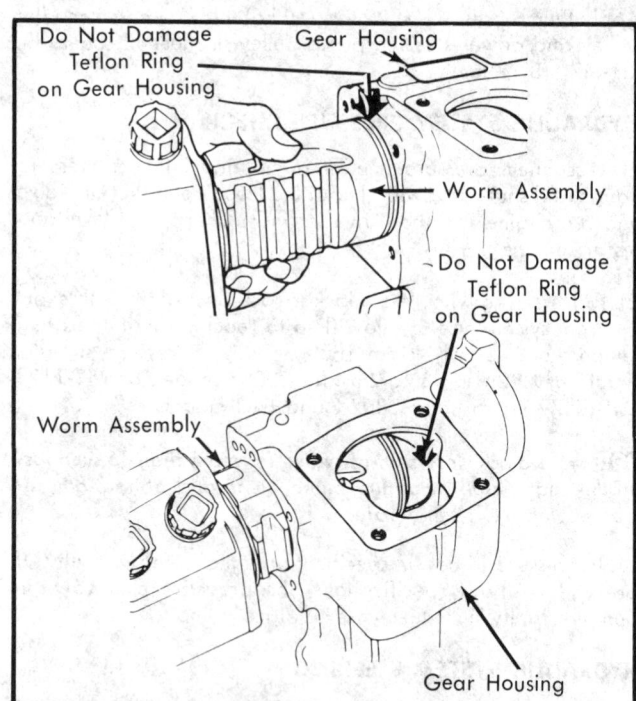

Fig. 2　Installing Worm Assembly to Gear Housing

2) Tighten rear cover bolts in a crisscross pattern. Install sector shaft. See *Sector Shaft Seal Replacement* for installation procedures. Make sure steering gear operates smoothly, then check and adjust turning torque.

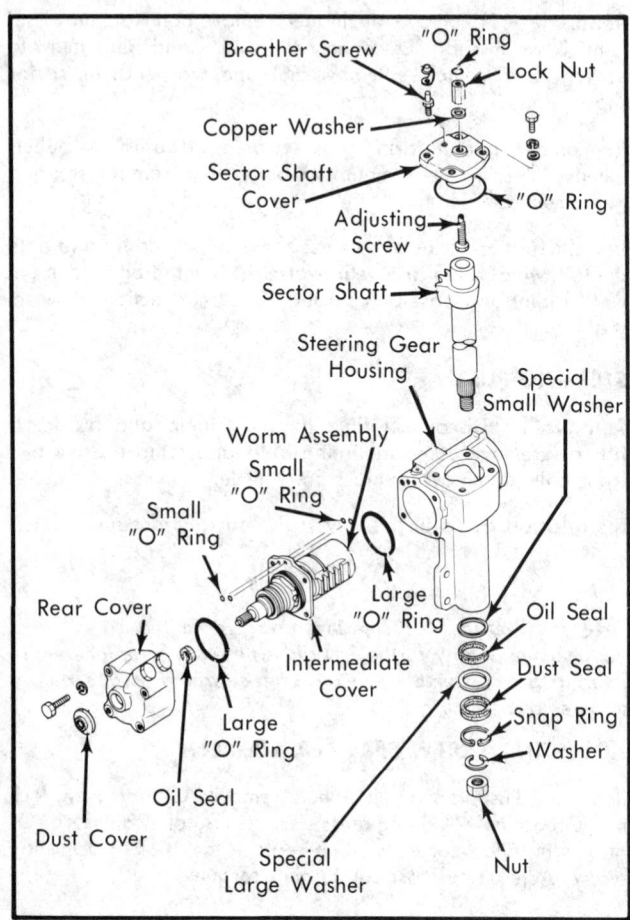

Fig. 1　Exploded View of Datsun Power Steering Gear

TIGHTENING SPECIFICATIONS

Application	Ft. Lbs. (mkg)
Hose-to-Gear Housing	36-51 (5.0-7.0)
Rear Cover Bolts	20-24 (2.7-3.3)
Sector Shaft-to-Pitman Arm Nut	94-108 (13.0-15.0)

FIAT POWER-ASSISTED RACK & PINION

Brava

DESCRIPTION

A power-assisted rack and pinion steering gear is optional on Fiat Brava models. The system consists of a vane pump, rotary piston pinion gear assembly and an oil reservoir. The vane pump draws fluid from the reservoir and supplies it to the flow control valve. The control valve supplies fluid to the proper side of the rack/piston as the steering wheel is turned. The pump is belt driven and mounted on the lower right front side of the engine. The reservoir is located near the battery.

GENERAL SERVICE

Capacity — 1.9 pt.

Lubricant — ATF Type A

Oil Level Check — Remove wing nut and cover from reservoir. With engine stopped, level should reach mark on side of reservoir. With engine idling, level must not be more than .39" (10 mm) below mark.

Hydraulic System Bleeding — Start engine and allow to idle. Check that fluid is at proper level. Turn steering wheel from lock to lock several times quickly. Continue until fluid level remains at reservoir mark. Make sure that no bubbles appear in reservoir when steering wheel is turned. Shut off engine and check that oil level does not rise more than ⅜" above mark.

Oil Filter Replacement — Remove wing nut, outer cover, gasket and spring from reservoir. Remove inner filter cover and filter insert. Replace filter. Install new filter, replace filter cover, spring, gasket, cover and wing nut. Check fluid level.

REMOVAL & INSTALLATION

STEERING GEAR

Removal — **1)** Remove nut securing tie rod end in steering knuckle. Using appropriate tool (A-47033), remove ball joint from steering knuckle. Repeat operation for other side. Loosen clamp and remove fluid return line from steering gear. Allow fluid to drain. Remove banjo bolt and washers from supply line and allow fluid to drain.

2) Remove bolt and nut securing universal joint to steering gear. Remove left steering gear mounting bolt at crossmember. Remove 2 right steering gear mounting bolts at crossmember. Remove power steering gear.

Installation — To install, reverse removal procedure and tighten. Fill system with fluid and bleed system if necessary.

VANE PUMP

Removal — Remove vane pump tensioner bolt and mounting bolt. Remove vane pump drive belt. Remove vane pump.

Installation — To install, reverse removal procedure and fill system with fluid. Bleed system if necessary.

OVERHAUL

NOTE — *Manufacturer does not recommend overhaul of steering gear.*

TIGHTENING SPECIFICATIONS

Application	Ft. Lbs. (mkg)
Steering Arm Ball Joint Nut	25 (3.5)
Steering Gear-to-Body Bolt	18 (2.5)
Ball Joint Collar	36 (5.0)
Universal Joint Clamp Nut	18 (2.5)

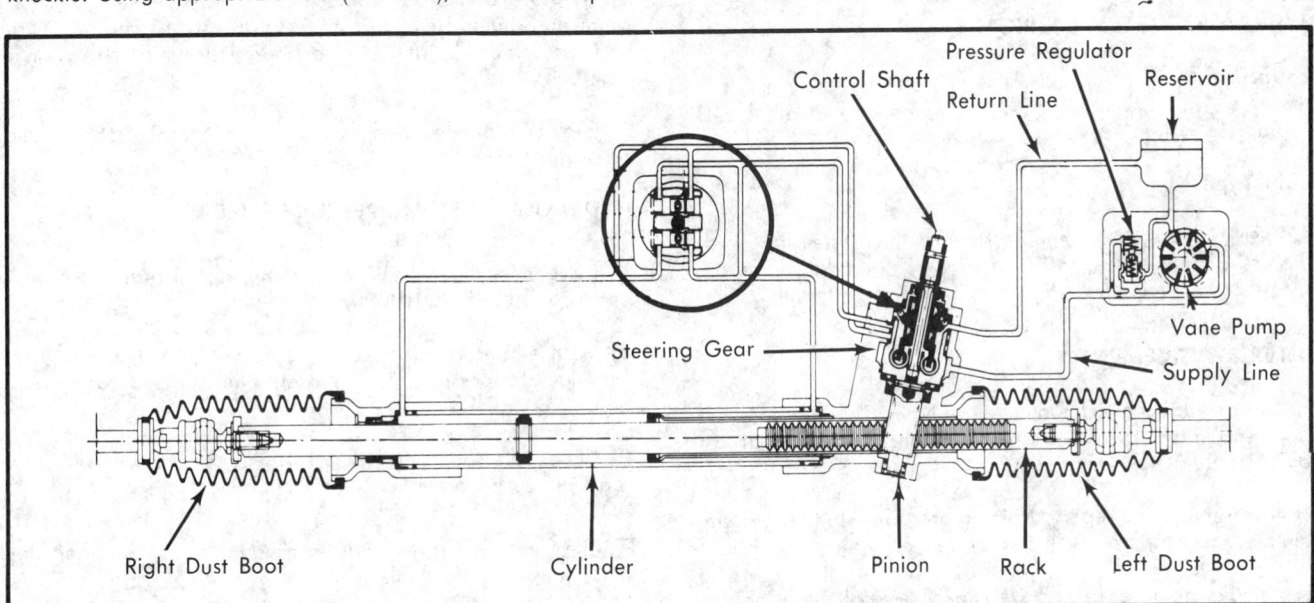

Fig. 1 Schematic of Fiat Brava Power Steering System

HONDA POWER-ASSISTED RACK & PINION

Accord
LX
4-Door

DESCRIPTION

Power steering is rack and pinion with the power assist proportional to both vehicle speed and steering load. Power assist is high when vehicle speed is low and reduces as vehicle speed increases. The system consists of a power rack and pinion steering gear, steering pump, fluid reservoir, fluid cooler, vehicle speed sensor and connecting lines and hoses.

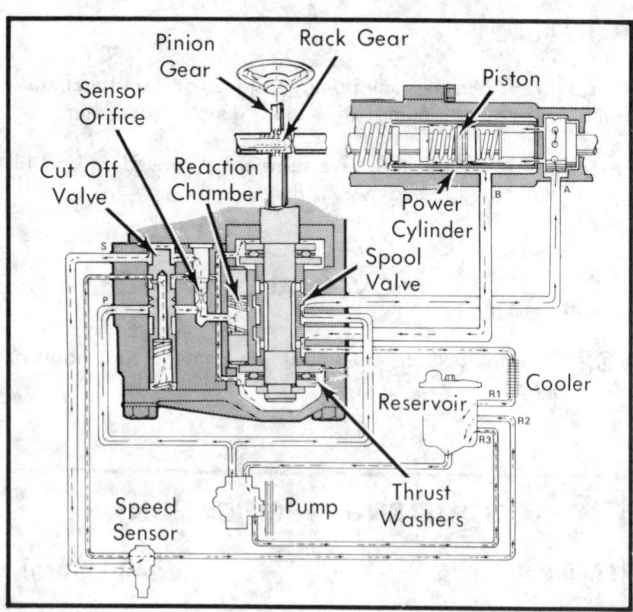

Fig. 1   Sectional View of Power Steering Pump and Power Steering Gear

GENERAL SERVICE

HYDRAULIC SYSTEM LUBRICANT

Capacity

Reservoir	.85 qts. (.8 liter)
Complete System	2.1 qts. (2 liters)

Fluid Type

CAUTION – Use only genuine Honda power steering fluid. The use of any other fluids, such as ATF or other manufacturer's power steering fluid, will cause damage to the system.

FILTER REPLACEMENT

1) To drain, disconnect cooler return hose from reservoir and place end in a suitable container. Start engine and run at fast idle until fluid flow stops.

2) Fill reservoir and repeat draining procedure to flush system. Remove reservoir from vehicle before removing guide bolt.

3) Remove guide bolt. Remove clip on end of guide bolt to remove filter and remaining components, noting their respective positions.

4) Clean and inspect all parts. Replace worn or defective parts. Carefully reassemble components to reservoir, making sure that retaining clip seats in filter recess. Install reservoir in vehicle.

5) Fill reservoir with fluid, start engine and run at fast idle. Turn steering wheel lock-to-lock several times to bleed air from system. Check fluid and add, if necessary.

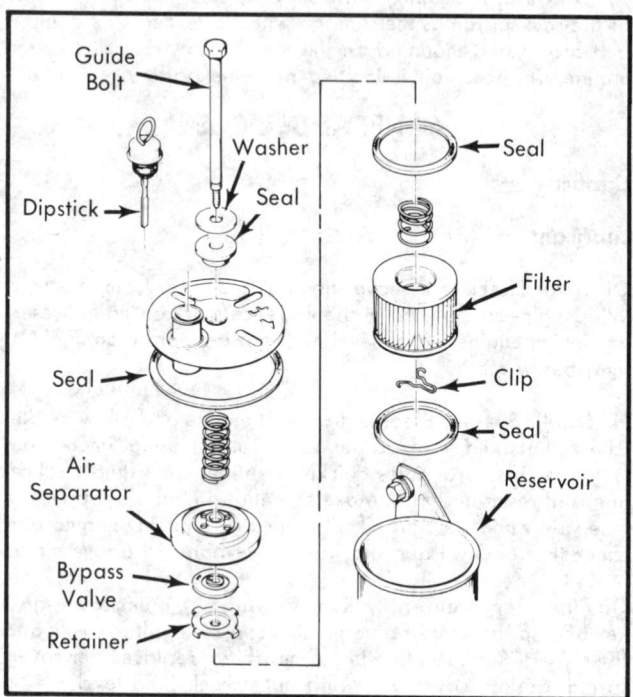

Fig. 2   Power Steering Reservoir Components

BELT TENSION ADJUSTMENT

1) Measure pump belt deflection midway between pulleys. Deflection should be 9/16" at 22 lbs. pressure (13 mm at 10 kg) on used belt or 7/16" at 22 lbs. pressure (11 mm at 10 kg) on a new belt.

2) Replace belt when pump adjusting bolt reaches "bump" on adjusting bracket.

HYDRAULIC SYSTEM PRESSURE CHECK

1) Disconnect outlet hose from pump. Install pressure gauge and valve (07406-0010000).

2) With engine running, open valve and turn steering wheel from lock to lock several times until fluid is at operating temperature.

3) Check idle speed and adjust if necessary. Close valve and read pressure gauge.

CAUTION – Do not keep valve closed for more than 5 seconds or pump could be damaged by overheating.

4) Pump pressure should be at least 980 psi (70 kg/cm²). If pump pressure is too low, replace pump.

HONDA POWER-ASSISTED RACK & PINION (Cont.)

5) Open valve fully and turn steering wheel to full left lock. Read gauge, then turn wheel to full right lock and read gauge. Both readings should be at least 980 psi (70 kg/cm²). A low reading indicates rack and pinion housing or speed sensor is defective. Check speed sensor (as described later), if sensor is OK, replace steering gear assembly.

SPEED SENSOR CHECK

Low Speed Assist — 1) Start engine and let idle. Attach spring tension scale to steering wheel (outer end of spoke). Vehicle should be on a clean dry surface. Turn steering wheel with the tension gauge and check reading.

2) Reading should be no more than 6 lbs. (2.7 kg). If reading is higher than specified, disconnect and plug large diameter hose running from steering gear to speed sensor.

3) Measure pull as described above. If scale reads less than with hose connected, the sensor is defective and should be replaced.

High Speed Assist — 1) With power steering fluid at normal operating temperature, stop engine and disconnect all 3 sensor hoses (at speed sensor) and connect special by-pass tool (07406-0010100) to the 3 hoses. This tool simulates driving speeds over 30 MPH. Start engine.

2) Measure steering effort as described previously. If turning force is 11 lbs. (5.0 kg) or more, replace speed sensor. If turning force is less than 11 lbs. (5.0 kg), speed sensor is OK. Check for a restriction in sensor feed line. If sensor feed line is OK, replace steering gear assembly.

STEERING SHAFT MOVEMENT CHECK

1) With engine not running, turn steering wheel to left and then to right. Steering wheel cover should move closer to or further away from turn signal cover.

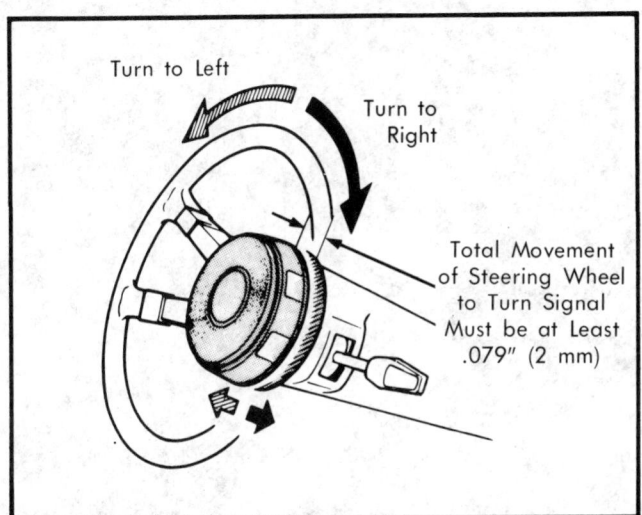

Fig. 3 Checking Steering Shaft Movement

Turn to Left

Turn to Right

Total Movement of Steering Wheel to Turn Signal Must be at Least .079" (2 mm)

2) Movement of steering wheel should be at least .079" (2 mm) for proper spool valve operation.

3) If the steering wheel moves only in or only out, but not both, loosen the 3 bolts in the steering shaft connector. Adjust shaft and make sure that shaft slides freely in column. Retighten bolts.

4) If adjustment does not allow correct movement of steering wheel, replace rack and pinion gears.

ADJUSTMENT

RACK PISTON ADJUSTMENT

Loosen rack screw lock nut. Tighten rack screw until rack piston is lightly bottomed. Loosen rack screw 45° from bottomed position, then tighten lock nut while holding rack screw from turning.

REMOVAL & INSTALLATION

STEERING GEAR

Removal — 1) Disconnect tie rods from steering knuckles. Disconnect exhaust pipe at manifold.

2) On manual transmission models only, shift transmission to 1st or 3rd gear. Disconnect shift linkage by removing shift rod yoke bolt. Remove crossmember (center). Disconnect shift lever torque arm from transmission.

3) On automatic transmission models only, remove center engine mount and transmission splash guard. Disconnect control cable from transmission.

4) Disconnect the following lines from power steering gear:

- Hose to right side of power cylinder.
- Hose to left side of power cylinder.
- Hose from power steering pump.
- Hose to power steering cooler.
- Hose to speed sensor.
- Hose from speed sensor.

5) Turn steering wheel to full left and remove bottom bolt in steering shaft connector. Remove steering gear brackets.

6) Lower steering gear to pull pinion out of connector, then move to right until left tie rod drops out of subframe. Remove steering gear to left.

Installation — To install steering gear, reverse removal procedure.

STEERING PUMP

Removal — 1) Drain fluid from system. Disconnect inlet and outlet hoses at pump. Remove power steering belt by loosening the pump pivot and adjusting bolts.

2) Remove pump mounting bolts, bracket and power steering pump.

Power Steering

HONDA POWER-ASSISTED RACK & PINION (Cont.)

Installation — **1)** To install steering pump, reverse removal procedures. Full reservoir to full mark on dipstick with new fluid.

CAUTION — *Use only genuine Honda power steering fluid. The use of other fluids, such as ATF or other manufacturer's power steering fluid, will cause damage to the system.*

2) Start engine and let run at fast idle while turning the steering wheel lock to lock several times to bleed air from system.

SPEED SENSOR

Removal — **1)** Lift speedometer cable boot up to gain access to retaining clip. Remove retaining clip and pull out cable.

2) Disconnect and plug speed sensor hoses, back off speedometer gear set bolt. Lift speed sensor out.

Installation — After installing new sensor, turn steering wheel from lock to lock several times (engine idling), to bleed air from system.

OVERHAUL

NOTE — *Power steering pump, steering gear and speed sensor cannot be overhauled. These items must be replaced as an assembly. Steering pump shaft seal can be replaced.*

POWER STEERING PUMP SHAFT SEAL

Remove power steering pump belt. Remove pump pulley. Remove oil seal. Coat new seal and pump shaft with clean fluid and install seal on pump shaft. Be careful not to scratch or damage inner part of seal.

TIGHTENING SPECIFICATIONS

Application	Ft. Lbs. (mkg)
Rack Screw Lock Nut	32 (4.4)
Steering Shaft Clamp Bolt	22 (3.0)
Tie Rod Nut	32 (4.4)

Power Steering

JAGUAR & TRIUMPH POWER-ASSISTED RACK & PINION

Jaguar
XJ6
Triumph
TR8

DESCRIPTION

Vehicles are equipped with a power assisted rack and pinion type steering system. The system consists of two main components: the rack and pinion steering gear and the power assist pump. The two components are connected by flexible fluid lines. The power assist pump and fluid reservoir are combined.

LUBRICANT

Type — ATF Dexron II

Intervals — Check power steering fluid every 3,000 miles.

TESTING

Control Valve & Pinion (Jaguar Only) — 1) Connect a 100 psi (7 kg/cm²) pressure gauge into pump return line, start engine and allow to idle. Pressure reading should be approximately 40 psi (2.8 kg/cm²). Turn steering gear left and right a small amount.

CAUTION — *Excessive turning of steering gear will cause gauge damage.*

2) Pressure should increase equal amounts as wheel is turned in either direction. A slight fall in pressure occurring before rise in pressure indicates a defective control valve. Stop and restart engine and check that steering does not kick to one side.

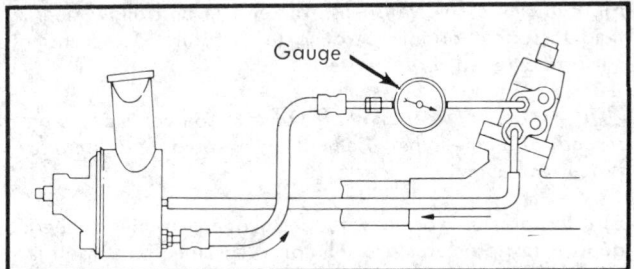

Fig. 1 Pressure Gauge Connection

Hydraulic System — 1) Connect a 1500 psi (100 kg/cm²) pressure gauge into the pump pressure line, start engine and allow to idle.

2) Turn steering to full lock and exert pressure on steering gear. On Jaguar, pressure should be 1100-1200 psi (77.5-84.4 kg/cm²) at idle. On Triumph, pressure should be a minimum of 450 psi (32 kg/cm²) at idle and 950-1000 psi (67-70 kg/cm²) at 1000 RPM.

NOTE — *On Jaguar models, if pressure is below 1100 psi (77.5 kg/cm²) at idle, but rises with engine speed increase, problem is either a defective pump control valve or internal leakage in rack and pinion.*

3) On Triumph, release steering wheel and allow to come off full lock position. Pressure reading should be a maximum of 55 psi (4 kg/cm²) at idle.

4) If system pressure readings were not to specifications, connect a shut-off valve (JD. 10-2) between pump and pressure gauge. This will isolate steering pump from steering gear and determine if problem is in gear or pump.

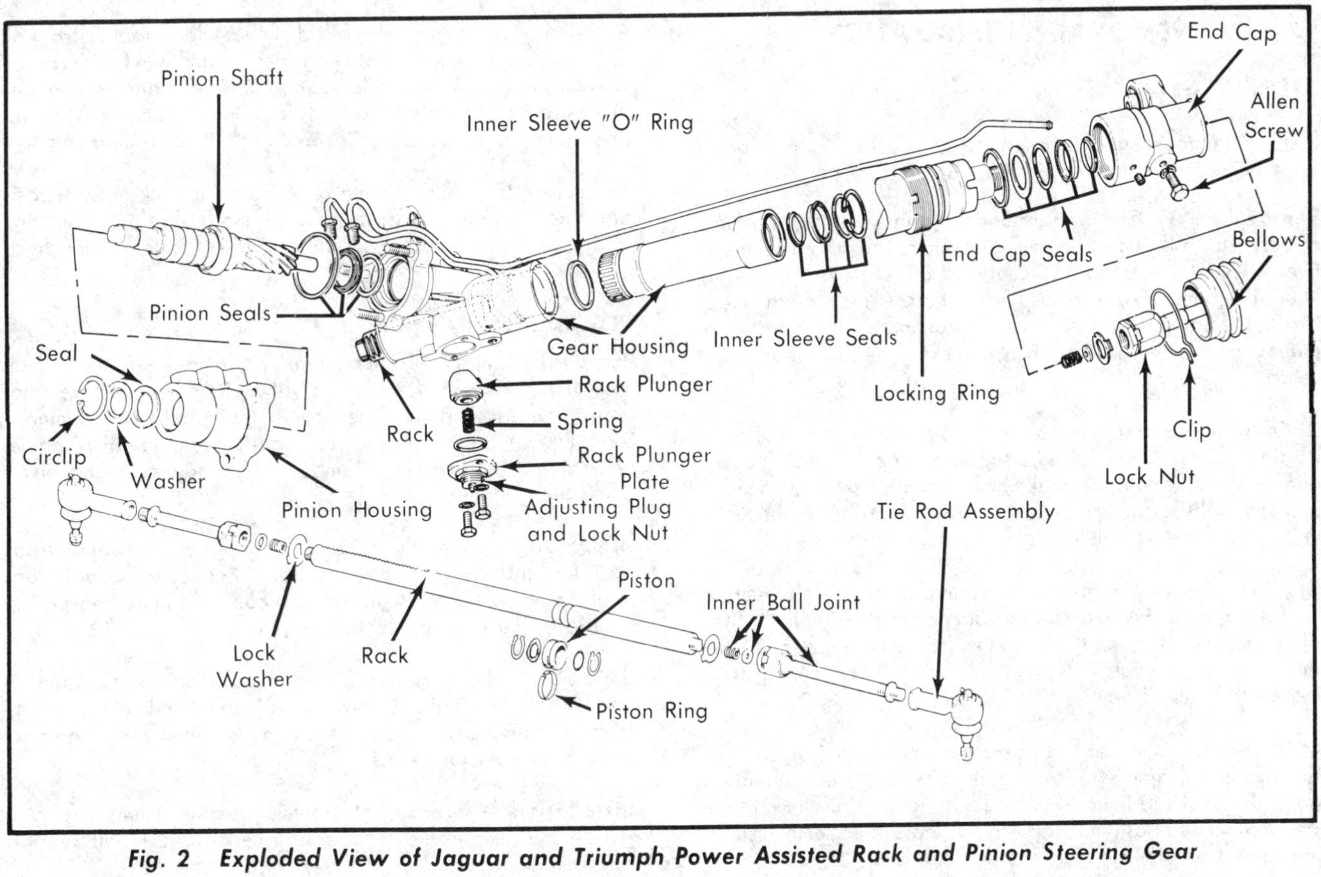

Fig. 2 Exploded View of Jaguar and Triumph Power Assisted Rack and Pinion Steering Gear

JAGUAR & TRIUMPH POWER-ASSISTED RACK & PINION (Cont.)

5) With shut-off valve open, start engine and allow steering fluid to reach normal operating temperature. Close shut-off valve and repeat pressure tests.

NOTE – *Do not keep shut-off valve closed for more than 5 seconds at a time, otherwise fluid will overheat and damage to system could occur.*

6) If test pressures are now to specifications, fault is in steering gear. If test pressures are still not to specifications, fault is in pump. *Refer to OVERHAUL in this article.*

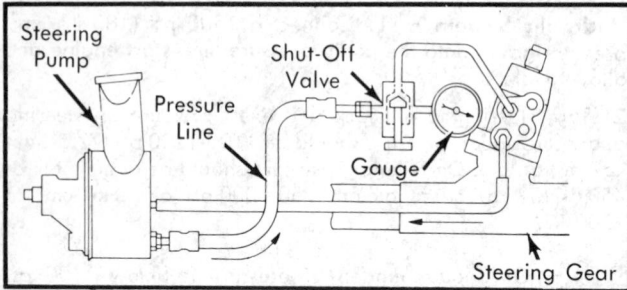

Fig. 3   Pressure Gauge and Shut-Off Valve Connections

SYSTEM BLEEDING

Turn wheels to full left lock, add fluid to "COLD" level mark on dipstick. Start engine and idle. Turn steering wheel lock to lock to expell air. Check fluid level. Straighten wheels and run engine for several minutes. Turn off engine, check fluid level. Fluid should be up to "HOT" mark on dipstick.

REMOVAL & INSTALLATION

STEERING GEAR

NOTE – *Amount and location of all washers and spacers must be noted for correct installation.*

Removal – **1)** On Jaguar models, remove lower steering column. Drain fluid from pump, disconnect pressure and return lines then cap openings. Disconnect ball joints from steering knuckles. Remove rack-to-suspension bolt. Remove heat shield bracket and spacers. Remove remaining bolts from rack mounting, save washers, then remove steering gear from vehicle.

2) On Triumph models, remove fresh air duct from engine compartment. Install an engine support bracket and support engine. Remove cold air intake hoses from temperature valves. Remove bolts attaching engine mounts to sub frame. Raise vehicle so front wheels are off ground.

3) Disconnect ball joints from steering knuckles and steering shaft from gear. Remove clamp from power steering lines, then disconnect pressure and return lines from steering gear. Drain fluid and cap openings. Remove nuts and bolts attaching steering gear to sub frame.

4) Position a jack under sub frame then remove bolts attaching sub frame-to-frame and lower sub frame until rear mounting bolts just clear sub frame. Turn steering to full right lock. Move steering gear to right until left tie rod clears, then remove steering gear from vehicle.

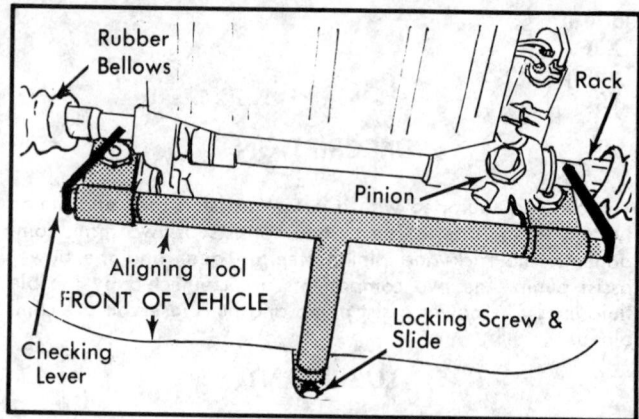

Fig. 4   Installing Rack and Pinion Gear

Installation – **1)** On Triumph models, to install steering gear assembly, reverse removal procedures. On Jaguar models, position rack against mounting brackets and center lugs on bracket. Insert shims between lug and bracket to insure a gap of .05" (1.3 mm) on both sides of rack lug and mounting bracket. Insert mounting bolts but do not tighten.

2) Repeat centering procedure on upper and lower mountings on pinion side of rack. Make sure heat shield mounting bracket is located on upper mounting bolt. Remove clip securing rubber bellows to rack housing and fold bellows back to expose inner ball joints.

3) Install attachment brackets, of alignment tool JD. 36A, over large hex head bolts on lower control arms. It may be necessary to bend shields slightly to locate tool correctly. See Fig. 4.

4) Release locking screw and slide collar along tool to front of suspension unit until slot engages front weld flange of crossbeam. Lock slide in this position. Rotate alignment tool until legs rest on tie rods. To adjust slack, loosen lock nut of single bolt mounting and raise or lower same side of rack assembly.

5) Remove tool, fully tighten rack mounting lock nuts. Reposition bellows and secure clips. On all models, reinstall tie rods and power steering hoses. Refill and bleed system, then check wheel alignment.

POWER STEERING PUMP

Removal – **1)** On Triumph models, remove left air intake hose from temperature control valve. Remove pressure and return lines from pump, then drain fluid and cap openings. Loosen pivot and adjusting nuts, push pump toward engine and take belt off pulley. Remove pump adjusting and pivot bolts, then remove pump.

2) On Jaguar models, remove air cleaner. Partially drain radiator and remove upper radiator hose. Drain fluid from steering pump, then disconnect and cap fluid lines. Loosen nut securing adjusting rod to timing cover.

3) Remove bolt securing adjuster rod to pump, swing adjuster clear of pump. Remove lower pump pivot nut. Move pump toward engine and remove belt. Remove lower pivot bolt and remove pump from vehicle.

Installation – To install power steering pump, reverse removal procedures. After replacement, adjust belt tension and bleed system.

JAGUAR & TRIUMPH POWER-ASSISTED RACK & PINION (Cont.)

CONTROL VALVE AND PINION

NOTE — *No adjustment or repair is possible except the replacement of the pinion seal.*

Removal — Remove steering gear assembly. Clean rack and pinion housing. Note position of pinion housing ports-to-valve cylinder pipes for reassembly reference. Loosen rack plunger lock nut and adjusting screw to remove spring tension. Remove pinion housing bolts and remove pinion housing with pinion shaft.

Installation — To install control valve and pinion, reverse removal procedure. Make sure pinion housing ports are aligned with cylinder pipes. On Jaguar models, make sure recess on pinion shaft are in correct position with pinion housing.

OVERHAUL

RACK ASSEMBLY

Disassembly — **1)** Clean rack and pinion housing, drain assembly of fluid. Remove clips attaching bellows to tie rods and fold bellows back, exposing tie rod inner ball joint. Straighten lock tab of tie rod inner ball joint.

2) Remove tie rods from rack by loosening lock nut on inner ball joint. Note position of pinion housing-to-valve cylinder pipes, then remove pipes. Remove air transfer pipe. On Jaguar models, remove Allen screw from end cap. On all models, remove locking ring from end housing and remove end housing.

3) Remove rack plunger lock nut, adjusting nut, spring and plunger. Remove pinion housing cover, then remove pinion housing from rack housing. Remove pinion from pinion housing. Remove snap ring, washer and seal from pinion housing. Remove rack from rack housing.

4) Remove porting adapter and slide porting ring along cylinder until feed hole is exposed. Using a scribe (or similar tool) pry seal until seal can be removed from cylinder with a hooked wire. Remove all seals, "O" rings and sleeves from rack housing.

NOTE — *Do not remove seals from pinion piston.*

Inspection — Clean all parts in solvent and blow dry or air dry. Do not wipe dry as lint could contaminate parts and cause malfunction when assembled. Check all parts for excessive wear, scratches, nicks or scoring. Replace parts as necessary. Check rack teeth and pinion teeth for chips, burrs and other damage. Always replace all "O" rings and seals upon reassembly. Check rubber bellows for cracks, splits or holes, replace as necessary.

Reassembly — **1)** Lubricate all "O" rings, seals and sleeves before installation. Also lubricate all moving parts before installation. Install seal and "O" ring to end housing.

2) Install new center feed porting adapter to porting ring. Position ring to allow conical seating on adapter to engage with seating on cylinder, then tighten. Install rack seal over rack teeth up against piston. Install anti-extrusion ring to recess in back of rack seal.

3) Lubricate inside of rack housing and grease rack. Insert rack into rack housing with firm steady pressure until seal seats against abutment face. Make sure piston ring collapses and enters rack housing without damage.

4) Install new seal, washer and snap ring to pinion housing. Install new pinion valve seal to pinion shaft (located against pinion bearing). Lubricate pinion shaft, piston seals and bearing. Carefully install pinion shaft to pinion housing, tapping gear end of shaft lightly to make sure it is seated.

5) Grease pinion teeth and small journal of pinion then install pinion and housing (use new gasket) to rack housing. Make sure rack teeth and pinion teeth mate correctly. Make sure pinion housing ports are correctly aligned so cylinder-to-valve pipes can be installed.

6) Install seals to end housing. Install end housing-to-rack housing and screw locking ring into end housing just enough to hold mounting feet in parallel alignment. With end housing and mounting feet in alignment, tighten locking ring.

7) Install rack plunger, spring, adjusting plug and lock nut. Tighten adjusting plug, while moving rack through full stroke, until rack is hard to move then back off adjusting nut just enough to obtain a smooth rack movement (approximately ⅛ turn). Tighten lock nut while holding adjusting plug from turning.

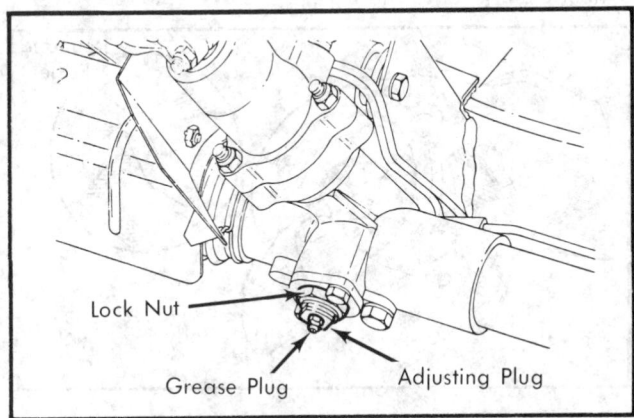

Fig. 5   Rack End Play Adjustment

8) Install air transfer pipe and cylinder-to-valve pipes. Place bellows onto tie rods, small opening towards outer ball joint. Install tie rod inner ball joint to rack. Make sure lock washer tab is aligned with slot in rack end. Pull rack out until rack teeth can be held in soft jawed vise, then tighten tie rod inner ball joint lock nut. Repeat procedure for other tie rod. Bend lockwasher tab into rack slots with punch.

9) Place 1 to 2 oz. of grease to each bellows then attach bellows to rack housing and tie rod with wire clips. Remove plug in rack plunger adjusting plug and install grease nipple. Using a hand grease gun, fill with approximately 5 strokes of grease gun. Remove grease nipple and replace plug.

POWER STEERING PUMP

Disassembly — **1)** Remove rear mounting plate and pulley from pump. Remove front mounting plate from pump and clean pump body. Remove pressure outlet union and mounting plate studs from rear of pump. Tip pump and remove flow control valve and spring.

2) Place pump in padded vise and tap pump casing from body. Remove "O" rings from pump body and magnet from flange. With suitable pin punch, push retaining ring free from groove and lever from body. Remove spring retaining plate and spring. Remove "O" ring from recess in pump body.

JAGUAR & TRIUMPH POWER-ASSISTED RACK & PINION (Cont.)

3) Remove Woodruff key from shaft. Tap roller spindle toward body and remove pump assembly from body. Remove "O" ring from recess in pump body. Remove dowel pins.

4) Remove rotor housing top plate and rotor housing. Remove rotor vanes and circlip securing rotor to drive shaft. Remove drive shaft oil seal from pump body.

Cleaning and Inspection — Clean all parts with lint-free cloth. Replace all "O" rings and seals. Check all parts for scratches, nicks, burrs or excessive wear. Replace rotor ring and vanes if excessive wear or chatter marks are present. Check flow control valve for free movement in bore. Lubricate all parts with power steering fluid before reassembly. Check interference fit between pump shaft and pulley. Replace parts if interference fit is less than .001" (.025 mm) or more than .0026" (.066 mm).

Reassembly — 1) Lubricate drive shaft seal and fit into pump shaft housing. Fit "O" ring to lower recess in pump body. Place dowel pins in locating holes. With cutaway face uppermost, fit bottom plate to drive shaft.

2) Fit rotor over splines of drive shaft (countersunk face towards thrust plate) and secure with snap ring. Insert vanes in rotor with curved edge out. Fit drive shaft and rotor to pump body, ensuring that dowel pins locate through smallest holes of bottom plate. With arrow towards rear of housing, place pump ring chamber over rotor and dowel pins.

3) With spring recess up, fit chamber top plate over dowel pins. Push complete pump assembly home. Fit "O" ring into upper recess of pump body. Fit spring to recess in top plate. Place retaining plate over spring and push into body. Fit "O" rings to port recess, and large "O" ring to outside pump body and magnet to flange.

4) Place pump casing over body. Locate mounting studs into outer casing and into pump body. Place outer casing over pump body. Tighten mounting studs. Install spring and flow control valve. Fit pressure outlet union. Place Woodruff key in drive shaft spindle. Replace pulley and mounting plates. Refill system with fluid and bleed system.

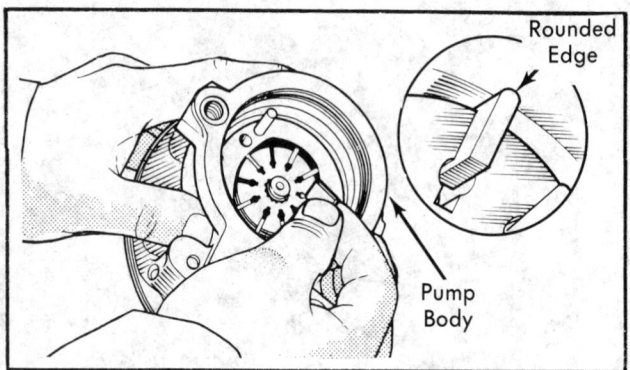

Fig. 6 *Placing Vanes in Rotor Plate*

TIGHTENING SPECIFICATIONS

Application	Ft. Lbs. (mkg)
Center Feed Porting Adapter Ring	22-25 (3.0-3.5)
Pump High Pressure Fitting	25-40 (3.5-5.5)
Rack Housing End Plate Lock Ring	80-90 (11.1-12.4)
Rack Housing Mounting Bolts	
Jaguar	49-55 (6.8-7.6)
Triumph	30 (4.1)
Tie Rod Inner Ball Joint Lock Nut	
Jaguar	45-55 (6.2-7.6)
Triumph	66-81 (9.1-11.2)

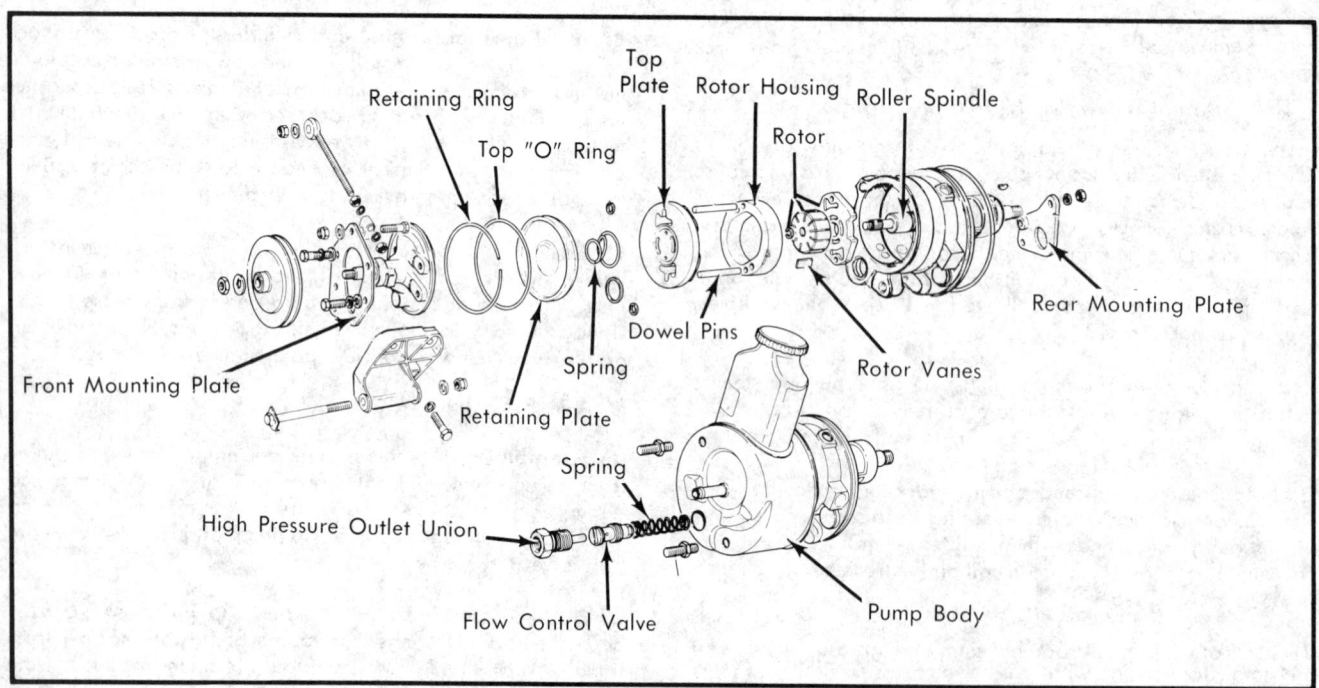

Fig. 7 *Exploded View of Jaguar and Triumph Power Steering Pump*

MERCEDES-BENZ POWER-ASSISTED RECIRCULATING BALL

240D
280 Series
300 Series
450 Series

DESCRIPTION

Power steering system is composed of power steering pump, steering gear and connecting hoses. All pumps have integral reservoirs. Both ZF and VT49 type pumps are used; some of these pumps are made of a light alloy material. The light alloy pumps are interchangeable with the cast iron type.

All power steering pumps are engine driven vane type with a control valve. The purpose of the power steering gear pump is to supply fluid (under pressure) to the steering gear.

Steering gear has integral piston/steering nut. Fluid pressure to each side of piston/steering nut is controlled by a control valve which is moved by a lever from steering column shaft.

LUBRICATION

Capacity — 2.6 pts. automatic transmission fluid.

REMOVAL & INSTALLATION

POWER STEERING PUMP

Removal — 1) Remove power steering tank cover, spring and damping plate. Drain tank with a syringe. Disconnect and plug high pressure and return hoses.

2) Loosen fastening bolts and push pump towards engine, remove "V" belts from pulley. Remove remaining bolts and remove pressure pump with carrier.

Installation — To install power steering pump, reverse removal procedures. Fill system with recommended fluid.

POWER STEERING GEAR

NOTE — *All models are equipped with a modified power steering gear. The stop for the full lock position is incorporated into the housing itself, not on the steering arms as before. When replacing steering gears, install only the newer type gear. This gear can be recognized by an "A" * stamped on the housing.*

Removal — 1) Drain fluid from power steering pump. Disconnect and plug pressure line and return line from steering gear. Remove bolts from steering coupling. Remove rear exhaust system and left hand exhaust pipe at manifold (all 450 models). Disconnect center link and tie rod from pitman arm. Remove bolts securing steering gear to frame, force steering gear from steering column shaft, in a downward direction.

2) Drain fluid from steering gear, remove steering coupling and pitman arm from gear (be sure to mark pitman shaft-to-pitman arm position for proper assembly).

Installation — To install steering gear, reverse removal procedure. Replace locking nuts and bolts, tighten to specifications. Fill system with recommended fluid.

OVERHAUL

POWER STEERING PUMP

Disassembly (VT49 Pump) — 1) Remove wing nut and cover from reservoir. Remove compression spring, 2 damping plates and filter ring. Remove Woodruff key from input shaft.

2) Install puller 1104-7251 on input shaft. Screw bolt back on puller enough to install clamping shoes 11004-6304 between puller and seal. Turn clamping cone of puller to the right up to stop and remove seal ring out of housing.

3) On rear of housing, push in cover and insert a punch through hole in housing. See Fig. 1. Push in on punch and remove circlip and cover. Remove spring and "O" ring from housing. Push input shaft with pressure plate at cover end, rotor, cam ring and pressure plate at input end out of housing in rearward direction.

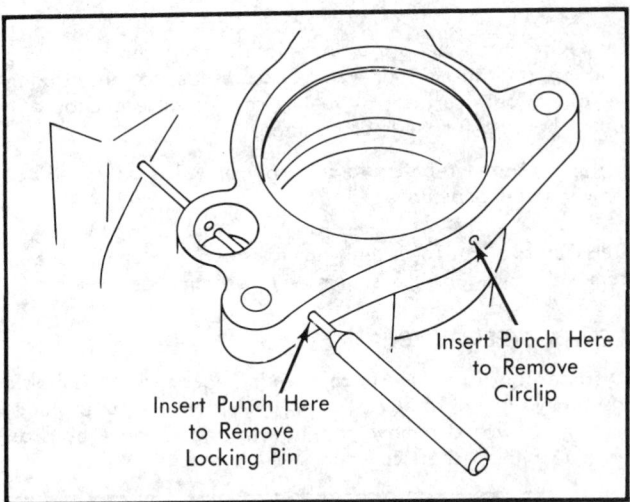

Fig. 1   Circlip Punch Hole Location and Removing Locking Pin on VT49 Pump

4) Remove pressure plate, cam ring and blades. Remove locking clip from input shaft, then remove rotor and pressure plate. Remove cylinder pins from housing. Using a punch, knock out locking pins in housing. See Fig. 1.

5) Remove closing plug, volume control valve and compression spring from housing. Clamp volume control valve in vise and disassemble valve. Check spacer washer, valve cone and compression spring.

Inspection — Check pressure plates, input shaft, and bearing bushing for wear. Check blades for easy sliding in rotor. Check surfaces of volume control valve and bore in pump housing for wear or damage.

NOTE — *Never replace volume control valve only, replace power steering pump.*

Reassembly — To install power steering pump, reverse removal procedure. Fill system with recommended fluid.

Disassembly (ZF Pump) — 1) Remove Woodruff key from input shaft. Install puller (1104-7251) on shaft. Screw bolt back on puller enough to install clamping shoes (1104-6304) between puller and seal.

MERCEDES-BENZ POWER-ASSISTED RECIRCULATING BALL (Cont.)

2) Turn clamping core of puller to the right up to stop, remove tool, seal and washer from housing. Remove knurled nut and cover from housing. Remove retaining and compression springs. Remove upper damping plate, filter ring, and lower damping plate.

3) On rear of housing, push in cover plate and using a screwdriver remove circlip and cover. Remove "O" ring, compression spring, and pressure plate. Remove rotor with blades from input shaft and "O" ring and cam ring.

4) Remove lock ring from forward end of shaft. Press out input shaft from rear of housing. Remove circlip from shaft and remove bearing by pressing off toward rear of shaft. Remove needle bearing from housing.

5) Remove closing plug from housing. Remove compression spring and volume control valve. Clamp volume control valve in vise, disassemble and check spacer washers, ball, and compression spring.

Inspection — Check pressure plates, input shaft, bearing housing, and bushing for wear. Check blades for easy sliding in rotor. Check surfaces of volume control valve and bore in pump housing for wear or damage.

NOTE — *Never replace volume control valve only, replace power steering pump.*

Reassembly — To install power steering pump, reverse removal procedure. Fill system with recommended fluid.

POWER STEERING GEAR

Disassembly — **1)** Attach steering gear to a suitable assembly plate (116 589 01 59 00). Remove lock nut from adjusting screw and remove copper seal ring. Remove bolts attaching pitman shaft cover to steering case.

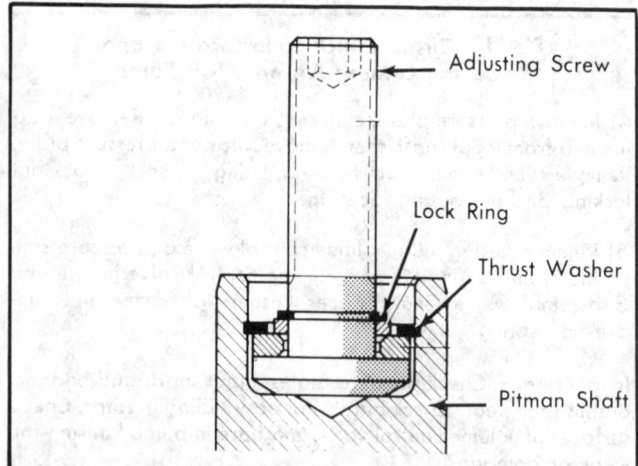

Fig. 2   Sectional View of Adjusting Screw

2) With steering in center position, turn adjusting screw clockwise. This forces pitman shaft, with housing, from steering gear case. Remove pitman shaft with cover. Remove "O" rings from cover. Remove lock ring and seal ring. Remove lock ring from pitman shaft and remove adjusting screw with thrust washers See *Fig. 2*.

3) Remove bolts securing bearing cap to steering gear case. Turn worm gear counterclockwise until bearing cap is forced out of steering gear case.

NOTE — *Balls will fall out of ball guide if worm gear is turned too far.*

4) Remove bearing cap and worm gear with piston/steering nut from steering gear case.

5) Unscrew worm gear with bearing cap from piston/steering nut.

CAUTION — *Do not lose circulator balls.*

6) Remove "O" ring from bearing cap and attach bearing cap to a suitable assembly fixture.

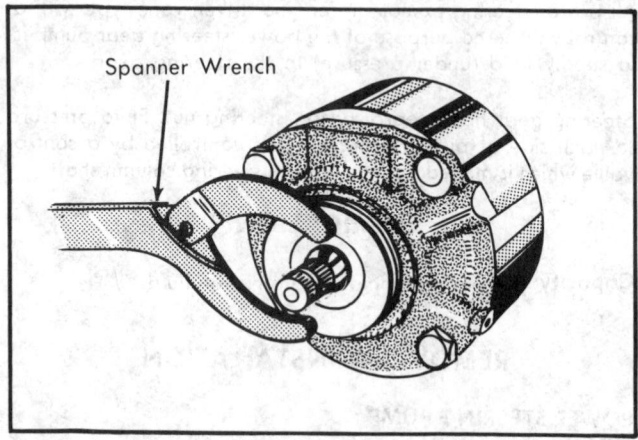

Fig. 3   Removing Bearing Insert from Bearing Cap

7) Unscrew slotted nut, using hook wrench, from bearing insert.

8) Remove bearing insert from bearing cap using spanner wrench. See *Fig. 3*. Remove steering worm and washer from bearing cap. Remove roller cage from steering worm, along with seal and "O" rings.

9) Remove bearing and disc from bearing cap. Remove bolts, clamp, and both ball guide halves from piston/steering nut.

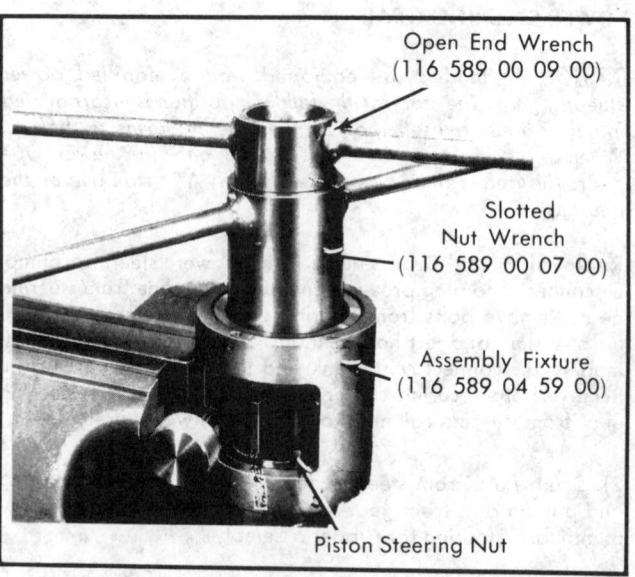

Fig. 4   Removing Worm Gear Nut from Piston Steering Nut

MERCEDES-BENZ POWER-ASSISTED RECIRCULATING BALL (Cont.)

10) Using suitable clamp and tools, remove worm gear nut from piston/steering nut. See *Fig. 4*. Remove seal ring and "O" ring from worm gear nut.

11) Remove bearings from piston/steering nut, then remove lock ring, cover and control valve from steering gear case. See *Fig. 5*.

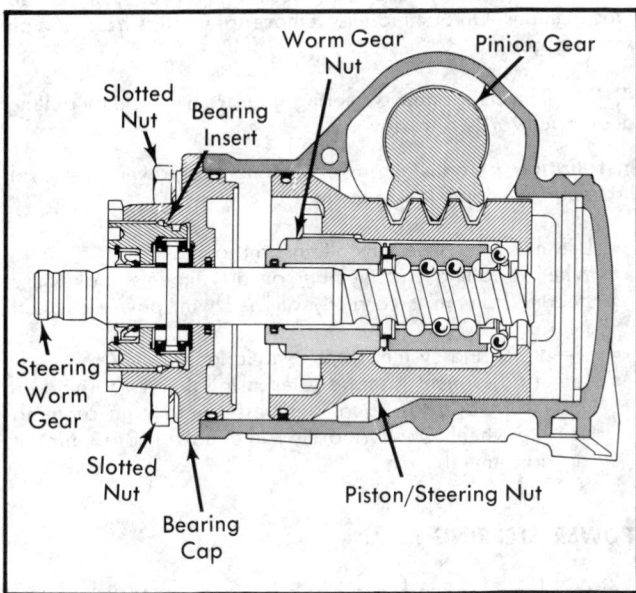

Fig. 5 Cross Sectional View of Steering Gear

Inspection — 1) On worm gear, check ball paths and bearings surfaces for wear and damage, replace if necessary.

2) On piston/steering nut, remove seal rings, "O" rings, bearings and races, and worm gear nut. Inspect for wear or damage and replace as necessary.

3) Check pitman shaft for wear or damage on bearing surfaces, check for bent or warped shaft and replace as necessary. Check steering case, cover, and bearing insert for wear or damage and replace as necessary.

4) On control valve, check reaction piston in control valve for free movement. If necessary remove pistons from control valve by removing lock rings.

Reassembly — To reassemble steering gear, reverse disassembly procedure. Replace all "O" rings and sealing rings with new ones. Adjust gear to specifications.

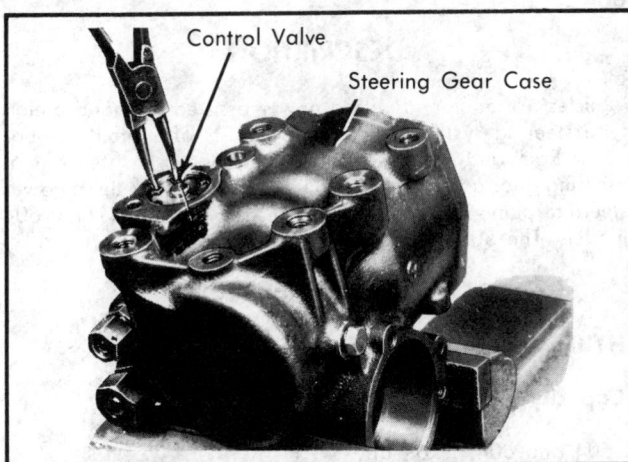

Fig. 6 Removing Control Valve from Steering Gear Case

STEERING SPECIFICATIONS

Application	Dimensions
Steering Wheel Free Play	1" Maximum
Pump Circulation Pressure	28.4-71 psi
Number of Balls in Ball Circuit	24
End Play of Pump Shaft	
New	.028" Maximum
Used	.039" Maximum

TIGHTENING SPECIFICATIONS

Application	Ft. Lbs. (mkg)
Steering Gear to Frame	50-57 (7-8)
Pitman Arm to Pitman Shaft	116-145 (16-19)
Slotted Nut to Bearing Cap	101-115 (14-16)
Adjusting Screw Nut	22-25 (3-3.5)
Pump Housing Bolts	25-29 (3.5-4)

Power Steering

PEUGEOT POWER-ASSISTED RACK & PINION

504
505
604

DESCRIPTION

Vehicles are equipped with a power assisted rack and pinion type steering system. The system consists of 2 main components: Rack and steering gear, and the power assisted pump. Steering gear and pump are connected by flexible lines. Power steering pump has an integral reservoir on 504 and 604 models. The 505 model has a separate reservoir.

GENERAL SERVICE

HYDRAULIC SYSTEM LUBRICANT

Capacity

504 and 604 — .69 qts.
505 — .74 qts.

SYSTEM BLEEDING

Fill reservoir to full mark on dipstick. Start engine and turn steering wheel from lock-to-lock several times (to expel all air). Recheck fluid level and refill as required.

REMOVAL & INSTALLATION

STEERING GEAR

Removal — 1) Drain steering system and disconnect pressure lines between pump and gear. Disconnect bolt at flexible coupling. Disconnect tie rod ball joints at steering knuckle.

2) On 604 models, remove rear bolts of front crossmember and install longer bolts. Remove front crossmember from bolts, then loosen rear bolts until a gap of approximately 1.5" (40 mm) exists between crossmember and frame.

3) On all models, remove steering gear to crossmember mounting bolts. Remove bolt securing power cylinder to crossmember. On 604 models, remove safety clips from pins on steering gear.

4) On all models, remove steering gear from vehicle by pulling gear backwards and down.

Installation — To install power steering gear, reverse removal procedures, noting the following:

- Use new nuts when installing ball joints.
- When installing crossmember on 604 models, make sure steering column is correctly aligned with power assisted steering valve.
- Bleed steering system after installation.
- Toe-in adjustment is made after installation by turning tie rods. Turn tie rods equal amounts to maintain centered steering wheel. One turn of tie rod equals .118" (3 mm) of toe adjustment.

POWER STEERING PUMP

Removal — 1) Remove air cleaner and connecting hoses. Remove pressure lines from pump. Loosen drive belt tensioner bolts and remove drive belt.

2) Remove pump attaching bolts. On 505 models, disconnect hose from reservoir to pump. On all models, remove pump from vehicle.

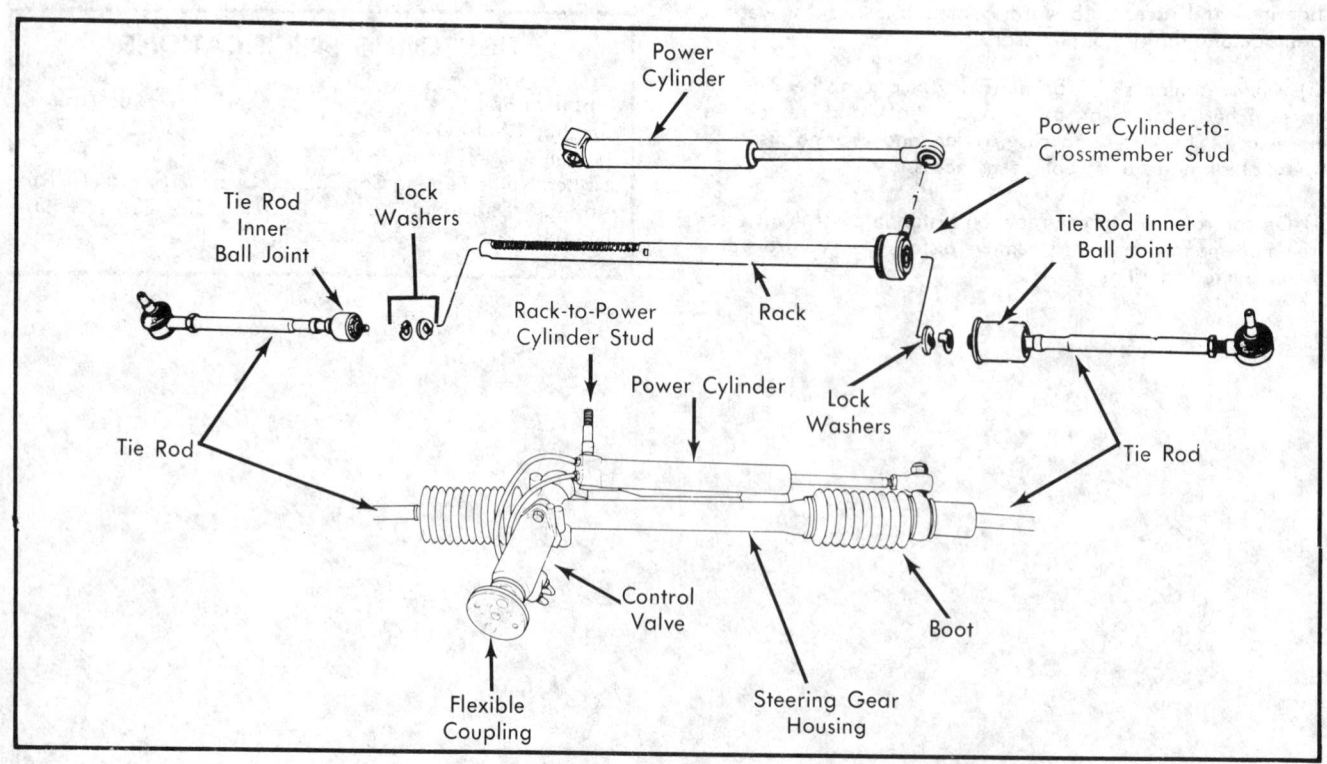

Fig. 1 Peugeot Power Assisted Rack and Pinion Steering Gear

PEUGEOT POWER-ASSISTED RACK & PINION (Cont.)

3) On 504 models, remove pump pulley with suitable gear puller (555 TAX). On 505 models, remove pulley by removing 4 bolts attaching pulley to pump. On 604 models, on pumps with extractor groove, use extractor tool (80706 H1, H2, H5) and pull pulley out as far as possible. Then tap pulley off with mallet. On 604 models without extractor groove, use suitable gear puller (555 TAX) and remove pulley.

Installation — To install steering pump, reverse removal procedures noting the following: Make sure hose connections are clean before installing. Fill system with fluid, then bleed system. *See System Bleeding in this article.*

OVERHAUL

POWER STEERING PUMP

NOTE — *Manufacturer does not recommend overhaul of power steering pump.*

POWER STEERING GEAR

Disassembly — 1) Clean steering gear assembly before starting disassembly. Place steering gear assembly in a padded vise. Disconnect pressure pipes from power cylinder and plug ports in power cylinder and cap pressure pipes.

NOTE — *Do not disconnect pressure pipes from control valve if valve is to be reused. Do not loosen lock nut on power cylinder attaching joint.*

2) Remove nut securing power cylinder to rack and remove power cylinder. Loosen lock nut on right tie rod inner ball joint, then disconnect tie rod from rack.

3) If control valve is to be replaced, remove pressure pipe connections.

NOTE — *Be careful not to bend or twist pipes connecting control valve to power cylinder.*

4) Remove left boot clamp and push boot toward steering gear. Disconnect left tie rod inner ball joint from rack. Remove rack piston cover, spring and rack piston from steering gear housing.

5) Remove control valve bearing cap cover, then remove nut. Remove bolts attaching control valve-to-steering gear. Carefully remove control valve from gear housing. Carefully withdraw rack from housing. Remove snap ring and remove pinion gear bearing.

6) If control valve is to be rebuilt, proceed as follows: Remove flexible coupling. Remove snap ring and thrust washer, then withdraw control valve piston from control valve housing.

NOTE — *Do not tap on shaft to aid removal or damage to shaft will occur. Do not remove piston rotor segments from shaft.*

7) From control valve housing, remove snap ring, scraper seal and oil seal.

Inspection — Check steering gear housing and rack for any damage, scoring or any signs of excessive wear. Check control valve housing and shaft for damage, wear or scoring. Replace components as necessary. Always replace all washers, nuts, seals and bearings when reassembling steering gear.

Reassembly — 1) If control valve was disassembled, install oil seal (soaked in oil) to piston/pinion gear assembly with seal lip facing pinion gear. Install piston in control valve. Install thrust washer and snap ring on pinion end of control valve housing. Install oil seal, scraper ring, and snap ring on flexible coupling end of valve housing. Install flexible coupling to control valve housing.

2) Install new pinion gear bearing into steering gear housing, then install snap ring. Insert rack into housing, align rack teeth with pinion gear/control valve mounting hole. Align flexible coupling pinch bolt with pressure pipe holes (holes that connect control valve with power cylinder) on control valve.

3) Insert control valve/pinion gear into steering gear housing. To make sure control valve is properly aligned with rack, line up control valve flange bolt holes with gear box holes. Then rotate control valve 90° counterclockwise. Insert control valve into gear box while rotating control valve 90° clockwise. this will properly align rack teeth with pinion teeth.

4) Hold flexible coupling and install pinion nut, grease bearing location and install grease cap. Temporarily place plunger and spring in housing. Install rack plunger cover, upper bolt and dial indicator mount into lower bolt hole. Install dial indicator on mount and tighten down cover.

5) Using flexible coupling, turn steering rack from lock-to-lock and zero dial indicator on maximum deflection indicated. Using lever, push steering rack in direction of plunger and record dial indicator reading. Remove dial indicator, rack cover and rack plunger from housing.

6) Install stop to rack plunger and lay straight edge over stop and plunger. Select shim pack to eliminate clearance between stop and straight edge.

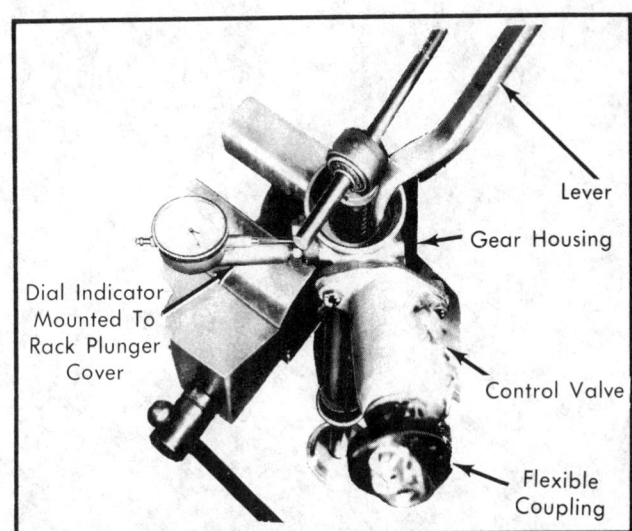

Fig. 2 *Measuring Steering Rack Plunger Clearance*

PEUGEOT POWER-ASSISTED RACK & PINION (Cont.)

7) Steering rack plunger clearance should be .004±.002" (.1±.05 mm) at maximum point along rack travel. To obtain required clearance, subtract .004" (.1 mm) from dial indicator reading obtained in step 5), this measurement indicates the thickness of shim washers needed in plunger.

8) Install shim pack selected, stop and spring to rack plunger. Install rack plunger assembly to gear housing. Install grease nipple to cover then install cover over rack plunger assembly and tighten bolts. Install rubber boots, with clamps, to steering gear housing. Push boots out of way when installing tie rod inner ball joints.

9) Install stop plate and lock washer, then install tie rod inner ball joints to rack. Insert bolt into power cylinder. Attach power cylinder to bolt on rack end and tighten nut finger tight. Install pressure pipes from control valve to power cylinder. Do not bend or deform pressure pipes when installing and tightening connections.

10) With pressure pipes installed, tighten rack bolt nut. Install pressure lines to control valve. Before steering gear installation in vehicle, install spacer on power cylinder to crossmember bolt.

TIGHTENING SPECIFICATIONS

Application	Ft. Lbs. (mkg)
Ball Joint Nut	31 (4.3)
Crossmember-to-Frame	31 (4.3)
Engine Mount-to-Crossmember	25 (3.5)
Gear Housing-to-Crossmember	24 (3.3)
Inner Ball Joint Lock Nut	33 (4.5)
Inner Ball Joint-to-Rack	36 (5.0)
Power Cylinder-to-Crossmember	40 (5.5)
Power Cylinder-to-Rack	33 (4.5)
Tie Rod Lock Nut (Outer)	58 (8.0)

Power Steering

PORSCHE POWER-ASSISTED RACK & PINION

928

DESCRIPTION

A power-assisted rack and pinion steering gear is used as standard equipment on Porsche 928 models. The power assistance decreases with engine speed to provide a better road feel at high speeds. The system consists of a belt driven vane pump mounted on the engine, a fluid reservoir located in the left front engine compartment, and a rotary piston pinion steering gear.

GENERAL SERVICE

Lubricant — ATF Dexron Type

Oil Level Check — Remove reservoir cap and start engine. Check that fluid level is up to embossed mark on inside of reservoir.

Hydraulic System Bleeding — Start engine, set to idle. Check fluid level. Turn steering wheel lock to lock several times quickly. Do not turn wheel harder than necessary. Check fluid and add if needed. No air bubbles should rise in reservoir. Shut off engine. Check that fluid level does not rise more than ⅜″ (10 mm). If level rises, repeat procedure.

ADJUSTMENTS

PUMP BELT

Check belt deflection at center of belt between pump pulley and crankshaft pulley. Correct deflection is ⅜″ (10 mm). Adjust by loosening pump mounting bolts and moving pump.

SYSTEM LEAKS

With engine running, turn steering to full lock position and hold. This produces maximum pressure in lines. Check all hose connections and tighten if necessary.

REMOVAL & INSTALLATION

STEERING GEAR

Removal — 1) Drain fluid from system. Raise front of vehicle and support on safety stands. Press out tie rods with standard extractor. Remove bolt holding hose strap, and pull back hose and harness.

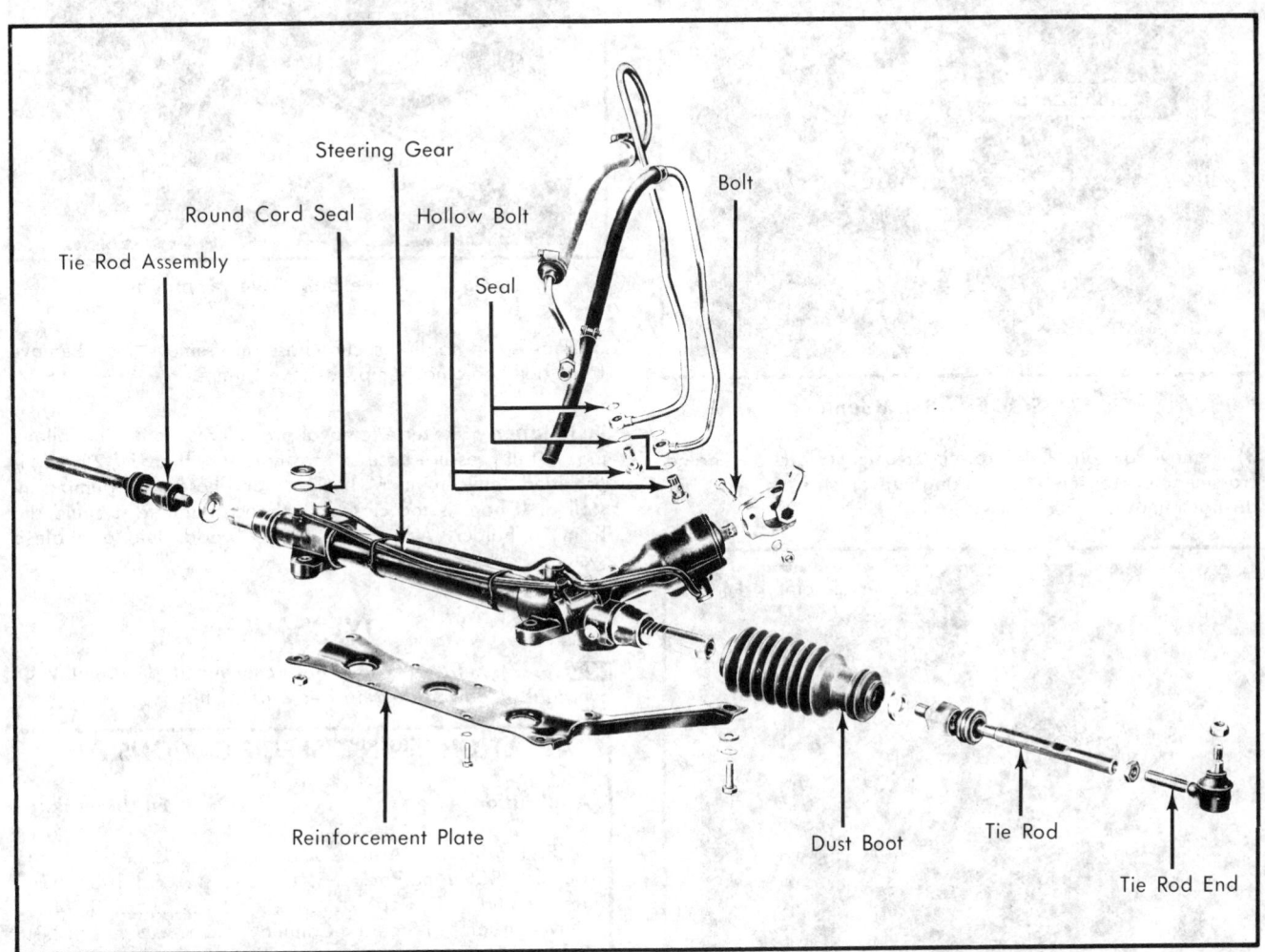

Fig. 1 Power Steering Gear Porsche 928

Power Steering

PORSCHE POWER-ASSISTED RACK & PINION (Cont.)

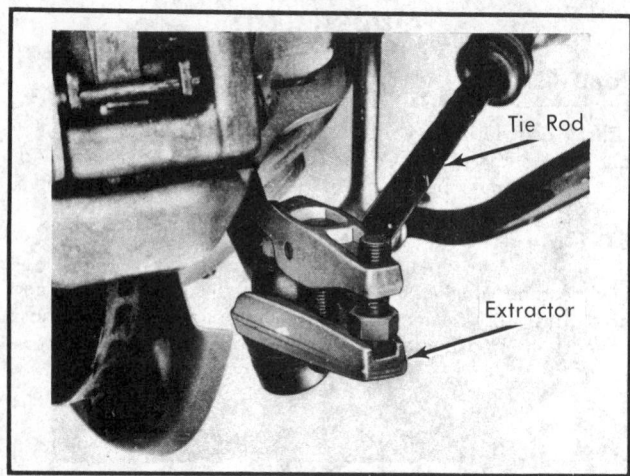

Fig. 2   Tie Rod Removal

2) Remove bolts from stabilizer bar mounts. Allow stabilizer to hang down. Disconnect pressure and return lines from steering gear.

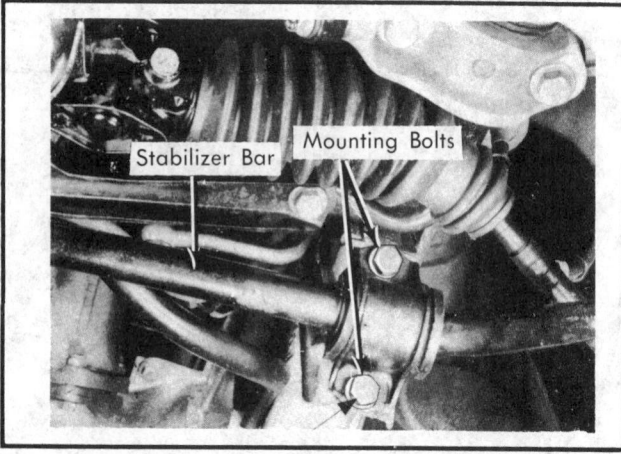

Fig. 3   Stabilizer Bar Mounting

3) Remove 5 bolts holding reinforcement plate on engine crossmember. Loosen 4 self-locking nuts on steering gear, but do not remove.

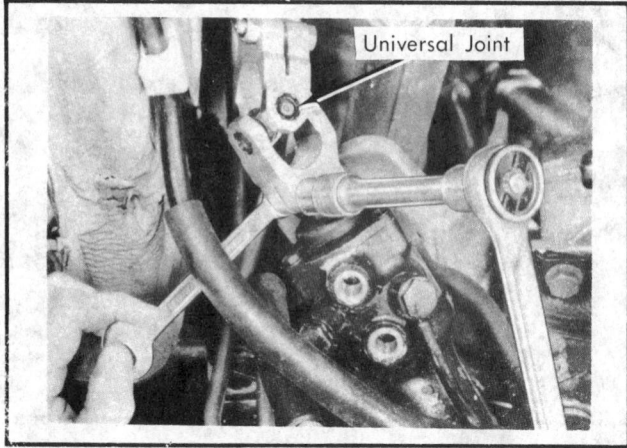

Fig. 4   Steering Intermediate Shaft Removal

4) Remove bolt on universal joint which connects to steering intermediate shaft and pull off shaft. Remove 4 nuts on steering gear and lower steering gear out of studs on engine crossmember.

Installation — 1) Reverse removal procedures, noting the following: Position steering intermediate shaft correctly and install bolt to universal shaft. Add fluid to reservoir. Check for leaks after reinstalling. Adjust toe if necessary.

STEERING PUMP

Removal — 1) Detach intake hose from air cleaner on left side. Drain fluid from reservoir. Remove splash shield. Loosen front bolts on pump, but do not remove.

2) Remove rear bolt from pump. Remove "V" belt. Take off upper left section of drive belt cover. Disconnect pressure hose from pump.

Fig. 5   Drive Belt Cover Removal

3) Loosen clip holding suction hose and remove hose. Remove front bolts holding pump. Remove pump.

Installation — Reverse removal procedures, noting the following: Install pressure hose so that not more than 1" (25 mm) is provided between inner wheel well and hose when pump is installed. If hose is too close to exhaust manifold it could slip from its holder. Adjust belt tension, add fluid and bleed system. Check for leaks.

OVERHAUL

NOTE — *Manufacture does not recommend disassembly or overhaul of power steering gears or pumps.*

TIGHTENING SPECIFICATIONS

Application	Ft. Lbs. (mkg)
Tie Rod-to-Steering Arm	61 (8.5)
Tie Rod-to-Steering Rack	108 (15.0)
Tie Rod End-to-Tie Rod	33 (4.5)
Universal Joint-to-Steering Column	17 (2.3)
Steering Rack-to-Crossmember	33 (4.6)
Pressure/Return Lines-to-Steering Rack	22 (3.0)

Power Steering

SAAB POWER-ASSISTED RACK & PINION — 99

99

DESCRIPTION

Power steering is added to some vehicles as optional equipment. The assembly consists of a rack and pinion steering gear with a servo valve which regulates the oil flow to a servo plunger on the rack. The hydraulic pressure is generated by an oil pump which is driven by a belt attached to the crankshaft pulley. A separate oil reservoir located by the left wheel housing supplies the system with hydraulic oil. A tube running between the two ends of the steering gear housing leads the oil past the hydraulic portion of the rack.

REMOVAL & INSTALLATION

Removal — 1) Loosen servo pump and lift away from mounting. Turn steering wheel a full turn left and remove clamping screw holding universal joint to steering gear. Block up the engine and remove left side engine mounting. Remove left cover under instrument panel and remove bearing bracket mounting from body.

2) Lift steering column with universal joint and support out of way. Raise and support front of vehicle. Remove front wheels. Using tie rod remover tool (8995409), detach tie rod end assemblies from control arms. Unscrew left tie rod end assembly from tie rod.

3) Disconnect speedometer cable from transmission. Disconnect left side handbrake cable at brake yoke and vehicle housing. Remove right side handbrake cable clamp on steering gear. Remove steering gear mounting from body.

4) From left side, remove two retaining screws from steering gear, and remove intermediate piece. On right side, remove yoke and intermediate piece. Disconnect delivery and return lines from servo valve.

5) Move steering gear over to right far enough so left tie rod can be pulled down through the body opening while twisting the valve housing backward. Take steering assembly out by moving it down and to the left.

Installation — Installation, is a reversal of removal procedure; however, tie rod ends are to be connected after gear assembly has been fully installed. Adjust toe-in.

OVERHAUL

POWER STEERING GEAR

Disassembly — 1) Clean exterior of gear assembly thoroughly before beginning work. Back off lock nut and remove tie rod end assemblies. Loosen clamps and take off rubber bellows. Bend up lock plate between end piece and rack.

2) Clamp toothed end of rack in a vise. Unscrew lock nut and adjusting screw. Withdraw adjusting screw retaining plate, spring "O" ring, and plunger. Remove tubes between servo valve and servo cylinder.

3) Unscrew three lock nuts, then detach valve housing and servo valve with pinion. Keep servo valve in a clean plastic bag. Remove ring nut locking screws. Clamp gear end of housing vertically in padded vise and remove ring nut using a suitable spanner (8995961).

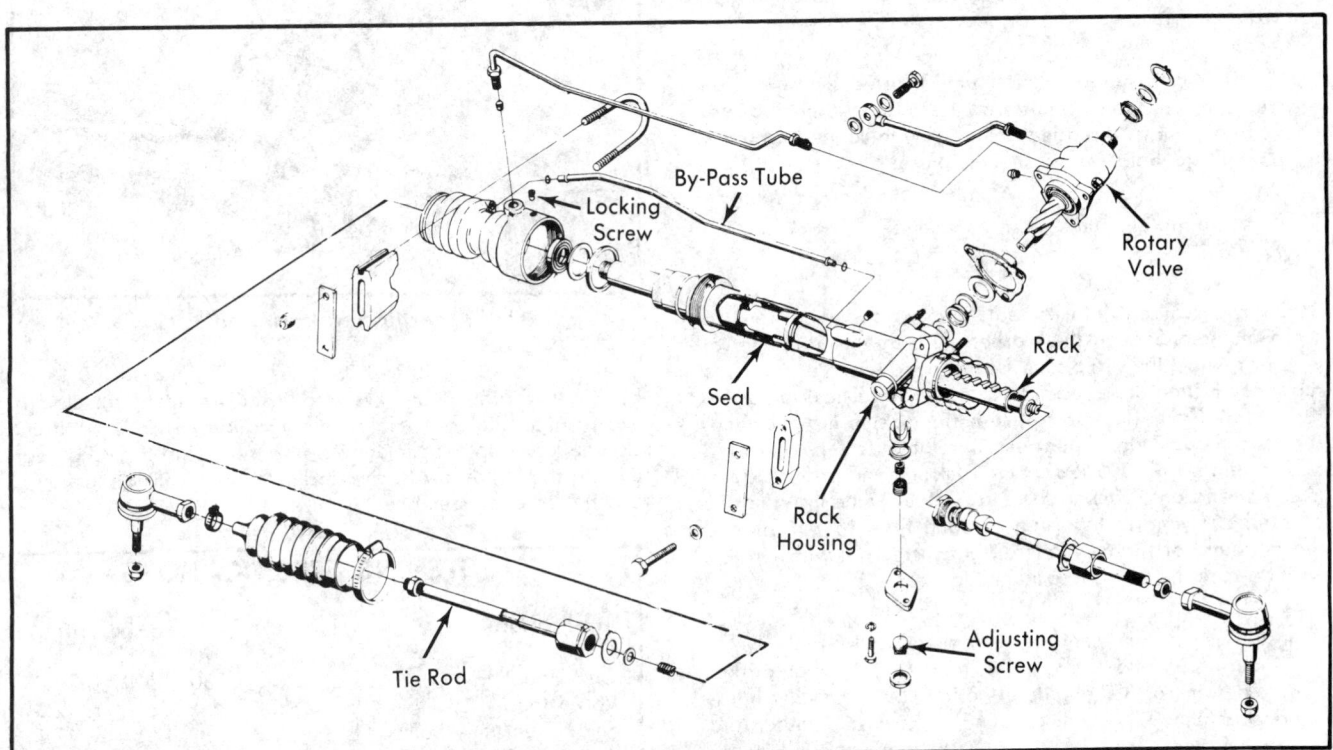

Fig. 1   Exploded View of Saab Power Steering Components

SAAB POWER-ASSISTED RACK & PINION — 99 (Cont.)

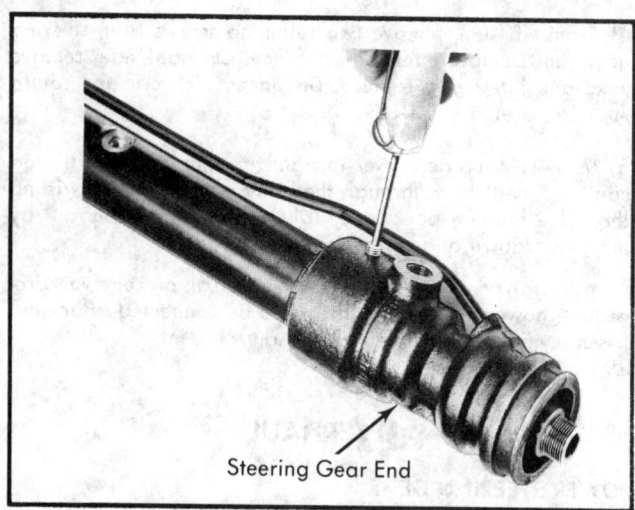

Fig. 2 *Removing Ring Nut Locking Screw from Steering Gear End*

4) Remove steering gear end from the cylinder and the rack while removing the bleeder tube. Set aside loose cone in hole for oil tube. Remove sealing ring, washer, and servo seal from steering gear end. Pull rack out of steering gear housing. Remove knurled sleeve, servo seal, and washer from cylinder. Remove plunger seal and snap ring.

NOTE — *Plunger cannot be detached from rack.*

Reassembly — 1) Apply Loctite to needle bearing seat and push in the needle bearing, if it has been removed. Fit snap ring and new teflon ring onto rack plunger. Slide knurled sleeve onto rack. Fit servo seal on fitting sleeve using the special cone tools (8995938 and 8995946). Slide sleeve with seal past teeth on rack. Remove tools. Turn notch in seal toward servo plunger.

2) Push rack into servo cylinder until knurled sleeve can be seen in hole for tube connection. Use a screwdriver to turn sleeve to expose its threaded hole. Screw in connecting screw temporarily to hold the washer in place.

NOTE — *Do not tighten screw completely, or rack will be damaged.*

3) Insert servo seal into its seat. Turn notch in seal toward servo plunger. Slip on the washer. Turn smaller diameter of washer toward the servo seal. Fit flat sided seal. Put cone into tube connection hole and lock cone using special screw (8995953). Cylindrical part of cone (inside steering gear end) serves to fix position of gear end in relation to servo cylinder. Screw fitting cone (8995987) onto rack end and position steering gear end onto rack and servo cylinder while inserting the vent tube. Cylindrical portion of cone fits into "U" shaped recess in end of servo cylinder. Tighten ring nut with suitable wrench. Lock the nut with socket head screw.

4) Install washer and seal between pinion and servo valve in gear housing. Position servo valve in housing. Position gasket (earlier design), or "O" ring (later design), between valve housing and gear housing. Insert sealing ring, plastic washer and lock ring in valve housing. Place installation tool (8995979), over shaft end of valve. Attach valve housing.

5) Remove special locking screw (8995953) from connection hole in steering gear end. Install tubes between servo valve and two sides of cylinder. Position new gaskets on banjo connection of the shorter tube to the cylinder. Install rack plunger, "O" ring, spring, cover, adjusting screw, and lock nut for radial adjustment of rack.

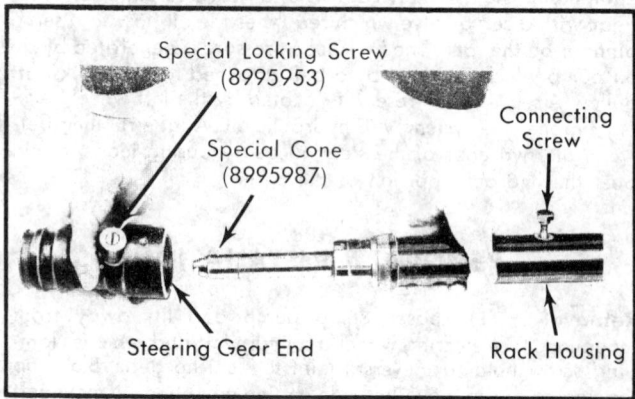

Fig. 3 *Fitting Steering Gear End to Rack Housing*

6) Clamp toothed end of rack in a padded vise, and install complete end pieces with thrust washer, spring, and lock washer. Lock the washer.

7) Adjust the radial play of the rack as follows: Screw in adjusting screw until resistance of the gear is felt. Back off screw $1/12$ of a turn. Check that steering gear can be turned from lock-to-lock without jamming. Tighten adjusting screw lock nut.

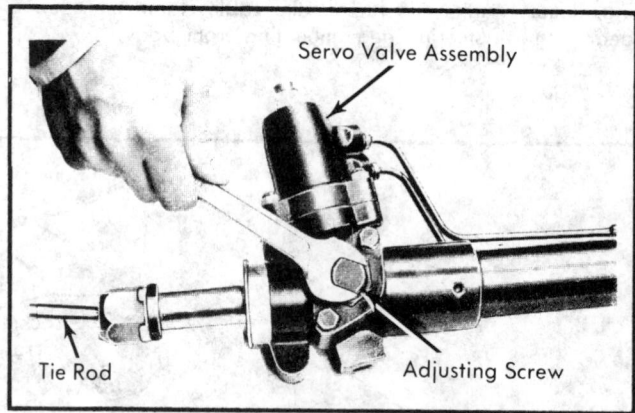

Fig. 4 *Adjusting Rack Radial Play*

8) Position rubber bellows and install (tighten) all clamps except one outer one. Hold steering gear vertically, with unclamped end up, and inject 6.5 fl. oz. of suitable EP 90 gear oil into the bellows. Attach remaining clamp. Install lock nuts and tie rod end assemblies.

TIGHTENING SPECIFICATIONS

Application	Ft. Lbs. (mkg)
Gear End Ring Nut	130-135 (18.0-19.0)
Valve Housing Lock Nuts	17 (2.3)
End Pieces (Inner Ball Joints)	47-54 (6.5-7.5)
Adjusting Screw Lock Nut	50-60 (7.0-8.0)

SAAB POWER-ASSISTED RACK & PINION – 900

900

DESCRIPTION

Power steering is available as optional equipment. The assembly consists of a rack and pinion steering gear with a servo valve which regulates the oil flow to a servo plunger on the rack. The hydraulic pressure is generated by an oil pump which is driven by a belt attached to the crankshaft pulley. The pump is integrated in a steel container that also serves as the hydraulic reservoir. In addition to pump unit itself, the pump also contains a control valve which regulates the pressure and flow.

REMOVAL & INSTALLATION

Removal – 1) Clean areas around hydraulic connections and disconnect return and pressure lines from steering gear. Plug lines and steering gear to prevent dirt from entering system. This will also prevent fluid from draining out.

2) Remove steering gear-to-intermediate shaft clamp bolt. Raise and support vehicle. Remove front wheels. Separate tie rods from steering knuckles.

3) Remove steering gear attaching bolts. Separate steering column (intermediate shaft) joint from steering gear, lift steering gear to the side and remove by guiding it diagonally downwards through opening in engine compartment.

Installation – Installation is a reversal of removal procedure; however, tie rod ends are to be connected after gear assembly has been fully installed. Adjust toe-in.

OVERHAUL

POWER STEERING GEAR

Disassembly – 1) With steering gear removed from vehicle, remove lock nuts and tie rod ends. Remove rubber bellows and breather tube. Remove hydraulic lines from steering valve and steering housing. Remove lock nut, adjusting nut, spring and piston from steering housing.

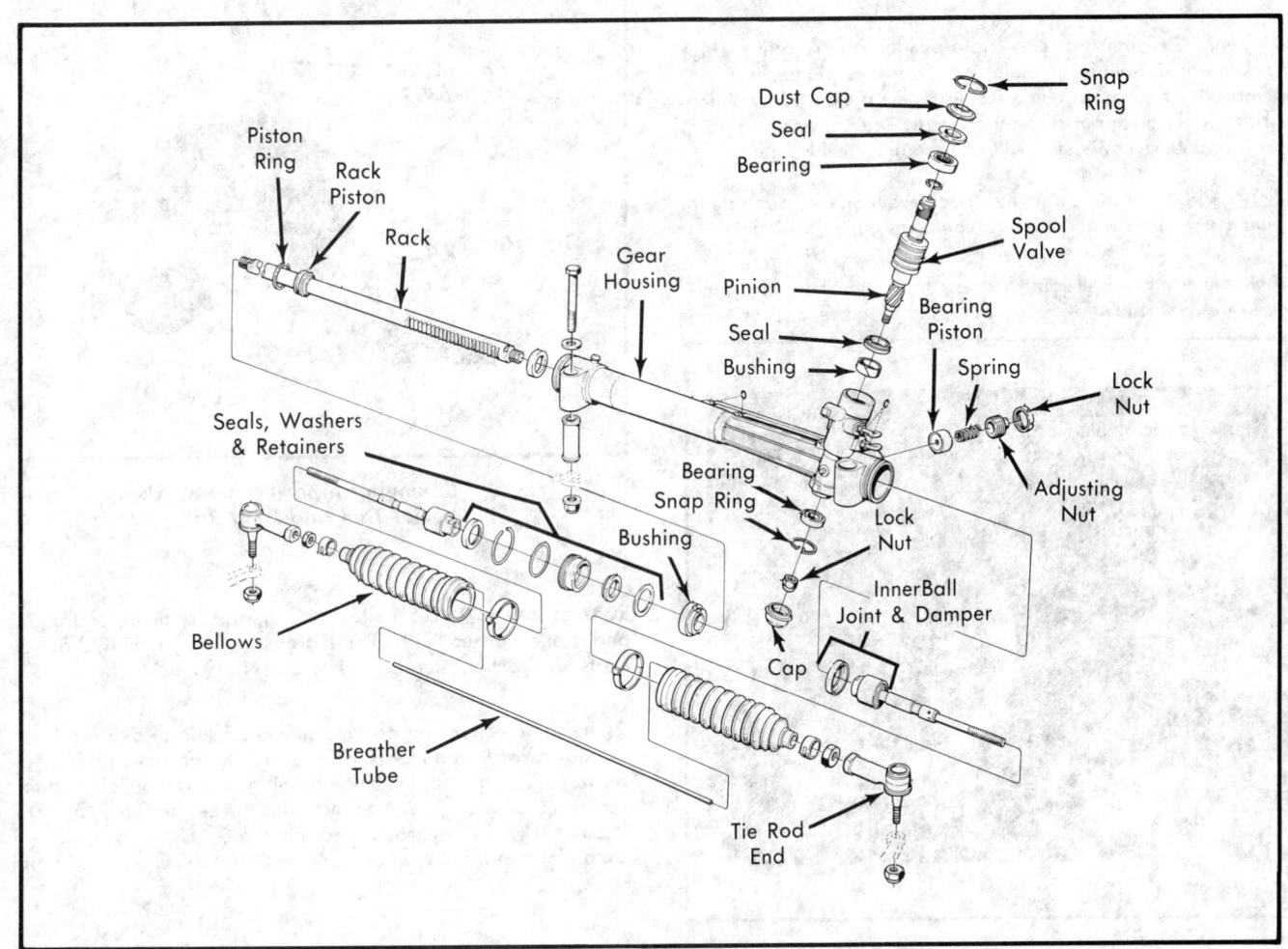

Fig. 1 Exploded View of Saab 900 Power Steering Components

SAAB POWER-ASSISTED RACK & PINION — 900 (Cont.)

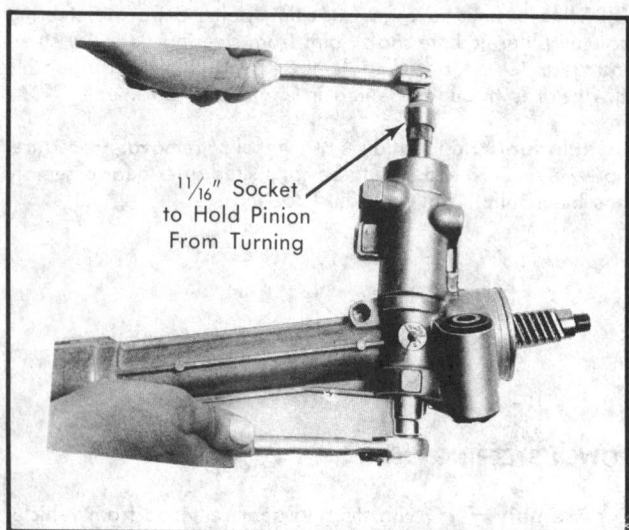

Fig. 2   *Removing Pinion Lock Nut from Pinion Gear and Spool Valve*

NOTE — *Tapping steering housing lightly against wooden block will aid in removing bearing piston.*

2) Remove pinion dust cap. Hold pinion from rotating ($^{11}/_{16}$" socket will fit splines of pinion) and remove pinion lock nut. Remove dust cover lock ring from (upper) pinion. Press pinion (with spool valve) out of steering gear. The bearing, support, seal, and dust cover seal will come out with the pinion.

NOTE — *Do not use a hammer to remove pinion or damage to pinion, spool valve or housing could result.*

3) Remove inner ball joint farthest from pinion by clamping rack in a soft-jawed vise. Push plastic sleeve out of way

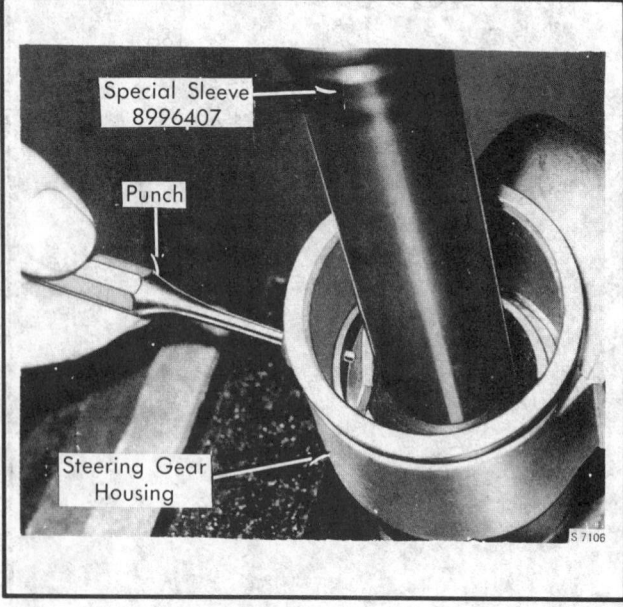

Fig. 3   *Removing Wire Lock Ring from Steering Gear Housing*

unscrew ball joint. Remove lock ring in end of gear housing as follows: Push rack into gear housing as far as it will go, install special sleeve (8996407) over rack and use inner ball joint (tighten) to press seal housing in. Then, use a punch to depress wire end of locking ring. Pry out ring with two screwdrivers. With ring removed, remove ball joint and special sleeve (8996407).

4) Remove ball joint nearest pinion as other ball joint was removed. Press out rack together with seal, washer and bushing. Remove seal and bushing from rack. Make sure there are no burrs on rack to damage seal or bushing before removing.

5) Remove inner rack using special tool (8996399) and a long punch or rod. Insert tool lips under seal, then from other end of housing insert long rod and drive seal out. Remove lock ring and lower pinion bearing. Remove sealing ring and bushing from top of pinion housing.

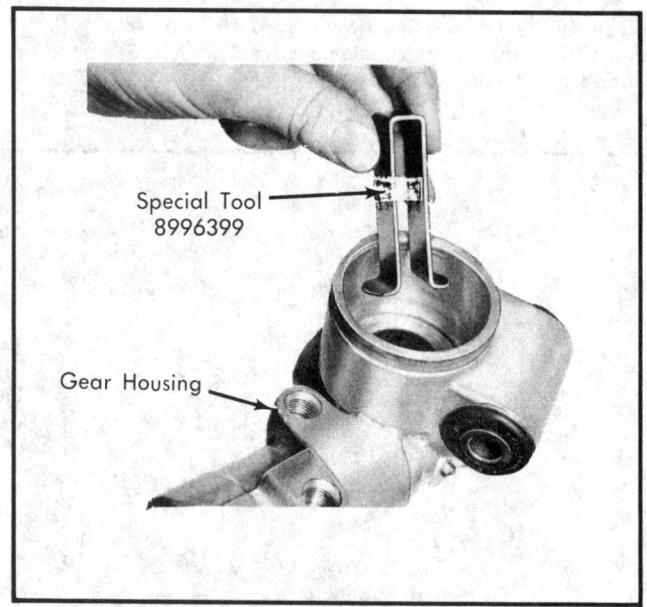

Fig. 4   *Removing Inner Rack Seal Using Special Tool and Long Rod*

Reassembly — **1)** Lubricate pinion gear, rack teeth, bearings and dust cover seal with lithium grease. Lubricate all hydraulic parts with power steering fluid. DO NOT use ATF fluid.

2) Install lower pinion bearing (enclosed side of bearing facing downward) and lock ring (with chamfer on lock ring facing outwards). Install upper pinion bushing and hydraulic seal into pinion housing of gear housing using special tool (8996407). Install rack inner hydraulic seal onto rack. Use a thin plastic sheath or metal foil to cover rack teeth to protect sealing lip of seal.

3) Install rack into housing. Install inner hydraulic seal into housing using rack piston as a press. Do not use more than 500 lbs. (227 kg) force. Install bushing in gear housing (smaller

Power Steering

SAAB POWER-ASSISTED RACK & PINION — 900 (Cont.)

bore facing in), then washer against bushing. Install new "O" ring on outer hydraulic seal support. Install old seal (if not damaged).

4) Slide sealing ring support carefully onto rack to avoid damaging sealing lip. Press sealing ring support into housing using suitable sleeve (8390148). Center rack so same amount extends from each end of housing. Rotate rack so that rack teeth will mesh with pinion gear teeth when it is installed.

5) Install pinion gear and spool valve in gear housing as follows: Hold pinion gear (with spool valve) so groove in end of shaft (for tensioning screw) points toward the left (9 o'clock

position) when the pinion teeth engage the rack teeth. Insert pinion. Pinion should rotate so that groove in end of pinion points toward front (12 o'clock position) with rack centered. *See Fig. 5.*

6) Install pinion lock nut and tighten. Install cover. Install washer, needle bearing, sealing ring, dust cover and lock ring onto top of pinion gear (spool valve). Protect seal lips with tape or plastic sleeve over splines of pinion.

7) Install bearing piston, spring and adjusting nut in gear housing. Tighten adjusting nut until bearing piston firmly contacts rack, then back off adjusting nut 30-50°. Install and tighten lock nut.

8) Install plastic sleeves (endstops) and inner ball joints, with tie rods, to rack ends. Hold rack in soft-jawed vice and tighten ball joints. Lock inner ball joints by tapping tab on ball joint into rack.

9) Install lock ring for sealing ring support in end of gear housing. Turn pinion until inner ball joint presses against sealing ring support. Press in support and, at same time, install sealing ring in groove with thin screwdriver. Install rubber bellows, breathing tube and hydraulic lines.

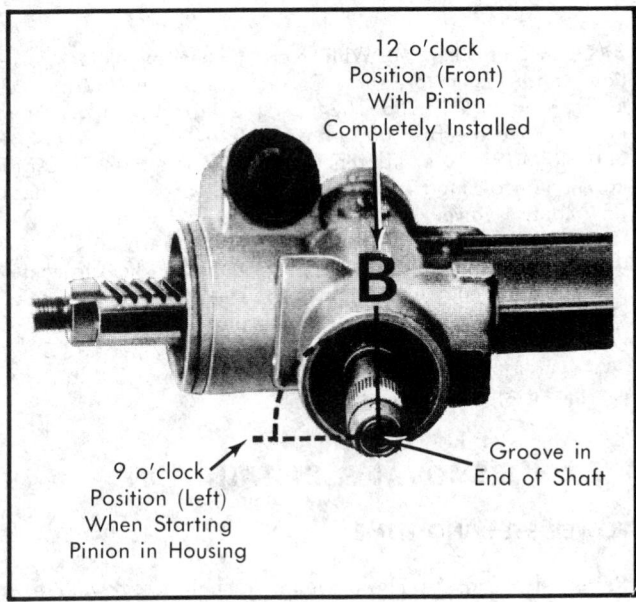

Fig. 5 Installing Pinion Gear (with Spool Valve) Into Gear Housing with Rack Installed

TIGHTENING SPECIFICATIONS

Application	Ft. Lbs. (mkg)
Ball Joint-to-Steering Arm	37-44 (5.0-6.0)
Pinion Gear Lower Lock Nut	22-34 (3.0-4.5)
Bearing Piston Lock Nut	48-55 (6.5-7.5)
Inner Ball Joint-to-Rack	59-72 (8.0-10.0)
Gear Housing-to-Crossmember	44-60 (6.0-8.0)

Power Steering

TOYOTA POWER-ASSISTED RECIRCULATING BALL

Celica
Corolla
Corona
Cressida

Supra
Land Cruiser
4-WD Pickup

POWER STEERING PUMP

The power steering pump is a vane type composed of an engine driven eccentric rotor, a fixed ring (having six slotted grooves), and a flow control valve (to regulate maximum oil pressure and amount of oil flow). Slippers are fitted in each slotted groove and are pressed against rotor outside surface by pressure produced in adjoining slots and by spring tension. As rotor rotation increases or decreases, then space between the rotor and fixed ring changes accordingly, in order to control oil flow.

POWER STEERING GEAR

Power steering gear consists of a mechanism which converts steering wheel torque to cross shaft torque by means of worm and power piston nut, and of a mechanism which detects hydraulic pressure developed by vane pump and controls this pressure in proportion to the steering effort.

GENERAL SERVICE

HYDRAULIC SYSTEM LUBRICANT

Capacity
Pickup 4-WD — 1.8 pts.
All Other Models — 1.7 pts.

Type — ATF Dexron

BELT TENSION ADJUSTMENT

With 22 lbs. (10 kg) pressure applied, belt deflection between idler pulley and pump pulley (crank pulley and pump pulley on Cressida) should be as follows: Corona, .28-.35" (7-9 mm); Cressida, .71-.85" (18-21.5 mm); Land Cruiser, .43-.55 (11-14 mm). On all other models, use a belt tension gauge and adjust belt tension to 100-150 lbs. (45-68 kg) for new belt or to 60-100 lbs. (27-45 kg) for used belt.

SYSTEM BLEEDING

1) Jack up front of vehicle and support with safety stands. Fill fluid to proper level in vane pump reservoir (turn wheels fully in both directions and recheck fluid level).

2) Start engine and let idle. Turn steering from lock to lock 2 or 3 times. Lower vehicle. Run engine at 1000 RPM or less. Turn wheel from lock to lock 2 or 3 times. Center steering wheel. If fluid level does not rise and no foaming of fluid is evident, bleeding is complete. If level rises, or foaming is evident, repeat procedure until air is released.

FLUID REPLACEMENT

Raise and support front of vehicle. Disconnect return hose and drain fluid into container. Turn steering wheel from lock to lock while draining. Connect return hose, add fresh fluid and bleed system.

HYDRAULIC PRESSURE TESTING

1) Disconnect pressure lines from steering gear case and vane pump. Attach pressure gauge with gauge side connected to vane pump. Attach valve side of gauge to pressure line. Bleed air from system and check fluid level.

2) With engine at idle, check fluid pressure reading with pressure gauge valve closed. Correct pressure should be 882 psi (62 kg/cm²) on Pickup and 1024 psi (72 kg/cm²) on all other models.

NOTE — *Do not keep pressure gauge valve closed for more than 10 seconds. Fluid testing temperature should be 176°F (80°C).*

3) Open pressure valve. With steering wheel at full lock position, check system pressure. Correct pressure is 882 psi (62 kg/cm') on Pickup and 1024 psi (72 kg/cm²) on all other models. Measure pressure with engine at idle and again at 3000 RPM. Pressure difference should be less than 71 psi (5 kg/cm') on all models. If pressure difference is more, check flow control valve.

4) With vehicle on flat surface, turn steering wheel to center position. With engine idling, measure steering turning force at steering wheel outer rim over a full rotation on both sides of center point. Turning force should not exceed 7.7 lbs. (3.5 kg) on Pickup, 13.2 lbs. (6.0 kg) on Land Cruiser or 8.8 lbs. (4.0 kg) on all other models.

REMOVAL & INSTALLATION

POWER STEERING PUMP

Removal — Loosen pulley mounting nut before removing drive belt. Disconnect and plug pressure line at pump housing. Disconnect and plug return line at pump housing on Celica, Supra, Corona and Pickup or at reservoir on Corolla, Cressida and Land Cruiser. Remove pump mounting bolts, then remove pump.

NOTE — *Keep disconnected hoses elevated to prevent fluid from draining out.*

Installation — To install, reverse removal procedure and note: Adjust drive belt tension and bleed system.

POWER STEERING GEAR

Removal — Disconnect and plug pressure and return lines at gear housing. Mark steering gear shaft to flexible coupling or universal joint, then disconnect flexible coupling or universal joint. Mark pitman arm to sector shaft, then disconnect pitman arm. Disconnect steering gear housing from heat shield on Land Cruiser. Remove steering gear mounting bolts, then remove steering gear.

Installation — To install, reverse removal procedure and note: Align all marks during installation. Bleed system and perform pressure test.

TOYOTA POWER-ASSISTED RECIRCULATING BALL (Cont.)

OVERHAUL

POWER STEERING PUMP

Disassembly — 1) Attach pump to suitable holding tool and mount in vise. On Corolla, Cressida and Land Cruiser models, remove bolts attaching reservoir to housing and remove reservoir. Be careful not to lose sealing "O" ring located in pump housing. Remove pulley if not already removed.

2) Mark front and rear housings for reassembly reference. Remove front housing bolts and tap front housing off. On Corolla models, remove rotor, cam ring and rotor shaft with front cover. On all other models, make sure rotor shaft remains with rear housing.

3) On Corolla models, tap plate and spring out of rear housing. Remove snap ring, seal, spring and flow control valve from rear housing. From other side of rear housing, remove other snap ring and seal of flow control valve. On front housing, remove cam ring, rotor and vanes. Remove snap ring and then tap rotor shaft out of front housing.

4) On all other models, pull rotor shaft from rear housing while holding slipper assemblies in (to prevent slippers from flying out). Tap rear housing off of fixed ring. Remove flow control valve screw, tab washer and snap ring. Reinsert screw into plug and pull plug, spring and flow control valve out.

Inspection — 1) On Corolla models, check rotor shaft bearing and replace if necessary. Check rotor shaft and housing bushing diameters. Clearance should be .0004-.0028" (.01-.07

mm). On all other models, place rotor shaft in vise with front housing installed. Mount dial indicator so plunger is against housing; then move housing side-to-side and measure bushing clearance. Turn rotor shaft around and install rear housing to measure bushing clearance. Both clearances should be .0004-.001" (.01-.03 mm).

2) On all models except Corolla, measure overall length of rotor (between end faces) and overall length of fixed ring. If overall length of rotor is more than fixed ring, replace with new rotor shaft sub-assembly.

3) On Corolla models, check rotor, cam ring and rear plate for wear or scratches. Measure vanes for minimum value of following specifications: Length, .589" (14.97 mm); height, .307" (7.8 mm); width, .067" (1.7 mm). Check clearance between rotor and vane. Should be maximum of .0026" (.06 mm). If any measurement is not to specifications, replace components as necessary.

4) On all other models, inspect slipper for wear: Measure length and thickness. If thickness is less than .055" (1.4 mm) or if length is less than 1.572" (39.92 mm), replace entire set. Check free length of slipper spring. If length is less than .51" (13 mm), replace springs.

5) On all models, use special tool (SST 09630-30030) to test flow control valve for leaks. With valve installed inside of tool, apply 58-73 psi (4.1-5.1 kg/cm²). Place a small amount of oil in top of tool and watch for air bubbles. If air bubbles appear, replace flow control valve. Measure flow control valve spring for free length of 1.9-2.0" (47-50 mm). Replace if necessary.

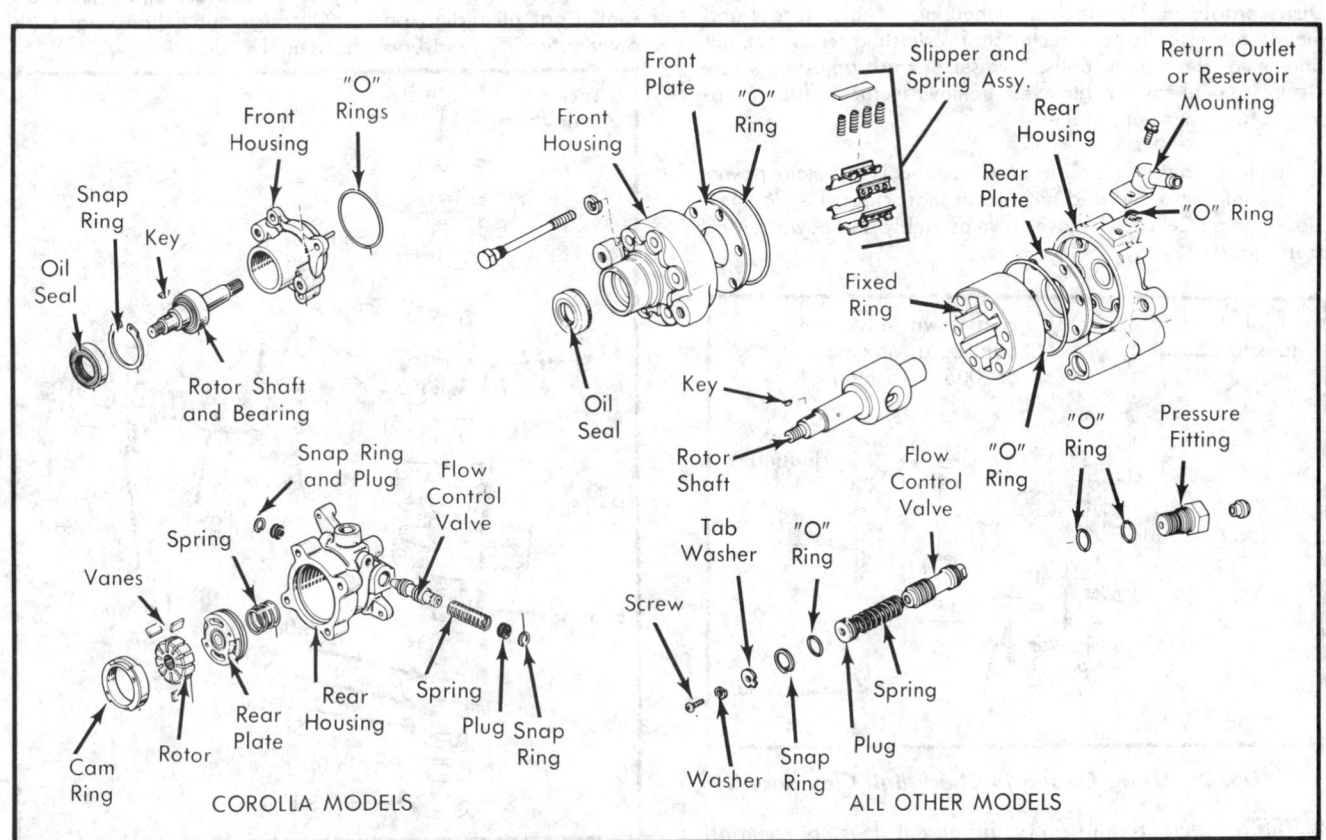

Fig. 1   Exploded View of Toyota Power Steering Pump Assemblies

TOYOTA POWER-ASSISTED RECIRCULATING BALL (Cont.)

Reassembly – 1) Coat all moving parts with power steering fluid. Install flow control valve assembly in reverse order of disassembly. If flow control valve was replaced, make sure mark on flow control valve matches mark on pump housing.

2) On Corolla models, install rotor shaft and snap ring to front housing. Install cam ring and rotor (with chamfered side of hub facing front housing). Install rotor vanes with rounded edge facing out. Install rear plate and spring to cam ring, then install rear housing to front housing.

3) Install 2 housing bolts to hold housings in place; then install reservoir to rear housing. Install rest of housing bolts and tighten.

4) On all other models, install rear plate (with large beveled side facing rear housing) to rear housing. Install fixed ring to rear housing, using 2 bolts as guides. Install rotor shaft to rear housing. Make sure code marks on rotor shaft, fixed ring and slipper assemblies match. Install slipper assemblies to fixed ring and rotor shaft.

5) Install front plate (with large beveled side facing front housing). Install front housing to rear housing. On models with separate reservoir, install return fitting. On models with integral mounted reservoir, install reservoir to pump. Install housing bolts and tighten.

6) On all models, temporarily install pulley. Using a spring gauge, measure turning force of pump. Corolla turning force should be less than 1.1 lbs. (.5 kg). All other models should be less than 6.2 lbs. (2.8 kg).

POWER STEERING GEAR

Disassembly – 1) Attach gear housing to holding tool and mount in a vise. Remove sector shaft adjusting screw lock nut and sector shaft cover bolts. Turn sector shaft adjusting screw clockwise until cover is removed. Remove sector shaft by tapping bottom end with mallet.

2) Remove valve housing-to-gear housing bolts. Hold power piston nut with hand and turn worm shaft clockwise (counterclockwise on Celica). Remove valve assembly and power piston from gear housing.

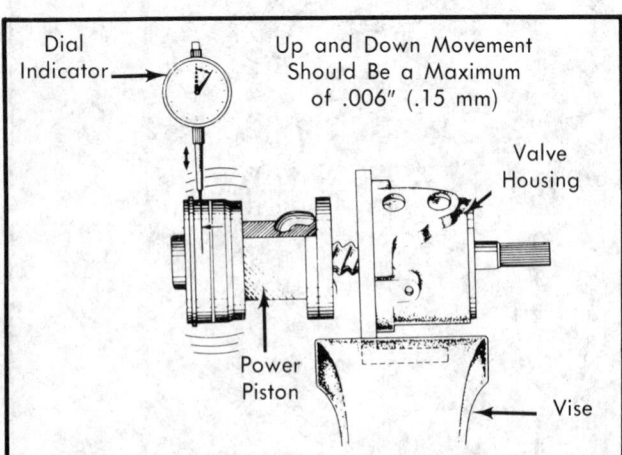

Fig. 2   Using Gauge to Check Ball Clearance

CAUTION – *Ensure that power piston nut does not come off worm shaft. Do not disassemble valve body or remove power piston from worm shaft.*

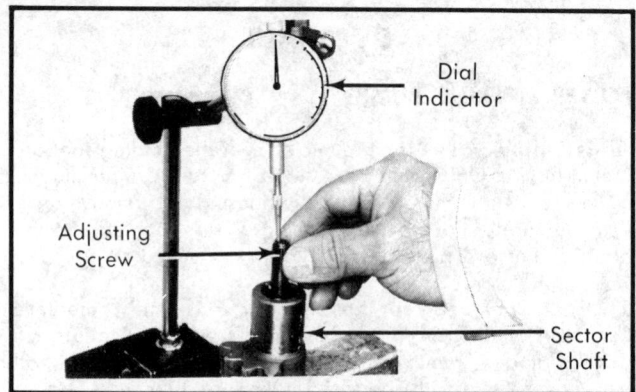

Fig. 3   Using Dial Indicator to Check Sector Shaft Thrust Clearance

3) Install valve assembly in vise. Using a dial indicator measure ball clearance. If clearance exceeds .006" (.15 mm) replace valve assembly.

4) Install sector shaft in a vise. Using dial indicator, check sector shaft adjusting screw for thrust clearance of .001-.002" (.03-.05 mm). To adjust thrust clearance, remove stake on adjusting nut. Turn adjusting nut to obtain correct thrust clearance, then stake out.

5) Temporarily install valve assembly in gear housing and install mounting bolts. Using lock nut tool, remove lock nut and adjusting bolt from gear assembly. Remove and replace as needed, oil seal, "O" ring, and bearing assembly. Install lock nut and tighten. Remove valve assembly from gear housing.

Cleaning & Inspection – 1) Clean and dry all parts in solvent. Coat all sliding parts, "O" rings and teflon rings with power steering fluid upon reassembly.

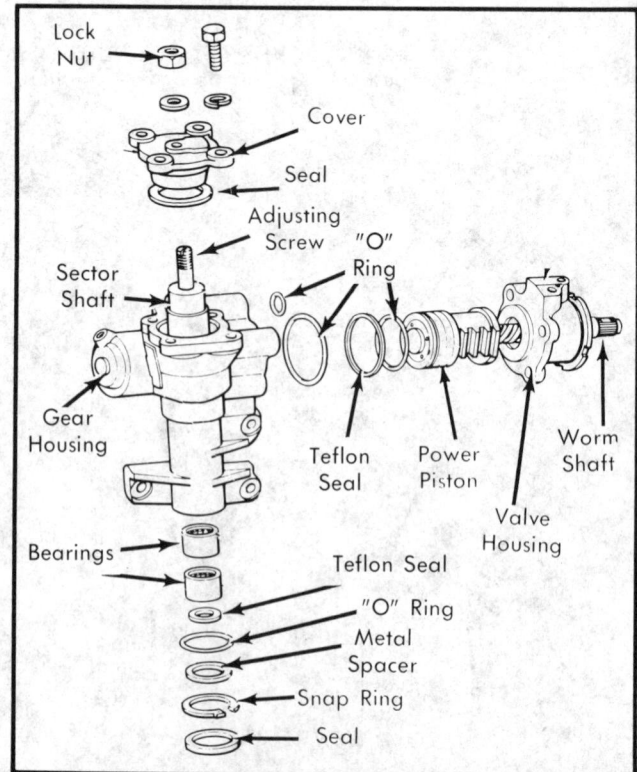

Fig. 4   Exploded View of Toyota Power Steering Gear Assembly

Power Steering

TOYOTA POWER-ASSISTED RECIRCULATING BALL (Cont.)

2) Inspect sector shaft for peeling or pitting at ball rolling surface. Check power piston nut mesh with sector shaft. Look for damaged tooth surfaces or ball rolling surfaces.

3) Gear housing bearings must be replaced if bearing rollers are pitted or peeled. Also replace housing bearings if it was noticed that sector shaft bearing surfaces had been scored or pitted.

4) Remove teflon ring and "O" ring from gear housing. Using needle bearing removing tool, remove needle bearings.

Reassembly — 1) Install needle bearings with longer edge of outer race facing outwards and make sure bearing top end aligns with housing end surface. Install lower bearing so that it is positioned .93" (23.6 mm) on Land Cruiser and Pickup models, or .76" (19.4 mm) on all other models, away from housing inner end surface.

2) Install "O" ring and Teflon ring to power piston. Install large and small "O" rings to gear housing, then install power piston assembly to gear housing. Tighten bolts.

3) To adjust worm shaft preload, loosen lock nut and install adjusting wrench to adjusting plug. Install torque wrench to wormshaft and tighten adjusting plug until preload is 3.5-5.6 INCH lbs. (4.0-6.5 cmkg) on all models. Hold adjusting plug and tighten lock nut.

4) Wrap a piece of tape around spline area of sector shaft. Align sector shaft gear teeth with power piston teeth (centered) and insert sector shaft into gear housing. Do not turn sector shaft during installation, as damage to "O" ring could result.

5) Install sector shaft cover, with seal, to sector shaft adjusting screw. Turn screw counterclockwise until cover will fit completely down on gear housing. Install bolts and tighten. To adjust total preload of steering gear, place steering gear in center postion and attach torque wrench to worm shaft.

6) Turn sector shaft adjusting screw until correct total preload is obtained. Total steering gear preload should be 6.1-9.1 INCH lbs. (7.0-10.5 cmkg) for Corona and Cressida models or 5.2-8.2 INCH lbs. (6.0-9.5 cmkg) for all other models. Install sector shaft adjusting lock nut and tighten.

TIGHTENING SPECIFICATIONS

Application	Ft. Lbs. (mkg)
Pump Housing Bolts	
Corolla	30-40 (4.1-5.5)
All Other Models	24-30 (3.3-4.1)
Sector Shaft Adjusting Screw Lock Nut	30-40 (4.1-5.5)
Sector Shaft Cover Bolts	30-40 (4.1-5.5)
Sector Shaft-to-Pitman Arm Nut	
Pickup, Land Cruiser	116-137 (16.0-19.0)
All Other Models	80-101 (11.0-14.0)
Worm Gear Adjusting Plug Lock Nut	33-40 (4.5-5.5)

Power Steering

VOLVO POWER-ASSISTED RACK & PINION

DL   GLE
GL   Coupe
GT   Diesel

DESCRIPTION

Power steering is rack and pinion cam gear type. Power steering consists of a rack and pinion steering gear and a power assist pump interconnected by flexible lines. The DL, GL and GT models use a ZF type pump. The GLE, Coupe and Diesel models use a Saginaw type of pump. Both types of pumps use separate reservoirs.

GENERAL SERVICE

STEERING GEAR LUBRICANT

Type — Engine oil SAE 20W-50 or SAE 20W-40.

Capacity — 6¾ oz.

HYDRAULIC SYSTEM LUBRICANT

Type — ATF
Capacity
  DL, GL, GT — 1.5 pts.
  GLE, Coupe, Diesel — 2.5 pts.

STEERING GEAR FILLING

Remove inner clamp on right side rubber bellows, and using a suction gun, fill gear with recommended lubricant through side of bellows. Reinstall clamp, then carefully compress bellows so some oil will flow to other side.

HYDRAULIC OIL FILLING AND BLEEDING

Fill the reservoir with approved oil, then start engine and allow to idle, adding oil as level drops. Turn steering wheel left and right lock to lock in a slow even motion to allow the pump to operate at low pressure. Continue turning steering wheel until oil in reservoir is almost free of air bubbles. Check that oil is at the level mark, then install reservoir cap.

SERVO BALANCE TESTING AND ADJUSTING

Testing — 1) Connect a pressure gauge as shown in *Fig. 1*. Make sure oil in reservoir is at level mark. Place pressure gauge so it can be seen from the drivers seat.

2) Remove steering wheel impact guard by compressing sides slightly. Install a torque wrench on steering wheel nut.

3) With engine at idle, turn steering wheel (using torque wrench) slowly to right and read torque the moment pressure reaches 170 psi (12 kg/cm²). Repeat operation turning steering wheel to left. Torque should be 30-40 INCH lbs. (35-46 cmkg) as pressure approaches 170 psi (12 kg/cm²). The difference between right and left sides may not exceed 8 INCH lbs. (9 cmkg).

4) If the difference between the sides exceeds this amount, use the following procedures for correction.

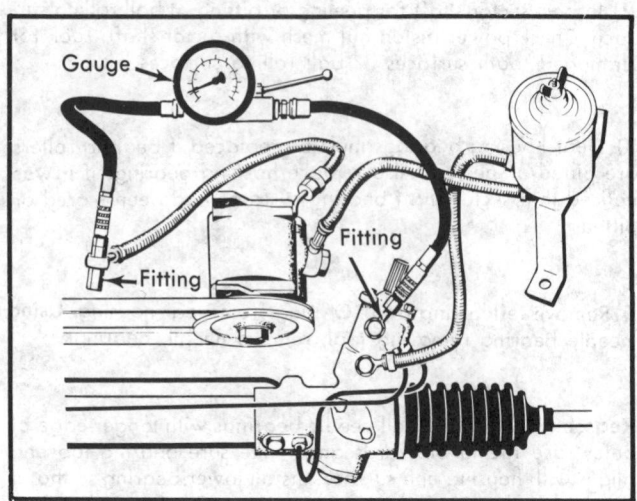

Fig. 1 Pressure Gauge Test Set Up

Adjusting — 1) Turn off engine and remove lock nut and lock washer from pinion lower bearing (See Fig. 2) Lock washer will have one tab bent down to lock adjustment nut (bearing race).

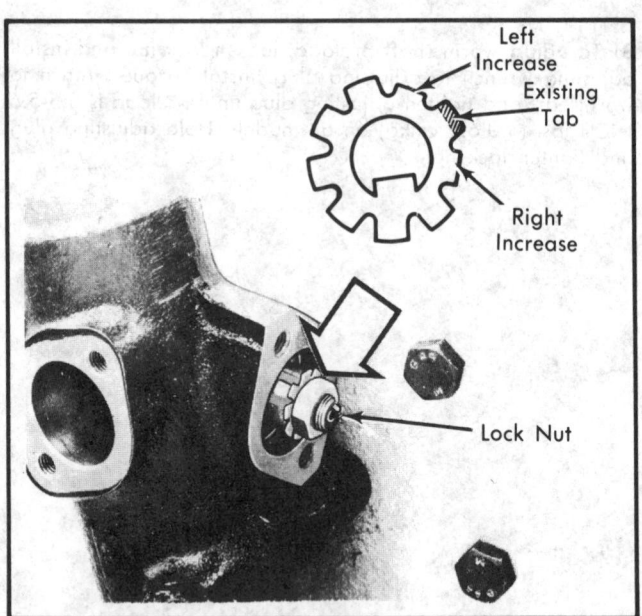

Fig. 2 Lock Washer Adjustment

2) To increase torque for left side, straighten existing bent tab and bend first tab to left. To increase torque for right side, bend first tab to right.

NOTE — *Changing tabs increases torque for one side and decreases torque an equal amount on the other side. The value of torque increase or decrease is 4 INCH lbs. (4.6 cmkg).*

3) After bending tab, use suitable tool (9995049) to turn adjustment nut until groove fits lock washer tab. Reinstall lock washer and lock nut. Install pinion cover and gasket.

VOLVO POWER-ASSISTED RACK & PINION (Cont.)

PUMP PRESSURE TEST

1) — With pressure gauge connected as shown in *Fig. 1*, and engine at idle, turn steering wheel fully to left, then fully to right, pressing at end position for a maximum of 10 seconds. Correct pressure should be 895-995 psi (63-69 kg/cm^2) for the Saginaw pump and 825 psi (58 kg/cm^2) for the ZF pump.

2) To test system maximum pressure, close pressure gauge valve and block oil flow for maximum of 10 seconds. If pressure does not reach the values in the preceeding paragraph, the pump is defective and must be repaired or replaced, *see Overhaul in this article.*

NOTE — *The manufacturer does not recommend repair of the Saginaw pump, replace if defective.*

REMOVAL & INSTALLATION

STEERING GEAR

Removal — **1)** Remove lock bolt and nut from pinion flange. Bend flange apart slightly. Raise and support front of vehicle and remove wheels. Remove tie rod nuts and disconnect ball studs from spindle using suitable ball joint removal tool (5043). Remove splash guard.

2) Disconnect hoses at steering gear and install plugs in hose connections to protect against contamination. Remove bolts securing steering gear to front axle member. Pull steering gear down until free of steering shaft flange, then remove steering gear on left side of vehicle.

Installation — **1)** To install, reverse removal procedure, noting the following: Make sure recess on pinion shaft is aligned toward lock bolt opening in flange.

2) Install right side "U" bolt and flange, but do not tighten. Install and tighten left side bolts, then tighten right side "U" bolt.

3) Connect steering rods, making sure rods are same length. Difference should not exceed $\frac{1}{16}$" (2 mm). Install lock bolt on flange and reconnect hoses.

POWER STEERING PUMP (ZF)

Removal — Place a container below the pump to receive drain oil, then disconnect hydraulic connections. Remove nuts on two long bracket bolts and tensioner locking screws on both sides of pump. Remove drive belt.

2) Turn pump up and remove three screws retaining bracket to engine block, then remove pump and bracket.

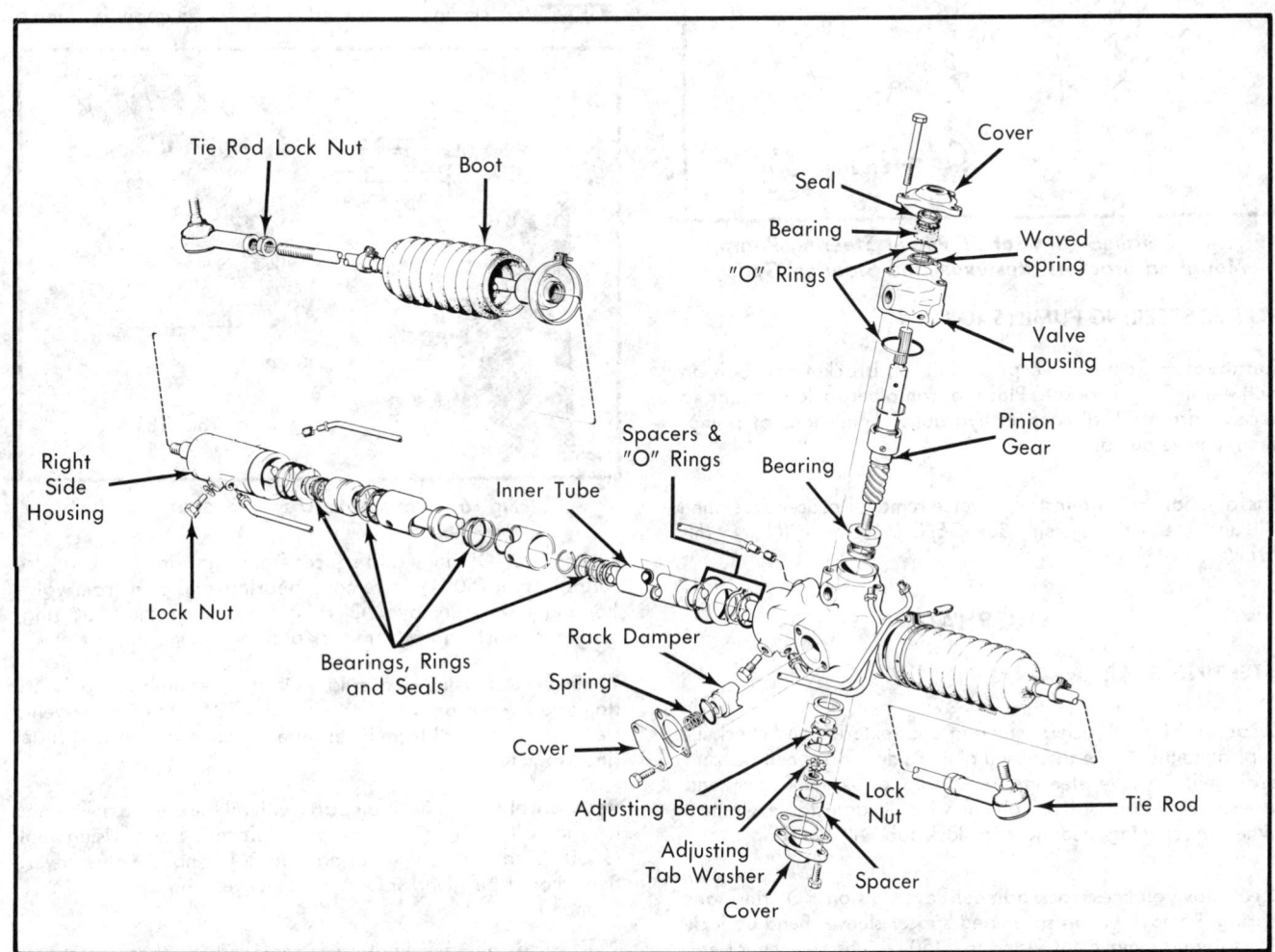

Fig. 3 Exploded View of Volvo Power Steering Components

VOLVO POWER-ASSISTED RACK & PINION (Cont.)

Installation — 1) To reinstall, reverse removal procedures, noting the following: Use new copper washers when reconnecting pump hoses. Fill the system with new oil that meets specifications. See *GENERAL SERVICING* in this article.

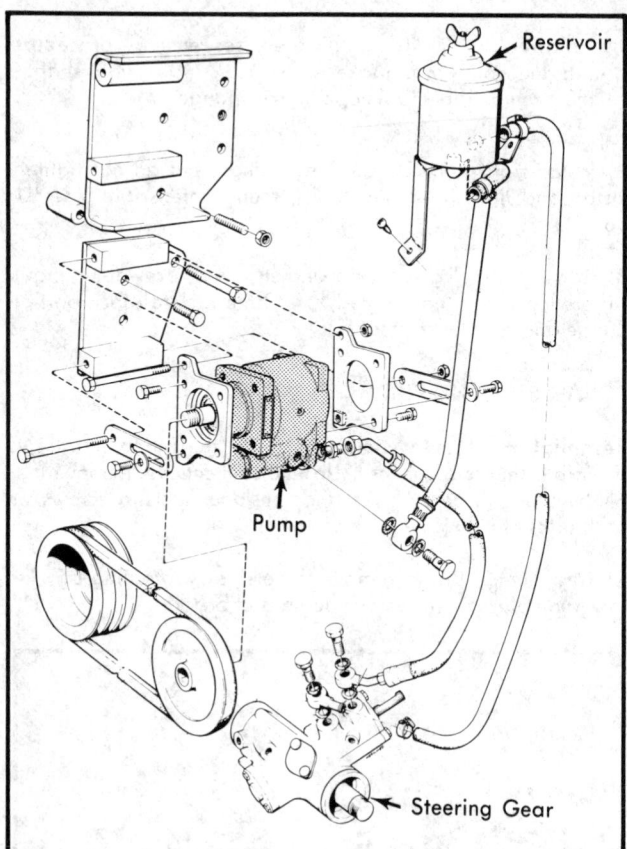

Fig. 4   Detailed View of ZF Power Steering Pump, Mounting Brackets, Reservoir and Steering Gear

POWER STEERING PUMP (SAGINAW)

Removal — Remove two pivot bolts on bracket and bolt on belt tensioning bracket. Place a container below pump to receive drain oil, disconnect hydraulic connections at pump, then remove pump.

Installation — To reinstall, reverse removal procedures, then fill and bleed the system, See *GENERAL SERVICING* in this article.

OVERHAUL

STEERING GEAR

Disassembly — 1) Clean steering gear exterior and check inner ball joints for wear. Loosen pinion side rubber bellows and drain oil. Remove steering rod using a 32 mm open end wrench, take load off of pinion with an adjustable wrench. When unscrewing steering rod, lock tab will bend up.

2) Remove oil lines, rack damper cover, piston, "O" ring, and spring. Remove pinion cover and spacer sleeve. Bend up locking tab and remove nut. Using tool (5049), unscrew inner bearing race with ball retainer and outer race from pinion.

3) Unscrew three screws from valve housing cover and remove cover and spring, then lift off valve housing and lift out pinion.

4) Unscrew right side housing lock bolt and remove housing and connecting tube from outer tube, then pull out rack and bearing sleeve. Remove bearing sleeve rack.

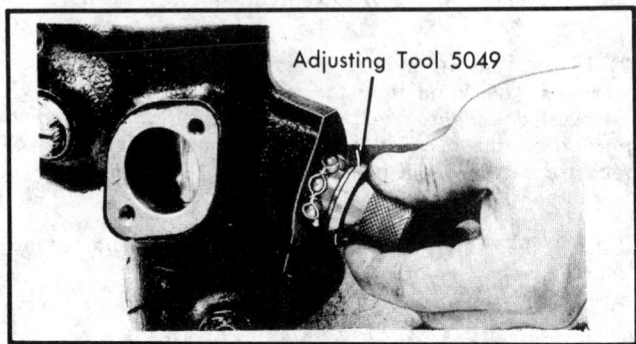

Fig. 5   Removing Inner Bearing Race from Steering Gear using Special Adjusting Tool 5049

5) Unscrew left side housing lock bolt, then remove outer and inner tube from housing. Using suitable tool (1819) remove upper bushing from housing. Use two narrow screwdrivers and remove lower pinion bearing outer race. Remove left side housing from fixture.

CAUTION — *Do not use tool (5051) to remove upper bushing.*

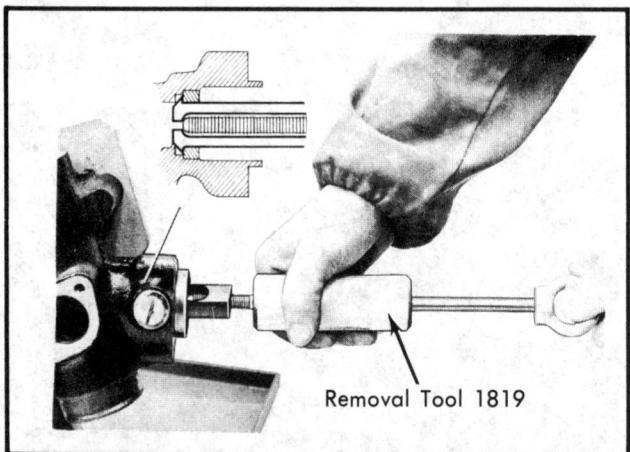

Fig. 6   Removing Upper Bushing

6) Remove "O" rings and spacer from right side housing. Use suitable tool (5051) to remove bearing and seal from valve housing cover. Remove "O" ring from cover and "O" ring, seal, and plastic rings from rack bearing sleeve.

7) Remove plastic ring and "O" ring from rack only if, damaged, worn or rack has more than 24,000 miles on vehicle. Remove oil seal from inner tube. Remove washer and snap ring from tube.

Reassembly — 1) Coat all parts with oil before reassembling. Replace all seals, "O" rings, and defective parts. Using tool (5050) install oil seal, bearing and "O" ring in valve cover. Seal should be glued into cover or cover and seal should be changed.

NOTE — *If the rack bearing is replaced, the bearing sleeve should also be replaced.*

VOLVO POWER-ASSISTED RACK & PINION (Cont.)

2) Install plastic ring and "O" ring on rack bearing sleeve with "O" ring on tapered side of sleeve. Install snap ring on inner tube, then install "O" ring and plastic ring on rack piston with the "O" ring under the plastic ring.

3) Assemble spacer sleeve, oil seal, and plastic ring on rack (from tooth side). Use tape over teeth to avoid damaging oil seal, then remove tape and install spacer sleeve on rack.

4) Insert seal in left side housing with lip facing out, then press in bushing using suitable tool. Install two "O" rings in left side housing, then install the two "O" rings and spacer washer in right side housing.

5) Lubricate end of inner tube and install with spacer into left housing, then push rack (with seal and spacer rings) into inner tube. Place tool (5056) on rack and using rack and tool, press seal and spacer rings into housing. Withdraw rack approximately ¾" (20 mm) and remove tool, install lock ring.

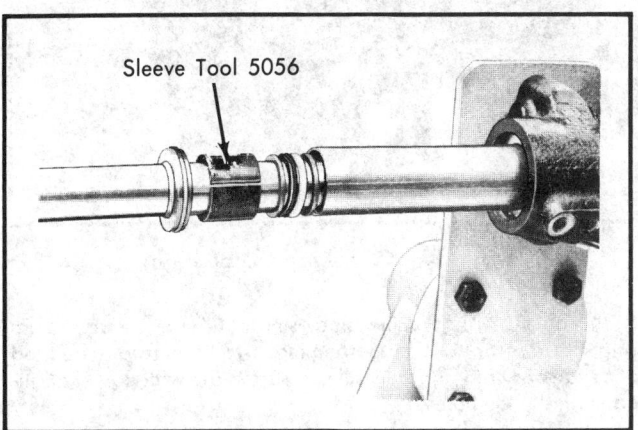

Sleeve Tool 5056

Fig. 7   Installing Seals & Spacer Rings

6) Insert outer tube in left housing, align lock bolt holes in housing and tube, lubricate tube and plastic seal on rack piston, then insert lock bolt with seal. Torque bolt to 9-12 ft. lbs. (1.24-1.66 mkg). Lubricate and insert bearing sleeve in outer tube.

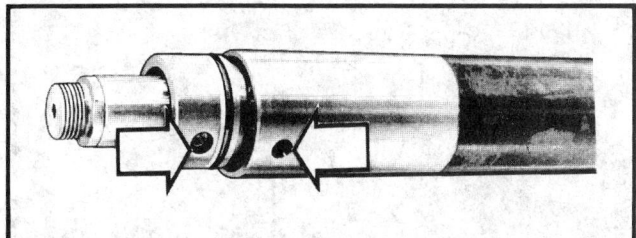

Fig. 8   Lock Bolt Hole Alignment

7) Align sleeve hole with outer tube hole, tape threaded edges and install seal. Remove tape and install plastic ring in bearing sleeve. Lubricate end of connecting tube and insert tube with rubber seal in right side of housing.

8) Install right housing with connecting tube and rubber seal. Align hole in right side of housing with hole in outer tube and install lock bolt. Torque bolt to 9-12 ft. lbs. (1.24-1.66 mkg).

9) Install upper race for pinion lower bearing and insert pinion. To avoid readjusting the steering wheel, center the rack. Insert the pinion with the flat outwards (to the left). Screw on sleeve tool (5049) until .31" (8 mm) of the axle end comes through the retainer. Remove tool.

10) Install outer race and spacer sleeve in housing. Press down spacer sleeve so it bottoms on bearing race, then use feeler gauge and straight edge to measure distance between spacer ring and housing. Select gasket(s) of proper thickness, then temporarily install gaskets and cover plate. Gaskets range in thickness from .008-.028" (.2-.7 mm).

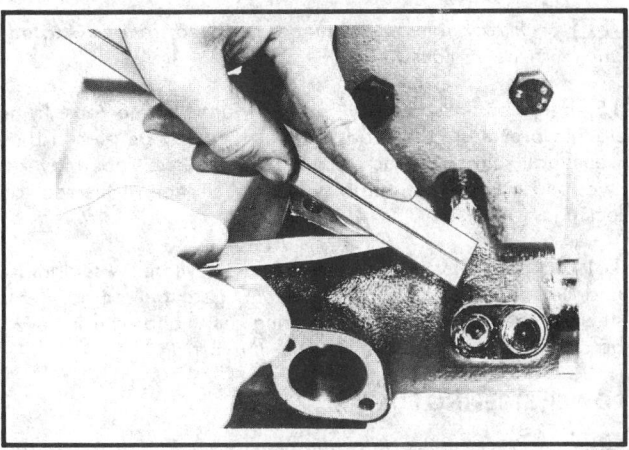

Fig. 9   Measuring for Gasket(s)

NOTE – Cover plate will have to be removed to make servo balance adjustment after steering gear is installed on vehicle. See GENERAL SERVICING in this article.

11) Insert "O" ring in valve housing, then install valve housing on gear. Install tool (5171) over splines. Place coil spring in valve housing, large end first. To eliminate the possibility of spring being caught in top groove of valve housing, adjust pinion upwards until spool covers the groove completely.

12) Install valve housing cover, check that coil spring is not squeezed between cover and housing. Pinion shaft shoulder should be .06" (1.5 mm) above cover face. Adjust by using tool (5049) and moving lower bearing inner race. Install lock ring and lock nut.

.088"
(1.5 mm)

Fig. 10   Pinion Shaft Shoulder Measurement

VOLVO POWER-ASSISTED RACK & PINION (Cont.)

13) Install damper piston (without "O" ring) in housing. Press piston against rack, then use feeler gauge and straight edge to measure clearance between piston face and housing. Adjust by using shims equal to measured clearance plus .002-.006" (.05-.15 mm). Shims are available in the following thicknesses: .002" (.051 mm), .0035" (.089 mm), .005" (.127 mm), and .010" (.254 mm).

14) Install "O" ring damper, spring, shims, and cover on housing. Use brass shims as the outer ones in stack. Connect an INCH lbs. torque wrench to pinion shaft and rotate shaft in both directions to stop. Torque should be 8-14 INCH lbs. (9-16 cmkg). If torque is excessive at any point, stop rack in that position and readjust by adding shims.

NOTE — *If rack jams with damper removed, rack is warped, and must be replaced.*

15) Install oil lines, reinstall left and right steering rods. If installing previously used rods, a thin shim may be placed between ball joint and rack shoulder or the two rods may be swapped in order to obtain an unused portion of the rod for locking.

16) Lock ball joint in rack recess and install bellows, clamps, and tie rod ends, then install steering gear on vehicle. Refill steering gear and power steering unit and check servo balance. *See General Servicing in this article.*

POWER STEERING PUMP

NOTE — *Procedures are for the ZF type pump only, manufacturer recommends replacement of the Saginaw type pump if found defective.*

Disassembly — 1) With pump removed from vehicle, pry front seal from housing. Remove rear cover snap ring and cover. Take out pressure plate and spring.

2) Turn pump over and tap on end until parts fall free. Remove ball bearing retaining ring, then push shaft out of housing. Push out thrust plate and cam ring, if still in housing.

3) Remove plug, control valve, spring and all "O" rings from housing. Check all parts for wear and scratches. Replace all worn or damaged parts and all "O" rings.

NOTE — *If pump housing bushing is defective, replace housing assembly. Rotor, vanes and cam ring are also replaced as an assembly.*

Reassembly — 1) Install bearing on shaft (if replaced). Bearing is held by rings on each side. Press bearing and shaft into housing.

2) Snap bearing retaining ring into housing. Install thrust plate in housing making sure dowel is through one of the holes in thrust plate, then place cam ring on dowel, arrow facing up.

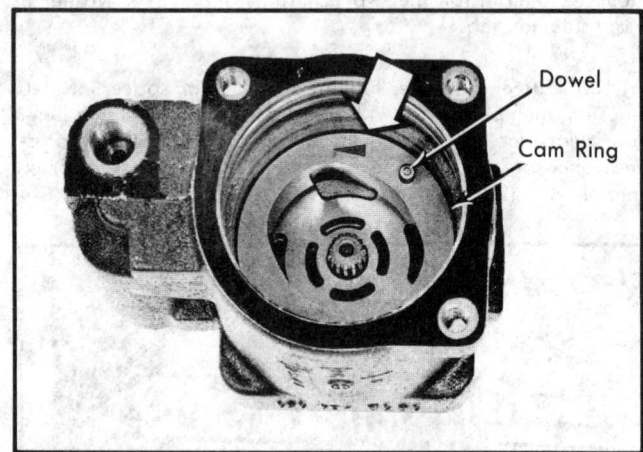

Fig. 11 Cam Ring Installation

3) Install "O" rings in housing, small "O" ring nearest cam ring. Place rotor in housing, then insert vanes in rotor (rounded ends toward cam ring). Install pressure plate with dowel aligned in one of the holes.

4) Insert "O" ring, spring and cover, then press in cover and install retaining ring. Install control valve, spring and plug, then place shaft seal into housing and tap seal lightly until properly seated.

5) Install pump assembly on vehicle, then refill and bleed system. *See GENERAL SERVICING in this article procedure.*

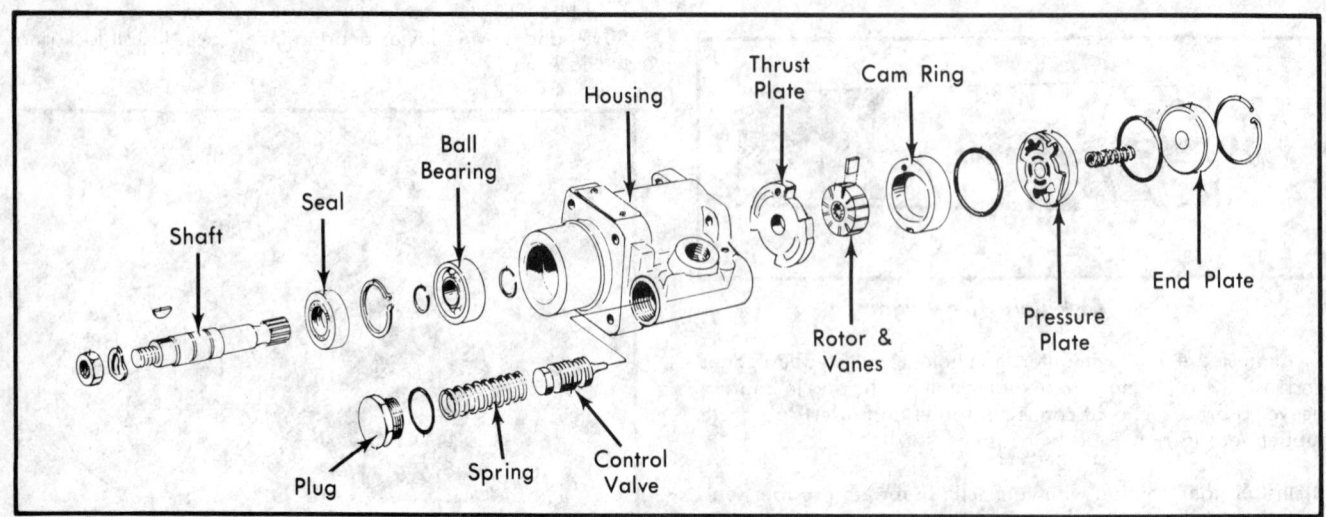

Fig. 12 Exploded View of ZF Power Steering Pump

English-Metric Conversion Chart

FRACTIONS TO INCHES & METRIC EQUIVALENTS

Fractions	Inches	MM	Fractions	Inches	MM
1/64	.016	.397	33/64	.516	13.097
1/32	.031	.794	17/32	.531	13.494
3/64	.047	1.191	35/64	.547	13.891
1/16	.063	1.588	9/16	.563	14.288
5/64	.078	1.984	37/64	.578	14.684
3/32	.094	2.381	19/32	.594	15.081
7/64	.109	2.778	39/64	.609	15.478
1/8	.125	3.175	5/8	.625	15.875
9/64	.141	3.572	41/64	.641	16.272
5/32	.156	3.969	21/32	.656	16.669
11/64	.172	4.366	43/64	.672	17.066
3/16	.188	4.763	11/16	.687	17.463
13/64	.203	5.159	45/64	.703	17.859
7/32	.219	5.556	23/32	.719	18.256
15/64	.234	5.953	47/64	.734	18.653
1/4	.250	6.350	3/4	.750	19.050
17/64	.266	6.747	49/64	.766	19.447
9/32	.281	7.144	25/32	.781	19.844
19/64	.297	7.541	51/64	.797	20.241
5/16	.313	7.938	13/16	.813	20.638
21/64	.328	8.334	53/64	.828	21.034
11/32	.344	8.731	27/32	.844	21.431
23/64	.359	9.128	55/64	.859	21.828
3/8	.375	9.525	7/8	.875	22.225
25/64	.391	9.922	57/64	.891	22.622
13/32	.406	10.319	29/32	.906	23.019
27/64	.422	10.716	59/64	.922	23.416
7/16	.438	11.113	15/16	.938	23.813
29/64	.453	11.509	61/64	.953	24.209
15/32	.469	11.906	31/32	.969	24.606
31/64	.484	12.303	63/64	.984	25.003
1/2	.500	12.700			

CONVERSION FACTORS

Unit	To	Unit	Multiply By	Unit	To	Unit	Multiply By
LENGTH				**WEIGHT**			
Millimeters		Inches	.03937	Grams		Ounces	.03527
Inches		Millimeters	25.4	Ounces		Grams	28.34953
Meters		Feet	3.28084	Kilograms		Pounds	2.20462
Feet		Meters	.3048	Pounds		Kilograms	.45359
Kilometers		Miles	.62137	**WORK**			
Miles		Kilometers	1.60935	Centimeter Kilograms		Inch Pounds	.8676
AREA				Inch Pounds		Centimeter Kilograms	1.15262
Square Centimeters		Square Inches	.155	Meter Kilograms		Foot Pounds	7.23301
Square Inches		Square Centimeters	6.45159	Foot Pounds		Meter Kilograms	.13826
VOLUME				**PRESSURE**			
Cubic Centimeters		Cubic Inches	.06103	Kilograms/ Sq. Centimeter		Pounds/Sq.Inch	14.22334
Cubic Inches		Cubic Centimeters	16.38703	Pounds/Sq.Inch		Kilograms/Sq.Centimeter	.07031
Liters		Cubic Inches	61.025	Bar		Pounds/Sq.Inch	14.504
Cubic Inches		Liters	.01639	Pounds/Sq.Inch		Bar	.06895
Liters		Quarts	1.05672	Atmosphere		Pounds/Sq.Inch	14.696
Quarts		Liters	.94633	Pounds/Sq.Inch		Atmosphere	.06805
Liters		Pints	2.11344	**TEMPERATURE**			
Pints		Liters	.47317	Centigrade Degrees		Fahrenheit Degrees	$(C° \times \frac{9}{5})+32$
Liters		Ounces	33.81497	Fahrenheit Degrees		Centigrade Degrees	$(F° - 32) \times \frac{5}{9}$
Ounces		Liters	.02957				

English-Metric Conversion Chart

MILLIMETERS TO INCHES

Conversion Factor — Multiply known millimeter figure by .03937

MM	Inches	MM	Inches	MM	Inches	MM	Inches	MM	Inches
1	.039	21	.827	41	1.614	61	2.402	81	3.189
2	.079	22	.866	42	1.654	62	2.441	82	3.228
3	.118	23	.906	43	1.693	63	2.480	83	3.268
4	.157	24	.945	44	1.732	64	2.520	84	3.307
5	.197	25	.984	45	1.772	65	2.559	85	3.346
6	.236	26	1.024	46	1.811	66	2.598	86	3.386
7	.276	27	1.063	47	1.850	67	2.638	87	3.425
8	.315	28	1.102	48	1.890	68	2.677	88	3.465
9	.354	29	1.142	49	1.929	69	2.717	89	3.504
10	.394	30	1.181	50	1.969	70	2.756	90	3.543
11	.433	31	1.220	51	2.008	71	2.795	91	3.583
12	.472	32	1.260	52	2.047	72	2.835	92	3.622
13	.512	33	1.299	53	2.087	73	2.874	93	3.661
14	.551	34	1.339	54	2.126	74	2.913	94	3.701
15	.591	35	1.378	55	2.165	75	2.953	95	3.740
16	.630	36	1.417	56	2.205	76	2.992	96	3.780
17	.669	37	1.457	57	2.244	77	3.031	97	3.819
18	.709	38	1.496	58	2.283	78	3.071	98	3.858
19	.748	39	1.535	59	2.323	79	3.110	99	3.898
20	.787	40	1.575	60	2.362	80	3.150	100	3.937

INCHES TO MILLIMETERS

Conversion Factor — Multiply known inch figure by 25.40

Inches	MM	Inches	MM	Inches	MM	Inches	MM	Inches	MM
.001	.025	.040	1.016	.340	8.636	.640	16.256	.940	23.876
.002	.051	.050	1.270	.350	8.890	.650	16.510	.950	24.130
.003	.076	.060	1.524	.360	9.144	.660	16.764	.960	24.384
.004	.102	.070	1.778	.370	9.398	.670	17.018	.970	24.638
.005	.127	.080	2.032	.380	9.652	.680	17.272	.980	24.892
.006	.152	.090	2.286	.390	9.906	.690	17.526	.990	25.146
.007	.178	.100	2.540	.400	10.160	.700	17.780	1.000	25.400
.008	.203	.110	2.794	.410	10.414	.710	18.034	2.000	50.800
.009	.229	.120	3.048	.420	10.668	.720	18.288	3.000	76.200
.010	.254	.130	3.302	.430	10.922	.730	18.542	4.000	101.600
.011	.279	.140	3.556	.440	11.176	.740	18.796	5.000	127.000
.012	.305	.150	3.810	.450	11.430	.750	19.050		
.013	.330	.160	4.064	.460	11.684	.760	19.304		
.014	.356	.170	4.318	.470	11.938	.770	19.558		
.015	.381	.180	4.572	.480	12.192	.780	19.812		
.016	.406	.190	4.826	.490	12.446	.790	20.066		
.017	.432	.200	5.080	.500	12.700	.800	20.320		
.018	.457	.210	5.334	.510	12.954	.810	20.574		
.019	.483	.220	5.558	.520	13.208	.820	20.828		
.020	.508	.230	5.842	.530	13.462	.830	21.082		
.021	.533	.240	6.096	.540	13.716	.840	21.336		
.022	.559	.250	6.350	.550	13.970	.850	21.590		
.023	.584	.260	6.604	.560	14.224	.860	21.844		
.024	.610	.270	6.858	.570	14.478	.870	22.098		
.025	.635	.280	7.112	.580	14.732	.880	22.352		
.026	.652	.290	7.366	.590	14.986	.890	22.606		
.027	.686	.300	7.620	.600	15.240	.900	22.860		
.028	.711	.310	7.874	.610	15.494	.910	23.114		
.029	.737	.320	8.128	.620	15.748	.920	23.368		
.030	.762	.330	8.382	.630	16.002	.930	23.622		

NOTE — The latest changes and corrections represent a collection of last minute 1980 information which arrived too late to be incorporated into the regular data pages. In addition, we have included information on prior year models which we have received since the production of last year's edition.

TUNE-UP & FUEL SYSTEMS — SECTIONS 1 & 2

1 ▶ *1979 COLT & CHAMP: OIL IN AIR CLEANER* — A small amount of oil in the air cleaner is considered normal. In cases of excessive oil in the air cleaner, replace valve cover on 1400 cc engine with part number MD30274. On 1600 cc engines, install washer, part number MDO 07746 under left front camshaft bearing cap bolt and install new valve cover, part number MDO 07496, and retainer screw, part number MF 100065.

2 ▶ *1979 STRADA AND X1/9: IGNITION TIMING* — Some 1979 Fiat Strada and X1/9 models may experience a shifting of the ignition timing pointer at the crankshaft pulley, resulting in improper timing settings. To ensure correct timing setting, check the timing marks at both the crankshaft pulley and the flywheel. Correct timing for standard transmission models should be 5°BTDC at 800-850 RPM, and 5°BTDC at 700-750 RPM for automatic transmission models.

3 ▶ *1980 FIESTA WITH FEDERAL EMISSIONS AND CALIBRATION NUMBERS 0-5B-R1 AND 0-5B-R2: EXHAUST BACKFIRE DURING UPSHIFT AND DECELERATION* — A condition of minor, but noticeable, exhaust backfire that occurs when shifting gears or during deceleration can be corrected by installing a new thermactor air by-pass valve and revised vacuum controls as described below.

1) Disconnect single vacuum hose from thermactor air by-pass valve. Remove and discard existing by-pass valve. Install a new timed air by-pass valve (Part No. D5ZZ-9B289F).

2) Install a new thermactor idle vacuum valve (Part No. D6DZ-9G328A) by connecting vacuum hose removed from original by-pass valve to idle vacuum valve connector port marked "VAC".

3) Connect 3" length of vacuum hose to other port of idle vacuum valve. Connect other end of this hose to vacuum reservoir (Part No. D6TZ-9E453A).

4) Connect remaining port of vacuum reservoir to upper port of air by-pass valve with a 4" piece of vacuum hose. Unfasten air cleaner and raise it slightly.

5) Locate vacuum hose running between air cleaner bi-metal sensor and vacuum tee and insert a new 3-way tee (Part No. 378830-S) into line.

6) Connect open end of tee to one end of an 18" length of vacuum hose. Connect opposite end of hose to lower port on air by-pass valve.

7) Refasten air cleaner. Use plastic straps to secure vacuum hoses and ensure there are no kinks in hoses. Install emission modification decal in engine compartment.

4 ▶ *1978-80 FIESTA: CARBURETOR THROTTLE DASHPOT SPECIFICATION* — The specification for adjustment of throttle dashpot to obtain proper clearance between dashpot plunger and throttle lever is .197" (5 mm). The measurement should be made with throttle lever set at specified engine curb idle speed and dashpot plunger in fully collapsed position. Loosen dashpot locknut and adjust dashpot position as required to obtain proper clearance.

5 ▶ *1979 MERCEDES DIESEL: PRECHAMBER TIP* — 1979 Turbo Diesel models use a cup shaped prechamber. This prechamber is not interchangeable with the wedge shaped prechamber used in earlier models.

6 ▶ *1979 PEUGEOT 504 (GASOLINE): IGNITION SYSTEM* — 1979 models are equipped with electronic ignition, replacing contact points. The distributor advance curve remains the same for both ignition systems. Champion N 288 spark plugs are used on all models.

7 ▶ *1979 & EARLIER PORSCHE 928 & TURBO MODELS: ENGINE MISFIRING* — Engine misfiring may be caused by fuel restriction to one or more of the fuel injectors. Check for loose fuel filter screens in fuel outlet ports of the fuel distributor. If the screens are loose, replace all 8 bolts which hold down the fuel distributor with new bolts (part number 930-110-547-00). Do not replace the outlet port filter screens or fuel distributor unless replacement of bolts fails to correct the misfiring. Always replace the gasket on the bolts when replacing bolts.

8 ▶ *SAAB MODELS WITH BREAKERLESS IGNITION: DISTRIBUTOR HOLD DOWN CLIPS* — On these models, the ignition distributor contains an electromagnetic pulse generator. Care must be exercised when cranking an engine with the distributor cap removed. The magnetism in the unit will attract the distributor hold-down clips. When the engine is cranked over the clips will interfere with the metal timing rotor and may cause bending or breakage of either the rotor or the clips.

9 ▶ *SAAB MODELS WITH LAMBDA CONROL AND ALL SAAB TURBOS: USING EXHAUST GAS ANALYZERS* — When using an exhaust gas analyzer for checking/adjusting idle air fuel mixture on these models, the oxygen sensor wire plug must ALWAYS be disconnected. Failure to disconnect wire will result in excessively rich mixtures, high emissions, poor fuel economy, oil dilution and possible long term durability problems. After using exhaust gas analyzers, reconnect oxygen sensor wire.

TUNE-UP & FUEL SYSTEMS — SECTIONS 1 & 2 (Cont.)

▶ *1980 TOYOTA COROLLA MODELS: CARBURETOR FLOAT CHANGE* — The shape of carburetor float used on these models has been changed for parts standardization as shown in the illustration. In addition, float adjusting levels have been changed. The upper level adjustment has changed from .255" (6.5 mm) to .362" (9.2 mm). The lower level adjustment remains the same at .047" (1.2 mm). The new float and old float are interchangeable.

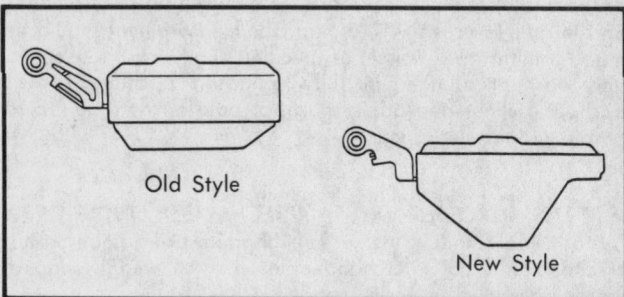

Toyota Corolla Float Modification

▶ *1980 VOLVO MODELS WITH DIESEL ENGINES: DELIVERY VALVE* — Whenever it is necessary to loosen or replace a diesel injection pump delivery valve, a new packing washer MUST be installed. The packing washer is installed behind spring seat in pump housing. *See illustration.* After packing washer (Volvo Part No. 243558-4) is installed, nipple should be tightened to 37 ft. lbs. (5.1 mkg).

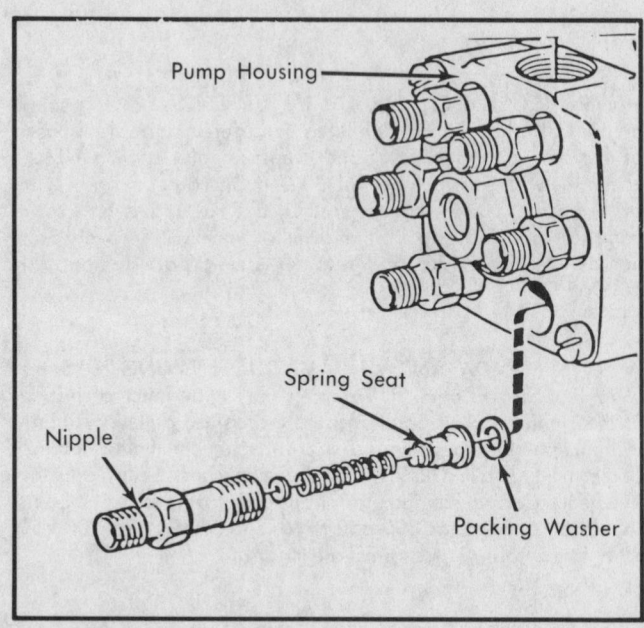

Installing Packing Washer on Volvo Injection Pump

ELECTRICAL — SECTION 3

▶ *1978-80 FIESTA MODELS: INSTRUMENT VOLTAGE REGULATOR* — A condition of erratic operation of fuel and temperature gauges where indicator needle momentarily flicks upward, then returns to normal position, may be serviced by installing a new electronic instrument voltage stabilizer (Part No. EORZ-10804-A). When installing the new stabilizer on Sport and Ghia models, the radio suppressor must be removed and discarded.

▶ *ALL SAAB MODELS: ALTERNATOR REGULATOR USAGE* — Do not attempt to interchange alternator regulators between Turbo and non-Turbo alternators. Turbo alternator has smaller diameter slip rings and longer brushes. Use of non-Turbo regulator in Turbo alternator will result in very short brush life.

ENGINES — SECTION 5

▶ *ALL AUDI 500 DIESEL MODELS: COMBUSTION CHAMBER INSERTS* — Combustion chamber inserts in the cylinder heads on diesel engines are no longer supplied as a service replacement. If inserts are damaged, the cylinder head must be replaced.

▶ *1978 AND EARLIER CHYSLER CORP. IMPORT VEHICLES: ENGINE BLOCK-TO-TRANSMISSION DOWEL PINS* — When replacing engine block, transmission case or clutch housing on these models, the following dowel pin precautions should be observed.

Manual Transmission — If dowel pin surface of bolt hole in transmission case or clutch housing is smaller than .276" (7 mm), replace dowel pin in new engine block with replacement pin (Chrysler Part No. MS471108). If this area is greater than .276" (7 mm), do not replace dowel pin.

Automatic Transmission — It is not necessary to replace dowel pins on automatic transmissions.

Engine Block — If dowel pins project more than .256" (6.5 mm) from engine block, no replacement is required. If pins project less than .256" (6.5 mm), replace pins with new pins (Chrysler Part No. MD020260).

FOR 1980 & PREVIOUS MODELS

ENGINES — SECTION 5 (Cont.)

3 ► *1979 CHRYSLER CORP. IMPORTS WITH 2000 OR 2600 cc ENGINES: ROCKER ARM CHANGES* — The rocker arms on these engines were changed from cast iron to aluminum to improve engine sound. In addition, an oil groove was added to rocker arm shaft oil hole to improve rocker arm lubrication. Aluminum rocker arms cannot be used with rocker arm shafts that do not have the added oil groove.

4 ► *ALL CHRYSLER CORP. COLT & ARROW MODELS WITH 2000 cc OR 2600 cc ENGINES: COUNTERBALANCE AND TIMING CHAIN NOISE* — Before replacing either of these chains on subject models, the following procedures should be performed. On counterbalance chains, make sure chain is properly adjusted. If adjustment does not correct problem, then replace chain. On timing chains, start engine and listen for noise. If the chain chatters on starting, a rubber washer (part number MD021242) should be added to the tensioner sleeve to prevent the noise. If the chain is noisy at idle, an improved tensioner spring (part number MD022235) should be installed to provide proper tension. The new spring has green paint on one end, and white paint on the other end.

5 ► *ALL 1979 CHRYSLER IMPORT CARS & TRUCKS: CRANKSHAFT MAIN BEARING CHANGE* — On subject models, the oil grooves of the lower main bearing and cap have been removed to improve engine sound. Modifications were also made to the crankshaft oil holes. When using the lower main bearing and cap with the oil groove, either the old or new crankshaft may be used. When using the lower main bearing and cap without the oil groove, only the new crankshaft can be used.

6 ► *1979-80 COURIER MODELS WITH 2300 cc ENGINE, CALIFORNIA EMISSIONS AND ALL CHASSIS CAB MODELS: EXHAUST LEAK AT CYLINDER HEAD* — On these models built before April, 1980, an exhaust leak may be noticed when starting a cold engine. The leak comes from below the No. 4 cylinder exhaust port and thermactor port. The leak is a result of warpage of exhaust manifold due to extreme operating conditions. This can be corrected as follows:

1) With air cleaner in place, remove exhaust manifold heat stove. Disconnect thermactor hose from check valve without removing check valve and pipe assembly from manifold. Disconnect EGR line from manifold.

2) Disconnect manifold from exhaust pipe, saving stainless steel gasket. Remove exhaust manifold.

3) Clean exhaust side of cylinder head and face of exhaust manifold. Insert a brass plug (Part No. E07Z-6026-A) into No. 4 thermactor port in cylinder head. Insert small end first and drive it in using small drift and hammer until plug stops moving, being careful not to damage gasket surface.

4) Apply a light film of graphite grease to mounting surface of cylinder head and exhaust manifold. Reinstall exhaust manifold using new gaskets (Part No. E07Z-9448-A).

5) Torque manifold mounting bolts to 35-40 ft. lbs. (4.8-5.5 mkg) in two steps. Reconnect exhaust pipe to manifold, using gasket saved from removal.

6) Connect EGR tube to manifold and tighten connector. Install thermactor/check valve assembly to exhaust manifold. Reconnect thermactor hose to check valve.

7) Start engine and allow it to warm-up. After engine is hot, retorque exhaust manifold bolts. Install manifold heat stove and air cleaner hot air tube.

7 ► *1979 FIAT STRADA: COOLING FAN* — 1979 Fiat Strada models may exhibit a condition where the engine cooling fan does not stay energized when the ignition key is removed. This is possibly due to reversed wire connections at the cooling fan relay. Proper wire color code connections for the fan relay are:

Color	Relay Terminal No.
Black	30
Gray/Black	85
Black/Violet	86
White/Black	87
Gray/Red	87A

8 ► *1980 FIAT BRAVA AND SPIDER 2000 MODELS: TIMING BELT TENSIONER PULLEY* — To maximize usage of timing belt, the width of timing belt tensioner pulley has been increased from .944" (24 mm), to 1.102" (28 mm). Old and new tensioner pulleys are interchangeable. Part number for new pulley is 4443446.

9 ► *1978-79 FIAT SPIDER AND BRAVA: ENGINE TIGHTENING SPECIFICATIONS* — The following specifications should be added to the Fiat Brava and Spider engine article in 1978 and 1979 editions of Mitchell's Imported Car and Truck Manual. The Center Main Bearing Cap Bolt should be tightened to 83 ft. lbs. (11.4 mkg). The Main Bearing Cap Self-Locking Bolts should also be tightened to 83 ft. lbs. (11.4 mkg).

10 ► *All FIAT MODELS: RETORQUING CYLINDER HEAD* — Whenever a cylinder head gasket is replaced on Fiat engines, it is essential that cylinder head be retorqued after vehicle has been driven for 700 to 1000 miles. This will ensure proper seating of cylinder head to crankcase. Torquing of cylinder head should only be performed when cylinder head is cool to touch.

11 ► *ALL FIAT X1/9: PISTON AND ROD INSTALLATION* — Revised factory information states that X1/9 piston and rod assemblies must be installed in block with numbers stamped on connecting rods and rod caps facing AWAY from auxiliary shaft. Original procedure stated that numbers must face toward auxiliary shaft.

FOR 1980 & PREVIOUS MODELS

ENGINES — SECTION 5 (Cont.)

► *1978-80 FIESTA: TIMING CHAIN FRONT COVER GASKET REPLACEMENT* — The timing chain front cover gasket can be removed and replaced without removing the engine by following the procedure below.

1) Open hood and cover fenders. Loosen thermactor pump pivot bolt and adjusting bolt and remove drive belt. Remove adjusting and pivot bolts, and remove thermactor pump.

2) Remove 3 bolts securing water pump pulley to water pump and remove pulley. Raise vehicle on hoist. Remove alternator drive belt, pivot and adjusting bolts and alternator.

3) Remove crankshaft damper retaining bolt and remove damper. Remove 10 bolts securing front cover to engine, and remove cover.

4) Throroughly clean gasket mating surfaces of front cover, block and oil pan. Position a new gasket and oil pan front seal on front cover.

5) Position front cover on block and secure with original bolts. Tighten bolts evenly to 5-7 ft. lbs. (.69-.96 mkg). Position crankshaft damper pulley on crankshaft and tighten attaching bolts to 40-44 ft. lbs. (5.5-6.0 mkg).

6) Place alternator in position and install adjusting and pivot bolts finger tight. Lower vehicle.

7) Place water pump pulley in position and tighten bolts evenly to 6-8 ft. lbs. (.82-1.1 mkg). Place drive belt over crankshaft, water pump inner groove and alternator pulleys. Adjust belt tension to specifications and tighten alternator adjusting and pivot bolts.

8) Place thermactor pump in position and install mounting bolts finger tight. Place drive belt over water pump pulley outer groove and thermactor pump pulley. Adjust belt tension to specifications and tighten thermactor adjusting and pivot bolts.

► *1980 MERCEDES-BENZ 300SD MODELS: VIBRATION DAMPER FOR INJECTION PUMP* — Since February, 1980, a vibration damper is installed on governor linkage of injection pump. This damper greatly reduces problem of engine vibration at idle. Damper is not set at factory, because setting and adjustment must take place on a run-in engine. If complaints of engine vibration at idle exist, the following procedure should be used to set and adjust damper.

1) Bring engine to operating temperature. Loosen lock nut on vibration damper.

2) With engine idling at 750 RPM, turn screw on damper until engine vibration is at its lowest point.

3) Tighten lock nut to 15-18 ft. lbs. (2.0-2.4 mkg).

NOTE — *Do not turn damper adjusting screw in too far as this will have an adverse effect on cold engine idle.*

► *ALL MERCEDES-BENZ 240D AND 300 SERIES MODELS WITH DIESEL ENGINES: CAP AND LOCK NUTS FOR VALVES* — When adjusting valve clearance or repairing valve mechanism on these engines, check that cap nut is securely locked by lock nut. Loose cap nuts can lead to engine damage. The following items should be noted when performing valve work.

1) Check cap and lock nuts for tightness. Check that there is a secure seating between cap and lock nuts.

2) Check nuts for wear. If thickness of lock nut is less than .197" (5 mm), it should be replaced with a new lock nut with a thickness of .236" (6 mm).

3) If nuts are worn out, check threads on valve stems for damage and repair or replace as required.

4) Check temper cast camshafts for wear. An exceedingly worn surface on camshaft lobe can result in loosening of lock nuts. In case of worn cam lobes, replace camshaft, rocker arms, valve springs and cap and lock nuts. Check general condition of valves and replace as required.

► *SAAB MODELS WITH SODIUM-FILLED EXHAUST VALVES: PROPER DISPOSING OF SCRAP VALVES* — Special procedures must be taken when disposing of sodium-filled exhaust valves used on some Saab models. The following procedure should be followed exactly for proper disposal. These valves must never be mixed with ordinary scrap without first performing this procedure. Failure to do so may incur danger of explosions and personal harm.

1) Drill a hole through the valve disc as far as the sodium content, as shown in the illustration.

2) Drill a second hole through the shaft, or saw off the shaft, about 1" (25 mm) from end of valve as shown in illustration.

CAUTION — *During drilling, sawing or other action which exposes the sodium, extreme care must be taken so that no water is allowed to come into contact with sodium. If water is mixed with sodium, an explosion will result.*

3) Stand at least 10 ft. away from a bucket of water and throw valve into bucket. This will cause a powerful explosive reaction which will last about one or two minutes. Valves may then be mixed with ordinary scrap for disposal.

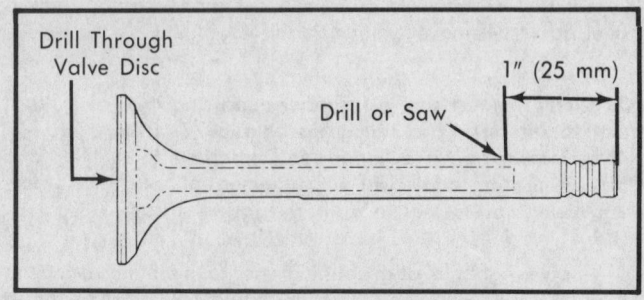

Drilling Saab Sodium-Filled Exhaust Valves

FOR 1980 & PREVIOUS MODELS

ENGINES — SECTION 5 (Cont.)

[16] ▶ *SAAB TURBO ENGINES: PISTON "ROCK" IN CYLINDER —* When evaluating cylinder wear in Turbo engines, do not be mislead by piston "rock" after cylinder head is removed. This is normal. Turbo pistons are manufactured with considerable taper as compared with normal engine pistons. The taper, toward piston crown, allows for increased heat and expansion when operating under boost. The crown and bottom piston skirt may measure up to .025" (.646 mm) difference. Therefore, the only valid measuring point for turbo pistons is between bottom of piston skirt and cylinder wall.

[17] ▶ *ALL SAAB MODELS WITH CONTINUOUS INJECTION SYSTEM (CIS): THERMOSTAT REMOVAL —* When changing thermostat on CIS-equipped engines, it is very important that coolant be drained below level of thermostat housing. If themostat housing is removed with coolant level high, coolant may spill over into warm-up regulator vent. Coolant saturation on warm-up regulator may lead to corrosion of regulator and possible malfunction.

[18] ▶ *ALL VOLKSWAGEN RABBIT & SCIROCCO MODELS: CRANKSHAFT OIL SEAL —* When replacing crankshaft oil seals at the flywheel end, always measure crankshaft diameter and select the seal to match. Seals come in 2 sizes, 82 and 85 millimeters.

[19] ▶ *1979 VOLKSWAGEN RABBIT & SCIROCCO: CAMSHAFT SPROCKET BOLT —* If engine is turned by crankshaft sprocket bolt counter to engine rotation when adjusting valve clearances, bolt may come loose. If this occurs, remove bolt and clean threads. Coat bolt with suitable locking compound and tighten to 58 ft. lbs. (8.0 mkg).

CLUTCHES — SECTION 6

[1] ▶ *1978-80 CHRYSLER CORP. IMPORT VEHICLES WITH KM 130 AND KM 132 MANUAL TRANSMISSIONS: NEW CLUTCH RELEASE BEARING —* A new style clutch release bearing with an integral carrier has been released for servicing these vehicles. The new style release bearing is self-aligning and replaces the separate release bearing and carrier set. The appropriate part numbers are listed below.

Application	Part No.
KM 130	MD700257
KM 132	MD703270

[2] ▶ *1978-79 FORD FIESTA WITH MANUAL TRANSMISSIONS: CLUTCH RELEASE FORK ATTACHING BOLT BREAKAGE —* If clutch pedal feels spongy and the friction point for clutch engagement moves toward lower end of pedal travel causing difficult noisy gear changes, it may be caused by the release fork bolt breaking.

The bolt breaking can be caused by one of the following: If bolt is insufficiently tightened, or bolt shank is not flush to release fork mating surface. If there is a misalignment of shaft threaded hole-to-fork counterbore. If bolt bottoms in fork due to insufficient thread depth. If any of these conditions exist, the following procedure can be used to correct it.

1) Remove transaxle assembly from vehicle.

2) Drill out and remove broken bolt. Dismantle fork, shaft and lever assembly.

3) Hand check new bolt into fork prior to assembly on shaft and lever assembly.

4) Hand start new bolt until shank is fully seated in counterbore. If bolt fails to seat by hand, replace shaft and lever assembly.

5) Insure that bolt is fully seated and properly tightened to 19-24 ft. lbs. (2.6-3.3 mkg).

[3] ▶ *MERCEDES-BENZ 240D AND ALL 300 SERIES MODELS WITH AUTOMATIC TRANSMISSIONS: MODIFIED CLUTCH DISCS FOR K2 CLUTCH —* Since September of 1979, clutch discs without grooves have been installed in 722.117/118/120 transmissions. At the same time, the number of pressure springs for clutch piston was reduced from 20 to 16. The modified clutch discs possess a greater coefficient of friction, resulting in prevention of occasional slippage on 3rd to 4th upshifts. When rebuilding transmissions, it is possible to install new clutch discs on transmissions which do not have them. In addition, the number of pressure springs should be reduced to 16, from 20. The modified clutch discs were placed in production after the following transmission numbers.

Application	Transmission No.
300SD	14921
240D	30916
300D, CD & TD	86933

[4] ▶ *VOLVO MODELS WITH MANUAL TRANSMISSIONS: PRESSURE PLATES AND RELEASE BEARINGS —* Two different designs of pressure plates and release bearings are used on Volvo 240 and 260 models. The two designs are easily recognizable by the fingers of the pressure plate. Plates for 260 models have fingers that are raised approximately 9/32" (7 mm) at the center. Plate fingers on 240 model plates are straight. Because of the finger difference, there are two different release bearings for these models. Release bearings for 260 models are approximately 1-7/16" (36.5 mm) long. Release bearings for 240 models are approximately 1-11/16" (43 mm) long. Pressure plates and release bearings must be used in the correct combination and should not be mixed.

Latest Changes & Corrections

FOR 1980 & PREVIOUS MODELS

BRAKES — SECTION 7

▶ *1980 CHRYSLER CORP. SAPPORO, CHALLENGER, COLT STATION WAGON AND ARROW MODELS WITH 9" REAR BRAKES: REAR BRAKE VIBRATION* — If vibration of rear brakes at low speed application occurs, the shoe-to-shoe retaining springs should be replaced using following procedures.

Shoe-to-Shoe Spring — Attach one end of shoe-to-shoe spring to hole in trailing shoe, then install hook of other end of spring to hole in leading shoe with a screwdriver.

Shoe Retainer Spring — Installation procedure remains unchanged for retaining spring; however, spring ends must point away from backing plate when installing new retaining springs (Chrysler Part No. MD151334). When replacing retaining springs, new parts should be used.

▶ *1978 AND 1979 DATSUN: BRAKE DRUM TOLERANCE* — Revised specifications for brake drums are .0047" (.12 mm) maximum out of round for pickups and .0039" (.10 mm) maximum out of round for passenger cars. Maximum allowable inner diameter of drums is as follows: Pickup — 10.06" (255.5 mm); 210 and F10 — 8.05" (204.5 mm); all remaining models — 9.06" (230.0 mm).

▶ *ALL FIAT MODELS WITH DISC BRAKES: ALTERNATE METHOD OF BLEEDING BRAKE CALIPERS* — If bleeder screws cannot be turned on disc brake models, the following alternate method may be used to bleed brake system.

1) Remove caliper from support bracket. Place a 2" x 4" block of wood between caliper and piston.

2) Using brake pedal, pump piston against block of wood. Invert caliper so bleeder and inlet brake line are facing downward.

3) Bleed air from caliper by loosening inlet fitting at caliper. With caliper in this position, air is forced to inlet passage.

4) Use normal bleeding procedures for remainder of system.

▶ *1978 AND 1979 FIESTA: BRAKE ROTOR REPLACEMENT* — Previously it was required that both front disc rotors have the same engineering number stamped on the outer periphery of the rotor. This procedure has been revised so that it is now permissible to mix any of the 4 engineering numbered discs so long as minimum thickness of .34" (8.7 mm) is observed.

▶ *ALL MERCEDES-BENZ MODELS: BRAKE PADS* — The following items should be noted when servicing brake pads on Mercedes vehicles.

1) In vehicles with brake pad wear indicators, brake pad sensor need only be replaced if damaged, if conductor is exposed or if insulation of sensor pin has been worn off by brake disc.

2) White numbers stamped on brake pad backing plate identify batch from which brake lining material originated. It is important that only pads having the same batch number be installed in both front calipers. This helps to avoid pulling tendencies, due to different friction coefficients of pads.

3) Brake caliper pistons should only be retracted with Piston Return Pliers (MB Part No. 123 589 00 37 00). If other tools are used, there is a danger of damaging piston or dust seal. On vehicles with wear indicators, avoid pinching cable or cable guard.

4) Brake pads should only be removed with an Impact Puller (MB Part No. 115 589 14 33 00). If pads are stuck in caliper, use Seize Puller (MB Part No. 116 589 04 33 00).

5) Before installing new pads, discs that are grimy, rusted or discolored must be sanded to a bright finish with a cleaning pad.

6) Apply a light coat of heat-proof lubricant (Molykote, or equivalent) to edges of backing plate, before installing in brake pad. This will reduce squealing and ease brake and disassembly in next service.

7) When replacing a cross spring (ATE) or pad retaining spring (Bendix or Girling), make sure that correct spring is installed.

▶ *LATE MODEL SAAB: SEMI-METALLIC BRAKE PADS* — When installing semi-metallic brake pads on front brakes of subject models, the semi-metallic pads must only be installed on the outside of the disc toward the wheel. Installing the pads on the inside results in excessive heat transfer to the wheel cylinder, which may result in damage to the dust covers and seals under hard driving conditions.

WHEEL ALIGNMENT — SECTION 8

▶ *1980 AUDI 5000: WHEEL ALIGNMENT* — Late model 1980 Audi 5000 vehicles have front suspension parts that are the same as Audi 5000 Turbo models. These vehicles have non-adjustable caster. Early model 5000 vehicles had adjustable caster. The acceptable caster range for checking is as follows: Caster — 1° 10′+40′.

▶ *VOLVO DL, GL, GLE AND GT DIESEL MODELS: CAMBER SPECIFICATION CHANGE* — The correct specification for camber on these vehicles should be as follows: DL, GL and GTE diesel models, +1° to +1-1/2°, with an allowable difference between right and left of 1/2°. GT models should be set at +1/4° to 3/4°.

FOR 1980 & PREVIOUS MODELS

SUSPENSION — SECTION 9

1 ▶ *1978 DATSUN 620: LOWER BALL JOINT INSPECTION* —The lower ball joints were formerly checked by measuring turning torque. Revised procedure is to check for axial end play. Standard end play is .004-.039" (.1-1.0 mm).

2 ▶ *1978-1979 FIESTA: FRONT SUSPENSION MOUNTING* — A "clunking" noise heard when making either right or left hand turns may be caused by the front coil spring responding to rotational movement of the top strut mount bearing. To eliminate this noise, install new thrust plate and bearing (part numbers DR8Z-3K048-A and D8RZ-3K099-B) as a pair.

3 ▶ *1978 VOLKSWAGEN RABBIT & SCIROCCO: FRONT SUSPENSION CHANGES* — Mid-way through the 1978 model year, the front ball joint pin diameter was increased from 15 to 17mm. The clamping hole in the front wheel bearing housing was also enlarged to match the ball joint change. 15 mm ball joints will still be available, but only 17 mm wheel bearing housings will be supplied as replacement parts. In the event one wheel bearing housing must be changed, manufacturer allows the use of old, 15 mm housing on the other side of vehicle. New tightening torque for clamping bolt is 37 ft. lbs. (5 mkg).

4 ▶ *ALL VOLVO MODELS WITH NIVOMAT SHOCK ABSORBERS: PROPER DISPOSAL PROCEDURES* — Whenever Nivomat shock absorbers must be discarded, they must first be depressurized. This is done by loosening the lower screw in shock body slowly and then loosening upper screw. Shock absorber is pressureless when piston rod can easily be pushed in by hand.

STEERING — SECTION 10

1 ▶ *ALL 1980 FIAT MODELS EXCEPT SPIDER 2000: MANUAL RACK AND PINION STEERING BOX LUBRICANT* — The lubricant used in Fiat manual rack and pinion steering boxes has been changed from SAE 80W/90 EP Oil, to Lithium Base Grease containing Molybdenum Disulphide. The new lubricant may be used for servicing steering boxes on models which were originally filled with oil.

2 ▶ *1975 THROUGH 1979 LUV: STEERING KNUCKLE REPLACEMENT* — When replacing the steering knuckle on 1975 and newer LUV trucks, it is necessary that the spacer be removed from the old knuckle and installed on the replacement knuckle.

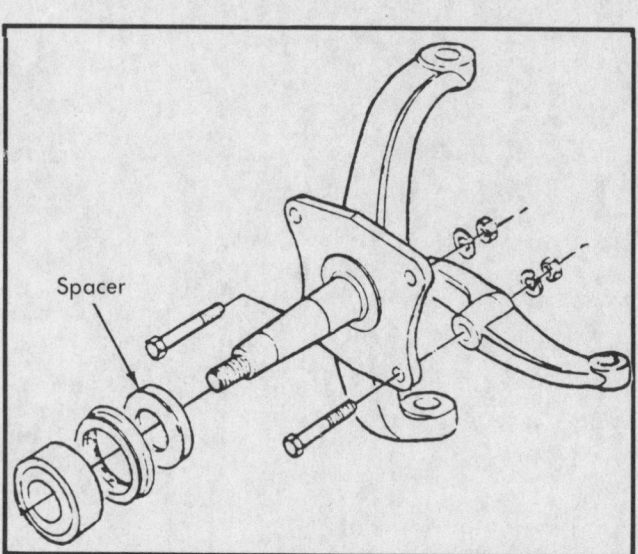

Spacer

LUV Steering Knuckle

3 ▶ *1977 AND LATER MERCEDES-BENZ: STEERING STOP CHANGE* — A new power steering unit has been installed on 230, 280E, 240D & 300D models. New unit has internal steering stops located in steering gear housing. Previously stops were on crossmember and pitman arm. New unit part number is preceeded with "A*". Note that 300CD and 280CE models are equipped with new unit from start of production. When new unit was introduced slight modifications to steering linkage were made. Make certain an early version system is never installed into a vehicle that does not have stops on crossmember, pitman arm, and idler arm.

4 ▶ *1977 AND LATER MERCEDES-BENZ: UPPER CONTROL ARM BUSHING CHANGE* — As of 1/77 all models except 450 SL and 450 SLC have been fitted with a two piece upper control arm bushing. Make sure when repair is required that only one type of bushing is used (either one-piece or two-piece version). Make sure two-piece bushing is installed if vehicle has steel (not aluminum) upper control arms.

5 ▶ *ALL SAAB MODELS WITH SAGINAW POWER STEERING RACKS: REINSTALLING ORIGINAL TIE RODS* — Removal of tie rods on Saab models with Saginaw power steering racks has required replacement of tie rods due to distortion of staked area of ball joint locking flange. A new shim (Saab Part No. 89 46 360) has been introduced that eliminates need to replace tie rods. By placing shim between end of rack and inner ball joint, the locking flange is repositioned 90° from previously staked area after tightening. This places strong undamaged metal over flats of rack for a new secure staking of locking flange.

Latest Changes & Corrections

STEERING — SECTION 10 (Cont.)

▶ *1977 AND LATER VOLKSWAGEN TYPE 2: ROLLER SHAFT OIL SEAL REPLACEMENT* — It is now possible to replace a leaking roller shaft oil seal instead of replacing steering gear. Perform seal replacement as follows:

1) Remove steering drop arm. Use a sharp tool to pry out oil seal. DO NOT scratch or damage roller shaft.

2) Clean oil seal seats in housing and shaft. Clean splines on shaft. Cover splines with cardboard or tape to prevent new seal from being damaged during installation.

3) Coat oil seal lip with multi-purpose grease. Slide seal on roller shaft and carefully drive into place.

4) Reinstall drop arm, install new lock plate and tighten nut to 100 ft. lbs. (14 mkg). Check oil level and add if needed.

▶ *1977 AND LATER VOLVO 260 MODELS: POWER STEERING HOSE CHAFING CAUTION* — The location of the power steering reservoir has been changed. This relocating changes the fluid hose routing so it runs close to the battery purchase. To prevent premature hose failure, ensure the strip clamp mounting hose is adequately positioned.

▶ *1977 VOLVO 240: POWER STEERING SERVO NOISE* — Some subject vehicles may encounter a vibration or audible noise coming from the power steering servo area. Noise usually occurs between 3,100 and 4,100 RPM. The noise may even be heard when vehicle is stationary. Volvo has released a new pump mounting bracket with rubber grommets to eliminate this noise. Part number for new bracket is 1219522-8. Bracket was introduced in production at approximately the following chassis numbers: 242, 76000; 244, 120000; 245, 76000.

▶ *1976 AND LATER VOLVO MODELS: STEERING WHEEL NOISE* — Models equipped with the new design "off center cover pad" are subject to a "creaking" noise during maneuvers where excessive steering effort is required. Proceed as follows to eliminate noise:

- Remove steering wheel padding.
- Lubricate the four sleeves where pad attaches to steering wheel.
- Refit padding.

"WE LISTEN"

We will greatly appreciate receiving your comments or corrections so that we may continue to publish the world's best automotive manuals. **Mail this card today. We'd like to hear from you!**

☐ Domestic   ☐ Imported   ☐ Trucks
☐ A/C Service   ☐ Tune-Up   ☐ Mechanical   ☐ Transmissions   ☐ Emission Control

Section No._____ Page No._____ Vehicle Model, year _____

Comments: _____

_____

_____

Company Name _____ Phone ( )

Address _____ Zip _____

"WE LISTEN"

We will greatly appreciate receiving your comments or corrections so that we may continue to publish the world's best automotive manuals. **Mail this card today. We'd like to hear from you!**

☐ Domestic   ☐ Imported   ☐ Trucks
☐ A/C Service   ☐ Tune-Up   ☐ Mechanical   ☐ Transmissions   ☐ Emission Control

Section No._____ Page No._____ Vehicle Model, year _____

Comments: _____

_____

_____

Company Name _____ Phone ( )

Address _____ Zip _____

"WE LISTEN"

We will greatly appreciate receiving your comments or corrections so that we may continue to publish the world's best automotive manuals. **Mail this card today. We'd like to hear from you!**

☐ Domestic   ☐ Imported   ☐ Trucks
☐ A/C Service   ☐ Tune-Up   ☐ Mechanical   ☐ Transmissions   ☐ Emission Control

Section No._____ Page No._____ Vehicle Model, year _____

Comments: _____

_____

_____

Company Name _____ Phone ( )

Address _____ Zip _____

BUSINESS REPLY CARD

FIRST CLASS   PERMIT NO. 3701   SAN DIEGO, CA

POSTAGE WILL BE PAID BY ADDRESSEE

MITCHELL MANUALS, INC.

P.O. BOX 26260
San Diego, California 92126

BUSINESS REPLY CARD

FIRST CLASS   PERMIT NO. 3701   SAN DIEGO, CA

POSTAGE WILL BE PAID BY ADDRESSEE

MITCHELL MANUALS, INC.

P.O. BOX 26260
San Diego, California 92126

BUSINESS REPLY CARD

FIRST CLASS   PERMIT NO. 3701   SAN DIEGO, CA

POSTAGE WILL BE PAID BY ADDRESSEE

MITCHELL MANUALS, INC.

P.O. BOX 26260
San Diego, California 92126

Now . . . Save Time, Expand Your Business, Increase Profits

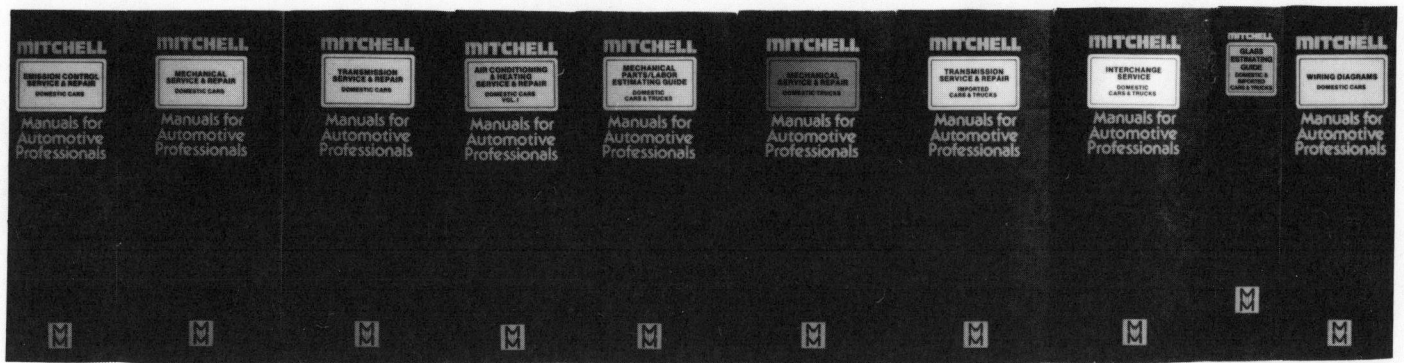

with Mitchell's time-saving profit builders!

Turn Page ↗

AIR CONDITIONING AND HEATING SERVICE MANUAL

The manual that's used and respected by the people who KNOW the air conditioning industry. Now service any air conditioning or heating system profitably! You get everything you need to make system servicing quick and easy: in-depth trouble shooting and diagnosis...servicing, repair and overhaul data...thousands of illustrations...hundreds of spec tables and charts...factory bulletins...labor estimating section...and more! Coverage for all U.S. factory-installed systems since 1972. **Price: only $60.00**

AIR CONDITIONING OLDER MODELS

Covers vehicles from 1966-1971. **Price: only $25.00**

AIR CONDITIONING BASIC TRAINING MANUAL

Now you can have the most complete basic training manual available for air conditioning systems! Covers all the important aspects of air conditioning service: Theory, components, operation, diagnosis, servicing and compressor repair. Includes handy trouble-shooting wall chart. **Price: only $6.95**

DOMESTIC EMISSION CONTROL SERVICE MANUAL

Tough new pollution laws mean big profits for you in emission control servicing! Cash in on it with Mitchell! You get the most complete and current data available...anywhere! Description, operation, trouble-shooting, maintenance, repair and overhaul info for all domestic car emission systems produced since 1966! PLUS—you get a complete fuel system section, engine I.D., all system wiring and vacuum diagrams. Application charts. **Price: only $50.00**

IMPORTED EMISSION CONTROL/SERVICE MANUAL

Imported cars need pollution control servicing too...and that means more profit opportunities for your shop! Cash in on it with this fantastic coverage—over 30 foreign manufacturers are covered, in complete detail, since 1968. Description, operation, trouble-shooting, maintenance, repair, and overhaul—you get it all with Mitchell. PLUS...you get a complete carburetion and fuel injection section, emission system wiring and vacuum diagrams and more! Over 3,400 pages—it's the most in-depth, money-making repair tool you'll find. Start enjoying big emission profits today! **Price: only $50.00**

LT. TRUCK EMISSION CONTROL SERVICE MANUAL

New edition! Now profit from the growing emission control business in domestic light trucks! Has it all—description, operation, maintenance, repair, trouble-shooting and overhaul information for all domestic light truck emission systems since 1968. Complete fuel system section and wiring and vacuum diagrams for all systems. Handy application charts. **Price: only $50.00**